Your Daily Shakespeare

To Paul and William

Copyright © 2001 by Jimmie Moglia
First Edition

All rights reserved. No part of this book shall be reproduced, stored in a retrieval system, or transmitted by any means without written permission from the author.
Printed in Korea.

International Standard Book Number: ISBN-1-59872-644-7

INDEX

Preface   7

How to Use Your Daily Shakespeare   13

Abbreviations   15

Your Daily Shakespeare   19

Analytical Index   1039

Summary of Plays and Poems   1375

> But pardon, gentles all
> The flat, unraised spirits, that have dared,
> On this unworthy scaffold, to bring forth
> So great an object
>
> Henry V, Prologue.

Preface

Writing yet another book on Shakespeare, given the abundance of related works, may seem presumptuous - or perhaps a well-known trick to seduce the reader into attention, by relying on the universal appeal of the name of a Giant. A preface is therefore necessary to offer, alas, an explanation short of an apology, well remembering that "… **excusing of a fault doth make the fault the worse by the excuse**" (King John, act 4, scene 2). But, if you will "**lend thy serious hearing to what I shall unfold**" (Hamlet, act 1, scene 5), I will demonstrate why this book had to be written and why (I hope) you will find it the most useful reference work of its kind. The assertion smacks terribly of self-praise or worse, vanity – a sin, however, easily avoided by remembering the line, "**For it will come to pass that every braggart shall be found an ass**" (All's Well that Ends Well, act 4, scene 3)

Though based on serious and thorough research, 'Your Daily Shakespeare' is NOT another book of quotations. One technical definition could be 'Dictionary of Shakespearean Situations' or 'Reverse Dictionary of Shakespearean Quotations'. Neither definition, however, conveys the spirit, purpose and soul of the book. Hence the title. The genesis and evolution of 'Your Daily Shakespeare' will (I like to think), justify the claim to its usefulness.

My formal education is in Engineering - a branch of study that, in literary circles, confines me to the rank of the actors in Midsummer Night's Dream ("**A crew of patches, rude mechanicals, that work for bread upon the Athenian walls**" (act 3, scene 2). Still, I define myself a "Shakespearean *Road* Scholar". The italics are mine, the spelling is wilful and the meaning literal.

After graduation, following the inscrutable paths of chance ("**What can be avoided whose end is purpos'd by the mighty Gods**?" (Julius Caesar, act 2, scene 2), I was employed by a large corporation and became a manager, sometimes referred to as an 'executive' ("**I hate the word as I hate hell and all Montagues**" (from Romeo & Juliet, act 1, scene 1)) Two circumstances triggered the interest that led to the book, extended travel time during which I read intensely and frequent participation in corporate meetings.

While traveling, Shakespeare's "**fair discourse hath been as sugar, making the hard way sweet and delectable**" (King Richard II, act 2, scene 3). At meetings I concluded that relatively few (corporate) speakers have respect for their own words. The statement seems presumptuous but often it was a case of "**senseless speaking or speaking such as sense cannot untie**" (Cymbeline, act 5, scene 4), or "**Be plain, good son, and homely in thy drift; riddling confession finds but riddling shrift**." (Romeo & Juliet, act 2, scene 3)

Then I discovered the obvious ("**… a great cause of the night is lack of the sun**" (As You Like It, act 3, scene 2)) – i.e. that Shakespeare is an excellent trainer in concision and clarity of expression. The following and equally obvious discovery was the positive effect on an audience of a befitting Shakespearean quotation. Next I searched for a comprehensive work that would match everyday situations to appropriate Shakespearean lines. I found none - Thomas Dolby, in 1832, captured the idea but his work (if I may say so) is limited.

As the wanted dictionary did not exist I wrote one. My goal was (is) to help the reader find and deliver the 'killing' Shakespearean answer or comment, quickly and easily. The book title conveys the idea that there are frequent (yes, daily), practical uses for a good Shakespeare quote. Each entry in 'Your Daily Shakespeare' includes the situation, the associated quote and frequent examples of where, when and how to use it. Each entry also includes a brief description of the context of the quote, in the actual play.

Quotations have been used ever since someone said words worth remembering. The words may or may not have contained universal truths, but there was something in their meaning, sound, rhythm (or in all three together), that triggered an emotional response in the hearer(s). The response to a good quote can be acceptance of your message, a confirmation of your specific knowledge or the establishing of a friendly atmosphere. It is generally assumed that quotations are used in formal presentations or written essays. But a good quote can be, for example, an effective and elegant way out of a potentially embarrassing situation.

Take the fairly common instance when someone asks you, "How much money do you make?". It is a tricky and (in the view of many) impolite question. The same question is even trickier if you are not wealthy but are concerned that a frank admission of the truth may 'lower your rating' – as we say today in our monetary, personal-worth-driven society. In general you could,

- Answer that you do not want to disclose that information. If so, you indirectly imply that the questioner is impolite and this creates an unfriendly atmosphere.
- Say that you don't know or remember. You are a liar.
- Give out a number. If the number is correct you surrender to impoliteness. If the number is incorrect you (again) are lying and the truth usually comes out sooner or later.

Try instead, **"They are but beggars that can count their worth"** (Romeo and Juliet, Act 2, Scene 5). Let's examine the virtues of this answer.

a) For one, you have given the questioner a way out. The question is impolite but you have not told the questioner that he/she is impolite. Rather, your answer implicitly acknowledges that he does not want to think of you as a 'beggar'. If you disclosed the information you would have caused him to consider you a 'beggar' and embarrassed him. In other words, a situation potentially uncomfortable for you has changed completely - it is now you who are relieving the questioner from embarrassment.
b) The sentence has rhythm, with the accents falling on the 'e' of 'beggars' and the 'o' of 'count' and 'worth'. The combination of rhythm and the old-sounding word 'beggar' gives the sentence a charge of humor. That is, a potential source of tension has become instead an occasion for amusement or at least light-heartedness.
c) The word 'worth' shifts the idea of money (prosaic and impolite) to that of individual value (respectful and elegant), as if to say, "I appreciate your interest - it implies that you assume me a person of worth as an individual and yet….etc."

In general and depending, of course, on the nature of the subject and of your audience, a Shakespearean quotation achieves the following objectives,

- It proves implicitly that you are educated, that you value the importance and the intriguing power of words. It prompts a recognition that transcends your actual social status, title or position, it shows that you are not exclusively interested in things material. It suggests that you have a balanced view of events or transactions. It instantly establishes the presence of a bond between you and a higher spirit. All these are symptoms of personal reliability. No need to explain why reliability is an asset in business, on the job and generally in personal relations.

   Sometimes the effect is immediate. When in high school, my son William was addressed and directed by a teacher to perform a task. The command was abrupt, forceful and did not call for a response (other than the execution of the command). Having just finished reading 'Julius Caesar', William replied, **"If Caesar says 'do this', it is performed"** (act 1, scene 2). William reports that the teacher's expression indicated real surprise. And from that day onward, the teacher treated him with noticeable consideration.

   Sometimes the positive effect is unpredictable. For example, two quotes convinced two different judges to dismiss a traffic ticket. One for unwittingly turning left from the wrong lane (**"I am a man more sinned against than sinning**" (King Lear, act 3, scene 2), the other for having forgotten to renew my licence plate (**"When the age is in the wit is out**" (Much Ado About Nothing, act. 3, scene 5).

- It will often lead your audience to smile or even laugh, thus establishing that you have a sense of humor. The humor in the quote is often independent of the quote's meaning - it derives from the contrast between the modernity of the situation and the amusing antiquity of the language. Try this quick test. Did you smile at least once at the quotes cited so far? If yes, you have proven the point, if not I will be tempted to repeat with Falstaff, **"…nor a man cannot make him laugh: but that's no marvel, he drinks no wine…"** (King Henry IV, part 2, act 4, scene 3). Assuming, of course, that you be a member of the less gentle sex.

- It implies a certain degree of respect towards the receiver, especially if the quote is easily understandable (most are), and is delivered in a familiar, rather than professorial, tone. The amusing and clever quote implies that the recipient is equally clever by appreciating it. He/she may feel flattered. Oscar Wilde remarked that flattery is the infantry of negotiations (of any kind!). And we all know that intelligent humor is a catalyst for dialog. It follows that intelligent humor and elegant flattery make a winning combination.

A few words about Shakespeare's romantic quotations. Love looms large in his plays, sonnets and poems in all its aspects, sentimental, passionate, platonic, sexual, marital, filial, brotherly, friendly, compassionate, heroic and all shades in-between.

Perhaps you are like the character Proteus who, referring to his friend Valentine, said '**He after honour hunts, I after love'** (Two Gentlemen of Verona, act 1, scene 1). More likely, you know or realize that in our contemporary market-driven life there is more to life than market.

Whatever your intentions, you will find in Shakespeare a wealth of lines usable and adaptable to just about all situations that have a romantic overtone, from introducing yourself to a yet unknown and appealing lady, to handling or even reversing rejections. The unexpected quote will qualify you as romantic without being ridiculous, original without being odd, elegant without being eccentric and witty without being wacky.

A summary of practical uses for 'Your Daily Shakespeare'? Introductions, epilogues, reports, speeches, lines for blank cards, and any type or kind of (as the experts would say), interpersonal communications. Besides, to quote Thomas Dolby but referring to 'Your Daily Shakespeare', *"As a table book, it is presumed this work will be found no less pleasing, than as a book of reference it will be useful"*. And he continued, *"...the devoted admirer of Shakespeare will not, it is hoped, be displeased at occasionally meeting beauties which had long been familiar to him, suddenly presenting themselves from behind coverts where he had not expected to see them"*.

It took a long time to complete 'Your Daily Shakespeare', considering that, at various stages, I decided to change its structure, leading to radical re-writes and re-work. But **"To business that we like we rise betimes and go to it with delight"** (Antony and Cleopatra, act 4, scene 4). Echoing my personal experience, the original title was 'Shakespeare for the Busy Executive'. Later I changed it to 'Your Daily Shakespeare', reflecting the broader audience addressed. The analytical index (over 9400 entries), is sorted by situations. The situations are described by a concise, descriptive sentence and supported by a short extract of the complete quote. The reader can then refer to the full quote in the body of the book, where he will find in order,

- The title of the quote
- The quote itself
- Suggestions for applications. Sometimes, (may Purists and Literature Professors forgive me), I suggested minor modifications of the original quote to fit the application. The modifications in no way alter the rhythm or the sense of the original.
- A short description of what actually happens in the play in connection with the specific quotation. This helps with use and memorization. The quotation does not float in mid mind with no other reference but that the line is from Shakespeare. Tracking the context of the quote helps store the quote in the correct mental repository and facilitates recollection.

At the end of the book you will also find a summary of each play.

I could say more good things about 'Your Daily Shakespeare' but **'... there's not a wise man in twenty that will praise himself.'** (Much Ado About Nothing, act 5, scene 2). I hope you will discover the value of the book by your very personal use. And I will be grateful if you will tell me when your use of a Shakespearean quote has had the positive effects you hoped for.

It is commonly assumed that poetry is the antithesis of business, but there is ample evidence that this is not true. Charles Stearns, an American physician and business man wrote in 1860, "*The mental discipline induced by learning Shakespeare is even better than mathematics, because it exercises more of the separate mental faculties, and, at the same time, by stirring the emotions, places us in close relations with our fellow men; which pure science does not do, but, on the contrary, tends to cut off and obstruct.*"

Finally, though I tried to include all usable quotes and aphorisms, I will not claim that the work is complete (nor any work on Shakespeare could ever be complete). I will ask of the reader**, "If hearty sorrow be a sufficient ransom for omission, I tender it here**" (from 'Two Gentlemen of Verona', act 5, scene 4). Still, for good measure, I will seek refuge under the ample mantle of the famous compiler of the first Dictionary of the English Language, Samuel Johnson. At the onset of his dictionary he declared, "N*o dictionary is perfect, but any is better than none".*

How to use 'Your Daily Shakespeare'

There are two main parts in the book, the TEXT and the ANALYTICAL INDEX. In the TEXT each entry contains:

1. The title of the citation, followed (after the hyphen), by an extract of the quote and its usage. Short quotes are part of the title entirely.
2. The complete quote, followed by the listing of the play, (with act and scene), poem or sonnet it comes from.
3. Suggestion(s) or hints on use of the citation and reference(s) to other entries and quotes with a similar or related meaning. You will also find occasional anecdotal information or reference to how other authors or historical characters have handled the same issue, question or situation.
4. A description of the context in which the lines are used in the original play or poem. Sometimes a quote can be applied in a sense different from the original intent.

In the ANALYTICAL INDEX you will find,

- The title of each quotation, reported verbatim from the TEXT.
- Entries as questions and answers, referring to the applicable complete quotation in the TEXT.
- The initial line of the most popular quotes, to help locate the complete quote in the TEXT. For example, "O hard condition, twin born of greatness. See 'Power, the downside of p. - .. . subject to the breath of every fool, whose sense no more can feel, but his own wringing.'"
- Multiple ways of referring to one specific quote. For example, you can find the quote 'Break, my heart, for I must hold my tongue' listed as
    - Break, my heart…
    - Invocation, reluctance to shut up
    - It is not nor it cannot come to good…
    - Silence, self-enforced - It is not nor it cannot come to good: but break, my heart; for I must hold my tongue.

- Reference to potential different answers for the same question. For example, **What do you do for a living?** See "Life, l. as a battle - Strives in his little world of man to out-scorn the to-and-fro-conflicting wind and rain.' *** 'Profession, what do you do for a living? - As my imagination bodies forth the forms of things unknown…' *** 'Title, job t. magnified - Thou art a cobbler, art thou?… I am, indeed, sir, a surgeon to old shoes.' *** 'Labor, description of repetitive work – … from the rise to set sweats in the eye of Phoebus and all night…' *** 'Personnel, crew, a motley crew - A crew of patches, rude mechanicals, that work for bread upon the Athenian walls.'

Conventionally, quotes are used as verbal ammunition to strengthen your point, or to lighten a presentation, or to support your argument by appealing to an uncontested authority (such as Shakespeare), or to add elegance to your speech, and so on.

You will find an extensive collection of introductions and epilogues to presentations. For the body of your speech, simply search (starting with the analytical index), for the idea that most closely reflects the point(s) you wish to make. For example: you wish to convey the irrational response and behavior of crowds. You will find (21) entries for 'Opinion, your op. on crowds and masses', as well as various multiple entries for 'Opinion, your op. on authority', lawyers, doctors, politicians, etc.

A less conventional method is to use 'Your Daily Shakespeare' as a source of inspiration, as a trigger of ideas. Just open the book at random, as I-Ching practitioners do, locate a quote and make it the start of your creative thinking. Visualize situations where the message or the description contained in the quote ring true to your own life, or your relatives', or friends', or lovers'. Or recollect real life episodes or observations of nature where the lines may apply. Associating a quote with a personal, real or imagined situation also helps memorize the citation.

Many quotes can be used routinely in everyday situations as answers, for example, to 'How are you'?, 'What do you do for a living?', 'What do you drink?', 'What do you know of him?' 'What is your experience?' etc. - or to deliver salutations and express wishes, (see entries for 'Salutations and wishes'). Most people can easily retain and apply 20 to 50 quotes as the occasion demands. It is easier than you think.

Finally, all medical and psychology experts concur that a mind kept active via intelligent memorization is excellent insurance for maintaining our spirit young and our memory strong. What better way than selecting a cluster of favorite Shakespearean quotes and make them part of your memory fitness kit! You will profit by the exercise and find pleasure in the use. After all, "**No profit grows where is no pleasure taken...**" (TOS.1.1). Not only, but as you gracefully advance in years you will not have to admit that, "**When the age is in, the wit is out**" (MAAN.3.1).

Happy quoting!

Abbreviations

All's Well That Ends Well	AWEW
Antony and Cleopatra	AC
As You Like It	AYLI
Comedy of Errors	COE
Coriolanus	COR
Cymbeline	CYM
Hamlet	HAM
Julius Caesar	JC
King John	KJ
King Henry IV part 1	HIV,1
King Henry IV part 2	HIV,2
King Henry VI part 1	HVI,1
King Henry VI part 2	HVI,2
King Henry VI part 3	HVI,3
King Henry VIII	HVIII
King Lear	KL
King Richard II	R2
King Richard III	R3
Love's :Labours Lost	LLL
Macbeth	M
Measure for Measure	MFM
Merchant of Venice	MOV
Midsummer Night's Dream	MND
Much Ado About Nothing	MAAN
Othello	OTH
Pericles, Prince of Tyre	PER
Romeo and Juliet	RJ
Sonnets	SON
The Merry Wives of Windsor	MWW
The Taming of the Shrew	TOS
The Tempest	TEM
The Winter's Tale	WT
Timon of Athens	TOA
Titus Andronicus	TA
Troilus and Cressida	TC
Twelfth Night	TN
Two Gentlemen from Verona	TGV
Ovid 'Art of Loving'	AOL

YOUR DAILY
SHAKESPEARE

| Why do you need a raise? | *"I can get no remedy against this consumption of the purse..."* | Do you pay cash or credit? | *"I'll pay cash as far as my coin would stretch; and, where it would not, I will use my credit."* |

| Will you do this for me? | *"Being your slave what should I do but tend upon the hours and times of your desire?"* | What do you think of him? | *"God made him, therefore let him pass for man."* |

JIMMIE MOGLIA

Ability, magic abilities claimed - I can call spirits from the vasty deep.
GLENDOWER: I can call spirits from the vasty deep.
HOTSPUR: Why, so can I: or so can any man;
But will they come, when you do call for them? (KHIV p1.3.1)
A comparison to debunk any type of exaggerated claim. E.G. 'This reminds me of a dialog between two characters in King Henry IV. Glendower says, 'I can call…deep' and Hotspur replies, 'So can I but will…for them?'
In the play. *Hotspur antagonizes Glendower who fancies himself a magician.*

Ability, questionable - a horse that's the more capable creature.
ACHILLES. Come, thou shalt bear a letter to him straight.
THERSITES. Let me bear another to his horse; for that's the more capable creature. (TC.3.3)
Give your indirect opinion on XY. For example, someone says 'I will send him a fax' and you can counter, quoting the source, 'Send another to his horse; for that's the more capable creature'.
In the play. *Achilles' letter is for Ajax of whose intelligence Thersites does not think much.*

Ability, a. strength and courage displayed - … doing, in the figure of a lamb, the feats of a lion
"…he hath borne himself beyond the promise of his age, doing, in the figure of a lamb, the feats of a lion" (MAAN.1.1)
In the play. *A messenger describes to Leonato the performance of Claudio in a recent war.*

ABSENCE
Ladies like to think they hold an important place in your mind, or that you think of them. Thought (along with imitation) is the best form of flattery. Think of your mind as a television screen – if she is on your mind, she is on the screen. Television equals popularity and by inference (most of the times and often unfortunately) admiration. Therefore she loves to know you think of her, particularly if you tell her so with an elegant turn of phrase. It always works, whether she is part of an established relationship or if she is a new acquaintance in whose graces you wish to fall.

Letters are evidence that you are thinking of her. See 'Writing, excusing your poor means to extol her charms - I grant (sweet love) thy lovely argument deserves the travail of a worthier pen...' ***
'Writing, power of printed message - … in black ink my love may still shine bright'.
If a gift accompanies a letter, the evidence is tangible (see 'Jewelry, gifts large and small'). In a letter to Ann Boleyn, his second wife, married after divorcing Catherine of Aragon, King Henry VIII writes, '…and seeing I cannot be present in person with you, I send you the nearest thing to that possible, that is my picture set in bracelets, wishing myself in their place, when it shall please you.'
And in another letter to the same Ann Boleyn….'You may judge what an effect the presence of that person must have on me, whose absence has made a greater wound in my heart than either words or writing can express, and which nothing can cure but her return.'

Absence, 'Will you miss me?' – Or call it winter, which being full of care, makes summer's welcome thrice more wished, more rare.

"Or call it winter, which being full of care,
Makes summer's welcome thrice more wished,
              More rare." (SON 56)
You are leaving and when she asks the question answer, 'I'll call being away from you a winter, which being full of care, makes summer's welcome, thrice more wished, more rare.'

Absence, a. felt - Is it thy will, thy image should keep open my heavy eyelids to the weary night?
"Is it thy will, thy image should keep open
My heavy eyelids to the weary night?" (SON.61)
Compliment, equates to 'I can't live without you', 'you deprive me of sleep', 'your power is so strong that it interferes with one of the fundamental necessities of life'. After a pause you may follow up with the famous lines on sleep from Macbeth, 'Sleep, that knits up the ravell'd sleeve of care,' (see **'Sleep, soothing properties of s.'**). See also 'Anxiety, obsession, missing her presence - how can I then return in happy plight, that am debarred the benefit of rest?' *** 'Mind, always on your m. - Weary with toil, I haste me to my bed, the dear repose for limbs with travel tired...'
In the play. *Macbeth begins to feel remorse after killing King Duncan in his sleep*

Absence, a. from an event - ... our absence makes us unthrifty to our knowledge...
"...our absence makes us unthrifty to our knowledge.
Let's along." (WT.5.2)
In the play. *Some gentlemen in Sicilia want to be present at the extraordinary final events occurring at the court of Leontes, king of Sicilia.*

Absence, a. worse than death - if I depart from thee I cannot live: and in thy sight to die, what were it else...
"If I depart from thee I cannot live: And in thy sight to die, what were it else,
But like a pleasant slumber in your lap?" (KHVI.p2.3.2)
Either of these two options (first or second line) will demonstrate the magnetic and absolute hold she has on you. See also 'World. She is the w. - ... for where thou art, there is the world itself.'
– 'Death, d. preferable to be away from her - ... To die is to be banish'd from myself'.
In the play. *The banished Suffolk addresses Queen Margaret whose lover he probably was, though she was married to the pious King Henry VI.*

Absence, a. worse than death - to die by thee, were but to die in jest; from thee to die, were torture more than death.
"To die by thee, were but to die in jest;
From thee to die, were torture more than death." (KHVI.p2.3.2)
In the play. *The banished Suffolk takes leave of Queen Margaret.*

Absence, being away from her felt like winter - How like a winter hath my absence been from thee...
"How like a winter hath my absence been
From thee, the pleasure of the fleeting year!
What freezings have I felt, what dark days seen!
What old December's bareness every where!" (SON 97)

Absence, hoping that a. may not be detrimental – ... I hope my absence doth neglect no great designs...

"…I hope,
My absence doth neglect no great designs,
Which by my presence might have been concluded." (KRIII.3.4)
In the play. *Richard joins an ongoing meeting of lords and courtiers who were waiting for him.*

Absence, invitation to make one's presence felt – appear thou in the likeness of a sigh speak but one rhyme, and I am satisfied.
"Appear thou in the likeness of a sigh,
Speak but one rhyme, and I am satisfied." (RJ.2.1)
Call someone who is absent or who, being present, says nothing or appears to have his mind somewhere else. Alternative to the question 'Where are you?'
In the play. *Benvolio and Mercutio try to find out where Romeo has gone. Romeo has climbed a wall dividing the road from the Capulets' house. Mercutio calls for Romeo.*

Absent, cannot find him - I think he be transform'd into a beast for I can no where find him like a man.
"I think he be transform'd into a beast;
For I can no where find him like a man." (AYLI.2.7)
Answer to 'Where is he?'
In the play. *Duke Senior inquires where Jacques may be.*

Abstinence, consequences of a. when turned into law – … the ungenitured agent will unpeople the province with continency…
"…the ungenitured agent will unpeople the province with continency; sparrows must not build in his house-eaves, because they are lecherous" (MFM.3.2)
In the play. *Lucio's comment on Deputy-Duke Angelo's new law enforcement of abstinence.*

Abstinence, some distance advisable – such separation…becomes a virtuous bachelor and a maid.
"Lie further off; in human modesty,
Such separation, as may well be said,
Becomes a virtuous bachelor and a maid." (MND.2.2)
Use at your discretion.
In the play. *The night has arrived while Lysander and Hermia are lost in the woods. Lysander proposes to share accommodations. Hermia in modesty refuses.*

Abuse, someone is being abused – you are abused beyond the mark of thought.
"…You are abused
Beyond the mark of thought" (AC.3.6)
Change 'you' to 'I' if it applies.
In the play. *Octavian to his sister, abused by Antony who has abandoned her.*

Abuse, verbal a. - … what man of good temper would endure this tempest of exclamation?
"…what man of good temper would endure this tempest of exclamation?" (KHIV.p2.2.1)
Retort to the railing of an opponent. See also 'Argument, a. between to contending parties – The bitter clamour of two eager tongues.'
In the play. *The Chief Justice reprimands Falstaff who defends himself against accusation of exploitation, abuse and lying from Mistress Quickly*

Academic qualification not necessarily equating to intelligence - … for, besides that he is a fool, he's a great quarreler.
SIR TOBY (of Aguecheek). ... and speaks three or four languages word for word without book, and hath all the good gifts of nature.
MARIA. He hath indeed, - almost natural; for, besides that he is a fool, he's a great quarreler." (TN.1.3)

Downplay the value of being multilingual, in self-effacing mode or as irony towards a multilingual fool.
In the play. *The subject referred to is Sir Andrew Aguecheek, a friend of Sir Toby and a notorious drunkard*

Accent, not recognizing the a. - ... pardon me, that any accent breaking from thy tongue should 'scape the true acquaintance of mine ear
"... pardon me,
That any accent breaking from thy tongue
Should 'scape the true acquaintance of mine ear." (KJ.5.6)
In the play. *Hubert does not immediately recognize Ph. Faulconbridge from his accent.*

Acceptance, a. and resignation to the will of Heaven - ... but heaven hath a hand in these events...
"But heaven hath a hand in these events,
To whose high will we bound our calm contents" (KRII.5.2)
See also entries for 'Destiny, beyond our control'
In the play. *The Duke of York gives an account to his wife of the crowds' reception to the procession of the usurper Bolingbroke and the usurped King Richard. Bolingbroke is the favorite by a long shot.*

Acceptance, a. of what may come - I do find it cowardly and vile for fear of what might fall...
"... I do find it cowardly and vile,
For fear of what might fall, so to prevent
The time of life; arming myself with patience
To stay the providence of some high powers
That govern us below." (JC.5.1)
In the play. *Brutus' answer to Cassius who asks what they should do should they lose the battle of Philippi. 'Prevent the time of life' means ending one's own life for fear of the future.*

Accounting, a. above board, request for an audit -... call me before the exactest auditors...
"If you suspect my husbandry or falsehood,
Call me before the exactest auditors,
And set me on the proof." (TOA.2.2)
If anyone suspects your accounting or accounting practices.
In the play. *Informed by servant- accountant Flavius of the poor financial conditions Timon asks Flavius how this could have happened. Flavius assures Timon that the problem is not with the accounting.*

Accusation, a. rejected – I have a thousand spirits in my breast to answer twenty thousand such as you.
"I have a thousand spirits in my breast,
To answer twenty thousand such as you." (KRII.4.1)
A retort to an accusation or to an improper remark.
In the play. *Aumerle to courtier who accuses him of having slain Gloucester in Calais.*

Accusation, a. unfair – take good heed you charge not in your spleen a noble person.
"... take good heed
You charge not in your spleen a noble person,
And spoil your nobler soul!" (KHVIII.1.2)
Persuade not to lodge an unfair accusation against an honest person.
In the play. *Queen Kathryn pleads for Buckingham, accused by Wolsey through a surveyor who had previously been fired by Buckingham for bribery.*

Accusation, answer to a. - The blood is hot that must be cool'd for this.

"The blood is hot that must be cool'd for this:
Yet can I not of such tame patience boast
As to be hush'd and nought at all to say." (KRII.1.1)
Interrupt an unfair statement that affects you directly.
In the play. *Mowbray responds to the accusations of treason by Bolingbroke.*

Accusation, false a. engendered by rancor - ... It issues from the rancour of a villain
"...as for the rest appeal'd,
It issues from the rancour of a villain,
A recreant and most degenerate traitor" (KRII.1.1)
In the play. *Mowbray admits to one previous fault already forgiven by the King and now defends himself against Bolingbroke's accusations of treason for having killed the duke of Gloucester.*

Accusation, false a., innocence will triumph – innocence shall make false accusation blush.
"I doubt not then but innocence shall make
False accusation blush." (WT.3.2)
Modify to 'I doubt not but innocence shall make false accusation blush' if she indeed accuses you of something you have not done.
In the play. *The virtuous Hermione, wife of Leontes, king of Sicilia is unjustly accused of adultery by her over-jealous husband.*

Accusation, false a. or false suspicion – you do me shameful injury falsely to draw me...
"My lord, you do me shameful injury
Falsely to draw me in these vile suspects." (KRIII.1.3)
Reject any accusation. See also entries for 'Defense from accusation'.
In the play. *Richard tries to imply that Elizabeth is responsible for Clarence's imprisonment – while Richard is actually plotting to have Clarence killed.*

Accusation, personal a. (here of corruption and treason), prompted by evidence not malice – ... whom from the flow of gall I name not but from sincere motions...
"... this top-proud fellow,
Whom from the flow of gall I name not but
From sincere motions...I do know
To be corrupt and treasonous" (KHVIII.1.1)
In the play. *Buckingham confides with Norfolk about the corruption of Cardinal Wolsey, currently a favorite of the King (and Buckingham's sworn enemy).*

Accusations, explanation for the false a. - And that engenders thunder in his breast and makes him roar these accusations forth.
"And that engenders thunder in his breast,
And makes him roar these accusations forth." (KHVI p1.3.1)
Retort to a false accusation, e.g. "Your own guilt engenders thunder in your breast and makes you roar...forth'. Also a colorful definition of anger, 'does this engender thunder in your breast?'
In the play. *Bishop of Winchester accuses Gloucester of not wanting anyone but himself near the king.*

Accusations, preventing sting of a. – Comest thou with deep premeditated lines...
"Comest thou with deep premeditated lines,
With written pamphlets studiously devised
Humphrey of Gloucester?" (KHVI.p1.3.1)
In the play. *The Bishop of Winchester and Gloucester are enemies and are ready to square out in front of the king.*

Accusers, attitude towards a. and you are innocent - I am richer than my base accusers.
"Yet, I am richer than my base accusers,
That never knew what truth meant."
(KHVIII.2.1)
Take a noble stance after you have lost as a result of false accusations.
In the play. *Buckingham' last words after he is condemned to death upon charges of treason trumped up by Cardinal Wolsey*

Ache, stomach ache - There is so hot a summer in my bosom…
"There is so hot a summer in my bosom,
That all my bowels crumble up with dust." (KJ.5.7)
When the restaurant food was not so good. See also entries for 'Health-care', 'Dieting', 'Apologies for behavior caused by indisposition'
In the play. *King John has allegedly been poisoned by a monk.*

Achievement, a. requires effort - Pain pays the income of each precious thing…
"Pain pays the income of each precious thing;
Huge rocks, high winds, strong pirates, shelves and sands,
The merchant fears, ere rich at home he lands." **(ROL)**
In the poem. *Tarquin's rationalization of the difficulties he met in reaching Lucrece's chamber. 'Ere' = 'Before'*

Achievement, happily married to the woman of choice – And happily I have arrived at last unto the wished haven of my bliss.
"And happily I have arrived at the last
Unto the wished haven of my bliss." (TOS.5.1)
Answer to 'Are you happy with your marriage?' or equivalent – assuming, of course, that you are happy.
In the play. *Lucentio, now happily married to Bianca discloses his true identity to his father in law Baptista.*

Achievements, a. worth praising - … And make her chronicle as rich with praise as is the ooze and bottom of the sea with sunken wreck and sunless treasuries.
"….And make her chronicle as rich with praise
As is the ooze and bottom of the sea
With sunken wreck and sunless treasuries" (KHV.1.2)
Introduction to a speaker enumerating his/her achievements. E.G. 'Of him we can say that his chronicle is as rich with praise… treasuries'.
In the play. *Canterbury allays Henry's fear of a Scottish attack by reminding how previously a King of Scotland had been captured by the English, therefore making England's chronicles 'as rich as praise'.*

Achievements, value of past a. not to be forgotten - the service of the foot being once gangrened…
"The service of the foot
Being once gangrened, is not then respected
For what before it was?" (COR.3.1)
Bring to attention the previous services of a now maligned person (employee, manager, politician etc.). See also 'Perseverance, in praise of p.' - 'Remembering, the bad more remembered than the good'.
In the play. *Menenius attempts to reason with the citizens who are enraged at Coriolanus. By means of an example Menenius means that Coriolanus had saved Rome and should be respected in any event, even if now the citizens are mad at him.*

Acknowledgment, a. and appreciation of help given – Thou art all the comfort the gods will diet me with.
"Thou art all the comfort
The gods will diet me with" (CYM.3.4)
In the play. *Imogen to Pisanio who assists with her escape from the pursuit of the evil Cloten.*

Acquaintance, a. superficial - we know each other faces; but for our hearts...
"We know each other faces;
But for our hearts, he knows no more of mine
Than I of yours; nor I no more of his, than you of mine." (KRIII.3.4)
Answer to the question, 'How well do you know him?'
In the play. *The Bishop of Ely questions Buckingham on the leanings of Richard III as regards the coronation of the Prince of Wales, (after Edward IV has died). Buckingham answers evasively.*

Acquaintance, a. unpleasant - and long to know each other worse...
AENEAS. We know each other well.
DIOMEDES. We do; and long to know each other worse." (TC.4.1)
Answer to 'Do you know each other?'
See also 'Dislike, mutual d. expressed'.
In the play. *Diomedes is in Troy to deliver the Trojan prisoner Antinor and to pick up Cressida in exchange.*

Acquaintance, worth of a. recognized - I am blest in your acquaintance.
"I am blest in your acquaintance." (MWW.2.2)
In the play. *Falstaff likes to have come across Master Brook (alias Mr. Ford).*

Act, a. not done under any condition - ... Not the world's mass of vanity could make me.
"To do the act that might the addition earn
Not the world's mass of vanity could make me." (OTH.4.2)
Emphatic refusal to do something you judge dishonorable.
In the play. *Accused by Othello of being a whore, Desdemona, still believing Iago honest, complains with him that she would not to an adulterous act ever.*

Act, dreadful a. that will come to haunt his authors - too many curses on their heads...
"... it calls,
I fear, too many curses on their heads,
That were the authors." (KHVIII.2)
Predict (or justify) the disasters that often follow injustice. See also 'Sleeplessness, nightmares caused by impending critical decision'.
In the play. *A citizen commenting on the unjust execution of Buckingham*

Act, extreme a. shaping all things to come - ... this blow be the be-all and the end-all here.
"...that but this blow
Might be the be-all and the end-all here" (M.1.7)
In the play. *Macbeth meditates on his impending crime of murder.*

Action, a. contrary to purpose - So play the foolish throngs with one that swoons...
"So play the foolish throngs with one that swoons;
Come all to help him, and so stop the air
By which he should revive" (MFM.2.4)
See also 'Intentions, good i. gone awry - We are not the first who with best meaning have incurred the worst.'
In the play. *Isabel calls again on Angelo to plead for Claudio's (her brother) life. Angelo by now obsessed with Isabel compares his situation to that where a good intent (Isabel's love for her brother) has a bad effect (Angelo's increased obsession).*

Action, a. contrary to purpose - That were to blow at fire in hope to quench it.
CLEON. My Dionyza, shall we rest here,
And by relating tales of griefs,
See if it will teach us to forget our own?
DIONYZA. That were to blow at fire in hope to quench it." (PER.1.4)
Use the last line, when you believe that proposed action will have results contrary to the intended effect.
In the play. *The scene is in Tharsus, ruled by King Cleon and wife Dionyza. The city is in the grip of a famine and Cleon does not know what to do.*

Action, a. contrary to purpose - That were to enlard his fat already pride and add more coals to Cancer when he burns…
"That were to enlard his fat already pride
And add more coals to Cancer when he burns
With entertaining great Hyperion." (TC.2.3)
In the play. *Ulysses explains why Ajax should not plead with Achilles to rejoin the fight against the Trojans. The sun is in Cancer from June 22 to July 22, at the peak of summer.*

Action, a. contrary to what needed - you rub the sore when you should bring the plaster.
"The truth you speak doth lack some gentleness
And time to speak it in: you rub the sore,
When you should bring the plaster." (TEM.2.1)
Point out a rude and untimely remark. Or indicate that words or behavior hurt rather than help, 'You rub the sore when… plaster.'
In the play. *Gonzalo addresses Sebastian who, believing Ferdinand to be lost and dead, talks about the matter without concern over the pain it may bring to others.*

Action, a. critical and urgent - And 'tis no little reason bids us speed…
"And 'tis no little reason bids us speed,
To save our heads by raising of a head" (KHIVp1.1.3)
In the play. *Worcester explains the critical need to rebel rather than acquiesce to the will of King Henry.*

Action, a. made useless by its timing - … this is like the mending of highways in summer, where the ways are fair enough.
"Why, this is like the mending of highways
In summer, where the ways are fair enough" (MOV.5.1)
In the play. *In an extremely improbable plot Portia and Nerissa are not recognized in their man-disguise by their respective husbands, Bassanio and Gratiano. Therefore the two ladies can respectively claim to have slept with men (i.e. themselves). In a somewhat stretched analogy Gratiano compares the apparent cuckoldry to an unnecessary action, such as (in Shakespeare's times) fixing the roads when it was not necessary.*

Action, a. preferable to inaction - A stirring dwarf we do allowance give before a sleeping giant.
"A stirring dwarf we do allowance give
Before a sleeping giant. Tell him so" (TC.2.3)
In the play. *Agamennon gives Patroclus a message for Achilles.*

Action, a. requiring urgent and strong response – 't is not sleepy business but must be look'd to speedily…
"'T is not sleepy business;
But must be look'd to speedily and strongly." (CYM.3.5)

Prompt and reinforce the need for action. See also entries for 'Urgent business, u. action required'
In the play. *The Queen prompts her husband Cymbeline to get ready for war with the Romans after the ultimatum delivered by Lucius.*

Action, a. requiring urgent and strong response – The affair cries haste and speed must answer it.
"The affair cries haste,
And speed must answer it." (OTH.1.3)
Indicate urgency. See also 'Urgent business, u. action required'
In the play. *The Duke commands Othello to leave for Cyprus immediately to defend the island from an imminent attack by the Turks*

Action, a. that cannot be delayed - This weighty business will not brook delay.
"This weighty business will not brook delay." (KHVI p2.1.1)
Emphasize urgency
In the play. *The business urged by the Cardinal is the unseating of the duke of Gloucester from the position of protector to the King.*

Action, a. that promises to be successful - ... rich advantage of a promised glory as smiles upon the forehead of this action.
"So rich advantage of a promised glory
As smiles upon the forehead of this action" (TC.2.2)
Make the lines part of a toast for example at the conclusion of an agreement or after a decision is reached to pursue a new course of action.
In the play. *Hector wants to return Helen to the Greeks but Troilus exhorts him to keep her. By doing so the war would continue with opportunities for glory.*

Action, a. vs. speculation – Thoughts speculative their unsure hopes relate but certain issue strokes must arbitrate.
"Thoughts speculative their unsure hopes relate,
But certain issue strokes must arbitrate" (M.5.4)
In the play. *Siward to Macduff as the decisive battle with Macbeth is imminent.*

Action, abominable a. - the deed you undertake is damnable.
"The deed you undertake is damnable." (KRIII.1.4)
Emphatically denounce your opposition.
In the play. *Clarence tries to stop his murderers without success.*

Action, concurrence in the proposed action - ... if you say ay, the king will not say no.
"Strong reasons make strong actions: let us go:
If you say ay, the king will not say no." (KJ.3.4)
Change 'the king' for your name. – See also 'Agreeing, a. with the majority'.
In the play. *Lewis agrees with the plan promoted by Cardinal Pandulph to attack England.*

Action, doing the best with the means available - The means that heaven yields must be embraced and not neglected.
"The means that heaven yields must be embraced,
And not neglected..." (KRII.3.2)
In the play. *The Bishop of Carlysle tries to encourage King Richard, who has been abandoned by most Lords.*

Action, eagerness for a. – let the hours be short, till fields, and blows, and groans applaud our sport!
"O, let the hours be short,
Till fields, and blows, and groans applaud our sport!" (KHIV p1.1.3)

Conclusion of a motivational speech to promote an aggressive project.
In the play. *Hotspur looks forward to battling King Henry IV (Bolingbroke).*

Action, eloquence in a. – for in such business action is eloquence.
"… For in such business
Action is eloquence, and the eyes of the ignorant
More learned than the ears."
(COR.3.2)
Explain the need for advertising that is flashy and has action, to appeal to the masses. See also entries for 'Opinion, your op. on crowds and masses'.
In the play. *Coriolanus' mother counsels Coriolanus to soften his approach to the citizens and make gestures of deference and concern (action).*

Action, immediate a. lest resolution will falter - I must be brief, lest resolution drop out of mine eyes, in tender womanish tears.
"I must be brief, lest resolution drop
Out of mine eyes, in tender womanish tears." (KJ.4.1)
Alternative to 'I must do it while I am determined or I will not do it'.
In the play. *Hubert has pangs of conscience before murdering young Arthur.*

Action, invitation to a. - … with that spur as he would to the lip of his mistress.
"Each man to his stool, with that spur as he would to
the lip of his mistress" (TOA.3.5)
Conclusion after describing the task at hand.
In the play. *Timon urges his parasitic guests to their last dinner.*

Action, invitation to take corrective a. - Speak, strike, redress!
"Speak, strike, redress!" (JC.2.1)
In the play. *Brutus reads from a letter addressed to him by other conspirators. The redress referred to is the alleged abuse of power by Caesar.*

Action, justifying honorable a. - … what I did, I did in honour, led by the impartial conduct of my soul…
"...what I did, I did in honour,
Led by the impartial conduct of my soul:
And never shall you see that I will beg
A ragged and forestall'd remission."
(KHIV.p2.5.2)
When, after having done your duty, you are upbraided for having done so. Or when you acted honorably, though against your interests.
In the play. *The Chief Justice does not regret having judged sternly the Prince of Wales, now king.*

Action, let's go – our corn's to reap for yet our tithe's to sow.
"…Come, let us go:
Our corn's to reap, for yet our tithe's to sow." (MFM.4.1)
In the play. *The 'corn to reap' is the unmasking of Angelo's hypocrisy and foiling of his scheme to have Claudio executed.*

Action, need to act notwithstanding possible censure – If we shall stand still in fear our motion...
"… If we shall stand still,
In fear our motion will be mock'd or carp'd at,
We should take root here where we sit, or sit
State-statues only." (KHVIII.1.1)
Encourage action and dispel fears of ensuing criticism ('mocked or carped at') by portraying the effects of inaction ('take root here where we sit…'). See also 'Custom, c. as an obstacle to positive change - What custom wills, in all things should we do't, the dust of antique time would lie unswept…'

In the play. *Wolsey is defending his levying of higher taxes against the criticism of Queen Catherine.*

Action, need to act notwithstanding possible censure – We must not stint our necessary actions...
"We must not stint
Our necessary actions, in the fear
To cope with malicious censurers."
(KHVIII.1.2)
Encourage action and dispel fears of ensuing criticism.
In the play. *Wolsey is prompting the king to action.*

Action, quick a. needed as time goes by quickly - let's take the instant by the forward top.
"Let's take the instant by the forward top,
For we are old, and on our quick'st decrees
The inaudible and noiseless foot of time
Steals, ere we can effect them."
(AWEW.5.3)
Exhort the audience to prompt action with minor adaptation, e.g. 'Let's take the instant by the forward top, because… on our quick'st decrees the inaudible and noiseless foot of time steals, ere we can effect them.' See also 'Procrastination to be avoided'.
In the play. *The King has forgiven Bertram for his mistakes and now suggests that Bertram marry Lafeu's daughter*

Action, ready for a. - I am settled, and bend up each corporal agent to this terrible feat.
"I am settled, and bend up
Each corporal agent to this terrible feat." (M.1.7)
Answer to 'Are you ready?'
In the play. *Macbeth declares himself ready to murder King Duncan.*

Action, ready for a. if mind is ready - All things are ready, if our minds be so.
"All things are ready, if our minds be so." (KHV.4.3)
A final persuading statement at end of presentation.
In the play. *Henry V is ready for battle.*

Action, reason for a. made public - ... and public reasons shall be rendered of Caesar's death.
"... and public reasons shall be rendered
Of Caesar's death." (JC.3.2)
Answer to a journalist when you wish to delay to announce the reason for some policy or deliberation, e.g. 'and public reason shall be rendered of (occurrence)'.
In the play. *Brutus manages the mode and procedure of explaining to the people Caesar's death.*

Action, request for advice on how or what to do - let your own discretion be your tutor.
"…let your own discretion be your tutor; suit the action to the word, the word to the action; with this special observation, that you o'erstep not the modesty of nature… " (H.3.2)
Answer to "What shall I do?"
In the play. *Hamlet gives advise to the players for the oncoming production, not to saw the air too much with their hands, not to be too wild or too tame, just use discretion.*

Action, resolution to act quickly - ay, that's the way, dull not device by coldness and delay.
"…ay, that's the way
Dull not device by coldness and delay." (OTH.2.3)
In the play. *The perfidious Iago has finalized his plan to doom everyone but himself.*

Action, senseless a. - What a pretty thing man is when he goes in his

doublet and hose and leaves off his wit!
"What a pretty thing man is when he goes in his doublet and hose and leaves off his wit!" (MAAN.5.1)
In the play. *Don Pedro comments on the challenge that Benedick has thrown to Claudio.*

Action, urgent a. required against enemy - The land is burning; Percy stands on high, and either we or they must lower lie.
"The land is burning; Percy stands on high;
And either we or they must lower lie." (KHIV.3.3)
Change 'Percy' to the name of the enemy you are facing. It could also be the name of your competitor, or competing company.
In the play. *Prince Henry to Falstaff as the rebels are gathering strength*

Actions, a. not corresponding to words - ... your words and performance are no kin together.
IAGO. Will you hear me Roderigo?
RODERIGO. Faith, I have heard too much; for your words and performance are no kin together." (OTH.4.3)
Extract, 'Your words and performance are no kin together.' Good for a politician fighting the incumbent.
In the play. *Roderigo complains with Iago that, notwithstanding Iago's promises, Desdemona is farther away than ever.*

Actions, a. speak more than words - Words to the heat of deeds too cold breath gives.
"Words to the heat of deeds too cold breath gives." (M.2.1)
The apparent discrepancy ('gives' instead of 'give') is also found elsewhere in Shakespeare. Use 'give' for consistency of meaning. See also 'Words, w. that are no

deeds - ... 'tis a kind of good deed to say well and yet words are no deeds.'
In the play. *Macbeth's soliloquy observing the dagger with which he will shortly kill King Duncan. Macbeth has some reservations but is edge forward towards the murder by a force he cannot resist.*

Actions, nobility in a. and thoughts - my actions are as noble as my thoughts, that never relish'd of a base descent.
My actions are as noble as my thoughts,
That never relish'd of a base descent." (PER.2.5)
Declare the honorability of your intentions. See also entries for 'Reliability' - 'Honor' – 'Reputation, value placed on own r., spotless r. an asset'.
In the play. *To test Pericles, Simonides accuses him of treachery for having bewitched Thaisa into loving him (Pericles). Pericles rejects the accusation with noble words.*

Actions, past a. cannot be remedied – Look, what is done cannot be now amended, men shall deal unadvisedly sometimes...
"Look, what is done cannot be now amended:
Men shall deal unadvisedly sometimes,
Which after hours give leisure to repent." (KRIII.4.4)
A good line of self defense when reminded of some past action you should regret. See also entries for 'Regret' *** 'Remorse' *** 'Repentance'
In the play. *Richard III talks with Queen Elizabeth, widow of Henry IV. After having killed her sons he now wants to marry her daughter and pretends to regret the murders.*

Actor, capable of feigning as needed - ... ghastly looks are at my service, like enforced smiles…

"... ghastly looks
**Are at my service, like enforced smiles;
And both are ready in their offices,
At any time, to grace my stratagems."**
(KRIII.3.5)
Answer to 'Can you put up a good show?' E.G. 'I have various tricks, ghastly looks....stratagems'
In the play. *Buckingham to Richard. Buckingham will put up a show with the mayor of London to ensure that the mayor and the citizens approve of Richard becoming king (instead of the rightful successor.*

**Actors, their quality in acting – The best in this kind are but shadows…
"The best in this kind are but shadows; and the worst are no worse, if imagination amend them."**
(MND.5.1)
In the play. *Theseus moderates Hyppolita's criticism of the amateur actors who have produced a play for them.*

ADMIRATION

The wish to be admired is universal. Those who say they don't either lie or hope (maybe subconsciously) to be admired for their being an exception. It is an un-resolvable dilemma with some similarity to the paradox of Epimenides of Crete who said that all Cretans are liars.

The frontier between admiration and flattery is a verbal no man's land, when you address directly the object of your admiration (or flattery). We could argue, somewhat arbitrarily, that if you tell her that she is an object of admiration by you as well as others (even better by VIPs or, as in the case of Cleopatra, a king), your admiration is objective. See entry 'Admiration, worth to be admired by kings – I was a morsel for a monarch...'

You must, of course, assess her character. If she is looking for the proverbial white knight in shining armor (or his modern equivalent) and you do not measure up to her expectation, the compliment may backfire. If she takes your statement of collective admiration at face value, she may decide to look for the knight you say she is worthy of.

In most cases, however, telling her that she is an object of admiration by many (including yourself), can be a form of re-assurance and it has the ring of objectivity. It helps dispel a potential concern that yours is just an infatuation, based purely on the exclusive attraction she has on you.

**Admiration, a. and love without flattery - I cannot flatter; I do defy the tongues of soothers but…
"I cannot flatter; I do defy
The tongues of soothers; but a braver place
In my heart's love hath no man than yourself"** (HIV.p1.4.1)
When you actually wish to flatter without appearing to do so. Most people enjoy flattery even when they deny that they do, as Julius Caesar. See 'Flattery, flattered for hating flatterers - ...when I tell him he hates flatterers he says he does, being then most flattered'
In the play. *Hotspur to the Earl of Douglas at a camp near Shrewsbury.*

**Admiration, a. for adversary unconditional - And were I any thing but what I am, I would wish me only he.
"And were I any thing but what I am, I would wish me only he."** (COR.1.1)
Express your respect or sportive admiration for an enemy or competitor.
In the play. *Coriolanus admires his enemy, the chief of the Volsces (and an enemy of Rome) for his courage*

Admiration, not flattery – I do defy the tongues of soothers; but a braver place in my heart's love …
"*… I do defy
The tongues of soothers; but a braver place
In my heart's love hath no man than yourself*" (KHIVp1.4.1)
In the play. *Hotspur to comrade in arms, the Earl of Douglas.*

Admiration, she is top of the list – … the top of admiration! Worth what's dearest to the world!
"*Admired Miranda!
Indeed the top of admiration! worth What's dearest to the world!*" (TEM.3.1)
Change 'Miranda' to the name of the applicable lady. To continue the compliment see 'Best, compliment, you are the best – full many a lady I have eyed with best regards…'
In the play. *Ferdinand asks Miranda what is her name. Her reply prompts him to utter a compliment.*

Admiration, worth to be admired by kings – I was a morsel for a monarch…
"*…Broad fronted Caesar,
When thou wast here above the ground, I was
A morsel for a monarch; and great Pompey
Would stand and make his eyes grow in my brow;
There would he anchor his aspect, and die
With looking on his life.*" (AC.1)
Shorten it to 'you are a morsel for a monarch' and she will feel like royalty.
In the play. *Cleopatra to Alexas, commenting on her past conquests.*

Adoration, a. not just friendship - I profess myself her adorer, not her friend.
"*I profess myself her adorer, not her friend.*" (CYM.1.4)
Answer to 'What do you think of her?' or change 'her' to 'you' for a direct answer to the party involved.
In the play. *The subject of adoration is Imogen and the adorer is Posthumous Leonatus, who is embarking on a debate about the degree of faithfulness of ladies in England and Italy.*

Adultery, a. not punished - Thou shalt not die: die for adultery! No: the wren goes to 't…
"*I pardon that man's life. What was thy cause? Adultery?
Thou shalt not die: die for adultery! No:
The wren goes to 't, and the small gilded fly
Does lecher in my sight.*" (KL.4.6)
In the play. *King Lear addresses the blinded Gloucester at Dover.*

Advance, applying for an advance or raise - I do beseech you, as in the way of taste to give me now a little benefit…
"*I do beseech you, as in the way of taste,
To give me now a little benefit,
Out of those many registered in promise.*" (TC.3.3)
Ask for a raise after accomplishing what was requested of you. See also 'Patience, asking for p. or a raise - I am much too venturous in tempting of your patience…' – Entries for 'Financial status, challenging' – 'Love, prosperity an essential ingredient for l. - Prosperity's the very bond of love, whose fresh complexion and whose heart together affliction alters.'
In the play. *The traitor Calchas who has defected to the Greeks now wants a reward, namely that his daughter Cressida be exchanged for a Trojan prisoner held by the Greeks.*

Advantage, better taking a. than trusting - 'Tis better using France than trusting France
MONTAGUE But the safer when 'tis back'd with France.
HASTINGS 'Tis better using France than trusting France (KHVI.p3.4.1)
Apply to a person or any other state by changing 'France' as appropriate.
In the play. *The new king Edward IV has slighted France by reneging on a marriage commitment to the Lady Bona of France. Montague and Hastings debate the pros and cons of a French alliance*

Advantage, edge, planning for strategic a. - ... advantage is a better soldier than rashness.
"Though we seemed dead, we did but sleep: advantage is a better soldier than rashness." (KHV.3.6)
When you oppose taking rash action without planning or thinking about it.
In the play. *Montjoy tells Henry V why the French did not check and stop him at Harfleur for strategic purposes.*

Adventure, move prompted by a sense of a. – Such wind as scatters young men through the world.
HORTENSIO. - What happy gale Blows you to Padua here, from old Verona?
PETRUCHIO. Such wind as scatters young men through the world,
To seek their fortunes farther than at home." (TOS.1.2)
Answer to 'What made you come here?'
In the play. *Hortensio meets Petruchio and asks him what prompted him to relocate to Padua from Verona.*

Adventure, travelling for a. and learning - ... as he that leaves a shallow plash to plunge him in the deep ...
"...I have Pisa left
And am to Padua come, as he that leaves
A shallow plash to plunge him in the deep
And with satiety seeks to quench his thirst." (TOS.1.1)
In the play. *Lucentio tell his servant Tranio what led him to leave native Pisa for Padua. 'Plash' = 'A pool, a collection of water'.*

Adversary, defeat of a. crucial for survival – ... the welfare of us all hangs on the cutting short that fraudful man.
"Take heed, my lord; the welfare of us all
Hangs on the cutting short that fraudful man" (KHVI.p2.3.1)
In the play. *Q. Margaret to King Henry referring to Gloucester whom she hates.*

Adversary, inhuman and pitiless - A stony adversary, an inhuman wretch, uncapable of pity...
"A stony adversary, an inhuman wretch
uncapable of pity, void and empty
From any dram of mercy." (MOV.4.1)
In the play. *The Duke of Venice, tells Antonio what kind of adversary (Shylock), he will have to deal with.*

Adversary, noble a. – He is a lion that I am proud to hunt.
"... he is a lion
That I am proud to hunt." (COR.1.1)
Express your respect or sportive admiration for an enemy or competitor.
In the play. *Coriolanus admires his enemy, the chief of the Volsces (and an enemy of Rome) for his courage.*

Adversary, paying homage to a valiant a. - His valour shown upon our crests to-day hath taught us to cherish such high deeds even in the bosom of our adversaries.
"His valour shown upon our crests to-day

Hath taught us how to cherish such high deeds
Even in the bosom of our adversaries." (KHIV.p1.5.5)
Introduction of a political adversary when for once his action helps you or your cause.
In the play. *The Prince of Wales refers to Douglas, valiant fighter caught prisoner at the battle of Shrewsbury.*

Adversary, political a. to be defeated – He's a rank weed… and must root him out.
"…He's a rank weed, Sir Thomas, And we must root him out. From your affairs
I hinder you too long: good night, Sir Thomas" (KHVIII.5.1)
In the play. *Gardiner to Lovell referring to Cardinal Cranmer.*

Adversity, a. as a test of the spirit - Where is your ancient courage…
…extremity was the trier of spirits.
"Where is your ancient courage? You were us'd
To say extremity was the trier of spirits". (COR.4.1)
Sustain the spirit in critical circumstances, e.g. 'They say extremity is the trier of spirits'.
In the play. *Coriolanus says farewell to mother and wife and scolds them because they are crying.*

Adversity, a. assembles strange characters - … misery acquaints a man with strange bedfellows.
"… misery acquaints a man with strange bedfellows." (TEM.2.2)
Describe a questionable character met in adverse conditions.
In the play. *Trinculo has repaired to a cave to shelter himself from a storm. In the cave he finds the foul Caliban, who smells like fish. See 'Odor, unpleasant – indignation to the nose'.*

Adversity, a. put to good use - Sweet are the uses of adversity…
"Sweet are the uses of adversity, Which, like the toad, ugly and venomous,
Wears yet a precious jewel in his head." (AYLI.2.1)
Deliver a positive message in negative circumstances. — See also 'Philosophy, p. as a remedy'
In the play. *In the forest of Arden, Duke S. comments positively on the turn of events whereby an adversity (his being pushed out by the usurping brother) has made it possible for Duke S. to appreciate the beauty of living with nature. The lines describing life in the woods make a beautiful copy for a tourist brochure or as a comment on the dramatic difference between simple living and corporate life.*
Hath not old custom made this life more sweet
Than that of painted pomp? Are not these woods
More free from peril than the envious court?
Here feel we but the penalty of Adam,
The seasons' difference, as the icy fang
And churlish chiding of the winter's wind,
Which, when it bites and blows upon my body,
Even till I shrink with cold, I smile and say
'This is no flattery: these are counsellors
That feelingly persuade me what I am.'
Smile and remember the lines when you are shrinking with cold following a change in seasons, the penalty of Adam.

Adversity, affected by a. – A man I am cross'd with adversity.
"Then know that I have little wealth to lose:
A man I am cross'd with adversity" (TGV.4.1)
Try to persuade the traffic court judge to reduce your traffic fine.

In the play. *Valentine, banned from Milan is ambushed by robbers and declares his poverty.*

Adversity, attitude towards a. - Let me embrace these sour adversities, for wise men say it is the wisest course.
"Let me embrace these sour adversities,
For wise men say it is the wisest course." (KHVI p3.3.1)
Answer to remarks of sympathy or to the question, 'What will you do now?'
In the play. *Henry VI reflects on the lost battle of Towton and after having been taken prisoner.*

Adversity, positive attitude towards a. - Some falls are means the happier to arise.
"...Be cheerful; wipe thine eyes
Some falls are means the happier to arise." (CYM.4.2)
Put a positive spin after you have been fired.
In the play. *The Roman Consul Caius Lucius comforts Imogen, who is wearing a boy's disguise and has arrived dejected at the Roman camp.*

Adversity, some g. can be found in a. - There is some soul of goodness in things evil...
"There is some soul of goodness in things evil,
Would men observingly distil it out.
For our bad neighbour makes us early stirrers,
Which is both healthful and good husbandry."** (KHV.4.1)
Find reasons to uplift the spirits of your audience in case of a temporary setback or retrenchment. See also 'Good, finding good in bad' - 'Complaint after problems useless' – 'Complaint useless'.
In the play. *King Henry to Bedford before the battle of Agincourt. The 'things evil' are the French who, however, cause the English to prepare themselves early for battle (thus distilling a 'soul of goodness').*

Adversity, spirit of acceptance of a. eases the spirit - 'Tis good for men to love their present pains upon example; so the spirit is eased…
"'Tis good for men to love their present pains
Upon example; so the spirit is eased:
And when the mind is quicken'd, out of doubt,
The organs, though defunct and dead before,
Break up their drowsy grave and newly move,
With casted slough and fresh legerity." (KHV.4.1)
Answer to comments of the type 'I am sorry you have to do this'. See also 'Work, it does not matter if it is hard w. provided we like it - The labour we delight in physics pain.'
In the play. *K. Henry's answer to Erpingham who gallantly claims to actually see value in hard times and even in finding agreeable the poor accommodations (near Agincourt). 'Slough' is the dry, shed (casted) skin of a snake. 'Legerity' is lightness.*

Adversity, turning a. around - ... that can translate the stubbornness of fortune into so quiet and so sweet a style.
"Happy is your grace,
That can translate the stubbornness of fortune
Into so quiet and so sweet a style." (AYLI.2.1)
Adapt as an example of ability to adapt to circumstances. See also 'Philosophy, p. as a remedy to adversity.'
In the play. *Amiens, a member of Duke Senior' entourage, praises the Duke.*

Advertising - To things of sale a seller's praise belongs…
"To things of sale a seller's praise belongs" (LLL.4.3)
See also 'Bargaining, dispraising the value of what you wish to buy - ... you do as

chapmen do dispraise the thing that you desire to buy...'
In the play. *Biron is so enamoured of Rosaline and almost fears that any praise of her may be inferior to her actual worth. See 'Speech, introduction to a flattering or praising s. - Lend me the flourish of all gentle tongues'. 'Chapman' = 'Buyer'*

Advertising, false a. – Thus credulous fools are caught.
"Thus credulous fools are caught" (OTH.4.1)
In the play. *The credulous Othello has bought completely Iago's tale about Desdemona's infidelity.*

Advice, a. from a world hater - Hate all, curse all, show charity to none…
"Hate all, curse all, show charity to none,
But let the famish'd flesh slide from the bone,
Ere thou relieve the beggar; give to dogs
What thou deny'st to men..." (TOA.4.3)
In the play. *Timon relinquishes his lately found gold to his faithful servant Flavius with the words of advice of a misanthrope.*

Advice, a. hopeless to a lover or a sensualist - …that art a votary to fond desire.
VALENTINE (to Proteus). But wherefore waste I time to counsel thee,
That art a votary to fond desire?" (TGV.1)
Decline to give advice to a lover.
In the play. *Valentine's skeptical view of love.*

Advice, a. not to be rude or patronizing – (Haughtiness) …leaves behind a stain…
"(Haughtiness) … leaves behind a stain
Upon the beauty of all parts besides
Beguiling them of commendation." (KHIV p1.3)
A word of advice to whomever may profit from it.
In the play. *Worcester admonishes and counsels Hotspur to be less rude towards others.*

Advice, a. not wanted - … cease thy counsel which falls into mine ear as profitless as water in a sieve.
"I pray thee, cease thy counsel,
Which falls into mine ear as profitless
As water in a sieve." (MAAN.5.1)
Indicate that you have had enough of being given advice or that you will in any event disregard it.
In the play. *Antonio counsels his brother Leonato not to torture himself after the events that led to the accusations against Hero, but Leonato shrugs the advice away.*

Advice, a. on cultivating friendship - Those friends thou hast, and their adoption tried, grapple them to thy soul with hoops of steel.
"Those friends thou hast, and their adoption tried,
Grapple them to thy soul with hoops of steel;
But do not dull thy palm with entertainment
Of each new-hatch'd, unfledged comrade" (H.1.3)
A comment on friendship in a speech. Or apply the first two lines to yourself to indicate your feeling about friendship or in answer to general questions about friendship. E.G. 'The friends I have and their adoption tried, I grapple…steel'
In the play. *Polonius to son Laertes who leaves for Paris.*

Advice, a. on general behavior in life - Keep thy foot out of brothels, thy hand out of plackets, thy pen from lenders' books…
"…keep thy foot out of brothels, thy hand out of plackets, thy pen from

lenders' books, and defy the foul fiend" (KL.3.4)
In the play. *Edgar, pretending to be mad, tells of himself and his philosophy to K. Lear and fool.*

Advice, a. on general behavior with others and way of life – give your thoughts no tongue...
"…Give your thoughts no tongue,
Nor any unproportionate thought his act.
Be thou familiar, but by no means vulgar." (H.1.3)
Turn it around and use it as an answer to the following questions: 'What do you think about it?', if you do not want to answer, e.g. 'I give my thoughts no tongue'. Or 'What can you tell me about yourself?' or 'Are you gregarious?' E.G. 'I give my thoughts no tongue, nor any unproportionate thought his act. I am familiar but by no means vulgar.'
In the play. *Polonius launches a volley of counsels to his son Laertes who leaves for Paris.*

Advice, a. on general behavior with others and way of life - Love all, trust a few, do wrong to none.
"Love all, trust a few,
Do wrong to none...
 ...keep thy friend
Under thy own life's key: be check'd for silence,
But never tax'd for speech."
(AWEW.1.1)
Answer to 'Tell me something about yourself.' 'I love all, trust a few, do wrong to none'. Embellish by adding 'I usually check myself for silence but I am never taxed for speech.'
In the play. *Bertram is leaving Roussillon for the court of Paris and his mother offers some words of advice.*

Advice, a. on how to apply knowledge and the arts - Music and poesy use to quicken you…
"Music and poesy use to quicken you;
The mathematics and the metaphysics,
Fall to them as you find your stomach serves you" (TOS.1.1)
In the play. *Tranio counsels his master Lucentio on applied knowledge.*

Advice, a. on how to stand out – … put thyself into the trick of singularity.
"'Cast thy humble slough,' says she; 'be opposite with a kinsman, surly with servants; let thy tongue tang with arguments of state; put thyself into the trick of singularity" (TN.3.4)
In the play. *Malvolio recalls the very words of the fake letter sent by Olivia to him (but he believes the letter to be authentic). 'Slough' is the discarded skin of a snake.*

Advice, a. on men's wear and fashion - Costly thy habit as thy purse can buy, but not express'd in fancy; rich, not gaudy…
"Costly thy habit as thy purse can buy,
But not express'd in fancy; rich, not gaudy;
For the apparel oft proclaims the man,
And they in France of the best rank and station
Are of a most select and generous chief in that." (H.1.3)
Answer when you are complimented about your attire. E.G. 'My habit is as costly as my purse can buy, but not expresses…gaudy'. Answer to question(s) about your taste on clothing, e.g. 'Costly my habit as my purse can buy…man'. For a different view see entries for 'Appearances, a. deceptive' – 'Character, c. all in his clothes - … the soul of this man is in his clothes...'

In the play. *Polonius gives his son Laertes a set of precepts to follow while in Paris. See note to 'Opinion, your op. on money, handling of, borrowing and lending' for the complete list.*

Advice, a. on strength of character - ... to thine own self be true, and it must follow, as the night the day, thou canst not then be false to any man
"This above all: to thine own self be true,
And it must follow, as the night the day,
Thou canst not then be false to any man" (H.1.3)
Answer to question about yourself or 'Can I rely on you?' E.G. 'I follow the classic advice, to thine own self…man'. In the XXI century the advice sounds terribly out of date, when 'image' has supreme predominance over substance.
In the play. *Polonius to son Laertes who leaves for Paris.*

Advice, a. on talking and listening - Give every man thy ear, but few thy voice, take each man's censure, but reserve thy judgment.
"Give every man thy ear, but few thy voice;
Take each man's censure, but reserve thy judgment." (H.1.3)
Answer to 'How do you react to criticism?' 'I give every man mine ear…my judgment'. Answer to 'Tell me something about yourself'. E.G. 'I give every man my ear, but few my voice…judgment'
In the play. *Polonius to son Laertes who leaves for Paris.*

Advice, a. to a sharp-tongued woman - ... if thou be so shrewd of thy tongue.
"By my word, niece, thou will never get thee a husband, if thou be so shrewd of thy tongue." (MAAN.2.1)
Retort to a sharp remark from a young woman. Or extract, 'Thou are so shrewd of thy tongue'. See also 'Woman, spiteful and sharp tongued - She speaks poniards, and every word stabs…'
In the play. *Leonato counsels Beatrice to control her sharp tongue.*

Advice, a. to be modest with no boasting or wild behavior - …take pain to allay with some cold drops of modesty…
"…pray thee, take pain
To allay with some cold drops of modesty,
Thy skipping spirits." (MOV.2.2)
A substitute for 'calm down', or apply to yourself as a retort, e.g., to someone who tells you to calm down, 'OK, I will allay with some cold drop… my skipping spirits.'
In the play. *Bassanio asks the exuberant Gratiano to moderate his extroverted behavior during an impending visit to Portia's.*

Advice, a. to love moderately and to avoid excess - ... too swift arrives as tardy as too slow.
"The sweetest honey
Is loathsome in his own deliciousness,
And in the taste confounds the appetite:
Therefore, love moderately; long love doth so;
Too swift arrives as tardy as too slow." (RJ.2.6)
Use the first three lines as an invitation to restrain from any excess in general. Or to state that you love in moderation in answer to a personal question on the subject. 'The sweetest…appetite: therefore I love moderately; long love…too slow.'
For limits on sugar intake see also 'Health, too much sweet is bad'.

In the play. *Romeo is on pins and needles at Fr. Lawrence's cell, waiting for Juliet's arrival so that the wedding can be celebrated. Fr. Lawrence attempts to give Romeo some words of advice*

Advice, a. to proceeds slowly - Wisely and slow; they stumble that run fast.
"Wisely and slow; they stumble that run fast." (RJ.2.3)
In the play. *Friar Lawrence counsels Romeo to slow down in his hurry to marry Juliet.*

Advice, asking for a. – Bestow your needful counsel to our business.
"…bestow
Your needful counsel to our businesses,
Which craves the instant use."
(KL.2.1)
Address the expert. See also 'Advice, request for a. from capable person'
In the play. *Regan asks advice from Gloucester regarding letters received both from Lear and from her sister Goneril.*

Advice, asking for a. – What counsel give you in this weighty cause?
"What counsel give you in this weighty cause?" (KHVI.p2.3.1)
In the play. *Cardinal Beaufort asks York how to handle the rebellion in Ireland.*

Advice, be true to yourself - … to thine own self be true…
"…To thine own self be true;
And it must follow, as the night the day,
Thou canst not then be false to any man." (H.1)
Answer to question about yourself or "Can I rely on you?" As Shakespeare says…"To thine own self be true…"
In the play. *Polonius' advice to son Laertes.*

Advice, general a. - Have more than thou showest, speak less than thou knowest, lend less than thou owest.
"Have more than thou showest,
Speak less than thou knowest,
Lend less than thou owest" (KL.1.4)
Answer to question 'Tell me something about yourself', e.g. 'I have more than I show, speak less than I know and lend less than I owe'.
In the play. *Lear's fool translates some wit or wisdom into a song for Lear's benefit.*

Advice, good a. – When a wise man gives thee better counsel, give me mine again.
"…When a wise man gives thee better counsel, give me mine again" (KL.2.4)
In the play. *The fool to Kent after Kent has just been released from the stocks.*

Advice, his a. would be helpful now - his counsel now might do me golden service.
"His counsel now might do me golden service" (TN.4.3)
In the play. *Sebastian, still stunned at the turn of events (whereby he finds himself the instant subject of love by Olivia), looks for the lost Antonio who may give him some advice in the circumstances.*

Advice, listen more than speak - give every man thine ear, but few thy voice…
"Give every man thine ear, but few thy voice.
Take each man's censure, but reserve my judgement." (H.1)
Answer to 'How do you react to criticism?' 'I give every man mine ear…my judgment'.
In the play. *Polonius advice to son Laertes.*

Advice, listen to my a. - … fasten your ear on my advisings…
"… fasten your ear on my advisings: to the love I have in doing good a remedy presents itself." (MFM 3.1)

Give a mildly satirical slant to your request to be heard. See also 'Win-win situation through a stratagem'.
In the play. *The friar (Duke Vicentio in disguise) hatches a plot to save Claudio and asks Isabel (Claudio's sister) to listen.*

Advice, listen to experienced a. - Knit all the Greekish ears to his experienced tongue.
"…knit all the Greekish ears
To his experienced tongue" (TC.1.3)
Introduction, introducing an expert. Change 'Greekish' to the citizens of the applicable city or state.
In the play. *Ulysses addresses Nestor to whose experienced tongue all Greeks should listen.*

Advice, project needing friend's assistance - ... some sport in hand wherein your cunning can assist me much.
"I have some sport in hand,
Wherein your cunning can assist me much." (TOS.ind 1)
An opening when you are seeking someone's advice on an idea or project. See also 'Welcome, w. to our house' - Entries for 'Party'.
In the play. *A prankster lord addresses the players who will actually play the prank on Sly*

Advice, refusal to give a. - I will not cast away my physic, but on those that are sick.
"I will not cast away my physic, but on those that are sick. " (AYLI.3.2)
When you do not want to answer, particularly if you are requested to provide an answer or a solution to a problem you do not think exists.
In the play. *Rosalind (in disguise as a boy) exchanges some banter with Orlando. He insists that Rosalind name some of general women's faults.*

Advice, request for a. from capable person - Counsel me Tranio, for I know thou canst…
"Counsel me Tranio, for I know thou canst;
Assist me Tranio, for I know thou wilt." (TOS.1.1)
When asking for advice. Substitute for 'Tranio' the name of the person you are addressing. See also 'Advice, asking for a.'.
In the play. *Lucentio declares to have been possessed by a strong passion for Bianca.*

Advice, safety a. - better avoid than question the nature of the problem - 'tis safer to avoid what's grown than question how 't is born.
"I am sure 'tis safer to
Avoid what's grown than question how 't is born." (WT.1)
Better to avoid the issue than attempting to discuss it by raising questions.
In the play. *Camillo advises Polixenes to immediately leave the court of Sicilia*

Advice, suggestion to banish strange ideas - Arm thy constant and thy nobler parts... giddy loose suggestions.
"And better conquest never canst thou make,
Than arm thy constant and thy nobler parts
Against these giddy loose suggestions." (KJ.3.1)
Oppose proposals (giddy suggestions) that you rate harmful.
In the play. *The giddy loose suggestions, which Pandulph refers to, are the idea of peace between France and England, which the pope opposes.*

Advice, take best advantage of the opportunity - ... frame the season for your own harvest.
" ... it is needful that you frame the season for your own harvest." (MAAN.1.3)

Alternative to 'let's exploit the opportunity'. See also 'Opportunity, why it should not be missed' – 'Astrology, astrological conditions favorable'
In the play. *Don John is a blood but evil brother of Don Pedro. Recently there has been a reconciliation between the two and Conrade (a follower of Don John) suggests that Don John make the best of it.*

Advice, useful and approved a. - ... Now I begin to relish thy advice…
"Ulysses,
Now I begin to relish thy advice;
And I will give a taste of it forthwith
To Agamemnon" (TC.1.3)
Change 'Agamemnon' to the name of the person to whom you wish to convey the received advice.
In the play. *Nestor understands the scheme Ulysses proposes to get Achilles moving by exciting his desire to emulate Ajax. Nestor compares Ajax and Achilles to two dogs,*
"Two curs shall tame each other: pride alone
Must spur the mastiffs on, as 'twere their bone".

Advice, uselessness of a. when in pain - Every one can master a grief, but he that has it.
"… every one can master a grief, but he that has it." (MAAN.3.2)
Express the uselessness of consolations.
In the play. *Benedick is sad and claims the cause is a toothache but Claudio and Don Pedro know better. Claudio is in love.*

Advice, a. welcome and praised, along with praise of learning - I could have stay'd here all the night to hear good counsel: O, what learning is!
"I could have stay'd here all the night
To hear good counsel: O, what learning is!" (RJ.3.3)
Use if it applies or sarcastically.

In the play. *Juliet's nurse is impressed by the soothing words of advice that Friar Laurence has given Romeo in her presence.*

Advice, you like her a. - I like thy counsel; well hast thou advised…
"I like thy counsel; well hast thou advised:
And that thou mayst perceive how well I like it,
The execution of it shall make known." (TGV.1.3)
The first line conveys the idea already.
In the play. *Panthino suggests to Antonio, Proteus' father, to send Proteus to Milan to gain experience in social skills. Antonio likes the idea.*

Affair, symptoms of ongoing a. – …Is leaning cheek to cheek? is meeting noses?…
"Is whispering nothing?
Is leaning cheek to cheek? is meeting noses?
Kissing with inside lip? stopping the career
Of laughing with a sigh?--a note infallible
Of breaking honesty--horsing foot on foot?
Skulking in corners? wishing clocks more swift?
Hours, minutes? noon, midnight?" (WT.1.2)
Pull the leg of a friend, e.g. 'I saw you horsing foot on foot'
In the play. *Leontes is mad with unwarranted jealousy towards his wife Hermione and expounds on the signs that signal an affair.*

Affectation – the lady doth protest too much, methinks.
HAMLET. How like you this play?
QUEEN. The lady doth protest too much, methinks." (H.3.2)
Comment on the affectation of anyone. Substitute 'man' for 'lady' or the name of

anyone to whom the statement may apply.
In the play. *Hamlet tests the reaction to the play of the queen his mother.*

After-life, how to deal with the a-l. - … for the life to come, I sleep out the thought of it.
"…for the life to come, I sleep out the thought of it." (WT.4.3)
Answer to a biblical or Jehovah Witness preacher and evangelist, who prompts you to join his church out of concern for the after-life.
In the play. *Autolycus, a scoundrel but not completely so, expounds his philosophy to a shepherd in Bohemia.*

AGE – all the world's a stage…
A most difficult issue to handle for the young-at-heart seducer, especially in our times when to be old is but one step away from it being a crime. It is no accident that age discrimination has reached the realm of law.
What constitutes 'being old' is both absolute and relative and the difficulty (applied to romance) lies in this uncertainty. For Dante, Italy's Shakespeare's equivalent, old age begins at 46. But a subdivision of the ages of man into agreed-upon categories has ever been a thorny issue. According to two different theories the ages of man are four (in analogy with the seasons of the year) or seven (in correspondence with the seven planets).
Dante (1265-1321) believed in the four-age theory and says:
"...human life is scanned into four ages. The first is called Adolescence, that is "a growing of life"; the second is called Youth (Gioventute), that is 'age that can be of benefit' ('etade che puo' giovare'), meaning that can grant perfection and therefore (youth) is the perfect age. The third is called Old Age in its initial stage (Senettute), the fourth is the Old Age, no questions about it (Senio). We can then conclude that youth is over in the forty-fifth year. And therefore, just as Adolescence consists in the twenty-five years that, in the ascent, precede Youth, it follows that the descent, contains the same number of years that follow youth; hence, by calculation twenty-five plus forty-five is seventy and Old Age ends at seventy."
Are you an extremely well preserved, vigorous and active mature adult or senior? If so, you may be ready to hate Dante who has so unceremoniously confined you into hopeless inactivity and, by inference, excluded you from any chance of romance. But do not despair because Dante himself adds, "these four ages can be longer or shorter according to our complexion and composition." (Convivio, IV, 24).
Shakespeare, on the other hand, subscribed to the seven-age theory, as shown in As You Like It, when he has the character Jaques say:

**All the world's a stage,
And all the men and women merely players:
They have their exits and their entrances,
And one man in his time plays many parts,
His act being seven ages. At first the infant,
Mewling and puking in the nurse's arms:
Then the whining school-boy, with his satchel
And shining-morning face, creeping like snail
Unwillingly to school. And then the lover,
Sighing like furnace, with a woeful ballad,
Made to hi mistress' eyebrow. Then a soldier,
Jealous in honour, sudden, and quick in quarrel,**

Seeking the bubble reputation,
Even in the cannon mouth. And then the justice,
In fair round belly with good capon lin'd,
With eyes severe and beard of formal cut,
Full of wise saws and modern instances;
And so he plays his part. The sixth age shifts
Into the lean and slipper'd pantaloon,
With spectacles on nose and pouch on side;
His youthful hose, well sav'd, a world too wide
For his shrank shank; and his big manly voice,
Turning again towards childish treble, pipes
And whistles in his sound. Last scene of all,
That ends this strange, eventful history,
Is second childishness, and mere oblivion,
Sans teeth, sans eyes, sans taste, sans everything. (AYLI.2.7)

The real secret of remaining young, of course, is to lie about your age. And that can work sometimes, particularly if you envision a short or casual relationship. In all other cases, dealing with your or her age requires extreme care and consummate skill. I strongly recommend that age related quotes be among the first you memorize. The techniques (as evidenced by the quotes themselves) can be sound bited as follows:
- Deflecting the question
- Old but still strong
- Young looking and by extensions as good as young
- Laughing about it
Choice of technique depends on you, on her and, oddly enough, on her parents. Parents are traditionally hostile to daughters becoming involved with older men. Their first fear is that he is but an over-aged satyr, a dirty old man who has not given up on what he should have let go long ago.

Another worry, particularly if she is quite young, is that she may forego better and more attractive opportunities. They also fear that he may have mesmerized her by some kind of mental alchemy. Or they worry about what will happen if he survive and get old. Will their daughter be reduced to the role of a live-in nurse? Whatever your age may be, you may keep in mind the observation by Juan Ruiz, Archdeacon of Hita (Spain, 1280-1350 ad). "(Love) keeps the young in youth and in old folks it reduces significantly their sense of seniority; it transforms into white and beautiful what is as dark as tar; and gives great value to what is actually worth less than one walnut".

When, on the other hand, we are dealing with an older she, the age issue is even more delicate.

Ladies' concerns make up a trinity, age, skin care and weight control. Skin care and weight control are (usually but not always, especially weight), attendant issues of age. With age itself, here is the scenario.

- You have not seen her for a long time and, however much her looks may have changed, you must immediately make her feel that for you she has not changed at all. See 'Ageless - Age cannot wither her, nor custom stale her infinite variety ...'
- She is young but is already concerned about how you will feel towards her after a few years and
the effects of age will have become visible. See Ageless - To me fair friend you never can be old, for as you were...'
*** 'Beauty, b. preservation and its relationship with goodness of character - the hand that hath made you fair hath made you good...'

For a similar reference to life as a state see 'Life, l. as a stage for fools - When we are born we cry that we are come to this great stage of fools.'
In the play. *Jacques philosophizes in the forest of Arden. 'Capon' is a castrated chicken and a typical gift to a judge. 'Capon-justice' was a term used to indicate a judge who could be bribed with a capon. 'Sans' = 'Without'. 'Saws'= 'Maxims, sentences'.*

Age, a. and hunger - Oppress'd with two great evils, age and hunger
"There is an old poor man
…
Oppress'd with two great evils, age and hunger… " (AYLI.2.7)
In the play. *Orlando, having escaped to the Forest of Arden with his faithful servant Adam, asks for food from the table of the Duke.*

Age, a. and hypocrisy – A man can no more separate age and covetousness than he can part young limbs and lechery.
"A man can no more separate age and covetousness, than he can part young limbs and lechery." (KHIVp2.1.2)
In the play. *Falstaff's harsh (and unjustified) comments on the Chief Justice with whom he had an exchange.*

Age, a. and insomnia - Care keep his watch in every old man's eye, and where care lodges, sleep will never lie…
"Care keep his watch in every old man's eye,
And where care lodges, sleep will never lie:
But where unbruised youth with unstuff'd brain
Doth couch his limbs, there golden sleep doth reign." (RJ.2)
Explain or justify why you don't sleep many hours or to justify why you sleep a lot.

In the play. *Fr. Lawrence generalizes on the relationship between age and sleep patterns*

Age, a. and its byproducts - … the unruly waywardness that infirm and choleric years bring with them.
"…must we look to receive from his age, not alone the imperfections of long-engraffed condition, but therewithal the unruly waywardness that infirm and choleric years bring with them." (KL.1.1)
In the play. *After obtaining their inheritance in advance, Goneril and Regan default on their commitments to King Lear. 'Engraffed' = 'rooted'*

Age, a. and its way of thinking - … it is as proper to our age to cast beyond ourselves in our opinions…
"… it is as proper to our age
To cast beyond ourselves in our opinions
As it is common for the younger sort
To lack discretion" (H.2.1)
In the play. *Polonius attributes to his own age his excess of caution regarding Hamlet's feelings for Ophelia.*

Age, a. and lying - Lord, lord, how subject we old men are to this vice of lying.
"Lord, lord, how subject we old men are to this vice of lying!" (KHIV p2.3.2)
Modify slightly and use as an alternative to 'you re a liar'. "O Lord, how subject old men are to this vice of lying."
In the play. *Falstaff referring to Justice Shallow from whom he will be able to pill a good sum of money.*

Age, a. and lying - … old men of less truth than tongue (SON 23)

Age, a. and related waywardness - … must we look to receive from his age,

not alone the imperfections of long-engraffed condition…
"The best and soundest of his time hath been but rash; then must we look to receive from his age, not alone the imperfections of long-engraffed condition, but therewithal the unruly waywardness that infirm and choleric years bring with them." (KL.1.1)
In the play. *Crafty daughter Goneril, after her ample declarations of love towards Lear immediately plots with sister Regan how to completely dis-empower him.*

Age, a. and retirement savings – … Five hundred crowns…which I did store to be my foster-nurse when… service should in my old limbs lie lame.
"… I have five hundred crowns,
The thrifty hire I saved…
Which I did store to be my foster-nurse
When service should in my old limbs lie lame
And unregarded age in corners thrown" (AYLI.1.3)
In the play. *Adam offers his modest retirement savings to Adam*

Age, a. causing childishness - Old fools are babes again.
"Old fools are babes again" (KL.1.3)
In the play. *Goneril, who is temporarily hosting her father Lear, begins to resent him.*

Age, a. causing childishness - They say an old man is twice a child.
"…they say an old man is twice a child" (H.2.2)
In the play. *Rosencrantz to Hamlet referring to the oncoming Polonius.*

Age, a. causing taste to change - A man loves the meat in his youth, that he cannot endure in old age…
"Does not the appetite alter? A man loves the meat in his youth, that he cannot endure in old age: shall quips, and sentences, and these paper bullets of the brain, awe a man from the career of his humour?"
(MAAN.2.3)
Comment on changes of taste. 'A man…old age.' You can also use 'paper bullet of the brain' as a quip on a funny and unexpected comment from a colleague.
In the play. *Benedick meditates about his own change of attitude towards love now that he begins to love Beatrice.*

Age, a. discrimination on the part of a woman - ... and he that is less than a man, I am not for him.
"…. He that hath a beard is more than a youth, and he that hath no beard is less than a man: and he that is more than a youth is not for me, and he that is less than a man, I am not for him" (MAAN.1.1)
If you are a woman and you want to say no.
In the play. *Beatrice makes her opinion known about men. She is the spiritual sister of the Shrew Katharina in the 'Taming of the Shrew'.*

Age, a. incapable of enjoying wealth – 'The aged man that coffers-up his gold is plagued with cramps and gouts and painful fits…
"'The aged man that coffers-up his gold
Is plagued with cramps and gouts and painful fits;
And scarce hath eyes his treasure to behold,
But like still-pining Tantalus he sits,
And useless barns the harvest of his wits;
Having no other pleasure of his gain
But torment that it cannot cure his pain." (ROL)
In the poem. *Evil Tarquin knows he is committing a crime and meditates on it with various arguments.*

Age, a. inevitably engenders wisdom - ... instructed by the antiquary times, he must be, he is, he cannot be but wise.
"… here's Nestor, -
Instructed by the antiquary times,
He must, he is, he cannot be but wise." (TC.2.3)
Flattering introduction of the next speaker. Depending on the person, you may modify the second line to read: 'instructed by valuable experience'. The second and third line supports the value of knowing history.
In the play. *In praise of the wisdom that supposedly comes with age.*

Age, a. placing a limit to the display of gallantry - … One that is well-nigh worn to pieces with age to show himself a young gallant.
"One that is well-nigh worn to pieces with age to show himself a young gallant." (MWW.2.1)
Apply jokingly to yourself if you are suspected of courting a young woman.
In the play. *Mrs. Ford comments on the love letter sent to him by the aging Romeo Falstaff.*

Age, admitting to being old - ... I am declined into the vale of years.
"... I am declined
Into the vale of years" (OTH.3.3)
In the play. *Othello, now tricked into believing Desdemona's adultery, meditates on the causes of her dislike, including his age.*

Age, admitting to being old - Myself am struck in years, I must confess.
"Myself am struck in years, I must confess" (TOS.2.1)
In the play. *Gremio, one of Bianca's suitors knows he is old. However, should he die he would leave all his possessions to Bianca if she were to marry him.*

Age, admitting to being old - That time of year thou mayst in me behold…
"That time of year thou mayst in me behold
When yellow leaves, or none, or few, do hang
Upon those boughs which shake against the cold,
Bare ruin'd choirs where late the sweet birds sang.
In me thou seest the twilight of such day
As after sunset fadeth in the west,
Which by and by black night doth take away,
Death's second self, that seals up all in rest.
In me thou see'st the glowing of such fire
That on the ashes of his youth doth lie,
As the death-bed whereon it must expire
Consumed with that which it was nourish'd by.
   This thou perceivest, which makes thy love more strong,
   To love that well which thou must leave ere long." (SON.73)
See also 'Autumn, winter – When lofty trees I see barren of leaves…'

Age, advantages and disadvantages in the eyes of a woman - ... youth in ladies' eyes that flourisheth.
GREMIO Skipper, stand back: 'tis age that nourisheth.
TRANIO But youth in ladies' eyes that flourisheth.
In the play. Old *Gremio and young Tranio, extol the virtues of their respective age as seen through the eyes of women.*

Age, dangerous to be old – It is as dangerous to be aged in any kind of course…

"…it is as dangerous to be aged in any kind of course, as it is virtuous to be constant in any undertaking…" (MFM.3.2)
In the play. *The Duke (in disguise) gives Escalus his comments on the world at large after having observed it from the point of view of an ordinary man*

Age, debilitating effects of a. - … When sapless age and weak unable limbs should bring thy father to his drooping chair.
"…When sapless age and weak unable limbs
Should bring thy father to his drooping chair" (KHVI.4.5)
In the play. *Talbot Sr. to Talbot Jr. who has joined his father at the siege of Bordeaux.*

Age, declaration of old a. – every part of you blasted with antiquity…
"…every part of you blasted with antiquity…" (KHIV.p2.1.2)
Apply to yourself in an ironic way, e.g. 'Every part of me is blasted with antiquity. See 'Age, signs of aging'
In the play. *The Chief Justice questions Falstaff's pretense to youth.*

Age, defending old a. and a happy disposition - If to be old and merry be a sin, then many an old host that I know, is damned.
"If to be old and merry be a sin, then many an old host that I know, is damned." (KHIV p1.2.4)
Use in mock self-defense, e.g. 'Yes, I am old, but merry and if to be old…damned.'
In the play. *Falstaff, pretending to be Prince Henry in a mock play, defends himself.*

Age, difference in a. – Octavius, I have seen more days than you…
"Octavius, I have seen more days than you" (JC.4.1)

When you feel that your age and experience carry weight.
In the play. *Antony, with the experience of age, tells Octavius that Lepidus is not worth much and compares him to an ass, assigned to carry loads.*

Age, difference in judgment between young and old – … it is as proper to our age to cast beyond ourselves in our opinions…
"… it is as proper to our age
To cast beyond ourselves in our opinions
As it is common for the younger sort
To lack discretion" (H.2.1)
In the play. *Polonius reflects on Hamlet's odd behavior still believing it to be the effect of Hamlet's passion for Ophelia.*

Age, graying hair does not imply less brain power - … though grey do something mingle with our younger brown, yet have we a brain…
"… though grey
Do something mingle with our younger brown, yet ha' we
A brain that nourishes our nerves, and can
Get goal for goal of youth" (AC.4.8)
When and if she notices your grey hair. Or if you wish to declare that your aging has not impaired your effectiveness. Change 'with our' to 'with my' and 'have we' to 'have I'
In the play. *Antony is happy to have (temporarily) pushed back and defeated the forces of the younger Octavian.*

Age, how old are you? - … Not so young, sir, to love a woman for singing…
KING LEAR How old art thou?
KENT Not so young, sir, to love a woman for singing, nor
so old to dote on her for any thing (KL.1.4)
Answer to question.

In the play. *Banished Kent disguises himself and his accent and tries to be hired by Lear to actually protect him.*

Age, life at its limit - Nature in you stands on the very verge of her confine.
"O, sir, you are old.
Nature in you stands on the very verge
Of her confine" (KL.2.4)
Apply ironically to yourself – change 'in you' to 'in me'. See also 'Life, end of l. - My life is run his compass…'
In the play. *Regan, one of the two evil daughters, to her father K. Lear.*

Age, making man redundant - … I confess that I am old, age is unnecessary.
"…I confess that I am old;
Age is unnecessary" (KL.2.4)
Apply ironically to yourself.
In the play. K. Lear ironically confirming to Regan her rude remark about his old age.

Age, observation on old age by a young person - … old folks, many feign as they were dead; unwieldy, slow, heavy and pale as lead.
"…old folks, many feign as they were dead;
Unwieldy, slow, heavy and pale as lead." (RJ.2.5)
In the play. *Juliet is anxiously waiting for the return of the Nurse. She sent the Nurse in search of Romeo.*

Age, old a. and hunger, two concurrent evils - … Oppressed with two weak evils, age and hunger.
"… Oppressed with two weak evils, age and hunger." (AYLI.2.7)
In the play. *Orlando pleads for some food for Adam who has been left temporarily behind.*
Should you be hungry and past your prime, 'I am oppressed with…hunger'.

Age, old a. should be more serious - Now ill white hairs become a fool and jester.
"How ill white hairs become a fool and jester!" (KHIV.p2.5.5)
In the play. *The Prince of Wales, now king Henry V, will not have anything more to do with Falstaff.*

Age, old a. without wisdom – Thou shouldst not have been old till thou hadst been wise.
"Thou shouldst not have been old till thou hadst been wise" (KL. 1.5)
In the play. *The fool confronts King Lear with the folly Lear displayed in assigning his inheritance.*

Age, old and unhappy – You see me here, you gods, a poor old man, as full of grief as age; wretched in both.
"You see me here, you gods, a poor old man,
As full of grief as age; wretched in both!" (KL.2.4)
When you wish to exaggerate your conditions, answer to 'who are you?' maybe a police officer who harasses you for a minor, so called, traffic violation.
In the play. *King Lear to daughter Regan who treats him worse than a beggar.*

Age, question about a. – Not old enough to be a man and…
OLIVIA. Of what personage and years is he?
MALVOLIO. Not yet old enough to be a man, nor young enough for a boy. (TN.1.5)
Describe a candidate whom you rate too young and immature.
In the play. *Viola/Cesario has arrived at Olivia's abode and was first met by Malvolio. Olivia questions Malvolio about the visitor's age.*

Age, pretending to be young - Do you set down your name in the scroll of youth…
"Do you set down your name in the scroll of youth, that are written down old with all the characters of age? Have you not a moist eye? a dry hand? A yellow cheek? a white beard? a decreasing leg? An increasing belly? is not your voice broken? Your wind short? your chin double? your wit single? And every part about you blasted with antiquity? And will you yet call yourself young?" (KHIVp2.1.2)
Admit to your age, e.g. 'I am written down with… age', 'Every part about me is blasted with antiquity'.
In the play. *Falstaff pretends to be young and the Chief Justice who tells him the truth.*

Age, recognition of one's old a. and plea for understanding - Pray you now, forget and forgive: I am old and foolish.
"Pray you now, forget and forgive: I am old and foolish." (KL.4.7)
In the play. *King Lear to Cordelia who offers to guide him in a walk.*

Age, sex and aging - Is it not strange that desire should so many years outlive performance?
"Is it not strange that desire should so many years outlive performance?" (KHIVp2.2.4)
Comment on an aging Romeo
In the play. *Poins referring to Falstaff.*

Age, signs of aging - Have you not a moist eye? a dry hand? a yellow cheek?…
CHIEF JUSTICE (to Falstaff). Have you not a moist eye? a dry hand? a yellow cheek? a white beard? a decreasing leg? an increasing belly? Is not your voice broken? your wind short? Your chin double? Your wit single? and every part of you blasted with antiquity; and will you yet call yourself young?" (KHIVp2.1.2)
You may find a character who just fits this description and apply the quotation directly. Or you may ironically modify the quote slightly and turn its meaning around in your favor.
'Yes, my eye is moist, my hand dry, my cheek yellow…but I call myself young'.
In the play. *The Chief Justice questions Falstaff's pretense to youth.*

Age, too old to learn– … Too far in years to be a pupil now.
"I am too old to fawn upon a nurse, Too far in years to be a pupil now" (KRII.1.3)
In the play. *Mowbray, exiled by Richard II is not or cannot learn a foreign language.*

Age, too old to love – You cannot call it love; for at your age, the hey-day in the blood is tame…
"You cannot call it love; for at your age
The hey-day in the blood is tame, it's humble,
And waits upon the judgment: and what judgment
Would step from this to this?" (H.3.2)
In the play. *Hamlet to his mother.*

Age, young defeat the old - The younger rises when the old doth fall.
"The younger rises when the old doth fall" (KL.3.3)
Could be part of your retirement speech when your successor is younger.
In the play. *Evil son Edmund plots the downfall of his father.*

Age, young in a. but old in judgment - "…I am only old in judgment and understanding.
"…I am only old in judgment and understanding." (KHIV.p2.1.2)
Answer to 'How old are you?'

In the play. The judge ridicules Falstaff for his claims of being young. Falstaff replies that he is old only in judgment and understanding.

Age. Its effects on intelligence - When the age is in, the wit is out.
"When the age is in, the wit is out." (MAAN.3.5)
Self-effacing statement to justify your not having understood or not remembering something.
In the play. *Verges, a city officer has some difficulty in explaining to Don John how he has arrested the two knaves that slandered Hero. Dogberry accounts for the difficulty.*

Age. Its effects on memory - ... And as, with age, his body uglier grows, so his mind cankers.
"And as, with age, his body uglier grows,
So his mind cankers." (TEM.4.1)
Attribute your instance of forgetfulness (or forgetting in general) to the effects of age. This can work, in principle, irrespective of your age. If you are indeed old, the answer is an example of your taking your age in stride and laughing about it. For example, 'I am sorry I forgot. You see, as with age my body uglier grows, so my mind cankers'.
In the play. *The magical spirit Ariel has just informed Prospero of the absurd plot of Caliban and Prospero comments.*

Age. Its effects on memory and warm feelings – ... Nature, as it grows again towards earth, is fashion'd for the journey, dull and heavy.
"And Nature, as it grows again towards earth,
Is fashion'd for the journey, dull and heavy." (TOA.2.2)
Again, attribute your instance of forgetfulness to the effects of age. Here you are connecting your age to Nature and its universal and unavoidable laws.

In the play. *The weakness referred to is one of lack of warmth, or sympathy. A first group of previous old friends of Timon refuse to answer his call for help. Timon attributes the ingratitude to their old age. 'T is lack of kindly warmth they are not kind'*

Age. Its effect on wrinkles - When forty winters shall besiege thy brow, and dig deep trenches in thy beauty's field.
"**When forty winters shall besiege thy brow,
And dig deep trenches in thy beauty's field.**" (SON.2)
Applications.

- If you are a woman (and in the unlikely case that you are asked about your age), modify the lines slightly and apply them to yourself as an evasive answer to 'How old are you?' For example, 'Too many winters have besieged my brow and dug deep trenches in my beauty's field'.
- If you are a man and wants to answer evasively, change 'beauty's field' to 'body and soul', i.e. 'Too many winters have besieged my brow and dug deep trenches in my body and soul.'
- A reminder that youth has narrow time limits.

Ovid says, 'Now already be mindful of the old age which is to come; thus no hour will slip wasted by you...for the years pass like flowing water; the wave that has gone cannot be called back, the hour that has gone by cannot return.....Serpents put off their age with their frail skins, nor are stags made old by casting their horns: our charms flee without our aid' (AOL.2)
See also comments to 'Beauty and its relationship with goodness of character.'

- Appearance, a remarkable (negative) change in appearance due to the strokes of fortune.

Age. Longevity promoted by lightheartedness - a light heart lives long.
"A light heart lives long." (LLL.5.2)
Use as a piece of advice or to explain why you take matters lightly.
In the play. *Katherine praises Rosaline for her sprightly spirit.*

Age. Looking good for your age - …but flowers distilled though they with winter meet, lose but their show, their substance still lives sweet.
"Those hours, that with gentle work did frame
The lovely gaze where every eye doth dwell,
Will play the tyrants to the very same
And that unfair which fairly doth excel;
For never-resting time leads summer on
To hideous winter, and confounds him there;
Sap checked with frost, and lusty leaves quite gone,
Beauty o'er-snowed and bareness every where:
Then were not summer's distillation left,
A liquid prisoner pent in walls of glass,
Beauty's effect with beauty were bereft,
Nor it, nor no remembrance what it was:
But flowers distilled though they with winter meet,
Lose but their show, their substance still lives sweet." (SON.5)

Use the last two lines to answer a compliment that you look young for your age, for example, 'Thank you for your compliment, you could say that I have been distilled by time, just as 'flowers distilled, though they with winter meet, loose but their show, their substance still lives sweet.' Follow up with words hinting that your 'substance' (by the way, when quoting, raise your voice a little and really stress the word 'substance') that is, your strength is still as good as ever.
Use the second line, 'The lovely gaze where every eye doth dwell' as a compliment to her face or eyes. See also 'Face, expression, beauty, imitating Nature.' And any of the eight entries for 'Eyes'.
'Pent' is the participle of 'to pen' = 'to confine'.

Age. Man who has walked hand in hand with time - ... good old chronicle, that hast so long walked hand in hand with time.
" ... good old chronicle,
That hast so long walked hand in hand with time." (TC.4.1)
Use during a retirement speech. Or to say that you feel old. E.G.'I feel as an old chronicle, that has so long walked…time.'
In the play. *Hector has arrived to the Greek camp to deliver his challenge and greets Nestor.*

Age. Reasons for men to marry younger women - Then let thy love be younger than thyself, or thy affection cannot hold the bent...
"Then let thy love be younger than thyself,
Or thy affection cannot hold the bent;
For women are as roses, whose fair flower
Being once display'd, doth fall that very hour." (TN.1.4)
This could be a reply to "Don't you think I am too young for you?" though the

statement reflects a very obsolete double standard.
In the play. *The Duke Orsino asks Cesario (who is actually Viola strategically dressed in a man's disguise) if he Cesario loves a woman and what type of woman is she. Cesario, secretly in love with Duke Orsino says that her type of woman is of Orsino's age. 'Too old', he says and then continues giving reasons why men (in this case Cesario) should always marry women younger than themselves.*

Age. Time showing the effect of time and care - … careful hours with time's deformed hand have written strange defeatures in my face.
"…And careful hours with time's deformed hand
Have written strange defeatures in my face" (COE.5.1)
When a friend or acquaintance does not recognize you after seeing you last time years ago.
In the play. *Antipholus does not recognize his father Aegeon and Aegeon explains why.*

Age, wisdom expected out of a. – … As you are old and reverend, you should be wise.
"…I do beseech you
To understand my purposes aright:
As you are old and reverend, you should be wise" (KL.1.4)
In the play. *As soon as King Lear empowers his evil daughter Goneril she starts rejecting limiting Lear's requests and freedom.*

Age. You admit that you are old but explain why and how you have maintained your youthful strength – Though I look old yet I am strong and lusty…
"Though I look old, yet I am strong and lusty:
For in my youth I never did apply
Hot and rebellious liquor in my blood,
Nor did not with unbashful forehead woo
The means of weakness and debility;
Therefore my age is as lusty as winter,
Frosty, but kindly" (AYLI.2.3)
In the play. *Adam is old but still strong to follow his master Orlando. Orlando is concerned whether Adam could take the hardship of exile and attendant escape to the forest of Arden.*

Age. You admit that you are old but explain why and how you have maintained your youthful intellect – … yet hath my night of life some memory.
"Though now this grained face of mine be hid
In sap-consuming winter's drizzled snow,
And all the conduits of my blood froze up
Yet hath my night of life some memory,
My wasting lamps some fading glimmer left,
My dull deaf ears a little use to hear." (COE.5.1)
In the play. *Neither Dromio E. or Ant. E. recognize Aegeon. Aegeon restates to himself that, notwithstanding his age, he has still a warm blood, memory etc.*

Age. You admit that you are old but explain why and how you have maintained your youthful strength – Time hath not yet so dried up this blood of mine…
"Time hath not yet so dried this blood of mine,
Nor age so eat up my invention." (MAAN.4.1)
Leonato can still avenge the honor of his daughter Hero, if the accusations made against her are false.

Age. You admit that you are old but there is still substantial sparkle in you - ... some smack of age in you, some relish of the saltness of time.
"Your lordship, though not clean past your youth, hath yet some smack of age in you, some relish of the saltness of time." (KH4.2.2)
Modify this one a little, "Though not clean past my youth, yet there is yet some smack of age in me, some relish of the saltness of time."
In the play. *Falstaff addresses the Chief Justice and tries to ingratiate himself with him*

Age. You are a bit older than she is - My glass shall not persuade me I am old as long as youth and thou are of one date.
"My glass shall not persuade me I am old
As long as youth and thou are of one date." (SON.22)
Answer to "How old are you?" when you intend to deflect the question. Turn the situation around and make it an occasion for a compliment, how young she is or how young she looks.

Age. You are old and you may as well admit it – when my glass shows me myself indeed.
"But when my glass shows me my self indeed
Beated and chopt with tanned antiquity… " (SON.62)
You have two ways of using these lines. One, admit your age with realism and a touch of modesty. Two, deflect the question - admit that you look old but still leave her with a doubt. That is, you may be younger than you look but you have played rough with your life. If so, you imply or declare that it is better to be burnished with use than rusty from principle.

Age. You are old and you may as well admit it – ... the silver livery of advised age.
"…to achieve
The silver livery of advised age"
(KHVI p2.5.2)
Change to, 'I have achieved the silver livery of advised age.'
In the play. *Young Clifford meditates on the death of his father, slain at the battle of St. Alban's. He asks,*
Wast thou ordain'd, dear father,
To lose thy youth in peace, and to achieve
The silver livery of advised age,
And, in thy reverence and thy chair-days, thus
To die in ruffian battle?

Age. You are old, you know it, she tells you that you are young and you pretend to believe it - When my love swears that she is made of truth…
When my love swears that she is made of truth,
I do believe her though I know she lies,
That she may think me some untutored youth,
Unlearned in the world's false subtelties.
Thus vainly thinking that she thinks me young,
Although she knows my days are past the best,
Simply I credit her false speaking tongue,
On both sides thus is simple truth suppressed.
But wherefore says she not she is unjust?
And wherefore say I not that I am old.
O love's best habit is in seeming trust
And age in love loves not to have years told.
　　　　Therefore I lie with her and she with me

And in our faults by lies we flattered be. (SON.138)
You have several additional options here by simply extracting specific lines. For example let's say she asks that terrible question "How old are you?". You are reluctant to answer but do not want her to think that you lie about your age. Yet you want to give strong hints that you like her. Try "Age in love loves not to have years told."
Or maybe she says that you are young as a compliment. You want to make it clear that you do not believe her. Look into the distance (or at the ceiling) and utter with a sigh…."Thus vainly thinking that she thinks me young, although she knows my days are past their best, simply I credit her false speaking tongue." Of course, if the moment makes you so anxious as to completely forget the lines there are some alternative options. For example:
'Age is a question of mind over matter, if you don't mind it doesn't matter'
Or (better),
'I am old enough to have good taste and young enough to still have an appetite'

Ageless - Age cannot wither her, nor custom stale her infinite variety …
"**Age cannot wither her, nor custom stale**
Her infinite variety. Other women cloy
The appetite they feed, but she makes Hungry, where most she satisfies."
(AC.2.2)

Answer to "Will you always love me even when I am old?" Change the case of the particle from 'her' to you and from 'she makes' to 'you make' and from 'she' to 'you'. 'Age cannot wither you, nor custom stale / Your infinite variety. Other women cloy / The appetite they feed, but you make / Hungry where most you satisfy.' See also 'Writing. Confidence in your writing power.'
In the play. *Enobarbus, while in Rome accompanying Antony to a meeting with Octavian and Lepidus, extols to a friend Cleopatra's talents.*

Ageless - To me fair friend you never can be old, for as you were…
"**To me fair friend you never can be old**
For as you were when first your eye I eyed,
Such seems your beauty still."
(SON.104)
Answer to 'Do you think I look old?' or 'How old do you think I look'.
This answer works wonders, especially with women extremely concerned about their appearance. That women dread aging is a truism already established in ancient times and mythology.
So Ovid, 'Ask not how old she be, nor under what consul she was born; these are the duties of the stern Censor: particularly so if she is past her prime, if the flower of her age is over, and already she is plucking out the whitening hair.' (AOL.2)
Any compliment or remark that emphasizes a woman's young age, however untrue, will gain you points.

Agree or prove me wrong - Reprove my allegations if you can; or else conclude my words effectual.
"**Reprove my allegations if you can;**
Or else conclude my words effectual."
(KHVI p2.3.1)

Alternate to 'Agree with me or prove me wrong'
In the play. *Queen Margaret tries to put Humphrey, duke of Gloucester in a bad light with Henry VI and elicits the support of her allies to sustain her allegations.*

Agreeing, a. with the majority - As will the rest, so willeth Winchester.
"As will the rest, so willeth Winchester." (KHVI.p1.3.1)
Modify using your own name. Answer to 'What do you think?' – See also 'Action, strong r. for action'.
In the play. *Winchester agrees with the King's proposal to restore the rights of Richard Plantagenet.*

Agreeing, a. with wish or proposal - My vows are equal partners with thy vows.
"My vows are equal partners with thy vows." (KHVI p1.3.2)
In the play. *Burgundy agrees with Talbot on their renewed commitment to retake Rouen.*

Agreement, a. formalized - Let specialties be therefore drawn between us...
"Let specialties be therefore drawn between us,
That covenants may be kept on either hand." (TOS.2.1)
Follow up to ratify an agreement already reached verbally.
In the play. *Petruchio has asked Baptista for the hand of his daughter Katharina.*

Agreement, a. on a course of action – Strong reasons make strong actions.
"Strong reasons make strong actions. Let's go.
If you say ay, the king will not say no." (KJ.3.4)
Use the first line to justify forceful actions. Modify the second line substituting your name for 'the king' to indicate consent.

In the play. *King Lewis follows the advice of the Pope's legate.*

Agreement, a. on the choice - ... your choice agrees with mine, I like it well.
"... your choice agrees with mine; I like it well." (PER.2.5)
Indicate your agreement.
In the play. *In Pentapolis, Thaisa has made up her mind that she will marry Pericles, the winner of the tourney. Her father Simonides agrees with her choice.*

Agreement, a. or contract, quick implementation of a. - ... lest the bargain should catch cold and starve.
"Your hand; a covenant: we will have these things set down by lawful counsel, and straight away for Britain, lest the bargain should catch cold and starve" (CYM.1.4)
Suggest to quickly consign the agreement to paper.
In the play. *The evil Iachimo concludes the terms of the wager questioning the faithfulness of Imogen.*

Agreement, a. or contract concluded - I'll have this knot knit up to-morrow morning.
"I'll have this knot knit up to-morrow morning." (RJ.4.2)
In the play. *Capulet senior is determined to have Juliet married to Paris the next day.*

Agreement, a. quickly concluded - Was ever match clapp'd up so suddenly?
"Was ever match clapp'd up so suddenly?" (TOS.2.1)
Comment on a quick and unexpected conclusion to a debate that was anticipated as extended or controversial.
In the play. *Gremio is very surprised at how quickly Petruchio has managed to get Katharina to marry him.*

Agreement, a. reached to be quickly made official - ... since it is but green, it should be put to no apparent likelihood of breach.
"Yet, since it is but green, it should be put
To no apparent likelihood of breach" (KRIII.2.3)
When the agreement was reached after lengthy or arduous and complicated negotiations – so much so that there may be a chance that one part or another may change their minds.
In the play. *What is green is the statement of peace between Richard III and the party of the widowed Queen Elizabeth. Rightly so, Rivers suggests that the queen's young son be immediately proclaimed king. Rivers senses that Richard of Gloucester is up to no good.*

Agreement, a. with advice to reach a specific location – When Gloucester says the word, King Henry goes...
"When Gloucester says the word, King Henry goes;
For friendly counsel cuts off many foes." (KHVI.p1.3.1)
Change names accordingly.
In the play. *King Henry VI will follow Gloucester's advice to be crowned in France*

Agreement, abiding by the majority decision or a., even if you do not like the terms - ... although I seem so lotah, I am the last that will last keep his oath.
"But, I believe, although I seem so loath,
I am the last that will last keep his oath." (LLL.1.1)
Reinforce the idea that you will stand by the agreement even if you may not like it.
In the play. *Biron reassures his companion that, notwithstanding his reservations, he will not break the commitment to learning in isolation from the world.*

Agreement, full a. and friendship – Then you love us, we you, and we'll clasp hands...
"Then you love us, we you, and we'll clasp hands:
When peers thus knit, a kingdom ever stands" (PER.2.4)
In the play. The peers of Tyre agree with the proposals of Helicanus who is temporarily in charge of the kingdom as Pericles is absent.

Agreement, half-hearted a. – I have no great devotion to the deed and yet...
"I have no great devotion to the deed;
And yet he hath given me satisfying reasons..." (OTH.5.1)
In the play. *Roderigo's answer to Iago's directive that he, Roderigo, kill Cassio.*

Agreement, incidental a. with an enemy - ... If thou couldst please me with speaking to me...
"If thou couldst please me with speaking to me, thou mightst have hit upon it here: the commonwealth of Athens is become a forest of beasts." (TOA.5.3)
In the play. *Apemantus and Timon exchange an arsenal of insults*

Agreement, rhetorical expression of a. - To cry amen to that, thus we appear.
"To cry amen to that, thus we appear." (KH.5.2)
In the play. *K. Henry's agreement to the words of peace and the wishes uttered by Queen Isabel of France.*

Agreement, signing the a. - Give me the paper, let me read the same and to the strict'st decrees I'll write my name.
BIRON. Give me the paper, let me read the same;
And to the strict'st decrees I'll write my name." (LLL.1.1)
Use prior to signing the agreement

In the play. *Notwithstanding some initial reluctance, Biron agrees to the proposed time of learning with king and associates.*

Agreement, wholeheartedly in a. - May I never, to this good purpose, that so fairly shows dream of impediment.
"May I never
To this good purpose, that so fairly shows,
Dream of impediment." (AC.2.2)
Answer to 'Do you agree?', particularly if the agreement is an important compromise.
In the play. *Antony agrees to the proposal, put forward by Agrippa, that he, Antony, marries Octavia, Octavian's sister, thus sealing the peace between the two political enemies.*

Agreement, you agree in principle with the other party - What wills lord Talbot, pleaseth Burgundy.
"What wills lord Talbot, pleaseth Burgundy." (KHVI.p1.3.2)
Change 'Lord Talbot' to the name of the person you agree with, and Burgundy to your name.
In the play. *After a victory at Rouen in which the Pucelle participated, Talbot proposes to go to Paris for the coronation of Henry VI.*

Air, excellent a. quality - The air breathes upon us here most sweetly.
"The air breathes upon us here most sweetly." (TEM.2.1)
See also 'Place, a nice p. to stay – cottage'
In the play. *Adrian comments on the air quality of the island.*

Air, invigorating a. stimulating the appetite - the air is quick there, and pierces and sharpens the stomach.
"…the air is quick there,
And it pierces and sharpens the stomach" (PER.4.1)
See also 'Place, a nice p. to stay'

In the play. *Dionyza invites Marina to take a walk in the invigorating air along the seashore, though Dionyza actually plans Marina's murder.*

Alive, being a. - … living blood doth in these temples beat
"…living blood doth in these temples beat" (KJ.2.1)
In the play. *King Philip of France accuses King John of England of having usurped the crown from young Arthur whose blood beats in his temples.'*

Allegiance, a. emphatically stated – longer than I prove loyal to your grace.
"Longer than I prove loyal to your grace
Let me not live to look upon your grace" (TGV.3.2)
In the play. *Proteus emphatically declares allegiance to the Duke of Milan while preparing a dirty trick for Valentine.*

Allegiance, a. firmly promised - … while life upholds this arm, this arm upholds…
"No, Warwick, no; while life upholds this arm,
This arm upholds the house of Lancaster" (KHVI.p3.3.3)
In the play. *Warwick prompts Oxford to switch allegiance and Oxford responds.*

Allegiance, a. questionable when government is rotten – Brutus had rather be a villager than to repute himself a son of Rome under these hard conditions as this time...
"Brutus had rather be a villager
Than to repute himself a son of Rome
Under these hard conditions as this time
Is like to lay upon us." (JC.1)
When misguided 'patriots' accuse you of being anti-american or (in general) against

your country, simply because the government is rotten.
In the play. Cassius outlines to Brutus the reasons for a needed change in government, as Cassius considers Caesar a dictator. Brutus will mull over Cassius' proposal, while already indirectly agreeing on the assessment of the situation.

Allegiance, criterion for determining a. - ... who's your king? The king of England; when we know the king.
KING PHILIP Speak, citizens, for England; who's your king?
First Citizen The king of England; when we know the king. (KJ.2.1)
An example of an uncertain situation.
In the play. The citizens of Angiers declare themselves subjects of the King of England, except that who is the actual king, John or Arthur will be decided by battle and murder later on.

Allegiance, determining a. - I rather wish you foes than hollow friends.
"I rather wish you foes than hollow friends" (KHVI p3.4.1)
In the play. Edward IV abandoned by his brother Clarence and Somerset, addresses Hastings and Montague. In Richard III, Richard will have Hastings murdered.

Allegiance, feigned a. – In following him, I follow but myself...
"In following him, I follow but myself;
Heaven is my judge, not I for love and duty" (OTH.1.1)
In the play. Iago explains to Roderigo his feelings towards Othello.

Allegiance, how to secure a. from subjects - I stole all courtesy from heaven and dress'd myself in such humility...
"... I stole all courtesy from heaven, And dress'd myself in such humility

That I did pluck allegiance from men's hearts" (KHIVp1.3.2)
See also 'Strategy, s. for kingly popularity - ... my state, seldom but sumptuous, showed like a feast...'
In the play. King Henry gives lessons to Prince Harry on how to win allegiance from the subjects.

Alliance, a. and peace established between old enemies – Smile heaven upon this fair conjunction that long have frown'd upon their enmity!
"We will unite the white rose and the red:
Smile heaven upon this fair conjunction,
That long have frown'd upon their enmity!" (KRIII.5.5)
In the play. The historical and official end of the War of the Roses, officially declared by Richmond who has just won the battle against Richard III.

Alliance, a. between two strong companies - ... two such silver currents, when they join do glorify the banks that bound them in.
"O, two such silver currents, when they join,
Do glorify the banks that bound them in." (KJ.2.2)
Comment on a merger or alliance. A comparison when an important contract has just been signed.
In the play. Hubert of Angiers suggests a marriage that may deflect the threat of war. Lady Blanch is suggested as a wife for the Dauphin of France. The two will make up the 'silver currents'.

Alliance, a. not to be severed - ... 'twere pity to sunder them that yoke so well together.
"... ay, and 'twere pity
To sunder them that yoke so well together." (KHVI p3.4.1)

In the play. *Richard of Gloucester's comment on the marriage between Edward IV and the Lady Grey.*

Alliance, a. reinforced by marriage - … to knit your hearts with an unslipping knot…
"To hold you in perpetual amity,
To make you brothers, and to knit your hearts
With an unslipping knot…"(AC.2.2)
See also 'Fear, mutual f. eliminated by a marriage'
In the play. In the play. *Agrippa explains the benefits of Antony marrying Octavia, Octavian's sister. Antony and Octavian will be like brothers, though it will not turn out that way.*

Alliance, a. weak in power but heartfelt - I give you welcome with a powerless hand but with a heart full of unstained love.
"I give you welcome with a powerless hand,
But with a heart full of unstained love." (KJ.2.1)
Offer an alliance even if practically you cannot be of great immediate help.
In the play. *Arthur, exiled heir to the throne of England to the Archduke of Austria.*

Alliance, questionable a. only based on profit – … a lordly nation that will not trust thee but for profit's sake.
"Who joint'st thou with but with a lordly nation
That will not trust thee but for profit's sake?" (KHVI.p1.3.3)
In the play. *La Pucelle persuades Burgundy to abandon the English and join in with the French.*

Alliance, great and wonderful a. - … two such silver currents, when they join, do glorify the banks that bound them in.
"O, two such silver currents, when they join,
Do glorify the banks that bound them in" (KJ.2)
A comparison when an important contract has just been signed.
In the play. *The first citizen of Angiers propose a marriage between Lady Blanche and the Dauphin of France, the two 'silver currents'*

Alliance, unholy a. - O inglorious league!
"O inglorious league!" (KJ.5.1)
Invocation against an improper alliance.
See also 'Group, g. of bad people agreeing on something bad - Shameful is this league!'
In the play. *The alliance between K. John and the Pope's legate says Faulconbridge to King John.*

Ally, shaky a. - What shalt thou expect, to be depender on a thing that leans.
"…What shalt thou expect,
To be depender on a thing that leans" (CYM.1.5)
In the play. *The Queen finds a rational justification for Imogen's depression. The 'thing that leans' is her husband Posthumous Leonatus, who has been exiled to Rome by Imogen's father, king Cymbeline.*

Alone, a. but busy - I, measuring his affections by my own, that most are busied when they are most alone.
"I, measuring his affections by my own, -
That most are busied when they are most alone." (RJ.1.1)
Answer to question 'Are you busy?' See also 'Solitude, need to be alone for a while, need for space' – 'Solitude, wanting to be alone'.
In the play. Benvolio explains to Lady Montague why he has left Romeo alone with his thoughts.

Alternative, dismal a. - Thus have I shunned the fire for fear of burning; and drench'd me in the sea, where I am drown'd...
"Thus have I shunned the fire for fear of burning;
And drench'd me in the sea, where I am drown'd." (TGV.1.3)
Alternate to 'From the pan into the fire'. See also 'Situation, from one bad s. to another - ... Thus must I from the smoke into the smother...'
In the play. *Proteus wanted to remain in Verona to court Julia and finds himself shipped to Milan by his father Antonio.*

Alternatives, sarcastic, dramatic a. still better than original option - I had rather be set quick i' the earth and bowl'd to death with turnips.
"I had rather be set quick i' the earth, And bowl'd to death with turnips." (MWW.3.4)
Emphatically underscore your refusal to an idea or proposal.
In the play. *Anne Pages' reaction at the idea of being married with Dr. Caius, one of her suitors.*

Amazement, admiring a. - ... every wink of an eye some new grace will be born.
"... every wink of an eye some new grace will be born" (WT.5.2)
Answer to 'What is your impression?' Change 'will be' to 'is' as applicable.
In the play. *A gentleman refers to the unfolding sequence of miraculous events at the court of Leontes.*

Amazement, perceived a. - ... and scarce think their eyes do offices of truth, their words are natural breath.
"...they devour their reason and scarce think
Their eyes do offices of truth, their words
Are natural breath:" (TEM.5.1)
Apply to others as is or to yourself, e.g. 'I scarce think my eyes do offices of truth'.
In the play. *Prospero begins to disclose to the shipwrecked party the history of his arrival in the island with his daughter Miranda and of all subsequent magic.*

Amazement, unbelievable a. - ... makes me more amazed than had I seen the vaulty top of heaven figured quite o'er with burning meteors.
"My heart hath melted at a lady's tears,
Being an ordinary inundation;
But this effusion of such manly drops,
This shower, blown up by tempest of the soul,
Startles mine eyes, and makes me more amazed
Than had I seen the vaulty top of heaven
Figured quite o'er with burning meteors." (KJ.5.2)
In the play. *King Lewis of France to the doubt ridden and crying Lord Salisbury.*

Amazement, waiting for verification of truth - ... doubtful whether what I see be true until confirm'd, sign'd, ratified by you.
"So, thrice fair lady, stand I, even so;
As doubtful whether what I see be true,
Until confirm'd, sign'd, ratified by you." (MOV.3.2)
Make it part of a compliment of her beauty. E.G. 'I am doubtful whether what I see be true...by you'.
In the play. *Bassanio has solved the riddle but waits for Portia's confirmation.*

Amazon, an a. - ... thou art an Amazon and fightest with the sword of Deborah.
"Stay, stay thy hands! thou art an Amazon
And fightest with the sword of Deborah." (KHVI p1.1.2)

Comment on a belligerent woman, e.g. 'She is an Amazon and fights with the sword of Deborah.
In the play. *Charles, test fighting with Joan of Arc is impressed with her strength. Deborah was a prophetess and judge of the Old Testament. She defeated Sisera, a general of the army of Jabin, king of Canaan in one of the endless broils involving the Jews and their neighbors.*

Ambiguity, a deliverer of a. - This is a riddling merchant for the nonce…
"This is a riddling merchant for the nonce;
He will be here, and yet he is not here:
How can these contrarieties agree?" (KHVI.p1.2.4)
See also 'Character, a quibbler. See 'Words, rehearsed w. planted in memory - The fool hath planted in his memory an army of good words.' *** 'Words, silly w., playing with w., - …and discourse will grow commendable only in parrots.'
In the play. *The Countess of Auvergne's judgment on Talbot who understands her tricks and behaves accordingly. 'Nonce' = 'occasion' meaning 'just as the occasion requires'.*

Ambition, a. as a scarlet sin – Thy ambition, thou scarlet sin…
"Thy ambition,
Thou scarlet sin, robb'd this bewailing land
Of noble Buckingham" (KHVIII.3.2)
Attack your political adversary and expose the object and nature of his robbery(ies).
In the play. *Surrey accuses Cardinal Wolsey who had Buckingham (Surrey's father in law), executed.*

Ambition, a. for greatness self-destructing - Thou seek'st the greatness that will o'erwhelm thee.
"O foolish youth!
Thou seek'st the greatness that will o'erwhelm thee." (KHIV p2, 4.5)
In the play. *Ailing King Henry IV upbraids Prince Henry (the future Henry V) due to a misunderstanding.*

Ambition, a. maintained to the point of death – I better brook the loss of brittle life than those proud titles thou hast won of me…
"I better brook the loss of brittle life
Than those proud titles thou hast won of me;
They wound my thoughts worse than sword my flesh" (HIV p1.5.4)
In the play. *Hotspur, mortally wounded by the Prince of Wales in the battle of Shrewsbury, reflects on his pain at having lost his titles. See 'Thought, t. as the slave of life, expressing pessimism - … thought's the slave of life, and life time's fool; and time, that takes survey of all the world, must have a stop.'*

Ambition, a. spurring to action - … I have no spurs to prick the sides of my Intent, but only vaulting ambition…
"…I have no spurs
To prick the sides of my Intent, but only
Vaulting Ambition, which o'erleaps itself,
And falls on the other." (M.1.7)
Modify to describe a character of excessive ambition. 'He needs no spurs to prick the sides of his intent… other'
In the play. *Amidst reservations, Macbeth tries to rationalize to himself the impending assassination of King Duncan*

Ambition, ambitious thoughts - Thoughts tending to ambition, they do plot unlikely wonders…
"Thoughts tending to ambition, they do plot
Unlikely wonders …
And, for they cannot, die in their own pride." (KRII.5.5)
In the play. *Richard II, in prison at Pomfret Castle imagines his thoughts to be people who*

can keep him company in his confinement. In this case, thoughts of ambition.

Ambition, banish the thought - Banish the canker of ambitious thoughts!
"Banish the canker of ambitious thoughts!
And may that thought, when I imagine ill
Against my king and nephew, virtuous Henry,
Be my last breathing in this mortal world." (KHVI p2.1.2)
Defend yourself from accusations of ambitions or similar. Use the first line
In the play. *Gloucester to his wife who urges him on to take advantage of the weak king.*

Ambition, dangerous - Cromwell, I charge thee, fling away ambition: by that sin fell the angels...
"Cromwell, I charge thee, fling away ambition:
By that sin fell the angels; how can man, then,
The image of his Maker, hope to win by it?" (KVIII.3.2)
See also 'Character, ambition. Answer to 'Are you ambitious?'
In the play. *Cardinal Wolsey, fallen and out of favor with the king, advises Cromwell, who replaced Wolsey, not to commit the same mistakes that caused Wolsey's demise. He also tells Cromwell,*
"Say, Wolsey, that once trod the ways of glory,
And sounded all the depths and shoals of honour,
Found thee a way, out of his wreck, to rise in"
'... trod the ways of glory and sounded all the depths and shoals of honour' is a good line of introduction for an illustrious speaker.

Ambition, moderate a. – (You) art not without ambition, but without the illness should attend it...
"...thou wouldst be great;
Art not without ambition, but without
The illness should attend it: what thou wouldst highly,
That wouldst thou holily; wouldst not play false,
And yet wouldst wrongly win" (M.1.5)
Answer to 'What are your ambitions?'
E.G. 'I am not without ambition...attend it'. This may assure the interviewer, especially if you are going to work for him/her.
In the play. *Lady Macbeth's assessment of her husband's character.*

Ambition, not satisfied with the plenty already available - Hast thou not worldly pleasure at command, above the reach and compass of thy thought?
"Hast thou not worldly pleasure at command,
Above the reach and compass of thy thought?
And wilt thou still be hammering treachery,
To tumble down thy husband and thyself
From top of honour to disgrace's feet?
Away from me, and let me hear no more!" (KHVI.p2.1.2)
Refuse an advancement or what appears as an advancement or a questionable advantage. E.G., 'I have worldly pleasures at my command above the reach and compass of my thought'. With the last line, "away from me..." express disgust at what you have been told or proposed.
In the play. *Gloucester to his wife who urges him on to take advantage of the weak king*

Amen, prompt concurrence with a wish – Let me say 'amen' betimes, lest the devil cross my prayer...

**SALARINO I would it might prove the end of his losses.
SALANIO Let me say 'amen' betimes, lest the devil cross my prayer, for here he comes in the likeness of a Jew.** (MOV.3.1)
In the play. *The losses (of Antonio) referred to are his allegedly sunken ships and the chance that he, Antonio, may not be able to repay Shylock's bond.*

Amends, impossible to make amends but... - I cannot make you what amends I would, therefore accept such kindness as I can.
"I cannot make you what amends I would,
Therefore accept such kindness as I can." (KRIII.4.4)
In the play. *Richard III in conversation with Queen Elizabeth, widow of Henry IV. After having killed her sons he now wants to marry her daughter and pretends to regret the murders.*

Angel, complete identity to an a. - An angel is like you, Kate; and you are like an angel.
"**An angel is like you, Kate; and you are like an angel**." (KHV.5.2)
Modify according to the name of the lady
In the play, *Henry V woos Kathryn of France after having defeated the French at Agincourt.*

Angel, or very close to one - By Jupiter an angel, or if not, an earthly paragon.
"**By Jupiter an angel, or if not, an earthly paragon**." (CYM.3.6)
Show your astonishment at such a perfection. Or use to soothe her feelings if you were not so kind to her beforehand and she believes that you do not think too highly of her.
In the play. *Imogen, disguised in man's attire, shows up at Belarius' place in the country. But her beauty shows through anyway and leaves Belarius and company astounded.*

**Angel, (saint) or very close to one - is she not a heavenly saint?... No, but she is an earthly paragon.
VALENTINE Even she; and is she not a heavenly saint?
PROTEUS No; but she is an earthly paragon.** (TGV.2.4)
Combine, e.g. 'she may not be a heavenly saint but she is an earthly paragon'.
In the play. *Now both in Milan, Valentine extols the praises of Julia.*

Angels, a. are a. even if some of them become rotten - Angels are bright still, though the brightest fell...
"That which you are my thoughts cannot transpose:
Angels are bright still, though the brightest fell;
Though all things foul would wear the brows of grace,
Yet grace must still look so." (M.4.3)
The first line can be an answer to 'What do you think of me?'
In the play. *Malcolm to Macduff after commenting on the changes that made Macbeth a tyrant.*

Angels, an army of a. – ... if angels fight, weak men must fall, for heaven still guards the right.
"...if angels fight,
Weak men must fall, for heaven still guards the right" (KRII.3.2)
In the play. *Self-delusional King Richard, still hopes in a reversal of the rebellion started by Bolingbroke.*

ANGER
Call it anger, call it irritation, it is humanly impossible to always avoid it. In the play Timon of Athens Alcibiades, in attempting to excuse a friend's behavior says to the Athenian senators, "To be angry is impiety; / But who is man that is not angry?" And in the same play, Shakespeare has even one of the characters quote the Latin philosopher

Seneca, the private tutor of Roman Emperor Nero, "Ira furor brevis est", or "Anger is a short lived fury". It is inevitable, no relationship is ever and always completely smooth. A fact well illustrated by the lines uttered by Lysander in Midsummer Night's Dream, "LYSANDER. ... for aught that I could ever read, /Could ever hear by tale or history, /The course of true love never did run smooth." Considering Seneca's finding that repressed anger hurts both mind and body ("Ira quae tegitur nocet" (De Ira)), you may adopt Mark Twain's technique "When angry count until four, when very angry swear" (Pudd'nhead Wilson). In a relationship, it would seem advisable to hold a middle course, that is, neither repression nor fury. Words told can never come back.

There are two key distinctions or cases - whether she is angry at you or whether you are angry at her. Here we deal primarily with the case when she is angry at you - the best technique is to deflect the anger with a compliment. Carefully observe, however, whether she gets red or white when she gets angry. In his Treatise on Passion, the French philosopher Descartes (1596 – 1650) maintains that "Those who grow pale with anger are more to be feared than those who grow red". Check her color and choose your lines accordingly.

Ovid compares love to war. 'Love is a kind of warfare; on ye laggards! These banners are not for the timid men to guard. Night, storm, long journeys, cruel pains, all kind of toil are in this dainty camp. Oft will you put up with rain from melting clouds of heaven, and oft you'll lie cold on the bare ground.' AOL.2.

Anger - My heart for anger burns; I cannot brook it.
"My heart for anger burns; I cannot brook it." (KHVI p3.1.1)
Express your anger forcefully

In the play. *Westmoreland's reaction at the thought of Richard Plantagenet, duke of York, becoming king instead of Henry VI. York is defiantly already sitting on the throne.*

Anger, a. aroused with difficulty and quickly extinguished – ... That carries anger as the flint bears fire, who... shows a hasty spark and straight is cold again.
"O Cassius, you are yoked with a lamb
That carries anger as the flint bears fire;
Who, much enforced, shows a hasty spark,
And straight is cold again" (JC.4.3)
Answer to 'Do you get angry easily?'
E.G. 'I carry anger as the flint bears fire... cold again'
In the play. *Brutus has accused Cassius of bribe taking but now his anger has subsided.*

Anger, a. at authorities - ... woe upon ye, and all such false professors!
"... woe upon ye,
And all such false professors!"
(KHVIII.3.1)
A good mix of insult and curse. Use against false accusers
In the play. *Katherine is angry at Wolsey and Campeius.*

Anger, a. at news that makes the blood curdle, invocation - ... then my best blood turn to an infected jelly.
"... O, then my best blood turn
To an infected jelly, my name
Be yoked with his that did betray the Best!
Turn then my freshest reputation to
A savour that may strike the dullest nostril
Where I arrive, and my approach be shunned." (WT.1.2)
Express your disgust at being unjustly accused of a despicable act.

In the play. *Polixenes is astounded at the idea of having been accused of an improper relationship with Leonte's wife Hermione.*

Anger, a. barely repressed - Scarce can I speak, my choler is so great. O, I could hew up rocks and fight with flint.
"Scarce can I speak, my choler is so great:
O, I could hew up rocks and fight with flint." (KHVI p2.5.1)
In the play. *Ready to battle the forces of King Henry VI, York is angry at the terms of peace offered by the king.*

Anger, a. boiling up to the point of explosion - The bow is bent and drawn, make from the shaft.
"The bow is bent and drawn, make from the shaft." (KL.1.1)
In the play. *Lear to Kent who intervenes in favor of Cordelia, the sincere and only truly reliable daughter.*

Anger, a. caused by sustained unjust treatment or injuries - ... great Northumberland, whose bosom burns with an incensed fire of injuries.
"... great Northumberland, whose bosom burns
With an incensed fire of injuries."
(KHIV.p2.1.3)
Make a dramatic statement, 'My bosom burns with an incensed fire of injuries'.
In the play. *After the defeat at Shrewsbury, the rebels regroup. Hastings believes that Northumberland has an ax to grind with the King Henry IV and will join the rebel's cause.*

Anger, a. detected but inexplicable – I understand a fury in your words but not the words.
"...what doth your speech import?
I understand a fury in your words.
But not the words." (OTH.4.2)

In the play. *Desdemona, unaware of Iago's plot, cannot understand why her husband Othello seems so angry with her.*

Anger, a. increased by pleading - ... if thou dost plead for him, thou wilt but add increase unto my wrath.
"... if thou dost plead for him,
Thou wilt but add increase unto my wrath." (KHVI p2.3.2)
In the play. *K. Henry to Q. Margaret who is pleading for Suffolk's cause.*

Anger, a. justified - ... know you no reverence? ... Yes, sir; but anger hath a privilege.
CORNWALL Peace, sirrah!
You beastly knave, know you no reverence?
KENT Yes, sir; but anger hath a privilege. (KL.2.2)
In the play. *Kent is mad at the rascally and cowardly Oswald,, a servant and accomplice of the Duke of Cornwall and of the two evil sisters, Regan and Goneril.*

Anger, a. more easily provoked by depression or bad luck – ... When my good stars, that were my former guides have empty left their orbs...
"And at this time most easy 'tis to do't,
When my good stars, that were my former guides,
Have empty left their orbs, and shot their fires
Into the abysm of hell." (AC.3.13)
In the play. *Antony to envoy from the victorious Caesar Octavian.*

Anger, a. not constructive – ... more is to be said and to be done than out of anger can be uttered.
"For more is to be said and to be done,
Than out of anger can be uttered."
(KHIV p1.1.1)

Counsel calm when the argument is turning into a brawl.
In the play. *Henry IV has called for Harry Percy (Hotspur) to come to Windsor. Percy is accused of impudence or subordination.*

Anger, a. not good for safety – … never anger made good guard for itself.
"… never anger
Made good guard for itself." (AC.4.1)
In the play. *Mecaenas comments on Antony's state of mind after losing the sea battle to Octavian.*

Anger, a. not to be repressed - My tongue will tell the anger of my heart, or else my heart concealing it will break.
"My tongue will tell the anger of my heart,
Or else my heart concealing it will break." (TOS.4.3)
When you have finally decided not to be quiet any longer. See also 'Pain, mental p. relieved by talking about it - Give sorrow words: the grief that does not speak…'
*** 'Grievances, g. aired out - windy attorneys to their client's woes …. let them have scope.'
In the play. *Katharina is mad at Petruchio over a hat of hers that she likes and he doesn't.*

Anger, a. or superciliousness simulated and not real - How eagerly I taught my brow to frown when inward joy enforc'd my heart to smile.
"How eagerly I taught my brow to frown,
When inward joy enforc'd my heart to smile!" (TGV.1.2)
When you (or she) said no but really meant yes.
In the play. *Julia pretends not to love Proteus.*

Anger, a. self-destructive - … She'll gallop fast enough to her destruction.
"She's tickled now; her fume can need no spurs,
She'll gallop fast enough to her destruction." (KHVI p2.1.3)
Show how anger can lead to destruction. Change 'she' to 'he' and 'her' to 'him' as applicable.
In the play. *Buckingham on the Duchess of Gloucester who has left angry at Queen Margaret. The Queen, to provoke her, had hit her in the head.*

Anger, a. vented - My tongue will tell the anger of my heart…
"My tongue will tell the anger of my heart;
Or else my heart, concealing it, will break." (TOS.4.3)
An introduction to justify your anger. See also 'Pain, mental p. relieved by talking about it' – 'Hunger, feeling incredibly hungry'
In the play. *Katharina cannot take any more the corrective treatment handed out to her by her husband Petruchio and complains to him.*

Anger, acknowledge her a. – … since I am near slain, kill me outright with looks and rid my pain.
"…since I am near slain,
Kill me outright with looks and rid my pain." (SON 39)
Acknowledge her anger, as well as the hatred conveyed by her expression.

Anger, advice to contain a. - … let your reason with your choler question...
"... let your reason with your choler question
What 't is you go about; ... to climb steep hills,
Requires slow pace at first: anger is like
A full hot horse, who, being allowed his way,
Self mettle tires him." (KHVIII.1.1)

Warn and persuade not to make hasty decisions out of anger.
In the play. *Norfolk advises Buckingham to cool it off.*

Anger, are you patient? - Patience is sottish, and impatience does become a dog that's mad.
"…All's but naught
Patience is sottish, and impatience does
Become a dog that's mad" (AC.4.15)
Try for example, "Good question - to suffer in patience is bad but to show impatience will not improve the situation. I hold the view of Cleopatra, "Patience is sottish, and impatience does become a dog that's mad." With this or a similar answer you leave your options open to choose between using patience or expressing your impatience.
In the play. *Caesar has defeated Antony and Cleopatra ponders whether to ride the course of events or seek an early death.*

Anger, bad but natural - To be in anger is impiety but who is man that is not angry?
"To be in anger is impiety;
But who is man that is not angry?" (TOA.3.5)
In the play. *Alcibiades tries to explain to the unmovable Athenians senators why am otherwise good soldier killed another soldier in a fit of anger.*

Anger, behavior of crowd's anger - … like an angry hive of bees that want their leader, scatter up and down…
"The commons, like an angry hive of bees
That want their leader, scatter up and down
And care not who they sting in his revenge." (KHVI p2.3.2)
See also entries for 'Masses' ***
'Opinion, your op. on crowds and masses'

In the play. *Warwick reports to King Henry VI on the mood of the Commons, who are angry at Suffolk, rightly suspected of Gloucester's death.*

Anger, consequences of not contained a. - This tiger-footed rage, when it shall find the harm of unscann'd swiftness…
"This tiger-footed rage, when it shall find
The harm of unscann'd swiftness, will too late
Tie leaden pounds to's heels. Proceed by process" (COR.3.1)
Counsel restraint and the following of grievance redress procedures.
In the play. *Menenius counsels calm to the enraged tribunes who want Coriolanus immediately condemned.*

Anger, even her a. is an occasion for admiration - … wonderful when angels are so angry.
"More wonderful when angels are so angry". (R3.2.2)
After delivering the compliment, keep in mind and remember the principle of compliance, consisting in (apparent) compliance with all her wishes. On this issue Ovid suggests, 'I do not bid you arm and climb the forests of Maenalus*, nor carry nets upon your neck; nor do I bid you offer your breasts to flying arrows; a cautious lover will find the precepts of my art easy. Yield if she resists; by yielding you will depart the victor; only play the part she bids you to play. Blame if she blames; approve whatever she approves. Affirm what she affirms and deny what she denies. If she laughs, laugh with her; if she weeps, remember to weep; let her impose her laws upon your countenance' (Ovid, AOL.2)
* The Maenalus mountain range is in Arcadia in the center of the Peloponnese (Greece). The mountains were said to be

sacred to the God Pan. Pan, son of Zeus, was the Greek God who looked after shepherds and their flocks.
In the play. *Richard of Gloucester, who has slain Clarence, Anne's husband, is now trying to woo her. The exchange in itself has some quoting possibilities.*
ANNE. No beast so fierce but knows some touch of pity.
RICHARD. But I know none, and therefore am no beast
ANNE O wonderful, when devils tell the truth
RICHARD. More wonderful when angels are so angry.
'**O wonderful, when devils tell the truth**' may apply sarcastically or amicably to a statement which you recognize true by a person whom you wish to poke friendly fun at.

Anger, her a. an occasion for a compliment - Never came poison from so sweet a place.
"Never came poison from so sweet a place" (R3.1.2)
An excellent way to deflect the shafts of her anger by turning the situation into an occasion for a compliment. See also 'Beautiful, even when expressing contempt - o, what a deal of scorn looks beautiful in the contempt and anger of his lip.' *** 'Anger, even her a. is an occasion for admiration -. .. wonderful when angels are so angry.' *** 'Rejection, rebuttal to rejection or harsh words - Teach not thy lip such scorn; for it was made for kissing, lady, not for such contempt.'
In the play. *Anne has just spit at Richard.*

Anger, rage compared to a river at flood stage – Like an unseasonable stormy day which makes the silver rivers drown their shores…
"Like an unseasonable stormy day, Which makes the silver rivers drown their shores,
As if the world were all dissolved to tears,
So high above his limits swells the rage
Of Bolingbroke…"** (KRII.3.2)
In the play. *Lord Scroop reports to King Richard on the doings of Bolingbroke in England*

Anger, rage extreme and calling for blood - A rage whose heat that this condition, that nothing can allay, nothing but blood.
"… I am burn'd up with inflaming wrath,
A rage whose heat that this condition, That nothing can allay, nothing but blood." (KJ.3.1)
Express your outrage.
In the play. *King John is angry at the French, who have broken the treaty under the influence injunctions of the Pope's legate.*

Anger, state of a. - The fire of rage is in him.
"The fire of rage is in him" (CYM.1.1)
Describe an angry person.
In the play. *The queen refers to King Cymbeline's anger with his daughter Imogen for marrying Leonatus against the king's will.*

Anger, two characters angry at each other - in rage deaf as the sea, hasty as fire.
"High-stomach'd are they both, and full of ire,
In rage deaf as the sea, hasty as fire." (KRII.1.1)
Comment on two characters who hate each other.
In the play. *Bolingbroke and Mowbray, angry at each other, appeal to the King Richard II, who calls for them.*

Anger, unable to refrain from expressing a. - my tongue will tell the anger of my heart.

"My tongue will tell the anger of my heart,
Or else my heart concealing it will break," (TOS.4.3)
See also 'Pain, mental p. relieved by talking about it' – 'Grievances, g. aired out - windy attorneys to their client's woes ... let them have scope.'
In the play. *Katharina is at the end of her resistance after having put up with her husband Petruchio's strange antics.*

Angry, a. and furious to the point of tears – Mad ire and wrathful fury makes me weep
"Mad ire and wrathful fury makes me weep" (KHVI.p1.4.3)
In the play. *York is angry at Somerset for not having brought military help to the encircled Talbot.*

Angry, a. and unable to maintain silence - ... Yet can I not of such tame patience boast as to be hash's, and nought at all to say.
"The blood is hot that must be cool'd for this.
Yet can I not of such tame patience boast,
As to be hash's, and nought at all to say." (KRII.1.1)
Retort to an unfair accusation.
In the play. *Mowbray answers Bolingbroke's accusations of treason.*

Angry, a. at her compared to a she-wolf - She-wolf of France, but worse than wolves of France, whose tongue more poisons than the adder's tooth.
"She-wolf of France, but worse than wolves of France,
Whose tongue more poisons than the adder's tooth!
How ill-beseeming is it in thy sex
To triumph, like an Amazonian trull,
Upon their woes whom fortune captivates!" (KH6 p3.1.4)

Change 'France' to another applicable place, e.g. Minneapolis-St. Paul, etc. Expressing anger is not a tool of seduction. However, as it is inevitable that at times she may be angry at you, so you will be angry at her some times. A poetical outburst is at least elegant, if not, maybe, more effective than a standard or vulgar outburst. See also the next entries from the same address.
In the play. *Queen Margaret, who now leads the forces of Lancaster, has defeated the Yorkist army at a battle conducted near Wakefield. The dying York (defeated by Clifford) has obviously still enough strength to rail at Queen Margaret. 'Trull'='a lewd and worthless woman'.*

Angry, a. at her, compared to a tiger in disguise - O tiger's heart wrapt in a woman's hide!...
"O tiger's heart wrapt in a woman's hide!
…
"Women are soft, mild, pitiful and flexible;
Thou stern, obdurate, flinty, rough, remorseless."
….
you are more inhuman, more inexorable,
O, ten times more, than tigers of Hyrcania." (KH6 p3.1.4)
In the play. *See entry for 'Anger. Angry at her - compared to a she-wolf.'*

Angry, a. at her, the opposite of every good - Thou art as opposite to every good as the Antipodes are unto us or as the south to the septentrion.
"Thou art as opposite to every good
As the Antipodes are unto us,
Or as the south to the septentrion." (KH6 p3.1.4)
In the play. *See entry for 'Anger. Angry at her - compared to a she-wolf.'*

Angry, too a. to speak - boiling choler chokes the hollow passage of my prison'd voice.
"Speak Winchester; for boiling choler chokes
The hollow passage of my prison'd voice,
By sight of these our baleful enemies" KHVI.p1.5.4)
When you are too angry to speak out, e.g. 'I cannot speak because boiling choler chokes…voice'.
In the play. *York asks Winchester to answer Charles of France who, along with other French lords, has come over to arrange a truce. Winchester's anger stems from just seeing his former enemies.*

Animal, man acting like an a. or woman - thy wild acts denote the unreasonable fury of a beast…
"Thy wild acts denote
The unreasonable fury of a beast.
Unseemly woman in a seeming man!" (RJ.3.3)
Use in a meeting or debate when your adversary behaves or speaks irrationally.
In the play. *Romeo draws his sword suggesting an attempted suicide and Fr. Lawrence boldly reprimands him.*

Animals, a. better than men - … give it the beasts, to be rid of the men.
TIMON. What wouldst thou do with the world,
Apemantus, if it lay in thy power?
APEMANTUS Give it the beasts, to be rid of the men." (TOA.4.3)
See also entries for 'Man and its wicked nature' - 'Dogs, d. preferable to men'.
In the play. *The cantankerous Apemantus answers a question from Timon.*

Animals, a. better than men - the unkindest beast more kinder than mankind.
"Timon will to the woods; where he shall find
The unkindest beast more kinder than mankind." (TOA.4.1)
See also entries for 'Man and its wicked nature' – 'Dogs, d. preferable to men'.
In the play. *The overgenerous Timon, abandoned by all friends when in need of their help, retires to the wilderness.*

Announcement, self-a. via a third party - …importunes personal conference with his grace…
"Tell him, the daughter of the King of France,
On serious business, craving quick dispatch,
Importunes personal conference with his grace:
Haste, signify so much; while we attend,
Like humble-visaged suitors, his high will." (LLL.2.1)
In the play. *The Princess instructs Boyet on what to say to the King of Navarre.*

Annoyance, enemies creating more a. than damage - The eagle suffers little birds to sing…
"The eagle suffers little birds to sing,
And is not careful what they mean thereby,
Knowing that with the shadow of his wings
He can at pleasure stint their melody:" (TA.4.4)
In the play. *Tamora cheers up dejected emperor Saturninus who has just heard that his enemies are marching on Rome.*

Annoyance, enemies creating more a. than damage - …though they cannot greatly sting to hurt…
"For though they cannot greatly sting to hurt,
Yet look to have them buzz, to offend thine ears." (KHVI p3.2.6)
Comment on an enemy that cannot hurt but still can annoy.

In the play. *Warwick will get the Lady Bona of France to marry Edward so as to ensure the amity of France, therefore Edward's enemies won't have France to rely on for support. Those that 'cannot greatly sting', at the moment, are the defeated Henry VI and allies.*

Annoying, arrogant and unpleasant to hear – she does abuse our ears…
"She does abuse our ears: to prison with her." (AWEW.5.3)
Change 'she' to 'you' as applicable and delete 'to prison with her' unless you are a policeman.
In the play. *The King cannot as yet believe Diana's story of how she came to possess the ring she is wearing.*

Anonymity, pleasures of a. -
Methinks it were a happy life to be no better than a homely swain…
"O God! methinks it were a happy life
To be no better than a homely swain;
To sit upon a hill, as I do now,
To carve out dials quaintly, point by point,
Thereby to see the minutes how they run." (KHVI p3.2.5)
Answer to a question about the reasons for your secluded life. Why you enjoy a life made up of simple and peaceful pleasures. See also entries for 'Life, simple l.'.
In the play. *Henry VI's thoughts as a battle rages that will affect his destiny.*

Answer, a. clear and unequivocal -
What plain proceeding is more plain than this?
"What plain proceeding is more plain than this?" (KHVI p2.2.2)
Counter an objection of obscurity of meaning.
In the play. *Warwick agrees with York's explanation that he, York, has a right to the throne of England.*

Answer, a. delayed due to melancholy – … My mind was troubled with deep melancholy.
"... Pardon me,
That I have given no answer all this while,
My mind was troubled with deep melancholy." (KHVI p2.5.1)
Delay your answer and prepare the audience to accept that you will raise objections.
In the play. *York to Buckingham who is asking why the display of armed force so near the king. York is containing his anger as he is actually plotting to overthrow the king.*

Answer, a. fitting all questions – It is like a barber's chair, that fits all buttocks…
COUNTESS. Marry, that's a bountiful answer, that fits all questions.
CLOWN. It is like a barber's chair, that fits all buttocks. the pin-buttock, the quatch-buttock, the brawn buttock, or any buttock. (AWEW.2.3)
Demolish your adversary when he answers evasively. E.G. 'your answer is like a barber's chair, that fits all buttocks'. For another semi-poetical use of 'buttocks' see the comment to 'Characters, similarity of c.'
In the play, *In Rousillon, the clown and the Countess exchange some banter. "Quatch-buttock = flat buttock".*

Answer, a, with one word impossible – …to say ay and no to these particulars is more than to answer in a catechism.
ROSALIND. Answer me in one word.
CELIA You must borrow me Gargantua's mouth first: 'tis a word too great for any mouth of this age's size. To say ay and no to these particulars is more than to answer in a catechism. (AYLI.3.2)
In the play. *Rosalind asks all sorts of questions about Orlando and expects a one-word answer from Celia. Gargantua was a large man, fond of eating and equipped with a large mouth.*

Answer, an a. you would wish you could give - That answer might have become Apemantus.
"That answer might have become Apemantus." (TOA.2.2)
Alternate to 'I wish I said that', change 'Apemantus' with your name.
In the play. *The fool gives a witty reply to a servant of Varro (Varro is one of Timon's questionable friends). Apemantus is impressed.*

Answer, answerer is not obliged to please the questioner - I am not bound to please thee with my answers.
"I am not bound to please thee with my answers." (MOV.4.1)
Answer to 'I don't like your answer'.
In the play. *Shylock replies to a comment by Bassanio as to Shylock's answer to the Duke of Venice.*

Answer, difficulty to a. a base man - What answer shall I make to this base man?…
"Princes and noble lords,
What answer shall I make to this base man?
Shall I so much dishonour my fair stars,
On equal terms to give him chastisement?" (KRII.4.1)
In the play. *Aumerle rhetorically asks his audience scornfully how should he answer Bagot's accusations. See 'Denial, difficulty to deny previous statement – I know your daring tongue scorns to unsay what once it hath deliver'd…'*

Answer, hesitating to a. - … But how to make ye suddenly an answer… to such men of gravity and learning, in truth, I know not.
"But how to make ye suddenly an answer,
In such a point of weight, so near mine honour,--
More near my life, I fear,--with my weak wit,
And to such men of gravity and learning,
In truth, I know not" (KHVIII.3.1)
In the play. *Q. Kathryn to Cardinals Wolsey and Campeius.*

Answer, injunction to stop giving silly a. – No more light answers.
"No more light answers" (AC.1.2)
In the play. *Antony to Enobarbus who makes light of political and military threats to Antony's position.*

Answer, irrelevant a. - … put your discourse into some frame and start not so wildly from my affair.
"Good my lord, put your discourse into some frame and start not so wildly from my affair." (H.3.2)
In the play. *Guilderstern asks Hamlet not to misunderstand his message referring to the anger of the king and the dismay of the Queen, after watching the play produced by Hamlet.*

Answer, on the point of giving reluctantly a nasty answer - will you tear impatient answers from my gentle tongue?
"….What, will you tear
Impatient answers from my gentle tongue? (MND.3.2)

Try 'Do not force impatient answers from my gentle tongue.'
In the play. *Helena replies to Hermia who accuses Helena of having stolen her boyfriend.*

Answer, request to have an a. - ... O, answer me! Let me not burst in ignorance.
"…O, answer me!
Let me not burst in ignorance" (H.1.4)
In the play. *Hamlet pleads with the Ghost to reveal himself.*

Answer, retort to irrational a. - Your reasons are too shallow and too quick.
"Your reasons are too shallow and too quick." (KRIII.4.4)
In the play. *After having murdered her sons, Richard has the gall to ask Queen Elizabeth to marry her younger daughter Anne. She answers scornfully and Richard pushes on with his request.*

Answer, unable to a. tit for tat - I am so full of businesses, I cannot answer thee acutely.
"I am so full of businesses, I cannot answer thee acutely." (AWEW.1.3)
In the play. *Parolles to Helena who has ridiculed his cowardice.*

Answer, witty but unconvincing a. - you are full of pretty answers…
"You are full of pretty answers. ….
You have a nimble wit;
I think it was made of Atalanta's heels." (AYLI.3.2)
A sarcastic comment on what said.
In the play. *Jaques to Orlando, they dislike each other.*

Answering, buying time to answer - the charm dissolves apace… mantle their clearer reason.
". … The charm dissolves apace;
And as the morning steals upon the night,
Melting the darkness, so their rising senses
Begin to chase the ignorant fumes that mantle
Their clearer reason." (TEM.5.1)
Whatever she may ask and you cannot find an answer, e.g. 'Just a moment, let my rising senses begin to chase the ignorant fumes that mantle their clearer reason'. Applicable also when you wake up dazed or have just recovered from a hangover. See also 'Speech, gaining time before speaking up - ... he's winding up the watch of his wit' by and by it will strike.'
In the play. *With the help of Ariel, Antonio and others find themselves dazed and in a circle but now Prospero decides that the magic will come to an end.*

Antagonism, a. strategically provoked - Two curs shall tame each other…
"Two curs shall tame each other: pride alone
Must tarre the mastiffs on, as 'twere their bone." (TC.1.3)
In the play. *The two mastiffs are Ajax and Achilles. Ulysses lays a plot whereby they will vie for supremacy and in so doing fight harder for the Greeks. 'To tarre' = 'To provoke'.*

Anticipation and increased heart beat - my heart beats thicker than a feverous pulse…
"My heart beats thicker than a feverous pulse;
And all my powers do their bestowing lose,
Like vassalage at unawares encountering
The eyes of majesty." (TC.3.2)
She just said that she will be back soon – you can just use the first line.

Sometimes the feeling of anticipation is associated with gory and macho images of (anticipated) complete possession, equal in spirit and impact, for example, in the killing of an animal. In writing to Ann Boleyn, King Henry VIII explains the circumstances that will make possible her rejoining him in London and his feelings of anticipation, '…no more to you, at this present, mine awne darling, for lake of time; but that I would you were in myne arms, or I in yours; for I think it long since I kyseth you. Written after the killing of a hart (a deer), at XI of the clock; minding with God's grace tomorrow, mightily tymely to kill another, by the hand of him, which I trust shortly shall be yours, Henry Rex'.
In the play. *Troilus awaits the arrival of Cressida in the orchard.*

Anticipation and time passing slowly - Time goes on crutches till love have all his rites.
"Time goes on crutches till love have all his rites." (MAAN.2.1)
Your comment when she excuses herself for being late.
In the play. *Claudio is passionately in love with Hero.*

Anticipation, day tedious waiting for night - so tedious is the day as is the night before some festival to an impatient child…
"So tedious is the day,
As is the night before some festival
To an impatient child that has new robes
And may not wear them." (RJ.3.2)
Good line for a card. Precede with 'Until I see you…"So tedious …wear them."
In the play. *Juliet eagerly awaits the night when Romeo will arrive.*

Anticipation, giddy - I am giddy; expectation whirls me round…
"I am giddy; expectation whirls me round.
The imaginary relish is so sweet
That it enchants my sense; what will it be,
When that the watery palate tastes indeed
Love's thrice reputed nectar?" (TC.3.2)
A good line at a romantic dinner – possibly a follow up when she says 'I am late'. But Ovid cautions against feverish haste, 'Believe me, love's bliss must not be hastened, but gradually lured on by slow delay.' (AOL.2)
In the play. *Troilus awaits the arrival of Cressida in the orchard.*

Anticipation, love's shadows alluring - how sweet is love itself possess'd, when but love's shadows are so rich in joy.
"Ah me! How sweet is love itself possess'd,
When but love's shadows are so rich in joy." (RJ5.1)
Declare on the phone your pleasure at the idea of seeing her this evening, with a strong hint at your intentions. Use these lines after she says, 'This evening then' or equivalent.
In the play: *Romeo, who escaped to Mantua after killing a Capulet in a duel, longs for and dreams of Juliet.*

Anticipation, wishing for the appointed day to be next - … I would that Thursday were to-morrow.
"My lord, I would that Thursday were to-morrow." (RJ.3.4)
Answer to 'Let's meet on day xx' assuming that 'xx' is later than the next day.
In the play. *Lord Capulet fixes for Thursday the wedding date for Paris and Juliet. Paris cannot wait for the day.*

Anxiety, a. about what may happen at the office while you are away – I am questioned by my fears, of what may chance or breed upon our absence.
"I am questioned by my fears, of what may chance
Or breed upon our absence." (WT.1)
Explain why you have to return to base. See also 'Leadership, consequences of an absent leader'.
In the play. *Leontes wants Polixenes to stay longer but Polixenes is concerned about what may be going on in his own kingdom of Bohemia.*

Anxiety, a. at doing something you don't like but must do - Since I receiv'd command to do this business I have not slept a wink.
"Since I receiv'd command to do this business,
I have not slept one wink." (CYM.3.4)
You have been given an assignment that keeps you on the edge
In the play. *Pisanio was instructed by Posthumous to kill Imogen on account of her alleged infidelity.*

Anxiety, obsession, missing her presence - how can I then return in happy plight, that am debarred the benefit of rest?...
"How can I then return in happy plight,
That am debarred the benefit of rest?
When day's oppression is not eased by night,
But day by night and night by day oppressed." (SON.28)
Tell her that you need her constant presence and you miss her when she is absent. And when she asks "How are you?", reply (if it applies), "My day's oppression is not eased by night, but day by night and night by day oppressed."

Anxiety, a. perceived and questioned - what is't that takes from thee thy stomach, pleasure and thy golden sleep?
"Tell me, sweet lord, what is't that takes from thee
Thy stomach, pleasure and thy golden sleep?" (KHIV.p1.2.3)
In the play, *Lady Percy asks her husband Hotspur the motives for his sleeplessness and anxiety*

Anxiety, state of a., concern - with my vex'd spirits I cannot take a truce.
"And though thou now confess thou didst but jest,
With my vex'd spirits I cannot take a truce,
But they will quake and tremble all this day." (KJ.3.1)
Alternative to "I am concerned" - "With my vexed...... truce."
In the play. *Constance to Salisbury who has tentatively informed Constance of the pending agreement between the king of France and King John to which she bitterly objects.*

Anxiety, state of a., hope and fear mixed - I feel such sharp dissension in my breast...
"I feel such sharp dissension in my breast
Such fierce alarums both of hope and fear,
As I am sick with working with my thoughts." (KHVI.p1.5.5)
Answer to 'how are you' or 'what do you think?' if the subject is one on which you cannot decide.
In the play. *In conversation with Suffolk Henry VI declares to be edgy and anxious while waiting to e for the first time his future bride, Margaret.*

Anxiety, a. till return - ... till you do return, I rest perplexed with a thousand cares.
"...till you do return,
I rest perplexed with a thousand cares." (KHVI p1.5.5)

Comment after she says that she goes out shopping. Answer to 'How are you?'
In the play. *Henry VI to Suffolk, the cares refer to Henry's anxiety until Margaret, his future wife and queen, will arrive from France.*

Anxious and undecided - I rest perplexed with a thousand cares.
"I rest perplexed with a thousand cares" (KHVI.p1.5.5)
See also entries for 'indecision'. Answer to 'Are you worried?'
In the play. *Henry VI is torn between wanting to marry Margaret of France and the other English lords who object to the marriage*

Anxious while waiting for her answer – thus ready for the way of life or death I wait the sharpest blow.
"Thus ready for the way of life or death,
I wait the sharpest blow." (PER.1.1)
You have just asked her to marry you and are waiting for her answer. Or it could be her answer to any other important or critical question. See also 'Reply, anxiously awaiting for her r. - ... expecting thy reply, I profane my lips on thy foot...'
– 'Character, not afraid of taking chances - I have set my life upon a cast and I will stand the hazard of the die.'
In the play. Antiochus, king of Antiochia will give her daughter in marriage to whoever will answer a riddle – if the solution is incorrect, the prospect will be killed. King Pericles answers the challenge and is 'ready for the sharpest blow.'

Anything, a. but this – ...I had rather be a toad, and upon the vapour of a dungeon, than...
"...I had rather be a toad,
And live upon the vapour of a dungeon,
Than ..." (OTH.3.3)
In the play. *Worked on by the perfidious Iago, Othello begins to doubt of Desdemona's fidelity.*

Anything but seeing this – I had rather have skipp'd from sixteen years of age to sixty...
" ... I had rather
Have skipp'd from sixteen years of age to sixty,
To have turn'd my leaping-time into a crutch,
Than have seen this." (CYM.4.2)
In the play. *Arviragus on seeing the seemingly dead Imogen.*

APHRODISIACS
The idea that a man's sex appeal may be increased by mechanical or chemical alterations of his anatomy is frankly disgusting. It lowers man to the level of animals, actually even below them. Cows would not, by themselves, take hormones to produce more milk. And God only knows what will be the long-term effect on humans of hormone-laced milk.
But through history a myth has been kept alive that certain foods, medicines or preparations may enhance the romantic mood of the partaker. Old recipes or remedies, however ineffective, have at least the gift of originality.
In the play 'Clizia' by Machiavelli (the same author who also wrote "The Prince"), we find this dietary recommendation - 'First of all a salad of boiled onions to which a mixture of lima beans and spices should be added. These onions, lima beans and spices, as they are hot and windy, would have enough power to propel a Genoese galleon. Along with this salad take care to eat a large pigeon, medium rare, with some of its blood still in it."
In the Middle Ages all food classified as 'windy' was supposed to have aphrodisiac powers. Besides onions, an aphrodisiac diet would include chestnuts and, even better, eggplants. For old men with young wives the recommended stimulant

food were truffles (assuming they could afford them).

But King Henry VIII may have found useful a diet that would reduce rather than increase his amorous propensities. A foreign diplomat reporting on the king to the government of Venice wrote, "he has seen few young women whom he did not desire - and very few he desired whom he did not rape." (quod paucas vidit pulchriores quas non concupierit, et paucissimas non concupierit quas non violarit".

Number one among aphrodisiac foods were sparrows. In his 'Very Useful Treatise for the Maintenance of Health' - written by Michele Savonarola in 1554 for Niccolo' Borso, Duke of Ferrara in Italy - he recommends a sparrow-based diet, on the authority of Aristotle's observation that sparrows make love 83 times an hour.

Actually, Duke Borso may not have needed stimulants. A popular pun of his time went, 'On this side and on the other side of the river Po, everybody is a son of Niccolo' ('al di qua e al di la' del Po, tutti figli di Niccolo'). He may have benefited from a diet of lettuce, "Lettyse doth extynct veneryous actes" (Andrew Boorde, 1490-1549 in 'A dietary of health'). The same 'Dietary of Health' rates figs as a stimulant. Should you wish to try them, however, be aware of the potential side effects, "Figs doth steere a man to veneryous actes, for they encourage and increase the sede of generacyon. And also they prouoke a man to sweate; wherfore they doth engender lyce."

Aphrodisiac, a. food and logical consequences - he eats nothing but doves, love; and that breeds hot blood...

"He eats nothing but doves, love; and that breeds hot blood, and hot blood begets hot thoughts, and hot thoughts beget hot deed s, and hot deeds is love." (TC.3.1)

If you find the idea of eating doves revolting, remove the doves and use, instead for example, wine. You may hint at your passion during a dinner for example, after the waiter has brought in the bottle, you have tasted the wine, accepted it and he has left the table. "This is excellent wine, and that breeds hot blood…. etc." Or as an answer to the question, "Why are you so passionate?" In the play. *Following a song sung by Pandarus, Paris gives his own definition of love.*

Apologies for absent-mindedness - ... my dull brain was wrought with things forgotten.

"…my dull brain was wrought With things forgotten" (M.1.3)

Answer to 'Are you with us?' when you are lost in your train of thought.
In the play. *Macbeth excuses his absent-mindedness*

Apologies for behavior caused by indisposition - ... we are not ourselves when nature being oppress'd commands the mind to suffer with the body.

**"Infirmity doth still neglect all office Whereto our health is bound; we are not ourselves
When nature, being oppress'd, commands the mind
To suffer with the body: I'll forbear."** (KL.2.4)

See also 'Indisposition, minor i. affecting overall behavior - ... let our finger ache, and it indues our other healthful members even to that sense of pain' – 'Recognizing, reason for not r. someone – ... I fear I am not in my perfect mind' A good justification for harsh words or rudeness or otherwise unkind behavior.

In the play. *Lear thinks that the very poor treatment he got from his daughter Regan may be due to her being ill.*

Apologies for comment - Forgive the comment that my passion made…
"Forgive the comment that my passion made
Upon thy feature; for my rage was blind,
And foul imaginary eyes of blood
Presented thee more hideous than thou art" (KJ.4.2)
In the play. *King John apologizes to Hubert who, the king thought, had murdered Prince Arthur.*

Apologies for comment - Our griefs, and not our manners, reason now.
"Our griefs, and not our manners, reason now" (KJ.4.3)
In the play. *Salisbury to Faulconbridge instructed to King John of that he, Salisbury and others, will defect to the French.*

Apologies for delay - … not I but my affairs have made you wait.
"… your patience for my long abode,
Not I but my affairs have made you wait." (MOV.2)
In the case (to be avoided) that you are late at a meeting.
In the play. *Lorenzo is late at a meeting he set up with Gratiano and Salarino, near the house of Shylock, the merchant of Venice.*

Apologies for having drunk too much – it perfumes the blood ere one can say, what's this?
"But I' faith, you have drunk too much canaries; and that's a marvelous searching wine, and it perfumes the blood ere one can say, what's this?
(KHIV p2.2.4)
This can be used to excuse, perhaps, your excessive talkativeness at dinner. Or if you are called on to say something at an after-dinner speech, you may point to the wine served and say, 'I think I have drunk a bit too much of this (lift the bottle and pronounce the name on the label) wine; and, as Shakespeare said, 'that's a marvelous searching wine, and it perfumes the blood before one can say, what's this?"
In the play. *At the Boar's Head Tavern in Eastcheap the Hostess tells Doll Tearsheet that by her color ("and your colour, I warrant you, is as red as any rose in good truth") and demeanor she, Doll Tearsheet, has drunk too much. The tavern, the hosts and the patrons, among whom the idle and fun loving Falstaff, is the historical equivalent of a modern strip joint.*

Apologies for leaving without notice - … my business was great; and in such a case as mine a man may strain courtesy.
"Pardon, good Mercutio, my business was great; and in such a case as mine a man may strain courtesy." (RJ.2.4)
In the play. *Romeo apologizes to Mercutio and Benvolio for having suddenly left them the previous evening. He went to look for Juliet.*

Apologies for poor manners due to haste - … my haste made me unmannerly.
"I humbly do entreat your highness' pardon;
My haste made me unmannerly."
(KHVIII.4.2)
Use as an apology whenever you have been hasty or rash. You may use just the second line or delete 'highness"
In the play. *Messenger enters without being announced.*

Apologies for unruly words caused by indisposition - … impute his words to wayward sickliness and age in him.
"…impute his words
To wayward sickliness and age in him" (KRII.2.1)

78

In the play. *Gaunt, on his deathbed, has been quite blunt with visiting King Richard.*

Apologies to lady for having caused offense - ... to make a sweet lady sad is a sour offence.
"…to make a sweet lady sad is a sour offence." (TC.3.1)
Use to add strength to your apologies if you indeed did something to make her sad.
In the play. *Helen and Pandarus exchange some pleasantries and banter.*

Apologies unnecessary, on the contrary – Thou mak'st faults graces that to thee resort…
"Thou mak'st faults graces that to thee resort.
As on the finger of a throned queen, The basest jewel will be well esteemed." (SON.46)
Answer with these lines after whatever incident or occurrence that caused her to say 'excuse me'.
Grasp an occasion to tell her unexpectedly that she is actually a queen. Surprise works wonders in love and war. See also 'Perfection, p. even in her shortcomings.' – 'Value, v. of object enhanced by owner'.
A forgiving, let-go attitude is always recommended. So Ovid, 'Chief above all does tactful indulgence win the mind; harshness causes hatred and angry wars. We hate the hawk because he ever lives in a warring mood, and the wolves that are wont to go against the timorous flock…the dowry of a wife is quarrelling: but let your mistress ever hear welcome sounds.'

Equally, if you are poor, you should be prepared to tolerate from her more than you would otherwise. So Ovid, 'I am the poet of the poor, because I was poor when I loved; since I could not give gifts, I gave words. Let the poor man love with caution; let the poor man fear to speak harshly; let him bear much that the rich would not endure.' (AOL.2)
See also 'Value, v. of object enhanced by owner - ... things of like value differing in the owners are prized by their masters…'
*** 'Perfection, p. even in her shortcomings - She spoke and panted that she made defect perfection.'

Apologies unnecessary, on the contrary - Who takes offence at that would make me glad?
"Who takes offence at that would make me glad?" (PER.2.5)
Answer to 'Sorry' when what done actually pleases you. You may also change the conditional to the present tense, i.e. 'Who takes offence at that that makes me glad?'
In the play. *Thaisa would actually have welcomed love overtures by Pericles. Her father king Simonides has accused Pericles of bewitching Thaisa.*

Appeal, a. to bear witness - bear witness, all that have not hearts of iron…
"Bear witness, all that have not hearts of iron,
With what a sorrow Cromwell leaves his lord." (KHVIII.3.2)
Introduction to emphasize your distress, 'Bear witness, all that have not hearts of iron…' and continue with whatever point you wish to make about your feelings.
In the play. *Cromwell, faithful to the fallen Wolsey, makes a rhetorical statement.*

Appearance, a. deceiving – All hoods make not monks.
"They should be good men; their affairs as righteous:
But all hoods make not monks." (KHVIII.3.1)
For a contrary perspective on the relationship between attire and character see 'Opinion, your op. on fashion. See 'Advice, a. on men's wear and fashion - Costly thy habit as thy purse can buy, but not express'd in fancy; rich, not gaudy…' In the play. *Queen Katherine sees Cardinals Wolsey and Campeius approaching and is suspicious of their motives.*

Appearance, a. improving with age, ugliness in men as an advantage - I was created with a stubborn outside…
"I was created with a stubborn outside, with an aspect of iron, that, when I come to woo the ladies, I frighten them. But in faith, Kate, the elder I wax, the better I shall appear: my comfort is that old age, that ill layer-up of beauty, can do no more spoils upon my face." (KHV.5.2)
In general, modesty is good, but it is absolutely necessary when you are not (or do not consider yourself to be) Mr. America material. Slightly modify and try this, "When I come to woo the ladies I frighten them. But in faith, (name of lady), the older I wax… upon my face." In the play. *Henry V woos Katharine of France*

Appearance, as if just out of hell – … a look so piteous in purport as if he had been loosed out of hell
"Pale as his shirt; his knees knocking each other;
And with a look so piteous in purport As if he had been loosed out of hell To speak of horrors." (H.2.1)
In the play. *Ophelia describes her latest sighting of Hamlet.*

Appearance, a. of truth hiding a deeper and malicious purpose - … to win us to our harm the instruments of darkness tell us truths…
"… But 't is strange:
And oftentimes, to win us to our harm,
The instruments of darkness tell us truths;
Win us with honest trifles, to betray 's In deepest consequence." (M.1.3)
Questioning the wisdom of acting on limited information. See also Hypocrisy, false conclusion from a righteous example - The devil can cite scriptures for his purpose… ' *** 'Ignorance, i. of what is really good for us - We, ignorant of ourselves beg often our own harms…' ** 'Hypocrisy, vice and h. – There is no vice so simple, but assumes some mark of virtue…' *** Devil, d. appearing in a deceivingly pleasing shape - … the devil hath power to assume a pleasing shape… *** 'Dissimulation, devils' technique - When devils will the blackest sins put on, they do suggest at first with heavenly shows…'
In the play. *Banquo reflecting on the words of the witches after they left.*

Appearance, dejected a., crying - why holds thine eye that lamentable rheum…
"Why holds thine eye that lamentable rheum,
Like a proud river peering over his bounds?
Be these sad signs confirmers of thy words?" (KJ.3.1)
Alternative to "Why are you crying?" (first two lines). Or downplay the emotions that have caused you to cry. "…that lamentable rheum, like…bounds." In the play. *Constance to Salisbury who has informed Constance of the pending agreement between the king of France and King John to which she bitterly objects.*

Appearance, did you see how you look? – No…. for the eye sees not itself but by reflection, by some other things.
"No, Cassius; for the eye sees not itself,
But by reflection, by some other things" (JC.1.2)
Change 'Cassius' to the name of the person who asks the question - when it is pointed out to you that your hair is uncombed, your tie crooked etc.
In the play. *Brutus answers Cassius who asked him if he saw his own face. Cassius is trying to lead Brutus to admit his desire to revolt against Caesar. See 'Proposal, dangerous p.'*

Appearance, disgusting a. - … not honour'd with a human shape.
"…not honour'd with
A human shape." (TEM.1.2)
An insult or to make the point you may apply to yourself if you show up in dirty attire or similar due to unforeseen circumstances. E.G. 'You may think I am not honored with human shape'
In the play. *Prospero describes Caliban.*

Appearance, kingly - … every inch a king.
GLOUCESTER The trick of that voice I do well remember:
Is 't not the king?
KING LEAR Ay, every inch a king (KL.4.6)
Confirm the exceptional standing of a person. You can change 'king' to 'queen', 'prince' or other equivalent (preferably monosyllabic) titles with equal effect.
In the play. *Gloucester, blinded by the Duke of Cornwall rejoins Lear and his party at Dover.*

Appearance, haggard, fat – my skin hangs about me like an old lady's loose gown…
"…my skin hangs about me like an like an old lady's loose gown; I am withered like an old apple-john."
(KHIV.1 3.3)
Self-effacing statement with a touch of humor. Humor can soften the impact of the inevitable. See also entries for 'Age'.
In the play. *Falstaff confides his reservations about his personal appearance to servant Bardolph.*

Appearance, honest a. - … knavery cannot, sure, hide himself in such reverence
"… knavery cannot, sure, hide himself in such reverence"
(MAAN.2.3)
You may use the quote in its opposite sense, i.e. 'Knavery can hide himself… reverence'.
In the play. *Benedick is confident that the mature Leonato is telling the truth about the affection of Beatrice (towards Benedick).*

Appearance, negative change in a. due to misfortune – I know not what counts harsh fortune cast upon my face…
OCTAVIAN: Since I saw you last
           There's a change upon you
POMPEY: Well, I know not
           What counts harsh fortune cast upon my face,
           But in my bosom shall she never come
           To make my heart her vassal (AC.2.6)
Answer to "You have changed" or "You have put on weight" or "You look older" etc. See also 'Age. Its effect on wrinkles'.
In the play. *Octavian meets Pompey near Misenum.*

Appearance, unexpected a. - What unaccustom'd cause procures her hither?
"What unaccustom'd cause procures her hither?" (RJ.3.5)
Alternative to the question, 'Why do you come here?' or 'What is it that you want?'

In the play. *Juliet is startled by the arrival of her mother, who, unaware of Juliet's secret marriage to Romeo comes in with the proposal for Juliet to marry Paris.*

Appearance. She is not pretty but… - love looks not with the eyes, but with the mind...
"Love looks not with the eyes, but with the mind,
And therefore is winged Cupid painted blind.
Nor hath love's mind of any judgement taste,
Wings, and no eyes, figure unheedy haste;
And therefore is love said to be a child,
Because in choice he is so oft beguiled." (MND.1.1)
You like her even if she is not all that pretty. She is conscious of it and wants some reassurance. You will tell her first that she is absolutely beautiful, see '**Beauty**'. But in the unlikely case that she may not believe your flattery, follow up with the first two lines, 'Love looks not with the eyes…painted blind'.
In the play: *Helena thinks she is as pretty as Hermia, but Demetrius (Helena's love) likes Hermia better. Helena comments on the irrationality of love.*

Appearances, a. in men betraying women - … our frailty is the cause, not we.
"How easy is it for the proper-false
In women's waxen hearts to set their forms!
Alas, our frailty is the cause, not we!" (TN.2.2)
Justifying or excusing the passion of a lady for a bad man. See also 'Woman, female frailty, invocation'.
In the play. *Viola/Cesario meditates on the events that caused Olivia to fall in love with her (Viola) thinking she is a man (Cesario). The 'proper-false' applies to anyone who may look* proper but is false. And this proper-false has its way due to the frailty of women as a whole.

Appearances, a. deceiving – All that glisters is not gold.
All that glisters is not gold,
Often have you heard that told."
(MOV.2.7)
Admonition not to be taken in by appearances.
In the play. *One of the puzzles presented to the Prince of Morocco, one of Portia's suitors.*

Appearances, a. deceiving - So may the outward shows be least themselves, the world is still deceived with ornament…
"So may the outward shows be least themselves:
The world is still deceived with ornament.
In law, what plea so tainted and corrupt,
But, being seasoned with a gracious voice,
Obscures the show of evil? In religion,
What damned error, but some sober brow
Will bless it and approve it with a text,
Hiding the grossness with fair ornament?" (MOV.3.2)
In the play. *Bassanio comments on the caskets one of which contains the solution to the puzzle that will let the winner marry Portia.*

Appearances, a. deceiving - When devils will the blackest sins put on…
"When devils will the blackest sins put on,
They do suggest at first with heavenly shows,
As I do now" (OTH.2.3)
In the play. *Iago plies his course aimed at destroying Othello.*

Appearances, a. deceiving – Who makes the fairest show means most deceit.
"Who makes the fairest show, means most deceit" (PER.1.4)
General comment whenever you see or detect hypocrisy
In the play. *A lord has brought news of the sighting of approaching ships. The lord thinks the ship seems to come in peace, but Cleon is suspicious. The fleet is Pericles' who, having heard of the problems at Tharsus, has arrived with supplies.*

Appearances, a. deceiving (usually), but not in this case - ... thou hast a mind that suits with this fair and outward character.
"There is a fair behaviour in thee, captain;
And though that nature with a beauteous wall
Doth oft close in pollution, yet of thee
I will believe thou hast a mind that suits
With this fair and outward character." (TN.1.2)
Express trust. 'Of thee I will believe… character.'
In the play. *Shipwrecked after a storm, Viola asks the captain to help her acquire the disguise of a man, after which she will apply for a servant's position at the Duke's court.*

Appearances, a. deceptive or false – look like the innocent flower but be the serpent under it.
"…look like the innocent flower,
But be the serpent under't." (M.1.5)
The 'snake' defined, as found in politics and corporations. Apply the sentence to the third person, 'He looks like the innocent flower, but he is the serpent under it.'
In the play. *Lady Macbeth gives some instructions to her husband while waiting for King Duncan to arrive at their castle.*

Appearances, a. deceptive or false – Ornament... the seeming truth which cunning times put on to entrap the wisest.
"Thus ornament is but the guiled shore
To a most dangerous sea; the beauteous scarf
Veiling an Indian beauty; in a word,
The seeming truth which cunning times put on
To entrap the wisest." (MOV.3.2)
When you see the truth and others do not. E.G. 'This is but the guiled shore….'
In the play. *Prior to selecting which basket to choose (the correct basket will entail marrying Portia), Bassanio meditates on some truths which will lead him to discard the gold basket.*

Appearances, a. deceptive or false – O, what may man within him hide, though angel on the outward side!
"O, what may man within him hide,
Though angel on the outward side!" (MFM.3.2)
Comment on hypocrisy and hypocrites. See also 'Character, false, cunning, shifting and perverse' – 'Character, deceitful, treacherous'.
In the play. *The Duke makes some general considerations about power, corruption and hypocrisy, arising from the behavior of Angelo.*

Appearances, a. deceptive or false – Seems he a dove? his feathers are but borrowed…
"Seems he a dove? his feathers are but borrowed,
For he's disposed as the hateful raven:
Is he a lamb? his skin is surely lent him,
For he's inclined as is the ravenous wolf." (KHVI.p2.3.1)
In the play. *Queen Margaret tries to discredit the good Humphrey duke of Gloucester with the king.*

Appearances, a. deceptive or false –
… that deceit should steal such gentle shape and with a virtuous visor hide deep vice!
"Ah, that deceit should steal such gentle shape
And with a virtuous visor hide deep vice!" (KRIII.2.2)
Denounce hypocrisy. See also entries for 'Hypocrisy' *** 'Person, deceitful but beautiful - O that deceit should dwell in such a gorgeous palace.'
In the play. *Richard has told Clarence's son that the king (Edward) and not he himself had Clarence assassinated. The duchess of York comments.*

Appearances, a. deceptive or false –
… the world is still deceived with ornament.
"So may the outward shows be least themselves:
The world is still deceived with ornament" (MOV.3.2)
Use in every instance when you suspect that glamour and pomp are the veneer to cover fraud and deception.
In the play. *Prior to selecting which basket to choose (the right basket will entail marrying Portia), Bassanio meditates on some truths which will lead him to discard the gold basket.*

Appearances, a. deceptive or false – what a goodly outside falsehood hath.
O, what a goodly outside falsehood hath." (MOV.1.3)
See also 'Hypocrisy, false conclusion from a righteous example'.
In the play. *Antonio cautions Bassanio not to take seriously Shylock's quotations of the Bible. Shylock uses a biblical anecdote to justify the levying of interest on borrowed money*

Appearances, a. deceptive or false –
Who cannot steal a shape that means deceit?
"Who cannot steal a shape that means deceit?" (KHVI p2.3)

See also entries for 'Hypocrisy'
In the play. *Queen Margaret tries to discredit the good Humphrey duke of Gloucester with the king.*

Appearances, a. deceptive or false –
Ye have angels' faces, but heaven knows your hearts.
"Ye have angels' faces, but heaven knows your hearts." (KHVIII.3.1)
Address deceitful and devious enemies. See also entries for 'Hypocrisy'
In the play. *Queen Katherine to Cardinals Wolsey and Campeius.*

Appearances, feigning love but harboring hatred - though I do hate him as I do hell pains…
"Though I do hate him as I do hell pains,
Yet for necessity of present life
I must show out a flag and sign of love,
Which is indeed but sign." (OTH.1.1)
Describe a hypocritical and pharisaic attitude. 'They show out a flag and sign of love, which is indeed but sign.'
In the play. *Iago hates Othello but for the moment he must feign it.*

Appearances, outside a. leading to false judgment - Opinion's but a fool, that makes us scan the outward habit by the inward man.
" Opinion's but a fool, that makes us scan
The outward habit by the inward man." (PER.2.2)
Counteract a biased opinion based on appearance. See also 'Advice, a. on men's wear and fashion - Costly thy habit as thy purse can buy, but not express'd in fancy; rich, not gaudy…'
In the play. *A courtier comments on Pericles' rusty armor and shoddy attire. Pericles has decided to participate in the tourney. Simonides, the king rebuts him.*

Appearances, seeing through a. - … thy casement I need not open, for I look through thee.
"So, my good window of lattice, fare thee well; thy casement I need not open, for I look through thee." (AWEW.2.3)
Alternative to express that you can see through a person without going any further. See also 'Intuition, seeing through appearance'.
In the play. *Lafeu loathes Parolles. Parolle is an open window, whose character can be judged without further inquiries.*

Appetite, good a. improving the quality of a humble meal – … our stomachs will make what's homely savoury.
"… Come; our stomachs
Will make what's homely savoury" (CYM.3.6)
In the play. *Belarius prepares a meal in the cave for Guiderius and Arviragus.*

Appetite, sexual a. as a motive denied – (I) therefore beg it not, to please the palate of my appetite…
"… (I) therefore beg it not,
To please the palate of my appetite,
Nor to comply with heat--the young affects
In me defunct--and proper satisfaction." (OTH.1.3)
In the play. *Othello pleads with the Venetian senate to let Desdemona accompany him to Cyprus.*

Applause, large a. promised if feat accomplished – I would applaud thee to the very echo that should applaud again.
"… I would applaud thee to the very echo,
That should applaud again" (M.5.3)
In the play. *Macbeth makes a rhetorical statement to the doctor as the enemy forces approach Duncinane. The expected feat is the disappearance of the enemy.*

Appointment, a. from above, appointee expected to work miracles - … chosen from above by inspiration of celestial grace to work exceeding miracles on earth.
"… chosen from above,
By inspiration of celestial grace,
To work exceeding miracles on earth." (KHVI.p1.5.4)
Introduction or a form of flattery. E.G., 'Here is a man of whom it could be said, 'chosen from above… earth."
In the play. *La Pucelle defends herself while being tried by the English.*

Appointment, next a. tomorrow night – … we must starve our sight from lovers' food till morrow deep midnight.
"Keep word, Lysander: we must starve our sight
From lovers' food till morrow deep midnight." (MND.1.1)
See also 'Meeting, scheduling the next m. - When shall we three meet again? In thunder, lightning or in rain?
In the play. *Hermia and Lysander will elope the next night, to escape the threats of her father if she does not marry Demetrius.*

Appointment, tomorrow night – … when Phoebe doth behold her silver visage in watery glass.
" Tomorrow night, when Phoebe doth behold
Her silver visage in the watery glass,
Decking with liquid pearl the bladed grass." (MND.1.1)
Answer when asked when she can see you again or viceversa, if the roles are reversed.

In the play. *Lysander discloses to Helena his marriage plans with Hermia. Phoebe is the moon – today, however, Phoebe is the name of the outermost satellites of Saturn.*

Appreciation coming too late - ... for it so falls out that what we have we prize not the worth…
"… for it so falls out,
That what we have we prize not the worth,
Whiles we enjoy it; but being lacked and lost,
Why, then we rack the value; then we find
The virtue that possession would not show us
While it was ours." (MAAN.4.1)
Robert Browning expresses a similar concept in the poem 'Fra Lippo Lippi',
"…we're made so that we love
First when we see them painted, things we have passed
Perhaps a hundred times nor cared to see."
In the play. *The friar counsels to move Hero temporarily away and to make it appear that she is dead. The idea is that the accusers and in particular Claudio will miss her and come to their senses regarding the false accusations against her.*

Appreciation coming too late - Our rash faults make trivial price of serious things we have…
"Our rash faults
Make trivial price of serious things we have,
Not knowing them, until we know their grave." (AWEW.5.3)
Persuade not to undervalue the current strengths of the group or, for example, the assets of the company.
In the play. *Bertram realizes that he loves Helen but it appears it is too late. The King comments that we do not appreciate what we have until it is too late.*

Appreciation coming too late - The idea of her life shall sweetly creep…
"The idea of her life shall sweetly creep
Into his study of imagination,
And every lovely organ of her life
Shall come apparell'd in more precious habit,
More moving-delicate and full of life,
Into the eye and prospect of his soul,
Than when she lived indeed"
(MAAN.3.5)
In the play. *Friar Francis has organized the disappearance of Hero and she is believed dead. He tells Leonato, her father, that Claudio will now see her in a new light. Hero had wrongly been accused of infidelity by the evil Don John.*

Appreciation coming too late - What our contempt doth often hurl from us we wish it ours again…
"What our contempt doth often hurl from us,
We wish it ours again; the present pleasure,
By revolution lowering, does become
The opposite of itself:" (AC.1.2)
In the play. *Antony becomes aware of the death of Fulvia's his estranged wife and has a sudden change of heart. For a moment he even considers leaving Cleopatra "(I must from this enchanting queen break off") but it will not happen.*

Appreciation, a. expressed without prompting - The time was once when thou unurged wouldst vow that never words were music to thine ear… unless I spake.
"The time was once when thou unurged wouldst vow
That never words were music to thine ear,
That never object pleasing in thine eye,
That never touch well welcome to thy hand,
That never meat sweet-savor'd in thy

taste,
Unless I spake, or look'd, or touch'd, or carved to thee." (COE.2.2)
Carve sections for compliments, e.g. 'Never words are music to mine ear, unless you speak' etc.
In the play. *Adriana is baffled by the reaction of Antipholus E whom she believes to be her husband, whereas he is his twin Antipholus S.*

Apprehension, generalized a. of danger – When clouds appear, wise men put on their cloaks…
"When clouds appear, wise men put on their cloaks;
When great leaves fall, the winter is at hand;
When the sun sets, who doth not look for night?
Untimely storms make men expect a dearth.
All may be well; but, if God sort it so, 'Tis more than we deserve, or I expect.
…
Truly, the souls of men are full of dread:
Ye cannot reason almost with a man That looks not heavily and full of fear." (KRIII.2.3)
See also 'Danger, imminent d. and reaction on men – … By a divine instinct men's minds mistrust ensuing dangers…'
In the play. *Citizens comment among themselves about the sense of dangers signaling the imminent coronation of the evil Richard III.*

APPROACH, SECURING A WAY OUT.

You are preparing the ground and she understands that you are interested in her. Some ladies will let you go on with your verbal preparations until you declare what you want them to do. Others, especially professional women, tend to be more abrupt. She may ask, "What do you want?". You wish to make your intentions known but with a vein of irony. Hence, if she says no forcefully you can bow out elegantly under the cover of humor. See next,

Approach, securing a way out - Gentle thou art, therefore to be won…
"Gentle thou art, therefore to be won, Beautiful thou art, therefore to be assailed" (SON)
Careful though, you should precede the quote with 'As Shakespeare said', lest she may think that you are bent on raping her. Be even more careful if she is totally illiterate. According to Ovid force works (at least sometimes), 'You may use force; women like you to use it; they often wish to give unwillingly what they like to give. She whom a sudden assault has taken by storm is pleased, and counts the audacity as a compliment.' (AOL.2)
An almost identical in spirit but somewhat milder quote could be the next:

Approach, securing a way out - She's beautiful, and therefore to be woo'd…
"She's beautiful, and therefore to be woo'd;
She is a woman, therefore to be won." (KHVI p1.5.3)
Answer to 'What do you want?' Change 'she' to 'you'. See also 'Macho man or unstoppable skirt chaser'.
In the play. *Suffolk has just captured Margaret in France and is struck by her beauty. He will arrange her marriage to king Henry VI. Suffolk and Margaret may become lovers though the play, but he only hints at their mutual feelings without going any further.*

Appropriateness, the right thing at the right time – At Christmas I no more desire a rose...
"At Christmas I no more desire a rose,
Than wish a snow in May's new fangled mirth,
But like of each thing as in season grows." (LLL.1.1)
Emphasize the importance of appropriateness - each thing in its own place and time. See also 'Time, everything in good t. – … there's a time for all things.' – 'Time, give it time to mature - How many things by season season'd are…'
In the play. *Prompted to give a reason for his disapproval of the king's proposal, Biron suggests that learning is out of place and season.*

Approval, a. with mixed feelings - considerations infinite do make against it.
"And, Prince of Wales, so dare we venture thee,
Albeit considerations infinite
Do make against it." (KHIV.p1.5.1)
Try, 'I'll go ahead with your plan albeit considerations infinite do make against it'.
In the play. *The Prince of Wales announces that he will fight Hotspur in single combat and his father, King Henry IV reluctantly consents.*

April day - A day in April never came so sweet to show how costly summer was at hand…
"A day in April never came so sweet,
To show how costly summer was at hand,
As this fore-spurrer comes before his lord." (MOV.2.9)
See also 'Love, l. compared to an April day - O, how this spring of love resembleth the uncertain glory of an April day' - 'Character, a dandy – he speaks holiday, he smells April and May' - Life, married l. affecting negatively behavior of men and women - Men are April when they woo, December when they wed. – 'Tears, t. of love – The April 's in her eyes: it is love's spring…'
In the play. *Portia's servant announces the arrival of Bassanio's steward. The steward is April and Bassanio the summer'.* 'Fore-spurrer' = *'One that rides ahead of another'*

April, A. suggesting youth - … proud-pied April dress'd in all his trim hath put a spirit of youth in every thing...
"From you have I been absent in the spring,
When proud-pied April dress'd in all his trim
Hath put a spirit of youth in every thing,
That heavy Saturn laugh'd and leap'd with him." (SON 98)

April, A. welcome by young men - … Such comfort as do lusty young men feel when well-apparell'd April on the heel of limping winter treads...
"…look to behold this night
Earth-treading stars that make dark heaven light:
Such comfort as do lusty young men feel
When well-apparell'd April on the heel
Of limping winter treads, even such delight
Among fresh female buds shall you this night
Inherit at my house" (RJ.1.2)
In the play. *Capulet announces the party he will give in the evening at his house to the kinsman Paris.*

Arbitration, intervening for a. - Let me be umpire in this doubtful strife.
"Let me be umpire in this doubtful strife." (KHVI p1.4.1)
Intervene when the disagreement seems to expand into an outright conflict.

In the play. *Henry VI will arbitrate on the issue of whether it is more appropriate to wear a white or a red rose. This has to do with the War of the Roses.*

Ardor, military a. – O, let the hours be short, till fields and blows and groans applaud our sport!
"Uncle, Adieu: O, let the hours be short
Till fields and blows and groans applaud our sport!" (KHIV.p1.1.3)
As a metaphor it could be used as a call to action. See also entries for 'Exhortation, e. to act'.
In the play. *Hotspur is eager to start the rebellion against ungrateful Henry IV.*

Arguing, exhortation to stop a. - to leave this keen encounter of our wits…
"…But, gentle Lady Anne,
To leave this keen encounter of our wits
And fall something into a slower method." (KRIII.1.2)
Use with mild modification, "But, gentle Lady (name of lady), let's leave this keen encounter of our wits and fall something into a slower method". See also 'Quarrel'
In the play. *Richard, who has slain Edward, duke of Clarence and Anne's husband, is now trying to woo her (and will succeed in the end!).*

Argument, a. between to contending parties – The bitter clamour of two eager tongues.
"The bitter clamour of two eager tongues" (KRII.1.1)
Comment on a useless debate. See also 'Abuse, verbal a. - … what man of good temper would endure this tempest of exclamation?'
In the play. *Mowbray responds to Bolingbroke's accusations levied in the presence of King Richard II*

Argument, a. degenerating into conflict - this spark will prove a raging fire, if wind and fuel be brought to feed it with.
"…this spark will prove a raging fire,
If wind and fuel be brought to feed it with" (KHVI p2.3.1)
Intervene in a dispute before it overheats.
In the play. *Q. Margaret attempts to stop and argument between Somerset and York.*

Argument, avoiding it – … if I longer stay we shall begin our ancient bickerings.
"…proud prelate, in thy face
I see thy fury: if I longer stay,
We shall begin our ancient bickerings." (KHVI p2.1.1)
A way out to avoid an argument
In the play. *Gloucester to Cardinal well established enemies of each other.*

Argument, good a. but honest dealing is best - didst thou never hear that things ill got had ever bad success?
"Full well hath Clifford play'd the orator,
Inferring arguments of mighty force,
But Clifford, tell me didst thou never hear
That things ill got had ever bad success?" (KHVI p3.2.2)
An argument for fair and honest dealing. The first two lines can be used as a prelude to an objection after your opponent has apparently made a decent or oratorically appealing argument. Exchange 'Clifford' for the name of the applicable party. See also 'But yet, everything is well but yet - I do not like 'but yet', it does allay the good precedence...'
In the play. *King Henry VI to Clifford near York after the victory during which York has been beheaded.*

Argument, heated a. and you are determined to stop it - Content you,

gentlemen: I will compound this strife.
"Content you, gentlemen: I will compound this strife" (TOS.2.1)
In the play. *Baptista intervenes to stop the argument between Gremio and Tranio as to whether age is or isn't a detriment in the eyes of the object of their romantic endeavours (Bianca). Baptista will give Bianca to him who has the greater dowry.*

Argument, proving the contrary - I'll prove the contrary, if you'll hear me speak.
"I'll prove the contrary, if you'll hear me speak" (KHVI.p3.1.2)
In the play. *Richard attempts to convince his father (also Richard Plantagenet) to renege on the oath he took with Henry VI.*

Argument, subject not worth arguing about - ... it is too starved a subject for my sword.
"I cannot fight upon this argument; It is too starved a subject for my sword." (TC.1)
State that you do not think the subject worth arguing about.
In the play. *The argument that cannot be resolved with a fight (starved a subject) is whether Helen is fairer than Cressida or viceversa.*

Argument, value in the a. - Methinks there is much reason in his sayings.
"Methinks there is much reason in his sayings." (JC.3.2)
Change 'his' to 'your' as applicable.
In the play. *A citizen agrees with the points made by Antony in his oration.*

Arguments, a. of equal merit - Both merits poised, each weighs nor less nor more.
"Both merits poised, each weighs nor less nor more; But he as he, the heavier for a whore" (TC.4.1)

Answer to which one is the better? See also 'Characters, similarity of c.'
In the play. *Paris has asked Diomedes who, in his opinion, more deserves Helen, he Paris or her husband Menelaus. Diomedes is non-committal in his reply.*

Arms, her a. – ... sweet ornaments, whose circling shadows kings have sought to sleep in
"...sweet ornaments, Whose circling shadows kings have sought to sleep in" (TA.2.5)
Compliment.
In the play. *Marcus comments on the gory scene of Lavinia raped and mutilated by the evil Chiron and Demetrius. Making a lady an object of desire even kings is also found in 'Hand, worthy to be kissed by kings – ... a hand that kings have lipped, and trembled kissing.'*

Army, a. not in good shape - ... half of the which dare not shake snow from off their cassocks...
"...fifteen thousand poll; half of the which dare not shake snow from off their cassocks, lest they shake themselves to pieces." (AWEW.4.3)
See also 'Funding, inadequate funding for the project – but a shirt and a half in all my company'. – 'Personnel, p. not in good shape - The stuff we have, a strong wind will blow to pieces'
In the play. *Interrogated by presumed enemies Parolles gives out all sort of information, disparaging his own master Bertram and other Frenchmen, who have prepared the trap for him.*

Army, ragged a. or unruly mass - ... His army is a ragged multitude of hinds and peasants, rude and merciless.
"His army is a ragged multitude Of hinds and peasants, rude and merciless" (KHVI p2.4.4)
See also 'Personnel, crew, a motley crew'
In the play. *A messenger gives an account of John Cade and his force of rebels.*

Arrival, a. in haste – ... bloody with spurring, fiery-red with haste.
"Here come the Lords of Ross and Willoughby,
Bloody with spurring, fiery-red with haste." (KRII.2.3)
Comment on arrival of person with quickened breath.
In the play. *Northumberland announces the hasty arrival of two noblemen who join Henry Bolingbroke's party to seize the throne from Richard.*

Arrival, a. of individual voiding the need to search him - he saves my labour by his own approach.
"He saves my labour by his own approach." (AYLI.2.7)
When you are asked to locate someone and first you cannot find him, but then he shows up unexpectedly.
In the play. *The Duke S dispatches the first lord to look for Jacques, when Jacques suddenly shows up.*

Arrival, a. of unpleasant or unwelcome character - By the pricking of my thumbs, something wicked this way comes.
"By the pricking of my thumbs, Something wicked this way comes." (M.4.1)
Gently ironic comment on the arrival of a friend (or enemy)
In the play. *One of the witches alerts the others to the arrival of Macbeth who has come to question them about the meaning and accuracy of their forecast.*

Arrival, a. with noise and fanfare - ... in fierce tempest is he coming, in thunder and in earthquake, like a Jove.
"...in fierce tempest is he coming, In thunder and in earthquake, like a Jove" (KHV.2.4)
In the play. *Exeter, spokesman for King Henry tells Charles of France, the Dauphin and others of the intents of Henry V to conquer France and get the crown.*

Arrival, fearful a. - He came in thunder; his celestial breath was sulphurous to smell.
"He came in thunder; his celestial breath
Was sulphurous to smell." (CYM.5.4)
In the play. *Leonatus, in prison, has a prophetic dream full of symbolic values. The 'he' here is Jupiter.*

Arrival, possibly unexpected a. of friend - Now is the winter of our discontent, made glorious summer by this sun of York.
"Now is the winter of our discontent
Made glorious summer by this sun of York;
And all the clouds that lour'd upon our house
In the deep bosom of the ocean buried..." (RIII.1.1)
Change 'by this sun of York' to name of oncoming friend. See also 'Arrival, a. with noise and fanfare - ... in fierce tempest is he coming, in thunder and in earthquake, like a Jove.'
In the play. *Richard III comments on the ascent to the throne (for the second time) of Edward IV. 'To lour'= 'To hang'*

Arrival, quiet a. and by night - Who comes so fast in silence of the night?
"Who comes so fast in silence of the night?" (MOV.5.1)
In the play. *Lorenzo asks Stephano, Portia's servant just arriving from Venice.*

Arrival, unexpected a. - what wind blew you hither.
FALSTAFF What wind blew you hither, Pistol?
PISTOL Not the ill wind which blows no man to good (KHIV.p2.5.3)

Change 'Pistol' with the name of the unexpectedly incoming party.
In the play. *Pistol travelled to meet Falstaff in Gloucestershire and to announce that King Henry IV is dead and that the new king is Henry V.*

Arrogance, a. behind false modesty - ... but your heart is cramm'd with arrogancy, spleen and pride.
"You sign your place and calling, in full seeming,
With meekness and humility; but your heart
Is cramm'd with arrogancy, spleen and pride." (KHVIII.2.4)
Use with an adversary (or describe a character) who hides arrogance behind a homely demeanor or a veil of modesty. Change slightly, 'behind meekness and humility, his heart is crammed with...pride'.
In the play. *Q Katherine assesses Cardinal Wolsey's character.*

Arrogance, a. promoted by submission - supple knees feed arrogance, and are the proud man's fees.
" ... pride hath no other glass
To show itself but pride; ... for supple knees
Feed arrogance, and are the proud man's fees." (TC.3.3)
An argument for avoiding a submissive attitude.
In the play. *Ulysses tells the Greek generals to stroll in front of Achille's tent and ignore him. This will hurt his pride - whereas if they showed respect (by, for example, bending their knees in homage), they would feed his arrogance.*

Art and theatrical representation – ... the purpose of playing... to hold, the mirror up to nature...
"...the purpose of playing, whose end, both at the first and now, was and is, to hold, as 'twere, the mirror up to nature; to show virtue her own feature, scorn her own image, and the very age and body of the time his form and pressure" (H.3.1)
In the play. *Hamlet gives advise to the players on how to perform in the oncoming production.*

Artist, compliment to an artist or anyone who won a contest where skills are shown - ... In framing an artist, art hath thus decreed...
"In framing an artist, art hath thus decreed,
To make some good, but others to exceed;
And you are her labour's scholar." (PER.2.3)
By stretching it out a little, you can use the statement with a woman who is as beautiful as intelligent.
In the play. *Pericles has won the tourney and Simonides acknowledges his superiority.*

Artists, a. as a representing their times - ... they are the abstract and brief chronicles of the time...
"...Do you hear, let them be well used; for they are the abstract and brief chronicles of the time: after your death you were better have a bad epitaph than their ill report while you live" (H.2.2)
Introduction of a journalist or of a media personality.
In the play. *Hamlet to Polonius referring to the players he (Hamlet) has called in for the production of the 'play within the play'*

Asking, a. a question with reverence and ready for a blush - I ask, that I might waken reverence...
" I ask, that I might waken reverence,
And bid the cheek be ready with a blush
Modest as morning when she coldly eyes
The youthful Phoebus." (TC.1.3)

When you inadvertently address an authority familiarly, not realizing whom you are talking to. E.G. 'I bid my cheek be ready…Phoebus'.
In the play. *Hector, visiting the Grecian camp, does not know Agamennon and asks how he may recognize him and then proceeds to say why he asks - that is so they he may 'waken reverence'.*

Ass, written record of being one – …remember that I am an ass; though it be not written down…
"But, masters, remember that I am an ass; though it be not written down, yet forget not that I am an ass" (MAAN.4.2)
Alternative to 'I made an ass of myself'.
In the play. *The well meaning Dogberry has arrested the scoundrel Conrade who tells Dogberry that he is an ass. Dogberry refers to a written statement or confession by Conrade.*

Assassination, a. of king or enemy – … though I did wish him dead, I hate the murderer, love him murdered.
"…though I did wish him dead,
I hate the murderer, love him murdered.
The guilt of conscience take thou for thy labour" (KRII.5.6)
Example of supreme deniability and hypocrisy.
In the play. *Bolingbroke hinted openly at wanting Richard II murdered. Exton does it and as reward obtains Bolingbroke's hatred.*

Assassination, a. under the guise of law - That he should die is worthy policy; but yet we want a colour for his death…
"That he should die is worthy policy;
But yet we want a colour for his death:
'Tis meet he be condemn'd by course of law." (KHVI p2.3.1)
The code of operation by the CIA and sometimes by the FBI. See also 'Pretext, p. for personal attack - … my pretext to strike at him admits a good construction.'
In the play. *Cardinal Beaufort's contribution to the assassination of Gloucester. Suffolk convenes that*
…. And yet we have but trivial argument,
More than mistrust, that shows him worthy death

Assets, a. not worth holding on to - … she is not worth what she doth cost the holding.
"Brother, she is not worth what she doth cost
The holding." (TC.2.2)
Dump a company, shares or a product. Change 'she' to 'it' as applicable. See also 'Value, v. resides in perception - What is aught, but as 'tis valued?' A man who wanted to stress his ignorance in economics said once "The first time I heard of assets I thought they were little donkeys'.
In the play *Hector tells Troilus that the cost of holding Helen is not worth the cost of the war. For Troilus' opinion see 'Fear, f. induced by desire to conform - … reason and respect make livers pale and lustihood deject.'*

Assets, liquidation of a. acquired with great effort – …and are the cities that I got with wounds…
"And are the cities, that I got with wounds,
Deliver'd up again with peaceful words?" (KHVI p2.1.1)
Comment to a loss of assets or power via an unfavorable agreement.
In the play. *Warwick's pain at the terms of the agreement with France.*

Assignment or responsibility, turning it down - better head her glorious body fits…
"A better head her glorious body fits
Than his that shakes for age and feebleness" (TA.1.1)

In the play. *Titus A. refuses to be a candidate for emperor.*

Assignment or responsibility, turning it down - Your love deserves my thanks; but my desert unmeritable shuns your high request.
"Your love deserves my thanks; but my desert
Unmeritable shuns your high request." (KRIII.3.7)
In the play. *Richard answers Buckingham in a hypocritical refusal to accept the throne.*

Assistant - I was a pack-horse in his great affairs, a weeder-out of his proud adversaries...
"I was a pack-horse in his great affairs;
A weeder-out of his proud adversaries,
A liberal rewarder of his friends:
To royalize his blood I spilt mine own." KRIII.1.3
If you are an assistant to a VIP and are asked what you exactly do. E.G. "I am a pack-horse in his great affairs, a weeder-out of his proud adversaries…'
In the play. *Richard to the soon-to-be-widowed wife of Edward IV, king and Richard's brother.*

Association, a. with person or organization only partial – A little more than kin, and less than kind
"A little more than kin, and less than kind" (H.1.2)
Answer to whether you belong to a party or association, when you do but only formally. In the play. *Hamlet's silent thought in response to a call from King Claudius who addresses him as cousin and son.*

Assurance, double a. - I'll make assurance double sure and take a bond of fate.
"But yet I'll make assurance double sure,
And take a bond of fate" (M.4.1)
Answer to 'Are you sure?' when an important outcome is at stake.
In the play. *Though the witches have reassured Macbeth with their predictions Macbeth wants to have total assurance by killing Macduff.*

Astrology, astrological conditions favorable - I find my zenith doth depend upon a most auspicious star...
"I find my zenith doth depend upon
A most auspicious star, whose influence
If now I court not, but omit, my fortunes
Will ever after droop." (TEM.1.2)
Explain or justify why the action or project you are proposing must be acted on immediately. See also 'Opportunity, why it should not be missed' – 'Advice, take best advantage of the opportunity'.
In the play. *Prospero, endowed with magic powers has raised a sea storm as part of a larger objective. He decided on this action based on astrological observations and explains the matter to his daughter Miranda.*

Astrology, astrological influence on personality – my nativity was under Ursa major; so that it follows, I am rough and lecherous.
"…my nativity was under Ursa major; so that it follows, I am rough and lecherous" (KL.1.2)
In the play. *The evil brother Edmund meditates on his own character.*

Astrology, how long have you believed in a. – How long have you been a sectary astronomical?
"How long have you been a sectary astronomical?" (KL.1.2)
In the play. *Edgar questions brother Edmund on the subject.*

Astronomy, pernicious influence on events - These late eclipses in the sun and moon portend no good to us.

"These late eclipses in the sun and moon portend
no good to us: though the wisdom of nature can
reason it thus and thus, yet nature finds itself
scourged by the sequent effects: love cools,
friendship falls off, brothers divide: in cities, mutinies; in countries, discord; in
palaces, treason; and the bond cracked 'twixt son
and father." (KL.1.2)
Comment on the wickedness of the times.
In the play. *Gloucester, duped by son Edmund attributes the alleged treason by his other son Edgar to astronomical effects. For clever/evil Edmund's comment see 'Philosophical considerations. Unwillingness to take responsibility for our mistakes'.*

Astronomy, pointlessness of a. and erudition in general - Those earthly godfathers of heaven's lights...
"Those earthly godfathers of heaven's lights,
That give a name to every fixed star,
Have no more profit of their shining nights,
Than those that walk, and know not what they are." (LLL.1.1)
Put down erudition. See also 'Eyes, e. as a source of knowledge'.
In the play. *Biron support his argument against erudition by using astronomers as an example, who derive no profit from their pursuit.*

Astronomy, the teaching of a., astronomy 101 - ... and teach me how to name the bigger light, and how the less...
"...and teach me how
To name the bigger light, and how the less,
That burn by day and night." (TEM.1.2)
An introduction to a speech or presentation, when you wish to downplay the expectations of the audience. E.G. 'I am not here to reveal extraordinary things but simply 'to name the bigger light and how the less...night'
In the play. Ca*liban acknowledges to Prospero that he (Prospero) taught Caliban Astronomy 101.*

Athenians, A. as scoundrels - why dost thou call them knaves?
TIMON. Why dost thou call them knaves? thou know'st them not.
APEMANTUS. Are they not Athenians?
TIMON. Yes.
APEMANTUS. Then I repent not." (TOA.1.1)
Change "Athenians" to citizens of any other city as applicable. You may also change 'knaves' to 'scoundrels'. See also 'Honesty, an honest Athenian as a physical impossibility - ... if doing nothing be death by the law.'
In the play. *The grouchy Apemantus understands the character of Athens' citizens.*

Athens, imprecation against A. - ... sink, Athens! henceforth hated be of Timon, man and all humanity!
"... sink, Athens! henceforth hated be
Of Timon, man and all humanity!" (TOA.3.6)
Change "Athens' to applicable city or location or company. Change 'Timon' to name of imprecating person.
In the play. *After the party of parasites has gathered, Timon dismisses them angrily throwing plates at them and condemning them along with all the Athenians.*

Attention deficit, questioning lack of a. – ... how is't with you, that you do bend your eye on vacancy...
"Alas, how is't with you,
That you do bend your eye on vacancy

And with the incorporal air do hold discourse?" (H.3.4)
Reproach an inattentive student or subordinate.
In the play. *The Queen cannot see the Ghost who speaks to Hamlet. Therefore Hamlet appears as looking into a void and talking to the air.*

Attention, object of a., unconcerned about being the object of a. – Men's eyes were made to look, and let them gaze.
"Men's eyes were made to look, and let them gaze" (RJ.3.1)
In the play. *Mercutio refuses an invitation by Benvolio to go into a more secluded place to resolve the grievances with Tybald, a Capulet*

Attention, undivided a. - Had I three ears, I'd hear thee.
Second Apparition Macbeth! Macbeth! Macbeth!
MACBETH Had I three ears, I'd hear thee. (M.4.1)
Answer to 'Do you hear me?' or 'Are you paying attention?'
In the play. *The second apparition materializes while Macbeth consults with the witches about his next prospects, now that he killed Duncan and is king.*

Attire, a. or general appearance questionable – so … unfashionable that dogs bark at me as I halt by them.
"so … unfashionable
That dogs bark at me as I halt by them" (KRIII.1.1)
See also 'Disregard, completely disregarded – … they pass'd by me as misers do by beggars…'
In the play. *Richard meditates about his own options for life and for achieving the crown.*

Attire, justification or excuse for the poor appearance of your clothing - … Jove sometimes went disguised, and why not I?
WHITMORE The Duke of Suffolk muffled up in rags!
SUFFOLK Ay, but these rags are no part of the duke:
Jove sometimes went disguised, and why not I? (KH6.p2.4)
Try, 'Yes my clothes are tattered but as Suffolk said, 'These rags are no part of the duke…why not I?
In the play. *The Duke of Suffolk attempts to board a ship to France after having been banned from the court of Henry VI.*

Attire, justifying your curious a. or transformation - the gods themselves… have taken the shapes of beasts upon them.
"…The gods themselves,
Humbling their deities to love, have taken
The shapes of beasts upon them: Jupiter
Became a bull, and bellow'd; the green Neptune
A ram, and bleated; and the fire-robed god,
Golden Apollo, a poor humble swain" (WT.4.3)
When she makes a comment, perhaps not too positive, about how you look, or your garment(s), etc. Also answer to 'you are a beast'
In the play. *Florizel took up the garment of a shepherd to meet shepherdess Perdita. He assures he that his intents are noble. His put-on garments are just an expedient – the Gods transformed themselves into various disguises but never for 'a peace of beauty rare' as Perdita. See note to 'Reliability. "Am I going to be safe with you? Can I trust you? Etc.'*

Attire, nobility behind a humble a. – … though thy tackle's torn. Thou show'st a noble vessel.

"... though thy tackle's torn.
Thou show'st a noble vessel"
(COR.4.5)
Retort to an apology for being dressed poorly or casually.
See also '**Identification, characteristics - More than I seem, and less than I was born to...**'
In the play. *The Volscian leader Aufidius to Coriolanus who has arrived to join the Volsces against ungrateful Rome.*

Attire, outlandish or wacky - ... so wild in their attire, that look not like the inhabitants o' the earth
"What are these
So wither'd and so wild in their attire,
That look not like the inhabitants o' the earth" (M.1.3)
When you have soiled your dress or when everyone is dressed formally and you are not. Or ironic and mildly self-effacing retort to anyone who comments negatively on your suit or dress. E.G.'I know I look not like an inhabitant of the earth' Or address a person strangely dressed.
In the play. *Banquo comments on the apparition of the three witches.*

Attitude, a. of strength towards challenges ahead - ... And meet the time as it seeks us.
"I thank you. Let's withdraw;
And meet the time as it seeks us. We fear not
What can from Italy annoy us"
(CYM.4.3)
Epilogue to a presentation, e.g. 'The tasks are daunting, but we need to 'meet the time as it seeks us.'
In the play. *King Cymbeline to an attendant who warned him that Roman forces have landed in Britain.*

Attitude, a. towards pain felt by ourselves or by others - ... But were we burdened with like weight of pain...
"A wretched soul, bruised with adversity,
We bid be quiet when we hear it cry;
But were we burdened with like weight of pain,
As much or more would we ourselves complain" (COE.2.1)
Justify complaints or lamentations.
In the play. *Adriana, wide of Antipholus E. to her sister Luciana*

Attitude, a. towards the world, hating it – one...whom the vile blows and buffets of the world...
SECOND MURDERER: I am one, my liege,
Whom the vile blows and buffets of the world
Have so incens'd, that I am reckless what I do
To spite the world.
FIRST MURDERER: And I another,
So weary with disasters, tugg'd with fortune,
That I would set my life on any chance,
To mend it, or be rid of it." (M.3.1)
Use either of the two quotes to explain or justify why you are ready to take on a risky assignment. See also 'Life, tired of l. – I am so out of love with life that I will sue to be rid of it.'
In the play. *Two murderers hired by Macbeth explain why they have no qualms in murdering Banquo. 'To tug' = 'To be drawn and shaken about by fortune while trying to grapple with her'.*

Attitude, a. towards what is past and cannot be changed - Not one word more of the consumed time.
"**Not one word more of the consumed time**" (AWEW.5.3)
See also 'Time, let's concentrate on the present – Let's take the instant by the forward top' S*** 'Regret, r. corrosive for

things that cannot be changed' and entries for 'Complaint'
In the play. *The King of France has forgiven Bertram for his mistakes and now suggests that Bertram marry Lafeu's daughter.*

Attitude, a. towards what is past and cannot be changed - Things past redress are now with me past care.
"Things past redress are now with me past care." (KRII.2.3)
You have done everything you can to correct a situation but met too much opposition. See also 'Regret, r. corrosive for things that cannot be changed' and entries for 'Complaint'
In the play. *York at the end of a meeting with Bolingbroke and his allies. York is helpless to stop their rebellious acts.*

Attitude, a. towards what is past and cannot be changed - Things that are past are done with me.
"Things that are past are done with me." (AC.1.2)
Your attitude or a way to say that you have forgotten a past quarrel or misunderstanding or animosity. See also 'Regret, r. corrosive for things that cannot be changed' and entries for 'Complaint'
In the play. *Antony in conversation with a messenger from Rome, who is afraid to speak, as the news he reports is bad (Antony's wife Fulvia is dead). But Antony still thinks that the messenger may refer to something else.*

Attitude, a. towards what is past and cannot be changed – Things without all remedy should be without regard. .
"…Things without all remedy, Should be without regard: what's done is done." (M.3.1)
Cut short explanations or excuses for prior failures. See also 'Regret, r. corrosive for things that cannot be changed' and entries for 'Complaint'.

In the play. *Lady Macbeth to husband noticing his dejected looks*

Attitude, a. towards what is past and cannot be changed - To mourn a mischief that is past and gone…
"When remedies are past, the griefs are ended
By seeing the worst, which late on hopes depended.
To mourn a mischief that is past and gone
Is the next way to draw new mischief on
…The robbed that smiles steals something from the thief;
He robs himself that spends a bootless grief." (OTH.1.3)
Encouragement to forget the past. See also 'Regret, r. corrosive for things that cannot be changed' *** Entries for 'Complaint'
In the play. *Othello has succeeded in marrying Desdemona. This is the mischief that the Duke refers to, while talking to the distraught Brabantio. Brabantio is Desdemona's father.*

Attitude, a. towards what is past and cannot be changed - What's gone and what's past help should be past grief.
" ... what's gone and what's past help Should be past grief." (WT.3.2)
An alternative to 'Bygones are bygones'. See also 'Regret, r. corrosive for things that cannot be changed' and entries for 'Complaint'
In the play. *Now that Leontes recognizes his folly Paulina will stop reminding him of painful memories since nothing can be done about it.*

Attitude, mercenary a. - Believe't, that we'll do any thing for gold.
"Well, more gold: what then?
Believe't, that we'll do any thing for gold" (TOA.4.3)
Point out the mercenary nature of a transaction or character. E.G. As Phrynia said to Timon 'Believe't, that we'll do any

thing for gold". See also 'Gold, g. as powerful tool of corruption'.
In the play. *Phrynia, Alcibiades' girlfriend or whore completely overlooks an insulting tirade by Timon. Timon has found some gold by chance and all she interested in is, obviously, the gold.*

Attitude, negative a. of a person rejecting ideas - ... like an envious sneaping frost that bites the first born infants of the spring.
"Biron is like an envious sneaping frost,
That bites the first born infants of the spring." (LLL.1.1)
Apply to a person who immediately rejects your idea. Change 'Biron' to applicable person.
In the play. *The king disapproves of Biron's negative attitude towards the proposed time of learning and abstinence. 'Sneaping' = 'biting, nipping'*

Attitude, positive a. in reversals - The robb'd that smiles steals something from the thief...
"The robb'd that smiles steals something from the thief;
He robs himself that spends a bootless grief." (OTH.1.3)
See also 'Complaint after problems useless' - 'Actions, past a. cannot be remedied' – 'Relationship beyond repair'.
In the play. *The Duke of Venice counsels Brabantio, Desdemona's father, to put a smile on the fact that she is marrying Othello against his wish.*

Attitude, positive and defiant towards adversity – in poison there is physic' and these news...
"In poison there is physic; and these news,
Having been well, that would have made me sick;
Being sick, have in some measure made me well." (KHIVp2.1.1)

Show your resolve to fight back. See also 'Determination, d. to fight back after a setback - ... make my ill th'advantage of my good.'
In the play. *Northumberland puts a positive spin on a bad case - it will quicken his resolve to revenge Hotspur.*

Attitude, posture and its importance - Let not the world see fear and sad distrust... threaten the threatener...
Ph. FAULCONBRIDGE (to King John).
Let not the world see fear and sad distrust,
Govern the motion of a kingly eye
...
Threaten the threatener, and outface the brow
Of bragging horror: so shall inferior eyes,
That borrow their behaviour from the great,
Grow great by your example, and put on
The dauntless spirit of resolution." (KJ.5.1)
Persuade how important is to show an image of strength.
In the play. *Encouragement to K. John to face up to the situation.*

Attitude, stoic a. towards reversal – ... do not please sharp fate to grace it with your sorrows... and we punish it seeming to bear it lightly.
"... do not please sharp fate
To grace it with your sorrows: bid that welcome
Which comes to punish us, and we punish it
Seeming to bear it lightly" (AC.4.14)
In the play. *Antony to his troops after defeat at the hand of Octavian.*

Attitude, unexplainable change in a. - …what is breeding that changeth thus his manners.
"…So leaves me to consider what is breeding
That changeth thus his manners."
(WT.1.2)
In the play. *Polixenes cannot explain the sudden hostile behavior of Leontes.*

Attraction, fatal, her voice and shape - mine ear is much enamoured of thy note…
"Mine ear is much enamoured of thy note,
So is mine eye enthralled to thy shape.
"(MND.3.1)
A good compliment but find out first if she knows about the play lest she may misinterpret your compliment. In Midsummer Night's Dream, it is Titania who says these lines to a character meaningfully called Bottom. In a play-within-the-play Bottom is reciting the part of an ass and is attired accordingly. Through a magic trick Oberon manages to have Titania fall in love with an ass.
In the play. *The drops have worked their magic and Titania, on waking up sees Bottom (masquerading as a donkey) and falls in love with him.*

Attraction, it is obvious that she likes him - … she did so course o'er my exteriors with such a greedy intention…
"O, she did so course o'er my exteriors with such a greedy intention, that the appetite of her eye did seem to scorch me up like a burning glass!"
(MWW.1.3)
Most of the time this is wishful thinking, just as Falstaff thinks so is in the actual play.
In the play. *Falstaff thinks (has the illusion) that Mistress Ford finds him irresistibly attractive.*

Attraction, physical a. observed - … who even now gave me good eyes too…
"I have writ me here a letter to her: and here
another to **Page's** wife, who even now gave me good
eyes too, examined my parts with most judicious
oeillades; sometimes the beam of her view gilded my
foot, sometimes my portly belly."
(MWW.1.3)
Start from '(she) gave me good eyes…' Change 'oeillades' to 'looks'.
In the play. *Centuries ahead of mass mailing, Falstaff has written the same love letter to Mrs. Ford and Mrs. Page, changing only name and address.*

Attraction, visual a. and nothing else - … young men's love then lies not truly in their hearts, but in their eyes.
"**Is Rosaline, that thou didst love so dear,
So soon forsaken? Young men's love then lies,
Not truly in their hearts, but in their eyes.**" (RJ.2.3)
Explanation for an unlikely match or a passing flirt. 'Young men's love…their eyes' can be used as a general statement or an expression of opinion.
In the play. *Fr. Lawrence is clearly aware of Romeo's various romantic involvements.*

Audience, determined to have an a. or be received by elusive party or VIP - … tell them, there thy fixed foot shall grow till thou have audience.
"And tell them, there thy fixed foot shall grow,
Till thou have audience." (TN.1.4)
Use with secretary when she says that the person you wish to see is not available, e.g. 'my fixed foot shall grow will I have audience'.

In the play. *The Duke dispatches Cesario to talk to Olivia on his (the Duke's) behalf and wants him not to take no for an answer.*

Audience, quiet or unreceptive - …like dumb statues or breathing stones.
"…they spake not a word;
But, like dumb statues or breathing stones,
Star'd on each other and looked deadly pale." (KRIII.3.7)
In the play. *Buckingham reports that the aldermen of London gave him a very cold reception when he told them that Richard should be the next king of England instead of the lawful heir, son of Edward.*

Audience, request for an a. - shall I vouchsafe your worship a word or two?
MISTRESS QUICKLY Shall I vouchsafe your worship a word or two?
FALSTAFF Two thousand, fair woman: and I'll vouchsafe thee the hearing. (MWW.2.2)
Answer to 'Can I have a word with you?'
In the play. *Mistress Quickly, keeper of the Garter Inn, acts on behalf of Mrs. Ford who wants to play a trick on Falstaff.*

August, A's heat tiring - You sunburnt sicklemen, of August weary…
"You sunburnt sicklemen, of August weary,
Come hither from the furrow and be merry:
Make holiday; your rye-straw hats put on
And these fresh nymphs encounter every one
In country footing." (TEM.4.1)

In the play. *Prospero has agreed to let his daughter Miranda marry Ferdinand. Now Prospero demonstrates his power to evoke spirits, nymphs etc. Iris, a spirit, invites certain nymphs to enter the scene and (presumably) provide good company to miscellaneous farm-workers, read 'sunburnt sicklemen'*

Austerity, a. program - The grosser manner of these world's delights…
"The grosser manner of these world's delights
He throws upon the gross world's baser slaves" (LLL.1.1)
Change 'he' to 'I' if you apply the lines to yourself. Food, giving priority to spiritual over material f. - The mind shall banquet, though the body pine
In the play. *Dumain subscribes to a program of learning, dieting and abstinence that will actually never be followed.*

Authority, a. can get away with sin - … authority, though it err like others hath yet a kind of medicine in itself, that skins the vice o' the top.
ANGELO Why do you put these sayings upon me?
ISABELLA Because authority, though it err like others,
Hath yet a kind of medicine in itself,
That skins the vice o' the top.
(MFM.2.1)
In the play. *Isabella pleads with Angelo for mercy for her brother Claudio. Her point is that if Angelo, who is an authority, had committed the same fault he would escape punishment.*

Authority, a. of king derived from God – … that supernal judge, that stirs good thoughts…
"…that supernal judge, that stirs good thoughts
In any breast of strong authority,
To look into the blots and stains of right" (KJ.2.1)

In the play. *King Philip answers a question from King John as to John's usurpation of the English throne.*

Authority, a. of princes and signs of respect due to them - ... for princes are a model, which heaven makes like to itself...
"... for princes are
A model, which heaven makes like to itself:
As jewels lose their glories if neglected,
So princes their renown, if not respected." (PER.2.2)
A retort when a guest asks you not to go to any trouble for him/her. 'I must, because as jewels lose…respected'.
In the play. *Simonides (to Thaisa). Respect shown to princes reinforces their nobility. The principle applies equally to other authorities.*

Authority, a. proclaimed – Let them obey, that know not how to rule…
"Let them obey, that know not how to rule;
This hand was made to handle nought but gold:
I cannot give due action to my words,
Except a sword or sceptre balance it."
(KHVI p2.5.1)
Use the first line to enforce your right wing opinions.
In the play. *York before the battle at Blackheath*

Authority, a. restricted or slave to interests - To be a queen in bondage is more vile than is a slave…
"To be a queen in bondage is more vile
Than is a slave in base servility;
For princes should be free"
(KHVI.p1.5.3)
Applicable to ministers or political leaders driven by corporate interests.

In the play. *Margaret, captured by Suffolk, misinterprets at first Suffolk's suggestion that she become queen of England*

Authority, a. using its power to discredit accusers and whistle blowers - ... no particular scandal once can touch but it confounds the breather.
"For my authority bears of a credent bulk,
That no particular scandal once can touch
But it confounds the breather."
(MFM.4.6)
In the play. *Angelo, strong in his position of authority, thinks (and hopes) that nobody will believe Isabel when she will accuse him of corruption*

Authority, beneficial effect of the presence of a. - the presence of a king engenders love…
"The presence of a king engenders love
Amongst his subjects and his loyal friends;
As it disanimates his enemies."
(KHVI.p1.3.1)
A good flattering tool to persuade your boss to join you in a business trip. For a contrary view see 'Visibility. Advantages, for authorities of not being seen too often.
In the play. *Gloucester suggests to Henry VI that he be crowned in France to reinforce the image of a caring ruler.*

Authority, consequences of lack of a. and management - ... And this neglection of degree it is that by a pace goes backward, with a purpose it hath to climb.
"…And this neglection of degree it is
That by a pace goes backward, with a purpose
It hath to climb" (TC.1.3)

In the play. *Ulysses upbraids the Greeks for their weakness and lack of unified authority (degree).*

Authority, consequences of lack of a. and management - ... when degree is shaked, which is the ladder to all high designs, then enterprise is sick.
"…O, when degree is shaked,
Which is the ladder to all high designs,
Then enterprise is sick!
…
Take but degree away, untune that string,
And, hark, what discord follows! each thing meets
In mere oppugnancy: the bounded waters
Should lift their bosoms higher than the shores
And make a sop of all this solid globe:
Strength should be lord of imbecility,
And the rude son should strike his father dead:
Force should be right; or rather, right and wrong,
Between whose endless jar justice resides,
Should lose their names, and so should justice too.
Then every thing includes itself in power,
Power into will, will into appetite;
And appetite, an universal wolf,
So doubly seconded with will and power,
Must make perforce an universal prey,
And last eat up himself. " (TC.1.3)
See also 'Management, m. and leadership crucial - The heavens themselves, the planets and this centre'
In the play. *Ulysses upbraids the Greeks for their weakness and lack of unified authority (degree).*

Authority, consequences when a. is afraid - …and what was first but fear what might be done grows elder now and cares it be not done.
"…the passions of the mind,
That have their first conception by mis-dread,
Have after-nourishment and life by care;
And what was first but fear what might be done,
Grows elder now and cares it be not done." (PER.1.2)
See also 'Cover up, planned - and what may make him blush in being known, he'll stop the course by which it might be known'. See also 'Authority, consequences when a. is afraid - …and what was first but fear what might be done grows elder now and cares it be not done'.
In the play. *Back in Tyre, Pericles reflects on what Antioch may do as his fear (of Pericles divulging his incest) may cause Antioch to take extreme measures to make sure the matter does not become known.*

Authority, corrupted by gold - ... and though authority be a stubborn bear, yet he is oft led by the nose with gold.
"… And though authority be a stubborn
bear, yet he is oft led by the nose with gold." (WT.4.3)
Use to comment on applicable instances of corruption. See also 'Justice, purchased and corrupted by money' - 'Opinion, your op. on authority' – 'Money, m opening the way' – 'Gold, g. as powerful tool of corruption'.
In the play. *The clown confers with the sly Autolycus on how to get some concessions from the authority.*

Authority, executive position, suffered, not wanted - was never subject long'd to be a king...

"Was never subject long'd to be a king
As I do long and wish to be a subject." (KHVI p2.4.9)
Why you refuse an important position or title or responsibility
In the play. *Henry VI reflects on his position at Kenilworth Castle.*

Authority, fear in a. grows with time – ... tyrants' fears decrease not, but grow faster than the years.
"… tyrants' fears
Decrease not, but grow faster than the years" (PER.2.1)
Rational explanation for various measures of authoritarian regimes, e.g. Offices of Homeland Security, Patriot Acts etc.
In the play. *Pericles tells Helicanus about his meeting with tyrannous King Antioch.*

Authority, king no different from other men - ... the king is but a man, as I am: the violet smells to him as it doth to me.
"I think the king is but a man, as I am: the violet smells to him as it doth to me: the element shows to him as it doth to me" (KHV.4.1)
In the play. *Bates (a soldier) to King Henry (incognito).*

Authority, limits to its importance - ... for within the hollow crown that rounds the mortal temples of a king keeps death its watch…
... for within the hollow crown
That rounds the mortal temples of a king
Keeps Death his court and there the antic sits,
Scoffing his state and grinning at his pomp,
Allowing him a breath, a little scene,
To monarchize, be fear'd and kill with looks,

Infusing him with self and vain conceit…" (KRII.3.2)
See also 'Pessimism, limits of self-importance - … Infusing him with self and vain conceits, as if this flesh, which walls about our life were brass impregnable.'
In the play. *Richard reflection after Bolingbroke has seized in effect the kingdom.*

Authority, rarely to be questioned - for few men rightly temper with the stars.
"For few men rightly temper with the stars" (KHVI p3.4)
Soften the impact of your objections, e.g. 'I know that few men rightly temper with the stars'. Or if dealing with a lady add '...and I know you are a star but…'.
In the play. *Warwick gently argues with Henry VI because the king has chosen Warwick as a kind of prime minister instead of Clarence, who should have been the natural appointee. By so objecting, Warwick 'tempers with the stars.'*

Authority, smiling authorities to be feared - 'T is time to fear, when tyrants seem to kiss.
"'T is time to fear, when tyrants seem to kiss." (PER.1.2)
Express your mistrust of authorities who appear pleasant but whom you suspect of wickedness. See also 'Opinion, your op. on authority'.
In the play. *Pericles comments on the feigned courtesy displayed by Antioch.*

Authority, using the power of a. for cover-up – ... you shall stifle in your own report and smell of calumny.
"Who will believe thee, Isabel?
My unsoil'd name, the austereness of my life,
My vouch against you, and my place i' the state,
Will so your accusation overweigh,
That you shall stifle in your own report
And smell of calumny" (MFN.2.4)

Established black mail tactics used by authority to cover up their misdeeds.
In the play. *The hypocrite Angelo warns Isabel that her report about his sexual advances will not be believed.*

Authorization, hope you have a. - I hope your warrant will bear out the deed.
"I hope your warrant will bear out the deed." (KJ.4.1)
In the play. *An executioner to Hubert. Hubert is set to blind young Prince Arthur, captured by King John.*

Autumn, season of plenty – The teeming autumn, big with rich increase…
"The teeming autumn, big with rich increase,
Bearing the wanton burden of the prime,
Like widow'd wombs after their lords' decease." (SON 97)

Autumn, winter – When lofty trees I see barren of leaves…
"…When lofty trees I see barren of leaves
Which erst from heat did canopy the herd,
And summer's green all girded up in sheaves" (SON 12)
See also 'Age, admitting to being old - That time of year thou mayst in me behold…'

Avalanche, formation of an a., metaphor for a revolution - … as a little snow, tumbled about anon becomes a mountain.
"Or as a little snow, tumbled about, Anon becomes a mountain." (KJ.3.4)
In the play. *The image refers to the effect of a few French forces sent to England. They would gather English forces around them to overthrow the murderous King John.*

Awakening, too early to get up - … it argues a distempered head so soon to bid good morrow to thy bed.
"What early tongue so sweet saluteth me?
Young son, it argues a distempered head,
So soon to bid good morrow to thy bed." (RJ.2.3)
When someone unexpectedly calls on you early in the morning.
In the play. *Fr. Lawrence returns Romeo's introductory salutations.*

Awareness, a. declared and pointed out – I see things too although you judge I wink.
"I see things too, although you judge I wink." (TGV.1.2)
Use with anyone who acts as if you did not know what is going on.
In the play. *Lucetta sees through the pretence of Julia, who loves Proteus but does not want to admit it.*

Bachelorhood, b. recanted – When I said I would die a bachelor, I did not think I should live till I were married.
"When I said I would die a bachelor, I did not think I should live till I were married" (MAAN.2.3)
Answer to 'I did not know you were married'.
In the play. *Benedick, contrary to his previous assertions, has fallen in love with Beatrice.*

Bachelorhood, consolation of b. – … broom -groves, whose shadow the dismissed bachelor loves…
"…broom-groves,
Whose shadow the dismissed bachelor loves,
Being lass-lorn" (TEM.4.1)
In the play. *Iris makes an invocation to the Goddess Ceres to approach and list all Cere's assets, including the groves of brooms.*

Bachelorhood, justification for b. - Because I will not do them the wrong to mistrust any, I will do myself the right to trust none…
"… all women shall pardon me. Because I will not do them the wrong to mistrust any, I will do myself the right to trust none; and the fine is, for the which I may go the finer, I will live a bachelor." (MAAN.1.1)
In the play. *Benedick explains to his friend Claudio why he is or thinks he will remain a bachelor.*

Background, checkered professional b. - … having flown over many knavish professions…
" … and, having flown over many knavish professions, he settled only in rogue: some call him Autolycus." (WT.4.2)
Describe a character of dubious background, with minor paraphrasing, e.g. '… after having flown over many knavish professions, he settled only in being a rascal."
In the play. *Autolycus pretends to have been robbed and beaten and while the clown helps him up he robs the clown. The clown asks him who was he that robbed him. Autolycus says he knew the robber and tells of the alleged robber's somewhat checkered background.*

Bad, from bad to good better than from good to bad - … The lamentable change is from the best; the worst returns to laughter.
"…To be worst,
The lowest and most dejected thing of fortune,
Stands still in esperance, lives not in fear:
The lamentable change is from the best;
The worst returns to laughter." (KL.4.1)

See also "Last, not being the l. better than nothing - not being the worst stands in some rank of praise"
In the play. *The good son Edgar joins the motley group around King Lear to whom Edgar's father, blinded by the duke of Cornwall, also belongs. In the next lines Edgar toasts the fresh air. See 'Nature, air, welcome to the air - … Welcome, then, thou unsubstantial air that I embrace'.*

Balance of power, examination of – I have in equal balance justly weigh'd…and find our griefs heavier than our offences.
"I have in equal balance justly weigh'd
What wrongs our arms may do, what wrongs we suffer,
And find our griefs heavier than our offences" (KHIV.p2.3.1)
In the play. *Archbishop of York answers Westmoreland as to his position in the rebellion against Henry IV. See associated entry, 'Rebellion, reasons and occasions for a r.'*

Balance, in praise of balanced life - … they are as sick that surfeit with too much, as they that starve with nothing.
"… for aught I see, they are as sick that surfeit with too much, as they that starve with nothing; it is no mean happiness therefore to be seated in the mean - superfluity comes sooner by white hair, but competency lives longer." (MOV.3.2)
Fight the compulsive push to get ahead, an answer to "Don't you want to have more?", 'It is no mean happiness to be seated in the mean.
In the play. *Nerissa counsels Portia who, notwithstanding all her fortunes, is weary of the world*

Baldness, dealing with hair issues, praise of b. -... it is a blessing that times bestows on beasts...
ANTIPHOLUS of Syracuse. Why is Time such a niggard of hair, being, as it is, so plentiful an excrement?
DROMIO of Syracuse. Because it is a blessing that times bestows on beasts; and what he has scanted men in hair, he hath given them in wit.
ANTIPHOLUS OF SYRACUSE Why, but there's many a man hath more hair than wit.
DROMIO OF SYRACUSE Not a man of those but he hath the wit to lose his hair. (COE.2.2)
Depending on your hair condition use Dromio's comment as a statement in self-defense or as a self-effacing, tone-down comment - should anyone comment on your luxuriant hair.
If you have plenty of hair and groom it with care, you may keep in mind the word of caution that Ovid gives to women regarding men who style their hair, "But avoid men who profess elegance and good looks and who arrange their hair in their proper place. What they tell you they have told a thousand women; their fancy wanders, and has no fixed abode.' (AOL.3)
In the play. *After having been beaten by Antipholus from Syracuse, Dromio S. enters into a semi-serious disquisition on baldness with Antipholus from Ephesus. Dromio S asserts that time itself is bald ("a rule as plain as the bald pate of Father Time itself"). 'Niggard' = 'Stingy provider'.*

Baldness, hair restoring procedures questionable - There's no time for a man to recover his hair that grows bald by nature.
"There's no time for a man to recover his hair that grows bald by nature" (COE.2.2)

Express your skepticism about hair restoration advertisements and procedures.
In the play. *Dromio S to Antipholus S as they discuss problems connected with mistaken identity.*

Baldness, statistical advantages of b. - there's many a man hath more hair than wit.
"…there's many a man hath more hair than wit." (COE.2.2)
Another retort to a comment to the scantiness of your hair.
In the play. *Antipholus and Dromio of Syracuse speculate on the connection between hair and intelligence.*

Bankruptcy, consequences of b. - ... and of all my lands is nothing left me but my body's length.
"…and of all my lands
Is nothing left me but my body's length." (KHVI.p3.5.2)
Give a *dramatic representation to the loss of assets, divorce, medical bills etc.*
In the play. *Warwick, wounded to death in the battle against the York forces near Barnet, reflects on his life.*

Bankruptcy, forced b. - He hath eaten me out of house and home...
"…He hath eaten me out of house and home; he hath put all my substance into that fat belly of his" (KHIV.p2.2.1)
In the play. *Mistress Quickly complains with the Chief Justice about Falstaff's unpaid bills*

Bar, going to b. to find solace in alcohol and company - I will see what physic the tavern affords.
"I will see what physic the tavern affords." (KHVI.p1.3.1)
Answer to 'where are you going?'
In the play. *After a skirmish, servants of Gloucester and Winchester go their own ways*

and one decides to go to a tavern. Gloucester and Winchester have agreed to a tenuous peace

Bargaining, dispraising the value of what you wish to buy - ... you do as chapmen do dispraise the thing that you desire to buy...
"Fair Diomed, you do as chapmen do,
Dispraise the thing that you desire to buy:
But we in silence hold this virtue well,
We'll not commend what we intend to sell." (TC.4.1)
When someone disparages what you have to sell. Or to moderate your sale pitch.
In the play. *Diomedes has said some disparaging words on Helen and Paris replies.*

Bated breath - With bated breath and whispering humbleness…
"With bated breath and whispering humbleness…" (MOV.1.3)
In the play. *Shylock rhetorically asks Antonio how he, Shylock, should respond to Antonio's request for a loan of 3000 ducats. 'Bated' s the participle of 'to bate'='to weaken'*

Battle, b. of the wits - there is no such sport, as sport by sport overthrown.
"There is no such sport, as sport by sport overthrown." (LLL.5.2)
Sportingly admit defeat in a battle of words or wits. See also 'Reply, unable to sustain the verbal attack'.
In the play. *The Princess and company will answer in kind the masquerade set up by king and company*

Battle, b. strategy, diplomacy first, arms later - ... let's fight with gentle words…
"…let's fight with gentle words
Till time lend friends and friends their helpful swords." (KRII.3.3)
Stall when you are not strong enough to accept a direct battle.

In the play. *King Richard II suddenly proposes to be defiant towards Bolingbroke, Aumerle suggests instead a different tactics.*

Battle, b. to the end - swords and lances arbitrate the swelling difference of your settled hate.
"There shall your swords and lances arbitrate
The swelling difference of your settled hate:" (KRII.1.1)
Change 'your' to 'our' and emphasize that the battle must be continued to the bitter end.
In the play. *Richard II decrees that Bolingbroke and Mowbray will settle their hatred and arguments in a duel at Coventry.*

Battle, mental preparation of a warmonger – I shall prove a lover of thy drum, hater of love.
"Great Mars, I put myself into thy file:
Make me but like my thoughts, and I shall prove
A lover of thy drum, hater of love. " (AWEW.3.3)
Quote as an example of a macho statement of intent.
In the play. *Bertram conditions himself mentally for the battles.*

Battle, outcome of b. uncertain – so is the equal poise of this fell war.
"Now sways it this way, like a mighty sea
Forced by the tide to combat with the wind;
Now sways it that way; like the selfsame sea
Forced to retire by fury of the wind
Sometimes the flood prevails, and then the wind;
Now, one the better, then, another best;
Both tugging to be victors, breast to breast,
Yet neither conqueror nor conquered:

So is the equal poise of this fell war." (KHVI p3.2.5)
Use the last two lines to comment on an inconclusive battle or turn of events
In the play. *Henry VI commenting on the development of the battle of Towton where his forces will lose.*

Battle, prepared for b. - ... why he cometh hither plated in habiliments of war.
"Marshal, ask yonder knight in arms,
Both who he is and why he cometh hither
Thus plated in habiliments of war," **(KRII.1.3)**
Comment on two known adversaries, e.g. 'Here they come, plated in their habiliments of war.
In the play. *At Coventry, Bolingbroke and Mowbray are ready for a mortal duel.*

Beach, entertainment on the beach - ... chase the ebbing Neptune and do fly him when he comes back
"And ye that on the sands with printless foot
Do chase the ebbing Neptune and do fly him
When he comes back" (TEM.5.1)
In the play. *Part of Prospero the Magician's parting words to the audience.*

Beard, a professional shave after extended neglect – This ornament makes me look dismal will I clip to form...
"This ornament
Makes me look dismal will I clip to form;
And what this fourteen years no razor touch'd,
To grace thy marriage-day, I'll beautify." (PER.5.3)
In the play. *Pericles, re-united with earlier presumed lost wife and daughter, will shave beard and (probably) cut his 'unscissored' hair, see 'Haircut, no h. for a while'*

Beard, b. and moustaches, barber needed - methinks I am marvellous hairy about the face.
"I must to the barber's, monsieur; for methinks I am marvellous hairy about the face" (MND.4.1)
When you were too rushed to shave and someone comments on it.
In the play. *Bottom, actor in a theater company made of 'rude mechanicals' comments about the status of his own grooming. Bottom is playing the part of an ass in the production. The full lines are:*
I must to the barber's, monsieur; for methinks I am marvellous hairy about the face; and I
am such a tender ass, if my hair do but tickle me, I must scratch.

Beard, b. long and substantial - Thou hast got more hair on thy chin than Dobbin my fill-horse has on his tail.
"...what a beard hast thou got! thou hast got more hair on thy chin than Dobbin my fill-horse has on his tail." (MOV.2.2)
In the play. *Blind Gobbo finds his son Launcelot in Venice after a long time and is surprised at the length or feel of Launcelot's beard.*

Beard, b. shaved – ... the old ornament of his cheek hath already stuffed tennis-balls.
"...the barber's man hath been seen with him, and the old ornament of his cheek hath already stuffed tennis-balls." (MAAN.3.2)
In the play. *Claudio reports that Benedick went to the barber, a sign that Benedick is in love.*

Beard, b. unkempt (but also hair) - ...beard made rough and rugged, like to the summer's corn by tempest lodged.

**"His well-proportion'd beard made rough and rugged,
Like to the summer's corn by tempest lodged."** (KHVIp2.3.2)
Adjust to 'My beard (or hair) is rough and rugged…lodged'.
In the play. *Warwick gives King Henry evidence that Duke Humphrey was murdered, including the state of the Duke's beard.*

**Beard, white b. or b. with strands of white - … whose beard the silver hand of peace hath touch'd.
"…Whose beard the silver hand of peace hath touch'd"** (KHIV.p2.4.1)
Answer to comment on the white strands of your beard, e.g. 'I am one whose beard…touched'.
In the play. *In the forest of Gaultree in Yorkshire. Westmoreland meets the rebels addressing the archbishop of York with flattering and flowery words. This will prove a trick and when the rebels agree to disband they will be arrested and executed.*

**Beast, unreasoning b. would make better decision - … a beast, that wants discourse of reason…
"O, God! a beast, that wants discourse of reason,
Would have…."** (H.1.2)
In the play. *Hamlet is distressed at the unreasonable haste with which Queen Gertrude has decided to marry Hamlet's uncle after the death of Hamlet's father.*

BEAUTY

In general, compliments on her beauty work better if she is intelligent but not beautiful. On the other hand, if she is beautiful, (intelligent or not), she is probably used to be told so by all the guys over and over again, with almost identical words and expressions, such as 'you are beautiful' or (worse) 'what a doll', 'what a babe', etc. If so, however silly she may otherwise be, you will gain some points with a judicious choice of any of the quotes referring to her beauty.
Beauty's Maintenance. Ladies are extremely concerned about retaining their beauty and youthful appearance, fearing that they may lose you if their beauty fades away. (See Age). In the 1600, throughout the Baroque period and down to the beginning of the 1800 doctors prescribed viper based dishes, broth and other viper products to enhance, maintain and restore beauty. It was widely believed that viper flesh would restore beauty withered through time. The same viper flesh had the magical virtue of delivering charm and seductive powers to young ladies. Eventually, the Italian doctor Francesco Redi (1626-1697) proto-physician at the court of the Dukes of Tuscany, studied the matter and concluded that:
"Whether eating viper flesh and viper-based foods produces in youthful ladies' bodies (as many scientists affirm) that pleasing harmony of parts and colors, which is called beauty - and whether the same food may restore their lost beauty, when the ladies have reached a senile age, I have not been able to determine clearly…." (Francesco Redi, 'Observations on Vipers')
Ovid addresses the ladies as follows, 'Beauty is a heaven's gift: but few can boast of beauty! A great part of you lacks a gift so precious. Care will give good looks: looks neglected go to waste though they resemble the Idalian* goddess. (AOL.3)

* Aphrodite was the patron goddess of many cities of Cyprus, and for this reason she is testified with epithets like: Paphian, Idalian, Goglian.

And how about men?

Today beauty salons are often unisex and some men undergo plastic surgery to either (supposedly) increase their sex appeal or, more often, reverse the effects of age (see AGE). But for Ovid, 'An uncared-for beauty is becoming to men. Theseus carried off Minos' daughter, though no ring clasped his nose or earrings his ears. Phaedra loved Hippolytus, and yet he was not a dandy.... Let your person please by cleanliness…let your toga fit and be spotless…let your feet not float about in shoes too loose; let hair and beard be handled by a practiced hand. Do not let your nails project, and let them be free of dirt; nor let any hair be in the hollow of your nostrils. Let not the breath of your mouth be sour and unpleasing.' (See 'Breath, how to avoid bad breath' and 'Breath excellent. Also answer to 'Do I have bad breath?')

Beautiful, b. work of nature - the most replenished sweet work of nature…
"The most replenished sweet work of nature,
That from the prime creation e'er she framed." (KRIII.4.3)
(You are) the most etc. etc – a compliment.
In the play. *Tyrrel the contract killer has killed the young princes while they were asleep and now meditates on the heinous act.*

Beautiful, beyond any praise - You will find she will outstrip all praise…
"You will find she will outstrip all praise,
And make it halt behind." (TEM.4.1)

Change the 'she' to a 'you' and shorten to 'You outstrip all praise' if you tell her directly. Or use the line in its entirety if you wish to describe beforehand a lady (to whom the description may apply) to others who may have the occasion to meet with her later.
In the play. *Prospero has submitted Ferdinand to various physical and psychological tests to verify that he be a suitable match for Prospero's exquisite daughter Miranda. Ferdinand passed the tests and now Prospero describes to him Miranda's qualities. This is utterly unnecessary (other than for poetical purposes), because Ferdinand is already in love head over heels with Miranda*

Beautiful, beyond comparison - If lusty love should go in quest of beauty, where should he find it fairer than in Blanch?
"If lusty love should go in quest of beauty,
Where should he find it fairer than in Blanch?" (KJ.2.2)
Change 'Blanch' to any applicable name. One more optional answer to the question, 'Do you like me?'. Remember also Ovid, 'But whoever you are who are anxious to keep your mistress, be sure she thinks you spellbound by her beauty. AOL.2
In the play. *Hubert suggests a marriage that may deflect the threat of war between England and France. Lady Blanch as a wife for the Dauphin of France. The next two lines are an equal praise of the Lady Blanch's virtues,*
"If zealous love should go in search of virtue,
Where should he find it purer than in Blanch?"
You can use these lines too as applicable, though they may be found ironic.

Beautiful, beyond description - Fairer than tongue can name thee…
"Fairer than tongue can name thee." (KRIII.1.2)

Compliment.
See also 'Defense, d. from general accusation – let me have some patient leisure to excuse myself.'
In the play. *Richard is wooing the widowed Lady Anne.*

Beautiful, beyond description - For her own person, it beggar'd all description.
"…For her own person,
It beggar'd all description" (AC.2.2)
Answer to 'Is she beautiful?', 'It beggars all description'
In the play. *Enobarbus, after having extolled to Agrippa the beauty of Cleopatra's yacht, lacks words to describe her charm.*

Beautiful, even when expressing contempt – O, what a deal of scorn looks beautiful in the contempt and anger of his lip.
**"O, what a deal of scorn looks beautiful
In the contempt and anger of his lip!"** (TN.3.1)
Change 'his lip' to 'your lip' and use the quote when she is nasty and/or angry at you. See also 'Rejection, rebuttal to rejection or harsh words - Teach not thy lip such scorn; for it was made for kissing, lady, not for such contempt.' ***
'Anger, even her a. is an occasion for admiration - ...how wonderful when angels are so angry.'.
In the play. *Olivia is madly in love with Cesario, but Cesario is but Viola disguised in man's garments.*

Beautiful, particularly yesterday - ... she looked yesternight fairer than ever I saw her look, or any woman else.
"Well, she looked yesternight fairer than ever I saw her look, or any woman else." (TC.1.1)
Apply as is to an observed beauty or change 'she' to 'you' and make it a direct compliment. Also answer to 'How do I look?' E.G. 'Fairer than ever I saw you, or any woman else'.
In the play. *Troilus has asked Pandarus if he saw Cressida recently and Pandarus gives a description.*

Beautiful, sweet - in mine eye she is the sweetest lady that ever I looked on.
"In mine eye she is the sweetest lady that ever I looked on." (MAAN.1.1)
Can be used as an observation on a specific lady- or an answer to 'Do you like me?' Change to: 'In mine eye you are the sweetest lady that ever I looked on'.
In the play. *Claudio describes to his friend Benedick the impression gained by meeting with Hero.*

Beauty, artificial b. obtained with heavy make-up - ... Look on beauty and you shall see 'tis purchased by the weight…
**"… Look on beauty,
And you shall see 'tis purchased by the weight;
Which therein works a miracle in nature,
Making them lightest that wear most of it."** (MOV.3.2)
Your comment on a heavily made-up lady.
In the play. *Prior to selecting which basket to choose (the correctly chosen basket will entail marrying Portia), Bassanio meditates on some truths which will lead him to discard the gold basket.*

Beauty, b. above all others - Beauty too rich for use, for earth too dear…
**"Beauty too rich for use, for earth too dear!
So shows a snowy dove trooping with crows,
As yonder lady o'er her fellows shows.
So shows a snowy dove trooping with crows,**

As yonder lady o'er her fellows shows." (RJ.1.5)
Do not say this in the presence of ladies other than that whom you admire, unless you want to make yourself some (female) enemies.
In the play. *At the Capulet party Romeo is stunned by Juliet's beauty exceeding all others.*

Beauty, b. and education and social standing worthy of a princess - ... in beauty, education, blood, holds hand with any princess of the world.
"... she in beauty, education, blood, Holds hand with any princess of the world." (KJ.2.1)
Change 'she' to 'you' and 'holds' to 'hold'. Answer to 'Do you like me?'
In the play. *King John proposes a marriage between the Dauphin of France and the Lady Blanche, the holder of beauty, education and (noble) blood, as indicated by the lines.*

Beauty, b. and evil don't mix – ... the beauteous-evil are empty trunks, o'erflourish'd by the devil.
"...the beauteous-evil
Are empty trunks, o'erflourish'd by the devil." (TN.3.5)
In the play. *Antonio has been arrested by the Duke's men and addresses Viola for help mistaking her (in her man's disguise) for her twin brother Sebastian. Of course she knows nothing of what is going on. Antonio decries her unkindness.*

Beauty, b. and honesty incompatible? – ... for honesty coupled to beauty is to have honey a sauce to sugar.
AUDREY Would you not have me honest?
TOUCHSTONE No, truly, unless thou wert hard-favoured; for honesty coupled to beauty is to have honey a sauce to sugar. (AYLI.3.3)
'To have honey a sauce to sugar' is a fitting analogy for excess.

In the play. *Touchstone banters with Audrey whom he will eventually marry.*

Beauty, b. and personality, she deserves the best - ... her beauty claims no worse a husband than the best of men...
"...her beauty claims no worse a husband than the best of men,
Her virtue and her general graces speak that which none else can utter." (AC.2.2)
Change the possessives when answering to 'What do you think of me?' that is, '...your beauty claims no worse a husband than the best of men, Your virtue... utter.' If you are not yet ready for marriage, make it clear that the statement is Shakespeare's and should be taken somewhat figuratively.
Some ladies have instinctive 'virtues and general graces', other attend expensive finishing schools in Switzerland or elsewhere for the same purpose. But it is not guaranteed that training or instruction may have an effect, especially in stubborn cases. Chesterfield wrote a book "Advice to a Son". The book became popular but it had little actual effect on the general character of his son. Still, inspired by Chesterfield's idea, George Savile, Marquess of Halifax (1633-1695) wrote a book in the same spirit, "Advice to his Daughter". She turned out quite an untamable shrew. Her husband, Horace Walpole, in his complimentary copy of the book, wrote, "Wasted effort".
In the play. *This is how Agrippa describes Octavia, sister of Octavian and a potential bride of Antony.*

Beauty, b. and wisdom - her sight did ravish; but her grace in speech...
"Her sight did ravish; but her grace in speech,
Her words clad with wisdom's majesty,

Makes me, from wandering, fall to weeping, joys;
Such is the fullness of my heart's content." (KHVI.2.1.1)
Compliment for something she said that you like or is particularly well expressed. Change 'her sight did ravish' to 'Your sight does ravish'.
In the play. *Lady Margaret of France has just arrived at the English court where she will marry Henry VI. Her expressions and salutations to the king prompt him to commend her for her beauty and wisdom.*

Beauty, b. as a determining factor - your beauty was the cause of that effect...
Your beauty was the cause of that effect -
Your beauty, that did haunt me in my sleep
To undertake the death of all the world,
So I might live one hour in your sweet bosom. (RIII.1.2)
She asks "Why do you go after me?" or "Why do you like me?" or "Why did you do this?" where 'it' could be a range of things, for example, giving her a bouquet of flowers, a gift or a surprise.
In the play: *Crafty Richard, Duke of Gloucester, turns things around and implies that his killing (of Edward, Anne's husband) was prompted by his passion for Anne.*

Beauty, b. beats any learning - for where is any author in the world teaches such beauty as a woman's eye?...
"For where is any author in the world,
Teaches such beauty as a woman's eye?
Learning is but an adjunct to ourselves,
And where we are, our learning likewise is." (LLL.4.3)
Use the first two lines to praise women. Use the third line in praise of learning.

In the play. *Biron continues to rationalize breaking the king's oath of study, seclusion and abstinence.*

Beauty, b. contending with that of lilies and roses – Of Nature's gifts thou mayst with lilies boast and with the half-blown rose.
"Of Nature's gifts thou mayst with lilies boast,
And with the half-blown rose" (KJ.3.1)
In the play. *Constance states the conditions of her son young Prince Arthur, blessed by Nature but betrayed by Fortune.*

Beauty, b. declining with age or unforeseen circumstances - And every fair from fair sometime declines...
"And every fair from fair sometime declines,
By chance or nature's changing course untrimm'd" (SON 18)
Answer to 'You have changed' when the statement or the tone of voice implies that you look worse than you did when you were last met.

Beauty, b. eliciting admiration - With more than admiration he admired her azure veins...
"With more than admiration he admired
Her azure veins, her alabaster skin,
Her coral lips, her snow-white dimpled chin" (ROL)
In the poem. *Tarquin observes the unsuspecting, sleeping Lucrece.*

Beauty, b. enhanced by truth - O, how much more doth beauty beauteous seem by that sweet ornament which truth doth give!...
"O, how much more doth beauty beauteous seem
By that sweet ornament which truth doth give!
The rose looks fair, but fairer we it deem

For that sweet odour which doth in it live." (SON 54)
See also 'Beauty, b. preservation and its relationship with goodness of character - The hand that hath made you fair hath made you good…'

Beauty, b. exceeding power of the pen to describe it - … a maid that paragons description and wild fame; one that excels the quirks of blazoning pens…
MONTANO But, good lieutenant, is your general wived?
CASSIO Most fortunately: he hath achieved a maid
That paragons description and wild fame;
One that excels the quirks of blazoning pens,
And in the essential vesture of creation
Does tire the ingener. (OTH.2.1)
Compliment.
In the play. *In Cyprus, Cassio gives a glowing description of Desdemona to the inquiring Montano. 'Ingener' is synonym of 'inventor', 'creator'.*

Beauty, b. exceeding that of all others - … like the stately Phoebe 'mongst her nymphs dost overshine…
"…lovely Tamora, queen of Goths,
That like the stately Phoebe 'mongst her nymphs
Dost overshine the gallant'st dames of Rome" (TA.1.1)
Change 'Tamora' for the lady of your choice and 'Rome' to the name of the applicable location.
In the play. *Emperor Saturninus proposes marriage to Tamora, queen*

Beauty, b. grace and majesty all in one - a maid of grace and complete majesty.
"A maid of grace and complete majesty." (LLL.1.1)

Compliment.
In the play: *The King and companions have set for themselves strict rules for the total avoidance of women for a period of (3) years dedicated exclusively to learning and self-improvement. Biron is reading the rules, which include never to speak to a woman. He tells the King the he will have to break this rule right away because the daughter of the King of France is arriving for a visit.*

Beauty, b. greater than stars - … will make the face of heaven so fine that all the world will be in love with night…
"…he will make the face of heaven so fine
That all the world will be in love with night
And pay no worship to the garish sun." (RJ.3.2)
Compliment, applicable to either sex with minor modifications, e.g. 'If you were a star, you would make the face of heaven…sun'.
In the play. *Juliet is eagerly waiting for the arrival of Romeo, whom she has just married.*

Beauty, b. meditated on and kept in mind - bethink thee on her virtues that surmount...
"Bethink thee on her virtues that surmount,
And natural graces that extinguish art." (KHVI p1.5)
A compliment or an alternative answer to "Do you like me?" For example 'I think on your virtues that surmount and natural graces that extinguish art.' Or just 'your natural graces extinguish art.'
In the play. *Suffolk, on his way to England to arrange the marriage between King Henry VI and Margaret of France tells himself to keep Margaret's beauty and grace in mind.*

Beauty, b. needing no verbal description – my beauty though but

mean needs not the painted flourish of your praise…
"My beauty, though but mean,
Needs not the painted flourish of your praise;
Beauty is bought by judgement of the eye,
Not uttered by base sale of chapmen's tongue." (LLL.2.1)
Use the last two lines not to answer a question on whether one specific woman is beautiful or not, 'Beauty is bought…. tongue.'
In the play. *Boyet, a lord attending the Princess of France flatters her and she responds somewhat harshly.*

Beauty, b. of a queen - O queen of queens! how far dost thou excel, no thought can think, nor tongue of mortal tell.
"O queen of queens! how far dost thou excel,
No thought can think, nor tongue of mortal tell." (LLL.4.3)
Compliment. See also 'Queen, woman with all the traits of a queen – She had all the royal makings of a queen…'
In the play. *Ferdinand reads the letter he has prepared for the visiting Princess.*

Beauty, b. of face – …Her face the book of praises, where is read nothing but curious pleasures.
"… Her face the book of praises, where is read
Nothing but curious pleasures…" (PER.1.1)
Compliment, change 'her' to 'your' when directly addressing the object of your admiration.
In the play. *Pericles on seeing the daughter of Antiochus for the first time.*

Beauty, b. of face majestical - What peremptory eagle-sighted eye… that is not blinded by her majesty?
"What peremptory eagle-sighted eye
Dares look upon the heaven of her brow,
That is not blinded by her majesty?" (LLL.4.3)
In the play. *Biron praises his love Rosaline.*

Beauty, b. of face plus sweetness, angelic disposition and worth a kingdom - Thou hast the sweetest face I ever look'd on.
"Thou hast the sweetest face I ever look'd on.
Sir, as I have a soul, she is an angel;
Our king has all the Indies in his arms,
And more and richer…" (KHVIII.4.1)
Answer to 'Do you like me?' E.G. 'Thou hast… on, as I have a soul, you are an angel, I have all the Indies in my arms.'
In the play. *A gentleman expresses his opinion on Anne Boleyn at her coronation.*

Beauty, b. overwhelming even savages - Who sees the heavenly Rosaline… bows not his vassal head…
"Who sees the heavenly Rosaline,
That, like a rude and savage man of Inde,
At the first opening of the gorgeous east,
Bows not his vassal head and strucken blind
Kisses the base ground with obedient breast?" (LLL.4.3)
In the play. *Biron praises his love Rosaline.*

Beauty, b. preservation and its relationship with goodness of character - the hand that hath made you fair hath made you good…
"The hand that hath made you fair hath made you good. The goodness that is cheap in beauty makes beauty brief in goodness; but grace, being the soul of your complexion, shall

keep the body of it ever fair."
(MFM.3.1)
See also 'Beauty, b. and evil don't mix – … the beauteous-evil are empty trunks, o'erflourish'd by the devil.' *** 'Beauty, b. enhanced by truth - O, how much more doth beauty beauteous seem by that sweet ornament which truth doth give!…'
In the play. *The Duke of Vienna (in disguise) compliments Isabel and comments on the relationship of goodness and lasting beauty.*
Use to praise a lady that has really captured your heart (if it applies).
A similar concept is found in the introduction of Ovid's 'Art of Love' where he warns about the ephemeral nature of beauty'…Think first, ye women, to look to your behavior. The face pleases when character commands. Love of character is lasting: beauty will be ravaged by age, and the face that charmed will be ploughed by wrinkles…Goodness endures and lasts for many a day, and throughout its years love securely rests thereon.' (AOL.1)
However, this did not mean that Latin ladies were not expected to take care of their aesthetics. 'Learn, o women – he says – what pains can enhance your looks and how your beauty may be cultivated…Cultivation improves the bitter juices of fruit, and the cleft tree gains adopted riches.' (AOL.1)
Rather than today's ready-to-apply cosmetics, Roman ladies were expected to be do-it-yourself make-up manufacturers. For this they had to have a decent knowledge of agricultural products and mineralogy - plus adequate mathematics to accurately prepare their moisturizing and rejuvenating creams. 'Remove the chaff from the barley which Lybian husbandmen have sent in ships. Let an equal measure of vetch be moistened in ten eggs, but let the skinned barley weigh two pounds. When this has dried in the blowing breezes, bid the slow she-ass break it on the rough millstone: grind therewith too the first horns that fall from a nimble stag (of the grinding let the sixth part of a pound be added). And now when it is mixed with the dusty grain, sift it all straightway in hollow sieves. Add twelve narcissus-bulbs without their skins, and let a strenuous hand pound them on pure marble. Let gum and Tuscan seed weigh the sixth part of a pound, and let nine times as much honey go to that. Whoever shall treat her face with such a prescription wilt shine smoother than her own mirror.' (AOL.1)
See also 'Beauty, b. that is evil, an empty trunk - virtue is beauty, but the beauteous evil…

Beauty, b. shown in color of lips and cheeks - … beauty's ensign… is crimson in thy lips and in thy cheeks.
"…beauty's ensign yet
Is crimson in thy lips and in thy cheeks…" (RJ.5.3)
Compliment. Assume that the recipient is unaware of the somewhat macabre circumstances in which these lines appear in the play. Omit 'yet'
In the play. *Romeo thinks that Juliet is dead but she is only asleep under the influence of the sleeping potion provided by Friar Lawrence.*

Beauty, b. such as to generate wonder in the onlookers - … like beauty's child, whom nature gat for men to see…
"…our daughter,
In honour of whose birth these triumphs are,
Sits here, like beauty's child, whom nature gat
For men to see, and seeing wonder at." (PER.2.2)
Modify into a compliment, 'You are like beauty's…wonder at'.

In the play. *King Simonides has thrown a birthday party in Pentapolis for his daughter Thaisa and invited noblemen to a tourney.*

Beauty, b. superior even to a goddess - Thou for whom Jove would swear Juno but an Ethiope were…
"Thou for whom Jove would swear
Juno but an Ethiope were;
And deny himself for Jove,
Turning mortal for thy love" (LLL.4.3)
In the play. *Dumain reads from the letter he has prepared for one of the Princess' ladies in waiting.*

Beauty, b. that deprives man of reason - … thou mayst bereave him of his wits with wonder.
"…when thou comest to kneel at Henry's feet,
Thou mayst bereave him of his wits with wonder." (KHVI p1.5.3)
Answer to 'What do you think of me?' E.G. 'You have bereaved me of my wits and wonder'. Also generic expression of astonishment, 'I am bereaved of my wits with wonder'.
In the play. *Suffolk will describe the beauty of queen-to-be Margaret in such a glowing terms that King Henry VI will agree to the marriage 'sight unseen'.*

Beauty, b. that is evil, an empty trunk - virtue is beauty, but the beauteous evil…
"Virtue is beauty, but the beauteous evil
Are empty trunks o'erflourish'd by the devil." (TN.3.4)
Comment on a woman pleasant in appearance but ugly in character. See also 'Beauty preservation and its relationship with goodness of character - the hand that hath made you fair hath made you good...'

In the play. *Antonio believes that Viola/Cesario is actually her twin Sebastian towards whom Antonio has been most kind and generous. Antonio needs urgent help but Viola/Cesario knows nothing about the matter. Antonio then rails against beauty that is evil.*

Beauty, b. transcending the limitations of time – When in the chronicle of wasted time…
"When in the chronicle of wasted time,
I see description of the fairest wights,
And beauty making beautiful old rhyme,
In praise of ladies dead, and lovely knights,
Then in the blazon of sweet beauty's best,
Of hand, of foot, of lip, of eye, of brow,
I see their antique pen would have expressed,
Even such beauty as you master now.
So all their praises are but prophesies
Of this our time, all you prefiguring." (SON.106)
Tell her that when the ancient poets were describing a beautiful woman they were unconsciously anticipating her arrival on the scene. A good script for a card – you may wish to change the halloweenish 'ladies dead' to 'ladies past'. A 'wight', roughly speaking is a medieval knight. 'Chronicle of wasted time' can be an elegant, modest and humorous self-effacing statement about (at least parts of) your life.

Beauty, b. without intelligence – her beauty and her brain go not together…
"… her beauty and her brain
go not together: she's a good sign, but I have seen
small reflection of her wit." (CYM.1.2)

In the play. *A lord comments with the foolish Cloten on Imogen who, far from what is being said of her, is both beautiful and intelligent.*

Beauty, b. worth commending and wondering at - Well learned is that tongue that well can thee commend...
"Well learned is that tongue that well can thee commend,
All ignorant that soul that sees thee without wonder" (LLL.4.2)
Compliment.
In the play. *Holofernes reads from a letter addressed to the pretty wench Jacquenetta.*

Beauty, b., voice and perfection - ... whose beauty did astonish the survey of the richest eyes...
"...Whose beauty did astonish the survey
Of richest eyes, whose words all ears took captive,
Whose dear perfection hearts that scorn'd to serve
Humbly call'd mistress." (AWEW.5.3)
Compliment. Answer to 'Do you like me?' E.G. 'Your beauty astonishes the survey of the richest eyes…' See also entries for 'Voice, her v. delightful, harmonious, feminine etc.'
In the play. *Lafeu describes Helena whom people at this point still give for dead*

Beauty, black is beautiful – And therefore is she born to make black fair...
"And therefore is she born to make black fair.
Her favour turns the fashion of the days,
For native blood is counted painting now;
And therefore red, that would avoid dispraise,
Paints itself black, to imitate her brow." (LLL.4.3)
In the play. *Biron praises his love Rosaline.*

Beauty, black is beautiful - Is ebony like her? O wood divine!
FERDINAND "By heaven, thy love is black as ebony".
BIRON "Is ebony like her? O wood divine!
A wife of such wood were felicity."
(LLL.4.3)
Quote the short dialog in its entirety or adapt it slightly. E.G. 'If you are black and ebony is like you I'll say 'O wood divine!'" Particularly applicable if your girlfriend is African-American.
In the play. *Ferdinand teases Biron who is in love with the black Rosaline. Biron answers appropriately.*

Beauty, black is beautiful – No face is fair that is not full so black
"No face is fair that is not full so black." (LLL.4.3)
In the play. *Biron praises his love Rosaline.*

Beauty, comparing beauties - ... exceeds her as much in beauty as beauty as the first of May doth the last of December.
"...there's her cousin, an she were not possessed with a fury, exceeds her as much in beauty as the first of May doth the last of December"
(MAAN.1.1)
In the play. *Claudio thinks that Hero is wonderful. According to Benedick, her cousin Beatrice is more beautiful, but for her unapproachable character.*

Beauty, dangers of b. - b. more tempting than gold - Beauty provoketh thieves sooner than gold.
"Beauty provoketh thieves sooner than gold." (AYLI.1.3)
Point out the dangers of being beautiful.
In the play. *Celia suggests to Rosalind to escape to the forest of Arden. Rosalind questions whether they - two young and pretty girls - would be safe. Later Rosalind will suggest that they disguise themselves as boys.*

Beauty, her b. and virtue praised everywhere - hearing thy mildness praised in every town...
"Hearing thy mildness praised in every town,
Thy virtues spoke of, and thy beauty sounded." (TOS.2.1)
Try this instead of 'Can I buy you a drink?' 'I heard thy mildness praised….sounded' See also 'Ego boosting. She is a sought after prize' – other entries for 'Admiration'
In the play. *Petruchio flatters Katharina and tells her he wants to marry her.*

Beauty, her b. compared to a cheering sun - As all the world is cheered by the sun, so I…
"As all the world is cheered by the sun,
So I by that; it is my day, my life." (KRIII.1.2)
In 'so I by that', 'that' is her beauty. Substitute 'that' with 'your beauty'. Answer to 'Do you like me?'
In the play. *Richard has the gall of wooing the recently widowed Ann, whose husband Edward he himself has killed*

Beauty, her b. exceeding power of poetic description - For to no other pass my verses tend than of your graces and your gifts to tell…
"For to no other pass my verses tend Than of your graces and your gifts to tell;
And more, much more than in my verse can sit
Your own glass shows you when you look in it." (SON 103)
'Pass'='Course, objective'.

Beauty, her b. outperforms Venus' - ...
O'er-picturing that Venus where we see the fancy outwork nature.
"… For her own person,
It beggar'd all description: she did lie
In her pavilion--cloth-of-gold of tissue--
O'er-picturing that Venus where we see
The fancy outwork nature" (AC.2.2)
Compliment, e.g. 'You are overwhelming that Venus where…nature'
In the play. *Now in Rome with Antony, Enobarbus gives Agrippa an account of Cleopatra's shenanigans, here specifically how Cleopatra arranged to meet Antony so as to impress him.*

Beauty, impossible to say 'no' to it - All orators are dumb when beauty pleadeth.
"All orators are dumb when beauty pleadeth" (ROL)
Answer to 'Will you do this for me？' See also entries for 'Service, at her complete s.'
In the poem. *Tarquin rationalizes for his own benefit his impending rape of Lucrece.*

Beauty, male b. - Describe Adonis, and the counterfeit is poorly imitated after you.
"Describe Adonis, and the counterfeit Is poorly imitated after you" (SON 53)
If he asks you, 'Do you like me?' and you know that he likes flattery.

Beauty, mathematical comparison - thrice-fairer than myself.
"Thrice-fairer than myself" (V&A)
Compliment.
In the poem. *Venus sees Adonis for the first time. With all V&A entries we have to take some license and invert the roles.*

Beauty, no match, unseen up to this moment - ...the all seeing sun ne'er saw her match since first the world began.
"… the all seeing sun
Ne'er saw her match, since first the world began." (RJ.1.2)

Use as a compliment, "...the all seeing sun never saw your match since first the world began."
In the play. *Benvolio has tried to downplay Rosaline's beauty (current Romeo's flame) and Romeo retorts. This happens before he met Juliet.*

Beauty, no question you are beautiful etc. - by heaven, that thou art fair is most infallible...
"'By heaven, that thou art fair is most infallible; true that thou art beauteous; truth itself that thou art lovely. More fairer than fair, beautiful than beauteous, truer than truth itself, have commiseration on thy heroical vassal." (LLL.4.1)
Compliment.
In the play. *Boyet reads a letter from Biron to Rosaline.*

Beauty, one exceedingly more beautiful than the other (girl) - ... so with the dove of Paphos might the crow vie feathers white.
"...so
With the dove of Paphos might the crow
Vie feathers white." (PER.3.Gower)
When she thinks that you like another girl – e.g. 'To compare you with her would be the same as if with the dove of Phaphos…white.'
In the play. *Pericles leaves his baby daughter Marina in the custody of the wicked Cleon. Cleon has a daughter, Philoten. As they grow up Marina outshines Philoten in grace and natural beauty. Gower, the commentator suggests that for Philoten to compete with Marina would be the same as for a crow to compete with a dove in whiteness. The dove of Paphos (Cyprus) was whiter than white.*

Beauty, ornament of the world – Thou that art now the world's fresh ornament.

"Thou that art now the world's fresh ornament" (SON 01)
Compliment

Beauty, outside is wonderful, what about the inside? - All of her that is out of door most rich!...
" All of her that is out of door most rich!
If she be furnished with a mind so rare,
She is alone the Arabian bird."
(CYM.1.5)
Use the first line as a beauty compliment, in case the meaning of the next does not apply, "All of you that is out of door most rich!"
In the play. *The perfidious Iachimo has got a first glimpse at Imogen. The Arabian bird referred to is the Phoenix.*

Beauty, persuasive power of b. - Beauty itself doth of itself persuade the eyes of men without an orator.
"Beauty itself doth of itself persuade
The eyes of men without an orator."
(ROL)
In the poem. *Lucrece's beauty needs no explanation or (in this case) the unhappy advertising by her husband Collatine.*

Beauty, power of b. - ... beauty hath his power and will, which can as well inflame as it can kill.
"…beauty hath his power and will,
Which can as well inflame as it can kill." (PER.2.3)
See also 'Lust, intemperance leading to disaster'.
In the play. *King Simonides and daughter Thaisa comment on the insignia of a passing knight. The Latin motto is 'Quod me alit, me extinguit', what inflames me extinguishes me.*

Beauty, radiant - most radiant, exquisite, unmatchable beauty.
"Most radiant, exquisite, unmatchable beauty." (TN.1.5)

A good way to greet your girlfriend.
In the play. *Taking the assignment seriously, Viola/Cesario addresses Olivia with flattering terms so as to gain her good will.*

Beauty, rejuvenating effects of b. - beauty doth varnish age, as if new born…
"Beauty doth varnish age, as if new born,
And gives the crutch the cradle's infancy.
O 't is the sun that maketh all things shine." (LLL.4.3)
Explain why you have fallen in love with a much younger woman.
In the play. *Biron in love sings the praises of Rosaline.*

Beauty, the flower of the city - Verona's summer hath not such a flower.
"Verona's summer hath not such a flower" (RJ.1.3)
Compliment, change Verona to the name of the applicable city. Answer to 'Do you like me?'
In the play. *Lady Capulet praises the charm of Paris for the benefit of Juliet. Paris wants to marry Juliet.*

Beauty, three times more beautiful than the complimenter - Thrice-fairer than myself…
"Thrice-fairer than myself,' …
The field's chief flower, sweet above compare,
Stain to all nymphs…
More white and red than doves or roses are" (V&A)
Compliment – ignore that in the original it's a woman complimenting a man.
In the poem. *Venus' initial address to Adonis*

Beauty, true b. observed for the first time - … for I ne'er saw true beauty till this night.

"Did my heart love till now? forswear it, sight!
For I ne'er saw true beauty till this night." (RJ.1.5)
When she makes an appearance in her spectacular evening gown or dress.
In the play. *Romeo catches sight of Juliet for the first time at the Capulets' party and immediately forgets Rosaline, whom he previously thought unmatchable.*

Beauty, well endowed by Nature - … Framed in the prodigality of nature…
"Framed in the prodigality of nature" (KRIII.1.2)
Compliment, answer to 'Do you like me?'
E.G. 'You are framed in…'
In the play. *Richard describes young Edward whom he slain at Tewksbury*

Beauty, you as the virtual painter of her beauty- Mine eye hath play'd the painter…
"Mine eye hath play'd the painter and hath stell'd
Thy beauty's form in table of my heart;
My body is the frame wherein 'tis held,
And perspective it is the painter's art" (SON 24)
Compliment.
'To stell'='To place'

Beer, do you like b.? - … a quart of ale is a dish for a king.
"… a quart of ale is a dish for a king." (WT.4.2)

Beer is less classy than wine but there is no reason you should give up the pleasure of it, if she does not like it or if she wrinkles her nose at your taste. Therefore at a restaurant, for example, if she takes wine and you take beer, she may ask you 'do you like beer?, implying a certain surprise at the inelegance of your taste compared to hers. By using this quote you raise in a few words the standing of beer and the elegance of your taste. By the way, ale is (was) the simple amalgam or fermentation of malt, yeast and water, before hops were introduced. In England, the strength of an ale was controlled by ale inspectors. In the test, according to lore, the inspector poured some ale on an oak bench and sat down on the wetted oak. If the bench did not get stuck to his trousers when he got up, the ale was logged as weak.
In the play. *Autolycus appears on the scene singing a song.*

Begging, first time b. - A beggar begs that never begg'd before.
"A beggar begs that never begg'd before." (KRII.5.3)
See also 'Request, emphatic r. due to strained circumstances - He asks of you that never used to beg.'
In the play. *The Duchess of York, pleading with Bolingbroke (now Henry IV) for her son's (duke of Aumerle) life.*

Beginning – ... here, upon this bank and shoal of time...
"... here, upon this bank and shoal of time,
We'll jump the life to come" (M.1.4)
Give emphasis to the beginning of a new venture.
In the play. *Macbeth makes a clear analysis of the consequences of a crime. Fear, let alone remorse, is the price to pay for crime.*

Beginning, abrupt or violent b. foreshadowing unfortunate end – ... it was a violent commencement, and thou shalt see an answerable sequestration.
"... it was a violent commencement, and thou shalt see an answerable sequestration" (OTH.1.3)
The line can apply to marriage or any undertaking begun in haste.
In the play. *The perfidious Iago plays on Roderigo's passion for Desdemona, married to the Moor. Their marriage was secret and abrupt and, according to Iago, destined to a premature end.*

Behavior, b. appropriate to circumstances - ... good manners at court, are as ridiculous in the country.
CORIN. ... those that are good manners at court, are as ridiculous in the country, as the behaviour of the country is most mockable at the court. (AYLI.3.2)
Express the idea that everything has its place.
In the play. *The courtly Touchstone engages the shepherd Corin into an exchange of ideas and opinions.*

Behavior, b. appropriate to peace and war - ... modest stillness and humility....then imitate the action of the tiger...
"In peace, there's nothing so becomes a man,
As modest stillness and humility:
But when the blast of war blows in our ears,
Then imitate the action of the tiger:
Stiffen the sinews, summon up the blood." (KHV.3.1)
Use in motivational speech, comparing the project to a war where no effort must be spared.
In the play. *K. Henry addressing the troops before the siege of Harfleur.*

Behavior, b. cowardly and infamous, unworthy of a nobleman - ... this fact

was infamous and ill beseeming any common man…
"To say the truth, this fact was infamous
And ill beseeming any common man,
Much more a knight, a captain and a leader" (KHVI.p1.4.1)
In the play. *Gloucester comments on the reported cowardly behavior of Fastolfe at the battle of Patay.*

Behavior, minor irritation affecting overall b. - ... and in such cases men's natures wrangle with inferior things, though great ones are their object…
"…and in such cases
Men's natures wrangle with inferior things,
Though great ones are their object.
'Tis even so;
For let our finger ache, and it indues
Our other healthful members even to that sense
Of pain" (OTH.3.4)
In the play. *Desdemona cannot know about the evil plot that Iago is weaving for her destruction. She speculates that something other than jealousy caused Othello to be upset and change his normal behavior.*

Behavior, saucy and affected b. - ... having been praised for bluntness, doth affect a saucy roughness. "This is some fellow
Who, having been praised for bluntness, doth affect
A saucy roughness." (KL.2.2)
Apply to anyone who is cheeky or arrogant
In the play. *Cornwall referring to Kent who told him what he thought of Cornwall's entourage.*

Behavior, tyrannical b. of a newly appointed leader – Whether it be fault and glimpse of newness…
"Whether it be the fault and glimpse of newness,
Or whether that the body public be
A horse whereon the governor doth ride,
Who, newly in the seat, that it may know
He can command, lets it straight feel the spur" (MFM.1.2)
Attribute the shortcomings of a new manager to 'the fault and glimpse of newness'.
In the play. *Claudio comments on the reasons why the newly appointed duke Angelo may have condemned him to death for having seduced the willing Juliet.*

Behavior, wise or honest b.?- I should be wise, for honesty's a fool and loses that it works for.
OTHELLO Nay, stay: thou shouldst be honest.
IAGO I should be wise, for honesty's a fool
And loses that it works for. (OTH.3.3)
Answer to a somewhat embarrassing comment that you are honest.
In the play. *Iago continues his cunning plot to make Othello jealous and destroy him.*

Believability, complete b. – If Jupiter should from yond cloud speak divine things…
"…If Jupiter
Should from yond cloud speak divine things,
And say 'Tis true,' I'ld not believe them more
Than thee, all noble Marcius" (COR.4.5)
Change 'Marcius' to the name whose believability you do not dispute.
In the play. *Aufidius, leader of the Volsces, believes Coriolanus who left the Roman side out of anger at how he was treated.*

Belief, consistency of b. - ... were he meal'd with that which he corrects, then were he tyrannous…

"…were he meal'd with that
Which he corrects, then were he tyrannous;
But this being so, he's just."
(MFM.4.2)
In the play. *Duke Vicentio attempts to justify Angelo's condemnation of Claudio for fornication. If Angelo were abstinent (which he is not) then he would be just in the condemnation.* 'Mealed' = 'Tainted'.

Benevolence and benefices misapplied - ... wonder of good deeds evilly bestow'd
"…O monument
And wonder of good deeds evilly bestow'd!" (TOA.4.3)
In the play. *Faithful servant Flavius goes to meet Timon, now living in a cave.*

Best, compliment, she is the best wife – … kings might be espoused to more fame but king nor peer to such a peerless dame.
"… kings might be espoused to more fame,
But king nor peer to such a peerless dame. " (ROL)
In the poem. *Lucrece's beauty exceeds (in comparison) the fame inherent in a king.*

Best, compliment, you are the best – … a gallant creature, and complete in mind and feature.
"She is a gallant creature, and complete
In mind and feature" (KHVIII.3.2)
In the play. *Suffolk, conversing with Norfolk, refers to Ann Boleyn.*

Best, compliment, you are the best – Full many a lady I have eyed with best regards…
"Full many a lady
I have eyed with best regards; and many a time
The harmony of their tongues hath into bondage

Brought my too diligent ear: for several virtues
Have I lik'd several women; never any
With so full a soul, but some defect in her
Did quarrel with the noblest grace she ow'd,
And put it to the foul." (TEM.3.1)
Say this slowly or she may have a hard time to follow. Use to tell her that she is the best of all. All women like to be #1 at least for you if you love them.
In the play. *Ferdinando is deeply in love with Miranda and explains why.*

Best, compliment, you are the best – … Nor can imagination form a shape, beside yourself, to like of.
"… I would not wish
Any companion in the world but you,
Nor can imagination form a shape,
Besides yourself, to like of" (TEM.3.1)
Applicable from her to him or viceversa,
In the play. *Miranda to Ferdinand with whom she has instantly fallen in*

Best, compliment, you are the best – … o you, so perfect and so peerless…
" … but you, O you,
So perfect and so peerless, are created
Of every creature's best!" (TEM.3.1)
If quotation 'Best, compliment You are the best - full many a lady' is a bit too hard to remember, just use this one to tell her that she is the best. See also 'Pretty, the prettiest of all' – 'Love, the best of all (applies to both woman and man)'
In the play. *Ferdinando is deeply in love with Miranda. After having explained the shortcomings of all the women that he has met (before Miranda), he concludes by telling her of her superiority.*

Beware, b. of the enemy - Take heed o' the foul fiend!
"Take heed o' the foul fiend!" (KL.3.1)

In the play. *One of the unconnected utterances by Edgar who joins Lear's party in the forest. Edgar pretends to be mad. 'Take heed'='Take care'.*

Bewitched by her words - Either she has bewitch'd me with her words, or nature makes me suddenly relent.
"Either she has bewitch'd me with her words,
Or nature makes me suddenly relent." (KHVI.I.1)
Change to "Either you have bewitched me with your words…relent" - when you have decided to give in gracefully to her demands.
In the play. *Joan of Arc has convinced the Duke of Burgundy to join the French camp.*

Big Brother – … Keeps place with thought and almost, like the gods, does thoughts unveil in their dumb cradles.
"The providence that's in a watchful state
Knows almost every grain of Plutus' gold,
Finds bottom in the uncomprehensive deeps,
Keeps place with thought and almost, like the gods,
Does thoughts unveil in their dumb cradles" (TC.3.3)
In the play. *Achilles is surprised that Ulysses knows he loves one of Priam's daughters. Ulysses explains the superb intelligence characteristic, according to him, of a well-run state.*

Biographer, chosen b. - After my death I wish no other herald… But such an honest chronicler as Griffith.
"After my death I wish no other herald,
No other speaker of my living actions,
To keep mine honour from corruption,
But such an honest chronicler as Griffith." (KHVIII.4.2)
Comment when someone says something good about you to a third party in your presence. Change 'Griffith' to the name of the praiser.
In the play. *Griffith tells Queen Katharine that Cardinal Wolsey, her enemy is dead. Griffith asks permission to point out some of Wolsey's virtues and Katharine is impressed.*

Biographical sketch - In war was never lion raged more fierce, in peace …
"In war was never lion raged more fierce,
In peace was never gentle lamb more mild
…
His hands were guilty of no kindred blood,
But bloody with the enemies of his kin" (KRII.2.1)
In the play. *The Duke of York reminds King Richard of the virtues of his father in the hope that Richard may correct his dissolute ways*

Biography, invitation to tell his/her life story – I long to hear the story of your life…
"I long
To hear the story of your life, which must
Take the ear strangely." (TEM.5.1)
Show your interest in hearing a person talk about him/herself, particularly if the person in question has an unusual curriculum. See also 'Dinner, have it precede a meeting' – 'Ceremony, no time for it even if friends meet again after a long time'.
In the play. *After the happy ending, reunion and reconciliation of the parties involved, Alonso would like to hear of Prospero's life.*

Biography, life story will be told - …for this one night; which, part of it, I'll waste with such discourse as, I not doubt, shall make it go quick away; the story of my life.

"Sir, I invite your highness and your train
To my poor cell, where you shall take your rest
For this one night; which, part of it, I'll waste
With such discourse as, I not doubt, shall make it
Go quick away; the story of my life..." (TEM.5.1)
Introducing your biographical words.
In the play. *Prospero will give a detailed account of his life to Alonso.*

Black, advantages of the color b. - Coal-black is better than another hue...
"Coal-black is better than another hue,
In that it scorns to bear another hue." (TA.4.2)
In the play. *The evil Aaron comments on his black baby adulterously born to the evil queen Tamara. He will kill midwife and nurse who witnessed the birth.*

Black, if you dislike the color - ... black is the badge of hell...
"... Black is the badge of hell,
The hue of dungeons and the suit of night." (LLL.4.3)
In the play. *Ferdinand pulls Biron's leg who is in love with the dark Rosaline. See Biron's retort at 'Beauty, black is beautiful'.*

Blindness, b. of lovers to themselves - But love is blind and lovers cannot see the pretty follies they themselves commit.
"But love is blind and lovers cannot see
The pretty follies they themselves commit." (MOV2.6)
Love seen from the outside. Justifying the behavior of friends in love who appear silly. People, especially ladies, like to gossip about their friends in love.

In the play: *Jessica escapes from Shylock's house dressed in man's clothes, a 'folly' she commits out of her love for Lorenzo.*

Blinking idiot - What's here? the portrait of a blinking idiot
"What's here? the portrait of a blinking idiot" (MOV.2.9)
Aphorism slipped in the language.
In the play. *The prince of Arragon has chosen the wrong casket.*

Blood, b. covering earth - ... and temper clay with blood of Englishmen.
"The uncivil kerns of Ireland are in arms
And temper clay with blood of Englishmen." (KHVI.p2.3.1)
Answer to 'Will you get the order?' E.G. 'Yes, I'll temper clay with the blood of the competition'
In the play. *Cardinal Beaufort to York questioning and encouraging him to go and fight the Irish.*

Blood, cold or hot? - Shall our quick blood, spirited with wine, seem frosty?
"... shall our quick blood, spirited with wine,
Seem frosty?" (KHV.3.5)
See also entries for wine. A rhetorical question to a group from which you expect action, at the end of a good dinner accompanied by abundant wine.
In the play. *The constable of France poses a rhetorical question after remarking that the English are full of mettle notwithstanding their notorious cold climate.*
where have they this mettle?
Is not their climate foggy, raw and dull,
On whom, as in despite, the sun looks pale,
Killing their fruit with frowns?

Blood, lady as dear as own b. - ... as dear to me as the ruddy drops that visit my sad heart.
" (You are) **as dear to me as the ruddy drops**
That visit my sad heart" (JC.2.1)
Answer to any question probing the depth of your affection. But careful, that 'dear' sounds close to 'endearment' and this does not usually fly very well. In general, ladies expect passion, not endearment. Besides, if your heart is sad, you have to be ready to explain why. However, this may be a good line if you are planning to get out of the relationship. You are telling that she is dear to you but that your heart is sad because you think that the relationship must end.
In the play. *Brutus addresses Portia's doubts as to why Brutus keeps secrets from her.*

Blood, power acquired with b. unstable - There is no sure foundation set on blood... No certain life achieved by others' death.
"...I repent:
There is no sure foundation set on blood,
No certain life achieved by others' death." (KJ.4.2)
A reminder to imperialist warmongers.
In the play. *King John repents of having given orders to Hubert to kill young Prince Arthur, a murders that is triggering a rebellion.*

Blushing, b. as evidence - ... thy cheeks confess it, th' one to th' other; and thine eyes see it so grossly shown in thy behaviors...
"...**thy cheeks**
Confess it, th' one to th' other; and thine eyes
See it so grossly shown in thy behaviors
That in their kind they speak it: only sin

And hellish obstinacy tie thy tongue,
That truth should be suspected" (AWEW.1.3)
In the play. *The Countess benevolently upbraids Helena who does not want to admit to her love for Bertram.*

Blushing, b. made invisible by night - thou know'st the mask of night is on my face, else would a maiden blush bepaint my cheek...
"**Thou know'st the mask of night is on my face,**
Else would a maiden blush bepaint my cheek
For that which thou hast heard me speak to-night." (RJ.2.2)
Preparing the ground for a question that might be thought as too direct or somewhat indiscrete.
In the play. *At her window Juliet has declared her love for Romeo not knowing that he was listening.*

Boat, not in great conditions - ...the very rats instinctively have quit it!
"**A rotten carcass of a boat ... the very rats**
Instinctively had quit it!" (TEM.1.2)
Describe an uncomfortable boat or ship.
In the play. *Prospero describes to his daughter Miranda the boat that led them both to the island.*

Body, b. language – ... sometimes from her eyes I did receive fair speechless messages.
"... **sometimes from her eyes I did receive fair speechless messages."** (MOV.1.1)
Answer to 'does she like you?' or to justify your self-introduction. "My name is Jones and sometimes from your eyes, I have received fair, speechless messages?". Be ready to say 'never mind' if she says she does not know what you are talking about.

The situation may be different at a dinner especially if accompanied by good wine. So Ovid, 'Therefore when the bounty of Bacchus is set before you and a woman shares your convivial couch*, beseech the king and the spirits of the night that they bid not the wines to hurt your head. Here may you say many things in covered speech, so that she may feel they are said to her…you may gaze at her eyes with eyes that confess their flame: there are often voice and words in a silent look.'(AOL.2)
See also 'Wine, positive effects of.'
* For reasons poorly understood by historians, instead of using benches or chairs, Romans insisted on eating laying down stretched on their side in a most uncomfortable position.
In the play. *Bassanio tells Antonio of his intention to pursue Portia, the sender of the speechless messages.*

Body, b. language - Her eye discourses; I will answer it.
"Her eye discourses; I will answer it" (RJ.2.2)
Not a bad self-introduction if you notice that she noticed you. Change 'her' to 'your'
In the play. *Romeo sneaked into Juliet's garden and observes her at her window.*

Body, b. language - There was speech in their dumbness, language in their very gestures.
GENTLEMAN (to Autolycus)
"There was speech in their dumbness, language in their very gestures." (WT.5.2)
Describe the astonishment of a silent audience.
In the play. *Autolycus has managed to travel to Sicilia and inquires of the Gentleman what was Polixenes' (and Camillo's) reaction once they found the information contained in the shepherd's package – Perdita is King Leonte's daughter.*

Body, celestial b. - ... body as a paradise, to envelop and contain celestial spirits.
"… body as a paradise,
To envelop and contain celestial spirits." (HV.1.1)
Though this applies to a man (the reformed Henry V), the lines can be used as a compliment to a gorgeous lady.
In the play. *The Archbishop of Canterbury describes to the Bishop of Ely the astounding reformation of Henry V, who, when Prince of Wales preferred wine, women and song to the duties of a king-to-be.*

Body, charming b. imperfection - ... a mole, right proud of that most delicate lodging.
"… under her breast--
Worthy the pressing--lies a mole, right proud
Of that most delicate lodging" (CYM.2.4)
In the play. *The evil Iachimo who surreptitiously sneaked into Imogen's bedroom to take a good look at her while she was asleep, pretends with Leonatus, her husband, that he had sex with her.*

Body, every part of her b. excellent - ... some natural notes about her body... would testify, to enrich mine inventory.
"Ah, but some natural notes about her body,
Above ten thousand meaner moveables
Would testify, to enrich mine inventory" (CYM.2.2)
Lay it thick. E.G. 'The natural notes about your body enrich mine inventory'.
In the play. *The evil Jachimo has sneaked into Imogen's bedroom while she is asleep. He makes note of every object is there. Back in Rome, he will claim he had sex with Imogen.*

Body, our bodies as gardens and our wills as gardeners - ... Our bodies are our gardens...
"'tis in ourselves that we are thus or thus. Our bodies are our gardens, to the which our wills are gardeners: so that if we will plant nettles, or sow lettuce, set hyssop and weed up thyme, supply it with one gender of herbs, or distract it with many, either to have it sterile with idleness, or manured with industry, why, the power and corrigible authority of this lies in our wills." (OTH.1.3)
A powerful image to inspire self-control and temperance. If you wish to use the last sentence, i.e. 'the power and corrigible authority...' you may want to substitute the bulk of the preceding 'plants' sown with 'whatever we plant...'
In the play. *Roderigo has confessed t Iago his passion for Desdemona and Iago gives Roderigo a lesson in philosophy. See also 'Human nature – thank heaven that reason balances instinct'.*

Boldness, sudden inflow of b. - Boldness comes to me now, and brings me heart.
"Boldness comes to me now, and brings me heart." (TC.3.2)
After a pause while you are collecting yourself for an answer to an unexpected question.
In the play. *Cressida declares to Troilus that she has loved him for months.*

Books, b. as tools and utensils - he has brave utensils, for so he calls them...
" ... burn but his books;
He has brave utensils, - for so he calls them, --
Which, when he has a house, he'll deck withal." (TEM.3.2)
Alternative to the same idea expresses in 'Books, key to power'. Or justify why you fill your house with books, '...my books are my brave utensils, - for so I call them, which, when I have a house, I'll deck withal'.
In the play. *Caliban is hatching a plot against Prospero and tells his co-conspirators to burn Prospero's books first.*

Books, key to power – remember first to possess his books...
"Remember,
First to possess his books; for without them
He's but a sot, as I am, nor hath not
One spirit at his command."
(TEM.3.2)
Emphasize the importance of reading, as a tool to acquire strength or power.
Narrate the episode in full and terminate with Caliban's quote.
In the play. *Caliban is hatching a plot against Prospero along with Stephano, a drunken butler and Trinculo, a jester. The plot should result in Stephano becoming king of the island and marrying Miranda.*

Boomerang effect, effect opposite to intentions, without adequate power to sustain attack -- ... my arrows, too slightly timber'd for so loud a wind...
"...so that my arrows,
Too slightly timber'd for so loud a wind,
Would have reverted to my bow again,
And not where I had aim'd them"
(H.4.7)
Dissuade from undertaking an action without adequate power.
In the play. *The King gives various reasons to Laertes why Hamlet was not immediately punished for the death of Polonius. The people love Hamlet and any action against Hamlet (arrows) would have reverted itself against the King.*

Boredom, b. with great position, desire for change - ... could I with boot change for an idle plume which the air beats for vain.

"…The state, whereon I studied
Is like a good thing, being often read,
Grown fear'd and tedious; yea, my gravity,
Wherein--let no man hear me--I take pride,
Could I with boot change for an idle plume,
Which the air beats for vain." (MFM.2.4)
Answer to 'How do you like your job?' – if you carry heavy responsibilities.
In the play. *Tempted by the charm of virtuous Isabel, Angelo reflects on his own nature, vanity and conceit.*

Bosom, her b. as a coveted place of rest - I might live one hour in your sweet bosom.
"… I might live one hour in your sweet bosom." (RIII.1.2)
Try 'I would do anything to live …sweet bosom.' Answer to 'Do you like me?' - See also 'Beauty as a determining factor.'
In the play. Richard courts Anne.

Boss, b. calls you in and you imagine the worst – … Hear it not, Duncan; for it is a knell that summons thee to heaven or to hell.
"I go, and it is done; the bell invites me.
Hear it not, Duncan; for it is a knell
That summons thee to heaven or to hell." (M.2.1)
You are afraid that the boss may have bad news for you, a reprimand or maybe dismissal. Change 'Duncan' to your name.
In the play. *Lady Macbeth gives a signal with a bell for Macbeth to go and kill King Duncan in his sleep.*

Boss, never outshine b. - Better to leave undone, than by our deed acquire too high a fame when him we serve's away.
"Better to leave undone, than by our deed
Acquire too high a fame when him we serve's away." (AC.3.1)
In the play. *Ventidius in Syria gives some of words of advice to Silius.*

Boss, never out-do your b., modesty strategically applied - Who does in the wars more than his captain can, becomes his captain's captain…
"Who does in the wars more than his captain can
Becomes his captain's captain; and ambition
(The soldier's virtue) rather makes choice of loss
Than gain which darkens him."
(AC.3.1)
Advice for the appropriate party or justify your hesitation to go over the bounds of your responsibility.
In the play. *In the plains of Syria, Ventidius, an officer of Antony, explains to a Silius, a Roman, why he has not completely destroyed the Parthians after obtaining a victory.*

Brain, no more raking of the b. - Cudgel thy brains no more about it…
"Cudgel thy brains no more about it, for a dull ass will not mend his pace with beating" (H.5.1)
In the play. *The first clown to the second clown. The second clown was not able to solve a riddle posed by the first clown. See 'Wit, w. admired - I like thy wit well, in good faith'.*

Breasts, beauty of her b. - Her breasts, like ivory globes circled with blue
"Her breasts, like ivory globes circled with blue"
In the poem. *Tarquin observes the unsuspecting, sleeping Lucrece.*

Breath excellent, inviting to love - ... comes breath perfumed that breedeth love by smelling.
"For from the stillitory of thy face excelling
Comes breath perfumed that breedeth love by
smelling." (V&A)
Answer to 'Do I have bad breath?'
In the poem. *Adones' breath alone would be sufficient to drive Venus into love's madness, she says. 'Stillitory' = 'Alambic, distiller, still'*

Breath excellent, stolen from the violet - the forward violet thus did I chide..
"The forward violet thus did I chide:
Sweet thief, whence didst thou steal thy sweet that smells,
If not from my love's breath?" (SON 49)
Answer to 'Do I have bad breath?'

Breath excellent - the leaf of eglantine, whom not to slander out-sweetens not thy breath
"The leaf of eglantine, whom not to slander,
Out-sweetens not thy breath." (CYM.4.1)
Answer to 'Do I have bad breath?' The answer, actually, can be, 'No, your breath is better than the leaf of eglantine, whom… breath.' 'Eglantine' is 'sweet briar'. You may substitute, for example, 'the leaf of lavender, whom not to slander…'
In the play. *Arviragus talks to Imogen who appears dead but is only asleep.*

Breath like honey - ...suck'd the honey of your breath...
"… that hath suck'd the honey of thy breath,
Hath had no power yet upon thy beauty" (RJ.5.3)
Applying the original lines word by word would be gruesome. She that hath not removed the honey of Juliet's breath is death. However, 'I am sucking the honey of your breath' is a good compliment.
In the play. *Romeo arrives from Mantua and finds Juliet in the tomb, drugged by Friar Lawrence's potion, but not dead.*

Breath like sugar - here are sever'd lips parted with sugar breath...
"…Here are sever'd lips,
Parted with sugar breath: so sweet a bar
Should sunder such sweet friends." (MOV.3.2)
Answer to 'What do you think of my picture?' when she handles you a picture of herself and asks your comment on it. Change 'bar' to 'line' to make the meaning clearer. See also 'Hair as cobweb to entrap the heart of men'
In the play. *Bassanio has won Portia's hand by making the right choice in a quiz contest that Portia's deceased father had established as a condition for her inheritance. Bassanio chooses the right leaden casket and inside he finds Portia's picture along with an announcement that he has won the contest. In a monologue, he comments on the details of the picture.*

Breath that perfumes the air – and with her breath she did perfume the air..
"Tranio, I saw her coral lips to move
And with her breath she did perfume the air:
Sacred and sweet was all I saw in her." (TOS.1.1)
Extract the first two lines and change to, 'As your coral lips move, with your breath you do perfume the air', or 'with her breath she did perfume the air' if you are referring to another beauty.
In the play. *Lucentio describes to Tranio the charms of Bianca.*

Breath, bad b. attributable to unhealthy diet - ... in their thick breaths rank of gross diet...
"…In their thick breaths,
Rank of gross diet, shall we be enclouded,
And forced to drink their vapor."
(AC.5.2)
Describe being in close range of people with bad breath.
In the play. *Cleopatra foresees what would happen if she decided to accompany Octavian to Rome as a prisoner.*

Breath, bad b. chronic- She is not to be kissed fasting in respect of her breath.
"'Item: She is not to be kissed fasting in respect of her breath."(TGV.3.1)
In the play. *In the company of Launce, Speed makes an analysis of the pros and cons of a milkmaid with whom he believes to be in love.*

Breath, b. like a balm, irresistible – Ah balmy breath, that dost almost persuade justice to break her sword!
"Ah balmy breath, that dost almost persuade
Justice to break her sword!" (OTH.5.2)
Compliment. Answer to 'Do I have bad breath?'
In the play. *Desdemona is asleep and Othello almost hesitates whether to kill her or not.*

Breath, b. perfuming the air – ... sweeten with thy breath this neighbour air…
"…sweeten with thy breath
This neighbour air and let rich music's tongue
Unfold the imagined happiness that both
Receive in either by this dear encounter" (RJ.2.6)
Compliment. Answer to 'Do I have bad breath?'
In the play. *Romeo on meeting Juliet at Friar Lawrence's where he will officiate the marriage.*

Breath, b. perfuming the air - 'Tis her breathing that perfumes the chamber thus
"...'Tis her breathing that
Perfumes the chamber thus"
(CYM.2.2)
Compliment on excellent breath.
In the play. *The evil Jachimo has sneaked into Imogen's bedroom.*

Breath, divine b. - ... And calls it heavenly moisture, air of grace.
"She feedeth on the steam as on a prey,
And calls it heavenly moisture, air of grace;
Wishing her cheeks were gardens full of flowers,
So they were dew'd with such distilling showers" (V&A)
Answer to 'Do I have bad breath?' E.G. 'No, it's a heavenly moisture… I wish my cheeks…flowers'
In the poem. *Venus is instantly infatuated with Adonis*

Breath, how to avoid bad b. - ... eat no onion, nor garlic, for we are to utter sweet breath.
"And most dear actors, eat no onion, nor garlic, for we are to utter sweet breath." (MND.4.2)
You both are at dinner and the waiter suggests or praises a dish that contains garlic or onions. Rather than say 'no' try, "Sorry, no onion, nor garlic, for we are to utter sweet breath." You may truly hate garlic or onions, still you are giving hints about your romantic disposition or intents.
Most people are put off by bad breath. Cleopatra herself, for example, chose death by snake poison, rather than suffering the risk of being exposed to the bad breath of the victorious Romans. See entry for 'Breath, bad b. attributable to unhealthy diet'.

In the same spirit, Ovid recommends, 'Let not the breath of your mouth be sour and unpleasing and offend the nose' (AOL.1) and….' 'She whose breath is tainted should never speak before eating, and she should always stand at a distance from her lover's face' (AOL. 3)
In the play. *The actor Bottom addresses his amateur acting companions before the play begins.*

Breath, out of b. - How art thou out of breath, when thou hast breath to say to me that thou art out of breath?
"How art thou out of breath, when thou hast breath
To say to me that thou art out of breath?
The excuse that thou dost make in this delay
Is longer than the tale thou dost excuse." (RJ.2.5)
Comment to 'I am out of breath'.
In the play. *Juliet hurries the Nurse to give an account of the outcome of her search for Romeo*

Brevity, b. in communications - I will imitate the honourable Romans.
"'I will imitate the honourable Romans in
brevity:', 'I commend me to thee, I commend
thee, and I leave thee." (KHIV.p2.2.2)
See also 'Introduction. I want to be brief - since brevity is the soul of wit'– 'also 'Speech, brevity of s. promised - my short date of breath is not so long as is a tedious tale'.
In the play. *Poins reads the beginning of a letter sent by Falstaff to the Prince of Wales*

Bribery, accusation of b. - … an itching palm to sell and mart your offices for gold to undeservers.
"…you yourself
Are much condemn'd to have an itching palm;
To sell and mart your offices for gold
To undeservers." (JC.4.3)
Comment on the activity of lobbyists. See also 'Authority, corrupted by gold - … and though authority be a stubborn bear, yet he is oft led by the nose with gold.'
In the play. *Brutus accuses Cassius of taking bribes.*

Bribery, b. detestable – … shall we now contaminate our fingers with base bribes…
"…shall we now
Contaminate our fingers with base bribes,
And sell the mighty space of our large honours
For so much trash as may be grasped thus?" (JC.4.3)
In the play. *Brutus to Cassius upbraiding him for his acquiescence towards bribe taking.*

Bribery, b. suggested – … show the inside of your purse to the outside of his hand.
"…show the inside of your purse to the outside of his hand, and no more ado" (WT.4.4)
Characterize a lobbyist.
In the play. *The clown suggests to the shepherd to pay Autolycus who pretends to be a courtier who can introduce the shepherd to court.*

Bribery, not tempted by bribes - For I can raise no money by vile means…
For I can raise no money by vile means:
By heaven, I had rather coin my heart,
And drop my blood for drachmas,
than to wring
From the hard hands of peasants their vile trash
By any indirection" (JC.4.3)
In the play. *Brutus to Cassius, accused of taking bribes. 'Indirection' = 'Dishonest practice'*

Brotherhood, b. acquired by sharing common danger - For he to-day that sheds his blood with me shall be my brother.
"For he to-day that sheds his blood with me
Shall be my brother" (KHV.4.3)
When you are looking for supporters in a battle (physical or political).
In the play. *King Henry to the troops before the battle of Agincourt.*

Brows, women's b., standards of excellence - ... black brows, they say, become some women best...
"...black brows, they say,
Become some women best, so that there be not
Too much hair there, but in a semicircle
Or a half-moon made with a pen" (WT.2.1)
In the play. *Mamilius, Leonte's son in conversation with ladies of the court.*

Bubbles - The earth hath bubbles, as the water has and these are of them.
"The earth hath bubbles, as the water has,
And these are of them." (M.1.3)
Metaphor for inconsequential people or matters.
In the play. *Banquo's comment to Macbeth after the three witches disappeared.*

Budge an inch - I'll not budge an inch, boy: let him come, and kindly.
"I'll not budge an inch, boy: let him come, and kindly." (TOS, induction)
In the play. *Sly will not pay for the glasses he broke at the inn when drunk.*

Budget deficit – ... his coffers sound with hollow poverty and emptiness.
"...his coffers sound
With hollow poverty and emptiness." (KHIV.p2.1.3)
See also 'Financial status, challenging - no remedy for consumption of the purse'
In the play. *The rebels get some confidence from the fact that the King's budget shows a big deficit, which may affect his ability to spend in military operations.*

Budget, exceeding b. with extravagant expenses - for our coffers, with too great a court and liberal largess are grown somewhat light.
"... for our coffers, with too great a court
And liberal largess, are grown somewhat light,
We are inforced to farm our royal realm;
The revenue whereof shall furnish us
For our affairs in hand:" (KRII.1.4)
Attack the incumbent administration with charges of extravagant expenses. See also entries for 'Financial status'. Change 'our coffers' to 'your coffers' or use the quote as an example to support your condemnation of increased taxation.
In the play. *Richard II thinks of new taxes and collection to finance his war against Ireland.*

Building, cold and stony - ... ill-erected tower to whose flint bosom...
"...this is the way
To Julius Caesar's ill-erected tower,
To whose flint bosom my condemned lord
Is doom'd a prisoner" (KRII.5.1)
Use 'flint bosom' to describe a cold building resembling a prison.
In the play. *The Queen refers to the prison in the Tower of London where King Richard should have first resided. However, he was instead sent to Pomfret Castle.*

Bunch of no good – ...you, that are polluted with your lusts, stain'd with the guiltless blood of innocents...
Stain'd with the guiltless blood of innocents

"…you, that are polluted with your lusts,
Stain'd with the guiltless blood of innocents,
Corrupt and tainted with a thousand vices" (KHVI.p1.5.4)
In the play. *Joan of Arc upbraids the scornful English who captured her in battle.*

Business travel expenses, pretty nifty - … as 't is ever common, that men are merriest when they are from home.
"… as 't is ever common,
That men are merriest when they are from home." (KHV.1.2)
Comment on a hefty travel expense record after a business trip
In the play. *Henry V makes a comment to his previous dissolute life, also hinted at by the Dauphin of France.*

Business trip, reason for taking them - The world and my great office will sometimes divide me from your bosom.
"The world and my great office will sometimes
Divide me from your bosom" (AC.2.3)
In the play. *Antony tells newly wedded wife Octavia that he may have to absent for important reasons.*

Business trip, temporary separation - The strong necessity of time commands our services a while…
"The strong necessity of time commands
Our services a while; but my full heart Remains in use with you." (AC.1.3)

Reassure her before you leave for a trip. Or use it as a reason or excuse for leaving, or as an answer to "Where are you going?" 'The strong necessity of time … our a while.' *** See Departure, reason for having to leave - I take it, your own business calls on you and you embrace the occasion to depart." ***
'Departure, d. difficult - Can I go forward when my heart is here?'
In the play. *Antony tells Cleopatra that his impending trip to Rome is necessary but not a symptom of his lack of love for her.*

Business, b. conducted at night suspect - … affairs, that walk as they say spirits do, at midnight…
"…affairs, that walk,
As they say spirits do, at midnight, have
In them a wilder nature than the business
That seeks dispatch by day." (KVIII.5.2)
In the play. *Gardiner questions Lovell, whom he found casually roaming at night.*

Business, b. cares upsetting – … every object that might make me fear misfortune to my ventures…
"…every object that might make me fear
Misfortune to my ventures, out of doubt
Would make me sad" (MOV.1.1)
In the play. *Salanio attempts a logical explanation for Antonio's sadness.*

Business, serious b. - … our graver business frowns at this levity.
"…our graver business
Frowns at this levity." (AC.2.7)
In the play. *Octavian takes leave of Pompey after a party when all got drunk.*

Busy and alone - …most are busied when they're most alone.
"…most are busied when they're most alone" (RJ.1.1)
Answer to 'Are you busy?' When you are busy but apparently other do not think so. He/she may ask you if you are busy, implying that you are not and are available for chat or equivalent.
In the play. *Benvolio reports on Romeo who seemed concerned with himself and not to want to be disturbed.*

But me no Buts (not a Shakespeare quote but…)
In the 1980s popular series 'Yes, Prime Minister', the otherwise un-literary Prime Minister Hacker tells his secretary Bernard, "But me no buts!" and adds "That's from Shakespeare". The literary Bernard then says, "No Prime Minister, "but me no buts" is a 19th century quotation, about 1820. Mrs. Centlivre used the phrase in 1708 (her play *The Busy Body)*, but it was Scott's employment of it in *The Antiquary* which popularized it."
And Bernard continues, "I think you are confusing Mrs. Centlivre with Old Capulet in Romeo and Juliet…"
In any event, as Prof. Chris Ferns says, "If Shakespeare didn't actually write it, it's the kind of thing he might have written". Therefore, with some liberty, you can, without offense to literature, use the quote to give a Shakespearean flavor to your objecting to objections.
Note. *See 'Thanks rejected - thank me no thankings, nor, proud me no prouds.'*

But yet, everything is well but yet - I do not like 'but yet', it does allay the good precedence…
"I do not like 'but yet', it does allay The good precedence: fie upon 'but yet',
'But yet' is as a jailer to bring forth Some monstrous malefactor." (AC.2.5)

When she is almost ready to say yes but there is still some hesitation. Or in any occasion where a positive statement is followed by a 'but' or 'and yet'. See also 'Argument, good a. but honest dealing is best - didst thou never hear that things ill got had ever bad success?'
In the play. *Cleopatra to messenger who hesitates (knowing Cleopatra's character) to tell her that Antony married Octavia while in Rome.*

Cakes and ale - Dost thou think, because thou art virtuous, there shall be no more cakes and ale?
"Dost thou think, because thou art virtuous, there shall be no more cakes and ale?" (TN.2.3)
In the play. *Toby Belch to the Clown.*

Call, your girlfriend calls you - It is my soul that calls upon my name.
"It is my soul that calls upon my name" (RJ.2.2)
If the setting is suitable follow up with the lines found at 'Music, words of love like m - How silver sweet sound lovers' tongues by night like softest music to attending ears!'
In the play. *In the Capulet's orchard Romeo hears Juliet talking to herself about him*

Candor, c. declared – In simple and pure soul I come to you.
"In simple and pure soul I come to you" (OTH.1.1)
See also entries for 'Credentials, sincerity'.
In the play. *Roderigo, accompanied by Iago has called on Brabantio at night to tell him that his daughter Desdemona has married Othello in secret. Brabantio at first is not amused and Roderigo makes a statement of candor.*

Capital, no raising capital by corruption - ... I can raise no money by vile means...
"...I can raise no money by vile means:
By heaven, I had rather coin my heart,
And drop my blood for drachmas, than to wring
From the hard hands of peasants their vile trash
By any indirection" (JC.4.3)
Answer to 'Why do you not get venture capital money?' See also 'Corruption for the sake of money - ...shall we now contaminate our fingers with base bribes...'
In the play. *Brutus upbraids Cassius for his corruption. After killing Caesar to restore freedom and remove arbitrary government, Cassius has accepted bribes and sold offices.*

Capitalism, rationale for c. - The sweat of industry would dry and die, but for the end it works to.
"The sweat of industry would dry and die,
But for the end it works to" (CYM.3.6)
In the play. *Belarius rationalizes his forthcoming culinary efforts (sweat of industry).*

Capitalists, c. and plutocrats described – I can compare our rich misers to nothing so fitly as to a whale...
"I can compare our rich misers to nothing so fitly as to a whale; a' plays and tumbles, driving the poor fry before him, and at last devours them all at a mouthful: such whales have I heard on o' the land, who never leave gaping till they've swallowed the whole parish, church, steeple, bells, and all." (PER.2.1)
In the play. *Fishermen standing on the shore of Pentapolis engage in sociological analysis.*

Care, c. and concerns a threat to life - The incessant care and labour of his mind hath wrought the mure that should confine it in...
"The incessant care and labour of his mind
Hath wrought the mure that should confine it in
So thin that life looks through and will break out." (KHIVp2.4.4)
In the play. *Clarence is pessimistic about the recovery of King Henry affected by apoplexy. 'Mure'= 'Wall'*

Care, too much c. about worldly opinion counterproductive - You have too much respect upon the world, they lose it that do buy it with much care.
"You have too much respect upon the world:
They lose it that do buy it with much care" (MOV.1.1)
In the play. *Gratiano tries to cheer up Antonio who declares himself constitutionally sad.*

Careful now, the ides of March, impending danger – beware the ides of March.
"Beware the ides of March." (JC.1.2)
Possible danger on March 15. Or use as an example of a presentiment, e.g. 'As the soothsayer said, beware the ides of (name of month as it applies)'. See also 'Safety warning - if thou beest not immortal, look about you'.
In the play. *A soothsayer tries to warn Caesar about impending danger*

Catholic, anti-c. statement - ... you and all the rest so grossly led, this juggling witchcraft with revenue cherish...
"Though you and all the rest so grossly led
This juggling witchcraft with revenue cherish,
Yet I alone, alone do me oppose
Against the pope and count his friends my foes" (KJ.3.1)

In the play. *King John reacting to Bishop Pandulph, an envoy of the Pope*

Cause and effect explained - ... And now remains that we find the cause of this effect.
"…And now remains
That we find the cause of this effect,
Or rather say, the cause of this defect,
For this effect defective comes by cause:
Thus it remains, and the remainder thus" (H.2.2)
In a speech you have described the situation. Use the phrase (first two lines), to revive the attention. Quote the source if you use all the lines.
In the play. *Polonius continues in his rhetorical rendering of Hamlet's state of mind, which he attributes to hamlet's passion for Ophelia.*

Cause, lost c. - past hope, past cure, past help.
"... Come weep with me!
Past hope, past cure, past help!"
(RJ.4.1)
Indicate the finality of the situation. See also 'Attitude, a. towards what is past and cannot be changed'
In the play. *Juliet has come to Fr. Lawrence to seek help. She is expected to marry Paris, as her parents do not know that she has already married Romeo in secret.*

Cause, rotten c. beyond any discussion – A rotten cause abides no handling.
"That argues but the shame of your offence:
A rotten cause abides no handling."
(KHIV.p2.4.1)
When you do not want to discuss further an issue that you find worthless or disgusting.
In the play. *The rebel Mowbray does not want to discuss grievances with Westmoreland (a lord in the King's retinue). Westmoreland replies. 'To abide' = 'To put up with, to admit'.*

Caution, c. in fighting the enemy – heat not a furnace for your foe so hot that it do singe yourself.
"Heat not a furnace for your foe so hot
That it do singe yourself; we may outrun,
By violent swiftness, that which we run at,
And lose by over-running."
(KHVIII.1.1)
An analogy to warn off and persuade not to make hasty decisions out of anger.
In the play. *Norfolk advises Buckingham to cool it off in his declared anger at Cardinal Wolsey*

Caution, c. in fighting the enemy – the fire that mounts the liquor till it run over, in seeming to augment it wastes it.
"… Know you not,
The fire that mounts the liquor till it run over
In seeming to augment it wastes it."
(KHVIII.1.1)
Use as an analogy to warn off and persuade not to make hasty decisions out of anger.
In the play. *Norfolk advises Buckingham to cool it off in his declared anger at Cardinal Wolsey*

Caution, c. required - it is the bright day that brings forth the adder…
"It is the bright day that brings forth the adder;
And that craves wary walking."
(JC.2.1)
Advocate prudence in the midst of excessive optimism. See also 'Scoundrels, s. around – … there are cozeners abroad; therefore it behooves men to be wary.'
In the play. *Brutus meditates on the forthcoming crowning of Caesar as king.*

Celebration, day of c. when even the sun contributes to the glory - ... to solemnize this day, the glorious sun stays his course…
"To solemnize this day, the glorious sun
Stays his course, and plays the alchymist;
Turning, with splendour of his precious eye,
The meagre cloddy earth to glittering gold." (KJ.3.1)
Introduction to a happy event (if the weather cooperates). Or inject the quote into the toast.
In the play. *The event is the marriage of the Dauphin Lewis and the Lady Blanch. King Philip is making a speech and a toast.*

Celebrations, c. for victory or any happy event - And he that throws not up his cap for joy…
"And he that throws not up his cap for joy,
Shall for the fault make forfeit of his head." (KHVI p3.2.1)
Opening speech for a party. See also entries for 'Party, p. time, celebration' ** 'Wishes, w. of joy – Let grief and sorrow still embrace his heart that doth not wish you joy.' ** 'Welcome, rhetorical w. – Welcome, a curse begin at very root on's heart…' *** 'Victory, v. celebrations -... and let's away, to part the glories of this happy day.'
In the play. *Warwick will proclaim Edward the new king and people will have to be happy and accept it*

Celebrity, c. who dislikes cheering crowds - I love the people, but do not like to stage me to their eyes…
"I love the people,
But do not like to stage me to their eyes" (MFM.1.1)
See also 'Lifestyle, shunning crowds – … I have ever loved the life removed and held in idle price to haunt assemblies…'
In the play. *The Duke will leave Vienna privately to avoid the cheering masses.*

Censure, presence required to avoid rumors and censure - ... to avoid the censures of the carping world.
"And to that end we wish'd your lordship here,
To avoid the censures of the carping world." (KRIII.3.4)
Use the last line to justify formalities or actions required to conform to the norm or preserve appearances.
In the play. *Richard makes up flimsy excuses for having hastily executed Hastings. He has asked the Mayor of London to visit with him in the Tower so as to prepare him both to the death of Hasting and to the proclamation of Richard as King.*

Ceremonies, no time for c. even if friends meet again after a long time - ...the leisure and the fearful time cuts off the ceremonious vows of love...
"Farewell: The leisure and the fearful time
Cuts off the ceremonious vows of love,
And ample interchange of sweet discourse,
Which so long sundered friends should dwell upon." (KRIII.4)
Urgency in parting words among friends - substitute for 'I would like to spend more time but…' See also 'Biography, invitation to tell his/her life story'.
In the play. *Derby has come to visit with Richmond the night before the final battle with Richard III at Bosworth Field.*

Ceremony, ceremonial salutations dispensed with – … rebukeable and worthy shameful cheque it were, to stand on more mechanic compliment.
"…rebukeable
And worthy shameful cheque it were, to stand

On more mechanic compliment"
(AC.4.4)
In the play. *Antony, already in arms, simply kisses Cleopatra before leaving for the decisive battle against the forces of Caesar Octavian.*

Ceremony, c. unnecessary among friends - Ceremony was but devised at first to set a gloss on faint deeds...
"Ceremony was but devised at first
To set a gloss on faint deeds, hollow welcomes,
Recanting goodness, sorry ere 'tis shown;
But where there is true friendship, there needs none." (TOA.1.2)
When a guest or guests or friends appear to be overly formal.
In the play. *A score of parasites stand ceremoniously in front of Timon after he refuses to take back the talents he previously gave to Ventidius, another parasite.*

Ceremony, c., pomp and flattery useless - ... and what are thou, thou idol ceremony?...
"And what are thou, thou idol ceremony?
...
What drink'st thou oft, instead of homage sweet,
But poison'd flattery?" (KHV.4.1)
Use to dismiss ceremonies or formalities, or as an ironic response to a compliment, i.e. 'Is it homage sweet or poisoned flattery?'
In the play. *King Henry V meditates before the battle on the downside of power.*

Ceremony, properties of c. - O ceremony, show me but thy worth!...
"O ceremony, show me but thy worth!
What is thy soul of adoration?
Art thou aught else but place, degree and form,
Creating awe and fear in other men?
...

What drink'st thou oft, instead of homage sweet,
But poison'd flattery? " (HV.4.1)
In the play. *Henry V, the night before the battle of Agincourt, meditates on the characteristics of power.*

Certainty, absolutely certain on pain of self-damnation – I were damn'd beneath all depth in hell but...
"O, I were damn'd beneath all depth in hell,
But that I did proceed upon just grounds
To this extremity." (OTH.5.2)
In the play. *Othello is still convinced of Desdemona's guilt just before Emilia reveals the plot by Iago, her husband.*

Certainty, sure of it - ...as certain as I know the sun is fire.
SICINIUS Art thou certain this is true? is it most certain?
SECOND MESSENGER As certain as I know the sun is fire. (COR.5.6)
Answer to 'Are you sure?'
In the play. *The messenger announces that Coriolanus will no longer fight with the Volsces against the Romans.*

Challenge, c. by an unworthy enemy - shall I be flouted thus by dunghill grooms?
"Shall I be flouted thus by dunghill grooms?" (KHVI.p1.1)
Use with any stupid or obnoxious official who harasses you
In the play. *The Duke of Gloucester is denied access to the Tower by order of Winchester.*

Challenge, prepared to meet the c. - ...I am fresh of spirit and resolved to meet all perils very constantly.
"... I am fresh of spirit and resolved
To meet all perils very constantly." (JC.5.1)
In the play. *Cassius is ready to fight at Philippi, notwithstanding various bad omens.*

Challenge, the greater the c. the greater the victory - The harder match'd, the greater victory.
"The harder match'd, the greater victory" (KHVI.p3.5.1)
See also 'People, the fewer the better for a great enterprise - ... the fewer men, the greater share of honour.'
In the play. *Edward IV harangues his soldiers as he approaches Warwick and his forces at Coventry.*

Chance, let c. decide - If chance will have me king, why, chance may crown me, without my stir.
"If chance will have me king, why, chance may crown me,
Without my stir." (M.1.3)
Answer to 'Do you think you will be elected?' or 'What is your ambition?'
In the play. *The seeds of ambition to be king begin to develop in the soul of Macbeth, with yet some reservations.*

Chance, taking your c. for a while - ... let myself and fortune tug for the time to come.
"... let myself and fortune
Tug for the time to come" (WT.4.3)
Answer to 'What are you going to do next?' 'I will let myself...to come'
See also 'Character, not afraid of taking chances - I have set my life upon a cast and I will stand the hazard of the die.'
In the play. *Florizel will try his chances and elope with Perdita after renouncing to the throne of Bohemia.*

Chance, temper of man shown when handling reversals – In the reproof of chance lies the true proof of men.
"In the reproof of chance
Lies the true proof of men: the sea being smooth,
How many shallow bauble boats dare sail
Upon her patient breast, making their way
With those of nobler bulk!" (TC.1.3)
Good words to inspire yourself or others, especially 'in the reproof of chance lies the true proof of men'. 'Bauble' stands for 'insignificant'.
In the play. *Things are not going too well for the Greeks besieging Troy. Nestor follows up on inspiring words by Agamennon.*

Change, desire for radical c. – Contending with the fretful element...that things might change or cease...
"Contending with the fretful element:
Bids the winds blow the earth into the sea,
Or swell the curled water 'bove the main,
That things might change or cease
…
Strives in his little world of man to out-scorn
The to-and-fro-conflicting wind and rain." (KL. 3.1)
In the play. *A gentleman describes to Kent the state of mind of King Lear, who is indeed battling a real storm, but also a rage towards his ungrateful daughters Goneril and Regan.*

Character (yours), habitually changing your mind - thus change I like the moon.
"Thus change I like the moon." (LLL.5.1)
Answer to 'Why did you change your mind?' See also 'Power, privilege of p. to give no explanations -...the cause is in my will'.
In the play. *Rosaline first asks her companions to play then changes her mind and suggests dancing.*

Character, a cold fish – ... a man whose blood a snow-broth...
"...a man whose blood
Is very snow-broth; one who never feels

The wanton stings and motions of the sense,
But doth rebate and blunt his natural edge
With profits of the mind, study and fast." (MFM.1.4)
Answer to question, 'What do you think of (so and so)?'
In the play. *Lucio describes to Isabella the character of Angelo, the new interim governor of Vienna.*

Character, a cold fish - ... scarce confesses that his blood flows…
"… scarce confesses
That his blood flows, or that his appetite
Is more to bread than stone" (MFM.1.2)
Answer to question, 'What do you think of (so and so)?'
In the play. *Duke Vicentio describes the character of Angelo, newly appointed (by the Duke) ruler of Vienna.*

Character, a cold fish - ... when he makes water his urine is congealed ice.
"Some report a sea-maid spawned him; some, that he was begot between two stock-fishes. But it is certain that when he makes water his urine is congealed ice." (MFM.3.2)
Answer to question, 'What do you think of (so and so)?' of a cold person. E.G. 'I don't know but it is certain… ice'.
In the play. *Lucio gives Duke Vicentio an assessment of Angelo's character and make up. Lucio says that Angelo was not created the usual way and the Duke asks him 'How should he be made, then?'*

Character, a dandy – he speaks holiday, he smells April and May.
"… he capers, he dances, he has eyes of youth, he writes verses, he speaks holiday, he smells April and May" (MWW.3.2)

In the play. *The Host refers to young Master Fenton, the most likely candidate to carry away the pretty Ann.*

Character, a humorous c. - … When I am dull with care and melancholy lightens my humour with his merry jests.
"A trusty villain, sir, that very oft,
When I am dull with care and melancholy,
Lightens my humour with his merry jests." (COE.1.2)
Skip the first line and simply define a character with a sense of humor.
In the play: *Antipholus S. defines and describes his servant Dromio S to a merchant.*

Character, a hypocrite and a filthy c. - … His filth within being cast, he would appear a pond as deep as hell.
"This outward –sainted deputy…
… is yet a devil,
His filth within being cast, he would appear
A pond as deep as hell.
…'t is the cunning livery of hell,
The damned'st body to invest and cover
In prenzie guards!" (MFM.3.1)
Describe a hypocrite and a pervert. 'Prenzie' stands for 'too nice' with a derogatory tone.
In the play. *Isabel tells Claudio of Angelo who tried to seduce her in exchange for her brother Claudio's life.*

Character, a hypocrite with a false smile - … he does smile his face into more lines than are in the new map, with the augmentation of the Indies.
"... he does smile his face into more lines than are in the new map, with the augmentation of the Indies." (TN.3.2)
Define an ever-smiling hypocrite. The 'augmentation of the Indies' refers to the discovery of America and the attendant

enlargement of geographic maps. Or use to explain the need for a face-lift, e.g. (my face) has more lines than…Indies'.
In the play. *Malvolio has fallen for the trick to make him believe that Olivia loves him and Maria comments on Malvolio's behavior.*

Character, a milk-sop - A milk-sop, one that never in his life felt so much cold as over shoes in snow.
"And who doth lead them but a paltry fellow,
Long kept in Bretagne at our mother's cost?
A milk-sop, one that never in his life
Felt so much cold as over shoes in snow?" (KRIII.5.3)
In the play. *Richard's opinion of the Earl of Richmond, his opponent at the battle of Bosworth field.*

Character, a respectable person - common speech gives him a worthy pass.
"Yes, I do know him well; and common speech
Gives him a worthy pass."
(AWEW.2.5)
Answer to 'What do you know of him?' when you want to express a guarded opinion on a person you do not completely or necessarily endorse.
In the play. *Parolles' only defense against the correct judgment of Lafeu is to try to discredit Lafeu. Hence he asks if Bertram knows Lafeu and Bertram answers.*

Character, a ruffian and total loss – … and commits the oldest sins the newest kind of ways.
"Have you a ruffian that will swear, drink, dance,
Revel the night, rob, murder, and commit
The oldest sins the newest kind of ways?" (KHIV.p2.4.4)
In the play. *London, the Jerusalem chamber at court. The ailing King upbraids his son for keeping bad company. The ruffian specifically referred to is Falstaff.*

Character, all show no substance - dissuade me from believing thee a vessel of too great a burthen.
" … the scarfs and the bannerets about thee, did manifoldly dissuade me from believing thee a vessel of too great a burthen." (AWEW.2.3)
Show that you are unimpressed. E.G. 'His attire and general manners did manifoldly dissuade me from believing him a vessel of too great a burden'.
In the play. *Lafeu openly discloses his contempt for Parolles.*

Character, always laughing and does not taking things seriously - are of such sensible and nimble lungs that they always use to laugh at nothing.
"These gentlemen, who are of such sensible and nimble lungs that they always use to laugh at nothing." (TEM.2.1)
Use with buffoons that always laugh and never take anything seriously, 'You are of such sensible…nothing' – See also 'Jokes, no time for joking'.
In the play. *Gonzalo is rebuffed by Alonso and defends himself. He wanted the expose 'those gentlemen' as goons.*

Character, ambitious - for the very substance of the ambitious is merely the shadow of a dream.
GUILDENSTERN. "… for the very substance of the ambitious is merely the shadow of a dream."
ROSENCRANTZ. "…and I hold ambition of so airy and light a quality that it is but a shadow's shadow." (H.2.2)
Answer to 'Are you ambitious? When you wish to position yourself as a non ambitious or over-grabbing.

In the play. *Hamlet and his dubious friends ROSENCRANTZ and GUILDENSTERN engage in a dialog on the subject of ambition.*

Character, ambitious and greedy - ... no man's pie is freed from his ambitious finger.
"… No man's pie is freed
from his ambitious finger." (KHVIII.1.1)
Apply to your greedy political enemy.
In the play. *Buckingham refers to Cardinal of York.*

Character, ambitious and weaving his own web for success - ... the force of his own merit makes his way.
…being not propped by ancestry, whose grace
Chalks successors their way; nor call'd upon
For high feats done to the crown; neither allied
To eminent assistants; but, spider like,
Out of his self drawing web, - he gives us note -
The force of his own merit makes his way." (KHVIII.1.1)
Describe an ambitious and scheming person
In the play. *Buckingham describes the abilities of Cardinal Wolsey who is always able to 'buy a place next to the king'*

Character, ambitious, with a swelling ambition - ... swell'd so much that it did almost stretch the sides of the world.
"… Caesar's ambition,
Which swell'd so much that it did almost stretch
The sides of the world." (CYM.3.1)
Describe an ambitious individual, "His ambition is like Caesar's, which swell'd so much that it did stretch…world."

In the play. *Cymbeline makes reference to Caesar while addressing Caius Lucius who has arrived from Rome to claim overdue taxes. It was Caesar to subdue the Britons who now refuse to pay more tributes.*

Character, annoying - ... you do me most insupportable vexation.
"…you do me most insupportable vexation." (AWEW.2.3)
Alternative to 'You annoy me.'
In the play. *Parolles' reaction at Lafeu's string of (actually deserved) insults.*

Character, arrogant and dishonest – … we think him over-proud and under-honest…
"... and you shall not sin,
If you do say we think him over-proud
And under-honest; in self-assumption greater
Than in the note of judgment."
(TC.2.3)
Describe a proud and dishonest person.
In the play *Agamennon tells Patroclus how the other Greeks feel about Achilles*

Character, arrogant behind a display of humility – … but your heart is cramm'd with arrogancy, spleen, and pride.
"You sign your place and calling, in full seeming,
With meekness and humility; but your heart
Is cramm'd with arrogancy, spleen, and pride" (KHVIII.2.4)
In the play. *Queen Catherine to Cardinal Wolsey as she is called to a trial that should legalize her divorce from the king.*

Character, arrogant, supercilious, hateful - I do hate a proud man, as I hate the engendering of toads.
" I do hate a proud man, as I hate the engendering of toads." (TC.2.3)
Express your feelings about an arrogant person.

In the play. *Ajax thinks that Achilles is proud without realizing that he is just the same.*

Character, baseness of c. displayed by the expression – … an eye base and unlustrous as the smoky light that's fed with stinking tallow.
"…an eye
Base and unlustrous as the smoky light
That's fed with stinking tallow" (CYM.1.6)
In the play. *The perfidious Iachimo attempts to slander Imogen's absent husband by implying that he is having affairs with girls of base character (in Rome). Hence, the image of 'peeping in an eye…'*

Character, blind to own faults - … the raven chides blackness.
AJAX (of Achilles). Can he not be sociable?
ULYSSES (aside). The raven chides blackness (TC.2.3)
Comment when someone criticizes in others his own very faults.
In the play *Ajax is a blockhead and accuses Achilles of being antisocial but Ajax he is just as antisocial - hence Ulysses' remark.*

Character, bombastic and cowardly - … so confidently seems to undertake this business, which he knows is not to be done…
"…Is not this a strange fellow, my lord, that so confidently seems to undertake this business, which he knows is not to be done; damns himself to do and dares better be damned than to do't?" (AWEW.3.6)
In the play. *A lord comments on Parolles who claims outwardly to want to recover a drum lost in enemy hands while it is clear that he wants to get out of the enterprise.*

Character, bookworm – …my library was dukedom large enough.

"…Me, poor man, my library
Was dukedom large enough" (TEM.1.2)
If you are a bookworm, use to express the well-defined range of your ambitions, 'my library is dukedom large enough'. Or you are annoyed at the world and find refuge and solace in books.
In the play. *Prospero explains to daughter Miranda the events that forced him into exile in the island where they both are now.*

Character, bookworm – … volumes that I prize above my kingdom.
"Knowing that I lov'd my books, he furnish'd me,
From mine own library, with volumes that
I prize above my dukedom." (TEM.1)
State your love of books. E.G. 'As Prospero said in the Tempest, I prize my books above my dukedom'
In the play. *Prospero details the events that led to his escape from Milan. The man who furnished the books is Gonzalo.*

Character, brainless – not Hercules could have knock'd out his brains, for he had none.
"…not Hercules
Could have knock'd out his brains, for he had none" (CYM.4.2)
Turn the similitude to a hypothetical present '…not Hercules could knock out his brain, for he has none'.
In the play. *Belarius referring to the foolish son of the Queen, Cloten, whom he has just slain in a fight.*

Character, brutish and ugly - He is as disproportion'd in his manners as in his shape.
"He is as disproportion'd in his manners
As in his shape" (TEM.5.1)
In the play. *Prospero referring to Caliban.*

Character, c. acting quickly on decision - He's sudden, if a thing comes in his head.
"He's sudden, if a thing comes in his head." (KHVI p3.5.5)
In the play. *Edward IV of Richard of Gloucester who suddenly left Coventry for London with the intent of killing Henry VI, prisoner at the Tower.*

Character, c. all in his clothes - ... the soul of this man is in his clothes…
"... the soul of this man is in his clothes: trust him not in matter of heavy consequence." (AWEW.2.3)
Describe a man who is all appearance and no substance. See also 'Image building or restoration - I'll be at charges for a looking glass and entertain a score or two of tailors…' *** 'Image, happy about your i. - Shine out, fair sun, till I have bought a glass, that I may see my shadow as I pass.' *** 'Advice, a. on men's wear and fashion - Costly thy habit as thy purse can buy, but not express'd in fancy; rich, not gaudy…'
In the play. *Bertram is leaving for Italy with Parolles and Lafeu tells Bertram that Parolles is a fluke.*

Character, c. always angry – ira furor brevis est, but yond' man is ever angry.
"They say, my lords, ira furor brevis est,
But yond' man is ever angry." (TOA.1.2)
Describe a man who is always angry.
In the play. *Timon's assessment of Apemantus, the only man present who is not a parasite.*

Character, c. and qualities intergenerational - O noble strain! O worthiness of nature! breed of greatness!
"O noble strain!
O worthiness of nature! breed of greatness!
Cowards father cowards and base things sire base:
Nature hath meal and bran, contempt and grace" (CYM.4.2)
Use the first two lines to praise, the second two to disparage.
In the play. *Belarius, adoptive father of Guiderius and Arviragus wonders at their nobility as observed in dealing with Fideles/Imogen, who turns out to be their sister.*

Character, c. bound to make mistakes but not devious – …(one that) errs in ignorance and not in cunning.
"…(one that) errs in ignorance and not in cunning" (OTH.3.3)
In the play. *Unaware of Iago's plot, Desdemona pleads with Othello on behalf of Cassio.*

Character, c. capable of saying only a few and identical words - That ever this fellow should have fewer words than a parrot, and yet the son of a woman!
"That ever this fellow should have fewer words than a parrot, and yet the son of a woman! " (KHIV.p1.2.4)
In the play. *Prince Henry's opinion of Francis, a servant who always says 'anon'.*

Character, c. changes explained - There is differency between a grub and a butterfly…
"There is differency between a grub and a butterfly; yet your butterfly was a grub" (COR.5.4)
In the play. *Menenius use the similitude of the butterfly to explain the changes in character of Coriolanus who has turned from a man into a dragon.*

Character, c. deceitful, treacherous - treacherous man! Thou hast beguiled my hopes…
"…treacherous man!
Thou hast beguiled my hopes; nought

but mine eye
Could have persuaded me:" (TGV.5.4)
You completely misjudged the man. See also 'Physiognomy, p. unreliable - ... there's no art to find the mind's construction in the face…'
In the play. *Valentine has discovered the treachery of his alleged friend Proteus.*

Character, c. easily deceived about the nature of men - ... of a free and open nature that thinks men honest that but seem to be so…
"The Moor is of a free and open nature,
That thinks men honest that but seem to be so,
And will as tenderly be led by the nose
As asses are." (OTH.1.3)
In the play. *Iago plies his hateful plot against Othello.*

Character, c. fierce in war and mellow in peace - In war was never lion raged more fierce, in peace was never gentle lamb more mild.
"In war was never lion raged more fierce,
In peace was never gentle lamb more mild" (KRII.2.1)
In the play. *York eulogizes Edward, King Richard's father.*

Character, c. helpful to excess – … she holds it a vice in her goodness not to do more than she is requested
"…she holds it a vice in her goodness not to do more than she is requested" (OTH.2.3)
In the play. *Iago pushes Cassio to ask Desdemona to intercede with Othello on his behalf. This is part of the plot to inflame Othello's jealousy.*

Character, c. given to extremes - The middle of humanity thou never knewest, but the extremity of both ends.
"The middle of humanity thou never knewest, but the extremity of both ends" (TOA.4.3)
Change 'knewest' to 'knowest' or 'thou' to 'he' if you extend the comment to a third person.
In the play. *Timon, now living in a cave, receives an unwanted visit by Apemantus, who reminds Timon of his extreme behavior in all circumstances.*

Character, c. history showing rashness - The best and soundest of his time hath been but rash.
"The best and soundest of his time hath been but rash" (KL.1.1)
In the play. *Goneril begin finding faults with her father Lear now that she got the inheritance.*

Character, incapable of paying compliments or praising – He would not flatter Neptune for his trident…
"He would not flatter Neptune for his trident,
Or Jove for his power to thunder…" (COR.3.1)
In the play. *Menenius describes Coriolanus to Sicinius.*

Character, c. not used to ask favors - Suffolk's imperial tongue is stern and rough, used to command, untaught to plead for favour...
"Suffolk's imperial tongue is stern and rough,
Used to command, untaught to plead for favour.
Far be it we should honour such as these
With humble suit: no, rather let my head
Stoop to the block than these knees bow to any
Save to the God of heaven and to my king" (KHVI p2.4.1)

Be sarcastic with an arrogant person or bureaucrat. E.G. 'I see that your imperial tongue is…plead for favor'.
In the play. *Suffolk banished and on a ship bound for France is accused of treason by the captain and will not ask for any mercy.*

Character, c. observed in a person that reveals his history - … there is a kind of character in thy life…
"Angelo,
There is a kind of character in thy life
That to the observer doth thy history
Fully unfold." (MFM.1.1)
Leave the other party uncertain as to whether you trust him/her or not
In the play. *The Duke of Vienna is planning to let Angelo in charge as he, the Duke, absents himself from the city.*

Character, c. occasionally honest - though I am not naturally honest, I am so sometimes by chance.
"Though I am not naturally honest, I am so sometimes by chance."
(WT.4.3)
Comment on the exception, a good deed by a dishonest person, 'Though he is not naturally honest, he is so sometimes by chance'.
In the play. *Autolycus admits to a weakness for occasional honesty. He will make himself pass for a courtier and play a part in the meeting with Polixenes, where Polixenes will learn that Perdita is not a shepherdess but rather the daughter of Leontes.*

Character, c. of a person who seems truthful - … thou seem'st a palace for the crown'd truth to dwell in.
"Prithee, speak:
Falseness cannot come from thee; for thou look'st
Modest as Justice, and thou seem'st a palace
For the crown'd Truth to dwell in."
(PER.5.1)

State your belief in the honesty of the teller and of what he is going to say. Answer to "are you telling the truth?'
E.G. 'I am a palace for the crowned…in'
In the play. *Pericles invites Marina to tell her history, but she is afraid that, though true, the history may sound unbelievable. Pericles reassures her.*

Character, c. of integrity, not afraid to be politically incorrect - … knew the true minute when exception bid him speak.
"…and his honour,
Clock to itself, knew the true minute when
Exception bid him speak."
(AWEW.1.2)
Describe a man of honor not afraid to take on critical issues even if unpopular. Or to justify opposition. E.G. 'We should imitate that character whose honor (I quote), clock to himself, knew the true minute when exception bid him speak. And this is the true minute…etc.'
In the play. *The King speaks of Helen's father, the most celebrated and respected doctor of his time.*

Character, c. of questionable qualities - … a tried and valiant soldier …So is my horse.
OCTAVIUS You may do your will;
But he's a tried and valiant soldier.
ANTONY So is my horse; So is my horse, Octavius; and for that
I do appoint him store of provender"
(JC.4.1)
Change animal as needed. E.G. 'But he is faithful…' – 'so is my dog'.
In the play. *Antony does not think much of Lepidus, the third consul and says so to Octavian. 'Provender' = 'Dry food for animals'*

Character, c. only interested in gain and therefore unreliable - That sir which serves and seeks for gain, and

follows but for form, will pack when it begins to rain…
"That sir which serves and seeks for gain,
And follows but for form,
Will pack when it begins to rain,
And leave thee in the storm" (KL.2.4)
When you question the reliability and loyalty of an appointee. See also 'Flattery, f. and praise tied to reward - … when the means are gone that buy this praise, the breath is gone whereof this praise is made.'
In the play. *The Fool gives Lear a piece of wisdom – the reference is to Lear's two evil daughters Regan and Goneril*

Character, c. quarrelous – … As quarrelous as the weasel.
"… As quarrelous as the weasel" (CYM.3.4)
In the play. *Pisanio tells Imogen to dress like a man and as such be quick to quarrel (among other things).*

Character, c. pessimistic by nature - His discontents are unremoveably coupled to nature.
"His discontents are unremoveably Coupled to nature." (TOA.5.1)
Answer to 'Why are you unhappy?' Change 'his' to 'my'.
In the play. *A senator came to Timon's cave begging for his lobbying Alcibiades not to attack Athens. Timon rejects the senators and answers with a prediction of his own doom. See 'Invocation, end - Sun, hide thy beams! Timon hath done his reign.'*

Character, c. proud and disdainful of others – … Such a nature, tickled with good success, disdains the shadow which he treads on at noon.
"… Such a nature,
Tickled with good success, disdains the shadow
Which he treads on at noon:" (COR.1.1)
Emphasize how your political adversary, when elected has forgotten his promises to the electorate.
In the play. *Brutus, a tribune of the people, comments on the character of Coriolanus.*

Character, proud and petty – Things small as nothing, for request's sake only, he makes important…
"Things small as nothing, for request's sake only,
He makes important: possess'd he is with greatness,
And speaks not to himself but with a pride
That quarrels at self-breath" (TC.2.3)
In the play. *Ulysses gives an account of Achilles's character to Agamennon.*

Character, c. reformation more dramatic given the precedents – My reformation, glittering o'er my fault shall show more goodly…
"My reformation, glittering o'er my fault,
Shall show more goodly and attract more eyes
Than that which hath no foil to set it off" (KHIV.p1.1.2)
In the play. *Prince Henry plans to reform from his hippie life style.*

Character, c. reliable who keeps our promises – ever precise in promise keeping.
"…and he was ever precise in promise-keeping." (MFM.1.2)
Change 'was' to 'is' for compliment or praise. Or to 'I' to strongly support your promise-keeping nature.
In the play. *Lucio is surprised that Claudio has not showed up at an agreed time. Claudio has been arrested by order of Angelo the vice-duke of Vienna.*

Character, c. self-centered - … you speak like one besotted on your sweet delights…

"Paris, you speak
Like one besotted on your sweet delights:
You have the honey still, but these the gall;
So to be valiant is no praise at all."
(TC.2.2)
In the play. *Priam's answer to Troilus' bombastic statement that he alone would fight to retain Helen in Troy.*

Character, c. self-described as not sociable - ... society is no comfort to one not sociable.
IMOGEN. I am ill, but your being by me
Cannot amend me: society is no comfort
To one not sociable." (CYM.4.1)
Answer to suggestions to join clubs or group activities, e.g. 'Society is no comfort to one not sociable'. Or if you are not well but prefer to be left alone, 'I am ill but your being…amend me.'
In the play. *Imogen is sad and does not want any company.*

Character, c. shaped by own mistakes - they say best men are moulded out of faults…
"They say best men are moulded out of faults,
And, for the most, become much more the better
For being a little bad." (MFM.5.1)
Turn a setback or a character liability into an asset. Answer to 'Why did you do this?' You can say, 'I realize now it was bad but…they say best men….bad.' It could be a concluding line to get the matter (e.g. an objectionable action or a despicable act), over and done with. See also "Character, promise of self-reformation - …that to come hall all be done by the rule'.

In the play *The Duke declares that Angelo will die in reparation for the death of Claudio. Actually, the Duke already saved Claudio's life. It is just a plot to see how the various protagonists will react. Mariana asks Isabel to plead with the Duke to save Angelo – however rotten Angelo has been just about with everyone.*

Character, c. showing natural traits - how hard it is to hide the sparks of nature.
"How hard it is to hide the sparks of nature." (CYM.3.3)
Use it positively or negatively. If a fool behaves like a fool, 'How hard it is…. Nature'. – See also 'Instinct, i. revealing of character'
In the play. *Guiderius and Arviragus are in reality the king's sons - they do not know it but Belarius, their adoptive father, remarks about their instinctive nobility.*

Character, c. slippery and opportunist - ... a slipper and subtle knave, a finder of occasions.
"... a slipper and subtle knave, a finder of occasions" (OTH.2.1)
In the play. *Iago describes (unfairly) Cassio to Roderigo to put Cassio in a bad light.*

Character, c. softer than shown by appearances - ... of a better nature, sir, then he appears by speech.
" My father's of a better nature, sir,
Then he appears by speech."
(TEM.1.2)
When you need to soften the impression left on a third party by the attitude or words of a colleague. Change 'my father's' to 'so and so is'.
In the play. *Prospero purposely puts on a rough demeanor with Ferdinand and Miranda, Prospero's daughter, comments.*

Character, c. somewhat pretentious and wordy – A man …that hath a mint of phrases in his brain…

"A man in all the world's new fashion planted,
That hath a mint of phrases in his brain"
....
A man of complements, whom right and wrong
Have chosen as umpire of their mutiny." (LLL.1.1)
In the play. *The King of Navarre speaks of the pompous and wordy Armado.*

Character, c. surly and independent -
... his surly nature, which easily endures not article tying him to aught
"...his surly nature,
Which easily endures not article
Tying him to aught" (COR.2.3)
In the play. *The tribune Sicinius describes Coriolanus' character.*

Character, c. that acts more than speak - ... speaking in deeds and deedless in his tongue...
"...firm of word,
Speaking in deeds and deedless in his tongue;
Not soon provoked nor being provoked soon calm'd" (TC.4.5)
In the play. *Ulysses describes Troilus to the inquiring Agamennon.*

Character, c. that disregards riches -
... (he) look'd upon things precious as they were the common muck of the world...
" (he) look'd upon things precious as they were
The common muck of the world: he covets less
Than misery itself would give; rewards
His deeds with doing them, and is content
To spend the time to end it."
(COR.2.2)
When you want to convey your disregard for external symbols of wealth. E.G. 'I look upon things precious....muck of the world.'
In the play. *Cominius describes the character of Coriolanus, a true fanatic.*

Character, c. treacherous and false -
... and be ever double in his words and meaning.
"... He was a man
Of an unbounded stomach, ever ranking
Himself with princes; one that, by suggestion,
Tied all the kingdom: simony was fair-play,
His own opinion was his law; and in the presence
He would say untruths; and be ever double,
Both in his words and meaning."
(KHVIII.4.2)
Change the tense from past to present and use to describe a schemer and double dealer.
In the play. *Queen Katherine assessment's of Wolsey whose death has just been announced to her.*

Character, c. truthful and simple - I am as true as truth's simplicity and simpler than the infancy of truth.
" I am as true as truth's simplicity,
And simpler than the infancy of truth." (TC.3.2)
Emphasize your absolute truthfulness. Alternative answer to 'Are you telling the truth?' See also 'Truth, answer to "Are you telling the truth?'
In the play. *Troilus and Cressida argue as to whom is the winner in a context as who is the truer of the two.*

Character, c. unpredictable when angry - ... And, touched with choler, hot as gunpowder.
"For I do know Fluellen valiant
And, touched with choler, hot as gunpowder" (KHV.4.7)

In the play. *King Henry tells Warwick to follow Fluellen.*

Character, c. very religious – ... all his mind is bent to holiness...
"...all his mind is bent to holiness,
To number Ave-Maries on his beads;
His champions are the prophets and apostles,
His weapons holy saws of sacred writ
His study is his tilt-yard, and his loves
Are brazen images of canonized saints" (KHVI.p2.1.2)
In the play. *Queen Margaret complains with Suffolk that King Henry her husband is too religious.*

Character, c. who rarely or never smiles – ... Seldom he smiles, and smiles in such a sort...
"Seldom he smiles, and smiles in such a sort
As if he mock'd himself and scorn'd his spirit
That could be moved to smile at any thing." (JC.1.2)
In the play. *Caesar to Antony referring to Cassius.*

Character, c. who says a lot of nonsense - Gratiano speaks an infinite deal of nothing...
"Gratiano speaks an infinite deal of nothing, more than any man in all Venice. His reasons are as two grains of wheat hid in two bushels of chaff: you shall seek all day ere you find them, and when you have them, they are not worth the search." (MOV.1.1)
Apply to any (of many) to whom the statement applies, i.e. those who say nothing in the largest number of words. See also entries for 'Speech, nonsensical or meaningless'
In the play. *The loquacious Gratiano has just left Bassanio and Antonio. Bassanio expresses his opinion of Gratiano.*

Character, c. with a melancholy disposition - I can suck melancholy out of a song, as a weasel sucks eggs.
"I can suck melancholy out of a song, as a weasel sucks eggs." (AYL1.2.5)
Define yourself if you fit the profile or define the character who does.
In the play. *In another part of the forest, Jacques is a self-proclaimed constitutionally melancholy character.*

Character, c. with a bad temper compared to a weasel – A weasel hath not such a deal of spleen as you are toss'd with.
"A weasel hath not such a deal of spleen
As you are toss'd with" (KHIVp1.2.3)
In the play. *Lady Percy to her husband who is riding away to start a rebellion against Henry IV.*

Character, c. with a strong religious disposition - But all his mind is bent on holiness...
"But all his mind is bent on holiness,
To number Ave Maria on his beads:
His champions are his prophets and apostles;
His weapons, holy saws of sacred writ;
His study is tilt-yard, and his loves
Are brazen images of canonized saints." (KHVI p2.1.3)
Characterize a religious person – use the first 3 lines.
In the play. *Margaret of her husband the king.*

Character, c. without malice - I lack iniquity some times to do me service.
"I lack iniquity
Sometimes to do me service"
(OTH.1.2)
Define yourself. See also "Credentials, sincerity, one tongue - What I think I utter and spend my malice in my breath'.

In the play. *Knowing what Iago will do and be the cause of in the play, this declaration by him is hypocritical at best.*

Character, compound of all faults - a man who is the abstract of all faults that all men follow.
"A man who is the abstract of all faults
That all men follow." (AC.1.4)
Flail a bad man, politician, boss or employee.
In the play. *Octavian sums up to Lepidus the content of a letter describing the behavior of Antony in Alexandria.*

Character, conceited - ... the best persuaded of himself, so crammed, as he thinks, with excellencies, that it is his grounds of faith that all that look on him love him.
" ... the best persuaded of himself, so crammed, as he thinks, of excellencies, that it is ground of faith, that all that look on him love him." (TN.2.3)
Describe a conceited person who thinks he is best.
In the play. *Maria describes Malvolio on whom she is planning a revenge to expose his sense of excessive self-importance.*

Character, conservative - old fashions please me best...
"Old fashions please me best: I am not so nice,
To change true rules for odd inventions." (TOS.3.1)
State your conservative values or stance. See also 'Custom, c. as an obstacle to positive change' – entries for 'Custom' – 'Image building or restoration'
In the play. *Bianca does not particularly like the new-style song Hortensio has composed for her.*

Character, constancy, a desirable trait - ... were man but constant, he were perfect. That one error fills him with faults; makes him run through all the sins.
"O heaven! were man
But constant, he were perfect. That one error
Fills him with faults; makes him run through all the sins" (TGV.5.4)
Applies not necessarily and exclusive to occasional infidelities. Use in an ironic, self-effacing way, when you said you would do something and then you didn't. See also 'Credentials. Establishing your credentials'.
In the play. *Proteus recognizes his folly at pursuing Sylvia instead of being faithful and truthful to the equally beautiful Julia, who (unbelievably) still loves him. In fact he continues,* What is in Silvia's face, but I may spy / More fresh in Julia's with a constant eye?

Character, constant –... now from head to foot I am marble constant.
"...now from head to foot
I am marble-constant; now the fleeting moon
No planet is of mine." (AC.5.2)
See also 'Credentials, establishing your c. - constancy.' One of several answers to 'Tell me something about yourself?' or, 'What happens if you find an obstacle in your way'.
In the play. *Cleopatra is determined to end her life with the bite of the adder brought in a basket of figs.*

Character, coward - and you find so much blood in his liver as will clog the foot of a flea.
"... and you find so much blood in his liver as will clog the foot of a flea." (TN.3.2)
Define a coward. See also 'Insult, cowards'
In the play. *Sir Toby's opinion of Aguecheek.*

Character, coward and thieving – ... They will steal any thing, and call it purchase.
"...for a' never broke any man's head but his own, and that was against a post when he was drunk. They will steal any thing, and call it purchase." (KHV.3.4)
In the play. *An attendant boy's evaluation of Pistol and Nym*

Character, coward - ... has no man's blood in's belly than will sup a flea.
"...(he) has no man's blood in's belly than will
sup a flea." (LLL.5.2)
In the play. *Biron's opinion of Armado.*

Character, coward - A coward, a most devout coward, religious in it
"A coward, a most devout coward, religious in it" (TN.3.4)
In the play. *Fabian refers to Viola/Cesario, mistakenly identified with her twin brother Sebastian.*

Character, cunning and needing no assistance - a crafty knave does need no broker.
"They say, - a crafty knave does need no broker." (KHVI p2.1.2)
Apply to a scheming person who will be perfectly able to carry out his plans without assistance.
In the play. *Hume reflecting on his own plans.*

Character, deceitful - ... a quicksand of deceit.
"What Clarence but a quicksand of deceit?" (KHVI.p3.5.4)
In the play. *Q. Margaret arraigns the troops before the battle of Tewksbury against the forces of Edward IV.*

Character, devious behind a façade of plainness - ... in this plainness harbour more craft and more corrupter ends than twenty silly ducking observants...
"These kind of knaves I know, which in this plainness
Harbour more craft and more corrupter ends
Than twenty silly ducking observants
That stretch their duties nicely."
(KL.2.2)
In the play. *The Duke of Cornwall makes light of Kent's directness.*

Character, direct - for what his heart thinks, his tongue speaks.
" ... he hath a heart as sound as a bell, and his tongue is the clapper; for what his heart thinks, his tongue speaks." (MAAN.3.2)
Indicate your being direct, e.g. 'what my heart thinks my tongue speaks.' – see also 'Credentials, sincerity, one tongue'.
In the play. *Don Pedro's general assessment of Benedick. Benedick is present and claims to have changed.*

Character, direct to the extreme - ... what his breast forges, that his tongue must vent.
"He would not flatter Neptune for his trident,
Or Jove for his power to thunder. His heart's his mouth:
What his breast forges, that his tongue must vent." (COR.3.1)
Describe an overly outspoken character.
In the play. *Menenius describes Coriolanus to Sicinius.*

Character, dishonest and worthless - ... he has everything that an honest man should not have...
" ... he has everything that an honest man should not have; of what an honest man should have, he has nothing." (AWEW.4.3)
Define a dishonest man.

In the play. *Believing his capturers to be the enemy, Parolles does not hesitate to badmouth Bertram.*

Character, dramatic change in c. - This tyrant, whose sole name blisters our tongues was once thought honest.
"This tyrant, whose sole name blisters our tongues
Was once thought honest." (M.4.3)
Apply to a politician who has become very arrogant. Define someone you really dislike, '…. His sole name blisters my tongue' – See also 'Name, hateful n. - The devil himself could not pronounce a title more hateful to mine ear'.
In the play. *Malcolm referring to Macbeth.*

Character, drunkard, drunkenness described - … like a drowned man, a fool and a madman…
OLIVIA. What's a drunken man, like, fool?
CLOWN. Like a drowned man, a fool and a madman: one drought above heat makes him a fool; the second mads him; and a third drowns him." (TN.1.5)
Demonstrate the effects of drinking. Or insert as a comment if you are requested to speak after a generous libation. E.G. 'I am not saying that I am drunk and to prove it I wish to give you a literary definition of a drunken man. A drunken man is like…drowns him.'
In the play. *Sir Toby has arrived on the scene, drunk as usual. This prompts Olivia to ask the clown for a definition of a drunkard.*

Character, drunkard, symptoms and effects - … drunkenness is his best virtue…
" … drunkenness is his best virtue, for he will be swine drunk, and in his sleep he does little harm, save to his bed clothes about him." (AWEW.4.3)
Define a drunkard. See also entries on wine and its effects *** 'Opinion, your

op. on specific man, bad in himself and worse when drunk - … when he is best, he is a little worse than a man and when he is worst, he is little better than a beast.'
In the play. *Believing his capturers to be the enemy, Parolles, to save his own skin, does not hesitate to badmouth Bertram, his friend and protector.*

Character, dull but honest - … his wits are not so blunt as, God help, I would desire they were…
"…his wits are not so blunt as, God help, I would desire they were; but, in faith, honest as the skin between his brows." (MAAN.3.5)
Mildly ironic definition of a simple but honest man, 'honest as the skin between his brows'.
In the play. *Constable Dogberry introduces officer Verges to Leonatus.*

Character, evil and beyond description - … For mischiefs manifold and sorceries terrible to enter human hearing.
"…This damn'd witch Sycorax,
For mischiefs manifold and sorceries terrible
To enter human hearing" (TEM.1.2)
Ironic remark, e.g. 'He is a man for mischief manifold… hearing'.
In the play. *Prospero reminds spirit Ariel that he, Prospero, freed him from the clutches of the witch Sycorax, mother of Caliban.*

Character, evil c. in a woman worse than in an enemy – Proper deformity seems not in the fiend so horrid as in woman.
"Proper deformity seems not in the fiend
So horrid as in woman." (KL.4.2)
Bad attitude and character showing even more in a woman.
In the play. *Albany discovers the evil in his wife Goneril.*

Character, evil, totally and absurdly e. – if one good deed in all my life I did, I do repent it from my very soul.
"If one good deed in all my life I did, I do repent it from my very soul." (TA.5.3)
An example of utter evil, or attribute such probable behavior or attitude to a profoundly evil person.
In the play. *The evil Aaron has been condemned to death, remorseless to the end.*

Character, excellent person and one in a thousand – we may pick a thousand salads ere we light on such another herb.
"... we may pick a thousand salads, ere we light on such another herb." (AWEW.4.5)
Change to 'I may pick a thousand salads before I light on such another herb'. It can be an original answer to the question 'Do you like me?' Words of commendation, for example, for someone leaving a position to assume another.
In the play. *Lafeu extols the virtues of Helena who at this moment is still thought as dead.*

Character, false or unbelievable – there's no more faith in thee than in a stewed prune.
"There's no more faith in thee than in a stewed prune; nor no more truth in thee than in a drawn fox" (KHIV.p1.3.3)
Change 'thee' to 'him' or 'her' as applicable.
In the play. *Falstaff accuses the innocent keeper of a tavern in Eastcheap to have stolen from him.*

Character, false, cunning – Alencon! that notorious Machiavel!
"Alencon! that notorious Machiavel!" (KHVI.p1.5.4)
Change 'Alencon' to applicable name.
In the play. *York's comment after Joan of Arc said she is pregnant with Alencon's child.*

Character, false, cunning, shifting and perverse – I can smile and murder whiles I smile.
"Why, I can smile, and murder whiles I smile,
And cry 'Content' to that which grieves my heart,
And wet my cheeks with artificial tears,
And frame my face to all occasions.
…
I can add colours to the chameleon,
Change shapes with Proteus for advantages,
And set the murderous Machiavel to school." (KHVI p3.3.2)
Change the sentence to the third person, use the lines in their entirety or extract as needed, e.g. 'He can add colors to the chameleon' or 'He can frame his face to all occasions' etc. See also 'Counterfeit, c. skills – … ghastly looks are at my service, like enforced smiles and both are ready in their offices at any time, to grace my stratagems'
In the play. *Gloucester, the future Richard III, lists in a monologue his own set of political skills.*

Character, faked simplicity – These kind of knaves I know, which in this plainness…
"These kind of knaves I know, which in this plainness
Harbour more craft and more corrupter ends
Than twenty silly ducking observants
That stretch their duties nicely." (KL.2.2)
In the play. *Cornwall does not believe in the simplicity and direct character of Kent.*

Character, fatalistic – We profess ourselves to be the slaves of chance, and flies of every wind that blows.
"… Not any yet;

But as the unthought-on accident is guilty
To what we wildly do, so we profess
Ourselves to be the slaves of chance, and flies
Of every wind that blows". (WT.4.3)
Evasive answer to 'what are your plans?' if you don't have any or have not made any yet or do not want to disclose them. 'I profess myself to be the slave of chance and fly of every wind that blows'. Equally, quote without modifications to explain your fatalistic attitude.
In the play. *Camillo asks Florizel where he plans to go. Florizel replies, then Camillo proposes to Florizel and bride-to-be Perdita to join him in his return journey to Sicilia.*

Character, funny c. - I warrant thou art a merry fellow.
"I warrant thou art a merry fellow." (TN.3.1)
Comment or answer to him who gave a good joke or reply.
In the play. *Viola is impressed by the clown's wit.*

Character, gentle but resolute - ... as gentle as zephyrs blowing below the violet...
"They are as gentle
As zephyrs blowing below the violet,
Not wagging his sweet head; and yet as rough,
Their royal blood enchafed, as the rudest wind,
That by the top doth take the mountain pine,
And make him stoop to the vale" (CYM.4.1)
See also 'Honor, meaning of h. and standing up when h. is at stake'. For the image of shaken mountain pines see also 'Impossibility to soften a hard heart - You may as well forbid the mountain pines...'

In the play. *Belarius comments on the characters of adopted sons Guiderius and Arviragus.*

Character, gentlemanly and kind - A kinder gentleman treads not the earth.
"A kinder gentleman treads not the earth." (MOV.2.8)
In the play. *Salarino to Solanio commenting on Antonio.*

Character, good overwhelming evil - I must not think there are evils enow to darken all his goodness…
"I must not think there are
Evils enow to darken all his goodness:
His faults in him seem as the spots of heaven,
More fiery by night's blackness" (AC.1.4)
Come to the defense of a friend
In the play. *In Rome, Lepidus rebuts Octavian's negative comments on Antony.*

Character, greedy and ambitious - no man's pie is freed from his ambitious fingers.
"The devil speed him! no man's pie is freed
From his ambitious fingers." (KHVIII.1.1)
Describe or warn against an ambitious person. 'No man's pie is freed…fingers.'
In the play. *Buckingham referring to Cardinal Wolsey who organized the meeting in France between Henry VIII and Francis I*

Character, habit can change c. - for use almost can change the stamp of nature and either quell the devil, or throw him out with wondrous potency.
"For use almost can change the stamp of nature,
And either quell the devil, or throw him out
With wondrous potency." (H.3.4)

Indicate that you can change and acquire good habits. Or she can (change habits) if she says that she cannot. Or counteract the opposition to a person you like when others say that he/she cannot change his/her character. See also 'Habit, h. formation – How use doth breed a habit in a man!'
In the play. *Hamlet upbraids his mother Gertrude and prompts her not to have anything to do with her husband Claudius. She married Claudius without knowing that he had killed Hamlet's father, former king of Denmark.*

Character, hot and ebullient - As full of spirits as the month of May and gorgeous as the sun at midsummer.
"As full of spirits as the month of May,
And gorgeous as the sun at midsummer,
Wanton as youthful goats, wild as young bulls" (KHIV.p1.4.1)
Moderate enthusiasm, 'Hey, you are as full of spirits as the month of May'.
In the play. *Vernon's account of the Prince of Wales. Vernon is with rebels.*

Character, incompatibility of c. - No contraries hold more antipathy than I and such a knave.
"No contraries hold more antipathy Than I and such a knave." (KL.2.2)
In the play. *Kent speaking of the cowardly and rascally Oswald.*

Character, judgment of c. incorrect - I am sorry that with better heed and judgment I had not quoted him
"I am sorry that with better heed and judgment
I had not quoted him" (H.2.1)
When you assumed that the person you assigned a task to perform showed lack of judgment.
In the play. *Polonius referring to Hamlet and to Hamlet's passion for Ophelia. But that is not the cause for Hamlet's apparently erratic behavior.*

Character, kind, perhaps too much - ... it is too full o' the milk of human kindness...
"... yet do I fear thy nature;
It is too full o' the milk of human kindness
To catch the nearest way:" (M.1.5)
You can say 'I am full of the milk of human kindness' as a way of defining yourself, or as a comment to 'Oh you are so kind' to add a light ironic touch and elegantly soften the impact of the compliment or mild flattery.
In the play. *Lady Macbeth has received a letter from Macbeth where he tells her that the witches have predicted that he will be king. Lady Macbeth is concerned that her husband may not have enough ambition to achieve the goal 'the nearest way'.*

Character, knowledge of c. and how to get to him - you know the very road into his kindness.
"You know the very road into his kindness." (COR.5.1)
Ask a friend to interpose, recommend you or introduce to a powerful higher up.
In the play. *Brutus acknowledges that Menenius knows how to handle Coriolanus, though it will not prove so*

Character, liar - ... he will lie, sir, with such volubility, that you would think truth were a fool.
"... he will lie, sir, with such volubility, that you would think truth were a fool" (AWEW.3.7)
Define a habitual liar. See also entries for 'Liar' and 'Insult, liar'.
In the play. *Believing his capturers to be the enemy, Parolles, to save his own skin, does not hesitate to badmouth Bertram, his friend and protector. Besides of lying, Parolles also accuses him of drunkenness. See 'Character, drunkard,*

symptoms and effects - ... drunkenness is his best virtue.'

Character, liar but amusing - ... I love to hear him lie and I will use him for my minstrelsy.
"But, I protest, I love to hear him lie
And I will use him for my minstrelsy.'
(LLL.1.1)
In the play. *Ferdinand's account of Armado, a Spanish character that Ferdinand entertains for amusement.*

Character, like mother like sons - ...the raven doth not hatch a lark.
"...the raven doth not hatch a lark"
(TA.2.3)
Can apply to next of kin or to political protégé.
In the play. *Lavinia cannot ask for pity of Tamora's sons. The equally evil Tamora is the raven who cannot hatch a lark.*

Character, likes and dislikes, a temperate man immune to mass media and events - rather rejoicing to see another merry...
DUKE (to Escalus) What pleasures was he given to?
ESCALUS. Rather rejoicing to see another merry, than merry at anything that professed to make him rejoice: a gentleman of all temperance"
(MFM.3.2)
Answer to 'What do you like?' E.G. 'I rather rejoice at seeing another merry than merry at anything that professes to make me rejoice.'
In the play. *The Duke (in disguise) prompts Escalus to express an opinion about himself (the Duke that is).*

Character, malicious with everyone - ...the king... is not quite exempt from envious malice of thy swelling heart.
"The king, thy sovereign, is not quite exempt

From envious malice of thy swelling heart. ."* (KHVI.p1.3.1)
Defend yourself against an accusation, 'this is but the envious malice...heart'. Or warn others, e.g. '(No one) is quite exempt...heart'.
In the play. *Winchester and Gloucester are at each other heels. Here Gloucester accuses Winchester.*

Character, man of good c. - ... he is of noble strain, of approved valour, and confirmed honesty.
"... he is of noble strain, of approved valour, and confirmed honesty."
(MAAN.2.1)
When asked about your opinion of a person whom you would recommend (or of a good friend).
In the play. *Don Pedro, in conversation with Hero suggests that the two of them may concoct a plan whereby Beatrice and Benedick will fall in love with each other. Don Pedro refers the remark to Benedick.*

Character, man with a jovial disposition - ... a merrier man, within the limit of becoming mirth, I never spent an hour's talk withal.
"...a merrier man,
Within the limit of becoming mirth,
I never spent an hour's talk withal"
(LLL.2.1)
Use also to define yourself, e.g. 'I am a merry man, within the limit of becoming mirth'.
In the play. *Rosaline characterizes Biron.*

Character, melancholy - He did incline to sadness, and oft-times not knowing why.
"He did incline to sadness, and oft-times
Not knowing why." (CYM.1.4)
See also "Melancholy, personal m. explained - ... it is a melancholy of mine own, compounded of many simples...'

In the play. *Imogen refers to the character of her husband Leonatus.*

Character, mellowed by time - ... mellow'd by the stealing hours of time.
"…mellow'd by the stealing hours of time" (RIII.3.7)
When you wish to characterize yourself as mellow but not a wash-out – especially if you are reminded of some rash, unexpected or violent episodes of yours, e.g. 'I have been mellowed…time'.
In the play. *Richard, hypocritically pretends that he endorses the young legitimate heir to the royal throne, King Edward's son. Instead he is already planning for his murder. The complete lines are:*
"The royal tree hath left us royal fruit,
Which, mellow'd by the stealing hours of time,
Will well become the seat of majesty."

Character, merciless - ... there is no more mercy in him than there is milk in a male tiger.
"... there is no more mercy in him than there is milk in a male tiger" (COR.5.4)
Describe a hard character. See also 'Expression, vinegary, sour.'
In the play. *Menenius did not succeed in changing Coriolanus' mind and comments accordingly.*

Character, modest but strong and reliable - I cannot gasp out my eloquence, nor I have no cunning in protestation…
"I cannot gasp out my eloquence, nor I have no cunning in protestation: only downright oaths, which I never use till urged, nor never break for urging." (KHV.5.2)
A claim of modesty.
In the play. *Henry V modestly woos Kathryn of France.*

Character, must always be the first in starting something - ... For he will never follow any thing that other men begin.
"... For he will never follow any thing That other men begin." (JC.2.1)
In the play. *Brutus' opinion of Cicero.*

Character, noble and naïve - ... whose nature is so far from doing harms that he suspects none…
"…a brother noble,
Whose nature is so far from doing harms,
That he suspects none: on whose foolish honesty
My practises ride easy!" (KL.1.2)
Change 'whose' to 'my' and 'he' to 'I' and reply with tongue in cheek when you are questioned if you believe a statement or a person.
In the play. *Evil brother Edmund's comment on Edgar.*

Character, noble though poor, of noble lineage - though wayward fortune did malign my state...
"Though wayward fortune did malign my state,
My derivation was from ancestors Who stood equivalent with mighty kings." (PER.5.1)
Express that you were not always in such as bad a predicament as you are now in.
In the play. *In Mytilene, they decide to see if Marina can get Pericles to speak. She starts singing and he seems somewhat revived. She is actually Pericle's daughter, separated from him at birth after a shipwreck.*

Character, not afraid of taking chances - I have set my life upon a cast and I will stand the hazard of the die.
"I have set my life upon a cast,
And I will stand the hazard of the die." (KRIII.5.4)

When you are asked why you are pursuing a certain course when the outcome is uncertain. See also 'Determination, d. to face the inevitable - I am tied to the stake, and I must stand the course'. – 'Anxious while waiting for her answer – thus ready for the way of life or death I wait the sharpest blow.' – 'Decimation - … by the hazard of the spotted die let die the spotted.' – 'Risks, not afraid to take r. - I do not set my life in a pin's fee.' *** 'Determination, d. to overcome obstacles - … that is a step on which I must fall down, or else o'er-leap…'

In the play. *At Bosworth Field Richard III has remained without a horse. Catesby offers to help Richard escape but Richard refuses with these words and calls Catesby 'Slave'. This is unfair to Catesby as just before this expostulation Richard had cried out the famous line:*

A horse, a horse, my kingdom for a horse!

Character, not easily moved to compassion - … it is no little thing to make mine eyes to sweat compassion.
"… it is no little thing to make
Mine eyes to sweat compassion."
(COR.5.3)
State that you are not moved easily.
In the play. *Coriolanus shares his emotions with Aufidius who witnessed the meeting of Coriolanus with wife and mother.*

Character, not very bright – … his wit is as thick as Tewksbury mustard.
"…his wit is as thick as Tewksbury mustard!" (KHIVp2.2.4)
A good put down.
In the play. *Falstaff's opinion of Poins' intelligence. Tewksbury is a town in Gloucestershire, at the confluence of the rivers Avon and Severn. Tewksbury mustard is horseradish mustard.*

Character, one that always speaks and does not let anyone else put a word in - … keep me company but two years more thou shalt not know the sound of thine own tongue.
LORENZO: … Gratiano never lets me speak
GRATIANO: Well keep me company but two years more
Thou shalt not know the sound of thine own tongue." (MOV.1.1)
When someone complains that you do not let him speak. Use as a graceful self-effacing sentence. 'Keep me company…tongue.'
In the play. *Gratiano gracefully acknowledges that he never stops talking.*

Character, one who pretends to be thought clever by saying nothing - There are a sort of men whose visages…
"There are a sort of men whose visages
Do cream and mantle like a standing pond,
And to a wilful stillness entertain,
With purpose to be dress'd in an opinion
Of wisdom, gravity, profound conceit,
As who should say, "I am sir Oracle,
And when I ope my lips, let no dog bark.
O, my Antonio, I do know of there,
That therefore only are reputed wise
For saying nothing; when, I am very sure
If they should speak, would almost damn those ears
Which (hearing them) would call their brothers fools." (MOV.1.1)
There are characters like these – I met with some - especially in large corporations, '…that therefore are reputed wise for saying nothing'. You can modify the somewhat obscure last line, '… when, if they should speak, would

almost damn those ears that hear them', or leave the line entirely out.
In the play. *Gratiano's describes to Antonio a well define type of conceited person.*

Character, overweight and underfunded - our means are very slender, and your waist is great...
CHIEF JUSTICE: Your means are very slender, and your waist is great
FALSTAFF: I would it were otherwise: I would my means were greater and my waist slenderer.
(KHIVp2.1.2)
Ironic self effacing statement, 'My means are slender and my waist great. I would it were otherwise. I would my means …slenderer'.
In the play. *Falstaff in an exchange with the chief justice.*

Character, passion, c. immune to passion - ... Ere I would say, I would drown myself for the love of a guinea-hen, I would change my humanity with a baboon.
"…Ere I would say, I would drown myself for the love of a guinea-hen, I would change my humanity with a baboon." (OTH.1.3)
In the play. *Iago's opinion of love and passion.*

Character, passion, c. that cannot resist passion - I confess it is my shame to be so fond; but it is not in my virtue to amend it.
"I confess it is my shame to be so fond; but it is not in my virtue to amend it." (OTH.1.3)
In the play. *Roderigo admits to his unruly but irresistible passion for the married Desdemona.*

Character, person who does not keep his promises - ... the sun borrows of the moon, when Diomed keeps his word.

"... the sun borrows of the moon, when Diomed keeps his word."
(TC.5.1)
Change 'Diomed' to the name of the person who habitually does not keep his word.
In the play. *Thersites on Diomedes.*

Character, pompous, an ass - for it will come to pass that every braggart shall be found an ass.
"Who knows himself a braggart,
Let him fear this, for it will come to pass
that every braggart shall be found an ass." (AWEW.4.3)
Explain why you do not want to advertise your merits, '…for it will come to pass…ass'. Or whisper quietly as a comment to a boring and pompous speaker.
In the play. *The pompous and cowardly Parolles has been unmasked and reflects on his own undoing.*

Character, positive assessment – I see virtue in his looks.
"…Harry,
I see virtue in his looks."
(KHIV.p1.2.4)
Mildly ironic answer to the question, 'Can we trust him?' when the party in question is present, e.g. 'I see virtue in his looks'.
In the play. *Falstaff pretends to be King Henry IV scene talking to the Prince of Wales in a mocking scene. The man whose virtue is visible in his looks is Falstaff himself.*

Character, promise of self-reformation - ... that to come hall all be done by the rule.
"Read not my blemishes in the world's report:
I have not kept my square; but that to come
Shall all be done by the rule" (AC.2.3)

See also 'Apologies for past poor behavior - they say best men are moulded out of faults...'
In the play. *Having just married Octavia, Octavian's sister, Antony makes an apology for his past notorious behavior – behavior that, in reality, he does not plan to change. The marriage is purely political.*

Character, proud – ... I can see his pride peep through each part of him...
"I cannot tell
What heaven hath given him,--let some graver eye
Pierce into that; I can see his pride
Peep through each part of him: whence has he that?
If not from hell, the devil is a niggard." (KHVIII.1.1)
Describe an arrogant person.
In the play. *Lord Abergavenny adds his bit to the sketch of Cardinal Wolsey's character.* 'Niggard'='Miser'.

Character, proud, quarrelsome, not worthy of his position - ... as stout and proud as he were lord of all.
"(he is) as stout and proud as he were lord of all
Swears like a ruffian and demean himself
Unlike the ruler of a commonweal." (KHVI p2.1.1)
There are characters in many organizations that fit this description perfectly.
In the play. *Salisbury (of the Cardinal of Winchester).*

Character, quiet but crafty - smooth runs the water where the brook is deep.
"Smooth runs the water where the brook is deep
And in his simple show he harbours treason." (KHVI p2.3.1)
In the play. *Q. Margaret tries to portray Gloucester as traitorous to the king, when he is not. To further make her point she says later,* "Is he a lamb? his skin is surely lent him,
For he's inclined as is the ravenous wolf.
Who cannot steal a shape that means deceit?"

Character, radical change in c. - presume not that I am the thing I was.
"Presume not that I am the thing I was;
For God doth know, so shall the world perceive,
That I have turn'd away my former self" (KHIV.p2.5.5)
See also 'Reform, determination to r. – to mock the expectations of the world'
In the play. *Henry V tells Falstaff that he (Falstaff) will be banished as Henry V's character has changed.*

Character, reformed - consideration, like an angel came and whipp'd the offending Adam out of him.
"Consideration, like an angel came,
And whipp'd the offending Adam out of him
Leaving his body as a paradise,
To envelop and contain celestial spirits" (KHV.1.1)
Make a positive statement about a person who improved himself notwithstanding murky precedents. If referring to yourself, change to 'Consideration, like an angel… out of me.' When she brings out your earlier faults and/or shortcomings. See also 'Reform, determination to r. – to mock the expectations of the world'
In the play. *The Archbishop of Canterbury describes to the Bishop of Ely the astounding reformation of Henry V, who, when Prince of Wales preferred wine, women and song to the duties of a king-to-be.*

Character, rough but gentle – … he is not the flower of courtesy but, I'll warrant him, as gentle as a lamb.
"…he is not the flower of courtesy, but, I'll warrant him, as gentle as a lamb" (RJ.2.5)
In the play. *The Nurse gives to Juliet her first impression of Romeo.*

Character, self-commitment to radical change and improvements in c. – Yet herein will I imitate the sun…
"Yet herein will I imitate the sun,
Who doth permit the base contagious clouds
To smother up his beauty from the world,
That, when he please again to be himself,
Being wanted, he may be wonder'd at,
By breaking through the foul and ugly mists
Of vapours, that did seem to strangle him." (KHIV p1.1.2)
Use as a statement of intent when you plan a radical change in policy, e.g., 'I will imitate the sun and break through the foul and ugly mists of vapours, that did seem to strangle him.' See also "Reform, determination to r. – to mock the expectations of the world'.
In the play. *Prince Henry's mission statement.*

Character, self-declared lighthearted – …I thank it, poor fool, it keeps on the windy side of care.
DON PEDRO. In faith my lady, you have a merry heart.
BEATRICE. Yea, my lord; I thank it, poor fool, it keeps on the windy side of care." (MAAN.2.1)
Alternate way to indicate that you take things lightheartedly. 'My heart keeps on the windy side of care.'
In the play. *Beatrice prompts Hero to say something or if not at least to kiss Claudio, now that Leonato has consented to their marriage.*

Don Pedro comments on Beatrice's words and suggestion.

Character, self-declared lighthearted – I was born to speak all mirth, and no matter.
"I was born to speak all mirth, and no matter." (MAAN.2.1)
Answer in modesty to a remark about your sense of humor.
In the play. *Beatrice and Don Pedro exchange some banter. At one point Don Pedro asks Beatrice if she would have him, she says no on the ground that he, Don Pedro, is too expensive. She then tones down the comment by suggesting that it was a joke (mirth).*

Character, self-defined, straight, direct and who does not like any of the company around him - … 'tis my occupation to be plain…
"…'tis my occupation to be plain
I have seen better faces in my times
Than stands on any shoulder that I see
Before me at this instant." (KL.2.2)
Use ''tis my occupation to be plain' as an opening or as a mission statement. Or answer the question, 'Do you like these people?' when you don't.
In the play. *Kent to Cornwall who asked Kent what is the issue with Oswald, a pawn of the wicked sisters.*

Character, self-loathing - … Apemantus, that few things loves better than to abhor himself.
"... Apemantus, that few things loves better
Than to abhor himself" (TOA.1.1)
In the play. *The freeloader poet lists to the equally freeloading painter the characters who frequent Timon's house, including the pessimistic, cantankerous but least corrupt Apemantus.*

Character, signs of destructive c. clear from the beginning - Teeth hadst thou in thy head when thou wast

born, to signify thou camest to bite the world.
"Teeth hadst thou in thy head when thou wast born,
To signify thou camest to bite the world" (KHVI.p3.5.6)
If describing a third party change 'hadst thou' to 'had he', 'thy' to 'his' and 'thou camest' to 'he came'.
In the play. *The soon to be murdered King Henry VI confronts Richard of Gloucester (later Richard III)*

Character, similarity between parent and offspring - ... the raven doth not hatch the lark.
" 'T is true, the raven doth not hatch the lark." (TA.2.3)
Alternative to 'like parent, like offspring'.
In the play. *Lavinia pleads in vain for her life with Demetrius, by suggesting that though their mother is a monster, her sons do not have necessarily to be so. The plea is not successful. In the comparison the raven (bad) does not hatch a lark (good).*

Character, sincerity of c. advocated – Men should be what they seem; or those that be not, would they might seem none!
"Men should be what they seem; Or those that be not, would they might seem none!" (OTH.3.3)
In the play. *Iago pretends to be honest with Othello.*

Character, skirt chaser - He woos both high and low, both rich and poor...
"He woos both high and low, both rich and poor,
Both young and old, one with another." (MWW.2.1)
Define a skirt chaser
In the play. *Pistol shares with Mrs. Ford his knowledge of Falstaff's habits.*

Character, skirt chaser, anything that moves - ... he would mouth with a beggar, though she smelt brown bread and garlic.
...I say to thee, he would mouth with a beggar, though she smelt brown bread and garlic" (MFM.3.2)
In the play. *Not recognizing the disguise, Lucio makes extravagant comments on the Duke to the Duke himself.*

Character, slanderer, habitual slanderer - a slave whose gall coins slanders like a mint.
"A slave whose gall coins slanders like a mint." (TC.1.3)
Describe a gossip monger and a slanderer
In the play. *Thersites is the quintessential complainer among the Greeks and Nestor defines him.*

Character, softness of c. leading to insubordination - ... smooth as oil, soft as young down...
"Which, hath been smooth as oil, soft as young down,
And therefore lost that title of respect
Which the proud soul ne'er pays but to the proud." (KHIV p1.1.3)
Use as a preamble to show why you have been underestimated c- e.g. 'I know, I am as smooth as oil, soft as young down, and therefore have lost the respect ...proud.'
In the play. *King Henry IV addresses Worcester and others who have proven disobedient.*

Character, steady and ready to face unfriendly reception - ... to the proof, as mountains are for winds...
BAPTISTA. But be thou armed for some unhappy words.
PETRUCHIO. Ay, to the proof, as mountains are for winds,
That shake not, though they blow perpetually." (TOS.2.1)
A statement of your power of endurance. 'I am as mountains are...perpetually.'

In the play. *Baptista warns Petruchio not to expect a friendly reception from Katharina.*

Character, steady c., as a rock - ... he's the rock, the oak not to be wind-shaken.
"The worthy fellow is our general: he's the rock, the oak not to be wind-shaken." (COR.5.2)
Use for praise. "He is the rock…shaken."
In the play. *Two Volscian guards talk with themselves soon after Menenius left. The rock referred to is their general Aufidius.*

Character, straight-forward - I have no gift at all in shrewishness.
"I have no gift at all in shrewishness." (MND.3.2)
Stress your openness and sincerity. See also 'Credentials, sincerity, one tongue'.
In the play. *Helena thinks that everyone is poking fun at her and accuses Hermia of shrewishness.*

Character, strong, unable to weep - I am a soldier, and unapt to weep, or to exclaim on fortune's fickleness.
"I am a soldier, and unapt to weep, Or to exclaim on fortune's fickleness." (KHVI.p1.5.3)
Show strength in adversity
In the play. *Reigner to Suffolk who has captured Reigner's daughter.*

Character, stubborn - ... and perversely she persevers so.
"Ay, and perversely she persevers so" (TGV.3.2)
Answer to 'Does he (or she) still do it?'
In the play. *The Duke is angry at her daughter Silvia who perseveres in disobeying him.*

Character, sudden c. reformation – ... Never came reformation in a flood...
"Never was such a sudden scholar made;
Never came reformation in a flood,
With such a heady currance, scouring faults"** (KHV.1.1)
Express your surprise at an unexpected change in character of a person you know.
In the play. *Archbishop of Canterbury discusses with the Archbishop of Ely the changes in Henry V's character. 'Heady Currance'='Impetuous Current'*

Character, supercilious - ... you are sick of self-love, Malvolio, and taste with a distempered appetite.
"... you are sick of self-love, Malvolio, and taste with a distempered appetite. To be generous, guiltless and of free disposition, is to take those things for bird-bolts that you deem cannon-bullets" (TN.1.5)
There are characters like Malvolio to whom you can use the line or say 'you take bird-bolts for cannon-bullets'.
In the play. *Olivia tells Malvolio that to become upset at the sallies of the clown is exaggerated and a symptom of superciliousness.*

Character, suspicious c, admitted – ... it is my nature's plague to spy into abuses...
"…it is my nature's plague
To spy into abuses, and oft my jealousy
Shapes faults that are not…" (OTH.3.3)
In the play. *Conversing with Othello, Iago skillfully instills the seeds of jealousy in him, while pretending to be overcautious about accusing Cassio.*

Character, trusting c. – ... Whose nature is so far from doing harms that he suspects none.
"…a brother noble,
Whose nature is so far from doing harms,
That he suspects none" (KL.1.2)

Characterize yourself with tongue in cheek, e.g. 'My nature is so far… I suspect none'.
In the play. *Evil Edmund is plotting against his brother and father.*

Character, transformed dramatically - … nor the exterior nor the inward man resembles that it was.
"…nor the exterior nor the inward man
Resembles that it was." (H.2.2)
In the play. *King Claudius asks Guildenstern and Rosencranz to go and find out the motive of Hamlet's transformation.*

Character, trustworthy - … would not betray the devil to his fellow…
"At no time broke my faith, would not betray
The devil to his fellow and delight
No less in truth than life" (M.4.3)
Define yourself. Answer to question 'What can you tell me about yourself?' or 'Can I trust you?'
In the play. *Malcolm tests Macduff's reactions by first claiming to be totally rotten – then he corrects himself and declares his true nature.*

Character, truthful and plain self-described - … alas, it is my vice, my fault, whiles others fish with craft for great opinion…
"… alas, it is my vice, my fault:
Whiles others fish with craft for great opinion,
I with great truth catch mere simplicity;
Whilst some with cunning gild their copper crowns,
With truth and plainness I do wear mine bare." (TC.4.4)
In the play. *Troilus describes his own character to the departing Cressida, meaning that he will be true to her.*

Character, unable to flatter, pretend and deceive - Because I cannot flatter and speak fair…
"Because I cannot flatter and speak fair,
Smile in men's faces, smooth, deceive and cog,
Duck with French nods and apish courtesy,
I must be held a rancorous enemy.
Cannot a plain man live and think no harm,
But thus his simple truth must be abused
By silken, sly, insinuating Jacks?" (KRIII.1.3)
Define yourself. "I cannot flatter …apish courtesy, but I am not an enemy'. See also 'Flattery, tools of f. - …sweet words, low-crooked court'sies and base spaniel-fawning' *** 'Habit, not yet used to flattery and submission – … hardly yet have learn'd to insinuate, flatter, bow, and bend my limbs'.
In the play. *Richard III pretends that it is Queen Elizabeth and her allies who wrongly consider him an enemy. In fact he is their enemy and is set on destroying them.*

Character, unable to say 'no' to women - … whom ne'er the word of 'No' woman heard speak.
"…our courteous Antony,
Whom ne'er the word of 'No' woman heard speak" (AC.2.2)
Answer to 'will you do this for me?' E.G. 'Of course, never the word 'No' woman herd me speak'. See also 'Women, requests from w. bound to be gratified - … when maidens sue, men give like gods; but when they weep and kneel…'
In the play. *Enobarbus explains to Agrippa how Cleopatra ensnared Antony in Egypt.*

Character, uncouth and discourteous - The elephant hath joints, but none for courtesy...
"The elephant hath joints, but none for courtesy: his legs are legs for necessity, not for flexure." (TC.2.3)
In the play. *Ulysses makes a remark about Achilles.*

Character, uncouth, uncoordinated, confused – ... he hath the joint of every thing; but every thing so out of joint...
"... he hath the joint of every thing; but every thing so out of joint, that he is a gouty Briareus, many hands and no use; or purblind Argus, all eyes and no sight." (TC.1.2)
Describe a man fitting this profile.
In the play. *Alexander, a servant, tells Cressida what he thinks of Ajax. Briareus was a mythical giant with one hundred hands. Argus was a mythical dog assigned to guard Io. In turn Io was a young girl loved by Jupiter - he turned her into a cow so that he could sneak her into the Olympus without upsetting his jealous wife Hera.*

Character, unfriendly – ... nothing but himself which looks like man is friendly with him.
"For he is set so only to himself
That nothing but himself which looks like man
Is friendly with him" (TOA.5.1)
In the play. *Flavius, Timon's servant, explains to the poet and the painter that they will not get a friendly reception from Timon.*

Character, unrepentant - ... I have done a thousand dreadful things as willingly as one would kill a fly...
"...I have done a thousand dreadful things
As willingly as one would kill a fly,
And nothing grieves me heartily indeed
But that I cannot do ten thousand more." (TA.5.1)
In the play. *The unrepentant and evil Aaron prepares to die with no regret for his sociopathic past.*

Character, unshakable - ... I do know but one that unassailable holds on his rank...
"And men are flesh and blood, and apprehensive;
Yet in the number I do know but one
That unassailable holds on his rank,
Unshaked of motion: and that I am he," (JC.3.1)
Rhetorical answer to pressures to change your mind. See also 'Credentials, establishing your c. - I am as constant as the northern star...'
In the play. *Caesar confirms to Brutus that he will not relent and have Publius Cimber banished.*

Character, untruthful and dishonest - ...there's no room for faith, truth, nor honesty in this bosom of thine.
"... there's no room for faith, truth, nor honesty in this bosom of thine; it is all filled up with guts and midriff." (KHIV.p1.3.3)
Use as an insult to a fat and dishonest person or change 'in this bosom of thine' to 'in that bosom of his' as applicable.
In the play. *The Prince of Wales upbraids Falstaff. 'Midriff' stands for 'diaphragm'.*

Character, vane, arrival of a vane c. - ... here he comes, swelling like a turkey-cock.
"Why, here he comes, swelling like a turkey-cock" (KHV.5.1)
In the play. *Captain Gower announces to Fluellen the arrival of Pistol.*

Character, vane, a turkey-cock - contemplation makes a rare turkey-cock of him...

"Contemplation makes a rare turkey-cock of him; how he jets under his advanced plumes!" (TN.2.5)
Describe a vane person.
In the play. *Malvolio believes that Olivia is in love with him but it was a joke organized by Maria. Fabian observes Malvolio's behavior.*

Character, vane, likes his own speech- ... One whom the music of his own vain tongue doth ravish like enchanting harmony.
"One whom the music of his own vain tongue
Doth ravish like enchanting harmony" (LLL.1.1)
Apply to a suitable character, e.g. 'he is one whom…harmony'.
In the play. *The King of Navarre speaks of the pompous and wordy Armado.*

Character, villainous with an Oscar for villainy - ... he hath out-villained villainy so far, that the rarity redeems him.
"He hath out-villained villainy so far, that the rarity redeems him." (AWEW.4.3)
Define a particularly obnoxious person.
In the play. *Both Bertram and the first lord could listen in to Parolles' performance when under pressure and to the lies he invented to save his skin. The first lord defines Parolles.*

Character, violent – ...the foot that leaves the print of blood.
"… nor attend the foot
That leaves the print of blood." (KJ.4.3)
Ironic comment, 'You have the foot that leaves the print of blood'.
In the play. *Salisbury tells Faulconbridge that he will not follow the King after the murder of young Prince Arthur.*

Character, wild - for he is given to sports, to wildness and much company
"... for he is given
To sports, to wildness and much company." (JC.2.1)
In the play. *Brutus' opinion of Antony.*

Character, wishing for a poetical c. – Truly, I would the gods had made thee poetical.
"Truly, I would the gods had made thee poetical." (AYLI.3.3)
In the play. *Touchstone is courting Audrey but she does not understand his sallies.*

Character, with a sense of humor - ... the world's large tongue proclaims you for a man replete with mocks.
"…the world's large tongue
Proclaims you for a man replete with mocks." (LLL.5.2)
A way out when you cannot immediately come up with a retort to a witticism of which you are subject. See also, 'Insult, lips to rot off'
In the play. *Rosaline addresses the witty Biron, who is in love with her.*

Character, woman, ambitious w. - ... being a woman, I will not slack to play my part in Fortune's pageant.
"Were I a man, a duke, and next of blood,
I would remove these tedious stumbling blocks,
And smooth my way upon their headless necks:
And, being a woman, I will not slack
To play my part in Fortune's pageant." (KHVI.p2.1.2)
Possible woman's answer to the question 'What is your ambition?' '…Being a woman, I will not slack… pageant.' Or ironically address those who oppose your plans, 'I will remove your tedious stumbling blocks and smooth my way upon your headless necks'.
In the play. *The Duchess of Gloucester reflects on her ambition after her husband refuses to go along with her treacherous plans.*

Character, wordy - ... what a spendthrift is he of his tongue!
"Fie, what a spendthrift is he of his tongue!" (TEM.2.1)
In the play. *Antonio comments on Gonzalo.*

Characters, of all sorts - ... Nature hath framed strange fellows in her time...
"Nature hath framed strange fellows in her time:
Some that will evermore peep through their eyes
And laugh like parrots at a bag-piper,
And other of such vinegar aspect
That they'll not show their teeth in way of smile,
Though Nestor swear the jest be laughable." (MOV.1.1)
Particularly applicable (first line), after an odd character has just left the meeting. In the play. *Salarino tries to cheer up the constitutionally sad Antonio whom he just met along the streets of Venice. Nestor was the wise man of the Greeks at Troy, whose judgment was universally trusted.*

Characters, similarity of c. - ... both of you are birds of selfsame feather.
"For both of you are birds of selfsame feather." (KHVI.p3.3.3)
Emphasize the concomitance of negative traits. You may change to 'Both of them are birds of selfsame feather'. In more modern terms try also 'They are two buttocks of the same bum.' Though never found in any of his plays, the definition has a certain Shakespearean legitimacy. See also 'Growing up together - ... Like to a double cherry, seeming parted, but yet an union in partition' - 'Similarity between two people, twins - An apple cleft in two is not more twin than these two creatures.'
In the play. *At the court of French King Louis XI, Margaret compares the Warwick, (who is present), to the absent Edward IV, both being capable of 'sly conveyance' and 'false love'.*

Characters, similarity of c. – ... in companions...there must be needs a like proportion of lineaments...
"...in companions
That do converse and waste the time together,
Whose souls do bear an equal yoke Of love,
There must be needs a like proportion Of lineaments, of manners and of spirit" (MOV.3.4)
In the play. *Portia will help Antonio as he is Bassanio's (her husband) friend considering the assumed affinity of character.*

Characters, similarity of c. - ... the weight of a hair will turn the scales between their avoirdupois.
"...the weight of a hair will turn the scales between their avoirdupois." (KHIV p2.2.4)
In the play. *According to Falstaff there is little difference between the Prince of Wales and Poins. 'Avoirdupois' is a French form for 'weight'*

Characters, similarity of c. - ... you weigh equally; a feather will turn the scale.
"... you weigh equally; a feather will turn the scale." (MFM.4.2)
In the play. *The prison's provost judges the hangman Abhorson and the bawd Pompey to be equals in the scale of ethical values.*

Chase, enjoyment greater in the chase - All things that are, are with more spirit chased than enjoyed.
"... All things that are,
Are with more spirit chased than enjoyed." (MOV.2.6)
You may not want to tell her this but it is a fact of life. And you may use this very fact of life, perhaps, to explain a certain lack of enthusiasm or zest on your part as the relationship unfolds.

In the play. *Gratiano and Salarino converse while waiting for Lorenzo. The comparison refers to love pursued versus love conquered. See 'Dinner, not hungry after dinner'.*

Chastity, c. in men not to be expected - I will find you twenty lascivious turtles, ere one chaste man.
"I will find you twenty lascivious turtles, ere one chaste man." (MWW.2.1)
Should your philandering ever be brought against you or should you suspect an alleged righteousness of someone you do not trust.
In the play. *Mrs. Ford shares with Mrs. Page her opinion on men.*

Chastity, effects of enforced c. - the moon, methinks, looks with watery eye…
"The moon, methinks, looks with watery eye,
And when she weeps, weeps every little flower,
Lamenting some enforced chastity." (MND.3.1)
Inducement to love. See also entries for 'Abstinence' and 'Virginity'
In the play. *Titania expresses poetically her passion for Bottom.*

Chastity, supreme c. - … Chaste as the icicle that's curdled by the frost from purest snow.
"The moon of Rome; chaste as the icicle,
That's curdled by the frost from purest snow." (COR.5.3)
If applicable, use as answer to the question, "What type of girl is she?"
In the play. *The lady referred to is Valeria, friend of Virgilia, Coriolanus' wife.*

Cheek, wishing to be o a glove to fit her hand to touch her c. … o, that I were a glove upon that hand…
"See, how she leans her cheek upon her hand!
O, that I were a glove upon that hand, That I may touch her cheek!" (RJ.2.2)
Be ready with these lines when she leans her head on her hand. Usable for a note on a card.
In the play. *Romeo has sneaked into Juliet's garden and she appears at her window, pensive.*

Cheeks and eyes as objects of compliment - … such war of white and red within her cheeks.
"Such war of white and red within her cheeks!
What stars do spangle heaven with such beauty,
As those two eyes become that heavenly face?" (TOS.4.5)
Change 'her cheeks' to 'your cheeks' and 'that heavenly' to 'your heavenly'. Usable for a note on a card.
In the play. *Petruchio pretends that the oncoming Vincentio is a woman endowed with the graces expressed by these lines. The idea is to have Katharina agree with Petruchio that Vincentio is actually a woman – the agreement representing her will finally tamed to do always her husband's bidding, whatever it may be.*

Cheeks and hands - … this cheek to bathe my lips upon… this hand, whose touch… would force the feeler to an oath of loyalty… this object which takes prisoner the wild motion of mine eye.
"…this cheek
To bathe my lips upon; this hand, whose touch,
Whose every touch, would force the feeler's soul
To the oath of loyalty; this object, which
Takes prisoner the wild motion of mine eye,
Fixing it only here." (CYM.1.6)

Use in its entirety or select sections, e.g. 'You take prisoner the wild motion of mine eye, fixing it only on you.' or 'This cheek to bathe my lips upon' etc.
In the play. *The perfidious Iachimo is trying unsuccessfully to seduce the beautiful and virtuous Imogen.*

Cheeks, c. becoming pale - ... Their cheeks are paper.
"Look ye, how they change!
Their cheeks are paper." (HV.2.2)
In the play. *Reaction of 3 traitors in the train of Henry V when they read the evidence of their own treachery.*

Cheeks, their brightness - the brightness of her cheek would shame those stars...
"The brightness of her cheek would shame those stars,
As daylight doth lamp; her eyes in heaven
Would through the airy region stream so bright,
That birds would sing, and think it were not night. (RJ.2.2)
Change 'her' to 'you' when one to one. Lay it thick and try, "I can say of you what Romeo said of Juliet when he saw her in her garden, ...the brightness of her cheek...think it were not night."
Are the lady's cheeks not as naturally white as she would like them to be? Does she apply make up? Ovid suggests that her make-up process should not be watched by anyone. 'So while you are at your parlor let us think you are asleep; it is more fitting that you should be seen only when the last touch has been applied. Why must I know the cause of the whiteness of your cheeks? Close your chamber door: why show the unfinished work? There is much that it befits men not to know; most of your doings would offend, did you not hide them within.' (AOL.3)

In the play. *Romeo sees Juliet at her balcony while he is down in her garden.*

Cheer up – ... cast thy nighted colour off and let thine eye look like a friend on Denmark.
"Good Hamlet, cast thy nighted colour off,
And let thine eye look like a friend on Denmark." (H.1.2)
In the play. *The Queen to the sullen Hamlet.*

Cheer up - Cheer your heart, be you not troubled with the time...
"... Cheer your heart;
Be you not troubled with the time, which drives
O'er your content these strong necessities;
But let determined things to destiny
Hold unbewail'd their way" (AC.3.6)
In the play. *Octavian to sister Octavia, who, abandoned by husband Antony returns somewhat dejected to Rome.*

Cheer up – clear up, fair queen, that cloudy countenance.
"Clear up, fair queen, that cloudy countenance." (TA.1.1)
An exhortation to lift the spirit of the lady you are addressing. See also 'Expression of sadness misconstrued - My heart is ten times lighter than my looks.' – 'Expression, come on relax'.
In the play. *Saturninus has told Titus Andronicus that he will marry his daughter but secretly he loves Tamora, captured queen of the Goths. He now attempts to cheer Tamora up.*

Cheer up - lay aside life-harming heaviness and entertain a cheerful disposition.
"... lay aside life-harming heaviness
And entertain a cheerful disposition." (KRII.2.2)
In the play. *Bushy tries to lift up the mood of the Queen, sad at the departure of Richard II for*

Ireland. See 'Fear, f. unwarranted - Each substance of a grief hath twenty shadows…'

Cheer up – live a little, comfort a little; cheer thyself a little.
"Live a little, comfort a little; cheer thyself a little." (AYLI.2.6)
Cheer up the audience.
In the play. *Orlando attempts to cheer up the starving and tired Adam.*

Cheer-up - … make not your thoughts your prisons.
"…Therefore be cheer'd;
Make not your thoughts your prisons" (AC.5.2)
In the play. *Octavian reassures Cleopatra that she will be well treated in Rome.*

Cheer up – Unknit that sorrow-wreathen knot.
" …unknit that sorrow-wreathen knot." (TA.3.2)
In the play *Titus converts sorrow and rage into an irrepressible desire for revenge.*

Chicken hawk - Show me one scar character'd on thy skin: men's flesh preserved so whole do seldom win.
"Show me one scar character'd on thy skin:
Men's flesh preserved so whole do seldom win" (KHVI.p2.3.1)
In the play. *York accuses Somerset not to have defended the English possessions in France adequately, evidence being that he did not fight any battle and therefore has no scars to show.*

Chivalry, lack of c. towards a woman - If you were men, as men you are in show…
"If you were men, as men you are in show,
You would not use a gentle lady so;
To vow, and swear, and superpraise my parts,
When I am sure you hate me with your hearts." (MND.3.2)
In the play. *Helena upbraids Lysander, Demetrius for poking (unwittingly) fun at her.*

Choice, deprived of c. – I may neither choose whom I would nor refuse whom I dislike.
"…I may neither choose whom I would nor refuse whom I dislike" (MOV.1.2)
Applies perfectly to the current two party system.
In the play. *At Belmont in her palace, Portia comments with servant Nerissa about her (Portia's) dilemma. She must accept to marry him who solves the riddle, hence limiting her choice of a husband.*

Choices, c. dictated by likes and dislikes - … for affection, mistress of passion, sways it to the mood of what it likes or loathes.
"… for affection,
Mistress of passion, sways it to the mood
Of what it likes or loathes" (MOV.4.1)
Explain why a certain event is unexplainable.
In the play. *In an answer to the Duke of Venice Shylock says he wants his bond (a pound of flesh from Antonio) for no other reason that he wants it so.*

Circumstances, adapting course to c. - Let go thy hold when a great wheel runs down a hill…
"Let go thy hold when a great wheel runs down a hill, lest it break thy neck with following it" (KL.2.4)
When the cause is lost and any further effort useless and counterproductive. See also 'Siding with the losing party - …though my reason sits in the wind against me.'
In the play. *The fool to Kent after Kent has just been released from the stocks.*

Circumstances, c. and status, a complete turn-around - A man may

fish with a worm that had eat of a king...
"A man may fish with a worm
That had eat of a king
And eat of the fish
That had fed on that worm." (H.4.3)
Show that life and fortunes always change for anyone. Suggest that nothing in life always remains fixed and impregnable even if it may appear so at some time.
In the play. *The king asks Hamlet where is the body of the slain Polonius. Hamlet sarcastically that Polonius' body is at supper where rather then eating, it is eaten by a worm.*

Circumstances, favored by c. – (standing in) ...the smile of heaven.
"...First, methought
I stood not in the smile of heaven" (KHVIII.2.4)
Use it negatively or positively, i.e. 'I stand in...' or 'I stand not in...' Also part of a salutation, e.g. 'May you all stand in the smile of heaven'.
In the play. *King Henry strives to find rational reasons for divorcing Queen Katherine, including the idea that his first marriage did not sit well with the heavenly powers.*

Circumstances, resignation to current c. - ... what I have I need not to repeat and what I want it boots not to complain.
"...what I have I need not to repeat;
And what I want it boots not to complain" (KRII.3.4)
See also entries for 'Resignation, r. to fate'.
In the play. *The Queen to her ladies in waiting. 'To boot' = 'to avail'*

Citizen, private c. powerless against authority - ... That's a perilous shot out of an elder-gun, that a poor and private displeasure can do against a monarch!"
"... That's a perilous shot out of an elder-gun, that a poor and private displeasure can do against a monarch!" (HV.4.1)
It applies to authority in general
In the play. *Soldier Williams is skeptical about any redress that a low class citizen (or soldier) may have against a monarch. For a comparison of the chances see 'Impossibility, cooling the sun with a fan'.*

Claim, rational reason for c. - ... nor from the dust of old oblivion raked.
"...Nor from the dust of old oblivion raked" (KHV.2.4)
In the play. *Exeter, ambassador to the King of France explains that Henry V's claim to the crown of France has legal roots and it is not based undusted and old pretensions.*

Class, c. consciousness - Strange is it, that our bloods of colours, weight, and heat, pour'd all together...
"Strange is it, that our bloods,
Of colours, weight, and heat, pour'd all together,
Would quite confound distinction, yet stand off
In differences so mighty."
(AWEW.2.3)
Support the idea that class-consciousness is deeply rooted, notwithstanding the many claims to equality. See also 'Opinion, your op. on sociological issues - minimum wage' – 'Equality among men impossible'.
In the play. *A curious (though indirect) plea for equality by the King of France while talking to Helena. All the lords at court have refused her as a wife because she belongs to a lower class.*

Class, c. distinction even in death - When beggars die, there are no comets seen...
"When beggars die, there are no comets seen;
The heavens themselves blaze forth the death of princes" (JC.2.2)

Make it a rallying cry against class distinction. See also 'Invocation, i. against the heavens for their doings - Hung be the heavens with black, yield day to night!'
In the play. *Calpurnia tells husband Caesar that extraordinary and unnatural events (see 'Events, strange and extraordinary and given ominous meaning') signify the impending doom of a VIP.*

Class, c. warfare - Well, I say it was never merry world in England since gentlemen came up.
HOLLAND Well, I say it was never merry world in England since gentlemen came up.
BEVIS. O miserable age! virtue is not regarded in handicrafts-men.
HOLLAND. The nobility think scorn to go in leather aprons
BEVIS. Nay, more, the king's council are no good workmen.
HOLLAND. True; and yet it is said, labour in thy vocation; which is as much to say as, let the magistrates be labouring men; and therefore should we be magistrates.
BEVIS. Thou hast hit it; for there's no better sign of a brave mind than a hard hand. (KHVI.p1.4.2)
In the play. *Two commoners in John Cade's rabble-rebel army comment on class distinction in England.*

Class, poorer c. – ... we, the poorer born whose baser stars do shut us up in wishes.
"...we, the poorer born,
Whose baser stars do shut us up in wishes" (AWEW.1.1)
See also 'Opinion, your op. on sociological issues, minimum wage - O, reason not the need: our basest beggars are in the poorest thing superfluous…'
In the play. *Helena wishes she could follow Bertram whom she loves.*

Classification, c. of man uncertain – That which you are my thoughts cannot transpose.
"That which you are my thoughts cannot transpose" (M.4.3)
In the play. *Malcolm to Macduff.*

Classification, unclassifiable - 'Tis neither here nor there.
"'Tis neither here nor there." (OTH.4.3)
One everyday's sentence descending directly from Shakespeare.
In the play. *Emilia's answer to a question from Desdemona whether itching eyes are a precursor of tears.*

Cleopatra, indirectly equating her to C. – Where's my serpent of old Nile?
"…He's speaking now,
Or murmuring 'Where's my serpent of old Nile?' (AC.1.5)
When you are calling wife or girlfriend at home.
In the play. *Antony being absent in Rome, Cleopatra fantasizes as to whether Antony is thinking of her.*

Climate, northern c. - ... the north, where shivering cold and sickness pines the clime.
"…I toward the north,
Where shivering cold and sickness pines the clime" (KRII.5.1)
In the play. *King Richard leaves for Pomfret Castle in the North and says farewell to the Queen.*

Clock, sound of c. striking hours painful - ... the sound that tells what hour it is…
"…the sound that tells what hour it is
Are clamorous groans, which strike upon my heart,
Which is the bell: so sighs and tears and groans
Show minutes, times, and hours " (KRII.5.5)

In the play. *Richard II, in prison at Pomfret Castle alone with his thoughts.*

Clothing, foul and in need of changing, a bath needed too - I have held some familiarity with fresher clothes...
"I have held some familiarity with fresher clothes, but I am now, sir, muddied in fortune's moat, and smell somewhat strong of her strong displeasure." (AWEW.5.1)
An alternative to explain that you need to change your clothes, for example after a long trip.
In the play. *The humbled Parolles addresses the clown and tries to enlist his help in getting some new clothes.*

Cloud, mutation in c. shapes – That which is now a horse, even with a thought the rack dislimns, and makes it indistinct...
"That which is now a horse, even with a thought
The rack dislimns, and makes it indistinct,
As water is in water" (AC.4.14)
See also 'Illusions, constructs of the mind - Sometimes we see a cloud that's dragonish...'
In the play. *Antony addresses assistant Eros in a roundabout way, comparing himself to a cloud, and will eventually ask Eros to kill him.* 'Rack' = 'Rush of wind, collision'.

Codependence, c. to be avoided - There lives within the very flame of love...
"There lives within the very flame of love
A kind of wick or snuff that will abate it...
For goodness, growing to a plurisy,
Dies in its own too much." (H.4.7)

Excessive attention, excessive acts of kindness could scare her away, considering that this kind of attention cannot be maintained indefinitely.
In the play: *The king wants to inflame Laertes to revenge his father death at the hands of Hamlet. Therefore the king asks Laertes if he loves his father, implying that perhaps he does not.*

Cold, feeling very c. and possible remedy for it - Let me pour in some sack to the Thames water...
"Let me pour in some sack to the Thames water; for my belly's as cold as if I had swallowed snowballs for pills to cool the reins." (MWW.3.5)
Answer to 'Are you cold?' E.G. 'I feel as cold as if I had...reins'.
In the play. *After surviving an escape in a basket of dirty laundry, Falstaff comforts himself with a draft of brandy.*

Collection, c. efforts - Importune him for my moneys; be not ceased with slight denial.
"Importune him for my moneys; be not ceased
With slight denial, nor then silenced when--
'Commend me to your master'--and the cap
Plays in the right hand, thus:" (TOA.2.1)
In the play. *A senator dispatches his servant to collect Timon's debt.*

Comfort, c. arriving too late – ... that comfort comes too late; 't is like a pardon after execution...
"O, my good lord, that comfort comes too late;
'T is like a pardon after execution;
That gentle physic, given in time, had cur'd me;
But now I am past all comforts here, but prayers." (KHVIII.4.2)

Use in a situation where the decision you were expecting has arrived too late.
In the play. *Capucious, ambassador from Emperor Charles V enters with greetings and good words from the king to Katherine.*

Comfort, c. useless - Charm ache with air and agony with words
"Charm ache with air and agony with words" (MAAN.5.1)
In the play. *Leonato's reaction to the words of comfort offered by his brother Antonio*

Comfort, exhortation to see things positively – Put color in thy cheek.
"Put colour in thy cheek." (AC.4.14)
In the play. *A defeated Antony) asks Eros kill by him as Antony cannot find the strength to commit suicide. Seeing his hesitation Antony reassures Eros that it is a good deed.*
Thou strikest not me, 'tis Caesar thou defeat'st.
Put colour in thy cheek.

Comfort, false c. based on rumor – They bring smooth comforts false, worse than true wrongs.
"…From Rumour's tongues
They bring smooth comforts false, worse than true wrongs"
(KHIVp2.1.intro)
In the play. *'They' are the people who repeat the wrong news that the rebels have won rather than lost the battle of Shrewsbury.*

Comfort, recognizing a person for his/her help - Thou art all the comfort the gods will diet me with.
"Thou art all the comfort
The gods will diet me with."
(CYM.3.4)
In the play. *Distressed Imogen thanks her faithful servant Pisanio.*

Command, answer to c. – Anything … that my ability may undergo and nobleness impose.
"Any thing, my lord,
That my ability may undergo
And nobleness impose" (WT.2.3)
Answer to 'Will you do this?'
In the play. *Leontes will finally relent and not kill his queen's baby believing the baby no his. Archidamus answer Leonte's request to expose the baby.*

Command, answer to c. - Your bidding shall I do effectually.
"Your bidding shall I do effectually." (TA.4.4)
In the play. *Aemilius answers a command by Saturninus to deliver a message to Titus A.*

Command, c. given with some arrogance, reaction to - When Caesar says 'do this,' it is perform'd.
"When Caesar says 'do this,' it is perform'd." (JC.1.2)
The reference to Caesar will suggest the tyrannical implication of his/her request or injunction. See also 'Obedience, o. and execution – … Performance shall follow'
In the play. *Antony answers a request from Caesar. Caesar's curious request is that Antony, during some kind of ceremony or procession, touch Calphurnia therefore removing her sterility.*

Command, c. imperative – Do it at once or thy precedent services are all but accidents unpurposed.
"…Do it at once;
Or thy precedent services are all
But accidents unpurposed" (AC.4.14)
In the play. *Antony orders Eros to kill him and Eros understandably hesitates.*

Command, peremptory c. with execution unavoidable - Do't and thou hast the one half of my heart; do't not, thou split'st thine own.
"Do't and thou hast the one half of my heart;
Do't not, thou split'st thine own" (WT.1.2)

In the play. *Leontes orders Camillo to poison Polixenes or else.*

Command, quick, no talk - Waste no time in words but get thee gone.
"…Waste no time in words,
But get thee gone" (MOV.3.4)
In the play. *Portia to servant Balthasar as she must instructs him to deliver an urgent message to Doctor Bellario in Padua.*

Comment, no c. - … what he is indeed, more suits you to conceive than I to speak of.
"…what he is indeed,
More suits you to conceive than I to speak of." (AYLY.1.2)
Answer to 'What type of person is he?' when you do not want to disclose your opinion. Equally, when you are requested to confirm or deny a statement, try the non-shakespearean but excellent 'You might think that, I couldn't possibly comment'.
In the play. *Le Beau advises Orlando to leave quickly as the duke is angry but Le Beau does not want to expand on the issue.*

Commitment, c. to always consult before taking important action - And never will I undertake the thing wherein thy counsel and consent is wanting.
"And never will I undertake the thing
Wherein thy counsel and consent is wanting." (KHVI.p3.2.6)
In the play. *Edward of York, soon to be king (in place of Henry VI) submits himself to the will of Warwick the king-maker. It won't be long before Edward reneges on his commitment.*

Commitment, c. to execute o. to the fullest - … thy commandment all alone shall live within the book and volume of my brain, unmix'd with baser matter.
"… thy commandment all alone shall live
Within the book and volume of my brain,
Unmix'd with baser matter" (H.1.5)
Answer to 'Will you do exactly what I told you to do?'
In the play. *Hamlet commits himself to the Ghost of his father to revenge his murder.*

Commitment, c. to writing frequently - Who's born that day when I forget to send to Antony shall die a beggar.
"Who's born that day
When I forget to send to Antony,
Shall die a beggar." (AC.1.5)
Use also when you commit to something else but writing, e.g. 'Who's born that day when I forget to (do equivalent action), shall die a beggar.
In the play. *Cleopatra commits herself to write Antony every day while he is in Rome.*

Commitment, full c. to the enterprise, no half measures - Either our history shall, with full mouth, speak freely of our acts; or else…
"Either our history shall, with full mouth,
Speak freely of our acts; or else our grave,
Like Turkish mute, shall have a tongueless mouth,
Not worshipp'd with a waxen epitaph." (KHV.1.2)
An ending to a planning speech. E.g., 'This then is the plan we wish to implement. And either our history shall, …epitaph.'
In the play. *Henry V has decided to attack France*

Commitment, you will maintain the c. - … and when I break that oath, let me turn monster.
"… and when I break that oath, let me turn monster." (AYLI.1.2)
Confirm that you will keep your promise(s). See also ' Credentials. Establishing your credentials.' –

'Credentials, sincerity, one tongue. –
'Politicians' promises, habitual'
In the play. *Celia commits to be the eternal friend of Rosalind whatever the circumstances.*

Commitments, purposeful c. must be limited in number - It is the purpose that makes strong the vow but vows to every purpose must not hold.
"It is the purpose that makes strong the vow;
But vows to every purpose must not hold." (TC.5.3)
Dissuade a person from going ahead with a plan just because he (or she) said he would do so.
In the play. *Cassandra and Andromache plead with Hector not to fight with Achilles.*

Committee, portrait of a c. and its characteristic confusion – ... truly I think if all our wits were to issue out of one skull, they would fly east, west...
"We have been called so of many; not that our heads are some brown, some black, some auburn, some bald, but that our wits are so diversely coloured: and truly I think if all our wits were to issue out of one skull, they would fly east, west, north, south, and their consent of one direct way should be at once to all the points o' the compass." (COR.2.3)
In the play. *The 'third citizen' describes the multitude and its habits – a multitude of which he is part and which he acknowledges as having been called the 'many-faced multitude'*

Common sense, would say no but perhaps... - And what impossibility would slay in common sense, sense saves another way.
"And what impossibility would slay
In common sense, sense saves another way." (AWEW.2.1)
You will go along with the idea though you rate the success unlikely. Possibly add a 'perhaps', '...in common sense, perhaps sense saves another way.'
In the play. *Helena has staked her life against her power to cure the King. That is, either the cure is effective or she is prepared to die. The King begins to yield to Helen's attempt at a cure.*

Communications, clarity and honesty go together - An honest tale speeds best being plainly told.
"An honest tale speeds best being plainly told." (KRIII.4.4)
In the play. *Now Richard wants to marry young Elizabeth, daughter of Queen Elizabeth, widow of Edward IV and prompts the mother to present his suit to the daughter* (Be eloquent on my behalf!) *Q. Elizabeth responds with this line.*

Communism, communist manifesto – ... there shall be no money; all shall eat and drink on my score.
"...there shall be no money; all shall eat and drink on my score; and I will apparel them all in one livery, that they may agree like brothers and worship me their lord." (KHVI p2.4.2)
In the play. *The rebel John Cade, after the first successful stage of his rebellion, expounds his political-economic program.*

Company, c. downsizes, effect on employees - ... leak'd is our bark and we, poor mates, stand on the dying deck...
"... leak'd is our bark,
And we, poor mates, stand on the dying deck,
Hearing the surges threat: we must all part
Into this sea of air." (TOA.4.2)
When waiting for the pink slip.
In the play. *One of Timon's servants comments on the imminent bankruptcy of his master.*

Company, commercial c. in poor but recoverable shape - it is but as a body

yet distemper'd, which to his former strength may be restored...
"It is but as a body yet distemper'd;
Which to his former strength may be restored
With good advice and little medicine" (KHIV.p2.3.1)
In the play. *The body is England, where rebellion is brewing. Warwick gives some comfort to the worried king.*

Company, good c. making time and travel seem shorter - ... And yet your fair discourse hath been as sugar, making the hard way sweet and delectable.
"These high wild hills and rough uneven ways
Draws out our miles, and makes them wearisome,
And yet your fair discourse hath been as sugar,
Making the hard way sweet and delectable." (KRII.2.3)
In the play. *Northumberland to Bolingbroke on their way to Ravenspurgh where they will confront King Richard II.*

Company, rationalization for having frequented the wrong crowd - The strawberry grows underneath the nettle... fruit of baser quality.
"The strawberry grows underneath the nettle,
And wholesome berries thrive and ripen best,
Neighboured by fruit of baser quality." (HV.1.1)
Answer to, 'How could you possibly associate with people like that?' or equivalent. See also, 'Apologies for past poor behavior.'
In the play. *The bishop of Ely concurs with the archbishop of Canterbury in the praises of the reformed Prince of Wales, now Henry V.*

Company, the c. of men apt to easily change their mind - I am betrayed, by keeping company with men-like men, of strange inconstancy.
"I am betrayed, by keeping company
With men-like men, of strange inconstancy." (LLL.4)
Blame your associates for not doing what they have agreed to do.
In the play. *As all the company, including the king, has fallen in love, Biron says he feels betrayed (though he himself has fallen in love with Rosaline).*

Comparison, night beyond c. - ... My young remembrance cannot parallel a fellow to it.
MACBETH 'Twas a rough night.
LENNOX My young remembrance cannot parallel
A fellow to it. (M.2.3)
In the play. *The night when Duncan was killed (by Macbeth).*

Compassion, perfunctory c. cannot exempt from responsibility – ... And water cannot wash away your sin.
"Though some of you with Pilate wash your hands
Showing an outward pity; yet you Pilates
Have here deliver'd me to my sour cross,
And water cannot wash away your sin." (KRII.4.1)
When you are the victim of a gross injustice.
In the play. *At Westminster Hall in London, Richard II upbraids Northumberland and others who plotted or consented with Bolingbroke to depose him.*

Compassion, stones better than people - ... a stone is as soft wax, tribunes more hard than stones...
"I tell my sorrow to the stones,
Who, though they cannot answer my distress,
Yet in some sort they are better than the tribunes,

For that they will not interrupt my tale;
When I do weep, they, humbly at my feet,
Receive my tears and seem to weep with me.
A stone is as soft wax, - tribunes more hard than stones;
A stone is silent, and offendeth not; -
And tribunes with their tongues doom men to death." (TA.3.1)
Use to convey your feeling of sadness and contempt of mankind. See also entries for 'Pity', 'Mercy', and 'Indifference'.
In the play. *The stones are better than the Tribunes who refuse to hear Titus' plea for his sons' innocence.*

Competition, driving away the c. - so bees with smoke, and doves with noisome stench are from their hives and houses driven away.
"So bees with smoke, and doves with noisome stench,
Are from their hives and houses driven away." (KHVIp1.1.5)
Use as a comparison
In the play. *Talbot compares the effect of La Pucelle on the English whom she has driven away from Orleans.*

Competition, unexpected surge of the c. - Where slept our scouts, or how are they seduced that we could hear no news of his repair?
"Where slept our scouts, or how are they seduced,
That we could hear no news of his repair?" (KHVI p3.5.1)
In the play. *Near Coventry, Warwick is surprised to find that Edward escaped from York and is now close at hand and with an army.*

Complaint, c. after problems useless - ... wise men ne'er sit and wail their loss, but cheerly seek how to redress their harms.
"...wise men ne'er sit and wail their loss,
But cheerly seek how to redress their harms." (KHVI p3.5.4)
Promote a positive attitude in front of a setback. See also entries for 'Positive thinking'. *** 'Exhortation, e. not to yield to enemy – We will not from the helm to sit and weep, but keep our course, though the rough wind say no…'
In the play. *Queen Margaret tries to lift the spirits of her allies after the defeat at Coventry.*

Complaint, c. after problems useless - ... wise men ne'er sit and wail their woes, presently prevent the ways to wail.
"...wise men ne'er sit and wail their woes,
But presently prevent the ways to wail." (KRII.3.2)
Promote a constructive attitude, as opposed to fear or feeling of defeat, when handling difficult situation
In the play. *The Bishop of Carlyle offers words of encouragement to the beleaguered Richard II, who returning from a campaign in Ireland, finds the country in rebellion and siding with his rival Bolingbroke, the future Henry IV.*

Complaint, c. after problems useless - all of us have cause to wail the dimming of our shining star...
"…All of us have cause
To wail the dimming of our shining star;
But none can help our harms by wailing them." (KRIII.2.2)
Exhort to look at the future rather than the past.
In the play. *Richard has the gall to comfort the duchess of York after he has had her son Clarence killed.*

Complaint, c. after problems useless - cease to lament for that thou canst not

help, and study help for that which thou lament'st...
"Cease to lament for that thou canst not help,
And study help for that which thou lament'st.
To fear the foe, since fear oppresseth strength,
Gives, in your weakness, strength unto our foe." (TGV.3.1)
See also 'Relationship beyond repair.' – 'Complaint after problems useless.' Use third and fourth line to allay fear of the competition.
In the play. *The treacherous and hypocritical Proteus gives advice to Valentine after succeeding in having him banned from Milan. Proteus will then (unsuccessfully) try to steal Silvia's affection.*

Complaint, c. of unfair treatment - ... all his faults observed, set in a notebook, learn'd, and conn'd by rote to cast into my teeth.
"...Cheque'd like a bondman; all his faults observed,
Set in a note-book, learn'd, and conn'd by rote,
To cast into my teeth." (JC.4.1)
In the play. *Upbraided by Brutus for taking bribes, Cassius becomes defensive and talks of himself in the third person, possibly to induce pity in Brutus.*

Complaint, c. to the point of breaking, union's grievances – Know that our griefs are risen to the top and now at length they overflow their banks.
"Know that our griefs are risen to the top,
And now at length they overflow their banks." (PER.2.4)
Bring your complaints to management.
In the play. *In Tyre, the noblemen demand the presence of a leader and want Helicanus to assume all the responsibilities of the absent king Pericles. The second lord addresses Helicanus, second in command to the king.*

Complaint, c. very loud and excessive - ... thy groans did make wolves howl, and penetrate the breasts of ever-angry bears...
"... thy groans
Did make wolves howl, and penetrate the breasts
Of ever-angry bears; it was a torment
To lay upon the damn'd." (TEM.1.2)
Point out the excess of complaint. 'Your groans make wolves howl and penetrate the breasts...bears; it is a torment...damned'
In the play. *Prospero reminds Ariel of the condition he (Ariel) was in when prisoner of Sycorax a witch and mother of Caliban. Therefore his loud complaints are unjustified.*

Complexion, alternating colors - This silent war of lilies and of roses.
"This silent war of lilies and of roses" (ROL)
Remark on her blushing, e.g. 'I can see a silent war of lilies and roses'.
In the poem. *Lucrece's beautiful complexion has bewitched the evil Tarquin.*

Complexion, c. of a criminal - ... his complexion is perfect gallows.
"...his complexion is perfect gallows" (TEM.1.1)
In the play. *Gonzalo's assessment on one of the sailors of the boat where they both are on.*

Complexion, excellent c. - ... That excellent complexion which did steal the eyes of young and old.
"... That excellent complexion which did steal
The eyes of young and old." (PER.4.1)
Answer to 'What is that you liked in me?

If she has a fine complexion this will not fail but please her tremendously. After all, ladies spend (aggregately) billions to improve their complexion. Yours is but a very modest acknowledgement, given their effort. On the other hand, if her complexion is so-so, or marginal, or if she has acne, this works even better. If then she says to you, 'But you did not notice my pimples?' you have two options, lie and deny that you saw anything wrong with her complexion. Or (a better solution), ignore the question and follow up with another powerful line (see 'Best. Compliment. You are the best'.)
In the play. *Feigning kindness and complimenting her for her complexion, Dionyza lures Marina into going out of the house where servant Leonine is supposed to kill her.*

Complexion, good c. – …your colour, I warrant you, is as red as any rose, in good truth.
"…your colour, I warrant you, is as red as any rose, in good truth" (KHIVp2.2.4)
In the play. *Mistress Quickly assesses Falstaff's physical conditions after he drank a large amount of wine. See 'Apologies for having drunk too much'*

Compliments, a volley of c. - … mine own self's better part, mine eye's clear eye…
"… mine own self's better part,
Mine eye's clear eye, my dear heart's dearer heart,
My food, my fortune and my sweet hope's aim,
My sole earth's heaven and my heaven's claim." (COE.3.2)
In the play. *Antipholus of Ephesus showers Luciana with a rain of compliments. Luciana thinks that A. Ephesus is instead A. of Syracuse, in which case the compliments are out of line as A. Syracuse is married to Luciana's sister.*

Compliments, exchange of c. and formalities - … too mean a servant… Leave off discourse of disability.
SILVIA Too low a mistress for so high a servant.
**PROTEUS Not so, sweet lady: but too mean a servant
To have a look of such a worthy mistress.**
**VALENTINE Leave off discourse of disability:
Sweet lady, entertain him for your servant.** (TGV.2.2)
Follow up to 'Nice meeting you', e.g. 'Too mean a servant…. Mistress'.
In the play. *Now in Milan, Proteus and Silvia exchange formalities and compliments.*

Compliments, c. reserved for dinner time – … let me praise you while I have a stomach -- … No, pray thee, let it serve for table-talk…
**JESSICA Nay, let me praise you while I have a stomach.
LORENZO No, pray thee, let it serve for table-talk;
' Then, howso'er thou speak'st, 'mong other things
I shall digest it**. (MOV.3.5)
In the play. *Jessica and Lorenzo house-sit for Portia who is temporarily in Venice. In a partially joking way Lorenzo has suggested that he (Lorenzo) represents for her (Jessica) what Portia represents for Bassanio.*

Compliments, string of paradoxical compliments - Beautiful tyrant! fiend angelical! Dove-feather'd raven!…
"**Beautiful tyrant! fiend angelical! Dove-feather'd raven! wolvish-ravening lamb!**" (RJ.3.2)
Answer to her angry words. See also 'Anger, her a. an occasion for a compliment - Never came poison from so sweet a place.'

In the play. *News that Romeo killed Tybald, Juliet's cousin has reached her. Not knowing that the killing was unprovoked and in self-defense, Juliet draws the wrong conclusions about Romeo*

Conceit, as when a wise person pretends not to understand – Thus wisdom wishes to appear most bright when it doth tax itself...
"Thus wisdom wishes to appear most bright
When it doth tax itself; as these black masks
Proclaim an enshielded beauty ten times louder
Than beauty could, display'd."
(MFM.2.4)
Attack your conceited opponents, e.g. 'They are like those black masks…displayed'. See also entries for 'Hypocrisy' *** 'Understanding, sincerity of lack of u. questioned - Your sense pursues not mine or seem so craftily; and that's not good.' *** 'See 'Character, one who pretends to be thought clever by saying nothing - there are a sort of men whose visages…'
In the play. *Angelo tries to accuse Isabel of conceit because she does not understand his advances couched in weasel words.*

Conceit, hiding the real intent – … with forged quaint conceit to set a gloss upon his bold intent.
"…he seem with forged quaint conceit
To set a gloss upon his bold intent"
(KHVI.p1.4.1)
In the play. *Vernon (a Gloucester's supporter), is at odds with Basset (a Somerset's supporter).*

Conceit, you do not say what you mean - You speak not as you think, it cannot be.
"You speak not as you think, it cannot be." (MND.3.2)
Express disbelief in the arguments of an opponent.
In the play. *Unaware of why Lysander rejects her, Hermia cannot believe it.*

Concern, c. about having upset someone - … I hope my words disbench'd you not.
"Sir, I hope
My words disbench'd you not"
COR.2.2)
See also entries for 'Apologies'.
In the play. *The tribute Brutus attempts a friendly tackle with the imperious Coriolanus.*

Concession, little initial c. leading to eventual defeat - … when the fox hath once got in his nose...
"…when the fox hath once got in his nose,
He'll soon find means to make the body follow." (KHVI p3.4.7)
When you have reason not to make the smallest concession.
In the play. *Edward IV asks for entry into York and tells the mayor of York that he, Edward, has only arrived to claim his dukedom. Gloucester knows it is not so, Edward aims at the throne, hence the similitude with the fox' action.*

Concession, tolerate your adversary's temporary glory - Let frantic Talbot triumph for a while and like a peacock sweep along his tail…
"Let frantic Talbot triumph for a while
And like a peacock sweep along his tail;
We'll pull his plumes and take away his train" (KHVI.p1.3.3)
Also a representation of vanity, e.g. 'He, like a peacock, sweeps along his tail.
In the play. *Joan of Arc to the French leaders after Talbot has re-conquered Rouen*

Conclusion, c. does not follow from premise - ... there is no consonancy in the sequel.
"... there is no consonancy in the sequel" (TN.2.5)
In the play. *Malvolio disputing Fabio's conclusion.*

Conclusions, wrong c. drawn by a giddy person - He that is giddy thinks the world turns round.
"He that is giddy thinks the world turns round." (TOS.5.2)
Imply the unreliability of an opinion, statement or judgment.
In the play. *The widow's statement refers to Petruchio. Petruchio said that Hortensio is afraid of the widow. She means that Petruchio thinks so because earlier on he was afraid of the shrewish Katharina ('troubled with a shrew', she says).*

Concordance between belief and words used to express it - For things are often spoke and seldom meant...
"For things are often spoke and seldom meant:
But that my heart accordeth with my tongue." (KHVI p2.3.1)
Answer to 'Do you mean it?' 'My heart accordeth with my tongue'. See also, 'Credentials, sincerity, one tongue.'
In the play. *Suffolk means to get rid of the good Duke Humphrey, Lord Protector to Henry VI, on the ground that Humphrey is a traitor. Suffolk actually double crosses himself, by indicating his sincerity of intent, while the intent is insincere.*

Condemnation, c. of an innocent man through prejudice – ... that dye is on me which makes my whitest part black.
"It will help me nothing
To plead mine innocence; for that dye is on me
Which makes my whitest part black" (KHVIII.1.1)
In the play. *Wolsey has plotted to have Buckingham executed for treason by providing false evidence (the stain making dye).*

Conditions, current place and c. not as bad as others' - This wide and universal theatre presents more woeful pageants...
"Thou seest we are not all alone unhappy:
This wide and universal theatre
Presents more woeful pageants than the scene
Wherein we play in." (AYLY.2.7)
Encouragement to see the positive side of a situation.
In the play. *Duke S. points to Orlando that there are worst places and events than the Forest of Arden and the events of which the Duke S and Orlando are part.*

Conditions, political c intolerable – Brutus had rather be a villager than to repute himself a son of Rome...
"Brutus had rather be a villager
Than to repute himself a son of Rome
Under these hard conditions as this time
Is like to lay upon us." (JC.1.2)
Paraphrase changing 'Brutus' to your name and 'son of Rome' to 'son of the country with whose government you disagree'
In the play. *Cassius, conversing with Brutus, has very clearly hinted that Caesar is a tyrant to be eliminated.*

Conditions, tough c. to be in - ... the condition of the time, which cannot look more hideously upon me than I have drawn it in my fantasy.
"(I) do arm myself
To welcome the condition of the time,
Which cannot look more hideously upon me
Than I have drawn it in my fantasy." (KHIV.p2.5.2)

Answer to 'How does it look?' when it doesn't look too good.
In the play. *The Lord Chief Justice acknowledges that the Prince of Wales, now king, does not like him.*

Confession, confessing to lust - ... served the lust of my mistress' heart, and did the act of darkness with her.
"A serving-man, proud in heart and mind; that curled my hair; wore gloves in my cap; served the lust of my mistress' heart, and did the act of darkness with her" (KL.3.4)
Interesting alternative to the question, 'Did you make love?' E.G. 'You mean I did the act of darkness?'
In the play. *Edgar, pretending to be mad, tells of himself to K. Lear and fool.*

Confession, confessing to sins - ...false of heart, light of ear, bloody of hand; hog in sloth, fox in stealth, wolf in greediness...
"Wine loved I deeply, dice dearly: and in woman out-paramoured the Turk: false of heart, light of ear, bloody of hand; hog in sloth, fox in stealth, wolf in greediness, dog in madness, lion in prey." (KL.3.4)
A good line of epithets for your most disfavored politician
In the play. *Edgar, pretending to be mad, tells of himself to K. Lear and fool.*

Confidence, c. among trusted friends - ... We three are but thyself; and, speaking so, thy words are but as thoughts; therefore, be bold.
"Be confident to speak, Northumberland:
We three are but thyself; and, speaking so,
Thy words are but as thoughts; therefore, be bold." (KRII.2.1)
When you sense some reluctance to reveal possibly sensitive information.

In the play. *Lord Ross to Northumberland, who has heard that the exiled Bolingbroke plans to sail from Brittany to England with a military force to regain his lost possessions.*

Confidence, c. in victory and subsequent reward - doubt not of the day, and, that once gotten, doubt not of large pay.
"Come on, brave soldiers, doubt not of the day,
And, that once gotten, doubt not of large pay." (KHVI p3.4.7)
Promise reward to inspire action.
In the play. *Edward IV to soldiers before fighting Warwick and the forces of Henry VI.*

Confidence, c. that overcomes any fear – ... all too confident to give admittance to a thought of fear.
"...all too confident
To give admittance to a thought of fear" (KHIV.p2.4.1)
In the play. *Westmoreland (of the king's party) addresses the rebel Mowbray.*

Confidence, overconfidence challenges the frailty of our powers - And sometimes we are devils to ourselves...
"And sometimes we are devils to ourselves,
When we tempt the frailty of our powers,
Presuming on their changeful potency." (TC.4.4)
Use to moderate overconfidence – See also 'Woman, female frailty, invocation'.
In the play. *Cressida must leave Troilus. Troilus tells her not to be tempted. Do you think I will be tempted? - she asks - No, says Troilus but...*

Confidence, overconfidence dangerous and misguided - The man that once did sell the lion's skin...
"The man that once did sell the lion's skin

While the beast lived, was killed with hunting him." (KHV.4.3)
When you want to inspire caution and prudence.
In the play. *The overconfident Montjoy spokesman for the French, demands surrender from the English before the battle (of Agincourt). King Henry V answers accordingly.*

Confidence, overconfidence not a sign of wisdom - ... your wisdom is consumed in confidence.
"Alas my lord,
Your wisdom is consumed in confidence." (JC.2.2)
Inspire caution where you observe excessive wishful thinking. See also 'Security, false sense of s. - ... If thou beest not immortal look about you: security gives way to conspiracy.'
In the play. *Calphurnia has a hard time to convince Caesar, her husband, to be prudent.*

Confirmation, c. of statement – I said so and I must not blush to affirm it.
"I said so, dear Katharine; and I must not blush to affirm it." (KHV.5.2)
In the play. *King Henry told Katherine that she is an angel and on her asking what he meant, Henry confirms it.*

Conflict, not a time for c. – 'Tis not a time for private stomaching…
LEPIDUS 'Tis not a time
For private stomaching.
DOMITIUS ENOBARBUS Every time
Serves for the matter that is then born in't. (AC.2.2)
Use Enobarbus' comment as an answer to 'Is this a good time?'
In the play. *Enobarbus, Antony's Lieutenant meets with Lepidus in Rome.*

Conflict resolution, advice to proceed with caution - ... temperately proceed to what you would thus violently redress.

" … temperately proceed to what you would
Thus violently redress." (COR.3.1)
Counsel moderation rather than force to solve a problem.
In the play. *Menenius counsels moderation to the tribune Brutus in order to achieve the desired result. In other words, Menenius calls for civil disobedience. For Brutus' counter-reply see 'Revolution, call for violent action when peaceful demonstrations ineffective'.*

Conflict resolution, calming down the debate - ... When we debate our trivial differences loud, we do commit murder in healing wounds.
"…When we debate
Our trivial differences loud, we do commit
Murder in healing wounds. (AC.2.2)
Use to calm a heated debate during which participants hurl accusations at each other.
In the play. *Lepidus opening an electric meeting during which it is expected that Antony and Octavian will argue.*

Conflict resolution, inflaming not cooling off the conflict - This is the way to kindle, not to quench.
"This is the way to kindle, not to quench." (COR.3.1)
Disapprove a move that exasperates animosities rather than bringing peace. See also 'Quarrel. Dispute and arguments to be avoided, peace making, conflict resolution' – 'Action, a. contrary to what needed - you rub the sore when you should bring the plaster'.
In the play. *Menenius upbraids the Tribune Sicinius for his inflaming words - Sicinius has told the people that Coriolanus is about to take away their liberties.*

Conflict resolution, relative importance of arguments in dispute - But small to greater matters must give way.
"But small to greater matters must give way." (AC.2.2)
Use to dismiss a debate on trivia. See also 'Quarrel. Dispute and arguments to be avoided, peace making, conflict resolution'.
In the play. *Lepidus asks Enobarbus to prompt Antony to moderate his tone during the impending meeting with Octavian.*

Conflict resolution, use of wit with those who have little - I'll try whether my old wit be in request with those that have but little.
" I'll try whether my old wit be in request
With those that have but little." (COR.3.1)
You volunteer to be the mediator between two stubborn parties.
In the play. *Menenius will attempt to mediate between Coriolanus and the tribunes.*

Conflict, c. smoldering between two parties - ... there is division although as yet the face of it is covered with mutual cunning.
"…There is division,
Although as yet the face of it is covered
With mutual cunning." (KL.3.1)
You have discovered hidden discord or disagreement between two parties, notwithstanding a façade of harmony, agreement and cooperation. See also 'Peace, shaky p.'
In the play. *Kent tells a gentleman that there is smoldering conflict between the dukes of Albany and Cornwall. Albany is the more decent of the two.*

Confusion, c. following management upheaval - ... and vast confusion waits, as doth the raven on a sick fallen beast, the imminent decay of wrested pomp.
"Now powers from home, and discontents at home,
Meet in one line, and vast confusion waits,
As doth the raven on a sick fallen beast,
The imminent decay of wrested pomp." (KJ.4.3)
Underscore a state of confusion, e.g. "Vast confusion waits…pomp."
In the play. *Faulconbridge predicts that the death/murder of young Arthur and the danger of war with France may lead to the fall of K. John and cabinet.*

Confusion, how quickly things become confused -... so quick bright things come to confusion.
"Making it momentary as a sound,
Swift as a shadow, short as any dream,
Brief as the lightning in the collied night,
That, in a spleen, unfolds both heaven and earth,
And ere a man hath power to say, -- Behold!
The jaws of darkness do devour it up:
So quick bright things come to confusion." (MND.1.1)
A comment on how quickly events can change unpredictably. 'Just like a lightning in the night, the jaws of darkness…confusion'. 'The jaws of darkness' is a good alternative for 'night', e.g. 'He disappeared into the jaws of darkness'.
In the play. *Obstacles have suddenly arisen preventing Hermia to marry Lysander, hence the reference to bright things coming to confusion. What has become 'momentary as a sound' is the love between Hermia and Lysander. 'Collied' means 'darkened'.*

Confusion, remedy for c. is not more c. - ... confusion's cure lives not in these confusions.
"Peace, ho, for shame! confusion's cure lives not
In these confusions." (RJ.4.5)
Bring a loud arguing group to silence and/or reason.
In the play. *Juliet appears dead (but is only heavily drugged) and the house of the Capulets is in understandable great confusion. Fr. Lawrence invites them to order and reason.*

Confusion, state of c. – all is uneven and every thing is left at six and seven.
"…all is uneven,
And every thing is left at six and seven." (KRII.2.2)
In the play. *The Duke of York is concerned at the state of confusion and simmering feeling of rebellion brewing at the court of Richard II.*

Confusion, state of c. at its zenith - Confusion now hath made his masterpiece!
"Confusion now hath made his masterpiece!" (M.2.3)
In the play. *After a cry of horror at the sight of slain Duncan (See 'Invocation, horror'), Macduff summarizes the situation.*

Connections, importance of good c. - A friend in the court is better than a penny in purse.
"A friend in the court is better than a penny in purse." (KHIV.p2.5.1)
Why you are seeking the friendship of a powerful person. See also 'Help, asking to put a word on your behalf - … let me have thy voice in my behalf.'
In the play. *Justice Shallow counts on Falstaff to be his friend at the court of Henry V, but events will prove otherwise.*

Conquest accomplished, totally overwhelmed - … My heart and hands thou hast at once subdued.
"Impatiently I burn with thy desire;
My heart and hands thou hast at once subdued." (KH6.1.1.2)
You can also use this as an opening compliment, after you have spoken with her for a few minutes, or after she has said something witty or paid you a compliment.
In the play. *Charles of France is convinced of Joan of Arc's superior abilities.*

Conquest, determination to conquer - Now, Rouen, I'll shake thy bulwarks to the ground.
"Now, Rouen, I'll shake thy bulwarks to the ground." (KHVI p1.3.2)
Change 'Rouen' to name of city, or organization, or corporation that may be the object(s) of your wrath.
In the play. *Joan of Arc confident of victory, has climbed on the battlements of the city.*

Conscience, c. as an obstacle – I'll not meddle with it: it is a dangerous thing…
"I'll not meddle with it: it is a dangerous thing: it makes a man a coward: a man cannot steal, but it accuseth him; he cannot swear, but it cheques him; he cannot lie with his neighbour's wife, but it detects him: 'tis a blushing shamefast spirit that mutinies in a man's bosom; it fills one full of obstacles" (KRIII.1.4)
See also 'Conscience, c. lost to money - … in the Duke of Gloucester's purse.'
In the play. *Prior to killing the Duke of Clarence in the tower the two contract killers digress about conscience*

Conscience, c. as power when fighting against evil - Every man's conscience is a thousand swords…
"Every man's conscience is a thousand swords,

To fight against that bloody homicide" (KRIII.5.2)
In the play. *At Tamworth, Lord Oxford, an ally of Richmond, prompts the troops to fight valiantly against Richard*

Conscience, c. lost to money - ... in the Duke of Gloucester's purse.
FIRST MURDERER. Where's thy conscience now?
SECOND MURDERER. In the Duke of Gloucester purse (KRIII.1.4)
Verbal tool against corrupt politician. Change 'the Duke of Gloucester's' to the name of the person in whose payroll the politician is. E.G. 'Your conscience is in the XXX' purse'.
In the play. *On order of Richard III, Duke of Gloucester, two murderers have come to the Tower to Kill the Duke of Clarence, his brother and brother of King Edward. A few seconds earlier one of the killers felt some pangs in his conscience and said* 'certain dregs of conscience are yet within me'.

Conscience, c. moved by speech heard - How smart a lash that speech doth give my conscience!
"How smart a lash that speech doth give my conscience!
 In the play.. *The King, overhearing Polonius' words to Ophelia, finds their dramatic relevance to his own murderous actions.*

Conscience, c. or fear – ... conscience is but a word that cowards use devised at first to keep the strong in awe…
"Let not our babbling dreams affright our souls
Conscience is but a word that cowards use,
Devised at first to keep the strong in awe.
Our strong arms be our conscience, swords and law!" (KRIII.5.3)

Illustrate the concept of conscience for some people. Also rationalization for US foreign policy.
In the play. *Richard addressing the troops before the final battle with Richmond's forces at Bosworth field.*

Conscience, c. or fear – Thus conscience does make cowards of us all…
"Thus conscience does make cowards of us all;
And thus the native hue of resolution
Is sicklied o'er with the pale cast of thought.
And enterprises of great pith and moment
With this regard their currents turn awry,
And lose the name of action" (H.3.1)
When the arguments for inaction are flimsy or don't hold water. Some invoke their conscience as a justification for their action or inaction. Use when it is questionable whether it is a matter of conscience or just an excuse. See also 'Depression, general depression leading to total pessimism'.
In the play. *Life is so inherently laden with problems and pain that suicide may appear the most logical solution. But men are afraid of what they will find in their afterlife.*

Conscience, clear c. when fighting for a just cause - ... the arms are fair when the intent of bearing them is just.
"Now, for our consciences, the arms are fair,
When the intent of bearing them is just." (KHIV.p1.5.2)
See also "Invocation, i. to God - God befriend us, as our cause is just!'
In the play. *Hotspur's final words to his allies before the battle of Shrewsbury in which he will be killed.*

**Conscience, debating within one's c.
– … Thus hulling in the wild sea of my conscience…**
"…Thus hulling in
The wild sea of my conscience, I did steer
Toward this remedy" (KHVIII.2.4)
Make it a preamble to your proposal or plan, particularly if the plan involves curing a problem.
In the play. *King Henry strives to find rational reasons for divorcing Queen Katherine. The 'remedy' is the consultation with 2 cardinals as to the legitimacy of his marriage.*

Conscience, dilemma, torn between duty and desire - … well, my conscience says, Launcelot, budge not…
"… well, my conscience says, Launcelot, budge not: budge, says the fiend; budge not, says my conscience: Conscience, say I, you counsel well; fiend, say I, you counsel well… my conscience is but a hard conscience, to offer to counsel me to stay with the Jew; the fiend gives me more friendly counsel: I will run, fiend, my heels are at your commandment, I will run." (MOV.2.2)
Quote it entirely as an example of the inherent difficulty of some decisions, where there are plausible reasons for making one choice or its opposite.
In the play. *Shylock's servant, Launcelot, is torn between duty and opportunity.*

Conscience, false c. - … their best conscience is not to leave it undone, but keep it unknown.
"I know our country disposition well;
In Venice they do let heaven see the pranks
They dare not show their husbands; their best conscience
Is not to leave't undone, but keep't unknown." (OTH.3.3)
Retort to a crooked politician that brings conscience into the debate or claims to have a conscience
In the play. *Iago works Othello into believing Desdemona unfaithful. Here he generalizes about the general habits of Venetian women to hide their secret deeds.*

Conscience, guilt of c. as a reward – The guilt of conscience take thou for thy labour…
"The guilt of conscience take thou for thy labour,
But neither my good word nor princely favour:
With Cain go wander through shades of night,
And never show thy head by day nor light." (KRII.5.5)
Quote the episode as a supreme example of deniability – see also other entries for 'Deniability'.
In the play. *To ensure deniability, Exton killed Richard at Pomfret Castle following an indirect injunction by Bolingbroke. In a supreme act of hypocrisy, now Bolingbroke pretends to have had nothing to do with the murder.*

Conscience, no scruples of c. – … where lies that? if 'twere a kibe, 'twould put me to my slipper…
SEBASTIAN But, for your conscience?
ANTONIO Ay, sir; where lies that? if 'twere a kibe,
'Twould put me to my slipper: but I feel not
This deity in my bosom: twenty consciences,
That stand 'twixt me and Milan, candied be they
And melt ere they molest! (TEM.2.2)
In the play. *The perfidious Antonio prompts Sebastian to plot against Alonso, king of Naples. 'Kibe' is an open sore on the heel, hence the need for a slipper.*

Conscience, pangs of guilty c. - My conscience hath a thousand several tongues...
"My conscience hath a thousand several tongues,
And every tongue brings in a several tale,
And every tale condemns me for a villain." (RIII.5.3)
With a touch of irony in your voice use the lines to confess to your multiple guilts.
In the play. *Richard III at Bosworth Field the night before the battle, is assailed by the remorse that he attempted to disguise earlier on.*

Conscience, pangs of guilty c. - My conscience, thou art fetter'd more than my shanks and wrists.
"...My conscience, thou art fetter'd More than my shanks and wrists" (CYM.4.4)
In the play. *Leonatus is jailed as a Roman after the battle between Romans and Britons. His conscience bites him as he ordered Pisanio to kill Imogen.*

Conscience, rationale for disregarding it - I'll not meddle with it: it is a dangerous thing...
"I'll not meddle with it: it is a dangerous thing: it makes a man a coward: a man cannot steal, but it accuseth him; he cannot swear, but it cheques him; he cannot lie with his neighbour's wife, but it detects him: 'tis a blushing shamefast spirit that mutinies in a man's bosom; it fills one full of
obstacles: it made me once restore a purse of gold that I found; it beggars any man that keeps it: it
is turned out of all towns and cities for a dangerous thing; and every man that means to live
well endeavours to trust to himself and to live without it." (KRIII.1.4)

Almost a custom tailored formula for many politicians. Try the last three lines to accuse your opponent of having no conscience. After having exposes his misdeeds conclude with 'He applies the formula of Shakespeare's killers, 'and every man...without conscience'.
In the play. *Two contract killers meditate on a touchy subject prior to executing the Duke of Clarence.*

Conscience, rhetorical question - and hast a thing within thee called conscience...
AARON (to Lucius). "...And hast a thing within thee called conscience..." (TA.5.1)
Turn the sentence from a statement to an interrogative and address a person without scruples, 'Hast thou a thing within thee called conscience?'
In the play. *Aaron pleads with Lucius to swear to spare the life of the baby, fruit of the adulterous relationship with Tamara. In exchange Aaron will provide information. Lucius asks Aaron what he, Lucius, should swear by since Aaron has no gods and therefore cannot believe an oath. Aaron suggests that Lucius has a conscience.*

Conscience, seeing the blackness of one's c. – ... And there I see such black and grained spots as will not leave their tinct.
"Thou turn'st mine eyes into my very soul;
And there I see such black and grained spots
As will not leave their tinct." (H.3.4)
In the play. *Queen Gertrude after Hamlet's string of accusations following her marriage to King Claudius.*

Conscience, shaking of c. - This respite shook the bosom of my conscience, enter'd me, yea, with a splitting power...

"...This respite shook
The bosom of my conscience, enter'd me,
Yea, with a splitting power, and made to tremble
The region of my breast" (KHVIII.2.4)
Shorten to for example, 'This shakes the bosom of my conscience'
In the play. *King Henry confers with Cardinal Wolsey. The shaking of the king's conscience has to do with the idea that his marriage to Kathryn, widow of his dead brother may not have been legitimate – also a good excuse for divorcing her and marrying Anne Bullen.*

Conscience, stilling of c. - So much my conscience whispers in your ear...
"Your strong possession much more than your right,
Or else it must go wrong with you and me:
So much my conscience whispers in your ear,
Which none but heaven and you and I shall hear." (KJ.1.1)
In the play. *Q. Elinor to her son King John on the legitimacy of his claim to the throne of France.*

Conscience, tormenting c. – O coward conscience, how dost thou afflict me.
"O coward conscience, how dost thou afflict me!" (KRIII.5.3)
In the play. *The night before the final battle, King Richard finally cannot escape the bites of conscience.*

Consensus, acknowledging hearty c. - I am glad that my weak words have struck but thus much show of fire from Brutus.
"I am glad that my weak words
Have struck but thus much show of fire from Brutus." (JC.1.2)
Change 'Brutus' to the name of the party who enthusiastically agrees with you.

In the play. *Cassius convinces Brutus that Caesar is a tyrant to be eliminated. Brutus responds with a tirade against living under tyranny. Cassius acknowledges Brutus' oratory.*

Consequences, c. imaginable based on previous narrative - ... let me say no more! Gather the sequel by that went before.
"... O, let me say no more!
Gather the sequel by that went before." (COE.1.1)
In the play. *Aegeon ends his narrative to the Duke of Ephesus (or the first part of it).*

Consequences, c. of a bad decision - You pluck a thousand dangers on your head...
"You pluck a thousand dangers on your head,
You lose a thousand well-disposed hearts
And prick my tender patience, to those thoughts
Which honour and allegiance cannot think." (KRII.2.1)
In the play. *The Duke of York admonishes King Richard as to what will happen if he insists on confiscating Gaunt's estate.*

Consequences, dangerous c. predicted - I told ye all, when ye first put this dangerous stone a-rolling, 'twould fall upon ourselves.
"I told ye all,
When ye first put this dangerous stone a-rolling,
'Twould fall upon ourselves." (KHVIII.5.3)
In the play. *The Duke of Suffolk commenting on Cranmer. Accused by Gardiner and others to be a heretic, Cranmer pulls out his ring of office signaling that he leaves the judgment of his position at the discretion and mercy of the king.*

Consolation, thoughts of c. in sharing misfortunes - ... that they are not the first of fortune's slaves...

"Thoughts tending to content flatter themselves
That they are not the first of fortune's slaves,
Nor shall not be the last;
...
And in this thought they find a kind of ease,
Bearing their own misfortunes on the back
Of such as have before endured the like " (KRII.5.5)
In the play. *Richard II, in prison at Pomfret Castle imagines his thoughts to be people who can keep him company in his confinement. In this case, comforting thoughts thinking that other people had similar misfortunes.*

Conspiracy – ... Open-eyed conspiracy his time doth take ...
"While you here do snoring lie,
Open-eyed conspiracy
His time doth take.
If of life you keep a care,
Shake off slumber, and beware:
Awake, awake!" (TEM.2.2)
In the play. *The spirit Ariel sings a tune with warning lyrics in the ear of the sleeping Gonzalo.*

Conspiracy, aware of c. against yourself – Myself had notice of your conventicles....
"Myself had notice of your conventicles --
And all to make away my guiltless life" (KHVI.p2.3.1)
In the play. *Gloucester is aware that his enemies have conspired to see him dead.*

Conspiracy, c. suitable for dark hours night - O, then by day where wilt thou find a cavern dark enough to mask thy monstrous visage?
"...O conspiracy!
Sham'st thou to show thy dangerous brow by night,
When evils are most free? O, then by day

Where wilt thou find a cavern dark enough
To mask thy monstrous visage? Seek none, Conspiracy;
Hide it in smiles and affability:
For if thou have thy native semblance on,
Not Erebus itself were dim enough
To hide thee from prevention."
(JC.2.1)
Use extracts to address your enemy, e.g. 'Where wilt thou find a cavern dark enough to mask thy monstrous visage?'
In the play. *Brutus is drawn into the conspiracy against Caesar but is also aware of its horror.*

Constancy, c. of wifely love – ...like a jewel, has hung twenty years about his neck, yet never lost her lustre...
"... a loss of her
That, like a jewel, has hung twenty years
About his neck, yet never lost her lustre;
Of her that loves him with that excellence
That angels love good men with; even of her
That, when the greatest stroke of fortune falls,
Will bless the king: and is not this course pious?" (KHVIII.2.2)
In the play. *Norfolk comments on the virtue of Queen Catherine of Aragon, whom the King will shortly divorce.*

Contempt, c. for a person compared to another - ... his meanest garment that ever hath but clipped his body...
"...His meanest garment,
That ever hath but clipp'd his body, is dearer
In my respect than all the hairs above thee" (CYM.2.2)
See also 'Dislike, d. mixed with contempt - ... I care not for you and am so near the

lack of charity to accuse myself--I hate you.'
In the play. *Imogen despises Cloten who woos her. The reference is to the garment of her beloved and exiled husband Leonatus.*

Contempt, c. for manual labor – The nobility think scorn to go in leather aprons.
"The nobility think scorn to go in leather aprons" (KHVI.p2.4.2)
In the play. *Holland comments to a comrade in rebellion with the rabble of John Cade.*

Contentment, c. assured if insensitive to poverty - Poor and content is rich and rich enough...
"Poor and content is rich and rich enough,
But riches fineless is as poor as winter
To him that ever fears he shall be poor." (OTH.3.3)
An argument showing the reason of continual psychological unrest and dissatisfaction when exposed to the display of extravagant wealth. See also 'Ignorance, i. of events a blessing - … There may be in the cup a steep'd, and one may drink, depart and yet partake no venom…' *** 'Ignorance, advantage of not knowing – He that is robbed, not wanting what is stolen…'
In the play. *The evil Iago tries successfully to instill the seeds of jealousy in Othello's mind.*

Contentment, c. as the best asset – our content is our best having.
**OLD LADY. Our content
Is our best having."** (KHVIII.2.3)
Justify a philosophy of life - that to be content with oneself is our best asset.
In the play. *Anne Bullen and assistant comment on K. Henry and soon to be divorced Queen Catherine.*

Contentment, c. observed among lower middle class - How well this honest mirth become their labour.
"How well this honest mirth become their labour!" (PER.2.1)
Comment on the sporting mood of your personnel.
In the play. *After leaving Tharsus, a devastating storm destroys Pericles' fleet and he manages to swim ashore where he meets with 3 fishermen. He begs for help, which they offer while engaging in innocent and inconsequential banter.*

Contentment, the art of c. - I could be bounded in a nutshell, and count myself a king of infinite space.
"I could be bounded in a nutshell, and count myself a king of infinite space, were it not that
I have bad dreams" (H.2.2)
Answer to accusation of ambition.
In the play. *Hamlet debates with Rosencrantz and Guildenstern. Hamlet says that Denmark is a prison, Rosencrantz attributes Hamlet's perception to ambition. Hamlets rebuts.*

Contest, no contest - So first the harmless sheep doth yield his fleece and next his throat unto the butcher's knife.
"So first the harmless sheep doth yield his fleece
And next his throat unto the butcher's knife." (KHVI p3.5.6)
When what happen is clear but the authors of the crime want to give it a cover of officialdom or justice.
In the play. *Henry VI knows that Richard of Gloucester has come to kill him.*

Continuation, going to the next step - … to perform an act whereof what's past is prologue.
"And by that destiny to perform an act
Whereof what's past is prologue, what to come

In yours and my discharge."
(TEM.2.1)
In a presentation, extract 'what's past is prologue.... discharge' when presenting or introducing the next phase of a project. See also 'Life, l.'s history of a person as a predictor of future performance – there is a history in all men's lives.'
In the play. *Antonio suggests a plot to Sebastian to deprive Alonso of the kingdom of Naples.*

Conversation, c. begun in jest and continued seriously - ... since we are stepp'd thus far in, I will continue that I broach'd in jest.
"Petruchio, since we are stepp'd thus far in,
I will continue that I broach'd in jest." (TOA.1.2)
In the play. *Hortensio will continue to explain to Petruchio how he, Petruchio, can get himself a wealthy wife.*

Conviction, unshakable c. – (He) swears his thought over by each particular star in heaven…
"Swear his thought over
By each particular star in heaven and
By all their influences" (WT.1.2)
See also 'Impossibility to make a man change his mind - ... you may as well forbid the sea for to obey the moon…'
In the play. *Camillo explains to Polixenes the deranged jealousy that has taken hold of Leontes.*

Convinced, convincing argument - His words do take possession of my bosom.
"His words do take possession of my bosom." (KJ.4.1)
You can admit to being persuaded by him/her by chancing 'his' to 'your'.
In the play. *The executioner Hubert is moved by the plea of young Prince Arthur, the intended victim.*

Cooking test - 't is an ill cook that cannot lick his own fingers.
"Marry, sir, 't is an ill cook that cannot lick his own fingers." (RJ.4.2)
If you are cooking at a party and someone sees you tasting the food.
In the play. *Capulet assigns a servant to look for twenty cooks for the impending marriage of Paris and Juliet. The servant attempts a witty remark.*

Cooling off observed, general truth - When love begins to sicken and decay, it useth an enforced ceremony.
"When love begins to sicken and decay,
It useth an enforced ceremony." (JC.4.2)
She may still appear friendly and courteous but you notice the coldness. If you are sure that the relationship is in a crisis you may wish to face the situation directly. Use the quote as an opening statement. See also 'Expression, change in e. denoting loss of favor - ... see already how he doth begin to make us strangers to his looks of love.
In the play: *In a camp near Sardis Brutus to Lucilius commenting on Cassius' behavior.*

Cooling off observed, question for verification - dwell I but in the suburbs of your good pleasure?
"Dwell I but in the suburbs of your good pleasure?" (JC.2.1)
Things have gone along pretty smoothly. Lately, you have asked two or three times if she wants to go out with you, or you have proposed some activities. She has turned you down every time. Use as a poetic substitute for 'Have I done anything wrong?'
In the play. *Portia questions Brutus as to why he does not wish to confide in her.*

Cooperation, c. requested in tricky situation - ...Make not impossible that which but seems unlike.

"…Make not impossible
That which but seems unlike"
(MFM.5.1)
In the play. *Isabella to the Duke who pretends to believe Angelo's allegation that Isabella is insane.*

Correction, correcting the assessment of a person - …'Good Gloucester' and 'good devil' were alike…
"Ay, my good lord:--my lord, I should say rather;
Tis sin to flatter; 'good' was little better:
'Good Gloucester' and 'good devil' were alike,
And both preposterous; therefore, not 'good lord.'" (KHVI.p3.5.6)
Whenever a positive adjective is tackled on to the name of despicable adversary.
In the play. *With a slip of the tongue, out of habit, King Henry addresses Gloucester with 'My good Lord and then corrects himself.*

Correction, regret for having to take corrective action – O cursed spite, that ever I was born to set it right.
"The time is out of joint: O cursed spite,
That ever I was born to set it right!"
(H.1.5)
When you are called on to solve a problem and the solution may be hurtful.
In the play. *The ghost of Hamlet's father just vanished and Hamlet meditates on the meaning and the effect of the apparition and its message.*

Corruption, agent of c. – … she that sets seeds and roots of shame and iniquity.
"…she that sets seeds and roots of shame and iniquity" (PER.4.6)
In the play. *Lysimachus, governor of Mytilene refers to the matron of the brothel where the spotless Marina has been sold by kidnapping pirates.*

Corruption, c. for the sake of money - … shall we now contaminate our fingers with base bribes…
"…What, shall one of us
That struck the foremost man of all this world
But for supporting robbers, shall we now
Contaminate our fingers with base bribes,
And sell the mighty space of our large honours
For so much trash as may be grasped thus?" (JC.4.3)
See also 'Capital, no raising capital by corruption - … I can raise no money by vile means…'
In the play. *Brutus upbraids Cassius for his corruption. After killing Caesar to restore freedom and remove arbitrary government, Cassius has accepted bribes and sold offices.*

Corruption, c. no better than honesty - corruption wins no more than honesty.
"Corruption wins no more than honesty.
Still in thy right hand carry gentle peace,
To silence envious tongues."
(KHVIII.3.2)
An encouragement to be honest.
In the play. *Words of advice from the fallen Wolsey to Cromwell.*

Corruption, c. of a man - And whatsoever cunning fiend it was… hath got the voice in hell for excellence.
"And whatsoever cunning fiend it was
That wrought upon thee so preposterously
Hath got the voice in hell for excellence:" (KHV.2.2)
Use 'voice in hell for excellence' to characterize the author of a despicable act.

In the play. *K. Henry chastises Lord Scroop. Henry cannot understand what fiend could lead Scroop to be a traitor, given his otherwise reliable character.*

**Corruption, c. of young person –
Thou hast … abused her delicate youth with drugs or minerals that weaken motion.**
"That thou hast practised on her with foul charms,
Abused her delicate youth with drugs or minerals
That weaken motion" (OTH.1.2)
In the play. *Brabantio accuses Othello to have taken advantage of Desdemona.*

Corruption, corrupted witnesses - … at what ease might corrupt minds procure knaves as corrupt to swear against you?…
"… and not ever
The justice and the truth o' the question carries
The due o' the verdict with it: at what ease
Might corrupt minds procure knaves as corrupt
To swear against you? such things have been done." (KHVIII.5.1)
In the play. *K. Henry to Cranmer who is opposed and attacked by powerful enemies*

Corruption, the price of c. - Is it possible that any villany should be so dear?…
CONRADE Is it possible that any villany should be so dear?
BORACHIO Thou shouldst rather ask if it were possible any villany should be so rich; for when rich villains have need of poor ones, poor ones may make what price they will (MAAN.3.3)
Apply by extension to episodes of imperialism (villany) – when an imperialist power, for example, establishes a puppet government and the puppets (poor ones) can ask the price they will for their puppetry.
In the play. *Don John has paid Borachio 1000 ducats to organize the plot to slander Hero.*

Counsel, c. useless for stubborn hearer - … for all in vain comes counsel to his ear.
"Vex not yourself, nor strive not with your breath;
For all in vain comes counsel to his ear." (KRII.2.1)
See also ' Invocation, i. to flattery, men's ears deaf to good sense but not to flattery'.
In the play. *At Ely's castle, the Duke of York tells John of Gaunt that Richard II's ear is deaf to counsel.*

Counsel, impact of c. from a man nearing death - More are men's ends mark'd than their lives before…
"More are men's ends mark'd than their lives before:
The setting sun, and music at the close,
As the last taste of sweets, is sweetest last,
Writ in remembrance more than things long past" (KRII.2.1)
The lines may apply to the last statement or remark by a writer, politician, etc.
In the play. *Gaunt hopes that his last words may have a good influence on King Richard*

Counsel, refusal of c. - … give me no counsel, my griefs cry louder than advertisement.
"…give me no counsel:
My griefs cry louder than advertisement" (MAAN.5.1)
In the play. *Leonato's reaction to the words of comfort offered by his brother Antonio.*

Counsel, too late for c. - … all too late comes counsel to be heard.

"…all too late comes counsel to be heard,
Where will doth mutiny with wit's regard." (KRII.2.1)
Comment on profligate character.
In the play. *The Duke of York comments on the profligate ways of Richard II's court.*

Counterfeit, c. skills – … ghastly looks are at my service, like enforced smiles and both are ready in their offices at any time, to grace my stratagems
"… I can counterfeit the deep tragedian;
Speak and look back, and pry on every side,
Tremble and start at wagging of a straw,
Intending deep suspicion: ghastly looks
Are at my service, like enforced smiles;
And both are ready in their offices,
At any time, to grace my stratagems" (KRIII.3.5)
See also 'Character, false, cunning, shifting and perverse – I can smile and murder whiles I smile'
In the play. *Buckingham answers a question by Richard as to Buckingham's skills in counterfeit and pretension.*

Country living, in praise of country living - … Here can I sit alone, unseen of any and to the nightingale's complaining notes…
"This shadowy desert, unfrequented woods,
I better brook than flourishing peopled towns:
Here can I sit alone, unseen of any,
And to the nightingale's complaining notes
Tune my distresses and record my woes." (TGV.5.4)
Use the last three lines to tell her that you miss her. Answer to 'What will you do this weekend? E.G. 'I will go where I can sit alone… woes'. See also 'Pleasures, p, of a simple life – If I kept sheep, I should be as merry as the day is long.'
In the play. *Valentine banished to a forest outside of Milan reflects on the advantages of country living while sad because he is away from Silvia.*

Country, c. in poor state, only the ignorant smile - … where nothing, but who knows nothing, is once seen to smile.
"Alas, poor country!
Almost afraid to know itself. It cannot
Be call'd our mother, but our grave;
where nothing,
But who knows nothing, is once seen to smile
Where sighs and groans and shrieks that rend the air
Are made, not mark'd; where violent sorrow seems
A modern ecstasy; the dead man's knell
Is there scarce ask'd for who" (M.4.3)
In the play. *Ross comments on the state of Scotland under Macbeth.*

Country, c. under yoke - I think our country sinks beneath the yoke…
"I think our country sinks beneath the yoke;
It weeps, it bleeds; and each new day a gash
Is added to her wounds" (M.4.3)
If you believe that true freedom has been lost.
In the play. *Malcolm to Macduff referring to Scotland.*

Courage, c. an asset in women's eyes. - … there is no love-broker in the world can more prevail in man's commendation with woman than report of valour.
"… there is no love-broker in the world can more prevail in man's

commendation with woman than report of valour." (TN.3.2)
In the play. *Sir Toby tells Fabian how he could conquer Olivia by challenging Viola/Cesario to a duel.*

Courage, c. displayed in a state of weakness - … that's a valiant flea, that dare eat his breakfast on the lip of a lion.
"…that's a valiant flea, that dare eat his breakfast on the lip of a lion." (KHV.3.7)
Retort to a bragging statement such as "we will beat them" when you know that the party to be beaten is strong
In the play. *The Duke of Orleans banters with Lord Rambures about the valor of the English.*

Courage, c. the number one virtue - … valour is the chiefest virtue and most dignifies the haver.
"… the deeds of Coriolanus
Should not be utter'd feebly. – It is held,
That valour is the chiefest virtue
And most dignifies the haver." (COE.2.2)
Introduction to a speech in honor of a person. E.G. 'The deeds of XX should not be …haver.'
In the play. *Although Coriolanus refuses praise for his victory at Corioli, Cominius says he deserves it.*

Courage, circumstances inspiring c. – Courage mounteth with occasion.
"Courage mounteth with occasion: Let them be welcome then, we are prepared." (KJ.2.1)
Inspire courage and confidence in the shy.
In the play. *King John has arrived in France from England to challenge Arthur's alleged right to the English throne*

Courage, exhortation to c. - what cannot be avoided, 't were childish weakness to lament or fear.
Why, courage then! what cannot be avoided,
'T were childish weakness to lament or fear." (KHVI p3.5.4)
Exhort courage and a stoic and manly attitude towards events. See also entries for 'Complaint after problems useless'.
In the play. *Queen Margaret to allies before the battle of Tewksbury*

Courage, no fear of risk to gain the prize - … think death no hazard, in this enterprise.
"I have, Antiochus, and with a soul
Embolden'd with the glory of her praise,
Think death no hazard, in this enterprise. (PER.1.1)
Answer to, 'Are you ready for the project, (or enterprise, or assignment)?' - 'I am and with a soul…enterprise'
In the play. *King Antiochus has warned Pericles of what would happen if he did not solve the riddle. Antiochus would give his daughter in marriage to him who will solve a riddle. Should the answer be wrong the punishment is death.*

Courage, reward goes to the courageous - … fearless minds climb soonest unto crowns.
"... fearless minds climb soonest unto crowns." (KHVI p3.4.7)
Use to inspire courage
In the play. *Gloucester advises Edward to proclaim himself again king after escaping imprisonment. That announcement is likely to procure immediately new allies.*

Courage, the advantages of c., dying only once - …Cowards die many times before their deaths...
"Cowards die many times before their deaths,
The valiant never taste of death but once.

**Of all the wonders that I yet have heard,
It seems to me most strange that men should fear;
Seeing that death, a necessary end,
Will come when it will come "** (JC.2.2)
Motivate or inspire courage. An argument for avoiding been kept alive as a vegetable though modern machinery.
In the play. *Caesar rejects the efforts of his wife Calphurnia to keep him from going to the Capitol on March 15.*

**Courtesy, c. shown to the wrong person - Why strew'st thou sugar on that bottled spider, whose deadly web ensnareth thee about?
"Poor painted queen, vain flourish of my fortune!
Why strew'st thou sugar on that bottled spider,
Whose deadly web ensnareth thee about?"** KRIII.1.3
In the play. *In a heated exchange of insults and curses, Q. Elizabeth, wife of dying Edward IV, takes the side of Richard and Queen Margaret warns her about Richard's character, warning that will prove too true.*

**Courtesy, false c. - Grace me no grace, nor uncle me no uncle.
"Grace me no grace, nor uncle me no uncle."** (KRII.2.3)
Manly retort to someone who is trying to shaft you while veiling the shaft with words, e.g. 'I regret to say this, but equally…' Answer, 'Regret me no regrets, nor equal me no equals. etc. See also 'Thanks rejected - thank me no thankings, nor, proud me no prouds.'– 'Opinion, your op. on profusely given thanks - … when a man thanks me heartily...'
In the play. *Bolingbroke has returned to England and York (his uncle) suspecting a plot, is leery about Bolingbroke's display of courtesy.*

**Courtesy, false c. - … how fine this tyrant can tickle where she wounds.
'Dissembling courtesy! How fine this tyrant
Can tickle where she wounds"** (CYM.1.1)
In the play. *Imogen refers to the queen, her stepmother. The king is angry with his daughter Imogen for marrying Leonatus against the king's will.*

**Courtesy, false c. - … this courtesy is not of the right breed.
"Nay, good my lord, this courtesy is not of the right breed."** (H.3.2)
Comment on false or commercially motivated courtesy, or courtesy from a suspicious character, '(His) courtesy is not of the right breed'
In the play. *The queen has sent Guildenstern and Rosencranz to meet with Hamlet as both king and queen are very distressed. Hamlet has just welcomed them very sarcastically and Guildenstern points it out to him.*

**Courtesy, people not trained to c. - … Turks and Tartars, never train'd to offices of tender courtesy.
"… stubborn Turks and Tartars, never train'd
To offices of tender courtesy."** (MOV.4.1)
In the play. *The Duke of Venice tells Antonio his opinion about Shylock.*

**Courtship, no time for c. - These times of woe afford no time to woo.
"These times of woe afford no time to woo."** (RJ.3.4)
In the play. *Paris, who wishes to marry Juliet, acknowledges that the time is not ripe for courtship, as the Capulets mourn the death of Tybalt, slain by Romeo.*

Cover up, planned - and what may make him blush in being known, he'll stop the course by which it might be known.

"And what may make him blush in being known,
He'll stop the course by which it might be known." (PER.1.2)
Characterize a hypocrite. "He is like a hypocrite, … sight."
In the play. *Pericles perceives immediately that Antioch's feigned courtesy is suspicious and he will immediately run away.*

Cover up, sins self compounding - … one sin, I know, another doth provoke…
" Antioch, farewell! for wisdom sees, those men
Blush not in actions blacker than the night,
Will shun no course to keep them from the light.
One sin, I know, another doth provoke;
Murder's as near to lust, as flame to smoke." (PER.1.1)
Illustrate the dangers of knowing something you wish you didn't, 'Those men…from the light'. Or point out the connection between lust and further crimes, including murder.
In the play. *In a monologue Pericles perceives immediately that Antioch's feigned courtesy is suspicious and therefore it's time to run.*

Coward, c. by instinct - Instinct is a great matter; I was now a coward on instinct.
"Instinct is a great matter; I was now a coward on instinct" (KHIV.p1.2.4)
In the play. *Falstaff claims that he instinctively recognized the Prince in the staged robbery at Gadshill and that is why he ran away, thus appearing a coward.*

Coward, hoping your fears may be unfounded - Pray God, I say, I prove a needless coward.
"Pray God, I say, I prove a needless coward!" (KRIII.3.2)
When your concerns have been disregarded or dismissed.
In the play. *Stanley is concerned about Richard's ambitions and hopes to be wrong, as Hastings does not believe him.*

Cowardice, c. disguised with a martial outside - we'll have a swashing and a martial outside...
"We'll have a swashing and a martial outside;
As many other mannish cowards have,
That do outface it in their semblances." (AYLI.1.3)
Describe people who are all show and no substance. 'Sometimes cowards have a 'swashing and a martial outside' which they 'outface it in their semblances'.
In the play. *Rosalind will suggest that she and Celia disguise themselves as men and travel incognito towards the forest of Arden where the de-throned Duke S. (Rosalind's father) has taken refuge along with his exiled court.*

Cowardice, c. evident – … there's no more valour in that Poins, than in a wild duck.
"…there's no more valour in that Poins, than in a wild duck." (KHIV p1.2.2)
Substitute for Poins the name of your favorite coward
In the play. *At Gadshill Falstaff robs some travelers and then is robbed by the Prince of Wales, who had organized the caper. Falstaff accuses Poins of cowardice.*

Cowardice, c. hidden in loud threats - … coward dogs most spend their mouths when what they seem to threaten…
"…coward dogs
Most spend their mouths when what they seem to threaten
Runs far before them." (KHV.2.4)

In the play. *A comment by the Dauphin of France as he tries to dispel the French's concern about the real power of Henry V who has landed in France with an army.*

Cowardice, c. justified - honor hath no skills in surgery...
"Honour hath no skill in surgery then? No. What is Honour? A word. What is that word, Honour?"
(KHIVp1.5.1)
Promote peace and point out the death and destruction caused by war.
In the play. *Falstaff outlines his philosophy to the Prince of Wales.*

Cowardice, c. or discretion - The better part of valour is, discretion...
"The better part of valour is discretion; in the which better part I have saved my life." (KHIV p1.5.4)
In an ironic tone, justify why you pulled out of a tricky situation or gamble.
In the play. *Falstaff has pretended to participate in the battle of Shrewsbury, won by the Prince of Wales, but in reality he has avoided any contact with the enemy. In an attempt to justify his own actions (and his pretending to be dead during the battle) Falstaff also says*
"I am no counterfeit: to die, is to be a counterfeit; for he is but the counterfeit of a man who hath not the life of a man: but to counterfeit dying, when a man thereby liveth, is to be no counterfeit, but the true and
perfect image of life indeed".

Cowardice, c. shown by running away – ... Your legs did better service than your hands.
"When you and I met at Saint Alban's last,
Your legs did better service than your hands." (KHVI.p3.2.2)
In the play. *Near York, Queen Margaret reminds enemy Warwick that he fled during the battle of St. Albans', won by the Lancastrians.*

Cowards - The mouse ne'er shunn'd the cat as they did budge from rascals worse than they.
"The mouse ne'er shunn'd the cat as they did budge
From rascals worse than they."
(COR.1.6)
In the play. *Coriolanus' own opinion of Roman common soldiers and people.*

Cowards, c. defined - I know them to be as true-bred cowards as ever turned back.
"I know them to be as true-bred cowards as ever turned back." (KHIV p1.1.2)
In the play. *Poins has devised a caper to frighten Falstaff and company. The true-bred cowards are Falstaff and Bardolph.*

Credentials, establishing your c. - I am as constant as the northern star...
"If I could pray to move, prayers would move me:
But I am as constant as the northern star,
Of whose true fixed and resting quality
There is no fellow in the firmament.
The skies are painted with unnumber'd sparks,
They are all fire, and every one doth shine;
But there is but one in all doth hold his place." (JC.3.1)
Sometimes constancy is not necessarily a virtue of universal appreciation. There may be a danger that constancy be misjudged as stiffness of character. Still, the quote may work as an opening line, for example as an answer to the question, "what can you tell me about yourself? "I am…firmament". Could work as well in a job interview – it establishes at least some literary credentials.

In the play. *Cassius and Brutus approach Caesar requesting that he pardons Publius Cimber but he says no on the ground of hi unshakable character.*

Credentials, questionable – by birth a pedlar, by education a card-maker…
"… (am I not) by birth a pedlar, by education a card-maker, by transmutation a bear-herd, and now by present profession a tinker?" (TOS.IND.)
A sarcastic answer to 'Who are you?'
In the play. *As part of the prank, Sly is addressed as a person of high standing and he cannot believe it.*

Credentials, sincerity, one tongue - I have no tongue but one
"I have no tongue but one." (MFM.2.4)
Answer to any question of the type, 'Are you sure?', 'Is this really true?' etc.
In the play. *Isabel attempts to plead mercy for her brother Claudio's life from the wicked and hypocritical Angelo, temporary ruler of Vienna.*

Credentials, sincerity, one tongue - What I think I utter and spend my malice in my breath.
"What I think I utter and spend my malice in my breath". (COR.2.1)
A good way to declare both your sincerity, particularly if there is a hint or innuendo that you may be hiding something. See also 'Character, straight-forward, no shrewishness'.
In the play. *Menenius speaks with the tribunes and wants to make clear that he speaks as he sees it.*

Credibility, c. reduced - my credit now stands on such slippery ground...
"…what shall I say?
My credit now stands on such slippery ground,
That one of two bad ways you must conceit me,

Either a coward or a flatterer." (JC.3.1)
The internal political situation has changed dramatically and you find yourself in the opposing and winning field.
In the play. *Antony to Brutus. Antony was an ally of Caesar and now is befriended by Brutus who has just killed Caesar. Antony is actually pretending to be a friend in order to plan a revenge.*

Credibility, lack of c. - … will you credit this base drudge's words, that speaks he knows not what?
"And will you credit this base drudge's words,
That speaks he knows not what?" (KHVI.p2.4.2)
In the play. *In Blackheath, Sir William Stafford addresses the rebels led by John Cade.*

Credit worthiness spoiled by uncollected debts - … my reliance on his fracted dates have smit my credit…
"…my reliances on his fracted dates
Have smit my credit: I love and honour him;
But must not break my neck to heal his finger." (TOA.2.1)
Explain the reason for refusing to extend the credit any further. See also entries for 'Financial Status' – 'Receivables, r. must be collected immediately'
In the play. *One creditor (actually a Senator), has had enough of Timon's delays to pay his invoices.*

Creditors, c. cruel - my creditors grow cruel...
"...my creditors grow cruel..." (MOV.3.2)
See also 'Insult, creditors, imprecation – They have e'en put my breath from me, the slaves...'
In the play. *Bassanio reads from a letter of Antonio.*

Crime, authority-contracted c. unsafe for the contractor - ... if a king bid a man be a villain, he's bound by the indenture of his oath to be one.
"…he was a wise fellow, and had good discretion, that, being bid to ask what he would of the king, desired he might know none of his secrets: now do I see he had some reason for't; for if a king bid a man be a villain, he's bound by the indenture of his oath to be one" (PER.1.3)
In the play. *Thaliard, dispatched by Antioch to Tyre to kill Pericles has second thoughts and recalls how Pericles behaved when*

Crime, c. emboldened by clemency - ... nothing emboldens sin so much as mercy.
FIRST SENATOR. ... nothing emboldens sin so much as mercy." (TOA.3.5)
When you feel pitiless.
In the play. *A soldier in Alcibiades' army is accused of murder. The senators want to condemn him to death. Alcibiades, his captain, maintains that the killing was done in self-defense and pleads for mercy to no avail.*

Crime, c. of unspeakable proportions, indignation - The earth hath not a hole to hide his deed.
LORD PEMBROKE. The earth had not a hole to hide this deed.
…
LORD SALISBURY. … This is the very top,
The height, the crest, or crest unto the crest,
Of murder's arms.
….
FAULCONBRIDGE. It is a damned and a bloody work;
The graceless action of a heavy hand,
If that it be the work of any hand." (KJ.4.3)
In the play. *Lord Pembroke stumbles on the dead body of young Prince Arthur, believed murdered by King John. Lord Salisbury and Faulconbridge follow up with their own assessment*

Crime, c. of unspeakable proportions, indignation - This is the very top the height, the crest, or crest onto the crest of murder's arms.
"This is the very top,
The height, the crest, or crest onto the crest,
Of murder's arms; this is the bloodiest shame,
The wildest savagery, the vilest stroke,
That ever wall-eyed wrath, or staring rage,
Presented to the tears of soft remorse." (KJ.4.3)
Use the first two lines to show that whatever act it was, it was the worst of the worst. You can change 'of murder's arm' to whatever the act was, e.g., thievery, treachery, folly etc.
In the play. *Salisbury comments on the murder of young Arthur.*

Crime, c. or villainy, who did it - The practise of it lives in… whose spirits toil in frame of villanies.
"The practise of it lives in John the bastard,
Whose spirits toil in frame of villanies." (MAAN.4.1)
In the play. *Benedick points to John the Bastard as the author of the villainous accusation of the chaste Hero.*

Crime, c. prompted by opportunity - How oft the sight of means to do ill deeds makes ill deeds done.
"How oft the sight of means to do ill deeds
Makes ill deeds done." (KJ.4.2)
Point out how the effects of temptation.
In the play. *King John reflects on the killing of young Arthur. Though John asked Hubert to kill the prince, now he faults him for having done*

it. See a similar situation in 'Assassination, a. of king or enemy – … though I did wish him dead, I hate the murderer, love him murdered.'

Crime, c. sex and murder connected – Murder's as near to lust as flame to smoke.
"Murder's as near to lust as flame to smoke" (PER.1.1)
In the play. *Pericles decides to live Antioch ASAP after discovering Antioch's incestuous practices.*

Crime, evidence of c. provided – If imputation and strong circumstance which lead directly to the door of truth…
"If imputation and strong circumstance
Which lead directly to the door of truth,
Will give you satisfaction, you might have it." (OTH.3.3)
Announce that you will provide the required evidence. 'The door of truth' is a powerful image you may also use in other contexts, e.g. 'Open the door of truth'.
In the play. *Iago will provide false evidence of Desdemona's alleged adultery to destroy both her and Othello.*

Crime, evidence of who is the criminal unmistakable - Who finds the heifer dead and bleeding fresh…
"Who finds the heifer dead and bleeding fresh,
And sees fast by a butcher with an axe,
But will suspect, 't was he that made the slaughter?
Who finds the partridge in the puttock's nest,
But may imagine how the bird was dead,
Although the kite soar with unbloodied beak?
Even so suspicious is this tragedy" (KHVI p2.3.2)

Explain the reason for your suspicions and accusations.
In the play. *Warwick after the discovery of Gloucester's dead body, points the finger at Suffolk. 'Puttock' = 'bird of prey'*

Crime, extreme c. - O, my offence is rank it smells to heaven.
"O, my offence is rank it smells to heaven;
It hath the primal eldest curse upon't, A brother's murder" (H.3.3)
Apply to an action you rate bad or criminal, e.g. 'The offense is rank…'
In the play. *King Claudius reflects on the extremity of his crime.*

Crime, planning the unspeakable c. – … if that thou couldst see me without eyes, hear me without thine ears, and make reply without a tongue…
"… if that thou couldst see me without eyes,
Hear me without thine ears, and make reply
Without a tongue, using conceit alone,
Without eyes, ears and harmful sound of words;
Then, in despite of brooded watchful day,
I would into thy bosom pour my thoughts" (KJ.3.3)
See also entries for 'Deniability'
In the play. *Superb example of government sponsored crime and deniability. King John wants Huber to assassinate young Prince Arthur without telling him to do so.*

Crime, why knowledge of c. is dangerous – Since he's so great can make his will his act will think me speaking, though I swear to silence…
"Since he's so great can make his will his act,
Will think me speaking, though I swear to silence;
Nor boots it me to say I honour him.

If he suspect I may dishonour him" (PER.1.1)
In the play. Pericles decides to live Antioch ASAP after discovering Antioch's incestuous practices. 'To boot' = 'to avail'

Crimes, unspeakable c. - 'Twill vex thy soul to hear what I shall speak; for I must talk of murders…
"'Twill vex thy soul to hear what I shall speak;
For I must talk of murders, rapes and massacres,
Acts of black night, abominable deeds,
Complots of mischief, treason, villanies
Ruthful to hear, yet piteously perform'd" (TA.5.1)
It could be the start of a report from the chief of the CIA.
In the play. The evil Aaron responds to a request from Lucius to give an account of his (Aaron's) crimes and Aaron starts with this declaration. In exchange Lucius will spare the life of Aaron's baby born from the adulterous relation with Queen Tamara.

Criminal, who is the real c.? - It is an heretic that makes the fire, not she which burns in't.
"It is an heretic that makes the fire, Not she which burns in't." (WT.2.3)
Applies to all those who are punished and condemned for their beliefs, when the beliefs reflect a desire to better mankind according to acceptable standards, or standards agreed upon by rational minds.
In the play. Paulina defends defiantly the innocence of Leonte's wife. Leontes the king is incensed and threatens Paulina. She replies stoically.

Criminals, c. acting in the dark - …
Then thieves and robbers range abroad unseen in murders and in outrage bloody…
That when the searching eye of heaven is hid,
Behind the globe, that lights the lower world,
Then thieves and robbers range abroad unseen
In murders and in outrage bloody, here,
But when from under this terrestrial ball
He fires the proud tops of the eastern pines…" (KRII.3.2)
In the play. King Richard to Aumerle and Carlysle, referring to the rebel Bolingbroke and his allies.

Criticism, better a little c. than a lot of heart-break - … better a little chiding, than a great deal of heart-break.
"… better a little chiding, than a great deal of heart-break," (MWW.5.3)
A retort to criticism on your facetiousness
In the play. Mrs. Page has in mind a husband for her daughter Anne. Her choice differs from her husband's. Eventually Anne will marry her own choice, Master Fenton. The chiding could refer to the tricks played previously on Falstaff or to how Mrs. Page will handle her husband when the news of his daughter's marriage will become known. 'Chiding' = 'Scolding'.

Criticism, c. of dead people to be avoided - … beat not the bones of the buried…
"… beat not the bones of the buried: when he breathed he was a man." (LLL.5.2)
Try 'Let's beat not the bones of the buried…' See also 'Remembering, the bad more remembered than the good'.
In the play. The wordy Armado in defense of Hector, the Trojan warrior who was indeed dead.

Criticism, c. of powerful government figure dangerous – … who dare speak one syllable against him?

"…The archbishop
Is the king's hand and tongue; and who dare speak
One syllable against him?" (KHVIII.5.1)
In the play. *Lovell, speaking of Cranmer, the Archbishop who replaced the disgraced Cardinal Wolsey*

Criticism, c. suspect - … such may rail against great buildings.
"Who can speak broader than he that has no house to put his head in? such may rail against great buildings." (TOA.3.4)
An argument to deny the complaints of the disenfranchised.
In the play. *A spiteful servant of a Timon's creditor comments on a remark by Flavius, Timon's servant who, justly, called the other servant's master a knave.*

Criticism, exposed to c. by fools. See 'Opinion, your op. on crowds and masses - … subject to the breath of every fool, whose sense no more can feel but his own wringing!

Criticism, handling of c. – Take each man's censure but reserve thy judgment.
"Give every man thy ear, but few thy voice;
Take each man's censure, but reserve thy judgment." (H.1.3)
Answer to 'How do you react to criticism?' 'I take each man's censure but reserve my judgment'
In the play. *Polonius gives his son Laertes a set of precepts to follow while in Paris. See note to 'Opinion, your op. on money, handling of, borrowing and lending.' for the complete list.*

Criticism, psychological strategy for c. – Chide him for faults, and do it reverently…
"Chide him for faults, and do it reverently,
When thou perceive his blood
inclined to mirth" (KHIVp2.4.4)
In the play. *King Henry advises Thomas of Clarence on how to reprimand or counsel Prince Harry.*

Criticism, self-c. rejected – …Nor shall you … make it truster of your own report against yourself.
"Nor shall you do mine ear that violence,
To make it truster of your own report
Against yourself" (H.1.2)
Response to a self-effacing remark. E.G. 'I will not be truster of…yourself'.
In the play. *Hamlet rejects the notion that his friend Horatio is truant, as Horatio said of himself to explain his presence in Elsinore.*

Crowd, dense c. – … where a finger could not be wedged in more.
"…where a finger
Could not be wedged in more: I am stifled
With the mere rankness of their joy." (KHVIII.4.1)
See also entries for 'Opinion, your op. On crowds and masses'.
In the play. *A citizen referring to his watching with the crowd the coronation of Anne Boleyn.*

Crows, s. impatient for their preys – … the knavish crows fly o'er them, all impatient for their hour.
"And their executors, the knavish crows,
Fly o'er them, all impatient for their hour" (HV.4.2)
In the play. *Grandpre (a Frenchman) believes the English to be done for (at Agincourt) but will be proven wrong.*

Cruel to be kind - I must be cruel, only to be kind…
"I must be cruel, only to be kind:
Thus bad begins and worse remains behind" (H.3.4)

When you are accused of cruelty and yet you have your good reasons – use the first line only.
In the play. *Hamlet rationalizes his actions after upbraiding his mother and killing Polonius*

Cruel, heartbreaker, slain by her - Fly away, fly away breath; I am slain by a fair cruel maid.
"Fly away, fly away breath;
I am slain by a fair cruel maid."
(TN.2.4)
Dramatize her rejection or if she says no to something you asked of her.
In the play: *The clown begins to sing a sad love song at the prompting of Duke Orsino.*

Cruel, pierced through the heart - Pierced through the heart with your stern cruelty.
"Pierced through the heart with your stern cruelty." (MND.3.2)
Dramatic *reaction when she says 'no', 'I am pierced…cruelty'.*
In the play. Demetrius tells Hermia that she is cruel to him.

Cruelty, c. in Rome - Rome is but a wilderness of tigers.
"Rome is but a wilderness of tigers." (TA.3.1)
Apply to any city or country that fits the profile.
In the play. *Lucius attempts to rescue his brothers Quintus and Martius and is banished from Rome. Titus judges Rome accordingly.*

Cruelty, c. on a man fallen from grace - …'tis a cruelty to load a falling man.
"…'tis a cruelty
To load a falling man." (KHVIII.5.3)
In the play. *Cromwell to Gardiner who was very hard on the fallen Cranmer.*

Cruelty, invocation to c. by a woman – Come, you spirits that tend on mortal thoughts, unsex me here…

"Come, you spirits
That tend on mortal thoughts, unsex me here:
And fill me from the crown to the toe top-full
Of direst cruelty! make thick my blood;
Stop up the access and passage to remorse,
That no compunctious visitings of nature
Shake my fell purpose, nor keep peace between
The effect and it!" (M.1.5)
See also 'Anger. Angry at her, compared to a she-wolf - She-wolf of France, but worse than wolves of France, whose tongue more poisons than the adder's tooth.'
In the play. *Lady Macbeth wants to feel no remorse for the forthcoming slaying of King Duncan.*

Cry, c. of encouragement - A Talbot! a Talbot! cried out amain and rush'd into the bowels of the battle.
"A Talbot! a Talbot! cried out amain
And rush'd into the bowels of the battle" (KHVI p1.1.1)
Answer to 'Will you do it?' E.G. 'I'll rush into the bowels of the battle'.
In the play. *A messenger reports of the feats of Talbot in France.*

Cry, do not cry – fall not a tear, I say; one of them rates all that is won and lost…
"Fall not a tear, I say; one of them rates
All that is won and lost: give me a kiss;
Even this repays me." (AC.3.11)
If she start crying believing to be at fault for whatever reason.
In the play. *Antony comforts Cleopatra, whom he scolded for her role in the loss of the sea battle.*

Cry, starting to cry - Then can I drown an eye, unused to flow…
"Then can I drown an eye, unused to flow…." (SON 30)
Change to 'Now I can drown…flow' See also 'Disappointment, d. expressed in dramatic terms – … make dust our paper and with rainy eyes…'

Crying not called for, on the contrary - the tears live in an onion that should water this sorrow.
"…the tears live in an onion that should water this sorrow." (AC.1.2)
When something that technically should make you sad, actually doesn't.
In the play. *Enobarbus comments on the death of Fulvia, Antony's estranged wife. Antony is temporarily sad and Enobarbus says he shouldn't be.*

Crying, c. impossible notwithstanding the pain but…– …weep I cannot, but my heart bleeds…
"Weep I cannot,
But my heart bleeds, and most accursed am I
To be by oath enjoined to do this." (WT.3.3)
Alternative to 'I hate to do this'. Start from 'most accursed I am'
In the play. *In a dream Hermione, believed dead, tells Antigonus to abandon the child in a remote place in Bohemia. He was bound to kill the infant but instead decides to follow the indications of the dream and abandons the baby. Still he regrets it. The baby will be found and raised by a shepherd.*

Crying, c. prevented by re-distribution of moisture - I cannot weep; for all my body's moisture scarse serves to quench my furnace-burning heart.
"I cannot weep; for all my body's moisture
Scarce serves to quench my furnace-burning heart:
Nor can my tongue unload my heart's great burthen;
For selfsame wind that I should speak withal
Is kindling coals that fires all my breast,
And burns me up with flames that tears would quench." (KHVI.p3.2.1)
Add emphasis to your rage.
In the play. *Richard of Gloucester commenting on his father Richard, slain by Clifford.*

Crying, competition at who cries more – And with the southern clouds contend in tears…
"And with the southern clouds contend in tears,
Theirs for the earth's increase, mine for my sorrows" (KHVI.p2.3.1)
In the play. *Queen Margaret cries at Suffolk having been banished from court.*

Crying, invitation to a lady to stop c. - … weep no more, lest I give cause to be suspected of more tenderness than doth become a man.
"O lady, weep no more, lest I give cause
To be suspected of more tenderness
Than doth become a man" (CYM.1.1)
See also 'Tears, unmanly and prompted by moving scene - these foolish drops do something drown my manly spirit'.
In the play. *Leonatus to wife Imogen as he leaves for Rome, exiled by her father, King Cymbeline.*

Crying, on the point of crying - Mine eyes smell onions, I shall weep anon.
"Mine eyes smell onions, I shall weep anon." (AWEW.5.3)
Lighten the emotional mood, if you happen to be moved to tears by an event. See also 'Tears, unmanly and prompted by moving scene.' – 'Crying not called for, on the contrary'.

In the play. *Helena enters the scene and discloses the secret behind her wearing the ring. Lafeu is moved by the happy outcome.*

Crying, why are you crying? - ... that this distemper'd messenger of wet… rounds thine eye?
"What's the matter,
That this distemper'd messenger of wet,
The many colour'd Iris, rounds thine eye?" (AWEW.1.3)
Ask the question, 'why are you crying?' if you already suspect that the reasons are not that critical.
In the play. *The Countess finds Helen crying. Helen cries because she loves Bertram and he does not know it.*

Crying, with unhappiness - I am great with woe, and shall deliver weeping.
"I am great with woe, and shall deliver weeping." (PER.5.1)
Use satirically, you will now start crying.
In the play. *Pericles, moved by Marina's words and not yet knowing she is his daughter, starts crying.*

Culture, c. conditioning the characters of men – ... men are as the time is.
"... men
Are as the time is" (KL.5.3)
In the play. *Evil Edmund instructs a captain to murder the captured Cordelia. The rationale, to kill any remorse, is that the times, not the evil of man, call for the slaughter.*

Cunning, c. observed - ... practices of cunning hell.
"... practices of cunning hell"
(OTH.1.3)
Put down the doings of your opposition.
In the play. *Brabantio does not accept Othello's version of events that led to his marriage with Desdemona and attributes the event to witchcraft.*

Cunning, c. observed - The fox barks not when he would steal the lamb.
"The fox barks not when he would steal the lamb." (KHVI p2.3.1)
When you suspect a hidden purpose.
In the play. *Suffolk tells King Henry VI his opinion of Gloucester whom he and others try to do in.*

Cunning, using a partial truth to make a bigger lie – You do advance your cunning more and more when truth kills truth.
"You do advance your cunning more and more
When truth kills truth" (MND.3.2)
Use during election debate or equivalent.
In the play. *Helena cannot understand the sudden passion for her of Lysander, bewitched by the magic potion applied to him by Puck.*

Cupid, C. can make ladies mad - Cupid is a knavish lad thus to make poor females mad.
"Cupid is a knavish lad,
Thus to make poor females mad." (MND.3.2)
In the play. *Puck on observing Hermia. The confusion caused by Puck, Oberon and their potions has upset Hermia.*

Cupid, C's arrows - ... Of this matter is little Cupid's crafty arrow made…
"…Of this matter
Is little Cupid's crafty arrow made,
That only wounds by hearsay."
(MAAN.3.1)
In the play. *Hero suggests to Ursula a little trick aimed at informing Beatrice that Benedick actually loves her.*

Cupid, C's varied mode of operation - ... loving goes by haps, some Cupid kills with arrows, some with traps.
"…loving goes by haps:
Some Cupid kills with arrows, some with traps" (MAAN.3.1)

In the play. *Hero's comment at the success of her 'trap' to make Beatrice fall in love with Benedick.*

Cupid, love, definition - The anointed sovereign of sighs and groans.
"The anointed sovereign of sighs and groans" (LLL.3.1)
Use this definition to indicate your pessimism about love in general. For example, 'Cupid is the god of love, the anointed sovereign of sighs and groans'. Alternatively, use the quote somewhat theatrically to indicate that you are in love.
Among the places where an aspiring lover may be able to find his match, Ovid recommends the Coliseum especially when they hold (held) gladiatorial games. The pleasure (or pain) of romantic conquest are mixed with the excitement of gambling. 'Such openings will the Circus afford to a new courtship, and the melancholy sand scattered on the busy ring. Often has Cupid fought upon that sand, just like the gladiator who watched the wounds has inflicted on his adversary is himself wounded. Similarly, while (the aspiring lover) is speaking and touching her hand and asking for the book, and inquiring who is winning as he places his bet, he feels the winged barb and groans with the wound, and is himself part of the show which he is watching". (AOL.2)
If you are a mass sport watcher, I would still suggest that you do not mix sport watching and/or gambling with romantic advances. You may lose your gamble, miss the sport action and not get very far with your advances.
In the play. *Biron meditates on his love for Rosaline.*

Curse, arthritis - aches contract and starve your supple joints!
"Aches contract and starve your supple joints!" (TOA.1.1)
In the play *Apemantus decries Timon's company and wishes arthritis upon them. If they contracted arthritis they would be prevented from bending their knees in faked respect and flattery of Timon.*

Curse, asking permission to c. - I pr'ythee, give me leave to curse awhile.
"I pr'ythee, give me leave to curse awhile." KHVI.p1.5.3)
Use to create contrast just before uttering a four letter word
In the play. *La Pucelle has been captured by the English near in the town of Angiers, after a fight with the duke of York. She addresses her captor, York.*

Curse, c. against a city - O thou wall that girdlest in those wolves, dive in the earth and fence not Athens.
"O thou wall,
That girdlest in those wolves, dive in the earth,
And fence not Athens!" (TOA.4.1)
Change 'Athens' for the appropriate city. With the US the city is Washington.
In the play. *Timon's angry at his parasitic, ungrateful and greedy friends*

Curse, asking gods to confirm curses - I would the gods had nothing else to do...
"I would the gods had nothing else to do,
But to confirm my curses! Could I meet 'em
But once a day, it would unclog my heart
Of what lies heavy to it." (COR.4.2)
In the play. *Volumnia curses Sicinius and the citizens.*

Curse, cursing a murderous hand - Cursed be the hand that made these fatal holes!...
"Cursed be the hand that made these fatal holes!

Cursed be the heart that had the heart to do it!
Cursed the blood that let this blood from hence!
More direful hap betide that hated wretch,
That makes us wretched by the death of thee,
Than I can wish to adders, spiders, toads,
Or any creeping venom'd thing that lives!" (KRIII.1.2)
In the play. *Lady Anne, widow of the son of Henry VI, slain by Richard curses the killer.*

Curse, c. and prediction for a traitor - his treasons will sit blushing in his face...
"His treasons will sit blushing in his face,
Not able to endure the sight of day,
But self-affrighted tremble at his sin." (KRII.3.2)
Change 'his' to 'your' if you address directly the traitor who betrayed you.
In the play. *Richard II refers to the usurping Bolingbroke. His hope that Bolingbroke may fail in his attempt will be shattered.*

Curse, c. on unsympathetic associates – Sorrow on thee and all the pack of you that triumph thus upon my misery!
"Sorrow on thee and all the pack of you,
That triumph thus upon my misery!" (TOS.4.3)
In the play. *Katharina is mad at Grumio for not having brought any food.*

Curse, c. piercing the clouds - Can curses pierce the clouds and enter heaven?
"Can curses pierce the clouds and enter heaven?
Why, then, give way, dull clouds, to my quick curses!" (KRIII.1.3)
Express your indignation.

In the play. *Queen Margaret is mad at Richard and just about everyone else.*

Curse, c. to a liar - ... may his pernicious soul rot half a grain a day! He lies to the heart.
"...may his pernicious soul
Rot half a grain a day! he lies to the heart" (OTH.5.2)
In the play. *Emilia, on hearing from Othello that her husband Iago was the instigator of the jealousy and the events that led to Desdemona's murder, inveighs against Iago.*

Curse, c. to both Democrats and Republicans - A plague o' both your houses!
"A plague o' both your houses!
They have made worms' meat of me." (RJ.3.1)
Apply to Democrats and Republicans, to the Congress and the Senate if you are unhappy with the two party system.
In the play. *Mercutio's reaction at being hurt by the Capulet Tybalt while fighting on behalf of the Romeo and the Montagues.*

Curse, c. to enemy - More direful hap betide that hated wretch...
"More direful hap betide that hated wretch
Than I can wish to wolves, to spiders, toads,
Or any creeping venom'd thing that lives!" (KRIII.1.2)
Curse an enemy.
In the play. *The body of the slain Henry VI has just been brought in. Anne, daughter in law of Henry VI curses his assassin.*

Curse, c. to him who brings unpleasant news - Accursed be that tongue that tells me so.
"Accursed be that tongue that tells me so" (M.5.7)

In the play. *In the battlefield outside Dunsinane, Macduff has just told Macbeth that he (Macduff) was born via a Cesarean delivery; hence he 'was not born of a woman'.*

Curse, c. to the slanderers - Sink Rome, and their tongues rot that speak against us.
"Sink Rome, and their tongues rot
That speak against us!" (AC.3.7)
Change Rome to any other city or applicable organization.
In the play. *Cleopatra is determined to join Antony in the sea battle against Octavian, a move that Enobarbus discourages and that will prove fatal.*

Curse, c. to the unfair winners - Beshrew the winners, for they play'd me false.
"Beshrew the winners, for they play'd me false." (KHVI p2.3.1)
Comment on your undeserved defeat
In the play. *Gloucester is resigned to his fate. His enemies have arrested him on false pretences.* 'Beshrew' = *'mild imprecation meaning 'woe to'.*

Curse, c. to wars and sex - ... wars and lechery; nothing else holds fashion: a burning devil take them!
"...wars and lechery; nothing else holds fashion: a burning devil take them!" (TC.5.2)
In the play. Thersites' conclusion after observing Cressida and her dealings with Diomed.

Curse. canker - The canker gnaw thy heart for showing me again the eyes of man.
ALCIBIADES. What art thou there? Speak.
TIMON. The canker gnaw thy heart, For showing me again the eyes of man!" (TOA.4.3)
You have retired to a solitary place and do not want to see anyone. "Canker gnaw the heart of him who shows me again the eyes of man!"

In the play. *Alcibiades is actually a rare and honest friend of Timon and is also the first man who calls on him in the woods where he retired after declaring bankruptcy.*

Curse, damnation - Let molten coin be thy damnation, thou disease of a friend, and not himself!
"Let molten coin be thy damnation, Thou disease of a friend, and not himself!" (TOA.3.1)
In the play. *Flaminius, faithful servant to Timon, curses Lucullus, who refuses to lend any money to Timon.*

Curse, darkness and lack of sun - May never glorious sun reflex his beams upon the country where you make abode...
"May never glorious sun reflex his beams
Upon the country where you make abode;
But darkness and the gloomy shade of death
Environ you, till mischief and despair
Drive you to break your necks or hang yourselves!" (KHVI p1.5.4)
In the play. *Joan of Arc to the English before being burned at the stake.*

Curse, desire to c. under any circumstances - Well could I curse away a winter's night...
"Well could I curse away a winter's night,
Though standing naked on a mountain top,
Where biting cold would never let grass grow,
And think it but a minute spent in sport" (KHVI p2.3.2)
In the play. *Suffolk to Q. Margaret on his wish to curse the enemies that had him banished.*

Curse, fog - The south-fog rot him!
"The south-fog rot him!" (CYM.2.3)

In the play. *Cloten curses Leonatus whose praise Imogen has just extolled.*

Curse, go to hell - Hie thee to hell for shame, and leave the world, thou cacodemon! there thy kingdom is.
"Hie thee to hell for shame, and leave the world,
Thou cacodemon! there thy kingdom is" KRIII.1.3
In the play. *Q. Margaret, widow of Henry VI, sees through the scheme and evil soul of Richard of Gloucester.*

Curse, infectious diseases - All the infections that the sun sucks up from bogs...
"All the infections that the sun sucks up
From bogs, fens, flats, on Prosper fall and make him
By inch-meal a disease!" (TEM.2.1)
In the play. *Caliban is chronically disaffected with his master Prospero.*

Curse, lung eating vultures - Let vultures vile seize on his lungs.
"Let vultures vile seize on his lungs also!" (KHIVp2.5.3)
In the play. *The object of the curse is the Lord Chief Justice, whom Pistol and Falstaff think will be fired by Henry V. But he will not.*

Curse, may that dog die - Cancel his bond of life, dear God, I pray, that I may live to say, the dog is dead.
"Cancel his bond of life, dear God, I prey,
That I may live to say, The dog is dead!" (KRIII.4.4)
In the play. *Queen Margaret hopes that Richard (the dog) will die for all his murders.*

Curse, minister of hell - Break thou in pieces and consume to ashes thou foul accursed minister of hell.
"Break thou in pieces and consume to ashes,
Thou foul accursed minister of hell!" (KHVI.p1.5.4)
In the play. *The Duke of York replies in kind to the curses of the captured Joan of Arc (Pucelle)*

Curse, misery – your misery increase with your age!
"…your misery increase with your age!" (COR.5.2)
In the play. *Menenius to Volscean Senators after his unsuccessful visit with Coriolanus.*

Curse, plague – ... all the plagues that in the pendulous air hung fated over men's faults...
"Now, all the plagues that in the pendulous air
Hang fated o'er men's faults light on thy daughters." (KL.3.4)
Change 'thy daughters' to the person(s) who are the object of the curse.
In the play. *King Lear, partially out of his mind imagines that the troubles Edgar is in, were caused by Edgar's own daughters, though Edgar has no daughters.*

Curse, plague - ... and would send them back the plague could I but catch it for them.
FIRST SENATOR. The senators of Athens greet thee, Timon.
TIMON. I thank them; and would send them back the plague,
Could I but catch it for them (TOA.5.1)
In the play. *Hoping to enlist Timon's help, Athenian senators come to visit him in his cave. They hope he will intercede with his friend Alcibiades who wants to attack Athens.*

Curse, plague on murderers - A plague upon you, murderers, traitors all!
"A plague upon you, murderers, traitors all!
I might have saved her; now she's gone for ever!" (KL.5.3)

In the play. *King Lear on discovering the murdered body of his good daughter Cordelia.*

Curse, plague plus - Plagues, incident to men, your potent and infectious fevers heap on Athens…
"…Plagues, incident to men,
Your potent and infectious fevers heap
On Athens, ripe for stroke!" (TOA.4.1)
In the play. *Timon expresses his dissatisfaction at the Athenian Senate and Athenians in general.*

Curse, poison - Poison be their drink!…
"… Poison be their drink!
Gall, worse than gall, the daintiest that they taste!" (KHVI p2.3.2)
In the play. *Suffolk' wish for the enemies who had him banished.*

Curse, poison - Would poison were obedient and knew my mind…
TIMON Would poison were obedient and knew my mind!
APEMANTUS Where wouldst thou send it?
TIMON To sauce thy dishes.
(TOA.4.3)
Convert to 'If poison were obedient and knew my mind I would send it to sauce thy dishes'.
In the play. *Timon, now living in a cave, receives an unwanted visit by Apemantus*

Curse, quick course on cursing. - …
Forbear to sleep the nights, and fast the days…
"Forbear to sleep the nights, and fast the days;
Compare dead happiness with living woe;
Think that thy babes were fairer than they were,
And he that slew them fouler than he is:
Bettering thy loss makes the bad causer worse:
Revolving this will teach thee how to curse." (KRIII.4.4)
In the play. *On request by Queen Elizabeth,* ('O thou well skill'd in curses, stay awhile, And teach me how to curse mine enemies!) *Queen Margaret gives her a quick lesson. in cursing.*

Curse, sciatica - Thou cold sciatica cripple our senators…
"Thou cold sciatica,
Cripple our senators, that their limbs may halt
As lamely as their manners."
(TOA.4.1)
In the play. *Timon angry at his parasitic and ungrateful wolfish friends.*

Curse, sterility - Into her womb convey sterility! Dry up in her the organs of increase.
"Into her womb convey sterility!
Dry up in her the organs of increase" (KL.1.4)
In the play. *King Lear is angry at his daughter Goneril, one of the two evil daughters.*

Curse, variety of skin conditions - …
Itches, blains, sow all the Athenian bosoms; and their crop be general leprosy!
"…Itches, blains,
Sow all the Athenian bosoms; and their crop
Be general leprosy!" (TOA.4.1)
Change 'Athenian' to the category you wish to curse.
In the play. *Timon expresses his dissatisfaction at the Athenian Senate and Athenians in general.*

Curse, wishing ignorance and stupidity - The common curse of mankind, folly and ignorance…
" … The common curse of mankind, folly and ignorance, be thine in great revenue, heaven bless thee from a

tutor, and discipline come not near thee!" (TC.2.3)
In the play *Thersites is not very social by nature and curses Patroclus.*

Curse, you cause me to c. - ... thou, I fear, has given me cause to curse.
" ... thou, I fear, has given me cause to curse." (MND.3.2)
Comment to nonsense that has just been uttered, or to a mishap or error (e.g. spilling of coffee on your shirt).
In the play. *Hermia is upset with Demetrius who is in love with Hermia.*

Curse, your enemy shipped to hell - would thou wert shipped to hell, rather than rob me of the people's hearts.
"Andronicus, would thou wert shipped to hell,
Rather than rob me of the people's hearts." (TA.1.1)
Use the first line as appropriate, by changing 'Andronicus' to the name of the recipient (of the curse).
In the play. *Saturninus aspires to become emperor of Rome and is concerned about a challenge from Titus. Actually, Tutus does not want to be emperor.*

Curses, antidote to c. - ... curses never pass the lips of those that breathe them in the air.
"...curses never pass
The lips of those that breathe them in the air." (KRIII.1.3)
In the play. *Buckingham puts an end to Queen Margaret's string of curses by claiming that they are ineffective.*

Curses, if curses would work - Would curses kill, as doth the mandrake's groan...
"Would curses kill, as doth the mandrake's groan,
I would invent as bitter-searching terms,

As curst, as harsh and horrible to hear,
Deliver'd strongly through my fixed teeth,
With full as many signs of deadly hate,
As lean-faced Envy in her loathsome cave" (KHVIp2.3.2)
In the play. *Suffolk's thought as he prepared to leave Queen Margaret after having been banished from England.*

Custom, c. as an obstacle to positive change - What custom wills, in all things should we do't, the dust of antique time would lie unswept...
"What custom wills, in all things should we do't,
The dust on antique time would lie unswept,
And mountainous error be too highly heapt
For truth to o'er-peer." (COR.2.3)
Retort when someone says '...but we have always done it this way.'
In the play. *Coriolanus, forced by custom to stand in front of the people to garner their affection and gain popularity, decries the obligations of custom and (by inference) the continuation of error.*

Custom, c. making heart (or mind) impenetrable to sense – ... damned custom have not brass'd it so that it is proof and bulwark against sense.
"And let me wring your heart; for so I shall,
If it be made of penetrable stuff,
If damned custom have not brass'd it so
That it is proof and bulwark against sense." (H.3.4).
Apply to the minds of people refractory to reason, e.g. 'Damned custom has brass'd their minds so that...sense'.
In the play. *Hamlet upbraids his mother for having married King Claudius.*

Custom, c. more ignored than followed - … it is a custom more honour'd in the breach than the observance.
"… though I am native here
And to the manner born, it is a custom
More honour'd in the breach than the observance." (H.1.4)
A typical example is reading a company's operation manual.
In the play. *Horatio asks if it is the local custom to hold a celebration party, which is just being given by the king. Hamlet replies.*

Custom, how to reverse a c. or bad habit - That monster, custom, who all sense doth eat…
"That monster, custom, who all sense doth eat,
Of habits devil, is angel yet in this,
That to the use of actions fair and good
He likewise gives a frock or livery,
That aptly is put on" (H.3.4)
See also 'Virtue, how to acquire it - Assume a virtue, if you have it not.'
In the play. *After a tempestuous volley of accusations, Hamlet tells his mother to forego the nuptial bed that evening. This would be a reversal of a bad habit and the beginning of some kind of redemption.*

Damage (unexpected) received from a supposedly helpful source - … from that spring whence comfort seem'd to come discomfort swells.
"…from that spring whence comfort seem'd to come
Discomfort swells" (M.1.2)
In the play. *A sergeant, back from the battlefield narrates the events of the day. The metaphorical spring referred to here is a Norwegian lord who suddenly sided with the rebels*

Damage, d. minimal, only annoyance. See 'Annoyance, enemies creating more a. than damage'.

Dance, invitation to d. - … with measure heap'd in joy, to the measure fall.
"Play music! - and you, brides and bridegrooms all,
With measure heap'd in joy, to the measure fall." (AYLI.5.4)
Declare the party started. Substitute, "ladies and gentlemen" for 'brides and bridegrooms'. See also 'Party, let's party.'
In the play. *The Duke S throws a party for the several couples recently married.*

Dancing, reason for not d. – … I have a soul of lead so stakes me to the ground I cannot move.
"Not I, believe me: you have dancing shoes
With nimble soles: I have a soul of lead
So stakes me to the ground I cannot move." (RJ.1.4)
Answer to 'Why don't you dance?'
In the play. *Romeo insists that he will attend but not dance at the Capulet party.*

Dandy, arrival of a d. - Came there a certain lord, neat, and trimly dress'd, fresh as a bridegroom.
"Came there a certain lord, neat, and trimly dress'd,
Fresh as a bridegroom…"(KHIVp1.1.3)
Friendly ironic comment on a neatly attired colleague, e.g. 'Here comes XY, neat…bridegroom' See also 'Greetings, end of unhappiness – Now is the winter of our discontent, made glorious summer by this sun of York…'
In the play. *Hotspur recounts to King Henry an encounter with a dandy sent by the King*

Danger, avoiding unnecessary d. - ... nor seek for danger where there's no profit.
"We'll hunt no more to-day, nor seek for danger
Where there's no profit" (CYM.4.1)
Strengthen your argument about rejecting a dangerous venture that has little possibilities of profit.
In the play. *Belarius calls an end to a hunt during which Guiderius met with Cloten (the Queen's son), and killed him in a fight.*

Danger, courage needed in d. - 'tis true that we are in great danger, the greater therefore should our courage be.
"Gloucester, 'tis true that we are in great danger;
The greater therefore should our courage be" (KHV.4.1)
In the play. *King Henry prior to the battle of Agincourt.*

Danger, d. compared t an approaching storm – When tempest of commotion, like the south…
"When tempest of commotion, like the south
Borne with black vapour, doth begin to melt
And drop upon our bare unarmed heads" (KHIVp2.2.4)
In the play. *Prince Harry feels guilty at wasting time with Falstaff and company while the rebels are gathering strength and are compared to an approaching storm.*

Danger, d. necessary to achieve safety – out of this nettle, danger, we pluck this flower, safety.
"…Out of this nettle, danger, we pluck this flower, safety." (KHIV p1.2.3)
A reference to promote a daring plan, 'Yes, there are dangers, but out of this nettle, danger, we pluck this flower, safety.

In the play. *Hotspur comments on a letter he is reading aloud from George Dunbar, Earl of Scotland.*

Danger, d. undertaken for someone else's benefit - Much danger do I undergo for thee.
"Much danger do I undergo for thee" (KJ.4.1)
In the play. *Hubert to young Prince Arthur. Hubert has been persuaded not to kill the prince after all.*

Danger, dismissing d. unwise – You take a precipice for no leap of danger and woo your own destruction.
"You take a precipice for no leap of danger,
And woo your own destruction." (KHVIII.5.1)
In the play. *K. Henry to Cranmer who takes lightly the opposition of powerful enemies*

Danger, facing d. as best option - I must go and meet with danger there…
"I must go and meet with danger there,
Or it will seek me in another place
And find me worse provided." (KHIV.p2.2.3)
In the play. *Northumberland decides to join the rebels in the second battle, but then will change his mind.*

Danger, fearing d. before any evidence, creates danger - To fly the boar before the boar pursues were to incense the boar to follow us…
"To fly the boar before the boar pursues,
Were to incense the boar to follow us,
And make pursuit where he did mean no chase." (KRIII.3.2)
Exhortation not to display signs of weakness.

In the play. *Hastings disregards the dream-conveyed warning message given by Stanley. The message involved a fierce and aggressive boar. Stanley was right, though.*

Danger, facing up to d. – (we) boldly did outdare the dangers of the time
"…boldly did outdare
The dangers of the time."
(KHIVp1.5.1)
In the play. *Worcester reminds King Henry that he, his brother and Hotspur ensured that Henry could dethrone Richard II.*

Danger, imminent d. and reaction on men – … By a divine instinct men's minds mistrust ensuing dangers…
"Before the times of change, still is it so:
By a divine instinct men's minds mistrust
Ensuing dangers; as by proof, we see
The waters swell before a boisterous storm." (KRIII.2.3)
In the play. *Citizens comment among themselves about the sense of dangers signaling the imminent coronation of the evil Richard III.*

Danger, mind's ability to sense danger - By a divine instinct men's minds mistrust ensuing dangers…
"By a divine instinct men's minds mistrust
Ensuing dangers; as by proof, we see
The waters swell before a boisterous storm." (KRIII.2.3)
Justify your concerns and your perception of looming danger.
In the play. *King Edward is dead and two citizens share their view on the current uncertain political situation in England and the impending changes.*

Danger, on being pre-warned of a danger - For many men that stumble at the threshold are well foretold that danger lurks within.
"For many men that stumble at the threshold,
Are well foretold that danger lurks within." (KHVI.p3.4.7)
Counsel prudence or restraint when the danger ahead is known beforehand.
In the play. *Gloucester to the temporarily dethroned Edward IV who intends to fight and enter into York.*

Dangers, assessment and priority of d. – Thou'ldst shun a bear; but if thy flight lay toward the raging sea…
"…Thou'ldst shun a bear;
But if thy flight lay toward the raging sea,
Thou'ldst meet the bear i' the mouth. When the mind's free,
The body's delicate: the tempest in my mind
Doth from my senses take all feeling else
Save what beats there." (KL.3.4)
See also 'Pain, mental p., greater suffering makes us insensitive to the lesser - … where the greater malady is fix'd the lesser is scarce felt.'
In the play. Lear to Kent. *The greatest pain for Lear is the ingratitude of his daughters.*

Dangers, images of mortal d. - Thou mayst hold a serpent by the tongue.
"France, thou mayst hold a serpent by the tongue,
A chafed lion by the mortal paw,
A fasting tiger safer by the tooth,
Than keep in peace that hand which thou dost hold." (KJ.3.1)
Graphically depict situations or people you consider dangerous.
In the play. *Cardinal Pandulph orders King Philip to wage war on England or else.*

Daring, d. but to a limit - I dare do all that may become a man; who dares do more is none.
"I dare do all that may become a man; Who dares do more is none." (M.1.7)

Possible answer to job interview questions of the type 'What can you do for us?'
In the play. *Macbeth has second thoughts about killing Duncan, though his wife, Lady Macbeth will find arguments to spur him on to execute the murder.*

Darkness, fear of d. - In the night, imagining some fear, how easy is a bush supposed a bear.
"... in the night, imagining some fear
How easy is a bush supposed a bear." (MND.5.1)
Allay concerns or fears.
In the play. *Theseus comments on the power and the effects of imagination.*

Date, looking forward to a second d. – This bud of love…may prove a beauteous flower when we next meet.
"Sweet, good night! This bud of love, by summer's ripening breath,
May prove a beauteous flower when next we meet." (RJ.2.2)
Use at the end of the first date, especially if nothing much happened.
In the play. *Juliet attempts to cool Romeo's outburst of declared love and passion.*

Dating, a long time without d. - … For long agone I have forgot to court, besides the fashion of the time is changed.
"For long agone I have forgot to court;
Besides, the fashion of the time is changed" (TGV.3.1)
Make allowance for any possible shortcomings, if the situation applies to you.
In the play. *The mature Duke of Milan pretends to be in love again with a Milanese lady and to need Valentine's instructional assistance in the matter.*

Day, black day, beginning of dark period - This day's black fate on more days doth depend; this but begins the woe, others must end.
"This day's black fate on more days doth depend;
This but begins the woe, others must end." (RJ.3.1)
Comment on a bad decision, an attack, an insult or other event to which unpleasant occurrences follow.
In the play. *Benvolio tells Romeo that Mercutio (of the Montague faction) has been slain by Tybalt (a Capulet). Romeo comments on the event and shortly later he will kill Tybalt in a duel.*

Day, d. of shame to be eliminated from the calendar – … Nay, rather turn this day out of the week…
"What hath this day deserved? what hath it done,
That it in golden letters should be set
Among the high tides in the calendar?
Nay, rather turn this day out of the week,
This day of shame, oppression, perjury." (KJ.3.1)
In the play. *Constance refers to the day of the wedding between the Dauphin of France and Lady Blanche, a marriage that will void the right of her young son Arthur to the throne of England.*

Deafness, d. to heavenly harmony caused by corrupted nature of man - Such harmony is in immortal souls…
"Such harmony is in immortal souls;
But whilst this muddy vesture of decay
Doth grossly close it in, we cannot hear it." (MOV.5.1)
Use as a comparison when inviting the audience to let go of gross or material considerations and to listen to higher voices or ideas.
In the play. *Lorenzo, house-sitting for Portia and in the company of his wife Jessica, is inspired to meditation by the spectacle of a starry heaven.*

The harmony he refers to is the rhythmic motion of the stars
"There's not the smallest orb which thou behold'st
But in his motion like an angel sings."
A good line to quote when observing the heavens in the company of the lady of your choice.

Deafness, strategic d. – ... my master is deaf ... I am sure he is, to the hearing of any thing good.
PAGE. You must speak louder; my master is deaf.
LORD CHIEF JUSTICE I am sure he is, to the hearing of any thing good.
Go, pluck him by the elbow; I must speak with him. (KHIV.p2.1.2)
Generalize, e.g. 'Like Falstaff, they are deaf to the hearing of anything good'.
In the play. *Falstaff feigns deafness to avoid having to deal with the judge.*

Deal, d. with credulous party almost done - I have him already tempering between my finger and my thumb.
"I have him already tempering between my finger and
my thumb, and shortly will I seal with him" (KHIV.p2.4.3)
Answer to 'How are the negotiations progressing?' - when you sense that the party you are dealing with is ready to yield to your request.
In the play. *Falstaff anticipates the pleasure of tricking Justice Shallow into giving him money with the promise of advancing him at court.*

Death by inches – ... They'll give him death by inches.
"...if
The Roman ladies bring not comfort home,
They'll give him death by inches." (COR.5.4)
Use as a metaphor for mental torture.

In the play. *A messenger reports on the plebeians who are now angry at a tribune. Coriolanus ha defected to the Volsces and hold the tribune responsible for it.*

Death, advantages of d. - Though death be poor, it ends a mortal woe.
"Though death be poor, it ends a mortal woe" (KRII.2.1)
In the play. *The Duke of York's comment upon hearing of Gaunt's death.*

Death, attitude towards d. – ... To throw away the dearest thing he owed as 'twere a careless trifle.
"...he died
As one that had been studied in his death
To throw away the dearest thing he owed,
As 'twere a careless trifle." (M.1.4)
In the play. *Malcolm relates to King Duncan how the previous Thane of Cowdor faced his execution for treason.*

Death, d. after an evil life – ... what a sign it is of evil life where death's approach is seen so terrible!
"Ah, what a sign it is of evil life,
Where death's approach is seen so terrible!" (KHVI.p2.3.3)
In the play. *Cardinal Beaufort, on point of death, is terrified by it and King Henry comments on the fear.*

Death, d. and suffering equal for any creature – ... The sense of death is most in apprehension...
"... Dare'st thou die?
The sense of death is most in apprehension;
And the poor beetle that we tread upon,
In corporal suffering fins a pang as great
As when a giant dies." MFM.3.1)
Express a general truth about suffering

In the play. *Isabel is pessimistic that Angelo will pardon her brother Claudio and change the death sentence. She attempts to prepare him spiritually.*

Death, d. as a cave – ... the blind cave of eternal night.
"...bid him bring his power
Before sunrising, lest his son George fall
Into the blind cave of eternal night." (KRIII.5.3)
In the play. *George, Stanley's son, is hostage and Richard wants Stanley to bring in his forces to fight at Bosworth Field.*

Death, d. not feared - ... he that hath a will to die by himself fears it not from another.
"... He that hath a will to die by himself fears it not from another." (COR.5.2)
A statement of total contempt of life. See also 'Sleep, s. of death considered as rest'.
In the play. *Menenius addresses two guards in Aufidius' camp while leaving it after his unsuccessful attempt to persuade Coriolanus not to fight the Romans.*

Death, d. not felt by a habitual drunkard - ... insensible of mortality, and desperately mortal.
"A man that apprehends death no more dreadfully but as a drunken sleep; careless, reckless, and fearless of what's past, present, or to come; insensible of mortality, and desperately mortal" (MFM.4.2)
In the play. *The Provost describes to Duke Vicentio (in disguise) a prisoner held in the same prison as the condemned Claudio.*

Death, d. as a means to beat collectors - ... But the comfort is, you shall be called to no more payments...
"...But the comfort is,
you shall be called to no more payments, fear no more tavern-bills; which are often the sadness of
parting, as the procuring of mirth" (CYM.4.4)
In the play. *A jailer demonstrates to condemned prisoner Leonatus the positive side of death.*

Death, d. as a relief to despair - ... my joy is death, death at whose name I oft have been afear'd...
"...my joy is death;
Death, at whose name I oft have been afear'd,
Because I wish'd this world's eternity." (KHVI.p2.2.4)
In the play. *The Duchess of Gloucester, disgraced and bound for her exile in the Isle of Man, ponders on her own condition.*

Death, d. as liberation – ... my long sickness of health and living now begins to mend...
"...my long sickness
Of health and living now begins to mend,
And nothing brings me all things" (TOA.5.1)
In the play. *While writing his own epitaph, Timon confides his thoughts to the faithful Flavius.*

Death, d. as the end of despair - ... the arbitrator of despairs, just death, kind umpire of men's miseries.
"... the arbitrator of despairs,
Just death, kind umpire of men's miseries" (KHVI.p1.2.5)
In the play. *Old Mortimer, prisoner for having stood by the deposed king Richard comments on his own impending death.*

Death, d. attacking the mind - O vanity of sickness! fierce extremes in their continuance will not feel themselves...
"O vanity of sickness! fierce extremes
In their continuance will not feel

themselves.
Death, having prey'd upon the outward parts,
Leaves them invisible, and his siege is now
Against the mind, the which he pricks and wounds
With many legions of strange fantasies." (KJ.5.7)
In the play. *Prince Henry comments on the out-of-mind behavior of poisoned and moribund King John.*

Death, d. common to high and low – But kings and mightiest potentates must die, for that's the end of human misery.
"But kings and mightiest potentates must die,
For that's the end of human misery" (KHVI.p1.3.2)
In the play. *Talbot comments on the death of the Duke of Bedford at Rouen*

Death, d. defined – … the blind cave of eternal night.
"…the blind cave of eternal night." (KRIII.5.3)
In the play. *King Richard command to Stanley to bring about his forces at Bosworth Field or his son George will be killed, i.e. 'fall in the blind cave…'.*

Death, d. defined - …the kingdom of perpetual night.
"…then began the tempest to my soul,
Who pass'd, methought, the melancholy flood,
With that grim ferryman which poets write of,
Unto the kingdom of perpetual night" (KRIII.1.4)
In the play. *The Duke of Clarence recounts his nightmare to guard and guardian Brakenbury. The nightmare continued even after Clarence dreamed that he died.*

Death, d. in imperialistic wars useless - … for a fantasy and trick of fame go to their graves like beds…
"…I see
The imminent death of twenty thousand men,
That, for a fantasy and trick of fame,
Go to their graves like beds…" (H.4.4)
In the play. *Hamlet compares his condition (hesitating about how to revenge the murder of his father) with the passing Norwegian troops that are going to lose their life for questionable glory.*

Death, d. indifferent to status - A man may fish with the worm that hath eat of a king…
"A man may fish with the worm that hath eat of a king, and cat of the fish that hath fed of that worm." (H.4.3)
In the play. *Hamlet philosophizes on kings, fish and worms.*

Death, d. inevitable – All lovers young, all lovers must consign to thee, and come to dust.
"All lovers young, all lovers must Consign to thee, and come to dust" (CYM.4.2)
In the play. In the play. *Guiderius and Arviragus think that Imogen/Fidele is dead and sing a meditative song (actually a dirge) as an obsequy.*

Death, d. inevitable – And live we how we can, yet die we must.
"And, live we how we can, yet die we must." (KHVI p3.5.2)
In the play. *Warwick, mortally wounded and defeated by the forces of Edward IV, reflects on the relative worthlessness of coveted ambitions. For another usable part of this monologue see 'Defeat, admitting electoral.'*

Death, d. inevitable – Death will have his day.
"Death will have his day" ((KRII.3.2)
In the play. *King Richard II is ready to hear the news that Lord Scroop has come to deliver, namely that many lords have defected to the usurping Bolingbroke.*

Death, d. inevitable – Golden lads and girls all must, as chimney-sweepers, come to dust.
"Golden lads and girls all must,
As chimney-sweepers, come to dust"
...
"Fear no more the frown o' the great;
Thou art past the tyrant's stroke;
Care no more to clothe and eat;
To thee the reed is as the oak:
The sceptre, learning, physic, must
All follow this, and come to dust.
"(CYM.4.2)
In the play. *Guiderius and Arviragus think that Imogen/Fidele is dead and sing a meditative song (actually a dirge) as an obsequy.*

Death, d. not more painful than separation - There cannot be a pinch in death more sharp than this.
"There cannot be a pinch in death
More sharp than this." (CYM.1.1)
Magnify a disappointment. Also answer to: "Do you mind this?"
In the play. *Posthumus is banned from Cymbeline's court and his newly wed wife Imogen is distraught.*

Death, d. preferable if event is true – ... if thou teach me to believe this sorrow teach thou this sorrow how to make me die...
"O, if thou teach me to believe this sorrow,
Teach thou this sorrow how to make me die,
And let belief and life encounter so
As doth the fury of two desperate men
Which in the very meeting fall and die" (KJ.3.1)

In the play. *Lady Constance to Salisbury after he tells her that the French have made peace with King John and this voids the chances that her young son Arthur may affirm his rights as legitimate heir to the English throne.*

Death, d. preferable to be away from her - ... To die is to be banish'd from myself...
"And why not death rather than living torment?
To die is to be banish'd from myself;
And Silvia is myself" (TGV.3.1)
See also 'World. She is the w. - ... for where thou art, there is the world itself.' – 'Absence worse than death - if I depart from thee I cannot live.'
In the play. *Valentine's reaction at having been banned from Milan.*

Death, d. preferable to the rule of a wicked politician - More welcome is the stroke of death to me than Bolingbroke to England.
"More welcome is the stroke of death to me
Than Bolingbroke to England."
(KRII.3.1)
In the play. *Bushy, faithful to King Richard and condemned to death by the usurping Bolingbroke states his opinion.*

Death, d., sleep and dreams - To sleep: perchance to dream: ay, there's the rub...
"To sleep: perchance to dream: ay, there's the rub;
For in that sleep of death what dreams may come
When we have shuffled off this mortal coil,
Must give us pause..." (H.3.1)
Use 'when I have shuffled off this mortal coil', as a metaphor for 'when I am dead'.
In the play. *Part of the follow up to the 'To be or not to be' monologue*

Death, d. wish - ... with thy sharp teeth this knot intrinsicate of life at once untie.
"With thy sharp teeth this knot intrinsicate
Of life at once untie" (AC.5.2)
In the play. *Cleopatra addresses the serpent that she uses to kill herself.*

Death, d. with dignity – ... The stroke of death is as a lover's pinch, which hurts, and is desired.
"If thou and nature can so gently part,
The stroke of death is as a lover's pinch,
Which hurts, and is desired" (AC.5.2)
See also "Life, l. unbearable, death as a physician – It is silliness to live when to live is torment…'
In the play. *Cleopatra kisses Iras her lady in waiting for the last time. The snake's poison already in Cleopatra's blood cause Iras to gently fall and die. Cleopatra comments on her death.*

Death, effects of d. – ... and shake the yoke of inauspicious stars from this world-wearied flesh.
"… and shake the yoke of inauspicious stars
From this world-wearied flesh." (RJ.5.3)
Use 'the yoke of inauspicious stars' as a metaphor for bad fortune, e.g. 'I could not escape the yoke…stars' or 'Let's shake off the yoke…. Stars'.
In the play. *Romeo prepares for his own death, while close to the apparently dead Juliet and after having slain Paris in a duel inside the Capulet tomb.*

Death, egalitarian nature of d. - ... mean and mighty, rotting together, have one dust.
"BELARIUS …though mean and mighty, rotting
Together, have one dust, yet reverence,
That angel of the world, doth make distinction
Of place 'tween high and low
…
GUIDERIUS. Thersites' body is as good as Ajax',
When neither are alive." (CYM.4.1)
An argument for cremation.
In the play. *Guiderius killed Cloten, the Queen's son and Belarius suggests to give him a princely burial, though an enemy to them.*

Death, fear and other problems eliminated by d. - Fear no more the heat o' the sun...
"Fear no more the heat o' the sun,
Nor the furious winter's rages;
Thou thy worldly task hast done,
Home art gone, and ta'en thy wages" (CYM.4.2)
In the play. *Guiderius commenting on the (presumed) death of Imogen/Fidele.*

Death, fear of d. – The weariest and most loathed worldly life…
"Ay, but to die, and go we know not where;
To lie in cold obstruction and to rot;
This sensible warm motion to become
A kneaded clod…
… The weariest and most loathed worldly life
That age, ache, penury and imprisonment
Can lay on nature is a paradise
To what we fear of death." (MFM.3.1)
An argument for the idea that the fear of death is worse than death itself.
In the play. *Claudio, wavering between fear and courage, shares his feelings with his sister Isabella.*

Death, fear of d. strange - Of all the wonders that I yet have heard...
"Of all the wonders that I yet have heard.
It seems to me most strange that men should fear;

Seeing that death, a necessary end,
Will come when it will come." (JC.2.2)
In the play. *Caesar rejects the efforts of his wife Calphurnia to keep him from going out on March 15.*

Death, fearful d. versus shamed life -
Death is a fearful thing… And shamed life a hateful
CLAUDIO Death is a fearful thing.
ISABELLA And shamed life a hateful (MFM.3.1)
See also 'Life, rationalization against 'death with dignity' advocates - … The weariest and most loathed worldly life…is a paradise to what we fear of death'
In the play. *Claudio, condemned to death by Angelo, shares thoughts on life and death with his sister Isabella.*

Death, grave as a place of peace - … here are no storms, no noise, but silence and eternal sleep.
"Here lurks no treason, here no envy swells,
Here grow no damned grudges; here are no storms,
No noise, but silence and eternal sleep" (TA.1.1)
In the play. *Titus' words before burying the Romans dead in battles against the Goths.*

Death, happy to d. - I am merrier to die than thou art to live.
"I am merrier to die than thou art to live." (CYM.5.4)
In the play. *Leonatus to his jailer.*

Death, lightning before d. – How oft when men are at the point of death have they been merry!
"How oft when men are at the point of death
Have they been merry! which their keepers call
A lightning before death" (RJ.5.3)

In the play. *Romeo observes the beauty of Juliet lying in the tomb – he thinks she is dead while she is only deeply out from the potion administered by Friar Lawrence. He plans to kill himself while his spirit is lifted by observing Juliet.*

Death, mortuary – … palace of dim night.
"…palace of dim night" (RJ.5.3)
Comment on a poorly lit room
In the play. *Romeo is in the sepulchral chapel of the Capulets, where Juliet appears dead, though she is only asleep.*

Death, no escape from d. - … this fell sergeant, death is strict in his arrest.
"…Had I but time--as this fell sergeant, death,
Is strict in his arrest" (H.5.2)
In the play. *The dying Hamlet has no more time to speak with Horatio.*

Death, noble d. – Mount, mount, my soul! thy seat is up on high…
"Mount, mount, my soul! thy seat is up on high;
Whilst my gross flesh sinks downward, here to die." (KRII.5.5)
In the play. *Richard dies stabbed by the envoy of the King, Exton.*

Death, not afraid to die - … what blessings I have here alive, that I should be afraid to die?
"… what blessings I have here alive,
That I should fear to die?" (WT.3.2)
In the play. *Hermione unfairly accused of infidelity by her husband Leontes is not afraid to die.*

Death, only d. certain, the interim is not - That we shall die, we know; 'tis but the time and drawing days out, that men stand upon.
"That we shall die, we know; 'tis but the time

And drawing days out, that men stand upon." (JC.3.1)
In the play. *In the confusion following Caesar's assassination Brutus comments on the uncertainty of what may follow.*

Death, positive view on d. – ... he that cuts off twenty years of life cuts off so many years of fearing death.
"Why, he that cuts off twenty years of life
Cuts off so many years of fearing death." (JC.1.3)
In the play. *Cassius' comments shortly after Caesar's assassination.*

Death, ready for d. - ... gaunt as a grave, whose hollow womb inherits nought but bones.
"Gaunt am I for the grave, gaunt as a grave,
Whose hollow womb inherits nought but bones." (KRII.2.1)
In the play. **John of Gaunt to King Richard who has come to visit.**

Death, the right way how to face it – If I must die, I will encounter darkness as a bride...
"Think you I can a resolution fetch
From flowery tenderness? If I must die,
I will encounter darkness as a bride,
And hug it in mine arms." (MFM.3.1)
In the play. *Claudio takes a courageous stand now that he knows that there will be no remission of his sentence by the evil Angelo.*

Debate, angry and refusal to d. - I will not bandy with thee word for word.
"I will not bandy with thee word for word
But buckle with thee blows, twice two for one." (KHVI p3.1.4)
Refuse to argue with a fool. See also entries for 'Quarrel'
In the play. *Clifford to York in the plains near Sandal Castle before killing him.*

Debate, disagreeing with skill - but Brutus says he was ambitious, and Brutus is an honourable man.
"But Brutus says he was ambitious;
And Brutus is an honourable man." (JC.3.2)
Use the same tactic when you wish to undermine the arguments of your opponent. E.G. 'XY says that we should not increase our expenses on education... and XY is an honorable man'
In the play. *Antony's powerful oratory destroys the plebe's support for Brutus and his conspirators.*

Debate, feisty but friendly d. - strive mightily, but eat and drink as friends.
TRANIO (to Hortensio). "And do as adversaries do in law, -
Strive mightily, but eat and drink as friends." (TOS.1.2)
Introduction to a debate.
In the play. *Tranio, disguised as Lucentio will pretend to court Bianca. Hortensio, an old gentleman also likes Bianca. They (Tranio and Hortensio) will compete for Bianca's hand in a fair contest.*

Debate, skillful destruction of opponent's argument - I speak not to disprove what Brutus spoke but here I am to prove what I do know.
"I speak not to disprove what Brutus spoke
But here I am to prove what I do know." (JC.3.2)
Destroy your opponent's argument, before you give yours, 'I speak not to disprove what XX spoke, but here I am ...know.' The technique is similar to that used in the quote 'Debate, disagreeing with skill'.
In the play. *Antony addresses the crowd and begins his verbal plot to turn the crowd against Brutus.*

Debates, d. instead of action – You are disputing of your generals, one would have lingering wars with little cost...
"You are disputing of your generals:
One would have lingering wars with little cost;
Another would fly swift, but wanteth wings;
A third thinks, without expense at all,
By guileful fair words peace may be obtain'd." (KHVI.p1.1.1)
In the play. *A messenger from France reports on the mood of the English troops who are waiting for reinforcements.*

Debriefing, d. postponed due to length - ... For 'tis a chronicle of day by day not a relation for a breakfast nor befitting this first meeting.
"...No more yet of this;
For 'tis a chronicle of day by day,
Not a relation for a breakfast nor
Befitting this first meeting" (TEM.5.1)
In the play. *Prospero introduces himself to the party stranded on the island and postpones the disclosure of the events that caused the party's shipwreck.*

Debt, insisting on repaying a courtesy - In common worldly things, 'tis call'd ungrateful, with dull unwillingness to repay a debt.
"In common worldly things, 'tis call'd ungrateful,
With dull unwillingness to repay a debt" (KRIII.2.2)
A friend did you a favor and refuses to be repaid but you want to.
In the play. *Dorset tries to comfort Queen Elizabeth remained widow after the death of Edward IV. The debt referred to is the fact that her son will be king – though Richard III will prevent this from happening by murdering the boy.*

Deceit, d. and treachery rationalized - ... for that is good deceit which mates him first that first intends deceit.
"... for that is good deceit
Which mates him first that first intends deceit." (KHVI p2.3.1)
Rationalize an otherwise questionable decision.
In the play. *Suffolk rationalizes the murder of Gloucester. The real deceivers are Suffolk and company.*

Deceit, learning the tricks of d. to avoid it - to avoid deceit, I mean to learn, for it shall strew the footsteps of my rising.
' ...(I will) deliver
Sweet, sweet poison for the age's tooth:
Which, though I will not practise to deceive,
Yet, to avoid deceit, I mean to learn;
For it shall strew the footsteps of my rising." (KJ.1.1)
In the play. *Faulconbridge meditates on the steps to take and the type of learning to acquire, to make his way in the world.*

Deceit, no reason to deceive – What in the world should make me now deceive...
"What in the world should make me now deceive,
Since I must lose the use of all deceit?" (KJ.5.4)
In the play. *Melun, mortally wounded, advises the English Lords to quit the Dauphin Lewis' side to save their lives.*

Deception, d. by friends - ... that in alliance, amity and oaths, there should be found such false dissembling guile?
"O monstrous treachery! Can this be so,
That in alliance, amity and oaths,
There should be found such false dissembling guile?" (KHIV.p1.4.1)

In the play. *Gloucester's reaction at the news that Burgundy has left the English and joined the French*

Deception, d. from false teachers - Thus may poor fools believe false teachers…
"Thus may poor fools
Believe false teachers: though those that are betray'd
Do feel the treason sharply, yet the traitor
Stands in worse case of woe"
(CYM.3.4)
It may not always be so, but it makes us feel good to think it. See also 'Speak, double-speak – And be these juggling fiends no more believed, that palter with us in a double sense'
In the play. *Imogen's reaction to the letter from husband Posthumous Leonatus requesting Pisanio to kill her for presumed adultery. The poor fool is Leonatus.*

Deception, d. to cover foul objectives – … With colours fairer painted their foul ends.
"…With colours fairer painted their foul ends." (TEM.1.2)
Applies especially to politicians.
In the play. *Antonio, usurper of Prospero's dukedom, tried to put a less damning spin on the usurpation.*

Decimation - … by the hazard of the spotted die let die the spotted.
"And by the hazard of the spotted die
Let die the spotted." (TOA.5.4)
See also 'Character, not afraid of taking chances - I have set my life upon a cast and I will stand the hazard of the die.'
In the play. *The Athenian senators negotiate with Alcibiades on possible decimation of the Athenians as opposed to wholesale execution.*

Decision, acceptance of a d. - Be it as your wisdom will.
"Be it as your wisdom will."
(MFM.2.1)
In the play. *Escalus must accept with grace Angelo's firm decision to have Claudio executed for fornication.*

Decision, bad d. – thou hast pared thy wit o' both sides, and left nothing i' the middle.
"…thou hast pared thy wit o' both sides, and left nothing i' the middle"
(KL.1.4)
In the play. *The Fool tell Lear how bad was his way of accessing who, among his three daughters, loved him most.*

Decision, bad personnel or management d. - Ah! thus King Henry throws away his crutch before his legs be firm to bear his body.
"Ah! thus King Henry throws away his crutch
Before his legs be firm to bear his body." (KHVI p2.3.1)
In the play. *Gloucester, lord Protector, accused of trumped up charges and arrested by his political enemies, warns King Henry VI while being carried away.*

Decision, bad personnel or management d. - Thus is the shepherd beaten from thy side, and wolves are gnarling who shall gnaw thee first.
"Thus is the shepherd beaten from thy side,
And wolves are gnarling who shall gnaw thee first" (KHVI.p2.3.1)
In the play. *Gloucester warns King Henry VI that he too is in danger from the political enemies that caused Gloucester's arrest.*

Decision, concern about a decision taken too quickly - It is too rash, too unadvise'd, too sudden, too like the lightning…
"It is too rash, too unadvise'd, too sudden,

**Too like the lightning, which doth cease to be,
Ere one can say - it lightens."** (RJ.2.2)
State your concern at any decision taken too quickly.
In the play. *In a moment of reflection and partial composure, Juliet encourages Romeo not to swear his love right away as the sequence of events seems somewhat rash.*

Decision, d. guided by sight and hearing - ...mine eyes and ears, two traded pilots 'twixt the dangerous shores of will and judgement.
**"… and my election
Is led on in the conduct of my will;
My will, enkindled by mine eyes and ears,
Two traded pilots 'twixt the dangerous shores
Of will and judgement."** (TC.2.2)
Answer to 'Did you see it happen?' 'Yes, with mine eyes and ears, two traded pilots…judgment'. Or affirm that you will only make a decision after a direct assessment of the situation.
In the play. *In a somewhat intricate exchange Troilus and Hector debate on the role of the will in our decision making - in this case whether to hold on to Helen or not. The 'election' Troilus refers to as an example is his decision to take a wife. His will guide the choice of a wife assisted by the 'pilot' eyes and ears.*

Decision, d. making, important matters to be considered before taking a d. - … we would be resolv'd … of some things of weight that task our thoughts…
**"Not yet, my cousin; we would be resolv'd,
Before we hear him, of some things of weight,
That task our thoughts, concerning us and France."** (KHV.1.2)
Change a little, e.g. 'We would be resolved, before deciding, of some things of weight, that task our thoughts, concerning (matter of concern)'.
In the play. *The 'not yet' refers to the calling in of the French ambassador.*

Decision, d. prompted by passion or revenge - The reasons you allege do more conduce to the hot passion of distempered blood…
**"The reasons you allege do more conduce
To the hot passion of distempered blood
Than to make a free determination
Twixt right and wrong; for pleasure and revenge
Have ears more deaf than adders to the voice
Of any true decision."** (TC.2.2)
Question the reasons for an irrational proposal. Your comment on questionable reasons for a questionable decision.
In the play *The reasons alleged by Troilus and Paris for keeping Helen are shaky at best, being pleasure and revenge and Hector tells them so.*

Decision, d. that would require more research but even so it would not help - More should I question thee, and more I must, though more to know could not be more to trust…
**"More should I question thee, and more I must,
Though more to know could not be more to trust."** (AWEW.2.1)
Say that more information should or could be gathered, though you know that more information would not help you make up your mind.
In the play. *The King accepts to be cured by Helen with some lingering reservations.*

Decision, self-defeating d. – What is it, but to make thy sepulchre and creep into it far before thy time?
**"What is it, but to make thy sepulchre
And creep into it far before thy time?"** (KHVI.p3.1.1)

232

In the play. *The Queen reprimands King Henry for having promised York the throne (after Henry's death).*

Decision, you decide - Frame the business after your own wisdom.
"Frame the business after your own wisdom." (KL.1.2)
When you are asked to make a decision for someone else and you can't. Or when it is impossible to give specific instructions
In the play. *Gloucester falls in Edmund's trap. Edmund tries to frame his brother Edgar, by writing a phony letter in which Edgar discloses plans to kill his father (Gloucester) so as to have access to the inheritance.*

Decisions, decisions – to be or not to be...
"To be or not to be - that is the question,
Whether 'tis nobler in the mind to suffer
The slings and arrows of outrageous fortune,
Or to take arms against a sea of troubles,
And by opposing end them? - To die - to sleep -
No more; and by a sleep to say we end
The heart-ache, and the thousand natural shocks
That flesh is heir to; 'tis a consummation
Devoutly to be wished." (H.3.1)
The first line is known by just about everyone, therefore you can customize it at will - yet everyone will recall or perhaps feel the impact of the original - e.g. "To buy or not to buy", "To sell or not to sell" etc.
Turn some lines into an oratorical question mark, "Is it nobler in the mind, to suffer the slings and arrows…or to take arms against a sea of troubles and by opposing end them?

Use as a biographical statement, "(I have suffered) the slings and arrows of outrageous fortune and the thousand natural shocks that flesh is heir to." Or to express agreement, "'tis a consummation devoutly to be wished"
In the play. *Hamlet meditates.*

Decisions, bad d. yielding bad results - ... But by bad courses may be understood that their events can never fall out good.
"…farewell:
What will ensue hereof, there's none can tell
But by bad courses may be understood
That their events can never fall out good." (KRII.2.1)
See also 'Hypocrisy, h. and dishonesty exposed - foul deeds will rise though all the world o'erwhelm them, to men's eyes'.
In the play. *The Duke of York rebukes King Richard II for appropriating the land and goods of John of Gaunt who just died.*

Decisions, rash d. - What to ourselves in passion we propose, the passion ending, doth the purpose lose.
"What to ourselves in passion we propose,
The passion ending, doth the purpose lose." (H.3.2)
Oppose a decision that seems to have been taken on the spur of the moment.
In the play. *The play that Hamlet has produced is full of direct and indirect references to the recent real-life events. Gonzago recites these lines.*

Declaration, d. of admiration and respect - … Burgundy enshrines thee in his heart…

"Warlike and martial Talbot, Burgundy
Enshrines thee in his heart and there erects
Thy noble deeds as valour's monuments." **(KHVI.p1.3.2)**
In the play. *Burgundy, soon to defect to the French here declares his unending admiration for Talbot.*

Dedication, d. and spirituality - … Not dallying with a brace of courtezans, but meditating with two deep divines…
"Not dallying with a brace of courtezans,
But meditating with two deep divines,
Not sleeping, to engross his idle body,
But praying, to enrich his watchful soul." **(KRIII.3.7)**
Use the last two lines as an answer to 'What are you doing?' especially if the questioner seems to imply that you are idling, 'I am not sleeping to engross my idle body, but praying to enrich my watchful soul'.
In the play. *In a masterful image-building charade, Richard III arrives at the meeting of the London council accompanied by two priests, all in prayer.*

Dedication, total and complete d. - … And all my fortunes at thy foot I'll lay and follow thee…
"And all my fortunes at thy foot I'll lay
And follow thee my lord throughout the world" **(RJ.2.2)**
Change 'my lord' to 'my lady' if the object of your dedication is a lady.
In the play. *Parting words by Juliet to Romeo as he leaves her garden.*

Deduction, the power of d. - … therefore thou art a sheep.
PROTEUS. The sheep for fodder follows the shepherd, the shepherd for food follows not the sheep; thou for wages followest thy master, thy master for wages follows not thee: therefore, thou art a sheep.
SPEED. Such another proof will make me cry baa." **(TGV.1.1)**
Use as an example of Aristotelian chop-logic. This is a poetic variant of the classic, 'The Apostles were twelve, these pears are twelve, therefore the Apostles were pears'. Speed's answer can also be a retort to very questionable verbal evidence.
In the play. *Proteus and Speed engage in some banter*

Deed, a good d. shines in a bad world - … So shines a good deed in a naughty world.
"That light we see is burning in my hall.
How far that little candle throws his beams!
So shines a good deed in a naughty world." **(MOV.5.1)**
In the play. *Arriving back to Belmont, Portia compares the light produced by a candle to a good deed.*

Deed, damned and bloody - It is a damned and a bloody work; the graceless action of a heavy hand…
"It is a damned and a bloody work;
The graceless action of a heavy hand,
If that it be the work of any hand" **(KJ.4.3)**
In the play. *Ph. Faulconbridge commenting on the discovery of Prince Arthur's body*

Deed, horrible d. - … such a deed as from the body of contraction plucks the very soul….
"…O, such a deed
As from the body of contraction plucks
The very soul, and sweet religion makes
A rhapsody of words. **(H.3.4)**

In the play. *Hamlet confronts the Queen his mother with her responsibilities, having married her brother in law Claudius after Claudius murdered him.*

Deed, d. so vile to be unmentioned - The deed, which both our tongues held vile to name.
"The deed, which both our tongues held vile to name." (KJ.4.2)
In the play. *King John, extremely hypocritical, addresses Hubert, whom he had assigned to kill young Prince Arthur*

Defeat, admitting electoral d. – Thus yields the cedar to the axe's edge…
"Thus yields the cedar to the axe's edge,
Whose arms gave shelter to the princely eagle,
Under whose shade the ramping lion slept,
Whose top-branch overpeer'd Jove's spreading tree
And kept low shrubs from winter's awful wind." (KHVI p3.5.2)
In the play. *Warwick, mortally wounded and defeated by the forces of Edward IV, reflects on his own defeat.*

Defeat, d. acknowledged – … My blood, my want of strength, my sick heart shows, that I must yield my body to the earth.
"… who is victor, York or Warwick?
Why ask I that? my mangled body shows,
My blood, my want of strength, my sick heart shows,
That I must yield my body to the earth
And, by my fall, the conquest to my foe." (KHVI.p3.5.2)
Acknowledge defeat with a dramatic tone.
In the play. *Warwick, wounded to death in the battle against the York forces near Barnet, reflects on his life.*

Defeat, d. acknowledged – Reproach and everlasting shame sits mocking in our plumes.
"Reproach and everlasting shame
Sits mocking in our plumes" (HV.4.5)
In the play. *The Dauphin acknowledges defeat at Agincourt.*

Defeat, d. acknowledged – Our enemies have beat us to the pit: it is more worthy to leap in ourselves, than tarry till they push us.
"Our enemies have beat us to the pit:
It is more worthy to leap in ourselves,
Than tarry till they push us." (JC.5.5)
Tough decisions needed promptly after being defeated
In the play. *Brutus after losing the battle of Philippi.*

Defeat, d. against overwhelming forces – But Hercules himself must yield to odds; and many strokes…fell the hardest-timber'd oak.
"But Hercules himself must yield to odds;
And many strokes, though with a little axe,
Hew down and fell the hardest-timber'd oak." (KHVI p3.2.1)
Words of encouragement when the task seems large at first, but not so if subdivided into smaller steps, ('many strokes').
In the play. *A messenger reports that the duke of York fell in battle against the Lancastrians, notwithstanding a brave fight at Mortimer's Cross.*

Defeat, d. converted into triumph over oneself – … not Caesar's valour hath overthrown Antony, but Antony's hath triumph'd on itself.
"Peace!
Not Caesar's valour hath o'erthrown Antony,

But Antony's hath triumph'd on itself." (AC.4.15)
Converting defeat into a self-achieved triumph.
In the play. *The dying Antony is brought to the monument where Cleopatra has taken refuge and he utters words of defiance. Cleopatra agrees, So it should be, that none but Antony Should conquer Antony; but woe 'tis so!*

Defeat, d. imminent - … our throats are sentenced and stay upon execution.
"…our throats are sentenced and stay upon execution." (COR.5.4)
In the play. *Menenius holds little hope that an attack on Rome by the Volsces and Coriolanus may be averted.*

Defeat, d. or retribution, a metaphor – Thus hath the candle singed the moth…
"Thus hath the candle singed the moth.
O, these deliberate fools!" (MOV.2.9)
In the play. *Portia comments on the unsuccessful attempts by suitors to solve the riddle that wold enable the first solver to marry her.*

Defeat, d. that does not mean dishonor - A scar nobly got, or a noble scar, is a good livery of honour; so, belike, is that.
"A scar nobly got, or a noble scar, is a good livery of honour; so, belike, is that." (AWEW.4.5)
Put a positive spin on an event that left you metaphorically scarred.
In the play. *The clown at Rousillon enters to announce that Bertram is arriving with a patch on his face, possibly a battle scar. Lafeu comments accordingly.*

Defeat, putting a good face on d. - I here do give thee that with all my heart which, but thou hast already…
"I here do give thee that with all my heart
Which, but thou hast already, with all my heart
I would keep from thee" (OTH.1.3)
In the play. *Brabantio must accept defeat after Othello explained how he won Desdemona's hands without tricks or black magic.*

Defense, d. from accusation, justification for rash words - I was provoked by her slanderous tongue…
"I was provoked by her slanderous tongue,
which laid their guilt upon my guiltless shoulders." (KRIII.1.2)
In the play. *The slanderous tongue Richard speaks of is that of Queen Margaret, who accused him of murder, a murder that he actually committed and now denies.*

Defense, d. from general accusation – let me have some patient leisure to excuse myself.
"Fairer than tongue can name thee, let me have
Some patient leisure to excuse myself." (KRIII.1.2)
You can also use part of the first line as a compliment, 'Fairer than tongue can name thee.' The compliment prepares the ground for a forgiveness.
In the play. *Richard of Gloucester, who has slain Edward, Anne's husband, is now trying to woo her.*

Defense, d. from general accusation - … Till I have told this slander of his blood how God and good men hate so foul a liar.
"O, let my sovereign turn away his face
And bid his ears a little while be deaf,
Till I have told this slander of his blood,
How God and good men hate so foul a liar" (KRII.1.1)
In the play. *Mowbray accuses back Bolingbroke of being a liar.*

Defense, d. from general accusation, look who's talking - ... if thy offences were upon record...
"...Gentle Northumberland,
If thy offences were upon record,
Would it not shame thee in so fair a troop
To read a lecture of them?" (KRII.4.1)
In the play. *Northumberland pushes King Richard to confess his alleged crimes so as to justify the usurpation of the throne by Bolingbroke. The King responds.*

Defense, d. from general accusations – I am a man more sinned against than sinning.
"I am a man
More sinned against than sinning." (KL.3.2)
Your reputation as an incorrigible skirt chaser has preceded you and your new date says something like "I have heard bad things about you" or equivalent. As with the issue of age, the key is to deflect the arrow and leave the questioner wondering, intrigued or baffled. The answer applies just about to any type of real or alleged accusation - for example if you were arrested for DUI, or if you are an Enron, Worldcom or Anderson ex-executive, accused of stealing or of faking the balance sheet.
Also answer to 'Who are you?' See also 'Man, m. shipwrecked (materially or metaphorically) - A man whom both the waters and the wind.' – "Attitude, a. towards the world, hating it – one…whom the vile blows and buffets of the world…'
In the play. *King Lear, dispossessed of everything and forced to hide in a forest during a storm, compares himself with the sinful and hypocrite daughters and accomplices. He then concludes that he has few crimes to conceal and yet he is made to suffer.*

Defense, d. from general accusations - ... my name be blotted from the book of life.
"No Bolingbroke; if ever I were traitor
My name be blotted from the book of life,
And I from heaven banish'd, as from hence!" (KRII.1.3)
Change 'Bolingbroke' to name of person whom you are addressing.
In the play. *Mowbray answers Bolingbroke who asked Mowbray to admit to treason. King Richard II has banished both of them from England*

Defense, d. from general accusations - pierced to the soul with slander's venom spear.
"I am disgrac'd, impeached, and baffled here;
Pierced to the soul with slander's venom spear,
The which no balm can cure but his heart-blood
Which breathed this poison." (KRII.1.1)
Use all lines or the second line only, depending on the nature and circumstances of the accusation.
In the play. *Norfolk's reaction at Bolingroke's accusation of treason.*

Defense, d. from slander – it's slander, whose edge is sharper than the sword...
"No it's slander,
Whose edge is sharper than the sword; whose tongue
Outvenoms all the worms of Nile; whose breath
Rides on the posting winds, and doth belie
All corners of the world." (CYM.3.4)
Given the inherently wicked nature of man, slander and calumny are common. See also 'Man and its wicked nature ' – entries for 'Slander'

In the play. *Pisanio reflects on the fact that the accusations about Imogen's infidelity to Posthumous are pure slander. In the Winter's Tale (act 2.3) we also find* 'slander, whose sting is sharper than the sword'.

Defense, d. of criminal demeaning - ... every word you speak in his behalf is slander to your royal dignity.
"Madam, be still; with reverence may I say;
For every word you speak in his behalf
Is slander to your royal dignity."
(KHVI p2.3.2)
In the play. *Warwick attempts to tell Q. Margaret to shut up as she continues to defend Suffolk, who murderer Gloucester, the lord Protector.*

Defense, d. of loved ones natural - ... for the poor wren, the most diminutive of birds, will fight, her young ones...
"...He loves us not;
He wants the natural touch: for the poor wren,
The most diminutive of birds, will fight,
Her young ones in her nest, against the owl." (M.4.2)
See also "Prevarication on anyone will prompt vengeance - the smallest worm will turn being trodden on.'
In the play. *Lady Macduff, abandoned with infant son in her castle, justly complains against her husband who has fled to England out of fear of Macbeth. She is now defenseless.*

Defiance, d. based on the merit of your services – ... My services which I have done the signiory shall out-tongue his complaints.
"Let him do his spite:
My services which I have done the signiory
Shall out-tongue his complaints."
(OTH.1.2)

Defend yourself against your political opponent's false accusations, e.g. 'The services I have done in my tenure do out-tongue your complaints'.
In the play. *Othello's remark after Iago warns him that Desdemona's father, Brabantio, could harm him (Othello) for having married Brabantio's daughter.*

Defiance, d. declared - Defiance, traitors, hurl we in your teeth.
"Defiance, traitors, hurl we in your teeth" (JC.5.1)
In the play. *Before the momentous battle of Philippi, Octavius shows defiance towards his enemy Cassius.*

Defiance, d. declared in unpleasant circumstances - Though what I am I cannot avoid, yet to be what I would not shall not make me tame.
"Though what I am I cannot avoid, yet to be what I would not shall not make me tame" (MWW.3.5)
In the play. *Mr. Ford is convinced that his wife has made him what he cannot avoid (cuckold), but is determined to fight (Falstaff, the presumed seducer).*

Defiance, refusal to yield - I had rather chop this hand off at a blow, and with the other fling it at thy face.
"I had rather chop this hand off at a blow,
And with the other fling it at thy face"
(KHVI p3.5.1)
In the play. *In a sudden reversal of fortune, Warwick is requested to swear allegiance (by Richard of Gloucester), to Edward IV whom he previously dethroned. Warwick answers defiantly.*

Definition, calling things by their names - We call a nettle but a nettle; and the faults of fools, but folly.
"We call a nettle but a nettle; and
The faults of fools, but folly."
(COE.2.1)

State clearly the reality of the situation, when someone wants to put a spin to it.
In the play. *Menenius knows that Coriolanus is not popular with a section of Rome's citizens. He uses this sentence to indirectly acknowledge the facts and imply the folly of Coriolanus' enemies.*

Definition, offensive d, cannot be named - What I cannot name but I shall offend.
MARINA. What trade, sir?
LYSIMACHUS. What I cannot name but I shall offend." (PER.4.6)
When you do not want to be specific. Answer to 'What did he say?' or 'What words did he use?'
In the play. *Lysimachus, Mytilene's governor, is impressed with Marina's beauty and asks how long she has been in the trade that he 'cannot name'. Of course she has nothing to do with it. See* 'Woman, totally incorruptible'.

Delay, avoid d. - Defer no time, delays have dangerous ends.
"Defer no time, delays have dangerous ends." (KHVI.p1.3.2)
Expedite action. See also 'Exhortation, e. to discipline and expeditiousness' – 'Procrastination to be avoided'
In the play. *Alencon prompts Charles to enter the city of Rouen where Joan of Arc has already climbed on the battlements.*

Delay, d. is time wasted - … in delay we waste our lights in vain, like lamps by day.
"I mean, sir, in delay
We waste our lights in vain, like lamps by day." (RJ.1.4)
Urge action and cutting out delay. See also 'Time, t. management, time wasted.' – 'Time, let's do it now' – 'Procrastination to be avoided' – 'Action, a. requiring urgent and strong response'

In the play. *Mercutio attempts to draw Romeo out from his longings for Rosaline and convinces him to attend instead the party or mask given by Lord Capulet. It is the party where Romeo will meet Juliet.*

Demeanor, wondering at a sudden change of d. – (this) leaves me to consider what is breeding that changeth thus his manners.
"So leaves me to consider what is breeding
That changeth thus his manners." (WT.1.2)
Reporting an as yet inexplicable change in demeanor by someone you know.
In the play. *Polixenes is perplexed at the sudden change of humor of his friend and host Leontes.*

Demonstration, d. of love prevented by circumstances - … have prevented the ostentation of our love, which, left unshown, is often left unloved.
"… and have prevented
The ostentation of our love, which, left unshown,
Is often left unloved." (AC.3.6)
Insist on her accepting your gift if she seems reluctant to accept it. Change it slightly in a one to one situation, i.e., 'Do not prevent the ostentation of my love, which, left unshown, is often left unloved.'
In the play. *Octavia, abandoned by Antony not long after their marriage, returns all alone to Rome and Octavian, her brother regrets not having met her at the gates of Rome with the honors due to her.*

Deniability, d., politics and crime - … Being done unknown I should have found it afterwards well done but must condemn it now.
"Ah, this thou shouldst have done,
And not have spoke on't! In me 'tis villany;
In thee't had been good service."

…
"Repent ever thy tongue
Hath so betrayed thine act. Being done unknown,
I should have found it afterwards well done,
But must condemn it now." (AC.2.7)
In the play. *If Menas had killed Pompey's adversaries without informing him, Pompey could have approved of the crime.*

Denial - … contradict thyself and say it is not so.
"Dear Duff, I prithee, contradict thyself,
And say it is not so." (M.2.2)
In the play. *Banquo on knowing that King Duncan was found slain.*

Denial, absolute d. - As faithfully as I deny the devil.
LADY FAULCONBRIDGE Hast thou denied thyself a Faulconbridge?
BASTARD As faithfully as I deny the devil. (KJ.1.1)
Answer to 'Do you deny this?'
In the play. *Philip is indeed a Plantagenet and not a Faulconbridge, being the son of Richard I.*

Denial, complete d. (of a husband) - … Not till God make men of some other metal than earth.
LEONATO Well, niece, I hope to see you one day fitted with a husband.
BEATRICE Not till God make men of some other metal than earth. (MAAN.1.3)
In the play. *Beatrice displays her angular temper.*

Denial, d. of wrongdoing - The gods throw stones of sulphur on me, if...
"The gods throw stones of sulphur on me, if..."
In the play. *Imogen thinks that her faithful servant Pisanio attempted to poison her, but the poison came from the now dead queen. Pisanio defends himself.*

Denial, difficulty to deny previous statement – I know your daring tongue scorns to unsay what once it hath deliver'd…
"My Lord Aumerle, I know your daring tongue
Scorns to unsay what once it hath deliver'd…" (KRII.4.1)
In the play. *According to Bagot (a Bolingbroke's man), Aumerle admitted earlier on to have taken part in the assassination of the Duke of Gloucester, earlier attributed to Mowbray, duke of Norfolk.*

Denial, when you have to say no to a lady - I beseech you, punish me not with your hard thoughts...
"I beseech you, punish me not with your hard thoughts; wherein I confess me much guilty, to deny so fair and excellent lady anything." (AYLI.1.2)
When you are regrettably compelled to deny the requests of a fine lady.
In the play. *Rosalind, who is beginning to fall in love with Orlando, pleads with him that he not fight the wrestler Charles, but Orlando refuses to quit the fight.*

Departure, d. difficult - Can I go forward when my heart is here?
"Can I go forward when my heart is here?" (RJ.2.1)
When you are about to take off. See also 'Business trip, temporary separation' - 'Departure, reason for having to leave'.
In the play. *Romeo is reluctant to leave the Capulets' premises after being struck by the beauty of Juliet.*

Departure, d. expedited – … aboard, aboard, for shame! The wind sits in the shoulder of your sail…
"…aboard, aboard, for shame! The wind sits in the shoulder of your sail…" (H.1.3)
Expedite group or company to leave or move on. You can change to 'Aboard,

aboard. The wind sits in the shoulder of our sail'.
In the play. *Polonius prompts his son Laertes to board the ship directed to France. Then he gives him the famous string of advises. See 'Opinion, your op. on money, handling of, borrowing and lending - Neither a borrower nor a lender be…'*

Departure, d. necessary - … though parting be a fretful corrosive, it is applied to a deathful wound.
"Away! though parting be a fretful corrosive,
It is applied to a deathful wound."
(KHVI p2.3.2)
In the play. *Q. Margaret to the banished Suffolk, though parting be painful, if he stays longer he will be killed.*

Departure, d. of unwelcome guest welcome - You cannot, sir, take from me any thing that I will more willingly part withal: except my life
POLONIUS I will most humbly take my leave of you.
HAMLET You cannot, sir, take from me any thing that I will more willingly part withal: except my life (H.2.2)
Not many will say 'I take my leave of you'. But you can say 'if you take your leave of me you cannot take from me…withal'.
In the play. *End of Polonius' interview with Hamlet, to determine if Hamlet's madness is due to his love for Ophelia.*

Departure, forceful d. from a slaughtering place or abandonment of sin in general.
"Away with me, all you whose souls abhor
The uncleanly savours of a slaughter-house;
For I am stifled with this smell of sin." (KJ.4.3)
Apply to any place where you find arrogance, back-stabbing etc.

Once in London I passed in front of a church. A banner outside said 'If you are tired of sin, come inside'. Below someone had written, 'If not, telephone 01 788 etc.'
In the play. *Salisbury, disgusted at the death of Arthur by King John defects to the French.*

Departure, reason for having to leave - I take it, your own business calls on you and you embrace the occasion to depart.
"I take it, your own business calls on you
And you embrace the occasion to depart." (MOV.1.1)
Apply the statement to yourself, '…my business calls on me and I embrace the occasion to depart'. Maybe someone calls you on the cellular phone or you try to find excuses for leaving.
In the play. *Salarino makes apologies for leaving Antonio and Antonio suggests a rational explanation, i.e. you must leave because of your business.*

Depression, general depression leading to total pessimism – to-morrow and to-morrow and to-morrow…
"To-morrow, and to-morrow, and to-morrow,
Creeps in this petty pace from day to day
To the last syllable of recorded time,
And all our yesterdays have lighted fools
The way to dusty death. Out, out, brief candle!
Life's but a walking shadow, a poor player
That struts and frets his hour upon the stage
And then is heard no more: it is a tale
Told by an idiot, full of sound and fury,
Signifying nothing." (M.5.5)

Well describes a probable view of life when you are down in the dumps.
In the play. *Seyton has just announced to Macbeth that the queen is dead.*

Depression, general depression leading to total pessimism - ... if this were seen, the happiest youth, viewing his progress through...
"... if this were seen,
The happiest youth, viewing his progress through,
What perils past, what crosses to ensue,
Would shut the book, and sit him down and die." (KHIVp2.3.1)
In the play. *The depressing 'this' is found in 'Destiny, d. inscrutable – ... how chances mock, and changes fill the cup of alteration with divers liquors!'*

Depression, general depression leading to total pessimism – ... the whips and scorns of time, the oppressor's wrong, the proud man's contumely...
"... To die, to sleep;
To sleep: perchance to dream: ay, there's the rub;
For in that sleep of death what dreams may come
When we have shuffled off this mortal coil,
Must give us pause: there's the respect
That makes calamity of so long life;
For who would bear the whips and scorns of time,
The oppressor's wrong, the proud man's contumely,
The pangs of despised love, the law's delay,
The insolence of office and the spurns
That patient merit of the unworthy takes,
When he himself might his quietus make
With a bare bodkin? who would fardels bear,
To grunt and sweat under a weary life,
But that the dread of something after death,
The undiscover'd country from whose bourn
No traveller returns, puzzles the will
And makes us rather bear those ills we have
Than fly to others that we know not of?
Thus conscience does make cowards of us all;
And thus the native hue of resolution
Is sicklied o'er with the pale cast of thought,
And enterprises of great pith and moment
With this regard their currents turn awry,
And lose the name of action " (H.3.1)
This is the most accurate and concise description of all the evils that load life with unhappiness, power, arrogance, rejection, insolence, contempt. The quotation may not have a direct use but can be kept in mind as a reminder that misery is not an isolated phenomenon, including the 'pangs of despised love'. 'Bodkin' means knife. However, you can turn the sentence from a question to a statement on the inevitable hardships of life, "(We are all subject to) the whips and scorns of time...merit of the unworthy takes."
In the play. *The lines are part of the universally known monologue that starts with 'To be, or not to be: that is the question'. See 'Decisions, decisions'.*

Depression, in a state of d. – I have... lost all my mirth, forgone all custom of exercises...
Answer to 'Why do you not come to the gym?' or more in general 'How do you feel?' See also 'World, pessimistic view of the w., a congregation of vapors – it goes

so heavily with my disposition that this goodly frame, the earth...'
"…I have of late—but wherefore I know not--lost all my mirth, forgone all custom of exercises…" (H.2.2)
In the play. *Anticipating the investigative efforts of Rosencrantz and Guilderstern, Hamlet gives the an account of his disposition.*

Depression, self-deprecation - I am nothing: or if not nothing to be were better.
"I am nothing: or if not,
Nothing to be were better." (CYM.4.2)
In the play. *Imogen/Fidele finds her/himself in the camp of the Romans.*

Depression, state of d. – a heart as full of sorrows as the sea of sands.
"… a heart
As full of sorrows as the sea of sands" (TGV.4.3)
Answer to the question, 'Why do you look so sad?'
In the play. *Silvia asks Eglamour to accompany her in her travel and quest for the banished Valentine.*

Depression, state of d. – I am wrapped in dismal thinkings.
"I am wrapped in dismal thinkings." (AWEW.5.3)
Answer to the question, 'Why do you look so sad?' See also 'Expression of sadness misconstrued - My heart is ten times lighter than my looks.'
In the play. *The King is perplexed at the turn of events and does not know why Bertram refuses to recognize the ring.*

Description, beyond d. - I never heard of such another encounter, which lames report to follow it and undoes description to do it.
"I never heard of such another encounter, which lames report to follow it and undoes description to do it." (WT.5.2)

Besides encounters you can apply the reference to any other extraordinary event.
In the play. In the play. *A gentleman refers to the sight when Leontes and Polixenes reunite and discover that Florizel and Perdita are at hand and that Perdita is the lost daughter of Leontes.*

Description, self-evident d. - What manner o' thing is your crocodile?…
LEPIDUS What manner o' thing is your crocodile?
MARK ANTONY It is shaped, sir, like itself; and it is as broad
as it hath breadth: it is just so high as it is,
and moves with its own organs: it lives by that
which nourisheth it; and the elements once out of
it, it transmigrates.
LEPIDUS What colour is it of?
MARK ANTONY Of it own colour too.
LEPIDUS 'Tis a strange serpent.
MARK ANTONY Tis so. And the tears of it are wet. (AC.2.7)
The first lines by Antony, 'it is shaped like itself' etc. can be used as an ironic reply to the question 'What kind of man is he?'
In the play. *Hosts of Pompey and almost completely drunk, Mark Antony is conscious enough to give a lesson in obviousness to Lepidus. Lepidus asked Antony to describe a crocodile – an animal found in the Nile river and therefore familiar to Antony who comes from Egypt and Cleopatra.*

Description, d. of her perfection would fill volumes - The chief perfections of that lovely dame … would make a volume of enticing lines.
"…this superficial tale
Is but a preface of her worthy praise:

The chief perfections of that lovely dame,
(Had I sufficient skill to utter them,)
Would make a volume of enticing lines,
Able to ravish any dull conceit."
(KH6.p1.5.5)
Accurate written description of her perfection tough to accomplish. Change the first line to 'Your perfections are such that…(had I sufficient skill to utter them)…conceit.'
In the play. *Returning to London from France, Suffolk describes to Henry VI the beauty of Margaret of France, chosen wife for the king.*

Desire, d. expressed – To taste the fruit of yon celestial tree…
"To taste the fruit of yon celestial tree…"
Use 'Celestial tree' as a compliment.
In the play. *Pericles invokes the Gods to help him solve the riddle and therefore marry the daughter of King Antiochus.*

Despair, d. and desperation - … And if I die, no soul will pity me. Nay wherefore should they, since that I myself find in myself, no pity to myself?
"I shall despair: - there is no creature loves me;
And if I die, no soul will pity me.
Nay, wherefore should they, since that I myself
Find in myself, no pity to myself?"
(KRIII.5.3)
Use to inspire pity and sympathy
In the play. *Richard at war with himself, the night before the final battle with Richmond at Bosworth Field.*

Despair, d. and determination to go down fighting – … Blow, wind! come, wrack At least we'll die with harness on our back
"Ring the alarum-bell! Blow, wind! come, wrack!
At least we'll die with harness on our back." (M.5.5)
In the play. *Macbeth's reaction on learning that a wood is approaching his castle at Duncinane.*

Despair, d. as the result of a horrible act - If thou didst but consent to this most cruel act, do but despair.
"If thou didst but consent
To this most cruel act, do but despair;
And if thou want'st a cord, the smallest thread
That ever spider twisted from her womb
Will serve to strangle thee" (KJ.4.3)
In the play. *Faulconbridge to Hubert whom he believes to be the murderer of young Prince Arthur.*

Despair, let the world go to pieces – … let order die! … And darkness be the burier of the dead!
"…let order die!
And let this world no longer be a stage
To feed contention in a lingering act;
But let one spirit of the first-born Cain
Reign in all bosoms, that, each heart being set
On bloody courses, the rude scene may end,
And darkness be the burier of the dead!" (KHIV.p2.1.1)
In the play. *Northumberland upon receiving the news that the King's forces won at Shrewsbury and that Hotspur is dead.*

Desperation, d. as the only defense policy – … desperation is all the policy, strength and defence …
"…desperation
Is all the policy, strength and defence,
That Rome can make against them." (COR.4.6)
In the play. *Cominius gives an update about the poor defensive position of Rome against the Volsces (and Coriolanus).*

Desperation, d. at the easily predictable course of events - ... Which is so plain, that Exeter doth wish his days may finish ere that hapless time.
"...Which is so plain, that Exeter doth wish
His days may finish ere that hapless time." (KHVI.p1.3.1)
A feeling not uncommon when observing the relentless destruction of the environment. Change 'Exeter' to your name if that is how you feel.
In the play. *What is plain to see is that Henry VI will lose all the conquests made by his father Henry V in France.*

Desperation, d. leading to desperate acts - O mischief! thou art swift to enter the heart of desperate men.
"O mischief! thou art swift
To enter the heart of desperate men!" (RJ.5.1)
Remind your audience that desperate men can act in desperate ways.
In the play. *Balthasar has arrived from Verona and, unaware of the business arranged by Fr. Lawrence, thinks that Juliet is dead and tells Romeo about it. Romeo immediately plans to poison himself.*

Desperation, d. out of repressed anger - Now could I drink hot blood, and do such bitter business as the day would quake to look on.
"Now could I drink hot blood,
And do such bitter business as the day
Would quake to look on" (H.3.2)
In the play. *Hamlet reflects and gathers strength to attack his mother with an aggressive and punitive speech.*

Desperation, total d. – ... Holding the eternal spirit against her will in the vile prison of afflicted breath.

"...a grave unto a soul;
Holding the eternal spirit against her will,
In the vile prison of afflicted breath." (KJ.3.4)
In the play. *King Philip's comment as observing Constance. Constance is dejected because an agreement between Philip of France and King John of England will quash the rights to the throne of her son Arthur.*

Desperation, ready to die - ... Thou desperate pilot, now at once run on the dashing rocks thy sea-sick weary bark!
"Come, bitter conduct, come, unsavoury guide!
Thou desperate pilot, now at once run on
The dashing rocks thy sea-sick weary bark!" (RJ.5.3)
In the play. *Romeo, near Juliet presumed dead and holding a poisoned drink in his hand, utter his last words before drinking it.*

Destiny - What must be shall be. ...That's a certain text.
JULIET what must be shall be.
FRIAR LAURENCE That's a certain text. (RJ.4.1)
Combine the two sentences to underscore inevitability, 'That what must be shall be is a certain text'
In the play. *Paris has just asked Juliet to marry her very shortly. Juliet gives a true but evasive answer, supported by F. Lawrence.*

Destiny, accepting the inevitability of d. - ... let determined things to destiny hold unbewail'd their way.
"...let determined things to destiny
Hold unbewail'd their way" (AC.3.6)
In the play. *Octavia, for a short time wife to Antony, returns dejected to Rome as he abandoned her. Octavian, her brother comforts her.*

Destiny, accepting the inevitability of d. - Are these things then necessities? Then let us meet them like necessities.
"Are these things then necessities? Then let us meet them like necessities" (KHIVp2.3.1)
In the play. *The 'necessities' King Henry refers to are the rebellion and particularly Northumberland, who betrayed Richard II and now rebels against King Henry.*

Destiny, accepting the inevitability of d. - But He, that hath the steerage of my course direct my sail!
"But He, that hath the steerage of my course,
Direct my sail!" (RJ.1.4)
In the play. *Romeo resigns himself to be driven by heavenly powers, here he will go along and attend the Capulet's party where he will meet Juliet.*

Destiny, accepting the inevitability of d. – Heaven has an end in all.
"Heaven has an end in all" (KHVIII.2.1)
In the play. *Buckingham, condemned to death for treason offers words of advice. See 'Ingratitude, i. tied to loss of fortune - ... when they once perceive the least rub in your fortunes, fall away like water from ye...'*

Destiny, accepting the inevitability of d. - What cannot be eschew'd, must be embraced
" What cannot be eschew'd, must be embraced." (MWW.5.5)
Indicate your acceptance or resignation to the course of events.
In the play. *Mr. Page is resigned at Anne Page having married her love Master Fenton.*

Destiny, at odd with our wills - ... Our wills and fates do so contrary run that our devices still are overthrown, our thoughts are ours, their ends none of our own.

"But, orderly to end where I begun,
Our wills and fates do so contrary run
That our devices still are overthrown;
Our thoughts are ours, their ends none of our own." (H.3.2)
In the play. *The player king sums up and ends the play-within-the-play, that Hamlet has produced to check what effects the production has on King Claudius, who is in the audience.*

Destiny, beyond our control - ...ourselves we do not owe; what is decreed must be, and be this so.
"...ourselves we do not owe;
What is decreed must be, and be this so." (TN.1.5)
Commenting on the futility of fighting the decrees of destiny. See also 'Acceptance, a. and resignation to the will of Heaven'.
In the play. *Olivia has fallen in love with Cesario who is none else than Viola in man's attire. Fortunately, Viola has an identical twin and all will end well.*

Destiny, beyond our control - ...the lottery of my destiny bars me the right of voluntary choosing.
"...the lottery of my destiny
Bars me the right of voluntary choosing." (MOV.2.1)
Indicate that the choices you made were inevitable.
In the play. *Portia answers the advances of the Prince of Morocco*

Destiny, beyond our control – A greater power than we can contradict hath thwarted our intents.
"A greater power than we can contradict
Hath thwarted our intents." (RJ.5.3)
When you, however reluctantly must give up.
In the play. *Juliet wakes up from the effect of the drug after she has been presumed dead. But in the meantime Romeo is dead. This is why Fr. Lawrence's intents have been thwarted.*

Destiny, beyond our control – What can be avoided whose end is purposed by the mighty gods?
"What can be avoided
Whose end is purposed by the mighty gods?
Yet Caesar shall go forth" (JC.2.2)
When she warns you about the danger of your enterprise(s) but you will not budge. Change 'Caesar' to your name.
In the play. *Calpurnia, Caesar's wife, attempts to convince him not to go to the Senate on March 15 on the ground of strange observed events, but Caesar does not change his mind.*

Destiny, d. inscrutable – ... how chances mock, and changes fill the cup of alteration with divers liquors!
God! that one might read the book of fate,
And see the revolution of the times
Make mountains level, and the continent,
Weary of solid firmness, melt itself
Into the sea! and, other times, to see
The beachy girdle of the ocean
Too wide for Neptune's hips; how chances mock,
And changes fill the cup of alteration
With divers liquors! (KHIV.p2.3.1)
Comment on a complaint that events proved different from what expected. See also 'Expectations often fail - Oft expectation fails, and most oft there, and most oft there where it most promises...' – 'Expectations, e. fed by hope often frustrated by reality'.
In the play. *King Henry, knowing that revolution is brewing in the realm, expresses his distress to Warwick.*

Destiny, d. of the weak – The weakest kind of fruit drop earliest to the ground.
"...the weakest kind of fruit
Drop earliest to the ground."
(MOV.4.1)
Self-effacing statement to gracefully accept defeat
In the play. *Antonio is resigned to his fate after Shylock refuses to renounce to the payment of the bond (a pound of Antonio's flesh, in practice Antonio's life).*

Destiny, d. shaping our ends - ...
There's a divinity that shapes our ends, rough-hew them how we will.
"Our indiscretions sometimes serves us well,
When our dear plots do pall; and that should teach us
There's a divinity that shapes our ends,
Rough-hew them how we will."
(H.5.2)
Surrendering to circumstances beyond your control.
In the play. *By indiscreetly opening an envelope Hamlet discovered the king's plot to have Hamlet assassinated in England. Therefore he could foil the plot.*

Destiny, d. unavoidable – All unavoided is doom of destiny.
RICHARD. All unavoided is the doom of destiny.
Q. ELIZABETH. True, when avoided grace makes destiny."
(KRIII.4.4)
In the play. *Richard in conversation with Queen Elizabeth, whose daughter he now would like to marry, (his previous wife, Lady Anne, wife of Clarence is dead).*

Destiny, d. unavoidable – 'Tis destiny unshunnable, like death.
"'Tis destiny unshunnable, like death" (OTH.3.3)
In the play. *Gnawed by jealousy, Othello reflects on his own condition.*

Destiny, d. uncontrollable – O vain boast! Who can control his fate?
"... O vain boast!
Who can control his fate?" (OTH.5.2)

In the play. *Othello, who has just killed Desdemona and realized her total innocence, answers a question from Gratiano in Cyprus. Othello recollects his valiant feats in war and realizes that his boast is vain.*

Destiny, evil event triggering a series of subsequent disasters. Day, black day, beginning of dark period - This day's black fate on more days doth depend; this but begins the woe, others must end.

Destiny, inappropriate to resist to d. - What fates impose, that men must needs abide, it boots not to resist both wind and tide.
"What fates impose, that men must needs abide;
It boots not to resist both wind and tide." (KHVI p3.4.3)
In the play. *Warwick, disgusted by Edward IV, deposes him, takes him prisoner and re-established King Henry VI on the throne. Edward reacts philosophically. 'To boot' = 'to avail'*

Destiny, mastership of our own d. - Men at some time are masters of their fates, the fault, dear Brutus, is not in our stars…
"Men at some time are masters of their fates:
The fault, dear Brutus, is not in our stars,
But in ourselves, that we are underlings." (JC.1.2)
Change 'Brutus' with the name of the person (or the audience) you are addressing. Good to stir a group into aggressive action.
In the play. *Cassius makes a dramatic plea to Brutus on the necessity to eliminate tyranny (i.e. eliminate Caesar).*

Destiny, resignation to d. - … there's a special providence in the fall of a sparrow…
"… we defy augury: there's a special providence in the fall of a sparrow. If it be now, 'tis not to come; if it be not to come, it will be now; if it be not now, yet it will come: the readiness is all: since no man has aught of what he leaves, what is't to leave betimes? Let be." (H.5.2)
Words of stoic inspiration and courage during trying times.
In the play. *Horatio attempts to discourage Hamlet from engaging in a duel with Laertes, but Hamlet decides to go on with this final trial.*

Destiny, revolving - The wheel is come full circle.
"The wheel is come full circle: I am here." (KL.5.3)
Put emphasis on the truth of your predictions.
In the play. *Edmund to Edgar. Edgar has just mortally wounded the evil brother Edmund in a duel. Edmund recognizes that all parties involved in some guilt (the father, Gloucester and the son Edmund) have been punished.*

Destiny, the stars in charge of us - It is the stars, the stars above us, govern our conditions…
"It is the stars,
The stars above us, govern our conditions;
Else one self mate and mate could not beget
Such different issues." (KL.4.3)
In the play. *Kent's conclusion on hearing a report from a gentleman about the care that Cordelia, Lear's previously banned daughter, has given to her father.*

Destruction, d. and undoing of previous achievements - Undoing all, as all had never been!
"Undoing all, as all had never been!" (KHVI.p2.1.1)
Express your disapproval of a decision that you feel destructive.

In the play. *Gloucester believes that the agreement between England and France will erase all the previous conquests of England in France.*

Detective work to find out the scoundrel. – … we'll unkennel the fox.
"... we'll unkennel the fox." (MWW.3.3)
Indicate your determination to discover plot and plotter.
In the play. *The 'fox' is Falstaff who will be the object of an unpleasant trick for having wooed Mrs. Ford and Mrs. Page*

Determination - What man dare, I dare.
"What man dare, I dare" (M.3.1)
In the play. *Macbeth addressing the ghost of the slain Banquo while the guests are baffled at Macbeth's apparent insanity.*

Determination and resolution. - My will is back'd with resolution, thoughts are but dreams till their effects be tried…
"… Love and Fortune be my gods, my guide!
My will is back'd with resolution:
Thoughts are but dreams till their effects be tried" (ROL)
Here the intent is bad but the concept applies universally.
In the poem. *Tarquin's thoughts as he debates whether to commit rape or not.*

Determination and resolution - we have no friend but resolution, and the briefest end.
"…Come; we have no friend
But resolution, and the briefest end." (AC.4.15)
Exhortation to fight, "We have no friends but resolution".
In the play. *Cleopatra to her women after Antony's death.*

Determination and strength failing, common weakness of human nature - … I melt, and am not of stronger earth than others.
"... I melt, and am not
Of stronger earth than others."
(COR.5.3)
Indicate that you are ready to accept the offer or proposal that you have previously rejected or fought against.
In the play. *Coriolanus' wife and mother have now arrived to persuade him not to fight against the Romans. He begins to melt*

Determination, d. in anger – … my intents are savage-wild, more fierce and more inexorable far than empty tigers or the roaring sea.
"… My intents are savage-wild,
More fierce and more inexorable far
Than empty tigers or the roaring sea" (RJ.5.3)
Demonstrate and publicize your anger
In the play. *Romeo, out of himself at the news (incorrect) of Juliet's death, develops desperate intents.*

Determination, d. never to retreat - Him I forgive my death that killeth me when he sees me go back one foot or fly.
"Him I forgive my death that killeth me,
When he sees me go back one foot or fly." (KHVI p1.1.2)
In the play. *Charles of France rallies his allies before the city of Orleans.*

Determination, d. or agreement to do anything honorable - I have spirit to do any thing that appears not foul in the truth of my spirit.
"… I have spirit to do any thing that appears not foul in the truth of my spirit." (MFM.3.1)
Answer to 'Are you going to do this?' when you wish to hedge your bets. See

also '**End, e. justifies means** – All with me's meet that I can fashion fit.'
In the play. *The Duke (in disguise) proposes to Isabel a solution that will unmask Angelo's hypocrisy and save Claudio, her brother.*

Determination, d. shown even in extreme circumstances - I shall show the cinders of my spirits through the ashes of my chance.
"I shall show the cinders of my spirits
Through the ashes of my chance:" (AC.5.2)
Answer to 'What are you going to do now that you have been fired?'
In the play. *Seleucus, the administrator, implies that Cleopatra has hidden some of her treasures from the conquering Romans. Cleopatra denies the charge and sends Seleucus away or else…*

Determination, d. to accept suffering - henceforth I'll bear affliction till it do cry out itself 'enough, enough' and die.
"… henceforth I'll bear
Affliction till it do cry out itself
'Enough, enough,' and die." (KL.4.6)
In the play. *Gloucester, encouraged by his son Edgar (still in disguise) will no longer attempt to take his own life.*

Determination, d. to act - To crown my thoughts with acts, be it thought and done.
"…from this moment
The very firstlings of my heart shall be
The firstlings of my hand. And even now,
To crown my thoughts with acts, be it thought and done" (M.4.1)
In the play. *Macbeth is determined to destroy Macduff who fled to England. Macbeth repents for not having it done sooner. He will start by destroying Macduff's castle and killing his whole family.*

Determination, d. to be remorseless - … make thick my blood, stop the access and passage of remorse…
"(Spirits) …make thick my blood,
Stop the access and passage of remorse;
That no compunctions visitings of nature
Shake my fell purpose." (M.1.5)
You are asked to fire many employees at once and are asked 'Are you sure you can do it?'. 'I'll make thick my blood, stop the access and passage of remorse… purpose'. Omit 'fell' as applicable. Equally, use in any situation where what you are asked to do is unpleasant but you want to show you will do it.
In the play. *Lady Macbeth invokes the spirits that 'tend on mortal thoughts' to unsex her (sic) and make her ready for any foul play that may help Macbeth become king.*

Determination, d. to face the inevitable - I am tied to the stake, and I must stand the course.
"I am tied to the stake, and I must stand the course" (KL.3.7)
See also 'Character, not afraid of taking chances - I have set my life upon a cast and I will stand the hazard of the die.
In the play. *Gloucester, in his own castle is tortured and interrogated by the evil Cornwall and Regan.*

Determination, d. to fight back after a setback - … make my ill th'advantage of my good.
"Or make my ill th'advantage of my good." (KHVI.p1.2.5)
Pep up talk and motivational talk after a set back. 'Let us not be discouraged by circumstances and 'we'll make our ills th'advantage of our good.' See also entries for 'Adversity'
In the play. *Plantagenet is on his way to parliament for a redress of his rights or, hence the line, to convert an adversity into an advantage.*

Determination, d. to fight on - I'll set my teeth and send to darkness all that stop me.
"…I'll set my teeth,
And send to darkness all that stop me" (AC.3.13)
In the play. *Defeated by Octavian, Antony is determined to have another go at war.*

Determination, d. to fight to the very end - And here will Talbot mount, or make his grave
"And here will Talbot mount, or make his grave" (KHVI.p1.2.1)
Change 'Talbot' with your name.
In the play. *Talbot of himself as he begins his assault on the city of Orleans*

Determination, d. to fight to the very end - I'll fight, till from my bones my flesh be hack'd.
"I'll fight, till from my bones my flesh be hack'd." (M.5.3)
Can be applied to any number of situations to express your determination to overcome obstacles.
In the play. *Macbeth is determined to fight to the end at Dunsinane.*

Determination, d. to overcome obstacles - … that is a step on which I must fall down, or else o'er-leap…
"The prince of Cumberland! - that is a step
On which I must fall down, or else o'er-leap,
For in my way it lies." (M.1.4)
A difficult assignment that must be completed before anything else can be accomplished, 'That is a step on which…lies'. See also 'Character, not afraid of taking chances - I have set my life upon a cast and I will stand the hazard of the die.'
In the play. *The prince of Cumberland is Malcolm. Macbeth begins to concoct the plan (and the murders) that will lead him to become king of Scotland, as the witches had predicted.*

Determination, d. to participate to an event or a party even if ill - … Not sickness should detain me.
"Noble Antony,
Not sickness should detain me." (AC.2.2)
Answer to 'Will you come?' when you are determined to go. See also 'Apologies for behavior caused by indisposition'.
In the play. *Lepidus answers very cordially to an invitation by Antony to join in a meeting with Octavian.*

Determination, d. to proceed against tenuous odds - … my project may deceive me but my intents are fix'd and will not leave me.
"… my project may deceive me,
But my intents are fix'd and will not leave me." (AWEW.1.1)
See also 'Self-reliance, remedies to be found within ourselves', 'Impossible, nothing i. to the daring'
In the play. *Helena will go to Paris to cure the King and win Bertram's love.*

Determination, d. to take care alone of your own affairs - I will be master of what is mine own.
"I will be master of what is mine own" (TOS.4.2)
When you wish to cut out interference in a personal decision.
In the play. *Petruchio re-affirms his right to steal away with his new bride Katharina immediately after the ceremony.*

Determination, d. to the bitter end, no trading dignity for life - I am resolved for death or dignity.
"I am resolved for death or dignity." (KHVI p2.5.1)
Answer to 'What do you want to do?' when you wish to give emphasis to your answer, meaning that you will go ahead with it, even if you know the risks.

In the play. *York is resolved to snatch the throne from Henry VI or die.*

Determination, d. to turn the situation around - Or make my ill the advantage of my good.
"Or make my ill the advantage of my good." (KHVI.p1.2.5)
See also "Adversity, some g. can be found in a. - There is some soul of goodness in things evil…'
In the play. *Plantagenet, after visiting the dying imprisoned Mortimer, is determined to redress the torts endured by the York family.*

Determination, insisting may yield results - He plies her hard; and much rain wears the marble.
"He plies her hard; and much rain wears the marble." (KHVI.p3.3.2)
A rationalization of insisting in your pursuit. See also 'Justification for insisting even after she said 'no".
In the play. *Richard of Gloucester comments to Clarence on their brother, now King Edward IV, who is trying to seduce (unsuccessfully) the Lady Grey. To have her Edward will marry her.*

Determination, lapses in d. occurring often - … But what we determine oft we break. Purpose's but the slave to memory, of violent birth, but poor validity.
"I do believe you think what now you speak;
But what we do determine oft we break
But what we determine oft we break. Purpose's but the slave to memory, Of violent birth, but poor validity." (H.3.2)
Soften the belief or complete assurance that something will happen or that someone will keep an unrealistic commitment. See also 'Procrastination to be avoided – ... for this 'would' changes, hath abatements and delays as many as there are tongues, are hands, are accidents.'
In the play. *The play that Hamlet has produced is full of direct and indirect references to recent real-life events. Gonzago recites these lines.*

Determination, no boasting - No boasting like a fool, this deed I'll do before this purpose cool.
"No boasting like a fool;
This deed I'll do before this purpose cool." (M.4.1)
Show the opposing party or the audience at large that you are determined to do what you need to do and quickly.
In the play. *Macbeth is determined to assault Fife and exterminate Macduff's family. Macduff has fled to England after Macbeth murdered King Duncan.*

Determination, sign of d. until goal accomplished - I vow by heaven these eyes shall never close
"Before I see thee seated in that throne…
I vow by heaven these eyes shall never close." (KHVI p3.1.1)
Emphasize dramatically your concern and dedication to see the project through.
In the play. *Warwick will not close his eyes until Richard Plantagenet, duke of York, will replace Henry VI on the throne.*

Determination, simile - … and much rain wears the marble.
"… and much rain wears the marble." (KHVI.p3.3.2)
In the play. *Richard of Gloucester comments to Clarence on their brother, now King Edward IV, who is trying to seduce (unsuccessfully) the Lady Grey.*

Determination, simile – … many strokes, though with a little axe, hew down and fell the hardest-timbered oak.
"But Hercules himself must yields to odds;

And many strokes, though with a little axe,
Hew down and fell the hardest-timbered oak." (KHVI p3.2)
An example to show the result of persistence and determination
In the play. *A messenger describes Richard, duke of York's fruitless resistance in the battle.*

Determination, stubbornness, no change of mind – There is no power in the tongue of man to alter me.
"There is no power in the tongue of man
To alter me." (MOV.4.1)
Declare your unwavering determination. Answer to 'Will you change your mind?'
See also 'Invitation, i. impossible to resist - ... There is no tongue that moves, none, none in the world so soon as yours could win me.'
In the play. *Shylock is determined to have his bond (pound of Antonio's flesh), paid in blood as agreed.*

Detraction, reaction to detraction or exposure of your faults – ... happy are they that hear their detractions and can put them to mending.
"...happy are they that hear their detractions and can put them to mending" (MAAN.2.3)
In the play. *Benedick, who repeatedly vowed to remain a bachelor, is secretly in love with Beatrice. The expected detractions will come from those who will chide him for having so suddenly changed his mind.*

Devil, a creature from hell - I think this Talbot be a fiend of hell.
"I think this Talbot be a fiend of hell" (KHVI.p1.2.1)
Change 'Talbot' to applicable name.
In the play. *The bastard of Orleans commenting on the feat of arms by Talbot at Orleans*

Devil, d. appearing in a deceivingly pleasing shape - ... the devil hath power to assume a pleasing shape.
"...the devil hath power
To assume a pleasing shape" (H.2.2)
See also 'Appearance, a. of truth hiding a deeper and malicious purpose - ... to win us to our harm the instruments of darkness tell us truths...'
In the play. *Hamlet has still some last minute doubt that the Ghost may be a creature from Hell, rather than his own father.*

Devil, how to recognize the d. – by his horns.
Mrs. PAGE (referring to Falstaff) "No man means evil but the devil, and we shall know him by his horns." (MWW.5.2)
Assure party or audience that you are capable of recognizing danger in time.
In the play. *Mrs. Page concocts a plan whereby Falstaff will wear a disguise including a set of horns. At the right moment he will be beaten and recognized as the horns as the object of the beating.*

Devil, who are you? - What devil art thou, that dost torment me thus?
"What devil art thou, that dost torment me thus?" (RJ.3.2)
Answer to a telemarketer. Or when contacting again a party who should have already replied but who didn't – e.g. 'I know you may ask 'What devil art thou, that dost torment me thus?' but... etc.
In the play. *The nurse comes in with disconnected news about Romeo and the duel he had during which he slain Tybalt. On pins and needles, Juliet asks the nurse why she, the nurse, seems to want to torment her.*

Diagnosis, d. based on Galen - ... I have read the cause of his effects in Galen
"It hath its original from much grief, from study and perturbation of the

brain: I have read the cause of his effects in Galen" (KHIVp2.1.2)
In the play. *In an attempt to evade questions from the Chief Justice Falstaff attempts to diagnose at a distance the reason for King Henry's illness.*

Dialog, d. postponed when hearer in better mood - ... I will talk to you when you are better temper'd to attend.
"Farewell kinsman! I will talk to you, When you are better temper'd to attend." (KHIV p1.1.3)
When you cannot get your message across due to the impatience of the hearer, 'I will talk to you when… attend.'
In the play. *Worcester to the impatient Hotspur.*

Dictatorship, in praise of d. - ...at once pluck out the multitudinous tongue, let them not lick the sweet which is their poison.
"... at once pluck out
The multitudinous tongue; let them not lick
The sweet which is their poison." (COR.3.1)
Justify denying a voice to a large group of people.
In the play. *Coriolanus explains the reasons for his dictatorial view of politics. The people are ignorant and should not have any say in government. To make his point he appeals to those who prefer*
'A noble life before a long, and wish
To hazard a body with a dangerous physic
That's sure of death without it'

Die, desire to d. - ... he hates him much that would upon the rack of this tough world stretch him out longer.
"…he hates him much
That would upon the rack of this tough world
Stretch him out longer." (KL.5.3)

Refusing to be kept alive in a vegetative state via state-of-the-art life support systems.
In the play. *Kent, speaking of King Lear who is dying of grief at the news that Cordelia was killed under order from Edmund.*

Dieting, d. advice – Make less thy body hence, and more thy grace, leave gormandizing
"Make less thy body hence, and more thy grace;
Leave gormandizing; know the grave doth gape
For thee thrice wider than for other men" (KHIV.p2.5.2)
See also entries for 'Obesity'
In the play. *Parting advice from the now reformed Prince of Wales to his former companion of revelries and hearty eater-drinker Falstaff.*

Dieting, how to refuse when offered more food - ... dainty bits make rich the ribs, but bankrupt quite the wits.
"The mind shall banquet, though the body pine:
Fat paunches have lean pates, and dainty bits
Make rich the ribs, but bankrupt quite the wits." (LLL.1.1)
You can just say, 'No thank you, dainty bits make rich the ribs, but bankrupt quite the wits.'
In the play. *Loganville subscribes to a program of learning, dieting and abstinence that will actually never be followed.*

While Loganville's program, in Love's Labours Lost, was perhaps too ambitious, cultivation of the mind, for Ovid, should be an accompanying goal of the seducer. 'And to thee, o handsome youth, will soon come hoary hairs, soon will come wrinkles to make furrows in your body, (See 'Age. Its effect on wrinkles.'). Now make thee a soul that will abide and add it to thy beauty; only that endures to the ultimate *pyre (i.e. until you are dead)*. Nor let it be a slight care to cultivate your mind in liberal arts, or to learn the two languages well (i.*e. Latin and Greek at the time of course - today you may consider French)*. Ulysses was not comely, but he was eloquent and he fired with love two goddesses of the sea.' (AOL.2). You may also consider taking up German, but not for singing. Said Frederick, King of Prussia (1712-1786), "A German singer! I should as soon expect to get pleasure from the neighing of a horse." In those times, to be fair, operas were as popular as country music is today and only Italians were thought to be able to sing well.

Dieting, too much sugar, excess brings distaste - ... a surfeit of the sweetest things the deepest loathing to the stomach brings.
"… a surfeit of the sweetest things
The deepest loathing to the stomach brings." (MND.2.2)
A metaphor to guard against excess, or to decline to eat more dessert. See also entries for 'Health-care' *** 'Advice, a. to love moderately and to avoid excess in general' – *** 'Excess, e. leads to loathing – They surfeited with honey and began to loathe the taste of sweetness…'
In the play. *Lysander compares his suddenly lost love for Hermia to a stomachache brought about by his excessive passion.*

Difference, d. in type of actions or offices - To offend, and judge, are distinct offices and of opposite nature. "To offend, and judge, are distinct offices
And of opposed natures." (MOV.2.9)
Applicable to a range of actions or ideas other than offending and judging.
In the play. *The Prince of Arragon has chosen the wrong casket and is offended. Portia makes a point to him.*

Diffidence as a form of cowardice - I hold it cowardice to rest mistrustful where a noble heart hath pawn'd an open hand in sign of love.
"I hold it cowardice
To rest mistrustful where a noble heart
Hath pawn'd an open hand in sign of love." (KHVI p3.4.2)
In the field. *Clarence, brother to Edward IV and Somerset have defected to Warwick's camp. Shortly before they were Edward's allies. Some suspicion would be warranted but Warwick rates it unnecessary and cowardly.*

Dinner invitation, answer to - Ay, if I be alive and your mind hold and your dinner worth the eating.
CASSIUS Will you dine with me tomorrow?
CASCA Ay, if I be alive and your mind hold and your dinner worth the eating. (JC.1)
In the play. *Cassius invites Casca to dinner. The apparent rude reply is explained by Casca to Brutus. See 'Rudeness, r. explained - This rudeness is a sauce to his good wit…'*

Dinner time, d.t. as an opportunity to remove attention - ... that you might kill your stomach on your meat and not upon your maid.
JULIA Is't near dinner-time?
LUCETTA I would it were,
That you might kill your stomach on

your meat
And not upon your maid. (TGV.1.2)
In the play. *Lucetta's frank opinion on Julia's character.*

Dinner, have d. precede a meeting - Discourse is heavy, fasting; when we have supp'd we'll mannerly demand thee of thy story so far as thou wilt speak it.
"Discourse is heavy, fasting; when we have supp'd,
We'll mannerly demand thee of thy story,
So far as thou wilt speak it." (CYM.3.6)
Negotiations or conversations are notoriously more successful after a good dinner accompanied by good wine. Wine also prompts drinkers to be more truthful or less mendacious. See also 'Biography, invitation to tell his/her life story'
Note Browning's (BISHOP BLOUGRAM'S APOLOGY.)
'Truth that peeps
Over the glasses' edge when dinner's done,
See also 'Negotiations, n. better after dinner' *** Biography, invitation to tell his/her life story – I long to hear the story of your life...' *** 'Dinner, have d. precede a meeting - Discourse is heavy, fasting; when we have supp'd we'll mannerly demand thee of thy story so far as thou wilt speak it.'
In the play. *Imogen, in a man's disguise, has fled to Wales where he/she meets with Belarius and her two (as yet unknown to her) brothers, Guiderius and Arviragus. Belarius suggest to first have dinner.*

Dinner, invitation to a working d. - ... let us sup betimes, that afterwards we may digest our complots in some form.
"Come, let us sup betimes, that afterwards
We may digest our complots in some form." (RIII.3.1)

See also 'Negotiations, n. better after dinner' – 'Invitation, i. to dinner and to freedom from care'.
In the play. *Richard invites Buckingham to dinner during which he (Richard) may concoct further murderous plans.*

Dinner, not hungry after d. - Who riseth from a feast with that keen appetite that he sits down?
"… who riseth from a feast
With that keen appetite that he sits down?" (MOV.2.6)
Impossible to reconcile appetite with a full stomach. Answer to 'You are not hungry any more?'
In the play. *Gratiano and Salarino converse while waiting for Lorenzo. The comparison refers to love pursued versus love conquered. See 'Chase, enjoyment greater in the chase'*

Dinner. How to pay for dinner, cash or credit card – (I'll pay cash) as far as my coin would stretch…
"(I'll pay cash) as far as my coin would stretch; and, where it would not, I have used my credit."
(KHIV.p1.1.2)
Answer to 'How would you wish to pay?' If you go out on a date you should always pay for dinner. Dinners for two where parties 'go dutch' are unromantic. It may well happen that you do not have a credit card or that your credit card has maxed out. It is absolutely terrible for the waiter to come back to your table and announce that your credit card is no good. Should this ever happen, use this line before actually paying. The statement may be interpreted to mean that you prefer to pay cash than with a credit card for whatever reason.
In the play. *The Prince of Wales add-on to Falstaff's remark that the Prince of Wales has always paid for everything.*

Diplomacy, adjusting d. - O, pardon me…that I am meek and gentle with these butchers!
"O, pardon me, thou bleeding piece of earth,
That I am meek and gentle with these butchers!" (JC.3.1)
In the play. *Antony, facing the body of murdered Julius Caesar, must adjust his diplomacy. The butchers are Brutus, Cassius and associates.*

Direction, wrong d. – by a pace goes backward, with a purpose it hath to climb.
"…by a pace goes backward, with a purpose
It hath to climb…" (TC.1.3)
Sarcastically describe the political or social achievements of the incumbent adversary.
In the play. *Part of Ulysses' motivational speech to the disaffected Greeks.*

Disagreement, d. costly - … we'll no longer stay; these words will cost ten thousand lives this day.
Q. MARGARET. Stay Edward.
EDWARD. No, wrangling woman, we'll no longer stay;
These words will cost ten thousand lives this day." (KHVI p3.2)
A meeting has ended without resolution and you are afraid of the consequences. Start from 'we'll no longer stay'.
In the play. *At Towton in Yorkshire the meeting has ended without a peaceful resolution between the party of King Henry VI and the party of Edward of York, supported by Warwick.*

Disappearance – … they made themselves air, into which they vanished.
"…When I burned in desire to question them further, they made themselves air, into which they vanished." (M.1.5)
Answer to 'Where did he go? 'He made himself air… ….vanished'.
In the play. *Lady Macbeth reads a letter from her husband, who reports about his fateful meeting with the witches.*

Disappearance, where is he? - …melted into air, into thin air…
"…melted into air, into thin air…" (TEM.5.1)
Answer to 'Where is he?' See also 'Vanished, persons v. - … Into the air; and what seem'd corporal melted as breath into the wind.'
In the play. *Prospero has accomplished all his goals with his acquired skills in magic. He takes leave of the audience reminding them that the spirits who acted in the play have melted away.*

Disappointment, d. anticipated - … this may prove food to my displeasure.
"… this may prove food to my displeasure." (MAAN.1.3)
Alternative to 'I don't think I like this'.
In the play. *Don John hears from Borachio that Claudio, a great friend of Don Pedro is in love with Hero and Don John does not like the idea.*

Disappointment, d. expressed in dramatic terms – … make dust our paper and with rainy eyes…
"(Let's) make dust our paper and with rainy eyes
Write sorrow on the bosom of the earth" (RII.3.2)
Works well to emphasize your reaction at her disappointment with you. Give a dramatic tone to her 'no', e.g. 'I'll make dust my paper and with rainy eyes…earth'. Equally, alternative to 'I am sorry'. See also, 'Anger, she is really angry.' *** 'Anger, her a. an occasion for a compliment.' – 'Rejection, reaction to r., emphatic and mildly theatrical' *** 'Speech, disappointment or despair at her words' *** 'Cry, starting to cry'

In the play. *Richard II has been dethroned by Bolingbroke who will be crowned Henry IV.*

Disaster, too late to avoid d. - We see the very wreck that we must suffer and unavoided is the danger now…
"We see the very wreck that we must suffer;
And unavoided is the danger now,
For suffering so the causes of our wreck" (KRII.2.1)
See also 'Storm, s. (metaphor for vexation) unavoidable - … we hear this fearful tempest sing, yet see no shelter to avoid the storm.'
In the play. *Lord Ross confirms with another metaphor the dangerous state of the realm under King Richard.*

Disasters, rationalizing d. – … checks and disasters grow in the veins of actions highest rear'd.
"…checks and disasters
Grow in the veins of actions highest rear'd" (TC.1.3)
See also 'Expectations, e. fed by hope often frustrated by reality - The ample proposition that hope makes in all designs begun on earth below fails in the promised largeness…'
In the play. *Agamemnon addresses the Grecian troops who have besieging Troy for a long time without victory. He invites them to consider the temporarily failed expectations as trials to test the Greeks' fiber.*

Disbelief, d. about one's mental state and perception - Or sleep I now and think I hear all this?
"Or sleep I now and think I hear all this?
What error drives our eyes and ears amiss?" (COE.2.2)
See also 'Mind, state of m. 'where am I?' - Am I in earth, in heaven or in hell….'
Entries for 'Unbelievable'

In the play. *Antipholus S. cannot explain why Adriana (wife of Antipholus E. takes him for her husband.*

Discipline, measured approach in establishing d. - We shall be call'd purgers, not murderers.
"We shall be call'd purgers, not murderers." (JC.2.1)
Clear example of putting the politically correct spin to murder.
In the play. *Brutus outlines a strategy for killing Caesar and for providing the right spin for public opinion.*

Disclaimer - … if I were disposed to stir your hearts and minds to mutiny and rage…
"… if I were disposed to stir
Your hearts and minds to mutiny and rage" (JC.3.2)
Before you start your attack on the establishment, e.g. 'I am not here to stir your hearts and minds to mutiny and rage.'
In the play. *Antony begins his eulogy of Caesar.*

Disclaimer, dramatic d. - The gods throw stones of sulphur on me, if…
"The gods throw stones of sulphur on me, if…" (CYM.5.5)
In the play. *Pisanio rejects the accusation that he intended to poison Imogen*

Disclosure, complete d. - … I have unclasped to thee the book even of my secret soul.
"Thou know'st no less but all; I have unclasped
To thee the book even of my secret soul." (TN.1.4)
Use to end a conversation where the matter was confidential.
In the play. *The Duke has confessed to Cesario his love for Olivia.*

Discontent, inability to see the good and its pernicious effects – Thou pout'st upon thy fortune and thy love: take heed, take heed, for such die miserable.
"Happiness courts thee in her best array;
But, like a misbehaved and sullen wench,
Thou pout'st upon thy fortune and thy love:
Take heed, take heed, for such die miserable" (RJ.3.3)
In the play. *Friar Lawrence upbraids Romeo who rails about being banished from Verona, when the Friar is still optimistic about Romeo and Juliet being happily re-united in the near future.*

Discretion, invitation not to exceed the limits of d. - Let's teach ourselves that honourable stop not to outsport discretion.
"Let's teach ourselves that honourable stop,
Not to outsport discretion." (OTH.2.3)
In the play. *Othello counsels his lieutenant Cassio to keep the festivities in Cyprus within limits*

Discretion, relying on d. - your discretions better can persuade than I am able to instruct or teach.
"…your discretions better can persuade
Than I am able to instruct or teach" (KHVI.p1.4.1)
Evasive answer to 'What shall we do?'
In the play. *King Henry attempts to reconcile Basset with Vernon.*

Discrimination, nature does not discriminate – The selfsame sun that shines upon his court hides not his visage…
"The selfsame sun that shines upon his court
Hides not his visage from our cottage but
Looks on alike" (WT.4.3)
In the play. *Perdita is distraught after a conversation with Polixenes, who insulted her by telling her that she is of low birth and unsuitable to marry his son Florizel.*

Discrimination, no racial d. – Mislike me not for my complexion…
"Mislike me not for my complexion,
The shadowed livery of the burnish'd sun
To whom I am a neighbour, and near bred." (MOV.2.1)
When you suspect race bias, 'I trust you will not mislike me for my complexion…near bred'. See also 'Beauty, black is beautiful'.
In the play. *At Belmont the Prince of Morocco has arrived to take part in the quiz that will deliver Portia as a wife to the winner.*

Disguise, d. and pretence, tools of wicked enemy - Disguise, I see, thou art a wickedness, wherein the pregnant enemy does much…
"Disguise, I see, thou art a wickedness,
Wherein the pregnant enemy does much.
How easy is it for the proper-false
In women's waxen hearts to set their forms!" (TN.2.2)
Apply to the evil plots of your political opponents or party.
In the play. *Olivia, having met Viola disguised as Cesario, falls in love with her/him. Viola, conscious of the equivocal situation, exclaims against disguise and philosophizes about women's character.*

Disguise, d. discovered - there is a kind of confession in your looks.
"… there is a kind of confession in your looks which your modesties have not craft enough to colour" (H.2.2)

In the play. *Rosencranz and Guilderstern have been sent by the King to spy on Hamlet and he tells them that he knows.*

Disguise, hypocrisy - ... some that smile have in their hearts, I fear, millions of mischiefs.
"…some that smile have in their hearts, I fear,
Millions of mischiefs." (JC.4.1)
See also 'Hypocrisy, range and scope of h.'
In the play. *Octavius and Antony are planning on how to beat Brutus and Cassius. Octavius agrees with Antony that the matter must be planned secretly, given that the enemies smile but have mischiefs in mind.*

Disguise, taking on a d. - ... disliken the truth of your own seeming.
"... and, as you can, disliken
The truth of your own seeming" (WT.4.3)
Change 'your' to 'my' if you apply the statement to yourself. See also 'Ornaments, to make a goddess angry'
In the play. *Camillo advises Perdita to wear a disguise so that she may not be recognized while in the company of Florizel, with whom she elopes.*

Disgust, d. and hatred expressed - Tempt not too much the hatred of my spirit for I am sick when I do look on thee.
"Tempt not too much the hatred of my spirit;
For I am sick when I do look on thee." (MND.2.1)
In the play. *Demetrius does not want to have anything to do with Helena who, instead, loves him.*

Disgust, d. at words heard - I do condemn mine ears that have so long attended thee
"I do condemn mine ears that have
So long attended thee." (CYM.1.6)

Retort to a negative comment or to a nasty statement or speech from adversary.
In the play. *Imogen reject the abject advances of Iachimo.*

Disgust, d. at words heard - Mine ears, that to your wanton talk attended…
"Mine ears, that to your wanton talk attended,
Do burn themselves for having so offended" (V&A)
In the poem. *Adonis flatly rejects Venus' repeated advances.*

Dislike, d. and antagonism - ... for I desire nothing but odds with England.
"…for I desire
Nothing but odds with England" (KHV.2.4)
Answer to your opinion about a person or a party. Change 'England' to the same of a political party, a nation or organization.
In the play. *The Dauphin answers a remark by Exeter, the English ambassador.*

Dislike, d. mixed with contempt - ... I care not for you and am so near the lack of charity to accuse myself--I hate you.
"…I care not for you,
And am so near the lack of charity--
To accuse myself--I hate you" (CYM.2.2)
Alternative to 'I hate to say this but…'
See also 'Contempt, c. for a person compared to another - ... his meanest garment that ever hath but clipped his body.'
In the play. *Imogen despises Cloten who woos her.*

Dislike, d. of speech and person - 'T is not my speeches that you do

mislike, but 't is my presence that doth trouble ye.
"My lord of Winchester, I know your mind;
'T is not my speeches that you do mislike,
But 't is my presence that doth trouble ye." (KHVI p2.1.1)
Use in a situation when you want it to be known that you know who is your enemy.
In the play. *Gloucester to Cardinal, they are well established enemies of each other.*

Dislike, I don't like him - His countenance likes me not.
CORNWALL Why dost thou call him a knave? What's his offence?
KENT His countenance likes me not. (KL.2.2)
Answer to 'Why don't you like him?' On a one-to-one encounter you may express the same idea with these lines by Groucho Marx, 'I never forget a face but in your case I'll make an exception'.
In the play. *The subject in question is the vile Oswald, a servant and accomplice of the Duke of Cornwall. Kent does not like him.*

Dislike, intense d. of a person – I see, lady, the gentleman is not in your books...
MESSENGER. I see, lady, the gentleman is not in your books.
BEATRICE. No; and if he were, I would burn my study." (MAAN.1.1)
Express displeasure and distance. E.G. 'He is not in my books and if he were, I would burn my study'.
In the play. *The gentleman in question is Benedick.*

Dislike, liking what you don't like - That that likes not you pleases me best.
DIOMEDES. I do not like this fooling.
THERSITES (aside). Nor I, by Pluto: that that likes not you pleases me best. (TC.5.2)
Express your antagonistic attitude.
In the play. *The fooling that Diomedes does not like is Cressida's teasing. Thersites is a witness*

Dislike, mutual d. expressed - I do desire we may be better strangers.
" I do desire we may be better strangers." (AYLI.3.2)
Politely indicate your dislike of the person you are dealing with or jokingly, if he/she has said something you do not like or approve of. See also 'Acquaintance, a. unpleasant'.
For an opposite feeling see 'Interest, personal i. in knowing person better'.
In the play. *Orlando and Jacques do not get along very well, as expressed by this wish by Orlando.*

Dismissal, cold d. - ... when we need your use and counsel, we shall send for you.
"You have good leave to leave us: when we need
Your use and counsel, we shall send for you" (KHIV.p1.1.3)
This is a variant of "We do not know what we can do without you but from tomorrow we are going to try'
In the play. *Henry IV dismisses Worcester.*

Disobedience, civil d. useless – ... those cold ways that seem like prudent helps, are very poisonous...
"...those cold ways,
That seem like prudent helps, are very poisonous
Where the disease is violent." (COR.3.1)
In the play. *After an outburst of Coriolanus who shows his contempt of the common people, the tribunes recoil from simple complaint and want harsher measures against him.*

Disobedience, d. justified on moral grounds – Every good servant does not all commands
"… O Pisanio!
Every good servant does not all commands" (CYM.5.1)
In the play. *Back in Britain Leonatus thinks that Pisanio has really executed the command of killing Imogen, Leonatus' wife.*

Disobedience, d. perceived -
Worcester, get thee gone, for I do see danger and disobedience in thine eye.
"Worcester, get thee gone, for I do see
Danger and disobedience in thine eye." (KHIV p1.1.3)
When you perceive an undeclared opposition, 'I do see danger and disobedience in thine eye.'
In the play. *King Henry IV addresses Worcester and others who have proven disobedient.*

Disobedience, the cost of d. - … You have obedience scanted and well are worth the want that you have wanted.
"… You have obedience scanted,
And well are worth the want that you have wanted." (KL.1.1)
In the play. *Cordelia, banned by her silly father Lear is reprimanded by Goneril, one of the evil sisters.*

Displeasure, d. reduced by knowledge of circumstances - If you did know for what I gave the ring you would abate the strength of your displeasure.
"If you did know for what I gave the ring
…
You would abate the strength of your displeasure." (MOV.5.1)
You may use the last line alone, ('Abate the strength of your displeasure'), or the complete quote modifying the description of the action. E.G., 'If you knew why I did it, you would abate…. displeasure'.

In the play. *Bassanio responds to the upbraiding* by Portia. In a very improbable plot, Bassanio gives the ring to Portia who is disguised as a man. Though he is her husband, he does not recognize her.

Dispute, d. and disagreement on right and wrong - If that be right which Warwick says is right, there is no wrong, but everything is right.
"If that be right which Warwick says is right,
There is no wrong, but everything is right." (KHVI p3.2.2)
Express your strong disagreement. Change 'Warwick' with the name of the person you are disagreeing with. See also 'Law, anarchy as a consequence of unjust law – When law can do no right, let it be lawful that law bar no wrong.'
In the play. *The Prince of Wales, rightful heir to the throne comments on Warwick's reasons why Henry VI should abdicate (whereby the Prince of Wales would lose his rights).*

Dispute, d. that cannot be peacefully resolved - … the wound that bred this meeting here cannot be cured by words.
"…. the wound that bred this meeting here
Cannot be cured by words." (KHVI p3.2.2)
Indicate that action not words will resolve the issue.
In the play. *Edward, Warwick, Q. Margaret and Clifford argue after the battle of York.*

Disregard, completely disregarded –
… they pass'd by me as misers do by beggars…
"…they pass'd by me
As misers do by beggars, neither gave to me
Good word nor look" (TC.3.3)
See also 'Attire, a. or general appearance questionable – so … unfashionable that dogs bark at me as I halt by them.'

Rhetorical affirmation that you are being ignored, e.g. 'You pass by me as misers…. neither give to me… look.'
In the play. *Achilles agrees that the other Greeks take no notice of him. Ulysses is trying to convince Achilles to rejoin the fight against the Trojans.*

Dissension, strife dangerous - Civil dissension is a viperous worm, that gnaws the bowels of the commonwealth.
"Civil dissension is a viperous worm, That gnaws the bowels of the commonwealth." (KHVI.p1.3.1)
Calm tempers during a tumultuous meeting. See also entries for 'Quarrel'
In the play. *K. Henry VI tries to bring some peace between Winchester, Gloucester.*

Dissimulation - … and wonder greatly that man's face can fold in pleasing smiles such murderous tyranny.
" …and wonder greatly that man's face can fold
In pleasing smiles such murderous tyranny." (TA.2.4)
Describe a dissimulator, e.g., 'His face can fold in pleasing smiles murderous tyranny'.
In the play. *The arch-evil Tamora concocts a plot whereby she accuses two of Titus' sons of having murdered Bassianus.*

Dissimulation, devils' technique - When devils will the blackest sins put on, they do suggest at first with heavenly shows…
"…Divinity of hell!
When devils will the blackest sins put on,
They do suggest at first with heavenly shows,
As I do now" (OTH.2.3)
See also 'Appearance, a. of truth hiding a deeper and malicious purpose - … to win us to our harm the instruments of darkness tell us truths…' and entries for 'Appearances'.
In the play. *Iago plans his move to drive Othello into mad jealousy.*

Dissimulation, enchanting with sweets but poisonous words - I will enchant the old Andronicus with words more sweet, and yet more dangerous…
"I will enchant the old Andronicus
With words more sweet, and yet more dangerous,
Than baits to fish, or honey-stalks to sheep,
When as the one is wounded with the bait,
The other rotted with delicious feed." (TA.4.4)
Describing a dangerous enchantress, '(she) enchants with words more sweet, and yet more dangerous…feed'.
In the play. *Tamora plots against Titus A., but he will outsmart her in the end.*

Dissimulation, facial expression not giving away intention – (We will) make our faces vizards to our hearts, disguising what they are.
"(We will) make our faces vizards to our hearts,
Disguising what they are." (M.3.2)
Invitation to a group of conspirators not to give away the game. 'Vizard' is 'mask'. You can use 'masks' or perhaps 'curtains' to keep the rhythm.
In the play. *Macbeth prompts Lady Macbeth to show friendliness to Banquo so that he may not suspect that Macbeth plans to kill him.*

Dissimulation, lesson in d. - Your face, my thane, is as a book where men may read strange matters…
"Your face, my thane, is as a book where men
May read strange matters - to beguile the time,

Look like the time; bear welcome in your eye,
Your hand, your tongue: look like the innocent flower,
But be the serpent under it." (M.1.5)
Question the intent of a potential adversary with slight modifications, e.g. 'Your face, Mr. Carson, is as a book, where men do read strange matters'. Or describe the classic corporate snake, 'He bears welcome in his eye, his hand, his tongue; he looks like the innocent flower but he is a serpent under it.'
In the play. *Lady Macbeth tutors her husband before he kills King Duncan who is visiting Macbeth's castle.*

Dissimulation, pretence, put a show, as if nothing were happening - ...and mock the time with fairest show...
"... And mock the time with fairest show;
False face must hide what the false heart doth know!" (M.1.7)
Apply to an adversary who is literally putting up a show, 'Your false face must hide what the false heart doth know', or use the sentence completely.
In the play. *Macbeth's word of advise to his wife (a bitch herself who does not need any). Macbeth is on his way to murdering King Duncan.*

Dissimulation, pretence, put a show, as if nothing were happening – ... look fresh and merrily let not our looks put on our purposes.
"...look fresh and merrily;
Let not our looks put on our purposes" (JC.2.1)
Advise to co-conspirators.
In the play. *Brutus recommends to Cassius and other conspirators not to give away by their looks their intent to kill Caesar.*

Dissipation, d. of assets for a woman - ... .He hath given his empire up to a whore...

"… He hath given his empire
Up to a whore…"(AC.3.6)
In the play. *Octavian to his sister, rejected Antony's wife, referring to Antony and Cleopatra.*

Dissipation, loss of assets through poor management - Pirates may make cheap worth of their pillage...
"Pirates may make cheap worth of their pillage, And purchase friends, and give to courtesans,
Still revelling, like lords, till all be gone." (KHVI p2.1.1)
Describe big spenders or poor managers who spend money because it is not their own, just like pirates. Often the case with venture capital companies.
In the play. *York reflects on the conditions that led to the loss of English power in France*

Distance (physical) not a problem.
"But it is such long way away!" or "Do you mind?" - A true devoted pilgrim is not weary to measure kingdoms with his feeble steps.
"A true devoted pilgrim is not weary
To measure kingdoms with his feeble steps." (TGV.2.7)
Apply any time she asks you to do something that implies going (and returning from) anywhere. Answer to her question, 'Do you mind to do this?'
In the play: *In Verona, Julia misses Proteus who earlier went to Milan. Julia and decides to travel to Milan. Lucetta, her servant points out the dangers of such a trip and Julia counters Lucetta's arguments.*

Distance, keeping a long d. due to personal dislike - ... if there be breadth enough in the world, I will hold a long distance.
"... if there be breadth enough in the world, I will hold a long distance." (AWEW.3.2)
Show your dislike, by wanting to be as far as possible from the disliked person.

In the play. *The words come from a letter Bertram has written to his mother explaining why he dos not want to be Helen's husband and why, therefore, he will 'hold a distance'.*

Distinction, d. or promotion misplaced or unbecoming – It lies as sightly on the back of him as great Alcides' shows upon an ass.
"It lies as sightly on the back of him
As great Alcides' shows upon an ass" (KJ. 2.1)
In the play. *Faulconbridge's opinion of the enemy Austria.*

Distraction, no d. please – When holy and devout religious men are at their beads…
"When holy and devout religious men
Are at their beads, 'tis hard to draw them thence,
So sweet is zealous contemplation." (KRIII.3.7)
Suggest ironically that you do not want to lose your concentration.
In the play. *In a masterful image-building charade, Richard III arrives at the meeting of the London council accompanied by two priests, all in prayer.*

Distress, d. emphasized dramatically - …if the river were dry, I am able to fill it with my tears…
"…if the river were dry, I am able to fill it with my tears; if the wind were down, I could drive the boat with my sighs." (TGV.2.3)
Mockingly express your dismay. Possible answer to 'how are you?' when and if you are feeling down.
In the play *Launce, Proteus' servant and Panthino, servant to Proteus' father exchange some banter.*

Distress, deep d. and reason of- why, say, fair queen, whence springs this deep despair?
KING LEWIS XI Why, say, fair queen, whence springs this deep despair?
QUEEN MARGARET From such a cause as fills mine eyes with tears. And stops my tongue, while heart is drown'd in cares. (KHVI p3.3)
Answer to 'What is the problem?' 'It's a cause that fills … cares'.
In the play. *Queen Margaret has traveled to the French king's court to lobby for help after King Henry VI, her husband, has been dethroned by Edward IV with the support of Warwick.*

Disturbance, d. and noise - But with thy brawls thou hast disturb'd our sport.
"But with thy brawls thou hast disturb'd our sport." (MND.2.1)
In the play. *Fairy Queen Titania dismisses Oberon's insinuations about her supposed infidelities. The real issue is the possession of a page boy, claimed by both.*

Divine, exceeding all natural excellence - I might call him a thing divine, for nothing natural I ever saw so noble.
"I might call him
A thing divine, for nothing natural
I ever saw so noble." (TEM.1.2)
Can be applied to a woman too. Answer to 'What do you think of me?' 'I might call you a thing divine…noble'
In the play. *Miranda is impressed by Ferdinand's looks.*

Divine, goddess of my idolatry - Do not swear at all… or by thy gracious self, which is the god of my idolatry.
"Do not swear at all;
Or, if thou wilt, swear by thy gracious self,
Which is the god of my idolatry." (RJ.2.2)

Swearing oaths is optional. 'Goddess of my idolatry' is a good self-standing compliment.
In the play. *Romeo and Juliet exchange vows of love in her garden.*

Do not tell me what to do - Prescribe not us our duties
"Prescribe not us our duties" (KL.1.1)
In the play. *Cordelia, banned by silly father Lear, still recommends him to the care of her evil sisters. Regan responds haughtily*

Doer, d. of no good – ... The close contriver of all harms...
"And I, the mistress of your charms,
The close contriver of all harms,
Was never call'd to bear my part,
Or show the glory of our art?" (M.3.5)
Define a scheming obnoxious character, e.g. 'He is a close contriver of all harms'.
In the play. *Hecate, supervisor of the 3 witches complains that they made a deal with Macbeth without first consulting with her and having a part in it too.*

Doctors, d. that procured the illness - ... careless patient as thou art, commit'st thy anointed body to the cure of those physicians that first wounded thee.
"And thou, too careless patient as thou art,
Commit'st thy anointed body to the cure
Of those physicians that first wounded thee" (KRII.2.1)
The doctors can be actual physicians or a metaphor.
In the play. *Gaunt reproaches nephew King Richard II for being too eager for flattery.*

Document, policy statement, message filled with questionable reasons for a dreadful act - ... Larded with many several sorts of reasons.

"...an exact command,
Larded with many several sorts of reasons" (H.5.4)
Express your contempt for the content of a document justifying a despicable policy. See also 'Words, despicable w. but well crafted - ignominious words, though clerkly couched.'
In the play. *Hamlet explains to Horatio the content of a sealed message from the King to England. The instruction was to kill Hamlet immediately, but Hamlet discovered this by chance.*

Dog, beware of venomous dog (figuratively) - O Buckingham, take heed of yonder dog; look, when he fawns he bites...
"O Buckingham, take heed of yonder dog;
Look when he fawns he bites; and when he bites
His venom tooth will rankle to the death." (KRIII.1.3)
Apply to any snake in the company.
In the play. *Margaret warns Buckingham, currently allied to Richard - she will prove right in the end.*

Dogs, d. preferable to men - ... I do wish thou wert a dog that I might love thee something.
"I am misanthropos and hate mankind.
For thy part, I do wish thou wert a dog,
That I might love thee something." (TOA.4.3)
Express your complete contempt of mankind. See also entries for 'Animals, a. better than men' *** 'Misanthropy – ... nothing but himself which looks like man is friendly with him.'
In the play. *Timon' gruff greeting of Alcibiades.*

Doing good - I never did repent for doing good, nor shall not now.

"I never did repent for doing good, Nor shall not now:" (MOV.3.4)
Insist on an act of kindness when the recipient is concerned about your going out of your way to help him.
In the play. *Portia is determined to help Antonio, friend of Bassanio.*

Double-crosser - Weigh oath with oath, and you will nothing weigh…
"Weigh oath with oath, and you will nothing weigh;
Your vows to her and me, put in two scales,
Will even weigh, and both as light as tales" (MND.3.2)
In the play. *Helena is mad at Lysander for his double crossing.*

Double-speak – And be these juggling fiends no more believed, that palter with us in a double sense
"And be these juggling fiends no more believed,
That palter with us in a double sense" (M.5.8)
When the government invades other countries inflicting thousands or millions of deaths to bring 'freedom and democracy'. See also 'Deception, d. from false teachers - Thus may poor fools believe false teachers…'
In the play. *In the final battle at Dunsinane, Macbeth inveighs against the witches and their quimsical predictions, specifically that a man born via a Caesarian delivery was not 'of woman born'. 'To palter' = 'to equivocate'.*

Doubt, d. as a symptom of wisdom - … modest doubt is call'd the beacon of the wise.
"… modest doubt is call'd
The beacon of the wise." (TC.2.2)
Justify reservation about the certainty of a positive outcome. See also 'Wisdom, modest w. suggesting caution in expectations'.

In the play. *Hector, Troilus and Priam discuss whether they should Helen go. Although confident of the strength of Troy, Hector joins Priam in proposing that Helen be returned to the Greeks.*

Doubt, d. or remorse, or awareness of crime - … this even-handed justice commends the ingredients of our poison'd chalice to our own lips.
"… if the assassination
Could trammel up the consequence, and catch
With his surcease success; that but this blow
Might be the be-all and the end-all here,
But here, upon this bank and shoal of time,
We'd jump the life to come. But in these cases
We still have judgment here; that we but teach
Bloody instructions, which, being taught, return
To plague the inventor: this even-handed justice
Commends the ingredients of our poison'd chalice
To our own lips" (M.1.7)
Remind highly placed criminals that their crime will return to haunt them, e.g. 'Remember that justice commends the ingredient of your poisoned chalice to your own lips'.
The line 'here, upon this bank and shoal of time' is a powerful image to give emphasis to a beginning, of a project, new era or equivalent.
In the play. *Macbeth makes a clear analysis of the consequences of a crime. Fear, let alone remorse, is the price to pay for crime.*

Doubt, seeding d. and fears – He dives into the king's soul, and there scatters…
"He dives into the king's soul, and there scatters

**Dangers, doubts, wringing of the conscience,
Fears, and despairs"** (KHVIII.2.2)
In the play. *Norfolk comments on Cardinal Wolsey's plan to make King Henry divorce Queen Catherine.*

Doubts, d. as traitors - Our doubts are traitors and make us lose the good we oft might win by fearing to attempt.
"Our doubts are traitors,
And make us lose the good we oft might win
By fearing to attempt." (MFM.1.4)
Dispel doubt and prompt audience to action. See also 'Fear, f. causing treason - ... when our actions do not our fears do make us traitors.'
In the play. *Isabel doubts of her power to sway Angelo to be merciful to her brother Claudio.*

Dowry, not marrying for m. – Henry is able to enrich his queen…
"Henry is able to enrich his queen
And not seek a queen to make him rich
So worthless peasants bargain for their wives
As market-men for oxen, sheep, or horse" (KHVI.p1.5.5)
In the play. *Suffolk rebuts Exeter's criticism that Margaret, future wife of Henry VI is penniless.*

Dream and illusion - Thus have I had thee as a dream doth flatter, in sleep a king, but waking, no such matter.
"Thus have I had thee as a dream doth flatter,
In sleep a king, but waking, no such matter." (SON.87)
Maybe you are writing to her or sending her a note while you are on a business trip or away from her for some time.

Dream or madness - 'Tis still a dream, or else such stuff as madmen tongue and brain not.

**"'Tis still a dream, or else such stuff as madmen
Tongue and brain not"** (CYM.5.4)
Apply the attributes of madness to a mad speech or reasoning, e.g. 'This is stuff that madmen tongue and brain not.'. See also entries for 'Speech, nonsensical or meaningless'
In the play, *Posthumus Leonatus, jailed and condemned to death has a dream where he is told that his fortunes will brighten up and he is skeptical. The lines that follow are in 'Speech, nonsensical or meaningless - ... senseless speaking or a speaking such s sense cannot untie.'*

Dream, American d realized - I have lived to see inherited my very wishes…
"I have lived
To see inherited my very wishes
And the buildings of my fancy" (COR.2.1)
In the play. *Volumnia, Coriolanus' mother expressing her satisfaction at her son's accomplishments.*

Dream, bad d. put it down to a bad d. - … think no more of this night's accidents but as the fierce vexation of a dream.
"And think no more of this night's accidents,
But as the fierce vexation of a dream." (MND.4.1)
Express disbelief by attributing your conclusion to the effects of a dream – e.g. 'Perhaps it was the fierce vexation of a dream'.
In the play. *Oberon gets ready to release Titania from the spell that made her fall in love with Bottom.*

Dream, d. past recollection or not to be explained – I have had a dream, past the wit of man to say what dream it was…
"I have had a dream, past the wit of man to say what dream it was: man is

but an ass, if he go about to expound this dream
… The eye of man hath not heard, the ear of man hath not seen, man's hand is not able to taste, his tongue to conceive, nor his heart to report, what my dream was" (MND.4.1)
In the play. *Bottom, the actor wakes up.*

Dream, d. that inspires confidence and well being - If I may trust the flattering truth of sleep, my dreams presage some joyful news at hand…
"If I may trust the flattering truth of sleep,
My dreams presage some joyful news at hand:
My bosom's lord sits lightly in his throne;
And all this day an unaccustom'd spirit
Lifts me above the ground with cheerful thoughts." (RJ.5.1)
Answer to 'How are you?' if you feel particularly happy or zesty, e.g. '…al this day…cheerful thoughts'. Or – if applicable – answer to 'How did you sleep?', e.g. 'If I may trust the flattering…hand'. For a more skeptical view or statement on the meaning of dreams see 'Dreams, not believing in them'
In the play. *In Mantua, unaware of the turmoil in Verona dreamt of a happy ending to his and Juliet's ordeal.*

Dream, d. with pleasant forebodings – If I may trust the flattering truth of sleep my dreams presage some joyful news at hand.
"If I may trust the flattering truth of sleep,
My dreams presage some joyful news at hand" (RJ.5.1)
In the play. *Romeo, exiled to Mantua, has great hopes to rejoin Juliet.*

Dream, it feels like a dream - How like a dream is this I see and hear!
"How like a dream is this I see and hear!" (TGV.5.4)
Can be used with a positive or negative event.
In the play. *Silvia is chased by the treacherous Proteus, false friend of Valentine. And it just so happens that Valentine overhears Proteus' advances to Silvia who fled to the forest in search of Valentine.*

Dream, it feels like a dream- all this is but a dream, too flattering sweet to be substantial.
"Being in night, all this is but a dream,
Too flattering sweet to be substantial." (RJ.2.2)
When the outcome of your action or hope went well beyond your expectations. Omit 'Being in night' if the dream-like experience occurs during the day-time.
In the play. *Romeo, head over heels on Juliet, cannot believe the incredibly favorable turn of events, meaning that Juliet reciprocates his love with equal passion.*

Dream, waking from a d., true or pretended - O, where am I?' quoth she, 'in earth or heaven, or in the ocean drench'd, or in the fire?
"O, where am I?' quoth she, 'in earth or heaven,
Or in the ocean drench'd, or in the fire?" (V&A)
In the poem. *Venus, fainting at Adonis' perceived coldness, wakes up.*

Dreams, delusions – … I talk of dreams, which are the children of an idle brain, begot of nothing but vain fantasy.
ROMEO. Peace, peace, Mercutio, peace,
Thou talk'st of nothing.
MERCUTIO. True, I talk of dreams,

Which are the children of an idle brain,
Begot of nothing but vain fantasy." (RJ.1.4)
State your opposition to an unrealistic project or expectation, e.g. 'These are but dreams, the children...fantasy.'
In the play. *Romeo has tried to stop a meandering monologue by Mercutio.*

Dreams, illusions and nightmares - ... it is the weakness of mine eyes that shapes his monstrous apparition.
"I think it is the weakness of mine eyes
That shapes his monstrous apparition." (JC.4.3)
Something preposterous is presented to you and you do not want to acknowledge it.
In the play. *Brutus has a nightmare in which the ghost of slain Caesar appears.*

Dreams, not believing in them - ... to trust the mockery of unquiet slumbers.
"And for his dreams, I wonder he is so fond
To trust the mockery of unquiet slumbers." (KRIII.3.2)
Answer to, 'Do you believe in dreams?' 'I don't trust the mockery of unquiet slumbers'.
In the play. *Lord Stanley sends a message to Hastings that he, Stanley, had a frightful dream about a fierce boar. He saw in their dream signs of impending danger (and he was right). But Hasting does not believe in dreams.*

Dress, adorned d. eliciting the idea of May and Spring – ...she came adorned hither like sweet May...
"My wife to France: from whence, set forth in pomp,
She came adorned hither like sweet May,
Sent back like Hallowmas or short'st of day" (KRII.5.1)
Compliment, e.g. 'She comes adorned ...sweet May'.
In the play. *King Richard says farewell to the Queen, as he is led prisoner to Pomfret Castle.*

Dress, compliment for a sparkling dress - The intertissued robe of gold and pearl...
"The intertissued robe of gold and pearl..." (KHV.4.1)
Try 'What an intertissued robe...pearl".
In the play. *King Henry V has just heard, incognito, his troops' complaints against him the night before the battle of Agincourt and meditates on the disadvantages of majesty (greatness).*

Dress, fitting the d. - The tailor stays thy leisure to deck thy body with his ruffling treasure.
"The tailor stays thy leisure,
To deck thy body with his ruffling treasure." (TOS.4.3)
Answer to her request, 'Will you come with me to the department store (to get a dress)?' E.G. 'Of course, the tailor will stay his leisure...treasure'.
In the play. *Petruchio has called in a tailor and haberdasher to try their designs on soon wife-to-be Katharina.*

Dress, long d. to be held up - ... lest the base earth should from her vesture chance to steal a kiss.
"She shall be dignified with this high honour--
To bear my lady's train, lest the base earth
Should from her vesture chance to steal a kiss" (TGV.2.4)
She may ask you to, if so say, 'I shall be dignified... kiss.' Or you do it without being asked. If so, say, '(I will bear) my lady's train.... Kiss.'
In the play. *Valentine, totally and unwisely trusting his friend Proteus, tells him that Julia (Proteus' girlfriend), will have the honor to bear*

Silvia's dress (when Valentine and Silvia will get married).

Dress, white, beautiful and worthy of a fairy queen - ... the queen of all the fairies, finely attired in a robe of white.
"… the queen of all the fairies,
Finely attired in a robe of white."
(MWW.4.4)
Compliment for when she shows up in a white dress. 'Here comes the queen of all fairies… white'.
In the play. *Mistress Page describes her daughter.*

Drink, d. or liquid, disgusting and poisonous - ... leperous distilment; whose effect holds such an enmity with blood of man...
"And in the porches of my ears did pour
The leperous distilment; whose effect
Holds such an enmity with blood of man
That swift as quicksilver it courses through
The natural gates and alleys of the body,
And with a sudden vigour doth posset
And curd, like eager droppings into milk,
The thin and wholesome blood:"
(H.1.5)
Cast your opinion on a bad wine or a bad soup or anything liquid unpleasant to taste or unhealthy.
In the play. *The Ghost describes his own murder at the hands of his brother to the attentive Hamlet. 'To posset'= 'To curdle'*

Drinking, heavy d. and its effect on the purse - ... you come in flint for want of meat, depart reeling with too much drink…
"… You come in flint for want of meat, depart reeling with too much drink; sorry that you have paid too much, and sorry that you are paid too much; purse and brain both empty; the brain the heavier for being too light, the purse too light, being drawn of heaviness: of this contradiction you shall now be quit" (CYM.5.4)
Answer to 'How are you?' after you got out of a bar where you overindulged in drinking.
In the play. *The jailer puts a positive spin on death for the benefit of the condemned Leonatus – no more bills to pay. He then expands on the concept.*

Drinking, knowing when to stop (drinking) – Let's teach ourselves that honorable stop, not to out-sport discretion.
"Let's teach ourselves that honorable stop,
Not to out-sport discretion."
(OTH.2.3)
At a party when you decline another drink. See also entries for 'Wine, negative effects of w.' – 'Wine, drinking, unable to tolerate strong drinks'
In the play. *There is a feast in Cyprus and Othello cautions Cassio not to overdo it. Cassio does not take to drink easily.*

Driving under the Influence, not DUI – ... I am not drunk now; I can stand well enough, and speak well enough.
"Do not think, gentlemen. I am drunk: this is my ancient; this is my right hand, and this is my left: I am not drunk now; I can stand well enough, and speak well enough." (OTH.2.3)
In the play. *Cassio, who does not tolerate wine, assures his companions that he is not drunk, while he actually is. The 'ancient' Cassio refers to is Iago.*

Drunkenness, d. as a source of illusion – the world turns round.
WIDOW. "He that is giddy thinks the world turns round.

PETRUCHIO. Roundly replied. " (TOS.5.2)
Attribute to drunkenness the mistaken perceptions of your adversary or imply that he thinks like a drunkard. 'Roundly replied' is a good positive comment to a good answer.
In the play. *A widow, freshly married to Hortensio, answers wittily to a remark by Petruchio while sitting down at a wedding feast.*

Drunkenness, d. as a source of illusion – I believe drink gave thee the lie last night'
"I believe drink gave thee the lie last night." (M.2.3)
See also 'Wine, negative effects of w.'
In the play. *The porter came late to open the door for Macduff. As an excuse, he says he had been drinking too much the night before.*

Drunkenness, d. of group described – … they were red-hot with drinking…
"… they were red-hot with drinking;
So fun of valour that they smote the air
For breathing in their faces; beat the ground
For kissing of their feet" (TEM.4.1)
In the play. *Spirit Ariel reports to Prosper on the state of Caliban, Stephano and Trinculo as he last saw them.*

Duty, d. performed formally only - … Others there are who, trimm'd in forms and visages of duty, keep yet their hearts attending on themselves…
"   Others there are
Who, trimm'd in forms and visages of duty,
Keep yet their hearts attending on themselves,
And, throwing but shows of service on their lords,
Do well thrive by them and when they have lined their coats
Do themselves homage: these fellows have some soul;
And such a one do I profess myself." (OTH.1.1)
In the play. *Iago plans his strategy of revenge after he did not get the promotion to lieutenant*

Duty, sense of d. and straightforwardness leading to good results – For never anything can be amiss when simpleness and duty tender it.
"For never anything can be amiss,
When simpleness and duty tender it." (MND.5.1)
Support the values of straight talk and integrity. See also ' Speech, simple s. and sense of duty better than pompous eloquence'.
In the play. *Theseus insists on watching the play set up by the amateur team of 'rude mechanicals', notwithstanding the negative review by the critic Philostrate.*

Eagerness for action, eager and ready to go – I see you stand like greyhounds in the slips, straining upon the start.
"I see you stand like greyhounds in the slips,
Straining upon the start…" (KHV.3.1)
In the play. *K. Henry addresses the troops before the siege of Harfleur.*

Eating, good food, antipasto - … Epicurean cooks sharpen with cloyless sauce his appetite.
"… Epicurean cooks
Sharpen with cloyless sauce his appetite.
Compliment the cook for an excellent antipasto. 'An Epicurean cook has sharpened with cloyless sauce my appetite.' Also answer to 'How do you like the food?'
In the play. *Pompey speaking of Antony in Egypt.*

Eccentricity, above the crowd –... I will not jump with common spirits and rank me with the barbarous multitude.
"I will not choose what many men desire,
Because I will not jump with common spirits,
And rank me with the barbarous multitudes." (MOV.2.9)
Use of these lines depends on your character or on the image you wish to project with her or with others. Many of us are troubled or puzzled by an inner contradiction, the wish to belong to a group and the simultaneous desire to be different. These are good lines in answer to questions of the type "Why don't you drive a Mercedes?" particularly if you cannot afford it. See also entries for 'Opinion, your op. on crowds and masses' *** 'Praise, self-p. or praise of speaker – And all the courses of my life do show I am not in the roll of common men.'
In the play. *The prince of Arragon, one of Portia's suitors meditates on the meaning of a puzzle. He who solves the puzzle will be able to marry Portia.*

Echo, e. defined - ... the babbling gossip of the air.
"Halloo your name to the reverberate hills
And make the babbling gossip of the air
Cry out 'Olivia!'" (TN.1.5)
Emphatic expression of unwavering passion, e.g. 'I'll cry your name...cry out (name of pertinent lady).'
In the play. *Part of an answer of Viola/Cesario to Olivia.*

Economy, price of hogs affected by religious conversions - this making of Christians will raise the price of hogs...
"... This making of Christians will raise the price of hogs: if we grow all to be pork-eaters we shall not shortly have rasher on the coals for money." (MOV.3.5)
An example of supply and demand economics.
In the play. *Launcelot speculates on the potential increase of the price of bacon if Jews will mass convert to Christianity, just as Jessica (Shylock's daughter) did, to marry Lorenzo.*

Education, e. and knowledge, limits of. - ... all delights are vain; but that most vain, which with pain purchased doth inherit pain...
"Why, all delights are vain; but that most vain,
Which with pain purchased doth inherit pain:
As, painfully to pore upon a book
To seek the light of truth; while truth the while
Doth falsely blind the eyesight of his look:
Light seeking light doth light of light beguile" (LLL.1.1)
Originally applied to the obsessive search for knowledge, can also be applied to any activity conducted with pain and yielding pain.
In the play. *Biron tempers the enthusiasm of his companions as to the merits of excessive study and abstinence.*

Education, a less orthodox view - Thou hast most traitorously corrupted the youth of the realm in erecting a grammar school.
"Thou hast most traitorously corrupted the youth of the realm in erecting a grammar school." (KHVI p2.4.7)
See also 'Judgment, unfair sentence and war on literacy'.
In the play. *One of the rebel John Cade's accusations against Lord Say. He goes on to list the other associated accusations,*

'...and whereas, before, our forefathers had no other books but the score and the tally, thou hast caused printing to be used, and, contrary to the king, his crown and dignity, thou hast built a paper-mill. It will be proved to thy face that thou hast men about thee that usually talk of a noun and a verb, and such abominable words as no Christian ear can endure to hear.

Education, continued e. - ... continue your resolve to suck the sweets of sweet philosophy.
"Glad that you thus continue your resolve,
To suck the sweets of sweet philosophy." (TOS.1.1)
Potentially evasive answer to the question, 'What are you doing now?' 'I am continuing my resolve to suck the sweets of sweet philosophy'.
In the play. *Tranio approves of his master Lucentio's idea of continuing his studies in Padua*

Education, e. and lack thereof - ... he that hath learned no wit by nature nor art, may complain of good breeding or comes of a very dull kindred.
CORIN. ... he that hath learned no wit by nature nor art, may complain of good breeding or comes of a very dull kindred. (AYLI.3)
Example of self-evident truth.
In the play. *The courtly Touchstone engages the shepherd Corin into an exchange of ideas and opinions.*

Education, importance of good company. - It is certain that either wise bearing or ignorant carriage is caught, as men take diseases, one of another...
"It is certain that either wise bearing or ignorant carriage is caught, as men take diseases, one of another:

therefore let men take heed of their company"** (KHIV.p2.5.1)
In the play. *Falstaff impression of Shallow and his company, while trying to get some money from him.*

Education, lack of formal education - (I) have been an idle truant, omitting the sweet benefit of time to clothe mine age with angel-like perfection.
"(I) have been an idle truant,
Omitting the sweet benefit of time
To clothe mine age with angel-like perfection". (TGV.2.4)
Use to explain why you do not have a master's degree or a PhD.
In the play. *Proteus arrives in Milan and Valentine, in modesty, rates Proteus better than himself. Valentine admits to not having made the best use of his time.*

Education, literature, results of teaching - You taught me language and my profit on it is, I know how to curse.
"You taught me language and my profit on it
Is, I know how to curse." (TEM.1.2)
Introduction, irony on education. E.G. 'Not everybody agrees that education is a good thing, As Caliban told his teacher Prospero, 'You taught me language and my profit on it is that I know how to curse'.
In the play. *Caliban reports the results of the education imparted by Prospero.*

Education, not an asset - The clerk of Chatham: he can write and read and cast accompt… O monstrous.
SMITH The clerk of Chatham: he can write and read and cast accompt.
CADE O monstrous. (KHVI p2.4.2)
Quote the episode in its entirety in occasions when education is being berated or thought unimportant. See also 'Politics, qualification for office'.

In the play. *The rebel John Cade and associates set themselves up to govern the realm according to all new standards.*

Education, principles of e. – If I had a thousand sons, the first human principle I would teach them…
"If I had a thousand sons, the first human principle I would teach them should be to forswear thin potations, and to addict themselves to sack." (KHIV.p2.2.3)
In the play. *Pleased with himself, Falstaff extols the virtues of sherry. For a complete rendering see 'Wine, positive effects of w. – A good sherri-sack hath a two fold operation in it…'*

Education, profitable if pleasurable – No profit grows where is no pleasure taken…
"No profit grows where is no pleasure taken; -
In brief, sir, study what you most affect." (TOS.1.1)
An argument for education that inspires pleasure in learning.
In the play. *Tranio approves of Lucentio's idea of continuing his studies in Padua and advises his master to study what he really likes.*

Effect, quick, strong and violent - As violently, as hasty powder fired doth hurry from the fatal cannon's womb.
"As violently, as hasty powder fired Doth hurry from the fatal cannon's womb." (RJ.5.1)
A comparison for the type of action or reaction required. Answer to 'How quick do you want it?'
In the play. *Romeo describes to the apothecary in Mantua the type of poison he is looking for - that is a poison that kills quickly.*

Effort, hard e. – Double, double toil and trouble; fire burn, and cauldron bubble.
"Double, double toil and trouble; Fire burn, and cauldron bubble." (M.4.1)
Comment to 'Working hard?'
In the play. *The three witches toil with their implements in a cavern, waiting for Macbeth who wants another forecast.*

Effort, making an effort to share her taste - I'll look to like, if looking liking move.
"I'll look to like, if looking liking move." (RJ.1.3)
When she likes something you heartily dislike and yet you wish to be amenable and not controversial. Uncommitted answer to 'Do you think you will like it?'
In the play. *Juliet's parents want her to marry Paris – she is not keen on him but does not want to antagonize her mother. The mother asks, 'Speak briefly, can you like of Paris' love?' and Juliet answers modestly,*
'I'll look to like, if looking liking move:
But no more deep will I endart mine eye
Than your consent gives strength to make it fly.'
'To endart'= 'To let fly and pierce like an arrow'.

Effort, overwhelmed by opposing forces - … as I have seen a swan with bootless labour swim against the tide…
"…as I have seen a swan
With bootless labour swim against the tide
And spend her strength with over-matching waves" (KHVI p3.1.4)
Apply to yourself when you are stalled notwithstanding your efforts. E.G. 'I am like a swan who with bootless labor swims…waves' or 'I swim against the tide and spend my labor…waves'. See also 'Task, t. impossible and unrealistic - … the task he undertakes is numbering sands and drinking oceans dry.'

In the play. *York describes the useless efforts to repel the forces of Henry VI at the battle of Sandal Castle.*

Effort, trying does not hurt - What I can do, can do no hurt to try.
"What I can do, can do no hurt to try." (AWEW.2.1)
Convince a reluctant party to try a specific remedy or idea. See also 'Hope, h. never hurts'.
In the play. *Helena wishes to cure the King but he continues to be skeptical. She presses her point.*

Effort, useless and detrimental - You lay too much pains for purchasing but trouble.
"You lay too much pains
For purchasing but trouble. (CYM.2.2)
Comment to an unsound solicitation for a business that does more harm than good.
In the play. *Imogen fends off the advances of the foolish Cloten.*

Efforts, e. unrewarded or punished – ... and like the bees are murdered for our pains.
"…like the bee, culling from every flower
The virtuous sweets,
Our thighs pack'd with wax, our mouths with honey,
We bring it to the hive, and, like the bees,
Are murdered for our pains"
(KHIVp2.4.5)
In the play. *King Henry reproaches his son Prince Harry, having misinterpreted Harry's action when he tried on the crown.*

Efforts, hard e. disregarded or unappreciated - ... Have broke their sleep with thoughts, their brains with care, their bones with industry.
"For this the foolish over-careful fathers
Have broke their sleep with thoughts, their brains with care,
Their bones with industry"
(KHIVp2.4.5)
In the play. *King Henry reproaches his son Prince Harry, having misinterpreted Harry's action when he tried on the crown.*

Ego boosting, she is a sought after prize - Nor is the wide world ignorant of her worth…
"**Nor is the wide world ignorant of her worth,**
For the four winds blow in from every coast,
Renowned suitors." (MOV.1.1)
She is the type who wants you to know that many men are after her and that by selecting you she is doing you a great favor or honor. Change 'her' to 'you'. You can say, "I know, nor is the world ignorant of your worth…suitors." Acknowledge that she is a prize sought after and follow up by outlining some of your qualifications. For example "I know that the world is not ignorant of your worth… suitors." but "I am as constant as the Northern star of whose true fixed and vesting quality there is no fellow in the firmament" (see **Credentials**) or other. She may think you are totally mad or fall in love with you instantly.

Conversely, it may be that you who are God's given gift to women and wish to tell her that you are ready to give up all your other female connections for her sake. This is a technique tried by Henry VIII with Ann Boleyn. In a letter to her he writes '… if you please to do the duty of a true and loyal mistress, and to give up yourself, body and heart, to me, who will be, as I have been your most loyal servant (if your rigour does not forbid me), I promise that not only the name shall be given you, but also that I will take you for my mistress, casting off all others that are in competition with you, out of my thoughts and affection, and serving you only." – See also other entries for 'Admiration' – 'Beauty, her b. and virtue praised everywhere'
In the play. *Bassanio tells his friend Antonio about Portia. Bassanio needs to borrow some money so as not look cheap, compared to the other contenders when he will meet with Portia.*

Elbow room – … now my soul hath elbow-room…
"…now my soul hath elbow-room" (KJ.5.7)
In the play. *King John, poisoned by a monk and at the end of its rope gets some relief from seeing Salisbury, who has returned to the English camp.*

Elections, democratic e. - … let desert in pure election shine, and, Romans, fight for freedom in your choice.
"… let desert in pure election shine,
And, Romans, fight for freedom in your choice" (TA.1.1)
In the play. *Bassanius campaigns for free elections of the new Roman Emperor. The other candidate, Saturninus wants to be appointed based on alleged descendant rights. Eventually Titus Andronicus, returning victorious from a campaign against the Goths will propose Saturninus as emperor.*

Elections, electoral commitment – I would with such perfection govern, sir, to excel the golden age.
"I would with such perfection govern, sir,
To excel the golden age" (TEM.2.1)
In the play. *Gonzalo speculates about what he wold do if he were king of the island where he has been stranded along with Antonio and companions.*

Eloquence, characteristic of the eloquent – … on the tip of their persuasive tongue carry all arguments and questions deep…
"Some there are
Who on the tip of their persuasive tongue
Carry all arguments and questions deep;
And replication prompt, and reason strong,
To make the weeper smile, the laugher weep" (Poems)
See also 'Words, despicable w. but well crafted - ignominious words, though clerkly couched.' *** 'Spin, how to re-interpret reality - You undergo too strict a paradox striving to make an ugly deed look fair.'

Embrace, rationale for embracing lady – … the nobleness of life is to do thus…
"…the nobleness of life
Is to do thus; when such a mutual pair
And such a twain can do't" (AC.1.1)
Make sure that she agrees to it.
In the play. *Antony embraces Cleopatra declaring (as well) his preference and allegiance to her and Egypt.*

Embrace, style of embracing - So doth the woodbine the sweet honeysuckle…
"So doth the woodbine the sweet honeysuckle

Gently entwist; the female ivy so
Enrings the barky fingers of the elm.
O, how I love thee! how I dote on
thee!" (MND.4.1)
In the play. *Titania holds Bottom in her arms after he has been charmed to sleep. Magic has temporarily transformed Bottom into an ass.*

Emotion, overpowered by e. – My tears will choke me, if I ope my mouth.
"My tears will choke me, if I ope my mouth." (TA.5.3)
See also 'Tears, difficult to hold back t. - Beshrew me, but his passions move me so, that hardly can I check my eyes from tears.
In the play. *Young Lucius as older Lucius recounts how Titus A. was kind towards his grandson (young Lucius).*

Emotional reaction - Who can be wise, amazed, temperate and furious…
"Who can be wise, amazed, temperate and furious,
Loyal and neutral, in a moment?" (M.2.2)
Justify an emotional reaction.
In the play. *Macbeth answers with an lame explanation Macduff's pointed question as to why he (Macbeth) killed the guards who, supposedly, killed Duncan.*

Employees, e. stuck in their career or simple opportunists – You shall mark many a duteous and knee-crooking knave…
"…You shall mark
Many a duteous and knee-crooking knave,
That, doting on his own obsequious bondage,
Wears out his time, much like his master's ass,
For nought but provender, and when he's old, cashier'd:
Whip me such honest knaves" (OTH.1.1)
In the play. *Iago explains to Roderigo why he, Iago, will follow Othello, only to do advance himself, as opposed to the majority that serve their master and do as they are told.*

Employment, quick resume - … that which ordinary men are fit for, I am qualified in; and the best of me is diligence.
KING LEAR What services canst thou do?
KENT I can keep honest counsel, ride, run, mar a curious
tale in telling it, and deliver a plain message
bluntly: that which ordinary men are fit for, I am
qualified in; and the best of me is diligence. (KL.1.4)
Answer to 'What are your strengths?'
In the play. *Banished Kent disguises himself and his accent and tries to be hired by Lear to actually protect him. Previously Lear dismissed and fired Kent in anger.*

Employment, reason for seeking alternative e. – … their villany goes against my weak stomach and therefore I must cast it up.
"…their villany goes against my weak stomach, and therefore I must cast it up." (HV.3.2)
In the play. *The boy in the service of Pistol, Nym and Bardolph does not think much of his employers.*

Employment, working for a company as opposed to being self-employed -
… I am shepherd to another man and do not shear the fleeces that I graze.
"But I am shepherd to another man,
And do not shear the fleeces that I graze." (AYLI.2.4)
Answer to question, "Do you work for yourself?" (When you do not). Or to

indicate that you do not share the profits generated by your talent or efforts.
In the play. *Rosalind asks Corin for help in finding accommodations but the help that Corin can offer is limited, as Silvius is the owner of the lodgings Rosalind has set her eyes on.*

Employment, working for someone else - My affairs are servanted to others.
"... My affairs
Are servanted to others." (COR.5.2)
Answer to 'what work do you do?' if you are working for a company. See also 'Employment, working for a company as opposed to being self-employed'.
In the play. *Coriolanus rejects Menenius' plea not to fight the Romans.*

Encouragement, e. uncalled for given the valiant nature of the encouraged – ... And yet I do thee wrong to mind thee of it...
"... fight valiantly to-day:
And yet I do thee wrong to mind thee of it,
For thou art framed of the firm truth of valour" (HV.4.3)
In the play. *Exeter to Salisbury before the battle of Agincourt.*

Encouragement, e. during distress - let not discontent daunt all your hopes.
"...let not discontent
Daunt all your hopes" (TS.1.1)
In the play. *Emperor Saturninus cheers up Tamora queen of Goths.*

Encouragement, self-e. to change doubt to resolution. - Now, York, or never, steel thy fearful thoughts, and change misdoubt to resolution...
"Now, York, or never, steel thy fearful thoughts,
And change misdoubt to resolution.
...

Let pale faced fear keep with the mean born man,
And find no harbour in a royal heart."
(KHVI p2.3.1)
Use in motivational speech or directly address the party you wish to encourage. Change 'York' to applicable name.
In the play. *York to himself, hatching a plan to destroy his enemies*

End, beginning of the e. – now prosperity begins to mellow and drop into the rotten mouth of death.
"So, now prosperity begins to mellow
And drop into the rotten mouth of death" (KRIII.4.4)
In the play. *Q. Margaret comments on the unraveling of the fortunes of her former enemies.*

End, e. crowns the deed – La fin couronne les oeuvres.
"La fin couronne les oeuvres" (KHVI.p2.5.2)
In the play. *Clifford, slain by York at the battle of St. Albans' utters his last words in French.*

End, e. justifies means – All with me's meet that I can fashion fit.
"All with me's meet that I can fashion fit." (KL.1.2)
See also 'Determination, d. or agreement to do anything honorable - I have spirit to do any thing that appears not foul in the truth of my spirit.'
In the play. *Edmund justifies to himself the diabolical scheme for appropriating his father's estate.*

End, e. justifies means – ... some kinds of baseness are nobly undergone...
"...some kinds of baseness
Are nobly undergone and most poor matters
Point to rich ends" (TEM.3.1)
Answer to a remark on the apparent humbleness of your pursuits.

In the play. *Ferdinand meditates – his carrying of logs (baseness) on behalf of his future father-in-law Prospero, may help him win his consent to marrying his daughter Miranda (rich ends).*

End, e. justifies means – All with me's meet that I can fashion fit.
"All with me's meet that I can fashion fit." (KL.1.2)
In the play. *Edmund justifies to himself the diabolical scheme for appropriating his father's estate.*

Endurance, your e. at an end - I will no longer endure it, though yet I know no wise remedy how to avoid it.
"I will no longer endure it, though yet I know no wise remedy how to avoid it." (AYLI.1.1)
When you want to get out of a situation but do not as yet know how.
In the play. *Orlando can no longer live under the humiliating conditions set by elder brother Oliver.*

Enemies, abandoned by friend in the hands of the e. - So flies the reckless shepherd from the wolf…
"So flies the reckless shepherd from the wolf;
So first the harmless sheep doth yield his fleece
And next his throat unto the butcher's knife" (KHVI.p3.5.6)
In the play. *King Henry, prisoner in the Tower, comments after visiting Richard of Gloucester (later Richard III) dismisses the keeper to kill Henry.*

Enemies, how e. work - know'st thou not that when the searching eye of heaven is hid…
"…know'st thou not
That when the searching eye of heaven is hid,
Behind the globe, that lights the lower world,
Then thieves and robbers range abroad unseen
In murders and in outrage." (KRII.3.2)
A metaphor for the CIA's mode of operation.
In the play. *King Richard II answers a comment by the Duke of Aumerle on how the usurping Bolingbroke took advantage of the absence of the king in Ireland.*

Enemies, planning traps for your e. - My brain more busy than the labouring spider…
My brain more busy than the labouring spider
Weaves tedious snares to trap mine enemies." (KHVI.p2.3.1)
Use as is or ironically apply the statement to a present pensive colleague, e.g. 'His brain more busy…to entrap us'.
In the play. *York to himself, hatching a plan to destroy his enemies*

Enemies, smiling e. - … some that smile have in their hearts, I fear, millions of mischiefs.
"…for we are at the stake,
And bay'd about with many enemies;
And some that smile have in their hearts, I fear,
Millions of mischiefs." (JC.4.1)
In the play. *A comment by Octavian, in this play an ally to Antony.*

Enemies, unthinking and unreasonable – … like to village curs bark when their fellows do.
"…You are not to be taught
That you have many enemies, that know not
Why they are so, but, like to village-curs,
Bark when their fellows do."
(KHVIII.2.4)
Blanket criticism of the ignorance behind prejudice and hatred. If you are a problem solver and make some enemies try, 'I have many enemies…fellows do'

280

In the play. *K. Henry VIII to Cardinal Wolsey, who has expressed to the King concern about Q. Katherine. She thinks Wolsey is her enemy.*

Enemies, weak but annoying e. - For though they cannot greatly sting to hurt, yet look to have them buzz to offend thine ears.
"For though they cannot greatly sting to hurt,
Yet look to have them buzz to offend thine ears." (KHVI.p3.2.6)
In the play. *Warwick, the kingmaker has won the battle of Towton and prepares to crown Edward of York king. He will consolidate the victory by having Edward marry the sister of the French King Louis. This will make it impossible for the former enemies (King Henry VI etc.) to challenge the crown.*

Enemies, why e. are better than friends - ... my friends praise me and make an ass of me...
DUKE (to Clown). ...how dost thou, my good fellow?
CLOWN. Truly, sir, the better for my foes, and the worse for my friends.
DUKE. Just the contrary
CLOWN. No, sir, my friends praise me, and make an ass of me; now my foes tell me plainly I am an ass: so that, by my foes, sir, I profit in the knowledge of myself; and by my friends I am abused." (TN.5.1)
A satirical example of the value of opposition.
In the play. *The Duke and the clown exchange some banter.*

Enemies, you are all my e., don't trouble me any more - My foes I do repute you every one; so, trouble me no more, but get you gone.
"My foes I do repute you every one;
So, trouble me no more, but get you gone." (TA.1.1)
Show your disgust.

In the play. *Titus is mad at his own family who has upset the plans to make Lavinia wife of Saturninus and empress of Rome. He does not know that Saturninus had other plans anyway.*

Enemy, bitter e. - The devil himself could not pronounce a title more hateful to mine ear.
"The devil himself could not pronounce a title
More hateful to mine ear." (M.5.7)
When hearing the name of a hated enemy.
In the play. *Macbeth has revealed himself to young Siward and Siward reacts.*

Enemy, e. hurt but not destroyed - We have scotch'd the snake, not kill'd it...
"We have scotch'd the snake, not kill'd it:
She'll close and be herself, whilst our poor malice
Remains in danger of her former tooth" (M.3.2)
In the play. *Macbeth commenting on the fact that Banquo's son escaped assassination.*

Enemy, e. shamed - ... now shall the devil be shamed.
"... now shall the devil be shamed." (MWW.4.2)
In the play. *Mr. Ford still thinks that Falstaff may have succeeded with Mrs. Ford and hopes for revenge*

Enemy, e. to be eliminated - ... the welfare of us all hangs on the cutting short that fraudful man.
"Take heed, my lord; the welfare of us all
Hangs on the cutting short that fraudful man." (KHVI.p2.3.1)
Rail against your political opponent
In the play. *The shrewish Queen Margaret exhorts Henry VI to get rid of his uncle and Lord Protector the Duke of Gloucester.*

Enemy, know your real e., don't hurt your friends - ... strike those that hurt, and hurt not those that help.
"O turn thy edged sword another way; Strike those that hurt, and hurt not those that help!" (KHVI.p1.3.3)
Answer to a misguided enemy.
In the play. *La Pucelle tries to convince the Duke of Burgundy to join the French camp.*

Enemy, my e. and e. of the truth - ... whom, yet, once more I hold my most malicious foe, and think not at all a friend to truth.
"(Cardinal Wolsey) …whom, yet, once more,
I hold my most malicious foe, and think not
At all a friend to truth." (KHVIII.2.4)
Use to address an enemy who is not completely stupid, e.g. 'I hold you my most malicious foe… truth.'
In the play. *Queen Katherine to Cardinal Wolsey, who is weaving a plot.*

Enemy, recognizing honor in e. - For though mine enemy thou hast ever been high sparks of honour in thee have I seen.
"For though mine enemy thou hast ever been,
High sparks of honour in thee have I seen." (KRII.5.6)
In the play. *Bolingbroke, now Henry IV spares the life of the Bishop of Carlisle who was his declared enemy. Every other enemy has been killed.*

Enemy, resurgence of e. - … Thrusts forth his horns again into the world, which were inshell'd…
"(Aufidius) … hearing of our Marcius' banishment,
Thrusts forth his horns again into the world;
Which were inshell'd when Marcius stood for Rome,
And durst not once peep out."
(COR.4.6)
In the play. *Menenius thinks that the reported activity of the Volsces stems from their awareness that Coriolanus has been banned form Rome. Coriolanus has actually joined in with the Volsces.*

Engineering, civil e. - ...much more... should we survey the plot of the situation and the model...
"...Much more, in this great work,
Which is almost to pluck a kingdom down
And set another up, should we survey
The plot of situation and the model,
Consent upon a sure foundation,
Question surveyors, know our own estate,
How able such a work to undergo,
To weigh against his opposite; or else
We fortify in paper and in figures,
Using the names of men instead of men:
Like one that draws the model of a house
Beyond his power to build it; who, half through,
Gives o'er and leaves his part-created cost
A naked subject to the weeping clouds
And waste for churlish winter's tyranny." (KHIV.p2.1.3)
A metaphor to show that much more revision, thought and considerations are necessary before launching the project. See also 'Weak, feeling w. and unprotected'
In the play. *Bardolph continues with his exposition by comparison of the skills required to plan a great enterprise.*

England – E. and her connection with the sea - …your isle, which stands as Neptune's park…
"…your isle, which stands
As Neptune's park, ribbed and paled

in
With rocks unscalable and roaring waters," (CYM.2.1)
In the play. *The Queen reminds Cymbeline about the history of England and that Caesar did not subdue the island easily.*

England, E. never conquered – This England never did, nor never shall lie at the proud foot of a conqueror...
"This England never did, nor never shall,
Lie at the proud foot of a conqueror,
But when it first did help to wound itself." (KJ.5.7)
In the play. *The dissentions among the nobles being settled and King John dead, Faulconbridge makes a closing and uplifting pronouncement*

England, in praise of E. – The natural bravery of your isle, which stands as Neptune's park...
"The natural bravery of your isle, which stands
As Neptune's park, ribbed and paled in
With rocks unscalable and roaring waters,
With sands that will not bear your enemies' boats,
But suck them up to the topmast..." (CYM.3.1)
In the play. *The Queen reminds King Cymbeline of England's tradition of bravery to convince him to refuse paying taxes to the Romans.*

England, in praise of E. while deploring the current state of affairs – This fortress...This precious stone...bound in with triumphant sea...
This royal throne of kings, this scepter'd isle,
This earth of majesty, this seat of Mars,
This other Eden, demi-paradise,
This fortress built by Nature for herself
Against infection and the hand of war,
This happy breed of men, this little world,
This precious stone set in the silver sea,
Which serves it in the office of a wall,
Or as a moat defensive to a house,
Against the envy of less happier lands
...
This fortress, built by nature for herself,
Against infection and the hand of war.
...
This precious stone set in the silver sea,
Which serves it in the office of a wall,
Or as a mote defensive to a house,
Against the envy of less happier lands.
...
England, bound in with triumphant sea,
Whose rocky shore beats back the envious siege
Of watery Neptune, is now bound in with shame,
With inky blots, and rotten parchment bonds;
This England that was wont to conquer others,
Hath made a shameful conquest of itself." (KRII.2.1)
Apply in a speech directed at the current performance of management when the stocks of the company tumble. "This (name of company" that was wont to... itself."
In the play. *While praising England as a nation, Gaunt bewails the state into which the country has fallen under Richard II.*

England, in praise of the greatness of E. - O England! model to thy inward greatness, like little body with a mighty heart.
"O England! model to thy inward greatness,

Like little body with a mighty heart"
(HV.2.chorus)
Suggest that greatness does not depend on size or power.
In the play. *The chorus fills the gaps of time in the play and the absence of special effects technology.*

England, nationalistic statement - Come the three corners of the world in arms and we shall shock them…
"Come the three corners of the world in arms,
And we shall shock them. Nought shall make us rue,
If England to itself do rest but true" (KJ.5.7)
In the play. *Ph. Faulconbridge supports the nationalistic statements of Prince Henry. Usually the determination to 'defense' is an excuse for attack.*

England, protected by the sea against foreign invasion - England, hedged in with the main… that water-walled bulwark…
"…England, hedged in with the main,
That water-walled bulwark, still secure
And confident from foreign purposes." (KJ.2.1)
In the play. *Austria reassures Constance that England will recognize the rights of her son Arthur to the English throne. 'Main' here means 'ocean'.*

England, that will never be conquered - This England never did, nor never shall lie at the proud foot of a conqueror…
"This England never did, nor never shall,
Lie at the proud foot of a conqueror,
But when it first did help to wound itself.

… Nought shall make us rue,
If England to itself do rest but true."
(KJ.5.7)
In the play. *The rebels have rejoined the English side and Faulconbridge praises England.*

England, the cliffs of Dover - There is a cliff whose high and bending head looks fearfully in the confined deep.
"There is a cliff whose high and bending head
Looks fearfully in the confined deep."
(KL.4.1)
Colorful description also applicable to landscapes of similar appearance (to Dover's)
In the play. *Gloucester (blind) asks his son Edgar to lead him to the edge of the cliffs. Edgar has not yet revealed himself to Gloucester.*

England, the shores of E. - … that pale, that white faced shore, whose foot spurns back the ocean's roaring tides.
"…Together with that pale, that white faced shore,
Whose foot spurns back the ocean's roaring tides
And coops from other lands her islanders." (KJ.2.1)
Define the area of England near Dover. See also 'England, the cliffs of Dover' - 'England, in praise of E. while deploring the current state of affairs'
In the play. *The archduke refers to the rights of young Arthur, son of Constance, to the throne of England, occupied by King John. The archduke commits himself not to return home until Arthur will have his rights restored, including the claims to the throne of England.*

Englishman, proud to be an E. – Where'er I wander, boast of this I can… a trueborn Englishman.
"Where'er I wander, boast of this I can,

284

Though banish'd, yet a trueborn Englishman" (KRII.1.3)
In the play. *Bolingbroke's parting words after the exile imposed King Richard.*

Enmity, e. declared - I do believe induced by potent circumstances, that you are mine enemy.
"... I do believe
Induced by potent circumstances, that
You are mine enemy." (KHVIII.2.4)
Address an enemy who is not completely stupid.
In the play. *Queen Katherine to Cardinal Wolsey, who is weaving a plot.*

Enterprise, a daring e. - ... an enterprise of honourable-dangerous consequence.
"...an enterprise
Of honourable-dangerous consequence" (JC.1.3)
In the play. *Cassius tells Casca of the impending meeting during which the plot to assassinate Caesar will be discussed.*

Entertainment, e. of an honored guest - ... your entertain shall be as doth befit our honour and your worth.
"And until then your entertain shall be,
As doth befit your honor and your worth." (PER.1.1)
Use with important guest whom you wish to entertain before getting down to business, 'until then…worth'. See also 'Welcome, w. to our house'.
In the play. *Antiochus tells Pericles that he will be entertained for one month until he can solve a riddle. Pericles guessed the answer but refuses to say it because it incriminates Antiochus. Antiochus plans to have Pericles killed.*

Entertainment, moderation in e. - It will be pastime passing excellent if it be husbanded with modesty.
"It will be pastime passing excellent If it be husbanded with modesty." (TOS.ind 1)
Agree on the proposed form of recreation or amusement.
In the play. *A lord designs a prank to be played on Sly the Tinker.*

Entrapment - I am angling now, though you perceive me not how I give line.
"I am angling now,
Though you perceive me not how I give line" (WT.1.2)
In the play. *Jealous Leontes tries to find reasons to justify his obsessive and mad jealousy.*

Envy, above the reach of e. - Advanced above pale envy's threatening reach, as when the golden sun salutes the morn…
"Advanced above pale envy's threatening reach.
As when the golden sun salutes the morn,
And, having gilt the ocean with his beams,
Gallops the zodiac in his glistering coach,
And overlooks the highest-peering hills." (TA.2.1)
In a sentence of praise or commendation, e.g. 'With his merits he has advanced above pale envy's threatening reach'.
In the play. *Aaron meditates on the luck of Tamora (his lover and now wife of Emperor Saturninus). Her sudden elevation takes her out of the reach of envy.*

Envy, addressing envious accusers – Now I feel of what coarse metal ye are molded, - envy!
"Now I feel

Of what coarse metal ye are molded, - envy!" (KHVIII.3.2)
Show that envy is the source of the accusations leveled at you.
In the play. *Wolsey has fallen from grace and reflects on the cause of his misfortune.*

Envy, e. as a monster - That monster envy, oft the wrack of earned praise.
"That monster envy, oft the wrack
Of earned praise..." (PER.3.Gower)
In the play. *Gower summarizes the events for the audience. Envy prompts Dionyza to plan the murder of Marina who outperforms Dionyza's own daughter in everything. See 'Beauty, one exceedingly more beautiful than the other (girl)'*

Envy, e. as practiced by the envious - ... Men that make envy and crooked malice nourishment, dare bite the best.
"... Men that make
Envy and crooked malice nourishment,
Dare bite the best." (KHVIII.5.2)
Defense against unfair attack and criticism of your achievements.
In the play. *Cranmer referring to his accusers.*

Envy, e. coupled with ambition - Such men as he be never at heart's ease whiles they behold a greater than themselves, and therefore are they very dangerous.
"Such men as he be never at heart's ease
Whiles they behold a greater than themselves,
And therefore are they very dangerous." (JC.1.2)
General assessment of a certain type of individuals.
In the play. *Caesar gives Antony an assessment of Cassius' character that is equally tied up to Cassius' lean and hungry psychosomatic characteristics.* See 'Fat, f. men less dangerous than thin.'

Envy, e. mixed with hypocrisy – Follow your envious courses, men of malice…
"Follow your envious courses, men of malice;
You have Christian warrant for 'em, and, no doubt,
In time will find their fit rewards" (KHVIII.3.2)
In the play. *Cardinal Wolsey to his accusers, Suffolk and Norfolk.*

Envy, e. shown in speech - Sharp Buckingham unburthens with his tongue the envious load that lies upon his heart.
"Sharp Buckingham unburthens with his tongue
The envious load that lies upon his heart" (KHVI p2.3)
Change 'Buckingham' with the applicable name or change pronoun, e.g. "You unburthen with your tongue… your heart.'
In the play. *The virtuous Gloucester (Duke Humphrey) observes his enemies at work – they want him out and will succeed in killing him.*

Envy, words or speech prompted by envy – The envious barking of your saucy tongue…
"The envious barking of your saucy tongue…" (KHVI.p1.3.4)
Suggest envy as the reason for adversarial remarks or speech.
In the play. *Basset (allied to Somerset) upbraids Vernon (allied to York)*

Epitaph, e. kind to the memory of an evil man - Thy ignominy sleep with thee in the grave but not remember'd in thy epitaph!
"Thy ignominy sleep with thee in the grave,
But not remember'd in thy epitaph!" (KHIV.p1.5.4)

In the play. *Prince Henry to Harry Percy whom he has just killed in the battle of Shrewsbury.*

**Epitaph, e. of a disgruntled man –
Here lies a wretched corse, of wretched soul bereft: seek not my name…**
"'Here lies a wretched corse, of wretched soul bereft:
Seek not my *name: a plague consume you wicked caitiffs left!*" *(TOA.5.4)*
In the play. *Alcibiades reads the epitaph that his friend Timon wrote for himself. 'Caitiff' = 'Wretched or miserable person'*

**Equality among men impossible -
…but clay and clay differs in dignity, whose dust is both alike.
ARVIRAGUS Are we not brothers?
IMOGEN So man and man should be;
But clay and clay differs in dignity, Whose dust is both alike."** (CYM.4.1)
Use it as a philosophical argument to support your anti-leftist and anti-socialist views. See also 'Class consciousness'
In the play. *Imogen escaped from court and her evil stepmother. Imogen is wearing a man's disguise and has been quickly adopted by the two brothers Arviragus and Belarius as another brother.*

Equivocation - … here's an equivocator, that could swear in both the scales against either scale.
"Faith, here's an equivocator, that could swear in both the scales against either scale" (M.2.2)
Show your adversary that he is for or against a measure or a policy depending on whether measure or policy fit his own interest.
In the play. *The porter comments on the repeated knocks he hears at the door. Macduff is at the door. To justify his delay in opening the Porter will give an amusing explanation – see* 'Wine, negative effects of w.' For reactions to loud knocking see 'Knock, hard k. on door'

Equivocation, misunderstanding, need for accurate wording or expression – … we must speak by the card or equivocation will undo us.
"How absolute the knave is! We must speak by the card or equivocation will undo us." (H.5.1)
Clarifying a point when someone misunderstood, 'We must speak…us'.
See also 'Words, silly w., playing with w., parrots.
In the play. *Hamlet to Horatio, referring to a witty gravedigger who is preparing Ophelia's grave. Ophelia having become mad has drowned herself in a river nearby.*

Error, e. admitted and due to youthful inexperience – Those were my salad days when I was green in judgement.
"Those were my salad days,
When I was green in judgement."
(AC.1.5)
Unless you are really old (see AGE) you can often attribute your errors to inexperience and get away with it.
Lettuce, the paramount ingredient of a salad was considered an anti-aphrodisiac (See Aphrodisiacs) as well as a potent medicine. In his XVth century book "Honest Pleasures and Good Health", Platina relates how the Roman Emperor Augustus was healed from a threatening illness by eating exclusively salads. "Nor this should cause any surprise – he writes – because lettuce helps digestion and creates good blood more than any other vegetable." The two views on the effects of salads seem contradictory. But equally conflicting views are held today on various diets.
See also entries for 'Naivete'
In the play. *Cleopatra commenting on her younger years in conversation with attendant Charmian.*

Error, e. due to ignorance, not cunning - ... if he be not one that truly loves you that errs in ignorance, and not in cunning...
"For if he be not one that truly loves you,
That errs in ignorance, and not in cunning,
I have no judgment in an honest face." (OTH.3.3)
Defense of a trustworthy person who has made inadvertently a mistake. Or to excuse your mistake, e.g. 'I may err in ignorance and not in cunning'
In the play. *Under advisement from Iago Cassio seeks the intercession of Desdemona to try to get back into Othello's favor. She does not know that by doing so she will further Othello's jealousy, prompted at first by Iago's innuendoes and accusations.*

Error, e. due to misapprehension or misrepresentation - O, hateful error, Melancholy's child! Why dost thou show to the apt thoughts of men the things that are not?
"O, hateful error, Melancholy's child! Why dost thou show to the apt thoughts of men
The things that are not? O, Error, soon conceived,
Thus never com'st unto a happy birth, But kill'st the mother than engendered thee." (JC.5.3)
Show that the advantages of the proposed course of action are illusory and that the result will be a disaster.
In the play. *Messala wails the tactical error that caused Brutus and Cassius to lose the battle of Philippi to Antony.*

Error, e. in character judgment, acknowledged - What a thrice-double ass was I to take this drunkard for a god...
"...What a thrice-double ass
Was I, to take this drunkard for a god
And worship this dull fool!" (TEM.5.1)
Extend the characterization to a third party as an insult, e.g. 'He is a thrice-double ass'.
In the play. *Caliban recognizes the futility of having relied in Stephano and Trinculo as co-conspirators.*

Error, fault, mixed feelings about a fault - There's something in me that reproves my fault...
"There's something in me that reproves my fault;
But such a headstrong potent fault it is
That it but mocks reproof." (TN.3.4)
Explain an inner conflict. In the play. *Olivia has declared her love for Viola/Cesario, who for various reasons (besides being a woman disguised as a man), cannot reciprocate. This is why Olivia regrets the declaration of love she just made to Viola/Cesario.*

Errors, e. as a source of experience, sarcastic – ... to wilful men the injuries they themselves procure must be their schoolmasters.
"O sir, to wilful men,
The injuries they themselves procure
Must be their schoolmasters."
(KL.2.4)
Show how to take and accept responsibility and to learn from one's own mistakes.
In the play. *Regan forces her old father Lear to leave her house and brave a storm and this is her comment to Gloucester.*

Erudition, master of e. – ... Thrice famed, beyond all erudition.
"Famed be thy tutor, and thy parts of nature
Thrice famed, beyond all erudition" (TC.2.3)
In the play. *Ulysses pulls Ajax' leg by attributing to him qualities he does not possess, but Ajax sucks it all in.*

Escape, fleeing - … fly, like ships before the wind or lambs pursued by hunger-starved wolves.
"…and fly, like ships before the wind
Or lambs pursued by hunger-starved wolves" (KHVI.p3.1.4)
Metaphor describing the retreat of an enemy or adversary. See also entries for 'Cowards' and 'Cowardice'
In the play. *The forces of Queen Margaret have defeated the forces of York and followers near Sandal Castle.*

Establishment, e. run down and poorly managed - … epicurism and lust make it more like a tavern or a brothel than a graced palace.
"…our court, infected with their manners,
Shows like a riotous inn: epicurism and lust
Make it more like a tavern or a brothel
Than a graced palace. The shame itself doth speak
For instant remedy" (KL.1.4)
In the play. *Goneril blames her father King Lear for the excesses of his court and companions.*

Esteem, return to a statement of esteem - Your worth is very dear in my regard.
"Your worth is very dear in my regard." (MOV.1.1)
Answer to an expression of esteem
In the play. *Antonio thanks Salerio who has attempted to cheer Antonio up.*

Estimation, e. of people or objects differing among people - I never knew man hold vile stuff so dear.
"I never knew man hold vile stuff so dear." (LLL.4.3)
See also 'Necessity, n. changing the appearance of things – The art of our necessities is strange, that can make vile things precious.'

In the play. *Dumain is surprised at the attraction that Rosaline exerts on Biron.*

Eulogy – He was a man, take him for all in all, I shall not look upon his like again.
"He was a man, take him for all in all, I shall not look upon his like again." (H.1.2)
In the play. *Hamlet to Horatio speaking of the murdered King.*

Eulogy – Now cracks a noble heart. Good night sweet prince…
"Now cracks a noble heart. Good night sweet prince:
And flights of angels sing thee to thy rest!" (H.5.2)
In the play. *Horatio's comment soon after Hamlet dies.*

Eulogy, e. for a sinner – So may he rest; his faults lie gently on him!
"So may he rest; his faults lie gently on him!" (KHVIII.4.2)
In the play. *Q. Catherine, in seclusion at Kimbolton, comments on the report of Wolsey's death by Griffith.*

Eulogy, praises - His life was gentle: and the element so mixed in him..
"His life was gentle: and the elements
So mixed in him, that Nature might stand up,
And say to all the world, This was a man!" (JC.5.2)
Turn the past to the present tense and use as a flattering statement, 'He is gentle and the elements so mixed in him that Nature might stand up and say to all the world, this is a man!'
In the play. *Antony recognizes the value of Brutus, his fallen enemy.*

Event, course of e. completely changing your outlook on life - Had I but died an hour before this chance I had lived a blessed time…

"Had I but died an hour before this chance,
I had lived a blessed time; for, from this instant,
There 's nothing serious in mortality:
All is but toys: renown and grace is dead;
The wine of life is drawn, and the mere lees
Is left this vault to brag of." (M.2.2)
'Lees' is a synonym for 'dregs'. Start from 'All is but toys' to comment on your state of mind and your assessment of the situation. See also entries for 'Repentance'.
In the play. *Macbeth has just killed King Duncan and feels the pangs of remorse.*

Event, deprecating an unhappy e. - ... unhappy was the clock that struck the hour.
"Upon a time,--unhappy was the clock
That struck the hour!" (CYM.5.4)
In the play. *Jachimo begins the story of his perfidious plots and false accusations to Imogen.*

Event, e. of historical importance - How many ages hence shall this, our lofty scene be acted over, in states unborn…
"How many ages hence
Shall this, our lofty scene be acted over,
In states unborn and accents yet unknown." (JC.3.1)
A very important event has taken place. Use the quote to emphasize its importance via tasteful exaggeration. See also 'Time, almost forever – when time has forgot itself' *** 'Prediction, dire p. - the woe's to come; the children yet unborn...' *** 'Story, sad s. to be told - ... And in this harsh world draw thy breath in pain, to tell my story' *** 'Victory, v. remembered in future ages – Saint Alban's battle won by famous York shall be eternized in all age to come.'

In the play. *Cassius referring to Caesar's assassination just committed.*

Event, e. or fact, confirmation of it - If this were so, so were it uttered.
"If this were so, so were it uttered." (MAAN.1.1)
Answer to 'Is it true?' when you wish to confirm but with mild reservation.
In the play. *Claudio confirms that Benedick's statement is true, Claudio is in love with Hero.*

Event, e. remembered even in old age - ... all shall be forgot but he'll remember with advantages…
"Old men forget: yet all shall be forgot,
But he'll remember with advantages
What feats he did that day…" (KHV.4.2)
In the play. *King Henry addresses the troops before the battle of Agincourt*

Event, e. that can only be told with shame - may not be without much shame retold.
"…as may not be
Without much shame retold or spoken of." (KHIV p1.1.1)
Preparing the audience to listen to a disgraceful event in which you or others have been involved.
In the play. *Westmoreland relates to King Henry IV how Glendower has capture Mortimer in Wales with slaughter of 1000 of Mortimer's troops. Dead corpses were abused by Welshwomen in an unspeakable way.*

Event, e. that should have excited more reaction - The breaking of so great a thing should make a greater crack.
"The breaking of so great a thing should make
A greater crack" (AC.5.1)
In the play. *Octavian's reaction to the news that Antony is dead.*

Event, extraordinary astronomical event called for – Methinks it should be now a huge eclipse…
"O, insupportable! O heavy hour!
Methinks it should be now a huge eclipse
Of sun and moon, and that the affrighted globe
Should yawn at alteration." (OTH.5.2)
In the play. *Having killed Desdemona Othello realizes the enormity of his act, such as to call for, or comparable to some extraordinary astronomical event.*

Event, greatness of event, next day better than the last - … Each following day became the next day's master, till the last made former wonders its.
"…Each following day
Became the next day's master, till the last
Made former wonders its."
(KHVIII.1.1)
Lavishly praise a turn of events.
In the play. *The Duke of Norfolk refers to the historic meeting in France between Henry VIII and Francis I (at the field of the Cloth of Gold)*.

Event, new and amazing e. – 'tis wondrous strange, the like yet never heard of.
"'Tis wondrous strange, the like yet never heard of." (KHVI p3.2.1)
Give special emphasis to your amazement – perhaps she has agreed to an idea of yours and it seemed impossible before.
In the play. *Richard of Gloucester and Edward see extraordinary events in nature as a sign of their success. Specifically, as reported by Richard:*
Three glorious suns, each one a perfect sun;
Not separated with the racking clouds,
But sever'd in a pale clear-shining sky.
See, see! they join, embrace, and seem to kiss,
As if they vow'd some league inviolable:
Now are they but one lamp, one light, one sun.
In this the heaven figures some event.

Event, potentially incredible e. - That would be ten days' wonder at the least.
"That would be ten days' wonder at the least" (KHVI.p3.3.2)
In the play. *The wonder refers to the marriage of King Edward to the Lady Grey. That is, brothers Clarence and Richard of Gloucester would consider it a wonder.*

Event, strange e. explained - All this amazement can I qualify…
"All this amazement can I qualify:
…
Meantime let wonder seem familiar"
(MAAN.5.4)
In the play. *The friar recognizes the amazement of the audience at seeing Hero, whom everyone believed dead.*

Events, e. turning out as you wanted - every thing lies level to our wish.
"And every thing lies level to our wish,
Only, we want a little personal strength" (KHIV.p2.4.4)
Answer to 'How are things?' when things are going well. Add the second line if things go well but you are not in the best of health.
In the play. *London, the Jerusalem chamber at court. The rebels defeated, everything lies level to King Henry IV's wishes and now he wants to launch a crusade in the Holy Land, but his weakness will make it impossible.*

Events, interpretation of e., how the doubtful draw their conclusions - … how such an apprehension may turn the tide of fearful faction and breed a kind of question in our cause.
"…think how such an apprehension
May turn the tide of fearful faction

And breed a kind of question in our cause" (HIV. P1.4.1)
In the play. *Worcester points out how the absence of Hotspur's father from the battle may be interpreted negatively by the undecided.*

Events, mass hysteria turning natural e. distorted into supernatural phenomena - ... they will pluck away his natural cause and call them meteors, prodigies and signs...
"No natural exhalation in the sky,
No scope of nature, no distemper'd day,
No common wind, no customed event,
But they will pluck away his natural cause
And call them meteors, prodigies and signs,
Abortives, presages and tongues of heaven,
Plainly denouncing vengeance upon John" (KJ.3.4)
See also 'Opinion, your o. on crowds and masses.
In the play. *After the assassination of Prince Arthur by King John the people will attribute ominous meanings to any natural event.*

Events, strange and extraordinary and given favorable interpretation - 'tis wondrous strange, the like yet never heard of...
"'T is wondrous strange, the like yet never heard of." (KHVI p3.2)
Give special emphasis to your amazement – perhaps she has agreed to an idea of yours and it seemed impossible before.
In the play. *Edward commenting on the simultaneous appearance of (3) suns. Here is a live description of the phenomenon,*
"Three glorious suns, each one a perfect sun;
not separated with the racking clouds,
But sever'd in a pale clear-shining sky.
See, see! they join, embrace, and seem to kiss,
As if they vow'd some league inviolable:
Now are they but one lamp, one light, one sun.
In this the heaven figures some event."

Events, strange and extraordinary and given ominous meaning - ...And meteors fright the fixed stars of heaven.
"'Tis thought the king is dead; we will not stay.
The bay-trees in our country are all wither'd
And meteors fright the fixed stars of heaven" (KRII.2.4)
In the play. *The Captain of Welsh soldiers loyal to King Richard disbands his army on the assumption that Richard is dead in Ireland – suspicion confirmed by dead trees and the meteor shower.*

Events, strange and extraordinary and given ominous meaning - ... The graves stood tenantless and the sheeted dead...
"A little ere the mightiest Julius fell,
The graves stood tenantless and the sheeted dead
Did squeak and gibber in the Roman streets
... and the moist star
Upon whose influence Neptune's empire stands
Was sick almost to doomsday with eclipse" (H.1.1)
In the play. *Horatio's interpretation of the appearance of the Ghost.*

Events, strange and extraordinary and given ominous meaning - ... stars with trains of fire and dews of blood ...
"As stars with trains of fire and dews of blood,
Disasters in the sun; and the moist star
Upon whose influence Neptune's

empire stands
Was sick almost to doomsday with eclipse" (H.1.1)
In the play. *Horatio, after seeing the Ghost for himself, compares the strange events to those reportedly occurred in Rome before the assassination of Julius Caesar.*

Events, strange and extraordinary and given ominous meaning – ... The bay-trees in our country are all wither'd and meteors fright the fixed stars of heaven...
"'Tis thought the king is dead; we will not stay.
The bay-trees in our country are all wither'd
And meteors fright the fixed stars of heaven;
The pale-faced moon looks bloody on the earth
And lean-look'd prophets whisper fearful change
...
These signs forerun the death or fall of kings" (KRII.2.4)
In the play. *In Wales, a captain waiting for the return of King Richard from Ireland, sees signs portending to the demise of Richard.*

Events, strange and extraordinary and given ominous meaning - ... they say five moons were seen tonight; four fixed and the fifth...
"... they say five moons were seen tonight;
Four fixed and the fifth did whirl about
The other four, in wondrous motion." (KJ.4.2)
Use as an example of unfounded superstitious reasons.
In the play. *Panic at the court of King John where Hubert reports on strange events.*

Events, strange and extraordinary and given ominous meaning - A lioness hath whelped in the streets and graves have yawn'd, and yielded up their dead.
"A lioness hath whelped in the streets; And graves have yawn'd, and yielded up their dead." (JC.2.1)
Question the relevance or believability of observation, 'Come on, now you will tell me that a lioness hath whelped in the streets and graves have yawned…dead.' See also 'Nature, extraordinary natural events - ... and I have seen the ambitious ocean swell and rage and foam...' – 'Night, n. holding record of strange events - ... I have seen hours dreadful and things strange; but this sore night...'
In the play. *Calphurnia tries to persuade Caesar to stay at home, given the reports of strange events*

Events, stranger and stranger - These are not natural events; they strengthen from strange to stranger.
"These are not natural events; they strengthen,
From strange to stranger." (TEM.5.1)
You cannot believe what's happening - express your approval or disapproval, depending on the circumstances. See also 'Explanation, e. of strange events needing oracle - ... some oracle must rectify our knowledge.' *** Entries for 'Events, strange'
In the play. *The other members of the crew from the shipwrecked boat have arrived and Alonso is flabbergasted.*

Event, unbelievable - ... it is past the infinite of thought.
"By my troth, my lord, I cannot tell what to think of it… it is past the infinite of thought." (MAAN.2.3)
In the play. *Leonato has learned that the seemingly unapproachable and intractable Beatrice actually loves Benedick and confirms the news to him.* 'Troth' = 'faith'

Evidence, additional supporting e. –
... And this may help to thicken other proofs that do demonstrate thinly.
"And this may help to thicken other proofs
That do demonstrate thinly."
(OTH.3.3)
In the play. *The alleged supporting evidence is the fabrication of what Iago has heard spoken of Desdemona by Cassio in a dream.*

Evidence, desire to disbelieve the e. -
Yet there is a credence in my heart... that doth invert the utmost of eyes and ears...
" ... yet there is a credence in my heart,
An esperance so obstinately strong,
That doth invert the utmost of eyes and ears;
As if those organs had deceptious functions,
Created only to calumniate." (TC.5.2)
You desire not to believe what is actually happened.
In the play. *Though Troilus has ample evidence of Cressida's betrayal he does not want to believe it.*

Evidence, disputing incriminating written e. – My heart is not confederate with my hand.
"...read not my name there
My heart is not confederate with my hand" (KRII.5.3)
In the play. *The Duke of York is bent on having his son Aumerle killed for treason by presenting a latter written by Aumerle before repenting.*

Evidence, e. lacking or circumstantial – To vouch this, is no proof, without more wider and more overt test.
"To vouch this, is no proof,
Without more wider and more overt test" (O.1.3)
In the play. *The Duke of Venice to Brabantio. Brabantio suggests that Othello has charmed Desdemona into marrying him with sorcery or similar.*

Evidence, e. required before confirming doubt- ... I'll see before I doubt; when I doubt, prove.
"...to be once in doubt
Is once to be resolved
...
... No, Iago;
I'll see before I doubt; when I doubt, prove;
And on the proof, there is no more but this,--
Away at once with love or jealousy!"
(OTH.3.3)
In the play. *Othello makes one last effort to shake off the gnawing jealousy inspired by the evil Iago.*

Evidence, e. very clear – ... proofs as clear as founts in July when we see each grain of gravel...
"...by intelligence,
And proofs as clear as founts in July when
We see each grain of gravel, I do know
To be corrupt and treasonous"
(KHVIII.1.1)
Add strength to your summing up of the evidence.
In the play. *Buckingham confides with Norfolk about the corruption of Cardinal Wolsey, currently a favorite of the King (and Buckingham's sworn enemy).*

Evidence, e. from the vice squad - ... We have here recovered the most dangerous piece of lechery that ever was known in the commonwealth.
"....We have here recovered the most dangerous piece of lechery that ever was known in the commonwealth." (MAAN.3.4)
Apply to sex scandals of politicians.
In the play. *The First Watch has discovered the plot to slander good Hero.*

Evidence, e, heard directly – … and by an auricular assurance have your satisfaction.
"If your honour judge it meet, I will place you where you shall hear us confer of this, and by an auricular assurance have your satisfaction" (KL.1.2)
Try 'Do you want to have auricular assurance?' as an alternate to 'Do you want to hear it yourself?'
In the play. *Evil Edmund hatches a crafty plot to have his good brother Edgar hated by their father Gloucester. Edgar is innocent but Edmund arranges matters so that what Gloucester hear (auricular assurance') may seem to confirm Edgar's bad intentions.*
'Meet'='proper'

Evidence, e. of your worth or action - Well, let my deeds be witness of my worth.
"Well, let my deeds be witness of my worth." (TA.4.1)
Possible answer to 'What are your strengths?' E.G. 'I'll let my deeds be witness of my worth'. Or when enemies try to undermine your position with phony arguments.
In the play. *The evil Aaron gleefully recounts his exploits of murder.*

Evidence, e. requested will be provided – … strong circumstances which lead directly to the door of truth…
"If imputation and strong circumstances,
Which lead directly to the door of truth,
Will give you satisfaction, you may have't." (OTH.3.3)
In the play. *Iago will give Othello (fabricated) evidence of Desdemona's infidelity.*

Evidence, e. required or else - Give me the ocular proof: or by the worth of man's eternal soul…
"…give me the ocular proof:
Or by the worth of man's eternal soul,
Thou hadst been better have been born a dog
Than answer my waked wrath!" (OTH.3.3)
In the play. *Othello, agitated but still disbelieving that Desdemona can be unfaithful, warns Iago to provide proof.*

Evidence, e. showing shame and guilt - that argues but the shame of your offence.
"That argues but the shame of your offence:
A rotten case abides no handling" (KHIV.p2.4.1)
See also 'Disguise, d. discovered - there is a kind of confession in your looks'.
In the play. *The rebel Mowbray refuses the offer of negotiation by Westmoreland and Westmoreland replies angrily.*

Evidence, example of self-e. - that, that it is, is.
"Bonos dies, sir Toby; for as the old hermit of Prague, that never saw pen and ink, very wittily said to a niece of king Gordobuc, That, that it is, is." (TN.4.2)
Prepare the audience to your stating the obvious that, however, needs to be stated…
In the play. *Sir Toby addresses the Clown as master parson. Malvolio, secluded in a dark prison is supposed to hear the conversation. The Clown replies. This is all part of a trick played on Benvolio.*

Evidence, let e. prove the point – Let proof speak.
"Let proof speak" (CYM.3.1)
In the play. *Caius Lucius to Leonatus who is in Rome and hints at the Britons rebelling against Rome.*

Evidence, we have the e. - the particular confirmation, point to point, to the full arming of the verity.
" (we have) the particular confirmation, point to point, to the full arming of the verity." (AWEW.4.3)
Stress that you have all the required information and evidence.
In the play. *The verity referred to is the alleged death of Helena, as reported in the Countess' letter to Bertram and here reported by the First Lord.*

Evident, clear and e. - 'Tis probable and palpable to thinking.
"'Tis probable and palpable to thinking." (OTH.1.2)
In the play. *Brabantio is dismayed at his daughter Desdemona who eloped with the Moor. What is 'palpable to thinking' is that he somehow bewitched her.*

Evil, consorting with evil to understand and avoid it - ... studies his companions like a strange tongue, wherein, to gain the language...
"The prince but studies his companions
Like a strange tongue, wherein, to gain the language,
'Tis needful that the most immodest word
Be look'd upon and learn'd; which once attain'd,
Your highness knows, comes to no further use
But to be known and hated."
(KHIVp2.4.4)
In the play. *Westmoreland gives a positive spin to Prince Harry's escapades and association with the hedonistic Falstaff.*

Evil, e. that calls for curses on its doers - ... it calls I fear, too many curses on their heads that were the authors.
"O, this is full of pity! Sir, it calls,
I fear, too many curses on their heads
That were the authors" (KHVIII.2.1)
In the play. *A citizen comments on Buckingham, unjustly condemned to death by the King, on instigation from Cardinal Wolsey.*

Evil, doing e. to do good - A little harm done to a great good end...
"A little harm done to a great good end
For lawful policy remains enacted.
The poisonous simple sometimes is compacted
In a pure compound; being so applied,
His venom in effect is purified."
(ROL)
Example for the all the war crimes committed by imperialist powers in the name of some often unspecified 'good'.
In the poem. *Tarquin attempts to rationalize his evil intention to Lucrece.*

Evil, e. compounding with e. - Things bad begun make strong themselves by ill.
"Things bad begun make strong themselves by ill." (M.3.2)
In the play. *Macbeth in conversation with his wife. He refers to' things bad begun', i.e. the murder of Duncan that are reinforced by more evil (here the imminent murder of Banquo).*

Evil, e. destroying virtue – ... The adder hisses where the sweet birds sing; what virtue breeds iniquity devours.
"Unruly blasts wait on the tender spring;
Unwholesome weeds take root with precious flowers;
The adder hisses where the sweet birds sing;
What virtue breeds iniquity devours"
(ROL)

Evil, e. rebounding against its inventor - … Bloody instructions, which, being taught, return, return to plague the inventor.
"… But in these cases
We still have judgment here; that we but teach
Bloody instructions, which, being taught, return
To plague the inventor: this even-handed justice
Commends the ingredients of our poison'd chalice
To our own lips" (M.1.7)
In the play. *Macbeth meditates on the consequences of his planned murder of King Duncan.*

Evil, no e. intended – No man means evil but the devil, and we shall know him by his horns.
"No man means evil but the devil, and we shall know him by his horns" (MWW.5.2)
In the play. *Mr. Page to Shallow as they prepare to watch the trick and mask played on the unwary Falstaff.*

Evil, piling e. on e. – … And do not spread the compost on the weeds, to make them ranker.
And do not spread the compost on the weeds,
To make them ranker" (H.3.4)
Alternative to 'Do not make matters worse'.
In the play. *Hamlet tells his mother the Queen not to attribute his words to madness and thus continue to justify her behavior*

Evils, self-created e. - And this same progeny of evils comes from our debate, from our dissension…
"And this same progeny of evils comes
From our debate, from our dissension;
We are their parents and original." (MND.2.1)
Calm a heated debate.
In the play. *Fairy Queen Titania accuses Oberon of creating a dissension that alters the course of seasons and various other evils*

Exaggeration, resentment not called for – taking bird bolts for cannon bullets
"O, you are sick of self-love, Malvolio, and taste with distempered appetite. To be generous, guiltless, and of free disposition, is to take things for bird bolts, that you deem cannon bullets." (TN.1.5)
Persuade a person not to take small incidents too seriously, 'To be generous…bullets'
In the play. *Olivia invites Malvolio not to be so supercilious and not to react so angrily at the banter and arrow-shafts of the clown.*

Example, bad e. and/or bad education – … a' had him from me Christian; and look, if the fat villain have not transformed him ape
"And the boy that I gave Falstaff: a' had him from me Christian; and look, if the fat villain have not transformed him ape." (KHIV.p2.2.1)
A metaphor for poor education, e.g. we send them Christians, they transformed them apes'.
In the play. *The Prince of Wales refers to a page he has assigned to Falstaff and clearly does not put much trust in Falstaff's educational or training skills.*

Example, power of e. – … inferior eyes, that borrow their behaviour from the great…
"…inferior eyes,
That borrow their behaviour from the great…" (KJ.5.1)

In the play. *Faulconbridge encourages K. John to face up to a difficult situation.*

Example, role model – For from his metal was his party steel'd…
"For from his metal was his party steel'd;
Which once in him abated, all the rest
Turn'd on themselves, like dull and heavy lead." (KHIVp2.1.1)
Emphasize the importance of example, e.g. A role model is very important in the life of an individual as well as a group or a party, as in the lines, …for from his metal was his party… lead.' Use the idea constructively, to promote the election of an ally or destructively, to call for the resignation of a poor role model.
In the play. *Morton relates the events of the battle after Hotspur fell at the hands of the Prince of Wales.*

Examples, e. leading to decisions – Examples gross as earth exhort me…
"Examples gross as earth exhort me:
Witness this army of such mass and charge
Led by a delicate and tender prince…" (H.4.4)
In the play. *Undecided still on how or whether to carry out his revenge against King Claudius, Hamlet considers the Norwegian army going to battle for almost no gain.*

Excellence, e. has no fear – things done well and with a care exempt themselves from fear.
"Things done well,
And with a care, exempt themselves from fear." (KHVIII.1.2)
Counter criticism or opposition to action on the ground of possible consequences.
In the play. *King Henry VIII answers a comment from Wolsey.*

Excess, a comparison - Light seeking light doth light of light beguile.
"Light seeking light doth light of light beguile" (LLL.1.1)
In the play. *Biron warns against the counterproductive effects of excessive learning.*

Excess, e. bad even in excellence - striving to better, oft we mar what's well.
"How far your eyes may pierce I can not tell:
Striving to better, oft we mar what's well." (KL.1.4)
Expedite action when others still want to delay it because more needs to be done.
In the play. *Goneril has reproached her husband Albany for being too soft with Lear and he replies.*

Excess, e. leads to loathing – They surfeited with honey and began to loathe the taste of sweetness…
"…They surfeited with honey and began
To loathe the taste of sweetness, whereof a little
More than a little is by much too much." (KHIV.p1.3.2)
See also 'Dieting, too much sugar, excess brings distaste - …a surfeit of the sweetest things the deepest loathing to the stomach brings.'
In the play. *King Henry has a talk on royal policy and behavior with son Harry, Prince of Wales.*

Excess, e. leading to corruption - most subject is the fattest soil to weeds.
"Most subject is the fattest soil to weeds." (KHIVp2.4.4)
Use to warn against useless expenses.
In the play. *King Henry is concerned about the company P. Henry keeps, that is Falstaff, who is notoriously fat, and crew.*

Excess, e. not necessary and wasteful once objective is reached - To gild

refined gold, to paint the lily… is wasteful and ridiculous excess.
" To gild refined gold, to paint the lily
To throw a perfume on the violet,
To smooth the ice, or add another hue
Unto the rainbow, or with taper-light
To seek the beauteous eye of heaven to garnish,
Is wasteful and ridiculous excess."
(KJ.4.2)
Call for economy and disallow excessive expenses on trivial matters See also the first two lines in 'Excuse, e. often worse than the fault - … And oftentimes excusing of a fault, …discredit more in hiding of the fault than did the fault before it was so patched.'
In the play. *Salisbury advises against additional ceremonies after King John returns to England from France.*

Excess, effects of e. - Sweets grown common lose their dear delight.
"Sweets grown common lose their dear delight.
Therefore like her I sometime hold my tongue,
Because I would not dull you with my song" (SON 102)
The 'her' referred to is a singing bird.

Exchange, e. for the better - … what fool is not so wise to lose an oath to win a paradise?
"… what fool is not so wise
To lose an oath to win a paradise?" (LLL.4.3)
In the play. *Longaville reads from a letter he has prepared for Maria. The oath referred to is the oath of abstinence and study, concocted by the King of Navarre.*

Exclamation, false conclusion - O most lame and impotent conclusion!
"O most lame and impotent conclusion!" (OTH.2.1)
In the play. *Desdemona's response to some comments by Iago.*

Exclamation, falsehood – Excellent falsehood!
"Excellent falsehood!" (AC.1.1)
In the play. *Cleopatra pretends not to believe the attestation of unending love by Antony.*

Exclamation, what the dickens - I cannot tell what the dickens his name is…
"I cannot tell what the dickens his name is my husband had him of. What do you call your knight's name, sirrah?" (MWW.3.2)
See also entries for 'Invocation'
In the play. *Questioned by Mr. Ford, Mrs. Page does not remember the name of the person through whom she obtained a weather-cock admired by Mr. Ford. The person is actually Falstaff. 'Dickens' is synonym for 'devil'*

Excuse, e. often worse than the fault - … And oftentimes excusing of a fault, …discredit more in hiding of the fault than did the fault before it was so patched.
"When workmen strive to do better than well,
They do confound their skills in covetousness.
And oftentimes excusing of a fault
Doth make the fault the worse by the excuse;
As patches, set upon a little breach,
Discredit more in hiding of the fault,
Than did the fault before it was so patched." (KJ.4.2)
Use the third and fourth line "Oftentimes…excuse." or continue with the comparison. See also 'Virtue, sin and their interrelationship, maxim - Any thing that's mended is but patched…'
In the play. *Pembroke and Salisbury advise King John to limit additional parades and ceremonies*

Excuse, no e. plus insult – Fouler than heart can think thee, thou canst make no excuse current, but to hang thyself.
"Fouler than heart can think thee, thou canst make
No excuse current, but to hang thyself." KRIII.1.2
In the play. *Lady Anne to Richard who tries to find some lame excuses for having killed her husband.*

Excuses, attempt to cover-up with excuses - Why seek'st thou to cover with excuse that which appears in proper nakedness?
"Why seek'st thou to cover with excuse,
That which appears in proper nakedness?" (MAAN.4.1)
Express your disappointment at attempts to a cover up.
In the play. *The friar advises Leonato not to believe the accusations against Hero. Leonato believes that the friar is trying to cover things up.*

Executioner, refusing to be the e. - though I wish thy death I will not be the executioner.
"Arise, dissembler: though I wish thy death,
I will not be the executioner."
(KRIII.1.2)
You can apply this also in the third person, e.g. 'I may wish his death but will not be his executioner'.
In the play. *Richard offers Anne his sword and pretends to ask Anne to kill him but she refuses to be an executioner.*

Exercise, enough e. for now - Thy exercise hath been too violent for a second course of fight.
"Thy exercise hath been too violent for
A second course of fight." (COR.1.5)
In the play. *Lartius prompts Coriolanus not to attack (again) the Volsces after being wounded, but Coriolanus will disregard the advice.*

Exhortation, e. not to aggravate a man who is desperate - Tempt not a desperate man.
"… tempt not a desperate man" (RJ.5.3)
In the play. *Romeo meets with Paris in the tomb where Juliet seemingly lies dead. Paris challenges Romeo and Romeo responds.*

Exhortation, e. not to feed a delusion - … Lay not that flattering unction to your soul, that not your trespass, but my madness speaks….
"… for love of grace,
Lay not that flattering unction to your soul,
That not your trespass, but my madness speaks:
It will but skin and film the ulcerous place,
Whilst rank corruption, mining all within,
Infects unseen
…
And do not spread the compost on the weeds,
To make them ranker" (H.3.4)
In the play. *Hamlet tells his mother the Queen not to attribute his words to madness and thus continue to justify her behavior*

Exhortation, e. not to yield to enemy - … And he that will not fight for such a hope, go home to bed…
"And he that will not fight for such a hope.
Go home to bed, and like the owl by day,
If he arise, be mock'd and wonder'd at." (KHVI p3.5.4)
In the play. *Somerset joins Q. Margaret in encouraging the troops to fight on at the battle of Coventry notwithstanding initial reversals.*

Exhortation, e. not to yield to enemy – We will not from the helm to sit and weep, but keep our course, though the rough wind say no...
"We will not from the helm to sit and weep,
But keep our course, though the rough wind say no,
From shelves and rocks that threaten us with wreck." (KHVI p3.5.4)
See also entries for 'Complaint, c. after problems useless'
In the play. *Q. Margaret, undaunted by the loss of Warwick at the battle of Coventry, incites her forces.*

Exhortation, e. not to yield to enemy - ... With tearful eyes add water to the sea and give more strength to that which hath too much?
"(Is it meet).. .With tearful eyes add water to the sea
And give more strength to that which hath too much?" (KHVI p3.5.4)
In the play. *Q. Margaret, undaunted by the loss of Warwick at the battle of Coventry, incites her forces. 'Meet'='proper'.*

Exhortation, e. not to stir up trouble - Your speech is passion: but, pray you, stir no embers up. '
"Your speech is passion:
But, pray you, stir no embers up." (AC.2.2)
In the play. *Lepidus asks Enobarbus to tell Antony to go easy with words when meeting Caesar Octavian in the impending meeting.*

Exhortation, e. redundant - ...and yet I do thee wrong to mind thee of it…
"Farewell, kind lord; fight valiantly to-day:
And yet I do thee wrong to mind thee of it,
For thou art framed of the firm truth of valour." (KHV.4.3)
An alternative to a wish for success.

In the play. *Exeter to Salisbury before the battle of Agincourt.*

Exhortation, e. to act - ... be a soldier to thy purpose.
"…but be
A soldier to thy purpose." (PER.4.1)
In the play. *The evil Dionyza, envious that Marina excels her own daughter in everything, hires a contract killer and prompts him to take out Marina.*

Exhortation, e. to act according to intent expressed - ... And let your mind be coupled with your words.
"...And let your mind be coupled with your words." (TC.5.2)
In the play. *Diomed reminds Cressida of a previous unspecified promise.*

Exhortation, e. to act manfully and forcefully – Be great in act, as you have been in thought
"Be great in act, as you have been in thought;
Let not the world see fear and sad distrust
Govern the motion of a kingly eye" (KJ.5.1)
In the play. *Faulconbridge exhorts King John not to appear weak and fearful, now that many English lords have forsaken him. They suspect him (and rightly so) to have killed or caused to be killed young Prince Arthur.*

Exhortation, e. to act quickly – ... make no delay: we may effect this business yet ere day.
"…make no delay:
We may effect this business yet ere day." (MND.3.2)
In the play. Oberon to Puck. *The business is the reversal of the charm that everyone in the play confused.*

Exhortation, e. to action with stealth - ... let's on our way in silent sort: for

Warwick and his friends, God and Saint George!
"Why, then, let's on our way in silent sort:
For Warwick and his friends, God and Saint George!" (KHVI.p3.4.2)
Change 'Warwick' with your name or the name of the party whose cause you espouse.
In the play. *Warwick leads the party to capture the forsworn King Edward IV.*

Exhortation, e. to action - ... Better consider what you have to do than I, that have not well the gift of tongue can lift your blood up with persuasion.
"And fellow soldiers, friends,
Better consider what you have to do,
Than I, that have not well the gift of tongue,
Can lift your blood up with persuasion." (KHIVp1.5)
Stress the importance of the task itself, requiring no persuasion to be undertaken. 'Friends, better consider… persuasion'
In the play. *Hotspur addresses his allies before the battle of Shrewsbury with the forces of King Henry IV and of the Prince of Wales.*

Exhortation, e. to be brave - Hang those that talk of fear.
"Hang those that talk of fear" (M.5.3)
In the play. *Under siege at Dunsinane, Macbeth prepares for the last battle*

Exhortation, e. to be friendly – ... put off these frowns and ill-beseeming semblance for a feast.
"Show a fair presence and put off these frowns,
And ill-beseeming semblance for a feast." (RJ.1.5)
Extract '…put off these frowns, and ill-beseeming semblance'
In the play. *Capulet exhorts Tybald to allay his anger after seeing Romeo, a Montague, at the Capulet's party.*

Exhortation, e. to calm to reduce confusion - Peace, ho, for shame! confusion's cure lives not in these confusions.
"Peace, ho, for shame! confusion's cure lives not
In these confusions." (RJ.4.5)
Exhort to use rationality and moderation.
In the play. *Juliet has drunk the potion provided by Fr. Lawrence. She is asleep but appears dead to her father Capulet. Capulet is now desperate and Fr. Lawrence attempts to calm him down.*

Exhortation, e. to change opinion - ... remove the root of his opinion which is rotten as ever oak or stone was sound.
"… remove
The root of his opinion, which is rotten
As ever oak or stone was sound." (WT.2.3)
See also "Opinion, emphatic exhortation to discard an o. – ... be cured of this diseased opinion.'
In the play. *Paulina is outraged at the suspicion that Leontes has on his virtuous wife Hermione and says that thought (opinion) is rotten.*

Exhortation, e. to change opinion - Remove your thought; it doth abuse your bosom.
"Remove your thought; it doth abuse your bosom." (OTH.4.2)
In the play. *Emilia to Othello, the thought is the nonexistent infidelity of Desdemona.*

Exhortation, e. to change opinion - ... weed your better judgments of all opinion that grows rank in them.
"…weed your better judgments
Of all opinion that grows rank in them" (AYLI.2.7)
In the play. *Jacques exchanges opinions with Duke Senior in the forest of Arden. The opinion*

in question relates to Jacques himself, reputed wise.

Exhortation, e. to change opinion - I do beseech you, gracious madam, to unthink your speaking…
"… I do beseech you, gracious madam, to unthink your speaking, And to say no more." (KHVIII.2.4)
Elegantly deny an allegation.
In the play. *Cardinal Wolsey responds to Q. Katherine, who accuses him of lying and malice.*

Exhortation, e. to consider the issue - I would your highness would give it quick consideration, for there is no primer business.
"I would your highness
Would give it quick consideration, for
There is no primer business." (KHVIII.1.2)
You can also phrase as 'Let us give it quick…business'
In the play. *Q. Katherine to King Henry, referring to the grievances of the subjects about excessive taxation.*

Exhortation, e. to discipline and expeditiousness - Let's want no discipline, make no delay for, lords, tomorrow is a busy day.
"Call for some men of sound direction,
Let's want no discipline, make no delay,
For, lords, tomorrow is a busy day." (KRIII.5.3)
End of speech and/or motivator for action. See also 'Delay, avoid d. - Defer no time, delays have dangerous ends…'*** 'Procrastination to be avoided – … for this 'would' changes, hath abatements and delays as many as there are tongues, are hands, are accidents' *** Planning, call for strategic p. by experts - Call for our chiefest men of discipline to cull the plots of best advantages.

In the play. *Richard speaks to his forces near Bosworth Field before the impending battle with Richmond.*

Exhortation, e. to dispel fear - Nay, good my lord, be not afraid of shadows.
"Nay, good my lord, be not afraid of shadows." (KRIII.5.3)
In the play. *Ratcliff reassures a suddenly fearful Richard III before the final battle at Bosworth Field.*

Exhortation, e. to fairness - We turn not back the silks upon the merchant, when we have soil'd them…
"We turn not back the silks upon the merchant,
When we have soil'd them, nor the remainder viands
We do not throw in unrespective sieve,
Because we now are full" (TC.2.3)
In the play. *Troilus' argument for not returning Helen to the Greeks.*

Exhortation, e. to fight - Now put your shields before your hearts, and fight…
"Now put your shields before your hearts, and fight
With hearts more proof than shields." (COR.1.4)
In the play. *Coriolanus exhorting the troops before attacking the Volsces*

Exhortation, e. to get started and go – Let us go, our corn's to reap, for yet our tithe's to sow.
"… Come, let us go:
Our corn's to reap, for yet our tithe's to sow." (MFM.4.1)
'Tithe' = 'land'. Use 'land' for better comprehension.
In the play. *Duke Vicentio to Mariana and Isabella as they proceed with the plot to unravel and expose Angelo's hypocrisy.*

Exhortation, e. to limit facetiousness - … do not play in wench-like words with that which is so serious.
"Prithee, have done;
And do not play in wench-like words with that
Which is so serious" (CYM.4.2)
In the play *Arviragus reprimands Guiderius who spends words at the sight of (presumed) dead Imogen.*

Exhortation, e. to listen and understand a plain message - I pray thee, understand a plain man in his plain meaning.
"… I pray thee, understand a plain man in his plain meaning" (MOV.3.5)
In the play. *Lorenzo is annoyed at Launcelot's sallies and prompts him to listen seriously.*

Exhortation, e. to listen for a little longer – Hear a little further and then I'll bring thee to the present business…
"Hear a little further
And then I'll bring thee to the present business
Which now's upon's; without the which this story
Were most impertinent" (TEM.1.2)
When you sense some restlessness among the audience as you explain the background that will lead you to make your point.
In the play. *Prospero is giving daughter Miranda the history of their escape and exile in the island.*

Exhortation, e. to passion - … put fire in your heart and brimstone in your liver.
"… put fire in your heart and brimstone in your liver." (TN.3.2)
This can be a rhetorical exhortation to action, e.g. 'Put fire… liver'
In the play. *Fabian explains to Aguecheek that the apparent show of liking to Viola/Cesario by Olivia was an attempt on Olivia's part to stir passion or anger in Aguecheel's soul. 'Brimstone' = 'Sulphur'. 'Fire and brimstone' is an expression also found in the Bible (Revelation 14:10).*

Exhortation, e. to patience - Be patient, for the world is broad and wide.
"Hence from Verona art thou banished:
Be patient, for the world is broad and wide" (RJ.3.3)
Answer to 'what will you do?' after you have resigned or were fired. E.G. '…the world is broad and wide…' hinting that you will do something else.
In the play. *Friar Lawrence to Romeo who must quickly leave for Mantua.*

Exhortation, e. to question our motives - Go to your bosom; knock there, and ask your heart what it doth know…
"Go to your bosom;
Knock there, and ask your heart what it doth know
That's like my brother's fault: if it confess
A natural guiltiness such as is his,
Let it not sound a thought upon your tongue
Against my brother's life." (MFM.2.2)
In the play. *Isabella pleads with Angelo for mercy for her brother Claudio.*

Exhortation, e. to rational behavior - Seal up the mouth of outrage for a while, till we can clear these ambiguities…
"Seal up the mouth of outrage for a while,
Till we can clear these ambiguities
And know their spring, their head, their true descent." (RJ.5.3)
Defuse a tense situation, when the parties are outraged and each suspect the other of being the cause of the outrage

In the play. *Unfortunately, Juliet, Romeo and Paris are dead. Montague is beyond himself in grief and the Prince attempts to calm Montague.*

Exhortation, e. to redouble the effort – Once more unto the breach, dear friends, once more
"Once more unto the breach, dear friends, once more,
Or close the wall up with our English dead" (KHV.3.1)
In the play. *K. Henry addresses the troops before the siege of Harfleur.*

Exhortation, e. to unite powers against common foe – … and join our powers and seek how we may prejudice the foe.
"Now let us on, my lords, and join our powers,
And seek how we may prejudice the foe." (KHVI.p1.3.3)
In the play. *Joan of Arc has persuaded Burgundy to defect to the French and now Charles exhorts lords and peers to unite their efforts against the English.*

Exhortation, e. to use reason - Sweet earl, divorce not wisdom from your honour.
"Sweet earl, divorce not wisdom from your honour." (KHIV.p2.1.1)
In the play. *Lord Bardolph tries to calm down the Earl of Northumberland*

Exhortation, e. to understand the limitations imposed by circumstances - Construe the times to their necessities.
"O my good Lord Mowbray! Construe the times to their necessities." (KHIVp2.4.1)
Convey the idea that in the circumstances there is only so much that can be done.
In the play. *Westmoreland prepares a trap for the rebels while quieting down the suspicious Mowbray.*

Exile, going into e. - … He'll shape his old course in a country new.
"Thus Kent, O princes, bids you all adieu;
He'll shape his old course in a country new." (KL.1.1)
See also 'Return, r. from a foreign assignment - (I) sighed my English breath in foreign clouds, eating the bitter bread of banishment.' ** 'Imagination, not a substitute of reality - O, who can hold a fire in his hand by thinking on the frosty Caucasus?…'
In the play. *Faithful Kent has been banished by King Lear for objecting to his treatment of Cordelia.*

Existence, e. and being proven - … as the old hermit of Prague… said to a niece of King Gorboduc, 'That that is is".
"… as the old hermit of
Prague, that never saw pen and ink, very wittily
said to a niece of King Gorboduc, 'That that is is;'" (TN.4.2)
In the play. *The Clown banters with Sir Toby. The Clown assumes the part of a parson to further continue the trick Maria, Toby and the Clown have played on Malvolio.*

Expectations, e. and rapid sequence of events – … every minute is expectancy of more arrivance.
"For every minute is expectancy
Of more arrivance." (OTH.2.1)
In the play. *A gentleman in Cyprus anxiously awaits with others the arrival of Othello's ship.*

Expectations, e. fed by hope often frustrated by reality - The ample proposition that hope makes in all designs begun on earth below fails in the promised largeness…
"The ample proposition that hope makes
In all designs begun on earth below
Fails in the promised largeness:

checks and disasters
Grow in the veins of actions highest rear'd,
As knots, by the conflux of meeting sap,
Infect the sound pine and divert his grain
Tortive and errant from his course of growth." (TC.1.3)
Explain that it is the very nature of expectations that makes them chancy, as described in these lines. And yet they should be considered as a stimulus for persistence. See also 'Persistence, failure. positive attitude - ... the protractive trials of great Jove to find persistive constancy in men.'
In the play. *Agamennon addresses the Grecian troops who have besieging Troy for a long time without victory. He invites them to consider the temporarily failed expectations as trials to test the Greeks' fiber.*

Expectations, e. often fail - Oft expectation fails, and most oft there, and most oft there where it most promises…
"**Oft expectation fails, and most oft there
Where most it promises; and oft it hits
Where hope is coldest, and despair most fits.**" (AWEW.2.1)
You went on a blind date with pessimistic expectations and then it turns out that she is a superlative beauty with a friendly disposition and she likes you.
On the other hand, should you have a date and she fails to show up, you may remember Oscar Wilde's line "It is always nice to be expected and not to arrive" (An Ideal Husband, act 4)
See also 'Destiny, d. inscrutable – ... how chances mock, and changes fill the cup of alteration with divers liquors!'
In the play. *Helen wishes to cure the King but he continues to be skeptical. She continues to presses her point suggesting exceptions to the general outcome of expectations.*

Expectations, e. poorly placed - ... briefly die their joys that place them on the truth of girls and boys.
"**…briefly die their joys
That place them on the truth of girls and boys.**" (CYM.5.4)
In the play. *Caius Lucius believes that Imogen/Fidele will not help save him as he has helped save Imogen/Fidele from death by Cymbeline's forces.*

Expectations, your e. unreasonable – ... till all graces be in a woman, one woman shall not come in my grace.
"**…Till all graces be in one woman, one woman shall not come in my grace.**" (MAAN.2.3)
You may turn this around and use the line to explain your philosophy and that she fulfills your expectations.
In the play. *The determinate bachelor Benedick explains in a monologue, his reasons for not falling in love.*

Expedience - Who dares not stir by day must walk by night.
"**Who dares not stir by day must walk by night**" (KJ.1.1)
In the play. Philip Faulconbridge in reply to a comment by Queen Elinor that he, Philip, shows the spirit of the Plantagenets. *The reference to 'walk by night' has to do with Philip's illegitimacy.*

Expedience, e. not sincerity involved - ... it proceeds from policy, not love.
"**But he hath forced us to compel this offer;
And it proceeds from policy, not love**" (KHIV.p2.4.1)
In the play. *Mowbray is suspicious of the peace offer by Westmoreland, King Henry IV's ambassador.*

Expenses, excessive e. and personal gain – How, i' the name of thrift, does he rake this together!

"What piles of wealth hath he accumulated
To his own portion! and what expense by the hour
Seems to flow from him! How, i' the name of thrift,
Does he rake this together!"
(KHVIII.3.2)
In the play. *King Henry has discovered the expenses and personal gains of Cardinal Wolsey.*

Experience, direct e. disproving official reports - Experience, O, thou disprov'st report!
"Experience, O, thou disprov'st report!" (CYM.4.1)
See also 'Observation, direct o. more trustworthy than official reports – Let every eye negotiate for itself and trust no agent.'
In the play. Imogen is favorably impressed by the kindness and courtesies bestowed upon country dwellers Belarius, Arviragus and Guiderius, whom she met in the forest, contrary to previous reports about people living in the country.

Experience, e. acquired through observation - How hast thou purchased this experience? By my penny of observation.
ADRIANO DE ARMADO How hast thou purchased this experience?
MOTH By my penny of observation. (LLL.3.1)
In the play. *Moth has always a quick retort to Armado's flowering expressions. The experience referred to here is that of courting ladies.*

Experience, e. or evidence disproving commonly held notions – Experience, O, thou disprov'st report!
"Experience, O, thou disprov'st report!" (CYM.4.1)
In the play. *Imogen is favorably impressed by the kindness and courtesies bestowed upon her by Belarius, Arviragus and Guiderius, whom she met in the forest. This is contrary to the notion that good things are only found at court.*

Experience, expensive e. and no other benefit - ... unless experience be a jewel that I have purchased at an infinite rate.
"...But whatsoever I have merited, either in my mind or, in my means, meed, I am sure, I have received none; unless experience be a jewel that I have purchased at an infinite rate" (MWW.2.2)
In the play. *Master Brook (alias Mr. Ford) pretends not to have had any success with Mrs. Ford other than experience.*

Experience, lack of e. alleged for refusing to take on a responsibility - Let there be some more test made of my metal...
ANGELO. Let there be some more test made of my metal,
Before so noble and so great a figure
Be stamped upon it.
DUKE. No more evasion:
We have with a leaven'd and prepared choice
Proceeded to you." (MFM.1.1)
Use (see Angelo's statement) as a delaying tactic to postpone the acceptance of an assignment.
In the play. *Angelo is reticent about taking the job offered by the Duke.*

Experience, let e. speak - ... give experience tongue.
"Peace, peace, and give experience tongue" (PER.1.2)
In the play. *Helicanus, King Pericles' minister addresses the lords of Tyre.*

Experience, value of e. and how it is acquired - Experience is by industry achieved and perfected by the swift course of time.

"Experience is by industry achieved
And perfected by the swift course of
time." (TGV.1.3)
Answer to question 'What is your
experience?' during a job interview.
In the play. *Antonio chats with Pantino and
discusses where to send Proteus (Antonio's son)
to achieve experience.*

Experience, worldly experience
makes a perfect man- ... he cannot be
a perfect man, not being tried and
tutored in the world.
"I have consider'd well his loss of
time
And how he cannot be a perfect man,
Not being tried and tutored in the
world." (TGV.1.3)
An alternate to claiming that you have
experience. E.G. 'I have been tried and
tutored in the world'.
In the play. *Antonio thinks that Proteus, his
son, would benefit from time spent abroad.*

Experimentation, e. harmless and
worth trying – What I can do can do
no hurt to try.
"What I can do can do no hurt to try"
(AWEW.2.1)
In the play. *Helena attempts to convince the
skeptical King to try her medicine.*

Explanation, difficult matter made
easy by expert - What impossible
matter will he make easy next?
"What impossible matter will he make
easy next?" (TEM.2.1)
Relate the line anecdotally when
introducing an expert.
In the play. *Antonio mocks Gonzalo who has
noted that something strange is happening after
the tempest that landed Antonio, Gonzalo and
others in a magic island.*

Explanation, do you want to know
why? - Ay sir, and wherefore; for, they
say, every why hath a wherefore.
ANTIPHOLUS S. Shall I tell you
why?
DROMIO S. Ay sir, and wherefore;
for, they say, every why hath a
wherefore. (COE.2.2)
Answer to any question of the type, 'do
you want to know why?'
In the play. *Ant S has beaten Dromio S.
Dromio S does not why and answers yes when
asked if he would like an explanation.*

Explanation, e. by way of an example
- ...I shall tell you a pretty tale; it may
be, you have heard it...
"… I shall tell you
A pretty tale; it may be, you have
heard it;
But, since it serves my purpose, I will
venture
To stale it a little more." (COR.1.1)
Introduction to an example or a story.
In the play. *Menenius attempts to soothe the
rebellious citizens and bring them to reason by
way of an example.*

Explanation, e. of strange events
needing oracle - … some oracle must
rectify our knowledge.
"This is as strange a maze as e'er men
trod
And there is in this business more
than nature
Was ever conduct of: some oracle
Must rectify our knowledge."
(TEM.5.1)
See also 'Events, stranger and stranger -
These are not natural events; they
strengthen from strange to stranger'
In the play. *Alonso cannot make heads or tail
of all the strange events that occurred in the
island.*

Explanation, further e. required - This
fierce abridgement hath to it
circumstantial branches...
"This fierce abridgement
Hath to it circumstantial branches,
which

Distinction should be rich in." (CYM.5.4)
In the play. *A quick run of events uncovers a sequence of extraordinary facts. Cymbeline is overjoyed but is aware of only a small part of all that happened.*

Explanation, pleading for an e. – Lay open…the folded meaning of your words' deceit.
"Lay open to my earthy-gross conceit, Smother'd in errors, feeble, shallow, weak,
The folded meaning of your words' deceit." (COE.3.2)
In the play. *Antipholus S to Luciana, sister of Adriana – Adriana is the wife of Antipholus E*

Explanation, rational e. and miracles excluded - … for miracles are ceased…
"It must be so: for miracles are ceased;
And therefore we must needs admit the means
How things are perfected." (KHV.1.1)
Before you attempt an explanation of an unusual or extraordinary event.
In the play. *Bishops of Canterbury and Ely confer on the subject of King Henry V. Canterbury agrees with Ely's analysis of King Henry V's reformation after his early wild years.*

Exploits, young and ready for e. - … in the very May-morn of his youth, ripe for exploits and mighty enterprises.
"... And my thrice-puissant liege
is in the very May-morn of his youth, Ripe for exploits and mighty enterprises." (KHV.1.2)
In the play. *The Bishop of Ely prompts Henry to invade France*

Exploitation - … He hath eaten me out of house and home.
"…He hath eaten me out of house and home; he hath put all my substance into that fat belly of his" (KHIV.p2.2.1)
In the play. *Mistress Quickly complains about Falstaff's abuse.*

Exposition, clear e. - your exposition hath been most sound.
"You know the law, your exposition Hath been most sound" (MOV.4.1)
In the play. *Shylock is convinced that Portia (disguised as an attorney) will uphold his rights to Antonio's pound of flesh.*

Exposure, e. of face - … we will draw the curtain and show you the picture…
"… We will draw the curtain and show you the picture…" (TN.1.5)
Turn the statement into a well-meant injunction equally applicable to other garments than a veil.
In the play. *Olivia, upon request by Viola/Cesario shows her face, previously hidden behind a veil.*

Expression of sadness misconstrued - My heart is ten times lighter than my looks.
RICHARD III. My Lord of Surrey, why look you so sad?
SURREY. My heart is ten times lighter than my looks. (RIII.5.3)
Sometimes your expression does not accord with your feelings. Answer to 'Why do you look so sad?' or equivalent, if and when you do not want to give the impression that indeed you are sad. See also 'Depression, state of d.' – 'Look, appearance, worried l.'
In the play. *Richard III polls his generals' mood at Bosworth Field before the final battle.*

Expression of sadness unsuitable for a p. - … put off these frowns, and ill-beseeming semblance for a feast.
"Show a fair presence and put off these frowns,

And ill-beseeming semblance for a feast" (RJ.1.5)
In the play. *Capulet Senior tells Tybalt to put off his anger against the presence of Romeo and friends at the Capulet's party.*

Expression, come on relax - ... unknit that threatening unkind brow.
"... unknit that threatening unkind brow
And dart not scornful glances from those eyes..." (TOS.5.2)
When your girlfriend appears angry. See also 'Cheer up – clear cloudy countenance'.
In the play. *The totally transformed Katharina prompts Bianca and Widow to listen to advice on how to be or become a good, obedient wife. It is a triumph of male chauvinistic principles, though with some grains of truth. For a complete listing of the traits of an ideal wife see 'Husband, declaration of husband's rights - Such duty as the subject owes the prince even such a woman oweth to her husband.'*

Expression, change in e. denoting loss of favor - ... see already how he doth begin to make us strangers to his looks of love.
"And see already how he doth begin
To make us strangers to his looks of love." (KHIV.p1.1.3)
You can signify directly to the party involved that you noticed the change. E.G. 'I see how you begin to make us strangers to your looks of love'. Or you can tell your girlfriend that you noticed her cooling off. See also entries for 'Cooling off observed'.
In the play. *Worcester comments on the mood of Henry IV.*

Expression, change in e. giving away evidence of misdeeds – I'll observe his looks; I'll tent him to the quick: if he but blench...
"...I'll observe his looks;
I'll tent him to the quick: if he but blench,
I know my course." (H.2.2)
In the play. *Hamlet plans to produce the show that replicates the murder scene as described by the Ghost, Hamlet's father. 'To tent'='To probe' (here to probe the King's conscience). Tent was a piece of lint or linen used to open and clean a wound. 'To blench'='To shrink or to startle'*

Expression, e. indicating an offense received - You throw a strange regard upon me, and by that I do perceive it hath offended you.
"You throw a strange regard upon me, and by that
I do perceive it hath offended you:" (TN.5.1)
In the play. *Sebastian is puzzled by Olivia's look, puzzlement justified by the effect of mistaken identities.*

Expression, e. indicating bad n. – ... this man's brow, like to a title-leaf foretells the nature of a tragic volume.
"Yea, this man's brow, like to a title-leaf,
Foretells the nature of a tragic volume" (KHIV.p2.1.1)
In the play. *Northumberland observes the expression of Morton who returns from Shrewsbury where the rebels have lost their battle.*

Expression, e. indicating concealment - ... didst contract and purse thy brow together, as if thou then hadst shut up in thy brain some horrible conceit.
"... Didst contract and purse thy brow together,
As if thou then hadst shut up in thy brain
Some horrible conceit" (OTH.3.3)
Try 'Why did you contract and purse your brow together, as if…conceit?' and throw adversary off guard by anticipating his thought.

In the play. *Othello remarks on Iago's expression. Iago aims at raising Othello's suspicions on the infidelity of Desdemona.*

Expression, e. indicating troubled conscience - The colour of the king doth come and go between his purpose and his conscience…
"The colour of the king doth come and go
Between his purpose and his conscience,
Like heralds 'twixt two dreadful battles set:
His passion is so ripe, it needs must break." (KJ.4.2)
In the play. *Lord Salisbury observes the expression of King John as he debates the pros and cons of having young Prince Arthur murdered.*

Expression, e. indicating urgency - How now, good Blunt? thy looks are full of speed.
"How now, good Blunt? thy looks are full of speed." (KHIVp1.3.2)
In the play. *Blunt arrives at court to announce the advancing of the rebels, led by Hotspur*

Expression, e. portending the witnessing of extraordinary events - … So should he look that seems to speak things strange.
"What a haste looks through his eyes! So should he look
That seems to speak things strange" (M.1.2)
In the play. *Lennox comments on the expression of the incoming Thane of Ross.*

Expression, facial e. articulating its meaning - …to speak that in words which his eye hath disclosed, I only have made a mouth of his eye…
"… to speak that in words which his eye hath disclosed.
I only have made a mouth of his eye,
By adding a tongue which I know will not lie." (LLL.2.1)
Convey the idea that the expression you observed was unmistakable.
In the play. *Boyet reports to the Princess of France evidence of the King's admiration for her.*

Expression, facial e. clearly supporting the suspicion of bad news – hath by instinct knowledge from others' eyes.
"See what a ready tongue suspicion hath!
He that but fears the thing he would not know
Hath by instinct knowledge from others' eyes
That what he fear'd is chanced" (KHIV.p2.1.1)
See also entries for 'News, bad n. inferred by the look of the messenger'.
In the play. *The rebel Morton arrives from Shrewsbury announcing the defeat of the rebels. He hesitates to tell Northumberland that Harry Percy, his son, was killed in the battle. Northumberland guesses the news from Morton's expression.*

Expression, facial e. indicating anger - He knits his brow and shows an angry eye…
"He knits his brow and shows an angry eye,
And passeth by with stiff unbowed knee,
Disdaining duty that to us belongs." (KHVI p2.3.1)
Use the first line to diffuse and soften the perceived anger or resentment at something you said.
In the play. *Q. Margaret to Henry VI referring to Gloucester whom unjustly she aims to do in.*

Expression, facial e. indicating anger - Here comes the queen, whose looks bewray her anger
"Here comes the queen, whose looks bewray her anger:
I'll steal away." (KHVI p3.1.1)
In the play. *Feisty Queen Margaret arrives at the meeting between the opposing factions of Lancastrians and Yorkists and Exeter decides to leave. 'To bewray' = 'to discover, to be evidence of'.*

Expression, facial e. indicating anger - ... The angry spot doth glow on Caesar's brow.
"…But, look you, Cassius,
The angry spot doth glow on Caesar's brow" (JC.1.2)
Mildly ironic way to soften a friend's restrained anger.
In the play. *Caesar senses that Cassius is a dangerous man and Brutus notices the frown on Caesar's face. Caesar then makes an interesting statement (to Antony) about the dangers of people who think (i.e. Cassius). See 'Fat, f. men less dangerous than thin – a lean and hungry look.'*

Expression, facial e. indicating discontent, why? See 'Mood, why are you in a bad mood? - ... what's the matter that you have such a February face…'

Expression, facial e. indicating positive traits – ... in thy face I see the map of honour, truth and loyalty.
"Ah, uncle Humphrey! in thy face I see
The map of honour, truth and loyalty" (KHVI p2.3.1)
In the play. *Henry VI is distraught at the arrest and trial of Gloucester whom he, the King was not strong enough to avoid.*

Expression, facial e. indicating positive traits - ... There is written in your brow, provost, honesty and constancy…
"...There is written in your brow, provost, honesty and constancy: if I read it not truly, my ancient skill beguiles me" (MFM.4.2)
In the play. *The Duke enlists the Provost into a scheme to undo the machinations and the hypocrisy of Angelo.*

Expression, facial e. indicating sadness, why? - Why are thine eyes fixed to the sullen earth, gazing on that which seems to dim thy sight?
"Why are thine eyes fixed to the sullen earth,
Gazing on that which seems to dim thy sight?" (KHVI p2.1.2)
Inquire on reasons for sadness.
In the play. *The Duchess of Gloucester (Eleanor) to her husband.*

Expression, facial e. indicating sadness, why? – Why droops my lord, like over-ripened corn…
"Why droops my lord, like over-ripened corn,
Hanging the head at Ceres' plenteous load?" (KHVI p2.1.2)
Inquire on reasons for sadness. Modify, 'Why droop you like over-ripened corn… load?'
In the play. *The Duchess of Gloucester to her husband*

Expression, facial e. indicating tyranny – Upon thy eye-balls murderous tyranny sits in grim majesty, to fright the world.
"Upon thy eye-balls murderous tyranny
Sits in grim majesty, to fright the world" (KHVI.p2.3.2)
In the play. *Henry VI to the Duke of Suffolk who killed Henry's protector Humphrey of Gloucester and who will be banned from court and killed by pirates.*

Expression, facial e. knitting of brows – ... knit his brows, as frowning at the favours of the world?
"Why doth the great Duke Humphrey knit his brows,
As frowning at the favours of the world?" (KHVI.p2.1.2)
In the play. *The Duchess of Gloucester queries her husband, the Lord Protector*

Expression, facial e. misinterpreted - Interpretation will misquote our looks.
"Look how we can, or sad or merrily, Interpretation will misquote our looks,
And we shall feed like oxen at a stall, The better cherish'd, still the nearer death" (KHIV.p1.5.2)
In the play. *The Earl of Worcester does not trust the offer of peace by the King. Once suspected of treason that suspicion will continue on any small cause.*

Expression, facial e. of unhappiness detected - I see your brows are full of discontent...
"I see your brows are full of discontent,
Your hearts of sorrow and your eyes of tears" (KRII.4.1)
In the play. *Abbot, faithful to the deposed King Richard II confers with other lords of the same faction, unhappy at the turn of events.*

Expression, facial e. unfriendly - ... the tartness of his face sours ripe grapes.
"...The tartness of his face sours ripe grapes" (COR.5.4)
Describe a sour character. See 'Man, m. causing heartburn at sight - ... I never can see him, but I am heart burned an hour after.'
In the play. *On returning to Rome Menenius reports to his senator colleagues that Coriolanus' sour mood cannot be changed.*

Expression, frowning to be expected - Prepare thy brow to frown.
"Prepare thy brow to frown." (COR.4.5)
Answer to "What is your name?" when meeting a competitor or former enemy. Or use when you expect an unfavorable reaction to what you have to say.
In the play. *Aufidius has not yet recognized Coriolanus. Coriolanus prepares and warns him.*

Expression, invitation to a more cheerful e. - Clear up, fair queen, that cloudy countenance.
"Clear up, fair queen, that cloudy countenance" (TA.1.1)
Change 'queen' to the name of the person whose countenance you are inviting to clear up.
In the play. *Saturninus addresses Tamora, the captured queen of the Goths. He likes her and will end up marrying her.*

Expression, perplexed and amazed e. detected at seeing your attire - ... wherefore gaze this goodly company as if they saw some wondrous monument...
"...wherefore gaze this goodly company,
As if they saw some wondrous monument,
Some comet or unusual prodigy?" (TOS.3.2)
Comment in the way of a question, when you detect an expression of amazement in your audience.
In the play. *Petruchio shows up in a very strange attire at his wedding to Katharina and comments on the startled expression of the audience.*

Expression, power of e. tremendous– ... these brows of mine, whose smile and frown...able with the change to kill and cure.
"...these brows of mine,
Whose smile and frown, like to

Achilles' spear,
Is able with the change to kill and cure." (KHVI.p2.5.1)
In the play. *Rebellious York defies and insults King Henry.*

**Expression, sour facial e. habitual when seeing a (figurative) crab - ... you must not look so sour ... It is my fashion when I see a crab.
PETRUCHIO. Nay, come Kate, you must not look so sour.
KATHARINA. It is my fashion when I see a crab.** (TOS.2.1)
Answer to impolite question of the type, 'why do you look so sad, or upset or serious?'
In the play. *Petruchio makes a valiant attempt to subdue Katharina with pleasant words and compliments. So far the success is marginal.*

**Expression, sour look - Why look you still so stern and tragical?
"Why look you still so stern and tragical? "** (KHVI.p1.3.1)
Question party as applicable.
In the play. *Warwick questions Winchester. Gloucester has taken the initiative to make peace (with Winchester).*

**Expression, telling e. – ...I saw his heart in his face.
"I do believe thee;
I saw his heart in his face."** (WT.1.2)
Use as a concise statement of the truth of physiognomy.
In the play. *Polixenes believes Camillo's report on Leonte's newly acquired hatred of Polixenes, as shown in his face.*

**Expression, why so serious, what are you thinking about? - ... What serious contemplation are you in?
"How now brother Edmund! What serious contemplation are you in?"** (KL.1.2)
Observing a colleague in deep meditation. Substitute as appropriate, for example, How now Jones, what serious contemplation are you in?
In the play. *Edmund is laying a trap for his brother Edgar but Edgar does not know it.*

**Expression, why so solemn an e.? - Why do you bend such solemn brows on me?...
"Why do you bend such solemn brows on me?
Think you I bear the shears of destiny?
Have I commandment on the pulse of life?"** (KJ.4.2)
'I do not bear the shears of destiny' is a good expression to convey that you could not affect the turn of events.
In the play. *King John to Pembroke who hints very clearly that King John actually killed Arthur – King John wants to pretend he is not guilty.*

**Expression, wild e. observed - Forth at your eyes your spirits wildly peep.
"Forth at your eyes your spirits wildly peep"** (H.3.4)
In the play. *The Queen cannot see the Ghost who speaks to Hamlet. Therefore Hamlet appears as looking into a void and talking to the air.*

**Eyebrows, aesthetic considerations – ... black brows, they say, become some women best...
"...black brows, they say,
Become some women best, so that there be not
Too much hair there, but in a semicircle
Or a half-moon made with a pen."** (WT.2.1)
In the play. *Mamillius, Leonte's son banters with the ladies in waiting to Hermione, Leonte's wife.*

Eyelids - ...behold her eyelids, cases to those heavenly jewels.

"… behold,
Her eyelids, cases to those heavenly jewels." (PER.3.2)
Change to 'your eyelids… jewels'.
In the play: *Doctor Cerimon has just revived Queen Thaisa who was shipwrecked and feared drown.*

Eyes and voice together - Your eyes are lodestars; and your tongue's sweet air more tunable than lark to shepherd's ear.
"Your eyes are lodestars; and your tongue's sweet air
More tunable than lark to shepherd's ear,
When wheat is green, when hawthorn buds appear." (MND.1.1)
Flatter and praise.
In the play. *Helena loves Demetrius but Demetrius likes Hermia better. Helena acknowledges the beauty that causes Demetrius' passion.*

Eyes that partake of the miraculous - … in her eye I find a wonder, or a wondrous miracle.
"… In her eye I find
A wonder, or a wondrous miracle." (KJ.2.1)
Change to "In your eye I find a wonder, or a wondrous miracle."
In the play: *The Dauphin Lewis is mesmerized by the beauty of Blanch's eyes.*

Eyes with the sparkle of diamonds - I see how thine eye would emulate the diamond: thou hast the right arched beauty of the brow.
"I see how thine eye would emulate the diamond: thou hast the right arched beauty of the brow." (MWW.3.3)
Change 'thine' to 'your' and 'thou hast' to 'you have'. Compliment, eyes as sparkling as diamonds.
In the play. *Falstaff woos Mrs. Ford.*

Eyes, beauty of e. and eyelids – Her eyelids, cases to those heavenly jewels…
"Her eyelids, cases to those heavenly jewels
…
Begin to part their fringes of bright gold;
The diamonds of a most praised water
Do appear, to make the world twice rich" (PER.3.2)
In the play. *Cerimon, a famous doctor brings Queen Thaisa back to life by applying miraculous remedies.*

Eyes, beauty of e. to be written about - If I could write the beauty of your eyes, and in fresh numbers number all your graces…
"If I could write the beauty of your eyes,
And in fresh numbers number all your graces,
The age to come would say this poet lies,
Such heavenly touches never touched earthly faces." (SON.17)
Beauty beyond written description - eyes to be written about, unbelievably beautiful.

Eyes, e. and cheeks - The lustre in your eye, heaven in your cheek, pleads your fair usage.
"The lustre in your eye, heaven in your cheek,
Pleads your fair usage" (TC.4.4)
Compliment
In the play. *Diomedes greets Cressida in Troy.*

Eyes, e. as a source of knowledge - Not from the stars do I my judgment pluck, and yet methinks I have astronomy…
"Not from the stars do I my judgment pluck,
And yet methinks I have astronomy…

But from thine eyes my knowledge I derive." (SON.14)
Compliment. Her eyes are a source of inspiration better than any knowledge derived from astronomy, astrology or any other science.
Archdeacon Ruiz starting from very similar premises reaches quite different conclusions. 'I do not know much about astrology, nor I know the astrolabe very little just as I know how to distinguish an ox from its harness. (Note: the astrolabe is a very ancient astronomical mechanical device and computer for solving problems relating to time and the position of the Sun and stars in the sky). But I have seen and verified that many are born under the sign of Venus, therefore they spend most of their life chasing women. They never forget their star-conditioned life mission and continuously trouble themselves about it. Yet the majority never reaches their goal. I myself think that I was born under this sign because I have consistently gone after women. I never disliked the good they did to me, I courted many but never got exactly what I wanted.' (Libro de Bueno Amor #152).

Eyes, e. as instruments of persuasion - Did not the heavenly rhetoric of thine eye, 'gainst whom the world cannot hold argument…
"Did not the heavenly rhetoric of thine eye,
'Gainst whom the world cannot hold argument,
Persuade my heart to this false perjury?" (LLL.4.2)
Reinforcing sentence to prove that she has persuaded you on whatever she wished to persuade you to. 'The heavenly rhetoric of thine eye' can stand alone as a compliment.
In the play. *Longaville reads a message that reveals how he himself (persuaded by the lady's eyes) broke the vow of abstinence made with king and friends at the beginning of the play.*

Eyes, e. as painters of her beauty - Mine eye hath play'd the painter and drawn thy beauty's form in table of my heart…
Mine eye hath play'd the painter and drawn
Thy beauty's form in table of my heart …
Mine eyes have drawn thy shape, and thine for me
Are windows to my breast, where-through the sun
Delights to peep, to gaze therein on thee" (SON 24)

Eyes, e. as spies – If these be true spies which I wear in my head, here's a goodly sight.
"If these be true spies which I wear in my head, here's a goodly sight." (TEM.5.1)
In the play. *The spirit Ariel drives Trinculo, Caliban and Stephano to the place where all the other displaced crowd is assembled.*

Eyes, e. as teachers - For where is any author in the world teaches such beauty as a woman's eye?
"For where is any author in the world Teaches such beauty as a woman's eye?" (LLL.4.1)
Give philosophical and intellectual reasons to explain why you like women.
In the play. *Having by now given up on all pretence of study and abstinence Biron gives one explanation of his philosophy, equally shared, no doubt, by his friends.*

Eyes, e. emitting bright light - … her eye in heaven would through the airy region stream so bright, that birds would sing, and think it were not night.
"…her eye in heaven

Would through the airy region stream so bright,
That birds would sing, and think it were not night." (RJ.2.2)
Change 'her' to 'your' when delivering the compliment.
In the play. *Romeo has sneaked into Juliet's garden and she just appeared at her window.*

Eyes, e. like stars – Two of the fairest stars in all the heaven, having some business, do entreat her eyes to twinkle in their spheres till they return.
"Two of the fairest stars in all the heaven,
Having some business, do entreat her eyes
To twinkle in their spheres till they return." (RJ.2.1)
Change 'her eyes' to 'your eyes' for a direct compliment
In the play. *Unseen and in her orchard, Romeo observes Juliet who has appeared at her window.*

Eyes, e. like stars – What stars do spangle heaven with such beauty as those two eyes become that heavenly face?
"What stars do spangle heaven with such beauty,
As those two eyes become that heavenly face? (TOS.4.5)
Compliment in question form, eyes like stars. Change 'become that heavenly face' to 'become your heavenly face'
In the play. *Petruchio has so tamed Katharina that she is ready to agree to anything Petruchio says, even (in this case) to the point of believing that the just arrived Vincentio is a woman (to whom the quoted statement applies).*

Eyes, e. made red by pain and rage - ... With eyes as red as new-enkindled fire.

"I met Lord Bigot and Lord Salisbury,
With eyes as red as new-enkindled fire" (KJ.4.2)
In the play. *Faulconbridge reporting to King John. The lords' eyes are red due to pain and anger at seeing the body of the murdered young Prince Arthur.*

Eyes, e. of a man compared to the e. of an eagle – ... an eagle, madam hath not so green, so quick, so fair an eye as Paris hath.
"Romeo's a dishclout to him: an eagle, madam,
Hath not so green, so quick, so fair an eye
As Paris hath" (RJ.3.5)
In the play. *The Nurse attempts to convince Juliet that Paris is a better party than Romeo. 'Dishclout'='Dishcloth'.*

Eyes, e. on lookout for the ladies - My eyes, my lord, can look as swift as yours...
"My eyes, my lord, can look as swift as yours:
You saw the mistress, I beheld the maid" (MOV.3.1)
In the play. *Gratiano, who accompanied Bassanio in his quest for Portia, falls in love with Portia's maid Nerissa.*

Eyes, her e. and lids - ... the enclosed lights, now canopied under these windows, white and azure laced with blue of heaven's own tinct.
"...To see the enclosed lights, now canopied
Under these windows, white and azure laced
With blue of heaven's own tinct." (CYM.2.2)
Compliment. When her eyes are closed but she is not yet asleep...Start with '...those enclosed eyes...own tinct.'
In the play. *The perfidious Iachimo observes Cymbeline who is fast asleep and cannot but be impressed by her beauty.*

Eyes, her e. as windows to your breast - Mine eyes have drawn thy shape, and thine for me are windows to my breast…
"Mine eyes have drawn thy shape, and thine for me
Are windows to my breast, wherethrough the sun
Delights to peep, to gaze therein on thee" (SON 24)

Eyes, her e. weapons of mass destruction - … there lies more peril in thine eye, than twenty of their swords.
JULIET. If they do see thee, they will murder thee.
ROMEO. Alack! there lies more peril in thine eye,
Than twenty of their swords (of the Capulets) - (RJ.2.2)
Lay it thick. Introduce this in the way of a comparison, to praise her eyes, e.g. 'There lies more peril in thine eye than twenty of the Capulets' swords'. Or 'There lies more peril in thine eye than twenty swords'. See also comment to 'Insult, lips – thy lips to rot off.'
In the play. *Defying danger (he is a Montague, she is a Capulet and the Capulets hate the Montagues), Romeo manages to sneak up to Juliet and court her.*

Eyes, incomparably beautiful, shinier than crystal - To what, my love shall I compare thine eye? Crystal is muddy.
"Helena, goddess, nymph, perfect, divine!
To what, my love shall I compare thine eye? Crystal is muddy." (MND.3.2)
Compliment, incomparably beautiful eyes clearer than crystal. Change 'Helena' to the name of the addressed lady.
In the play. *Demetrius awakes and erupts in loving words of praise of Helena.*

Eyes, ladies e. as a source of philosophical learning - From women's eyes this doctrine I derive…
"From women's eyes this doctrine I derive;
They are the ground, the books, the academes
From whence doth spring the true Promethean fire." (LLL.4.3)
Give philosophical and intellectual reasons to explain why you like women.
In the play. *Having by now given up on all pretence of study and abstinence, Biron gives one explanation of his philosophy, equally shared, no doubt, by his friends.*

Eyes, open e. but unable to see - You see, her eyes are open. Ay, but their sense is shut.
Doctor: You see, her eyes are open
Gentlewoman: Ay, but their sense is shut." (M.5.1)
Negative comment on a bungler, 'His eyes are open but their sense is shut'.
In the play. *The patient is Lady Macbeth who has gone insane.*

Eyes, sun interfering with good vision - … my mistaking eyes that have been so bedazzled with the sun.
"…my mistaking eyes,
That have been so bedazzled with the sun" (TOS.4.5)
In the play. *Katharina is put to the test by Petruchio and is ready to agree with him on anything – here that a man was a woman and then a man when Petruchio changed his mind about it.*

Eyes, their rejuvenating power – … might shake off fifty, looking in her eyes.
"A withered hermit, five score winters worn,
Might shake off fifty, looking in her eyes." (LLL.4.3)
Change 'her' to your' and lay it on thick.

In the play. *Biron in love sings the praises of Rosaline.*

Face shown or visible after she removes her mask, or a hat or anything which partially or completely hides her face - Fair ladies mask'd are roses in their bud...
"Fair ladies mask'd are roses in their bud;
Dismask'd, their damask sweet commixture shown,
Are angels vailing clouds, or roses blown." (LLL.5.2)
You can substitute 'trailing' for 'vailing' without altering the sense of the quote.
In the play. *Boyet in a dialog with the Princess. Admirers of Princess showed up in masks at first. The ladies were wearing masks too. In a second round of this caper Boyet suggests that the ladies remove their masks.*

Face, beautiful beyond wonder - Her face was to mine eye beyond all wonder.
"Her face was to mine eye beyond all wonder." (PER.1.2)
Change to 'Your face is to mine eye beyond all wonder'. Answer to 'Do you like me?'
In the play. *On his return from Antioch, King Pericles explains to Helicanus the ordeal he (Pericles) went through. The 'face beyond all wonder' belonged to the daughter of the king of Antioch, Antiochus. She was indeed beautiful but wicked and tied by incest to her father.*

Face, brighter than the moon - Nor shines the silver moon one half so bright...as doth thy face through tears of mine give light.
"Nor shines the silver moon one half so bright
Through the transparent bosom of the deep,
As doth thy face through tears of mine give light." (LLL.4.3)

In the play. *Ferdinand reads from a letter he has prepared for the princess of France.*

Face, expression., beauty, imitating Nature - 'T is beauty truly blent, whose red and white, nature's own sweet and cunning hand laid on.
"'T is beauty truly blent, whose red and white
Nature's own sweet and cunning hand laid on." (TN.1.5)
Laying it thick.
In the play. *Olivia pulls off a veil from her face and Cesario/Viola, who came to deliver a love message on behalf of Count Orsino comments on Olivia's beauty.*

Face, f. saving - How well this yielding rescues thee from shame!
"How well this yielding rescues thee from shame!" (LLL.1.1)
When a person has corrected himself or has taken the action that you think proper.
In the play. *Notwithstanding some initial reluctance, Biron agrees to the proposed time of learning with king and associates. The king approves and comments*

Face, heavenly f. as a cause of various acts, desperate or otherwise - ... 'twas thy heavenly face that set me on.
"...But 'twas thy heavenly face that set me on." (KRIII.1.2)
Answer to 'Why did you do this?' 'It was your heavenly face that set me on'.
In the play. *Wooing Lady Anne, Richard claims that his infatuation for her beauty drove him to kill her husband.*

Face, relative value of a f. - Your face hath got five hundred pound a year yet sell your face for five pence and 'tis dear.
"Brother, take you my land, I'll take my chance.
Your face hath got five hundred pound a year,

Yet sell your face for five pence and 'tis dear." (KJ.1.1)
In the play. *Philip Faulconbridge addresses his half-brother of Robert Faulconbridge, the legitimate son.*

Face, sweet expression - Thou hast the sweetest face I ever look'd on.
"Thou hast the sweetest face I ever look'd on." (KHVIII.4.1)
In the play. *A gentleman in attendance pays a gallant compliment to Anne Boleyn, now queen. He goes on to say,*
"Sir, as I have a soul, she is an angel;
Our king has all the Indies in his arms,
And more and richer."
from which you can extract a line for 'thank you', i.e. 'As I have a soul, you are an angel'.

Fact, a common f. - …is as common as any the most vulgar thing to sense.
"For what we know must be and is as common
As any the most vulgar thing to sense,
Why should we in our peevish opposition
Take it to heart?" (H.1.2)
See also entries for 'Destiny, accepting the inevitability of d.'
In the play. *King Claudius craftily tries to lift Hamlet's spirits (believed to be depressed by the death of his father), by stating that mortality is common.*

Fact, just repeating a well known f. - I speak no more than everyone doth know.
I speak no more than everyone doth know." (KRII.3.4)
Answer to 'How can you say this?'
In the play. *A gardener tells the queen that her husband Richard is in the hands of Bolingbroke. The Queen is so upset as to cast a micro-curse,*
Gardener, for telling me these news of woe,
Pray God the plants thou graft'st may never grow.

Facts, knowledge of f. by audience implied - I tell you that which you yourselves do know.
"I tell you that which you yourselves do know" (JC.3.2)
Add a modest touch to your presentation, particularly if you know that the audience does NOT know the content of what you are going to say next.
In the play. *One of Antony's masterly rhetorical touches in his speech all designed to inflame the crowds against Brutus and accomplices. See 'Oratory, lack of o. claimed - … I have neither wit, nor words, nor worth..'*

Failure, dealing with fear of f. - … screw your courage to the sticking-place and we'll not fail.
MACBETH If we should fail?
LADY MACBETH We fail!
But screw your courage to the sticking-place,
And we'll not fail." (M.1.7)
Exhortation to be bold.
In the play. *Lady Macbeth rebuts her husband's fear of failure.*

Fair play - … and I would call it, fair play
"Yes, for a score of kingdoms you should wrangle,
And I would call it, fair play." (TEM.5.1)
Common aphorism.
In the play. *Ferdinand and Miranda exchange some banter while playing chess.*

Faith, broken f. causing rebellion – … unkind usage, dangerous countenance and violation of all faith and troth…
"… we stand opposed by such means
As you yourself have forged against yourself
By unkind usage, dangerous countenance,

And violation of all faith and troth
Sworn to us in your younger
enterprise" (KHIVp1.5.1)
In the play. *Worcester explains to King Henry the reason for the rebellion.*

Faithfulness, faithful after saying yes -
… they are constant being won: they are burs, I can tell you; they'll stick where they are thrown.
"…our kindred, though they be long ere they are wooed, they are constant being won: they are burs, I can tell you; they'll stick where they are thrown." (TC.3.2)
Reassurance that once you have said yes you will stick with it as part of a genetic trait.
In the play. *Pandarus to Troilus referring to his niece Cressida*

Faithfulness, f. restated - While others fish with craft for great opinion, I with great truth catch more simplicity…
CRESSIDA. My lord, will you be true?
TROILUS. Alas, it is my vice, my fault:
While others fish with craft for great opinion,
I with great truth catch more simplicity;
Whilst some with cunning gild their copper crowns,
With truth and plainness I do wear mine bare. (TC.4.4)
Answer to 'Will you be true?' Or as an answer to the question, 'What is your strength?', 'Truth, it is my vice, my fault…bare'. Of course the quote applies only if you determine that truth is appreciated, often it is not. See also "Love, l. preferred over power - He after honour hunts, I after love…'
In the play. *Troilus reasserts that he will be faithful to Cressida.*

Faithlessness - better have none than plural faith which is too much by one.
"Thou hast no faith left now, unless thou'dst two;
And that's far worse than none; better have none
Than plural faith which is too much by one" (TGV.5.4)
Extract 'better have none than plural faith' and apply to wholesale flatterers.
In the play. *Silvia, chased and attacked by Proteus upbraids him for his faithlessness to Julia, that is his double-faith.*

Fall, f. from greatness - Take but good note, and you shall see in him…
"Take but good note, and you shall see in him.
The triple pillar of the world transform'd
Into a strumpet's fool:" (AC.1.1)
See also 'Lust, intemperance leading to disaster - Boundless intemperance in nature is a tyranny…'
In the play. *Philo in Alexandria points Antony to Demetrius' attention.*

Fall from greatness described – … then was I as a tree whose boughs did bend with fruit: but in one night…
"…then was I as a tree
Whose boughs did bend with fruit: but in one night,
A storm or robbery, call it what you will,
Shook down my mellow hangings, nay, my leaves,
And left me bare to weather." (CYM.3.3)
In the play. *Belarius gives a biographical account to his (adopted sons) and describes his fall from grace with King Cymbeline. In comparison, he praises the advantages of country life, see 'Life, l. inside a corporation or the Washington belt – … the art of the court as hard to leave as keep…'*

Fall from greatness painful, better not have pomp to begin with – … 'tis a sufferance panging as soul and body's severing.
"O, God's will! much better
She ne'er had known pomp: though't be temporal,
Yet, if that quarrel, fortune, do divorce
It from the bearer, 'tis a sufferance panging
As soul and body's severing" (KHVIII.2.3)
See also 'Greatness, advantages of g. questionable – … 'tis better to be lowly born and range with humble livers in content…'
In the play. *Anne Boleyn to a lady in waiting. They are referring to Queen Catherine whom Henry VIII is divorcing. This is before Henry proposes to Anne. 'Panging'= 'To torment', 'to afflict with great pain'.*

Fall from greatness, meditation on f. from greatness – … And when you would say something that is sad, speak how I fell.
"…Farewell:
And when you would say something that is sad,
Speak how I fell." (KHVIII.2.1)
In the play. *Buckingham, condemned to death for treason, addresses his enemies Lovell and Vaux.*

Fall from greatness and general reaction - 'Tis certain, greatness, once fall'n out with fortune must fall out with men too…
'What, am I poor of late?
'Tis certain, greatness, once fall'n out with fortune,
Must fall out with men too: what the declined is
He shall as soon read in the eyes of others
As feel in his own fall; for men, like butterflies….
Show not their mealy wings" (TC.3.3)
In the play. *Achilles comments on an observation by Patroclus, that the other Greeks do not seem to show their respect (to Achilles) as they used to.*

Fall, f. from greatness sudden - … then in a moment, see how soon this mightiness meets misery.
"The very persons of our noble story
As they were living; think you see them great,
And follow'd with the general throng and sweat
Of thousand friends; then in a moment, see
How soon this mightiness meets misery" (KHVIII.PRO)
Use for an introduction to a related, topic presentation. See also 'Time, t. and the inherent limited duration of everything - When I consider everything that grows holds in perfection but a little moment…'
In the play. *The Chorus introduces the play.*

Fall, season - … the year growing ancient, not yet on summer's death, nor on the birth of trembling winter.
" Sir, the year growing ancient,
Not yet on summer's death, nor on the birth
Of trembling winter" (WT.4.4)
In the play. *Polixenes, king of Bohemia and friend Camillo visit the humble home of a shepherd and of his adopted daughter Perdita. Perdita responds to a comment by Polixenes on flowers presented to him by her.*

Fall, season - That time of year thou mayst in me behold…
That time of year thou mayst in me behold
When yellow leaves, or none, or few, do hang
Upon those boughs which shake against the cold,
Bare ruin'd choirs, where late the sweet birds sang.
In me thou seest the twilight of such

day
As after sunset fadeth in the west,
Which by and by black night doth take away,
Death's second self, that seals up all in rest.
In me thou see'st the glowing of such fire
That on the ashes of his youth doth lie,
As the death-bed whereon it must expire
Consumed with that which it was nourish'd by.
This thou perceivest, which makes thy love more strong,
To love that well which thou must leave ere long. (SON 73)
When you wish to convey a melancholy tone to your relationship. Also answer to 'How old are you'. See entries for 'Age'.

False claim, claiming a non existent achievement or feat - ... the knave bragged of that he could not compass.
"…may be the knave bragged of that he could not compass." (MWW.3.3)
Applies especially well to politician's promises. See also 'Politicians' promises, wine for all'
In the play. *Mr. Ford cannot locate Falstaff who should have come to Mr. Ford's house for a rendez-vous with Mrs. Ford.*

False, as f. as - ... As false as dicers' oaths.
"Such an act
… makes marriage-vows
As false as dicers' oaths" (H.3.4)
See also 'Man, m. false - … falser than vows made in wine'
In the play. *Hamlet upbraids his mother for having married Claudius soon after Hamlet's father died.*

Falsehood, f. of the powerful. stronger than truth of the poor - ... Say what you can, my false o'erweighs your true.
"… As for you,
Say what you can, my false o'erweighs your true." (MFM.2.4)
An example of how those in power can escape responsibility by denial.
In the play. *The hypocrite Angelo believes that no one will believe Isabel when she will accuse him of sexual harassment.*

Falsehood, f. worse in higher ups than common people - ... and falsehood is worse in kings than beggars.
"…no wonder,
When rich ones scarce tell true. To lapse in fulness
Is sorer than to lie for need, and falsehood
Is worse in kings than beggars" (CYM.3.6)
In the play. *Imogen asked some beggars for road instructions and thinks that the instructions were incorrect.*

Fame, f. and achievements - Great is the rumor of this dreadful knight and his achievements of no less account.
"Great is the rumor of this dreadful knight,
And his achievements of no less account" (KHVI.p1.2.3)
Could be part of a friendly ironic introduction. E.G. 'Of the next speaker I could say, 'Great…account' and here he is'.
In the play. *The Countess of Auvergne has invited Lord Talbot to her castle hoping to entrap him.*

Fame, f. defeating death and time - … And make us heirs of all eternity.
"Let fame, that all hunt after in their lives,
Live register'd upon our brazen tombs
And then grace us in the disgrace of death;

When, spite of cormorant devouring Time,
The endeavor of this present breath may buy
That honour which shall bate his scythe's keen edge
And make us heirs of all eternity." (LLL.1.1)
See also 'Writing, fame and immortality through w. - Death makes no conquest of this conqueror for now he lives in fame, though not in life.'
In the play. *King Ferdinand proposes to his friends a course of study whose aim is the acquisition of immortal fame.*

Fame, looking for f. in war - ... to win renown even in the jaws of danger and of death.
"...to win renown
Even in the jaws of danger and of death." (KJ.5.2)
In the play. *The Dauphin Lewis of France is determined to fight the English on their soul notwithstanding the sudden reversal of position of Cardinal Pandulph.*

Fame, no claim to f. – ... our grave, like Turkish mute, shall have a tongueless mouth...
"...our grave,
Like Turkish mute, shall have a tongueless mouth,
Not worshipp'd with a waxen epitaph." (KHV.1.2)
In the play. *Henry V has decided to attack France and gain fame and recognition there or die unsung.*

Farewell, f. - ... farewell, and better than I fare.
"Sheriff farewell, and better than I fare, -
Although thou hast been conduct of my shame!" (KHVI p2.2)
You are leaving for good, not angry but somewhat disappointed, 'Farewell and better than I fare.' You can live the 'sheriff' in when you drive off again after if a policeman has given you a traffic ticket.
In the play. *The Duchess of Gloucester to the sheriff who will take her in exile to the Isle of Man.*

Farewell, f. to beautiful but cruel woman - ... Farewell, fair cruelty.
"... Farewell, fair cruelty." (TN.1.1)
When leaving a girl who has steadfastly said no. See also entries for 'Rejection'.
In the play. *Viola/Cesario's mission was not successful, Olivia continues to refuse the advances of the Duke on whose behalf Viola/Cesario came to plead. Viola/Cesario takes her leave with this salutation.*

Fashion, f. making suits or dresses useless – ... the fashion wears out more apparel than the man
"... the fashion wears out more apparel than the man..." (MAAN. 3.3)
In the play. *Conrade to Borachio. Both have been hired by Don John to slander Hero to spite her and create trouble.*

Fashion, f. or custom setting – ... we are the makers of manners, Kate...
"...we are the makers of manners, Kate; and the liberty that follows our places stops the mouth of all find-faults." (HV.5.2)
When and if she refuses to go along with any of your romantic requests. Change 'Kate' to the appropriate name.
In the play. *Henry V woos Princess Katherine. She refuses to kiss him on the grounds of French customs.*

Fashion, new or ridiculous f. easily adopted – New customs, though they be ever so ridiculous... yet they are followed.
"New customs,
Though they be ever so ridiculous,
Nay, let them be unmanly, yet they are followed." (KHVIII.1.3)

Warn against adopting a procedure or a course of action just because it is new.
In the play. *Lord Sands referring to fashions adopted from France.*

Fasting, f. after dinner – when you fasted it was presently after dinner… "…When you fasted, it was presently after dinner..." (TGV.2.1)
Sarcastic comment on fasting, applicable to yourself or others with suitable change of pronouns.
In the play. *Servant Speed points out to his master Valentine the extraordinary changes in eating habits prompted by Valentine's love for Silvia.*

Fat, being f. as a justification for weakness of character or errors - Thou seest I have more flesh than another man does, and therefore more frailty.
"Thou seest I have more flesh than another man, and therefore more frailty." (KHIV.p1.3.3)
Try this with an officer that pulls you over for a traffic stop or with a judge in a traffic court. See also 'Misbehavior, m. justified – … in the state of innocency Adam fell…'
In the play. *Falstaff finds an excuse for his weaknesses as he is upbraided by the Prince of Wales.*

Fat. f. man and flotation - … you may know by my size that I have a kind of alacrity in sinking.
"… you may know by my size that I have a kind of alacrity in sinking." (MWW.3.5)
In the play. *Falstaff meditating on the events that led him to be thrown into the river.*

Fat, f. man and lust - … till the wicked fire of lust have melted him in his own grease.
"I think the best way were to entertain him with hope, till the wicked fire of lust have melted him in his own grease" (MWW.2.1)
You can change 'lust' to any other vice to stigmatize the subject
In the play. *Mistress Ford plans a trick on Falstaff.*

Fat, f. men less dangerous than thin – … Yond Cassius has a lean and hungry look.
"Let me have men about me that are fat;
Sleek-headed men and such as sleep o' nights:
Yond Cassius has a lean and hungry look;
He thinks too much: such men are dangerous." (JC.1.2)
Use the last two lines to cast an ironic and not unfriendly comment on a colleague, 'Yond (name of colleague) has a lean and…dangerous.'
In the play. *Caesar expresses to Antony his reservations about Cassius.*

Fatalism, fatalistic a. to life – … let determined things to destiny hold unbewail'd their way.
"...let determined things to destiny Hold unbewail'd their way" (AC.3.6)
A statement of your philosophy, it if applies.
In the play. *Octavian to sister Octavia, who, abandoned by husband Antony returns somewhat dejected to Rome.*

Fault, admitting to your fault - I have deserved all tongues to talk their bitterest.
"I have deserved
All tongues to talk their bitterest." (WT.3.2)
The fault was one of mad jealousy, but the admission of guilt can apply to any number of faults or shortcomings, especially if you wish to be somewhat theatrical about it.

In the play. *Finally Leontes, king of Bohemia, recognizes that his jealousy was but folly and says so to Paulina.*

Fault, condemning the f., not the perpetrator – Condemn the fault and not the actor of it.
"Condemn the fault and not the actor of it?" (MFM.2.3)
Use the line without the interrogation mark to plea for leniency.
In the play. *Angelo rejects the Provost's plea to forgive Claudio's sin of fornication.*

Fault, f. from which good results occurred - I cannot wish the fault undone, the issue of it being so proper.
" I cannot wish the fault undone, the issue of it being so proper." (KL.1.1)
Use in any situation where something good came out of what was at first thought bad.
In the play. *Gloucester refers to his extramarital affair and his son Edmund and Kent comments on the 'issue', that is Edmund.*

Fault, one f. obscuring all other virtues - ... the stamp of one defect... shall in the general censure take corruption from that particular fault.
"So, oft it chances in particular men,
That for some vicious mole of nature in them,
As, in their birth--wherein they are not guilty,
Since nature cannot choose his origin--
By the o'ergrowth of some complexion,
Oft breaking down the pales and forts of reason,
Or by some habit that too much o'er-leavens
The form of plausive manners, that these men,
Carrying, I say, the stamp of one defect,
Being nature's livery, or fortune's star,--
Their virtues else--be they as pure as grace,
As infinite as man may undergo--
Shall in the general censure take corruption
From that particular fault" (H.1.4)
See also 'Taint, a fault that obscures other virtues - ... the dram of base doth all the noble substance often dout to his own scandal.'
In the play. *Hamlet explains to Horatio that the heavy drinking of the Danes at their feasts taints their other virtues in the eyes of other people. 'Plausive' = 'Pleasing'.*

Faults, man with many f. – ... he hath faults, with surplus, to tire in repetition.
"…I need not be barren of accusations; he hath faults, with surplus, to tire in repetition" (COR.1.1)
In the play. *Citizens commenting on the character of Coriolanus.*

Faults, f. redeemed by spirit of generosity - ... faults that are rich are fair.
"... faults that are rich are fair" (TOA.1.2)
It applies also to the ability of the rich to get away with their crimes or sins.
In the play. *Timon responds to thanks from Ventidius. See 'Generosity, true g. - there's none can truly say he gives, if he receives...'*

Favor, begging for a f. - ... But if a humble prayer may prevail
"…But if a humble prayer may prevail…" (KHVI.p3.4.6)
In the play. *Henry VI is freed from the Tower and his former guard and keeper asks for forgiveness of Henry.*

Favor, begging for a f. while declaring your total subservience - and if thy poor devoted servant may but beg one favour at thy gracious hand...
"And if thy poor devoted servant may
But beg one favour at thy gracious hand,
Thou dost confirm his happiness forever." (RIII.1.2)
You choose what the favor should be. Use the first two lines to ask any other favor of a lady.
In the play. *Richard III is wooing Anne, whose husband, Clarence he has just killed.*

Favor, f. of the powerful risky – how wretched is that poor man that hangs on princes' favours.
"O, how wretched
Is that poor man that hangs on princes' favours." (KHVIII.3.2)
A warning against relying on the protection by authorities or their help
In the play. *Wolsey meditates on his own fall from the grace of the King.*

Favor, f. of the wicked easily turns to hate - the love of wicked men converts to fear...
"The love of wicked men converts to fear;
That fear to hate, and hate turns one or both
To worthy danger and deserved death." (KRII.5.1)
Why it is dangerous to be accomplices of crimes, even if committed by powerful persons.
In the play. *Deposed King Richard II predicts to Northumberland his downfall – a prediction that will occur in the play King Henry IV p1. The 'love' of the wicked Bolingbroke will turn to hate and Northumberland will fall. Here are the lines that illustrate how crooks often end up hating each other over the division of the spoils obtained by crime*
"thou shalt think,
Though he divide the realm and give thee half,
It is too little, helping him to all;
And he shall think that thou, which know'st the way
To plant unrightful kings, wilt know again,
Being ne'er so little urged, another way
To pluck him headlong from the usurped throne"

Favor, out of f. with lady - ... you are now sailed into the north of my lady's opinion...
"...you are now sailed into the north of my lady's opinion; where you will hang like an icicle on a Dutchman's beard" (TN.3.2)
Asking her 'Have I now sailed into the north of your opinion?' may sooth her displeasure.
In the play. *Fabian tries to encourage Toby Belch to pursue his courtship of Lady Olivia.*

Favor, unable to plead for favors - ... Used to command, untaught to plead for favour.
"Suffolk's imperial tongue is stern and rough,
Used to command, untaught to plead for favour." (KHVI.p2.4.1)
In the play. *Suffolk replies to his enemy Walter Whitmore, who will shortly later cut Suffolk's head.*

Favorite, f. through oratory - ... he hath a witchcraft over the king ...
"...he hath a witchcraft
Over the king in's tongue."
(KHVIII.3.2)
Accompany your acceding to a request with 'You have a witchcraft over me with your tongue'.
In the play. *The Chamberlain, in conversation with Suffolk, refers to Cardinal Wolsey.*

Favorite, crawling into being a f. – ...one hath crawl'd into the favour of the king...

"…one
Hath crawl'd into the favour of the king,
And is his oracle." (KHVIII.3.2)
In the play. *Cardinal Wolsey referring to Cranmer.*

Fed up with comforting efforts - I'll hate him everlastingly that bids me be of comfort any more.
"By heaven, I'll hate him everlastingly
That bids me be of comfort any more." (KRII.3.2)
See also 'Flattery, f. rejected - he does me double wrong that wounds me with the flatteries of his tongue.'
In the play. *Richard II abandoned and dejected refuses to hear any optimistic statement.*

Fear, afraid of not pleasing – … Ever in fear to kindle your dislike
"…Ever in fear to kindle your dislike" (KHVIII.2.4)
In the play. *Queen Katherine makes a strenuous self-defense in the trial that prepares the historical divorce from the King.*

Fear, f. arising poor judgment - … for defect of judgment is oft the sauce of fear.
"…for defect of judgment
Is oft the sauce of fear." (CYM.4.2)
Suggest that fear is unjustified.
In the play. *Belarius and Arviragus are concerned about Guiderius' absence. Guiderius is OK.*

Fear, f. causing treason - When our actions do not our fears do make us traitors.
"….when our actions do not,
Our fears do make us traitors." (M.4.2)
See also 'Doubts, d. as traitors - Our doubts are traitors and make us lose the good we oft might win by fearing to attempt.'

In the play. *Lady Macduff comments on her husband who has left his castle for England leaving it open to attack from Macbeth.*

Fear, f. contemptible and cursed passion - Of all base passions, fear is most accursed.
"Of all base passions, fear is most accursed." (KHVI.p1.5.2)
Imply that you are not afraid.
In the play. *La Pucelle does not fear the advance of the English army in the plains of Anjou.*

Fear, determination to conquer f. - The mind I sway by, and the heart I bear, shall never shake with doubt nor shake with fear.
"The mind I sway by and the heart I bear
Shall never sag with doubt nor shake with fear." (M.5.3)
Conclusion to a presentation of your plan - a plan in which you believe in and want to carry out to the very end.
In the play. *The witches predicted that no man born of a woman will win over Macbeth, but Malcolm was born with a Cesarean delivery. At this moment Macbeth still does not know it.*

Fear, display of f. a stimulus for coward enemies – … coward dogs most spend their mouths when…
"…coward dogs
Most spend their mouths when what they seem to threaten
Runs far before them." (HV.2.4)
In the play. *The Dauphin of France refers to the English who are 'chasing' the French thinking that the French are afraid of them.*

Fear, effects of f. - … distilled almost to jelly with the act of fear.
"… distilled
Almost to jelly with the act of fear." (H.1.2)
Explaining the escape from a fearful situation, or a comment to an idea or a

dangerous proposal, "(I am) distilled almost to jelly with the act of fear".
In the play. *Horatio tells Hamlet how frightened were the guards when the ghost showed up.*

Fear, f. as a corrupting agent – Fears make devils of cherubims; they never see truly.
"Fears make devils of cherubims; they never see truly" (TC.3.2)
Dismiss fears or excessive concerns.
In the play. *Troilus comments on Cressida's observations.*

Fear, f. as a factor in safety – … best safety lies in fear.
"…best safety lies in fear" (H.1.3)
In the play. *Part of the string of advice from Laertes to his sister Ophelia. See 'Youth, a dangerous time, prudence counseled'*

Fear, f. as the reason for defeat - … nothing routs us but the villany of our fears.
"We have the advantage of the ground;
the lane is guarded: nothing routs us but
the villany of our fears." (CYM.5.2)
Use in motivational speech
In the play. *The Britons suffer a temporary setback in the battle against the Roman. Belarius comes in with brother Arviragus to help the Britons to victory.*

**Fear f. engendered by wrongdoing –
… fears, which, as they say, attend the steps of wrong.**
"…Your fears, which, as they say, attend
The steps of wrong…" (KJ.4.2)
In the play. *Lord Pembroke attempts to convince King John it is bad and inadvisable to kill young Prince Arthur.*

Fear, f. generates delay and failure – fearful commenting is leaden servitor to dull delay…
"Come, I have heard that fearful commenting
Is leaden servitor to dull delay;
Delay leads impotent and snail-paced beggary." (KRIII.4.3)
In the play. *Richard cheers up his associates after the bad news that former allies have changed front and joined the enemy Richmond.*

Fear, f. generates disorder - Fear frames disorder, and disorder wounds where it should guard…
"Fear frames disorder, and disorder wounds
Where it should guard. O war, thou son of hell,
Whom angry heavens do make their minister,
Throw in the frozen bosoms of our part
Hot coals of vengeance." (KHVI p2.5)
Dispel fear - e.g. 'Fear frames disorder and disorder…. Guard. Therefore….'
In the play. *Young Clifford sees that the battle of St.. Alban's is turning in favor of the Yorkists, as the Lancastrian forces are fearful.*

Fear, f. guided by reason better than fearless blind reason - Blind fear, that seeing reason leads, finds safer footing than blind reason stumbling without fear…
"Blind fear, that seeing reason leads, finds safer footing than blind reason stumbling without fear; to fear the worst oft cures the worst." (TC.3.2)
Counsel restraint and discourage rash decisions.
In the play. *Troilus prompts Cressida not to fear him and she replies with a piece of philosophy.*

Fear, f. in leader demeaning - If Caesar hide himself, shall they not whisper… Caesar is afraid'?

"If Caesar hide himself, shall they not whisper
'Lo, Caesar is afraid'?" (JC.2.2)
In the play. *Conspirator Decius Brutus wants to make sure that Caesar will go to the Senate on March 15 and asks him a strategic and motivating question*

Fear, f. induced by desire to conform - … reason and respect make livers pale and lustihood deject.
"…reason and respect
Make livers pale and lustihood deject." (TC.2.2)
When you wish to shake off concerns and reservations – see also 'Conscience, c. or fear?'
In the play. *Troilus pleads for retaining Helen at Troy suggesting that cowardice disguised under 'reason and respect' prompts the other Trojans to want to let her go.*

Fear, f. of death, attitude towards it - That life is better life, past fearing death than that which lives to fear.
"That life is better life, past fearing death,
Than that which lives to fear."
(MFM.5.1)
Somewhat dramatic and perhaps ironic answer to 'Are you afraid?' – also depending on the situation that prompts the question. See also entries for 'Death, fear of d.'
In the play. *Duke Vincentio of Vienna pretends that Claudio, Isabel's brother, is already dead, to watch the reactions of the parties involved.*

Fear, f. of obstacle unjustified - … every cloud engenders not a storm.
"… every cloud engenders not a storm." (KHVI.p3.5.3)
In the play. *Edward IV's forces have won but news arrives that Queen Margaret is arriving from France with an army to defend her interests. Edward is concerned*

"…in the midst of this bright-shining day,
I spy a black, suspicious, threatening cloud"
but Clarence dismisses the concern.
"A little gale will soon disperse that cloud
And blow it to the source from whence it came:
The very beams will dry those vapours up,
For every cloud engenders not a storm."

Fear, f. or compunction – Art thou afeard to be the same in thine own act and valour as thou art in desire?
"…Art thou afeard
To be the same in thine own act and valour
As thou art in desire?" (M.1.7)
In the play. *Lady Macbeth scolds her husband who hesitates before murdering King Duncan.*

Fear, f. prompted by imagination - …'tis the eye of childhood that fears a painted devil.
"…the sleeping and the dead
Are but as pictures: 'tis the eye of childhood
That fears a painted devil." (M.2.1)
Dismiss unwarranted fears.
In the play. *Lady Macbeth reproaches her husband for his fear to return to the murder room to reposition the daggers.*

Fear, f. unwarranted - Each substance of a grief hath twenty shadows…
"Each substance of a grief hath twenty shadows,
Which shows like grief itself, but is not so
…
Which, look'd on as it is, is nought but shadows" (KRII.2.2)
In the play. *Bushy attempts to cheer the Queen up thinking that her fears stem from Richard having left to fight in Ireland. See 'Premonition, fearful p. – … methinks, some unborn sorrow, ripe in fortune's womb is coming towards me…'*

Fear, mutual f. eliminated by a marriage - ... truths would be tales where now half tales be truths.
"... By this marriage,
All little jealousies, which now seem great,
And all great fears, which now import their dangers,
Would then be nothing: truths would be tales,
Where now half tales be truths." (AC.2.2)
See also 'Alliance, a. reinforced by marriage'.
In the play. *Agrippa explains the benefits of Antony marrying Octavia, Octavian's sister.*

Fear, nobility, a noble soul is fearless - True nobility is exempt from fear: more can I bear than you dare execute.
"True nobility is exempt from fear:
More can I bear than you dare execute." (KHVI p2.4.1)
Self defense and retort to a threat.
In the play. *Suffolk to the captain of a ship who captured him.*

Fear, not afraid as compared to an instinctual coward - ... Not a whit, i' faith; I lack some of thy instinct.
FALSTAFF. Art thou not horribly afraid? doth not thy blood thrill at it?
PRINCE HENRY Not a whit, i' faith; I lack some of thy instinct. (KHIV.p1.2.4)
In the play. *The fear has to do with the impending war with the rebels.*

Fear, questioning inappropriate f. - ... why do you start; and seem to fear things that do sound so fair?
"Good sir, why do you start; and seem to fear
Things that do sound so fair? (M.1.3)
Question your adversary who rejects your proposal.
In the play. *Banquo queries Macbeth as to why he seems distraught at hearing the positive forecast the witches make about his future?*

Fear, reason for defying f. - ... and fight and die, is death destroying death.
"Fear and be slain? No worse can come, to fight;
And fight and die, is death destroying death,
Where fearing dying, pays death servile breath." (KRII.3.2)
Justify why you will continue to fight for the right cause at the danger of losing.
In the play. *Carlisle encourages the depressed King Richard.*

Fear, sweating in f. See 'Time, midnight, sweating at m. - fearful drops stand on my trembling flesh'.

Fear, symptoms or evidence of f. – ... these linen cheeks of thine are counsellors to fear.
"...these linen cheeks of thine
Are counsellors to fear." (M.5.3)
Teasing a colleague who does not want to go along with the plan.
In the play. *Macbeth upbraids a servant who is understandably shaken after having seen a large English force approach Macbeth's castle.*

Fear, type of f. that is common - ... 'twas a fear which oft infects the wisest.
"...if ever fearful
To do a thing, where I the issue doubted,
Where of the execution did cry out
Against the non-performance, 'twas a fear
Which oft infects the wisest" (WT.1.2)
A line of defense if you are accused of being too cautious.
In the play. *Responding to an insinuation of his master Leontes, Camillo responds admitting to negligence, folly and fear but not to dishonesty.*

Fear, useless and an advantage to the enemy – To fear the foe, since fear oppresseth strength, gives in your weakness strength unto your foe.
"To fear the foe, since fear oppresseth strength,
Gives in your weakness strength unto your foe" (KRII.3.2)
Encouragement and words of advice.
In the play. *The Bishop of Carlyle advises Richard II on the detrimental effects of fear.*

Fear, whom to f. and whom not to f. - Those that I reverence those I fear, the wise: at fools I laugh, not fear them.
"Those that I reverence those I fear, the wise:
At fools I laugh, not fear them." (CYM.4.2)
In the play. *Belarius to the arrogant Cloten.*

Fears, f. unsubstantiated - ... his fears are shallow, wanting instance.
"...his fears are shallow, wanting instance" (KRIII.3.2)
In the play. *Hastings does not believe in the fears of Richard by Lord Stanley. Lord Stanley will prove to be right.*

Feat, f. to be rewarded with honor and commendations - ... the duke shall both speak of it and extend to you what further becomes his greatness...
"...the duke shall both speak of it and extend to you what further becomes his greatness, even to the utmost syllable of your worthiness." (AWEW.3.7)
Emphatic recognition, e.g. 'I recognize your worth even to the utmost syllable of your worthiness'.
In the play. *Bertram encourages the coward Parolles to recapture a drum lost to the enemy, promising rewards and honor from the duke of Florence. A plot is in place to prove Parolle's cowardice.*

Feeling, f. of loss and deprivation by enemies - Thus are my blossoms blasted in the bud...
"Thus are my blossoms blasted in the bud
And caterpillars eat my leaves away;
But I will remedy this gear ere long," (KHVI p2.3.1)
Your reaction at a negative course of events.
In the play. *York, at the news of England's losses in France. The remedy hinted to is getting the crown.*

Feeling, f. very sorry - It strains me past the compass of my wits.
"It strains me past the compass of my wits." (RJ.4.1)
Show empathy and sympathy
In the play. *Fr. Lawrence is sympathetic to Juliet's predicament.*

Feelings, true f. as opposed to hollow f. - Nor are those empty-hearted whose low sound reverbs no hollowness.
"Nor are those empty-hearted whose low sound
Reverbs no hollowness." (KL.1.1)
Retort to someone who says you are not demonstrating enthusiasm.
In the play. *Kent tells Lear that simplicity or modesty do not indicate a lack of feelings. He refers to Cordelia who really loves her father but does not want to join her sisters in their false declarations.*

Feelings, true f. instead of affectation - ... I am sure my love's more richer than my tongue.
"... poor Cordelia!
And yet not so, since I am sure my love's
More richer than my tongue." (KL.1.1)
Justify the lack of proper words for the occasion. You may apply to concepts, ideas or situations other than love, for

example 'commitment', 'dedication', 'ability' etc.
In the play. *Cordelia listens to the exaggerated and false declarations of love towards their father by sisters Regan and Goneril.*

Feet, f. in pain due to long walk or rough path - The ruthless flint doth cut my tender feet.
"The ruthless flint doth cut my tender feet." (KHVI p2.2.4)
When you refuse to walk any longer, if your companion is a determined sportsman or jogger
In the play. *The Duchess of Gloucester is paraded through the streets after having been condemned for abetting sorcery. She complains with her husband about her condition.*

Feet, tired f. - these feet, whose strengthless stay is numb, unable to support this lump of clay.
"...Yet are these feet, whose strengthless stay is numb,
Unable to support this lump of clay" (KHVI.p1.2.5)
When you do not want to walk any longer, e.g. 'My feet are unable…clay'.
In the play. *Mortimer is brought in a chair in the Tower of London for a meeting with Richard Plantagenet who will later become Duke of York.*

Female, a f. defined - ... with a child of our grandmother Eve a female; or, for thy more sweet understanding, a woman.
"...with a child of our grandmother Eve a female; or, for thy more sweet understanding, a woman." (LLL.1.1)
Put some irony in the identification of a woman.

In the play. *The king reads a letter written by Armado and delivered by Dull, a constable. In the letter, written in flowery and pompous words Armado discloses to the king that Costard, a clown was discovered in the company of Jaquenetta, a wench, against the disposition of the king.*

Femininity and genetics - Why are our bodies soft and weak and smooth, unapt to toil and trouble in the world…
"Why are our bodies soft and weak and smooth,
Unapt to toil and trouble in the world,
But that our soft conditions and our hearts
Should well agree with our external parts?" (TOS.5.2)
When you want to relieve her of a tiring task or a task that should be performed by a man. Change 'our' to 'your'. See also 'Labor, heavy lifting, offer to carry her suitcase' -
In the play. *The fully tamed Katharina has just won a bet for her husband Petruchio whereby she is the most obedient wife of all. She now delivers a speech for the benefit of the other (less obedient) wives.*

Feminism, feminist plea for equality of rights in marriage – … Let husbands know their wives have sense like them…
"…Let husbands know
Their wives have sense like them: they see and smell
And have their palates both for sweet and sour,
As husbands have. " (OTH.4.3)
In the play. *Emilia, Iago's wife, explains her philosophy on marriage to Desdemona.*

Fetish, f. that takes prisoner the eye - ... this object, which takes prisoner the wild motion of mine eye, fixing it only here.
"… this object, which

Takes prisoner the wild motion of mine eye,
Fixing it only here." (CYM.1.6)
See also 'Cheeks and Hands'. If she likes to have for example, her pretty foot admired, apply the words accordingly - or any other part, within taste, of course.
In the play. *The perfidious Iachimo is trying unsuccessfully to seduce the beautiful and virtuous Imogen.*

Fight, determination to f. on - ... I cannot fly, but, bear-like, I must fight the course.
".... I cannot fly,
But, bear-like, I must fight the course." (M.5.7)
Show that you are not prepared to give way at all.
In the play. *Macbeth is surrounded by enemy forces but still hangs on to the hope based on one of the witches' predictions – that Macbeth can only be vanquished by a man not born of a woman.*

Fight, determined to f. for your rights - By words or blows here let us win our right.
"By words or blows here let us win our right." (KHVI p3.1.1)
In the play. *Duke of York referring to the imminent council held by Queen Margaret, wife of Henry VI still king.*

Fight, fighting to be right – o virtuous fight when right with right wars who shall be most right.
" O, virtuous fight,
When right with right wars who shall be most right." (TC.3.2)
Assuage or moderate the contention between two fiercely arguing parties. Suggest that two apparently disagreeing parties actually say the same thing. E.G. 'This is a cease when right ... most right.'
In the play. *Troilus and Cressida argue as to who is the winner in truth and Troilus suggests an elegant exit.*

Fight, f. among equals – Blood hath bought blood and blows have answered blows.
"Blood hath bought blood and blows have answered blows" (KJ.2.1)
In the play. *The Citizens of Angiers hesitate whether to declare themselves subjects of King John or King Philip as the armies seem of equal strength.*

Fight, f. to the end - I'll fight till from my bones my flesh be hack'd.
"I'll fight till from my bones my flesh be hack'd." (M.5.3)
In the play. *Under siege at Dunsinane, Macbeth prepares for the last battle.*

Fight, f. to the end. - Ring the alarum-bell! Blow, wind! come, wrack! At least we'll die with harness on our back.
"Ring the alarum-bell! Blow, wind! come, wrack!
At least we'll die with harness on our back." (M.5.5)
In the play. *At Dunsinane, Macbeth defiantly prepares for the last battle. 'Alarum-bell'='A bell used to call men to arms'.*

Fighter, a. committed f. – A stouter champion never handled sword.
"A stouter champion never handled sword." (KHVI.p1.3.4)
In the play. *Henry VI recalls the opinion of his father Henry V on Lord Talbot.*

Financial analysis discouraging - ... Lord Timon's happy hours are done and past, and his estate shrinks from him.
"… now Lord Timon's happy hours are done and past, and his estate shrinks from him." (TOA.3.2)
In the play. *A stranger comments to Lucilius about rumors concerning Timon's financial situation.*

Financial assistance, f.a. offered for honorable cause - My purse, my person, my extremest means, lie all unlock'd to your occasions.
"let me know it;
And if it stand, as you yourself still do,
Within the eye of honour, be assured,
My purse, my person, my extremest means,
Lie all unlock'd to your occasions." (MOV.1.1)
Use also if it is you applying for financial assistance. Try 'my request stands in the eye of honor etc.'
In the play. *Antonio declares himself ready to continue to bankroll Bassanio.*

Financial contribution denied - Who bates mine honour shall not know my coin.
"Who bates mine honour shall not know my coin" (TOA.3.3)
Denying requests for contribution by questionable charities.
In the play. *With a pitiful excuse, Sempronius denies any help to Timon.*

Financial Status - They are but beggars that can count their worth.
"They are but beggars that can count their worth" (RJ.2.5)
In the play. *The lines are used in a different sense (See corresponding entry for 'Love, how much?'). Romeo has declared his overwhelming happiness at the shortly to be celebrated wedding to Juliet. Juliet gives an account of her love with an outburst of emotion.*

Financing, f. denied - They have all been touch'd and found base metal…
"They have all been touch'd and found base metal, for
They have all denied him." (TOA.3.3)
In the play. *Answering a question from Sempronius, Timon's servant replies that all other friends have denied Timon help.*

Financing, lending denied - … this is no time to lend money, especially upon bare friendship, without security.
"… this is no time to lend money, especially upon bare friendship, without security." (TOA.2.1)
See also 'Opinion, your op. on money, handling of, borrowing and lending - Neither a borrower nor a lender be...'
In the play. *The ungrateful Lucullus refuses to lend money to relieve Timon's financial distress.*

Financial status, cash flow critical – …his means most short means, his creditors most strait.
"…His means most short, his creditors most strait." (TOA.1.1)
Use if applicable to answer the question 'What are his financial conditions?'
In the play. *A servant of Ventidius has called on Timon to ask for some relief as Ventidius is in jail for debt. Timon obliges but Ventidius will refuse when it is his turn to help.*

Financial status, cash flow critical – His promises fly so beyond his state that what he speaks is all in debt…
"His promises fly so beyond his state
That what he speaks is all in debt; he owes
For every word." (TOA.1.2)
Describe a spendthrift or financially irresponsible person.
In the play. *Flavius, Timon's faithful servant comments on his master's penchant for profligacy and ignorance of basic economics.*

Financial status, challenging – I can get no remedy against this consumption of the purse…
"I can get no remedy against this consumption of the purse; borrowing only lingers and lingers it out, but the disease is incurable." (KHIV.p2.1.2)

Use the first part of the sentence, 'I can get no remedy from this consumption of the purse' when you find yourself temporarily out of cash for whatever reason and must ask her to pay, with the idea of refunding her for the borrowed amount. She may interpret your line as a witty explanation of why you have to ask her for the small loan required for the immediate necessity to pay a bill. Should you have a female boss and you notice that she likes you (see 'Body, b. language'), you can use the sentence completely when the subject is your salary, a prospective raise or similar. Sometimes the stark reality of economics contrasts with the tender airiness of love. In 1697 John Hervey, First Earl of Bristol, fondly writes to his wife Elizabeth from Newmarket, 'My ever-new delight, Knowing how kind a welcome all my scribbles meet with where they are addressed, neither heart nor hand can forbear, when any opportunity offers, to tell thee how much I long to be in the place of this my harbinger…for all time is worse than lost that's spent where thou art not… 'Tis you alone that sweetens life, and makes one wish the wings of time were clipt…'
But Elizabeth, in writing back from Bury, while acknowledging her love for her husband has pressing financial matters to deal with.
'My dear dear love, Ye hundred things I had to say when you left me, must be only to repeat how much and dearly I love you….

Though I could dwell for ever on this subject (i.e. love), yet I am sure you would be angry with me if I did not tell ye wants those bills you left me to pay has put me in more then I thought for; but 20 pounds will effectually do my bisness, which sum, if it is not easy for you to send, a note from Mr. Cook to receive it at London will do as well; for he can let me have that or any other sum I want; but I shall need no more.'
See also 'Budget deficit – coffers sound with hollow poverty and emptiness'.
In the play. *Falstaff's assessment of his own finances.*

Financial status, challenging - 't is deepest winter in Lord Timon's purse.
"'t is deepest winter in Lord Timon's purse;
That is, one may reach deep enough, and yet
Find little". (TOA.3.4)
If the admission applies to you, change 'Lord Timon' to your name.
Admitting straightness of means does not imply necessarily a loss in your romantic credit rating. The key, as reflected in other quoted instances, is to admit the condition but elegantly. This is even more important if you know she is wealthy. A stylish poor can often compete successfully against an uncouth rich. An elegant statement or explanation (of your financial conditions) suggests a variability of situation, a temporary reversal attributable more to chance than design.

Historically, there have been times where obstacles to a relationship were due to her financial conditions more than his. In England in 1477, for example, Margery Brews was in love with John Paston, her cousin and wanted to marry him. But it seems that he would only do so if her father would agree to a specific money value on her dowry. She writes to him as follows around Valentine day and she calls him 'Valentine' in the spirit of the occasion.

'Right worshipful and well-beloved Valentine, in my most humble wise I recommend me unto you etc… And if ye come, and the matter take no effect, then should I be much more sorry and full of heaviness…and I let you plainly understand that my father will no more money part withal in that behalf, but 100 and 50 marks, which is right far from the accomplishment of your desire. Wherefore, if that ye could be content with that good and my poor person, I would be the merriest maiden on ground.'

In the play. *Philotus, servant of a Timon's creditors gather at his house and comment on his financial conditions.*

Financial status, financial irresponsibility - … the world is but a word: were it all yours to give it in a breath…
"O my good lord, the world is but a word:
Were it all yours to give it in a breath,
How quickly were it gone?" (TOA.2.2)
Describe financial irresponsibility. E.G. 'For him (them) the world is but a word, were it all his (theirs) to give…gone?'
In the play. The servant *Flavius makes Timon aware of the poor financial conditions.*

Financial status, foreseen weakness in financial position - When every feather sticks in his own wing, Lord Timon will be left a naked gull…

"When every feather sticks in his own wing,
Lord Timon will be left a naked gull,
Which flashes now a phoenix."
(TOA.2.1)
Point out your suspicions about the real financial status of a person (or company) who outwardly appear very successful. Change 'Lord Timon' to the name of the applicable party.
In the play. *An Athenian senator (and Timon's creditor), correctly assesses Timon's financial conditions and prospects.*

Financial status, on the edge of ruin - … leaked is our bark and we stand on the dying deck, hearing the surges threat.
"… leaked is our bark;
And we, poor mates, stand on the dying deck,
Hearing the surges threat." (TOA.4.2
When the company is sinking.
In the play. *Timon's servants assess their situation.*

Financial status, poverty, evidence of poverty - … for I have no more stockings than legs, nor no more shoes than feet…
"… for I have no more stockings than legs, nor no more shoes than feet; nay, sometime, more feet than shoes, or such shoes as my toes look through the over-leather." (TOS.ind 2)
When asking your boss for a raise. See also entries reported at 'Salary, s. issues'.
In the play. *Sly, the object of the prank on which hinges the play 'Taming of the Shrew' speaks about himself.*

Financial status, poverty, evidence of poverty - The naked truth of it is, I have no shirt
"The naked truth of it is, I have no shirt" (LLL.5.2)
In the play. Armado tries to evade a contest with Costard by means of a silly excuse.

Financial status, poverty obvious - ... famine is in thy cheeks, need and oppression starveth in thine eyes...
"... famine is in thy cheeks,
Need and oppression starveth in thine eyes,
Contempt and beggary hangs upon thy back;
The world is not thy friend nor the world's law;
The world affords no law to make thee rich;
Then be not poor, but break it, and take this." (RJ.5.1)
Sarcastic answer to 'What is his (or your) financial condition?' Change 'thy' to 'his', or 'my' as applicable.
In the play. *Romeo, desperate because he believes Juliet to be dead, calls on an apothecary to buy a death-inducing drug for himself. The apothecary tells Romeo that the sale of drugs is illegal. Romeo offers a counter-argument. On accepting the argument the apothecary will say* 'My poverty, but not my will, consents'.

Financial status, pressure from collectors - the future comes apace: what shall defend the interim?
"...the future comes apace:
What shall defend the interim?" (TOA.2.2)
In the play. *Servant and accountant Flavius questions Timon on how to handle the precarious financial situation.*

Financial status, strained due to overspending - ... By something showing a more swelling port than my faint means would grant continuance...'
"'Tis not unknown to you, Antonio,
How much I have disabled mine estate,
By something showing a more swelling port
Than my faint means would grant continuance

...the great debts
Wherein my time something too prodigal
Hath left me gaged" (MOV.1.1)
Admit with a smile your economic woes. E.G. 'Yes, these are debts wherein my time... gaged'.
In the play. *Bassanio tells Antonio about the reduced size of his (Bassanio's) estate.*

Fingers, their enchanting touch - his stubborn buckles, with these your white enchanting fingers touch'd...
"...his stubborn buckles,
With these your white enchanting fingers touch'd,
Shall more obey than to the edge of steel
Or force of Greekish sinews." (TC.3.1)
After, say, a shoulder massage – e.g. '...with these your white enchanting fingers touch'd...I feel better already.
In the play. *Paris exhorts Helena to help Hector to undo his armor an by so doing to reduce his disenchantment at the war (started because of Helena).*

Fishing, metaphorically speaking - Bait the hook well; this fish will bite.
"Bait the hook well; this fish will bite." (MAAN.2.3)
In the play. *The fish here is Beatrice who shows signs of love for Benedick.*

Fishing, pleasures of f. (also metaphorically) - The pleasant'st angling is to see the fish... greedily devour the treacherous bait.
"The pleasant'st angling is to see the fish
Cut with her golden ears the silver stream,
And greedily devour the treacherous bait." (MAAN.3.1)
Use when you are metaphorically expecting someone to eat the bait, of whatever type.

In the play. *Ursula is a gentlewoman attending on Beatrice. The fish is actually Beatrice. The bait is what Ursula and Hero are scheming to make Beatrice fall in love with Benedick.*

Flatterers, character of f. is always the same - ... this is the world's soul; and just of the same piece is every flatterer's spirit.
"Why, this is the world's soul; and just of the same piece
Is every flatterer's spirit" (TOA.3.2)
In the play. *A stranger comments on the flatterers who abandoned Timon completely at time of need.*

Flatterers, f. as sponges – take you me for a sponge my lord?
ROSENCRANTZ. Take you me for a sponge, my lord?
HAMLET. Ay, sir, that soaks up the king's countenance, his rewards, his authorities." (H.4.2)
Comment on anyone openly subservient to authority for personal benefit, "He soaks up…authorities". Substitute the name of the authority for 'king'.
In the play. *Rosencrantz asks Hamlet where has he put the slain Polonius' body. Hamlet in turn asks why he, the son of a king, should answer a question from a sponge.*

Flatterers, many and stupid - A thousand flatterers sit within thy crown, whose compass is no bigger than thy head.
"A thousand flatterers sit within thy crown,
Whose compass is no bigger than thy head." (KRII.2.1)
Change 'thy' to 'his' or 'within thy crown' to 'around him' to make the same point.
In the play. *At Ely Castle, the dying John of Gaunt reprimands nephew and King Richard II.*

Flattery - ... you are a gentleman of excellent breeding, admirable discourse…
"…you are a gentleman of excellent breeding, admirable discourse, of great admittance, authentic in your place and person, generally allowed for your many war-like, court-like, and learned preparations." (MWW.2.2)
In the play. *Ford flatters Falstaff so as to use him to test the faithfulness of Ford's wife.*

Flattery, extreme f. – ... in action how like an angel! in apprehension how like a god…
"…in form and moving how express and admirable! in action how like an angel! in apprehension how like a god…" (H.2.2)
Also usable sarcastically in answer to the question 'What do you think of me?' or 'What do you think of him?'
In the play. *Hamlet in conversation with Rosencrantz and Guildenstern.* 'Express' = 'well made'

Flattery, f. and praise tied to reward - ... when the means are gone that buy this praise, the breath is gone whereof this praise is made.
"Ah, when the means are gone that buy this praise,
The breath is gone whereof this praise is made:
Feast-won, fast-lost; one cloud of winter showers,
These flies are couch'd." (TOA.2.2)
General statement about flattery. Change 'this' to 'the' in the generalization. See also 'Prudence, p. in giving confidence and being generous - ...where you are liberal of your loves and counsels be sure you be not loose...' *** 'Character, c. only interested in gain and therefore unreliable - That sir which serves and seeks for gain, and follows but for form, will pack when it begins to rain…'

In the play. *The faithful servant Flavius sees through the shallow based loyalties of Timon's friends.*

Flattery, f. by the intellectual to the rich - ...the learned pate ducks to the golden fool: all is oblique...
"… The learned pate
Ducks to the golden fool: all is oblique;
There's nothing level in our cursed natures,
But direct villainy" (TOA.4.3)
In the play. *Timon, retired to a cave reflects and concludes that all men are flatterers and villains.*

Flattery, f. counterproductive - They do abuse the king that flatter him...
"They do abuse the king that flatter him:
For flattery is the bellows blows up sin;
The thing which is flatter'd, but a spark,
To which that blast gives heat and stronger glowing;
Whereas reproof, obedient and in order,
Fits kings, as they are men, for they may err " (PER.1.2)
In the play. *Helicanus to various lords of Tyre who came to wish a good trip to the departing Pericles.*

Flattery, f. crime, hypocrisy - No vizor does become black villainy so well as soft and tender flattery.
"No vizor does become black villainy,
So well as soft and tender flattery." (PER.4.4)
Comment on the general smooth talk of constitutional hypocrites. See also entries for 'Hypocrisy'.
In the play. *Pericles has returned to Tharsus to claim daughter Marina. Cleon and Dionyza make him believe that Marina is dead with 'soft and tender flattery'. A voice off stage comments on the epitaph inscribed on the tomb of the presumed dead Marina, marked to die out of envy for Marina's perfections.*

Flattery, f. exposed - you play the spaniel and think with wagging of your tongue to win me.
"To me you cannot reach, you play the spaniel,
And think with wagging of your tongue to win me;
But, whatsoe'er thou takest me for, I'm sure
Thou hast a cruel nature and a bloody" (KHVIII.5.2)
Response from a lady to a cunning pursuer who flatters her. Also generic retort from anyone to a cunning flatterer.
In the play. *Henry VIII addresses Gardiner, the Bishop of Winchester.*

Flattery, f. in hope of reward - No, let the candied tongue lick absurd pomp, and crook the pregnant hinges of the knee where thrift may follow fawning.
"…Why should the poor be flatter'd?
No, let the candied tongue lick absurd pomp,
And crook the pregnant hinges of the knee
Where thrift may follow fawning" (H.3.2)
In the play. *Hamlet to Horatio, who thought that Hamlet flattered him by saying that he is honest.*

Flattery, f. justified – … when the sweet breath of flattery conquers strife.
" 'T is holy sport to be a little vain,
When the sweet breath of flattery conquers strife." (COE.3.2)
When your flattery is well intentioned and someone accuses you of duplicity or insincerity.
In the play. *Antipholus S is after Luciana, sister of Adriana, Antipholus E's wife. Luciana is upset and reminds Ant S (thinking that he is*

Ant E) of his duties to his wife Adriana. Therefore she suggests to Ant S to comfort and flatter his (presumed) wife.

Flattery, f. observed – ... rain sacrificial whispering in his ears.
"All which were his fellows but of late,
Follow his strides, his lobbies fill with tendance,
Rain sacrificial whispering in his ears." (TOA.1.1)
Comment on lobbyists.
In the play. The poet gives a quick description of Timon's entourage.

Flattery, f. observed and used for advancement – You shall mark many a duteous and knee-crooking knave...
"...You shall mark
Many a duteous and knee-crooking knave,
That, doting on his own obsequious bondage,
Wears out his time, much like his master's ass,
For nought but provender" (OTH.1.1)
In the play. Iago to Roderigo referring to the promotion of Cassius. 'Doting' = 'To be fond in excess'. 'Provender' = 'Dry food for animals'

Flattery, f. overlooks sin - A friendly eye could never see such faults...
CASSIUS A friendly eye could never see such faults.
BRUTUS A flatterer's would not, though they do appear
As huge as high Olympus. (JC.4.3)
In the play. Brutus and Cassius had an argument. Cassius quiets down and moans that Brutus should either not see or perhaps condone Cassius' faults

Flattery, f. rejected - he does me double wrong that wounds me with the flatteries of his tongue.
"He does me double wrong,
That wounds me with the flatteries of his tongue." (KRII.3.2)

Mildly ironic answer to a praise. See also 'Fed up with comforting efforts - I'll hate him everlastingly that bids me be of comfort any more.'
In the play. Richard to Aumerle and Carlisle after knowing that even York has joined the enemy.

Flattery, f. useless – ... blood that will be thaw'd from the true quality with that which melteth fools...
"...Be not fond,
To think that Caesar bears such rebel blood
That will be thaw'd from the true quality
With that which melteth fools; I mean, sweet words..." (JC.3.1)
In the play. Caesar's response to a plea by Metellius Cimber to rescind the banishment of Cimber's brother.

Flattery, flattered for hating flatterers - ...when I tell him he hates flatterers he says he does, being then most flattered.
"But when I tell him he hates flatterers,
He says he does, being then most flattered." (JC.2.1)
In the play. Decius Brutus thinks he knows how to make sure that Caesar will not fail to go to the Capitol and provides a sketch of Caesar's character.

Flattery, leave f. to servile people - ... let the candied tongue lick absurd pomp...
"...let the candied tongue lick absurd pomp,
And crook the pregnant hinges of the knee
Where thrift may follow fawning." (H.3.2)
Why it is that you do not flatter. See also 'Character, unable to flatter, pretend and deceive'

In the play. *Hamlet in conversation with his friend Horatio.*

Flattery, let there be no limit to your f. - Flatter and praise, commend, extol their graces, though ne'er so black, say they have angels' faces.
"Flatter and praise, commend, extol their graces,
Though ne'er so black, say they have angels' faces." (TGV.3.1)
On flattery there is a general consensus, it works. So Ovid, '...each woman thinks herself lovable; hideous though she be, there is none her own looks do not please…Now be the time to ensnare the mind with crafty flatteries, as the water eats away an overhanging bank. Nor be weary of praising her looks, her hair, her shapely fingers, her small foot: even honest maids love to have their charms extolled; even to the chaste their beauty is a care and a delight.' (AOL.2)
You may object that a compliment does not necessarily constitute flattery. The frontier between flattery and compliments is undefined. Let the object of the compliment (or the flattery) decide for herself.
According to Archdeacon Ruiz, flattery can take the place of gifts, 'If you will not give gifts to her, be generous with your words, do not be silly in your speech: who does not hold honey in a container let him have honey on his mouth – so does the merchants when he wants to sell or to barter well' (Book of Good Love).
In the play. *The Duke pretends to have lost his seducing skills and enlists the help of Valentine to learn how to conquer the heart of a lady the Duke is after.*

Flattery, love of f. leading to financial ruin - Methinks false hearts should never have sound leg, thus honest fools lay out their wealth on courtsies.
"Methinks false hearts should never have sound legs,
Thus honest fools lay out their wealth on courtsies." (TOA.1.2)
Decry flatterers and characterizes those who enjoy to be flattered. See also 'Opinion, your op. on flattery'
In the play. *If hypocrites had bad legs they could not bow in flattery, thus preventing the flattered to give away his estate in payment – so says the cantankerous but accurate Apemantus.*

Flattery, no f. – … do not think I flatter, for what advancement may I hope from thee…
"Nay, do not think I flatter;
For what advancement may I hope from thee
That no revenue hast but thy good spirits,
To feed and clothe thee?" (H.3.2)
You may omit the lines about the lack of revenue. Or apply the line to yourself if you are unemployed, i.e. 'I have no revenue but my good spirits'.
In the play. *Hamlet to loyal but poor friend Horatio.*

Flattery, power yielding to f. and the obligations of honor - Think'st thou that duty shall have dread to speak when power to flattery bows?…
"Think'st thou that duty shall have dread to speak,
When power to flattery bows? To plainness honour's bound,
When majesty stoops to folly." (KL.1.1)
Modify. E.g., 'To plainness honor is bound when authority stoops to folly' when you try to prevent insanity or a stupid decision.
In the play. *Kent will not be put down by Lear's unjustified anger towards Cordelia and Kent himself.*

Flattery, the dews of f. – … with dews of flattery seducing so my friends.

"He water'd his new plants with dews of flattery,
Seducing so my friends" (COR.5.6)
In the play. *Aufidius plots the reasons for assassinating Coriolanus, including how Coriolanus changed his rough character and used flattery to ingratiate himself with the Volsces.*

Flattery, tools of f. - Serving of becks and jutting-out of bums.
"Serving of becks and jutting-out of bums!" (TOA.1.2)
See also 'Character, unable to flatter, pretend and deceive - because I cannot flatter and speak fair...' 'Becks' is a synonym for 'nods' as in 'nod of approval'.
In the play. *Apemantus' comment on Timon's company.*

Flattery, tools of f. - ...sweet words, low-crooked court'sies and base spaniel-fawning.
" ... sweet words,
Low-crooked court'sies and base spaniel-fawning" (JC.3.1)
See also 'Character, unable to flatter, pretend and deceive - because I cannot flatter and speak fair...'
In the play. *Caesar rejects the plea by Metellius Cimber to stop the banishment of Cimber's brother. The 'sweet words' etc. appear flattery to Caesar.*

Fly, killing a f. - ... A deed of death done on the innocent.
TITUS ANDRONICUS. A deed of death done on the innocent
Becomes not Titus' brother: get thee gone:
I see thou art not for my company.
MARCUS ANDRONICUS Alas, my lord, I have but kill'd a fly.
TITUS ANDRONICUS But how, if that fly had a father and mother?
How would he hang his slender gilded wings,
And buzz lamenting doings in the air!
Poor harmless fly,
That, with his pretty buzzing melody,
Came here to make us merry! and thou hast kill'd him. (TA.3.2)
Utter while killing fly or bug, e.g. 'I am doing a deed of death on the innocent'.
In the play. *Titus A. is loosing his mind and deplores the killing of a fly. He will change his mind when Marcus A. reminds him that the color of the fly is the same as that of evil Aaron.*

Flower, compliment – ... no shepherdess, but Flora peering in April's front.
"...no shepherdess, but Flora Peering in April's front." (WT.4.4)
Try 'you are like Flora, peering in April's front. Or 'you are a flower, peering on April's front'
In the play. *Florizel finds Perdita and recognizes that she is more than a simple shepherdess, daughter of a shepherd.*

Flower, the sweetest flower - ... the sweetest flower of all the field.
"...the sweetest flower of all the field." (RJ.4.5)
Answer to 'what do you think of me?' '(You are) the sweetest flower of all the field.'
In the play. *Capulet Sr. discovers Juliet who appears dead due to the potent controlled substance given to her by Fr. Lawrence (to avoid bigamy, as Juliet would have been forced to marry Paris). The previously irate father of Juliet is now all in tears,*
"Death lies on her like an untimely frost
Upon the sweetest flower of all the field"

FLOWERS
Flowers are indissolubly linked to romance and the association woman-flower is almost instinctive. A flower is perfection. Therefore giving flowers to a lady is to give her a symbol of herself at her best, of the perfection of femininity. With this in mind, the poet Neville Fleeson in 1917 wrote,

"Say it with flowers from love's sweetest bowers,
And you'll find her waiting, waiting for you."
Ever hungry for your buck, the Society of American Florists in 1919 adopted the slogan, 'Say it with Flowers', thereby debasing even the most romantic of symbols to the level of trade - suggesting optional McDonalds of roses ('over 50 billion sold)' or Coca Colas of daffodils ('Daffodil is the real thing').
Perish the thought.
Still, compare your lady to flowers or skillfully bring them into the conversation, implying an association between her and your favorite flower. It will inevitably improve your rating in her chart.
Shakespeare had good knowledge of wild and cultivated flowers and of their particular meaning and symbolic value. King Richard II forces into exile Bolingbroke, the future Henry IV. Bolingbroke is very unhappy and his father John of Gaunt gives him an injection of positive thinking,
(when in exile)….**Suppose the singing birds musicians,**
The flowers fair ladies, and thy step no more
Than a delightful measure or a dance" (KRII.1.3)
With some license you can say (or write), "Fair lady you are a flower, and your step no more than a delightful measure or a dance."
You can introduce flowers when praising her good breath, see 'Breath excellent', where you compare her breath to the scent of eglantine (sweet briar). And if she asks you 'what is eglantine'? You have the option of telling that it is a wild rose or quote the definition given by Parkinson in his 'Garden of Pleasant Flowers' (1629), '(Eglantine) has exceedingly large green shoots, armed with the cruellest sharpe and strong thornes, and thicker set than in any rose, either wilde or tame; the leaves are small, very greene, and sweet in smell, above the leaves of any other kind of rose'.
If you plan a walk in a garden or a meadow, in March or at the beginning of Spring, and there are daffodils, comment with,
"**Daffodils, that come before the swallows dare, and take**
The winds of March with beauty" (WT.4.4)
or maybe
"**When daffodils begin to peer,**
Why then comes in the sweet o' the year;
For the red blood reigns in the winter's pale." (WT.4.2)
where that 'red blood' suggests a lingering passion unaffected by coldness or winter.
Or bring in the woodbine, also called honeysuckle, that suggests fidelity and affection but weigh the situation carefully so as not to go overboard,
"**So doth the woodbine, the sweet honeysuckle,**
Gently entwine." (MND.4.1)
On the other hand, if she is a vixen to live with, or has been really rotten and dealt with you unfairly, you can tell her (or write her a note with) the following
"**For sweetest things turn sourest by their deeds,**
Lilies that fester, smell far worse than weeds." (SON 94).

Flowers, compliment, like spring-time f. - For thou are pleasant, gamesome… yet sweet as spring-time flowers.
"**For thou are pleasant, gamesome, passing courteous,**
But slow in speech, yet sweet as spring-time flowers" (TOS.2.2)
Compliment, e.g. 'you are as sweet as spring-time flowers'.

In the play. *Petruchio tries to approach the unapproachable Katharina. She refuses the approach saying that she is terrible ('I chafe you if I tarry'). Petruchio dismisses her resistance and showers her with compliments.*

Flowers, fields in flower and romance - Away before me to sweet beds of flowers, Love-thoughts lie rich when canopied with bowers.
"Away before me to sweet beds of flowers:
Love-thoughts lie rich when canopied with bowers." (TN.1.1)
In the play. *Duke Orsino fantasizes about Olivia whom he desperately loves. 'Bower' = 'A shady area amidst flowers and trees'*

Flowers, honeysuckle providing shade - ... honeysuckles, ripen'd by the sun, forbid the sun to enter...
"…the pleached bower,
Where honeysuckles, ripen'd by the sun,
Forbid the sun to enter, like favourites,
Made proud by princes, that advance their pride" (MAAN.3.1)
In the play. *Hero tells Margaret to go to the 'pleached bower'. Bower' = 'A shady area amidst flowers and trees'. 'Pleached' = 'Intertwined'. Therefore 'Pleached bower' = 'A shady area made up of thick bushes'.*

Flowers, marigolds and other f. indicated for middle age men - ... Here's flowers for you, hot lavender...
"….Here's flowers for you;
Hot lavender, mints, savoury, marjoram;
The marigold, that goes to bed wi' the sun
And with him rises weeping: these are flowers
Of middle summer, and I think they are given
To men of middle age. You're very welcome." (TN.4.4)

If you are a man of middle age this would be a reply to the question, 'What kind of flowers you like?'
In the play. *Camillo, just arrived in Bohemia meets with the shepherdess Perdita (alias daughter of Leontes, king of Sicilia). Perdita in kindness offers flowers to him. Camillo answers with a pointed compliment – see 'Shepherdess, if she were a shepherdess'.*

Flowers, primrose and harebell - … thou shalt not lack the flower that's like thy face, pale primrose, nor the azured harebell, like thy veins.
"…thou shalt not lack
The flower that's like thy face, pale primrose, nor
The azured harebell, like thy veins." (CYM.4.1)
As soon as she says 'primrose' try 'ah, the flower that's like thy face'
In the play. *Arviragus thinks that Imogen (Fidele) is dead and describes the flowers he will bring her/him. Imogen is actually heavily sedated after having drunk a potion prepared by the Queen to kill her. But the Queen's doctor had altered the potion to make it not lethal.*

Flowers, primroses - ... pale primroses that die unmarried ere they can behold bright Phoebus in his strength.
"…pale primroses,
That die unmarried ere they can behold
Bright Phoebus in his strength." (WT.4.4)
In the play. *Polixenes and Camillo, disguised, arrive at the shepherd's house where they find Florizel and Perdita. Polixenes and Camillo engage Perdita into a dialog on flowers.*

Flowers, homage of f - Sweets to the sweet
"Sweets to the sweet" (H.5.1)
In the play. *Queen Gertrude throws flowers to the body of Ophelia who drowned from despair.*

Flowers, violets - … a violet in the youth of primy nature…
"A violet in the youth of primy nature,
Forward, not permanent, sweet, not lasting,
The perfume and suppliance of a minute." (H.1.3)
You may make a love declaration by the use of contrast. E.G. "I do not consider you just a violet in the youth…suppliance of a minute'. Or use the first line as a compliment. Answer to 'Do you like me?'
In the play. *Laertes warns his sister Ophelia that Hamlet's love may be short term and temporary.*

Flowers, violets - …dim but sweeter than the lids of Juno's eyes…
"…violets dim,
But sweeter than the lids of Juno's eyes
Or Cytherea's breath" (WT.4.4)
Compliment, 'a flower… sweeter than… breath'. See also entries for 'Breath'.
In the play. *Polixenes and Camillo disguised arrive at the shepherd's house where they find Florizel and Perdita. Polixenes and Camillo engage Perdita into a dialog on flowers*

Flowers, violets – Who are the violets now that strew the green lap of the new come spring?
"…who are the violets now
That strew the green lap of the new come spring?" (KRII.5.2)
Alternative way for the question 'How is your love life?' Or a compliment, 'you are the violet that strews… Spring.'
In the play. *The Duke of Aumerle, son of the Duke of York arrives home and his mother asks him an innocent question.*

Flowers, her beauty exceeding all flowers - More flowers I noted, yet none I could see, but sweet, or colour it had stolen from thee.
"More flowers I noted, yet none I could see,
But sweet, or colour it had stolen from thee." (SON.99)
Works perfectly if both of you are attending a flower show. It also fits if you are taking a walk in the country.

Flowers, lilies and roses - Nor did I wonder at the lily's white, nor praise the deep vermilion in the rose….
"**Nor did I wonder at the lily's white,
Nor praise the deep vermilion in the rose.
They were but sweet, but figures of delight,
Drawn after you, you pattern of all those**.
Yet seem'd it winter still, and, you away,
As with your shadow I with these did play." (SON.98)
Keep it in store when you sense that she is ready for more compliments (use the first four lines). Or maybe she has been away for a long time. You send her some flowers – include a note saying "Yet seem'd it winter still, and, you away… with these did play."

The association of love with rose is familiar. Less common is the association of love and cities. French novelist Honore' de Balzac had twenty-three 'sacred' towns. In writing to Countess Hanska he says 'I do not know what they (the 23 cities) mean to you but for me, when one of these names enters my thoughts, it is as if a Chopin were touching a piano key; the hammer awakens sounds which reverberate through my soul, and a complete poem takes shape…And St. Petersburg? The blue salon on the Neva! The first initiation of my sweetheart, the first step in her education. What a union: it lasted for two months without a false note, unless one is to count that argument over the hat and the one about the expense of engaging a cook.'

Flowers, white rose - ... the milk-white rose, with whose sweet smell the air shall be perfumed.
"Then will I raise aloft the milk-white rose,
With whose sweet smell the air shall be perfumed." (KHVI.p2.1.1)
Say this when you lift her up, provided she fits the profile. Or you can write the lines on a card if you send her a bunch of white roses. Or maybe if you happen to pick up a white rose during a walk.
In the play. *The duke of York, representative of the White or Yorkist faction in the War of the Roses, meditates in a soliloquy on how to make his party prevail over the Red or Lancastrian faction.*

Fly, murder of a f. and considerations thereof - Poor harmless fly! That with his pretty bussing melody...
"Poor harmless fly!
That, with his pretty bussing melody, Came here to make us merry! and thou hast killed him." (TA.3.2)
Use as an example on how quickly it is possible to rationalize any act depending on the premises.
In the play. *Marcus has killed a fly. The overwrought Titus upbraids him but Marcus says he killed the fly because it was black as the empress' moor lover Aaron. Titus then regrets having reprehended Marcus.*

Folly maybe but not childishness - Though age from folly could not give me freedom it does from childishness.
"Though age from folly could not give me freedom,
It does from childishness. " (AC.1.3)
When anyone wants to make you believe the unbelievable.
In the play. *Cleopatra does not believe the news that Fulvia, Antony's wife, is dead in Rome.*

Folly or malice - Either you must confess yourselves wondrous malicious or be accus'd of folly.
"Either you must
Confess yourselves wondrous malicious,
Or be accus'd of folly." (COR.1.1)
Alternative to 'You are criminal or stupid'
In the play. *Menenius attempts to soothe the rebellious citizens and bring them to reason by way of an example and an explanation. See 'Explanation by the way of an example'.*

Food, fast f. distaste for it – On what I hate I feed not.
"On what I hate I feed not." (TOA.4.3)
Answer to 'Let's have a bite at (fast food or restaurant type you dislike)'
In the play. *Apemantus, visiting Timon in his cave, offers him a medlar (orange-yellow fruit) and Timon refuses it.*

Food, giving priority to spiritual over material f. - The mind shall banquet, though the body pine
"The mind shall banquet, though the body pine" (LLL.1.1)
When you are the last in line and there is no more food left for you. Adopt an lofty expression of resignation.
In the play. *Loganville subscribes to a program of learning, dieting and abstinence that will actually never be followed.*

Food, questionable f. - ... strange flesh which some did die to look on.
"....on the Alps
It is reported thou didst eat strange flesh,
Which some did die to look on:" (AC.1.4)
My (or perhaps your) feelings on fast food.
In the play. *In Rome Octavian recounts to Antony some of his (Antony's) previous exploits*

Food, virtual f. – (Who can) cloy the hungry edge of appetite by bare imagination of a feast?
"**Or cloy the hungry edge of appetite By bare imagination of a feast?**" (KRII.1.3)
See also "Hunger, when in love not important but…- ... though the chameleon love may feed on air, I am one that is nourished by my victuals, and would fain have meat.'
In the play. *Bolingbroke rejects the suggestions by his father John of Gaunt on positive thinking regarding Bolingbroke's impending exile.*

Fool, do you think I am a fool? – … bear some charity to my wit: do not think it so unwholesome.
"**…bear some charity to my wit: do not think it so unwholesome.**" (OTH.4.1)
In the play. *Cassio's response to Iago's question as to whether Cassio will marry Bianca, his promiscuous lover. Othello overhears this and thinks that Cassio refers to Desdemona.*

Fool's paradise – …if ye should lead her into a fool's paradise…
"**…if ye should lead her into a fool's paradise, as they say, it were a very gross kind of behavior, as they say**" (RJ.2.4)
In the play. *The nurse gives words of advise and warning to Romeo (as regards Juliet)*

Foolery, clever f. requiring some wit - … to do that well craves a kind of wit.
"**This fellow is wise enough to play the fool; And to do that well craves a kind of wit.**" (TN.3.1)
Explain that there is such a thing as clever foolery, which, to be clever, requires intelligence. See also 'Insult, answer to insult of being a fool'
In the play. *Viola is impressed by the fool.*

Foolery, skill in f. and men who make fools of themselves – … a practice as full of labour as a wise man's art…
"**…This is a practice, As full of labour as a wise man's art: For folly, that he wisely shows, is fit; But wise men, folly fallen, quite taint their wit.**" (TN.3.1)
Explain that there is such a thing as clever foolery, which, to be clever, requires intelligence. That is, there is wise folly and foolish wisdom. 'Folly, wisely shown, is fit, but wise men…their wit.'
In the play. *Viola, after listening to the fool, concludes that the art of foolery (or rather wit) requires as mush skill as the art of wisdom.*

Fools, dullness of f. as an opportunity for the clever - … for always the dulness of the fool is the whetstone of the wits.
"**… for always the dulness of the fool is the whetstone of the wits.**" (AYLI.1.2)
Sporting self-effacement line when you fail to understand either a joke or a double meaning.
In the play. *Celia concludes a brief dissertation on nature, wit and Fortune*

Fools, f. making bad choices - O, these deliberate fools! when they do choose…
"**Thus hath the candle singed the moth. O, these deliberate fools! when they do choose, They have the wisdom by their wit to lose.**" (MOV.2.9)
In the play. *Portia comments on the unsuccessful attempts by suitors to solve the riddle that wold enable the first solver to marry her.*

Fools, two of them observed approaching - Here comes a pair of very strange beasts which in all tongues are called fools.

"Here comes a pair of very strange beasts, which in all tongues are called fools." (AYLI.5.4)
In the play. *The ornery Jaques sees Touchstone and his recently married peasant wife Audrey arriving.*

Foot, a light f. - O, so light a foot will ne'er wear out the everlasting flint.
"Here comes the lady: O, so light a foot
Will ne'er wear out the everlasting flint." (RJ.2.5)
In the play. *Fr. Lawrence sees (and hears) Juliet who arrives at the convent to be married to Romeo.*

Force, f. imposing action - for do we must what force will have us do.
"For do we must what force will have us do." (KRII.3.3)
In the play. *King Richard is forced to resign the crown.*

Forecast, f. looks good - If consequence do but approve my dream, my boat sails freely, both with wind and stream.
"If consequence do but approve my dream,
My boat sails freely, both with wind and stream" (OTH.2.3)
In the play. *Iago speculates on the outcome of his malicious and murderous plan.*

Forecast, gloomy f. - ... lend me ten thousand eyes and I will fill them with prophetic tears.
" ... lend me ten thousand eyes,
And I will fill them with prophetic tears." (TC.2.2)
Predict negative results if a course of action is maintained and not changed.
In the play *Cassandra prophesies doom (by keeping Helen) but it is her fate not to be believed.*

Forecast, positive f. - Last night the very gods show'd me a vision...
"Last night the very gods show'd me a vision--
I fast and pray'd for their intelligence--thus
I saw Jove's bird, the Roman eagle, wing'd
From the spongy south to this part of the west,
There vanish'd in the sunbeams: which portends--
Unless my sins abuse my divination
Success to the Roman host" (CYM.4.2)
After having given argument as to the reason for your optimism conclude with (e.g.) '(this) portends, unless my sins abuse my divination, success to (our venture)'
In the play. *A soothsayer with the Roman army gives positive predictions about the outcome (for the Romans) of the war with Britain.*

Forecasting ability - In nature's infinite book of secrecy a little I can read.
"In nature's infinite book of secrecy
A little I can read." (AC.1.2)
In the play. *Cleopatra's ladies in waiting interrogate the soothsayer about their future.*

Forecasting and prophetic ability - Methinks I am a prophet new inspired…
"Methinks I am a prophet new inspired
And thus expiring do foretell of him…" (KRII.2.1)
Use the first line unless you really feel you are at the end of your rope – in which case you use both.
In the play. *At Ely's House, John of Gaunt launches into a tirade against the extravagance and vanity of Richard II and prophesies hell for England under his rule.*

Forecasting requested - If you can look into the seeds of time and say

which grain will grow and which will not…
"If you can look into the seeds of time,
And say which grain will grow and which will not,
Speak then to me, who neither beg nor fear
Your favours nor your hate." (M.1.3)
Try the first two lines when she asks questions of the type 'What will happen to us?' or equivalent and you are not really sure.
In the play. *Banquo prompts the witches to make a forecast of future events as they affect Banquo and Macbeth.*

Forecasting skills – The spirit of deep prophecy she hath, exceeding the nine sibyls of old Rome...
"The spirit of deep prophecy she hath,
Exceeding the nine sibyls of old Rome:
What's past and what's to come she can descry." (KHVI p1.1.2)
In the play. *The Bastard of Orleans describes the abilities of Joan of Arc, in the play somewhat vulgarly called 'Puzelle', to spite the French.*

Forecasting, expressing doubts about someone's forecasts – How far your eyes may pierce I can not tell…
"How far your eyes may pierce I can not tell…" (KL.1.4)
In the play. *Goneril has reproached her husband Albany for being too soft with Lear and he replies*.

Forecasting, if I am correct… – If secret powers suggest but truth to my divining thoughts…
"If secret powers
Suggest but truth to my divining thoughts…" (KHVI.p3.4.6)
In the play. *Henry VI predicts that Richmond will heal the bloody rift between the houses of York and Lancaster.*

Forecasting, not good at f. – … much too shallow to sound the bottom of the after-times.
"You are too shallow, Hastings, much too shallow,
To sound the bottom of the after-times." (KHIVp2.4.2)
Use with someone who disputes your assessment of future developments, e.g. 'You are too shallow, (name of person), much too shallow…after-times'.
In the play. *Prince John of Lancaster, son of Henry IV puts down Hasting's remarks about what will or may happen in a confrontation between the forces of King Henry and the rebels.*

Forecasting, positive f. - My mind presageth happy gain and conquest.
"My mind presageth happy gain and conquest." (KHVI p3.5.1)
In the play. *Edward IV before the battle of Coventry against Warwick and the forces of Henry VI.*

Forecasting, total confidence in the forecaster - No prophet will I trust, if she prove false.
"No prophet will I trust, if she prove false." (KHVI p1.1.2)
In the play. *After some tests, Charles has now complete confidence in Joan of Arc.*

Foregone conclusion - But this denoted a foregone conclusion.
"But this denoted a foregone conclusion" (OTH.3.3)
Common aphorism.
In the play. *Othello's reaction to Iago's account of (invented) Cassio's dream about Desdemona. Othello believes everything.*

Foreign girl, f.g. whom you like and she speaks some English – …for thy tongue makes Welsh as sweet as ditties highly penn'd…
"… For thy tongue

Makes Welsh as sweet as ditties highly penn'd,
Sung by a fair queen in a summer's bower,
With ravishing division, to her lute."
(KHIV p1.3.1)
Use it even with a native English speaker - substitute 'English' for 'Welsh'. A compliment or a retort to an apology for inaccurate wording. For example, 'On the contrary, thy tongue makes English as sweet ... her lute.'
In the play. *Mortimer's assessment of Lady Mortimer's Welsh.*

Foreign girls, admitting to limited knowledge of the lady's native tongue - I shall never move thee in French, unless it be to laugh at me.
"I shall never move thee in French, unless it be to laugh at me." (KHV.5.2)
Your French is clearly not up to par but you hope it will not be a barrier. If she is foreign but not French, just change 'French' to the applicable language.
In the play. *Henry V woos Kathryn of France after having defeated the French at Agincourt.*

Foreign girls, effort at speaking in the lady's native tongue - ... in French; which, I am sure, will hang upon my tongue like a new-married wife about her husband's neck...
" I will tell thee in French; which, I am sure, will hang upon my tongue like a new-married wife about her husband's neck; hardly to be shook off." (KHV.5.2)
Change 'French' to the applicable tongue. Be prepared to the fact that, depending on her level of English and education, she may not understand you or know what you are talking about. If so, simply say that the lines are from Shakespeare. The name itself carries weight worldwide.
In the play. *Henry V woos Kathryn of France after having defeated the French at Agincourt.*

Foreign girls, love overcoming language barriers - ... if you will love me soundly with your French heart...
"... if you will love me soundly with your French heart, I will be glad to hear you confess it brokenly with your English tongue." (KHV.5.2)
Modify in accordance to the nationality of the lady. E.g. '.... If you will love me soundly with your Moldavian heart, I will be glad to hear you confess it brokenly with your English tongue'. Eliminate 'brokenly' if her English is good.
In the play. *Henry V is wooing Katherine of France after having defeated the French at Agincourt.*

Foreign girls, Italian girls, irresistible - Those girls of Italy, take heed of them...
"Those girls of Italy, take heed of them;
They say, our French lack language to deny,
If they demand." (AWEW.2.1)
Praise the attraction of Italian ladies. Or change 'Italy' to the applicable country and 'French' to the applicable nationality. E.g. 'Those girls of Belgium,...them; they say our Dutch lack...demand'
In the play. *The Florentines are at war with the Sienese and the French lend support to the Florentines. As some French lords leave for Italy, the king offers words of warning.*

Foreign girls, kissing overcoming language barriers – I understand thy kisses and thou mine...
"I understand thy kisses and thou mine,
And that's a feeling disputation"
(KHIV.p1.3.1)
In the play. *Mortimer to the daughter of Glendower who speaks in Welsh. The disputation has to do with her wanting to follow Mortimer in battle.*

Foreign language, disadvantages of speaking a f.l. - ... can he that speaks with the tongue of an enemy be a good counselor, or no?
"I ask but this: can he that speaks with the tongue of an enemy be a good counselor, or no?" (KHVI.p2.4.2)
In the play. *John Cade's assessment of Lord Say, who, by knowing how to speak French, disqualifies himself as an English counselor.*

Foreign language, f.l. expert – (he) speaks three or four languages word for word without book.
"...speaks three or four languages word for word without book" (TN.1.3)
In the play. *Toby Belch extols the virtues of his friend Andrew Aguecheek.*

Foreign language, knowledge of French a liability - ... he can speak French and therefore he is a traitor.
JOHN CADE ...and more than that, he can speak French; and therefore he is a traitor."
SIR HUMPHREY. O gross and miserable ignorance! (KHVI p2.4)
Use to pull the leg of French speakers or quoting Sir Humphrey's comment take a shot at those who seem to have a contempt for culture.
In the play. *John Cade attempts to start a communist revolution in London and the poor Lord Say (the French speaker) is accused of this and other crimes.*

Foreign language, knowledge of Latin a liability - Away with him, away with him! he speaks Latin.
"Away with him, away with him! he speaks Latin." (KHVI.p2.4.7)
In the play. *Lord Say uttered a Latin sentence (bona terra, mala gens = good land, bad people). For the rebel John Cade speaking Latin is an admission of guilt.*

Foreign policy, war to cover up internal problems - Be it thy course to busy giddy minds with foreign quarrels.
"Be it thy course to busy giddy minds with foreign quarrels." (KHIVp2.4.5)
Criticize or unmask the justification for an aggressive foreign policy. 'History gives us plentiful examples of foreign wars conducted to distract attention from domestic problems. Even Henry IV advised his son, "Be it thy course...quarrels"'.
In the play. *King Henry IV, on point of death, gives some final advice to his son, the future Henry V.*

Foreigner - Not of this country, though my chance is now to use it for my time.
ESCALUS Of whence are you?
DUKE VINCENTIO Not of this country, though my chance is now To use it for my time. (MFM.3.2)
Answer to 'Where are you from?' You can change 'country' to 'city', 'region' etc.
In the play. *Duke-Vicentio's disguise is perfect as citizen Escalus thinks that the Duke is a foreigner.*

Forewarning, f. advisable – To acquaint you with this evil, that you might the better arm you to the sudden time...
"To acquaint you with this evil, that you might
The better arm you to the sudden time,
Than if you had at leisure known of this." (KJ.5.6)
In the play. *Hubert alerts Faulconbridge that King John has been poisoned.*

Forgetting - I have forgot all men; then, if thou grant'st thou'rt a man, I have forgot thee.
FLAVIUS Have you forgot me, sir?

TIMON Why dost ask that? I have forgot all men;
Then, if thou grant'st thou'rt a man, I have forgot thee. (TOA.4.3)
Answer to 'Have you forgotten me?' when you are in a bad mood.
In the play. *Faithful servant Flavius goes to meet Timon, now living in a cave.*

Forgetting and consequences - I shall forget, to have thee still stand there, remembering how I love thy company.
ROMEO Let me stand here till thou remember it.
JULIET I shall forget, to have thee still stand there,
Remembering how I love thy company. (RJ.2.2)
In the play. *Juliet calls Romeo back to tell him something. Then she forgets what she wanted to say. The occasion offers Romeo and Juliet the opportunity to spend some more time together.*

Forgetting, cannot forget what not remembered – That is not forgot which never did I remember.
"... that is not forgot
Which ne'er did I remember." (KRII.2.3)
Answer to 'Have you forgotten this or so & so?'
In the play. *Northumberland asks Percy if he has forgotten the duke of Hereford, but Percy never met Hereford and replies accordingly.*

Forgetting, f. common to men - But men are men; the best sometimes forget.
"But men are men; the best sometimes forget" (OTH.2.1)
In the play. *Affecting to defend Cassio, Iago is actually hurting his cause and prepares the trap for Othello to believe that Cassio has an affair with Desdemona.*

Forgetting, f. the good under the influence of anger - All this from my remembrance brutish wrath sinfully pluck'd...
"All this from my remembrance brutish wrath
Sinfully pluck'd..." (KRIII.2.1)
See also entries for 'Remembering, the bad more than the good'.
In the play. *King Edward, earlier on angry at Clarence now upbraids his court for not having reminded him of how kind Clarence had been with Edward.*

Forgetting, f. the most important – Great thing of us forgot!
"Great thing of us forgot!" (KL.5.3)
In the play. *A rapid sequence of events has let Kent, Albany and Edgar forget for a moment where is King Lear.*

Forgetting, questioning rhetorically - May this be wash'd in Lethe, and forgotten?
"May this be wash'd in Lethe, and forgotten?" (KHIV.p2.5.2)
When you want to stress that the matter in question should not be forgotten.
In the play. *King Henry V addresses the Chief Justice, who once had Henry arrested for misbehavior.*

Forgetting, time helps f - ... some more time must wear the print of his remembrance out.
"...some more time
Must wear the print of his remembrance out,
And then she's yours." (CYM.2.2)
Apply to an event that will be forgotten with time, e.g. 'Some more time must wear the print of his remembrance out.'
In the play. *King Cymbeline wants her daughter to marry the foolish Cloten, but she cannot forget her exiled and beloved Leonatus, whom she already married against the will of the king.*

Forgetting, tools for f. See 'Wine, w. as a tool for forgetting and making others forget - ... memory, the warder of the brain, shall be a fume...'

Forgetting, wishing to forget - ... that I could forget what I have been...
"...O that I were as great
As is my grief, or lesser than my name!
Or that I could forget what I have been,
Or not remember what I must be now!" (KRII.3.3)
See also 'Madness, wishing to be mad to forget/avoid pain'.
In the play. *King Richard is desperate as he sees his crown lost.*

Forgiveness, f. advisable for little faults - If little faults, proceeding on distemper, shall not be wink'd at...
"If little faults, proceeding on distemper,
Shall not be wink'd at, how shall we stretch our eye,
When capital crimes, chew'd, swallow'd and digested,
Appear before us?" (KHV.2.2)
When you are pleading indulgence for someone's minor slip(s) of conduct.
In the play. *King Henry V will pardon a man who criticized the king while drunk.*

Forgiveness, f. and forgetting - ... it hath the excuse of youth and heat of blood
"My nephew's trespass may be well forgot; it hath the excuse of youth and heat of blood" (KHIVp1.5.2)
In the play. *Worcester compares his situation to that of his nephew Hotspur, should the peace terms offered by the king be accepted.*

Forgiveness, f. asked for rashness –
Forgive my general and exceptless rashness, you perpetual-sober gods!
"Forgive my general and exceptless rashness,
You perpetual-sober gods!" (TOA.4.3)

In the play. *Timon does not at first recognize his trustful servant Flavius who came to visit and addressed him rudely.*

Forgiveness, f. at something she has done - No more be grieved at that which thou hast done, roses have thorns, and silver mountains mud...
"No more be grieved at that which thou hast done,
Roses have thorns, and silver mountains mud,
Clouds and eclipses stain both moon and sun,
And loathsome canker lives in sweetest bud.
All men make faults." (SON.35)
Answer to "Do you forgive me?" (if you are so inclined). Keep Ovid's words in mind, 'Particularly forbear to reproach a woman with her faults, faults which many have found useful to feign otherwise. ... All thought Andromache too big: Hector alone deemed her of moderate size. Grow used to what you bear ill: you will bear it well; a love of long standing will discount many faults, whereas when new it notices all...With names you can soften shortcomings; let her be called swarthy, whose blood is blacker than Illyrian pitch; if cross-eyed, let her be like Venus: gray-haired, like Minerva: and call her slender whose thinness impairs her health; if short call her trim; if stout, of full body; let its nearness to a virtue conceal a fault.' (AOL.2)
For the mythologically curious, Andromache was Hector's wife. Illyria was a district of the Balkan Peninsula, which, at the time of Ovid, was the eastern shore of the Adriatic. I have been unable to find why the pitch of Illyria was thought blacker than other pitches.
'See also 'Apologies unnecessary'

Forgiveness, f. by a king, request for f. - Who am I, ha? ... A gracious king,

that pardons all offences malice never meant.
K.HENRY. How dare you thrust yourselves
Into my private meditations? Who am I, ha?
NORFOLK. A gracious king, that pardons all offences
Malice ne'er meant." (KHVIII.2.2)
Soften an intrusion or an unannounced visit, e.g., 'you are a gracious person, that pardons all offenses malice never meant'.
In the play. *Norfolk and others present themselves, unannounced to the king's presence*

Forgiveness, f. following adversary's repentance – ... these words have turn'd my hate to love; and forgive and quite forget old faults.
"Warwick, these words have turn'd my hate to love;
And I forgive and quite forget old faults" (KHVI.p3.3.3)
In the play. *Queen Margaret forgives Warwick after he turns against the Yorkists and becomes an ally of King Henry.*

Forgiveness, f. for looking at other women - ... A sin prevailing much in youthful men who give their eyes the liberty of gazing.
"Hath not, else, his eye
Stray'd his affections in unlawful love?
A sin prevailing much in youthful men,
Who give their eyes the liberty of gazing." (COE.5.1)
She tells you (a friend) that her boyfriend or husband has cast looks of unmistakable meaning to other women. Your comment, 'It's a sin prevailing much…gazing', could help soften her resentment by realizing that the practice is universal with solid historical roots.

In the play. *Everyone thinks that Antipholus from Ephesus has lost his wits. The Lady Abbess questions Adriana as to the possible causes of his madness. Perhaps he was taken in by sudden passion (for someone else than Adriana).*

Forgiveness, f. granted - The nature of his great offence is dead and deeper than oblivion we do bury the incensing relics of it.
"The nature of his great offence is dead,
And deeper than oblivion we do bury
The incensing relics of it."
(AWEW.5.3)
Elegant declaration of forgiveness and/or to state that you hold no grudges. Change 'his' to 'yours' if you are dealing with the offender directly.
In the play. *The King has forgiven Bertram for his mistakes.*

Forgiveness, f. to a recreant – ... ten times more beloved than if thou never hadst deserved our hate
"…ten times more beloved,
Than if thou never hadst deserved our hate." (KHVI.p3.4.5)
In the play. *Edward IV welcomes his brother Clarence who had earlier on defected to Warwick and the Lancastrians.*

Forgiveness, no f. possible. See 'Pity, p. not to be hoped for – as the wolf does of the shepherd' – 'Pity, p. prevented by resentment at offense or injury'.

Forgiveness, plea to be forgiven - ... if hearty sorrow be a sufficient ransom for offence, I tender it here.
"Forgive me, Valentine; if hearty sorrow
Be a sufficient ransom for offence,
I tender it here." (TGV.5.4)
An alternate to 'excuse me' or 'forgive me'. Change 'Valentine' for your name.

In the play. *Proteus asks Valentine for forgiveness after having tried his utmost to snatch Sylvia, Valentine's girlfriend.*

Forgiveness, injuries forgotten - The record of what injuries you did us...as done by chance'
"The record of what injuries you did us,
Though written in our flesh, we shall remember
As things done by chance." (AC.5.2)
Forgive with class.
In the play. *Octavian to the defeated Cleopatra.*

Forgiveness, see entries for 'Defense, d. from accusation'.

Forgiveness, self-f. - ... at the last do as the heavens have done, forget your evil; with them forgive yourself.
"...at the last,
Do as the heavens have done, forget your evil;
With them forgive yourself." (WT.5.1)
Advise to a redeemed friend.
In the play. *Cleomenes exhorts Leontes to forgive himself after the penance that he, Leontes, has undergone to repent of his former evil.*

Formality asserted, austere regard of control - ... quenching my familiar smile with an austere regard of control.
"I extend my hand to him thus, - quenching my familiar smile with an austere regard of control." (TN.2.5)
Question a change in behavior from familiar to distant. E.G. 'Why do you quench your familiar smile with an austere regard of control?' For the opposite of formality see 'Ceremony, c. unnecessary among friends - Ceremony was but devised at first to set a gloss on faint deeds...'

In the play. *Malvolio fantasizes aloud on how to handle Sir Toby should he (Malvolio) ever marry Olivia whose steward he currently is.*

Formality, no f. in love – Love is not love when it is mingled with regards, that stand aloof from the whole point.
"Love is not love when it is mingled with regards
That stand aloof from the whole point." (KL.1.1)
Show your sincerity. Answer to comments or questions of the type "What will the others think?" For example, she is in a different class than yours, but you really love her.
In the play. *The King of France will marry Cordelia even if her father Lear has disinherited her.*

Fortune cruel f. that usually lets man outlive his wealth – ... To view with hollow eye and wrinkled brow an age of poverty...
"For herein Fortune shows herself more kind
Than is her custom: it is still her use
To let the wretched man outlive his wealth,
To view with hollow eye and wrinkled brow
An age of poverty; from which lingering penance
Of such misery doth she cut me off." (MOV.4.1)
In the play. *Antonio, considering his impending death (pound of flesh to be cut near his heart) sees the positive side of it. He will not be forced to live poor and regret his lost wealth.*

Fortune, defying f. - ... Fortune knows we scorn her most when most she offers blows.
" ...Fortune knows
We scorn her most when most she offers blows." (AC.3.11)
Inspire a determination to fight when circumstances appear difficult. See also

'Person, worthiness of a p. shown under trial - … in the wind and tempest of her frown, distinction…'
In the play. *After having lost a battle to Octavian, Antony tries to make the best of a bad situation.*

Fortune, down with f. - Affliction is enamour'd of thy parts…
"Affliction is enamour'd of thy parts,
And thou art wedded to calamity" (RJ.3.3)
Quote the first line and change 'thy' to 'my' to add some emphasis to your state of mind.
In the play. *Fr. Lawrence announces to Romeo that he, Romeo, has been banished from Verona.*

Fortune, f. biased and unfair - … for those that Fortune makes fair, she scarce makes honest…
"… for those that Fortune makes fair, she scarce makes honest: and those that she makes honest, she makes very ill-favouredly." (AYLI.1.2)
Complaint about Fortune.
In the play. *Celia agrees with Rosalind's assessment of the intrinsic unfairness of Fortune.*

Fortune, f. has taken a turn for the worse – Thus hath the course of justice wheel'd about, and left thee but a very prey to time…
"Thus hath the course of justice wheel'd about,
And left thee but a very prey to time;
Having no more thought of what you wert
To torture thee the more for what you art." (KRIII.4.4)
'I am prey to time' is a good expression to convey a certain resignation to the turn of events.
In the play. *Wronged and vengeful Queen Margaret reminds Queen Elizabeth that her (Elizabeth's) fortunes have taken (indeed) a turn for the worst.*

Fortune, f. never complete - will fortune never come with both hands full…
"Will fortune never come with both hands full,
But write her fair words still in foulest letters?
She either gives a stomach and no food;
Such are the poor, in health; or else a feast
And takes away the stomach; such are the rich,
That have abundance and enjoy it not." (KHIV.p2.4.4)
In the play. *London, the Jerusalem chamber at court. Harcourt brings in more good news. The fleeing rebel Northumberland has been defeated and dispatched by the sheriff of York. Now all possible rebellious embers are spent, but the King is sick and cannot enjoy the bounty of fortune.*

Fortune, f. re-interpreted, she is acting in disguise - … when fortune means to men most good she looks upon them with a threatening eye.
" … when fortune means to men most good,
She looks upon them with a threatening eye." (KJ.3.4)
Suggest a less negative interpretation of a sticky situation.
In the play. *Pandulph, the Pope's legate sees some positive developments even after the loss of the battle of Angier by the French.*

Fortune, f. so far good but… - Thus far our fortune keeps an upward course …but… I spy a black, suspicious, threatening cloud…
"Thus far our fortune keeps an upward course,
And we are graced with wreaths of victory.
But, in the midst of this bright-shining day,
I spy a black, suspicious, threatening cloud,

That will encounter with our glorious sun,
Ere he attain his easeful western bed" (KHVI p3.5.3)
In the play. *Edward IV at Coventry. Warwick has been killed but the threatening cloud refers to the announced oncoming French reinforcements of Queen Margaret.*

Fortune, f. to be praised for good turnout of events - Well, if Fortune be a woman, she's a good wench for this gear.
"Well, if Fortune be a woman, she's a good wench for this gear." (MOV.2)
Acknowledge the influence of luck on the positive outcome. Change 'gear' to 'business'.
In the play. *Launcelot has drawn good omens by a quick examination of his palm. He is ready with his father Gobbo, to enter Bassanio's service. 'Gear' stands for 'business'.*

Fortune, fickle - O fortune, fortune! all men call thee fickle.
"O fortune, fortune! all men call thee fickle." (RJ.3.5)
Comment on the variability of fortune.
In the play. *Romeo, regrettably, must leave for Mantua and Juliet does not like it.*

Fortune, friendship and their relationship - When Fortune, in her shift and change of mood, spurns down her late beloved...
"When Fortune, in her shift and change of mood,
Spurns down her late beloved, and all his dependants,
Which laboured after him to the mountain's top,
Even on their knees and hands, let him slip down,
Not one accompanying his declining foot." (TOA.1.1)
Comment on the aftermath of declining fortunes.

In the play. *The poet, though a parasite himself, predicts the behavior of the other parasites, should Timon's fortunes change.*

Fortune, gifts of f. uneven and unequal - ... the bountiful blind woman doth most mistake in her gift.
CELIA. Let us sit and mock the good housewife Fortune from her wheel, that her gifts may henceforth be bestowed equally.
ROSALIND. I would we could do so; for her benefits are mightily misplaced; and the bountiful blind woman doth most mistake in her gift. (AYLI.1.2)
Complaint about Fortune.
In the play. *Celia attempts to cheer Rosalind up*

Fortune, invocation - Fortune, good night: smile once more: turn thy wheel!
"Fortune, good night: smile once more: turn thy wheel!" (KL.2.2)
In the play. *Kent makes an invocation to Fortune to be more benevolent to himself and King Lear after the horrible treatment received by King Lear's bad daughters Regan and Goneril.*

Fortune, invocation - O lady Fortune, stand auspicious!
"O lady Fortune,
Stand you auspicious!" (WT.4.3)
In the play. *Perdita, pursued by Florizel hopes for the best.*

Fortune, luck found in number 3 or in odd numbers - I hope good luck lies in odd numbers.
"...This is the third time; I hope good luck lies in odd numbers. ...They say there is divinity in
odd numbers, either in nativity, chance, or death" (MWW.5.1)

In the play. *Would be lover Falstaff makes a third attempt at his conquests, but the merry wives of Windsor have prepared another and final trick for him.*

Fortune, luck will do the selection - ... in a moment, fortune shall call forth out of one side her happy minion...
"Then, in a moment, fortune shall call forth
Out of one side her happy minion;
To whom in favour she shall give the day,
And kiss him with a glorious victory." (KJ.2.2)
Comment while waiting for the resolution of an event, a competition or a contest or a raffle.
In the play. *Meditations by Philip F. in front of the walls of Angiers.*

Fortune, meditation on the fall of f. - This is the state of man; today he puts forth the tender leaves of hope...
"Farewell, a long farewell, to all my greatness!
This is the state of man; today he puts forth
The tender leaves of hope; tomorrow blossoms,
And bears his blushing honours thick upon him;
The third day comes a frost, a killing frost;
And, when he thinks, good easy man, full surely
His greatness is a-ripening, - nips his root,
And then he falls, as I do."
(KHVIII.3.2)
Introduction to a presentation containing examples of rise and fall, success followed by defeat, the inevitable destiny of man etc.
In the play. *Wolsey meditates on his own fall from the grace of the King.*

Fortune, men show respect and loyalty only to the rich and fortunate - ... for men, like butterflies show not their mealy wings but to the summer.
"... for men, like butterflies,
Show not their mealy wings but to the summer
And not a man, for being simply man,
Hath any honour, but honour for those honours
That are without him, as place, riches, favour,
Prizes of accident as oft as merit:
Which when they fall, as being slippery standers,
The love that lean'd on them as slippery too,
Do one pluck down another and together
Die in the fall " (TC.3.3)
See also 'Flattery, f and praise tied to reward'.
In the play. *Patroclus tells Achilles that the other Greeks do not seem to show their respect (to Achilles) as they used to. 'Mealy' = 'made of particles'.*

Fortune, mistreated by f. - A man whom both the waters and the wind...have made a ball for them to play upon.
"A man whom both the waters and the wind,
In that vast tennis-court, have made the ball
For them to play upon." (PER.2.1)
Answer to 'Who are you?' when you wish to place emphasis on the negative side of life or to make an ironic, self-effacing statement.
In the play. *Some fishermen find Pericles shipwrecked on their shore and ask who is he. 'What a drunken knave was the sea to cast thee in our way!' Pericles replies and introduces himself with the lines above.*

**Fortune, modest attitude towards f. –
Since you will buckle fortune on my back... I must have patience to endure the load.**
"Since you will buckle fortune on my back,
To bear her burthen, whether I will or no,
I must have patience to endure the load" (KRIII.3.7)
In an acceptance speech after you have given a new responsibility, title or equivalent.
In the play. *Richard of Gloucester pretends to reluctantly accept the crown at the hands of Buckingham and others in a coup engineered by Richard himself.*

Fortune, moment of unfavorable conditions due to astrological influences - There's some ill planet reigns...
"There's some ill planet reigns.
I must be patient till the heavens look
With an aspect more favorable." (WT.2.1)
Statement of patience and acceptance of circumstances.
In the play. *Leontes sends his wife Hermione to prison on charges of infidelity. She rejects the accusations but patiently accepts the unjust punishment.*

Fortune, on the good side of f. - ... Fortune is merry and in this mood will give us any thing.
"...Fortune is merry,
And in this mood will give us any thing." (JC.2.3)
Make it part of an uplifting speech.
In the play. *Antony receives the welcome news that Caesar Octavian is at hand in Rome. Octavian will be an ally in the battle against Brutus and followers.*

Fortune, recollection of former f. - ... The ruin speaks that sometime it was a worthy building.
"...The ruin speaks that sometime
It was a worthy building" (CYM.4.2)
Comment on someone who recounts his former glories.
In the play. *Roman general Caius Lucius stumbles upon the beheaded body of the slain Cloten. The image of the 'worthy building' refers to the man when he was alive.*

Fortune, reversal of f. - ... my good stars, that were my former guides, have empty left their orbs...
"...my good stars, that were my former guides,
Have empty left their orbs, and shot their fires
Into the abysm of hell" (AC.3.13)
Admitting that things are not so good at the moment.
In the play. *Antony has whipped Thyreus, a messenger from the victorious Octavian who addressed Antony in arrogant tone. Antony recognizes, however, that his luck is down.*

Fortune, reversal of f. and abandonment by friends - Thy friends are fled to wait upon thy foes and crossly to thy good all fortune goes.
"Thy friends are fled to wait upon thy foes,
And crossly to thy good all fortune goes." (KRII.2.4)
See also 'Flattery, f. and praise tied to reward - ... when the means are gone that buy this praise, the breath is gone whereof this praise is made.'
In the play. *Lord Salisbury waiting for Richard to land in Wales from Ireland while enemies gather around Bolingbroke*

Fortune, reversal of f. and the bright side of it - ... and found the blessedness of being little.
"His overthrow heap'd happiness upon him;
For then, and not till then, he felt himself,

And found the blessedness of being little." (KHVIII.4.2)
See the bright side of being fired, e.g. 'Like Cardinal Wolsey I found the blessedness of being little'.
In the play. *Griffith gives to ex-queen Katharine an account of the last days of Cardinal Wolsey. Cardinal Wolsey was instrumental in the divorce of Q. Katharine, after which Henry VIII married Anne Boleyn.*

Fortune, reversal of f. observed - ... I see thy glory like a shooting star fall to the base earth from the firmament.
"Ah, Richard, with the eyes of heavy mind
I see thy glory like a shooting star
Fall to the base earth from the firmament.' (KRII.2.4)
In the play. *Lord Salisbury waiting for Richard to land in Wales from Ireland while enemies gather around Bolingbroke.*

Fortune, reversal of f. vs. earlier ambitious claims– Now Phaethon hath tumbled from his car...
"Now Phaethon hath tumbled from his car,
And made an evening at the noontide prick." (KHVI.p3.1.4)
In the play. *Clifford's sarcastic comment on the captured York, who was confident of dethroning King Henry thus (figuratively) becoming a new sun.*

Fortune, scratched by f. - ... I am a man whom fortune hath cruelly scratched.
"... I am a man whom fortune hath cruelly scratched." (AWEW.5.2)
In the play. *Parolles partially acknowledges his own faults to the nobleman Lafeu, who always saw through him. Lafeu replies, 'And what would you have me to do? 't is too late to pair her nails now.'*

Fortune, sequence of events too good to be true - ... (I) am ready to distrust mine eyes, and wrangle with my reason...
"Yet, doth this accident and flood of fortune
So far exceed all instance, all discourse,
That I am ready to distrust mine eyes,
And wrangle with my reason, that persuades me
To any other trust, but that I am mad." (TN.4.3)
Describe your happiness as beyond belief. See also 'Happiness, h. overwhelming – drowned in sweetness, needing some pain to be reminded of mortality'
In the play. *Sebastian, mistaken for his twin sister/ brother Viola/ Cesario, is still shocked at the love and reception given him by Olivia.*

Fortune, she is your total f. - ... the continent and summary of my fortune.
"...Here's the scroll,
The continent and summary of my fortune" (MOV.3.2)
Compliment, e.g. 'You are the continent...fortune'. See also 'Modesty, total m. – the full some of me is sum of nothing.'
In the play. *The scroll fund in the correctly guessed casket contains Portia's picture and Bassanio will then be able to marry her.*

Fortune, unfriendly to the poor –
Fortune, that arrant whore, ne'er turns the key to the poor.
"Fortune, that arrant whore,
Ne'er turns the key to the poor." (KL.2.4)
A realistic assessment of fortune who is notoriously stingy with the poor.
In the play. *Lear's fool reflecting on the circumstances that he and Lear are in.*

Fortune, wish of good f. - ... and fortune play upon thy prosperous helm as thy auspicious mistress!

"Then go forth;
And fortune play upon thy prosperous helm,
As thy auspicious mistress! "
(AWEW.3.3)
Delivering good wishes at the onset of a project.
In the play. *The Duke of Florence wishes Bertram good luck in the forthcoming battles.*

Fortune's fool – O, I am fortune's fool.
"O, I am fortune's fool!" (RJ.3.1)
In the play. *Romeo after he slay Tybald in a brawl.*

Foul play suspected – all is not well; I doubt some foul play.
"…all is not well;
I doubt some foul play: would the night were come!" (H.1.2)
In the play. *Hamlet suspects foul play even before actually seeing the Ghost of his Father.*

France, French air prompts bragging - … this your air of France hath blown that vice in me…
"Yet, forgive me,
That I do brag thus! - this your air of France
Hath blown that vice in me; I must repent." (KHV.3.6)
Soften the impact of some self-serving assertion, e.g. ' 'Yet, forgive me…I must repent'. Modify 'this your air of France' to the circumstances that caused you to brag.
In the play. *K. Henry V talking to the French envoy and extolling the superior military skill and courage of the English*

France, uncomplimentary remark on F. or any place - France is a dog hole, and it no more merits the thread of a man's foot.
" France is a dog hole, and it no more merits

The thread of a man's foot."
(AWEW.2.3)
When you don't like the place you are in for whatever reason, by changing 'France' to the applicable location or country.
In the play. *Bertram has just told Parolles how he was forced to marry Helena. Bertram decides to join the other Frenchmen fighting at Florence in Italy. Parolles, still smitten by all the insults received by Lafeu, agrees with the idea and adds a disparaging remark on France.*

Freedom, as free as - … as free as heart can wish or tongue can tell.
"…and we charge and command that their
wives be as free as heart can wish or tongue can tell." (KHVI.p2.4.5)
Answer to 'Are you free?'
In the play. *This is part of the political and reform program announced by the rebel John Cade.*

Freedom, as free as - … free as mountain winds.
"Thou shalt be free
As mountain winds" (TEM.1.2)
In the play. *Prospero promises freedom to Ariel after completion of the project.*

Freedom, f. as a personal achievement - … every bondman in his own hand bears the power to cancel his captivity.
"… every bondman in his own hand bears
The power to cancel his captivity." (JC.1.3)
In the play. *Cassius elaborates on the ideas and reasons that lead to the assassination of Caesar.*

Freedom, f. fighters or terrorists? - … So often shall the knot of us be call'd the men that gave their country liberty.
BRUTUS How many times shall Caesar bleed in sport,

That now on Pompey's basis lies along
No worthier than the dust!
CASSIUS So oft as that shall be,
So often shall the knot of us be call'd
The men that gave their country liberty. (JC.3.1)
In the play. *After having assassinated Caesar the conspirators meditate on the historical importance of their act. See also 'Event, e. of historical importance - how many ages hence shall this, our lofty scene be acted over, in states unborn...'*

Freedom, f. of the soul – Every subject's duty is the king's; but every subject's soul is his own.
"Every subject's duty is the king's; but every subject's soul is his own" (HV.4.1)
In the play. *King Henry V incognito speaks with Williams, one of his soldiers, who holds somewhat unorthodox views.*

Freedom, f. of the spirit has no obstacles - ... Nor stony tower, nor walls of beaten brass...
".... Nor stony tower, nor walls of beaten brass,
Nor airless dungeon, nor strong links of iron,
Can be retentive to the strength of spirit" (JC.1.3)
In the play. *Cassius to Casca advocating the power of the spirit to beat all obstacles, while elaborating on the ideas and reasons that lead to the assassination of Caesar.*

Freedom, relocation in search of f. – Now go we in content to liberty...
"Now go we in content
To liberty, and not to banishment" (AYLI.1.3)
In the play. *Celia, along with friend Rosalind, is banished from court and quite happy to pursue a life of freedom in the country (actually the Forest of Arden).*

French, a warning against their seductive techniques - Beware of them, Diana; their promises... are not the things they go under.
"Beware of them, Diana; their promises, enticements, oaths, tokens, and all these engines of lust, are not the things they go under" (AWEW.3.5)
A warning affecting the French or modify to any target nationality.
In the play. *Mariana, a friend of Diana, a Florentine young lady, warns her against the courting tactics of the French.*

French, f. language not understood - Speak 'pardon' as 'tis current in our land; the chopping French we do not understand.
"Speak 'pardon' as 'tis current in our land;
The chopping French we do not understand" (KRII.5.3)
Skip 'pardon' and exhort relevant parties to speak in understandable language.
In the play. *The Duchess of York has pleaded with King Henry IV for her son's life. Her husband suggests to the king a French formula for pardon. The Duchess object to French being used.*

French, the French are unreliable - Done like a Frenchman: turn, and turn again!
"Done like a Frenchman: turn, and turn again!" (KHVI.p.1.3.3)
In the play. *Joan of Arc comments aside on the Duke of Burgundy who has turned and joined her side. Needless to say, Shakespeare is not exactly objective in his portrayal of English-French wars.*

French, the French are unreliable - ... we are in France, amongst a fickle wavering nation.
"...remember where we are,
In France, amongst a fickle wavering nation" (KHVI.p1.4.1)

In the play. *Henry VI reminds Basset and Vernon who are arguing amongst themselves, that the enemies are the French.*

Freshness, like a rose - she looks as clear as morning roses newly wash'd with dew.
"… she looks as clear
As morning roses newly wash'd with dew" (TOS.2.1)
Compliment on her freshness.
In the play. *Petruchio has a plan of action on how to woo Katharina. He will praise her defects.*

Freshness, like dew - ... As fresh as morning dew distilled on flowers.
"…. As fresh as morning dew distilled on flowers." (TA.2.4)
Compliment on her freshness.
In the play. *Titus Andronicus is the goriest of Shakespeare's plays. The line here refers actually to drops of blood found by Martius on leaves in a wood. They are evidence of the horrible crimes committed by Tamara's sons.*

Friend, f. or enemy? - ... But what compact mean you to have with us? Will you be prick'd in number of our friends…
"But what compact mean you to have with us?
Will you be prick'd in number of our friends;
Or shall we on, and not depend on you?" (JC.3.1)
Alternate to 'Are you with us or not?' I.E. 'Will you be prick'd in number of our friends?'
In the play. *Cassius questions Antony if he will be friends or enemy of the conspirators, now that Caesar has been murdered.*

Friend, one's soul chooses or elects someone to be a f. – Since my dear soul was mistress of her choice and could of men distinguish…
"Since my dear soul was mistress of her choice
And could of men distinguish, her election
Hath seal'd thee for herself" (H.3.2)
Also an answer to the generic question, 'What made you decide?' when the decision was made on instinct more than analysis, e.g. 'My dear soul was mistress of her choice'
In the play. *Hamlet selected Horatio to be a friend.*

Friend, trusted f. – (he was) my book wherein my soul recorded the history of all her secret thoughts.
"…my book wherein my soul recorded
The history of all her secret thoughts" (KRIII.3.5)
Answer to 'Do you trust me?' E.G. 'You are the book wherein my soul records…thoughts.'
In the play. *After cutting Lord Hastings' head (for not wanting to endorse him as king), Richard puts on a charade pretending that Hastings was his trusted friend.*

Friends, f. amazed and perplexed - ... wild amazement hurries up and down the little number of your doubtful friends.
"And wild amazement hurries up and down
The little number of your doubtful friends." (KJ.5.1)
In the play. *Ph. Faulconbridge tells King John that most noblemen have rallied around the Dauphin of France and old friends are doubtful. This follows the death of young Prince Arthur, attributed to the king's will.*

Friends, f. as wealth – I am wealthy in my friends
"I am wealthy in my friends" (PER.2.2)
In the play. *Timon harbors the illusion that his well-benefited friends may come to his help.*

Friends, not many words needed among f. - ... 'twixt such friends as we few words suffice.
"Signor Hortensio, 'twixt such friends as we
Few words suffice." (TOS.1.2)
Indicate friendship and that not many words are necessary for mutual understanding.
In the play. *Hortensio has proposed to Petruchio the idea of getting a rich wife (meaning the impossible Katharina) and Petruchio replies*

Friends, ungrateful and mercenary f. - ... left me open, bare for every storm that blows.
"... numberless upon me stuck as leaves
Do on the oak, hive with one winter's brush
Fell from their boughs and left me open, bare
For every storm that blows."
(TOA.4.3)
See also entries for 'Ingratitude' – 'Weak, feeling w. and unprotected – a naked subject to the weeping clouds' - Pessimism, fleetness of life – As flies to wanton boys are we to the gods, they kill us for their sport'
In the play. *Timon's friends have left him and he reflects on them with Apemantus who came to visit Timon in his cave.*

Friendship, continued help required and extended to friend - 'T is not enough to help the feeble up, but to support him after.
"'T is not enough to help the feeble up,
But to support him after." (TOA.1.1)
Support the idea of providing continued assistance when needed.
In the play. *Timon will continue to help Ventidius even after Ventidius gets out of jail to help him rebuild his position.*

Friendship, disappointed and disillusionment with friends - O time most accurst, 'mongst all foes that a friend should be the worst!
"...O time most accurst,
'Mongst all foes that a friend should be the worst!" (TGV.5.4)
In the play. *Valentine expressing his indignation at the treachery of his friend Proteus.*

Friendship, extreme f. - Methinks, I could deal kingdoms to my friends and ne'er be weary.
"Methinks, I could deal kingdoms to my friends,
And ne'er be weary" (TOA.1.2)
In the play. *Timon carried away by his own enthusiasm, expands on the meaning of friendship.*

Friendship, f. and help assured - ... If I do vow a friendship, I'll perform it to the last article.
"...assure thee,
If I do vow a friendship, I'll perform it
To the last article" (OTH.3.3)
In the play. *Desdemona assures Cassio that she will do her utmost to restore him in Othello's good book.*

Friendship, f. declared. - I have professed me thy friend, and I confess me knit to thy deserving with cables of perdurable toughness.
"I have professed me thy friend, and I confess me knit to thy deserving with cables of perdurable toughness." (OTH.1.3)
Emphatically declare your friendship or allegiance. – See also 'Advice, make and keep good friends'
In the play. *The perfidious Iago will use Roderigo in his scheme to destroy Othello.*

Friendship, f. guaranteed by wisdom - The amity that wisdom knits not, folly may easily untie.
"The amity that wisdom knits not, folly may easily untie." (TC.2.3)
Support the idea that alliances between crooks (lacking wisdom) are bound to be broken by their own follies.
In the play. *Ulysses' comment to Nestor. Achilles and Ajax are the ones who lack wisdom.*

Friendship, f. restoring optimism - But if the while I think on thee, dear friend, all losses are restored and sorrows end.
"But if the while I think on thee, dear friend,
All losses are restored and sorrows end." (SON 30)

Friendship, f. should show some understanding - A friend should bear his friend's infirmities…
"A friend should bear his friend's infirmities,
But Brutus makes mine greater than they are" (JC.4.3)
In the play. *Cassius' retort to Brutus' charges of bribe taking.*

Friendship, f. shown and extended in difficult circumstances - I am not of that feather to shake off my friend when he most needs me.
"I am not of that feather to shake off
My friend when he most needs me." (TOA.1.1)
When you agree to help a friend.
In the play. *Timon is ready to help Ventidius who is in a bind with creditors.*

Friendship, f. with woman leading to physical relationship - … to mingle friendship far is mingling bloods.
"…Too hot, too hot!
To mingle friendship far is mingling bloods." (WT.1.2)
Pull the leg of your friend when he says that he and she are just friends.
In the play. *Leontes has developed the crazy notion that his faithful wife Hermione has an affair with his guest Polixenes.*

Friendship, questionable and insincere f. – For who not needs shall never lack a friend…
"…For who not needs shall never lack a friend,
And who in want a hollow friend doth try,
Directly seasons him his enemy" (H.3.2)
In the play. *Part of the play within the play, 'The Murder of Gonzago' – the lines here recited by the player king.*

Friendship, strategic f. and tied to wealth - Every man will be thy friend whilst thou hast wherewith to spend…
"Every man will be thy friend
Whilst thou hast wherewith to spend;
But if store of crowns be scant,
No man will supply thy want" (Pass. Pilgrim)

Friendship, value of f. – …would most resembled instruments hung up in their cases.
"…(friends, if not needed at some time) would most resemble sweet instruments hung up in their cases, that keep their sounds to themselves." (TOA.1.2)
Convince your friend that you are really glad to do him a favor.
In the play. *Timon explains his philosophy on friendship. Friendship is to be shown at moments of need. He will soon find that his parasitic friends do not have the same view.*

Frigidity, plea to cold lady – Titled goddess… you are no maiden, but a monument…
" Titled goddess;

And worth it, with addition! But, fair soul,
In your fine frame hath love no quality?
If the quick fire of your youth light not your mind,
You are no maiden, but a monument:
When you are dead you should be such a one
As you are now, for you are cold and stern." (AWEW.4.2)
When you have tried everything but she does not budge.
In the play. *Bertram tries to seduce Diana, a Florentine lady.*

Frown, f. by a powerful m. - ... And who durst smile when Warwick bent his brow?
"And who durst smile when Warwick bent his brow?" (KHVI.p3.5.2)
Soften the bad mood of your boss. See also the entry for 'Power, p. broker' for use of the preceding lines.
In the play. *Warwick, wounded to death in the battle against the York forces near Barnet, reflects on his life*

Frustration, f. relieved at the cost of retribution - ... I will ease my heart, albeit I make a hazard of my head.
"...I will ease my heart,
Albeit I make a hazard of my head."
(KHIV.p1.1.3)
You are going to tell them like it is at the cost of being fired.
In the play. *Hotspur, angered by the king is tempted to tell him that he will not send him the requested prisoners.*

Fully equipped – With all appliances and means to boot…
"With all appliances and means to boot…" (KHIV.p2.3.1)

In the play. *King Henry cannot sleep. See 'Sleep, s. denied to persons with great power and responsibility - Canst thou, O partial sleep, give thy repose to the wet sea-boy in an hour so rude…*

Fun, f. behind one's back - … persevere, counterfeit sad looks, make mouths upon me when I turn my back…
"Ay do, persevere, counterfeit sad looks,
Make mouths upon me when I turn my back,
Wink each at the other, hold the sweet jest up." (MND.3.2)
When you think you are being made fun of.
In the play. *Helena thinks that everyone is making fun of her.*

Funding, inadequate funding for the project – There's but a shirt and a half in all my company…
"There's but a shirt and a half in all my company: and the half-shirt is two napkins tacked together and thrown over the shoulders like an herald's coat without sleeves." (KHIVp1.4.2)
Dramatize that assets have been reduced to a minimum. See also 'Personnel, p. not in good shape - The stuff we have, a strong wind will blow to pieces.' ***
'Weakness, group w., in a weak position - … our lances are but straws, our strength as weak, our weakness past compare…'
In the play. *Falstaff's inventory of his resources and supplies as he approaches the battle with the rebels.*

Furniture, comfortable couch - … couch softer and sweeter than the lustful bed…
"…couch
Softer and sweeter than the lustful bed
On purpose trimm'd up for Semiramis" (TOS.ind)

Comment on new furniture in the house of friends.
In the play. *The Lord who organized the play (and prank) for the peddler Sly promises to provide among other things excellent furniture to him. 'Semiramis' was the queen of Assyria and famous for her voluptuousness, as well as cruelty.*

Fury, f. prevents rational thinking – Now he'll outstare the lightning … in that mood the dove will peck the estridge.
"Now he'll outstare the lightning …
…To be furious,
Is to be frighted out of fear; and in that mood
The dove will peck the estridge
… when valour preys on reason,
It eats the sword it fights with." (AC.3.13)
See also entries for 'Anger'.
In the play. *Enobarbus comments on Antony's intent to challenge Octavian to a hand to hand duel to resolve the war. Antony shows poor judgment, as the victorious Octavian has no reason to accept Antony's challenge.*

Future, attitude towards the f. - … for the life to come, I sleep out the thought of it.
"…for the life to come, I sleep out the thought of it." (WT.4.2)
In the play. *Small crook Autolycus expounds his philosophy on life.*

Future, marred by the effect of current events - The woe's to come; the children yet unborn.
"The woe's to come; the children yet unborn.
Shall feel this day as sharp to them as thorn." (KRII.4.1)
Hint at the future consequences of a decision or policy with which you disagree.
In the play. *Carlisle refers to the day when Bolingbroke was crowned king after having deposed Richard II.*

Future, sensing the f. in one moment - …and I feel now the future in the instant.
"…and I feel now
The future in the instant." (M.1.5)
Applies to those moments occurring in many, when you sense the development of all subsequent events from one key one. For example, the moment and Reagan's election triggered the sequence of events that led to the attacks of September 11, 01.
In the play. *Lady Macbeth greets her returning husband. The future she sees is the crown, after Macbeth assassinates King Duncan.*

Future, the f. will tell – There are many events in the womb of time, which will be delivered.
"There are many events in the womb of time, which will be delivered." (OTH.1.3)
Use as a truism when you really do not know what is going to happen. – See also 'Forecasting requested', 'Forecasting ability'. A good evasive answer when you wish to be uncommitted in your answer. Answer to 'What do you think will happen?'
In the play. *Roderigo is after Desdemona and hopes that Iago may help in the intent.*

Gain, g. assured under any circumstance – Sort how it will, I shall have gold for all.
"Hume's knavery will be the duchess' wreck,
And her attainture will be Humphrey's fall:
Sort how it will, I shall have gold for all" (KHVI.p2.1.2)
In the play. *Hume, the crafty knave gets money from the Duchess of Gloucester to consult with a witch and money from Gloucester's enemies to betray her for consorting with witches.*

Gain, g. from crime illusory - ... Who buys a minute's mirth to wail a week? Or sells eternity to get a toy?
"'What win I, if I gain the thing I seek?
A dream, a breath, a froth of fleeting joy.
Who buys a minute's mirth to wail a week?
Or sells eternity to get a toy?
For one sweet grape who will the vine destroy?" (ROL)
In the poem. *The evil Tarquin is conscious of the gravity of the crime he is about to commit.*

Gains, ill gotten g. to be maintained with ill deeds - ... and he that stands upon a slippery place must be as boisterously maintain'd as gain'd.
"A sceptre snatch'd with an unruly hand
Must be as boisterously maintain'd as gain'd;
And he that stands upon a slippery place
Makes nice of no vile hold to stay him up" (KJ.3.4)
The problem with imperialist policies. See also 'Remedies, extreme r. required - ... Diseases desperate grown by desperate appliances are relieved or not at all'.
In the play. *Cardinal Pandulph tells Lewis of France that King John will probably kill Arthur, legitimate heir to the English throne. This in turn will embitter the people and King John will be deposed, hence favoring the political position of France.*

Games, dice - ... and by the hazard of the spotted die...
"...And by the hazard of the spotted die
Let die the spotted." (TOA.5.4)
Answer to 'What have you been doing?' when you went to Las Vegas or equivalent, e.g. 'I tried the hazard of the spotted die'. See also 'Character, not afraid of taking chances - I have set my life upon a cast and I will stand the hazard of the die'.
In the play. *Athenian Senators propose to Alcibiades that his revenge may be affected by decimation as opposed to total destruction. The 'spotted' are those marked to die by decimation.*

Gardening, weed pulling – ...I will go root away the noisome weeds, which without profit suck the soil's fertility from wholesome flowers.
"... I will go root away
The noisome weeds, which without profit suck
The soil's fertility from wholesome flowers." (KRII.3.4)
In the play. *The Queen's gardener detailing his next course of action. The garden will offer other metaphors for government and politics, such as weeds, un-pruned trees, superfluous branches etc.*

Garments needing to be worn to fit well - ... garments, cleave not to their mould but with the aid of use.
"New honours come upon him
Like our strange garments, cleave not to their mould
But with the aid of use." (M.1.3)
Can be equally applied to shows. Or answer to a question about your reaction to new procedures. E.G. 'They feel like strange garments, that cleave…use'
In the play. *Banquo observes Macbeth who appears still in awe after the witches' predictions of current and future honors.*

Gaze, turning away your g. - I am no loathsome leper; look on me.
"What, dost thou turn away and hide thy face?
I am no loathsome leper; look on me." (KHVI p2.3.2)
Answer to 'Why don't you look at me?'
In the play. *Q. Margaret puts up a pretence that she was not responsible for Gloucester's death. King Henry VI does not look at her, hence her question.*

Gem, she is a g. - But 'tis that miracle and queen of gems…
"But 'tis that miracle and queen of gems
That nature pranks her in attracts my soul."(TN.2.4)
Compliment. Answer, 'why do you love me?' Change 'her' to 'you'.
In the play. *The Duke Orsino conveys to Viola/Cesario the reasons why he is so attracted to Olivia (a love that she does not reciprocate).*

Gesturing, acting - … do not saw the air too much with your hand, thus, but use all gently.
"… do not saw the air too much with your hand, thus, but use all gently; for in the very torrent, tempest, and, as I may say, the whirlwind of passion, you must acquire and beget a temperance that may give it smoothness." (H.3.2)
An observation applicable to Italians, those among them who do saw the air too much with their hands.
In the play. *Hamlet gives acting hints to the band of actors that will perform at court.*

Gift, unexpected g. - I see, a man here needs not live by shifts, when in the street he meets such golden gifts.
"I see, a man here needs not live by shifts,
When in the street he meets such golden gifts." (COE.3.2)
Comment on a city or place or company where you have been treated especially well.
In the play. *Angelo brings in a chain that Ant E had ordered for his wife Adriana. But Angelo gives the chain to Ant S (thinking he is Ant E). Ant S is taken aback and reacts positively to a city where one receives such unexpected, expensive gifts.*

Gifts, g. sometimes not welcome - … to the noble mind rich gifts wax poor when givers prove unkind.
"Take these again, for to the noble mind
Rich gifts wax poor when givers prove unkind." (H.3.1)
When a gift or free something appears motivated rather than sincere.
In the play. *Ophelia, who is at a loss to explain Hamlet's earlier harsh words and change of behavior towards her, wants to return his gifts.*

Gifts, poor g. due to poor fortune– … one out of suits with fortune, that could give more, but that her hand lacks means.
"Wear this for me, one out of suits with fortune,
That could give more, but that her hand lacks means" (AYLI.1.2)
Explain the small size of your contribution, e.g. 'I am one…lacks means'. See also 'Attitude, a. towards the world, hating it – one…whom the vile blows and buffets of the world…'
In the play. *Rosalind gives Orlando a chain to wear after his victorious bout with the wrestler Charles.*

Gifts, g. as means to a young woman's heart - … trifles, nosegays, sweetmeats, messengers of strong prevailment in unharden'd youth.
"With bracelets of thy hair, rings, gawds, conceits,
Knacks, trifles, nosegays, sweetmeats, messengers
Of strong prevailment in unharden'd youth" (MND.1.1)
In the play. *Egeus, father of Hermia, accuses Lysander of having won her heart with gifts.* 'Gawds'='useless things, toys'

Girl (wench), looking forward to a chat - …I love her ten times more than e'er I did: I love her ten times more than e'er I did: O, how I long to have some chat with her!
"Now, by the world, it is a lusty wench;

I love her ten times more than e'er I did:
O, how I long to have some chat with her!" (TOS.2.1)
When someone has berated a girl you do not know and that criticism has instead sparked your interest.
In the play. *Music teacher Hortensio had his head smacked and bruised by Katharine, and this intrigues and motivates Petruchio to meet with the lady ('lusty wench').*

Girl, bad g. – I have sworn thee fair and thought thee bright who art as black as hell, as dark as night.
"For I have sworn thee fair and thought thee bright,
Who art as black as hell, as dark as night." (SON 147)

Girls, easy going g. warning about them - … they appear to men like angels of light…
" It is written, they appear to men like angels of light; light is an effect of fire, and fire will burn; ergo, light wenches will burn." (COE.4.3)
Soften or tone down the excessive praise of a woman. For example,
- "…. So you say she is an angel of light?"
- "Yes"
- " Now then, it is written that light wenches appear… will burn."
In the play. *A courtesan approaches Ant S (mistaken for Ant E) and claims the jewelry chain she expected from Ant E. Ant S strongly rejects her. Dromio S expands on a crafted syllogism on easygoing girls.*

Give the devil his due – … the devil shall have his bargain… : he will give the devil his due.
"…the devil shall have his bargain; for he was never yet a breaker of proverbs: he will give the devil his due" (KHIV.p1.1.2)

Use 'We should give the devil his due' to acknowledge in good humor an unexpected positive action by an adversary.
In the play. *The Prince of Wales answers a question by Poins. The giver of the due to the devil is Falstaff. The occasion is thepurse-snatching caper at Gadshill, where Falstaff will also prove a coward.*

Giving up - … deeper than did ever plummet sound I'll drown my book.
"…deeper than did ever plummet sound
I'll drown my book" (TEM.5.1)
You have supported your point with written and well-documented information. Yet, your claim or suggestion or argument is denied. Throw away your documents with an air of disgust while uttering the quote.
In the play. *Prospero has accomplished all his goals with his acquired skills in magic. Before retiring he gives up his tools and book of magic.*

Glories, the time of past g. – … in former golden days…
"I was, I must confess,
Great Albion's queen in former golden days:
But now mischance hath trod my title down" (KHVI.p3.3.3)
Adapt to explain that the negative change in your circumstances was due to mischance. Or use 'in former golden days' to make reference to a more prosperous past in general.
In the play. *Queen Margaret has traveled to France to seek military assistance from King Lewis.*

Glory, there is g. in dying for a good cause - He lives in fame that died in virtue's cause.
"He lives in fame that died in virtue's cause." (TA.1.1)

A rhetorical conclusion to an unsuccessful project conducted with good intentions.
In the play. *Mutius is laid to rest after having been slain by Titus. Mutius died in a virtuous cause and the mourners comment on his death.*

God, g. responsible for victory - thy arm was here; and not to us, but to thy arm alone, ascribe we all.
"...God, thy arm was here;
And not to us, but to thy arm alone,
Ascribe we all! " (KHV.4.8)
In the play. *King Henry's comment on the victory at Agincourt.*

Gods, their qualified assistance - If the great gods be just, they shall assist the deeds of justest men.
"If the great gods be just, they shall assist
The deeds of justest men." (AC.2.1)
In the play. *Pompey to assistant Menecrates while pondering his claims on Octavian, Lepidus and Antony.*

Gold, corrupting effects of g. - O thou sweet king-killer, and dear divorce 'twixt natural son and sire!...
"O thou sweet king-killer, and dear divorce
'Twixt natural son and sire! thou bright defiler
Of Hymen's purest bed! thou valiant Mars!
Thou ever young, fresh, loved and delicate wooer,
Whose blush doth thaw the consecrated snow
That lies on Dian's lap! thou visible god,
That solder'st close impossibilities,
And makest them kiss! that speak'st with every tongue,
To every purpose!" (TOA.4.3)
In the play. *Timon rhetorically addresses the gold he has casually found while digging for roots in the woods. He lists the gold's properties and power to corrupt, desecrate and make the unthinkable possible.*

Gold, corrupting effects of g. – Thus much of this will make black white, foul fair, wrong right, base noble, old young, coward valiant....
"Thus much of this will make black white, foul fair,
Wrong right, base noble, old young, coward valiant.
Ha, you gods! why this? what this, you gods? Why, this
Will lug your priests and servants from your sides,
Pluck stout men's pillows from below their heads:
This yellow slave
Will knit and break religions, bless the accursed,
Make the hoar leprosy adored, place thieves
And give them title, knee and approbation
With senators on the bench: this is it
That makes the wappen'd widow wed again;
She, whom the spital-house and ulcerous sores
Would cast the gorge at, this embalms and spices
To the April day again." (TOA.4.3)
In the play. *Timon happens to stumble on some hidden gold while looking for edible roots in the woods and philosophizes on its pernicious effects.*
'Hoar'= 'Whitish as an indication of sickness'.
'Wappened'='Over-worn, stale, unattractive'

Gold, effects of g. in overlooking a person's liabilities – Hortensio, peace! thou know'st not gold's effect...
"Hortensio, peace! thou know'st not gold's effect:
Tell me her father's name and 'tis enough;
For I will board her, though she chide as loud

As thunder when the clouds in autumn crack" (TOS.1.2)
In the play. *Petruchio is not concerned if Katharina is a shrew.*

Gold, g. as an object of idolatry – What a god's gold, that he is worshipp'd in a baser temple than where swine feed!
"What a god's gold,
That he is worshipp'd in a baser temple
Than where swine feed!" (TOA.5.1)
In the play. *Timon's reaction at overhearing the schemes of the poet and the painter to extract money from him, who is now in the woods.*

Gold, g. as powerful tool of corruption – … gold were as good as twenty orators and will, no doubt, tempt him to anything.
RICHARD. Know'st thou not any whom corrupting gold
Would tempt to a close exploit of death?
PAGE. I know a discontented gentleman,
Whose humble means match not his haughty spirit.
Gold were as good as twenty orators,
And will, no doubt, tempt him to anything." (KRIII.4.2)
Describe a person of modest means and high ambitions, e.g. 'his humble means match not his haughty spirits". Or a corruptible person, 'Gold were as good as twenty orators and… anything'. See also 'Money, m opening the way' – 'Authority, corrupted by gold' – 'Attitude, mercenary a. - Believe't, that we'll do any thing for gold.'
In the play. *Richard wants to dispose of the two princes in the Tower who in time may prove a challenge to his throne. Buckingham is backing out. This is why Richard has to ask the page to locate a contract killer.*

Gold, power of g. to buy access. – 'Tis gold which buys admittance…
"…'Tis gold
Which buys admittance…
… and 'tis gold
Which makes the true man kill'd and saves the thief;
Nay, sometime hangs both thief and true man: what
Can it not do and undo?" (CYM.2.3)
See also 'Authority, corrupted by gold - … and though authority be a stubborn bear…'
In the play. *The foolish Cloten plans to bribe Imogen's chambermaids.*

Good and bad, inability to distinguish between g. and bad - … can we not partition make with spectacles so precious 'twixt fair and foul?
"What, are men mad? Hath nature given them eyes
To see this vaulted arch, and the rich crop
Of sea and land, which can distinguish 'twixt
The fiery orbs above and the twinn'd stones
Upon the number'd beach? and can we not
Partition make with spectacles so precious
'Twixt fair and foul?" (CYM.1.6)
In the play. *The evil Iachimo tries to portray Leonatus as an unfaithful husband to the trusting and spotless Imogen.*

Good night – as sweet repose and rest come to thy heart as that within my breast!
"Good night, good night! as sweet repose and rest
Come to thy heart as that within my breast!" (RJ.2.2)
In the play. *After mutual declarations of love, Romeo leaves Juliet's garden and she wishes him good night.*

Good night - Enjoy the honey-heavy dew of slumber.
"Enjoy the honey-heavy dew of slumber" (JC.2.1)
Also alternative for "I am going to sleep', e.g. 'I am going to enjoy… slumber'
In the play. *Brutus sees his servant Lucius asleep and after a moment of thought decides to let him continue to sleep. Presumably Lucius does not hear what Brutus says and sleeps soundly as he has no cares. See 'Sleep, lack of care promoting sound sleep'*

Good night – fair thoughts be your fair pillow.
" ... fair thoughts be your fair pillow!" (TC.3.1)
In the play *Pandarus knows how to ingratiate himself with women. This is his good night to Helen.*

Good night – sleep dwell upon thine eyes, peace in thy breast!
"Sleep dwell upon thine eyes, peace in thy breast!
Would I were sleep and peace, so sweet to rest!" (RJ.2.2)
A parting salutation. See also 'Salutations, wishing the good of the night' – 'Separation temporarily postponed, good night.
In the play. *Romeo to Juliet (she on the balcony, he down in the garden) - they just cannot let go of each other.*

Good, finding good in bad - Thus may we gather honey from the weed and make a moral of the devil himself.
"Thus may we gather honey from the weed,
And make a moral of the devil himself." (KHV.4.1)
See also 'Adversity, some g. can be found in a. - there is some soul of goodness in things evil...'
In the play *King Henry to Bedford before the battle of Agincourt. The French have made much noise during the night (useless, i.e. the weed). In turn this causes the English to rise early (good thing, i.e. the honey), and prepare themselves for battle.*

Good, one out of ten - Among nine bad if one be good, there's yet one good in ten.
"Among nine bad if one be good,
There's yet one good in ten" (AWEW.1.3)
See also '**Last, not being the l. better than nothing - not being the worst stands in some rank of praise**'.
In the play. *The clown sings a song for the Countess of Rousillon.*

Good, what g. does not need propping – Good alone is good without a name. Vileness is so…
"…Good alone
Is good without a name. Vileness is so:
The property by what it is should go,
Not by the title." (AWEW.2.3)
In the play. *The King attempts to convince Bertram that Helena would be a good wife for him.*

Good-bye, cordial - If we do meet again, why, we shall smile; if not, why then, this parting was well made.
"And whether we shall meet again I know not.
Therefore our everlasting farewell take:
….
If we do meet again, why, we shall smile;
If not, why then, this parting was well made" (JC.5.1)
In the play. *Brutus to Cassius before the battle of Philippi.*

Goodbye, when she is leaving for a short or long trip, or a shopping excursion - Let all the number of the stars give light to thy fair way.

"Let all the number of the stars give light
To thy fair way!" (AC.3.2)
You can use it with her or she can use it with you whenever you leave for a business trip. – See also entries for 'Salutations'.
In the play. *After a summit meeting in Italy Lepidus wishing a good trip to departing Antony and Octavian*

Goodbye, when you really hate to leave - Good night, good night! parting is such sweet sorrow...
"Good night, good night! parting is such sweet sorrow,
That I shall say-good night till it be morrow!" (RJ.2.1)
In the play. *Romeo and Juliet (she on the balcony, he down in the garden) just cannot let go of each other.*

Goodness, g. poorly repaid - Undone by goodness! Strange, unusual blood, when man's worst sin is, he does too much good!
"Undone by goodness! Strange, unusual blood,
When man's worst sin is, he does too much good!" (TOA.4.2)
In the play. *Flavius, faithful Timon's servant comments on the demise of his master.*

Goodness' sake - For goodness' sake, consider what you do...
"For goodness' sake, consider what you do,
How you may hurt yourself " (KHVIII.3.1)
Common aphorism.
In the play. *Cardinal Wolsey to Queen Katherine trying to convince her to go along with the King's request for a divorce.*

Gossip, g. about celebrities - What great ones do, the less will prattle of.
"What great ones do, the less will prattle of." (TN.1.2)
Introduce a personality who will talk about his life. E.G. ". Until now we have been prattling about our speaker, now let's hear from his very voice – what great ones do the less will prattle of'. See also entries for 'Rumor'
In the play. *Viola asks the Captain about the duke Orsino. Rumor has it, answers the Captain, that Orsino is in love with Olivia.*

Government, foreign g. support of home tyranny - For how can tyrants safely govern home, unless abroad they purchase great alliance?
"His demand
Springs not from Edward's well-meant honest love,
But from deceit bred by necessity;
For how can tyrants safely govern home,
Unless abroad they purchase great alliance?" (KHVI p3.3.3)
Use in support of your criticism of imperialist foreign policies. See the many Latin American dictators sustained in power through history by the US Administration.
In the play. *Queen Margaret to King Lewis of France and his sister lady Bona. Margaret sees through Warwick's plot to have the usurping Edward marry Lady Bona of France.*

Government, good ruler defined by the goodness of his g. - ... He is a happy king, since he gains from his subjects the name of good by his government.
FIRST FISHERMAN Why, I'll tell you: this is called Pentapolis, and our king the good Simonides. and he deserves so to be called for his peaceable reign and good government
PERICLES The good King Simonides, do you call him…. He is a happy king, since he gains from his subjects the name of good by his government. (PER.2.1)

In the play. *Pericles is shipwrecked in front of Pentapolis and he meets three fishermen on the shore.*

Grace, compared to the best herb in a salad - she was the sweet marjoram of the salad, or rather, the herb of grace.
"Indeed, sir, she was the sweet marjoram of the
salad, or rather, the herb of grace." (AWEW.4.5)
Compliment. Change to '(You are) the sweet marjoram of the salad, or rather, the herb of grace." A compliment that may work well at dinner, especially if she is a vegetarian.
In the play: *Helena is believed dead (she is not) and the Clown agrees with Lafeu in praising Helena and extending the comparison (to a precious herb) that Lafeu initiated.*

Grace, presence, speech - ... Possess'd with such a gentle sovereign grace, of such enchanting presence and discourse.
"…Possess'd with such a gentle sovereign grace,
Of such enchanting presence and discourse." (COE.3.2)
Answer to 'Do you like me?', 'What do you like in me?' or similar.
In the play. *Antipholus of Syracuse cannot understand why the wife of Antipholus of Ephesus called him (Syracuse) husband. That is of course because the two Antipholus are identical twins. Yet, while he does not like Luciana (the once who called him husband, he really likes her sister who has 'gentle sovereign grace' etc.*

Graces, her g. and virtues - Her virtues graced with external gifts do breed love's settled passions in my heart…
"Her virtues graced with external gifts
Do breed love's settled passions in my heart:
And like as rigor of tempestuous gusts
Provokes the mightiest hulk against the tide,
So am I driven by breath of her renown
Either to suffer shipwreck or arrive
Where I may have fruition of her love." (KHV.p1.5.5)
Use the first two lines and change to 'Your virtues graced with external gifts do breed love's settled passions in my heart.' Also an alternate to the question 'Do you like me?'
In the play: *Suffolk has arrived to London from France where he has identified in Margaret a suitable bride for young King Henry VI. King Henry is quite impressed by Suffolk's presentation. Other English Peers are not so impressed and indeed Margaret will prove quite a character. 'She-wolf' of France, York will address her so later.*

Graffiti, g. on tree barks - … and in their barks my thoughts I'll character.
" O Rosalind! these trees shall be my books,
And in their barks my thoughts I'll character." (AYLI.3.2)
Indicate the type of material on which you will inscribe your love lines.
In the play. *Orlando seeks a written means to express his love for Rosalind.*

Graphics, picture as a substitute - Vouchsafe me yet your picture for my love, picture that is hanging in your chamber.
"Madam, if your heart be so obdurate,
Vouchsafe me yet your picture for my love,
The picture that is hanging in your chamber." (TGV.4.2)
This is really a last resort if she has turned you down. It is a compliment to her vanity so perhaps she may still keep you in mind.

Ladies are extremely concerned about how they look in pictures. Fortunately today, with cheap and quick digital photography it is possible to take as many pictures as needed until she finds the one of herself she likes most. It was not that easy in the age of portraits, before the advent of photography. The famous American portrait painter John Sargent (1865-1925) had to admit, 'Every time I paint a portrait, I lose a friend' See also 'Love, consolation prize - ... but one fair look; a smaller boon than this I cannot beg...'
In the play. *Proteus makes a pass at Sylvia who rejects him utterly. Proteus asks at least to have a picture of her.*

Graphology, g and an occasion for a compliment – ...and whiter than the paper it writ on is the fair hand that writ.
"I know the hand: in faith, 'tis a fair hand;
And whiter than the paper it writ on
Is the fair hand that writ." (MOV.2.4)
In the play. *Lorenzo recognizes the handwriting of Jessica in a letter delivered to him by Launcelot.*

Gratitude - ... only I have left to say more is thy due than more than all can pay.
"... only I have left to say,
More is thy due than more than all can pay." (M.1.4)
Express gratitude.
In the play. *Duncan expresses gratitude to Macbeth for having discovered and stopped Cawdor's treason.*

Gratitude, beyond g. – ... thou art so far before that swiftest wing of recompense is slow...
"The sin of my ingratitude even now
Was heavy on me: thou art so far before
That swiftest wing of recompense is slow
To overtake thee" (M.1.3)
In the play. *Duncan, still unaware of what Macbeth has in store for him profusely thanks him.*

Gratitude, commitment to demonstrate g. - ... and creep time ne'er so slow, yet it shall come from me to do thee good.
"... and creep time ne'er so slow,
Yet it shall come from me to do thee good" (KJ.3.3)
In the play. *King John to Hubert after the battle at Angiers.*

Gratitude, extent of g. limited by circumstances - ... all my treasury is yet but unfelt thanks.
"...all my treasury
Is yet but unfelt thanks" (KRII.2.3)
In the play. *Bolingbroke to the just arrived Lords Ross and Willoughby.*

Gratitude, extent of g. limited by circumstances - My recompense is thanks, and that's all, yet my good will is great, though the gift small.
"My recompense is thanks, and that's all;
Yet my good will is great, though the gift small." (PER.3.4)
Use any time when you believe that what she has done for you is more than what you can do in recompense or value.
In the play. *In Ephesus, the physician-magician Cerimon has revived Queen Thaisa. Having lost all at sea Queen Thaisa can only say thanks.*

Gratitude, g. and promise of reward - ... If fortune serve me, I'll requite this kindness.
"... thanks unto you all:
If fortune serve me, I'll requite this kindness." (KHVI p3.4.7)

In the play. *Freed from his confinement in York, Edward IV proclaims himself king again and thanks his supporters.*

Gratitude, g. expressed and responded to - ... **To be acknowledged, madam, is o'erpaid.**
CORDELIA O thou good Kent, how shall I live and work,
To match thy goodness? My life will be too short,
And every measure fail me.
KENT To be acknowledged, madam, is o'erpaid. (KL.4.7)
Answer to 'How can I thank you?' See also 'Welcome, w. to our house - All our services in every point twice done, and then done double...' *** 'Work, it does not matter if it is hard w. provided we like it - The labour we delight in physics pain'
In the play. *Cordelia acknowledges the service and loyalty of Kent towards his master and her father King Lear.*

Gratitude, g. expressed and responded to. - Too little payment for so great a debt.
"**Too little payment for so great a debt**" (TOS.5.2)
Answer to an expression of gratitude for the gratitude that you, in turn, have expressed for a previous favor. See also 'Welcome, w. to our house - All our services in every point twice done, and then done double...'
In the play. *Katharina refers to is a wife's debt to her husband. See 'Husband, declaration of husband's rights '.*

Gratitude, g. expressed and responded to - Your presence makes us rich, most noble lord and far surmounts our labour to attain it.
"**Your presence makes us rich, most noble lord.**
And far surmounts our labour to attain it." (KRII.2.3)

In the play. *Ross and Willoughby reply to Bolingbroke who expressed hi appreciation at their joining him.*

Gratitude, g. and promise of reward to good friends – I count myself in nothing else so happy as in a soul remembering my good friends.
"**I count myself in nothing else so happy**
As in a soul remembering my good friends
...
My heart this covenant makes, my hand thus seals it." (KRII.2.3)
In the play. *Bolingbroke to Harry Percy.*

Gratitude, g. expressed for welcome - ... **I am not of many words, but I thank you.**
"**I thank you: I am not of many words, but I thank you.**" (MAAN.1.1)
In the play. *Don John thanks Leonato for the welcome.*

Gratitude, g. expressed to team for good work - I thank you all, For doughty-handed are you, and have fought not as you served the cause...
"**I thank you all;**
For doughty-handed are you, and have fought
Not as you served the cause, but as 't had been
Each man's like mine; you have shown all Hectors." (AC.4.8)
In the play. *Antony thanks his general and soldiers after they won a temporary victory against Octavian.*

Gratitude, g. expressed with accompanying tears - I have a kind soul, that would give you thanks and knows not how to do it, but with tears.
"**I have a kind soul, that would give you thanks,**

And knows not how to do it, but with tears." (KJ.5.7)
Express profound and heart-felt gratitude In the play. *King John is dead and Henry III, his son is now king - he thanks Salisbury and other allies.*

Gratitude, g. expressed with commitment to a reward - I give thee thanks in part of thy deserts and will with deeds requite thy gentleness.
"I give thee thanks in part of thy deserts,
And will with deeds requite thy gentleness" (TA.1.1)
When you cannot immediately reciprocate the favor or the concession. In the play. *Andronicus has refused the Roman Emperor's crown in favor of Saturnine who says words of thanks.*

Gratitude, g. for good news – the gods bless you for your tidings, next ...
"First, the gods bless you for your tidings; next,
Accept my thankfulness." (COR.5.4)
In the play. *The tribune Sicinius to the messenger who announces that Coriolanus has relented and will not attack Rome.*

Gratitude, g. for honor received – I have received much honour by your presence and ye shall find me thankful.
"I have received much honour by your presence,
And ye shall find me thankful." (KHVIII.5.4)
In the play. *King Henry to lords and attendants to the christening of daughter Elizabeth, the future Elizabeth I.*

Gratitude, g. recognized and expressed – ... within this wall of flesh there is a soul that counts thee her creditor.
"...within this wall of flesh There is a soul that counts thee her creditor." (KJ.3.1)
A bit emphatic but it will leave a mark in her memory and she will remember later on. Works equally well for any occasion when you wish to be a bit more original in expressing gratitude than with the universal 'thank you'.
In the play. *King John thanks Hubert for his contribution to the happy outcome of the battle of Angiers.*

Gratitude, g. to Jupiter and stars – Jove and my stars be praised!"
"Jove and my stars be praised!" (TN.2.5)
In the play. *Malvolio falls for the trick played by Maria and believes a love letter by Olivia to be true and not a fake.*

Gratitude, g. towards noble men - ... and thanks to men of noble minds is honourable meed.
"My faction if thou strengthen with thy friends,
I will most thankful be; and thanks to men
Of noble minds is honourable meed." (TA.1.1)
In the play. *Bassianus to Titus Andronicus.*

Gratitude, modesty in expressing g. – Too little payment for so great a debt
"Too little payment for so great a debt." (TOS.5.2)
In the play. *The fully tamed Katharina has acknowledged her husband Petruchio as her lord – the payment consists of love, fair looks and true obedience.*

Gratitude, no need to return favor - The service and the loyalty I owe in doing it, pays itself.
"The service and the loyalty I owe, In doing it, pays itself. " (M.1.4)
When you wish to be noble and generous. Answer to 'I owe you' or 'How much do I owe you?' See also

'Satisfaction, s. as payment. - He is well paid that is well satisfied…'
In the play. *Macbeth answers the expressions of gratitude from King Duncan.*

Gratitude, refusing payment or recompense for a previous favor or act of kindness - … there's none can truly say he gives, if he receives.
"I gave it freely ever; and there's none
Can truly say he gives, if he receives:
If our betters play at that game, we must not dare
To imitate them; faults that are rich are fair" (TOA.1.2)
Refuse a gift in return of your gift. Alternatively, free the recipient of your gift from having to reciprocate.
In the play. *Ventidius, shortly before helped by Timon to get out of jail for debt, wants (or pretends) to reciprocate. Timon refuses to accept*

Greatness, acquisition of g. - Some are born great, some have greatness thrust upon them.
MALVOLIO (reading letter). In my stars I am above thee; but be not afraid of greatness: some are born great, some achieve greatness, and some have greatness thrust upon them." (TN.2.5)
Use satirically to explain your exploits, 'Some are born great… upon them'. Or encourage a reluctant participant, e.g. 'Be not afraid of greatness'.
In the play. *Maria has prepared a fake letter in which Olivia declares her love for Malvolio and he falls for it.*

Greatness, advantages of g. questionable – … 'tis better to be lowly born and range with humble livers in content…
"… Verily,
I swear, 'tis better to be lowly born,
And range with humble livers in content
Than to be peer'd up in a glistening grief,
And wear a golden sorrow.
(KHVIII.2.3)
See also 'Fall from greatness painful, better not have pomp to begin with – … 'tis a sufferance panging as soul and body's severing.'
In the play. *Anne Bullen comments on the fate of Queen Catherine soon to be divorced by Henry VIII.*

Greatness, g. falling with falling fortune - 'T is certain, greatness, once fall'n out with fortune must fall out with men too.
" 'T is certain, greatness, once fall'n out with fortune,
Must fall out with men too." (TC.3.3)
State an inevitable truth.
In the play. *Feeling ignored, Achilles muses on the turn of events.*

Greatness, g. self-conscious - … greatness knows itself…
"…greatness knows itself…"
(KHIV.p1.4.3)
Ironic comment when you are congratulated for a small achievement.
In the play. *At Shrewsbury, Hotspur tell Sir Walter Blunt what are the grievances of the rebels. The 'greatness' refers to King Henry supercilious handling of his former allies.*

Greed, g. disclaimed - … I would not have you to think that my desire of having is the sin of covetousness.
"…I would not have you to think that my desire of having is the sin of covetousness" (TN.5.1)
In the play. *Duke Orsino promises additional tips to the clown if he succeeds in persuading Olivia to meet with him.*

Greed, g., covetousness and desire for more - Those that much covet are with gain so fond…

"Those that much covet are with gain so fond,
For what they have not, that which they possess
They scatter and unloose it from their bond,
And so, by hoping more, they have but less;
Or, gaining more, the profit of excess
Is but to surfeit, and such griefs sustain,
That they prove bankrupt in this poor-rich gain.
...
... we do neglect
The thing we have; and, all for want of wit,
Make something nothing by augmenting it." (ROL)
In the poem. *A reference to the lusty and insatiable Tarquin, who, having everything still plots to have Lucrece.*

Greed, gold provokes g. – how quickly nature falls into revolt, when gold becomes her object!
"How quickly nature falls into revolt, When gold becomes her object!" (KHIVp2.4.4)
Alternative to the statement that people will do anything for a buck. – See also 'Authority, corrupted by gold' - 'Money, poisonous and murderous effects of m.'
In the play. *The ailing King Henry thinks that P. Henry stole the crown and considers himself king.*

Greed, more calling for more - ... and my more having would be as a sauce to make me hunger more... "And my more having would be as a sauce
To make me hunger more: that I should forge
Quarrels unjust against the good and loyal,
Destroying them for wealth." (M.4.3)

Use as an example and a warning against greed, on the ground that greed feeds on itself.
In the play. *Malcolm portrays himself worse than what he is to test the ground.*

Greed, wanting more - Hast thou not worldly pleasure at command, above the reach or compass of thy thought?
"Hast thou not worldly pleasure at command,
Above the reach or compass of thy thought?" (KHVI p2.1.2)
Rhetorical reminder to a well-paid employee who still wants more.
In the play. *Humphrey of Gloucester reprimands his ambitious wife who prompts him to acquire the crown*

Greeting, g. an unexpected visitor while you are down in the dumps - what art thou? and how comest thou hither...
"What art thou? and how comest thou hither,
Where no man never comes but that sad dog
That brings me food to make misfortune live?" (KRII.5.5)
In the play. *Richard II, in prison at Pomfret Castle greets the porter who brings him food.*

Greetings, answer to early morning greetings – What early tongue so sweet saluteth me?
"What early tongue so sweet saluteth me?" (RJ.2.3)
In the play. *Fr. Lawrence returns Romeo's introductory salutations. Romeo visits with Fr. Lawrence to arrange for the wedding with Juliet.*

Greetings, end of unhappiness – Now is the winter of our discontent, made glorious summer by this sun of York...
"Now is the winter of our discontent
Made glorious summer by this sun of York;

And all the clouds that lour'd upon our house,
In the deep bosom of the ocean buried." (KRIII.1.1)
Someone arrives and joins an assembled group, e.g. 'Now is the winter of our discontent made glorious summer by the arrival of 'name of person'. See also 'Dandy, arrival of a d. - Came there a certain lord, neat, and trimly dress'd, fresh as a bridegroom.' *** 'War, end of war or quarrel - Grim-visaged war hath smooth'd his wrinkled front…'
Quote the last two lines at the end of a difficult negotiations between opposing parties.
In the play. *Richard meditates sarcastically on the current state of affairs at the court of his brother Henry IV. 'To lour' means 'to hang'*

Greetings, g. and wishes - Most excellent accomplished lady, the heavens rain odours on you!
"Most excellent accomplished lady, the heavens rain odours on you!" (TN.3.1)
Compliment. If you are concerned that the term 'odours' may be misinterpreted and turn your greeting into an insult, rather than a compliment, try 'rain balms' or 'rain flowers'.
In the play. *Viola, in the disguise of Cesario, rehearses how she will address Olivia.*

Grief, burning g. - …I have that honourable grief lodged here which burns worse than tears drown.
"I am not prone to weeping, as our sex
Commonly are; the want of which vain dew
Perchance shall dry your pities: but I have
That honourable grief lodged here which burns
Worse than tears drown" (WT.2.1)
See also entries for 'Pain, mental p.'

In the play. *Hermione, accused of non-existing adultery by her husband Leontes faces her judges*

Grief, g. at being forced to resign - You may my glories and my state depose, but not my griefs; still am I king of those.
"You may my glories and my state depose,
But not my griefs; still am I king of those." (KRII.4.1)
In the play. *Richard II to Bolingbroke after Richard has been forced to resign the throne.*

Grief, demonstrations of g. - And some will mourn in ashes, some coal-black…
"And some will mourn in ashes, some coal-black,
For the deposing of a rightful king." (KRII.5.1)
In the play. *King Richard imagining his woeful tale narrated by his wife to a hypothetical audience.*

Grief, g. and anxiety magnifying fears - … shapes of grief, more than himself, to wail which, look'd on as it is, is nought but shadows of what it is not.
"Each substance of a grief hath twenty shadows,
Which shows like grief itself, but is not so;
For sorrow's eye, glazed with blinding tears,
Divides one thing entire to many objects;
Like perspectives, which rightly gazed upon
Show nothing but confusion, eyed awry
Distinguish form: Looking awry upon your lord's departure,
Find shapes of grief, more than himself, to wail;
Which, look'd on as it is, is nought

but shadows
Of what it is not" (KRII.2.2)
In the play. *Bushy attempts to cheer the Queen up thinking that her fears stem from Richard having left to fight in Ireland.*

Grief, g. excessive - Some grief shows much of love but much of grief shows some want of wit.
"… some grief shows much of love;
But much of grief shows some want of wit." (RJ.3.5)
Use as a word of encouragement towards someone who is made sad by the turn of events.
In the play. *Juliet's mother thinks Juliet is sad because Tybalt is dead but that is not the reason.*

Grief, g. immeasurable - … my particular grief is of so flood-gate and o'erbearing nature …
"…my particular grief
Is of so flood-gate and o'erbearing nature
That it engluts and swallows other sorrows
And it is still itself." (OTH.1.3)
In the play. *Brabantio to the Duke of Venice. The grief is the fact that Desdemona, his daughter, has married Othello.*

Grief, g. kept inside – … my grief lies all within and these external manners of laments…
"'Tis very true, my grief lies all within;
And these external manners of laments
Are merely shadows to the unseen grief
That swells with silence in the tortured soul" (KRII.4.1)
In the play. *Richard to Bolingbroke who has usurped the throne.*

Grief, g. makes time seem long. - … grief makes one hour ten.
JOHN OF GAUNT What is six winters? they are quickly gone.
HENRY BOLINGBROKE To men in joy; but grief makes one hour ten (KRII.1.3)
In the play. *Richard II banished Bolingbroke from England. John of Gaunt tries to show Bolingbroke, his son, the less negative side of temporary banishment from England.*

Grief, g. softens the mind - Oft have I heard that grief softens the mind…
"Oft have I heard that grief softens the mind,
And makes it fearful and degenerate;
Think therefore on revenge and cease to weep." (KHVI.p2.4.4)
In the play. *Q. Margaret, distressed at the killing of Suffolk tells herself not to weep and meditates further revenges.*

Grief, g. soothed by grieving, and not cheerful company – Grief best is pleased with grief's society…
"Sad souls are slain in merry company;
Grief best is pleased with grief's society:
True sorrow then is feelingly sufficed
When with like semblance it is sympathized. " (ROL)
In the poem. *Lucrece is desperate after having been assaulted by Tarquin.*

Grief, g. that outlasts death – … my grief stretches itself beyond the hour of death… the unguided days and rotten times that you shall look upon…
"…my grief
Stretches itself beyond the hour of death:
The blood weeps from my heart when I do shape
In forms imaginary the unguided days
And rotten times that you shall look

upon
When I am sleeping with my ancestors" (KHIV.p2.4.4)
In the play. *Ailing King Henry IV's reaction at being informed that his heir, the Prince of Wales, is in the company of Poins and others. Actually, unbeknown to the king, the Prince has already changed his course of conduct.*

Grief, real g. is all inside - ... my grief lies all within, and these external manners of laments...
"...my grief lies all within;
And these external manners of laments
Are merely shadows to the unseen grief
That swells with silence in the tortured soul;
There lies the substance" (KRII.4.1)
Answer to 'How do you feel?'
In the play. *K. Richard to Bolingbroke who has just deposed him.*

Grievances, g. aired out - Windy attorneys to their client's woes .... let them have scope.
DUCHESS OF YORK. Why should calamity be full of words?
Q. ELIZABETH. Windy attorneys to their client's woes,
Airy succeeders of intestate joys,
Poor breathing orators of miseries,
Let them have scope! Though what they impart
Help nothing else, yet do they ease the heart. (KRIII.4.4)
Comment on the therapeutic value of venting complaints or verbalize suffering. See also 'Complaint after problems useless', 'Pain, mental p. relieved by talking about it.' *** Entries for 'Positive thinking' *** 'Pain, p. repressed more hurtful - Sorrow concealed, like an oven stopped, doth burn the heart to cinders where it is.'*** 'Anger, unable to refrain from expressing a. - my tongue will tell the anger of my heart.'

In the play. *With all his killings Richard III has caused much grief everywhere.*

Grievances, ready to listen to g. - ... Then in my tent, Cassius, enlarge your griefs and I will give you audience.
"...Then in my tent, Cassius, enlarge your griefs,
And I will give you audience." (JC.4.2)
In the play. *Cassius thinks that Brutus' criticism is uncalled for. Brutus invites Cassius to tell of his grievances privately and not in front of the soldiers at Sardi.*

Group, g. of bad people agreeing on something bad - Shameful is this league!
"Shameful is this league!" (KHVI p2.1.1)
Express your disapproval of a decision reached by your enemies or people you despise. See also 'Alliance, unholy a.'
In the play. *Gloucester is unhappy with the terms of the agreement between England and France and with the agreement itself.*

Growing up together - ... Like to a double cherry, seeming parted, but yet an union in partition.
"...So we grow together,
Like to a double cherry, seeming parted,
But yet an union in partition;
Two lovely berries moulded on one stem." (MND.3.2)
Use 'two berries moulded on one stem' to indicate identity of character. See also entries for 'Characters, similarity of c. - ...both of you are birds of selfsame feather'.
In the play. *Hermia, unaware of Oberon and Puck tricks, upbraids Helena and reminds her that they grew up together.*

Guarantee, personal g. – ... let the forfeit be nominated for an equal pound of your fair flesh...

384

"…let the forfeit
Be nominated for an equal pound
Of your fair flesh…" (MOV.1.3)
In the play. *Shylock will not ask for interest on the loan to Shylock but a pound of flesh if Shylock does not pay back in time.*

Guessing, refusal to g. due to previous mistakes (in guessing) - …I have found my self in my uncertain grounds to fail as often as I guessed.
". …(I) dare not
Say what I think of it, since I have found
My self in my uncertain grounds to fail
As often as I guessed." (AWEW.3.1)
Justify why you do not wish to guess, given previous failures.
In the play. *The Duke of Florence wonders why the King of France has not yet sent reinforcements for the war against Siena. An attending lord refuses to provide an opinion and explains why.*

Guilt, admission of g. and remorse - O Brakenbury, I have done those things, which now bear evidence against my soul.
"O Brakenbury, I have done those things,
Which now bear evidence against my soul" (KRIII.1.4)
In the play. *Clarence, prisoner in the Tower to his guard Brakenbury, describing a nightmare. Richard will soon have Clarence killed to prevent a possible Clarence's claim to the crown.*

Guilt, admit your g. and be honest - Now if you can blush and cry guilty, cardinal, you'll show a little honesty.
" Now, if you can blush and cry guilty, cardinal,
You'll show a little honesty."
(KHVIII.3.2)
Address your enemy and substitute his/her name in place of 'cardinal'. See also 'Impudence, shamelessness – you never blush at this? -
In the play. *Surrey and Wolsey in a heated exchange.*

Guilt, extreme admission of g. - … Wrong hath but wrong, and blame the due of blame
"… convey me to the block of shame;
Wrong hath but wrong, and blame the due of blame" (KRIII.5.1)
In the play. *The disgraced Buckingham who had earlier helped Richard in his evil plans is resigned to his fate.*

Guilt, g. evident without need for a verbal confession - … guiltiness will speak, though tongues were out of use.
"…guiltiness will speak,
Though tongues were out of use." (OTH.5.1)
In the play. *The perfidious Iago tries to make Bianca part of the plot that he himself has organized so that Roderigo attacks Cassio.*

Guilt, g. generates fear - So full of artless jealousy is guilt, it spills itself in fearing to be spilt.
"So full of artless jealousy is guilt,
It spills itself in fearing to be spilt."
(H.4.5)
See also 'Suspicion, s. sign of guilty mind - Suspicion always haunts the guilty mind, the thief doth fear each bush an officer.'
In the play. *The Queen first refuses to see Ophelia, distracted by the death of her father Polonius, then changes her mind and receives her. She was at first afraid that Ophelia may have had something against the Queen herself, that is,* To my sick soul, as sin's true nature is, Each toy seems prologue to some great amiss.

Guilt, evidence of g. visible in expression - The image of a wicked heinous fault lives in his eye.

"The image of a wicked heinous fault
Lives in his eye; that close aspect of his
Does show the mood of a much troubled breast." (KJ.4.2)
Change the third to the second person and mockingly tell the party that you think him responsible. 'The image of guilt lives in your eye; that closed aspect of yours…breast'.
In the play. *Hubert, the executioner enters the room. Pembroke tells Salisbury that Hubert may have already killed Arthur, judging by his looks.*

Guilt, guilty but not through recklessness - … your fault was not your folly.
"…your fault was not your folly". (KJ.1.1)
Change the pronouns and apply to yourself when you happen to have done something wrong, due to circumstances that you could not control.
In the play. *Lady Faulconbridge explains to her son that she was seduced by Richard Lionheart against her will and Faulconbridge acknowledges the event.*

Guilt, invitation to admit g. - … bear not along the clogging burthen of a guilty soul…
"Since thou hast far to go, bear not along
The clogging burthen of a guilty soul." (KRII.1.3)
Prompt the admission of error, for example, '(Name of person), admit it, bear not along…soul'.
In the play. *Bolingbroke and Mowbray have been banished. Bolingbroke still keeps accusing Mowbray and prompts him to admit to treason.*

Guilt, sense of g. – … Though inclination be as sharp as will…
"Pray can I not,
Though inclination be as sharp as will:

My stronger guilt defeats my strong intent" (H. 3.3)
In the play. *King Claudius is torn by the sense of his guilt and the desire to pray for comfort.*

Guilt, tempter or tempted guiltier - The tempter or the tempted, who sins most, ha?
"The tempter or the tempted, who sins most, ha?" (MFM.2.2)
Soften your responsibility for a mistake on the ground that you were drawn to commit it.
In the play. *Isabel ends her honest plea for her brother Claudio's life. The hypocrite Angelo meditates as he tries to justify to himself whether he should or should not try to seduce the virtuous Isabel.*

Habit, h. formation – How use doth breed a habit in a man!
"How use doth breed a habit in a man!" (TGV.5.4)
To counter the idea that people's habits cannot be changed. See also "Character, habit can change c. - for use almost can change the stamp of nature and either quell the devil, or throw him out with wondrous potency.'
In the play. *Valentine learns to accept his exile in the forest. For the lines that follow see 'Country living, in praise of country living'.*

Habit, not yet used to flattery and submission – … hardly yet have learn'd to insinuate, flatter, bow, and bend my limbs
"…hardly yet have learn'd
To insinuate, flatter, bow, and bend my limbs:
Give sorrow leave awhile to tutor me
To this submission." (KRII.4.1)
See also 'Character, unable to flatter, pretend and deceive - Because I cannot flatter and speak fair…'
In the play. *King Richard, soon to be dethroned, to his rival Bolingbroke.*

Habit, personal h. - ...(I am) one that converses more with the buttock of the night than with the forehead of the morning.
"...(I am) one that converses more with the buttock of the night than with the forehead of the morning." (COR.2.1)
See also 'Sleep, s. patterns and logic whereby late sleep is actually early rising - ... not to be abed after midnight is to be up betimes.'
In the play. *Menenius gives an account of his own habits to the tribune Sicinius. Menenius goes on to tell a bit more about himself. See 'Credentials, sincerity, one tongue - What I think I utter and spend my malice in my breath.'*

Hair, a blonde – ... her sunny locks hang on her temples like a golden fleece.
"...her sunny locks
Hang on her temples like a golden fleece"
Modify. ".... Your sunny locks hang on your temple like a golden fleece".
On hair here is Ovid's opinion, 'Let one girl's locks hang down on either shoulder; thus art thou, tuneful Phoebus (1), when thou hast taken up the lyre. Let another braid her hair like girt-up Diana, as she is wont to be when she hunts the frightened beasts. This one beseems to let her waving locks lie loose; let that one have her tight-drawn tresses close confined.... Even neglected hair is becoming to many; often you would think it lay loose from yesterday; this very moment it has been combed afresh....
Ah how kind is nature to your beauty, you whose defects may be made good in so many ways!... 'Tis with elegance we are caught: let not your locks be lawless: a touch of the hand can give or deny beauty... an oval face prefers a parting upon the head left unadorned. Round faces would fain have a small knot left on top of the head, so that the ears show'.

As for wigs 'a woman walks beneath a burden of purchased tresses, and money buys new locks for old. Nor does she blush to buy: publicly do we see them sold before the eyes of Hercules and the Virgin band /
(1) Phoebus, also called Apollo, was the Greek God of Enlightenment, with multiple responsibilities, god of the sun, music, poetry, prophecy, agricultural and pastoral life, as well as the leader of the nine Muses.
(2) The 'eyes of Hercules and the 'Virgin band' is a reference to the temple of Hercules and the Muses built in Rome by Fulvius Nobilior, 189 BC. Apparently wigs were available at a market in front of the temple.
In the play. *Bassanio describes Portia's beauties.*

Hair, artificial hair - So are those crisped snaky golden locks ...the skull that bred them in the sepulchre.
"So are those crisped snaky golden locks
Which make such wanton gambols with the wind,
Upon supposed fairness, often known
To be the dowry of a second head,
The skull that bred them in the sepulchre" (MOV.3.2)
Answer to 'What do you think of her hair' when you suspect a wig or some other equivalent. Use the last line, 'The skull that bred them (is) in the sepulchre'.
In the play. *Prior to selecting which basket to choose (the right basket will entail marrying Portia), Bassanio meditates on some truths which will lead him to discard the gold basket.*
'Gambols'='skips, jumps'

Hair, as tempting cobweb - a golden mesh to entrap the hearts of men...
"... Here in her hairs
The painter plays the spider and hath woven
A golden mesh to entrap the hearts of

men,
Faster than gnats in cobwebs."
(MOV.3.2)
Answer to 'What do you think of my hair? – Or if she handles you a picture of herself and asks your comment on it. Change to '…here in your hair it is as if a painter….' To account that it is a photograph, unless, of course, it is an actual painting. You can also use the last two lines as a straight compliment on her hair after she returns from the hairdresser. See also 'Breath like sugar'
In the play. In the play. *Bassanio has won Portia's hand by making the right choice in a frankly silly contest that Portia's deceased father had established as a condition for her inheritance. Bassanio chooses the right leaden casket and inside he finds Portia's picture along with an announcement that he has won the contest. In a monologue, he comments on the details of the picture.*

Hair, h. color as a tool for seduction –
Her hair is auburn, mine is perfect yellow: if that be all the difference in his love…
"Her hair is auburn, mine is perfect yellow:
If that be all the difference in his love,
I'll get me such a colour'd periwig"
(TGV.4.4)
In the play. *Julia observes the picture of Silvia with whom Julia's unfaithful Proteus is infatuated.*

Hair, some gray in it, but you still have the vigor of youth - … though grey do something mingle with our younger brown…
"What, girl! though grey
Do something mingle with our younger brown, yet have we
A brain that nourishes our nerves, and can
Get goal for goal of youth." (AC.4.8)
You may say this if she lightheartedly or seriously points out at your grey hair showing. Change 'with our' to 'with my' and 'have we' to 'have I'. See also entries for 'Age'.
In the play. *Antony has gained a temporary victory against the forces of Augustus.*

Haircut, no h. for a while –
Unscissor'd shall this hair of mine remain.
"Unscissored shall this hair of mine remain." (PER.3.3)
When someone suggests you have a haircut and you reject the suggestion.
In the play. *Pericles leaves Marina with Cleon and Dionyza and vows he will not cut his hair until Marina is happily married.*

Halcyon days – Expect Saint Martin's summer, halcyon days…
"Assign'd am I to be the English scourge.
…
Expect Saint Martin's summer, halcyon days,
Since I have entered into these wars"
(KHVI.p1.1.2)
In the play. *Joan of Arc will bring calm (peace) to France after defeating the English, she says to Charles of France. 'Halcyon' refers to the ancient belief that fourteen days of calm weather were to be expected around the winter solstice. 'Halcyon' means calm and tranquil, or 'happy or carefree'. The name of the legendary bird was actually alcyon, the 'h' was added in regard to the supposed association with the sea ('hals' in Greek).*

Halloween, h. material - … Nature seems dead, and wicked dreams abuse the curtain'd sleep…
"…Now o'er the one half world
Nature seems dead, and wicked dreams abuse
The curtain'd sleep; witchcraft celebrates
Pale Hecate's offerings, and wither'd murder,
Alarum'd by his sentinel, the wolf,

Whose howl's his watch, thus with his stealthy pace.
With Tarquin's ravishing strides, towards his design
Moves like a ghost." (M.2.1)
See also 'Time, night t. - Tis now the very witching time of night, when churchyards yawn…'
In the play. *Macbeth meditates before murdering Duncan.*

Halloween, h. material - Upon the corner of the moon there hangs a vaporous drop profound…
"Upon the corner of the moon
There hangs a vaporous drop profound;
I'll catch it ere it come to ground" (M.3.5)
In the play. *Hecate to the witches.*

Hand and hand kissing - If I profane with my unworthiest hand this holy shrine, the gentle sin is this - my lips, two blushing pilgrims, ready stand…
"If I profane with my unworthiest hand
This holy shrine, the gentle sin is this, -
My lips, two blushing pilgrims, ready stand
To smooth that rough touch with a tender kiss." (RJ.1.5)
Change to, 'My lips, two blushing pilgrims, ready stand to smooth my rough touch with a tender kiss.' Hand kissing was very popular at one time. Used now, it adds a touch of class to your greetings to a lady. If she may not be used to it and be mildly overwhelmed. Just in case… keep in mind the answer that a XVIIIth century gentleman gave to the lady who asked him, "Why are you kissing my hand?". "Madam – he replied – one has to start from somewhere."
In the play. *Romeo has sneaked into the party organized by the archenemy family of the Capulets and introduces himself to Juliet.*

Hand, her h. an occasion to extol her beauty - The fairest hand I ever touched! O beauty, till now I never knew thee.
"The fairest hand I ever touched! O beauty, till now I never knew thee." (KHVIII.1.4)
Follow up after kissing the hand of a particularly beautiful lady.
Ovid offers some advise to her if her hands are not perfect. 'Let her whose fingers are fat, or nails rough, mark what she says with but little gesture' (AOL.3)
In the play, *King Henry pays a compliment to Ann Boleyn.*

Hand, her h. epitome of whiteness - O, that hand, in whose comparison all whites are ink…
"O, that hand,
In whose comparison all whites are ink,
Writing their own reproach…" (TC.1.1)
Change 'that' to 'your'
In the play. *Troilus sings the praise of Cressida's hands.*
Before the age of tanning, natural or artificial, whiteness was considered one of the supreme standards of beauty. In 1788 the Institute of Science in Bologna (Italy) published a Manual for Newlyweds with entries from various contributors. One short poem by Abbott Clementino Vannetti recommends garments (to be worn by the bride in the intimacy of the house), that simultaneously let the husband have a glimpse of the beauty of her whiteness.

"Oh how a short dressing gown succeeds in showing all the pretty limbs to their best, by just providing their outline. How it manages not to hide completely to the inquisitive look the live and warm ivories of a heaving breast. And how it uncovers part of the extended, lovely, beautiful and snowy leg, along with the pretty foot!" ("*Oh come esprimer tutte / Le vezzosette membra, / E disegnarle sembra / La gonnelletta appien! / Come non tutti asconde / A' guardi altrui furtivi / I caldi avori, e vivi / Del palpitante sen! / E come parte scopre / De la distesa e bella / Nevosa gamba snella / Col breve pie' gentil!*"

And Ovid, "Nevertheless let the lower part of your shoulder and the upper part of your arm be bare and easily seen from the left hand. This becomes you especially, you who have snowy skins; when I see this, fain would I kiss that shoulder (*oscula ferre umero*), whenever it is exposed.' (AOL.2)

Hand, kissing of h. as a means to be remembered - O, could this kiss be printed in thy hand, that thou mightst think upon this as a seal…
"O, could this kiss be printed in thy hand,
That thou mightst think upon this as a seal,
Through whom a thousand sighs are breathed for thee!" (KHVI.p2.3.2)
When you are leaving for a long trip.
In the play. *The Duke of Suffolk has been banished from England for having killed Humphrey of Gloucester. Queen Margaret is very fond of Suffolk and possibly her lover. She takes leave of him with regret.*

Hand, request to kiss her h. - Behold this man, commend unto his lips thy favouring hand.
" Behold this man;
Commend unto his lips thy favouring hand." (AC.4.8)

In the play. *Antony has gained a temporary victory against the forces of Augustus. He addresses Cleopatra and speaks of himself in the third person as some people sometimes do (e.g. former presidential candidate and speaker of the senate Bob Dole). Antony continues and says of himself,*
He hath fought to-day
As if a god, in hate of mankind, had
Destroy'd in such a shape.

Hand, snow-white - … To the snow-white hand of the most beauteous Lady Rosaline.
"'To the snow-white hand of the most beauteous Lady Rosaline." (LLL.4)
Change 'Lady Rosaline' to the name of the applicable lady.
In the play. *Holofernes reads the address of a letter from Biron to Rosaline.*

Hand, white– as soft as dove's down and as white as it…
"I take thy hand, this hand,
As soft as dove's down and as white as it,
Or Ethiopian's tooth, or the fann'd snow that's bolted
By the northern blasts twice o'er."
(WT.4.4)
Compliment.
In the play. *Florizel declares his unending love to Perdita against the protestations of his father the king of Bohemia, who objects because Perdita is below Florizel's station.*

Hand, worthy to be kissed by kings – … a hand that kings have lipped, and trembled kissing.
" … a hand that kings
Have lipped, and trembled kissing" (AC.2.5)
Unless you and she are hobnobbing with royalty quote may not be applied directly. But, while holding her hand precede the ceremonial hand kissing with slightly modified lines, '…a hand that kings may lip and tremble kissing.'

In the play. *A messenger has arrived from Rome with news of Antony. The messenger's expression is not reassuring and Cleopatra is afraid that Antony be dead. But if he isn't she will allow the messenger to kiss her hand. But when the messenger informs her that Antony has actually married Octavia, Caesar's sister, Cleopatra goes into a rage and almost kills the messenger.*

Handling, proper h. of an execution or firing - Let's carve him as a dish fit for the gods..
"Let's carve him as a dish fit for the gods,
Not hew him as a carcass fit for hounds." (JC.2.1)
A metaphor for firing some important fellow.
In the play. *Brutus' idea of how Caesar should be killed, a kind of sacrificial offering as opposed to a butchery out of hatred.*

Hands, beautiful, like lilies - ... those lily hands tremble, like aspen-leaves, upon a lute, and make the silken strings delight to kiss them.
"… those lily hands
Tremble, like aspen-leaves, upon a lute,
And make the silken strings delight to kiss them" (TA.2.4)
Complimenting her hands.
In the play. *Andronicus says that only a monster could have cut Lavinia's hands.*

Hands (metaphor) unstained with kindred blood - His hands were guilty of no kindred blood, but bloody with the enemies of his kin.
"His hands were guilty of no kindred blood,
But bloody with the enemies of his kin." (KRII.2.1)
In the play. *York eulogizes Edward, King Richard's father, who clearly was a better person than his son.*

Hands, white - That pure congealed white, high Taurus' snow… turns to a crow, when thou hold'st up thy hand.
"That pure congealed white, high Taurus' snow,
Fanned with the eastern wind, turns to a crow,
When thou hold'st up thy hand: O, let me kiss
This impress of pure white, this seal of bliss!" (MND.3.2)
Compliment.
In the play. *Demetrius awakes and erupts in loving praise of Helena.*

Happiness, feigned h. - I am not merry; but I do beguile the thing I am, by seeming otherwise.
"I am not merry; but I do beguile
The thing I am, by seeming otherwise" (OTH.2.1)
In the play. *Desdemona to Iago. She has no idea of Iago's cunning and hatred.*

Happiness, h. at last - And happily I have arrived at the last unto the wished haven of my bliss.
"And happily I have arrived at the last,
Unto the wished haven of my bliss." (TOS.5.1)
Comment after she said yes.
In the play. *Lucentio has succeeded in marrying Bianca*

Happiness, h. beyond description - I cannot speak enough of this content; it stops me here; it is too much of joy.
"I cannot speak enough of this content;
It stops me here; it is too much of joy." (OTH.2.1)
Answer to 'Are you happy?'.
In the play. *Othello and Desdemona are finally together in Cyprus. They were married in Venice but reached Cyprus in separate ships.*

Happiness, h. beyond endurance - If this be so, the gods do mean to strike me to death with mortal joy.
"If this be so, the gods do mean to strike me
To death with mortal joy." (CYM.5.5)
In the play. *Cymbeline's happiness at finding that his daughter Imogen is alive.*

Happiness, h. described as a human figure dressed in best garments - Happiness courts thee in her best array.
"Happiness courts thee in her best array" (RJ.3.3)
You could make a statement about a seemingly overhappy person, e.g. 'I can see that happiness is courting you in her best array'. Or, if you yourself are somewhat unhappy, answer to 'How are you?' with 'Happiness does not court me with her best array.' Or convert the line into a wish, 'Happiness court thee...'
In the play. *Friar Lawrence upbraids Romeo who rails about being banished from Verona, when the Friar is still optimistic about Romeo and Juliet being happily re-united in the near future.*

Happiness, h. in simplicity - ... my crown is called content: a crown it is that seldom kings enjoy.
"My crown is in my heart, not on my head;
Not decked with diamonds and Indian stones,
Nor to be seen: my crown is called content:
A crown it is that seldom kings enjoy." (KHVI p3.3.1)
Potential alternative response to questions of the type, 'What is your title?' or 'What makes you happy? Etc.
In the play. *Henry VI, captured by keepers ready to switch allegiance to the new king, answers their sarcastic question as to where is his crown.*

Happiness, h. not secured by titles or fame - Princes have but their tides for their glories... an outward honour for an inward toil.
"Princes have but their tides for their glories,
An outward honour for an inward toil
…
They often feel a world of restless cares:
So that, betwixt their tides and low names,
There's nothing differs but the outward fame " (KRIII.1.4)
In the play. *The Duke of Clarence, prisoner in the Tower of London, reflects on the predicament*

Happiness, h. or peace of mind, farewell to - Farewell the tranquil mind! farewell content!
"Farewell the tranquil mind! farewell content!
Farewell the plumed troop, and the big wars,
That make ambition virtue!
…
The royal banner, and all quality,
Pride, pomp and circumstance of glorious war!" (OTH.3.2)
In the play. *Othello, now stung with jealousy via Iago's slander of Desdemona, says farewell to all that made him happy, including the pomp and circumstance connected with war.*

Happiness, h. overwhelming – ...this great sea of joys.... drown me with their sweetness.
"O, Helicanus, strike me, honored sir,
Give me a gash, put me to present pain;
Lest this great sea of joys rushing upon me
Overbear the shores of my mortality
And drown me with their sweetness." (PER.5.1)
Describe a moment of irresistible happiness. See also 'Fortune, sequence of events too good to be true'.

392

In the play. *Pericles is on the brink of extreme happiness having found his daughter Marina. Rhetorically he wants to suffer enough pain so as to balance the weight of the happiness that may otherwise overwhelm him. Hence the invitation to Helicanus to strike him.*

Happiness, h, overwhelming and incredible - If it be thus to dream, still let me sleep!
"What relish is this? how runs the stream?
Or I am mad, or else this is a dream: --
Let fancy still my sense in Lethe steep;
If it be thus to dream, still let me sleep!" (TN.4.1)
Use to externalize your happiness. The fourth line is enough by itself to convey the idea (of your happiness), if it applies.
In the play. *Sebastian, the twin of Viola/Cesario listens to Olivia's love declarations. She thinks that Sebastian is his/her twin Viola/Cesario. Pleasantly shocked, Sebastian thinks to be dreaming. In Greek mythology, the Lethe is one of the rivers that flow through the realm of Hades and is also called the River of Oblivion.*

Happiness, h. seen through another man's eyes a bitter experience - ... how bitter a thing it is to look into happiness through another man's eyes.
" O, how bitter a thing it is to look into happiness through another man's eyes!" (AYLI.5.2)
Comment, if it applies to your current circumstances.
In the play. *In an unexpected turn of events, Oliver, Orlando's evil brother, repents and marries Aliena. Orlando, who has not yet discovered Rosalind's true identity, meditates on Oliver's happiness at marrying Aliena.*

Happiness, contrast of happiness with personal unhappiness - the apprehension of the good gives but the greater feeling to the worse.
"O, no! the apprehension of the good
Gives but the greater feeling to the worse:
Fell sorrow's tooth doth never rankle more
Than when he bites, but lanceth not the sore." (KRII.1.3)
In the play. *Bolingbroke rejects the suggestions by his father John of Gaunt on positive thinking regarding Bolingbroke's impending exile.*

Happiness, in a state of h. - ... turns to a wild of nothing, save of joy...
"Where every something, being blent together,
Turns to a wild of nothing, save of joy,
Express'd and not express'd" (MOV.3.2)
Elaborate on your happiness. Answer to 'Are you happy?' E.G. 'I am turned to a wild of nothing, save of joy, expressed and not expressed'.
In the play. *This is Bassanio's description of the feeling of a crowd after it has listened to a speech from a beloved prince. See 'Happiness, in a state of happy confusion'*

Happiness, in a state of happy confusion - ... there is such confusion in my powers...
"... there is such confusion in my powers,
As after some oration fairly spoke
By a beloved prince, there doth appear
Among the buzzing pleased multitude" (MOV.3.2)
Use the first time after she said she loves you. Also, your beginning statement when you are the next to follow up a good speech. See also 'Speech, speaking after a well known or skillful speaker'.
In the play. *Bassanio has won the contest and will marry Portia. Portia gives him a ring and*

asks Bassanio to promise that he will never part with it. Bassanio replies.

Happiness, promise of return to h. - ...The liquid drops of tears that you have shed shall come again, transform'd to orient pearl...
"...we have many goodly days to see:
The liquid drops of tears that you have shed
Shall come again, transform'd to orient pearl,
Advantaging their loan with interest
Of ten times double gain of happiness." ((KRIII.4.4)
When she reminds you of how much she has suffered because of you – and you are on the road of reformation.
In the play. *Richard III talks with Queen Elizabeth, widow of Henry IV whose son he has murdered. But now he wants to marry her daughter to ensure the legitimacy oh his crown. The event, according to him, will transform the previous sorrow (tears) into happiness.*

Happiness, road to h. via applied philosophy - ... that part of philosophy will I apply that treats of happiness by virtue specially to be achieved.
"...for the time I study,
Virtue and that part of philosophy
Will I apply that treats of happiness
By virtue specially to be achieved" (TOS.1.1)
In the play. *Lucentio informs his servant Tranio about his course of studies in Padua.*

Happiness, supreme and unsurpassable - ... If it were now to die, 't were now to be most happy...
"... If it were now to die,
'Twere now to be most happy; for, I fear,
My soul hath her content so absolute
That not another comfort like to this
Succeeds in unknown fate." (OTH.2.1)
In the play. *Othello has landed safely in Cyprus after escaping a storm and finds Desdemona there waiting for him.*

Happiness, unbearable h. - ... the gods do mean to strike me to death with mortal joy.
"...the gods do mean to strike me
To death with mortal joy." (CYM.5.4)
In the play. *Cymbeline cannot believe that he has found his daughter Imogen well and alive.*

Happy with leftovers - ... I shall think it a most plenteous crop to glean the broken ears after the man that the main harvest reaps.
"...I shall think it a most plenteous crop,
To glean the broken ears after the man
That the main harvest reaps." (AYLI.3.5)
She has rejected you but you love her so much that you hope to have another shot if and when your rival gets tired of her. (See also entries for 'Rejection')
In the play. *In a display of total devotion, Silvius accepts the task of carrying Phebe's letter to the disguised Rosalind, whom Phebe believes to be a boy and with whom she has fallen in love.*

Happy with yourself - Shine out, fair sun, till I have bought a glass, that I may see my shadow, as I pass.
"Shine out, fair sun, till I have bought a glass,
That I may see my shadow, as I pass." (R3.1)
One of the ways to make her feel that she has made you happy.
In the play. *Richard has convinced Anne to marry him. Surprised at his success, Richard makes a somewhat curious request from the sun – later he decides to equip himself with a brand new set of suits.* See also 'Image building or restoration.'

Harassment, handling of sexual h. - ... I am too mean to be your queen, and yet too good to be your concubine.
"... I am too mean to be your queen,
And yet too good to be your concubine." (KHVI p3.3.2)
See also 'Sexual harassment'
In the play. *The Lady Grey fends off the advances of King Edward IV, who will eventually marry him.*

Harassment, handling of sexual h. - What love, think'st thou, I sue so much to get?...
KING EDWARD IV Ay, but, I fear me, in another sense.
What love, think'st thou, I sue so much to get?
LADY GREY My love till death, my humble thanks, my prayers;
That love which virtue begs and virtue grants. (KHVI p3.3.2)
Elegant way for a lady to fend off the advances of her boss, granted and not given that he may have the intelligence to understand.
In the play. *Edward has developed a passion for the Lady Grey, and she handles the situation skillfully.*

Harassment, stop harassing me - ... leave to afflict my heart: sorrow and grief have vanquished all my powers.
"Ambitious churchman, leave to afflict my heart:
Sorrow and grief have vanquished all my powers." (KHVI p2.2.1)
Plea to stop harassment, particularly in a situation where you are already in distress.
In the play. *With a cunning plot the Cardinal has succeeded to disgrace the otherwise virtuous Gloucester. Gloucester addresses the Cardinal.*

Hardiness, h. acquired via a rough life - Plenty and peace breeds cowards: hardness ever of hardiness is mother.
"Plenty and peace breeds cowards: hardness ever
Of hardiness is mother." (CYM.3.5)
Show the positive side of a rough assignment.
In the play. *Imogen, now alone and in a man's attire, thinks how to psychologically combat hunger pains.*

Harpy, h. of a woman. See 'Woman, evil w. like a harpy - ... to betray, dost, with thine angel's face seize with thine eagle's talons'. *** 'Woman, anything but talking with her – (anything) rather than hold three words' conference with this harpy.'

Haste, counting what has not yet been achieved - But yet I run before my horse to market...
"But yet I run before my horse to market
Clarence still breathes." (KRIII.1.1)
Cool over-enthusiastic projections - "just a moment, we run before our horse to market." See also 'Prudence, p. advisable instead of unrealistic optimism – the lion's skin'
In the play. *Richard meditates on his murderous plans.*

Haste, over h. – The mellow plum doth fall, the green sticks fast...

Hate, h. not deserved - To plead for love deserves more fee than hate.
"To plead for love deserves more fee than hate." (TGV.1.2)
When she is really nasty to you.
In the play. *Julia pretends not to accept a letter sent by Proteus via a servant and Lucetta answers back.*

Hate, h. removed and changed in love - ... my heart is purged from grudging hate: and with my hand I seal my true heart's love.

"By heaven, my heart is purged from grudging hate:
And with my hand I seal my true heart's love" (KRIII.2.1)
Emphatically make peace with enemy.
In the play. *Rivers, prompted by the dying King Edward makes peace with Hastings.*

Hate, you cannot stand any of them - The sight of any of the house of York is as a fury to torment my soul.
"The sight of any of the house of York
Is as a fury to torment my soul" (KHVI.p3.1.3)
Change 'the house of York' to applicable party(ies)
In the play. *Clifford to his soon-to-be- victim, the young Rutland of York.*

Hateful, I hate you as I hate hell - I hate the word, as I hate hell, all Montagues and thee.
"What, drawn and talk of peace? I hate the word,
As I hate hell, all Montagues and thee" (RJ.1.1)
Express your disgust at an idea conveyed or encapsulated into a word. You may omit 'and thee' if not needed.
In the play. *Servants of the Montagues and Capulets enter into a brawl. Benvolio, friend of Romeo, tries to restore piece, Tybald, nephew of Lady Capulet is not of the same idea.*

Hateful - ... she did confess was as a scorpion to her sight.
"...she did confess
Was as a scorpion to her sight" (CYM.5.4)
In the play. *Physician Cornelius tells Cymbeline about the true feeling of the Queen towards Cymbeline's daughter Imogen.*

Hating just to look at it - It is a basilisk unto mine eye, kills me to look on't.
"It is a basilisk unto mine eye,
Kills me to look on't" (CYM.2.4)

In the play. *In Rome Leonatus cannot believe that Imogen gave her ring to the treacherous Iachimo and cannot even look at it. Iachimo stole the ring.*

Hatred, h. declared - I do hate him as I do hell pains.
"I do hate him as I do hell pains..." (OTH.1.1)
In the play. *Iago hates Othello but for the moment he must feign it.*

Hatred, h. expressed in terms of opposites - All form is formless, order orderless, save what is opposite to England's love.
"All form is formless, order orderless,
Save what is opposite to England's love." (KJ.3.1)
Change 'England' with name of relevant power, which you oppose.
In the play. *Card. Pandulph wants at all cost that King Philip battle King John of England*

Hatred, h. mixed with pity - ... but that I hate thee deadly I should lament thy miserable state.
"Alas poor York! but that I hate thee deadly,
I should lament thy miserable state." (KHVI p3.1.4)
Commiserate the defeated competition.
In the play. *Queen Margaret to the captured York.*

Hatred, h. of the world - ... had I power, I should pour the sweet milk of concord into hell…
"…Nay, had I power, I should
Pour the sweet milk of concord into hell,
Uproar the universal peace, confound
All unity on earth." (M.4.3)
Apply to your political opponent as a statement of what would happen if he were elected.
In the play. *In a strange statement Malcolm declares himself as boundlessly intemperate and*

hateful Malcolm wants to test Macduff's reaction.

Hatred, mutual h. - ... Not Afric owns a serpent I abhor more than thy fame and envy.
"We hate alike:
Not Afric owns a serpent I abhor
More than thy fame and envy." (COR.1.7)
The subject of hatred can also be anything besides fame and envy.
In the play. *The Volscian general Aufidius to Coriolanus.*

Hatred, shared h. – All the commons hate him perniciously... wish him ten fathom deep.
"All the commons
Hate him perniciously, and, o' my conscience,
Wish him ten fathom deep" (KHVIII.2.1)
In the play. *Two citizens' opinion of Cardinal Wolsey.*

Hawk, h. or falcon observed – A falcon, towering in her pride of place.
"A falcon, towering in her pride of place" (M.2.4)
In the play. *An old man reports to Ross an unnatural event, a hawk killed by an owl, a symptom of evil times (read the killing of King Duncan by Macbeth).*

Head-piece, heavy hp - ... if their heads had any intellectual armour, they could never wear such heavy head pieces.
CONSTABLE If the English had any apprehension, they would run away.
ORLEANS That they lack; for if their heads had any intellectual armour, they could never wear such heavy head pieces (KHV.3.7)
In the play. *The French Constable and Orleans (unduly optimistic before the battle of Agincourt) exchange jokes about the English.*

Health, banning of obesity - I'll exhibit a bill in parliament for the putting down of fat men.
"I'll exhibit a bill in parliament for the putting down of fat men." (MWW.2.1)
Sarcastic comment on fat men.
In the play. *Mistress Page has just received a love letter from Falstaff and reacts accordingly. The letter is the same sent to Mrs. Ford. Falstaff is notoriously corpulent.*

Health, care an enemy to good h. - I am sure care's an enemy to life.
"I am sure care's an enemy to life." (TN.1.3)
Explain away your general lightheartedness using Shakespeare as an authority.
In the play. *Sir Toby Belch denounces his niece's sadness.*

Health, good eating habits, good digestion disrupted by arguing - Unquiet meals make ill digestion.
"Unquiet meals make ill digestion." (COE.5.1)
Suggest to postpone the discussion of a thorny issue after eating, lest the dinner may not be well digested.
In the play. *The Lady Abbess attributes Ant E's madness to Adriana's jealousy that, in turn, caused Ant E not to digest his meals properly.*

Health, laughter as a medicine - With mirth and laughter let old wrinkles come and let my liver rather heat with wine...
"With mirth and laughter let old wrinkles come,
And let my liver rather heat with wine
Than my heart cool with mortifying groans,
Why should a man whose blood is warm within
Sit like his grandsire cut in alabaster?" (MOV.1.1)

Answer to a question on your philosophy of life. Or a rationalization for your liking of wine or in praise of wine itself, e.g. 'I'll let my liver rather heat with this wine than my heart cool with mortifying groans.')
In the play. *Gratiano attempts to cheer up Antonio who is melancholy by nature or disposition.*

Health, physical and mental h. of leader key to safety - The lives of all your loving complices lean on your health...
"The lives of all your loving complices
Lean on your health; the which, if you give o'er
To stormy passion, must perforce decay" (KHIV.p2.1.1)
In the play. *Morton counsels reason to the incensed Northumberland.*

Health care, a good psychologist – ... The quiet of my wounded conscience, thou art a cure fit for a king.
"… O my Wolsey,
The quiet of my wounded conscience;
Thou art a cure fit for a king."
(KHVIII.2.2)
Comments on some comforting words from a trusted friend. Change 'O my Wolsey' to name of friend. See also 'Health-care, request for psychological remedy – Canst thou not minister to a mind diseased…'
In the play. *King Henry believes in the sincerity and disinterestedness of Cardinal Wolsey. The 'wounded conscience' has to do with the impending divorce from Queen Catherine.*

Health-care, ease at getting upset as a cause for hepatitis – Why should a man sleep when he wakes and creep into the jaundice by being peevish?
"(Why should a man)
Sleep when he wakes and creep into the jaundice
By being peevish?" (MOV.1.1)
In the play. *Gratiano attempts to cheer up Antonio who is melancholy by nature or disposition.*

Health-care, effects of a bad diet - O, he hath kept an evil diet long, and overmuch consumed his royal person...
HASTINGS The King is sickly, weak and melancholy,
And his physicians fear him mightily.
GLOUCESTER Now, by Saint Paul, this news is bad indeed.
O, he hath kept an evil diet long,
And overmuch consumed his royal person:
'Tis very grievous to be thought upon.
(KRIII.1.1)
Answer to 'Are you OK? You don't look good'. 'I have kept an evil diet that has overmuch consumed my person'
In the play. *The sickly (and overweight) king is Edward IV.*

Health-care, exposure to night cold air unadvisable if already affected by a respiratory ailment – To dare the vile contagion of the night.
"What, is Brutus sick,
And will he steal out of his wholesome bed,
To dare the vile contagion of the night
And tempt the rheumy and unpurged air
To add unto his sickness?" (JC.2.1)
In the play. *Brutus' wife, Portia attempts to discourage Brutus from leaving his home at night. 'Rheumy' = 'Causing rheumatism'.*

Health-care, herbal remedies – Within the infant rind of this small flower ...
"Within the infant rind of this small flower
Poison hath residence and medicine power." (RJ.2.3)
In the play. *Fr. Lawrence is a naturopath and dabbles in chemistry and herbal pharmacology.*

Health-care, nutrition - things sweet to taste prove in digestion sour.
"Things sweet to taste prove in digestion sour." (KRII.1.3)
Denying partaking of dessert. See also entries for 'Dieting'
In the play. *Gaunt answers a remark by Richard II.*

Health-care, nutrition – a little more than a little, is by much too much.
"… and began
To loathe the taste of sweetness, whereof a little
More than a little, is by much too much." (KHIV p1.3)
Answer to 'Do you take sugar', e.g. 'I loathe the taste of sweetness…much' – See also 'Advice, a. to love moderately and to avoid excess in general' -
In the play. *K. Henry explains to his son the advantages to be seen rarely but sumptuously. To be seen often is like too much sugar. Being seldom seen induces a sense of awe as expressed by the 'extraordinary gaze'*

Health, recreation necessary for healthy life - Sweet recreation barred, what doth ensue…
"Sweet recreation barred, what doth ensue,
But moody and dull melancholy,
Kinsman to grim and comfortless despair,
And, at her heels, a large infectious troop
Of pale distemperatures and foes to life?
In food, in sport, and life-preserving rest,
To be disturb'd, would mad or man or beast." (COE.5.1)
Justify your need of a vacation or time off.
In the play. *The Lady Abbess diagnoses Ant E's madness. Adriana's jealousy deprived Ant E's of a good digestion and of a zest for life. The here described consequences follow.*

Health-care, request for psychological remedy – Canst thou not minister to a mind diseased…
MACBETH. Canst thou not minister to a mind diseased,
Pluck from the memory a rooted sorrow,
Raze out the written troubles of the brain
And with some sweet oblivious antidote
Cleanse the stuff'd bosom of that perilous stuff
Which weighs upon the heart?
DOCTOR. Therein the patient
Must minister to himself. (M.5.5)
See also 'Health care, a good psychologist – … The quiet of my wounded conscience, thou art a cure fit for a king.'
In the play. *Macbeth asks the doctor if he can do anything about his mentally sick wife.*

Health-care, rest as medicine - Our foster-nurse of nature is repose, the which he lacks…
"Our foster-nurse of nature is repose,
The which he lacks, that to provoke in him,
Are many simples operative, whose power
Will close the eye of anguish" (KL.4.4)
Change 'he' to 'you' when you wish to recommend rest to a fatigued colleague or friend. See also 'Sleep, lack of sleep creating anxiety - You lack the season of all natures, sleep'.
In the play. *A doctor prescribes sleep and sleeping pills for the ailing Lear.*

Health-care, ritual denial of death - … sick men, when their deaths be near…
"…sick men, when their deaths be near,

No news but health from their physicians know" (SON 140)
Use to support instances of misleading medical care.

Health-care, upset stomach - Prithee, do not turn me about; my stomach is not constant.
"Prithee, do not turn me about; my stomach is not constant." (TEM.2.2)
Ask the driver to go more slowly in a windy road after a large meal.
In the play. *Stephano to Trinculo after both have been lost in the storm.*

Hearing, do you hear me? – Your tale, sir, would cure deafness.
PROSPERO Dost thou hear?
MIRANDA Your tale, sir, would cure deafness (TEM.1.2)
Answer to 'Do you hear me?' or 'Are you following me?'
In the play. *Prospero has started narrating to his daughter Miranda the sequence of events that led to his being deposed as duke of Milan and being exiled to their current residence.*

Heart, h. corrupted by custom – … if damned custom have not brass'd it so that it is proof and bulwark against sense.
"…let me wring your heart; for so I shall,
If it be made of penetrable stuff,
If damned custom have not brass'd it so
That it is proof and bulwark against sense." (H.3.4)
"If his heart be made of penetrable stuff' can be a qualifier before you undertake your task of persuasion. See also entries for 'Man, m. and his wicked nature'.
In the play. *Hamlet to Polonius whom he has just slain. Polonius was hiding behind a curtain as part of a scheme to observe Hamlet's behavior.*

Heart, h. in misery - … my heart, all mad with misery, beats in this hollow prison of my flesh.
" … my heart, all mad with misery,
Beats in this hollow prison of my flesh." (TA.2.1)
Indicate your state of disarray.
In the play. *When Titus' heart beats in sorrow, he will thump it down.*

Heart, h. in turmoil - … the windy tempest of my heart
"… see what showers arise,
Blown with the windy tempest of my heart" (KHVI p3.2.5)
In the play. *In the battle of Towton a father has just killed his son.*

Heart, heartbreaking discovery - This blows my heart if swift thought break it not, a swifter mean shall outstrike thought.
"…This blows my heart:
If swift thought break it not, a swifter mean
Shall outstrike thought" (AC.4.6)
In the play. *Enobarbus repents of having abandoned Antony and finding that Antony had left him his treasure on account of Enobarbus' good service.*

Heart, voice of the h. - What my tongue dares not, that my heart shall say…
"What my tongue dares not, that my heart shall say." (KRII.5.5)
See also 'Silence, self-enforced - It is not nor it cannot come to good: but break, my heart; for I must hold my tongue.'
In the play. *Richard's faithful groom says farewell to the King, prisoner in Pomfret Castle.*

Heart, positive self appraisal and advertisement - … a good heart, Kate, is the sun and the moon…
"A good leg will fall; a straight back will stoop; a black beard will turn white; a curled pate will grow bald; a

fair face will wither; a full eye will wax hollow: a good heart, Kate, is the sun and the moon; or rather, the sun, and not the moon; for it shines bright, and never changes, but keeps its course truly." (HV.5.2)
You are trying to sell yourself as a valuable companion. This is what King Henry V said to Katherine of France on meeting her.
In the play. *After victory at the Battle of Agincourt, Henry V plans to marry Kathryn of France, thus expanding the size of his Kingdom.*

Heart, question about heartlessness – Is there any cause in nature that makes these hard hearts?
"Is there any cause in nature that makes these hard hearts?" (KL.3.6)
In the play. *King Lear asks a rhetorical question thinking that a study of Regan's actual heart may yield an answer.*

Heartbreak - O heart, heavy heart, why sigh'st thou without breaking?
"-- O heart, heavy heart,
Why sigh'st thou without breaking?" (TC.4.2)
See also 'Silence, self-enforced - It is not nor it cannot come to good: but break, my heart; for I must hold my tongue.'
In the play. *Pandarus observes the farewell hug between Troilus and Cressida.*

Heat, virtual h. – (Who can) wallow naked in December snow by thinking on fantastic summer's heat?
"…wallow naked in December snow
By thinking on fantastic summer's heat?" (KRII.1.3)
In the play. *Bolingbroke rejects the suggestions by his father John of Gaunt on positive thinking regarding Bolingbroke's impending exile.*

Heaven on earth - A heaven on earth I won, by wooing thee.
"A heaven on earth I won, by wooing thee." (AWEW.4.2)

Good in a number of occasions, as a compliment or as a tool of discovery. For example, if she has agreed to go out with you but you are uncertain about her feelings towards you, you can try the line and see how she reacts. If she smiles and says nothing you are on the right track. If she says, " you have won nothing" or equivalent, you know you have some more work to do. Or you can pull back and give a defensive line (see Reliability). See also 'Pride, p. in possession'.
In the play. *Diana pretends to agree to go to bed with Bertram, but at the last moment Helena (Bertram's estranged wife), who also has arrived in Florence, will switch places with Diana. Therefore Bertram will end up going to bed with his (so far) estranged wife. Bertram throws a compliment at Diana thinking that he has succeeded.*

Heaven walking on earth - Here comes the countess: now heaven walks on earth.
"Here comes the countess: now heaven walks on earth." (TN.5.1)
Substitute for 'the countess' the name of the applicable lady. A greeting when she enters the room.
In the play. *Duke Orsino sees Olivia coming in.*

Heavenly powers, obedience to h. powers - We cannot but obey the powers above us.
"We cannot but obey
The powers above us." (PER.3.3)
Accepting the inevitable. See also entries for 'Destiny'.
In the play. *Pericles ends up again in Tharsus with his infant daughter Marina after a shipwreck at sea. He asks King Cleon and queen Dionyza to look after Marina. Tyre is not safe due to the previous business and the wrath of Antiochus.*

Heavens, h. restraining the extremes of in-humanity - … Humanity must

perforce prey on itself like monsters of the deep.
"If that the heavens do not their
visible spirits
Send quickly down to tame these vile offences,
It will come,
Humanity must perforce prey on itself,
Like monsters of the deep." (KL.4.2)
In the play. *The Duke of Albany to his wicked wife Goneril. The offences are those perpetrated by Goneril and her sister Regan against their father Lear.*

Heavens, tempting the h. - But wherefore did you so much tempt the heavens?...
"But wherefore did you so much tempt the heavens?
It is the part of men to fear and tremble,
When the most mighty gods by tokens send
Such dreadful heralds to astonish us." (JC.1.3)
In the play. *Casca asks Cassius why he tempted the heavens by walking into the storm. Cassius knows the cause of the fires, i.e. the tyranny of Caesar, that is Caesar is the object of heavens' wrath.*

Hell, automatic insurance protection - ... the devil will not have me damned, lest the oil that's in me should set hell on fire.
"I think the devil will not have me damned, lest the oil that's in me should set hell on fire" (MWW.5.5)
In the play. *Falstaff, tricked and pinched by masked fairies and magic creatures, meditates about his own fate.*

Hell, you make earth hell - ...Thou camest on earth to make the earth my hell.
"No, by the holy rood, thou know'st it well,
Thou camest on earth to make the earth my hell" (KRIII.4.4)
In the play. *The Duchess of York to her evil son Richard.*

Help, asking to put a word on your behalf - ... let me have thy voice in my behalf.
"...let me have thy voice in my behalf" (MWW.1.4)
When asking for a recommendation. See also 'Connections, importance of good c. - a friend in the court is better than a penny in purse.'
In the play. *Fenton is in love with Anne Page and enlists the help of Mistress Quickly to further his plans*

Help, determination to h. beyond what one would do for him/herself – What I can do I will; and more I will than for myself I dare.
"What I can do I will; and more I will
Than for myself I dare: let that suffice you." (OTH.3.4)
In the play. *Desdemona will continue to help Cassio to be reconciled with Othello who, by now, firmly believes that she has an affair with Cassio.*

Help, h. assured - what I can help thee to, thou shalt not miss.
"... and be sure of this,
What I can help thee to, thou shalt not miss." (AWEW.1.3)
Assure the addressed party of your support and help.
In the play. *Helen plans to go to the court in Paris (where Bertram is already) and attempt to cure the king. The Countess will help her in any way she can.*

Help, h. inadequate - The help of one stands me in little stead.
"The help of one stands me in little stead" (KHVI.p1.4.6)
In the play. *Talbot Sr. surrounded by the French attempts (unsuccessfully) to convince his*

son to flee, as the help of one more soldier is not sufficient against the overwhelming French forces.

Help, h. offered - ... tell thy grief, it shall be eased, if France can yield relief.
"Be plain, Queen Margaret, and tell thy grief;
It shall be eased, if France can yield relief" (KHVI.p3.3.3)
Change 'Queen Margaret' to the name of the supplicant and 'France' to your name. In the *play. King Louis to Queen Margaret who has come to seek help against the Yorkists in England.*

Help, h. on the way - Be not dismay'd for succour is at hand.
Be not dismay'd for succour is at hand." (KHVIp1.1.2)
In the play. *The Bastard of Orleans comforts Charles who has been pushed back by the English in the siege of Orleans. The forthcoming help is Joan of Arc.*

Help, h. sought from heavens to escape from dreadful place - ... some heavenly power guide us out of this fearful country.
"All torment, trouble, wonder and amazement
Inhabits here: some heavenly power guide us
Out of this fearful country!" (TEM.5.1)
Answer to 'Do you like this place?' when you really do not like it.
In the play. *Gonzalo has had enough of the magic island and its strange creatures.*

Help, request for h. unexpectedly rejected - ... shut his bosom against our borrowing prayers.
"We marvel much, our cousin France
Would, in so just a business, shut his bosom
Against our borrowing prayers." (AWEW.3.1)

Modify slightly, e.g. 'We marvel much that (name of person in question), would, in so just a business, shut his bosom against... prayers.'
In the play. *The Duke of Florence wonders why the King of France has not yet sent reinforcements for the war against Siena.*

Help, seeking h. in secret - ... and thence it is that I to your assistance do make love: masking the business from the common eye for sundry weighty reasons.
"...and thence it is
That I to your assistance do make love:
Masking the business from the common eye
For sundry weighty reasons." (M.3.1)
You have shared your plan, idea, or project in confidence to a colleague, use the quote as a conclusion and to request his/her cooperation. If the contacted party is a female, make sure you quote the source and the context to avoid accusations of sexual harassment.
In the play. *Macbeth in conversation with the hired murderers (of Banquo).*

Helter-Skelter – And helter-skelter have I rode to thee…
"And helter-skelter have I rode to thee,
And tidings do I bring and lucky joys
And golden times and happy news" (KHIVp2.5.3)
In the play. *Pistol has arrived from London in Gloucestershire to tell Falstaff that now Prince Harry is King Henry V.*

Hiding something - ... the quality of nothing hath not such need to hide itself…
"...the quality of nothing hath not such need to hide itself. Let's see:" (KL.1.2)
In the play. *Edmund hatches a terrible plot against his brother Edgar. Gloucester refuses to*

think that the letter in the hands of Edmund is 'nothing'. Edmund has penned the letter himself to accuse Edgar.

History, incredible h. – If I should tell my history, it would seem like lies disdained in the reporting.
"If I should tell my history, it would seem
Like lies disdained in the reporting."
(PER.5.1)
Prepare the audience to what appears an incredible story.
In the play. *Pericles invites Marina to tell her history, but she is afraid that, though true, the history may sound unbelievable.*

History, short period of h. but pregnant with consequences - Small time, but in that small most greatly lived this star of England.
"Small time, but in that small most greatly lived
This star of England"
(KHV.5.epilogue)
Adapt to the scope of events that you wish to emphasize.
In the play. *Final comment of the chorus after apologies for the lack of special effects.*

Honesty, an honest Athenian as a physical impossibility - ... if doing nothing be death by the law.
TIMON. Whither art going?
APEMANTUS. To knock out an honest Athenian's brain.
TIMON. That's a deed thou'lt die for.
APEMANTUS. Right, if doing nothing be death by the law."
(TOA.1.1)
Change 'Athenian' to the name of citizens of any other applicable city.
In the play. *The grouchy Apemantus does not think that there is one single honest Athenian.*

Honesty, h. a rare quality - ... to be honest, as this world goes, is to be one man picked out of ten thousand.

"... to be honest, as this world goes, is to be one man picked out of ten thousand." (H.2.2)
A comment on widespread dishonesty.
In the play. *Polonius confronts Hamlet who pretends not to know him and actually tells him that he is a fishmonger. When Polonius denies it Hamlet wishes that he (Polonius) were at least as honest as a fishmonger. This causes Polonius to conclude with the famous lines,*
"Though this be madness, yet there is method in it."

Honesty, h. as a fault - Every man has his faults, and honesty is his; I have told him on it; but I could never get it from it.
"Every man has his faults, and honesty is his; I have told him on it; but I could never get it from it."
(TOA.3.1)
Apply to an honest man who has been taken advantage of.
In the play. *Lucullus refuses to help Timon.*

Honesty, h. as a questionable virtue - ... what a fool Honesty is! and Trust, his sworn brother, a very simple gentleman!
"... what a fool Honesty is! and Trust, his sworn brother, a very simple gentleman!" (WT.4.4)
Code of behavior of many politicians.
In the play. *The thief Autolycus congratulates himself for his successful exploits of theft.*

Honesty, h. best legacy - ... and no legacy is so rich as honesty.
"...and no legacy is so rich as honesty. (AWEW.3.5)
In the play. *In Florence Mariana (alias Helena) advises Diana to beware of the courtship by Bertram.*

Honesty, h. in the world presaging doomsday – ... the world's grown honest... Then is doomsday near.
HAMLET ... What's the news?

ROSENCRANTZ None, my lord, but that the world's grown honest.
HAMLET Then is doomsday near (H.2.2)
In the play. *Hamlet exchanges some banter with spies-to-be Rosencrantz and Guilderstern.*

Honesty, h. not safe – Take note, take note, O world, to be direct and honest is not safe.
"…Take note, take note, O world,
To be direct and honest is not safe." (OTH.3.3)
See also 'World, pessimistic view of the w. and its inherent evil - I am in this earthly world; where to do harm is often laudable…'
In the play. *False Iago pretends that Othello be mad because he, Iago, told him the truth about Desdemona's infidelity*

Honesty, h. over wisdom - … Methinks thou art more honest now than wise..
"Methinks thou art more honest now than wise;
For, by oppressing and betraying me,
Thou mightst have sooner got another service:
For many so arrive at second masters,
Upon their first lord's neck" (TOA.4.3)
In the play. *Timon to faithful servant Flavius*

Honesty, h. unsuspecting of dishonesty – … unstain'd thoughts do seldom dream on evil.
"… unstain'd thoughts do seldom dream on evil." (ROL)
See also 'Innocence, i. and naivete - … we knew not the doctrine of ill-doing, nor dream'd that any did.'
In the poem. *The honest Lucrece does not suspect the evil intention of Tarquin.*

Honor, a man of exemplary h. – Honour stuck upon him as the sun in the grey vault of heaven.
"(honour) stuck upon him as the sun
In the grey vault of heaven, and by his light
Did all the chivalry of England move
To do brave acts" (KHIVp2.2.3)
A term of reference for anything good that is particularly suited for a person.
In the play. *Lady Percy referring to her husband, slain in battle by the Prince of Wales.*

Honor, a man of h. to whom praise is due - the theme of honour's tongue.
"A son who is the theme of honour's tongue;
Amongst a grove, the very straightest plant;
Who is sweet fortune's minion, and her pride" (KHIV.p1.1.1)
In the play. *K. Henry IV sadly compares the feats of Harry Percy (Hotspur), 'the very straightest plant' versus the dissolute life of the Prince of Wales, future Henry V. Henry V will mend his ways though.*

Honor, can h. and politics co-exists? – … In peace what each of them by the other lose that they combine not there.
"…have heard you say,
Honour and policy, like unsever'd friends,
I' the war do grow together: grant that, and tell me,
In peace what each of them by the other lose,
That they combine not there." (COR.3.2)
In the play. *Volumnia attempts to convince her son to soften his tone with the Tribunes and the people.*

Honor, h. above all – 'tis not my profit that does lead mine honor, mine honour, it.
"'Tis not my profit that does lead mine honour;
Mine honour, it." (AC.2.7)

In the play. *A wonderful example of dirty/clean politics. Menas suggests to Pompey that, as all his competitors are on board his ship for a banquet, that is a wonderful occasion to get rid of them. Pompey declines with a very interesting argument. See 'Deniability, d., politics and crime - … Being done unknown I should have found it afterwards well done but must condemn it now.'*

Honor, h. above all – I love the name of honor more than I fear death.
"For, let the gods so speed me as I love
The name of honour more than I fear death." (JC.1.2)
Use as a statement of integrity, "I love the name … fear death"
In the play. *Brutus tells Cassius that he will not do anything dishonorable. 'To speed' = 'to assist'*

Honor, h. above all – if I lose mine honor I lose myself.
"…if I lose mine honour,
I lose myself: better I were not yours
Than yours so branchless" (AC.3.4)
In the play. *Antony replies to Octavia, hi wife and Octavian's sister, who realizes the enmity between the two.*

Honor, h. above all – … But, if it be a sin to covet honor I am the most offending soul alive.
"I am not covetous for gold,
It yearns me not, if men my garments wear;
Such outward things dwell not in my desires:
But, if it be a sin to covet honour,
I am the most offending soul alive." (KHV.4.3)
Use in defense of honor, e.g. 'Even in these times when the sense of honor has lost luster I can say, 'Outward things dwell not in my desires… alive".
In the play. *Henry V addressing the troops.*

Honor, h. above all – … honour we love, for who hates honor hates the gods above.
"… honour we love,
For who hates honour, hates the gods above." (PER.2.3)
Stress your honorable intentions.
In the play. *Pericles has won the tourney and Simonides expresses his appreciation.*

Honor, h. above all – Life every man holds dear; but the dear man holds honour far more precious dear than life.
"Mine honour keeps the weather of my fate.
Life every man holds dear; but the dear man
Holds honour far more precious dear than life" (TC.5.3)
Emphasize your commitment to honor and/or honorable behavior.
In the play. *Hector will fight Achilles notwithstanding Cassandra's and Andromache's plead that he do not do so.*

Honor, h. and credit at stake - Thereon I pawn my credit and mine honour.
"Thereon I pawn my credit and mine honour." (KHVI p3.3.3)
Answer to 'Are you sure?'
In the play. *Answering a question from King Lewis of France, Warwick pawns credit and honor on the fact that Edward IV is the true king of England, rather than the deposed Henry VI.*

Honor, h. as motive for murder, not hate – … For nought I did in hate, but all in honour.
"An honourable murderer, if you will;
For nought I did in hate, but all in honour." (OTH.5.2)
In the play. *Othello dictates his own epitaph to Lodovico, who inquires what should be said of Othello in Venice.*

**Honor, h. inseparable part of life -
Mine honour is my life; both grow in one: take honour from me, and my life is done.**
"Mine honour is my life; both grow in one:
Take honour from me, and my life is done" (KRII.1.1)
In the play. *To defend his reputation, Mowbray (Norfolk) will challenge the accusing Bolingbroke.*

Honor, h. inspiring what chances to take – Mine honour keeps the weather of my fate.
"Mine honour keeps the weather of my fate" (TC.5.3)
In the play. *Hector will fight Achilles notwithstanding Cassandra's and Andromache's plead that he do not do so.*

Honor, h. potentially lost – (It) would bark your honour from that trunk you bear…
"(It) would bark your honour from that trunk you bear,
And leave you naked" (MFM.3.1)
In the play. *Isabella tells her brother Claudio what Angelo expects of her to save Claudio from execution – if accepted Claudio (as well as Isabella) would lose their honor.*

Honor, if you have h. show it - If you were born of honour, show it now, if put on you…
"If you were born of honour, show it now,
If put upon you, make the judgement good
That thought you worthy of it." (PER.4.6)
Exhort a person to behave honorably.
In the play. *Lysimachus, Mytilene's governor, is impressed with Marina's beauty and does not know the circumstances that brought her to the brothel. Her demeanor and behavior end up converting to virtue even the governor. This is how she addresses him.*

Honor, man who is tops for h. – …Upon his brow shame is ashamed to sit, for 'tis a throne where honour…
"…he was not born to shame:
Upon his brow shame is ashamed to sit;
For 'tis a throne where honour may be crown'd
Sole monarch of the universal earth." (RJ.3.2)
In the play. *Juliet reprimands her nurse for having called Romeo shameful.*

Honor, meaning of h. and standing up when h. is at stake - Rightly to be great is not to stir without great argument…
"…Rightly to be great
Is not to stir without great argument,
But greatly to find quarrel in a straw
When honour's at the stake." (H.4.4)
Push for action from principle, when others may be willing to let the matter rest.
In the play. *Alone again, Hamlet meditates.*

Honor, sense of h. paramount - I beg mortality, rather than life preserved with infamy.
"I beg mortality,
Rather than life preserved with infamy." (KHVI p1.4.5)
Emphasize your commitment to honorable behavior or when you have to admit that you are the culprit of something and have decided to come forward with it.
In the play. *Talbot father and Talbot son are surrounded by enemies near Bordeaux. Talbot Sr. asks his son to leave but Talbot Jr. refuses, as it would be infamy.*

Honor, the narrow path of h. - …honour travels in a strait so narrow, where one but goes abreast…
"Take the instant way;

For honour travels in a strait so narrow,
Where one but goes abreast: keep, then, the path;
For emulation hath a thousand sons,
That one by one pursue: if you give way,
Or hedge aside from the direct forthright,
Like to an enter'd tide, they all rush by,
And leave you hindmost;
Or like a gallant horse fall'n in first rank,
Lie there for pavement to the abject rear,
O'er-run and trampled on: then what they do in present,
Though less than yours in past, must o'ertop yours " (TC.3.3)
Stress the value of honor and honorable behavior. Or quote while explaining why you have chosen a certain course of action that was not profitable but honorable.
In the play. *Ulysses suggests that time has caused the Greeks to forget Achilles and his past deeds. But by 'taking the instant way' Achilles can recover his position and glory.*

Hope, abandoning h. -…I will put off my hope and keep it no longer for my flatterer.
"….I will put off my hope and keep it
No longer for my flatterer" (TEM.3.3)
In the play. *Alonso has no hope to find Ferdinand whom he fears drowned.*

Hope, caution about unwarranted h. – … a cause on foot lives so in hope as in an early spring we see the appearing buds…
"…a cause on foot
Lives so in hope as in an early spring
We see the appearing buds; which to prove fruit,
Hope gives not so much warrant as despair

That frosts will bite them"
(KHIV.p2.1.3)
In the play. *Lord Bardolph cools the optimism of fellow rebels for the success in the forthcoming war against Henry IV. Follows Lord Bardolph's presentation on the value of planning. See 'Planning, importance of p. - When we mean to build, we first survey the plot, then draw the model…'*

Hope, concern about h., will it really happen? - I sometimes do believe, and sometimes do not, as those that fear they hope, and know they fear.
DUKE SENIOR Dost thou believe, Orlando, that the boy
Can do all this that he hath promised?
ORLANDO I sometimes do believe, and sometimes do not;
As those that fear they hope, and know they fear. (AYLI.5.4)
Express your cautious apprehension regarding a positive event promised by someone else.
In the play. *Rosalind, disguised as a boy, has promised a sequence of miracles that will end in everyone being satisfied, including Orlando who is madly in love with Rosalind. Orlando does not know as yet if to believe that it will happen.*

Hope, glimmer of h. spied – … even through the hollow eyes of death I spy life peering…
"… even through the hollow eyes of death
I spy life peering; but I dare not say
How near the tidings of our comfort is." (KRII.2.1)
In the play. *Northumberland cheers up the dejected English Lords. Bolingbroke may return to England.*

Hope, glimmer of h. spied - I do spy a kind of hope which craves as desperate an execution as that is desperate which we would prevent.
"I do spy a kind of hope

Which craves as desperate an execution
As that is desperate which we would prevent." (RJ.4.1)
Prelude to presenting your daring idea on how to remedy or correct a dangerous situation. See also 'Remedies, extreme r. required - ... Diseases desperate grown by desperate appliances are relieved or not at all.'
In the play. *Fr. Lawrence has a plan to spirit away Juliet and avoid her marriage to Paris.*

Hope, h. as a flatterer and parasite - I will despair, and be at enmity with cozening hope: he is a flatterer.
BUSHY Despair not, madam.
QUEEN Who shall hinder me?
I will despair, and be at enmity
With cozening hope: he is a flatterer,
A parasite, a keeper back of death,
Who gently would dissolve the bands of life,
Which false hope lingers in extremity" (KRII.2.1)
'Cozening' means 'cheating'.
In the play. *Lord Green has given the news that many English lords have defected to the Bolingbroke, who has returned form exile.*

Hope, h. as a weapon against adversity - Till then fair hope must hinder life's decay.
"Till then fair hope must hinder life's decay." (KHVI p3.4.4)
In the play. *Queen Elizabeth resigns herself to hope, now that Warwick has captured and dethroned her husband Edward of York.*

Hope, h. as the refuge of the distressed - The miserable have no other medicine but only hope.
"The miserable have no other medicine
But only hope:
I've hope to live, and am prepared to die." (MFM.3.1)

In the play. *Claudio has been condemned to death by Angelo, Vienna's temporary ruler, for having seduced a girl in Vienna. Duke Vicentio queries Claudio whether he hopes in a reprieve. Angelo is a class one hypocrite. Later, commenting on the punishment, the saucy Lucio says,*
Why, what a ruthless thing is this in him, (*Angelo*) for the rebellion of a codpiece to take away the life of a
man!

Hope, h. comparable to actual enjoyment - And hope to joy is little less in joy than hope enjoy'd.
"And hope to joy is little less in joy
Than hope enjoy'd" (KRII.2.3)
In the play. *Northumberland referring to the hope of his absent friends of joining the forces collecting around the rebellious Bolingbroke.*

Hope, h. in a person crashed - the hopes we have in him touch ground.
"Thus do the hopes we have in him touch ground
And dash themselves to pieces." (KHIV.p2.4.1)
In the play. *In the Gaultree forest in Yorkshire, Mowbray comments on the news that Northumberland will not join the rebel forces after all.*

Hope, h. in a new president - shall convert those tears by number into hours of happiness.
"But Harry lives, that shall convert those tears
By number into hours of happiness." (KHIV.p2.5.2)
Part of the speech at the change of the guard or president. Change 'Harry' to name of new president. E.G. 'Some are sad that I am living, but (name of new president) lives…etc. '
In the play. *Henry IV is dead. The Prince of Wales, now Henry V, joins other princes and courtiers and reassures them of his good intents.*

Hope, h. making kings out of common men - True hope is swift, and flies with swallow's wings.
"True hope is swift, and flies with swallow's wings:
Kings it makes gods, and meaner creatures kings." (KRIII.5.2)
Encouraging remark in a morale-boosting speech.
In the play. *Richmond props up his troops' morale at his camp in Tamworth, prior to battling the forces of Richard III at Bosworth.*

Hope, h. misplaced - ... do not satisfy your resolution with hopes that are fallible.
"... do not satisfy your resolution with hopes that are fallible:" (MFM.3.1)
In the play. *Duke Vicentio tells Claudio not to have false hope that Angelo will reverse hi verdict of death. Lucio was condemned for having seduced a girl in Vienna.*

Hope, h. never hurts -... it never yet did hurt to lay down likelihoods and forms of hope.
"But, by your leave, it never yet did hurt
To lay down likelihoods and forms of hope." (KHIV p2.1.3)
When she insists on giving you no hope. Or when she is dejected about a seemingly hopeless situation.
In the play. *At the bishop of York's palace the rebels discuss their prospects in the war against the forces of Henry IV Bolingbroke. Lord Bardolph is pessimistic, Hastings, instead, suggests that it does not hurt to hope (i.e. be optimistic).*

Hope, h. revived - how thy words revive my heart.
"O Clifford, how thy words revive my heart." (KHVI p3.1.1)
Express gratitude for a piece of unexpected good news
In the play. *King Henry VI to Clifford who will fight in defense of the king.*

Hope, h. shattered, exclamation - O my breast, thy hope ends here.
"...O my breast,
Thy hope ends here!" (M.4.3)
In the play. *Malcolm portrays himself as unfit to govern (after the probable defeat of Macbeth) and Macduff who counts on Malcolm to be king, feels a pang of desperation. But Malcolm was only pretending.*

Hopelessness, beyond help - "(We must not)... esteem a senseless help when help past sense we deem.
"(We must not)... esteem
A senseless help when help past sense we deem." (AWEW.2.1)
In the play. *The King is skeptical about the remedies proposed by Helena after the doctors have given up hope of a cure.*

Hopelessness, h. and helplessness - Hopeless and helpless doth Aegeon wend....
"Hopeless and helpless doth Aegeon wend,
But to procrastinate his lifeless end" (COE.1.1)
Change 'Aegeon' with your name when you are requested to keep searching for something (or a solution) that you know it is impossible to find.
In the play. *Aegeon must pay a fine of one thousand marks for having set foot in Ephesus. Therefore he is hopeless to find his son and helpless to raise the thousand marks.*

Horizon, h. at sea, sky and water blended – ... to throw out our eyes...even till we make the main and the aerial blue an indistinct regard.
"...to throw out our eyes for brave Othello,
Even till we make the main and the aerial blue
An indistinct regard." (OTH.2.1)
In the play. *Montano, in Cyprus anxiously awaits with others the arrival of Othello's ship.*

Horse, excellent h. - It is the prince of palfreys; his neigh is like the bidding of a monarch…
"It is the prince of palfreys; his neigh is like the bidding of a monarch and his countenance enforces homage." (KHV.3.7)
Answer to a question on your opinion of a horse (when you expect the horse to be praised).
In the play. *The Dauphin of France joins comrades in praising the excellence of the horse of the Duke of Orleans.*

Horse, happy h. because of its rider – O happy horse, to bear the weight of Antony!
"O happy horse, to bear the weight of Antony!" (AC.1.5)
Admittedly a stretch but it could be turned into a compliment for a lady, e.g. 'O happy car seat, to bear the weight of (name of lady'.
In the play. *While Antony is in Rome, Cleopatra imagines where he could be and draws her conclusions.*

House, dwelling, not necessarily reflecting the mind of the dwellers - … nor measure our good minds by this rude place we live in.
"…nor measure our good minds By this rude place we live in" (CYM.3.6)
When you do not exactly reside in a trophy house.
In the play. *Belarius invites Imogen not to underrate him and adopted sons because of the dwelling they have.*

House, compliment on a h. you are visiting – 'Fore God, you have here a goodly dwelling and a rich
"'Fore God, you have here a goodly dwelling and a rich." (KHIV.p2.5.3)
Compliment your guest's house.
In the play. *Falstaff, entering the house of Master Shallow, justice of the peace, whom he plans to swindle.*

House, reason for going somewhere else when not welcome in your own h. - … Since mine own doors refuse to entertain me…
"Since mine own doors refuse to entertain me,
I'll knock elsewhere, to see if they'll disdain me" (COE.3.1)
In the play. *Antipholus E. barred from entering his own house due to confusions arising from his twin already been inside, elects to go somewhere else.*

Household words - …our names, familiar in his mouth as household words…
"…Then shall our names,
Familiar in his mouth as household words…" (HV.4.3)
In the play. *Henry V addresses the troops on St. Crispin day before the battle of Agincourt. That day and the name of the participants to the battle will become household words forever. 'His mouth' is that of the (now old) warrior who will tell the story to his descendants.*

Housing, h. unsuitable to rank or circumstance, poor living conditions, hotel comment, travel - … call you that keeping… that differs not from the stalling of an ox?
"For call you that keeping, for a gentleman of my birth, that differs not from the stalling of an ox?" (AYLI.1.1)
Describe poor living conditions. "Call you that keeping that… ox?"
In the play. *Elder brother Oliver has a grudge or envy against the younger Orlando, who describes his own conditions.*

Hotel, looking for a h. in the evening – Now spurs the lated traveller apace to gain the timely inn.

"Now spurs the lated traveller apace
To gain the timely inn." (M.3.3)
In the play. *Macbeth's hired killers get ready to murder Banquo as he returns to Macbeth's castle after a horse-ride in the country.*

How are you? Answer to question, better now that you ask - The better that it pleases your good worship to ask.
FENTON How now, good woman? how dost thou?
MISTRESS QUICKLY The better that it pleases your good worship to ask. (MWW.1.4)
In the play. *Fenton is in love with Anne Page and enlists the help of Mistress Quickly to further his plans.*

How are you? Answer to question, in the middle - Happy, in that we are not overhappy; on Fortune's cap we are not the very button.
"HAMLET. How do ye both?
ROSENCRANTZ. As the indifferent children of the earth.
GUILDENSTERN. Happy, in that we are not overhappy;
On Fortune's cap we are not the very button." (H.2.2)
The answer can be the poetic equivalent to 'not too bad'. 'Very button' refers to the button at the top, meaning that the top button represents the best of fortune. Substitute 'top' to 'very', "…on Fortune's cap we are not the top button." You can substitute the singular for the plural and apply the answer to yourself, 'As the indifferent child of the earth, happy in that I am not overhappy; on Fortune's cap I am not the very button'
In the play: *Hamlet meets with Guildenstern and Rosencrantz, who are following his moves. Hamlet engages them into semi-serious disquisitions.*

How are you? Answer to question, in the middle - Like to the time of the year between the extremes of hot and cold, he was nor sad nor merry.
"Like to the time of the year between the extremes
Of hot and cold, he was nor sad nor merry." (AC.1.5)
Modify to '(I am like) to the state of the year between the extremes of hot and cold, neither sad, nor merry'. You can exchange 'happy' for 'merry' without altering the tone of the quote.
In the play: *Antony must go to Rome and temporarily leave Cleopatra. Cleopatra asks a maid in waiting (Alexas), to observe Antony's mood before he departs and refer back to her. Antony's mood shows that he is not happy to leave Cleopatra but also not sad because he must go to Rome to fulfill a duty. And in fact on hearing Alexa's report Cleopatra exclaims, "Oh well divided disposition!"*

Human nature, follow the fortunate, abandon the unfortunate - Men shut their doors against the setting sun.
"Men shut their doors against the setting sun." (TOA.1.2)
Express one very known fact.
In the play. *Apemantus rightly predicts the ingrate behavior of the parasites who are now happy to feast at Timon's table.*

Human nature, h.n. common to even kings - I live with bread like you, feel want, taste grief, need friends..
"I live with bread like you, feel want,
Taste grief, need friends: subjected thus,
How can you say to me, I am a king?" (KRII.3.2)
Modest retort to a praise of your position or standing.
In the play *Dejected Richard II questions the real difference in status between himself and other mortals.*

Human nature, reason balancing instinct - If the balance of our lives had not one scale of reason to poise another of sensuality…
"If the balance of our lives had not one scale of reason to poise another of sensuality, the blood and baseness of our natures would conduct us to most preposterous conclusions: but we have
reason to cool our raging motions, our carnal stings, our unbitted lusts" (OTH.1.3)
Somewhat pessimistic but realistic considerations on human nature.
In the play. *Roderigo confesses his passion for Desdemona to Iago. This prompts Iago to deliver a general statement on the nature of man.*

Human nature, despicable and similar to the spirit that inspires flattery.
"Why this is the world's soul; and just of the same piece
Is every flatterer's spirit." (TOA.3.2)
Comment on an act of selfishness.
In the play. *Some men who witnessed Lucius' refusal to help Timon comment and generalize on the event.*

Human nature, pessimism about h.n. – all is oblique, there is nothing level in our cursed natures but direst villainy.
"... the learned pate
Ducks to the golden fool: all is oblique;
There is nothing level in our cursed natures,
But direst villainy." (TOA.4.2)
Express your general disappointment in humanity.
In the play. *Timon's rating of humanity.*

Human nature, pessimism about h.n. – I set it down, that one may smile, and smile, and be a villain; at least I'm sure it may be so in Denmark.
"…I set it down,
That one may smile, and smile, and be a villain;
At least I'm sure it may be so in Denmark" (H.1.5)
In the play. *Hamlet's conclusion after the meeting with the Ghost.*

Humanity, common trait of h. – One touch of nature makes the whole world kin…
"One touch of nature makes the whole world kin
That all with one consent praise new-born gawds,
Though they are made and moulded of things past,
And give to dust that is a little gilt
More laud than gilt o'er-dusted.
The present eye praises the present object" (TC.3.3)
In the play. *Ulysses tries to convince Achilles to re-join the Greek forces against the Trojans. Here the common habit of men is to be impressed by what is new and forget past achievements. 'Gawds'='worthless things that provide amusement, toys'.*

Humiliation, reaching the bottom of h. – I have sounded the very base-string of humility.
"I have sounded the very base-string of humility" (KHIV.p1.2.4)
In the play. *The Prince of Wales of himself, referring to his association with Falstaff and other companions of the same ilk.*

Humility, h. leading to safer life - And often, to our comfort, shall we find the sharded-beetle in a safer hold…
"And often, to our comfort, shall we find
The sharded beetle in a safer hold
Than is the full-wing'd eagle" (CYM.3.3)
In the play. *Belarius reminds his two adoptive sons of his instructions and the relative values of*

life at court versus a simple life. 'Sharded'='Hard shell'.

Humor, truth in h. - Jesters do oft prove prophets.
"Jesters do oft prove prophets." (KL.5.3)
When your remark is dismissed as silly.
In the play. *Evil sisters Regan and Goneril jostle as to which one has a claim to marry the evil Edmund. Regan responds to an ironic remark by Goneril.*

Hunger, feeling incredibly hungry – I am so hungry that if I might have a lease of my life for a thousand years I could stay no longer.
"...I (am) so
hungry that if I might have a lease of my life for a
thousand years I could stay no longer." (KHVI p2. 4.10)
In the play. *John Cade, fleeing London finds himself very hungry and weak in a garden belonging to Mr. Iden, who will kill Cade in a fight.*

Hunger, feeling hungry - I am weak with toil, yet strong in appetite.
" I am weak with toil, yet strong in appetite." (CYM.3.6)
In the play. *Arviragus is hungry.*

Hunger, h. not appeased by imagining food - "(who can) cloy the hungry edge of appetite by bare imagination of a feast?
"(who can) cloy the hungry edge of appetite
By bare imagination of a feast?" (KRII.1.3)
In the play. *Bolingbroke rejects the suggestions by his father John of Gaunt on positive thinking regarding Bolingbroke's impending exile.*

Hunger, h. to be appeased, food coming - ...but if thou diest before I come, thou art a mocker of my labour.
"... if I bring thee not something to eat, I'll give thee leave to die; but if thou diest before I come, thou art a mocker of my labour." (AYLI.2.6)
Before you go out to get the pizza for a hungry group.
In the play. *Orlando leaves Adam to find and bring him back something to eat.*

Hunger, hungry and looking for anything as long as it is healthy food - ... get me some repast; I care not what so it be wholesome food.
"I prithee go, and get me some repast;
I care not what so it be wholesome food." (TOS.4.3)
Ask for something to eat
In the play. *Katharina, starving, asks Grumio for something to eat.*

Hunger, poverty and resentment - ... for the gods know, I speak in hunger for bread, not in thirst for revenge...
" ... for the gods know, I speak in hunger for bread, not in thirst for revenge..." (COR.1.1)
Dramatize your predicament, it applicable.
In the play. *Working class citizens plot a riot*

How old are you? Various answers in the entries for 'Age'.

Hunger, when in love not important but...- ... though the chameleon love may feed on air, I am one that is nourished by my victuals, and would fain have meat. (TVG.2.1)

When you fall in love, other issues, however essential, seem utterly unimportant, eating, for example. As you well know when someone says that he/she is not hungry, it is common to ask, "Are you in love?" But if love has made you lose your appetite, your friends haven't. One of them could pointedly quote this line.

You can change 'fain' to 'rather' or 'gladly'. 'Fain' actually means 'gladly' and in Shakespeare is always used in conjunction with 'would'.

In another unrelated application, say you are in a meeting, you are hungry, it is lunchtime and your colleagues seem to have completely forgotten about it. You can use the quote to raise their attention – even if you are a vegetarian, it's the idea that counts. See also 'Food, virtual f. – (Who can) cloy the hungry edge of appetite by bare imagination of a feast?'
In the play: *Valentine, in love with Sylvia, is not hungry but his servant Speed is.*

**Hurricane, more noise than a h. – …
the dreadful spout which shipmen do the hurricano call …**
"…not the dreadful spout
Which shipmen do the hurricano call,
Constringed in mass by the almighty sun,
Shall dizzy with more clamour Neptune's ear
In his descent than shall my prompted sword
Falling on Diomed." (TC.5.1)
In the play. *Witnessing unseen Cressida's betrayal with Diomed, Troilus vows revenge.*

Hurt, you hurt me - Thou stickest a dagger in me.
"Thou stickest a dagger in me" (MOV.3.1)
See also 'Rejection, she says no with a smile that hurts more than soothes - Thou cuttest my head with a golden axe and smil'st upon the stroke that murders me.'
In the play. *Shylock to fellow brethren Tubal who announced that Jessica, Shylock's daughter, eloped to Genoa and spent all his money.*

Husband, declaration of husband's rights - Such duty as the subject owes the prince even such a woman oweth to her husband.
"Thy husband is thy lord, thy life, thy keeper,
Thy head, thy sovereign; one that cares for thee,
And for thy maintenance commits his body
To painful labour both by sea and land,
To watch the night in storms, the day in cold,
Whilst thou liest warm at home, secure and safe;
And craves no other tribute at thy hands
But love, fair looks and true obedience;
Too little payment for so great a debt.
Such duty as the subject owes the prince
Even such a woman oweth to her husband" (TOS.5.2)
Terribly out of fashion in the 21st century but you may use the lines to say how stood matters in the good old times. Answer to 'What do you want from me?' E.G. 'Love, fair looks and true obedience'
In the play. *The fully tamed Katharina has just won a bet (on behalf of her husband Petruchio) that she is the most obedient wife of all. She now delivers a speech for the benefit of other (less obedient) wives.*

Hygiene, good manners require hand-washing – When good manners shall lie all in one or two men's hands and they unwashed…

"When good manners shall lie all in one or two men's hands and they unwashed too, 'tis a foul thing." (TJ.1.5)
In the play. *Capulet's servants scramble to prepare for the party in which Romeo will meet Juliet.*

Hypocrisy, accusing others of one's mischiefs - The secret mischiefs that I set abroach I lay unto the grievous charge of others.
"The secret mischiefs that I set abroach
I lay unto the grievous charge of others." (KRIII.1.3)
In the play. *Richard outlines his strategy in a monologue. 'Abroach' refers to a barrel that has been opened or 'broached'.*

Hypocrisy, criticizing one's own faults in others - wilt thou whip thine own faults in other men?
TIMON (to poet). ... wilt thou whip thine own faults in other men?" (TOA.5.1)
Use with anyone who criticizes in others what he does himself.
In the play. *The poet tells the painter that he will deliver to Timon a poem describing satirically the flattery that is associated with wealth. Timon, unseen, listens and comments.*

Hypocrisy, deceit and cunning - O, what authority and show of truth can cunning sin cover itself withal.
"O, what authority and show of truth Can cunning sin cover itself withal." (MAAN.4.1)
Comment on hypocrisy in general. See also 'Character, a hypocrite and filthy' – entries for 'Appearances, a. deceptive or false.'
In the play. *Claudio, unaware of the evil plot of Don John, believes Hero to be a slut and is angry at her.*

Hypocrisy, determination to stamp it out - Now step I forth to whip hypocrisy.
"Now step I forth to whip hypocrisy."(LLL.4.3)
Prepare the audience to your next subject making clear your intentions.
In the play. *Biron will uncover the hypocrisy of his fellow students and friends.*

Hypocrisy, devils mask sin with good appearance - When devils will the blackest sins put on, they do tempt at first with heavenly shows...
"When devils will the blackest sins put on,
They do tempt at first with heavenly shows,
As I do now." (OTH.2.3)
Caution assembly or party on excessive reliance on a character you do not trust. See also entries for "Appearances'
In the play. *Iago begins to carry out his diabolic plot against Othello and first pretends to be his true friend. He will suggest that Desdemona is secretly in love with Cassio.*

Hypocrisy, false conclusion from a righteous example - The devil can cite scriptures for his purpose...
"The devil can cite scriptures for his purpose.
An evil soul, producing holy witness
Is like a villain with a smiling cheek;
A goodly apple, rotten at the heart;
O, what a goodly outside falsehood hath." (MOV.1.3)
Retort to an assertion by a self-righteous individual, 'The devil can cite scriptures for his purpose'. Or as an observation when you know that under a veneer of apparent truth there is rotten falsehood. See also entries for 'Appearances, a. deceptive or false'.
In the play. *Antonio cautions Bassanio not to take seriously Shylock's quotations of the Bible. Shylock uses a biblical anecdote to justify the levying of interest on borrowed money.*

Hypocrisy, flimsy excuses to deny help - How fairly this lord strives to appear foul.
"How fairly this lord strives to appear foul!" (TOA.3.3)
Objecting to the spin given to a situation.
In the play. *A servant comments on Sempronius' sleazy way to deny Timon help.*

Hypocrisy, h. and cunning will eventually be discovered - Time shall unfold what pleated cunning hides, who cover faults at last shame them derides.
"Time shall unfold what pleated cunning hides;
Who cover faults at last shame them derides." (KL.1.1)
Apply to a flawed scheme which, however, may cause you damage. A situation in which others attempt to accuse you for their failure.
In the play. *Cordelia referring to her cunning sisters. 'Pleated'='convoluted', 'folded'*

Hypocrisy, h. and dishonesty exposed - foul deeds will rise though all the world o'erwhelm them, to men's eyes.
"… Foul deeds will rise,
Though all the world o'erwhelm them, to men's eyes." (H.1.2)
Put a positive spin and a hope of justice to punish or at least expose something bad done by others. See also 'Whisperings, w. about bad deeds' – 'Decisions, bad d. yielding bad results'
In the play. *Hamlet has a presentment after Horatio's report about the appearance of the ghost.*

Hypocrisy, h. and double standards condemned - Shame to him whose cruel striking kills for faults of his own liking!
"Shame to him whose cruel striking Kills for faults of his own liking!" (MFM.3.2)
In the play. *In a monologue the Duke refers to Angelo who condemned Claudio for a fault that he himself, Angelo, is or would like to commit.*

Hypocrisy, h. and feigned kindness - How courtesy would seem to cover sin when what is done is like a hypocrite….
"How courtesy would seem to cover sin,
When what is done is like a hypocrite
The which is good in nothing but in sight!" (PER.1.1)
Characterize a hypocrite. "He is like a hypocrite, … sight."
In the play. *Pericles perceives immediately that Antioch's feigned courtesy is suspicious and he will immediately run away.*

Hypocrisy and self-illusion - … with devotion's visage and pious action we do sugar o'er the devil himself.
POLONIUS We are oft to blame in this, --
'Tis too much proved--that with devotion's visage
And pious action we do sugar o'er
The devil himself.
KING CLAUDIUS [Aside] O, 'tis too true!
How smart a lash that speech doth give my conscience!
The harlot's cheek, beautied with plastering art
Is not more ugly to the thing that helps it
Than is my deed to my most painted word (H.3.1)

Examples of the application of the principles are endless – just think of how many times the US administration has invaded other countries killing thousands to bring 'freedom and democracy'.
In the play. *Polonius tells Ophelia to read or pretend to read a book while waiting for the arrival of Hamlet. This is part of the scheme to find out what is really bothering Hamlet. The King, overhearing Polonius' words to Ophelia, finds their dramatic relevance to his own actions.*

Hypocrisy, h. covering vice - There is no vice so simple but assumes some mark of virtue on his outward parts.
"There is no vice so simple but assumes
Some mark of virtue on his outward parts" (MOV.2.2)
When your political adversary tries to cover up or put a spin on a crime.
In the play. *The fair Portia will marry him who solves a riddle. Before attempting to do so, Bassanio meditates on some important truths.*

Hypocrisy, h. defined - your virtue hath a licence in't.
"I know your virtue hath a licence in't, which seems a little fouler than it is, to pluck on others.
Which seems a little fouler than it is,
To pluck on others." ((MFM.2.4)
In the play. *Angelo's license, which Isabel mentions, refers to the request for sex by Angelo, the same person that has condemned Claudio to death for having had sex with Juliet.*

Hypocrisy, h. in prayers – His prayers are full of false hypocrisy…
"His prayers are full of false hypocrisy;
Ours of true zeal and deep integrity.
Our prayers do out-pray his"
(KRII.5.3)
In the play. *The Duchess of York pleads with Bolingbroke to pardon her son, whereas her husband and father of Aumerle would rather have him executed for treason.*

Hypocrisy, h. in religion - … In religion, what damned error… hiding the grossness with fair ornament?
"…In religion,
What damned error, but some sober brow
Will bless it and approve it with a text,
Hiding the grossness with fair ornament?" (MOV.2.1)
See also 'Religion, religious hypocrites – … and sweet religion makes a rhapsody of words.'
In the play. *The fair Portia will marry him who solves a riddle. Before attempting to do so, Bassanio meditates on some important truths.*

Hypocrisy, h. in religion. - How canst thou urge God's dreadful law to us when thou hast broke it in so dear degree?
"How canst thou urge God's dreadful law to us,
When thou hast broke it in so dear degree?" (KRIII.1.4)
In the play. *A murderer rebuts the soon-to-be-slain Clarence. Clarence urges the two contract killers to respect the law of God.*

Hypocrisy, h. in seeming a saint - … And thus I clothe my naked villany… and seem a saint, when most I play the devil…
"And thus I clothe my naked villany
With old odd ends stolen out of holy writ;
And seem a saint, when most I play the devil." (KRIII.1.3)
Denounce hypocrisy and extend to the plural via a minor modification. 'And so they clothe their naked villany…and seem saints, when most they play the devil.
In the play. *Talking to himself, Richard describes his evil plans to acquire the crown.*

Hypocrisy, h. in writing - A huge translation of hypocrisy, vilely compiled….
"A huge translation of hypocrisy,
Vilely compiled, profound simplicity" (LLL.5.2)
In the play. *Katharine does not think much of the letter sent to her by her admirer Dumain.*

Hypocrisy, h. masking vice - There is no vice so simple but assumes some mark of virtue.
"There is no vice so simple but assumes
Some mark of virtue on his outward parts" (MOV.2.1)
When your adversary tries to cover ups or put a spin on a crime.
In the play. *The fair Portia will marry him who solves a riddle. Before attempting to do so, Bassanio meditates on some important truths.*

Hypocrisy, h. to cover treason - How smooth and even they do bear themselves!…
"How smooth and even they do bear themselves!
As if allegiance in their bosoms sat,
Crowned with faith and constant loyalty" (HV.2.2)
In the play. *Westmoreland comments on the behavior of 3 traitors paid to kill Henry V. The king and Westmoreland are aware of the plot.*

Hypocrisy, practice what you preach - Do not, as some ungracious pastors do… The primrose path of dalliance threads and recks not his own reed.
"… But good my brother,
Do not, as some ungracious pastors do,
Show me the steep and thorny way to heaven,
Whilst, like a puffed and reckless libertine,
The primrose path of dalliance threads,
And recks not his own reed." (H.1.3)

Paraphrase the 'do-as-I-say and not-as-I-do' behavior of many, or comment on difference between words and deeds, e.g. 'He tells others to do so and so but he recks not his own reed'.
In the play. *Ophelia tell Laertes' not to be a hypocrite, after all the advice he has given her.*

Hypocrisy, show of virtue - So smooth he daub'd his vice with show of virtue… he lived from all attainder of suspect.
"So smooth he daub'd his vice with show of virtue,
That, his apparent open guilt omitted,
I mean, his conversation with Shore's wife,
He lived from all attainder of suspect" (KRIII.3.5)
In the play. *Richard accuses the (already executed) Hastings of treason and hypocrisy whereas the real arch-devil and hypocrite is Richard himself.*

Hypocrisy, unfelt sorrow - To show an unfelt sorrow is an office which the false man does easy.
"To show an unfelt sorrow is an office
Which the false man does easy." (M.2.2)
In the play. *Malcolm suggests to Donalbain not to attend Macbeth's meeting after Duncan was slain. Having himself killed Duncan, Macbeth's sorrow is false.*

Hypocrisy, vice and h. – There is no vice so simple, but assumes some mark of virtue in its outward parts…
"There is no vice so simple, but assumes
Some mark of virtue in its outward parts.
How many cowards, whose hearts are all as false
As stairs of sand, wear yet upon their chins
The beards of Hercules and frowning Mars,

Who, inward searched, have livers white as milk." (MOV.3.2)
Use the first two lines to debunk an argument where a foul action is introduced under the pretense of doing good. Use the last four lines as an argument against hypocrisy. See also 'Appearance, a. of truth hiding a deeper and malicious purpose - … to win us to our harm the instruments of darkness tell us truths...'
In the play. *It is Bassanio's turn to ponder on the puzzle the solution of which will lead to marrying Portia.*

Hypocrite, address to a h. - thou wolf in sheep's array.
"… thou wolf in sheep's array." (KHVI.p1.1.3)
Ironic response to a proposal made with a smile but where you are or would be the loser.
In the play. *Gloucester addresses his archenemy and unchurchlike Bishop of Winchester.*

Ideas, heretical i. - … new opinions, divers and dangerous; which are heresies…
"…new opinions,
Divers and dangerous; which are heresies,
And, not reform'd, may prove pernicious" (KHVIII.5.3)
Sarcastic retort to critics of your opinions.
In the play. *The Chancellor opens his statement as a prosecutor against Cranmer, accused of holding heretical views. He was leaning towards Protestantism when England had not yet detached herself from Rome.*

Ideas, new i. to be rewarded - Search out thy wit for secret policies, and we will make thee famous through the world.
"Search out thy wit for secret policies
And we will make thee famous through the world." (KHVI.p1.3.3)
Elicit new ideas from a group.
In the play. *The Bastard of Orleans prompts La Pucelle to come up with new expedients to defeat the English. The French maintain their trust in the Pucelle notwithstanding the defeat at Rouen.*

Identification, are you so and so? - If I do not usurp myself, I am.
VIOLA/CESARIO. Are you the lady of the house?
OLIVIA. If I do not usurp myself, I am.
VIOLA/CESARIO. Most certain, if you are she, you do usurp yourself; for what is yours to bestow is not yours to reserve." (TN.1.5)
Use the second line as an answer to 'Are you so and so?' Use the line 'what is yours to bestow… reserve.' to prompt her to yield. See also 'Pregnancy. 'I don't want to get pregnant'' – 'Virginity, time dependent value of v.
In the play. *If Olivia is the lady the house there is no 'usurping'. Viola/Cesario calls on Olivia on behalf of Duke Orsino.*

Identification, characteristics - More than I seem, and less than I was born to…
"More than I seem, and less than I was born to:
A man at least, for less I should not be" (KHVI p3.3.1)
Answer to 'Who are you?'
In the play. *Henry VI's answers a question by two keepers, ready to profit by capturing Henry now that the Lancastrians have lost at Towton.*

Identification, who is who? – How may a stranger to those most imperial looks know them from the eyes of other mortals?
"… How may
A stranger to those most imperial looks
Know them from the eyes of other mortals?" (TC.1.3)

Alternative to 'How can I recognize you at the airport?' – See also 'Manager, how to recognize the m.'
In the play. *Aeneas travels to the Greek camp bringing Hector's challenge to a contest with a Greek warrior of the Greeks' choice. He does not know Agamemnon, the Greek leader, and asks how he may recognize him.*

Idleness, i. harmful - Ten thousand harms, more than the ills I know my idleness doth hatch.
"Ten thousand harms, more than the ills I know,
My idleness doth hatch" (AC.1.2)
In the play. *Antony meditates and realizes the harms that his idleness in Alexandria procures to himself.*

Idolatry, i. misplaced - ...idol of idiot worshippers.
"...thou picture of what thou seemest, and idol of idiot worshipper" (TC.5.1)
In the play. *Thersites delivers a letter to Achilles.*

If, the power of 'If' as a peacemaker - Your 'If' is the only peacemaker; much virtue in 'If'.
JAQUES Can you nominate in order now the degrees of the lie?
TOUCHSTONE O sir, we quarrel in print, by the book; as you have books for good manners: I will name you the degrees. The first, the <u>Retort Courteous</u>; the second, the <u>Quip Modest</u>; the third, the <u>Reply Churlish</u>; the fourth, the <u>Reproof Valiant</u>; the fifth, the <u>Countercheque Quarrelsome</u>; the sixth, the <u>Lie with Circumstance</u>; the seventh, the <u>Lie Direct</u>. All these you may avoid but the Lie Direct; and you may avoid that too, with an If. I knew when seven justices could not take up a quarrel, but when the parties were met themselves, one of them thought but of an If, as, 'If you said so, then I said so;' and they shook hands and swore brothers. Your If is the only peacemaker; much virtue in If."
(AYLI.5.4)
See also 'Lies, the seven degrees of lying'. When you hear a platitude or a statement said with questionable conviction, bring in the 'if'. E.G. Other party, 'We will win this election'. You, 'If we convey the right message, much virtue in an 'if'.
In the play. *Touchstone has previously listed a progression of disagreements between two parties (See 'Lies, the seven degrees of lying'). Now, at the request of Jaques, he gives a summary of the list, adding that even at the point of starting a real quarrel, the contenders remember to qualify their statements with an 'if'.*

Ignorance, advantage of not knowing - ... There may be in the cup a steep'd, and one may drink, depart and yet partake no venom...
"Alack, for lesser knowledge! how accursed
In being so blest! There may be in the cup
A spider steep'd, and one may drink, depart,
And yet partake no venom, for his knowledge
Is not infected: but if one present
The abhorr'd ingredient to his eye, make known
How he hath drunk, he cracks his gorge, his sides,
With violent hefts. I have drunk, and seen the spider." (WT.2.1)
In the play. *Leontes (totally wrongly), suspects his wife of adultery and sees presumed evidence in everything he sees. Paradoxically he explains to himself how better it would be if he did not know.*

Ignorance, advantage of not knowing – He that is robbed, not wanting what is stolen...
"He that is robbed, not wanting what is stolen,

Let him not know it and he is not robbed at all." (OTH.3.3)
Alternative to 'I wish I did not know this.' See also 'Contentment, c. assured if insensitive to poverty - Poor and content is rich and rich enough...'
In the play. *Othello, gnawed by jealousy, now wishes he had not been made aware (by Iago) of Desdemona's alleged adultery. However, he has still some doubt.*

Ignorance, i. decried – O gross and miserable ignorance!
"O gross and miserable ignorance!" (KHVI p2.4)
In the play. *Sir Humphrey is accused by John Cade of being a traitor for being able to speak French.*

Ignorance, i. observed in person - there is no darkness but ignorance.
"I say, there is no darkness but ignorance; in which thou art more puzzled than the Egyptians in their fog." (TN.4.2)
Decry ignorance. Or use the complete sentence to accuse someone of ignorance.
In the play. *The clown to Malvolio. The clown pretends not to understand or to misunderstand Malvolio's requests. Malvolio has been confined into a very dark cell.*

Ignorance, i. of what is really good for us - We, ignorant of ourselves beg often our own harms, which the wise powers deny us for our good...
"We, ignorant of ourselves,
Beg often our own harms, which the wise powers
Deny us for our good: so we find we profit
By losing of our prayers." (AC.2.1)
Authoritative reference showing that often we do not know what is good or bad for us. See also 'Self-destruction, s.d. compounded by incorrect judgment - ...when we in our own viciousness grow hard.. the wise Gods seal our eyes...' *** 'Appearance, a. of truth hiding a deeper and malicious purpose - ... to win us to our harm the instruments of darkness tell us truths...' *** 'Shortcomings, sometimes s. prove useful - ...full oft 'tis seen, our means secure us, and our mere defects prove our commodities.'
In the play. *Menecrates to Pompey suggesting a different point of view on the course of events.*

Ignorance, i. shown - you speak, Lord Mowbray, now you know not what.
"You speak, Lord Mowbray, now you know not what." (KHIV.p2.4.1)
Change 'Lord Mowbray' to the name of the ignorant party.
In the play. *Westmoreland rebuts a comment from the rebel Mowbray.*

Ignorance, i. vs. knowledge - ... ignorance is the curse of God, the wing wherewith we fly to heaven.
"And seeing ignorance is the curse of God,
Knowledge the wing wherewith we fly to heaven." (KHVI p2.4.7)
See also entries for 'Learning' *** 'Knowledge'.
In the play. *Lord Say mounts a useless self-defense against the rebel John Cade and associates, by declaring his (Lord Say's) merits in the field of education. This argument actually backfires, given John Cade's unorthodox and contemptuous views on education.*
"Thou hast most traitorously corrupted the youth of the realm in erecting a
grammar school."

Ignorance, pain of knowing too little - I swear 'tis better to be much abused than but to know't a little.
"...thou hast set me on the rack:
I swear 'tis better to be much abused
Than but to know't a little" (OTH.3.3)

In the play. *Othello to Iago who skillfully meters out information on Desdemona's supposed infidelity.*

Ignorance, planned i. to escape guilt - I will not reason what is meant hereby, because I will be guiltless of the meaning.
"I will not reason what is meant hereby,
Because I will be guiltless of the meaning." (KRIII.1.4)
Another tool of deniability.
In the play. *Brakenbury, guarding Clarence in the Tower, reads the message to deliver Clarence in the hands of the murderers.*

Ignorance, you don't know what you are talking about - thou knowest not what thou speak'st.
"…thou knowest not what thou speak'st" (MFM.5.1)
Retort to a garbled and misconstrued sentence or speech.
In the play. *The Duke pretends to believe Angelo's (false) story and not Isabella's (true) story.*

Illusion, i. leading to confusion – … the strength of their illusion shall draw him on to his confusion.
"…the strength of their illusion
Shall draw him on to his confusion" (M.3.5)
See also entries for 'Tyrant'.
In the play. *Hecate predicts that the illusion of grandeur fostered into Macbeth by the witches and Hecate's magic will lead Macbeth to confusion, or rather perdition.*

Illusion, optical i. - Mine eyes are made the fools o' the other senses.
"Mine eyes are made the fools o' the other senses" (M.2.1)
In the play. *Macbeth waits for a signal from his wife to go and murder King Duncan. The illusion refers to the dagger that Macbeth will use for the murder.*

Illusion, state of i., invocation - … and here we wander in illusions some blessed power deliver us from hence.
"And here we wander in illusions;
Some blessed power deliver us from hence." (COE.4.3)
Indicate (with the first line), your pessimism and objection to the line of reasoning or proposals, typically in a meeting or panel discussion.
In the play. *The distraught Ant S is mistaken for Ant E by servant Dromio S.*

Illusions, constructs of the mind - Sometimes we see a cloud that's dragonish…
"Sometimes we see a cloud that's dragonish;
A vapour sometime like a bear or lion,
A tower'd citadel, a pendent rock,
A forked mountain, or blue promontory
With trees upon't, that nod unto the world,
And mock our eyes with air: thou hast seen these signs;
They are black vesper's pageants" (AC.4.14)
Use as a comparison to demolish a quixotic expectation or opinion. See also 'Cloud, mutation in c. shapes – That which is now a horse, even with a thought the rack dislimns, and makes it indistinct…
In the play. *Antony addresses assistant Eros in a roundabout way, comparing himself to a cloud, and will eventually ask Eros to kill him.* 'Pendent'='hanging'

IMAGE
Image is to a man what spin is to the news. You rely on image to show what you are not, as you rely on spin to modify reality and transform it into a lie.

Views on image differ depending on a person's cast of thought. For Aesop "Outside show is a poor substitute for inner worth" (Fables, The Fox and the Mask").

An epigram by the Latin poet Martial (ad 86) suggests "Be content to seem what you really are".

But for Oscar Wilde (1891) "It is only shallow people who do not judge by appearances. The true mystery of the world is the visible, not the invisible." (The Picture of Dorian Gray).

Image building or restoration - I'll be at charges for a looking glass and entertain a score or two of tailors...
"I'll be at charges for a looking glass
And entertain a score or two of tailors
To study fashions to adorn my body.
Since I am crept in favour with myself,
I will maintain it with a little cost." (RIII.1.2)
Use if she does not like the way you dress, or if she says that you should change your image.
Here are Ovid's words of advice on the subject. 'White is a shameful color in a sailor; swarthy should he be, both from the sea-waves and from heaven's beams; shameful too in a farmer who ever beneath the sky turns up the ground with curved ploughshare and heavy implements. Thou too, who seekest the prize of Pallas' garland (i.e. crown of olive leaves given to the athlete who won the match), art shamed if thy body be white. Let every lover be pale; this is the lover's hue. Such looks become him.' (AOL.1)
In the play. *Richard has won Anne over and she has agreed to marry him. Richard did not see himself as too much of a lover, but now he is encouraged and will even considering adopting a fashionable attire.*

Image building, too much effort - You might have been enough the man you are with striving less to be so.
"You might have been enough the man you are,
With striving less to be so." (COR.3.2)
Counsel restraint with ambition. See also 'Ambition, dangerous'
In the play. *Volumnia, Coriolanus' mother attempts to counsel Coriolanus to soften his approach to the citizens and life in general.*

Image, happy about your i. - Shine out, fair sun, till I have bought a glass, that I may see my shadow as I pass.
"Shine out, fair sun, till I have bought a glass,
That I may see my shadow as I pass." (KRIII.1.2)
In the play. *Having won Anne over and she having agreed to marry him, Richard is quite happy with himself, as he did not expect or trust his seducing skills.*

Image, i. appearing as seen at first - ... thy image doth appear in the rare semblance that I loved it first.
"Sweet Hero! now thy image doth appear
In the rare semblance that I loved it first." (MAAN.5.1)
Use it positively or negatively when you discover that she is really the opposite of the image she projected at first.
In the play. *Claudio realizes how wrong he was to believe the accusations against Hero.*

Image, the power of i. to deceive and corrupt - O place! O form! How often dost thou with thy case, thy habit, wrench awe from fools...
"... O place! O form!
How often dost thou with thy case, thy habit,
Wrench awe from fools, and tie the wisest souls
To thy false seeming." (MFM.2.4)

Comment on the general vice of trusting in appearances, to the detriment of truth.
In the play. *Angelo is attracted by Isabel and meditates with himself on what to do.*

Imagination, appeal to the i. to visualize events when graphics are missing - ... Still be kind and eke out our performance with your mind.
"…Still be kind,
And eke out our performance with your mind." (KHV.3.prologue)
Use in a presentation, when describing something grand but lack graphics or props.
In the play. *At the beginning of act III the chorus asks again the audience to supply with the imagination what the actors cannot provide with props.*

Imagination, conceit, lack of realism - Conceit in weakest bodies strongest works.
"Conceit in weakest bodies strongest works." (H.3.4)
Here conceit stands for 'imagination', substitute the word for clarity and adapt accordingly to put down in one stroke an unrealistic idea as evidence of a weak mind.
In the play. *Hamlet has reprimanded his mother the Queen and she is shaken. The ghost appears to Hamlet only, has sympathy for her and tells Hamlet to talk to her.*

Imagination, figment of the i. – This the very coinage of your brain…
"This the very coinage of your brain…" (H.3.4)
In the play. *The Queen cannot see the Ghost who speaks to Hamlet. Therefore Hamlet appears as if he were talking to himself.*

Imagination, i. is rich with strange images – So full of shapes is fancy that it alone is high-fantastical.
"... so full of shapes is fancy,
That it alone is high-fantastical."
(TN.1.1)
Emphasize the unrealistic ideas generated by a strong imagination.
In the play. *The Duke ponders about his unreturned love to Olivia.*

Imagination, imagining that thoughts are people – My brain I'll prove the female to my soul…
"My brain I'll prove the female to my soul,
My soul the father; and these two beget
A generation of still-breeding thoughts,
And these same thoughts people this little world,
In humours like the people of this world,
For no thought is contented"
(KRII.5.5)
In the play. *A lone prisoner at Pomfret Castle, Richard gives free reign to his troubled imagination.*

Imagination, man of i. - ... these are begot in the ventricle of memory…
"This is a gift that I have, simple, simple; a foolish extravagant spirit, full of forms, figures, shapes, objects, ideas, apprehensions, motions, revolutions: these are begot in the ventricle of memory, nourished in the womb of pia mater, and delivered upon the mellowing of occasion." (LLL.4.2)
Use 'Ventricle of memory' when you are trying to remember, e.g. 'I am searching my ventricle of memory...'
In the play. *The pompous Holofernes praises his own wit. 'Pia mater' is the membrane that protects the brain. 'Pia mater' = 'Membrane that surrounds the brain'.*

Imagination, not a substitute of reality - O, who can hold a fire in his

hand by thinking on the frosty Caucasus?...
"O, who can hold a fire in his hand
By thinking on the frosty Caucasus?
Or cloy the hungry edge of appetite
By bare imagination of a feast?
Or wallow naked in December snow
By thinking on fantastic summer's heat?
O, no! the apprehension of the good
Gives but the greater feeling to the worse:
Fell sorrow's tooth doth never rankle more
Than when he bites, but lanceth not the sore." (KRII.1.3)
Compare the reality of the present condition against the positive pictures usually presented by governments.
In the play. *Bolingbroke rejects the suggestions by his father John of Gaunt on positive thinking regarding Bolingbroke's impending exile.*

Imagination, product of the i. - ... the baseless fabric of your vision.
"...And, like the baseless fabric of this vision
... Leave not a rack behind" (TEM.4.1)
A preamble to your showing that your adversary is wrong, e.g. 'Let me show how what you call facts are but the baseless fabric of your vision'
In the play. *At the conclusion of the play (and plot), Prospero discloses that all was but a product of magic and illusion. 'Rack' = 'floating vapor', 'cloud'.*

Imagination, seeing a fleet - ... behold the threaden sails, borne with the invisible and creeping wind...
"...behold the threaden sails,
Borne with the invisible and creeping wind,
Draw the huge bottoms through the furrow'd sea,
Breasting the lofty surge"
(KHV.3.prologue)
When you make a presentation without graphics.
In the play. *K Henry's fleet is bound for France landing at Harfleur. 'Threaden'='Made of thread'*

Imagination, use of i. prompted - ... the quick forge and working-house of thought.
"... behold,
In the quick forge and working-house of thought,
How London doth pour out her citizens." (KHV.5.prologue)
Extract the second line, e.g. 'Use 'the quick forge and working house of thought' to visualize this'.
In the play. *The chorus before the 5th act, again makes up for the lack of props.*

Imitation, i. of foreign fashion - ... whose manners still our tardy apish nation limps after in base imitation.
"The open ear of youth doth always listen;
Report of fashions in proud Italy,
Whose manners still our tardy apish nation
Limps after in base imitation"
(KRII.2.1)
Criticize the imitation of stupid foreign habits.
In the play. *The Duke of York comments on the profligate ways of Richard II's court.*

Immortality, desire for i. – I have immortal longings in me.
"Give me my robe, put on my crown; I have
Immortal longings in me" (AC.5.2)
Answer to 'Why are you doing this?' referring to a political career or a particularly selfless act.

In the play. *Cleopatra asks attendant Iras for the insignia of regality while getting ready for death by an adder's poison.*

Impartiality, I'll be impartial -... nor partialize the unstooping firmness of my upright soul.
"...impartial are our eyes and ears:
Were he my brother, nay, my kingdom's heir,
As he is but my father's brother's son,
Now, by my sceptre's awe, I make a vow,
Such neighbour nearness to our sacred blood
Should nothing privilege him, nor partialize
The unstooping firmness of my upright soul." (KRII.1.1)
Answer to 'Are you sure you can be objective?'... 'Nothing will partialize the …soul.'
In the play. *Richard II will be an impartial judge between Bolingbroke and Mowbray, though Bolingbroke is Richard's cousin.*

Impatience, its privilege - ... impatience hath his privilege.
"Sir, sir, impatience hath his privilege." (KJ.4.3)
In the play. *Lord Salisbury to Ph. Faulconbridge who came to sooth the lords' anger on behalf of King John. The unpleasant Faulconbridge answers, in this instance with a pointed comment,*
'Tis true, to hurt his master, no man else'.

Impatience, i. for action - Imagination of some great exploit drives him beyond the bounds of patience.
"Imagination of some great exploit
Drives him beyond the bounds of patience" (KHIVp1.1.3)
In the play. *Hotspur justifies his impatience at listening quietly to serious proposals for a rebellion against King Henry.*

Impatience, i. observed – ... a very little thief of occasion will rob you of a great deal of patience
"…a very little thief of occasion will rob you of a great deal of patience" (COR.2.1)
Tone down the observed impatience of an impatient man.
In the play. *Menenius (friend of Coriolanus) to the two Tribunes, angry at Coriolanus for his air of disdain and contempt.*

Impatience, signs of i. – Hoping it was but an effect of humour, which sometimes hath his hour with every man.
"…And withal
Hoping it was but an effect of humour,
Which sometimes hath his hour with every man." (JC.2.1)
Apply to yourself to explain impatience or brush it off, 'It was but an effect of humor, which sometimes hath his hour with every man'. Or in general when you cannot explain an irrational answer or behavior.
In the play. *Portia tells husband Brutus why she kept quiet even if she saw something changed in Brutus' behavior. She thought it was the effect of a temporary mood.*

Implementation, careful i. - by cold gradation and well-balanced form.
"By cold gradation and well-balanced form" (MFM.4.2)
In the play. *The Duke plans his return to Vienna when 'By cold gradation and well-balanced form' he will deal with Angelo, his hypocrite deputy.*

Impossibility to make a man change his mind - ... you may as well forbid the sea for to obey the moon…
"…You may as well
Forbid the sea for to obey the moon
As or by oath remove or counsel shake

The fabric of his folly, whose foundation
Is piled upon his faith and will continue
The standing of his body." (WT.1.2)
Use the first two lines as an expression of dramatic impossibility.
In the play. *Camillo warns Polixenes that it is impossible to eradicate from Leonte's mind the absurd idea that Polixenes has an affair with Leonte's wife.*

Impossibility to soften a hard heart - You may as well forbid the mountain pines…
"You may as well use question with the wolf
Why he hath made the ewe bleat for the lamb;
You may as well forbid the mountain pines
To wag their high tops and to make no noise,
When they are fretten with the gusts of heaven" (MOV.4.1)
See also 'Pity, pitiless man'.
In the play. *Shylock wants Antonio's contracted pound of flesh and will not accept any other alternative and more rewarding offer.*
'Fretten' = 'Agitated'

Impossibility, cooling the sun with a fan - … you may as well go about to turn the sun to ice…
"…you may as well go about to turn the sun to ice with fanning in his face with a peacock's feather." (KHV.4.1)
Answer to an absurd proposal or suggestion.
In the play. *Soldier William addresses King Henry V, who walks in disguise among his troops. William is skeptical about the willingness of the king to die with his troops.*

Impossible, dreaming on the i. – Flattering me with impossibilities…
"Flattering me with impossibilities.
My eye's too quick, my heart o'erweens too much,
Unless my hand and strength could equal them" (KHVI.p3.3.2)
In the play. *Richard of Gloucester meditates on his next move, to achieve the crown*

Impossible, nothing i. to the daring - Impossible be strange attempts to those that weigh their pains in sense…
"Impossible be strange attempts to those
That weigh their pains in sense and do suppose
What hath been cannot be"
(AWEW.1.1)
In the play. *Helena meditates on her plan to go to Paris to achieve her noble ends, however weighed against her be the odds.*

Impressed, amazed (positively) - This is a most majestic vision, and harmoniously charming.
"This is a most majestic vision, and Harmoniously charming" (TEM.4.1)
Your reaction (for example) to the view from your friend's house, or anything that he/she/they may enjoy hearing praised. Could apply to a girl too. See also 'Place, a nice p. to stay – cottage' – 'Air, excellent a. quality'.
In the play. *Ferdinand is impressed by the performance produced by spirits that Prospero directed. Prospero says of them,*
'Spirits, which by mine art
I have from their confines call'd to enact
My present fancies."

Impudence, shamelessness – What, canst thou say all this, and never blush?
"What, canst thou say all this, and never blush?" (TA.5.1)
Make him/her aware of the shame there is in what he/she is saying. See also 'Guilt, admit your g. and show a little honesty'. - 'Invocation, shamelessness'

In the play. *Aaron has confessed to various murders etc. without any remote hint of remorse. This prompts a Goth to ask the question.*

Indecision, i. between two courses of action - ... I am at war 'twixt will and will not.
"There is a vice that most I do abhor,
And most desire should meet the blow of justice;
For which I would not plead, but that I must;
For which I must not plead, but that I am
At war 'twixt will and will not."
(MFM.2.2)
Use the last line, 'I am at war 'twixt will and will not'.
In the play. *Isabel introduces herself to Angelo, newly appointed ruler of Vienna and prepares the ground to plea for Claudio's – her brother – life.*

Indecision, i. between two courses of action - ... 't is with my mind as with the tide... running either way.
"... 't is with my mind,
As with the tide swell'd up unto his height,
That makes a still-stand, running neither way." (KHIVp2.2.3)
Alternative to 'I don't know which way to go'.
In the play. *At Warkworth Castle, Northumberland is undecided whether to go and join the forces of the archbishop of York or prudently retire to Scotland and wait to see how events develop.*

Indecision, i. between two courses of action - ... like a man to double business bound, I stand in pause where I shall first begin and both neglect.
"And, like a man to double business bound,
I stand in pause where I shall first begin,
And both neglect." (H.3.3)
When you are undecided about an issue. Or when you need to explain why you have not taken action on something you promised you would do.
In the play. *King Claudius begins to suffer the pains of conscience after the murder of his brother, Hamlet's father.*

Indecision, i. due to confusion in the mind - My thoughts are whirled like a potter's wheel; I know not where I am, nor what I do.
"My thoughts are whirled like a potter's wheel;
I know not where I am, nor what I do." (KHVIp1.1.5)
Use to take time to decide when in a difficult situation.
In the play. *Talbot after seeing the Pucelle in action.*

Indecision, state of i. – Her tongue will not obey her heart nor can her heart inform her tongue.
"Her tongue will not obey her heart, nor can
Her heart inform her tongue. (AC.3.2)
Comment on hesitation to answer your question. Change 'her' to 'your' or 'his' as applicable.
In the play. *Antony detects that his newly married wife Octavia, brother of Octavian, is hesitant between allegiances to her brother or to her husband.*

Indecision, i. to act,, wisdom or fear? - ... A thought which, quarter'd, hath but one part wisdom and ever three parts coward, I do not know.
"...Now, whether it be
Bestial oblivion, or some craven scruple
Of thinking too precisely on the event,
A thought which, quarter'd, hath but one part wisdom

And ever three parts coward, I do not know
Why yet I live to say 'This thing's to do;'
Sith I have cause and will and strength and means
To do't." (H.4.4)
In the play. *Hamlet does not know himself why he is still hesitating to enact his revenge.*

Indifference, heartlessness – ... you recount your sorrows to a stone.
"... you recount your sorrows to a stone." (TA.3.1)
A characterization of a cold person, 'It's like recounting your sorrow to a stone'. See also entries for 'Pity, pitiless'.
In the play. *The stones are Rome's tribunes who do not want to hear Titus plead that Quintus and Martius are innocent of Bassianus' murder. The comment is by Lucius.*

Indifference, indifferent to someone's praise or hatred - ... his curses and his blessings touch me alike, they're breath I not believe in
"…his curses and his blessings
Touch me alike, they're breath I not believe in." (KHVIII.5.1)
In the play. *Suffolk's opinion of Cardinal Wolsey.*

Indifference, seeming indifferent at tragedy - ... And look upon, as if the tragedy were play'd in jest by counterfeiting actors?
"Why stand we like soft-hearted women here,
Wailing our losses, whiles the foe doth rage;
And look upon, as if the tragedy
Were play'd in jest by counterfeiting actors?" (KHVI.p3.2.3)
In the play. *Warwick upbraids allies during a setback in the battle of Towton between the forces of Henry VI and those of the Yorkists.*

Indignation – ... his indignation derives itself out of a very competent injury
"… his indignation derives itself out of a very competent injury" (TN.3.4)
In the play. *Viola/Cesario has been challenged to a duel by Aguecheek and Toby Belch tells Viola that Aguecheek's indignation is justified.*

Indignation, hold back outrage until facts are clear - seal up the mouth of outrage for a while..
"Seal up the mouth of outrage for a while,
Till we can clear these ambiguities,
And know their spring, their head, their true descent." (RJ.5.3)
Addressing an audience who is predisposed to be angry because of incorrect or partially received information.
In the play. *The Prince of Verona has been called on to investigate and unravel the reasons for the death of Romeo, Juliet and Paris.*

Indignation, i. at a bad deed – O, forfend it, God, that souls refined should show so heinous, black, obscene a deed.
"…O, forfend it, God,
That in a Christian climate souls refined
Should show so heinous, black, obscene a deed!" (KRII.4.1)
In the play. *The Bishop of Carlysle, faithful to the deposed King Richard II, upbraids usurper Bolingbroke and company. 'Forfend' = 'Forbid'.*

Indignation, i. at the idea – Throw your vile guesses in the devil's teeth…
"Throw your vile guesses in the devil's teeth,
From whence you have them" (OTH.3.4)
In the play. *Cassio to his lover Bianca. Bianca thinks that the handkerchief that Cassio unwittingly gave her belong to some other Cassio's lover.*

Indignation, i. mixed with threats - the cannons have their bowels full of wrath...
"The cannons have their bowels full of wrath,
And ready mounted are they, to spit forth
Their iron indignation against your walls." (KJ.2.1)
Indicate that you are ready and determined to fight.
In the play. *King John has brought the battle to France and addresses the citizens of the city of Angiers.*

Indignities, i. not recounted for decency – Many more there are which … I will not taint my mouth with.
"…Many more there are;
Which, since they are of you, and odious,
I will not taint my mouth with." (KHVIII.3.2)
In the play. *Surrey to Cardinal Wolsey now fallen from grace.*

Indiscretion, sometimes i. pays off – Our indiscretion sometimes serves us well.
"Our indiscretion sometimes serves us well" (H.5.2)
In the play. *Hamlet opened the message he carried to England. The message instructed the receiver to kill immediately the carrier of the message. Therefore an indiscrete act saved Hamlet's life.*

Indisposition, confined by i. – An untimely ague stay'd me a prisoner in my chamber...
"An untimely ague
Stay'd me a prisoner in my chamber when
Those suns of glory, those two lights of men,
Met in the vale of Andren" (KHVIII.1.1)
If it is a cold, for example, change 'ague' to 'cold', etc.
In the play. *Buckingham regrets that he could not attend the historic meeting of King Henry VIII and Francis I of France. Buckingham was confined to bed by the gout.*

Indisposition, feeling out of sorts -... to deal plainly, I fear I am not in my perfect mind.
"Pray, do not mock me:
I am a very foolish fond old man,
Fourscore and upward, not an hour more nor less;
And to deal plainly,
I fear I am not in my perfect mind." (KL.4.7)
In the play. *K. Lear sees Kent and Cordelia but does not recognize them.*

Indisposition, major i. or illness - ... my cloud of dignity is held from falling with so weak a wind that it will quickly drop.
"…my cloud of dignity
Is held from falling with so weak a wind
That it will quickly drop: my day is dim." (KHIV p2, 4.4)
'My cloud of dignity' could be a metaphor when you acknowledge you are about to lose your face.
In the play. *Ailing Henry IV to the Prince of Wales.*

Indisposition, minor i. - ... I am not very sick since I can reason of it.
"…I am not very sick,
Since I can reason of it." (CYM.4.1)
Answer to 'Do you feel OK?'
In the play. *In a forest near Milford Haven, Imogen (in man's attire) does not feel well but allays the concerns of her new company, Guiderius and Arviragus and their adopted father Belarius.*

Indisposition, minor i. affecting overall behavior - ... let our finger

ache, and it indues our other healthful members even to that sense of pain.
"For let our finger ache, and it indues
Our other healthful members even to that sense
Of pain" (OTH.3.4)
See also 'Apologies for behavior caused by indisposition - ... we are not ourselves when nature being oppressed...'
In the play. *Desdemona cannot know about the evil plot that Iago is weaving for her destruction. She speculates that something other than jealousy caused Othello to be upset and change his behavior.*

Indisposition, momentary i. – The fit is momentary; upon a thought he will again be well.
"The fit is momentary; upon a thought
He will again be well." (M.1.4)
Your answer to words of concern by others if and when you suddenly feel not well and then recover.
In the play. *Lady Macbeth tries to excuse with the other guests the odd behavior of Macbeth at dinner. Macbeth is haunted by the ghost of the slain Banquo.*

Indivisible, always together – No more can I be sever'd from your side than can yourself yourself in twain divide.
"No more can I be sever'd from your side,
Than can yourself yourself in twain divide" (KHVI.p1.4.5)
In the play. *Talbot Jr., though prompted by his father Talbot Sr. to flee the battlefield for safety, refuses*

Infidelity, lax views on i. - ... who would not make her husband a cuckold to make him a monarch?
"...who would not make her husband a cuckold to make him a monarch? I should venture purgatory for't." (OTH.4.3)
In the play. *Emilia's answer to Desdemona's question if she, Emilia, would betray her husband for the world.*

Infidelity, no tolerance for i. - I had rather be a toad and live upon the vapour of a dungeon, than …
"I had rather be a toad,
And live upon the vapour of a dungeon,
Than keep a corner in the thing I love
For others' uses" (OTH.3.3)
In the play. *Othello's views when thinking about the possibility that Desdemona may be unfaithful.*

Information, amusing i. delivered while walking - And, as we walk along, I dare be bold with our discourse to make your grace to smile.
"And, as we walk along, I dare be bold
With our discourse to make your grace to smile" (TGV.5.4)
In the play. *After a most happy and final denouement Valentine on the way back to Milan will describe to the Duke the machinations of Proteus and the disguise of Julia.*

Information, confidential i. and for one person only - My matter hath no voice, lady, but to your own most pregnant and vouchsafed ear.
"My matter hath no voice, lady, but to your own most pregnant and vouchsafed ear." (TN.3.1)
In the play. *Viola/Cesario, on a mission from Count Orsino, addresses Olivia.*

Information, dangerous and sensitive i. – … matter deep and dangerous, as full of peril and adventurous spirit…
"I'll read you matter deep and dangerous,
As full of peril and adventurous spirit
As to o'er-walk a current roaring loud

On the unsteadfast footing of a spear"
(KHIVp1.1.3)
In the play. *Worcester prepares to disclose to the impatient Hotspur sensitive information about a brewing rebellion.*

Information, fishing for i. - I am angling now, though you perceive not how I give line.
"I am angling now,
Though you perceive not how I give line." (WT.1.2)
A diplomatic ruse in a plot to pretend that you are giving away your game. Maybe you are, maybe you are not.
In the play. *Leontes begins to suspect that Hermione and Polixenes have an affair and develops a deep jealousy.*

Information, i. annoying and unpleasant - Tedious it were to tell, and harsh to hear, sufficeth…
"Tedious it were to tell, and harsh to hear:
Sufficeth I am come to keep my word" (TOS.3.2)
Answer to 'Tell me about it' when you really do not want to.
In the play. *Petruchio arrives late for his marriage to Katharina – it's all part of his plot to subdue her irksome character.*

Information, i. is money - Open your purse, that the money and the matter be at once delivered.
PROTEUS. Come, come, open the matter in belief, what said she?
SPEED. Open your purse, that the money, and the matter be at once delivered." (TGV.1.1)
Answer to "What is the matter about?"
In the play. *Proteus has charged Speed with delivering a love letter to Julia. He did so but wants money before reporting Julia's reactions at the letter.*

Information, i. not wanted or sought (in the past) - More to know did never meddle with my thoughts.
"More to know
Did never meddle with my thoughts." (TEM.1)
When dealing with a delicate situation in which it is better not to know than to know.
In the play. *Prospero has explained to his daughter Miranda how they came about to end up in an island. Miranda acknowledges the information realizing that she did not ask for it before.*

Information, i. requested and believed interesting - Inform us of thy fortunes; for it seems they crave to be demanded.
"Inform us of thy fortunes; for it seems
They crave to be demanded." (CYM.4.3)
Asking for a quick verbal report from someone who has come back from a business trip or a meeting
In the play. *Lucius and company stumble on Imogen (disguised as a boy) and questions him/her.*

Information, i. to be made public for security - This must be known, which, being kept close, might move more grief to hide…
"This must be known, which, being kept close, might move
More grief to hide than hate to utter love." (H.2)
Urge disclosure of critical information - stop at 'more grief to hide'.
In the play. *Polonius thinks that the assumed Hamlet's passion for Ophelia must be made known to the king and queen.*

Information, importance of packaging I. - I fear my Julia would not deign my lines receiving them from such a worthless post.

"I fear my Julia would not deign my lines
Receiving them from such a worthless post." (TGV.1.1)
With some stretching example to justify the additional expenses to create a good package for the product.
In the play. *Somewhat miffed by Speed's greedy request for money, now Proteus doubts whether it was a good idea to have Speed deliver the love letter to Julia.*

Information, important i. not to be withheld from friend – ... and makest his ear a stranger to thy thoughts.
"Thou dost conspire against thy friend, Iago,
If thou but think'st him wrong'd and makest his ear
A stranger to thy thoughts." (OTH.3.3)
In the play. *Othello falls completely for the innuendoes and crafty ways of Iago.*

Information, last to know - Nimble mischance, that art so light of foot... and am I last that knows it?
"Nimble mischance, that art so light of foot,
Doth not thy embassage belong to me,
And am I last that knows it? " (KRII.3.4)
In the play. *The Queen knows from the gardener the downfall of King Richard.*

Information, no i. disclosed about what you intend to do next - ... What course I mean to hold shall nothing benefit your knowledge.
"...What course I mean to hold
Shall nothing benefit your knowledge, nor
Concern me the reporting." (WT.4.4)
Answer to question, 'What will you do next?'
In the play. *Florizel is eloping with Perdita and cannot or does not want to tell Camillo where he is planning ton go.*

Information, no more i. - Seek to know no more.
"Seek to know no more." (M.4.1)
When you are pressed but not ready to tell more.
In the play. *The witches to Macbeth who continues to poll them as to whether Banquo's sons will be kings.*

Information, plea to be given critical i. - If you know aught which does behoove my knowledge...
" ...I beseech you,
If you know aught which does behoove my knowledge
Thereof to be informed, imprison it not
In ignorant concealment." (WT.1.2)
Exhort party disclose all and complete information.
In the play. *Polixenes pleads with Camillo to be informed as to what may have caused the displeasure of Leontes.*

Information, questioning the source of the i. - ... from whence you owe this strange intelligence?
"...Say from whence
You owe this strange intelligence?" (M.1.3)
In the play. *Banquo queries the witches as to the ground for their predictions (Macbeth will be king and Banquo will be the father of kings).*

Information, revealing so far kept secret personal i. - ... who shall be true to us when we are so unsecret to ourselves?
"...who shall be true to us,
When we are so unsecret to ourselves?" (TC.3.2)
Add after 'Now you know all', implying that you have placed unusual trust in the receiver of the information.
In the play. *Cressida concludes her confession of her love to Troilus.*

Information, sensitive and to remain secret - I am to break with thee of some affairs that touch me near…
"I am to break with thee of some affairs
That touch me near, wherein thou must be secret." (TGV.3.1)
In the play. *The Duke of Milan to Valentine, an exchange during which the Duke will ban Valentine.*

Information, sensitive i. - that which I would discover, the law of friendship bids me to conceal.
"My gracious lord, that which I would discover
The law of friendship bids me to conceal" (TGV.3.1)
I do hope no one has to use these lines. But if you substitute 'friendship' with, for example, 'propriety', there may be occasions where the lines fit.
In the play. *The rascally Proteus snitches on his bosom friend Valentine with the Duke of Milan. He does so to remove Valentine from Silvia and make a pass at her*

Information, twisted in one's favor - … your manner of wrenching the true cause the false way.
"Sir John, I am well acquainted with your manner of wrenching the true cause the false way" (KHIV p2.2.1)
In the play. *The Chief Justice to Falstaff who tries to wiggle his way out of a suit brought against him by the Hostess of a Tavern.*

Ingratitude, addressing the ingrate as wasps - Injurious wasps! to feed on such sweet honey and kill the bees, that yield it, with your sting.
"Injurious wasps! to feed on such sweet honey,
And kill the bees, that yield it, with your sting." (TGV.1.2)
Attack the ingratitude of your colleagues.

In the play. *The wasps are Julia's very hands that earlier on had torn a letter from Proteus. Julia loves Proteus.*

Ingratitude, i. as a deformity - In nature there's no blemish but the mind…
"In nature there's no blemish but the mind,
None can be call'd deformed but the unkind.
Virtue is beauty; but the beauteous-evil
Are empty trunks, o'erflourish'd by the devil." (TN.3.5)
Decry ingratitude and a bad act by a good-looking person. See also 'Beauty, b. preservation and its relationship with goodness of character - the hand that hath made you fair hath made you good…'
In the play. *Antonio has been arrested by the Duke's men and addresses Viola for help mistaking her (in her man's disguise) for her twin brother Sebastian. Of course she knows nothing of what is going on. Antonio decries her unkindness.*

Ingratitude, i. despicable and beyond description - … and cannot cover the monstrous bulk of this ingratitude with any size of words.
POET … I am rapt, and cannot cover
The monstrous bulk of this ingratitude
With any size of words.
TIMON Let it go naked, men may see't the better (TOA.5.1)
Decry ingratitude.
In the play. *The poet pretends to chastise the ingratitude shown to Timon by all the others.*

Ingratitude, i. dishonorable - My honour would not let ingratitude so much besmear it.
"My honour would not let ingratitude
So much besmear it" (MOV.5.1)

In the play. *Bassanio explains why he gave the ring to Portia (disguised as a judge). In that disguised Portia had forces her husband to relinquish a ring he had sworn to keep forever.*

Ingratitude, i. from friends - What viler thing upon the earth than friends...
"What viler thing upon the earth than friends
Who can bring noblest minds to basest ends!" (TOA.4.3)
In the play. *Faithful servant Flavius goes to meet Timon, now living in a cave and exclaims against Timon's ungrateful friends.*

Ingratitude, i. hateful – I hate ingratitude more in a man, than lying, vainness, babbling, drunkenness...
"I hate ingratitude more in a man,
Than lying, vainness, babbling, drunkenness,
Or any taint of vice, whose strong corruption
Inhabits our frail blood." (TN.3.5)
State your loathing of ingratitude
In the play. *Antonio has been arrested by the Duke's men and addresses Viola for help mistaking her (in her man's disguise) for her twin brother Sebastian. Of course she knows nothing, he accuses her of ingratitude and Viola replies.*

Ingratitude, i. observed - ... 'tis called ungrateful, with dull unwillingness to repay a debt which with a bounteous hand was kindly lent.
"... 'tis call'd ungrateful,
With dull unwillingness to repay a debt
Which with a bounteous hand was kindly lent" (KRIII.2.2)

In the play. *Dorset attempts to console or lift the spirits of her mother, King Edward's queen, also known as the Lady Grey, shortly to remain a widow. Dorset does not see the hand of Richard III in the recent killing of the king's brother Clarence and considers only the circumstances that led to his mother being Queen. She should be grateful for it.*

Ingratitude, i. of the masses monstrous – Ingratitude is monstrous and for the multitude to be ungrateful...
"Ingratitude is monstrous, and for the multitude to be ungrateful were to make a monster of the multitude." (COR.2.3)
Why the group must be grateful for a good and difficult deed done by someone. See also 'entries for 'Opinion, your op. on crowds and masses'.
In the play. *A spokesman for the people acknowledges that Coriolanus deserves thanks for his military exploits.*

Ingratitude, i. tied to aging - These old fellows have their ingratitude in them hereditary...
"... These old fellows
Have their ingratitude in them hereditary:
Their blood is caked, it is cold, it seldom flows." (TOA.2.2)
Describe an old and stingy donor.
In the play. *A first group of previous friends of Timon refuse to answer his call for help. Timon attributes the ingratitude to their older age.*

Ingratitude, i. tied to loss of fortune - ... when they once perceive the least rub in your fortunes, fall away like water from ye...
"Where you are liberal of your loves and counsels
Be sure you be not loose; for those you make friends
And give your hearts to, when they once perceive

436

The least rub in your fortunes, fall away
Like water from ye, never found again
But where they mean to sink ye"
(KHVIII.2.1)
In the play. *Buckingham, unjustly condemned to death for treason, addresses his few friends.*

Ingratitude, i. to be deprecated - … see the monstrousness of man when he looks out in an ungrateful shape.
"…O, see the monstrousness of man
When he looks out in an ungrateful shape!" (TOA.3.2)
In the play. *A stranger comments on the ingratitude of Timon's friends who, after partaking of Timon's generosity, leave him in the lurch when he needs them.*

Ingratitude, i. towards parents despicable - How sharper than a serpent's tooth it is to have a thankless child!
"How sharper than a serpent's tooth it is
To have a thankless child!" (KL.1.4)
In the play. *Enraged at her ingratitude, King Lear wishes Goneril to be sterile or, if not, to have a thankless child.*

Ingratitude, i. worse than treason - Ingratitude, more strong than traitors' arms…
"Ingratitude, more strong than traitors' arms,
Quite vanquish'd him" (JC.3.2)
In the play. *Antony plies the crowd and will turn the mood against Caesar's killers.*

Ingratitude, invocation to filial i. - Ingratitude, thou marble-hearted fiend…
"Ingratitude, thou marble-hearted fiend,
More hideous when thou show'st thee in a child
Than the sea-monster!" (KL.1.4)
See also 'Ingratitude, i. towards parents'.

In the play. *K. Lear furious about the behavior oh his daughter Goneril.*

Ingratitude, invocation to i. - And thou, all-shaking thunder, smite flat the thick rotundity o' the world…
"And thou, all-shaking thunder,
Smite flat the thick rotundity o' the world!
Crack nature's moulds, an germens spill at once,
That make ingrateful man!" (KL.3.2)
In the play. *K. Lear addressing the thunder while weathering the storm.* "Germens" = 'germs' and 'seeds'.

Ingratitude, invocation to i. - Blow, blow, thou winter wind. Thou art not so unkind as man's ingratitude.
"Blow, blow, thou winter wind.
Thou art not so unkind
As man's ingratitude." (AYLI.2.7)
In the play. *Amiens sings a song on the subject of ingratitude.*

Ingratitude, show of i. - … small thanks for my labour.
"… small thanks for my labour" (TC.1.1)
In the play. *Pandarus resents or pretends to resent Troilus' lack of appreciation for Pandarus' pandering efforts with Cressida.*

Injunction, do no return empty handed - Be clamorous and leap all civil bounds, rather than make unprofited return.
"Be clamorous and leap all civil bounds,
Rather than make unprofited return." (TN.1.4)
Use as is or modify it to fit your situation. E.G. 'I will be clamorous and leap…. unprofited return.' A good slogan for a collection agency.

In the play. *The Duke dispatches Cesario to talk to Olivia on his (the Duke's) behalf and wants her not to take no for an answer. Cesario must meet with Olivia.*

Injunction, stay away - come not within the measure of my wrath.
"Come not within the measure of my wrath." (TGV.5.4)
Use it as a warning.
In the play. *The spineless Thurio is quickly put down by Valentine and the Duke finally agrees to the marriage between his daughter Silvia and Valentine.*

Injunction, stay out of this - Come not between the dragon and his wrath.
"Come not between the dragon and his wrath." (KL.1.1)
Command to anyone who tries to meddle in a business that must be resolved exclusively between the two parties involved.
In the play. *Kent tries to calm Lear down but he does not want to listen and reacts angrily. Lear is angry at his daughter Cordelia for refusing to express her filial love in words.*

Injustice, justice unequally applied - Some rise by sin and some by virtue fall…
"Some rise by sin, and some by virtue fall:
Some run from brakes of ice, and answer none:
And some condemned for a fault alone." (MFM.2.1)
Comment on the incredible inequalities in the application of justice.
In the play. *Escalus comments on the death sentence meted by Angelo on Claudius, condemned for having seduced a girl. See also in-the-play comments to 'Hope as the refuge of the distressed.'*

Injustice, revenge for injustices - … even for revenge mock my destruction!
"… all that have miscarried
By underhand corrupted foul injustice,
If that your moody discontented souls
Do through the clouds behold this present hour,
Even for revenge mock my destruction!" (KRIII.5.1)
Change 'my' destruction to 'his' destruction or to the name of the foul miscarrier of justice.
In the play. *Buckingham, captured and shortly to be beheaded, reflects on his own bad deeds.*

Injustice, unjust accusations and attack on the weak – … A staff is quickly found to beat a dog.
"I shall not want false witness to condemn me,
Nor store of treasons to augment my guilt;
The ancient proverb will be well effected, -
A staff is quickly found to beat a dog." (KHVI p2.3.1)
Denounce abuse and injustice.
In the play. *The innocent Gloucester to the king.*

Injustice, using tools of injustice to correct wrongs – But such is the infection of the time that for the health and physic of our right…
"But such is the infection of the time,
That, for the health and physic of our right,
We cannot deal but with the very hand
Of stern injustice and confused wrong" (KJ.5.2)
In the play. *Salisbury must wage war in England alongside the Dauphin of France to revenge the wrongs carried out by King John.*

Innocence, claim of no responsibility for violent crime - This hand of mine is yet a maiden and an innocent hand,

not painted with the crimson spots of blood.
"This hand of mine
Is yet a maiden and an innocent hand,
Not painted with the crimson spots of blood." (KJ.4.2)
State your innocence with a pinch of exaggeration, e.g. 'My innocent hand is not painted…blood'.
In the play. *Hubert refers to young Arthur who at the moment is still alive. Eventually Arthur was not technically killed by Hubert, though Hubert was held responsible. Arthur died in a fall from the walls of the prison while attempting to escape.*

Innocence, declaration of i. - … as innocent… as is the sucking lamb or harmless dove.
"Our kinsman Gloucester is as innocent
From meaning treason to our royal person
As is the sucking lamb or harmless dove" (KHVI.p2.3.1)
Declare your innocence, e.g. I am as innocent as is the sucking lamb… dove'
In the play. *King Henry VI defends Gloucester (Duke Humphrey) from the accusations of treason levied against him by his enemies.*

Innocence, declaration of i. - A heart unspotted is not easily daunted.
"A heart unspotted is not easily daunted.
The purest spring is not so free from mud,
As I am clear from treason to my sovereign." (KHVI p2.3.1)
Defend yourself against accusations.
In the play. *Suffolk arrests Humphrey (Gloucester), but Humphrey is conscious of his innocence.*

Innocence, declaration of i. – I here protest, in sight of heaven, and by the hope I have of heavenly bliss, that…
"I here protest, in sight of heaven,
And by the hope I have of heavenly bliss,
That I am clear from this misdeed …" (KHVI.p3.3.3)
In the play. *Warwick tells King Lewis of France of being unaware of Edward's. Warwick is Edward's ambassador.*

Innocence, declaration of i. - These hands are free from guiltless bloodshedding…
"These hands are free from guiltless bloodshedding,
This breast from harbouring foul deceitful thoughts." (KHVI.p2.4.5)
In the play. *Facing the rebel crowd of John Cade, Lord Says still hopes that they may spare his life.*

Innocence, i. unsuspecting - … unstain'd thoughts do seldom dream on evil.
"…unstain'd thoughts do seldom dream on evil;
Birds never limed no secret bushes fear" (ROL)
Defense from a charge of conspiracy.
In the poem. *Lucretia does not suspect evil intentions in the visit by Tarquin.*

Innocence, i. and naivete - … we knew not the doctrine of ill-doing, nor dream'd that any did.
"…we knew not
The doctrine of ill-doing, nor dream'd
That any did." (WT.1.2)
See also 'Error, e. admitted and due to youthful inexperience – Those were my salad days when I was green in judgement.' *** 'Honesty, h. unsuspecting of dishonesty – … unstain'd thoughts do seldom dream on evil.'
In the play. *Polixenes tells Hermione of his childhood years growing up with Leontes, king of Sicilia.*

Innocence, i. claimed - Heaven lay not my transgression to my charge!
"Heaven lay not my transgression to my charge!" (KJ.1.1)
Express your innocence against false accusers.
In the play. *Lady Faulconbridge explains to her son that she was by Richard Lionheart, against her will.*

Innocence, i. claimed and complaint about slander - ... howsoever rude exteriorly, is yet the cover of a fairer mind ...
"And you have slander'd nature in my form,
Which, howsoever rude exteriorly,
Is yet the cover of a fairer mind
Than to be butcher of an innocent child" (KJ.4.2)
In the play. *Hubert defends himself against the accusations of hypocrite King John of having murdered young Prince Arthur.*

Innocence, i. giving courage - The trust I have is in my innocence and therefore am I bold and resolute.
"The trust I have is in my innocence,
And therefore am I bold and resolute." (KHVI p2.4)
Words preceding your self-defense
In the play. *Lord Say to K. Henry. Lord Say goes to meet John Cade's rebels, trusts in his own innocence and therefore he believes (wrongly) to be able to persuade them.*

Innocence, i. not immune from undeserved punishment – Some innocents 'scape not the thunderbolt.
"Some innocents 'scape not the thunderbolt." (AC.2.5)
In the play. *Cleopatra just punished a messenger from Rome for having told her of Antony's marriage to Cleopatra. This is her answer to an attendant who points out the innocence of the messenger.*

Innocence, i. of murder and treason - These hands are free from guiltless blood-shedding...
"These hands are free from guiltless blood-shedding,
This breast from harbouring foul deceitful thoughts." (KHVI p2.4.7)
In the play. *Lord Say begs for his life from John Cade's rebels.*

Innocence, i. will be proven - ... innocence shall make false accusation blush and tyranny and tyranny tremble at patience.
"...But thus: if powers divine
Behold our human actions - as they do -
I doubt not then but innocence shall make
False accusation blush and tyranny
Tremble at patience." (WT.3.2)
Use to state your complete innocence including or excluding the intervention of the divine powers depending on your religious convictions. '…I doubt not… patience.'
In the play. *Now Leontes calls for a public trial of Hermione accusing her of infidelity and conspiracy against Leontes' life. Hermione, protesting her complete innocence, responds calmly and forcefully to the accusations.*

Innocence, innocent and not ashamed to denounce crime - ... my true eyes have never practised how to cloak offences with a cunning brow.
"...my true eyes have never practised how
To cloak offences with a cunning brow. " (ROL)
In the play. *Tarquin raped Lucrece and she does not want to hide the event for fear of shame.*

Innocence, innocent of any wrongdoing and non violent of character - I never killed a mouse, nor hurt a fly…
"I never killed a mouse, nor hurt a fly;

I trod upon a worm against my will,
But I wept for it." (PER.4.1)
A good line of defence when you are accused you of heinous deeds, thoughts or intentions. Particularly suitable if the accuser is your wife or girlfriend. See also entries under 'Defence'
In the play. *Marina asks Leonine what has she done to deserve to be killed. Leonine, who was to kill Marina under contract from the evil Dionyza, hesitates. Right at that moment a band of pirates show up. They kidnap Marina and bring her to Mytilene. There they sell her to a brothel.*

Innocence, naïveté due to youth - ... the untainted virtue of your years hath not yet dived into the world's deceit...
"Sweet prince, the untainted virtue of your years
Hath not yet dived into the world's deceit
Nor more can you distinguish of a man
Than of his outward show; which, God he knows,
Seldom or never jumpeth with the heart.
Those uncles which you want were dangerous;
Your grace attended to their sugar'd words,
But look'd not on the poison of their hearts " (KRIII.3.1)
Extract and modify to make a statement of fact, '…man's outward show which, God knows, seldom jumpeth with the heart'. Another possibility, 'These are sugared words, but there is poison in your heart'.
In the play. *Richard III attempts to convince young Prince Edward about the real nature of his friends. The Prince has said good words about his uncles whom Richard has already put to death.*

Innocence, the strength of i. - The trust I have is in mine innocence and therefore am I bold and resolute.
"The trust I have is in mine innocence,
And therefore am I bold and resolute." (KHVI.p2.4.5)
In the play. *Facing the rebel crowd of John Cade, Lord Says still hopes that they may spare his life.*

Innocence, what is my fault? – What is my offence? Where are the evidence that do accuse me?…
"…What is my offence?
Where are the evidence that do accuse me?
What lawful quest have given their verdict up
Unto the frowning judge?" (KRIII.1.4)
In the play. *The Duke of Clarence to the contract murderers sent by his brother Richard.*

Insist, do not i. - Harp not on that string, madam; that is past.
"Harp not on that string, madam; that is past." (KRIII.4.4)
In the play. *Richard exhorts Queen Elizabeth to stop talking or referring to his murders.*

Insistence, warning about further insisting - ... urge it no more on height of our displeasure…
"… urge it no more,
On height of our displeasure: friend or brother,
He forfeits his own blood that spills another" (TOA.3.5)
In the play. *The Senators ask Alcibiades to stop arguing in defense of a soldier who killed in self-defense.*

Insisting, request not to insist on the same subject – harp not on that string.
"Harp not on that string, madam; that is past." (KRIII.4.4)

Change 'madam' with the name of the person who is harping.
In the play. *Queen Elizabeth has reminded Richard about her young son slain by Richard.*

Insolence, intolerable i. – … His insolence is more intolerable than all the princes in the land beside.
"…let us watch the haughty cardinal: His insolence is more intolerable Than all the princes in the land beside" (KHVI.p2.1.1)
In the play. *York meditates his strategy to unseat King Henry VI. The Cardinal of Winchester can be an obstacle in York's strategy.*

Insolence, questioning with i. - With many holiday and lady terms he question'd me.
"With many holiday and lady terms He question'd me" (KHIVp1.1.3)
Sarcastic comment on distorted words, e.g. 'I like your holiday and lady terms…'
In the play. *Hotspur recounts to King Henry an encounter with a dandy sent by the King to collect the prisoners.*

Insolence, reaction to i. - … his insolence draws folly from my lips.
"You wisest Grecians, pardon me this brag,
His insolence draws folly from my lips." (TC.4.5)
Justify some hasty words said in anger at an unjustified attack.
In the play. *Hector replies in kind but more nobly to the insolence of Achilles and then apologizes to the hosting Greeks.*

Insomnia – not enjoying the golden dew of sleep.
"For never yet one hour in his bed Have I enjoy'd the golden dew of sleep,
But have been waked by his timorous dreams." (KRIII.4.1)

The second line can also be used as an alternative to going to bed, e.g. 'I am going to enjoy the golden dew of sleep'. See also entries for 'sleep'
In the play. *Lady Anne, married to Richard repents of having done so.*

Inspiration, a powerful Muse required before starting a speech - O for a Muse of fire, that would ascend the brightest heaven of invention!
"O for a Muse of fire, that would ascend
The brightest heaven of invention!
A kingdom for a stage, princes to act,
And monarchs to behold the swelling scene" (KHV.prologue)
Introduction to a presentation, when the importance of the subject you will cover requires above average inspiration. E.G. 'To deal adequately for our subject tonight I require a Muse of fire…' Or, with a lady, claim you need special inspiration to describe all her qualities.
In the play. *Much action takes place in Henry V. Special effect technology being limited, theater goers are invited to make up with their mind the images suggested by the action of the play.*

Inspiration, how i. works - … the fire i' the flint shows not till it be struck.
"…the fire i' the flint
Shows not till it be struck." (TOA.1.1)
Answer to an insistent request that you produce ideas, or a write-up or anything creative that requires a mixture of thought and inspiration.
In the play. *The poet, caught in a rapture by his friend the painter, both parasites of Timon, explains to the painter the process of poetic inspiration*

Inspiration, she is a source of i. and poetry - Never durst poet touch a pen to write…
"Never durst poet touch a pen to write,

Until his ink were tempered with Love's sighs;
O, then his lines would ravish savage ears,
And plant in tyrants mild humility. " (LLL.4.3)
Tell her that she is such a source of inspiration that you may begin to write to her. Or that her effect has been so positive that she has inspired and enable you to write. You may change 'durst' with 'does'
In the play: *Biron continues to rationalize breaking the king's oath.*

Inspiration, she is a superb source of i. - How can my Muse want subject to invent, while thou dost breathe...
"How can my Muse want subject to invent,
While thou dost breathe, that pour'st into my verse
Thine own sweet argument, too excellent
For every vulgar paper to rehearse?" (SON.38)
Laying it thick.

Inspiration, she is capable of performing miracles - ... chosen from above, by inspiration of celestial grace...
"…chosen from above,
By inspiration of celestial grace,
To work exceeding miracles on earth." (KHVI.p1.5.4)
Congratulate her for something extraordinary she has done, completing a difficult project or similar. 'You were chosen from above… earth.'
In the play. *The English have captured Joan of Arc (Pucelle) and she defends herself against their accusation that she is a witch.*

Inspiration, she is the 10th Muse - Be thou the tenth Muse, ten times more in worth than those old nine which rhymers invocate...

"Be thou the tenth Muse, ten times more in worth
Than those old nine which rhymers invocate" (SON 38)
And if she expresses admiration for the lines that you just recalled and recited try,
**If my slight Muse do please these curious days,
The pain be mine, but thine shall be the praise** (same Sonnet 38)

Instinct, i. revealing character - ... 'Tis wonder that an invisible instinct should frame them to royalty unlearn'd.
"…'Tis wonder
That an invisible instinct should frame them
To royalty unlearn'd" (CYM.4.1)
See also 'Character, c. showing natural traits - how hard it is to hide the sparks of nature.'
In the play. *Belarius comments on the instinctively noble character of his adopted sons who are actually the sons of King Cymbeline.*

Instinct, i. prevailing over the dictates of law - …the brain may devise laws for the blood…
"…the brain may devise laws for the blood, but a hot temper leaps o'er a cold decree." (MOV.1.1)
Explain behavior inspired by passion. See also entries for 'Promises. Love promises unreliable' *** 'Youth, restricting y. ineffective - young blood doth not obey an old decree.' *** 'Necessity, n. overriding commitments and other concerns – Necessity will make us all forsworn…'
In the play. *Portia candidly admits to a common weakness. The character or disposition of a man, called temper, was supposed to depend on the mixture of basic four humours, hot, cold, dry and wet. A hot temper would have an excess of choler (hot and dry) or of blood (hot and wet). Blood was associated with high spirits, prompt action and youth.*

Insubordination, youthful i. - ... bristle up the crest of youth against your dignity.
"This is his uncle's teaching; this is Worcester,
Malevolent to you in all aspects;
Which makes him prune himself, and bristle up
The crest of youth against your dignity." (KHIV.p1.1.1)
Excuse youthful lack of dutiful respect.
In the play. *Westmoreland attributes to Worcester the reason why young Hotspur 'bristle up' against Henry IV.*

Insult, a dog, a bloodhound - ... That dog, that had his teeth before his eyes, to worry lambs and lap their gentle blood.
"From forth the kennel of thy womb hath crept
A hell-hound that doth hunt us all to death:
That dog, that had his teeth before his eyes,
To worry lambs and lap their gentle blood" (KRIII.4.4)
In the play. *Q. Margaret addresses the Duchess of York, mother of Clarence, slain by Richard III, and of Richard himself.*

Insult, a longwinded speaker of nonsense - What cracker is this ass, that deafs our ears with this abundance of superfluous breath.
What cracker is this ass, that deafs our ears
With this abundance of superfluous breath." (KJ.2.1)
Comment on a boring and loud speaker
In the play. *The Archduke of Austria and Philip F. (on whom he pronounces the judgment), don't get along well.*

Insult, absolute devil - Not in the legions of horrid hell can come a devil more damn'd in evil...
"Not in the legions
Of horrid hell, can come a devil more damn'd
In evils to top Macbeth!" (M.34)
Substitute for 'Macbeth' the name of a suitable enemy.
In the play. *Madcap expresses his opinion of Macbeth.*

Insult, abuser of the world – (I) do attach thee for an abuser of the world, a practices of arts inhibited...
"... do attach thee
For an abuser of the world, a practiser
Of arts inhibited and out of warrant." (OTH.1.2)
In the play. *Brabantio, Desdemona's father accuses Othello of having bewitched her.*

Insult, all noise, no substance - The empty vessel makes the greatest sound.
"I did never know so full a voice issue from so empty a heart: but the saying is true, 'The empty vessel makes the greatest sound'." (KHV.4.4)
Sarcastic comment about a loud character. Answer to "What do you think of (name of person)?"
In the play. *An attendant boy's opinion of Pistol.*

Insult, answer to insult of being a fool - Thou art not altogether a fool ...
Nor thou altogether a wise man...
VARRO'S SERVANT Thou art not altogether a fool.
FOOL Nor thou altogether a wise man: as much foolery as I have, so much wit thou lack'st. (TOA.2.2)
It could go as follows, 'You are a fool'. Answer, 'As much foolery I have, so much intelligence you are short of'. See also 'Foolery, clever f. requiring some wit'.
In the play. *Varro's servant, who came to collect debts from Timon on behalf of their respective masters, exchange barbs with the*

resident fool and with Apemantus. On hearing the Fool's reply Apemantus says, 'That answer might have become Apemantus.'

Insult, arch-villain and more – ... but he's more, had I more name for badness.
"...an arch-villain... but he's more, Had I more name for badness" (MFM.5.1)
In the play. *Isabella attempts to expose the criminal hypocrisy of Angelo to the Duke.*

Insult, ass - Asses are made to bear, and so are you.
PETRUCHIO Thou hast hit it: come, sit on me.
KATHARINA Asses are made to bear, and so are you. (TOS.2.1)
In the play. *Katharina's charming side shows up but Petruchio is not deterred.*

Insult, ass, i. delivered sarcastically - ... what a thing it is to be an ass!
"... what a thing it is to be an ass!" (TA.4.2)
Use sarcastically, e.g. 'Of him I can say, 'what a thing it is to be an ass''.
In the play. *Aaron does not think much of Chiron and Demetrius, sons of Tamora. Chiron has been given a scroll in which there is written in Latin the discovery of Aaron's plot. Chiron thinks it is a verse by Horace.*

Insult, lack of self-knowledge - ... asses... that you ask me what you are, and do not know yourselves.
ALL SERVANTS. What are we Apemantus?
APEMANTUS. Asses.
ALL SERVANTS. Why?
APEMANTUS. That you ask me what you are, and do not know yourselves." (TOA.2.2)
Quote the example in its entirety and apply it to those who do not know what they are or what they want.

In the play. *Servants of various Timon's creditors test Apemantus' wit and sour character.*

Insult, beast – The very best at a beast, my lord, that ever I saw.
THESEUS. ... A very gentle beast, and of good conscience.
DEMETRIUS. The very best at a beast, my lord, that ever I saw." (MND.5.1)
A reinforcer when comparing a person to an animal. 'He is an animal and the very best at a beast that I ever saw'.
In the play. *In the play by amateur actors one of them wears the mask of a lion and the spectators comment.*

Insult, beshrew your heart.
"...beshrew your heart!" (TC.4.2)
In the play. *Cressida to her uncle after he mocked her for her affair with Troilus. 'Beshrew' = 'woe to'.*

Insult, better be a dog - I had rather be a dog and bay the moon than such a Roman.
"I had rather be a dog and bay the moon
Than such a Roman." (JC.4.3)
Insult or retort to offensive statement, e.g. 'I had rather be a dog and bay the moon that XX" See also 'Insults, a medley of i.'
In the play. *Brutus upbraids Cassius for his acquiescence towards bribe taking.*

Insult, better to be an animal than Menelaus - ... but to be Menelaus - I would conspire against destiny.
"To be a mule, a cat, a fitchew, a toad, a lizard, an owl, a puttock, or a herring without a roe, I would not care; but to be Menelaus - I would conspire against destiny." (TC.5.1)
Alternative to "I'd rather be anything but you," Change 'Menelaus' to the name of the person in question.

445

In the play. Thersite's opinion of Menelaus. 'Fitchew' is a pole-cat, 'puttock' is a kite or bird of prey.

Insult, blisters on tongue - blistered by thy tongue, for such a wish!
"Blistered be thy tongue,
For such a wish!" (RJ.3.2)
In the play. *The nurse, poorly predicting Juliet's state of mind, after Juliet's initial comment on Romeo's deeds, calls Romeo shameful. Juliet vehemently objects.*
Strongly object to an idea or a wish. Change 'wish' to 'idea' as applicable. Or just use 'Blistered by thy tongue'. See also 'Insult, lips to rot off'.

Insult, blood-suckers - A knot you are of damned blood-suckers!
"A knot you are of damned blood-suckers!" (KRIII.3.3)
In the play. *Lord Grey to Ratcliff and his executioners. Richard has planned the death of Grey and other allies of the Queen to clear his own path to the crown.*

Insult, brain - ... as dry as the remainder biscuit after a voyage....
"... and in his brain,
Which is as dry as the remainder biscuit
After a voyage - he hath strange places crammed
With observation, the which he vents
In mangled forms." (AYLI.2.7)
A figure of comparison for a confused verbal (or written) report.
In the play. *Jacques' assessment of Touchstone.*

Insult, brainless - ... in such a barren rascal... that has no more brain than a stone.
OLIVIA. How say you to that, Malvolio?
MALVOLIO. I marvel your ladyship takes delight in such a barren rascal... that has no more brain than a stone. (TN.1.5)
Put down an unworthy fellow who, in your opinion, does not deserve to be heard.
In the play. *The clown has told Malvolio that he is a fool. Olivia prompts Malvolio to reply to the clown*

Insult, brainless – ... thou hast no more brain in thy head than I have in mine elbows.
"... thou hast no more brain in thy head than I have in mine elbows." (TC.2.1)
Apply directly or modify to dramatize your adversary's lack of qualifications, e.g. 'He has no more brain...elbows'.
In the play. *Thersites' opinion of Ajax.*

Insult, butcher, blood thirsty - Thou wast provoked by thy bloody mind, that never dreamt on aught but butcheries.
"Thou wast provoked by thy bloody mind,
That never dreamt on aught but butcheries." (KRIII.1.2)
Comment on a cruel person, 'he never dreamt on aught but butcheries'.
In the play. *Richard says he killed Clarence, Anne's husband under provocation and Anne replies.*

Insult, chicken hawk - Foul-spoken coward, that thunder'st with thy tongue...
"Foul-spoken coward, that thunder'st with thy tongue,
And with thy weapon nothing darest perform!" (TA.2.1)
In the play. *Chiron to his brother Demetrius during an argument should have Lavinia.*

Insult, cow in June - ... The breese upon her, like a cow in June, hoist sails and flies.
"... i' the midst o' the fight,
When vantage like a pair of twins appear'd,

Both as the same, or rather ours the elder,
The breese upon her, like a cow in June,
Hoists sails and flies." (AC. 3.10)
Set a disparaging tone to her leaving you, e.g. 'Like a cow in June she hoisted sails and flied'.
In the play. *Scarus reports to Enobarbus the development of the sea battle between the fleets of Antony and Caesar Octavian. Things were even until Cleopatra set sail away from the battle and Antony followed her.*

Insult, coward - Coward, that thunder'st with thy tongue, and with thy weapon nothing darest perform!
"Foul-spoken coward, that thunder'st with thy tongue,
And with thy weapon nothing darest perform!" (TA.2.1)
In the play. *Tamora's sons argue with each other and Chiron responds to Demetrius' threats*

Insult, coward - You are the hare of whom the proverb goes, whose valour plucks dead lions by the beard.
"You are the hare of whom the proverb goes,
Whose valour plucks dead lions by the beard" (KJ.2.1)
In the play. *Ph. Faulconbridge to Austria. The two dislike each other intensely.*

Insult, cowards - souls of geese, that bear the shapes of men.
"You souls of geese,
That bear the shapes of men." (COR.1.4)
See also, 'Cowards, c. defined - I know them to be as true-bred cowards as ever turned back. ' *** Entries for 'Character, coward'.
In the play. *Coriolanus continues to show his contempt for the people.*

Insult, cowards, thief, thieves - ... he hath a killing tongue and a quiet sword... steal anything, and call it purchase... few bad words are matched with few good deeds.
"For Pistol, - he hath a killing tongue and a quiet sword...
...
(Nym's) few bad words are matched with few good deeds: for 'a never broke any man's head but his own; and that was against a post when he was drunk. They will steal anything, and call it purchase." (KHV.3.2)
Define a seller of smoke, 'He hath a quiet sword ... and his few bad words... deeds.' As for his achievements we could say that he never broke a man's head but his own, and that was against a post when he was drunk.' Or accuse of inappropriate appropriation. "I know, you will steal anything and call it purchase."
In the play. *An unnamed boy's assessment of Pistol, Bardolph and Nym who are part of the retinue of K. Henry V's army.*

Insult, creditors, imprecation – They have e'en put my breath from me, the slaves...
TIMON. They have e'en put my breath from me, the slaves.
Creditors! - devils." (TOA.3.4)
Show contempt for harassing creditors.
In the play. *Timon feels helpless against his creditors.*

Insult, crooked - ... foul indigested lump, as crooked in thy manners as thy shape.
"... heap of wrath, foul indigested lump,
As crooked in thy manners as thy shape!" (KHVI p2.5.1)
In the play. *Clifford to Richard Plantagenet (later Richard III) at the battle of St. Alban's.*

Insult, curse – Let vultures gripe thy guts!
"Let vultures gripe thy guts." (MWW.1.3)

Retort to an accusation or insolence when you do not immediately have an answer.
In the play. *Falstaff has just left and Pistol is unhappy.*

Insult, curse of universal illness - Of man and beast the infinite malady crust you quite o'er!
"Of man and beast the infinite malady
Crust you quite o'er!" (TOA.3.5)
In the play. *In his last fake banquet, Timon throws warm water in the face of all his ungrateful friends and parasites.*

Insult, deceit, compared to actions by crocodile - ... as the mournful crocodile with sorrow snares relenting passengers...
"... and Gloucester's show
Beguiles him, as the mournful crocodile
With sorrow snares relenting passengers;
Or, as the snake, rolled in a flowering bank,
With shining checkered slough, doth sting a child,
That for the beauty thinks it excellent." (KHVI p2.3.1)
Try 'You are like the mournful crocodile that with sorrow snares relenting passengers....'
In the play. *Margaret, the really deceitful one accuses the innocent Gloucester of deceit.* 'Slough'='Skin of a snake'.

Insult, devil - hell's black intelligencer.
"Richard yet lives, hell's black intelligencer" (KRIII.4.4)
In the play. *Queen Margaret makes a tally of who killed whom, for the benefit of the Duchess of York. Of the murderous teams, only Richard is still alive.*

Insult, dog - Away, inhuman dog! unhallow'd slave.
"Away, inhuman dog! unhallow'd slave." (TA.5.3)
In the play. *Lucius dispatches the super-evil Aaron.*

Insult, dog - It is the most impenetrable cur hat ever kept with men.
"It is the most impenetrable cur
That ever kept with men" (MOV.3.3)
In the play. *Salarino's opinion of Shylock.*

Insult, dog and abuser of patience - Out dog! out, cur! thou drivest me past the bounds of maiden's patience.
"Out dog! out, cur! thou drivest me past the bounds
Of maiden's patience." (MND.3.2)
Use when he really makes you mad. Maidenhood here is a figure of speech and you do not necessarily need to be a maiden to use the quote.
In the play. *Hermia is very upset with Demetrius' remarks on Lysander with whom Hermia is still in love.*

Insult, dog and retort - Thy mother's of my generation: what's she, if I be a dog?
Painter. You're a dog.
APEMANTUS. Thy mother's of my generation: what's she, if I be a dog? (PER.1.1)
In the play. *Apemantus passed a disparaging remark on the painter, one of the parasites in Timon's retinue.*

Insult, dog and viper - ... egregious dog? O viper vile!
"... egregious dog? O viper vile!" (KHV.2.1)
In the play. *Pistol to Nym in a tavern of London's Eastcheap.*

Insult, dog from Crete - O hound of Crete!

"O hound of Crete!" (KHV.2.1)
In the play. *Pistol to Nym in a tavern of London's Eastcheap. Pistol surmises that Nym is after his wife.*

Insult, either ignorant by decrepitude or a fool - Either thou art most ignorant by age or thou wert born a fool.
"Either thou art most ignorant by age, Or thou wert born a fool. " (WT.2.1)
Address a stubborn and ignorant individual.
In the play. *Leontes accuses Antigonus of decrepitude or stupidity simply because he does not want to join the king in the unfounded accusations towards Hermione.*

Insult, envious tongue - ... the envious barking of thy saucy tongue.
"... The envious barking of thy saucy tongue." (KHVI.p1.3.4)
Change to, 'This is but the envious barking of a saucy tongue.'
In the play. *In Paris Vernon argues with Basset. Vernon is a supporter of the duke of York, whereas Basset supports the duke of Somerset. This has to do with the history-famous hatred between the houses of York and Lancaster that produced the War of the Roses.*

Insult, evil, one for whom goodness is poison – All goodness is poison to thy stomach.
"All goodness
Is poison to thy stomach."
(KHVIII.3.2)
In the play. *Lord Surrey to Cardinal Wolsey, fallen from grace now galled by his enemies.*

Insult, fat –... thou globe of sinful continents...
"Why, thou globe of sinful continents, what a life dost thou lead?" (KHIV p2.2.4)
Define a sloth, e.g. 'He is a globe of sinful continents'.
In the play. *Henry to Falstaff.*

Insult, fit only for hell - ... thou unfit for any place but hell.
"And thou unfit for any place but hell." (KRIII.1.2)
In the play. *Lady Anne to Richard, who after having slain Clarence, her husband has the gall to say that Clarence was more fit for heaven than earth – that's why Richard killed him.*

Insult, fool, response and maxim - Better a witty fool than a foolish wit.
"… for what says Quinapalus? Better a witty fool than a foolish wit." (TN.1.5)
Retort when accused of folly or when your idea is put down as foolish.
In the play. *The clown uses himself as a subject to assert a truth. Quinapalus sounds like the name of a Greek philosopher, but it is an invention, no such wit existed.*

Insult, goat - Thou damned and luxurious mountain goat.
"Thou damned and luxurious mountain goat" (KHV.4.4)
In the play. *Pistol to French prisoner captured in the battle of Agincourt.*

Insult, go away - Go, base intruder! overweening slave!
"Go, base intruder! overweening slave!
Bestow thy fawning smiles on equal mates" (TGV.3.1)
In the play. *The Duke bans Valentine after discovering his plans to elope with Silvia, the Duke's daughter.*

Insult, go away - ... mend my company, take away thyself.
TIMON ... mend my company, take away thyself.
APEMANTUS So I shall mend mine own, by the lack of thine. (TOA.4.3)
Dismiss a very unpleasant company.

In the play. *Apemantus who has also called on Timon must be prepared to receive a volley of insults.*

Insult, go away, direct your feet - ... but direct thy feet where thou and I henceforth may never meet.
"…but direct thy feet
Where thou and I henceforth may
never meet." (TN.5.1)
Use satirically with person who pulled your leg.
In the play. *Olivia has married Sebastian and the priest confirms it. The duke believes Viola/Cesario to be the groom whilst Viola is flabbergasted. In anger the duke tells Viola to go away and never show up again.*

Insult, go away, I cannot stand you - Fellow, be gone: I cannot brook thy sight, this news hath made thee a most ugly man.
"Fellow, be gone: I cannot brook thy sight,
This news hath made thee a most ugly man." (KJ.3.1)
Dismiss the bearer of bad news especially when he was also a participant, besides being a messenger.
In the play. *Constance to Salisbury, who has informed her of the pending agreement between the king of France and King John – an agreement to which she bitterly objects.*

Insult, go away – Take thy face hence.
"Take thy face hence." (M.5.3)
In the play. *Macbeth to a servant who, frightened, has come in to report the sighting of 10,000 English enemy soldiers.*

Insult, good for nothing - To say nothing, to do nothing, to know nothing, and to have nothing...
" To say nothing, to do nothing, to know nothing, and to have nothing, is to be a great part of your title; which is within a very little of nothing." (AWEW.2.4)

Change 'your title' to 'his title' and use as a scathing remark to define a worthless person.
In the play. *Even the clown of Roussillon sees through Parolles and insults him.*

Insult, hang thyself or equivalent - No, I will do nothing at thy bidding; make thy request to thy friend.
FIRST LORD. Hang thyself.
APEMANTUS. No, I will do nothing at thy bidding; make thy request to thy friend." (TOA.1.1)
Answer or retort to any sentence that has a tone of injunction or insult
In the play. *A member of Timon's retinue, having just been insulted by Apemantus, replies back. Apemantus has a retort ready.*

Insult, hatred plus - I hate thee, pronounce thee a gross lout, a mindless slave.
"I hate thee,
Pronounce thee a gross lout, a mindless slave." (WT.1.2)
In the play. *Leontes is angry at Camillo who does not want to agree that Hermione is betraying Leontes.*

Insult, hell as a destination - ...would thou wert shipp'd to hell.
"Andronicus, would thou wert shipp'd to hell" (TA.1.1)
In the play. *Saturnine thinks that Andronicus wants to deprive him of the Roman throne, which instead Andronicus will refuse.*

Insult, i. and curse - Blasts and fogs upon thee!
"Blasts and fogs upon thee!" (KL.1.4)
An easy way out when you are at a loss for a retort to an unpleasant remark.
In the play. *Lear to his ungrateful daughter Goneril.*

Insult, i. and curse – you herd of boils and plagues ... that you may be abhorr'd further than seen...

"All the contagion of the south light on you,
You shames of Rome! you herd of --
Boils and plagues
Plaster you o'er, that you may be abhorr'd
Further than seen and one infect another
Against the wind a mile!" (COR.1.4)
In the play. *Coriolanus to Roman soldiers beaten back by the Volsces.*

Insult, i. followed by threat - Base dunghill villain and mechanical...
"Base dunghill villain and mechanical,
I'll have thy head for this thy traitor's speech." (KHVI.p2.1.3)
In the play. *York is angry at Horner, accused by assistant Peter of treacherous speech.*

Insult, i. given and returned – Dost dialog with your shadow?
VARRO'S SERVANT. How dost, fool?
APEMANTUS. Dost dialogue with thy shadow?" (TOA.2.2)
Any time you are directly insulted with an epiteth or attribute.
In the play. *Apemantus has a retort always ready.*

Insult, i. plus threat - Abominable Gloucester, guard thy head; for I intend to have it ere long.
"Abominable Gloucester, guard thy head;
For I intend to have it ere long." (KHVI.p1.1.3)
In the play. *The bishop of Wincester and Gloucester do not get along very well.*

Insult, i. to a group, incapable of thought - ...when you speak best unto the purpose, it is not worth the wagging of your beards.
"... When you speak best unto the purpose, it is not worth the wagging of your beards. (COE.2.1)
Show that they don't know what they are talking about. Or change 'beards' to 'beard' if your address is to one person rather than a crowd.
In the play. *Menenius upbraids the tribunes.*

Insult, i. to a group, sickening conversation - ... more of your conversation would infect my brain, being the herdsmen of the beastly plebeians.
"... more of your conversation would infect my brain, being the herdsmen of the beastly plebeians. I will be bold to take my leave of you." (COE.2.1)
You have had enough. "More of your conversation…brain."
In the play. *Menenius upbraids the tribunes.*

Insult, i. to flattering parasites - Live loathed and long, ...affable wolves...
"Live loathed and long,
Most smiling, smooth, detested parasites,
Courteous destroyers, affable wolves, meek bears,
You fools of fortune, trencher-friends, time's flies,
Cap and knee slaves, vapours, and minute-jacks!" (TOA.3.5)
See also 'Insult, curse of universal illness'.
In the play. *Timon to his parasitic guests.*

Insult, i. to individual and his followers - (Thou) idol of idiot-worshippers.
" (Thou) idol of idiot-worshippers." (TC.5.1)
Comment applied to a well-known personality you do not respect.
In the play. *Thersites' further assessment of Achilles.*

Insult, i. to masses considered as despicable - You common cry of curs!

whose breath I hate as reek of the rotten fens...
"You common cry of curs! whose breath I hate
As reek of the rotten fens, whose loves I prize
As the dead carcasses of unburied men." (COR.3.3)
See also entries for 'Opinion, your op. on crowds and masses'.
In the play. *Coriolanus addresses the citizens, somewhat un-diplomatically.*

Insult, i. to rebellious group - ... dissentious rogues that, rubbing the poor itch of your opinion, make yourselves scabs.
"What's the matter, you dissentious rogues,
That, rubbing the poor itch of your opinion,
Make yourselves scabs?" (COR.1.1)
Address a disorganized and bickering group or define them, e.g. 'they are but dissentious rogues, that rubbing the poor itch of their opinions, make themselves scabs.'
In the play. *Coriolanus has a deep-seated contempt for the common people and it shows.*

Insult, ignorance - ... Would the fountain of your mind were clear again, that I might water an ass at it.
ACHILLES. My mind is troubled, like a fountain stirred
And I myself see not the bottom of it.
THERSITES. Would the fountain of your mind were clear again, that I might water an ass at it! I had rather be a tick in a sheep than such a valiant ignorance." (TC.3.3)
Extract. 'I had rather be a tick... ignorance'. Or use the first sentence to describe your state of mind.
In the play. *After the reproaches and lectures of Ulysses' Achilles is confused. Thersites does not miss the occasion to comment on Achilles' confusion (or ignorance)*

Insult, ignorant – there will be little learning die, then, that day thou art hanged.
APEMANTUS (to Page). Canst not read?
PAGE. No.
APEMANTUS. There will little learning die, then, that day thou art hanged." (TOA.2.2)
Describe an ignorant person by quoting the exchange in its entirety, e.g. 'To xxx the following lines apply..."
In the play. *An oncoming, illiterate page makes the mistake of enlisting Apemantus' help in reading the address of a letter addressed to Timon.*

Insult, in your place I would dispose of myself - Were I like thee, I'd throw away myself.
"Were I like thee, I'd throw away myself." (TOA.4.3)
Use with anybody who says something bad about you.
In the play. *This time the cantankerous Apemantus receives a barbed retort from his host Timon.*

Insult, injurer of heaven and earth - Thou monstrous injurer of heaven and earth!
"Thou monstrous injurer of heaven and earth!" (KJ.2.1)
In the play. *The two mothers of the kings, one true one usurper depending on the point of view, exchange insults. Constance, mother of Arthur says this to Elinor.*

Insult, lascivious, wanton, a shame to the profession - ... Lascivious, wanton, more than well beseems a man of thy profession and degree.
"Thou art a most pernicious usurer,
Forward by nature, enemy to peace;
Lascivious, wanton, more than well beseems

452

A man of thy profession and degree" (KHVI p1.3.1)
In the play. *Gloucester to Bishop of Winchester.*

Insult, last letter of the alphabet - Thou whoreson zed, thou unnecessary letter…
"Thou whoreson zed, thou unnecessary letter! My lord, if you will give me leave, I will turn this unbolted villain into mortar and daub the walls of a jakes with him." (KL.2.2)
You may go easy on the whoreson bit, unless you are ready to use your fists, or the insulted really deserves it.
In the play. *Kent to Oswald. Oswald is carrying letters against King Lear.*

Insult, liar – … the lyingest knave in Christendom.
"Then, Saunder, sit there, the lyingest knave in Christendom. If thou hadst been born blind, thou mightest as well have known all our names as thus to name the several colours we do wear" (KHVI.p2.2.1)
See also entries for 'Liar'
In the play. *Humphrey of Gloucester unmasks the imposture of a self-declared blind man miraculously healed of blindness at St. Alban's. This expression is also found in the Taming of the Shrew, uttered by the character Sly.*

Insult, liar – … Within these forty hours Surrey durst better have burnt that tongue than said so.
"… thou liest:
Within these forty hours Surrey durst better
Have burnt that tongue than said so." (KHVIII, 3.2)
Change 'Surrey' to the name of the liar.
In the play. *Card. Wolsey to Surrey, who has accused the cardinal of treason*

Insult, liar - I say, thou liest and will maintain what thou hast said is false…
"I say, thou liest,
And will maintain what thou hast said is false
In thy heart-blood, though being all too base
To stain the temper of my knightly sword." (KRII.4.1)
See also entries for 'Liar'
In the play. *Aumerle to Bagot who as accused him of complicity in the slaying of the Duke of Gloucester.*

Insult, liar - In thy foul throat thou liest.
"In thy foul throat thou liest." (KRIII.1.2)
In the play. *Richard, who has slain Edward, Lady Anne's husband and Prince of Wales, now says he has not and Anne responds with a double insult.*

Insult, liar - Thou liest, malignant thing!…
"Thou liest, malignant thing! Hast thou forgot
The foul witch Sycorax…" (TEM.1.2)
In the play. *Prospero reprimands the spirit Ariel who had just presented him with some work-related grievances. Sycorax was the witch who imprisoned Ariel and subsequently was liberated by Prospero.*

Insult, liar – Through the false passage of thy throat thou liest.
"Through the false passage of thy throat, thou liest!" (KRII.1.1)
In the play. *Mowbray's retort to Bolingbroke's accusation of treason.*

Insult, liar - You lie, up to the hearing of the gods.
"You lie, up to the hearing of the gods." (AC.5.2)
In the play. *Cleopatra to Dolabella, a Roman envoy from Octavian.*

Insult, liar, defense from accusation - Thou speakest it falsely, as I love mine honour.
"Thou speakest it falsely, as I love mine honour." (AWEW.5.3)
Reject a false accusation. See also entries for 'Liar'.
In the play. *Lafeu gives Bertram a ring that belonged to Helena. The King recognizes the ring. Bertram knows that he gave the ring to Diana and cannot accept that the ring was actually worn by Helena*

Insult, lips – thy lips to rot off.
"Thy lips rot off" (TOA.4.3)
One of the way out when you cannot immediately come up with a retort to a witticism of which you are the subject. See also 'Insult, blisters on tongue - blistered by thy tongue, for such a wish!'
In the play. *Phrynia, Alcibiades' girlfriend replies to Timon's insult who called her a whore. In fact Timon had said,*
"This fell whore of thine
Hath in her more destruction than thy sword,
For all her cherubim look."
You will find the same concept, expressed more romantically and less coarsely in Romeo and Juliet – see 'Eyes, her e. weapons of mass destruction'

Insult, man like animal according to the theories of Pythagoras - thou almost make'st me waver in my faith, to hold opinion with Pythagoras...
"Thou almost mak'st me waver in my faith,
To hold opinion with Pythagoras,
That souls of animals infuse themselves
Into the trunks of men." (MOV.4.1)
Answer to verbal attack from adversary – See also 'Man, m. in shape but with traits of an animal - Never did I know a creature, that did bear the shape of man...'

In the play. *Bassanio to Shylock.*

Insult, minister of hell - ... thou dreadful minister of hell!"
"... thou dreadful minister of hell!" (KRIII.1.2)
In the play. *Lady Anne, widow of the son of Henry VI, to Richard, the assassin.*

Insult, miscellany of I, liar, hound, braggart.
CORIOLANUS (to Aufidius) Measureless liar!
CORIOLANUS (to Aufidius) False hound!
AUFIDIUS (to Coriolanus) Unholy braggart. (COR.5.6)
Select and use as applicable.
In the play. *Coriolanus and Aufidius exchange a volley of insults at Coriolis before a band of conspirators finally kills Coriolanus.*

Insult, murderer - Pernicious blood-sucker of sleeping men!
"Pernicious blood-sucker of sleeping men!" (KHVI p2.3.2)
In the play. *Warwick to Suffolk who indeed had Gloucester killed in his sleep.*

Insult, negative qualification, ass - ... if thou be'st not an ass, I am a youth of fourteen.
"...if thou be'st not an ass, I am a youth of fourteen" (AWEW.2.3)
Apply to your favorite political enemy, 'If he is not an ass, I am a youth of fourteen'
In the play. *Lafeu has assessed the real character of Parolle.*

Insult, no honesty, no honor - You have as little honesty as honour.
"If I loved many words, lord, I should tell you
You have as little honesty as honour." (KHVIII.3.2)
In the play. *Wolsey has fallen from grace and galled by his enemies addresses Surrey.*

Insult, not fit to be in the company of honest men - Fie on thee wretch! 'tis pity that thou livest to walk where any honest men resort.
"Fie on thee wretch! 'tis pity that thou livest
To walk where any honest man resort." (COE.5.1)
A retort to an attack by indirectly but forcefully saying that the opposing party is dishonest.
In the play. *Ant S., wearing the chain sold by Angelo, walks in on Angelo and Merchant. Ant S says he never denied having received the chain. Angelo and Merchant confront him, thinking he is Ant E*

Insult, not worth another word - You are not worth another word, else I'd call you knave.
"You are not worth another word, else I'd call you knave." (AWEW.2.3)
Use the quotation also in the third person, e.g.. 'He is not worth another word.' Or change 'knave' to an other equivalent disqualifying word. See also 'Insult, worth less than dust - … You are not worth the dust which the rude wind blows in your face.'
In the play. *Lafeu has just informed Parolles that Bertram is married (to Helen) and then dismisses him.*

Insult, nymphomaniac – … you are more intemperate in your blood than Venus…
"…But you are more intemperate in your blood
Than Venus, or those pamper'd animals
That rage in savage sensuality" (MAAN.4.1)
In the play. *Deceived through a plot engineered by the evil Don John, Claudio thinks that Hero is a slut.*

Insult, opinion defining the man - … An all men were o' my mind wit would be out of fashion.
AJAX An all men were o' my mind, --
ULYSSES Wit would be out of fashion. (TC.2.3)
In the play. *Ulysse's side remark is intended not to be heard by Ajax. 'An all men' means 'If all men'*

Insult, opinion of a person - God made him, and therefore let him pass for a man.
"God made him, and therefore let him pass for a man." (MOV.1.2)
Answer to 'What do you think of him?' See also 'Men, one word catch all - … in the catalogue ye go for men…'
In the play. *Nerissa's opinion of Monsieur LeBon, one of Portia's suitors.*

Insult, owl of death – Thou ominous and fearful owl of death.
"Thou ominous and fearful owl of death" (KHVI.p1.4.2)
In the play. *The French general at Bordeaux responding to the threats by besieging Lord Talbot.*

Insult, out of my sight - Out of my sight! Thou dost infect mine eyes.
"Out of my sight! Thou dost infect mine eyes." (KRIII.2.2)
Get rid of an unpleasant person
In the play. *Richard is trying to woo Lady Anne who does not yield (for the moment).*

Insult, pestilence - A pestilence on him!
"…A pestilence on him!" (TC.4.2)
In the play. *Cressida to Troilus referring to her uncle Pandarus. She anticipates his mocking her for her affair with Troilus.*

Insult, pestilence – The most infectious pestilence upon thee.
"The most infectious pestilence upon thee! (AC.2.5)

In the play. *Cleopatra curses the messenger who arrived from Rome and told her that Antony has married Octavia, sister of Octavian.*

Insult, plague – ... thou wast born to be a plague to men.
"... thou wast born to be a plague to men." (KHVI p3.5.4)
In the play. *Q. Margaret to Richard of Gloucester after she and her son have been captured at the battle of Coventry.*

Insult, poison - Thou'rt poison to my blood.
"Thou'rt poison to my blood." (CYM.1.1)
In the play. *King Cymbeline to Leonatus who married his daughter Imogen against the king's will.*

Insult, retort to i. – Look in a glass, and call thy image so.
CLIFFORD Why, what a brood of traitors have we here!
YORK Look in a glass, and call thy image so (KHVI.p2. 5.1)
In the play. *Richard Plantagenet, father of Richard III, returns from Ireland with troops bent upon dethroning Henry VI and becoming king. Clifford calls him and his allies traitors.*

Insult, reversing the direction of the i. - Look in a glass, and call thy image so.
CLIFFORD Why, what a brood of traitors have we here!
YORK Look in a glass, and call thy image so (KHVI.p2.5.1)
In the play. *York claims the throne and wants to depose King Henry VI.*

Insult, scorn, insult, arrogant villain, pretender - Small things make base men proud...
"Small things make base men proud; this villain here,
Being captain of a pinnace, threatens more

Than Bargulus, the strong Illyrian pirate." (KHVI p2.4.1)
Put down someone who pretends too much
In the play. *Suffolk to the captain of a ship who captured him.*

Insult, seeing your face is like hell - I never see thy face, but I think of hell-fire.
"I never see thy face, but I think of hell-fire." (KHIV p1.3.3)
Retort to a any criticism while you search for the right response. The more modern version of this line is 'I never forget a face, but in your case I will make an exception'. See also 'Insult, lips to rot off'.
In the play. *Falstaff to Bardolph.*

Insult, slanderers and injurers - Thou monstrous slanderer of heaven and earth! ...
ELINOR (to Constance). Thou monstrous slanderer of heaven and earth!
CONSTANCE (to Elinor). Thou monstrous injurer of heaven and earth!" (KJ.2.1)
In the play. *Elinor, mother of King John, the usurper and Constance, mother of young Arthur, the rightful heir to the throne of England, do not get along.*

Insult, snake - ... with doubler tongue than thine, thou serpent, never adder stung.
" An adder did it: for with doubler tongue
Than thine, thou serpent, never adder stung." (MND.3.2)
Apply to a devious character and a traitor. E.G. "An adder did it and that adder is you: for with… stung."
In the play. *Hermia is very upset with Demetrius' remarks on Lysander with whom Hermia is still in love. She accuses Demetrius of*

having killed Lysander and compares him to a particularly poisonous snake.

Insult, son of a bitch and villain plus an ass - Thou art sensible in nothing but blows, and so is an ass.
ANTIPHOLUS E. (to Dromio E). Thou whoreson, senseless villain.
DROMIO E. I would I were senseless, sir, that I might not feel your blows.
ANTIPHOLUS E. (to Dromio E). Thou art sensible in nothing but blows, and so is an ass. (COE.4.4)
When an appeal to sensibility is inappropriately made. E.G. 'Some people are sensible in nothing…..ass.'
In the play. *Ant. E. beats servant Dromio E. following the continued mix-ups due to mistaken identities.*

Insult, stupid – .. . who wears his wit in his belly and his guts in his head.
"Ajax, who wears his wit in his belly and his guts in his head" (TC.2.1)
In the play. *Thersites' opinion of Ajax.*

Insult, totally unmannered - ... ungracious wretch, fit for the mountains and the barbarous caves… out of my sight!
"… Ungracious wretch,
Fit for the mountains and the barbarous caves,
Where manners never were preached! out of my sight!" (TN.4.1)
Define a rude and uncouth person, 'He is an ungracious wretch… preached'.
In the play. *Olivia is mad at Sir Toby. She arrives on the scene as Sir Toby has finished wrangling with the real Sebastian, whom Toby thinks still to be Viola/Cesario.*

Insult, traitor - … from the extremest upward of thy head to the descent and dust below thy foot…
"… from the extremest upward of thy head
To the descent and dust below thy foot,
A most toad-spotted traitor" (KL.5.3)
The colorful definition of the delimiting area to which the insult applies can be extended to other faults, e.g. lying, cheating, stealing etc.
In the play. *Edgar to traitor and brother Edmund before the duel.*

Insult, traitors - O villains, vipers, damn'd without redemption!…
"O villains, vipers, damn'd without redemption!
Dogs, easily won to fawn on any man!
Snakes, in my heart-blood warm'd, that sting my heart!" (RII.3.2)
Use as is in a desperate situation or modify or apply to a third party. E.G. '(Name of person) is a viper, damned without redemption'.
In the play. *Back from Ireland, Richard II inveighs against some previous allies whom he thinks passed to the side of his enemy Bolingbroke. But Bolingbroke actually beheaded them, they did not betray Richard II.*

Insult, untrustworthy - ... of no more trust than love that's hired.
"…O slave, of no more trust
Than love that's hired!" (AC.5.2)
In the play. *Cleopatra to Seleucus, her accountant who hinted that she had hidden some of her treasures.*

Insult, venomous toad or lizard - ... mark'd by the destinies to be avoided as venom toads, or lizards' dreadful stings.
"… (you are) mark'd by the destinies to be avoided,
As venom toads, or lizards' dreadful stings." (KHVI p3.2.2)
In the play. *Q. Margaret to Richard (the future Richard III) as they exchange insults before the town of York.*

Insult, villain - I know thee well: a serviceable villain…
"I know thee well: a serviceable villain;
As duteous to the vices of thy mistress
As badness would desire" (KL.4.6)
Characterize a servant or subject executing the evil will of his/her master. Change 'thy mistress' to 'your master' or 'his master' as applicable.
In the play. *Edgar recognizes the dying Oswald, servant to Goneril.*

Insult, villain and murderer - … thou bloodier villain than terms can give thee out!
"… thou bloodier villain
Than terms can give thee out!" (M.5.8)
In the play. *Macduff to Macbeth before the final duel at the battle of Dunsinane.*

Insult, wicked man – A very tainted fellow and full of wickedness.
"A very tainted fellow, and full of wickedness." (AWEW.3.2)
Characterize a person that deserves contempt, or jokingly, apply the quote to a friend who is actually neither tainted nor full of wickedness. E.G. 'Some may say that he is a very tainted fellow and full of wickedness but actually instead, he…etc.'
In the play. *The Countess' opinion of Parolles. She is informed that Parolles is accompanying Bertram in his travel to Italy.*

Insult, wishing never to see a person again - If I hope well, I'll never see thee more.
"If I hope well, I'll never see thee more." (TOA.4.3)
In the play. *Timon is angry at mankind, even at his good friend Alcibiades, who came to visit him in the woods.*

Insult, worth less than dust - … You are not worth the dust which the rude wind blows in your face.
"O Goneril!
You are not worth the dust which the rude wind
Blows in your face." (KL.4.2)
When you are ready to cut all bridges and all further communications. Use directly with caution or apply to man/woman deserving of the statement. See also 'Insult, not worth another word - You are not worth another word, else I'd call you knave.'
In the play. *The duke of Albany begins to discover what stuff his wife Goneril is made of.*

Insult, worthless - … vile thing, let loose…
"…Vile thing, let loose,
Or I will shake thee from me like a serpent!" (MND.3.2)
In the play. *Lysander to Hermia after Puck mistakenly has administered the wrong potion to Lysander. The potion makes him hate Hermia with whom he was previously in love.*

Insult, worthy of indignity - … with all my heart; and thou art worthy of it.
PAROLLES My lord, you give me most egregious indignity.
LAFEU Ay, with all my heart; and thou art worthy of it. (AWEW.2.3)
In the play. *Lafeu sees Parolle's true character behind the façade.*

Insult, you are vane and untrustworthy - I trust I may not trust thee; for thy word is but the vain breath of a common man.
"I trust I may not trust thee; for thy word
Is but the vain breath of a common man." (KJ.3.1)
Alternative to "I do not trust you."
In the play. *Constance to Salisbury who has informed Constance of the pending agreement*

between the king of France and King John to which she bitterly objects.

Insults, a medley of i. – I had rather a beggar's dog, clean enough to spit upon.
APEMANTUS. I'll see thee again
TIMON. When there is nothing living but thee, thou shalt be welcome. I had rather be a beggar's dog, than Apemantus.
TIMON (to Apemantus). Would thou wert clean enough to spit upon!
APEMANTUS (to Timon). A plague on thee, thou art too bad to curse.
TIMON (to Apemantus). All villains that do stand by thee are pure.
APEMANTUS (to Timon). There is no leprosy but what thou speakest." (TOA.4.3)
Select according to mood and circumstance.
In the play. *Timon and Apemantus engage in a battle of insults.*

Insults, a volley of i. – ... cunning but in craft, crafty but in villany.
"...Wherein is he good, but to taste sack and drink it? wherein neat and cleanly, but to carve a capon and eat it? wherein cunning, but in craft? wherein crafty, but in villany? wherein villainous, but in all things? wherein worthy, but in nothing?"
(KHIV.p1.2.4)
Attack your political adversary.
In the play. *In a mock-up scene the Prince of Wales pretends to be his father Henry IV talking to Falstaff who pretends to be the Prince of Wales. This gives the occasion to the Prince of Wales to define Falstaff himself for what he is.*

Insults, a volley of i. - Slave, soulless villain, dog.
"...slave, soulless villain, dog! O rarely base!" (AC.5.2)
In the play. *Cleopatra to Seleucus, her accountant who hinted that she had hidden some of her treasures.*

Insults, volley of i. plus curses – Stay dog for thou shalt hear me, deadly eye, troubler of world's peace etc.
"...stay, dog, for thou shalt hear me.
If heaven have any grievous plague in store
Exceeding those that I can wish upon thee,
O, let them keep it till thy sins be ripe,
And then hurl down their indignation
On thee, the troubler of the poor world's peace!
The worm of conscience still begnaw thy soul!
Thy friends suspect for traitors while thou livest,
And take deep traitors for thy dearest friends!
No sleep close up that deadly eye of thine,
Unless it be whilst some tormenting dream
Affrights thee with a hell of ugly devils" (KRIII.1.3)
In the play. *Queen Margaret unloads her curses on Richard III. who killed her husband (King Henry VI) and her son Edward.*

Insults, volley of i. – Trunk of humours, hutch of beastliness, parcel of dropsies etc.
"Why dost thou converse with that trunk of humours, that bolting hutch of beastliness, that swoll'n parcel of dropsies, that huge barrel of sack, that stuffed cloak-bag of guts, that roasted Manningtree ox with the pudding in his belly, that reverend vice, that grey iniquity, that father ruffian, that vanity in years?" (KHIV.p1.2.4)
Take your pick, whole or partial.
In the play. *P. Henry pretends to imitate his father who obviously disapproves of Henry's friendship with Falstaff. Manningtree is a place*

in Essex famous for the size of its oxen.
'Dropsies'='Diseased collection of water in the body'.

Insurance, self-i. to pay for requirements of old age - … When service should in my old limbs lie lame and unregarded age in corners thrown.
"When service should in my old limbs lie lame
And unregarded age in corners thrown" (AYLI.2.3)
Also an ironic way to question why you have been excluded from a task, e.g. 'You think that service…lame'.
In the play. *Old Adam offers his saved 500 crowns to his master Orlando who is in temporary difficulties.*

Integrity or second stage after introduction - … my integrity never knew the craft that you do charge men with…
"… my integrity never knew the craft,
That you do charge men with: stand no more off,
But give thyself unto my sick desires, Who then recovers. " (AWEW.4.2)
She does not trust you and thinks that you are just the same as the others. Or perhaps she wants you to believe that she may trust you if you demonstrate, or at least declare, integrity. Often she could not care less but this innocent ploy is a good face-saver. If, for whatever reason, you do not turn out to be what she thinks or likes, she can safely put it down to mistaken integrity. Careful however. You may wish to use, rather than 'sick desires', for example, 'strong passion'. In the original sick stands for 'passionate'.
In the play: *Bertram in Florence attempts to seduce Diana, a buxom Florentine.*

Integrity, no change of mind – … nothing alter'd: what I was, I am

"…delay'd,
But nothing alter'd: what I was, I am" (WT.4.3)
In the play. *Florizel to his father King Polixenes who is angry at Florizel for wanting to marry Perdita who is only a shepherd's daughter (though in reality she is the daughter of the king of Sicilia.*

Intellectuals, i. as caterpillars - All scholars, lawyers, courtiers, gentlemen, they call false caterpillars…
"All scholars, lawyers, courtiers, gentlemen,
They call false caterpillars, and intend their death." (KHVI p2.4.4)
In the play. *A messenger gives an account of John Cade's ideas and of his rebels' force.*

Intellectuals, the opposite of i. - Hard-headed men, that work in Athens here, which never laboured in their minds till now.
"Hard-headed men, that work in Athens here,
Which never laboured in their minds till now." (MND.5.1)
Comment on a bunch of not very bright people. Change 'Athens' to the applicable location.
In the play. *Philostrate gives his reaction and a critical account of the play rehearsal by the amateurs acting group.*

Intelligence services, vacuum in the i. s. - where hath our intelligence been drunk? Where hath it slept?
"O, where hath our intelligence been drunk?
Where hath it slept?" (KJ.4.2)
Apply to intelligence lapses by FBI, CIA or equivalent.
In the play. *K. John's reaction after a messenger from France brings in the bad news that the French are ready to attack and no one knew anything before hand.*

Intelligence, i. available and confirmed - … and the particular confirmations, point from point, to the full arming of verity.
SECOND LORD. Hath the count all this intelligence?
FIRST LORD. Ay, and the particular confirmations, point from point, so to the full arming of the verity.
(AWEW.4.3)
In the play. *The intelligence mentioned in the lines is the information about Bertram's wife who allegedly is dead (but it will turn out that she is alive and well).*

Intelligence, gathering and sifting i. - Your bait of falsehood takes this carp of truth…. By indirections find directions out.
"See you now;
Your bait of falsehood takes this carp of truth:
And thus do we of wisdom and of reach,
With windlasses and with assays of bias,
By indirections find directions out." (H.2.1)
When you are trying to discover the truth by making an inaccurate statement.
In the play. *Polonius instructs Reynaldo on how to spy on Laertes, while the latter is in Paris. Laertes is Polonius' son.*
"Windlass"="A device for raising weights by winding a rope round a cylinder, here a metaphor for roundabout ways". "Assays of reach"="Giving a spin or curve to a bowl in the game of bowling, again a metaphor for 'curved' or roundabout ways".

Intemperance, i. without limits - … But there is no bottom, none to my voluptuousness.
"But there is no bottom, none,
In my voluptuousness" (M.4.3)
Should this be the case, you may want to be quiet about it. Or it could be an ironic answer to questions of the type, 'Are you passionate?'
In the play. *Malcolm tests Macduff's reaction by pretending that he (Malcolm) is a greedy libertine without a conscience.*

Intent, evil i. to remain hidden – Stars hide your fires, let not light see my black and deep desires.
"… **Stars, hide your fires!**
Let not light see my black and deep desires." (M.1.4)
Change 'my' to 'your'. Throw it in with nonchalance when you suspect your adversary of perfidious intents.
In the play. *Macbeth begins to concoct the plan (and the murders) that will lead him to become king of Scotland, as the witches had predicted.*

Intentions, do you mean it? – Fair Margaret knows that Suffolk doth not flatter, face, or feign.
REIGNIER Speaks Suffolk as he thinks?
SUFFOLK Fair Margaret knows
That Suffolk doth not flatter, face, or feign. (KHVI.p1.5.3)
Answer to 'Do you mean it?' E.G. 'Everybody knows that (your name) doth not… feign'.
In the play. *Reigner verifies if Suffolk really intends to have Margaret marry Henry VI.*

Intentions, good i. gone awry - We are not the first who with best meaning have incurred the worst.
"We are not the first
Who with best meaning have incurred the worst." (KL.5.3)
Justify a failure or use for generic damage control. See also 'Action, a. contrary and with opposite effect to original intentions - So play the foolish throngs with one that swoons...'
In the play. *Cordelia has just been taken prisoner along with her father Lear.*

Intentions, i. misinterpreted - ... some about him have too lavishly wrested his meaning and authority.
"My father's purposes have been mistook,
And some about him have too lavishly
Wrested his meaning and authority"
(KHIV p2.4.2)
In the play. *Lancaster, Henry IV's son downplays the actions and intentions of his father towards the rebels. Actually he is laying down a trick that will result in the rebels' downfall.*

Intentions, i. that did not materialize – thoughts are no subjects, intents but merely thoughts.
"His acts did not overtake his bad intent;
And must be buried as an intent
That perished by the way: thoughts are no subjects,
Intents but merely thoughts."
(MFM.5.1)
Avoid putting intentions on trial, 'Thoughts are no subjects… thoughts.
In the play *Isabel pleads with the Duke to spare Angelo's life for the sake of Mariana. After all Angelo's plans were foiled by the Duke's plot and his intent to do evil did not materialize.*

Intentions, wicked i. shown in the type of question and type of answer - ... you question with a wicked tongue.
QUEEN. Come, come you answer with an idle tongue
HAMLET. Go, go, you question with a wicked tongue (H.3.4)
A retort to any loaded question or answer.
In the play. *The queen tells Hamlet that he has offended his stepfather. Hamlet retorts that she has offended his father.*

Interest, i. in knowing person better - ... I desire more acquaintance of you.
"Good Master Brook, I desire more acquaintance of you." (MWW.2.2)
To add a touch of mild irony, change 'Brook' to the name of the person addressed. E.G. 'Good Master (name of person) ...of you'. For an opposite feeling see 'Dislike, mutual d. expressed'
In the play. *Master Brook (alias Mr. Ford) lends money and hints promises of romantic success to Falstaff who reacts positively. Actually the jealous Mr. Ford is using Falstaff to test the fidelity of Mrs. Ford.*

Interest, personal i. reply to statement indicating interest - ... I shall study deserving
KENT. I must love you and sue to know you better
EDMUND. I shall study deserving." (KL.1.1)
An answer when someone suggest an act of kindness to come, for example, 'I want to be your friend', or 'I want to know more about you' etc.
In the play. *Edmund has been introduced to Kent by his father Gloucester.*

Interpretation, i. is all - So our virtues lie in the interpretation of the time... One fire drives out one fire; one nail, one nail...
"So our virtues
Lie in the interpretation of the time:
And power, unto itself most commendable,
Hath not a tomb so evident as a chair
To extol what it hath done.
One fire drives out one fire; one nail, one nail;
Rights by rights falter, strengths by strengths do fail." (COR.4.7)
Use as an example (the first two lines) when you want to justify a point of view different from the mainstream. Use the last two lines to indicate the volatility and temporary nature of power. Daniel Defoe, the author of Robinson Crusoe wrote an 'Ode to Pillory' – he was indeed

unjustly pilloried for something he had written. In the Ode to Pillory we find, 'Actions receive their tincture from the times,
And as they change are virtues made of crimes'
In the play. *Aufidius, leader of the Volscii comments on Coriolanus.*

Interpretation, i. of events depending on the interpreter - ... but men may construe things after their fashion clean from the purpose of the things themselves.
"Indeed, it is a strange-disposed time:
But men may construe things after their fashion,
Clean from the purpose of the things themselves." (JC.1.3)
Explain why your words or action were interpreted differently than what you intended.
In the play. *Casca told Cicero about strange and unnatural events and Cicero comments in a somewhat non-committal way.*

Interpretation, wrong interpretation of events - ... you take things ill which are not so...
"I learn, you take things ill which are not so,
Or being, concern you not." (AC.2.2)
In the play. *Antony addresses Octavian at the beginning of an electric meeting in Lepidus' house.*

Introduction, exhortation to the audience to use their imagination - ...Yet sit and see, minding true things by what their mockeries be.
"...Yet sit and see,
Minding true things by what their mockeries be." (KHV.4.prologue)
In the play. *Again the virtual producer of the play exhorts the audience to make up with the imagination for the lack of special effects and technology required to properly show the battle of Agincourt.*

Introduction, i. of a VIP - ... But pardon, gentles all the flat unraised spirits...
"... But pardon, gentles all,
The flat unraised spirits, that have dar'd,
On this unworthy scaffold, to bring forth
So great an object." (KHV.1 Prologue)
When introducing an important guest, e.g. 'Given the stature of the guest it befell to me to introduce I must, just like the chorus in Shakespeare, ask pardon, gentles all, ...so great an object'. See also 'Inspiration, a powerful Muse required before starting a speech'
In the play. *The chorus, realizing the greatness of the subject apologizes for the limited choreography.*

Introduction, i. to a point or an argument, with irony and sarcastic affectation - ... in good faith, in sincere verity, under the allowance of your great aspect...
KENT: Sir, in good faith, in sincere verity,
Under the allowance of your great aspect,
Whose influence, like a wreath of radiant fire
On flickering Phoebus' front
CORNWALL: What mean'st by this?
KENT: To go out of my dialect, which you discommend so much." (KL.2.2)
Use a sarcastically bombastic opening. In the play the sentence is interrupted by Cornwall. To make a complete sentence modify line 3 to read '...Whose influence is like a wreath of radiant fire on flickering Phoebus front'
Equally let it be an answer to a request to speak more formally, 'OK I will go out of my dialect, which you discommend so much.'

In the play. *Cornwall upbraids Kent for his direct manners and Kent retorts sarcastically with hyperbolic praises of Cornwall.*

Introduction, i. to a presentation - ... And let me speak to the yet unknowing world how these things came about.
"...And let me speak to the yet unknowing world
How these things came about: so shall you hear
Of carnal, bloody, and unnatural acts,
Of accidental judgments, casual slaughters,
Of deaths put on by cunning and forced cause,
And, in this upshot, purposes mistook
Fall'n on the inventors' heads: all this can I
Truly deliver." (H.5.2)
In the play. *Horatio, only survivor of the mass carnage at the Danish court, will explain the events of the Hamlet tragedy to the Danish ambassador to England and to the Norwegian captain Fortinbras, the latter returning from Poland.*

Introduction, i. to a presentation - As an unperfect actor on the stage, who with his fear is put besides his part...
"As an unperfect actor on the stage
Who with his fear is put besides his part,
Or some fierce thing replete with too much rage,
Whose strength's abundance weakens his own heart..." (SON 23)
Indicate how passionately you feel about the subject, your only fear is that you may not inspire an equal passion in your audience.

Introduction, i. to a presentation - If you have tears, prepare to shed them now...
"If you have tears, prepare to shed them now.

You all do know this mantle: I remember
The first time ever Caesar put it on"
(JC.3.2)
In the play. *Antony plies the crowd and will turn the mood against Caesar's killers.*

Introduction, i. to a speaker of great reputation – (A) man whose glory fills the world with loud report.
"...That she may boast she hath beheld the man
Whose glory fills the world with loud report" (KHVI.p1.2.2)
In the play. *A messenger on behalf of the Countess of Auvergne invites Talbot to visit her.*

Introduction, i. to a speaker with an impressive background – ... that once trod the ways of glory and sounded all the depths and shoals of honour.
"Wolsey, that once trod the ways of glory,
And sounded all the depths and shoals of honour" (KHVIII.3.2)
Try 'We can say of (name of speaker) that he/she has trod the ways of glory...honour'
In the play. *Parting words from Cardinal Wolsey to protegee' Cromwell who, unlike Wolsey is in favor with the king. Wolsey talks of himself in the style of former presidential candidate Bob Dole.*

Introduction, i. to the last part of a presentation - ... To show our simple skill that is the true beginning of our end.
"...To show our simple skill,
That is the true beginning of our end." (MND.5.1)
In the play. *The actors' introduction to their play within the play.*

Introduction, request to accept the limitations of the presentation and choreography - Piece out our imperfections with your thoughts...

"Piece out our imperfections with your thoughts;
Into a thousand parts divide one man,
And make imaginary puissance:
Think, when we talk of horses, that you see them
Printing their proud hoofs in the receiving earth." (KHV.prologue)
Use entirely or just the first line in an introduction to a presentation. Should you, for whatever reason, have lost or mislaid the graphic material for your presentation but cannot delay it, then use the line 'Think, when we talk of horses, that you see them'
In the play. *The chorus, given the limited number of props must rely on the imagination of the audience to visualize the action of this action-packed play.*

Introduction, impossible to describe all her/his accomplishments in a short time - Turning the accomplishment of many years into an hour-glass...
"Turning the accomplishment of many years
Into an hour-glass" (KHV.prologue)
Introduce a speaker or use it as your introduction when the subject (of your presentation) is a man or a woman who has accomplished many things. You can also use the following lines as a point of kindness to the audience.
"Admit me Chorus to this history;
Who prologue-like your humble patience pray,
Gently to hear, kindly to judge, our play."
For example, with minor modification, '…therefore prologue-like I your humble patience pray, gently to hear, kindly top judge, my presentation.'
It also works well as a preamble especially if you are not so young and therefore your history is extended (see also 'age'). You could start with 'I have to turn the accomplishment of many years into an hour glass'.
In the play. *Lacking Hollywood's resources of special effects, the Chorus asks the audience to visualize some of the action scenes or backgrounds that occur in the play, horses, battles, French landscapes etc.*

Introduction, self-introduction – Am bold to show myself a forward guest… to make mine eye the witness of that report which I so oft have heard.
"Am bold to show myself a forward guest
Within your house, to make mine eye the witness
Of that report which I so oft have heard." (TOS.2.1)
It can apply to the beauty of the house or to any other reported marvel in the place or abode you are visiting. You may skip the introduction and declare the reasons for your visit. E.G. 'I came to make mine eyes the witness… heard.'
In the play. *Petruchio introduces himself to Baptista. What Petruchio claims to have often heard of is the beauty and virtues of the shrewish Katharina.*

Introduction, self-introduction - I prithee, pretty youth, let me be better acquainted with thee.
"I prithee, pretty youth, let me be better acquainted with thee." (AYLI.4.1)
Use as a substitute to 'Did I not see you before?' or any other repeated, hacked way of approaching a girl.
In the play. *In the forest of Arden Jacques meets Rosalind and likes her*

Introduction, self-introduction to pretty lady - … Be not offended, nature's miracle, thou art allotted to be ta'en by me.
"An earl I am, and Suffolk am I call'd.
Be not offended, nature's miracle,

Thou art allotted to be ta'en by me"
(KHVI.p1.5.3)
Possible answer to 'Who are you?' at a blind date. Change to A man I am, and (your name) am I called etc. You may use the third line as is after having assessed the situation – meaning if you think she may be amenable. Otherwise try, 'Be not offended, nature's miracle by my bold self-introduction' or equivalent.
'Nature's miracle' can stand on its own as a compliment.
In the play. *Suffolk has captured the beautiful Margaret in a battle near Angers (France) and he plans to have her marry King Henry VI in England.*

Introduction, self-introduction, modest – If one so rude and of so mean condition may pass into the presence of a king.
"If one so rude and of so mean condition
May pass into the presence of a king"
(KHVI.p2.5.1)
See also entries for 'Modesty'.
In the play. *Squire Iden shows up at court with the head of the slain rebel Cade.*

Introduction, you will be brief - I will be brief, for my short date of breath is not so long as is a tedious tale.
"I will be brief, for my short date of breath
Is not so long as is a tedious tale."
(RJ.5.3)
In the play. *Fr. Lawrence explains the sequence of events that let to the death of Romeo, Juliet, and Paris.*

Introduction, you will be brief - O' Sir, 't is better to be brief than tedious.
"O' Sir, 't is better to be brief than tedious." (KRIII.1.4)
Reassure the audience that your speech will be short. E.G. 'As the murderer said to the guardian of the Tower of London, "'t is better to be brief than tedious"'.
In the play. *The murderers sent by Richard of Gloucester to the Tower to kill Clarence are met by Brakenbury, the Tower's lieutenant. He asks them the reason for their coming. The second murdered replies.*

Introduction, you will be brief - Since brevity is the soul of wit and tediousness the limbs and outward flourishes, I will be brief.
"... since brevity is the soul of wit,
And tediousness the limbs and outward flourishes,
I will be brief." (H.2.2)
Use as an introduction to any speech or presentation. It gives comfort to the audience. See also 'also 'Speech, brevity of s. promised - my short date of breath is not so long as is a tedious tale'– 'Brevity, b. in communications - I will imitate the honourable Romans'
In the play. *Polonius believes he has identified the cause of Hamlet's erratic behavior, namely that Hamlet is in love with Ophelia. Proud of his (actually wrong) diagnosis, Polonius delivers a lengthy and pompous introduction to the attending king and queen.*
"My liege, and madam, to expostulate
What majesty should be, what duty is,
Why day is day, night night, and time is time,
Were nothing but to waste night, day and time.
Therefore, since brevity is the soul of wit,
And tediousness the limbs and outward flourishes,
I will be brief: your noble son is mad:
Mad call I it; for, to define true madness,
What is't but to be nothing else but mad?
But let that go."
To which Queen Gertrude replies with the line 'More matter, with less art', words you can use when you wish to invite a verbose person to come to the bone of the matter
.

Intuition, general i. - There is a thing within my bosom tells me…

"There is a thing within my bosom
tells me
That no conditions of our peace can
stand" (KHIV p2.4.1)
In the play. *Mowbray is suspicious of the peace offer by Henry IV (and he was right).*

Intuition, seeing through appearance
- It may be so; but yet my inward soul
persuades me it is otherwise.
"It may be so; but yet my inward soul
Persuades me it is otherwise."
(KRII.2.2)
Answer to a question on your opinion. You disagree but have not enough evidence to dispute the findings. See also 'Presentment, premonition'.
In the play. *Richard has left for Ireland and the Queen has a presentiment that Richard's enemies will take advantage of the king's absence. She does not buy the confidence that Bushy shows while cheering her up.*

Invention, extraordinary power of i. required to properly describe her – O for a Muse of fire, that would ascend the brightest heaven of invention.
"O for a Muse of fire, that would ascend
The brightest heaven of invention"
(KHV.prologue)
Answer to 'What do you like in me?' before you start the descriptions. Also usable as an introduction to a presentation, when the presented subject is lofty.
In the play. *Lacking Hollywood's power to generate special effects, the Chorus asks the audience to imagine some of the action scenes or backgrounds that occur in the play, horses, battles, French landscapes etc.*

Inventiveness, i., wit and geniality rewarded - ...wit shall not go unrewarded while I am king of this country.
"... wit shall not go unrewarded while I am king of this country." (TEM.4.1)
Show your appreciation of a good repartee. E.G. 'See me later, wit shall not go…. Country'.
In the play. *Stephano, who fancies himself already as king of the island, will reward the wit of the jester Trinculo who just produced a word pun.*

Investments, diversification of i. - … my ventures are not in one bottom trusted.
"My ventures are not in one bottom trusted,
Nor to one place; nor is my whole estate
Upon the fortune of this present year" (MOV.1.1)
In the play. *Antonio has diversified his investments and is not concerned about losing one or two ships at sea.* 'Bottom' = 'Ship' You may use 'ship' to avoid misunderstandings.

Invincibility - I will not be afraid of death and bane till Birnam forest come to Dunsinane.
"I will not be afraid of death and bane,
Till Birnam forest come to Dunsinane" (M.5.3)
You may qualify the use of 'bottom' as a synonym of 'boat' to avoid misinterpretations.
In the play. *Though the enemy is at hand and allies abandon him, Macbeth still clings to the prediction of the witches about the moving forest.*

Invitation, i. impossible to resist - …
There is no tongue that moves, none, none in the world so soon as yours could win me.
"Press me not, beseech you, so.
There is no tongue that moves, none, none in the world,
So soon as yours could win me."
(WT.1.2)

Two situation where you can use it. When you wish to deny the invitation gracefully, e.g. 'There is no tongue that moves, none… win me, but I cannot because… etc.'
Or if you wish to accept the invitation and add a compliment to your acceptance.
In the play. *Leontes, king of Sicily insists that Polixenes stay longer as a guest in Sicily but Polixenes wants to go back to his kingdom, Bohemia.*

Invitation, i. not to mourn – No longer mourn for me when I am dead…
"No longer mourn for me when I am dead
Then you shall hear the surly sullen bell
Give warning to the world that I am fled
From this vile world, with vilest worms to dwell" (SON 71)

Invitation, i. refused - I have heard it said, unbidden guests are often welcomest when they are gone.
TALBOT. Will not your honours bear me company?
BEDFORD. No truly; it is more than manners will:
And I have heard it said, unbidden guests
Are often welcomest when they are gone." (KHVIp1.2.2)
Exempt yourself from attending a meeting where you know you will not feel comfortable for whatever reason.
In the play. *Bedford and Talbot exchange courtesies. The countess of Auvergne has invited Talbot to her castle and Talbot has invited Bedford to come along.*

Invitation, i. refused (to dinner) – I will buy with you, sell with you…but I will not eat with you…

"I will buy with you, sell with you, talk with you, walk with you, and so following; but I will not eat with you, drink with you, nor pray with you." (MOV.1.3)
In the play. *Shylock refuses an invitation to a business dinner by Bassanio and Antonio.*

Invitation, i. to be frank and plain - Therefore with frank and with uncurbed plainness tell us the Dauphin's mind'.
"Therefore with frank and with uncurbed plainness
Tell us the Dauphin's mind." (KHV.1.2)
Change 'the Dauphin's' to the name or title of the applicable person. Solicit someone to really say what troubles him. 'Now then, with frank and with uncurbed plainness, tell us your mind'.
In the play. *King Henry V prompts the French ambassadors to explain the position of the Dauphin of France.*

Invitation, i. to butchery - The lamb entreats the butcher: where's thy knife?
"The lamb entreats the butcher: where's thy knife?" (CYM.3.4)
In the play. *Imogen tells Pisanio to kill her, though Pisanio has already decided that he will not carry out Leonatus' instructions to murder her.*

Invitation, i. to cold lady to warm up – … descend; be stone no more; approach.
"'Tis time; descend; be stone no more; approach" (WT.5.2)
In the play. *The loyal Paulina addresses the statue of the wrongly accused Hermione and tells her to come alive. This magic is also made possible by the perfection of the sculpture, executed by "that rare Italian master, Julio Romano".*

Invitation, i. to dinner and to freedom from care - Let's to supper, come, and drown consideration.
"... Let's to supper, come,
And drown consideration." (AC.4.2)
See also 'Dinner, invitation to a working d.'
In the play. *Antony will revive his generals after the lost battle at sea and the impending land battle with Octavian.*

Invitation, i. to give information about self. See 'Life, longing to hear her life story - I long hear the story of your life, which must take the ear strangely.' - 'Dinner, have d. precede a meeting - Discourse is heavy, fasting; when we have supp'd we'll mannerly demand thee of thy story so far as thou wilt speak it.'

Invitation, i. to leave out all niceties and pretenses - Lay by all nicety and prolixious blushes that banish what they sue for.
"Lay by all nicety and prolixious blushes,
That banish what they sue for." (MFM.2.4)
In the play. *Angelo's last attempt to seduce Isabel whom she accuses of affected modesty.*

Invitation, i. to return soon – O thou that dost inhabit in my breast, leave not the mansion so long tenantless.
"O thou that dost inhabit in my breast,
Leave not the mansion so long tenantless" (TGV.5.4)
Tell her that you cannot live without her.
In the play. *Alone in the forest and banned from Milan, Valentine fantasizes about being with his beloved Silvia.*

Invitation, i. to speak openly - Say as you think, and speak it from your souls.

"Say as you think, and speak it from your souls" (KHVI.p2.3.1)
In the play. *York addresses Suffolk and Cardinal Beaufort. All plot to kill Duke Humphrey (Gloucester) each for different motives.*

Invitation, i to travel - I rather would entreat thy company to see the wonders of the world abroad.
"I rather would entreat thy company
To see the wonders of the world abroad" (TGV.1.1)
Try 'May I entreat your company to see...abroad?'
In the play. *Valentine would invite his friend Proteus to travel abroad but Proteus is in love with Julia and would not consider leaving Verona.*

Invitation, i. to your place when you know that your place is in a state of disarray - We will give you sleepy drinks, that your senses, unintelligent of our insufficience...
"We will give you sleepy drinks, that your senses, unintelligent of our insufficience, may, though they cannot praise us, as little accuse us" (WT.1.1)
Change the 'we' to 'I', 'our' to 'my' and 'us' to 'me'. "I will give you sleepy drinks, that your senses, unintelligent of my insufficience, may, though they cannot praise me, as little accuse me". Also applicable when she lives in a mansion and you invite her for the first time to your miniscule studio apartment.
In the play. *Next summer Camillo will visit Archidamus in his native Bohemia's. Archidamus is concerned that the reception could not possibly match the hospitality and magnificence displayed in Sicily at his arrival.*

Invitation, i. to wife to sit near you - Come, madam wife, sit by my side and let the world slip: we shall ne'er be younger.

"…Come, madam wife, sit by my side and let the world slip: we shall ne'er be younger." (TOS. Ind.)
The invitation is extendable to other people in the same spirit.
In the play. Sly, *the drunkard subject of a prank and for whose benefit the play is staged, addresses his newly appointed wife and invites her to watch the play itself, 'Taming of the Shrew'.*

Invitation, your hand - Your hand, my Perdita, so turtles pair, that never mean to part.
"**Your hand, my Perdita, so turtles pair, that never mean to part**" (WT.4.4)
Change 'Perdita' with her name. Clearly you must have already a strong relationship going to use these lines.
In the play. *Florizel loves Perdita. Meanwhile Polixenes and Camillo are concerned that Florizel may be tempted to marry Perdita, a girl of unacceptable lower rank or, as Camillo points out,* 'queen of curds and creams'. *But in fact and unbeknown to Camillo, Perdita is the daughter of Leontes, king of Sicilia.*

Invocation - Fire and brimstone!
"**Fire and brimstone!**" (TN.2.5)
In the play. *Toby Belch is indignant on overhearing Malvolio talking to himself.* 'Brimstone' is sulphur. 'Fire and brimstone' is an expression also found in the Bible (Revelation 14:10)

Invocation, accursed hour - Let this pernicious hour stand aye accursed in the calendar.
"**Let this pernicious hour
Stand aye accursed in the calendar!**" (M.4.1)
In the play. *Macbeth is distressed after yet another apparition of Banquo's ghost, this time with the witches.* 'Aye' = 'Always'.

Invocation, anger - O, were mine eyeballs into bullets turned, that I, in rage, might shoot them at your faces.
"**O, were mine eyeballs into bullets turned,
That I, in rage, might shoot them at your faces.**" (KHVI.p1.4.7).
Express your anger. See also 'Speech, unable to speak due to vexation and frustration' – 'Anger - too angry to speak'.
In the play. *Lord Lucy's anger at the French for having slain John Talbot.*

Invocation, by this and by that - By Jove that thunders!
"**… by Jove that thunders!**" (AC.3.13)
In the play. *Antony is mad at Thyreus, ambassador from Octavian.*

Invocation, by this and by that - By that fair sun which shows me where thou stand'st.
"**By that fair sun which shows me where thou stand'st**" (KRII.4.1)
In the play. *At Westminster Hall, Lord Fitzwater accuses the Duke of Aumerle of having killed Gloucester.*

Invocation, by this and by that - By the roses of the spring.
"**…by the roses of the spring…**" (TN.3.1)
In the play. *Olivia declares her love to Viola/Cesario, or rather to Cesario who is actually Viola dressed as a boy as part of the play's plot.*

Invocation, by this and by that – By my troth.
In the plays. *This invocation occurs in many plays.* 'Troth' = 'faith, belief'.

Invocation, by this and by that – By the fire that quickens Nilus' slime.
"**…By the fire
That quickens Nilus' slime.**" (AC.1.3)
Make it precede a statement indicating surprise or use instead of an expletive just when you are ready to lose your patience.
In one of Socrate's dialogs you will find

the equally effective exclamation, 'By the dog of Egypt'.
In the play. *Antony is on the point of leaving for Rome and close to losing his patience while being harassed by Cleopatra.*

Invocation, by this and by that – By the grace of Grace
"… by the grace of Grace… (M.5.8)
Use as is or as part of a statement of intent to accomplish a task. See 'Task, t. will be accomplished'.
In the play. *Malcolm, winner of the battle of Dunsinane, addresses his allies before moving to be crowned at Scone.*

Invocation, by this and by that – By the sacred radiance of the sun.
"… By the sacred radiance of the sun,
The mysteries of Hecate, and the night;
By all the operation of the orbs
From whom we do exist, and cease to be." (KL.1.1)
Have these words precede emphatically what you say you are going to do next.
In the play. *Lear is mad at Cordelia because she does not want to compete with her hypocrite sisters in declaring her filial love with words. Lear will therefore disinherit* **her.**

Invocation, by this and by that – By the salt wave of the Mediterranean.
"By the salt wave of the Mediterranean." (LLL.5.1)
Elegant expletive-less invocation.
In the play. *Moth teases Armado and Armado answers in his style.*

Invocation, by this and by that - By the sky that hangs above our heads I like it well.
"Now, by the sky that hangs above our heads,
I like it well." (KJ.2.1)
Declare your approval.
In the play. *The Bastard advises King John to attack the city of Angiers.*

Invocation, by this and by that - By these blessed candles of the night…
"… by these blessed candles of the night" (MOV.5.1)
In the play. *Bassanio justifies to Portia why he had to part with the ring that she gave him.*

Invocation, by this and by that – By two-headed Janus.
"…Now, by two-headed Janus,
Nature hath framed strange fellows in her time" (MOV.1.1)
In the play. *Salarino comments on the alleged sadness of Antonio.*

Invocation, by this and by that - By yond marble heaven.
"Now, by yond marble heaven,
In the due reverence of a sacred vow
I here engage my words." (OTH.3.3)
In the play. *Othello is determined to be avenged of Desdemona's infidelity.*

Invocation, by this and by that – For all the mud in Egypt…
"For all the mud in Egypt: have you heard it?" (KHVIII.2.3)
In the play. *A lady courtier chides Anne Boleyn about her denying a craving to be a queen. The king has just appointed Anne as Marchioness of Pembroke.*

Invocation, by this and by that - Now, by the death of Him that died for all…
"Now, by the death of Him that died for all,
These counties were the keys of Normandy…" (KHVI.p2.1.1)
In the play. *Lord Salisbury participates in the dismay of the English Lords at the cession of the duchies of Anjou and Maine back to France.*

Invocation, damned letter - O damn'd paper! Black as the ink that's on thee!
"…O damn'd paper!
Black as the ink that's on thee!" (CYM.3.2)
See also 'Words, carrying bad news or offensive or poorly written'.
In the play. *Pisanio cannot believe what Leonatus has asked him to do, i.e. kill Imogen.*

Invocation, delivery from illusions – See 'Illusion, state of i., invocation - … and here we wander in illusions some blessed power deliver us from hence.'

Invocation, despair – Now let hot Aetna cool in Sicily and be my heart an ever-burning hell!
" Now let hot Aetna cool in Sicily,
And be my heart an ever-burning hell!" (TA.3.1)
In the play. *A messenger has just brought in the heads of Marcus and Quintus, unjustly accused and executed for the murder of Bassianus.*

Invocation, deviant mood – Can it be that so degenerate a strain as this should once set footing in your generous bosoms?
"Can it be
That so degenerate a strain as this,
Should once set footing in your generous bosoms?" (TC.2.2)
Decry outrageous ideas, words, or proposal. For an opposite argument see the following 'In the play'.
In the play. *Paris appeals to Hector's and Priam's generosity of soul as an argument to hold on to Helen. Troilus' point is an example illustrated in the quote 'Appearance, a. of truth hiding a deeper and malicious purpose'. The purpose is malicious (keeping Helen), but the appeal is to a noble sentiment, i.e. generosity.*

Invocation, despicable administration - hell is empty and all the devils are here.
"…Hell is empty
And all the devils are here." (TEM.1.2)
Apply to an administration whose deeds are particularly despicable.
In the play. *As reported by Ariel, this is what Ferdinand said as he quit the ship during the tempest that gives name to the play.*

Invocation, end - Sun, hide thy beams! Timon hath done his reign.
"Sun, hide thy beams! Timon hath done his reign." (TOA.5.1)
Make it part of your retirement or resignation speech.
In the play. *Timon's final voice of defiance to the world.*

Invocation, i. after feeling shame - Let life be short; else shame will be too long.
"Let life be short; else shame will be too long." (KHV.4.4)
In the play. *The French Bourbon commenting on the defeat of the French in the battle of Agincourt.*

Invocation, i. against adverse Fortune - … let me rail so high that the false housewife Fortune break her wheel, provoked by my offence.
"…let me rail so high,
That the false housewife Fortune break her wheel,
Provoked by my offence" (AC.4.15)
In the play. *Cleopatra's defying stance against bad fortune as Antony is dying and asks to speak.*

Invocation, i. against enemies – earth, yield stinging nettles to mine enemies…
"…earth
Yield stinging nettles to mine enemies;
And when they from thy bosom pluck a flower,

Guard it, I pray thee, with a lurking adder,
Whose double tongue may with a mortal touch
Throw death upon thy sovereign's enemies." (KRII.3.2)
In the play. *Richard II lands on the coast of Wales from Ireland, in the meantime the rebels led by Bolingbroke are ready to depose Richard.*

Invocation, i. against the heavens for their doings - Hung be the heavens with black, yield day to night!...
"Hung be the heavens with black, yield day to night!
Comets, importing change of times and states,
Brandish your crystal tresses in the sky,
And with them scourge the bad revolting stars,
That have consented...."
(KHVI.p1.1.1)
Applicable to any event that in your view is detrimental to your cause. See also 'Class, c. distinction even in death - When beggars die, there are no comets seen...'
In the play. *The Duke of Bedford begins the play with an invocation to the stars that have consented to the death of King Henry V.*

Invocation, i. against time – ... Thou ceaseless lackey to eternity...
'Mis-shapen Time, copesmate of ugly Night,
Swift subtle post, carrier of grisly care,
Eater of youth, false slave to false delight,
Base watch of woes, sin's pack-horse, virtue's snare;
Thou nurses all and murder'st all that are:
O, hear me then, injurious, shifting Time!
....
'Thou ceaseless lackey to eternity, "
(ROL)

In the poem. *Assaulted Lucrece inveighs against time. 'Copesmate'='Companion'*

Invocation, i. against rascals – ... And put in every honest hand a whip to lash the rascals naked through the world...
"O heaven, that such companions thou'ldst unfold,
And put in every honest hand a whip
To lash the rascals naked through the world
Even from the east to the west!"
(OTH.4.2)
In the play. *Emilia, still unaware that the rascal she is inveighing against is her husband Iago.*

Invocation, i. against unfair heaven - ... that heaven should practise stratagems upon so soft a subject as myself!
"Alack, alack, that heaven should practise stratagems
Upon so soft a subject as myself!"
(RJ.3.5)
When you consider yourself unjustly targeted by inexplicable events.
In the play. *Juliet's invocation after discovering that her father wants her to marry Paris right away. He does not know that Juliet has already married Romeo in secret.*

Invocation, i. against war and current times. - O, pity, God, this miserable age!...
"O, pity, God, this miserable age!
What stratagems, how fell, how butcherly,
Erroneous, mutinous and unnatural,
This deadly quarrel daily doth beget!"
(KHVI.p3.2.5)
In the play. *A father fighting with the Yorkists unwittingly has killed his son who was fighting for the Lancastrians.*

Invocation, i. and curse to the baseness of human nature - Fly,

damned baseness to him that worships thee.
"Is it possible the world should so much differ;
And we alive that lived? Fly, damned baseness,
To him that worships thee." (TOA.3.1)
Decry baseness in general.
In the play. *Flaminius, Timon's servant is outraged at Lucullus' refusal to help Timon.*

Invocation, i. and satisfaction at the success of your scheme – Work on, my medicine, work!
"Work on,
My medicine, work! Thus credulous fools are caught" (OTH.4.1)
If your scheme was honest omit the line about the fools.
In the play. *Othello has bought completely Iago's tale about Desdemona's infidelity (the medicine, as Iago calls it).*

Invocation, i. for inspiration - Assist me, some extemporal god of rhyme…
"Assist me, some extemporal god of rhyme, for I am sure I shall turn sonnet. Devise, wit; write, pen; for I am for whole volumes in folio" (LLL.1.2)
In the play. *Armado calls for inspiration.*

Invocation, i. for lover to come – …come, thou day in night; for thou wilt lie upon the wings of night whiter than new snow on a raven's back.
"… come, thou day in night;
For thou wilt lie upon the wings of night
Whiter than new snow on a raven's back." (RJ.3.2)
Applicable to either sex. Compliment on perfect skin – exaggerate a little to allay her concern about acne symptoms.

In the play. *Juliet, earlier on hastily married to Romeo, pines for the night to arrive so that Romeo may come.*

Invocation, i. for night to come - … Come, thick night, and pall thee in the dunnest smoke of hell…
"…Come, thick night,
And pall thee in the dunnest smoke of hell,
That my keen knife see not the wound it makes,
Nor heaven peep through the blanket of the dark,
To cry 'Hold, hold!'" (M.1.4)
In the play. *Lady Macbeth prepares to direct and manage the assassination of King Duncan, guest at her and Macbeth's castle. 'Dun'='dark, black'.*

Invocation, i. for patience, need for p. - You heavens, give me that patience, patience I need!
"You heavens, give me that patience, patience I need!" (KL.2.4)
Suggest that his/her behavior is a nuisance, his/her words a disappointment, his/her work insufficient. See also entries for 'Patience'
In the play. *Lear to himself.*

Invocation, i. for the world to end - O, let the vile world end and the premised flames of the last day…
"O, let the vile world end,
And the premised flames of the last day
Knit earth and heaven together!" (KHVI.p2.5.2)
In the play. *Young Clifford at discovering the body of his father slain in the battle of St. Albans'*

Invocation, i. for thunder - O that I were a god, to shoot forth thunder upon these paltry, servile, abject drudges!

"O that I were a god, to shoot forth thunder
Upon these paltry, servile, abject drudges!" (KHVI.p2.4.1)
In the play. *Suffolk to the captain of a ship and comrades who captured him.*

Invocation, i. that faults of kings be not hidden - … heaven forbid that kings should let their ears hear their faults hid!
"…heaven forbid
That kings should let their ears hear their faults hid! (PER.2.2)
In the play. *Pericles to Helicanus, a faithful minister who does not flatter.*

Invocation, i. to angels and superior powers – Angels and ministers of grace defend us!
"Angels and ministers of grace defend us!" (H.1.4)
In the play. *Hamlet's reaction at the first appearance of the Ghost*

Invocation, i. to an oath maintained - Let nature crush the sides o' the earth together and mar the seeds within!
"Let nature crush the sides o' the earth together
And mar the seeds within!" (WT.4.3)
Answer to 'Are you sure?' E.G. 'Yes, if not, let nature…within'.
In the play. *Florizel will renounce his succession to the throne of Bohemia rather than violate his oath (and love) to Perdita.*

Invocation, i. to God - God befriend us, as our cause is just!
"God befriend us, as our cause is just!" (KHIV.p1.5.1)
In the play. *King Henry IV moments before the start of the battle of Shrewsbury.*

Invocation, i. to hard times – O heavy times, begetting such events!
"O heavy times, begetting such events!" (KHVI.p3.2.5)

In the play. *In the battle of Towton, a son fighting with the Lancastrians has slain unwittingly his father who was fighting with the Yorkists.*

Invocation, i. to heavens that tolerate the victory of hell – Heavens, can you suffer hell so to prevail?
"Heavens, can you suffer hell so to prevail?" (KHVI.p1.1.5)
In the play. *Talbot, after his first bout with Joan of Arc.*

Invocation, i. to ignorance - O thou monster Ignorance, how deformed dost thou look!
"O thou monster Ignorance, how deformed dost thou look!" (LLL.4.2)
In the play. *Holofernes, referring to the ignorance of Dull who completely misconstrued or misunderstood Holoferne's highly intricate wording.*

Invocation, i. to one's own power of prediction - O my prophetic soul!
"O my prophetic soul!" (H.1.5)
In the play. *Hamlet's reaction at the revelation by his father's Ghost who discloses the details of his own murder.*

Invocation, i. to the Gods – Gods and goddesses, all the whole synod of them!
"Gods and goddesses,
All the whole synod of them!"
(AC.3.10)
In the play. *Scarus exclaims after Antony has lost the battle against Octavian*

Invocation, i. to the world and its vicissitudes – World, world, O world! But that thy strange mutations make us hate thee…
"…World, world, O world!
But that thy strange mutations make us hate thee,
Lie would not yield to age." (KL.4.1)

In the play. *Edgar's reaction on seeing his blinded father Gloucester led by an old man.*

Invocation, i. to heaven, that what is feared be not true - Grant, heavens, that which I fear prove false!
"…Grant, heavens, that which I fear Prove false!" (CYM.3.5)
In the play. *Cymbeline fears that Imogen has run away, she has.*

Invocation, i. to Jove for hope – Great Jove… give renew'd fire to our extincted spirits.
"Great Jove…
Give renew'd fire to our extincted spirits" (OTH.2.1)
In the play. *Cassio hopes for the safe arrival of Othello in Cyprus.*

Invocation, i. to Neptune to calm a sea and thunder storm - … rebuke these surges, which wash both heaven and hell…
"Thou god of this great vast, rebuke these surges,
Which wash both heaven and hell; and thou, that hast
Upon the winds command, bind them in brass,
Having call'd them from the deep! O, still
Thy deafening, dreadful thunders; gently quench
Thy nimble, sulphurous flashes!" (PER.3.1)
In the play. *Pericles in a storm at sea, while returning to Tyre with wife Thaisa who has just delivered infant daughter Marina.*

Invocation, happiness in love – O Love, be moderate, allay thy ecstasy… make it less for fear I surfeit.
"…O love,
Be moderate; allay thy ecstasy,
In measure rein thy joy; scant this excess.
I feel too much thy blessing: make it less,
For fear I surfeit." (MOV.3.2)
On the subject of moderation in love see also 'Love and moderation. In praise of moderation in l.' - 'Happiness, unbearable h. - … the gods do mean to strike me to death with mortal joy'.
In the play. *Portia is over herself. She loves Bassanio and is overjoyed that he has chosen the right basket containing her picture, has won the quiz and therefore will marry her.*

Invocation, horror. - … Tongue nor heart cannot conceive nor name thee!
"O horror, horror, horror! Tongue nor heart
Cannot conceive nor name thee!" (M.2.2)
In the play. *Macduff discovers the slain body of Duncan.*

Invocation, i. about honesty - O wretched fool, that livest to make thine honesty a vice!
"O wretched fool.
That livest to make thine honesty a vice!
O monstrous world! Take note, take note, O world,
To be direct and honest is not safe.
I thank you for this profit; and from hence
I'll love no friend, sith love breeds such offence." (OTH.3.3)
In the play. *False Iago pretends that Othello be mad because he, Iago, told him the truth about Desdemona's infidelity. 'Sith'='Since'.*

Invocation, i. to heaven to send down justice. See 'Justice, no j. on earth – invocation to heaven to send down justice'.

Invocation, if real merit were rewarded and not theft.
"O, that estates, degrees and offices,
Were not deriv'd corruptly!   And that clear honour

Were purchas'd by the merit of the wearer!
How many then should cover that stand bare!" (MOV.2.9)
In a speech use as a contrast, in praise of a person who is both successful and honorable, e.g. 'Shakespeare wonders whether clear honor is purchased by the merit of the wearer. Here we have a real example when this is so...' Or as a comment on the deception of appearances and the reward of demerit.
In the play. *The prince of Arragon, one of Portia's suitors meditates on the meaning of a puzzle. People in authority do not cover their heads, subordinates do. The point is that if true merit were to be rewarded many roles would be reversed.*

Invocation, if this happens then... - Then let the pebbles on the hungry beach fillip the stars...
"Then let the pebbles on the hungry beach
Fillip the stars; then let the mutinous winds
Strike the proud cedars 'gainst the fiery sun;
Murdering impossibility, to make
What cannot be, slight work"
(COR.5.3)
Comparing an absurd with an impossible event
In the play. *Coriolanus at the sight of his mother kneeling and pleading that he do not fight against Rome.*

Invocation - ... in the names of all the gods at once
"... in the names of all the gods at once" (JC.1.2)
In the play. *Cassius gives Brutus reasons for getting rid of Caesar and questions the ground of Caesar's popularity.*

Invocation - In the name of something holy...
"I' the name of something holy, sir, why stand you
In this strange stare?" (TEM.3.3)
In the plat. *Gonzalo questions Alonso who has been shocked by perceiving messages in waves and songs in winds.*

Invocation, ironic i. applicable to fools – God give them wisdom that have it; and those that are fools, let them use their talents.
"God give them wisdom that have it; and those that are fools, let them use their talents."
See also 'Insult, fool, response and maxim - Better a witty fool than a foolish wit.'
In the play. *The Clown banters with Maria, Olivia's servant.*

Invocation, let the sky rain potatoes - Let the sky rain potatoes; let it thunder to the tune of Green Sleeves.
"Let the sky rain potatoes; let it thunder to the tune of Green Sleeves" (MWW.5.5)
In the play. *Falstaff has been tricked once more into believing that Mrs. Ford and Mrs. Page will accept his courtship, but ends up being the butt of a funny caper.*

Invocation, i. in amazement - All seeing heaven, what a world is this!
"All seeing heaven, what a world is this!" (KRIII.2.1)
In the play. *Queen Elizabeth is shocked to hear the news that Clarence has been executed in the tower of London.*

Invocation, i. in the name of truth - As there comes light from heaven, and words from breath, as there is sense in truth, and truth in virtue...
"As there comes light from heaven, and words from breath,

As there is sense in truth, and truth in virtue,
I am affianc'd this man's wife."
(MFM.5.1)
Use the first two lines to support the validity of your following statement.
In the play. *The plot unfolds - Mariana testifies that it was she and not Isabel that Angelo slept with. Mariana had been jilted by Angelo because she was not as rich or important as he thought she should be.*
'Affianced'= 'Betrothed'.

Invocation, i. in the way of assurance - Heaven and fortune bar me happy hours! … if …
"Heaven and fortune bar me happy hours!
Day, yield me not thy light; nor, night, thy rest!
Be opposite all planets of good luck
To my proceedings, if, with pure heart's love…" (KRIII.4.4)
What follows your 'if' is what you are promising or committing yourself to do unfailingly.
In the play. *After having murdered her sons, Richard has the gall to ask Queen Elizabeth to marry her younger daughter Anne. He uses his rhetoric to prove that his motives are good, if…*
"with pure heart's love,
Immaculate devotion, holy thoughts,
I tender not thy beauteous princely daughter!"

Invocation, i. not to bear or tolerate the horrible - O, horrible! O, horrible! most horrible! If thou hast nature in thee, bear it not.
"O, horrible! O, horrible! most horrible!
If thou hast nature in thee, bear it not" (H.1.5)
Your comment on an intolerable event, occurrence or statement of policy.
In the play. *The Ghost to Hamlet, reinforcing the exhortation to seek revenge.*

Invocation, i. of desperation - Hath no man's dagger here a point for me?
"Hath no man's dagger here a point for me?" (MAAN.4.1)
In the play. *Leonato is out of himself after hearing of the accusations levied against his daughter Hero.*

Invocation, i. prompted by government's evil deeds - Woe, woe for England! not a whit for me.
"Woe, woe for England! not a whit for me" (KRIII.3.4)
Change 'England' to name of applicable state.
In the play. *Richard has just condemned Hastings to death on charges of witchcraft. Hastings realizes the accuracy of Stanley's earlier forebodings and predictions.*

Invocation, i. to comets and physical phenomena - yield day to night! Comets, importing changes of times and states…
"… yield day to night!
Comets, importing changes of times and states,
Brandish your crystal tresses in the sky." (KHVIp1.1.1)
Underscore with an invocation an important occasion.
In the play. King *Henry V has died and Bedford gives a eulogy.*

Invocation, i. to constancy - O constancy, be strong upon my side, set a huge mountain 'tween my heart and tongue!
"O constancy, be strong upon my side,
Set a huge mountain 'tween my heart and tongue!" (JC.2.4)
In the play. *Calpurnia, Caesar's wife is torn between her presentiment that something horrible will occur to Caesar and her duty to obey Caesar who decided to go to the Senate anyway.*

Invocation, i. to cruelty. See 'Cruelty, invocation to c. by a woman – Come, you spirits that tend on mortal thoughts, unsex me here…'

Invocation, i. to flattery - O, that men's ears should be to counsel deaf, but not to flattery.
"O, that men's ears should be
To counsel deaf, but not to flattery!" (TOA.1.2)
Describe persons who enjoy flattery to the detriment of wisdom. See also 'Counsel, c. useless for stubborn hearer - all in vain comes counsel to his ear'.
In the play. *Apemantus witnesses Timon's weakness and foresees his imminent downfall.*

Invocation, i. to heaven not to see men's evil acts - O, you powers! that give heaven countless eyes to view men's acts…
"O, you powers!
That give heaven countless eyes to view men's acts,
Why cloud they not their sights perpetually." (PER.1.1)
Underscore the perversity of man.
In the play. *Pericles solved the riddle but the solution coincides with the discovery of the incestuous relationship between King Antiochus and his daughter. Pericles is horrified.*

Invocation, i. to heaven that I am telling the truth - Heaven be the record to my speech
"… heaven be the record to my speech." (KRII.1.1)
Place emphasis on the truth of your statement. See also 'Statement, making a formal s. - Let me be recorded by the righteous gods…'
In the play. *Bolingbroke starts his attack on Mowbray, duke of Norfolk, in the presence of Richard II.*

Invocation, i. to nature as a supreme ruler, also answer to a request from your girlfriend - Thou, nature, art my goddess; to thy law my services are bound.
"Thou, nature, art my goddess; to thy law
My services are bound." (KL.1.2)
Answer to 'what is your philosophy?'. Or substitute for 'nature' the name of a girl you fancy and want her to know it. See also 'Service. You are at her complete service.'
In the play. *Edmund justifies to himself his next (evil) course of action.*

Invocation, i. to bullets, do not hit - O, you leaden messengers, that ride upon the wicked speed of fire…
"O, you leaden messengers,
That ride upon the wicked speed of fire,
Fly with false aim." (AWEW.3.2)
Wish the party to whom you address the remark that he may escape real (or metaphorical) bullets.
In the play. *The devoted Helena, aware of the dangers of war, prays that the bullets may not hit Bertram, her estranged husband.*

Invocation, i. to self-safety in combat - God keep lead out of me! I need no more weight than mine own bowels.
"God keep lead out of me! I need no more weight than mine own bowels." (KHIVp1.5.3)
Indicate that you will abstain or not join the fight.
In the play. *Falstaff's invocation at the battle of Shrewsbury.*

Invocation, i. to success in the pursuit of love - Love, lend me wings to make my purpose swift…
"Love, lend me wings to make my purpose swift,
As thou hast lent me wit to plot this drift!" (TGV.2.5)
In the play. *Proteus hatches a plan to steal Silvia from Proteus.*

Invocation, i, to poetical inspiration - Assist me, some extemporal god of rhyme…
"Assist me, some extemporal god of rhyme, for, I am sure, I shall turn sonnets. Devise, wit, write, pen; for I am for whole volumes of folio." (LLL.1.2)
A call for inspiration.
In the play. *Enthralled by the sight of Jacquenetta, Armado drops his plans to forego the company of women. He asks the assistance of poetical inspiration (god of rhyme) to write love sonnets.*

Invocation, i. to predict the future. See entries for 'Prediction, desire to know in advance'

Invocation, i. to revenge - Arise, black vengeance, from thy hollow cell!
"Arise, black vengeance, from thy hollow cell!" (OTH.3.3)
In the play. *Othello is determined to avenge the (totally false) infidelity of Desdemona and Cassio.*

Invocation, i. to stormy skies - Yet cease your ire, you angry stars of heaven!…
"Yet cease your ire, you angry stars of heaven!
Wind, rain, and thunder, remember, earthly man
Is but a substance that must yield to you" (PER.2.1)
Applicable when in the middle of a hurricane, tornado or similar.
In the play. *Pericles is shipwrecked in front of Pentapolis.*

Invocation, i. to the gods for justice - We will solicit heaven and move the gods to send down Justice for to wreak our wrongs.
"And since there's no justice in earth or hell,
We will solicit heaven and move the gods
To send down Justice for to wreak our wrongs." (TA.4.3)
Express the idea that sometimes only heaven can provide justice in an unjust world.
In the play. *Titus is ready to deliver the just revenge for the various preceding murders, rapes etc.*

Invocation, i. to utter falsehood - Let all untruths stand by thy stained name and they'll seem glorious.
"Let all untruths stand by thy stained name,
And they'll seem glorious." (TC.5.2)
Address a liar.
In the play. *Troilus curses Cressida.*

Invocation, i. to the moon, massive depression - O sovereign mistress of true melancholy,…
"O sovereign mistress of true melancholy,
The poisonous damp of night disponge upon me,
That life, a very rebel to my will,
May hang no longer on me." (AC.4.9)
Use the first line as an alternative description of the moon, or turn it around as a curse, "May the sovereign mistress of true melancholy disponge the poisonous damp of night upon you."
In the play. *Enobarbus repents for having abandoned Antony.*

Invocation, i. to thunder - And thou, all-shaking thunder, smite flat the thick rotundity o' the world!
"…. And thou, all-shaking thunder, Smite flat the thick rotundity o' the world!" (KL.3.2)
In the play. *Lear, evicted by his evil daughters, inveighs against the weather.*

Invocation, i. to time as a problem solver - O time, thou must untangle

this, not I; it is too hard a knot for me to untie.
"O time, thou must untangle this; not I;
It is too hard a knot for me to untie!" (TN.2.2)
Suggest that only time can resolve the matter as it is too entangled or complicated.
In the play. *Viola has fallen in love with the Duke, but the Duke is in love with Olivia. Olivia, thinking Viola/Cesario to be a man, has fallen in love with him. It is a tangle.*

Invocation, thunder in the mouth – O, that my tongue were in the thunder's mouth! Then with a passion would I shake the world.
"O, that my tongue were in the thunder's mouth!
Then with a passion would I shake the world." (KJ.3.4)
In the play. *After the lost battle of Angiers, young Arthur, Constance' son, has been captured by the English and she is desperate.*

Invocation, let's go, I am upset - O, come away! My soul is full of discord and dismay.
"... O, come away!
My soul is full of discord and dismay." (H.4.1)
Express internal conflict and disarray, "My soul... dismay" or an exhortation to quit a bad meeting, "Come away... dismay"
In the play. *After the recent turn of events and now the slaying of Polonius by Hamlet, the king is distraught.*

Invocation, madness generalized - Mad world! mad kings! mad disposition!
"Mad world! mad kings! mad disposition!" (KJ.2.2)
Sarcastic comment on the world or on a series of events that show man's genetically inherited madness

In the play. *Ph. Faulconbridge reflects and objects to the terms of the proposed agreement between France and England.*

Invocation, misplaced ambition, see the results - Ill-weav'd ambition, how much art thou shrunk!
"Ill-weav'd ambition, how much art thou shrunk!
When that this body did contain a spirit,
A kingdom for it was too small a bound;
But now two paces of the vilest earth
Is room enough" (KHIVp1.5.4)
Reinforce the moral of an example where excessive ambition has proven destructive.
In the play. *The Prince of Wales meditates on the fallen Hotspur.*

Invocation, mistrust in human nature – Grant I may never prove so fond, to trust man on his oath or bond.
"Grant I may never prove so fond,
To trust man on his oath or bond." (TOA.1.2)
Assert your total distrust of just about everyone.
In the play. *Apemantus does not spare an occasion to deliver messages of skepticism or contempt for mankind. This is his version of 'Grace' before sitting down at Timon's dinner.*

Invocation, no honesty among thieves - ... a plague upon it when thieves cannot be true one to another!
"... a plague upon it when thieves cannot be true one to another!" (KHIV.p1.2.2)
In the play. *Falstaff complains of hardship while he prepares to ambush and some travelers at Gadshill.*

Invocation, no pity in the clouds - Is there no pity sitting in the clouds that sees into the bottom of my grief?
"Is there no pity sitting in the clouds,

That sees into the bottom of my grief?" (RJ.3.5)
Rhetorically show your disgust or pain at the way events develop.
In the play. *Capulet has delivered an ultimatum to his daughter, marry Paris or else and Juliet reacts*

Invocation, obstinacy - Let it be virtuous to be obstinate.
"Let it be virtuous to be obstinate" (COR.5.3)
In the play. *Coriolanus to himself hoping that he will not relent to his mother's and his wife's plea that he do not attack Rome.*

Invocation, protection from shame - The gods defend him from so great a shame!
"The gods defend him from so great a shame!" (JC.5.4)
Change 'him' to 'me' if you wish to emphatically denies an allegation levied against you.
In the play. *Lucilius tells Antony that Brutus will not be taken alive at the battle of Philippi.*

Invocation, rain as tears - Dissolve, thick cloud, and rain; that I may say, the gods themselves do weep!
"Dissolve, thick cloud, and rain; that I may say,
The gods themselves do weep!" (AC.5.2)
In the play. *Charmian, on seeing Iras, Cleopatra's other lady in waiting die of poison.*

Invocation, rascals to be punished - And put in every honest hand a whip to lash the rascals naked through the world...
"O heaven, that such companions thou should unfold,
And put in every honest hand a whip
To lash the rascals naked through the world,
Even from the east to the west." (OTH.4.3)

Generic wish for punishment of a specific type of people.
In the play. *Emilia correctly suspects that some evil character (actually Iago, her husband) has made false accusations to ruin Othello's marriage and mind.*

Invocation, rather this than... - May that ground gape and swallow me alive...
"May that ground gape and swallow me alive,
Where I shall kneel to him that slew my father!" (KHVI.p3.1.1)
Invocation is followed by 'rather than...' and description of the abhorred alternative.
In the play. *Clifford Junior vows revenge against York who killed Clifford Senior and asserts to be the rightful king of England.*

Invocation, revenge - I am Revenge: sent from the infernal kingdom, to ease the gnawing vulture of thy mind...
"I am Revenge: sent from the infernal kingdom,
To ease the gnawing vulture of thy mind,
By working wreakful vengeance on thy foes" (TA.4.2)
Try 'Come Revenge, sent from the infernal kingdom... my foes'. Change 'thy mind' to 'my mind'
In the play. *The evil Tamora, thinking that Titus A. is mad, pretends to soothe his desire for revenge by pretending to be herself the goddess of revenge.*

Invocation, shame - Live in thy shame, but die not shame with thee!
"Live in thy shame, but die not shame with thee!" (KRII.2.1)
In the play. *Gaunt's parting words to visiting King Richard.*

Invocation, shamelessness - O shame, where is thy blush!

"O shame, where is thy blush!" (H.3.4)
Comment on any action, word or proposal with which you strongly disagree.
In the play. *Hamlet confronts the Queen his mother.*

Invocation, skepticism about human nature - O, what men dare do! what men may do! what men daily do! not knowing what they do!
"O, what men dare do! what men may do! what men daily do! not knowing what they do!" (MAAN.4.1)
Comment on the inherent ignorance and therefore inhumanity of humanity. See also entries for "Man and its wicked nature'
In the play. *Claudio, unaware of the evil plot of Don John, believes Hero to be a slut and refuses to marry her.*

Invocation, state of country – Bleed, bleed, poor country! Great tyranny! lay thou thy basis sure…
"Bleed, bleed, poor country!
Great tyranny! lay thou thy basis sure,
For goodness dare not cheque thee!" (M.4.3)
See also 'State of affairs, rotten state of affairs - Something is rotten in the state of Denmark'
In the play. *Macduff, in conversation with Malcolm comments on the state of Scotland under Macbeth.*

Invocation, stones in heaven - Are there no stones in heaven but what serve for thunder?
"Are there no stones in heaven
But what serve for thunder?" (OTH.5.2)
Express indignation.
In the play. *Iago has just stabbed and killed his wife Emilia who had uncovered his diabolic plot to destroy Othello. Othello is beyond indignation.*

Invocation, sun – O sun, Burn the great sphere thou movest in!
"O sun,
Burn the great sphere thou movest in!" (AC.4.15)
In the play. *Cleopatra on seeing Antony brought in. He inflicted himself a mortal wound.*

Invocation, that heaven may not see disgusting acts - O you powers that give heaven countless eyes to view men's acts…
"…O you powers
That give heaven countless eyes to view men's acts,
Why cloud they not their sights perpetually,
If this be true, which makes me pale to read it?" (PER.1.1)
In the play. *Pericles reads the text of the riddle showing clearly the incestuous relationship involving the daughter of Antioch.*

Invocation, time, short time for goodbyes - Injurious time now with a robber's haste…
"Injurious time now with a robber's haste
Crams his rich thievery up, he knows not how:
As many farewells as be stars in heaven,
With distinct breath and consign'd kisses to them,
He fumbles up into a lose adieu,
And scants us with a single famish'd kiss,
Distasted with the salt of broken tears" (TC.4.4)
Use the first two lines.
In the play. *Troilus must say farewell to Cressida who is delivered to the Greeks in exchange for the Trojan prisoner Antinor. There is little time for farewells, hence Troilus' invocation.*

Invocation, unkind hour - Ah, what an unkind hour is guilty of this lamentable chance!
"... Ah, what an unkind hour
Is guilty of this lamentable chance!"
(RJ.5.3)
In the play. *Friar Lawrence discovers the bodies of Romeo and Paris in the tomb where both went to see the (presumed dead) Juliet. Just then Juliet wakes up from the effect of the drugs earlier administered by Friar Lawrence.*

Invocation, why does it fall to me to do this! - The time is out of joint - O cursed spite, that ever I was born to set it right.
"The time is out of joint - O cursed spite,
That ever I was born to set it right."
(H.1.5)
Express the idea that you don't like to do something but it must be done.
In the play. *Hamlet's reflections after meeting with Ghost.*

Irrelevance, bound to i. - ... snapper-up of unconsidered trifles.
"My father named me Autolycus; who, being as I am, littered under Mercury, was likewise a snapper-up of unconsidered trifles." (WT.4.3)
Soften the reaction to news that you know important but others may not.
E.G. 'I may be a snapper-up of unconsidered trifles...but you should know that...'
In the play. *Autolycus introduces himself and somewhat convolutedly explains why he is a thief by profession.*

Issue, outcome of political i. or debate uncertain – This battle fares like to the morning's war...
"This battle fares like to the morning's war,
When dying clouds contend with growing light,
What time the shepherd, blowing of his nails,
Can neither call it perfect day nor night.
Now sways it this way, like a mighty sea
Forced by the tide to combat with the wind;
Now sways it that way, like the selfsame sea
Forced to retire by fury of the wind"
(KHVI.p3.2.5)
In the play. *King Henry's assessment on the ongoing battle near Towton between his forces and the Yorkists.*

Issue, very clear i. - ... as clear as is the summer's sun.
"... as clear as is the summer's sun."
(KHV.1.2)
Powerful comparison to conclude your argument or reasoning.
In the play. *After a long and contorted listing of events and genealogies the Bishop of Canterbury optimistically concludes that it is clear that Henry has a right to invade France. The reasoning is anything but clear, but this is the rationale of all imperialists. The priests in England want Henry to pillar in France what he could obtain in England by taxing the church.*

Jargon, people who use jargon - They have been at a great feast of languages, and stolen the scraps.
"They have been at a great feast of languages, and stolen the scraps."
(LLL.5.1)
In the play. *Moth, referring to the strange parlance of Armado and Holofernes'*

Jealousy, a standard accompaniment of love - ... love, thou know'st, is full of jealousy.
"... love, thou know'st, is full of jealousy" (TGV.2.4)
In the play. *Valentine to Proteus. Valentine has a rival for the hand of Julia in the foolish but rich Thurio.*

Jealousy, characteristic of j. and of the jealous – … They are not ever jealous for the cause but jealous for they are jealous…
DESDEMONA Alas the day! I never gave him cause.
EMILIA But jealous souls will not be answer'd so;
They are not ever jealous for the cause,
But jealous for they are jealous: 'tis a monster
Begot upon itself, born on itself. (OTH.3.4)
Illustrate that jealousy feeds on itself, almost incurable.
In the play. *Desdemona confides with Emilia about Othello's worrisome state of mind and Emilia diagnoses it correctly. Desdemona cannot believe it because she is completely innocent.*

Jealousy, effects of j. - … the food that to him now is as luscious as locusts, shall be to him shortly as bitter as coloquintida.
"…the food that to him now is as luscious as locusts, shall be to him shortly as bitter as coloquintida" (OTH.1.3)
In the play. *Iago, for Roderigo's benefit, predicts the effects of jealousy on Othello. 'Coloquintida' = 'Colocynth' is a type of bitter apple or cucumber.*

Jealousy, evidence of deceit invented - These are the forgeries of jealousy.
"These are the forgeries of jealousy" (MND.2.1)
In the play. *Fairy Queen Titania dismisses Oberon's insinuations about her supposed infidelities. The real issue is the possession of a page boy, claimed by both.*

Jealousy, j. as a monster and to be avoided - T'is the green-eyed monster, which doth mock the meat it feeds on.
"O beware, my lord, of jealousy!
T'is the green-eyed monster, which doth mock
The meat it feeds on." (OTH.3.3)
Exhortation to repel or not to harbor jealousy.
In the play. *The cunning Iago plants seeds of jealousy into Othello's mind and Othello falls for it.*

Jealousy, j. as a poison - The venom clamour of a jealous woman poisons more deadly than a mad dog's tooth.
"The venom clamour of a jealous woman
Poisons more deadly than a mad dog's tooth." (COE.5.1)
Maybe you want to counsel a friend against being jealous, as obsessive jealousy can destroy a relationship.
In 1782 Mozart wrote to Constance Weber to express his annoyance at an incident related by her to her sisters in his presence - 'I love you far too well… I entreat you, therefore, to ponder and reflect upon the cause of all this unpleasantness, which arose from my being annoyed that you were so impudently inconsiderate as to say to your sisters – and, be noted, in my presence, that you had let an admirer measure the calves of your legs at a party. No woman who cares for her honor, can do such a thing…'
In the play. *The Lady Abbess attributes Antipholus of Ephesus's madness to the effect of Adriana's jealousy.*

Jealousy, j. barring sleep - … Nor all the drowsy syrups of the world shall ever medicine thee to that sweet sleep which thou owed'st yesterday.
"Not poppy, nor mandragora,
Nor all the drowsy syrups of the world,
Shall ever medicine thee to that sweet sleep
Which thou owed'st yesterday" (OTH.3.3)

In the play. *Iago has sown the seeds of jealousy in the heart of Othello and describes the ensuing effects. 'Mandragora =A mood-changing herb inducing sleep and relaxation'.*

Jealousy, j. beyond the reach of judgment - ... a jealousy so strong that judgment cannot cure.
"...a jealousy so strong
That judgment cannot cure"
(OTH.2.1)
In the play. *Iago describes the jealousy he will (successfully) be able to instill into Othello.*

Jealousy, j. left to the fools - How many fond fools serve mad jealousy.
"How many fond fools serve mad jealousy" (COE.2.1)
A punchline if the subject of conversation happens to be jealousy.
In the play. *Antipholus of Syracuse has developed a liking for Luciana, sister of Adriana, Antipholus of Ephesus' wife. But Adriana, thinking that Antipholus of Syracuse is actually Antipholus of Ephesus, is jealous.*

Jealousy, j. prompting madness in the man subjected to it. - ... thy jealous fits have scared thy husband from the use of wits.
"The consequence is then thy jealous fits
Have scared thy husband from the use of wits." **(COE.5.1)**
In the play. *The Lady Abbess diagnoses Ant E's madness. Adriana's jealousy deprived Ant E's of a good digestion and of a zest for life. The here described consequences follow.*

Jealousy, jealous and passionate - I will be more jealous of thee than a Barbary cock-pigeon over his hen...
"I will be more jealous of thee than a Barbary cock-pigeon over his hen...more giddy in my desires than a monkey." (AYLI.4.1)

This line is definitely more suitable to be uttered by a woman. If so, lady, go ahead with the Barbary rooster but go easy on the jealousy bit, depending also on his character.
In the play. *Rosalind disguised as a man (and incredibly unrecognized by Orlando) now pretends to be a woman and in a humorous way asks Orlando to show his courting skills. A mock marriage follows and Rosalind describes her own disposition and inclinations.*

Jealousy, no j. – Nor dare I question with my jealous thought...
"Nor dare I question with my jealous thought
Where you may be, or your affairs suppose,
But, like a sad slave, stay and think of nought
Save, where you are how happy you make those." (SON 57)
Answer to 'Are you jealous?'

Jealousy, trifles make the jealous jealous - Trifles light as air are to the jealous confirmation strong as proofs of holy writ.
"Trifles light as air
Are to the jealous confirmation strong
As proofs of holy writ." (OTH.3.3)
Illustrate jealousy at work.
In the play. *Iago tells his wife Emilia that Othello is jealous of Desdemona.*

Jewel, like an expensive jewel - ... she hangs upon the cheek of night as a rich jewel in an Ethiop's ear...
"O, she doth teach the torches to burn bright
It seems she hangs upon the cheek of night
As a rich jewel in an Ethiop's ear
Beauty too rich for use, for earth too dear!" (RJ.1.5)

One of the many answers to 'What do you think of me?' E.G. 'You are like a beauty too rich for use, for earth too dear' - that is just use the last line, unless you want to compare her to a jewel in an Ethiop's ear. But then you would have to explain why and how Ethiops had a penchant for large jewels and ear pendants.
In the play. *Romeo's first impressions of Juliet after seeing her at a party given by the Capulets.*

Jewelry, gifts large and small - ... Dumb jewels often, in their silent kind, more than quick words, do move a woman's mind.
DUKE. "(Tell me) how and which way, I may bestow myself
To be regarded in her sun-bright eye.
VALENTINE. Win her with gifts, if she respects not words,
Dumb jewels often, in their silent kind,
More than quick words, do move a woman's mind." (TGV.3.1)
As always, it depends on the type of lady you have or you are after. Theories on the nature, type and worth of gifts to be bestowed on ladies are many and varied. Ovid recommends "Nor do I bid you give your mistress costly gifts: let them be small, but choose your small gifts cunningly and well. While lands are fertile, and your branches droop with their burden, let a slave bring rustic tributes in a basket. You can say they were sent to you from your suburban property, though you bought them at the nearest market." (AOL.2).
Should you not have a slave at hand to carry your gifts to her, try Western Union or any of the commonly available city courier services.

Some gifts are unusual, escape classification and I would not recommend them. Such is the case with the gift Henry VIII sent to Ann Boleyn, included or I should say, accompanying the letter,
'God may continue as long as in prosperity, as I with my own; and, that you may the oftener remember me, I send you by this bearer, a buck killed late last night by my hand, hoping, when you eat of it, you will think on the hunter; and thus, for want of more room I will make an end of this letter. Written by the hand of your servant, who often wishes you in his room.'
In the play. *The Duke pretends to have lost his seducing skills and enlists the help of Valentine to learn how to conquer the heart of the lady the Duke is after. But in reality the Duke is plotting a trick to find Valentine guilty of planning to elope with Sylvia. Sylvia is the Duke's daughter.*

Jewelry, value of j. depending on fancy - ... Or stones whose rates are either rich or poor as fancy values them.
"...Or stones whose rates are either rich or poor
As fancy values them." (MFM.2.2)
Cast doubt on the value of an object, material or metaphorical.
In the play. *Isabel offers prayers (rather than ...stones whose rates...) if Angelo will spare her sister Claudio's life.*

Jewelry, value of discount jewel increased by the charm of the wearer – You mend the jewel by the wearing it.
"You mend the jewel by the wearing it" (TOA.1.1)
You have given an ornament to your girlfriend. Try, '... believe it, dear lady, you mend the jewel by the wearing of it.'

In the play. *A jewelry salesman and at the same time a parasite, feigning modesty, offers for sale a jewel to Timon.*

Joining the party – The swallow follows not summer more willing than we your lordship.
"The swallow follows not summer more willing than we your lordship."(TOA.3.6)
Answer to 'Will you come with me?' Change 'your lordship' to other name or title, as appropriate.
In the play. *Angry at the stinginess and pitilessness of his former friends, Timon invites them again to a banquet (unbeknown to them), of warm water. On hearing this statement Timon says aside,*
"Nor more willingly leaves winter; such summer-birds are men"

Joke, a j. you don't find funny - This jest is dry to me.
"This jest is dry to me" (LLL.5.2)
In the play. *Biron's answer to a Rosaline's comment. Biron and company had previously made asses of themselves by showing up in Russian masks.*

Joke, determining if a j. is good or not - A jest's prosperity lies in the ear of him that hears it…
" A jest's prosperity lies in the ear
Of him that hears it, never in the tongue
Of him that makes it." (LLL.5.2)
One way to avoid repeating a joke when asked to. Answer to 'What is that good joke that you said last night?'
In the play. *Rosaline expresses an opinion to Biron.*

Joke, more nonsense than a j. - These are old fond paradoxes, to make fools laugh in the alehouse.
"These are old fond paradoxes, to make fools laugh in the alehouse." (OTH.2.1)

Comment to a poor joke.
In the play. *Desdemona comments on Iago's mildly out of line witticisms.*

Joke, poor j. - His jest will savour but of shallow wit, when thousands weep, more than did laugh at it.
"His jest will savour but of shallow wit,
When thousands weep, more than did laugh at it." (KHV.1.2)
Retort to anyone who has ridiculed your idea or tried to make a joke of it. See also, 'Insult, lips to rot off'.
In the play. *The Dauphin of France has sent a set of tennis balls in jest as a gift to Henry V.*

Joke, semi-ironic reaction to j. – I will bite thee by the ear for that jest.
"I will bite thee by the ear for that jest." (RJ.2.4)
In the play. *Mercutio to Romeo who has cracked a joke at Mercutio's expense.*

Jokes, j. inappropriate to the moment or situation - … these jests are out of season; reserve them till a merrier hour than this.
"… these jests are out of season;
Reserve them till a merrier hour than this." (COE.1.2)
See also 'Merriment, m. not a good response to situation - … this merry inclination accords not with the sadness of my suit'.
In the play. *Antipholus of Ephesus asks Dromio of Syracuse a question. Dromio of Syracuse is the identical twin of Dromio of Ephesus. Dromio S. gives an irrelevant answer and Antipholus of Ephesus becomes upset.*

Jokes, no time for joking - … 't is no time to jest, and therefore frame your manners to the time.
"… 't is no time to jest,
And therefore frame your manners to the time." (TOS.1.1)

Use as a call to seriousness. See also 'Character, one who always laugh and does not take things seriously'.
In the play. *Lucentio upbraids Biondello another of his servants. Lucentio has exchanged clothes with Tranio as part of the plot to gain the hand of Bianca. Biondello laughs at Lucentio's attire.*

Jokes, no time for joking - ... do not play in wench-like words with that which is so serious.
"... do not play in wench-like words with that
Which is so serious" (CYM.4.2)
In the play. *Fideles/Imogen appears dead and Guiderius tells his brother Arviragus to stop his (otherwise innocent) encomium of him/her.*

Jokes, no time for joking - Reply not to me with a fool-born jest...
"Reply not to me with a fool-born jest Presume not that I am the thing I was" (KHIV.p2.5.5)
In the play. *Prince Harry, now Henry V admonishes Falstaff that times have changed.*

Jokes, not in the mood for j. - I am not in a sportive humour now; tell me and dally not, where is the money?
"I am not in a sportive humour now; Tell me and dally not, where is the money?" (COE.1.2)
Reject untimely humor. See also 'Jokes inappropriate to the moment or situation'.
In the play. *Antipholus (Syracuse) questions Dromio of Ephesus thinking Dromio E is actually Dromio of Syracuse. Dromio E gives a funny answer and Antipholus S is not amused.*

Jokes, the butt of others' jokes - ... the brain of this foolish-compounded clay, man, is not able to invent...
"... the brain of this foolish-compounded clay, man, is not able to invent anything that tends to laughter, more than I invent or is invented on me: I am not only witty in myself, but the cause that wit is in other men. (KHIV.p2.1.2)
In the play. *Falstaff comments on himself*

Joking, leave me out of it - Make yourself mirth with your particular fancy, and leave me out on it.
"Make yourself mirth with your particular fancy,
And leave me out on it." (KHVIII.2.3)
Dismiss innuendoes and sly talks regarding yourself or your private life.
In the play. *Anne upbraids an assistant who is trying to get Anne to say something about K. Henry and his attitude to Anne.*

Judge, thief, which is which? - ... change places; and, handy-dandy, which is the justice, which is the thief?
"...see how yond justice rails upon yond simple thief. Hark, in thine ear: change places; and, handy-dandy, which is the justice, which is the thief?" (KL.4.6)
See also 'Opinion, your op. on authority – ...There thou mightst behold the great image of authority: a dog's obeyed in office.'
In the play. *King Lear expounds to the blinded Gloucester his amended views on justice and authority.*

Judges, j. as thieves - Thieves for their robbery have authority when judges steal themselves.
"Thieves for their robbery have authority,
When judges steal themselves." (MFM.2.2)
Comment on corrupt justice.
In the play. *Angelo is attracted to Isabel and meditates with himself on what to do. If he pursues her, he is breaking the very law, which he is trying to enforce.*

Judgment, agreeing with the judge –
A Daniel come to judgment! yea, a Daniel!
"A Daniel come to judgment! yea, a Daniel!
O wise young judge, how I do honour thee!" (MOV.4.1)
Emphatic praise of him who said that you are right in an argument.
In the play. *Shylock is excited that Portia (disguised as a judge) concurs that Shylock's bond must be enforced and a pound of flesh cut off from Antonio.*

Judgment, fear of final j. – The urging of that word 'judgment' hath bred a kind of remorse in me.
SECOND MURDERER The urging of that word 'judgment' hath bred a kind
of remorse in me.
FIRST MURDERER What, art thou afraid?
SECOND MURDERER Not to kill him, having a warrant for it; but to be damned for killing him, from which no warrant can defend us (KRIII.1.4)
In the play. *The two contract killers sent by Richard to do Clarence out discuss the killing.*

Judgment, inability to assess the situation - You smell this business with a sense as cold as is a dead man's nose.
"You smell this business with a sense as cold
As is a dead man's nose." (WT.2.1)
Show a man's lack of perception, e.g. 'his sense is as cold… nose'.
In the play. *Now Leontes wants Antigonus to acknowledge that Hermione was unfaithful. Antigonus does not and Leontes accuses him of having lost the sense of perception.*

Judgment, j. and offence are not the same thing – To offend, and judge, are distinct offices and of opposed natures.

"To offend, and judge, are distinct offices
And of opposed natures." (MOV.2.9)
In the play. *Portia soothes the feelings of the Prince of Arragon, who having chosen the wrong answer (showing him the picture of a blinking idiot), takes the matter personally.*

Judgment, j. as the mark of man - … poor Ophelia, divided from herself and her fair judgment, without the which we are pictures, or mere beasts.
"…poor Ophelia
Divided from herself and her fair judgment,
Without the which we are pictures, or mere beasts" (H.4.5)
Comment on lack of judgment, '...judgment, without the which…mere beasts'. See also 'Opinion, your op. on sociological issues, minimum wage'.
In the play. *The King comments on Ophelia's senseless utterings indicating that she has become mad with her grief.*

Judgment, j. tempted by desire – Yet I confess that often ere this day, mine ear hath tempted judgment to desire.
"Yet I confess that often ere this day,
When I have heard your king's desert recounted,
Mine ear hath tempted judgment to desire" (KHVI.p3.3.3)
In the play. *Lady Bona, sister to the French King Lewis, answers a question from Warwick who came to propose her marriage to King Edward IV of England.*

Judgment, j. vanished - O judgment, thou art fled to brutish beasts and men have lost their reason.
"O judgment, thou art fled to brutish beasts,
And men have lost their reason." (JC.3.2)
Use to express your utter and total opposition.

In the play. *Antony to the crowd. Why can they not mourn Caesar whom they loved only a short time before?*

Judgment, men's j. affected by circumstances and showing their character - …I see men's judgments are a parcel of their fortunes…
"…I see men's judgments are
A parcel of their fortunes, and things outward
Do draw the inward quality after them
To suffer all alike." (AC.3.13)
Show that circumstances may cloud a person's ability to reason, as well as demonstrating the weakness of his judgment. See also 'Misfortune, m. affecting manners and judgment - … for his wits are drown'd and lost in his calamities.'
In the play. *Enobarbus commenting on Antony. Antony has the illusion that Octavian will accept a one-to-one duel to decide who wins.*

Judgment, no fear of j. - What judgment shall I dread, doing no wrong?
"What judgment shall I dread, doing no wrong?" (MOV.3.1)
In the play. *Shylock answers a question from the Duke of Venice.*

Judgment, poor j. compared to nor seeing well - … our very eyes are sometimes like our judgments, blind!
"…our very eyes
Are sometimes like our judgments, blind!" (CYM.4.1)
A comment on a poor decision.
In the play. *Imogen wakes up from a deep sleep and finds herself near the corpse of the slain Cloten She is confused and afraid.*

Judgment, refraining from j. – … in these nice sharp quillets of the law, good faith, I am no wiser than a daw.
"… Between two horses, which doth bear him best;
Between two girls, which hath the merriest eye: -
I have perhaps, some shallow spirit of judgement:
But in these nice sharp quillets of the law,
Good faith, I am no wiser than a daw." (KHVI.p1.2.4)
When you wish not to answer or take sides in a dispute.
In the play. *Warwick declines to judge on an argument between Somerset and Plantagenet.*

Judgment, skepticism about people's j. – All that follow their noses are led by their eyes but blind men…
"…All that follow their noses are led by their eyes but blind men; and there's not a nose among twenty but can smell him that's stinking" (KL.2.4)
See also "Siding with the losing party - …though my reason sits in the wind against me.'
In the play. *The Fool gives advice to Kent who has remained faithful to Lear after Lear lost power.*

Judgment, suspending j. for we all are at fault - Forbear to judge, for we are sinners all.
"Forbear to judge, for we are sinners all." (KHVI p2.3.2)
In the play. *King Henry softening Warwick's remarks on Cardinal Beaufort who just died.*

Judgment, unfair sentence and war on literacy - … because they could not read, thou hast hanged them…
"Moreover, thou hast put poor men in prison; and because they could not read, thou hast hanged them; when, indeed, only for that cause they have been most worthy to live." (KHVI p2.4.7)
An ironic example for those who put down culture. See also 'Education, a less orthodox view - Thou hast most

traitorously corrupted the youth of the realm in erecting a grammar school.'
In the play. *The rebel Cade accuses Lord Say.*

Judgment, without j. - Sense, sure, you have, else could you not have motion, but…
"…Sense, sure, you have,
Else could you not have motion; but sure, that sense
Is apoplex'd" (H.3.2)
In the play. *Hamlet to his mother*

Justice, bringing offenders to j. - … and poise the cause in justice's equal scales, whose beam stands sure, whose rightful cause prevails.
"… call these foul offenders to their answers;
And poise the cause in justice's equal scales,
Whose beam stands sure, whose rightful cause prevails." (KHVI p2.2.1)
Begin a peroration or an arbitration, e.g., 'Let's poise the cause… prevails."
In the play. *Henry VI calls for a trial of the alleged offenders, in particular Gloucester's wife who had been, in turn, betrayed by the Cardinal in a sting operation.*

Justice, corruption of j. by commercial interests - In the corrupted currents of this world, offence's gilded hand may shove by justice…
"May one be pardon'd and retain the offence?
In the corrupted currents of this world,
Offence's gilded hand may shove by justice,
And oft is seen the wicked prize itself
Buys out the law." (H.3.3)
Use to illustrate, for example, how contributions by powerful interest groups buy the politicians who craft laws benefiting the contributors. Or as a comment on any situation where money prevails on justice.

In the play. *The king meditates. He is torn by the remorse for the killing of his brother - money may buy justice but not soothe the pangs of conscience.*

Justice, fitting the law to the will of the powerful - … Bidding the law make court'sy to their will, hooking both right and wrong to the appetite…
"O perilous mouths,
That bear in them one and the self-same tongue,
Either of condemnation or approof;
Bidding the law make court'sy to their will:
Hooking both right and wrong to the appetite,
To follow as it draws!" (MFM.2.4)
See also 'Justice, misapplied and arbitrary – time for revolution'.
In the play. *Isabel meditates on the arrogance of power. In this case the subject is Angelo who 'bids the law to make court'sy to his will.'*

Justice, God as incorruptible judge - Heaven is above all yet; there sits a judge that no king can corrupt.
"Heaven is above all yet; there sits a judge,
That no king can corrupt."
(KHVIII.3.1)
Appeal to divine justice.
In the play. *Queen Katherine to Cardinal Campeius who examines her along with Cardinal Wolsey.*

Justice, gold buys j. - Plate sin with gold and the strong lance of justice hurtless breaks…
"Through tatter'd clothes small vices do appear;
Robes and furr'd gowns hide all Plate sin with gold
And the strong lance of justice hurtless breaks,
Arm it in rags, a pigmy's straw does pierce it." (KL.4.6)

The poor always get a raw deal. Justice unevenly applied. With gold people can get away with murder, perjury etc. Use 'Plate sin with gold and the strong lance of justice hurtless breaks' to comment on applicable instances of corruption.
In the play. *King Lear launches in a scathing attack on authority while talking to Gloucester.*

Justice, hope in j. after death – My comfort is that heaven will … plague injustice with the pains of hell.
"My comfort is that heaven will take our souls
And plague injustice with the pains of hell" (KRII.3.1)
In the play. *Green, faithful to King Richard and condemned to death by the usurping Bolingbroke states his opinion.*

Justice, misapplied and arbitrary, time for revolution - … now breathless wrong shall sit and pant in your great chairs of ease…
"Till now you have gone on and fill'd the time
With all licentious measure, making your wills
The scope of justice; till now myself and such
As slept within the shadow of your power
Have wander'd with our traversed arms and breathed
Our sufferance vainly: now the time is flush,
When crouching marrow in the bearer strong
Cries of itself 'No more:' now breathless wrong
Shall sit and pant in your great chairs of ease,
And pursy insolence shall break his wind
With fear and horrid flight." (TOA.5.4)
Comment on law passed by corrupt politicians. Use as a call for revolution.

See also 'Justice, fitting the law to the will of the powerful'.
In the play. *Alcibiades addresses the dishonest Athenian senators. 'Pursy'= 'fat' referring to the excess weight of the Athenian Senators.*

Justice, no j. possible from the very author of the crime - … You bid me seek redemption of the devil.
"O worthy duke,
You bid me seek redemption of the devil" (MFM.5.1)
In the play. *Duke Vicentio prompts Isabella to ask Angelo for the redress of her grievances. But Angelo is the very author of the crimes for which Isabella is seeking redress.*

Justice, pretence of j. to justify selfish gain - … and by this face this seeming brow of justice, did he win..
"…and by this face,
This seeming brow of justice, did he win
The hearts of all that he did angle for" (HIV.p1.4.3)
Today the 'seeming brow of justice' is found in formulas such as 'freedom and democracy' used to invade and plunder other countries.
In the play. *Hotspur rejects an offer of negotiations by Blunt, envoy of Henry IV. To support his denial, Hotspur recalls how just Henry wanted to appear when he deposed the rightful king Richard II.*

Justice, right and wrong lost when there is no principle - Force should be right; or rather, right and wrong, between whose endless jar justice resides…
"Force should be right; or rather, right and wrong,
Between whose endless jar justice resides,
Should lose their names, and so should justice too" (TC.1.3)
Ulysses refers to the consequences of lack of authority, but the meaning can

equally be applied to cases where principle is lost.
In the play. *Ulysses upbraids the Greeks for their weakness and lack of unified authority (degree).*

Justice, j. tainted - ... craft, being richer than innocency, stands for the facing
"...of two usuries, the merriest was put down, and the worser allowed by order of law a furred gown to keep him warm; and furred with fox and lamb-skins too, to signify, that craft, being richer than innocency, stands for the facing." (MFM.3.2)
In the play. *Pompey the Pimp gives his interpretation of tainted justice. 'Facing' = 'Trimming, something put outside for decoration'.*

Justification for insisting after a rejection - A woman sometimes scorns what best contents her.
"A woman sometimes scorns what best contents her." (TGV.3.1)
In the play. *At the Duke's request, Valentine gives him a courting lesson.*

Justification for insisting even after she said 'no' - ... maids in modesty, say 'No' to that which they would have the profferer construe 'Ay''.
"... maids in modesty, say 'No' to that Which they would have the profferer construe 'Ay'." (TGV.1.2)
This may not get you too far if you keep insisting after she said no. Still, it provides a good excuse and an elegant way to get out of a tight spot. Besides, elegance has always charm and she may even change her mind, who knows? See also 'Rejection, reason for not taking 'no' for an answer – For scorn at first makes after-love the more…' – 'Pretence, no for yes - Play the maid's part, still answer nay, and take it.'

According to Ovid you should never be afraid of asking.
'That you may gain her, ask. She only wishes to be asked; provide the cause and starting point of your desire. Jupiter went as a suppliant to his women… Yet, if you find that your prayers cause swollen pride, stop what you have begun, draw back a pace. Many women desire what flees them; they hate what is too forward; moderate your advance, and save them from getting tired of you.' (AOL.1)
But he also says,
'See that she grows used to you: Nothing is mightier than her assuefaction to you. Till you secure that, shun no weariness. Let her be always seeing you, always giving you her ear; let night and day show her your features. When you are quite confident that you can be missed, when your absence is likely to be regretted, suffer her to rest; a field that is rested will repay its trust, and a dry soil drinks up heaven's rain.'. (AOL.2).
See also entries for 'Rejection' – 'Playing hard-to-get and why - ... If I confess much, you will play the tyrant. – 'Pretence, no for yes - Play the maid's part, still answer nay, and take it.'
In the play. *Julia reflects and admits to herself that she said no (to reading a letter from Proteus) but she really meant the contrary.*

Justification for insisting even after she said 'no' – Things out of hope are compass'd oft with venturing, chiefly in love.
"Things out of hope are compass'd oft with venturing,
Chiefly in love, whose leave exceeds commission
…
What though the rose have prickles, yet 'tis pluck'd:
Were beauty under twenty locks kept fast,
Yet love breaks through and picks them all at last." (V&A)

In the poem. *Through intense insistence Venus manages to deliver some kisses to the icy-cold Adonis.*

Justification, request for j. for change of heart and feeling - ... when was the hour I ever contradicted your desire...
"... when was the hour
I ever contradicted your desire,
Or made it not mine too?"
(KHVIII.2.4)
Usually, if the situation has reached this point, your previous kindness or condescension will not have much effect, but it never hurts to try.
In the play. *King Henry VIII has decided to divorce Katherine of Aragon and sets up a trial to establish a legal reason for his act (other than having fallen in love with Anne Boleyn). Katherine naively tries to defend herself.*

Justification, self j. - I hope this reason stands for my excuse.
"I hope this reason stands for my excuse." (TOS.Induction, 2)
In the play. *A page (man dressed as a woman) tells the drunken Sly that she (the page) cannot be with him due to doctor's orders.*

Kill him - ... Off with the crown, and with the crown his head...
"Off with the crown, and with the crown his head;
And, whilst we breathe, take time to do him dead." (KHVI.p3.1.4)
Ironic answer to 'What should we do with him?' when dealing with an overbearing person or manager about to be fired.
In the play. *Queen Margaret scoffs at the captured Gloucester in the battle at Sandal Castle.*

Kill him – ... to the Tower and chop away that factious pate of his.
"He is a traitor; let him to the Tower,
And chop away that factious pate of his." (KHVI.p2.5.1)

In the play. *Clifford referring to York who claims he is the real king and not Henry VI*

Killing, unjust k. breeds revenge - ... to end one doubt by death revives two greater in the heirs of life.
"... For he hath found to end one doubt by death
Revives two greater in the heirs of life," (KHIV p2.4.1)
In the play. *The Archbishop of York is more inclined to believe that Henry IV wants peace, as opposed to the suspicious (but correctly so) Mowbray.*

Reprimand, complaint about being reprimanded - ... it is not meet that every nice offence should bear his comment.
CASSIUS In such a time as this it is not meet
That every nice offence should bear his comment.
BRUTUS Let me tell you, Cassius, you yourself
Are much condemn'd to have an itching palm (JC. 4.3)
In the play. *Brutus and Cassius have a debate in Brutus' tent prior to the battle of Philippi.*

Kindness always, I am always kind - For Caesar cannot live to be ungentle.
"For Caesar cannot live
To be ungentle." (AC.5.1)
Substitute your name for Octavian and indicate that you will oblige with a request.
In the play. *Octavian declares that he will be kind towards the defeated Cleopatra.*

Kindness conducive to love more than external appearance - Kindness in women, not their beauteous looks shall win my love.
"Kindness in women, not their beauteous looks,
Shall win my love." (TOS.4.2)

Compliment to a not-so-pretty lady who does not want to be lied to and told that she is beautiful.
In the play. *Hortensio leaves the contest for the hand of Bianca.*

Kindness, false k. - ... what a candy deal of courtesy this fawning greyhound then did proffer me!
"Why, what a candy deal of courtesy
This fawning greyhound then did proffer me!" (KHIV p1.1.3)
Modify, e.g. ' What a candy deal of courtesy did he proffer me, but still he is but a fawning greyhound." See also 'Courtesy, false c.'
In the play. *Hotspur referring to his first encounter with Bolingbroke when Hotspur was needed to sustain Bolingbroke's rebellion against King Richard II.*

Kindness, k. applied even to the wicked - ... for I am one of those gentle ones that will use the devil himself with courtesy.
" Fie, thou dishonest Satan! I call thee by the most modest terms; for I am one of those gentle ones that will use the devil himself with courtesy."
(TN.4.2)
Use to say that you treat everybody kindly. 'I am one of… courtesy. See also entries for 'Courtesy, false c.'
In the play. *The clown pretends not to understand or to misunderstand Malvolio's requests.*

Kindness, k. misplaced and bestowed on a snake - Why strew'st thy sugar on that bottled spider…
"Why strew'st thy sugar on that bottled spider
Whose deadly web ensnareth thee about?
Fool, fool! Thou whett'st a knife to kill yourself." (KRIII.1.3)

Counsel not to believe that a positive approach may change the attitude of a son of a bitch.
In the play. *Margaret warns Elizabeth about Richard as Elizabeth attempts to reason with him.*

Kindness, k. more effective than rudeness to achieve results - What thou wilt, thou rather shalt enforce it with thy smile, than hew to it with thy sword.
"What thou wilt,
Thou rather shalt enforce it with a smile,
Than hew to it with thy sword." (TOA.5.4)
Answer when she is angry or asks for something with a violent and angry tone of voice. Little is more annoying than arrogance in women, it reduces their charm and kills femininity. Still, some (or more than we may think) may have to deal with a woman's arrogance in their relationship. Use in general to point out that kindness achieves more results than arrogance.
In the play. *An Athenian senator suggests to Alcibiades that his wishes will be more likely accomplished if he uses kindness rather than force*

Kindness, k. more effective than rudeness to achieve results - Your gentleness shall force more than your force move us to gentleness.
"…Your gentleness shall force
More than your force move us to gentleness" (AYLI.2.7)
In the play. *In the Forest of Arden the Duke answers Orlando's threatening request for food*

Kindness, k. poorly repaid - Who, then, dares to be half so kind again? For bounty, that makes gods, does still mar men.
"Who, then, dares to be half so kind again?

For bounty, that makes gods, does still mar men." (TOA.4.2)
In the play. *Flavius, faithful Timon's servant comments on the demise of his master.*

King, how nice to be a k. – ... how sweet a thing it is to wear a crown.
"Therefore to arms! and, father, do but think,
How sweet a thing it is to wear a crown;
Within whose circuit is Elysium
And all that poets feign of bliss and joy" (KHVI p3.1.2)
The second line can be a compliment for someone who has just got a promotion.
In the play. *Edward prompts his father to usurp the throne of England.*

King, k. that shares the pain of his subjects – Much is your sorrow; mine ten times so much.
"Was ever king so grieved for subjects' woe?
Much is your sorrow; mine ten times so much." (KHVI.p3.2.5)
In the play. *King Henry has just witnessed a heart-wrenching scene where a father has unwittingly slain his son in battle and a son a father.*

King, k's approval ratings to a minimum – ... For yet may England curse my wretched reign
"Come, wife, let's in, and learn to govern better;
For yet may England curse my wretched reign" (KHVI.p2.4.9)
In the play. *After Cade's rebellion is quenched, the Duke of York arrives in force to unseat Henry VI.*

King, k.'s power in the name itself – Is not the king's name twenty thousand names?
"Is not the king's name twenty thousand names?" (KTII.3.2)

In the play. *Prompted by the Duke of Aumerle, King Richard, besieged and weakened by usurper Bolingbroke, tries to find courage relying on the inherent power or charisma of a king.*

Kings, authority, making their own laws - Kings are the earth's gods: in vice their law is their will...
"Kings are the earth's gods: in vice their law is their will,
And if Jove stray, who dares say Jove doth ill?
It is enough you know; and it is fit,
What being more known grows worse, to smother it." (PER.1.1)
Justify why you did not complain when you saw some wrong being done. See also entries on 'Authority' and 'Opinion, your op. on authority'.
In the play. *Pericles lets Antiochus know indirectly that he understood the meaning of the riddle.*

Kings, authority, vices of k. better kept secret - Who has a book of all that monarchs do, he's more secure to keep it shut, than shown...
"Who has a book of all that monarchs do,
He's more secure to keep it shut, than shown.
For vice repeated's like the wandering wind,
Blows dust in others' eyes, to spread itself." (PER.1.1)
Explain why the matter should be kept quiet. See also entries for 'Opinion, your op. on authority'.
In the play. *Pericles solved the riddle but the solution is the discovery of the incestuous relationship between King Antiochus and his daughter. Pericles declines to explain the true meaning of the riddle but lets Antiochus know indirectly that he understood very well what is going on.*

Kings, supreme power of k. - ... such is the breath of kings
"How long a time lies in one little word!
Four lagging winters and four wanton springs
End in a word: such is the breath of kings" (KRII.1.3)
Mildly ironic comment to a command by your boss.
In the play. *Bolingbroke comments on his four-year exile as decreed by Richard II. The 'little word' is 'banishment'.*

Kiss of death, figuratively speaking – Thus with a kiss I die.
"Thus with a kiss I die." (RJ.5.3)
Pretend that her kiss was something out of this world.
In the play. *Poisoned by the potion that he just drank, Romeo gives one last kiss to the sleeping Juliet.*

Kiss, longing for a k. – Never did passenger in summer's heat more thirst for drink than...
"Never did passenger in summer's heat
More thirst for drink than she for this good turn" (V&A)
Change 'she for this good turn' to 'I for your kiss'.
In the poem. *Venus is infatuated with Adonis*

Kisses, cold k. – ... a nun of winter's sisterhood kisses not more religiously...
"...a nun of winter's sisterhood kisses not more religiously; the very ice of chastity is in them." (AYLI.3.4)
In the play. *Celia refers to the kisses of the somewhat shy Orlando.*

Kissing, compared to the sun kissing a rose - So sweet a kiss the golden sun gives not to those fresh morning drops upon the rose.
"So sweet a kiss the golden sun gives not
To those fresh morning drops upon the rose." (LLL.4.3)
Use to praise her kissing skills.
In the play. *Ferdinand reads from a letter he has prepared for the princess of France.*

Kissing, invitation to kiss - Touch but my lips with those fair lips of thine...
"Touch but my lips with those fair lips of thine,
Though mine be not so fair, yet are they red
The kiss shall be thine own as well as mine." (V&A)
In the poem. *Venus' advances to Adonis.*

Kissing, invitation to mix kissing with gentle words - ... speak fair words, or else be mute: give me one kiss...
"Speak, fair; but speak fair words, or else be mute:
Give me one kiss, I'll give it thee again,
And one for interest, if thou wilt have twain." (V&A)

Kissing, invitation to sit down and kiss - Here come and sit, where never serpent hisses...
"Here come and sit, where never serpent hisses,
And being set, I'll smother thee with kisses" (V&A)

Kissing, k. a princess – O, le me kiss this princess of pure white, this seal of bliss!
"O, let me kiss
This princess of pure white, this seal of bliss!" (MND.3.2)
In the play. *Demetrius wakes up, sees Helena and falls immediately in love with her*

Kissing, prepared extremities for kissing - I know a lady in Venice would have walked barefoot

to Palestine for a touch of his nether lip.
"I know a lady in Venice would have walked barefoot
to Palestine for a touch of his nether lip." (OTH.4.3)
Change to 'I would walk barefoot to Palestine for a touch of your nether lip.'
In the play. *Emilia sings the praises of Ludovico to the unwary Desdemona.*

Kissing, the first kiss – The tender spring upon thy tempting lip shows thee unripe; yet mayst thou well be tasted.
"The tender spring upon thy tempting lip
Shows thee unripe; yet mayst thou well be tasted:" (V&A)
You may try the lines also with a more seasoned lover.
In the poem. *Venus is infatuated with Adonis.*

Kneeling, k. for request - … with no softer cushion than the flint, I kneel before thee.
"…with no softer cushion than the flint,
I kneel before thee" (COR.5.3)
Use for a request padded with rhetoric.
In the play. *Coriolanus' mother Volumnia pleads with her son not to attack Rome.*

Knock, hard k. on door - … That spirit's possessed with haste that wounds the unsisting postern with these strokes.
"what noise? That spirit's possessed with haste
That wounds the unsisting postern with these strokes" (MFM.4.2)
In the play. *Duke Vicentio is startled by the hasty and hurried knocking at the door by a messenger reminding the provost not to delay Claudio's execution.*

Knock, hard k. on door - What's he that knocks as he would beat down the gate?
"What's he that knocks as he would beat down the gate?" (TOS.5.1)
Comment on loud knocking
In the play. *Petruchio, Katharina and others beat loudly at Lucentio's door. A pedant inside is startled and asks who it could be.*

Knock, knock! - Knock, knock, knock! Who's there, i' the name of Beelzebub?
"…Knock, knock, knock! Who's there, i' the name of Beelzebub?" (M.3.3)
In the play. *The porter is late in answering the vehement knocking at the door by Macduff and Lennox*

Knowledge, bookish k. ineffective – Small have continual plodders ever won save base authority from others' books.
"Small have continual plodders ever won
Save base authority from others' books" (LLL1.1)
In the play. *Biron makes a point against bookish learning*

Knowledge, man well known in town - Thy very stones prate of my whereabout…
"Thy very stones prate of my whereabout,
And take the present horror from the time,
Which now suits with it." (M.2.1)
When you want to retire to a less obvious place to discuss a delicate matter because 'here the very stones …whereabouts'.
In the play. *Macbeth is tormented by conscience and fear just before murdering Duncan. 'Prate' = 'To tattle' and by metaphor 'to declare'. He makes an invocation to the earth that it may not hear his steps for fear of being discovered.*
"…Thou sure and firm-set earth,
Hear not my steps, which way they walk,

for fear
Thy very stones prate of my whereabout,
And take the present horror from the time,
Which now suits with it"

Knowledge, k. by fame, hearsay and reputation - this famous Duke of Milan of whom so often I have heard renown but never saw before.
"…She
Is daughter to this famous Duke of Milan,
Of whom so often I have heard renown,
But never saw before." (TEM.5.1)
When you are introduced to someone of whom you knew already something before hand (and you wish to flatter him/her a little). E.G. '(Name of person), of whom so often…before.'
In the play. *Ferdinand, re-united with the rest of the company begins to tell them about his encounter with Prospero and Miranda.*

Knowledge, search for k. - … and with satiety seeks to quench his thirst.
"Tell me thy mind, for I have Pisa left,
And am to Padua come, as he that leaves
A shallow place, to plunge him in the deep,
And with satiety seeks to quench his thirst." (TOS.1.1)
Answer to a college interviewer who asks you why you would like to enroll in one particular college. E.G. 'I have come from Padua to Princeton, as he that leaves…thirst'. See also entries for 'Education'
In the play. *Lucentio seeks Tranio's opinion on the idea of applying himself (Lucentio), to serious studies in Padua.*

Knowledge, she is the absolute source of your k. - **But thou art all my art, and dost advance as high as learning, my rude ignorance.**
"But thou art all my art, and dost advance
As high as learning, my rude ignorance" (SON 78)
You have a college education and she hasn't. She is concerned that the difference in education may affect your relationship. It could also work the other way around, when she has a degree and you haven't. Your accurate and emphatic rendition of these lines will erase the perception of any inequality in intellectual standards. See also 'Eyes, e. as a source of knowledge'.

Label, power of the label – … the king's name is a tower of strength.
"…the king's name is a tower of strength" (KRIII.5.3)
Use in an introduction as a comparison to praise the speaker if he/she indeed has been a tower of strength in the pursuit of a special and beneficial cause. Change 'the king's name' to the name of the praised speaker.
In the play. *At Bosworth Field Richard points out to his commanders that he, being the king, has a natural advantage over his adversaries in the pending battle.*

Labor, description of repetitive work – … from the rise to set sweats in the eye of Phoebus and all night…
"… like a lackey, from the rise to set
Sweats in the eye of Phoebus and all night
Sleeps in Elysium; next day after dawn,
Doth rise and help Hyperion to his horse,
And follows so the ever-running year,
With profitable labour, to his grave" (KHV.4.1)
Ironic answer to describe your daily toil, e.g. 'From the rise to set, I sweat in the eye of Phoebus and next day I help

Hyperion to his horse, and….ever-running year' Answer to 'What do you do for a living?'
In the play. *Part of King Henry's meditation on the life of the common man, compared to the life of a king, the night before the battle of Agincourt.*

Labor, heavy lifting, offer to carry her suitcase - I'd rather crack my sinews, break my back than you such dishonour undergo as I sit lazy by.
"I'd rather crack my sinews, break my back
Than you such dishonour undergo
As I sit lazy by." (TEM.3.1)
Offer to carry her suitcase, or do any other type of manual labor even if she insist on doing it herself.
The desire to achieve feats of valor as a tribute to the lady of one's heart is a recurrent theme in love relationships. Unable to think of one such feat, the composer Robert Schumann writes to Clara Wiek (1838), 'What would I not do for you, my own Clara! The knights of old were better off; they could go through fire or slay dragons and win their ladies, but we of today have to content ourselves with more prosaic methods, such as smoking fewer cigars, and the like. After all, though, we can love, knights or no knights; and so, as ever, only the times change, not men's hearts.'
See also 'Femininity and genetics.'
In the play. *Miranda plans to help Ferdinando move and stack some logs, a job or penance that Prospero, Miranda's father, has imposed upon him. Ferdinando gallantly refuses her offer of help.*

Labor, value of manual l. – … for there's no better sign of a brave mind than a hard hand.
"… for there's no better sign of a brave mind than a hard hand." (KHVI.p1.4.2)

In the play. *Bevis, a commoner in John Cade's rabble-rebel army comments on class distinction in England and the lack of labor representation in government.*

Labor, ultimate uselessness of patient l. – … they say, all the yarn she spun in Ulysses' absence did but fill Ithaca full of moths.
"You would be another Penelope: yet, they say, all the yarn she spun in Ulysses' absence did but fill Ithaca full of moths. (COR.1.3)
Prompt your lady friend to forgo her domestic duties for some fun in town.
In the play. *Valeria, a friend of Virgilia, wife of Coriolanus, prompts the reluctant and modest Virgilia to go out with her and celebrate the impending election of Coriolanus to high office. Valeria chides Virgilia who prefers to go on knitting.*

Ladies, l's man and yet not – I'll make my heaven in a lady's lap, and deck my body in gay ornaments…
"I'll make my heaven in a lady's lap,
And deck my body in gay ornaments,
And witch sweet ladies with my words and looks.
O miserable thought!" (KHVI.p3.3.2)
See also 'Love, making l. not war. - … He capers nimbly in a lady's chamber to the lascivious pleasing of a lute.' The first three lines can be an answer to 'What is your hobby?' E.G. 'I make my heaven in a lady's lap.'
In the play. *Richard III monologues and considers the options available to gain the crown from Edward, as well as the alternatives.*

Lady, l. killer – … a lady in Venice would have walked barefoot to Palestine for a touch of his nether lip.
"I know a lady in Venice would have walked barefoot to Palestine for a touch of his nether lip." (OTH.4.2)
In the play. *Emilia's opinion of Ludovico, an envoy from Venice to Cyprus.*

Lady, l. killer - ... sometimes the beam of her view gilded my foot, sometimes my portly belly.
"...(Page's wife) who even now gave me good eyes too, examined my parts with most judicious oeillades; sometimes the beam of her view gilded my foot, sometimes my portly belly" (MWM.1.5)
In the play. *Falstaff values his seductive power very highly. 'Oeillades' = 'Looks'.*

Lady, l. killer - This gallant pins the wenches on his sleeve; had he been Adam, he had tempted Eve.
"This gallant pins the wenches on his sleeve;
Had he been Adam, he had tempted Eve" (LLL.5.2)
See also entries for 'Character, skirt-chaser'.
In the play. *Biron's opinion of Boyet a lord in attendance to the Princess*

Lady, l. killer - This is the flower that smiles on every one to show his teeth as white as whale's bone.
"...the ladies call him sweet;
The stairs, as he treads on them, kiss his feet:
This is the flower that smiles on every one,
To show his teeth as white as whale's bone" (LLL.5.2)
In the play. *Biron's opinion of Boyet a lord in attendance to the Princess*

Lady, l. who behaved rottenly towards you - For sweetest things turn sourest by their deeds...
"For sweetest things turn sourest by their deeds,
Lilies that fester, smell far worse than weeds." (SON 94).
'To fester' = 'to rot'.

Laid on with a trowel - Well said: that was laid on with a trowel.
"Well said: that was laid on with a trowel" (AYLI.1.2)
In the play. *Touchstone is mimicking Le Beau in his pompous speech. Celia notices and comments.*

Lamentation, no need for help in l. - Give me no help in lamentation; I am not barren to bring forth complaints...
"Give me no help in lamentation;
I am not barren to bring forth complaints,
All springs reduce their currents to mine eyes,
That I, being govern'd by the watery moon,
May send forth plenteous tears to drown the world!" (KRIII.2.2)
In the play. *Q. Elizabeth, widow of Edward IV to Clarence's children. Clarence has been murdered by Richard III's hired assassins.*

Lamentations, generating l. - I am your sorrow's nurse, and will pamper it with lamentations.
"... I am your sorrow's nurse,
And I will pamper it with lamentations." (KRIII.2.2)
In the play. *The Duchess of York has lost son and King Edward IV, died of illness, as well as Clarence, killed by order of her other son Richard III.*

Land, l. preferable to sea - ... would I give a thousand furlongs of sea for an acre of barren ground...
"Now would I give a thousand furlongs of sea for an acre of barren ground, long heath, brown furze, any thing... I would fain die a dry death." (TEM.1.1)
In the play. *Gonzalo views on the sea in the middle of a sea storm.*

Land, value of l. lowered - ... you may buy land now as cheap as stinking mackerel.
"… you may buy land now as cheap as stinking mackerel" (KHIV.p1.2.4)
It can apply to any cheap commodity or a commodity that suddenly lost value.
In the play. *The perceived imminence of a war (between King Henry IV and the rebels) has cheapened the value of fixed assets.*

Language, hackers of English – ... let them question: let them keep their limbs whole and hack our English.
"…let them question: let them keep their limbs whole and hack our English" (MWW.3.1)
In the play. *The Host intervenes to bring peace in angry debate between Dr. Caius (a Frenchman), and Hugh Evans (a Welshman). Both of them make fritters of English'*

Language, his English marginal – ... at the taunt of one that makes fritters of English.
PARSON EVANS. Seese is not good to give putter; your pelly is all putter.
FALSTAFF. Sees and putter! have I lived to stand at the taunt of one that makes fritters of English?" (MWW.5.5)
Use Falstaff's answer to rebut an accusation from a political enemy with questionable communication skills, e.g. 'He is one that makes fritters of English.' If you cannot imitate the Welsh accent you can try German.
In the play. *Falstaff's reply to a remark by Hugh Evans, a Welshman, whose English pronunciation is questionable, ('Sees' is 'cheese'). Hugh Evans pokes fun at Falstaff after the pranks played on Falstaff by Mrs. Ford and Mrs. Page.*

Language, insubordination in l. - ... Language unmannerly, yea, such which breaks the sides of loyalty and almost appears in loud rebellion.
"… even he escapes not
Language unmannerly, yea, such which breaks
The sides of loyalty, and almost appears
In loud rebellion." (KHVIII, 1.2)
In the play. *Q. Katherine tells the King about his subjects' anger about taxation - they vent their anger at Cardinal Wolsey but also at the King.*

Language, l. of peasants – Talk like the vulgar sort of market men…
"Talk like the vulgar sort of market men
That come to gather money for their corn." (KHVI.p1.3.2)
In the play. *Joan of Arc instructs French soldiers how to adopt the disguise (and speech) of peasant while entering the city of Rouen.*

Language, no correct l. adequate to describe the fault - ... There is not chastity enough in language without offence to utter them.
"…they are not to be named, my lord, Not to be spoke of;
There is not chastity enough in language
Without offence to utter them" (MAAN.4.1)
In the play. *Don Pedro refers to the alleged encounters between Hero and her lover. Actually it was not Hero but Margaret*

Language, risque' l. justified - ... If I chance to talk a little wild, forgive me, I had it from my father.
"By your leave, sweet ladies:
If I chance to talk a little wild, forgive me;
I had it from my father." (KHVIII, 1.4)

You may change the figure or character from whom you alleged to have acquired your freedom in expression.
In the play. *Lord Sands to the ladies between whom he has seated himself.*

Lascivious remark – That's a lascivious apprehension…. So thou apprehendest it: take it for thy labour.
TIMON. That's a lascivious apprehension.
APEMANTUS. So thou apprehendest it: take it for thy labour. (PER.1.1)
Applicable to generic remarks on your statements. E.G. 'That's a bad remark' Answer, 'So thou remark's it, take it for thy labor'.
In the play. *Apemantus made a generic and mildly scurrilous remark on women.*

Last, not being the l. better than nothing - Not being the worst stands in some rank of praise.
"… not being the worst
Stands in some rank of praise." (KL.2.4)
Put a good face on a mediocre outcome. See also 'Bad, from bad to good better than from good to bad - … The lamentable change is from the best; the worst returns to laughter.'
In the play. *Lear thinks that Goneril is better than Regan therefore Goneril stands in some rank of praise.*

Latin, adequacy in L. - Satis quod sufficit.
"Satis quod sufficit." (LLL.5.1)
Latin alternate to 'enough is enough'.
In the play. *Holofernes and Nathaniel engage in another exchange of pompous platitudes.*

Latin, few words as a sign of wisdom - Vir sapit, qui pauca loquitur.
"Vir sapit, qui pauca loquitur." (LLL.4.2)
Answer the question, 'Why do you not speak?' See also entries for 'Silence'

In the play. *Nathaniel and Holofernes exchange words of wisdom. The Latin sentence means 'That man who speaks little is wise'.*

Latin, incorrect L. - I smell false Latin.
"I smell false Latin." (LLL.5.1)
Express your skepticism at a proposal or idea even if expressed in English. And if he says 'But I am speaking English' reply 'Perhaps, but I cannot understand you.'
In the play. *Holofernes comments on a sarcasm by Costard.*

Latin, L. for the lower middle classes - 'Hang-hog' is Latin for bacon, I warrant you.
EVANS. I pray you, have your remembrance, child; Accusativo, hing, hang, hog.
MISTRESS QUICKLY. Hang hog is Latin for bacon, I warrant you." (MWW.4.1)
Use as an analogy to describe ignorance and report the exchange in full.
In the play. *The Welsh Master Evans (whose accent is reproduced by the misspellings) teaches Latin to William Page, son of Mr. and Mrs. Page. But the Welsh pronunciation prompts Mistress Quickly to deliver a sarcastic remark and to give her own interpretation to Evan's Latin lesson.*

Latin, no l. please we are British – … no Latin; I am not such a truant since my coming as not to know the language I have lived in…
"…no Latin;
I am not such a truant since my coming,
As not to know the language I have lived in:
A strange tongue makes my cause more strange, suspicious;
Pray, speak in English" (KHVIII.3.1)
In the play. *Queen Katherine to Cardinal Wolsey who is her political enemy and addresses her in Latin.*

Laugh, laughable matter or character - If you desire the spleen, and will laugh yourself into stitches, follow me.
"If you desire the spleen, and will laugh yourself into stitches, follow me." (TN.3.2)
In the play. *Maria refers to the conceited Malvolio who has been led to believe that his mistress loves him. He completely falls for the spoof and shows up wearing ridiculous yellow stockings.* 'Spleen' here stands for 'fits of laughter'.

Laughing, l. matter for a long time - …argument for a week, laughter for a month and a good jest for ever.
"… it would be argument for a week, laughter for a month and a good jest for ever." (KHIVp1.2.2)
In the play. *Prince Harry meditates on the prank that he has played on Falstaff.*

Laughing, reasons for not l. - … and for mine own part, I durst not laugh, for fear of opening my lips and receiving the bad air.
"…and for mine own part, I durst not laugh, for fear of opening my lips and receiving the bad air." (JC.1.2)
Scold your political adversary for his laughable and ridiculous statements.
In the play. *Cassius did not laugh at the exalted flatteries to Caesar as displayed and uttered by the adoring masses with a 'a deal of stinking breath '*

Laughter, fit of l. - I am stabbed with laughter.
"O, I am stabbed with laughter." (LLL.5.2)
Elegant alternate to 'it makes me laugh'.
In the play. *Boyet announces that king and company is arriving attired in various disguises and masks and making asses of themselves. The king and his company organize a ridiculous masquerade to approach and gain the attention of the Princess of Navarre and her attendant ladies.*

Laughter, forced l. - … the heaving of my lungs provokes me to ridiculous smiling.
"... the heaving of my lungs provokes me to ridiculous smiling." (LLL.3.1)
Sarcastic alternate to 'It makes me laugh' or when you wish to deny that you are laughing.
In the play. *Armado makes himself ridiculous with his speech.*

Laughter, l. not called for - Laughest thou, wretch? thy mirth shall turn to moan.
"Laughest thou, wretch? thy mirth shall turn to moan." (KHVI.p1.2.3)
In the play. *The Countess of Auvergne to Talbot whom she thinks to have lured into a trap.*

Laughter, laughing to tears - … I must confess, made nine eyes water; but more merry tears the passion of loud laughter never shed.
"… I must confess,
Made mine eyes water, but more merry tears
The passion of loud laughter never shed." (MND.5.1)
Sarcastic answer to the question, 'Did you like the joke?'
In the play. *Philostrate gives his reaction and a critical account of the play rehearsal by the amateurs acting group.*

Laughter, opportunity for l. not to be missed - I will not give my part of this sport for a pension of thousands to be paid by the Sophy.
"I will not give my part of this sport for a pension of thousands to be paid by the Sophy." (TN.2.5)
Alternative to 'I won't miss this for the world'

In the play. *Fabian prepares himself to the laughter that Malvolio will provide by acting on the belief that Olivia loves him, Malvolio. The Sophy refers to an impossibly rich Persian king.*

Law, anarchy as a consequence of unjust law – When law can do no right, let it be lawful that law bar no wrong.
"When law can do no right,
Let it be lawful that law bar no wrong."
(KJ.3.1)
Justify taking the law into your own hands. See also 'Values, perversion of v. - Fair is foul, and foul is fair'. *** 'Dispute, d. and disagreement on right and wrong - If that be right which Warwick says is right, there is no wrong, but everything is right.'
In the play. *Constance fights for the rights of her young son Arthur to the throne of England.*

Law, authorities making their will the l. - ... bidding the law make court'sy to their will...
"... O perilous mouths,
That bear in them one and the self-same tongue,
Either of condemnation or approof;
Bidding the law make court'sy to their will:
Hooking both right and wrong to the appetite,
To follow as it draws!" (MFM.2.4)
In the play. *Isabella is disgusted with the hypocrisy of Angelo.*

Law, corruption of the l, - what plea so tainted and corrupt... being seasoned with a gracious voice.
"In law, what plea so tainted and corrupt,
But, being seasoned with a gracious voice,
Obscures the show of evil?"
(MOV.2.1)
Make a point about law-sanctioned injustice.

In the play. *The fair Portia will marry him who solves a riddle. Before attempting to do so, Bassanio meditates on some important truths.*

Law, l. acts on what is visible – What's open made to justice, that justice seizes... The jewel that we find, we stoop and take't...
"... What's open made to justice,
That justice seizes: what know the laws
That thieves do pass on thieves? 'Tis very pregnant,
The jewel that we find, we stoop and take't
Because we see it; but what we do not see
We tread upon, and never think of it."
(MOV.2.1)
In the play. *Angelo justifies to Escalus the legal point that the law punishes what it sees. That is, unseen crime goes unpunished.*

Law, l. and order – There is a law in each well-order'd nation to curb those raging appetites...
"There is a law in each well-order'd nation
To curb those raging appetites that are
Most disobedient and refractory."
(TC.2.2)
In the play. *Hector argues for returning Helen to the Greeks, after all the 'moral laws of nature and of nations' call for a woman (Helen) to stay with her husband.*

Law, l. and precedent – 'Twill be recorded for a precedent, and many an error by the same example...
"'Twill be recorded for a precedent,
And many an error by the same example
Will rush into the state: it cannot be."
(MOV.4.1)
In the play. *Portia (disguised as a male lawyer) skillfully argues her case to entrap Shylock.*

Law, l. discriminatory and against the poor - ... here's a fish hangs in the net....
"... here's a fish hangs in the net, like a poor man's right in the law; 't will hardly come out." (PER.2.1)
An example of the disproportionate balance of power between the common citizen and the state.
In the play. *A wave carries to shore Pericles' armor and this prompts the fisherman to deliver a satire on costume.*

Law, l. maybe right but judges questionable - ... (the law) has done upon the premises, but justice; but those that sought it I could wish more Christians.
"... (the law) has done upon the premises, but justice;
But those that sought it I could wish more christians." (KHVIII.2.1)
Question the judicial process, the questionable evidence and the harshness of the sentence
In the play. *Buckingham' last words after he is condemned to death upon charges of treason trumped up by Cardinal Wolsey.*

Law, l. must be enforced - We must not make a scarecrow of the law...
"We must not make a scarecrow of the law,
Setting it up to fear the birds of prey,
And let it keep one shape, till custom make it
Their perch and not their terror." (MFM.2.1)
In the play. *Angelo explains to Escalus his intended law enforcement policies.*

Law, l. not allowing for justification - I cannot justify whom the law condemns.
"I cannot justify whom the law condemns." (KHVI p2.2.3)
If this is your opinion, you may also keep in mind the other different point of view, see 'Law, anarchy as a consequence of unjust law.'
In the play. *Humphrey of Gloucester to wife Eleanor, arrested for witchcraft and sedition after a setup by Gloucester's enemies. Gloucester only partly realizes that his enemies will do him in shortly.*

Law, l. to repress base passions - There is a law in each well ordered nation, to curb these raging appetites...
"There is a law in each well ordered nation,
To curb these raging appetites that are
Most disobedient and refractory." (TC.2.2)
Explain the presence of laws to restrain man from 'raging appetites'
In the play. *Hector appeals to a universal law intended to reign in dangerous tendencies.*

Law, l. vs. personal will - I have been a truant to the law....
"I have been a truant to the law,
And never yet could frame my will to it;
And therefore, frame the law unto my will." (KHVI.p1.2.4)
An assertive statement when someone brings out a questionable legal argument or cavil to derail your plans
In the play. *Somerset and Plantagenet are involved in a dispute and Suffolk declines to pronounce judgement.*

Law, precedent in l. – ... no power in Venice can alter a decree established: 'twill be recorded for a precedent...
"...there is no power in Venice
Can alter a decree established:
'Twill be recorded for a precedent,
And many an error by the same example
Will rush into the state: it cannot be" (MOV.4.1)

In the play. *Portia (disguised as a male lawyer) states that Shylock's bond cannot be reversed.*

Law, punishment as a deterrent – Those many had not dared to do that evil…
"The law hath not been dead, though it hath slept:
Those many had not dared to do that evil,
If the first that did the edict infringe
Had answer'd for his deed" (MFM.2.1)
In the play. *Angelo explains why he must enforce the law against Claudio as a deterrent.*

Law, rules of law abolished - the wild dog shall flesh his tooth on every innocent.
"For the fifth Harry from curbed licence plucks
The muzzle of restraint, and the wild dog
Shall flesh his tooth on every innocent." (KHIV.p2.4.4)
Decry the implementation of a more liberal law.
In the play. *London, the Jerusalem chamber at court. The ailing King upbraids his son ('fifth Harry') not knowing that Harry is completely reformed.*

Law, trial jury may include criminals – The jury, passing on the prisoner's life, may in the sworn twelve have a thief or two…
"The jury, passing on the prisoner's life,
May in the sworn twelve have a thief or two
Guiltier than him they try" (MOV.2.1)
In the play. *Angelo justifies to Escalus the legal point that the law punishes what it sees. That is, unseen crime, even by members of the jury, goes unpunished.*

Law, unjust l. - … if I shall be condemn'd upon surmises… I tell you 'tis rigor and not law.
"…if I shall be condemn'd
Upon surmises, all proofs sleeping else
But what your jealousies awake, I tell you
'Tis rigor and not law." (WT.3.2)
In the play. *Leontes, king of Sicilia, and raving mad of jealousy, indicts his virtuous wife Hermione. She claims her innocence and condemns the unjust law that condemned her.*

Laws, l. on the book but not enforced – … the enrolled penalties which have, like unscour'd armour, hung by the wall…
"…the enrolled penalties
Which have, like unscour'd armour, hung by the wall
So long that nineteen zodiacs have gone round
And none of them been worn" (MFM.1.2)
In the play. *Claudio, condemned for fornication, explains to friend Lucio his theory as to the reason for the condemnation. See 'Behavior, tyrannical b. of a newly appointed leader – Whether it be fault and glimpse of newness…'*

Laws, l. disregarded – I have seen corruption boil and bubble till it o'er-run the stew…
"I have seen corruption boil and bubble
Till it o'er-run the stew; laws for all faults,
But faults so countenanced, that the strong statutes
Stand like the forfeits in a barber's shop,
As much in mock as mark." (MFM.5.1)
In the play. *Duke Vicentio took a leave of absence to observe life in Vienna and reaches some uncomfortable conclusions. 'Forfeits' in a barber's shop stands for 'conditions of operation', not to be taken seriously.*

Laws, l. to be enforced - …our decrees, dead to infliction, to themselves are dead…
"… our decrees,
Dead to infliction, to themselves are dead
And liberty plucks justice by the nose.
The baby beats the nurse, and quite athwart
Goes all decorum." (MFM.1.3)
Use as a leverage to enforce a policy that is now lax
In the play. *The Duke makes a position statement to Friar Thomas.*

Laws, questionable effects of repressive l. against licentious behavior - …. it is impossible to extirp it quite, friar, till eating and drinking be put down.
"… it is impossible to extirp it quite, friar, till eating and drinking be put down." (MFM.3.2)
In the play. *Claudio's opinion about Angelo's laws prohibiting unlawful sex.*

Lawyers, tricks of l. - Is not this a lamentable thing, that of the skin of an innocent lamb… should undo a man?
"Is not this a lamentable thing, that of the skin of an innocent lamb should be made parchment? That parchment, being scribbled o'er, should undo a man?" ((KHVI p2.4.2)
In the play. *The rebel John Cade gives reasons for why all lawyers should be killed.* See entry for 'Opinion, your op. on lawyers - The first thing we do, let's kill all the lawyers.'

Leader, metaphor for a l. – When that the general is not like the hive…what honey is expected?
"When that the general is not like the hive
To whom the foragers shall all repair,
What honey is expected?" (TC.1.3)

See also "Anxiety, a. about what may happen at the office while you are away - I am questioned by my fears, of what may chance or breed upon our absence'.
In the play. *After Agamennon and Nestor, it is Ulysses' turn to address the unruly Greek forces.*

Leadership, consequences of a lack of l. – Strength should be lord of imbecility…right and wrong…should lose their names…
"Strength should be lord of imbecility,
And the rude son should strike his father dead:
Force should be right; or rather, right and wrong,
Between whose endless jar justice resides,
Should lose their names, and so should justice too." (TC.1.3)
Strength as a lord of imbecility is a good put-down for any bully or for arrogance in general. Justice's residence is an elegant characterization.
In the play. *Ulysses delivers a motivational speech to the disaffected Greeks.*

Leadership, consequences of an absent leader - Indeed a sheep doth very often stray if the shepherd be awhile away.
SPEED. … And I have played the sheep in losing him
PROTEUS. Indeed a sheep doth very often stray,
If the shepherd be awhile away." (TGV.1.1)
Explain why you have to get back to the office. 'A sheep doth often stray, away'. See also 'Anxiety, a. about what may happen at the office while you are away.'
In the play. *Speed is Valentine's master and doesn't know where his master is.*

Leadership, l. indispensable - … and knowing this kingdom is without a head…

"...And knowing this kingdom is without a head
Like goodly buildings left without a roof
Soon fall to ruin." (PER.2.4)
Prompt the appointment of a capable manager.
In the play. *In Tyre, the noblemen demand the presence of a leader. They want Helicanus to assume all the responsibilities of the absent king to preserve the kingdom from 'fall to ruin'.*

Leadership, wishing for a l. change - ... a swift blessing may soon return to this our suffering country...
"...a swift blessing
May soon return to this our suffering country
Under a hand accursed!" (M.3.6)
In the play. *Lennox wishes for a change in leadership in the country now ruled by the tyrant Macbeth.*

Learning, a man of commendable l. - ... learning, the greatness whereof I cannot enough commend.
"...his own learning, the greatness whereof I cannot enough commend." (MOV.4.1)
Introduction for a scholar, e.g. 'What can I say of his learning?' 'His learning...commend'.
In the play. *A court clerk reads a letter from Bellario, an attorney from Padua. Bellario commends the learning and the ability of his assistant whom he has dispatched to Venice to arbitrate the case of Shylock vs. Antonio. The assistant is actually Portia in disguise.*

Learning, l. as an addition to our personality – Learning is but an adjunct to ourselves, and where we are, our learning likewise is.
"Learning is but an adjunct to ourselves,
And where we are, our learning likewise is" (LLL.4.3)
In the play. *Biron gives his opinion on the king's proposed oath of learning and abstinence.*

Learning, power of l. - O this learning, what a thing it is.
"O this learning, what a thing it is!" (TOS.1.2)
Sarcastic comment to a stupid statement.
In the play. *Gremio comments on words well delivered by Lucentio.*

Learning, power of l. better displayed after a drink – ... and learning a mere hoard of gold kept by a devil, till sack commences it and sets it in act and use."
"...and learning a mere hoard of gold kept by a devil, till sack commences it and sets it in act and use."
(KHIV.p2.4.3)
In the play. *Falstaff on the several virtues of wine. See 'Wine, positive effects of w. – A good sherris-sack hath a two fold operation in it...'*

Leaving the country - then thus I turn me from my country's light.
"Then thus I turn me from my country's light,
To dwell in solemn shades of endless night." (KRII.1.3)
Parting speech when your international assignment brings you away from your base for some time. See also entries for 'Travel'.
In the play. *Mowbray's answer to the King who has banished Mowbray from England forever.*

Leg pulling, response to l.p.– Make yourself mirth with your particular fancy and leave me out on't.
"Make yourself mirth with your particular fancy,
And leave me out on't" (KHVIII.2.3)
In the play. *Anne Boleyn to lady courtier who is chiding Anne for having been appointed Marchioness of Pembroke by King Henry.*

Lesson, l. given was understood - I shall th'effect of this good lesson keep as watchman to my heart.
"I shall th'effect of this good lesson keep
As watchman to my heart." (H.1.3)
Answer to an advice or admonition or counsel.
In the play. *Ophelia acknowledging Laertes' advice.*

Let's do it quickly. See 'Expeditiousness - let's do it quickly'.

Let's get out of here – ... To seek the empty, vast and wandering air.
"...To seek the empty, vast and wandering air..." (KRIII.1.4)
Answer to 'where are you going?' when you are leaving the meeting.
In the play. *Clarence recounts his nightmare to guard Brakenbury.*

Letter, ending of l. - Your ladyship's in all desired employment.
"...Your ladyship's in all desired employment" (LLL.4.2)
In the play. *Holofernes reads from a letter written by Biron to Rosaline.*

Letter, l. too long - The letter is too long by half a mile.
"The letter is too long by half a mile." (LLL.5.2)
Comment on a verbose and lengthy report. See also 'Man, a verbose m.'
In the play. *Maria's comment on the letter sent her by Longaville.*

Letter, l. written immediately fresh from receiving ideas and inspiration - I'll write straight; the matter's in my head and in my heart.
"I'll write straight;
The matter's in my head and in my heart. " (AYLI.3.5)
Take the time and write down what is in your mind before you forget it.
In the play. *Phebe remembers the scorning words the disguised Rosalind used with Phebe. Phebe did not reply then but will reply now with a letter.*

Letter, silly l. - What plume of feathers is he that indited this letter?
"What plume of feathers is he that indited this letter?
What vane? what weathercock."(LLL.4.1)
In the play. *The Princess' reaction after her assistant Boyet ends reading a letter written by Armado.*

Liar, a breaker of promises - He professes no keeping of oaths; in breaking them he is stronger than Hercules.
"He professes no keeping of oaths; in breaking them he is stronger than Hercules." (AWEW.4.3)
Define a liar.
In the play. *Believing his capturers to be the enemy, Parolles, to save his own skin, does not hesitate to badmouth Bertram, his friend and protector.*

Liar, a well known l. - He's quoted for a most perfidious slave, whose nature sickens, but to speak the truth.
"He's quoted for a most perfidious slave,
Whose nature sickens, but to speak the truth." (AWEW.5.3)
Characterize a scoundrel and a liar.
In the play. *Parolles is back again, now called in as a witness to Bertram's shenanigans with Diana in Florence and Bertram has now learned what Parolles really is.*

Liar, an endless l. - An infinite and endless liar.
"... an infinite and endless liar, an hourly promise-breaker, the owner of no one good quality worthy your lordship's entertainment."
(AWEW.3.6)

When you want to be hard on a liar.
In the play. *A French lord who knows Parolles alerts Bertram as to Parolles' true nature.*

Liar, an endless l. who once makes an exception - This is the first truth that ever thine own tongue was guilty of.
"This is the first truth that ever thine own tongue was guilty of."
(AWEW.4.1)
When a habitual liar tells something true for a change.
In the play. *Unseen by a French lord, Parolles tells himself that his bragging has placed him into danger, and that is the truth.*

Liar, habitual l. –... and every third word a lie.
"… and every third word a lie."
(KHIV.p2.3.2)
In the play. *Now in Gloucestershire at Justice Shallow's house, Falstaff meditates on Shallow's lies about his own youth.*

Liar, imaginative l. - ... return with an invention and clap upon you two or three probable lies.
"…return with an invention and clap upon you two or three probable lies"
(AWEW.3.6)
In the play. *A lord predicts the predictable cowardly outcome of Parolle's exploit to recover a drum lost to the enemy.*

Liar, making allowances for some lies and punishment for an incorrigible l. – ... and uses a known truth to pass a thousand nothings…
"A good traveller is something at the latter end of a dinner; but one that lies three thirds, and uses a known truth to pass a thousand nothings with, should be once heard and thrice beaten." (AWEW.2.5)
Stigmatize a habitual liar. E.G. 'He is a liar and a man that lies three thirds of the time and uses … beaten'.

In the play. *Bertram is leaving for Italy with Parolles and Lafeu does not miss the occasion to point out to Bertram that Parolles is a liar.*

Liar, pathologic l. - ... and swear the lies he forges.
"…and swear the lies he forges."
(AWEW.4.1)
Condemn an untrustworthy adversaries or a group, e.g. 'Not only they lie but they swear the lies they forge'
In the play. *A French lord near Florence comments on Parolles, the notorious liar*

Liar, twenty times a l. – If thou deny'st it twenty times, thou liest…
"If thou deny'st it twenty times, thou liest;
And I will turn thy falsehood to thy heart,
Where it was forged, with my rapier's point" (KRII.4.1)
See also 'Accusation, a. rejected – I have a thousand spirits in my breast to answer twenty thousand such as you.'
In the play. *Lord Fitzwater confirms Bagot's accusations of lying aimed at Lord Aumerle.*

Liars – men of less truth than tongue.
"…old men of less truth than tongue"
(SON 17)
Apply to any liar when you want to define him indirectly, e.g. 'He is a man of less truth than tongue'

Liberality, l. excessive - ... Plutus the God of gold is but his steward.
"... He outgoes
The very heart of kindness. Plutus the God of gold
Is but his steward." (TOA.1.1)
Describe a big spender or how your ex-wife describes your status when applying for alimony.
In the play. *Timon's character described by a character called 'First Lord'.*

Liberty, fighting to maintain one's l. - We'll mingle our bloods together in the earth, from whence we had our being and our birth.
PERICLES I do not doubt thy faith; But should he wrong my liberties in my absence?
HELICANUS We'll mingle our bloods together in the earth, From whence we had our being and our birth. (PER.1.2)
In the play. *The potential killer of liberty is Antioch.*

License, l. to use humor limited - Great men may jest with saints; 'tis wit in them but in the less foul profanation.
"Great men may jest with saints; 'tis wit in them,
But in the less foul profanation." (MFM.2.2)
In the play. *Isabella pleads with Angelo for mercy for her brother Claudio. The jest consists in equating Claudio with Angelo.*

License, l. without punishment - ... when evil deeds have their permissive pass and not the punishment.
"... for we bid this be done,
When evil deeds have their permissive pass
And not the punishment" (MFM.1.3)
If you are a red neck conservative
In the play. *The Duke will let Angelo be the hard law enforcer as opposed to the Duke himself, who was quite tolerant during his tenure.*

Lies, l. from a fat man - These lies are like the father that begets them; gross as a mountain, open, palpable.
"These lies are like the father that begets them; gross as a mountain, open, palpable.

…this huge hill of flesh." (KHIV p2.4)
When the liar is fat.

In the play. *After Falstaff gives a completely false account of what happened at Gadshill, the Prince of Wales intervenes to expose Falstaff for the liar that he is.*

Lies, l. well constructed - ... lies well steeled with weighty arguments.
" ...to urge his hatred more of Clarence
With lies well steeled with weighty arguments. " (KRIII.1.1)
Use as a charge of lying, e.g. 'these are lies well steeled with weighty arguments, but still lies'
In the play. *Richard plans to further inflame the king against his brother Clarence. Richard will then assassinate Clarence and pretend to have done so to follow the directives of the king.*

Lies, letter or document filled to the brim with l. - ... and as many lies as will lie in thy sheet of paper, although the sheet were big enough for the bed of Ware...
"... and as many lies as will lie in thy sheet of paper, although the sheet were big enough for the bed of Ware in England, set them down." (TN.3.2)
Denounce the report or document as being full of lies. 'There are as many lies in thy sheet of paper, as if the sheet were big enough for the bed of Ware in England.' The bed of Ware, in Hertfordshire, was a Guinness record holder in its category, being ten feet square, and able to accommodate twelve people.
In the play. *Sir Toby counsels Aguecheek to send a letter to Viola/Cesario challenging her/him to a duel. The letter should be filled with lies about the prowess and rage of the (otherwise coward) Aguecheek.*

Lies, manufacturing l. – ... Made such a sinner of his memory to credit his own lie.
"... like one

Who having unto truth, by telling of it,
Made such a sinner of his memory,
To credit his own lie." (TEM.1.2)
Elegant way to point to a liar. 'You have made such a sinner of your memory to credit your own lie.'
In the play. *Prospero refers to Antonio, his brother, who surreptitiously usurped the dukedom that belonged to Prospero.*

Lies, marketing l. – Let me have no lying: it becomes none but tradesmen.
"…Let me have no lying: it becomes none but tradesmen"(WT.4.3)
Try 'this is typical marketing lying and I say 'let me have…tradesmen'
In the play. *Autolycus, a liar and a thief himself, engages the clown in some banter.*

Lies, quaint l. - ... and tell quaint lies how honourable ladies sought my love.
"…and tell quaint lies,
How honourable ladies sought my love" (MOV.3.4)
See also 'Lies, l. well constructed'. Combine the two, e.g. 'There are quaint lies and lies steeled with weighty arguments.'
In the play. *Portia anticipates what pretences she will come up with when wearing a man's attire. This, the man's attire, is part of her scheme to foil Shylock's effort at exacting a pound of flesh from Antonio.*

Lies, the seven degrees of lying – Reply churlish... reproof valiant... counter-cheque quarrelsome…
JAQUES But, for the seventh cause; how did you find the
quarrel on the seventh cause?
TOUCHSTONE Upon a lie seven times removed:--…- as thus, sir. I did dislike the cut of a certain courtier's beard: he sent me word, if I said his beard was not cut well, he was in the mind it was: this is called the <u>Retort Courteous</u>.
If I sent him word again 'it was not well cut,' he would send me word, he cut it to please himself: this is called the <u>Quip Modest</u>.
If again 'it was not well cut,' he disabled my judgment: this is called the <u>Reply Churlish</u>.
If again 'it was not well cut,' he would answer, I spake not true: this is called the <u>Reproof Valiant</u>.
If again 'it was not well cut,' he would say I lied: this is called the <u>Counter-cheque Quarrelsome</u>:
and so to the Lie Circumstantial and the Lie Direct. (AYLI.5)
You may read the quote in a presentation to illustrate the fine degrees among lies and how people respond to them. Or you can extract as needed. E.g. if someone questions your judgment you may say, 'Yours is called the 'reply churlish'', etc. See also 'If, the power of 'if''
In the play. *Touchstone gives a precise step-by-step analysis of the development of a quarrel. It evolves from a person having a differing opinion to the same person being accused of straight lying. In Touchstone's analysis contenders come to blows once they get to the 'Lie Circumstantial and the Lie Direct'. A quarrel, however, can still be avoided by using the particle 'If', see 'If, the power of 'if''*

Life, a combination of good and bad - The web of our life is of a mingled yarn, good and ill go together...
"The web of our life is of a mingled yarn, good and ill go together: our virtues would be proud, if our faults whipped them not, and our crimes would despair, if they were not cherished by our virtues" (AWEW.3.3)
Add a philosophical explanation to the alternation of pleasant and unpleasant events in life.
In the play. *Two French Lords comment on the virtues and faults of Bertram, the French count who has deserted his wife. The mingled yarn*

referred to here is the valor Bertram has displayed in battle at Florence (the good) and the shame he has incurred by his behavior towards Helen (the ill) - behavior that has cost him the (alleged) death of his wife and the displeasure of the King.

Life, an alternation of joys and sorrows - Thus sometimes hath the brightest day a cloud; and after summer evermore succeeds…
"Thus sometimes hath the brightest day a cloud;
And after summer evermore succeeds
Barren winter, with his wrathful nipping cold:
So cares and joys abound, as seasons fleet." (KHVI p2.2.4)
Use the first line to soften the impact of a mildly unpleasant event.
In the play. *Gloucester takes a philosophical view on the events that caused his ambitious wife to be arrested and banished to the Isle of Man. Queen Margaret hated her and also plots against the unwary Gloucester.*

Life, desire for a l. with love and honor – Love they to live that love and honour have.
"Love they to live that love and honour have" (KRII.2.1)
In the play. *Gaunt's parting words to visiting King Richard.*

Life, end of l. - My life is run his compass…
"This day I breathed first: time is come round,
And where I did begin, there shall I end;
My life is run his compass" (JC.5.1)
In the play. *Cassius senses that the battle at Philippi against Antony's forces is lost and comments on his own end.*

Life, everything has an end - all that lives must die passing through nature to eternity.
"Thou know'st 'tis common - all that lives must die,
Passing through nature to eternity.** (H.1.2)
Comment on the end of a project or an era or a procedure. Or a reply to someone who is complaining about change, 'but before we did it differently'. See also 'Custom, c. as an obstacle to positive change - What custom wills, in all things should we do't, the dust of antique time would lie unswept…' – 'Death, questions about the afterlife - … When we have shuffled off this mortal coil…'
In the play. *Hamlet continues to mourn the death of the king his father and the Queen tries to make him see the matter rationally.*

Life, everything has an end – We cannot hold mortality's strong hand.
"We cannot hold mortality's strong hand" (KJ.4.2)
In the play. *Young Prince Arthur is dead and King John gives the news to his court. He ordered Hubert to kill Arthur but now he pretends that sickness was the cause of Arthur's death.*

Life, getting to the Autumn of life - I have lived long enough: my way of life is fallen into the sear, the yellow leaf.
I have lived long enough: my way of life
Is fall'n into the sear, the yellow leaf" (M.5.3)
Part of your retirement speech
In the play. *Under siege at Dunsinane, Macbeth begins to perceive that the end is near. 'Sear' is the state or condition of a yellow leaf.*

Life, longing to hear her life story - I long hear the story of your life, which must take the ear strangely.
"…I long
To hear the story of your life, which must
Take the ear strangely." (TEM.5.1)

She had an apparently varied life including travels, different jobs etc. Indicate strong interest in her biography. Possible use for an introduction to a speaker reputed for interesting adventures, e.g. 'And now…we long to hear…strangely'.
In the play. *Prospero gets ready to tell Alonso the story of his life in the island where he, Prospero, landed a long time ago. Alonso indicates his keen interest to listen and know more.*

Life, manly approach to unexpected events, however rough - Come what come may, time and the hour runs through the roughest day.
"Come what come may,
Time and the hour runs through the roughest day." (M.1.3)
See also 'Prediction, desire to know in advance.'
In the play. *Macbeth does not what to make of the prediction of the witches and takes a stoic approach to the situation.*

Life, married l. affecting negatively behavior of men and women - Men are April when they woo, December when they wed.
"…men are April when they woo, December when they wed: maids are May when they are maids, but the sky changes when they are wives." (AYLI.4.1)
Select the applicable section depending on whether you are a he or a she. Or if you are constitutionally opposed to the institution of marriage use the quote in its entirety to support your point.
In the play. *Rosalind banters with Orlando with whom she is madly in love and whom she will end up marrying anyway.*

Life, not really a l. - Canst thou believe thy living is a life, so stinkingly depending?
"Canst thou believe thy living is a life, So stinkingly depending?" (MFM.3.2)
In the play. *Duke-Vicentio in disguise questions the bawd Pompey.*

Life, personal view of l., afraid of oneself - I had as lief not be, as live to be in awe of such a thing as I myself.
"I cannot tell what you and other men Think of this life; but, for my single self,
I had as lief not be as live to be
In awe of such a thing as I myself."
(JC.1.2)
In the play. *Cassius explains his views on life to Brutus. 'I had as lief' = 'I should like as much'*

Life, pessimistic view of l. - … each hour's joy wrecked with a week of teen.
"… each hour's joy wrecked with a week of teen." (KRIII.4.1)
In the play. *The Duchess of York, Richard's mother, reflects on her sorrowful life. 'Teen' = 'grief, vexation'.*

Life, pessimistic view of l. - Comfort's in heaven; and we are on the earth.
"Comfort's in heaven; and we are on the earth" (KRII.2.2)
In the play. *Invited rhetorically by the Queen to give news that may comfort her, the Duke of York cannot, given the circumstances. See 'Expression, facial e. indicating bad news - … full of careful business are his looks!'*

Life, pessimistic view of l. - This world to me is like a lasting storm.
"This world to me is like a lasting storm" (PER.4.1)
In the play. *Marina meditating on her own life.*

Life, rationalization against 'death with dignity' advocates - ... The weariest and most loathed worldly life…is a paradise to what we fear of death'
"Ay, but to die, and go we know not where;
To lie in cold obstruction and to rot;
This sensible warm motion to become
A kneaded clod; and the delighted spirit
To bathe in fiery floods, or to reside
In thrilling region of thick-ribbed ice;
To be imprison'd in the viewless winds,
And blown with restless violence round about
The pendent world; or to be worse than worst
Of those that lawless and incertain thought
Imagine howling: 'tis too horrible!
The weariest and most loathed worldly life
That age, ache, penury and imprisonment
Can lay on nature is a paradise
To what we fear of death" (MFM.3.1)
Also a source for imagery of death, e.g. 'to lie in cold obstruction…', 'reside in thrilling region…' etc.
In the play. *Claudio to Sister Isabella who claims that a 'shamed life is hateful'. 'Pendent' = 'Hanging'.*

Life, reasons for hanging on to l. - O, our lives' sweetness! That we the pain of death would hourly die…
"…O, our lives' sweetness!
That we the pain of death would hourly die
Rather than die at once!--taught me to shift
Into a madman's rags…" (KL.5.3)
See also 'Depression, general depression leading to total pessimism – ... the whips and scorns of time, the oppressor's wrong, the proud man's contumely…'
In the play. *Edgar explains how he pretended to be mad and camouflaged himself to save his life to enjoy the perceived 'lives' sweetness!'*

Life, short and therefore to be well lived - ... the time of life is short! To spend that shortness basely were too long.
"O gentlemen, the time of life is short!
To spend that shortness basely were too long" (KHIV p1.5.2)
Your (possible) philosophy of life.
Answer to a question on the reason of a bold action of yours.
In the play. *Hotspur's words just before the beginning of the battle of Shrewsbury where he will be killed by the Prince of Wales, the future Henry V.*

Life, simple l. - ... and the greatest of my pride is to see my ewes graze, and my lambs suck.
CORIN (to Touchstone). Sir, I am true labourer; I earn that I eat; get that I wear; owe no man hate, envy no man's happiness; glad of other men's good, content with my harm: and the greatest of my pride is to see my ewes graze, and my lambs suck. (AYLI.3.2)
Answer to 'What can you tell me about yourself?'
In the play. *The courtly Touchstone engages the shepherd Corin into an exchange of ideas and opinions.*

Life, simple country l., advantages of – Here feel we but the penalty of Adam…
"Here feel we but the penalty of Adam,
The seasons' difference, as the icy fang
And churlish chiding of the winter's wind,
Which, when it bites and blows upon my body,

Even till I shrink with cold, I smile"
(AYLI.2.1)
In the play. *Duke S. comments positively on the turn of events that led him to the exile in the forest of Arden.*

Life, simple country l., advantages of – ... Is far beyond a prince's delicate... when care, mistrust, and treason waits on him.
"And to conclude, the shepherd's homely curds
...
All which secure and sweetly he enjoys,
Is far beyond a prince's delicates,
His viands sparkling in a golden cup,
His body couched in a curious bed,
When care, mistrust, and treason waits on him." (KHVI.p3.2.5)
In the play. *King Henry VI meditates while the battle of Towton is fought between Lancastrians and Yorkists, battle that will decide his fate as king.*

Life, simple l. preferable - Hath not old custom made this life more sweet than that of painted pomp?
"Hath not old custom made this life more sweet
Than that of painted pomp?" (AYLI.2)
Explain why you prefer the simple life in the country.
In the play. *In the forest of Arden, Duke S. praises the value of a pastoral and rural life.*

Life, simple country life preferable to rat-race - Gives not the hawthorn bush a sweeter shade... to shepherds, looking on their silly sheep...
"Gives not the hawthorn bush a sweeter shade
To shepherds, looking on their silly sheep,
Than doth a rich embroidered canopy
To kings, that fear their subjects' treachery?
O yes it doth; a thousand-fold it doth." (KHVI p3.2.5)
Explain the advantages of simplicity. See also 'Country living, in praise of country living - ... Here can I sit alone, unseen of any and to the nightingale's complaining notes...' – 'Life, l. inside a corporation or the Washington belt – ... the art of the court as hard to leave as keep.'
In the play. *King Henry VI meditates while the battle of Towton is fought between Lancastrians and Yorkists, battle that will decide his fate as king.*

Life, l. and death, values reversed - To sue to live, I find I seek to die...
"To sue to live, I find I seek to die;
And, seeking death, find life: let it come on." (MFM.3.1)
In the play. *The friar (the Duke in disguise) convinces Claudio of the futility of life and Claudio is convinced.*

Life, l. as a battle - Strives in his little world of man to out-scorn the to-and-fro-conflicting wind and rain.
"Strives in his little world of man to out-scorn
The to-and-fro-conflicting wind and rain." (KL.2.4)
Metaphorical answer to 'What do you do for a living?' or similar.
In the play. *A gentleman describes the predicament Lear is in, battling a storm in a forest.*

Life, l. as a stage for fools - When we are born we cry that we are come to this great stage of fools.
"When we are born we cry that we are come
To this great stage of fools." (KL.4.6)
Skeptical opinion on life
In the play. *Lear's opinion on life.*

Life, l. as an hourly progress towards death – ... That we the pain of death would hourly die, rather than die at once!
"...O, our lives' sweetness!
That we the pain of death would hourly die
Rather than die at once!" (KL.5.3)
In the play. *Edgar laments the circumstances that led to the blindness and death of his father Gloucester.*

Life, l. at court or in a corporation compared to country life - ... what lies I have heard! Our courtiers say all's savage but at court...
"... Gods, what lies I have heard! Our courtiers say all's savage but at court:
Experience, O, thou disprov'st report!" (CYM.4.1)
Explain why you have left the large corporation or to enjoy a simpler life.
In the play. *Imogen is favorably impressed by the kindness and courtesies bestowed upon her by Belarius, Arviragus and Guiderius, whom she met in the forest.*

Life, l. better ended if her l. is missing - My life were better ended by their hate, than death prorogued, wanting of thy love.
"My life were better ended by their hate,
Than death prorogued, wanting of thy love." (RJ.2.2)
Remove 'by their hate' if it does not apply and add drama to her rejection or to emphasize the depth of your affection.
In the play. *Romeo speaks with Juliet in her garden and answers her words of warning (of the danger he is in being where he is).*

Life, l. in the country as opposed to l. in a corporation - ... and we will fear no poison, which attends In place of greater state.
"And we will fear no poison, which attends
In place of greater state" (CYM.3.3)
In the play. *Belarius to adopted sons – there will be no poison in their venison, as opposed to the poison that could be found in meals served at court.*

Life, l. in the country as opposed to l. in a corporation - ... prouder than rustling in unpaid-for silk.
"...O, this life
Is nobler than attending for a cheque,
Richer than doing nothing for a bauble,
Prouder than rustling in unpaid-for silk" (CYM.3.3)
See also 'Life, l. inside a corporation or the Washington belt – ... the art of the court as hard to leave as keep...' – 'Place, a nice p. to stay – ...the air nimbly and sweetly recommends itself unto our gentle senses'.
In the play. *Belarius tells his adopted sons about the advantages of a simple life away from court.*

Life, l. in the country, advantages of –
Lord, who would live turmoiled in the court, and may enjoy such quiet walks as these?...
"Lord, who would live turmoiled in the court,
And may enjoy such quiet walks as these?
This small inheritance my father left me
Contenteth me, and worth a monarchy.
I seek not to wax great by others' waning,
Or gather wealth, I care not, with what envy:
Sufficeth that I have maintains my

state
And sends the poor well pleased from my gate." (KHVI.p2.4.10)
In the play. *Squire Iden, who will soon acquire glory by slaying the rebel Cade, meditates on the benefits of a simple country life.*

Life, l. inherently short and lasting but a moment – … And a man's life's no more than to say 'One.'
"…The interim is mine;
And a man's life's no more than to say 'One.'" (H.5.2)
Another milder way to express your general pessimism. See also 'Warning, gratitude for the w. – I thank thee who hath taught my frail mortality to know itself…'
In the play. *Horatio advises Hamlet that shortly the king will know what happened in England to Rosencrantz and Guildenstern.*

Life, l. inside a corporation or the Washington belt – … the art of the court as hard to leave as keep…
"…the art of the court,
As hard to leave as keep; whose top to climb
Is certain falling, or so slippery that
The fear's as bad as falling."
(CYM.3.3)
Give this as a reason why you have left politics or resigned from a big corporation. See also 'Management, m's chronic stress'.
In the play. *Belarius speaks to Guiderius and Arviragus who are anxious to leave the country life to lead a more active life at court.*

Life, l. is but a questionable commodity - Reason thus with life - If I do lose thee, I do lose a thing that none but fools would keep…
"Reason thus with life; --
If I do lose thee, I do lose a thing
That none but fools would keep: a breath thou art,
Servile to all the skyey influences
That do this habitation, where thou keep'st,
Hourly afflict: merely, thou art death's fool" (MFM.3.1)
Use as a consideration on the volatility of life and anything earthly. 'Reason thus with life, a breath thou art, servile to all skyey influences.'
In the play. *The duke (in disguise) converses with Claudio who has been condemned to death by Angelo.*

Life, l. lived according to nature - … tongues in trees, books in the running brooks.
"And this, our life, exempt from public haunt,
Finds tongues in trees, books in the running brooks,
Sermons in stones, and good in every thing." (AYLI.2.1)
Extol the advantages of an eco-friendly life.
In the play. *In the forest of Arden, Duke Senior praises the living of life according to nature.*

Life, l. unbearable, death as a physician – It is silliness to live when to live is torment…
"It is silliness to live when to live is torment; and then have we a prescription to die when death is our physician." (OTH.1.3)
In the play. *Roderigo to Iago. Roderigo cultivates a morbid passion for Desdemona and Iago uses him to further his own objectives of hatred*

Life, l's chronic unhappiness - Happy thou art not; for what thou hast not, still thou strivest to get…
"Happy thou art not;
For what thou hast not, still thou strivest to get,
And what thou hast, forget'st."
(MFM.3.1)

In the play. *Duke Vicentio in disguise gives some philosophical lessons to the condemned Claudio.*

Life, l.'s history of a person as a predictor of future performance –
There is a history in all men's lives.
"There is a history in all men's lives,
Figuring the nature of the times deceased;
The which observed, a man may prophesy,
With a near aim, of the main chance of things
As yet not come to life, which in their seeds
And weak beginnings lie intreasured.
Such things become the hatch and brood of time" (KHIV p2.3.1)
Explain why you anticipate a behavior or reaction to events by a person whose life's history or pattern you know. Or give a positive spin to the plan and action that must be undertaken to make the company profitable again. See also 'Outcome of events detectable in small details at the beginning - And in such indexes, although small pricks to their subsequent volumes…' – 'Continuation, going to the next step - to perform an act whereof what's past is prologue.'
In the play. *Warwick meditates on a prediction by King Richard II. Northumberland had helped Bolingbroke take over the crown. Richard II predicted that the same Northumberland wold betray the new king. 'Main' here means 'general'.*

Life, l's inherent fleetingness, comforts for the concept of mortality -
… a breath thou art, servile to all the skyey influences, that dost this habitation…
"Reason thus with life:
If I do lose thee, I do lose a thing
That none but fools would keep: a breath thou art,
Servile to all the skyey influences,
That dost this habitation, where thou keep'st,
Hourly afflict." (MFM.3.1)
In the play. *Duke Vicentio (disguised) passes words of wisdom to Claudio, unfairly condemned to death by the evil Angelo.*

Life, l's objectives and the consequences of excessive ambition for wealth - Honour for wealth; and oft that wealth doth cost the death of all, and all together lost.
"The aim of all is but to nurse the life
With honour, wealth, and ease, in waning age;
And in this aim there is such thwarting strife,
That one for all, or all for one we gage;
As life for honour in fell battle's rage;
Honour for wealth; and oft that wealth doth cost
The death of all, and all together lost" (ROL)
In the poem. *Tarquin, who has everything, will lose everything by wanting to seduce the virtuous and married Lucretia.*

Life, l's story, invitation to speak about his/her/their l. – Part performed in this wide gap of time.
"… Good Paulina,
Lead us from hence, where we may leisurely
Each one demand an answer to his part
Perform'd in this wide gap of time" (WT.5.3.)
When various friends meet after a long time and you want to invite each to tell the other about their history. See also 'Dinner, have it precede a meeting.'
In the play. *After an extraordinary sequence of events has resuscitated Queen Hermione previously believed dead, Polixenes is reconciled forever with Leontes and their respective son and daughter are married. Leontes suggests a leisure*

meeting where everyone involved may recount the story of his/her life during the preceding years.

Life, l's uncertainties - …(The) other incident throes that nature's fragile vessel doth sustain in life's uncertain voyage.
"…incident throes
That nature's fragile vessel doth sustain
In life's uncertain voyage" (TOA.5.1)
In the play. *Extract of Timon's response to the Athenian senators who came to ask for help with Alcibiades. Timon will intercede with Alcibiades and ease the senators of their griefs and the 'incident throes…'*

Life, life-style – … whose humble means match not his haughty spirit.
"I know a discontented gentleman, Whose humble means match not his haughty spirit." (KRIII.4.2)
In the play. *A Page replies to Richard's request to locate a contract killers for the two young princes held at the Tower. See 'Gold, g. as powerful tool of corruption – … gold were as good as twenty orators and will, no doubt, tempt him to anything.'*

Life, life-style not commensurate with means - … whose large style agrees not with the leanness of his purse.
"Unto poor king Reignier, whose large style
Agrees not with the leanness of his purse." (KHVI p2.1.1)
Comment on a show-off, 'His large style agrees not… purse'.
In the play. *Gloucester on Reignier, imminent father in law of Henry VI.*

Life, longevity and unusual way of expressing love for it – I love long life better than figs.
"O excellent! I love long life better than figs." (AC.1.2)
In the play. *Charmian's reaction after a soothsayer has predicted that she will outlive Cleopatra.*

Life, surrounded by sleep and partaking of dream experience - We are such stuff as dreams are made on, and our little life is rounded with a sleep.
"…We are such stuff
As dreams are made on, and our little life
Is rounded with a sleep." (TEM.4.1)
Express a feeling of unreality and of the fleetingness of life.
In the play. *Prospero utters a philosophical consideration for Miranda and Ferdinand's benefit. Prospero is getting ready to fire the spirits and goblins that have helped him make the point with his dastardly power-hungry brother.*

Life, tired of l. – I am so out of love with life that I will sue to be rid of it.
"I am so out of love with life that I will sue to be rid of it." (MFM.3.1)
See also 'Attitude, a. towards the world, hating it – one…whom the vile blows and buffets of the world…'
In the play. *Claudio to his sister, after a last moment of hesitation whether she should try to save him or not by yielding to the deputy Duke Angelo.*

Life, the act of living – … live the lease of nature, pay his breath to time and mortal custom.
"… Macbeth
Shall live the lease of nature, pay his breath
To time and mortal custom" (M.4.1)
In the play. *The third apparition materializes while Macbeth consults with the witches and tells him that he will never be vanquished till the Birnam wood will physically move to Dunsinane. Macbeth feels reassured that he will live a normal live and speaks of himself in the third person.*

Life, uncertainty of l. – What surety of the world, what hope, what stay, when this was now a king, and now is clay?
"What surety of the world, what hope, what stay,
When this was now a king, and now is clay?" (KJ.5.7)
See also entries for 'Destiny, beyond our control'
In the play. *Prince Henry who succeeds the poisoned King John generalizes on the inherent volatility of life.*

Lifestyle, desired l. not commensurate to available means - ... a discontented gentleman whose humble means match not his haughty spirit.
"I know a discontented gentleman, Whose humble means match not his haughty spirit" (KRIII.4.2)
In the play. *Richard asks a page to locate a contract killer as Buckingham bucks out from the idea of murdering the two young princes. The page has an idea.*

Lifestyle, not bothered by ambition for public office – Let those who are in favour with their stars...
"Let those who are in favour with their stars
Of public honour and proud titles boast,
Whilst I..." (SON 25)
Answer to 'Why are you not running for office' or similar. See also entries for 'Modesty'

Life, uncertainty of the afterlife and its influence on our behavior - The undiscovered country from whose bourn no traveler returns - puzzles the will...
"The undiscovered country from whose bourn
No traveler returns - puzzles the will.
And makes us rather bear those ills we have,
Than fly to others that we know not of." (H.3.1)
Use to justify your rejection of a proposal or remedy that you deem dangerous or reckless, "(I would) rather bear those ills we have, than fly to others that we know not of." ('Bourn' means boundary, frontier)
In the play. *Hamlet meditates.*

Lifestyle, shunning crowds – ... I have ever loved the life removed and held in idle price to haunt assemblies...
"...I have ever loved the life removed
And held in idle price to haunt assemblies
Where youth, and cost, and witless bravery keeps." (MFM.1.3)
See also 'Celebrity, c. who dislikes cheering crowds - I love the people, but do not like to stage me to their eyes...'
In the play. *The Duke, in disguise as a friar, explains to another friar the reasons for his temporary absence from the government of Vienna.*

Light, l. through a window – ... what light through yonder window breaks? It is the east...
"But, soft! what light through yonder window breaks?
It is the east, and Juliet is the sun." (RJ.2.2)
Compliment material, e.g. 'It is the east and you are the sun'.
In the play. *In Juliet's garden, Romeo notices a light in her window.*

Lion, dying l. still shows his rage - ... and wounds the earth, if nothing else, with rage.
"The lion dying thrusteth forth his paw,
And wounds the earth, if nothing else, with rage
To be o'erpower'd..." (KRII.5.1)

Explain the desperation of those who, unjustly treated and defeated react with rage and commit desperate acts. See also 'Reprimand, r. for going down and not fighting – … wilt thou, pupil-like, take thy correction mildly…'
In the play. *The Queen meets the deposed Richard II and encourages him if he has to fall, to fall like a lion.*

Lips, bewitching - you have witchcraft in your lips…
"You have witchcraft in your lips, Kate: there is more eloquence in a sugar touch of them, than in the tongues of the French council." (HV.5.2)
Be prepared to explain why the French council comes into it, depending on her literary background. Refer to the summary of the play.
In the play. *Henry V woos Kathryn of France.*

Lips, delivering immortal blessings - … and steal immortal blessing from her lips…
"…dear Juliet's hand
And steal immortal blessing from her lips,
Who even in pure and vestal modesty,
Still blush, as thinking their own kisses sin." (RJ.3.3)
'Let me steal immortal blessings from your lips' makes a good line.
In the play. *Romeo is banished from Verona and in despair envies animals and insects that somehow may see Juliet's hands or taste her lips.*

Lips, doors of breath – o you the doors of breath, seal with a righteous kiss a dateless bargain.
"…lips, O you
The doors of breath, seal with a righteous kiss
A dateless bargain.." (RJ.5.3)
Use the expression 'the doors of breath' together with a compliment about her good breath.

In the play. *The occasion for these lines is not very cheerful. Romeo has returned from Mantua and finding Juliet in deep sleep in a mausoleum, thinks that she is dead.*

Lips, l. and fresh breath - Here are sever'd lips parted with sugar breath…
"…Here are sever'd lips,
Parted with sugar breath: so sweet a bar
Should sunder such sweet friends" (MOV.3.2)
In the play. *Bassanio comments on the picture of Portia found in the correct basket.*

Lips, l. like roses - Their lips were four red roses on a stalk.
"Their lips were four red roses on a stalk" (KRIII.4.3)
Reduce four to two and turn the line into a compliment, 'Your lips are two roses on a stalk'.
In the play. *Tyrrel the contract killer has killed the young princes while they were asleep and now meditates on the heinous act.*

Lips, moving in discontent - …whose restraint doth move the murmuring lips of discontent.
"… Arthur; whose restraint
Doth move the murmuring lips of discontent
To break into this dangerous argument." (KJ.4.2)
Answer to question 'What is the mood of the workers?' Or, if it applies, 'I can see murmuring lips of discontent'.
In the play. *Pembroke advises King John to release young Prince Arthur lest discontent breaks into rebellion.*

Lips, plus nose plus cheeks – lily lips, this cherry nose, these yellow cowslip cheeks.
"These lily lips,
This cherry nose,

These yellow cowslip cheeks."
(MND.5.1)
In the play. *Thisbe tries to revive Pyramus.*

Lips, smooth - ... Diana's lip is not more smooth and rubious.
"... Diana's lip
Is not more smooth and rubious; thy small pipe
Is as the maiden's organ, shrill and sound,
And all is semblative of a woman's part." (TN.1.4)
Use to praise her lips.
In the play. *The Duke thinks that Cesario's feminine manners may succeed with Olivia after previous attempts failed. He points out to Cesario his (Cesario's) feminine traits. And in fact Cesario is actually Viola in man's garb.*

Lips, tempting - O, how ripe in show thy lips, those kissing cherries, tempting grow!
"O, how ripe in show,
Thy lips, those kissing cherries, tempting grow!" (MND.3.2)
Flatter and praise
In the play. *Demetrius awakes and erupts in loving praise of Helena.*

Listening, are you l.? - ... how is't with you, that you do bend your eye on vacancy and with the incorporal air do hold discourse?
"Alas, how is't with you,
That you do bend your eye on vacancy
And with the incorporal air do hold discourse?" (H.3.4)
A teacher to student(s) whose mind is seemingly vacant during a lecture.
In the play. *Hamlet talks with the Ghost, his mother, unable to see the Ghost herself thinks that Hamlet is mad*

Listening, eager l. – and with a greedy ear devour up my discourse.

"...and with a greedy ear
Devour up my discourse" (OTH.1.3)
Answer to 'Are you listening?' E.G. ' With greedy ears I devour up your discourse'. See also 'Biography, invitation to tell his/her life story – I long to hear the story of your life...' – 'Dinner, have d. precede a meeting - Discourse is heavy, fasting; when we have supp'd we'll mannerly demand thee of thy story so far as thou wilt speak it.'
In the play. *Othello explains how Desdemona was mesmerized by the adventures he told her. This was the trigger that moved her to love him.*

Listening, prepared to listen - What you have said I will consider; what you have to say I will with patience hear.
"...What you have said
I will consider; what you have to say
I will with patience hear, and find a time
Both meet to hear and answer such high things." (JC.1.2)
In the play. *Brutus replies to Cassius who is laying the seeds for the conspiracy against Julius Caesar.*

Listening, unable to listen as a disease – ... it is the disease of not listening... that I am troubled withal.
"...it is the disease of not listening, the malady of not marking, that I am troubled withal." (KHIV.p2.1.2)
In the play. *Falstaff pretends to be troubled with hearing in an effort not to answer the Chief Justice at court.*

Listening, you are not l. - You start away and lend no ear unto my purposes.
"You start away
And lend no ear unto my purposes." (KHIVp1.1.3)
In the play. *Worcester to the impatient Hotspur.*

Little, content with very little, a smile sufficient - ... loose now and then a scattered smile, and that I'll live upon.
"... loose now and then
A scattered smile, and that I'll live upon." (AYLI.3)
She has turned you down - this is an elegant way to remain in her graces.
In the play. *Silvius loves Phebe but Phebe has a crush on the disguised Rosalind whom she (Phebe) believes to be a boy.*

Living means - ... you take my life when you do take the means whereby I live...
"Nay, take my life and all; pardon not that:
You take my house when you do take the prop
That doth sustain my house; you take my life
When you do take the means whereby I live..." (MOV.4.1)
If and when the judge wants to take away your driving licence, or equivalent situation.
In the play. *Shylock rails against the sentence that suddenly turned the table against him.*

Load, heavy (metaphorical) load to carry - I was not made a horse and yet I bear a burthen like an ass.
"Forgiveness, horse! why do I rail on thee,
Since thou, created to be awed by man,
Wast born to bear? I was not made a horse;
And yet I bear a burthen like an ass" (KRII.5.5)
Answer to 'How are you doing?' when things are not going your way.
In the play. *Richard II, in prison at Pomfret Castle is visited by the faithful groom who took care of the royal horse Barbary. Richard meditates on the fortunes of his horse now owned and ridden by Bolingbroke.*

Lobbying, expression of lobbying intent – I come to whet your gentle thoughts on his behalf.
"I come to whet your gentle thoughts
On his behalf." (TN.3.1)
Introduce your lobbying efforts or expedition.
In the play, *Viola/Cesario attempts to plead with Olivia on the Duke's behalf.*

Lobbyist, l. defined – (he who has access to)... the perfumed chambers of the great...
"... in the perfumed chambers of the great,
Under the canopies of costly state" (KHIV.p2.3.1)
Boost the ego of a lobbyist.
In the play. *King Henry cannot sleep.*

Location, remote l. - ... some forlorn and naked hermitage, remote from all the pleasures of the world...
"...some forlorn and naked hermitage,
Remote from all the pleasures of the world" (LLL.5.2)
Answer to 'Where do you live?' or use to describe your somewhat recluse life style.
In the play. *The Princess leaves for her home in Aquitaine and counsels the King of Navarre and friends about what to do for the next twelve months.*

Location, secluded l. where to discuss private matter – We are too open here to argue this, let's think in private more.
"We are too open here to argue this;
Let's think in private more" (KVIII.2.1)
In the play. *The matter discussed by two citizens is the impending divorce between Henry VIII and Catherine, organized by Cardinal Wolsey. Wolsey was miffed at Emperor Charles V (uncle to Catherine) for not assigning to him the archbishopric of Toledo.*

Logic, lack of l. – How now, how now, chop-logic!
"How now, how now, chop-logic!" (RJ.3.5)
In the play. *Capulet is confused at Juliet's word. She tries to get out of her established marriage with Paris.*

Loneliness, feeling alone – Now my soul's palace is become a prison.
"Now my soul's palace is become a prison:
Ah, would she break from hence, that this my body
Might in the ground be closed up in rest!" (KHVI p3.2.1)
Describe your state of mind as it applies.
In the play. *Edward commenting on the death of the Duke of York in the battle of St. Alban's.*

Look carefully! – The fringed curtain of thine eye advance and say what thou seest yond.
"The fringed curtains of thine eye advance
And say what thou seest yond." (TEM.1.2)
Answer to 'What do I do next?'
In the play. *Prospero invites Miranda to look and describe whom she sees, who happens to be Ferdinand.*

Look, angry l. – ... so looks the chafed lion upon the daring huntsman that has gall'd him...
"...so looks the chafed lion
Upon the daring huntsman that has gall'd him,
Then makes him nothing." (KHVIII.3.2)
In the play. *Cardinal Wolsey referring to the King who is reading a letter that compromises Wolsey.*

Look, angry l. not justified. - Why do you bend such solemn brow on me? Think you I bear the shears of destiny?...
"Why do you bend such solemn brow on me?
Think you I bear the shears of destiny?
Have I commandment on the pulse of life?" (KJ.4.2)
Alternative to question, 'Why do you give me such a nasty look?'
In the play. *Young Arthur died in suspicious circumstances and Pembroke demands an explanation of K. John, the party most likely to be responsible. K. John senses Pembroke's thought by his expression.*

Look, appearance, worried l. - What watchful cares do interpose themselves betwixt your eyes and night?
"What watchful cares do interpose themselves
Betwixt your eyes and night?" (JC.2.1)
Question friend or colleague about his troubled expression. See also 'Expression of sadness misconstrued - My heart is ten times lighter than my looks.'
In the play. *Brutus observes Cassius look.*

Looks, killing l. - ... my love well knows her pretty looks have been mine enemies...
"ah! my love well knows
Her pretty looks have been mine enemies,
And therefore from my face she turns my foes,
That they elsewhere might dart their injuries:
Yet do not so; but since I am near slain,
Kill me outright with looks and rid my pain. " (SON 134)
When she either does not look at you or looks at you with a hateful expression.

**Lose, every which way you lose –
Whoever wins, on that side shall I lose…**
"Whoever wins, on that side shall I lose
Assured loss before the match be play'd" (KJ.3.1)
In the play. *Lady Blanche, niece of King John of England and married to the Dauphin of France, laments that if the French win the oncoming battle she will lose an uncle, if the English win, she will lose a husband.*

Losing, l. gracefully - … adieu. I have too grieved a heart to take a tedious leave: thus losers part.
"Portia, adieu. I have too grieved a heart
To take a tedious leave: thus losers part" (MOV.2.7)
Admit your defeat, especially applicable if she said 'no' to your advances.
In the play. *The Prince of Morocco did not guess right at the quiz for the hand of Portia*

Losses due to ignorance - With very ignorance; we have kiss'd away kingdoms and provinces.
"With very ignorance we have kiss'd away
Kingdoms and provinces" (AC.3.10)
Comment on general squandering of good resources.
In the play. *Scarus, returning from the sea battle between the fleets of Antony and Caesar Octavian, tells Enobarbus that Antony has lost.*

Lost, l. in the world - I to the world am like a drop of water that in the ocean seeks another drop.
"I to the world am like a drop of water
That in the ocean seeks another drop" (COE.1.2)
In the play. *Antipholus S. is pessimistic about finding lost brother and mother in Ephesus.*

Love, a folly – Love is a folly bought with wit, or else a wit with folly vanquished.
Love is but a folly bought with wit,
Or else a wit with folly vanquished.
(TGV.1.1)
Explain why you do no easily fall in love.
In the play: *Proteus is in love with Julia whereas Valentine is skeptical about love in general. But later Valentine will fall in love hand over heels with the pretty Sylvia.*

Love, a folly supported by written evidence – And writers say, as the most forward bud is eaten by the canker ere it blow…
"And writers say, as the most forward bud
Is eaten by the canker ere it blow,
Even so by love the young and tender wit
Is turn'd to folly, blasting in the bud,
Losing his verdure even in the prime
And all the fair effects of future hopes" (TGV.1.1)
Justify your skepticism about love. Start with '…by love the young and tender wit…'
In the play. *Valentine is leaving for Milan and upbraids his friend Proteus, who is retained in Verona by his love for Julia.*

Love, a masochistic exercise – To be in love, where scorn is bought with groans…
"To be in love, where scorn is bought with groans;
Coy looks with heart-sore sighs; one fading moment's mirth
With twenty watchful, weary, tedious nights:" (TGV.1.1)
If you find her cold to your approaches, try to play the part of the romantically unhappy, sometimes it works. See also 'Masochism, m. for love – cut me to pieces with thy keen conceit'.
In the play. *Valentine, leaving Verona for Milan tells Proteus his negative opinion about*

love. But in Milan Valentine will immediately fall in love with Silvia.

Love, account of your love life boring - My tales of love were wont to weary you; I know you joy not in a love discourse.
"My tales of love were wont to weary you;
I know you joy not in a love discourse." (TGV.2.4)
Potential answer to 'How is your love life?'
In the play. *Forced by his father in Verona, Proteus has reluctantly joined his friend Valentine in Milan. The tales refer to Proteus' love for Julia.*

Love, acknowledging signs of l. reciprocated - ... yet my blood begins to flatter me that thou dost...
"By mine honour, in true English, I love thee, Kate: by which honour I dare not swear thou lovest me; yet my blood begins to flatter me that thou dost, notwithstanding the poor and untempering effect of my visage" (HV.5.2)
In the play. *Henry V woos Princess Katherine of France.*

Love, always thinking of her – My thoughts do harbour with my Silvia nightly and slaves they are to me that send them flying...
"'My thoughts do harbour with my Silvia nightly,
And slaves they are to me that send them flying:" (TGV.3.1)
Change Silvia to the name of the beloved party. Particularly suitable for a line on a card sent by airmail.
In the play. *Part of a letter proposing elopement, sent by Valentine to Silvia and discovered by the Duke her father*

Love, appeal of l. inversely proportional to appeal of books to schoolboys - Love goes toward love, as schoolboys from their books...
"Love goes toward love, as schoolboys from their books,
But love from love, toward school with heavy looks." (RJ.2.2)
Answer to 'Why are you still here?' or justification to the same effect.
In the play. *Romeo has a hard time to take leave of Juliet his first meeting with her.*

Love, argument for accepting your courtship - Torches are made to light, jewels to wear...
"Torches are made to light, jewels to wear...
Things growing to themselves are growth's abuse" (V&A)
One argument for her to open up to your invitations.

Love, argument for her saying yes without extended delays – ... Thou by thy dial's shady stealth mayst know time's thievish progress to eternity.
"Thy glass will show thee how thy beauties wear,
Thy dial how thy precious minutes waste
...
The wrinkles which thy glass will truly show
Of mouthed graves will give thee memory;
Thou by thy dial's shady stealth mayst know
Time's thievish progress to eternity." (SON 77)
See also 'Time, admitting to having wasted it - I wasted time and now doth time waste me' – 'Time, consciousness of wasted t. - The clock upbraids me with the waste of time'.

Generosity, an excess in g. a fine weakness - ...faults that are rich are fair.

"…faults that are rich are fair'
(TOA.1.2)
In the play. *See comment to 'Gratitude, refusing payment or recompense for a previous favor or act of kindness'*

Love, being in l., virtue or fault? -
…'T is a fault I will not change for your best virtue.
JACQUES. The worst fault you have is to be in love.
ORLANDO. 'T is a fault I will not change for your best virtue. (AYLI.3.2)
Actually you can use this in any occasion when someone tells you 'your fault is…etc.', especially if the alleged fault is not a fault at all.
In the play. *Orlando and Jacques do not get along very well.*

Love, beware of hasty proposals - … A time, methinks, too short to make a world-without-end bargain in.
"… A time, methinks, too short
To make a world-without-end bargain in." (LLL.5.2)
In the play. *The King and his company propose (respectively) to the Princess and her company. She is not ready yet for a 'world-without-end' commitment.*

Love, blindness of l. impairing clear vision - If you love her, you cannot see her…
SPEED If you love her, you cannot see her.
VALENTINE Why?
SPEED Because love is blind.
(TGV.2.1)
Expand poetically on the well know truth that love is blind.
In the play. *Valentine, after having upbraided Proteus for falling in love, is now falling in love himself with Silvia.*

Love, case of reversed roles – The dove pursues the griffin…
"The dove pursues the griffin; the mild hind
Makes speed to catch the tiger"
(MND.2.1)
In the play. *Helena chases Demetrius who does not want to have anything to do with her.*

Love, l. and its detrimental effect on education - Thou, Julia, thou hast metamorphosed me, made me neglect my studies, lose my time…
"Thou, Julia, thou hast metamorphosed me,
Made me neglect my studies, lose my time,
War with good counsel, set the world at nought;
Made wit with musing weak, heart sick with thought." (TGV.1.1)
Change 'Julia' to the name of the applicable lady. With minor modification turn the line into an answer to 'How is your love life?'. E.G. '(Name of lady) has metamorphosed me… thought'. Or you may tell her this to show the extraordinary power she has over you.
In the play. *Valentine, who proclaims himself to be resistant to the allurements of love, has left Verona for Milan to seek a career in the retinue of the Duke of Milan. Proteus remains in Verona and meditates on his own situation and attraction to Julia and its consequences.*

Love, characteristics of a man in love – … and every thing about you demonstrating a careless desolation.
"…then your hose should be ungartered, your bonnet unbanded, your sleeve unbuttoned, your shoe untied and every thing about you demonstrating a careless desolation" (AYLI.3.2)
In the play. *Rosalind (in a boy's disguise) banters with Orlando with whom she is in love.*

Love, characteristics of l. - … love is full of unbefitting strains, all wanton as a child…

"… love is full of unbefitting strains,
All wanton as a child, skipping and vain,
Form'd by the eye and therefore, like the eye,
Full of strange shapes, of habits and of forms,
Varying in subjects as the eye doth roll
To every varied object in his glance" (LLL.5.2)
In the play. *Biron owns to the silly capers that he, the king of Navarre and friends have acted with the Princess and her attendants.*

Love, characteristics of l., both gentle and rough – Alas, that love, so gentle in his view, should be so tyrannous and rough in proof!
"Alas, that love, so gentle in his view,
Should be so tyrannous and rough in proof!" (RJ.1.1)
In the play. *Benvolio in conversation with Romeo.*

Love, cold l. easily supplanted - This weak impress of love is as a figure trenched in ice…
"This weak impress of love is as a figure
Trenched in ice, which with an hour's heat
Dissolves to water and doth lose his form.
A little time will melt her frozen thoughts
And worthless Valentine shall be forgot." (TGV.3.2)
In the play. *The Duke of Milan still believes that he can force his daughter to marry the spineless Thurio and forget Valentine.*

Love, command to l. - Put off your maiden blushes, avouch the thoughts of your heart…
"Put off your maiden blushes; avouch the thoughts of your heart with the looks of an empress; take me by the hand, and say 'Harry of England I am thine'" (HV.5.2)
You may change 'empress' into 'queen' and use your name instead of 'Harry of England'.
In the play. *Henry V woos Princess Katherine of France.*

Love, compared to an impatient and acquisitive child –… Love is like a child, that longs for every thing that he can come by.
"…Love is like a child,
That longs for every thing that he can come by." (TGV.3.1)
When she upbraids you for your impatience. In the play the 'every thing' referred to is actually a ladder, but you can change and apply the reference as needed.
In the play. *Proteus has betrayed his friend Valentine. The Duke asks Valentine for a ladder that he, the Duke, will supposedly use to climb to the window of a virtual lady. But it is a trick to expose Valentine. Valentine loves Silvia and the Duke opposes the relationship.*

Love, compared to being thirsty in a summer's day - Never did passenger in summer's heat…
"Never did passenger in summer's heat
More thirst for drink than she for this good turn." (V&A)
Change 'she' to 'I' to pay her a compliment about the power she has on you.
In the poem. *Venus pursues Adonis, The 'good turn' referred to is Adonis' never coming consent.*

Love, complete l. - I love you with so much of my heart that none is left to protest.
"I love you with so much of my heart that none is left to protest." (MAAN.4.1)

531

In the play. *Beatrice to Benedick after they engage in a witty exchange on protestations of love.*

Love, complete possession - One half of me is yours, the other half yours...
"One half of me is yours, the other half yours,
Mine own, I would say; but if mine, then yours,
And so all yours" (MOV.3.2)
In the play. *Portia to Bassanio while he is on the point of solving the riddle (or choosing the casket with the right answer).*

Love, completely ruled by her – ... this lovely face ruled like a wandering planet, over me.
"...this lovely face
Ruled, like a wandering planet, over me" (KHVI.p2.4.2)
Change 'ruled' to 'rules' and make it a compliment while you yield to her request(s).
In the play. *Queen Margaret presented with the severed head of Suffolk comments while her husband Henry VI deals with the rebellion of John Cade.*

Love, consolation prize - ... but one fair look; a smaller boon than this I cannot beg...
"Vouchsafe me, for my meed, but one fair look;
A smaller boon than this I cannot beg
And less than this, I am sure, you cannot give." (TGV.5.4)
See also 'Graphics. Picture as a substitute - Vouchsafe me yet your picture for my love, picture that is hanging in your chamber'.
In the play. *Proteus, rejected, still pursues Silvia in the forest.*

Love, darkness more suitable for l. - Blind is his love and best befits the dark.

"Blind is his love and best befits the dark." (RJ.2.1)
Answer to 'why do you want it so dark?' Change 'his' with 'my'. See also 'Love, blindness of l.'
In the play. *Mercutio and Benvolio are at a loss on where to find Romeo. They suspect him to be in love.*

Love, declaration of l. - ... And run through fire I will for thy sweet sake...
"...And run through fire I will for thy sweet sake.
Transparent Helena! Nature shows art,
That through thy bosom makes me see thy heart." (MND.2.2)
Also answer to 'Do you love me?'
In the play. *Lysander wakes up and immediately falls in love with Helena, forgetting Hermia. This is the result of the potion mistakenly applied to his eyes while asleep by Puck.*

Love, declaration of. l. - ... behold the window of my heart, mine eye...
"Mistress, look on me,
Behold the window of my heart, mine eye,
What humble suit attends thy answer there;
Impose some service on me for thy love." (LLL.5.2)
You may just use the last line, possibly when she asks 'Do you really love me?' Or use it verbatim as a love declaration.
In the play. *Biron declares his love to Rosaline.*

Love, declaration of l. - I speak no more than what my soul intends...
"I speak no more than what my soul intends;
And that is, to enjoy thee for my love" (KHVI.p3.3.2)
In the play. *Edward woos the widow Lady Grey*

Love, declaration of l. – Doubt thou the stars are fire…
"'Doubt thou the stars are fire;
Doubt that the sun doth move;
Doubt truth to be a liar;
But never doubt I love." (H.2.2)
Answer to 'Do you love me?'
In the play. *Polonius reads an extract from a Hamlet's letter to Ophelia.*

Love, declaration of. l. - … mine own self's better part; mine eye's clear eye, my dear heart's dearer heart…
"It is thyself, mine own self's better part;
Mine eye's clear eye, my dear heart's dearer heart,
My food, my fortune, and my sweet hope's aim,
My sole earth's heaven, and my heaven's claim." (COE.3.2)
In the play. *Antipholus of Syracuse addresses his affection to Luciana and she is distressed as she thinks that he is Antipholus of Ephesus. Therefore he should say this to her sister Adriana.*

Love, deep in it, denial useless - Invention is ashamed, against the proclamation of thy passion
"Invention is ashamed, against the proclamation of thy passion"
(AWEW.1.3)
Use with a friend whom you know to be desperately in love but tries to deny it. Or change 'thy' to 'my', if you wish to state that there is no way you can hide your all-consuming passion.
In the play. *Up to now Helen has tried (unsuccessfully) to disguise her love for Bertram. Now the Countess prompts Helen not to try to disguise her love any longer.*

Love, detection possible without verbal evidence - O learn to read what silent love hath writ…
"O learn to read what silent love hath writ,

To hear with eyes belongs to love's fine wit." (SON 23)
Answer to 'How did you guess that I wanted this?' or 'How did you guess that I love you?' E.G. 'I have learnt to read what silent love… fine wit.'

Love, determination to win her - He plies her hard; and much rain wears the marble.
"He plies her hard; and much rain wears the marble." (KHVI.p3.3.2)
In the play. *Richard of Gloucester comments to Clarence on their brother, now King Edward IV, who is trying to seduce (unsuccessfully) the Lady Grey.*

Love, difference between l. and lust – Love comforteth like sunshine after rain…
"Call it not love, for Love to heaven is fled,
Since sweating Lust on earth usurp'd his name;
Under whose simple semblance he hath fed
Upon fresh beauty, blotting it with blame;
Which the hot tyrant stains and soon bereaves,
As caterpillars do the tender leaves
…
Love comforteth like sunshine after rain,
But Lust's effect is tempest after sun;
Love's gentle spring doth always fresh remain,
Lust's winter comes ere summer half be done;
Love surfeits not, Lust like a glutton dies;
Love is all truth, Lust full of forged lies" (V&A)
In the poem. *The super-chaste Adonis reprimands Venus for her continuing harassment.*

Love, determination to win her – (I would)… mock the lion when he roars for prey to win thee, lady.
"(I would)… Pluck the young sucking cubs from the she-bear,
Yea, mock the lion when he roars for prey,
To win thee, lady" (MOV.2.1)
In the play. *The Prince of Morocco will try to guess the right casket and therefore marry Portia.*

Love, different points of view on whether darkness is conducive to l. -
… If love be blind, love cannot hit the mark.
BENVOLIO. Blind is his love and best befits the dark.
MERCUTIO. If love be blind, love cannot hit the mark. (RJ.2.1)
See also "Time, t. for love, night more suitable -… if love be blind, it best agrees with night.'
In the play. *Benvolio and Mercutio cannot find where Romeo is but they know that he is in love and has absconded somewhere in the evening.*

Love, direct declaration of l. - … I know no ways to mince it in love, but directly to say 'I love you'
"…I know no ways to mince it in love, but directly to say 'I love you' "
(KHV.5.2)
When you are repeatedly asked for reassurance of your feelings. Answer to "Do you love me?"
In the play. *King Henry V wants to marry Katherine of France after winning the battle of Agincourt against
the French.*

Love, effects of l. overpowering - The strongest, love ill instantly make weak…
"The strongest, love ill instantly make weak:
Strike the wise dumb and teach the fool to speak" **(V&A)**

Love, effects of l. recollected, drive to extremity - … and truly in my youth I suffered much extremity for love…
"…and truly in my youth I suffered much extremity for love; very near this." (H.2.1)
In the play. *Polonius' thoughts as he listens to Hamlet's ravings.*

Love, effects of l., empowerment – … love, first learned in a lady's eyes… gives to every power a double power, above their functions and their offices.
"… love, first learned in a lady's eyes,
Lives not alone immured in the brain;
But, with the motion of all elements,
Courses as swift as thought in every power,
And gives to every power a double power,
Above their functions and their offices" (LLL.4.2)
In the play. In the play. *Part of Biron's rationalization for breaking the king's oath of study, seclusion and abstinence.*

Love, effects of l., ennoblement – Things base and vile, holding no quantity, love can transpose to form and dignity.
"Things base and vile, holding no quantity,
Love can transpose to form and dignity" (MND.1.1)
In the play. *Helena's comments as she considers her position. She loves Demetrius but Demetrius loves Hermia.*

Love, effects of l., reversal of physical phenomena - All days are nights to see till I see thee, and nights bright days when dreams do show thee me.
"All days are nights to see till I see thee,
And nights bright days when dreams do show thee me." (SON.43)

See also 'Passion, effects of strong p. - This is the very ecstasy of love, whose violent property fordoes itself and leads the will to desperate undertakings.'

Love, effects on words and expression - ... his words are a very fantastical banquet, just so many strange dishes.
"He was wont to speak plain and to the purpose, like an honest man and a soldier; and now is he turned orthographer; his words are a very fantastical banquet, just so many strange dishes" (MAAN.2.3)
In the play. *Benedick describes the remarkable changes in his friend Claudio, after having fallen in love with Hero.*

Love, endurance of l. through poetry - Not marble, nor the gilded monuments of princes…
"Not marble, nor the gilded monuments
Of princes, shall outlive this powerful rhyme" (SON.55)
Answer to 'Will you always love me? Take some liberty and change to, 'Not marble, nor the gilded monuments of princes, shall outlive my love'.
With minor variation, use the same line when you hand your trip report to your boss, e.g. 'Not marble…this powerful prose'.
Marble holds an interesting place in the history of love. Venus de Milo (even if you have to complete the figure by adding her missing arms and hands with your imagination) is considered the supreme ideal in the art of female representation. It also symbolizes the somewhat morbid voluptuousness of perennial and invariable beauty. In Greek mythology, Amicleus from Athens fell in love with the statue of Venus and during the night he sneaked into the temple to make love to the statue. Apprehended by Athens' vice police he defended himself as follows: "I wanted to love a stone because I know how to love and I am not such a vile and selfish person who only loves so that he be loved in return. Though my love is to be blamed, I should be applauded for my being discrete, even if by nature I am incontinent. And where better could I display my constitutional incontinence than with marble that cannot laugh or blush at my 'dishonesties', if you wish to call them that way. Loving a woman means sacrificing one's heart to inconstancy. It is common knowledge that a woman's mood is variable and she can dump a lover in an instant. But the statue knows no mutability… O blind Athenians, you do not know the miracles of your Venus. We cannot really worship the power of Venus, if we do not accept that even with her marble (image) she can fire the spirit of lust in the breast of man"
If you think that this myth is an exaggeration, walk into any sex shop and you will have ample opportunities to cry in horror.
With…abundant license you may use the line as a praise or satiric/ironic comment on a report, e.g. 'Not marble… outlive this excellent report'

Love, evidence suggesting that he is in l. - Methinks he looks as though he were in love.
"Methinks he looks as though he were in love" (TOS.3.1)
In the play. *Hortensio thinks that Lucentio is in love with Bianca.*

Love, fickle l. recognized - O, she knew well thy love did read by rote and could not spell.
"O, she knew well
Thy love did read by rote and could not spell." (RJ.2.3)
In the play. *The one who knew about the lightness of Romeo's love was his former girlfriend Rosaline, a fact observed by Fr. Lawrence.*

Love, food to the mind - So are you to my thoughts as food to life, or as sweet-seasoned showers are to the ground.
"So are you to my thoughts as food to life,
Or as sweet-seasoned showers are to the ground." (SON.75)
Compliment, note for a card.

Love, geographical distance no barrier - … yet, wert thou as far as that vast shore wash'd with the farthest sea…
"I am no pilot; yet, wert thou as far
As that vast shore wash'd with the farthest sea,
I would adventure for such merchandise." (RJ.2.2)
Answer to 'Do you like me?'
In the play. *In Juliet's garden Romeo tells her about his feelings.*

Love, great l. concerned about little things - Where love is great, the littlest doubts are fear…
"Where love is great, the littlest doubts are fear;
Where little fears grow great, great love grows there" (H.3.2)
In the play. *The Player Queen in the play-within-a-play produced by Hamlet*

Love, her extraordinariness as a reason for your loving her - What made me love thee? let that persuade thee, there's something extraordinary in thee.
"What made me love thee? let that persuade thee, there's something extraordinary in thee." (MWW.3.3)
Change 'thee' to 'you' and give it as an answer when she asks, "What made you love me?"
In the play. *Falstaff is wooing Mrs. Ford, unsuccessfully in his case.*

Love, how l. betrayed turns to hate – Sweet love, I see, changing his property turns to the sourest and most deadly hate.
"Sweet love, I see, changing his property,
Turns to the sourest and most deadly hate" (KRII.3.2)
In the play. *Richard thinks that his allies Bagot, Bushy and Green have joined in with Bolingbroke, but in fact Bolingbroke executed them.*

Love, how much? – Doubt thou the stars are fire…
"'Doubt thou the stars are fire;
Doubt that the sun doth move;
Doubt truth to be a liar;
But never doubt I love" (H.2.2)
In the play. *Polonius reads to King and Queen from a letter sent by Hamlet to Ophelia.*

Love, how much? - I love you with so much of my heart that none is left to protest.
"I love you with so much of my heart that none is left to protest." (MAAN.4.1)
In the play. *Beatrice to Benedick after they engage in a witty exchange on protestations of love.*

Love, how much? – let him (Cupid) be judge how deep I am in love.
"(Cupid), that wicked bastard of Venus, that was begot of thought, conceived of spleen, and born of madness… let him be judge how deep I am in love." (AYLI.4.1)
Answer to 'How much are you in love?' or similar. You can shorten it to: 'Cupid, let him be judge…'
In the play. *Orlando has left and Rosalind confides the depth of her passion for Orlando, who is just as much in love with Rosalind. Rosalind attempts to measure the depth of her love but on second thoughts she thinks that Cupid is better qualified for this measurement.*

Love, how much? – My bounty is as boundless as the sea, my love as deep…
"My bounty is as boundless as the sea,
My love as deep; the more I give to thee,
The more I have, for both are infinite" (RJ.2.2)
In the play. *Juliet from her window to Romeo in her garden.*

Love, how much? - Neither rhyme nor reason can express so much.
ROSALIND. But are you so much in love as your rhymes speak?
ORLANDO. Neither rhyme nor reason can express so much. (AYLI.3.2)
Answer to 'How much do you love me?'
In the play. *Rosalind (in disguise as a boy) exchanges some banter with Orlando.*

Love, how much? - There's beggary in the love that can be reckoned.
CLEOPATRA. If it be love indeed, tell me how much
ANTONY. There's beggary in the love that can be reckoned (AC.1.1)
Answer to "How much do you love me?"
In the play. *Antony and Cleopatra in romantic conversation.*

Love, how much? - With admirations, with fertile tears, with groans that thunder love, with sighs of fire.
OLIVIA. How does he love me?
VIOLA. With admirations, with fertile tears, with groans that thunder love, with sighs of fire. (TN.1.5)
Maybe someone asks you, 'Are you sure that he loves her?' Answer 'I am sure, he loves her with admirations …of fire.'
Also alternative answer to 'How much do you love me?' 'With admiration... etc.'
In the play. *Viola/Cesario sent by the Duke to woo Olivia on his behalf has declared the Duke's love for her. Olivia asks a generic question*

Love, how much? Deflecting the question - They are but beggars that can count their worth, but my love…
"They are but beggars that can count their worth;
But my love is grown to such excess,
I cannot sum up sum of half my wealth." (RJ.2.6)
Use the quote in its entirety or just the last two lines. The first line can also be an answer to the question 'How much money do you make? See 'Financial Status. "Are you rich?" or "How much money do you make?"
In the play. *Romeo has declared his overwhelming happiness at the shortly to be celebrated wedding with Juliet and Juliet gives an account of her own love.*

Love, how much? Exceeding power of words to express it - … more than words can witness, or your thoughts can guess.
"And I am one that loves Bianca more
Than words can witness, or your thoughts can guess." (TOS.2.1)
Answer to 'How much do you love me?'
Change 'Bianca' to the name of the applicable lady.
In the play. *Tranio, one of Bianca's competing suitors, claims he loves her most of all.*

Love, how much? Immeasurable - I love you more than words can wield the matter…
"…I love you more than words can wield the matter
…
A love that makes breath poor and speech unable." (KL.1.1)
Answer to 'How much do you love me?'
Try it when you are not afraid of going overboard.

537

In the play. *The scheming Goneril knows that the more outlandishly she declares her love towards her father Lear, the more land she will get as he retires and parses out his possessions.*

Love, how much? Very deeply - … it cannot be sounded; my affection hath an unknown bottom, like the bay of Portugal.
"… that thou didst know how many fathom deep am I in love! But it cannot be sounded; my affection hath an unknown bottom, like the bay of Portugal" (AYLI.4.3)
Answer to "How much do you love me?" You may acquaint yourself beforehand as to the actual water depth in the Bay of Portugal, should you perceive that she has a penchant for statistics. You may shorten the first line to, 'How much I am in love? It cannot be sounded… Portugal.'
In the play. *Orlando has just left the scene and Rosalind expresses to Celia the depth of her passion for Orlando, who is just as much in love with Rosalind. 'Fathom' = a unit of measure equal to six feet, used to measure depth'.*

Love, I would do anything for you – What dangerous action, stood it next to death, would I not undergo for one calm look!
"What dangerous action, stood it next to death,
Would I not undergo for one calm look!" (TGV.5.4)
In the play. *Proteus laments that Silvia does not love him.*

Love, if you love tell me what you think - … If thou dost love me, show me thy thought.
"… If thou dost love me,
Show me thy thought." (OTH.3.3)
Prompt the release of information from a reluctant party.
In the play. *The cunning Iago plants seeds of jealousy into Othello's mind and he falls for it.*

Love, in l. but unpossessive - That god forbid that made me first your slave…
"That god forbid that made me first your slave,
I should in thought control your times of pleasure,
Or at your hand the account of hours to crave,
Being your vassal, bound to stay your leisure!" (SON 58)
Answer to 'Do you mind if I do this?' (when 'this' could be anything in which you would expect perhaps to be involved). See also "Jealousy, no j. – Nor dare I question with my jealous thought…'

Love, includes making a fool of yourself - If thou remember'st not the slightest folly that ever love did make thee run into thou hast not loved.
"If thou remember'st not the slightest folly
That ever love did make thee run into,
Thou hast not loved." (AYLI.2.4)
A friend is being criticized because of his odd behavior, due to his being in love. Use this as his defence.
In the play. *Silvius loves Phebe and rebuts Corin's criticism.*

Love, l. affecting mental and physical condition - … stabbed with a white wench's black eye…
"Alas, poor Romeo, he is already dead! stabbed with a white wench's black eye; shot through the ear with a love song; the very pin of his heart cleft with the blind bow-boy's butt-shaft." (RJ.2.4)

Change 'Romeo' to the name of the applicable party. Or you can apply section of the quote to you by a slight change, e.g. 'thanks to you the very pin of my heart has been cleft with the blind bow-boy's butt-shaft'. Or, if you think that that butt shaft is mildly out of taste, use 'arrow' instead, e.g. 'with the blind bow-boy's arrow'. Needless to say, the bow-boy is Cupid. See also 'Love, effects of l. – reversal of physical phenomena'.
In the play. *Mercutio and Benvolio speculate as to whether Romeo may be and Mercutio guesses it right. Romeo is in love.*

Love, l. and flattery, plea to be flattered - O flatter me, for love delights in praises.
"O flatter me, for love delights in praises." (TGV.2.4)
Follow up on a compliment that he has just made to you, if you are a woman. See also 'Praise, importance of p.' – 'Praise, how praise can accomplish objectives more easily than reprimands.'
In the play. *Valentine asks Proteus to call Sylvia 'divine' so that he, Valentine, may be indirectly flattered by the compliment.*

Love, l. and folly as a natural association - ... but as all is mortal in nature, so is all nature in love, mortal in folly.
"We, that are true lovers, run into strange capers; but as all is mortal in nature, so is all nature in love, mortal in folly." (AYLI.2.4)
Become philosophical if someone teases you about being in love, e.g. 'I know, I know, but as all is mortal in nature…in folly."

In the play. *Touchstone, who has joined Celia and Rosalind, has heard Silvius' expression of love (for Phebe) and comments accordingly.*

Love, l. and folly - ... what folly I commit, I dedicate to you.
"**…what folly I commit, I dedicate to you.**" (TC.3.2)
Use this as a counter in any situation where you undertake a task for her, maybe dangerous and she says 'don't do it' (but she secretly hopes that you will (do it)).
In the play. *The folly is Cressida's love of Troilus. She dedicates her folly to Pandarus because he is responsible for having 'pandered' to the affair.*

Love, l. and its association with flowers - Away before me to sweets beds of flowers; love-thoughts lie rich, when canopied with bowers.
"Away before me to sweets beds of flowers;
Love-thoughts lie rich, when canopied with bowers. "(TN.1.1)
Answer to 'Where are you going?' especially if you are in a romantic disposition.
In the play. *The Duke cannot remove from his mind Olivia with who he is deeply in love.*

Love, l. and moderation. In praise of moderation in l. - ... Therefore, love moderately; long love doth so; too swift arrives as tardy as too slow.
"… The sweetest honey
Is loathsome in his own deliciousness,
And in the taste confounds the appetite:
Therefore, love moderately; long love doth so;
Too swift arrives as tardy as too slow." (RJ.2.6)
A line of defense should she accuse you of lacking fire or passion. "The sweetest…appetite: therefore I love

moderately…too slow." See also
'Invocation, happiness in love – love be
moderate, allay thy ecstasy... make it less
for fear I surfeit'
In the play. *Romeo is on pins and needles at Fr. Lawrence's cell, waiting for Juliet's arrival so that the wedding can be celebrated. Fr. Lawrence attempts to give Romeo some words of advice.*

Love, l. and priorities - ...this is my answer, not that I loved Caesar less, but that I loved Rome more.
"…this is my answer, --
Not that I loved Caesar less, but that I loved Rome more." (JC.3.2)
Justify your choice, for example, for what you perceive is/was the good of the company (or the nation), e.g. 'Not that I loved X less, but that I loved Y more
In the play. *Brutus addresses the crowd and justifies the assassination of Caesar.*

Love, l. and silence - Fire, that's closest kept, burns most of all.
JULIA. His little speaking shows his love but small.
LUCETTA. Fire, that's closest kept, burns most of all. (TGV.1.2)
Utter this line whenever you are defined as or accused of being cold. See also 'Silence, s. as a symptom of happiness' – 'Love, obstacles increase passion'.
In the play. *Julia is in love with Proteus and drives the conversation in such a direction that Lucetta, her servant, will praise him.*

Love, l. as a fever – My love is as a fever, longing still for that which longer nurseth the disease..
My love is as a fever, longing still
For that which longer nurseth the disease,
Feeding on that which doth preserve the ill,
The uncertain sickly appetite to please.
My reason, the physician to my love,
Angry that his prescriptions are not kept,
Hath left me, and I desperate now approve
Desire is death, which physic did except.
Past cure I am, now reason is past care,
And frantic-mad with evermore unrest;
My thoughts and my discourse as madmen's are,
At random from the truth vainly express'd;
   For I have sworn thee fair and thought thee bright,
   Who art as black as hell, as dark as night. (SON 147)
When you just cannot give her up. Use the first (4) lines to describe your state, the last (2) to tell her how nasty she is or has been to you.

Love, l. as a fiery spirit – Love is a spirit all compact of fire
"Love is a spirit all compact of fire" (V&A)
In the poem. *Venus, infatuated with Adonis brings a number of arguments to make him yield.*

Love, l. as a joining of hearts - ... my heart unto yours is knit so that but one heart we can make of it.
"…my heart unto yours is knit
So that but one heart we can make of it." (MND.2.2)
Answer to "Do you love me?"
In the play. *Lysander, bewitched by the magic ointment administered by Puck declares his love to the reluctant Hermia.*

Love, l. as a location finder - By whose direction found'st thou out this place? ... By love, that first did prompt me to inquire...
JULIET. By whose direction found'st thou out this place?
ROMEO. By love, that first did prompt me to inquire;

He lent me counsel, and I lent him eyes.
I am no pilot, yet, wert thou as far
As that vast shore washed with the farthest sea,
I would adventure for such merchandise." (RJ.2.2)
Answer to question from female, 'How did you find me?' E.G. 'Love lent me counsel and I lent him eyes'.
In the play. *Romeo lays it thick on Juliet.*

Love, l. as an antidepressant. - ... thy sweet love remembered such wealth brings...
"...thy sweet love remembered such wealth brings,
That then I scorn to change my state with kings" (SON 29)

Love, l. as madness - Love is merely a madness, and, I tell you...
"Love is merely a madness, and, I tell you, deserves as well a dark house and a whip as madmen do: and the reason why they are not so punished and cured is, that the lunacy is so ordinary that the whippers are in love too." (AYLI.3.2)
In the play. *Rosalind to Orlando.*

Love, l. as the birth of conscience – Love is too young to know what conscience is; yet who knows not conscience is born of love?
"Love is too young to know what conscience is;
Yet who knows not conscience is born of love?" (SON 151)

Love, l. asserted unenthusiastically - ... nothing do I see in you... that I can find should merit any hate.
"... nothing do I see in you,
Though churlish thoughts themselves should be your judge,
That I can find should merit any hate." (KJ.2.1)

This is for her. Answer to 'Do you like him?' when you are not sure you do. E.G. 'Nothing do I see in him, that I can find should merit any hate'.
In the play. *Lady Blanche to Lewis who has raptly fallen in love with her.*

Love, l. at first sight - ... How now! Even so quickly may one catch the plague?
"...How now!
Even so quickly may one catch the plague?
Methinks I feel this youth's perfections
With an invisible and subtle stealth
To creep in at mine eyes" (TN.1.5)
In the play. *Olivia falls instantly in love with the disguised Viola/Cesario, thinking that she is a he.*

Love, l. at first sight - ...that maid whose sudden sight hath thrall'd my wounded eye.
"And let me be a slave, to achieve that maid
Whose sudden sight hath thrall'd my wounded eye." (TOS.1.1)
Compliment to a lady who has immediately bewitched you.
In the play. *Lucentio has fallen in love with Bianca and is devising a scheme to get to her. Part of the scheme is to exchange roles between himself and his servant Tranio. 'To thrall'= 'To enslave'.*

Love, l. at first sight - ...the very instant that I saw you, did my heart fly to your service.
"Hear my souls speak:
The very instant that I saw you, did My heart fly to your service" (TEM.3.1)
She asks, "When did you start to love me?" or 'How did you find me?' Also a reply to the eternal question, 'Do you really love me?'

In the play: *Ferdinando is deeply in love with Miranda.*

Love, l. at first sight – …there was never any thing so sudden but…
"…there was never any thing so sudden but the fight of two rams and Caesar's thrasonical brag of 'I came, saw, and overcame:' for your brother and my sister no sooner met but they looked, no sooner looked but they loved, no sooner loved but they sighed, no sooner sighed but they asked one another the reason, no sooner knew the reason but they sought the remedy" (AYLI.5.2)
In the play. *Ganimede relates to Orlando the meeting of Orlando's (repented) brother Oliver and Celia. 'Thrasonical'='Boastful'. Thrason is a character appearing in a Latin comedy by Terence.*

Love, l. at first sight - Who ever loved that loved not at first sight?
"Who ever loved that loved not at first sight?" (AYLI.3.5)
'When did you first like me?', 'When did you begin to love me' are questions often asked. Ladies often like to think that they made an immediate appeal, irrespective of how long it took for the relationship to develop.
In the play. *Silvius loves Phebe but Phebe has a crush on the disguised Rosalind whom she (Phebe) believes to be a boy*

Love, l. at first sight, effects of – O, when mine eyes did see Olivia first, methought she purged the air of pestilence!…
"O, when mine eyes did see Olivia first,
Methought she purged the air of pestilence!
That instant was I turn'd into a hart;
And my desires, like fell and cruel hounds,
E'er since pursue me." (TN.1.1)

Change 'Olivia' to the name of the lady that made a similar effect on you.
In the play. *Duke Orsino reflects on his first encounter with Olivia, with whom he is in (unreciprocated) love. 'Hart'='male deer'.*

Love, l. blind to lover's shortcomings - So true a fool is love that in your will, though you do any thing, he thinks no ill.
"So true a fool is love that in your will,
Though you do any thing, he thinks no ill." (SON 57)
Answer to 'Will you forgive me? See also 'Jealousy, no j. – Nor dare I question with my jealous thought…'

Laughter, l. cannot destroy pain - Mirth cannot move a soul in agony.
"Mirth cannot move a soul in agony" (LLL.5.2)
Answer to 'Why don't you laugh?'
In the play. *Biron's answer to the tasks of love that Rosaline imposes on him for one year before she say yes to him.*

Love, l. causing sleeplessness - Love hath chased sleep from my enthralled eyes and made them watchers of mine own heart's sorrow.
"Love hath chased sleep from my enthralled eyes
And made them watchers of mine own heart's sorrow." (TGV.2.4)
When you want to admit that you are in love. Or rib a friend with 'I see, love hath chased sleep from your enthralled eyes'. Possibly a form of love declaration to a somewhat cold lady.
In the play. *Valentine, notorious for despising love, is now head over heels for Julia and confesses to his friend Proteus his new attitude and state of mind.*

Love, l. compared to a shadow - Love like a shadow flies when substance love pursues…

"Love like a shadow flies when substance love pursues;
Pursuing that that flies, and flying what pursues." (MWW.2.2)
In the play. *Mr. Ford disguises his real identity. He tells Falstaff that he, Mr. Ford, had no success as a seducer with his own wife.*

Love, l. compared to an April day - O, how this spring of love resembleth the uncertain glory of an April day…
"O, how this spring of love resembleth
The uncertain glory of an April day:
Which now shows all the beauty of the sun,
And by and by a cloud takes all away!" (TGV.1.3)
She is in a good mood but you know her to have a volatile character. It may not hurt to remind her.
In the play: *Proteus refers to the necessity to go abroad and be away from Julia. Proteus' father compels Proteus to go to Milan to acquire some experience of the world in a new settings. Proteus, who is a rascal, will eventually go. Once in Milan he immediately forgets Julia and tries to snatch Sylvia (unsuccessfully), from his friend Valentine.*

Love, l. compared to the magnetic center of the earth - … the strong base and building of my love is as the very centre of the earth…
"… the strong base and building of my love
Is as the very centre of the earth,
Drawing all things to it" (TC.4.2)
Answer to 'How much do you love me?' E.G., 'I can say that the strong base… to it.'
In the play. *Cressida declares her unwavering love and fidelity to Troilus, though she will prove false.*

Love, l. concealed. 'Shyness, love concealed - She never told her love, but let concealment, like a worm in the bud…'

Love, l. detected - I do spy some marks of love in her.
"I do spy some marks of love in her." (MAAN.2.3)
In the play. *Benedick begins to change his mind about Beatrice*

Love, l. enabling flight - A lover may bestride the gossamer, that idles in the wanton summer air, and yet not fall…
"A lover may bestride the gossamer
That idles in the wanton summer air,
And yet not fall; so light is vanity." (RJ.2.5)
Change 'a gossamer' for 'a feather' for clarity. Comment on the fact that love prompts or explains the most extraordinary occurrences.
In the play. *Fr, Lawrence's observation on the passion between Romeo and Juliet.*

Love, l. eternal – … eternal love in love's fresh case weighs not the dust and injury of age…
"…eternal love in love's fresh case
Weighs not the dust and injury of age,
Nor gives to necessary wrinkles place,
But makes antiquity for aye his page,
    Finding the first conceit of love there bred
        Where time and outward form would show it dead" (SON 108)
See also 'Love, l. made immortal by words - So long as men can breath or eyes can see, so long lives this and this gives life to thee.' *** 'Love, unshakable and beyond any obstacle - Let me not to the marriage of true minds admit impediments.' 'Aye'='Always'

Love, l. felt but kept hidden - I have loved you night and day for many weary months.

"…I have loved you night and day
For many weary months." (TC.3.2)
When she finally says yes. Answer to the question, "Do you love me?"
In the play. *Cressida declares her love to Troilus. When he asks her why she did appear so hard to win Cressida replies,*
"Hard to seem won: but I was won, my lord,
With the first glance …"
and
"My thoughts were like unbridled children, grown
Too headstrong for their mother."

Love, l. for her above all else – … were I crown'd the most imperial monarch… had force and knowledge more than was ever man's…
"…were I crown'd the most imperial monarch,
Thereof most worthy, were I the fairest youth
That ever made eye swerve, had force and knowledge
More than was ever man's, I would not prize them
Without her love; for her employ them all;
Commend them and condemn them to her service
Or to their own perdition" (WT.4.4)
In the play. *Florizel to his father and King Polixenes, reaffirming his unflinching determination to love and marry Perdita.*

Love, l. hidden and undeclared - … thus, Indian like, religious in mine error, I adore the sun…
"… thus, Indian like,
Religious in mine error, I adore
The sun, that looks upon his worshipper,
But knows of him no more."
(AWEW.1.3)
A compliment and/or as a passionate declaration of love to a girl who seems to ignore you. E.G. 'I think that you ignore me and yet… You are that sun and I adore the sun that looks… no more.'
In the play, *Helen confesses to the Countess that her love for Bertram is similar to an Indian who adores the sun but the sun does not know it. Equally, Bertram is not aware of Helen's feelings.*

Love, l. impossible but unavoidable - I know I love in vain, strive against hope…
"I know I love in vain, strive against hope;
Yet, in this dispute, and intenible sieve,
I still pour in the waters of my love." (AWEW.1.3)
She has turned you down but you want to tell her that you can't stop loving her.
In the play. *Helen confesses her love to Bertram to the Countess, who is his mother.*

Love, l. impossible to hide – A murderous guilt shows not itself more soon than love that would seem hid…
"A murderous guilt shows not itself more soon
Than love that would seem hid: love's night is noon" (TN.3.1)
In the play. *Olivia has fallen in love with the disguised Viola/Cesario, thinking that she is a he.*

Love, l. in any conditions – Had I no eyes but ears, my ears would love that inward beauty and invisible…
"Had I no eyes but ears, my ears would love
That inward beauty and invisible;
Or were I deaf, thy outward parts would move
Each part in me that were but sensible:
Though neither eyes nor ears, to hear nor see,
Yet should I be in love by touching thee" (V&A)
Answer to 'Do you love me?'

In the poem. *Venus to the ice cold Adonis*

Love, l. incompatible with reason - … to say the truth, reason and love keep little company together now-a-days.
". and yet, to say the truth, reason and love keep little company together now-a-days." (MND.3.1)
Comment on an unsuitable match. Or justify yourself, "I know but truth, reason and love keep little company."
In the play. *Bottom is somewhat perplexed by the love declarations of Titania but tries to rationalize the occurrence.*

Love, l. incompatible with wisdom - … for to be wise and love exceeds man's might; that dwells with gods above.
"… for to be wise and love,
Exceeds man's might; that dwells with gods above. (TC.3.2)
She is ready to say yes but wants to make sure that you want it too. So she asks, "Are you sure?" You want to subtly indicate that your passion drives you but that is part of the regular course of things.
Or, circumstances may suggest that falling in love with her (or marrying her) may be a risky proposition. But your desire or love overpowers your considerations of wisdom and prudence.
In the play: *Cressida teases Pandarus by pretending to yield to Troilus out of passion whereas if she were wise she would at least think about it.*

Love, l. inspired by dangerous accomplishments – She loved me for the dangers I had pass'd…
"She loved me for the dangers I had pass'd,
And I loved her that she did pity them" (OTH.1.3)
In the play. *Othello addresses the disbelieving audience, including Desdemona's father*

Brabantio, explaining how Desdemona fell in love with him.

Love, l. inspiring reactions opposite to what they should be – (Love) shall suspect where is no cause of fear, it shall not fear where it should most mistrust.
"It shall suspect where is no cause of fear;
It shall not fear where it should most mistrust" (V&A)
In the poem. *After Adonis' death, Venus predicts all that can go wrong in love's relationships.*

Love, l. inspiring wordiness - Thou wilt be like a lover, presently and tire the hearer with a book of words.
"Thou wilt be like a lover, presently,
And tire the hearer with a book of words." (MAAN.1.1)
Tease a person who is or is likely to be in love. Or use the second line to describe a verbose person, e.g. 'He tires the hearer… words'.
In the play. *Don Pedro has just heard from Claudio that he, Claudio is in love with Hero, Leonato's daughter.*

Love, l. keeps him enchained - … his mistress did hold his eyes locked in her crystal looks.
"This is the gentleman I told your ladyship,
Had come along with me, but that his mistress
Did hold his eyes locked in her crystal looks." (TGV.2.4)
Extract material for a short compliment, e.g. 'my eyes are locked in your crystal looks', perhaps as a neutral reply to 'What are you thinking?' Or use to justify (if applicable) the absence of a friend or colleague, e.g. 'He would have come along with me but… looks.'

In the play. *Valentine says this lines to Silvia to introduce his newly arrived friend Proteus in Milan.*

Love, l. kept platonic - I never tempted her with word too large… bashful sincerity and comely love.
"I never tempted her with word too large;
But, as a brother to his sister, show'd
Bashful sincerity and comely love."
(MAAN.4.1)
See also entries for 'Reliability, am I going to be safe with you? Can I trust you?'
In the play. *Claudio explains to Leonato that he kept a platonic relationship with Leonato's daughter Hero.*

Love, l. lessons - You must lay lime to tangle her desires by wailful sonnets…
"You must lay lime to tangle her desires
By wailful sonnets, whose composed rhymes
Should be full-fraught with serviceable vows" (TGV.3.2)
In the play. *Proteus pretends to instruct the hapless Thurio on how to win the heart of Silvia.*

Love, l. long lasting even after beauty is a thing of the past - Yet, do thy worst old Time; despite thy wrong, my love shall in my verse ever live young.
"Yet, do thy worst old Time; despite thy wrong,
My love shall in my verse ever live young." (SON.19)

With a bit of twisting use this to soften the impact of your being so much older than she is - e.g. 'I know I am old but I can say, yet do thy worst… young.' I leave it up to you how to answer if after this she asks you if you are a poet. If you are one, of course say 'yes'; if not you can say that, though you are not a poet, you will always find something nice to say to her. Follow up with any of the complimenting and flattering quotes, depending on your taste or her type of beauty. See also entries for 'AGE'.

Love, l. made immortal by words - So long as men can breath or eyes can see, so long lives this and this gives life to thee.
"So long as men can breath or eyes can see,
So long lives this and this gives life to thee." (SON.18)
A good line for a blank card. You leave her a bit hanging on the interpretation of the quote but this adds a pleasant and mildly intriguing or puzzled feeling. You can mean that she is worth to be immortal just as the subject for whom the sonnet was written. But it can also be read as a generic statement that your love transcends the limits of time.

Love, l. makes time pass quickly - A summer's day will seem an hour but short being wasted in such time-beguiling sport.
"A summer's day will seem an hour but short,
Being wasted in such time-beguiling sport." (V&A)
Metaphor for time spent in loving, a 'time-beguiling' sport.

Love, l. making with a divine lady – … not yet made wanton the night with her; and she is sport for Jove.

"…he hath not yet made wanton the night with her; and she is sport for Jove" (OTH.2.3)
In the play. *Iago injects a vulgar comment on Othello) who retired early after his arrival in Cyprus.*

Love, l. misplaced – …dotes in idolatry upon this spotted and inconstant man.
"…and she, sweet lady, dotes, Devoutly dotes, dotes in idolatry, Upon this spotted and inconstant man" (MND.1.1)
In the play. *Lysander explains to Theseus how Helena loves the undeserving Demetrius.*

Love, l. never smooth - … the course of true love never did run smooth.
"… for aught that I could ever read, Could ever hear by tale or history, The course of true love never did run smooth." (MND.1.1)
If you are a third party witnessing a quarrel between two lovers, deliver the lines as a way to indicate that the strength of true love is not to be measured by trivial disagreements. If you are a direct party in the quarrel and she tells you that you don't love her, use the lines to show her that you do.
In the play. *Obstacles have arisen preventing Hermia to marry Lysander.*

Love, l. not ambition as a driving force - No blown ambition doth our arms incite but love, dear love.
"No blown ambition doth our arms incite,
But love, dear love…." (KL.4.4)
Reasoning often adopted by right-wing politicians to justify attacking, invading or bombing other countries.
In the play. *Cordelia lands at Dover from France with an army to rescue her father Lear from the malicious clutches of his other wicked daughters Regan and Goneril.*

Love, l. of self prompted by seeing her – … I beheld myself drawn in the flattering table of her eye.
"I do protest I never loved myself
Till now infixed I beheld myself
Drawn in the flattering table of her eye." (KJ.2.1)
In the play. *Lewis of France at the prospect of marrying the beautiful Lady Blanche.*

Love, l. preferred over power - He after honour hunts, I after love…
"He after honour hunts, I after love:
He leaves his friends to dignify them more,
I leave myself, my friends and all, for love." (TGV.1.1)
Answer or explanation as to why your career is or has not been that brilliant. If you do not have an immediate person to compare yourself with, change 'He after honor hunts' to 'Some after honor hunt'.
In the play. *Valentine, who proclaims himself to be resistant to the allurements of love, has left Verona for Milan to seek a career in the retinue of the Duke of Milan. Proteus remains in Verona and meditates on the difference between himself and Valentine.*

Love, l. prevailing over friendship - Friendship is constant in all other things, save in the office and affairs of love…
"Friendship is constant in all other things,
Save in the office and affairs of love
… for beauty is a witch,
Against whose charms faith melteth into blood." (MAAN.2.1)
When you are going out with your friend's girlfriend, 'Beauty is a witch against whose charm…blood'
In the play. *For some reason Claudio has asked Don Pedro to woo Hero on his (Claudio's) behalf. Now Claudio is not so sure that it was a good idea. Perhaps Don Pedro will woo Hero for himself.*

Love, l. prevailing over friendship - O, but I love his lady too too much, and that's the reason I love him so little.
"O, but I love his lady too too much,
And that's the reason I love him so little" (TGV.2.4)
In the play. *Proteus is besotted with his bosom-friend Valentine's girlfriend Silvia. He explains to himself why now Valentine is no longer a friend.*

Love, l. prompting oratory - My tongue could never learn sweet smoothing words; but now thy beauty is propos'd my fee...
"My tongue could never learn sweet smoothing words;
But now thy beauty is propos'd my fee,
My proud heart sues, and prompts my tongue to speak." (KRIII.1.2)
A regal introduction if you asking her to marry you.
In the play. *King Richard III uses these very words to start the conversation with his future queen (Anne) leading to his proposal of marriage to her.*

Love, l. put to a test - ... If frosts and fasts, hard lodging and thin weeds nip not the gaudy blossoms of your love...
"If frosts and fasts, hard lodging and thin weeds
Nip not the gaudy blossoms of your love" (LLL5.2)
If she delays a decision on your proffers, e.g. 'Frosts and fasts etc. will not nip the gaudy blossom of my love'
In the play. *The Princess is leaving for France after the King's passionate love declaration. She will re-examine his suit after one year if her feelings are still the same.*

Love, l. so deep, chaos without it - ... and when I love thee not chaos is come again.

"But I do love thee! and when I love thee not,
Chaos is come again." (OTH.3.3)
Strong indication of the effect she has on you. Answer to "Do you love me?"
In the play. *Othello is beginning to be gnawed by jealousy, thinking unjustly that Desdemona is betraying him with Cassio.*

Love, l. spontaneous or sought - Love sought is good, but given unsought is better.
"Love sought is good, but given unsought is better." (TN.3.1)
Applicable more to a she than a he - when he is after her but she does not reciprocate the feeling.
In the play. *Olivia tries to come to terms with her love for Viola/Cesario.*

Love, l. tender or rough? - ... it is too rough, too rude, too boisterous; and it pricks like thorn.
"Is love a tender thing? it is too rough,
Too rude, too boisterous; and it pricks like thorn." (RJ.1.4)
A rebuttal if everyone else magnified or extols the beauties of love.
In the play. *Romeo's comments to a remark by Mercutio.*

Love, l. tested by time – ... love is begun by time and ...time qualifies the spark and fire of it.
"... I know love is begun by time;
And that I see, in passages of proof,
Time qualifies the spark and fire of it." (H.4.7)
In the play. *King Claudius tries to work up Laertes to kill Hamlet by hinting that perhaps Laertes did not love so much his father Polonius, slain by Hamlet.*

Love, l. tied to success or fortune? - For 'tis a question left us yet to prove whether love lead fortune, or else fortune love...

"This world is not for aye, nor 'tis not strange
That even our loves should with our fortunes change;
For 'tis a question left us yet to prove,
Whether love lead fortune, or else fortune love.
The great man down, you mark his favourite flies;
The poor advanced makes friends of enemies.
And hitherto doth love on fortune tend;
For who not needs shall never lack a friend,
And who in want a hollow friend doth try,
Directly seasons him his enemy." (H.3.2)
In the play. *The lines are part of the play 'The Murder of Gonzago' here recited by the player king.*

Love, l. travelling at the speed of thought - ... love's heralds should be thoughts, which ten times faster glide than the sun's beams...
"...love's heralds should be thoughts,
Which ten times faster glide than the sun's beams,
Driving back shadows over louring hills" (RJ.2.5)
See also 'Thought, power of t. and imagination to travel instantly - For nimble thought can jump both sea and land as soon as think the place where he would be.' *** 'Nearness, wishing to be near loved one - If the dull substance of my flesh were thought...'
In the play. *Juliet is anxiously awaiting the return of the Nurse whom she dispatched to deliver a message to Romeo. 'Louring' = 'Hovering'.*

Love, l. unrequited, how looking at other ladies does not help - ... What doth her beauty serve, but as a note where I may read who pass'd that passing fair?
"Show me a mistress that is passing fair,
What doth her beauty serve, but as a note
Where I may read who pass'd that passing fair?
Farewell: thou canst not teach me to forget." (RJ.1.1)
You cannot forget a woman with whom your relationship has ended. Your answer to friends who suggest that you should look at other women.
In the play. *Benvolio suggests that Romeo considers other female options, other than unconquerable Rosaline, with whom Romeo is currently infatuated. But Romeo rebuts with the notion that any pretty girl looked at would cause him to think of the original prettier one.*

Love. l. unrequited, technique for forgetting - O, teach me how I should forget to think, ... By giving liberty unto thine eyes...
ROMEO O, teach me how I should forget to think.
BENVOLIO By giving liberty unto thine eyes;
Examine other beauties. (RJ.1.1)
In the play. *Prior to meeting with Juliet Romeo was in love with a lady of a conservative disposition. See 'Love unrequited. How looking at other ladies does not help'.*

Love, l. unstoppable, beyond any limit - For stony limits cannot hold love out, and what love can do, that dares love attempt.
"For stony limits cannot hold love out;
And what love can do, that dares love attempt." (RJ.2.2)

Your relationship is made difficult by circumstances out of your control, but you wish to state your unswerving determination to love her. The second line may be an answer to 'Will you do this for me?'
In the play. *Romeo reveals that he climbed Juliet's garden walls (stony limits) to be near her.*

Love, l. waning or melted away -- … my love is thaw'd, which, like a waxen image, 'gainst a fire bears no impression of the thing it was.
"…now my love is thaw'd;
Which, like a waxen image, 'gainst a fire,
Bears no impression of the thing it was." (TGV.2.4)
See also 'Replacement, you loved her first and suddenly you love another - Even as one heat another heat expels, or as one nail by strength drives out another…'
In the play. *Proteus tries to explain to himself how come that he has suddenly forgotten his love Julia and is now suddenly in love with Silvia.*

Love, l.'s downside - Love is a smoke made with the fume of sighs…
Love is a smoke made with the fume of sighs;
Being urged, a fire sparkling in lovers' eyes;
Being vexed, a sea nourished with loving tears." (RJ.1.1)
Give your cold and somewhat pessimistic opinion during a topic discussion.
In the play: *Romeo's skeptical comments on love.*

Love, l's effects on young and old respectively – How love makes young men thrall and old men dote…
"How love makes young men thrall and old men dote;
How love is wise in folly, foolish-witty" (V&A)
In the poem. *Comment on the pining by Venus after Adonis has flatly refused her advances. 'Thrall'='Enslaved', 'To dote'='to love in excess'*

Love, l.'s letter ending – Thine own true knight, by day or night…
"Thine own true knight,
By day or night,
Or any kind of light,
With all his might" (MWW.2.1)
In the play. *Ending of Falstaff's letter(s) respectively to Mrs. Ford and Mrs. Page.*

Love, l.'s pains not to be laughed at - He jests at scars that never felt a wound.
"He jests at scars that never felt a wound." (RJ.2.2)
Should anyone poke fun at you because you are madly in love. See also 'Unhappiness, impossible to be understood by those who do not feel it - thou canst not speak of that thou dost not feel.' – 'Love, l's yearnings not abated by words'.
In the play. *Wounded by his love for Juliet, Romeo enters the Capulets' garden in the hope of seeing Juliet.*

Love, l.'s pleasures recalled - Eternity was in our lips and eyes, bliss in our brows' bent.
"Eternity was in our lips and eyes,
Bliss in our brows' bent." (AC.1.3)
When you are trying to rekindle a long past passion. Or a compliment, e.g. 'Eternity is in your lips and eyes…'
In the play. *Antony must leave Alexandria for Rome and has come to say good-bye. Cleopatra takes the occasion to recall former happy times.*

Love, l.'s power to wound when feelings are not reciprocated - … then shall you know the wounds invisible that love's keen arrows make.
"If ever (as that ever may be near)
You meet in some fresh cheek the power of fancy,

Then shall you know the wounds invisible
That love's keen arrows make." (AYL.3.5)
Try it if all else has failed. Who knows, she may even in time change her mind. In the actual play, Silvius, who says this line ends up marrying the very girl whom he addresses and that so far has scorned him.
In the play. *Silvius loves Phebe but Phebe has a crush on the disguised Rosalind whom she (Phebe) believes to be a boy.*

Love, l.'s psychological effects, generator of poetical spirit - ... it hath taught me to rhyme, and to be melancholy...
"By heaven, I do love; and it hath taught me to rhyme, and to be melancholy; and here is part of my rhyme, and here my melancholy." (LLL.4.3)
In the play. *Biron ponders sending additional romantic messages to Rosaline.*

Love, l.'s redemptive effects on men of questionable character - ... base men being in love have then a nobility in their natures more than is native to them.
"...base men being in love have then a nobility in their natures more than is native to them." (OTH.2.1)
Advance your theory for the inexplicable good behavior of a man whom you normally find despicable.
In the play. *Iago in conversation with Roderigo. It is not clear whether the comment refers to Roderigo or, more likely to Cassio. As part of this diabolic plot, Iago wants Roderigo to believe that Desdemona is in love with Cassio.*

Love, l.'s remarkable power of transformation - O powerful love! that, in some respects, makes a beast a man, in some other, a man a beast.

"O powerful love! that, in some respects, makes a beast a man, in some other, a man a beast." (MWW.5.4)
A comment.
In the play. *Falstaff has subjected himself to all sorts of pranks, abuse and transformations in order to get to Mistress Page. Dressed now like a horned deer, he will be subject to one last prank.*

Love, l.'s revenge for having undervalued it – ... it is a plague that Cupid will impose for my neglect...
"...it is a plague
That Cupid will impose for my neglect
Of his almighty dreadful little might.
Well, I will love, write, sigh, pray, sue and groan" (LLL.3.1)
In the play. *Biron's reflections after having fallen in love with Rosaline.*

Love, l.'s revenge for having undervalued it - I have done penance for contemning love...
"I have done penance for contemning love;
Whose imperious thoughts have punished me
With bitter fasts, with penitential groans,
With nightly tears, and daily heart-sore sighs." (TGV.4.2)
It may apply to you or to a friend who rails against love. You may remind him of what happens to people who speak or think like him.
In the play. *Valentine confides to Proteus to be madly in love with Sylvia.*

Love, l' s strategy when courting a rich woman – ... I found thee of more value than stamps in gold or sums in sealed bags...
"... wooing thee, I found thee of more value
Than stamps in gold or sums in sealed bags;

And 'tis the very riches of thyself
That now I aim at." (MWW.3.4)
In the play. *Master Fenton plans to marry Anne Page (and will succeed).*

Love, l.'s trials - …if frosts and fasts, hard lodging and thin weeds nip not the gaudy blossoms of your love…
"If frosts and fasts, hard lodging and thin weeds
Nip not the gaudy blossoms of your love…" (LLL.5.2)
Give emphasis to the strength of your affection, e.g. 'Not frosts and fasts will nip …of my love'.
In the play. *The Princess counsels the King to adopt a recluse and austere life for one year to test the strength of his love for her.*

Love, l.'s voice and its divine harmony - when Love speaks, the voice of all the gods makes heaven drowsy with the harmony.
"…. when Love speaks, the voice of all the gods
Makes heaven drowsy with the harmony." (LLL.4.3)
Use after a quarrel has been settled.
In the play. *Biron provides his friends with a final, lengthy and eloquent string of arguments to abandon their vows and the oath of an ascetic and studious life and instead chase the girls that have just come by. In fact he concludes his peroration with these lines,*
"Then fools you were these women to forswear,
Or keeping what is sworn, you will prove fools.
For wisdom's sake, a word that all men love,
Or for love's sake, a word that loves all men,
Or for men's sake, the authors of these women,
Or women's sake, by whom we men are men,
Let us once lose our oaths to find ourselves,
Or else we lose ourselves to keep our oaths."

Love, l's vows like music – And I… that suck'd the honey of his music vows…
"And I, of ladies most deject and wretched,
That suck'd the honey of his music vows…" (H.3.1)
Compliment, e.g. 'The honey of your music words'
In the play. *Ophelia cannot explain Hamlet's madness and rude behavior.*

Love, l's yearnings not abated by words - Didst thou but know the inly touch of love…
"Didst thou but know the inly touch of love,
Thou wouldst as soon go kindle fire with snow,
As seek to quench the fire of love with words." (TGV.2.7)
This explains why to dissuade anyone from pursuing his/her passion for someone else (however unsuited) is useless.
In the play. *Lucetta attempts to persuade Julia to wait for Proteus' return rather than chasing him in Milan, but Julia's love cannot be abated with words.*

Love, lack of attraction suggesting abandonment of pursuit - …if there be no great love in the beginning…
"… if there be no great love in the beginning, yet heaven may decrease it upon better acquaintance."
(MWW.1.1)
Reason for not pursuing her if you detect a lack of interest.
In the play. *Shallow questions Slender on whether he (Slender) could love Anne Page, should he be married to her.*

Love, lack of l. for own self prevents loving others - Love loving not itself none other can.
"O king, believe not this hard-hearted man!
Love loving not itself none other can." (KRII.5.3)
In the play. *The Duke of York pleads with the King (Bolingbroke, now Henry IV), to punish his own (York's) son, the Duke of Aumerle, who joined plotters against Bolingbroke. His mother instead pleads with the King for a pardon and points out the inhumanity of her husband's attitude.*

Love, lover compared to a book - This precious book of love, this unbound lover, to beautify him, only lacks a cover.
"This precious book of love, this unbound lover,
To beautify him, only lacks a cover." (RJ.1.3)
A mildly stretched but always elegant way to tell her that you are interested and that you can be the cover to beautify the book."
In the play. *Lady Capulet praises Paris in absentia and suggests him as a perfect match for Juliet who, in this metaphor, is the 'cover' to the 'book of love'.*

Love, lovers' looks as food - O, know'st thou not his looks are my soul's food?
"O, know'st thou not his looks are my soul's food?" (TGV.2.7)
A compliment usable by both sexes, 'Your looks are my soul's food'. See also 'Love, food to the mind - So are you to my thoughts as food to life, or as sweet-seasoned showers are to the ground'
In the play. *Julia to Lucetta referring to Proteus.*

Love, l. making fools of people. ... he that is so yoked by a fool, methinks should not be chronicled for wise.
"Love is your master, for he masters you:
And he that is so yoked by a fool,
Methinks, should not be chronicled for wise." (TGV.1.1)
Generalize, e.g. 'Love enslaves people and he that is… wise'. Or, with a self-effacing sentence, admit that you have been taken in by a fool and therefore you carry some blame yourself.
In the play. *Valentine scoffs at Proteus who is in love with Julia.*

Love, making l. not war. - ... He capers nimbly in a lady's chamber to the lascivious pleasing of a lute..
"Grim-visaged war hath smooth'd his wrinkled front;
And now, - instead of mounting barbed steeds,
To fight the souls of fearful adversaries, -
He capers nimbly in a lady's chamber
To the lascivious pleasing of a lute." (KRIII.1.1)
Talk ironically about yourself or justify your unwillingness to fight – 'instead of mounting barbed steeds… (I prefer to) caper nimbly in a lady's chamber … lute'.
In the play. *Richard meditates sarcastically on the end of war. War is personalized, instead of fighting war pursues more pleasurable and peaceful activities. 'Barbed'='armed and harnessed (horses)'*

Love, more under the control of heavens than anything else - In love, the heavens themselves do guide the state. Money buys land and wives are sold by fate.
"In love, the heavens themselves do guide the state. Money buys land and wives are sold by fate." (MWW.5.5)
State that love cannot be managed.

In the play. *Anne Page has married her love Master Fenton and not the party her father had in mind. A resigned Mr. Page comments on the event.*

Love, mutual l. visible – …or both dissemble deeply their affections.
"…your son Lucentio here
Doth love my daughter and she loveth him,
Or both dissemble deeply their affections" (TOS.4.4)
In the play. *Baptista referring to his daughter Bianca who loves Lucentio.*

Love, never so much l. - I never loved myself, till now infixed I beheld myself, drawn in the flattering picture of her eye.
"I do protest, I never loved myself,
Till now infixed I beheld myself,
Drawn in the flattering picture of her eye." (KJ.2.2)
Women like to hear that either they are your first love, or if that is not possible, that you never loved anyone else so strongly and passionately. Good as a sophisticated alternative to "I am attracted to you."
In the play. *The Dauphin Lewis is mesmerized by the beauty of Blanch's eyes.*

Love, no trial too difficult – … to weep seas, live in fire, eat rocks…
"…when we vow to weep seas, live in fire, eat rocks, tame tigers; thinking it harder for our mistress to devise imposition enough than for us to undergo any difficulty imposed" (TC.3.2)
In the play. *Troilus explains to Cressida the state of mind when a man is in love.*

Love, not a sign of wisdom - … he that is so yoked by a fool, methinks should not be chronicled for wise.
"Love is your master, for he masters you:
And he that is so yoked by a fool,
Methinks, should not be chronicled for wise." (TGV.1.1)
Generalize, e.g. 'Love enslaves people and he that is… wise'. Or, with a self-effacing sentence, admit that you have been taken in by a fool and therefore you carry some blame yourself.
In the play. *Valentine scoffs at Proteus who is in love with Julia.*

Love, obstacles increase passion - … the current that with gentle murmur glides, thou know'st, being stopp'd, impatiently doth rage…
"The more thou damm'st it up, the more it burns.
The current that with gentle murmur glides,
Thou know'st, being stopp'd, impatiently doth rage;
But when his fair course is not hindered,
He makes sweet music with the enamell'd stones,
Giving a gentle kiss to every sedge
He overtaketh in his pilgrimage,
And so by many winding nooks he strays
With willing sport to the wild ocean." (TGV.2.7)
One possible answer to 'How is your love life?'. The first line can suffice. In another context the image of the unimpeded versus the constricted current, can be used as a metaphor to insist that freedom is more productive than constriction.
In the play. *Julia burns with passion for the philandering and inconstant Proteus. Her servant and advisor Lucetta attempts to counsel Julia who responds with this aquatic analogy*

Love, offerings of sacrifices - Say that upon the altar of her beauty you sacrifice your tears, your sighs, your heart.

"Say that upon the altar of her beauty
You sacrifice your tears, your sighs, your heart" (TGV.3.2)
Could work as an initial love declaration with minor changes, 'Upon the altar of your beauty, I sacrifice my tears, my sighs, my heart.'
In the play. *Proteus pretends to give courting lessons to Thurio so as to win the hand of Silvia. In addition to sacrificial tears Proteus recommends writing and make the ink last longer by moistening it again with more tears,*
Write till your ink be dry, and with your tears
Moist it again

Love, plea for l. not to be ridiculed - … but, good Kate, mock me mercifully…
"…but, good Kate, mock me mercifully; the rather, gentle princess, because I love thee cruelly" (KHV.5.2)
In the play. *King Henry woos Katharine of France.*

Love, pleading for l's sake, a play on words - For wisdom's sake, a word that all men love..
"For wisdom's sake, a word that all men love,
Or for love's sake, a word that loves all men." (LLL.4.3)
Use as a supporting argument when you ask for something, e.g. 'Do this for wisdom's sake…or for love's sake, a word that loves all men'.
In the play. *At the end of a lengthy argument Biron persuades his friends that their vow of a secluded life of learning and abstinence was foolish.*

"Then fools you were these women to forswear,
Or keeping what is sworn, you will prove fools.
For wisdom's sake, a word that all men love,
Or for love's sake, a word that loves all men,
Or for men's sake, the authors of these women,
Or women's sake, by whom we men are men"

Love, poetry and madness - The lunatic, the lover and the poet are of imagination all compact.
"The lunatic, the lover and the poet,
Are of imagination all compact." (MND.5.1)
Counter with this when she says, "Are you mad?" after you have made a suggestion that shocked or amused her well enough to ask you the question.
In the play. *Theseus, in conversation with Hippolyta makes some important philosophical statements*

Love, pregnancy and agricultural references – … As those that feed grow full, as blossoming time …
"Your brother and his lover have embraced:
As those that feed grow full, as blossoming time
That from the seedness the bare fallow brings
To teeming foison, even so her plenteous womb
Expresseth his full tilth and husbandry." (MFM.1.4)
In the play. *Lucio reports to Isabella that her brother Claudio has been arrested for having seduced Juliet. 'Seedness'='The act of sowing'. 'Foison' = 'Plentiful harvest'. 'Tilth' = 'Tillage' and a synonym for 'husbandry'.*

Love, prosperity an essential ingredient for l. – Prosperity's the very

bond of love, whose fresh complexion and whose heart together affliction alters.
"Prosperity's the very bond of love,
Whose fresh complexion and whose heart together
Affliction alters." (WT.4.3).
Use to justify a request for salary increase now that you are married. See also 'Advance, applying for an advance or raise' - Patience, asking for p. or a raise'
In the play. *Camillo offers words of advice to Florizel while prompting him to take the risk and travel to Sicilia. The outcome is uncertain. However, if Florizel does not take the risk, he is certain to live precariously and without the prosperity that necessary for a steady relationship.*

Love, ready to take any abuse for her l. – Such is my love, to thee I so belong, that for thy right myself will bear all wrong.
"Such is my love, to thee I so belong,
That for thy right myself will bear all wrong." (SON 88)

Love, reasons for l. uncertain – … love's reason's without reason.
"I know not why I love this youth, and I have heard you say, love's reason's without reason" (CYM.4.2)
Answer to 'Why do you love her?' or 'What do you find in her?' If, on hearing your answer, the other party says that he never said that (i.e. that love's reason without reason) tell him that he is right but that you are just quoting Shakespeare.
In the play. *Arviragus cannot explain his feeling for Imogen. Imogen at that moment is disguised as a boy, having fled from the king, her father. It turns out that Imogen is the sister of Arviragus.*

Love, reasons for l. unexplainable – Ask me no reason why I love you.
"Ask me no reason why I love you; for though Love use Reason for his physician, he admits him not for his counsellor." (MWW.2.1)
Answer to 'Why do you love me?' if you wish to remain vague.
In the play. *Mistress Page reads from a letter received from Falstaff.*

Love, reasons for not refusing it - Affection is a coal that must be cool'd…
"Affection is a coal that must be cool'd;
Else, suffer'd, it will set the heart on fire:
The sea hath bounds, but deep desire hath none" (V&A)
In the poem. *Adone's horse fled to chase a mare and Venus draw a motivating comparison.*

Love, reasons for not refusing it – Beauty within itself should not be wasted…
"Beauty within itself should not be wasted:
Fair flowers that are not gather'd in their prime
Rot and consume themselves in little time" (V&A)
See also 'Age. Its effect on wrinkles - When forty winters shall besiege thy brow, and dig deep trenches in thy beauty's field.' *** Entries for 'Virginity, negative characteristics of v.'
In the poem. *Venus is infatuated with Adonis but he is very shy.*

Love, reasons for not refusing it – Torches are made to light, jewels to wear…
"Torches are made to light, jewels to wear,
Dainties to taste, fresh beauty for the use,
Herbs for their smell, and sappy plants to bear:
Things growing to themselves are growth's abuse:

Seeds spring from seeds and beauty breedeth beauty" (V&A)
In the poem. *Venus finds reasons to prompt a positive response from Adonis*

Love, restating your love with a touch of modesty – So all my best is dressing old words new.
"O, know, sweet love, I always write of you,
And you and love are still my argument;
So all my best is dressing old words new,
Spending again what is already spent:
For as the sun is daily new and old,
So is my love still telling what is told." (SON.76)
Good as words for a note to a loved one or to one whom you love but to whom you have not disclosed your feelings.

Love, selection criteria for choosing between two loves established - The will of man is by his reason sway'd...
"The will of man is by his reason sway'd;
And reason says you are the worthier maid" (MND.2.2)
When she knows your previous girlfriend well and is uncertain as to the strength of your affection. If she still insists on the issue use the lines immediately following,
"And touching now the point of human skill,
Reason becomes the marshal to my will
And leads me to your eyes, where I o'erlook
Love's stories written in love's richest book."
In the play. *See next entry.*

Love, selection criteria for choosing between two loves established - Who will not change a raven for a dove?

"Not Hermia but Helena I love:
Who will not change a raven for a dove?" (MND.2.2)
Change Hermia to the other girl's name and Helena to the name of the girl you now love. Useful when she accuses you of still loving your previous girlfriend.
In the play. *Lysander who was in love with Hermia has a sudden change of preferences after being affected by a magical concoction prepared and delivered by Puck. The concoction is a flower extract that, when deposited on the lips of a sleeping subject, causes the subject to fall in love with the first person (of the opposite sex) seen after opening his/her eyes.*

Love, she said yes – As doubtful whether what I see be true until confirm'd, sign'd, ratified by you.
"As doubtful whether what I see be true,
Until confirm'd, sign'd, ratified by you." (MOV.3.2)
Change 'see' to 'hear' for effect. Or apply to any positive outcome of an event.
In the play. *Bassanio, still in mild disbelief, has guessed the right basket thereby winning Portia's hand.*

Love, showing signs of being in l. - Methinks he looks as though he were in love.
"Methinks he looks as though he were in love" (TOS.3.1)
Possible explanation for irrational behavior of friend or acquaintance. Answer to 'Why do you think he behaves this way?'
In the play. *Hortensio suspects (correctly) that Lucentio is in love with Bianca.*

Love, sign of l. unexpected when abandoned by all - For 'tis a sign of love; and love to Richard is a strange brooch in this all-hating world.
"For 'tis a sign of love; and love to Richard

Is a strange brooch in this all-hating world." (KRII.5.5)
Give recognition to friends who have not abandoned you when everyone else has. Change 'Richard' to your name.
In the play. *Imprisoned at Pomfret, Richard II meditates that the music played for him is a sign of love or deference. 'Brooch' is a jewel worn in a hat or elsewhere, here the word is used figuratively.*

Love, signs of l. unmistakable - ... he is far gone, far gone: and truly in my youth I suffered much extremity for love; very near this.
"...he is far gone, far gone: and truly in my youth I suffered much extremity for love; very near this." (H.2.2)
In the play. *Polonius is sure that Hamlet loves his daughter Ophelia, which would explain his apparent madness.*

Love, signs of l. unmistakable – ... if he love her not and be not from his reason fall'n thereon...
"...if he love her not
And be not from his reason fall'n thereon,
Let me be no assistant for a state,
But keep a farm and carters." (H.2.2)
In the play. *Polonius is sure that Hamlet loves his daughter Ophelia, which would explain his apparent madness. 'Carters'='Drivers of carts'*

Love, signs or evidence of being in l. – If he be not in love with some woman, there is no believing old signs...
"If he be not in love with some woman, there is no believing old signs: a' brushes his hat o' mornings; what should that bode?" (MAAN.3.2)
In the play. *Claudio comments on the changed behavior of Benedick, a one-time staunch skeptic on love.*

Love, signs or evidence of l. - ... he might not beteem the winds of heaven visit her face too roughly.
"... so loving to my mother,
That he might not beteem the winds of heaven
Visit her face too roughly." (H.1.2)
Answer to the question, 'Do you love me?' Instead of just saying 'yes', pump up the answer a bit by saying that you will even protect her from the harshness of the weather. E.G. 'I will not even beteem the winds of heaven visit your face too roughly'. Also an answer to the question 'Will you take care of me?'
In the play: *Hamlet remembers how much his murdered father, king of Denmark, was kind and loving to his wife who did not wait very long to marry the evil Claudius, Hamlet's stepfather. 'To beteem' = 'to allow'. See also 'Passion, obvious.'*

Love, sincerity in expressing it – I am too fond, and therefore thou mayst think my 'havior light: but trust me...
"In truth, fair Montague, I am too fond,
And therefore thou mayst think my 'havior light:
But trust me, gentleman, I'll prove more true
Than those that have more cunning to be strange" (RJ.2.2)
'I'll prove more true than...strange' can be an answer to 'Can I trust you?' See also entries for 'Playing hard-to-get'.
In the play. *Juliet to Romeo.*

Love, strength of l. in youth - ... Our blood to us, this to our blood is born...
"... This thorn
Doth to our rose of youth belong:
Our blood to us, this to our blood is born;
It is the show and seal of nature's truth,
Where love's strong passion is impressed in youth." (AWEW.1.3)

Good for a card, especially if you had an argument (hence the thorn). Make sure that you indicate the author of the lines. Use the last two lines to tell her that it is natural that you love her.
In the play. *The countess meditates that she herself felt the thorns of love in her youth, just as now Helen loves Bertram.*

Love, string of compliments - … bright eyes, by her high forehead and her scarlet lip, by her fine foot, straight leg and quivering thigh…
"I conjure thee by Rosaline's bright eyes,
By her high forehead and her scarlet lip,
By her fine foot, straight leg and quivering thigh
And the demesnes that there adjacent lie,
That in thy likeness thou appear to us!" (RJ.2.1)
Select the good features and attribute them to the lady of your choice when you ask her for some favor or other. You may stop at the thighs depending on your degree of familiarity with her.
In the play. *Mercutio, unaware of Romeo's sudden passion for Juliet and not finding him devises an invocation, based on Rosaline's alleged charms. The idea is to use the invocation to track down Romeo. Prior to meeting Juliet Romeo loved Rosaline.*

Love, strong l. but unwise – (I am) one that loved not wisely but too well.
"… one that loved not wisely but too well" (OTH.5.2)
Justify your failed marriage(s).
In the play. *Othello tells to Ludovico, who is returning to Venice, what to say to the Venetian Senators about the business who led to Desdemona's murder by Othello and his death by his own hand.*

Love, sudden l. realized only after personal experience - … till I found it to be true I never thought it possible or likely.
TRANIO I pray, sir, tell me, is it possible
That love should of a sudden take such hold?
LUCENTIO O Tranio, till I found it to be true,
I never thought it possible or likely (TOS.1.1)
In the play. *Lucentio has fallen in love with Bianca, Katharina's sister.*

Love, symptoms of something going on – … whispering… meeting noses… horsing foot on foot…
"Is whispering nothing?
Is leaning cheek to cheek? is meeting noses?
Kissing with inside lip? stopping the career
Of laughing with a sigh?--a note infallible
Of breaking honesty--horsing foot on foot?
Skulking in corners? wishing clocks more swift?
Hours, minutes? noon, midnight?
…
Why, then the world and all that's in't is nothing;
The covering sky is nothing; Bohemia nothing;
My wife is nothing; nor nothing have these nothings,
If this be nothing. (WT.1.2)
Pull the leg of a friend, e.g. 'I saw you horsing foot on foot' See also 'Relationship, indications of a deeper r. - … to be paddling palms and pinching fingers … and making practised smiles…'
In the play. *Jealous Leontes upbraids counselor Camillus for refusing to see Hermione's alleged adultery. Hermione is Leonte's wife.*

Love, the right man not yet found (or woman by changing one word) - … I never yet beheld that special face

which I could fancy yet more than any other.
"Believe me, sister, of all the men alive,
I never yet beheld that special face
Which I could fancy yet more than any other." (TOS.2.1)
If you are a woman, use as an answer to the question, 'Do you have a boyfriend?' Believe me, of all men alive… other. If you are a man change 'of all the men' to 'of all the women'.
In the play. *Bianca answers a question by her sister Katharina as to whether she (Bianca) has found a man she really likes.*

Love, the state of being in l. – It is to be all made of sighs and tears…
"It is to be all made of sighs and tears
It is to be all made of faith and service
It is to be all made of fantasy,
All made of passion and all made of wishes,
All adoration, duty, and observance,
All humbleness, all patience and impatience,
All purity, all trial, all observance"
(AYLI.5.2)
Possibly a mildly ironic answer when asked about an opinion on love.
In the play. *Silvius answers a question from Phebe as to what it is or means to be in love.*

Love, to die for l. not proven by historical evidence - … men have died from time to time and worms have eaten them, but not for love.
"… men have died from time to time and worms have eaten them, but not for love." (AYLI.4.1)
In the play. *Rosalind, in a man's disguise, pretends to be a woman and try Orlando's skills at wooing Rosalind-the-man, pretending that Rosalind-the-man is actually a woman. Rosalind contradicts Orlando on how far can love drive a man.*

Love, transfixed by l. – for never gazed the moon upon the water as he'll stand and read as 'twere my daughter's eyes.
"He says he loves my daughter:
I think so too; for never gazed the moon
Upon the water as he'll stand and read
As 'twere my daughter's eyes."
(WT.4.4)
Comment on a friend in love. Change 'my daughter' to name of lady loved. 'I think he loves (name of lady); for never… eyes'. Or adapt for yourself, e.g. 'Never gazed the moon…'twere your eyes.'
In the play. *Polixenes, king of Bohemia and wearing a disguise, inquires of the shepherd about 'Doricles'. Doricles is actually Polixenes' son, wearing a shepherd's disguise in order to woo Perdita, the shepherd's adopted daughter. Perdita's adoptive father comments on how much Doricles loves her.*

Love, unshakable and beyond any obstacle - Let me not to the marriage of true minds admit impediments.
"Let me not to the marriage of true minds
Admit impediments. Love is not love
Which alters when it alteration finds,
Or bends with the remover to remove:
O, no! it is an ever-fixed mark,
That looks on tempests and is never shaken;
It is the star to every wandering bark,
Whose worth's unknown, although his height be taken.
Love's not Time's fool, though rosy lips and cheeks
Within his bending sickle's compass come;
Love alters not with his brief hours and weeks,
But bears it out even to the edge of doom.
If this be error and upon me prov'd,
I never writ, nor no man ever lov'd.
(SON 116)
Use 'Love alters not with his brief hours and weeks…doom' as a reply to 'Will you always love me?'

Love, waiting for your l. to arrive - I'll go find a shadow and sigh till he come.
"I'll go find a shadow and sigh till he come." (AYLI.4.1)
Change 'he' to 'she' if it is you who is waiting for her.
In the play. *Rosalind is waiting for Orlando with whom she is passionately in love.*

Love, your l. and her pride - I love thee so, that, maugre all thy pride, nor wit nor reason can my passion hide.
"I love thee so, that, maugre all thy pride,
Nor wit nor reason can my passion hide." (TN.3.1)
Change 'maugre' for 'notwithstanding'
In the play. *Olivia tries to come to terms with her love for Viola/Cesario. 'Maugre' = 'notwithstanding'*

Love, your l. as your empress - …empress of my soul, which never hopes more heaven than rests in thee.
"…empress of my soul,
Which never hopes more heaven than rests in thee" (TA.2.3)
See also 'Writing. Decision to write in prose after questioning your own poetical skills', where Longaville, the writer, calls Maria 'empress of my love'.
In the play. *The evil Aaron addresses his lover queen Tamora in a forest outside Rome where he has come for a rendezvous.*

Lover, absence of l. unbearable - …and lovers' absent hours more tedious than the dial eight score times? O weary reckoning.
"What, keep a week away? seven days and nights?
Eight score eight hours? and lovers' absent hours,
More tedious than the dial eight score times?
O weary reckoning!" (OTH.3.4)
When she says she will be absent for some days (or hours). Suggest you will count days or hours and end with 'O weary reckoning!'.
In the play. *Bianca, Cassio's lover, complains about his extended absence from her.*

Lover, l's absence justified - I have this while with leaden thoughts been pressed…
"I have this while with leaden thoughts been pressed:
But I shall, in a more continue time,
Strike off this score of absence" (OTH.3.4)
See also 'Mood, in a poor m. - Vexed I am, of late, with passions of some difference, conceptions only proper to

561

myself, which give some soil, perhaps to my behaviours.'
In the play. *Cassio explains to his lover Bianca why he has not called on her recently.*

Lover, sighing characteristics of a l. - ... as true a lover as ever sigh'd upon a midnight pillow.
"No, Corin, being old, thou canst not guess,
Though in thy youth thou wast as true a lover
As ever sigh'd upon a midnight pillow" (AYLI.2.4)
In the play. *Silvius is in love with the supercilious Phebe and confides in the somewhat skeptical Corin.*

Lovers, l. always punctual – ... for lovers ever run before the clock.
"And it is marvel he out-dwells his hour,
For lovers ever run before the clock." (MOV.2.6)
In the play. *Gratiano comments on Lorenzo's unexpected delay. Lorenzo has enrolled Gratiano's and others' help to kidnap and elope with Jessica, Shylock's daughter.*

Lovers, l. always punctual – Lovers break not hours unless it be to come before their time.
"... lovers break not hours,
Unless it be to come before their time." (TGV.5.1)
In the play. *Chaperon Eglamour expects Silvia to be punctual as he will accompany her in her search for the Valentine who escaped into a forest.*

Lovers, l. arriving holding hands - ... Like to a pair of loving turtle-doves that could not live asunder day or night.
"...arm in arm they both came swiftly running,
Like to a pair of loving turtle-doves
That could not live asunder day or night" (KHVI.p1.2.1)
See also 'Invitation, your hand - Your hand, my Perdita, so turtles pair, that never mean to part.'
In the play. *Burgundy referring to Charles of France and Joan of Arc at the siege of Orleans.*

Lovers, eloquent lovers not reliable - ... these fellows of infinite tongue that can rhyme themselves into ladies' favours...
"...these fellows of infinite tongue, that can rhyme themselves into ladies' favours, they do always reason themselves out again. What! A speaker is but a prater; a rhyme is but a ballad." (KHV.5.2)
By uttering these lines you may attempt to rhyme yourself into the lady's favor by using the tactics that the very lines are discommending,…..but you decide. See also "Man, a verbose m. – He draweth out the thread of his verbosity finer than the staple of his argument'.
In the play. *Henry V woos Kathryn of France after having defeated the French at Agincourt.*
'Prater' = 'A twaddler, speaker of nonsense'.

Lovers, l. observed fostering romantic inclinations - The sight of lovers feedeth those in love.
"The sight of lovers feedeth those in love." (AYLI.3.4)
When you are with her and see another couple giving signs of mutual attachment.
In the play. *Rosalind answers a comment from Corin*

Lovers, odd behavior of l. - It is as easy to count atomies as to resolve the propositions of a lover.
"It is as easy to count atomies as to resolve the propositions of a lover" (AYLI.4.1)
In the play. *Celia responds to the barrage of questions by Rosalind who inquires about Orlando with whom she is in love.*

Loving skills, apologizing for lack of l.s. – For I am rough and woo not like a babe.
"For I am rough and woo not like a babe." (TOS.2.1)
In the play. *Petruchio explains to Baptista his tactic for subduing her fiery daughter Katharina.*

Loyalty, l. to fools an act of folly, pros and cons - The loyalty well held to fools does make our faith mere folly, yet…
"Mine honesty and I begin to square.
The loyalty well held to fools does make
Our faith mere folly; yet he that can endure
To follow with allegiance a fall'n lord
Does conquer him that did his master conquer
And earns a place i' the story" (AC.3.13)
In the play. *Enobarbus, reluctantly, begins to consider abandoning Antony after Antony's loss at sea and display of very poor judgment. A messengers from Caesar unceremoniously approaches Cleopatra. Enobarbus, Antony's lieutenant, observes the event and draws some conclusions.*

Loyalty, no l. left – O, where is loyalty? If it be banish'd from the frosty head, where shall it find a harbour in the earth?
"…O, where is loyalty?
If it be banish'd from the frosty head,
Where shall it find a harbour in the earth?" (KHVI.p2.5.1)
In the play. *King Henry VI upbraids the aged Salisbury (Warwick's father) for having switched allegiance to York.*

Lust, evidence of lustful intents – … an index and obscure prologue to the history of lust and foul thoughts.
"…an index and obscure prologue to the history of lust and foul thoughts" (OTH.2.1)
In the play. *Iago attempts to convince Roderigo that Cassio's mode of hand kissing of Desdemona is a sign of Cassio's lust for her.*

Lust, intemperance leading to disaster - Boundless intemperance in nature is a tyranny…
"Boundless intemperance
In nature is a tyranny; it hath been
The untimely emptying of the happy throne,
And fall of many kings." (M.4.3)
See also 'Fall, f. from greatness - Take but good note, and you shall see in him…'
A suitable comment to any event (usually a disaster), shows the effects of intemperance.
In the play. *Macduff's comments after Malcolm in a strange statement declares himself as boundlessly intemperate. Malcolm wants to test Macduff's reaction.*

Lust, l. checked by reason – … but we have reason to cool our raging motions…
"…but we have reason to cool our raging motions, our carnal stings, our unbitted lusts, whereof I take this that you call love to be a sect or scion." (OTH.1.3)
In the play. *Iago to Roderigo who lusts for Desdemona.*

Lust, l. compared to virtue - … So lust, though to a radiant angel link'd, will sate itself in a celestial bed and prey on garbage.
"But virtue, as it never will be moved,
Though lewdness court it in a shape of heaven,
So lust, though to a radiant angel link'd,
Will sate itself in a celestial bed,
And prey on garbage." (H.1.5)

In the play. *The Ghost commenting on the lust that he attributes to his now widowed wife.*

Lust, l. triggered by first kisses – And having felt the sweetness of the spoil, with blindfold fury she begins to forage...
"And having felt the sweetness of the spoil,
With blindfold fury she begins to forage;
Her face doth reek and smoke, her blood doth boil,
And careless lust stirs up a desperate courage,
Planting oblivion, beating reason back,
Forgetting shame's pure blush and honour's wrack" (V&A)
Change 'she begins to forage' to 'I begin to forage' to signal your state or intentions.
In the poem. *Notwithstanding Adonis' reluctance, Venus has managed to sneak a kiss off him.*

Lust, perhaps reprehensible but inevitable - All this the world well knows yet none knows well to shun the heaven that leads men to this hell.
"Th'expense of spirit in a waste of shame
Is lust in actin, and till action, lust
Is perjured, murd'rous, bloody, full of shame,
Savage, extreme, rude, cruel, not to trust,
Enjoyed no sooner but despised straight,
Past reason hunted, and no sooner had,
Past reason hated, as a swallowed bait,
On purpose laid to make the taker mad.
Mad in pursuit and in possession so,
Had, having and in quest, to have extreme,
A bliss in proof, and proved, a very woe
Before a joy proposed behind a dream.
  All this the world well knows yet none knows well
  To shun the heaven that leads men to this hell". (SON.129)
Use the last two lines as a rationalization of masochism.

Lust, seemingly rational reasons for justifying l – O strange excuse, when reason is the bawd to lust's abuse!
"...O strange excuse,
When reason is the bawd to lust's abuse!" (V&A)
In the poem. *Adonis coldly refuses Venus' advances. The excuse brought up by Venus is the need for Adonis to reproduce himself through love.*

Lying or rather admitting to it - If I could add a lie unto a fault, I would deny it.
"If I could add a lie unto a fault, I would deny it." (MOV.5.1)
This would have been a much better answer from Clinton, instead of "I never had sex with that woman". The fault you are admitting to does not have to be, necessarily, of a specific type. The answer applies in all cases where there is a measure of embarrassment in the fault, whether admitted or not.
In the play. *Bassanio gave away the ring to the lawyer who defended Antonio in court, but the lawyer was Bassanio's wife herself, Portia, in disguise. Now the 'true' Portia asks him if he, Bassanio, gave away the ring and he is in trouble.*

Lying, am I compelled to lie? - Must I, with my base tongue give to my noble heart a lie, that I must bear?
"Must I, with my base tongue give to my noble heart
A lie, that I must bear?" (COR.3.2)

Rhetoric question in substitution of "Must I really lie?"
In the play. *Notwithstanding Volumnia's advice, Coriolanus is reluctant to soften his approach and hide his contempt for the citizens.*

Lying, I do not mean to say you're lying - Now much beshrew my manners and my pride if Hermia meant to say Lysander lied.
"Lysander riddles very prettily:
Now much beshrew my manners and my pride,
If Hermia meant to say Lysander lied." (MND.2.2)
Change 'Hermia' to your name and 'Lysander' to the name of the person addressed.
In the play. *Lysander has made some cautious and well-crafted advances towards Hermia. She, however, sticks to a defensive stance. See 'Reliability and innocence claimed - O, take the sense, sweet, of my innocence!...' 'Beshrew' = 'woe to".*

Lying, l. about impossibility and fear - ... Cannot, is false, and that I dare not, falser...
"..tell them that I will not come to-day:
Cannot, is false, and that I dare not, falser:
I will not come to-day: tell them so, Decius." (JC.2.2)
See also 'Power, privilege of p. to give no explanations- ....the cause is in my will'.
In the play. *Caesar, seemingly persuaded by his wife Calpurnia decides for a moment not to go to the Senate but does not want to lie to Decius on the reason why.*

Lying, l. based on equivocation – ... and begin to doubt the equivocation of the fiend that lies like truth.
"...and begin
To doubt the equivocation of the fiend
That lies like truth" (M.1.5)

See also 'Equivocation, misunderstanding, need for accurate wording or expression – ... we must speak by the card or equivocation will undo us.'
In the play. *Malcolm's soldiers screened by branches advance on Dunsinane, hence verifying the prediction of the witches. Macbeth did not grasp the equivocation.*

Lying, penalty for l. – If thou speak'st false, upon the next tree shalt thou hang alive till famine cling thee...
"If thou speak'st false,
Upon the next tree shalt thou hang alive,
Till famine cling thee..." (M.5.5)
In the play. *Macbeth to the messenger who said he saw the Birnam wood approaching, thus confirming one of the witches' predictions.*

Lying, will you lie for me? - If a lie may do thee grace, I'll gild it with the happiest terms I have.
"For my part, if a lie may do thee grace,
I'll gild it with the happiest terms I have." (KHIV.p1.5.4)
In the play. *Prince Henry will support the notion that Falstaff behaved valiantly at the battle of Shrewsbury, an obvious overstatement.*

Macho man or unstoppable skirt chaser - She is a woman, therefore may be woo'd; she is a woman, therefore may be won..
She is a woman, therefore may be woo'd;
She is a woman, therefore may be won;
She is Lavinia, therefore must be loved." (TA.2.1)

Use to characterize him (if he is indeed a skirt chaser). 'His philosophy with any woman goes like this, she is a woman…..won' (use the first two lines). Or perhaps the line describes your character to a 'T'. See also 'Approach, securing a way out'.
In the play. *Demetrius and Chiron, Tamora's sons plan the gruesome murder-rape of Lavinia and of her husband, Bassanio.*

Macho man, successful with women - … a dangerous and lascivious boy, who is a whale to virginity..
"(he is) a dangerous and lascivious boy, who is a whale to virginity, and devours up all the fry it finds." (AWEW.4.3)
A humorous characterization of a Casanova or of a self-defined macho man.
In the play. *Believing his capturers to be the enemy, Parolles does not hesitate to badmouth Bertram. 'Fry' refers to a swarm of small fish after spawning.*

Mad, how mad? - Mad as the sea and wind, when both contend which is the mightier.
"Mad as the sea and wind, when both contend
Which is the mightier…" (H.4.1)
In the play. *Queen Gertrude's answer to King Claudius' question on Hamlet's state of mind.*

Madness, charge of madness rejected - … it is not madness that I have utter'd: bring me to the test…
"My pulse, as yours, doth temperately keep time,
And makes as healthful music: it is not madness
That I have utter'd: bring me to the test,
And I the matter will re-word; which madness
Would gambol from" (H.3.4)
In the play. *Hamlet rejects his mother's statement that he is mad. He was addressing the ghost while meeting with her. 'Gambol'='to skip'*

Madness, evidence of m. due to perceived lack of understanding or ability to listen - .. O, then I see that madmen have no ears.
"..O, then I see that madmen have no ears." (RJ.3.3)
Give your opinion on a stubborn person who refuses to listen.
In the play. *Romeo is insensitive to the Friar Lawrence's suggested use of philosophy as a psychological palliative.*

Madness, isn't this m.? – … have we eaten on the insane root that takes the reason prisoner?
"…have we eaten on the insane root
That takes the reason prisoner?" (M.1.3)
Repeat the question as is, if you are at odd with the ideas or proposals brought forward by the group. Or apply to yourself to deny your madness, e.g. 'No, I have not taken of the insane root…..prisoner'. Or change 'we' to 'you' to limit the range of those to whom the question applies.
In the play. *In a heath near Forres, the three witches appear to Macbeth and Banquo. Banquo speculates that the vision is prompted by their insanity (Macbeth's and Banquo's).*

Madness, m. confirmed rhetorically - That he's mad, 'tis true; 'tis true, 'tis pity. And pity 'tis 'tis true.
"That he's mad, 'tis true; 'tis true, 'tis pity.
And pity 'tis 'tis true; a foolish figure." (H.2.2)
Can be applied to madness or other states of mind or unpleasant quality. Or as an example of verbosity.

In the play. *After being asked by the queen for 'more matter, with less art' Polonius cannot resist to deliver another verbal sally.*

Madness, m. in men due to astronomical factors - It is the very error of the moon; she comes more nearer earth than she was wont and makes men mad.
"It is the very error of the moon;
She comes more nearer earth than she was wont,
And makes men mad." (OTH.5.2)
When you wish to shift your responsibility or explain away an unexplicable behavior. See also 'Weather, hot w. and its effects on temper'. For a radically different and more realistic view on the subject see 'Philosophical considerations. Unwillingness to take responsibility for our mistakes'
In the play. *Othello has killed Desdemona out of unjustified jealousy.*

Madness, m. in VIPs of concern - Madness in great ones must not unwatch'd go.
"It shall be so;
Madness in great ones must not unwatch'd go." (H.3.1)
In the play. *The King concurs with Polonius' suggestion to send Hamlet to England hoping for his mental recovery.*

Madness, m. inspiring feats of intelligence - ... a happiness that often madness hits on, which reason and sanity ...
"How pregnant sometimes his replies are! a happiness that often madness hits on, which reason and sanity could not so prosperously be delivered of" (H.2.2)
In the play. *Polonius' comment on an answer by Hamlet.*

Madness, m. that has all the traits of sanity - ... her madness hath the oddest frame of sense..
"If she be mad--as I believe no other--
Her madness hath the oddest frame of sense,
Such a dependency of thing on thing,
As e'er I heard in madness."
(MFM.5.1)
A retort to an incorrect pronunciation of madness on a person or on a matter. Answer to 'This is madness'. See also 'Madness, method in m. - Though this be madness, yet there is method in it'
In the play. *Angelo wants the Duke to believe that Isabel is mad. The Duke pretends to believe Angelo though he comments on the strange sanity of Isabel's madness.*

Madness, m. conclusively defined - .. Mad I call it; for, to define true madness, what is 't but to be nothing else but mad?
"....your noble son is mad.
Mad I call it; for, to define true madness,
What is 't but to be nothing else but mad?
But let that go." (H.2.2)
Emphatic declaration that someone is mad. Or use as an ironic example of saying something obvious.
In the play. *After a pompous and long preamble, Polonius equally pompously delivers the news about Hamlet's madness.*

Madness, m. typical of summer, but applicable or attributable to other seasons -... this is very midsummer madness.
"... this is very midsummer madness." (TN.3.4)
Comment an odd behavior or idea or action.
In the play. *Olivia is puzzled at Malvolio's behavior, He mistakenly believes that she loves him.*

Madness, method in m. - Though this be madness, yet there is method in it
"Though this be madness, yet there is method in it." (H.2.2)
Retort to anyone who defines your ideas, suggestions or projects as mad. Or comment on the positive and otherwise well organized ideas of a mad plan.
In the play. *Polonius rates Hamlet, who pretending to be mad has made some wise remarks.*

Madness, obvious mad behavior prompting lack of manners - be Kent unmannerly when Lear is mad.
"….be Kent unmannerly,
When Lear is mad." (KL.1.1)
Substitute your name for 'Kent' as applicable when your boss (change 'Lear' for his name) is demonstrably insane
In the play. *Kent stands up in defense of Cordelia and Lear reprimands him.*

Madness, you are mad - … thou art essentially mad, without seeming so.
"… thou art essentially mad, without seeming so" (KHIV.p1.2.4)
A direct allegation or applicable to a third party, e.g. 'He is essentially mad without seeming so'.
In the play. *Falstaff to the Prince of Wales in a tavern of Eastcheap.*

Madness, exhortation not to be considered mad - … neglect me not, with that opinion that I am touch'd with madness.
"O prince, I conjure thee
…
That thou neglect me not, with that opinion
That I am touch'd with madness!" (MFM.5.1)
In the play. *Isabella to the Duke who pretends to believe Angelo's allegation that Isabella is insane.*

Madness, wishing to be mad to forget/avoid pain - I am not mad, I would to heaven I were…
"I am not mad - I would to heaven I were!
For then, 't is like I should forget myself!" (KJ.3.4)
Express distress. See also 'Sleep, wish that s. could erase worries - I wish mine eyes would, with themselves, shut up my thoughts.'
In the play. *After the lost battle of Angiers, young Arthur, Constance' son, has been captured by the English and she is desperate.*

Madness, wishing to be mad to forget/avoid pain -… better I were distract, so should my thoughts be severed from my griefs…
"… Better I were distract.
So should my thoughts be severed from my griefs,
And woes, by wrong imaginations lose
The knowledge of themselves." (KL.4.6)
Emphatic alternative to 'I wish I did not know this'
In the play. *Gloucester is extremely depressed, after having been blinded by the Duke of Cornwall and his evil wife Regan.*

Madness, wishing to be mad to forget/avoid pain – Preach some philosophy to make me mad…
"Preach some philosophy to make me mad,
And thou shalt be canonized, cardinal;
For being not mad but sensible of grief,
My reasonable part produces reason
How I may be deliver'd of these woes,
And teaches me to kill or hang myself" (KJ.3.4)

In the play. *Lady Constance to Cardinal Pandulph who imposes a policy on the King of France inimical to Constance's aspirations.*

Magic, a wonderful art to be sanctioned by law - If this be magic, let it be an art as lawful as eating.
"If this be magic, let it be an art
As lawful as eating." (WT.5.3)
Show your (positive) amazement at a successful and somewhat unexpected result.
In the play. *Paulina, using extraordinary magic, has made Hermione's statue come alive to the understandable happiness of all concerned. The repented Leontes is on top of the world*

Magic, black m. - ... practises of cunning hell.
"...practises of cunning hell" (OTH.1.3)
In the play. *According to Brabantio Desdemona was driven to marry Othello thanks to the latter's black magic.*

Magic, black m., a practitioner of black m. - ... an abuser of the world, a practiser of arts inhibited and out of warrant.
"...an abuser of the world, a practiser
Of arts inhibited and out of warrant" (OTH.1.2)
In the play. *Brabantio wants Othello arrested for (alleged) corruption of Desdemona.*

Magnanimity, gentlemanship, lack of envy - ... for we are gentlemen that neither in our hearts nor outward eyes, envy the great, nor the low despise.
"... for we are gentlemen,
That neither in our hearts nor outward eyes,
Envy the great, nor the low despise." (PER.2.3)
Statement of unbiased and non envious admiration.
In the play. *Pericles has won the tourney and the other knights acknowledge his excellence without envy.*

Mailing, mass m. - ... Thousand of these letters, writ with blank space for different names.
"I warrant he hath a thousand of these letters, writ with blank space for different names." (MWW.2.1)
In the play. *Mrs. Page and Mrs. Ford discover that Falstaff has sent the same love letter to both of them.*

Make-up, neglected – ... since she did neglect her looking glass.
"But since she did neglect her looking-glass" (TGV.4.4)
Justification for your unkempt appearance, e.g. 'I did neglect my looking glass.'
In the play. *Julia, dressed as a boy-page answers a question from Silvia on what the real Julia looks like. The boy-page Julia says that Julia would be as fair as Silvia would had she not neglected her make up, masks, sunscreen etc.*
And threw her sun-expelling mask away,
The air hath starved the roses in her cheeks
And pinch'd the lily-tincture of her face,
That now she is become as black as I.

Malcontent, primacy in unhappiness – Thou art the Mars of malecontents.
"Thou art the Mars of malecontents" (MWM.1.5)
In the play. *Pistol to Nym.*

Malice, m. and hate – Beaufort's red sparkling eyes blab his heart's malice...
"Beaufort's red sparkling eyes blab his heart's malice,
And Suffolk's cloudy brow his stormy hate" (KHVI p2.3.1)
Change names as applicable or use the last two lines addressing directly your enemy, e.g. '(Name of enemy), you

unburden with your tongue the envious load that lies upon your heart.'
In the play. *Gloucester comments on his sworn enemies, Cardinal Beaufort and Suffolk. 'Brow' = 'Countenance'*

Malice, m. expressed - ... the venomous malice of my swelling heart.
"Some devil whisper curses in mine ear,
And prompt me, that my tongue may utter forth
The venomous malice of my swelling heart!" (TA.5.3)
Use as an example of utter evil.
In the play. *Captured by Lucius, the super-evil Aaron maintains his defiant stance.*

Malice, m. expressed in sarcastic remarks - Ill will never said well.
"Ill will never said well." (HV.3.7)
In the play. *The Constable of France does not thing highly of the Dauphin and Orleans accuses him of ill will.*

Man and his wicked nature - ... use every man after his desert, and who should 'scape whipping?
"....use every man after his desert, and who should 'scape whipping?" (H.2.2)
In the play. *Hamlet to Polonius after Polonius said he will treat the incoming players, hired by Hamlet, according to their desert.*

Man and his wicked nature - ... what is this quintessence of dust? Man delights not me.
"And yet, to me, what is this quintessence of dust? Man delights not me, no, nor woman neither, though by your smiling you seem to say so"(H.2.2)
You may even add the next sentence 'no, nor woman neither, though by your smiling
you seem to say so' if you wish to reinforce your position. See also 'Man, m. as dust – Would it not grieve a woman to be overmastered with a piece of valiant dust?'
In the play. *Hamlet in conversation with Rosencrantz and Guildenstern.*

Man and his wicked nature – All is oblique, there is nothing level in our cursed natures but direst villainy.
" ..the learned pate
Ducks to the golden fool: all is oblique;
There is nothing level in our cursed natures,
But direst villainy." (TOA.4.3)
Express your general disappointment in humanity.
In the play. *Timon's rating of humanity.*

Man and his wicked nature - Who lives that's not depraved or depraves?
"Who lives that's not depraved or depraves?" (TOA.1.2)
In the play. *Apemantus' moralizing statement as a group of dancing ladies joins Timon's ongoing party.*

Man and his wicked nature – Is man no more than this?
"Is man no more than this?.... Thou art the thing itself: unaccommodated man is no more but such a poor bare, forked animal as thou art" (KL.3.4)
Sobering consideration (Is man no more than this?) on any of the multiple follies and crimes occurring daily.
In the play. *King Lear to Edgar who feigns madness and appears undressed in the forest where Lear and a few companions escaped from Lear's evil daughters. 'Forked' stands for 'two-legged'.*

Man, m's nature, faults inevitable – ... but we all are men, in our own natures frail...
"...but we all are men,
In our own natures frail, and capable

Of our flesh; few are angels…"
(KHVIII.5.3)
In the play. *The Chancellor opens his statement as a prosecutor against Cranmer, accused of holding heretical views. He was leaning towards Protestantism when England had not yet detached herself from Rome.*

Man and his wicked nature - There's no trust, no faith, no honesty in man..
"There's no trust,
No faith, no honesty in man; all perjured,
All forsworn, all naught, all dissemblers." (RJ.3.2)
In the play. *Juliet's nurse comments on Romeo, after knowing that he slain Tybald and extends her criticism to all men.*

Man, a bad m. all around - From forth the kennel of thy womb hath crept a hell-hound….
"From forth the kennel of thy womb hath crept
A hell-hound that doth hunt us all to death
…
That foul defacer of God's handiwork" (KRIII.4.4)
In the play. *Queen Margaret to the Duchess of York referring to her son, bloody Richard.*

Man, a brave m. - … to grace this latter age with noble deeds.
"I do not think a braver gentleman, … is now alive
To grace this latter age with noble deeds." (KHIV.p1.5.1)
In the play. *With an act of sporting chivalry, the Prince of Wales pays homage to the absent Hotspur, head of the rebel forces.*

Man, a dangerous m. – …full of danger is the Duke of Gloucester.
"O, full of danger is the Duke of Gloucester!" (KRIII.2.3)
Change 'the Duke of Gloucester' to the name of the applicable person. Good humored answer to 'What do you think of him?' if the person of whose opinion you are asked is present.
In the play. *King Edward is dead and two citizens share their view on the current political situation and who will succeed Edward.*

Man, a drunkard – … drunk many times a day, if not many days entirely drunk.
"(He is) drunk many times a day, if not many days entirely drunk."
(MFM.4.2)
See also 'Opinion, your op. on specific man, bad in himself and worse when drunk - … when
he is best, he is a little worse than a man and when he is worst, he is little better than a beast.'
In the play. *The provost's characterization of the inmate Barnardine.*

Man, a hated m. – All the commons hate him perniciously and … wish him ten fathom deep.
"All the commons
Hate him perniciously, and, o' my conscience,
Wish him ten fathom deep"
(KHVIII.2.1)
In the play. *Two gentlemen comment on Cardinal Wolsey. Fathom' = a unit of measure equal to six feet, used to measure depth'.*

Man, a m. called Pompey Bum – … and your bum is the greatest thing about you…
"Troth, and your bum is the greatest thing about you; so that in the beastliest sense you are Pompey the Great." (MFM.2.1)
Convert it into a scathing remark about a man with large buttocks.
In the play. *Escalus to Pompey, a pimp.*

Man, a noble m. - The noblest mind he carries that ever govern'd man.

"The noblest mind he carries
That ever govern'd man." (TOA.1.1)
In the play. *A lord's comment on Timon.*

Man, a verbose and annoying m. – ... such a deal of skimble-skamble stuff as puts me from my faith.
"I cannot choose: sometime he angers me
With telling me of the mouldwarp and the ant
...
And such a deal of skimble-skamble stuff
As puts me from my faith..."
(KHIV.p1.3.1)
In the play. *Hotspur expresses to Mortimer his opinion of Glendower. 'Mouldwarp'='An insect'. 'Skimble-skamble'='condused'.*

Man, a verbose m. – He draweth out the thread of his verbosity finer than the staple of his argument.
"He draweth out the thread of his verbosity finer than the staple of his argument." (LLL.5.1)
Characterize a boring, wordy and inconclusive man. See also, 'Speech, why giving me the run around?'
In the play. *Holofernes describes Armado though they are two buttocks of the same bum.*

Man, a verbose or fast talking m. – a gentleman... that loves to hear himself talk, and he will speak more in a minute...
"A gentleman, nurse, that loves to hear himself talk; and will speak more in a minute, than he will stand to in a month." (RJ.2.4)
Characterize a verbose person whose thoughts are shallow.
In the play. *In an attempt to soften the impact of Mercutio's sarcastic remarks on Juliet's nurse, Romeo makes a somewhat disparaging mini-sketch of Mercutio..*

Man, able to stir things up - .. when he meant to quail and shake the orb he was as rattling thunder.
"But when he meant to quail and shake the orb,
He was as rattling thunder" (AC.5.2)
Flattering or ironic statement about a powerful man. Change verb tense from past to present.
In the play. *Cleopatra tells Dolabella about a dream she had of dead Antony.*

Man, all show, no brain - What a pretty thing man is, when he goes in his doublet and hose..
"What a pretty thing man is, when he goes in his doublet and hose, and leaves off his wit!" (MAAN.5.1)
Comment on an apparently normal but stupid person.
In the play. *Don Pedro and Claudio make light of Benedick who has challenged Claudio to avenge Hero's honor.*

Man, an absolutely trustworthy and loving m. - His words are bonds, his oaths are oracles...
"His words are bonds, his oaths are oracles; his love sincere, his thoughts immaculate; his tears, pure messengers from his heart." (TGV.2.7)
The guy to whom these words apply (Proteus) proved to be in reality nothing of the sort. You can, however, use the lines by making yourself the subject of them, e.g. "My words are bonds, my oaths are oracles, my love sincere, my thoughts immaculate, my tears, pure messengers from my heart." A possible answer to 'Can I trust you?' See also entries for 'Reliability'
In the play. *Lucetta suggests that all men are deceitful. Julia believes that Proteus is an exception but she will prove too optimistic.*

Man, antisocial - ...he does neither affect company, nor is he fit for't, indeed.

"… he does neither affect company, nor is he fit for't, indeed." (TOA.1.2)
In the play. *Timon assigns the grumpy Apemantus to a separate table, given Apemantus' antisocial character.*

Man, bad m. exceedingly so – … a thing too bad for bad report.
"He that hath miss'd the princess is a thing
Too bad for bad report" (CYM.1.1)
In the play. *A gentleman defines Cloten, vain pretender to Imogen.*

Man, base and worthless - … from whose so many weights of baseness cannot a dram of worth be drawn.
"Is she with Posthumus?
From whose so many weights of baseness cannot
A dram of worth be drawn." (CYM.3.5)
Characterize a worthless man as one '..from whose….drawn'.
In the play. *The foolish Cloten insults Posthumus Leonatus, Imogen's husband.*

Man, best m. of all – Thou art the ruins of the noblest man that ever lived in the tide of times.
"Thou art the ruins of the noblest man
That ever lived in the tide of times." (JC.3.1)
A sarcastic preamble, "Of course you are the noblest man that ever lived in the tide of times but…….." See also 'Person, p. best of all (applies to both woman and man) - … and was the best of all among the rar'st of good ones.'
In the play. *Antony to the slain body of Caesar.*

Man, capable m. able to discern deceit – These eyes… as piercing as the mid-day sun, to search the secret treasons of the world…
"These eyes, that now are dimm'd with death's black veil,
Have been as piercing as the mid-day sun,
To search the secret treasons of the world" (KHVI.p3.5.2)
In the play. *Warwick, wounded to death in the battle against the York forces near Barnet, reflects on his life.*

Man, cheap, stingy and vulgar bargain hunter - So worthless peasants bargain for their wives…
"So worthless peasants bargain for their wives
As market-men for oxen, sheep, or horse" (KHVI.p1.5.5)
In the play. *Suffolk rebuts Exeter's criticism that Margaret, future wife of Henry VI is penniless, as if a queen were on the same level of peasants.*

Man, clearly not an intellectual - He is only an animal, only sensible in the duller parts.
"Sir, he hath never fed of the dainties that are bred in a book, he hath not eaten paper, as it were; he hath not drunk ink: his intellect is not replenished; he is only an animal, only sensible in the duller parts." (LLL.4.2)
Describe an ignoramus, e.g. 'He is only an animal…parts'.
In the play. *Holofernes accuses Dull of ignorance. Nathaniel explains Dull's background.*

Man, compared to a bird soaring high - … man and birds are fain of climbing high.
"To see how God in all his creatures works!
Yea, man and birds are fain of climbing high." (KHVI p2.2.1)
Generic comment on man's aspiration to greatness or a specific comment on the ambition of an individual (second line).
In the play. *Henry VI at a hunt observes a falcon.*

Man, comparing unfavorably one m. to another - Romeo's a dishclout to him.
"Romeo's a dishclout to him" (RJ.3.5)
Change 'Romeo' to the name of the applicable party.
In the play. *The Nurse attempts to convince Juliet that Paris is a better party than Romeo. 'Dishclout'='Dishcloth'.*

Man, convinced, almost c. - ... three parts of him is ours already, and the man entire upon the next encounter yields him ours.
"...three parts of him
Is ours already, and the man entire
Upon the next encounter yields him ours." (JC.1.3)
In the play. *Cassius tells Casca that Brutus is almost convinced about the need to get rid of Caesar.*

Man, corrupt m. - ... smacking of every sin that has a name.
"I grant him bloody,
Luxurious, avaricious, false, deceitful,
Sudden, malicious, smacking of every sin
That has a name" (M.4.3)
In the play. *Malcolm describes Macbeth to Macduff.*

Man, cruel and a pest since birth - Teeth hadst thou in thy head when thou wast born to signify thou camest to bite the world.
"Teeth hadst thou in thy head when thou wast born,
To signify thou camest to bite the world:" (KHVI p3.5.6)
To refer to a third party change to 'Teeth had he in his head when he wast born to signify he came to bite the world.
In the play. *Henry VI, prisoner in the Tower, addresses his killer Richard of Gloucester, later Richard III*

Man, dangerous and to be avoided – ... if my name were liable to fear, I do not know the man I should avoid so soon as that spare Cassius.
"... But I fear him not:
Yet if my name were liable to fear,
I do not know the man I should avoid
So soon as that spare Cassius." (JC.1.2)
In the play. *Caesar's opinion of Cassius, after expressing the wish that Cassius were fatter. See 'Fat, f. men less dangerous than thin – ... Yond Cassius has a lean and hungry look.*

Man, despicable m. and a danger to the nation – ... whose filth and dirt troubles the silver spring where England drinks.
"...whose filth and dirt
Troubles the silver spring where England drinks" (KHVI.p2.4.1)
In the play. *A sea-captain to the soon to be executed Suffolk, banished by the King.*

Man, disconnected – ... he hath the joints of every thing, but everything so out of joint...
"... he hath the joints of every thing, but everything so out of joint that he is a gouty Briareus, many hands and no use, or purblind Argus, all eyes and no sight." (TC.1.2)
Modify to ...everything is out of joint'
In the play. ***The subject in question is the Greek Ajax as described by Alexander to Cressida in Troy.***

Man, dissimulating m. – O serpent heart, hid with a flowering face!
"O serpent heart, hid with a flowering face!
…..
Was ever book, containing such vile matter,
So fairly bound?" (RJ.3.2)
Express indignation at unexpected behavior from an apparently trustworthy

person. See also multiple entries for 'Appearances, deceiving, feigning etc.'
In the play. *Juliet's reaction at the news that Romeo has killed Tybalt.*

Man, dissolute m. - … he fishes, drinks, and wastes the lamps of night in revel…
"This is the news: he fishes, drinks, and wastes
The lamps of night in revel; is not more man-like
Than Cleopatra; nor the queen of Ptolemy
More womanly than he" (AC.1.4)
In the play. *Octavian tells Lepidus of Antony.*

Man, easily irritated - .. thou wilt quarrel with a man that hath a hair more, or a hair less, in his beard, than thou hast.
"…thou wilt quarrel with a man that hath a hair more, or a hair less, in his beard, than thou hast." (RJ.3.1)
Describe a quarrelsome character, e.g. 'he will quarrel with a man………..than he has'
In the play. *Mercutio brings out a trait of Benvolio's character.*

Man, easily quarrelsome after a few drinks – … as full of quarrel and offence as my young mistress' dog.
"…as full of quarrel and offence
As my young mistress' dog" (OTH.2.3)
In the play. *Iago describes Cassio's change of behavior after drinking.*

Man, evil m. - .. he is born with teeth!'
and so I was; which plainly signified that I should snarl and bite and play the dog.
That I should snarl and bite and play the dog
"The midwife wonder'd and the women cried
'O, Jesus bless us, he is born with teeth!'
And so I was; which plainly signified
That I should snarl and bite and play the dog." (KHVI.p3.5.4)
Modify to 'he was born with teeth which plainly signifies that he should snarl and bite and play the dog.'
In the play. *Gloucester (the soon to be Richard III), has just killed Henry VI in the Tower and reflects on the accidents of his own birth.*

Man, extraordinary m. - He sits 'mongst men like a descended god..
"He sits 'mongst men like a descended god:
He hath a kind of honour sets him off,
More than a mortal seeming" (CYM.1.6)
In the play. *The scoundrel Iachimo pulls back from slandering Imogen's husband and now feigns to praise him.*

Man, extremely undernourished man, but lusty – He was the very genius of famine…
"He was the very genius of famine, yet lecherous as a monkey, and the whores called him mandrake" (KHIV.p2.3.4)
In the play. *Falstaff's opinion of Master Shallow a country justice of the peace whom Falstaff plans to fleece.*

Man, gentleman described - A gentleman of noble parentage, of fair demesnes..
"A gentleman of noble parentage,
Of fair demesnes, youthful and nobly grained
Stuffed, as they say, with honorable parts,
Proportioned as one's heart could wish a man." (RJ.3.5)
With a dash of irony, a positive description of, for example, a job candidate.

In the play. *Capulet attempts to entice Juliet to marry Paris by praising him. 'Demesnes' = 'estate in lands'.*

Man, good man meaning commercially reliable or solvent – … my meaning in saying he is a good man is to have you understand me that he is sufficient.
"…my meaning in saying he is a good man is to have you understand me that he is sufficient." (MOV.1.3)
In the play. Prompted by a question from Bassanio, Shylock clarifies what he meant when he said that Antonio was a 'good man'

Man, harmless m. - I took him for the plainest harmless creature….
"I took him for the plainest harmless creature
That breathed upon this earth a Christian" (KRIII.3.5)
In the play. After putting Lord Hastings to death (for not wanting to endorse Richard as king),, Richard puts on a charade of false regret.

Man, honest and acute judge of human nature – (a fellow) of exceeding honesty and knows all qualities with a learned spirit…
"This fellow's of exceeding honesty, And knows all qualities, with a learned spirit,
Of human dealings" (OTH.3.3)
In the play. Othello could not be more wrong but this is how he rates Iago at first.

Man, honest but not very intelligent - .. an honest fellow enough… but he has not so much brain as earwax.
"Here's Agamemnon, an honest fellow enough and one that loves quails; but he has not so much brain as earwax:" (TC.5.1)
In the play. Thersite's opinion of Agamennon.

Man, honorable Italian m. – … one in whom the ancient Roman honour more appears…
"…one in whom
The ancient Roman honour more appears
Than any that draws breath in Italy." (MOV.3.2)
For other nations change accordingly, e.g. 'Teutonic' for 'Roman' and 'Germany' for 'Italy'.
In the play. Bassanio characterizes his friend Antonio to Portia, at her house in Belmont.

Man, m's inherent oddity – … every man is odd.
"An odd man, lady! every man is odd." (TC.4.5)
In the play. Cressida to Menelaus after a bantering exchange as to how many kisses by Menelaus is one of Cressida's kisses worth.

Man, inhuman - He's opposite to humanity.
"He's opposite to humanity" (TOA.1.1)
In the play. An unidentified parasite at Timon's table comments on the sour-spoken Apemantus.

Man, m. and his qualities, salt and spice – Is not birth, beauty… the spice and salt that seasons a man?
" .. Is not birth, beauty, good shape, discourse, manhood, learning, gentleness, virtue, youth, liberality, and such like, the spice and salt that seasons a man?" (TC.1.2)
Extract the qualities according to your taste. Or ironically ask the rhetorical question, "Do I not have the spice and salt that seasons a man?"
In the play. Pandarus extols the virtues and qualifications of Troilus to Cressida.

Man, m. arriving in force and fanfare - … In thunder and in earthquake, like a Jove…

"…in fierce tempest is he coming, In thunder and in earthquake, like a Jove…" (H V.2.4)
In the play. *Exeter tells the King of France to give up the crown as Henry V is approaching tempestuously.*

Man, m. as dust – Would it not grieve a woman to be overmastered with a piece of valiant dust?
"Would it not grieve a woman to be overmastered with a pierce of valiant dust?
Usable by a woman to explain why she is not yet married or why she does not plan to.
See also 'Man and its wicked nature - ..what is this quintessence of dust? Man delights not me.'
In the play. *To Leonato's wish that Beatrice find a good husband she replies she will have one when men will be made of something nobler than dust.*

Man, m. as paragon of animals – What a piece of work is a man!…
"What a piece of work is a man! how noble in reason! how infinite in faculty! in form and moving how express and admirable! in action how like an angel! in apprehension how like a god! the beauty of the world! the paragon of animals! And yet, to me, what is this quintessence of dust? man delights not me: no, nor woman neither, though by your smiling you seem to say so." (H.2.2)
In the play. *Hamlet in conversation with Rosencrantz and Guildenstern.* 'Express' = 'well made'

Man, m. believed to be plain and harmless - I took him for the plainest harmless creature..
"I took him for the plainest harmless creature
That breathed upon this earth a Christian" (KRIII.3.4)
Express your surprise at acts of a person whom you rated harmless. Or make an emphatic declaration about yourself, 'I am the plainest harmless creature that breathes upon this earth (a Christian)' If you are not a Christian quote the lines in full and then add, e.g. 'Actually I am an agnostic but still harmless'.
In the play. *Richard III pretends to cry at the death of Hastings whom he himself had killed.*

Man, m. causing heartburn at sight - … I never can see him, but I am heart burned an hour after.
"How tartly that gentleman looks! I never can see him, but I am heart burned an hour after." (MAAN.2.1)
Stronger alternative to 'He is a bothersome person'. See also 'Expression, facial e. unfriendly - .. the tartness of his face sours ripe grapes."
In the play. *Beatrice aims her sharp (but accurate) comments at the evil Don John.*

Man, m. courageous to the end – Undaunted spirit in a dying breast!"
"Undaunted spirit in a dying breast!" (KHVI.p1.3.2)
In the play. *Talbot comments on the old Duke of Bedford, who, though on the point of death, does not want to leave the field.*

Man, m. damned – Mark'd with a blot, damn'd in the book of heaven.
"Mark'd with a blot, damn'd in the book of heaven" (KRII.4.1)
In the play. *Northumberland pushes King Richard to confess his alleged crimes so as to justify the usurpation of the throne by Bolingbroke. The King responds.* See 'Defense, d. from general accusation, look who's talking - … if thy offences were upon record…'

Man, m. discredited and speaking nonsense - … will you credit this base drudge's words that speaks he knows not what?

"And will you credit this base drudge's words,
That speaks he knows not what?" (KHVI p2.4.2)
See also entries for 'Speech, nonsensical or meaningless'.
In the play. *Sir Stafford to the rabble that follows the rebel John Cade.*

Man, m. eating man, just like fish –
..the great ones eat up little ones.
3rd FISHERMAN. I marvel how the fishes live in the sea.
1st FISHERMAN. Why, as men do a-land; the great ones eat up the little ones." (PER.2.1)
Express a general law of mankind by relating the exchange in its entirety. See also entries for 'Man and its wicked nature'.
In the play. *After leaving Tharsus, a devastating storm destroys Pericles' fleet and he manages to swim ashore, near Pentapolis, where he meets with 3 fishermen.*

Man, m. false - ... falser than vows made in wine
"I am falser than vows made in wine" (AYLI.3.5)
See also 'False, as f. as - ... As false as dicers' oaths.'
In the play. *Rosalind, in a man's attire, fends off the advances of Phebe who, believing Rosalind to be a boy, has fallen in love with him/her.*

Man, m. heaped with honors – And sounded all the depths and shoals of honour...
"Say, Wolsey, that once trod the ways of glory,
And sounded all the depths and shoals of honour,
Found thee a way, out of his wreck, to rise in..." (KHVIII.3.2)
In the play. *The disgrace Wolsey to his successor Cromwell.*

Man, m. honest if slow witted - ... his wits are not so blunt as, God help, I would desire they were...
"...his wits are not so blunt as, God help, I would desire they were; but, in faith, honest as the skin between his brows." (MAAN.3.5)
In the play. *Officer Dogberry to Leonato referring to officer Verges.*

Man, m. genetically predisposed to crime - A fellow ... quoted and sign'd to do a deed of shame.
"A fellow by the hand of nature mark'd,
Quoted and sign'd to do a deed of shame" (KJ.4.2)
In the play. *King John attempts to shift on Hubert the responsibility of Arthur's murder by saying that he, Hubert, inspired him to the murder.*

Man, m. in full form and perfect shape - As full of spirit as the month of May.
"Glittering in golden coats, like images;
As full of spirit as the month of May,
And gorgeous as the sun at midsummer;
Wanton as youthful goats, wild as young bulls" (KHIV.p1.4.1)
Mildly ironic flattery, e.g. 'Here comes (name of party) as full of spirits as the month of May)
In the play. *The rebel Vernon gives Hotspur an account of the Prince of Wales and his allies.*

Man, m. in general, constitutionally unreliable – Man is a giddy thing and this is my conclusion.
"....for man is a giddy thing, and this is my conclusion." (MAAN.5.4)
Comment on the changing and fickle nature of humanity.
In the play. *Don Pedro pulls Benedick's leg for first declaring himself against marriage while now he plans to marry Beatrice. Benedick*

578

answers that yes he has changed his mind and it can happen because man is by nature a changeling (giddy).

Man, m. in shape but with traits of an animal - Never did I know a creature, that did bear the shape of man..
"Never did I know
A creature, that did bear the shape of man,
So keen and greedy to confound a man" (MOV.3.2)
Your opinion on a person with the traits of Shylock - there are many. See also 'Insult, man like animal according to the theories of Pythagoras'.
In the play. *Salerio comments on the nature of the Merchant of Venice, keen to exact a pound of flesh from Antonio.*

Man, m. larger than life, doer of good and poorly repaid - O monument and wonder of good deeds evilly bestow'd!
"O monument
And wonder of good deeds evilly bestow'd!" (TOA.4.3)
In the play. *Faithful servant Flavius goes to visit Timon in the woods.*

Man, m. never completely above board - Who has a breast so pure, but some uncleanly apprehensions…
"Utter my thoughts? Why, say they are vile and false;
As where's that palace whereinto foul things
Sometimes intrude not? Who has a breast so pure,
But some uncleanly apprehensions
Keep leets and law-days and in session sit
With meditations lawful?" (OTH.3.3)
In the play. *Iago drives Othello into jealousy by a mildly self-effacing statement, as if the hints about Desdemona's infidelity were attributable to a natural weakness. 'Leet' = a day when court is held'. 'Leet' means 'manor, court'.*

Man, m. not enslaved by passion a commendable exception - Give me that man that is not passion's slave…
"Give me that man
That is not passion's slave, and I will wear him
In my heart's core, ay, in my heart of heart." (H.3.2)
See also entries for 'Man and its wicked nature.'
In the play. *Hamlet in conversation with his friend Horatio after recognizing that Horatio is a true friend. The lines continue after Hamlet praises those men who 'are not a pipe for fortune's fingers'. See 'Man, m. to be praised who can stand up to fortune'.*

Man, m. not shaken by extraordinary natural phenomena – Are not you moved, when all the sway of earth shakes like a thing unfirm?
"Are not you moved, when all the sway of earth
Shakes like a thing unfirm?" (JC.1.3)
In the play. *Casca asks the imperturbable Cicero if he is not impressed by the extraordinary natural phenomena that supposedly signal a historic event, i.e. the assassination of Caesar.*

Man, m. of good qualities - a man of good repute, carriage, bearing, and estimation
"… a man of good repute, carriage, bearing, and estimation." (LLL.1.1)
Compliment with built-in a dash of irony
In the play. *Armado describes in a letter to Ferdinand the character of the letter carrier, Anthony Dull*

Man, m. of good qualities - A man of sovereign parts he is esteem'd, well fitted in arts, glorious in arms.
"A man of sovereign parts he is esteem'd;
Well fitted in arts, glorious in arms" (LLL.2.1)
In the play. *Maria's description of Longaville.*

Man, m. of honorable mind and of behavior with women - … he bears an honourable mind and will not use a woman lawlessly.
"Fear not; he bears an honourable mind,
And will not use a woman lawlessly." (TGV.5.3)
Answer to 'Can I trust you?'
In the play. *An outlaw in the retinue of Valentine stumbles upon Silvia and chaperon Eglamour and will bring them to Valentine (the 'honorable' man in the quote).*

Man, m. of noble character - .. a nobler sir ne'er lived 'twixt sky and ground.
"… a nobler sir ne'er lived
'Twixt sky and ground" (CYM.5.4)
In the play. *Jachimo begins his confession and he refers here to Leonatus.*

Man, m. of perfection - … the sole inheritor of all perfections that a man may owe…
"… the sole inheritor
Of all perfections that a man may owe,
Matchless Navarre" (LLL.2.1)
In the play. *Boyet, a courtier describes to the Princess, the qualities of the King of Navarre who will shortly call on her.*

Man, m. of physical substance – … think of that,--a man of my kidney …
"…think of that,--a man of my kidney,--think of that,--that am as subject to heat as butter; a man of continual dissolution and thaw" (MWW.3.5)
In the play. *Falstaff describes to Mr. Ford the adventure that landed him in the water.*

Man, m. of quick wit - I do say thou art quick in answers…
"I do say thou art quick in answers: thou heatest my blood." (LLL.1.2)
In the play. *Armado answers Moth.*

Man, m. of solid character and fiber – … whose solid virtue the shot of accident, nor dart of chance…
"…whose solid virtue
The shot of accident, nor dart of chance,
Could neither graze nor pierce?" (OTH.4.1)
In the play. *Ludovico, an envoy from the Venetian Government to Cyprus is amazed at Othello's change in demeanor, not consonant to his reputation as a man of 'solid virtue' etc.*

Man, m. particularly skillful in his profession or trade and still OK - … most profound in his art and yet not damnable.
"Believe then, if you please, that I can do strange things: I have, since I was three year old, conversed with a magician, most profound in his art and yet not damnable." (AYLI.5.2)
Answer to a request for reference about someone's skills, 'Yes…he is most profound…not damnable). Or you can apply it to yourself, 'I can say I am most profound in my art and yet not damnable.'
In the play. *Rosalind, disguised as a man, will miraculously return to be a woman, thanks to the skills of the non-existent magician (i.e. herself).*

Man, m. passionate and fiery - Why should a man whose blood is warm within…
"Why should a man whose blood is warm within
Sit like his grandsire cut in alabaster?" (MOV.1.1)
A justification for your (perhaps) fiery advances. See also "Intemperance, i. without limits - … But there is no bottom, none to my voluptuousness.'
In the play. *Gratiano attempts to cheer up Antonio who is melancholy by nature or disposition.*

Man, m. prone to mischief – … as prone to mischief as able to perform it.
"… for he is equal ravenous
As he is subtle, and as prone to mischief
As able to perform it." (KHVIII.1.1)
Change 'he' for 'she' if the subject is a woman.
In the play. *Buckingham of Wolsey.*

Man, m. prone to mischief - There's mischief in this man.
"There's mischief in this man" (KHVIII.1.2)
Ironic retort to a barb by a friend said in the presence of others. See also 'Sin, s. not occasional, but chronic - Thy sin's not accidental, but a trade', entries for 'Mischief'.
In the play. *An informant spies on Buckingham. King Henry VIII believes the accusations and pronounces a judgment on Buckingham.*

Man, qualified only for menial responsibilities – This is a slight unmeritable man, meet to be sent on errands.
"This is a slight unmeritable man,
Meet to be sent on errands" (JC.4.1)
In the play. *Antony's opinion of Lepidus who has just left the meeting with Antony and Octavian.*

Man, m. restraining himself against his won advantage - I lack iniquity sometimes to do me service.
"… I lack iniquity
Sometimes to do me service" (OTH.1.2)
In the play. *Iago pretends to have fought against an unknown man who was disparaging Othello.*

Man, m. shipwrecked (materially or metaphorically) - A man whom both the waters and the wind…
"A man whom both the waters and the wind,
In that vast tennis-court, have made the ball
For them to play upon" (PER.2.1)
Answer to 'Who are you?' when you feel under the weather or in difficult circumstances. See also 'Defence, d. from general accusations - more sinned against than sinning' – 'Attitude, a. towards the world, hating it – one…whom the vile blows and buffets of the world…'
In the play. *Pentapolis' fishermen come across the shipwrecked and stranded Pericles.*

Man, m. subject to constant mood changes - … his humour was nothing but mutation…
"… his humour
Was nothing but mutation, ay, and that
From one bad thing to worse" (CYM.4.2)
In the play. *Belarius speculates on what may have brought Cloten in the forest where Belarius lives with his adoptive sons.*

Man, m. thin and lusty – … was the very genius of famine; yet lecherous as a monkey…
"… (he) was so forlorn, that his dimensions to any thick sight were invincible: a' was the very genius of famine; yet lecherous as a monkey, and the whores called him mandrake" (KHIVp2.3.2)
In the play. *Falstaff describes Master Shallow in his youth in London.*

Man, m. to be praised who can stand up to the vagaries of fortune - … blest are those whose blood and judgment are so well commingled..
"A man that fortune's buffets and rewards

Hast ta'en with equal thanks: and blest are those
Whose blood and judgment are so well commingled,
That they are not a pipe for fortune's finger
To sound what stop she please. (H.3.2)
You can apply the idea to yourself, e.g. 'I am not a pipe for fortune's finger…..she please'.
In the play. *Hamlet in conversation with his friend Horatio after recognizing that Horatio is a true friend, who..*
'That no revenue hast but thy good spirits,
To feed and clothe thee.'

Man, m. wealthy and generous - O, he's the very soul of bounty.
"O, he's the very soul of bounty!" (TOA.1.2)
In the play. *A party-attending lord comments on Timon's generosity.*

Man, m. wealthy and powerful – … realms and islands were as plates dropp'd from his pocket.
"…realms and islands were
As plates dropp'd from his pocket" (AC.5.2)
Change 'were' to 'are' and describe a tycoon.
In the play. *Cleopatra eulogizes Antony.*

Man, m. well connected who knows what is going on in politics - … those that know the very nerves of state.
"… but we do learn
By those that know the very nerves of state…" (MFM.1.4)
Mild irony or flattery, e.g. 'You are one who knows the very nerves of state'
In the play. *Lucio talks with Isabel, sister of the condemned Claudio, and brings her up to speed with current events in Vienna.*

Man, m. who anticipates our very ideas - My other self, my counsel's consistory, my oracle, my prophet!
"My other self, my counsel's consistory,
My oracle, my prophet! " (KRIII.2.2)
In the play. *Richard's reaction at Buckingham's plan to separate the queen from her relatives so as to isolate them (and eventually kill them). 'Consistory' = 'meeting place'*

Man, m. who does not want to be found - … 'tis in vain to seek him here that means not to be found.
"…'tis in vain
To seek him here that means not to be found." (RJ.2.1)
In the play. *After leaving the Capulets' party where Romeo instantly fell in love with Juliet, Benvolio looks helplessly for him.*

Man, m. who never retreats - … Whose warlike ears could never brook retreat
"…the great Lord of Northumberland,
Whose warlike ears could never brook retreat" (KHVI.p3.1.1)
Change 'whose' to 'my' and apply to yourself or use as a comparison to extol the virtue of a man who fights on against unfavorable odds.
In the play. *York comments on the behavior of Lord Northumberland (one of his enemies) after the battle of St. Albans.*

Man, m. who promises but does not deliver - .. he writes brave verses, speaks brave words, swears brave oaths, and breaks them bravely.
" O, that's a brave man! he writes brave verses, speaks brave words, swears brave oaths, and breaks them bravely." (AYLI.3.4)
Sarcastic answer to, "What do you think of him?"

In the play. *Rosalind points out to Celia that Orlando swore his love for Rosalind. Celia offers words of warning.*

Man, m. wielding great political power – (No one) dares stir a wing, if Warwick shake his bells.
"…
Dares stir a wing, if Warwick shake his bells" (KHVI.p3.1.1)
Change 'Warwick' with the name whose power you are referring to.
In the play. *Warwick speaks about himself. No one dares contradict him. Here he plans to depose King Henry VI and install York as a monarch.*

Man, m. with a big mouth - Here's a large mouth indeed that spits forth death, and mountains, rocks, and seas..
" …Here's a large mouth indeed,
That spits forth death, and mountains, rocks, and seas,
Talks as familiarly of roaring lions,
As maids of thirteen of puppy dogs!" (KJ.2.2)
Comment or description of a big mouth
In the play. *Philip F. takes issue with the mayor of Angiers' suggestions for settling pending issues between King John of England and King Philip of France. The mayor points out the dire consequences for all parties involved if the suggestions are not carried out. Faulconbridge tells him he is a 'large mouth'*

Man, m. with a keen sense of humor - His eye begets occasion for his wit…
"His eye begets occasion for his wit;
For every object that the one doth catch,
The other turns to a mirth-moving jest;
Which his fair tongue (conceit's expositor)
Delivers in such apt and gracious words,
That aged ears play truant at his tales,
And younger hearings are quite ravished;
So sweet and voluble is his discourse." (LLL..2.1)
Flatter a notorious wit or extract whatever lines apply to you. E.G. 'I deliver words in such apt and gracious words that aged ears……my tales'.
In the play. *Rosaline, who knows Biron having once danced with him, describes him to her friends as a man with a sense of humor.*

Man, m. with self-asserted composition skills – … motions, revolutions: these are begot in the ventricle of memory…
"This is a gift that I have, simple, simple; a foolish extravagant spirit, full of forms, figures, shapes, objects, ideas, apprehensions, motions, revolutions: these are begot in the ventricle of memory, nourished in the womb of pia mater, and delivered upon the mellowing of occasion" (LLL.1.2)
In the play. *The pompous Holofernes has no qualms in self-praise.*

Man, m's nature but a collection of dust – Thou art not thyself, for thou exist'st on many a thousand grains that issue out of dust.
"…Thou art not thyself;
For thou exist'st on many a thousand grains
That issue out of dust." (MFM.3.1)
See also 'Life, surrounded by sleep and partaking of dream experience - We are such stuff as dreams are made on, and our little life is rounded with a sleep.' *** 'Man and his wicked nature - … what is this quintessence of dust? Man delights not me.' *** 'Wealth, w. unloaded by death – If thou art rich, thou'rt poor for, like an ass whose back with ingots bows…'

In the play. *The duke (in disguise) converses with Claudio who has been condemned to death by Angelo.*

Man, m.'s nature disappointing– Is man no more than this?
"Is man no more than this? Consider him well" (KL.3.4)
In the play. *King Lear's reaction at seeing the stark naked and apparently mad Edgar who joined Lear's party in a forest.*

Man, m's nature subject to unpredictable changes – Thou art not certain, for thy complexion shifts to strange effects after the moon.
"… Thou art not certain;
For thy complexion shifts to strange effects,
After the moon." (MFM.3.1)
In the play. *The duke (in disguise) converses with Claudio who has been condemned to death by Angelo*

Man, m.'s nature unpredictable - .. we know what we are, but know not what we may be.
"Lord, we know what we are, but know not what we may be" (H.4.5)
In the play. *Ophelia, now mad, utters unconsciously important truths.*

Man, m.'s nature volatile - … such summer-birds are men.
"… such summer-birds are men" (TOA.3.6)
In the play. *Timon's skeptical comment to an expression of allegiance by a parasite flatterer. See 'Joining the party – The swallow follows not summer more willing than we your lordship.'*

Man, m's nature, a conflict of good and bad - … Two such opposed kings encamp them still in man as well as herbs, grace and rude will…
Within the infant rind of this small flower
Poison hath residence and medicine power:
For this, being smelt, with that part cheers each part;
Being tasted, slays all senses with the heart.
Two such opposed kings encamp them still
In man as well as herbs, grace and rude will;
And where the worser is predominant,
Full soon the canker death eats up that plant." (RJ.2.2)
A comparison when describing the character of a man with good and bad qualities. For concision extract 'Two such opposed kings…..rude will'. See also 'Life, a combination of good and bad - The web of our life is of a mingled yarn, good and ill go together…'
In the play. *Friar Lawrence compares the opposite good and bad qualities of plants to the conflict between good and bad qualities in man. See also 'Virtue, vice and their relationship'*

Man, m's nature, his faults separate him from the Gods - … but you, gods, will give us some faults to make us men.
"A rarer spirit never
Did steer humanity; but you, gods, will give us
Some faults to make us men" (AC.5.2)
Alternative to no-one is perfect, 'The gods give us some faults to make us men'. See also 'Forgiveness, f. at something she has done'.
In the play. *Agrippa eulogizing Antony.*

Man, m's qualifications questioned - But he's a tried and valiant soldier… So is my horse, Octavius…
OCTAVIUS You may do your will;
But he's a tried and valiant soldier.
ANTONY So is my horse, Octavius; and for that
I do appoint him store of provender:
It is a creature that I teach to fight,
To wind, to stop, to run directly on,

His corporal motion govern'd by my spirit.
And, in some taste, is Lepidus but so (JC.4.1)
In the play. *Clearly Antony does not think much of Lepidus*

Man, new rich and self-made - ... a man, they say, that from very nothing, and beyond the imagination of his neighbours, is grown into an unspeakable estate.
"...a man, they say, that from very nothing, and beyond the imagination of his neighbours, is grown into an unspeakable estate" (WT.4.1)
Introducing to a successful entrepreneur.
In the play. *Polixenes confides to Camillo that Florizel (Polixenes' son) has been seen often visiting the house of a new-rich shepherd. The reason is that Florizel has fallen in love with Perdita, who is the shepherd's adoptive daughter.*

Man, perception establishing his value - And not a man, for being simply a man hath any honour...
"And not a man, for being simply a man,
Hath any honour; but honour for those honours
That are without him, as places, riches and favour,
Prizes of accident as oft as merit:
Which when they fall, as being slippery standers,
The love that leaned on them is slippery too,
Do one pluck down another, and together
Die in the fall." (TC.3.2)
State an inevitable truth.
In the play. *Feeling ignored, Achilles muses on the turn of events.*

Man, politically broken and seeking a quiet life – ... An old man, broken with the storms of state...
"... he gave these words, 'O, father abbot,
An old man, broken with the storms of state,
Is come to lay his weary bones among ye;
Give him a little earth for charity!"
(KHVIII.4.2)
In the play. *Griffith reports to the divorced Queen Katharine how the disgraced Cardinal Wolsey retired to a convent.*

Man, politically powerful and dangerous man – ... this imperious man will work us all from princes into pages...
"...this imperious man will work us all
From princes into pages: all men's honours
Lie like one lump before him, to be fashion'd
Into what pitch he please."
(KHVIII.2.2)
In the play. *Norfolk tells Suffolk his opinions and fears about powerful Cardinal Wolsey.*

Man, politically very powerful - ... this is he that moves both wind and tide.
"... now begins a second storm to rise;
For this is he that moves both wind and tide." (KHVI p3.3.3)
Humor with a dash of flattery. E.G. 'I ask you because it is you that moves both wind and tide'. Or if you wish to be creative and make your own rhyme, 'Let me ask you, let me take you aside, for it is you that moves both wind and tide.'
Introduction to a powerful politician, e.g. the chairman of the House and Means committee.
In the play. *Warwick has arrived at the court of King Louis XI of France to arrange a marriage between Edward IV of England and the Lady Bona, sister of King Louis. Queen Margaret, his enemy, recognizes the political power of Warwick.*

Man, qualities of a complete m. - ... they are both the varnish of a complete man.
MOTH You are a gentleman and a gamester, sir.
ARMADO I confess both: they are both the varnish of a complete man. (LLL.1.2)
In the play. *Moth pulls the leg of Armado.*

Man, question about man's stability of mind – Are his wits safe? is he not light of brain?
"Are his wits safe? is he not light of brain?" (OTH.4.1)
In the play. *Ludovico's reaction at observing Othello's odd behavior with Desdemona. :Ludovico is an envoy from Venice and Desdemona's uncle.*

Man, self-conscious and somewhat full of himself - Full of wise saws and modern instances.
"Full of wise saws and modern instances" (AYLI.2.7)
Use as a starter in the rebuttal of your adversary. E.G. 'My learned friend is full of wise saws and modern instances, but…'
In the play. *Jacques characterizes the typical judge, as representative of one of the seven stages of life. 'Saw' is synonym for 'wise maxim', 'sentence'. For the complete description of the seven ages of man see the introduction to the quotes on 'AGE'.*

Man, self-supporting and living within his means – I earn that I eat; get that I wear.
"…I earn that I eat; get that I wear…"(AYLI.3.2)
In the play. *Shepherd Corin tells Touchstone about himself and his philosophy. See also 'Life, simple l. - … and the greatest of my pride is to see my ewes graze, and my lambs* **suck.***'.*

Man, simple-minded m. – How green you are and fresh in this old world!
"How green you are and fresh in this old world!" (KJ.3.4)
In the play. *Cardinal Pandulph to King Lewis of France as the Cardinal tries to convince him to follow Vatican policy in dealing with England.*

Man, something wrong with his brain - .. for, sure, the man is tainted in's wits.
"… he does nothing but smile: your ladyship were best to have some guard about you, if he come; for, sure, the man is tainted in's wits." (TN.3.4)
In the play. *Maria pre-warns Olivia about the oncoming visit by Malvolio. Maria has tricked Malvolio into believing that Olivia is in love with him.*

Man, strain of m. debased - The strain of man's bred into baboon and monkeys.
"The strain of man's bred
Into baboon and monkeys." (TOA.1.1)
Indicate your disgust of certain people.
In the play. *Apemantus decries Timon's company and wishes arthritis upon them. If they contracted arthritis they would be prevented from their bending in faked demonstrations of respect and flattery. The lines go,*
"Aches contract and starve your supple joints!
That there should be small love 'mongst these sweet knaves,
And all this court'sy! The strain of man's bred
Into baboon and monkeys."
See 'Curse, arthritis'

Man, type of m. better to a friend than enemy - I had rather have such men my friends than enemies.
"…I had rather have
Such men my friends than enemies" (JC.5.4)

In the play. *Antony commenting on the captured Lucilius, whom a soldier had mistakenly assumed to be Brutus.*

Man, tyrannical - ... and like the tyrannous breathing of the north shakes all our buds from growing.
"… comes in my father
And like the tyrannous breathing of the north
Shakes all our buds from growing." (CYM.1.3)
Metaphor for having projects disrupted by an uncouth and tyrannical person.
In the play. *Imogen reflects about the hasty parting from her husband when King Cymbeline walked in like the tyrannous wind. Cymbeline has exiled her husband to Italy.*

Man, very emotional m., characteristics of - Where joy most revels, grief doth most lament; grief joys, joy grieves, on slender accident.
"The violence of either grief or joy
Their own enactures with themselves destroy:
Where joy most revels, grief doth most lament;
Grief joys, joy grieves, on slender accident." (H.3.2)
In the play. *Part of the lines recited by the player king in the play produced by Hamlet to test King Claudius' reactions.*

Man, very thin out of constitution or hunger - ... was so forlorn, that his dimensions to any thick sight were invincible…
"..was so forlorn, that his dimensions to any thick sight were invincible: a' was the very genius of famine; yet lecherous as a monkey, and the whores called him mandrake" (KHIV p2.3.2)
In the play. *Falstaff reflects on the youth of his host Master Shallow, whom he plans to bilk with the promise of preferment at court.*

Man, well poised m. - ... stuffed with all honourable virtues
"…stuffed with all honourable virtues." (MAAN.1.1)
In the play. *The subject in question is Benedick as described to Beatrice by a messenger.*

Man, wicked and villainous - The multiplying villanies of nature do swarm upon him.
"The multiplying villanies of nature
Do swarm upon him" (M.1.2)
In the play. *A sergeant narrates the events that led to the victory over the Scottish rebels, one of whom, referred to here, was Mcdonald.*

Man, worse than the worst of devils – Not in the legions of horrid hell can come a devil more damn'd to top Macbeth.
"Not in the legions
Of horrid hell can come a devil more damn'd
In evils to top Macbeth" (M.4.3)
Change 'Macbeth' with the name of the applicable villain.
In the play. *Malcolm in conversation with Macduff, pretends to be worse than Macbeth. Macduff disagrees.*

Man, m. with a cutting wit - ... a sharp wit matched with too blunt a will…
"…a sharp wit matched with too blunt a will;
Whose edge hath power to cut, whose will still wills
It should none spare that come within his power." (LLL.2.1)
In the play. *Maria's description of the cutting wit of Loganville.*

Man, young and always sad - I fear he will prove the weeping philosopher when he grows old…
"I fear he will prove the weeping philosopher when he grows old, being

so full of unmannerly sadness in his youth" (MOV.1.2)
In the play. *Portia describes one of her suitors, the County Palatine.*

Man, young and intelligent - ... I never knew so young a body with so old a head.
"…I never knew so young a body with so old a head." (MOV.4.1)
In the play. *A court clerk reads a letter from Bellario, an attorney from Padua. Bellario commends the learning and the ability of his assistant whom he has dispatched to Venice to arbitrate the case of Shylock vs. Antonio. The assistant is Portia, wearing a man's disguise.*

Man, young but experienced – his years but young, but his experience old..
"His years but young, but his experience old;
His head unmellow'd, but his judgment ripe" (TGV.2.4)
With tongue in cheek apply to yourself in answer to comments of the type, 'you are too young'. 'My years but young, but my experience old'.
In the play. *Valentine sings the praises of Proteus to the Duke of Milan.*

Man, young but experienced - How much more elder art thou than thy looks!
"…O wise and upright judge!
How much more elder art thou than thy looks!" (MOV.4.1)
In the play. *Believing that he will have his bond, Shylock compliments the attorney (that is the disguised Portia).*

Management structure, hierarchical – Obedience: for so work the honey bees…
"Obedience: for so work the honey bees,
Creatures that, by rule in nature, teach
The act of order to a peopled kingdom.
They have a king, and officers of sorts." (KHV.1)
In a pep talk to explain the reason for a hierarchical structure, 'We must have obedience: for so work… sorts.' See also "Planning, importance of p. - When we mean to build, we first survey the plot, then draw the model...'
In the play. *Canterbury uses the comparison of bees to illustrate his thoughts about an ideal management structure. His syrupy and self-serving praise of hierarchy goes as follows:*
for so work the honey-bees,
Creatures that by a rule in nature teach
The act of order to a peopled kingdom.
They have a king and officers of sorts;
Where some, like magistrates, correct at home,
Others, like merchants, venture trade abroad,
Others, like soldiers, armed in their stings,
Make boot upon the summer's velvet buds,
Which pillage they with merry march bring home
To the tent-royal of their emperor;
Who, busied in his majesty, surveys
The singing masons building roofs of gold,
The civil citizens kneading up the honey,
The poor mechanic porters crowding in
Their heavy burdens at his narrow gate,
The sad-eyed justice, with his surly hum,
Delivering o'er to executors pale
The lazy yawning drone. I this infer,
That many things, having full reference
To one consent, may work contrariously:
As many arrows, loosed several ways,
Come to one mark; as many ways meet in one town;
As many fresh streams meet in one salt sea;
As many lines close in the dial's centre;
So may a thousand actions, once afoot.
End in one purpose, and be all well

borne
Without defeat.

Management style, fear and government - In time we hate that which we often fear.
"In time we hate that which we often fear." (AC.1.3)
Suggest a soft rather than a hard hand in handling people.
In the play. *Charmian, attendant girl to Cleopatra, suggests that she (Cleopatra) may lose Antony's love if she continues to disappoint him with erratic behavior.*

Management, m. and leadership crucial - The heavens themselves, the planets and this centre…
"The heavens themselves, the planets and this centre
Observe degree, priority and place,
Insisture, course, proportion, season, form,
Office and custom, in all line of order." (TC.1.3)
See also 'Authority, consequences of lack of a. and management - .. when degree is shaked, which is the ladder to all high designs, then enterprise is sick
In the play. *Ulysses points out to Agamennon the weakness among the Greeks arising from exercising weak leadership.*

Management, m. and managers - We cannot all be masters, nor all masters cannot be truly follow'd.
"We cannot all be masters, nor all masters
Cannot be truly follow'd" (OTH.1.1)
Evasive answers to 'Do you want to be president?'
In the play. *Iago gives his opinion to Roderigo about the promotion of Othello to General and Cassius' promotion to Lieutenant.*

Management, m. changes at the top and consequences – The cease of majesty, but, like a gulf doth draw what's near it with it…
"The cease of majesty
Dies not alone; but, like a gulf, doth draw
What's near it with it: it is a massy wheel,
Fix'd on the summit of the highest mount,
To whose huge spokes ten thousand lesser things
Are mortised and adjoin'd; which, when it falls,
Each small annexment, petty consequence,
Attends the boisterous ruin." (H.3.3)
In the play. *Rosencranz concurs with the king that Hamlet's alleged madness is dangerous to the king and everyone else.*

Management, m. conflict, conflicting personalities – Two stars keep not their motion in one sphere…
"Two stars keep not their motion in one sphere;
Nor can one England brook a double reign,
Of Harry Percy and the Prince of Wales." (KHIV.p1.5.3)
When you resign or cause your opponents to resign due to personality conflicts.
In the play. *Moments before their final duel, the Prince of Wales tells Harry Percy that there cannot be two parties in the same role, meaning that Harry is the rebel and the Prince of Wales the rightful heir to the throne.*

Management, m. strength shown in trying circumstances - (Did you not say) …That common chances common men could bear…
" (Did you not say) …That common chances common men could bear;
That, when the sea was calm, all boats alike
Show'd mastership in floating." (COR.4.1)

Show that managerial skills are tested and proven when the situation is difficult.
In the play. *Coriolanus says farewell to mother and wife and reminds his crying mother of the precepts she imparted to him.*

Management, m's chronic stress – I leap into the seas, where's hourly trouble for a minute's ease.
"Take I your wish, I leap into the seas,
Where's hourly trouble for a minute's ease" (PER.2.4)
See also 'Life, l. inside a corporation or the Washington belt'
In the play. *Helicanus is solicited by Tyre's lords to step into the throne of the missing and given for lost Pericles. But he asks for a delay of another 12 months before 'leaping into the sea'.*

Management, metaphor for good management and good manager - His bark is stoutly timbered, and his pilot of very expert and approved allowance.
"His bark is stoutly timber'd, and his pilot
Of very expert and approved allowance." (OTH.2.1)
A metaphor for a good manager. 'Of his management we can say 'his bark is stoutly timbered and his pilot…..allowance'.
In the play. *Othello is due to arrive in Cyprus for a military mission.*

Management, mixed m. and conflicting authorities - .. and my soul aches to know, when two authorities are up, neither supreme…
" .. and my soul aches
To know, when two authorities are up,
Neither supreme, how some confusion
May enter 'twixt the gap of both, and take
The one by the other." (COR.3.1)

Oppose split management
In the play. *Coriolanus in conversation with Cominius, decried the structure of shared responsibility.*

Management, multiple lines of command unmanageable - How in one house should many people under two commands hold amity?
"… How in one house
Should many people under two commands
Hold amity? 'Tis hard, almost impossible." (KL.2.4)
To implement your plan you cannot afford interference.
In the play. *Regan to Lear suggesting a further reduction in Lear's staff.*

Management, poor m. coupled with bitter in-fighting - … when envy breeds unkind division, there comes the ruin, there begins confusion.
"'T is much when sceptres are in children's hands
But more, when envy breeds unkind division;
There comes the ruin, there begins confusion." (KHVI.p1.4.1)
Pinpoint envy as the cause of the trouble, '…when envy breeds…confusion'.
In the play. *Exeter comments on the current state of affair among the English.*

Management, unfit for m. - … how should you govern any kingdom,
"Alas! how should you govern any kingdom,
That know not how to use ambassadors,
Nor how to be contented with one wife,
Nor how to use your brothers brotherly,
Nor how to study for the people's welfare,
Nor how to shroud yourself from enemies?" (KHVI p3.4.3)

In the play. *Warwick has captured Edward, guilty of botching up Warwick's effort at establishing an alliance with France, in order to marry the Lady Grey with whom Edward was infatuated.*

Management, upward mobility stunted - ... Farewell the hopes of court! my hopes in heaven do dwell
"... Farewell
The hopes of court! my hopes in heaven do dwell." (KHVIII.3.2)
Use in closing a retirement or resignation speech.
In the play. *Wolsey leaves the worldly scene.*

Manager, how to recognize the m. - ... which is the head lady?
COSTARD God dig-you-den all! Pray you, which is the head lady?
PRINCESS Thou shalt know her, fellow, by the rest that have no heads. (LLL.4.1)
Answer to 'Who is the manager?' if you restate the question first as, 'You mean who is the head person?' See also 'Identification, who is who?' – 'Identification, are you so and so?'
In the play. *Costard must speak with the princess and does not know that he is actually talking to her. The Princess tends to be sarcastic as a character.*

Manager, m. that is followed without enthusiasm - Those he commands move only in command, nothing in love...
"Those he commands move only in command,
Nothing in love: now does he feel his title
Hang loose about him, like a giant's robe
Upon a dwarfish thief." (M.5.2)
Comment about an authoritarian boss or a management style leading to the same results, task performed because requested but without enthusiasm.

In the play. *Angus, a Scottish nobleman, reports on the state of affairs at Macbeth's court.*

Mankind, admiration of m. (ironic) - ... O brave new world that has such people in it.
MIRANDA. "... O brave new world, That has such people in it!" (TEM.5.1)
Answer ironically the question, 'How do you like these people'. See also 'Opinion, your op. on specific man - bad in himself and worse when drunk'
In the play. *Miranda is moved at a scene in which Ferdinand kneels to get a blessing from his father Alonso.*

Manners, I thought you more gentleman than you are - ... perforce I must confess I thought you lord of more true gentleness.
"But fare you well: perforce I must confess,
I thought you lord of more true gentleness." (MND.2.2)
Elegantly pointing out rudeness, '...perforce I must confess... gentleness.'
In the play. *Helena rejects the advances of Lysander.*

Manners, m. over murder (part of a threat) – ... the cool and temperate wind of grace o'erblows the filthy and contagious clouds...
"Whiles yet the cool and temperate wind of grace
O'erblows the filthy and contagious clouds
Of heady murder, spoil and villany" (HV.3.3)
In the play. *Henry V tells the people of Harfleur, under siege, to surrender or else.*

Manners, self-training in m. - ...he has been yonder i' the sun practising behavior to his own shadow...
"... he has been yonder i' the sun practising behavior to his own shadow this half hour." (TN.2.5)

When you are advised to improve your communication skills, e.g. 'OK I'll practice behavior to my own shadow'.
In the play. *Maria refers how the vane Malvolio practices the gestures and the demeanor of a gentleman.*

Marriage, combination unusual or plainly mad - Such a mad marriage never was before.
"Such a mad marriage never was before." (TOS.3.2)
Comment to an unlikely association or marriage
In the play. *The marriage Gremio refers to is between Petruchio and Katharina.*

Marriage, in praise of m. – But earthly happier is the rose distill'd….
"But earthly happier is the rose distill'd,
Than that, which, withering on the virgin thorn,
Grows, lives and dies, in single blessedness." (MND.1.1)
Overcome the restraints of a reluctant lady.
In the play. *Theseus prompts Hermia to face up to the alternatives, to be a nun or follow her father's wishes and marry Demetrius. Theseus compares marriage to the distilling of a rose.*

Marriage, joys of m. – … the sweet silent hours of marriage joys.
"… acquaint the princess
With the sweet silent hours of marriage joys" (KRIII.4.4)
If you are madly in love with her try 'let me acquaint you with the sweet hours of marriage joys'
In the play. *The super-crafty Richard now asks Queen Elizabeth, widow of dead king Edward IV, to marry her daughter and to prepare her for this event.*

Marriage, m. and sentencing subjects to destiny - The ancient saying is no heresy, hanging and wiving goes by destiny.
"The ancient saying is no heresy, Hanging and wiving goes by destiny." (MOV.2.9)
In the play. *Nerissa's comment after the prince of Arragon chose the wrong picture and leaves dejected.*

Marriage, m. between upper and lower class - … we marry a gentler scion to the wildest stock…
"You see, sweet maid, we marry
A gentler scion to the wildest stock,
And make conceive a bark of baser kind
By bud of nobler race: this is an art
Which does mend nature, change it rather, but
The art itself is nature." (WT.4.4)
Your rebuttal to a remark about the difference in class or wealth between bride and groom
In the play. *Florizel, son of the king of Bohemia, rationalizes to Perdita, now a shepherdess, why he can marry her.*

Marriage, m. unsuited to military life - A soldier is better accommodated than with a wife.
"A soldier is better accommodated than with a wife." (KHIV.p2.3.2)
If you are single, answer to why you are not married, or to whether you are married.
See also 'Single - … thou consumest thyself in single life.'
In the play. *Bardolph answers Shallow's question as to how is Falstaff's wife. Falstaff is single.*

Marriage, negative view of m. - A young man married is a man that's marr'd.
"A young man married is a man that's marr'd" (AWEW.2.3)

In the play. *Bertram was forced to marry the virtuous Helena and wants to leave immediately for the war in Tuscany. Parolles agrees with Bertram on the issue of marriage.*

Marriage, not marrying her under any circumstance – ... were my state far worser than it is, I would not wed her for a mine of gold.
"Her only fault, and that is faults enough,
Is that she is intolerable curst
And shrewd and froward, so beyond all measure
That, were my state far worser than it is,
I would not wed her for a mine of gold." (TOS.1.2)
In the play. *Hortensio explains to Petruchio why he dislikes Katharina. 'Froward' stands for 'unbearable'.*

Marriage, quick m. statistically unsuccessful - ... hasty marriage seldom proveth well.
"... hasty marriage seldom proveth well." (KHVI p3.4.1)
In the play. *Richard of Gloucester's opinion on the marriage of his brother Edward IV with the Lady Grey.*

Marriage, spontaneous vs. forced m. - For what is wedlock forced but a hell, an age of discord and continual strife?
"Marriage is a matter of more worth
Than to be dealt in by attorneyship;
For what is wedlock forced but a hell,
An age of discord and continual strife?
Whereas the contrary bringeth bliss,
And is a pattern of celestial peace."
(KHVI.p1.5.5)
Use in a similar context or as a metaphor for a fruitful and concordant agreement between two parties.

In the play. *Suffolk answers a point by Exeter that Margaret, proposed wife to Henry VI, has no dowry. The marriage will be a happy one, Suffolk contends thus making up for the lack of a dowry.*

Marriage, the state of being m. – ... the true concord of well-tuned sounds, by unions married.
"...the true concord of well-tuned sounds,
By unions married..." (SON 8)
Answer to 'Are you married?' E.G. 'Yes, I experience the true concord...sounds.'

Masochism, against m. - all delights are vain; but that most vain, which with pain purchased doth inherit pain.
"Why, all delights are vain; but that most vain,
Which with pain purchased doth inherit pain" (LLL.1.1)
Question the value of pleasures that involve pain. Answer to questions about types of entertainment that you utterly dislike, e.g. 'Why don't you like to go to a discotheque?'
In the play. *Biron tempers the enthusiasm of his companions as to the merits of excessive study and abstinence.*

Masochism, m. for love – ... dart thy skill at me... cut me to pieces with thy keen conceit.
"...dart thy skill at me;
Bruise me with scorn, confound me with a flout;
Thrust thy sharp wit quite through my ignorance;
Cut me to pieces with thy keen conceit." (LLL.5.2)
When you admit that you deserve punishment and by admitting it you hope to be forgiven without damage. 'Thrust thy sharp wit quite through my ignorance' is enough if and when she wants to prove you ignorant. See also

'Love, a masochistic exercise – where scorn is bought with groans'.
In the play. *Biron admits to a previous piece of foolery and mockingly and masochistically asks Rosaline to hurt him. 'Flout' = 'mock'*

Mass, m. behavior – … they threw their caps as they would hang them on the horns o' the moon…
"…they threw their caps
As they would hang them on the horns o' the moon,
Shouting their emulation." (COR.1.1)
In the play. *Coriolanus disdainfully comments on the happiness of the masses at being granted some corn.*

Mass, m. manipulation - … patient fools, whose children he hath slain their base throats tear …
"… patient fools,
Whose children he hath slain, their base throats tear
With giving him glory." (COR.5.6)
In the play. *Aufidius commenting on the Volsces who love Coriolanus though he previously had slain many of them.*

Mass, m. psychology – Look, how the world's poor people are amazed at apparitions, signs and prodigies…
"Look, how the world's poor people are amazed
At apparitions, signs and prodigies,
Whereon with fearful eyes they long have gazed,
Infusing them with dreadful prophecies" (V&A)
In the poem. *Venus wishes to disregard signs that seem to indicate that Adonis is dead. But she observes a number of dogs wounded by a boar and fears for Adonis' life.*

Mass, m. psychology, following thoughtlessly - They'll take suggestion as a cat laps milk; they'll tell the clock to any business that we say befits the hour.

"…For all the rest,
They'll take suggestion as a cat laps milk;
They'll tell the clock to any business that
We say befits the hour." (TEM.2.1)
In the play. *Antonio, shipwrecked in the island, hatches a plot against Alonso, king of Naples, also shipwrecked in the island. Once the plot is carried out, he thinks the others will obey without questioning.*

Mass, m. psychology, masses needing excitement - … And quietness, grown sick of rest, would purge by any desperate change.
"… And quietness, grown sick of rest, would purge
By any desperate change." (AC.1.3)
A historic reference. Justify the need for some excitement or change of pace or procedures to maintain employees' morale. See also entries for 'Opinion, your op. on crowds and masses'
In the play. *Antony tells Cleopatra about the political situation in Rome.*

Masses, crowds at all windows driven by curiosity – You would have thought the very windows spake…
"You would have thought the very windows spake,
So many greedy looks of young and old
Through casements darted their desiring eyes
Upon his visage…" (KRII.5.2)
In the play. *The Duke of York gives an account to his wife about the coronation march for Bolingbroke.*

Masses, grumbling m. defined – This inundation of mistemper'd humour.
"… This inundation of mistemper'd humour" (KJ.5.1)

In the play. *King John pleads with Cardinal Pandulph to stop the French from attacking. The English people are upset with King John and threaten to defect to the French.*

Masses, m. contemptible - ...The breath of garlic-eaters!
"...you that stood so up much on
The breath of garlic-eaters!" (COR.4.6)
See also 'Breath, bad b. attributable to unhealthy diet - ... in their thick breaths rank of gross diet...'
In the play. *Menenius upbraids the tribunes of the people for having enraged Coriolanus against Rome.*

Masses, m. in confusion – ... like a flight of fowl, scatter'd by winds and high tempestuous gusts
"... like a flight of fowl
Scatter'd by winds and high tempestuous gusts" (TA.5.3)
In the play. *Marcus A. addresses the Roman citizens, after Lucius returns at the heads of the Goths and the evil emperor Saturninus and queen Tamora are done away with.*

Masses, mass excitement - ... so many greedy looks of young and old...
"You would have thought the very windows spake,
So many greedy looks of young and old
Through casements darted their desiring eyes
Upon his visage" (KRII.5.2)
See also entries for 'Opinion, your opinion on crowds and masses'.
In the play. *The Duke of York gives an account to his wife of the crowds' reception to the procession of the usurper Bolingbroke and the usurped King Richard. Bolingbroke is the favorite by a long shot.*

Masses, pitiless - ... had not God, for some strong purpose, steel'd the hearts of men...

"...had not God, for some strong purpose, steel'd
The hearts of men, they must perforce have melted
And barbarism itself have pitied him."
KRII.5.2)
In the play. *The Duke of York gives an account to his wife of the crowds' reception to the procession of the usurper Bolingbroke and the usurped King Richard. Bolingbroke is the favorite by a long shot.*

Masses, working the m - ... Wooing poor craftsmen with the craft of smiles.
"Observed his courtship to the common people;
How he did seem to dive into their hearts
With humble and familiar courtesy
....
Wooing poor craftsmen with the craft of smiles " (KRII.1.4)
In the play. *Richard II comments on the behavior of Bolingbroke seemingly already intent to ingratiate himself with the people (and eventually to usurp the throne)*

Masses, working the m. using applause as a tool – This general applause and loving shout argues your wisdoms and your love to Richard.
"'Thanks, gentle citizens and friends,' quoth I;
'This general applause and loving shout
Argues your wisdoms and your love to Richard" (KRIII.3.7)
In the play. *Buckingham has paid some cheerleaders to applaud Richard as the new king, while the mayor of London and all the others are perplexed at the turn of events.*

Master of ceremonies, calling for the m.o.c. - Where is our usual manager of mirth?"

"Where is our usual manager of mirth?" (MND.5.1)
In the play. *Theseus calls for Philostrate, master of ceremony, to produce a play or stage some entertainment waiting for the wedding day between Theseus and Hippolyta.*

Match, m. beyond hope or impossible - The hind that would be mated by the lion must die for love.
"The hind that would be mated by the lion
Must die for love" (AWEW.1.1)
Change 'lion' to 'lioness' if you are the pursuer of an unreachable lady.
In the play. *Helena comments on her love for Bertram, impossible due to her lower condition or status.*

Match, mad m. - Of all mad matches never was the like.
"Of all mad matches never was the like." (TOS.3.2)
In the play. *Gremio and Tranio comment on the marriage of Petruchio and Katharina, two very dissonant characters.*

Mathematics, elegant m. - … one more than two…which the base vulgar do call, three.
MOTH. I am sure you know how much the gross sum of deuce and ace amounts to.
ARMADO. It doth amount to one more than two.
MOTH Which the base vulgar do call, three." (LLL.1.2)
Inject some irony in a conversation that centers on numbers. Adapt as needed, e.g.. 'This is like saying that two and two is three plus one which the base vulgar do call four'.
In the play. *Moth pulls the leg of his master Armado by parroting Armado's mode of speaking.*

Mathematics, error in calculations - … it were pity you should get your living by reckoning.
BIRON. By Jove, I always took three threes for nine.
COSTARD. O Lord, sir, it were pity you should get your living by reckoning, sir." (LLL.5.2)
Ironic comment when someone makes an error in calculations.
In the play. *Biron and Costard banter.*

Mathematics, not a strength - …cannot take two from twenty, for his heart and leave eighteen
"…a woman that
Bears all down with her brain; and this her son
Cannot take two from twenty, for his heart,
And leave eighteen." (CYM.2.1)
In the play. *A lord comments on the stupidity of Cloten, the queen's son. He also says,*
That such a crafty devil as is his mother
Should yield the world this ass!

Mathematics, not a strength - I am ill at reckoning: it fitteth the spirit of a tapster.
MOTH. How many is one thrice told?
ARMADO. I am ill at reckoning: it fitteth the spirit of a tapster." (LLL.1.2)
Explain away your dislike of numbers.
In the play. *The page Moth banters with his master Armado.*

Mathematics, questionable m. - A horse and a man is more than one and yet not many.
"Nay, by Saint Jamy,
I hold you a penny,
A horse and a man
Is more than one,
And yet not many." (TOS.3.2)
Try, 'Your mathematics remind me of the line, 'Nay, by Saint Jamy …not many.'
In the play. *Biondello and Baptista engage on a discussion of simple mathematics. Petruchio is*

seen approaching on a horse. Does the horse plus rider count as one or two?

Matters, leave m. as they are - ...wake not a sleeping wolf.
"... wake not a sleeping wolf."
(KHIV.p2.1.2)
In the play. *Chief Lord Justice will not prosecute Falstaff. His presence or 'contribution' at the battle of Shrewsbury makes up for his robbery at Gadshill.*

Matters, weighty m. to consider - ...some things of weight that task our thoughts...
"...we would be resolved,
Before we hear him, of some things of weight
That task our thoughts, concerning us and France." (KHV.1.2)
When you are urged to take a decision and your are not ready. E.G. 'there are some things of weight...thoughts, concerning us and (whatever subject or whoever person be on your mind'.
In the play. *King Henry waits before receiving the French Ambassador.*

Maturity, m. is everything - Men must endure their going hence, even as their coming hither. Ripeness is all.
... Men must endure
Their going hence, even as their coming hither.
Ripeness is all." (KL.5.2)
Express that the situation is critical or unpleasant but that the mark of strength is in the facing the challenge.
In the play. *The battle with the French forces that came to help King Lear has been lost and Lear taken prisoner. Edgar wants to save his father Gloucester but Gloucester wants to hasten his own death. Edgar attempts to lift the spirits of his father. Men must wait for their death just as they waited to go as far as they went. There is a right time (ripeness) for everything.*

May, M. as the month of love - Love, whose month is ever May.
"On a day--alack the day!--
Love, whose month is ever May
Spied a blossom passing fair
Playing in the wanton air..." (LLL.4.3)
In the play. *So begins a poem written by Dumain that he reads to his colleagues.*

Meadow, m. in bloom – I know a bank where the wild thyme blows...
"I know a bank where the wild thyme blows,
Where oxlips and the nodding violet grows,
Quite over-canopied with luscious woodbine,
With sweet musk-roses and with eglantine" (MND.2.1)
Use to compliment a well-kept garden.
In the play. *Oberon explains to the spirit Puck where to find Titania asleep and play a trick of magic, whereby she will fall in love with first creature she sees upon waking up. 'Eglantine '= 'eucalyptus'*

Meaning, m. misinterpreted – ... to have what we would have we speak not what we mean.
"...it oft falls out,
To have what we would have, we speak not what we mean:" (MFM.2.4)
Apologies when you have been misinterpreted.
In the play. *Isabel is concerned that her words may have been misinterpreted by the crafty and conceited Angelo.*

Meaning, m. misinterpreted, invocation - Now the witch take me, if I meant it thus!
"Now the witch take me, if I meant it thus!" (AC.4.2)
When you vehemently disagree with the interpretation given to your words.
In the play. *Antony to his comrades. A soulful message he delivered to them was misinterpreted as acceptance of defeat.*

Meaning, m. misinterpreted, plea not to misinterpret m. – Construe my speeches better, if you may.
"Construe my speeches better, if you may" (LLL.5.2)
In the play. *Ferdinand asks the Princess not to misinterpret his words. The Princess is mocking him.*

Means, idolizing means rather than end, wrong - …'tis mad idolatry to make the service greater than the god.
"…value dwells not in particular will;
It holds his estimate and dignity
As well wherein 'tis precious of itself
As in the prizer: 'tis mad idolatry
To make the service greater than the god" (TC.2.3)
A glaring example is to make secondary the welfare of man to the needs of the market.
In the play. *Hector counters Troilus' assertion that Helen is worth keeping for the value that the Trojans attribute to her, rather than for her intrinsic value.*

Means, m. appropriate to objectives - What need the bridge much broader than the flood?
"What need the bridge much broader than the flood? The fairest grant is the necessity." (MAAN.1.1)
When someone apologizes for not having provided enough reasons or material whereas you find the reasons or material sufficient, 'What need the bridge much broader than the flood?'
In the play. *Don Pedro to Claudio who speculates on imaginary efforts required to secure the hand of Hero whom he loves passionately.*

Measure, inevitable m. - There is no help; the bitter disposition of the time will have it so.
"There is no help;
The bitter disposition of the time
Will have it so." (TC.4.1)

In the play. *The regrettable event that Paris refers to is the exchange of Cressida from Troy with Antinor a Trojan prisoner of the Greeks.*

Media, m. control – (Antonio) set all hearts i' the state to what tune pleased his ear.
"…set all hearts i' the state
To what tune pleased his ear"
(TEM.1.2)
In the play. *Prospero tells Miranda how surreptitiously Antonio set himself to usurp the dukedom of Milan.*

Medicine, alternative m, efficacy of - mickle is the powerful grace, that lies in plants, herbs, stones, and their true qualities…
"O, mickle is the powerful grace, that lies
In plants, herbs, stones, and their true qualities:
For naught so vile that on the earth doth live,
But to the earth some special good doth give." (RJ.2.3)
Promote natural medicine and in general, the importance of everything natural and simple.
In the play. *Fr. Lawrence is a bit of a naturopath and dabbles in chemistry and herbal pharmacology. 'Mickle' means 'great'.*

Medicine, beyond the power of m. - This disease is beyond my practise.
"This disease is beyond my practise" (M.5.1)
In the play. *The Doctor to a gentlewoman in attendance to Lady Macbeth who, while sleepwalking, utters sentences related to the bloody deeds she was involved in. She cannot be cured.*

Medicine, bitter m. but necessary - They love not poison, that do poison need.
"They love not poison, that do poison need,

Nor do I thee, though I did wish him dead." (KRII.5.6)
Justify the expected reaction by those who need the very medicine that causes the reaction.
In the play. *The poison that Bolingbroke (now King Henry IV) refers to is the execution of Richard II by Pierce of Exton. In his zeal, Exton executed Bolingbroke's will, though Bolingbroke never directly told Pierce of Exton to kill Richard, though he strongly hinted at it.*

Medicine, effective within 24 hours - (before) four and twenty times the pilot's glass hath told the thievish minutes how they pass…
"…(before) four and twenty times the pilot's glass
Hath told the thievish minutes how they pass;
What is infirm, from your sound parts shall fly,
Health shall be free, and sickness freely die. (AWEW.2.1)
\ Use the first two lines as the equivalent of "in 24 hours" or the complete sentence for a get-well card.
In the play. *The King begins to relent his resistance and asks Helen how long would it take for her cure to show results (should he accept to be cured). Less than a day, she says.*

Medicine, doctor, an excellent and honest doctor – … whose skill … would have made nature immortal.
"…whose skill was
almost as great as his honesty; had it stretched so
far, would have made nature immortal" (AWEW.1.1)
In the play. *Lafeu praises the medical skills of Helena's father*

Medicine, doctors, skeptical about doctors - … under whose practises he hath persecuted time with hope…
"He hath abandoned his physicians, madam; under whose practises he hath persecuted time with hope, and finds no other advantage in the process but only the losing of hope by time" (AWEW.1.1)
Equally applicable to any hopeless situation, e.g. 'I have persecuted time with hope and find …by time'.
In the play. *Lafeu relates to the Countess the conditions of the King.*

Medicine, excellent m. - … that's able to breathe life into a stone.
"… I have seen a medicine,
That's able to breathe life into a stone,
Quicken a rock, and make you dance canary,
With sprightly fire and motion." (AWEW.2.1)
Extol the virtues of a special medicine, alternatively, apply the sentence to praise wine, at a dinner or party – e.g. 'This wine… is able to breathe… motion.'
In the play. *The King is reluctant to be cured but the nobleman Lafeu tries to convince him that there is indeed a cure. Lafeu is from Roussillon and is at court to introduce Helen to the King.*

Medicine, good for patient but refused by the doctor - …a potion unto me, that thou wouldst tremble to receive thyself.
HELICANUS. To bear with patience
Such griefs as you yourself do lay upon yourself.
PERICLES. Thou speakest like a physician, Helicanus;
That ministerest a potion unto me,
That thou wouldst tremble to receive thyself." (PER.1.2)
Comment to unpleasant advice, 'Thou speakest like a physician…thyself'.
In the play. Pericles has returned to Tyre from Antioch. *Helicanus, Pericle's faithful minister counsels patience and acceptance.*

Medicine, healing, confidence in one's ability to heal - My art is not past power nor you past cure.
"My art is not past power nor you past cure." (AWEW.2.1)
Convince your audience (of one or many as applicable), that you have the solution to the problem (or the cure, if you are a physician).
In the play. *After a series of arguments and counter-arguments, Helen finishes her address to the King with a powerful one-liner.*

Medicine, hypothetical m. requested – If thou couldst, doctor... find her disease and purge it to a sound and pristine health...
"...If thou couldst, doctor, cast
The water of my land, find her disease,
And purge it to a sound and pristine health,
I would applaud thee to the very echo,
That should applaud again - Pull't off, I say.--
What rhubarb, cyme, or what purgative drug,
Would scour these English hence?" (M.5.3)
In the play. *Macbeth makes a rhetorical statement to the doctor as the enemy forces approach Duncinane. "Cyme"="A purgative drug".*

Medicine, illness beyond power of m. - ... labouring art can never ransom nature.
"The congregate college have concluded
That labouring art can never ransom nature
From her unaidable estate." (AWEW.2.1)
Express the concept that human powers are limited against the laws of nature.
In the play. *Helen wishes to cure the King but he is skeptical considering the advice of his other doctors.*

Medicine, limits of m. - ... By medicine life may be prolong'd, yet death will seize the doctor too.
"Whom worse than a physician
Would this report become? But I consider,
By medicine life may be prolong'd, yet death
Will seize the doctor too." (CYM.5.5)
Pinpoint the limits of medicine
In the play. *Cornelius the physician comes in to announce that the queen is dead.*

Medicine, limits of m., it cannot defeat mortality - ...if knowledge could be set up against mortality
"...he was skilful enough to have lived still, if knowledge could be set up against mortality." (AWEW.1.1)
In the play. *Lafeu comments on the medical skills of the now defunct Helena's father.*

Medicine, metaphor, m. against costume - ... 'Tis time to give 'em physic, their diseases are grown so catching
"...'Tis time to give 'em physic, their diseases
Are grown so catching." (KHVIII, 1.3)
In the play. *Lord Sands in conversation with Lord Lovell. The 'diseases' are the new French fashions, such as tall stockings, buckled breeches etc.*

Medicine, prescription, effective, take it – ... prescriptions of rared and proved effects.
"You know, my father left me some prescriptions
Of rare and proved effects." (AWEW.1.3)
Recommend a remedy you believe effective. "Take this, it is a prescription of rare and proved effects." In a proposal use the sentence as a metaphor to enhance the value of your idea – e.g. 'I

have a prescription of rare and proved effects.'
In the play. *The king is ill. Helen thinks that some of her father's prescriptions may cure the king and tells the Countess.*

Medicine, skeptical about medicinal remedy – Throw physic to the dogs; I'll none of it.
"Throw physic to the dogs; I'll none of it." (M.5.3)
In the play. *Macbeth is skeptical about the cure that the doctor seems to recommend for the mental disorder of Lady Macbeth*

Medicine, swallowing a bitter medicine or unpleasant drink – O true apothecary! Thy drugs are quick.
"O true apothecary!
Thy drugs are quick." (RJ.5.3)
In the play. *Romeo poisons himself near Juliet whom he believes dead.*

**Meditating on the mystery of things -
... and take upon's the mystery of things…**
"…so we'll live,
And pray, and sing, and tell old tales, and laugh
At gilded butterflies, and hear poor rogues
Talk of court news; and we'll talk with them too,
Who loses and who wins; who's in, who's out;
And take upon's the mystery of things,
As if we were God's spies: and we'll wear out,
In a wall'd prison, packs and sects of great ones,
That ebb and flow by the moon." (KL.5.3)
Use sections separately to make different specific points. Refer to politicians as 'gilded butterflies', to members of the media as 'poor rogues that talk of court news', to people who believe to be important as 'packs and sects of great ones, that ebb and flow by the moon' and to the complex web of everything and everybody that makes up the world as the 'mystery of things'.
In the play. *King Lear and good daughter Cordelia are confined to a prison by the evil Edmund. But Lear, happy to have finally found Cordelia and recognized her worth and virtue, finds the good of life even in a prison.*

Meditation, lamenting an interrupted m. - How dare you thrust yourselves into my private meditations?
"How dare you thrust yourselves
Into my private meditations?" (KHVIII.2.2)
See also lines 3,4 in 'Request, r. to be heard – Lend favourable ear to our requests…'
In the play. *Norfolk and others present themselves, unannounced to the king's presence*

Meeting, announcing an important m. - Let's briefly put on manly readiness and meet in the hall together.
"Let's briefly put on manly readiness
And meet in the hall together." (M.2.2)
Corralling somewhat sleepy or sheepish colleagues.
In the play. *Macbeth calls a meeting as to investigate King Duncan's death. Macbeth actually killed Duncan.*

Meeting, calling a m. at night – Now sit we close about this taper here and call in question our necessities.
"Now sit we close about this taper here,
And call in question our necessities." (JC.4.3)
In the play. *Brutus calls a meeting with Messala and Titinius, as Antony's troops approach Philippi.*

**Meeting, difficult but not impossible to get participants together - ... but

mountains may be removed with earthquakes, and so encounter.
" O lord!, o lord!! it is a hard matter for friends to meet; but mountains may be removed with earthquakes, and so encounter." (AYLI.3.2)
An example to show that even intractable problems can be resolved, e.g. 'I know it's difficult but mountains…encounter'.
In the play. *Celia jokingly refers to Orlando and Rosalind and the circumstances that make their meeting difficult.*

Meeting, electric and stormy m. predicted - ... fire and water, when their thundering shock at meeting tears the cloudy cheeks of heaven.
"Methinks King Richard and myself should meet
With no less terror than the elements
Of fire and water, when their thundering shock
At meeting tears the cloudy cheeks of heaven." (KRII.3.3)
Describe an impending meeting between two political enemies.
In the play. *Outside Flint Castle in Wales, Bolingbroke predicts the type of meeting that will shortly occur between himself and the King.*

Meeting, invitation to sit down and talk - Then sit we down, and let us all consult.
"Then sit we down, and let us all consult." (TA.4.2)
In the play. *A black baby born to Tamara is proof of her adultery with the evil Aaron. Aaron and the other 2 murderous sons of Tamara will consult on what to do.*

Meeting, joining a contentious m. when is finished – To the latter end of a fray and the beginning of a feast…
"To the latter end of a fray and the beginning of a feast
Fits a dull fighter and a keen guest" (KHIV.p1.4.2)

In the play. *Falstaff's personal plans regarding the imminent battle of Shrewsbury.*

Meeting, m. of strong characters - ... where two raging fires meet together, they do consume the thing that feeds upon.
"And where two raging fires meet together,
They do consume the thing that feeds upon.
Though little fire grows great with little wind,
Yet extreme gusts will blow out fire and all" (TOS.2.1)
Counterargument to the general idea that similar characters do not get along with each other
In the play. *Baptista does not know if Petruchio may make Katharina love him. Petruchio says that his character is not unlike Katharina's. Therefore chances are good that they will get along. Baptista is Katharina's father.*

Meeting, m. of VIPs - Here is like to be a good presence of Worthies.
"Here is like to be a good presence of Worthies" (LLL.5.2)
In the play. *Ferdinand's ironic comment on various characters joining him and his friends.*

Meeting, quiet m. where no one speaks - We meet like men that have forgot to speak.
PRINCE OF LANCASTER. - We meet like men that have forgot to speak.
WARWICK. We do remember; but our argument
Is all too heavy to admit much talk." (KHIVp2.5.2)
Alternative to 'This is a very quiet meeting'. See also entries for 'Silence'
In the play. *In London, the Prince of Lancaster joins a quiet and moody group of courtiers soon after Henry IV's death.*

**Meeting, scheduling the next m. -
When shall we three meet again? In thunder, lightning or in rain?**
"When shall we three meet again?
In thunder, lightning or in rain?"
(M.1.1)
If the meeting party is two or more than three, omit the 'three'. See also 'Appointment, next a. tomorrow night – ... we must starve our sight from lovers' food till morrow deep midnight.'
Change number three according to the number of persons who may attend the next meeting.
In the play. *First witch to the others.*

Meeting, she arrives for the appointment before you do - It gives me wonder great as my content to see you here before me.
"It gives me wonder great as my content
To see you here before me. (OTH.2.1)
Be ready just in case you are a bit late for the appointment.
In the play. *Othello and Desdemona arrive in Cyprus in different ships. Due to unpredictable weather and sea conditions, Othello arrives later than Desdemona.*

Meeting, surprise at meeting him/her unexpectedly – In the name of truth, are you fantastical or that indeed which outwardly you show?
"In the name of truth,
Are you fantastical, or that indeed
Which outwardly you show?"
(MAC.1.3)
You have not seen her for a long time and you are surprised and startled by her appearance, or her appearing so suddenly. Follow up with a compliment, for example, on how young she looks. See entries for 'Ageless'.
In the play. *Banquo is startled by the appearance of the three witches.*

Meeting, surprise at meeting him/her unexpectedly – ... is it fantasy that plays upon our eyesight?
"Or is it fantasy that plays upon our eyesight?" (KHIV.p1.5.3)
In the play. *The Prince of Wales is surprised at finding Falstaff alive. Prudently and cowardly Falstaff had pretended to be dead during the battle.*

Meeting, the fourth participant arrives late at the m. - The fox, the ape and the bumble bee..
ARMADO. The fox, the ape and the bumble bee,
Were still at odds being but three.
MOTH. Until the goose came out of door,
And stayed the odds by adding four."
(LLL.3.1)
The fourth expected participant to the meeting (or dinner or celebratory occasion) has just arrived.
In the play. *Armado and Moth exchange nonsense.*

Melancholy, m. an evil influence and an enemy to health – ... frame your mind to mirth and merriment, which bars a thousand harms, and lengthens life.
"For so your doctors hold it very meet,
Seeing too much sadness hath congeal'd your blood,
And melancholy is the nurse of frenzy:
Therefore they thought it good you hear a play
And frame your mind to mirth and merriment,
Which bars a thousand harms, and lengthens life." (TOS.ind 2.)
Philosophical statement for promoting a tranquil and happy frame of mind. See also entries for 'Character, self-declared lighthearted' – 'Health, laughter as a medicine' – entries for 'Health-Care'

In the play. *A servant addresses Sly and tells him that some players have arrived to stage a play for him to pull him out of his melancholy*

Melancholy, personal m. explained -
… it is a melancholy of mine own, compounded of many simples…
"I have neither the scholar's melancholy, which is emulation, nor the musician's, which is fantastical, nor the courtier's, which is proud, nor the soldier's, which is ambitious, nor the lawyer's, which is politic, nor the lady's, which is nice, nor the lover's, which is all these: but it is a melancholy of mine own, compounded of many simples, extracted from many objects, and, indeed, the sundry contemplation of my travels, which, by often rumination, wraps me in a most humourous sadness." (AYLI.4.1)
Explain your chronic melancholy. See also 'Character, melancholy - He did incline to sadness, and oft-times not knowing why.'
In the play. *Jacques explains his own character to Rosalind.*

Melancholy, sadness, invocation. - O, melancholy, who ever yet could sound thy bottom?
"O, melancholy -
Who ever yet could sound thy bottom?" (CYM.4.1)
Evasive answer to "How come are you sad?".
In the play. *Arviragus brings in Imogen who seems dead (but isn't).*

Melancholy, in a m. mood -
…besieged with sable-coloured melancholy…
"…besieged with sable-coloured melancholy…" (LLL.1.1)
In the play. *Ferdinand reads from a letter written by Biron.*

Memory, impossible to forget - Why should I write this down, that's riveted, screw'd to my memory.
"Why should I write this down, that's riveted,
Screw'd to my memory?" (CYM.2.2)
Answer to 'Will you remember?' or 'Why are you not taking notes?' Or you can make reference to a beautiful body whose details you cannot forget. See also 'Eyes, beauty of e. to be written about - If I could write the beauty of your eyes, and in fresh numbers number all your graces…'
In the play. *The evil Jachimo has sneaked into Imogen's bedroom while she is asleep and makes note of everything is there to then claim that he had sex with Imogen. He has noticed a mole on her breast – no need to write this detail down. He defines it as*
A mole cinque-spotted, like the crimson drops
I' the bottom of a cowslip.

Memory, indistinct and vague recollections - I remember a mass of things, but nothing distinctly.
"I remember a mass of things, but nothing distinctly" (OTH.2.3)
In the play. *Cassio does not remember what happened when he was drunk and got into a quarrel.*

Memory, m. recollections - What seest thou else in the dark backward and abysm of time?
"What seest thou else
In the dark backward and abysm of time?" (TEM.1.2)
Alternative answer to 'what do you remember?' See also 'Recollection, vague r. only – T'is far off and rather like a dream than an assurance that my remembrance warrants.' *** 'Forecasting requested - If you can look into the seeds of time and say which grain will grow and which will not… 'The dark backward

and abysm of time' is a good image for 'time'.
In the play. *Prospero asks his daughter Miranda if she remembers the events that brought them both to the island where they live now*

Memory, praising good m. – ... praise be given to your remembrance.
"...praise
Be given to your remembrance" (CYM.2.4)
In the play. *In Rome Iachimo begins a description of the interior of Imogen's bedchamber to Leonatus, her husband. He ironically congratulates Iachimo for his memory still unaware of his imposture.*

Men, characteristics of hollow m. - ... hollow men, like horses hot at hand make gallant show and promise of their mettle...
"There are no tricks in plain and simple faith:
But hollow men, like horses hot at hand,
Make gallant show and promise of their mettle,
But when they should endure the bloody spur,
They fall their crest and like deceitful jades,
Sink in the trial." (JC.4.2)
An ally has not delivered as promised
In the play. *Brutus to Lucilius after being advised of Cassius' change of heart.*

Men, contempt for men in general to the point of purposely forgetting their existence - ... if thou grantest thou art a man, I have forgot thee.
TIMON (to Flavius). ... I have forgot all men;
Then, if thou grantest thou art a man, I have forgot thee." (TOA.4.3)
Show your annoyance with mankind. See also entries for 'Human nature' and 'Man and its wicked nature'

In the play. *The faithful Flavius calls on Timon in the woods.*

Men, fallen men with a noble mind to be respected - ... men so noble, however faulty, yet should find respect for what they have been...
"...men so noble,
However faulty, yet should find respect
For what they have been: 'tis a cruelty
To load a falling man." (KHVIII.5.3)
In the play. *Cromwell defends Cranmer who is attacked for his heretical Protestant views by Catholic members of the court.*

Men, fat m. are harmless, lean m. are dangerous - ... Yond Cassius hath a lean and hungry look; he thinks too much: such men are dangerous.
"Let me have men about me that are fat;
Sleek-headed men, and such as sleep o'nights':
Yond Cassius hath a lean and hungry look;
He thinks too much: such men are dangerous." (JC.1)
If you are fat use the first two lines to emphasize the point that being fat you are not dangerous, e.g. 'Caesar himself said, let me have... and such as sleep at night.' If your opponent is thin, use the last two lines as an ironic comment, e.g. 'Yon (name of opponent) has a lean and hungry look, he thinks too much, such men are dangerous'.
In the play. *Caesar's opinions on the matter explained to Antony.*

Men, fat m. disliked - I shall think the worse of fat men, as long as I have an eye to make difference of men's liking.
"I shall think the worse of fat men, as long as I have an eye to make difference of men's liking" (MWW.2.1)

In the play. *Mistress Ford's reaction after discovering Falstaff's plot to seduce her.*

Man, fat m., questions on his arrival – … this whale, with so many tuns of oil in his belly…
"What tempest, I trow, threw this whale, with so many tuns of oil in his belly, ashore at Windsor?" (MWW.2.1)
In the play. *Mrs. Ford, a recipient of Falstaff's advances, expresses clearly her opinion on him.*

Men, m. blind to their own faults - Men's faults do seldom to themselves appear, their own transgressions partially they smother…
"Men's faults do seldom to themselves appear;
Their own transgressions partially they smother:
This guilt would seem death-worthy in thy brother.
O, how are they wrapp'd in with infamies
That from their own misdeeds askance their eyes!" (ROL)
In the poem. *Evil Tarquin knows he is committing a crime and meditates on it.*

Men, m. generally unreliable - Trust none, for oaths are straws, men's faiths are wafer-cakes…
Trust none, for oaths are straws, men's faiths are wafer-cakes,
And hold-fast is the only dog, my duck." (KHV.2.3)
Retort to a general endorsement or approval of a person because whom you do not trust.
In the play. *Pistol's general philosophy. The 'duck' receiving the advice is the hostess, Mistress Quickly, who is visiting Pistol's house in Eastcheap.*

Men, m. inspiring an age and moment - … the choice and master spirits of this age.

"The choice and master spirits of this age." (JC.3.1)
Introduction of a panel of distinguished speakers.
In the play. *Antony makes a rhetorical but clever speech to Brutus and Cassius as the body of slain Caesar is on the ground. He concludes the speech by giving himself up in their hands, 'choice and master spirits of this age'.*

Men, m. of few words - … he hath heard that men of few words are the best men …
"… For Nym, he hath heard that men of few words are the best men; and therefore he scorns to say his prayers, lest a' should be thought a coward" (HV.3.2)
Retort or comment on a man of few words. See also 'Character, one who pretends to be thought clever by saying nothing - there are a sort of men whose visages.'
In the play. *The boy comments on the character of Nym while in France before the town of Harfleur.*

Men, m. of strong temper - …brave conquerors… that war against your own affections
"… brave conquerors,--for so you are,
That war against your own affections
And the huge army of the world's desires" (LLL.1.1)
In the play. *The King sets up the questionable program of learning, seclusion and abstinence for himself and friends.*

Men, m. subjected to women – Why, this it is, when men are ruled by women…
"Why, this it is, when men are ruled by women:
'Tis not the king that sends you to the Tower:
My Lady Grey his wife, Clarence, 'tis she

That tempers him to this extremity." (KRIII.1.1)
In the play. *Richard pretends that Clarence is in the tower due to the actions of the Lady Grey.*

Men, m. superior to women – ... Men, more divine, the masters of all these...
"The beasts, the fishes, and the winged fowls,
Are their males' subjects and at their controls:
Men, more divine, the masters of all these,
Lords of the wide world and wild watery seas,
Indued with intellectual sense and souls,
Of more preeminence than fish and fowls,
Are masters to their females, and their lords:
Then let your will attend on their accords" (COE.2.1)
See also entries for 'Women, anti-feminist statement and anti-feminist logic'
In the play. *Luciana tries to comfort her sister Adriana who is distressed at the behavior of her husband Antipholus E.*

Men, m. taking advantage of women – 'Tis not a year or two shows us a man: they are all but stomachs, and we all but food...
"'Tis not a year or two shows us a man:
They are all but stomachs, and we all but food;
To eat us hungerly, and when they are full,
They belch us." (OTH.3.4)
In the play. *Emilia to Desdemona. Desdemona cannot understand the sudden change of behavior in Othello, no knowing that he suspects her of infidelity.*

Men, m. versus women, women more steady than m. - However we do praise ourselves, our fancies are more giddy and unfirm...
DUKE (to Viola Cesario).
"... however we do praise ourselves, Our fancies are more giddy and unfirm,
More longing, wavering, sooner lost than worn,
Than women's are." (TN.2.4)
When you wish to praise women as being more steady and firmly grounded than men.
In the play. *The Duke has asked Viola/Cesario if he loves a woman and what kind of woman she is. Cesario says the woman he loves has the same age as the Duke. The Duke objects that the supposed woman loved (by Viola/Cesario) is too old and provides reasons why a man should always love a younger woman. Actually Viola loves the Duke.*

Men, mad men to be recovered in a mental institution - ... I know it by their pale and deadly looks; they must be bound and laid in some dark room.
"...both man and master is possess'd;
I know it by their pale and deadly looks:
They must be bound and laid in some dark room" (COE.4.4)
In the play. *Pinch, a schoolmaster, assesses the state of mind of Antipholus E and Dromio E.*

Men, malicious m. - Follow your envious courses, men of malice.
"Follow your envious courses, men of malice" (KHVIII, 3.2)
In the play. *Cardinal Wolsey to his accusers who wanted him to fall from grace with the King.*

Men, one word catch all - ... in the catalogue ye go for men...
FIRST MURDERER We are men, my liege.
MACBETH Ay, in the catalogue ye go for men;
As hounds and greyhounds, mongrels, spaniels, curs,

Shoughs, water-rugs and demi-wolves, are clept
All by the name of dogs: …
… from the bill
That writes them all alike: and so of men. (M.3.1)
Answer to 'What do you think of them?' when you want to convey contempt with your answer. E.G. 'In the catalog they go for men as hounds and greyhounds, mongrels, spaniels and curs go by the name of dogs'. See also 'Insult, opinion of a person - God made him, and therefore let him pass for a man.'
In the play. *Macbeth contracts two murderers to kill Banquo and pricks their sense of pride by prompting them to stand out from the pack and the uniformity of other dogs in a virtual dog catalog.*

Men, their folly - Lord, what fools these mortals be!
"Lord, what fools these mortals be!" (MND.3.2)
In the play. *Puck to Oberon commenting on the shenanigans affecting the mortals in the play.*

Men, volatile by nature - … such summer-birds are men.
"… such summer-birds are men." (TOA.3.5)
In the play. *Timon's comment to the parasites who pledge to follow Timon hoping to get rewards. See 'Joining the party – following swallows'.*

Mercy, benefits of using mercy with justice - … and earthly power doth then show likest God's when mercy seasons justice.
"And earthly power doth then show likest God's
When mercy seasons justice" (MOV.4.1)
In the play. *Portia (disguised as a male attorney) expands on the benefits and quality of mercy.*

Mercy, exhortation not to hit a falling man - Press not a falling man too far! 'tis virtue...
"… Press not a falling man too far! 'tis virtue:
His faults lie open to the laws; let them,
Not you, correct him." (KHVIII, 3.2)
In the play. *Lord Chamberlain to Lord Surrey, the latter an arch enemy of Card. Wolsey who has fallen from grace from the King*

Mercy, m. a sign of nobility - sweet mercy is nobility's true badge.
"Sweet mercy is nobility's true badge." (TA.1.1)
Use to suggest leniency.
In the play. *Tamora pleads with Titus not to sacrifice her Gothic son in homage to the Gods. Titus will not relent.*

Mercy, m. becoming to the great – No ceremony…become them with one half so good a grace as mercy does.
"No ceremony that to great ones belongs,
Not the king's crown, nor the deputed sword,
The marshal's truncheon, nor the judge's robe,
Become them with one half so good a grace
As mercy does." (MFM.2.2)
Answer to the judge when, before the sentence on your traffic ticket (or worse), he asks if you have anything to say.
In the play. *Isabella pleads with Angelo for mercy for her brother Claudio.*

Mercy, m. dangerous - … And what makes robbers bold but too much lenity?
"For what doth cherish weeds but gentle air?
And what makes robbers bold but too much lenity?
Bootless are plaints, and cureless are my wounds" (KHVI p3.2.6)

In the play. *Clifford, mortally wounded at the battle of Towton, blames King Henry VI for his lenity towards the house of York.*

Mercy, m. engendering more sin or rebellion - ...more sins for this forgiveness prosper may.
"If thou do pardon, whosoever pray,
More sins for this forgiveness prosper may" (KRII.5.3)
When you favor punishment.
In the play. *The Duke of York pleads with the King (Bolingbroke, now Henry IV), to punish hi own (York's) son, the Duke of Aumerle, who joined plotters against Bolingbroke.*

Mercy, m. obtained with honest methods - Ignomy in ransom and free pardon are of two houses...
"Ignomy in ransom and free pardon
Are of two houses: lawful mercy
Is nothing kin to foul redemption."
(MFM.2.4)
In the play. *Isabella refuses the sex-for-pardon (to her brother), exchange offered by Angelo.*

Mercy, no m. for killers – Mercy but murders, pardoning those that kill.
"Mercy but murders, pardoning those that kill" (RJ.3.1)
In the play. *The Prince of Verona is angry at finding Mercutio and Tybalt slain after he had banned dueling.*

Mercy, plead for m. - ... behold my sighs and tears and will not once relent?
"Can you, my Lord of Winchester, behold
My sighs and tears and will not once relent?" (KHVI p1.3.1)
Change 'my lord of Winchester' to name of applicable party.
In the play. *King Henry VI pleads with the Bishop of Winchester to stop his feuding with Gloucester.*

Mercy, quality of m. - ... It droppeth as the gentle rain from heaven...
"The quality of mercy is not strain'd,
It droppeth as the gentle rain from heaven
Upon the place beneath; it is twice blest;
It blesseth him that gives and him that takes:
'Tis mightiest in the mightiest: it becomes
The throned monarch better than his crown;
His sceptre shows the force of temporal power,
The attribute to awe and majesty,
Wherein doth sit the dread and fear of kings;
But mercy is above this sceptred sway;
It is enthroned in the hearts of kings,
It is an attribute to God himself " (MOV.4.1)
Possible answer to question from the judge of the type 'Have you anything to say?' E.G. 'The quality of mercy becomes the throned monarch better than his crown'.
In the play. *Portia (disguised as a male attorney) answers an objection from Shylock, why should he compelled to be merciful (towards Antonio)*

Mercy, reasons against m. – Mercy is not itself, that oft looks so, pardon is still the nurse of second woe.
"Mercy is not itself, that oft looks so;
Pardon is still the nurse of second woe" (MFM.2.1)
In the play. *Escalus commenting on the rigor of the deputy duke Lord Angelo.*

Mercy, reasons for m. – ... in the course of justice, none of us should see salvation...
"... consider this,
That, in the course of justice, none of us

Should see salvation: we do pray for mercy;
And that same prayer doth teach us all to render
The deeds of mercy" (MOV.4.1)
In the play. *Portia offers Shylock cogent reasons to be merciful towards Antonio.*

Merit, m., skills or talent excite envy - … to some kind of men their grace serve them as enemies.
"Know you not, master, to some kind of men
Their grace serve them as enemies?" (AYLI.2.3)
Why merit is often a liability more than an asset.
In the play. *Orlando has been banned and Adam, his faithful servant, generalizes that grace (in this case Orlando's valor and character) can be a man's enemy.*

Meritocracy advocated - From lowest place when virtuous things proceed…
"From lowest place when virtuous things proceed,
The place is dignified by the doer's deed:
Where great additions swell us, and virtue none,
It is a dropsied honour: good alone
Is good, without a name; vileness is so." (AWEW.2.3)
Show that virtue and dignity dignify a person independently of his class or social status. Or apply to yourself if you are denied something because you are not famous or well known. Extract 'Good alone is good, without a name.'
In the play. *The King reminds Bertram that actions are more important than titles or nobility. Bertram is ashamed at being forced to marry Helena, whom he considers below his status, being a physician's daughter.*

Meritocracy advocated – … honours thrive when rather from our own acts we them derive than our fore-goers.

"... honours thrive,
When rather from our own acts we them derive
Than our fore-goers." (AWEW.2.3)
Use to demonstrate that acquiring honor is an equal opportunity.
In the play. *The King of France comments on the medical success of Helena and her being kept at a distance by the lords because she comes from a lower class.*

Merriment, m. not a good response to situation - … this merry inclination accords not with the sadness of my suit.
"But, mighty lord, this merry inclination
Accords not with the sadness of my suit." (KHVI.p3.3.2)
Start from 'this merry inclination…suit'. See also 'Jokes, j. inappropriate to the moment or situation - … these jests are out of season; reserve them till a merrier hour than this.'
In the play. *The Lady Grey to the King who wants to take advantage of her request foe reinstatement of her land rights and asks for sex.*

Merriment, m. preferable to melancholy - …I had rather have a fool make me merry than experience to make me sad.
"And your experience makes you sad: I had rather have a fool make me merry than experience to make me sad." (AYLI.4.1)
Declare your support for laughter as opposed to gloom
In the play. *Rosalind's comments on Jacques' melancholy, melancholy derived from experience acquired through extensive travels.*

Message or request, same m. or request annoying - If it be aught to the old tune… it is as fat and fulsome to mine ear…
"If it be aught to the old tune, my lord,

It is as fat and fulsome to mine ear
As howling after music." (TN.5.1)
When you have had enough of a repeated request or of a stale subject. You can eliminate the first line.
In the play. *Olivia addresses Viola/Cesario thinking mistakenly that he is his twin Sebastian. The old tune is the suit on behalf of Duke Orsino, who loves (unrequited) Olivia.*

Message, acknowledging pleasant m. - Thou sing'st sweet music.
"Thou sing'st sweet music" (KRIII.4.2)
In the play. *Richard to the hired murderer Tyrrel who will be a contract killer of the young princes in the Tower.*

Message, ignoring written m. irrelevant - … I know they are stuff'd with protestations and full of new-found oaths…
"I will not look upon your master's lines:
I know they are stuff'd with protestations
And full of new-found oaths; which he will break
As easily as I do tear his paper." (TGV.4.4)
In the play. *Proteus has charged his new servant (actually Julia disguised as a man) to deliver a message to Silvia.*

Message, m. or news that are good to hear – Thou sing'st sweet music.
"Thou sing'st sweet music." (KRIII.4.2)
In the play. *Tyrrel the contract killer has agreed to murder the young princes in the Tower, music for Richard.*

Message, serious but delivered lightly - If seriously I may convey my thoughts in this my light deliverance.
" If seriously I may convey my thoughts
In this my light deliverance.

….
That done, laugh well at me" (AWEW.2.1)
Suggest that there is a serious message in your address, though you do not want to bore or annoy your audience with a heavy delivery.
In the play. *Lafeu proposes to the skeptical King to meet Helen and to let her cure him.*

Messenger, advise to a breathless m. - Let your breath cool yourself, telling your haste.
"Let your breath cool yourself, telling your haste." (PER.1.1)
In the play. *A messenger arrives to tell Antioch that Pericles is fled.*

Messenger, exhortation to m. to deliver information quickly - Thou comest to use thy tongue; thy story quickly.
"Thou comest to use thy tongue; thy story quickly." (M.5.5)
See also 'Speech, why giving me the run around? - What need'st thou run so many miles about when thou mayst tell thy tale the nearest way?' *** 'Speech, lengthy and annoying - This will last out a night in Russia when nights are longest there.'
In the play. *Macbeth to a messenger who hesitates to report that he saw a forest on the move (as predicted by the witches). The forest is actually the camouflage of Malcolm's army, but still a close rendition of the prophecy.*

Messenger, guiltless m. - I am but as a guiltless messenger.
"I am but as a guiltless messenger" (AYLI.4.3)
When you seem the target for resentment for having delivered an unpleasant news.
In the play. *Silvius delivers a supposedly angry letter written by Phebe to Ganimede (who is actually Rosalind in man's attire).*

611

Messenger, m. better than the author of the message - a horse to be ambassador to an ass.
ARMADO. Fetch hither the swain; he must carry me a letter.
MOTH. A message well sympathized; a horse to be ambassador to an ass." (LLL.3.1)
When an ass sends a message to someone by means of a carrier (not necessarily a horse'. E.G. 'This is like a horse being ambassador to an ass.'
In the play. *Armado banters with his smart page and the page tells Armado he is an ass.*

Messenger, m. fearful to report information - I should report that which I say I saw but know not how to do it.
"I should report that which I say I saw,
But know not how to do it" (M.5.5)
In the play. *A messenger saw a wood moving towards Dunsinane and is reluctant to report the event to Macbeth. The messenger does not know about the witches' prediction.*

Messenger, m. not needed – I shall not need transport my words by you, here comes his grace in person.
"I shall not need transport my words by you;
Here comes his grace in person" (KRII.2.3)
In the play. *Bolingbroke to Lord Berkeley delivering a message from the Duke of York who arrives just as Berkeley is talking.*

Messenger, punishing the m - ... reason with the fellow before you punish him...
"...But reason with the fellow,
Before you punish him, where he heard this,
Lest you shall chance to whip your information
And beat the messenger who bids beware
Of what is to be dreaded." (COR.4.6)
This would have been proper advice (for example) to those democratic congressmen who were harassing a congressional investigator. The investigator found that the president and executives of Fannie Mae a government banking institution set up to help the poor, had cooked the books and paid themselves 450 million dollars in bonuses.
In the play. *Menenius counsel the Tribunes to verify the information of a messenger who said that Coriolanus has defected to the Volsces and is marching against Rome.*

Messenger, reprimanding the m. for the bad n. - How dares thy harsh rude tongue sound this unpleasing news?
"How dares thy harsh rude tongue sound this unpleasing news?" (KRII.3.4)
See also 'But yet, everything is well but yet - I do not like 'but yet', it does allay the good precedence...'
In the play. *At Langley, the Queen overhears the gardener talk about the deposition of her husband Richard II.*

Middle ground, no middle ground – no midway 'twixt these extremes at all.
"... No midway
'Twixt these extremes at all." (AC.3.4)
Emphasize that there are only two options and no compromise.
In the play. *Octavia, Antony's wife is struggling between her love of Antony her husband and her love of Octavian, her brother. Antony and Octavian are enemies with no 'midway' in between.*

Militarism, reputation as a volatile commodity - ... Seeking the bubble reputation even in the cannon's mouth.

"… A soldier,
**Full of strange oaths and bearded like the pard,
Jealous in honour, sudden and quick in quarrel,
Seeking the bubble reputation
Even in the cannon's mouth.** " (AYLI.2.7)
Soldiers have often been puppets and pawns giving their lives to increase the power and wealth of the few. However, you may apply the line to someone who runs a great risk in order to acquire some kind of reputation. E.G. 'He reminds me of those who sought the bubble reputation even in the cannon's mouth'
In the play. *Jaques the philosopher expounds his theory about the seven ages of men, of which soldiering is one. 'Bearded like the pard'='Having a bristly beard, or more literally 'As hairy as a leopard'*. See the first entry for 'Age' for the complete theory of the ages of men and other entries for 'Reputation'.

Mind, always on your m. - Weary with toil, I haste me to my bed, the dear repose for limbs with travel tired...
"**Weary with toil, I haste me to my bed,
The dear repose for limbs with travel tired,
But then begins a journey in my head
To work the mind, when body's work expired.**" (SON.27)
Alternative with a twist to "I cannot stop thinking of you". See also 'Presence, 'Do you miss me?' - … Save that my soul's imaginary sight presents thy shadow to my sightless view…' *** 'Absence, a. felt - Is it thy will, thy image should keep open my heavy eyelids to the weary night?'

Mind, change of m. after words heard directly - Either she hath bewitch'd me with her words or nature makes me suddenly relent.
"**Either she hath bewitch'd me with her words,
Or nature makes me suddenly relent.**" (KHVI.p1.3.3)
Explain your change of mind after an argument has been made for you to do so. Change 'she' and 'her' as appropriate.
In the play. *La Pucelle has convinced Burgundy to abandon the English.*

Mind, decision to change your mind on something very important - Let us once lose our oaths to find ourselves…
"**Let us once lose our oaths to find ourselves,
Or else we lose ourselves to keep our oaths.**" (LLL.4.3)
Change to 'Let me once lose my oath to find myself, or else I lose myself to keep an oath'. It may not have to be an oath but something on which you were or seemed to be very firm and unmovable. See also entries for 'Oath, excuse for breaking an o.'
In the play. *Biron's final peroration to his friends to forego their earlier vows of a secluded life, learning and abstinence.*

Mind, muddled m. due to problems unspoken of - … and in such cases men's natures wrangle with inferior things, though great ones are their object.
"**… some unhatch'd practise
Made demonstrable here in Cyprus to him,
Hath puddled his clear spirit: and in such cases
Men's natures wrangle with inferior things,
Though great ones are their object.**" (OTH.3.4)
Justify or explain the strange behavior of your boss.
In the play. *Desdemona has an explanation for Othello's strange and altered behavior, (an*

'unhatched practise'), not realizing that Othello believes she is having an affair with Cassio.

Mind, out of his mind – ... his pure brain ... doth, by the idle comment that it makes, foretell the ending of mortality.
"...his pure brain
(Which some suppose the soul's frail dwelling house)
Doth, by the idle comments that it makes,
Foretell the ending of mortality." (KJ.5.7)
Say that what you heard is sheer madness, e.g. 'His brain doth, by the idle comments that it makes, foretell the ending of sanity'.
In the play. *Prince Henry announces that King John is on the point of death.*

Mind, state of m. – Are his wits safe? is he not light of brain?
"Are his wits safe? is he not light of brain?" (OTH.4.1)
In the play. *Ludovico queries Iago as to the odd state of mind of Othello. Iago responds with these non-committing lines.*

Mind, state of m. 'where am I?' - Am I in earth, in heaven or in hell....
"Am I in earth, in heaven or in hell, - Sleeping or walking - mad or well advised?" (COE.2.2)
Express your disbelief at a strange turn of events or situation. See also 'Disbelief about one's condition - Or sleep I now and think I hear all this?'
In the play. *Adriana, wife of Ant E invites Ant S to dinner (thinking that he is Ant E) and Ant S is at a loss for an explanation.*

Mind, state of mind, full of doubts and fears – ... now I am cabin'd, cribb'd, confined, bound in to saucy doubts and fears.
"But now I am cabin'd, cribb'd, confined, bound in
To saucy doubts and fears" (M.3.4)
In the play. *Macbeth's state of mind after knowing that Fleance escaped the assassination attempt by Macbeth's murderers.*

Mind, state of m. in good spirits – ... all this day an unaccustom'd spirit lifts me above the ground with cheerful thoughts.
"And all this day an unaccustom'd spirit
Lifts me above the ground with cheerful thoughts" (RJ.5.1)
In the play. *In Mantua, unaware of the turmoil in Verona dreamt of a happy ending to his and Juliet's ordeal.*

Mind, state of m. in mutiny - There is a mutiny in his mind.
"There is a mutiny in his mind" (KHVIII, 3.2)
Declare your state of uncertainty and indecision by changing 'his' to 'my'.
In the play. *King Henry refers to Wolsey who, inadvertently has given the King papers showing all the riches accumulated by the cardinal*

Mind, state of mind, in turmoil - ... the tempest in my mind doth from my senses take all feeling else save what beats there.
"...When the mind's free,
The body's delicate:
the tempest in my mind
Doth from my senses take all feeling else
Save what beats there." (KL.3.4)
In the play. *K. Lear, exposed to the storm, feels a greater storm in his heart realizing the wickedness of his two daughters Regan and Goneril.*

Mind, state of mind, thinking about nothing and sad - ... though, in thinking, on no thought I think.

"...howe'er it be,
I cannot be but sad; so heavy sad,
As, though, in thinking, on no thought I think,
Makes me with heavy nothing faint and shrink." (KRII.2.2)
Answer to 'What are you thinking about?' when you elegantly do not wish to disclose the nature of your thought. E.G. 'Though I am thinking, on no thought I think'.
In the play. *The Queen at her palace has a presentment that matters will not turn out well for King Richard.*

Mind, state of m. troubled - My mind is troubled, like a fountain stirred and I myself see not the bottom of it.
ACHILLES. "My mind is troubled, like a fountain stirred
And I myself see not the bottom of it"
THERSITES. Would the fountain of your mind were clear again, that I might water an ass at it! I had rather be a tick in a sheep than such a valiant ignorance" (TC.3.3)
For a comparison of clarity see "Evidence, e. very clear – ... proofs as clear as founts in July when we see each grain of gravel...'
In the play. *Achilles, talked to, upbraided, counseled and insulted by various Greeks feels somewhat lost*

Mind, state of m. weariness as a weakness - ... it discolours the complexion of my greatness to acknowledge it.
"... it (weariness) discolours the complexion of my greatness to acknowledge it" (KHIVp2.2.2)
Answer to 'Are you tired?'
In the play. *In an exchange with Poins Prince Harry admits to weariness as a psychological distemper*

Mine own flesh and blood - ... if thou be Launcelot, thou art mine own flesh and blood
"...if thou be Launcelot, thou art mine own flesh and blood" (MOV.2.2)
In the play. *Gobbo, old and blind, to his son Launcelot, who in jest pretended to be someone else.*

Miracles, possibility of m. not to be excluded - They say miracles are past...
They say miracles are past; and we have our philosophical persons, to make modern and familiar, things supernatural and causeless. Hence it is that we make trifles of terrors, ensconcing ourselves into seeming knowledge, when we should submit ourselves to an unknown fear." (AWEW.2.3)
Argument to uphold the importance of the supernatural. Or use 'We have our philosophical persons to make ...causeless' as an indication of presumption in knowledge.
In the play. *Helen, against all predictions has succeeded in healing the King and Lafeu delivers a philosophical commentary.*

Mirror, m. showing her beauty better than your words can express – And more, much more than in my verse can sit...
"And more, much more than in my verse can sit
Your own glass shows you when you look in it". (SON 103)
Answer to 'Do you like me?' after your first tentative description in prose.

Misanthropy, m. questioned – Is man so hateful to thee that art thyself a man?
"...Is man so hateful to thee,
That art thyself a man?" (TOA.4.3)

In the play. *Alcibiades, Timon's old friend questions him as a retort to an initial gruff greeting.*

Misanthropy, self as the only friend – … nothing but himself which looks like man is friendly with him.
"…he is set so only to himself
That nothing but himself which looks like man
Is friendly with him." (TOA.4.3)
To declare your own misanthropy try, 'Nothing but myself…with me.'
In the play. *Alcibiades explains to his girlfriends the reason for the rude words by Timon to them.*

Mischief, m. turning on the miscreant - What mischiefs work the wicked ones heaping confusion on their own heads thereby.
"O God, what mischiefs work the wicked ones,
Heaping confusion on their own heads thereby!" (KHVI p2.2.1)
If you believe in the universality of justice, use to show that the wicked ones will be repaid in their own coin. See also 'Hypocrisy, h. and dishonesty exposed - foul deeds will rise though all the world o'erwhelm them, to men's eyes.'
In the play. *Henry VI's comment on the events that have led to the downfall of Gloucester*

Miscommunications - … we understand not one another: I am too courtly and thou art too cunning.
"Friend, we understand not one another: I am too courtly and thou art too cunning" (TC.3.1)
In the play. *Pandarus to a servant who gives smart-ass answers to plain questions.*

Misconduct, m. as a front - I'll so offend, to make offence a skill; redeeming time when men think least I will.

"I'll so offend, to make offence a skill;
Redeeming time when men think least I will." (KHIV.p1.1.2)
In the play. *Prince Henry's mission statement.*

Misconduct, m. justified – … in the state of innocency Adam fell…
"…in the state of innocency Adam fell; and what should poor Jack Falstaff do in the days of villany?" (KHIVp1.3.2)
See also 'Fat, being f. as a justification for weakness of character or errors - Thou seest I have more flesh than another man, and therefore more frailty.'
In the play. *Falstaff tries to justify himself with Prince Harry for lying about an alleged theft by an inn hostess.*

Misfortune, affected by m. – … wayward fortune did malign my state…
"… Though wayward fortune did malign my state…" (PER.5.1)
In the play. *Marina begins to tell her story to Pericles.*

Misfortune, determination to overcome m. - Though fortune's malice overthrow my state, my mind exceeds the compass of her wheel.
"Though fortune's malice overthrow my state,
My mind exceeds the compass of her wheel." (KHVI p3.4.3)
In the play. *Warwick has captured Edward, dethroned him and reduced him to the rank of Duke of York – Edward takes a stoic attitude towards it.*

Misfortune, m. affecting manners and judgment - … for his wits are drown'd and lost in his calamities.
"Pardon him, sweet Timandra; for his wits
Are drown'd and lost in his calamities." (TOA.4.3)

See also 'Judgment, men's j. affected by circumstances and showing their character - ...I see men's judgments are a parcel of their fortunes...
In the play. *Alcibiades, one of few of Timon's friends left comes to visit him in the woods in the company of some girlfriends.*

Misfortune, setback - My stars shine darkly over me
"… My stars shine darkly over me." (TN.2.1)
In the play. *Sebastian, stranded after a shipwreck, expresses his feelings to Antonio the captain.*

Misfortunes piling up - When sorrows come, they come not single spies, but in battalions!
"When sorrows come, they come not single spies,
But in battalions!" (H.4.5)
Comment when many problems come at once. See also 'Sorrow, one s. after another - One sorrow never comes but brings an heir, that may succeed as his inheritor.'
In the play. *King Claudius to Queen Gertrude after Polonius has been slain by Hamlet and now Ophelia, Polonius' daughter, has become mad.*

Misgivings, bad feelings about an occurrence - ... in the gross and scope of my opinion this bodes some strange eruption to our state.
"In what particular thought to work I know not;
But in the gross and scope of my opinion,
This bodes some strange eruption to our state." (H.1.1)
In the play. *Horatio's conclusions after witnessing the appearance of the Ghost.*

Misgivings, gutsy negative feelings - I know not what may fall; I like it not.

"I know not what may fall; I like it not." (JC.3.1)
Explain your concern and disapproval of a plan. See also 'Plan, p. disapproved'.
In the play. *Cassius is very uneasy about Antony speaking at Julius Caesar's funeral. His concern will prove justified. Antony's famous speech ('...and Brutus is an honorable man', see 'Debate, disagreeing with skill') will prove fatal to the conspirators.*

Misgivings, m. about the future - ... my mind misgives some consequence yet hanging in the stars.
"...my mind misgives
Some consequence yet hanging in the stars" (RJ.1.4)
In the play. *Romeo has bad feelings about attending the Capulet's party where he will meet Juliet.*

Misinterpretation, exhortation not to misinterpret meaning - Be not so hasty to confound my meaning.
"Be not so hasty to confound my meaning" (KRIII.4.4)
In the play. *Richard in conversation with Queen Elizabeth.*

Misinterpretation, wrong interpretation of events - ... you take things ill which are not so.
"...you take things ill which are not so" (AC.2.2)
In the play. *Antony, arrived in Rome for a meeting, finds an angry Octavian who has misinterpreted events and believes Antony to be in league with his enemies.*

Misjudgment, m. in the selection of a controller, overseer, accountant or similar - ... thou hast entertained a fox, to be the shepherd of thy lambs.
"Alas, poor Proteus! thou hast entertained
A fox, to be the shepherd of thy lambs." (TGV.4.4)

Show your mistrust for the person who has been appointed to look after the interests of your operations. 'We have entertained a fox to be the shepherd of our lambs.'
In the play. *Julia, disguised as a man, becomes Proteus' page and he hopes to use her to get at Sylvia.*

Misjudgement, transposition of values - ... What we oft do best... is not ours, or not allow'd; what worst … is cried up for our best act.
"…What we oft do best,
By sick interpreters, once weak ones, is
Not ours, or not allow'd; what worst, as oft,
Hitting a grosser quality, is cried up
For our best act" (KHVIII, 1.2)
See also entries for 'Remembering, the bad more than the good' *** 'Virtue, perception of v. depending on contemporary culture – So our virtues lie in the interpretation of the time.'
In the play. *Cardinal Wolsey ably deflects criticism (from the King) on taxation that has brought discontent among the subjects.*

Misnomer – Benefactors? Well; what benefactors are they? Are they not malefactors?
"Benefactors? Well; what benefactors are they? Are they not malefactors?" (MFM.2.1)
In the play. *Constable Elbow has some difficulty in describing his arrested charges to Angelo and calls them 'benefactors' Angelo corrects him.*

Mission, going alone if companions fearful - ... But if you faint, as fearing to do so, stay and be secret, and myself will go.
"But if you faint, as fearing to do so, Stay and be secret, and myself will go" (KRII.2.1)
In the play. *Northumberland to Ross and Willoughby. Northumberland will travel to Ravenspurgh to meet with the returning Bolingbroke and confront the king.*

Mission, m. accomplished - If to have done the thing you gave in charge beget your happiness…
"If to have done the thing you gave in charge
Beget your happiness, be happy then,
For it is done, my lord." (KRIII.4.2)
Answer when your boss asks 'Did you do it?'
In the play. *Tyrrel confirms that he slew the young princes in the Tower on instructions from Richard.*

Mission, m. important and confidential - ... And my appointments have in them a need, greater than shows itself at the first view...
" And my appointments have in them a need,
Greater than shows itself at the first view,
To you that know them not." (AWEW.2.5)
Justify or explain why you must leave.
In the play. *Unwilling to be Helena's husband, Bertram tells her that he has urgent business to attend elsewhere and therefore he will leave. He is actually going to Florence with the unsavory Parolles.*

Mistake me? No it's you who are mistaken - ... But thou mistakest me much to think I do.
"I do not mistake;
But thou mistakest me much to think I do." (KHVI p2.5.1)
Retort to 'You are making a mistake'
In the play. *York tells Clifford that he (Clifford) is mistaken in keeping his allegiance to Henry VI instead of York who sets himself up as king. Clifford tells York that it is he who is mistaken.*

**Mistake, admitting m. without lying -
If I could add a lie unto a fault, I would deny it.**
"If I could add a lie unto a fault,
I would deny it." (MOV.5.1)
Admission to your weakness or error.
In the play. *Bassanio admits to having disposed of the ring that Portia gave him, though for a good cause.*

Mistrust, total – I will no more trust him when he leers, than I will a serpent when he hisses.
"I will no more trust him when he leers, than I will a serpent when he hisses." (TC.5.1)
Express mistrust. Change 'leers' with 'smile or 'laugh' for impact.
In the play. *Thersites of Diomedes.*

Mockery, displaying one's scars deserving ridicule - ... to such as boasting show their scars a mock is due.
"…to such as boasting show their scars
A mock is due." (TC.4.5)
In the play. *Troilus to Ulysses who asked him if Cressida, now in the Greek camp and completely oblivious of Troilus, had a lover in Troy.*

Mockery, reaction to mild mockery - You do blaspheme the good in mocking me.
"You do blaspheme the good in mocking me" (MFM.1.4)
In the play. *Lucio overly compliments Isabel on her virtues and she mildly resents it.*

Moderation, m. urged in criticism - ... deal mildly with his youth; for young hot colts being raged do rage the more.
"... deal mildly with his youth;
For young hot colts being raged do rage the more." (KRII.2.1)
In the play. *York advises Gaunt to go easy with King Richard who has come to visit.*

Moderation, m. urged in upbraiding - Forbear sharp speeches to her…
"Forbear sharp speeches to her: she's a lady
So tender of rebuke, that words are strokes,
And strokes death to her." (CYM.3.5)
Counsel a soft approach to criticism. Or jokingly ask to moderate the tone of the speech towards yourself, e.g. 'Forbear sharp speeches to me: I am a person so tender of rebuke, that words are strokes, and strokes death to me.'
In the play *The Queen prompts the king to be soft when dealing with his daughter Imogen, who has been distraught since the departure of Posthumous.*

Modesty, admitted m. of personal looks – ... so lamely and unfashionable that dogs bark at me as I halt by then.
" (I am)…so lamely and unfashionable
That dogs bark at me as I halt by then." (KRIII.1.1)
Self effacing statement.
In the play. *Richard meditates on his image, the current state of affairs and his plans to steal the throne of England.*

Modesty, admitted m. of personal looks – ... not shaped for sportive tricks, nor made to court an amorous looking-glass…
"But I, that am not shaped for sportive tricks,
Nor made to court an amorous looking-glass;
I, that am rudely stamp'd, and want love's majesty
To strut before a wanton ambling nymph." (KRIII.1.1)
Modesty always works, even if you are or were an Adonis.

In the play. *Richard III (in a monologue) acknowledges his lack of sex appeal. But later he will succeed in wooing Anne, daughter of former enemy Warwick. Richard killed both Warwick and her husband.*

Modesty, admitted m. of personal looks – I am as ugly as a bear, for beasts that meet me run away in fear.
"No, no, I am as ugly as a bear,
For beasts that meet me run away in fear." (MND.2.2)
A self-effacing or modesty statement, to dispel concerns about your vanity.
In the play. *Helena thinks she is ugly and therefore finds a reason why Demetrius does not love her.*

Modesty, admitted m. of personal looks - (a fellow)… that never looks in his glass for love of any thing he sees there…
"(a fellow)… that never looks in his glass for love of any thing he sees there…" (HV.5.2)
In the play. *Henry V woos with modesty Princess Katherine of France.*

Modesty, admitting to m. of descent or skill - … I am by birth a shepherd's daughter, my wit untrain'd in any kind of art.
"Dauphin, I am by birth a shepherd's daughter,
My wit untrain'd in any kind of art." (KHVI.p1.1.2)
Modesty of descent is a cultural point of pride especially in America. It particularly affects those who have become rich, as it points out to the listener the strength of their achievements. If you are the recipient of this momentous information (and you are a male), try for example 'I am by birth a farmer's son… etc.' A modern and alternate rejoinder I found effective with those who boast of their modest beginnings is 'My family was so poor that even my brother had to be made in Hong Kong'
In the play. *Joan of Arc is introduced to the Dauphin of France.*

Modesty, comment on a modest comment of hers - Words sweetly placed and modestly directed.
"Words sweetly placed and modestly directed." (KHVI.p1.5.3)
Your comment to a statement you approve of or of which you want to make fun mildly. It also applies to any comment that is neutral or to words that are supposed to be answers to a question but do not really answer it.
In the play. *Suffolk has asked Margaret if she has any message (commendations) for the king (Henry VI) to whom she will be married and Margaret replied very diplomatically,*
"Such commendations as becomes a maid,
A virgin and his servant, say to him."

Modesty, commitment expressed with m. - … We'll strive to bear it for your worthy sake to the extremest edge of hazard.
"… Sir, it is
A charge too heavy for my strength; but yet
We'll strive to bear it for your worthy sake,
To the extremest edge of hazard." (AWEW.3.3)
A comment when you have just been assigned an important task or responsibility.
In the play. *The Duke of Florence expresses his confidence in Bertram's valor and Bertram responds modestly but firmly.*

Modesty, deeds as their own reward - … rewards his deeds with doing them, and is content to spend the time to end it.
"…rewards
His deeds with doing them, and is

content
To spend the time to end it."
(COR.2.2)
Apply the sentence to yourself in answer to the question, 'What's in it for you?' E.G.'I reward my deeds with doing them'. Could also work well in a job interview as an answer to 'What are your expectations?'
In the play. *Cominius describes the modesty of Coriolanus.*

Modesty, absence not felt - My worth unknown, no loss is known in me.
"My worth unknown, no loss is known in me." (KHVI p1.4.5)
Talbot junior refers to the consequences of his possible death in the imminent battle. Absence is equally a kind of loss for which the statement is applicable.
In the play. *Near Bordeaux Talbot senior and junior are surrounded by the French. Talbot junior tells Talbot senior to escape, Talbot Junior would not be such a great loss to the English than the famous Talbot senior.*

Modesty, Jupiter is responsible for my success, not I. - Well, Jove, not I, is the doer of this, and he is to be thanked.
"Well, Jove, not I, is the doer of this, and he is to be thanked." (TN.3.4)
Deflect praise in modesty.
In the play. *Malvolio is thankful to the gods that they (as he wrongly believes) have caused Olivia to fall in love with him.*

Modesty, just a scratch - Scratches with briers, scars to move laughter only.
"Scratches with briers,
Scars to move laughter only"
(COR.3.3)
Answer to 'Did you hurt yourself?' when the damage is minor.
In the play. *Coriolanus tones down Menenius' praises of Coriolanus feats in battle and consequent wounds and scars.*

Modesty, justifying the display of some skill - Heaven doth with us as we with torches do, not light them for themselves…
"Heaven doth with us as we with torches do,
Not light them for themselves, for if our virtues
Did not go forth of us, 'twere all alike
As if we had them not." (MFM.1.1)
Answer to a compliment where your unique and particular skills are praised.
In the play. *Angelo is reticent about taking the job offered by the Duke and the Duke retorts with a good reason.*

Modesty, m. about your achievements - … my endeavors have ever come too short of my desires.
"… my endeavours
Have ever come too short of my desires." (KHVIII.3.2)
Convey modesty when recounting your actions or achievements, 'I have done this and that… but my endeavors have ever come short of my desires'.
In the play. *Wolsey is talking with the king.*

Modesty, m. at a ceremony to celebrate your achievements - … It is a part that I shall blush in acting.
"…It is a part
That I shall blush in acting."
(COR.2.2)
Use the present tense as an introduction, e.g. 'Speaking about or praising myself is a part that I blush in acting'.
In the play. *Coriolanus is uneasy about the pending ceremony whereby he will be made consul.*

Modesty, m. at a compliment - It is your grace's pleasure to commend, not my desert.
"… It is your grace's pleasure to commend;
Not my desert." (PER.2.5)

Soften the impact of praise and use as a token of modesty.
In the play. *Besides being a winner of the tourney, Pericles is a skilled musician. Pericles acknowledges in modesty Simonide's praise.*

Modesty, m. at recounting one's exploits - I have some wounds upon me, and they smart to hear themselves remember'd.
"I have some wounds upon me, and they smart
To hear themselves remember'd." (COR.1.9)
See also 'Modesty, self-praise, knowing the limitations of self-praise - lose by telling.'
In the play. *The super-modest but over-proud Coriolanus does not want to hear his merits praised.*

Modesty, m. at your new high responsibility - This new and gorgeous garment, majesty…
"This new and gorgeous garment, majesty,
Sits not so easy on me as you think:" (KHIVp2.5.2)
In the play. *King Henry V, soon after the succession addresses his brothers and to the Chief Justice.*

Modesty, m. by denial of personal merit - … But most it is presumption in us when the help of heaven we count the act of men.
"Inspired merit so by breath is barred:
It is not so with him that all things knows,
As it is with us that square our guess by shows:
But most it is presumption in us when
The help of heaven we count the act of men." (AWEW.2.1)
Display modesty by deflecting merit while at the same time retaining it. E.G. '…but most it is presumption… act of

men. I was but the instrument of an action whose merit I cannot claim.'
In the play. *Helena offers a barrage of counter-arguments to demolish the King's skepticism about the possibility that she may cure her.*

Modesty, m. characteristic of a wise person - … there's not one wise man among twenty that will praise himself. "…there's not one wise man among twenty that will praise himself." (MAAN.5.2)
A qualifier when you are called to say something about yourself, e.g. 'I realize that there is not one wise man among twenty that will praise himself but etc.'
See also, 'Character, pompous' - 'Modesty, self-praise to be avoided' – 'Modesty, self-praise, knowing the limitations of self-praise - … Though I lose the praise of it by telling…' - 'Modesty, self-praise, awareness of self-praise and enough of it - … methinks I do digress too much citing my worthless praise...'
In the play. *Beatrice replies to a comment of Benedick.*

Modesty, m. expressed - Your praises are too large.
"Your praises are too large:" (WT.4.4)
In the play. *Perdita responds to compliments from Florizel.*

Modesty, m. gently reprimanded – Too modest are you, more cruel to your good report…
"Too modest are you;
More cruel to your good report than grateful
To us that give you truly." (COR.1.9)
In the play. *Coriolanus almost scorns at the praises given him by the crowd and Cominius reprimands him in a friendly way.*

Modesty, m. hurt by disclosure of feats - … we wound our modesty and make foul the clearness of our

deservings, when of ourselves we publish them.
"Madam, the care I have had to even your content, I wish might be found in the calendar of my past endeavours; for then we wound our modesty and make foul the clearness of our deservings, when of ourselves we publish them." (AWEW.1.3)
In the play. *The Steward answers a question from the Countess with this preamble.*

Modesty, m. in a woman as temptation for a seducer - … modesty may more betray our sense than woman's lightness?
"… Can it be
That modesty may more betray our sense
Than woman's lightness?" (MFM.2.3)
See also 'Women, modest and virtuous w. have greater appeal than lascivious ones - Most dangerous is that temptation that doth goad us on to sin in loving virtue…'.
In the play. *The virtue of Isabel tempts the hypocrite Angelo.*

Modesty, m. in introduction - … Further to boast were neither true nor modest, unless I add, we are honest.
"In Cambria are we born, and gentlemen
Further to boast were neither true nor modest,
Unless I add, we are honest." (CYM.5.5)
Usable in a job interview. Describe your achievement and conclude with 'Further…add, I am honest'
In the play. *Belarius answer a question from Cymbeline*

Modesty, m. in possession – … this thing of darkness acknowledge mine.
"…Two of these fellows you
Must know and own; this thing of darkness!
Acknowledge mine." (TEM.5.1)
Self-effacing statement about an item you own but do not value much e.g. an old car, a tattered executive briefcase, a stained coffee mug etc. e.g. 'This thing of darkness I acknowledge mine'. 'Thing of darkness' can also be applied to a contemptible character.
In the play. *Prospero addresses the re-united company. The two fellows are the drunkard conspirators Stephano and Trinculo. The 'thing of darkness' is Caliban.*

Modesty, m. in victory - Praised be God, and not our strength, for it!
"Praised be God, and not our strength, for it!" (KHV.4.7)
In the play. *Montjoy has arrived to the English Camp and announces to King Henry that the English are the victors at Agincourt.*

Modesty, m. observed – It is the witness still of excellency to put a strange face on his own perfection.
"It is the witness still of excellency
To put a strange face on his own perfection" (MAAN.2.3)
In the play. *Don Pedro has prompted his attendant Balthazar to sing and Balthazar modestly refuses.*

Modesty, refusal to be praised - I had rather have my wounds to heal again, than hear say how I got them.
"I had rather have my wounds to heal again,
Than hear say how I got them." (COE.2.2)
In the play. *Coriolanus, true to his character, is sincerely an enemy of flattery.*

Modesty, refusal to teach an expert - To teach a teacher ill beseemeth me.
"But pardon me, I am too sudden-bold
To teach a teacher ill beseemeth me." (LLL.2.1)

Answer to a request for advice when you do not want to give it, e.g. 'To teach... beseemeth me'.
In the play. *The Princess teases the King who has come to visit her. She has heard of his oath and tells him that to keep that oath is a sin as it is a sin to break it. Then she corrects herself suggesting that it is not proper for her to advise a teacher.*

Modesty, responding to praise of your good company - Of much less value is my company than your good words.
"Of much less value is my company
Than your good words" (KRII.2.3)
In the play. *Bolingbroke responds to a compliment by Northumberland, who enjoyed Bolingbroke's company.*

Modesty, self-doubt - ... I do not call your faith in question so mainly as my merit...
"...I do not call your faith in question
So mainly as my merit: I cannot sing,
Nor heel the high lavolt, nor sweeten talk,
Nor play at subtle games; fair virtues all,
To which the Grecians are most prompt and pregnant:" (TC.4.4)
You can change 'faith' to 'confidence' when you wish to project modesty – for example when you have received an important assignment or responsibility.
In the play. *Cressida must be exchanged for a Trojan prisoner. Troilus fears that she will be tempted by the prowess of the Greeks with whom he fears not to be able to compete. 'Lavolt' was a dance involving high jumps and acrobatics.*

Modesty, self-praise to be avoided - The worthiness of praise distains his worth, if that the praised himself bring the praise forth.
"The worthiness of praise distains his worth,
If that the praised himself bring the praise forth:

But what the repining enemy commends,
That breath fame blows; that praise, sole sure, transcends." (TC.1.3)
In the play. *Aeneas, visiting the Trojan camp answers a question from Agamennon.*

Modesty, self-praise to be avoided - This comes too near the praising of myself, no more of it.
"This comes too near the praising of myself,
Therefore no more of it." (MOV.3.4)
Use at the end of a narrative of something good you may have done or have to report – See also 'Modesty, self-praise, knowing the limitations of self-praise'
In the play. *Portia is determined to help Antonio, friend of her soon husband-to-be Bassanio.*

Modesty, self-praise, awareness of self-praise and enough of it - ... methinks I do digress too much citing my worthless praise...
"But, soft! methinks I do digress too much,
Citing my worthless praise: O, pardon me;
For when no friends are by, men praise themselves." (TA.5.3)
When you had to speak about yourself and your exploits. You may stop at 'worthless praise'. See also, 'Character, pompous' - 'Modesty, self-praise to be avoided' – 'Modesty, self-praise, knowing the limitations of self-praise - lose by telling' – 'Pride, p. misguided - ... He that is proud eats up himself: pride is his own glass, his own trumpet, his own chronicle...'
In the play. *Lucius explains to the Romans all the events that led him to take refuge among the Goths. However, he has always kept in mind the welfare of Rome - including eliminating her enemies (Saturninus, Tamora and company). This is the self-praise he refers to.*

Modesty, self-praise, knowing the limitations of self-praise - ... Though I lose the praise of it by telling...
"...Though I lose
The praise of it by telling, you must know..." (AC.2.3)
Soften the implied lack of modesty in speaking well about yourself or in having to remind one or more people about what you have done. See also 'Modesty, self-praise to be avoided' – 'Pride, p. misguided and canceling the value of the deed that inspired the pride'
In the play. *Pompey reminds Antony that he (Pompey) offered shelter to Antony's mother during difficult times.*

Modesty, shying away from excessive praise - You shout me forth in acclamation hyperbolical...
"You shout me forth in acclamation hyperbolical;
As if I loved my little should be dieted
In praises sauced with lies." (COR.1.9)
A statement of modesty if and when you are praised.
In the play. *Coriolanus shuns the praise.*

Modesty, total m. – The full some of me is sum of nothing.
"... but the full sum of me
Is sum of nothing." (MOV.3.2)
Use in any occasion when it is good to be modest See also 'Fortune, your total f. - ... the continent and summary of my fortune.'
In the play. *Portia assumes a modest tone after Bassanio has solved the puzzle and therefore will marry her.*

Money, m. covers up faults or liabilities - O, what a world of vile ill-favoured faults looks handsome in three hundred pounds a year!
"O, what a world of vile ill-favoured faults
Looks handsome in three hundred pounds a year!" (MWW.3.4)
Comment on the corrupting power or on the influence of money.
In the play. *Anne Page resigns herself to exchange a few words with Slender, the wealthy suitor chosen by her father. She dislikes him but recognizes the power of wealth.*

Money, m. only partial motive - For me, the gold of France did not seduce...
"For me, the gold of France did not seduce;
Although I did admit it as a motive
The sooner to effect what I intended" (KHV.2.2)
When you want to make the hearer understand that money is an incentive to accelerate the doing of what you had in mind before. Change the verb to the present tense if applicable. E.G. 'For me the gold does not seduce... intended'.
In the play. *Cambridge intended to kill the king (Henry V) and money was (relatively) a minor inducement.*

Money, m. opening the way - ... for they say, if money go before, all ways do lie open.
"... for they say, if money go before, all ways do lie open." (MWW.2.2)
Comment on the inherent corruptibility of the world. See also 'Authority, corrupted by gold - ... and though authority be a stubborn bear, yet he is oft led by the nose with gold. ' *** 'Gold, g. as powerful tool of corruption – ... gold were as good as twenty orators and will, no doubt, tempt him to anything.'
In the play. *Mr. Ford (disguised as Master Broom) wants to lend money to Falstaff as part of a plot to test Mrs. Ford's fidelity.*

Money, m. overrides any other consideration – ... nothing comes amiss, so money comes withal.

"…give him gold enough and marry him to an old trot with ne'er a tooth in her head, … though she have as many diseases as two and fifty horses: why, nothing comes amiss, so money comes withal." (TOS.1.2)
In the play. *Grumio (Petruchio's servant) explains to Hortensio Petruchio's intent and philosophy.*

Money, m. poisonous and murderous effects of m. - There is thy gold, worse poison to men's souls…
"There is thy gold, worse poison to men's souls,
Doing more murders in this loathsome world,
Than these poor compounds that thou mayst not sell." (RJ.5.1)
Comment on the damaging side effects of money. See also 'Greed, gold provokes g.' – 'Authority, corrupted by gold'.
In the play. *The gold Romeo refers to is used by him to purchase the poison with which he plans to end his life now that Juliet (he believes incorrectly) is dead. The apothecary cannot (technically) sell poisons but will bend the law for money.*

Monitoring, you are observing someone's behavior – I have eyes upon him and his affairs come to me on the wind.
"I have eyes upon him,
And his affairs come to me on the wind." (AC.3.6)
Change 'him' to 'you' and 'his' to 'your' when you mean, jocularly, to imply that you know what is going on with the life of a friend.
In the play. *Octavia has just returned to Rome and talks with her brother Octavian who monitors long distance Antony's activities and whereabouts.*

Monster (figurative) that leads man to madness – … some other horrible form which might deprive your sovereignty of reason…
"…some other horrible form,
Which might deprive your sovereignty of reason
And draw you into madness?" (H.1.4)
An analogy for people drawn into mad or criminal behavior by a mental monstruosity or obsession.
In the play. *Horatio counsels Hamlet not to approach the Ghost fearing that the Ghost may make Hamlet mad.*

Mood, aloofness due to personal reasons - … if I have veil'd my look, I turn the trouble of my countenance merely upon myself.
"… if I have veil'd my look,
I turn the trouble of my countenance
Merely upon myself." (JC.1.2)
Answer to 'You seem distressed' or equivalent.
In the play. *Cassius has noted a coldness in Brutus and Brutus replies*

Mood, bad m epidemic – It is foul weather in us all, good sir when you are cloudy.
"It is foul weather in us all, good sir,
When you are cloudy." (TEM.2.1)
In the play. *Gonzalo comments on the bad mood of Sebastian.*

Mood, change in m. observed - … I have not from your eyes that gentleness and show of love as I was wont to have.
"Brutus, I do observe you now of late:
I have not from your eyes that gentleness
And show of love as I was wont to have" (JC.1.2)
In the play. *Cassius noticed a change in mood in his old friend Brutus.*

Mood, combative m. – I am fire and air; my other elements I give to baser life.

"I am fire and air; my other elements I give to baser life." (AC.5.2)
Answer to 'Are you ready for this?' when 'this' is a challenging or an exciting task.
In the play. *Cleopatra thinks of the courage of Antony and takes inspiration for his memory while she prepares herself to die.*

Mood, depressed m. followed by an uplifting – When in disgrace with fortune and men's eyes…
"When in disgrace with Fortune and men's eyes,
I all alone beweep my outcast state,
And trouble deaf heaven with my bootless cries,
And look upon my self and curse my fate,
Wishing me like to one more rich in hope,
Featured like him, like him with friends possessed,
Desiring this man's art, and that man's scope,
With what I most enjoy contented least,
Yet in these thoughts my self almost despising,
Haply I think on thee, and then my state,
(Like to the lark at break of day arising
From sullen earth) sings hymns at heaven's gate,
For thy sweet love remembered such wealth brings,
That then I scorn to change my state with kings". (SON.29)
You can shorten it to, 'When in disgrace with Fortune and men's eyes,
I all alone beweep my outcast state, thy sweet love remembered such wealth brings,
That then I scorn to change my state with kings'.

Mood, in a good m. and ready to say yes - I am in a holiday humour, and like enough to consent.
"I am in a holiday humour, and like enough to consent." (AYLI.4.1)
Turn this into a question, if you perceive the time to be right, 'Are you in a holiday humor, and like enough to consent?' Depending on whether she is used to your quotations or not she may say 'What?' This will give you an entry point and you can go on explaining why she should consent.
Ovid agrees that a good mood in a lady will enhance your chances of success. 'When hearts are glad, and not fast bound by grief, then do they lie open, and Venus steals-in with persuasive art.' (AOL.1)
In the play. *Rosalind in a man's disguise (and incredibly unrecognized by Orlando) now pretends to be a woman and in a humorous way asks Orlando to show his courting skills.*

Mood, in a merry m. - I am glad to see you in this merry vein…
"I am glad to see you in this merry vein:
What means this jest? I pray you, master, tell me." (COE.2.2)
In the play. *Dromio S. to Antipholus S who accuses Dromio S. of deceit due to mistaken identity.*

Mood, in a poor m. - Vexed I am, of late, with passions of some difference, conceptions only proper to myself, which give some soil, perhaps to my behaviours.
"… Vexed I am,
Of late, with passions of some difference,
Conceptions only proper to myself,
Which give some soil, perhaps to my behaviours" (JC.1.2)

Answer to 'Is there something wrong with you?' Explain your apparent distance, aloofness or avoidance of social interaction. See also 'Lover, l's absence justified - I have this while with leaden thoughts been press'd…'
In the play. *Brutus explains why he appears reserved to his friends.*

Mood, in a poor m. – … my lord leans wondrously to discontent: his comfortable temper has forsook him…
"…my lord leans wondrously to discontent: his comfortable temper has forsook him; he's much out of health, and keeps his chamber" (PER.3.4)
Applied to yourself it can be an answer to 'How are you?' E.G. 'I lean wondrously to discontent.'
In the play. *Servant Servilius fends off Timon's creditor at the door.*

Mood, pessimistic, life tedious - There's nothing in this world can make me joy: life is as tedious as a twice-told tale, vexing the dull ear of a drowsy man.
"There's nothing in this world can make me joy:
Life is as tedious as a twice-told tale
Vexing the dull ear of a drowsy man" (KJ.4.4)
Pessimistic answer to 'How is it going?'
In the play. *Lewis' comment after the battle of Angiers has been lost by the French*

Mood, tormented and seeking a way out of a problem or dilemma - … like one lost in a thorny wood, that rends the thorns and is rent with the thorns, seeking a way and straying from the way…
"…like one lost in a thorny wood,
That rends the thorns and is rent with the thorns,
Seeking a way and straying from the way;
Not knowing how to find the open air,
But toiling desperately to find it out." (KHVI p3.3.2)
An answer to 'How are you?' if the conditions apply.
In the play. *Richard of Gloucester is already planning the misdeed and murders he will commit to acquire the crown. In fact he continues saying,*
"…Torment myself to catch the English crown:
And from that torment I will free myself,
Or hew my way out with a bloody axe."

Mood, unhappy - … I show more mirth than I am mistress of.
CELIA. I pray thee, Rosalind, be merry.
ROSALIND. Dear Celia, I show more mirth than I am mistress of. (AYLI.1.2)
When you are prompted to be happy but you cannot.
In the play. *Rosalind, daughter of banished Duke Senior is an inseparable friend of Celia, daughter of the usurping Duke Frederick. Rosalind, in the circumstances, is melancholy.*

Mood, why are you in a bad mood? - … what's the matter that you have such a February face…
"…what's the matter,
That you have such a February face,
So full of frost, of storm and cloudiness?" (MAAN.5.4)
Alternative to 'What's wrong with you?' Or 'why do you look so sad?' For a counter-reply see 'Expression of sadness misconstrued - My heart is ten times lighter than my looks.'
In the play. *Don Pedro asks the question of Benedick, who comes in with a dark and sad expression.*

Mood, why are you still in a bad mood? - How is it that the clouds still hang on you?
"How is it that the clouds still hang on you?" (H.1.1)
In the play. *King Claudius queries Hamlet about Hamlet's sour looks.*

Moon, m. envious of her beauty - Arise, fair sun, and kill the envious moon, who is already sick with grief, that thou her maid art far more fair than she.
"Arise, fair sun, and kill the envious moon,
Who is already sick with grief,
That thou her maid art far more fair than she." (RJ.2.2)
Alternative answer to "do you like me?" or "do you think I am pretty?" Example, "What could I say, if I were Romeo I would say, 'Arise fair sun, and kill the envious moon… than she.'
In the play. *Romeo sees Juliet at her balcony while he is down in the garden.*

Moonlight, by the m. – How sweet the moonlight sleeps upon this bank!
"How sweet the moonlight sleeps upon this bank!
Here will we sit and let the sounds of music
Creep in our ears: soft stillness and the night
Become the touches of sweet harmony.
Sit, Jessica. Look how the floor of heaven
Is thick inlaid with patines of bright gold" (MOV.5.1)
Change 'Jessica' to the name of the applicable lady.
In the play. *Lorenzo and newly married Jessica have been house-sitting for Bassanio and Portia who in turn are separately involved in a law suit brought in by the merchant of Venice, Shylock. Shylock wants a pound off Antonio's flesh.*

While waiting for the masters' return, Lorenzo waxes romantic.

Morning, an early start - This morning, like the spirit of a youth that means to be of note, begins betimes.
"This morning, like the spirit of a youth
That means to be of note, begins betimes." (AC.4.4)
Introduction to an early morning meeting.
In the play. *Antony to generals and Cleopatra the morning of the battle.*

Mortality, m. recognized – Even so must I run on, and even so stop…
"Even so must I run on, and even so stop.
What surety of the world, what hope, what stay,
When this was now a king, and now is clay?" (KJ.5.7)
In the play. *King John has just died and Prince John, heir to the throne, takes the occasion to reflect on the inevitability of death.*

Mortality, m. recognized - Thou know'st 'tis common; all that lives must die passing through nature to eternity.
"Thou know'st 'tis common; all that lives must die,
Passing through nature to eternity" (H.1.1)
A philosophical statement or a comment to any ending, to express together a note of sadness and a note of resignation.
In the play. *Queen Gertrude asks Hamlet why he continues to be so upset following his father's death, considering that mortality is the fate of all mankind.*

Mortality, m. recognized - Well, we were born to die.
"Well, we were born to die." (RJ.3.4)

In the play. *Capulet Senior to Paris who has called on him to ask for Juliet's hand in marriage.*

Mortality, m. to be kept in mind - For death remembered should be like a mirror…
"For death remembered should be like a mirror,
Who tells us, life's but a breath, to trust it, error." (PER.1.1)
In the play. *Antiochus has reminded Pericles of all those who died because they did not solve the riddle. Pericles takes the admonishment in stride, as an occasion to remember a general truth.*

Motion, what moves catches the attention - … things in motion sooner catch the eye than what not stirs.
"Since things in motion sooner catch the eye
Than what not stirs." (TC.3.3)
Explain the need for more visibility.
In the play. *Ulysses appeals to Achilles' vanity, envy of Ajax and desire for emulation. Ajax is 'what moves' and gets more attention by the Greeks.*

Motivation, m. to stand up to ill fortune - Yield not thy neck to fortune's yoke, but let thy dauntless mind still ride in triumph over all mischance.
"Yield not thy neck
To fortune's yoke, but let thy dauntless mind
Still ride in triumph over all mischance." (KHVI p3.3.3)
Words of encouragement.
In the play. *King Lewis XI of France comforts Queen Margaret of England who is calling on him for help against the Yorkists.*

Mountains, high m. described – … rocks and hills whose heads touch heaven.
"…rocks and hills whose heads touch heaven" (OTH.1.3)

In the play. *Othello explains how Desdemona fell in love with him by listening to his stories.*

Mouth, sweet and heavenly - The heavenly moisture, that sweet coral mouth…
"The heavenly moisture, that sweet coral mouth,
Whose precious taste her thirsty lips well knew" (V&A)
In the poem. *Adonis stops kissing Venus.*

Murder, foul m. – Murder most foul, as in the best it is; but this most foul, strange and unnatural
"Murder most foul, as in the best it is;
But this most foul, strange and unnatural" (H.1.5)
One way of expressing your disgust, whether the murder is real or metaphorical.
In the play. *The ghost makes his case with Hamlet.*

Murder, m. cannot be concealed – For murder, though it have no tongue, will speak with most miraculous organ.
"For murder, though it have no tongue, will speak
With most miraculous organ…" (H.2.2)
In the play. *In a soliloquy Hamlet explains the rationale for staging the play within the play*

Murder, m. cannot be erased - Here's the smell of the blood still: all the perfumes of Arabia will not sweeten this little hand.
"Here's the smell of the blood still: all the perfumes of Arabia will not sweeten this little hand." (M.1.5)
In the play. *Lady Macbeth, sleepwalking, utters sentences related to the bloody deeds she was involved in.*

Murder, m. discovered – For murder, though it have no tongue, will speak with most miraculous organ.
"For murder, though it have no tongue, will speak
With most miraculous organ" (H.2.2)
In the play. *Hamlet organizes a play where the murder of his father by the present king will be re-enacted.*

Murder, m. has no excuses - ... he forfeits his own blood that spills another.
"On height of our displeasure: friend or brother,
He forfeits his own blood that spills another" (TOA.3.5)
See also 'Revenge, request to r. murder.'
In the play. *The Athenian Senate is unmoved at the request by Alcibiades for mercy for one of his soldiers who killed another in self-defense.*

Murder, no m. of boys or civilians - ... murder not this innocent child, lest thou be hated both of God and man!
"Ah, Clifford, murder not this innocent child,
Lest thou be hated both of God and man!" (KHVI.p3.1.3)
In the play. *Rutland's tutor pleads with Clifford not to murder the boy.*

Music, a superb artist – Every thing that heard him play...
"Every thing that heard him play,
Even the billows of the sea,
Hung their heads, and then lay by.
In sweet music is such art..."
(KHVIII.3.1)
Answer to 'Did you like his performance?'
In the play. *This is part of a song played for the sulking and dejected Queen Katherine.*

Music, beautiful and restful - Most heavenly music! It nips me unto listening...
"Most heavenly music!
It nips me unto listening, and thick slumber
Hangs upon my eyes; let me rest."
(PER.5.1)
The music is beautiful and restful to the point of inducing sleep in you.
In the play. *Overwhelmed by happiness Pericles thinks he can hear the heavenly music of the heavenly spheres and falls asleep. In a dream Pericles is informed that his wife Thaisa is alive and safe in Ephesus*

Music, calling for m. while depressed – Let there be no noise made…will whisper music to my weary spirit.
"Let there be no noise made, my gentle friends;
Unless some dull and favourable hand
Will whisper music to my weary spirit." (KHIV.p2.4.5)
Try 'Let there be no noise made but whispered music to my weary spirit.
In the play. *Ailing King Henry calls for music.*

Music, contempt for music, pop, rap or country - I had rather be a kitten, and cry - mew, than one of these same metre ballad-mongers.
"I had rather be a kitten, and cry - mew,
Than one of these same metre ballad-mongers." (KHIV p1.3.1)
Express your distaste of rap music or equivalent.
In the play. *Hotspur is not impressed by the self-asserted musical ability of Glendower.*

Music, delightful m. and performance - ... my ears were never better fed with such delightful pleasing harmony.
"... I do
Protest, my ears were never better fed
With such delightful pleasing harmony." (PER.2.5)
Answer to 'Did you like the music?' This can work either when you are performing (she would extend the compliment to you), or you are listening to her playing.

Or in baroque style you can attribute to her voice the quality of a 'delightful pleasing harmony'.
In the play. *Besides being a winner of the tourney, Pericles is a skilled musician and Simonides, the king of Pentapolis congratulates him*

Music, disharmony, lack of balance, metaphor - …how sour sweet music is, when time is broke, and no proportion kept.
"…how sour sweet music is,
When time is broke, and no proportion kept." (KRII.5.5)
A metaphor for lack of coordination, wasted efforts, conflicting projects.
In the play. *King Richard in the dungeon of Pomfret Castle hears some music.*

Music, dislike for bag-pipes - … and others, when the bagpipe sings i' the nose cannot contain their urine.
"Some men there are love not a gaping pig;
…
And others, when the bagpipe sings i' the nose
Cannot contain their urine."
(MOV.4.1)
Answer to, "Do you like bagpipes?" or interject it as a comment if and when the subject turns to bagpipes. Or take an artistic license and substitute bagpipes for any music genre you may not like.
In the play. *Shylock finds arguments (with the Duke of Venice), to have his forfeit paid, the famous pound of flesh culled from Antonio.*

Music, distasteful or that you do not like - … 'tis like the howling of Irish wolves against the moon.
"Pray you, no more of this; 'tis like the howling
of Irish wolves against the moon."
(AYLI.5.3)
In the play. *Rosalind finds herself at the center of a tangled web involving her lover Orlando, Phebe and Silvius. The weaning by the parties involved causes Rosalind to plead with them to shut up.*

Music, distrust for men who do not like music - The man that hath no music in himself … is fit for treasons, stratagems and spoils.
"The man that hath no music in himself,
Nor is not moved by concord of sweet sounds,
Is fit for treasons, stratagems and spoils;
The motions of his spirit are dull as night
And his affections dark as Erebus:
Let no such man be trusted"
(MOV.5.1)
Sting your adversary should he declare a dislike for music. Or modify 'of sweet sounds' to 'of these sweet sounds' if the party shows contempt for the music that you (instead) like.
Even Shakespeare, however, does not endorse the sound of music wholesale. In the same play, Merchant of Venice, Shylock pronounces:
"Others, when the bag pipe sings I' the nose,
Cannot contain their urine." (MOV.4.1)
On the other hand, if music is not your forte you can always bring out the fact that "Music helps not the toothache" (George Herbert, 1593-1633).
And should you decide to volunteer to sing for her, try to record yourself on tape first and listen to how you sound, because…
"Swans sings before they die – 'twere no bad thing
Should certain people die before they sing."
(Samuel Coleridge, 1772-1834, epigram on a volunteer singer).
In the play. *Lorenzo is at Belmont with his newly married Jessica, babysitting Portia's house*

while Portia has gone to Venice to attend to urgent business.

Music, effect of m. recalling images and scent of violets - … like the sweet sound that breathes upon a bank of violets.
"That strain again; it had a dying fall:
O, it came over my ear, like the sweet sound
That breathes upon a bank of violets." (TN.1.1)
Answer to 'Do you like this music?' or a compliment to her voice, 'It came over…. Violets'. See also entries for 'Voice'
In the play. *Count Orsino pines over the unreturned love of Olivia.*

Music, excellent performance - …true concord of well tuned sounds.
"…true concord of well tuned sounds" (SON 8)
Also usable as a comment at the end of a meeting where the conclusions were reached in unanimous agreement. E.G. 'O true concord of well tuned sounds'. Or apply ironically to situations where all stoop to flattery in hope of reward.

Music, extraordinary power of m. to humanize even things - Since nought so stockish, hard and full of rage…
"…therefore the poet
Did feign that Orpheus drew trees, stones and floods
Since nought so stockish, hard and full of rage,
But music for the time doth change his nature" (MOV.5.1)
In the play. *Lorenzo explains to his wife Jessica his theory on the power of music after she confessed that*
'I am never merry when I hear sweet music'.

Music, lady who plays or sings to you – (I am) lulled with the sound of sweetest melody.
"…lulled with the sound of sweetest melody?" (KHIV.p2.3.1)
Compliment. Answer to 'How do you like my singing (or playing)?'
In the play *King Henry IV compares his insomnia to the sleeping ease of his subjects. His insomnia is not cured even by soothing music.*

Music, m. and its mixed power to be good and bad - … music oft hath such a charm to make bad good, and good provoke to harm.
"'T is good; though music oft hath such a charm
To make bad good, and good provoke to harm." (MFM.4.1)
In the play. *The Duke (in disguise) calls on Mariana, jilted lover of Angelo - as he arrives, a boy was singing and the Duke comments on the song and the music played.*
Answer to 'Do you like music?' E.G. 'It depends, music oft… harm.'

Music, m. as solace - In sweet music is such art; killing care and grief of heart
In sweet music is such art;
Killing care and grief of heart." (KHVIII.3.1)
In praise of music
In the play. *A lady in attendance sings a song at the command of Q. Katherine*

Music, m. as solace - Take thy lute, wench my soul grows sad with troubles: sing and disperse them.
" Take thy lute, wench; my soul grows sad with troubles:
Sing and disperse them." (KHVIII.3.1)
You want to listen to some music, possibly played by a pleasing lady.
In the play. *Katherine tries to find solace in music knowing of the impending divorce trial*

Music, m. composer complimenting himself - ...I framed to the harp...and gave the tongue a helpful ornament.
"...I framed to the harp
Many an English ditty, lovely well,
And gave the tongue a helpful ornament." (KHIV p1.3.1)
Announce your singing, 'I will give the tongue a helpful ornament'. See also entries for 'Praise, self-p.'
In the play. *Glendower extols his own achievements to the skeptical Hotspur.*

Music, m. dramatically improving when it stops – ... the general so likes your music, that he desires you... to make no more noise with it.
"But, masters, here's money for you: and the general so likes your music, that he desires you, for love's sake, to make no more noise with it"
(OTH.3.1)
In the play. *A clown banters with musicians who play on the occasion of the arrival of Othello in Cyprus.*

Music, m. even tames animals - ... Their savage eyes turn'd to a modest gaze by the sweet power of music.
"Their savage eyes turn'd to a modest gaze
By the sweet power of music"
(MOV.5.1)
In the play. *Lorenzo explains to Jessica the emotional power of music that stops even horses when they hear a trumpet.*

Music, m. of the lark – the lark, whose notes do beat the vaulty heaven so high above our heads.
"...the lark, whose notes do beat
The vaulty heaven so high above our heads" (RJ.3.5)
In the play. *Romeo and Juliet dispute as to whether birds heard outside their room are larks (signaling dawn) or nightingales (signaling it is still dark).*

Music, m. or singing produced by a mermaid calming the sea - ... the rude sea grew civil at her song and certain stars shot madly from their spheres....
"...Thou rememberest
Since once I sat upon a promontory,
And heard a mermaid on a dolphin's back
Uttering such dulcet and harmonious breath
That the rude sea grew civil at her song
And certain stars shot madly from their spheres,
To hear the sea-maid's music."
(MND.2.1)
Answer to 'How did you like the music or singing? 'It was such a dulcet and harmonious breath that...song' etc.
In the play. *Oberon reminds Puck of a previous experience. 'Dulcet' is synonym of 'sweet'.*

Music, m. ordered to relieve sadness - Take thy lute, wench: my soul grows sad with troubles; sing and disperse 'em...
"Take thy lute, wench: my soul grows sad with troubles;
Sing, and disperse 'em, if thou canst"
(KHVIII, 3.1)
In the play. *Queen Katherine to lady in attendance.*

Music, m. queen – This is the patroness of heavenly harmony.
"...this is
The patroness of heavenly harmony"
(TOS.3.1)
If you are a musician, flatter your (female) sponsor. Or refer to harmony in general and compliment a lady for the harmony she is capable of diffusing or inspiring among those who know her.
In the play. *Hortensio and Lucentio, suitors of Bianca, become her tutors to have better opportunities of being near her. Hortensio teaches*

music and declares Bianca to be 'patroness of heavenly harmony'.

Music, m. suitable to evening - How still the evening is, as hush'd on purpose to grace harmony.
DON PEDRO Come, shall we hear this music?
CLAUDIO Yea, my good lord. How still the evening is,
As hush'd on purpose to grace harmony! (MAAN.2.3)
In the play. *Don Pedro invites Claudio to listen to some music provided by Balthazar.*

Music, m. that induces sadness - I am never merry when I hear sweet music.
"I am never merry when I hear sweet music" (MOV.5.1)
In the play. *Jessica to Lorenzo in the garden of Portia's house.*

Music, m. that inspires sadness –
Music to hear, why hear'st thou music sadly?
"Music to hear, why hear'st thou music sadly?
Sweets with sweets war not, joy delights in joy" (SON 9)

Music, m. that speaks to the heart –
… It gives a very echo to the seat where Love is throned.
DUKE ORSINO How dost thou like this tune?
VIOLA It gives a very echo to the seat
Where Love is throned. (TN.2.4)
In the play. *Duke Orsino elicits Viola/Cesario's opinion about a song.*

Music, m. to be played during a lottery extraction or similar - Let music sound while he doth make his choice…
"Let music sound while he doth make his choice;
Then, if he lose, he makes a swan-like end,
Fading in music:" (MOV.3.1)
Apply to yourself if you are the extractor.
In the play. *It's Bassanio's turn to choose the right casket. Portia wants the choice accompanied by music*

Music, m. without rhythm compared to life misspent - … how sour sweet music is, when time is broke and no proportion kept!! So is it in the music of men's lives
"…how sour sweet music is,
When time is broke and no proportion kept!
So is it in the music of men's lives." (KRII.5.5)
In the play. *King Richard, prisoner at Pomfret castle, detects a lack of rhythm in some music he overhears and compares the disharmony to his own life when he did not detect his own errors.*
"To cheque time broke in a disorder'd string;
But for the concord of my state and time
Had not an ear to hear my true time broke.
I wasted time, and now doth time waste me"

Music, melody lulling to sleep - lull'd with sound of sweetest melody.
"Under the canopies of costly state,
And lull'd with sound of sweetest melody?" (KHIV.p2.3.1)
Answer to 'How do you feel?' when relaxing after a meal and listening to music, e.g. 'I am lulled with sound of sweetest melody'. Especially good if the player is the lady of the house.
In the play. *The King meditates on the sleeplessness of the great even if when lulled by music.*

Music, power of m. - …whose golden touch could soften steel and stones.
"For Orpheus' lute was strung with poets' sinews;

Whose golden touch could soften
steel and stones,
Make tigers tame, and huge
leviathans
Forsake unsounded deeps to dance
on sands." (TGV.3.2)
Answer to 'Did you like the music?" E.G.
'Its golden touch could soften steel and
stones'.
In the play. *Proteus pretends to give courting lessons to the spineless Thurio. By so doing Proteus plans to get access to Sylvia. Here we deal with music and song as courting tools. See the context of 'Poetry, power of p. - much is the force of heaven-bred poesy' for a more extended explanation.*

Music, power of m. to soothe the
spirit – (When) doleful dumps the
mind oppress then music with her
silver sound with speedy help doth
lend redress.
'When griping grief the heart doth
wound,
And doleful dumps the mind oppress
Then music with her silver sound
With speedy help doth lend redress"
(RJ.4.5)
In the play. *Musicians are called at Juliet's house to celebrate a wedding turned into a (presumed) funeral. They banter as to whether the silver sound of music is attributable to the music or to the silver they are paid for it.*

Music, purpose of m. - ... to refresh
the mind of man after his studies or
his usual pain.
"...why music was ordain'd!
Was it not to refresh the mind of man
After his studies or his usual pain?"
(TOS.3.1)
In the play. *Lucentio argues with Hortensio as to who should be first to instruct Bianca, the literature teacher (Lucentio) or the music teacher (Hortensio)*

Music, questionable musical
execution - ... I count it but time lost
to hear such a foolish song.
FIRST PAGE You are deceived, sir:
we kept time, we lost not our time.
TOUCHSTONE By my troth, yes; I
count it but time lost to hear such a
foolish song (AYLI.5.3)
In the play. *Touchstone and Page have different opinions about musical execution.*

My heart upon my sleeve - But I will
wear my heart upon my sleeve....
"But I will wear my heart upon my
sleeve.
For daws to peck at. I am not what I
am." (OTH.1.1)
In the play. *Iago convinces Roderigo that he, Iago, will work for Roderigo's goal, namely to seduce Desdemona. In fact, Iago's aim is to dupe Roderigo and extract from him as much gold as possible. 'Daw' is a foolish bird.*

Music, request for m. as food of love –
... music, moody food of us that trade
in love.
"Give me some music; - music,
moody food
Of us that trade in love." (AC.2.5)
Answer to "What can I offer you?" or
"What would you like to have?" or
similar.
In the play. *Antony had to leave Alexandria for Rome to take stock of the political and military situation. Cleopatra is sad due to his absence and asks her attendants to arrange for some music to be played.*

Music, request for m. as food of love –
If music be the food of love, play on...
"If music be the food of love, play on;
Give me excess of it; that surfeiting
The appetite may sicken and so die.
O, it came o'er my ear like the sweet
sound,
That breathes upon a bank of violets,
Stealing and giving odour!" (TN.1.1)
Answer to 'Would you like some music?'

In the play. *Orsino, the Duke of Illyria loves Olivia who does not return his love. He asks attending musicians to play for him.*

Music, singing and the effect of string instruments - Is it not strange, that sheep's guts, should hale souls out of men's bodies.
" Is it not strange, that sheep's guts, should hale souls out of men's bodies." (MAAN.2.3)
Comment on your guitar playing.
In the play. *Balthazar is going to sing a song and Benedick comments on the strange effect of sound, considering the sound's somewhat lowly origin, i.e. sheep's guts. 'Hale' means 'to draw', 'to draw out'.*

Music, singing, refusal to sing - … tax not so bad a voice, to slander music any more than once…
BALTHAZAR. O good my lord, tax not so bad a voice,
To slander music any more than once.
DON PEDRO. It is the witness still of excellency,
To put a strange face on his own perfection: --
I pray thee, sing and let me woo no more." (MAAN.2.3)
Say no to a request to perform - it could be singing but it may stretch to other arts.
In the play. *Don Pedro has prompted his attendant Balthazar to sing and Balthazar modestly refuses.*

Music, singing, warning that music or singing will be below standards - … There's not a note of mine that's worth the noting.
"Note this before my notes;
There's not a note of mine that's worth the noting" (MAAN.2.3)
In the play. *Don Pedro has prompted his attendant Balthazar to sing and Balthazar modestly refuses.*

Music, uneducational type of m. - Lascivious metres, to whose venom sound the open ear of youth doth always listen.
"Lascivious metres, to whose venom sound
The open ear of youth doth always listen" (KRII.2.1)
In the play. *York commenting on King Richard's penchant for flattery.*

Music, unpleasant and discordant - …Straining harsh discords and unpleasing sharps.
"It is the lark that sings so out of tune
Straining harsh discords and unpleasing sharps" (RJ.3.5)
Your comment on a poor musical execution.
In the play. *Juliet refers to the singing of the lark that signals the arrival of the morning when Romeo must flee for Mantua or be captured by the Verona police. Hence the music of the lark is discordant. For a better evaluation of the lark's singing see 'Psychological uplifting, her positive effect when you are down in the dumps. See 'Love, l. as an antidepressant. - … thy sweet love remembered such wealth brings…'*

Music, why good music has a silver sound – I say 'silver sound,' because musicians sound for silver.
"I say 'silver sound,' because musicians sound for silver" (RJ.4.5)
In the play. *Musicians due to play for Juliet's wedding to Paris must now play dirges for the (only apparent) death of Juliet. Peter, the bandmeister teases the players with a question.*

Music, why good music has a silver sound – I say 'silver sound,' because musicians sound for silver.
"I say 'silver sound,' because musicians sound for silver" (RJ.4.5)
In the play. *Musicians due to play for Juliet's wedding to Paris must now play dirges for the (only apparent) death of Juliet. Peter, the bandmeister teases the players with a question.*

Music, words of love like m - How silver sweet sound lovers' tongues by night like softest music to attending ears!
"How silver sweet sound lovers' tongues by night,
Like softest music to attending ears!" (RJ.2.2)
Drop this in passing after she has said something nice, at night of course.
In the play. *Romeo and Juliet (she on the balcony, he down in the garden) just cannot let go of each other.*

Musician, extraordinary m. - ... To his music, plants and flowers ever sprung...
Orpheus with his lute made trees,
And the mountain tops that freeze,
Bow themselves, when he did sing.
To his music, plants and flowers
Ever sprung; as sun and showers
There had made a lasting spring.
Every thing that heard him play,
Even the billows of the sea,
Hung their heads, and then lay by.
(KHVIII.3.1)
Lines for praise, e.g. '(He is like) Orpheus (who) with his lute....)
In the play. *Melancholy Queen Katharine asks a lady in waiting to sing for her and the lady obliges.*

Musicians, 'in' joke for m. – ... Marry, sir, because silver hath a sweet sound.
PETER. why 'music with her silver sound'? What say you, Simon Catling?
SIMON C. Marry, sir, because silver hath a sweet sound.
MUSICIAN. I say 'silver sound,' because musicians sound for silver.
(RJ.4.5)
In the play. *Musicians due to play for Juliet's wedding to Paris must now play dirges for the (only apparent) death of Juliet. Peter, the band-meister teases the players with a question..*

Naivete, innocence - You speak like a green girl, unsifted in such perilous circumstance.
"... you speak like a green girl,
Unsifted in such perilous circumstance." (H.1.3)
See also 'Error, e. admitted and due to youthful inexperience – Those were my salad days when I was green in judgement'.
In the play. *Polonius to daughter Ophelia who has told him of Hamlet's interest and love of her.*

Naivete, n. observed - How green you are and fresh in this old world!
"How green you are and fresh in this old world!" (KJ.3.4)
See also 'Error, e. admitted and due to youthful inexperience – Those were my salad days when I was green in judgement.'
In the play. *Card. Pandulph to Lewis of France who does not agree with the rosy forecasts of the cardinal.*

Name, n. or label, irrelevant - ... That which we call a rose by any other name would smell as sweet.
"What's in a name? That which we call a rose,
By any other name would smell as sweet." (RJ.2.2)
In the play. In the play. *Unbeknownst to Juliet, Romeo, after sneaking into her garden, listens to her monologue in which she muses about Romeo's last name, Montague. The Montagues are mortal enemies of her family, the Capulets.*

Put a stop to arguments about controversial definitions. Sometimes people like to give odd names, different from the original to the objects of their affection. In a 1787 letter to Agnes Maclehose, the poet Robert Burns addresses her as 'Clarinda' and extols the virtue of blending love and friendship, 'Such a composition is like adding cream to strawberries; it not only gives the fruit a more elegant richness, but has a peculiar deliciousness of its own… You cannot imagine, Clarinda (I like the idea of Arcadian names in a commerce of this kind) how much store I have set by the hopes of your future friendship….'

Name, hateful n. - The devil himself could not pronounce a title more hateful to mine ear.
MACBETH My name's Macbeth.
YOUNG SIWARD The devil himself could not pronounce a title
More hateful to mine ear. (M.5.7)
See also 'Hateful, I hate you as I hate hell - I hate the word, as I hate hell, all Montagues and thee.'
In the play. *In the battlefield the two enemies meet. Siward ion this instance will be the loser.*

Name, n. appropriately chosen - O how that name befits my composition!
KING RICHARD II What comfort, man? how is't with aged Gaunt?
JOHN OF GAUNT O how that name befits my composition! (KRII.2.1)
In the play. *Richard has come to visit the ailing John of Gaunt with a view to confiscate his domains after his death.*

Name, hearing n. is a source of pleasure - … and every tongue that speaks but Romeo's name, speaks heavenly eloquence.
"… and every tongue that speaks But Romeo's name, speaks heavenly eloquence." (RJ.3.2)

It could be an answer to 'Have you heard of So and So?' where So and So is a lady of interest to you, e.g. 'every tongue that speaks but (So and So's) name…'eloquence''. So and So could even be yourself if you by chance catch your name mentioned in the conversation of others and want to introduce a little irony.
In the play. *Juliet sees her nurse arriving and hopes she will bring news of Romeo.*

Name, hesitation to self-introduction – By a name I know not how to tell thee who I am.
"By a name I know not how to tell thee who I am" (RJ.2.2)
Answer to 'Who are you?' when you either wish to be somewhat mysterious or know that the person who asks holds entirely different views from yours.
In the play. *Romeo hesitates to introduce himself by name to Juliet as he is a Montague and she a Capulet.*

Name, is this your name? - Simple, you say your name is? Ay, for fault of a better.
MISTRESS QUICKLY. Peter Simple, you say your name is?
SIMPLE. Ay, for fault of a better." (MWW.1.4)
Answer to 'Is your name so and so?' Or, if you wish to imply irony, 'My name is XXX for fault of a better'.
In the play *Mistress Quickly acknowledges the presence of Simple*

Name, play on n., Pompey the Great - … your bum is the greatest thing about you; so that, in the beastliest sense
POMPEY. (My name is Pompey Bum)
ESCALUS. Truth, and your bum is the greatest thing about you; so that, in the beastliest sense, you are Pompey the Great (MFM.2.1)

Use the dialog entirely to size down a pompous guy, 'This reminds me of etc. etc.'
In the play. *Pompey is the servant to Mistress Overdone, keeper of a brothel. Her business, given the enforced morality standard of the new governor Angelo, is going down hill.*

Name, psychosomatic and/or negative reaction at just hearing a n. - I am whipp'd and scourg'd with rods, with pismires...
"I am whipp'd and scourg'd with rods,
Nettled and stung with pismires, when I hear
Of this vile politician, Bolingbroke." (KHIV p1.1.3)
Substitute for 'Bolingbroke' the hated politician or corporate technician of your choice. You can use 'ants' instead of 'pismires'.
In the play. *Hotpur justifies his impatience. 'Pismire' is another word for ant.*

Name, unpleasant n. due to past occurrences - ... A name unmusical to the Volscians' ears and harsh in sound to thine.
AUFIDIUS. What is thy name?
CORIOLANUS. A name unmusical to the Volscians' ears,
And harsh in sound to thine."
(COR.4.5)
Answer to "What is your name?" when meeting a competitor or a former enemy.
In the play. *Coriolanus passes to the Volsces and is met by their chief Aufidius.*

Narration, beginning of a narration of a fact - ... And let me speak to the yet unknowing world how these things came about.
"And let me speak to the yet unknowing world
How these things came about."
(H.5.2)

Introduction to a narrative, "Let me speak ... came about."
In the play. *Horatio explains to the just arrived Fortinbras, prince of Norway, the sequence of events that got just about everyone killed but Horatio.*

Nature, air, welcome to the air - ... Welcome, then, thou unsubstantial air that I embrace.
"...Welcome, then,
Thou unsubstantial air that I embrace!
The wretch that thou hast blown unto the worst
Owes nothing to thy blasts" (KL.4.1)
When you get out of a stuffy room with poor air circulation.
In the play. *Edgar in the heath where he meets with his father Gloucester who has been blinded by evil Cornwall and wife Goneril. See "Bad, from bad to good better than from good to bad - ... The lamentable change is from the best; the worst returns to laughter'.*

Nature, clouds spoiling a clear sky - the more fair and crystal is the sky the uglier seem the clouds that in it fly.
"Since the more fair and crystal is the sky,
The uglier seem the clouds that in it fly." (RII.1.1)
Comment on the cloud(s) that spoil your picnic or as use it as a comparison to accuse a foul contender.
In the play. *Bolingbroke accuses Mowbray of treason and challenges him to combat.*

Nature, dawn approaching - ... night's swift dragons cut the clouds full fast, and yonder shines Aurora's harbinger...
"...night's swift dragons cut the clouds full fast,
And yonder shines Aurora's harbinger;
At whose approach, ghosts, wandering here and there,

Troop home to churchyards"
(MND.3.2)
In the play. *Before the night is out Puck must remedy to the error he made in delivering a magic ointment to the wrong subject.*

Nature, dawn approaching - ... the gentle day before the wheels of Phoebus, round about dapples the drowsy east with spots of grey.
"...the gentle day,
Before the wheels of Phoebus, round about
Dapples the drowsy east with spots of grey." (MAAN.5.3)
In the play. *Don Pedro announces the dawn of the day of the wedding.*

Nature, dawn approaching – The glow-worm shows the matin to be near...
"The glow-worm shows the matin to be near,
And 'gins to pale his uneffectual fire" (H.1.5)
In the play. *Parting words from the Ghost to Hamlet. ('gins=begins).*

Nature, dawn at sea - ... the eastern gate ... turns into yellow gold his salt green streams.
"...the eastern gate, all fiery-red,
Opening on Neptune with fair blessed beams,
Turns into yellow gold his salt green streams" (MND.3.2)
In the play. *Oberon describes his habit of jogging on the beach waiting for the sun to rise to the spirit Puck*

Nature, dawn of a cloudy day - ... yon grey clouds that fret the clouds are messengers of day.
"...yon grey lines,
That fret the clouds, are messengers of day." (JC.2.1)
The meeting has extended until dawn and you remark accordingly

In the play. *Cinna and others dispute where is the East - which will determine the direction of the Capitol, where they will go and carry out the attack on Caesar.*

Nature, dawn, an hour before dawn - ... an hour before the worshipped sun...
"Madam, an hour before the worshipped sun
Peer'd forth the golden window of the east...." (RJ.1.1)
To make a nature statement, very early in the morning, modify slightly, '. The worshipped sun peers forth the golden window of the east.' Or use to announce that you will wake up early. "I'll get up an hour...east."
In the play. *Lady Montague asks Benvolio if he has seen Romeo.*

Nature, dawn, aurora - ... the all-cheering sun should in the furthest east begin to draw...
"... all so soon as the all-cheering sun
Should in the furthest east begin to draw
The shady curtains from Aurora's bed." (RJ.1.1)
Alternative for 'tomorrow morning' when answering the question 'when?' E.G. 'As soon as the all-cheering sun...bed.'
In the play. *Montague reflects and describes Romeo's behavior.*

Nature. dawn, before d. - Ere the sun advance his burning eye, The day to cheer and night's dank dew to dry...
"...ere the sun advance his burning eye,
The day to cheer and night's dank dew to dry,
I must fill up this osier cage of ours
With baleful weeds and precious-juiced flowers" (RJ.2.3)

In the play. *Friar Laurence makes a list of 'to do' things before the sun is up. 'Osier' is a basket made with strands of willow.*

Nature, dawn, just breaking - The silent hours steal on and flaky darkness breaks within the east.
"…The silent hours steal on,
And flaky darkness breaks within the east." (RIII.5.3)
In the play. *Derby confers with Richmond at Bosworth Field, the day of the battle that will see the end of Richard III.*

Nature, dawn, lights showing on clouds - … what envious streaks do lace the severing clouds in yonder east.
"…look, love, what envious streaks
Do lace the severing clouds in yonder east." (RJ.3.5)
In the play. *Romeo must hurry up and leave Juliet – he has been banished from Verona and besides Juliet's mother is arriving.*

Nature, dawn, smiling morning - The grey-eyed morn smiles on the frowning night, chequering the eastern clouds with streaks of light…
"The grey-eyed morn smiles on the frowning night,
Chequering the eastern clouds with streaks of light,
And flecked darkness like a drunkard reels
From forth day's path and Titan's fiery wheels:" (RJ.2.3)
Shorten to the first two lines. Beside as a nature statement, use as an alternative to "I must go" (if you must go), when it is early morning.
In the play, *Romeo calls on Father Lawrence to hastily organize the marriage with Juliet.*

Nature, dawn, night fled - The day begins to break, and night is fled…
"The day begins to break, and night is fled,
Whose pitchy mantle over-veil'd the earth." (KHVI p1.2.2)
In the play. *The duke of Bedford suggests to interrupt the pursuit of the French outside the town of Orleans.*

Nature, dawn, one hour before dawn - The hour before the heavenly-harness'd team…
"The hour before the heavenly-harness'd team
Begins his golden progress in the east." (KHIV p1.3)
In the play. *Glendower translates for Mortimer what Lady Mortimer said in Welsh.*

Nature, dawn, planet Venus waking up shepherd – Look, the unfolding star calls up he shepherd.
"Look, the unfolding star calls up he shepherd." (MFM.4.2)
The meeting has protracted into early morning
In the play. *The Duke (in disguise) is directing a plot designed to unmask the hypocrisy of Angelo*

Nature, dawn, sun and its gracious light – Lo in the orient when the gracious light…
"Lo in the orient when the gracious light
Lifts up his burning head." (SON.7)
It's a bit of a stretch, but hint that you wish to stay with her until breakfast so as to observe 'the gracious light that lifts up his burning head". Or, as the case applies, make a poetic comment on the rising sun.

Nature, dawn, sun on the mountains - Full many a glorious morning have I seen, flatter the mountain top with sovereign eye…
"Full many a glorious morning have I seen,
Flatter the mountain top with sovereign eye,

Kissing with golden face the meadows green;
Gilding pale streams with heavenly alchemy." (SON.33)

Nature, dawn, uncertainty or conflict between dark and light – ... When dying clouds contend with growing light...
"This battle fares like to the morning's war,
When dying clouds contend with growing light,
What time the shepherd, blowing of his nails,
Can neither call it perfect day nor night." (KHVI.p3.2.5)
In the play. *Henry VI comments on the uncertain development of the battle of Towton.*

Nature, deep forest – The trees, though summer, yet forlorn and lean...
"The trees, though summer, yet forlorn and lean,
O'ercome with moss and baleful mistletoe:
Here never shines the sun; here nothing breeds,
Unless the nightly owl or fatal raven" (TA.2.3)
In the play. *The evil Queen Tamora is found in a remote part of the forest with her lover Aaron.*

Nature, earthquakes explained - Diseased nature oftentimes breaks forth in strange eruptions...
"Diseased nature oftentimes breaks forth
In strange eruptions; oft the teeming earth
Is with a kind of colic pinch'd and vex'd
By the imprisoning of unruly wind Within her womb" (KHIV.p1.3.1)

Use the first line as a comment on violent thunder or apply metaphorically to the action of a person you despise.
In the play. *Hotspur disputes with Glendower whether an earthquake occurred when Glendower was born marked or not the importance of his nativity.*

Nature, extraordinary exceptional events - ... and I have seen the ambitious ocean swell and rage and foam...
"... and I have seen
The ambitious ocean swell and rage and foam,
To be exalted with the threatening clouds:
But never till to-night, never till now,
Did I go through a tempest dropping fire.
Either there is a civil strife in heaven,
Or else the world, too saucy with the gods,
Incenses them to send destruction." (JC.1.3)
See also 'Events, strange and extraordinary and given ominous meaning'
In the play. *Casca tells Cicero (a senator) about the unusual natural events witnessed portending to some impending drama, (in this case the assassination of Caesar).*

Nature, frost on flowers - ... hoary-headed frosts fall in the fresh lap of the crimson rose.
"...hoary-headed frosts
Fall in the fresh lap of the crimson rose" (MND.2.1)
In the play. *Titania describes the alterations of nature and seasons due to the bad mood of Oberon, jealous about the possession of a page boy. 'Hoary'='White'. 'Hoary-headed'='Having a white head, as typically brought about by age'.*

Nature, in between night and morning - What is the night?...

Almost at odds with morning, which is which.
MACBETH What is the night?
LADY MACBETH Almost at odds with morning, which is which (M.3.4)
In the play. *The end of the late dinner during which Macbeth fell ill by seeing the ghost of the slain Banquo.*

Nature, only n. has the power of improving itself - ... nature is made better by no mean but nature makes that mean.
"...nature is made better by no mean
But nature makes that mean" (WT.4.3)
In the play. *Polixenes, king of Bohemia, converses with Perdita and by means of analogies explains to her that she (of a lower stock) should not marry Florizel, Polixenes' son.*

Nature, light through the trees – The green leaves quiver with the cooling wind.
"The green leaves quiver with the cooling wind,
And make a chequered shadow on the ground." (TA.2.2)
Describe a familiar enough event in glowingly poetic tone.
In the play. *Taking advantage of the hunt Tamora secludes herself with Aaron in the woods.*

Nature, lightning - Jove's lightnings, the precursors of the dreadful thunder-claps.
Jove's lightnings, the precursors
Of the dreadful thunder-claps, more momentary,
And sight-out-running were not." (TEM.1.2)
Describe this common natural event.
In the play. *Ariel gives Prospero an account of his (well-intended but yet terrorist) acts performed on Prospero's order.*

Nature, moon shining bright and creating romantic environment - The moon shines bright: in such a night as this, when the sweet wind did gently kiss the trees…
"The moon shines bright: in such a night as this,
When the sweet wind did gently kiss the trees
And they did make no noise, in such a night
Troilus methinks mounted the Troyan walls
And sigh'd his soul toward the Grecian tents,
Where Cressid lay that night."
(MOV.5.1)
Enhance the quality of the time with this description. You may stop at 'did make no noise'. See also 'Sounds, gentle sounds propitious to love - Whiles hounds and horns and sweet melodious birds be unto us as is a nurse's song…'
In the play. *Lorenzo - alone with Jessica and babysitting Portia's house while Portia is absent – meditates on the nature of the moment.*

Nature, morning – But, soft! methinks I scent the morning air.
"But, soft! methinks I scent the morning air" (H.1.4)
In the play. *The Ghost in conversation with Hamlet*

Nature, morning, announced by the crows - …the busy day, waked by the lark, hath roused the ribald crows…
"…the busy day,
Waked by the lark, hath roused the ribald crows…" (TC.4.2)
In the play. *Troilus comments on the dawn of the day when Cressida will be sent to the Greeks*

Nature, morning - ... the morning steals upon the night melting the darkness...
"... the morning steals upon the night,
Melting the darkness" (TEM.5.1)

In the play. *With the help of Ariel Antonio and others find themselves dazed and in a circle but now Prospero decides that the magic will come to an end.*

Nature, morning giving way to afternoon - See how the morning opes her golden gates…
"See how the morning opes her golden gates,
And takes her farewell of the glorious sun!" (KHVI p3.2.1)
In the play. *Richard discusses with Edward the outcome of the battle that just took place.*

Nature, morning - … from whose silver breast the sun ariseth in his majesty.
"Lo, here the gentle lark, weary of rest,
From his moist cabinet mounts up on high,
And wakes the morning, from whose silver breast
The sun ariseth in his majesty;
Who doth the world so gloriously behold
That cedar-tops and hills seem burnish'd gold." (V&A)
In the play. *Venus has complained through one whole night about her rejection by Adonis.*

Nature, n. at its best - The birds chant melody on every bush… green leaves quiver with the cooling wind…
"The birds chant melody on every bush,
The snake lies rolled in the cheerful sun,
The green leaves quiver with the cooling wind
And make a chequer'd shadow on the ground" (TA.2.3)
In the play. *Tamora invites Aaron to love in the forest.*

Nature, night - … horrid night, the child of hell.
"…horrid night, the child of hell" (KHV.4.1)
See also entries for 'Time, night'.
In the play. *K Henry V meditates on the prerogatives of a king, who is (often) awake in the night, as opposed to the relaxed life of the average subject.*

Nature, night - … when the searching eye of heaven is hid behind the globe…
"…when the searching eye of heaven is hid,
Behind the globe" (KRII.3.2)
In the play. King Richard to the few remaining allies Aumerle and Carlysle, See 'Criminals, c. acting in the dark'

Nature, night - The dragon wing of night o'erspreads the earth.
"The dragon wing of night o'erspreads the earth." (TC.5.9)
In the play. *Achille has slain Hector and the battle between Greeks and Trojans draws to a temporary stop at the end of the day.*

Nature, night - … the night comes on, and the bleak winds do sorely ruffle…
"Alack, the night comes on, and the bleak winds
Do sorely ruffle; for many miles about
There's scarce a bush." (KL.2.4)
In the play. *Gloucester uselessly tries to inspire some pity for their father in the two evil daughters Regan and Goneril.*

Nature, night, decreases visibility and sharpens hearing - Dark night that from the eye his function takes, the ear more quick of apprehension makes…
"Dark night that from the eye his function takes,
The ear more quick of apprehension makes;
Wherein doth impair the seeing sense,

It pays the hearing double recompense." (MND.3.2)
An argument to suggest that a weakness can be compensated by a mirroring strength.
In the play. *Hermia arrives in the night - following sounds she finds Lysander who had run away from her following the effect of the drug poured by Puck in Lysander's ear.*

Nature, northern star - The skies are painted with unnumber'd sparks... but there is but one in all doth hold his place.
"The skies are painted with unnumber'd sparks,
They are all fire, and every one doth shine;
But there is but one in all doth hold his place." (JC.3.1)
Could be used as an alternative to pinpoint your strengths, (see 'Credentials, establishing your c. - I am as constant as the northern star...'). Answer to question 'Why should you be different from others?'
In the play. *Caesar compares himself to the Northern star as a symbol of firmness and stability of purpose.*

Nature, not quite dawn, not quite night – Almost at odds with morning, which is which.
MACBETH What is the night?
LADY MACBETH Almost at odds with morning, which is which. (M.3.4)
In the play. *At a late dinner with guests Macbeth is troubled by the appearance of Banquo's ghost. The dinner over, Macbeth will re-consult the witches.*

Nature, portentous events explained - ... they are portentous things unto the climate that they point upon.
"...When these prodigies
Do so conjointly meet, let not men say 'These are their reasons; they are natural;'

For, I believe, they are portentous things
Unto the climate that they point upon." (JC.2.3)
In the play. *Cassius gives Cicero a theory to explain the portentous natural events occurred the night before the Ides of March.*

Nature, sea and crested waves - The watery kingdom, whose ambitious head spits in the face of heaven.
"The watery kingdom, whose ambitious head
Spits in the face of heaven" (MOV.2.7)
In the play. *The Prince of Morocco has crossed the sea in the hope of solving the riddle and claiming the hand of Portia.*

Nature, shadow of honeysuckles - ... honeysuckles, ripen'd by the sun...
"...honeysuckles, ripen'd by the sun,
Forbid the sun to enter, like favourites,
Made proud by princes, that advance their pride
Against that power that bred it" (MAAN.3.1)
In the play. *Hero coaxes Margaret to meet in a secluded place so as to be overheard purposely by Beatrice.*

Nature, signs of tempest - The southern wind doth play the trumpet to his purposes.
"The southern wind
Doth play the trumpet to his purposes,
And by his hollow whistling in the leaves
Foretells a tempest and a blustering day." (KHIV.p1.5.1)
In the play. *At Shrewsbury and prior the decisive battle the Prince of Wales gives a report on weather conditions.*

Nature, sky - The skies are painted with unnumber'd sparks...

"The skies are painted with unnumber'd sparks,
They are all fire and every one doth shine,
But there's but one in all doth hold his place" (JC.3.1)
In the play. *Caesar elaborates and compares himself to a star that is untouched by motion, a metaphor for stability and clarity for purpose. See also 'Credentials, establishing your c. – constancy'.*

Nature, storm brewing - ... yond same black cloud, yond huge one, looks like a foul bombard that would shed his liquor.
"...another storm brewing;
I hear it sing i' the wind: yond same black
cloud, yond huge one, looks like a foul
bombard that would shed his liquor" (TEM.2.2)
In the play. *Trinculo observes the arriving of a storm.*

Nature, storm, the creation of a s. – For raging wind blows up incessant showers and when the rage allays, the rain begins.
"For raging wind blows up incessant showers,
And when the rage allays, the rain begins." (KHVI.p3.1.4)
In the play. *York, captured in the battle at Sandal Castle, compares the tears he will shed for his slain son Rutland to the evolution of a storm.*

Nature, stormy day - ... like an unseasonable stormy day which makes the silver rivers drown their shores...
"Like an unseasonable stormy day,
Which makes the silver rivers drown their shores,
As if the world were all dissolved to tears." (KRII.3.2)

Use as a comment on a stormy day or as an image and comparison for a sudden and unexpected turn of events.
In the play. *Lord Scroop compares the rage and terror of the usurping Bolingbroke to the effects of a bad storm.*

Nature, stormy sea – ... the sea puff'd up with winds rage like an angry boar chafed with sweat. "... the sea puff'd up with winds
Rage like an angry boar chafed with sweat." (TOS.1.2)
In the play. *See comment to 'Resistance, power of r. acquired via repeated trials'.*

Nature, stormy sea – ... the visitation of the winds who take the ruffian billows by the top...
"...the rude imperious surge
And in the visitation of the winds,
Who take the ruffian billows by the top,
Curling their monstrous heads and hanging them
With deafening clamour in the slippery clouds" (KHIVp2.3.1)
Suitable remark when your host is afraid that noise in the house may have disturbed your sleep. E.G. 'I can even sleep during the visitation of the winds...clouds'
In the play. *King Henry IV cannot sleep and wonders how can sailors manage to sleep even during a storm.*

Night, stormy sea - ... the wrathful skies gallow the very wanderers of the dark and make them keep their caves...
"...the wrathful skies
Gallow the very wanderers of the dark,
And make them keep their caves:
since I was man,
Such sheets of fire, such bursts of horrid thunder,
Such groans of roaring wind and rain,

I never
Remember to have heard" (KL.3.2)
In the play. *Kent comments on the storm endured by King Lear thrown out of doors by his evil daughters.*

Nature, stormy sea – When I have seen the hungry ocean gain advantage on the kingdom of the shore.
"When I have seen the hungry ocean gain
Advantage on the kingdom of the shore." (SON.44)

Nature, sunrise - The morn, in russet mantle clad walks o'er the dew of yon high eastern hill
"The morn, in russet mantle clad,
Walks o'er the dew of yon high eastern hill." (H.1.1)
A meeting has extended through the night and the early hour of the morning. Could be used as a prompt to end the meeting. Alternatively use it in a romantic setting.
In the play. *Horatio at the end of the watch when he too has seen the ghost.*

Nature, sunrise with threatening clouds - ... as doth the blushing discontented sun from out the fiery portal of the east...
"King Richard doth himself appear,
As doth the blushing discontented sun
From out the fiery portal of the east,
When he perceives the envious clouds are bent
To dim his glory and to stain the track
Of his bright passage to the occident." (KRII.3.3)
Answer to 'How are you?' when you are not too happy. E.G. 'Here I am, as doth the blushing… occident.'.
In the play. *The usurping Bolingbroke comments on the appearance of King Richard II coming out of Flint Castle in Wales*

Nature, sunset – ... the world's comforter, with weary gait his day's hot task hath ended in the west.
"Look, the world's comforter, with weary gait,
His day's hot task hath ended in the west" (V&A)
In the poem. *With the excuse of saying 'Good Night', Venus tries to steal a kiss from Adonis.*

Nature, sunset delayed - The sun of heaven methought was loath to set but stay'd and made the western welkin blush.
"The sun of heaven methought was loath to set,
But stay'd and made the western welkin blush" (KJ.5.5)
Enhance the description of an extraordinary day.
In the play. *King Lewis of France comments after an essentially victorious day of battle*

Nature, sunset, almost night - Night, whose black contagious breath already smokes about the burning crest…
"... this night, - whose black contagious breath
Already smokes about the burning crest
Of the old, feeble, and day-wearied sun." (KJ.5.4)
Alternative to 'it's night already'
In the play. *An English nobleman, Melun, wounded in battle has come to advise the English rebels to quit their rebellion against King John.*

Nature, sunset, at sea – The gaudy, blabbing and remorseful day is crept into the bosom of the sea.
"The gaudy, blabbing and remorseful day
Is crept into the bosom of the sea…" (KHVI.p2.4.1)

In the play. *The captain of a ship gets ready to receive the ransom for some captive prisoners. Soon Suffolk will go aboard the ship and be killed by the captain.*

Nature, sunset, before s. - … ere the weary sun set in the west.
"…ere the weary sun set in the west." (COE.1.2)
In the play. *An Ephesian merchant tells of a Syracusan merchant execution's (in Ephesus) before sunset.*

Nature, sunset, beginning of - the sun begins to gild the western sky.
"The sun begins to gild the western sky" (TGV.5.1)
In the play. *Old Eglamour gets ready to accompany Silvia in her search for the banished Valentine.*

Nature, sunset, golden s. boding well for tomorrow - The weary sun hath made a golden set and by the bright track of his fiery car…
"The weary sun hath made a golden set
And by the bright track of his fiery car
Gives token of a goodly day tomorrow." (KRIII.5.3)
Use as a positive note at end of speech
In the play. *Just before the battle at Bosworth Field, Richard sees in the golden sunset a good token of success.*

Nature, sunset, light dimming – Light thickens and the crow makes wing to the rooky wood.
"…Light thickens; and the crow Makes wing to the rooky wood" (M.3.3)
In the play. *Macbeth plans to have Banquo murdered when darkness comes.*

Nature, sunset, immediately after s. - The sun no sooner shall the mountains touch.
"The sun no sooner shall the mountains touch…" (H.4.1)
In the play. *King Claudius will dispatch Hamlet to England at sunset.*

Nature, sunset, still some light - The west yet glimmers with some streaks of day…
"The west yet glimmers with some streaks of day:
Now spurs the lated traveller apace
To gain the timely inn" (M.3.3)
In the play. *A contract-killer who will soon murder Banquo, considers the time of day.*

Nature, sunset, with signs of impending storm - Thy sun sets weeping in the lowly west, witnessing storms to come, woe and unrest.
"Thy sun sets weeping in the lowly west,
Witnessing storms to come, woe and unrest." (KRII.2.4)
In the play. *Lord Salisbury, still of king Richard's party senses the impending doom of the king while waiting for him to land in Wales from Ireland.*

Nature, things observed from above - … the murmuring surge, that on the unnumber'd idle pebbles chafes cannot be heard so high.
"…the murmuring surge,
That on the unnumber'd idle pebbles chafes,
Cannot be heard so high." (KL.4.6)
In the play. *Edgar, not recognized by his blind father Gloucester, pretends to lead him to the edge of Dover's cliffs where Gloucester really wanted to go.*

Nature, things seen from above – The crows… show scarce so gross as beetles.
"The crows and choughs that wing the midway air
Show scarce so gross as beetles" (KL.4.6)

'Choughs' are a species of crows, you can safely substitute with 'birds' for comprehension without altering the rhythm.
In the play. *Edgar not recognized by his blind father Gloucester, pretends to lead him to the edge of Dover's cliffs where Gloucester really wanted to go.*

Nature, tides – … the beached verge of the salt flood who once a day with his embossed froth…
"Timon hath made his everlasting mansion
Upon the beached verge of the salt flood;
Who once a day with his embossed froth
The turbulent surge shall cover" (TOA.5.1)
Change 'who' to 'that' to transform the quote into a poetical description of the tide.
In the play. *Timon's message to the Athenian senators. He will make his tomb at the edge of the sea.*

Nature, thunder - … as thunder when the clouds in autumn crack.
"For I will board her, though she chide as loud
As thunder when the clouds in autumn crack." (PER.1.2)
In the play. *Notwithstanding her shrewiness, Petruchio is not deterred from approaching Katharina.*

Nature, weather, cold - The air bites shrewdly; it is very cold.
"The air bites shrewdly; it is very cold" (H.1.4)
In the play. *Hamlet to Horatio while waiting on the platform for the appearance of the Ghost.*

Nature, weather, fearful w. – the strange impatience of the heavens.
"…and cast yourself in wonder,
To see the strange impatience of the heavens." (JC.1.3)
Passing comment to lightning and thunder, "O the strange impatience of the heavens."
In the play. *Cassius to Casca. Casca does not understand the reason of the strange un-natural phenomena that are taking place, including the impatience of the heavens. The reason for the unnatural events is the tyranny of Caesar,*
Why all these things change from their ordinance
Their natures and preformed faculties
To monstrous quality,--why, you shall find
That heaven hath infused them with these spirits,
To make them instruments of fear and warning
Unto some monstrous state.

Nature, weather, very foul weather, hurricane etc. – Diseased nature oftentimes breaks forth in strange eruptions.
"Diseased nature oftentimes breaks forth
In strange eruptions" (KHIV.p1.3.1)
Comment to particularly foul or nasty weather.
In the play. *Glendower claims that exceptional natural events marked his own nativity. Hotspur contradicts him.*

Nature, weather, very foul weather, hurricane etc. – Diseased nature oftentimes breaks forth in strange eruptions.

Nearness, wishing to be near loved one - If the dull substance of my flesh were thought…
"If the dull substance of my flesh were thought,
Injurious distance should not stop my way;
For then despite of space I would be brought,

From limits far remote where thou dost stay. " (SON 44)
See also 'Thought, power of t. and imagination to travel instantly - For nimble thought can jump both sea and land as soon as think the place where he would be.'

Necessity, brother to n. - I am sworn brother, sweet, to grim Necessity….
I am sworn brother, sweet,
To grim Necessity, and he and I
Will keep a league till death"
(KRII.5.1)
See also 'Past, happy p. as a dream - … learn, good soul, to think our former state a happy dream… '
In the play. *Richard II, deposed from the throne and on his way to prison, addresses his wife.*

Necessity, n. as a virtue - Teach thy necessity to reason thus; there is no virtue like necessity.
"Teach thy necessity to reason thus; There is no virtue like necessity." (KRII.1.2)
In the play. *Bolingbroke (the future Henry IV) has been exiled by Richard II and John of Gaunt, Bolingbroke's father, offers words of advice to cope with the banishment.*

Necessity, n. changing the appearance of things – The art of our necessities is strange, that can make vile things precious.
"The art of our necessities is strange, That can make vile things precious." (KL.3.2)
Retort to anyone who is belittling something modest but useful to you, for example, the old cup you use to drink your coffee. See also 'Estimation, e. differing among people - I never knew man hold vile stuff so dear.'
In the play. *Lear lost in a storm finds value in straw to protect himself from the cold.*

Necessity, n. overriding commitments and other concerns – Necessity will make us all forsworn…
"Necessity will make us all forsworn Three thousand times within this three years' space;
For every man with his affects is born, Not by might master'd but by special grace" (LLL.1.1)
See also 'Instinct, i. prevailing over the dictates of law - …the brain may devise laws for the blood…'
In the play. *Realistic Biron foresees the outcome of the oaths of study and abstinence undertaken by the King of Navarre and his friends.*

Necessity, n. as a sharp reminder – Necessity's sharp pinch!
"Necessity's sharp pinch!" (KL.2.4)
In the play. *Regan, one of the evil sisters suggests that Lear return to stay with Goneril, the other evil sister, but Lear makes it clear that he won't. Necessity's sharp pinch is being homeless.*

Necessity, political n. and drive for power - … necessity so bow'd the state that I and greatness were compell'd to kiss.
"…God knows, I had no such intent, But that necessity so bow'd the state That I and greatness were compell'd to kiss:" (KHIV p2.3.1)
Comment on your promotion.
In the play. *Henry IV recalls the events that led him to depose Richard II and ascend to the throne.*

Neglect, n. explained - Nor construe any further my neglect that poor Brutus…
"Nor construe any further my neglect, That poor Brutus with himself at war, Forgets the shows of love to other men." (JC.1.2)

Change 'Brutus' to your name. Answer or comment to statements of the type, 'You have not called me, why?' or 'You have not written to me' or 'You seem distant'. See also, "Mood, in a poor m. - Vexed I am, of late, with passions of some difference, conceptions only proper to myself, which give some soil, perhaps to my behaviours.'
In the play. *In conversation with Cassius, Brutus accepts that his inner turmoil prevents him to be sociable to his friends.*

Negligence, invocation - O negligence! Fit for a fool to fall by!
"…O negligence!
Fit for a fool to fall by!" (KHVIII.3.2)
In the play. *Cardinal Wolsey has betrayed himself by inadvertently allowing King Henry VIII to see a compromising letter that he (Wolsey) sent to the Pope.*

Negotiations, delegating power to negotiate - ... take with you free power to ratify, augment, or alter, as your wisdoms best ...
"… go with the king;
And take with you free power to ratify, Augment, or alter, as your wisdoms best
Shall see advantageable for our dignity" (KHV.5.2)
In the play. *King Henry V appoints Exeter and others to craft agreements with King Charles of France.*

Negotiator, a hard n. and petty to the penny - ... in the way of bargain, mark ye me, I'll cavil on the ninth part of a hair.
"But, in the way of bargain, mark ye me,
I'll cavil on the ninth part of a hair." (KHIV p1.3.1)
Indicate that you are a hard negotiator. Or change 'I'll' to 'he'll' to describe a pedantic or stingy negotiator.

In the play. *Hotspur's view of bargaining explained to Glendower.*

Neighbor, unreliable n. - ... the Scot, who hath been still a giddy neighbour to us.
"… the Scot,
Who hath been still a giddy neighbour to us" (KHV.1.2)
In the play. *King Henry V is afraid that the Scots attack England while he is attacking France.*

Negotiations, n. better after dinner –
... but when we have stuffed these pipes and these conveyances of our blood with wine and feeding…
"The veins unfilled, our blood is cold, and then
We pout upon the morning, are unapt
To give or forgive, but when we have stuffed
These pipes and these conveyances of our blood
With wine and feeding, we have suppler souls
Than in our priest like fasts."
(COR.5.1)
Postpone a business discussion till after lunch or dinner. See also 'Dinner, have it precede a meeting' – 'Dinner, invitation to a working d.'
In the play. *The Romans send Menenius to the Volscean camp in an attempt to persuade Coriolanus not to fight his own citizens. Menenius exposes his plan to talk business with Coriolanus after dinner.*

Negotiations, n. craftily conducted -
... this swift business I must uneasy make, lest too light winning make the prize light.
"... this swift business I must uneasy make, lest too light winning
Make the prize light." (TEM.1.2)
Use as an example to explain why a done deal is held up by the other party. See also entries for 'Playing hard-to-get'.

In the play. *Ferdinand, landed in the island as a result of the storm, has met Miranda and it is love at first sight. Prospero, talking to himself, favors the marriage of the two but not too hastily*.

Negotiations, no deal - No, he shall not knit a knot in his fortunes with the fingers of my substance.
"No, he shall not knit a knot in his fortunes with the fingers of my substance." (MWW.3.2)
Explain why you did not enter in an unprofitable agreement
In the play. *Anne Page loves Master Fenton but her father, Page Senior, who utters these lines, prefers a wealthier suitor. The 'he' is Master Fenton.*

New rich, weaknesses of the new rich - ... beggars mounted run their horse to death.
"…the adage must be verified, beggars mounted run their horse to death." (KHVI p3.1.4)
In the play. *The defeated York (in a battle near Wakefield), rails against Queen Margaret. Because she wasn't rich to begin with, York insults her, implying that her ambition will destroy her, just as beggars who become rich cannot manage their wealth.*

News, bad n. – ... uneven and unwelcome news…
"…more uneven and unwelcome news
Came from the north " (KHIVp1.1.1)
In the play. *Westmoreland tells King Henry of the rebels in the North.*

News, bad n. and reluctance to deliver it - Let not your ears despise my tongue for ever, which shall possess them with the heaviest sound that ever yet they heard.
"Let not your ears despise my tongue for ever,
Which shall possess them with the heaviest sound
That ever yet they heard." (M.4.3)
In the play. *Ross hesitates to deliver the news (to Macduff and Malcolm) that Macbeth has slain Macduff's wife and child.*

News, bad n. bearer - … thou art the midwife to my woe.
"So, Green, thou art the midwife to my woe,
And Bolingbroke my sorrow's dismal heir" (KRII.2.2)
In the play. *Green reports to the Queen the defection of various English Lords to Bolingbroke.*

News, bad n. causing the reader to pale - … that steals the colour from Bassanio's cheek.
"There are some shrewd contents in yon same paper,
That steals the colour from Bassanio's cheek" (MOV.3.2)
If you do not like the content of the message you can try, 'This steals the color from my cheek' See also 'Words, carrying bad news or offensive or poorly written'
In the play. *In Belmont, Bassanio pales at reading a letter from Venice from friend Antonio. The letter contains bad news about Antonio's sunken ships.*

News, bad n. circulating – There's villanous news abroad.
"There's villanous news abroad." (KHIV.p1.2.4)
In the play. *Falstaff refers to the news that a rebellion is brewing in England led by Percy.*

News, bad n. fitting the night - ... news fitting to the night, black, fearful, comfortless and horrible.
BASTARD Brief, then; and what's the news?
HUBERT O, my sweet sir, news fitting to the night,
Black, fearful, comfortless and horrible. (KJ.5.6)

In the play. *The news is that King John has been poisoned by a monk*

News, bad n. inferred by the look of the messenger - ... full of careful business are his looks!
"O, full of careful business are his looks!
Uncle, for God's sake, speak comfortable words" (KRII.2.2)
See also 'Speech, invitation to speak in mild tone - Speak sweetly, man, although thy looks be sour.'
In the play. *The Queen to the Duke of York who will confirm that most of the nobles have defected to Bolingbroke.*

News, bad n. inferred by the look of the messenger – ... whose heavy looks foretell some dreadful story hanging on thy tongue?
"But what art thou, whose heavy looks foretell
Some dreadful story hanging on thy tongue?" (KHVI p3.2.1)
Question someone who even before starting to speak has a very dismal and dejected look.
In the play. *Richard (Gloucester) to messenger who comes to announce that Gloucester's father Richard Plantagenet, duke of York has been slain.*

News, bad n. inferred by the look of the messenger - A fearful eye thou hast. Where is that blood, that I have seen inhabit in those cheeks?
"A fearful eye thou hast. Where is that blood,
That I have seen inhabit in those cheeks?
So foul a day clears not without a storm;
Pour down thy weather." (KJ.4.2)
Alternative to question, 'Why that dejected expression?'

In the play. *K. John to messenger arrived from France who brings the bad news that the French are ready to attack.*

News, bad n. inferred by the look of the messenger and delivered slowly – men judge by the complexion of the sky the state and inclination of the day...
"Men judge by the complexion of the sky
The state and inclination of the day;
So may you, by my dull and heavy eye,
My tongue hath but a heavier tale to say.
I play the torturer, by small and small
To lengthen out the worst that must be spoken" (KRII.3.2)
Prepare the audience to accept the loss of a contract to the competition. Or as a metaphor to predict the behavior of an audience, 'As men...day, so by looking at this audience I can say...' If the news you are bringing is good, keep the first two lines and modify the remainder – e.g. '...so may you from my expression gather that I have good news for you'.
In the play. *King Richard queries Lord Scroop on the expected reinforcements of the Duke of York, needed to battle the usurping Bolingbroke. But York himself has defected to Bolingbroke.*

News, bad n. inferred by the look of the messenger - the nature of bad news infects the teller
"The nature of bad news infects the teller." (AC.1.2)
Soften or prepare the delivery of unpleasant information.
In the play. *A messenger from Rome is reluctant to tell Antony that his wife Fulvia died.*

News, bad n. inferred by the look of the messenger - ... the whiteness in thy cheek is apter than thy tongue to tell thy errand.

"Thou tremblest; and the whiteness in thy cheek
Is apter than thy tongue to tell thy errand" (KHIV.p2.1.1)
In the play. *Northumberland greets Morton arriving from Shrewsbury where the rebels lost the battle and Hotspur was killed.*

News, bad n. like a cold wave - ... as flowers with frost or grass beat down with storms.
These tidings nip me, and I hang the head
As flowers with frost or grass beat down with storms." (TA.4.4)
In the play. *Matters begin to turn sour for the dreadful Emperor Saturnine. Lucius Andronicus is at the head of the Goths' army.*

News, bad n. recounted – ... at each word's deliverance, stab poniards in our flesh till all were told...
"Great Lord of Warwick, if we should recount
Our baleful news, and at each word's deliverance,
Stab poniards in our flesh till all were told,
The words would add more anguish than the wounds." (KHVI p3.2.1)
Comment on a bad turn of events
In the play. *Richard (Gloucester) to Warwick referring to the death of Richard (York).*

News, bad n. unwelcome – Though it be honest, it is never good to bring bad news...
"Though it be honest, it is never good
To bring bad news: give to a gracious message
An host of tongues; but let ill tidings tell
Themselves when they be felt."
(AC.2.5)
In the play. *Cleopatra calls back the messenger whom she previously beat for having reported that Antony married Octavia in Rome, clearly bad news for Cleopatra.*

News, barely capable to hear the n. – My heart hath one poor string to stay it by...
"My heart hath one poor string to stay it by,
Which holds but till thy news be uttered" (KJ.5.7)
In the play. *King John to Faulconbridge who will report that the French are ready to invade England after the English Lords have defected to the Dauphin.*

News, believability of a story - ... And let us once again assail your ears that are so fortified against our story.
"Sit down a while
And let us once again assail your ears
That are so fortified against our story." (H.1.1)
Convince a person about a piece of news, an event or a situation when you know that he/she must convince is a skeptic by definition or character. See also entries for 'Request, r. to be heard'
In the play. *The guard Bernardo has seen the ghost of the slain king of Denmark and Horatio does not believe it.*

News, better than expected - ... I have better news in store for you than you expect.
"... I have better news in store for you
Than you expect." (MOV.5.1)
In the play. *Portia tells Antonio that three of his ships that were thought lost at sea have actually arrived safely in Venice along with their cargo.*

News, chilling n. - Ay, by my faith, that bears a frosty sound.
"Ay, by my faith, that bears a frosty sound." (KHIV.p1.4.1)
In the play. *The rebel Worcester comments on the news that Glendower and his forces will be delayed and may not be arrive in time for the battle (Shrewsbury).*

News, condensing the n. - Short tale to make...
"Short tale to make, we at Saint Alban's met..." (KHVI.p3.2.1)
A poetical alternative to 'In summary'.
In the play. *Warwick recounts to the York brothers the loss of a battle near St. Alban's fought against the Lancastrians.*

News, conflicting n., not knowing how to react - Such welcome and unwelcome things at once 't is hard to reconcile.
"Such welcome and unwelcome things at once
'T is hard to reconcile." (M.4.3)
Comment on conflicting pieces of information arriving rapidly in succession.
In the play. *Macduff does not know what to make of Malcolm's conflicting declarations. At first Malcolm portrayed himself as unfit to reign because of his uncontrollable passions but later he recants and denies the charges he levied on himself. It was just a test.*

News, difficult to be delivered - ... the news I bring is heavy in my tongue.
"... the news I bring
Is heavy in my tongue." (LLL.5.2)
In the play. *Mercade interrupts the jolly meeting of the princess and her entourage with the King of Navarre and friends. Mercade has received the news that her ailing father died. See also 'Expression, facial expression as indication of impending utterings, compared to visual weather forecasting.'*

News, encouraging n. - ... Lines of fair comfort and encouragement.
"... here receive we from our father Stanley
Lines of fair comfort and encouragement" (KRIII.5.2)
Answer to 'What's in the letter?' or fax, memo, email. Change 'father Stanley' to the name of the writing person, or just use the second line.
In the play. *Richmond, disembarked at Tamworth, received comforting news from his father Stanley who is, however, in a hostage position with Richard.*

News, enough of bad n., dangers of ignoring it - ... if you be afeard to hear the worst then let the worst unheard fall on your bead.
KING JOHN. ...do not seek to stuff
My head with more ill news, for it is full.
PH. FAULCONBRIDGE. But if you be afeard to hear the worst,
Then let the worst unheard fall on your bead." (KJ.4.2)
Alternative to "No more of this" (first two lines) and retort (last two lines)
In the play. *King John senses the mounting of rebellion after the killing of young Prince Arthur and does not want to hear any more bad news –* that is a *messenger from France reports that the French are ready to attack.*

News, everybody knows it already - I speak no more than every one doth know.
"... you will find it so;
I speak no more than every one doth know." (KRII.3.4)
Answer to 'Is it really true?' when the matter is already known by many.
In the play. *The Queen overheard the gardener telling about King Richard II's abdication. The Queen is startled and at first angry with the gardener who defends himself.*

News, exhortation to deliver the n. - Pour out the pack of matter to mine ear, the good and bad together.
"Pour out the pack of matter to mine ear,
The good and bad together" (AC.2.5)
Answer to 'Do you want to hear first the good news or the bad news?'
In the play. *Cleopatra to messenger arriving from Rome with news of Antony.*

News, extraordinary n. beyond the power of songwriters – … such a deal of wonder is broken out within this hour that ballad-makers cannot be able to express it
"… such a deal of wonder is broken out within this hour that ballad-makers cannot be able to express it." (WT.5.2)
In the play. *A gentleman conveys to other gentlemen the news of the miracles happening at the court of Leontes, Leontes' lost daughter found, Hermione statue come to life etc.*

News, good and bad - … that is the best news … is colder tidings, yet they must be told.
"My liege, the Duke of Buckingham is taken;
That is the best news: that the Earl of Richmond
Is with a mighty power landed at Milford,
Is colder tidings, yet they must be told." (KRIII.4.5)
Follow up to question, 'Do you want first the good and next the bad news?'
In the play. *Catesby delivers good and bad news to Richard.*

News, good n. – (News) such as fill my heart with unhoped joys.
"(News) such as fill my heart with unhoped joys" (KHVI.p3.3.3)
In the play. *Q. Margaret has just heard that Edward has reneged on his commitment to marry the Lady Bona, sister of King Lewis of France.*

News, good news brought in by messenger – … he hath brought us smooth and welcome news.
"And he hath brought us smooth and welcome news" (KH.IV.p1.1.1)
In the play. *Sir Blunt has reported to the king the defeat of the Earl of Douglas by the King's forces.*

News, good n. delivered by a bad guy - Did ever raven sing so like a lark, that gives sweet tidings of the sun's uprise?
"Did ever raven sing so like a lark,
That gives sweet tidings of the sun's uprise?" (TA.3.1)
When you question the truth or the unexpected kindness from a questionable and usually deceitful person. See also 'Suspicion, s. at terms offered by a crook - I like not fair terms and a villain's mind.'
In the play. *The evil Aaron tells Titus his sons will be spared their life if he Titus chops his hand off. However dreadful the idea, Titus welcomes it and the voice of the raven (Aaron) sound like that of the lark.*

News, heavy n. and a heavy heart - … this heavy act with heavy heart relate.
"Myself will straight aboard: and to the state
This heavy act with heavy heart relate" (OTH.5.2)
In the play. *Ludovico leaves Cyprus for Venice where he will give an account of the tragic events regarding Othello, Desdemona etc.*

News, hesitation to give the n. - I am loath to tell you what I would you knew.
"I am loath to tell you what I would you knew." (AC.5.2)
In the play. *Dolabella hesitates to confirm to Cleopatra that she will be paraded in triumph in Rome by Octavian.*

News, I have reported all I know - The sum of all I can I have disclosed.
"The sum of all I can I have disclosed." (KRIII.2.4)
Answer to additional request of information. Alternative to "this is all I can do" or "this is all I know"

In the play. *Friends and relatives of Queen Elizabeth have been arrested by Richard - she asks the messenger who came with the news why and he does not know. Richard simply wanted to get rid of them.*

News, information, hesitation to deliver - I should report that which I say I saw but know not how to do it.
"I should report that which I say I saw,
But know not how to do it." (M.5.5)
In the play. *A messenger hesitates to report to Macbeth that he saw a forest on the move (as predicted by the witches). The forest is actually the camouflage of Malcolm's army, but still a close rendition of the prophecy.*

News, invitation to disclose (good) news - Ram though thy fruitful tidings in mine ears, that long time have been barren.
"Ram thou thy fruitful tidings in mine ears,
That long time have been barren." (AC.2.5)
Answer to 'Do you want to hear some good news?'
In the play. *Cleopatra prompts a messenger just arrived form Rome to give her news of Antony.*

News, messenger bringing good news at a bad time - O Westmoreland, thou art a summer bird.
"O Westmoreland, thou art a summer bird,
Which ever in the haunch of winter sings
The lifting up of day" (KHIV.p2.4.4)
Change 'Westmoreland to the name of the party who brings in the good news.
In the play. *London, the Jerusalem chamber at court. Ailing King Henry IV thinks Westmoreland who brings the news that all rebels are defeated and peace reigns in the land. 'Haunch' means 'in the latter part', here the latter part of winter.*

News, n. already known and not extraordinary – There needs no ghost, my lord, come from the grave to tell us this.
"There needs no ghost, my lord, come from the grave
To tell us this." (H.1.5)
Comment to information delivered as portentous or confidential but not really so.
In the play. *Hamlet has made a generalized statement and Horatio takes it to be a message from the Ghost to Hamlet. The statement is 'There's ne'er a villain dwelling in all Denmark but he's an arrant knave.'*

News, n. already known to everybody who is not deaf - … every one hears that who can distinguish sound
"…every one hears that,
Who can distinguish sound." (KL.4.6)
Comment on something branded as new or important, but in reality obvious. Or use as a reply to "Did you hear that?"
Answer to 'Did you hear'.
In the play. *A gentleman answers a question from Edgar. The referred to noise is the noise of a battle fought nearby between the French forces led by Cordelia's husband and the English.*

News, n. carrier spotted and a notorious gossip - …(news) which he will put on us as pigeons feed the young.
CELIA. Here comes Monsieur Le Beau.
ROSALIND. With his mouth full of news.
CELIA. Which he will put on us as pigeons feed the young. (AYLI.1.2)
Point out the expected behavior of an incoming gossip, 'with his mouth full of news which he will put…young'
In the play. *Le Beau brings news from court to the two ladies.*

News, n. delivered without spin – I will a round unvarnish'd tale deliver…
"I will a round unvarnish'd tale deliver…" (OTH.1.3)
In the play. *Othello skillfully uses modesty before delivering an accurate explanation of how Desdemona fell in love with him.*

News, n. depressing – I hang the head as flowers with frost.
"These tidings nip me; and I hang the head
As flowers with frost, or grass beat down with storms." (TA.4.4)
Comment to depressing news.
In the play. *Lucius, Titus' son, is advancing on Rome at the head of the Goths. Saturninus is dejected because he knows that the Romans will rather stand with Lucius than with him.*

News, n. eagerly expected and requested - I stand on fire, come to the matter.
" I stand on fire:
Come to the matter." (CYM.5.4)
Prompt to speak a slow or reluctant carrier of information.
In the play. *Cymbeline is eager to know from Iachimo what he knows about Imogen.*

News, n. fast reaching destination – Thither go these news, as fast as horse can carry them.
"Thither go these news, as fast as horse can carry them:" (KHVI.p2.1.4)
In the play. **The news York refers to is the arrest of the Duchess of Gloucester, accused of abetting sorcery. The news will be carried to the king at St. Albans'.**

News, n. gathered from hearsay - … this from rumour's tongue I idly heard; if true or false, I know not.
"… but this from rumor's tongue I idly heard; if true or false, I know not." (KJ.4.2)
Answer to "Where did you hear of this?"
In the play. *The messenger refers to the news that both Elinor (King John's mother) and Constance (mother of young Prince Arthur), are dead.*

News, n. hard and unpleasant to report - Such as my heart doth tremble to unfold
KING HENRY VI What tidings with our cousin Buckingham?
BUCKINGHAM Such as my heart doth tremble to unfold (KHVIp2.2.1)
Answer to 'What news?'
In the play. *Buckingham reports to the king about the discovery of witchcraft activities involving the wife of the Lord Protector. This was part of a set up to discredit and eliminate the Protector himself. Buckingham was one of the engineers of the plot.*

News, n. hotly and widely discussed – … men's mouths are full of it.
"…men's mouths are full of it." (KJ.4.2)
In the play. *Faulconbridge reports to King John on the arrival of the French and the stir the news has generated.*

News, n. incorrect - … many tales devis'd, which oft the ear of greatness needs must hear by smiling pick-thanks and base newsmongers.
"This extenuation let me beg,
As, in reproof of many tales devis'd, -
Which oft the ear of greatness needs must hear,
By smiling pick-thanks and base newsmongers." (KHIV p1.3.2)
Argument for self-defense, 'These are but tales devised by smiling pick-thanks and base newsmongers'.
In the play. *King Henry IV reprimands the Prince of Wales and he defends himself.*

News, n. leaked but not public - ... and may be left to some ears unrecounted.
"... this (news) is yet but young, and may be left
To some ears unrecounted."
(KHVIII.3.2)
Suggest that it is not time yet to divulge the news.
In the play. *The news is the impending marriage between K. Henry VIII and Anne Bullen.*

News, n. of an insurrection - ... and all goes worse than I have power to tell.
"...both young and old rebel,
And all goes worse than I have power to tell" (KRII.3.2)
Reporting on unhappiness among employees or troops.
In the play. *Lord Scroop tells King Richard II that the people of the realm are defecting to Bolingbroke.*

News, n. reported faithfully - All my reports go with the modest truth, nor more nor clipp'd, but so.
"All my reports go with the modest truth;
Nor more nor clipp'd, but so."
(KL.4.7)
In the play. *The faithful Kent to Cordelia who has come to England to save her father.*

News, n. strange almost a tale - his is the strangest tale that ever I heard.

"This is the strangest tale that ever I heard." (KHIVp1.5.4)
In the play. *Lancaster cannot believe Falstaff's tale about having wounded Hotspur in the thigh.*

News, n. that lacks credibility - There is no composition in these news that gives them credit.
"There is no composition in these news
That gives them credit." (OTH.1.2)

In the play. *The Duke of Venice disputes the accuracy of an assessment of size of the Turkish fleet near Cyprus.*

News, n. that is neither good nor bad - None good, my liege, to please you with the hearing...
RICHARD III Stanley, what news with you?
STANLEY. None good, my liege, to please you with the hearing,
Nor none so bad but well may be reported." (KRIII.4.4)
Announce news that is neither good or bad.
In the play. *Richmond is arriving by sea to fight Richard. For King Richard's comment see* 'Speech, why giving me the run around?'

News, no pleasure in delivering it - Little joy have I to breathe this news, yet what I say is true.
"Pardon me, madam: little joy have I
To breathe this news; yet what I say is true." (KRII.3.4)
In the play. *The Queen overheard the gardener telling about King Richard II's abdication. The Queen is startled and at first angry with the gardener who defends himself.*

News, not speculation but fact - I speak not this in estimation as what I think might be...
"I speak not this in estimation,
As what I think might be, but what I know
Is ruminated, plotted and set down..." (KHIVp1.1.3)
In the play. *Worcester announces that the archbishop of York may participate in the rebellion.*

News, nothing new - there is no news at court, sir; but the old news.
"There is no news at court, sir; but the old news." (AYLI.1.1)

660

Answer to "what's new with you?" or similar – e.g. 'There is no news with me but the old news'.
In the play. *Oliver summons the wrestler Charles and asks him of the news at court.*

News, promise requested to advise of one's whereabouts - ... let me hear from thee, for wheresoe'er thou art in this world's globe...
"... let me hear from thee;
For wheresoe'er thou art in this world's globe,
I'll have an Iris that shall find thee out." (KHVIp2.3.2)
In the play. *Queen Margaret to Suffolk who leaves for France after having been banished from England. Iris was the daughter of Thaumas, a sea god and of Electra, a sea nymph. Iris personified the rainbow and was a messenger of then Gods, a kind of Federal Express messenger.*

News, questionable – ... is so like an old tale, that the verity of it is in strong suspicion.
"... this news, which is called true, is so like an old tale, that the verity of it is in strong suspicion." (WT.5.2)
Cast doubt about some questionable information. A variant to 'it's too good to be true'.
In the play. *Leontes has found out who Perdita really is, (his own daughter), with great happiness of course and an anonymous gentleman comments on the event.*

News, ready to receive the bad n. – Glad am I that your highness is so arm'd to bear the tidings of calamity.
"Glad am I that your highness is so arm'd
To bear the tidings of calamity." (KRII.3.2)
In the play. *Lord Scroop starts a report to King Richard on the doings of Bolingbroke in England*

News, ready to receive the bad n. - Mine ear is open and my heart prepared.
"Mine ear is open and my heart prepared
....
The worst is death, and death will have his day." (KRII.3.2)
Answer to 'Do you want to hear the news?'
In the play. *King Richard II is ready to hear the news that Lord Scroop has come to deliver, namely that many lords have defected to the usurping Bolingbroke.*

News, refusal to listen to any more n. good or bad - My ears are stopt and cannot hear good news, so much of bad already hath possess'd them.
"My ears are stopt and cannot hear good news,
So much of bad already hath possess'd them" (TGV.3.1)
In the play. *Proteus reaches Valentine to tell him that he is banned from Milan but Valentine knows that already.*

News, source of it apparently reliable – A gentleman well bred and of good name...
"A gentleman well bred and of good name,
That freely render'd me these news for true." (KHIVp2.1.1)
In the play. *Bardolph quotes the source of information who said that the rebels had won than lost the battle of Shrewsbury.*

News, the n. is true – It is true, without any slips of prolixity or crossing the plain highway of talk.
"...But it is true, without any slips of prolixity or crossing the plain highway of talk." (MOV.3.1)
Answer to 'Is it true?'
In the play. *Salanio, conversing with Salarino, confirms the news of the shipwreck of one of Antonio's ships.*

News, unbelievable n. were it not for the evidence - ...That which I shall report will bear no credit, were not the proof so nigh.
"Most noble sir,
That which I shall report will bear no credit,
Were not the proof so nigh." (WT.5.1)
Use before announcing an important or striking finding or conclusion.
In the play. *Florizel, son of the king of Bohemia, has traveled to Sicilia with Perdita, the daughter of Leontes, king of Sicilia and a Lord announces the (at first hand unbelievable) event to Leontes.*

News, uncertain nature of the n. detected by the expression of the messenger - Though news be sad, yet tell them merrily; if good, thou shamest the music of sweet news...
"Though news be sad, yet tell them merrily;
If good, thou shamest the music of sweet news
By playing it to me with so sour a face." (RJ.2.5)
Prompt the messenger to deliver the news if you detect some hesitation.
In the play. *The nurse arrives from her encounter with Romeo and Juliet is anxious to hear news.*

News, unwelcome n. makes messenger unwelcome - ... the first bringer of unwelcome news hath but a losing office.
"Yet, the first bringer of unwelcome news
Hath but a losing office; and his tongue
Sounds ever after as a sullen bell,
Remember'd tolling a departing friend." (KHIVp2.1.1)
Soften the impact of the news you are about to give, 'I well know that the first bringer...office'.
In the play. *Northumberland to Morton who hesitates to report about the lost battle of Shrewsbury.*

News, unwelcome n. makes messenger unwelcome - ... harm within itself so heinous is as it makes harmful all that speak of it.
SALISBURY What other harm have I, good lady, done,
But spoke the harm that is by others done?
CONSTANCE Which harm within itself so heinous is
As it makes harmful all that speak of it. (KJ.3.1)
In the play. *The harm referred to is an agreement between Lewis of France and John of England that would exclude Arthur from his rights to the English throne.*

Night and morning reversed by her presence - 'tis fresh morning with me when you are by at night.
"...'Tis fresh morning with me,
When you are by at night." (TEM.3.1)
She turns the night into morning. Compliment.
In the play. *Ferdinand is madly in love with Miranda.*

Night, best suited for work at hand - Deep night, dark night, the silent of the night...
"Deep night, dark night, the silent of the night,
The time of night when Troy was set on fire;
The time when screech-owls cry and ban-dogs howl,
And spirits walk and ghosts break up their graves,
That time best fits the work we have in hand." (KHVI.p2.1.4)
In the play. *The Duchess of Gloucester, prompted by Bolingbroke, starts witching ceremonies intended to help her revenge against Queen Margaret. 'Ban-dog'='Watch-dog'*

Night, effects of a cold n. - This cold night will turn us all to fools and madmen.
"This cold night will turn us all to fools and madmen." (KL.3.4)
In the play. *The fool commenting on the cold and stormy night.*

Night, face of lover eliminating night's darkness - "It is not night when I do see your face…
"It is not night when I do see your face,
Therefore I think I am not in the night" (MND.2.1)
See also 'Night and morning reversed by her presence - 'tis fresh morning with me when you are by at night.
In the play. *Demetrius reproaches Helena for having followed him in the wood at night and Helena responds*

Night, n. and reduced visibility – (the) smoke and dusky vapours of the night…
"…as far as I could well discern
For smoke and dusky vapours of the night…" (KHVI.p1.2.2)
In the play. *Burgundy, still in the English field could not see where Joan of Arc went after she left Orleans.*

Night, n. holding record of strange events - … I have seen hours dreadful and things strange; but this sore night..
"…I have seen
Hours dreadful and things strange;
but this sore night
Hath trifled former knowings." (M.2.4)
See also 'Events, strange and extraordinary and given ominous meaning'
In the play. *An old man comments on the night at Macbeth castle, following the slaying of King Duncan by Macbeth.*

Night, n. to think it over - A night is but small breath and little pause to answer matters of this consequence.
"A night is but small breath and little pause
To answer matters of this consequence." (KHV.2.4)
In the play. *The King of France will deliver next day his answer to K. Henry's ultimatum.*

Night, nightmare – O, I have pass'd a miserable night, so full of ugly sights, of ghastly dreams.
"O, I have pass'd a miserable night,
So full of ugly sights, of ghastly dreams,
That, as I am a Christian faithful man,
I would not spend another such a night,
Though 'twere to buy a world of happy days,
So full of dismal terror was the time!" (RIII.1.4)
Answer to 'Did you sleep well?' when you didn't. See also 'Sleep, troubled s. - I have been troubled in my sleep this night, but dawning day new comfort hath inspired.'
In the play. *The Duke of Clarence tells his keeper Brakenbury about his very recent dream and nightmare.*

Night, nightmare, waking up from a n. - I trembling waked, and for a season after could not believe but that I was in hell…
"I trembling waked, and for a season after
Could not believe but that I was in hell,
Such terrible impression made the dream." (KRIII.1.4)
Applicable to a nightmare but possibly to a place you did not like, omitting 'I trembling waked'

In the play. *Held in the tower of London, Clarence has a prophetic nightmare which he relates to his keeper Brakenbury.*

Night, preferring n. to day – … let us be Diana's gentlemen of the shade, minions of the moon.
"…let us be Diana's foresters, gentlemen of the shade, minions of the moon" (KHIV p1.1.2)
You wish to declare yourself as a night lover, e.g. 'I am Diana's forester, a gentleman of the shade, a minion of the moon.
In the play. *Falstaff in conversation with the Prince of Wales.*

Night, preferring n. to day - … we that take purses go by the moon and the seven stars.
"… for we that take purses go by the moon and the seven stars, and not by Phoebus, he ,'that wandering knight so fair.'" (KHIV p1.1.2)
You wish to declare yourself as a night lover, e.g. 'I go by the moon and the seven starts… fair'.
In the play. In the play. *Falstaff proposes a new categorization of himself and the Prince of Wales, once the prince will be king.*

Night, slowly passing - … the cripple tardy-gaited night, who … doth limp so tediously away.
"And chide the cripple tardy-gaited night
Who, like a foul and ugly witch, doth limp
So tediously away". (KHV.4.prologue)
In the play. *The chorus describes the night before the battle of Agincourt. 'Gait' = 'the way of walking'. To chide' = 'To rebuke, to scold', here used figuratively.*

Night, starry n. – the floor of heaven is thick inlaid with patines of bright gold…

"…the floor of heaven
Is thick inlaid with patines of bright gold" (MOV.5.1)
See also lines 'this majestical roof fretted with golden fire' in 'World, pessimistic view of the w., a congregation of vapors – it goes so heavily with my disposition that this goodly frame, the earth…'
In the play. *Lorenzo and newly married Jessica have been housesitting for Bassanio and Portia and Lorenzo waxes romantic. See also 'Moonlight, by the m. – How sweet the moonlight sleeps upon this bank!'*

Night, stormy or unpleasant, no suitable for going out - … things that love night love not such nights as these.
"…things that love night
Love not such nights as these"
(KL.3.2)
Comment on a stormy night.
In the play. *Kent commenting on the storm to which he and King Lear are exposed.*

Night, stormy n. hard to bear - The tyranny of the open night's too rough for nature to endure.
"The tyranny of the open night's too rough
For nature to endure" (KL.3.4)
Why you do not go outside in such bad weather or suggest to a guest not to. Alternative to 'Let's go inside'.
In the play. *Kent invites K. Lear to take shelter from the stormy night.*

Night, wish for n. to come – Come, civil night, thou sober-suited matron, all in black.
**Gallop apace, you fiery-footed steeds,
Towards Phoebus' lodging: such a wagoner
As Phaethon would whip you to the west,
And bring in cloudy night immediately.**
…

**Come, gentle night, come, loving, black-brow'd night,
Give me my Romeo…**
…
**…Come, civil night,
Thou sober-suited matron, all in black** (RJ.3.2)
Substitute 'Romeo' for the object of your desires. See also 'Invocation, i. for lover to come – … come, thou day in night; for thou wilt lie upon the wings of night whiter than new snow on a raven's back.' *** 'Anticipation, day tedious waiting for night - so tedious is the day as is the night before some festival to an impatient child…'
In the play. *Juliet is eagerly awaiting for Romeo.*

Nightmares, no fear from nightmares - Let not our babbling dreams affright our souls…
"**Let not our babbling dreams affright our souls:
Conscience is but a word that cowards use,
Devised at first to keep the strong in awe.**" (KRIII.5.3)
At the end of the description of your own nightmare. Use the first line to inspire courage when you detect pessimism.
In the play. *Richard III rallies his troops prior to the battle of Bosworth, though he knows he has a bad conscience. See also 'Conscience, imperialistic attitude.'*

Noise, injunction to cut out noise - Silence that dreadful bell: it frights the isle from her propriety.
"**Silence that dreadful bell: it frights the isle
From her propriety.**" (OTH.2.3)
When the meeting is continuously interrupted by a ringing phone or similar. Change 'bell' to 'noise' or 'music' as applicable.

In the play. *The perfidious Iago has engineered a brawl involving Cassio and Montano. An alarm bell sounds and the intervening Othello wants the noise (of the bell) to stop. The 'isle' is Cyprus where the action occurs.*

Noise, loud n. generated via arguing – … mortal ears might hardly endure the din.
"**… mark'd you not, how her sister
Began to scold; and raise up such a storm,
That mortal ears might hardly endure the din?**" (TOS.1.1)
Point out a noisy person or a noise. E.G. '(He/she) raises up such a storm… din'. Or, 'This is so noisy that mortal ears…din'. See also 'Nature, stormy day - …like an unseasonable stormy day which makes the silver rivers drown their shores…'
In the play. *Tranio points out to Lucentio Katharina's asperity of character.*

Noise, make absolutely no n. - … tread softly, that the blind mole may not hear a footfall.
"**…tread softly, that the blind mole may not
Hear a foot fall**" (TEM.4.1)
In the play. *Caliban to co-conspirators Stephano and Trinculo. They have arrived close to Prospero's cell.*

Nonsense, stop talking n. – Peace, peace, Mercutio, peace! Thou talk'st of nothing
"**Peace, peace, Mercutio, peace!
Thou talk'st of nothing**" (RJ.1.4)
Change 'Mercutio' with the name of the nonsense speaking party. You may follow up using the lies from 'Dreams, delusions – … I talk of dreams, which are the children of an idle brain, begot of nothing but vain fantasy.' Changing 'I' to 'You'.

In the play. *Mercutio is delivering a long-winded description of fairy Queen Mabe and Romeo pleads for a halt to the nonsense.*

Nonsense, stop the n. - ... leave thy vain bibble babble.
"...leave thy vain bibble babble." (TN.4.2)
In the play. *The clown to Malvolio, who, as a consequence of a prank, has been confined to a dark cellar.*

Nose, importance of the olfactory sense - ... a good nose is requisite also, to smell out work for the other senses.
"... a good nose is requisite also, to smell out work for the other senses" (WT.4.3)
Should you ever be congratulated for your keen sense of smell.
In the play. *The scoundrel Autolycus describes his own strengths as a thief.*

Nostalgia, regret - When to the session of sweet silent thought, I summon up remembrance of things past...
"When to the session of sweet silent thought,
I summon up remembrance of things past,
I sigh the lack of many a thing I sought,
And with old woes new wail my dear time's waste." (SON.30)
Use the first two lines to introduce your description or narration of a memory or the quote completely to sound a melancholy note about lost time and happier times gone by.

Notes, note-taking – Fery goot: I will make a prief of it in my note-book.
"Fery goot: I will make a prief of it in my note-book..." (MWW.1.1)

In the play. *Sporting a heavy Welsh accent, Master Evans takes notes on comments by Master Page.*

Notes, note-taking – I will set down what comes from her, to satisfy my remembrance the more strongly.
"...I will set down what comes from her, to satisfy my remembrance the more strongly." (M.5.1)
In the play. *The doctor takes notes of what Lady Macbeth says during sleepwalking.*

Numbers, n. unnecessary - Spare your arithmetic.
"Spare your arithmetic" (CYM.2.4)
When your adversary attacks you with questionable statistics.
In the play. *Leonatus refuses to hear more (actually contrived) evidence of Imogen's adultery.*

Oak, old o. also metaphor for old age – ... an oak, whose boughs were moss'd with age and high top bald with dry antiquity.
"...an oak, whose boughs were moss'd with age
And high top bald with dry antiquity" (AYLI.4.2)
In the play. *The repented Oliver narrates an adventure in the forest involving his brother Orlando.*

Oath - ... by this pale queen of night I swear...
"... by this pale queen of night I swear" (TGV.4.2)
In the play. *Silvia proclaims vehemently that she does not want to have anything to do with the pursuing Proteus.*

Oath, all sort of bad things may happen to me if... - ... myself myself confound!... if
"...myself myself confound!
Heaven and fortune bar me happy hours!
Day, yield me not thy light; nor, night,

thy rest!
Be opposite all planets of good luck
To my proceedings, if, with pure heart's love,
Immaculate devotion, holy thoughts,
I tender not thy beauteous princely daughter!" (KRIII.4.4)
In the play. *Now king, Richard wants to marry Elizabeth's daughter after slaughtering Elizabeth's young son.*

Oath, curse should an o. not be kept - ... And let him ne'er see joy that breaks that oath!
"We all have strongly sworn to give him aid;
And let him ne'er see joy that breaks that oath!" (KRII.2.3)
In the play. *Northumberland to York. The oath of aid was made to Bolingbroke.*

Oath, excuse for breaking an o. - ... but, for a kingdom, any oath may be broken
YORK. I took an oath that he should quietly reign "
EDWARD But, for a kingdom, any oath may be broken: I'd break a thousand oaths to reign one year." (KHVI p3.1.2)
Cite the example to justify skepticism that some commitment or other will be kept if a better opportunity arises that conflicts with the commitment Common tool of politicians to further their advancement, though never openly admitted.
In the play. *At Sandal Castle Edward prompts his father York to break the oath according to which York would be the successor when Henry VI would die.*

Oath, excuse for breaking an o. - ...The truth is then most done not doing it
"What since thou sworest is sworn against thyself
And may not be performed by thyself,
For that which thou hast sworn to do amiss
Is not amiss when it is truly done,
And being not done, where doing tends to ill,
The truth is then most done not doing it" (KJ.3.1)
In the play. *Cardinal Pandulph moves King Philip of France on reneging on his pact of alliance with England.*

Oath, excuse for breaking an o. - An oath is of no moment, being not took before a true and lawful magistrate...
"An oath is of no moment, being not took
Before a true and lawful magistrate,
That hath authority over him that swears" (KHVI p3.1.2)
Governments use similar arguments to justify their own crimes.
In the play. *Richard finds a rationale for York to break an oath.*

Oath, excuse for breaking an o. - It is great sin to swear unto a sin...
"It is great sin to swear unto a sin,
But greater sin to keep a sinful oath." (KHVI p2.5.1)
Cheap excuses by politicians to confuse the people or (worse) to appease their conscience over their crimes and the crimes of their government.
In the play. *Salisbury turns his coat against King Henry VI who reminds Salisbury about his oath of allegiance. Salisbury gives this answer and continues, inventing reasons that make no sense because King Henry VI is the epitome of peace, goodness and lack of violence.*
'Who can be bound by any solemn vow
To do a murderous deed, to rob a man,
To force a spotless virgin's chastity,
To reave the orphan of his patrimony,
To wring the widow from her custom'd right,
And have no other reason for this wrong
But that he was bound by a solemn oath?'

at which Queen Margaret comments, 'A subtle traitor needs no sophister.'

Oath, excuse for breaking an o. - To keep that oath were more impiety than Jephthah's, when he sacrificed his daughter.
"To keep that oath were more impiety
Than Jephthah's, when he sacrificed his daughter." (KHVI p3.5.1)
In the play. *Clarence arrives at Coventry and suddenly reneges on his allegiance to Warwick. Warwick is his father in law. Clarence will remember his treachery and repent in the play Richard III, while imprisoned in the tower of London. Jephthah was a Jewish leader who fought the Ammonites. He had vowed that, should he win the battle, he would sacrifice the first person whom he met afterwards. And the first person he met was his daughter.*

Oath, no o. needed - do not stain the even virtue of our enterprise...
"Swear priests and cowards and men cautelous,
Old feeble carrions and such suffering souls
That welcome wrongs...
...but do not stain
The even virtue of our enterprise,
Nor the insuppressive mettle of our spirits,
To think that or our cause or our performance
Did need an oath" (JC.2.1)
In the play. *Brutus tells Cassius that no oaths are necessary to undertake the task of freeing Rome from the danger of dictatorship.*

Oath, no reason could make me break this o. - ... (not) for all the sun sees or the close earth wombs...
"...(not) for all the sun sees or
The close earth wombs or the profound sea hides
In unknown fathoms, will I break my oath
To this my fair beloved:" (WT.4.3)

Answer to 'Can I trust you?' or 'Do you really mean it?' For an opposite view see 'Oath, excuse for breaking an o.'
In the play. *Polixenes commands Camillo to advise Florizel to break his engagement with Perdita on penalty of losing his inheritance and title to the throne. Florizel refuses. Fathom' = a unit of measure equal to six feet, used to measure depth'.*

Oaths, not easily given to pronounce o. but maintaining them when given – ... I never use till urged, nor never break for urging.
"...oaths, which I never use till urged, nor never break for urging" (KHV.5.2)
Modify to 'Oaths I never use till urged... urging',
In the play. *Henry V modestly woos Kathryn of France.*

Oath, resolution broken - ... Breaking his oath and resolution, like a twist of rotten silk.
"...Breaking his oath and resolution, like
A twist of rotten silk." (COR.5.6)
Characterize anyone on whose word cannot be relied on
In the play. *Aufidius is angry at Coriolanus who has abandoned the Volsces, following the prayers of Coriolanus' wife and mother.*

Oath, solemn o. taken – ... In the due reverence of a sacred vow I here engage my words.
"Now, by yond marble heaven,
In the due reverence of a sacred vow
I here engage my words." (OTH.3.3)
In the play. *Othello's oath of revenge against Cassio and Desdemona for their alleged (and false) infidelity.*

Oath, sworn o. invalid if the premises of the o. are false – ... if you swear by that that is not, you are not forsworn.
"...if you swear by that that is not, you are not forsworn' (AYLI.1.2)

In the play. *The Clown says that if Celia (a beardless girl) were to swear by her beard, her o. would be invalid. His example explains a previous clownish pronouncement of his.*

Oaths, o. unnecessary between gentlemen - I'll take thy word for faith, not ask thine oath…
"I'll take thy word for faith, not ask thine oath;
Who shuns not to break one, will sure crack both." (PER.1.2)
When you think that trust is adequate and that an agreement is not necessary.
In the play. *Fearing the reprisal of the powerful Antioch, Pericles will leave Tyre for a while, leaving the government in the hands of Helicanus. An oath of allegiance is not needed due to the Helicanus' integrity.*

Oaths, unreliable o. or vows - … those mouth-made vows which break themselves in swearing.
"…Riotous madness,
To be entangled with those mouth-made vows,
Which break themselves in swearing!" (AC.1.3)
In the play. *As Antony cheated on Fulvia, Cleopatra mistrusts (and rightly so) Antony's oaths of faithfulness.*

Obedience, complete o. - I am your shadow, my lord; I'll follow you
"I am your shadow, my lord; I'll follow you." (KHIVp2.2.2)
Answer to 'Will you come with me?', omit 'my lord' or leave it in for irony.
In the play. *Prince Harry proposes to Poins another prank to be played on Falstaff and Poins agrees in obedience.*

Obedience, immediate o. - Proud of employment, willingly I go.
"Proud of employment, willingly I go." (LLL.2.1)
Show your willingness to obey the order. See also 'Command given with some arrogance, reaction to - When Caesar says 'do this,' it is perform'd.'
In the play. *The Princess has told Boyet to deliver a message to the King and Boyet complies.*

Obedience, o. and execution – … Performance shall follow.
BAWD Get this done as I command you.
BOULT Performance shall follow
(PER.4.2)
Answer to 'do this' from your boss. See also 'Command given with some arrogance, reaction to - When Caesar says 'do this,' it is perform'd.'
In the play. *The command refers to advertising the beauties of Marina to the male population of Mytilene.*

Obedience, o. and the ideal capitalist system - … for so work the honey-bees…
"Obedience: for so work the honey-bees,
Creatures that by a rule in nature teach
The act of order to a peopled kingdom.
They have a king and officers of sorts;
Where some, like magistrates, correct at home,
Others, like merchants, venture trade abroad,
Others, like soldiers, armed in their stings,
Make boot upon the summer's velvet buds,
Which pillage they with merry march bring home
To the tent-royal of their emperor;
Who, busied in his majesty, surveys
The singing masons building roofs of gold,
The civil citizens kneading up the honey,
The poor mechanic porters crowding in
Their heavy burdens at his narrow

gate,
The sad-eyed justice, with his surly hum,
Delivering o'er to executors pale
The lazy yawning drone" (KHV.1.2)
See also 'Organization, perfect management o. such as the bees - … So may a thousand actions, once afoot. end in one purpose…'
In the play. *The Bishop of Canterbury lectures the King on the perfect organizational structure.*

Obedience, o. declared - my voice shall sound as you do prompt mine ear.
"My voice shall sound as you do prompt mine ear,
And I will stoop and humble my intents
To your well-practised wise directions" (KHIV.p2.5.2)
Answer to 'Will you do as I say?' when you wish to agree and inject some mild irony.
In the play. *King Henry V, repenting of his youthful follies, humbly acknowledges the wisdom and rectitude of the Chief Justice.*

Obedience, o. or responsibility? - … our obedience to the king wipes the crime of it out of us
"for we know enough, if we know we are the king's subjects: if his cause be wrong, our obedience to the king wipes the crime of it out of us." (KHV.4.1)
The argument to sustain crimes against humanity by armies and similar.
In the play. *Soldier Bates to King Henry (incognito) who said that the cause is just and the quarrel honorable (meaning the invasion of France).*

Obedience, o. to authority as justification of crime - My commission is not to reason of the deed, but do it.
"My commission
Is not to reason of the deed, but do it." (PER.4.1)
Universal *reason through the ages to cast conscience in the toilet and commit all sort of crimes.*
In the play. *Contract killer Leonine is deaf to Marina's pleadings.*

Obedience, passive o. expected – It fits thee not to ask the reason why because we bid it…
"It fits thee not to ask the reason why, Because we bid it. Say, is it done?" (PP.1.1)
In the play. *Antiochus instructs Thaliard to go and kill Pericles who has solved the riddle and knows of Antiochus' incest.*

Obedience, we'll do as you say - Well hast thou lesson'd us; this shall we do.
"Well hast thou lesson'd us; this shall we do." (TA.5.2)
See also 'Command given with some arrogance, reaction to - When Caesar says 'do this,' it is perform'd.' *** Entries to 'Command, answer to c.'
In the play. *Tamora pretends to do what Titus A. tells her. In turn Titus A. pretends to be mad.*

Obesity, hell no place for fat men - I think, the devil will not have me damned, less the oil that is in me should set hell on fire.
" I think, the devil will not have me damned, less the oil that is in me should set hell on fire." (MWW.5.5)
If you are overweight, use as a rebut to 'go to hell'. See also 'Dieting, d. advice – Make less thy body hence, and more thy grace, leave gormandizing'
In the play. *Falstaff is ridiculed and abandoned. He thinks the devil did it but then he speculates that the devil himself would not accept Falstaff in hell to avoid oil (fat) induced extra fire.*

Obesity, o. caused by stress - … when I was about thy years… I was not an eagle's talon in the waist…
"…when I was about thy years, Hal, I was not an eagle's talon in the waist; I could have crept into any alderman's thumb-ring: a plague of sighing and grief! it blows a man up like a bladder." (KHIV.p1.2.4)
In the play. *Falstaff to Prince Henry who constantly chides Falstaff for obesity.*

Obesity, obese man in Windsor - … What tempest, I trow, threw this whale, with so many tons of oil in his belly, ashore in Windsor?
"What tempest, I trow, threw this whale, with so many tons of oil in his belly, ashore in Windsor?" (MWW.2.1)
Negative (if ungenerous) comment on the arrival of a nasty (and fat) character. Substitute the place of arrival for 'Windsor'.
In the play. *Mrs. Ford, pursued by Falstaff, shares with Mrs. Page her opinion on him after reading the love letters he has written to them both. 'Trow' means 'I dare say', you may substitute for clarity.*

Objective, examining the folly required to achieve an o. - … in everything the purpose must weigh with the folly.
"… in everything the purpose must weigh with the folly" (KHIV.p2.2.2)
Call to attention the risk of a folly enterprise
In the play. *The Prince of Wales and companions are planning another trick on Falstaff.*

Objective, now I understand your o. – Now I see the bottom of your purpose.
"Now I see
The bottom of your purpose." (AWEW.3.7)
Use when the objective you see has an element of sneakiness in it.
In the play. *The widow understands the scheme wherewith Helena will try to recapture her husband Bertram and make him abide by his promises.*

Objectives, finally stating your o. - … here is the heart of my purpose.
"… here is the heart of my purpose" (MWW.2.2)
After describing the background you come to the core of the proposal.
In the play. *Mr. Ford engages Falstaff to test Ford's wife's faithfulness (or lack of).*

Objectives, focus on the o. – … let every man now task his thought that this fair action may on foot be brought.
"… let every man now task his thought,
That this fair action may on foot be brought." (HV.1.2)
Inspirational note before starting a campaign.
In the play. *Henry V to his allies prior to undertaking the invasion of France.*

Objectives, means to achieve o. – … to load our purposes with what they travail for.
"… and is very likely to load our purposes with what they travail for" (TOA.5.1)
In the play. *Believing that Timon is still wealthy, the parasitic poet and painter approach him by his cave.*

Objectives, o. of a plea - Was't not to this end that thou began'st to twist so fine a story?
"…Was't not to this end
That thou began'st to twist so fine a story?" (MAAN.1.1)
In the play. *Don Pedro to Claudio, the story is Claudio's love for Hero.*

Objectives, o. achieved with humble tools - What poor an instrument may do a noble deed!
"What poor an instrument
May do a noble deed!" (AC.5.2)
If they question the resources or the means available to achieve the stated objectives.
In the play. *A clown brings in a basket of figs among which there is the adder ordered by Cleopatra to end her life – the adder is 'the poor instrument' that does a noble deed.*

Objectives, o. versus conscience - The colour of the king doth come and go between his purpose and his conscience…
"The colour of the king doth come and go
Between his purpose and his conscience,
Like heralds 'twixt two dreadful battles set." (KJ.4.2)
Simile for uncertainty. To apply to yourself change 'of the king' to 'My color doth come and go' and 'his' to 'my'. See also 'Indecision, i. between two courses of action'
In the play. *The dilemma is between killing or not killing young Arthur who is the legitimate heir to the throne. Salisbury reports on the mood of King John.*

Obligations, no o. and no love - I owe him little duty, and less love.
"I owe him little duty, and less love" (KHVI p1.4.4)
In the play. *Somerset tells Lucy about his dislike of York.*

Oblivion, insurance against o. – … A forted residence 'gainst the tooth of time and razure of oblivion.
"…A forted residence 'gainst the tooth of time
And razure of oblivion" (MFM.5.1)
In the play. *Duke Vicentio returning to Vienna pretends that Angelo has done a good job of governing while Vicentio was abroad. In fact, Angelo was a liar and a lecher.* 'Forted' = 'fortified', 'razure' = 'erasure'.

Oblivion, o. as a gulf - … in the swallowing gulf of blind forgetfulness and dark oblivion.
"…in the swallowing gulf
Of blind forgetfulness and dark oblivion" (KRIII.3.7)
Oratorical for 'I forgot', e.g. 'Sorry, it fell in the swallowing gulf…dark oblivion'. Equally a good image when you want to impress that the matter should not be forgotten. E.G. 'Let not the matter fall into the swallowing gulf…oblivion'.
In the play. *Buckingham in a pre-arranged charade addresses Richard explaining to him that he, Richard is the real heir to the throne as his brother (allegedly) was illegitimate. The efforts of Buckingham have prevented the ignominy that the genuine royal stock be 'swallowed in the gulf of forgetfulness'.*

Observation, concurring with an o. - Thou but rememberest me of mine own conception…
"Thou but rememberest me of mine own conception: I have perceived a most faint neglect of late" (KL.1.4)
When you agree with an observation.
In the play. *An accompanying knight has pointed out to Lear the perceived neglect by Lear's daughter and he agrees that it is true.*

Observation, careful o. by a person - But there's more in me than thou understand'st. Why dost thou so oppress me with thine eye?
"But there's more in me than thou understand'st.
Why dost thou so oppress me with thine eye?" (TC.4.5)
Alternative to 'Why are you looking at me?'

In the play. *Hector to Achilles who is trying to locate in a bragging way the point where to hit Hector and kill him in the ensuing battle.*

Observation, careful o. of a person – I have with exact view perused thee…
"I have with exact view perused thee, Hector,
And quoted joint by joint." (TC.4.5)
It could work with a girl. Answer to 'Why are you looking at me?'
In the play. *Achilles examines Hector accurately to determine where to hit him and kill him.*

Observation, direct o. more trustworthy than official reports – Let every eye negotiate for itself and trust no agent.
"Let every eye negotiate for itself
And trust no agent" (MAAN.2.1)
See also 'Experience, direct e. disproving official reports - Experience, O, thou disprov'st report!'
In the play. *For some reason Claudio has asked Don Pedro to woo Hero on his (Claudio's) behalf. Now Claudio is not so sure that it was a good idea. He should have done the wooing himself.*

Observation, insincere or exaggerated reaction - The lady protests too much, methinks.
"The lady protests too much, methinks." (H.3.2)
Answer to "What do you think of so-and-so?" when you do not trust her. Or him – if so change 'the lady' to 'the man'.
In the play. *Hamlet has asked his mother, Queen Gertrude, her opinion on the play that Hamlet has just produced and staged. The Queen gives her opinion about the main actress.*

Observation, intelligent o. always yield some benefit – … to apprehend thus, draws us a profit from all things we see.
"…to apprehend thus,
Draws us a profit from all things we see" (CYM.3.3)
In the play. *Belarius gives some philosophical advice to his adoptive sons. See 'Perception, p. determining judgment – This service is not service, so being done but being so allow'd.'*

Obstacles, all o. removed – … And all the clouds that lour'd upon our house, in the deep bosom of the ocean buried.
"…And all the clouds that lour'd upon our house,
In the deep bosom of the ocean buried." (KRIII.1.1)
Statement at the successful end of complex negotiations, especially political.
In the play. *Richard meditates sarcastically on the current state of affairs at the court of his brother Henry IV.* 'To lour' = 'to hang'.

Obstacles, o. increasing desire --… as all impediments in fancy's course are motives of more fancy.
"She knew her distance, and did angle me, madding my eagerness with her restraint, as all impediments in fancy's course are motives of more fancy." (AWEW.5.3)
This is a tactic that (perhaps) was popular more in the past than today. Keep it in mind, however, if you detect in her a similar behavior.
In the play. *Bertram attempts to discredit Diana saying that she obtained the ring he gave her by craft.*

Occupation, stock breeding - …to get your living by the copulation of cattle.
"That is another simple sin in you, to bring the ewes and the rams together and to offer to get your living by the copulation of cattle." (AYLI.3.2)
Ironic description of a cattle breeder.
In the play. *Touchstone banters with Corin the shepherd.*

Occurrence, rare o. - It is no act of common passage, but a strain of rareness.
"It is no act of common passage, but
A strain of rareness" (CYM.3.5)
In the play. *Imogen reflects on her genuine love for Leonatus and her allegiance to him, having refused all other suitors and incurred the wrath of her father Cymbeline.*

Odds, o. overwhelmingly unfavorable - ... But now 't is odds beyond arithmetic.
"... But now 't is odds beyond arithmetic." (COR.3.1)
Justify giving up against overwhelming odds.
In the play. *Cominius, Coriolanus and a few friends cannot take on the mass of the revolting people.*

Odor, unpleasant – ... I do smell all horse-piss; at which my nose is in great indignation.
"…I do smell all horse-piss; at which my nose is in great indignation."
(TEM.4.1)
It can be any unpleasant smell at which you can say, 'I do smell (nature of smell) l at which my nose is in great indignation.' The indignation of your nose will give the statement the necessary weight. See also 'Adversity, a. assembles together strange characters'.
In the play. *Caliban and wanna-be conspirators Stephano and Trinculo find themselves in a stink pond.*

Odor, unpleasant and offensive to nostrils - ... there was the rankest compound of villanous smell, that ever offended nostril.
"... there was the rankest compound of villanous smell, that ever offended nostril." (MWW.3.5)
Describe foul a foul odor, literal or figurative, 'This is the rankest…nostril.'
In the play. *Mrs. Ford had arranged to have Falstaff carried away in a basket of dirty linen and other garbage. Falstaff describes the adventure.*

Offense, charge of o. rejected - Never so much as in a thought unborn did I offend your highness.
"Never so much as in a thought unborn,
Did I offend your highness."
(AYLI.1.3)
A semi-ironic retort to someone who states you offended him/her. Change 'your highness' with the name of the party whom you never offended
In the play. *The usurping Duke Frederick now decides to ban Rosalind from court. Rosalind states that she never offended Frederick in anything.*

Offense, if any o. done that's the end of it - I will no further offend you than becomes me for my good.
" I will no further offend you than becomes me for my good." (AYLI.1.1)
A retort if you are accused to be offensive.
In the play. *Orlando to Oliver after a confrontation in which Orlando grabbed Oliver by the neck.*

Offense, no o. done to anyone - ... my remembrance is very free and clear from any image of offence done to any man.
"... my remembrance is very free and clear from any image of offence done to any man."(TN.3.4)
You do not recall offending intentionally anyone.
In the play. *Sir Toby arrives to warn Viola/Cesario that Aguecheek is angry and wants a duel. Viola/Cesario cannot recall any offense given.*

Offence, o. forgotten – ... his great offence is dead and deeper than oblivion we do bury...
"...his great offence is dead,
And deeper than oblivion we do bury
The incensing relics of it"
(AWEW.5.3)
In the play. *The King forgives Bertram for his behavior towards Helen.*

Offense, o. will not be rewarded - Who bates mine honour, shall not know my coin.
"Who bates mine honour, shall not know my coin." (TOA.3.3)
Use as applicable to refuse a request.
In the play. *To avoid helping Timon, Sempronius invents an imaginative excuse. He will not help Timon because Timon did not call first on him for help but only after others refused to help him.*

Office, o. functions better when you are not there - They prosper best of all when I am thence.
"Margaret my queen, and Clifford too,
Have chid me from the battle; swearing both
They prosper best of all when I am thence." (KHVI.p3.2.5)
In the play. *Margaret and Clifford have persuaded the peaceful Henry to stay away from the battle, as he tends to do more harm than good.*

Offer, o. unacceptable - This proffer is absurd and reasonless.
"This proffer is absurd and reasonless" (KHVI p1.5.5)
When they make you an offer that they think you cannot refuse.
In the play. *Alencon refuses the conditions placed by Winchester on the French*

Office holders, often of questionable merit or qualifications - O, that estates, degrees and offices were not derived corruptly...
"...Let none presume
To wear an undeserved dignity.
O, that estates, degrees and offices
Were not derived corruptly, and that clear honour
Were purchased by the merit of the wearer!
How many then should cover that stand bare!
How many be commanded that command!
How much low peasantry would then be glean'd
From the true seed of honour! and how much honour
Pick'd from the chaff and ruin of the times
To be new-varnish'd!" (MOV.2.9)
Applies to many government and private appointments.
In the play. *The Prince of Arragon will not pick the right answer in the contest for the hand of Portia. But the puzzle he is asked to solve prompts him to make a consideration on the questionable qualification of meritless persons. In the last four lines Arragon says that among the true sons of nobility (seed of honour), some would just rank as peasant whereas there is honour among the reputedly worthless (chaff and ruin of the times).*

Omen, o. characterizing an evil man – The owl shriek'd at thy birth, --an evil sign...
"The owl shriek'd at thy birth,--an evil sign;
The night-crow cried, aboding luckless time;
Dogs howl'd, and hideous tempest shook down trees;
The raven rook'd her on the chimney's top,
And chattering pies in dismal discords sung" (KHVI.5.6)

Use any line against an evil adversary or political enemy. Change 'thy' to 'his'. See also entries for 'Events, strange'.
In the play. *Henry VI to Richard III who has come to the Tower with the specific purpose of killing Henry*

Omission, o. does not mean giving up - Omittance is no quittance.
"... omittance is no quittance." (AYLI.3.5)
Reaffirm your commitment to the cause even though you may have omitted to do whatever was required at one point.
In the play. *Phebe remembers the scorning words the disguised Rosalind used with her (Phebe). Phebe did not reply then (omittance) but will reply now.*

Omission, o. of responsibility dangerous - Omission to do what is necessary seals commission to a blank of danger...
"Omission to do what is necessary
Seals commission to a blank of danger,
And danger, like an ague, subtly taints
Even then when we sit idly in the sun." (TC.3.3)
Force a reluctant audience to accept your proposal because it is necessary and cannot be avoided.
In the play. *Now Patroclus joins Achilles in prompting him to do 'what is necessary' or else.*

One fell swoop (M.4.3)
In the play. *Macduff reflects in horror and disbelief how Macbeth killed his wife and children at once,*
Did you say all? O hell-kite! All?
What, all my pretty chickens and their dam
At one fell swoop?

One thing after another - Like to a ship that, having 'scaped a tempest is straightway calm'd and boarded with a pirate.
"Like to a ship that, having 'scaped a tempest,
Is straightway calm'd and boarded with a pirate" (KHVI.p2.4.9)
In the play. *King Henry, having just escaped the tempest of the John Cade rebellion, now faces the uprising of York, who claims the throne for himself.*

Openness, invitation to o. - Out with it boldly; truth loves open dealing.
"Out with it boldly; truth loves open dealing." (KHVIII.3.1)
Reinforce your intention to have matters dealt with in the open, 'Truth loves open dealing'. See also 'Communications, clarity and honesty go together - An honest tale speeds best being plainly told.'
In the play. *Queen Katherine to Cardinal Wolsey whom she mistrusts.*

Openness, no need for secrecy - There's nothing I have done yet, of my conscience, deserves a corner.
"Speak it here;
There's nothing I have done yet, of my conscience,
Deserves a corner." (KHVIII.3.1)
Explain why you intend to have things discussed in the open.
In the play. *Cardinal Wolsey, arrived with Cardinal Campeius, suggests a private meeting but Katherine wants it in the open.*

Opinion, acquired excellent o. - ... I have bought golden opinions from all sorts of people.
"...I have bought
Golden opinions from all sorts of people" (M.1.7)
See also 'Report, he is doing very well - report speaks goldenly of his profit.'
In the play. *Macbeth hesitates and finds arguments to cancel the plans to kill Duncan.*

But his wife, Lady Macbeth will find arguments to spur him on to execute the murder.

Opinion, o. of others to be disregarded – A plague of opinion! a man may wear it on both sides, like a leather jerkin.
"A plague of opinion! a man may wear it on both sides, like a leather jerkin" (TC.3.3)
Retort to 'What will other people think?'
In the play. *Thersites, conversing with Achilles, gives his negative assessment of Ajax, who is held in high opinion by other Greeks.*

Opinion, comparing o. - I will hear Cassius; and compare their reasons, when severally we hear them rendered.
FIRST CITIZEN I will hear Brutus speak.
SECOND CITIZEN I will hear Cassius; and compare their reasons, When severally we hear them rendered. (JC.3.2)
In the play. *Brutus and Cassius will both address the people to explain the reasons for Caesar's assassination.*

Opinion, emphatic exhortation to discard an o.– ... be cured of this diseased opinion.
"Good my lord, be cured
Of this diseased opinion, and betimes,
For it is most dangerous." (WT.1.2)
Correct an incorrect opinion. See also 'Exhortation, e. to change opinion - ... remove the root of his opinion which is rotten as ever oak or stone was sound.'
In the play. *Camillo tells Leontes that his jealousy is totally unjustified and dangerous.*

Opinion, false o. strangely acquired - ...what a strange infection is fall'n into thy ear!
"...what a strange infection
Is fall'n into thy ear!" (CYM.3.2)

In the play. *Pisanio wonders what may have convinced Leonatus in Rome that Imogen betrayed him.*

Opinion, good op. lost - ... you are now sailed into the north of my lady's opinion.
"... you are now sailed into the north of my lady's opinion where you will hang like an icicle on a Dutchman's beard..." (TN.3.2)
Use to indicate that he/she does not like you. Change 'you are' to 'I have' as applicable.
In the play. *Fabian tries to provide Aguecheek with an explanation for Olivia's rude treatment of Aguecheek. To redeem himself Aguecheek, according to Fabian, should challenge Viola/Cesario to a duel.*

Opinion, good op. regained - Thou hast redeem'd thy lost opinion.
"Thou hast redeem'd thy lost opinion." (KHIVp1.5.4)
When a political enemy turns suddenly friendly
In the play. *K. Henry IV to his son the Prince of Wales after the Prince made Douglas run for his life.*

Opinion, op. directs the course of events - ... opinion, a sovereign mistress of effects...
"...opinion, a sovereign mistress of effects, throws a more safer voice on you" (OTH.1.3)
Answer to a statement of the type 'that's just an opinion', e.g. 'Yes, but opinion is the sovereign mistress of effects'. Or explain why a biased media creates a biased opinion with negative effects.
In the play. *Though there is a substitute commander in Cyprus, the Duke of Venice states that by general opinion Othello is a better commander. Therefore, he and his wife Desdemona will be dispatched to Cyprus.*

Opinion, op. or idea, stuck on an op. or idea and unable to change it - ... you may as well forbid the sea to obey the moon...
"... you may as well
Forbid the sea to obey the moon
As, or by oath remove, or counsel shake
The fabric of his folly, whose foundation
Is piled upon his faith, and will continue
The standing of his body." (WT.1.2)
Use all or in part to express that the party referred will stick to his opinions, however wrong they may be. To convey the idea of utter impossibility see also 'Success, s. impossible given the man and the circumstances.' *** Entries for 'Impossibility'
In the play. *Camillo advises Polixenes that it would be impossible to reason with Leontes and make him see that the accusations to Polixenes are totally unfounded. Leontes thinks that his wife Helena is having an affair with guest Polixenes.*

Opinion, o. poll negative - I find the people strangely fantasied... not knowing what they fear, but full of fear.
"I find the people strangely fantasied;
Possess'd with rumours, full of idle dreams,
Not knowing what they fear, but full of fear" (KJ.4.2)
In the play. *Faulconbridge reports to King John on the mood of the English masses.*

Opinion, op. poll worse than before - The faiths of men ne'er stained with revolt, fresh expectation troubled not the land ...
"The faiths of men ne'er stained with revolt;
Fresh expectation troubled not the land
With any long'd-for change or better state" (KJ.4.2)
In the play. *Pembroke to King Arthur who, unexplainably and against his counselors' opinion, has scheduled a second coronation.*

Opinion, public o. gained by the appearance of maturity in the shape of an elder person - ... his silver hairs will purchase us a good opinion...
"...his silver hairs
Will purchase us a good opinion
And buy men's voices to commend our deeds" (JC.2.1)
Apply to yourself when, if you are no youngster, apply for a job, implying that your image of implied maturity may be beneficial to your employer.
In the play. *Metellius Cimber proposes to enroll Cicero in the conspiracy against Caesar and gives reasons why.*

Opinion, what is your o? (case when you approve) - The image of it gives me content already...
DUKE VICENTIO. What think you of it?
ISABELLA The image of it gives me content already; and I trust it will grow to a most prosperous perfection." (MFM.3.1)
Answer to 'What do you think of my idea?' when you approve of it. See also 'Win-win situation through a stratagem'.
In the play. *The Duke has hatched a plan to save Claudio and asks Isabel for her opinion. Claudio has been condemned to death for fornication by Angelo, the temporary Duke's substitute.*

Opinion, your op. delivered simply - I'll show my mind according to my shallow simple skills.
"I'll show my mind
According to my shallow simple skills." (TGV.1.2)

Answer to a request for explanation or information, especially if you sense a mild tone of distrust.
In the play. *Julia is in love with Proteus and asks Lucetta about her opinion of Proteus, which Lucetta will now give.*

Opinion, your op. firm and immovable - ... is the opinion, that fire cannot melt out of me; I will die in it at the stake.
"That I neither feel how she should be loved, nor know how she should be worthy, is the opinion, that fire cannot melt out of me; I will die in it at the stake." (MAAN.1.1)
Express the firmness of your opinion. 'It is an opinion that fire cannot melt out of me.'
In the play. *Benedick's opinion of Beatrice.*

Opinion, your op. on a man who could be better - He's that he is: I may not breathe my censure, what he might be...
"He's that he is: I may not breathe my censure
What he might be: if what he might he is not,
I would to heaven he were!" (OTH.4.1)
If you wish to be cryptic and politically correct.
In the play. *Ludovico queries Iago as to the odd state of mind of Othello and Iago responds with these ambiguous lines*

Opinion, your op. on a man who is rich but shallow - Well of his wealth; but of himself, so, so.
JULIA. What thinks't thou of the rich Mercutio?
LUCETTA. Well of his wealth; but of himself, so, so." (TGV.1.2)
Express your opinion of a rich but shallow character.
In the play. *Julia reviews the roster of her potential suitors with her servant Lucetta.*

Opinion, your op. on a man whose clothing lacks coordination – How oddly he is suited! I think he bought his doublet in Italy, his round hose in France...
NERISSA: What say you then to Faulconbridge, the young baron of England?
PORTIA: ...How oddly he is suited! I think he bought his doublet in Italy, his round hose in France, his bonnet in Germany, and his behavior everywhere." (MOV.1.2)
Characterize a person with some contrasting character traits
In the play. *Nerissa and Portia review the roster of Portia's suitors.*

Opinion, your op. on a specific man – ... know him noble, of great estate, of fresh and stainless youth...
"Yet I suppose him virtuous, know him noble,
Of great estate, of fresh and stainless youth;
In voices well divulged, free, learn'd and valiant;
And in dimension and the shape of nature
A gracious person." (TN.1.5)
Answer to 'what do you think of him?
In the play. *Olivia feels no attraction for the Duke Orsino who is actively pursuing her, here via the offices of Viola/Cesario.*

Opinion, your op. on an inarticulate man – dull of tongue.
I think so, Charmian: dull of tongue, and dwarfish!" (AC.3.3)
In the play. *On hearing from the messenger that Octavia, Antony's newly wed wife is 'dull of tongue' and short, Cleopatra feels reassured that Antony's marriage won't last long.*

Opinion, your op. on authority – ...
There thou mightst behold the great image of authority: a dog's obeyed in office.
K. LEAR Thou hast seen a farmer's dog bark at a beggar?
GLOUCESTER Ay, sir.
K. LEAR And the creature run from the cur? There thou mightst behold the great image of authority: a dog's obeyed in office. (KL.4.6)
See also entries on 'Authority' and 'Authority, a. corrupted by gold'.
In the play. *The blind Gloucester and (ex) King Lear find themselves in a field near Dover.*

Opinion, your op. on authority –
...man, proud man, dressed in a little brief authority...
"... man, proud man,
Drest in a little brief authority,
Most ignorant of what he's most assured,
His glassy essence, like an angry ape,
Plays such fantastic tricks before high heaven
As make the angels weep." (MFM.2.2)
In the play. *The virtuous Isabella comments on the stupidity, hypocrisy and double standards of Angelo, the temporary ruler of Vienna.*

Opinion, your op. on crowds and masses - ... Commanded always by the greater gust; such is the lightness of you common men.
"Look, as I blow this feather from my face,
And as the air blows it to me again,
Obeying with my wind when I do blow,
And yielding to another when it blows,
Commanded always by the greater gust;
Such is the lightness of you common men." (KHVI p3.3.1)
The last two lines well convey the concept. You can change to
'Commanded always by the greater gust; such is the lightness of the common men.'
In the play. *King Henry VI has been deposed by Edward of York and two keepers use the occasion to take Henry VI prisoner in the hope of a reward. Only a little time earlier they had been his subjects.*

Opinion, your op. on crowds and masses – ... your affections are a sick man's appetite ...
"... your affections are
A sick man's appetite, who desires most that
Which would increase his evil" (COR.1.1)
In the play. *Coriolanus to the plebe.*

Opinion, your op. on crowds and masses – An habitation giddy and unsure hath he, that buildeth on the vulgar heart.
"An habitation giddy and unsure
Hath he, that buildeth on the vulgar heart." (KHIVp2.1.3)
Define questionable, unreliable and uncouth allies, or unstable masses.
In the play. *The archbishop of York commenting on the support base of Henry IV.*

Opinion, your op. on crowds and masses – He that trusts to you, where he should find you lions, finds you hares...
"...He that trusts to you,
Where he should find you lions, finds you hares;
Where foxes, geese..." (COR.1.1)
Describe a disorganized and unreliable group. Change 'you' to 'them' when not addressing the group directly. See also entries for 'Opinion, your opinion on crowds and masses'.
In the play. *Coriolanus has a deep-seated contempt for the people and it shows.*

Opinion, your op. on crowds and masses – The beast with many heads...
"...the beast
With many heads butts me away" (COR.4.1)
In the play. *Coriolanus says farewell to wife and mother after having been forced to flee Rome by the people.*

Opinion, your op. on crowds and masses – The blunt monster with uncounted heads.
"...the blunt monster with uncounted heads,
The still-discordant wavering multitude..." (KHIV.p2.intro)
In the play. In the play. *Rumor, made a character, defines the masses in whose unthinking mind he can plant slander and lies. For more declarations by Rumor see 'Rumor, r. fabricating slander – upon my tongue continual slanders ride, the which in every language I pronounce.'*

Opinion, your op. on crowds and masses - The fool multitude, that choose by show...
"...the fool multitude, that choose by show,
Not learning more than the fond eye doth teach;
Which pries not to the interior, but, like the martlet,
Builds in the weather on the outward wall,
Even in the force and road of casualty." (MOV.2.9)
The first line is sufficient to convey the idea. See also 'Eccentricity, above the crowd – ... I will not jump with common spirits and rank me with the barbarous multitude.'
In the play. *The prince of Arragon, one of Portia's suitors meditates on the meaning of a puzzle. He who solves the puzzle will be able to marry Portia. 'Martlet' is a swallow.*

Opinion, your op. on crowds and masses - The mutable, rank-scented many.
"... the mutable, rank-scented many" (COR.3.1)
See also "Insult, i. to masses considered as despicable'
In the play. *Coriolanus refuses to do anything to please the Roman populace*

Opinion, your op. on crowds and masses – (They) can judge as fitly of his worth as I can of those mysteries which heaven will not have earth to know.
"(They) can judge as fitly of his worth
As I can of those mysteries which heaven
Will not have earth to know." (COR.4.2)
In the play. *Volumnia, Coriolanus' mother, referring to the masses who are angry with him for his pride.*

Opinion, your op. on crowds and masses - This common body, like to a vagabond flag upon the stream, goes to and back...
"I should have known no less.
It hath been taught us from the primal state,
That he which is was wish'd until he were;
And the ebb'd man, ne'er loved till ne'er worth love,
Comes dear'd by being lack'd. This common body,
Like to a vagabond flag upon the stream,
Goes to and back, lackeying the varying tide,
To rot itself with motion." (AC.1.4)
In the play. *A messenger has announced to Octavius Caesar that Pompey's fortunes are rising. Octavius Caesar comments on the quickly changing allegiance or favor of the masses.*

Opinion, your op. on crowds and masses – Was ever feather so lightly blown to and fro as this multitude?
"Was ever feather so lightly blown to and fro as this multitude?" (KHVI p2.4.8)
In the play. *John Cade's rebel rabble is quickly turned against him by a better prepared speaker (Clifford) with an appealing message (the recollection of the exploits of Henry V), as well as the (invented for the purpose) fear of the French.*

Opinion, your op. on crowds and masses – With every minute you do change a mind
"With every minute you do change a mind;
And call him noble that was now your hate,
Him vile that was your garland." (COR.1.1)
Describe the general behavior of masses.
In the play. *Coriolanus has a deep-seated contempt for the people and it shows.*

Opinion, your op. on crowds and masses - Worship shadows and adore false shapes.
"I am very loath to be your idol, sir;
But since your falsehood shall become you well
To worship shadows and adore false shapes,
Send to me in the morning and I'll send it" (TGV.4.2)
In the play. *The false Proteus, rejected by Silvia, asks at least for a picture of her and she will give the picture to him.*

Opinion, your op. on crowds and masses, mass psychology - ... if they love they know not why, they hate upon no better a ground.
"Faith, there have been many great men that have flattered the people, who never loved them; and there be many that have loved, they know not wherefore; so that, if they love they know not why, they hate upon no better a ground." (COE.2.2)
In the play. *The comment by an officer underscores an almost universal characteristic of masses, to love and hate without a logical cause or connection.*

Opinion, your op. on crowds and masses, always siding with the winner - The common people swarm like summer flies and whither fly the gnats but to the sun?
"The common people swarm like summer flies;
And whither fly the gnats but to the sun?" (KHVI.p3.2.6)
In the play. *Clifford laments the ease with which masses switch allegiance in favor of the victorious party.*

Opinion, your op. on crowds and masses, blindly applauding the last mountebank - ... when you saw his chariot but appear, have you not made an universal shout...
"And when you saw his chariot but appear,
Have you not made an universal shout,
That Tiber trembled underneath her banks,
To hear the replication of your sounds
Made in her concave shores?" (JC.1.1)
In the play. *Marullus, a tribune, confronts some commoners about their infatuation with Caesar, expressed by loud acclamations.*

Opinion, your op. on crowds and masses, never depend on their favor - He that depends upon your favours, swims with fins of lead...
"... He that depends
Upon your favours, swims with fins of lead,
And hews down oaks with rushes." (COR.1.1)

Why not to rely on the support of the masses.
In the play. *Coriolanus has a deep-seated contempt for the people and it shows. 'Rush' is a plant of the genus 'Juncus', used to make strands of brooms.*

Opinion, your op. on crowds and masses, slippery, unable to know who is good - – whose love is never linked to the deserver.
" …Our slippery people
Whose love is never linked to the deserver
Till his deserts are past" (AC.1.2)
Target the questionable allegiance of employees or stockholders. E.G. "They are slippery people, whose love…till his desert are past."
In the play. *Antony to friend Enobarbus, reflecting on the dangerous (to Antony) political situation in Rome. The people are beginning to side with Pompey's son.*

Opinion, your op. on crowds and masses, using eyes, not judgment - He is loved of the distracted multitude, who like not in their judgement, but their eyes.
"He is loved of the distracted multitude,
Who like not in their judgement, but their eyes." (H.4.3)
Dismiss the poor judgement of the masses.
In the play. *King Claudius reflects on Hamlet, who is loved by the people of Denmark. Therefore Claudius must be careful on his plans to get rid of him.*

Opinion, your op. on doctors, you do not trust them - … trust not the physician; his antidotes are poison.
"… trust not the physician;
His antidotes are poison, and he slays More than you rob." (TOA.4.3)
In the play. *Two robbers stumble upon Timon who has retreated and retired to a wood. He talks with robbers and almost converts them away by their profession, by inciting them to pursue it.*

Opinion, your o. on fashion – Seest thou not, I say, what a deformed thief this fashion is?…
" Seest thou not, I say, what a deformed thief this fashion is? how giddily a' turns about all the hot bloods between fourteen and five-and-thirty?" (MAAN.3.3)
In the play. *Borachio to Conrade. Both have been hired by Don John to slander Hero to spite her and create trouble.*

Opinion, your op. on fashion (new, foreign and trendy) - … is not this a lamentable thing, grandsire, that we should be thus afflicted with these strange flies…
"Why, is not this a lamentable thing, grandsire, that we should be thus afflicted with these strange flies, these fashion-mongers, these perdona-mi's, who stand so much on the new form, that they cannot at ease on the old bench?" (RJ.2.4)
In the play. *Mercutio's opinion of new fashions and trendiness*

Opinion, your op. on flattery - … he that loves to be flattered is worthy of the flatterer.
"… he that loves to be flattered is worthy of the flatterer." (TOA.1.1)
Express your opinion on flattery
In the play. *Apemantus has no qualms in telling it as he sees it.*

Opinion, your op. on lawyers - The first thing we do, let's kill all the lawyers.
"The first thing we do, let's kill all the lawyers." (KHVI p2.4.2)
This may not be your opinion or you may be a lawyer yourself. If so you may quote the line anyway to indicate your

awareness of how hateful may be the profession to some. See also entries for 'Politicians' promises'.
In the play. *Dick, a companion of the rebel leader John Cade makes a proposal agreed upon by the leader.*

Opinion, your op. on money, handling of, borrowing and lending - Neither a borrower nor a lender be…
"Neither a borrower nor a lender be;
For loan oft loses both itself and friend,
And borrowing dulls the edge of husbandry." (H.1.3)
Explain with this example your philosophy about borrowing and lending. See also 'Financing, lending denied - … this is no time to lend money, especially upon bare friendship, without security.'
In the play. *Polonius gives his son Laertes a set of precepts to follow while in Paris.*
Here is the list of counsels:
"And these few precepts in thy memory
See thou character. Give thy thoughts no tongue,
Nor any unproportioned thought his act.
Be thou familiar, but by no means vulgar.
Those friends thou hast, and their adoption tried,
Grapple them to thy soul with hoops of steel;
But do not dull thy palm with entertainment
Of each new-hatch'd, unfledged comrade. Beware
Of entrance to a quarrel, but being in,
Bear't that the opposed may beware of thee.
Give every man thy ear, but few thy voice;
Take each man's censure, but reserve thy judgment.
Costly thy habit as thy purse can buy,
But not express'd in fancy; rich, not gaudy;
For the apparel oft proclaims the man,
And they in France of the best rank and station
Are of a most select and generous chief in that.
Neither a borrower nor a lender be;
For loan oft loses both itself and friend,
And borrowing dulls the edge of husbandry.
This above all: to thine own self be true,
And it must follow, as the night the day,
Thou canst not then be false to any man."
More usable lines can be extracted from this list. See 'Criticism. Handling of c.' - 'Opinion, your op. on friendship and its value.' - 'Advice, a. on men's wear and fashion - Costly thy habit as thy purse can buy, but not express'd in fancy; rich, not gaudy…'

Opinion, your op. on politicians in general - The devil knew not what he did when he made man politic, he crossed himself by 't.
"The devil knew not what he did when he made man politic; he crossed himself by 't." (TOA.3.3)
In the play. *Sempronius, along with other supposed friends, denies any help to Timon and says so to Timon's faithful servant.*

Opinion, your op. on power, pomp and prestige - … what is pomp, rule, reign, but earth and dust?… "Why, what is pomp, rule, reign, but earth and dust?
And, live we how we can, yet die we must." (KHVI p3.5.2)
In the play. *Warwick, mortally wounded and defeated by the forces of Edward IV, reflects on the relative worthlessness of coveted goals. For another usable part of this monologue see 'Defeat, admitting electoral d.'*

Opinion, your op. on profusely given thanks - … when a man thanks me heartily…
"…when a man thanks me heartily, methinks I have given him a penny

and he renders me the beggarly thanks." (AYLI.2.5)
When someone overly insists on thanking you and you become mildly uncomfortable.
In the play. *The skeptical and witty Jaques addresses Amiens a companion in the forest of Arden.*

Opinion, your op. on salesmen and merchants - Traffic's thy god; and thy god confound thee!
"Traffic's thy god; and thy god confound thee!" (TOA.1.1)
Address an insistent sales person.
In the play. *Apemantus to the merchant.*

Opinion, your op. on sociological issues, minimum wage - O, reason not the need: our basest beggars are in the poorest thing superfluous…
"O, reason not the need: our basest beggars
Are in the poorest thing superfluous:
Allow not nature more than nature needs,
Man's life's as cheap as beast's" (KL.2.4)
Use it unless you are a staunch right winger and believer in 'trickle down economics'. See also 'Class, poorer class – … we, the poorer born whose baser stars do shut us up in wishes.'
In the play. *The two ugly sisters Regan and Goneril want to deny Lear his request for servants, after he has bequeathed to them all his assets and properties. Lear counters their argument.*

Opinion, your op. on specific man, bad in himself and worse when drunk - … when
he is best, he is a little worse than a man and when he is worst, he is little better than a beast.
NERISSA How like you the young German, the Duke of Saxony's nephew?
PORTIA. Very vilely in the morning, when he is sober, and most vilely in the afternoon, when he is drunk: when he is best, he is a little worse than a man, and when he is worst, he is little better than a beast" (MOV.1.2)
See also 'Man, a drunkard – … drunk many times a day, if not many days entirely drunk.'
In the play. *The duke of Saxony is one of Portia's suitor who arrived in hope to solve the riddle.*

Opinion, your op. on the choice - how like you our choice that you stand pensive, as half malcontent?
"Now, brother of Clarence, how like you our choice,
That you stand pensive, as half malcontent?" (KHVI p3.4.1)
When the facial expression of the person whose opinion you ask indicates disapproval.
In the play. *Edward IV asks Clarence what does he think of the Lady Grey whom Edward has decided to marry and make her his queen.*

Opinion, your op. on the newly rich - … 'tis a common proof that lowliness is young ambition's ladder…
"…'tis a common proof,
That lowliness is young ambition's ladder,
Whereto the climber-upward turns his face;
But when he once attains the upmost round,
He then unto the ladder turns his back,
Looks in the clouds, scorning the base degrees
By which he did ascend." (JC.2.1)
Tease a friend who has become important and now does not want to acknowledge you or help you in some way.

In the play. *Brutus comments on what usually happens when circumstances elevate a man well above the level he started from.*

Opinion, your op. on who is the best man - ... of many good I think him best.
JULIA Why not on Proteus, as of all the rest?
LUCETTA Then thus: of many good I think him best. (TGV.1.2)
In the play. *Julia reviews the roster of her potential suitors with her servant Lucetta.*

Opportunity, advice to seize on the o. – Sell when you can: you are not for all markets.
"...mistress, know yourself: down on your knees,
And thank heaven, fasting, for a good man's love:
For I must tell you friendly in your ear,
Sell when you can: you are not for all markets" (AYLI. 3.5)
In the play. *Rosalind (in man's disguise) to Phebe who thinks that Rosalind is a man and has fallen in love with him.*

Opportunity, crime of o. - O Opportunity, thy guilt is great!
'O Opportunity, thy guilt is great!
'Tis thou that executest the traitor's treason:
Thou set'st the wolf where he the lamb may get
...
And in thy shady cell, where none may spy him,
Sits Sin, to seize the souls that wander by him.
...
Thy secret pleasure turns to open shame,
Thy private feasting to a public fast,
Thy smoothing titles to a ragged name,
Thy sugar'd tongue to bitter wormwood taste:
Thy violent vanities can never last.
How comes it then, vile Opportunity,
Being so bad, such numbers seek for thee?" (ROL)
In the poem. *Evil Tarquin knows he is committing a crime and meditates on it*

Opportunity, men's different behavior with o. - ... O heavens, what some men do, while some men leave to do!.
"...O heavens, what some men do,
While some men leave to do!
How some men creep in skittish fortune's hall,
Whiles others play the idiots in her eyes!" (TC.3.3)
In the play. *Ulysses works on Achille's sense of pride and emulation*

Opportunity, o. dependent on right time and availability - ... advantage, which doth ever cool in the absence of the needer.
"...And lose advantage, which doth ever cool
I' the absence of the needer." (COR.4.1)
In the play. *Cominius will accompany Coriolanus so that if he (Coriolanus) is needed (by Rome), he may be quickly and easily found.*

Opportunity, o. missed through lack of judgment - ... defect of judgement to fail in the disposing of those chances which he was lord of'.
"... defect of judgement,
To fail in the disposing of those chances
Which he was lord of." (COR.4.7)
Explaining a lack of success. E.G. 'It was defect of judgment that failed ... of which I was lord of'. See also 'Opportunity, why it should not be missed - There is a tide in the affairs of men, which, taken at the flood, leads on to fortune, omitted...'

In the play. *Aufidius discusses with his lieutenant the reasons why Coriolanus could not make the best of his chances with the Romans, that is to become their leader.*

Opportunity, o. offered and rejected - Who seeks, and will not take when once 'tis offer'd shall never find it more'.
"Who seeks, and will not take when once 'tis offer'd,
Shall never find it more." (AC.2.7)
In the play. *Menas proposes to his boss Pompey to kill Antony, Octavian and Lepidus while they are hosts at Pompey's party. Pompey has refused and Menas is upset. See 'Honor, h. above all – 'tis not my profit that does lead mine honor'.*

Opportunity, o. offered and rejected - Who seeks, and will not take when once 'tis offered, shall never find it more.
"Who seeks, and will not take when once 'tis offered,
Shall never find it more." (AC.2.7)
Persuade a reluctant party to jump at the opportunity. See also 'Opportunity, why it should not be missed.'
In the play *Menas is disappointed that Pompey has rejected the idea of killing guests Antony and Octavian during a banquet thus acquiring supreme power.*

Opportunity, poor chance of paying back for goods or services received - ... thou prun'ST a rotten tree that cannot so much as a blossom yield...
"... thou prun'st a rotten tree,
That cannot so much as a blossom yield,
In lieu of thy pains and husbandry." (AYLI.2.3)
When you would like to help or reciprocate but currently you cannot.
In the play. *Orlando is not very optimistic at his prospects now that he too must escape to the forest of Arden. He says so to his faithful servant Adam who offers to follow Orlando in exile.*

Opportunity, the world as a source of o - ...then the world's mine oyster.
FALSTAFF I will not lend thee a penny.
PISTOL Why, then the world's mine oyster,
Which I with sword will open. (MWW.2.2)
The line 'The world is mine oyster' has become symbolic of a certain attitude – meaning that the holder of the opinion and/or the utterer of the phrase considers the world as a vigorous challenge and a source of opportunities.
In the play. *Pistol requests a loan of Falstaff and Falstaff refuses.*

Opportunity, the world as a source of o. - There's place and means for every man alive.
"There's place and means for every man alive.
I'll after them" (AWEW.4.4)
In the play. *Parolles, shamed for his cowardice reflects on his next options.*

Opportunity, waiting for the o. - ... there I am till time and vantage crave my company.
"...there am I,
Till time and vantage crave my company" (KHIVp2.2.3)
Answer to 'What will you do now?' E.G. 'I will wait till… company'
In the play. *Northumberland heeds Lady Percy's advice to wait for developments before committing his forces to fight the army of King Henry.*

Opportunity, why it should not be missed - There is a tide in the affairs of men, which, taken at the flood, leads on to fortune, omitted….
"There is a tide in the affairs of men,
Which, taken at the flood, leads on to

fortune;
Omitted, all the voyage of their life
Is bound in shallows and in miseries.
….
On such a full sea we are now afloat;
And we must take the current as it serves,
Or lose our ventures." (JC.4.3)
Why you cannot miss the opportunity even if it may have unpleasant sentimental side effects, such as living town, changing job etc. See also 'Advice, take best advantage of the opportunity - ...frame the season for your own harvest...' – 'Astrology, astrological conditions favorable - I find my zenith doth depend upon a most auspicious star...' '
In the play. *Brutus and Cassius get ready at Philippi to fight the decisive battles against the forces of Antony.*

Opposition, o. without reason – … though you bite so sharp at reasons you are so empty of them.
"No marvel, though you bite so sharp at reasons,
You are so empty of them" (TC.2.2)
In the play. *Helenus, Troilus' brother, rebuts Troilus' empty arguments as to why Helen should be not returned to the Greeks.*

Opposition, strong and malicious – … potently opposed; and with a malice of as great size.
"You are potently opposed; and with a malice
Of as great size." (KHVIII.5.1)
In the play. *K. Henry to Cranmer who is opposed and attacked by powerful enemies*

Oppression, o. and unfair working conditions – … I have served him from the hour of my nativity to this instant…
"I am an ass, indeed; you may prove it by my long ears. I have served him from the hour of my nativity to this instant, and have nothing at his hands for my service but blows" (COE.4.4)
In the play. *Dromio E. complains at the treatment he receives from his master*

Optimism, overly optimistic - Description cannot suit itself in words to demonstrate the life of such a battle.
"Description cannot suit itself in words
To demonstrate the life of such a battle." (KHV.4.2)
Two uses, to imply that the impact of the event is greater than any words used to describe it, or to caution against excessive optimism. E.G. 'I would be careful before claiming victory. The French thought themselves invincible before the battle of Agincourt and someone even said, 'Description…battle' and then see what happened.' The first line can indicate that the impact of the event you refer to is greater than words can convey. See also 'Prudence, p. advisable instead of unrealistic optimism'.
In the play. *The French Granpre is overly optimistic about the outcome of the battle.*

Optimism, over o. disastrous - … And so, with great imagination proper to madmen, led his powers to death and winking leap'd into destruction.
"It was, my lord; who lined himself with hope,
Eating the air on promise of supply,
Flattering himself in project of a power
Much smaller than the smallest of his thoughts:
And so, with great imagination
Proper to madmen, led his powers to death
And winking leap'd into destruction." (KHIV.p.2.1.3)
Slip the last three lines nonchalantly as your comment to a mad idea.

In the play. *Bardolph comments on the circumstances leading to the defeat and death of Hotspur at the battle of Shrewsbury.*

Oratory, a subtle orator and a pliable listener - ... For Warwick is a subtle orator, and Lewis a prince soon won with moving words.
"For Warwick is a subtle orator,
And Lewis a prince soon won with moving words" (KHVI p3.3.1)
Exaggerate ironically the oratorical chances of success, change names accordingly.
In the play. *Henry VI questions himself whether Margaret may be able to get reinforcements from France, now that Warwick is also calling on King Lewis with an alluring proposal on behalf of Henry's enemies – that is, to marry Lewis' sister to Edward of England.*

Oratory, lack of o. claimed - ... I have neither wit, nor words, nor worth...
"...I have neither wit, nor words, nor worth,
Action, nor utterance, nor the power of speech,
To stir men's blood: I only speak right on;
I tell you that which you yourselves do know." (JC.3.2)
An introduction to imply that what you say is already known by the audience and they only need to be reminded. – See also 'Love, l. prompting oratory - My tongue could never learn sweet smoothing words; but now thy beauty is propos'd my fee…'
In the play. *Antony addressing the crowd after Caesar's assassination starts with a modest comparison of his oratorical skills with those of Brutus, knowing full well that he, Antony will be able to stir the populace,*
I come not, friends, to steal away your hearts:
I am no orator, as Brutus is;
But, as you know me all, a plain blunt man,

This is the speech where Antony artfully resorts to the phrase '… but Brutus is an honourable man.' See 'Debate, disagreeing with skill - … but Brutus says he was ambitious, and Brutus is an honourable man.'

Oratory, lack of o. claimed - Rude am I in my speech, and little bless'd with the soft phrase of peace.
"…Rude am I in my speech,
And little bless'd with the soft phrase of peace" (OTH.1.3)
In the play. *Othello begins his speech admitting that he has married Desdemona and explaining how it came about.*

Oratory, lack of o. claimed but … - … little shall I grace my cause in speaking for myself. Yet, by your gracious patience…
"…little shall I grace my cause
In speaking for myself. Yet, by your gracious patience,
I will a round unvarnish'd tale deliver…" (OTH.1.3)
The beginning of your defense speech against unfair accusations.
In the play. *Othello skillfully uses modesty before delivering an effective explanation of how Desdemona fell in love with him.*

Oratory, working up the crowd – You are not wood, you are not stones, but men …
"You are not wood, you are not stones, but men;
And, being men, bearing the will of Caesar,
It will inflame you, it will make you mad…" (JC.3.2)
In the play. *Antony pretends not to want to read Caesar's will to the crowd so as to inflame them until he will read it. This will further inflame the anger of the crowd towards Brutus and accomplices.*

Orders, disobeying o. for the safety of the orderer - They say, in care of your

most royal person... and therefore do they cry, though you forbid.
"They say, in care of your most royal person,
That if your highness should intend to sleep
And charge that no man should disturb your rest
In pain of your dislike or pain of death,
Yet, notwithstanding such a strait edict,
Were there a serpent seen, with forked tongue,
That slily glided towards your majesty,
It were but necessary you were waked,
Lest, being suffer'd in that harmful slumber,
The mortal worm might make the sleep eternal;
And therefore do they cry, though you forbid." (KHVI p2.3.2)
Give a positive twist to employee's complaint and use the last line at the end of your comment.
In the play. *Salisbury tells King Henry VI what the Commons say to justify their claim for Suffolk's punishment. Suffolk had Gloucester murdered.*

Organization, creativity of an o. - ... This teeming womb of royal kings ...
"... This teeming womb of royal kings..." (KRII.2.1)
Praise the creativity of a research or development team or similar other, e.g. 'This teeming womb of spectacular idea'
In the play. *John of Gaunt rails against the excesses of King Richard II while praising England as a nation and the English as a people'*

Organization, o. on the point of sinking - ... leak'd is our bark and we, poor mates, stand on the dying deck...

"... leak'd is our bark,
And we, poor mates, stand on the dying deck,
Hearing the surges threat: we must all part
Into this sea of air." (TOA.4.2)
Applicable to any Titanic type situation.
See also "Siding with the losing party - ...though my reason sits in the wind against me.'
In the play. *Timon's suddenly unemployed servants reflect on their situation.*

Organization, perfect management o. such as the bees - ... So may a thousand actions, once afoot. end in one purpose...
"I this infer,
That many things, having full reference
To one consent, may work contrariously:
As many arrows, loosed several ways, Come to one mark; as many ways meet in one town;
As many fresh streams meet in one salt sea;
As many lines close in the dial's centre;
So may a thousand actions, once afoot.
End in one purpose, and be all well borne
Without defeat." (KHV.1.2)
Show an example of co-operative, well-directed action.
In the play. *After giving a description of the several tasks assigned to bees the Bishop of Canterbury sums up his presentation to convince King Henry to invade France. The bees are the perfect arrangement for an imperialistic and capitalist society. See 'Obedience, the ideal capitalist system - ... for so work the honey-bees...'*

Ornaments, enhancing a divine beauty - Sweet ornament, that decks a thing divine.

"Sweet ornament, that decks a thing divine." (TGV.2.1)
Compliment you can use whenever she wears something new or unusual, in any event, something that surprises you or that she wants you to surprise you with - a new hat, a pair of gloves, maybe even a tanga.
In the play. *The ornament is Silvia's glove, Valentine's newly found love in Milan.*

Ornaments, to make a goddess angry - Your laboursome and dainty trims, wherein you made great Juno angry.
"….and forget
Your laboursome and dainty trims, wherein
You made great Juno angry." (CYM.3.4)
Minor modifications required. Try this while observing in awe her dress, ornaments and attire, '… these are the laboursome and dainty trims wherein you would make even great Juno angry.' Juno was Jupiter's wife. With this line you are indirectly tell her that she is better than a goddess. Also answer to questions of the type, 'Do you like this necklace, or these earrings, or cameo, etc.' See also 'Disguise, taking on a d.'
Advising ladies on this subject Ovid says, 'Tis with elegance we are caught: let not your lock be lawless: a touch of the hand can give or deny beauty. Nor is there one form of adornment: let each choose what becomes her, and take counsel before her own mirror. An oval face prefers a parting upon the head left unadorned: the tresses of Laodamia* were so arranged. Round faces would fain have a small knot on top of the head, so that the ears show.' (AOL.3)
Laodamia was the wife of the first Greek to be slain by the Trojans, Protesilaus. She managed to get Hades to grant her a final meeting with her dead husband, but when he had to return to Hades she committed suicide and joined him.
* Hades is the lord of the dead and ruler of the nether world, also called the domain of Hades or in short, Hades.
In the play. *For her own safety Imogen must escape from her father's royal palace and dress as a man. This includes, as Pisanio suggests, leaving out all feminine decorations and frills.*

Outburst, puzzled at o. – … what means this passionate discourse…
"…what means this passionate discourse,
This peroration with such circumstance?" (KHVI.p2.1.1)
In the play. *Bishop of Wincester's comment at Gloucester's railing against the loss of lands in France.*

Outcome of events detectable in small details at the beginning - And in such indexes, although small pricks to their subsequent volumes…
"And in such indexes, although small pricks
To their subsequent volumes, there is seen
The baby figure of the giant mass
Of things to come at large." (TC.1.3)
Why you attribute great importance to the beginning of a relationship (or any project in general). See also 'Life, l.'s history of a person as a predictor of future performance – there is a history in all men's lives.'
In the play. *Hector has proposed a sporty duel with 'the best of the Greeks'. Nestor and Ulysses discuss who should answer Hector's challenge to an interim and sporty duel. Nestor says that the Trojans will draw their won conclusions on the strength or conditions of the Greeks based on which challenger they will present.*

Outcome, happy o. after a hard trial - …and if it end so meet, the bitter past, more welcome is the sweet.
"All yet seems well, and if it end so meet,
The bitter past, more welcome is the sweet." (AWEW.5.3)
Show your satisfaction at the successful end of a long struggle. See also 'Results, positive results in the end.'
In the play. *The King has the last word on the happy ending.*

Ovid, in praise of O. – The elegancy, facility, and golden cadence of poesy…
"…for the elegancy, facility, and golden cadence of poesy, caret, Ovidius Naso was the man" (LLL.1.2)
In the play. *The wordy and flowery Holofernes praises Ovid. 'Caret' comes from the Latin verb 'carere', that is, 'it misses'. Holofernes refers to poetry that he compares to Ovid. In other words, the poetry he refers to misses the elegancy, facility etc. which are instead characteristics of Ovid.*

Ownership by implication - ... when France is mine and I am yours, then yours is France and you are mine.
"... I love France so well that I will not part with a village of it; I will have it all mine: and, Kate, when France is mine and I am yours, then yours is France and you are mine." (KHV.5.2)
A good argument to claim the wealth of your future wife.
In the play. *King Henry pursues his suit with Katherine of France, even if it is just a formality. Katherine is part of the loot after Henry's victory at Agincourt.*

Ownership pre-established and without question - ... To try if that our own be ours or no.
"Belike your lordship takes us then for fools,
To try if that our own be ours or no." (KHVI p1.3.2)

In the play. *Joan of Arc is defiant towards Talbot.*

Pain, p. better endured by him who does nor feel it – He bears the sentence well that nothing bears…
"He bears the sentence well that nothing bears
But the free comfort which from thence he hears,
But he bears both the sentence and the sorrow
That, to pay grief, must of poor patience borrow.
These sentences, to sugar, or to gall,
Being strong on both sides, are equivocal" (OTH.1.5)
See also 'Philosophy, p. and tooth ache - ... there was never yet philosopher, that could endure the tooth-ache patiently.'
In the play. *Brabantio responds with a realistic statement to the Duke of Venice. The Duke counseled Brabantio to put a smile on the fact that she has married Othello against his wish.*

Pain, mental p. - … I am bound upon a wheel of fire, that mine own tears do scald like moulten lead.
"Thou art a soul in bliss; but I am bound
Upon a wheel of fire, that mine own tears
Do scald like moulten lead." (KL.4.7)
See also entries for 'Grief'
In the play. *King Lear on seeing his good daughter Cordelia in Dover, whom he previously wronged by banning her and leaving without inheritance.*

Pain, mental p. - These miseries are more than may be borne. To weep with them that weep doth ease some deal…
"These miseries are more than may be borne.
To weep with them that weep doth ease some deal;

But sorrow flouted at is double death." (T.A.3.1)
In the play. *Marcus Andronicus o n seeing the heads of Andronicus' sons and Andronicus' severed hand – all this being the result of arch-evil Aaron's deed. 'Flouted at' = 'jeered at'*

Pain, mental p. absolute - Nothing so heavy as these woes of mine.
"Nothing so heavy as these woes of mine" (KHVI.p2.5.2)
In the play. *York has killed Clifford Senior in battle at St. Alban's. Young Clifford vows revenge.*

Pain, mental p. aggravated by being concealed - Sorrow concealed, like an oven stopp'd doth burn the heart to cinders where it is.
"Sorrow concealed, like an oven stopp'd,
Doth burn the heart to cinders where it is." (T.A.2.5)
In the play. *Marcus, Lavinia's uncle, discovers her mutilated of her hands and tongue. Marcus is helpless as he cannot find the authors of the crime.*

Pain, mental p. at thinking of the future – ... when I do shape in forms imaginary the unguided days and rotten times...
"The blood weeps from my heart when I do shape
In forms imaginary the unguided days
And rotten times that you shall look upon" (KHIVp2.4.4)
In the play. *Ailing King Henry is concerned about the state of the kingdom after his death.*

Pain, mental p. leading to madness - Extremity of griefs would make men mad.
"Extremity of griefs would make men mad" (T.A.4.1)
In the play. *Young Lucius refers to Lavinia, who, deprived of tongue and hands tries desperately to communicate the name of her assailants.*

Pain, mental p. not realized by other party – ... thou wouldst not think how ill all's here about my heart.
"...thou wouldst not think how ill all's here about my heart: but it is no matter." (H.5.2)
In the play. *Hamlet to Horatio who thinks that Hamlet may hesitate to accept a fencing challenge by Laertes.*

Pain, mental p. reduced by seeing other sufferers - When we our betters see bearing our woes, we scarcely think our miseries our foes...
"When we our betters see bearing our woes,
We scarcely think our miseries our foes.
Who alone suffers suffers most i' the mind,
Leaving free things and happy shows behind:
But then the mind much sufferance doth o'er skip,
When grief hath mates, and bearing fellowship.
How light and portable my pain seems now" (KL.3.6)
In the play. *Edgar meditates on the state of Lear and compares Lear's predicament to his own*

Pain, mental p. relieved by talking about it - Give sorrow words: the grief that does not speak...
"Give sorrow words: the grief that does not speak
Whispers the o'er-fraught heart and bids it break." (M.4.3)
Comment to situations leading to sentences of the type, 'I am sorry if I annoy you with my troubles'. See also 'Grievances, g. aired out - windy attorneys to their client's woes ... let them have scope.'

In the play. *Hamlet has killed Macduff's wife and baby and Malcolm invites Macduff not to bottle his sorrow inside.*

Pain, mental p. that is both proud and cannot be supported by anything smaller than the earth.
"I will instruct my sorrows to be proud;
For grief is proud and makes his owner stoop.
To me and to the state of my great grief
Let kings assemble; for my grief's so great
That no supporter but the huge firm earth
Can hold it up." (KJ.3.1)
Add some drama, for example to your disappointment – use the last three lines, 'My grief's so great…hold it up'.
In the play. *Constance is dismayed at the news of the wedding of the Dauphin with the Lady Blanche. It means the loss of the English crown for young Arthur, Constance's son.*

Pain, mental p., greater suffering makes us insensitive to the lesser - … where the greater malady is fix'd the lesser is scarce felt.
"…where the greater malady is fix'd,
The lesser is scarce felt" (KL.3.4)
Explain why you can tolerate an apparent pain because you are tormented by a greater one. See also 'Dangers, assessment and priority of d. – Thou'ldst shun a bear; but if thy flight lay toward the raging sea…
In the play. *K. Lear to Kent who tries to get Lear to take cover from the fierce storm. 'Fixed' here means 'immovable' or 'not cured'. The storm is small matter compared to the Lear's pain due to filial ingratitude*

Pain, mental p. increased by impossibility to verbalize it - … the heart hath treble wrong when it is barr'd the aidance of the tongue…
"For lovers say, the heart hath treble wrong
When it is barr'd the aidance of the tongue.
…
Free vent of words love's fire doth assuage;
But when the heart's attorney once is mute,
The client breaks, as desperate in his suit. " (V&A)

Pain, mental p. leading to incoherent speech - Sorrow and grief of heart makes him speak fondly, like a frantic man.
"Sorrow and grief of heart
Makes him speak fondly, like a frantic man" (KRII.3.3)
In the play. *Northumberland reports to Henry Bolingbroke on the state of mind of King Richard.*

Pain, mental p., stones as a better audience than people - … I tell my sorrows to the stones; who, though they cannot answer my distress, yet in some sort they are better than the tribunes…
"Therefore I tell my sorrows to the stones;
Who, though they cannot answer my distress,
Yet in some sort they are better than the tribunes,
For that they will not intercept my tale:
When I do weep, they humbly at my feet
Receive my tears and seem to weep with me" (TA.3.1)
Tell an unfeeling audience what you think of them. See also 'Stones, s. more sympathetic than people – A stone is soft as wax,--tribunes more hard than stones…'
In the play. *The tribunes will not hear Titus A. Shattered by the murder of his sons and the*

mutilations of his daughter Lavinia, Andronicus finds the stones a more amenable audience

Pain, mental p., use of reason as a palliative - … If not a present remedy, at least a patient sufferance.
DON JOHN And when I have heard it, (reason),what blessing brings it?
CONRADE If not a present remedy, at least a patient sufferance.
(MAAN.1.3)
In the play. *Don John is constitutionally sad and wicked*

Pain, p. and sorrow altering perceptions - Sorrow breaks seasons and reposing hours, makes the night morning, and the noon-tide night.
"Sorrow breaks seasons and reposing hours,
Makes the night morning, and the noon-tide night." (KRIII.1.4)
In the play. *Clarence, imprisoned in the tower of London responds to a goodnight wish given to him by a guard.*

Pain, p. at having to say this – I grieve at what I speak and am right sorry to repeat what follows.
"…I grieve at what I speak,
And am right sorry to repeat what follows" (KHVIII.5.1)
In the play. *King Henry to Cardinal Cranmer, accused by fierce political opponents.*

Pain, p. internalized and invisible – …the unseen grief that swells with silence in the tortured soul…
"…the unseen grief
That swells with silence in the tortured soul;
There lies the substance" (KRII.4.1)
Comment on the suspected pain of a friend or person, or apply to your case if applicable.
In the play. *Richard II now deposed speaks to the (technically) usurper Bolingbroke.*

Pain, p. limiting power of expression - I'll utter what my sorrows give me leave.
"I'll utter what my sorrows give me leave." (COE.1.1)
Answer to 'How do you feel?' when you are hurt.
In the play. *Aegeon explains to the Duke of Syracuse the reasons why he came from Ephesus to Syracuse.*

Pain, p. or wrong, describing it not a cure – …if it should be told, the repetition cannot make it less…
"…if it should be told,
The repetition cannot make it less;
For more it is than I can well express:
And that deep torture may be call'd a hell
When more is felt than one hath power to tell." (ROL)
In the poem. *Lucrece answers a maid who inquires as to why Lucrece appears so sad.*

Pain, p. repressed more hurtful - Sorrow concealed, like an oven stopped, doth burn the heart to cinders where it is.
"Sorrow concealed, like an oven stopped,
Doth burn the heart to cinders where it is." (TA.2.4)
Prompt party to speak freely about his/her grievances. See also "Pain, mental p. relieved by talking about it.', 'Sorrow, disappointment, attitude towards s.' Grievances, g. aired out - windy attorneys to their client's woes … let them have scope.'
In the play. *Marcus discovers the mutilated Lavinia whose tongue has been cut. He does not know who did the evil act and cannot channel his anger, therefore 'sorrow is concealed'*

Pain, p. scorned at doubly painful - … sorrow flouted at is double death
"…sorrow flouted at is double death" (TA.3.1)

In the play. *Titus sacrifices his hand to save his sons wrongly accused of murder but they are executed anyway.*

Pain, p. soothed when shared with others - Grief best is pleased with grief's society...
"Grief best is pleased with grief's society:
True sorrow then is feelingly sufficed
When with like semblance it is sympathized
...
And fellowship in woe doth woe assuage" (ROL)

Pain, p. suffered by accused party contradicting alleged motives - Never did base and rotten policy colour her working with such deadly wounds.
"Never did base and rotten policy
Colour her working with such deadly wounds" (KHIV.p1.1.3)
In the play. *Hotspur tells Henry IV of the wounds suffered by Mortimer in battle for Henry's sake. Hence the king's insinuation that Mortimer is rebellious is false.*

Pain, p. that cannot be comforted - ...men can counsel, and speak comfort to that grief which they themselves do not feel... Charm ache with air and agony with words.
"... men
Can counsel, and speak comfort to that grief
Which they themselves do not feel;
but, tasting it,
Their counsel turns to passion, which before
Would give preceptial medicine to rage,
Fetter strong madness in a silken thread,
Charm ache with air and agony with words" (MAAN.5.1)
Reject attempts to comfort or solace you.

In the play. *Antonio counsels his brother Leonato not to lighten up but Leonato answers that it is impossible for Antonio to feel the pain the he (Leonato) is suffering.*

Pain, painful event, seeing it has greater impact than hearing about it - - To see sad sights moves more than hear them told...
"To see sad sights moves more than hear them told;
For then eye interprets to the ear
The heavy motion that it doth behold" (ROL)
One of the reason why governments are so careful to prevent to show on television the results of their crimes.
In the poem. *Lucrece decides to ask her husband and her family to come and see her so that they can witness her state and state of mind after the assault by the evil Tarquin.*

Pain, tears repressed but heart aches - Weep I cannot, but my heart bleeds.
"...Weep I cannot,
But my heart bleeds." (WT.3.3)
When she says 'no'. See also entries for 'Rejection'.
In the play. *Antigonus has been ordered by the king of Sicilia to kill the Hermione's baby. The king suspects unjustly that the baby isn't his. Antigonus does not kill the baby, instead he abandons it while regretting to have to do so.*

Painting, inherent value of the art of p. – ... the painting is almost the natural man...
"Painting is welcome.
The painting is almost the natural man;
For since dishonour traffics with man's nature,
He is but outside: these pencill'd figures are
Even such as they give out." (TOA.1.1)
Support the value of painting. Answer to 'Do you like painting?'

In the play. *A score of parasites, one of whom is a painter, come to feast at Timon's table and sell him their stuff, knowing that he is overgenerous.*

Painting, p. better than words to explain a concept - A thousand moral paintings I can show...
"A thousand moral paintings I can show,
That shall demonstrate these quick blows of fortune's
More pregnantly than words." (TOA.1.1)
Insert, 'A picture will show what I am talking about more pregnantly than words'.
In the play. *The painter claims he can represent events with paintings better than words do.*

Painting, your positive opinion on a p. – I will say of it, it tutors nature...
"Admirable: how this grace
Speaks his own standing! what a mental power
This eye shoots forth! how big imagination
Moves in this lip!
...
I will say of it,
It tutors nature: artificial strife
Lives in these touches, livelier than life." (TOA.1.1)
Answer to 'Do you like this painting?' (or graphics), especially if you have already assessed that she likes it.
In the play. *The poet praises the painter's painting. Both expect to extract some advantages by presenting their productions to the overgenerous Timon.*

Paleness, inquiring about the reasons of her p. - How chance the roses there do fade so fast?
"Why is your cheek so pale?
How chance the roses there do fade so fast?" (MND.1.1)
Inquire about the motive of whatever apprehension caused a lady's color to pale.
In the play. *Obstacles have arisen preventing Hermia to marry Lysander. Hermia pales and Lysander asks why.*

Paleness, the act of becoming pale – chased your blood out of appearance?
"... and chased your blood
Out of appearance?" (KHV.2.2)
In the play. *Traitor's Lords Grey, Scroop and Richard read the letters they wrote, that were seized and prove their treason.*

Paradise, a comparison - ... O nature! What hadst thou to do in hell when thou didst bower the spirit of a fiend...
"O nature! What hadst thou to do in hell,
When thou didst bower the spirit of a fiend
In mortal paradise of such sweet flesh?" (RJ.3.2)
Extract 'paradise of such sweet flesh' as a compliment.
In the play. *News that Romeo killed Tybald, Juliet's cousin has reached her. Not knowing that the killing was unprovoked and in self-defense, Juliet draws the wrong conclusions. 'Bower' stands for 'to cover', 'to attire'.*

Paradox, criticism followed by imitation - ... after he hath laughed at such shallow follies in others... will become the argument of his own scorn, by falling in love.
"I do much wonder that one man, seeing how much another man is a fool when he dedicates his behaviours to love, will, after he hath laughed at such shallow follies in others, become the argument of his own scorn, by falling in love." (MAAN.2.3)
In the play. *Benedick comments on Claudio's sudden love for Hero.*

Paradox, explaining a failure, infinite will, finite reality - This is the monstruosity in love, lady - that the will is infinite, and the execution confined…
"This is the monstruosity in love, lady - that the will is infinite, and the execution confined; that the desire is boundless, and the act a slave to limit." (TC.3.2)
Use any time she asks you something that you just cannot do. See also 'Age, sex and aging - Is it not strange that desire should so many years outlive performance?'
In the play. *Troilus admits that of all the promises that passion inspires to make only a limited number can be maintained.*

Paranoia - There is a plot against my life, my crown; all's true that is mistrusted.
"There is a plot against my life, my crown;
All's true that is mistrusted" (WT.2.1)
An argument to set up another office of homeland security.
In the play. *Paranoid Leontes now suspects everything and everybody.*

Pardon, p. befitting a king – The word is short, but not so short as sweet…
"The word is short, but not so short as sweet;
No word like 'pardon' for kings' mouths so meet." (KRII.5.3)
In the play. *The Duchess of York pleads with Bolingbroke to pardon her son Aumerle.*

Pardon, p. granted to thief while he retains the loot – May one be pardon'd and retain the offence?
"May one be pardon'd and retain the offence?" (H.3.3)
Apply to the many trials of mega-thieves who are discharged with minimal penalties and no clause of restitution.

In the play. *The king meditates. He is torn by the remorse for the killing of his brother Can he repent and still keep the usurped throne?*

Pardon, p. reasonable – I do think that you might pardon him and neither heaven nor man grieve at the mercy.
"…I do think that you might pardon him,
In the play. *Isabella pleads with Angelo to pardon her brother Claudio for his sin of fornication.*

Pardon, royalty of p. - … how royal 'twas to pardon when it was less expected.
"I minded him how royal 'twas to pardon
When it was less expected" (COR.5.1)
Answer to 'Why did you let it go at that?'
In the play. *Cominius reports to Rome about his efforts to convince Coriolanus to desist from fighting for the Volsces.*

Part, p. forgotten, like an actor forgetting his p. - Like a dull actor now, I have forgot my part…
"Like a dull actor now,
I have forgot my part, and I am out,
Even to a full disgrace." (COR.5.3)
When you suddenly forget what you wanted to say. See also entries for 'Forgetting'
In the play. *Coriolanus' wife and mother have now arrived to persuade him not to fight against the Romans. He sinks in a mood of self-deprecation.*

Part, easy p. to learn and play, roaring lion - … You may do it extempore, for it is nothing but roaring.
SNUG. Have you the lion's part written? pray you, if it be, give it to me for I am slow of study.
QUINCE. You may do it extempore, for it is nothing but roaring."
(MND.1.1)

Use as an anecdote to explain that the task you are assigned to do is in reality quite simple.
In the play. *A company of amateurs will stage a play and the actor Snug has an easy task of reciting.*

Part, unsuitable p. in a play – ... let not me play a woman; I have a beard coming.
Nay, faith, let not me play a woman; I have a beard coming." (MND.1.1)
Refuse to do something or play a role that is not in line with your disposition or character.
In the play. *A company of amateurs will stage a play and Flute thinks that the part he is assigned to play is unbecoming.*

Participation, p. in the scheme or debate inevitable - I see the play so lies that I must bear a part.
"I see the play so lies
That I must bear a part." (WT.4.3)
Use just before you are called into question or action or are asked for an opinion.
In the play. *The rogue Autolycus shows up. Camillo arranges for Florizel to exchange his clothes with those of Autolycus and for Perdita to be disguised as a man. The idea is not to get noticed on the ship that will take them to Sicilia. Perdita acknowledges that she must go along with the plot.*

Parting, p. with promise of fidelity –
Here is my hand for my true constancy...
"Here is my hand for my true constancy;
And when that hour o'erslips me in the day
Wherein I sigh not, Julia, for thy sake,
The next ensuing hour some foul mischance
Torment me for my love's forgetfulness!" (TGV.2.2)

In the play. *Proteus takes leave of Julia in Verona. He will quickly renege on his promise.*

Party, invitation to p. - ... let's take hand till the conquering wine hath steeped our sense in soft and delicate Lethe.
"Come, let's take hand
Till that the conquering wine hath steeped our sense
In soft and delicate Lethe." (AC.2.7)
Invitation to start the dance after the dinner party.
In the play. *Antony takes up an invitation to dance while already quite tipsy at a party hosted by Pompey.* In Greek mythology, Lethe is one of the rivers that flow through the realm of Hades. Called the River of Oblivion, the shades of the dead had to drink from this river to forget about their past lives on earth.

Party, let's party - ... we will begin these rites as we do trust they'll end in true delights.
" Proceed, proceed, we will begin these rites,
As we do trust they'll end in true delights." (AYLI.5.4)
Declare the party open.
In the play *The Duke gives an official start to the party for the married couple after Jacques has declined participation.*

Party, many fine ladies expected - look to behold this night earth treading stars, that make dark heaven light.
"At my poor house, look to behold this night
Earth treading stars, that make dark heaven light". (RJ.1.2)
Pull out the last line and turn it to singular, 'You are an earth trading star, that makes dark heaven light."
In the play. *Capulet Senior announces a party at his house in Verona. It is the party when Romeo will meet Juliet and instantly fall in love*

with her. For a complete rendition of the announcement including other quotes see 'April, A. welcome by young men - ... Such comfort as do lusty young men feel when well-apparell'd'

Party, not attracted to parties - ... so to your pleasures I am for other than for dancing measures.
" ... So, to your pleasures;
I am for other than for dancing measures." (AYLI.5.4)
Decline to join the party, 'Let them to their pleasures; I am... measures.'
In the play. *True to his own self, Jacques does not join the party for the married couples.*

Party, opening the p. - Prepare for mirth, for mirth becomes a feast...
"Prepare for mirth, for mirth becomes a feast:
You are princes and my guests." (PER.2.3)
Announce that the party under way. If 'princes' is too much change with 'gentlemen'
In the play. *The party for Thaisa's birthday is about to begin and her father King Simonides makes the announcement.*

Party, p. attended by fools and parasites - ... to see meat fill knaves, and wine heat fools
SECOND LORD. Thou art going to lord Timon's feast?
APEMANTUS. Ay; to see meat fill knaves, and wine heat fools."
(TOA.1.1)
Answer to question, "Will you go to XY's party?" when diplomacy suggests you go even if you loath most of the other party-goers
In the play. *Apemantus assesses the worth of Timon's company.*

Party, p. sounds out - Let not the sound of shallow foppery enter my sober house.
"Let not the sound of shallow foppery enter
My sober house" (MOV.2.5)
Could apply to other areas other than strictly partying. E.G. answer to 'Do you watch television?' 'I do not let the sound... house'.
In the play. *Shylock recommends to daughter Jessica to lock doors and windows while he is out. A masked parade is scheduled in Venice.*

Party, p. spoiler - You have displaced the mirth, broke the good meeting...
"You have displaced the mirth, broke the good meeting,
With most admired disorder." (M.3.4)
In the play. *Lady Macbeth to Macbeth who, during dinner, erupted in exclamations and fits leveled at Banquo's ghost, leaving the guests baffled and mystified.*

Party, p. time, celebration - ... let us banquet royally after this golden day of victory.
"... let us banquet royally,
After this golden day of victory."
(KHVIp1.1.5)
Announce a victory party
In the play. *Charles gives a party after the conquest of Orleans.*

Party, p. time, celebration - My banquet is to close our stomachs up... sit down; for now we sit to chat as well as eat.
"My banquet is to close our stomachs up,
After our great good cheer. Pray you, sit down;
For now we sit to chat as well as eat" (TOS.5.2)
In the play. *Lucentio to Hortensio and others as they attend his banquet.*

Party, partying till and after midnight - ... fill our bowls once more; let's mock the midnight bell.

"…fill our bowls once more;
Let's mock the midnight bell."
(AC.3.13)
In the play. *After his initial defeat at sea, Antony plucks some spirit and drinks to the next battle against Caesar Octavian.*

Party, partying with good wine, welcome and company - … good company, good wine, good welcome can make good people.
"… he would have all us merry
As, first good company, good wine, good welcome,
Can make good people." (KHVIII.1.4)
Introduction to a party. 'Our host would have all us merry… people'. Or 'I want you all to be merry as… people.'
In the play. *Sir Guildford announces the king's wishes to the ladies at the beginning of a party.*

Party, speeding to p. considering the charm of the participants – The very thought of this fair company clapp'd wings to me.
"The very thought of this fair company
Clapp'd wings to me." (KHVIII.1.4)
In the play. *K. Henry VIII organizes a party and it is at this party that he will meet with Ann Boleyn, his second wife (out of six). 'To clap' = 'to thrust, to do anything with fast motion'. Here 'applied wings to me'.*

Party, toasts and request to be merry - … that noble lady or gentleman that is not freely merry…
"You're welcome, my fair guests: that noble lady,
Or gentleman, that is not freely merry,
Is not my friend: this, to confirm my welcome;
And to you all, good health"
(KHVIII.1.4)
See also entries for 'Punishment, p. for not celebrating'

In the play. *Cardinal Wolsey welcomes guests and drinks a toast at a party organized by Henry VIII.*

Party, victory p. - And now what rests but that we spend the time with stately triumphs, mirthful comic shows…
"And now what rests but that we spend the time
With stately triumphs, mirthful comic shows,
Such as befits the pleasure of the court?
Sound drums and trumpets! farewell sour annoy!
For here, I hope, begins our lasting joy." (KHVI p3.5.7)
In the play. *All enemies defeated Edward IV declares it's time to party.*

Passion, behavior inspired by p. - … the brain may devise laws for the blood, but a hot temper leaps o'er a cold decree.
"…the brain may devise laws for the blood, but a hot temper leaps o'er a cold decree." (MOV.1.1)
Use to excuse or explain behavior inspired by passion, particularly if you have gone a bit overboard in the expression or materialization of your feelings. See also 'Theory and practice, their difference - if to do were as easy as to know what were good to do…'
In the play. *Portia candidly admits to a common weakness. The character or disposition of a man, called temper, was supposed to depend on the mixture of basic four humours, hot, cold, dry and wet. A hot temper would have an excess of choler (hot and dry) or of blood (hot and wet). Blood was associated with high spirits, prompt action and youth.*

Passion, desire to hear and to see her eyes - … do I love her, that I desire to hear her speak again and feast upon her eyes?

"…What, do I love her,
That I desire to hear her speak again,
And feast upon her eyes?" (MFM.2.3)
In the play. *Angelo cannot take Isabel out of his mind.*

Passion, effects of strong p. - This is the very ecstasy of love, whose violent property fordoes itself and leads the will to desperate undertakings.
"This is the very ecstasy of love,
Whose violent property fordoes itself,
And leads the will to desperate undertakings
As oft as any passion under heaven
That does afflict our natures" (H.2.1)
Use as a comment when the odd, silly or extraordinary action of someone in love become the subject of conversation. See also 'Blindness, b. of lovers to themselves - but love is blind and lovers cannot see the pretty follies they themselves commit.'
In the play. *Polonius concludes that Hamlet's apparent madness is attributable to Hamlet's passion for Ophelia.*

Passion, generating irrational belief (in oneself or in what said) - Methinks his words do from such passion fly, that he believes himself.
"Methinks his words do from such passion fly,
That he believes himself." (TN.3.5)
When someone, stubbornly and vehemently, sustains the wrong argument.
In the play. *Antonio has been arrested by the Duke's men and addresses Viola for help mistaking her (in her man's disguise) for her twin brother Sebastian. Of course she knows nothing of what is going on. Antonio is mad and Viola attempts an explanation.*

Passion, noble p. observed – … this noble passion, child of integrity …
"Macduff, this noble passion,
Child of integrity, hath from my soul
Wiped the black scruples, reconciled my thoughts
To thy good truth and honour" (M.4.3)
Explain your commitment, determination or passion for a good cause, e.g. 'I am passionate about this but it this passion that is child of integrity…'
In the play. *Malcolm pretends to be a very corrupt person to test Macduff's reaction. Macduff's noble reaction prompts Malcolm to say that his words were a test*

Passion, p. instantly developed - … if he be married, my grave is like to be my wedding bed.
"…if he be married.
My grave is like to be my wedding bed." (RJ.1.5)
If it is you that are awestruck by her, change 'if he' to 'if she'.
In the play. *Juliet is instantly taken by Romeo, who is now leaving the Capulet's party.*

Passion, overwhelming the heart - Why does my blood thus muster to my heart…
"Why does my blood thus muster to my heart,
Making both it unable for itself,
And dispossessing all my other parts
Of necessary fitness?" (MFM.2.4)
Tell her the influence she is having on you.
In the play. *Angelo is fired with passion for Isabella.*

Passion, power of p. to overcome obstacles - … passion lends them power, time means, to meet, tempering extremities with extreme sweet.
"… passion lends them power, time means, to meet,
Tempering extremities with extreme sweet." (RJ.1.5)
Remove 'them' to make a general statement or observation, e.g. 'Passion lends power…extreme sweet.'

In the play. *The chorus comments on the instant falling in love of Romeo and Juliet.*

Passion, self-compounding, clearly in love with him - ... she would hang on him as if increase of appetite had grown by what it fed on.
"… she would hang on him
As if increase of appetite had grown
By what it fed on." (H.1.2)
Turn it around and apply it to yourself to declare the strength of your passion, "My increase of appetite grows by what it feeds on."
In the play: *Hamlet reminisces how much his mother loved the dead king - in contrast she married her brother in law within a month after her husband died. The brother in law, unbeknown to her, actually murdered her husband (and his brother) and became the new king of Denmark.*

Passion, tied up by p. - ... faster bound to Aaron's charming eyes than is Prometheus tied to Caucasus.
"(she is) faster bound to Aaron's charming eyes
Than is Prometheus tied to Caucasus." (TA.2.1)
Here it is a woman who is tied to a man. In case of a man tied in the same fashion to a woman, change Aaron into the name of the woman and 'she' into the name of the man.
In the play. *Aaron knows that Tamora loves him and is tied to him 'faster than Prometheus to Caucasus'. Prometheus stole fire from the gods and gave it to mortals, carrying it away from Mount Olympus. As a consequence, Zeus chained Prometheus to a rock in the Caucasus area where each day an eagle pecked out his liver (which grew back each night).*

Passion, too strong, almost unbearable - ... some joy too fine, too subtle potent, turned too sharp in sweetness, for the capacity of my ruder powers…
"... some joy too fine,
Too subtle potent, turned too sharp in sweetness,
For the capacity of my ruder powers:
I fear it much; and I do fear besides,
That I shall lose distinctions of my joys:
As doth a battle, when they charge on heaps
The enemy flying." (TC.3.2)
An answer to "Do you like me? Or "Do you like this?" Stop at 'ruder powers'.
In December 1795 Napoleon Bonaparte wrote to Josephine de Beauharnais, his soon first-wife-to-be, '...You are leaving at noon; I shall see you in three hours. Until then, mio dolce amor, a thousand kisses; but give me none in return, for they set my blood on fire.'
And in another letter to Josephine, in 1796, he says, '...whether I am at the head of my army or inspecting the camps, my beloved Josephine stands alone in my heart, occupies my mind, fills my thoughts. If I am moving away from you, it is only that I may see you again more quickly.'
In the play. *Troilus awaits the arrival of Cressida in the orchard.*

Past, happy p. as a dream - ... learn, good soul, to think our former state a happy dream...
"…learn, good soul,
To think our former state a happy dream;
From which awaked, the truth of what we are
Shows us but this (KRII.5.1)
See also 'Necessity, brother to n. - I am sworn brother, sweet, to grim Necessity….'

In the play. *Richard II, deposed from the throne, addresses his wife.*

Patience, against p. – Patience is for poltroons.
"Patience is for poltroons"
(KHVI.p3.1.1)
In the play. *Clifford is angry at the pretences to the throne of Plantagenet (York).*

Patience, asking for a little p. - ... I shall crave your forbearance a little.
"...I shall crave your forbearance a little." (MFM.4.1)
In the play. *The Duke (disguised) to Mariana to whom he will shortly disclose the plot he has in mind.*

Patience, asking for p. or a raise - I am much too venturous in tempting of your patience...
"I am much too venturous
In tempting of your patience; but am boldened
Under your promised pardon."
(KHVIII.1.2)
Introduce a request or warn that what you say next is a request, for example a request for a raise. See also "Advance, applying for an advance or raise' – 'Financial status, challenging'.
In the play. *Queen Kathryn addresses the king regarding her grievances*

Patience, calm down - ... Sheath thy impatience; throw cold water on thy choler.
" ... but first sheath thy impatience; throw cold water on thy choler." (MWW.2.3)
Calm down an excitable character
In the play. *The Host counsels patience to Doctor Caius who is in competition with Slender to win the hand of Miss Anne Page.*

Patience, calm down – ... Upon the heat and flame of thy distemper sprinkle cool patience.
"...Upon the heat and flame of thy distemper
Sprinkle cool patience." (H.3.4)
Ask one or many to calm down. See also entries for 'Conflict resolution'.
In the play. *Queen Gertrude sees Hamlet seemingly addressing the Ghost and thinks that he is 'distempered' or mad.*

Patience, compared to a tired horse - ... though patience be a tired mare, yet she will plod.
"...though patience be a tired mare, yet she will plod." (KHV.2.1)
When you reluctantly will continue to have patience. Try, '...though patience... she will plod, I'll be patient for a bit longer'.
In the play. *Nym's philosophy of life. Nym and Bardolph, tavern and brothel companions of Falstaff discuss their own affairs.*

Patience, counseling p. to sorrow useless - ... 'tis all men's office to speak patience to those that wring under the load of sorrow...
"...'tis all men's office to speak patience
To those that wring under the load of sorrow,
But no man's virtue nor sufficiency
To be so moral when he shall endure
The like himself" (MAAN.5.1)
See also 'Comfort, c. useless - Charm ache with air and agony with words'
In the play. *Leonato's reaction to the words of comfort offered by his brother Antonio.*

Patience, endowed with the utmost p. - Were I as patient as the midnight sleep, by Jove, 'twould be my mind!
"Were I as patient as the midnight sleep,
By Jove, 'twould be my mind!"
(COR.3.1)
Answer to, 'Are you patient?' or retort to 'You are so impatient'. Try, 'I am as

patient as the midnight sleep.'. See also entries for 'Anger'.
In the play. *Coriolanus is anything but patient and is mad at the tribunes and the people. He is the quintessential far right winger.*

Patience, exhortation to p. - ... with patience calm the storm while we bethink a means to break it off.
"Renowned queen, with patience calm the storm,
While we bethink a means to break it off." (KHVI.p3.3.3)
In the play. *King Louis to Queen Margaret who has come to seek help against the Yorkists in England.*

Patience, exhortation to p. - I pray thee, sort thy heart to patience...
"The greatest help is quiet, gentle Nell
I pray thee, sort thy heart to patience;
These few days' wonder will be quickly worn." (KHVI p2.2.4)
Use as words of comfort.
In the play. *The Duchess of Gloucester, prisoner after her trial for treason and witchcraft, warns her husband to beware of his enemies. Gloucester responds exhorting her to be patient in the circumstances. She has been sent in exile and prison to the Isle of Man.*

Patience, p. and time management required - How poor are they that have not patience!...
"How poor are they that have not patience!
What wound did ever heal but by degrees?
Thou knowest we work by wit, and not by witchcraft;
And wit depends on dilatory time." (OTH.2.3)
Answer to, "Haven't you finished yet?' E.G. 'I work by wit and not by witchcraft'. Use only the last two lines to explain why you need more time. See also

'Anger. Answer to "Are you patient?" or "Do you get angry easily?"
In the play. *Iago counsel patience to the impatient Roderigo.*

Patience, p. as a palliative – I have her sovereign aid and rest myself content.
"... I have her sovereign aid
And rest myself content." (TEM.5.1)
In the play. *Prospero counsels Alonso to use patience.*

Patience, p. as a weapon against bad fortune – What cannot be preserved when fortune takes...
"What cannot be preserved when fortune takes
Patience her injury a mockery makes" (OTH.1.5)
See also, 'Attitude, positive a. in reversals - The robb'd that smiles steals something from the thief...'
In the play. *The Duke of Venice counsels Brabantio, Desdemona's father, to put a smile on the fact that she has married Othello against his wish.*

Patience, p. lost - ... quite besides the government of patience
"Quite besides
The government of patience!" (CYM.2.4)
In the play. *In Rome, Philario notes that Leonatus is distraught after Jachimo's false revelations about the alleged dishonesty of Imogen*

Patience, p. or cowardice? - That which in mean men we entitle patience is pure cold cowardice in noble breasts.
"That which in mean men we entitle patience,
Is pure cold cowardice in noble breasts" (KRII.1.2)
Retort to 'Have patience'. Explain why you cannot longer have patience when you are invited to continue to use it. Use 'entitle' instead of 'intitle'.

In the play. *The duchess of Gloucester upbraiding Gaunt for not seeking revenge for the killing of the Duke of Gloucester, her brother.*

Patience, p. requested - ... If you'll bestow a small (of what you have little) patience...
"I will tell you;
If you'll bestow a small (of what you have little)
Patience…." (COR.1.1)
Prompt patience when insistently asked a question.
In the play. *Menenius attempts to soothe the rebellious citizens and bring them to reason.*

Patience, p. required until horoscope improves. See 'Fortune, moment of unfavorable conditions due to astrological influences'.

Patience, p. should rule misfortune - … let mischance be slave to patience.
"… let mischance be slave to patience" (RJ.5.3)
It can be an exhortation to others, as well as an act of self-encouragement.
In the play. *The Prince invites Montague to have patience while he (the Prince) will sort out the events that led the death of both Romeo and Juliet.*

Patience, p. strained - Who can be patient in such extremes?
KING HENRY VI Be patient, gentle queen, and I will stay.
QUEEN MARGARET Who can be patient in such extremes? (KHVI p3.1.1)
In the play. *Q. Margaret upbraids the husband for his weakness towards the Yorkists.*

Patience, p. with authority strained - How long shall I be patient? ah, how long shall tender duty make me suffer wrong?
"How long shall I be patient? ah, how long

Shall tender duty make me suffer wrong?" (KRII.2.1)
In the play. *The Duke of York to King Richard on hearing that the king wants to confiscate Gaunt's estate.*

Patience, reluctantly silent – I will be the pattern of all patience, I will say nothing.
"... I will be the pattern of all patience;
I will say nothing." (KL.3.2)
When you want to make it clear that your silence is an act of will not of inclination. Or you want to reassure that you will be patient, when prompted to be so.
In the play. *King Lear will say nothing at the sarcastic comments of the Fool who points out Lear's shortcomings.*

Patience, resigned to the situation and bearing it with p. and melancholy - … And with a green and yellow melancholy, she sat like Patience on a monument…
"... she pined in thought;
And with a green and yellow melancholy,
She sat like Patience on a monument,
Smiling at grief." (TN.2.4)
Answer to 'What have you done about it so far?' Turn the third to the first person, 'I have pined in thought… grief'.
In the play. *Viola tells the Duke a story in which a woman loved a man but concealed her love. The love is actually real, but Viola, being disguised as Cesario, cannot make it known.*

Patience, rhetorical self-analysis - Why have I patience to endure all this?
"Why have I patience to endure all this?" (TA.2.3)
In the play. *Tamora's reaction at Lavinia who has discovered Tamora's adultery.*

Patience, running out of p. - The devil take Henry of Lancaster and thee! patience is stale, and I am weary of it.
"The devil take Henry of Lancaster and thee!
Patience is stale, and I am weary of it." (KRII.5.5)
Change 'Henry of Lancaster' to the name of him who harasses you.
In the play. *Richard to his keeper at Pomfret Castle. The keeper refuses to taste the (poisoned) meat designed to kill Richard. Richard will not eat, but Exton, a leader of assassins will finish Richard who puts up a good fight.*

Patriotism – … But yet I love my country, and am not one that rejoices in the common wreck…
"But yet I love my country, and am not
One that rejoices in the common wreck,
As common bruit doth put it." (TOA.5.1)
Change 'bruit' to 'noise' or 'word'
In the play. *Timon to the flattering senators who, now meek and afraid, have come to plead with Timon to return to Athens. Timon loathes them, will refuse to go but will do whatever in his power to save the city from the ire of his friend Alcibiades.*

Pause, relaxation after victorious struggle - … good fortune bids us pause, and smooth the frowns of war with peaceful looks.
"Now breathe we, lords; good fortune bids us pause,
And smooth the frowns of war with peaceful looks." (KHVI p3.2.6)
Introduction to a victory speech
In the play. *Edward after the enemy retreats at the battle of Towton.*

Payment, p. after service – When I have chased all thy foes from hence, then will I think upon a recompense.
"When I have chased all thy foes from hence,
Then will I think upon a recompense" (KHVI.p1.1.2)
Answer to 'How much do your services cost?' E.G. 'Once I have resolved your problems, or rather, as Joan of Arc said…When I have chased…recompense'.
In the play. *The Dauphin of France hints at marrying Joan of Arc but her priority is the liberation of France from the English.*

Payment, refusing to be p. – All gold and silver rather turn to dirt, as 'tis no better reckon'd, but of those who worship dirty gods.
"All gold and silver rather turn to dirt!
As 'tis no better reckon'd, but of those
Who worship dirty gods." (CYM.3.6)
In the play. *Imogen, now attired as a man, wants to pay for her food, but Arviragus says no.*

Payroll, meeting the p. – … there is remuneration; for the best ward of mine honour is rewarding my dependents.
"…there is remuneration; for the best ward of mine honour is rewarding my dependents." (LLL.3.1)
See also See 'Salary, meager s. - Remuneration! O, that's the Latin word for three farthings'
In the play. *Armado gives a letter to Costard to be delivered to Jaquenetta, loved by Armado.*

Peace, calling for p. - … let your drums be still for here we entertain a solemn peace.
"Hang up your ensign, let your drums be still,
For here we entertain a solemn peace." KHVI.p1.5.5)
Silence an argumentative and uncompromising person.

In the play. *York to Charles of France after a peace agreement has been signed. Reignier and Alencon have convinced Charles to accept the terms offered by the English.*

Peace, calling for p. - Peace, peace, for shame, if not for charity.
BUCKINGHAM. Peace, peace, for shame, if not for charity.
QUEEN MARGARET. Urge neither charity, nor shame to me." (KRIII.1.3)
'For xxx, if not for yyy' where x and y may vary is a sentence occasionally used for exhortation. Reply by saying 'Urge neither xxx, nor yyy to me.'
In the play. *Margaret is mad at Richard, Buckingham and their entourage. She calls them 'wrangling pirates'.*

Peace, exhortation to stop arguing - ... cease these jars, and rest your minds in peace.
"Cease, cease these jars, and rest your minds in peace! " (KHVIp1.1.1)
See also, 'Conflict resolution, calming down the debate' – Entries for 'Quarrel'
In the play. *The duke of Bedford tries to soothe the animosity between the Bishop of Winchester and the Duke of Gloucester.*

Peace, in praise of p. - ... dear nurse of arts, plenties and joyful births.
"... peace,
Dear nurse of arts, plenties and joyful births." (KHV.5.2)
Calm people down. 'Let's have peace, dear nurse of arts… births.'
In the play. *The duke of Burgundy makes a plea for peace.*

Peace, inconsistency of p. proposal – What, drawn and talk of peace?
"What, drawn and talk of peace?" (RJ.1.1)
In the play. *Servants of the Montagues and Capulets enter into a brawl. Benvolio, friend of Romeo, tries to restore piece, Tybald, nephew of Lady Capulet is not of the same idea.*

Peace, inner p. felt. - ... I feel within me a peace above all earthly dignities, a still and quiet conscience.
" I know myself now, and I feel within me
A peace above all earthly dignities,
A still and quiet conscience."
(KHVIII.3.2)
Put a good countenance in the face of events, or consider the other side of the coin.
In the play. *Wolsey to his servant Cromwell after Wolsey's fall from grace*

Peace, inner p., self-created disruption of one's inner peace -... put rancours in the vessel of my peace.
"For them the gracious Duncan have I murdered:
Put rancours in the vessel of my peace" (M.3.1)
Use as is to justify your sour attitude or modify it into an explanation for a negative reply, e.g. 'I do not want to put rancours in the vessel of my peace'.
In the play. *Macbeth has lost his inner peace after having killed King Duncan and yet he realizes that he has done all this for the benefit of Banquo's issue, according to the prediction of the witches.*

Peace, invitation to p. - ... tame the savage spirit of wild war
"... tame the savage spirit of wild war" (KJ.5.2)
In the play. *Cardinal Pandulph exhorts Lewis of France to drop his war plans against England*

Peace, invocation and wishes for p. - ... poor and mangled peace, dear nurse of arts and joyful births...
"...let it not disgrace me,
If I demand, before this royal view,
What rub or what impediment there is.

Why that the naked, poor and mangled Peace,
Dear nurse of arts and joyful births,
Should not in this best garden of the world
Our fertile France, put up her lovely visage?
...
And as our vineyards, fallows, meads and hedges,
Defective in their natures, grow to wildness,
Even so our houses and ourselves and children
Have lost, or do not learn for want of time,
The sciences that should become our country;
But grow like savages,--as soldiers will
That nothing do but meditate on blood,--
To swearing and stern looks, diffused attire
And every thing that seems unnatural.
Which to reduce into our former favour
You are assembled: and my speech entreats
That I may know the let, why gentle Peace
Should not expel these inconveniences
And bless us with her former qualities" (KHV.5.2)
In the play. *In the royal French palace the duke of Burgundy makes a plea for peace between France and England – peace shortly to be formalized and strengthened the marriage between Henry V and Katharine of France.*

Peace, offer of p. - His glittering arms he will commend to rust...
"His glittering arms he will commend to rust,
His barbed steeds to stables, and his heart
To faithful service of your majesty."
(KRII.3.3)
Change 'his' to 'my' and 'he' to 'I' when you are ready to make peace, e.g. 'My glittering arms I will commend to rust etc.' If you are making peace with your wife or girlfriend change 'majesty' to grace'.
In the play. *Flint Castle. Bolingbroke affirms that he will not challenge the rightful King Richard II though he is already planning to do so.*

Peace, p. advocated between France and England - ... combine the blood of malice in a vein of league and not to spend it so unneighbourly.
"O nation, that thou couldst remove!
That Neptune's arms, who clippeth thee about,
Would bear thee from the knowledge of thyself,
And grapple thee unto a pagan shore;
Where these two Christian armies might combine
The blood of malice in a vein of league,
And not to spend it so unneighbourly" (KJ.5.2)
Use the last two lines to exhort to peace, e.g. 'Let's convert this blood of malice in a vein of league and not spend it so unneighborly'.
In the play. *Lord Salisbury to King Lewis of France. Salisbury has reluctantly and temporarily joined the French forces against the murderous King John of England.*

Peace, p. after rebellion - Our peace will, like a broken limb united grow stronger for the breaking.
"Our peace will, like a broken limb united,
Grow stronger for the breaking." (KHIVp2.4.1)
In the play. *The Archbishop of York hopes that the supposed peace terms offered by the King*

may be real and good for the rebels' aims. It will not be so.

Peace, p. among equals - ... It was both impious and unnatural, that such cruelty and bloody strife should reign among professors of one faith.
"...for I always thought
It was both impious and unnatural,
That such cruelty and bloody strife
Should reign among professors of one faith." (KHVI.p1.5.1)
A reason for promoting peace among equals. Faith can be extended to other areas than religion, e.g. the faith of reason.
In the play. *Henry VI concurs with Gloucester's proposal to make peace with the French.*

Peace, p. and harmony sanctioned by the highest powers - The fingers of the powers above do tune the harmony of this peace.
"The fingers of the powers above do tune
The harmony of this peace."
(CYM.5.4)
A final remark after an agreement has been reached, to resolve a thorny or controversial issue.
In the play. *The British and the Romans make peace and the soothsayer comments accordingly.*

Peace, p. and reconciliation - ... to the brightest beams distracted clouds give way...
"... to the brightest beams
Distracted clouds give way; so stand thou forth,
The time is fair again." (AWEW.5.3)
A recovery is in full swing, e.g. 'We have now turned the corner and 'to the brightest beams, distracted clouds give way; so stand we forth, the time is fair again'.
In the play. *The King has forgiven Bertram for his mistakes and all is on the point of ending well.*

Peace, p. as the goal of war - ... cheerly on, courageous friends to reap the harvest of perpetual peace by this one bloody trial of sharp war.
"In God's name cheerly on, courageous friends,
To reap the harvest of perpetual peace
By this one bloody trial of sharp war."
(KRIII.5.2)
Use to motivate action or as a reminder that all wars have peace as a goal.
In the play. *Richmond in a plain near Tamworth pumps up the troops before the battle with the forces of Richard III.*

Peace, p. at last - Now civil wounds are stopp'd, peace lives again that she may long live here, God say amen.
"Now civil wounds are stopp'd, peace lives again:
That she may long live here, God say amen!" (KRIII.5.5)
Comment when a dispute has been settled.
In the play. *Final words by the victorious Richmond. The civil wounds are those brought about by the slain Richard III and in general by the civil war of the Roses between the House of Lancaster and the House of York. The battle of Bosworth Field officially puts an end to the civil war.*

Peace, p. considered as a conquest and a victory – A peace is of the nature of a conquest ; for then both parties nobly are subdued...
"A peace is of the nature of a conquest;
For then both parties nobly are subdued,
And neither party loser." (KHIVp2.4.2)
Comment on an important agreement between management and trade unions, reached after heavy debates.

In the play. *The archbishop of York is ready to accept the peace terms offered by the King's representatives, but it will turn out to be a deadly trap.*

Peace, p. declared – The edge of war, like an ill-sheathed knife, no more shall cut his master.
"The edge of war, like an ill-sheathed knife,
No more shall cut his master" (KHIV p1.1.1)
At the end of a dispute peacefully concluded.
In the play. *Aged K. Henry IV believes peace reigns on his land and plans a trip to Jerusalem. His belief will be proven wrong.*

Peace, p. making efforts - Let's purge this choler without letting blood.
"Let's purge this choler without letting blood!
This we prescribe, though no physician;
Deep malice makes too deep incision:
Forget, forgive, conclude and be agreed;
Our doctors say, this is no month to bleed." (KRII.1.1)
Intervene when the debate becomes too hot and tempers and anger rise. If a lady is angry just use the first line. Keep in mind that if she is really angry she may have little patience for Shakespeare, but the power of words is often unpredictable and it is worth the try.
In the play. *Richard II tries to mediate (unsuccessfully) between Mowbray and Bolingbroke who accuses Mowbray of treason.*

Peace, p. of the soul, only learning to become nothing can provide some comfort - Nor I nor any man that but man is, with nothing shall be pleased, till he be eased with being nothing.
"… but whate'er I be,
Nor I nor any man that but man is,
With nothing shall be pleased, till he be eased
With being nothing" (KRII.5.5)
In the play. *Richard II, in prison at Pomfret Castle alone with his thoughts.*

Peace, p. promised - My tongue shall hush again this storm of war and make fair weather in your blustering land.
"My tongue shall hush again this storm of war,
And make fair weather in your blustering land." (KJ.5.1)
Support peace and declare that you are no longer angry ('my tongue….war')
In the play. *Pandulph has switched sides and wants to prop up K. John, by promising peace, providing K. John fights a war first.*

Peace, shaky p. - This late dissension, grown betwixt the peers burns under feigned ashes of forged love…
"This late dissension, grown betwixt the peers,
Burns under feigned ashes of forged love,
And will at last break out into flame." (KHVI.p1.3.1)
Describe a shaky peace. E.G. "This late dissension burns …flame.' See also 'Conflict, c. smoldering between two parties.'
In the play. *Exeter comments on recent events and the brawl between the peers at the court of Henry VI, each one of which has a separate personal agenda.*

Peerless, without comparison - … the most peerless piece of earth, I think, e'er the sun shone bright on.
"….the most peerless piece of earth, I think,
That e'er the sun shone bright on." (WT.5.1)
Answer to her question 'What do you think of me?' '(You are) the most…bright on.'

In the play. *Answering an inquiry from Leontes, a gentleman comments on the beauty of Perdita who is approaching Leontes' court.*

People, love of the p. to a limit – ... I love the people but do not like to stage me to their eyes...
"...I love the people,
But do not like to stage me to their eyes:
Through it do well, I do not relish well
Their loud applause and Aves vehement;
Nor do I think the man of safe discretion
That does affect it." (MFM.1.1)
In the play. *Duke Vicentio will leave Vienna incognito and leave the government temporarily in the hands of Angelo. 'Aves' is Latin for salutations to an emperor.*

People, the fewer the better for a great enterprise - ... the fewer men, the greater share of honour.
"If we are mark'd to die, we are enough
To do our country loss; and if to live,
The fewer men, the greater share of honour." (KHV.4.3)
Use as a comparison when you start a project with limited resources. See also 'Challenge, the greater the c. the greater the victory - The harder match'd, the greater victory.'
In the play. *Henry V addresses the troops before the battle of Agincourt.*

People, there are all sorts of p. – Nature hath meal and bran, contempt and grace.
"Nature hath meal and bran, contempt and grace" (CYM.4.2)
In the play. *Belarus, adoptive father of Guiderius and Arviragus wonders at their nobility as observed in dealing with Fideles/Imogen, who turns out to be their sister.*

Perception, craftiness can make bad appear good - ... His countenance, like richest alchemy will change to virtue and to worthiness.
"O, he sits high in all the people's hearts:
And that which would appear offence in us,
His countenance, like richest alchemy,
Will change to virtue and to worthiness" (JC.1.3)
One has but to look at Ronald Reagan's disasters that he caused to the very people who actually thought high of him. With mild modification you can apply the statement to the media, e.g. '...that which would appear offence in us, the media, like richest alchemy ...worthiness.' See entries for 'Opinion, your o. on the masses' *** 'Interpretation, i. of events depending on the interpreter'
In the play. *Cassius explains to Casca how Caesar can make people believe that what is bad for them is actually good.*

Perception, giving the right spin to an event by using the right words – ... but now the bishop turns insurrection to religion.
"This word, rebellion, it had froze them up,
As fish are in a pond: but now the bishop
Turns insurrection to religion:
Suppos'd sincere and holy in his thoughts,
He's follow'd both with body and with mind." (KHIVp2.1.1)
Illustrate different perceptions of the same event. When the government decides to invest trillions in defense spending, they will not say that the money will end into the pocket of the contractors who elected the government with their campaign contribution. Rather they will say that this is crucial to defend the American citizen. In other words, to

make war, they call it peace or democracy. Hence, e.g. 'This word, war, it would freeze them up as fish are in a pond: but now the cabinet turns war to peace, supposed sincere and holy and people follow both with body and mind'. If you are still not convinced, remember that one model of nuclear missile was called 'Peace Maker'. Or read Orwell's '1984' where the ministry of war is called the ministry of peace.
In the play. *Morton shows the advantages of a rebellion supported by religious motives. The bishop referred to is Scroop, archbishop of York who has turned against Henry IV. To further illustrate the uncomfortable or undecided state of mind of the rebel forces Morton also says these lines,*
For that same word, rebellion, did divide
The action of their bodies from their souls.

Perception, p. determining judgment – This service is not service, so being done but being so allow'd.
"This service is not service, so being done,
But being so allow'd" (CYM.3.3)
In the play. *Belarius tells his adoptive sons that no action is servile unless they think it so.*

Perception, you want me dead - Thou hidest a thousand daggers in thy thoughts…
"Thou hidest a thousand daggers in thy thoughts,
Which thou hast whetted on thy stony heart,
To stab at half an hour of my life" (KHIV.p2.4.4)
Ironically suggest to a colleague that he hates you or is conspiring against you. See also 'Place, a dangerous p. – where we are there's daggers in men's smiles'
In the play. *London, the Jerusalem chamber at court. Mistakenly, King Henry thinks that his son Prince Henry wants him dead.*

Perfection, astrological contribution to her perfection - … The senate-house of planets all did sit to knit in her their best perfections.
"…to glad her presence,
The senate-house of planets all did sit,
To knit in her their best perfections." (PER.1.1)
Compliment; change to 'when you were born, to glad your presence, the senate-house…perfections'.
In the play. *Pericles has arrived in Antioch and Antiochus is ready to present his daughter and describes her perfection.*

Perfection, conditions to avoid in order to achieve p. - For he's no man on whom perfections wait….
"For he's no man on whom perfections wait
That, knowing sin within, will touch the gate" (PER.1.1)
In the play. *Pericles reflects after solving the riddle presented by King Antioch, riddle that clearly showed evidence of incest.*

Perfection, her p. unbelievable - Who will believe my verse in time to come…
"Who will believe my verse in time to come,
If it were fill'd with your most high deserts? " (SON 27)

Perfection, her p. unparalleled - … her, whom, we know well the world's large spaces cannot parallel.
"Well may we fight for her, whom, we know well,
The world's large spaces cannot parallel." (TC.2.2)
Dress it up a little, for example, 'You are as beautiful as Helen of Troy of whom Paris said, 'Well may we fight for her…"parallel.'

713

In the play. *Paris, the most interested party, is all for keeping Helen with the Trojans, rather than giving her back to the Greeks.*

Perfection, p. compounding with p. - ... each your doing, so singular in each particular... that all your acts are queens.
"...each your doing,
So singular in each particular,
Crowns what you are doing in the present deed,
That all your acts are queens." (WT 4.4)
The fourth line is enough. Answer to question whether you like what she has done.
In the play. *Florizel praises Perdita's perfection. Everything Perdita does is a royal act, or each of her actions is invested with supreme (royal) perfection.*

Perfection, p. even in her shortcomings - She spoke and panted that she made defect perfection.
"She spoke and panted,
That she made defect perfection."
(AC.2.2)
Change to 'You make defect perfection'. Follow up to her saying "I am sorry" for whatever reason. See also 'Apologies unnecessary, on the contrary – Thou mak'st faults graces that to thee resort...'
In the play. *Enobarbus, Antony's soldier and bodyguard describes Cleopatra to another soldier in Rome and says of her, "And having lost her breath, she spoke, and panted that she did make defect perfection".*

Perfection, p. in action, speech, dance etc. – What you do, still betters what is done. When you speak, sweet, I'd have you do it ever...
"What you do,
Still betters what is done. When you speak, sweet,
I'd have you do it ever ....when you dance,
I wish you a wave of the sea, that you may do nothing but that." (WT.4.4)
Compliment or flattery. See also entries for 'Flattery'.
In earlier times woman was often compared to or associated with the sea. In an essay written in 1629 we read, "It is Simonide's opinion that woman is similar to the sea. And perhaps it is because of this that antiquity believed that Venus was born in and from the sea. And truly, a woman is nothing less than a sea, if we consider the instances of happiness and the instances of bitterness she can inflict on us. When in a good mood she prompts us to pleasure, when surly she threatens us, when angry she assails us. These are phenomena identical to those of the sea. The sea invites us when calm, frightens us with tempests and prepares our tomb in its vortexes. Inconstant, untamable and insatiable is woman. Unfathomable, proud and endless is the sea. In summary, sea and woman, woman and sea are the same thing." (Loredano, "Academic Fancies" (1629).
If she likes dancing and/or is especially fond of ballet and you are not, you may remind her of Checkov's related assessment, "I don't understand anything about ballet. All I know is that during the intervals, the ballerinas stink like horses" (Anton Checkov, 1860-1904).
In the play. *Florizel is head over heels in love with Perdita.*

Perfection, p. never total – ... no perfection is so absolute, that some impurity doth not pollute
"But no perfection is so absolute,
That some impurity doth not pollute"
(ROL)
In the poem. *Evil Tarquin knows he is committing a crime and meditates on it with various arguments.*

Perfection, p. that excludes any possibility of evil - There's nothing ill can dwell in such a temple…
"There's nothing ill can dwell in such a temple:
If the ill spirit have so fair a house,
Good things will strive to dwell with't." (TEM.1.2)
Use the first line to show that you believe her claims of innocence.
In the play. *Miranda vouchsafes for the nobility and honor of Ferdinand against the accusations of her father.*

Perfection, the description of her p. would fill volumes - The chief perfections of that lively dame… would make a volume of enticing lines…
"The chief perfections of that lively dame,
(Had I sufficient skill to utter them,)
Would make a volume of enticing lines,
Able to ravish any dull conceit." (KHVI p1, 5.5)
Answer to 'What do you think of her?' Or, if you wish to extend the lines to her directly as a compliment, change the first line to, 'Your chief perfections.'
In the play. *The earl of Suffolk has described to the young King Henry VI the beauty of Lady Margaret soon to arrive in England. Lady Margaret will marry Henry and the marriage, supposedly, should ensure a lasting peace between England and France. It will turn out otherwise.*

Perfection, wishing no one else but her - … nor can imagination form a shape beside yourself, to like of.
"… I would not wish
Any companion in the world but you,
Nor can imagination form a shape,
Besides yourself, to like of." (TEM.3.1)
This is a she-to-him compliment, but it would seem more suitable as a he-to-her pronouncement.
In the play. *This amounts to a declaration of love by Miranda to Ferdinand.*

Perfection, worthy of a king - … all her perfections challenge sovereignty; one way or other, she is for a king.
"Her looks do argue her replete with modesty;
Her words do show her wit incomparable;
All her perfections challenge sovereignty:
One way or other, she is for a king;" (KH6 p3.2.1)
Change 'her' to 'your' and 'she' to 'you', i.e. 'Your looks do argue you replete with modesty…all your perfections challenge sovereignty: one way or other, you are for a king.'
In the play. *Edward, now king Edward IV is supposed to marry Lady Bona, sister of the King of France. But in a sudden reversal of intent and burst of passion, Edward falls in love with the widow Lady Gray and marries her. This will upset many people who supported him, including Warwick the king-maker. Edward will even temporarily lose the throne. In some ways the Lady Gray was to Edward IV what Mrs. Simpson was to Edward VIII.*

Performance, effectiveness of p. depending on quality of choreography or suitable setting. - The nightingale, if she should sing by day…
"The nightingale, if she should sing by day,
When every goose is cackling, would be thought
No better a musician than the wren." (MOV.5.1)
Explain why you require special conditions or equipment for your performance to be successful.
In the play. *Portia comments on an observation on music by her servant Nerissa. Portia will then generalize, see 'Time, give it time to mature, t. as a seasoning agent - How many things by season season'd are…'*

Performance, outdoing previous p. -
... he hath in this action outdone his former deeds doubly.
"...he hath in this action outdone his former deeds doubly" (COR.2.1)
In the play. *Volumnia, Coriolanus' mother, reports the opinion of the Senate on her son.*

Performance, p. beyond description -
... his deeds exceed all speech.
"What should I say? his deeds exceed all speech." (KHVIp1.1.1)
Introduction a top performer. See also entries for 'Introduction'
In the play. King *Henry V has died and Gloucester gives a eulogy.*

Perfume, excellent scent – A delicate odour... as ever hit my nostrils.
SECOND GENTLEMAN. A delicate odour
CERIMON. As ever hit my nostrils." (PER.3.2)
Answer to the question, 'Do you like my perfume?' E.G. 'This is the most seductive scent that ever hit my nostrils'. Or just say it without being asked. It usually has a good effect.
In the play. *Two servants have brought in a chest that actually contains the seemingly lifeless Thaisa, beautiful and delicately scented even in her lifeless state.*

Perfume, p. that even makes the winds love-sick – ... and so perfumed that the winds were love-sick with them.
"...and so perfumed that
The winds were love-sick with them" (AC.2.2)
Comment on her perfume or answer to 'Do you like this perfume or scent?' E.G. 'You are so perfumed that the winds are love-sick with you'.
In the play. *Enobarbus extols the extraordinary features of Cleopatra's yacht, including the perfume of the sails.*

Perjury, p. punished – Thus pour the stars down plagues for perjury.
"Thus pour the stars down plagues for perjury.
Can any face of brass hold longer out?" (LLL.5.2)
In the play. *Biron is on the point to drop the mask in the ridiculous attempt to disguise himself to Rosaline. This was a prank devised by Biron's friends.*

Perjury, what punishment for p. -
What scourge for perjury can this dark monarchy afford false Clarence?
"'What scourge for perjury
Can this dark monarchy afford false Clarence?
...
Seize on him, Furies, take him to your torments!"
Upbraid a political enemy who suddenly changes his story or denies what he earlier said about a critical issue
In the play. *Clarence, soon to be killed by his brother Richard III (of Gloucester), has a nightmare and recounts it to his keeper in the Tower of London, Brackenbury.*

Perseverance, in praise of p. - ... perseverance, dear my lord keeps honour bright...
"... perseverance, dear my lord
Keeps honour bright: to have done is to hang
Quite out of fashion, like a rusty mail
In monumental mockery." (TC.3.3)
Emphasize the value of perseverance. Use to answer the question 'why do you insist' where the object of your insistence could be, for example, something that qualifies you as a workaholic or a fanatic or a compulsive over-achiever. See also 'Achievements, value of past a. not to be forgotten - the service of the foot being once gangrened... – Entries for

'Remembering, r. the bad more than the good'
In the play. *Ulysses tries to appeal to Achilles' superciliousness by making him believe that the Greeks like Ajax better than him. See 'Honor, the narrow path of h.'*

Perseverance, p. against a set back -
Do not, for one repulse, forego the purpose that thou resolved to effect.
"Do not, for one repulse, forego the purpose
That thou resolved to effect."
(TEM.3.3)
Encouragement after a setback. See also entries for 'Determination'.
In the play. *Antonio to Sebastian. Antonio is hatching a plot against his brother Alonso.*

Persistence, failure. positive attitude -
… the protractive trials of great Jove to find persistive constancy in men.
"Why then, you princes,
Do you with cheeks abash'd behold our works,
And call them shames? which are indeed nought else
But the protractive trials of great Jove
To find persistive constancy in men."
(TC.1.3)
Change to 'Our difficulties are but the protractive trials of great Jove…in men'. Make the lines follow an observation on expectations, if conditions apply. See 'Expectations, e. fed by hope often frustrated by reality.' - 'Chance, temper of man shown when handling reversals.' – 'Venture, v. delivered what predicted - … what hath then befallen, or what hath this bold enterprise brought forth...'
In the play. *Agamennon addresses the Grecian troops who have besieged Troy for a long time without victory. He invites them to consider the temporarily failed expectations as trials to test the Grecians' fiber.*

Persistence, your persistence has paid off - He that will have a cake out of the wheat, must tarry the grinding.
"He that will have a cake out of the wheat, must tarry the grinding." (TC.1.1)
Two ways of applying this. Romantically if you are making a special effort to get her. She may ask you why you are going to all the trouble or she may congratulate you for all the efforts you have undertaken to win her heart. Your answer suggests that she was well worth it. Or answer to a complaint about the difficulty or hardness of a task.
In the play. *Troilus laments his state of mind to Pandarus who answers with a general truth.*

Person, a rude p. - … a rude despiser of good manners, that in civility thou seem'st so empty.
(Are you) a rude despiser of good manners,
That in civility thou seem'st so empty?" (AYLI.2.7)
Stigmatize a rude person. "He is a rude despiser of good manners, that in civility seems quite empty?"
In the play. *Orlando rudely shows up and claims the food that Duke S and company are eating.*

Person, arrival of a gullible p. to be made fun of - … here comes the trout that must be caught with tickling.
" … here comes the trout that must be caught with tickling." (TN.2.5)
Describe the strategy necessary to convince a somewhat gullible person. E.G. 'He is a trout that …tickling'.
In the play. *Maria has planned a nasty trick on the approaching Malvolio.*

Person, compliments to a witty p. -
…forms… begot in the ventricle of memory…
"…(I have an) extravagant spirit, full of forms, figures, shapes, objects,

ideas, apprehensions, motions, revolutions: these are begot in the ventricle of memory, nourished in the womb of pia mater, and delivered upon the mellowing of occasion." (LLL.2.2)
Turn to the third person, e.g. 'his fine sparkles are begot in the ventricle…occasion'.
In the play. *The pompous Holofernes defines himself.*

Person, deceitful but beautiful - O that deceit should dwell in such a gorgeous palace.
"Was ever book containing such vile matter
So fairly bound? O that deceit should dwell
In such a gorgeous palace!" (RJ.3.2)
When the beautiful she (or the handsome he) has really been rotten to you in all possible ways.
In the play. *Juliet has just been informed that Romeo slain Tybald and is not yet aware of other details that would exculpate Romeo.*

Person, p. best of all (applies to both woman and man) - … and was the best of all among the rar'st of good ones.
"…and was the best of all
Among the rar'st of good ones." (CYM.5.4)
Positive assessment or compliment (to a woman). 'You are the best of all among the rarest of good ones' or answer to 'Do you like me?' If you are a woman use it as a compliment (directly) or as a statement of appreciation for a man you like. See also entries for 'Best, compliment, you are the best'– 'Pretty, the prettiest of all - the prettiest Kate in Christendom' – 'Man, best m. of all – Thou art the ruins of the noblest man that ever lived in the tide of times.'

In the play. *The repentant Iachimo refers to Posthumous on whom earlier on he played a dirty trick.*

Person, p. undefinable - … Why an otter?… she's neither fish nor flesh…
PRINCE HENRY An otter, Sir John! Why an otter?
FALSTAFF Why, she's neither fish nor flesh; a man knows not
where to have her." (KHIVp1.3.2)
In the play. *Falstaff has called his hostess an otter and explains why.*

Person, p. who inspires hope - … Their very heart of hope.
"…o'er them Aufidius,
Their very heart of hope." (COR.1.6)
In the play. *Cominius' account of the Volsces' army. Aufidius is the Volsces' leader.*

Person, P's comparative worth - To me he seems like diamond to glass.
"To me he seems like diamond to glass." (PER.2.3)
Statement could equally apply to a woman. If so, change 'he' to 'she'.
In the play. *Thaisa expresses her opinion on Pericles who has won the tournament in her honor.*

Person, worthiness of a p. shown under trial - … in the wind and tempest of her frown, distinction…
"The fineness of which metal is not found
In fortune's love; for then the bold and coward,
The wise and fool, the artist and unread,
The hard and soft seem all affined and kin:
But, in the wind and tempest of her frown,
Distinction, with a broad and powerful fan,
Puffing at all, winnows the light away;
And what hath mass or matter, by

itself
Lies rich in virtue and unmingled."
(TC.1.3)
The metal referred to is constancy. See also 'Fortune, defying f. - ... Fortune knows we scorn her most when most she offers blows.'
In the play. *Agamennon attempts to cheer up the demoralized Greek forces. The 'frown' is Fortune's.*

Personality, multiple p. - thus play I in one person many people and none contented.
"Thus play I in one person many people,
And none contented" (KRII.5.5)
Retort to statements of the type, 'I did not know you were like this'.
In the play. *Richard II, in prison at Pomfret Castle alone with his thoughts. To see how Richard reached rationally this conclusion see "Ambition, ambitious thoughts - Thoughts tending to ambition, they do plot unlikely wonders...' and 'Consolation, thoughts of c. in sharing misfortunes - ... that they are not the first of fortune's slaves...'*

Personnel, crew, a motley crew - A crew of patches, rude mechanicals, that work for bread upon the Athenian walls.
"A crew of patches, rude mechanicals,
That work for bread upon the Athenian walls." (MND.3.2)
Comment on a very poor team of workers or employees. Answer to 'Who is working on this?' Also answer to 'What do you do for a living?', i.e. 'I work for bread upon the Athenian walls'.
In the play. *Returning from his assignment, Puck explains to Oberon how it came that Titania fell in love with Bottom. Bottom is a member of the amateur crew of actors who are rehearsing a play. 'Patch' = 'Worthless fellow'.*

Personnel, downsizing - ... superfluous branches we lop away, that bearing boughs may live...
"...superfluous branches
We lop away, that bearing boughs may live:
Had he done so, himself had borne the crown,
Which waste of idle hours hath quite thrown down." (KRII.3.4)
In the play. *The Queen's gardener draws from his profession parallels applicable to the ill-fated reign of Richard II.*

Personnel, more people needed - Never so few, and never yet more need.
"Never so few, and never yet more need." (KHIVp2.1.1)
Promote the addition of new personnel.
In the play. *The rebels, as stated by Northumberland, need as many allies as they can.*

Personnel, p. not in good shape - The stuff we have, a strong wind will blow to pieces.
"The stuff we have,
A strong wind will blow to pieces." (PER.4.2)
Emphasize the poor quality of personnel and/or the poor conditions of the establishment. See also 'Funding, inadequate funding for the project – There's but a shirt and a half in all my company.'
In the play. *Bawd, one of the brothel's conductors, complain of the poor quality of the current personnel.*

Personnel, unskilled p. - Hard-handed men... which never labour'd in their minds till now.
"Hard-handed men that work in Athens here,
Which never labour'd in their minds till now" (MND.5.1)

In the play. *Philostrate, master of ceremonies at Theseus' court, describes the band of actors who will shortly stage a play in Theseus' honor*

Persuader, absolute p. - This is a creature, would she begin a sect, might quench the zeal…
"This is a creature,
Would she begin a sect, might quench the zeal
Of all professors else, make proselytes
Of who she but bid follow." (WT.5.1)
Describe a person with the gift of persuasion. Change 'she' to 'he' if applicable.
In the play. *A gentleman explains to Paulina the charm and (potential) inspiring power of Perdita, who has just arrived in Sicilia with Florizel.*

Persuasion, all efforts to persuade useless – I have laboured for the poor gentleman to the extremest shore of my modesty.
"…I have laboured for the poor gentleman to the extremest shore of my modesty" (MFM.3.2)
In the play. *Escalus tells Duke Vicentio he tried unsuccessfully to persuade Deputy Duke Angelo to spare Claudio's life, condemned for fornication.*

Persuasion, p. and sugared words - … By fair persuasions, mix'd with sugar'd words, we will entice the duke of Burgundy…
"…this doth Joan devise:
By fair persuasions, mix'd with sugar'd words,
We will entice the duke of Burgundy
To leave the Talbot and to follow us." (KHVI.p1.3.3)
Try, 'Convince him with fair persuasion mixed with sugared words' or 'I will convince him…sugared words'. See also 'Wine, w. as a tool for forgetting and making others forget - … memory, the warder of the brain, shall be a fume…'

In the play. *La Pucelle announces her plan to the French princes.*

Persuasion, p. obtained with honey words - … my woman's heart grossly grew captive to his honey words.
"… my woman's heart
Grossly grew captive to his honey words." (KRIII.4.1)
The last line is neutral. Pretend that you begin to believe the tale you are hearing, e.g. 'I am growing captive to your honey words'.
In the play. *Lady Anne reflects on the circumstances that led her to accept to marry Richard.*

Persuasion, p. or suggestion that achieves the opposite result - Has almost charmed me from my profession, by persuading me to it
"Has almost charmed me from my profession, by persuading me to it." (TOA.4.3)
In the play. *Two robbers stumble upon Timon who has retreated and retired to a wood. He talks with robbers and almost converts them away by their profession, by inciting them to pursue it.*

Persuasion, persuaded by a woman - … As prisoners to her womanly persuasion.
"As prisoners to her womanly persuasion" (TOS.5.2)
When you give in to her requests, e.g. 'I am prisoner to your womanly persuasion'.
In the play. *The now tamed Katharina won a wage for her husband Petruchio to prove herself as the most obedient wife. She has also persuaded the two other wives in the play, Bianca and an unnamed widow, to join her and return to the wedding dinner. Petruchio observes their arrival as 'prisoners' of Katharina's persuasion.*

Perversion, p. of the imagination - O, deeper sin than bottomless conceit can comprehend in still imagination!
"O, deeper sin than bottomless conceit
Can comprehend in still imagination!" (ROL)
In the poem. *Evil Tarquin knows he is committing a crime and meditates on it*

Pessimism, comfort only in heaven - Comfort's in heaven; and we are on earth where nothing lives, but crosses, cares and grief.
"Comfort's in heaven; and we are on earth,
Where nothing lives, but crosses, cares and grief." (KRII.2.2)
Express skepticism about palliatives.
In the play. *York cannot comfort the queen, who responds to his consoling words.*

Pessimism, down in the dumps remembering the past - And weep afresh love's long since cancell'd woe…
"…Then can I drown an eye, unused to flow,
For precious friends hid in death's dateless night,
And weep afresh love's long since cancell'd woe,
And moan the expense of many a vanish'd sight:
Then can I grieve at grievances foregone,
And heavily from woe to woe tell o'er
The sad account of fore-bemoaned moan,
Which I new pay as if not paid before." (SON 30)
See also 'World, pessimistic view of the w., a congregation of vapors – it goes so heavily with my disposition that this goodly frame, the earth…'

Pessimism, fleetness of life - … Yet in this life lie hid more thousand deaths…
"…What's yet in this
That bears the name of life? Yet in this life
Lie hid more thousand deaths: yet death we fear,
That makes these odds all even." (MFM.3.1)
Comment on the nature of man and his contradictions.
In the play. *The duke (in disguise) converses with Claudio who has been condemned to death by Angelo.*

Pessimism, fleetness of life – As flies to wanton boys are we to the gods, they kill us for their sport.
"As flies to wanton boys are we to the gods;
They kill us for their sport." (KL.4.1)
Express generic skepticism. See also 'Weak, feeling w. and unprotected – a naked subject to the weeping clouds.' – 'Friends, ungrateful and mercenary f. - … left me open, bare for every storm that blows'.
In the play. *Gloucester meets with the good son Edgar*

Pessimism, life – O world, but that thy strange mutations make us hate thee life would not yield to age.
"…World, world, O world!
But that thy strange mutations make us hate thee,
Life would not yield to age." (KL.4.1)
Maybe your view, we would not easily submit to old age and decadence if the world were a bit better than what it is.
In the play. *Edgar sees oncoming his blinded father*

Pessimism, life - O, that this too too solid flesh would melt thaw and resolve itself into a dew!

"O, that this too too solid flesh would melt
Thaw and resolve itself into a dew!" (H.1.2)
In the play. *Hamlet is distressed even before seeing the Ghost.*

Pessimism, limits of self-importance - ... Infusing him with self and vain conceits, as if this flesh, which walls about our life were brass impregnable.
"... (Death)
Infusing him with self and vain conceits,
As if this flesh, which walls about our life,
Were brass impregnable." (KRII.3.2)
Use as a comment about the volatility of everything, e.g. 'We behave as if this flesh, which walls about our life were brass impregnable.' A retort to someone who says you don't look too well, 'Well, this flesh, which walls about my life, is not brass impregnable.' See also 'Authority, limits to its importance - ... for within the hollow crown that rounds the mortal temples of a king keeps death its watch...'
In the play. *Richard reflection after Bolingbroke has seized in effect the kingdom.*

Pessimism, not even caring about being deceived – ... I do not greatly care to be deceived, that have no use for trusting.
"Antony
Did tell me of you, bade me trust you; but
I do not greatly care to be deceived,
That have no use for trusting" (AC.5.2)
In the play. *Cleopatra, resigned to her destiny after Antony's death, talks to Proculeius, an envoy from Caesar Octavian.*

Pessimism, nothing left that is important after an important person gone - ... and there is nothing left remarkable beneath the visiting moon.
"... The odds is gone,
And there is nothing left remarkable
Beneath the visiting moon." (AC.4.15)
Emphatic comment when a colleague or am important person changes jobs or position or location. See also 'Mood, pessimistic, life tedious' – Entries for 'Man and its wicked nature'
In the play. *Cleopatra's feelings after Antony's death.*

Pessimism, p. on life and personal property - ... And nothing can we call our own but death and that small model of the barren earth...
"And nothing can we call our own but death,
And that small model of the barren earth,
Which serves as paste and cover to our bones." (KRII.3.2)
In the play. *Richard II's reflections after Bolingbroke has seized everything, including the throne.*

Pessimism, p. to the point that death is tolerable - The stroke of death is as a lover's pinch, which hurts, and is desired.
"The stroke of death is as a lover's pinch,
Which hurts, and is desired." (AC.5.2)
Explain why sometimes death appears desirable. See also 'Absence worse than death, torture when away from her' – 'Absence worse than death, dying near her just like taking a nap'.
In the play. *Cleopatra is on the verge of letting herself be bitten by the viper she has ordered.*

Pessimism, sadness on a grand scale - How weary, stale, flat and unprofitable seem to me all the uses of this world!...
"How weary, stale, flat and unprofitable

Seem to me all the uses of this world!
Fie on't! O, fie! fie! 'Tis an unweeded garden
That grows to seed; things rank and gross in nature
Possess it merely." (H.1.2)
An ending to a speech criticizing a bad action or proposal or a group of people, "'Tis an unweeded garden that grows to seed…."
A comment on what is bad in the world, "Weary, stale, flat and unprofitable, seem to me…."
A semi-sarcastic answer to the question, "How are things", "Weary, stale, flat and unprofitable…"
In the play. *The king and queen have just left the scene after reproaching Hamlet for his moodiness. Hamlet meditates and despises the world.*

Pessimism, unable to be happy - He that commends me to mine own content, commends me to do the thing I cannot get.
"He that commends me to mine own content,
Commends me to do the thing I cannot get." (COE.1.2)
When you are not in the mood for positive thinking, e.g., as an answer to "I wish you happiness".
In the play. *A merchant makes a parting wish to the saddened Antipholus of Syracuse, who is skeptical about the possibility of being or becoming content.*

Pessimism, world will not feel my loss - … I shall do my friends no wrong, for I have none to lament me…
"… I shall do my friends no wrong, for I have none to lament me; the world no injury, for in it I have nothing." (AYLI.1.2)
Comment on a very risky proposition, 'If I don't come back, I shall do… nothing.'

In the play. *Orlando assesses the consequences of the impending match with the bone-breaking wrestler Charles, should Orlando be killed in it. But Orlando will win the match.*

Philosophical considerations. Unwillingness to take responsibility for our mistakes - This is the excellent foppery of the world…
"This is the excellent foppery of the world, that,
when we are sick in fortune,--often the surfeit
of our own behavior,--we make guilty of our
disasters the sun, the moon, and the stars: as
if we were villains by necessity; fools by
heavenly compulsion; knaves, thieves, and
treachers, by spherical predominance; …
an admirable evasion
of whoremaster man, to lay his goatish
disposition to the charge of a star!" (KL.1.2)
Poetical rendering of those who having committed a crime impute it to the will of the devil.
In the play. *Edmund comments on a statement by Gloucester that attributed the unfavorable course of events to 'late eclipses in the sun and moon'.*

Philosophical considerations, uselessness of coveting patronage as patronage is so prone to change - O momentary grace of mortal men which we more hunt for than the grace of God…
"O momentary grace of mortal men,
Which we more hunt for than the grace of God!
Who builds his hopes in air of your fair looks,
Lives like a drunken sailor on a mast,

Ready, with every nod, to tumble down
Into the fatal bowels of the deep."
(KRIII.3.4)
See also entries for 'Character, ambitious' *** 'Ambition' *** 'Reliance, r. on the favor of the great a source of disappointment. - Poor wretches that depend on greatness' favour dream as I have done, wake and find nothing.'
In the play. *Richard III has condemned Hastings on the spot on a trumped up accusation of sorcery. Hastings did not agree to Richard becoming king instead of the legitimate heir.*

Philosophy, p. and common sense -
… and that he that wants money, means and content is without three good friends.
TOUCHSTONE. Hast thou any philosophy in thee, shepherd?
CORIN. No more but that I know, the more one sickens, the worse at ease he is; and that he that wants money, means and content is without three good friends. (AYLI.3.2)
…
"…That the property of rain is to wet, and fire to burn; that good pasture makes fat sheep; and that a great cause of the night is lack of the sun. (AYLI.3.2)
Example of simple truths exposed simply. Answer to 'What is your philosophy of life?'
In the play. *The courtly Touchstone engages the shepherd Corin into an exchange of ideas and opinions.*

Philosophy, p. and tooth ache - … there was never yet philosopher, that could endure the tooth-ache patiently.
" For there was never yet philosopher, That could endure the tooth-ache patiently." (MAAN.5.1)
Use to express your criticism of pain counselors or of theoretical training in general. See also 'Pain, p. that cannot be comforted - …men can counsel, and speak comfort to that grief which they themselves do not feel' *** 'Pain, p. better endured by him who does nor feel it – He bears the sentence well that nothing bears…'
In the play. *Antonio counsels his brother Leonato to lighten up but Leonato answers that it is impossible for Antonio to feel the pain the he (Leonato) is suffering.*

Philosophy, p. as a remedy to adversity - I'll give thee armour to keep off that word, adversity's sweet milk, philosophy.
"I'll give thee armour to keep off that word;
Adversity's sweet milk, philosophy." (RJ.3.3)
Answer to 'what shall we do now?' 'The only remedy seems to be adversity's sweet milk, philosophy'
In the play. *The prince of Verona has banished Romeo and Fr. Lawrence brings the news to Romeo. Romeo is desperate and Fr. Lawrence offers some counseling. The feared word is 'banishment'*

Philosophy, simple p. - Thou art a scholar; let us therefore eat and drink.
SIR TOBY. Does not our life consists of the four elements?
SIR AGUECHEEK. Faith, so they say, but I think it rather consists of eating and drinking.
SIR TOBY. Thou art a scholar; let us therefore eat and drink." (TN.2.3)
Use as an example of twisted reasoning or make fun of complicated practices or philosophies. Sarcastic comment after someone has made a silly statement, 'Thou art a scholar'.
In the play. *Toby and Aguecheek, two sybarites find a philosophical foundation to their common taste as they exchange some banter. The four elements of life were considered by the ancient to be fire, water, air, and earth.*

Philosophy, simple p. of life - ... I will live so long as I may, that's the certain of it...
"Faith, I will live so long as I may, that's the certain of it; and when I cannot live any longer, I will do as I may: that is my rest, that is the rendezvous of it." (HV.2.1)
In the play. *Nym's philosophy of life.*

Philosophy, theory vs. practice - Of your philosophy you make no use, if you give place to accidental evils.
"Of your philosophy you make no use,
If you give place to accidental evils." (JC.4.3)
Use with him who, after advocating optimism, is or appears very depressed.
In the play. *Cassius to Brutus after Brutus has stated to be 'sick of many griefs'.*

Philosophy, there is a reason for everything - There is occasions and causes why and wherefore in all things.
"There is occasions and causes why and wherefore in all things." (KHV.5.1)
An alternate for a reason for everything. See also "Supernatural, existence of the s. a clear fact'.
In the play. *Fluellen continues his discussion with Gower.*

Phrases, good p. appreciated – good phrases are surely, and ever were, very commendable.
"...good phrases are surely, and ever were, very commendable" (KHIV.p2.3.4)
See also 'Words, w. that are no deeds - ... 'Tis a kind of good deed to say well and yet words are no deeds.
In the play. *Master Shallow attempts to ingratiate himself with Bardolph, Falstaff's assistant.*

Physician, a p. faithful to the calling and not attracted by riches - ... a more content in course of true delight than to be thirsty after tottering honour...
"I can speak of the disturbances
That nature works, and of her cures; which doth give me
A more content in course of true delight
Than to be thirsty after tottering honour,
Or tie my treasure up in silken bags,
To please the fool and death." (PER.3.2)
Possibly a quote to hang in a doctor's office.
In the play. *Cerimon to two gentlemen who came in to summon for his help*

Physiognomy, a person whose feelings are easily detected by his expression - ... For by his face straight shall you know his heart.
"I think there's never a man in Christendom
That can less hide his love or hate than he;
For by his face straight shall you know his heart." (KRIII.3.4)
In the play. *Hastings thinks he knows Richard by his facial expression but he is grossly misguided. A few lines later Richard will have Hastings decapitated for trumped up charges of treason and witchcraft.*

Physiognomy, expression telling – In many's looks the false heart's history is writ in moods and frowns and wrinkles strange...
"In many's looks the false heart's history
Is writ in moods and frowns and wrinkles strange,
But heaven in thy creation did decree
That in thy face sweet love should ever dwell" (SON 93)
Explain how you can judge the character of a person by his expression. Use the

Physiognomy, p. unreliable - There's no art to find the mind's construction in the face…
"There's no art
To find the mind's construction in the face:
He was a gentleman on whom I built
An absolute trust." (M.1.4)
Use the first two lines to counteract statements of the type, 'He has an honest face' or similar or to comment on the deceit committed by someone you thought trustworthy.
In the play. *Duncan did not suspect that his vassal Cawdor was a traitor. Macbeth discovered the treachery. Duncan, besides instantly making Macbeth, Thane of Cawdor (in recognition and gratitude), reflects on the unreliability of his (Duncan's) assessment of Cawdor's character.*

Picture, loving her p. to extremes – O thou senseless form, thou shalt be worshipp'd, kiss'd, loved and adored!
"…O thou senseless form,
Thou shalt be worshipp'd, kiss'd, loved and adored!" (TGV.4.4)
Compliment when she has given you a picture of hers
In the play. *Julia observes a portrait of Silvia and muses about her unfaithful Proteus who is infatuated with Silvia.*

Pirates, thieves who argue on how to split the loot - Hear me, you wrangling pirates, that fall out in sharing that which you have pill'd from me!
"Hear me, you wrangling pirates, that fall out
In sharing that which you have pill'd from me!" (KRIII.1.3)
Use in full to let yourself be heard or define those whom you deem pirates or thieves, e.g. '…those wrangling pirates, that fall out in sharing that which they have pilled from the commonwealth'.
In the play. *The zesty, feisty and old Queen Margaret addresses the 'wrangling pirates', i.e. Richard III and the noblemen in the party of King Edward and his queen – who, admittedly deprived her of the throne having killed Henry VI, see KHVI.p3.*

Pity, hints of p. observed - My friend, I spy some pity in thy looks… a begging prince what beggar pities not?
"My friend, I spy some pity in thy looks
… A begging prince what beggar pities not?" (KRIII.1.4)
Try this with a police officer after you have run out of your reasons and explanations.
In the play. *In vain Clarence tries to dissuade his murderers from killing him.*

Pity, no feeling of p. - Think but upon the wrong he did us all and that will quickly dry thy melting tears.
"Think but upon the wrong he did us all,
And that will quickly dry thy melting tears." (KHVI p3.1.4)
When people try to put a favorable spin on the actions of a scoundrel
In the play. *Queen Margaret says that the fallen York deserves no pity, considering the harm he did to Henry VI whose wife Margaret is.*

Pity, no other help possible but p. - No good at all that I can do for him, unless you call it good to pity him.
"No good at all that I can do for him;
Unless you call it good to pity him,
Bereft and gelded of his patrimony" (KRII.2.1)
In the play. *Lord Ross to Lord Willoughby, referring to the disenfranchised Bolingbroke.*

Pity, no pity? – Will nothing turn your unrelenting hearts?
"Will nothing turn your unrelenting hearts?" (KHVI.p1.5.4)
In the play. *Joan of Arc, captured by the English in battle, pleads for her life.*

Pity, no p. expected - ...O let no noble eye profane a tear for me, if I be gored with Mowbray's spear.
"O let no noble eye profane a tear
For me, if I be gored with Mowbray's spear" (KRII.1.3)
Before participating in a tournament, tennis match, boxing match or similar. Change 'Mowbray' to name of opponent.
In the play. *Bolingbroke's rhetorical statement before the duel with Mowbray.*

Pity, pitiful case moving even a monster – ... it is a pity would move a monster.
"...it is a pity
Would move a monster." (KHVIII.2.3)
In the play. *Anne Boleyn to a lady in waiting. The pity refers to Queen Catherine whom Henry VIII is divorcing. This is before Henry makes a marriage proposal to Anne.*

Pity, p. and the law - ... pity is the virtue of the law and none but tyrants use it cruelly.
"... pity is the virtue of the law,
And none but tyrants use it cruelly." (TOA.3.5)
Use to suggest mercy.
In the play. *A soldier in Alcibiades' army is accused of murder. The Athenian senators want to condemn him to death. Alcibiades, his captain, maintains that the killing was done in self-defense and pleads for mercy. The senators are unmoved.*

Pity, p. leading to a pardon - Say 'pardon,' king; let pity teach thee how; the word is short, but not so short as sweet...

"Say 'pardon,' king; let pity teach thee how:
The word is short, but not so short as sweet;
No word like 'pardon' for kings' mouths so meet." (KRII.5.3)
In the play. *The Duchess of York pleading with Bolingbroke (now Henry IV) to pardon her son, the duke of Aumerle for a youthful act of rebellion.*

Pity, p. not to be hoped for – ... the people deserve such pity of him as the wolf does of the shepherd.
"...the people
Deserve such pity of him as the wolf
Does of the shepherds." (COR.4.6)
When you do not want to forgive, e.g. 'He (she, they) deserves such pity of me as the wolf does of the shepherds'.
In the play. *Cominius' comment. It is not likely that Coriolanus will have any pity for the people now that he has been banned from Rome and joined the Volscii.*

Pity, p. or tenderness, how to prevent it - Not of a woman's tenderness to be, requires nor child nor woman's face to see.
"Not of a woman's tenderness to be,
Requires nor child nor woman's face to see." (COR.5.3)
In the play. *The sight of his family moves Coriolanus, including his young son.*

Pity, p. prevented by resentment at offense or injury - ... his injury the gaoler to his pity.
"...His injury
The gaoler to his pity." (COR.5.1)
In the play. *Cominius returns from an unsuccessful attempt to convince Coriolanus not to fight with the Volscii against the Romans.*

Pity, pitiless – ... be your heart to them as unrelenting flint to drops of rain.
"... Let it be our glory

To see her tears, but be your heart to them
As unrelenting flint to drops of rain."
(TA.2.2)
A comparison for heartlessness, 'his heart is unrelenting as …rain'.
In the play. *Demetrius and Chiron show up in the forest during a hunt organized by Emperor Saturninus - first they kill Bassianus then rape and mutilate the poor Lavinia.*

Pity, pitiless, heart turned to stone and hurting hands when struck - My heart is turned to stone; I strike it, and it hurts my hand.
"…my heart is turned to
Stone; I strike it, and it hurts my hand." (OTH.4.1)
When you will not relent.
In the play. *Othello, convinced of Desdemona's infidelity is determined to kill her.*

Pity, pitiless, heart turned to stone and remaining stony - My heart is turn'd to stone, and, while't is mine it shall be stony.
"My heart is turn'd to stone, and, while't is mine,
It shall be stony." (KHVI p2.5.2)
Answer to someone who thinks you will be swayed by pity
In the play. *York has killed Clifford Senior in battle at St. Alban's. Young Clifford vows revenge*

Pity, pitiless – … and pluck commiseration of his state from brassy bosoms and rough hearts of flint.
"… (losses such as to) pluck commiseration of his state
From brassy bosom and rough hearts of flint
From stubborn Turks and Tartars, never train'd
To offices of tender courtesy."
(MOV.4.1)

Turn it into a question to an apparently pitiless man, "Do you have a brassy bosom and a rough heart of flint? Are you a stubborn Tartar or a Turk, never trained to offices of tender courtesy?"
(Do not use in the presence of Turkish nationals). You can also apply it to yourself, 'I do not have a brassy bosom …flint. I am not a stubborn Turk or Tartar…courtesy
In the play. *The duke of Venice tries to convince Shylock to be merciful.*

Pity, pitiless – … no hoped-for mercy with the brothers more than with ruthless waves, with sands and rocks.
"That there's no hoped-for mercy with the brothers
More than with ruthless waves, with sands and rocks." (KHVI.p3.5.4)
In the play. *Queen Margaret speaks to the soldiers and encourages them to fight victoriously, as they cannot expect pity from the enemy (the Yorkists) in case the battle is lost.*

Pity, pitiless – Tear-falling pity dwells not in this eye.
"Uncertain way of gain! But I am in
So far in blood that sin will pluck on sin:
Tear-falling pity dwells not in this eye." (KRIII.4.2)
In the play. *To ensure his tenure of the throne, Richard now plans to marry the daughter of his brother, while still planning to murder her brothers. He is indeed very 'far in blood'.*

Pity, pitiless as shown by deeds – Were thy heart as hard as steel as thou hast shown it flinty by thy deeds...
"Then, Clifford, were thy heart as hard as steel
(As thou hast shown it flinty by thy deeds),
I come to pierce it, - or to give thee mine." (KHVI p3.2.1)

Judgment on a pitiless person, 'Thy heart is as hard as steel, as thou hast shown it flinty by thy deeds'.
In the play. *Richard (Gloucester) is determined to avenge the death of York.*

Place, a dangerous p. – Where we are there's daggers in men's smiles.
"…where we are,
There's daggers in men's smiles" (M.2.2)
'Let's go talk away from here – where we are… smiles' – a setting typical of large corporations. See also 'Perception, you want me dead - thou hidest a thousand daggers in thy thoughts'.
In the play. *At Macbeth's castle, after Duncan has been killed, Donalbain agrees with Malcolm that it is better to leave very quickly, for safety.*

Place, haunted p. to get away from - There's none but witches do inhabit here and therefore 'tis high time that I were hence.
"There's none but witches do inhabit here;
And therefore 'tis high time that I were hence" (COE.3.2)
…
"Lapland sorcerers inhabit here" (COE.4.3)
A good line when you wish to depart from a place filled with unpleasant women.
In the play. *Antipholus S. mistaken for Antipholus E. is flabbergasted and rates Ephesus a den of witches.*

Place, a nice p. to go to - I know a bank where the wild thyme blows…
"I know a bank where the wild thyme blows,
Where oxlips and the nodding violet grows,
Quite over-canopied with luscious woodbine,
With sweet musk-roses and with eglantine" (MND.2.1)

Answer to 'Where are you taking me?
In the play. *Oberon describes to Puck a place where Titania rests.*

Place, a nice p. to stay – … the air nimbly and sweetly recommends itself unto our gentle senses.
"This castle hath a pleasant seat; the air
Nimbly and sweetly recommends itself
Unto our gentle senses." (M.1.6)
When you visit her house (or apartment) for the first time. See also 'Air, excellent a. quality - The air breathes upon us here most sweetly' – 'Impressed, amazed (positively) - This is a most majestic vision, and harmoniously charming. '
In the play. *King Duncan has arrived as a guest at Macbeth's castle unaware and unsuspicious that Macbeth plans to kill him.*

Place, a nice p. to stay – I like this place and willingly could waste my time in it.
"I like this place.
And willingly could waste my time in it." (AYLI.2.4)
Indicate your liking of a place or location.
In the play. *Celia and Rosalind have escaped to the forest of Arden and have located a cottage to live in. Celia likes it and expresses her opinion.*

Place of birth, if nearby, where were you born? - Not three hours' travel from this very place.
"I was bred and born
Not three hours' travel from this very place." (TN.1.2)
You may modify 'three hours' according to the applicable distance. If you include air travel in the computations the reply may apply to any place in the country,
In the play. *Viola asks the captain of a ship if he knows the place where they landed and he replies accordingly.*

Place, p. suitable to melancholy musings - Let us seek out some desolate shade and there weep our sad bosoms empty.
"Let us seek out some desolate shade, and there
Weep our sad bosoms empty." (M.4.3)
In the play. *Malcolm to Macduff in England waiting to gather the forces to fight Macbeth.*

Place, residence, temporary safe heaven - ... we'll feast here awhile, until our stars that frown lend us a smile.
"...we'll feast here awhile,
Until our stars that frown lend us a smile." (PER.1.4)
The lines could equally apply when you are taking refuge from a storm somewhere
In the play. *Pericles accepts the hospitality of Cleon, governor of Tharsus.*

Plainness moving more than eloquence - Thy plainness moves me more than eloquence.
"Thy plainness moves me more than eloquence." (MOV.3.2)
Sometimes ladies, sincerely or to flatter you a little may say something like, "I am just a simple country girl" or "I am not as good as you are" etc. Therefore this line works as a positive retort to any girl who apologizes for being plain or not enough educated or for not speaking well or as well as yourself.
In the play. *A puzzle involves a choice of metal caskets. The puzzle solver will marry Portia. Bassanio is considering choosing lead and talks to the lead as if it were human.*

Plan, contingency p. - ... since the affairs of men rest still uncertain let's reason with the worst that may befall.
"But since the affairs of men rest still uncertain,
Let's reason with the worst that may befall." (JC.5.1)
In the play. *Before the battle of Philippi, Cassius questions Brutus about contingency plans should the battle be lost.*

Plan, contingency p. – ... this project should have a back or second, that might hold, if this should blast in proof.
"... this project
Should have a back or second, that might hold,
If this should blast in proof" (H.4.7)
When you are advocating a contingency plan.
In the play. *The King to Laertes. The primary plan is for Laertes to wound Hamlet in a duel with a poisoned rapier. If that were to fail and Hamlet win unscathed, the King will give Hamlet a poisoned cup of wine to celebrate his victory.*

Plan, p. disapproved – Uneven is the course, I like it not.
"Uneven is the course, I like it not." (RJ.4.1)
When you disagree with a proposal, idea or plan. Or when you do not like the situation in general. See also 'Misgivings, gutsy negative feelings - I know not what may fall; I like it not.'
In the play. *Fr. Lawrence is in a pickle. Paris has called on him to schedule the marriage ceremony with Juliet. Fr. Lawrence attempts to put off the event by pointing out to Paris that Juliet has not yet made up her mind. In fact Juliet has already married (in secret) to Romeo.*

Plan, p. must have no holes to succeed - ... and stop all sight-holes, every loop from whence the eye of reason may pry in upon us.
"For well you know we of the offering side
Must keep aloof from strict arbitrement,
And stop all sight-holes, every loop from whence

The eye of reason may pry in upon us" (KHIV.p1.4.1)
This is the routine tactic of the CIA and secret services, 'stop all sight-holes, every loop from whence the eye of reason may pry in upon us'
In the play. *Hotspur's father is sick and cannot join the rebels. The Earl of Worcester tells Hotspur that this turn of events may raise fear among the uncertain and make them question the rebels' cause.*

Plan, p. of deceit – ... Knavery's plain face is never seen till used.
"…'Tis here, but yet confused: Knavery's plain face is never seen till used." (OTH.2.1)
In the play. *Iago architects his plan to destroy Othello.*

Plan, p. to be carried out with care and secrecy - And that's not suddenly to be performed, but with advise and silent secrecy.
"And that's not suddenly to be performed,
But with advise and silent secrecy." (KHVI p2.2.2)
Explain to your co-conspirators that the plan has to be carried out secretly.
In the play. *The duke of York plans to acquire the throne of England after Cardinal Beaufort and other plotters, in turn, have deposed Henry VI.*

Plan, p. to remain confidential - What course I mean to hold shall nothing benefit your knowledge, nor concern me the reporting.
"... What course I mean to hold
Shall nothing benefit your knowledge, nor
Concern me the reporting." (WT.4.3)
Decline to divulge any further information about your plans.
In the play. *Polixenes, king of Bohemia tells Camillo to advise Florizel to break his engagement with Perdita on penalty of losing his inheritance and title to the throne. Florizel refuses nor will tell Camillo what he plans to do instead.*

Plan, strategy for upward mobility - ... And, when I spy advantage, claim the crown for that's the golden mark I seek to hit.
"And, when I spy advantage, claim the crown,
For that's the golden mark I seek to hit." (KHVI p2.1.1)
Expose his plans. E.G. '... he spies advantage and will claim the crown, for that's the golden mark he seeks to hit'. See also, 'Upward mobility. Learning the tools for u.m.' *** 'Deceit, learning the tricks of d. to avoid it' *** 'Opinion, your op. on the newly rich - ... 'tis a common proof that lowliness is young ambition's ladder…'
In the play. *An agreement with France, disadvantageous to England has shifted political positions and allegiances at court. Gloucester plans to take advantage of the situation.*

Plans, evil p. fall back on the evil planners - ... purposes mistook fall'n on the inventors' heads.
"…purposes mistook
Fall'n on the inventors' heads" (H.5.2)
In the play. *Horatio tells Prince Fortinbras about the plot by King Claudius that ended up in a carnage of just about all involved.*

Planning, call for strategic p. by experts - Call for our chiefest men of discipline to cull the plots of best advantages.
"Call for our chiefest men of discipline,
To cull the plots of best advantages" (KJ.2.1)
See also 'Exhortation, e. to discipline and expeditiousness - Let's want no

discipline, make no delay for, lords, tomorrow is a busy day.'
In the play. *King Philip of France is preparing to lay siege to the city of Angiers in France.*

Planning, importance of p. - When we mean to build, we first survey the plot, then draw the model..
"When we mean to build,
We first survey the plot, then draw the model;
And when we see the figure of the house,
Then must we rate the cost of the erection;
Which if we find outweighs ability,
What do we then but draw anew the model
In fewer offices, or at last desist
To build at all." (KHIV p2.1.3)
When you want to encourage planning a venture rather than thoughtlessly diving into it.
In the play. *Lord Bardolph cheers up the rebels by describing how planning is important in any enterprise. He compares planning to the construction of a house.*

Preparations, p. for action - ... (let) all things thought upon ... add more feathers to our wings.
"(let) all things thought upon
That may with reasonable swiftness add
More feathers to our wings" (HV.1.2)
Alternative for 'let's get ready'. When the project has been approved and it's the time to start with organization and implementation.
In the play. *Henry V prepares to invade France.*

Presence, 'Are you here?' – No, no, I am but shadow of myself.
"No, no, I am but shadow of myself" (KHVI.p1.2.3)
In the play. *Talbot's answer to the Countess of Auvergne who hoped to entrap him at her castle.*

Planning, p. and reflection advised before action - ... determine on some course, more than a wild exposture to each chance that starts i' the way before thee.
"...determine on some course,
More than a wild exposture to each chance
That starts i' the way before thee."
(COR.4.1)
In the play. *Volumnia counsels her son Coriolanus to use wisdom in planning his next move after he, enraged, has decided to leave Rome. 'Exposture' = 'Exposure'*

Planning, putting it on paper - Give me some ink and paper in my tent: I'll draw the form and model of our battle.
"Give me some ink and paper in my tent:
I'll draw the form and model of our battle." (KRIII.5.3)
Start to a planning meeting or session. See also 'Planning, importance of p.'
In the play. *Richmond prepares the battle plan against Richard III at Bosworth Field.*

Playing hard-to-get and why - ... If I confess much, you will play the tyrant.
TROILUS Why was my Cressid then so hard to win?
CRESSIDA Hard to seem won: but I was won, my lord,
With the first glance that ever--pardon me--
If I confess much, you will play the tyrant (TC.3.2)
In the play. *Cressida had played 'hard to get' with Troilus.*

Playing hard-to-get - Or if thou think'st I am too quickly won, I'll frown, and be perverse, and say thee nay.
"Or if thou think'st I am too quickly won,

I'll frown, and be perverse, and say thee nay." (RJ.2.2)
Make reference to Romeo and Juliet in case she has reservations about being 'quickly won'. Even Juliet - you may say - gave in pretty quickly and their love was unquestionably strong. Then recite the quote. See also 'Justification for insisting even after she said 'no' - ... maids in modesty, say 'No' to that which they would have the profferer construe 'Ay". – 'Negotiations, n. craftily conducted - ... this swift business I must uneasy make, lest too light winning make the prize light.'
In the play. *Juliet questions whether the acknowledgment of her love to Romeo gives him some kind of unfair advantage.*

Plea, introduction to a 'not guilty' p. - ... it shall scarce boot me to say 'not guilty:' mine integrity being counted falsehood...
"Since what I am to say must be but that
Which contradicts my accusation and
The testimony on my part no other
But what comes from myself, it shall scarce boot me
To say 'not guilty:' mine integrity
Being counted falsehood, shall, as I express it,
Be so received" (WT.2.3)
In the play. *Hermione is on trial for alleged and totally false adultery charges.*

Plea, p. for being understood - If ever from your eyelids wiped a tear, and know what it is to pity and be pitied...
"If ever from your eyelids wiped a tear,
And know what it is to pity and be pitied,
Let gentleness my strong enforcement be
In the which hope I blush, and hide my sword." (AYLI.2.7)
Use the first two lines as an introduction to a request.
In the play. *Orlando addresses Duke S and company in the forest of Arden and explains the distress he is in.*

Plea, plea of not guilty of questionable use – ... it shall scarce boot me to say 'not guilty:' mine integrity being counted falsehood...
"Since what I am to say must be but that
Which contradicts my accusation and
The testimony on my part no other
But what comes from myself, it shall scarce boot me
To say 'not guilty:' mine integrity
Being counted falsehood, shall, as I express it,
Be so received. " (WT.3.2)
In the play. *Hermione, unjustly accused of infidelity by her husband Leontes has little faith in the effectiveness of her plea. She relies on divine powers. See 'Innocence, i. will be proven - ... innocence shall make false accusation blush and tyranny and tyranny tremble at patience.'*

Plea, pleading for a good cause - If his occasions were not virtuous, I should not urge it half so faithfully.
"If his occasions were not virtuous,
I should not urge it half so faithfully." (TOA.3.2)
Put strength and emphasis about your request. Modify 'his' to 'my' if applicable.
In the play. *Lucius, another of Timon's friends, refuses to help, notwithstanding that Servilius pleads for Timon on the ground that the reasons for the request are 'virtuous'.*

Pleasure, excessive p. unsafe - These violent delights have violent ends and in their triumph die, like fire and powder, which as they kiss consume.
"These violent delights have violent ends
And in their triumph die, like fire and

powder,
Which as they kiss consume" (RJ.2.5)
In the play. *Romeo is anxious to marry Juliet and Friar Lawrence utters unheeded words of wisdom. This is the preamble to the counsel to Romeo to love moderately, see 'Advice, a. to love moderately and to avoid excess.'*

Pleasure, p. and revenge as great motivators - ... pleasure and revenge have ears more deaf than adders to the voice of any true decision.
"... for pleasure and revenge
Have ears more deaf than adders to the voice
Of any true decision." (TC.2.2)
Give a rational explanation to apparently irrational behavior
In the play. Hector comments on Troilus' and Paris' reasons not to return Helen to the Greeks, reasons dictated by pleasure (Paris) and revenge (Troilus). See 'Decision, d. prompted by passion or revenge - The reasons you allege do more conduce to the hot passion of distempered blood...'

Pleasure, p. offered and misinterpreted - ... your pleasure?... That you might know it, would much better please me...
ISABELLA I am come to know your pleasure.
ANGELO That you might know it, would much better please me
Than to demand what 'tis (MFM.2.4)
Answer to 'What would you like me to do?'
In the play. *Isabella meets again with Angelo to plead for her brother's life.*

Pleasures, brief p. of life - The sweet degrees that this brief world affords.
"The sweet degrees that this brief world affords" (TOA.4.3)
In the play. *Timon, now living in a cave digresses and exchanges insults with Apemantus. Apemantus reprimands Timon for his earlier profligate life-style. Timon retorts that if he, Apemantus, had enjoyed 'the sweet degrees... etc.', rather than being a beggar he would have behaved the same way.*

Pleasures, p, of a simple life – If I kept sheep, I should be as merry as the day is long.
"(If I) ... kept sheep,
I should be as merry as the day is long" (KJ.4.1)
See also 'Country living, in praise of country living - ... Here can I sit alone, unseen of any and to the nightingale's complaining notes...'
In the play. *King Arthur to his jailer Hubert.*

Pleasures, priorities in p. - But that a joy past joy calls out on me, it were a grief, so brief to part with thee.
"But that a joy past joy calls out on me,
It were a grief, so brief to part with thee." (RJ.3.3)
Use, mildly sarcastically, when you need to leave the meeting. Change 'thee' to 'you all'.
In the play. *The joy past joy refers to Romeo's impending visit to Juliet. Romeo takes his leave of Friar Lawrence.*

Plot, a p. and a set-up - A pretty plot, well chosen to build upon!
"A pretty plot, well chosen to build upon!" (KHVI.p2.1.4)
Your comment on a set-up whether or not you are the victim.

In the play. *York to Buckingham who, with other enemies of the King's Protector, have engineered a plan to entrap the Protector's wife and discredit her husband.*

Plot, p. and motives clear to see but no one speaks out of fear - ... Who is so gross that cannot see this palpable device?...
"… Who is so gross
That cannot see this palpable device?
Yet who's so bold but says he sees it not?
Bad is the world and all will come to nought,
When such ill dealings must be seen in thought." (KRIII.3.6)
Everybody knows what is going on but pretends not to see and ignore it to protect their position
In the play. *The scrivener refers to the trumped up charges against Hasting by Richard III, which he must record and knows to be false. Yet the scrivener must be quiet about the truth.*

Plot, political p. clear to anyone that is interested - ... all that dare look into these affairs see this main end...
"…These news are every where; every tongue speaks 'em,
And every true heart weeps for't: all that dare
Look into these affairs see this main end,
The French king's sister"
(KHVIII.2.2)
In the play. *The Chamberlain speaks with Norfolk and Suffolk about the impending divorce of King Henry from Catherine of Aragon.*

Plutocrats, p. as whales - I can compare our rich misers to nothing so fitly as to a whale...
"I can compare our rich misers to nothing so fitly as to a whale; a' plays and tumbles, driving the poor fry before him, and at last devours them all at a mouthful: such whales have I heard on o' the land, who never leave gaping till they've swallowed the whole parish, church, steeple, bells, and all." (PER.2.1)
In the play. *Pericles is shipwrecked in front of Pentapolis and he meets three fishermen on the shore.*

Poem, ready p. for the purpose - I have a sonnet that will serve the turn...
"I have a sonnet that will serve the turn
To give the onset to thy good advice" (TGV.3.2)
In the play. *Thurio heeds Proteus' advice as to the means to conquer Silvia's heart. The advice is to resort to poetry and music as tools of seduction.*

Poetry, bad p. – This is the very false gallop of verses; why do you infect yourself with them?
"This is the very false gallop of verses; why do you infect yourself with them?" (AYLI.3.2)
In the play. *Orlando inscribed silly love lines on barks of trees for the benefit of Rosalind. When the fool/wit Touchstone happens to read those lines he delivers his critique.*

Poetry, contempt of poetry or lyrics in general - ... Nothing so much as mincing poetry, 't is like the forced gait of a shuffling nag.
"... a dry wheel grate on the axle-tree;
And that would set my teeth nothing on edge,
Nothing so much as mincing poetry:
'Tis like the forced gait of a shuffling nag" (KHIVp1.3.1)
In the play. *Hotspur declares his distaste for Glendower's self-described artistic skills.*

Poetry, difficulty in finding a suitable rhyme - ... I can find out no rhyme to 'lady' but 'baby...

"Marry, I cannot show it in rhyme; I have tried: I can find out no rhyme to 'lady' but 'baby,' an innocent rhyme; for 'scorn,' 'horn,' a hard rhyme; for, 'school,' 'fool,' a babbling rhyme; very ominous endings: no, I was not born under a rhyming planet, nor I cannot woo in festival terms." (MAAN.5.2)
Extract 'I can find out no rhyme to 'lady' but 'baby' or 'I was not born under a rhyming planet, nor I cannot woo in festival terms' to show modesty should you be asked to improvise a speech, a statement or a song to befit a special occasion. See also entries for 'Modesty'.
In the play. *Benedick improvises a song after a bantering exchange with Margaret.*

Poetry, disavowal of poetical skills compensated by general strength in other areas - I have no strength in measure, yet a reasonable measure in strength.
"I have no strength in measure, yet a reasonable measure in strength." (HV.5.2)
Your claim of modesty in poetical powers is compensated by masculine strength.
In the play, *Henry V informs Katharine of France of his falling short in poetry (measure).*

Poetry, equally applicable to women or horses - I once writ a sonnet in his praise and began thus: 'Wonder of nature'...
"DAUPHIN. I once writ a sonnet in his praise and began thus: 'Wonder of nature,'—
ORLEANS I have heard a sonnet begin so to one's mistress.
DAUPHIN. Then did they imitate that which I composed to my courser, for my horse is my mistress." (HV.3.7)
Recall the exchange to give your opinion on poor lyrics.
In the play. *The Dauphin of France and the Duke of Orleans exchange their views on the subject while waiting to begin the battle of Agincourt with the English forces of King Henry V.*

Poetry, futility of p. – A speaker is but a prater; a rhyme is but a ballad.
"What! A speaker is but a prater; a rhyme is but a ballad." (KHV.5.2)
In the play. *Henry V woos Kathryn of France after having defeated the French at Agincourt and declines to admit to any skill in romantic speech or poetry.*

Poetry, good p. – the elegancy, facility, and golden cadence of poesy.
"...for the elegancy, facility, and golden cadence of poesy" (LLL.4.2)
In the play. *Holoferne's critique while reading a poem written by Sir Nathaniel.*

Poetry, love p. not necessarily true –
... the truest poetry is the most is most feigning...
AUDREY I do not know what 'poetical' is: is it honest in deed and word? is it a true thing?
TOUCHSTONE No, truly; for the truest poetry is the most feigning; and lovers are given to poetry, and what they swear in poetry may be said as lovers they do feign. (AYLI.3.3)
In the play. *Touchstone is courting Audrey and told her, 'Truly, I would the gods had made thee poetical' and the dialog ensues.*

Poetry, p. as a tool for seduction - You must lay lime to tangle her desires by wailful sonnets...
"You must lay lime to tangle her desires
By wailful sonnets, whose composed rhymes
Should be full-fraught with serviceable vows." (TGV.3.2)
In the play. *Proteus gives advise to Thurio on how to conquer Silvia, knowing full well that Thurio has no chance, but Proteus hopes to profit from the situation and get to Silvia. Lime is a*

viscous substance that used to be laid on twigs to catch birds.

Poetry, p. of very questionable taste - Let no face be kept in mind but the face of Rosalind.
"Let no face be kept in mind
But the face of Rosalind". (AYLI.3.2)
An example of very poor love poetry or poor copy.
In the play. *Rosalind discovers Orlando's childish graffiti.*

Poetry, power of p. - much is the force of heaven-bred poesy.
"Ay, much is the force of heaven-bred poesy." (TGV.3.2)
While this is true in general, consider also its limitation. See comments to 'Writing. Power of printed message.'
In 1839 Nathaniel Hawthorne wrote to Sophia Peabody, "I wish I had the gift of making rhymes, for methinks there is poetry in my head since I have been in love with you. You are a Poem. Of what sort? Epic? Mercy on me, no! A sonnet? No; for that is too labored and artificial. You are a sort of sweet, simple, gay, pathetic ballad, which Nature is singing sometimes with tears, sometimes with smiles, and sometimes with intermingling smiles and tears."
In the play. *The Duke reinforces and concurs with the advice Proteus gives to Thurio. It's a complicated quadrangle. Valentine loves Sylvia, the Duke's daughter, and so does Valentine's treacherous friend Proteus, who fiendishly succeeded in placing Valentine on the Duke's black book. The Duke wants Sylvia to marry the sheepish (but rich) Thurio. Sylvia does not want to have anything to do with Thurio and Proteus pretends to teach Thurio how to win the heart of Sylvia.*

Poetry, very poor verses or text - some of them had in them more feet than verses would bear.
CELIA. Didst thou hear these verses?
ROSALIND. O, ye, I heard them all, and more too; for some of them had in them more feet than verses would bear. (AYLI.3.2)
A comment on very poor copy.
In the play. *Rosalind agrees on to the questionable literary value of Orlando's verses.*

Poison, poisonous drink - … in the porches of my ears did pour the leperous distilment.
"…in the porches of my ears did pour
The leperous distilment; whose effect
Holds such an enmity with blood of man…" (H.1.5)
In the play. *The Ghost gives Hamlet details on how the Ghost, his father was killed by Hamlet's uncle.*

Police officer, a hard p.o. - One whose hard heart is button'd up with steel…
"One whose hard heart is button'd up with steel;
A fiend, a fury, pitiless and rough" (COE.4.2)
In the play. *Dromio S. relates to Adriana how his master was arrested by a police officer.*

Police officer, response to a p.o. - What wilt thou do, peevish officer? Hast thou delight to see a wretched man do outrage and displeasure to himself?
"What wilt thou do, p officer?
Hast thou delight to see a wretched man
Do outrage and displeasure to himself?" (COE.4.4)
Use only if you detect in the police officer a measure of humanity and/or intelligence.
In the play. *A police officer has just arrested Antipholus E. who went into a rage due to continued instances of mistaken identity with his twin Antipholus S. 'Peevish' = 'silly, childish'*

Policy, imperialistic p. – France being ours, we'll bend it to our awe, or break it all to pieces...
"France being ours, we'll bend it to our awe,
Or break it all to pieces: or there we'll sit,
Ruling in large and ample empery" (KHV.1.2)
In the play. *King Henry will attack France*

Politeness, p. in asking for pardon - Pardon me, if you please; if not, I, pleased not to be pardon'd, am content withal.
"Pardon me, if you please; if not, I, pleased
Not to be pardon'd, am content withal" (KRII.2.1)
In the play. *The Duke of York's preamble to his plea with King Richard no to confiscate Gaunt's estate.*

Political appeal for the discontented - ... creeps apace into the hearts of such as have not thrived upon the present state...
"...condemn'd Pompey,
Rich in his father's honour, creeps apace,
Into the hearts of such as have not thrived
Upon the present state, whose numbers threaten" (AC.1.3)
In the play. *Antony explains to Cleopatra whey he must go to Rome.*

Political (and personal) double standards - whiles I am a beggar, I will rail... there is no sin but to be rich...
"Well, whiles I am a beggar, I will rail
And say there is no sin but to be rich;
And being rich, my virtue then shall be
To say there is no vice but beggary." (KJ.2.2)

When a politician completely reverses his opinions and commitments to further his own personal gains. Also prove that people change their political views according to their self-interest. See also 'Politicians' promises, habitual.'
In the play. *Faulconbridge is dismayed that King John has come to an agreement with the French thus reversing former decisions for his own personal gain. The line by the Bastard is a natural extension of gain over principle. 'Gain' in the play is used together with 'Commodity' as synonyms.* He continues,
"Commodity, the bias of the world -
The world, who of itself is peised well,
Made to run even upon even ground,
Till this advantage, this vile-drawing bias,
This sway of motion, this Commodity"

'Since kings break faith upon commodity,
Gain, be my lord, for I will worship thee.'
... proving, if it were needed, that the example of the leader influence the behavior of the nation. 'Peised' = 'Poised'

Political convictions, shaky' - I am a feather for each wind that blows.
"I am a feather for each wind that blows." (WT.2.3)
Applied to others. Characterize a person who easily changes his opinion or allegiance. Applied to yourself, hint that you go along with the crowd or that you do not have the strength or power to influence a situation in which you have been asked to intervene.
In the play. *The insanely jealous Leontes, king of Sicilia, suspects that his wife Hermione's baby is not his. He wants to kill the baby but his courtiers plead not to do so and Leontes is torn about what to do.*

Political correctness and political skills – ... manhood is melted into courtesies, valour into compliment, and men are only turned into tongue...

"…manhood is melted into courtesies, valour into compliment, and men are only turned into tongue, and trim ones too: he is now as valiant as Hercules that only tells a lie and swears it" (MAAN.4.1)
In the play. *Beatrice, angry at the accusations levied on her cousin Hero, vents her frustration with Benedick.*

Political situation, pessimism about present ruler - It is a reeling world, indeed, my lord; and I believe twill never stand upright…
"It is a reeling world, indeed, my lord;
And I believe t'will never stand upright
Till Richard wear the garland of the realm." (KRIII.3.2)
Change 'Richard' to the name of applicable current ruler or president whom you despise.
In the play. *Lord Catesby visits with Lord Hastings and expresses his opinion. 'Reeling' means 'staggering while drunk', 'unstable'.*

Political staffers – … gallants, that fill the court with quarrels, talk, and tailors.
"…gallants,
That fill the court with quarrels, talk, and tailors" (KHVIII.1.3)
In the play. *Lovell informs the Chamberlain about a proclamation intended to reign in extravagance of the courtiers.*

Political stand, an extreme right winger - … he is a very dog to the communalty.
"… he is a very dog to the communalty. (COR.1.1)
Chastise a bad politician.
In the play. *Working class citizens see Coriolanus as the embodiment of the arrogance of power.*

Political strategies, common enemy abating intestine differences – … how the fear of us may cement their divisions and bind up the petty difference…
"… they have entertained cause enough
To draw their swords: but how the fear of us
May cement their divisions and bind up
The petty difference, we yet not know" (AC.2.1)
In the play. *Pompey speculates with his men as to what hie enemies may do.*

Politician, honest p. as an exception - He's one honest enough: would all the rest were so!
"He's one honest enough: would all the rest were so!" (COR.1.1)
In the play. *A citizen's opinion of Senator Menenius Agrippa*

Politician, p. who fleeced the treasury - … Lord Say hath gelded the commonwealth, and made it an eunuch.
"Fellow kings, I tell you that that Lord Say hath gelded the commonwealth, and made it an eunuch" (KHVI p2.4.2)
In the play. *Rebel John Cade harangues his fellow rebels. Lord Say was a royal minister.*

Politician, young aspiring p. - The expectancy and rose of the fair state… the observed of all observers.
"The expectancy and rose of the fair state,
The glass of fashion and the mould of form,
The observed of all observers" (H.3.1)
'You are the observed of all observers' can be equally a compliment for a lady. Introduction of a young politician running for office. See also entries for 'Introduction'

739

In the play. *Ophelia realizes that all the hopes in Hamlet are shattered as he appears to her definitely mad.*

Politicians, deceitful - … And like a scurvy politician, seem to see the things thou dost not.
"…Get thee glass eyes;
And like a scurvy politician, seem
To see the things thou dost not."
(KL.4.6)
'Scurvy' is a synonym for 'contemptible' and 'vile'. We could argue that 'scurvy' politicians pretend to ignore 'things' more than seeing them. But the meaning is consistent, that is pretence is a trait of contemptible politicians. In a debate try 'I'll say to you as King Lear said, 'Get thee glass eyes…. etc.'
In the play. *K. Lear utters words of wisdom while being mad. Here he addresses the blind Gloucester after having described to him the image of authority (see 'Opinion, your op. on authority') and the corruptibility of justice (see 'Justice, gold buys j. - Plate sin with gold and the strong lance of justice hurtless breaks…'*

Politicians' promises, habitual - Promising is the very air o' the time: it opens the eyes of expectation…
"Promising is the very air o' the time: it opens the eyes of expectation: performance is ever the duller for his act;
…To promise is most courtly and fashionable: performance is a kind of will or testament which argues a great sickness in his judgment that makes it." (TOA.5.1)
Use it one to one when she or he has a track record of promise without performance. Or use to attack a specific politician or politicians in general. Remark sarcastically that promising is much better than delivering.

In the play. *The poet and the painter, believing that Timon is still rich decide to go and see him in the forest where he retired after declaring bankruptcy. To ingratiate himself with Timon the painter will promise to give him a painting. The poet, as good a parasite as the painter, comments sarcastically that promising is better than delivering.*

Politicians' promises, wine for all - … I charge and command that, of the city's cost, the pissing-conduit run nothing but claret wine…
"And here, sitting upon London-stone, I charge and command that, of the city's cost, the pissing-conduit run nothing but claret wine this first year of our reign."(KHVI p2.4.5)
See also 'False claim, claiming a non existent achievement or feat'.
In the play. *John Cade, financed by Gloucester, attempts to start a communist revolution in London. The plan was designed to equally appeal to lovers of beer, because John Cade adds*

Politicians' promises, price reductions and more plentiful manufactured products - There shall be in England seven halfpenny loaves sold for a penny…
"There shall be in England seven halfpenny loaves sold for a penny: the three-hooped pot; shall have ten hoops." (KHVI p2.4)
In the play. *John Cade, financed by Gloucester, attempts to start a communist revolution in London. The plan was designed to equally appeal to lovers of beer, because John Cade adds,*
"…. and I will make it felony
to drink small beer: all the realm shall be in
common".
'Small beer' is beer with little alcoholic strength.

Politics, democracy, defects of d., lack of clear objectives - … purpose so

barred, it follows, nothing is done to purpose.
"... it must omit
Real necessities, and give way the while
To unstable lightness: purpose so barred, it follows,
Nothing is done to purpose." (COR.3.1)
An argument for restricting the responsibility of management.
In the play. *Coriolanus explains the reasons for his dictatorial view of politics. The people are ignorant and unstable and should not have any say in government.*

Politics, democracy, evils of d. - ... Where one part does disdain with cause, the other insult without all reason...
" This double worship -
Where one part does disdain with cause, the other
Insult without all reason; where gentry, title, wisdom,
Cannot conclude but by yea and no
Of general ignorance." (COR.3.1)
An argument for restricting the responsibility of management.
In the play. *Coriolanus explains the reasons for his choice of dictatorship over democracy. The people are ignorant and should not have any say in government.*

Politics, hating p. - ...for policy I hate: I had as lief be a Brownist as a politician.
"...for policy I hate: I had as lief be a Brownist as a politician." (TN.3.2)
In the play. *Andrew Aguecheek comments on a proposition by Toby Belch. Robert Browne founded a separate branch or organization of the Church of England in 1560. The idea was controversial. 'I had as lief' = 'I should like as much'*

Politics, p. above conscience - Men must learn now with pity to dispense, for policy sits above conscience.
"... but I perceive,
Men must learn now with pity to dispense,
For policy sits above conscience." (TOA.3.2)
Comment when you see that profit or politics prevail over a just cause.
In the play. *Some observers who witnessed Lucius' refusal to help Timon comment and generalize on the event. Lucius had previously benefited from Timon's generosity.*

Politics, p. as a gift from hell - ... the devil knew not what he did when he made man politic, he crossed himself by it.
"...The devil knew not what he did when he made man politic - he crossed himself by it." (TOA.3.3)
Decry office politics or politics in general.
In the play. *Servilius comments bitterly on Sempronius' lame and 'political' excuse for not helping Timon.*

Politics, p. in a well run state - There is a mystery (with whom relation durst never meddle) in the soul of state...
"There is a mystery (with whom relation
Durst never meddle) in the soul of state;
Which hath an operation more divine,
Than breath, or pen can give expression to." (TC.3.3)
Show the importance of a well-ordered management structure, by comparing it to a well-run state.
In the play. *Ulysses gives Achilles a lecture in politics. Actually this seems an apology for the Greek CIA and is covert operation. Ulysses tells Achilles that the 'state' has found out that he (Achilles) likes the Trojan Polixena.*

Politics, power, role of foul play - A sceptre, snatched with an unruly hand...
"A sceptre, snatched with an unruly hand,
Must be boisterously maintained as gained:
And he that stands upon a slippery place
Makes nice of no vile hold to stand him up." (KJ.3.4)
State that scoundrels will go to any length to maintain their position.
In the play. *Pandulph, the Pope's legate refers to King John who occupies the throne illegally instead of young Arthur.*

Politics, qualification for office –
...Outcake or Seacoal for they can read and write.
DOGBERRY. ... who think you the most deserving man to be constable?
FIRST WATCH. Hugh Outcake, sir, or George Seacoal; for they can read and write." (MAAN.3.3)
When you refuse to answer a question as to whom you think should be elected. Quote the lines anecdotally. See also 'Education, not an asset'.
In the play. *Dogberry is a city officer who will uncover the evil plan of Don John to slander and discredit Hero.*

Politics, representatives of the people despised - The tongues of the common mouth: I do despise them
"Behold, these are the tribunes of the people,
The tongues of the common mouth: I do despise them." (COR.3.1)
Show that what you say represents the view of the majority, e.g. 'I am but the tongue of the common mouth'. Or define the popular media as 'the tongues of the common mouth'.
In the play. *The tribunes arrive to confer with Coriolanus.*

Politics, right wing p. - I tell you, friends, most charitable care have the patricians of you...
MENENIUS I tell you, friends, most charitable care
Have the patricians of you. For your wants,
Your suffering in this dearth, you may as well
Strike at the heaven with your staves as lift them
Against the Roman state, whose course will on
The way it takes, cracking ten thousand curbs
Of more strong link asunder than can ever
Appear in your impediment. For the dearth,
The gods, not the patricians, make it, and
Your knees to them, not arms, must help. Alack,
You are transported by calamity
Thither where more attends you, and you slander
The helms o' the state, who care for you like fathers,
When you curse them as enemies.
FIRST CITIZEN Care for us! True, indeed! They ne'er cared for us yet: suffer us to famish, and their store-houses
crammed with grain; make edicts for usury, to
support usurers; repeal daily any wholesome act
established against the rich, and provide more
piercing statutes daily, to chain up and restrain
the poor. If the wars eat us not up, they will; and
there's all the love they bear us. (COR.1.1)
Use the argument of Menenius or of the Citizen to make your point, depending of course on your political orientation.

In the play. *Menenius Agrippa, friend of Coriolanus gives the people a lesson in Reaganomics. The Citizen gives evidence destroying Menenius' claims. 'Staves' = staffs or clubs. 'Dearth' = scarcity of food or famine.*

Pomp, the p. that surrounds power – … the tide of pomp that beats upon the high shore of this world.
"…the tide of pomp
That beats upon the high shore of this world" (HV.4.1)
In the play. Henry V, the night before the battle of Agincourt, meditates on the characteristics of power.

Pope, the p's rotten policies and sale of indulgences - … are led so grossly by the meddling priest.
"… you and all the kings in Christendom,
Are led so grossly by the meddling priest,
Dreading the course that money may buy out;
And by the merit of vile gold, dress, dust,
Purchase corrupted pardon of a man,
Who, in that sale, sells pardon for himself." (KJ.3.1)
A historical reminder of the corruption of the clerical establishment.
In the play. *King John comments on Pandulph, the pope's legate has arrived with an injunction to the French not to make peace to the English.*

Popularity, achieving p. with the common man - How he did seem to dive into their hearts with humble and familiar courtesy.
"…Bagot here and Green
Observed his courtship to the common people;
How he did seem to dive into their hearts
With humble and familiar courtesy,
What reverence he did throw away on slaves,

Wooing poor craftsmen with the craft of smiles" (KRII.1.4)
Policy of various politicians who wish to appear folksy to the common people but when elected will sock it to them.
In the play. *King Richard II comments on the attitude of Bolingbroke. Richard has exiled him but suspects that he is after the throne – it will prove a correct suspicion.*

Popularity, p. questioned - Upon what meat doth this our Caesar feed, that he is grown so great?
"… in the names of all the gods at once,
Upon what meat doth this our Caesar feed,
That he is grown so great?" (JC.1.2)
Use the example to illustrate the dangers of misplaced and irrational media appeal and charisma.
In the play. *Cassius gives Brutus reasons for getting rid of Caesar and questions the ground of Caesar's popularity.*

Portrait, p. of a lady observed with mild vanity – … And yet the painter flattered her a little, unless I flatter with myself too much.
"And yet the painter flattered her a little,
Unless I flatter with myself too much." (TGV.4.4)
An example of feminine vanity mixed with a bit of jealousy.
In the play. *On observing Silvia's picture, Julia finds faults with her features.*

Position, p. achieved through crooked means - God knows… by what by-paths and indirect crooked ways I met this crown.
"God knows, my son,
By what by-paths and indirect crook'd ways
I met this crown; and I myself know well

How troublesome it sat upon my head" (KHIV.p2.4.5)
In the play. *London, the Jerusalem chamber at court. Ailing King Henry IV gives his final words to the Prince of Wales and recognizes the 'indirect and crooked ways' by which he took the throne away from Richard II.*

Position, p. felt secure due to tenure - Not all the water in the rough, rude sea can wash the balm from an anointed king…
"Not all the water in the rough, rude sea
Can wash the balm from an anointed king;
The breath of worldly men cannot depose
The deputy elected by the Lord" (KRII.3.2)
Show that everything seemingly unshakable can still be removed or destroyed, by citing this example of Richard II, deposed by Henry IV. Or with tongue in cheek use it to show that you are above the fray and cannot be touched by events.
In the play. *King Richard unwisely trusts that his royalty and throne cannot be challenged (by Bolingbroke).*

Position, precarious p. physical and metaphorical – … I stand as one upon a rock environ'd with a wilderness of sea…
"… I stand as one upon a rock,
Environ'd with a wilderness of sea,
Who marks the waxing tide grow wave by wave,
Expecting ever when some envious surge
Will in his brinish bowel swallow him." (TA.3.1)
Forcefully express that you are surrounded by enemies, 'I stand upon……sea.' – or that you are in a precarious political position.
In the play. *Titus A. is pained to the point of madness after seeing the status his daughter Lavinia is in.*

Position, solid and secure p. defined - Whole as the marble, founded as the rock…
"Whole as the marble, founded as the rock,
As broad and general as the casing air" (M.3.4)
In the play. *Macbeth defines what his own position would be if besides killing Banquo, the murderers also had killed Fleance, Banquo's son, who has instead escaped. 'Founded' = 'immovable', 'Casing' = 'surrounding'.*

Position, well positioned at court – (He) sits within a monarch's heart and ripens in the sunshine of his favour.
"…sits within a monarch's heart,
And ripens in the sunshine of his favour" (KHIV.p2.4.2)
Comment on a colleague favored by boss, e.g. 'he ripens in the sunshine of his favor'
In the play. *The Prince of Lancaster, son of King Henry IV addresses the rebel Archbishop of York implying that the king favors the archbishop (sits within the monarch's heart). It is a trap, the Archbishop will take the bait.*

Positive outcome - All's well that ends well.
All's well that ends well; still the fine's the crown;
Whate'er the course, the end is the renown." (AWEW.4.4)
The first line is known to almost everyone and usable universally. See also 'Results, positive r. in the end - All's well that ends well, yet; though time seems so adverse, and means unfit'

In the play. *Title of one of the plays and used (in the play itself) by Helena as she departs from Florence towards France with Diana, the Florentine·girl whom Bertram believes to have seduced.*

Positive thinking about exile - ... suppose devouring pestilence hangs in our air and thou art flying to a fresher clime.
"...suppose
Devouring pestilence hangs in our air
And thou art flying to a fresher clime:
Look, what thy soul holds dear, imagine it
To lie that way thou go'st, not whence thou comest" (KRII.1.3)
Could apply to a situation where your job requires relocation.
In the play. *Gaunt tries to cheer up his son Bolingbroke, banished from England.*

Positive thinking and defiance towards setbacks – For gnarling sorrow hath less power to bite the man that mocks at it and sets it light.
"For gnarling sorrow hath less power to bite
The man that mocks at it and sets it light." (KRII.1.3)
Use to infuse after a setback. See also entries for 'Complaint, c. after problems useless' Pain, mental p. relieved by talking about it - Give sorrow words: the grief that does not speak...' *** 'Sorrow concealed, like an oven stopped, doth burn the heart to cinders where it is.'
In the play. *John of Gaunt advises son Bolingbroke on how to weather the exile from England.*

Positive thinking and defiance towards setbacks – Woe doth the heavier sit, where it perceives it is but faintly borne.
"...woe doth the heavier sit,
Where it perceives it is but faintly borne." (KRII.1.3)

Words of encouragement.
In the play. *Gaunt tries to cheer up his banished son Bolingbroke.*

Positive thinking ineffective - who can hold a fire in his hands by thinking on the frosty Caucasus?...
"O, who can hold a fire in his hands,
By thinking on the frosty Caucasus?
Or cloy the hungry edge of appetite,
By bare imagination of a feast?
... the apprehension of the good
Gives but the greater feeling to the worse." (KRII.1.3)
Retort to soothing thoughts and words.
In the play. *Bolingbroke is not convinced that difficulties will be lightened by a positive attitude, as advised by his father Gaunt.*

Positive thinking, how to acquire it, the art of it – All places… are to a wise man ports and happy havens.
"All places that the eye of heaven visits,
Are to a wise man ports and happy havens:
Teach thy necessity to reason thus;
There is no virtue like necessity." (KRII.1.3)
Encouraging to see the good side of events and the virtue of understanding necessity. Use the third and fourth line
In the play. *Gaunt tries to cheer up his banished son Bolingbroke*

Positive thinking, how to acquire it, the art of it – Suppose the singing birds musicians... the flowers, fair ladies...
"Suppose the singing birds musicians;
The grass whereon thou thread'st, the presence strew'd;
The flowers, fair ladies; and thy steps, no more
Than a delightful measure, or a dance." (KRII.1.3)

How to learn to accept a place you or someone else dislikes originally.
In the play. *Gaunt tries to cheer up his banished son Bolingbroke. 'Presence' stands for 'presence-chamber' or 'state room'. That is imagine the grass in the field as the carpet of an executive conference room.*

Poverty, a case for p. - Who would not wish to be from wealth exempt…
"Who would not wish to be from wealth exempt,
Since riches point to misery and contempt?" (TOA.4.2)
In the play. *Timon's faithful servant Flavius reflects on the downside of wealth.*

Poverty, p. as a social disease – … A dedicated beggar to the air, with his disease of all-shunn'd poverty…
"…leave their false vows with him,
Like empty purses pick'd; and his poor self,
A dedicated beggar to the air,
With his disease of all-shunn'd poverty,
Walks, like contempt, alone"
(TOA.4.2)
Use as a remark on sociology, inequality, fear of poverty etc.
In the play. *Timon's servants comment on the turn of events that have left him penniless and devoid of (false) friends.*

Poverty, p. prevailing over will – My poverty, but not my will, consents.
"My poverty, but not my will, consents" (RJ.5.1)
In the play. *The apothecary accepts to sell a poisonous drug to Romeo, though against the law.*

Power, abuse of p. - The abuse of greatness is, when it disjoins remorse from power.
"The abuse of greatness is, when it disjoins
Remorse from power." (JC.2.1)
Use in any situation where you see this happening, as a conclusion to your explanation.
In the play. *Brutus meditates on the dangers of excessively concentrated power.*

Power, declining p. – Now my charms are all o'erthrown and what strength I have's mine own…
"Now my charms are all o'erthrown,
And what strength I have's mine own,
Which is most faint
… Now I want
Spirits to enforce, art to enchant,
And my ending is despair,
Unless I be relieved by prayer,
Which pierces so that it assaults
Mercy itself and frees all faults "
(TEM.epilogue)
Answer to 'Why can't you do this?' E.G. 'Sorry, but my charms…most faint'. Add a touch of modesty after successfully completing a project. E.G. 'My charms are all overthrown and what strength I have's mine own'. Also usable as an ending to a retirement speech.
In the play. *Prospero addressing the audience and confirming he has given his magic powers.*

Power, disappointment with p. - I'll give my jewels for a set of beads, my gorgeous palace for a hermitage…
"I'll give my jewels for a set of beads,
My gorgeous palace for a hermitage,
My gay apparel for an almsman's gown,
My figured goblets for a dish of wood,
My sceptre for a palmer's walking staff,
My subjects for a pair of carved saints
And my large kingdom for a little grave" (KRII.3.3)
In the play. *King Richard's reaction at the situation he finds himself in, at the mercy of Bolingbroke, soon-to-be usurper and new king Henry IV.*

Power, dreaming of p. - ... I do but dream on sovereignty; like one that stands upon a promontory...
"... I do but dream on sovereignty;
Like one that stands upon a promontory,
And spies a far-off shore where he would tread,
Wishing his foot were equal with his eye" (KHVI p3.3.2)
Skip the first line and apply to yourself when you have a goal in mind but (as yet) lack the means to achieve it.
In the play. *Richard of Gloucester (later Richard III) musing on his dreams of acquiring the crown.*

Power, effects of uncontrolled p. – ... And appetite, an universal wolf ... must make perforce an universal prey...
"Then every thing includes itself in power,
Power into will, will into appetite;
And appetite, an universal wolf,
So doubly seconded with will and power,
Must make perforce an universal prey,
And last eat up himself" (TC.1.3)
A concise and accurate description of late 20th century US foreign policy.
In the play. *Ulysses delivers a motivational speech to the disaffected Greeks.*

Power, high places, long falls, powerful shattered to pieces - They that stand high have many blasts to shake them...
"They that stand high have many blasts to shake them;
And if they fall, they dash themselves to pieces." (KRIII.1.3)
Historically true, though not at the end of the XXth century and beginning of the XXIst. Now big crooks wear golden parachutes. You can use the quote as a historical reference to point out the contrast to current culture.
In the play. *Queen Margaret fell from where she was 'standing high'. She addresses the Marquess of Dorset who is in a position of power, but threatened by the ambition of Richard.*

Power, invocation for honestly acquired p. - O, that estates, degrees and offices were not derived corruptly...
"O, that estates, degrees and offices
Were not derived corruptly, and that clear honour
Were purchased by the merit of the wearer!" (MOV.2.9)
In the play. *The prince of Arragon meditates on the meaning of the puzzle the solution to which will entitled the puzzle solver to marry Portia.*

Power, lust for p. as a psychological compensation - Then, since this earth affords no joy to me... I'll make my heaven to dream upon the crown.
"Then, since this earth affords no joy to me,
But to command, to cheque, to o'erbear such
As are of better person than myself,
I'll make my heaven to dream upon the crown" (KHVI p3.3.2)
Apply to a ruler or manager who is significantly worse than those whom he/she manages.
In the play. *Conscious of his unappealing looks, Richard of Gloucester (later Richard III), rationalizes his greed for power as some kind of compensation.*

Power, magic p. - I have bedimm'd the noontide sun, call'd forth the mutinous winds...
"... I have bedimm'd
The noontide sun, call'd forth the mutinous winds,
And 'twixt the green sea and the azured vault
Set roaring war" (TEM.5.1)

Invert the sense of the quote in answer to rhetorical questions of the type 'What can you do?' E.G. "I cannot bedim the nooontide sun, nor call forth the mutinous winds.... But... continue describing what you can do.
In the play. *Prospero, his goals accomplished, recalls some of his feats before giving up his magic powers.*

Power, misapplied or abused p. is self-defeating - ... The hardest knife ill-used doth lose his edge.
"Take heed, dear heart, of this large privilege;
The hardest knife ill-used doth lose his edge." (SON 95)

Power, one way to use p. - And when the lion fawns upon the lamb, the lamb will never cease to follow him.
"And when the lion fawns upon the lamb,
The lamb will never cease to follow him." (KHVI p3.4.8)
Though this theory is proven false in the play, it may still have some validity. Helping the weak may foster their allegiance.
In the play. *Self-delusional and naïve Henry VI believes that the people will be loyal to him because he was good to them.*

Power, p. broker - ... For who lived king, but I could dig his grave?
"The wrinkles in my brows, now filled with blood,
Were liken'd oft to kingly sepulchres;
For who lived king, but I could dig his grave?
And who durst smile when Warwick bent his brow?" (KHVI.p3.5.2)
Describe a power broker, one who acts in the shadow. For use of the last line see 'Frown, f. by a powerful m.'
In the play. *Warwick, wounded to death in the battle against the York forces near Barnet, reflects on his life.*

Power, p. broker - Proud setter up and puller down of kings!
"Proud setter up and puller down of kings!" (KHVI.p3.3.3)
In the play. *Queen Margaret addresses her (for now) enemy Warwick who has just arranged for the married of the Lady Bona of France to the newly installed Edward IV of England.*

Power, p. broker - Thou setter up and plucker down of kings.
"Thou setter up and plucker down of kings" (KHVI.p3.2.3)
In the play. *Edward of York to Warwick prior to a battle with the Lancastrians near Towton.*

Power, p. in the hands of the contemptible - More pity that the eagle should be mew'd, while kites and buzzards prey at liberty.
"More pity that the eagle should be mew'd,
While kites and buzzards prey at liberty." (KRIII.1.1)
When politics stunt the good and promote the despicable. See the (successful) efforts of both the Democratic and Republican parties to prevent a third independent candidate to content for the presidency.
In the play. *Hastings has been sent to the Tower by the machinations of the Queen's courtiers (kites and buzzards) while a nobler character (eagle) cannot express himself. So says Richard who will eventually get rid of Hastings too. 'To mew' = 'To shut up'.*

Power, p. provokes fear – ... great men tremble when the lion roars.
"Small curs are not regarded when they grin;
But great men tremble when the lion roars." (KHVI p2 3.1)
Comment on a command given you by your boss and uttered with emphasis, '... great men tremble ...roars'

In the play. *Q. Margaret tells King Henry VI that Duke Humphrey shows a defiant attitude – actually she is plotting to have him eliminated.*

Power, p. used appropriately and inappropriately – ... it is excellent to have a giant's strength...
"... O, it is excellent
To have a giant's strength, but it is tyrannous
To use it like a giant." (MFM.2.2)
Criticism on the injudicious use of power.
In the play. *Isabel attempts to plead for her brother's life with Angelo, the governor.*

Power, p. used to war and plunder - ... had I power, I should pour the sweet milk of concord into hell...
"...had I power, I should
Pour the sweet milk of concord into hell,
Uproar the universal peace, confound
All unity on earth." (M.4.3)
In the play. *Malcolm pretends that - should he become king - he would be worse than Macbeth.*

Power, p.'s precedence over custom - ... nice customs curtsy to great kings ...
"O Kate, nice customs curtsy to great kings. Dear Kate, you and I cannot be confined within the weak list of a country's fashion: we are the makers of manners, Kate; and the liberty that follows our places stops the mouth of all find-faults." (KHV.5.2)
Try this if she objects to your attentions.
In the play. *Henry offers an argument to overrun Katherine's objections to kissing before an official engagement.*

Power, privilege of p. to give no explanations - The cause is in my will.
"The cause is in my will" (JC.2.2)
Answer to 'What is the cause (or reason) for this?'
In the play. *Caesar's first answer to Decius Brutus who asks why he will not go to the senate. Decius, one of the conspirators, will eventually persuade Caesar to go. Before answering Caesar makes it clear that his decision is not dictated by impossibility or fear. See 'Lying, l. about impossibility and fear - ... Cannot, is false, and that I dare not, falser...'*

Power, source of p. more pain than joy - ... As brings a thousand-fold more care to keep than in possession any jot of pleasure.
"For all the rest is held at such a rate,
As brings a thousand-fold more care to keep,
Than in possession any jot of pleasure." (KHVI p3.2.2)
Explain the refusal of a privilege or of an expensive luxury. 'It brings a thousand-fold...pleasure.'
In the play. *King Henry VI to Clifford near York.*

Power, special p. of affection - Affection! thy intention stabs the centre...
"Affection! thy intention stabs the centre:
Thou dost make possible things not so held,
Communicatest with dreams" (WT.1.2)
In the play. *Leontes is obsessed with irrational jealousy now doubts that the boy Mamilius is really his son. What makes 'possible things not so held' is the affection he has developed towards the boy.*

Power, the downside of p. - ... subject to the breath of every fool, whose sense no more can feel, but his own wringing.
"O hard condition! Twin-born of greatness,
Subject to the breath of every fool, whose sense
No more can feel, but his own wringing!" (KHV.4.1)

When your boss complains about the inconveniences of power. Or suggest that your decisions cannot be influenced by the changing moods of many, "We cannot be subject to the breath of every fool…wringing!" Defend yourself when you are still criticized after having done well for the welfare of the community. See also 'Management, challenges of top m. – uneasy lies the head' - 'Opinion, your op. on crowds and masses'.
In the play. *King Henry V has just heard, incognito, his troops' complaints against him the night before the battle of Agincourt and meditates on the disadvantages of majesty (greatness).*

Power, where real power is - … As doth a sail, fill'd with a fretting gust, command an argosy to stem the waves.
"…the bloody-minded queen,
That led calm Henry, though he were a king,
As doth a sail, fill'd with a fretting gust,
Command an argosy to stem the waves" (KHVI.p3.2.6)
In the play. *After a field victory on Henry VI's forces, Edward pauses and instructs some soldiers to chase the fugitive enemy army.*
'Argosy' = 'Sailing cargo ship'

Power, where real power is - … for, as I hear you that are king, though he doth wear the crown.
"… for, as I hear,
You that are king, though he doth wear the crown." (KHVI p3.2.2)
Show that you know where real power lays, particularly applicable if the holder of power is a woman
In the play. *Edward claims the throne and accuses Henry VI of perjury for continuing to be king notwithstanding his previous commitment to abdicate. Edward says 'You that are king' sarcastically addressing Queen Margaret, wife of Henry VI and aggressive 'she-wolf of France'.*

Praise - … I never heard a man of his place, gravity and learning…
"I have lived fourscore years and upward; I never heard a man of his place, gravity and learning, so wide of his own respect." (MWW.2.3)
In the play. *Shallow extols the virtues of Doctor Caius.*

Praise for performance - … his deeds exceed all speech: he ne'er lift up his hand but conquered.
"…his deeds exceed all speech:
He ne'er lift up his hand but conquered." (KHVI p1.1)
In the play. *Gloucester eulogizes Henry V.*

Praise, accepted and returned, responding to praise - I will praise any man that will praise me.
"I will praise any man that will praise me." (AC.2.6)
Answer to praise received. A good opening after you have received a praising introduction. You may quote as is or with a brief narrative. See 'in the play' for this quote.
In the play. *Enobarbus, Antony's lieutenant meets with Menas, Pompey's lieutenant. Menas praises Enobarbus for his exploits and Enobarbus answers with this sentence.*

Praise, agreement in p. - Quick is mine ear to hear of good towards him.
"…out with it boldly, man
Quick is mine ear to hear of good towards him." (KRII.2.1)
In the play. *Lord Willoughby, referring to the exiled Henry Bolingbroke. A rebellion is brewing*

Praise, how p. can accomplish objectives more easily than reprimand - Our praises are our wages…
"Our praises are our wages: you may ride's
With one soft kiss a thousand furlongs

ere
With spur we beat an acre.*"* (WT.1.2)
Explain the value and effectiveness of praise. See also 'Love and flattery. Plea to be flattered.' – 'Kindness, k. more effective than rudeness to achieve results'.
In the play. *Hermione, in a semi-humorous tone, prompts her husband Leontes to praise her for her efforts at retaining a guest (Polixenes), who instead wanted to leave.*

Praise, importance of p., insisting in praising her - ... one good deed, dying tongueless slaughters a thousand waiting upon that.
"… one good deed dying tongueless
Slaughters a thousand waiting upon that." (WT.1.2)
Explain why you want to praise a person who seems to be overly modest. Introduction to a speaker whose exploits you wish to praise. Insist in praising her. for something good she has done, though she appears modestly reluctant to accept the praise.
In the play. *Hermione, in a semi-humorous tone, prompts her husband Leontes to praise her for her efforts at retaining a guest (Polixenes), who instead wanted to leave.*

Praise, indirect self-praise by accusing another of poor judgment - You praise yourself by laying defects of judgement to me...
"You praise yourself
By laying defects of judgement to me, but
You patched up your excuses."
(AC.2.2)
A retort to anyone who directly or indirectly accuses you of having misjudged a situation. E.G. 'You praise yourself…to me.'
In the play. *Octavian upbraids Antony for having lacked respect to the messenger sent to Egypt from Rome by Octavian. Antony says that the incident was unintentional and of small importance. Octavian is unconvinced.*

Praise, p. and endorsement - I know the gentleman to be of worth and worthy estimation and not without desert so well reputed.
"… I know the gentleman
To be of worth and worthy estimation
And not without desert so well reputed" (TGV.2.2)
In the play. *Valentine, gullibly as it turns out, endorses his friend Proteus with the Duke of Milan*

Praise, p. and gratitude - A god on earth thou art.
"A god on earth thou art." (KRII.5.3)
In the play. *The Duchess of Aumerle to King Henry IV for having pardoned her son Aumerle.*

Praise, p. as well as defense from accusation - To banish him that struck more blows for Rome than thou hast spoken words?
"To banish him that struck more blows for Rome
Than thou hast spoken words?"
(COR.4.2)
Defend an improperly accused, valuable and meritorious colleague.
In the play. *Volumnia, Coriolanus' mother, upbraids the tribunes who want to banish her son after all that he has done for the safety of Rome.*

Praise, p. by comparison - ... and make your chronicles as rich with praise as is the ooze and bottom of the sea with sunken wreck and sumless treasuries.
"... and make your chronicles as rich with praise,
As is the ooze and bottom of the sea,
With sunken wreck and sumless treasuries." (KHV.1.2)

Introduction to a person who has many accomplishments to his credit. E.g., 'My guest has made his chronicles as rich with praise as is the ooze…treasuries."
In the play. *Canterbury prods Henry V to attack France by recalling previous successful engagements in France, that made the chronicles 'rich with praise' etc. 'Ooze' is the soft mud sediment collecting at the bottom of a glass of muddy water.*

Praise, p. cannot create beauty - Where fair is not, praise cannot mend the brow.
"Where fair is not, praise cannot mend the brow" (LLL.4.1)
In the play. *The Princess banters with a Forester.*

Praise, p. deserved – You shall not be the grave of your deserving… 'twere a concealment worse than a theft… to hide your doings…
"You shall not be
The grave of your deserving; Rome must know…
The value of her own: 'twere a concealment
Worse than a theft, no less than a traducement,
To hide your doings; and to silence that,
Which, to the spire and top of praises vouch'd,
Would seem but modest." (COR.1.9)
When he/she modestly refuses to be praised, or praise and acknowledge a worthy action or brilliant career.
In the play. *Cominius insists with Marcius Coriolanus that he accept the praise and rewards earned with his victory at Coriolis (against the Volscii).*

Praise, deserved and not to be hidden - O, your desert speaks loud; and I should wrong it…
"O, your desert speaks loud; and I should wrong it,
To lock it in the wards of covert bosom,
When it deserves, with characters of brass,
A forted residence 'gainst the tooth of time
And razure of oblivion" (MFM.5.1)
When he/she modestly refuses to be praised. Good for an introduction. E.G. 'We know that you do not want to have your achievement praised but… 'your desert speaks loud… of oblivion'. Or counteract a statement of modesty and why the exploits of the subject in question should be made known to the audience.
In the play. *Duke Vicentio returning to Vienna pretends that Angelo has done a good job of governing while Vicentio was abroad. In fact, Angelo was a liar and a lecher. 'Forted' = 'fortified', 'razure' = 'erasure'.*

Praise, p. for achievements - The heavens through you, increase our wonder and set up your fame forever.
"The heavens,
Through you, increase our wonder and set up
Your fame forever." (PER.3.2)
In the play. *Cerimon has just revived Thaisa who was given for dead and a gentleman praises Cerimon.*

Praise, p. for noble behavior - A noble temper dost thou show in this…
"A noble temper dost thou show in this;
And great affections wrestling in thy bosom
Doth make an earthquake of nobility.
O, what a noble combat hast thou fought
Between compulsion and a brave respect!" (KJ.5.2)
In the play. *King Lewis of France to the doubt ridden Lord Salisbury who has joined the French in revolt against King John.*

Praise, p. lavished - ... every one her own hath garnished with such bedecking ornaments of praise.
"...every one her own hath garnished
With such bedecking ornaments of praise" (LLL.2.1)
In the play. *The Princess comments on her (female) attendants who seem to be all in love with the courtiers of the King of Navarre.*

Praise, p. misapplied, paid to approve - When we for recompense have praised the vile...
"When we for recompense have praised the vile,
It stains the glory in the happy verse
Which aptly sings the good."
(TOA.1.1)
Express your disagreement about the praise of something you do not like.
In the play. *A jeweler plans to present some junk jewelry to Timon and shows it to the poet expecting praise. The poet makes a sarcastic remark to himself about the 'vile' piece of jewelry.*

Praise, p. not flattery - ... the words I utter let none think flattery, for they'll find 'em truth.
"Let me speak, sir,
For heaven now bids me; and the words I utter
Let none think flattery, for they'll find 'em truth" (KHVIII.5.2)
Should she ever refuse your praise.
In the play. *Cranmer praises the baby daughter of Henry VIII and Ann Boleyn and predicts that that child, the future Elizabeth I, will fill England with glory. Easy for Shakespeare to say because by the time the play was produced, Elizabeth was already on the throne.*

Praise, p. of friends - I have told more of you to myself...
"I have told more of you to myself than you can with modesty speak in your own behalf" (TOA.1.2)
In the play. *Timon outdoes himself in praise of his partying friends who will turn out ungrateful parasites.*

Praise, p. rekindling memory – praising what is lost makes the remembrance dear.
"Praising what is lost
Makes the remembrance dear."
(AWEW.5.3)
A comment on nostalgia or a retort to someone who says that it is useless to remember.
In the play. *Lafeu has just praised the still missing (and reported dead) Helen and the King, who is present, offers a comforting thought.*

Praise, praising the criminal if advantage drawn from him – A giving hand, though foul, shall have fair praise.
"A giving hand, though foul, shall have fair praise." (LLL.4.1)
This also explains the success of lobbying, often exerted, directly or indirectly by criminals. See Enron etc.
In the play. *The Princess banters with a Forester while a deer hunt is organized.*

Praise, proper response to praise – 'Tis the best brine a maiden can season her praise in.
LAFEU Your commendations, madam, get from her tears.
COUNTESS 'Tis the best brine a maiden can season her praise in. (AWEW.1.1)
Quote ironically when you cannot refrain from crying at praise or honor bestowed on you.
In the play. *The referred-to and crying subject is Helena.*

Praise, refusal to be p. – He had rather venture all his limbs for honour...
"He had rather venture all his limbs for honour

Than one on's ears to hear it"
(COR.2.2)
In the play. *Menenius to various Roman Senators, referring to Coriolanus.*

Praise, self-p. - So much for praising myself, who, I myself will bear witness, is praiseworthy.
"…So much for praising myself, who, I myself will bear witness, is praiseworthy" (MAAN.5.2)
Ironical ending to a statement.
In the play. *Benedick ends an exchange with Beatrice during which pros and cons of praising oneself have been debated.*

Praise, self-p justified - … to be the trumpet of his own virtues, as I am to myself.
"…therefore is it most expedient for the wise, if Don Worm, his conscience, find no impediment to the contrary, to be the trumpet of his own virtues, as I am to myself" (MAAN.5.2)
In the play. *Benedick justifies his self-praise.*

Praise, self-p. or praise of speaker – And all the courses of my life do show I am not in the roll of common men.
"These signs have mark'd me extraordinary;
And all the course of my life do show, I am not in the roll of common men." (KHIV p1.3.1)
Apply to yourself as a comment or explanation when someone says, 'I did not know you could do this.' Or use as an introduction to praise the speaker for his achievements, e.g. 'And all thee courses of his life, do show he is not in the roll of common men.' See also 'Eccentricity, above the crowd –... I will not jump with common spirits and rank me with the barbarous multitude.'
In the play. *Glendower has a high opinion of himself.*

Praise, tongue too earthly to sing of her celestial beauty - …this wrong that sings heaven's praise with such an earthly tongue.
"Celestial as thou art, O, pardon, love, this wrong,
That sings heaven's praise with such an earthly tongue." (LLL.4.2)
Alternate answer to 'Do you like me?'
In the play. *Sir Nathaniel reads from a letter of Don Armado and addressed to Jaquenetta.*

Praising, p. while blaming – …but breathe his faults so quaintly that they may seem the taints of liberty…
"…but breathe his faults so quaintly
That they may seem the taints of liberty,
The flash and outbreak of a fiery mind," (H.2.1)
In the play. *Polonius instructs Reynaldo to keep a watch on Laertes' deeds in Paris. Laertes is Polonius' son.*

Prayers, conflict of p. for opposite ends - … our prayers do out-pray his…
"Our prayers do out-pray his; then let them have
That mercy which true prayer ought to have" (KRII.5.3)
When your adversary pleads for a cause opposite to yours. Change 'our' to 'my' and 'his' to 'mine'.
In the play. *The Duke of York pleads with the King (Bolingbroke, now Henry IV), to punish hi own (York's) son, the Duke of Aumerle, who joined plotters against Bolingbroke. His mother instead pleads with the King for a pardon. She makes the point that her prayer for a pardon is more sincere than York's pleading for a condemnation.*

Preaching, p. versus practice - … will not you maintain the thing you teach but prove a chief offender in the same?
"…I have heard you preach,

That malice was a great and grievous sin;
And will not you maintain the thing you teach,
But prove a chief offender in the same?" (KHVI.p1.3.1)
Confront him who does not practice what he preaches.
In the play. *K. Henry to the bishop of Winchester who is sour against Gloucester.*

Precision, p. shooting - ... and like an arrow shot from a well-experienced archer hits the mark...
"...fly after: and like an arrow shot
From a well-experienced archer hits the mark
His eye doth level at" (PER.1.1)
Use as a comparison to show the need of precision in executing the plan. Or as a metaphorical compliment for one who has answered correctly or has made a good point.
In the play. *Antioch instructs Thaliard to go after the fleeing Pericles and kill him.*

Prediction, desire to know in advance - O God! that one might read the book of fate and see the revolutions of the times...
"O God! that one might read the book of fate,
And see the revolutions of the times
Make mountains level, and the continent,
Weary of solid firmness, melt itself
Into the sea!" (KHIV p2.3.1)
In the play. *King Henry IV to Warwick reflecting on the turn of events that led him to the throne and a prophecy uttered by King Richard II before he died.*

Prediction, desire to know in advance - O, that a man might know the end of this day's business ere it come...
"O, that a man might know
The end of this day's business ere it come!

But it sufficeth that the day will end,
And then the end is known." (JC.5.1)
Answer to 'What do you think will happen?' Justifying your anxiety while waiting for the outcome of an event. See also 'Life, manly approach to unexpected events, however rough.'
In the play. *Brutus before the battle at Philippi.*

Prediction, dire p. – The time will come, that foul sin shall break into corruption.
"'The time will come, that foul sin, gathering head,
Shall break into corruption' so went on,
Foretelling this same time's condition
And the division of our amity."
(KHIV.p2.3.1)
In the play. *King Henry IV recalls the prophetic words of Richard II to Northumberland. Northumberland helped Henry IV to the throne but now he himself has become a rebel.*

Prediction, dire p. - The time shall not be many hours of age…
"The time shall not be many hours of age
More than it is ere foul sin gathering head
Shalt break into corruption."
(KRII.5.1)
In the play. *Deposed King Richard II predicts to Northumberland his downfall – a prediction that will occur in the play King Henry IV p1. A prediction well remembered by King Henry IV (see previous entry).*

Prediction, dire p. - The woe's to come; the children yet unborn shall feel this day as sharp to them as thorn.
"The woe's to come; the children yet unborn.
Shall feel this day as sharp to them as thorn." (KRII.4.1)

Many historical references prove this to be true when a gross political injustice has been done against a people or a nation. See also 'Event, e. of historical importance'
In the play. *The Bishop of Carlisle predicts the consequences of the usurpation of the throne by Bolingbroke.*

Prediction, p. in the process of occurring – …Which is so plain that Exeter doth wish his days may finish ere that hapless time.
"…Which is so plain that Exeter doth wish
His days may finish ere that hapless time." **(KHVI.p1.3.1)**
In the play. *The prediction Exeter refers to is that Henry V will win all that his son Henry VI will lose.*

Prediction, predicting what party is going to say - … his embassy, which I could with a ready guess declare…
"…go we in, to know his embassy;
Which I could with a ready guess declare,
Before the Frenchman speak a word of it." (HV.1.1)
Try 'I know your message, which I could with a ready guess declare before you speak a word of it".
In the play. *Canterbury and Ely know already what the French ambassador will say to Henry V.*

Pregnancy, p. good - Lady, you are the cruel'st she alive, if you will lead these graces to the grave…
"Lady, you are the cruel'st she alive,
If you will lead these graces to the grave,
And leave the world no copy." (TN.1.1)
A good retort is she says 'I don't want to get pregnant'. Mildly out of fashion in XXI century popular culture. Weigh her character first before using the lines.

In the play. *Viola/Cesario continues to lead Olivia to listen to the forthcoming message from the Duke.*

Pregnancy, causes of p. and evidence – … it chances the stealth of our most mutual entertainment …
"…But it chances
The stealth of our most mutual entertainment
With character too gross is writ on Juliet." (MFM.1.2)
In the play. *Claudio, arrested on orders of Angelo, explains to Lucio the reasons for his arrest.*

Pregnancy, p. good - From fairest creatures we desire increase, that thereby beauty's rose may never die.
"From fairest creatures we desire increase,
That thereby beauty's rose may never die" (SON 1)
Answer to 'I don't want to get pregnant'. You may follow with a "besides…." and add a description of whatever other measures you are taking or are prepared to take to avoid the occurrence. See also 'Virginity, time dependent value of v.'

Prejudice, exhortation to clear p. - … weed your better judgements of all opinion that grows rank in them.
"... weed your better judgements
Of all opinion that grows rank in them." (AYLI.2.7)
Exhort your audience to abandon prejudices and old beliefs.
In the play. *In a deliberately self-effacing statement, Jacques tells the Duke S. not to consider him (Jacques) wise - this being incorrect (rank opinion).*

Prejudice, inability to believe in exceptional performance - You judge it straight a thing impossible to compass wonders but by help of devils.

"Because you want the grace that others have,
You judge it straight a thing impossible
To compass wonders but by help of devils." (KHVI.p1.5.4)
Retort to the accusation that a positive result was achieved via questionable means.
In the play. *La Pucelle defends herself while being tried by the English.*

Prejudice, warped view of reality - ... warp'd the line of every other favour scorn'd a fair colour ...
"Contempt his scornful perspective did lend me,
Which warp'd the line of every other favour;
Scorn'd a fair colour, or express'd it stolen;
Extended or contracted all proportions
To a most hideous object"
(AWEW.5.3)
Characterize prejudice as a 'scornful perspective '.
In the play. *Bertram explains tot he king how unjustified prejudice made him turn all virtues of Helena into contempt*

Preparations, p. for action - ... (let) all things thought upon ... add more feathers to our wings.
"(let) all things thought upon
That may with reasonable swiftness add
More feathers to our wings" (HV.1.2)
Alternative for 'let's get ready'
In the play. *Henry V prepares to invade France.*

Presence, her p. your light and only joy - What joy is joy if Sylvia is not by? Unless it be to think that she is by and feed upon the shadow of perfection…
"What light is light, if Silvia be not seen?
What joy is joy if Sylvia is not by?
Unless it be to think that she is by
And feed upon the shadow of perfection.
Except I be by Sylvia in the night,
There is no music in the nightingale;
Unless I look on Sylvia in the day,
There is no day for me to look upon:
She is my essence." (TGV.3.1)
Change 'Sylvia' with the name of your love. Or select and modify, e.g. 'When I am away from you I just think of you and feed upon the shadow of perfection.' Or 'Unless you are by me at night, there is no music in the nightingale'. Many options here and a wealth of opportunities.
In the play. *The Duke has banned Valentine from Milan and Valentine is distraught at not having Sylvia by him.*

Presence, inquiry on physical presence – Is Horatio there?... A piece of him
BERNARDO …is Horatio there
HORATIO A piece of him. (H.1.1)
See also entries for 'Disappearance'
In the play. *In the night fog during which the Ghost appears, guards see the shadow of Horatio and verify who is coming.*

Presence, p. that inspires confidence and conquers fear - …a largess universal like the sun his liberal eye doth give to every one, thawing cold fear.
"… every wretch, pining and pale before,
Beholding him, plucks comfort from his looks:
A largess universal like the sun

His liberal eye doth give to every one, Thawing cold fear" (KHV.4.pro)
In the play. *The chorus describes the settings at the English camp, before the battle of Agincourt.*

Presence, physical p. crucial for success - The present eye praises the present object.
"The present eye praises the present object." (TC.3.3)
Explain and justify the importance of presence and of the perception of novelty. See also 'Motion, what moves catches the attention.' - 'Time erasing impact of action, compared to a parting host.' – 'Time, t. and ingratitude, t, making contributions to oblivion'
In the play. *Ulysses tries to convince the supercilious Achilles to rejoin the fighting against the Trojans.*

Present, impact of the p. moment – Each present joy or sorrow seems the chief.
"Each present joy or sorrow seems the chief" (Poems)

Presentation, complimenting a member of the audience who asked a good question - Well demanded, wench: my tale provokes that question.
"Well demanded, wench:
My tale provokes that question" (TEM.1.2)
If the questioner is a male, substitute 'wench' with 'sir'.
In the play. *Prospero is giving daughter Miranda the history of their escape and exile in the island.*

Presentation, plea for patience from audience – … with patient ears attend, what here shall miss, our toil shall strive to mend.
"The which if you with patient ears attend,
What here shall miss, our toil shall strive to mend" (RJ.Prologue)
Use at the beginning of the presentation or as an answer to a petulant questioner who asks a question before you come to the point.
In the play. *The Chorus gives a brief synopsis of what happens in the play and graciously asks for the audience's patience.*

Presentation, skipping intermediate sections of a p. - Then brook abridgment, and your eyes advance…
"Then brook abridgment, and your eyes advance,
After your thoughts, straight back again to France." (KHV.5.prologue)
In the play. *The chorus gives a quick summary of the events following the victory of King Henry V at Agincourt.*

Presentation. Epilogues to p. - … As you from crimes would pardon'd be, let your indulgence set me free.
"… my ending is despair,
Unless I be relieved by prayer,
Which pierces so that it assaults
Mercy itself and frees all faults.
As you from crimes would pardon'd be,
Let your indulgence set me free" (TEM.5.1)
Change 'crimes' to 'faults' when addressing the general audience, unless you are delivering a speech in a prison.
In the play. *At the conclusion of the play (and plot), Prospero discloses that all was but a product of magic and illusion.*

Presentation. Epilogues to p. - … If I were a woman I would kiss as many of you as had beards that pleased me…
"…If I were a woman I would kiss as many of you as had beards that pleased me, complexions that liked me and breaths that I defied not." (AYLI.5.4)

In the play. *Rosalind recites the epilogue.*

Presentation. Epilogues to p. - ... thanks to all at once and to each one.
"... thanks to all at once and to each one" (M.5.8)
In the play. *Malcolm, now king, thanks all his allies and friends before his coronation at Scone.*

Presentation. Epilogues to p. - Gentles, do not reprehend, if you pardon, we will mend.
"Gentles, do not reprehend;
If you pardon, we will mend."
(MND.5.1)
An expression of modesty at the end of a speech
In the play. *The fairy Puck, left alone on the stage at the end of the real play, gives a parting message to the audience.*

Presentation. Epilogues to p. – If it be true that 'good wine needs no bush'...
If it be true that 'good wine needs no bush', 'tis true that a good play needs no epilogue; yet to good wine they do use good bushes, and good plays prove the better by the help of good epilogues..." (AYLI. Epilogue)
In the play. *'Bush' refers to the ivy bush hanging outside a vintner's premises. The idea, contrary to today's marketing principles, is that a good product requires no propaganda.*

Presentation. Epilogues to p. - If we shadows have offended think but this, (and all is mended)...
"If we shadows have offended,
Think but this, (and all is mended),
That you have but slumbered here,
While these visions did appear."
(MND.5.1)
Expression of modesty at the end of a speech
In the play. *The fairy Puck, left alone on the stage at the end of the real play, suggests to the audience a mental remedy to recover from any potential offense.*

Presentation. Epilogues to p. – my tongue is weary; when my legs are too, I will bid you good night. "...My tongue is weary; when my legs are too, I will bid you good night"
(KHIV.p2.5.5)
Insertion in speech ending.
In the play. *The producer addresses the audience.*

Presentation. Epilogues to p. - So, on your patience evermore attending...
"So, on your patience evermore attending,
New joy wait on you! Here our play has ending." (PER.5.3)
Conclusion to a presentation. Change 'play' to 'presentation'.
In the play. *The play is finished with the good people living happily hereafter. Gower takes leave of the audience.*

Presentation. Epilogues to p. – First my fear; then my courtesy; last my speech...
"First my fear; then my courtesy; last my speech.
My fear is, your displeasure; my courtesy, my duty;
and my speech, to beg your pardons." (KHIV.p2.5.5)
In the play. *A dancer addresses the audience at the end of the play.*

Presentation. Epilogues to p. – Gentle breath of yours my sails must fill, or else my project fails...
"Gentle breath of yours my sails
Must fill, or else my project fails,
Which was to please" (TEM.5.1)
The sails refer to the fact that Prospero will leave the island. The quote is particularly suited if you must leave for a trip or leave immediately after your presentation. E.G. 'After this presentation I will leave for xxx. To conclude...'

759

In the play. *Part of Prospero the Magician's parting words to the audience.*

Presentation. Epilogues to p. - Thus far, with rough and all-unable pen our bending author hath pursued the story..
"Thus far, with rough and all-unable pen,
Our bending author hath pursued the story,
In little room confining mighty men,
Mangling by starts the full course of their glory." (HV.5.2)
At the end of a presentation. 'I am getting to the end and 'thus far….story' -- Still I hope…'. Or mix and match extracting from introductions and epilogues. See, 'Introduction. Impossible to describe all her/his accomplishments in a short time'. E.G.
"Thus far, with rough and all-unable pen,
Our bending author hath pursued the story,
So that all may not be turned to nought,
Piece out our imperfections with your thought."
In the play. *The chorus ends the play with a touch of modesty and renewed apologies for the props. 'Bending author' refers to the act of writing or the natural bending of the body while writing.*

Presentation. Epilogues to p. - 'Tis ten to one this play can never please all that are here…
"'Tis ten to one this play can never please
All that are here: some come to take their ease,
And sleep an act or two; but those, we fear,
We have frighted with our trumpets; so, 'tis clear,
They'll say 'tis naught:" (K HVIII.5.5)
Ending of your presentation, even if a trumpet was not part of it. E.G. 'I will end with a quote that may apply to a play more than my presentation, 'Tis ten to one…'tis nothing'. Still I hope I have not made you go to sleep for the whole time.'
In the play. *The stage manager or the play director to the audience*

Presentation. Epilogues to p., asking for pardon – … my fear is your displeasure; my courtesy, my duty; and my speech, to beg your pardons.
"First my fear; then my courtesy; last my speech.
My fear is, your displeasure; my courtesy, my duty; and my speech, to beg your pardons" (KHIV.p2.5.5)
Insertion in speech ending.
In the play. *The producer addresses the audience.*

Presentation. Epilogues to p., end of magic. – … But this rough magic I here abjure…
"But this rough magic
I here abjure… I'll break my staff,
Bury it certain fathoms in the earth,
And deeper than did ever plummet sound
I'll drown my book" (TEM.5.
Usable also as a metaphor for retirement, e.g. 'I abjured my magic and broken my staff…I drowned my book'.
In the play. *Prospero has accomplished all his goals with his acquired skills in magic. Before retiring he gives up his tools and book of magic. Fathom' = a unit of measure equal to six feet, used to measure depth'.*

Presentation, Epilogues to p., should I run? – If my tongue cannot entreat you to acquit me, will you command me to use my legs?
"If my tongue cannot entreat you to acquit me, will
you command me to use my legs?" (KHIV.p2.5.5)
Insertion in speech ending.
In the play. *The producer addresses the audience.*

Presentation, lack of special effects for the p. - Think, when we talk of horses, that you see them…
"Think, when we talk of horses, that you see them
Printing their proud hoofs in the receiving earth." (KHV.prologue)
Should you, for whatever reason, have lost or mislaid the graphic material for your presentation but cannot delay it, then use the line 'Think, when we talk of horses, that you see them'
In the play. *The chorus, given the limited number of props must rely on the imagination of the audience to visualize the action of this action-packed play.*

Presentation, modesty in p. – If you look for a good speech now, you undo me: for what I have to say is of mine own making...
"If you look for a good speech now, you undo me: for what I have to say is of mine own making; and what indeed I should say will, I doubt, prove mine own marring." (KHIV.p2.epilogue)

Presentment, p. and fear - I have a faint cold fear thrills through my veins, that almost freezes up the heat of life.
"…God knows when we shall meet again.
I have a faint cold fear thrills through my veins,
That almost freezes up the heat of life" (RJ.4.3)
In the play. *Juliet has said good night to mother and nurse and is about to ingest the potion given her by Friar Lawrence.*

Presentment, premonition - I am surprised with an uncouth fear, a chilling sweat o'er-runs my trembling joints…

"I am surprised with an uncouth fear;
A chilling sweat o'er-runs my trembling joints
My heart suspects more than mine eye can see." (TA.2.3)
Use the third line when your instincts make you uncomfortable with a person or a situation though you cannot produce specific evidence for the feeling. See also 'Woman, w.'s intuition' – 'Intuition, seeing through appearance'
In the play. *Quintus, at the edge of a hole in the ground in a forest suspects that some horrible deed has been committed.*

Presentment, premonition.– … methinks, some unborn sorrow, ripe in fortune's womb is coming towards me…
"…methinks,
Some unborn sorrow, ripe in fortune's womb,
Is coming towards me, and my inward soul
With nothing trembles." (KRII.2.2)
In the play. *The Queen is still unaware that Bolingbroke landed again in England and is bent on dethroning Richard II. Bushy attempts to cheer her up thinking that her fears stem from Richard having left to fight in Ireland. See 'Fear, f. unwarranted - Each substance of a grief hath twenty shadows…'*

Pretence, no for yes - Play the maid's part, still answer nay, and take it.
"Play the maid's part, still answer nay, and take it." (KRIII.3.7)
Possible remark when you are offered a treat and decide to accept it, 'I'll play the maid's part…take it'.
See also 'Playing hard-to-get and why - … If I confess much, you will play the tyrant.'– 'Justification for insisting even after she said 'no' - … maids in modesty, say 'No' to that which they would have the profferer construe 'Ay'.
In the play. *Buckingham concocts the scene when Richard will appear to the councilmen of*

London between two priests and pretend not to have ambitions on the crown.

Pretence, pretending to be silly - … as gardeners do with ordure hide those roots that shall first spring...
"„„,Covering discretion with a coat of folly;
As gardeners do with ordure hide those roots
That shall first spring, and be most delicate." (KHV.2.4)
Explain why an apparently silly action of yours was really intended as a cover for a deeper motive, e.g. 'I know but I was simply covering discretion…folly'.
In the play. *The constable of France warns the Dauphin not to underestimate K. Henry V due to Henry's youthful escapades.*

Pretext, p. for personal attack - … my pretext to strike at him admits a good construction.
"…my pretext to strike at him admits
A good construction." (COR.5.6)
See also 'Assassination, a. under the guise of law - That he should die is worthy policy; but yet we want a colour for his death…'
In the play. *Aufidius plots the reasons for assassinating Coriolanus*

Pretty, answer to 'Am I pretty?' – … if ladies be but young and fair they have the gift to know it.
"…And says, if ladies be but young and fair,
They have the gift to know it"
(AYLI.2)
Equivalent to saying, 'You know that you are'.
In the play: *The cantankerous Jaques describes to the Duke Senior the fool whom he (Jaques) has just met. The fool will prove quite witty. In this introduction Jaques continues to define him as follows,*
'in his brain,
Which is as dry as the remainder biscuit
After a voyage, he hath strange places cramm'd
With observation, the which he vents
In mangled forms'
In a different occasion, for example when you have forgotten something you can say, 'My *brain is as dry as the remainder biscuit after a voyage'*

Pretty, as a summer day – as a fair day in summer…
"As a fair day in summer, wondrous fair." (PER.2.5)
Answer to 'Do you like me?' or 'Am I pretty' or a plain compliment.
In the play. *Pericles wins a tournament in Pentapolis and will gain the hand of Thaisa, daughter of King Simonides. Simonides, cautious prospective father in law wishes to reassure himself that Pericles will be a good husband for Thaisa and questions him about his daughter. Clearly Pericles likes Thaisa.*

Pretty, as well as wise – ... fair and wise is she; the heaven such grace did lend her, that she might admired be
"…fair and wise is she;
The heaven such grace did lend her,
That she might admired be."
(TGV.4.2)
Change 'she' to 'you'. 'Fair and wise you are; the heaven such grace did lend you that you might admired be." Answer to 'Am I pretty?' Change 'her' and 'she' to 'you'.
In the play. *Julia, disguised has arrived in Milan from Verona and inquires about Julia. The host answers with this information (about Julia).*

Pretty, more than the word can express plus - ... she is fair, and, fairer than that word, of wondrous virtues.
"…she is fair, and, fairer than that word,
Of wondrous virtues." (MOV.1.1)
Change to, 'You are fair, fairer than that word, of wondrous virtues/

In the play: *Bassanio describes to his friend Antonio how beautiful Portia is. Portia is equally attracted to Bassanio (see entry for 'Body, b. language').*

Pretty, the prettiest of all - the prettiest Kate in Christendom.
"… the prettiest Kate in Christendom." (TOS.2.1)
Change 'Kate' to the name of the applicable lady. See also 'Best, compliment, you are the best – full many a lady I have eyed with best regards….'
In the play. *Petruchio begins his romantic pursuit of the wild Katharina.*

Prevarication on anyone will prompt vengeance - the smallest worm will turn being trodden on.
"The smallest worm will turn being trodden on." (KHVI p3.2)
Show that negative reaction may be expected by anyone whose rights have been infringed. See also 'Defense, d. of loved ones natural - … for the poor wren, the most diminutive of birds, will fight, her young ones…'
In the play. *Clifford to Henry VI who appears lenient towards his enemies. See accompanying lines in entry 'Strike, pre-emptive s.'*

Prevention, p. as key to success and security- Fast bind, fast find, a proverb never stale in thrifty mind.
"Do as I bid you; shut doors after you
Fast bind, fast find;
A proverb never stale in thrifty mind." (MOV.2.5)
Alternative to 'don't forget to lock the door!'
In the play. *Shylock recommends to daughter Jessica to lock doors and windows while he is out. A masked parade is scheduled in Venice.*

Presence, 'Do you miss me?' - … Save that my soul's imaginary sight presents thy shadow to my sightless view…
"Save that my soul's imaginary sight
Presents thy shadow to my sightless view,
Which like a jewel (hung in ghastly night)
Makes black night beauteous, and her old face new.
Lo thus by day my limbs, by night my mind,
For thee and for myself no quiet find" (SON 27)
Answer to question, "Do you miss me?" Answer, 'Of course, not only but… by day my limbs, by night my mind for you and for myself no quiet find.' – See also 'Mind, always on your mind - Weary with toil, I haste me to my bed, the dear repose for limbs with travel tired..' – Entries for 'Absence'.
How, on the other hand, do you get her to miss you? Ovid explains the technique, 'See that she grows used to you: nothing works better than habit and a sense of need. Never tire until you sense that you have created this condition. Let her always be seeing you, always giving you her ear; let night and day show her your features. When you are quite confident that you can be missed, when your absence is likely to be regretted, suffer her to rest: a field that is rested well repays its trust, and a dry soil drinks up heaven's rain.'

The 'lack of quiet' in the mind can have curious consequences, particularly when the party in question must conduct or run a business. In a letter to Mary Scurlock (1707) Richard Steele says, 'Madam, It is the hardest thing in the world to be in love and yet attend to business. As for me, all who speak to me find me out…A gentleman asked me this morning, 'What news from Lisbon?' and I answered, 'She is exquisitely handsome.'…Methinks I could write a volume to you; but all the language on earth would fail in saying how much and with what disinterested passion I am ever yours.'

Presence, giving happiness and pleasure - Your presence glads our days.
SIMONIDES (to Pericles). Your presence glads our days." (PER.2.3)
Flatter an important guest.
In the play. *Pericles has won the tourney and Simonides expresses his appreciation to all the knights who participated.*

Pride, cooling effect of p. - … And, may I say to thee, this pride of hers, upon advice, hath drawn my love from her.
"And, may I say to thee, this pride of hers,
Upon advice, hath drawn my love from her" (TGV.3.1)
When you are asked why you two are no longer together, if that is the reason.
In the play. *The Duke is angry at his daughter Silvia because she does not want to marry the rich but spineless Thurio.*

Pride, downside of p. – … pride, which out of daily fortune ever taints the happy man.
"…pride,
Which out of daily fortune ever taints
The happy man" (COR.4.7)
In the play. *The Volscian Aufidius comments on the character of Coriolanus, whose pride (along with defect of judgment) will be his ruin.*

Pride, excessive p. a personal liability – Pride, haughtiness, opinion and disdain… loseth men's hearts and leaves behind a stain…
"Pride, haughtiness, opinion and disdain:
The least of which haunting a nobleman
Loseth men's hearts and leaves behind a stain
Upon the beauty of all parts besides,
Beguiling them of commendation" (KHIV.p1.3.1)
In the play. *The Earl of Worcester upbraids the haughty and hasty Hotspur.*

Pride, extreme p. - He wants nothing of a god but eternity and a heaven to throne in.
"He wants nothing of a god but eternity
and a heaven to throne in" (COR.5.4)
In the play. *Menenius gives an account of Coriolanus' attitude now that he has joined the Volsces.*

Pride, p., ambition and envy as agents of mutual hatred - … .the eagle-winged pride of sky-aspiring and ambitious thoughts…set on you to wake our peace...
"… we think the eagle-winged pride
Of sky-aspiring and ambitious thoughts,
With rival-hating envy, set on you
To wake our peace, which in our country's cradle
Draws the sweet infant breath of gentle sleep" (KRII.1.3)
In the play. *King Richard II to Mowbray and Bolingbroke*

Pride, poverty no barrier to personal p. - O, world, how apt the poor are to be proud!
"O, world, how apt the poor are to be proud!" (TN. 3.1)
In the play. *Olivia counters a remark by Viola/Cesario who pitied her (Olivia).*

Pride, p. and ambition - Pride went before, ambition follows him.
"Pride went before, ambition follows him." (KHVI p2.1.1)
Comment on an ambitious person leaving a meeting
In the play. *Salisbury opinion of Cardinal Beaufort, who has just left the meeting.*

Pride, p. as a trait of women - ... it was Eve's legacy, and cannot be ta'en from her.
SPEED 'Item: She is proud.
LAUNCE Out with that too; it was Eve's legacy, and cannot be ta'en from her. (TGV.3.1)
In the play. *In the company of Launce, Speed makes an analysis of the pros and cons of a milkmaid with whom he believes to be in love.*

Pride, p. in lacking hypocritical skills - ... for want of that for which I am richer, a still-soliciting eye...
"But even for want of that for which I am richer,
A still-soliciting eye, and such a tongue
As I am glad I have not" (KL.1.1)
In the play. *Cordelia asks Lear to explain to her French suitors the reasons why he has disenfranchised her, so they do not think it was something terribly evil.*

Pride, p. in possession. 'Are you glad that you married me?' – (I am) as rich in having such a jewel as twenty seas, if all their sand were pearl...
"... you are mine own;
And I as rich in having such a jewel As twenty seas, if all their sand were pearl,
The water nectar, and the rocks pure gold." (TGV.2.4)
It applies to marriage as well as to any well-established relationship.
In the play. *Valentine is deep in love with Sylvia and tells her so.*

Pride, p. maintained even during pain - I will instruct my sorrows to be proud, for grief is proud, and makes his owner stout.
"I will instruct my sorrows to be proud,
For grief is proud, and makes his owner stout." (KJ.3.1)
Express dignity while in pain, physical or emotional.
In the play. *Salisbury has informed Constance of the pending agreement between the king of France and King John, which saddens her.*

Pride, p. misguided - ... He that is proud eats up himself: pride is his own glass, his own trumpet, his own chronicle...
" ... He that is proud eats up himself: pride is his own glass, his own trumpet, his own chronicle; and whatever praises itself but in the deed, devours the deed in the praise." (TC.2.3)
See also 'Modesty, self-praise to be avoided' *** 'Modesty, self-praise, knowing the limitations of self-praise - lose by telling'
In the play *After upbraiding Achilles with Patroclus, Agamennon points to Ajax the negative effects of pride.*

Pride, p. reducing consideration (for the proud man) - ... could be content to give him good report fort, but that he pays himself with being proud
"...and could be content to give him good report fort, but that he pays himself with being proud." (COR.1.1)

In the play. *A citizen commenting on the services that Coriolanus has done for Rome and his pride and haughtiness.*

Priorities, choosing to stay here – let Rome in Tiber melt, and the wide arch of the ranged empire fall!…
"Let Rome in Tiber melt, and the wide arch
Of the ranged empire fall! Here is my space." (AC.1.1)
She wants you to stay even if you have good reasons to leave, at least temporarily, for a business trip, or an important meeting etc. But she insists that you stay and you relent. Or you would like to move to another city, whereas she wants to remain where she is. Or any other situation where you yield to her choice of space or location. Precede the quotation with, 'As Antony said to Cleopatra, Let Rome…space."
Use also *as an answer to, "Will you come back?"*
In the play. *Antony reassures Cleopatra that he has little to do with Rome and everything with Egypt.*

Prison, forgetting being in a prison - … it made my imprisonment a pleasure; ay, such a pleasure as incaged birds…
"…I'll well requite thy kindness,
For that it made my imprisonment a pleasure;
Ay, such a pleasure as incaged birds
Conceive when after many moody thoughts
At last by notes of household harmony
They quite forget their loss of liberty." (KHVI p3.4.6)
In the play. *A guard has freed Henry VI from prison, now that Warwick has switched sides. Henry thanks the guard for the good treatment*

Privacy, disregard for p. acknowledged - Saucy controller of our private steps.
"Saucy controller of our private steps!" (TA.2.3)
You can change 'our' to 'my' if you are dealing with a private investigator, or the CIA.
In the play. *Bassianus has stumbled on Tamora who is meeting in secret with her lover Aaron*

Problem solver - Turn him to any cause of policy, the Gordian knot of it he will unloose, familiar as his garter.
"Hear him but reason in divinity,
And all-admiring with an inward wish
You would desire the king were made a prelate:
Hear him debate of commonwealth affairs,
You would say it hath been all in all his study:
 …
Turn him to any cause of policy,
The Gordian knot of it he will unloose,
Familiar as his garter." (KHV.1.1)
You are asked a difficult question or a question or a question that cannot be answered in one sentence, hence the simile to a Gordian knot, e.g. 'The Gordian knot of this I will unloose, familiar as my garter.'
In the play. *The archbishop of Canterbury praises Henry V. The Gordian knot has to do with Gordius, who, born a peasant, became King of Phrygia (Asia Minor) after a miraculous event involving an eagle who landed on the yoke of the oxen he was using to till the land. When Gordius became king he bequeathed the now famous yoke to the local temple and tied it with a knot. The oracle then predicted that whoever untied that knot would become king of Asia. Alexander the Great cut the knot with his sword, therefore applying the prediction to himself.*

Problem, how by avoiding a p. you created one greater - Thus have I shunn'd the fire for fear of burning and drench'd me in the sea, where I am drown'd.
"Thus have I shunn'd the fire for fear of burning,
And drench'd me in the sea, where I am drown'd." (TGV.1.3)
A statement of fact that may help soften the consequences of the compounding problems you created.
In the play. *Proteus does not show his father a letter received from Julia with whom Proteus is in love, fearing that his father may disapprove. But Proteus' father has in mind to send Proteus to Milan and Proteus does not want to leave Julia. Hence the double-bind.*

Problem, gradual approach to p. solving – … to climb steep hills requires slow pace at first
"… to climb steep hills,
Requires slow pace at first…" (KHVIII.1.1)
When you are accused of being too slow in solving a problem. See also 'Caution, c. in fighting the enemy – heat not a furnace for your foe so hot that it do singe yourself.'
In the play. *Norfolk advises Buckingham to take it easy with Cardinal Wolsey, Buckingham's enemy. The advise comes too late and Wolsey will have Buckingham executed.*

Problem, p. solving, effort at solving problem appreciated but.. - … the care you have of us, to mow down thorns that would annoy our foot, is worthy praise…
"… the care you have of us,
To mow down thorns that would annoy our foot,
Is worthy praise, but shall I speak my conscience?" (KHVI p2.3.1)
Objection to a proposal which seems beneficial to you but only on the surface.

In the play. *Queen Margaret and her allies try to discredit the good Humphrey duke of Gloucester with the king, but the king is not convinced.*

Problem, p. solving – … all difficulties are but easy when they are known.
" … Put not yourself into amazement how these things should be. All difficulties are but easy when they are known. (MFM.4.2)
Answer or comment to an expression of amazement or incredulity.
In the play. *The Duke (in disguise) is directing a plot designed to unmask the hypocrisy of Angelo. The Duke reassures the somewhat puzzled prison provost.*

Problem, p. to be tackled before it gets bigger – A little fire is quickly trodden out, which being suffered, rivers cannot quench.
"A little fire is quickly trodden out,
Which being suffered, rivers cannot quench." (KHVI p3.4.8)
Persuade to take care of the problem before it becomes intractable.
In the play. *In London Clarence advises Warwick on the need to put down Edward. Edward is Clarence's brother.*

Problem, p. to be tackled before it gets bigger – Now 'tis the spring, and weeds are shallow-rooted…
"Now 'tis the spring, and weeds are shallow-rooted;
Suffer them now, and they'll over-grow the garden,
And choke the herbs for want of husbandry." (KHVI p2.3.1)
Give persuasive reasons for eliminating the problem before it becomes too large to handle.
In the play. *Queen Margaret tries to put Humphrey, duke of Gloucester in a bad light with Henry VI - he is the weed to be routed out.*

Problem, solution of p. found after meditation - Thus hulling in the wild sea of my conscience, I did steer towards this remedy.
"… Thus hulling in
The wild sea of my conscience, I did steer
Towards this remedy." (KHVIII.2.4)
Indicate that your decision has been well thought and meditated on.
In the play. King *Henry VIII tries to find a justification for the impending divorce from Q. Katherine*

Procrastination to be avoided – … for this 'would' changes, hath abatements and delays as many as there are tongues, are hands, are accidents.
"…that we would do
We should do when we would; for this 'would' changes
And hath abatements and delays as many
As there are tongues, are hands, are accidents;
And then this 'should' is like a spendthrift sigh,
That hurts by easing." (H.4.7)
Stimulate prompt action after an initial indication of consent. See also 'Action, quick a. needed as time goes by quickly - let's take the instant by the forward top.'
*** 'Determination, lapses in d. occurring often - … But what we determine oft we break. Purpose's but the slave to memory, of violent birth, but poor validity.'
In the play. *King Claudius prompts Laertes to act quickly in taking revenge against Hamlet, who killed Polonius, Laertes' father.*

Profession, argument to use to justify a disreputable p. – What would you have me do? go to the wars…
"What would you have me do? go to the wars, would you? where a man may serve seven years for the loss of a leg, and have not money enough in the end to buy him a wooden one?" (PER.4.6)
In the play. *Boult awkwardly tells Marina why he is in the disreputable trade he is in (servant to a pimp).*

Profession, not the top of professions – (I) work for bread upon the Athenian walls.
" … work for bread upon the Athenian walls." (MND.3.2)
Answer to 'What do you do for a living?'
In the play. *Returning from his assignment, Puck explains to Oberon how it came that Titania fell in love with Bottom. Bottom is a member of the amateur crew of actors who are rehearsing a play.*

Profession, what do you do for a living? - As my imagination bodies forth the forms of things unknown…
This is where you establish your standing in her eye. She may expect that you have a glamorous profession, e.g. a heart or brain surgeon, trial lawyer, a very visible (and crooked) Enron executive, or Worldcom or K-Mart, visible (and equally crooked) high profile Anderson auditor, Investment Firm Executive, (crooked) high profile Accountant etc. If you are none of the above or if your profession is inherently unglamorous or if you are unemployed, you have the same options as when dealing with age, lie or deflect the question. Here is one option, obtained from modifying mildly the original lines,
"The lunatic, the lover and the poet,
Are of imagination all compact.
And, as imagination bodies forth
The forms of things unknown, the poet's pen
Turns them into shapes, and gives to airy nothing
A local habitation and a name." (MND.5.1)
to the following,
"As my imagination bodies forth

The forms of things unknown, my pen
Turns them into shapes, and gives to airy nothing
A local habitation and a name."
Be prepared to repeat the same lines slowly – when they have sunk in she may ask you if you are a poet. Assuming you are not you can say that you take a poetic approach to life and that, in a sense, you partake of the spirit of poetry. Or that you would not stoop to conduct any profession that is alien to your high spiritual standards. She may be so baffled that she may not insist that you be more specific.
In the play. *Theseus, in conversation with Hippolyta makes some important philosophical statements.*

Profit, p. derived from understanding - ... to apprehend thus, draws us a profit from all things we see.
"…to apprehend thus,
Draws us a profit from all things we see" (CYM.3.3)
Understanding a key concept opens the way to larger understanding of other related (and) unrelated matters. Use to reinforce the point. For example, Government is not for the people or by the people, but rather for the interest of a moneyed elite. Understanding this explains the reason for their actions.
In the play. *Belarius in conversation with his adopted sons.*

Profit, p. worship – Gain, be my lord, for I will worship thee.
"Since kings break faith upon commodity,
Gain, be my lord, for I will worship thee" (KJ.2.1)
In the play. *Faulconbridge meditates on his plan of action to enrich or aggrandize himself.*

Profit, speaking against one's own interest - I speak against my present profit, but my wish hath a preferment in 't.
"…I speak against my present profit, but my wish hath a preferment in 't." (CYM.5.4)
In the play. *A jailer comments to himself that if people were not criminals he would be out of a job.*

Profligacy, p. blind - 'Tis pity bounty had not eyes behind…
"'Tis pity bounty had not eyes behind,
That man might ne'er be wretched for his mind" (TOA.1.2)
Comment on the fall from wealth due to excessive spending to maintain luxurious life-style.
In the play. *Servant Flavius comments on the blind profligacy of his master Timon.*

Profligacy, p. short lived - His rash fierce blaze of riot cannot last, for violent fires soon burn out themselves…
"His rash fierce blaze of riot cannot last,
For violent fires soon burn out themselves;
Small showers last long, but sudden storms are short;
He tires betimes, who spurs too fast betimes;
With eager feeding the food doth choke the feeder" (KRII.2.1)
In the play. *Gaunt chastises the spendthrift hedonistic behavior of King Richard.*

Progeny, p. worse than parents - Good wombs have borne bad sons.
"Good wombs have borne bad sons." (TEM.1.2)
Justify bad son and good mother or father.
In the play. *The good womb is that of Miranda's grandmother whose sons were Prospero (good), Miranda's father and Antonio (bad), his brother and usurper.*

Promise, commitment to maintain a p. - I am the master of my speeches, and would undergo what's spoken.
"I am the master of my speeches, and would undergo what's spoken" (CYM.1.4)
In the play. *In Rome the evil Iachimo challenges Leonatus – Iachimo claims that any woman can be seduced, including Leonatus' wife Imogen.*

Promise, commitment to maintain a p. - My hand to thee; mine honour on my promise.
"My hand to thee; mine honour on my promise." (TOA.1.1)
In the play. *Timon will give money to one of his servants so that he can marry the daughter of an Old Athenian who is otherwise against the marriage.*

Promise, p. to comply with command - I'll not fail, if I live.
"I'll not fail, if I live." (AYLI.5.2)
In the play. *The shepherd Silvius in response to a command by Ganimede, who soon will return to her own real self Rosalind.*

Promise, p. to remember what you have been told - ... 'Tis in my memory lock'd and you yourself shall keep the key of it.
LAERTES *"…and remember well What I have said to you"*
OPHELIA *"'Tis in my memory lock'd,
And you yourself shall keep the key of it"* (H.1.3)
Comment to any recommendation to remember something well.
In the play. *Laertes makes reference to his previous advice to Ophelia.*

Promise, p. to repay for help received - ... if that ever my low fortune's better I'll your bounties; till then rest your debtor.

*"…if that ever my low fortune's better,
I'll pay your bounties; till then rest your debtor."* (PER.2.1)
In the play. *The shipwrecked Pericles summons 3 fishermen to his help and promises to repay their goodness.*

Promise, solemn p. – And I will die a hundred thousand deaths, ere break the smallest parcel of this vow.
*"And I will die a hundred thousand deaths,
Ere break the smallest parcel of this vow."* (KHIV p1.3.2)
Reinforce your commitment, or answer to 'Will you really do it?' 'I will die a hundred…vow.'
In the play. *P. Henry promises he will defeat Hotspur.*

Oath, reason why oath will be broken – If I break faith, this word shall speak for me, I am forsworn on 'mere necessity'.
*"Necessity will make us all forsworn…
If I break faith, this word shall speak for me;
I am forsworn on 'mere necessity.'"* (LLL.1.1)
In the play. *Biron is skeptical that the oath of abstinence and learning will be kept by his colleagues and by himself.*

Promises, alluring p. to a mature adult - ... I can smooth and fill his aged ear with golden promises...
*"If Tamora entreat him, then he will:
For I can smooth and fill his aged ear
With golden promises; that, were his heart
Almost impregnable, his old ears deaf,
Yet should both ear and heart obey my tongue."* (TA.4.4)
Change 'Tamora' to the name of the topic enchantress.

In the play. *Tamora plots against Titus A. but he will outsmart her in the end.*

Promises, love p. unreliable - ... the oath of a lover is no stronger than the word of a tapster...
"... the oath of a lover is no stronger than the word of a tapster; they are both the confirmers of false reckonings" (AYL.3.4)
Advise to the ladies - remember this to temper the temptation to believe everything he says.
In the play. *Orlando swore his love to Rosalind and she tells Celia.*

Promises, love p. unreliable - ...the strongest oaths are straw to the fire in the blood.
"... the strongest oaths are straw
To the fire in the blood." (TEM.4.1)
Use as a comment to the power of sexual attraction.
Historically, promises are standard mental equipment of a would-be lover. So Ovid, 'See that you promise: what harm is there in promises? In promises anyone can be rich... Nor be timid in your promises; by promises women are betrayed; call as witnesses what gods you please. Jupiter from Mt. Olympus smiles at the perjuries of lovers, and bids the winds of Aeolus carry them unfulfilled away.' (AOL).
In the play. *Prospero is concerned that Ferdinando may seduce Miranda before a formal marriage.*

Promises, love p. unreliable - ... Thou mayst prove false; at lovers' perjuries they say, Jove laughs.
"...yet if thou swear'st,
Thou mayst prove false; at lovers' perjuries
They say, Jove laughs." (RJ.2.2)
In the play. *Juliet suggests to Romeo not to swear about the strength of his love.*

Promises, love p. unreliable - I do know when the blood burns, how prodigal the soul lends the tongue vows.
"I do know,
When the blood burns, how prodigal the soul
Lends the tongue vows." (H.1.3)
A cautionary statement. Or explain why a passion that seemed endless actually ended so quickly. See also 'Instinct, i. prevailing over the dictates of law'.
In the play. *Polonius is skeptical about Hamlet's declared love for Ophelia.*

Promises, love p. unreliable - Men's vows are women's traitors.
"Men's vows are women's traitors." (CYM.3.4)
In the play. *Cymbeline is dismayed after reading a letter from her husband Posthumus to his servant Pisanio. In the letter Posthumus instructs Pisanio to kill Imogen due to her (non-existing) infidelity. Imogen questions her husband's previous vows and promises of love.*

Promises, more than can be delivered - They say all lovers swear more performance than they are able...
"They say all lovers swear more performance than they are able, and yet reserve an ability that they never perform; vowing more than the perfection of ten, and discharging less than the tenth part of one. They that have the voice of lions and the act of hares. Are they not monsters?" (TC.3.2)
In general this would apply more to her than you. But you can use it to make a positive statement about yourself. For example, 'there are some who vow more than the perfection of ten and discharge less than the tenth part of one. I, instead....' And you can go on praising your own trustworthiness or whatever else good you want to say about yourself.
In the play. *Cressida teases Troilus.*

Promises, p. not delivered - His promises were, as he then was, mighty, but his performance…'
"His promises were, as he then was, mighty;
But his performance, as he is now, nothing" (KHVIII.4.2)
In the play. *Ill and confined in a convent at Kimbolton, Queen Katherine discusses with Griffith, her gentleman usher, the passing of her former enemy Cardinal Wolsey.*

Promises, p. not delivered – … your words and performances are no kin together.
"…I have heard too much, for your words and performances are no kin together." (OTH.4.2)
In the play. *Roderigo to Iago. The performance consisted in paving the way for Roderigo to become a lover of Desdemona.*

Promises, p. not kept - … That keep the word of promise to our ear and break it to our hope.
"And be these juggling fiends no more believed,
That palter with us in a double sense;
That keep the word of promise to our ear,
And break it to our hope" (M.5.8)
In the play. *In the final battle at Dunsinane, Macbeth inveighs against the witches and their quimsical predictions, specifically that a man born via a Caesarian delivery was not 'of woman born'. 'To palter' = 'to equivocate'.*

Promises, p. quickly delivered - Thy promises are like Adonis' gardens that one day bloom'd and fruitful were the next.
"Thy promises are like Adonis' gardens
That one day bloom'd and fruitful were the next" (KHVI.p1.1.6)
Congratulations on a job well done.
In the play. *King Charles of France is very pleased at the immediate military results delivered by Joan of Arc.*

Promotion, p. given according to whim - … Preferment goes by letter and affection, and not by old gradation…
"Why, there's no remedy; 'tis the curse of service,
Preferment goes by letter and affection,
And not by old gradation, where each second
Stood heir to the first" (OTH.1.1)
In the play. *Iago is bitter that he has not been given the promotion to lieutenant.*

Promotion, p. promised - … I will be the man yet that shall make you great.
"Fear not your advancements; I will be the man yet that shall make you great" (KHIV.p2.5.4)
See also 'Man, politically very powerful - … this is he that moves both wind and tide.' Answer to 'Can you help me?'
In the play. *Falstaff still tries to dupe Master Shallow about prospects at court.*

Promotion, p. refused – I had rather hide me from my greatness, being a bark to brook no mighty sea…
"I had rather hide me from my greatness,
Being a bark to brook no mighty sea,
Than in my greatness covet to be hid,
And in the vapour of my glory smother'd." (KRIII.3.7)
Try 'I don't want to be smothered in the vapor of my glory' if and when you say no to a questionable preferment or promotion.
In the play. *Richard pretends to shun the throne offered to him by Buckingham in a well-choreographed scene at Baynard's Castle.*

Promotion, p. through slander – ... many so arrive at second masters upon their first lord's neck.
"For many so arrive at second masters,
Upon their first lord's neck" (TOA.4.3)
In the play. *Timon to faithful servant Flavius, who did not abandon Timon when everyone else did.*

Propaganda, economy is great – Here is everything advantageous to life... save means to live.
GONZALO Here is everything advantageous to life.
ANTONIO True; save means to live. (TEM.2.1)
In the play. *Gonzalo and Antonio hold different views about their predicament*

Proposal, dangerous p. - Into what dangers would you lead me, Cassius...
"Into what dangers would you lead me, Cassius,
That you would have me seek into myself
For that which is not in me." (JC.1.2)
Change 'Cassius' to the name of the person you are addressing. Comment or ponder on a proposal or partnership.
In the play. *Cassius suggests indirectly to Brutus that he, Brutus should rebel against Caesar*

Proposal, detailed p. on sharing pillows - One turf shall serve as pillows to us both....
"One turf shall serve as pillows to us both,
One heart, one bed, two bosoms and one troth." (MND.2.2)
This of course depends on how far you wish to go with her.
In the play. *The night has arrived while Lysander and Hermia are lost in the woods. Lysander proposes to share accommodations.*

Proposal, difference between an exciting and an unexciting p. – ... the blood more stirs to rouse a lion than to start a hare.
"... the blood more stirs,
To rouse a lion than to start a hare." (KHIV p1.1.3)
Support a more appealing and daring proposal, e.g. 'This is exciting stuff, we like it better, the blood more stirs... hare.'
In the play. *Hotspur is ready to listen to the risky plans hinted at by Worcester.*

Proposal, meditated p. - ...'tis a studied, not a present thought by duty meditated.
"...Pardon what I have spoke;
For 'tis a studied, not a present thought,
By duty ruminated." (AC.2.2)
Answer to 'Did you just think of this?'
In the play. *Agrippa ends his speech in which he proposed the marriage between Antony and Octavia, sister of Octavian.*

Prosperity, a satire on p. – ... the softness of prosperity, with a discovery of the infinite flatteries that follow youth and opulency.
"...a satire against the softness of prosperity, with a discovery of the infinite flatteries that follow youth and opulency." (TOA.5.1)
In the play. *The parasite and poet thinks that Timon is still wealthy and plans to extract more rewards by writing a new poem for him.*

Prostitute – a creature of sale
"... the house you dwell in proclaims you to be a creature of sale." (PER.4.6)
Applicable equally to corrupt politicians or authorities.
In the play. *Lysimachus, governor of Mytilene is unaware of Marina's silver virtue and character.*

Protection, offer of p. - My bosom as a bed shall lodge thee till thy wound be thoroughly heal'd.
"…my bosom as a bed
Shall lodge thee till thy wound be thoroughly heal'd" (TGV.1.2)
In the play. *What the bed (or rather the bosom) will host is a love letter from Proteus.*

Providence, luck of possession - She is mortal, but, by immortal providence, she is mine.
"She is mortal, but, by immortal providence, she is mine." (TEM.5.1)
Maybe OK at a party. Use as an answer to the question "Who is she?" when the questioner does not know that she is your wife, e.g. 'She is mortal but… mine".
In the play. *Ferdinand answer his father's question as to who is Miranda.*

Provocation, response to p. – … we can (not) let our beard be shook with danger and think it pastime.
" … must not think
That we are made of stuff so flat and dull
That we can let our beard be shook with danger
And think it pastime" (H.4.7)
In the play. *King Claudius to Laertes referring to Hamlet's actions*

Prudence, better keep what we have than lose everything - …I'll rather keep hat which I have, than, coveting for more…
"…I'll rather keep
That which I have, than, coveting for more,
Be cast from possibility of all." (KHVI.p1.5.5)
Reinforce the argument that it is prudent to stop now rather than risking a loss by implementing a questionable plan.

In the play. *Charles of France refuses a dubious proposal by the English whereby he would retain the whole of France but be viceroy of the king of England.*

Prudence, do not wake a sleeping dog - This butcher's cur is venom mouthed and I have not the power to muzzle him; therefore…
"… This butcher's cur is venom mouthed and I
Have not the power to muzzle him; therefore best
Not wake him in his slumber." (KHVIII.1.1)
Suggest prudence in dealing with a scheming and powerful individual.
In the play. *Buckingham referring to an assistant to Wolsey.*

Prudence, never underestimate enemy or competition - In cases of defence, 't is best to weigh the enemy more mighty than he seems…
"In cases of defence, 't is best to weigh
The enemy more mighty than he seems,
So the proportions of defence are fill'd." (KHV.2.4)
When someone dismisses too glibly a threat by the competition.
In the play. *The Dauphin agrees with the Constable that it is better never to underestimate the enemy.*

Prudence, p. advisable rather than unrealistic optimism – The man that once did sell the lion's skin while the beast liv'd…
"The man that once did sell the lion's skin
While the beast liv'd, was kill'd with hunting him." (KHV.4.3)
Downplay a boasting statement of your adversary about his future achievements

In the play. *Henry V warns the French Montjoy who came to propose to the English to surrender.*

Prudence, p. advised - It fits us then to be as provident as fear may teach...
"It fits us then to be as provident
As fear may teach us out of late examples" (HV.2.4)
In the play. *The King of France counsels prudence to his nobles and generals considering that the English are invading France.*

Prudence, p. in giving confidence and being generous - ...where you are liberal of your loves and counsels be sure you be not loose...
"This from a dying man receive as certain: -
Where you are liberal of your loves and counsels,
Be sure you be not loose; for those you make friends,
And give your hearts to, when they once perceive
The least run in your fortunes, fall away
Like water from ye, never found again
But where they mean to sink ye."
(KHVIII.2.1)
Counsel to be careful about strength of friendships. '...for those you make friends, when they once perceive......sink you.' See also 'Flattery, f. and praise tied to reward - ... when the means are gone that buy this praise, the breath is gone whereof this praise is made.'
In the play. *Buckingham' last words of advise after he is condemned to death upon charges of treason trumped up by Cardinal Wolsey.*

Psychological, p. help needed - ... the immortal part needs a physician.
POINS And how doth the martlemas, your master?
BARDOLPH In bodily health, sir.

POINS Marry, the immortal part needs a physician (KHIV.p2.2.1)
Answer to 'how are you?' if you are well in body but spiritually depressed, e.g. 'In bodily health yes, but my immortal part needs a physician'
In the play. *Prince Henry, Poins, Bardolph discuss the fitness of Falstaff, Bardolph's master. 'Martlemas' is the last festivity of the year and indicates metaphorically a person in decline or at the last stage of his life. Poins pokes fun at Falstaff.*

Psychological uplifting, positive effects of thoughts about a friend - ... But if the while I think on thee, dear friend, all losses are restored and sorrows end.
"But if the while I think on thee, dear friend,
All losses are restored and sorrows end." (SON 30)
When you have finished describing and narrating your vicissitudes to a true friend.

Psychology, doubt hurts more than certainty - Doubting things go ill often hurts more than to be sure they do.
"... doubting things go ill, often hurts more
Than to be sure they do; for certainties
Either are past remedies; or, timely knowing,
The remedy then born." (CYM.1.6)
Prompt a straight telling of the truth, however unpleasant "Tell us how things really are, for doubting things go ill, often... to be sure they do."
In the play. *Imogen prompts Iachimo to speak plainly regarding her husband's state of affairs in Italy*

Psychology, reverse p., turning her shortcomings into virtues and qualities - ... Say that she rails; why,

then I'll tell her plain she sings as sweetly as a nightingale...
"I will attend her here,
And woo her with some spirit when she comes.
Say that she rails; why, then I'll tell her plain
She sings as sweetly as a nightingale;
Say that she frown; I'll say, she looks as clear
As morning roses newly washed with dew:
Say she be mute and will not speak a word;
Then I'll commend her volubility,
And say she uttered piercing eloquence." (TOS.2.1)
Method for handling a difficult woman.
In the play. *Petruchio outlines his strategy to win the heart of Katharina.*

Psychology, self-encouragement to boldness - Boldness be my friend, arm me audacity from head to foot.
" ...Boldness be my friend!
Arm me audacity from head to foot!" (CYM.1.6)
Introduction to a bold proposal. "What I will say next may shock the audience but... 'boldness be my friend, arm me...foot'.
In the play. *Iachimo is planning a dirty trick.*

Psychology, self-knowledge key to knowing others - ... to know a man well, were to know himself.
"...to know a man well, were to know himself." (H.5.2)
Answer evasively when asked an opinion about someone.
In the play. *Osric has arrived to propose the duel between Laertes and Hamlet. Osric asks if Hamlet is aware of Laertes' skill with the sword and Hamlet answers.*

Psychology, winning encouraging - Winning will put any man into courage.
"Winning will put any man into courage." (CYM.2.3)
Motivating statement, victory gives man courage.
In the play. *Cloten responds to a comment by a courtier.*

Punctuality, p. important - better three hours too soon than a minute too late.
"... better three hours too soon than a minute too late." (MWW.2.2)
A reply to the comment that you arrived early to an appointment. See also 'Lovers routinely punctual.'
In the play. *Mr. Ford, fearing to be cuckholded by Falstaff will arrive sooner than expected at the place where the purported betrayal is supposed to occur.*

Punishment and condemnation - My hour is almost come, when I to sulphurous and tormenting flames must render up myself.
"My hour is almost come,
When I to sulphurous and tormenting flames
Must render up myself." (H.1.5)
When you are harassed with all sorts of accusations and recriminations. Turn the quote into a question, '(Must I) to sulphurous and tormenting flames render up myself?'
In the play. *The ghost must retire as daylight is near.*

Punishment, no p. strong enough - If it be true, all vengeance comes too short which can pursue the offender.
"If it be true, all vengeance comes too short
Which can pursue the offender." (KL.2.1)
Show your indignation
In the play. *Regan to Gloucester after learning of the (phony) letter written by Edmund to frame his brother Edgar. Gloucester has bought the lie.*

Punishment, p. announced - And where the offence is let the great axe fall.
"And where the offence is let the great axe fall." (H.4.5)
In the play. *King Claudius to Laertes, referring to the killing by Hamlet of Laerte's father Polonius*

Punishment, p. for bringing unpleasant news - Thou shalt be whipp'd with wire, and stew'd in brine, smarting in lingering pickle.
"Thou shalt be whipp'd with wire, and stew'd in brine,
Smarting in lingering pickle." (AC.2.5)
Apply the threat to any deserving character and situation.
In the play. *Cleopatra is upset with messenger who brought news from Rome of Antony's marriage to Octavia.*

Punishment, poison - If you have poison for me, I will drink it.
"If you have poison for me, I will drink it." (KL.4.7)
Answer to a reprimand. Perhaps Churchill had King Lear in mind during the famous exchange with the lady who disliked him. Lady, 'If you were my husband I would give you poison'. Churchill, 'If I were your husband I would drink it'.
In the play. *Lear to Cordelia in Dover. He was unjust to Cordelia and does not as yet realize that she has come to Diver to save him.*

Punishment, restraint advised in p. – Let us be keen, and rather cut a little than fall and bruise to death.
"…but yet
Let us be keen, and rather cut a little, Than fall, and bruise to death." (MFM.2.1)
In the play. *Escalus advises Lord Angelo not to condemn Claudio to death for having seduced Juliet.*

Punishment, selective p., only for the leaders - We, as the spring of all, shall pay for all
"We, as the spring of all, shall pay for all." (KHIVp1.5.2)
In the play. *Worcester gives Vernon reasons for not accepting the peace terms offered by King Henry.*

Punishment, suggested p. is castration - … An they were sons of mine, I'd have the whipped; or I would send them to the Turk, to make eunuchs of.
"Do they all deny her? An they were sons of mine, I'd have the whipped; or I would send them to the Turk, to make eunuchs of. " (AWEW.2.5)
Indicate a specific type of punishment for a class of people or a specific group of persons you take issue with. E.G. "If it were up to me, I'd have them whipped… eunuchs of."
In the play. *The King is still unaware that Helena wants Bertram as a husband (her reward for healing the King). Therefore he tells her to pick her choice among the young French noblemen currently at court. All refuse due to her lowly status. Lafeu erupts in anger. 'An' is synonym of 'if'.*

Puritans, dislike for p. - O, if I thought that I'ld beat him like a dog!
MARIA. Marry, sir, sometimes he is a kind of puritan.
SIR ANDREW. O, if I thought that I'ld beat him like a dog!
Sir Andrew's answer is equally applicable to any other category you dislike.
In the play. *The subject in question is the supercilious and affected Malvolio.*

Purpose, plea to guess an evil p. to be executed – … if that thou couldst see me without eyes, hear me without thine ears …
"Or if that thou couldst see me without eyes,

**Hear me without thine ears, and make reply
Without a tongue, using conceit alone,
Without eyes, ears and harmful sound of words"** (KJ.3.2)
See also entries for 'deniability'.
In the play. *King John to his faithful henchman Hubert. What John wants Hubert to hear without ears is the murder of young Arthur truly inheritor of the English crown.*

Purpose, unwavering p. – I am constant to my purpose.
"I am constant to my purpose" (H.5.2)
See also 'Credentials, establishing your c. - I am as constant as the northern star…'
In the play. *Hamlet answers a call from the King to have a fencing bout with Laertes*

**Qualifications, q. for office - … Hugh Otecake, sir, or George Seacole; for they can write and read.
DOGBERRY First, who think you the most desertless man to be constable?
FIRST WATCHMAN Hugh Otecake, sir, or George Seacole; for they can write and read.** (MAAN.3.3)
In the play. *Officer Dogberry consults with colleagues as to the best-qualified candidate for the office of constable.*

Quarrel, dispute and conflict resolution - … to leave this keen encounter of our wits and fall something into a slower method.
**"But, gentle Lady Anne,
To leave this keen encounter of our wits
And fall something into a slower method."** (KRIII.1.2)
Richard, who has slain Clarence, Anne's husband, is now trying to woo her
Exhortation to reason instead of arguing (second and third line) or use the full quote in case of a woman – change 'Lady Anne' with name of applicable lady.

Quarrel, dispute and conflict resolution - Now for the love of love and her soft hours let's not confound the time with conference harsh.
**"Now for the love of love and her soft hours,
Let's not confound the time with conference harsh."** (AC.1.1)
Soften or avoid a quarrel with her. Or use the second line as an exhortation to stop arguing when the atmosphere becomes too hot.
In the play. *Antony reassures Cleopatra. Cleopatra questions Antony's love and his life style.*

Quarrel, dissension, lack of harmony - How irksome is this music to my heart when such strings jar, what hope of harmony?
**"How irksome is this music to my heart
When such strings jar, what hope of harmony?
I pray, my lords, let me compound this strife"** (KHVI p2.2.1)
Use to settle a dissension.
In the play. *The Cardinal and Gloucester start arguing again during a hunt and Henry VI does not like it.*

Quarrel, exhortation to change attitude - O change thy thought, that I may change my mind…
**O change thy thought, that I may change my mind,
Shall hate be fairer lodged than gentle love?** (SON.10)
When she makes unfair and groundless accusations.

Quarrel, not really a q. - No quarrel, but a slight contention.
"No quarrel, but a slight contention." (KHVI p3.1.2)
Answer to invitation to stop a perceived quarrel.

In the play. *Edward in answer to York. The contention is about breaking or not an oath that York will not get the crown while Henry VI is still alive.*

Quarrel, plea for restraint from q. - Forbear sharp speeches to her: she's a lady so tender of rebukes that words are strokes…
"Forbear sharp speeches to her: she's a lady
So tender of rebukes that words are strokes
And strokes death to her." (CYM.3.5)
In the play. *The Queen pretends to intervene with the king on Imogen's behalf and asks him not to be too harsh with her. Imogen is the King's daughter.*

Quarrel, plea to stop q. – Cease, cease these jars and rest your minds in peace
"Cease, cease these jars and rest your minds in peace…" (KHVI.p1.1.1)
In the play. *Bedford exhorts Gloucester and the Bishop of Winchester to stop their arguing.*

Quarrel, plea to stop q. - Quarrel no more, but be prepared to know the purposes I bear.
"Quarrel no more, but be prepared to know
The purposes I bear" (AC.1.3)
In the play. *Antony to Cleopatra who thinks Antony will leave her and go to Rome.*

Quarrel, q. about trifles as a symptom of man's madness - … what madness rules in brainsick men, when for so slight and frivolous a cause…
"Good Lord, what madness rules in brainsick men,
When for so slight and frivolous a cause
Such factious emulations shall arise!" (KHVI p1.4.1)

In the play. *Henry VI commenting on the quarrel between Vernon and Basset regarding the display of a white or red rose.*

Quarrel, q. unjustified - In a false quarrel there is no true valour.
" In a false quarrel there is no true valour." (MAAN.5.1)
Indicate that the quarrel is not necessary or based on wrong reasons
In the play. *The quarrel is between Leonato and Claudio. Benedick is attempting to straighten the issue.*

Queen, like a Grecian Q. - He brought a Grecian queen, whose youth and freshness wrinkles Apollo's and makes stale the morning.
"He brought a Grecian queen, whose youth and freshness
Wrinkles Apollo's and makes stale the morning." (TC.2.2)
Compliment. In a one to one situation change to: "You are like a Grecian queen…morning." The god Apollo was considered an absolute standard of beauty.
In the play. *Troilus defends Paris for having stolen or taken Helen from the Greeks.*

Queen, so to speak - … she is the queen of curds and cream.
"… good sooth, she is
The queen of curds and cream." (WT.4.4)
Sarcastic remark to a woman who pretends to superiority.
In the play. *Camillo observes Perdita blushing after Florizel whispers something to her.*

Queen, woman with all the traits of a queen – She had all the royal makings of a queen…
"She had all the royal makings of a queen;
As holy oil, Edward Confessor's crown,
The rod, and bird of peace, and all

such emblems
Laid nobly on her" (KHVIII.4.1)
Compliment. See also 'Beauty, b. of a queen - O queen of queens! how far dost thou excel, no thought can think, nor tongue of mortal tell.'
In the play. *A gentleman comments on Anne Boleyn's demeanor during her coronation.*

Question, answering q. - Ask me what question thou canst possible, and I will answer unpremeditated.
"Ask me what question thou canst possible,
And I will answer unpremeditated." (KHVI.p.1.1.2)
Answer to 'can I ask you a question?' Especially useful when you sense beforehand that the question may be mildly embarrassing or deal with an issue you do not wish to immediately address. The mild irony prepares the ground for an answer (yours), that should be taken with a pinch of salt.
Useful also at end of presentation when you invite the audience to ask you questions. A modern alternative to invite questions is 'As the tower of London said to the tower of Pisa, if you have the inclination, I have the time'.
In the play. *Joan of Arc (in the play called simply 'Pucelle'), prompts the Dauphin of France, Charles to submit herself to any test or question regarding her skills or intentions.*

Question, apologizing for a posing a silly question - I will be a fool in question, hoping to be the wiser by your answer.
" I will be a fool in question, hoping to be the wiser by your answer. " (AWEW.2.2)
Alternative to 'Maybe this is a stupid question'.
In the play. *At Rousillon, the clown and the Countess exchange some banter. The Countess apologizes to the clown before asking him an irrelevant question.*

Question, insisting on receiving an answer - ...I pry'thee take the cork out of thy mouth, that I may drink thy tidings.
"... I would thou couldst stammer, that mightst pour this concealed man out of thy mouth, as wine comes out of a narrow mouthed bottle, - either too much at once, or not at all. I pry'thee take the cork out of thy mouth, that I may drink thy tidings." (AYLI.3.2)
Insist that he/she gives you the information. "I pry'thee take the cork ... thy tidings"
In the play. *Rosalind does not know or perhaps pretends not to know that the verses written on the tree were authored by Orlando and asks Celia about their author.*

Question, insisting on receiving an answer, who is it? – I pray thee now, with most petitionary vehemence...
"Nay, I pray thee now, with most petitionary vehemence, tell me who it is. " (AYLI.3.2)
Insist that the party tell you who is it.
In the play. *Rosalind does not know or perhaps pretends not to know that the verses written on the tree were authored by Orlando and asks Celia about their author.*

Question, q. that cannot be answered as it is outside the scope of the interview – I can say little more than I have studied, and that question's out of my part.
"I can say little more than I have studied, and that question's out of my part." (TN.1.5)
In the play. *Olivia has asked Viola/Cesario where she comes from. Viola/Cesario does not want to reveal as yet that he/she was dispatched by the duke Orsino to woo Olivia.*

Racket, a good racket – ... It is an honorable kind of thievery.

**"Master, be one of them:
It is an honorable kind of thievery."**
(TGV.4.1)
Justify a deed or a project, which may be somewhat questionable, though it is in general OK.
In the play. *The bandits who attacked Valentine, suddenly suggest that he become their leader. Speed prompts Valentine to accept the proposal as they are Robin Hood type characters, rather than typical criminals.*

Radiance, r. described – … like a wreath of radiant fire on flickering Phoebus' front.
"…like a wreath of radiant fire
On flickering Phoebus' front' (KL.2.2)
In the play. *Cornwall upbraids Kent for his direct manners and Kent retorts sarcastically with hyperbolic praises of Cornwall. See 'Introduction, i. to a point or an argument, with irony and sarcastic affectation - … in good faith, in sincere verity, under the allowance of your great aspect…'*

Rage, cool your language - Put not your worthy rage into your tongue one time will owe another.
"Put not your worthy rage into your tongue;
One time will owe another." (COR.3.1)
Counsel verbal restraint. See also entries for 'Conflict resolution'.
In the play. *Coriolanus is mad at the tribunes and at the people in general. Menenius tries to calm him down.*

Rage, effects of r. - … men in rage strike those that wish them best.
"…men in rage strike those that wish them best" (OTH.2.3)
In the play. *Iago, talking to Othello, tries to appear friendly to Cassio by justifying his actions when drunk.*

Rage, r. compared to a labyrinth - … lost in the labyrinth of thy fury!"

"… lost in the labyrinth of thy fury!"
(TC.2.3)
Point out the senselessness of an outburst by an adversary.
In the play. *Thersites in a monologue refers to himself, being angry at Ajax*

Rage, r. not conducive to wisdom – He's in his fit now and does not talk after the wisest…
"He's in his fit now and does not talk after the wisest. He shall taste of my bottle: if he have never drunk wine afore will go near to remove his fit."
(TEM.2.2)
In the play. *Stephano comments on the cantankerous Caliban.*

Raise, asking for a r. - Now, princes, for the service I have done you, the advantage of the time prompts me aloud to call for recompense.
"Now, princes, for the service I have done you,
The advantage of the time prompts me aloud
To call for recompense" (TC.3.3)
Skip 'princes' or use 'my lord'.
In the play. *Calcas asks the Greeks for a reward, that is, the exchange of Cressida for a Trojan prisoner.*

Ransom, r. terms dishonorable – … lawful mercy is nothing kin to foul redemption.
"Ignomy in ransom and free pardon
Are of two houses: lawful mercy
Is nothing kin to foul redemption."
(MFM.2.4)
In the play. *Isabella is horrified that Angelo demands sex n exchange for mercy for her brother who was condemned to die for having gotten Juliet pregnant.*

Reaction, cold r. – thou art all ice, thy kindness freezeth.
"…thou art all ice, thy kindness freezeth" (KRIII.4.2)

In the play. *Richard notes the coldness of Buckingham at the prospect of murdering the young princes held in the Tower.*

Reaction, negative r. – And on my face he turn'd an eye of death.
"And on my face he turn'd an eye of death…" (KHIVp1.1.3)
In the play. *Hotspur describes King Henry's reaction at his request to ransom Mortimer.*

Reaction, r. to a very strange suggestion - … whose horrid image unfix my hair and make my seated heart knock at my ribs.
"…why do I yield to that suggestion
Whose horrid image doth unfix my hair
And make my seated heart knock at my ribs,
Against the use of nature?" (M.1.3)
Try 'What? This doth unfix my hair ….nature'.
In the play. *The prediction by the witches that Macbeth will be king implies that he must kill King Duncan, a horrid suggestion.*

Reading, not being able to read on due to unhappiness - Some sudden qualm hath struck me at the heart…
"Some sudden qualm hath struck me at the heart,
And dimmed mine eyes, that I can read no further." (KHVI p2.1.1)
Whatever you are reading is disgusting you.
In the play. *Gloucester is disgusted at the announcement that Henry VI will marry Margaret of France and that, as part f the marriage agreement the duchy of Anjou and the county of Maine will pass to France.*

Reading, r. and writing natural - … to write and read comes by nature.
"…to write and read comes by nature." (MAAN.3.3)
Modest answer to a compliment on your writing.

In the play. *The constable Dogberry engages in a philosophical discussion with his watchmen.*

Reading, r. as a key to knowledge and understanding – He reads much; he is a great observer and he looks quite through the deeds of men.
"He reads much;
He is a great observer and he looks
Quite through the deeds of men"
(JC.1.2)
Use to draw by inference a practical truth. Tyrannical policies can be imposed on men who cannot or do not want to read and understand the very policies and abuse to which they are subjected.
In the play. *Caesar to Antony referring to Cassius.*

Reading, what are you r.? – Words, words, words.
POLONIUS. What do you read, my lord?
HAMLET Words, words, words.
In the play. *Polonius attempts to start a conversation with Hamlet.*

Reaganomics, trickle down economics, the belly as a metaphor for the super-rich - 'True is it, my incorporate friends,' quoth he, 'That I receive the general food at first'…
"'True is it, my incorporate friends,' quoth he,
'That I receive the general food at first,
Which you do live upon; and fit it is,
Because I am the store-house and the shop
Of the whole body: but, if you do remember,
I send it through the rivers of your blood,
Even to the court, the heart, to the seat o' the brain;
And, through the cranks and offices of man,
The strongest nerves and small

inferior veins
From me receive that natural competency
Whereby they live: and though that all at once,
You, my good friends,'--this says the belly, mark me,--" (COR.1.1)
Reagan could not have said it better.
In the play. *With a tale or metaphor, Menenius shows the citizens why it is proper that the rich (i.e. the belly) should accumulate all the wealth (food). They trickle it down to all others (the members of the body).*

Real, compliment, are you real? - But are you flesh and blood? Have you a working pulse?
"**But are you flesh and blood?**
Have you a working pulse?" (PER.5.1)
Suggest, with this rhetorical question, that she is so beautiful as to appear unreal.
In the play. *Pericles is on the brink of extreme happiness and coming to terms with the idea that he has found his daughter Marina.*

Realism, r. counseled - … speak with possibilities and do not break into these deep extremes.
"**…speak with possibilities,**
And do not break into these deep extremes." (TA.3.1)
In the play. *Marcus to brother Titus A. while plotting revenge against their murderous enemies.*

Reality and imagination - …art thou but a dagger of the mind, a false creation, proceeding from the heat-oppressed brain.
"**Is this a dagger which I see before me,**
The handle towards my hand?…
Art thou not, fatal vision, sensible
To feeling as to sight? or art thou but
A dagger of the mind, a false creation,
Proceeding from the heat-oppressed brain?" (M.2.1)
Refer to an obsessive thought (yours or of others) as a 'dagger of the mind'. Or refer to an odd idea or proposition as 'a false creation, proceeding from a heat-oppressed brain'.
In the play. *Macbeth is agitated prior to murdering King Duncan.*

Reality, not appearance - Seems, madam! nay it is; I know not 'seems'.
"**Seems, madam! nay it is; I know not 'seems.**" (H.1.2)
Use when the other party, by using the word 'seems' implies that your viewpoint or observation is not true.
In the play. *Queen Gertrude asks Hamlet why he continues to be so upset following his father's death, what seems so uncommon with the event.*

Reason, are you blind to reason? - … is your blood so madly hot, that no discourse of reason… can qualify the same?
" **… is your blood**
So madly hot, that no discourse of reason,
Nor fear of bad success in a bad cause,
Can qualify the same?" (TC.2.2)
Argue against a dangerous cause proposed with passion by your opponent.
In the play. *After Cassandra predicted doom caused by keeping Helen, Hector asks Troilus if he really does not want to listen to reason.*

Reason, doubts about one's reasoning – (What is) that makes me reasonless to reason thus?
"**Her true perfection, or my false transgression,**
That makes me reasonless to reason thus?" (TGV.2.4)
In the play. *Proteus is suddenly attracted to Julia and completely forgetting Julia with whom he was desperately in love but days before. He questions his own reasoning.*

Reason, lack of r. displayed - … is your blood so madly hot that no discourse of reason…

"… is your blood
So madly hot that no discourse of reason,
Nor fear of bad success in a bad cause,
Can qualify the same?" (TC.2.2)
In the play. *Hector questions Troilus who wants to retain Helen in Troy disregarding Cassandra's prophecy of doom.*

Reason, r. applied to passion - … For those that mingle reason with your passion…
"For those that mingle reason with your passion
Must be content to think you old" (KL.2.4)
In the play. *Regan continues to insult her father K. Lear.*

Reason, r. good enough – I have no exquisite reason but reason good enough.
SIR ANDREW. O, if I thought that, I'd beat him like a dog.
SIR TOBY. What, for being a puritan? thy exquisite reason, dear knight?
SIR ANDREW. I have no exquisite reason for it, but I have reason good enough." (TN.2.3)
Answer to 'what is your reason?' Use when you have good reasons for a specific action but have no time or inclination to report them. Change 'exquisite' to 'specific'. See also 'Woman, w.'s intuition - I have no other reason but a woman's reason.' – entries for 'Intuition'.
In the play. *Maria has told Aguecheek and Toby that Malvolio, on whom Maria is planning a nasty trick, is a puritan.*

Reasoning obvious, not an utterer of great truths - … a great cause of the night is lack of the sun.
"…a great cause of the night is lack of the sun." (AYLI.3.2)
Rephrase a meaningless statement to point out its meaninglessness. E.G. 'In other words what you are saying is that a great cause of the night is lack of the sun.
In the play. *Touchstone asks the shepherd Corin whether he has a philosophy of life or a 'Weltanschauung'. Corin gives a very common sense answer.*
CORIN No more but that I know the more one sickens the
worse at ease he is; and that he that wants money,
means and content is without three good friends;
that the property of rain is to wet and fire to
burn; that good pasture makes fat sheep, and that a
great cause of the night is lack of the sun; that
he that hath learned no wit by nature nor art may
complain of good breeding or comes of a very dull kindred.

Reasons, good and weighty - … if thou ask me why, sufficeth, my reasons are both good and weighty.
"… if thou ask me why, sufficeth, my reasons are both good and weighty." (TOS.1.1)
Answer to the question 'Why?' when you do not want to say.
In the play. *Lucentio gives last minute instructions to servant Tranio after their roles have been exchanged for reasons 'good and weighty'.*

Reasons, good r. yielding to better r. - Good reasons must, of course, give place to better.
"Good reasons must, of course, give place to better." (JC.4.3)
Acknowledge a better opinion or course of action.

In the play. *Brutus acknowledges the opinion of Cassius (with whom he is now reconciled), on the strategy of the upcoming battle. But Brutus thinks it is better to move from Sardis to Philippi rather than waiting for the enemy at Sardis, as Cassius suggested.*

Reassurance, answer to demands for r. – O, swear not by the moon, the inconstant moon, that monthly changes in her circle orb…
ROMEO. Lady, by yonder blessed moon I vow,
That tips with silver all these fruit tree tops…
JULIET. O, swear not by the moon, the inconstant moon,
That monthly changes in her circle orb,
Lest that thy love prove likewise variable. (RJ.2.2)
If she wants absolute assurance that you will marry her, or asks you to swear that you will do whatever you said you would do, or she asks you to do. Modify to: 'I will not swear by the moon, the inconstant moon, that monthly changes in her circle orb, lest that my love prove likewise variable.'
This may prove a subtle way to say that you are sure but not completely – that you need a bit more time to make up your mind for good.
In the play: *Romeo swears his love but Juliet objects to the structure of the swearing.*

Rebellion, exhortation against r. – Unthread the rude eye of rebellion…
"Unthread the rude eye of rebellion
And welcome home again discarded faith." (KJ.5.2)
In the play. *Count Melun, a French nobleman mortally wounded in battle, exhorts his English peers to quit their alliance with King Lewis of France.*

Rebellion, justification for r. – (he) broke oath on oath, committed wrong on wrong…
"Broke oath on oath, committed wrong on wrong,
And in conclusion drove us to seek out
This head of safety" (KHIV.p1.4.3)
In the play. *Hotspur reminds Sir Walter Blunt that the king (Henry IV) broke oaths and committed wrongs against those who helped him, causing them to rebel.*

Rebellion, justification for r. - … (we) find our griefs heavier than our offences.
"And find our griefs heavier than our offences" (KHIVp2.4.1)
In the play. *Archbishop of York, head of the rebellion to Westmoreland, from the King's side.*

Rebellion, measures to quench r. - Stop their mouths with stubborn bits and spur them till they obey the manage.
"… for those that tame wild horses
Pace'em not in their hands to make them gentle,
But stop their mouths with stubborn bits, and spur them
Till they obey and manage."
(KHVIII.5.2)
Advocate harsh measures to correct or change a situation.
In the play. *Gardiner refers to the presumed treacherous preaching of Cranmer and suggests quick and harsh punishment.*

Rebellion, r. as a vulture – … the vulture of sedition feeds in the bosom of such great commanders…
"Thus, while the vulture of sedition
Feeds in the bosom of such great commanders…" (KHVI.p1.4.3)
In the play. *Lord Lucy commenting on the brewing feud in King Henry's field, between the Lancastrians and the Yorkists.*

Rebellion, r. caused by heavy taxation – ... Unfit for other life, compell'd by hunger and lack of other means...
"The clothiers all, not able to maintain
The many to them longing, have put off
The spinsters, carders, fullers, weavers, who,
Unfit for other life, compell'd by hunger
And lack of other means, in desperate manner
Daring the event to the teeth, are all in uproar" (KHVIII.1.2)
Then the effect of taxation, now the effect of manufacturing jobs being moved overseas.
In the play. *Norfolk tells King Herny about the effects of the taxes proposed and forced by Cardinal Wolsey.*

Rebellion, r. promoted by perception of dissension - If they perceive dissension in our looks...
"If they perceive dissension in our looks,
And that within ourselves we disagree,
How will their grudging stomachs be provoked
To wilful disobedience, and rebel!" (KHVI.p1.4.1)
Urge a settlement of disputes and a united front against the opposing party
In the play. *Henry VI attempts to reconcile Vernon and Basset who want to duel against each other. The 'they' Henry VI refers to are the French.*

Rebellion, reasons and occasions for a r. - We see which way the stream of time doth run... the rough torrent of occasion.
"We see which way the stream of time doth run,
And are enforc'd from our most quiet there
By the rough torrent of occasion." (KHIVp2.4.1)
Indicate your awareness of the way things are gong, 'We have seen which way the stream of time doth run and are enforced... occasion'. Or express that circumstances got you to be where you are now, e.g. 'The rough torrent of occasion brings me here'.
In the play. *In the Gaultree forest in Yorkshire, the archbishop of York explains to Westmoreland the reasons for the rebellion.*

Rebellion, stirring a r. - ... ruffle up your spirits and put a tongue in every wound of Caesar...
"...there were an Antony
Would ruffle up your spirits and put a tongue
In every wound of Caesar that should move
The stones of Rome to rise and mutiny." (JC.3.2)
Use 'put a tongue in every wound of Caesar' with a mild modification, e.g. 'We will put a tongue in every wound you inflicted on us and move the stones of (city) in rise and mutiny'.
In the play. *Antony works up the crowd to rebel against Brutus and the other conspirators.*

Receivables, poor chances of collection - ... if money were as certain as your waiting, 't were sure enough.
TITUS. We wait for certain money here, sir.
FLAVIUS. Ay, if money were as certain as your waiting,
'T were sure enough." (TOA.3.4)
Comment on unrecoverable receivables. Change 'your waiting' to 'our waiting' if you are the creditor.
In the play. *Hopes by the creditors of collecting debts from Timon are dwindling. Flavius represents a collector.*

Receivables, r. must be collected immediately - Immediate are my needs; and my relief must not be tossed and turned to me in words...
"Immediate are my needs; and my relief
Must not be tossed and turned to me in words
But find supply immediate."
(TOA.2.1)
Dramatize your need to collect the receivables. See also 'Credit worthiness spoiled by uncollected debts' – Entries for 'Financial Status'.
In the play. *One creditor (actually a Senator), has had enough of Timon's delays to pay his debt and instructs his servant Caphus to call on Timon's to collect the payment.*

Recognition, unfair r. resulting from the passage of time- ... And give to dust that is a little gilt more laud than gilt o'er-dusted.
"…And give to dust that is a little gilt
More laud than gilt o'er-dusted"
(TC.3.3)
See also 'Time, t. and ingratitude - Time hath, my lord, a wallet at his back wherein he puts alms for oblivion…'
In the play. *Ulysses produces a string of arguments for Achilles to reconsider his abandoning the field. The image refers to 'gilt' covered with dust, i.e. Achilles, compared with other Greeks that are only dust covered with a little gilt.*

Recognizing, reason for not r. someone – ... I fear I am not in my perfect mind. Methinks I should know you.
"…to deal plainly,
I fear I am not in my perfect mind.
Methinks I should know you" (KL.4.7)
Use the first two lines if you have drunk a bit too much, cannot drive and need a ride. See also 'Apologies for behavior caused by indisposition'.

In the play. *King Lear does not recognize his daughter Cordelia who has arrived from France to assist him.*

Recollection, vague r. only – T'is far off and rather like a dream than an assurance that my remembrance warrants.
" T is far off
And rather like a dream than an assurance
That my remembrance warrants."
(TEM.1.2)
Indicate only a vague recollection, 'It is rather like a dream…. Warrants'.
In the play. *Prospero asks daughter Miranda if she remembers anything of her childhood – she is not sure.*

Reconciliation, r. effected with a smile - For looks kill love and love by looks reviveth; a smile recures the wounding of a frown.
"For looks kill love and love by looks reviveth;
A smile recures the wounding of a frown" (V&A)
In the poem. *Adonis' look of rejection at Venus' advances causes her to faint.*

Recreation, r. to put away care - What sport shall we devise here in this garden, to drive away the heavy thought of care?
"What sport shall we devise here in this garden,
To drive away the heavy thought of care?" (KRII.3.4)
Alternative for the question, 'What would you like to do now?' See also 'Time, searching for some entertainment to pass the t.'
In the play. *The queen to her ladies. The 'heavy thoughts' have to do with the precarious position of King Richard menaced by Bolingbroke.*

Recrimination, self-recrimination –
…my very hairs do mutiny, for the white reprove the brown for rashness…
"…My very hairs do mutiny; for the white
Reprove the brown for rashness, and they them
For fear and doting." (AC. 3.11)
In the play. *After having lost a critical sea battle with Octavian, Antony is mad at himself. 'Doting' = 'the act of speaking irrationally'.*

Redress, need for immediate r. - The shame itself doth speak for instant remedy.
"…The shame itself doth speak
For instant remedy" (KL.1.4)
In the play. *Goneril refers to the (alleged) misbehaving by the knights left in K. Lear's retinue.*

Redress, r. or positive a. promised - … and wherein it shall appear that your demands are just...
"… and wherein
It shall appear that your demands are just,
You shall enjoy them" (KHIV p2.4.1)
Answer calmly a (possibly reasonable) grievance or request made boisterously.
In the play. *Westmoreland to the rebels in Yorkshire.*

Redress, wish for the undoing of wrongs – (He) hath given me some worthy cause to wish things done, undone.
"(He)
Hath given me some worthy cause to wish
Things done, undone…" (JC.4.2)
In the play. *Cassius rejoins Brutus at Sardis. The 'things' referred to are alleged bribes or sales of offices by Cassius.*

Reform, determination to r. – ... I survive, to mock the expectations of the world; to frustrate prophecies…
"And with his spirit sadly I survive,
To mock the expectations of the world;
To frustrate prophecies, and to raze out
Rotten opinion, who hath writ me down
After my seeming." (KHIVp2.5.2)
You have just come back after a period of obscurity. 'Yes, I survived to mock the expectations of the world and to frustrate prophecies that have written me off.' See also 'Character, promise of self-reformation - ... that to come hall all be done by the rule.'
In the play. *Henry V is determined to change his ways and people's perception of him as an idle and profligate no-good.*

Reformation, symptoms of r. observed – I see some sparks of better hope…
"As dissolute as desperate; yet through both
I see some sparks of better hope, which elder years
May happily bring forth." (KRII.5.3)
In the play. *Bolingbroke to Percy referring to Bolingbroke's son Harry, Prince of Wales.*

Refusal, r. for a good reason – …I hope this reason stands for my excuse.
"For your physicians have expressly charged,
In peril to incur your former malady,
That I should yet absent me from your bed;
I hope, this reason stands for my excuse." (TOS.IND.)
Use to say no (fourth line), unless specific conditions call for the whole quote. See entries for 'Health-care'.
In the play. *An actor as part of the prank on which the play is based pretends to be Sly's wife.*

Refusal, r. of help or brokerage - ... give me leave to play the broker in mine own behalf ...
"In choosing for yourself, you show'd your judgment,
Which being shallow, you give me leave
To play the broker in mine own behalf;
And to that end I shortly mind to leave you" (KHVI.p3.4.1)
Use 'give me leave to play... behalf' to reject suggestions of help, not necessarily limited to finding a wife. See also 'Selection, desire to select independently - ... in such a business give me leave to use help of mine own eyes.'
In the play. *Clarence rebuts his brother's (and King Edward IV) suggestion that he Edward find a wife for Clarence. Edward married the Lady Grey thus creating resentment among his brothers and Warwick.*

Refusal, r. to budge - ... I will not budge for no man's pleasure.
"Men's eyes were made to look, and let them gaze;
I will not budge for no man's pleasure" (RJ.3.1)
Answer to 'Let's talk privately' when you don't want to.
In the play. *Mercutio refuses an invitation by Benvolio to go into a more secluded place to resolve the grievances with Tybald, a Capulet.*

Refusal, r. to compromise - ... nothing but death shall e'er divorce my dignities.
"...nothing but death
Shall e'er divorce my dignities." (KHVIII, 3.1)
In the play. *Q. Kathryn to Cardinal Wolsey, who discusses with her the possibility of a divorce from King Henry.*

Refusal, r. to do something distasteful – Not for all this land would I be guilty of so deep a sin.
"... not for all this land
Would I be guilty of so deep a sin."
(KRIII.3.1)
Refuse to participate in a project or to agree to an objectionable proposal.
In the play. *Q. Elizabeth, on knowing of the execution of her kin by Richard takes sanctuary with her son. Richard suggests to break the sanctuary and the cardinal vehemently refuses it. Richard will succeed in breaking the sanctuary clause with a technicality.*

Refusal, r. to give up – I was not born a yielder.
"I was not born a yielder"
(KHIV.p1.5.3)
In the play. *At the battle of Shrewsbury Sir Walter Blunt answers the challenge by Douglas. Douglas will kill Blunt in the ensuing fight.*

Refusal, r. to have patience or to yield to command - ... my tongue, though not my heart, shall have his will.
"I cannot, nor I will not, hold me still;
My tongue, though not my heart, shall have his will." (COE.4.2)
In the play. *Luciana tells her sister Adriana to be patience. Mistaken identities take their toll as Adriana thinks that her husband Antipholus E is unfaithful.*

Refusal, r. to serve a murderer - ... nor attend the foot that leaves the print of blood where'er it walks.
"We will not line his thin bestained cloak
With our pure honours, nor attend the foot
That leaves the print of blood where'er it walks" (KJ.4.3)
In the play. *Salisbury tells Faulconbridge that he and other English Lords will have nothing more to do with the murderous King John.*

Regret, r. at confirming truthfulness of event - I am sorry I should force you to believe that which I would to God I had not seen.

"I am sorry I should force you to believe
That which I would to God I had not seen" (KHIV.p2.1.1)
See also entries for 'News, unwelcome n.' – 'News, bad n.'
In the play. *Morton brings bad news to the remaining rebels from the field of Shrewsbury.*

Regret, r. corrosive for things that cannot be changed - Care is no cure, but rather corrosive, for things that are not to be remedied.
"Care is no cure, but rather corrosive, For things that are not to be remedied." (KHVI.p1.3.3)
Exhort the audience to look to the future rather than harping on the past. See also entries for 'Care' *** 'Complaint' *** 'Attitude, a. towards what is past and cannot be changed'
In the play. *La Pucelle addresses the French princes after their defeat at Rouen.*

Regret, r. past to be forgotten - Let us not burden our remembrance with a heaviness that's gone.
"Let us not burden our remembrance with
A heaviness that's gone." (TEM.5.1)
Exhortation to forget a painful past.
In the play. *Alonso is sorry at all that has passed before and Prospero invites him to forget about the past.*

Rejection, answer to rejecting words - ... Get thee to yond same sovereign cruelty.
"Once more, Cesario,
Get thee to yond same sovereign cruelty" (TN.2.4)
Try 'O sovereign cruelty'.
In the play. *Though his proposal was repeatedly rejected, the Duke Orsino sends Viola/Cesario again to Olivia, the sovereign cruelty to woe on his behalf.*

Rejection, curse of love - ... 'tis the curse in love, and still approved, when women cannot love where they're beloved!
"What dangerous action, stood it next to death,
Would I not undergo for one calm look!
O, 'tis the curse in love, and still approved,
When women cannot love where they're beloved!" (TGV.5.4)
In the play. *Proteus laments that Silvia does not love him.*

Rejection, cut it out - Dismiss your vows, your feigned tears, your flattery...
"Dismiss your vows, your feigned tears, your flattery;
For where a heart is hard they make no battery." (V&A)
In the poem. *Adonis rejects Venus' persistent and strong advances.*

Rejection, despair at her r. - ... thus I turn me from my country's light to dwell in solemn shades of endless night.
"Then thus I turn me from my country's light,
To dwell in solemn shades of endless night." (KRII.1.3)
Imply that her rejection will force you away from your current abode. Change 'country' to 'city' if you do not actually intend to move overseas. But just using the lines in their original will convey the idea.
In the play. *Thomas Mowbray has been forced into exile by Richard II.*

Rejection, despair at her words - ... if words be made of breath and breath of life, I have no life to breathe what thou hast said to me.
"Be thou assured, if words be made of breath,

And breath of life, I have no life to breathe
What thou hast said to me." (H.3.4)
Your reaction to her rejection or to any harsh or cruel words she may have said to you.
In the play. *Hamlet has just finished a bitter harangue to her mother Gertrude, Queen of Denmark.*

Rejection, despair, night and day reversed - ... dark shall be my light and night my day.
"... dark shall be my light and night my day" (KHVI.p2.2.4)
In the play. *The Duchess of Gloucester, forced into exile by enemies of her husband Duke Humphrey, pines over her condition. She rejects her husband's advice that counsels patience. Among other grievances she laments that,*
"The ruthless flint doth cut my tender feet"
and rhetorically asks her husband,
"Ah, Humphrey, can I bear this shameful yoke?
Trow'st thou that e'er I'll look upon the world,
Or count them happy that enjoy the sun?
No; dark shall be my light and night my day;
To think upon my pomp shall be my hell."

Rejection, handling of r. - Hope is a lover's staff, I'll walk hence with that and manage it against despairing thoughts.
"Hope is a lover's staff, I'll walk hence with that,
And manage it against despairing thoughts. (TGV.3.1)

Handling rejection requires skill. You need to assess immediately if her 'no' is final or staged (see 'Justification for insisting even after she said 'no'). If it is final you have to decide whether to give up for good or to retain a foot in the door, so to speak. If this is your intent, bow out gracefully but give her the impression that you are still hoping she will change her mind. History, literature and chronicles abound in examples of loves impossible at first and flourished later. So, when she says no, you may take on an expression of (temporary) resignation to her denial and follow up with:
Some girls secretly enjoy the idea of inspiring desperation in those whom they refuse. On the other hand, if the rejection is complete and final, you may keep in mind Tennyson's lines:
'T is better to have loved and lost
Than never to have loved at all.'
Ovid, in this matter, contradicts himself. On one hand he is confident that all women can be conquered, (see 'Word power, key to seduction'), and he adds 'women's lust is keener than ours, and has more of madness. Come then, doubt not that you may win all women.' But then he immediately injects some doubt, 'And, grant they or deny, yet are they pleased to have been asked'. (Ovid, AOL.1)
In the play: *The scoundrel Proteus pretends to console Valentine, who is unaware that Proteus caused his downfall.*

Rejection, no chance of a change of heart - Remove your siege from my unyielding heart; to love's alarms it will not ope the gate.
"Remove your siege from my unyielding heart;
To love's alarms it will not ope the gate" (V&A)

If she says 'no' and you wish to elegantly bow out try, 'I'll remove my siege from your unyielding heart'.
In the poem. *Adonis will have nothing to do with the pursuing Venus.*

Rejection, r. and dismissal - ... dismiss'd me this with his speechless hand.
"…dismiss'd me
Thus, with his speechless hand" (COR.5.1)
In the play. *Cominius relates on how poorly went his meeting with Coriolanus.*

Rejection, r. in all circumstances - Had I been seized by a hungry lion, I would have been a breakfast to the beast...
"Had I been seized by a hungry lion, I would have been a breakfast to the beast,
Rather than have false Proteus rescue me." (TGV.5.4)
See also 'Return? Not a chance - No, rather I abjure all roofs, and choose to wage against the enmity o' the air…'
In the play. *Silvia refuses Proteus' false protestations of love and care.*

Rejection, r. in principle - I had rather hear my dog bark at a crow, than a man swear he loves me.
"I had rather hear my dog bark at a crow, than a man swear he loves me." (MAAN.1.1)
When (f you are a woman), you have had enough of men and their antics. Or use some liberty and change 'man' to 'woman' and 'he' to 'she' as applicable.

Do not be overly discouraged if she dismisses you right away. So Ovid, 'Should she be neither kindly nor courteous to your wooing, persist and steel your resolve (*perfer et obdura*). One day she will be kind. By gradually applied effort is the curved bough bent away from the tree; you will break it if you try your strength. Gradual, determined effort tames the tigers and the Numidian lions; little by little the bull submits to the rustic plough.' (AOL.2)
In the play. *Beatrice is scornful of men who may profess to love her.*

Rejection, r. increasing rather than decreasing desire - If the scorn of your bright eyes have power to raise such love in mine…
"If the scorn of your bright eyes
Have power to raise such love in mine,
Alack, in me what strange effect
Would they work in mild aspect!" (AYLI.3)
Pass it as a rationalization of why you are still after her after she turned you down.
In the play. *Rosalind reads a letter from Phebe given to Rosalind by Silvius. Silvius loves Phebe. Rosalind, for safety, is disguised as a boy and Phebe has fallen in love with Rosalind not aware of the disguise. Understandably, Rosalind has rejected Phebe's approaches.*

Rejection, continuing to love her as a shadow - For since the substance of your perfect self is else devoted… to your shadow will I make true love.
"For since the substance of your perfect self
Is else devoted, I am but a shadow;
And to your shadow will I make true love." (TGV.4.2)
This assumes that you cannot get her out of your mind. See also 'Graphics, Picture as a substitute'
In the play. *Proteus does not want to give up on Julia and he has just asked for a picture.*

Rejection, heart of stone - I have said too much unto a heart of stone...
"I have said too much unto a heart of stone
And laid mine honour too unchary out" (TN.3.4)
'I have said too much to a heart of stone' is a good line if she very coldly rejects your advances.
In the play. *Olivia has declared her love for Viola/Cesario, who for various reasons (besides being a woman disguised as a man), cannot reciprocate. Now Olivia regrets the declaration of love she just made to Viola/Cesario.*

Rejection, plea for gentle refusal - Say that you love me not, but say not so in bitterness...
"Say that you love me not, but say not so
In bitterness. The common executioner,
Whose heart the accustomed sight of death makes hard,
Falls not the axe upon the humbled neck,
But first begs pardon: will you sterner be
Than he that dies and lives" (AYLI.3.5)
Try this when it seems that no matter what you do she refuses you.
In the play. *Silvius loves Phebe but Phebe has a crush on the disguised Rosalind whom she (Phebe) believes to be a boy.*

Rejection, plea not to be rejected - Rebuke me not for that which you provoke, the virtue of your eye must break my oath.
"Rebuke me not for that which you provoke:
The virtue of your eye must break my oath" (LLL.5.2)
When she says no but not conclusively. Substitute 'must break my oath' with whatever action or words prompted to declare your love or similar (that caused her rebuke).
In the play. *Ferdinand has fallen in love with the Princess and is ready to give up his oath of study and abstinence.*

Rejection, r. fostering even stronger passion - ...the more she spurns my love, the more it grows and fawneth on her still.
"Yet, spaniel-like, the more she spurns my love,
The more it grows and fawneth on her still." (TGV.4.2)
Sometimes it happens and you have to realize that you are not alone in experiencing this feeling.
In the play. *The devious Proteus tries unsuccessfully to supplant his friend Valentine in the heart of Silvia.*

Rejection, reaction to r., emphatic and mildly theatrical – ... like the lily, that once was mistress of the field and flourished I'll hang my head and perish.
"... like the lily,
That once was mistress of the field and flourished,
I'll hang my head and perish." (KHVIII.3.1)
When you have exhausted all your efforts and her no is final.
Not everyone can take a rejection so mildly. In 1757, Jean Jacques Rousseau apparently rejected by Countess Sophie d'Houdenot writes, 'Why should I spare you, whilst you robe me of reason, of honor, and life? Why should I allow your days to pass in peace, you, who make mine unbearable! Much less cruel would you have been, if you had driven a dagger in my heart.'
In the play. *Katherine realizes that she cannot oppose the king's will to divorce her. The King has decided to marry Anne Boleyn.*

Rejection, reason for not taking 'no' for an answer – For scorn at first makes after-love the more…
"For scorn at first makes after-love the more.
If she do frown, 'tis not in hate of you,
But rather to beget more love in you" (TGV.3.1)
Answer when she asks 'Why do you insist? See also 'Justification for insisting even after she said 'no' - … maids in modesty, say 'No' to that which they would have the profferer construe 'Ay''
In the play. *Valentine gives courting lessons to the Duke of Milan, who plans to unmask Valentine's machinations to elope with Silvia, the Duke's daughter.*

Rejection, rebuttal to rejection or harsh words - Teach not thy lip such scorn; for it was made for kissing, lady, not for such contempt.
"Teach not thy lips such scorn; for they were made
For kissing, lady, not for such contempt." (RIII.1.2)
She says no contemptuously and you want to try again. Since today we normally refer to 'lips' in the plural, you may change to 'Teach not thy lips such scorn; for they were made… contempt'
In the play. *Richard is trying to woo Anne who looks at him scornfully.*

Rejection, she says no with a smile that hurts more than soothes - Thou cuttest my head with a golden axe and smil'st upon the stroke that murders me.
"Thou cuttest my head with a golden axe,
And smil'st upon the stroke that murders me." (RJ.2.3)
Use in any occasion when she disappoints you but yet fakes a smile or tries to put a good face as she refuses your invitation, offering or advances. See also 'Hurt, you hurt me - Thou stickest a dagger in me'
In the play. *The prince of Verona has banished Romeo and Fr. Lawrence brings the bad news to Romeo, along with otherwise good news about Juliet.*

Rejection, warning about your character plus you don't like her - … do not fall in love with me, for I am falser than vows made in wine…
"…do not fall in love with me,
For I am falser than vows made in wine:
Besides, I like you not." (AYLI.3)
You may just use the first two lines. The qualification 'falser than vows made in wine' can be applied to any type of promise or commitment whose sincerity you question.
In the play. *Rosalind, in a man's disguise, fends off the advances of Phebe who, believing Rosalind to be a boy, has fallen in love with him/her.*

Relationship, indications of a deeper r. - … to be paddling palms and pinching fingers … and making practised smiles…
"But to be paddling palms and pinching fingers,
As now they are, and making practised smiles…" (WT.1.2)
Pull the leg of a friend, e.g. 'I saw you paddling palms and pinching fingers' See also 'Love, symptoms of something going on – … whispering… meeting noses… horsing foot on foot…'
In the play. *Jealous Leontes imagines that his wife Hermione has an affair with his visiting friend Polixenes.*

Relationship, r. beyond repair - … past hope, past cure, past help!
"…past hope, past cure, past help!" (RJ.4.1)
Apply to any situation that cannot be remedied.

In the play. *Juliet is in a bind. She has married Romeo secretly but her father has scheduled her marriage to the Capulet Paris the following Thursday.*

Reliability, r. and innocence claimed - O, take the sense, sweet, of my innocence!...
"O, take the sense, sweet, of my innocence!
Love takes the meaning in love's conference.
I mean, that my heart unto yours is knit
So that but one heart we can make of it;
Two bosoms interchained with an oath;
So then two bosoms and a single troth.
Then by your side no bed-room me deny;
For lying so, Hermia, I do not lie" (MND.2.2)
Use only the last two lines if you do not feel so innocent.
In the play. *Hermia, not yet married to Lysander, suggests he lay at a distance and Lysander responds with a tenable argument. Still, Hermia is not convinced.* See 'Lying, I do not mean to say you're lying' and 'Abstinence, some distance advisable – such separation…becomes a virtuous bachelor and a maid'.

Reliability, am I going to be safe with you? Can I trust you? Etc. – I shall never melt mine honour into lust.
"(I) shall never melt
Mine honour into lust" (TEM.4.1)
See also 'Love, l. kept platonic - I never tempted her with word too large… bashful sincerity and comely love.'
In the play. *Ferdinand replies to Prospero's injunction not to play around with Miranda before marriage.*

Reliability, am I going to be safe with you? Can I trust you? Etc. - … my desires run not before mine honour…
"… my desires
Run not before mine honour, nor my lusts
Burn hotter than my faith." (WT.4.3)
This works best if either you or she is religious.
In the play. *Chance makes Florizel, son of Polixenes king of Bohemia, meet Perdita who is being raised by a shepherd. He falls in love with her immediately while informing her of his innocent intentions.*

Reliability, am I going to be safe with you? Can I trust you? Etc. - … the strong'st suggestion… shall never melt mine honour into lust.
"…the strong'st suggestion.
Our worser genius can, shall never melt
Mine honour into lust" (TEM.4.1)
In the play. *Prospero urges Ferdinand to refrain from sex with Miranda until their marriage is celebrated and Ferdinand responds.*

Reliability, am I going to be safe with you? Can I trust you? Etc. - The white-cold virgin snow upon my heart abates the ardour of my liver.
"The white-cold virgin snow upon my heart
Abates the ardour of my liver." (TEM.4.1)
A good one if you wish to keep your options open. She will be so flabbergasted at your answer that she may forget her questions or concerns.
In ancient times, during the Middle Ages and the Renaissance, the liver was considered as the eminent organ responsible for sexual desire.

For some, love is a source of inspiration and creativity. For others it does not work as well. In a letter to Delphine Potocka, Chopin deals with the issue suggesting a masochistic solution for improving creativity, 'My one and only beloved, … I have slowly reflected on inspiration and creativity and slowly, slowly I think I have discovered the essential nature of these gifts. To me inspiration and creativity come only when I have abstained from a woman for a longish period…On the other hand unrequited love and unfulfilled passion, sharpened by the image of one's beloved and carrying unbearable frustration with it, can contribute to creativity… I have not composed anything for ever so long, immersed as I was in you and in love.'
In the play. *Answering Prospero's concerns, Ferdinand promises abstinence before marriage with Miranda. Prospero is Miranda's father.*

Reliability. am I going to be safe with you? Can I trust you? Etc. - O fairest beauty, do not fear or fly! for I will touch thee but with reverent hands…
" O fairest beauty, do not fear or fly! For I will touch thee but with reverent hands;
I kiss these fingers for eternal peace, And lay them gently on thy tender side." (KHVI.p1.5)
Reply to 'Do not hurt me!' or similar.
In the play. *Suffolk has taken prisoner Margaret, daughter of Reigner, a poor nobleman but with the titles of King of Naples and Jerusalem. Suffolk does not want to frighten Margaret and hatches a plan to have her marry King Henry VI.*

Reliable people needed - Natures of such deep trust we shall much need.
"Natures of such deep trust we shall much need" (KL.2.1)
In the play. *The Duke of Cornwall to Edmund who is actually the opposite of trustworthiness.*

Reliance, r. on the favor of the great a source of disappointment. - Poor wretches that depend on greatness' favour dream as I have done, wake and find nothing.
"…Poor wretches that depend
On greatness' favour dream as I have done,
Wake and find nothing." (CYM.5.4)
See also 'Philosophical considerations, uselessness of coveting patronage as patronage is so prone to change - O momentary grace of mortal men which we more hunt for than the grace of God…'
In the play. *Leonatus has a dream and a vision but on waking up he finds himself still the same and still in prison.*

Relief, cheering up - I'll take the winter from your lips, fair lady.
"I'll take the winter from your lips, fair lady:
Achilles bids you welcome." (TC.4.5)
Use to cheer up your girlfriend when she is in a bad mood. Try as an alternative, 'Let me take the winter….fair lady.' Change 'Achilles' to your own name. See also entries for 'Cheer up'.
In the play. *Cressida has arrived to the Greek field and all the Greek princes greet and kiss her. Achilles volunteers to kiss her and remove her anxiety (read 'winter'). Cressida proves to be a bit of a slut.*

Relief, r. at not to having to do what you dislike - I am best pleased to be from such a deed.
"I am best pleased to be from such a deed." (KJ.4.1)
In the play. *An executioner is excused from participating to the murder of young Prince Arthur.*

Religion, questionable religious character or motives – Name not religion, for thou lovest the flesh…

"Name not religion, for thou lovest the flesh,
And ne'er throughout the year to church thou go'st
Except it be to pray against thy foes."
(KHVI.p1.1.1)
In the play. *Gloucester to the Bishop of Winchester during the mourning for Henry V.*

Religion, religious hypocrites – ... and sweet religion makes a rhapsody of words.
"...and sweet religion makes
A rhapsody of words." (H.3.4)
Most applicable to some super-rich so called evangelists. See also 'Hypocrisy, h. in religion - ... In religion, what damned error....hiding the grossness with fair ornament?'
In the play. *Hamlet in the dramatic confrontation with his mother the Queen and during which he will slain the poor Polonius who was listening behind a curtain.*

Remedies, extreme r. required - ... Diseases desperate grown by desperate appliances are relieved or not at all.
"... Diseases desperate grown
By desperate appliances are relieved,
Or not at all." (H.4.3)
Dramatize the need for drastic measures. See also 'Gains, ill gotten g. to be maintained with ill deeds - ...and he that stands upon a slippery place must be as boisterously maintain'd as gain'd'.
In the play. *The King has decided to get rid of Hamlet by sending him to England and organizing to have him killed.*

Remedies, extreme r. required - ... The present time's so sick that present medicine must be ministered or overthrow incurable ensues.
"... pause not, for the present time's so sick,
That present medicine must be ministered,
Or overthrow incurable ensues."
(KJ.5.1)
Support strong corrective measures.
In the play. *K. Lewis addresses Pandulph, the Pope's legate. Pandulph actually caused the war and indirectly the death of young Arthur and all ensuing troubles. But now Pandulph has switched sides and wants to prop up K. John.*

Remedies, extreme r. required – ... those cold ways, that seem like prudent helps, are very poisonous where the disease is violent.
"Sir, those cold ways,
That seem like prudent helps, are very poisonous that
Where the disease is violent"
(COR.3.1)
In the play. *The tribune Brutus does not think that the pride and contempt for the people by Coriolanus can be reduced by diplomacy.*

Remedy, advice on possible r. after identifying a problem - The nature of the sickness found, Ulysses, what is the remedy?
"The nature of the sickness found, Ulysses,
What is the remedy?" (TC.1.3)
It is always much easier to find problems than solutions. Change 'Ulysses' with the name of the person who described the problem.
In the play. *Ulysses has made an accurate description and diagnosis of the problem. Agamennon now asks for a solution.*

Remedy, every r. will be tried - ... nothing we'll omit that bears recovery's name.
" ... nothing we'll omit
That bears recovery's name."
(PER.5.1)
Indicate that you will do whatever possible to remedy the situation.

In the play. *Pericles has arrived in Mytilene along with faithful minister Helicanus. Lysimachus comes on board the ship and inquires as to the nature of Pericles' distemper. Helicanus says that hey tried everything (ineffectively) and will continue to try everything to pull Pericles out of his mental depression.*

Remedy, r. painful but better than death – ... though parting be a fretful corrosive, it is applied to a deathful wound.
"...though parting be a fretful corrosive,
It is applied to a deathful wound." (KHVI.p2.3.1)
In the play. *Queen Margaret cries at Suffolk having been banished from court.*

Remedy, r. worse than the disease – So play the foolish throngs with one that swoons...
"So play the foolish throngs with one that swoons;
Come all to help him, and so stop the air
By which he should revive" (MFM.2.4)
In the play. *Troubled by his attraction to Isabella, Angelo questions his own fitness to uphold the law in Vienna where he is temporary governor.*

Remedy, taking r. before the problem spreads - ... and stop the rage betime, before the wound do grow uncurable...
"... and stop the rage betime,
Before the wound do grow uncurable;
For, being green, there is great hope of help." (KHVI p2.3.1)
Lend support to a campaign of repression.
In the play. *A messenger brings in news of a revolt in Ireland along with a request for help.*

Remembering, r. only the essential - ... from the table of my memory I'll wipe away all trivial fond records.

"...from the table of my memory
I'll wipe away all trivial fond records,
All saws of books, all forms, all pressures past,
That youth and observation copied there;
And thy commandment all alone shall live
Within the book and volume of my brain,
Unmix'd with baser matter" (H.1.5)
In the play. *Hamlet promises to the Ghost of his father to forget everything and concentrate on revenging his father's murder. 'Saws'='wise sentences'.*

Remembering, r. others' efforts on your behalf – ... your pains are register'd where every day I turn the leaf to read them.
"Kind gentlemen, your pains
Are register'd where every day I turn
The leaf to read them." (M.1.3)
In the play. *Macbeth to fellow soldiers and combatants who helped him win the battle against the rebel.*

Remembering, r. the bad more than the good - Men's evil manners live in brass; their virtues we write in water.
"Men's evil manners live in brass; their virtues
We write in water." (KHVIII.4.2)
See also 'Misjudgement, transposition of values'. – 'Forgetting, f. the good under the influence of anger - All this from my remembrance brutish wrath sinfully pluck'd.'
In the play. *Griffith tells Queen Katharine that Cardinal Wolsey is dead. Although Katharine had good reasons for disliking Wolsey, Griffith asks permission to point out some of Wolsey's virtues*

Remembering, r. the bad more than the good - The evil that men do lives after them, the good is oft interred with their bones.

"The evil that men do lives after them;
The good is oft interred with their bones." (JC.3.2)
When she is reminding you of all the (alleged) bad things you did to her.
In the play. *Antony begins the famous speech with which he will turn the mood of the Roman rabble against Brutus and other conspirators.*

Remorse - Will all great Neptune's ocean wash this blood clean from my hand?
"Will all great Neptune's ocean wash this blood
Clean from my hand? No, this my hand will rather
The multitudinous seas in incarnadine,
Making the green one red." (M.2.2)
Turn the sentence into an accusation, 'Not all great Neptune's ocean will wash this blood clean from your hand'
In the play. *Macbeth is assailed by remorse after having slain Duncan. 'Incarnadine' means 'dyed red'.*

Remorse, false r., false tears - Trust not those cunning waters of his eyes...
"Trust not those cunning waters of his eyes,
For villainy is not without such rheum;
And he, long traded in it, makes it seem
Like rivers of remorse and innocence." (KJ.4.3)
Throw suspicion on whether the culprit is really remorseful.
In the play. *Salisbury accuses Hubert of having caused the death of Arthur. 'Rheum' = 'Humid matter secreted by eyes, or nose, or mouth'.*

Remorse, r. and fear – I am afraid to think what I have done, look on't again I dare not.
"I'll go no more:
I am afraid to think what I have done;
Look on't again I dare not." (M.2.2)
In the play. *Macbeth is reluctant to return to the scene of his murder of King Duncan and guards.*

Remorse, r. and self-awareness - To know my deed, 'twere best not know myself.
"To know my deed, 'twere best not know myself." (M.2.2)
In the play. *Macbeth is assailed by remorse after having slain Duncan*

Remorse, r. at remembering - How sharp the point of this remembrance is!
"How sharp the point of this remembrance is!" (TEM.5.1)
Underscore the inevitability of the pain in remembering a painful event.
In the play. *Alonso thinks that his son Ferdinand drowned in the shipwreck.*

Remorse, wish to undo what done - Were I the chief lord of all this spacious world I'd give it to undo the deed.
DIONYZA. I think you'll turn a child again.
CLEON. Were I the chief lord of all this spacious world,
I'd give it to undo the deed." (PER.4.3)
Show your strong remorse and wish to undo what done.
In the play. *In Tharsus, Cleon repents of having agreed to Marina's killing.*

Repeat, ask her to r. what she said – … speak again, bright angel! for thou art as glorious to this night …
"O, speak again, bright angel! for thou art
As glorious to this night, being o'er my head
As is a winged messenger of heaven

Unto the white-upturned wondering eyes
Of mortals that fall back to gaze on him
When he bestrides the lazy-pacing clouds
And sails upon the bosom of the air" (RJ.2.2)
Remove 'being o'er my head' if the exchange occurs eye to eye, rather than from the ground floor to a window, as it is the case in the play.
In the play. *Romeo, in Juliet's garden, hears her speak.*

Repentance, insincere r. - My words fly up, my thoughts remain below, words without thoughts never to heaven go.
"My words fly up, my thoughts remain below:
Words without thoughts never to heaven go." (H.3.3)
When you question the sincerity of apologies, e.g. 'Your words fly up, your thoughts…go'.
In the play. *King Claudius attempts to pray in atonement of the murder oh his brother, Hamlet's father. But he himself knows that his words are not sincere.*

Repentance, invitation to repent – … Repent what's past; avoid what is to come…
"…Confess yourself to heaven;
Repent what's past; avoid what is to come;
And do not spread the compost on the weeds,
To make them ranker" (H.3.4)
In the play. *Hamlet at the end of his harangue to his mother.*

Repentance, pleasure of r. - … I do not shame to tell you what I was, since my conversion so sweetly tastes, being the thing I am.
"…I do not shame
To tell you what I was, since my conversion
So sweetly tastes, being the thing I am." (AYLI.4.3)
In the play. *Oliver repents of his evil designs against his brother Orlando and shares with Celia his new reformed feelings*

Repentance, r. accompanied by a request for punishment - … Choose your revenge yourself; impose me to what penance your invention…
"…Choose your revenge yourself;
Impose me to what penance your invention
Can lay upon my sin: yet sinn'd I not
But in mistaking." (MAAN.5.1)
Apologize for your mistake.
In the play. *Claudio repents for having unfairly accused Hero and tells Leonato, her father.*

Repentance, r. for brutal act - Were I chief lord of all this spacious world, I'ld give it to undo the deed.
"Were I chief lord of all this spacious world,
I'ld give it to undo the deed." (PER.4.3)
Show your remorse. See also 'Event, course of e. completely changing your outlook on life'.
In the play. *In Tharsus, Cleon repents of having agreed to have Marina murdered – she was actually captured by pirates on the seashore and later sold in Mytilene.*

Repentance, r. for despicable action - O would the deed were good, for now the devil, that told me I did well, says that this deed is chronicled in hell.
"… O, would the deed were good!
For now the devil, that told me I did well,
Says that this deed is chronicled in hell." (KRII.5.5)

800

Express your utmost disapproval of a decision or action.
In the play. *At Pomfret Castle Exton, a henchman of Bolingbroke has just killed King Richard II.*

Repentance, r. questionable – ... Words without thoughts never to heaven go.
"My words fly up, my thoughts remain below:
Words without thoughts never to heaven go." (H.3.3)
In the play. *King Claudius is torn between remorse and the need to deal with the present situation.*

Repentance, r. to be accepted - Who by repentance is not satisfied is nor of heaven nor earth...
"Who by repentance is not satisfied
Is nor of heaven nor earth, for these are pleased" (TGV.5.4)
In the play. *Valentine forgives Proteus for his attempts at Silvia.*

Repentance, r. useless and ineffective – ... betake thee to nothing but despair. A thousand knees...
"...O thou tyrant!
Do not repent these things, for they are heavier
Than all thy woes can stir; therefore betake thee
To nothing but despair. A thousand knees
Ten thousand years together, naked, fasting,
Upon a barren mountain and still winter
In storm perpetual, could not move the gods
To look that way thou wert" (WT.3.2)
In the play. *Paolina, faithful lady in waiting to Hermione reprimands Leontes who was the cause of Hermione's death.*

Repentance, willingness to repent questionable - ... if my wind were but long enough to say my prayers, I would repent.
"Well, if my wind were but long enough to say my prayers, I would repent." (MWW.4.4)
When you wish to communicate that although formally you must say you are sorry, in reality you are not.
In the play. *Falstaff meditates on his failed seduction efforts and the price he had to pay for it.*

Repetition, r. ineffective and counterproductive - This act is as an ancient tale new told and in the last repeating troublesome...
"This act is as an ancient tale new told,
And in the last repeating troublesome,
Being urged at a time unseasonable." (KJ.4.2)
For example, cutting taxes on the rich to stimulate the economy.
In the play. *Lord Pembroke to King John advising against a second repeated coronation.*

Replacement, you loved her first and suddenly you love another - Even as one heat another heat expels, or as one nail by strength drives out another...
"Even as one heat another heat expels,
Or as one nail by strength drives out another
So the remembrances of my former love
Is by a newer object quite forgotten." (TGV.2.4)
Explain your change of fancy and why now you like another girl. See also 'Star, s. versus sun, divided between two loves - At first I did adore a twinkling star, but now I worship a celestial sun.' *** 'Love, l. waning or melted away -- ... my love is thaw'd, which, like a waxen image, 'gainst

a fire bears no impression of the thing it was.'
In the play: *The rascally Proteus, now in Milan, finds that Sylvia has quickly displaced Julia as the center of his desires.*

Reply, anxiously awaiting for her r. - ... expecting thy reply, I profane my lips on thy foot...
"…Thus, expecting thy reply, I profane my lips on thy foot, my eyes on thy picture. and my heart on thy every part." (LLL.4.1)
Added comment when she says 'I'll let you know' to a critical question from you. See also 'Anxious while waiting for her answer – thus ready for the way of life or death I wait the sharpest blow.'
In the play. *Boyet reads to the Princess a letter from Armado.*

Reply, r. approved of – …'tis a loving and a fair reply.
"Why, 'tis a loving and a fair reply…" (H.1.2)
In the play. *King Claudius' comment on an answer by Hamlet to his mother the Queen 'I shall in all my best obey you, madam.'*

Reply, unable to sustain the verbal attack - You have too courtly a wit for me; I'll rest.
"You have too courtly a wit for me; I'll rest." (AYLI.3.2)
Acknowledge the superiority of your adversary in verbal wrestling. See also 'Insult, lips to rot off'.
In the play. *The courtly Touchstone engages the shepherd Corin into an exchange of ideas and opinions. Eventually Corin gives up.*

Report, false r. - … let not his report come current for an accusation…
"And I beseech you, let not his report Come current for an accusation Betwixt my love and your high majesty." (KHIVp1.1.3)

In the play. *Hotspur recounts to King Henry an encounter with a dandy sent by the King to collect the prisoners.*

Report, he is doing very well - Report speaks goldenly of his profit.
" ... report speaks goldenly of his profit." (AYLI.1.1)
Answer to 'What happened to so and so?' or 'How is he?'
In the play. *Orlando to Adam. The subject is Jacques, Orlando's brother, sent to school by the elder first born (and evil) Oliver.*

Repression, violent r. leading to vengeance - … to end one doubt by death revives two greater in the heirs of life.
"…to end one doubt by death Revives two greater in the heirs of life" (KHIVp2.4.1)
In the play. *The Archbishop of York thinks that the King has doubts about violent repression, for fear of its effects.*

Reprimand, invitation to r. – … taunt my faults with such full licence as both truth and malice have power to utter.
"…taunt my faults
With such full licence as both truth and malice
Have power to utter" (AC.1.2)
In the play. *Mark Antony to Messenger from Rome.*

Reporting, r. falling short of representing action - … the tract of every thing would by a good discourser lose some life, which action's self was tongue to.
"…the tract of every thing
Would by a good discourser lose some life,
Which action's self was tongue to" (KHVIII, 1.1)
Preface your narrative as an act of modesty.

In the play. *The Duke of Norfolk to the Duke of Buckingham. He refers to the historical meeting near Calais between King Henry VIII and King Francis I of France – meeting that was beyond the power of description. 'Tract' is synonym of 'course' or 'proceeding'.*

Reprimand, r. causing a fall in mental energy - you do draw my spirits from me, with new lamenting ancient oversights.
"…you do draw my spirits from me
With new lamenting ancient oversights." (KHIV.p2.3.1)
In the play. *Northumberland to Lady Percy who tries to discourage him from joining the rebel.*

Reprimand, r. for going down and not fighting – … wilt thou, pupil-like, take thy correction mildly…
"…wilt thou, pupil-like,
Take thy correction mildly, kiss the rod,
And fawn on rage with base humility,
Which art a lion and a king of beasts?" (KRII.5.1)
See also 'Lion, dying l. still shows his rage - … and wounds the earth, if nothing else, with rage.'
In the play. *The Queen upbraids King Richard who seems to accept the circumstances that led to his deposition from the throne and imprisonment.*

Reprimand, speed and the negligent - Celerity is never more admired than by the negligent.
"Celerity is never more admired
Than by the negligent." (AC.3.7)
Retort to expressed amazement at the advances of the competition. Also adapt to situations or qualities other than celerity. For example, "Clarity is never more admired than by the obscure" etc
In the play. *Cleopatra's critical comment to Antony. He is surprised that Octavian moved so quickly from Italy to Toryne across the Ionian sea. Antony acknowledges with 'a good rebuke'.*

Reproach, undeserved r. - I never knew yet but rebuke and cheque was the reward of valour.
"I never knew yet but rebuke and cheque was the reward of valour." (KHIV p2, 4.3)
When your boss reprimands you unfairly.
In the play. *Falstaff is ready to turn a reprimand against the reprimander.*

Reputation, man spoken of highly – … there's wondrous things spoke of him.
"…there's wondrous things spoke of him." (C.2.1)
In the play. *Valeria commenting on the Senate's decision to name Caius Marcius 'Coriolanus' after his victory on the Volsces at Corioli.*

Reputation, poor r. in the world – … we in the world's wide mouth live scandalized and foully spoken of.
"And for whose death we in the world's wide mouth
Live scandalized and foully spoken of." (KHIV.p1.1.3)
In the play. *Worcester refers to the death of Richard II. Worcester allied himself with Bolingbroke and help depose and murder Richard II. Now Worcester repents, given the treatment received by Bolingbroke, now Henry IV.*

Reputation, r. as a man with a sharp tongue - … the world's large tongue proclaims you for a man replete with mocks…
"Oft have I heard of you, my lord Biron,
Before I saw you; and the world's large tongue
Proclaims you for a man replete with mocks;

Full of comparisons and wounding flouts,
Which you on all estates will execute,
That lie within the mercy of your wit."
(LLL.5.2)
Soften the impact of a potential assault by a man known for his wit, e.g.. 'We lie within the mercy of your wit'.
In the play. *Rosaline expresses some reservation to Biron, who likes her.*

Reputation, r. as a questionable value - Reputation is an idle and most false imposition: oft got without merit, and lost without deserving...
"Reputation is an idle and most false imposition: oft got without merit, and lost without deserving: you have lost no reputation at all, unless you repute yourself such a loser." (OTH.2.3)
Use 'Reputation is an idle and most false imposition: oft got without merit' to put down an undeserved reputation. Add 'and lost without deserving' to emphasize the general fickle and questionable value of reputation. See also 'Militarism, reputation as a volatile commodity.'
In the play. *Cassio, while under the influence of wine engaged into a fight with Montano thus angering his boss Othello. Now sober, Cassio thinks he has lost his reputation but the perfidious Iago props Cassio up while hatching the plan that will doom Desdemona.*

Reputation, r. at stake - ... my reputation is at stake, my fame is shrewdly gored.
"I see my reputation is at stake
My fame is shrewdly gored." (TC.3.3)
Reaction to a sly remark about you or something you did or did not do. Use the first line when you are asked to speak when you really wouldn't but realize that you must.
In the play. *Achilles recognizes that his reputation is shaky, at the end of a speech from Ulysses who tried to stir again Achilles into action.*

Reputation, r. at stake - This touches me in reputation.
"This touches me in reputation.
Either consent to pay this sum for me
Or I attach you by this officer."
(COE.4.1)
In the play. *Angelo must pay a merchant with the money he is owed by Antipholus E. who is temporarily unable to pay.*

Reputation, r. established with the most reputable - ... your name is great in mouths of wisest censure.
"...your name is great
In mouths of wisest censure"
(OTH.2.3)
In the play. *Othello to Montano. Unaware of Iago's plot, Othello thinks that Montano was responsible for the brawl where Montano himself was wounded by Cassio, made drunk by Iago.*

Reputation, r. lost - ... I have lost the immortal part of myself and what remains is bestial.
"Reputation, reputation, reputation! O, I have lost my reputation! I have lost the immortal part of myself, and what remains is bestial. My reputation, Iago, my reputation!"
(OTH.2.3)
In the play. *Cassius to Iago. Cassius drank too much and became involved in a brawl.*

Reputation, r. more valuable than earthly goods – Good name in man and woman, dear my lord, is the immediate jewel of their souls...
"Good name in man and woman, dear my lord,
Is the immediate jewel of their souls:
Who steals my purse steals trash; 'tis something, nothing;
'Twas mine, 'tis his, and has been slave to thousands:
But he that filches from me my good name
Robs me of that which not enriches

him
And makes me poor indeed."
(OTH.3.3)
In the play. *Iago, by stealth, hints, cunning and slander, builds up Othello's jealousy.*

Reputation, r. ruined - ... the benefit which thou shalt thereby reap is such a name, whose repetition will be dogg'd with curses.
"The end of war's uncertain, but this certain,
That, if thou conquer Rome, the benefit
Which thou shalt thereby reap is such a name,
Whose repetition will be dogg'd with curses" (COR.5.3)
In the play. *Volumnia tells her son Coriolanus what would happen if he conquered Rome while fighting with the enemy.*

Reputation, tarnished by inaction - If thou wouldst not entomb thyself alive and case thy reputation in thy tent...
"If thou wouldst not entomb thyself alive
And case thy reputation in thy tent;
Whose glorious deeds, but in these fields of late,
Made emulous missions 'mongst the gods themselves." (TC.3.3)
Invitation in order to persuade a valiant but reluctant participant, e.g. 'Come on, do not case thy reputation in thy tent', just like Achilles.
In the play. *Ulysses tries to stir Achilles into action by pointing out that the start of the Greek camp is now Ajax, as Achilles has withdrawn himself from action out of pique (therefore 'cased' his reputation in his tent).*

Reputation, value placed on r. - The purest treasure mortal times afford...
"The purest treasure mortal times afford
Is spotless reputation; that away,

Men are but guilded loam or painted clay." (KRII.1.1)
Perhaps the word 'ethics' has, today, the ring of obsolescence. If not, resort to this answer when you are invited to something you deem unethical. Or stress the value you place on your honorability. Or why you will not stoop to sleazy tactics for personal gain or advantage.
In the play. *To defend his reputation, Norfolk will challenge Bolingbroke. Loam is a variety of clay.*

Reputation, what type of r. - How is the man esteemed here in the city?...
SECOND MERCHANT How is the man esteemed here in the city?
ANGELO Of very reverent reputation. (COE.5.1)
Answer to a question, 'He is a man of reverend reputation'
In the play. *A merchant asks Angelo what is the reputation of Antipholus of Ephesus. Angelo, actually, produces a string of positive attributes of Antipholus,*
"Of very reverend reputation, sir,
Of credit infinite, highly beloved,
Second to none that lives here in the city:
His word might bear my wealth at any time."

Reputation, wishing that r. could be purchased – I would to God thou and I knew where a commodity of good names were to be bought.
"...I would to God thou and I knew where a commodity of good names were to be bought" (KHIV.p1.1.2)
In the play. *Falstaff commenting to Prince Henry knowing what people think of both of them.*

Request, emphatic r. due to strained circumstances - He asks of you that never used to beg.
"He asks of you that never used to beg." (PER.2.1)

Emphasize the urgency or the critical nature of your request. See also 'Begging, first time b. - A beggar begs that never begg'd before.'
In the play. *After leaving Tharsus, a devastating storm destroys Pericles' fleet and he manages to swim ashore where he meets with 3 fishermen. He asks for their help.*

Request, negative response to r. - They froze me into silence.
"With certain half-caps and cold-moving nods
They froze me into silence." (PER.2.2)
In the play. *Servant Flavius reports to Timon the cold response of Athenian senators to Timon's request for help.*

Request, r. granted - I will both hear and grant you your requests.
"I will both hear and grant you your requests." (KJ.4.2)
Answer to 'Can I ask you a favor?'
In the play. *King John asks Salisbury what reforms or changes in policies he favors and King John will go along with Salisbury'' requests.*
"…meantime but ask
What you would have reform'd that is not well,
And well shall you perceive how willingly I will both hear and grant you your requests."

Request, more successful made with kindness than with arrogance – You may ride with one soft kiss a thousand furlongs ere with spur we heat an acre.
"You may ride
With one soft kiss a thousand furlongs ere
With spur we heat an acre." (WT.1.2)
Answer to a request made in a rude tone.
In the play. *Leontes asks his wife Hermione to use her charm or skills in persuading Polixenes to remain a bit longer as a guest in Sicilia.*
'Ere'='before'

Request, r. for dialog – … a word with you … A hundred, if they'll do you any good.
CLAUDIO One word, good friend. Lucio, a word with you.
LUCIO A hundred, if they'll do you any good. (MFM.1.2)
Answer to 'Can I have a word with you?
In the play. *Claudio, on his way to jail, sees his friend Lucio and wants to ask for help.*

Request, r. granted conditionally - Ay, if thou wilt say 'ay' to my request, no if thou dost say 'no' to my demand'
"Ay, if thou wilt say 'ay' to my request;
No if thou dost say 'no' to my demand" (KHVI.p3.3.2)
Answer to request for favor when you expect a trading of favors.
In the play. *King Edward IV will say yes (to returning her seized estate) to the Lady Grey is she will accept his advances.*

Request, r. of a lady not motivated by sexual motive or impropriety – I therefore beg it not to please the palate of my appetite…
"…I therefore beg it not,
To please the palate of my appetite,
Nor to comply with heat--the young affects
In me defunct--and proper satisfaction" (OTH.1.3)
In the play. *Othello pleads with the Duke of Venice to consent to Desdemona's wish to travel to Cyprus, accompanying Othello, her newly married husband.*

Request, r. or plan, is it reasonable? - Well, what is it? is it within reason and compass?
"Well, what is it? is it within reason and compass?" (OTH.4.3)
In the play. *Tired of promises Roderigo asks Iago if what he plans next (so that Roderigo can have Desdemona), is possible.*

Request, r. that can be easily accommodated – To do this is within the compass of man's wit...
"To do this is within the compass of man's wit: and therefore I will attempt the doing it." (OTH.3.4)
Mildly ironic answer to a simple request. In the play. *Desdemona asked the Clown to call on Cassio and the Clown complies.*

Request, r. to be heard – Friends, Romans, countrymen, lend me your ears.
"Friends, Romans, countrymen, lend me your ears
I come to bury Caesar, not to praise him" (JC.3.2)
If using the first line only change 'Roman' to the citizens of the place where you are speaking. You can also modify the second line to fit the objective of your speech or presentation. See also 'News, believability of a story'
In the play. *Antony begins the oration with which he will sway the mood of the masses. It is the stellar speech that will arouse the Roman rabble against Brutus.*

Request, r. to be heard – Hear me with patience but to speak a word
"Hear me with patience but to speak a word." (RJ.3.5)
In the play. *Juliet pleads with her father to let her speak.*

Request, r. to be heard – Lend favourable ear to our requests...
"...most famous prince,
Lend favourable ear to our requests;
And pardon us the interruption
Of thy devotion and right christian zeal." (KRIII.3.7)
Use the first three lines, "Most famous xxx, lend favourable ears to our requests; and pardon us the interruption." See also 'Meditation, lamenting an interrupted m. - How dare you thrust yourselves into my private meditations?'

In the play. *In a carefully orchestrated charade Buckingham sets the scene for persuading the London council that Richard is the legitimate heir to the throne.*

Request, r. to be heard - Sweet royalty, bestow on me the sense of hearing.
"Sweet royalty, bestow on me the sense of hearing" (LLL.5.2)
In the play. *Armado addresses the Princess.*

Request, r. to be heard – To my unfolding lend your gracious ear...
"To my unfolding lend your gracious ear,
And let me find a charter in your voice
To assist my simpleness." (OTH.1.3)
Introduction before making a request and suggesting humbleness. See also 'News, believability of a story.'
In the play. *Desdemona pleads with the Duke that he let her accompany Othello to Cyprus where he has been assigned.*

Request to be heard, important message coming - ... lend thy serious hearing to what I shall unfold.
"...lend thy serious hearing
To what I shall unfold." (H.1.5)
Alternative to 'Listen carefully'
In the play. *The Ghost prepares Hamlet to learn how he (the king his father) was assassinated.*

Reserve, rationale for being somewhat reserved at first - Therefore this maxim out of love I teach...
"Therefore this maxim out of love I teach, -
Achievement is command; ungained beseeched.
Then though my heart's content firm love doth hear,
Nothing of that shall from mine eyes appear." (TC.1.2)

In case she seems cold. Pose the question and let it slip in casually, "Are you following the maxim (and then recite the lines)?" Try to see from her response if she is really the type that puts you off so as to make herself more enticing as a prey.
In the play. *The crafty Cressida discloses in a monologue her theories on love and on how to keep a lover dangling. The immediately preceding lines offer a rational background for the maxim,*
"Men prize the thing ungain'd more than it is:
That she was never yet that ever knew
Love got so sweet as when desire did sue."
and
"Then though my heart's content firm love doth bear,
Nothing of that shall from mine eyes appear."

Rescue, refusing the rescuer – Had I been seized by a hungry lion, would have been a breakfast to the beast...
"Had I been seized by a hungry lion, I would have been a breakfast to the beast,
Rather than have false Proteus rescue me" (TGV.4.4)
In the play. *Proteus, chasing Silvia in the wood where she escaped in search of Valentine, becomes bold in his requests.*

Resignation, r. or revenge, rhetorical question - Shall we go throw away our coats of steel and wrap our bodies in mourning gowns...
"Shall we go throw away our coats of steel,
And wrap our bodies in mourning gowns,
Numbering our Ave-Marias with our beads?
Or shall we on the helmets of our foes
Tell our devotion with revengeful arms?" (KHVI p3.2.1)

Exhortation to fight against the unfavorable tide of events.
In the play. *Richard (Gloucester) to York, suggesting revenge for the death of Richard (York).*

Resignation, r. to fate - ... I embrace this fortune patiently since not to be avoided it falls on me.
"And I embrace this fortune patiently,
Since not to be avoided it falls on me." (KHIV.p1.5.5)
See also entries for 'Acceptance' and 'Destiny'
In the play. *Worcester's reaction at being condemned to death by King Henry IV.*

Resignation, r. to fate – ... stoop with patience to my fortune
"Nor I, but stoop with patience to my fortune" (KHVI.p3.5.5)
In the play. *Defeated by the forces of Edward IV, Oxford is exiled and Somerset condemned to be beheaded. This is Somerset's response on hearing his fate.*

Resignations, after resigning or being fired – I have touched the highest point of all my greatness, and from that full meridian of my glory...
"I have touched the highest point of all my greatness;
And, from that full meridian of my glory,
I haste now to my setting."
(KHVIII.3.2)
Use in a resignation speech or as a comment to your having been fired.
In the play. *Wolsey comments on his fall from grace.*

Resignations, going somewhere else - ... I turn my back: there is a world elsewhere.
"Despising,
For you, the city, thus I turn my back:
There is a world elsewhere."
(COR.3.3)

When you resign or leave in disgust. See also 'Retirement r. announced'.
In the play. *Disgusted with the Roman citizens, Coriolanus departs knowing that he must leave town as they (the beast with many heads – see 'Opinion, your op. on crowds and masses) send him packing.*

Resistance - A thousand more mischances than this one have learn'd me how to brook this patiently.
"A thousand more mischances than this one
Have learn'd me how to brook this patiently." (TGV.5.3)
Answer to statements of empathy for a relatively small mishap.
In the play. *Silvia meets with the outlaws that followed Valentine*

Resistance, female r. advisable - I see, a woman may be made a fool, if she had not the spirit to resist.
"I see, a woman may be made a fool,
If she had not the spirit to resist." (TOS.3.2)
Comment when (being a woman) your arguments are turned down but you want to be assertive.
In the play. *Petruchio wants to leave immediately after his wedding to Katharina and skip all the celebrations. Katharina insists on staying.*

Resistance, power of r. to noise acquired via repeated trials - Think you a little din can daunt mine ears?
"Think you a little din can daunt mine ears?
Have I not in my time heard lions roar?
Have I not heard the sea puff'd up with winds
Rage like an angry boar chafed with sweat?
Have I not heard great ordnance in the field,
And heaven's artillery thunder in the skies?
Have I not in a pitched battle heard
Loud 'larums, neighing steeds, and trumpets' clang?" (TOS.1.2)
When your ability to tolerate verbal attacks is questioned.
In the play. *Gremio and Grumio warn Petruchio of the intractable character of Katharina. Petruchio lists all his previous stints of sufferance compared to which even the prospect of Katharina is a relief. He says,*
And do you tell me of a woman's tongue,
That gives not half so great a blow to hear
As will a chestnut in a farmer's fire?

Resistance, r. to aggression – To whom do lions cast their gentle looks?
"To whom do lions cast their gentle looks?
Not to the beast that would usurp their den…" (KHVI p3.2)
See also 'Defense, d. of loved ones natural - ... for the poor wren, the most diminutive of birds, will fight, her young ones…'
In the play. *Clifford to Henry VI who appears lenient towards his enemies.*

Resistance, strong and unconquerable - As on a mountain top the cedar shows that keep his leaves in spite of any storm.
"… As on a mountain top the cedar shows
That keep his leaves in spite of any storm." (KHVI p2.5)
Apply the comparison to yourself to indicate your steadfastness.
In the play. *Warwick will wear his burgonet (a tight fitting helmet) in the forthcoming battle of St. Alban's to frighten his enemies, much as a cedar keeps hi leaves in a storm.*

Resources, physical r. strained. - As two spent swimmers, that do cling together and choke their art.
"Doubtful it stood,

As two spent swimmers, that do cling together
And choke their art" (M.1.2)
In the play. *A sergeant narrates the events that led to the victory over the Scottish rebels, one of whom, referred to here, was Mcdonwald.*

Resources, r. or weapons in the wrong hands - You put sharp weapons in a madman's hands.
"You put sharp weapons in a madman's hands." (KHVI p2.3.1)
In the play. *York to himself, the troops he will assemble in Ireland will be sharp weapons against his enemies when he returns to England.*

Respect and contempt - Those that I reverence, these I fear, - the wise...
"Those that I reverence, these I fear, - the wise:
At fools I laugh, not fear them." (CYM.4.1)
Answer to "Are you not afraid of me? Or similar."
In the play. *The fool Cloten meets Guiderius and tries to instill fear in him. Guiderius will kill Cloten in a duel.*

Respect, feigned r. - Love talks with better knowledge, and knowledge with dearer love.
LUCIO (to Duke) I know him and I love him
DUKE Love talks with better knowledge, and knowledge with dearer love. (MFM.3.2)
Cut through criticism disguised as friendship
In the play. *Lucio talks with the Duke (in disguise) and accuses the real Duke of ignorance and superficiality while declaring that he loves him.*

Respect, r. not learned - never learn'd the icy precepts of respect, but follow'd the sugar'd game before thee.
"... and never learn'd
The icy precepts of respect, but follow'd
The sugar'd game before thee." (TOA.4.3)
Characterize an uncouth person. See also 'Vanity, v. and heedlessness in a leader - he tires betimes, who spurs too fast betimes'
In the play. *Timon tells the beggar Apemantus that he Apemantus would have acted like Timon if roles and upbringings had been inverted.*

Response, available for a positive response - ... I am not made of stone but penetrable to your kind entreaties...
"Will you enforce me to a world of cares?
Call them again; I am not made of stone,
But penetrable to your kind entreaties,
Albeit against my conscience and my soul." (KRIII.3.7)
Indicate that you are prepared to yield on a request that you previously denied. See also 'Speech, unable to speak due to tears - My heart is not compact of flint and steel...'
In the play. *Richard pretends to yield to Buckingham's requests that he, Richard, be king.*

Response, explanation for a slow or lacking r. - ... a tardiness in nature which often leaves the history unspoke that it intends to do.
"Is it but this,--a tardiness in nature
Which often leaves the history unspoke
That it intends to do?" (KL.1.1)
In the play. *The king of France is surprised at the anger of Lear towards her daughter Cordelia. Cordelia has refused to compete with her two evil sisters in declaring her affection towards their father.*

Response, uncertain r. to a certain type of request - I cannot tell if to

depart in silence or bitterly to speak in your reproof...
"I cannot tell if to depart in silence
Or bitterly to speak in your reproof
Best fitteth my degree or your condition." (KRIII.3.7)
When you do not want to comment on a statement that refers to you and with which you disagree.
In the play. *Richard pretends not to accept Buckingham's plea that he, Richard, should be king.*

Responsibility, r. limited - ... your fault was not your folly.
"Some sins do bear their privilege on earth,
And so doth yours; your fault was not your folly" (KJ.1.1)
See also 'Perfection, p. even in her shortcomings - She spoke and panted that she made defect perfection.'
In the play. *Philip F. to his mother Lady Faulconbridge. The fault is her adultery with Richard I (Coeur de Lion) \, Philip's father.*

Responsibility, r. shifted, deniability - It is the curse of kings to be attended by slaves that take their humour as a warrant...
"It is the curse of kings to be attended,
By slaves that take their humour as a warrant
To break within the bloody house of life." (KJ.4.2)
Example of deniability at its best. Just like Pointdexter did with Reagan in the 80s on the Nicaragua Contras business. See also note on 'Honor, h. over profit.' *** Entries on 'Deniability'
In the play. *King John learns from Hubert that he (Hubert) killed young Arthur. K. John denies any responsibility.*

Responsibility, taking the fall - Upon mine honour, I will stand betwixt you and danger.
"Do not you fear. Upon mine honour, I will stand betwixt you and danger." (WT.2.2)
Reassure the party involved that you will assume the responsibility.
In the play. *Paulina tells the jailer that she will assume responsibility for removing Hermione's newly born baby girl and taking her to the king Leontes.*

Rest, r. badly needed – ... And spite of spite needs must I rest awhile
"For strokes received, and many blows repaid,
Have robb'd my strong-knit sinews of their strength,
And spite of spite needs must I rest awhile" (KHVI.p3.2.3)
In the play. *At Towton near York, Warwick must have some rest*

Rest, r. disturbed or interrupted - Who doth molest my contemplation?
"Who doth molest my contemplation?" (TA.5.2)
In the play. *Titus A.'s reaction at the knocking on his door by queen Tamora*

Rest, r. needed – ... and nature does require her times of preservation ...
"... and nature does require
Her times of preservation, which perforce
I, her frail son, amongst my brethren mortal,
Must give my tendence to." (KHVIII.3.2)
See also 'Sleep, s. or rest, time to adjourn the meeting - The deep of night is crept upon our talk and nature must obey necessity...' *** 'Health-care, rest as medicine - our foster-nurse of nature is repose, the which he lacks...' *** 'Time, t. for rest - ... times to repair our nature with comforting repose.'

In the play. *Cardinal Wolsey just before being fired converses with the king.*

Rest, r. needed. - I lay me down a little while to breath; …and, spite of spite, needs must I rest a while.
"I lay me down a little while to breath;
For strokes received, and many blows repaid,
Have robbed my strong-knit sinews of their strength.
And, spite of spite, needs must I rest a while." (KHVI p3.2.3)
Justify your need for a little rest. See also 'Health-care, rest as medicine - our foster-nurse of nature is repose, the which he lacks…' *** 'Sleep, s. after a hard day - … the long day's task is done and we must sleep.' *** 'Sleep, soothing properties of s. - … sleep that knits up the ravell'd sleeve of care…'
In the play. *Warwick gets some rest before the next battle of Towton.*

Rest, r. not to be interrupted - …life-preserving rest, to be disturb'd, would mad or man or beast.
"In food, in sport, and life-preserving rest,
To be disturb'd, would mad or man or beast." (COE.5.1)
Why you do not wish to be interrupted or called or disturbed during your siesta.
In the play. *The Lady Abbess diagnoses Ant E's madness. Adriana's jealousy deprived Ant E's of a good digestion and of a zest for life. The consequences here described follow.*

Restaurant, r. with bad food - … thy food is as hath been belched on by infected lungs.
"… thy food is such
As hath been belched on by infected lungs." (PER.4.6)
Stigmatize a bad restaurant and to answer what do you think of this restaurant?'
E.G., 'Their food is such as…. infected lungs'. See also 'Food, questionable f. -

… strange flesh which some did die to look on'.
In the play. *Marina upbraids one of the brothel's guardians by pointing out some of the pitfalls of the establishment. Boult is moved to help Marina escape.*

Restraint, r. caused by excess - As surfeit is the father of much fast…
"As surfeit is the father of much fast,
So every scope by the immoderate use
Turns to restraint." (MFM.1.2)
In the play. *Claudio, arrested by duke-in-charge Angelo for fornication, answers a question by Lucio.*

Results, great r. from small resources - He that of greatest works is finisher, oft does them by the weakest minister.
"He that of greatest works is finisher,
Oft does them by the weakest minister." (AWEW.2.1)
Argument against anyone who implies that you have not enough authority or standing to carry out the plan.
In the play. *Helen wishes to cure the King but he continues to be skeptical. She presses her point. Perhaps he does not trust the power of a simple girl - if so she offers a counter-argument.*

Results, poor personal r. acknowledged – How my achievements mock me!
"How my achievements mock me!" (TC.2.3)
In the play. *Troilus' reaction at the news that, after having won Cressida's love, he must give her up to the Greeks in exchange for a Trojan prisoner.*

Results, positive r. in the end - All's well that ends well, yet; though time seems so adverse, and means unfit.
"All's well that ends well, yet;
Though time seems so adverse, and means unfit." (AWEW.5.1)

The extremely popular first line can be a closing comment to any sequence of events that had a happy outcome. Use the full quotation to inspire confidence during temporarily adverse circumstances. See also 'Outcome, happy o. after a hard trial - ... if it end so meet the bitter past, more welcome is the sweet.'
In the play. *Helena wants to see the King but he is not at court. For a moment Helen is discouraged but then recovers. It turns out that the King is actually on his way to Rousillon, and that is even better for Helen.*

Results, positive results shown and a challenge to him who can do better - He that knows better how to tame a shrew, now let him speak: 'tis charity to show.
"Thus have I politicly begun my reign,
And 'tis my hope to end successfully."
...
This is a way to kill a wife with kindness;
And thus I'll curb her mad and headstrong humour.
He that knows better how to tame a shrew,
Now let him speak: 'tis charity to show." (TOS.4.1)
Use first two lines when you wish to express a little self-congratulation. Use the last two lines to challenge anyone to find a solution better than yours.
In the play. *Petruchio at the end of his first wedded day sums up the results of his efforts to tame the untamable Katharina.*

Results, r. prematurely assessed - ... the event is yet to name the winner.
"Sir, the event
Is yet to name the winner." (CYM.3.5)
Someone is assuming a victory (or a defeat) but the game has not yet ended

In the play. *Cloten assumes a belligerent tone towards Lucius who departs for Rome and Lucius replies that the game is not over yet.*

Retaliation, r. promised - ...we shall your tawny ground with your red blood discolour.
"If we may pass, we will; if we be hinder'd,
We shall your tawny ground with your red blood
Discolour:" (KHV.3.6)
Use 'We shall your tawny...discolour' as a rhetorical threat. See also entries for 'Revenge'.
In the play. *K. Henry's answer to Montjoy, the French emissary.*

Retaliation, threat of r. – and withal thrust these reproachful speeches down his throat...
"...and withal
Thrust these reproachful speeches down his throat..." (TA.2.1)
In the play. *Demetrius to his brother Chiron during an argument as to who of the two should have Lavinia.*

Retirement, desire to r. before becoming useless - ... let me not live, quoth he, after my flame lacks oil...
"... let me not live, quoth he,
After my flame lacks oil, to be the snuff
Of younger spirits, whose apprehensive senses
All but new things disdain; whose judgements are
Mere fathers of their garments; whose constancies
Expire before their fashion."
(AWEW.1.2)
Explain why you have decided to retire. E.G. "I don't want to go on, after my flame lacks oil...disdain."
In the play. *The King speaks of Helen's father was the most celebrated and respected doctor of his time, and remembers some of his sayings.*

813

Retirement, plans for r. - And thence retire me to my Milan, where every third thought shall be my grave.
"And thence retire me to my Milan, where
Every third thought shall be my grave" (TEM.5.1)
Change 'Milan' for your retirement location. Answer to 'What will you be doing after your retirement?
In the play. *Prospero will return to his original seat of dukedom.*

Retirement, r. announced - … and 'tis our fast intent to shake all cares and business from our age…
"…and 'tis our fast intent
To shake all cares and business from our age,
Conferring them on younger strengths, while we
Unburdened crawl towards death." (KL.1.1)
Introduction to a retirement speech.
In the play. *Lear announces his plan to abdicate and to divide his kingdom among daughters Regan, Goneril and Cordelia.*

Retirement, r. planned to be spent in peace – For mine own part, I could be well content to entertain the lag-end of my life with quiet hours.
"For mine own part, I could be well content
To entertain the lag-end of my life
With quiet hours." (KHIVp1.5.1)
Use in a retirement speech, 'I will be well content… with quiet hours'. Answer to 'What will you do when you retire?'
In the play. *The rebel Worcester answers a question from K. Henry.*

Retirement, r. to a secluded life – … to forswear the full stream of the world and to live in a nook merely monastic.

"…to forswear the full stream of the world, and to live in a nook merely monastic" (AYLI.3.2)
In the play. *Rosalind, disguised as a man, banter with her lover Orlando who, by the way, does not recognize the disguise.*

Retirement, retiring and giving up your secrets – … And deeper than did ever plummet sound I'll drown my book.
"**Our revels now are ended. These our actors,**
As I foretold you, were all spirits and
Are melted into air, into thin air:
And, like the baseless fabric of this vision,
The cloud-capp'd towers, the gorgeous palaces,
The solemn temples, the great globe itself,
Ye all which it inherit, shall dissolve
And, like this insubstantial pageant faded,
Leave not a rack behind
….
But this rough magic
I here abjure, and, when I have required
Some heavenly music, which even now I do,
To work mine end upon their senses that
This airy charm is for, I'll break my staff,
Bury it certain fathoms in the earth,
And deeper than did ever plummet sound
I'll drown my book." (TEM.5.1)
Part of your retirement speech. Compare yourself to Prospero the Magician in the Tempest, implying facetiously that with your retirement you will do away with your secret and tricks. Also adaptable to the end of a slide-show presentation. Or use the quote as a metaphor for life's elements of illusion. The first lines can reinforce the idea that what you said or

did before (an event or statement), was just a play.
See also 'Vanished, persons v. - … Into the air; and what seem'd corporal melted as breath into the wind.'
In the play. *Prospero has accomplished all his goals with his acquired skills in magic. Before retiring he gives up his tools and book of magic.* 'Rack' = *'floating vapor', 'cloud'*

Retouching of picture or painting - And yet the painter flatter'd her a little, unless flatter with myself too much.
"And yet the painter flatter'd her a little,
Unless I flatter with myself too much." (TGV.4.4)
In the play. *Julia comments on a picture of Silvia who has captured Proteus' fancy.*

Retreat? Never again - … Charge! upon our foes but never once again turn back and fly.
"… to London will we march amain;
And once bestride our foaming steeds,
And once again cry - Charge! upon our foes,
But never once again turn back and fly." (KHVI p3.2.1)
Exhortation to fight against the unfavorable tide of events. Use the third and fourth line.
In the play. *Warwick has decided to fight and revenge the death of Richard (York)*

Retreat? Never again - Never may he live to see a sunshine day that cries 'Retire', if Warwick bid him stay.
"Never may he live to see a sunshine day,
That cries - Retire, if Warwick bid him stay." (KHVI p3.2.1)
Exhortation to fight against the unfavorable tide of events. Change 'Warwick' with your own name.

In the play. *Richard (Gloucester) following up on Warwick's determination to fight.*

Retribution, divine r. - The gods are just, and of our pleasant vices make instruments to plague us.
"The gods are just, and of our pleasant vices.
Make instruments to plague us" (KL.5.3)
Support the idea that sin, however appealing, will be punished in the end (or at least this is the theory).
In the play. *Edgar, incognito, has challenged the traitorous Edmund to a duel and won, He then reveals his identity to the vanquished Edmund. The reference in the lines is to Gloucester's adulterous affair that ended in costing him his sight (via the treachery of his own son Edmund).*

Retribution, friends and enemies handled - … All friends shall taste the wages of their virtue.
"…All friends shall taste
The wages of their virtue, and all foes
The cup of their deservings." (KL.5.3)
Forceful ending to a speech announcing an ambitious program – omit the reference to 'foes' if not applicable.
In the play. *Albany at the end of a battle during which Lear and Cordelia were taken. Cordelia is killed by the evil Edmund. King Lear goes mad and die. The evil daughters Regan and Goneril die of poison and self-inflicted wounds, respectively.*

Retribution, time as an administrator of justice - … and thus the whirligig of time brings in his revenges.
"… and thus the whirligig of time brings in his revenges" (TN.5.1)
In the play. T*he Clown to Olivia referring to the prank and punishment inflicted to the conceited Malvolio. 'Whirligig' means 'rotation', literally the rotation that clowns perform in their gigs.*

815

Retribution, wish pronounced in jest has become true - ... And given in earnest what I begg'd in jest.
"That high All-Seer that I dallied with
Hath turn'd my feigned prayer on my head
And given in earnest what I begg'd in jest." (KRIII.5.1)
See also 'Ignorance, i. of what is really good for us - We, ignorant of ourselves beg often our own harms, which the wise powers deny us for our good…'
In the play. *Buckingham had prayed to be punished if he conspired against King Edward's relatives. He did and now is punished with death by King Richard*.

Return, r. from a foreign assignment - (I) sighed my English breath in foreign clouds, eating the bitter bread of banishment.
" … Till you did make him misinterpret me,
Have stoop'd my neck under your injuries,
Sighed my English breath in foreign clouds,
Eating the bitter bread of banishment. " (KRII.3.1)
You have returned after spending 2 years in a remote place to manage a subsidiary and you are asked an opinion about your assignment. Envy prevents many people from sharing in your contentment. It is always prudent to downplay the idea that you may have actually enjoyed an opportunity of any kind, in this case, a foreign assignment. Change 'English' to your actual nationality.
In the play. *Bolingbroke to the captured enemies Bushy and Green who apparently plotted against him with Bolingbroke.*

Return, r. home or to base – .. as the bark that hath discharged his fraught, return with precious lading to the bay...
"... as the bark that hath discharged his fraught,
Return with precious lading to the bay
From whence at first she weighed her anchorage." (TA.1.1)
Welcome home the conductor of a successful expedition. E.G.
'Welcome…as the bark… anchorage'.
In the play. *Titus returns to Rome after a victory over the Goths and compares himself to a boat (bark) returning to port laden with goods.*

Return, r. home or homebase - ... to England then: where ne'er from France arrived more happy men.
"…to England then:
Where ne'er from France arrived more happy men" (KHV.4.8)
Change 'England' and 'France' as appropriate.
In the play. *King Henry to his men after victory at Agincourt.*

Return? Not a chance - No, rather I abjure all roofs, and choose to wage against the enmity o' the air…
"Return to her, and fifty men dismiss'd?
No, rather I abjure all roofs, and choose
To wage against the enmity o' the air;
To be a comrade with the wolf and owl,--
Necessity's sharp pinch!" (KL.2.4)
Answer to 'Will you come back?' when you have strong reasons not to. See also 'Rejection, r. in all circumstances - Had I been seized by a hungry lion, I would have been a breakfast to the beast...'
In the play. *Regan, one of the evil sisters suggests that Lear return to stay with Goneril, the other evil sister, but Lear makes it clear that he won't.*

Revelation, startling r. – I could a tale unfold whose lightest word would harrow up thy soul, freeze thy young blood…
"… But that I am forbid
To tell the secrets of my prison-house
I could a tale unfold whose lightest word
Would harrow up thy soul, freeze thy young blood,
Make thy two eyes, like stars, start from their spheres,
Thy knotted and combined locks to part
And each particular hair to stand on end,
Like quills upon the fretful porcupine" (H.1.4)
Introduction to a presentation on the workings of the CIA or any fraudulent corporation.
In the play. *The Ghost begins the narration of the murder to Hamlet.*

Revenge, crime eliciting the vengeance of heaven – … Will cry for vengeance at the gates of heaven.
"Whose maiden blood, thus rigorously effused,
Will cry for vengeance at the gates of heaven." (KHVI.p1.5.4)
In the play. *Joan of Arc upbraids the scornful English who captured her in battle.*

Revenge, culprit should have thousands of lives - O, that the slave had forty thousand lives! One is too poor, too weak for my revenge.
"O, that the slave had forty thousand lives!
One is too poor, too weak for my revenge." (OTH.3.3)
In the play. *Othello buys the story that Cassio has an adulterous relationship with Desdemona.*

Revenge, determination to seek r. - … I'll never pause again, never stand still, till either death hath closed these eyes of mine or fortune given me measure of revenge.
"Here on my knee I vow to God above,
I'll never pause again, never stand still,
Till either death hath closed these eyes of mine,
Or fortune given me measure of revenge!" (KHVI p3.2.3)
Express your determination to fight. See also entries for 'Determination'.
In the play. *Warwick before the battle of Towton.*

Revenge, determination to seek r. - From this time forth my thoughts be bloody, or be nothing worth!
"O, from this time forth,
My thoughts be bloody, or be nothing worth!" (H.4.4)
In the play. *Hamlet is totally committed to seek revenge.*

Revenge, equal treatment when roles are reversed - The villany you teach me, I will execute…
"The villany you teach me, I will execute, and it shall go hard but I will better the instruction." (MOV.3.1)
In the play. *Shylock will apply the same standards of revenge to Antonio, a Christian, as presumably the Christians would apply to Jews, only harder.*

Revenge, exhortation to r. - O, let no words, but deeds, revenge this treason!
"O, let no words, but deeds, revenge this treason!" (KHVI.p1.3.2)
In the play. *Bedford to the English after the French have entered Rouen via a good ruse.*

Revenge, God's vengeance predicted – … my master, God omnipotent is mustering in his clouds on our behalf armies of pestilence.

"Yet know, my master, God omnipotent,
Is mustering in his clouds on our behalf
Armies of pestilence" (KRII.3.3)
In the play. *King Richard to the rebel Northumberland.*

Revenge, hope of r. - Hope of revenge shall hide our inward woe.
"Hope of revenge shall hide our inward woe." (TC.5.11)
Give vent to your feelings of revenge.
In the play. *The loss of Hector has devastated the Trojans and Troilus vows revenge.*

Revenge, justice from heaven - We will solicit heaven and move the gods to send down Justice for to wreak our wrongs.
"… sith there's no justice in earth nor hell,
We will solicit heaven and move the gods
To send down Justice for to wreak our wrongs." (TA.4.3)
In the play. *Titus A. plans his revenge on Tamora and her sons.*

Revenge, measure for measure – … like doth quit like and Measure still for Measure.
"Haste still pays haste, and leisure answer leisure;
Like doth quit like, and Measure still for Measure." (MFM.5.1)
Justify your action in retaliation of a wrong previously inflicted on you.
In the play. *The Duke declares that Angelo will die in reparation for the death of Claudio, but it is still a plot to see how the various protagonists will react.*

Revenge, measure for measure - Measure for measure must be answered.
"Measure for measure must be answered." (KHVI p3.2.6)

Explain the reason for the countermeasures.
In the play. *Edward's forces will pull down the displayed head of Richard Plantagenet and substitute it with the head of Clifford, who was slain in battle by Richard of Gloucester.*

Revenge, no limits to r. - Revenge should have no bounds.
"Revenge should have no bounds." (H.4.7)
In the play. *King Claudius prompts Laertes to avenge the death of Polonius (Laertes' father) at the hand of Hamlet.*

Revenge, no limits to the desire for r. - Had all his hairs been lives, my great revenge had stomach for them all.
"Had all his hairs been lives, my great revenge
Had stomach for them all" (OTH.5.2)
Use the present tense (e.g. 'If all his hair were lives…has stomach for them all').
In the play. *Othello, thinking that Desdemona is crying for the supposedly slain Cassio is bent on turning his revenge on her.*

Revenge, only satisfaction in r. – … I shall never come to bliss till all these mischiefs be return'd again…
"…I shall never come to bliss
Till all these mischiefs be return'd again
Even in their throats that have committed them" (TA.3.1)
In the play. *Titus reacts to the murder of his sons.*

Revenge, plea to refrain from r. – Stay thy revengeful hand; thou hast no cause to fear
"Stay thy revengeful hand; thou hast no cause to fear" (KRII.5.3)
In the play. *Aumerle to Bolingbroke, now King Henry IV. Aumerle's father, the Duke of York warns the King that Aumerle is a traitor.*

Revenge, prepared to die to seek r. - ... I'll empty all these veins and shed my dear blood drop by drop in the dust...
"...I'll empty all these veins,
And shed my dear blood drop by drop in the dust..." (KHIVp1.1.3)
In the play. *Angry Hotspur will defend the name of Mortimer, berated by King Henry*

Revenge, r. advocated – Be comforted: let's make us medicines of our great revenge, to cure this deadly grief.
"Be comforted:
Let's make us medicines of our great revenge,
To cure this deadly grief." (M.4.3)
In the play. *Malcolm to Ross and Macduff after learning that Macbeth has slain Macduff's wide and child*

Revenge, r. against a killer – Every man's conscience is a thousand swords...
"Every man's conscience is a thousand swords,
To fight against that bloody homicide." (KRIII.5.2)
In the play. *Oxford, in the field with Richmond, refers to the homicidal Richard III.*

Revenge, r. and justice – ... blood, like sacrificing Abel's, cries even from the tongueless caverns of the earth to me for justice and rough chastisement.
"Which blood, like sacrificing Abel's, cries,
Even from the tongueless caverns of the earth,
To me for justice and rough chastisement" (KRII.1.1)
In the play. *Bolingbroke refers to the death of the duke of Gloucester for which Norfolk is accused.*

Revenge, r. brewing - Vengeance is in my heart, death in my hand, blood and revenge are hammering in my head.
"Vengeance is in my heart, death in my hand,
Blood and revenge are hammering in my head." (TA.2.2)
In the play. *Aaron plans the murder of Bassianus and the rape and mutilation of Lavinia.*

Revenge, r. call for r. - ... shall we bite our tongues, and in dumb shows pass the remainder of our hateful days?
"... shall we bite our tongues, and in dumb shows
Pass the remainder of our hateful days?" (TA.3.1)
Incite to action after a setback.
In the play. *Titus asks a rhetorical question as to what to do next after the disfiguring and mutilation of Lavinia and other murders and mishaps. He will shortly plan a revenge.*

Revenge, r. on a fat man - ... for revenged I will be, as sure as his guts are made of puddings.
"...for revenged I will be, as sure as his guts are made of puddings" (MWW.2.1)
In the play. *Mrs. Page plans a revenge on Falstaff.*

Revenge, r. or tricks against lechers OK - Against such lewdsters and their lechery those that betray them do no treachery.
"Against such lewdsters and their lechery,
Those that betray them do no treachery." (MWW.5.3)
Justify a potentially questionable course of action to overcome the competition, metaphorically speaking.
In the play. *The lewdster referred to by Mistress Page is Falstaff who, once more, will be tricked and eventually ridiculed.*

Revenge, r. planned - My thoughts are ripe in mischief...
"My thoughts are ripe in mischief:
I'll sacrifice the lamb that I do love,
To spite a raven's heart within a dove." (TN.5.1)
Use the first line to indicate you are meditating revenge. Or the second and third line as an example of sacrificing an advantage for unprofitable returns.
In the play. *The duke is mad at Olivia, who has rejected him and is ready to do harm to Viola/Cesario who, he thinks, is responsible for Olivia's rejection.*

Revenge, r. promised - And they shall feel the vengeance of my wrath.
"And they shall feel the vengeance of my wrath" (KHVI.p3.4.1)
In the play. *Newly appointed King Edward IV answers his wife's concern about their enemies.*

Revenge, r. promised – I will have such revenges on you both... they shall be the terrors of the earth.
"I will have such revenges on you both,
That all the world shall -- I will do such things, --
What they are, yet I know not: but they shall be
The terrors of the earth." (K.L.2.4)
In the play. *King Lear to his ungrateful and wicked daughters Regan and Goneril.*

Revenge, r. promised on everyone - Clarence, thy turn is next, and then the rest, counting myself but bad till I be best.
"Clarence, thy turn is next, and then the rest,
Counting myself but bad till I be best." (KHVI.p3.5.4)
Address those who have played a prank on you.
In the play. *Gloucester (the soon to be Richard III), having just killed Henry VI, now plans the death of his own brother Clarence, who is an obstacle in the path to acquire the throne.*

Revenge, r. prompted by grief - Be this the whetstone of your sword: let grief convert to anger...
"Be this the whetstone of your sword: let grief
Convert to anger; blunt not the heart, enrage it." (M.4.3)
In the play. *Malcolm prompts Macduff to convert the pain for the slaughter of his wife and children (by Macbeth) into a thirst for revenge and retribution.*

Revenge, r. reminded - How all occasions do inform against me, and spur my dull revenge!
"How all occasions do inform against me,
And spur my dull revenge!" (H.4.4)
In the play. *Miscellaneous observation of events prompts Hamlet to execute his revenge.*

Revenge, r. threatened - I'll be revenged on the whole pack of you.
"I'll be revenged on the whole pack of you." (TN.5.1)
Use as a reaction to a prank or to a satire of which you are the object.
In the play. *Malvolio, victim of the prank organized by Maria and friends, promises revenge. However, Olivia and the Duke will try to soothe him. Olivia has already married Sebastian and the Duke will marry Viola. A happy ending.*

Revenge, raven as an emblem of r. - The croaking raven doth bellow for revenge.
"The croaking raven doth bellow for revenge." (H.3.2)
In the play. *Hamlet acts a commentator for Ophelia in the play-within-a-play ha has produced.*

**Revenge, request to r. murder -
Revenge this foul and most unnatural murder.**
GHOST "Revenge this foul and most unnatural murder"
HAMLET "Murder!"
GHOST "Murder most foul, as in the best it is;
But this most foul, strange and unnatural" (H.1.5)
Use as is, figuratively, or to express complete disgust, "This is most foul, strange and unnatural."
In the play. *The ghost makes his case with Hamlet.*

Revenge, sorrow preventing r. - I have not another tear to shed... then which way shall I find Revenge's cave?
"I have not another tear to shed:
Besides, this sorrow is an enemy,
And would usurp upon my watery eyes,
And make them blind with tributary tears:
Then which way shall I find Revenge's cave?" (TA.3.1)
In the play. *Titus A. is determined to avenge the death of his sons and the mutilation of his daughter Lavinia. He converts his sorrow into an irrepressible desire for revenge.*

Revenge, terrible r. threatened - Thou hadst been better have been born a dog than answer my waked wrath!
"Thou hadst been better have been born a dog
Than answer my waked wrath!" (OTH.3.3)
In the play. *Othello, agitated but still disbelieving that Desdemona can be unfaithful, warns Iago to provide proof.*

Revenge, total masochism until r. accomplished - ... Never to taste the pleasures of the world... till I have set a glory to this hand by giving it the worship of revenge.

The incense of a vow, a holy vow,
Never to taste the pleasures of the world,
Never to be infected with delight,
Nor conversant with ease and idleness,
Till I have set a glory to this hand,
By giving it the worship of revenge.
(KJ.4.3)
Quote the masochistic conditions as a premise for your vow, that may not be necessarily revenge. Or adapt the last two lines if revenge is what you have in mind, 'I will set a glory to this hand by... revenge'.
In the play. *Salisbury vows revenge after the assassination of young Prince Arthur by King John*

Revenge, vowing r. for unfair termination - My ashes, as the phoenix, may bring forth a bird that will revenge upon you all.
"My ashes, as the phoenix, may bring forth
A bird that will revenge upon you all:
And in that hope I throw mine eyes to heaven,
Scorning whate'er you can afflict me with" (KHVI.p3.1.4)
In the play. *York, defeated by the Lancastrians at Sandal Castle utters words of defiance before being killed.*

Revolution, call for violent action when peaceful demonstrations ineffective - ... those cold ways that seem like prudent helps, are very poisonous where the disease is violent.
"Sir, those cold ways,
That seem like prudent helps, are very poisonous
Where the disease is violent." (COR.3.1)
Support forceful or violent action. See also entries for 'Remedies, extreme r. required - ... Diseases desperate grown by

desperate appliances are relieved or not at all.'
In the play. *Menenius counsels moderation in order to achieve the desired result. Brutus disagrees given the critical situation.*

Revolution, discontent leading to r. - ... move the murmuring lips of discontent to break into this dangerous argument.
PEMBROKE. (We) heartily request The enfranchisement of Arthur; whose restraint Doth move the murmuring lips of discontent To break into this dangerous argument." (KJ.4.2)
Warn against the establishment of a new tax or unpopular change or measure, e.g. 'this tax doth move the murmuring…argument."
In the play. *Young Arthur is King John's prisoner and Pembroke suggests and requests that Arthur be freed to prevent a rebellion.*

Revolution, how a revolution gets started - ... kiss the lips of unacquainted change and pick strong matter of revolt and wrath...
"… and then the hearts Of all his people shall revolt from him, And kiss the lips of unacquainted change, And pick strong matter of revolt and wrath Out of the bloody fingers' end of John." (KJ.3.4)
Show the expected effects of an unjust or unpopular measure.
In the play. *Pandulph, the Pope's legate foresees a revolt among King John's subjects.*

Revolution, military strategy reversed - ... we in order when we are most out of order.
DICK They are all in order and march toward us.
CADE But then are we in order when we are most out of order. Come, march forward. (KHVI.p1.4.2)
In the play. *Those who march in order are the government forces of Stafford and Humphrey who will however, be defeated by the rebels led by John Cade.*

Revolution, r. ignited - Mischief, thou art afoot, take thou what course thou wilt.
"Mischief, thou art afoot, Take thou what course thou wilt!" (JC.3.3)
Indicate that you wash your hand of what happens next because you were not responsible for the decision. See also 'Start line, at the start line - the game's afoot…follow your spirit…' *** 'Times, hard t. ahead - the storm is up and all is on the hazard.'
In the play. *Antony has stirred the crowd against Brutus and Cassius after they murdered Caesar.*

Revolutions, why r. fail – ... and delight to live in slavery to the nobility.
"I thought ye would never have given out these arms till you had recovered your ancient freedom: but you are all recreants and dastards, and delight to live in slavery to the nobility" (KHVI.p2.4.8)
In the play. *The rabble roused by Cade listens to the message of Clifford, who quenches their revolutionary zeal by promising opportunity for pillage in French (as well as an imaginary invasion of London by the French.*

Reward, great r. promised – I'll set thee in a shower of gold, and hail rich pearls upon thee.
"I'll set thee in a shower of gold, and hail Rich pearls upon thee" (AC.2.5)
In the play. *A messenger from Rome struggles to find words to explain that in Rome Antony*

married Octavia, Caesar Octavian's sister. The messenger started with saying that Antony is well and that prompted Cleopatra to promise a reward.

Reward, promise of r. improving performance ... And if we thrive, promise them such rewards as victors wear at the Olympian games...
"And if we thrive, promise them such rewards
As victors wear at the Olympian games:
This may plant courage in their quailing breasts;
For yet is hope of life and victory."
(KHVI p3.2.3)
Justify a commission scheme for salesmen.
In the play. *George duke of Clarence to Warwick and colleagues before the battle of Towton against the forces of Henry VI.*

Reward, r. given only when merited - ... our head shall go bare till merit crown it.
"... our head shall go bare till merit crown it" (TC.3.2)
In the play. *Troilus will prove (and gain merit) with his faithfulness. It's all another story with Cressida.*

Reward, r. promised for success - ... If thou proceed as high as word, my deed shall match thy meed.
"... If thou proceed
As high as word, my deed shall match thy meed." (AWEW.2.1)
When you promise a reward if the project is successful.
In the play. *The King accepts to be cured by Helen. If the cure is successful the King will marry her to a nobleman of her choice, that is, the 'deed' of the king that matches her 'deed' of healing.*

Rhetoric, all smoke, no substance - Sweet smoke of rhetoric.

"Sweet smoke of rhetoric." (LLL.3.1)
After a pompous debater makes meaningless and unproven statements.
In the play. *Moth pulls the leg of verbose Armado, who gives this answer to a line from Moth.*

Rhetoric, imperialist r. - ... the signs of war advance, no king of England, if not king of France.
"...the signs of war advance:
No king of England, if not king of France" (HV.2.2)
In the play. *King Henry V to the troops before embarking for the invasion of France.*

Rhyme and Reason - ... in despite of the teeth of all rhyme and reason, that they were fairies.
"...in despite of the teeth of all rhyme and reason, that they were fairies" (MWW.5.5)
In the play. *Falstaff suspected that the fairies who 'attacked' him at Windsor Park were not really fairies, but he was guilty and for a moment he thought they were.*

Ridicule, being made an object of r. – A fixed figure for the time of scorn to point his slow unmoving finger at.
"A fixed figure for the time of scorn
To point his slow unmoving finger at!" (OTH.4.2)
In the play. *Othello opens up with Desdemona and considers himself an object of scorn.*

Ridicule, being made an object of r. - I see you all are bent to set against me for your merriment...
"... O hell! I see you all are bent
To set against me for your merriment:
If you we re civil and knew courtesy,
You would not do me thus much injury" (MND.3.2)
In the play. *Helena upbraids Lysander, Demetrius for poking (unwittingly) fun at her.*

Ridicule, recognizing that one is made object of r. - I do begin to perceive that I am made an ass…
FALSTAFF. I do begin to perceive that I am made an ass.
MISTER FORD. Ay, and an ox too; both the proofs are extant."
(MWW.5.5)
Gracefully admit defeat or a shortcoming. If you use the second line by Mrs. Ford, you will have to explain the dialog in the play.
In the play. *Falstaff recognizes his predicament. In a caper organized by Mrs. Ford to unmask him, he had been.*

Rise, an early rise to launch into an adventure - The day shall not be up so soon as I to try the fair adventure of tomorrow.
"The day shall not be up so soon as I,
To try the fair adventure of tomorrow." (KJ.5.5)
Motivate the crew to get up early next day.
In the play. *Lewis is ready for an early start for the second day of the battle near Bury St. Edmond's.*

Risk, desperate r. but confidence in its success – thou this to hazard, needs must intimate Skill infinite, or monstrous desperate…
"Thou this to hazard, needs must intimate
Skill infinite, or monstrous desperate,
Sweet practiser, thy physic I will try."
(AWEW.2.1)
State the highly risky nature of the idea but your willingness to go along with it. Explain the context before delivering the quote. Or extract 'This needs must intimate skill infinite, or monstrous desperate.' As a comment to the hazardous nature of the enterprise.
In the play. *Helena has staked her life against her power to cure the King. That is, either the cure is effective or she is prepared to die. The*

King accepts to be cured still somewhat questioning what prompts her to what would generally appear as a desperate act.

Risk, question about r. - … to set so rich a main on the nice hazard of one doubtful hour?
"(were it good) to set so rich a main
On the nice hazard of one doubtful hour?" (KHIVp1.4.1)
In the play. *Hotspur' reaction at the news that his father's forces will not be able to join him in the forthcoming battle with the king's forces.*

Risk, risking all on one speculation - to set so rich a main on the nice hazard of one doubtful hour.
"... to set so rich a main
On the nice hazard of one doubtful hour?" (HIV.p1.4.1)
Ask rhetorically if it is worth to risk everything based on an unproven assumption.
In the play. *Hotspur's father and his forces cannot take part in the forthcoming battle, but Hotspur is for continuing with the plan and give battle to the forces of Henry IV.*

Risks, not afraid to take r. - I do not set my life in a pin's fee.
"I do not set my life in a pin's fee"
(H.1.4)
See also 'Character, not afraid of taking chances - I have set my life upon a cast and I will stand the hazard of the die.'
In the play. *Hamlet's answer to Horatio who counsels not to approach the Ghost.*

Risks, r. inherent to transportation or trade at large – … but ships are but boards, sailors but men.
"… but ships are but boards, sailors but men: there be land-rats and water-rats, water-thieves and land-thieves…" (MOV.1.3)
Say it with nonchalance when someone seems cock-sure that everything will be OK even if there is risk.

In the play. *Shylock questions the security of Antonio's bond as ships can be shipwrecked and sailors are men, meaning that anything can happen.*

Roof decorations - The roof o' the chamber with golden cherubins is fretted.
"The roof o' the chamber
With golden cherubins is fretted"
(CYM.2.4)
Adapt for a compliment to a decorated ceiling, as 'fretted with golden fire'. See 'World, a congregation of vapors – it goes so heavily with my disposition…'
In the play. *Now in Rome the evil Jachimo tells Leonatus the details of his wife Imogen's room as evidence that he became her lover.*

Rudeness, apologies for r. – the thorny point of bare distress hath taken from me, the show of smooth civility…
"… the thorny point of bare distress hath taken from me, the show of smooth civility; yet am I inland bred,
And know some nurture." (AYL.1.2.7)
In the play. *Orlando apologized for the rudeness in demanding food. He has stumbled on the Duke and his company in the forest of Arden.*

Rudeness, r. explained - This rudeness is a sauce to his good wit…
"This rudeness is a sauce to his good wit,
Which gives men stomach to digest his words
With better appetite." (JC.1.2)
With a bit of ironic self-flattery excuse your previous potentially objectionable remarks, e.g. 'This rudeness is a sauce to my good wit… appetite.'
In the play. *Cassius rationalizes for Brutus' benefit Casca's apparent rudeness. See 'Dinner invitation, answer to - Ay, if I be alive and your mind hold and your dinner worth the eating.'*

Rudeness, r. undeserved - What have I done, that thou darest wag thy tongue in noise so rude against me?
QUEEN. What have I done, that thou darest wag thy tongue
In noise so rude against me?
HAMLET. Such an act
That blurs the grace and blush of modesty,
Calls virtue hypocrite, takes off the rose
From the fair forehead of an innocent love
And sets a blister there, makes marriage-vows
As false as dicers' oaths: O, such a deed
As from the body of contraction plucks
The very soul, and sweet religion makes
A rhapsody of words. (H.3.4)
Question the rudeness of the address.
In the play. *Hamlet in the dramatic confrontation with his mother the Queen, during which he will slain the poor Polonius who was listening from behind a curtain.*

Rule, authoritarian r. – … from them take their liberties; make them of no more voice than dogs…
"…a consul that will from them take
Their liberties; make them of no more voice
Than dogs that are as often beat for barking
As therefore kept to do so." (COR.2.3)
In the play. *The tribune Brutus instructs another tribune to convey to the electorate what kind of consul Coriolanus would make.*

Rule, authoritarian rule - … my mouth shall be the parliament of England
"Away, burn all the records of the realm: my mouth shall be the parliament of England." (KHVI.p2.4.7)

Use as a term of reference for presidents or senators who wish to change the Constitution.
In the play. *Rebel John Cade's idea of government.*

Rumor, effect of r. on fear - Rumour doth double, like the voice and echo, the numbers of the fear'd.
"Rumour doth double, like the voice and echo,
The numbers of the fear'd"
(KHIV.p2.3.1)
In the play. *Warwick reports to King Henry that the number of the rebels has been inflated by rumor.*

Rumor, r. defined and its effect on the masses - rumor is a pipe blown by surmises, jealousies, conjectures.
"Rumour is a pipe
Blown by surmises, jealousies, conjectures
And of so easy and so plain a stop
That the blunt monster with uncounted heads,
The still-discordant wavering multitude,
Can play upon it."
(KHIV.p2.introduction)
Elaborate on the dynamics and the effects of rumor mongering.
In the play. *Rumor introduces himself. The false rumor referred to is that Hotspur is alive and the battle of Shrewsbury won by the rebels*

Rumor, r. fabricating slander – Upon my tongue continual slanders ride, the which in every language I pronounce...
"Upon my tongue continual slanders ride,
The which in every language I pronounce,
Stuffing the ears of man with false reports." (KHIV.p2.introduction)
A good retort to any sentence of the type 'I have heard that you.... etc." and you

wish to deny whatever the rumor (or the statement) about you may be. Or to solicit accurate information, e.g. 'Don't bring me smooth comforts false, worse than true wrongs.' See also 'Defence, d. from slander – it's slander, whose edge is sharper than the sword.'
In the play. *Rumor introduces himself. The false rumor referred to is that Hotspur is alive and that the battle of Shrewsbury has been won by the rebels. Instead, Hotspur has been killed by the Prince of Wales and the king's forces are in pursuit of the rebels.*

Rumor, r. increases fear - Rumor doth double, like the voice and echo the numbers of the fear'd.
"It cannot be, my lord;
Rumor doth double, like the voice and echo,
The numbers of the fear'd."
(KHIVp2.3.1)
Reduce the concern or fear of action.
In the play. *Warwick reassures King Henry IV that the rebel Northumberland's forces are much weaker than rumor reports.*

Rumor, r. that must be stopped - ... stop the rumor, and allay those tongues that durst disperse it.
"...stop the rumor, and allay those tongues
That durst disperse it" (KHVIII.2.1)
In the play. *Two citizens discuss the rumor that King Henry VIII will separate from his wife Catherine. At first the King ordered the lord mayor to stop the rumor.*

Rumor, so far it is only r. - I mean the whispered ones, for they are yet but ear-kissing arguments.
"You have heard of the news abroad;
I mean the whispered ones, for they are yet but
ear-kissing arguments?" (KL.2.1)
Relate news as not yet certain and call it 'ear-kissing argument'.

In the play. *Curan to Edmund about the rumored disagreement between the Dukes of Albany and Cornwall.*

Rumor, wealth – It is noised he hath a mass of treasure.
"It is noised he hath a mass of treasure." (TOA.4.3)
In the play. *Bandits approach Timon in his cave supposing him to be rich.*

Run, time to r. - like a brace of greyhounds ... are at our backs.
"Edward and Richard, like a brace of greyhounds
Having the fearful flying hare in sight,
With fiery eyes sparkling for very wrath,
And bloody steel grasped in their ireful hands,
Are at our backs; and therefore hence amain." (KHVI p3.2.5)
The competition (or equivalent adversarial party) is catching up. "…like a brace of greyhounds…are at our backs."
In the play. *The battle at Towton turns against the forces of Henry VI and Margaret and Margaret advises Henry VI to run.*

Running as fast as you can - I drink the air before me, and return or ere your pulse twice beat.
"I drink the air before me, and return
Or ere your pulse twice beat." (TEM.5.1)
Change 'or ere' to 'before' for better comprehension.
In the play. *Ariel responds to one of the last commands by Prospero.*

Running as fast as you can – ... I have speeded here with the extremest inch of possibility.
"Do you think me a swallow, an arrow or a bullet? Have I, in my poor and old motion, the expedition of thought? I have speeded here with the extremest inch of possibility." (KHIVp2.4.3)
Explain that you only can run as fast as you can. See also entries for 'Speed, amazing s.'
In the play. *In Gaultree Forest in Yorkshire, Falstaff responds to P. Henry's reprimand that he, Falstaff, was slow.*

Sadness, imprisoned within oneself - Now my soul's palace is become a prison.
"Now my soul's palace is become a prison" (KHVI.p3.2.1)
In the play. *A messenger announces to Edward, the death of York in battle, to Edward's chagrin.*

Sadness, license to cry - Those that can pity, here may, if they think it well, let fall a tear; the subject will deserve it.
"Those that can pity, here
May, if they think it well, let fall a tear;
The subject will deserve it." (KHVIII, prologue)
Mildly satirical introduction to the description of an unpleasant episode. See also 'Presentation. Epilogues to p. - 'Tis ten to one this play can never please all that are here…'

Sadness, s. and misery - ... my heart, all mad with misery, beats in this hollow prison of my flesh.
"… my heart, all mad with misery,
Beats in this hollow prison of my flesh" (TA.3.2)
When you feel particularly sad or depressed. See also 'Depression, general depression leading to total pessimism.'
In the play. *Titus Andronicus is beyond himself at the enormity of the crime that was committed on his daughter Lavinia.*

Sadness, s. arising from business cares – ... had I such venture forth,

the better part of my affections would be with my hopes abroad…
"…had I such venture forth,
The better part of my affections would
Be with my hopes abroad. I should be still
Plucking the grass, to know where sits the wind,
Peering in maps for ports and piers and roads;
And every object that might make me fear
Misfortune to my ventures, out of doubt
Would make me sad." (MOV.1.1)
In the play. *Salanio attempts a logical explanation for Antonio's sadness.*

Sadness, s. detected - …even in the glasses of thine eyes I see thy grieved heart.
"…even in the glasses of thine eyes
I see thy grieved heart." (KRII.1.3)
Alternate to 'I see that you are sad'.
In the play. *Richard to Gaunt whose son Bolingbroke has been banished for 4 years.*

Sadness, s. not the natural condition for love - Venus smiles not in a house of tears,
"Venus smiles not in a house of tears." (RJ.4.1)
When you try to persuade to stop crying.
In the play. *Paris tells Friar Laurence that Juliet was always crying so he could not talk to her about marriage. He thinks that she cries because of Tybalt's death at the hands of Romeo, but she cries because she is already married to Rome and does not know how to get rid of Paris.*

Sadness, s. prompting tears - … my heart is drown'd with grief whose flood begins to flow within mine eyes.
"… my heart is drown'd with grief,
Whose flood begins to flow within mine eyes" (KHVI p2.3.1)
In the play. *The good Duke Humphrey of Gloucester has been killed by his enemies at Bury St. Edmonds and King Henry VI is distraught at an event that he was unable to stop.*

Sadness, sad and not knowing why - In sooth, I know not why I am so sad, it wearies me…
"In sooth, I know not why I am so sad:
It wearies me; you say it wearies you;
But how I caught it, found it, or came by it,
What stuff 'tis made of, whereof it is born,
I am to learn" (MOV.1.1)
In the play. *Meeting Salarino in Venice, Antonio cannot explain the reasons of his sadness*

Sadness, s. reinforced by inducing s. in others – Griefs of mine own lie heavy in my breast…
"Griefs of mine own lie heavy in my breast,
Which thou wilt propagate, to have it prest
With more of thine…" (RJ.1.1)
In the play. *Romeo rejects the sympathy of Benvolio for Romeo's love pains.*

Safety, escape for s. - … let us not be dainty of leave-taking, but shift away: there's warrant in that theft which steals itself, when there's no mercy left.
"This murderous shaft that's shot
Hath not yet lighted, and our safest way
Is to avoid the aim. Therefore, to horse;
And let us not be dainty of leave-taking,
But shift away: there's warrant in that theft
Which steals itself, when there's no mercy left." (M.2.2)
Alternative to 'Let's get out fop here'.

In the play. *Malcolm to Donalbain. King Duncan has been killed - they suspect that Macbeth did it and decide to leave the premises quickly.*

Safety, questionable s. - ... such safety finds the trembling lamb environed with wolves.
"… such safety finds
The trembling lamb environed with wolves." (KHVI p3.1.1)
In the play. *Q. Margaret is right. Appointing York as protector while King Henry VI remains king is not a safe measure. York aims at the crown.*

Safety, s. and beer preferable to fame – I would give all my fame for a pot of ale and safety.
"…I would give all my fame for a pot of ale and safety." (HV.3.2)
Use as a satire towards those who are afraid of change.
In the play. *Hearing Pistol bragging about acquiring fame in battle, the boy offers his counter point of view.*

Safety, s. first before questioning danger - …'tis safer to avoid what's grown than question how 'tis born.
"I am sure 'tis safer to
Avoid what's grown than question how 'tis born." (WT.1.2)
Cut down useless delays or discussion when safety measures are immediately required.
In the play. *Camillo warns Polixenes to leave quickly before Leontes has a chance to kill him. Leontes thinks that his wife Hermione has an affair with Polixenes.*

Safety, s. not achieved by task half accomplished - Nought's had, all's spent where our desire is got without content…
"Nought's had, all's spent,
Where our desire is got without content:

'Tis safer to be that which we destroy
Than by destruction dwell in doubtful joy." (M.3.2)
In the play. *Lady Macbeth has second thoughts about the events that led to the killing of Duncan and Banquo. She is concerned that Fleance, Banquo's son managed to escape.*

Salary, meager s. - Remuneration! O, that's the Latin word for three farthings
"Remuneration! O, that's the Latin word for three farthings." (LLL.3.1)
Comment on low pay. Answer to 'How much are you paid?' – 'You mean my remuneration? That's the Latin for three farthings'. See also 'Financial Status, 'Are you rich?' or 'How much money do you make?'
In the play. *Armado has asked Costard to bring a letter to Jacquenetta and gives him 'remuneration'. Costard re-dimensions the meaning of the name.*

Salary, meager s. and visible ribs - ….you may tell every finger I have with my ribs.
"I am famished in his service; you may tell every finger I have with my ribs." (MOV.2.2)
Modify to include the name of the employer or organization to which the statement applies, 'I am famished in this company's service: you may tell… ribs.'
In the play. *Launcelot explains to his blind father Gobbo the working conditions at Shylock's.*

Salutations – Hail, you anointed deputies of heaven!
"Hail, you anointed deputies of heaven!" (KJ.3.1)
Greeting some assembled VIPs with tongue in cheek.
In the play. *Cardinal Pandulph, the Pope's legate, arrives from Rome and greets King John of England and King Philip of France.*

Salutations and wishes - ... all joy befall your grace and you.
"Madam, all joy befall your grace, - and you!" (CYM.3.5)
Use when leaving your hosts' house after the party.
In the play. *Lucius takes leave of Cymbeline and Queen.*

Salutations and wishes - Be free, and fare thou well!
"Be free, and fare thou well!" (TEM.5.1)
Address individual or group (change 'thou' to 'you').
In the play. *At the end of his magician's exploits and career Prospero frees the spirit Ariel, who was instrumental in carrying out Prospero's instructions.*

Salutations and wishes - Bliss be upon you!
"Bliss be upon you!" (RJ.5.3)
Use as a salutation
In the play. *Balthasar has called on Fr. Lawrence and greets him.*

Salutations and wishes – ... fair be all thy hopes and prosperous be thy life in peace and war.
"And so farewell, and fair be all thy hopes
And prosperous be thy life in peace and war!" (KHVI.p1.2.5)
In the play. *Mortimer, prisoner of the Lancastrians and dying, takes leave of his nephew Plantagenet.*

Salutations and wishes - Health and fair time of day; joy and good wishes.
"Health and fair time of day; joy and good wishes" (KHV.5.2)
In the play. *Back in France K. Henry opens the meeting with the French court. The meeting will lead to his marriage to the French Princess Katharine.*

Salutations and wishes - Many years of happy days befal ...
"Many years of happy days befal
My gracious sovereign, my most loving liege!" (KRII.1.1)
In the play. *Bolingbroke on appearing in front of King Richard.*

Salutations and wishes - Sir, I commend you to your own content.
"Sir, I commend you to your own content." (COE.1.2)
Remove 'Sir' if you want to extend the wish to an audience.
In the play. *A merchant takes leave of Antipholus of Syracuse.*

Salutations and wishes – The best and wholesomest spirits of the night envelope you.
"The best and wholesomest spirits of the night
Envelope you." (MFM.4.2)
In the play. *The Duke greets the Provost.*

Salutations and wishes - Fair thoughts and happy hours attend on you.
"Fair thoughts and happy hours attend on you!" (MOV.3.4)
Alternative to 'so long'. See also entries for 'Good-bye'
In the play. *Lorenzo to Portia as she leaves for Venice.*

Salutations and wishes – The gentleness of all the gods go with thee.
"The gentleness of all the gods go with thee!" (TN.2.1)
See also 'Goodbye, when she is leaving for a short or long term trip, or a shopping excursion'
In the play. *Sebastian takes leave of Antonio, the sea captain who saved and befriended him.*

Salutations and wishes – The goodness of the night upon you, friends.

"The goodness of the night upon you, friends!" (OTH.1.2)
See also entries for 'Good night' – 'Separation temporarily postponed, good night'
In the play. *Othello in Venice greets Cassio and officers sent by the Duke*

Salutations and wishes - The grace of heaven, before, behind thee, and on every hand enwheel thee round!
"…the grace of heaven,
Before, behind thee, and on every hand,
Enwheel thee round!" (OTH.2.1)
In the play. *Cassio greets Desdemona as she lands in Cyprus.*

Salutations and wishes - The heavens give safety to your purposes!
"The heavens give safety to your purposes!" (MFM.1.1)
In the play. *Angelo, the Duke's deputy, wishes well to the departing Duke.*

Salutations and wishes, could also be sarcastic – ... I leave you to the protection of the prosperous gods…
"… I leave you
To the protection of the prosperous gods,
As thieves to keepers." (TOA.5.1)
In the play. *Timon at his cave dismisses the Athenian senators who came to enlist his help.*

Salutations, s and greetings quick due to time constraints - The time will not allow the compliment which very manners urges.
"The time will not allow the compliment
Which very manners urges." (KL.5.3)
Meeting an acquaintance in a rush, you must leave urgently and have no time for compliments and greetings
In the play. *Albany meets with Kent at a critical moment. Lear and Cordelia have been taken prisoners by Edmund's forces.*

Salutations, s. to a group - Good morrow to this fair assembly.
"Good morrow to this fair assembly" (MAAN.5.4)
Or good evening, afternoon etc.
In the play. *Don Pedro to Leonato and others.*

Salutations, s. to the earth – Dear earth, I do salute thee with my hand…
"Dear earth, I do salute thee with my hand,
Though rebels wound thee with their horses' hoofs." (KRII.3.2)
Use as an example of love of the country and contempt for government, equating the acts of a criminal government to the deeds of rebels.
In the play. *Richard II lands on the coast of Wales from Ireland, in the meantime the rebels led by Bolingbroke are ready to depose Richard.*

Salutations, s. with sadness - More health and happiness betide my liege than can my care-tuned tongue deliver him.
"More health and happiness betide my liege
Than can my care-tuned tongue deliver him!" (KRII.3.2)
In the play. *Scroop joins King Richard II on the coats of Wales.*

Salutations, till next time – This bud of love, by summer's ripening breath, may prove a beauteous flower when we next meet.
"This bud of love, by summer's ripening breath,
May prove a beauteous flower when we next meet." (RJ.2.2)
Parting remark after making an acquaintance with a lady whom you like and who likes you.
In the play. *Juliet attempts to cool Romeo's outburst of declared love and passion.*

Salutations, wishes for a rain of fragrances - ... the heavens rain fragrances on you.
"Most excellent accomplished lady, the heavens rain odours on you!" (TN.3.1)
As 'odours' does not sound as good as is the intent of the greeting in the play, change with – for instance – pleasant fragrances.
In the play. *Viola/Cesario greets Olivia who has entered the scene.*

Sarcasm, retort to s. – ... shall quips, and sentences, and these paper bullets of the brain...
"...shall quips, and sentences, and these paper bullets of the brain, awe a man from the career of his humour?" (MAAN.2.3)
In the play. *Benedick meditates about his own change of attitude towards love now that he begins to love Beatrice.*

Sarcasm – ... wit larded with malice.
"...wit larded with malice..." (TC.5.1)
Retort to a sarcasm, e.g. 'This is wit larded with malice' (TC.5.1)
In the play. *Thersites thinks of what kind of animal should Maenelaus turned into through the agency of nasty wit.*

Satire, impervious to s. – ... a college of wit-crackers cannot flout me out of my humour.
"I'll tell thee what, prince; a college of wit-crackers cannot flout me out of my humour" (MAAN.5.4)
In the play. *Don Pedro pulls Benedick's leg for first declaring himself against marriage while now he plans to marry Beatrice. Benedick answers that he does not care.*

Satisfaction, s. as payment. - He is well paid that is well satisfied...
"He is well paid that is well satisfied;
And I, delivering you, am satisfied
And therein do account myself well paid:" (MOV.4.1)
When you refuse to be paid for a favor or task you did for another. See also 'Gratitude, no need to return favor - The service and the loyalty I owe in doing it, pays itself.'
In the play. *Portia replies to a comment by Antonio. Antonio says he is in debt with Portia for her brilliant defense in court.*

Satisfaction, s. for the way things turned out – We have cause to be glad that matters are so well digested.
"We have cause to be glad that matters are so well digested." (AC.2.2)
In the play. *Maecenas (of the Octavian party) to Enobarbus commenting on the marriage of Antony with Octavian's sister, marriage intended to eliminate rivalries.*

Satisfaction, self s. - Thus have I politicly begun my reign.
"Thus have I politicly begun my reign,
And 'tis my hope to end successfully." (TOS.4.1)
In the play. *Petruchio has married the intractable Katharina and has won the first round in his attempt to tame her, the 'shrew' of the play.*

Satisfied, but wanting more - ... can one desire too much of a good thing?
"...can one desire too much of a good thing?" (AYLI.4.1)
Answer to, 'Did you not have enough?'
In the play. *Rosalind (in disguise) engages in a mock wooing performance and poses the question to Orlando. The 'good thing' referred to is obviously love.*

Saved, reasons to be grateful - ... then wisely, good sir, weigh our sorrow with our comfort.
"...but for the miracle,
I mean our preservation, few in millions

Can speak like us: then wisely, good sir, weigh
Our sorrow with our comfort." (TEM.2.1)
In the play. *Gonzalo cheers up the rest of the party after escaping alive from the tempest.*

Saving, s. as a virtue – And thrift is blessing, if men steal it not.
"And thrift is blessing, if men steal it not" (MOV.1.3)
In the play. *Shylock expounds the virtue of old biblical characters so as to justify to Antonio the legitimacy of interest.*

Saying, a s. well worth remembering – There was never a truer rhyme.
"'--O heart, heavy heart,
Why sigh'st thou without breaking?
where he answers again,
'Because thou canst not ease thy smart
By friendship nor by speaking.'
There was never a truer rhyme." (TC.4.4)
In the play. *Pandarus comments on the distress of Troilus and Cressida who must part as Cressida has been exchanged with a Trojan prisoner.*

Schedule, s. to adhere to - Stick to your journal course: the breach of custom is breach of all.
"Stick to your journal course: the breach of custom
Is breach of all" (CYM.4.1)
Alternative to 'I do not want to disrupt your schedule' See also 'Custom, c. more ignored than followed - more honour'd in the breach than the observance'.
In the play. *Guiderius wants to accompany Imogen (in man's attire) who goes hunting but she/ he wants to be alone.*

Scientists, s. explaining the supernatural – ... we have our philosophical persons, to make modern and familiar...

"...we have our philosophical persons, to make modern and familiar, things supernatural and causeless" (AWEW.2.3)
Introduction to a presentation by a scientist.
In the play. *Helen, against all predictions has succeeded in healing the King and Lafeu delivers a philosophical commentary.*

Scorn, reaction to s. - What means this scorn, thou most untoward knave?
"What means this scorn, thou most untoward knave?" (KJ.1.1)
In the play. *Lady Faulconbridge to her son Philip who scorns her for her adulterous relation with King Richard I.*

Scorpion, s's nest to be avoided - ... Seek not a scorpion's nest.
"What boded this, but well forewarning wind
Did seem to say 'Seek not a scorpion's nest" (KHVI p2.3.2)
In the play. *Q. Margaret puts up a charade implying that she made great sacrifices by coming to England (scorpion's nest) to be queen*

Scoundrel, s. constant to his calling – ... and therein am I constant to my profession.
"I hold it the more knavery to conceal it; and therein am I constant to my profession" (WT.4.4)
Apply to any notorious party, corporation man or politician.
In the play. *Autolycus, acting very logically, will tell the king of Florizel's flight. He does so because in this case it would be honest not to tell him.*

Scoundrels, s. around – ... there are cozeners abroad; therefore it behoves men to be wary.
"...there are cozeners abroad; therefore it behoves men to be wary." (WT.4.4)

See also 'Caution, c. required - it is the bright day that brings forth the adder…'
In the play. *The scoundrel Autolycus insincerely warns the Clown.*

Scruples, no s. - Let me, if not by birth, have lands by wit: all with me's meet that I can fashion fit.
"A credulous father! and a brother noble,
Whose nature is so far from doing harms,
That he suspects none: on whose foolish honesty
My practises ride easy! I see the business.
Let me, if not by birth, have lands by wit:
All with me's meet that I can fashion fit." (KL.1.3)
Use 'All with me is meet…. fit' in answer to a request for an intervention to the border of legality.
In the play. *Evil Edmund congratulates himself about the success of his ploy to have brother Edgar disinherited.*

Sculpture, divine s. – …a piece many years in doing and now newly performed by that rare Italian master, Julio Romano…
"…a piece many years in doing and now newly performed by that rare Italian master, Julio Romano, who, had he himself eternity and could put breath into his work, would beguile Nature of her custom, so perfectly he is her ape" (WT.5.2)
Praise of a sculpture or piece of art.
In the play. *A gentleman reports that Perdita went to observe the statue of her mother Hermione.*

Sea-crossing, virtual s.-c. - … charming the narrow seas to give you gentle pass…
"And thence to France shall we convey you safe,
And bring you back, charming the narrow seas
To give you gentle pass; for, if we may,
We'll not offend one stomach with our play." (KHV.2.prologue)
Use as a metaphor for the introduction to your presentation.
In the play. *The chorus makes up for the lack of special effects.*

Search, searching with no hope to find - … Hopeless to find, yet loath to leave unsought…
"…coasting homeward, came to Ephesus;
Hopeless to find, yet loath to leave unsought
Or that or any place that harbours men." (COE.1.1)
In the play. *Aegeon explain the reason for his coming to Ephesus, i.e. to search for his lost sons.*

Seclusion, total s. - Out of all eyes, tongues, minds and injuries.
"In some reclusive and religious life
Out of all eyes, tongues, minds and injuries." (MAAN.4.1)
Answer (as it applies) to 'Where are you going?' E.G. 'In a place out of… injuries'.
In the play. *The friar counsels to move Hero temporarily away and to make it appear that she is dead.*

Secrecy, impossible to break it if secret is not known - … thou wilt not utter what thou dost not know.
"… constant you are,
But yet a woman: and for secrecy,
No lady closer; for I well believe,
Thou wilt not utter what thou dost not know." (KHIV p1.2.3)
A reason for not disclosing a secret.
In the play. *Hotspur is acting secretly and is on the point of leaving. His wife tries to get information but Hotspur does not give any. He is organizing a rebellion with other conspirators.*

Secrecy, s. assured - ... the secrets of nature have not more gift in taciturnity.
"… the secrets of nature
Have not more gift in taciturnity." (TC.2.3)
In the play. *Aeneas reassures Troilus that he will not give out that he (Aeneas) saw him.*

Secrecy, s. assured - When you have spoken it, 't is dead, and I am the grave of it.
FIRST LORD. I will tell you a thing, but you shall let it well darkly with you.
SECOND LORD. When you have spoken it, 't is dead, and I am the grave of it. (AWEW.4.3)
Your answer to someone who asks you to keep the information confidential.
In the play. *The secret the two lords refer to is the reported tryst between Bertram and Diana, a Florentine lady. They do not know that at the last moment Helen switched places with Diana.*

Secrecy, s. demanded - ... such things that want no ear but yours.
"…I would commune with you of such things
That want no ear but yours." (MFM.4.3)
In the play. *The Duke will disclose to the prison provost the secret details of the plot to unmask Angelo's hypocrisy.*

Secrecy, s. essential - Seal up your lips, and give no words but mum!
"Seal up your lips, and give no words but - mum!
The business asketh silent secrecy." (KHVI p2.1.2)
Urge confidentiality.
In the play. *Hume, intent on nailing the Duchess of Gloucester with evidence of sorcery tells himself, in the meantime, to be quiet and secret about the matter.*

Secrecy, s. required, secret to be kept - ... stall this in your bosom.
"... stall this in your bosom." (AWEW.1.3)
Order secrecy or confidentiality.
In the play. *After discussing the newly discovered passion of Helen towards Bertram, the Countess invites the steward to be secret about it.*

Secret, I will keep the s. - ... your mute I'll be; when my tongue blabs, then let mine eyes not see!
" ... your mute I'll be;
When my tongue blabs, then let mine eyes not see!" (TN.1.2)
Commit yourself to the silence you have been asked to keep.
In the play. *The captain promises to Viola that he will not say anything about her disguise and her plans.*

Secret, information that must be kept s. – ... I will tell you a thing, but you shall let it dwell darkly with you.
"…I will tell you a thing, but you shall let it dwell darkly with you." (AWEW.4.3)
In the play. *Two French lords discuss matters near Florence. The secret that one discloses to the other is the effort by Bertram to seduce Diana.*

Secret, injunction to keep the matter s. - ... whatsoever else shall hap to-night, give it an understanding, but no tongue.
"And whatsoever else shall hap to-night,
Give it an understanding, but no tongue" (H.1.2)
In the play. *Hamlet exhorts Horatio and the guards not to talk about the apparition of the Ghost.*

Secret, s. information given away indirectly – Thou shalt never get such a secret from me but by a parable.
"Thou shalt never get such a secret from me but by a parable" (TGV.2.5)

In the play. *Servant Launce answers a question by Servant Speed.*

Secret, s. matters - For I would commune with you of such things that want no ear but yours.
"For I would commune with you of such things
That want no ear but yours."
(MFM.4.3)
In the play. *Duke-Vicentio will acquaint the Provost with the scheme to save Claudio and expose Angelo's hypocrisy.*

Secret, s. will be disclosed to her after the (successful) event - Be innocent of the knowledge, dearest chuck, till thou applaud the deed.
"Be innocent of the knowledge, dearest chuck,
Till thou applaud the deed." (M.3.2)
Answer to 'What have you done?' when for whatever reason you wish not to answer.
In the play. *Macbeth has killed Banquo but will postpone telling his (Macbeth's) wife.*

Secret, s. that must be well kept - ...'tis a secret must be locked within the teeth and the lips.
"...'tis a secret must be locked within the teeth and the lips" (MFM.3.2)
In the play. *Claudio pretends not to want to tell the friar (actually the Duke in disguise), why the Duke left Vienna.*

Secret, weighty s. - This secret is so weighty, 't will require a strong faith to conceal it.
This secret is so weighty, 't will require
A strong faith to conceal it."
(KHVIII.2.1)
Stress the importance of confidentiality.
In the play. *A citizen hints at an ensuing dreadful evil (to be kept secret) following the unjust execution of Buckingham, that is the separation between King Henry and Queen Kathryn.*

Secrets, s. of the heart, promise to reveal them - ... and by and by thy bosom shall partake the secrets of my heart.
"And by and by thy bosom shall partake
The secrets of my heart." (JC.2.1)
When they insist on your talking to them but you want to delay, 'By and by, your bosom(s) shall partake... heart.'
In the play. *Brutus tells Portia he will reveal his mind to her in time.*

Security, false sense of s. - ... If thou beest not immortal look about you: security gives way to conspiracy.
"... If thou beest not immortal, look about you: security gives way to conspiracy." (JC.2.3)
A reminder when your call for concern goes unheeded.
In the play. *Artemidorus gives a paper to Caesar in a street near the Capitol. The paper suggests to beware of the various conspirators (today we would call them terrorists) actually identified by name. But, as we all know, Caesar disregards the advice.*

Security, sense of s. always questionable - ...security is mortals' chiefest enemy.
"And you all know, security
Is mortals' chiefest enemy." (M.3.5)
Exhortation to the winning team not to sit on their laurels.
In the play. *The witch Hecate in conversation with the other witches while they verify the predictions regarding Macbeth.*

Seducer, great s. - He is the bluntest wooer in Christendom.
"He is the bluntest wooer in Christendom." (KHVI.p3.3.2)
In the play. *Richard of Gloucester to his brother Clarence comments on their other brother*

King Edward and his seducing efforts with the Lady Grey.

Seducer, requisites of a s. - ... the knave is handsome, young, and hath all those requisites in him...
"...the knave is handsome, young, and hath all those requisites in him that folly and green minds look after" (OTH.2.1)
In the play. *Iago describes Cassio to Roderigo.*

Seduction, a viewpoint on s. – ... when you have our roses, you barely leave our thorns to prick ourselves...
BERTRAM ... I love thee
By love's own sweet constraint, and will for ever
Do thee all rights of service.
DIANA Ay, so you serve us
Till we serve you; but when you have our roses,
You barely leave our thorns to prick ourselves
And mock us with our bareness (AWEW.4.2)
In the play. *Diana answers Bertram's advances in Tuscany where he was sent to fight by the King of France.*

Seduction, lesson in s. – ...you must seem to do that fearfully which you commit...
"...you must seem to do that fearfully which you commit willingly, despise profit where you have most gain" (PER.4.2)
In the play. *Bawd gives Marina a lesson in corruption.*

Seduction, tools of s. - ... a speeding trick to lay down ladies, a French song and a fiddle has no fellow.
"... the sly worsens
Have got a speeding trick to lay down ladies;
A French song and a fiddle has no fellow." (KHVIII, 1.3)
In the play. *Sir Lovell referring to the fashions affected by the young lords of the time, i.e. 'the sly whoresons'.*

Seeing, s. is believing - If there be truth in sight...
"If there be truth in sight, you are my daughter." (AYLI.5.4)
Emphasize that something is true because you yourself saw it. "If there be truth in sight. etc."
In the play. *The Duke meets Rosalind previously disguised as a boy.*

Seeing, s. is believing - If you dare not trust that you see, confess not that you know.
"If you dare not trust that you see, confess not that you know." (MAAN.3.2)
In the play. *The evil Don John has hatched a plot to slander Hero and will produce false evidence to the disbelieving Claudio.*

Selection, desire to select independently - ... in such a business give me leave to use help of mine own eyes.
"...I shall beseech your highness,
In such a business give me leave to use
The help of mine own eyes." (AWEW.2.3)
See also 'Refusal, r. of help or brokerage - ... give me leave to play the broker in mine own behalf ...'
In the play. *The King wants Bertram to marry Helena but Bertram balks.*

Selection, s. limited – ... there's small choice in rotten apples.
"Faith, as you say, there's small choice in rotten apples." (TOS.1.1)
Alternative to express that the selection is not good and the choice limited.
In the play. *Hortensio likes Bianca but cannot go any further because a husband must be found first for her older and intractable sister*

Katharina, to whom the rotten apple reference applies.

Self-accusation - ...I have done ill, of which I do accuse myself so sorely, that I will joy no more.
"...I have done ill;
Of which I do accuse myself so sorely,
That I will joy no more." (AC.4.6)
In the play. *Enobarbus repents of having abandoned Antony after Antony lost at sea against Octavian.*

Self-analysis, I wish you would look at yourselves - O, that you could turn your eyes towards the napes of your necks...
"O, that you could turn your eyes towards the napes of your necks, and make but an interior survey of your good selves!" (COE.2.1)
Criticism or sarcastic suggestion for some people to take a considered look at what they are doing.
In the play. *Menenius prompts the people's tribunes to examine themselves.*

Self-assertion encouraged - Self-love, my liege, is not so vile a sin as self-neglecting.
"Self-love, my liege, is not so vile a sin
As self-neglecting." (KHV.2.4)
A rebuttal when you are prompted to give up.
In the play. *The Dauphin of France exhorts the King not to be afraid of the English forces that landed with King Henry.*

Self-assertion to remove self-doubt - ... to be afeard of my deserving were but a weak disabling of myself.
"And yet to be afeard of my deserving
Were but a weak disabling of myself.
As much as I deserve!" (MOV.2.7)
In the play. *The prince of Morocco dispels (for his own benefit) some reservation he may have on whether he does or does not deserve Portia's hand in marriage.*

Self-assessment - A man that fortune's buffets and rewards hast ta'en with equal thanks.
"A man that fortune's buffets and rewards
Hast ta'en with equal thanks" (H.3.2)
Follow up to question 'What can you tell me about yourself?' Change 'hast' to 'has'.
In the play. *Hamlet of Horatio.*

Self-assessment - I am myself indifferent honest; but yet I could accuse me of such things that it were better my mother had not borne me...
"... I am myself indifferent honest; but yet I could accuse me of such things that it were better my mother had not borne me: I am very proud, revengeful, ambitious, with more offences at my beck than I have thoughts to put them in, imagination to give them shape, or time to act them in. What should such fellows as I do crawling between earth and heaven? We are arrant knaves, all; believe none of us." (H.3.1)
When you are pressed to tell about your weaknesses.
In the play. *Hamlet to Ophelia after suggesting that she gets herself to a nunnery.*

Self-assessment – I am not covetous for gold...
"I am not covetous for gold..." (KHV.4.3)
First answer during a job interview to 'How much money are you looking for?' It smoothes the ground before proceeding further on this important and yet delicate subject.
In the play. *Henry V addresses the troops before the battle of Agincourt.*

Self-assessment – Though I am not splenitive and rash, yet have I something in me dangerous.
"…though I am not splenitive and rash,
Yet have I something in me dangerous" (H.5.1)
In the play. *Hamlet tells Laertes to get off his fingers from Hamlet's throat.*

Self-defense, killing in s-d - To kill, I grant, is sin's extremest gust but, in defence, by mercy, 'tis most just.
"To kill, I grant, is sin's extremest gust;
But, in defence, by mercy, 'tis most just." (TOA.3.5)
In the play. *Alcibiades pleads with Athenian senators on behalf of a friend who killed in self-defence.*

Self-defense, killing in s-d. justified – Who cannot condemn rashness in cold blood?…
"Who cannot condemn rashness in cold blood?
To kill, I grant, is sin's extremest gust;
But, in defence, by mercy, 'tis most just." (TOA.3.5)
In the play. *Alcibiades pleads with Athenian senators to forego punishing a soldier who killed a fellow soldier in a brawl.*

Self-defence, s-d and parental defense - Unreasonable creatures feed their young… make war with him that climb'd unto their nest…
"Unreasonable creatures feed their young;
And though man's face be fearful to their eyes,
Yet, in protection of their tender ones,
Who hath not seen them, even with those wings
Which sometime they have used with fearful flight,
Make war with him that climb'd unto their nest,
Offer their own lives in their young's defence?" (KHVI.p.3.2.2)
In the play. *Clifford encourages Henry VI to stand up for his rights and the rights of his son against the usurpation of Richard Plantagenet of York.*

Self-denial, s.d. as a sign of wisdom – The greatest virtue of which wise men boast is to abstain from ill, when pleasing most
"The greatest virtue of which wise men boast,
Is to abstain from ill, when pleasing most" (Poems)

Self-destruction, s.d. compounded by incorrect judgment - … when we in our own viciousness grow hard.. the wise Gods seal our eyes…
"… When we in our own viciousness grow hard
(O misery on't) the wise gods seal our eyes,
In our own filth drop our clear judgments, make us
Adore our errors, laugh at us while we strut
To our confusion." (AC.3.13)
Comment on why men sometimes put themselves beyond redemption. See also 'Ignorance, i. of what is really good for us - We, ignorant of ourselves beg often our own harms, which the wise powers deny us for our good…'
In the play. *Antony in a mood of depression and self-criticism. 'To seel' = 'to close'*

Self-effacement and blame at having been betrayed by false appearances – What a thrice-double ass was I, to take this drunkard for a god…
"… What a thrice-double ass
Was I, to take this drunkard for a god,
And worship this dull fool!" (TEM.5.1)
Deprecate your having believed in the worth of an unworthy person.

In the play. *Caliban recognizes his own limitations, the drunkard is Stephano the would-be king of the island, and the dull fool is Trinculo.*

Self-effacement and pessimistic view of own self – What should such fellows as I do crawling between earth and heaven?
"…What should such fellows as I do crawling between earth and heaven? We are arrant knaves, all; believe none of us." (H.3.1)
In the play. In the play. *Hamlet to Ophelia after suggesting that she become a nun.*

Self-effacement, emphatic, beating your own head – … Beat at this gate, that let thy folly in.
"…O Lear, Lear, Lear!
Beat at this gate, that let thy folly in" (KL.1.4)
Leave 'Lear' or change to your first or last name.
In the play. *King Lear, appalled at the behavior of his evil daughter Goneril, realizes his folly at having banned the good Cordelia.*

Self-effacement, making sport of ones misery - … misery makes sport to mock itself
"… misery makes sport to mock itself" (KRII.2.1)
In the play. *John of Gaunt to King Richard who has come to visit. John has made a word play with 'Gaunt' used as a name or an adjective.*

Self-identity in question - Who is it that can tell me who I am?
"Who is it that can tell me who I am?" (KL.1.4)
Answer to the question, 'Who are you?' when you do not want to answer or prefer to be evasive.
In the play. *Lear, out in the cold and duped by his evil daughters has doubts about himself.*

Self-improvement - …all dedicated to closeness and the bettering of my mind.
"I, thus neglecting worldly ends, all dedicated
To closeness and the bettering of my mind." (TEM.1.2)
Answer to 'what are you doing now?' if, for example, you are unemployed.
In the play. *Prospero tells daughter Miranda about his life as duke of Milan.*

Self-interest, bias of the world - That smooth-fac'd gentleman, tickling commodity, commodity, the bias of the world.
"That smooth-fac'd gentleman, tickling commodity,
Commodity, the bias of the world." (KJ.2.2)
Change 'commodity' to 'self interest'. Answer to question, 'why did he do that?' E.G. 'It's self interest, that smooth faced … world.'
In the play. *Philip reflects and objects to the terms of the proposed agreement between France and England. Commodity stands (and can be substituted with) 'self interest'.*

Self-loathing – … one unperfectness shows me another, to make me frankly despise myself.
"…one unperfectness shows me another, to make me frankly despise myself" (OTH.2.3)
In the play. *Cassio sobers up after having been drunk (one unperfectness) and engaged into a quarrel (second unperfectness).*

Self-love, s-l admitted as a sin - Sin of self-love possesseth all mine eye, and all my soul, and all my every part…
"Sin of self-love possesseth all mine eye,
And all my soul, and all my every part;
And for this sin there is no remedy,
It is so grounded inward in the heart." (SON.62)

Use to justify or excuse your egotistical behavior.

Self-love, s-l. better than self-neglect - Self-love, my liege, is not so vile a sin as self-neglecting.
"Self-love, my liege, is not so vile a sin,
As self-neglecting." (KHV.2.4)
Answer an accusation of self-aggrandizement
In the play. *The Dauphin prompts the King of France to stand up to the English*

Self-punishment - thou gavest them the rod, and put'st down thine own breeches
"…thou gavest them the rod, and put'st down thine own breeches" (KL.1.4)
Comment on the results of a poor measure or maneuver. Change 'thou' to 'we' and 'thine' to 'our' if the event affects more than one person.
In the play. *The Fool tells Lear what he, Lear, metaphorically did when he entrusted power and inheritance to his fiendish daughters.*

Self-punishment, s.p. invoked – Hang there like a fruit, my soul, till the tree die!
"Hang there like a fruit, my soul,
Till the tree die!" (CYM.5.5)
In the play. *Leonatus' reaction at being embraced by his wife whom he thought dead, as he ordered Pisanio to kill her.*

Self-punishment, s.p. invoked – … roast me in sulphur! Wash me in steep-down gulfs of liquid fire!
"Whip me, ye devils,
….
Blow me about in winds! roast me in sulphur!
Wash me in steep-down gulfs of liquid fire! (OTH.5.2)

Dramatically over-emphasize that you recognize the extent of your mistake and are ready to pay for it.
In the play. *Othello has killed Desdemona and realizes the horror of the crime.*

Self-recrimination - My very hairs do mutiny, for the white reprove the brown for rashness…
"My very hairs do mutiny; for the white
Reprove the brown for rashness, and they them
For fear and doting." (AC.3.11)
In the play. *Antony reproaches himself for his conduct during the sea battle with Octavian.*

Self-reliance, remedies to be found within ourselves - Our remedies oft in ourselves do lie which we ascribe to heaven.
"Our remedies oft in ourselves do lie,
Which we ascribe to heaven."
(AWEW.1.3)
Use to inspire self-reliance when your team is downhearted or discouraged. See also entries for 'Complaint, c. after problems useless' *** 'Sorrow, disappointment, attitude towards s. - For gnarling sorrow hath less power to bite the man that mocks at it and sets it light'.
In the play. *Helen, helplessly in love with Bertram, meditates about a virtuous scheme whereby he may end up marrying her.*

Seminar, introduction to a s. - Here let us breathe, and haply institute a course of learning and ingenious studies.
"Here let us breathe, and haply institute
A course of learning, and ingenious studies." (TOS.1.1)
Introduction to a lecture or a training course. See also 'Beauty, b. beats any learning - for where is any author in the world teaches such beauty as a woman's eye?…' *** 'Education, profitable if

pleasurable – No profit grows where is no pleasure taken…'
In the play. *Lucentio and his servant Tranio have arrived in Padua. Lucentio speaks his mind.*

Sentence, reaction to a s. - He bears the sentence well that nothing bears…
"He bears the sentence well that nothing bears
But the free comfort which from thence he hears,
But he bears both the sentence and the sorrow
That, to pay grief, must of poor patience borrow" (OTH.1.3)
In the play. *Brabantio comments on the outcome of his suit with the Duke of Venice. Othello has been acquitted of wrong doing in marrying Desdemona and Brabantio must rely on patience to accept the verdict.*

Separation, s. between church and state – Where we do reign, we will alone uphold…
"Where we do reign, we will alone uphold,
Without the assistance of a mortal hand" (KJ.3.1)
In the play. *King John's reply to the requests of Cardinal Pandulph.*

Separation, s. concurrent with spiritual presence - Our separation so abides, and flies, that thou, residing here, go'st yet with me…
"Our separation so abides, and flies,
That thou, residing here, go'st yet with me,
And I, hence fleeting, here remain with thee." (AC.1.3)
In the play. *Antony must leave temporarily Cleopatra and go to Rome.*

Separation, s. in harrowing circumstances - I doubt it not; and all these woes shall serve for sweet discourses in our time to come.
JULIET O think'st thou we shall ever meet again?
ROMEO I doubt it not; and all these woes shall serve
For sweet discourses in our time to come. (RJ.3.5)
In the play. *Romeo must leave for Mantua where he has been exiled*

Separation, s. temporarily postponed - Good night, good night! parting is such sweet sorrow, that I shall say-good night till it be morrow!
"Good night, good night! parting is such sweet sorrow,
That I shall say-good night till it be morrow!" (RJ.2.2)
Use it if she doesn't want to let you go and yet you have to get up early in the morning. Add after the line, '…but tomorrow I am off to (the destination you are headed to).
In the play. *Romeo and Juliet (she on the balcony, he down in the garden) just cannot let go of each other.*

Separation, not wanting to leave - I have more care to stay than will to go.
"I have more care to stay than will to go" (RJ.3.5)
Make it clear that you would rather stay but cannot due to impending demands. See also 'Business trip, temporary separation - the strong necessity of time commands our services a while…' – Entries for 'Salutations' and 'Goodbye'
In the play. *Romeo must leave Juliet and Verona or he will die for having slain Tybald.*

Service, at her complete s. - … sworn by your command, which my love makes religion to obey…
"…sworn by your command,
Which my love makes religion to obey,
I tell you this" (AC.5.2)

You may or may not have something to tell. If not confirm you will do what asked, 'I am sworn by your command…. obey'.
In the play. *Dolabella announces to Cleopatra what are the designs of Octavian.*

Service, at her complete s. – Being thy slave what should I do but tend upon the hours and times of your desire?
"Being thy slave what should I do but tend
Upon the hours and times of your desire?
I have no precious time at all to spend,
Nor services to do till you require." (SON.57)
Answer to, 'Will you do this for me?' And/or a follow up after you already said yes to her request - you will gain some extra points. The two first lines already convey the idea perfectly, quote all four lines to make an absolutely lasting impression. See also 'Beauty, impossible to say 'no' to it - All orators are dumb when beauty pleadeth.'

Service, at her complete s. – I am thus early come to know what service it is your pleasure to command me in.
"I am thus early come to know what service
It is your pleasure to command me in" (TGV.4.3)
Answer to 'can you do something for me?' E.G. 'What service… command me in?'
In the play. *Eglamour arrives at the request of Silvia to accompany her in her journey and quest for the banished Valentine.*

Service, at her complete s. – I come to answer your pleasure.
"I come to answer thy pleasure; be't to fly,
To swim, to dive into the fire, to ride
On the curled clouds - to thy strong bidding, task
Ariel, and all his quality." (TEM.1.2)
Amusing way to indicate your availability.
In the play. *Ariel is a magic spirit owes a debt to Prospero and therefore will answer his commands*

Service, at her complete s. – I will live in thy heart, die in thy lap, and be buried in thy eyes…
"I will live in thy heart, die in thy lap, and be buried in thy eyes; and moreover I will go with
thee to thy uncle's." (MAAN.5.2)
Answer to, 'Will you do this for me?' and re-state what she has asked you to do, e.g. 'and moreover I will go with thee to see your in-laws' (or other as applicable).
In the play. *Benedick and Beatrice have finally discovered that they are in love with each other. Beatrice asks Benedick whether he will go with her to witness the discovery of the evil done to Hero by the evil Don John.*

Service, at the king's s. - … service shall with steeled sinews toil, and labour shall refresh itself with hope…
"… service shall with steeled sinews toil,
And labour shall refresh itself with hope,
To do your grace incessant services." (KHV.2.2)
Declare your willingness to serve or do the chore you are asked to carry out.
In the play. *Though plotting against the King, Scroop declares his allegiance.*

Service, at your s. – Thy humble servant vows obedience and humble service till the point of death.
"Thy humble servant vows obedience
And humble service till the point of death." (KHVI.p1.3.1)
In the play. *Plantagenet declares his (proven later false) allegiance to King Henry VI.*

Service, at your service - ... I will be correspondent to command and do my spiriting gently.
"Pardon, master;
I will be correspondent to command
And do my spiriting gently."
(TEM.1.2)
Change 'spiriting' to the gerund of the verb describing the specific task involved.
In the play. *Ariel, reminded of favors made to him by Prospero, will execute willingly Prospero's assignments.*

Service, at your service, ask me to do anything you want - I come to answer thy best pleasure; be't to fly, to swim, to dive into the fire…
"All hail, great master! grave sir, hail! I come
To answer thy best pleasure; be't to fly,
To swim, to dive into the fire, to ride
On the curl'd clouds, to thy strong bidding task
Ariel and all his quality." (TEM.1.2)
Ironic answer to a call for service.
In the play. *Ariel the fairy spirit arrives at Prospero's.*

Service, commitment to trustful service and looking forward to it - You never had a servant to whose trust your business was more welcome.
"You never had a servant to whose trust
Your business was more welcome." (AWEW.4.4)
Answer to 'Can you do this?' in a matter that requires discretion and confidence.
In the play. *The widow, mother of Diana, gives Helena assurances of reliability.*

Service, ready to provide best possible s. – ... we are ready to use our utmost studies in your service
"…if you please
To trust us in your business, we are ready

To use our utmost studies in your service." (KHVIII.3.1)
In the play. *Cardinal Campeius, who along with Cardinal Wolsey came to talk to Queen Catherine about her impending divorce.*

Service, s. offered as a token of love - … impose some service on me for thy love.
"… mistress, look on me;
Behold the window of my heart, mine eye,
What humble suit attends thy answer there:
Impose some service on me for thy love." (LLL.5.2)
Use to prompt an answer when you feel that she is hesitant.
In the play. *Biron loves Rosaline and wants her to say once and for all if she reciprocates her love.*

Service, s. requested and offered - I am thus early come, to know what service it is your pleasure to command me in.
"I am thus early come, to know what service
It is your pleasure to command me in." (TGV.4.3)
Your answer to "Can you please come here?" or similar.
In the play. *Sylvia plans to search for the banned Valentine (whom she loves) and asks the mature Eglamour to accompany her in her search.*

Service, s. without expectation of reward - ... do not look for further recompense than thine own gladness that thou art employed.
"... and I'll employ thee too:
But do not look for further recompense,
Than thine own gladness that thou art employed. " (AYLI.3.5)
If you are a woman state clearly that there are no rewards promised for

whatever services you ask him to render. Or, if you apply for an internship answer the question 'What are you looking for?' E.G. 'I do not look for further recompense than mine own gladness that I am employed'.
In the play. *In a display of total devotion, Silvius accepts the task of carrying Phebe's letter to the disguised Rosalind, whom Phebe loves not knowing of the disguise.*

Servility, following the leader – The swallow follows not summer more willing than we your lordship.
"The swallow follows not summer more willing than we your lordship." (TOA.3.6)
Answer to 'Will you follow me?'
In the play. *Timon will call on his unhelpful friends and pretend to throw another party. The parasites, thinking that Timon's problems are past flock again to his table.*

Sex identity difficult, masculine looking women - ... you should be women, and yet your beards forbid me to interpret that you are so.
"…you should be women,
And yet your beards forbid me to interpret
That you are so." (M.1.3)
Adapt to your narrative. E.G. 'They should have been women, but their beard forbade me to interpret that they were so.'
In the play. *Banquo addresses the witches.*

Sex, desire for s. – My poor body, madam, requires it: I am driven on by the flesh…
COUNTESS Tell me thy reason why thou wilt marry.
CLOWN My poor body, madam, requires it: I am driven on by the flesh; and he must needs go that the devil drives. (AWEW.1.3)
In the play. *The Countess and the Clown exchange some banter in the castle of Roussillon.*

Sex, hot s. - … till strange love, grown bold think true love acted simple modesty
"Hood my unmann'd blood, bating in my cheeks,
With thy black mantle; till strange love, grown bold,
Think true love acted simple modesty." (RJ.3.2)
In the play. *Wishing that night come sooner, Juliet, now married to Romeo, anxiously await his arrival*

Sex, indications of mutual attraction leading to s. - When these mutualities so marshal the way…
" When these mutualities so marshal the way, hard at hand comes the master and main exercise, it incorporates conclusion." (OTH.2.1)
Opinion on what is going on between a man and a woman of your acquaintance
In the play. *Iago suggests to Roderigo that the courtesy shown Cassio by Desdemona was actually a strong indication of an existing passion.*

Sex, s. as a restorer of spirits - … Make love's quick pants in Desdemona's arms give renew'd fire to our extincted spirits.
"Great Jove, Othello guard,
…
Make love's quick pants in Desdemona's arms,
Give renew'd fire to our extincted spirits" (OTH.2.1)
In the play. *Cassio hopes that Othello may reach Cyprus safely after a sea storm and be reinvigorated by making love to his wife Desdemona.*

Sex, s. having long historical precedents – All sects, all ages smack of this vice…

"All sects, all ages smack of this vice; and he
To die for't!" (MFM.2.2)
In the play. *The Provost cannot understand how Angelo can condemn Claudio to death for fornication.*

Sex, s. postponed - ... though Venus govern your desires, Saturn is dominator over mine.
"Madam, though Venus govern your desires,
Saturn is dominator over mine" (TA.2.3)
An alternate to 'I have a headache'
In the play. *Aaron has other thoughts in mind than Tamora's invitation.*

Sex, symptoms of mutual attraction - ... they met so near with their lips that their breaths embraced together.
"... an index and obscure prologue to the history of lust and foul thoughts. They met so near with their lips that their breaths embraced together" (OTH.2.1)
In the play. *Iago first tries to convince Roderigo that Desdemona loves Cassio. This is not true but the foolish Roderigo falls into the trap laid by Iago.*

Sex, when he does not seem interested – Why hast thou lost the fresh blood in thy cheeks and given my treasures and my rights of thee...
"Why hast thou lost the fresh blood in thy cheeks;
And given my treasures and my rights of thee
To thick-eyed musing and cursed melancholy" (KHIV.p1.2.3)
In the play. *Hotspur's wife, Lady Percy, questions him as to his mood. He is thinking of the pending rebellion against King Henry IV.*

Sexual desire waning – ... I begin to love, as an old man loves money, with no stomach.

"...the brains of my Cupid's knocked out, and I begin to love, as an old man loves money, with no stomach." (AWEW.3.2)
In the play. *The clown explains to the Countess how, after having seen the beauties at court, the beauties of the country do not impress him.*

Sexual education - ... the lesson is but plain and once made perfect, never lost again.
"O, learn to love; the lesson is but plain,
And once made perfect, never lost again." (V&A)
In the poem. *Adone's horse fled to chase a mare and Venus draw a motivating comparison.*

Sexual fantasy – That's a fair thought to lie between maids' legs.
"That's a fair thought to lie between maids' legs" (H.3.2)
In the play. *Hamlet, now at total odds with the world comments to Ophelia who said that she was thinking about nothing.*

Sexual harassment - Fit thy consent to my sharp appetite...
"Fit thy consent to my sharp appetite;
Lay by all nicety and prolixious blushes,
That banish what they sue for" (MFM.2.4)
Make your request clear, depending on the character of the party involved. See also entries for 'Harassment, handling of sexual h.'
In the play. *Angelo now harasses Isabella and pushes his sex-for-mercy offer.*

Sexual intercourse - ... conflict such as was supposed the wandering prince and Dido once enjoy'd.
"...conflict such as was supposed
The wandering prince and Dido once enjoy'd,

When with a happy storm they were surprised
And curtain'd with a counsel-keeping cave,
We may, each wreathed in the other's arms,
Our pastimes done, possess a golden slumber." (TA.2.1)
In the play. *The wicked queen Tamora prompts Aaron.*

Sexual intercourse – ... Groping for trouts in a peculiar river
MISTRESS OVERDONE But what's his offence?
POMPEY *Groping for trouts in a peculiar river.* (MFM.1.2)
In the play. *Brothel keeper and bawd discuss the arrest and condemnation of Claudio for fornication.*

Sexual intercourse - ... I liked her and boarded her i' the wanton way of youth.
"...certain it is I liked her,
And boarded her i' the wanton way of youth" (AWEW.5.3)
In the play. *Back at Rousillon Bertram has to explain how he gave away his ring to a lady who requested it from him.*

Sexual intercourse – ... the deed of darkness.
"If she'ld do the deed of darkness, thou wouldst say." (PER.4.6)
In the play. *Lysimachus comments on the praises of Marina as delivered by Bawd.*

Sexual intercourse – ... your daughter and the Moor are now making the beast with two backs.
"I am one, sir, that comes to tell you your daughter and the Moor are now making the beast with two backs" (OTH.1.1
In the play. *Iago comes to announce to the distraught Brabantio that his daughter Desdemona has married Othello.*

Sexual intercourse - He thinks ... that you have touch'd his queen forbiddenly.
"He thinks, nay, with all confidence he swears,
... that you have touch'd his queen Forbiddenly." (WT.1.2)
In the play. *Camillo, sent to poison Polixenes, tells him of the insane and deranged jealousy of Leontes.*

Sexual intercourse and related punishment - Why should he die, sir? ... filling a bottle with a tundish
DUKE VINCENTIO Why should he die, sir?
LUCIO Why? For filling a bottle with a tundish (MFM.3.2)
In the play. *The coarse Lucio answers Duke Vicentio who disguised himself as a friar. 'Tundish' = 'funnel'.*

Sexual intercourse suspected – I am doubtful that you have been conjunct...
"I am doubtful that you have been conjunct
And bosom'd with her, as far as we call hers" (KL.5.1)
In the play. *Jealous Regan to Edgar, referring to her sister Goneril.*

Shadows, rewarded with s. - Some there be that shadows kiss, such have but a shadow's bliss.
"Some there be that shadows kiss; Such have but a shadow's bliss" (MOV.2.9)
Comment on the poor results of a project that was an illusion.
In the play. *The prince of Arragon reads the message he found in the (wrong) silver casket. If had guessed right he would have married Portia.*

Shame, curious as to how the shameless can avoid s. – What trick,

what device, what starting-hole, canst thou now find out to hide thee…
"What trick, what device, what starting-hole, canst thou now find out to hide thee from this open and apparent shame?" (KHIV.p1.2.4)
In the play. *Prince Henry has exposed the lies of Falstaff and is curious as to how Falstaff will try to justify or clear himself.*

Shame, exempt from s. - … upon his brow shame is ashamed to sit.
"… he was not born to shame:
Upon his brow shame is ashamed to sit" (RJ.3.2)
In the play. *Juliet reprimands the Nurse who berated Romeo after he killed Tybalt.*

Shame, shameful acts and behavior – Heaven stops the nose at it and the moon winks…
"What committed!
Heaven stops the nose at it and the moon winks,
The bawdy wind that kisses all it meets
Is hush'd within the hollow mine of earth,
And will not hear it." (OTH.4.2)
In the play. *Othello accuses the faultless Desdemona of infidelity*

Shame, shameful acts by a shameless character – … Were shame enough to shame thee, wert thou not shameless.
"Were shame enough to shame thee, wert thou not shameless" (KHVI.p.3.1.4)
In the play. *York, captured in battle and taunted by Queen Margaret, responds to her*

Shepherdess, if she were a shepherdess - I should leave grazing, were I of your flock, and only live by gazing.
"I should leave grazing, were I of your flock,
And only live by gazing." (WT.4.4)

Compliment. Some ladies who proclaim that they like to live in the country. You can say, 'If you lived in the country and were a shepherdess…'I should leave… gazing.'
In the play. *Camillo, just arrived in Bohemia meets with the shepherdess Perdita (alias daughter of Leontes, king of Sicilia). Perdita in kindness offers flowers to him. Camillo answers with this pointed compliment.*

Ship, compliment, like Helen of Troy - ... she is a pearl, whose price hath launched above a thousand ships, and turn'd crown'd kings to merchants.
"…she is a pearl,
Whose price hath launched above a thousand ships,
And turn'd crown'd kings to merchants." (TC.2.2)
Answer to 'What do you think of me?' that is 'You are like Helen, a pearl…'
In the play. *Troilus defends Helen on questionable grounds, against those in the Trojan camp that would like to return her to the Greeks.*

Shoes, putting on s. on the wrong foot – … slippers, which his nimble haste had falsely thrust upon contrary feet.
"…slippers, which his nimble haste
Had falsely thrust upon contrary feet" (KJ.4.2)
See also 'Title, job t. magnified - Thou art a cobbler, art thou?… I am, indeed, sir, a surgeon to old shoes.'
In the play. *Hubert tells King John of the turmoil in the country, including a tailor who, in the excitement, misses the correct wearing of his slippers.*

Shop, s. not in tip-top conditions - … and about his shelves a beggarly account of empty boxes.
"… and about his shelves
A beggarly account of empty boxes" (RJ.5.1)

Describe your office with some irony and self-effacing. In one anonymous play the office occupier apologizes as follows, 'I should excuse the state of my office, but that would imply an exception'.
In the play. *Romeo's description of the pharmacist where he plans to acquire a poison for himself, as he believes that Juliet is dead.*

Short shrift - ... make a short shrift. (KRIII.3.4)
'To make a short shrift' is a common parlance line directly extracted from Shakespeare.
In the play. *Ratcliff (a lord in the service of Richard III) to Hastings who will be beheaded shortly for opposing Richard's claim to the throne. Ratcliff wants to dispatch the matter (execution) as soon as possible. 'Shrift' is a confession made to a priest.*

Shortcomings, admitting to one's own s. - If ever I were wilful-negligent it was my folly...
"If ever I were wilful-negligent,
It was my folly; if industriously
I play'd the fool, it was my negligence,
Not weighing well the end...
... these, my lord,
Are such allow'd infirmities that honesty
Is never free of" (WT.1.2)
In the play. *Leontes hints that his trusted counselor Camillo was negligent or perhaps dishonest and Camillo defends himself.*

Shortcomings, sometimes s. prove useful - ...full oft 'tis seen, our means secure us, and our mere defects prove our commodities.
"...full oft 'tis seen,
Our means secure us, and our mere defects
Prove our commodities" (KL.41)
See also 'Ignorance, i. of what is really good for us - We, ignorant of ourselves beg often our own harms, which the wise powers deny us for our good...'
In the play. *Gloucester, blinded by Regan, does not lament his state, because that very state has allowed him to recognize his previous faults (believing the accusations against his good son Edgar)*

Shyness and speechlessness, you are unable to speak - What passion hangs these weights upon my tongue?
"**What passion hangs these weights upon my tongue?**" (AYLI.1.2)
You are shy, you must say something but words just don't come out.
Not knowing what to say at a first encounter is a common problem. Archdeacon Ruiz gives a related biographical anecdote followed by some words of advice.
'Oh, how beautiful is Dona Endrina, what an egret's neck, what hair, little mouth, color! She wounds with love darts when she casts but a glance. But that place (the public square), was not suitable for romantic conversation, I lost confidence, my feet and hands were no longer masters of themselves. I lost courage and color. I had an introductory speech ready but could not deliver. Now, addressing a woman in a square is too obvious, sometimes an ugly rotweiler is ready to ambush you behind a perfidious open door. Therefore, when in a public square, limit your approach to neutral subjects, dropping hints perhaps, as in jest. I told her, 'My niece in Toledo, recommends herself to you and wants to meet you. My parents (in Toledo) want me to marry the daughter of Don Pepito, but I won't. My body will belong to her who owns my heart.' (Libro de Bueno Amor, #653-658).
In the play. *Orlando has won the wrestling match and has fallen in love with Rosalind to the point that he is tongue-tied.*

Shyness, love concealed - She never told her love, but let concealment, like a worm in the bud…
"She never told her love,
But let concealment, like a worm in the bud,
Feed on her damask cheek. " (TN.2.4)
It is clear that she likes him but somehow holds back.
Think before using this line. It may be politically incorrect if she has acne. Technically, you could reverse the gender and case of the articles and apply the statement to you. 'I never told her my love, but let concealment, like a worm in the bud, feed… cheek.' But to call your cheek 'damask' would be narcissistic or may be grossly misinterpreted. Choose another adjective instead of 'damask', e.g. 'coarse'
In the play: *Viola tells a story in which a woman loved a man but concealed her love. Her love for Duke Orsino is real, but Viola, being disguised as Cesario, cannot make it known to him.*

Sickness, s. doubtful - Many do keep their chambers are not sick.
"Many do keep their chambers are not sick" (TOA.3.4)
In the play. *Lucilius' servant questions whether Timon is really sick as reported by Servilius or if it is just an excuse.*

Sicily, (or any country) out of mind – Of that fatal country… pr'ythee speak no more; whose very naming punishes me with the remembrance.
"Of that fatal country Sicilia, pr'ythee speak no more; whose very naming punishes me with the remembrance." (WT.4.1)
Change 'Sicily' to whatever other country or city towards which you share Polixenes' feelings.

In the play. *After such a long time Camillo tells Polixenes of his intention to return to Sicilia. Polixenes does not want to lose Camillo's services but does not even want to hear of Sicilia, given his (Polixenes') unhappy experience last time he visited.*

Siding with the losing party - …though my reason sits in the wind against me.
" I'll yet follow
The wounded chance of Antony, though my reason
Sits in the wind against me." (AC.3.10)
Justify your loyalty before or, with modification, afterwards, e.g., 'I followed the wounded chance of (name of losing party) though my reason sat in the wind against me.' See also 'Judgment, skepticism about people's j. – All that follow their noses are led by their eyes but blind men…' *** 'Circumstances, adapting course to c. - Let go thy hold when a great wheel runs down a hill…' *** 'Organization, o. on the point of sinking - … leak'd is our bark and we, poor mates, stand on the dying deck...'
In the play. *Antony has lost a crucial battle against Octavian - his lieutenant Enobarbus remains faithful for the moment but with misgivings.*

Sigh - … adding to clouds more clouds with his deep sighs
"Many a morning hath he there been seen,
With tears augmenting the fresh morning's dew,
Adding to clouds more clouds with his deep sighs" (RJ.1.1)
Turn the lines into a question, 'Why are you adding to clouds more clouds with your deep sighs?' Or use them as a chronicle of your passion, e.g. 'With tears I have been augmenting the fresh… with my deep sighs'.

In the play. *Montague reports that Romeo has been seen repeatedly in the morning crying and sighing. Romeo is in love, Montague concludes, 'Black and portentous must this humour prove,*
Unless good counsel may the cause remove.'

Sigh - Wherefore breaks that sigh from the inward of thee?
"… Wherefore breaks that sigh
From the inward of thee?" (CYM.3.4)
Alternative to question, 'Why are you sighing?' See also 'Expression, why so serious, what are you thinking about? - … What serious contemplation are you in?'
In the play. *Imogen questions Pisanio about his uneasiness. He has not yet told her of the instructions to kill her, contained in a letter sent by Leonatus, her husband.*

Sigh, s. of distress fogging up the sky – … with our sighs we'll breathe the welkin dim…
"…with our sighs we'll breathe the welkin dim,
And stain the sun with fog, as sometime clouds
When they do hug him in their melting bosoms" (TA.3.1)
In the play. *Titus Andronicus to Lavinia, who was raped and mutilated by sociopaths Chiron and Demetrius. 'Welkin' = 'sky'.*

Sight, a horrible s. - … the object poisons sight; let it be hid.
"…the object poisons sight;
Let it be hid" (OTH.5.2)
In the play. *Ludovico, a relative of Desdemona's father Brabantio comments on the sight of the murdered Desdemona and Emilia and self-slain Othello.*

Sigh - (my heart) wounded it is, but with the eyes of a lady.

ROSALIND I thought thy heart had been wounded with the claws of a lion.
ORLANDO Wounded it is, but with the eyes of a lady. (AYLI.5.2)
Answer to 'Why are you sighing?' Try 'my heart is wounded by the eyes of a lady'.
In the play. *Orlando was not seriously wounded while battling a lioness who was stalking his elder (evil, but now repented) brother.*

Sight, heart-rendering - O thou side-piercing sight.
"O thou side-piercing sight!" (KL.4.6)
In the play. *Edgar at Dover on seeing King Lear in rags and demonstrably mad.*

Sight, heart warming and cheering s. - thy sight, which should make our eyes flow with joy, hearts dance with comfort.
"…thy sight, which should
Make our eyes flow with joy, hearts dance
with comforts…" (COR.5.3)
Turn into a compliment, e.g. 'Thy sight makes our hearts... comforts'
In the play. *Volumnia reprehends her son Coriolanus who, with his behavior, prevents her and his wife to be happy at seeing him.*

Sight, not seeing straight - Methinks I see these things with parted eye, when every thing seems double.
"Methinks I see these things with parted eye,
When every thing seems double." (MND.4.1)
In the play. *Hermia is not sure whether she is awake or asleep.*

Sight, pitiful s. especially in an authority – A sight most pitiful in the meanest wretch…

"A sight most pitiful in the meanest wretch,
Past speaking of in a king!" (KL.4.6)
In the play. *A gentleman comments on the mad state of King Lear in Dover.*

Sight, ugly s. – … most lamentable to behold.
"…is most lamentable to behold." (HV.2.1)
In the play. *The Hostess in Eastcheap refers to the physical conditions of Falstaff*

Sight, unbearable sight - The sight of any of the house of York is as a fury to torment my soul.
"The sight of any of the house of York
Is as a fury to torment my soul" (KHVI.p3.1.3)
Change 'the house of York' to other applicable tormenting subject.
In the play. *Clifford Junior (faithful to Henry VI of Lancaster) to the soon-to-be-slain young Rutland of York.*

Sight, unpleasant s. - … to see this sight, it irks my very soul.
Q. MARGARET. Doth not the object cheer your heart, my lord?
K. HENRY VI. Ay, as the rocks cheer them that fear their wreck;
To see this sight, it irks my very soul." (KHVI p3.2.2)
Express your dissatisfaction at an event that leaves other happy. Answer to 'Do you like this?'
In the play. *Margaret greets her husband outside the town of York. The object for which Henry should cheer is the severed head of Richard duke of York*

Sightseeing, acquiring knowledge of the town via s. - .. you beguile the time and feed your knowledge with viewing of the town.
"I will bespeak our diet,
Whiles you beguile the time and feed your knowledge

With viewing of the town." (TN.3.3)
Announce that you are going sightseeing, 'I will beguile the time… town'. Or use to say that you are organizing the dinner while the others are out.
In the play. *Sebastian wants to see the city before retiring to a hotel. Antonio instead, decided to go to the hotel and organize the dinner.*

Sightseeing, looking at people - … we'll wander through the streets and note the qualities of people.
"…To-night we'll wander through the streets and note
The qualities of people." (AC.1.1)
Signal your intentions to go for a walk downtown. Answer to 'What will you do this week end?' or equivalent. Change 'we'll' to 'I'll' as applicable
In the play. *Antony proposes to Cleopatra a sightseeing touring through town (Alexandria, Egypt). He is trying to find ways to calm her down.*

Sightseeing, s. suggestion, especially museums - … let us satisfy our eyes with the memorials and the things of fame…
"I pray you, let us satisfy our eyes
With the memorials and the things of fame,
That do renown this city." (TN.3.3)
Introduce a sightseeing tour. Or modify to answer the question 'Where are you going?' 'I am going to satisfy my eyes… this city'
In the play. *Sebastian suggests to Antonio a sightseeing walk through the city before retiring to a hotel.*

Sightseeing - … I'll view the manners of the town…
"…I'll view the manners of the town,
Peruse the traders, gaze upon the buildings,
And then return and sleep within mine inn" (COE.1.2)

In the play. *Aegeon plans to visit Syracuse before retiring to the hotel.*

Sightseeing - …I will go lose myself and wander up and down to view the city.
"…I will go lose myself,
And wander up and down to view the city." (COE.1.2)
How you will use your time off. See also 'Walk, a w. proposed – tonight we'll wander through the streets and note the qualities of people.'
In the play. *Antipholus of Syracuse takes temporary leave of a merchant and in the meantime he will go sightseeing in Ephesus.*

Silence, admired and meaningful – I like your silence, it the more shows off your wonder.
"I like your silence, it the more shows off
Your wonder" (TN.5.3)
When she seems temporarily at a loss for words after something you said, did or gave to her.
In the play. *Paulina pulls a curtain hiding the statue of Hermione, believed lost. As it will turn out the statue is the Hermione herself. This explains in part Leonte's wonder and speechlessness*

Silence, better keep quiet about the whole thing - It is enough you know; and it is fit what being known grows worse, to smother it.
"It is enough you know; and it is fit,
What being known grows worse, to smother it." (PER.1.1)
Explain why the matter should be kept quiet.
In the play. *Pericles lets Antiochus know indirectly that he understood the meaning of the riddle, concluding that it is better that the business does not become public knowledge. Antiochus is incestuous.*

Silence, criticized and unendorsed - … for silence is only commendable in a neat's tongue dried and a maid not vendible.
"Thank's i'faith, for silence is only commendable,
In a neat's tongue dried and a maid not vendible." (MOV.1.1)
Justify why you tend to speak a lot or a bit too much. A retort to 'Be quiet'
In the play. *Gratiano acknowledges Antonio's commitment to be more communicative. A neat's tongue was a delicacy in Shakespeare's time. However, it was not considered a wholesome food unless dried. In Salerno "Regimen Sanitatis" (Latin for 'health guide') a neat's tongue is defined as 'not very holsome when moyst'. It was necessary to stuff it with cloves "whereby the moystenes is dyminished".*

Silence, discretion, s. advised - … Bosom up my counsel, you'll find it wholesome.
"… Bosom up my counsel,
You'll find it wholesome."
(KHVIII.1.1)
Encourage to keep information confidential.
In the play. *Norfolk advises Buckingham that Cardinal Wolsey's sword has a sharp edge and his (Buckingham's) criticism may be dangerous*

Silence, exhortation to s. - Cry 'holla' to thy tongue, I prithee; it curvets unseasonably.
"Cry 'holla' to thy tongue, I prithee; it curvets unseasonably" (AYLI.4.1)
In the play. *Celia to Rosalind who incessantly inquires about Orlando with whom she is in love.*

Silence, frozen into s. - They froze me into silence.
"They froze me into silence."
(TOA.2.2)
See also 'Speechless, stunned by her beauty - you have bereft me of all words, lady.'

In the play. *Servant Flavius reports on the poor response of so called friends to the request for financial help by Timon.*

Silence, no answer to any question, remaining speechless - … From this time forth I never will speak word.
OTHELLO (to Cassio) Will you, I pray, demand that demi-devil,
Why he hat thus ensnar'd my soul and body?
IAGO (to Othello) Demand me nothing: what you know, you know; From this time forth I never will speak word." (OTH.5.2)
State that you will not answer any more questions.
In the play. *Othello, just before killing himself, tries to find out the reasons for Iago's diabolic actions but Iago refuses to answer.*

Silence, nothing else to say - The rest is silence.
"The rest is silence" (H.5.2)
Characterize the irrelevance of useless comments. Restate the point and end with 'The rest is silence'.
In the play. *Hamlet's last words to Horatio as he instructs him to tell Fortinbras about what happened in Elsinore.*

Silence, preferring s. to lying - I had rather seal my lips, than, to my peril, speak that which is not.
"I had rather seal my lips, than, to my peril,
Speak that which is not." (AC.5.2)
When you are asked to agree to something and you just can't.
In the play. *Cleopatra asks Seleucus, her treasurer to confirm that she has not hidden any treasure or valuable assets from the conquering Romans. By his reply Seleucus implies that she has.*

Silence, reason for s. – … our argument is all too heavy to admit much talk.

"…our argument
Is all too heavy to admit much talk."
(KHIVp2.5.2)
Answer to 'Why don't you talk?'
In the play. *In London, the Prince of Lancaster joins a quiet and moody group of courtiers soon after Henry IV's death.*

Silence, s. as a symptom or evidence of happiness - Silence is the perfectest herald of joy, I were but little happy, if I could say how much.
BEATRICE. Speak, count, it is your cue.
CLAUDIO. Silence is the perfectest herald of joy:
I were but little happy, if I could say how much. (MAAN.2.2)
Some ladies worry if you keep quiet and do not speak, especially so if you are usually talkative. Answer with Claudio's line when you are asked to explain your silence. See also 'Love, l. and silence - Fire, that's closest kept, burns most of all.'
On the same subject Ovid states that 'Keeping silence is but a small virtue, but to speak what should not be uttered is a heinous crime' AOL.2
In the play. *Leonato has just consented to Claudio marrying his daughter and Beatrice, who is present, prompts Claudio to speak. Claudio is speechless out of happiness.*

Silence, s. as proof of innocence - The silence often of pure innocence persuades, when speaking fails.
"The silence often of pure innocence
Persuades, when speaking fails."
(WT.2.2)
Answer to 'Why don't you say something?' when she has made an accusation to you and you do not want to answer, or have no justification if the accusation is true.
In the play. *Paulina will present to the king the newly born baby girl, born to Hermione while she is in jail. The foolish and jealous Leontes*

believes that the child is not his and will order the babe's killing.

Silence, s. commented on – ... methought her eyes had lost her tongue.
"…methought her eyes had lost her tongue," (TN.2.2)
Commenting on unexpected silence. If in the present try 'methinks your eyes have lost your tongue'.
In the play. *Viola/Cesario realizes that Olivia has fallen in love with her thinking she is a man – the symptom being that Olivia 'lost her tongue' after 'making good view of her'*

Silence, s. imposed - ... be you silent and attentive too, for he that interrupts him shall not live.
"… And be you silent and attentive too,
For he that interrupts him shall not live." (KHVI p3.1.1)
Change 'him' to 'me' if it is you who do not wish to wish to be interrupted.
In the play. *Warwick to audience which includes the rightful King Henry VI.*

Silence, s. not a symptom of indifference - I hear, yet say not much, but think the more.
"I hear, yet say not much, but think the more." (KHVI.p3.4.1)
Answer to 'Why do you not speak?' or 'Why are you so quiet?'
In the play. *King Edward made king by Warwick who, in turn, has deposed Henry VI, decides to marry the Lady Grey instead of the Lady Bona whom it had been assumed he would marry. This throws a wrench in the wheel of events. Some are upset, Richard says nothing but 'thinks the more' plotting his own course.*

Silence, s. observed in person - ... thou hast spoken no word all this while.

HOLOFERNES. Via, goodman Dull! thou hast spoken no word all this while.
DULL. Nor understood none neither, sir. (LLL.5.1)
In the play. *Holofernes notes Dull's silence.*

Silence, self-enforced - It is not nor it cannot come to good: but break, my heart; for I must hold my tongue.
"It is not nor it cannot come to good: But break, my heart; for I must hold my tongue." (H.1.2)
When you wish to signify your intense displeasure at what is being said or decided. The second line is sufficient. See also 'Heartbreak - O heart, heavy heart, why sigh'st thou without breaking?'
In the play. *Still unaware of his father's murder but upset at the quick nuptials of his widowed mother, Hamlet has bad presentiments but cannot as yet publicly express them.*

Silence, self-imposed in the circumstances - My heart is great; but it must break with silence…
"My heart is great; but it must break with silence,
Ere't be disburden'd with a liberal tongue." (KRII.2.1)
In the play. *Lord Ross is seething with anger at Richard II but will keep quiet until he be assured that his audience is on his side.*

Silence, unable to answer - I am perplex'd, and know not what to say.
"I am perplex'd, and know not what to say." (KJ.3.1)
In the play. *Bishop Pandulph has threatened King Philip of France with excommunication if the orders of the Pope are not followed.*

Silliness or foolery repeated - ... you see, sir, your fooling grows old, and people dislike it.
"Now you see, sir, your fooling grows old, and people dislike it." (TN.1.5)

When you are tired of the same jokes, or why you do not want to tell the same joke again. E.G. 'When the fooling grows old people dislike it'.
In the play. *Olivia reprimands the clown for having offended Malvolio.*

Similarity between two people, twins - An apple cleft in two is not more twin than these two creatures.'
" How have you made division of yourself? --
An apple cleft in two is not more twin Than these two creatures." (TN.5.1)
Indicate that two people are exactly the same, applicable equally to mode of thinking. See also entries for 'Characters, similarity of c.'
In the play. *The knot begins to untangle and Antonio realizes that the Sebastian whom he thought he was previously addressing was actually his twin sister disguised as a man.*

Simile, s. not appreciated – Thou hast the most unsavoury similes.
"Thou hast the most unsavoury similes" (KHIV.p1.1.2)
In the play. *Falstaff banters with Prince Henry*

Simile. s. OK but somewhat gross – A good swift simile, but something currish.
"A good swift simile, but something currish." (TS.5.2)
In the play. *Petruchio comments on a statement by Tranio, who, in turn said that he worked for Lucentio like a greyhound.*
'Currish'='Partaking of the characteristics of a dog'

Simony, assigning positions for bribes - … Cassius, you yourself are much condemn'd to have an itching palm.
"Let me tell you, Cassius, you yourself Are much condemn'd to have an itching palm." (JC. 4.3)
In the play. *Brutus and Cassius have a debate in Brutus' tent prior to the battle of Philippi.*

Simplicity, s. in giving away information – The flat transgression of a schoolboy…
"The flat transgression of a schoolboy, who, being overjoyed with finding a birds' nest, shows it his companion, and he steals it." (MAAN.2.1)
In the play. *Don Pedro has wooed Hero on Claudio's behalf and Claudio thinks that Don Pedro has stolen her affection. Benedick makes the comparison for Don Pedro's sake.*

Sin, cannot put a gloss on s. - You cannot make gross sins look clear
"You cannot make gross sins look clear" (TOA.3.5)
In the play. *Athenian senators reject Alcibiade's plea for clemency for one of his soldiers*

Sin, doubtful gains of s. - 'What win I, if I gain the thing I seek?…
"'What win I, if I gain the thing I seek?
A dream, a breath, a froth of fleeting joy.
Who buys a minute's mirth to wail a week?
Or sells eternity to get a toy?
For one sweet grape who will the vine destroy?" (ROL)
In the poem. *Tarquin meditates on his intention to rape the virtuous Lucrece.*

Sin, rationale for s. - … in the state of innocency Adam fell; and what should poor Jack Falstaff do in the days of villany?
"… thou knowest in the state of innocency Adam fell; and what should poor Jack Falstaff do in the days of villany?" (KHIV.p1.3.3)
In the play. *Falstaff answers a harangue of accusations and reprimands from Prince Henry*

Sin, s. not occasional, but chronic - Thy sin's not accidental, but a trade.
"Thy sin's not accidental, but a trade." (MFM.3.1)
Applicable to various sins and sinners, e.g. when accusing a political contender of corruption or similar.
In the play. *Isabella to her brother Claudio who has been condemned for fornication.*

Sincerity, doubts about s. - I would I knew thy heart. – 'tis figured in my tongue.
LADY ANNE I would I knew thy heart.
GLOUCESTER 'Tis figured in my tongue.
LADY ANNE I fear me both are false.
GLOUCESTER Then never man was true. (KRIII.1.2)
Assuming the other party may not know the plot, reinforce your plea of sincerity, e.g. 'My heart is figured in my tongue'.
In the play. *Richard woos the recently widowed Lady Anne, whose husband he slain.*

Sincerity, question about s. - Speakest thou from thy heart? ... And from my soul too; or else beshrew them both.
JULIET Speakest thou from thy heart?
NURSE And from my soul too; Or else beshrew them both. (RJ.3.5)
In the play. *The Nurse has just advised Juliet to marry Paris and forget Romeo. Juliet is, of course, astonished. 'Beshrew' = 'woe to'.*

Sincerity, s. as opposed to appearance – ... they are actions that a man might play, but I have that within which passeth show...
"...they are actions that a man might play,
But I have that within which passeth show;
These but the trapping and the suits of woe." (H.1.1)

Underscore the difference between your sincerity and the fake concern and/or hypocrisy of others - you may skip the last line or quote entirely by citing the source.
In the play. *Hamlet tells his mother that he is the only one who really mourns the death of the king.*

Sincerity, s. preferable to affected ceremony - Me rather had my heart might feel your love than my unpleased eye see your courtesy.
"Me rather had my heart might feel your love
Than my unpleased eye see your courtesy." (KRII.3.3)
In the play. *Richard to Bolingbroke who, in a show of feigned loyalty, has kneeled before him.*

Sincerity, s. stated - I want that glib and oily art to speak and purpose not...
"...I want that glib and oily art,
To speak and purpose not; since what I well intend,
I'll do't before I speak" (KL.1.1)
In the play. *Cordelia to Lear after he chastised her for not having expressed her love as emphatically as her (hypocrite) sisters have.*

Sincerity, spoken sincerely - ... and believe in heart that what you speak is in your conscience wash'd as pure as sin with baptism.
"For we will hear, note and believe in heart
That what you speak is in your conscience wash'd
As pure as sin with baptism." (KHV.1.2)
Apply to your statement, e.g. 'What I speak is in my conscience washed... baptism'
In the play. *King Henry to the Archbishop of Canterbury who wants Henry to conquer France to prevent him from collecting taxes from the Church of England.*

Sincerity, time to be sincere - The weight of this sad time we must obey, speak what we feel, not what we ought to say.
"The weight of this sad time we must obey,
Speak what we feel, not what we ought to say." (KL.5.3)
Use as is if, it applies, or just the line, '(We must) speak what we feel, not what we ought to say' when urging members of a committee to freely speak their mind.
In the play. *Sobering thoughts by Edgar at the end of a bloody battle followed by the death of Lear, Cordelia and just about everyone else.*

Sincerity, verifying a person's s. - But tell me true, for I must ever doubt…
"But tell me true,
For I must ever doubt, though ne'er so sure…" (TOA.4.3)
In the play. *Timon wants to verify the sincerity of his faithful servant Flavius.*

Singer, a poor s. - An he had been a dog that should have howled thus, they would have hanged him.
"An he had been a dog that should have howled thus, they would have hanged him." (MAAN.2.3)
Your opinion of a poor singer
In the play. *Benedick does not think much of Balthazar's singing. 'An' = 'if'.*

Singing, pleasure to be sung to - … and she will sing the song that pleaseth you…
"And rest your gentle head upon her lap,
And she will sing the song that pleaseth you,
And on your eyelids crown the god of sleep,
Charming your blood with pleasing heaviness;
Making such difference 'twixt wake and sleep,
As is the difference betwixt day and night,
The hour before the heavenly-harness'd team
Begins his golden progress in the east." (KHIV p1.3.1)
You can turn it around and make yourself the subject of the singing. 'Rest your gentle head upon my lap and I will sing the song that pleaseth you, and on your eyelids crown the god of sleep'.
In the play. *Glendower translates for Mortimer what Lady Mortimer said in Welsh.*

Single - … thou consumest thyself in single life.
"Is it for fear to wet a widow's eye
That thou consumest thyself in single life?" SON.9)
Answer to 'Are you married?' or 'Do you have a girlfriend?' 'No, I consume myself in single life' See also 'Marriage, m. unsuited to military life - A soldier is better accommodated than with a wife.'

Sinner, inventive s. – … commit the oldest sins the newest kind of ways…
"…and commit
The oldest sins the newest kind of ways…" (KHIV.p2.4.3)
In the play. *Ailing King Henry rhetorically imagines other countries dispatching scum and sinners to England in keeping with the behavior of the Prince of Wales. But the Prince has reformed.*

Sins, unpleasant to hear of one's own s - few love to hear the sins they love to act.
"Great King,
Few love to hear the sins they love to act;
'T would braid yourself too near for me to tell it." (PER.1.1)

Refuse saying something that may point out the pitfalls of him who asked you to speak.
In the play. *Pericles solved the riddle but the solution is the discovery of the incestuous relationship between King Antiochus and his daughter. Pericles declines to explain the true meaning of the riddle, out of concern for his own safety.* 'Braid' = 'Reproach'

Situation, acceptance (with some reservation) of a situation that cannot be changed - ... I must excuse what cannot be amended.
" ... I must excuse
What cannot be amended." (COR.4.7)
Acceptance a compromise solution.
In the play. *Coriolanus does not change his character even in the camp of Aufidius. But Coriolanus is useful and Aufidius accepts the situation.*

Situation, accurate assessment of the s. - ... Be it art or hap he hath spoken true.
"... Be it art or hap,
He hath spoken true." (AC.2.3)
Change 'hap' to 'chance' for better understanding. Use as a semi-sarcastic compliment, "Be it art or chance, thou hast spoken true."
In the play. *Antony reflecting on the soothsayer's pronouncement, who predicts that Octavian will overpower Antony.*

Situation, from one bad s. to another - ... Thus must I from the smoke into the smother...
"Thus must I from the smoke into the smother;
From tyrant duke unto a tyrant brother:" (AYLI.1.2)
Alternate to 'from the pan into the coals'. See also 'Alternative, dismal a. - Thus have I shunned the fire for fear of burning; and drench'd me in the sea, where I am drown'd...'

In the play. *Orlando, having defeated the wrestler Charles and incurred the hatred of his elder brother and of the usurping Duke, must flee for his life.*

Situation, general s. that you don't like - Uneven is the course, I like it not.
"Uneven is the course, I like it not." (RJ.4.1)
Could apply to a suggested hasty course or anything you are not clear about and yet you are pushed for a decision.
In the play. *Paris tells Father Laurence that the marriage between himself (Paris) and Juliet is scheduled in two days time. Friar Laurence, who has already married Juliet and Romeo is justifiably concerned.*

Situation, s. advantageous whatever the outcome - ... my end can make good use of either...
"... my end
Can make good use of either: she being down,
I have the placing of the British crown." (CYM.3.5)
In the play. *The one being down is Imogen who fled the paternal abode to escape her father who wants her to marry the loathsome Cloten.*

Situation, s. deteriorating, welcome overstayed - ... methinks my favour here begins to warp.
" ... methinks
My favour here begins to warp." (WT.1.2)
When you detect some dissension in the audience.
In the play. *Polixenes senses that he is no longer welcome at the court of Leontes.*

Situation, s. dire and without cure – Bootless are plaints, and cureless are my wounds.
"Bootless are plaints, and cureless are my wounds" (KHVI p3.2.6)

In the play. *Clifford, mortally wounded at the battle of Towton, blames King Henry VI for his lenity towards the house of York.*

Situation, s. redressed by hard means - ... for the health and physic of our right we cannot deal but with the very hand of stern injustice and confused wrong.
"But such is the infection of the time,
That, for the health and physic of our right,
We cannot deal but with the very hand
Of stern injustice and confused wrong." (KJ.5.2)
Describe situation calling for strong action.
In the play. *Salisbury must resort to ask France (King Lewis) to help redress the wrongs inflicted to England by King John.*

Situation, s. tangled - What an intricate impeach is this!
"What an intricate impeach is this!
I think you all have drunk of Circe's cup." (COE.5.1)
Your initial comment when handled a complex problem to resolve.
In the play. *The Duke of Ephesus steps in and is amazed at the intricate sequence of events. Circe's drink made people lose their memory.*

Situation, tense s. - ... every minute now should be the father of some stratagem: the times are wild.
"...every minute now
Should be the father of some stratagem:
The times are wild" (KHIV.p2.1.1)
In the play. *Northumberland to Lord Bardolph. The reference to the wild times has to do with the brewing rebellion against King Henry.*

Skepticism, s. on the current state of affairs - When clouds appear, wise men put on their cloaks...

"When clouds appear, wise men put on their cloaks;
When great leaves fall, the winter is at hand;
When the sun sets, who doth not look for night?
Untimely storms make men expect a dearth.
All may be well; but, if God sort it so,
'Tis more than we deserve, or I expect." (RIII.2.3)
Use the first line to approve a defensive measure or stand you may take.
In the play. *A citizen expresses the general fear and call for concern at the events triggered by Richard III's lust for power and the crown.* 'Dearth' = scarcity of food or famine.

Skepticism, s. on the value of offered help - ...to esteem a senseless help, when help past sense we deem.
"(We must not) dissever so
Our great self and our credit, to esteem
A senseless help, when help past sense we deem." (AWEW.2.1)
Express your skepticism at magic cures or solutions.
In the play. *Helen wishes to cure the King but he continues to be skeptical.*

Skin, her beautiful s. - That whiter skin of hers than snow, and smooth as monumental alabaster.
"...that whiter skin of hers than snow,
And smooth as monumental alabaster." (OTH.5.1)
Answer to 'What do you think of my new makeover?' Or just compliment her for her skin, change 'hers' to 'yours'. See also "Invocation, i. for lover to come – ... come, thou day in night; for thou wilt lie upon the wings of night whiter than new snow on a raven's back.'
In the play. *Othello, determined to kill Desdemona will do so without scarring her perfect skin.*

Skyscrapers, s. described – (Tarsus) Whose towers bore heads so high they kiss'd the clouds.
"(Tarsus) Whose towers bore heads so high they kiss'd the clouds" (PER.1.4)
In the play. *Cleon, king of Tarsus remarks on the dire straits the city is currently in.*

Slander, being the object of s. - So shall my name with slander's tongue be wounded.
"So shall my name with slander's tongue be wounded" (KHVIp2.3.2)
In the play. *Queen Margaret pretends to be dismayed that the common folks may think that she is the inspirer of Duke Humphrey's murder – she actually was.*

Slander, being the object of s. - To be a queen, and crown'd with infamy!
"To be a queen, and crown'd with infamy!" (KHVIp2.3.2)
Retort by a female executive, unjustly accused by board members.
In the play. *Queen Margaret pretends to be dismayed that the common folks may think that she is the inspirer of Duke Humphrey's murder – she actually was.*

Slander, calumny unavoidable – be thou as chaste as ice, as pure as snow, thou shalt not escape calumny.
"… be thou as chaste as ice, as pure as snow, thou shalt not escape calumny." (H.3.1)
Answer to unfounded or unjustified accusation.
In the play. *Hamlet warns Ophelia about the inevitability of escaping slander.*

Slander, calumny, unavoidable - No might nor greatness in mortality can censure 'scape…
"No might nor greatness in mortality Can censure 'scape: back-wounding calumny**

The whitest virtue strikes. What king so strong, Can tie the gall up in the slanderous tongue" (MFM.3.2)
Defend yourself from a slanderous attack.
In the play. *The Duke meditates on the slanderous comments by Lucio on the Duke himself (whose disguise Lucio has no recognized).*

Slander, killed by s. – Done to death by slanderous tongues…
"Done to death by slanderous tongues…" (MAAN.5.3)
Deny the allegations, e.g. 'I am done to death by slanderous tongues'. See also entries for 'Defence, d. from accusation'.
In the play. *Claudio reads from a scroll in front of the tomb of Hero, who is supposed dead (but is not). Malicious slander led to the forced disappearance of the good Hero.*

Slander, no s. can come from a fool - … there is no slander in an allowed fool, though he do nothing but rail.
"… there is no slander in an allowed fool, though he do nothing but rail" (TN.1.5)
Retort to an insult. Neutralize the sting from the attack of your opponent.
In the play. *Olivia tells Malvolio that he is too self-conceited to take issue at the barbs pronounced by the clown - the sallies of a clown contain no slander*

Slander, permanent characteristic of s. - For slander lives upon succession, for ever housed where it gets possession.
"For slander lives upon succession, For ever housed where it gets possession." (COE.3.1)
In the play. *The merchant Balthazar consoles Antipholus E. who suspects his wife. His wife, Adriana has mistaken Antipholus S for her husband.*

Slander, calumny, virtue not immune to s. - ...Virtue itself scapes not calumnious strokes...
"The chariest maid is prodigal enough,
If she unmask her beauty to the moon:
Virtue itself 'scapes not calumnious strokes:
The canker galls the infants of the spring,
Too oft before their buttons be disclosed,
And in the morn and liquid dew of youth
Contagious blastments are most imminent." (H.1.3)
Defend yourself or another from unjust accusations.
In the play. *Before leaving for France Laertes gives advice to his sister Ophelia, specifically to avoid temptations of all sorts, a typical macho distillate of double standards. 'Chariest' means 'nicest' as well as 'most heedful'.*

Slander, record of calumnies against you – ... none stands under more calumnious tongues than I myself.
"There's none stands under more calumnious tongues
Than I myself, poor man."
(KHVIII.5.1)
In the play. *Cranmer, Archbishop of Canterbury replies to King Henry who reports Cranmer's enemy's accusations.*

Slander, s. as a tool of self-advancement – ... some eternal villain... to get some office... have not devised this slander...
"I will be hang'd, if some eternal villain,
Some busy and insinuating rogue,
Some cogging, cozening slave, to get some office,
Have not devised this slander; I'll be hang'd else" (OTH.4.2)

In the play. *Emilia's opinion delivered to her husband Iago on the assumed adultery of Desdemona. Emilia is unaware that Iago is the villain.*

Slander, s. burning virtue – ... calumny will sear virtue itself.
"...calumny will sear
Virtue itself..." (WT.2.1)
In the play. *Leontes does not believe that the accusation of adultery levied against his wife Hermione is a calumny.*

Slander, sting of s. – ... slander, whose sting is sharper than the sword's...
"... slander,
Whose sting is sharper than the sword's" (WT.2.3)
Comment on slander.
In the play. *Paulina is outraged at the suspicion that Leontes has on his virtuous wife Hermione.*

Slander, transported like poison - ...slander whose whisper o'er the word's diameter, as level as the cannon to his blank...
"... slander
Whose whisper o'er the word's diameter,
As level as the cannon to his blank,
Transport his poisoned shot, may miss our name,
And hit the woundless air." (H.4.1)
Defense against rumor and accusations.
E.G.'This is slander... shot'.
In the play. *The king tells the queen that hopefully they will avoid the slander (meaning the implication (actually the truth) about the murder.*

Slanderer, reaction to a s. - O, fie upon thee, slanderer!
"O, fie upon thee, slanderer!" (OTH.2.1)
In the play. *Desdemona's reaction to Iago's disparaging comments on women. See 'Women,*

disparaging generalizations – … you are pictures out of doors…'

Sleep, s. creeping in - … o'er their brows death-counterfeiting sleep with leaden legs…
"… o'er their brows death-counterfeiting sleep
With leaden legs and batty wings doth creep" (MND.3.2)
In the play. *Oberon instructs Puck to induce sleep into Demetrius and Lysander.*

Sleep, s. or rest, time to adjourn the meeting - The deep of night is crept upon our talk and nature must obey necessity…
"The deep of night is crept upon our talk,
And nature must obey necessity;
Which we will niggard with a little rest." (JC.4.3)
The meeting has extended into the night and you need some rest. See also 'Time, t. for rest - … times to repair our nature with comforting repose.' *** 'Rest, need for r. – … and nature does require her times of preservation …' *** ***
'Health-care, rest as medicine - our foster-nurse of nature is repose, the which he lacks'
In the play. *After a conversation with Cassius the day before the battle at Philippi, Brutus is tired. 'To niggard'= 'To supply sparingly'.*

Sleep, 'Are you asleep?' - I have been broad awake two hours and more.
"I have been broad awake two hours and more." (TA.2.2)
Answer to the questions 'Are you asleep?' or 'Are you still asleep?' Change 'two' to any applicable other number.
In the play. *Bassianus questions Lavinia if he has awoken her up too early for a prospected hunting party. Lavinia replies that she was already awake.*

Sleep, before closing eyes and going to sleep – Ere I let fall the windows of mine eyes.
"Ere I let fall the windows of mine eyes" (KRIII.5.3)
Ask the question 'Anything I can do for you before I let fall…eyes?'
In the play. *Richmond recommends himself to the Almighty before going to sleep on the eve if the decisive battle at Bosworth Field against the forces of Richard III.*

Sleep, s. denied to persons with great power and responsibility - Canst thou, O partial sleep, give thy repose to the wet sea-boy in an hour so rude…
"Canst thou, O partial sleep, give thy repose
To the wet sea-boy in an hour so rude,
And in the calmest and most stillest night,
With all appliances and means to boot,
Deny it to a king?" (KHIV p2.3.1)
If you are not a big shot, use to explain to her some of the advantages of being little, such as a good sleeping pattern. See also, 'Fortune, reversal of f, and the bright side of it.'
In the play. *Henry, tormented with worries and pangs of conscience, meditates on one of the few disadvantages of royalty. In the same monologue are found the lines* 'Uneasy lies the head that wears a crown'. See 'Sleeplessness caused by the weight of your responsibilities.'

Sleep, drowsiness - What a strange drowsiness possesses them!
SEBASTIAN What a strange drowsiness possesses them!
ANTONIO It is the quality o' the climate. (TEM.2.1)
Try also 'A strange drowsiness possesses me'.
In the play. *The spirit Ariel has caused many of the shipwrecked party to fall asleep. Unaware*

of the intervening magic, Antonio attributes the reason to the climate.

Sleep, end of s. - ... shake off the golden slumber of repose.
"...at these early hours
Shake off the golden slumber of repose" (PER.3.2)
In the play. *Two gentlemen call on Dr. Cerimon's practice and are surprised to find him up so early as he does not need to. Cerimon gives a noble reply, see 'Virtue, v. and smartness as assets'.*

Sleep, excellent s. accompanied by pleasant dreams - The sweetest sleep, and fairest-boding dreams that ever enter'd in a drowsy head.
"The sweetest sleep, and fairest-boding dreams
That ever enter'd in a drowsy head
Have I since your departure had, my lords" (KRIII.5.3)
Answer to 'Did you sleep well?' 'I had the sweetest sleep...head.'
In the play. *Unlike Richard III, Richmond had the most pleasant dreams the night before the battle of Bosworth Field.*

Sleep, feeling sleepy - Night hangs upon mine eyes; my bones would rest, that have but labour'd to attain this hour.
"Night hangs upon mine eyes; my bones would rest,
That have but labour'd to attain this hour." (JC.5)
In the play. *Brutus after the lost battle of Philippi.*

Sleep, feeling sleepy - Thou art inclined to sleep; 'tis a good dulness...
"Thou art inclined to sleep; 'tis a good dulness,
And give it way: I know thou canst not choose." (TEM.1.2)
You can apply the statement to yourself, e.g. 'I am inclined to sleep, t'is a good dulness and will give it way'.
In the play. *Prospero to Miranda at the end of the history of their escape and exile in the island.*

Sleep, lack of care promoting sound sleep – Thou hast no figures nor no fantasies, which busy care draws in the brains of men...
"Enjoy the honey-heavy dew of slumber:
Thou hast no figures nor no fantasies,
Which busy care draws in the brains of men;
Therefore thou sleep'st so sound." (JC.2.1)
In the play. In the play. *Brutus sees his servant Lucius asleep and after a moment of thought decides to let him continue to sleep. Presumably Lucius does not hear what Brutus says.*

Sleep, lack of sleep creating anxiety - You lack the season of all natures, sleep.
"You lack the season of all natures, sleep." (M.3.4)
See also 'Health-care, rest as medicine - our foster-nurse of nature is repose, the which he lacks...'
In the play. *Macbeth is very agitated and Lady Macbeth diagnoses the agitation as caused by lack of sleep.*

Sleep, miserable and affected by nightmares - O, I have pass'd a miserable night, so full of ugly sights, of ghastly dreams.
"O, I have pass'd a miserable night,
So full of ugly sights, of ghastly dreams" (KRIII.1.4)
Answer to question 'Did you sleep well?' when you didn't
In the play. *The Duke of Clarence, prisoner in the Tower had nightmares. Richard III will shortly have him murdered.*

Sleep, s. after a hard day - … the long day's task is done and we must sleep.
"… the long day's task is done,
And we must sleep." (AC.4.14)
Why you must rest. Also usable as an epilogue to a presentation. E.G. "The long day's task is done… sleep – that is unless you have fallen asleep already…'
In the play. *After a lost battle at sea, Antony is tired.*

Sleep, s. as a tooth-ache reliever - Indeed, sir, he that sleeps feels not the tooth-ache.
"Indeed, sir, he that sleeps feels not the tooth-ache" (CYM.5.4)
Temporary postponement of a decision that is heavy on your mind. 'I'll go to sleep for the moment… he that…toothache.'
In the play. *A jailer engages the condemned Leonatus to discuss the advantages and disadvantages of being dead.*

Sleep, s. as rest - The crickets sing, and man's o'er-labour'd sense repairs itself by rest.
"The crickets sing, and man's o'erlabour'd sense
Repairs itself by rest." (CYM.2.2)
In the play. *Evil Jachimo exits from the trunk where he hid into Imogen's chamber.*

Sleep, heaviness of soul - My soul is heavy, and I fain would sleep.
"I pray thee, gentle keeper, stay by me;
My soul is heavy, and I fain would sleep." (KRIII.1.4)
When, for whatever reason, you need company as you are going to sleep. Change 'gentle keeper' to the name of the party you request the company of.
In the play. *Clarence, prisoner in the Tower is presaging his own demise (Richard III will actually have him killed) and asks the keeper to keep him company.*

Sleep, invocation to s. - …sleep… steal me awhile from mine own company.
"And sleep, that sometimes shuts up sorrow's eye,
Steal me awhile from mine own company." (MND.3.2)
In the sleep. *Helena is in distress and hopes to get some sleep before returning to Athens.*

Sleep, prayer before s. – To thee I do commend my watchful soul, let fall the windows of mine eyes.
"To thee I do commend my watchful soul,
Ere I let fall the windows of mine eyes:" (KRIII.5.3)
Alternative answer to 'Are you going to sleep?' E.G. 'Yes, I am going to let fall the windows of mine eyes'.
In the play. *Richmond recommends himself to God the night preceding the battle with King Richard at Bosworth Field.*

Sleep, soothing properties of s. - …sleep that knits up the ravell'd sleeve of care…
"… the innocent sleep;
Sleep that knits up the ravell'd sleeve of care,
The death of each day's life, sole labour's bath,
Balm of hurt minds, Great nature's second course,
Chief nourisher in life's feast." (M.2.2)
Answer to 'Are you sleepy?' An addition and/or an alternative to the answer 'I just need some sleep…the innocent sleep…feast."
In the play: *Macbeth begins to feel remorse. He killed King Duncan in his sleep.*

Sleep, soothing properties of s., when it comes – It seldom visits sorrow; when it doth, it is a comforter.
ALONSO What, all so soon asleep! I wish mine eyes
Would, with themselves, shut up my

thoughts: I find
They are inclined to do so.
SEBASTIAN Please you, sir,
Do not omit the heavy offer of it:
It seldom visits sorrow; when it doth,
It is a comforter. (TEM.2.1)
In the play. *Some survivors of the shipwrecked party have already fallen asleep thanks to the magic performed by the spirit Ariel.*

Sleep, s. habits influenced by lifestyle – Weariness can snore upon the flint, when resty sloth finds the down pillow hard.
"… weariness
Can snore upon the flint, when resty sloth
Finds the down pillow hard"
(CYM.3.6)
In the play. *Belarius' comments after a hard day acquiring food in the forest. 'Resty' = 'Torpid'*

Sleep, s. induced by a boring speaker - The best of rest is sleep and that thou oft provokest.
"The best of rest is sleep,
And that thou oft provokest; yet grossly fear'st
Thy death, which is no more."
(MFM.3.1)
See also, 'Speech, lengthy and annoying.' Change 'thou' to 'he' and 'provokest' to 'provoke' when referring to a boring speaker.
In the play. *Duke Vicentio holds a sobering conversation with Claudio who has been condemned to death*

Sleep, s. prevented by care, unimpeded in the young - … and where care lodges, sleep will never lie.
"Care keeps his watch in every old man's eye,
And where care lodges, sleep will never lie:
But where unbruised youth with unstuff'd brain

Doth couch his limbs, there golden sleep doth reign" (RJ.2.3)
Answer to, 'Why can't you sleep?' – '…where care lodges, sleep will never lie' In the play. *Friar Lawrence wonders why Romeo is up so early as little sleep is more typical of old men. See also 'Waking up, why so early?'*

Sleep, s. interruption common with soldiers - … 'tis the soldiers' life to have their balmy slumbers waked with strife.
"Come, Desdemona: 'tis the soldiers' life
To have their balmy slumbers waked with strife" (OTH.2.3)
When an associate or subordinate calls you at an ungodly hour to discuss an urgent matter and apologizes for it.
In the play. *Othello has been awaken by a brawl in Cyprus, engineered by Iago. Iago got Cassio drunk and a brawl ensued between Cassio and Montano.*

Sleep, s. of death considered as rest - … After life's fitful fever he sleeps well.
"Duncan is in his grave;
After life's fitful fever he sleeps well;
Treason has done his worst: nor steel, nor poison,
Malice domestic, foreign levy, nothing,
Can touch him further." (M.3.2)
In the play. *Macbeth's comment on King Duncan whom Macbeth has just slain. 'Fitful'=' Varying between extremes, full of paroxysms'*

Sleep, s. or nap required to restore strength - I'll strive with troubled thoughts to take a nap…
"I'll strive with troubled thoughts to take a nap,
Lest leaden slumbers weigh me down tomorrow,
When I should mount with wings of victory." (KRIII.5.3)

Justify your need for rest before the next day. See also 'Sleep, answer to 'Are you tired?'
In the play. *Richmond the night before the battle.*

Sleep, s. patterns and logic whereby late sleep is actually early rising - ... not to be abed after midnight is to be up betimes.
"To be up after midnight and to go to bed then, is early: so that to go to bed after midnight is to go
to bed betimes." (TN.3.1)
Answer to 'You came home too late'. See also 'Waking up early, possible reasons why - ... thy earliness doth assure me thou art up-roused by some distemperature…' – 'Time, up late, up early - I am glad I was up so late; for that's the reason I was up so early.' – 'Time, late night t. making it early morning - ... it is so very very late, that we may call it early by and by.'
In the play. *Sir Toby attempts to convince Sir Andrew that not going to bed after midnight is equivalent to getting up early. To support and demonstrate the argument he offers this clarification.*

Sleep, s. unprofitable - What is a man, if his chief good and market of his time be but to sleep and feed? a beast, no more.
"…What is a man,
If his chief good and market of his time
Be but to sleep and feed? a beast, no more. (H.4.4)
When you want to persuade that excessive sleep is not good. Also a follow up to the question, 'Why are you still in bed?'
In the play. *Hamlet reproaches himself for not taking more prompt action to revenge the death of his father.*

Sleep, singing her to s. - Many a time he danc'd thee on his knee sung thee asleep, his loving breast thy pillow.
"Many a time he danc'd thee on his knee
Sung thee asleep, his loving breast thy pillow." (TA.5.3)
Answer to, 'What are you going to do to me? E.G. 'I will sing thee asleep, my loving breast thy pillow'.
In the play. *Lucius reminds young Lucius of Titus' habit of playing with him and singing him to sleep.*

Sleep, sleeping remedy while lover is absent - Give me to drink mandragora that I might sleep out this great gap of time.
"Give me to drink mandragora,
That I might sleep out this great gap of time
My Antony is away" (AC.2.5)
In the play. *Cleopatra asks attendant Charmian for sleeping potion. Antony had to go to Rome on urgent business.' Mandragora' is derived from two Greek words implying 'hurtful to cattle' but was also a potent sleeping remedy.*

Sleep, someone fast asleep - As fast lock'd up in sleep as guiltless labour when lies starkly in the traveller's bones.
"As fast lock'd up in sleep as guiltless labour
When it lies starkly in the traveller's bones" (MFM.4.2)
Answer to 'Is he asleep?' when he is.
In the play. *The character fast asleep is the drunkard prisoner Barnardine.*

Sleep, sound s., invocation. - ... sleep, thou ape of death, lie dull upon her.
"… sleep, thou ape of death, lie dull upon her." (CYM.2.2)
Change 'her' to 'me' and use when you wish to go to sleep right away.
In the play. *The perfidious Iachimo observes Cymbeline who is fast asleep. He will make note*

of all the characteristics of the chamber and of Cymbeline to pretend with her husband that he (Iachimo) became Imogen's lover.

Sleep, talking while asleep - There are a kind of men so loose of soul, that in their sleeps will mutter their affairs.
"There are a kind of men so loose of soul,
That in their sleeps will mutter their affairs" (OTH.3.3)
In the play. *Iago drives Othello to jealousy by inventing a confession of Cassio heard while Cassio was asleep.*

Sleep, talking while asleep – ... infected minds to their deaf pillows will discharge their secrets.
"...infected minds
To their deaf pillows will discharge their secrets" (M.5.1)
In the play. *The doctor explains to a gentlewoman the reasons for Lady Makbeth's sleepwalking and sleeptalking.*

Sleep, tired and in need of immediate s. - ... Faintness constraineth me to measure out my length on this cold bed.
"...Faintness constraineth me
To measure out my length on this cold bed" (MND.3.2)
Remove 'cold' if you are tired at home and wish to announce that you are going to sleep.
In the play. *Demetrius is tired in the forest and lies down to sleep.*

Sleep, troubled s. but better in the morning - I have been troubled in my sleep this night, but dawning day new comfort hath inspired.
"I have been troubled in my sleep this night,
But dawning day new comfort hath inspired." (TA.2.2)
Answer to 'Did you sleep well?' See also 'Night, nightmare – O, I have pass'd a miserable night, so full of ugly sights, of ghastly dreams.'
In the play. *Titus A. before the hunt he has organized for emperor Saturninus*

Sleep, very sound s. - Though we seemed dead, we did but sleep.
"Though we seemed dead, we did but sleep." (KHV.3.6)
Change 'we' to 'I'. Comment to 'You were fast asleep', e.g. 'Yes, though I seemed dead, I did but sleep.'
In the play. *Montjoy tells Henry V why the French did not check and stop him at Harfleur in Picardy (France).*

Sleep, wish that s. could erase worries - I wish mine eyes would, with themselves, shut up my thoughts.
"I wish mine eyes
Would, with themselves, shut up my thoughts" (TEM.2.1)
See also 'Madness, wishing to be mad, to forget and avoid knowledge of what causes pain'
In the play. *The distressed Alonso wishes that sleep take away his concerns.*

Sleeplessness caused by inner conflict - ... in my heart there was a kind of fighting, that would not let me sleep.
"... in my heart there was a kind of fighting,
That would not let me sleep." (H.5.2)
Answer to 'Why can't you sleep?'
In the play. *Hamlet in conversation with Horatio, prior to the final and fatal duel with Laertes.*

Sleeplessness, s. caused by great responsibility - O polish'd perturbation! golden care! That keep'st the ports of slumber open wide...
"O polish'd perturbation! golden care!
That keep'st the ports of slumber open wide

To many a watchful night!" (KHIV p2.4.5)
In the play. *While King Henry is asleep or in apoplectic trance Prince Harry tries on the crown and addresses it.*

Sleeplessness caused by the weight of your responsibilities - ... Can sleep so soundly as the wretched slave, who with a body fill'd and vacant mind...
"Can sleep so soundly as the wretched slave,
Who with a body fill'd and vacant mind
Gets him to rest, cramm'd with distressful bread;
Never sees horrid night, the child of hell,
But, like a lackey, from the rise to set
Sweats in the eye of Phoebus and all night
Sleeps in Elysium; next day after dawn,
Doth rise and help Hyperion to his horse,
And follows so the ever-running year,
With profitable labour, to his grave" (KHV.4.1)
Rulers' argument to make the ruled feel content and unenvious.
In the play. *King Henry meditates on the life of the common man the night before the battle of Agincourt.*

Sleeplessness caused by the weight of your responsibilities - Uneasy lies the head that wears a crown.
"Uneasy lies the head that wears a crown." (KHIV p2.3)
Answer to 'Why can't you sleep?' if you wish to emphasize the force of your position.
In the play. *King Henry cannot sleep. See 'Sleep denied to big guys (that is, persons with great power and responsibility).' The same idea is conveyed later on in the play by the Prince of Wales, the future King Henry V. See next entry.*

Sleeplessness, invocation - O sleep, O gentle sleep, nature's soft nurse...
"O sleep, O gentle sleep,
Nature's soft nurse, how have I frighted thee,
That thou no more wilt weigh my eyelids down
And steep my senses in forgetfulness?
Why rather, sleep, liest thou in smoky cribs,
Upon uneasy pallets stretching thee
And hush'd with buzzing night-flies to thy slumber,
Than in the perfumed chambers of the great,
Under the canopies of costly state,
And lull'd with sound of sweetest melody?
O thou dull god, why liest thou with the vile
In loathsome beds, and leavest the kingly couch
A watch-case or a common 'larum-bell?
Wilt thou upon the high and giddy mast
Seal up the ship-boy's eyes, and rock his brains
In cradle of the rude imperious surge
And in the visitation of the winds,
Who take the ruffian billows by the top,
Curling their monstrous heads and hanging them
With deafening clamour in the slippery clouds,
That, with the hurly, death itself awakes?
Canst thou, O partial sleep, give thy repose
To the wet sea-boy in an hour so rude,
And in the calmest and most stillest night,
With all appliances and means to boot,
Deny it to a king? " (KHIV p2.3.1)

In the play. *King henry IV is worried about the cares of royalty and the threat of rebels.*

Sleeplessness, nightmares caused by impending critical decision - Between the acting of a dreadful thing and the first motion…
"I have not slept.
Between the acting of a dreadful thing
And the first motion, all the interim is
Like a phantasma, or a hideous dream:
The Genius and the mortal instruments
Are then in council; and the state of man,
Like to a little kingdom, suffers then
The nature of an insurrection."
(JC.2.1)
The day when an important decision is to be made. It could be a follow up answer to the question 'How are you?'
In the play. *Brutus reflects on the bad night and nightmares he had, prior to the fatal day when he and co-conspirators will do the 'dreadful thing', i.e. killing Caesar. The great Italian novelist of the XIXth century, A. Manzoni, refers to these lines in the 7th Chapter of 'The Promessi Sposi' (in English 'The Betrothed'). He calls Shakespeare 'a barbarian not without geniality'. The definition is actually of Voltaire's. Manzoni actually admired Shakespeare and the barb was directed at Voltaire.*

Sleepwalking. - … A great perturbation in nature, to receive at once the benefit of sleep and do the effects of watching.
"A great perturbation in nature, to receive at once
the benefit of sleep, and do the effects of
watching!" (M.5.1)
In the play. *A gentlewoman tells the doctor about Lady Macbeth's sleepwalking.*

Smile, hurtful. See 'Rejection. She says no with a smile that hurts more than soothes.'

Smile, mixed with a bit of sadness – Nobly he yokes a smiling with a sigh…
"Nobly he yokes
A smiling with a sigh, - as if the sigh
Was that it was, for not being such a smile;
The smile mocking the sigh, that it would fly
From so divine a temple, to commix
With winds that sailors rail at."
(CYM.4.1)
Extract and apply when you hear her sighing, 'O your sigh that flies from so divine a temple… rail at.'
In the play, *Arviragus comments on Imogen's sweet-sad disposition. Still unbeknown to Arviragus, Imogen is his sister.*

Snake, poisonous s. – His biting is immortal; those that do die of it do seldom or never recover.
"…his biting is immortal; those that do die of it do seldom or never recover." (AC.5.2)
Metaphor for a person who is devious, hurtful and conceited.
In the play. *The serpent ordered by Cleopatra has been brought at court and the clown comments on its qualities.*

Snake, s. preparing to attack - I fear me you but warm the starved snake, who, cherish'd in your breasts, will sting your hearts.
"I fear me you but warm the starved snake,
Who, cherish'd in your breasts, will sting your hearts" (KHVI p2.3.1)
Describe a snake in your organization, e.g. 'We but warm the starved snake…. our hearts'

In the play. *York to himself. He will use the soldiers given him to quell an Irish revolt to further his own aims.*

Snoring, snores with a meaning - Thou dost snore distinctly; there's meaning in thy snores
"Thou dost snore distinctly;
There's meaning in thy snores." (TEM.2.1)
In the play. *Sebastian to Antonio while spirit Ariel plays tricks on them.*

Social issues, exhortation to the better offs to think of the poor - ... Expose thyself to feel what wretches feel that thou mayst shake the superflux to them...
"...Take physic, pomp;
Expose thyself to feel what wretches feel,
That thou mayst shake the superflux to them,
And show the heavens more just." (KL.3.4)
In the play. *K. Lear's in distress is led to compare his current distressed position with that of others who are always distressed.*

Social issues, have the rich feel the sting of poverty - ... so distribution should undo excess, and each man have enough.
"...Let the superfluous and lust-dieted man,
That slaves your ordinance, that will not see
Because he doth not feel, feel your power quickly;
So distribution should undo excess,
And each man have enough." (KL.4.1)
A cure for social ills. See also 'Opinion, your op. on sociological issues, minimum wage - O, reason not the need: our basest beggars are in the poorest thing superfluous…'
In the play. *Blind Gloucester as he gives his purse to Edgar who will be his guide to Dover.*

Social issues, proletariat's point of view - ... the leanness that afflicts us, the object of our misery… our sufferance is a gain to them.
"… the leanness that afflicts us, the object of our misery, is an inventory to particularize their abundance; our sufferance is a gain to them." (COR.1.1)
If you are a left wing politician confirm the point that the rich are getting richer and enjoy the poverty of the poor.
In the play. *Citizens talk about unequal distribution of wealth.*

Social issues, strength in numbers and justice of claim - They say poor suitors have strong breaths; they shall know we have strong arms too.
"They say poor suitors have strong breaths; they shall know we have strong arms too." (COR.1.1)
Energize the rioters.
In the play. *Working class citizens plot a riot.*

Social position a handicap - ... whose state is such that cannot choose but lend and give where she is sure to lose.
"…her, whose state is such that cannot choose
But lend and give where she is sure to lose" (AWEW.1.3)
In the play. *Helena hopes the Countess will not be angry now that she knows that Helena loves Bertram, the Countess' son.*

Society, s. as the happiness of life - ... for society, saith the text, is the happiness of life
"… for society, saith the text, is the happiness of life." (LLL.4.2)
In the play. *Sir Nathaniel answers an invitation by Holofernes to socialize with him.*

Society, state of s. - ... there is so a great a fever on goodness, that the

dissolution of it must cure it. Novelty is only in request...
DUKE (answering a question from Escalus about what's new in the world)
None, but that there is so a great a fever on goodness, that the dissolution of it must cure it. Novelty is only in request; and it is as dangerous to be aged in any kind of course, as it is virtuous to be constant in any undertaking. There is scarse truth enough alive to make societies secure, but security enough to make fellowships accursed. Much upon this riddle runs the wisdom of the world. This news is old enough, yet it is every day's news." (MFM.3.2)
Use any of the statements to decry whatever reproachable aspect of contemporary society
In the play, *The Duke (in disguise) gives Escalus his comments on the world at large after having observed it from the point of view of an ordinary man.*

Soldier, life of a s. – ... all thy living lie in a pitched field.
"Thou art a soldier, therefore seldom rich;
It comes in charity to thee: for all thy living
Is 'mongst the dead, and all the lands thou hast
Lie in a pitch'd field." (TOA.1.2)
One out of many arguments to reduce the military budget.
In the play, *Timon addresses Alcibiades, one of his true friends, who has just joined the ongoing party.*

Solicitations, answer to telephone s. – I am not in the giving vein to-day.
"I am not in the giving vein to-day." (KRIII.4.2)
In the play, *Richard III, now king refuses to honor his commitment to Buckingham, who was instrumental in Richard's success.*

Solitude, need to be alone for a while, need for space - I and my bosom must debate awhile and then I would no other company.
"I and my bosom must debate awhile, And then I would no other company." (HV.4.1)
When you wish to remain or be left alone and yet do not want to be rude. See also 'Alone, a. but busy - I, measuring his affections by my own, that most are busied when they are most alone.'
In the play, *Henry V wants to be alone and meditate the night before the battle of Agincourt.*

Solitude, request to be left alone – I do beseech thee, grant me this, to leave me but a little to myself.
"...I do beseech thee, grant me this, To leave me but a little to myself" (OTH.3.3)
In the play, *Othello to Desdemona during her first intervention on Cassio's behalf.*

Soldier, s. and warring spirit – He that is truly dedicate to war hath no self-love...
"He that is truly dedicate to war Hath no self-love, nor he that loves himself
Hath not essentially but by circumstance
The name of valour." (KHVI.p2.5.2)
In the play, *Young Clifford on seeing his father killed in battle near St. Alban's*

Soldier, s. in love – ... we are soldiers, and may that soldier a mere recreant prove...
"... we are soldiers;
And may that soldier a mere recreant prove,
That means not, hath not, or is not in love!" (TC.1.3)
In the play, *Agamemnon replies to Hector who will challenge to a fight any Greek soldier who is truly in love.*

Solitude, s. preferable – ... I am best when least in company.
"... some four or five attend him;
All, if you will; for I myself am best,
When least in company." (TN.1.4)
Explain why you wish to remain alone. 'I myself...least in company'.
In the play. *The affair referred to (by Duke Orsino), is Viola/Cesario's mission to Olivia on the Duke's behalf.*

Solitude, wanting to be alone - ... I must think of that which company would not be friendly to.
"... Leave me alone;
For I must think of that which company
Would not be friendly to."
(KHVIII.5.1)
A request to be left alone.
In the play. *Henry asks Suffolk to be left alone.*

Solitude, wanting to be alone - ... leave me to my self to-night, For I have need of many orisons to move the heavens to smile upon my state.
"... leave me to my self to-night,
For I have need of many orisons
To move the heavens to smile upon my state" (RJ.4.3)
In the play. *Juliet asks the Nurse to be left alone. The real reason is that Juliet will take the medicine that will make her seem dead for 42 hours until Romeo will show up (if everything goes well).* 'Orisons' = 'prayers'

Solitude, wanting to be alone - ... she hath abjured the company and sight of men.
"They say, she hath abjured the company
And sight of men." (TN.1.2)
In the play. *A captain of a ship involved in a shipwreck explains to Viola why Olivia, a lady courted by Count Orsino has abjured the company of men, after the deaths of her father and brother.*

Solution, desperate s., anything better than this – Bid me lurk where serpents are, chain me with roaring bears.
"O, bid me leap, rather than marry Paris,
From off the battlements of yonder tower;
Or walk in thievish ways; or bid me lurk
Where serpents are; chain me with roaring bears." (RJ.4.1)
Use rhetorically to state that you would do anything but what you are asked to do. E.G. 'Bid me leap from off the battlements of yonder tower rather than (insert task you dislike).'
In the play. *For Juliet, clearly, marrying Paris is not even an option.*

Solution, masochistic solution to problem observed - Methinks you prescribe to yourself very preposterously.
"Methinks you prescribe to yourself very preposterously" (MWW.2.2)
Change 'you' to 'we' and 'yourself' to 'ourselves' if your comment applies to a group of which you are part.
In the play. *Falstaff to Mr. Ford who, in disguise, pays him to seduce his wife to test her fidelity.*

Sorrow, causing madness and misjudgment - ... grief hath so wrought on him, he takes false shadows for true substance.
"Alas, poor man! grief hath so wrought on him,
He takes false shadows for true substance." (TA.3.2)
Excuse lapses in judgment due to grief-induced stress.
Comment on opponent with whose silly ideas you strongly disagree.

In the play. *Titus dissects a fly with a knife pretending it be the archenemy Aaron. Marcus comments on Titus' state of mind.*

Sorrow, faked s. - … windy suspiration of forced breath.
"…windy suspiration of forced breath" (H.1.2)
See also entries for 'Tears, false t.' **
'Sincerity, s. as opposed to appearance –
… they are actions that a man might play, but I have that within which passeth show…'
In the play. *Hamlet refers to the show of sorrow at the death of his father by the court, especially King Claudius, the murderer of Hamlet's father.*

Sorrow, one s. after another - One sorrow never comes but brings an heir, that may succeed as his inheritor.
"One sorrow never comes but brings an heir,
That may succeed as his inheritor" (PER.1.4)
In the play. *The city of Tharsus is in the grip of a famine and a messenger tells the king that foreign ships have been sighted. Cleon thinks they may carry invaders, but they are Pericles' ships.*

Sorrow, one's s. greater than another's – If ancient sorrow be most reverend give mine the benefit of seniory…
"If ancient sorrow be most reverend,
Give mine the benefit of seniory,
And let my woes frown on the upper hand." (KL.4.4)
In the play. *Ex Queen Margaret to Ex Queen Elizabeth and the Duchess of York.*

Sorrow, s. concealed behind a smile - … sorrow, that is couch'd in seeming gladness…
"…sorrow, that is couch'd in seeming gladness,
Is like that mirth fate turns to sudden sadness" (TC.1.1)

In the play. *The contrived gladness and hidden sorrow has to do with Troilus' secret love for Cressida.*

Sorrow, s. inspiring desire for death – … Teach thou this sorrow how to make me die
"O, if thou teach me to believe this sorrow,
Teach thou this sorrow how to make me die,
And let belief and life encounter so
As doth the fury of two desperate men
Which in the very meeting fall and die." (KJ.3.1)
In the play. *Constance to Salisbury on knowing that the French Dauphin will marry Lady Blanche, thus voiding the right claim of her young son Arthur to the throne of England.*

Sorrows, graduation in s. - Great griefs, I see, medicine the less.
"Great griefs, I see, medicine the less" (CYM.4.2)
In the play. *The lesser grief is the slaying of Cloten by one of Belarius' sons, the greater grief is the (only apparent) of Fideles/Imogen.*

Soundness, different kind of s. - … not as one would say, healthy; but so sound as things that are hollow.
FIRST GENTLEMAN. Thou art always figuring diseases in me; but thou art full of error; I am sound.
LUCIO. Nay, not as one would say, healthy; but so sound as things that are hollow: thy bones are hollow; impiety has made a feast of thee. (MFM.1.2)
Sarcastic comment.
In the play. *Lucio banters with a gentleman*

Sounds, gentle sounds propitious to love - Whiles hounds and horns and sweet melodious birds be unto us as is a nurse's song…
"Whiles hounds and horns and sweet melodious birds

874

Be unto us as is a nurse's song
Of lullaby to bring her babe asleep." (TA.2.3)
Cut out the hounds and horns (unless you are participating to a foxhunt) and tell her '(Let) sweet melodious… asleep.'
See also 'Nature, moon shining bright and creating romantic environment - The moon shines bright: in such a night as this, when the sweet wind did gently kiss the trees…'
In the play. *The fiendish and adulterous Tamora visualizes an after-the-fact slumber with her lover Aaron in the forest where the Roman Emperor, her husband, is holding a hunt.*

Speak, double s. - And be these juggling fiends no more believed, that palter with us in a double sense…
"And be these juggling fiends no more believed,
That palter with us in a double sense;
That keep the word of promise to our ear,
And break it to our hope" (M.5.8)
In the play. *Macbeth finally understands the real meaning of the misinterpreted promises of the witches. 'To palter' = 'to equivocate'*

Speak, exhortation to s. – … If thou hast any sound, or use of voice, speak to me.
"…Stay, illusion!
If thou hast any sound, or use of voice,
Speak to me" (H.1.1)
In the play. *Horatio pleads with the Ghost to say something but the Ghost will only speak to Hamlet.*

Speak, s. openly, not to mince words - Give thy worst of thoughts the worst of words.
"I prithee, speak to me as to thy thinkings,
As thou dost ruminate, and give thy worst of thoughts
The worst of words." (OTH.3.3)

Invitation to be open and not to hide any unpalatable news.
In the play. *The cunning Iago plants seeds of jealousy into Othello's mind and he falls for it.*

Speaker, excellent s. - … we, almost with ravish'd listening, could not find his hour of speech a minute.
"… when we,
Almost with ravish'd listening, could not find
His hour of speech a minute." (KHVIII.1.2)
Praise the excellence of a speaker who has made a long but interesting presentation.
In the play. *King Henry VIII recalling Buckingham's speeches, but now Buckingham has fallen in disgrace.*

Speaker, pleasant and delightful – … your fair discourse hath been as sugar.
"…your fair discourse hath been as sugar" (KRII.2.3)
Compliment.
In the play. *Northumberland to Bolingbroke on their way to Ravenspurgh where they will confront King Richard II.*

Speaker, tedious s. - As tedious as a tired horse, a railing wife.
"… O, he is as tedious
As a tired horse, a railing wife:
Worse than a smoky house - I had rather live
With cheese and garlic, in a windmill, far,
Than feed on cates, and have him talk to me,
In any summer-house in Christendom." (KHIV p1.3.1)
Justify your avoiding to attend a conference or presentation by a bore. "I had rather live with cheese and garlic… Christendom",
In the play. *Hotspur's opinion of Glendower, 'Cates' means dainties or delicacies.*

Speaker, what discourages a s. - … that contempt will kill the speaker's heart and quite divorce his memory from his part
"… that contempt will kill the speaker's heart,
And quite divorce his memory from his part" (LLL.5.2)
When she is angry at you and you try to assuage her. E.G. 'This is the contempt….part'.
In the play. *Boyet comments on the proposed reaction of the ladies to the expected advances of the Prince of Navarre and friends.*

Speaking frankly - Speak frankly as the wind.
"Speak frankly as the wind." (TC.1.3)
Answer to the question 'Can I speak frankly?' By using the quote you give licence of free speech to the inquiring party, while at the same time mildly pre-distancing yourself from what he/she may have to say. See also, 'Credentials, sincerity'.
In the play. *Aeneas has reached the Grecian camp to deliver a message to Agamennon. Not having met him before Aeneas unaware, addresses Agamennon himself and Agamennon replies:*
"Speak frankly as the wind;
It is not Agamemnon's sleeping hour:
That thou shalt know."

Speaking to oneself - … with the incorporal air do hold discourse…
"…how is't with you,
That you do bend your eye on vacancy
And with the incorporal air do hold discourse?" (H.3.4)
In the play. *The Queen cannot see the Ghost who speaks to Hamlet. Therefore Hamlet appears as if he were talking to himself.*

Spectacle, a sad s. – The saddest spectacle that e'er I view'd.

"The saddest spectacle that e'er I view'd." (KHVI.p3.2.1)
Apply, for example, to slaughtered soldiers or to scenes of devastation such as New Orleans after Katrina.
In the play. *A messenger arrives at Mortimer Cross to report to the York brothers the earlier beheading of their father York by the Lancastrians.*

Spectacle, wonderful s. that cannot be described - … a sight, which was to be seen, cannot be spoken of.
"…Then have you lost a sight, which was to be seen, cannot be spoken of." (WT.5.2)
Give your rave review of the event.
In the play. *A gentleman refers to the sight when Leontes and Polixenes reunite and discover that Florizel and Perdita are at hand and that Perdita is the lost daughter of Leontes.*

Speculation, s. on uncertain help or aid, unwise – Conjecture, expectation, and surmise of aids incertain should not be admitted.
"… in a theme so bloody-fac'd as this,
Conjecture, expectation, and surmise
Of aids incertain should not be admitted." (KHIV.p2.1.3)
Temper the mood of those who want to undertake an ambitious project based on doubtful assistance or help from unreliable parties.
In the play. *Lord Bardolph injects some realism on the hopes of the rebels. 'Incertain' = 'uncertain'.*

Speech, annoying, boisterous and loud – You cram words into mine ear against the stomach of my sense.
"You cram these words into mine ears against
The stomach of my sense." (TEM.2.1)
Alternative to 'I'd really not like to hear about it again.' Or generic reaction to insistent demands.

In the play. *Gonzalo reminds Alonso of the occasion that made them travel and that eventually led to the storm and the shipwreck on Prospero's island. Alonso does not like it.*

Speech, be quiet – … for the benefit of silence would thou wert so too!
LUCIO He was drunk then, my lord: it can be no better.
DUKE VINCENTIO For the benefit of silence, would thou wert so too!
(MFM.5.1)
Should the speaker (that you wish to be quiet) not be drunk, try. 'For the benefit of silence, be quiet'.
In the play. *Lucio makes a silly remark while Mariana explains critical events and the Duke reprimands Lucio.*

Speech, be quiet - Be silent, boy; I profit not by thy talk
"Be silent, boy; I profit not by thy talk." (TC.5.1)
An alternative to 'shut up'.
In the play. *Thersites does not spare anyone, in this case he addresses Patroclus.*

Speech, clarity in language requested - Ay, is it not a language, I speak?
"Ay, is it not a language, I speak?" (AWEW.2.3)
Retort to a person who claims he/she does not understand what you are saying - but you feel they do and that their declared lack of understanding is a put-on.
In the play. *Parolles picks up the underlying contemptuous tone of Lafeu's words, who refers to Bertram as Parolles' lord and master. Parolles repeats the words 'lord' and 'master' as if he did not understand. Lafeu responds to the repetitions.*

Speech, clarity of language requested - A strange tongue makes my cause more strange, suspicious; pray, speak in English.
"No Latin…

…
A strange tongue makes my cause more strange, suspicious;
Pray, speak in English." (KHVIII.3.1)
Exhortation to clarity, 'A strange tongue makes the matter more strange… English.'
In the play. *Wolsey has just said something in Latin, a compliment to the queen. The Cardinal said in Latin,*
Tanta est erga te mentis integritas, regina serenissima -- that is '*So great is your integrity, most serene queen*'.

Speech, clarity of meaning requested – Be plain, good son, and homely in thy drift; riddling confession finds but riddling shrift.
"Be plain, good son, and homely in thy drift;
Riddling confession finds but riddling shrift." (RJ.2.3)
Urge clarity of words and expression as applicable
In the play. *Romeo answers indirectly and obscurely Fr. Lawrence's question as to where he (Romeo) has been the preceding night. Confused, Fr. Lawrence urges clarity.* 'Riddling' = 'spoken enigmatically'.

Speech, clarity of meaning requested - Be plainer with me; let me know my trespass by its own visage…
"Be plainer with me; let me know my trespass
By its own visage: if I then deny it,
'Tis none of mine." (WT.1.2)
In the play. *Counselor Camillo prompts Leontes to say clearly what is that supposedly Camillo has done wrong.*

Speech, comment on a good dinner s. - … your reasons at dinner have been sharp and sententious..
" … your reasons at dinner have been sharp and sententious; pleasant without scurrility, witty without affectation, audacious without

impudency, learned without opinion, and strange without heresy." (LLL.5.1)
Compliment a speaker.
In the play. *Holofernes and Nathaniel engage in another exchange of pompous platitudes.*

Speech, concision, be brief - If you be not mad, be gone; if you have reason, be brief:...
"If you be not mad, be gone; if you have reason, be brief: 't is not that time of the moon with me to make one in so skipping a dialogue." (TN.1.5)
Cut off the deliverer of a long and incoherent explanation.
In the play. *Olivia suspects that Viola/Cesario has come to plead for love on behalf of the Duke and is annoyed.*

Speech, content of s. wiser than speaker realizes - Thou speakest wiser than thou art 'ware of.
"Thou speakest wiser than thou art 'ware of." (AYLI.2.4)
When you want to agree with someone with whom you normally do not.
In the play. *Rosalind shows regard for a comment by Touchstone.*

Speech, determination to speak with courage - I'll use that tongue I have. If wit flows from it...
"I'll use that tongue I have. If wit flows from it
As boldness from my bosom, let't not be doubted
I shall do good. "(WT.2.2)
In the play. *Paulina to Emilia. Paulina will attempt to persuade the jail guard to let Hermione's baby be shown to Leontes – Leontes should recognize that the baby is his and that his wife Hermione was faithful.*

Speech, determined to speak and tell the truth - I will speak as liberal as the north, let heaven and men and devils, let them all...

"I will speak as liberal as the north: Let heaven and men and devils, let them all,
All, all, cry shame against me, yet I'll speak." (OTH.5.2)
When politics would suggest silence but you are determined to expose the truth.
In the play. *Iago told his wife Emilia to shut up but she is determined to prove that Desdemona was innocent.*

Speech, disappointment or despair at her words - ... thou hast cleft my heart in twain
"... thou hast cleft my heart in twain." (H.3.4)
Good for most occasions when she says something hurtful to you or if she rejects your advances. Add a dramatic stance, with your hand on your heart.
In the play. *Hamlet has reprimanded his mother in strong terms and she is distraught.*

Speech, dislike of manner of s. more than content - I do not much dislike the matter, but the manner of his speech.
"I do not much dislike the matter, but The manner of his speech" (AC.2.2)
When there is a tone of arrogance in your interlocutor's words.
In the play. *Octavian refers to Antony and the explanations Antony gave for having neglected Octavian's messages and requests.*

Speech, double speak or double tongue - you have a double tongue within your mask.
"You have a double tongue within your mask." (LLL.5)
Use with a known double dealer. See also 'Intentions, wicked and shown in the type of question and type of answer'
In the play. *Longaville recognizes Katherine's wit.*

Speech, exhortation to be brief to a girl-messenger - … be brief, my good she-Mercury.
"… be brief, my good she-Mercury." (MWW.2.2)
Drop the 'she' if the messenger is a male.
In the play. *Falstaff prompts Mistress Quickly to shorten her presentation.*

Speech, exhortation to speak and give information - Be not a niggard of your speech; how goes it?
"Be not a niggard of your speech; how goes it?" (M.4.3)
Prompt a reluctant speaker or holder of critical information to spill it out.
In the play. *Macduff prompts Ross who has just arrived to say what happened to Macduff's family left behind at their castle. Ross hesitates because Macbeth has murdered them.*
'Niggard'='Miser'.

Speech, exhortation to speak in mild tone - Speak sweetly, man, although thy looks be sour.
"Speak sweetly, man, although thy looks be sour." (KRII.3.2)
See also entries for 'News, bad n. inferred by the look of the messenger'
In the play. *King Richard to Lord Scroop whose looks betray the bad news that even the regent Duke of York has joined Bolingbroke's party.*

Speech, exhortation to speak properly - … keep a good tongue in your head.
"… keep a good tongue in your head" (TEM.3.2)
In the play. *Stephano to Trinculo who seemingly taunts Caliban – in reality the taunting is the work of the invisible spirit Ariel*

Speech, gaining time before speaking up - … he's winding up the watch of his wit, by and by it will strike.
"Look, he's winding up the watch of his wit;
By and by it will strike." (TEM.2.1)

When you are searching for an answer or a repartee and it does not come to mind immediately. 'I am winding up the watch of my wit…strike'. Or a comment when you see someone else doing the same. See also 'Answering, buying time to answer - the charm dissolves apace… mantle their clearer reason.' Entries for 'Speechless'
In the play. *Sebastian, brother of the King of Naples likes to pull Gonzalo's leg and see his reaction. Gonzalo is an old counselor to the King of Naples.*

Speech, her words have completely overcome your resistance - I am vanquished; these haughty words of hers have batter'd me like roaring cannon-shot…
"I am vanquished; these haughty words of hers
Have batter'd me like roaring cannon-shot,
And made me almost yield upon my knees." (KHVI.p1.3.3)
Change to 'these haughty words of yours…knees.' When, for example, she has asked you to do something, you have delayed doing it or delayed an answer and she is now angry. See also 'Mind, change of m. after words heard directly - Either she hath bewitch'd me with her words or nature makes me suddenly relent.'
In the play. *Burgundy commenting on La Pucelle's speech aimed at persuading him to change sides and fight with the French.*

Speech, how or where did you learn all this - Where did you study all this goodly speech?
"Where did you study all this goodly speech?" (TOS.2.1)
Sarcastic question to a speaker who normally expresses himself with difficulty.
In the play. *Katharina is surprised at having found someone (Petruchio) who is able to stand up to her shrewishness and tart remarks. Petruchio replies,*

"It is extempore, from my mother-wit."

Speech, hurtful s. but within limits - I will speak daggers to her, but use none.
"I will speak daggers to her, but use none" (H.3.2)
Adapt as a comment to hurtful speech, e.g. 'You speak daggers to me'.
In the play. *Hamlet before a dramatic confrontation with his mother the Queen*

Speech, hurtful s. - Runs not this speech like iron through your blood?
DON PEDRO Runs not this speech like iron through your blood?
CLAUDIO I have drunk poison whiles he utter'd it. (MAAN.5.1)
In the play. *No-good Borachio describes how he was part of the scheme to slander and dishonor Hero.*

Speech, incomprehensible s. and its correction - ... but wouldst gabble like a thing most brutish, I endow'd thy purposes with words that made them known.
"…when thou didst not, savage,
Know thine own meaning, but wouldst gabble like
A thing most brutish, I endow'd thy purposes
With words that made them known" (TEM.1.2)
A barb for someone whose speech is obscure, syntactically and grammatically incorrect.
In the play. *Prospero addresses Caliban reminding of how Prospero tried to improve his condition.*

Speech, insisting on delivering a s. - ... I would be loath to cast away my speech, for besides that it is excellently well penned…'
"…I would be loath to cast away my speech, for besides that it is excellently well penned, I have taken great pains to con it" (TN.1.5)
When you sense that, after all, you may not have a chance to speak at a meeting or convention.
In the play. *Viola/Cesario wants to assure herself that Olivia is the lady of the house so as not to waste her prepared speech on someone else.*

Speech, interruption of s. - Shall I hear more or shall I speak at this?
"Shall I hear more, or shall I speak at this?" (RJ.2.2)
Interrupt a conversation whose turn or content you do not like.
In the play. *Romeo, hidden in Juliet's garden hears her utter his name.*

Speech, interruption of s. impolite - It is not well done, mark you now, to take the tales out of my mouth, ere it is made an end and finished.
"It is not well done, mark you now, to take the tales out of my mouth, ere it is made an end and finished." (KHV.4.7)
Stop an interruption.
In the play. *Gower has interrupted Fluellen.* 'Ere' = 'before'.

Speech, introduction to a flattering or praising s. - Lend me the flourish of all gentle tongues.
" Lend me the flourish of all gentle tongues, --
Fie, painted rhetoric! O, she needs it not:
To things of sale a seller's praise belongs,
She passes praise; then praise too short doth blot." (LLL.4.3)
Introduction, prepare the audience to the announcement of a great event. See also 'Inspiration, a powerful Muse required before starting a speech'.
In the play. *Biron in love prepares to say good things about Rosaline.*

Speech, irritating content and incorrect English - … here will be an old abusing of God's patience, and the king's English.
"… here will be an old abusing of God's patience, and the king's English." (MWW.1.4)
Comment on a forthcoming speech from a person who does not speak well or properly. 'Here will be an old abusing of the king's English'.
In the play. *Mistress Quickly predicts the arrival of Doctor Caius, a Frenchman, and the consequent strain on her patience.*

Speech, language, watch your language - Take heed, be wary how you place your words.
"Take heed, be wary how you place your words." (KHVI.p1.3.2)
Caution adversary to watch what he says.
In the play. *La Pucelle to soldiers outside the city of Rouen – they are supposed to talk like farmers to misguide the English soldiers.*

Speech, lengthy and annoying - This will last out a night in Russia when nights are longest there.
"This will last out a night in Russia, When nights are longest there" (MFM.2.1)
See also 'Sleep, s. induced by a boring speaker - The best of rest is sleep and that thou oft provokest.'
In the play. *Angelo comments on the trivial and lengthy exchanges between Froth and Pompey.*

Speech, loud speaking, lower your voice - Thou but offend'st thy lungs to speak so loud.
"Thou but offend'st thy lungs to speak so loud." (MOV.4.1)
Answer to loud verbal attack from adversary. Try the following, 'First, thou but offendest thy lungs……loud. Second, thou almost mak'st me waiver in my faith…….trunks of men.' – See

'Insult, man like animal according to the theories of Pythagoras'.
In the play. *Shylock to Bassanio.*

Speech, melancholy mood not engendering cheerful s. - A heavy heart bears not a nimble tongue.
"A heavy heart bears not a nimble tongue." (LLL.5.2)
Explain why you appear so sad.
In the play. *The Princess of Navarre and her lady attendants take leave and say farewell to the King and his would-be studious companions.*

Speech, moving s. - This speech of yours hath moved me and shall perchance do good.
"This speech of yours hath moved me,
And shall perchance do good"
(KL.6.3)
In the play. *Edgar has revealed to the duke of Albany how he helped and sustained his blinded father*

Speech, nonsensical or meaningless - … senseless speaking or a speaking such s sense cannot untie.
"… senseless speaking or a speaking such
As sense cannot untie." (CYM.5.4)
See also 'Man, m. discredited and speaking nonsense - … will you credit this base drudge's words that speaks.'
In the play. *See context explanation for 'Dream or madness.'*

Speech, nonsensical or meaningless - … this learned constable is too cunning to be understood.
"… this learned constable is too cunning to be understood." (MAAN.5.1)
Comment to a memo or letter written in managerial lingo or to an incomprehensible spoken sentence.
In the play. *Dogberry has apprehended the rascals that have caused Hero to be unfairly*

accused, but his explanations are difficult to understand.

Speech, nonsensical or meaningless - This is the silliest stuff that ever I heard.
"This is the silliest stuff that ever I heard." (MND.5.1)
Comment to a wrong statement or statement with which you totally disagrees.
In the play. *Hippolyta's reaction to the play enacted by the amateur acting company.*

Speech, nothing said, silence, prompting to speak - Nothing will come of nothing, speak again.
"Nothing will come of nothing. Speak again." (KL.1.1)
Prompt a response that is not forthcoming.
In the play. *King Lear prompts Cordelia to speak – she refuses to join her sisters in their exaggerated and false declarations of love to their retiring father King Lear.*

Speech, blunt speaking - …but mark me: to be received plain, I'll speak more gross.
"…But mark me:
To be received plain, I'll speak more gross." (MFM.2.4)
Prepare the audience for your next direct and blunt statement.
In the play. *The hypocrite Angelo attempts to seduce Isabel, who at first did not understand what he was driving at.*

Speech, brevity of s. promised - My short date of breath is not so long as is a tedious tale.
"I will be brief, for my short date of breath
Is not so long as is a tedious tale." (RJ.5.3)
See also 'Introduction. I want to be brief'.
In the play. *Fr. Lawrence explains to Prince, Montagues and Capulets the events that led to the death of Juliet, Romeo and Paris. 'Short date of breath' means 'short period of life allowed' (here to the friar).*

Speech, bringing a message of peace and substance - I hold the olive in my hand: my words are full of praise as matter.
"I hold the olive in my hand: my words are full of praise as matter." (TN.1.5)
Introduction to a speech aimed at reconciliation and removing differences of perception or grudges.
In the play. *Viola/Cesario tries to prepare the ground with Olivia for the message from the Duke.*

Speech, change suggested in s. for the good of the speaker - … mend your speech a little lest you may mar your fortunes.
"… mend your speech a little,
Lest you may mar your fortunes." (KL.1.1)
Exhortation to modify a set position or idea.
In the play. *Cordelia insists on refusing to make affected declarations of filial love and King Lear still prompts her.*

Speech, painful to speak - My heart is heavy, and mine age is weak.
" My heart is heavy, and mine age is weak;
Grief would have tears, and sorrow bid me speak." (AWEW.3.4)
Introduction to a speech or statement that you feel may displease or disappoint some of the audience.
In the play. *The Countess is distressed at the turn of event that has led his son to war and her daughter in law to leave the castle.*

Speech, pessimistic and unpleasant to make - … discomfort guides my tongue and bids me speak of nothing but despair.

"... discomfort guides my tongue
And bids me speak of nothing but despair." (KRII.3.2)
In the play. *Salisbury to King Richard II. Salisbury is depressed because the armed forces that could have fought against the rebel Bolingbroke have already been dismissed.*

Speech, plea to stop hurtful s. - "O, speak to me no more; these words, like daggers, enter in mine ears.
"O, speak to me no more;
These words, like daggers, enter in mine ears" (H.3.4)
See also 'Perception, you want me dead - thou hidest a thousand daggers in thy thoughts.' - 'Place, a dangerous p. – where we are there's daggers in men's smiles.' - 'Speech, hurtful s. but within limits - I will speak daggers to her, but use none.'
In the play. *The Queen to Hamlet*

Speech, reaction (mildly ironic) at her reprimands or statements of principle - Well know they what they speak, that speak so wisely.
"Well they know they what they speak, that speak so wisely." (TC.3.2)
An alternate to 'well put'. But give the statement with a smile or maybe with blinking both eyes. You will signal that you acknowledge what she said but may not necessarily agree with her.
In the play. *Cressida teases Troilus and he answers with a compliment. She had ended her statement with* 'I know not what I speak'

Speech, refraining from making inflammatory statements - With silence, nephew, be thou politic...
"With silence, nephew, be thou politic;
Strong fixed is the house of Lancaster
And, like a mountain, not to be remov'd . ." (KHVI.p1.3.5)
Use as a comparison to indicate that a powerful man (or a group headed by him) has the upper hand at least for the moment. E.G., 'Strong fixed is the house of (name of group or man) and like a mountain not to be removed.'
In the play. *Mortimer cautions Plantagenet to be prudent. Plantagenet has just said that the execution of his father (by the Lancastrians) was an act of tyranny.*

Speech, request to speak - I'd crave a word or two, the which shall turn you to no further harm than so much loss of time.
" If, by the tribunes' leave, and yours, good people,
I may be heard, I'd crave a word or two;
The which shall turn you to no further harm,
Than so much loss of time."
(COR.3.1)
Use modesty to positively predispose the audience to hear what you have to say.
In the play. *Menenius attempts to reason with the citizens who are enraged at Coriolanus.*

Speech, restraint from use of expletives due to anger – More bitterly could I expostulate.
"More bitterly could I expostulate,
Save that, for reverence to some alive,
I give a sparing limit to my tongue." (KRIII.3.7)
Use to indicate that you have more bad things to say on the matter but that you will use restraint.
In the play. *Buckingham tries to prove that Richard is the legitimate candidate for the throne. The accusation is that the son of Edward by the Lady Grey, his wife is not legitimate.*

Speech, restraint from use of expletives due to anger – …the fair reverence of your highness curbs me from giving reigns and spurs to my free speech.
"…the fair reverence of your highness curbs me

From giving reigns and spurs to my free speech." (KRII.1.1)
Modify as applicable, e.g. 'The presence of ladies curbs me from…speech'. See also 'Speech, restraint'. Voltaire, in Candide, when having to mention the bottom defines it as 'a part of the body I'll forbear to mention out of my inviolable respect for the ladies'.
In the play. *Mowbray responds to Bolingbroke's accusations*

Speech, risks of free s. - … And stood within the blank of his displeasure for my free speech!
"As I have spoken for you all my best
And stood within the blank of his displeasure
For my free speech!" (OTH.3.4)
In the play. *Desdemona tells Cassio that she did what she could to attempt a reconciliation between Cassio and Othello.*

Speech, s. and opinion polling – … there shall I try in my oration, how the people take…
"… there shall I try
In my oration, how the people take
The cruel issue of these bloody men" (JC.3.1)
You can also turn the lines into a question, 'How the people take the cruel issue of these bloody men?'
In the play. *Antony will try to poll (and sway) the mood of the masses in his funeral eulogy of Caesar.*

Speech, s. can undo the speaker - … many a man's tongue shakes out his master's undoing.
"…many a man's tongue shakes out his master's undoing" (AWEW.2.4)
Explain why you are quite or do not want to answer.
In the play. *The fool confronts Parolles.*

Speech, s. completely unbecoming – You never spoke what did become you less than this.
"Shrew my heart,
You never spoke what did become you less
Than this." (WT.1.2)
Express your dismay and disagreement at what has been said or implied.
In the play. *Jealous Leontes, king of Sicilia thinks that his virtuous wife Hermione has an affair with Polixenes, king of Bohemia. This is not true at all and Camillus, a lord in Leonte's service says so to him.*

Speech, s. in silence - I'll speak to thee in silence.
"I'll speak to thee in silence." (CYM.5.4)
In the play. *Leonatus, prisoner in Britain imagines he can talk to Imogen.*

Speech, s. not easily forgotten – His speech sticks in my heart.
ALEXAS His speech sticks in my heart.
CLEOPATRA Mine ear must pluck it thence (AC.1.5)
In the play. *The speech is Antony's as he leaves Egypt and observed and heard by Alexas, Cleopatra's lady in waiting.*

Speech, s. that shows the lowliness of birth or status – Shamest thou not…to let thy tongue detect thy base-born heart?
"Shamest thou not, knowing whence thou art extraught,
To let thy tongue detect thy base-born heart?" (KHVI.p3.2.2)
In the play. *Richard responds in kind to insulting remarks by Queen Margaret.*

Speech, s. to further someone else's cause – … I'll play the orator as if the golden fee for which I plead were for myself.
"Fear not, my lord, I'll play the orator

As if the golden fee for which I plead
Were for myself." (KRIII.3.5)
Reassure party that you will plead his cause well.
In the play. *Buckingham reassures Richard. Buckingham will convince the mayor of London that Richard is the true heir to the throne.*

Speech, s. unpunished because of position of speaker - ... This tongue that runs so roundly in thy head, should run thy head from thy unreverent shoulders.
"Wert thou not brother to great Edward's son,
This tongue that runs so roundly in thy head
Should run thy head from thy unreverent shoulders." (KRII.2.1)
Use the last two lines as a retort following an offensive or absurd remark.
In the play. *King Richard reacts to the reproaches of his uncle John of Gaunt.*

Speech, saying the right thing at the wrong time - The truth you speak doth lack some gentleness and time to speak it in.
"The truth you speak doth lack some gentleness
And time to speak it in." (TEM.2.1)
In the play. *Gonzalo addresses Sebastian who, believing Ferdinand to be lost and dead, talks about the matter without concern over the pain it may bring to others.*

Speech, short and clear s. makes it well accepted - Your plainness and your shortness please me well.
"Your plainness and your shortness please me well." (TOS.4.4)
Comment on a clear and well-delivered message.
In the play. *Baptista approves of the speech by the pedant. The pedant is actually impersonating Lucentio's father. It's all a trick to have Baptista consent to his daughter Bianca marrying Lucentio.*

Speech, shortened by circumstances of urgency - More than I have said... the leisure and enforcement of the time forbids to dwell upon.
"More than I have said, loving countrymen,
The leisure and enforcement of the time
Forbids to dwell upon." (KRIII.5.3)
When you are in a rush and cannot speak for long. Eliminate 'loving countryman' or change with the name(s) of the addressed audience or with 'ladies and gentlemen'.
In the play. *Richmond addresses the troops before the battle against Richard III at Bosworth Field.*

Speech, showing impatience and a self-centered personality – ... tying thine ear to no tongue but thine own.
"Why, what a wasp-stung and impatient fool
Art thou, to break into this woman's mood:
Tying thine ear to no tongue but thine own?" (KHIV p1.1.3)
Use as is or change the question slightly, e.g. 'Why do you break into this woman's mood, tying thine ear to no tongue but thine own?' Or define a person of this type, e.g. 'He ties his ear to no tongue but his won.'
In the play. *Northumberland reprimands the impatient Hotspur.*

Speech, simple s. delivered with modesty better than pompous eloquence - ... in the modesty of fearful duty, I read as much, as from the rattling tongue of saucy and audacious eloquence.
"And in the modesty of fearful duty, I read as much, as from the rattling tongue
Of saucy and audacious eloquence." (MND.5.1)

Contrast the values of modesty and dedication versus arrogance. See also 'Duty, sense of d. and straightforwardness leading to good results'.
In the play. *Notwithstanding Philostrate's critical report, Theseus will hear the play enacted by modest but dutiful actors.*

Speech, speak no more - O, speak no more! for I have heard too much. O, speak no more! for I have heard too much." (KHVI p3.2.1)
When you have had enough of a speech that is dismal or painful for whatever reason
In the play. *Edward (other son of Plantagenet) to messenger who comes to announce that Richard Plantagenet has been killed.*

Speech, speaking after a well known or skillful speaker - As in a theatre, the eyes of men, after a well grac'd actor leaves the stage…
"As in a theatre, the eyes of men, After a well grac'd actor leaves the stage, Are idly bent on him that enters next, Thinking his prattle to be tedious." (KRII.5.2)
The audience applauded at length the last speaker just before it is your turn to speak. Introduction to your presentation now that it is your turn. See also entries for 'Introduction'
In the play. *In his palace, the duke of York answer the Duchess who asked the reaction of the people when they saw Richard after seeing Bolingbroke (here compared to the good actor).*

Speech, speaking simply and honestly - I speak as my understanding instructs me and as mine honesty puts it to utterance.
"I speak as my understanding instructs me, And as my honesty puts it to utterance." (WT.1.1)
When she questions if what you say is true either directly or by the intonation of her voice. Confirm that you speak according to your best knowledge and your honesty.
French writer Paul Valery defined conviction as "A good word, that allows to put the tone of force at the service our uncertainty". Or in French 'Bon mot, qui nous permet de mettre le ton de la force au service de l'incertitude'.
In the play. *Archidamus, a Bohemian Lord insists with his counterpart Camillo, a Sicilian Lord, that the welcoming facilities in Bohemia are inferior to those of Sicily.* See 'Invitation, i. to your place when you know that your place is in a state of disarray.'

Speech, speaking your mind emphatically - … unloose thy long-imprison'd thoughts and let thy tongue be equal with thy heart.
"Then, York, unloose thy long-imprison'd thoughts, And let thy tongue be equal with thy heart." (KHVI p2.5.1)
Cut through innuendoes and change 'York' with your name.
In the play. *York to himself in the presence of Q. Margaret. He is upset because the King did not imprison Lord Somerset. York is seeking excuses to unseat King Henry VI.*

Speech, stage-fright - As an unperfect actor on the stage who with his fear is put besides his part…
"As an unperfect actor on the stage Who with his fear is put besides his part, Or some fierce thing replete with too much rage, Whose strength's abundance weakens his own heart " (SON 23)
Possible introduction to a presentation in front of an august or very well qualified audience.

Speech, strange way of expressing oneself - He speaks not like a man of God's making.
PRINCESS. Doth this man serve God?
BIRON. Why ask you?
PRINCESS. He speaks not like a man of God's making." (LLL.5.2)
Comment on senseless or convoluted words or statements
In the play. *The princess gives her opinion of Armado.*

Speech, summarizing the sequence and course of events - I carry winged time post on the lame feet of my rhyme.
"… I carry winged time
Post on the lame feet of my rhyme" (PER.3.Gower)
During a presentation, when you must skip over a number of intervening events.
In the play. *Gower has given a summary of events occurring after Pericles left Cleon's house.*

Speech, tangled s. – His speech was like a tangled chain; nothing impaired, but all disordered.
"His speech was like a tangled chain; nothing impaired, but all disordered." (MND.5.1)
Comment to a disjointed speech or report. See also 'Speech, nonsensical or meaningless'.
In the play. *Theseus comments on the delivery of the prologue by one of the amateur actors.*

Speech, unable to speak due to tears - My heart is not compact of flint and steel…
"My heart is not compact of flint and steel,
Nor can I utter all our bitter grief,
But floods of tears will drown my oratory,
And break my very utterance, even in the time

When it should move you to attend me most." (TA.5.3)
Express your utter dismay. See also 'Response, available for a positive response - … I am not made of stone but penetrable to your kind entreaties…'
In the play. *Marcus addresses the Romans after the following. Titus has killed Chiron and Demetrius and cooked them for Tamora and Saturninus, whom he (Titus) had invited to dinner. At the end of the dinner Titus also kills Lavinia not to have her overlive her shame, then he proceeds to kill Tamora. The enraged Saturninus kills Titus, whereupon Lucius kills Saturninus. The only people remaining alive at the end of the play are Marcus, Titus' brother and Lucius, Titus' son.*

Speech, unable to speak due to vexation and frustration - Vexation almost stops my breath.
…Vexation almost stops my breath." (KHVI.p1.4.3)
When you want to make it known that you are angry and yet do not want to speak. See also 'Anger - too angry to speak.'
In the play. *York in Gascony on knowing that Talbot is fighting the French alone and without the support promised to him.*

Speech, unundestandable language or statement - You speak a language that I understand not.
"You speak a language that I understand not." (WT.3.2)
When what you hear makes no sense. See also 'Speech, clarity in delivery prompted.'
In the play. *Leontes accuses Hermione of knowing of Camillo's departure. Of course she doesn't and it is as if Leontes spoke another language.*

**Speech, undiplomatic mode of speaking - … (he) is ill school'd in boulted language; meal and bran

together he throws without distinction.
"… (he) is ill school'd
In boulted language; meal and bran together
He throws without distinction." (COR.3.1)
Describe a poor speaker.
In the play. *Menenius tries to minimize Coriolanus' rashness with the citizens. 'Boulted' here means 'refined' or 'polite and elegant'.*

Speech, using permission to speak - ... since you have given me leave to speak, freely will I speak.
"Well, my lord, since you have given me leave to speak.
Freely will I speak" (PER.1.2)
In the play. *Helicanus to Pericles suggesting that Pericles may travel for a while waiting for Antioch's anger to subside.*

Speech, warning an enemy not to shame himself with his s. - Be not thy tongue thy own shame's orator.
"Be not thy tongue thy own shame's orator." (COE.3.2)
Elegant warning to anyone whose statements you find preposterous or unbelievable.
In the play. *Ant S is after Luciana, sister of Adriana, Ant E's wife. Luciana is upset and reminds Ant S (thinking that he is Ant E) of his duties to his wife Adriana.*

Speech, well said – That's worthily as any ear can hear.
"That's worthily
As any ear can hear." (COR.4.1)
In the play. *Menenius comments on the farewell words said by Coriolanus to his family.*

Speech, well said - Thou dost speak masterly.
"Thou dost speak masterly." (TN.2.4)
Compliment for a good turn of phrase, speech or expression. See also 'Words, excellent and well put w.'
In the play. *Viola/Cesario has given articulate words of praise on music after the Duke asked her opinion. The Duke admires her answer.*

Speech, well said or very appropriate - ... thou never spokest to better purpose.
"... thou never spokest
To better purpose." (WT.1.2)
In the play. *Hermione has finally convinced Polixenes to extend his stay with Leontes, king of Sicilia.*

Speech, why giving me the run around? - What need'st thou run so many miles about when thou mayst tell thy tale the nearest way?
"What need'st thou run so many miles about,
When thou mayst tell thy tale the nearest way?" (KRIII.4.4)
Use with a wordy fellow or as a reference to support the value of concision and straight-talk in reporting. See also 'Man, a verbose man' – 'Messenger, exhortation to m. to deliver information quickly - Thou comest to use thy tongue; thy story quickly.'
In the play. *Richard asks Stanley for news on the military situation. Richmond is at hand and Stanley comes up with a sibylline answer, see* 'News, n. that is neither good nor bad - None good, my liege, to please you with the hearing...'

Speech, wine and its effect on women's speech - The red wine first must rise in their fair cheeks, my lord; then we shall have 'em talk us to silence.
"The red wine first must rise
In their fair cheeks, my lord; then we shall have 'em
Talk us to silence." (HVIII.1.4)
Persuade the ladies to partake of the wine more liberally. Or if it is just the two of you at dinner and she does not talk much, prompt her to drink a bit more

wine. Change slightly, e.g. "I see that you are quiet, have a bit more wine, as Shakespeare said, the red wine first must rise in your fair cheek; then I will have you talk me into silence.'
In the play. *Lord Sands at a party.*

Speech, witticism misplaced or to be stopped - This civil war of wits...
"This civil war of wits were much better used on Navarre and his book men; for here 't is abused." (LLL.2.1)
Use to stop an argument. "Let's stop this civil war of wits."
In the play. *The king being gone, Boyet banters with Maria one of the princess' ladies in waiting. The Princess suggests that the wit should be better aimed at the king of Navarre and company.*

Speech, words well said - 'Tis most nobly spoken.
"'Tis most nobly spoken." (TOA.5.4)
In the play. *Athenian senators commend Alcibiades' words at the end of negotiations*

Speechless - His tongue is now a stringless instrument.
"His tongue is now a stringless instrument" (KRII.2.1)
Announce that you will not speak anymore, e.g. 'from now on my tongue will be a stringless instrument'.
In the play. *Northumberland announces to Richard II that John of Gaunt is dead.*

Speechless - Within my mouth you have engaol'd my tongue.
"Within my mouth you have engaol'd my tongue
Doubly portcullis'd with my teeth and lips;
And dull unfeeling barren ignorance
Is made my gaoler to attend on me." (KRII.1.3)
'Doubly portcullis'd' stands for 'doubly locked'. A portcullis is a medieval castle door, sliding up and down adjacent guides and (usually) made up of a lattice of vertical and horizontal thick wooden bars.
In the play. *Mowbray's answer to the King who has banished Mowbray from England forever. 'Engaol'd' = 'imprisoned'*

Speechless, awed in wonder – I am so attired in wonder I know not what to say.
"I am so attired in wonder,
I know not what to say." (MAAN.4.1)
Use to express your amazement at her beauty, see also 'Speechless, stunned by her beauty or in general at a loss for words'. Good also when you face a situation you did not expect and you really do not know what to say. That 'attired in wonder' will predispose them either to wait for your answer or opinion or accept that you do not want to answer but want to do so gracefully.
In the play. *Benedick is shocked at hearing the accusations against Hero and witnessing Leonato's desperation.*

Speechless, plainly amazed - I am amazed and know not what to say.
"I am amazed and know not what to say." (MND.3.2)
When you cannot think of an answer
In the play. *Hermia is perplexed at the remarks and adversary attitude of Helena*

Speechless, made speechless by her princely beauty - ... beauty's princely majesty is such, confounds the tongue, and makes the senses rough.
"Ay, beauty's princely majesty is such,
Confounds the tongue, and makes the senses rough." (KHVI.p1.5.3)
In the play. *Suffolk has just met Lady Margaret of France, whom he will propose to the pious King Henry VI as future wife and queen of England.*

**Speechless, stunned by her beauty -
You have bereft me of all words, lady.**
"You have bereft me of all words, lady." (TC.3.2)
A good line to accompany or follow up immediately after complimenting her on her beauty, or when she steps into the room with a new dress etc.
With a slight modification you can use "I am bereft of words" when you are momentarily at a loss on how to comment or how to answer any question. See also 'Silence, frozen into s. - They froze me into silence.'
In the play. *Cressida has just arrived in the orchard where Troilus is waiting for her. For the record, in the play 'Merchant of Venice', act 3, Bassanio uses almost exactly the same words, see the next entry.*

Speechless, stunned by her love - Madam, you have bereft me of all words, only my blood speaks to you in my veins...
"Madam, you have bereft me of all words,
Only my blood speaks to you in my veins,
And there is such confusion in my powers,
As after some oration fairly spoke
By a beloved prince, there doth appear
Among the buzzing pleased multitude;
Where every something, being blent together,
Turns to a wild of nothing, save of joy,
Express'd and not express'd." (MOV.3.2)
In the play. *Bassanio has just won Portia's hand by solving a riddle. Portia gives him a ring accompanied by impassioned words of love.*

Speed, amazing s. - I go, I go; look, how I go swifter than arrow from the Tartar's bow.
"I go, I go; look, how I go;
Swifter than arrow from the Tartar's bow." (MND.3.2)
Emphasize that you will quickly go, come back and get the job done.
In the play. *Oberon orders Puck to go and find Helena.*

Speed, amazing s. - I'll put a girdle around the earth in forty minutes.
"I'll put a girdle around the earth
In forty minutes." (MND.2.1)
Answer 'When will you be back?' to indicate that you will accomplish a lot and quickly. See also 'Running as fast as you can – speeded with the extremest inch of possibility.'
In the play. *Oberon assigns a task to Puck and he is ready to execute it quickly. The task is to set a few drops in Titania's eyes while she is asleep. Whereupon on waking up she will fall in love with the first creature she sees.*

Speed, arriving very quickly at location - I am there before my legs.
"I am there before my legs." (AWEW.2.2)
Answer to 'How soon can you be there?' See also 'Running as fast as you can - I drink the air before me, and return or ere your pulse twice beat.'
In the play. *The Countess gives the clown a message to be delivered to Helen who is at Court in Paris curing the King and asks him to hurry up.*

Speed, command to be quick - Be Mercury, set feathers to thy heels ...
"Be Mercury, set feathers to thy heels,
And fly like thought from them to me again" (KJ.4.2)
In the play. *King John to Faulconbridge commanding him to reach the rebellious Lords before they join the French forces.*

Speed, let's do it quickly - If it were done when 't is done, then 't were well it were done quickly.

"If it were done when 't is done, then 't were well
It were done quickly: if the assassination
Could trammel up the consequence, and catch
With his surcease success; that but this blow
Might be the be-all and the end-all here,
But here, upon this bank and shoal of time,
We'ld jump the life to come." (M.1.7)
If an unpleasant measure must be taken, it may as well be done right away to avoid the anxiety of waiting. 'I am sitting on this bank and shoal of time' is an alternative answer to 'How are you?' or 'What are you doing?'
In the play. *Macbeth speculates about how he would feel (about the pending assassination of King Duncan), if we were sure that no adverse consequences would ensue. But he knows better. See 'Evil, e. rebounding against its inventor - … Bloody instructions, which, being taught, return, return to plague the inventor.' 'To trammel' = 'To tie up, to gather'. 'Trammel' was a contraption to regulate the motion of horses. 'Surcease' = 'Stop, cessation'.*

Speed, need for s. acknowledged - The spirit of the time shall teach me speed.
"The spirit of the time shall teach me speed." (KJ.4.2)
Answer to 'Be quick'.
In the play. *Ph. Faulconbridge answers a command of King John to seek and sooth the anger of sundry English dismayed at the death of young Prince Arthur, allegedly imputed to the king.*

Speed, speedy exit – as swift as swallow flies.
"Now to the Goths, as swift as swallow flies" (TA.4.2)
Determination to be quick, 'as swift as swallow flies'. See also 'Running as fast as you can'.
In the play. *Aaron will deliver his newborn black baby to the Goths to secure his safety. The baby is the result of his adulterous relationship with Tamara, wife of the Roman Emperor Saturninus.*

Spelling, poor s. - What call you the town's name where Alexander the pig was porn?
FLUELLEN: what call you the town's name where Alexander the pig was porn?
GOWER: Alexander the Great
FLUELLEN: Why, I pray you, is not pig, great? The pig, or the great, or the mighty, or the huge, or the magnanimous, are all one reckonings, save the phrase is a little variations. (KHV.4.7)
An example of poor spelling.
In the play. *Fluellen discusses matters with Gower.*

Spin, hypocrisy, posturing - … With colours fairer painted their foul ends
"…With colours fairer painted their foul ends" (TEM.1.2)
In the play. *Prospero is giving daughter Miranda the history of their escape and exile in the island and why evil Antonio did not kill Prospero fearing rebellion from the citizens*

Spin, how to re-interpret reality - You undergo too strict a paradox striving to make an ugly deed look fair.
"You undergo too strict a paradox Striving to make an ugly deed look fair." (TOA.3.5)
When spin is applied to change the nature of a crime or an 'ugly deed'. See also 'Information, twisted in one's favor - … your manner of wrenching the true cause the false way'. *** 'Eloquence, characteristic of the eloquent – … on the

tip of their persuasive tongue carry all arguments and questions deep…'
In the play. *A soldier in Alcibiades' army is accused of murder. The senators want to condemn him to death. Alcibiades maintains that the killing was done in self-defense and pleads for mercy. The senators do not want to listen.*

Spin, posturing - … with forged quaint conceit to set a gloss upon his bold intent…
"…with forged quaint conceit
To set a gloss upon his bold intent…" (KHVI.p1.4.1)
In the play. *Vernon rebuts a challenge from Basset concerning the virtues (or lack of) connected with the house of Lancaster (red rose) and York (white rose).*

Spirit, keeping up a good s. - And like the watchful minutes to the hour…
"And like the watchful minutes to the hour,
Still and anon cheer'd up the heavy time" (KJ.4.1)
In the play. *Prince Arthur reminds his jailer Hubert that he, Arthur, comforted him when he was sick.*

Sport, wrestling not a s. for ladies – … it is the first time that ever I heard breaking of ribs was sport for ladies.
"…it is the first time that ever I heard breaking of ribs was sport for ladies." (AYLI.1.2)
Applicable also to any sport that you judge unsuitable for ladies.
In the play. *Touchstone's comment at hearing that Celia and Rosalind will watch the wrestling match between Orlando and Charles.*

Spring, looking like the s. – See where she comes, apparell'd like the spring.
"See where she comes, apparell'd like the spring" (PER.1.1)
Compliment.
In the play. *King Antiochus introduces his daughter to Pericles*

Spring, s. and April - … the spring, when proud-pied April dress'd in all his trim..
"… the spring,
When proud-pied April dress'd in all his trim
Hath put a spirit of youth in every thing." (SON 98)

Spring, season for love and birds –
When birds do sing, hey ding a ding, ding: sweet lovers love the spring.
"When birds do sing, hey ding a ding, ding:
Sweet lovers love the spring." (AYLI.5)
Use when you are not in the mood for singing and you are still asked to sing a song.
In the play. *The song that concludes the play. That the lyrics were of questionable impact is confirmed by the fool/wise Touchstone who says, 'Truly, young gentlemen, though there was no great matter in the ditty, yet the note was very untuneable."*

Spy, private investigator - Saucy controllers of our private steps!
"Saucy controllers of our private steps!" (TA.2.2)
Apply to any snoopy or over-inquisitive person. Change 'controllers' to 'controlled'.
In the play. *Lavinia and Bassianus stumble on Tamora and Aaron. Tamora calls them spies.*

Stain, s. on a person's character - … it doth confirm another stain, as big as hell can hold …
"… it doth confirm
Another stain, as big as hell can hold,
Were there no more but it." (CYM.2.4)
In the play. *The perfidious Iachimo, with spurious evidence, has convinced Leonatus that his wife Imogen is unfaithful and Leonatus does not want to hear any more.*

Stalemate, s. between two equal powers - Blood hath bought blood, and blows have answered blows...
"Blood hath bought blood, and blows have answered blows;
Strength match'd with strength, and power confronted power:
Both are alike, and both alike we like." (KJ.2.2)
Describe a stalemate.
In the play. *Hubert, mayor of Angiers addresses the representatives of the French and English armies. Both the English and the French want the citizen of Angiers to declare themselves for one or the other. Hubert refuses to commit himself and the city.*

Star, s. versus sun, divided between two loves - At first I did adore a twinkling star, but now I worship a celestial sun.
"At first I did adore a twinkling star,
But now I worship a celestial sun" (TGV.2.5)
Explain why you like your latest girlfriend better than the previous one. Or change slightly to tell her how much your love has grown since you met her, e.g. 'When I met you I thought I adored a twinkling star, but now (that I have come to know you) I worship a celestial sun.' Or answer to 'Whatever happened to your girlfriend?' when they know that you have a new one. See also "Replacement, you loved her first and suddenly you love another - Even as one heat another heat expels, or as one nail by strength drives out another...'

In the play. *The rascally Proteus finds that Sylvia has quickly displaced Julia as the center of his desires. The twinkling star is Julia, the celestial sun Sylvia. Proteus now hatches a plot to have Valentine removed from Sylvia's life so that he can get to her. Valentine made the error of praising Sylvia's beauty to his friend Proteus, trusting him too much. An error, as Ovid pointedly explains,* 'Alas, it is not safe to praise to a friend the object of your love; so soon as he believes your praises, he slips into your place.' (AOL.1)

Star, compliment. See 'Party, many fine ladies expected - look to behold this night earth treading stars, that make dark heaven light.'

Start line, at the start line - the game's afoot…follow your spirit…
"I see you stand like greyhounds in the slips,
Straining upon the start. The game's afoot;
Follow your spirit: and, upon this charge,
Cry - God for Harry, England and Saint George!" (KHV.3.1)
Use at the end of a presentation or motivational speech when a new program or operation is started. "If I may borrow from some well known lines, the game's afoot, follow your spirit: and, upon this charge, cry - God for (name of company), (name of project) and St. George! See also 'Revolution, r. ignited - Mischief, thou art afoot, take thou what course thou wilt." *** 'War, call to battle – … set the teeth and stretch the nostril wide…'
In the play. *K. Henry addresses the troops before the siege of Harfleur.*

State of affairs, rotten state of affairs - Something is rotten in the state of Denmark
"Something is rotten in the state of Denmark." (H.1.4)

Apply to place, company or other by changing 'Denmark' to name of place, company or other. See also 'Invocation, state of country – Bleed, bleed, poor country! Great tyranny! lay thou thy basis sure…'
In the play. *Marcellus on seeing the Ghost again. The Ghost is Hamlet's father, slain by his brother Claudius now king of Denmark.*

State of affairs, state diseased - You perceive the body of our kingdom how foul it is …
"…you perceive the body of our kingdom
How foul it is; what rank diseases grow
And with what danger, near the heart of it." (KHIVp2.3.1)
In the play. *King Henry shares his thoughts with Warwick, the disease is the brewing rebellion.*

State of distress, cold and hungry - (I am) a man thronged up with cold, my veins are chill…
"(I am) a man thronged up with cold, my veins are chill,
And have no more of life that may suffice
To give my tongue that heat to ask your help." (PER.2.1)
Emphasize that you are cold, hungry and in need of restoration.
In the play. *After leaving Tharsus, a devastating storm destroys Pericles' fleet and he manages to swim ashore where he meets with 3 fishermen. He begs for their help.*

Statement, making a formal s. - Let me be recorded by the righteous gods…
"Let me be recorded by the righteous gods" (TOA.4.2)
See also 'Invocation, i. to heaven that I am telling the truth - heaven be the record to my speech'.

In the play. *Flavius, Timon's faithful servant to the other servants of the household, suddenly unemployed due to Timon's financial woes.*

Sting operation - ... the play's the thing wherein I'll catch the conscience of the king.
"…the play's the thing
Wherein I'll catch the conscience of the king." (H.2.2)
In the play. *Hamlet will observe the reaction of the king at the development of the murder plot in the play Hamlet has decided to produce.*

Stones, s. more sympathetic than people – A stone is soft as wax,-- tribunes more hard than stones…
"A stone is soft as wax,--tribunes more hard than stones;
A stone is silent, and offendeth not,
And tribunes with their tongues doom men to death" (TA.3.1)
See also 'Pain, mental p., stones as a better audience than people - .. I tell my sorrows to the stones'
In the play. *The tribunes will not hear Titus A. Shattered by the murder of his sons and the mutilations of his daughter Lavinia, Andronicus finds the stones a more amenable audience.*

Storm, braving a s. – … to stand against the deep dread-bolted thunder?
"…Was this a face
To be opposed against the warring winds?
To stand against the deep dread-bolted thunder?" (KL.4.7)
Refer to the storm you went through to get to destination. E.G. 'I was opposed…winds…I stood against…thunder.'
In the play. *Reunited with her father King Lear, Cordelia shudders at the suffering he felt in the storm after having been banned by his own daughters from their castle.*

Storm, s. (metaphor for vexation) unavoidable - ... we hear this fearful tempest sing, yet see no shelter to avoid the storm.
"But, lords, we hear this fearful tempest sing,
Yet see no shelter to avoid the storm;
We see the wind sit sore upon our sails,
And yet we strike not, but securely perish." (KRII.2.1)
Voice your criticism at the lack response or indifference to a critical situation.
In the play. *Northumberland referring to the vexation, the general excesses and the dissolution of King Richard II.*

Story, if same story I don't like it - If it be aught to the old tune, my lord, it is as fat and fulsome to mine ear, as howling after music.
" If it be aught to the old tune, my lord,
It is as fat and fulsome to mine ear,
As howling after music." (TN.5.1)
Explain that you are tired of the same thing or ideas. Eliminate 'my lord'.
In the play. *Olivia thinks that the Duke still wants to pursue her and is tired of it.*

Story, long boring s. and its effect on the audience – ... their copious stories oftentimes begun end without audience and are never done.
" (Men) If pleased themselves, others, they think, delight
In such-like circumstance, with suchlike sport:
Their copious stories oftentimes begun
End without audience and are never done." (V&A)
Use (as an antithesis), to reassure the audience that you will keep your report short.
In the poem. *Comment on the wailing songs by Venus, snubbed by Adonis.*

Story, a pitiful s. to tell – And if thou tell'st the heavy story right, upon my soul, the hearers will shed tears...
"And if thou tell'st the heavy story right,
Upon my soul, the hearers will shed tears;
Yea even my foes will shed fast-falling tears,
And say 'Alas, it was a piteous deed!'" (KHVI.p3.1.4)
In the play. *York, captured, taunted by Queen Margaret and on the point of being killed, addresses his enemies.*

Story, reaction to a lengthy account - The strangeness of your story put heaviness in me.
"The strangeness of your story put Heaviness in me." (TEM.1.2)
Change 'your' to 'his' and hint that you do not believe his story and are bored.
In the play. *Prospero has described to daughter Miranda all the vicissitudes from her birth to the current time in the island. Miranda is tired.*

Story, s. with record in painfulness – ... never was a story of more woe than this of Juliet and her Romeo.
"... never was a story of more woe Than this of Juliet and her Romeo." (RJ.5.3)
In the play. *The Prince of Verona makes a final remark after the festival of carnage and death involving Romeo, Juliet, and Tybalt. Mercutio, Paris and Juliet's mother.*

Story, sad s. to be told - ... And in this harsh world draw thy breath in pain, to tell my story.
"If thou didst ever hold me in thy heart
Absent thee from felicity awhile,
And in this harsh world draw thy breath in pain,
To tell my story." (H.5.2)
Introduction to a sad story. Change 'my' to 'this' as applicable.

See also 'Event, e. of historical importance - how many ages hence shall this, our lofty scene.' – Entries for 'Introduction'.
In the play. *Hamlet, dying, asks his faithful friend Horatio to tell the world about the tragedy*

Strange, isn't it strange? - As strange as the thing I know not.
BENEDICK. Is not that strange?
BEATRICE. As strange as the thing I know not." (MAAN.4.1)
Answer to a question about strangeness when you are expected to agree. See also 'Age, sex and aging - Is it not strange that desire should so many years outlive performance?'
In the play. *Benedick and Beatrice spar in friendship, the strangeness referred to is Benedick's love for Beatrice.*

Strategy, s. for kingly popularity - ... **my state, seldom but sumptuous, showed like a feast...**
"My presence, like a robe pontifical, Ne'er seen but wonder'd at: and so my state,
Seldom but sumptuous, showed like a feast
And won by rareness such solemnity" (KHIVp1.3.2)
See also 'Allegiance, how to secure a. from subjects - I stole all courtesy from heaven and dress'd myself in such humility...'
In the play. *King Henry gives lessons to Prince Harry on how to win allegiance from the subjects.*

Strategy, s. not to fight but fight if provoked - The sum of all our answer is but this...
"The sum of all our answer is but this: We would not seek a battle, as we are; Nor, as we are, we say we will not shun it" (KHV.3.6)
In the play. *K. Henry's answer to Montjoy, the French emissary before the battle of Agincourt.*

Strategy, s. requires to stop and avoid any uncertainty – ...**(stop) every loop from whence the eye of reason may pry in upon us.**
"(We must) stop all sight-holes, every loop from whence
The eye of reason may pry in upon us" (KHIVp1.4.1)
In the play. *Worcester's consideration on knowing that Hotpur's father's forces will not be able to join the fight against the King.*

Strength, s. deriving from doing the right thing - ...**Thrice is he arm'd, that hath his quarrel just...**
"What stronger breastplate than a heart untainted!
Thrice is he arm'd, that hath his quarrel just;
And he but naked, though lock'd up in steel,
Whose conscience with injustice is corrupted." (KHVI p2.3)
Stress the value of courage against injustice.
In the play. *K. Henry's comments on the events that led to the murder of Gloucester.*

Strength, s. in moderation – ... **if, with the sap of reason you would quench, or but allay, the fire of passion.**
"...there is no English soul
More stronger to direct you than yourself,
If with the sap of reason you would quench,
Or but allay, the fire of passion." (KHVIII.1.1)
Persuading someone to set aside anger and use reason instead. That is praise him ('There is no English (American?) soul more stronger to direct you than yourself') and then follow with a modifier, 'If with the sap of reason.... passion' Alternatively, modify for the same purpose, 'Quench the fire of passion with the sap of reason'.

In the play. *Norfolk advises Buckingham to tone down his anger at Cardinal Wolsey.*

Strength, s. relative – ... Troy in our weakness stands, not in her strength.
"To end a tale of length,
Troy in our weakness stands, not in her strength." (TC.1.3)
A comparison exhorting not to fear the competition and to motivate a change in attitudes, management or both.
In the play. *Ulysses ends a long monologue in which he demonstrates and attributes the weakness of the Greeks to a lack of respect for leadership.*

Strength, s. relative, wolf and sheep - ... I know he would not be a wolf but that he sees the Romans are but sheep.
"... I know he would not be a wolf,
But that he sees the Romans are but sheep:
He were no lion, were not Romans hinds." (JC.1.3)
Promote courage and a manly and strong response to threat.
In the play. *Cassius to Casca referring to Caesar.*

Strengths, s. neutralizing themselves - One fire drives out one fire: one nail, one nail.
"One fire drives out one fire: one nail, one nail;
Rights by rights founder, strengths by strengths do fail." (COR.4.7)
Remind your audience that nothing is permanent and that even apparently unshakable people or organization may fall or flounder.
In the play. *Aufidius discusses with his lieutenant the reasons why Coriolanus could not make the best of his chances with the Romans, that is, to become their leader.*

Strengthening, image of s. - ...join you with them, like a rib of steel to make strength stronger.
"...join you with them, like a rib of steel,
To make strength stronger"
(KHIVp2.2.3)
In the play. *Lady Percy counsels her father in law Northumberland to join the rebel forces only if they gain some initial victory against King Henry.*

Stress, influence of s. on longevity - Shorten my days thou canst with sullen sorrow.
"Shorten my days thou canst with sullen sorrow,
And pluck nights from me, but not lend a morrow" (KRII.1.3)
Example of how stress can shorten life.
In the play. *Richard II tells John of Gaunt he has many years to live. Gaunt, distressed at the banishment of Bolingbroke, his son, replies.*

Stress, s. caused by discontent - For what's more miserable than discontent?
"For what's more miserable than discontent?" (KHVI p2.3.1)
In the play. *His enemies have framed the good Duke Humphrey of Gloucester and King Henry VI is distraught at a turn of events he was not able to stop.*

Strike, pre-emptive s. - Who 'scapes the lurking serpent's mortal sting.
"To whom do lions cast their gentle looks?
Not to the beast that would usurp their den.
Whose hand is that the forest bear doth lick?
Not his that spoils her young before her face.
Who 'scapes the lurking serpent's mortal sting?
Not he that sets his foot upon her back.

The smallest worm will turn being trodden on." (KHVI p3.2)
Use the last line to show that negative reaction may be expected by anyone whose rights have been infringed. The first two lines are an encouragement to take preventive measures to secure safety.
In the play. *Clifford to Henry VI who appears lenient towards his enemies.*

Strong, as strong as - ... As doth a rock against the chiding flood...
"As doth a rock against the chiding flood
Should the approach of this wild river break,
And stand unshaken yours."
(KHVIII.3.2)
In the play. *Cardinal Wolsey's profession of continued allegiance to the king.*

Strong, feeling s. – A thousand hearts are great within my bosom...
"A thousand hearts are great within my bosom:
Advance our standards, set upon our foes
Our ancient word of courage, fair Saint George,
Inspire us with the spleen of fiery dragons!" (KRIII.5.3)
In the play. *At Bosworth Field, Richard III, after a restless night, tries to inspire himself with courage.*

Stubbornness, s. becoming folly after reaching a limit - ... And manhood is called foolery, when it stands against a falling fabric.
"... And manhood is called foolery, when it stands
Against a falling fabric." (COR.3.1)
Justify giving up against overwhelming odds.
In the play. *Cominius, Coriolanus and a few friends cannot take on the mass of the revolting people.*

Studying, against studying as mere erudition – Study is like the heaven's glorious sun that will not be deep-search'd with saucy looks...
BIRON Study is like the heaven's glorious sun
That will not be deep-search'd with saucy looks:
Small have continual plodders ever won
Save base authority from others' books
These earthly godfathers of heaven's lights
That give a name to every fixed star
Have no more profit of their shining nights
Than those that walk and wot not what they are.
Too much to know is to know nought but fame;
And every godfather can give a name.
FERDINAND How well he's read, to reason against reading! " (LLL.1.1)
In the play. *Biron presents his argument against the quest for erudition as proposed by Ferdinand. 'To wot'='To know'.*

Studying, bad effects of long s. - ... universal plodding poisons up the nimble spirits in the arteries...
"Why, universal plodding poisons up
The nimble spirits in the arteries,
As motion and long-during action tires
The sinewy vigour of the traveller." (LLL.4.3)
Your reply to your parents when they reproach you because you are not studying enough.
In the play. *Biron, after declaring that he gets his wisdom from women's eyes (see 'Eyes, ladies e. as a source of philosophical propositions'), points out the bad effects of long studying.*

Studying, limitation of s. and theoretical knowledge - ... while it

doth study to have what it would, it
doth forget to do the thing it should.
" So study evermore is overshot;
While it doth study to have what it
would,
It doth forget to do the thing it
should." (LLL.1.1)
Decry the danger of excesses.
In the play. *The 'forgetting of the thing it should' refers to the arrival of the Princess of France to whom the king must pay homage for reasons of politeness and politics.*

Studying, objective of s. - ... that to
know, which else we should not
know...
BIRON. What is the end of study?
KING. Why, that to know, which else
we should not know.
BIRON. Things hid and barr'd, you
mean, from common sense?
KING. Ay, that is study's god-like
recompense." (LLL.1.1)
Praise the value of studying
In the play. *Biron questions the wisdom of concentrated studying.*

Studying, passion for s. - ...
transported and rapt in secret studies.
"...being transported
And rapt in secret studies." (TEM.1.2)
Answer to 'What are you doing these
days?' 'I am rapt in secret studies'.
In the play. *Prospero tells daughter Miranda how he trusted his brother to run Milan while he dedicated himself to learning and secret studies.*

Stunned, mesmerized, in a trance -
My thoughts are whirled like a
potter's wheel; I know not where I
am, nor what I do.
"My thoughts are whirled like a
potter's wheel;
I know not where I am, nor what I
do." (KHVI.p1.1.5)

A state of mind that can describe either
your intense happiness and contentment
or, alternatively, your inability to think
clearly. See also entries for 'Speechless'
*** 'Trance, in a t. - ... Like our strange
garments, cleave not to their mould but
with the aid of use.'
In the play. *The state of mind of the famed English soldier, Sir Talbot, after an encounter in battle with Joan of Arc who is leading the French forces during the siege of Orleans.*

Stupidity, s. more striking in a person
not normally stupid - Folly in fools
bears not so strong a note...
"Folly in fools bears not so strong a
note,
As foolery in the wise, when wit doth
dote." (LLL.5.2)
Comment on a stupidity committed or
said by someone not expected to be
stupid.
In the play. *Maria's comment on Longaville. 'To dote' = 'to act irrationally'.*

Stupidity, s. not to be imitated, don't
copy the fool - If the enemy is an ass
and a fool, and a prating coxcomb...
"If the enemy is an ass and a fool, and
a prating coxcomb, is it meet, think
you, that we also, look you, be an ass,
and a fool, and a prating coxcomb?"
(KHV.4.1)
Retort to defensive statement such as
"They do it too" and what they do is
plainly stupid.
In the play. *Fluellen reproaches Gower who is noisy in the war camp at night on the ground that the enemy is also noisy. 'Meet'='proper'.*

Stupidity, s. universal, compared
sarcastically to the sun - Foolery, sir,
does walk about the orb, like the sun,
it shines everywhere.
VIOLA. I saw thee late at the count
Orsino's.

CLOWN. Foolery, sir, does walk about the orb, like the sun, it shines everywhere." (TN.3.1)
Answer to a rhetorical question of the type, 'How could this happen?' or 'How could they do this?'
In the play. *Viola and the clown continue to banter.*

Subservience - … and bend the dukedom yet unbow'd… to most ignoble stooping.
"… (to) Subject his coronet to his crown and bend
The dukedom yet unbow'd--alas, poor Milan!--
To most ignoble stooping." (TEM.1.2)
In the play. *An account by Prospero of how Antonio made Milan a puppet state of the Kingdom of Naples.*

Substance, come to the point - More matter, with less art.
"More matter, with less art." (H.2.2)
Alternative to 'cut it out and come to the point'.
In the play. *The Queen is annoyed at Polonius' wordiness.*

Substance, prevailing over form - … is the adder better than the eel, because his painted skin contents the eye?
"What is the jay more precious than the lark,
Because his fathers are more beautiful?
Or is the adder better than the eel, Because his painted skin contents the eye?" (TOS.4.3)
Reinforce the point that substance prevails over image. – See also 'Wealth relative. Real richness is in the mind'.
In the play. *In his planned and continued effort to tame his newly married wife Katharina (the shrew), Petruchio manages to have Katharina wear humble clothing not really suitable to her station and he answers to her objections.*

Subject, inquiring about secretly discussed s. – What were't worth to know the secret of your conference?
"What were't worth to know
The secret of your conference?" (KHVIII.2.3)
In the play. *The chamberlain, arriving to speak with Anne Boleyn, inquires about what is she talking about with her lady in waiting.*

Subject, obsessive subject of conversation, horse - … he doth nothing but talk of his horse…
"…he doth nothing but talk of his horse; and he makes it a great appropriation to his own good parts, that he can shoe him himself. I am much afeard my lady his mother played false with a smith" (MOV.1.2)
You can change 'horse' to 'car' or similar depending on the obsession of the party involved.
In the play. *Portia's opinion of one of her suitors, the Prince of Naples*

Success, promised s. certain - … doubt not but success will fashion the event in better shape than I can lay it down in likelihood.
"…doubt not but success
Will fashion the event in better shape
Than I can lay it down in likelihood." (MAAN.4.1)
In the play. *A friar hatches a counter-scheme to clear the innocent Hero of the accusations levied against her.*

Success, s. achieved through damaging policies - By devilish policy art thou grown great…
"By devilish policy art thou grown great…" (KHVI.p2.4.1)
See also entries for 'Upward Mobility'
In the play. *The captain of the ship on which Suffolk was hoping to escape to France is an enemy of his.*

Success, s. always temporary, dangers of over-extension - Glory is like a circle in the water, which never ceaseth to enlarge itself...
"Glory is like a circle in the water,
Which never ceaseth to enlarge itself,
Till, by broad spreading, it disperse to nought." (KHVIp1.1.2)
Warn against spreading too thinly the resources of the company. Example, "Growth like glory, is a circle...disperse to nought."
In the play. *The Pucelle refers to the waning glory of the English power, dramatically reduced after the death of Henry V.*

Success, s. depending on a specific condition - ... our fortune lies upon this jump.
"...our fortune lies
Upon this jump." (AC.3.9)
In the play. *Octavian instructs Taurus to execute his orders accurately.*

Success, s. impossible given the man and the circumstances - You may as well forbid the mountain pines...
"You may as well forbid the mountain pines
To wag their high tops, and to make no noise
When they are fretted with the gusts of heaven." (MOV.4.1)
Describe any occurrence, characteristic or person that cannot be changed.
In the play. *Antonio explains to Bassanio the meager chances of success when negotiating with Shylock.*

Success, s. impossible given the man and the circumstances – You may as well go stand upon the beach and bid the main flood bate his usual height...
"You may as well go stand upon the beach
And bid the main flood bate his usual height;
You may as well use question with the wolf
Why he hath made the ewe bleat for the lamb." (MOV.4.1)
In the play. *Antonio explains to Bassanio the meager chances of success when negotiating with Shylock. Two additional analogies of impossibility.*

Success, s. impossible given the man and the circumstances. See 'Impossibility, cooling the sun with a fan - ... you may as well go about to turn the sun to ice...'

Success, s. through deceit - ... their deceit, contrived by art and baleful sorcery
"...As fitting best to quittance their deceit,
Contrived by art and baleful sorcery" (KHVI.p1.2.1)
Cast doubt on an unexpected achievement. E.G. 'This has been contrived.... sorcery'.
In the play. *Talbot plans an attack on the French at Orleans after Joan of Arc's temporary victory. 'Baleful' = 'pernicious'.*

Successes, past s. irrelevant - O, let not virtue seek remuneration for the thing it was.
"O, let not virtue seek
Remuneration for the thing it was." (TC.3.3)
Use this in its reverse sense of the invitation. E.G., 'I don't want virtue seek remuneration for the thing it was but...', when you want to receive acknowledgement or a service in return for previous favors done. See also 'Time erasing impact of action, compared to a parting host.'
In the play. *Ulysses tries to convince the supercilious Achilles to rejoin the fighting against the Trojans.*

Suddenness as a string of comparisons - ... momentany as a

sound, swift as a shadow, short as any dream…
"…momentany as a sound,
Swift as a shadow, short as any dream;
Brief as the lightning in the collied night." (MND.1.1)
Change 'momentany' to 'momentary'.
In the play. *Lysander loves Hermia but her father wants her to marry Demetrius. Lysander comments on how quickly things can become confused.*

Suffering, insensible to s. – … if you can be merry then, I'll say a man may weep upon his wedding-day.
"…see
How soon this mightiness meets misery:
And, if you can be merry then, I'll say
A man may weep upon his wedding-day." (KHVIII.1.1)
See also entries for 'Pain', 'Sorrow'.
In the play. *The chorus anticipates to the audience the rise and falls of characters in the ensuing play.*

Suffering, s. as a badge of valor – He's truly valiant that can wisely suffer…
"He's truly valiant that can wisely suffer
The worst that man can breathe, and make his wrongs
His outsides, to wear them like his raiment, carelessly,
And ne'er prefer his injuries to his heart,
To bring it into danger" (TOA.3.5)
In the play. *An Athenian senator attempts to convince Alcibiades to drop his complaints against the Athenian senate.*

Suicide, ethical issues – … is it sin to rush into the secret house of death ere death dare come to us?
"…is it sin
To rush into the secret house of death,
Ere death dare come to us? " (AC.4.15)
In the play. *Cleopatra talks to her ladies in waiting after Antony just died and prior to her poisoning herself with an aspid. 'Ere'='Before'*

Suicide, s. always an option - …life, being weary of these worldly bars, never lacks power to dismiss itself…
"… life, being weary of these worldly bars,
Never lacks power to dismiss itself.
If I know this, know all the world besides,
That part of tyranny that I do bear
I can shake off at pleasure." (JC.1.3)
In the play. *Cassius' comments to Casca referring first to the strength of spirit prompting to fight against tyranny (see 'Freedom, f. of the spirit has no obstacles') then to suicide, an alternative method to escape the ills of the world.*

Suicide, s. as a liberation prevented – Is wretchedness deprived that benefit, to end itself by death?
"Is wretchedness deprived that benefit,
To end itself by death? 'Twas yet some comfort,
When misery could beguile the tyrant's rage,
And frustrate his proud will." (KL.4.6)
Argument against those who oppose assisted suicide.
In the play. *Blinded Gloucester thought to have fallen from the cliffs of Dover but was prevented from the act and saved from his good son Edgar.*

Suicide, s. as a way out – … it is great to do that thing that ends all other deeds …
"…it is great
To do that thing that ends all other deeds;
Which shackles accidents and bolts up change;
Which sleeps, and never palates more the dug,

The beggar's nurse and Caesar's." (AC.5.2)
In the play. *Cleopatra contemplates suicide after the death of Antony.*

Summarizing – There's the short and the long of it.
"…there's the short and the long of it" (MWW.2.2)
In the play. *Nym informs Mr. Page that Falstaff is after his wife.*

Summer, like a s. day but only better - Shall I compare thee to a Summer's day? Thou art more lovely and more temperate…
"Shall I compare thee to a Summer's day?
Thou art more lovely and more temperate.
Rough winds do shake the darling buds of May,
And summer's lease hath all too short a date.." (SON.18)
This is a classic and it always works. If she attended high school she is likely to remember it.

Summer, not yet fall, not yet winter - … the year growing ancient, not yet on summer's death, nor on the birth of trembling winter.
"… the year growing ancient,
Not yet on summer's death, nor on the birth
Of trembling winter." (WT.4.4)
In the play. *At her (adopted) shepherd father's party Perdita displays her entertaining skills and botanical knowledge. Here she discusses carnations and gillyvors, marigolds (see 'Flowers, marigolds') violets (See 'Flowers, violets'), primroses (see 'Flowers, primroses').*

Summer, s. turning into winter - For never-resting time leads summer on to hideous winter…

"For never-resting time leads summer on
To hideous winter, and confounds him there;
Sap checked with frost, and lusty leaves quite gone,
Beauty o'er-snowed and bareness every where" (SON.5)

Sunbeam, her beauty compared to the reflection of sunbeams on water - As plays the sun upon the glassy streams, twinkling another counterfeited beam…
"As plays the sun upon the glassy streams,
Twinkling another counterfeited beam,
So seems this gorgeous beauty to mine eyes." (KHVI.p1.5.3)
Compliment. Change the last line to 'So seems your gorgeous beauty to mine eyes.'
In the play. *Suffolk has just met Lady Margaret of France, whom he will propose to the pious King Henry VI as future wife and queen of England.*

Sunshine, her face like s. - Vouchsafe to show the sunshine of your face…
"Vouchsafe to show the sunshine of your face,
That we, like savages, may worship it." (LLL.5.2)
Change the second line to 'that I, like a savage, may worship it. Use this when she is upset and turns her face away so that you cannot see her. Or just cheer her up.
In the play. *Biron asks Rosaline to remove her mask.*

Supernatural, existence of the s. a clear fact. - There are more things in heaven and earth, Horatio, than are dreamt of in your philosophy.
"There are more things in heaven and earth, Horatio,

Than are dreamt of in your philosophy." (H.1.5)
Evasive answer to questions of the type, 'Why this?' or 'Why did you do this?' when you do not want to give a reason. Change 'Horatio' to name of party you are talking to. See also 'Philosophy, there is a reason for everything'.
In the play. *Hamlet, returning from the conversation with the Ghost, hints (to Horatio) at the reality of metaphysical phenomena.*

Supplement, s. to help imagination - Give me an ounce of civet, good apothecary, to sweeten my imagination.
"… Give me an ounce of civet, good apothecary, to sweeten my imagination" (KL.4.6)
In the play. *King Lear, partly out of himself, addresses the blinded Gloucester with a nonsensical speech that however contains some truths. 'Civet' = 'Perfume'.*

Sure, are you sure? - Yea, as sure as I have a thought, or a soul.
BENEDICK. Think you in your soul the count Claudio hath wronged Hero?
BEATRICE. Yea, as sure as I have a thought, or a soul." (MAAN.4.1)
Answer to 'Are you sure?'
In the play. *Beatrice is convinced that the accusations against Hero are false.*

Surprise, extreme s. – … (You) surprise me to the very brink of tears.
"You witch me in it;
Surprise me to the very brink of tears: Lend me a fool's heart and a woman's eyes,
And I'll beweep these comforts, worthy senators " (TOA.5.1)
When you sarcastically wish to express surprise at something really unexpected or something that should not surprise you at all.

In the play. *The Senators, fearful of being overthrown or punished by Alcibiades, now offer Timon recompense and the government of the city. Timon replies sarcastically.*

Surprise, hold your s. for a moment – season your admiration for a while with an attent ear…
"Season your admiration for a while
With an attent ear, till I may deliver,
Upon the witness of these gentlemen,
This marvel to you." (H.1.2)
An introduction to a speech or a presentation, in which you will provide evidence for a fact, or supporting a proposal - evidence supplied by the work of your associates. See also entries for 'Introduction'.
In the play. *Horatio wants Hamlet to hear what, the gentlemen (the guards) have to report about the ghost.*

Surprise, s. or wonder at meeting her or at her reaction - Am I in earth, in heaven, or in hell?…
"Am I in earth, in heaven, or in hell?
Sleeping or waking, mad or well-advis'd?" (COE.2.2)
Take away 'or in hell' and 'mad or well-advis'd'. 'Am I in earth, in heaven, sleeping or waking?' Use to indicate pleased wonder. Maybe she said 'yes' to something when you least expected it.
In the play. *Antipholus of Syracuse is taken for Antipholus of Ephesus and this creates all sorts of confusion.*

Suspicion, evidence of s. from expression - See, what a ready tongue suspicion hath!…
"See, what a ready tongue suspicion hath!
He, that but fears the thing he would not know,
Hath, by instinct, knowledge from others' eyes,
That what he fear'd is chanced." (KHIVp2.1.1)

Expose suspicion, 'See, what a ready tongue suspicion hath!'
In the play. *The rebel Morton arrives from Shrewsbury announcing the defeat of the rebels. He hesitates to tell Northumberland that his son, Harry Percy, was killed in the battle. Northumberland guesses the news from Morton's expression.*

Suspicion, I suspect it is you - I do suspect thee very grievously.
"I do suspect thee very grievously." (KJ.4.3)
Address the suspected person
In the play. *Faulconbridge suspects Hubert of having caused the death of young Prince Arthur.*

Suspicion, mutual s. - Each jealous of the other, as the stung are of the adder.
"Each jealous of the other, as the stung
Are of the adder." (KL.5.1)
See also 'Caution, c. required - it is the bright day that brings forth the adder....'
In the play. *Edmund comments on Regan and Cordelia.*

Suspicion, reason to be suspicious - The bird that hath been limed in a bush with trembling wings misdoubteth every bush.
"The bird that hath been limed in a bush,
With trembling wings misdoubteth every bush." (KHVI.p3.5.4)
In the play. *Henry VI in the Tower, to Gloucester (the soon to be Richard III), who has come to kill him. Gloucester had the gall to accuse Henry VI of being suspicious. See 'Suspicion, s. sign of guilty mind.'*

Suspicion, s. always follows a previous suspect - Suspicion all our lives shall be stuck full of eyes...
"Suspicion all our lives shall be stuck full of eyes;
For treason is but trusted like the fox,

Who, ne'er so tame, so cherish'd and lock'd up,
Will have a wild trick of his ancestors." (KHIV.p1.5.2)
In the play. *Henry IV has offered terms to the rebels. Worcester reasons why it would be unwise to accept the terms.*

Suspicion, s. as a biting hurt inside the body – ... the thought whereof doth, like a poisonous mineral, gnaw my inwards...
"...the thought whereof
Doth, like a poisonous mineral, gnaw my inwards;
And nothing can or shall content my soul
Till I am even'd with him" (OTH.2.1)
In the play. *The thought or suspicion is that Othello may have slept with Iago's wife Emilia. See also 'Suspicion, will to consider s. as truth – ...I know not if't be true; but I for mere suspicion in that kind will do as if for surety.*

Suspicion, shame on the suspicious – Honi soit qui mal y pense.
" Honi soit qui mal y pense." (MWW.5.5)
Counter an innuendo particularly if it involves love, sex or romance.
In the play. *Mistress Quickly is managing a caper directed at the misguided and credulous Falstaff. The sentence is the motto of the order of the garter, 'Dishonor to him who harbors a malignant thought'.*

Suspicion, will to consider s. as truth – ...I know not if't be true; but I for mere suspicion in that kind will do as if for surety.
"...I know not if't be true;
But I, for mere suspicion in that kind,
Will do as if for surety." (OTH.1.3)
In the play. *The suspicion, or rather the rumor, is that Othello may have slept with Iago's wife Emilia.*

Swearing, s. as a sign of strong manhood - ... a terrible oath, with a swaggering accent sharply twanged off...
"... for it comes to pass oft, that a terrible oath, with a swaggering accent sharply twanged off, gives manhood more approbation than ever proof itself would have earned him." (TN.3.4)
Comment on the frequent use of four letter words.
In the play. *Sir Toby advises Aguecheek on how to handle Viola/Cesario in the approaching duel. 'Twanged' = 'uttered with a shrill and sharp sound'.*

Sweat - ... sweats to death and lards the lean earth as he walks along...
"... Falstaff sweats to death,
And lards the lean earth as he walks along:
Were 't not for laughing, I should pity him." (KHIVp1.2.2)
In the play. *Prince Henry comments on the panting and sweating Falstaff made to flee by the Prince who pretended to be a robber incognito.*

Suspicion, s. at terms offered by a crook - I like not fair terms and a villain's mind.
"I like not fair terms and a villain's mind." (MOV.1.3)
Concern about a deal with a crook. See also 'News, good n. delivered by a bad guy'.
In the play. *Bassanio is suspicious about the unusually generous interest terms on a loan offered by Shylock - no interest but a pound of flesh in case of default by Antonio.*

Suspicion, s. in a person – ... but yet have I a mind that fears him much..
"... but yet have I a mind
That fears him much; and my misgiving still
Falls shrewdly to the purpose." (JC.3.1)
In the play. *Cassius does not trust Antony as much as Brutus. Cassius will prove right in his fears. 'Shrewdly' = 'quite in a high and mischievous degree'.*

Suspicion, s. in a person – ...our fears in Banquo stick deep.
"To be thus is nothing;
But to be safely thus.--Our fears in Banquo
Stick deep" (M.3.1)
In an ironic tone, change 'Banquo' to the name of the person you suspect.
In the play. *After having killed Duncan, Macbeth is now planning the second murder (of Banquo).*

Suspicion, s. rejected - Heaven make you better than your thoughts!
"Heaven make you better than your thoughts!" (MWW.3.3)
Reject or retort to an accusation or innuendo. Can be applied to any statement to which you object or find disturbing or offensive.
In the play. *Mr. Ford still suspects that Falstaff may succeed in seducing Mrs. Ford and she tells him off.*

Suspicion, s. removed and trust restored - I rather will suspect the sun with cold than thee with wantonness.
"I rather will suspect the sun with cold,
Than thee with wantonness." (MWW.4.4)
Express total trust. Change the tense as applicable, e.g. 'I'd rather suspect the sun with cold...wantonness.'
In the play. *Finally Mr. Ford believes in his wife's virtue. 'Wantonness' = 'lasciviousness'.*

Suspicion, s. sign of guilty mind - Suspicion always haunts the guilty mind, the thief doth fear each bush an officer.
"Suspicion always haunts the guilty mind;

The thief doth fear each bush an officer." (KHVI p3.5.6)
Comment on a suspicious person. See also 'Guilt, g. generates fear - So full of artless jealousy is guilt, it spills itself in fearing to be spilt'.
In the play. *After being defeated at Coventry, Henry VI is again prisoner at the Tower. Gloucester goes to the Tower with the clear intent to kill Henry VI. He is the real guilty party but shifts the guilt (of suspicion) to the hapless Henry VI.*

Suspicion, s. that show of love is insincere - ... you may think my love was crafty love and call it cunning.
"...you may think my love was crafty love
And call it cunning" (KJ.4.1)
In the play. *Young Prince Arthur pleading for his life with jailer Hubert.*

Syllogism, s. applied - ... if thou never wast at court, thou never sawest good manners...
CORIN. (I m damned) for not being at court? your reason?
TOUCHSTONE. Why, if thou never wast at court, thou never sawest good manners; if thou never sawest good manners, then thy manners must be wicked; and wickedness is sin, and sin is damnation. (AYLI.3.2)
An example of questionable syllogism.
In the play. *The courtly Touchstone engages the shepherd Corin into an exchange of ideas and opinions.*

Sympathy, false s. - Came he right now to sing a raven's note whose dismal tune bereft my vital powers.
"What, doth my Lord of Suffolk comfort me?
Came he right now to sing a raven's note,
Whose dismal tune bereft my vital powers" (KHVIp2.3.2)
Fit 'A raven's note' into your observation of false words of comfort or sympathy.
In the play. *Henry VI rejects the help of Suffolk who has just arranged the murder of Duke Humphrey, former Lord Protector*

Symptoms, s. observed but not conclusive - ... many likelihoods informed me of this before, which hung so tottering in the balance...
"... many likelihoods informed me of this before, which hung so tottering in the balance, that I could neither believe nor misdoubt." (AWEW.1.3)
Elegant, extended alternative to 'I got the same feeling or impression'
In the play. *The steward has discovered that Helen loves Bertram and tells the Countess. She acknowledges that she saw the symptoms before.*

Symptoms, s. of a potentially dangerous person - ... He reads much; he is a great observer, and he looks quite through the deeds of men.
"... He reads much;
He is a great observer, and he looks
Quite through the deeds of men."
(JC.1.2)
Apply to yourself facetiously, as an answer to 'What can you tell me about yourself?' e.g.. 'I read much, I am a good observer and I look quite through the deeds of men.' Or you can jokingly apply the lines to someone else. Follow up with '...this man is dangerous'. See 'Fat, f. men less dangerous than thin – ... Yond Cassius has a lean and hungry look.'
In the play. *Caesar's opinion of Cassius.*

System, corrupt s. cannot correct its own mistakes - ... correction lieth in those hands which make the fault we cannot correct...
"But since correction lieth in those hands
Which make the fault we cannot correct." (KRII.1.2)

The management structure created the situation and cannot correct it
In the play. *Gaunt to the duchess of Gloucester referring to the death of the duke of Gloucester. Gaunt is not in a position to avenge the duke of Gloucester's murder.*

System, s. or device suitable to your purpose – ... here an engine fit for my proceeding.
"And here an engine fit for my proceeding." (TGV.3.1)
In the play. *The Duke finds and confiscates the letter that Valentine was planning to send to Sylvia planning an elopement. The 'engine' is the letter itself. The Duke had been informed previously by the treacherous Proteus.*

Table talk - ... let it serve for table-talk' then... I shall digest it.
"...let it serve for table-talk;
' Then, howso'er thou speak'st,
'mong other things
I shall digest it." (MOV.3.5)
In the play. *Now in Belmont Lorenzo replies to a comment by his newly wedded wife Jessica.*

Taint, a fault that obscures other virtues - ... the dram of base doth all the noble substance often dout to his own scandal.
"...the dram of base
Doth all the noble substance often dout
To his own scandal." (H.1.4)
See also 'Fault, one f. obscuring all other virtues - ... the stamp of one defect... shall in the general censure take corruption from that particular fault.'
In the play. *Hamlet explains to Horatio that the heavy drinking of the Danes at their feasts taints their other virtues in the eyes of other people To dout'= 'to extinguish' 'Dram'='An old unit of measurement, about 1/16 of an ounce'*

Talents, t. or qualities misused – all his virtues, not virtuously on his own part beheld, do in our eyes begin to lose their gloss.
"... all his virtues, -
Not virtuously on his own part beheld, -
Do in our eyes begin to lose their gloss;
Yea, like fair fruit in an unwholesome dish,
Are like to rot untasted." (TC.2.3)
Show how misapplied talents or skills end up leaving an overall bad impression.
In the play. *Agamennon tells Patroclus the truth about Achilles.*

Talents, t. to be used – Heaven doth with us as we with torches do, not light them for themselves...
"Heaven doth with us as we with torches do,
Not light them for themselves, for if our virtues
Did not go forth of us, 'twere all alike
As if we had them not." (MFM.1.1)
Counteract the reticence of a well qualified person to undertake an action or to accept an assignment.
In the play. *Angelo is reticent about taking the job offered by the Duke and the Duke retorts with a good reason.*

Talk, all t. and no substance – ... mere prattle, without practise...
"...mere prattle, without practise,
Is all his soldiership" (OTH.1.1)
In the play. *Iago is envious of Cassio by whom he has been overtaken in promotion.*

Talk, I wish to talk to you - Vouchsafe me a word; it does concern you near.
"Vouchsafe me a word; it does concern you near." (TOA.1.2)
Ask for an audience or meeting where the matter is important to the person you are addressing.
In the play. *Flavius, Timon's faithful servant brings in the first message from creditors*

Talk, idle talk, let's put a stop to it - ... no more of this unprofitable chat.
"Come, come,
No more of this unprofitable chat."
(KHIV p1.3.1)
Call an end to useless talk. See also entries for 'Speech, nonsensical or meaningless'
In the play. *Mortimer calls for an end to the banter between Hotspur and Glendower.*

Talk, invitation to straight t. however negative - Speak to me home, mince not the general tongue...
"Speak to me home, mince not the general tongue"
...
"...taunt my faults
With such full licence as both truth and malice
Have power to utter" (AC.1.2)
In the play. *Antony invites a messenger from Rome not to mince words.*

Talk, let me talk to you - Hie thee hither that I may pour my spirits in thine ear.
"Hie thee hither,
That I may pour my spirits in thine ear,
And chastise with the valour of my tongue
All that impedes thee from the golden round,
Which fate and metaphysical aid doth seem
To have thee crown'd withal" (M.1.5)
In the play. *Lady Macbeth, monologuing, can't wait for her husband to return to his castle and guide him to kill King Duncan so as to take his place. 'Hie thee hither' = 'Come here quickly'*

Talk, subject t. when old - ... when we shall hear the rain and wind beat dark December
"What should we speak of
When we are old as you? when we shall hear
The rain and wind beat dark December, how,
In this our pinching cave, shall we discourse
The freezing hours away?" (CYM.3.3)
Introduce a biographical reference or story, e.g., 'Mine is a story for when the rain and wind beat dark December'.
In the play. *Guiderius and Arviragus are anxious to leave the forest where they live. The idea is to undertake adventures to recall and recount in old age.*

Talk, talk is no action - ... we will not stand to prate, talkers are no doers.
"... we will not stand to prate,
Talkers are no doers." (KRIII.1.3)
Response to concern about whether you will carry out a specific action or have doubts at the end. 'I will not stand to prate... doers'.
In the play. *Richard questions the candidate murderers (of Clarence) whether they may be swayed by Clarence's probable pleas. The first murderer responds.*

Talk, talking seriously now - But, turning these jests out of service, let us talk in good earnest.
"But, turning these jests out of service, let us talk in good earnest." (AYLI.1.3)
When you want the conversation to turn from idle to serious. – See also 'Message, serious but delivered lightly'.
In the play. *After this remark Celia will question Rosalind on the strength of Rosalind's sudden passion for Orlando.*

Talker, compulsive t. – ... what a spendthrift is he of his tongue!
"Fie, what a spendthrift is he of his tongue!" (TEM.2.1)
In the play. *Antonio referring to Gonzalo, both stranded by the tempest in Prospero's island.*

Taming of a shrew, any better solution to tame a woman? - He that knows better how to tame a shrew...
"He that knows better how to tame a shrew,
Now let him speak; 'tis charity to show." (TOS.4.1)
Concluding comment after you have described how you have tackled or solved a difficult problem. Answer to a criticism.
In the play. *With his strange tactics Petruchio succeeded in taming Katharina. Happy with his success Petruchio asks rhetorically whether any other tactics may have worked so well.*

Task, heavy t. imposed, to speak of your pain - A heavier task could not have been imposed than I to speak my griefs unspeakable.
"A heavier task could not have been imposed
Than I to speak my griefs unspeakable" (COE.1.1)
In the play. *Duke Solinus of Ephesus prompts Aegeon, merchant from Syracuse to explain how he got to Ephesus against a decree that bans all Syracusans.*

Task, need to finish the t. after initial success – let us not leave till all our own be won.
"And since this business so fair is done,
Let us not leave till all our own be won." (KHIV.p1.5.5)
In the play. *Henry IV, victorious against the rebels at Shrewsbury, wants to continue the fight and eliminate the remaining rebels at York.*

Task, proud to carry it out - This shall I undertake, and 't is a burden, which I am proud to bear.
"This shall I undertake, and 't is a burden
Which I am proud to bear." (TC.3.3)
Accept willingly and forcefully the assignment or task you have been given.

See also, 'Work, type of w. we like to go to' –'Work, it does not matter if it is hard w. provided we like it'
In the play. *Diomedes will deliver the Trojan prisoner back to Troy and bring back Cressida.*

Task, t. carried out but reluctantly - Thither I must, although against my will, for servants must their masters' minds fulfil.
"Thither I must, although against my will,
For servants must their masters' minds fulfil." (COE.4.1)
Ironically accept an assignment even if you do not like the place where you are posted.
In the play. *Ant E is arrested on perjury (following the continued mix-ups due to Ant E being taken for Ant S and viceversa). Ant E commands Dromio S (thinking Dromio S to be Dromio E) to go to Adriana's for help. Dromio S obeys though reluctantly. He knows that at Adriana's he will find Dowsabel, the large woman who claims him as a husband ("She is too big, I hope, for me to compass").*

Task, t. impossible and unrealistic - ... the task he undertakes is numbering sands and drinking oceans dry.
"...the task he undertakes
Is numbering sands and drinking oceans dry" (KRII.2.2)
See also 'Effort, overwhelmed by opposing forces - ... as I have seen a swan with bootless labour swim against the tide...'
In the play. *Green, a lord faithful to Richard II, comments on the impossible task of the Duke of York in gathering support for King Richard II, who will be dethroned by Henry IV Bolingbroke.*

Task, t. still incomplete - We are yet but young in deed.
"We are yet but young in deed." (M.3.4)

In the play. *After having slain King Duncan and killed Banquo Macbeth has more work to do.*

Task, t. that can be completed with very little effort - ... for very little pains will bring this labour to a happy end.
" But on my liege; for very little pains
Will bring this labour to a happy end." (KJ.3.1)
Show that the investment required is little compared with the anticipated results.
In the play. *The English have just won the battle in front of Angiers and Philip F. urges King John to finish the job.*

Task, t. will be accomplished – ... by the grace of Grace we will perform in measure, time and place.
"...and what needful else
That calls upon us, by the grace of Grace,
We will perform in measure, time and place." (M.5.8)
In the play. *Malcolm, winner of the battle of Dunsinane, addresses his allies before moving to be crowned at Scone.*

Task, willingness to undertake an unpleasant t. - Many can brook the weather, that love not the wind.
"Many can brook the weather, that love not the wind." (LLL.4.2)
Express your willingness to undertake the task even if it is unpleasant.
In the play. *After having explained Dull's ignorance, Nathaniel, by means of a metaphor, says he can put up with it.*

Taverns, drawback of t. - ... no more tavern bills; which are often the sadness of parting as the procuring of mirth...
"... no more tavern bills; which are often the sadness of parting, as the procuring of mirth; you come in faint for want of meat, depart reeling with too much drink; sorry that you have paid too much, and sorry that you are paid too much; purse and brain both empty, - the brain the heavier for being too light, the purse too light, for being drawn of heaviness." (CYM.5.4)
Explain why you do not like to drink and don't frequent bars.
In the play. *Posthumus is condemned to death. A jailer explains to Posthumous what he, Posthumus, will not have to endure, being dead.*

Tax, t. collection – We are inforced to farm our royal realm; the revenue whereof shall furnish us... large sums of gold
"We are inforced to farm our royal realm;
The revenue whereof shall furnish us
For our affairs in hand: if that come short,
Our substitutes at home shall have blank charters;
Whereto, when they shall know what men are rich,
They shall subscribe them for large sums of gold
And send them after to supply our wants" (KRII.1.4)
In the play. *Richard II needs money for his military campaign in Ireland.*

Tax, t. collector, how to handle a tax c. – My riches are these poor habiliments...
"My riches are these poor habiliments,
Of which if you should here disfurnish me,
You take the sum and substance that I have." (TGV.4.1)
Use with the IRS.
In the play. *Valentine, banned from Milan is attacked by bandits in the forest who want to rob him of all he has (actually he only has his clothes).*

Tax, t. revolt - we will nothing pay for wearing our own noses.
"…we will nothing pay
For wearing our own noses."
(CYM.3.1)
Reaction to the proposal of raising an extra tax on a universal commodity, or to any unjustified payment.
In the play. *Cloten rebukes Caius Lucius who has come from Rome to collect taxes from the English.*

Taxation, t. recipe of hatred – Their love lies in their purses and whoso empties them by so much fills their hearts with deadly hate.
"… their love
Lies in their purses, and whoso empties them,
By so much fills their hearts with deadly hate." (KRII.2.2)
Oppose an increase in fees or taxes, as applicable
In the play. *Bagot's reflection that the heavy taxation imposed by Richard has alienated the commons.*

Taxes, overbearing t. – … These exactions … are most pestilent to the bearing…
"…These exactions,
Whereof my sovereign would have note, they are
Most pestilent to the bearing; and, to bear 'em,
The back is sacrifice to the load."
(KHVIII.1.2)
In the play. *Queen Katherine presents the point of view of the taxpayers who are almost rebelling against the taxes imposed by Cardinal Wolsey.*

Teacher, a t. of teachers - She seems a mistress to most that teach.
"I cannot say 'tis pity
She lacks instructions, for she seems a mistress
To most that teach." (WT.4.4)
If it is pointed out to you that she does not compare to the standards of your education.
In the play. *Camillo concurs with Florizel that, though apparently a shepherdess' daughter, Perdita appears to know more than the teachers who (hypothetically) could teach her.*

Tears, drying off her t. - Let me wipe off this honorable dew that silverly doth progress on thy cheeks.
"Let me wipe off this honorable dew
That silverly doth progress on thy cheeks." (KJ.5.2)
Something happened to make her cry and you come to the rescue and comfort.
In the play. *Salisbury must resort to ask France (King Lewis) to help redress the wrongs inflicted to England by King John. Lewis nobly offers to wipe off Salisbury's tears.*

Tears, false t., induced by onions - An onion will do well for such a shift; which in a napkin being close conveyed, shall in despite force a watery eye.
"And if the boy have not a woman's gift,
To rain a shower of commanded tears,
An onion will do well for such a shift;
Which in a napkin being close conveyed,
Shall in despite force a watery eye."
(TOS.ind 1)
Comment on a hypocritical declaration. E.G. 'This reminds me of the onions used in plays to generate false tears', (follow with the quote). See also 'Crying not called for, on the contrary - the tears live in an onion that should water this sorrow.' **** 'Crying, on the point of crying - Mine eyes smell onions, I shall weep anon'
In the play. *Part of the prank to be played on Sly involves some form of crying. 'Shift' = Expedient, or stratagem'.*

Tears, flood of t. from a person who usually does not cry - ... drop tears as fast as the Arabian trees their medicinal gum.
"… one whose subdued eyes,
Albeit unused to the melting mood,
Drop tears as fast as the Arabian trees
Their medicinal gum." (OTH.5.2)
Put a humorous spin on your being moved for example at a movie or play. E.G. I drop tears as fast as the Arabian trees their medicinal gum.'
In the play. *Othello asks some Venetian lords to recount to the Venetian senate the events that led to his murdering his wife Desdemona and how he cried for it. In fact shortly later he will stab himself*

Tears, moved to t. - Beshrew me, but his passion moves me so that hardly can I cheque my eyes from tears.
"Beshrew me, but his passion moves me so
That hardly can I cheque my eyes from tears." (KHVI.p3.1.4)
See also 'Pity, no feeling of p. - Think but upon the wrong he did us all and that will quickly dry thy melting tears.'
In the play. *Northumberland, a Lancastrian is almost moved by the speech of the dying York defeated at Sandal Castle. 'Beshrew' = 'woe to'.*

Tears, not called for - Back, foolish tears, back to your native spring, your tributary drops belong to woe…
"Back, foolish tears, back to your native spring;
Your tributary drops belong to woe,
Which you, mistaking, offer up to joy." (RJ.3.2)
Some of us get emotional even when we do not want to. Throw some humor on the occurrence by saying 'Back foolish tears, back to your native springs.'

In the play. *Juliet cries and does not know if her tears should be of joy of pain. Romeo and not Tybald survived the deadly duel. Romeo is her husband, Tybald her cousin – a catch 22 situation.*

Tears, sarcastic promise of t. - Lend me a fool's heart and a woman's eyes and I'll beweep…
"Lend me a fool's heart and a woman's eyes,
And I'll beweep these comforts, worthy senators" (TOA.5.1)
Your reaction to a story of false pity, distress or interested change of heart. Change 'and I'll beweep' to 'and I will cry'.
In the play. *The Senators, fearful of being overthrown or punished by Alcibiades, now offer Timon recompense and the government of the city. Timon replies sarcastically.* See 'Surprise, extreme s. – … (You) surprise me to the very brink of tears.'

Tears, shedding t. - Let my tears stanch the earth's dry appetite.
Let my tears stanch the earth's dry appetite." (TA.3.1)
Mildly ironic indication that you sympathize with the problem or situation described to you.
In the play. *Titus A. is at the point of madness. Two of his sons, unjustly accused of crime, have been killed. 'To stanch' = 'To satiate'.*

Tears, t. banned and substituted by revenge - To weep is to make less the depth of grief: tears, then, for babes; blows and revenge for me.
"To weep is to make less the depth of grief:
Tears, then, for babes; blows and revenge for me." (KHVI p3.2.1)
Express your determination to revert and turn around the conditions that led the competition to success. See also entries

for 'Revenge', 'Pain, mental p. relieved by talking about it'
In the play. *Richard (Gloucester) after the news that Richard (York) has been slain.*

Tears, t. beginning to flow - my heart is drowned with grief whose flood begins to flow within mine eyes.
"…Margaret, my heart is drowned with grief,
Whose flood begins to flow within mine eyes." (KHVI p2.3)
Alternative to 'I am very sad'. Change 'Margaret' to the name of the person you are addressing.
In the play. *K. Henry is resigned to let stand the false accusations against his uncle Gloucester.*

Tears, t. brought in by tragedy – … what showers arise, blown with the windy tempest of my heart.
"…see what showers arise,
Blown with the windy tempest of my heart" (KHVI.p3.2.5)
In the play. *In the battle of Towton, a father fighting with the Yorkists has slain unwittingly his son who was fighting with the Lancastrians.*

Tears, t. down the beard - His tears run down his beard, like winter's drops from eaves of reeds.
"His tears run down his beard, like winter's drops
From eaves of reeds" (TEM.5.1)
In the play. *The spirit Ariel reports to Prospero on the state of Gonzalo.*

Tears, t. in great volume – … one whose subdued eyes drop tears as fast as the Arabian trees their medicinal gum.
"…one whose subdued eyes,
Albeit unused to the melting mood,
Drop tears as fast as the Arabian trees
Their medicinal gum." (OTH.5.2)
In the play. *Othello tells to Ludovico, who is returning to Venice, what to say to the Venetian Senators about the business who led to Desdemona's murder by Othello and his death by his own hand.*

Tears, t. ineffective though they show empathy - … tears show their love, but want their remedies…
"…dry your eyes,
Tears show their love, but want their remedies" (KRII.3.3)
In the play. *K. Richard II, soon to be deposed from the throne, to the Duke of York who cries at the event.*

Tears, t. of joy – Better to weep at joy than to joy at weeping.
"A kind overflow of kindness: there are no faces truer than those that are so washed.
How much better is to weep at joy, than to joy at weeping!" (MAAN.1.1)
When you cannot repress tears of joy.
In the play. *A messenger informs Leonato that Claudio's uncle is pleased about Claudio's performance in battle to the point of tears.*

Tears, t. of joy – I am a fool to weep at what I am glad of.
"I am a fool,
To weep at what I am glad of." (TEM.3.1)
When you are moved to the point of tears and are mildly embarrassed by it - see also 'Tears, unmanly and prompted by moving scene'.
In the play. *Ferdinando has just declared his love to the receptive Miranda and tears come to her eyes.*

Tears, t. of love – The April's in her eyes: it is love's spring…
"The April's in her eyes: it is love's spring,
And these the showers to bring it on" (AC.3.2)
In the play. *Octavian notices and comments on the tears of his sister Octavia. She has just married Antony and is leaving Rome with him.*

Tears, t. on hand - Give me thy hand that I may dew it with my mournful tears.
"Give me thy hand,
That I may dew it with my mournful tears" (KHVIp2.3.2)
In the play. *Queen Margaret takes Suffolk's hand before he leaves for good after having been banished from England.*

Tears, t. pouring out like heavy rain - And with the southern clouds contend in tears, theirs for the earth's increase, mine for my sorrows.
"And with the southern clouds contend in tears,
Theirs for the earth's increase, mine for my sorrows" (KHVI p2.3.2)
In the play. *Q. Margaret to the banished Suffolk, who was probably her lover.*

Tears, t. that prevent speech - … my tears, the moist impediments unto my speech.
"… my tears,
The moist impediments unto my speech." (KHIV.p2.4.4)
Lighten up the tone of your speech or presentation, if the subject is powerful enough to move you.
In the play. *London, the Jerusalem chamber at court. The Prince of Wales was crying as the ailing King reprimanded him (unjustly). Now he explains why he did let the king go on with his rebukes.*

Tears, t. that prevent speech – He has strangled his language in his tears.
"He has strangled
His language in his tears."
(KHVIII.5.1)
In the play. *King Henry comments on Cranmer, who is accused by political enemies.*

Tears unbecoming - … he weeps like a wench that hath shed her milk.
" … he weeps like a wench that hath shed her milk." (AWEW.4.3)
Apply jokingly to yourself when for whatever reason you get emotional and start crying.
In the play. *In a trick to expose his cowardice, Parolles has been captured by French soldiers disguised as enemies. The idea is to show Bertram how his friend Parolles will behave and what he will actually say under pressure. Parolles proves indeed a total coward.*

Tears, anger and thirst for revenge preventing t. and speech – For self-same wind that I should speak withal, is kindling coals that fire all my breast.
"I cannot weep; for all my body's moisture
Scarce serves to quench my furnace-burning heart:
Nor can my tongue upload my heart's great burden;
For self-same wind that I should speak withal,
Is kindling coals that fire all my breast." (KHVI p3.2.1)
Use the first two lines to express your indignation
In the play. *Richard (Gloucester) after the news that Richard (York) has been slain.*

Tears, compared to pearls – a sea of melting pearls.
"A sea of melting pearl, which some call tears" (TGV.3.1)
When she cries, especially if she cries for joy or as an emotional reaction to a special event.
In the play. *Proteus reports to the banned Valentine that Silvia cries bitterly at Valentine's banishment from Milan.*

Tears, difficult to hold back t. - Beshrew me, but his passions move me so, that hardly can I check my eyes from tears.
"Beshrew me, but his passions move me so,

That hardly can I check my eyes from tears." (KHVI p3.1.4)
When you cannot hold back tears. See also 'Emotion, overpowered by e. – My tears will choke me, if I ope my mouth.'
In the play. *Northumberland after listening to York 'Beshrew' = 'woe to'*

Tears, unmanly and prompted by moving scene - These foolish drops do something drown my manly spirit.
"… these foolish drops do something drown my manly spirit" (MOV.2.3)
Even the toughest macho man may at times become emotional. But if tears well up and you cannot stop them, locate the area right between the end of your wrist and the beginning of your hand. Then pass it casually against your eyes with a gesture that suggests you may take the occasion to simultaneously clear your eyes (as well as drying your tears) - and dispense the lines with a tone of unavoidable resignation.
Yet tears can be useful too, according to Ovid, '…with tears you can move iron; let her see, if possible, your moistened cheeks. If tears fail (for they do not always come at need), touch your eyes with a wet hand.' (AOL.2)
See also 'Crying, on the point of crying - Mine eyes smell onions, I shall weep anon.'
In the play. *The servant Launcelot takes an emotional leave from Jessica, Shylock's daughter.*

Tears, unstoppable - Mine eyes cannot hold out water, methinks.
"Mine eyes, cannot hold out water, methinks." (TOA.1.2)
It could be true or use to give the situation an ironic twist, if you sense that the other party wants you to feel sorry or emotional about an event that does not warrant it.
In the play. *Timon, in an enthusiastic mood praises the virtues of friendship and becomes emotional as he speaks.*

Tears, unstoppable t. at a moving sight – … And all my mother came into mine eyes and gave me up to tears.
"…I had not so much of man in me, And all my mother came into mine eyes
And gave me up to tears." (HV.4.6)
In the play. *Exeter narrates the moving death in battle of York and Suffolk.*

Tediousness, t. in everything being always the same – If all the year were playing holidays, to sport would be as tedious as to work.
"If all the year were playing holidays, To sport would be as tedious as to work." (KHIV p1.1.2)
Accept with a smile a laborsome task, e.g., 'I don't mind - if all the year were playing holidays… work.'
In the play. *P. Henry's end of his mission statement.*

Teen-agers, complaint against t-a. – I would there were no age between sixteen and three-and-twenty, or that youth would sleep out the rest…
"I would there were no age between sixteen and three-and-twenty, or that youth would sleep out the rest; for there is nothing in the between but getting wenches with child, wronging the anciently, stealing, fighting…" (WT.3.3)
In the play. *The Shepherd (who will adopt Perdita) makes a generalized complaints after some of his young workers after they neglected their duties.*

Telephone, who is calling – Your servant and your friend, one that attends your ladyship's command.
SILVIA Who calls?
EGLAMOUR Your servant and your friend;

One that attends your ladyship's command. (TGV.4.2)
When you are returning a call from your girlfriend and she says 'who is this?'
In the play. *Eglamour arrives following a request of Silvia to accompany her in quest of the banished Valentine.*

Temper, explaining a loss of t. - Thou must not take my former sharpness ill…
"Thou must not take my former sharpness ill;
I will employ thee back again; I find thee
Most fit for business." (AC.3.3)
A way of apologizing for having previously spoken harshly.
In the play. *Cleopatra had previously almost killed the messenger from Rome who reported Antony's marriage to Octavia. The same messenger later berated Octavia's beauty and Cleopatra repents.* See 'But yet. 'Everything is well but yet'.

Temperance, one who does not know it - Though you can guess what temperance should be, you know not what it is.
"Though you can guess what temperance should be,
You know not what it is." (AC.3.13)
The statement can be equally applied to other virtue of which the party you talk to or of is lacking, i.e. judgment, objectivity, honor etc. See also entries for 'Patience'.
In the play. *Antony upbraids Cleopatra whom he suspects of having or trying to make a deal with the victorious Octavian.*

Temperance, t. as a cure - … temperance; that's the appliance only which your disease requires.
"Ask God for temperance; that's the appliance only
Which your disease requires."
(KHVIII.1.1)

In the play. *Norfolk counsels patience to Buckingham in his dealing with Cardinal Wolsey, Buckingham's enemy.*

Temptation, t. arising from hearing tempting information - … For by our ears our hearts oft tainted be.
"Perchance his boast of Lucrece' sovereignty
Suggested this proud issue of a king;
For by our ears our hearts oft tainted be" (ROL)
In the poem. *The silly Collatinus praises his wife's beauty and this fives the evil Tarquin ideas.*

Temptation, t. by devil - Shall I be tempted of the devil thus?
QUEEN ELIZABETH Shall I be tempted of the devil thus?
KING RICHARD III Ay, if the devil tempt thee to do good. (KRIII.4.4)
Mildly ironic question posed to yourself while the 'tempter' listens. The best non-shakespearean quote about temptation is Oscar Wilde's, 'I can resist anything but temptation'.
In the play. *K. Richard has just finished making a long declaration to Queen Elizabeth about his good and pious intentions to marry her daughter.*

Temptation, t. different from sin - 'Tis one thing to be tempted, Escalus, another thing to fall.
"'Tis one thing to be tempted, Escalus,
Another thing to fall" (MFM.2.1)
Change 'Escalus' to the name of the person you are addressing.
In the play. *Angelo counters Escalus' argument that he, Angelo, may at some time have been tempted to the lust for which Claudio has now be condemned to death.*

Temptation, t. in the form of a fair and modest girl – O cunning enemy,

that, to catch a saint, with saints dost bait thy hook!
"O cunning enemy, that, to catch a saint,
With saints dost bait thy hook!" (MFM.2.1)
See also 'Women, modest and virtuous w. have greater appeal than lascivious ones - Most dangerous is that temptation that doth goad us on to sin in loving virtue…'
In the play. *Angelo will not prove exactly a saint. He excuses his temptation with the argument that a chaste girl presents a stronger temptation than a promiscuous one.*

Temptation, t. taking up false appearances - Devils soonest tempt, resembling spirits of light
"Devils soonest tempt, resembling spirits of light" (LLL.4.3)
In the play. *Biron responds to a comment by the king on Biron's girlfriend.*

Termination - … thus part we rich in sorrow, parting poor.
"… Not one word more:
Thus part we rich in sorrow, parting poor." (TOA.4.2)
When the company downsizes and eliminates jobs without severance payments.
In the play. *Flavius to Timon's other suddenly unemployed servants*

Terminator – … he was a thing of blood, whose every motion was timed with dying cries.
"He was a thing of blood, whose every motion
Was timed with dying cries." (COR.2.2)
Metaphorically praise a winning salesman who has destroyed the competition's efforts.
In the play. *Cominius praises the ability of Coriolanus as a killing machine at the battle of Coriolis.*

Testing, t. the skill or determination of a man – … now do I play the touch, if thou be current gold indeed.
"O Buckingham, now do I play the touch,
To try if thou be current gold indeed" (KRIII.4.2)
Change 'Buckingham' to the name of the person in question or use the last line only, e.g. 'Now I'll try if thou be current gold indeed'.
In the play. *Richard, now king with the indispensable help of Buckingham, will test him. Can Buckingham murder the young prices held in the Tower and still potential contenders to the throne? Buckingham totters and this will mean his end.*

Thank you for unexpected visit, answer or honor - My poor house to visit it is a surplus of your grace, which never my life may last to answer.
"…my poor house to visit
It is a surplus of your grace, which never
My life may last to answer." (WT.5.3)
In the play. *The repentant Leontes, king of Sicilia, visits the home of faithful servant Paulina for whom the visit constitutes a great honor.*

Thankful, great cause to be t. - … we have all great cause to give great thanks.
"Sir, we have all
Great cause to give great thanks." (COR.5.4)
When you start a meeting or presentation in which you will announce a success.
In the play. *The good news (announced by messenger to Sicinius) is that Coriolanus' mother and wife succeeded in making him change his mind*

Thanks but no thanks - Proffers not took, reap thanks for their reward.
"Proffers not took, reap thanks for their reward." (AWEW.2.1)
Use with telemarketers or obnoxious salesmen. Alternative to 'I think I'll pass'.
In the play. *The King refuses to try Helena's medicine after doctors have given up hope for a cure.*

Thanks profusely given. See 'Opinion, your o. on profusely given thanks'.

Thanks rejected - thank me no thankings, nor, proud me no prouds.
"Thank me no thankings, nor, proud me no prouds" (RJ.3.5)
When the thanking appears insincere or when you wish to deflect with some humor the potential embarrassment of excessive expressions of gratitude. See also "Opinion, your o. on profusely given thanks' and 'Courtesy, false c. rejected'.
In the play. *Juliet's father does not want any wiggling out of the planning wedding between Juliet and Paris.*

Thanks, multiple t. - I can no more answer make, but thanks and thanks, and ever thanks.
"I can no more answer make, but thanks,
And thanks, and ever thanks." (TN.3.1)
An expression of gratitude when you can do nothing more to show it than to use words.
In the play. *Sebastian is grateful to Antonio for his concern.*

The all of all - The very all of all is…
"The very all of all is,--but, sweet heart, I do implore secrecy,--that the king would have me
present the princess with some delightful ostentation…" (LLL.4.3)
In the play. *Armado is proud of the assignment given him by the king and says so to Holofernes.*

Theft, t. and proper terminology - 'Convey,' the wise call it. 'Steal!' foh! a fico for the phrase!
NYM The good humour is to steal at a minute's rest.
PISTOL 'Convey,' the wise call it. 'Steal!' foh! a fico for the phrase! (MWW.1.3)
In the play. *Bardolph has left the scene and Falstaff expresses the opinion that Bardolph is a thief. 'Fico' is Italian for 'fig' and a means to express contempt. 'Foh'= 'Exclamation of contempt or abhorrence'.*

Theft, t. probably unnoticed – … easy it is of a cut loaf to steal a shive, we know.
"…easy it is
Of a cut loaf to steal a shive, we know" (TA.2.1)
In the play. *Demetrius rationalizes how he could have Lavinia though she is married to Bassanius. 'Shive' = 'Slice'.*

Theory and practice, from one to the other - … the art and practic part of life must be the mistress to this theoric.
"So that the art and practic part of life
Must be the mistress to this theoric" (HV.1.1)
An alternative to 'now we must put this into practice'.
In the play. *Canterbury and Ely discuss Henry V's impressive acquired qualifications.*

Theory and practice, their difference - … they would be better if well followed.
PORTIA: Good sentences and well pronounced
NERISSA: They would be better if well followed." (MOV.1.2)

Modify to, 'good sentences and well pronounced but they would be better if well followed'. See also 'Hypocrisy, practice what you preach - Do not, as some ungracious pastors do... The primrose path of dalliance threads and recks not his own reed.'
In the play. *Nerissa has just ended giving some good advice to Portia*

Theory and practice, their difference - I can easier teach twenty what were good to be done..
"I can easier teach twenty what were good to be done, than be one of the twenty to follow mine own teaching." (MOV.1.2)
Statement of modesty. See also 'Hypocrisy, practice what you preach'.
In the play. *Portia candidly admits to a common weakness.*

Theory and practice, their difference - If to do were as easy as to know what were good to do..
"If to do were as easy as to know what were good to do, chapels had been churches and poor men's cottages princes' palaces - it is a good divine that follows his own instructions." (MOV.1.2)
Soften a didactic speech, e.g. 'I well realize that if to do were as easy......instructions'
In the play. *Portia acknowledges a universal truth.*

Thief, qualifications for a t. – ... to have an open ear, a quick eye, and a nimble hand, is necessary for a cut-purse...
"... to have an open ear, a quick eye, and a nimble hand, is necessary for a cut-purse; a good nose is requisite also, to smell out work for the other senses" (WT.4.3)
In the play. *The scoundrel Autolycus describes his own strengths as a thief.*

Thievery, t. universal – The sun's a thief, and with his great attraction...
"The sun's a thief, and with his great attraction
Robs the vast sea: the moon's an arrant thief,
And her pale fire she snatches from the sun:
The sea's a thief, whose liquid surge resolves
The moon into salt tears: the earth's a thief,
That feeds and breeds by a composture stolen
From general excrement: each thing's a thief:" (TOA.4.3)
In the play. *Two robbers stumble upon Timon who has retreated and retired to a wood. He talks with robbers and almost converts them away by their profession, by inciting them to pursue it.*

Thieves, comparing your winning enemies to t. - So triumph thieves upon their conquer'd booty...
"So triumph thieves upon their conquer'd booty;
So true men yield, with robbers so o'ermatch'd." (KHVI.p3.1.4)
In the play. *Defeated and captured near Sandal Castle, York is defiant towards Clifford, Queen Margaret and others who taunt him before killing him.*

Thieves, euphemistic definition - We are not thieves, but men that much do want.
"We are not thieves, but men that much do want." (TOA.4.3)
In the play. *Timon greet the thieves by their own appellation but they change their own definition. Before they defined themselves 'soldiers, not thieves', to which Timon sarcastically adds, "Both too, and women's sons".*

Thieves, t. in high places - ... there is boundless theft in limited professions.
"...Yet thanks I must you con
That you are thieves profess'd, that you work not
In holier shapes: for there is boundless theft
In limited professions" (TOA.4.3)
'To con thanks' = 'To be thankful' You can change to 'I must give you' without changing the impact, meaning or rhythm of the line.
In the play. *Timon to the robbers that plan to rob him on having heard that he has found some gold in the woods..*

Thieves, temptation to steal – Rich preys make true men thieves.
"Rich preys make true men thieves" (V&A)
In the play. *With her heated imagination. Venus speculates that if Adonis were to fall from his horse, the earth would take the occasion to steal a kiss from him.*

Things that do not go together - ... they do no more adhere and keep place together than the Hundredth Psalm to the tune of 'Green Sleeves'.
"...but they do no more adhere and keep place together than the Hundredth Psalm to the tune of 'Green Sleeves." (MWW.2.1)
In the play. *Mistress Ford comments on the coherence between the words and promises of Falstaff.*

Thinking, t. quickly - Faster than spring-time showers comes thought on thought...
Faster than spring-time showers comes thought on thought,
And not a thought but thinks on dignity" (KHVI.p2.3.1)
First line can be an alternative to 'let me think' or 'let us think quickly'.
In the play. *York to himself, hatching a plan to destroy his enemies*

Thirst, parched lips begging for water - ... entreat the north to make his bleak wind kiss my parched lips...
"... entreat the north
To make his bleak wind kiss my parched lips,
And comfort me with cold - I do not ask you much,
But beg cold comfort." (KJ.5.7)
When you are or feel very hot.
In the play. *King John feels the effects of poison in his stomach (see 'Ache, stomach ache - There is so hot a summer in my bosom.') and fantasizes about suitable remedies.*

Thought, forced to think the unthinkable – (You) prick my tender patience, to those thoughts which honour and allegiance cannot think.
"(You) prick my tender patience, to those thoughts
Which honour and allegiance cannot think." (KRII.2.1)

.

Thought, monstrous t. kept hidden - ... As if there were some monster in his thought too hideous to be shown.
"By heaven, he echoes me,
As if there were some monster in his thought
Too hideous to be shown" (OTH.3.3)
In the play. *Othello falls for the suspects on Desdemona implanted by the villainous Iago.*

Thought, power of t. and imagination to travel instantly - For nimble thought can jump both sea and land as soon as think the place where he would be.
'For nimble thought can jump both sea and land,
As soon as think the place where he would be." (SON 44)

See also 'Nearness, wishing to be near loved one - If the dull substance of my flesh were thought...' *** 'Love, l. travelling at the speed of thought - ... love's heralds should be thoughts, which ten times faster glide than the sun's beams...'

Thought, reticence to disclose or trust one's t. – Utter my thoughts? Why, say they are vile and false...
"Utter my thoughts? Why, say they are vile and false;
As where's that palace whereinto foul things
Sometimes intrude not?" (OTH.3.3)
In the play. *Iago drives Othello into jealousy. The thoughts referred to regard the alleged infidelity of Desdemona with Cassio.*

Thought, speed of t. - .. In motion of no less celerity than that of thought.
"Thus with imagined wing our swift scene flies
In motion of no less celerity
Than that of thought."
(KHV.3.prologue)
Emphasize or praise speed of execution or speed in general.
In the play. *The chorus bridges the intervening time between sailing from Southampton and the preparation for the attack on the city of Harfleur by the British. Henry refuses the offer of compromise by King Charles of France. Henry wants everything*

Thought, t. absent from non-thinkers - .. for cogitation resides not in that man that does not think it.
"(Have not you seen or thought), for cogitation
Resides not in that man that does not think it." (WT.1.2)
Sarcastic statement when someone is incapable of (correct) thought, e.g. 'cogitation resides not...think it'.

In the play. *Leontes sarcastically asks Camillo how he can have not observed that Hermione loves Polixenes.*

Thought, t. as the arbiter of good or bad - ... for there is nothing either good or bad, but thinking makes it so.
"...for there is nothing either good or bad, but thinking makes it so." (H.2.2)
When you try to rationalize a difference of opinion on a matter that can be judged one way or another.
In the play. *Hamlet quips with Rosencrantz and Guildenstern about whether Denmark is a prison or not.*

Thought, t. as the slave of life, expressing pessimism - ... thought's the slave of life, and life time's fool; and time, that takes survey of all the world, must have a stop.
"But thought's the slave of life, and life time's fool;
And time, that takes survey of all the world,
Must have a stop." (HIV p1.5.4)
Possible answer to 'What are you thinking?' or 'What is in your thoughts' when you wish to be purposely evasive.
In the play. *Hotspur, mortally wounded by the Prince of Wales in the battle of Shrewsbury, reflects on his pain at having lost his titles. See also 'Ambition, a. maintained to the point of death – I better brook the loss of brittle life than those proud titles thou hast won of me...'*

Thought, t. not to be considered - O monstrous fault, to harbour such a thought!
"O monstrous fault, to harbour such a thought!" (KHVI.p3.3.2)
In the play. *A monologue of Richard of Gloucester - the 'monstrous thought' is to believe that he can be loved by a woman or to pursue women in general.*

Thought, t. preceding action - so do all thoughts, they are winged.

ROSALIND. .. and certainly, a woman's thought runs before her action.
ORLANDO. So do all thoughts, they are winged." (AYLI.4.1)
Use the first line as a comment for feminine behavior. Or use the second line as a retort to "you go too fast" when applied to ideas. See also 'Women, impulsive character of w. - ... when I think, I must speak.'
In the play. Rosalind disguised as a man (and incredibly unrecognized by Orlando) now pretends to be a woman and in a humorous way asks Orlando to show his courting skills.

Thoughts, morbid or self-destructive t. to be avoided - You do unbend your noble strength, to think so brainsickly of things.
"You do unbend your noble strength, to think
So brainsickly of things. Go get some water,
And wash this filthy witness from your hand." (M.2.1)
In the play. *Lady Macbeth tries to sooth the mind of Macbeth. Returning from having slain King Duncan in his sleep, Macbeth is plagued with remorse. See 'Sleep, soothing properties of s. - ...sleep that knits up the ravell'd sleeve of care..'*

Thoughts, t. compared to people - ... And these same thoughts people this little world..
"... And these same thoughts people this little world,
In humours like the people of this world,
For no thought is contented."
(KRII.5.5)
Answer to 'What are you thinking?' E.G. 'My thoughts are like the people of this world....contented.'
In the play. *Richard II, in prison at Pomfret Castle imagines his thoughts to be people who can keep him company in his confinement.*

Thoughts, t. running wild - My thoughts were like unbridled children, grown too headstrong for their mother.
"My thoughts were like unbridled children, grown
Too headstrong for their mother."
(TC.3.2)
Men like to be told that they were loved at first sight – witness the prosperity of the male cosmetic industry.
In the play. *Cressida says or pretends to have fallen in love with Troilus at first sight.*

Threat, I will remember you - I'll note you in my book of memory to scourge for this apprehension.
"I'll note you in my book of memory,
To scourge for this apprehension."
(KHVI.p1.3.4)
Use it in an ironic tone, when someone makes you the target of an ironic criticism
In the play. *Plantagenet is angry at Somerset for accusations that Somerset levied against Plantagenet's father. Somerset makes a vague threat. 'To scourge' = 'To whip'.*

Threat, not an idle t. - It is the Prince of Wales that threatens thee who never promiseth but he means to pay.
"It is the Prince of Wales that threatens thee;
Who never promiseth but he means to pay." (KHIV.p1.5.4)
Change 'the Prince of Wales' to your name
In the play. *Prince Henry engages Douglas who flies and King Henry IV is saved.*

Threat, t. from an angered friend - Do not presume too much upon my love, I may do that I shall be sorry for.
"Do not presume too much upon my love;
I may do that I shall be sorry for"
(JC.4.3)

In the play. *Brutus blames Cassius for his bribe taking and Cassius replies back with a threat.*

Threat, t. of blood and revenge - ... I'll use the advantage of my power and lay the summer's dust with showers of blood...
"... I'll use the advantage of my power
And lay the summer's dust with showers of blood
Rain'd from the wounds of slaughter'd Englishmen" (KRII.3.3)
In the play. *Bolingbroke makes King Richard II an offer he cannot refuse, repeal of banishment, restoration of estate or else. The conveyor of the offer to Richard will be the Bishop of Carlysle.*

Threat, t. towards complaining employee - If thou more murmur'st, I will rend an oak and peg thee in his knotty entrails...
"If thou more murmur'st, I will rend an oak
And peg thee in his knotty entrails till
Thou hast howl'd away twelve winters" (TEM.1.2)
In the play. *Prospero threatens the spirit Ariel who demands freedom.*

Threat, t. useless - ... spare your threats; The bug which you would fright me with, I seek...
"Sir, spare your threats;
The bug which you would fright me with, I seek.
To me life can be no commodity." (WT.3.2)
Deflect the effect of a threat.
In the play. *Hermione is not afraid of dying, which to her is preferable than living being hated by her husband and king. The 'bug' she refers to is actually her death.*

Threat, t. useless - How I scorn these useless threats.
"How I scorn these useless threats." (KHVI p3.1)
Reject a threat
In the play. *Warwick to Clifford, Clifford is for Henry VI, Warwick for Richard Plantagenet, duke of York.*

Threat, verbal t. - I wear not my dagger in my mouth.
"Thy words, I grant, are bigger, for I wear not
My dagger in my mouth." (CYM.4.1)
Answer to a verbal threat.
In the play. *Cloten meets Guiderius and starts insulting him. Guiderius answers and then kills Cloten in a fight.*

Threats, idle t. - There is no terror, Cassius, in your threats...
"There is no terror, Cassius, in your threats;
For I am armed so strong in honesty,
That they pass by me as the idle wind,
Which I respect not." (JC.4.1)
Retort to threats. Substitute Cassius with name of opponent.
In the play. *Brutus answers to a veiled threat by Cassius after Brutus has upbraided him for taking bribes.*

Thrift, t. as a virtue under certain conditions - ... And thrift is blessing, if men steal it not.
"And thrift is blessing, if men steal it not." (MOV.1.3)
In the play. *The conclusion of an argument by which Shylock proves to Antonio the economic value of interest.*

Thunder, t. as a metaphor for loud voice - To tear with thunder the wide cheeks o' the air.
"...To tear with thunder the wide cheeks o' the air..." (COR.5.3)
Apply to person with a characteristically loud voice, e.g. 'He tears...air'

In the play. *Volumnia tells her son, somewhat sarcastically that he is trying to imitate the behavior of the gods.*

Time - ... the lazy foot of time
ORLANDO You should ask me what time o' day: there's no clock
in the forest.
ROSALIND Then there is no true lover in the forest; else sighing every minute and groaning every hour would detect the lazy foot of Time as well as a clock. (AYLI.3.2)
'The lazy foot of time' lends elegance to a time related answer to a question of the time 'What have you been doing?' E.G. 'I measured the lazy foot of time go by'.
In the play. *Orlando and Rosalind exchange pleasantries in the forest.*

Time, about nine o'clock -
...labouring for nine.
PHILOTUS What do you think the hour?
TITUS. Labouring for nine.(TOA.3.4)
Answer to question 'What is the time?' Change 'nine' to any other applicable hour of day.
In the play. *Two servants converse in Timon's house.*

Time, admitting to having wasted it -
I wasted time and now doth time waste me.
"I wasted time and now doth time waste me". (KRII.5.5)
Express regret at having wasted time, or to justify unemployment due to previous idleness. See also 'Education, lack of formal education' - Love, argument for her saying yes without extended delays –
.. Thou by thy dial's shady stealth mayst know time's thievish progress to eternity.
In the play. *King Richard II, dethroned by Bolingbroke (King Henry IV), is now in the dungeon of Pomfret Castle and reflects painfully on his life.*

Time, all encompassing power of t. –
It is in my power to o'erthrow law and in one self-born hour to plant and o'erwhelm custom.
"... it is in my power
To o'erthrow law and in one self-born hour
To plant and o'erwhelm custom Let me pass
The same I am, ere ancient'st order was
Or what is now received: I witness to
The times that brought them in; so shall I do
To the freshest things now reigning and make stale
The glistering of this present, as my tale
Now seems to it" (WT.4.chorus)
In the play. *Time, personified, asks permission of the audience to skip 16 years in the narrative. See 'Time, gap in the narrative'*

Time, almost forever – ... When time is old and hath forgot itself, when water drops have worn the stones of Troy..
"When time is old and hath forgot itself,
When water drops have worn the stones of Troy,
And blind oblivion swallow'd cities up,
And mighty states characterless are grated
To dusty nothing." (TC.3.2)
Introduction of speaker. Say that a special feat, for example accomplished by the speaker you introduce, will always be remembered, 'when time is old......'. Keep the audience in suspense with the quote and then describe the feat. See also 'Event, e. of historical importance, reenacted in successive centuries' – Entries for 'Introduction'
In the play. *Cressida answers the truth challenge. If she will be false let her falsehood be always remembered 'when time is old' etc.*

Time, appropriate t. for whatever needs to be done – Every time serves for the matter that is then born in it.
LEPIDUS 'Tis not a time
For private stomaching.
DOMITIUS ENOBARBUS Every time
Serves for the matter that is then born in't. (AC.2.2)
Answer to 'Is this a good time?', especially if you expect that the matter brought up by the questioner may not be all that pleasant.
In the play. *Lepidus prompts Enobarbus to cool Antony's aggressiveness when he (Antony) will meet with Caesar.*

Time, buying t. until conditions improve - .. there am I, till time and vantage crave my company.
"I will resolve for Scotland: there am I,
Till time and vantage crave my company" (KHIV p2.2.3)
In the play. *After some hesitation Northumberland will seek shelter in Scotland rather than joining the Archbishop of York and other rebels in the fight against Henry IV.*

Time, call back t. - O, call back yesterday, bid time return…
"O, call back yesterday, bid time return,
And thou shalt have twelve thousand fighting men!" (KRII.3.2)
In the play. *The Earl of Salisbury announces to Richard II the defection of the Welsh soldiers to Bolingbroke as rumor had it that Richard was dead.*

Time, characteristics of past and future – What's past and what's to come is strew'd with husks and formless ruin of oblivion…
"What's past and what's to come is strew'd with husks

And formless ruin of oblivion…" (TC.4.5)
In the play. *Agammenon's temporary welcome speech to Hector, who visits the Greek camp.*

Time, consciousness of wasted t. - The clock upbraids me with the waste of time
"The clock upbraids me with the waste of time." (TN.3.1)
Change 'me' to 'us' when you wish to steer your companions to stop wasting time.
In the play. *Olivia has just heard the clock strike while talking with Viola.*

Time, counting numbers to measure t. – Stay'd it long?… While one with moderate haste might tell a hundred.
HAMLET Very like, very like. Stay'd it long?
HORATIO While one with moderate haste might tell a hundred. (H.1.2)
Answer to 'How long did it last?'
In the play. *Horatio timed how long for the Ghost appeared.*

Time, defenseless against t. –
 Nothing 'gainst Time's scythe can make defence.
"… nothing 'gainst Time's scythe can make defence" (SON 12)
A reminder, for good or for bad, that nothing remains the same.

Time, destructive nature of t. – … Love, friendship, charity, are subjects all to envious and calumniating time…
"For beauty, wit,
High birth, vigour of bone, desert in service,
Love, friendship, charity, are subjects all
To envious and calumniating time." (TC.3.3)
In the play. *Ulysses attempts to persuade Achilles to rejoin the fight against the Trojans.*

Time, devastating effects of t. - …
And so, from hour to hour, we ripe and ripe, and then…
"…'It is ten o'clock:
Thus we may see,' quoth he, 'how the world wags:
'Tis but an hour ago since it was nine,
And after one hour more 'twill be eleven
And so, from hour to hour, we ripe and ripe,
And then, from hour to hour, we rot and rot;
And thereby hangs a tale.'" (AYLI.2.7)
Adapt the answer to answer the question, 'What is the time?'
In the play *Jacques philosophizes about the passage of time.*

Time, dinner t. about 6 PM – … when… men sit down to that nourishment which is called supper.
"About the sixth hour; when beasts most graze, birds best peck, and men sit down to that nourishment which is called supper.' (LLL.1.1)
In the play. *Ferdinand reads from a letter of the Armado.*

Time, everything in good t. – … there's a time for all things.
See also 'Appropriateness, the right thing at the right time – at Christmas I no more desire a rose…' *** Time, give it time to mature, t. as a seasoning agent - How many things by season season'd are…'
In the play. *Antipholus S. to servant Dromio S. who was jesting at the wrong time.*

Time, exhortation to t. not to damage her beauty - But I forbid thee one most heinous crime, o carve not with thy hours my love's fair brow..
But I forbid thee one most heinous crime,
O carve not with thy hours my love's fair brow.

….
Yet do thy worst old Time; despite thy wrong,
My love shall in my verse ever live young (SON.49)
See also 'Writing, confidence in your writing power - Your beauty shall in these black lines be seen, and they shall live, and you in them still green.'

Time, gap in the narrative - … Impute it not a crime to me or my swift passage… and leave the growth untried of that wide gap.
"… Impute it not a crime
To me or my swift passage, that I slide
O'er sixteen years, and leave the growth untried
Of that wide gap." (WT.4.chorus)
Use in a report or presentation when you must skip from one time period to another with a substantial lapse of time in between.
In the play. *Time is a fictional character appearing to announce that the play has now skipped 16 years.*

Time, give it time to mature, t. as a seasoning agent - How many things by season season'd are…
"How many things by season season'd are
To their right praise, and true perfection." (MOV.5.1)
Two possible uses. One, to justify the delay of a decision. "Give it time, how many things…. Perfection". Or as a compliment to a woman who is afraid of being too old, "Of you it can be said, how many things….. perfection." See also 'Age. "Do you think I look old?"'
In the play. *Portia commenting on a perfect evening during which everything falls into place.*

Time, healing properties of t. - Time is the nurse and breeder of all good.

"Time is the nurse and breeder of all good."(TGV.3.1)
Support and reinforce the well season advice of giving it time. Also, when she is putting pressure on you for whatever reason and you don't want to take a decision.
In the play. *The treacherous and hypocritical Proteus gives advice to Valentine after succeeding in having him banned from Milan. He hints vaguely that time may breed good (for Valentine) and perhaps make him forget Silvia.*

Time, his or her presence makes t. pass quickly - He makes a July's day short as December..
"He makes a July's day short as December." (WT.1.2)
Answer to 'Are you tired?' or 'Are you bored?'. Try 'On the contrary, you make a July's day as short as December.
In the play. *Polixenes explains to Leontes how Polixenes' young son with child's behavior makes the time pass quickly.*

Time, improvement expected with time - .. the time will bring on summer when briars shall have leaves as well as thorns..
"..the time will bring on summer, When briars shall have leaves as well as thorns;
And be as sweet as sharp."
(AWEW.4.4)
Promise improvements and lift the morale of the audience.
In the play. *In leaving Florence, Helen, using a metaphor, suggests to her newly acquired friends (widow with daughter Diana) that good times (the leaves) will come therefore offsetting the results from previous troubles (the thorns).*

Time, in one year - .. until the twelve celestial signs have brought about the annual reckoning.

"…until the twelve celestial signs Have brought about the annual reckoning." (LLL.5.2)
In the play. *The Princess suggests to the King of Navarre that one year pass before talking again of marriage proposals.*

Time, in the afternoon, a. redefined – …, in the posteriors of the day, which the rude multitude call afternoon.
" ..it is the king's most sweet pleasure and affection, to congratulate the princess at her pavilion, in the posteriors of the day, which the rude multitude call afternoon." (LLL.5.1)
Use sarcastically to indicate the afternoon, 'We can meet in the posterior……afternoon'.
In the play. *Armado in verbal action speaking to Holofernes.*

Time, in the early morning - ... look love, what envious streaks do lace the severing clouds in yonder east.
"... look love, what envious streaks Do lace the severing clouds in yonder east:
Night's candles are burnt out, and jocund day
Stands tiptoe on the misty mountain tops." (RJ.3.5)
When you must leave before breakfast.
In the play. *Romeo, regrettably, must leave Juliet and flee to Mantua.*

Time, in the early morning - The early village-cock hath twice done salutation to the morn.
"Ratcliff, my lord; 'tis I. The early village-cock
Hath twice done salutation to the morn;
Your friends are up, and buckle on their armour" (KRIII.5.3)
In the play. *Ratcliff alerts the startled King Richard III that the time for battle with the forces of Richmond is at hand.*

Time, in the morning - ... the cock, that is the trumpet to the morn, doth with his lofty and shrill-sounding throat awake the god of day.
"...I have heard,
The cock, that is the trumpet to the morn,
Doth with his lofty and shrill-sounding throat
Awake the god of day" (H.1.1)
In the play. *Horatio discussing the appearance and parting of the Ghost*

Time, in the morning - ...when the morning sun shall rise his car above the border of this horizon.
"... when the morning sun shall raise his car
Above the border of this horizon." (KHVI p3.4.7)
See also entries for 'Nature, dawn'.
In the play. *Edward tells his associates to rest for the night and in the morning they will go and battle Warwick.*

Time, in the morning, in the country with good weather - The hunt is up, the morn is bright and grey, the fields are fragrant, and the woods are green.
"The hunt is up, the morn is bright and grey,
The fields are fragrant, and the woods are green." (TA.2.2)
Comment on good weather in the country, skip 'the hunt is up'.
In the play. *Titus and company plan a hunt joined by Saturninus, Tamora, Aaron, Lavinia, her husband Bassianus and the two evil Demetrius and Chiron.*

Time, late night t. making it early morning - ... it is so very very late, that we may call it early by and by.
"...it is so very very late,
That we may call it early by and by." (RJ.3.4)
See also 'Sleep, s. patterns and logic whereby late sleep is actually early rising'

– Entries for 'Time, bedtime as a matter of interpretation'
In the play. *Capulet Senior tells his wife to go and alert Juliet that a date for her marriage with Paris has been set.*

Time, let's concentrate on the present – Let's take the instant by the forward top.... The inaudible and noiseless foot of time...
"Not one word more of the consumed time
Let's take the instant by the forward top,
For we are old, and on our quick'st decrees
The inaudible and noiseless foot of time
Steals, ere we can effect them." (AWEW.5.3)
Prompt action of any kind. If you are not old, modify somewhat the second line, "Let's take the instant by the forward top,/ Because on our quickest decrees...etc." Or eliminate the third line completely, e.g., 'Let's take the instant by the forward top, for the inaudible and noiseless foot of time steals on our chances.' See also 'Procrastination to be avoided – .. for this 'would' changes, hath abatements and delays as many as there are tongues, are hands, are accidents.'
In the play. *The King of France has forgiven Bertram for his mistakes and now suggests that Bertram marry Lafeu's daughter.*

Time, let's wait a bit longer - Let two summers wither in their pride..
"Let two summers wither in their pride,
Ere we may think her ripe for a bride." (RJ.1.2)
Use as a delaying tactic when you are pressured for a decision. The meaning is clear even if the quote refers to Juliet's wedding.
In the play. *Paris has asked Capulet for Juliet's hand.*

Time, long t. in a word - How long a time lies in one little word!...
"How long a time lies in one little word!
Four lagging winters and four wanton springs
End in a word: such is the breath of kings" (KRII.1.3)
In the play. *Bolingbroke comments on his four-year exile as decreed by Richard II.*

Time, midday - ..the bawdy hand of the dial is now upon the prick of noon.
" .. the bawdy hand of the dial is now upon the prick of noon." (RJ.2.4)
Alternative to 'It's midday'. Possibly follow with the suggestion or invitation to go to lunch.
In the play. *After some ironic comments, Mercutio comments sarcastically on Juliet's nurse clarification whether it is midday or not. 'Bawdy' = 'Unchaste', probably referring to the constant motion and therefore volubility of the dial-hand. 'Prick' = 'Mark'.*

Time, midday – Now is sun upon the highmost hill of this day's journey
"Now is the sun upon the highmost hill"
Alternative to 'It's midday'. Possibly follow with the suggestion or invitation to go to lunch.
In the play. *Juliet has sent her nurse on a mission to meet with Romeo. She has not yet returned and therefore Juliet is anxious.*

Time, midnight - The iron tongue of midnight hath told twelve.
"The iron tongue of midnight hath told twelve." (MND.5.1)
Bring to the attention of the participants that it is late and could they hurry up. See also 'Time, night, ..witching time.
In the play. *The play by the amateur actors group has finished.*

Time, midnight, close to midnight - ... it draws near the season wherein the spirit held his wont to walk.
"…it draws near the season
Wherein the spirit held his wont to walk." (H.1.4)
In the play. *Horatio waits for the appearance of the Ghost at midnight.*

Time, midnight, sweating at m. - It is now dead midnight. Cold fearful drops stand on my trembling flesh.
"It is now dead midnight.
Cold fearful drops stand on my trembling flesh.
What do I fear? myself? there's none else by:
Richard loves Richard; that is, I am I." (KRIII.5.3)
Answer to 'Are you cold?' (first two lines, or second line alone).
In the play. *The night before the decisive battle at Bosworth Field, Richard wakes up from a nightmare in which all his victims have appeared in turn.*

Time, morning, is it really morning? - Is the day so young?
BENVOLIO. Good morrow, cousin.
ROMEO. Is the day so young?" (RJ.1.1)
Answer to 'good morning'
In the play. *Benvolio greets Romeo who has just come in.*

Time, night t. – ... when creeping murmur and the poring dark fills the wide vessel of the universe.
"Now entertain conjecture of a time
When creeping murmur and the poring dark
Fills the wide vessel of the universe." (KHV.4.prologue)
Substitute for it's getting dark. Start from 'When creeping murmur…'
In the play. *The Chorus again makes up for the lack of props with a description.*

Time, night t. - In the dead vast and middle of the night.
"In the dead vast and middle of the night" (H.1.2)
In the play. *Horatio tells Hamlet of the nightly apparition of the Ghost.*

Time, night t.– 'Tis now the very witching time of night, when churchyards yawn…
"'Tis now the very witching time of night,
When churchyards yawn, and hell itself breaths out
Contagion to this world." (H.3)
The meeting has been going on way too long. Time to go home.
In the play. *Hamlet reflects and gathers strength to attack his mother with an aggressive and punitive speech..*

Time, n. time for rest – … times to repair our nature with comforting repose…
"These should be hours for necessities,
Not for delights; times to repair our nature
With comforting repose, and not for us
To waste these times" (KHVIII.5.1)
See also entries for 'Rest, r. needed'
In the play. *Gardiner, Bishop of Winchester comments on the late hour*

Time, no t. to be lost with an importune caller - … We hold our time too precious to be spent with such a babbler.
" We grant thou canst outscold us, fare thee well;
We hold our time too precious to be spent
With such a babbler." (KJ.5.2)
Use the last two lines to dismiss a long-winded person

In the play. *Faulconbridge has come to plead his cause with Lewis of France who is not impressed.*

Time, observing t. passing - When I do count the clock that tells the time…
"When I do count the clock that tells the time,
And see the brave day sunk in hideous night
When I behold the violet past prime,
And sable curls all silver'd o'er with white;
When lofty trees I see barren of leaves
Which erst from heat did canopy the herd,
And summer's green all girded up in sheaves" (SON.12)
Ironic answer to 'What are you doing?' – 'I do count the clock…time'.

Time, passing of t. inevitable –Like as the waves make towards the pebbled shore, so do our minutes hasten to their end…
"Like as the waves make towards the pebbled shore,
So do our minutes hasten to their end;
Each changing place with that which goes before,
In sequent toil all forwards do contend." (SON 60)
Romantic comment at the beach. Example of the inexorable passing of time and implied need to hurry up.

Time, passing t. carelessly - … and fleet the time carelessly, as they did in the golden world…
"…they say many young gentlemen flock to him every day, and fleet the time carelessly, as they did in the golden world." (AYLI.1.1)
Answer to 'What are you doing now?' or 'What are you doing in your retirement?' E.G. 'I fleet the time….world.'

In the play. *Charles the wrestler, reports to the usurping Duke that many people are following the rightful duke into the forest of Arden. 'To fleet' = 'to pass away quickly'.*

Time, precious short t. - .. The time 'twixt six and now must by us both be spent most preciously.
"…The time 'twixt six and now
Must by us both be spent most preciously." (TEM.1.2)
In the play. *Prospero assigns other magic tasks to spirit Ariel.*

Time, present bad, past and future OK – O thoughts of men accurst! Past and to come seem best, things present, worst.
"What trust is in these times?
…
O thoughts of men accurst!
Past and to come seem best; things present, worst." (KHIVp2.1.3)
Alternative to "I told you so"
In the play. *The Archbishop of York, in conference with the rebel lords refers to the times of King Richard II, deposed and killed by the present king Henry IV of Lancaster. Now the Archbishop thinks conditions better with Richard II.*

Time, relentlessly advancing, compared to a thief - Time comes stealing on by night and day.
"Nay, he's a thief too: have you not heard men say
 Time comes stealing on by night and day?" COE.4.2)
In the play. *Dromio S. in conversation with Adriana making some word play on time.*

Tine, sadness. extending the perception of time - … sad hours seem long.
"… sad hours seem long." (RJ.1.1)
In the play. *Love sick Romeo (not as yet with Juliet) comments to friend Benvolio.*

Time, sadness making hours long - what sadness lengthens Romeo's hours? Not having that…
BENVOLIO. What sadness lengthens Romeo's hours?
ROMEO. Not having that which, having, makes them short." (RJ.1.1)
Justify or explain your lack of merriment, e.g. 'Sadness lengthens my hours'.
In the play. *Romeo declares himself out of love, hence the sadness.*

Time, searching for some entertainment to pass the t. - How shall we beguile the lazy time, if not with some delight?
"Say, what abridgment have you for this evening?
What masque? what music? How shall we beguile
The lazy time, if not with some delight?" (MND.5.1)
At a party when you ask your guests if they have any preference in social games. See also 'Recreation, r. to put away care'
In the play. *Theseus, who has a time management problem, asks Philostrate how to solve it.*

Time, sense of guilt at wasting t. - I feel me much to blame so idly to profane the precious time…
"I feel me much to blame,
So idly to profane the precious time…" (KHIVp2.2.4)
In the play. *Prince Harry feels guilty at wasting time with Falstaff and company while the rebels are gathering strength (again).*

Time, spending it in a wood under the trees - … Under the shade of melancholy boughs lose and neglect the creeping hours of time.
"…But whate'er you are
That in this desert inaccessible,
Under the shade of melancholy boughs,

Lose and neglect the creeping hours of time." (AYLI.2.7)
What are you doing this week end?
'Under the shade of melancholy boughs I'll lose and neglect…time'
In the play. *Orlando in the forest and hungry bumps in on the Duke and friends who spend their time there.*

Time, sundown - The day begins to break, and night is fled whose pitchy mantle over-veiled the earth.
"The day begins to break, and night is fled,
Whose pitchy mantle over-veiled the earth." (KHVIp1.2.2)
Call an end to a long night meeting
In the play. *Bedford at Orleans.*

Time, survival t. limited - The sands are number'd that make up my life.
"The sands are number'd that make up my life" (KHVI.p3.1.4)
Apply rhetorically when waiting for the outcome of a decision or judgment that may significantly affect you.
In the play. *York is cornered by the forces of Queen Margaret near Warwick.*

Time, t. all encompassing ruler - …Time's the king of men, for he's their parent, and he is their grave and gives them what he will, not what they crave.
"…Time's the king of men,
For he's their parent, and he is their grave,
And gives them what he will, not what they crave." (PER.2.3)
Alternative comment to the inevitability of what destiny has decreed. That is consider time as having the same characteristics of destiny. See also entries for 'Destiny'
In the play. *Simonides and his court remind Pericles of his own father and his court. He then compares his own former glory to the present circumstances and ends with a statement of acceptance.*

Time, t. and ingratitude - Time hath, my lord, a wallet at his back wherein he puts alms for oblivion…
"Time hath, my lord, a wallet at his back,
Wherein he puts alms for Oblivion,
A great-sized monster of ingratitudes:
Those scraps are good deeds past;
Which are devoured as fast as they are made,
Forgot as soon as done." (TC.3.3)
Show that constant activity or presence is the only method not to be forgotten. See also 'Perseverance, in praise of p.' – 'Presence, physical p. crucial for success' – "Motion, what moves catches the attention.'
In the play. *Ulysses suggests that the passing of time has caused the Greek to forget Achilles and his past deeds.*

Time, t. and the inherent limited duration of everything - When I consider everything that grows holds in perfection but a little moment…
"When I consider everything that grows
Holds in perfection but a little moment,
That this huge stage presenteth nought but shows
Whereon the stars in secret influence comment". (SON.15)
Tell her that time is passing quickly and that nothing can go on forever.
"..everything that grows…but a little moment." See if you can make her hurry up and decide.

Time, t. and urgency - We are time's subjects, and time bids be gone.
"We are time's subjects, and time bids be gone." (KHIV.p2.1.3)
In the play. *After having conferred on the pros and cons of military operations to face the King's*

forces, Hastings reminds the others that time is running short.

Time, t. as a justice provider – Yet heavens are just, and time suppresseth wrongs.
"For though usurpers sway the rule awhile,
Yet heavens are just, and time suppresseth wrongs." (KHVI p3.3.3)
This is often more folklore than fact but the idea may find some resonance in the mind of some ill doers.
In the play. *At the court of Lewis of France, Q. Margaret attempts to fend off the efforts of Warwick to secure an alliance with the king.*

Time, t. as the test of love – .. I know love is begun by time, and that I see, in passages of proof, time qualifies the spark and fire of it.
"… I know love is begun by time;
And that I see, in passages of proof,
Time qualifies the spark and fire of it." (H4.7)
The lines apply both ways, whether you wish to confirm the constancy or strength of your feelings or their weakening.
In the play. *The King is concerned that Laertes' love for his slain father Polonius may not be as strong as to help Laertes carry out his revenge against Hamlet (who killed Polonius). See also 'Codependence, c. to be avoided - There lives within the very flame of love..' which is a follow up to this concern.*

Time, t. erasing impact of action - … time is like a fashionable host that slightly shakes his parting guest by the hand..
"For time is like a fashionable host
That slightly shakes his parting guest by the hand,
And with his arms outstretch'd, as he would fly,
Grasps in the comer: welcome ever smiles,

And farewell goes out sighing." (TC.3.3)
See also 'Motion, what moves catches the attention.'
In the play. *Ulysses tries to convince the supercilious Achilles to rejoin the fighting against the Trojans. The time he refers to is that of Achilles' former past glories.*

Time, t. for love, night more suitable - .. if love be blind, it best agrees with night.
"….if love be blind,
It best agrees with night." (RJ.3.2)
When she is stalling or when she asks 'Why do you only want to see me at night?' See also 'Love, different points of view on whether darkness is conducive to l. - … If love be blind, love cannot hit the mark.'
In the play. *Juliet awaits the arrival of Romeo and is not yet aware of the duel in which Romeo killed the Capulet Tybalt. As a consequence Romeo will be banned from Verona.*

Time, t. for meeting or request inappropriate - The time is unagreeable to this business..
"The time is unagreeable to this business:
Your importunacy cease till after dinner." (TOA.2.2)
Delay an answer or postpone a discussion.
In the play. *The good-willed servant Flavius attempts to stave off Timon's creditors.*

Time, t. for rest - … times to repair our nature with comforting repose.
"... times to repair our nature
With comforting repose" (KHVIII, 5.1)
See also 'Sleep or rest, time to adjourn the meeting - The deep of night is crept upon our talk and nature must obey necessity.'
In the play. *Gardiner to a page at the court of Henry VIII. It's one o'clock in the morning.*

Time, t. handled differently by different people - Time travels in divers paces with divers persons.
"Time travels in divers paces with divers persons. " (AYLI.3.2)
Retort to someone who reprimands you for being late.
In the play. *Rosalind (in disguise as a boy) exchanges some banter with Orlando.*

Time, t. helps to forget. See 'Forgetting, time helps f - .. some more time must wear the print of his remembrance out.

Time, t. management, t. wasted –
..thus we play the fools with the time and the spirits of the wise sit in the clouds and mock us.
"..thus we play the fools with the time; and the spirits of the wise sit in the clouds and mock us."
(KHIVp2.2.2)
Expedite action instead of idling. See also 'Delay, d. is time wasted' -
In the play. *The Prince of Wales to Poins.*

Time, t. of day - I see no reason why thou shouldst be so superfluous to demand the time of the day.
"What a devil hast thou to do with the time of the day? Unless hours were cups of sack and minutes capons and clocks the tongues of bawds and dials the signs of leaping-houses and the blessed sun himself a fair hot wench in flame-coloured taffeta, I see no reason why thou shouldst be so superfluous to demand the time of the day." (KHIVp1.1.1)
Answer to 'what is the time?' if you do not want to answer.
In the play. *Falstaff has asked Prince Henry what is the time and the Prince replies sarcastically.*

Time, t. passing and a sense of urgency - The hour steals on; I pray you, sir, dispatch
In the play. *Antipholus E. is urged to produce the money that inadvertently he gave to the servant of Antipholus E.*

Time, t. passing quickly - Four days will quickly steep themselves in nights…
"Four days will quickly steep themselves in nights;
Four nights will quickly dream away the time." (MND.1.1)
Use to calm haste and anxiety. Change 'four' to the number of applicable days. You can even generalize, e.g. 'days quickly steep themselves in nights, and nights….time.'
In the play. *Lysander will marry Hippolyta in four days and Hippolyta meditates on the intervening time.*

Time, t. passing without noise or trace - The inaudible and noiseless foot of time.
"The inaudible and noiseless foot of time". (AWEW.5.3)
Answer to 'What are you doing?'. 'I am listening to the inaudible and noiseless foot of time', when you are doing absolutely nothing or you do not want to go into details about what you are actually doing. See also 'Time, let's do it now', where the line is used in a different context.
In the play. *The King has forgiven Bertram for his mistakes and now suggests that Bertram marry Lafeu's daughter.*

Time, t. past for entertainment - … for you and I are past our dancing days.
"For you and I are past our dancing days" (RJ.1.5)
When you wish to refuse an invitation to wild entertainment, e.g. 'I am past my dancing days'. See also 'Error, e. admitted

and due to youthful inexperience – Those were my salad days when I was green in judgement'.
In the play. *Capulet invites his cousin to sit down as dancing would be inappropriate for both of them given their age.*

Time, t. past forgotten, future uncertain - What's past and what's to come is strew'd with husks…
"What's past and what's to come is strew'd with husks
And formless ruin of oblivion" (TC.4.5)
In the play. *Part of the welcome address by Agamennon to the visiting Hector. Agamennon means that for a moment past and future will be forgotten and give place to a welcome.*

Time, t. pregnant with news - With news the time's with labour, and throes forth each minute, some.
"With news the time's with labour, and throes forth,
Each minute, some." (AC.3.7)
In the play. *Canidius, a soldier in the service of Antony comments on the impending battle between the forces Octavian and of Antony.*

Time, t. seems short when passed in pleasurable undertakings - Pleasure and action make the hours seem short.
"Pleasure and action make the hours seem short." (OTH.2.3)
In the play. *Iago exhorts Roderigo to look on the brighter side of things.*

Time, t. self-described - I, that please some, try all, both joy and terror..
"I, that please some, try all, both joy and terror
Of good and bad, that makes and unfolds error" (WT.4.chorus)
In the play. *Time justifies the skipping of sixteen years in the development of the play. Baby Perdita is now a beautiful girl in Bohemia.*

Time, t. spent idly while danger at hand - .. When tempest of commotion, like the south borne with black vapour..
"…I feel me much to blame,
So idly to profane the precious time,
When tempest of commotion, like the south
Borne with black vapour, doth begin to melt
And drop upon our bare unarmed heads" (KHIV p2.2.4)
In the play. *Prince Henry to Poins confessing regret at idling away the time when rebel forces prepare for another attack.*

Time, t. spent leisurely - … under the shade of melancholy boughs lose and neglect the creeping hours of time.
"… But whatever you are,
That in this desert inaccessible,
Under the shade of melancholy boughs,
Lose and neglect the creeping hours of time." (AYLI.2)
An evasive answer to 'what do you do?' 'Under the shade of melancholy boughs I lose and neglect…time'.
In the play. *Orlando addresses Duke S and company and explain the distress he is in.*

Time, t. troublesome - The time is troublesome.
"The time is troublesome." (CYM.4.3)
Also an evasive answer to 'What is the time?'
In the play. *King Cymbeline is worried by an accumulation of bad reports.*

Time, t.'s tasks or characteristics - 'Time's glory is to calm contending kings…
"'Time's glory is to calm contending kings,
To unmask falsehood and bring truth to light,
To stamp the seal of time in aged things,

To wake the morn and sentinel the night,
To wrong the wronger till he render right,
To ruinate proud buildings with thy hours,
And smear with dust their glittering golden towers.
.....
To feed oblivion with decay of things
...
To cheer the ploughman with increaseful crops,
And waste huge stones with little water drops." (ROL)
In the poem. In the poem. *Evil Tarquin knows he is committing a crime and meditates on it. He shifts the blame of his crime on time and its servant opportunity. The quote lists all the good things that time is responsible for, as opposed to laying traps to the criminals (here Tarquin himself) via opportunity.*

Time, the great arbitrator - .... the end crowns all and that old common arbitrator, Time, will one day end it.
"....the end crowns all,
And that old common arbitrator, Time,
Will one day end it." (TC.4.5)
When the debate as to what may or may not happen cannot be resolved.
In the play. *Hector and Ulysses disagree about the outcome of the Trojan war. Hector makes a philosophical statement – time will decide on the outcome.*

Time, three years since last meeting - Three April perfumes in three hot Junes burn'd...
"Three April perfumes in three hot Junes burn'd,
Since first I saw you fresh, which yet are green" (Sonnet 104)

Time, two hours ago - Since when, my watch hath told me, toward my grave I have travelled but two hours.

"Since when, my watch hath told me, toward my grave
I have travelled but two hours."
(TN.5.1)
When referring to time past. Change 'two' to whatever applicable number.
In the play. *Olivia has married Sebastian and the priest confirms it with these lines. The duke believes Viola/Cesario to be the groom whilst Viola is flabbergasted.*

Time, unsuitable t. for receiving visits - If I might beseech you, gentlemen, to repair some other hour..
"If I might beseech you, gentlemen, to repair some other hour, I should derive much from't" (TOA.3.4)
In the play. *Servilius, Timon's servant, tells the creditors' servant to take a hike.*

Time, up late, up early - I am glad I was up so late; for that's the reason I was up so early.
"I am glad I was up so late; for that's the reason I was up so early"
(CYM.2.2)
See also 'Sleep, s. patterns and logic whereby late sleep is actually early rising - .. not to be abed after midnight is to be up betimes.' - 'Time, (in the) afternoon, a. redefined – posteriors of the day' - Awakening, too early to get up - .. it argues a distempered head so soon to bid good morrow to thy bed.'
In the play. *Cloten did not go to bed the previous night.*

Time, within one day - Ere twice the horses of the sun shall bring...
"Ere twice the horses of the sun shall bring
Their fiery torcher his diurnal ring,
Ere twice in murk and occidental damp
Moist Hesperus hath quench'd his sleepy lamp,
Or four and twenty times the pilot's glass

Hath told the thievish minutes how they pass" (AWEW.2.1)
You have three options to answer the question, 'When will it be ready?' – See also 'Medicine, effective within 24 hours.'
In the play. *This is the time within which Helena assure the King of France that he will be cured of his illness. Helena provides the medicine. 'Ere' = 'Before'*

Time, within one hour - ... ere the glass, that now begins to run finish the process of his sandy hour.
"For ere the glass, that now begins to run,
Finish the process of his sandy hour." (KHVI.p1.4.2)
In the play. *The General of the French forces addresses Talbot and threatens him with destruction within one hour 'Ere' = 'Before'*

Time, within two weeks - Ere a fortnight make me elder.
"Ere a fortnight make me elder" (KRIII.3.2)
In the play. *The gullible Hastings believes that within a fortnight some of his remaining enemies will be done in – but it will be Hasting himself to lose his head at the bequest of Richard.. 'Ere' = 'Before'*

Times, bad times – 'Tis the times' plague, when madmen lead the blind.
"'Tis the times' plague, when madmen lead the blind." (KL.4.1)
Your opinion of politicians or of the current political situation or of the management in your company.
In the play *Gloucester (blind) is led by Edgar who pretends to be mad.*

Times, bad times - ... these days are dangerous, virtue is chock'd with foul ambition...
"Ah, gracious lord, these days are dangerous!
Virtue is chock'd with foul ambition,
And charity chas'd hence by rancour's hand;
Foul subordination is predominant,
And equity exil'd your highness' land." (KHVI p2.3.1)
Illustrate the situation as applicable
In the play. *The innocent Gloucester, Lord Protector to the mild and naïve King Henry VI.*

Times, degeneracy of t. when values are reversed - .. the world is grown so bad that wrens make prey where eagles dare not perch..
"... the world is grown so bad,
That wrens make prey where eagles dare not perch:
Since every Jack became a gentleman,
There's many a gentle person made a Jack." (KRIII.1.3)
Comment to radical and dramatic management changes in the organization. Use the last two lines to express that there are too many poorly qualified managers and not enough doers.
In the play. *Richard is on the attack against his political enemies, Q. Elizabeth and Lord Grey. 'Jack' is a term of contempt for 'saucy' or 'silly'.*

Times, end of the good t. - ... the bright day is done and we are for the dark.
"... the bright day is done,
And we are for the dark" (AC.5.2)
In the play. *Lady in waiting Iras to Cleopatra after learning that Cleopatra will be led captive in a victory parade in Rome.*

Times, good old t, better then, less greed than now - ... how well in thee appears the constant service of the antique world...
"O good old man, how well in thee appears
The constant service of the antique world,
When service sweat for duty, not for meed!" (AYLI.2.3)

Contrast old to current attitudes towards duty.
In the play. *Orlando addressing his old and faithful servant Adam, contrasts the good times of old with the bad times of today. 'Meed' = 'resource' or 'recompense'.*

Times, good old t., less selfishness detectable in previous times - Thou art not for the fashion of these times, where none will sweat but for promotion.
"Thou art not for the fashion of these times,
Where none will sweat but for promotion." (AYLI.2)
Modify slightly to make the same point, "This is the fashion of these times…..promotion." In a job interview, use to emphasize that doing your job precedes expectations of advancement.
In the play. *Orlando addressing his old and faithful servant Adam, contrasts the good times of old with the bad times of today.*

Times, hard t. ahead - The storm is up and all is on the hazard.
"….blow, wind; swell, billow; and swim, bark!
The storm is up and all is on the hazard." (JC.5.1)
Prepare the troops for battle, physical or metaphorical. See also 'Revolution, r. ignited - Mischief, thou art afoot, take thou what course thou wilt.'
In the play. *Cassius's comment just before the battle of Philippi.*

Times, rebellious t. - Rich men look sad and ruffians dance and leap…
"The bay-trees in our country are all wither'd
And meteors fright the fixed stars of heaven;
The pale-faced moon looks bloody on the earth
And lean-look'd prophets whisper fearful change

Rich men look sad and ruffians dance and leap,
The one in fear to lose what they enjoy,
The other to enjoy by rage and war.
These signs forerun the death or fall of kings" (KRII.2.4)
In the play. *In Wales forces loyal to King Richard begin to despair of his return from Ireland. A captain points out to the Earl of Salisbury that rebellion and anarchy are in the air.*

Times, wild t. – contention like a horse.. bears down all before him.
"The times are wild: contention, like a horse
Full of high feeding, madly hath broke loose
And bears down all before him." (KHIV.p2.1.1)
Use as a comparison to illustrate the turbulence of the times.
In the play. *Northumberland, a rebel, asks the incoming Lord Bardolph about the outcome of the battle of Shrewsbury, as there is conflicting news about it. For Bardolph's (incorrect reply) see entry for 'Victory, v. that dignifies the times'.*

Timing, importance of being first - Fruits that blossom first will first be ripe.
"Though other things grow fair against the sun
Yet fruits that blossom first will first be ripe." (OTH.2.3)
Stress the importance of being first or starting ahead of others. The second line is enough.
In the play. *Iago suggests to the impatient Roderigo that things are well under way.*

Title, crown and content - My crown is call'd content, a crown is it that seldom kings enjoy.
"My crown is call'd content,
A crown is it that seldom kings enjoy." (KHVI p3.3.1)

Answer to 'What is your title?' E.G. 'My title is called content…'
In the play. *Henry VI to keepers who ask him where is his crown.*

Title, job t. magnified - Thou art a cobbler, art thou?… I am, indeed, sir, a surgeon to old shoes.
FLAVIUS. Thou art a cobbler, art thou?
SECOND CITIZEN. Truly, sir, all that I live by is with the awl… I am, indeed, sir, a surgeon to old shoes (JC.1.1)
Ironic answer to 'What do you do for a living?'. 'As the cobbler said, I am indeed a surgeon to old shoes'. Also quote as an example of inflated titles for menial or insignificant jobs. See also 'Shoes, putting on s. on the wrong foot – … slippers, which his nimble haste had falsely thrust upon contrary feet.'
In the play. *Flavius upbraids the idling rabble blaming the ease with which they idolize anyone. He addresses one of them, who happens to be a cobbler.*

Titles, all t. no substance – … no better than an earl. Although in glorious titles he excel.
"Her father is no better than an earl, Although in glorious titles he excel" (KHVI.p1.5.1)
In the play. *Gloucester objects to King Henry marrying Margaret as her father, Reignier has large titles but no substance.*

Toast, dinner and health - Now, good digestion wait on appetite and health on both!
"Now, good digestion wait on appetite,
And health on both!" (M.3.4)
In the play. *After having Banquo killed, Macbeth organizes a banquet in his castle, but Banquo's ghost is hovering about.*

Toast, drinking down unkindness - … I hope we shall drink down all unkindness.
"…I hope we shall drink down all unkindness." (MWW.1.1)
In the play. *Mr. Page invite a selected company to dinner.*

Toast, generic, drink - I drink to the general joy o' the whole table.
"I drink to the general joy o' the whole table" (M.3.4)
In the play. *After first killing Duncan and then Banquo Macbeth proposes a toasts to the other guests at his table and pretends that Banquo is missing for his (Banquo's) own reasons.*

Toast, joining in a t. - I'll drink to her, as long as there is a passage in my throat and drink in Illyria.
"I'll drink to her, as long as there is a passage in my throat and drink in Illyria." (TN.1.3)
When proposing a toast. Change 'drink' to 'wine' or other drink of your choice. Optionally, change Illyria to your country of residence.
In the play. *Aguecheek is reported as drinking to the health of Olivia, Sir Toby's niece. Toby reaffirms his commitment to continue drinking in the company of Aguecheek.*

Toast, proposing a t. - Be large in mirth; anon we'll drink a measure the table round.
"Be large in mirth; anon we'll drink a measure
The table round." (M.3.4)
In the play. *Macbeth proposes a toast at a dinner party he has organized for friends and guests, now that he is king.*

Toast, t. and wish, prosperity - Now the fair goddess, Fortune fall deep in love with thee. Prosperity be thy page!
"Now the fair goddess, Fortune,
Fall deep in love with thee.

Prosperity be thy page!" (COR.1.5)
In the play. *Roman General Lartius pays homage to Coriolanus.*

Toasts, t. to health and realization of wishes- Sweet health and fair desires consort your grace…
PRINCESS. Sweet health and fair desires consort your grace!
KING. Thy own wish wish I thee in every place! (LLL.2.1)
Answer to a pleasant wish wished on you. The King's answer can be an answer to any good wish.
In the play. *The king and associates leave the Princess, albeit, as it happens, temporarily.*

Toast, t. with water - … Here's that which is too weak to be a sinner, honest water…
"… Here's that which is too weak to be a sinner, honest water, which ne'er left man i' the mire" (TOA.1.2)
If you are a teetotaler but want to join the merry spirit of the drinking party, 'Here is to that which……mire'.
In the play. *The ornery Apemantus scorns the parasites who attend Timon's table and by his toast hints at what may come out of Timon's prodigality.*

Tongue, a witching t. - .. he has witchcraft over the king in his tongue.
CHAMBERLAIN ….. for he has witchcraft
Over the king in his tongue.
NORFOLK (of Cardinal Wolsey).
O, fear him not;
His spell is out: the king hath found
Matter against him that for ever mars
The honey of his language."
(KHVIII.3.2)
Introduction to an accusation, e.g., 'You may have witchcraft in your tongue but we have matters against you that forever mar the honey of your tongue.'. Or use as a compliment with a lady, e.g., 'There is witchcraft in your tongue, I cannot say no to you' - or, 'Oh, the honey of your language.'
In the play. *Cardinal Wolsey has fallen out of grace with the King.*

Tongue, leading speaker into peril - ….tongue… you prattle me into these perils.
"…Tongue, I must put you into a butter-woman's mouth and buy myself another of Bajazet's mule, if you prattle me into these perils."
(AWEW.4.2)
In the play. *In a monologue Parolles reprimands himself to have started his tongue before engaging the brain. He has committed himself to recover a lost drum from the enemy's camp. No explanation available as to the properties of Bajazet's mule. 'Bajazet' is the name of various Ottoman sultans and princes. Bajazet's mule would probably prevent its owner or rider from uttering follies.*

Tongue, malicious - … struck me with her tongue, most serpent-like, upon the very heart.
"(Regan)… struck me with her tongue,
Most serpent-like, upon the very heart" (KL.2.4)
You can address directly the hard-speaking lady, e.g. 'You strike me with your tongue…very heart'.
In the play. *King Lear of his daughter Regan.*

Tongue, native t. no longer of use - And now my tongue's use is to me no more than an unstringed viol or a harp…
"And now my tongue's use is to me no more
Than an unstringed viol or a harp,
Or like a cunning instrument cased up,
Or, being open, put into his hands
That knows no touch to tune the harmony" (KRII.1.3)

In the play. *Mowbray to King Richard after the sentence of permanent exile.*

Tongue, sharp t. – Thy wit is a very bitter sweeting; it is almost a sharp sauce.
"Thy wit is a very bitter sweeting; it is almost a sharp sauce." (RJ.2.4)
Retort to a sharp remark directed at you.
In the play. *Mercutio to Romeo as they exchange some banter.*

Tool, t. of destruction not used - Hence, vile instrument! Thou shalt not damn my hand.
"Hence, vile instrument!
Thou shalt not damn my hand" (CYM.3.4)
In the play. *Pisanio refuses to follow Leonatus' instructions and kill Imogen.*

Torment, mental t. – O, full of scorpions is my mind…
"O, full of scorpions is my mind, dear wife!" (M.3.2)
In the play. *Macbeth has killed Duncan but Banquo and son Fleece are still living and are an obstacle on his quest for domination, according to the prediction of the witches.*

Torture, inner torture - .. the thought whereof doth, like poisonous mineral, gnaw my innards.
" .. I do suspect the lusty Moor
Hath leaped into my seat, the thought whereof
Doth, like poisonous mineral, gnaw my innards." (OTH.2.1)
Describe something that hurts just thinking about it '…the thought whereof….. innards'.
In the play. *Iago monologues. He loves Desdemona too but more as a tool to destroy Othello, whom Iago hates out of envy.*

Touch, soft t. better than heavy hand - … when lenity and cruelty play for a kingdom, the gentler gamester is the soonest winner.
"… for when lenity and cruelty play for a kingdom, the gentler gamester is the soonest winner." (KHV.3.6)
Explain that better results can be obtained by projected kindness and understanding than by threats and perceived arrogance.
In the play. *In a plain in Picardy, Henry V orders that the English army behave civilly with the French population while moving through their country.*

Town, bad t, bad place. - They say this town is full of cozenage… dark working sorcerers…
"They say this town is full of cozenage;
As nimble jugglers, that deceive the eye,
Dark working sorcerers, that change the mind,
Soul killing witches, that deform the body,
Disguised cheaters, prating mountebanks,
And many such liberties of sin." (COE.1.2)
Put down a city or place you do not like.
In the play. *Antipholus (Syracuse) is mystified by the answers of Dromio E whom he thinks to be Dromio S. Antipholus S begins to suspect that the social environment of Ephesus is the source of the problem. 'Cozenage' is a synonym for 'deceit'.*

Trading security for untested chance - …and give up yourself merely to chance and hazard from firm security.
"…..and
Give up yourself merely to chance and hazard,
From firm security." (AC.3.7)
When you want to discourage to try new untested methods.

In the play. *Enobarbus tries to dissuade (unsuccessfully) Antony from battling Octavian at sea rather than on land.*

Traffic, long line of stalled cars – ... will the line stretch out to the crack of doom?
"What, will the line stretch out to the crack of doom?" (M.4.1)
In the play. *Macbeth's reaction at the apparition of an endless line of kings presented to him by the witches.*

Training, t. or good sense overcoming ignorance or folly - and let instructions enter where folly now possesses.
" ...Dost thou think in time
She will not quench, and let instructions enter
Where folly now possesses?"
(CYM.1.5)
Turn the question into a statement and apply it to a wayward employee to whom you wish to give another chance, "....let's hope that instructions enter where folly now possesses."
In the play. *The queen wonders if there may be any chance of Imogen changing her mind. Imogen has secretly married Posthumous but the queen would like Imogen to marry the idiotic Cloten, the queen's son.*

Traitor in full - By day and night he's traitor to the height.
"By day and night,
He's traitor to the height."
(KHVIII.1.2)
In the play. *King Henry VIII refers to the duke of Buckingham who will be tried and beheaded.*

Traitor, skilled at twisting the truth - A subtle traitor needs no sophister.
"A subtle traitor needs no sophister."
((KHVI p2.5.1)

Poor reasons for treason or betrayal. See also entries for 'Oath, excuse for breaking an o.'
In the play. *Salisbury turns his coat against King Henry VI using very specious arguments to break his allegiance. Queen Margaret comments in kind.*

Traitors, how to recognize them – ... Why, one that swears and lies...
SON. What is a traitor?
LADY MACDUFF. Why, one that swears and lies.
SON. And be all traitors that do so?
LADY MACDUFF. Every one that does so is a traitor, and must be hanged. (M.4.2)
In the play. *In Fife, at Macduff's castle Lady Macduff answers some pointed questions by her son.*

Traitors, t. corrupted by m. - A nest of hollow bosoms which he fills with treacherous crowns.
"A nest of hollow bosoms, which he fills
With treacherous crowns"
(HV.2.chorus)
A definition of puppet governments set up by imperialist powers.
In the play. *The chorus introduces three English traitors, paid by the French to assassinate Henry V. 'He' is the equivalent of the CIA in France.*

Traitors, t. purging treason with words - Thus do all traitors: if their purgation did consist in words they are as innocent as grace itself...
"Thus do all traitors:
If their purgation did consist in words,
They are as innocent as grace itself:
Let it suffice thee that I trust thee not." (AYLY.1.3)
In the play. *The Duke upbraids Rosalind who claimed she never offended him. See 'Offense, charge of o. rejected'*

Traitors, t. without knowing it. - But cruel are the times, when we are traitors and do not know ourselves…
"But cruel are the times, when we are traitors
And do not know ourselves, when we hold rumour
From what we fear, yet know not what we fear,
But float upon a wild and violent sea
Each way and move" (M.4.2)
'When we hold rumour from what we fear' has been interpreted as 'when our vague fears inspire rumour'. Use 'Cruel are the times… ourselves' to support your strong disagreement on a policy leading to self-destruction.
In the play. *At the castle of Macduff Ross follows up on a comment by Lady Macduff who complains that her husband has fled to London leaving her exposed to an attack by Macbeth*

Trance, in a t. - … Like our strange garments, cleave not to their mould but with the aid of use.
"New honours come upon him,
Like our strange garments, cleave not to their mould
But with the aid of use" (M.1.3)
See also 'Stunned, mesmerized, in a trance - My thoughts are whirled like a potter's wheel; I know not where I am, nor what I do.'
In the play. *Banquo comments on Macbeth who seems speechless after the predictions of the witches that he, Macbeth, will be king.*

Transformation, t. and new position in society – … And now is this vice's dagger become a squire.
"…And now is this Vice's dagger become a squire, and talks as familiarly of John a Gaunt as if he had been sworn brother to him." (KHIV.p2.3.2)
In the play. *In Gloucestershire at Justice Shallow's house, Falstaff meditates on Shallow's lies about his own youth. Shallow never was familiar with John of Gaunt.*

Transportation, fast t. needed – O, for a horse with wings!
"O, for a horse with wings!" (CYM.3.2)
In the play. *Leonatus writes that he has arrived in Milford-Haven and Imogen is anxious to see him.*

Transportation, t. needed quickly - A horse! A horse! My kingdom for a horse.
"A horse! A horse! My kingdom for a horse!" (KRIII.5.4)
Substitute any desired implement or conveyance for 'horse'.
In the play. *Richard II has lost his horse during the decisive and final battle with Richmond at Bosworth Field.*

Traps, t. for enemies - My brain more busy than the labouring spider weaves tedious snares to trap mine enemies.
"My brain more busy than the labouring spider
Weaves tedious snares to trap mine enemies." (KHVI p2.3.1)
Describe a snake by using the lines in the third person, e.g. 'His brain more busy….his enemies'.
In the play. *York to himself. He will use the soldiers given him to quell an Irish revolt to further his own aims.*

Travel, against t. – … to have seen much and to have nothing, is to have rich eyes and poor hands
"A traveller! By my faith, you have great reason to be sad: I fear you have sold your own lands to see other men's; then, to have seen much and to have nothing, is to have rich eyes and poor hands" (AYLI.4.1)
In the play. *Rosaline's opinion of Jacques' travels, considering that his acquired experience has not contributed to make him happy.*

Travel, better at home than travelling – ... when I was at home, I was in a better place: but travellers must be content.
"Ay, now am I in Arden; the more fool I; when I was at home, I was in a better place: but travellers must be content." (AYLI.2.4)
In the play. *Touchstone has accompanied Rosalind and Celia to the forest of Arden.*

Travel, have a good trip and return happy – Lead forth and bring you back in happiness!
ANGELO The heavens give safety to your purposes!
ESCALUS Lead forth and bring you back in happiness! (MFM.1.1)
In the play. *Duke Vicentio leaves (or pretends to leave) Vienna, Angelo, his deputy and Escalus, a courtier, extend their wishes.*

Travel, have a good trip and wish me with you - ... wish me partaker in thy happiness when thou dost meet good hap.
"Think on thy Proteus, when thou, haply, seest
Some rare note-worthy object in thy travel:
Wish me partaker in thy happiness,
When thou dost meet good hap." (TGV.1.1)
In the play. *Proteus will not go to Milan with Valentine but expresses appreciation for the trip and hope to be not forgotten by his friend.* 'Hap' = 'Fortune', 'Haply' = 'Fortunately'.

Travel, motivation for traveling to see her - .. my desire, more sharp than filed steel, did spur me on.
"...my desire, more sharp than filed steel, did spur me on." (TN.3.3)
Answer to questions such as, 'Why did you come so late?' or 'Why did you come so early?' Or 'Are you not tired after this long journey?' etc.

In the play. *Antonio has decided to follow Sebastian to protect him.*

Travel, seaport, airport, accompanying guest to seaport or airport - We'll bring your grace even to the edge o' the shore..
"We'll bring your grace even to the edge o' the shore
Then give you up to the mask'd Neptune, and
The gentle winds of heaven."
(PER.3.3)
Use as is for sea trip. Modify for air trip, e.g. 'We will bring your grace even to the edge of the field, then give you up to the masked gods of the air and the gentle winds of heaven.' See also entries for 'Salutations'.
In the play. *Pericles leaves takes leave of Cleon and Dionyza in care of whom he ahs left his infant daughter Marina. Cleon accompanies Pericles to the shore from where he departs.*

Travel, separation but you will think of her - .. the time shall not outgo my thinking of you.
" ...... the time shall not
Outgo my thinking of you." (AC.3.2)
You leave for a trip but will not forget her. See also 'Business trip, temporary separation' – 'Business trip abandoned for her sake. See 'World. Your world is where she is'
In the play. *Octavian says goodbye to his sister Octavia before a trip.*

Travel, statement of will to be a t. companion - The swallow follows not summer more willing than we your lordship.
"The swallow follows not summer more willing than we your lordship." (TOA.3.6)
Answer to 'Will you come with me?' Change the 'we' into 'I or (better) your name. Change 'your lordship' to her name or 'your grace'

In the play. *Timon will call on his unhelpful friends and pretend to throw another party. The parasites, thinking that Timon's financial problems are over flock again to his table.*

Travel, t. in youth an important educational tool - ...Which would be great impeachment to his age in having known no travel in his youth.
"(He) did request me to importune you
To let him spend his time no more at home
Which would be great impeachment to his age,
In having known no travel in his youth." (TGV.1.3)
In the play. *Panthino reports to Antonio (Proteus' father) Antonio's brother's opinion that Proteus needs to travel when young to gain worldly experience.*

Treachery, excellence in t. – And whatsoever cunning fiend... hath got the voice in hell for excellence.
"And whatsoever cunning fiend it was
That wrought upon thee so preposterously
Hath got the voice in hell for excellence" (HV.2.2)
In the play. *Henry V at traitor Lord Scroop paid by the French to assassinate the King in a foiled attempt.*

Treason, accusation of t. – ... never did insurrection want such water colours.
"These things, indeed, you have articulated,
Proclaim'd at market crosses, read in churches,
To face the garment of rebellion
With some fine color, that may please the eye
Of fickle changelings, and poor discontents
......
And never yet did insurrection want
Such water-colours, to impaint his cause." (KHIVp1.5.1)
When an ally is unexpectedly defecting. Try, 'I see, you attempt to trim the garment of rebellion....discontents. Never yet did insurrection want...cause.'
In the play. *K. Henry IV dismisses Worcester's grievances as an irrelevant trick to justify rebellion. 'To face' = 'To trim, to enhance'.*

Treason, condemnation for t. unjust – Condemn'd to die for treason, but no traitor.
"Condemn'd to die *for treason, but no traitor*" (KHVI.p1.2.4)
In the play. *Plantagenet (a Yorkist) to Somerset (a Lancastrian), referring to the death of Plantagenet's father at the hands of Henry IV.*

Treason, invocation, is this possible? - Can this be so, that in alliance, amity and oaths there should be found such false, dissembling guile?
"...Can this be so, --
That in alliance, amity and oaths,
There should be found such false, dissembling guile?" (KHVI.p1.4.1)
Treason or treachery that you did not expect.
In the play. *Gloucester's reaction at the news that Burgundy has left the English and joined the French*

Treason, t. and murder - Treason and murder ever kept together...
"Treason and murder ever kept together,
As two yoke-devils sworn to either's purpose" (KHV.2.2)
In the play. *King Henry V expostulates against the traitors who attempted to kill him for pay on behalf of the French.*

Treason, t. for money - That he should, for a foreign purse, so sell his sovereign's life to death and treachery.

"That he should, for a foreign purse, so sell
His sovereign's life to death and treachery." (KHV.2.2)
In the play. *A plot against King Henry has been discovered and Exeter comments on one of the plotters.*

Treason, treacherous intentions - ... so Judas kiss'd his master; and cried 'all hail!' whenas he meant all harm.
"To say the truth, so Judas kiss'd his master;
And cried 'all hail!' whenas he meant all harm." (KHVI p3.5.7)
Comment on an alleged change of allegiance by a suspicious character.
In the play. *In a monologue, Richard acknowledges that he has just kissed the son of Edward IV and Lady Grey, whom he already plans to kill (as it will happen in Richard III).* 'Whenas' = 'Where instead'.

Treason, unexpected t. from a friend hurting more - The private wound is deepest.
"The private wound is deepest." (TGV.5.4)
Show your disappointment and hurt.
In the play. *Proteus chases Sylvia and almost assails her were it not that Valentine appears at the right time to save her. The wound is Proteus' action and it is deep because Valentine never suspected his friend Proteus of treason.*

Treatment, care of details and pleasant t. promised - ... And pluck the wings from painted butterflies, to fan the moonbeams from his sleeping eye.
"...And pluck the wings from painted butterflies,
To fan the moonbeams from his sleeping eye." (MND.3.1)
Modify slightly and make it an answer to "Will you be good to me?", "I will pluck the wings..........to fan moonbeams from your sleeping eyes."

In the play. *Titania orders various fairies to show all kinds of courtesies to Bottom, including fanning him with butterflies' wings.*

Treatment, ignoble t. – ... noble uncle, thus ignobly used.
"...noble uncle, thus ignobly used" (KHVI.p1.2.5)
In the play. *Plantagenet visits his dying imprisoned uncle Mortimer.*

Treatment, pleasant treatment - ... and she will sing the song that pleaseth you, and on your eyelids crown the god of sleep.
"....and rest your gentle head upon her lap, and she will sing the song that pleaseth you, and on your eyelids crown the god of sleep" (H4.p1.3.1)
When she is tired try, 'Rest your gentle head upon my lap and I will sing the song that pleaseth you and on your eyelids crown the god of sleep."
In the play. *Glendower translates for Mortimer what Lady Mortimer said in Welsh.*

Treatment, reasons for treating her well - The lustre in your eye, heaven in your cheek pleads your fair usage.
"The lustre in your eye, heaven in your cheek,
Pleads your fair usage." (TC.4.1)
Alternative answer to 'Can I trust you?'. See also entries for 'Reliability' and 'Abstinence'
In the play. *Diomedes welcomes Cressida who has just arrived at the Greek camp.*

Treaty, t. unfavorable to the losing party – What good condition can a treaty find in the part that is at mercy?
"What good condition can a treaty find
I' the part that is at mercy?" (COR.1.10)
In the play. *Aufidius, leader of the Volsces, defeated by Coriolanus laments the inevitable.*

Trend setting by bucking the t. - To shame the guise o' the world, I will begin the fashion, less without and more within.
"To shame the guise o' the world, I will begin
The fashion, less without and more within." (CYM.5.1)
In the play. *Back in Britain, Leonatus vows to show his valor.*

Trend, trend setter - … the mark and glass, copy and book that fashion'd other.
"He was the mark and glass, copy and book,
That fashion'd other" (KHIVp2.2.3)
Changing to the present tense, make it part of an introduction for a trendsetter or someone who set a particular impressive example.
In the play. *Lady Percy reminds her father in law Northumberland that his son Hotspur (killed in battle at Shrewsbury) set the tone and the example for the whole army.*

Trick, good t. - … it is admirable pleasures, and fery honest knaveries.
"…it is admirable pleasures, and fery honest knaveries." (MWW.4.4)
Use in any occasion where you are metaphorically expecting someone to bite on the bait. If you cannot imitate the Welsh accent you can try German.
In the play. *Mrs. Page plans another nasty trick on Falstaff as a response to his amorous efforts. Parson Evans comments favorably on the idea – the misspelling is a rendering of Evan's Welsh accent.*

Trick, self-effacement after having been the butt of a prank – … if I be served such another trick, I'll have my brains ta'en out and buttered…
"Well, if I be served such another trick, I'll have my brains ta'en out and buttered, and give them to a dog for a new-year's gift" (MWW.3.5)
In the play. *Falstaff after being dumped out of a basket containing dirty laundry*

Trickster, t. unmasked - A subtle knave! but yet it shall not serve.
"A subtle knave! but yet it shall not serve" (KHVIp2.2.1)
Your defense against complex accusations showing a certain degree of cunning. See also 'Character, c. slippery and opportunist - .. a slipper and subtle knave, a finder of occasions.'
In the play. *While the king and court are hawking at St. Alban's a peasant shows up claiming that a miracle restored his sight. The idea was to get some rewards of sorts from the King. Duke Humphrey, the Protector unmasks the tricks of the impostor.*

Trippingly on the tongue - Speak the speech, I pray you, as I pronounced it to you, trippingly on the tongue.
"Speak the speech, I pray you, as I pronounced it to you, trippingly on the tongue" (H.3.2)
Emphasize that you are speaking calmly. E.G. 'I say this to you calmly, trippingly on the tongue'
In the play. *Hamlet, now a producer, instructs the players on how to recite the play 'The Murder of Gonzago'. Hamlet will note the reaction of King Claudius to the scene of the murder to validate the statements of the Ghost.*

Trivia, t. and trifles – … Triumphs for nothing and lamenting toys is jollity for apes and grief for boys.
"…All solemn things
Should answer solemn accidents. The matter?
Triumphs for nothing and lamenting toys
Is jollity for apes and grief for boys." (CYM.4.2)
In the play. *Guiderius' comments as Imogen is brought back from the wood and believed dead.*

True, absolutely and emphatically t. - As certain as I know the sun is fire.
SICINIUS. .. is it most certain?
SECOND MESSENGER. As certain as I know the sun is fire. " (COR.5.4)
Answer to "Is it true?"
In the play. *The good news is that Coriolanus' mother and wife succeeded in making him change his mind.*

True, as true as Troilus - ... truth tired with iteration, as true as steel, as plantage to the moon...
"... truth tired with iteration,
As true as steel, as plantage to the moon
As sun to day, as turtle to her mate,
As iron to adamant, as earth to centre, -
Yes, after all comparison of truth,
As truth's authentic author to be cited,
As true as Troilus shall crown up the verse,
And sanctify the numbers." (TC.3.2)
Extract at will. Use in its entirety or select the lines you like best suited to assure your truthfulness. Substitute your name for 'Troilus'.
In the play. *Troilus makes his final declaration of truth and faithfulness to Cressida. 'Plantage' = 'Plants'. Plants were supposed to grow larger with the increase of the moon.*

True, too good to be t., almost like a dream - This is the rarest dream that ever dull sleep did mock sad fools withal!
"This is the rarest dream that ever dull sleep
Did mock sad fools withal!" (PER.5.1)
Tell her that being in her presence is like a dream.
In the play. *Pericles is on the brink of extreme happiness and coming to terms with the idea that he has found his lost daughter Marina.*

Trust, no t. for him who has already proven untrustworthy - ... trust not him that hath once broken faith
"..trust not him that hath once broken faith" (KHVI.p3.4.1)
In the play. *Queen Elizabeth, wife of Edward IV will bring her children to sanctuary on hearing that Warwick, after having defected to the Lancastrians, is approaching London.*

Trust, skepticism in the face of deceitful friends - Who should be trusted, when one's own right hand is perjured to the bosom?
"Who should be trusted, when one's own right hand
Is perjured to the bosom?" (TGV.5.4)
In the play. *Valentine discovers Proteus' treachery.*

Trust, t. misplaced as a form of madness – He's mad that trusts in the tameness of a wolf....
"He's mad that trusts in the tameness of a wolf, a horse's health, a boy's love, or a whore's oath" (KL.3.6)
Why you do not trust politicians by way of comparison, i.e. 'He that trusts a politician is as mad as he that trusts in the tameness...oath'.
In the play. *The fool uttering a truth.*

Truth and lying accurately defined - ... whose tongue soe'er speaks false not truly speaks; who speaks not truly, lies.
"...whose tongue soe'er speaks false,
Not truly speaks; who speaks not truly, lies." (KJ.4.3)
Alternative to 'you are a liar' or to point out to your adversary that he cannot simultaneously lie and tell the truth.
In the play. *Hubert rebuts Salisbury's accusation of having murdered young Prince Arthur.*

Truth, assurance about one's own credibility - Believe my words for they are certain and unfallible.
"…Believe my words,
For they are certain and unfallible."
(KHVI p1.1.2)
Answer to 'Is it true?' or emphasize the strength of your convictions.
In the play. *The Bastard of Orleans is absolutely positive about the prophetic abilities of Joan of Arc. See 'Forecasting abilities'.*

Truth, assurance of t. emphatically stated – If I tell thee a lie, spit in my face, call me horse.
"If I tell thee a lie, spit in my face, call me horse." (KHIV.p1.2.4)
In the play. *The liar Falstaff pretends to tell the truth about a foray in Kent in which he proved a mighty coward.*

Truth, dangerous t., trying to prove it may be fatal – I have uttered truth which, if you seek to prove, I dare not stand by.
"… I
Have uttered truth; which, if you seek to prove,
I dare not stand by." (WT.1.2)
You are convinced of the accuracy of your assessment. The situation is dangerous enough for you to have decided to leave.
In the play. *Camillo assures Polixenes that the situation is as described and that Polixenes is in danger. Camillo himself will flee.*

Truth, emphatic statement of truth-telling - … for what I speak my body shall make good upon this earth or my divine soul answer it in heaven.
"…for what I speak
My body shall make good upon this earth,
Or my divine soul answer it in heaven." (KRII.1.1)
Answer to 'Are you sure?' or 'Is it true?' See also 'Invocation, i. to heaven that I am telling the truth - heaven be the record to my speech.'
In the play. *Bolingbroke preamble to his challenge to Norfolk whom he accuses of treason*

Truth, evident and yet unseen - … though the truth of it stands off as gross as black and white, my eye will scarcely see it.
"…'tis so strange,
That, though the truth of it stands off as gross
As black and white, my eye will scarcely see it." (KHV.2.2)
When using these lines, the truth you refer to may be pleasant or unpleasant – the quote applies in both cases.
In the play. *King Henry has just discovered a plot against himself by Lord Cambridge and Lord Scroop.*

Truth, extracting t. from falsehood via torture - Bitter torture shall winnow the truth from falsehood.
"….bitter torture shall
Winnow the truth from falsehood"
(CYM.5.4)
When you are given the word in a debate after your adversary has finished his speech. E.G. 'Now then, let's try to winnow the truth from falsehood.'
In the play. *Imogen/Fidele will interrogate the perfidious Jachimo who engineered the false accusations of infidelity towards Imogen. Cymbeline prompts him to tell the truth or else.*

Truth, extraordinary t. at first glance unbelievable - Most true, if ever truth were pregnant by circumstance…
"Most true, if ever truth were pregnant by circumstance: that which you hear you'll swear you see, there is such unity in the proofs." (WT.5.1)
Answer to the question, 'Is it true?'
In the play. *A gentleman confirms the extraordinary coincidence whereby the newly arrived Perdita wears attires and jewels belonging to Hermione who, unbeknown to the onlookers,*

is actually Perdita's mother. For another statement on the same event see notes to 'News, questionable – .. is so like an old tale..."

Truth, painful t. not told - ... sick men, when their deaths be near no news but health from their physicians know.
"...sick men, when their deaths be near,
No news but health from their physicians know" (SON 140)

Truth, t. passed on through the ages – Methinks the truth should live from age to age as 'twere retail'd to all posterity...
"Methinks the truth should live from age to age,
As 'twere retail'd to all posterity,
Even to the general all-ending day."
(KRIII.3.1)
In the play. *Young Prince Edward asks Buckingham whether there is a record of Caesar having undertaken the building of the Tower of London. Even if there were no record the truth should still be transmitted though the generations.*

Truth, simple t. not requiring oaths - 'T is not the many oaths that make the truth, but the plain single vow, that is vow'd true.
"'T is not the many oaths that make the truth,
But the plain single vow, that is vow'd true." (AWEW.4.2)
Indicate your skepticism at official, lengthy and pompous declarations of intent and statements of commitment.
In the play. *Diana, a Florentine lady, does not believe the promises and oaths of the would-be seducer Bertram.*

Truth, sometimes it cannot be told, conflict - ... That truth should be silent I had almost forgot.
ANTONY: Thou art a soldier only, speak no more.
ENOBARBUS: That truth should be silent I had almost forgot (AC.2.2)
A follow up when you are asked not to speak but you have a strong argument, 'That truth should…….almost forgot.'
See also "Silence, self-enforced - It is not nor it cannot come to good: but break, my heart; for I must hold my tongue.'
In the play. *Enobarbus has made a true but somewhat caustic remark.*

Truth, surprise at the devil telling the truth – What, can the devil speak true?
"What, can the devil speak true?" (M.1.3)
In the play. *Banquo's reaction at hearing that Ross addresses Macbeth as Thane of Cawdor, just as the witches predicted.*

Truth, t. confers calmness of spirit - Truth hath a quiet breast.
"As gentle and as jocund as to jest
Go I to fight: truth hath a quiet breast" (KRII.1.3)
Comment on a threat or an accusation, e.g. 'I don't care about what you say – truth hath a quiet breast'.
In the play. *Mowbray declares his confidence before the duel with Bolingbroke.*

Truth, t. destroyed by malice – ... it must appear that malice bears down truth.
"If this will not suffice, it must appear
That malice bears down truth." (MOV.4.1)
You have offered or tried to be cooperative as much as you can and yet the answer is still negative
In the play. *Bassanio's reaction when Shylock insists on having his bond on Antonio paid in blood with a pound of flesh.*

Truth, t. emphatically asserted – ... never man sigh'd truer breath.
"...never man
Sigh'd truer breath" (COR.4.5)
In the play. *Going somewhat overboard Aufidius, head of the Volsces compares the true love he has for his wife to the true love he now feels for Coriolanus who has just joined the Volsces.*

Truth, t. evident and on my side - By him that made me, I'll maintain my words on any plot of ground on Christendom.
"By him that made me, I'll maintain my words
On any plot of ground on Christendom." (KHVI.p1.2.4)
Reinforce your position as the holder of the correct idea or opinion.
In the play. *Somerset is convinced of holding the truth and denies Plantagenet's claims to the crown as descending from Edward III.*

Truth, t. evident and on my side – the truth appears so naked on my side, that any purblind eye may find it out.
PLANTAGENET. "The truth appears so naked on my side,
That any purblind eye may find it out."
SOMERSET. And on my side it is so well apparell'd,
So clear, so shining and so evident
That it will glimmer through a blind man's eye." (KHVI.p1.3.4)
Reinforce your position as the holder of the truth
In the play. *Plantagenet is convinced of being right as to his royal titles and rejects the apparent neutrality of judgment by Warwick.*

Truth, t. in economy of words - Where words are scarce, they are seldom spent in vain.
"O, but they say the tongues of dying men
Enforce attention like deep harmony:
Where words are scarce, they are seldom spent in vain,
For they breathe truth, that breathe their words in pain." (KRII.2.1)
Indicate that it pains you to say what nevertheless must be said.
In the play. *Gaunt to the Duke of York.*

Truth, t. incomplete or inaccurate - Though thou speak'st truth methinks thou speak'st not well.
"Though thou speak'st truth,
Methinks thou speak'st not well."
(COR.1.6)
Correct or point out that a statement that only appears true isn't.
In the play. *A messenger thinks he is telling the truth about the events of a battle between the citizens of Corioli and the Romans, but Cominius corrects him.*

Truth, t. is not slander - That is no slander, sir, which is a truth.
"That is no slander, sir, which is a truth" (RJ.4.1)
In the play. *Juliet modestly and indirectly tries to convince Paris that she is ugly naturally and not made ugly by tears. Unaware of her previous marriage to Romeo Paris thinks that he will marry her shortly.*

Truth, t. is on my side - ...And on my side truth so well apparell'd, so shining and so evident..
"... And on my side truth is so well apparell'd,
So clear, so shining and so evident
That it will glimmer through a blind man's eye." (KHVI.p1.2.4)
Also applies to truth in general, e.g. 'truth is so well'....eye', when you wish to stress that all doubts should be removed, due to the evidence being so clear.
In the play. *Somerset and Richard Plantagenet argue as to who has the right to succession to the*

English Crown, the Yorkists or the Lancastrians.

Truth, t. is t. however they may try to twist it - ... truth is truth to the end of reckoning.
"... this is all as true as it is strange: Nay, it is ten times true; for truth is truth
To the end of reckoning." (MFM.5.1)
When they try to discredit your rendition of facts with flimsy arguments.
In the play. *Isabel denounces Angelo to the Duke of Vienna even if Angelo tries to make her pass for mad.*

Truth, t. needs no embellishment – Truth needs no colour... beauty no pencil
"'Truth needs no colour, with his colour fix'd;
Beauty no pencil" (SON 101)

Truth, t. not seen or perceived - ...he doth but mistake the truth totally.
"No; he doth but mistake the truth totally." (TEM.2.1)
You can also use 'Thou dost but mistake the truth totally'. A more modern version can be 'Your truth is very inaccurate'
In the play. *Antonio, Sebastian and Gonzalo exchange some banter.*

Truth, t. only apparent - the seeming truth which cunning times put on.
"The seeming truth which cunning times put on
To entrap the wisest." (MOV.2.1)
In the play. *The fair Portia will marry him who solves a riddle. Before attempting to do so, Bassanio meditates on some important truths.*

Truth, t. supported by facts not words - ... truth hath better deeds than words to grace it.
"What, gone without a word?
Ay, so true love should do: it cannot speak;

For truth hath better deeds than words to grace it." (TGV.2.2)
Declare that you have facts more than words to prove your point.
In the play *Proteus has taken leave of Julia after intense protestations of faith. Julia has left without a word, a sign that Proteus interprets positively.*

Truth, t. that cannot be told - Truth's a dog must to kennel; he must be whipped out...
"Truth's a dog must to kennel; he must be whipped out, when Lady the brach may stand by the fire and stink." (KL.1.4)
In the play. *The Fool comments on a threat by King Lear after he, the fool has hinted at some painful truths. The brach was a female hound, or more coarsely, a bitch.*

Truth, t. told, end of story - Some such thing I said and said no more but what my thoughts did warrant me was likely.
"Some such thing I said,
And said no more but what my thoughts
Did warrant me was likely." (PER.5.1)
Conclude a presentation by implying that you have been as objective as possible.
In the play. *Marina has finished to tell her story.*

Truth, t. unexpectedly uttered - ...you have spoken truer than you purposed...
GONZALO ... you have spoken truer than you purposed.
SEBASTIAN You have taken it wiselier than I meant you should (TEM.2.1)
When your adversary trips himself and unwittingly agrees with your point.
In the play. *A quibble on words ('dollar' and 'dolour') prompts the exchange.*

Truth, this is the absolute t. - Mark what I say, which you shall find by every syllable a faithful verity.
"Mark what I say, which you shall find
By every syllable a faithful verity." (MFM.4.3)
Give strength to the information you are now giving out.
In the play. *The Duke (in disguise) does not disclose to Isabel that a man recently executed is not her brother but a condemned substitute. This is part of the plot to unmask Angelo's hypocrisy.*

Truth, you are determined to find the t. - If circumstances lead me, I will find where truth is hid, though it were hid indeed within the centre.
"If circumstances lead me, I will find
Where truth is hid, though it were hid indeed
Within the centre." (H.2.2)
A statement of intent when you are assigned any kind of investigation. Start from 'I will find….centre'.
In the play. *Polonius continues in his sermon to the king and queen about Hamlet's state of mind.*

Truthfulness, t. confirmed - … what truth can speak truest (shall be) not truer than Troilus.
"... what truth can speak truest not truer than Troilus." (TC.3.2)
Answer to 'Are you telling the truth?' Substitute your name instead of Troilus and emphasize your commitment to telling the truth. See also 'Character, c. truthful and simple - I am as true as truth's simplicity and simpler than the infancy of truth.'
In the play. *Troilus assures Cressida that he truly loves her.*

Truthfulness, t. confirmed - Heaven be re the record to my speech.
"Heaven be re the record to my speech." (KRII.1.1)
Answer to 'Are you telling the truth?'
In the play. *Bolingbroke, future Henry IV, accuses Mowbray of treason in front of the King Richard II.*

Turmoil, what is happening? – … Are we turn'd Turks, and to ourselves do that which heaven hath forbid the Ottomites?
"…from whence ariseth this?
Are we turn'd Turks, and to ourselves do that
Which heaven hath forbid the Ottomites?" (OTH.2.3)
In the play. *Othello's reaction to the squabbles and fights among the Venetians in Cyprus, squabbles planned and incited by Iago.*

Turpitude, rewarding t. - … my turpitude thou dost so crown with gold!
"… how wouldst thou have paid
My better service, when my turpitude
Thou dost so crown with gold!" (AC.4.6)
Rebuke or comment on an undeserved reward or benefit is bestowed on a particularly unsavory character, e.g. 'His turpitude we do so crown with gold'.
In the play. *Antony sends a bountiful treasure to Enobarbus even though he has abandoned him. Now Enobarbus repents.*

Tyranny, act of t. – … nothing less than bloody tyranny
"…nothing less than bloody tyranny" (KHVI.p1.2.5)
In the play. *Plantagenet visiting his imprisoned uncle Mortimer refers to the execution of Plantagenet's father by Henry IV.*

**Tyranny, invocation in helplessness -
O nation miserable, with an untitled tyrant bloody-scepter'd...**
"O nation miserable,
With an untitled tyrant bloody-scepter'd,
When shalt thou see thy wholesome days again" (M.4.3)
Invocation equally applies to those heads of state who claim to be 'democratic'.
In the play. *After the (untrue) self-admissions of deceit and greed by Malcolm, who should replace Macbeth on the throne of Scotland, Macduff is despairing about the fate of his country.*

Tyranny, t. of individual or corporations – ... and we petty men walk under his huge legs and peep about to find ourselves dishonourable graves...
"... he doth bestride the narrow world
Like a Colossus, and we petty men
Walk under his huge legs and peep about
To find ourselves dishonourable graves." (JC.1.2)
To apply to corporations change 'under his huge legs' to 'under their huge legs'.
In the play. *Cassius convinces Brutus that Caesar is a tyrant to be eliminated.*

Tyrant, almost a t. – ... I'll not call you tyrant but... something savours of tyranny and will ignoble make you...
"...I'll not call you tyrant;
But this most cruel usage of your queen,
Not able to produce more accusation
Than your own weak-hinged fancy, something savours
Of tyranny and will ignoble make you,
Yea, scandalous to the world."
(WT.2.3)
In the play. *Paulina to Leontes whose jealousy prompted him to have his wife killed.*

Tyrant, praying for deliverance from a t. – ... this imperious man will work us all from princes into pages...
"We had need pray,
And heartily, for our deliverance;
Or this imperious man will work us all
From princes into pages: all men's honours
Lie like one lump before him, to be fashion'd
Into what pitch he please."
(KHVIII.2.2)
In the play. *Norfolk referring to Cardinal Wolsey, who is in control of the political scene, while at the service of King Henry VIII.*

Tyrant, t. killing those who helped him succeed – One raised in blood, and one in blood establish'd...
"A bloody tyrant and a homicide;
One raised in blood, and one in blood establish'd
One that made means to come by what he hath,
And slaughter'd those that were the means to help him" (KRIII.5.3)
In the play. *Richmond addresses the troops before the final battle against Richard III and describes Richard's tyranny.*

Ugliness, u. not changed by praise - Where fair is not, praise cannot mend the brow.
"Where fair is not, praise cannot mend the brow" (LLL.4.1)
In a play. *The Princess engages the forester in a game of words. 'Brow' = 'countenance'.*

Unassailable - ... laugh to scorn the power of man for none of woman born shall harm Macbeth
"...laugh to scorn
The power of man, for none of woman born
Shall harm Macbeth." (M.4.1)
Brag with style when you are warned to be careful, e.g. 'I scorn the power of man.....shall harm (your name).'

In the play. *A witch reassures Macbeth about his invincibility – except that later in the play it turns out that Macduff had a Cesarean birth, hence technically he was 'not of woman born'. Macduff will defeat Macbeth.*

Unbelievable - .. 'tis but our fantasy, and will not let belief take hold of him.
"Horatio says 'tis but our fantasy,
And will not let belief take hold of him" (H.1.1)
Apply to third party or yourself, e.g. ''tis but a fantasy and will not let belief take hold of me.'
In the play. *The guards at the Castle have seen again the ghost of Hamlet's father.*

Unbelievable - I might not this believe without the sensible and true avouch of mine own eyes.
"I might not this believe
Without the sensible and true avouch
Of mine own eyes." (H.1.1)
See also 'News, questionable – .. is so like an old tale, that the verity of it is in strong suspicion.'
In the play. *Horatio has seen the Ghost himself.*

Unbelievable - If this were played upon a stage now I could condemn it as an improbable fiction.
"If this were played upon a stage now, I could condemn it as an improbable fiction." (TN.3.4)
Apply to very odd behavior or idea or action. See also 'Disbelief about one's mental state and perception - Or sleep I now and think I hear all this?'
In the play. *Fabian cannot contain his laughter at Malvolio's behavior.*

Unbelievable sight - ... speak; we will not trust our eyes without our ears...
"…is it fantasy that plays upon our eyesight?
I prithee, speak; we will not trust our eyes
Without our ears: thou art not what thou seem'st"** (KHIVp1.5.4)
In the play. *Prince Harry cannot believe that Falstaff is alive. Falstaff had counterfeited death during the battle of Shrewsbury.*

Unbelievable, can this be true? - Are these things spoken? or do I but dream?
"Are these things spoken? or do I but dream?" (MAAN.4.1)
Express your disbelief at something you just heard.
In the play. *Leonato cannot believe the accusations that Don Pedro is leveling against Hero, Leonato's daughter.*

Unbelievable, can this be true? - What fire is in my ears? can this be true?
"What fire is in my ears? can this be true?" (MAAN.3.2)
Express dramatically your disbelief.
In the play. *Beatrice has overheard the (staged) conversation between Hero and Ursula where they said that Benedick loves Beatrice.*

Unbelievable, cannot believe their (or my) eyes – ... scarse think their eyes do offices of truth, their words are natural breath.
"…I perceive these lords
At this encounter do so much admire
That they devour their reason and scarce think
Their eyes do offices of truth, their words
Are natural breath." (TEM.5.1)
Answer to 'What do you think?' after you have been shown the result of any remarkable feat, e.g. 'I scarce think my eyes do offices of truth.'
In the play. *Prospero has introduced himself to the shipwrecked party and they cannot believe their eyes.*

Unbelievable, can this be true? – Stand I, even so, as doubtful whether what I see be true…
"…thrice fair lady, stand I, even so;
As doubtful whether what I see be true,
Until confirm'd, sign'd, ratified by you" (MOV.3.2)
In the play. *Bassanio is overwhelmed by the emotion of having solved the riddle that will enable him to marry Portia.*

Uncertainty, end unknown - … and the end of it unknown to the beginning.
"It is the humane way: the other course
Will prove too bloody, and the end of it
Unknown to the beginning" (COR.3.1)
In the play. *The 'humane' way, suggested by Menenius is to try to reason with the proud Coriolanus as opposed to stirring an immediate confrontation between him and the people.*

Uncertainty, political u. - … I fear 'twill prove a giddy world.
"…I fear 'twill prove a giddy world." (KRIII.2.3)
In the play. *Some common citizens' opinion on the events following the death of Edward IV.*

Underrating, underestimation – … holding a weak supposal of our worth.
"…young Fortinbras,
Holding a weak supposal of our worth" (H.1.2)
In the play. *King Claudius gives instructions to his ambassador to Norway on how to react to the military sallies of the Norwegian Fortinbras.*

Understanding, discouraging attempt to sort out a strange business - Do not infest your mind with beating on the strangeness of this business.
"Do not infest your mind with beating on
The strangeness of this business." (TEM.5.1)
Persuade to accept facts and/or results as they are without further questions.
In the play. *Alonso tries to find an impossible rational explanation to magical events engineered by Prospero and Prospero prompts him not to bother.*

Understanding, limited u. - a knavish speech sleeps in a foolish ear.
ROSENCRANTZ I understand you not, my lord.
HAMLET I am glad of it: a knavish speech sleeps in a foolish ear. (H.4.2)
In the play. *Hamlet has explained, without success of understanding, to Rosencranz why he and Guilderstern are sponges.*

Understanding , maybe you understand now - But now you partly may perceive my mind.
LADY GREY Why, then you mean not as I thought you did.
KING EDWARD IV But now you partly may perceive my mind. (KHVI.p3.3.2)
Make clear that you are speaking indirectly but with a precise point in mind.
In the play. *Edward wants to have sex with the Lady Grey and after some double meaning that she ignores, he comes to the point.*

Understanding, one who does not understand…- I think his understanding is bereft!
"I think his understanding is bereft!" (KHVI.p3.2.6)
Change 'his' to 'your' when debating an adversary.
In the play. *After winning the battle of Towton, Warwick checks and verifies that the Lancastrian Clifford is dead.*

Understanding, sincerity of lack of u. questioned - Your sense pursues not

mine or seem so craftily; and that's not good.
"Your sense pursues not mine: either you are ignorant,
Or seem so craftily; and that's not good." (MFM.2.4)
In the play. *The lecherous, hypocrite Angelo to Isabella who does not understand his double meaning.*

Understanding, thick of u. - … thou wert not wont to be so dull…
"Cousin, thou wert not wont to be so dull
Shall I be plain? I wish the bastards dead" (KRIII.4.2)
Possible excuse for not understanding an apparently simple point, e.g. 'I was not wont to be so dull'.
In the play. *Richard to Buckingham, who does not want to take the hint about assassinating the heirs to the throne, kept in the Tower.*

Understanding, u. showing no specific education – …an understanding simple and unschooled.
"An understanding simple and unschooled." (H.1.1)
An opening or retort to a contorted and confused explanation that should be made simpler or clearer - e.g. 'My understanding is simple and unschooled, but…' or with a slight modification, "My understanding may be simple and unschooled, but…'
In the play. *The King reproaches Hamlet for his continued mourning and dark mood. It is this attitude that shows his alleged simplicity and ignorance.*

Undoing work previously accomplished with hardship - Undoing all, as all had never been!
"Undoing all, as all had never been!" (KHVI p2,1.1)

Emotional criticism of proposal that would set back company or enterprise.
In the play. *Gloucester commenting on the impending marriage between Henry VI and Margaret of France, marriage that secures excellent conditions for the French, reversing the gains made by Henry V.*

Unemployment, u. soon ending - … But long I will not be Jack out of office..
"I am left out; for me nothing remains.
 But long I will not be Jack out of office:
The king from Eltham I intend to steal
And sit at chiefest stern of public weal." (KHVI p1.1.1)
In the play. *The Bishop of Winchester plots his next career move. 'Jack out of office' is an expression of contempt for silly people.*

Unfairness, extreme u. – This was the most unkindest cut of all.
"This was the most unkindest cut of all" (JC.3.2)
In the play. *The 'cut' Antony refers to is the stab by Brutus that killed Caesar. Antony speaks to the citizens. This is part of the oration containing the lines 'And yet Brutus is an honourable man'.*

Unhappiness, asking for reasons of u. - … make me acquainted with your cause of grief.
"… Dear my lord,
Make me acquainted with your cause of grief." (JC.2.1)
In the play. *Portia asks husband Brutus the reason for his strange mood.*

Unhappiness, impossible to be understood by those who do not feel it - Thou canst not speak of that thou dost not feel.
"Thou canst not speak of that thou dost not feel." (RJ.3.3)

Answer anyone who downplays your argument or does not believe that you are suffering or that you have been damaged. See also 'Philosophy, p. and tooth ache - ..there was never yet philosopher, that could endure the tooth-ache patiently.' 'Love, l.'s pains not to be laughed at - He jests at scars that never felt a wound.' Entries for 'Pain'.
In the play. *Romeo tells Fr. Lawrence why his psychological counseling cannot work.*

Unhappiness, u. and desperation – O limed soul, that, struggling to be free, art more engaged!
"O wretched state! O bosom black as death!
O limed soul, that, struggling to be free,
Art more engaged!" (H.3.3)
In the play. *King Claudius is tormented by remorse at the murder of his brother.*

Unhappiness, u. and desperation - O, woe is me, to have seen what I have seen, see what I see!
"...O, woe is me,
To have seen what I have seen, see what I see!" (H.3.1)
In the play. *Ophelia realizes that all the hopes in Hamlet are shattered as he appears to her definitely mad.*

Unity, u. of effort – So may a thousand actions, once afoot end in one purpose…
"So may a thousand actions, once afoot
End in one purpose, and be all well borne
Without defeat." (HV.1.2)
In the play. *Canterbury declaims the merits of the ideal capitalist system (patterned after the bees), to Henry V. For the complete rendition see 'Management structure, hierarchical – Obedience: for so work the honey bees…'*

Unkindness, u. destructive – Unkindness may do much and his unkindness may defeat my life.
"…Unkindness may do much;
And his unkindness may defeat my life" (OTH.4.2)
In the play. *Desdemona, unaware of Iago's plotting, protests her unspotted love for Othello, who suspects her of adultery.*

Universe, rose, unique - For nothing this wide universe I call, save thou my rose, in it thou art my all.
"For nothing this wide universe I call,
Save thou my rose, in it thou art my all." (SON.109)
Compliment. Alternative answer to 'Do you love me?' See also 'World, she is the w. - .. for where thou art, there is the world itself.'

Unmentionable, u. something – Why, I cannot name't but I shall offend MARINA What trade, sir? LYSIMACHUS Why, I cannot name't but I shall offend (PER.4.6)
Answer to any question the reply to which would be inevitably offensive.
In the play. *Lysimachus, governor of Mytilene is unaware of Marina's silver virtue and character.*

Unnatural events as indication of the gravity of the times - .. they are portentous things unto the climate that they point upon.
"…For, I believe, they are portentous things
Unto the climate that they point upon." (JC.1.3)
It could be an unnatural event or an event sufficiently extraordinary for you to use it as a symptom of the temper of the times. See also 'Whisperings, w. about bad deeds - ..unnatural deeds do breed unnatural troubles' – entries for 'Events, strange and extraordinary'

In the play. *Casca lists a number of extraordinary and unnatural events that, in his opinion, signal the critical nature of the current state of affairs in Rome.*

Unpleasantness, tolerated for her sake - many can brook the weather that love not the wind.
"Many can brook the weather that love not the wind." (LLL.4)
She knows you do not like it (e.g. wash the dishes, clean the floor or anything unpleasant you may think of). Answer or comment to a statement from her of the type, 'Do you mind doing this, I know you don't like it?' or similar.
In the play. *Sir Nathaniel reflects on the ignorance of Dull and wishes that Dull could undertake some schooling to allay his ignorance. Dull may not like school (the wind) but may tolerate some exposure to learning (the weather).*

Unsalvageable, not worth looking for the salvageable - He could not stay to pick them in a pile of noisome musty chaff…
"He could not stay to pick them in a pile
Of noisome musty chaff: he said 'twas folly,
For one poor grain or two, to leave unburnt,
And still to nose the offence."
(COR.5.1)
In the play. *Cominius' report of Coriolanus attitude. Coriolanus thinks that the few friends he has in Rome do not warrant that Rome be saved.*

Unstoppable and ferocious - … from face to foot he was a thing of blood …
"…from face to foot
He was a thing of blood, whose every motion
Was timed with dying cries"
(COR.2.2)
A metaphor to celebrate a sport victory.

In the play. *Cominius describes to various Romans the feats in battle of Coriolanus.*

Unthinkable, u. that I would do this - If ever I did dream of such a matter, abhor me.
"If ever I did dream of such a matter, Abhor me" (OTH.1.1)
In the play. *Iago to Roderigo. Roderigo made reference to some alleged double-crossing by Iago in an event not explained in the play.*

Untrustworthy – I will trust as I will adders fang'd.
"…and my two schoolfellows
Whom I will trust as I will adders fang'd" (H.3.4)
In the play. *Hamlet, referring to Guildenstern and Rosencranz who accompany him to England.*

Urgency - It requires swift foot.
"It requires swift foot." (TOA.5.1)
In the play. *Athenians senators return from a visit to Timon in the woods. The purpose of the visit was to ask Timon to intercede with Alcibiades who wants to attack Athens with his troops. The senators must return quickly to Athens*

Urgent business, u. action required - … haste is needful in this desperate case.
"…haste is needful in this desperate case." (KHVI.p3.4.1)
In the play. *King Edward on hearing that even his brother Clarence plus Warwick have changed allegiance and now part with the Lancastrians.*

Urgent business, u. action required - Our hands are full of business: let's away..
"Our hands are full of business: let's away;
Advantage feeds him fat, while men delay." (KHIV p1.3.2)
Change slightly, 'Our hands are full of business: let's away; advantage feeds the

competition fat, while men delay'. See entries for 'Action, a. requiring urgent and strong response'
In the play. *The advantage referred to(by the Prince of Wales), is the enemy's, that is the English rebels lead by Hotspur.*

Valor, no v. in fighting a dog - What valour were it, when a cur doth grin for one to thrust his hands between his teeth…
"What valour were it, when a cur doth grin,
For one to thrust his hands between his teeth,
When he might spurn him with foot away?" (KHVI p3.1.4)
Justification for not arguing with an ass (or in this case a dog)
In the play. *Northumberland to Clifford, the dog referred to is the York who is on the point to be killed.*

Value, different v. placed on possession by thieves and rightful owners – Pirates may make cheap pennyworths of their pillage…
"Pirates may make cheap pennyworths of their pillage
And purchase friends and give to courtezans,
Still revelling like lords till all be gone;
While as the silly owner of the goods
Weeps over them and wrings his hapless hands
And shakes his head and trembling stands aloof…" (KHVI.p2.1.1)
In the play. *York meditates on the ease with which the English crown has abandoned French land to the French. York had a claim on those very lands.*

Value, perception of v. and relative v. of useful and useless things - …
Nature, what things there are most abject in regard, and dear in use!
".. Nature, what things there are, Most abject in regard, and dear in use!
What things again most dear in the esteem,
And poor in worth." (TC.3.3)
Praise or demonstrate the value of something (project, asset, device and even a person) that you know good but underestimated.
In the play. *Ulysses works at making Achilles feel challenged and be better than Ajax. Here, by means of a comparison, Ulysses implies that Ajax does not know his own worth.*

Value, v. of object enhanced by owner - … things of like value differing in the owners are prized by their masters…
"…but you well know,
Things of like value differing in the owners
Are prized by their masters: believe't, dear lord,
You mend the jewel by the wearing it." (TOA.1.1)
If she modestly tones down the praise of her own jewelry use the first two lines. See also 'Jewelry, value of discount jewel increased by the charm of the wearer – You mend the jewel by the wearing it.'
*** Entries for 'Apologies unnecessary, on the contrary'
In the play. *A jewelry salesman and at the same time a parasite, feigning modesty, offers for sale a jewel to Timon.*

Value, v. resides in perception - What is aught, but as 'tis valued?
"What is aught, but as 'tis valued?" (TC.2.2)
In the play. *Troilus, replying to Hector, argues that Helen is worth holding on to due to her perceived value. See 'Assets, a. not worth holding on to - … she is not worth what she doth cost the holding.'*

Value, valueless - … not worth my thinking.

961

TIMON. How dost thou like this jewel, Apemantus?
APEM. Not so well as plain-dealing, which will not cost a man a doit.
TIMON. What do you think 'tis worth?
APEM. Not worth my thinking." (TOA.1.1)
Answer to 'What do you think this is worth?'
In the play. *Timon asks Apemantus his opinion of the jewel offered by the parasite jeweler.*

Values, perversion of v. - Fair is foul, and foul is fair.
"Fair is foul, and foul is fair:
Hover through the fog and filthy air." (M.1.1)
When your opponents completely misrepresent facts. See also 'Law, anarchy as a consequence of unjust law – When law can do no right, let it be lawful that law bar no wrong. '
In the play. *Mumbo jumbo of the three witches.*

Values, v. reversed – In the fatness of these pursy times, virtue itself of vice must pardon beg…
"…in the fatness of these pursy times, Virtue itself of vice must pardon beg, Yea, curb and woo for leave to do him good." (H.3.4)
In the play. *Part of the speech in which Hamlet upbraids his mother Queen Gertrude for having married King Claudius. 'Pursy'='fat', meaning that the moral climate of the times is the opposite of what it should be.*

Vanished, persons v. - … Into the air; and what seem'd corporal melted as breath into the wind.
BANQUO Whither are they vanish'd?
MACBETH Into the air; and what seem'd corporal melted
As breath into the wind. Would they had stay'd! (M.1.3)

See also 'Disappearance, where is he? - …melted into air, into thin air…' ***
'Disappearance – … they made themselves air, into which they vanished.'
In the play. *After their first brief apparition, the witches vanish.*

Vanity, v. and heedlessness in a leader - … he tires betimes, who spurs too fast betimes.
"His rash fierce blaze of riot cannot last,
For violent fires soon burn out themselves;
Small showers last long, but sudden storms are short;
He tires betimes, who spurs too fast betimes;
With eager feeding the food doth choke the feeder;
Light vanity, insatiate cormorant,
Consuming means, soon preys upon itself." (KRII.2.1)
A good source of motivating metaphors. To suggest a slow down, 'He tires betimes, who spurs too fast betimes, with eager…. Feeder'. To deplore excess, 'This rash fierce blaze……themselves'. To chastise excessive spending for the sake of pomp, 'Light vanity……itself'.
In the play. *Gaunt chastises the spendthrift hedonistic behavior of King Richard.*

Vanity, v. displayed and observed - … what a sweep of vanity comes this way!
"Hoy-day, what a sweep of vanity comes this way!" (TOA.1.2)
In the play. *Apemantus' comments on the group of ladies (dressed as Amazons) who arrive to attend Timon's party.*

Vanity, v. or not? - it is not vain-glory for a man and his glass to confer in his own chamber.
"…… for it is not vain-glory for a man and his glass to confer in his own chamber." (CYM.4.1)

Admitting to talking to yourself.
In the play. *The foolish Cloten speaks to himself and will try to appear like Posthumous to impress or trick Imogen.*

Vanity, wanting others to believe to be sought after - .. You see, my good wenches, how men of merit are sought after...
"... You see, my good wenches, how men of merit are sought after: the undeserver may sleep, when the man of action is called on." (KHIV p2.2.4)
In the play. *Falstaff has been summoned at court and takes the occasion to display some vanity with the wenches in Eastcheap.*

Vegetables, unpalatable v. - ... mixture rank, of midnight weeds collected...
"Thou mixture rank, of midnight weeds collected..." (H.3.2)
In the play. *Actor Lucianus addresses the poison he will pour into the ear of the actor who plays the part of the king.*

Vegetarian, better to be a v. - ... but I am a great eater of beef, and I believe that does harm my wit.
"... but I am a great eater of beef, and I believe that does harm my wit." (TN.1.3)
An introduction when promoting the value of vegetarianism.
In the play. *Aguecheek suspects that his loss of wit is attributable to an excessive accumulation of proteins.*

Vegetarianism, plenty of natural nutrients available – ... The bounteous housewife, nature, on each bush lays her full mess before you...
"Your greatest want is, you want much of meat.
Why should you want? Behold, the earth hath roots;
Within this mile break forth a hundred springs;
The oaks bear mast, the briers scarlet hips;
The bounteous housewife, nature, on each bush
Lays her full mess before you. Want! why want?" (TO.A.4.3)
In the play. *Timon addresses a bunch of robbers who came to rob Timon in the woods.*
'Hips' = Fruit of the dogrose

Venom, v. useful under certain conditions – ... like the toad, ugly and venomous, wears yet a precious jewel in his head.
"...like the toad, ugly and venomous,
Wears yet a precious jewel in his head" (AYLI.2.1)
In the play. *In the forest of Arden, Duke S. comments positively on the turn of events whereby an adversity can be an advantage (see 'Adversity, a. put to good use - Sweet are the uses of adversity...' The toad was believed to conceal a jewel inside its head.*

Venture, risky v. but undertaken – We knew that we ventured on such dangerous seas that if we wrought our life 'twas ten to one...
"(We) knew that we ventured on such dangerous seas
That if we wrought our life 'twas ten to one;
And yet we ventured" (KHIV.p2.1.1)
In the play. *Bardolph comments on the defeat of the rebellious party at Shrewsbury.*

Venture, v. delivered what predicted - .. what hath then befallen, or what hath this bold enterprise brought forth..
"...what hath then befallen,
Or what hath this bold enterprise brought forth,
More than that being which was like to be?" (KHIV.p2.1.1)
See also 'Persistence, failure. positive attitude - .. the protractive trials of great Jove to find persistive constancy in men.'

963

In the play. *Morton states the obvious, that the rebels knew of their weak position before the battle they lost hence defeat should be no surprise.*

Venus, compared to V., worthy of worship - Bright star of Venus, fall'n down on earth, may I reverently worship thee enough?
"Bright star of Venus, fall'n down on earth,
How may I reverently worship thee enough?" (KHVIp1.1.2)
Compliment.
In the play. *Joan of Arc (the Pucelle), has defeated Charles, the Dauphin of France in a test fight and has proven beyond doubt her strength, ability and purpose. Charles is overwhelmed.*

Venus, love's soul - .. the heartbreak of beauty, love's invisible soul.
"…with him, the mortal Venus, the heartbreak of beauty, love's invisible soul" (TC.3.1)
Compliment. You can skip 'Venus' and just say, 'Oh you heartbreak of beauty'…etc.
Not everyone considered Venus, or at least her most classical sculptured representations, as overly seductive. In a letter from Florence, written to his sister, Checkov complains, "I have seen Venus de Medici, and I think that if she were dressed in modern clothes she would be hideous, especially about the waist. (Anton Checkov, 1860-1904).
In the play. *Music plays. Pandarus asks whom is it played for. For Paris and Helen, answers the Servant loading Helen with praise including a reference to Venus.*

Verbal self-defense, 'why don't you answer?' - Why bear you these rebukes and answer not?
"Why bear you these rebukes and answer not?" (COE.5.1)
Question and prompt an unjustly accused friend to answer back.

In the play. *The Lady Abbess accuses Adriana to be the cause of Ant E's apparent madness. Luciana knows it is not so and prompts her sister Adriana to defend herself.*

Vice, abhorrent v. - There is a vice that most I do abhor, and most desire should meet the blow of justice.
"There is a vice that most I do abhor,
And most desire should meet the blow of justice" (MFM.2.2)
The quote can apply to any aspect of behavior or any vice that you condemn.
In the play. *Isabella approaches Angelo to intercede for the life of her brother, condemned to die for fornication. She starts by agreeing with Angelo that the vice is abhorrent.*

Vice, v. counterbalanced by virtue – … his vice is to his virtue a just equinox…
"…his vice;
'Tis to his virtue a just equinox,
The one as long as the other." (OTH.2.3)
In the play. *Iago tells Montano, a Cyprus authority that Cassio's drunkenness balances out his virtues as a military leader.*

Vice, v. unchecked tends to spread - … vice repeated's like the wandering wind, blows dust in others' eyes, to spread itself.
"…**vice repeated's like the wandering wind,
Blows dust in others' eyes, to spread itself.**" (PER.1.1)
See also 'Kings, authority, vices of k. better kept secret - Who has a book of all that monarchs do, he's more secure to keep it shut, than shown…'
In the play. *Pericles solved the riddle but the solution is the discovery of the incestuous relationship between King Antiochus and his daughter. Pericles declines to explain the true meaning of the riddle but lets Antiochus know indirectly that he understood very well what is going on.*

Vice-President, VP's importance dimmed when President returns - So doth the greater glory dim the less...
NERISSA When the moon shone, we did not see the candle.
PORTIA So doth the greater glory dim the less:
A substitute shines brightly as a king
Unto the king be by, and then his state
Empties itself, as doth an inland brook
Into the main of waters ." (MOV.5.1)
'So doth the greater glory dim the less' can be a sporting way to acknowledge the better performance of your adversary.
In the play. *Arriving back to her home in Belmont Portia is in a philosophizing mood. The light of a candle inspires her with (2) generalizations. For the other see 'Deed, a good d. shines in a bad world'.*

Victory, a great v. - ... It is a conquest for a prince to boast of.
"In faith,
It is a conquest for a prince to boast of." (KHIV.p1.1.1)
Make it part of your congratulations for a splendid achievement.
In the play. *Westmoreland comments on the victories of the forces of Henry IV.*

Victory, confidence in v. against odds - ... though the odds be great, I doubt not, uncle, of our victory.
" Five men to twenty! -- though the odds be great,
I doubt not, uncle, of our victory." (KHVI p3.1.2)
Incite ardor when starting from an apparent weak position. Omit 'uncle'.
In the play. In the play. *At Sandal Castle, York is confident of victory (but he will prove wrong) and says so to his uncle Edward*

Victory, proud of one's v. - ... may justly say, with the hook-nosed fellow of Rome, 'I came, saw, and overcame.
"...he saw me, and yielded; that I may justly say, with the hook-nosed fellow of Rome, 'I came, saw, and overcame.'" (KHIVp2.4.3)
In the play. *Falstaff gives a greatly magnified account of his capture of the rebel Coleville to the Lancaster*

Victory, still not believing to have won - ... Giddy in spirit, still gazing in a doubt whether these pearls of praise be his or no...
"Like one of two contending in a prize,
That thinks he hath done well in people's eyes,
Hearing applause and universal shout,
Giddy in spirit, still gazing in a doubt
Whether these peals of praise be his or no;
So, thrice fair lady, stand I, even so" (MOV.3.2)
In the play. *Bassanio, still in mild disbelief, has guessed the right basket thereby winning Portia's hand.*

Victory, taking advantage of the v., pursuing the enemy – Let us score their backs ... 'Tis sport to maul a runner.
Let us score their backs,
And snatch 'em up, as we take hares, behind:
'Tis sport to maul a runner." (AC.4.7)
In the play. *Antony has temporarily defeated the forces of Caesar Octavian. Scarus prompts to chase the fleeing enemy.*

Victory, v. celebrations - ... and let's away, to part the glories of this happy day.
"call the field to rest; and let's away,
To part the glories of this happy day." (JC.5.5)

See also 'Celebrations, c. for victory or any happy event - And he that throws not up his cap for joy…'
In the play. *Octavian to Antony inviting to celebrate their joint victory against Brutus at Philippi.*

Victory, v. dedication – And with submissive loyalty of heart, ascribes the glory of his conquest…
"And with submissive loyalty of heart
Ascribes the glory of his conquest got
First to my God and next unto your grace" (KHVI.p1.3.4)
Try, 'Like Talbot after the victory at Rouen I ascribe the glory of this success to….etc.
In the play. *In Paris, English Lord Talbot talks of himself in the third person like Bob Dole, and dedicated the victory to God and King (Henry VI).*

Victory, v. makes everything seem good - nothing can seem foul to those that win.
"For nothing can seem foul to those that win." (KHIV.p1.5.1)
Although in the play the reference is to the weather, in history this is often the justification for incredible crimes and massacres by the militarily superior party.
In the play. *Henry IV commenting on the weather conditions that predict a stormy day at the battle of Shrewsbury.*

Victory, v. on the cheap - So great a day as this is cheaply bought.
"So great a day as this is cheaply bought." (M.5.8)
In the play. *Siward reflects on the final victory of Malcolm's forces over Macbeth. This was a first impression because there were many victims, including young Siward, in Malcolm's army.*

Victory, v. or nothing - Either our history shall with full mouth speak freely of our acts…
"Either our history shall with full mouth
Speak freely of our acts, or else our grave,
Like Turkish mute, shall have a tongueless mouth,
Not worshipp'd with a waxen epitaph" (HV.1.2)
In the play. *Henry V is determined to conquer France.*

Victory, v. proclaimed and confidence in the future – This day is ours, as many more shall be.
"This day is ours, as many more shall be." (KHVI.p1.1.5)
In the play. *Joan of Arc as she leaves the baffled Talbot.*

Victory, v. remembered in future ages – Saint Alban's battle won by famous York shall be eternized in all age to come.
"Saint Alban's battle won by famous York
Shall be eternized in all age to come." (KHVI.p2.5.2)
Change 'Saint Alban's battle' for the accomplished feat and 'York' for the name of the accomplisher. See also 'Event, e. of historical importance - how many ages hence shall this, our lofty scene be acted over, in states unborn..'
In the play. *Warwick comments on the victory of the Yorkists over the forces of King Henry VI.*

Victory, v. that dignifies the times – O, such a day, so fought, so follow'd and so fairly won came not till now to dignify the times…
"O, such a day,
So fought, so follow'd and so fairly won,
Came not till now to dignify the times,
Since Caesar's fortunes!" (KHIV.p2.1.1)

Celebrate a fairly won victory.
In the play. *Lord Bardolph announces victory for the rebels at Shrewsbury but the news will prove false.*

Victory, winner, w. takes all – ... the fall of either makes the survivor heir of all.
"... the fall of either
Makes the survivor heir of all." (COR.5.6)
In the play. *A conspirator tells Aufidius that the allegiance of the Volsces will go to whoever survives, either Aufidius or Coriolanus.*

Villain, lover or v. - ... since I cannot prove a lover ... I am determined to prove a villain
"... since I cannot prove a lover,
To entertain these fair well-spoken days,
I am determined to prove a villain" (KRII.1.1)
Comment on a defector or turncoat.
E.G. 'Since he cannot prove a lover, he is determined.. villain'
In the play. *Mission statement by Richard III.*

Villain, the word of a v. - Some villain, ay, and singular in his art, hath done you both this cursed injury.
"Some villain, ay, and singular in his art,
Hath done you both this cursed injury." (CYM.3.4)
In the play. *Pisanio believes that some villain tricked Leonatus into believing that Imogen was unfaithful*

Villany, extreme v. - A very excellent piece of villany.
"A very excellent piece of villainy." (TA.2.3)
In the play. *The vile Aaron hides some gold in order to frame two innocent Titus' sons and accuse them of murder.*

Villany, self-effacement – I am alone the villain of the earth.
"I am alone the villain of the earth" (AC.4.6)
Sarcastic comment when they try to unfairly accuse you.
In the play. *Enobarbus abandons Antony, but Antony rewards him by making him share Antony's treasure. Enobarbus adds,*
O Antony,
Thou mine of bounty, how wouldst thou have paid
My better service, when my turpitude
Thou dost so crown with gold!

Violence, v. and cruelty rationalized - ...men are as the time is: to be tender-minded does not become a sword.
"....men
Are as the time is: to be tender-minded
Does not become a sword" (KL.5.3)
Quote as an example of how and why 'democratic governments' justify their crimes.
In the play. *Evil Edmund instructs a captain to murder the captured Cordelia. The rationale, to kill any remorse, is that the times, not the evil of man, call for the slaughter.*

Violence, v. threatened - .. (I'll) make a quagmire of your mingled brains.
"Your hearts I'll stamp out with my horse's heels,
And make a quagmire of your mingled brains." (KHVIp1.1.4)
Apply to the competition. 'Their hearts we'll stamp out with out horses' heels and make a quagmire of their mingled brains.'
In the play. *Talbot's intentions towards the French. A messenger has just come in to announce the presence of the Pucelle among the French forces. Salisbury has been hit by French fire.*

Virginity as a waste - ..for beauty starved with her severity cuts beauty off from all posterity.
BENVOLIO Then she hath sworn that she will still live chaste?
ROMEO She hath, and in that sparing makes huge waste,
For beauty starved with her severity
Cuts beauty off from all posterity.
(RJ.1.1)
This is a recurring theme in Shakespeare's plays, see also entries on 'Pregnancy'. The notion seems outrageously out of fashion. Still, you may extract the last two lines changing 'her' to 'your' as it applies, 'For beauty starved with your severity….posterity'
In the play. *Romeo's current girlfriend Rosaline is unassailable.*

Virginity, determination to keep it at all costs - If fires be hot, knives sharp, or waters deep, untied I still my virgin knot will keep.
"If fires be hot, knives sharp, or waters deep,
Untied I still my virgin knot will keep." (PER.4.2)
In the play. *Notwithstanding the place where she was sold to by pirates, Marina is determined to maintain her virginity.*

Virginity, exhortation to v. - ..but if thou dost break her virgin-knot before all sanctimonious ceremonies…
"….take my daughter: but
If thou dost break her virgin-knot before
All sanctimonious ceremonies may
With full and holy rite be minister'd,
No sweet aspersion shall the heavens let fall
To make this contract grow: but barren hate,
Sour-eyed disdain and discord shall bestrew
The union of your bed with weeds so loathly
That you shall hate it both" (TEM.4.1)
In the play. *Prospero to Ferdinand who will marry Miranda. Ferdinand complies and adds that no place, occasion or temptation "shall never melt mine honour into lust".*

Virginity, loss of v. not recommended – … weigh what loss your honour may sustain …
"…weigh what loss your honour may sustain,
If with too credent ear you list his songs,
Or lose your heart, or your chaste treasure open
To his unmaster'd importunity"
(H.1.3)
In the play. *Words of advice from Laertes to his sister Ophelia.*

Virginity, negative characteristics of v. – … earthlier happy is the rose distill'd…
"…earthlier happy is the rose distill'd,
Than that which withering on the virgin thorn
Grows, lives and dies in single blessedness" (MND.1.1)
In the play. *Theseus threatens Hermia with a life in a nunnery if she does not follow her father's wishes and then stresses the limitation of life as a nun.*

Virginity, negative characteristics of v. - … virginity is peevish, proud, idle, made of self-love…
"Besides, virginity is peevish, proud, idle, made of self-love, which is the most inhibited sin in the canon. Keep it not; you cannot choose but loose by't: out with 't!" (AWEW.1.1)
In the play. *More arguments by Parolles against virginity. 'Peevish' = 'silly'*

Virginity, not politically correct - It is not politic in the commonwealth of nature, to preserve virginity.
"It is not politic in the commonwealth of nature, to preserve virginity. Loss of virginity is rational increase and there was never virgin got till virginity was first lost…..Virginity by being once lost
may be ten times found; by being ever kept, it is ever lost: 'tis too cold a companion; away with 't!"
(AWEW.1.1)
A possible argument in case the issue may come up.
In the play. *The worthless Parolle and the virtuous Helen exchange some banter.*

Virginity, time dependent value of v. - 'Tis a commodity will lose the gloss with lying; the longer kept, the less worth.
"'Tis a commodity will lose the gloss with lying; the longer kept, the less worth." (AWEW.1.1)
A further argument if the previous one failed. See 'Virginity, not politically correct'.
In the play. *The worthless Parolle and the virtuous Helen exchange some banter.*

Virginity, v. as a dried fruit – …your old virginity, is like one of our French withered pears, it looks ill, it eats drily…
"…your old virginity, is like one of our French withered pears, it looks ill, it eats drily; marry, 'tis a withered pear; it was formerly better; marry, yet 'tis a withered pear: will you anything with it?"
(AWEW.1.1)
In the play. *Parolle engages Helena on a silly discussion on this subject.*

Virginity, v. potentially traded for high life – I would… and so would you for all this spice of your hypocrisy.

ANNE By my troth and maidenhead,
I would not be a queen.
Old Lady Beshrew me, I would,
And venture maidenhead for't; and so would you,
For all this spice of your hypocrisy.
(KHVIII.2.3)
In the play. *Anne Boleyn compares her (so far) humble life with that of the soon to be divorced Queen Catherine.*

Virtue, how to acquire it - Assume a virtue, if you have it not.
"Assume a virtue, if you have it not."
(H.3.4)
See also 'Custom, how to reverse a c. or bad habit - That monster, custom, who all sense doth eat…'
In the play. *After a tempestuous volley of accusations, Hamlet tells his mother to forego the nuptial bed that evening. This would be a virtuous act, though by her previous marrying King Claudius, she proved not virtuous.*

Virtue, perception of v. depending on contemporary culture – So our virtues lie in the interpretation of the time.
"… So our virtues
Lie in the interpretation of the time."
(COR.4.7)
Show that even virtue is relative and depends on current cultural beliefs. See also 'Misjudgement, transposition of values - … What we oft do best… is not ours, or not allow'd; what worst … is cried up for our best act.' *** 'Thought, t. as the arbiter of good or bad - .. for there is nothing either good or bad, but thinking makes it so.'
In the play. *Aufidius discusses with his lieutenant the reasons why Coriolanus could not make the best of his chances with the Romans, that is, to become their leader.*

Virtue, sin and their interrelationship, maxim - Any thing that's mended is but patched : virtue that transgresses

is but patched with sin; and sin that amends is but patched with virtue. "Any thing that's mended is but patched: virtue that transgresses is but patched with sin; and sin that amends is but patched with virtue." (TN.1.5)
Use as an example of what appears to be different but is actually the same thing. See also 'Excuse, e. often worse than the fault - .. And oftentimes excusing of a fault, ...discredit more in hiding of the fault than did the fault before it was so patched.'
In the play. *The clown answers in jest to Olivia's somewhat angry address. She is angry because he is late.*

Virtue, v. and smartness as assets - ... Virtue and cunning were endowment greater than nobleness and riches...
"...I hold it ever,
Virtue and cunning were endowment greater
Than nobleness and riches: careless heirs
May the two latter darken and expend;
But immortality attends the former, Making a man a god." (PER.3.2)
Praise the inherent virtue of properly acquired merit. 'Cunning' here has a positive meaning, i.e. 'ability' or 'knowledge'.
In the play. *Pericles and Thaisa marry and sail back to Tyre. But another storm wrecks Pericles' ship. Thaisa gives birth to daughter Marina in the middle of the storm. Then Thaisa is given for lost and is swept ashore near Ephesus. Cerimon, who says these lines, is a renowned physician who will save and revive Thaisa.*

Virtue, v. as opposed to lust – But virtue, as it never will be moved...
"But virtue, as it never will be moved,
Though lewdness court it in a shape of heaven,
So lust, though to a radiant angel link'd,
Will sate itself in a celestial bed,
And prey on garbage." (H.1.5)
In the play. *The Ghost speaks to Hamlet, referring to his murderous brother's lust and to the too quickly yielding Queen.*

Virtue, v. inspires courage - Virtue is bold and goodness never fearful.
"Virtue is bold, and goodness never fearful." (MFM.3.1)
Expression of confidence in the outcome and of your determination to go ahead as your cause is just.
In the play. *The Duke reinforces Isabel's statement that she is prepared to do anything that is honorable to save her brother's life.*

Virtue, v. nobler than revenge - ..the rarer action is in virtue than in revenge.
" ..The rarer action is
In virtue than in vengeance." (TEM.5.1)
Make a point that revenge may not be the most advisable course of action.
In the play. *Prospero would have good reasons for revenge against the usurper Antonio but his aim is just to have him repent of his actions.*

Virtue, vice and their relationship - Virtue itself turns vice, being misapplied and vice sometimes is by action dignified.
"Virtue itself turns vice, being misapplied,
And vice sometimes is by action dignified.
Within the infant rind of this small flower
Poison hath residence and medicine power" (RJ.2.3)
Urge moderation against excess.

In the play. *Fr. Lawrence is a naturopath and dabbles in chemistry and herbal pharmacology. Here he reminds himself of a perennial truth that what is done properly is generally good and that even error or vice is somewhat redeemed by proper action. He then proceeds to give an analogy encompassing, nature, botany and medicine. See 'Man and his conflicting nature, a conflict of good and bad'. 'Rind' = 'Skin of vegetables'.*

Visibility, advantages for authorities of not being seen too often - … Such as is bent on sun-like majesty when it shines seldom in admiring eyes.
"…He was but as the cuckoo is in June,
Heard, not regarded; seen, but with such eyes
As, sick and blunted with community,
Afford no extraordinary gaze,
Such as is bent on sun-like majesty
When it shines seldom in admiring eyes." (KHIV.p1.3.2)
Ironic explanation for a boss rarely seen, e.g. 'Perhaps he is like Henry IV who showed himself rarely to the people so that they could "afford the extraordinary gaze such as is bent…… eyes.' Or an ironic reply to 'We haven't seen you too often lately'. Use the last two lines and follow with an explanation.
In the play. *K. Henry compares his style to that of his predecessor King Richard II. He explains to his son the advantages to be seen rarely but sumptuously. To be seen often is like too much sugar, (see also 'Dieting, too much sugar, excess brings distaste'). Being seldom seen induces a sense of awe as expressed by the 'extraordinary gaze'*

Vision, intuition - In my mind's eye, Horatio.
HAMLET. My father!--methinks I see my father
HORATIO Where, my lord?
HAMLET In my mind's eye, Horatio. (H.1.2)

Answer to 'Where did you see this?' when you just have a strong intuition.
In the play. *Hamlet confides to Horatio to have had the impression of seeing his (Hamlet's) deceased father (even before the actual apparition of the ghost)*

Visit, v. or call, reason for – I come, in kindness and unfeigned love…to crave a league of amity.
"I come, in kindness and unfeigned love,
First, to do greetings to thy royal person;
And then to crave a league of amity" (KHVI.p3.3.3)
Answer to 'What are you here for?'
In the play. *Warwick calls on King Lewis of France to arrange the marriage between the King's sister and the new King Edward of York.*

Vocation, following one's v. natural – 'tis no sin for a man to labour in his vocation.
"… 'tis no sin for a man to labour in his vocation." (KHIV.p1.1.2)
Answer to 'Why did you get into this business?' or similar.
In the play. *Falstaff responds to a quip by the prince of Wales. The 'vocation' here is purse-snatching. In turn, this will lead to the caper at Gadshill where Falstaff will also prove a coward.*

Voice, her excellent singing v. - … Uttering such dulcet and harmonious breath that the rude sea grew civil at her song…
"…once I sat upon a promontory,
And heard a mermaid on a dolphin's back
Uttering such dulcet and harmonious breath
That the rude sea grew civil at her song
And certain stars shot madly from their spheres,
To hear the sea-maid's music" (MND.2.1)

Extract a compliment, e.g. 'You utter such dulcet and harmonious breath…etc.'
In the play. *Oberon reminds Puck about a good singing mermaid.*

.Voice, her v. creating a heavenly harmony.
"…had he heard the heavenly harmony
Which that sweet tongue hath made" (TA.2.4)
Answer to 'Do you like my voice?' 'It's heavenly harmony which your sweet tongue does make'
In the play. *Andronicus says that only a monster could have cut Lavinia's tongue.*

Voice, her v. delightful, like a melodious bird - O, that delightful engine of her thoughts, that blabb'd with such pleasing eloquence…
"O, that delightful engine of her thoughts,
That blabb'd with such pleasing eloquence ..
Where, like a sweet melodious bird, is sung
Sweet varied notes, enchanting every ear!" (TA.3.1)
Changing the past tense to the present and 'blabb'd' into 'speaks' to prevent misunderstandings, you can use the lines as a compliment to a lady for her voice, conversation or both. Also answer to 'Do you like my voice?' – See also 'Music, flowers, voice, compliment - That strain again; it had a dying fall..'
In the play. *Marcus recalls the pleasing voice of Lavinia who can no longer speak, having her tongue been cut off by Tamora's sons. Technically, the reference is to Lavinia's tongue, but voice is a better attribute for a compliment.*

Voice, her v. feminine – … gentle and low, an excellent thing in a woman.
"… Her voice was ever soft,
Gentle and low, an excellent thing in a woman." (KL.5.3)
Use with fancied woman (if it applies) with minor changes, 'Your voice is ever soft, gentle and low…..woman'
In the play. *Lear of his daughter Cordelia..*

Voice, her v. harmonious and irresistible - The harmony of your tongue hath into bondage brought my too diligent ear.
"The harmony of your tongue hath into bondage
Brought my too diligent ear." (TEM.3.1)
This always works, especially if her voice is nothing to boast about. Ladies like you to appreciate in them what they know may not be so likeable. Select a few complimentary quotes. One for ears, hand, eyes, lips – your choice – and end with this one. That 'diligent' suggests discernment and great taste, that 'harmony' ennobles the 'tongue'. No damage will occur and the spirit and sense will be maintained if, instead of 'too diligent ear' you say 'two diligent ears'.
Dealing with ladies' manners and social demeanor Ovid says, 'Would you believe it? Women learn even how to laugh; here too seemliness is required of them. Let the mouth be but moderately opened, let the dimples on either side be small, and let the bottom of the lip cover the top of the teeth. Nor should they strain their sides with continuous laughter, but laugh with a feminine thrill.' (AOL.3)
In the play. *Ferdinand is deeply in love with Miranda and explains why.*

Voice, comparing her to a nightingale – My nightingale…
"My nightingale,
We have beat them to their beds…" (AC.4.8)

Compliment her voice, or, if she is dark, the address may indicate your appreciation for her dark hair.
In the play. *Antony, in a good mood after a temporary victory on Octavian's forces returns to Cleopatra's palace and greets her.*

Voice, her v. like music and with a foreign accent - ... for thy voice is music and thy English broken...
"Come, your answer in broken music; for thy voice is music and thy English broken; therefore, queen of all, Katharine, break thy mind to me in broken English; wilt thou have me?" (KHV.5.2)
See also entries for 'Foreign girls'.
In the play. *King Henry woos Katharine of France.*

Voice, her v. makes the ears hungry for it - ... another Juno, who starves the ears she feeds and makes them hungry, the more she gives them speech.
"....another Juno, who starves the ears she feeds
And makes them hungry, the more she gives them speech." (PER.5.1)
Answer to 'Do you like my singing?' Or get this ready for when she calls on the phone, "I am so glad you called, of your voice I can say you are like another Juno, who…..speech." Or you can shorten to, "your voice starves the ears she feeds….speech."
Says Ovid, 'A persuasive thing is song; let women learn to sing - with many, voice instead of face has been their procuress.' (AOL.3)
In the play. *Pericles, observing Marina as she sings, thinks she looks like his wife Thaisa who is believed dead. Her voice was like Juno's. It turns out that Marina is Pericle's daughter.*

Voice, her v. soothing - O! she will sing the savageness out of a bear.

"O! she will sing the savageness out of a bear" (OTH.4.1)
Answer to 'what do you think of my voice?' 'You will sing… bear'.
In the play. *Othello believes Iago's fabrications about Desdemona's alleged unfaithfulness but still thinks of her natural graces.*

Voice, provocative v. – And when she speaks, is it not an alarum to love?
"And when she speaks, is it not an alarum to love?" (OTH.2.3)
You may use 'call' instead of 'alarum'. See also entries for 'Woman, provocative w.'
In the play. *Iago discusses Desdemona with Cassio.*

Voice, v. as pleasure, honeyed sentences - ... when he speaks, the air, a charter'd libertine, is still...
"…when he speaks,
The air, a charter'd libertine, is still,
And the mute wonder lurketh in men's ears,
To steal his sweet and honeyed sentences." (HV.1.1)
Some extracting and gender change needed here. As a compliment to a lady who has said something you particularly like (or expect her to say), e.g. "O, what sweet and honeyed sentences." Or, 'when you speak, the air is still and the mute wonder lurketh in my ears to steal your sweet and honeyed sentences."
In the play. *The archbishop of Canterbury praises Henry V.*

Voice, v. unmistakable - The shepherd knows not thunder from a tabour...
"The shepherd knows not thunder from a tabour
More than I know the sound of Marcius' tongue
From every meaner man." (COR.1.6)
In the play. *Cominius has no difficulty in recognizing the voice of Coriolanus.* 'Tabour' = 'drum'

Voice, v. recognition - .. if you knew his pure heart's truth, you would quickly learn to know him by his voice.
SILVIA Who is that that spake?
PROTEUS One, lady, if you knew his pure heart's truth,
You would quickly learn to know him by his voice. (TGV.4.2)
Answer to 'Is it you?'
In the play. *The false and hypocritical Proteus has organized a sing-a-gram at Silvia's window and she inquires who addressed her when the music finished.*

Voice, v. recognition - My ears have not yet drunk a hundred words of that tongue's utterance, yet I know the sound.
"My ears have not yet drunk a hundred words
Of that tongue's utterance, yet I know the sound." (RJ.2.2)
Use romantically or sarcastically – the latter case particularly if someone has a funny voice.
In the play. *Romeo, until now, hidden in Juliet's garden, reveals his presence to her*

Voice, v. unmistakable - The shepherd knows not thunder from a tabour...
"The shepherd knows not thunder from a tabour
More than I know the sound of Marcius' tongue
From every meaner man." (COR.1.6)
In the play. *Cominius has no difficulty in recognizing the voice of Coriolanus. 'Tabour' = 'drum'⊤*

Wager, w. of life to sustain an opinion - ...to wager she is honest lay down my soul at stake.
"I durst, my lord, to wager she is honest,
Lay down my soul at stake" (OTH.4.2)
Reinforce your belief, e.g. 'To wager ...I would lay down my soul at stake'
In the play. *Emilia attempts to calm down Othello, who is inflamed with jealousy.*

Wake-up, invitation to an early rising - Stir with the lark to-morrow, gentle Norfolk.
"Stir with the lark to-morrow, gentle Norfolk" (KRIII.5.3)
In the play. *Richard III instructs Norfolk the night before the battle at Bosworth Field.*

Wake up, metaphor - Trumpet, blow loud, send thy brass voice through all these lazy tents.
"Trumpet, blow loud,
Send thy brass voice through all these lazy tents" (TC.1.3)
In the play. *Aeneas brings a message to the Greek camp to have a trial of strength between the nest of the Greeks and Hector.*

Waking up early, reaction to being woken up too early - What misadventure is so early up that calls our person from our morning's rest?
"What misadventure is so early up,
That calls our person from our morning's rest?" (RJ.5.3)
In the play. *The prince of Verona is waken up by watchmen who alert him about the dreadful business involving the Capulets and Montagues whereby Romeo, Juliet and Paris are all dead.*

Waking up early, possible reasons why - .. thy earliness doth me assure thou art up-roused by some distemperature; or if not so, then here I hit it right...
"...thy earliness doth me assure
Thou art up-roused by some distemperature;
Or if not so, then here I hit it right,
Our Romeo hath not been in bed to-night." (RJ.2.2)
See also 'Sleep, s. patterns and logic whereby late sleep is actually early rising -

.. not to be abed after midnight is to be up betimes.' – 'Sleep, prevented by care, unimpeded in the young - .. and where care lodges, sleep will never lie.'
In the play. *Friar Lawrence, based on his wide knowledge of human nature and the natural world diagnoses the reasons for Romeo's early arrival.*

Waking up, why so early? – It argues a distempered head so soon to bid good morrow to thy bed
"…it argues a distemper'd head
So soon to bid good morrow to thy bed" (RJ.2.3)
Make the observation when you question the need of getting up so early, as you would like to sleep a little bit more.
In the play. *Friar Lawrence wonders why Romeo is up so early as little sleep is more typical of old men. See 'Sleep, prevented by care, unimpeded in the young - .. and where care lodges, sleep will never lie.'*

Walk, a w. proposed. See 'Sightseeing, looking at people - … we'll wander through the streets and note the qualities of people.'

Walk, impossibility to w. any further - I can go no further, sir; my old bones ache.
"…I can go no further, sir;
My old bones ache" (TEM.3.3)
In the play. *Gonzalo has had enough of walking through the island.*

Walk, tiresome country w. – These high wild hills and rough uneven ways draws out our miles…
"These high wild hills and rough uneven ways
Draws out our miles, and makes them wearisome" (KRII.2.3)
In the play. *Northumberland to Bolingbroke on their way to Ravenspurgh where they will confront King Richard II.*

Walk, walking proudly by a horse, but applicable also to men – So proudly as if he disdain'd the ground.
"So proudly as if he disdain'd the ground" (KRII.5.5)
Body language of a pompous or self obsessed person.
In the play. *At Pomfret prison, Richard II inquires of his groom how Richard's horse ambled when ridden by Bolingbroke and the groom replies.*

Walking, tired of w. - My legs can keep no pace with my desires, here will I rest me…
"My legs can keep no pace with my desires,
Here will I rest me, till the break of day." (MND.3.2)
When you are tired and refuse to walk any further
In the play. *Hermia, tired in the wood decides to rest.*

Walking, w. as a relaxation exercise - … a turn or two I'll walk to still my beating mind.
"…a turn or two I'll walk,
To still my beating mind." (TEM.4.1)
In the play. *Prospero, resolved to thwart Caliban's plot against him tells Ferdinand and Miranda that he needs some time alone.*

War - … to open the purple testament of bleeding war…
"…he is come to open
The purple testament of bleeding war…" (KRII.3.3)
In the play. *King Richard to the rebel Northumberland referring to Bolingbroke.*

War, call to battle – … set the teeth and stretch the nostril wide…
"…set the teeth and stretch the nostril wide,
Hold hard the breath and bend up every spirit

To his full height. On, on, you noblest English." (HV.3.1)
See also 'Start line, at the start line - the game's afoot…follow your spirit…'
In the play. *Henry V to the troops before Harfleur in France.*

War, cold w. strategy – … frowns, words and threats shall be the war that Henry means to use.
"Cousin of Exeter, frowns, words and threats
Shall be the war that Henry means to use." (KHVI.p3.1.1)
In the play. *King Henry proposes a more subtle (and it will prove ineffective) way of handling the pretensions to the throne by York.*

War, cry to w. – … let our bloody colours wave! And either victory, or else a grave.
"Sound trumpets! let our bloody colours wave!
And either victory, or else a grave." (KHVI.p3.2.2)
In the play. *Edward's final words before the battle.*

War, declaring w. - Turning the word to sword and life to death.
"Turning the word to sword and life to death." (KHIV.p2.4.2)
Acknowledge that your adversary is bent on battle.
In the play. *The Prince of Lancaster, son of King IV addresses the rebel Archbishop of York implying that the king favors the archbishop (sits within the monarch's heart). It is a trap, the Archbishop will take the bait.*

Wars, destructive effects of w. – … wasteful war shall statues overturn and broils root out the work of masonry.
"…
When wasteful war shall statues overturn,
And broils root out the work of masonry" (SON 55)

War, do you want war? - … will you again unknit this curlish knot of all-abhorred war?
"… will you again unknit
This curlish knot of all-abhorred war?" (KHIVp1.5.1)
In the play. *King Henry makes a last offer of peace to the rebel Worcester.*

War, end of war or quarrel - Grim-visaged war hath smooth'd his wrinkled front…
"Grim-visaged war hath smooth'd his wrinkled front…" (KRIII.1.1)
In the play. *Richard's beginning monologue. See 'Greetings, end of unhappiness – Now is the winter of our discontent, made glorious summer by this sun of York…'*

War, in praise of w. – This peace is nothing, but to rust iron, increase tailors, and breed ballad-makers…
SECOND SERVANT This peace is nothing, but to rust iron, increase tailors, and breed ballad-makers.
FIRST SERVANT Let me have war, say I; it exceeds peace as far as day does night; it's spritely, waking, audible, and full of vent. Peace is a very apoplexy, lethargy; mulled, deaf, sleepy, insensible; a getter of more bastard children than war's a destroyer of men. (COR.4.5)
Sweet music to the ears of the 'defense' industry.
In the play. *Servants in the Volscean camp exchange opinions.*

War, let there be war - O war, thou son of hell, whom angry heavens do make their minister…
O war, thou son of hell,
Whom angry heavens do make their minister,

Throw in the frozen bosoms of our part
Hot coals of vengeance." (KHVI p2.5.2)
Call for war.
In the play. *Young Clifford after his father died in the battle at the hand of the duke of York.*

War, let there be war - Sound all the lofty instruments of war…
"Sound all the lofty instruments of war,
And by that music let us all embrace;
For, heaven to earth, some of us never shall
A second time do such a courtesy." (KHIV.p1.5.2)
In the play. *Hotspur rallies his forces before the battle of Shrewsbury.*

War, let there be war – Strike up the drums and let the tongue of war plead for our interest…
"Strike up the drums; and let the tongue of war
Plead for our interest, and our being here." (KJ.5.2)
Ending to a motivational speech calling for the beginning of a campaign (political, marketing etc.)
In the play. *Lewis is ready for one more battle between the English and the French.*

War, need to be certain that w. is necessary before declaring it - Therefore take heed… how you awake our sleeping sword of war'.
"Therefore take heed how you impawn our person,
How you awake our sleeping sword of war" (KHV.1.2)
Caution before declaring battle. E.G. 'Let us be certain before we awake our sleeping sword of war'.
In the play. *King Henry to the Bishop of Canterbury who will show how Henry has a right to the throne of France.*

War, outcome of w. uncertain – …Thou know'st, great son, the end of war's uncertain.
"…Thou know'st, great son,
The end of war's uncertain…" (COR.5.3)
In the play. *Volumnia to her son Coriolanus who is planing to attack Rome with the help of the Volscean army.*

War, ready for w. – the cannons have their bowels full of wrath.
"The cannons have their bowels full of wrath,
And ready mounted are they to spit forth
Their iron indignation 'gainst your walls" (KJ.2.1)
In the play. *King John to the besieged citizens of Angiers.*

War, who is responsible when participating in a criminal war - …But if the cause be not good, the king himself hath a heavy reckoning to make
BATES … we know enough, if we know we are the kings subjects: if his cause be wrong, our obedience to the king wipes the crime of it out of us.
WILLIAMS. But if the cause be not good, the king himself hath a heavy reckoning to make, when all those legs and arms and heads, chopped off in battle, shall join together at the latter day and cry all 'We died at such a place;' some swearing, some crying for a surgeon, some upon their wives left poor behind them, some upon the debts they owe, some upon their children rawly left. I am afeard there are few die well that die in a battle; for how can they charitably dispose of any thing, when blood is their argument? (KHV.4.1)

In the play. *Two soldiers, overheard by the King, discuss the key issues of personal responsibility in war crimes.*

War, w. bloody and unnatural - ... I always thought it was both impious and unnatural that such immanity and bloody strife…
"…I always thought
It was both impious and unnatural
That such immanity and bloody strife
Should reign among professors of one faith." (KHVI p1.5.1)
In the play. *Henry V to Gloucester referring to the struggle between the English and the French.*

War, warmongering breath - Your breath first kindled the dead coal of wars..
"Your breath first kindled the dead coal of wars
Between this chastised kingdom and myself,
And brought in matter that should feed this fire;
And now 'tis far too huge to be blown out
With that same weak wind which enkindled it." (KJ.5.2)
In the play. *King Lewis to Card. Pandulph who, having first promoted war with England under the threat of excommunication, now proposes peace*

War, w. and revenge - .. let slip the dogs of war that this foul deed shall smell above the earth…
"And Caesar's spirit, ranging for revenge,
With Ate by his side come hot from hell,
Shall in these confines with a monarch's voice
Cry 'Havoc,' and let slip the dogs of war;
That this foul deed shall smell above the earth

With carrion men, groaning for burial." (JC.3.1)
Declare your intention to fight bitterly for your trampled rights. E.G. 'We will let slip the dogs of war…burial'.
In the play. *Antony talking to himself visualizes the revenge for the slaying of Caesar. Ate was the God of Mischief.*

War, w. in progress – … the nimble gunner with linstock now the devilish cannon touches…
"…the nimble gunner
With linstock now the devilish cannon touches,
And down goes all before them" (KHV.3.PROL.)
In the play. *The chorus explains that Henry was not happy with the peace proposals offered by the French, hence the gunner(s) are at work again. 'Linstock' = 'A stick to hold the gunner's match'.*

War, w. justified for a noble cause – The peace of heaven is theirs, that lift their swords in such a just and charitable war.
"The peace of heaven is theirs, that lift their swords
In such a just and charitable war." (KJ.2.1)
Toast to a good cause. It may not necessarily be a military war, e.g. a war on ignorance, prejudice etc.
In the play. *The war referred to by Austria should restore the rights of young Arthur to the throne of England.*

War, w. justified if intent is just – The arms are fair when the intent of bearing them is just.
"…the arms are fair,
When the intent of bearing them is just." (KHIVp1.5.2)
Retort to someone who is questioning your methods or approach to solve a critical problem Usually the excuse of warmongers.

In the play. *Hotspur addressing his allies before the battle with the forces of the Prince of Wales*

War, w. leader and charismatic following – He is their god: he leads them like a thing made by some other deity than nature...
"He is their god: he leads them like a thing
Made by some other deity than nature,
That shapes man better; and they follow him,
Against us brats, with no less confidence
Than boys pursuing summer butterflies,
Or butchers killing flies" (COR.4.6)
In the play. *The Roman Cominius tells Memenius how Coriolanus has defected to the Volsces and the Volsces follow him*

War, w. predicted - I do believe, statist though I am none, nor like to be, that this will prove a war.
"I do believe,
Statist though I am none, nor like to be,
That this will prove a war" (CYM.2.4)
Add a touch of modesty to your prediction on international affairs. Stop at 'nor like to be' if your forecast is for developments other than wars and proceed with your assessment or prediction.
In the play. *Now in Rome and conversing with host Philario, Posthumous Leonatus anticipates (correctly) that there will be war between Rome and Britain.*

War, w. preferable to love - He wears his honour in a box unseen...
"He wears his honour in a box unseen,
That hugs his kicky-wicky here at home;
Spending his manly marrow in her arms,
Which should sustain the bounds and high curvet
Of Mars' fiery steed." (AWEW.2.3)
Use as an exhortation to war or to general belligerence.
In the play. *Though a complete coward, Parolles exalts the virtues of war. 'Kicky-wicky' is old English slang for 'wife'. 'Curvet' is a synonym of 'bounds', here the back of Mars' galloping horse.*

War, w. prevention - This might have been prevented and made whole with very easy arguments of love...
"This might have been prevented and made whole
With very easy arguments of love,
Which now the manage of two kingdoms must
With fearful bloody issue arbitrate" (KJ.1.1)
In the play. *Q. Elinor, mother of King John, referring to Constance, mother of young Prince Arthur, who wants France for her son.*

War, w. unsought but forced on us - made us doff our easy robes of peace.
"....... You have deceived our trust;
An made us doff our easy robes of peace,
To crush our old limbs in ungentle steel." (KHIVp1.5.1)
Modify. 'So, you want to make us doff our easy robes of peace to crush.....steel.'
In the play. *K. Henry to the rebel Worcester prior to the battle of Shrewsbury.*

War, w. useless – ... and shows no cause without why the man dies.
"Two thousand souls and twenty thousand ducats
Will not debate the question of this straw:
This is the imposthume of much wealth and peace,
That inward breaks, and shows no

cause without
Why the man dies." (H.4.4)
Make a statement about the uselessness of war, especially when it is triggered by boredom rather than need for defence.
In the play. *Hamlet comments on the explanation given by a Norwegian captain who is going to fight the Poles for a piece of land worth nothing. 'Imposthume' = 'corruption', i.e. the corruption caused by 'much wealth and peace'.*

War, w. useless - …the toil of war, a pain that only seems to seek out danger…
"…the toil of war,
A pain that only seems to seek out danger
I' the name of fame and honour; which dies i' the search,
And hath as oft a slanderous epitaph
As record of fair act" (CYM.3.3)
In the play. *Belarius speaks to Guiderius and Arviragus who are anxious to leave the country life to lead a more active life at court. For other Belarius' insights on political life see 'Life, l. inside a corporation or the Washington belt – … the art of the court as hard to leave as keep…'*

War, w. useless w. - … We go to gain a little patch of ground that hath in it no profit but the name.
"Truly to speak, and with no addition,
We go to gain a little patch of ground
That hath in it no profit but the name.
To pay five ducats, five, I would not farm it" (H.4.4)
In the play. *A Norwegian captain tells Hamlet his views on the conquering expedition against Poland.*

Warning, gratitude for the w. – I thank thee who hath taught my frail mortality to know itself…
"I thank thee who hath taught
My frail mortality, to know itself. …

For death remembered should be like a mirror,
Who tells us, life's but a breath, to trust it, error." (PER.1.1)
Express a general truth or use as a satirical retort to a threat, e.g. 'You are threatening me with death but you see, death remembered should be….error.'
See also 'Life, l. inherently short and lasting but a moment - … And a man's life's no more than to say 'One.' – 'Time, t. and the inherent limited duration of everything - When I consider everything that grows holds in perfection but a little moment..'
In the play. *Antiochus has reminded Pericles of all those who died because they did not solve the riddle. Pericles takes the admonishment in stride, as an occasion to remember a general truth.*

Warning, response to w. that indicates mistrust – Make me not offended in your distrust.
"Make me not offended
In your distrust…
You shall not find,
Though you be therein curious, the least cause
For what you seem to fear:" (AC.3.2)
You wish to advise him who warns him that the warning is unnecessary.
In the play. *Octavian warns Antony to be nice and respectful to Octavia, Octavian's sister and newly married to Antony. This was a marriage of convenience that will so. Antony replies to Octavian's warning.*

Warning, safety w. better leave this place - Hie thee from this slaughter-house, lest thou increase the number of the dead.
"… hie thee from this slaughter-house,
Lest thou increase the number of the dead" (KRIII.4.1)

Advise to a colleague before a pending massive firing at the company due to downsizing or other.
In the play. *Widowed Queen Elizabeth warns Stanley her son to flee from England and to reach Richmond (later Henry VII), in France, to escape the plots of Richard III. 'Hie thee'='Move, make haste'*

Warmonger, w's frame of mind - I, in this weak piping time of peace have no delight to pass away the time.
"…I, in this weak piping time of peace have no delight to pass away the time.
Have no delight to pass away the time" (KRIII.1.1)
In the play. *Richard meditates on his strategy to acquire the throne.*

Warning – Stop being a portent of broached mischief to the unborn times.
"(will you stop being)
A prodigy of fear and a portent
Of broached mischief to the unborn times?" (KHIV.p1.5.1)
When attacking an adversary whose actions will cause harm.
In the play. *The rebel Worcester has come to parley with the King who reproaches him.*

Warning, you'll hear from me - The thunder of my cannon shall be heard.
"The thunder of my cannon shall be heard." (KJ.1.1)
Stall an answer or warn contender that you will react forcefully as applicable.
In the play. *King John replies to the French ambassador.*

Warning, w. lest the pain inflicted on others may fall on the inflicters - Take heed, for heaven's sake, take heed, lest at once the burthen of my sorrows fall upon ye.
"Take heed, for heaven's sake, take heed, lest at once

The burthen of my sorrows fall upon ye." (KHVIII.2.4)
In the play. *Queen Catherine to Cardinal Wolsey and Campeius who are behind her impending divorce from the King.*

Warning, w. not to use the memory of great men to justify or add mischief - … let 'em look they glory not in mischief, nor build their evils on the graves of great men…
"Yet let 'em look they glory not in mischief,
Nor build their evils on the graves of great men;
For then my guiltless blood must cry against 'em" (KHVIII.2.1)
In the play. *Unjustly condemned Buckingham forgives his enemies and adds a warning.*

Warning, w. to a doer of evil deeds - … whilst I can vent clamour from my throat I'll tell thee thou dost evil.
"…whilst I can vent clamour from my throat,
I'll tell thee thou dost evil" (KL.1.1)
In the play. *Lear to Kent who intervenes in favor of Cordelia.*

Wash, in need of a w. - As black as Vulcan in the smoke of war.
"As black as Vulcan in the smoke of war" (TN.5.1)
Alternate to 'I must take a shower', e.g. I am as black as….war'.
In the play. *The Duke Orsino recognizes Antonio whose face he remembers from a previous encounter. His face was black at the time.*

Washing a persistent stain - Out, damned spot! out, I say.
"Out, damned spot! out, I say!" (M.5.1)
In the play. *Lady Macbeth is completely mad and hallucinating. The spot is the blood of King Duncan, killed by Macbeth so as to acquire the crown of Scotland.*

Waste, determination to eliminate w. - The caterpillars of the commonwealth, which I have sworn to weed and pluck away.
"... Bushy, Bagot, and their complices
The caterpillars of the commonwealth,
Which I have sworn to weed, and pluck away." (KRII.2.3)
Modify. In a political campaign substitute for Bushy, Bagot etc. the name of your adversaries. It could equally apply to the name of company or subsidiary that you wish to close down.
In the play. *Bolingbroke is heading to Bristol castle hosting Bushy, Bagot and their accomplices.*

Watch, without a w. at night - I cannot, by the progress of the stars give guess how near to day.
"..I cannot, by the progress of the stars,
Give guess how near to day" (JC.2.1)
If you say 'give guess what time it is' you can use the quote whenever you are asked the time and do not have a watch with you.
In the play. *Brutus has fallen asleep and admits to servant Lucius of not knowing what time of night it is.*

We have seen better days - True is it that we have seen better days..
"True is it that we have seen better days…" (AYLI.1.7)
In the play. *Duke Senior to Orlando who rushed on the company branding a sword and mistaking the nature of the company assembled in the forest of Arden.*

Weak, feeling w. and unprotected – A naked subject to the weeping clouds…
"…A naked subject to the weeping clouds

And waste for churlish winter's tyranny." (KHIVp2.1.3)
Pessimistic answer to 'How do you feel?'
See also 'Engineering, civil e. - ..much more.. should we survey the plot of the situation and the model…'
In the play. *Lord Bardolph actually cheers up the rebels by describing how planning is important in any enterprise. He compares planning to the construction of a house – without proper planning the house remains 'a naked subject to the weeping clouds'. For the lines about planning see 'Planning, importance of p. - When we mean to build, we first survey the plot, then draw the model..' 'Churlish' = 'brutal, rough'.*

Weakness, group w. , in a weak position - … our lances are but straws, our strength as weak, our weakness past compare…
"But now I see our lances are but straws,
Our strength as weak, our weakness past compare,
That seeming to be most which we indeed least are" (TOS.5.2)
When it more useful to admit weakness than cultivating ideas or illusions of strength. See also 'Funding, inadequate funding for the project – There's but a shirt and a half in all my company…'
In the play. *Part of the declaration of husbands' rights by the now reformed Kathari*

Weakness, perception of w. - This milky gentleness and course of yours…
"This milky gentleness and course of yours
Though I condemn not, yet, under pardon,
You are much more attask'd for want of wisdom
Than praised for harmful mildness" (KL.1.4)
In the play. *Evil Goneril accuses her husband, the Duke of Albany, of weakness in dealing*

Welcome, anything you want - ..
welcome: if thou wantest any thing,
and wilt not call, beshrew thy heart
"..welcome: if thou wantest any thing,
and wilt not call, beshrew thy heart"
(KHIV p2,5.3)
In the play. *Shallow to Bardolph who is visiting with Falstaff. Shallow hopes to get a preferment at court with the help of Falstaff. 'Beshrew' = 'woe to'*

Welcome, going behind formality -
You are very welcome to our house, it must appear in other ways than words...
"You are very welcome to our house:
It must appear in other ways than words,
Therefore, I scant this breathing courtesy." (MOV.5.1)
A hurried welcome when you do not have much time for formal greetings, for example if many people are coming..
In the play. *Portia welcomes Antonio to Belmont.*

Welcome, rhetorical w. – Welcome, a curse begin at very root on's heart…'
"Welcome.
A curse begin at very root on's heart,
That is not glad to see thee!"
(COR.2.1)
See also "Celebrations, c. for victory or any happy event - And he that throws not up his cap for joy…'
In the play. *Menenius welcomes Coriolanus back from the victory at Corioli.*

Welcome, sincere w. - … but when you depart from me, sorrow abides, and happiness takes his leave.
Never came trouble to my house in the likeness of your grace: for trouble being gone, comfort should remain; but when you depart from me, sorrow abides, and happiness takes his leave." (MAAN.1.1)

Response to a guest who is afraid of disturbing you with his/her presence
In the play. *Don Pedro, Prince of Aragon visits with Leonato, Governor of Messina, who welcomes Pedro wholeheartedly.*

Welcome, w. as spring to earth - …
Welcome hither, as is the spring to the earth.
"…Welcome hither,
As is the spring to the earth." (WT.5.1)
In the play. *The long repented Leontes welcomes Florizel and Perdita at the court of Sicilia.*

Welcome, w. kiss. - I can express no kinder sign of love, than this kind kiss.
"Welcome, queen Margaret:
I can express no kinder sign of love,
Than this kind kiss." (KHVI.p2.1.1)
In the play. *Queen Margaret arrives from France to the court of England to marry Henry VI and he welcomes her.*

Welcome, w. to our house - All our services in every point twice done, and then done double…
"All our services
In every point twice done, and then done double,
Were poor and single business to contend
Against those honours deep and broad wherewith
Your majesty loads our house."
(M.1.6)
Lay it in thick with your boss whom you have invited to dinner. See also 'Gratitude, g. expressed for the appreciation of your g. - Too little payment for so great a debt'.
In the play. *Lady Macbeth responds to the words of gratitude expressed by King Duncan who is visiting at her castle.*

Welcome, w. with friendly threat – ... welcome: if thou wantest any thing, and wilt not call, beshrew thy heart.
"...welcome: if thou wantest any thing, and wilt not call, beshrew thy heart." (KHIV.p2.5.3)
See also 'Celebrations, c. for victory or any happy event - And he that throws not up his cap for joy...'
In the play. *Hoping to gain from Falstaff's acquaintance, Master Shallow welcomes Falstaff and his assistant Bardolph to whom with these lines he extends his welcome.*

Welcoming compliments - ...the appurtenance of welcome is fashion and ceremony..
"...the appurtenance of welcome is fashion and ceremony: let me comply with you in this garb." (H.2.2)
When a guests tries to minimize your welcoming efforts or concern. See also 'Ceremony, c. unnecessary among friends - Ceremony was but devised at first to set a gloss on faint deeds...' – 'Welcome, w. kiss'.
In the play. *The players contracted by Hamlet to perform the play 'The Murder of Gonzago' arrive at the palace and Hamlet greets them. 'Garb' is a synonym of 'ceremony'.*

Welfare, excesses of w. - ... here's them in our country of Greece gets more with begging than we can do with working.
"No, friend, cannot you beg? here's them in our country of Greece gets more with begging than we can do with working." (PER.2.1)
Comment on costume as applicable.
In the play. *After leaving Tharsus, a devastating storm destroys Pericles' fleet and he manages to swim ashore where he meets with 3 fishermen. He begs for help and this allows one of the fishermen to express a satiric opinion on Greece.*

Well being, everything is OK if she is OK - ... for nothing can be ill, if she be well.
"How fares my Juliet? that I ask again;
For nothing can be ill, if she be well." (RJ.5.1)
Answer to 'How are you?'- 'Nothing can be ill if you are well.'
In the play. *Balthazar arrives in Mantua from Verona and Romeo eagerly inquires about Juliet.*

What have I done? – I should make very forges of my cheeks that would to cinders burn up modesty...
"... What committed!
Committed! O thou public commoner!
I should make very forges of my cheeks,
That would to cinders burn up modesty,
Did I but speak thy deeds" (OTH.4.2)
In the play. *Othello answers Desdemona's question 'what ignorant sin have I committed?'. She is unaware of Othello's mad jealousy.*

Where is he/she? - I know not where; but wheresoever, I wish him well.
LUCIO ... but where is he, think you?
DUKE VINCENTIO I know not where; but wheresoever, I wish him well. (MFM.3.2)
In the play. *Unaware of the disguise, Lucio asks Duke Vicentio where he (Duke Vicentio) is. Disguises are a recurring feature in WS' plays.*

Whisperings, w. about bad deeds - Foul whisperings are abroad, unnatural deeds do breed unnatural troubles.
"Foul whisperings are abroad: unnatural deeds
Do breed unnatural troubles." (M.5.1)
Sow the seeds of doubt or reinforce a general concern. The company has made

a bad investment and there is rumor that many will be fired or a division closed.
See also 'Hypocrisy, h. and dishonesty exposed - foul deeds will rise though all the world o'erwhelm them, to men's eyes.' – 'Unnatural events as indication of the gravity of the times - .. they are portentous things unto the climate that they point upon'.
In the play. *Unable to cure Lady Macbeth, the doctor explains. The illness (unnatural troubles) is a result of the unnatural events or deeds.*

Who are you? – …I am that merry wanderer of the night.
"Thou speak'st aright;
I am that merry wanderer of the night." (MND.2.1)
Remove 'that'
In the play. *Puck confirms the guess of a Fairy as to Puck's identity*

Who are you? - A most poor man, made tame to fortune's blows…
"A most poor man, made tame to fortune's blows;
Who, by the art of known and feeling sorrows,
Am pregnant to good pity" (KL.4.6)
See also ''Attitude, a. towards the world, hating it – one… whom the vile blows and buffets of the world…'
In the play. *Edgar's answers to his blinded father Gloucester's question, 'who are you?'.*

Who are you? - What man art thou that thus bescreen'd in night so stumblest on my counsel?
"What man art thou that thus bescreen'd in night
So stumblest on my counsel?" (RJ.2.2)
Alternative to the question 'who are you?' or 'what are you doing here?
In the play. *Hidden in the garden and hearing Juliet's monologue where she confesses her love for him, Romeo introduces himself and Juliet is surprised.*

Who are you? - What the devil art thou? One that will play the devil, sir, with you.
AUSTRIA What the devil art thou?
BASTARD One that will play the devil, sir, with you (KJ.2.1)
Answer to 'who the devil?', 'what the devil'" or equivalent.
In the play. *Austria meets Ph. Faulconbridge outside the walls of Angiers*

Wickedness, w. painted in fair colors - .. with colours fairer painted their foul ends.
MIRANDA Wherefore did they not
That hour destroy us?
PROSPERO Well demanded, wench:
My tale provokes that question. Dear, they durst not,
So dear the love my people bore me, nor set
A mark so bloody on the business, but
With colours fairer painted their foul ends. (TEM.1.2)
When imperialistic countries invade other countries and kill thousands (or millions as in Vietnam), they do it to bring 'freedom' and 'democracy'.
In the play. *Prospero is giving daughter Miranda the history of their escape and exile in the island.*

Wife, answer to an angry w. - To offer war where they should kneel for peace
"To offer war where they should kneel for peace;
Or seek for rule, supremacy and sway,
When they are bound to serve, love and obey." (TOS.5.2)
Your position when your wife is angry, disgruntled or peevish, e.g. 'Why do you offer war when you should kneel for peace… …obey?'
In the play. *Katharina delivers a speech for the benefit of the other (less obedient) wives.*

Wife, complaining w. 'You do nothing in the house' – … for thy maintenance commits his body to painful labour…
"…for thy maintenance commits his body
To painful labour both by sea and land,
To watch the night in storms, the day in cold,
Whilst thou liest warm at home, secure and safe." (TOS.5.2)
On receiving the statement 'You do nothing in the house' (or similar) answer 'For thy maintenance I commit my body…..secure and safe'.
In the play. *The reformed 'shrew' Katharina makes a statement in favor of all husbands.*

Wife, duties of a wife, obedience as a subject to a prince - .. such duty as the subject owes the prince..
"Such duty as the subject owes the prince,
Even such, a woman oweth to her husband." (TOS.5.2)
Justify your wish to be obeyed, if you still subscribe to this somewhat obsolete point of views.
In the play. *Katharina's acquired idea of wifely behavior.*

Wife, no trust in w. – I will rather trust a Fleming with my butter… than my wife with herself.
"I will rather trust a Fleming with my butter, Parson Hugh the Welshman with my cheese, an Irishman with my aqua-vitae bottle, or a thief to walk my ambling gelding, than my wife with herself." (MWW.2.2)
'Aqua-vitae' is brandy.
In the play. *The jealous Mr. Ford does not trust his wife's honesty.*

Wife, praise for a good w. – O ye gods, render me worthy of this noble wife
"O ye gods,
Render me worthy of this noble wife!" (JC.2.1)
In the play. *Brutus, at the conclusion of his wife's appeal to him for his own health and welfare.*

Wife, w. that routinely outspeaks her husband - When she will take the rein I let her run but she'll not stumble.
"When she will take the rein I let her run
But she'll not stumble." (WT.2.3)
See also 'Women, talkativeness of w. unstoppable - .. thou are worthy to be hang'd, that wilt not stay her tongue…'
In the play. *Antigonus cannot stop his wife Paulina from challenging King Leontes to forego his jealous obsessions.*

Wife, wives' merriment not incompatible with their honesty – Wives may be merry, and yet honest too.
"Wives may be merry, and yet honest too" (MWW.4.2)
In the play. *Mrs. Ford and Page comment on the pranks they have played on Falstaff.*

Wig, false hair – … the dowry of a second head, the skull that bred them in the sepulchre.
"So are those crisped snaky golden locks
…
Upon supposed fairness, often known
To be the dowry of a second head,
The skull that bred them in the sepulchre" (MOV.3.2)
See also entries for 'Baldness'.
In the play. *Bassanio reasons on what should be the casket to choose, whose correct guessing will allow him to marry Portia.*

Wild-goose chase - Nay, if thy wits run the wild-goose chase, I have done.

"Nay, if thy wits run the wild-goose chase, I have done, for thou hast more of the wild-goose in one of thy wits than, I am sure, I have in my whole five: was I with you there for the goose?" (RJ.2.4)
Refuse to follow up or respond to a silly suggestion. Also a reminder of the Shakespearean origin of the term 'wild-goose chase'.
In the play. *Mercutio responds to some banter by Romeo.*

Will, mind over matter notwithstanding a state of debility – And like the rich hangings in a homely house.
"And, like the rich hangings in a homely house,
So was his will in his old feeble body". (KHVI p2.5.3)
Modify and adapt to yourself to indicate your will remains strong. Change 'his' to 'my'
In the play. *Richard Plantagenet of his father Salisbury.*

Will, w. or fancy prevailing over reason - .. if my reason will thereto be obedient, I have reason…
"I am (advised), and by my fancy: if my reason
Will thereto be obedient, I have reason;
If not, my senses, better pleased with madness,
Do bid it welcome." (WT.4.3)
When you are determined not to change your mind.
In the play. *Florizel answers to a prompting by Camillo to reflect on his actions, 'be advised'. Florizel will renounce his succession to the throne of Bohemia rather than violate his oath (and love) to Perdita.*

Will, w. prevailing over reason – … that would make his will lord of his reason.

CLEOPATRA Is Antony or we in fault for this?
ENOBARBUS Antony only, that would make his will
Lord of his reason." (AC.3.13)
Comment when an event indicates that will prevailed over reason.
In the play. *Antony followed Cleopatra when she abandoned the field of battle with her ship. He did not have to but 'made his will lord of his reason'*

Wind, extremely strong w. – Methinks the wind hath spoke aloud at land…
"Methinks the wind hath spoke aloud at land;
A fuller blast ne'er shook our battlements:
If it hath ruffian'd so upon the sea,
What ribs of oak, when mountains melt on them,
Can hold the mortise? " (OTH.2.1)
In the play. *Montano, governor of Cyprus comments on the tempest that swept away the Turkish fleet that threatened the island.*

Wind, venture without profit - Ill blows the wind that profits nobody.
"Ill blows the wind that profits nobody" (KHVI p3.2.5)
In the play. *In the battle of Towton a son has just killed his father. He discovers the fact when he tries to get whatever money was in possession of the slain enemy, i.e. his father.*

Wine, drink as a warmer-upper - Come, let me pour some sack to the Thames water; for my belly's as cold..
"Come, let me pour some sack to the Thames water; for my belly's as cold, as if I had swallowed snow-balls for pills to cool the reins." (MWW.3.5)
Justify your drinking as a cold fighting measure. Change 'Thames; to the applicable river or skip the reference to a river altogether.

In the play. *Falstaff never misses an occasion for a strong drink, in this case because his stomach is cold..*

Wine, drinking, unable to tolerate strong drinks - ... I have very poor and unhappy brains for drinking...
"...I have very poor and unhappy brains for drinking: I could well wish courtesy would invent some other custom of entertainment." (OTH.2.3)
In the play. *Cassio wants to decline Iago's invitation to drink for the state reasons.*

Wine, drinking, unable to tolerate strong drinks - It's monstrous labor when I wash my brain and it grows fouler.
"It's monstrous labor when I wash my brain
And it grows fouler." (AC.2.7)
A starter when you have been asked to give a speech after a good meal, served with good wine that you have liberally drunk
In the play *Octavian at Pompey's banquet does not take well to drinking.*

Wine, effects of w. - ... it raises the greater war between him and his discretion
"...But it raises the greater war between him and his discretion. (AC.2.7)
You wish to decline to have another drink. Change 'him' to 'me' and 'his' to 'my'.
In the play. *The servant refers to Lepidus, who after having denied yet another drink in the end takes it becoming even more drunk. This follows the exchange with Antony when Antony described a crocodile. See "Description, self-evident d.*

Wine, effects of w. - ... mine own tongue splits what it speaks.
".....mine own tongue
Splits what it speaks" (AC.2.7)

In the play. *Octavian feels intoxicated by the wine at Pompey's party.*

Wine, evil effects of w. - O God, that men should put an enemy in their mouths to steal away their brains!...
"O God, that men should put an enemy in their mouths to steal away their brains! that we should, with joy, pleasance revel and applause, transform ourselves into beasts!" (OTH.2.3)
Suitable as an introduction or a general line while addressing an AA meeting.
In the play. *Cassio meditates on the effects of drinks he took but could not handle.*

Wine, good w. – Good wine is a good familiar creature if it be well used; exclaim no more against it.
"Come, come, good wine is a good familiar creature if it be well used; exclaim no more against it." (OTH.2.3)
In defense of wine when drinking is attacked by zealots.
In the play. *Cassio rails against wine and Iago speaks in its defense.*

Wine, negative effects of w. - ... and drink, sir, is a great provoker of three things.
PORTER. ...and drink, sir, is a great provoker of three things.
MACDUFF. What three things does drink especially provoke?
PORTER. Marry sir, nose-painting, sleep and urine. Lechery, sir, it provokes, and unprovokes: it provokes the desire, but it takes away the performance. (M.2.3)
A good line for an after dinner speech, especially if drinking has been abundant and you yourself have actively participated in the potations. Should you be abstemious you can use the porter's explanation to suggest that you avoid

alcoholic drinks in order to maintain your vitality.
In the play. *The porter came late to open the door for Macduff. As an excuse, he says he had been drinking too much the night before.*

Wine, no water in it - (I am) one that loves a cup of hot wine with not a drop of allaying Tiber in't.
" (I am) one that loves a cup of hot wine with not a drop of allaying Tiber in't" (COR.2.1)
Answer (if you like your drinks straight) to questions "Straight or on the rocks?" or "Do you with to add water?" etc. Applies to wine as well as liquor – if the latter delete 'hot' and substitute 'a cup of hot wine' with 'a glass of whisky' or equivalent.
In the play. *Menenius gives an account of his own habits to the tribune Sicinius. Menenius goes on to tell a bit more about himself. See entries for 'Credentials, sincerity'.*

Wine, positive effects of w. – A good sherri-sack hath a two fold operation in it…
"A good sherris-sack hath a two fold operation in it. It ascends me into the brain; dries me there all the crude, dull and foolish vapours which environ it: makes it apprehensive, quick, forgetive, full of quick, nimble, fiery and delectable shapes; which deliver'd over to the voice (the tongue) which is the birth, becomes excellent wit.
The second property of an excellent sherris is, - the warming of the blood, which, before cold and settled, left the liver white and pale, which is the badge of pusillanimity and cowardice: but the sherris warms it, makes it course from the inward to the parts extremes. It illumines the face: which, as a beacon, gives warning to all the rest of this little kingdom, man to arms.

… If I had a thousand sons, the first human principle I would teach them should be to forswear thin potations, and to addict themselves to sack. " (KHIV.p2.2.3)
Substitute 'wine' for sherry-sack. Quote the complete sentence when delivering a speech after a good dinner or in answer to "Do you like wine?"
Notwithstanding the potential negative side effects of drinking (see 'Wine, negative effects of w.'), there is general consensus that wine is, on the whole, an ally to romance. Ovid says,
'Often has bright-hued Love with soft arms drawn to him and held down the horns of Bacchus (i.e. wine divinity) as he there reclined. Wine gives courage and makes men apt for passion; care flees and is drowned in much wine. Then laughter comes, then even the timid find audacity, then sorrow and care and the wrinkles of the brow depart.' At such time often have women bewitched the minds of men, and Venus in the wine has been fire in fire.' (AOL.1)
Equally, 'As real drunkenness does harm, so will feigned bring profit: make your crafty tongue stumble into stammering talk, so that, whatever you do or say more freely than you should may be put down to too much wine.' (AOL.1)
Tobias Venner (1577-1660), in his book 'The right way to live long' concurs with the advise to stay away from water, 'Water doth very greatly deject the appetite, destroy the natural heat, and overthrow the strength of the stomach.' German wines are somewhat the exception. For Mark Twain (1835-1910) "The Germans are exceedingly fond of Rhine wines; they are put in tall, slender bottles, and are considered a pleasant beverage. One tells them from vinegar from the label'

In the play. *Falstaff, redoubtable companion of the young Prince of Wales (the future Henry V) extols the benefits and the effects that a good drink.*

Wine, refusing more e. or drink - I am unfortunate in the infirmity, and dare not task my weakness with any more.
"I am unfortunate in the infirmity, and dare not task my weakness with any more." (OTH.2.3)
In the play. *Cassio regrets that he cannot drink any more due to his poor resistance to alcohol.*

Wine, selecting the company with whom to get drunk - …if I be drunk, I'll be drunk with those that have the fear of God, and not with drunken knaves.
"…if I be drunk, I'll be drunk with those that have the fear of God, and not with drunken knaves." (MWW.1.1)
Comment on a good wind to be drunk in good company.
In the play. *Slender makes a personal resolution, showing a certain distaste for his present company.*

Wine, teetotaler, reasons for not drinking - Every inordinate cup is unblessed and the ingredient is a devil.
"Every inordinate cup is unblessed and the ingredient is a devil."
Explain why you do not drink. It can apply to other drinks besides wine.
In the play. *Cassio refuses Iago's exhortation to drink. Cassio knows he cannot take wine.*

Wine, unacceptable statements made under the effects of w. - … we consider it was excess of wine that set him on…
"…we consider it was excess of wine that set him on;
And on his more advice we pardon him" (HV.2.2)
In the play. *Henry V forgives a soldier who had railed against him.*

Wine, w. and forgetfulness - … though I cannot remember what I did when you made me drunk…
"… though I cannot remember what I did when you made me drunk, yet I am not altogether an ass." (MWW.1.1)
A lighthearted statements of self-defense.
In the play. *Slender to Nym as they banter.*

Wine, w. as a catalyst for reconciliation - Give me a bowl of wine. In this I bury all unkindness.
"Give me a bowl of wine.
In this I bury all unkindness, Cassius." (JC.4.3)
In the play. *Brutus to Cassius after the two had words about Cassius' alleged briberies*

Wine, w. as a psychosomatic remedy against anger or depression – He shall taste of my bottle: if he have never drunk wine afore…
"He shall taste of my bottle: if he have never drunk wine afore will go near to remove his fit." (TEM.2.2)
In the play. *Stephano comments on the cantankerous Caliban. 'Afore'='Before'*

Wine, w. as a support for speech - … give me some wine, and let me speak a little.
"I am dying, Egypt, dying:
Give me some wine, and let me speak a little." (AC.4.15)
Use emphatically to ask for wine or other drink of choice. Change 'Egypt' to the applicable country.
In the play. *Antony gathers his last strengths to give a message to Cleopatra.*

Wine, w. as a tool for forgetting and making others forget - … memory, the warder of the brain, shall be a fume…
"… his two chamberlains

Will I with wine and wassails so convince,
That memory, the warder of the brain,
Shall be a fume, and the receipt of reason
A limbeck only." (M.1.7)
'Limbeck' means 'alambic' or 'still'. Substitute 'still' for 'limbeck'. Should you have drunk a bit too much and not be able to remember something extract, 'My memory, the warder of the brain is a fume' 'Wassails' are 'large candles lighted up during or especially for a party'
In the play. *Lady Macbeth will distract the King Duncan's servant so that Macbeth can assassinate the king without their presence.*

Wine, w. as an anti-depressant - Give me a bowl of wine, I have not the alacrity of spirit nor cheer of mind that I as wont to have.
"…Give me a bowl of wine.
I have not the alacrity of spirit
Nor cheer of mind that I as wont to have." (KRIII.5.3)
A justification for a hearty drink.
In the play. *A somewhat depressed King Richard must draw the battle plan at Bosworth Field.*

Wine, w. as an ingredient for a sense of humor - … nor a man cannot make him laugh; but that's no marvel, he drinks no wine.
"…nor a man cannot make him laugh; but that's no marvel, he drinks no wine." (KHIV p2, 4.3)
Use as an anecdotal reference in praise of a good wine. Or to chide a teetotaler.
In the play. *Falstaff's opinion of Lancaster, younger brother of the Prince of Wales*

Wine, w. as an instrument of the devil – O thou invisible spirit of wine, if thou hast no name to be known by, let us call thee devil.
"O thou invisible spirit of wine, if thou hast no name to be known by, let us call thee devil." (OTH.2.3)
Use at a party when you decline another drink
In the play. *Cassio regrets his drinking to excess, which caused trouble with Othello.*

Wine, w. as the distillate of summer - But flowers distilled though they with winter meet…
"But flowers distilled though they with winter meet,
Lose but their show, their substance still lives sweet." (SON.5)
A metaphor included in praise of the wine served by your host.

Wine, w. or drink of horrible quality – (A) leperous distilment, whose effect holds an enmity with blood of man.
"…leperous distilment; whose effect Holds such an enmity with blood of man" (H.1.4)
In the play. *The Ghost gives Hamlet details on how the Ghost, his father was killed by Hamlet's uncle.*

Wine, w. preferred – The juice of Egypt's grape shall moist this lip.
"The juice of Egypt's grape shall moist this lip:" (AC.5.2)
Answer to 'What do you drink?'
In the play. *Prior to being bitten by the pre-ordered adder, Cleopatra arraigns herself in imperial clothes and moistens her lips with wine.*

Winners and losers, loser defeated by himself - Not Caesar's valor hath

o'erthrown Antony but Antony's hath triumphed on itself.
ANTONY. Not Caesar's valor hath o'erthrown Antony,
   But Antony's hath triumphed on itself
CLEOPATRA: So it should be, that none but Antony
   Should conquer Antony (AC.4.15)
Anticipating your enemy's victory you take whatever action to deprive him of the satisfaction of victory over you – e.g. if you know that you are going to be fired and resign before that happens.
In the play. *Antony has stabbed himself to prevent being taken prisoner by Octavian.*

Winter, it feels like w. when she is away – Yet seem'd it winter still, and, you away, as with your shadow I with these did play.
"Nor did I wonder at the lily's white,
Nor praise the deep vermilion in the rose;
They were but sweet, but figures of delight,
Drawn after you, you pattern of all those.
Yet seem'd it winter still, and, you away,
As with your shadow I with these did play" (SON 98)

Winter, w. as a tamer (mellowing agent) of spirits - ... thou know'st, winter tames man, woman and beast.
CURTIS. Is she so hot a shrew as she's reported?
GREMIO. She was, good Curtis before this frost; but, thou know'st, winter tames man, woman and beast. (TOS.4.1)
Explain a woman's change in character. Or make a positive comment on the effects of winter or cold in general.
In the play. *Gremio's assessment of Katharina before her marriage to Petruchio. Grumio,*

Petruchio's servant is freezing in the new abode of Petruchio and wife Katharina.

Winter, w. nights, a method of spending them – In winter's tedious nights sit by the fire…
"In winter's tedious nights sit by the fire
With good old folks and let them tell thee tales
Of woeful ages long ago betided…" (KRII.5.1)
Answer to 'What are you going to do this winter?'
In the play. *King Richard to his Queen as he is led to prison after his dethroning by Bolingbroke.*

Win-win situation through a stratagem - ... the doubleness of the benefit defends the deceit from reproof.
" … the doubleness of the benefit defends the deceit from reproof." (MFM.3.1)
Justify or rationalize your plot. See also 'Advice, listen to my a. - ... fasten your ear on my advisings…'
In the play. *The Duke (in disguise) hatches a plan that will unmask Angelo's hypocrisy and save Claudio's life.*

Wisdom, w. only apparent and misguided - 'The fool doth think he is wise but the wise man knows himself to be a fool.
"'The fool doth think he is wise, but the wise man
knows himself to be a fool.'" (AYLI.5.1)
In the play. *Touchstone quotes a saying for the benefit of William who declares himself to be witty.*

Wisdom, request to deliver w. – ... now unmuzzle your wisdom.
"…now unmuzzle your wisdom." (AYLI.1.2)

Mildly ironic alternative to "Let us know" or 'Talk!' or 'Tell us what you think.'
In the play. *The fool but not-so-foolish Touchstone approaches Celia and Rosalind. Rosalind consults him.*

Wisdom, showing lack of wisdom but not lack of nobility - Unwisely, not ignobly, have I given.
"Unwisely, not ignobly, have I given." (PER.2.2)
Soften the impact of your error(s). Change 'given' with 'acted' or other applicable verb participle.
In the play. *Timon responds to servant-accountant Flavius who presents Timon with the effects of reckless bounty.*

Wisdom, w. absorbed with nursing milk - Were not I thine only nurse, I would say thou hadst suck'd wisdom from thy teat.
"…An honour! were not I thine only nurse,
I would say thou hadst suck'd wisdom from thy teat." (RJ.1.3)
Comment on an unexpected piece of wisdom by an unwise fellow. E.G. 'As the nurse said to Juliet, were not I…thy teat'.
In the play. *The Nurse is impressed by the answer Juliet gave to her mother when asked her views about marriage.*

Wisdom, w. and goodness not for the vile - Wisdom and goodness to the vile seem vile, filths savour but themselves.
"Wisdom and goodness to the vile seem vile:
Filths savour but themselves."
(KL.4.2)
Why good or socially beneficial ideas are rejected by some politicians.
In the play. *The Duke of Albany to his wicked wife Goneril. See also 'Contempt, c. for a person - …you are not worth the dust which the rude wind.'*

Wisdom, w. beyond a doubt - I doubt not of your wisdom.
"I doubt not of your wisdom." (JC.3.1)
Ironic preamble to really mean that you doubt his wisdom, "I doubt not of your wisdom but…"
In the play. *Antony answers a remark by Brutus as to why Caesar was assassinated.*

Wisdom, w. exemplary – … whose wisdom was a mirror to the wisest
"…Henry the Fourth,
Whose wisdom was a mirror to the wisest" (KHVI.p3.3.3)
In the play. *Oxford reminds Warwick of the rights by merit of the house of Lancaster to the throne of England.*

Wisdom, w. hidden behind apparent folly - He uses his folly like a stalking horse, and under the presentation of that, he shoots his wit.
"He uses his folly like a stalking horse, and under the presentation of that, he shoots his wit." (AYLI.5.4)
A judgment on a person, or as a retort to someone who accuses you of not being serious. See also 'Rudeness, r. explained - This rudeness is a sauce to his good wit…'
In the play. *Impressed by Touchstone's argument and classification of lies, the Duke expresses his assessment of the fool Touchstone.*

Wisdom, w. in caution with expectations - …and modest wisdom plucks me from over-credulous haste.
"… and modest wisdom plucks me
From over-credulous haste." (M.4.3)
Caution against excessive confidence. See also 'Doubt, d. as a symptom of wisdom - … modest doubt is call'd the beacon of the wise.'

In the play. *Malcolm gives up the pretense of being a sinner, pretense he assumed to test Macduff's reaction. Malcolm had told Macduff that he (Malcolm) would prove a horrible ruler. He wanted to see if Macduff would still go along with the idea of Malcolm becoming king. If so, it would be a proof that Macduff was pursuing personal interests. Therefore 'modest wisdom' had prompted Malcolm to test Macduff's reactions.*

Wisdom, w. in the young dangerous to themselves - So wise so young, they say, do never live long.
"So wise so young, they say, do never live long." (KRIII.3.1)
In the play. *Prince Edward made a cogent remark on how historical records can be passed verbally from generation to generation. Richard comments silently.*

Wisdom, w. prevailing over chance - Wisdom and fortune combating together...
"Wisdom and fortune combating together,
If that the former dare but what it can,
No chance may shake it." (AC.3.13)
In the play. *Thyreus, Octavian's ambassador's comment to Cleopatra, who has accepted without resistance to relinquish her kingdom to the victorious Octavian.*

Wisdom, words of w. to oneself, avoiding messy situation – ... But, Suffolk, stay; thou mayst not wander in that labyrinth...
"...But, Suffolk, stay;
Thou mayst not wander in that labyrinth;
There Minotaurs and ugly treasons lurk" (KHVI.p1.5.3)
In the play. *Suffolk fantasizes about having Princess Margaret for himself instead of delivering her as a bride for King Henry VI. Then he checks his own intent.*

Wisdom, yielding to w. - To wisdom he's a fool that will not yield.
"To wisdom he's a fool that will not yield." (PER.2.4)
Signal your agreement to a suggestion you approve of.
In the play. *In Tyre, the noblemen demand the presence of a leader. They want Helicanus to assume all the responsibilities of the absent king. Helicanus does not want to but suggests a compromise and the noblemen accept.*

Wish, w. to possess the power of lightning-thunderbolt - If I had a thunderbolt in mine eye, I can tell who should down.
"If I had a thunderbolt in mine eye, I can tell who should down." (AYLI.1.2)
Answer to a quip of which you are the subject
In the play. *Celia watching the wrestling match between Orlando and Charles. Celia roots for Orlando.*

Wishes, good w. plus compliment - they are worthy to inlay heaven with stars.
"The benediction of these covering heavens
Fall on their heads like dew! for they are worthy
To inlay heaven with stars." (CYM.5.4)
Compliment, e.g. 'You are worthy to inlay heaven with stars'. Modify slightly for a more agnostic slant when wishing success to a group, 'The gifts of these covering heavens fall on your heads... stars.'
In the play. *Belarius delivers Arviragus and Guiderius to their father king Cymbeline*

Wishes, w. for a happy day - The gods make this a happy day to Antony!
"The gods make this a happy day to Antony!" (AC.4.5)
In the play. *A soldier greets Antony.*

Wishes, w. for a long life - ... let Aeneas live ... thousand complete courses of the sun!
"... let Aeneas live,
If to my sword his fate be not the glory,
A thousand complete courses of the sun!" (TC.4.1)
In the play. *Aeneas visits the Greek Camp and has an exchange with the Greek Diomed.*

Wishes, w. of a long life – ... may he live longer than I have time to tell his years!
"... may he live
Longer than I have time to tell his years!" (KVIII.2.1)
In the play. *Buckingham, condemned to death via the machinations of Cardinal Wolsey, still has good words for the King Henry VIII.*

Wishes, w. for a repetition of success - And more such days as these to us befall!
"...and to London all,
And more such days as these to us befall!" (KHVIp2.5.3)
In the play. *Warwick is toasting to victory in the field against the forces of Henry VI.*

Wishes, w. of happiness ever increasing - ... that our loves and comforts should increase even as our days do grow.
"...that our loves and comforts should increase,
Even as our days do grow!" (OTH.2.1)
In the play. *Othello declared that his happiness at being reunited with Desdemona in Cyprus could not be exceeded by any other occasion. Desdemona disagrees and wishes still for increased happiness.*

Wishes, w. of happiness - Let grief and sorrow still embrace his heart that doth not wish you joy!
"Let grief and sorrow still embrace his heart,
That doth not wish you joy!" (TEM.5.1)
In the play. *Alonso, king of Naples, to the newlywed Ferdinand and Miranda.*

Wishes, w. of getting what is desired - God send every one their heart's desire!
"God send every one their heart's desire!" (MAAN.3.4)
In the play. *Margaret to her company.*

Wishes, w. of joy – Let grief and sorrow still embrace his heart that doth not wish you joy.
"Let grief and sorrow still embrace his heart
That doth not wish you joy" (TEM.5.1)
See also 'Celebrations, c. for victory or any happy event - And he that throws not up his cap for joy...'
In the play. *The repented Alonso offers hearty wishes to the newly-weds Ferdinand and Miranda.*

Wishes, w. of peace and prosperity - Enrich the time to come with smooth-faced peace...
"Enrich the time to come with smooth-faced peace,
With smiling plenty and fair prosperous days!" (KRIII.5.5)
In the play. *A victory speech by Richmond after defeating and killing Richard III at Bosworth Field.*

Wishes, w. of success during a travel away from home - Upon your sword sit laurel victory and smooth success be strewed before your feet.
"... Upon your sword
Sit laurel victory, and smooth success
Be strewed before your feet!" (AC.1.3)
Address boss, friend or colleague who is leaving for a business trip.
In the play. *Cleopatra to Antony while he is leaving for Rome.*

Wishes, w. that facts may follow words – ... and ever may your highness yoke together... my doing well with my well saying.
"And ever may your highness yoke together,
As I will lend you cause, my doing well
With my well saying!" (KHVIII.3.2)
In the play. *Cardinal Wolsey answers a compliment on good words by the King. See the King's answer in 'Words, w. that are no deeds - ... 'tis a kind of good deed to say well and yet words are no deeds.'*

Wishes, w. that facts may follow words - ... And your large speeches may your deeds approve...
"And your large speeches may your deeds approve,
That good effects may spring from words of love." (KL.1.1)
In the play. *Lear has banished Kent who rose to defend Cordelia. Here Kent addresses the two other sisters whose sincerity he doubts.*

Wishes, w. to have the power of persuasion - God give thee the spirit of persuasion and him the ears of profiting.
"Well, God give thee the spirit of persuasion and him the ears of profiting" (KHIV.p1.1.2)
In the play. *Falstaff wishes Poins good luck as to the effect of the message Poins will deliver to the Prince of Wales.*

Wishful thinking, political w.t. – ... My pity hath been balm to heal their wounds...
"...my meed hath got me fame:
I have not stopp'd mine ears to their demands,
Nor posted off their suits with slow delays;
My pity hath been balm to heal their wounds,
My mildness hath allay'd their swelling griefs,
My mercy dried their water-flowing tears;
I have not been desirous of their wealth,
Nor much oppress'd them with great subsidies.
Nor forward of revenge, though they much err'd:
Then why should they love Edward more than me?" (KHVI.p3.4.5)
A quotable example on how a well meaning and proven honest politician may be eclipsed by a scoundrel using the right 'image' and media coverage or support.
In the play. *Henry VI is not concerned that the masses may turn to the usurper Edward – he will prove wrong and naïve.*

Wit, sarcasm on someone's wit - Thy wit is as quick as the greyhound's mouth; it catches.
BENEDICK Thy wit is as quick as the greyhound's mouth; it catches.
MARGARET (Your wit is) as blunt as the fencer's foils, which hit, but hurt not." (MAAN.5.2)
In the play. *Benedick comments on the sarcasm of Margaret.*

Wit, unaware of one's own wit – I shall ne'er be ware of mine own wit till I break my shins against it.
"I shall ne'er be ware of mine own wit till I break my shins against it." (AYLI.2.4)
Modest answer to 'You have a sense of humor'.
In the play. *Touchstone's answer to a semi-compliment by Rosalind. See 'Speech, content of s. wiser than speaker realizes - Thou speakest wiser than thou art 'ware of.'*

Wit, w. admired - I like thy wit well, in good faith.
"I like thy wit well, in good faith" (H.5.1)

In the play. *One clown's comment to another clown's witticism. Who builds constructions stronger than the mason's, shipwright's or carpenter's? The maker of gallows because they outlive a thousand tenants.*

Wit, w. ill directed and punished - See now, how wit may be made a Jack-a-lent, when 'tis upon ill employment.
"See now, how wit may be made a Jack-a-lent, when 'tis upon ill employment." (MWW.5.5)
Comment on an adversarial trick that did not succeed.
In the play. *Falstaff recognizes his own fault, to have tried to use his wit in good employment (the attempted seduction of the good wives of Windsor). 'Jack-a-lent' was a small, stuffed puppet tossed and thrown at during Lent.*

Wit, w. somewhat overwhelming - Your wit's too hot, it speeds too fast, 'twill tire.
"Your wit's too hot, it speeds too fast, 'twill tire." (LLL.2.1)
Retort to a verbal arrow cast at you.
In the play. *Biron to the witty Rosaline.*

Wit, w. that cannot be understood - When a man's verses cannot be understood, nor a man's good wit seconded with the forward child Understanding…
" When a man's verses cannot be understood, nor a man's good wit seconded with the forward child Understanding, it strikes a man more dead than a great reckoning in a little room. Truly, I would
the gods had made thee poetical." (AYLO.3.3)
In the play. *The simple country girl Audrey cannot understand the wit of Touchstone.*

Wit, wits that make fools of themselves – None are so surely caught, when they are catch'd, as wit turn'd fool…

"None are so surely caught, when they are catch'd,
As wit turn'd fool: folly, in wisdom hatch'd,
Hath wisdom's warrant and the help of school
And wit's own grace to grace a learned fool." (LLL.5.2)
In the play. *The princess comments on King and associates and their presenting themselves to the ladies in masks pretending to be Russians.*

Witchcraft, events attributable to w. - For nature so preposterously to err… sans witchcraft could not.
"For nature so preposterously to err,
Being not deficient, blind, or lame of sense,
Sans witchcraft could not." (OTH.1.3)
In the play. *Brabantio, on knowing that his daughter Desdemona has married Othello, can only assume that he employed witchcraft to seduce her. 'Sans' = 'without'*

Witchcraft, excellent w. - …fresh piece of excellent witchcraft.
"… fresh piece
Of excellent witchcraft" (WT.4.4)
Tell her so if she has bewitched you.
In the play. *Polixenes addresses himself to the fair ('fresh') Perdita who, he believes, has bewitched Florizel.*

Wits, w. willfully lost - … thou hast pared thy wit o' both sides and left nothing i' the middle.
"…thou hast pared thy wit o' both sides,
and left nothing i' the middle." (KL.1.4)
In the play. *The fool to Lear who has made himself a kind of hostage in the hands of two evil daughters.*

Witticism, humor as a double edges sword - A sentence is but a cheveril glove to a good wit; how quickly the wrong side may be turned outward!

CLOWN (to Viola/Cesario). A sentence is but a cheveril glove to a good wit; how quickly the wrong side may be turned outward!
VIOLA/CESARIO. Nay, that's certain; they, that dally nicely with words, may quickly make them wanton." (TN.3.1)
Try to excuse the way the audience has wrongly interpreted what you said by relating the quote as an anecdote.
In the play. *Viola and the clown exchange some banter. 'Cheveril' = 'goat'.*

Woman, a cold w. – I would have thought her spirit had been invincible against the assaults of affection.
"I would have thought her spirit had been invincible against the assaults of affection." (MAAN.2.3)
Define a cold w. Also a safe question to ask of a lady you like, e.g.. 'May I inquire as to whether your spirit is invincible against the assaults of affection?'
In the play. *Rumor has it that Beatrice is beginning to soften towards Benedick and Don Pedro is surprised.*

Woman, a cold w. – ... spoke with her but once and found her wondrous cold.
"... spoke with her but once
And found her wondrous cold."
(AWEW.3.7)
Your opinion on a girl cold in general or cold to your advances.
In the play. *Bertram attempts to seduce a Florentine girl who, however, has proven, so far, cold to his pursuit.*

Woman, amazement, a. at her change in character - ... I would have I thought her spirit had been invincible against all assaults of affection.
"You amaze me: I would have I thought her spirit had been invincible against all assaults of affection." (MAAN.2.3)

In the play. *The subject of the amazement is the impervious Beatrice who seems to fall for Benedick*

Woman, anything but talking with her – (Anything) rather than hold three words' conference with this harpy.
"...(Anything) rather than hold three words' conference with this harpy." (MAAN.2.1)
In the play. *Benedick's reaction at having to talk with Beatrice.*

Woman, assessment of a fair and silly w. – She never yet was foolish that was fair...
"She never yet was foolish that was fair;
For even her folly help'd her to an heir." (OTH.2.1)
In the play. *Iago in answer to a question by Desdemona.*

Woman, assessment of a fair and wise w. – If she be fair and wise, fairness and wit...
"If she be fair and wise, fairness and wit,
The one's for use, the other useth it." (OTH.2.1)
In the play. *Iago in answer to a question by Desdemona.*

Woman, assessment of an ugly and silly w. – There's none so foul and foolish thereunto...
"There's none so foul and foolish thereunto,
But does foul pranks which fair and wise ones do. (OTH.2.1)
In the play. *Iago in answer to a question by Desdemona.*

Woman, beautiful - ... As silver-voiced; her eyes as jewel-like and cased as richly...

"…wand-like straight;
As silver-voiced; her eyes as jewel-like
And cased as richly…" (PER.5.1)
In the play. *Pericles compares Marina to his wife (presumed dead) as he still does not know that Marina is actually his daughter.*

Woman, beautiful – … gorgeous as the sun at midsummer.
"…gorgeous as the sun at midsummer" (KHIV.p1.4.1)
Compliment, 'You are as gorgeous… midsummer'
In the play. *Vernon's account of the Prince of Wales. Vernon is with rebels.*

Woman, the opposite of a w. – Women are soft, mild… thou … rough, remorseless
"Women are soft, mild, pitiful and flexible;
Thou stern, obdurate, flinty, rough, remorseless." (KH6 p3.1.4)
Befitting characterization of C. Rice, Margaret Albright and perhaps other harpies in the Bush administrations. On hearing of the death by starvation of thousands of Iraqi children, Albright replied, 'The prize was worth it'.
In the play. *York to Queen Margaret who taunts him after he has been captured.*

Woman, trust in w. unjustified – Mine eyes were not in fault, for she was beautiful…
"Mine eyes
Were not in fault, for she was beautiful;
Mine ears, that heard her flattery; nor my heart,
That thought her like her seeming; it had been vicious
To have mistrusted her." (CYM.5.5)
In the play. *King Cymbeline refers to his wife who was trying to poison him little by little.*

Woman, w. admired for beauty and honor – I have perused her well, beauty and honour in her are so mingled…
"I have perused her well;
Beauty and honour in her are so mingled
That they have caught the king" (KHVIII.2.3)
Answer to 'Do you like me?' Change 'her' to 'you'. Or answer to 'What do you think of her?'
In the play. *The chamberlain came to deliver a message to Anne Boleyn from the King and is impressed by her general demeanor.*

Woman, w. beautiful, bewitching and sexy - Let witchcraft join with beauty, lust with both!
"Let witchcraft join with beauty, lust with both!" (AC.2.1)
In a compliment or a statement try, 'In you witchcraft joins with beauty'.
In the play. *Pompey hopes that Cleopatra's witchcraft and beauty will retain Antony in Egypt. See also 'Eating, good food, antipasto' for other comments by Pompey in the same spirit.*

Woman, w. beautiful, even the air would go and see her - … the air; which, but for vacancy had gone to gaze on Cleopatra too…
"…the air; which, but for vacancy,
Had gone to gaze on Cleopatra too,
And made a gap in nature." (AC.2.2)
Answer to 'Do you like me?' E.G. 'The air, but for vacancy, would go to gaze on you too, and make a gap in nature.'
In the play. *Enobarbus extols the extraordinary beauties of Cleopatra to Agrippa in Rome.*

Woman, best of all - She excels each mortal thing upon the dull earth dwelling.
"She excels each mortal thing
Upon the dull earth dwelling:" (TGV.4.2)
In the play. *A host accompanies Julia, former Proteus' girlfriend, to visit with Silvia, current*

object of Proteus' passion. While doing so the host unrealistically sings a song in praise of Julia.

Woman, correspondence between w.'s parts and countries' geography.
ANTIPHOLUS S. Where Scotland?
DROMIO S. I found it by the barrenness; hard in the palm of the hand
ANTIPHOLUS S Where France?
DROMIO S. In her forehead; armed and reverted, making war against her heir
ANTIPHOLUS S Where England?
DROMIO S. I looked for the chalky cliffs, but I could find no whiteness in them; but I guess it stood in her chin, by the salt rheum that ran between France and it
ANTIPHOLUS S Where Spain?
DROMIO S. Faith, I saw it not; but I felt it hot in her breath.
ANTIPHOLUS S Where America, the Indies?
DROMIO S. Oh, sir, upon her nose all o'er embellished with rubies, carbuncles, sapphires, declining their rich aspect to the hot breath of Spain; who sent whole armadoes of caracks to be ballast at her nose.
ANTIPHOLUS S Where stood Belgia, the Netherlands?
DROMIO S. Oh, sir, I did not look so low. (COE.3.2)
For Ireland see 'Woman, a very large w. - …in what part of her body stands Ireland'.
In the play. *Dromio S claims that he must go and see a woman and Antipholus S. asks for details.*

Woman, cruel - … Pierced through the heart with your stern cruelty…
"(I) Pierced through the heart with your stern cruelty:
Yet you, the murderer, look as bright, as clear,

As yonder Venus in her glimmering sphere" (MND.3.2)
In the play. *Demetrius responds to Hermia who accuses him unjustly to have slain Lysander.*

Woman, cruel, killer - Fly away, fly away breath, I am slain by a fair cruel maid.
"Fly away, fly away breath;
I am slain by a fair cruel maid."
(TN.2.4)
Act dramatically as you say this if she said 'no'.
In the play. *The Duke Orsino, disappointed in his pursuit of Olivia asks the Clown to sing a melancholy song. The lines are part of the song sung by the clown.*

Woman, cruel, serpent - O serpent heart, hid with a flowering face!
"O serpent heart, hid with a flowering face!" (RJ.3.2)
When you want to tell her the truth if she has really been cruel to you.
In the play. *News that Romeo killed Tybald, Juliet's cousin has reached her. Not knowing that the killing was unprovoked and in self-defense, Juliet draws the wrong conclusions about Romeo.*

Woman, dish for the Gods - A woman is a dish for the gods, if the devil dress her not.
"A woman is a dish for the gods, if the devil dress her not." (AC.5.2)
Generalization. See also 'Perfection, worthy of a king - … all her perfections challenge sovereignty; one way or other, she is for a king.' *** 'Hand, worthy to be kissed by kings – … a hand that kings have lipped, and trembled kissing.'
In the play. *Cleopatra banters with the clown who has just brought in a basket containing the aspic with whose venom Cleopatra intends to kill herself.*

Woman, evil w. – ... she hath lived too long to fill the world with vicious qualities.
"Take her away; for she hath lived too long,
To fill the world with vicious qualities." (KHVI.p1.5.4)
In the play. *York, referring to the captured Joan of Arc.*

Woman, evil w., like a harpy - ... with thine angel's face seize with thine eagle's talons.
"Thou art like the harpy,
Which, to betray, dost, with thine angel's face,
Seize with thine eagle's talons." (PER.4.3)
In the play. *Cleon to evil wife Dionyza who tried to have Marina murdered out of envy.*

Woman, female frailty – ... as the glasses where they view themselves; which are as easy broke as they make forms.
ANGELO Nay, women are frail too.
ISABELLA Ay, as the glasses where they view themselves;
Which are as easy broke as they make forms
....
...Nay, call us ten times frail;
For we are soft as our complexions are,
And credulous to false prints. (MFM.2.4)
In the play. *The evil Angelo tries to seduce the pious Isabella, who attempts to save her brother Claudio's life. He prompts her to admit that women are frail as part of his scheme of seduction.*

Woman, female frailty, invocation - Frailty, thy name is woman.
"Frailty, thy name is woman." (H.1.2)
Any situation in which a woman has done something wrong. It may get you into trouble if used with a feminist or with a feminist audience.
In the play. *After meditating about how quickly his mother married the new king, Hamlet inveighs against women.*

Woman, female frailty, invocation - ... how weak a thing the heart of woman is.
"...Ay me, how weak a thing
The heart of woman is!" (JC.2.4)
In the play. *Portia to herself as she worries about what Brutus may do.*

Woman, happy the man who will marry her - ... Happier the man, whom favourable stars allot thee for his lovely bed-fellow!
"Happy the parents of so fair a child;
Happier the man, whom favourable stars
Allot thee for his lovely bed-fellow!" (TOS.4.5)
In the play. *Katharina is put to the test by Petruchio and is ready to agree with him that a man pointed out by Petruchio is actually a woman.*

Woman, hard and harsh w. or crying - A woman mov'd is like a fountain troubled...
"A woman moved is like a fountain troubled,
Muddy, ill-seeming, thick, bereft of beauty;
And while it is so, none so dry or thirsty
Will deign to sip or touch one drop of it." (TOS.5.2)
Give reasons to your wife or girlfriend to be more cheerful.
In the play. *Katharina, now tamed by her husband Petruchio has words of advice for other women.*

Woman, ideal w. - ... a shop of all the qualities that man loves woman for.
"... for condition,

A shop of all the qualities that man Loves woman for" (CYM.5.4)
In the play. *Iachimo recounts the events that led him to play such a dirty trick on Leonatus and Imogen.*

Woman, impossible w. - Her only fault (and that is fault enough) is that she is intolerable curst... I would not wed her for a mine of gold.
"Her only fault (and that is fault enough)
Is, - that she is intolerable curst;
And shrew'd, and forward, so beyond all measure,
That, were my state far worser than it is;
I would not wed her for a mine of gold." (TOS.1.2)
Characterize a bossy or tyrannous woman.
In the play. *Hortensio delivers a character profile of Katharina to Petruchio.*

Woman, impregnable – She will not stay the siege of loving terms, nor bide...
"She will not stay the siege of loving terms,
Nor bide the encounter of assailing eyes,
Nor ope her lap to saint-seducing gold" (RJ.1.1)
In the play. *Questioned by Benvolio, Romeo describes the nature of the girl (not Juliet, but Rosaline), he is currently infatuated with. Juliet will quickly supplant Rosaline in Romeo's affections.*

Woman, in deep trouble – She is fallen into a pit of ink!
"O, she is fallen
Into a pit of ink! that the wide sea
Hath drops too few to wash her clean again;
And salt too little, which may season give
To her foul tainted flesh!" (MAAN.4.1)

Apply to either sex by changing articles and pronouns accordingly. Use to describe someone who has brought deep trouble upon him/herself.
In the play. *Leonato is ashamed of his daughter after hearing (and for a moment believing) the accusations leveled against her.*

Woman, inestimable and powerful – ... she is a pearl, whose price hath launch'd above a thousand ships...
"... she is a pearl,
Whose price hath launch'd above a thousand ships,
And turn'd crown'd kings to merchants" (TC.2.2)
Turn it into a compliment, change 'hath' to 'could' and 'turn'd' to 'turn'
In the play. *Troilus tries to convince the skeptical Hector to keep Helena rather than turning her to the Greeks*

Woman, large w. - ... in what part of her body stands Ireland?
ANTIPHOLUS S. Then she bears some breadth?
DROMIO S. No longer from head to foot than from hip to hip, she is spherical like a globe - I could find countries in her.
ANTIPHOLUS S. In what part of her body stands Ireland ?
DROMIO S. Marry sir, in her buttocks; I found it out by the bogs." (COE.3.1)
A somewhat rude but yet light hearted remark on a plump lady. See also entries for 'Obesity - 'Health, banning of obesity - I'll exhibit a bill in parliament for the putting down of fat men.'
In the play. *A fat woman claims Dromio S as her husband (thinking he is Dromio E). Dromio S relates the event to his master Ant. S. The two engage in a question and answer session on the physical attributes of the woman.*

Woman, large w. after an unwilling male - She is too big, I hope, for me to compass.
"To Adriana! that is where we dined,
Where Dowsabel did claim me for her husband:
She is too big, I hope, for me to compass" (COE.4.1)
The third line can be your answer to a question whether you like a lady of large constitution.
In the play. *Ant E commands Dromio S (thinking Dromio S to be Dromio E) to go to Adriana's for help. Dromio S obeys though reluctantly. He knows that at Adriana's he will find Dowsabel, a large woman who claims him as a husband.*

Woman, list of her lovable qualities - Beshrew me but I love her heartily, for she is wise, if I can judge of her...
"Beshrew me but I love her heartily;
For she is wise, if I can judge of her,
And fair she is, if that mine eyes be true,
And true she is, as she hath proved herself,
And therefore, like herself, wise, fair and true,
Shall she be placed in my constant soul." (MOV.2.6)
In the play. *Lorenzo explains to Gratiano why he loves Jessica. 'Beshrew me' is a form of assertiveness or a reinforcing remark equivalent to 'indeed'. 'Beshrew' = 'woe to'.*

Woman, moved by w's tears - At a few drops of women's rheum... he sold the blood and labour of our great action.
"At a few drops of women's rheum, which are
As cheap as lies, he sold the blood and labour
Of our great action" (COR.5.6)
When you see her crying and with some license, e.g. 'A few drops of woman's rheum and I am ready to sell the blood and labor of my actions'
In the play. *Aufidius, head of the Volsces, comments on how Coriolanus was moved by the tears of his mother and wife. 'Rheum' = 'tears'.*

Woman, perfect - divine perfection of a woman.
"Divine perfection of a woman." (KRIII.1.2)
Compliment, use as a preamble, especially useful when are asking for something.
Archdeacon Ruiz gives a rational explanation on the divine essence of woman. 'If God, when He created the world, had thought that woman was bad, He would not have given her to man for a companion, nor would He have created her from his rib. If God's intention had not been positive, she would not have turned out such a beautiful thing.' (Libro de Buen Amor, #109)
If you disagree with Ruiz' assessment, you may recall the anecdote of Adam who complained to God about Eve not being as good as he (Adam) would have liked. The replay was, 'What do you expect for a rib?'
In the play. *The evil Richard III, after having killed his own brother Clarence, woos Anne, Clarence's widowed wife in a scheme to acquire the throne.*

Woman, perfect w. everything OK with her - ... Whom every thing becomes, to chide, to laugh, to weep ...
"... Whom every thing becomes, to chide, to laugh,
To weep; whose every passion fully strives
To make itself, in thee, fair and admired!" (AC.1.1)
In the play. *Antony tries to stop Cleopatra's verbal wrangling with a compliment.*

Woman, pretty in foot, lip, eye and well spoken - We say that Shore's wife hath a pretty foot...
"We say that Shore's wife hath a pretty foot,
A cherry lip, a bonny eye, a passing pleasing tongue." (RIII.1.1)
Modify to say, "You have a pretty foot, a cherry lip... pleasing tongue."
In the play. *Richard makes a comment on the wife of Shore, while in conversation with Brakenbury a Lieutenant at the Tower, where Clarence, brother of the king has just been brought to. Shore's wife was a mistress of King Edward. 'Passing' = 'exceedingly'.*

Woman, pretty w, seen dancing, who is she? – What lady is that, which doth enrich the hand of yonder night?
"What lady is that, which doth enrich the hand
Of yonder knight?" (RJ.1.5)
In the play. *Romeo spots Juliet at the Capulets' party. 'Yonder' = demonstrative pronoun used to point an object or person at a distance*

Woman, pretty, witty and wild – I know a wench of excellent discourse, pretty and witty...
"I know a wench of excellent discourse,
Pretty and witty; wild, and yet, too, gentle" (COE.3.1)
In the play. *Antiphous E. to Balthazar, referring to a girlfriend.*

Woman, proud and haughty w. - Nature never framed a woman's heart of prouder stuff than that of Beatrice...
"...Nature never framed a woman's heart
Of prouder stuff than that of Beatrice;
Disdain and scorn ride sparkling in her eyes,
Misprising what they look on, and her wit

Values itself so highly that to her
All matter else seems weak"
(MAAN.3.1)
Change 'Beatrice' to the name of the woman to whom the statement applies.
In the play. *Hero describes Beatrice's character.*

Woman, provocative w. - there's language in her eye, her cheek, her lip, nay, her foot speaks...
"There's language in her eye, her cheek, her lip,
Nay, her foot speaks; her wanton spirits look out
At every joint and motive of her body." (TC.4.5)
Describe a provocative lady who seems available.
In the play. *Ulysses recognizes Cressida's character immediately. Cressida has just arrived with Diomedes to the Greek camp. 'Wanton' = 'lascivious'.*

Woman, provocative w. - What an eye she has! methinks it sounds a parley of provocation.
"What an eye she has! methinks it sounds a parley of provocation." (OTH.2.3)
See also 'Availability detected - I spy entertainment in her'.
In the play. *Iago at first tries to sound Cassio and get him interested in Desdemona.*

Woman, provocative w. and available - I spy entertainment in her.
"I spy entertainment in her"
(MWW.1.3)
Use this to give your opinion, if asked, on a lady easy to become friendly with. See also 'Woman, provocative w.'
In the play. *Somewhat optimistically Falstaff hopes to seduce Mistress Ford.*

Woman, real w. better than her picture – So far this shadow doth limp behind the substance.

"…so far this shadow
Doth limp behind the substance"
(MOV.3.2)
Answer to 'Do you like my picture?'
In the play. *Bassanio comments on the picture of Portia found in the correct basket.*

Woman, rich w. - … she is a region in Guiana, all gold and bounty.
"…she is a region in Guiana, all gold and bounty" (MWW.1.5)
In the play. *Falstaff refers to Mistress Page, whom he plans to seduce.*

Woman, search for a wealthy w. - … nothing comes amiss, so money comes withal.
"…though she have as many diseases as two and fifty horses: why, nothing comes amiss, so money comes withal." (PER.1.2)
In the play. *Grumio, Petruchio's servant states clearly to Hortensio Petruchio's aim in coming to Padua.*

Woman, spiteful and sharp tongued - She speaks poniards, and every word stabs…
"She speaks poniards, and every word stabs: if her breath were as terrible as her terminations, there were no living near her, she would infect to the north star." (MAAN.2.1)
Express your opinion of a vinegary woman. See also 'Advice, a. to a sharp-tongued woman - … if thou be so shrewd of thy tongue…'
In the play. *Benedick's opinion of Beatrice.*

Woman, splendid and majestic - What peremptory eagle-sighted eye dares look upon the heaven of her brow…
"What peremptory eagle-sighted eye
Dares look upon the heaven of her brow,
That is not blinded by her majesty?" (LLL.4.3)
Change 'her' to your' and lay it on thick.

In the play. *Biron of Rosaline with whom he in love. 'Peremptory' = 'bold, unawed'.*

Woman, sweet w. - … she is sweeter than perfume itself.
"… she is sweeter than perfume itself." (TOS.1.2)
In the play. *Tranio will arrange to have perfumed letter and books delivered to Bianca, in harmony with her sweetness.*

Woman, sweetest w. in the world - … the world hath not a sweeter creature
"…the world hath not a sweeter creature: she might lie by an emperor's side and command him tasks." (OTH.4.1)
Compliment.
In the play. *Othello, determined to kill Desdemona, still has pangs of love and despair thinking of her.*

Woman, task better left to a w. – The office becomes a woman best.
"… the office
Becomes a woman best; I'll take't upon me.
If I prove honey-mouth'd let my tongue blister
And never to my red-look'd anger be
The trumpet any more." (WT.2.2)
In the play. *Paulina decides to go and upbraid King Leontes that his jealousy is madness. She will bring to him his baby daughter just delivered by the jailed queen Hermione.*

Woman, thoughtful and gentle w. - You bear a gentle mind, and heavenly blessings follow such creatures.
"You bear a gentle mind, and heavenly blessings
Follow such creatures." (KHVIII.2.3)
In the play. *The Lord Chamberlain pays a compliment to Anne Boleyn.*

Woman, totally incorruptible –… she would make a puritan of the devil, if he should cheapen a kiss of her.

"... she would make a puritan of the devil, if he should cheapen a kiss of her." (PER.4.6)
Describe an unassailable woman.
In the play. *In Mytilene Marina manages to turn into a Salvation Army post the brothel she is compelled to be in.*

Woman, undaunted by w's shrewish character - Think you a little din can daunt mine ears?...
"Think you a little din can daunt mine ears?
...And do you tell me of a woman's tongue,
That gives not half so great a blow to hear
As will a chestnut in a farmer's fire?" (TOS.1.2)
In the play. *Petruchio to Grumio who discusses Katharina's fiery temper.*

Woman, unimaginably cunning w. – She is cunning past man's thought.
"She is cunning past man's thought." (AC.1.2)
In the play. *Antony describes Cleopatra.*

Woman, unique in perfection – Her whose worth makes other worthies nothing.
"... all I can is nothing
To her whose worth makes other worthies nothing;
She is alone." (TGV.2.4)
Compliment, 'You are one whose worth makes other worthies nothing'.
In the play. *Valentine, madly in love with Silvia, sings her praises to friend Proteus.*

Woman, unpredictable - Who is 't can read a woman?
"Who is 't can read a woman?" (CYM.5.4)
Justify unexpected action from a woman.

In the play. *King Cymbeline is flabbergasted at hearing the truth about the queen's deviousness. Had not Imogen fled, the queen was planning to poison her. Imogen is Cymbeline's daughter.*

Woman, what she is to you - The fountain from the which my current runs...
"The fountain from the which my current runs..." (OTH.4.2)
Compliment.
In the play. *Othello confronts Desdemona, this is what she is for him and that is why he cannot tolerate the idea that she is unfaithful to him.*

Woman, with mannish manners - A woman impudent and mannish grown...
"A woman impudent and mannish grown
Is not more loathed than an effeminate man
In time of action" (TC.3.3)
In the play. *Patroclus to Achilles after Ulysses has ended his speech exhorting Achilles to action.*

Woman, w. as a prize – ... the prize of all too precious you
"... the prize of all too precious you" (SON 86)
Answer to 'Why are you doing this?' when 'this' is a favor, a sacrifice etc.

Woman, w. beyond description - ... For her own person, it beggar'd all description.
"... For her own person,
It beggar'd all description" (AC.2.2)
Answer to 'What did you think of lady xx?'
In the play. *In Rome Enobarbus describes for Agrippa's benefit the first encounter between Antony and Cleopatra.*

Woman, w. believed chaste - ... as chaste as unsunn'd snow.

"...I thought her
As chaste as unsunn'd snow"
(CYM.2.5)
In the play. *Deceived by the evil Iachimo, Leonatus believes his wife deceitful.*

Woman, chaste – ... chaste as the icicle that curdied by the frost from purest snow...
"The moon of Rome, chaste as the icicle
That's curdied by the frost from purest snow
And hangs on Dian's temple"
(COR.5.3)
In the play. *Coriolanus on seeing his wife Virgilia who came to see him at the Volscean camp. 'To curdy' = 'To congeal'.*

Woman, w. defined - ... a child of our grandmother Eve, a female.
"... a child of our grandmother Eve, a female, a female; or, for thy more sweet understanding, a
woman " (LLL.1.1)
In the play. *An extract from a letter written to the King by Armado.*

Woman, w. difficult to read - You are such a woman! one knows not at what ward you lie...
"You are such a woman! one knows not at what ward you lie..." (TC.1.2)
In the play. *Pandarus to niece Cressida after she gives him somewhat evasive answers on her like or dislike of Troilus. 'Ward' is the district of a town. 'At what ward you lie' means 'where you stand' also metaphorically.*

Woman, w. helpful during negotiations – ... when maidens sue men give like gods...
"...when maidens sue,
Men give like gods; but when they weep and kneel,
All their petitions are as freely theirs
As they themselves would owe them"
(MFM.1.4)

See also 'Character, unable to say 'no' to women - ... whom ne'er the word of 'No' woman heard speak'. *** 'Woman, young w. and a natural persuader - ... for in her youth there is a prone and speechless dialect, such as move men.'
In the play. *Lucio advises Isabella to go to Lord Angelo and sue for her brother's life.*

Woman, w. helpful during negotiations – Haply a woman's voice may do some good...
"Haply a woman's voice may do some good,
When articles too nicely urged be stood on" (HV.5.2)
Apply to any situation, e.g. telephone calls, signing letters etc. where you think that a womanly touch may help smooth matters.
In the play. *Queen Isabel of France will participate in the negotiations between the English and the French, leading to the marriage of Henry V to Princess Katherine.*

Woman, w. loud and contentious w. - ... she chide as loud as thunder when the clouds in autumn crack.
"...though she chide as loud
As thunder when the clouds in autumn crack." (TOS.1.2)
In the play. *Petruchio is not concerned if Katharina is a shrew.*

Woman, lovely and fragrant to the extreme – (Thou) who art so lovely fair and smell'st so sweet...
"Who art so lovely fair and smell'st so sweet
That the sense aches at thee..."
(OTH.4.2)
In the play. *Othello to Desdemona regretting of having to kill her for her alleged infidelity.*

Woman, w. misjudged – Mine eyes were not in fault, for she was beautiful...

1011

"Mine eyes
Were not in fault, for she was beautiful;
Mine ears, that heard her flattery; nor my heart,
That thought her like her seeming; it had been vicious
To have mistrusted her" (CYM.5.5)
In the play. *King Cymbeline comments on the dead queen who, when alive, tried to poison him. Instead, he trusted her completely*

Woman, w. reserved and bashful – A pudency so rosy the sweet view on't might well have warm'd old Saturn.
"A pudency so rosy the sweet view on't
Might well have warm'd old Saturn" (CYM.2.5)
In the play. *Leonatus, believing that Imogen betrayed him rails against her and women in general.*

Woman, w. sun-tanned and/or with brown eyes - … as brown in hue as hazel nuts and sweeter than the kernels.
"…Kate like the hazel-twig
Is straight and slender and as brown in hue
As hazel nuts and sweeter than the kernels" (TOS.2.1)
Compliment or answer to 'Do you like my sun-tan?'
In the play. *Petruchio deploys his tactic to subdue the shrewish Katharina.*

Woman, w. super chaste – … in strong proof of chastity well arm'd…
"…in strong proof of chastity well arm'd,
From love's weak childish bow she lives unharm'd" (RJ.1.1)
In the play. *Romeo describes Rosaline to friend Benvolio.*

Woman, w. super chaste – He spake of her, as Dian had hot dreams…

"He spake of her, as Dian had hot dreams,
And she alone were cold" (CYM.5.5)
In the play. *The now defeated Iachimo recalls the events that led to his treachery towards Leonatus. The lady in question is Imogen, as described by Leonatus, her husband*

Woman, w. that keeps the books and is arbiter of economic decisions - … the report goes she has all the rule of her husband's purse.
"Now, the report goes she has all the rule of her husband's purse" (MWW.1.3)
Use if that is the case.
In the play. *Falstaff comments on Mrs. Ford, from whom he hopes to obtain love and extract money.*

Woman, w. unmarried and pregnant – … a gentlewoman of mine, who, falling in the flaws of her own youth hath blister'd her report.
"… a gentlewoman of mine,
Who, falling in the flaws of her own youth,
Hath blister'd her report: she is with child" (MFM.2.3)
In the play. *The Provost introduces Juliet to the disguised Duke Vicentio. Juliet has been led to prison for her transgression.*

Woman, w. unmoved by extraordinary events - … you can behold such sights and keep the natural ruby of your cheeks.
"When now I think you can behold such sights,
And keep the natural ruby of your cheeks" (M.3.4)
In the play. *Macbeth to his wife who, unlike him, shaken with fear at the sight of Banquo's ghost, has kept her cool. In fairness Banquo's ghost only appeared to Macbeth.*

Woman, w. who does not like bearded men - ... I could not endure a husband with a beard on his face...
"... I could not endure a husband with a beard on his face: I had rather lie in the woollen" (MAAN.1.3)
In the play. *Beatrice's attitude towards bearded men.*

Woman, w. who turns men off - So turns she every man the wrong side out ...
"So turns she every man the wrong side out
And never gives to truth and virtue that
Which simpleness and merit purchaseth." (MAAN.3.1)
In the play. *Hero referring to Beatrice and her character.*

Woman, w.'s character altered by anger - O, when she's angry, she is keen and shrewd!...
"O, when she's angry, she is keen and shrewd!
She was a vixen when she went to school;
And though she be but little, she is fierce" (MND.3.2)
Make a point to your wife or girlfriend when she is angry. Change 'she' to 'you'
In the play. *Helena describes how Hermia, a gentle lady of small frame, can become quite nasty when angry.*

Woman, w.'s intuition - I have no other reason but a woman's reason.
LUCETTA (of Proteus). Of many good I think him best.
JULIA. Your reason?
LUCETTA. I have no other but a woman's reason." (TGV.1.2)
Answer to 'Why?' or as an alternative to soften the impact, if you say that your 'reason' is your intuition – this assumes, of course, that you are a woman.

In the play. *Julia reviews the roster of potential suitors with her servant Lucetta*

Woman, w.'s power to move - ... Her sighs will make a battery in his breast, her tears will pierce into a marble heart.
"For she's a woman to be pitied much:
Her sighs will make a battery in his breast;
Her tears will pierce into a marble heart;
The tiger will be mild whiles she doth mourn;
And Nero will be tainted with remorse,
To hear and see her plaints, her brinish tears." (KHVI.p3.3.1)
When you relent and accept her request. Change 'her' to 'your' and 'his' to 'my'
In the play. *King Henry thinks of his wife Queen Margaret who has traveled to France to solicit military help from King Louis against the Yorkist usurpers.*

Woman, w.'s reputation, r. or character marred by sin – ... falling in the flaws of her own youth hath blister'd her report.
"... a gentlewoman of mine,
Who, falling in the flaws of her own youth,
Hath blister'd her report" (MFM.2.3)
In the play. *The Provost introduces to Duke Vicentio (in disguise) Juliet, whose reputation has been marred by having been seduced by Claudio.*

Woman, witty - Thou wert as witty a piece of Eve's flesh as any in Illyria.
"... thou wert as witty a piece of Eve's flesh as any in Illyria." (TN.1.5)
Compliment her on her sense of humor. Change 'Illyria' to the appropriate country.
In the play. *The Clown is impressed by Maria's wit and repartees.*

Woman, young w. and a natural persuader - ... for in her youth there is a prone and speechless dialect, such as move men.
"…for in her youth
There is a prone and speechless dialect,
Such as move men; beside, she hath prosperous art
When she will play with reason and discourse,
And well she can persuade."
(MFM.1.2)
See also entries for 'Woman, w. helpful during negotiations'
When you yield to her request(s), e.g. 'You have a prone and speechless dialect, such as move men'
In the play. *Claudio hopes that his sister Isabel can convince Angelo to spare his life and says so to friend Lucio. 'Prone' = 'expressive'.*

Womb, w. redefined - ... that nest of spicery…
"But in your daughter's womb I bury them:
Where in that nest of spicery they shall breed
Selves of themselves, to your recomforture." (KRIII.4.4)
Use of this image is left to your imagination.
In the play. *According to Richard, his begetting sons or daughters of young Anne, will make up for Anne's young brothers whom he has murdered. 'Recomforture' = 'new comfort'.*

Women as weapons of mass destruction - This fell whore of thine hath in her more destruction than thy sword, for all her cherubim look.
"This fell whore of thine
Hath in her more destruction than thy sword,
For all her cherubim look." (TOA.4.3)
Clearly not an expression to be used with ladies, but, in suitable circumstances, it can describe the potentially destructive effects of female attraction – historical examples are endless.
In the play. *Alcibiades comes to visit his old friend Timon who, after a reversal of fortunes, decides to abandon mankind completely and live in the woods. Alcibiades is accompanied by his girlfriend Phrynia to whom the topic comment applies. Phrynia, understandably offended by the remark brilliantly answer with a line universally applicable – when you answer back to an accusation, a misstatement or something plainly untrue. See 'Insult, lips – thy lips to rot off.'*

Women, a question about w's faults - …There were none principal; they were all like one another as half pence are…
ORLANDO. Can you remember any of the principal evils that he laid to the charge of women?
ROSALIND. There were none principal; they were all like one another as half pence are: every one fault seeming monstrous, till his fellow fault came to match it.
(AYLI.3.2)
Answer to a question of the type 'What's wrong with him/her?' or as a mild satire on women in general.
In the play. *Rosalind (in disguise as a boy) exchanges some banter with Orlando.*

Women, anti-feminist logic - Why are our bodies soft, and weak, and smooth, unapt to toil, and trouble in the world…
"Why are our bodies soft, and weak, and smooth,
Unapt to toil, and trouble in the world,
But that our soft conditions, and our hearts,
Should well agree with our external parts?" (TOS.5.2)
Show that feminism is incompatible with femininity.

In the play. *Maintain your femininity, is Katharina's advice to women.*

Women, anti-feminist statement - ... know he is the bridle of your will...
LUCIANA O, know he is the bridle of your will.
ADRIANA There's none but asses will be bridled so (COE.2.1)
In the play. *Luciana soothes Adriana's complaint about her husband's unreliability with an anti-feminist statement and Adriana replies.*

Women, light w. argument against them– It is written, they appear to men like angels of light...
"It is written, they appear to men like angels of light: light is an effect of fire, and fire will burn; ergo, light wenches will burn. Come not near her" (COE.4.3)
In the play. *Antipholus S. is approached by a courtesan who thinks that he is Antipholus E.*

Women, bill of rights for women - I'll exhibit a bill in the parliament for the putting down of men.
"I'll exhibit a bill in the parliament for the putting down of men." (MWW.2.1)
If you are a woman apply as is. If a man, quote as a possible sentence from a woman who displays a distinct aversion or rude manners to men, e.g. 'As the woman said, I'll exhibit a bill... men'
In the play. *Mrs. Ford's comment after reading in its entirety the love letter sent to her by Falstaff.*

Women, changelings even in vice - ... For even to vice they are not constant but are changing still...
"...For even to vice
They are not constant but are changing still
One vice, but of a minute old, for one
Not half so old as that." (CYM.2.5)
In the play. *Deceived by the evil Iachimo, Leonatus believes his wife deceitful.*

Women, contiguity of w. at table to be avoided - Two women placed together makes cold weather.
"Two women placed together makes cold weather:" (KHVIII, 1.4)
In the play. *The Lord Chamberlain prompts Lord Sands to sit between two ladies at a party given by the King. It is the party where King Henry will fall in love with Anne Bullen.*

Women, disparaging generalizations – ... you are pictures out of doors...
"... you are pictures out of doors,
Bells in your parlors, wild-cats in your kitchens,
Saints m your injuries, devils being offended,
Players in your housewifery, and housewives' in your beds" (OTH.2.1)
In the play. *Iago to his wife Emilia.*

Women, impulsive character of w. - ... when I think, I must speak.
"Do you not know I am a woman? when I think, I must speak."
(AYLY.3.2)
See also 'Thought, t. preceding action - so do all thoughts, they are winged.
In the play. *Rosalind to Celia who objected to being interrupted. Celia was giving information to Rosalind about Orlando.*

Women, modest and virtuous w. have greater appeal than lascivious ones - Most dangerous is that temptation that doth goad us on to sin in loving virtue...
"O cunning enemy, that, to catch a saint,
With saints dost bait thy hook! Most dangerous
Is that temptation that doth goad us on
To sin in loving virtue: never could the strumpet,
With all her double vigour, art and nature,

Once stir my temper; but this virtuous maid
Subdues me quite." (MFM.2.3)
See also 'Modesty, m. in a woman as temptation for a seducer - ... modesty may more betray our sense than woman's lightness?'
In the play. *The virtue of Isabel tempts the hypocrite Angelo.*

Women, over-feminist w. – I am ashamed that women are so simple to offer war where they should kneel for peace...
"...when she is froward, peevish, sullen, sour,
And not obedient to his honest will,
What is she but a foul contending rebel
And graceless traitor to her loving lord?
I am ashamed that women are so simple
To offer war where they should kneel for peace;
Or seek for rule, supremacy and sway,
When they are bound to serve, love and obey." (TOS.5.2)
See also 'Femininity and genetics - Why are our bodies soft and weak and smooth, unapt to toil and trouble in the world...'
In the play. *Katharina, now tamed by her husband Petruchio has words of advice for other women. 'Peevish' = 'annoyingly silly'*

Women, power of w's tongue - The tongues of mocking wenches are as keen as is the razor's edge invisible...
"The tongues of mocking wenches are as keen
As is the razor's edge invisible,
Cutting a smaller hair than may be seen
Above the sense of sense" (LLL.5.2)
Counter an insinuation or accusation by a woman, e.g. 'You tongue is as keen...sense'.

In the play. *Boyet, out of hearing reach, reflects on the conference held by the Princess and her ladies in attendance.*

Women, requests from w. bound to be gratified - ... when maidens sue, men give like gods; but when they weep and kneel...
"...when maidens sue,
Men give like gods; but when they weep and kneel,
All their petitions are as freely theirs
As they themselves would owe them." (MFM.1.5)
See also 'Character, unable to say 'no' to women - ... whom ne'er the word of 'No' woman heard speak'.
In the play. *Lucio's argument to convince Isabella to go and plead for Claudio's (her brother) life with deputy-governor Angelo.*

Women, submissive role of w. - I am asham'd that women are so simple to offer war, where they should kneel for peace..
"I am asham'd that women are so simple
To offer war, where they should kneel for peace;
Or seek for rule, supremacy and sway,
When they are bound to serve, love and obey." (TOS.5.2)
Express your opposition to feminist values.
In the play. *Katharina's acquired idea of wifely behavior.*

Women, talkativeness of w. unstoppable - ... thou are worthy to be hang'd, that wilt not stay her tongue...
LEONTES. ... thou are worthy to be hang'd,
That wilt not stay her tongue.
ANTIGONUS. Hang all the husbands
That cannot do that feat, you'll leave yourself

Hardly one subject. (WT.2.3)
Quote entirely to prove that historically, women always want to have the last word.
In the play. *Paulina continues to rail at Leontes who then accuses Antigonus, her husband, of being unable to make Paulina stop talking.*

Women, the fun is in the chase - Women are angels wooing, things won are done, joy's soul lies in the doing.
"Women are angels wooing;
Things won are done, joy's soul lies in the doing." (TC.1.2)
You may also not want to tell her this but it is the truth. Describe a common behavior. Or, if you are a woman, use to hold him off. See also 'Reserve, rationale for being somewhat reserved at first - Therefore this maxim out of love I teach…'
In the play. *The crafty Cressida discloses in a monologue her theories on love and on how to keep a lover dangling and eager.*

Women, their difficulty to keep things to themselves - How hard it is for women to keep counsel.
"How hard it is for women to keep counsel!" (JC.2.4)
In the play. *Portia, foreseeing and worried about upcoming events, is uncertain about what to do.*

Women, their judgment swayed by appearances - … the error of our eye directs our mind…
"Ah, poor our sex! this fault in us I find,
The error of our eye directs our mind;
What error leads, must err; O, then, conclude,
Minds swayed by eyes are full of turpitude." (TC.5.2)
Levy a general accusation to women, e.g. 'the error of their eyes directs their minds'. See also entries for 'Woman, female frailty'
In the play. *Cressida betrays Troilus and attributes the cause of her treason to the weakness of her sex.*

Women, their persuasive power greater than men's oratory - … when a world of men could not prevail with all their oratory, yet hath a woman kindness over-ruled.
"… when a world of men
Could not prevail with all their oratory,
Yet hath a woman's kindness over-ruled" (KHVI.p1.2.2)
An argument for assigning a responsible management position or task to a woman.
In the play. *The Countess of Auvergne has invited Talbot to visit her and Talbot thinks he may better negotiate with her than with the other Frenchmen.*

Women, their verbal persuasive skills - These women are shrewd tempters with their tongues.
"These women are shrewd tempters with their tongues." (KHVI.p1.1.2)
Words of advice for a negotiator whose counterpart is a woman
In the play. *Alencon suspects that King Charles may have fallen for Joan of Arc.*

Women, very uncomplimentary view - Down from the waist they are Centaurs, though women all above…
"Down from the waist they are Centaurs,
Though women all above:
But to the girdle do the gods inherit,
Beneath is all the fiends';
There's hell, there's darkness, there's the sulphurous pit,
Burning, scalding, stench, consumption" (KL.4.6)
In the play. *K. Lear's opinion of women. 'Girdle' = 'belt drawn around the waist'.*

Women, w. as repositories of vice - ... Could I find out the woman's part in me!
"...Could I find out
The woman's part in me! For there's no motion
That tends to vice in man, but I affirm
It is the woman's part:" (CYM.2.5)
In the play. *Leonatus, (completely duped by the evil Iachimo) believes that Imogen, his wife betrayed him with Iachimo and inveighs against women.*

Women, w. compared to German clocks - A woman, that is like a German clock, still a-repairing, ever out of frame, and never going a-right...
"A woman, that is like a German clock,
Still a-repairing, ever out of frame,
And never going aright, being a watch,
But being watch'd that it may still go right!" (LLL.3.1)
Answer to 'What do you think of women?' if you are partially misogynous. Keep in mind that during Shakespeare's times clocks were not digital nor accurate.
In the play. *Biron defines the type of woman he is seeking for a wife.* (LLL.3.1)

Women, w. compared to roses - For women are as roses, whose fair flower, being once displayed, doth fall that very hour.
"For women are as roses, whose fair flower
Being once display'd, doth fall that very hour." (TN.2.4)
This is a statement suggesting a double standard and a trace of 'macho' philosophy. You may just use 'Women are as roses'. But if she is an insufferable lady very full of herself who puts you down and off, quote the lines fully. Or explain why you prefer younger women.
In the play. *The Duke Orsino asks Cesario (who is actually Viola strategically dressed in a man's disguise) if he Cesario loves a woman and what type of woman is she. Cesario, secretly in love with Duke Orsino says that her type of woman is of Orsino's age. 'Too old', he says and then continues giving reasons why men (in this case Cesario) should always marry women younger than themselves.*

Women, w.'s reaction in trying circumstances – ... women are not in their best fortunes strong; but want will perjure...
"...women are not
In their best fortunes strong; but want will perjure
The ne'er touch'd vestal" (AC.3.12)
In the play. *Caesar Octavian has won a sea battle against Antony and Cleopatra and thinks that now Cleopatra will renege on Antony.*

Wonder, w. beyond power of written description – One that excels the quirks of blazoning pens.
"One that excels the quirks of blazoning pens." (OTH.2.1)
In the play. *In Cyprus, Cassio gives a glowing description of Desdemona to the inquiring Montano.*

Wonder, w. inducing news - 'tis the rarest argument of wonder that hath shot out in our latter times.
"...'tis the rarest argument of wonder that hath shot out in our latter times" (AWEW.2.3)
In the play. *Parolles follows up on Lafeu's comment on the miraculous healing of the King by the virtuous Helena.*

Wonders, w. to be described – Masters, I am to discourse wonders.
"Masters, I am to discourse wonders" (MND.4.2)

In the play. *Athenian actor Bottom to his co-actors during a play rehearsal.*

Word, compressing in itself and expressing a very long time - How long a time lies in one little word!
"How long a time lies in one little word!" (KRII.1.3)
Follow up on any word that she may use with an air of finality, e.g. retort to 'I don't want to see you any more, ever.'
In the play. *Richard II has just exiled Bolingbroke for 6 years from England. 'Banishment' is but a little word compared to 6 years.*

Word, convinced about the accuracy of the w. – I will maintain the word with my sword…
"…I will maintain the word with my sword to be a soldier-like word, and a word of exceeding good command, by heaven." (KHIV.p2.3.2)
In the play. *Bardolph's reply to a comment by Shallow on the semantic use of the word 'accommodate' as in 'accommodated with a wife'.*

Word, w. power, key to seduction - That man that hath a tongue, I say, is no man if with his tongue he cannot win a woman.
"That man that hath a tongue, I say, is no man
If with his tongue he cannot win a woman." (TGV.3.1)
Encouragement to a friend complaining that she does not want to say 'yes' to him. Or you want to win an argument on whether women in general may be easily gotten to and how.
The statement may appear an exaggeration, but Ovid concurs,
'First let assurance come to your minds, that all women can be caught; spread but your nets and you will catch them.
Sooner would birds be silent in spring, or grasshoppers in summer, or the hounds of Maenalus flee before the hare than a woman persuasively wooed resist a lover.'
(The Maenalus mountain range is in Arcadia in the center of the Peloponnese. The mountains were said to be sacred to Pan).
And… 'A woman, no less than populace, grave judge or chosen senate, will surrender, defeated, to eloquence.'
In the play: *Valentine teaches the Duke how to court a lady, in this case using words.* See also 'Jewelry, gifts large and small - … Dumb jewels often, in their silent kind, More than quick words, do move a woman's mind.'

Words, abuse and Orwellian use of w. – … they, that dally nicely with words, may quickly make them wanton.
That's certain; they, that dally nicely with words, may quickly make them wanton." (TN.3.1)
Apply to any Orwellian use of words, i.e. 'downsizing' for 'firing', 'flexibility' for 'job insecurity' etc.
In the play. *Viola and the clown exchange some banter.*

Words, acknowledgment of pleasing w.– I thank thee, Meg; these words content me much.
"I thank thee, Meg; these words content me much." (KHVI p2.3.2)
Change 'Meg' to name of applicable utterer of welcome and agreeable words.
In the play. *Henry VI credulously believes Margaret when she says that Gloucester will have a fair trial. It is a scam, Gloucester has already been killed.*

Words, array of good w. uttered by a fool - The fool has planted in his memory an array of good words.
"The fool has planted in his memory
An array of good words." (MOV.3.5)
Beginning of a statement opposed to the argument of your adversary. You can modify to, 'You have planted in your memory an array of good words'.

In the play. *Lorenzo's assessment of Launcelot's wit.*

Words, barrage of w. - I was never so bethump'd with words since I first call'd my brother's father dad
"Zounds! I was never so bethump'd with words
Since I first call'd my brother's father dad." (KJ.2.2)
In the play. *Faulconbridge's reaction to the words of the first citizen of Angiers.*

Words, barrage of w. - What craker is this same that deafs our ears with this abundance of superfluous breath?
"What craker is this same that deafs our ears
With this abundance of superfluous breath?" (KJ.2.1)
In the play. *Austria reacts to an insulting remark by Faulconbridge.*

Words, barrage of w, many and inconsequential - A fine volley of words, gentlemen, and quickly shot off.
"A fine volley of words, gentlemen, and quickly shot off." (TGV.2.4)
See also 'Love, l. inspiring wordiness - Thou wilt be like a lover, presently and tire the hearer with a book of words.' *** 'Man, a verbose m. – He draweth out the thread of his verbosity finer than the staple of his argument' *** "Speech, lengthy and annoying - This will last out a night in Russia when nights are longest there.'
In the play. *In the mansion of her father the Duke of Milan, Silvia comments on words and exchanges between Valentine and Thurio.*

Words, carrying bad news or offensive or poorly written - Here are a few of the unpleasant'st words that ever blotted paper.
"Here are a few of the unpleasant'st words
That ever blotted paper." (MOV.3.2)
Prepare the ground before announcing the unpleasant contents of a document. Or apply to a poorly written document. See also entries for 'Words, painful w.' - 'News, bad n.' - 'Invocation, damned letter - O damn'd paper! Black as the ink that's on thee!'
In the play. *Bassanio reads news from Antonio, who apparently has lost his ships at sea and must, therefore, pay his debt to the Merchant of Venice with blood (the famous pound of flesh).*

Words, deceiving w. – They shoot but calm words folded up in smoke…
"They shoot but calm words folded up in smoke,
To make a faithless error in your ears." (KJ.2.1)
Modify to 'They use calm words folded up in smoke to make a faithless error in our ears'.
In the play. *King John, addressing the citizens of Angiers, refers to the terms offered by the French.*

Words, despicable w. but well crafted - Ignominious words, though clerkly couched.
"… ignominious words, though clerkly couched." (KHVI p2.3.1)
Use to defend yourself. See also 'Eloquence, characteristic of the eloquent – … on the tip of their persuasive tongue carry all arguments and questions deep…' *** 'Document, policy statement, message filled with questionable reasons for a dreadful act - … Larded with many several sorts of reasons.'
In the play. *Suffolk accuses Gloucester.*

Words, devastating w. - I have words that would be howl'd out in the desert air…
"But I have words
That would be howl'd out in the desert air,

Where hearing should not latch them." (M.4.3)
In the play. *Ross has news that Macbeth destroyed and killed Macduff's wife and children. 'Latch' = 'catch' and you can substitute for better impact.*

Words, devious w. used in questioning - With many holidays and lady terms he question'd me.
"With many holidays and lady terms
He question'd me." (KHIV p1.1.3)
Get to the core of the matter with your question, e.g. 'Why all these holidays and lady terms, come to the point.'
In the play. *Hotspur refers to the king's officer who reported Percy's rebellious or disrespectful stance towards King Henry IV.*

Words, encouraging and acknowledged as such - O Clifford, how thy words revive my heart!
"O Clifford, how thy words revive my heart!" (KHVI p3.1)
Change 'Clifford' to the name of the actual reviver of your heart.
In the play. *Clifford decisively stands up against the York rebels and Henry VI feels revived.*

Words, encouraging and reviving w. – These words, these looks, infuse new life in me.
"These words, these looks, infuse new life in me." (TA.1.1)
In the play. *Tamora has interceded with the Emperor Saturninus on behalf of Andronicus who expresses his thanks.*

Words, encouraging and reviving – Those gracious words revive my drooping thoughts.
"Those gracious words revive my drooping thoughts
And give my tongue-tied sorrows leave to speak." (KHVI p3.3.3)

In the play. *King Lewis XI of France comforts Queen Margaret of England who is calling on him for help against the Yorkists.*

Words, evil w. aggravating weight of evil act - Ill deeds are doubled with an evil word.
"Ill deeds are doubled with an evil word." (COE.3.2)
A comment to any situation when malicious words accompany a bad action.
In the play. *Ant S is after Luciana, sister of Adriana, Ant E's wife. Luciana is upset and reminds Ant S (thinking that he is Ant E) of his duties to his wife Adriana. The evil word refers to the attention expressed to Luciana (by Ant S) in front of Adriana.*

Words, excellent and well put w. - These words become your lips as they pass through them.
"These words become your lips as they pass through them,
And enter in our ears like great triumphers
In their applauding gates." (TOA.5.1)
Use to commend a statement of retraction by someone who previously said something disagreeable. Change 'our' to 'my'. Or alter slightly to reprehend the speaker, e.g.. 'These words do NOT become your lips as they pass through them'. See also entries for 'Speech, well said'.
In the play. *As much as he despises the Athenians Timon does not refuse to help the senators, and by so doing to help his country, The senators commend his words.*

Words, false w. of peace - I speak of peace, while covert enmity under the smile of safety wounds the world.
"I speak of peace, while covert enmity
Under the smile of safety wounds the world" (KHIV.p2.Induction)
You can equally substitute 'freedom and democracy' for 'peace' and describe the

policies of certain governments or administrations.
In the play. *The fictitious character 'Rumor' describes himself in the play's introduction.*

Words, fed up with idle or self-serving w. - I can no longer brook thy vanities
"I can no longer brook thy vanities." (KHIV.p1.5.4)
In the play. *Hotspur to Prince Henry before their duel.*

Words, foul w. ending deductively into foul b. - Foul words is but foul wind…
"Foul words is but foul wind, and foul wind is but foul breath, and foul breath is noisome; therefore I will depart unkissed" (MAAN.5.2)
In the play. *Beatrice reacts to Benedick's reply that the exchanges between him and Claudio were just foul words.*

Words, good w. vs. bad action - Good words are better than bad strokes…
BRUTUS Good words are better than bad strokes, Octavius.
ANTONY In your bad strokes, Brutus, you give good words:
Witness the hole you made in Caesar's heart,
Crying 'Long live! hail, Caesar!'" (JC.5.1)
In the play. *Brutus and Cassius confront each other before the battle of Philippi.*

Words, hurting w. – … your words, they rob the Hybla bees and leave them honeyless
"…your words, they rob the Hybla bees,
And leave them honeyless." (JC.5.1)
In the play. *Brutus to Antony just before the battle of Philippi. Hybla was a town in Sicily whose bees were said to produce an especially sweet honey.*

Words, no mincing of w. - If I prove honey-mouth'd let my tongue blister…
"I'll take't upon me.
If I prove honey-mouth'd let my tongue blister
And never to my red-look'd anger be
The trumpet any more." (WT.2.2)
In the play. *Paulina decides to go and upbraid King Leontes that his jealousy is madness. She will bring to him his baby daughter just delivered by the jailed queen Hermione.*

Words, not w. for a woman - …'Tis not for you to hear what I can speak…
"O gentle lady,
'Tis not for you to hear what I can speak:
The repetition, in a woman's ear,
Would murder as it fell." (M.2.3)
In the play. *Macduff to Lady Macbeth referring to the murder of Duncan.*

Words, painful and pressing on memory – .. it presses to my memory like damned guilty deeds to sinners' minds.
"…. O, it presses to my memory,
Like damned guilty deeds to sinners' minds." (RJ.3.2)
Answer to 'What is worrying you?' if a specific word that she said (or someone else said) keeps haunting you.
In the play. *The word pressing on Juliet's memory is 'banished' referring to Romeo's banishment from Verona after he killed the Capulet Tybalt in a duel.*

Words, painful w. – These words are razors to my wounded heart.
"These words are razors to my wounded heart." (TA.1.1)
Reaction to unexpectedly unpleasant words.
In the play. *In a rapid change of scene Saturninus refuses to marry Lavinia (Titus A.'s daughter) and casts Titus A. out as an enemy. Titus is astounded. A few minutes earlier on he*

had fought to prevent Lavinia from being kidnapped by Bassianus. Bassianus, brother of Saturninus, loved Lavinia prior to the set-up whereby she would marry Saturninus. During that fight Titus slain his son Mutius, who sided with Bassianus.*

Words, painful w. – These words of yours draw life-blood from my heart.
"These words of yours draw life-blood from my heart" (KHVI.p1.4)
When she has been nasty, aggressive or insulting. See also 'Rejection, despair at her words.'
In the play. *John Talbot Jr. listens to his father suggestion that he, John Talbot Jr., flee the battlefield due to the impossibility of victory or rescue. But John Talbot Jr. will not fly.*

Words, perfunctory - ... (speak to them) with such words that are but roted in your tongue..
"… (speak to them) with such words
That are but roted in your tongue,
Though but bastards, and syllables
Of no allowance to your bosom's truth." (COR.3.2)
Acknowledge that what you will say will be dictated by policy and circumstance and does not represent what you really feel. Or make a comment on the perfunctory value of some third party statement, e.g. 'His words are of no allowance to his bosom's truth'.
In the play. *Volumnia, Coriolanus' mother, counsels Coriolanus to soften his approach to the Roman citizens and suggests that he tell them what they want to hear.*

Words, poisoned w. coated with false niceties - Hide not thy poison with such sugar'd words.
"Hide not thy poison with such sugar'd words." (KHVI p2.3.2)
Address an enemy who conspires against you but pretends he doesn't.

In the play. *King Henry to Suffolk who pretends to be sorry at the death of Duke Humphrey.*

Words, pompous w. - To divide him inventorially would dizzy the arithmetic of memory…
"Sir, his definement suffers no perdition in you; though, I know, to divide him inventorially would dizzy the arithmetic of memory… but in the verity of extolment, I take him to be a soul of great article…" (H.5.2)
Example of pompous talk. Also extract 'to divide him inventorially….memory' to introduce a guest with many credentials.
In the play. *Sent by the King, the pompous Osric used pompous and circumvoluted words to describe Laertes' fencing ability to Hamlet. Hamlet responds in kind.*

Words, power of w. to poison relationships - ... one doth not know how much an ill word may empoison liking.
"… one doth not know
How much an ill word may empoison liking." (MAAN.3.1)
Emphasize the importance of the right word and the danger of using an incorrect one.
In the play. *Hero and Ursula are acting out the plan whose aim is to get Benedick and Beatrice to fall in love.*

Words, quick wit recognized - I would my horse had the speed of your tongue, and so good a continuer.
"I would my horse had the speed of your tongue, and so good a continuer." (MAAN.1.1)
When you cannot immediately think of a reply to a sharp remark. 'I would my horse had the speed of your tongue'. See also entries for 'Speechless'.
In the play. *Beatrice has a sharp tongue which she employs against Benedick and Benedick tells*

her so. 'Continuer' = 'one who holds out without tiring'.

Words, reaction to w. without meaning or sincerity - Words, words, mere words, no matter from the heart..
"Words, words, mere words, no matter from the heart:
The effect doth operate another way.
Go, wind, to wind, there turn and change together." (TC.5.3)
See also "Sincerity, s. stated - I want that glib and oily art to speak and purpose not…'
In the play. *Troilus tears up a letter sent to him from Cressida, now in the Greek camp and lover of Diomed.*

Words, refraining from using abusive w., veiled insult - .. I know you what you are… am most loath to call your faults as they are named.
"I know you what you are;
And like a sister am most loath to call Your faults as they are named." (KL.1.1)
Change sister with, 'a discreet person' or 'a gentleman', 'a considerate person' or similar. See also entries for 'Speech, restraint from use of expletives due to anger'.
In the play. *Cordelia says farewell to her sisters after having been banned from her father Lear.*

Words, rehearsed w. planted in memory - The fool hath planted in his memory an army of good words.
"The fool hath planted in his memory An army of good words" (MOV.3.5)
In the play. *Lorenzo's opinion of Launcelot whom he previously called a parrot. See 'Words, silly w., playing with w.'*

Words, relative harmlessness of w. - But words are words, I never yet did hear…

"But words are words; I never yet did hear
That the bruised heart was pierced through the ear" (OTH.1.3)
In the play. *Brabantio's bitter comment on the Duke's pronouncement that has cleared Othello of wrong doing in marrying Desdemona.*

Words, silly w., playing with w., - …and discourse will grow commendable only in parrots.
"How every fool can play upon the word! I think, the best grace of wit will shortly turn into silence; and discourse will grow commendable only in parrots." (MOV.3.5)
In the play. *Launcelot is word sparring with Lorenzo in Belmont and Lorenzo reacts.* Retort to a any play of words, pun or joke of which you are the butt. See also 'Equivocation, misunderstanding, need for accurate wording or expression'.

Words, sincere w. - … his words come from his mouth, ours from our breast.
"… his prayers are in jest;
His words come from his mouth, ours from our breast" (KRII.5.3)
In the play. *The Duke of York pleads with the King (Bolingbroke, now Henry IV), to punish hi own (York's) son, the Duke of Aumerle, who joined other plotters against Bolingbroke. His mother instead pleads with the King for a pardon. She makes the point that her prayer for a pardon is more sincere than York's pleading for a condemnation.*

Words, smooth and treacherous - Let not his smoothing words bewitch your hearts; be wise and circumspect.
"… let not his smoothing words Bewitch your hearts; be wise and circumspect." (KHVI p2.1.1)
Caution against a smooth but deceitful talker
In the play. *Cardinal Beaufort warns other lords and political allies against Gloucester, protector of Henry VI.*

Words, stinging w. - Ah, what sharp sting are in her mildest words!
"Ah, what sharp sting are in her mildest words!" (AWEW.3.4)
Retort to a sharp tongue that remains sharp even when attempting kindness. 'What sharp stings are in your mildest words!'
In the play. *The Countess reads a letter from Helen, where she says she will renounce Bertram and hopes he will be happy and return safe from the wars in Italy*

Words, taking back words just uttered - What then he said, so he unsay it now.
"What then he said, so he unsay it now." (KHIV p1.1.3)
Change to 'What then I said, so I unsay it now.'
In the play. *Blunt comes to the rescue of Hotspur accused of improper words with King Henry IV.*

Words, t. before speaking - I know thou'rt full of love and honesty, and weigh'st thy words before thou giv'st them breath.
"... I know thou'rt full of love and honesty,
And weigh'st thy words before thou giv'st them breath." (OTH.3.3)
Comment or answer to someone who says 'I don't know whether I should say this.'
In the play. *The cunning Iago plants seeds of jealousy into Othello's mind and he falls for it.*

Words, unconvincing w. – Out idle words, servants to shallow fools!
"Out idle words, servants to shallow fools!
Unprofitable sounds, weak arbitrators!" (V&A)
In the poem. *Lucrece, assaulted by Tarquin meditates on the proper revenge or course of action.*

Words, weighing w. before speaking - …(Thou) weigh'st thy words before thou givest them breath…
"…weigh'st thy words before thou givest them breath…" (OTH.3.3)
In the play. *Othello naively values Iago's judgment and is concerned about his words and silences concerning the fidelity of Desdemona.*

Words, weight of w. depending on the their utterer - That in the captain's but a choleric word which in the soldier is flat blasphemy.
"That in the captain's but a choleric word,
Which in the soldier is flat blasphemy" (MFM.2.2)
In the play. *Isabella pleads with Angelo to spare her brother's life. She hints that authority can get away with what the common man may not.*

Words, w. comforting, true, honest – I do come with words as medicinal as true…
"… I
Do come with words as medicinal as true,
Honest as either, to purge him of that humour
That presses him from sleep." (WT.2.3)
Answer to 'What do you have to say?' Start with (e.g.) ' My words are as medicinal as true, honest as either…'
In the play. *Paulina is determined to convince Leontes to let go of his maddening and unwarranted jealousy.*

Words, w. of love, prompted by her beauty - My tongue could never learn sweet smoothing words…
My tongue could never learn sweet smoothing words;
But now thy beauty is propos'd my fee,

My proud heart sues, and prompts my tongue to speak
Use to plead for love and inject a good dose of false modesty.
In the play. *Richard, duke of Gloucester is trying to woo Anne who does not yield (for the moment)*

Words, wild and somewhat senseless - ... These are but wild and whirling words.
"These are but wild and whirling words, my lord." (H.1.5)
See also entries for 'Speech, nonsensical or meaningless'
In the play. *Horatio's comment at Hamlet's statements after the encounter with the Ghost.*

Words, wasted breath - Never did mockers waste more idle breath.
"Never did mockers waste more idle breath." (MND.3.2)
Show your contempt for what has just been said, especially if the remarks was sarcastic.
In the play. *Helena is confused and angry at both Demetrius and Lysander. She thinks they are mocking her.*

Words, w. not enough, truth is important - ... it is not enough to speak, but to speak true.
"... A good moral, my lord:
It is not enough to speak, but to speak true." (MND.5.1)
Introduction to a speech in which what you say may not please the audience, and yet it must be said. E.G. 'I am asked to speak on the subject of xxx. I am well aware that it is not enough to speak but to speak true." See also 'Words, w. that are no deeds'.
In the play. *Lysander comments and approves of the message contained in the prologue of a play - play enacted by the amateur acting company.*

Words, w. that are no deeds - ... 'Tis a kind of good deed to say well and yet words are no deeds.
"'Tis well said again;
And 'tis a kind of good deed to say well:
And yet words are no deeds."
(KHVIII.3.2)
Comment when you know that what you hear are just words. See also 'Words, w. not enough, truth is important' - 'Actions, a. speak more than words - Words to the heat of deeds too cold breath gives.' *** 'Phrases, good p. appreciated – good phrases are surely, and ever were, very commendable.'
In the play. *King Henry VIII replies to a statement by Cardinal Wolsey. Cardinal Wolsey has betrayed himself by inadvertently allowing King Henry VIII to see a compromising letter that he (Wolsey) sent to the Pope and the King gets ready to fire the Cardinal. Later on Wolsey recognizes his negligence in letting the King read the letter.* Negligence, invocation - O negligence! Fit for a fool to fall by!

Words, w. that please the audience - But what care I for words? yet words do well, when he that speaks them pleases those that hear.
"But what care I for words? yet words do well,
When he that speaks them pleases those that hear. " (AYLI.3.5)
Explain why you are careful in the choice of words.
In the play. *Phebe thinks aloud about the disguised Rosalind who speaks well, among other things.*

Words, w. that remove any resentment - Each word thou hast spoke hath weeded from my heart a root of ancient envy.
" Each word thou hast spoke hath weeded from my heart
A root of ancient envy.

… **A thousand welcomes!
And more a friend than e'er an enemy
"** (COR.4.5)
Indicate that you are prepared to be reconciled.
In the play. *Aufidius offers friendship to Coriolanus, his former enemy.*

Words, w. used to twist meaning - I can yield you no reason without words; and words are grown so false, I am loth to prove reason with them.
"…I can yield you no reason without words; and words are grown so false, I am loth to prove reason with them." (TN.3.1)
Give reasons why you do not want to give an explanation.
In the play. *Viola and the clown banter. Viola said that words turn wanton. Shortly later she asks the clown to explain the reason for something he said. He declines on the ground that words, being false, should not be used to provide reasons. 'Loth' = 'unwilling'.*

Words, w. uttered but not meant - … syllables of no allowance to your bosom's truth.
**"… syllables
Of no allowance to your bosom's truth."** (COR.3.2)
In the play. *Coriolanus' mother Volumnia encourages him to use soothing words with the plebes even if he does not mean what he says.*

Words, wounding w. - They wound my thoughts worse than sword my flesh.
"They wound my thoughts worse than sword my flesh" (KHIV p5.4)
Change to 'Your words wound my thoughts… flesh' to vividly paint the picture of the pain inflicted by her wounding words.
In the play. *The mortally wounded Hotspur pines at the loss of his titles. See 'In the play' section of 'Thought as the slave of life, expression of pessimism.'*

Words, your w. have no effect on me - Thy words move rage and not remorse in me.
"Thy words move rage and not remorse in me." (KHVI p2.4.1)
Use for self-defense or as a retort to a threat.
In the play. *Suffolk to the captain of a ship who captured him.*

Work, available for w. - … If it be man's work, I'll do 't.
**"I cannot draw a cart, nor eat dried oats;
If it be man's work, I'll do 't."** (KL.5.3)
In the play. *A captain answers Edgar's request to execute an order (to actually hang Cordelia and make it appear as a suicide).*

Work, enough of idle talk - … there are throats to be cut and works to be done
"…there are throats to be cut and works to be done." (KHV.3.4)
Motivate action to cut out or stop idle discussion.
In the play. *The Welsh Captain Fluellen wants to cut talk short and move to action just before the battle of Agincourt.*

Work, it does not matter if it is hard w. provided we like it - The labour we delight in physics pain.
**MACDUFF: I know this is a joyful trouble to you;
But yet't is one.
MACBETH: The labour we delight in physics pain."** (M.2.3)
Answer to boss who may kindly apologize for the extra work he/she lumbers on you. See also 'Work, type of w. we like to go to' – 'Task, proud to carry it out' – 'Adversity, spirit of acceptance of a. eases the spirit'
In the play. *Macduff has asked Macbeth to take him to the King, whom Macbeth has killed just a few hours before.*

Work, type of w. we like to go to - To business that we love we rise betime and go to it with delight.
"To business that we love we rise betime
And go to it with delight." (AC.4.4)
Answer to 'Do you like to go to work?' Or answer your boss if he asks you 'Hey, you are early at work.' See also 'Task, proud to carry it out - This shall I undertake, and 't is a burden, which I am proud to bear.'
In the play. *Antony is in optimistic mood before the final battle with the forces of Caesar Octavian (antony will lose).*

Work, what type of w. can you do? – ... If it be man's work, I'll do 't
"I cannot draw a cart, nor eat dried oats;
If it be man's work, I'll do 't" (KL.5.3)
Keep answer ready during a job's interview.
In the play. *A captain answers Edmund's request to deliver a letter. The letter is addressed to the jailers of Lear and Cordelia with instructions to kill them.*

Work, working overtime while other sleep -... constrain'd to watch in darkness, rain and cold.
"Thus are poor servitors
(When others sleep upon their quiet beds,)
Constrain'd to watch in darkness, rain and cold." (KHVI.p1.2.1)
Use in a mild ironic tone when someone comments on your working late at the office.
In the play. *A French sentinel at Orleans grumbles about his job.*

Workers' compensation for questionable disability - ... A good wit will make use of any thing: I will turn diseases to commodity.
"...A good wit will make use of any thing:
I will turn diseases to commodity." (KHIV.p2.1.2)
When you are questioning the truthfulness of illness claims.
In the play. *Falstaff feels some pangs of gout (A pox of this gout! or, a gout of this pox!) and immediately thinks of means of using the illness to increase his pension, or worker's compensation, by the use of his wit, of course.*

Working late or at night – ... some must watch, while some must sleep...
"For some must watch, while some must sleep:
So runs the world away." (H.3.2)
In the play. *Hamlet to Horatio after the king left angered by watching the play-within-the-play produced by Hamlet.*

World, w. a dangerous place – I am amazed, methinks, and lose my way among the thorns and dangers of this world.
"I am amazed, methinks, and lose my way
Among the thorns and dangers of this world." (KJ.4.3)
In the play. *Faulconbridge's conclusion after seeing the body of the dead young prince Arthur. His death will trigger an insurrection.*

World, a slippery place – O world, thy slippery turns!
"O world, thy slippery turns!" (COR.4.4)
In the play. *Coriolanus defects to the Volsces after the Romans turned their back on him.*

World, a tough w. to live in - O, how full of briers is this working-day world.
"O, how full of briers is this working-day world!" (AYLI.1.3)
Comment on the difficulties of every day life. See also 'Life, a combination of good and bad - The web of our life is of a

mingled yarn, good and ill go together..'
*** 'Pessimism, p. to the point that death is tolerable - The stroke of death is as a lover's pinch, which hurts, and is desired.' *** 'Pessimism, world will not feel my loss - ... I shall do my friends no wrong, for I have none to lament me...
*** Entries for 'World, pessimistic view of the w.'
In the play. *Rosalind sees difficulties in the development of her love for Orlando.*

World, medicine for the ills of the w. - ... and I will through and through cleanse the foul body of the infected world if they will patiently receive my medicine.
"... give me leave
To speak my mind, and I will through and through
Cleanse the foul body of the infected world,
If they will patiently receive my medicine." (AYLI.2.7)
Introduce your formula or plan to improve the world or any other topic condition that may be improved by implementing your suggestion
In the play. *Jacques claims to possess a sociological medicine to cure the ills of the world.*

World, pessimistic view of the w. – ... what is in this world but grief and woe?
"For what is in this world but grief and woe?" (KHVI.p3.2.5)
In the play. *King Henry, wishing he were dead, meditates while the battle of Towton is fought between his Lancastrian forces and the forces of York.*

World, pessimistic view of the w. – A bawdy planet, that will strike where 'tis predominant...
"It is a bawdy planet, that will strike Where 'tis predominant; and 'tis powerful, think it,

From east, west, north and south."
(WT.1.2)
In the play. *Believing that Polixenes is having an affair with his wife Hermione, Leontes rails against the world.*

World, pessimistic view of the w. - Earth, yield me roots! Who seeks for better of thee, sauce his palate thy most operant poison.
"...Earth, yield me roots!
Who seeks for better of thee, sauce his palate
With thy most operant poison"
(TOA.4.3)
In the play. *Timon retires to the woods after bankruptcy and expresses his pessimism about human nature*

World, pessimistic view of the w. - I am sick of this false world, and will love nought but even the mere necessities upon 't.
"I am sick of this false world, and will love nought
But even the mere necessities upon 't." (TOA.4.3)
In the play. *Timon starts digging his own grave in the woods.*

World, pessimistic view of the world – I 'gin to be aweary of the sun and wish the estate o' the world were now undone.
"I 'gin to be aweary of the sun,
And wish the estate o' the world were now undone." (M.5.5)
In the play. *Macbeth's reaction on learning that a wood is approaching his castle at Duncinane. 'gin'='begin'.*

World, pessimistic view of the w. – It wears as it grows.
POET How goes the world?
PAINTER. It wears, sir, as it grows."
(TOA.1.1)
Answer to 'How is it going?' if your mood reflects it.

In the play. *Poet and painter are two of the many parasites surrounding Timon of Athens.*

World, pessimistic view of the w. – There is enough written upon this earth to stir a mutiny in the most quiet.
"There is enough written upon this earth
To stir a mutiny in the mildest thoughts." (TA.4.1)
Sarcastic and pessimistic comment on the general state of affairs
In the play. *Using a piece of wood held in her mouth Lavinia writes the names of her rapists, Demetrius and Chiron, who also killed Bassianus. Marcus reacts.*

World, pessimistic view of the w. - We have seen the best of our time: machinations, hollowness, treachery, and all ruinous disorders…
"…We have seen the best of our time: machinations, hollowness, treachery, and all ruinous disorders, follow us disquietly to our graves." (KL.1.2)
In the play. *Gloucester's conclusion after reading the fake letter concocted by Edmund to entrap his brother Edgar. Gloucester believes the letter to be true.*

World, pessimistic view of the w., a congregation of vapors – It goes so heavily with my disposition that this goodly frame, the earth…
"…it goes so heavily with my disposition that this goodly frame, the earth, seems to me a sterile promontory, this most excellent canopy, the air, look you, this brave overhanging firmament, this majestical roof fretted with golden fire - why, it appears no other thing to me than a foul and pestilent congregation of vapours." (H.2.2)
You may shorten to 'The earth seems to me a sterile promontory and the air appears no other thing to me than a foul and pestilent congregation of vapours'. Use 'foul and pestilent congregation of vapours' to describe stagnant air, crowded meeting room with windows closed etc.
In the play. *Rosencrantz and Guildenstern admit that they were sent to spy on Hamlet. Hamlet proceeds to tell them himself what they were sent to discover, that is, why he is so sad. He goes on to say why.*

World, pessimistic view of the w., just a stage - I hold the world but as the world, Gratiano; a stage where every man must play a part…
"I hold the world but as the world, Gratiano;
A stage where every man must play a part,
And mine a sad one." (MOV.1.1)
See also Age – all the world's a stage…' – entries for 'Man and its wicked nature'. For an opposite attitude see 'Health, laughter as a medicine - With mirth and laughter let old wrinkles come and let my liver rather heat with wine…'
In the play. *Gratiano finds Antonio worried and sad. Antonio explains why.*

World, pessimistic view of the w., no honesty left - We need no grave to bury honesty: there is not a grain of it the face to sweeten of the whole dungy earth.
"If it be so
We need no grave to bury honesty:
There is not a grain of it the face to sweeten
Of the whole dungy earth." (WT.2.1)
In the play. *Antigonus tells Leontes that if, hypothetically, Hermione was unfaithful, then the very idea of honesty has disappeared from the earth. Hermione is the antithesis of any dishonesty.*

World, pessimistic view of the w. and its inherent evil - I am in this earthly

world; where to do harm is often laudable…
"I am in this earthly world; where to do harm
Is often laudable, to do good sometime
Accounted dangerous folly:" (M.4.2)
See also entries for 'Man and its wicked nature' *** 'Honesty, h. not safe – Take note, take note, O world, to be direct and honest is not safe.'
In the play. *Lady Macduff knows that her having done no harm to anyone will not save her from the murderers sent by Macbeth.*

World, she is the w. - ... for where thou art, there is the world itself.
"A wilderness is populous enough,
So Suffolk had thy heavenly company;
For where thou art, there is the world itself,
With every special pleasure in the world;
And where thou art not, desolation." (KHVI.p2.3.2)
Substitute your name instead of 'Suffolk'. Or just use lines 3, 4 and 5 possibly as an answer such questions as, 'Am I enough for you?' or similar. See also 'Death, d. preferable to be away from her - ... To die is to be banish'd from myself...' – 'Universe, rose, unique - For nothing this wide universe I call, save thou my rose, in it thou art my all.'
In the play. *Suffolk has been banished and he addresses Queen Margaret before leaving.*

World, w. hostile to goodness - O, what a world this is, when what is comely envenoms him that bears it.
"O, what a world this is, when what is comely
Envenoms him that bears it." (AYLI.2.3)
Deprecate that sometimes a worthy character is a liability rather than an asset. See also 'Merit, m., skills or talent excite envy - … to some kind of men their grace serve them as enemies.'
In the play. *Adam generalizes that 'what is comely', that is Orlando, can be a source of venomous envy*

Worm, w. or metaphor for small creature reacting in self-defense - The smallest worm will turn being trodden on.
"The smallest worm will turn being trodden on." (KHVI p3.2)
Use to show that negative reaction may be expected by anyone whose rights have been infringed. In the play. *Clifford to Henry VI who appears lenient towards his enemies*

Worship, question in the form of a compliment - Bright Star of Venus, fallen down on earth, how may I reverently worship thee enough?
"Bright Star of Venus, fallen down on earth,
How may I reverently worship thee enough? (HVI.p1.1.2)
If you really like her and you are not afraid that she may misinterpret you, use this line instead of the standard "Nice meeting you."
In the play. *This is how Henry VI, king of England, reacts when he meets with her bride-to-be Margaret of France for the first time.*

Worst, the extreme of w. - And worse I may be yet: the worst is not so long as we can say 'This is the worst'.
"I am worse than e'er I was…
And worse I may be yet: the worst is not
So long as we can say 'This is the worst.'" (KL.4.1)
In the play. *Edgar despairs at the sight of his father Gloucester made blind by Cornwall and Regan.*

Worth, w. depending on value – What is aught, but as 'tis valued?

"What is aught, but as 'tis valued?" (TC.2.2)
See also 'Means, idolizing means rather than end, wrong - …'tis mad idolatry to make the service greater than the god.'
In the play. *Troilus argues with Hector about keeping Helen rather than returning her to the Greeks.*

Wound, nothing to bother about - And God forbid a shallow scratch should drive the Prince of Wales from such a field as this...
"And God forbid a shallow scratch should drive
The Prince of Wales from such a field as this,
Where stain'd nobility lies trodden on, and rebels' arms triumph in massacres" (KHIV.p1.5.4)
When you cut yourself and your companion(s) insist on over-treating or dressing the wound.
In the play. *Prince Henry has been lightly wounded at Shrewsbury but will not stop fighting.*

Wounded, w. and in need of a band aid - But I am faint, my gashes cry for help.
"But I am faint, my gashes cry for help." (M.1.2)
Cut out 'I am faint' if the cut is only small.
In the play. *A wounded sergeant, just back from the battlefield has finished his narration to King Duncan of the events and of the bravery of Macbeth and Banquo.*

Wounds, w. self-inflicted hard to heel - Those wounds heal ill that men do give themselves.
"Those wounds heal ill that men do give themselves
Omission to do what is necessary Seals a commission to a blank of danger" (TC.3.3)

In the play. *Patroclus reinforces the message previously delivered by Ulysses to Achilles, prompting him to forego his pride (considered here as a self-inflicted wound).*

Writing, assurance of continued communications - I will omit no opportunity that may convey my greetings, love, to thee.
"I will omit no opportunity
That may convey my greetings, love, to thee." (RJ.3.5)
In the play. *Romeo has been banned from Verona after the killing of a Capulet and is taking his leave from Juliet.*

Writing, confidence in your w. power - Your beauty shall in these black lines be seen, and they shall live, and you in them still green.
Your beauty shall in these black lines be seen,
And they shall live, and you in them still green. (SON.63)
Alternative answer to 'Will you love me when I am old?', e.g. 'Yes but not only, your beauty… still green.' See also entries for 'Ageless'.

Writing, decision to write in prose after questioning your own poetical skills - I fear these stubborn lines lack power to move… These numbers will I tear, and write in prose.
"I fear these stubborn lines lack power to move:
O sweet Maria, empress of my love! These numbers will I tear, and write in prose." (LLL.4.3)
You can use it as the beginning of a letter, then follow with what you want to say.
In the play. *Longaville has doubts about his own poetical skills.*

Writing, excusing your poor means to extol her charms - "I grant (sweet love) thy lovely argument deserves the travail of a worthier pen..
"I grant (sweet love) thy lovely argument
Deserves the travail of a worthier pen." (SON.79)
Concluding lines at the end of a romantic letter, to show modesty and a touch of class.
On general correspondence with the ladies you may follow Ovid's advice. 'Your language should inspire trust and your words be familiar, yet coaxing too, so that you seem to be speaking in her presence.' In case your letter be returned to sender, do not despair, '....hold on to your purpose. In time refractory oxen come to the plough, in time horses are taught to bear the pliant reins; an iron ring is worn by constant use, and so is the blade of the plough, by constant ploughing of the ground.' If your letter does not come back but she does not reply, do not complain. 'She who has consented to read will consent to answer what she has read; that will come by its own stages and degrees. Perhaps even an angry letter will first come to you, asking you not to vex her. But what she asks she fears; what she does not ask, she desires – that you will continue; press on then and soon you will have gained your wish.' (Ovid, AOL.1).
Sometimes, especially professionals, cannot get away from the world and words of their trade and write with expressions more suitable to the recipients. Such is the case of the illustrious physicists Michael Faraday who while writing to Sarah Barnard in 1820 says,

'I want to say a thousand kind and, believe me, heartfelt things to you, but I am not a master of words fit for the purpose; and still, as I ponder and think of you, chlorides, trials, oil, Davy, steel, miscellanea, mercury and fifty other professional fancies swim in my mind and drive me further and further into the quandary of stupidness.'

Writing, fame and immortality through w. - Death makes no conquest of this conqueror, for now he lives in fame, though not in life.
"That Julius Caesar was a famous man:
With that his valour did enrich his wit,
His wit set down to make his valour live:
Death makes no conquest of this conqueror;
For now he lives in fame, though not in life." (KRIII.3.1)
Illustrate the long lasting value of literature as good literature gives the writer a kind of immortality.
In the play. *The Prince of Wales conversing with Richard III who secretly plans the Prince's assassination.*

Writing, letters anxiously awaited - ... and with mine eyes I'll drink the words you send though ink be made of gall.
"...thither write, my queen,
And with mine eyes I'll drink the words you send,
Though ink be made of gall."
(CYM.1.1)
In the play. *Posthumus Leonatus, Imogen's husband, has been banned from England – he asks the beautiful and loving Imogen to write to him in Italy.*

Writing, power of printed message - ... in black ink my love may still shine bright.
"O fearful meditation, where alack,

Shall Time's best jewel from Time's chest lie hid?
Or what strong hand can hold his swift foot back,
Or who his spoil of beauty can forbid?
O none, unless this miracle have might,
That in black ink my love may still shine bright." (SON.65)
Statement of unending love in subdued tone, e.g. 'We cannot fight or conquer time, unless this miracle have might…bright."
Be prepared to find ladies completely indifferent to the power of the word. Ovid admits, 'Though you come, Homer, and all the Muses with you, if you bring nothing, Homer, out you go!', meaning that you should supplement your fine words with more solid tokens of appreciation and endearment. On the other hand….'Yet there are learned women too, a scanty number and others are not learned, but wish to be so. Let either sort be praised in poems; his verses, whatever their quality, let the reader commend by the charm of his recital; and thus to the learned and the unlearned the poem fashioned in their praise will perchance seem like a little gift.' (Ovid, AOL 2).
In some other cases writing is power. Ovid, 'Therefore let a letter speed, laden with persuasive words - explore her feelings, and be the first to try the path. A letter carried in an apple betrayed Cydippe, and the maid was deceived unawares of her own words.' What happened is that Acontius, who was passionately in love with Cydippe, wrote on an apple, 'I swear by Diana to marry Acontius.' Cydippe read it aloud and so was bound by the vow to marry him. (AOL.2).
See also "Value, v. of object enhanced by owner - … things of like value differing in the owners are prized by their masters…'

Writing, using w. rather than speech - O let my books be then the eloquence…
"O let my books be then the eloquence
And dumb presagers of my speaking breast." (Sonnet 23)
When you decide to make your declaration of love in writing, as you are afraid that, being overwhelmed by your passion, you may not give correct expression to your feelings.

Writing, what are you w. – O, know, sweet love, I always write of you…
"O, know, sweet love, I always write of you,
And you and love are still my argument" (SON.76)

Writing, w. preferred to speech - I'll call for pen and ink, and write my mind.
"…I dare not speak:
I'll call for pen and ink, and write my mind." (KHVI p1.5.2)
See also, 'Speechless, made speechless by her princely beauty - … beauty's princely majesty is such, confounds the tongue, and makes the senses rough.'
In the play. *Suffolk is struck by the beauty of Margaret, daughter of the Duke of Angers.*

Writing, w. skills not always an asset - … I have been so well brought up that I can write my name…
CLERK… I have been so well brought up that I can write my name.
ALL He hath confessed: away with him! he's a villain and a traitor.' (KHVI p2.4.2)
See 'Reading, r. and writing natural - … to write and read comes by nature.' Or relate the short dialog from the play as an anecdote to show that not everyone appreciates the value of education. Also answer to 'What is your education?' (first line).

In the play. *A clerk confesses to John Cade of being able to write his name and by inference, to write – whereupon the rebels accuse him of treason.*

Wrong, w. compounded - ... thus to persist in doing wrong extenuates not wrong.
"...thus to persist
In doing wrong extenuates not wrong,
But makes it much more heavy." (TC.2.2)
Denounce the continuation of an evil act or program.
In the play. *Hector argues with Troilus and Paris about returning Helen to the Greeks.*

Young and ready for greatness - ... ripe for exploits and mighty enterprises.
"... and my thrice-puissant liege
Is in the very May-morn of his youth,
Ripe for exploits and mighty enterprises." (KHV.1.2)
Apply to yourself (if applicable) or to whom it may be. 'He is in the very May-morn of his youth, ripe for exploits... enterprises." Or when you agree and ready to go into action, 'I am ready for exploits and mighty enterprises'.
In the play. *Bishops Canterbury and Ely (who says these lines), have crafted a cause and invented a motive to make war to France and now Ely adds some flattery to Henry V to better motivate him. The bishops' intent is to prevent Henry V from taxing the church's income and to lure him to make up for the lost revenue with foreign plunders.*

Youth and rebellion - ... natural rebellion, done in the blaze of youth...
"I beseech your majesty to make it
Natural rebellion, done in the blaze of youth;
When oil and fire, too strong for reason's force,
O'erbears it, and burns it."
(AWEW.5.2)

Explain away your youthful errors or those of someone else.
In the play. *The Countess intercedes with the King on behalf of her son Bertram, suggesting that he erred on account of his youth.*

Youth, a dangerous time, prudence counseled - ... and in the morn and liquid dew of youth contagious blastments are most imminent.
"... And in the morn and liquid dew of youth
Contagious blastments are most imminent.
Be wary then; best safety lies in fear."
(H.1.3)
Advice to a young person, or encouragement to be cautious, "Be wary then; best safety lies in fear", or express a generalized concern, '...contagious blastments are most imminent, therefore best safety lies in fear'.
In the play. *Before leaving for France Laertes gives advice to his sister Ophelia, specifically to avoid temptations of all sorts.*

Youth, a dangerous time, prudence counseled - ... keep you in the rear of your affection...
"And keep you in the rear of your affection,
Out of the shot and danger of desire"
(H.1.3)
'He (or she) is in the rear of my affections' may be an answer as to whether you are still seeing her (or him' and you do not.
In the play. *Before leaving for France Laertes gives advice to his sister Ophelia, specifically to avoid temptations of all sorts.*

Youth, a young person – he wears the rose of youth upon him.
"...he wears the rose
Of youth upon him" (AC.3.13)
Alternative to 'how old is he?' or changing 'him' to 'her', 'how old is she?'

In the play. *In conversation with Cleopatra, Antony refers to the young age of his military rival, Octavian.*

Youth, carefree attitude in your younger days - ... two lads that thought there was no more behind...
"We were, fair Queen,
Two lads that thought there was no more behind
But such a day tomorrow as today,
And to be boy eternal." (WT.1.2)
Express your attitudes in youth, e.g. 'I thought there was no more…eternal.'
In the play. *Polixenes summarizes for Hermione his early friendship with Leontes.*

Youth, characteristics of youth's behavior - ... wanton, wild and usual slips as are companions noted...
"…wanton, wild and usual slips
As are companions noted and most known
To youth and liberty." (H.2.1)
In the play. *Polonius instructs Reynaldo to keep a watch on Laertes' deeds in Paris. Laertes is Polonius' son.*

Youth, levity of y. recollected - Our own precedent passions do instruct us…
"She is young and apt:
Our own precedent passions do instruct us
What levity's in youth." (TOA.1.1)
Soften criticism of the behavior of young people.
In the play. *Another parasite's daughter wants to marry a poor man and her father approaches Timon for help. Timon offers to match the value of the daughter's dowry and give it to the groom.*

Youth, lifestyle or regimen unsuitable to y. - To fast, to study and to see no woman.
"To fast, -- to study -- and to see no woman: --

Flat treason 'gainst the kingly state of youth." (LLL.4.3)
Use an ironic reply to 'What are you doing?' e.g., 'I fast, I study and see no women - flat treason… youth.'
In the play. *Biron gives reasons for breaking the king's oath of study, seclusion and abstinence.*

Youth, restricting y. ineffective - Young blood doth not obey an old decree.
"Young blood doth not obey an old decree:
We cannot cross the cause why we were born." (LLL.4.3)
Support the idea that love cannot be repressed. See entries for 'Promises, love p. unreliable' – 'Age, a. and hypocrisy - A man can no more separate age and covetousness, than he can part young limbs and lechery.' - Instinct, i. prevailing over the dictates of law - …the brain may devise laws for the blood…'
In the play. *Biron utters words of wisdom to rationalize why king and company cannot keep their oaths.*

Youth, stage of y. - His May of youth and bloom of lustihood.
"His May of youth and bloom of lustihood" (MAAN.5.1)
In the play. *Old Leonato is ready to revenge the honor of his daughter Hero against the insulting Claudio despite Claudio's youth to whom the line applies.*

Youth, y. always craving for novelty - … younger spirits, whose apprehensive senses all but new things disdain...
"…younger spirits, whose apprehensive senses
All but new things disdain…" (AWEW.1.2)
Characterize the fickle passion for novelty by young people.

In the play. *The King speaks of Helen's father, who was the most celebrated and respected doctor of his time, and remembers some of his sayings.*

Youth, y. potentially misspent - ... thou wouldst have plunged thyself in general riot; melted down thy youth in different beds of lust...
"...thou wouldst have plunged thyself
In general riot; melted down thy youth
In different beds of lust; and never learn'd
The icy precepts of respect, but follow'd
The sugar'd game before thee" (TOA.4.3)
Ironic answer to questions of the type 'What did you do at college?' or 'What did you do when you were young?' E.G. 'I plunged myself in general riot and melted down my youth…lust'.
In the play. *Apemantus visits Timon in the woods. Timon says that natural conditions and chance explain why Apemantus, an anarchist beggar, did not fall into disgrace as Timon himself did.*

Youth, y. shortened by recklessness - For though the camomile, the more it is trodden on, the faster it grows, yet youth, the more it is wasted, the sooner it wears.
"…for though the camomile, the more it is trodden on, the faster it grows, yet youth, the more it is wasted, the sooner it wears." (KHIV p1.2.4)
Apply to reckless behavior. Alternatively use partially as a term of reference. E.G. 'For though the camomile… it grows, here if we continue to let our rights be trodden on…'
In the play. *Falstaff explains his philosophy to Prince Henry.*

Youth, y. spent in prison – ... And hath detain'd me all my flowering youth within a loathsome dungeon…
"That cause, fair nephew, that imprison'd me
And hath detain'd me all my flowering youth
Within a loathsome dungeon, there to pine" (KHVI.p1.2.5)
In the play. *Mortimer explains the political reasons why he has spent his youth (and life) in prison.*

Youth, y. spent in idleness - ... wear out thy youth with shapeless idleness.
"… living dully sluggardized at home,
Wear out thy youth with shapeless idleness." (TGV.1.1)
Self-effacing answer to the question, 'What did you do when you were young?' E.G. 'I wore out my youth…idleness'.
In the play. *Valentine would invite his friend Proteus to travel abroad but Proteus is in love with Julia and would not consider leaving Verona. Valentine hints that Proteus lives in idleness.*

Youth, y. unable to follow good counsel – ... such a hare is madness the youth, to skip o'er the meshes of good counsel the cripple.
"… such a hare is madness the youth, to skip o'er the meshes of good counsel the cripple." (MOV.1.2)
In the play. *Portia comments on the difficulty of young people in general, by associating youth with a hare and good counsel with a cripple.*

Zero tolerance – I will be deaf to pleading and excuses, nor tears nor prayers shall purchase out abuses.
"I will be deaf to pleading and excuses;
Nor tears nor prayers shall purchase out abuses" (RJ.3.1)
In the play. *The Prince of Verona is angry at finding Mercutio and Tybalt slain after he had banned dueling.*

Analytical Index

A crew of patches. See 'Personnel, crew, a motley crew - A crew of patches, rude mechanicals, that work for bread upon the Athenian walls.'

A Daniel come to judgment! yea, a Daniel! See 'Judgment, agreeing with the judge'

A horse! A horse! My kingdom for a horse. See 'Transportation, t. needed quickly.'

A jest's prosperity lies in the ear of him that hears it… See 'Joke, determining if a j. is good or not'

A little fire is quickly trodden out … See 'Problem, p. to be tackled before it gets bigger – A little fire is quickly trodden out, which being suffered, rivers cannot quench.'

A man may fish with a worm … See 'Circumstances, c. and status, a complete turn-around - A man may fish with a worm that had eat of a king…'

A plague of opinion! a man may wear it on both sides, like a leather jerkin. See 'Opinion, o. of others to be disregarded'.

A pond as deep as hell. See 'Character, a hypocrite and a filthy c. - .. His filth within being cast, he would appear a pond as deep as hell.'

A rhapsody of words. See "Religion, r. allegiance just in words – … and sweet religion makes a rhapsody of words.'

A spotless reputation. See 'Reputation, value placed on r. - The purest treasure mortal times afford.'

Ability, magic abilities claimed - I can call spirits from the vasty deep.

Ability, questionable - A horse that's the more capable creature.

Ability, a. strength and courage displayed - … doing, in the figure of a lamb, the feats of a lion

Absence, 'Will you miss me?' – Or call it winter, which being full of care, makes summer's welcome thrice more wished, more rare.

Absence, a. felt - Is it thy will, thy image should keep open my heavy eyelids to the weary night?

Absence, a. from an event - … our absence makes us unthrifty to our knowledge…

Absence, a. from the office. See 'Anxiety, a. about what may happen at the office while you are away - I am questioned by my fears, of what may chance or breed upon our absence'

Absence, a. not felt. See 'Modesty, absence not felt - My worth unknown, no loss is known in me'.

Absence, a. worse than death - If I depart from thee I cannot live: and in thy sight to die, what were it else…

Absence, a. worse than death - To die by thee, were to die in jest; from thee to die, were torture more than death.

Absence, being away from her felt like winter - How like a winter hath my absence been from thee…

Absence, her a. makes it feel like winter. See lines in 'Flowers, lilies and roses - Nor did I wonder at the lily's white, nor praise the deep vermilion in the rose….'

Absence, hoping that a. may not be detrimental – … I hope my absence doth neglect no great designs…

Absence, invitation to make one's presence felt – Appear thou in the likeness of a sigh speak but one rhyme, and I am satisfied.

Absent, cannot find him - I think he be transform'd into a beast for I can no where find him like a man.

Absent-mindedness. See 'Apologies for absent-mindedness - … my dull brain was wrought with things forgotten.'

Abstinence, consequences of a. when turned into law – … the ungenitured agent will unpeople the province with continency…

Abstinence, some distance advisable – such separation…becomes a virtuous bachelor and a maid.

Abstinence. See entries for 'Reliability, am I going to be safe with you? Can I trust you?

Etc'

Abuse, a. not tolerated. See 'Zero tolerance – I will be deaf to pleading and excuses, nor tears nor prayers shall purchase out abuses.'

Abuse, a. occurring and increasing because it is tolerated. See 'Strength, s. relative, wolf and sheep - ... I know he would not be a wolf but that he sees the Romans are but sheep.'

Abuse, someone is being abused – You are abused beyond the mark of thought

Abuse, verbal a. - ... what man of good temper would endure this tempest of exclamation?

Abuses, looking into a. See 'Character, suspicious c, admitted – ... it is my nature's plague to spy into abuses…'

Academic qualification not necessarily equating to intelligence - For, besides that he is a fool, he's a great quarreler.

Accent, not recognizing the a. - ... pardon me, that any accent breaking from thy tongue should 'scape the true acquaintance of mine ear

Acceptance, a. and resignation to the will of Heaven - ... but heaven hath a hand in these events…

Acceptance, a. of a decision. See 'Decision, acceptance of a d. - Be it as your wisdom will.'

Acceptance, a. of what may come - I do find it cowardly and vile for fear of what might fall…

Accepting an invitation. See "Invitation, i. impossible to resist - ... There is no tongue that moves, none, none in the world so soon as yours could win me.'

Accident, as often as merit establishing a person's value. See 'Man, perception establishing his value'.

Accomplishment. See 'Feat, f. to be rewarded with honor and commendations'.

Accountant, poor a. See 'Mathematics, error in calculations - ... it were pity you should get your living by reckoning.' *** 'Mathematics, not a strength - I am ill at reckoning: it fitteth the spirit of a tapster.'

Accounting woman. See 'Woman, w. that keeps the books and is arbiter of economic decisions - ... the report goes she has all the rule of her husband's purse.'

Accounting, a. above board, request for an audit -... call me before the exactest auditors…

Accusation, a. based on a false report. See 'Report, false r. - ... let not his report come current for an accusation…'

Accusation, a. rejected – I have a thousand spirits in my breast to answer twenty thousand such as you.

Accusation, a. unfair – Take good heed you charge not in your spleen a noble person.

Accusation, answer to a. - The blood is hot that must be cool'd for this.

Accusation, defence from a. See entries for 'Defence, d. from accusation'

Accusation, false a. engendered by rancor - ... It issues from the rancour of a villain

Accusation, false a. innocence will triumph – Innocence shall make false accusation blush.

Accusation, false a. or false suspicion – You do me shameful injury falsely to draw me…

Accusation, personal a. (here of corruption and treason), prompted by evidence not malice – ... whom from the flow of gall I name not but from sincere motions…

Accusations, explanation for the false a. - And that engenders thunder in his breast and makes him roar these accusations forth.

Accusations, preventing sting of a. – Comest thou with deep premeditated lines…

Accusers, attitude towards a. and you are innocent - I am richer than my base accusers.

Ache, stomach ache - There is so hot a summer in my bosom…

Achievement, a. requires effort - Pain pays the income of each precious thing…

Achievement, a. requires effort. See 'Persistence, your persistence has paid off -

He that will have a cake out of the wheat, must tarry the grinding.'

Achievement, happily married to the woman of choice – And happily I have arrived at last unto the wished haven of my bliss.

Achievements, a. worth praising - ... And make her chronicle as rich with praise as is the ooze and bottom of the sea with sunken wreck and sunless treasuries.

Achievements, low a. See 'Results, poor personal r. acknowledged – How my achievements mock me!'

Achievements, value of past a. not to be forgotten - The service of the foot being once gangrened…

Acknowledgment, a. and appreciation of help given – Thou art all the comfort the gods will diet me with.

Acne, allaying concerns about a. See 'Invocation, i. for lover to come – ... come, thou day in night; for thou wilt lie upon the wings of night whiter than new snow on a raven's back'.

Acquaintance, a. superficial - We know each other faces; but for our hearts…

Acquaintance, a. unpleasant - And long to know each other worse…

Acquaintance, worth of a. recognized - I am blest in your acquaintance.

Act, a difficult a. to follow. See 'Speech, speaking after a well known or skillful speaker - As in a theatre, the eyes of men, after a well grac'd actor leaves the stage…'

Act, a. imposed by force. See 'Force, f. imposing action - for do we must what force will have us do'.

Act, a. not done under any condition - ... Not the world's mass of vanity could make me.

Act, dreadful a. that will come to haunt his authors - Too many curses on their heads…

Act, extreme a. shaping all things to come - ... this blow be the be-all and the end-all here.

Act, hellish a. See 'Repent

Act, uncommon a. and showing loyalty. See 'Occurrence, rare o. - It is no act of common passage, but a strain of rareness.'

Action, a. and accomplishment as their own reward. See 'Character, c. that disregards riches - ... (he) look'd upon things precious as they were the common muck of the world…'

Action, a. as its own reward. See 'Modesty, deeds as their own reward - ... rewards his deeds with doing them, and is content to spend the time to end it.'

Action, a. contrary to purpose - So play the foolish throngs with one that swoons...

Action, a. contrary to purpose - That were to blow at fire in hope to quench it.

Action, a. contrary to purpose - That were to enlard his fat already pride and add more coals to

Action, a. contrary to what needed - You rub the sore when you should bring the plaster.

Action, a. critical and urgent - And 'tis no little reason bids us speed…

Action, a. forced by circumstances. See 'Rebellion, reasons and occasions for a r. - We see which way the stream of time doth run… the rough torrent of occasion.'

Action, a. louder than words. See 'Character, c. that acts more than speak - ... speaking in deeds and deedless in his tongue…'

Action, a. made useless by the timing - ... this is like the mending of highways in summer, where the ways are fair enough.

Action, a. not taken without consent. See 'Commitment, c. to always consult before taking important action - And never will I undertake the thing wherein thy counsel and consent is wanting.'

Action, a. not talk. See 'Talk, talkers are no doers'.

Action, a. preferable to inaction - A stirring dwarf we do allowance give before a sleeping giant.

Action, a. requiring urgent and strong

response – 't is not sleepy business but must be look'd to speedily.

Action, a. requiring urgent and strong response – The affair cries haste and speed must answer it.

Action, a. that cannot be delayed - This weighty business will not brook delay.

Action, a. that promises to be successful - ... rich advantage of a promised glory as smiles upon the forehead of this action.

Action, a. vs. speculation – Thoughts speculative their unsure hopes relate but certain issue strokes must arbitrate.

Action, abominable a. - the deed you undertake is damnable.

Action, absurd a. See 'Task, t. impossible and unrealistic - ... the task he undertakes is numbering sands and drinking oceans dry.'

Action, concurrence in the proposed action - ... if you say ay, the king will not say no.

Action, doing the best with the means available - The means that heaven yields must be embraced and not neglected.

Action, eagerness for a. – Let the hours be short, till fields, and blows, and groans applaud our sport!

Action, eloquence in a. – For in such business action is eloquence.

Action, immediate a. lest resolution will falter - I must be brief, lest resolution drop out of mine eyes, in tender womanish tears.

Action, invitation to a. - ... with that spur as he would to the lip of his mistress.

Action, invitation to take corrective a. - Speak, strike, redress!

Action, justifying honorable a. - ... what I did, I did in honour, led by the impartial conduct of my soul…

Action, let's go – Our corn's to reap for yet our tithe's to sow.

Action, little a. better than none. See 'Action, a. preferable to inaction - A stirring dwarf we do allowance give before a sleeping giant.'

Action, need to act notwithstanding possible censure – If we shall stand still in fear our motion…

Action, need to act notwithstanding possible censure – We must not stint our necessary actions…

Action, quick a. needed as time goes by quickly - Let's take the instant by the forward top.

Action, ready for a. - I am settled, and bend up each corporal agent to this terrible feat.

Action, ready for a. if mind is ready - All things are ready, if our minds be so.

Action, reason for a. made public - ... and public reasons shall be rendered of Caesar's death.

Action, request for advice on how or what to do - Let your own discretion be your tutor.

Action, resolution to act quickly - Ay, that's the way, dull not device by coldness and delay.

Action, senseless a. - What a pretty thing man is when he goes in his doublet and hose and leaves off his wit!

Action, shameful a. calling for redress. See 'Redress, need for immediate r. - The shame itself doth speak for instant remedy.'

Action, urgent a. required against enemy - The land is burning; Percy stands on high, and either we or they must lower lie.

Actions, a. not corresponding to words - ... your words and performance are no kin together.

Actions, a. speak more than words - Words to the heat of deeds too cold breath gives.

Actions, a. that should be praised. See 'Praise, p. deserved and not to be hidden - O, your desert speaks loud; and I should wrong it…'

Actions, a. vs. intentions. See 'Intentions, i. are no actions'.

Actions, nobility in a. and thoughts - My actions are as noble as my thoughts.

Actions, past a. cannot be remedied – Look, what is done cannot be now amended, men shall deal unadvisedly sometimes…

Actor, a. that has forgotten his part. See 'Part, p. forgotten, like an actor forgetting his p. - Like a dull actor now, I have forgot my part…'

Actor, capable of feigning as needed - … ghastly looks are at my service, like enforced smiles…

Actors, amateur a. See 'Personnel, crew, a motley crew - A crew of patches, rude mechanicals, that work for bread upon the Athenian walls.'

Actors, their quality in acting – The best in this kind are but shadows…

Administration, a. run by incompetent people. See 'Times, bad times – 'Tis the times' plague, when madmen lead the blind.'

Admiration, a. and love without flattery - I cannot flatter; I do defy the tongues of soothers but…

Admiration, a. and respect stated. See 'Declaration, d. of admiration and respect - … Burgundy enshrines thee in his heart…'

Admiration, a. for adversary unconditional - And were I any thing but what I am, I would wish me only he.

Admiration, not flattery – I do defy the tongues of soothers; but a braver place in my heart's love …

Admiration, she is top of the list – … the top of admiration! Worth what's dearest to the world!

Admiration. See 'Ego boosting, she is a sought after prize - Nor is the wide world ignorant of her worth…'

Admiration, worth to be admired by kings – I was a morsel for a monarch…

Admired, a. by all. See 'Politician, young aspiring p. - The expectancy and rose of the fair state… the observed of all observers.'

Adonis. See 'Beauty, male b. - Describe Adonis, and the counterfeit is poorly imitated after you.' *** 'Promises, p. quickly delivered - Thy promises are like Adonis' gardens that one day bloom'd and fruitful were the next.'

Adoration, a. not just friendship - I profess myself her adorer, not her friend.

Adultery, a. not punished - Thou shalt not die: die for adultery! No: the wren goes to 't.…

Advance knowledge desired. See 'Prediction, desire to know in advance - O, that a man might know the end of this day's business ere it come…'

Advance, applying for an advance or raise - I do beseech you, as in the way of taste to give me now a little benefit…

Advancement. See entries for 'Promotion'.

Advantage, better taking a. than trusting - 'Tis better using France than trusting France

Advantage, edge, planning for strategic a. - … advantage is a better soldier than rashness.

Advantages, a. to be derived by a situation. See 'Situation, s. advantageous whatever the outcome - … my end can make good use of either…'

Adventure, move prompted by a sense of a. – Such wind as scatters young men through the world.

Adventure, thirst for a. See 'Rise, an early rise to launch into an adventure - The day shall not be up so soon as I to try the fair adventure of tomorrow.'

Adventure, travelling for a. and learning - … as he that leaves a shallow plash to plunge him in the deep …

Adversary, a. admired. See 'Admiration, a. for adversary unconditional'.

Adversary, defeat of a. crucial for survival – … the welfare of us all hangs on the cutting short that fraudful man.

Adversary, inhuman and pitiless - A stony adversary, an inhuman wretch, uncapable of pity…

Adversary, noble a. – He is a lion that I am proud to hunt.

Adversary, paying homage to a valiant a. - His valour shown upon our crests to-day hath taught us to cherish such high deeds

1045

even in the bosom of our adversaries.

Adversary, political a. to be defeated – He's a rank weed… and must root him out.

Adversity, a. as a test of the spirit - Where is your ancient courage... …extremity was the trier of spirits.

Adversity, a. assembles strange characters - … misery acquaints a man with strange bedfellows.

Adversity, a. put to good use - Sweet are the uses of adversity…

Adversity, affected by a. – A man I am cross'd with adversity.

Adversity, attitude towards a. - Let me embrace these sour adversities, for wise men say it is the wisest course.

Adversity, positive attitude towards a. See 'Attitude, positive and defiant towards adversity – in poison there is physic' and these news…'

Adversity, positive attitude towards a. - Be cheerful; wipe thine eyes, some falls are means the happier to arise.

Adversity, some g. can be found in a. - There is some soul of goodness in things evil…

Adversity, spirit of acceptance of a. eases the spirit - 'Tis good for men to love their present pains upon example; so the spirit is eased…

Adversity, turning a. around - … that can translate the stubbornness of fortune into so quiet and so sweet a style.

Advertising - To things of sale a seller's praise belongs…

Advertising, false a. – Thus credulous fools are caught.

Advice, a. from a world hater - Hate all, curse all, show charity to none…

Advice, a. hopeless to a lover or a sensualist - …that art a votary to fond desire.

Advice, a. not to be rude or patronizing - (haughtiness) … leaves behind a stain

Advice, a. not wanted - … cease thy counsel which falls into mine ear as profitless as water in a sieve.

Advice, a. on borrowing and lending. See 'Opinion, your op. on money, handling of, borrowing and lending - Neither a borrower nor a lender be...'

Advice, a. on cultivating friendship - Those friends thou hast, and their adoption tried, grapple them to thy soul with hoops of steel.

Advice, a. on general behavior in life - Keep thy foot out of brothels, thy hand out of plackets, thy pen from lenders' books…

Advice, a. on general behavior with others and way of life - Give thy thoughts no tongue, nor any unproportioned thought his act.

Advice, a. on general behavior with others and way of life - Love all, trust a few, do wrong to none.

Advice, a. on how to apply knowledge and the arts - Music and poesy use to quicken you…

Advice, a. on how to stand out – … put thyself into the trick of singularity.

Advice, a. on men's wear and fashion - Costly thy habit as thy purse can buy, but not express'd in fancy; rich, not gaudy…

Advice, a. on strength of character - … to thine own self be true, and it must follow, as the night the day, thou canst not then be false to any man

Advice, a. on talking and listening - Give every man thy ear, but few thy voice, take each man's censure, but reserve thy judgment.

Advice, a. to a sharp-tongued woman - … if thou be so shrewd of thy tongue.

Advice, a. to adapt to circumstances. See 'Circumstances, adapting course to c. - Let go thy hold when a great wheel runs down a hill…'

Advice, a. to be modest with no boasting or wild behavior - …take pain to allay with some cold drops of modesty…

Advice, a. to contain anger. See 'Anger,

advice to contain a.'

Advice, a. to love moderately and to avoid excess - ... too swift arrives as tardy as too slow.

Advice, a. to proceeds slowly - Wisely and slow; they stumble that run fast.

Advice, a. to stay away from dangerous persons or group. See 'Scorpion, s's nest to be avoided - ... Seek not a scorpion's nest.'

Advice, advising planning and reflection. See 'Planning, p. and reflection advised before action'

Advice, asking for a. – Bestow your needful counsel to our business.

Advice, asking for a. – What counsel give you in this weighty cause?

Advice, general a. - Have more than thou showest, speak less than thou knowest, lend less than thou owest.

Advice, good a. – When a wise man gives thee better counsel, give me mine again.

Advice, his a. would be helpful now - his counsel now might do me golden service.

Advice, listen more than speak - Give every man thine ear, but few thy voice...

Advice, listen to my a. - ... fasten your ear on my advisings…

Advice, listen to experienced a. - Knit all the Greekish ears to his experienced tongue.

Advice, project needing friend's assistance - ... some sport in hand wherein your cunning can assist me much.

Advice, promise to follow a. See 'Lesson, l. given was understood - I shall th'effect of this good lesson keep as watchman to my heart.'

Advice, refusal to give a. - I will not cast away my physic, but on those that are sick.

Advice, request for a. from capable person - Counsel me Tranio, for I know thou canst…

Advice, safety a. - better avoid than question the nature of the problem - 'Tis safer to avoid what's grown than question how 't is born.

Advice, suggestion to banish strange ideas - Arm thy constant and thy nobler parts... giddy loose suggestions.

Advice, take best advantage of the opportunity - ... frame the season for your own harvest.

Advice, useful and approved a. - ... Now I begin to relish thy advice…

Advice, uselessness of a. when in pain - Every one can master a grief, but he that has it.

Advice, a. welcome and praised, along with praise of learning - I could have stay'd here all the night to hear good counsel: O, what learning is!

Advice, you like her a. - I like thy counsel; well hast thou advised.

Affair, symptoms of ongoing a. – …Is leaning cheek to cheek? is meeting noses?…

Affectation – the lady doth protest too much, methinks.

Affection, power of a. See 'Power, special p. of affection - Affection! thy intention stabs the centre…

Affinities, a. of character. See entries for 'Characters, similarity of c.'

After life's fitful fever … See 'Sleep, s. of death considered as rest - … After life's fitful fever he sleeps well.'

After-life, how to deal with the a-l. - … for the life to come, I sleep out the thought of it.

Afternoon. See 'Time, (in the) afternoon, a. redefined – posteriors of the day'.

Age – all the world's a stage…

Age, a. and decrepitude. See lines in 'Indisposition, feeling out of sorts -. ... to deal plainly, I fear I am not in my perfect mind.'

Age, a. and hunger - Oppress'd with two great evils, age and hunger

Age, a. and hypocrisy – A man can no more separate age and covetousness than a' can part young limbs and lechery.

Age, a. and ingratitude. See 'Ingratitude, i. tied to aging - These old fellows have their ingratitude in them hereditary...'

Age, a. and insomnia - Care keep his watch in every old man's eye, and where care lodges, sleep will never lie…

Age, a. and its byproducts - … the unruly waywardness that infirm and choleric years bring with them.

Age, a. and its effects on beauty. See 'Beauty, b. declining with age or unforeseen circumstances - And every fair from fair sometime declines…'

Age, a. and its liabilities. See 'Insurance, self- i. to pay for requirements of old age - … When service should in my old limbs lie lame and unregarded age in corners thrown.'

Age, a. and its way of thinking - … it is as proper to our age to cast beyond ourselves in our opinions…

Age, a. and lying - Lord, lord, how subject we old men are to this vice of lying.

Age, a. and lying - … old men of less truth than tongue

Age, a. and related waywardness - … must we look to receive from his age, not alone the imperfections of long-engraffed condition…

Age, a. and retirement savings – … Five hundred crowns…which I did store to be my foster-nurse when… service should in my old limbs lie lame.

Age, a. causing childishness - Old fools are babes again.

Age, a. causing childishness - They say an old man is twice a child.

Age, a. causing taste to change - A man loves the meat in his youth, that he cannot endure in old age...

Age, a. discrimination on the part of a woman - … and he that is less than a man, I am not for him.

Age, a. incapable of enjoying wealth – 'The aged man that coffers-up his gold is plagued with cramps and gouts and painful fits…'

Age, a. inevitably engenders wisdom - … Instructed by the antiquary times, he must be, he is, he cannot be but wise.

Age, a. irrelevant to love, see entries for 'Ageless'.

Age, a. placing a limit to the display of gallantry - … One that is well-nigh worn to pieces with age to show himself a young gallant.

Age, admitting to being old - … I am declined into the vale of years.

Age, admitting to being old - Myself am struck in years, I must confess.

Age, admitting to being old - That time of year thou mayst in me behold…

Age, advantages and disadvantages in the eyes of a woman - … youth in ladies' eyes that flourisheth.

Age, aging gracefully due to lightness of heart. See 'Health, laughter as a medicine - With mirth and laughter let old wrinkles come and let my liver rather heat with wine…'

Age, dangerous to be old – It is as dangerous to be aged in any kind of course…

Age, debilitating effects of a. - … When sapless age and weak unable limbs should bring thy father to his drooping chair.

Age, declaration of old a. – every part of you blasted with antiquity…

Age, defending old a. and a happy disposition - If to be old and merry be a sin, then many an old host that I know, is damned.

Age, difference in a. – Octavius, I have seen more days than you…

Age, difference in judgment between young and old. See 'Age, a. and its way of thinking - … it is as proper to our age to cast beyond ourselves in our opinions…'

Age, graying hair does not imply less brain power - … though grey do something mingle with our younger brown, yet have we a brain…

Age, how old are you? - … Not so young, sir, to love a woman for singing…

Age, late in years, like the Fall. See 'Fall,

season - That time of year thou mayst in me behold…'

Age, late maturity. See 'Life, getting to the Autumn of life - I have lived long enough: my way of life is fallen into the sear, the yellow leaf'

Age, life at its limit - Nature in you stands on the very verge of her confine.

Age, making man redundant - … I confess that I am old, age is unnecessary.

Age, middle a., flowers suitable for middle a. See 'Flowers, marigolds and other f. indicated for middle age men - … Here's flowers for you, hot lavender…'

Age, observation on old age by a young person - … old folks, many feign as they were dead; unwieldy, slow, heavy and pale as lead.

Age, old a. and hunger, two concurrent evils - … Oppressed with two weak evils, age and hunger.

Age, old a. and wealth. See 'Wealth, w. of no use to old age - … when thou art old and rich, thou hast neither heat, affection, limb, nor beauty…'

Age, old a. compared to an oak. See 'Oak, old o. also metaphor for old age – … an oak, whose boughs were moss'd with age and high top bald with dry antiquity.'

Age, old a. should be more serious - How ill white hairs become a fool and jester.

Age, old a. without wisdom – Thou shouldst not have been old till thou hadst been wise.

Age, old and unhappy – You see me here, you gods, a poor old man, as full of grief as age; wretched in both.

Age, question about a. – Not old enough to be a man and…

Age, pretending to be young - Do you set down your name in the scroll of youth…

Age, recognition of one's old a. and plea for understanding - Pray you now, forget and forgive: I am old and foolish.

Age, rejuvenation, look up to 50 years younger. See 'Eyes, their rejuvenating power – … might shake off fifty, looking in her eyes.' *** 'Beauty, rejuvenating effects of b. - beauty doth varnish age, as if new born…'

Age, sex and aging - Is it not strange that desire should so many years outlive performance?

Age, signs of aging - Have you not a moist eye? a dry hand? a yellow cheek?…

Age, too old to learn – … Too far in years to be a pupil now.

Age, too old to love – You cannot call it love; for at your age, the hey-day in the blood is tame…

Age, weak body, strong will. See 'Will, mind over matter notwithstanding a state of debility – And like the rich hangings in a homely house.'

Age, wealth useless to a. See 'Wealth, w. of no use to old age - … when thou art old and rich, thou hast neither heat, affection, limb, nor beauty…'

Age, young defeat the old - The younger rises when the old doth fall.

Age, young in a. but old in judgment - "…I am only old in judgment and understanding.

Age. An asset under certain conditions. See 'Appearance, a. improving with age, ugliness in men as an advantage - I was created with a stubborn outside…'

Age. Its effects on intelligence - When the age is in, the wit is out.

Age. Its effects on memory - … And as, with age, his body uglier grows, so his mind cankers.

Age. Its effects on memory and warm feelings – … Nature, as it grows again towards earth, is fashion'd for the journey, dull and heavy.

Age. Its effects on wrinkles - When forty winters shall besiege thy brow, and dig deep trenches in thy beauty's field.

Age. Longevity affected by stress. See 'Stress, influence of stress on longevity - shorten my days thou canst with sullen sorrow.'

Age. Longevity promoted by

lightheartedness - A light heart lives long.

Age. Looking good for your age - ...but flowers distilled though they with winter meet, lose but their show, their substance still lives sweet.

Age. Man who has walked hand in hand with time - ... good old chronicle, that hast so long walked hand in hand with time.

Age. Reasons for men to marry younger women - Then let thy love be younger than thyself, or thy affection cannot hold the bent...

Age. Time showing the effect of time and care - ... careful hours with time's deformed hand have

Age. Value of a. in public relations. See 'Opinion, public o. gained by the appearance of maturity in the shape of an elder person - .. his silver hairs will purchase us a good opinion...'

Age. Wisdom expected out of a. – ... As you are old and reverend, you should be wise.

Age. You admit that you are old but explain why and how you have maintained your youthful intellect – ... yet hath my night of life some memory.

Age. You admit that you are old but explain why and how you have maintained your youthful strength – Time hath not yet so dried up this blood of mine...

Age. You admit that you are old but there is still substantial sparkle in you - ... some smack of age in you, some relish of the saltness of time.

Age. You are a bit older than she is - My glass shall not persuade me I am old as long as youth and thou are of one date.

Age. You are old and you may as well admit it – When my glass shows me myself indeed.

Age. You are old and you may as well admit it – ... the silver livery of advised age.

Age. You are old, you know it, she tells you that you are young and you pretend to believe it.

Ages, a. of man. See 'Age – all the world's a stage...'

Ageless - Age cannot wither her, nor custom stale her infinite variety ...

Ageless - To me fair friend you never can be old, for as you were...

Aggression, resistance to a. See 'Resistance, r. to aggression – To whom do lions cast their gentle looks?'

Aggressive and demanding lady. See 'Manners. Pleasant way of asking for something achieves better results than arrogance.'

Agree or prove me wrong - Reprove my allegations if you can; or else conclude my words effectual.

Agreeing, a. with the majority - As will the rest, so willeth Winchester.

Agreeing, a. with wish or proposal - My vows are equal partners with thy vows.

Agreement, a. formalized - Let specialties be therefore drawn between us...

Agreement, a. on a course of action – Strong reasons make strong actions.

Agreement, a. on the choice - ... your choice agrees with mine, I like it well.

Agreement, a. or contract concluded - I'll have this knot knit up to-morrow morning.

Agreement, a. or contract, quick implementation of a. - ... lest the bargain should catch cold and starve.

Agreement, a. quickly concluded - Was ever match clapp'd up so suddenly?

Agreement, a. reached to be quickly made official - ... since it is but green, it should be put to no apparent likelihood of breach.

Agreement, a. with advice to reach a specific location – When Gloucester says the word, King Henry goes...

Agreement, abiding by the majority decision or a., even if you do not like the terms - ... although I seem so loath, I am the last that will last keep his oath.

Agreement, complete a. reached. See 'Music, excellent performance - ...true concord of well tuned sounds.'

Agreement, full a. and friendship – Then you love us, we you, and we'll clasp hands…

Agreement, half-hearted a. – I have no great devotion to the deed and yet…

Agreement, incidental a. with an enemy - … If thou couldst please me with speaking to me…

Agreement, rhetorical expression of a. - To cry amen to that, thus we appear.

Agreement, signing the a. - Give me the paper, let me read the same and to the strict'st decrees I'll write my name.

Agreement, wholeheartedly in a. - May I never, to this good purpose, that so fairly shows dream of impediment.

Agreement, you agree in principle with the other party - What wills lord Talbot, pleaseth Burgundy.

Air, excellent a. quality. See 'Place, a nice p. to stay – … the air nimbly and sweetly recommends itself unto our gentle senses.

Air, excellent a. quality - The air breathes upon us here most sweetly.

Air, invigorating a. stimulating the appetite - the air is quick there, and pierces and sharpens the stomach.

Alcohol. See 'Wine, drinking, unable to tolerate strong drinks - … I have very poor and unhappy brains for drinking…'

Alive, being a. - … living blood doth in these temples beat.

All is oblique… See 'Man and his wicked nature – All is oblique, there is nothing level in our cursed natures but direst villainy.'

All my best is dressing old words new. See 'See 'Love, restating your love with a touch of modesty'

All the world's a stage. See "AGE – all the world's a stage…'

All things that are… See 'Chase, enjoyment greater in the chase - All things that are, are with more spirit chased than enjoyed.'

All this the world well knows… See 'Lust, perhaps reprehensible but inevitable - All this the world well knows yet none knows well to shun the heaven that leads men to this hell.'

Allegiance, a. based on money . See 'Taxation, t. recipe of hatred – their love lies in their purses and whoso empties them by so much fills their hearts with deadly hate.'

Allegiance, a. emphatically stated – longer than I prove loyal to your grace.

Allegiance, a. firmly promised - … while life upholds this arm, this arm upholds…

Allegiance, a. questionable when government is rotten – Brutus had rather be a villager than to repute himself a son of Rome under these hard conditions as this time.

Allegiance, criterion for determining a. - … who's your king? The king of England; when we know the king.

Allegiance, declared a. See 'Service, at the king's s. - … service shall with steeled sinews toil, and labour shall refresh itself with hope…'

Allegiance, determining a. - I rather wish you foes than hollow friends.

Allegiance, feigned a. – In following him, I follow but myself…

Allegiance, how to secure a. from subjects - I stole all courtesy from heaven and dress'd myself in such humility…

Alliance, a. and peace established between old enemies – Smile heaven upon this fair conjunction that long have frown'd upon their enmity!

Alliance, a. between two strong companies - … two such silver currents, when they join do glorify the banks that bound them in.

Alliance, a. not to be severed - … 'twere pity to sunder them that yoke so well together.

Alliance, a. reinforced by marriage - …. to knit your hearts with an unslipping knot,,

Alliance, a. weak in power but heartfelt - I give you welcome with a powerless hand but with a heart full of unstained love.

Alliance, questionable a. only based on

profit – … a lordly nation that will not trust thee but for profit's sake.

Alliance, unholy a. - O inglorious league!

All's well that ends well. See 'Results, positive r. in the end - All's well that ends well, yet; though time seems so adverse, and means unfit'

Ally, shaky a. - What shalt thou expect, to be depender on a thing that leans.

Alone, a. but busy - I, measuring his affections by my own, that most are busied when they are most alone.

Alone, wishing to be a. – See entries for 'Solitude'.

Alternative, dismal a. - Thus have I shunned the fire for fear of burning; and drench'd me in the sea, where I am drown'd.

Alternatives, sarcastic, dramatic a. still better than original option - I had rather be set quick i' the earth and bowl'd to death with turnips.

Amazement, a. as in a dream. See first two lines in 'Happiness, h, overwhelming and incredible - If it be thus to dream, still let me sleep!'

Amazement, a. at a change of character in a woman. See 'Woman, amazement, a. at her change in character - … I would have I thought her spirit had been invincible against all assaults of affection.'

Amazement, admiring a. - .. every wink of an eye some new grace will be born.

Amazement, expressing a. See 'Invocation, i. in amazement'.

Amazement, expressing a. at her beauty. See 'Beauty, b. that deprives man of reason - … thou mayst bereave him of his wits with wonder.'

Amazement, perceived a. - .. and scarce think their eyes do offices of truth, their words are natural breath.

Amazement, unbelievable a. - ... makes me more amazed than had I seen the vaulty top of heaven figured quite o'er with burning meteors.

Amazement, waiting for verification of truth - .. doubtful whether what I see be true until confirm'd, sign'd, ratified by you.

Amazon, an a. - .. thou art an Amazon and fightest with the sword of Deborah.

Ambiguity, a deliverer of a. - This is a riddling merchant for the nonce…

Ambition, a. as a scarlet sin – Thy ambition, thou scarlet sin…

Ambition, a. as the ruling principle. See 'Times, bad times - … these days are dangerous, virtue is chock'd with foul ambition…'

Ambition, a. blunted. See entries for 'Fortune, reversal of f.'

Ambiiton, a. defeated. See 'Invocation, misplaced ambition, see the results - Ill-weav'd ambition, how much art thou shrunk!'

Ambition, a. defined. See 'Character, ambition - for the very substance of the ambitious is merely the shadow of a dream.'

Ambition, a. for greatness self-destructing - Thou seek'st the greatness that will o'erwhelm thee.

Ambition, a. for wealth self-destructive. See 'Wealth, excessive ambition for w. self-destructing – …And this ambitious foul infirmity, in having much, torments us with defect…'

Ambition, a. maintained to the point of death – I better brook the loss of brittle life than those proud titles thou hast won of me…

Ambition, a. not the driving force. See 'Love, not ambition as a driving force - No blown ambition doth our arms incite but love, dear love'.

Ambition, a. spurring to action - … I have no spurs to prick the sides of my Intent, but only vaulting ambition..

Ambition, a's ladder. See 'Opinion, your op. on the newly rich - … 'tis a common proof that lowliness is young ambition's ladder…'

Ambition, ambitious thoughts - Thoughts

tending to ambition, they do plot unlikely wonders…

Ambition, banish the thought - Banish the canker of ambitious thoughts!

Ambition, dangerous - Cromwell, I charge thee, fling away ambition: by that sin fell the angels…

Ambition, moderate a. See 'Lifestyle, not bothered by ambition for public office – Let those who are in favour with their stars…'

Ambition, not satisfied with the plenty already available? - Hast thou not worldly pleasure at command, above the reach and compass of thy thought?

Amen, prompt concurrence with a wish – Let me say 'amen' betimes, lest the devil cross my prayer…

Amends, impossible to make amends but… - I cannot make you what amends I would, therefore accept such kindness as I can.

An honest tale speeds best being plainly told. See 'Communications, clarity and honesty go together.'

And Brutus is an honourable man. See 'Debate, disagreeing with skill - but Brutus says he was ambitious, and Brutus is an honourable man.'

And more, much more, than in my verse can sit… See 'Beauty, her b. exceeding power of poetic description - For to no other pass my verses tend than of your graces and your gifts to tell…'

And oftentimes to win us to our harms… See 'Appearance, a. of truth hiding a deeper and malicious purpose - … to win us to our harm the instruments of darkness tell us truths…'

And truly in my youth I suffered much extremity for love. See 'Love, effects of l. recollected, drive to extremity'

Anesthesia, argument for a. See 'Sleep, s. as a tooth-ache reliever - Indeed, sir, he that sleeps feels not the tooth-ache.'

Angel, complete identity to an a. - An angel is like you, Kate; and you are like an angel.

Angel, or very close to one - By Jupiter an angel, or if not, an earthly paragon.

Angel, (saint) or very close to one - is she not a heavenly saint?… No, but she is an earthly paragon.

Angels, a. are a. even if some of them become rotten - Angels are bright still, though the brightest fell…

Angels, an army of a. – … if angels fight, weak men must fall, for heaven still guards the right.

Anger - My heart for anger burns; I cannot brook it.

Anger, a. and rage, rage preventing crying. See 'Crying, c. prevented by re-distribution of moisture - I cannot weep; for all my body's moisture scarse serves to quench my furnace-burning heart'.

Anger, a. aroused with difficulty and quickly extinguished – … That carries anger as the flint bears fire, who… shows a hasty spark and straight is cold again.

Anger, a. at authorities - … woe upon ye, and all such false professors!

Anger, a. at news that makes the blood curdle, invocation - … then my best blood turn to an infected jelly.

Anger, a. barely repressed - Scarce can I speak, my choler is so great. O, I could hew up rocks and fight with flint.

Anger, a. boiling up to the point of explosion - The bow is bent and drawn, make from the shaft.

Anger, a. caused by sustained unjust treatment or injuries - … great Northumberland, whose bosom burns with an incensed fire of injuries.

Anger, a. detected but inexplicable – I understand a fury in your words but not the words.

Anger, a. detected by expression. See 'Expression, facial e. indicating anger - Here comes the queen, whose looks bewray her anger'.

Anger, a. increased by pleading - … if thou

1053

dost plead for him, thou wilt but add increase unto my wrath.

Anger, a. justified - ... know you no reverence? ... Yes, sir; but anger hath a privilege.

Anger, a. more easily provoked by depression or bad luck – ... When my good stars, that were my former guides have empty left their orbs...

Anger, a. not constructive – ... more is to be said and to be done than out of anger can be uttered.

Anger, a. not good for safety – ... never anger made good guard for itself.

Anger, a. not to be repressed - My tongue will tell the anger of my heart, or else my heart concealing it will break.

Anger, a. or superciliousness simulated and not real - How eagerly I taught my brow to frown when inward joy enforc'd my heart to smile.

Anger, a. repressed a. leading to desperation. See 'Desperation, d. out of repressed anger - Now could I drink hot blood, and do such bitter business as the day would quake to look on'

Anger, a. self-destructive - ... She'll gallop fast enough to her destruction.

Anger, a. vented - My tongue will tell the anger of my heart...

Anger, acknowledge her a. – ... since I am near slain, kill me outright with looks and rid my pain.

Anger, advice to contain a. - ... let your reason with your choler question...

Anger, angry expression. See 'Expression, e. of anger noticed - ... The angry spot doth glow on Caesar's brow'.

Anger, are you patient? - Patience is sottish, and impatience does become a dog that's mad.

Anger, bad but natural - To be in anger is impiety but who is man that is not angry?

Anger, behavior of crowd's anger - ... like an angry hive of bees that want their leader, scatter up and down...

Anger, cause for a. See 'Accusations, explanation for the false a. - And that engenders thunder in his breast and makes him roar these accusations forth.'

Anger, consequences of not contained a. - This tiger-footed rage, when it shall find the harm of unscann'd swiftness...

Anger, even her a. is an occasion for admiration - ... how wonderful when angels are so angry.

Anger, her a. an occasion for a compliment - Never came poison from so sweet a place.

Anger, plea for restraint. See 'Rejection, rebuttal to rejection or harsh words - Teach not thy lip such scorn; for it was made for kissing, lady, not for such contempt.'

Anger, rage compared to a river at flood stage – Like an unseasonable stormy day which makes the silver rivers drown their shores...

Anger, rage extreme and calling for blood - A rage whose heat that this condition, that nothing can allay, nothing but blood.

Anger, state of a. - The fire of rage is in him.

Anger, two characters angry at each other - In rage deaf as the sea, hasty as fire.

Anger, unable to refrain from expressing a. - my tongue will tell the anger of my heart.

Angry, a. and furious to the point of tears – Mad ire and wrathful fury makes me weep

Angry, a. and unable to maintain silence - ... Yet can I not of such tame patience boast as to be hash's, and nought at all to say.

Angry, a. at her compared to a she-wolf - She-wolf of France, but worse than wolves of France, whose tongue more poisons than the adder's tooth.

Angry, a. at her, compared to a tiger in disguise - O tiger's heart wrapt in a woman's hide!... "O tiger's heart wrapt in a woman's hide!

Angry, a. at her, the opposite of every good - Thou art as opposite to every good as the Antipodes are unto us or as the south to the septentrion.

Angry, a. but not using expletives. See entries for 'Speech, restraint from use of expletives due to anger.'

Angry, beautiful even when a. See 'Beautiful, even when expressing contempt - o, what a deal of scorn looks beautiful in the contem

Angry, she is really angry. See 'Peace, p. making efforts - Let's purge this choler without letting blood.'

Angry, too a. to speak - Boiling choler chokes the hollow passage of my prison'd voice.

Animal, man acting like an a. or woman - … thy wild acts denote the unreasonable fury of a beast.

Animals, a. better than men - … give it the beasts, to be rid of the men.

Animals, a. better than men - the unkindest beast more kinder than mankind.

Animals, a. sensitive to music. See 'Music, m. even tames animals - … Their savage eyes turn'd to a modest gaze by the sweet power of music

Animals, souls of animals in some men. See 'Insult, man like animal according to the theories of Pythagoras - thou almost make'st me waver in my faith, to hold opinion with Pythagoras…'

Announcement, self-a. via a third party - …importunes personal conference with his grace…

Annoyance, enemies creating more a. than damage - … though they cannot greatly sting to hurt..

Annoyance, enemies creating more a. than damage - The eagle suffers little birds to sing…

Annoyance. See 'Devil, who are you? - What devil art thou, that dost torment me thus?

Annoying, arrogant and unpleasant to hear – She does abuse our ears…

Anonymity, pleasures of a. - Methinks it were a happy life to be no better than a homely swain.

Answer, a. clear and unequivocal - What plain proceeding is more plain than this?

Answer, a. delayed due to melancholy – … My mind was troubled with deep melancholy.

Answer, a. fitting all questions – It is like a barber's chair, that fits all buttocks.

Answer, a, with one word impossible – …to say ay and no to these particulars is more than to answer in a catechism.

Answer, an a. you would wish you could give - That answer might have become Apemantus.

Answer, answerer is not obliged to please the questioner - I am not bound to please thee with my answers.

Answer, difficulty to a. a base man - What answer shall I make to this base man?…

Answer, hesitating to a. - … But how to make ye suddenly an answer… to such men of gravity and learning, in truth, I know not.

Answer, injunction to stop giving silly a. – No more light answers.

Answer, irrelevant a. - … put your discourse into some frame and start not so wildly from my affair.

Answer, on the point of giving reluctantly a nasty answer - will you tear impatient answers from my gentle tongue?

Answer, pleased at the a. See 'Words, acknowledgment of pleasing w.– I thank thee, Meg; these words content me much.'

Answer, request to have an a. - … O, answer me! Let me not burst in ignorance.

Answer, retort to irrational a. - Your reasons are too shallow and too quick.

Answer, summary of a. See 'Strategy, a not to fight but fight if provoked - The sum of all our answer is but this…'

Answer, unable to a. See 'Silence, unable to answer - I am perplex'd, and know not what to say'.

Answer, unable to a. tit for tat - I am so full

of businesses, I cannot answer thee acutely.

Answer, unsatisfactory or meaningless a. See 'Intentions, wicked i. shown in the type of question and type of answer - ... you question with a wicked tongue.'

Answer, witty but unconvincing a. - you are full of pretty answers…

Answering, buying time to answer - The charm dissolves apace… mantle their clearer reason.

Antagonism, a. strategically provoked - Two curs shall tame each other…

Anticipation and increased heart beat - My heart beats thicker than a feverous pulse…

Anticipation and time passing slowly - Time goes on crutches till love have all his rites.

Anticipation, day tedious waiting for night - so tedious is the day as is the night before some festival to an impatient child…

Anticipation, desire to know in advance. See entries for 'Prediction, desire to know in advance'

Anticipation, giddy - I am giddy; expectation whirls me round…

Anticipation, love's shadows alluring - How sweet is love itself possess'd, when but love's shadows are so rich in joy.

Anticipation, wishing for the appointed day to be next - ... I would that Thursday were to-morrow.

Anticipation. See also entries for 'Impatience', 'Expectations'

Anxiety, a. about outcome, wanting to know the result right away. See 'Prediction, desire to know in advance - o, that a man might know the end of this day's business ere it come…'

Anxiety, a. about what may happen at the office while you are away – I am questioned by my fears, of what may chance or breed upon our absence.

Anxiety, a. at doing something you don't like but must do - Since I receiv'd command to do this business I have not slept a wink.

Anxiety, a. caused by lack of sleep – See 'Sleep, lack of sleep creating anxiety - You lack the season of all natures, sleep'.

Anxiety, a. hurts more than reality. See 'Psychology, doubt hurts more than certainty'.

Anxiety, obsession, missing her presence - How can I then return in happy plight, that am debarred the benefit of rest?

Anxiety, a. perceived and questioned - What is't that takes from thee thy stomach, pleasure and thy golden sleep?

Anxiety, state of a., concern - With my vex'd spirits I cannot take a truce.

Anxiety, state of a., hope and fear mixed - I feel such sharp dissension in my breast.

Anxiety, a. till return - ... till you do return, I rest perplexed with a thousand cares.

Anxious and undecided - I rest perplexed with a thousand cares.

Anxious while waiting for her answer – Thus ready for the way of life or death I wait the sharpest blow.

Any questions? (at end of presentation). See 'Question, answering q. - Ask me what question thou canst possible, and I will answer unpremeditated.'

Anything, a. but this – …I had rather be a toad, and upon the vapour of a dungeon, than…

Anything, a. but this – I had rather have skipp'd from sixteen years of age to sixty…

Anything, a. but this. See 'Solution, desperate s., anything better than this – bid me lurk w

Aphrodisiac, a. food and logical consequences - He eats nothing but doves, love; and that breeds hot blood…

Apologies for absent-mindedness - … my dull brain was wrought with things forgotten.

Apologies for uncaring or angry behavior. See 'Impatience, signs of i. – hoping it was but an effect of humour, which sometimes hath his hour with every man.'

Apologies for behavior caused by indisposition - ... we are not ourselves when nature being oppress'd commands the mind to suffer with the body.

Apologies for comment - Forgive the comment that my passion made…

Apologies for comment - Our griefs, and not our manners, reason now.

Apologies for delay - … not I but my affairs have made you wait.

Apologies for having drunk too much – It perfumes the blood ere one can say, what's this?

Apologies, a. for lack of loving skills. See 'Loving skills, apologizing for lack of l.s. – For I am rough and woo not like a babe.'

Apologies for leaving without notice - … my business was great; and in such a case as mine a man may strain courtesy.

Apologies for past poor behavior. See 'Character, c. shaped by own mistakes - they say best men are moulded out of faults…'

Apologies for poor manners due to haste - … my haste made me unmannerly.

Apologies for poor manners or unconventional behavior by a third party. See 'Misfortune, m. affecting manners and judgment - … for his wits are drown'd and lost in his calamities.'

Apologies, a. for rashness. See 'Forgiveness, f. asked for rashness – Forgive my general and exceptless rashness, you perpetual-sober gods!'

Apologies for rudeness. See 'Rudeness, apologies for r. – the thorny point of bare distress hath taken from me, the show of smooth civility…'

Apologies for unruly words caused by indisposition - … impute his words to wayward sickliness and age in him.

Apologies to lady for having caused offense - … to make a sweet lady sad is a sour offence.

Apologies unnecessary, on the contrary – Thou mak'st faults graces that to thee resort.

Apologies unnecessary, on the contrary - Who takes offence at that would make me glad?

Apologies unnecessary, on the contrary. See 'Perfection, p. even in her shortcomings - She spoke and panted that she made defect perfection.'

Appeal, a. of novelty. See 'Novelty, appeal of n.

Appeal, a. to bear witness - Bear witness, all that have not hearts of iron…

Appearance, a. deceiving – All hoods make not monks.

Appearance, a. improving with age, ugliness in men as an advantage - I was created with a stubborn outside…

Appearance, a. and reality. See "Reality, not appearance - Seems, madam! nay it is; I know not 'seems'.'

Appearance, as if just out of hell – … a look so piteous in purport as if he had been loosed out of hell

Appearance, kingly - … every inch a king.

Appearance, a. of things changed by necessity. See 'Necessity, n. changing the appearance of things – The art of our necessities is strange, that can make vile things precious.'

Appearance, a. of truth hiding a deeper and malicious purpose - … to win us to our harm the instruments of darkness tell us truths…

Appearance, dejected a., crying - why holds thine eye that lamentable rheum…

Appearance, did you see how you look? – No…. for the eye sees not itself but by reflection, by some other things.

Appearance, disgusting a. - … not honour'd with a human shape.

Appearance, haggard, fat – My skin hangs about me like an old lady's loose gown…

Appearance, honest a. - … knavery cannot, sure, hide himself in such reverence

Appearance, negative change in a. due to misfortune – I know not what counts harsh fortune cast upon my face...

Appearance, unexpected a. - What

unaccustom'd cause procures her hither?

Appearance. She is not pretty but… - … love looks not with the eyes, but with the mind.

Appearances, a. in men betraying women - … our frailty is the cause, not we.

Appearances, a. deceiving – All that glisters is not gold.

Appearances, a. deceiving - So may the outward shows be least themselves, the world is still deceived with ornament…

Appearances, a. deceiving - When devils will the blackest sins put on…

Appearances, a. deceiving – who makes the fairest show means most deceit.

Appearances, a. deceiving (usually), but not in this case - … thou hast a mind that suits with this fair and outward character

Appearances, a. deceptive – adder better than the eel? See 'Substance prevailing over form.'

Appearances, a. deceptive or false – Look like the innocent flower but be the serpent under it.

Appearances, a. deceptive or false – Ornament… the seeming truth which cunning times put on to entrap the wisest.

Appearances, a. deceptive or false – O, what may man within him hide, though angel on the outward side!

Appearances, a. deceptive or false – Seems he a dove? his feathers are but borrowed…

Appearances, a. deceptive or false – … that deceit should steal such gentle shape and with a virtuous visor hide deep vice!

Appearances, a. deceptive or false – … the world is still deceived with ornament.

Appearances, a. deceptive or false – What a goodly outside falsehood hath.

Appearances, a. deceptive or false – Who cannot steal a shape that means deceit?

Appearances, a. deceptive or false – Ye have angels' faces, but heaven knows your hearts.

Appearances, a. deceptive or false. See 'Temptation, t. taking up false appearances - Devils soonest tempt, resembling spirits of light' *** 'Person, deceitful but beautiful - O that deceit should dwell in such a gorgeous palace.'

Appearances, feigning love but harboring hatred - Though I do hate him as I do hell pains…

Appearances, outside a. leading to false judgment - Opinion's but a fool, that makes us scan the outward habit by the inward man.

Appearances, preserving a. – See 'Censure, presence required to avoid rumors and censure - … to avoid the censures of the carping world.'

Appearances, rare public a. and why. See 'Visibility. Advantages, for authorities of not being seen too often - … Such as is bent on sun-like majesty when it shines seldom in admiring eyes.'

Appearances, seeing through a. - … thy casement I need not open, for I look through thee.

Appearances, seeing through a. See 'Intuition, seeing through appearance - It may be so; but yet my inward soul persuades me it is otherwise'.

Appearances, the outside, rarely corresponds to the inside. See last two lines of 'Innocence, naïveté due to youth'.

Appearances. See entries for 'Hypocrisy'

Appetite, a. as passion. See 'Passion, self-compounding, clearly in love with him - … she would hang on him as if increase of appetite had grown by what it fed on.'

Appetite, good a. improving the quality of a humble meal – … our stomachs will make what's homely savoury.

Appetite, sexual a. as a motive denied – (I) therefore beg it not, to please the palate of my appetite…

Applause, large a. promised if feat accomplished – I would applaud thee to the very echo that should applaud again.

Applause, using a. as a measure of popularity. See 'Masses, working the m. using applause as a tool – This general applause and loving shout argues your wisdoms and your love to Richard.'

Apples, rotten a. See "Selection, s. limited – Small choice in rotten apples.'

Appointment, a. from above, appointee expected to work miracles - ... chosen from above by inspiration of celestial grace to work exceeding miracles on earth.

Appointment, next a. tomorrow night – ... we must starve our sight from lovers' food till morrow deep midnight.

Appointment, tomorrow night – ... when Phoebe doth behold her silver visage in watery glass.

Appreciation coming too late - ... for it so falls out that what we have we prize not the worth...

Appreciation coming too late - Our rash faults make trivial price of serious things we have...

Appreciation coming too late - The idea of her life shall sweetly creep...

Appreciation coming too late - What our contempt doth often hurl from us we wish it ours again...

Appreciation, a. expressed without prompting - The time was once when thou unurged wouldst vow that never words were music to thine ear... unless I spake.

Apprehension, generalized a. of danger – When clouds appear, wise men put on their cloaks...

Approach, a. to a woman you are interested in. See comment to 'Woman, cold w. – invincible to affection'.

Approach, gentle a. more effective than rudeness. See 'Request, more successful made with kindness than with arrogance.'

Approach, securing a way out - Gentle thou art, therefore to be won...

Approach, securing a way out - She's beautiful, and therefore to be woo'd...

Appropriateness, the right thing at the right time – At Christmas I no more desire a rose...

Approval, a. with mixed feelings - Considerations infinite do make against it.

April day - A day in April never came so sweet to show how costly summer was at hand...

April, A. suggesting youth - ... proud-pied April dress'd in all his trim hath put a spirit of youth in every thing...

April, A. welcome by young men - ... Such comfort as do lusty young men feel when well-apparell'd April on the heel of limping winter treads...

April. See 'Spring, s and April - ...the spring, when proud-pied April dress'd in all his trim...

Aptitude. See 'Work, what type of w. can you do? – ... If it be man's work, I'll do 't'

Arbitration, intervening for a. - Let me be umpire in this doubtful strife.

Ardor, military a. – O, let the hours be short, till fields and blows and groans applaud our sport!

Are you afraid? See 'Fear, f. of death, attitude towards it - That life is better life, past fearing death than that which lives to fear.' *** Various entries for 'Fear'.

Are you ambitious? See entries for 'Ambition' *** 'Character'.

Are you cold? See 'Cold, feeling very c. and possible remedy for it - Let me pour in some sack to the Thames water...'

Are you free? See 'Freedom, as free as - ... as free as heart can wish or tongue can tell.'

Are you glad that you married me? See 'Pride, p. in possession. 'Are you glad that you married me?' – (I am) as rich in having such a jewel as twenty seas, if all their sand were pearl...'

Are you happy? See 'Happiness, h. beyond description - I cannot speak enough of this content; it stops me here; it is too much of joy.' *** Entries for 'Happiness'.

Are you happy with your marriage? See 'Achievement, happily married to the woman of choice – And happily I have arrived at last unto the wished haven of my bliss.'

Are you jealous? See 'Jealousy, no j. – Nor dare I question with my jealous thought…'

Are you married (if a bachelor)? See 'Single - … thou consumest thyself in single life.'

Are you married? (if married) See 'Marriage, the state of being m. – … the true concord of well-tuned sounds, by unions married.'

Are you not hungry any more? See 'Dinner, not hungry after d. - Who riseth from a feast with that keen appetite that he sits down?'

Are you passionate? See 'Intemperance, i. without limits - … But there is no bottom, none to my voluptuousness.'

Are you (physically) OK? See entries for 'Health Care' *** 'Indisposition'

Are you ready? See 'Action, ready for a. - I am settled, and bend up each corporal agent to this terrible feat.'

Are you ready for this? See 'Mood, combative m. – I am fire and air; my other elements I give to baser life.'

Are you ready for the project, (or enterprise, or assignment)? See 'Courage, no fear of risk to gain the prize - … think death no hazard, in this enterprise.'

Are you self-emp

Are you sure? See 'Honor, h. and credit at stake - Thereon I pawn my credit and mine honour.' *** 'Assurance, double a. - I'll make assurance double sure and take a bond of fate.' *** 'Credentials, sincerity, one tongue - I have no tongue but one'

Are you telling the truth? See 'Character, c. truthful and simple - I am as true as truth's simplicity and simpler than the infancy of truth.' *** Other entries for 'Truth', 'Character'.

Are you tired? See 'Mind, state of m. weariness as a weakness - … it discolours the complexion of my greatness to acknowledge it.'

Are you with us? See 'Apologies for absent-mindedness - … my dull brain was wrought with things forgotten.'

Are you working hard? See 'Effort, hard e. – Double, double toil and trouble; fire burn, and cauldron bubble.'

Are you worried? See 'Anxiety, a. till return - … till you do return, I rest perplexed with a thousand cares.' *** Entries for 'Fear'

Arguing, exhortation to stop a. - to leave this keen encounter of our wits.

Argument, a. between to contending parties – The bitter clamour of two eager tongues.

Argument, a. debated. See entries for 'Debate'.

Argument, a. degenerating into conflict - this spark will prove a raging fire, if wind and fuel be brought to feed it with.

Argument, avoiding it – … if I longer stay we shall begin our ancient bickerings

Argument, good a. but honest dealing is best - didst thou never hear that things ill got had ever bad success?

Argument, heated a. and you are determined to stop it - Content you, gentlemen: I will compound this strife.

Argument, invitation to end the a. See entries for 'Quarrel. Dispute and arguments to be avoided, peace making, conflict resolution'

Argument, proving the contrary - I'll prove the contrary, if you'll hear me speak.

Argument, subject not worth arguing about - … it is too starved a subject for my sword.

Argument, value in the a. - Methinks there is much reason in his sayings.

Arguments, a. of equal merit - Both merits poised, each weighs nor less nor more.

Arms, her a. – … sweet ornaments, whose circling shadows kings have sought to sleep in

Army, a. not in good shape - … half of the which dare not shake snow from off their cassocks..

1060

Army, ragged a. or unruly mass - ... His army is a ragged multitude of hinds and peasants, rude and merciless.

Arrival, a. in haste – ... bloody with spurring, fiery-red with haste.

Arrival, a. of a vane and pompous man. See 'Vanity, v. displayed and observed - ... what a sweep of vanity comes this way!'

Arrival, a. of individual voiding the need to search him - He saves my labour by his own approach.

Arrival, a. of unpleasant or unwelcome character - By the pricking of my thumbs, something wicked this way comes.

Arrival, a. with noise and fanfare - ... in fierce tempest is he coming, in thunder and in earthquake, like a Jove.

Arrival, fearful a. - He came in thunder; his celestial breath was sulphurous to smell.

Arrival, possibly unexpected a. of friend. See 'Greetings, end of unhappiness – Now is the winter of our discontent, made glorious summer by this sun of York…'

Arrival, quiet a. and by night - Who comes so fast in silence of the night?

Arrival, unexpected a. - what wind blew you hither.

Arrivederci, Aufwiedersehen, See ya, Ciao, Ta-ta etc. See 'Goodbye'

Arrogance, a. behind false modesty - ... but your heart is cramm'd with arrogancy, spleen and pride.

Arrogance, a. promoted by submission - Supple knees feed arrogance, and are the proud man's fees.

Arrogance, a. distasteful. See 'Character, arrogant, superficious, hateful - I do hate a proud man, as I hate the engendering of toads'.

Arrogance. See 'Manners. Pleasant way of asking for something achieves better results than arrogance.'

Art and theatrical representation – ... the purpose of playing… to hold, the mirror up to nature…

Art of magic. See 'Magic, a wonderful art to be sanctioned by law'.

Artist, compliment to an artist or anyone who won a contest where skills are shown - ... In framing an artist, art hath thus decreed…

Artist, excellent player or musical performer. See 'Music, a superb artist – Every thing that heard him play…'

Artists, a. as a representing their times - ... they are the abstract and brief chronicles of the time…

Ask, don't ask any more. See 'Insistence, warning about further insisting - ...urge it no more on height of our displeasure…'

Asking, a. a question with reverence and ready for a blush - I ask, that I might waken reverence...

Asking, unused to a. See 'Request, emphatic r. due to strained circumstances - He asks of you that never used to beg.'

Ass, treated like an a. See 'Oppression, o. and unfair working conditions – ... I have served him from the hour of my nativity to this instant…'

Ass, written record of being one – ... remember that I am an ass; though it be not written down…

Ass. See 'Character, pompous, an ass - for it will come t

Assassination, a. of king or enemy – ... though I did wish him dead, I hate hate the murderer, love him murdered.

Assassination, a. under the guise of law - That he should die is worthy policy; but yet we want a colour for his death...

Assassination. See entries for 'Murder'.

Assessment, a. of a person. See 'Correction, correcting the assessment of a person - ...'Good Gloucester' and 'good devil' were alike…'

Assets, a. as liabilities. See 'Merit, m., skills or talent excite envy - ... to some kind of men their grace serve them as enemies.'

Assets, a. not worth holding on to - ... she is

not worth what she doth cost the holding.

Assets, inherent limits of man's a. See 'Pessimism, p. on life and personal property - ... And nothing can we call our own but death and that small model of the barren earth…'

Assets, liquidation of a. acquired with great effort – …and are the cities that I got with wounds…

Assets, loss of a. See 'Bankruptcy, consequences of b. - … and of all my lands is nothing left me but my body's length.'

Assets, your clothes as your only assets. . See 'Tax collector, how to handle a tax c. – my riches are these poor habiliments'.

Assignment or responsibility, accepting it. See 'Fortune, modest attitude towards f. – Since you will buckle fortune on my back… I must have patience to endure the load'.

Assignment or responsibility, turning it down - Better head her glorious body fits…

Assignment or responsibility, turning it down - Your love deserves my thanks; but my desert unmeritable shuns your high request.

Assignment, see entries for 'Task'.

Assistant - I was a pack-horse in his great affairs, a weeder-out of his proud adversaries…

Association, a. with person or organization only partial – A little more than kin, and less than kind

Assume a virtue… See 'Virtue, how to acquire it - Assume a virtue, if you have it not.'

Assurance, double a. - I'll make assurance double sure and take a bond of fate.

Astonishment. See entries for 'Amazement'.

Astrology, astrological conditions favorable - I find my zenith doth depend upon a most auspicious star…

Astrology, astrological conditions unfavorable. See 'Fortune, moment of unfavorable conditions due to astrological influences'.

Astrology, astrological influence on personality – My nativity was under Ursa major; so that it follows, I am rough and lecherous.

Astrology, how long have you believed in a. – How long have you been a sectary astronomical?

Astronomy, knowledge derived from a. inferior to knowledge derived from beautiful eyes. See 'Eyes, e. as a source of knowledge'.

Astronomy, meteor shower. See 'Events, strange and extraordinary and given ominous meaning - …And meteors fright the fixed stars of heaven.'

Astronomy, pernicious influence on events - These late eclipses in the sun and moon portend no good to us.

Astronomy, pointlessness of a. and erudition in general - Those earthly godfathers of heaven's lights…

Astronomy, the teaching of a., astronomy 101 - … and teach me how to name the bigger light, and how the less…

Athenians, A. as scoundrels - Why dost thou call them knaves?

Athens, imprecation against A. - … sink, Athens! henceforth hated be of Timon, man and all humanity!

Attack, a. without adequate power. See 'Boomerang effect, effect opposite to intentions, without adequate power to sustain attack -- … my arrows, too slightly timber'd for so loud a wind…'

Attention deficit, questioning lack of a. – … how is't with you, that you do bend your eye on vacancy…

Attention, motion as an a. getter. See 'Motion, what moves catches the attention - … things in motion sooner catch the eye than what not stirs.'

Attention, object of a., unconcerned about being the object of a. – Men's eyes were made to look, and let them gaze.

Attention, requesting a. See 'Request to be heard, important message coming - … lend thy serious hearing to what I shall unfold.'

Attention, undivided a. - Had I three ears, I'd hear thee.

Attire, a. or general appearance questionable – so … unfashionable that dogs bark at me as I halt by them.

Attire, a. that lacks coordination. See 'Opinion, your op. on a man whose clothing lacks coordination – How oddly he is suited! I think he bought his doublet in Italy, his round hose in France…'

Attire, justification or excuse for the poor appearance of your clothing - … Jove sometimes went disguised, and why not I?

Attire, justifying your curious a. or transformation - the gods themselves… have taken the shapes of beasts upon them.

Attire, nobility behind a humble a. – … though thy tackle's torn. Thou show'st a noble vessel.

Attire, outlandish or wacky - … so wild in their attire, that look not like the inhabitants o' the earth

Attire. See also entries for 'Dress', 'Appearances'.

Attitude, a. of strength towards challenges ahead - … And meet the time as it seeks us.

Attitude, a. questioned. See 'Cooling off observed, question for verification'.

Attitude, a. towards defeated enemy. See 'Hatred, h. mixed with pity - … but that I hate thee deadly I should lament thy miserable state'.

Attitude, a. towards pain felt by ourselves or by others - … But were we burdened with like weight of pain…

Attitude, a. towards the future. See 'Future, attitude towards the f. - … for the life to come, I sleep out the thought of it.

Attitude, a. towards the world, hating it – one… whom the vile blows and buffets of the world…

Attitude, a. towards what is past and cannot be changed - Not one word more of the consumed time.

Attitude, a. towards what is past and cannot be changed - Things past redress are now with me past care.

Attitude, a. towards what is past and cannot be changed - Things that are past are done with me.

Attitude, a. towards what is past and cannot be changed – Things without all remedy should be without regard…

Attitude, a. towards what is past and cannot be changed - To mourn a mischief that is past and gone.

Attitude, a. towards what is past and cannot be changed - What's gone and what's past help should be past grief.

Attitude, carefree a. See 'Youth, carefree attitude in your younger days - Two lads that thought there was no more behind….'

Attitude, mercenary a. - Believe't, that we'll do any thing for gold.

Attitude, modest a. towards fortune. See 'Fortune, modest attitude towards f. – Since you will buckle fortune on my back… I must have patience to endure the load'.

Attitude, negative a. of a person rejecting ideas - … like an envious sneaping frost that bites the first born infants of the spring.

Attitude, positive a. beneficial to health. See 'Melancholy, m. an evil influence and an enemy to health – … frame your mind to mirth and merriment, which bars a thousand harms, and lengthens life.'

Attitude, positive a. in reversals - The robb'd that smiles steals something from the thief…

Attitude, positive a. towards failure. See 'Persistence, failure. positive attitude - … the protractive trials of great Jove to find persistive constancy in men.' *** Entries for 'Complaint, c. after problems useless '

Attitude, positive a. towards simple life. See 'Life, l. simple and in the open air, advantages of – Here feel we but the penalty of Adam…'

Attitude, positive and defiant towards adversity – In poison there is physic' and these news…

Attitude, posture and its importance - Let not the world see fear and sad distrust… threaten the threatener…

Attitude, stoic a. towards reversal – … do not please sharp fate to do not please sharp fate to grace it with your sorrows… and we punish it seeming to bear it lightly.

Attitude, unexplainable change in a. - …what is breeding that changeth thus his manners.

Attitude, when suffering a set back. See entries in 'Complaint, c. after problems useless'

Attraction, fatal, her voice and shape - mine ear is much enamoured of thy note…

Attraction, it is obvious that she likes him - … she did so course o'er my exteriors with such a greedy intention…

Attraction, physical a. observed - … who even now gave me good eyes too…

Attraction, visual a. and nothing else - … young men's love then lies not truly in their hearts, but in their eyes.

Audience, determined to have an a. or be received by elusive party or VIP - … tell them, there thy fixed foot shall grow till thou have audience.

Audience, quiet or unreceptive - … like dumb statues or breathing stones.

Audience, request for an a. - Shall I vouchsafe your worship a word or two?

Audit, see 'Accounting, a. above board, request for an audit'.

August, A's heat tiring - You sunburnt sicklemen, of August weary…

Austerity, a. program - The grosser manner of these world's delights…

Authority, a. can get away with sin - … authority, though it err like others hath yet a kind of medicine in itself, that skins the vice o' the top.

Authority, a. of king derived from God – … that supernal judge, that stirs good thoughts…

Authority, a. of princes and signs of respect due to them - … for princes are a model, which heaven makes like to itself…

Authority, a. proclaimed – Let those obey who do not know the rules.

Authority, a. restricted or slave to interests - To be a queen in bondage is more vile than is a slave…

Authority, a. self-serving. See 'Justice, fitting the law to the will of the powerful - … Bidding the law make court'sy to their will, hooking both right and wrong to the appetite…'

Authority, a. using its power to discredit accusers and whistle blowers - … no particular scandal once can touch but it confounds the breather.

Authority, abuse of a. See 'Justice, misapplied and arbitrary, time for revolution - … now breathless wrong shall sit and pant in your

Authority, authorities making their own laws. See 'Kings, authority, making their own laws - Kings are the earth's gods: in vice their law is their will…'

Authority, beneficial effect of the presence of a. - the presence of a king engenders love…

Authority, consequences of lack of a. and management - … And this neglect of degree it is that by a pace goes backward, with a purpose it hath to climb.

Authority, consequences of lack of a. and management - … when degree is shaked, which is the ladder to all high designs, then enterprise is sick.

Authority, consequences when a. is afraid - …and what was first but fear what might be done grows elder now and cares it be not done.

Authority, corrupted by gold - … and though authority be a stubborn bear, yet he is oft led by the nose with gold.

Authority, executive position, suffered, not wanted - … was never subject long'd to be a king…

Authority, fear in a. grows with time – … tyrants' fears decrease not, but grow faster than the years.

Authority, impatience with a. See 'Patience, p. with authority strained - How long shall I be patient? ah, how long shall tender duty make me suffer wrong?'

Authority, king, no different from other men - … the king is but a man, as I am: the violet smells to him as it doth to me.

Authority, limits to its importance - … for within the hollow crown that rounds the mortal temples of a king keeps death its watch…

Authority, rarely to be questioned - For few men rightly temper with the stars.

Authority, smiling authorities to be feared - 'T is time to fear, when tyrants seem to kiss.

Authority, u. the power of a. for cover-up – … you shall stifle in your own report and smell of calumny.

Authority, vices of a. better not disclosed. See 'Kings, authority, vices of kings better kept secret or they spread like the wind'.

Authority. See entries for 'Opinion, your op. on authority '

Authorization, hope you have a. - I hope your warrant will bear out the deed.

Autumn, season of plenty – The teeming autumn, big with rich increase…

Autumn, winter – When lofty trees I see barren of leaves…

Availability detected. See 'Woman, provocative w. and available - I spy entertainment in her.'

Avalanche, formation of an a., metaphor for a revolution - … as a little snow, tumbled about anon becomes a mountain.

Away with him. See 'Foreign language, knowledge of Latin a liability - Away with him, away with him! he speaks Latin.'

Awakening, too early to get up - … it argues a distempered head so soon to bid good morrow to thy bed.

Awareness, a. declared and pointed out – I see things too although you judge I wink.

Bachelorhood, b. recanted – When I said I would die a bachelor, I did not think I should live till I were married.

Bachelorhood, consolation of b. – … broom -groves, whose shadow the dismissed bachelor loves…

Bachelorhood, justification for b. - Because I will not do them the wrong to mistrust any, I will do myself the right to trust none…

Back in a jiffy. See 'Running as fast as you can - I drink the air before me, and return or ere your pulse twice beat.' – 'Speed, amazing s. - I'll put a girdle around the earth in forty minutes.'

Background, checkered professional b. - … having flown over many knavish professions…

Baboon and monkeys. See 'Man, strain of m. debased - The strain of man's bred into baboon and monkeys.'

Bad news. See entries for 'News'.

Bad smell, see entries for 'Odor, unpleasant'.

Bad, from bad to good better than from good to bad - … The lamentable change is from the best; the worst returns to laughter.

Bag-pipes. See 'Music, dislike for bag-pipes - … and others, when the bagpipe sings i' the nose cannot contain their urine.'

Balance, b. between purpose and means. See 'Objective, examining the folly required to achieve an o. - the purpose must weigh with the folly'.'

Balance, b.of power, examination of – I have in equal balance justly weigh'd…and find our griefs heavier than our offences.

Balance, in praise of balanced life - … they are as sick that surfeit with too much, as they that starve with nothing.

Baldness, dealing with hair issues, praise of b. -… it is a blessing that times bestows on beasts…

Baldness, hair restoring procedures questionable - There's no time for a man to recover his hair that grows bald by nature.

Baldness, statistical advantages of b. - There's many a man hath more hair than wit.

Bankruptcy, consequences of b. - … and of all my lands is nothing left me but my body's length.

Bankruptcy, forced b. - He hath eaten me out of house and home…

Bar, going to b. to find solace in alcohol and company - I will see what physic the tavern affords.

Barber, in need of a b. See 'Beard and moustaches, barber needed - methinks I am marvellous hairy about the face'.

Bargaining, dispraising the value of what you wish to buy - … you do as chapmen do dispraise the thing that you desire to buy…

Bated breath - With bated breath and whispering humbleness…

Battle, b. of the wits - There is no such sport, as sport by sport overthrown.

Battle, b. strategy, diplomacy first, arms later - … let's fight with gentle words…

Battle, b. to the end - Swords and lances arbitrate the swelling difference of your settled hate.

Battle, mental preparation of a warmonger – I shall prove a lover of thy drum, hater of love.

Battle, outcome of b. uncertain – So is the equal poise of this fell war.

Battle, prepared for b. - … why he cometh hither plated in habiliments of war.

Be quick. See 'Speed, command to be quick - Be Mercury, set feathers

Beach, entertainment on the beach - … chase the ebbing Neptune and do fly him when he comes back.

Beard, a professional shave after extended neglect – This ornament makes me look dismal will I clip to form…

Beard, b. and moustaches, barber needed - methinks I am marvellous hairy about the face.

Beard, b. long and substantial - Thou hast got more hair on thy chin than Dobbin my fill-horse has on his tail.

Beard, b. shaved – … the old ornament of his cheek hath already stuffed tennis-balls.

Beard, b. unkempt (but also hair) - …beard made rough and rugged, like to the summer's corn by tempest lodged.

Beard, presence or absence of as indicators of age. See lines in 'Age, a. discrimination on the part of a woman - .. and he that is less than a man, I am not for him.'

Beard, dislike of b. See 'Woman, w. who does not like bearded men - … I could not endure a husband with a beard on his face…'

Beard, white b. or b. with strands of white - … whose beard the silver hand of peace hath touch'd.

Beast, unreasoning b. would make better decision - … a beast, that wants discourse of reason…

Beasts better than men. See entries for 'Animals, a. better than men'.

Beautiful, b. work of nature - The most replenished sweet work of nature…

Beautiful, beyond any praise - You will find she will outstrip all praise…

Beautiful, beyond comparison - If lusty love should go in quest of beauty, where should he find it fairer than in Blanch?

Beautiful, beyond description - Fairer than tongue can name thee…

Beautiful, beyond description - For her own person, it beggar'd all description.

Beautiful, even when expressing contempt - O, what a deal of scorn looks beautiful in the contempt and anger of his lip.

Beautiful, like an angel. See 'Angel, or very close to one - By Jupiter an angel, or if not, an earthly paragon.'

Beautiful, particularly yesterday - .. she looked yesternight fairer than ever I saw her look, or any woman else.

Beautiful, sweet - In mine eye she is the

sweetest lady that ever I looked on.

Beauty, artificial b. obtained with heavy make-up - ... Look on beauty and you shall see 'tis purchased by the weight..

Beauty, b. above all others - Beauty too rich for use, for earth too dear…

Beauty, b. and education and social standing worthy of a princess - ... in beauty, education, blood, holds hand with any princess of the world.

Beauty, b. and evil don't mix – ... the beauteous-evil are empty trunks, o'erflourish'd by the devil.

Beauty, b. and honesty incompatible? – ... for honesty coupled to beauty is to have honey a sauce to sugar.

Beauty, b. and personality, she deserves the best - ... her beauty claims no worse a husband than the best of men..

Beauty, b. and ugliness opposed – Sky-clouds comparison. See 'Nature, clouds considered spoilers of an otherwise clear sky'.

Beauty, b. and wisdom - Her sight did ravish; but her grace in speech..

Beauty, b. as a destructive force. See 'Woman as a weapons of mass destruction.'

Beauty, b. as a determining factor - Your beauty was the cause of that effect..

Beauty, b. as embodied in her hands. See 'Hand, her h. an occasion to extol her beauty - The fairest hand I ever touched! O beauty, till now I never knew thee.'

Beauty, b. beats any learning - For where is any author in the world teaches such beauty as a woman's eye?…

Beauty, b. contending with that of lilies and roses – Of Nature's gifts thou mayst with lilies boast and with the half-blown rose.

Beauty, b. declining with age or unforeseen circumstances - And every fair from fair sometime declines…

Beauty, b. eliciting admiration - With more than admiration he admired her azure veins…

Beauty, b. enhanced by truth - O, how much more doth beauty beauteous seem by that sweet ornament which truth doth give!…

Beauty, b. exceeding power of the pen to describe it - ... a maid that paragons description and wild fame; one that excels the quirks of blazoning pens…

Beauty, b. exceeding that of all others - ... like the stately Phoebe 'mongst her nymphs dost overshine…

Beauty, b. grace and majesty all in one - A maid of grace and complete majesty.

Beauty, b. greater than stars - ... will make the face of heaven so fine that all the world will be in love with night…

Beauty making beautiful old rhyme. See 'Beauty, b. transcending the limitations of time – When in the chronicle of wasted time…'

Beauty, b. meditated on and kept in mind - Bethink thee on her virtues that surmount..

Beauty, b. needing no verbal description – My beauty though but mean needs not the painted flourish of your praise…

Beauty, b. of a queen - O queen of queens! how far dost thou excel, no thought can think, nor tongue of mortal tell.

Beauty, b. of face – …Her face the book of praises, where is read nothing but curious pleasures.

Beauty, b. of face majestical - What peremptory eagle-sighted eye… that is not blinded by her majesty?

Beauty, b. of face plus sweetness, angelic disposition and worth a kingdom - Thou hast the sweetest face I ever look'd on.

Beauty, b. of face. See 'Face, expression, beauty imitating Nature - 'T is beauty truly blent, whose red and white, nature's. own sweet and cunning hand laid on.'

Beauty, b. overwhelming even savages - Who sees the heavenly Rosaline… bows not his vassal head…

Beauty, b. preservation and its relationship with goodness of character - The hand that hath made you fair hath made you good…

Beauty, b. shown in color of lips and cheeks - … beauty's ensign… is crimson in thy lips and in thy cheeks.

Beauty, b. so striking that even air is attracted. See 'Woman, w. beautiful, even the air would go and see her - … the air; which, but for vacancy had gone to gaze on Cleopatra too…'

Beauty, b. such as to generate wonder in the onlookers - … like beauty's child, whom nature gat for men to see…

Beauty, b. superior even to a goddess' - Thou for whom Jove would swear Juno but an Ethiope were…

Beauty, b. supreme and for the world to wonder at. See 'Beauty, no match, unseen up to this moment.'

Beauty, b. that brightens the night and comparable to an angel. See 'Repeat, ask her to r. what she said – … speak again, bright angel! for thou art as glorious to this night …'

Beauty, b. that defies the power of words to describe it. See 'Eyes, beauty of e. to be written about.'

Beauty, b. that deprives man of reason - … thou mayst bereave him of his wits with wonder.

Beauty, b. that is evil, an empty trunk - Virtue is beauty, but the beauteous evil…

Beauty, b. that leaves you speechless. See 'Speechless, stunned by her beauty - You have bereft me of all words, lady.'

Beauty, b. transcending the limitations of time – When in the chronicle of wasted time…

Beauty, b. without intelligence – Her beauty and her brain go not together…

Beauty, b. worth commending and wondering at - Well learned is that tongue that well can thee commend…

Beauty, b., voice and perfection - … whose beauty did astonish the survey of the richest eyes…

Beauty, black is beautiful – And therefore is she born to make black fair…

Beauty, black is beautiful - Is ebony like her? O wood divine!

Beauty, black is beautiful – No face is fair that is not full so black

Beauty, celest

Beauty, comparing beauties - .. exceeds her as much in beauty as beauty as the first of May doth the last of December.

Beauty, dangers of b. - b. more tempting than gold - Beauty provoketh thieves sooner than gold.

Beauty, her b. and virtue praised everywhere - Hearing thy mildness praised in every town..

Beauty, her b. compared to a cheering sun - As all the world is cheered by the sun, so I…

Beauty, her b. exceeding art. See 'Beauty meditated on and kept in mind - bethink thee on her virtues that surmount..'

Beauty, her b. exceeding all flowers. See 'Flowers, her beauty exceeding all flowers - More flowers I noted, yet none I could see, but sweet, or colour it had stolen from thee.'

Beauty, her b. exceeding lilies and roses. See 'Flowers, lilies and roses - Nor did I wonder at the lily's white, nor praise the deep vermilion in the rose…'

Beauty, her b. exceeding power of poetic description - For to no other pass my verses tend than of your graces and your gifts to tell…

Beauty, her b. like Summer, only better. See 'Summer, like a s. day but only better - Shall I compare thee to a Summer's day? Thou art more lovely and more temperate…'

Beauty, her b. outperforms Venus' - .. O'er-picturing that Venus where we see the fancy outwork nature.

Beauty, impossible to say 'no' to it - All orators are dumb when beauty pleadeth.

Beauty, in praise of her b. See 'Praise, tongue too earthly to sing of her celestial beauty - ..this wrong that sings heaven's praise with such an earthly tongue.'

Beauty, male b. - Describe Adonis, and the counterfeit is poorly imitated after you.

Beauty, mathematical comparison - Thrice-fairer than myself

Beauty, no match, unseen up to this moment - .. the all seeing sun ne'er saw her match since first the world began.

Beauty, no question you are beautiful etc. - By heaven, that thou art fair is most infallible.

Beauty, one exceedingly more beautiful than the other (girl) - .. so with the dove of Paphos might the crow vie feathers white.

Beauty, ornament of the world – Thou that art now the world's fresh ornament.

Beauty, outside is wonderful, what about the inside? - All of her that is out of door most rich!..

Beauty, persuasive power of b. - Beauty itself doth of itself persuade the eyes of men without an orator.

Beauty, power of b. - .. beauty hath his power and will, which can as well inflame as it can kill.

Beauty, radiant - most radiant, exquisite, unmatchable beauty

Beauty, reality better than the picture. See 'Woman, real w. better than her picture – so far this shadow doth limp behind the substance.

Beauty, rejuvenating effects of b. - Beauty doth varnish age, as if new born…

Beauty, the flower of the city - Verona's summer hath not such a flower.

Beauty, three times more beautiful than the complimenter - Thrice-fairer than myself…

Beauty, true b. observed for the first time - .. for I ne'er saw true beauty till this night.

Beauty, unbelievable b. See 'Eyes, beauty of e. to be written about.'

Beauty, well endowed by Nature - … Framed in the prodigality of nature…

Beauty, you as the virtual painter of her beauty- Mine eye hath play'd the painter…

Beer, b. and safety a priority. See 'Safety, s. and beer preferable to fame – I would give all my fame for a pot of ale and safety.'

Beer, do you like b.? - …a quart of ale is a dish for a king.

Bees. See 'Obedience, o. and the ideal capitalist system - … for so work the honey-bees…'

Beggars. See 'Opinion, your op. on sociological issues, minimum wage - O, reason not the need: our basest beggars are in the poorest thing superfluous…' *** 'Class, c. distinction even in death - When beggars die, there are no comets seen…' *** 'Falsehood, f

Begging, first time b. - A beggar begs that never begg'd before.

Beginning – ... here, upon this bank and shoal of time…

Beginning, abrupt or violent b. foreshadowing unfortunate end – … it was a violent commencement, and thou shalt see an answerable sequestration.

Beginning, tell-tale sign about outcome. See 'Outcome of events detectable in small details at the beginning - And in such indexes, although small pricks to their subsequent volumes…'

Behavior, b. appropriate to circumstances - … good manners at court, are as ridiculous in the country.

Behavior, b. appropriate to peace and war - … modest stillness and humility….then imitate the action of the tiger…

Behavior, b. cowardly and infamous, unworthy of a nobleman - … this fact was infamous and ill beseeming any common man…

Behavior, b. of an animal or woman. See 'Animal, man acting like an a. or woman - thy wild acts denote the unreasonable fury of a beast…'

Behavior, change in b. noticed. See entries for 'Cooling off observed'.'

1069

Behavior, disrespectful b. See 'Respect, r. not learned - never learn'd the icy precepts of respect, but follow'd the sugar'd game before thee'

Behavior, evil or stupid b. See 'Folly or malice - Either you must confess yourselves wondrous malicious or be accus'd of folly.

Behavior, extreme b. See 'Character, c. given to extremes - The middle of humanity thou never knewest, but the extremity of both ends'.

Behavior, irrational b. attributed to bad mood. See Impatience, signs of i. – ... but an effect of humour, which sometimes hath his hour with every man'.

Behavior, minor irritation affecting overall b. - ... and in such cases men's natures wrangle with inferior things, though great ones are their object...

Behavior modification. See 'Habit, h. formation – use doth breed a habit in a man' – 'Character, habit can change c. - For use almost can change the stamp of nature and either quell the devil, or throw him out with wondrous potency.'

Behavior, observing someone's behavior. See 'Monitoring, you are observing someone's behavior – I have eyes upon him'.

Behavior, questioning barbarous b. See 'Turmoil, what is happening? – ... Are we turn'd Turks, and to ourselves do that which heaven hath forbid the Ottomites?'

Behavior, rationalization for bad b. See 'Apologies for past poor behavior - they say best men are moulded out of faults...'

Behavior, saucy and affected b. - ... having been praised for bluntness doth affect a saucy roughness.

Behavior, tyrannical b. of a newly appointed leader – Whether it be fault and glimpse of newness...

Behavior, wise or honest b.?- I should be wise, for honesty's a fool and loses that it works for.

Being thy slave... See 'Service, at her complete service – Being your thy slave what should I do but tend upon the hours and times of your desire?'

Belief, consistency of b. - ... were he meal'd with that which he corrects, then were he tyrannous...

Believability, complete b. – If Jupiter should from yond cloud speak divine things...

Believe me, self-assurance of truth in the report. See 'Truth, assurance about one's own credibility - Believe my words for they are certain and unfallible.'

Bell, stop the bell. See 'Noise, injunction to cut out noise - Silence that dreadful bell: it frights the isle from her propriety'.

Bell, summoned by the bell, 'the bell invites me'. See lines in 'Boss, b. calls you in and you imagine the worst – ... Hear it not, Duncan; for it is a knell that summons thee to heaven or to hell.'

Benevolence and benefices misapplied - .. wonder of good deeds evilly bestow'd

Best, compliment, she is the best wife – ... kings might be espoused to more fame but king nor peer to such a peerless dame.

Best, compliment, you are the best – ... a gallant creature, and complete in mind and feature.

Best, compliment, you are the best – Full many a lady I have eyed with best regards...

Best, compliment, you are the best – ... Nor can imagination form a shape, beside yourself, to like of.

Best, compliment, you are the best – ... O you, so perfect and so peerless...

Beware the ides of March. See 'Careful now, the ides of March, impending danger – beware the ides of March.'

Beware, b. of the enemy - Take heed o' the foul fiend!

Bewitched by her words - Either she has bewitch'd me with her words, or nature makes me suddenly relent.

Bible, quoting the b. See 'Hypocrisy, false

conclusion from a righteous example - The devil can cite scriptures for his purpose...'

Big Brother – ... Keeps place with thought and almost, like the gods, does thoughts unveil in their dumb cradles.

Bill of rights for women. See 'Women, bill of rights for women - I'll exhibit a bill in the parliament for the putting down of men.'

Biographer, chosen b. - After my death I wish no other herald... But such an honest chronicler as Griffith.

Biography, invitation to tell his/her life story – I long to hear the story of your life..

Biography, life story will be told - ..for this one night; which, part of it, I'll waste with such discourse as, I not

Black is beautiful. See 'Beauty, black is beautiful'.

Black, advantages of the color b. - Coal-black is better than another hue...

Black, if you dislike the color - ... black is the badge of hell..

Blemishes, only real b. are in the mind. See "Ingratitude, i. as a deformity - In nature there's no blemish but the mind...'

Blind date, see entries for 'Expectations'.

Blindness, b. in judgment. See 'Judgment, poor j. compared to not seeing well - .. our very eyes are sometimes like our judgments, blind!'

Blindness, b. of lovers to themselves - But love is blind and lovers cannot see the pretty follies they themselves commit.

Blinking idiot.

Bliss, lovers' b. See 'Love. L's pleasures recalled'.

Blood, b. covering earth - .. and temper clay with blood of Englishmen.

Blood, cold or hot? - Shall our quick blood, spirited with wine, seem frosty?

Blood, instinct balanced by judgment. See 'Man, m. to be praised who can stand up to the vagaries of fortune - .. blest are those whose blood and judgment are so well commingled..'

Blood, lady as dear as own b. - .. as dear to me as the ruddy drops that visit my sad heart.

Blood, power acquired with b. unstable - There is no sure foundation set on blood.. No certain life achieved by others' death

Blot, an infamous blot. See 'Man, m. damned – Mark'd with a

Blow, blow, thou winter wind. See 'Ingratitude, invocation to i. - Blow, blow, thou winter wind. thou art not so unkind as man's ingratitude.'

Bluntness, b. of behavior. See 'Behavior, saucy and affected b. - ... having been praised for bluntness, doth affect a saucy roughness.'

Blushing, b. as evidence - .. thy cheeks confess it, th' one to th' other; and thine eyes see it so grossly shown in thy behaviors..

Blushing, b. made invisible by night - thou know'st the mask of night is on my face, else would a maiden blush bepaint my cheek...

Boasting, b riduclous. See 'Mockery, displaying one's scars deserving ridicule - .. to such as boasting show their scars a mock is due.'

Boat, not in great conditions - ...the very rats instinctively had quit it!

Body, b. language – ... sometimes from her eyes I did receive fair speechless messages.

Body, b. language - Her eye discourses; I will answer it.

Body, b. language - There was speech in their dumbness, language in their very gestures.

Body, celestial b. - ... body as a paradise, to envelop and contain celestial spirits.

Body, charming b. imperfection - .. a mole, right proud of that most delicate lodging.

Body, every part of her b. excellent - .. some natural notes about her body.. would testify, to enrich mine inventory.

Body, our b as a fragile thing. See 'Life, l's uncertainties - ...(the) other incident throes that nature's fragile vessel doth sustain in life's uncertain voyage.'

Body, our bodies as gardens and our wills as gardeners - ... Our bodies are our gardens..

Boldness. See entries for 'Credentials, sincerity, one tongue'.

Boldness, invocation. See 'Psychology, self encouragement'

Boldness, sudden inflow of b. - Boldness comes to me now, and brings me heart.

Bombast. See 'Praise, self-p. or praise of speaker – And all the courses of my life do show I am not in the roll of common men.'

Book, I'll put you in my black book. See 'Threat, I will remember you - I'll note you in my book of memory to scourge for this apprehension.'

Books, b. as tools and utensils - he has brave utensils, for so he calls them..

Books, bookish knowledge questionable. See 'Knowledge, bookish k. ineffective – Small have continual plodders ever won save base authority from others' books.'

Books, bookworm. See entries for 'Character, bookworm'.

Books, key to power – Remember first to possess his books..

Boomerang effect, effect opposite to intentions, without adequate power to sustain attack -- .. my arrows, too slightly timber'd for so loud a wind..

Boredom, b. with great position, desire for change - .. could I with boot change for an idle plume which the air beats for vain.

Boring, b. and interminable event or speech. See 'Speech, lengthy and annoying - This will last out a night in Russia when nights are longest there.'

Born to be evil. See 'Man, evil m. - .. he is born with teeth!' and so I was; which plainly signified that I should snarl and bite and play the dog.'

Borrowing, b. and lend

Borrowing, b. not a solution to financial problems. See 'Financial status, challenging – I can get no remedy against this consumption of the purse…'

Bosom, her b. as a coveted place of rest - I might live one hour in your sweet bosom.

Boss, b. calls you in and you imagine the worst – ... Hear it not, Duncan; for it is a knell that summons thee to heaven or to hell.

Boss, never outshine b. - Better to leave undone, than by our deed acquire too high a fame when him we serve's away.

Boss, never out-do your b., modesty strategically applied - Who does in the wars more than his captain can, becomes his captain's captain…

Bragging, dangers of b. See 'Character, pompous, an ass - for it will come to pass that every braggart shall be found an ass.'

Brain, b. and blood at war. See 'Instinct, i. prevailing over the dictates of law - ...the brain may devise laws for the blood…'

Brain, no more raking of the b. - Cudgel thy brains no more about it….

Brain, something wrong with his b. See 'Man, something wrong with his brain - .. for, sure, the man is tainted in's wits.' – 'Insult, brain - ... as dry as the remainder biscuit after a voyage….'

Brainless. See 'Insult, brainless – ... thou hast no more brain in thy head than I have in mine elbows.' *** 'Character, brainless – not Hercules could have knock'd out his brains, for he had none.'

Brainwashing. See 'Prison, forgetting being in a prison - .. it made my imprisonment a pleasure; ay, such a pleasure as incaged birds…

Brave new world. See 'Mankind, admiration of m. (ironic) - ... O brave new world that has such people in it.

Bravery. See 'Man, a brave m. - To grace this latter age with noble deeds'.

Break, my heart… See 'Silence, self-enforced - It is not nor it cannot come to good: but break, my heart; for I must hold my tongue.'

Breakfast, nature, dawn. See 'Nature, dawn, sun and its gracious light'.

Breasts, beauty of her b. - Her breasts, like ivory globes circled with blue

Breath excellent, inviting to love - .. comes breath perfumed that breedeth love by smelling.

Breath excellent, stolen from the violet - The forward violet thus did I chide..

Breath excellent - The leaf of eglantine, whom not to slander out-sweetens not thy breath

Breath like honey - …suck'd the honey of your breath…

Breath like sugar - Here are sever'd lips parted with sugar breath..

Breath that perfumes the air – And with her breath she did perfume the air…

Breath, bad b. attributable to unhealthy diet - .. in their thick breaths rank of gross diet..

Breath, bad b. chronic- She is not to be kissed fasting in respect of her breath.

Breath, b. like a balm, irresistible – Ah balmy breath, that dost almost persuade justice to break her sword!

Breath, b. perfuming the air – … sweeten with thy breath this neighbour air…

Breath, b. perfuming the air – 'Tis her breathing that perfumes the chamber thus

Breath, divine b. - … And calls it heavenly moisture, air of grace.

Breath, fresh breath and lips. See 'Lips, l. and fresh breath - .. here are sever'd lips parted with sugar breath..

Breath, how to avoid bad b. - … eat no onion, nor garlic, for we are to utter sweet breath.

Breath, out of b. - How art thou out of breath, when thou hast breath to say to me that thou art out of breath?

Brevity is the soul of wit. See entries for 'Introduction, you will be brief'.

Brevity, b. in communications - I will imitate the honourable Romans

Bribery, accusation of b. - An itching palm to sell and mart your offices for gold to undeservers.

Bribery, appeal of b. disregards nature of giver. See 'Praise, praising the criminal if advantage drawn from him – A giving hand, though foul, shall have fair praise.'

Bribery, b. detestable – … shall we now contaminate our fingers with base bribes …

Bribery, b. suggested – … show the inside of your purse to the outside of his hand.

Bribery, not tempted by bribes - For I can raise no money by vile means…

Brotherhood, b. acquired by sharing common danger - For he to-day that sheds his blood with me shall be my brother.

Brows, women's b., standards of excellence - … black brows, they say, become some women best…

Brutality, b. and loss of judgment. See 'Judgment, j. vanished - O judgment, thou art fled to brutish beasts and men have lost their reason.'

Brutus is an honorable man. See 'Debate, disagreeing with skill - but Brutus says he was ambitious…'

Bubbles - The earth hath bubbles, as the water has and these are of them.

Budge an inch - I'll not budge an inch, boy: let him come, and kindly.

Budget deficit – … his coffers sound with hollow poverty and emptiness.

Budget, exceeding b. with extravagant expenses - For our coffers, with too great a court and liberal largess are grown somewhat light.

Building a house, how to plan for building a house. See ' Planning, importance of p. - When we mean to build, we first survey the plot, then draw the model…'

Building, cold and stony - … ill-erected tower to whose flint bosom…

Bunch of no good – …you, that are polluted with your lusts, stain'd with the guiltless blood of innocents…

Business travel expenses, pretty nifty - … as 't is ever common, that men are merriest when they are from home.

Business trip abandoned for her sake. See 'World, she is the w. - .. for where thou art, there is the world itself.'

Business trip, reason for taking them - The world and my great office will sometimes divide me from your bosom.

Business trip, temporary separation - The strong necessity of time commands our services a while..

Business, b. conducted at night suspect - … affairs, that walk as they say spirits do, at midnight…

Business, b. cares upsetting – … every object that might make me fear misfortune to my ventures…

Business, reason to leave. See 'Departure, reason for having to leave - I take it, your own business calls on you and you embrace the occasion to depart.'

Business, serious b. - … our graver business frowns at this levity.

Busy and alone - ….most are busied when they're most alone.

But if the while I think on thee. See 'Psychological uplifting, positive effects of thoughts about a friend - … But if the while I think on thee, dear friend, all losses are restored and sorrows end.'

But let determined things to destiny hold unbewail'd their way. See 'Cheer up - Cheer your heart, be you not troubled with the time…'

But me no Buts (not a Shakespeare quote but…)

But men may construe things…See 'Interpretation, i. of events depending on the interpreter - … but men may construe things after their fashion clean from the purpose of the things themselves.'

But that I hate thee deadly … See 'Hatred, h. mixed with pity - … but that I hate thee deadly I should lament thy miserable state.'

But yet, everything is well but yet - I do not like 'but yet', it does allay the good precedence...

Butterflies, gilded b. See lines in "Meditating on the mystery of things - … and take upon's the mystery of things…'

By indirections find directions out'. See 'Intelligence, gathering and sifting i. - Your bait of falsehood takes this carp of truth…. By indirections find directions out'

Bygones – let bygones be bygones. See 'Attitude, a. towards what is past and cannot be changed - consumed time'.

Caesar. See 'Command, c. given with some arrogance, reaction to - When Cae

Cakes and ale - Dost thou think, because thou art virtuous, there shall be no more cakes and ale?

Call, your girlfriend calls you - It is my soul that calls upon my name.

Campaign contribution, c.c. suspect. See 'Bribery, not tempted by bribes - For I can raise no money by vile means…'

Can I ask you a favor? See 'Request, r. granted - I will both hear and grant you your requests.' *** 'Service, at her complete service – Being your thy slave what should I do but tend upon the hours and times of your desire?' *** Entries for 'Service'.

Can I ask you a question? See 'Question, answering q. - Ask me what question thou canst possible, and I will answer unpremeditated.'

Can I have a word with you? See 'Request, r. for dialog – … a word with you … A hundred, if they'll do you any good.' *** 'Audience, request for an a. - shall I vouchsafe your worship a word or two?'

Can I speak frankly? See 'Speaking frankly - Speak frankly as the wind.'

Can I trust you? See 'Man, an absolutely trustworthy and loving m. - his words are bonds, his oaths are oracles…' *** 'Man, m. of honorable mind and of behavior with women - …

Can this be true? See 'Unbelievable, can this be true?'

1074

Can you put up a good show? See 'Actor, capable of feigning as needed - ... ghastly looks are at my service, like enforced smiles…'

Candor, c. declared – In simple and pure soul I come to you.

Capital, no raising capital by corruption - … I can raise no money by vile means…

Capitalism, rationale for c. - The sweat of industry would dry and die, but for the end it works to.

Capitalists, c. and plutocrats described – I can compare our rich misers to nothing so fitly as to a whale…

Care, c. and concerns a threat to life - The incessant care and labour of his mind hath wrought the mure that should confine it in…

Care, c. corrosive. See 'Regret, r. corrosive for things that cannot be changed - Care is no cure, but rather corrosive, for things that are not to be remedied.'

Care, c. preventing sleep. See 'Sleep, s. prevented by care, unimpeded in the young - ... and where care lodges, sleep will never lie.'

Care, too much c. about worldly opinion counterproductive - You have too much respect upon the world, they lose it that do buy it with much care.

Careful now, the ides of March, impending danger – beware the ides of March.

Carelessness, c. of youth. See "Youth, carefree attitude in your younger days - Two lads that thought there was no more behind….'

Carrying a heavy load. See 'Load, heavy (metaphorical) load to carry - I was not made a horse and yet I bear a burthen like an ass.'

Casanova, aged C. See 'Age, sex and aging - Is it not strange that desire should so many years outlive performance?'

Casanova, not a C. See entries for 'Modesty, admitted m. of personal looks.' *** 'Appearance, a. improving with age, ugliness in men as an advantage - I was created with a stubborn outside…'

Casanova. See entries for 'Lady, l. killer' *** 'Seducer, great s. - He is the

Cash flow critical. See 'Financial status, cash flow critical' – 'Financial status, cash flow challenging'

Catholic, anti-c. statement - ... you and all the rest so grossly led, this juggling witchcraft with revenue cherish…

Cause and effect explained - .. And now remains that we find the cause of this effect.

Cause, dying for a good c. See 'Glory, there is g. in dying for a good cause - He lives in fame that died in virtue's cause.'

Cause, just c. See 'Invocation, i. to God - God befriend us, as our cause is just!'.

Cause, lost c. - Past hope, past cure, past help.

Cause, rotten c. beyond any discussion – A rotten case abides no handling

Cause, what is the c.? See 'Power, privilege of p. to give no explanations- ….the cause is in my will'

Caution, c. characteristic of aging. See 'Age, a. and its way of thinking - ... it is as proper to our age to cast beyond ourselves in our opinions…'

Caution, c. in fighting the enemy – Heat not a furnace for your foe so hot that it do singe yourself.

Caution, c. in fighting the enemy – The fire that mounts the liquor till it run over, in seeming to augment it wastes it.

Caution, c. required - It is the bright day that brings forth the adder…

Celebration, day of c. when even the sun contributes to the glory - ... to solemnize this day, the glorious sun stays his course…

Celebrations, c. for victory or any happy event - And he that throws not up his cap for joy…

Celebrity, c. who dislikes cheering crowds - I love the people, but do not like to stage me to their eyes…

Censure, presence required to avoid rumors and censure - ... to avoid the censures of the carping world.

Censure, fear of c. not an obstacle. See 'Action, need to act notwithstanding possible censure – We must not stint our necessary actions…'

Censured. See 'Reputation, poor r. in the world – … we in the world's wide mouth live scandalized and foully spoken of.'

Centaurs, what women are from the waist down. See 'Women, very uncomplimentary view - Down from the waist they are Centaurs, though women all above…'

Ceremonies, no time for c. even if friends meet again after a long time - ..the leisure and the fearful time cuts off the ceremonious vows of love..

Ceremony, ceremonial salutations dispensed with – … rebukeable and worthy shameful cheque it were, to stand on more mechanic compliment.

Ceremony, c. unnecessary among friends - Ceremony was but devised at first to set a gloss on faint deeds..

Ceremony, c., pomp and flattery useless - … and what are thou, thou idol ceremony?…

Ceremony, properties of c. - O ceremony, show me but thy worth!…

Certainty, absolutely certain on pain of self-damnation – I were damn'd beneath all depth in hell but…

Certainty, sure of it - … as certain as I know the sun is fire.

Challenge, c. by an unworthy enemy - Shall I be flouted thus by dunghill grooms?

Challenge, everybody can appear great when there is no c.. See 'Chance, temper of man shown when handling reversals – in the reproof of chance lies the true proof of men.'

Challenge, prepared to meet the c. - …I am fresh of spirit and resolved to meet all perils very constantly.

Challenge, the greater the c. the greater the victory - The harder match'd, the greater victory

Challenges, meeting the c. (generic). See '

'Attitude, a. towards challenges ahead - … And meet the time as it seeks us.'

Chameleon. See 'Love, l. as an appetite suppressant. S

Chamomile, c. in opposite comparison to youth. See 'Youth, y. shortened by recklessness - for though the camomile, the more it is trodden on, the faster it grows, yet youth, the more it is wasted, the sooner it wears.'

Chance, let c. decide - If chance will have me king, why, chance may crown me, without my stir.

Chance, taking your c. for a while - … let myself and fortune tug for the time to come.

Chance, temper of man shown when handling reversals – in the reproof of chance lies the true proof of men.

Change your opinioni. See entries for 'Exhortation, e. to change opinion'

Change, c. constant. See 'Destiny, d. inscrutable – … how chances mock, and changes fill the cup of alteration with divers liquors!'

Change, c. in demeanor and attitude. See 'Demeanor, sudden change of d., disposition and attitude – wondering why'.

Change, desire for radical c. – Contending with the fretful element…that things might change or cease…

Change, need for c. from monotony. See 'Tediousness, t. in everything being always the same – If all the year were playing holidays, to sport would be as tedious as to work.'

Change, resistance to c. See 'Custom, c. as an obstacle to positive change - What custom wills, in all things should we do't, the dust of antique time would lie unswept…'

Changeling. See 'Man, m. subject to constant mood changes - … his humour was nothing but mutation…'

Chaos is come again . See Love, so deep, chaos without it - … and when I love thee not chaos is come again.

Character (yours), habitually changing your mind - thus change I like the moon.

Character, a cold fish – ... a man whose blood a snow-broth…

Character, a cold fish - ... scarce confesses that his blood flows…

Character, a cold fish - ... when he makes water his urine is congealed ice.

Character, a dandy – He speaks holiday, he smells April and May.

Character, a humorous c. - … When I am dull with care and melancholy lightens my humour with his merry jests.

Character, a hypocrite and a filthy c. - .. His filth within being cast, he would appear a pond as deep as hell.

Character, a hypocrite with a false smile - ... he does smile his face into more lines than are in the new map…

Character, a milk-sop - A milk-sop, one that never in his life felt so much cold as over shoes in snow.

Character, a quibbler. See 'Words, rehearsed w. planted in memory - The fool hath planted in his memory an army of good words.'

Character, a respectable person - Common speech gives him a worthy pass.

Character, a ruffian and total loss – … and commits the oldest sins the newest kind of ways.

Character, addicted to sin. See 'Sin, not occasional, but chronic - Thy sin's not accidental, but a trade'.

Character, all show, no substance - … dissuade me from believing thee a vessel of too great a burthen.

Character, always laughing and does not taking things seriously - … are of such sensible and nimble lungs that they always use to laugh at nothing.

Character, ambitious - For the very substance of the ambitious is merely the shadow of a dream.

Character, ambitious and greedy - … no man's pie is freed from his ambitious finger.

Character, ambitious and weaving his own web for success - ... the force of his own merit makes his way.

Character, ambitious but moderately so. See 'Ambition, moderate a. – (You) art not without ambition, but without the illness should attend it…'

Character, ambitious, with a swelling ambition - .. swell'd so much that it did almost stretch the sides of the world.

Character, annoying - .. you do me most insupportable vexation.

Character, arrogant and dishonest – ...we think him over-proud and under-honest…

Character, arrogant behind a display of humility – … but your heart is cramm'd with arrogancy, spleen, and pride.

Character, arrogant, supercilious, hateful - I do hate a proud man, as I hate the engendering of toads.

Character, baseness of c. displayed by the expression – … an eye base and unlustrous as the smoky light that's fed with stinking tallow.

Character, blind to own faults - ..the raven chides blackness.

Character, bombastic and cowardly - … so confidently seems to undertake this business, which he knows is not to be done..

Character, bookworm – …. my library was dukedom large enough.

Character, bookworm – ...volumes that I prize above my kingdom.

Character, brainless – not Hercules could have knock'd out his brains, for he had none.

Character, brutish and ugly - He is as disproportion'd in his manners as in his shape.

Character, c. acting quickly on decision - He's sudden, if a thing comes in his head.

Character, c. all in his clothes - ... the soul of this man is in his clothes…

Character, c. always angry – Ira furor brevis

est, but yond' man is ever angry.

Character, c. always unhappy. See 'Malcontent, primacy in unhappiness – Thou art the Mars of malecontents.' *** 'Pessimism, unable to be happy - He that commends me to mine own content, commends me to do the thing I cannot get.'

Character, c. and qualities inter-generational - O noble strain! O worthiness of nature! breed of greatness!

Character, c. bound to make mistakes but not devious – …(one that) errs in ignorance and not in cunning.

Character, c. capable of saying only a few and identical words - That ever this fellow should have fewer words than a parrot, and yet the son of a woman!

Character, c. changes explained - There is differency between a grub and a butterfly…

Character, c. deceitful, treacherous - treacherous man! Thou hast beguiled my hopes..

Character, c. easily deceived about the nature of men - … of a free and open nature that thinks men honest that but seem to be so…

Character, c. fierce in war and mellow in peace - In war was never lion raged more fierce, in peace was never gentle lamb more mild.

Character, c. helpful to excess – … she holds it a vice in her goodness not to do more than she is requested

Character, c. given to extremes - The middle of humanity thou never knewest, but the extremity of both ends.

Character, c. history showing rashness - The best and soundest of his time hath been but rash.

Character, c. incapable of hurting anyone. See 'Innocence, innocent of any wrongdoing and non violent of character - I never killed a mouse, nor hurt a fly…'

Character, incapable of paying compliments or praising – He would not flatter Neptune for his trident…

Character, c. insincere, equivocator. See 'Equivocation - here's an equivocator, that could swear in both the scales against either scale.'

Character, c. not used to ask favors - Suffolk's imperial tongue is stern and rough, used to command, untaught to plead for favour..

Character, c. observed in a person that reveals his history - … there is a kind of character in thy life...

Character, c. occasionally honest - though I am not naturally honest, I am so sometimes by chance.

Character, c. of a person who seems truthful - … thou seem'st a palace for the crown'd truth to dwell in.

Character, c. of integrity, not afraid to be politically incorrect - … knew the true minute when exception bid him speak.

Character, c. of questionable qualities - … a tried and valiant soldier …So is my horse.

Character, c. only interested in gain and therefore unreliable - That sir which serves and seeks for gain, and follows but for form, will pack when it begins to rain…

Character, c. quarrelous – … As quarrelous as the weasel.

Character, c. pessimistic by nature - His discontents are unremoveably coupled to nature.

Character, c. proud and ambitious. See 'Pride, p. and ambition - Pride went before, ambition follows him.'

Character, c. proud and disdainful of others – … Such a nature, tickled with good success, disdains the shadow which he treads on at noon.

Character, proud and petty – Things small as nothing, for request's sake only, he makes important…

Character, c. reformation more dramatic given the precedents – My reformation, glittering o'er my fault shall show more goodly…

Character, c. reformed - consideration, like an angel came and whipp'd the offending Adam out of him.

Character, c. reliable who keeps our promises – ever precise in promise-keeping.

Character, c. self-centered - … you speak like one besotted on your sweet delights…

Character, c. self-described as not sociable - …society is no comfort to one not sociable.

Character, c. shaped by own mistakes - They say best men are moulded out of faults..

Character, c. showing natural traits - how hard it is to hide the sparks of nature.

Character, c. slippery and opportunist - … a slipper and subtle knave, a finder of occasions.

Character, c. softer than shown by appearances - … of a better nature, sir, then he appears by speech.

Character, c. somewhat pretentious and wordy – A man …that hath a mint of phrases in his brain…

Character, c. surly and independent - … his surly nature, which easily endures not article tying him to aught

Character, c. that acts more than speak - … speaking in deeds and deedless in his tongue…

Character, c. that disregards riches - … (he) look'd upon things precious as they were the common muck of the world…

Character, c. treacherous and false - …and be ever double in his words and meaning.

Character, c. truthful and simple - I am as true as truth's simplicity and simpler than the infancy of truth.

Character, c. unpredictable when angry - … And, touched with choler, hot as gunpowder.

Character, c. very religious – … all his mind is bent to holiness…

Character, c. who rarely or never smiles – … Seldom he smiles, and smiles in such a sort…

Character, c. who says a lot of nonsense - Gratiano speaks an infinite deal of nothing…

Character, c. whose anger is short. See 'Anger, a. aroused with difficulty and quickly extinguished – … That carries anger as the flint bears fire, who… shows a hasty spark and straight is cold again.'

Character, c. with a melancholy disposition - I can suck melancholy out of a song, as a weasel sucks eggs.

Character, c. with a bad temper compared to a weasel – A weasel hath not such a deal of spleen as you are toss'd with.

Character, c. with a strong religious disposition - But all his mind is bent on holiness..

Character, c. without a sense of humor. See 'Wine, w. as an ingredient for a sense of humor - … nor a man cannot make him laugh; but that's no marvel, he drinks no wine'.

Character, compound of all faults - A man who is the abstract of all faults that all men follow.

Character, conceited, thinks that everyone loves and admires him - … the best persuaded of himself…

Character, conservative - Old fashions please me best..

Character, constancy, a desirable trait - … were man but constant, he were perfect. That one error fills him with faults; makes him run through all the sins.

Character, constant –… now from head to foot I am marble constant.

Character, constant. See Credentials. Establishing your credentials, constancy.

Character, coward - … has no man's blood in's belly than will sup a flea.

Character, coward - A coward, a most devout coward, religious in it

Character, coward - And you find so much blood in his liver as will clog the foot of a flea.

Character, coward and thieving – Never broke any man's head but his own and that was against a post when he was drunk

Character, cunning and needing no assistance - A crafty knave does need no broker.

Character, deceitful - … a quicksand of deceit.

Character, devious behind a façade of plainness - … in this plainness harbour more craft and more corrupter ends than twenty silly ducking observants…

Character, direct - for what his heart thinks, his tongue speaks.

Character, direct to the extreme - … what his breast forges, that his tongue must vent.

Character, dishonest and worthless - … he has everything that an honest man should not have..

Character, dramatic change in c. - This tyrant, whose sole name blisters our tongues was once thought honest.

Character, drunkard, drunkenness described - … like a drowned man, a fool and a madman..

Character, drunkard, symptoms and effects - … drunkenness is his best virtue..

Character, dull but honest - … his wits are not so blunt as, God help, I would desire they were..

Character, evil and beyond description - … For mischiefs manifold and sorceries terrible to enter human hearing.

Character, evil c. in a woman worse than in an enemy – Proper deformity seems not in the fiend so horrid as in woman.

Character, evil, totally and absurdly e. – If one good deed in all my life I did, I do repent it from my very soul.

Character, excellent person and one in a thousand – we may pick a thousand salads ere we light on such another herb,

Character, excitable c. - Imagination of some great exploit drives him beyond the bounds of patience.

Character, false or unbelievable – There's no more faith in thee than in a stewed prune.

Character, false, cunning – Alencon! that notorious Machiavel!

Character, false, cunning, shifting and perverse – I can smile and murder whiles I smile.

Character, faked simplicity – These kind of knaves I know, which in this plainness…

Character, fatalistic – We profess ourselves to be the slaves of chance, and flies of every wind that blows.

Character, funny c. - I warrant thou art a merry fellow.

Character, gentle but resolute - … as gentle as zephyrs blowing below the violet..

Character, gentlemanly and kind - A kinder gentleman treads not the earth.

Character, good overwhelming evil - I must not think there are evils enow to darken all his goodness…

Character, greedy and ambitious - No man's pie is freed from his ambitious fingers.

Character, habit can change c. - … for use almost can change the stamp of nature and either quell the devil, or throw him out with wondrous potency.

Character, honor above all. See 'Honor, h. above everything else'.

Character, honorable, capable of restraint. See 'Reliability. "Am I going to be safe with you? Can I trust you? Etc.'

Character, hot and ebullient - As full of spirits as the month of May and gorgeous as the sun at midsummer.

Character, improved by experience and mistakes. See 'Apologies for past poor behavior'

Character, incompatibility of c. - No contraries hold more antipathy than I and such a knave.

Character, judgment in critical circumstances as a show of c. See 'Judgment, men's j. affected by circumstances and showing their character'.

Character, judgment of a c. incorrect - I am sorry that with better heed and judgment I had not quoted him

Character, kind always. See 'Kindness always, I am always kind.'

Character, kind, perhaps too much - ... it is too full o' the milk of human kindness...

Character, knowledge of c. and how to get to him - You know the very road into his kindness.

Character, liar - .. he will lie, sir, with such volubility, that you would think truth were a fool.

Character, liar but amusing - ... I love to hear him lie and I will use him for my minstrelsy.

Character, light rather than somber. See 'Health, laughter as a medicine - With mirth and laughter let old wrinkles come and let my liver rather heat with wine…'

Character, like mother like sons - …the raven doth not hatch a lark.

Character, likes and dislikes, a temperate man immune to mass media and events - … rather rejoicing to see another merry…

Character, malicious with everyone - … the king.. is not quite exempt from envious malice of thy swelling heart.

Character, man of good c. - ... he is of noble strain, of approved valour, and confirmed honesty.

Character, man with a jovial disposition - … a merrier man, within the limit of becoming mirth, I never spent

Character, melancholy - He did incline to sadness, and oft-times not knowing why.

Character, mellowed by time - ... mellow'd by the stealing hours of time.

Character, merciless - ... there is no more mercy in him than there is milk in a male tiger.

Character, misanthrope. See 'Dogs, d. preferable to men - .. I do wish thou wert a dog that I might love thee something.'

Character, modest but strong and reliable - I cannot gasp out my eloquence, nor I have no cunning in protestation…

Character, must always be the first in starting something - … For he will never follow any thing that other men begin.

Character, noble and naïve - … whose nature is so far from doing harms that he suspects none…

Character, noble c. See 'Man, m. of noble character - .. a nobler sir ne'er lived 'twixt sky and ground'.

Character, noble though poor, of noble lineage - though wayward fortune did malign my state..

Character, non violent. See 'Innocence. Innocent of any wrongdoing and non violent of character.'

Character, not afraid of taking chances - I have set my life upon a cast and I will stand the hazard of the die.

Character, not easily moved to compassion - .. it is no little thing to make mine eyes to sweat compassion.

Character, not very bright – ... his wit is as thick as Tewksbury mustard.

Character, one that always speaks and does not let anyone else put a word in - ... keep me company but two years more thou shalt not know the sound of thine own tongue.

Character, one who likes to be flattered. See 'Opinion, your op. on flattery'.

Character, one who pretends to be thought clever by saying nothing - there are a sort of men whose visages…

Character, original, eccentric. See 'Eccentricity, above the crowd.'

Character, overweight and underfunded - our means are very slender, and your waist is great..

Character, passion, c. immune to passion - … Ere I would say, I would drown myself for the love of a guinea-hen , I would change my humanity with a baboon.

Character, passion, c. that cannot resist

Character, passion - I confess it is my shame to be so fond; but it is not in my virtue to amend it.

Character, person who does not keep his promises - .. the sun borrows of the moon, when Diomed keeps his word..

Character, pompous, an ass - For it will come to pass that every braggart shall be found an ass.

Character, positive assessment – I see virtue in his looks.

Character, promise of self-reformation - ...that to come hall all be done by the rule.

Character, proud – .. I can see his pride peep through each part of him..

Character, proud, quarrelsome, not worthy of his position - ... as stout and proud as he were lord of all.

Character, quiet but crafty - Smooth runs the water where the brook is deep.

Character, radical change in c. - Presume not that I am the thing I was.

Character, reliable and with the right sense of priorities. See 'Times, good old t., less selfishness detectable in previous times - Thou art not for the fashion of these times, where none will sweat but for promotion'

Character, religious by show only. See 'Religion, questionable religious character or motives – Name not religion, for thou lovest the flesh…'

Character, rough but gentle – … he is not the flower of courtesy but, I'll warrant him, as gentle as a lamb.

Character, rude c. See 'Courtesy, people not trained to c. - ... Turks and Tartars, never train'd to offices of tender courtesy.

Character, self-commitment to radical change and improvements in c. – Yet herein will I imitate the sun..

Character, self-declared lighthearted – ..I thank it, poor fool, it keeps on the windy side of care.

Character, self-declared lighthearted – I was born to speak all mirth, and no matter.

Character, self-defined, does not resent criticism. See 'Advice, a. on talking and listening - Give every man thy ear, but few thy voice, take each man's censure, but reserve thy judgment.

Character, self-defined, straight, direct and who does not like any of the company around him - .. 'tis my occupation to be plain…

Character, self-defined, true to one self. See 'Advice, a. on strength of character - .. to thine own self be true, and it must follow, as the night the day, thou canst not then be false to any man'.

Character, self-loathing - .. Apemantus, that few things loves better than to abhor himself.

Character, shortcomings, lack of constancy. See 'Character, constancy, a desirable trait'.

Character, signs of destructive c. clear from the beginning - Teeth hadst thou in thy head when thou wast born, to signify thou camest to bite the world.

Character, similarity between parent and offspring - ... the raven doth not hatch the lark.

Character, sincere. See entries for 'Credentials, sincerity'

Character, sincerity of c. advocated – Men should be what they seem; or those that be not, would they might seem none!

Character, skirt chaser - He woos both high and low, both rich and poor...

Character, skirt chaser, anything that moves - … he would mouth with a beggar, though she smelt brown bread and garlic.

Character, skirt-chaser. See 'Ladies, l's man and yet not – I'll make my heaven in a lady's lap, and deck my body in gay ornaments…'

Character, slanderer, habitual slanderer - A slave whose gall coins slanders like a mint.

Character, softness of c. leading to insubordination - .. smooth as oil, soft as young down..

Character, sour c. See 'Expression, facial e. unfriendly - ... the tartness of his face sours ripe grapes.'

Character, steady and ready to face unfriendly reception - ... to the proof, as mountains are for winds..

Character, steady c., as a rock - ... he's the rock, the oak not to be wind-shaken.

Character, straight-forward - I have no gift at all in shrewishness.

Character, strong, unable to weep - I am a soldier, and unapt to weep, or to exclaim on fortune's fickleness.

Character, stubborn - ... and perversely she persevers so.

Character, sudden c. reformation – ... Never came reformation in a flood…

Character, supercilious - ... you are sick of self-love, Malvolio, and taste with a distempered appetite.

Character, suspicious c, admitted – ... it is my nature's plague to spy into abuses…

Character, transformed dramatically - ... nor the exterior nor the inward man resembles that it was.

Character, trusting c. – ... whose nature is so far from doing harms that he suspects none.

Character, trustworthy - ... would not betray the devil to his fellow..

Character, truthful and plain self-described - ... alas, it is my vice, my fault, whiles others fish with craft for great opinion…

Character, truthful. See 'Truth, answer to 'Are you telling the truth?"

Character, unable to flatter, pretend and deceive - because I cannot flatter and speak fair..

Character, unable to say 'no' to women - ... whom ne'er the word of 'No' woman heard speak.

Character, uncouth – See 'Insult, totally unmannered - .. ungracious wretch, Fit for the mountains and the barbarous caves…'

Character, uncouth and discourteous - The elephant hath joints, but none for courtesy..

Character, uncouth, uncoordinated, confused – .. he hath the joint of every thing; but every thing so out of joint..

Character, unfriendly – ... nothing but himself which looks like man is friendly with him.

Character, unrepentant - .. I have done a thousand dreadful things as willingly as one would kill a fly..

Character, unshakable - .. I do know but one that unassailable holds on his rank..

Character, untruthful and dishonest - ..there's no room for faith, truth, nor honesty in this bosom of thine.

Character, vane, arrival of a vane c. - ... here he comes, swelling like a turkey-cock.

Character, vane, a turkey-cock - Contemplation makes a rare turkey-cock of him..

Character, vane, likes his own speech- .. One whom the music of his own vain tongue doth ravish like enchanting harmony.

Character, villainous with an Oscar for villainy - .. he hath out-villained villainy so far, that the rarity redeems him.

Character, violent – ... the foot that leaves the print of blood.

Character, weak c. easily affected by his/her imagination. See 'Imagination, conceit, lack of realism - Conceit in weakest bodies strongest works.'

Character, wild - For he is given to sports, to wildness and much company.

Character, wishing for a poetical c. – Truly, I would the gods had made thee poetical.

Character, with a sense of humor - ... the world's large tongue proclaims you for a man replete with mocks.

Character, woman, ambitious w. - ... being a woman, I will not slack to play my part in Fortune's pageant.

Character, wordy - ... what a spendthrift is he of his tongue!

Character, your c. misjudged or underestimated. See 'Observation, careful o. by a person - But there's more in me than thou understand'st. Why dost thou so oppress me with thine eye?'

Characters, interplay of two strong c. See 'Meeting, m. of strong characters - ... where two raging fires meet together, they do consume the thing that feeds upon.'

Characters, of all sorts - ... Nature hath framed strange fellows in her time...

Characters, similarity of c. - ... both of you are birds of selfsame feather.

Characters, similarity of c. – ... in companions...there must be needs a like proportion of lineaments...

Characters, similarity of c. - ... the weight of a hair will turn the scales between their avoirdupois.

Characters, similarity of c. - ... you weigh equally; a feather will turn the scale.

Chase, enjoyment greater in the chase - All things that are, are with more spirit chased than enjoyed.

Chase, the fun is in the c. See 'Women, the fun is in the chase - Women are angels wooing, things won are done, joy's soul lies in the doing.'

Chastity, c. in men not to be expected - I will find you twenty lascivious turtles, ere one chaste man.

Chastity, effects of enforced c. - The moon, methinks, looks with watery eye..

Chastity, supreme c. - ... chaste as the icicle that's curdled by the frost from purest snow.

Chastity. See entries for 'Woman, w. super chaste' *** Woman, chaste'.

Cheek, wishing to be o a glove to fit her hand to touch her c. - ... O, that I were a glove upon that hand...

Cheeks and eyes as objects of compliment - ... such war of white and red within her cheeks..

Cheeks and hands - ... this cheek to bathe my lips upon.. this hand, whose touch... would force the feeler to an oath of loyalty... this object which takes prisoner the wild motion of mine eye.

Cheeks, c. becoming pale - ... Their cheeks are paper.

Cheeks, their brightness - the brightness of her cheek would shame those stars..

Cheeks, whitening c. as a sign of bad news. See 'News, bad n. inferred by the look of the messenger - ... the whiteness in thy cheek is apter than thy tongue to tell thy errand.'

Cheer up – ... cast thy nighted colour off and let thine eye look like a friend on Denmark.

Cheer up - Cheer your heart, be you not troubled with the time...

Cheer up – Clear up, fair queen, that cloudy countenance.

Cheer up - Lay aside life-harming heaviness and entertain a cheerful disposition.

Cheer up – Live a little, comfort a little; cheer thyself a little.

Cheer-up - ... make not your thoughts your prisons.

Cheer up – Unknit that sorrow-wreathen knot.

Cheer up. See 'Expression, come on relax - ... unknit that threatening unkind brow.'

Chicken hawk - Show me one scar character'd on thy skin: men's flesh preserved so whole do seldom win.

Chickening out. See 'Cowardice, c. or discretion - the better part of valour is discretion'.

Childishness excluded. See 'Folly maybe but not childishness.'

Chivalry, lack of c. towards a woman - If you were men, as men you are in show,...

Chocolate, offering her a box of chocolates or note in a card accompanying them. See 'Flowers, homage of f - Sweets to the sweet'

Choice, agreeing with the c. See 'Agreement, a. on the choice - .. your choice agrees with mine, I like it well.'

Choice, deprived of c. – I may neither choose whom I would nor refuse whom I dislike.

Choice, limited c. See 'Selection, s. limited – small choice in rotten apples.'

Choice, you do not like my c.? See 'Opinion, your op. on the choice - how like you our choice that you stand pensive, as half malcontent?

Choices, c. dictated by likes and dislikes - ... for affection, mistress of passion, sways it to the mood of what it likes or loathes.

Chronicle of wasted time. See 'Beauty, b. transcending the limitations of time – When in the chronicle of wasted time…'

Circumstances, adapting course to c. - Let go thy hold when a great wheel runs down a hill…

Circumstances, ada

Circumstances, c. affecting judgment. See 'Judgment, men's j. affected by circumstances and showing their character - ..I see men's judgments are a parcel of their fortunes…'

Circumstances, c. and status, a complete turn-around - a man may fish with a worm that had eat of a king..

Circumstances, c. somewhat dire. See 'Past, happy p. as a dream - ... learn, good soul, to think our former state a happy dream... '

Circumstances, c. unfavorable and unpredicted. See 'Plan, p. disapproved – Uneven is the course, I like it not.'

Circumstances, favored by c. – (standing in) …the smile of heaven.

Circumstances, resignation to current c. - … what I have I need not to repeat and what I want it boots not to complain.

Citizen, private c. powerless against authority - … That's a perilous shot out of an elder-gun, that a poor and private displeasure can do against a monarch!"

Citizenship, rejection of c. See "Insult, better be a dog - I had rather be a dog and bay the moon than such a Roman.'

Claim, rational reason for c. - … nor from the dust of old oblivion raked.

Class, c. consciousness - Strange is it, that our bloods of colours, weight, and heat, pour'd all together…

Class, c. distinction even in death - When beggars die, there are no comets seen…

Class, c. inequality. See entries for 'Social Issues' *** 'Opinion, your op. on sociological issues, minimum wage - O, reason not the need: our basest beggars are in the poorest thing superfluous…'

Class, c. warfare - Well, I say it was never merry world in England since gentlemen came up.

Class, poorer c. – … we, the poorer born whose baser stars do shut us up in wishes.

Classification, c. of man uncertain – That which you are my thoughts cannot transpose.

Classification, unclassifiable - 'Tis neither here nor there.

Classification, not the last. See 'Last, not being the l. better than nothing - not being the worst stands in some rank of praise'.

Clay and Clay. See 'Equality among men impossible - …but clay and clay differs in dignity, whose dust is both alike.'

Cleopatra, indirectly equating her to C. – Where's my serpent of old Nile?

Climate, c. inducing drowsiness. See 'Sleep, drowsiness - What a strange drowsiness possesses them!'

Climate, northern c. - … the north, where shivering cold and sickness pines the clime.

Clock, sound of c. striking hours painful - ... the sound that tells what hour it is…

Clothes, all clothes and no substance. See 'Character, c. all in his clothes - The soul of this man is in his clothes…'

Clothing, c. is all I have. See 'Tax collector, how to handle a tax c. – my riches are these poor habiliments'

Clothing, foul and in need of changing, a bath needed too - I have held some familiarity with fresher clothes.

Clothing, justification for cheap looking a

Cloud, optical illusions. See "Illusions, constructs of the mind - Sometimes we see a cloud that's dragonish…'

Cloud, mutation in c. shapes – That which is now a horse, even with a thought the rack dislimns, and makes it indistinct…

Cloud, threatening c. See 'Nature, storm brewing - … yond same black cloud, yond huge one, looks like a foul bombard that would shed his liquor.'

Codependence, c. to be avoided - There lives within the very flame of love…

Cold and hungry. See 'Mind, state of m. in turmoil - … the tempest in my mind doth from my senses take all feeling else save what beats there'.

Cold comfort. See 'Thirst, parched lips begging for water - … entreat the north to make his bleak wind kiss my parched lips…'

Cold, feeling very c. and possible remedy for it - Let me pour in some sack to the Thames water…

Collection, c. efforts - Importune him for my moneys; be not ceased with slight denial..

College, search for good c. See 'Knowledge, search for k.'

Combat, c. between groups of equal strength. See 'Stalemate, s. between two equal powers'.

Combination, unlikely c. See 'Marriage, combination unusual or plainly mad - Such a mad marriage never was before.'

Come what come may. See 'Life, manly approach to unexpected events, however rough - Come what come may, time and the hour runs through the roughest day.'

Comfort, c. arriving too late – … that comfort comes too late; 't is like a pardon after execution…

Comfort, c. useless - Charm ache with air and agony with words

Comfort, exhortation to see things positively – Put color in thy cheek.

Comfort, false c. based on rumor – They bring smooth comforts false, worse than true wrongs.

Comfort, recognizing a person for his/her help - Thou art all the comfort the gods will diet me with.

Comfort, refusal of any c. See 'Advice, a. not wanted - … cease thy counsel which falls into mine ear as profitless as water in a sieve.' *** 'Advice, uselessness of a. when in pain - Every one can master a grief, but he that has it.'

Command, answer to c. – Anything … that my ability may undergo and nobleness impose.

Command, answer to c. - Your bidding shall I do effectually.

Command, c. given with some arrogance, reaction to - When Caesar says 'do this,' it is perform'd.

Command, c. imperative – Do it at once or thy precedent services are all but accidents unpurposed.

Command. See also entries for 'Obedience'.

Comment, no c. - … what he is indeed, more suits you to conceive than I to speak of.

Command, peremptory c. with execution unavoidable - Do't and thou hast the one half of my heart; do't not, thou split'st thine own.

Command, quick, no talk - Waste no time in words but get thee gone.

Commenting, fearful c. See 'Fear, f. generates delay and failure – fearful commenting is leaden servitor to dull delay…'

Commitment, c. not to break an oath. See 'Agreement, abiding by the majority decision or a., even if you do not like the terms - … although I seem so loath, I am the last that will last keep his oath.'

Commitment, c. to always consult before taking important action - And never will I undertake the thing wherein thy counsel and consent is wanting.

Commitment, c. to execute o. to the fullest - .. thy commandment all alone shall live within the book and volume of my brain, unmix'd with baser matter.

Commitment, c. to writing frequently - Who's born that day when I forget to send to Antony shall die a beggar.

Commitment, full c. to the enterprise, no half measures - Either our history shall, with full mouth, speak freely of our acts; or else...

Commitment, you will maintain the c. - .. and when I break that oath, let me turn monster.

Commitments, purposeful c. must be limited in number - It is the purpose that makes strong the vow but vows to every purpose must not hold.

Committee, portrait of a c. and its characteristic confusion – .. truly I think if all our wits were to issue out of one skull, they would fly east, west…

Commodity. See 'Self-interest, bias of the world - That smooth-fac'd gentleman, tickling commodity, commodity, the bias of the world'

Common sense, would say no but perhaps.. - And what impossibility would slay in common sense, sense saves another way.

Communications, clarity and honesty go together - An honest tale speeds best being plainly told.

Communism impossible. See 'Equality among men impossible - …but clay and clay differs in dignity, whose dust is both alike.'

Communism, communist manifesto – … there shall be no money; all shall eat and drink on my score.

Company, c. downsizes, effect on employees - .. leak'd is our bark and we, poor mates, stand on the dying deck…

Company, commercial c. in poor but recoverable shape - it is but as a body yet distemper'd, which to his former strength may be restored..

Company, good c. making time and travel seem shorter - .. And yet your fair discourse hath been as sugar, making the hard way sweet and delectable.

Company, not wanting any c. See 'Solitude, wanting to be a.'

Company, rationalization for having frequented the wrong crowd - The strawberry grows underneath the nettle… fruit of baser quality.

Company, the c. of men apt to easily change their mind - I am betrayed, by keeping company with men-like men, of strange inconstancy.

Company, type of company consorted with affecting behavior. See 'Education, importance of good company'.

Comparison, night beyond c. - … My young remembrance cannot parallel a fellow to it.

Comparison, no c. between the two. See 'Person, p's comparative worth - To me he seems like diamond to glass.

Compassion, perfunctory c. cannot exempt from responsibility – … And water cannot wash away your sin

Compassion, stones better than people - .. a stone is as soft wax, tribunes more hard than stones..

Competition, driving away the c. - So bees with smoke, and doves with noisome stench are from their hives and houses driven away.

Competition, unexpected surge of the c. - Where slept our scouts, or how are they seduced that we could hear no news of his repair?

Complaint, c. after problems useless - ... wise men ne'er sit and wail their loss, but cheerly seek how to redress their harms.

Complaint, c. after problems useless - … wise men ne'er sit and wail their loss, but cheerly seek how to redress their harms.

Complaint, c. after problems useless - All of us have cause to wail the dimming of our shining star…

Complaint, c. after problems useless - Cease to lament for that thou canst not help, and study help for that which thou lament'st..

Complaint, c. of unfair treatment - ... all his faults observed, set in a note-book, learn'd, and conn'd by rote to cast into my teeth.

Complaint, c. to the point of breaking, union's grievances – Know that our griefs are risen to the top and now at length they overflow their banks.

Complaint, c. very loud and excessive - ... thy groans did make wolves howl, and penetrate the breasts of ever-angry bears…

Complaint. See entries for 'Attitude, a. towards what is past and cannot be changed - To mourn a mischief that is past and gone…'

Completely and utterly, from head to foot. See 'Insult, traitor - … from the extremest upward of thy head to the descent and dust below thy foot…'

Complexion, alternating colors - This silent war of lilies and of roses.

Complexion, beautiful c. See 'Face, expression., beauty, imitating Nature. Blending of beautiful attributes imitating Nature at her best'.

Complexion, c. of a criminal - … his complexion is perfect gallows.

Complexion, excellent c. - .. That excellent complexion which did steal the eyes of young and old.

Complexion, good c. – …your colour, I warrant you, is as red as any rose, in good truth.

Compliment, c. on a house you are visiting. See 'Fore God, you have here a goodly dwelling and a rich'

Compliments, a volley of c. - ... mine own self's better part, mine eye's clear eye..

Compliments, exchange of c. and formalities - .. too mean a servant.. Leave off discourse of disability.

Compliments, c. reserved for dinner time – … let me praise you while I have a stomach - - … No, pray thee, let it serve for table-talk…

Compliments, c. to a woman. See entries for 'Face', 'Eyes', 'Lips', 'Cheeks', 'Hands', 'Skin', 'Beauty', 'Beautiful', 'Love', 'Ladies', 'Woman', 'Woman, beautiful', 'Woman, w. beautiful', 'Do you like me?', 'Dress'.

Compliments, string of paradoxical compliments - Beautiful tyrant! fiend angelical! Dove-feather'd raven!…

Comrade, strange c. See 'Adversity, a. assembles strange characters - .. misery acquaints man with strange bedfellows.

Conceit in weakest bodies strongest works. See 'Imagination, conceit, lack of realism'

Conceit, as when a wise person pretends not to understand – Thus wisdom wishes to appear most bright when it doth tax itself..

Conceit, hiding the real intent – … with forged quaint conceit to set a gloss upon his bold intent.

Conceit, you do not say what you mean - You speak not as you think, it cannot be.

Concentration, no distractions from c. See 'Distraction, no d. please – When holy and devout religious men are at their beads…'

Concern, c. about having upset someone - … I hope my words disbench'd you not.

Concession, little initial c. leading to eventual defeat - … when the fox hath once got in his nose…

Concession, tolerate your adversary's temporary glory - Let frantic Talbot triumph for a while and like a peacock sweep along his tail…

Conclusion, c. does not follow from premise - … there is no consonancy in the sequel.

Conclusion, false c. See 'Exclamation, false conclusion - O most lame and impotent conclusion!'

Conclusions, wrong c. drawn by a giddy person - He that is giddy thinks the world turns round.

Concordance between belief and words used to express it - For things are often spoke and seldom meant..

Condemnation, c. of an innocent man through prejudice – … that dye is on me which makes my whitest part black.

Condemning others for having your own faults. See 'Hypocrisy, criticizing one's own faults in others - Wilt thou whip thine own faults in other men?'

Condition, hard c. See 'Power, the downside of p. - ... subject to the breath of every fool, whose sense no more can feel, but his own wringing.'

Conditions, current place and c. not as bad as others - This wide and universal theatre presents more woeful pageants…

Conditions, political c intolerable – Brutus had rather be a villager than to repute himself a son of Rome…

Conditions, tough c. to be in - ... the condition of the time, which cannot look more hideously upon me than I have drawn it in my fantasy.

Conditions, unfair working c. See 'Oppression, o. and unfair working conditions – … I have served him from the hour of my nativity to this instant…'

Confess yourself to heaven… See 'Repentance, invitation to repent – … Repent what's past; avoid what is to come…'

Confession, confessing to lust - … served the lust of my mistress' heart, and did the act of darkness with her.

Confession, confessing to sins - …false of heart, light of ear, bloody of hand; hog in sloth, fox in stealth, wolf in greediness…

Confidence, c. among trusted friends - ... We three are but thyself; and, speaking so, thy words are but as thoughts; therefore, be bold.

Confidence, c. in victory and subsequent reward - …doubt not of the day, and, that once gotten, doubt not of large pay.

Confidence, c. that overcomes any fear – … all too confident to give admittance to a thought of fear.

Confidence, overconfidence challenges the frailty of our powers - And sometimes we are devils to ourselves…

Confidence, overconfidence dangerous and misguided - The man that once did sell the lion's skin..

Confidence, overconfidence not a sign of wisdom - ... your wisdom is consumed in confidence.

Confidence, self-confidence, see 'Opportunity, the world as a source of o - …then the world's mine oyster.'

Confirmation, c. of statement – I said so and I must not blush to affirm it.

Conflict, not a time for c. – 'Tis not a time for private stomaching…

Conflict resolution, advice to proceed with caution - ... temperately proceed to what you would thus violently redress.

Conflict resolution, calming down the debate - ...When we debate our trivial differences loud, we do commit murder in healing wounds.

Conflict resolution, inflaming not cooling off the conflict - This is the way to kindle, not to quench.

Conflict resolution, relative importance of arguments in dispute - But small to greater matters must give way.

Conflict resolution, use of wit with those who have little - I'll try whether my old wit be in request with those that have but little.

Conflict resolution. See 'Agreement, wholeheartedly in a. - May I never, to this good purpose, that so fairly shows dream of impediment.'

Conflict, c. smoldering between two parties - .. there is division although as yet the face of it is covered with mutual cunning.

Confused, in a state of confusion. See 'Indecision, i. due to confusion in the mind - My thoughts are whirled like a potter's wheel; I know not where I am, nor what I do.'

Confusion, c. following management upheaval - .. and vast confusion waits, as doth the raven on a sick fallen beast, the imminent decay of wrested pomp.

Confusion, c. generated by happiness. See 'Happiness, in a state of happy confusion - ..

there is such confusion in my powers..'

Confusion, how quickly things become confused -.. so quick bright things come to confusion.

Confusion, remedy for c. is not more c. - .. confusion's cure lives not in these confusions.

Confusion, state of c. – All is uneven and every thing is left at six and seven.

Confusion, state of c. at its zenith - Confusion now hath made his masterpiece!

Connections, importance of good c. - A friend in the court is better than a penny in purse.

Conquerors, c. of their own passions. See 'Men, m. of strong temper - …brave conquerors… that war against your own affections'

Conquest accomplished, in a dizzy. See 'Stunned, mesmerized, in a trance - My thoughts are whirled like a potter's wheel; I know not where I am, nor what I do.'

Conquest accomplished, totally overwhelmed - … My heart and hands thou hast at once subdued.

Conquest, determination to conquer - Now, Rouen, I'll shake thy bulwarks to the ground.

Conscience, c. as an obstacle – I'll not meddle with it: it is a dangerous thing…

Conscience, c. as power when fighting against evil - Every man's conscience is a thousand swords…

Conscience, c. lost to money - … in the Duke of Gloucester's purse.

Conscience, c. moved by speech heard - How smart a lash that speech doth give my conscience!

Conscience, c. or fear – …conscience is but a word that cowards use devised at first to keep the strong in awe…

Conscience, c. or fear – Thus conscience does make cowards of us all…

Conscience, c. second to politics. See 'Politics, p. above conscience - Men must learn now with pity to dispense, for policy sits above conscience.'

Conscience, c. vs. objectives. See 'Objectives, o. versus conscience - The colour of the king doth come and go between his purpose and his conscience…'

Conscience, clear c. See 'Openness, no need for secrecy - There's nothing I have done yet, of my conscience, deserves a corner.'

Conscience, clear c. when fighting for a just cause - … the arms are fair when the intent of bearing them is just.

Conscience, clear c. yielding piece of mind. See 'Peace, inner p. felt. - … I feel within me a peace above all earthly dignities, a still and quiet conscience.'

Conscience, debating within one's c. – … Thus hulling in the wild sea of my conscience…

Conscience, dilemma, torn between duty and desire - … well, my conscience says, Launcelot, budge not…

Conscience, exhortation to look into one's c. See 'Exhortation, e. to question our motives - Go to your bosom; knock there, and ask your heart what it doth know…'

Conscience, false c. - … their best conscience is not to leave it undone, but keep it unknown.

Conscience, guilt of c. as a reward – The guilt of conscience take thou for thy labour…

Conscience, guilty c. See 'Suspicion, s. sign of guilty mind - Suspicion always haunts the guilty mind, the thief doth fear each bush an officer.'

Conscience, imperialistic attitude. See 'Conscience, c. or fear – … conscience is but a word that cowards use devised at first to keep the strong in awe…'

Conscience, no scruples of c. – … where lies that? if 'twere a kibe, 'twould put me to my slipper…

Conscience, pangs of guilty c. - My conscience hath a thousand several tongues..

Conscience, pangs of guilty c. - My

conscience, thou art fetter'd more than my shanks and wrists.

Conscience, pangs of guilty c. See King Claudius' comment in 'Hypocrisy and self-illusion - .. with devotion's visage and pious action we do sugar o'er the devil himself.'

Conscience, rationale for disregarding it - I'll not meddle with it: it is a dangerous thing..

Conscience, rhetorical question - and hast a thing within thee called conscience?

Conscience, seeing the blackness of one's c. – ... And there I see such black and grained spots as will not leave their tinct.

Conscience, shaking of c. - This respite shook the bosom of my conscience, enter'd me, yea, with a splitting power..

Conscience, stilling of c. - So much my conscience whispers in your ear…

Conscience, tormenting c. – O coward conscience, how dost thou afflict me.

Consciousness, c. of doing wrong. See 'Intent, evil i. to remain hidden – stars hide your fires, let not light see my black and deep desires.'

Consensus, acknowledging hearty c. - I am glad that my weak words have struck but thus much show of fire from Brutus.

Consequences, c. imaginable based on previous narrative - … let me say no more! Gather the sequel by that went before.

Consequences, c. of a bad decision - You pluck a thousand dangers on your head…

Consequences, c. of not taking advantage of opportunities. See entries for 'Opportunity, o. offered and rejected'

Consequences, dangerous c. predicted - I told ye all, when ye first put this dangerous stone a-rolling, 'twould fall upon ourselves.

Consideration like an angel came …See 'Character, reformed - consideration, like an angel came and whipp'd the offending Adam out of him.'

Consolation, thoughts of c. in sharing misfortunes - .. that they are not the first of fortune's slaves..

Conspiracy – … Open-eyed conspiracy his time doth take …

Conspiracy, aware of c. against yourself – Myself had notice of your conventicles….

Conspiracy, c. brought about by unwarranted security. See 'Security, false sense of s. - … If thou beest not immortal look about you: security gives way to conspiracy'

Conspiracy, c. suitable for dark hours night - O, then by day where wilt thou find a cavern dark enough to mask thy monstrous visage?

Conspiracy, defense from charges of c. See 'Innocence, i. unsuspecting - … unstain'd thoughts do seldom dream on evil.' *** 'Intentions, i. that did not materialize – thoughts are no subjects, intents but merely thoughts.'

Constancy, a desirable trait. See 'Character, constancy, a desirable trait'.

Constancy, c. tested under trial. See 'Person, worthiness of a p. shown under trial - … in the wind and tempest of her frown, distinction…' *** 'Persistence, failure. positive attitude - ... the protractive trials of great Jove to find persistive constancy in men.'

Constancy, c. of wifely love – …like a jewel, has hung twenty years about his neck, yet never lost her lustre…

Consumerism, programmed unhappiness. See 'Life, l's chronic unhappiness - Happy thou art not; for what thou hast not, still thou strivest to get…'

Contempt, c. for a person worth less than dust. See 'Insult, worth less than dust - … You are not worth the dust which the rude wind blows in your face.'

Contempt, c. for a person compared to another - ... his meanest garment that ever hath but clipped his body…

Contempt, c. for manual labor – The nobility think scorn to go in leather aprons.

Contempt, c. for pain doubly hurtful. See 'Pain, mental p. - These miseries are more than may be borne. To weep with them that weep doth ease some deal…'

Contentment, c. as a title. See 'Happiness, h. in simplicity - … my crown is called content: a crown it is that seldom kings enjoy.'

Contentment, c. as the best asset – Our content is our best having.

Contentment, c. assured if insensitive to poverty - Poor and content is rich and rich enough...

Contentment, c. observed among lower middle class - How well this honest mirth become their labour.

Contentment, the art of c. - I could be bounded in a nutshell, and count myself a king of infinite space.

Contest, no contest - So first the harmless sheep doth yield his fleece and next his throat unto the butcher's knife.

Contingency, see entries for 'Plan, contingency p.'

Continuation, going to the next step - … to perform an act whereof what's past is prologue.

Contract terms, c.t. suspicious. See 'Suspicion, s. at terms offered by a crook - I like not fair terms and a villain's mind.'

Contract, see entries for 'Agreement, a. or contract'.

Conversation, c. begun in jest and continued seriously - .. since we are stepp'd thus far in, I will continue that I broach'd in jest.

Conversation, c. postponed. See 'Dialog, d. postponed when hearer in better mood'.

Conviction, 'Are you sure?. See 'Speech, speaking simply and honestly - I speak as my understanding instructs me and as mine honesty puts it to utterance.'

Conviction, unshakable c. – (He) swears his thought over by each particular star in heaven …

Convinced, almost c. See 'Man, convinced, almost c. - … three parts of him is ours already, and the man entire upon the next encounter yields him ours.

Convinced, convincing argument - His words do take possession of my bosom.

Convincing, attempt to convince. See 'News, believability of a story - … And let us once again assail your ears that are so fortified against our story.'

Cooking test - 'T is an ill cook that cannot lick his own fingers.

Cooling, virtual air conditioning. See 'Imagination, not a substitute of reality - O, who can hold a fire in his hand by thinking on the frosty Caucasus?…'

Cooling off observed, general truth - When love begins to sicken and decay, it useth an enforced ceremony.

Cooling off observed, question for verification - Dwell I but in the suburbs of your good pleasure?

Cooling off observer. See 'Mood, change in m. observed - … I have not from your eyes that gentleness and show of love as I was wont to have.'

Cooperation, c. requested in tricky situation - …make not impossible that which but seems unlike.

Corporate life. See 'Life, l. inside a corporation or the Washington belt – … the art of the court as hard to leave as keep…'

Correction, c. of mistakes impossible. See 'System, corrupt s. cannot correct its own mistakes - … correction lieth in those hands which make the fault we cannot correct…'

Correction, correcting the assessment of a person - …'Good Gloucester' and 'good devil' were alike

Correction, regret for having to take corrective action – O cursed spite, that ever I was born to set it right.

Corruption, agent of c. – … she that sets seeds and roots of shame and iniquity.

Corruption, c. caused by continued sinning. See 'Predictions, dire p. – foul sin shall break into corruption'.

Corruption, c. for the sake of money - … shall we now contaminate our fingers with base bribes…

Corruption, c. no better than honesty - Corruption wins no more than honesty.

Corruption, c. of a man - And whatsoever cunning fiend it was… hath got the voice in hell for excellence.

Corruption, c. of young person – Thou hast … abused her delicate youth with drugs or minerals that weaken motion.

Corruption, c. of justice by commercial interests. See 'Justice, corruption of j. by commercial interests'.

Corruption, c. rampant. See 'Laws, l. disregarded – I have seen corruption boil and bubble till it o'er-run the stew…'

Corruption, corrupted witnesses - … at what ease might corrupt minds procure knaves as corrupt to swear against you?…

Corruption, praising the corrupt. See 'Praise, praising the criminal if advantage drawn from him – A giving hand, though foul, shall have fair praise.'

Corruption, the price of c. - Is it possible that any villany should be so dear?..

Corruption, time to take measures against c. See 'Medicine, metaphor, m. against costume - … 'Tis time to give 'em physic, their diseases are grown so catching'

Counsel, c. useless for stubborn hearer - … for all in vain comes counsel to his ear.

Counsel, impact of c. from a man nearing death - More are men's ends mark'd than their lives before…

Counsel, refusal of c. - … give me no counsel, my griefs cry louder than advertisement.

Counsel, self-counseling. See 'Wisdom, words of w. to oneself, avoiding messy situation – … But, Suffolk, stay; thou mayst not wander in that labyrinth…

Counsel, too late for c. - … all too late comes counsel to be heard.

Counterfeit, c. skills – … ghastly looks are at my service, like enforced smiles and both are ready in their offices at any time, to grace my stratagems

Country living, in praise of country living - … Here can I sit alone, unseen of any and to the nightingale's complaining notes…

Country, c. in poor state, only the ignorant smile - … where nothing, but who knows nothing, is once seen to smile.

Country, c. living vs. corporate life. See 'Adversity, a. put to good use - Sweet are the uses of adversity…'

Country, c. under yoke - I think our country sinks beneath the yoke…

Country, see 'Leaving the country - Then thus I turn me from my country's light'.

Courage, c. against adversities. See entries for 'Complaint, c. after problems useless' *** 'Character, not afraid of taking chances - I have set my life upon a cast and I will stand the hazard of the die."

Courage, c. an asset in women's eyes. - … there is no love-broker in the world can more prevail in man's commendation with woman than report of valour.

Courage, c. derived from innocence. See 'Innocence, i. giving courage'.

Courage, c. displayed in a state of weakness - … that's a valiant flea, that dare eat his breakfast on the lip of a lion.

Courage, c. the number one virtue - … valour is the chiefest virtue and most dignifies the haver.

Courage, circumstances inspiring c. – Courage mounteth with occasion.

Courage, exhortation to c. - What cannot be avoided, 't were childish weakness to lament or fear.

Courage, no fear of risk to gain the prize - .. think death no hazard, in this enterprise.

Courage, reward goes to the courageous - .. fearless minds climb soonest unto crowns.

Courage, the advantages of c., dying only once - … Cowards die many times before their deaths...

Court, life at c. dangerous. See "Life, l. inside a corporation or the Washington belt – .. the art of the court as hard to leave as keep..'

Courtesy, c. shown to the wrong person - Why strew'st thou sugar on that bottled spider, whose deadly web ensnareth thee about?

Courtesy, false c. - Grace me no grace, nor uncle me no uncle.

Courtesy, false c. - ...how fine this tyrant can tickle where she wounds.

Courtesy, false c. - ...this courtesy is not of the right breed.

Courtesy, insisting to reciprocate c. See 'Debt, insisting on repaying a courtesy - In common worldly things, 'tis call'd ungrateful, with dull unwillingness to repay a debt.'

Courtesy, justifiable exception to c. See 'Apologies for leaving without notice - .. my business was great; and in such a case as mine a man may strain courtesy.'

Courtesy, people not trained to c. - ... Turks and Tartars, never train'd to offices of tender courtesy.

Courtiers, c. defined. See 'Flattery, f. observed and used for advancement – You shall mark many a duteous and knee-crooking knave…'

Courtship, no time for c. - These times of woe afford no time to woo.

Cover-up, c.-up for assassinations. See 'Assassination, a. under the guise of law - That he should die is worthy policy; but yet we want a colour for his death…'

Cover-up, planned - And what may make him blush in being known, he'll stop the course by which it might be known.

Cover-up, sins self compounding - ... one sin, I know, another doth provoke...

Cover-up, spin used as a c.-up. See 'Shame, curious as to how the shameless can avoid s. – What trick, what device, what starting-hole, canst thou now find out to hide thee…'

Cover-up. See 'Censure, presence required to avoid rumors and censure - ... to avoid the censures of the carping world.' *** 'lines 5 and

Covetousness. See 'Greed, g., covetousness and desire for more - Those that much covet are with gain so fond…'

Coward, c. by instinct - Instinct is a great matter; I was now a coward on instinct.

Coward, hoping your fears may be unfounded - Pray God, I say, I prove a needless coward.

Cowardice, c. bred by luxury and inaction. See 'Hardiness, h. acquired via a rough life - Plenty and peace breeds cowards: hardness ever of hardiness is mother.'

Cowardice, c. disguised with a martial outside - We'll have a swashing and a martial outside

Cowardice, c. evident – .. there's no more valour in that Poins, than in a wild duck.

Cowardice, c. hidden in loud threats - … coward dogs most spend their mouths when what they seem to threaten…

Cowardice, c. justified - Honor hath no skills in surgery..

Cowardice, c. or discretion - The better part of valour is, discretion…

Cowardice, c. shown by running away – … Your legs did better service than your hands.

Cowardice, c. vs. patience. See 'Patience, p. or cowardice? - That which in mean men we entitle patience is pure cold cowardice in noble breasts.'

Cowards - The mouse ne'er shunn'd the cat as they did budge from rascals worse than they.

Cowards, c. defined - I know them to be as true-bred cowards as ever turned back.

Cowards, c. dying multiple times. See 'Courage, the advantages of c., dying only once - ... Cowards die many times before their deaths…'

Cowards, c. in disguise. See lines in 'Hypocrisy, vice and h. – There is no vice so simple, but assumes some mark of virtue in its outward parts…'

Cowards. See entries for 'Insult, cowards'.

Crack of doom, endlessness.. See 'Traffic, long line of stalled cars – … will the line stretch out to the crack of doom?'

Creature, strange or contemptible c. See 'Modesty, m. in possession – … this thing of darkness acknowledge mine.'

Credentials, establishing your c. - I am as constant as the northern star…

Credentials, man with many c. See 'Words, pompous w. - to divide him inventorially would dizzy the arithmetic of memory…

Credentials, questionable – by birth a pedlar, by education a card-maker…

Credentials, sincerity, one tongue - I have no tongue but one.

Credentials, sincerity, one tongue - What I think I utter and spend my malice in my breath.

Credentials, steadiness. See 'Heart. Positive self appraisal and advertisement'.

Credentials, truthfulness. See 'Truth, answer to 'Are you telling the truth?"

Credibility, c. reduced - my credit now stands on such slippery ground..

Credibility, lack of c. - … will you credit this base drudge's words, that speaks he knows not what?

Credit card. See 'Dinner. How to pay for dinner, cash or credit card - I'll pay cash) as far as my coin would stretch…

Credit worthiness spoiled by uncollected debts - My reliances on his fracted dates have smit my credit.

Creditors, c. as devils. See 'Insult, creditors, imprecation – They have e'en put my breath from me, the slaves…'

Creditors, c. cruel - My creditors grow cruel…

Creditors. See 'Death, d. as a means to beat collectors - … But the comfort is, you shall be called to no more payments..'

Crickets, singing c. See 'Sleep, s. as rest - The crickets sing, and man's o'er-labour'd sense repairs itself by rest.'

Crime, authority contracted c. is unsafe for the contractor - … if a king bid a man be a villain, he's bound by the indenture of his oath to be one.

Crime, c. emboldened by clemency - … nothing emboldens sin so much as mercy.

Crime, c. not worth committing. See 'Gain, g. from crime illusory - … Who buys a minute's mirth to wail a week? Or sells eternity to get a toy?'

Crime, c. of opportunity. See 'Opportunity, crime of o. - O Opportunity, thy guilt is great!'

Crime, c. of unspeakable proportions, indignation - The earth hath not a hole to hide his deed.

Crime, c. of unspeakable proportions, indignation - This is the very top the height, the crest, or crest onto the crest of murder's arms.

Crime, c. or villainy, who did it - The practise of it lives in… whose spirits toil in frame of villanies.

Crime, c. prompted by opportunity - How oft the sight of means to do ill deeds makes ill deeds done.

Crime, c. returning to poison the criminal. See 'Doubt, d. or remorse, or awareness of crime - … this even-handed justice commends the ingredients of our poison'd chalice to our own lips.'

Crime, c. sex and murder connected – Murder's as near to lust as flame to smoke.

Crime, evidence of c. provided – If imputation and strong circumstance which lead directly to the door of truth..

Crime, evidence of who is the criminal unmistakable - Who finds the heifer dead and bleeding fresh..

Crime, extreme c. - O, my offence is rank it smells to heaven.

Crime, gain from c. illusory. See 'Gain, g. from crime illusory - … Who buys a minute's mirth to wail a week? Or sells eternity to get a toy?'

Crime, planning the unspeakable c. – … if that thou couldst see me without eyes, hear me without thine ears, and make reply without a tongue …

Crime, why knowledge of c. is dangerous – Since he's so great can make his will his act will think me speaking, though I swear to silence…

Crimes, unspeakable c. - 'Twill vex thy soul to hear what I shall speak; for I must talk of murders…

Criminal, who is the real c.? - It is an heretic that makes the fire, not she which burns in't.

Criminals, c. acting in the dark - … Then thieves and robbers range abroad unseen in murders and in outrage bloody…

Criticism, better a little c. than a lot of heart-break - … better a little chiding, than a great deal of heart-break.

Criticism, c. of dead people to be avoided - … beat not the bones of the buried…

Criticism, c. of powerful government figure dangerous – … who dare speak one syllable against him?

Criticism, c. suspect - .. such may rail against great buildings.

Criticism, exposed to c. by fools. See 'Opinion, your op. on crowds and masses - … subject to the breath of every fool, whose sense no more can feel but his own wringing!'

Criticism, fear of c. See 'Action, need to act notwithstanding possible censure – if we shall stand still in fear our motion…'

Criticism, handling of c. – Take each man's censure but reserve thy judgment.

Criticism, moderation in c. urged. See 'Moderation, m. urged in upbraiding - Forbear sharp speeches to her…'

Criticism, psychological strategy for c. – Chide him for faults, and do it reverently…

Criticism, self-c. rejected – …Nor shall you … make it truster of your own report against yourself.

Crocodile, insincere display or tears. See 'Insult, deceit, compared to actions by crocodile - … as the mournful crocodile with sorrow snares relenting passengers…' *** 'Remorse, false r., false tears - Trust not those cunning waters of his eyes…'

Crocodile. See 'Description, self-evident d. - What manner o' thing is your crocodile?…

Crooked ways to achieve power. See 'Position, p. achieved through crooked means - God knows… by what by-paths and indirect crooked ways I met this crown.'

Crowd, dense c. – … where a finger could not be wedged in more.

Crown, c. or high office preventing sleep. See entries for 'Sleeplessness, s. caused by great responsibility '

Crown, pleasure of wearing a c. See 'King, how nice to be a k. - … how sweet a thing it is to wear a crown.'

Crows, c. announcing the morning with their racket. See 'Nature, morning, announced by the crows - …the busy day, waked by the lark, hath roused the ribald crows…'

Crows, s. impatient for their preys – … the knavish crows fly o'er them, all impatient for their hour.

Cruel to be kind - I must be cruel, only to be kind…

Cruel words, reaction to cruel words. See 'Rejection, despair at her words.'

Cruel, heartbreaker, slain by her - Fly away, fly away breath; I am slain by a fair cruel maid.

Cruel, heartbreaker. See, 'Speech, disappointment or despair at her words - .. thou hast cleft my heart in twain'

Cruel, pierced through the heart - Pierced through the heart with your stern cruelty

Cruel, see 'Woman, cruel, serpent - O serpent heart, hid with a flowering face!'

Cruel, see 'Woman, cruel, killer - Fly away, fly away breath, I am slain by a fair cruel maid.'

Cruel, unmovable. See 'Impossibility to soften a hard heart - You may as well forbid the mountain pines…'

Cruelty, c. in Rome - Rome is but a wilderness of tigers.

Cruelty, c. on a man fallen from grace - …'tis a cruelty to load a falling man.

Cruelty, invocation to c. by a woman – Come, you spirits that tend on mortal thoughts, unsex me here…

Cruelty. See 'Violence, v. and cruelty rationalized - …men are as the time is: to be tender-minded does not become a sword.'

Cry, c. of encouragement - A Talbot! a Talbot! cried out Amman and rushed into the bowels of the battle.

Cry, do not cry – fall not a tear, I say; one of them rates all that is won and lost…

Cry, starting to cry - Then can I drown an eye, unused to flow…

Crying not called for, on the contrary - the tears live in an onion that should water this sorrow.

Crying, c. detrimental to woman's beauty. See 'Woman, hard and harsh w. - A woman moved is like a fountain troubled…'

Crying, c. impossible notwithstanding the pain but... – …weep I cannot, but my heart bleeds…

Crying, c. prevented by re-distribution of moisture - I cannot weep; for all my body's moisture scarse serves to quench my furnace-burning heart.

Crying, competition at who cries more – And with the southern clouds contend in tears…

Crying. See entries for 'Tears'

Crying, invitation to a lady to stop c. - … weep no more, lest I give cause to be suspected of more tenderness than doth become a man.

Crying, invitation to cry. See "Disappointment, d. expressed in dramatic terms – … make dust our paper and with rainy eyes…'

Crying, on the point of crying - Mine eyes smell onions, I shall weep anon.

Crying, on the point of c. See 'Sadness, s. prompting tears - … my heart is drown'd with grief whose flood begins to flow within mine eyes.' *** Entries for 'Tears unstoppable'.

Crying, unused to c. See 'Character, strong, unable to weep - I am a soldier, and unapt to weep, or to exclaim on fortune's fickleness.'

Crying, why are you crying? - … that this distemper'd messenger of wet… rounds thine eye?

Crying, with unhappiness - I am great with woe, and shall deliver weeping.

Cudgel thy brains.. See 'Brain, no more raking of the b - Cudgel thy brains no more about it….'

Culture, c. conditioning the characters of men – … men are as the time is.

Cunning, c. observed - The fox barks not when he would steal the lamb.

Cunning, using a partial truth to make a bigger lie – You do advance your cunning more and more when truth kills truth.

Cupid, C. can make ladies mad - Cupid is a knavish lad thus to make poor females mad.

Cupid, C's arrows - .. Of this matter is little Cupid's crafty arrow made…

Cupid, C's varied mode of operation - … loving goes by haps, some Cupid kills with arrows, some with traps.

Cupid, love, definition - The anointed sovereign of sighs and groans.

Curiosity, c. as the engine of the masses. See 'Masses, crowds at all windows driven by curiosity – You would have thought the very windows spake…'

Curse, arthritis - aches contract and starve your supple joints!

Curse, asking gods to confirm curses - I would the gods had nothing else to do..

Curse, asking permission to c. - I pr'ythee, give me leave to curse a while.

Curse, c. against a city - O thou wall that

girdlest in those wolves, dive in the earth and fence not Athens.

Curse, c. against a city. See 'Athens, imprecation against A. - ... sink, Athens! henceforth hated be of Timon, man and all humanity!'

Curse, c. against capitalists. See 'Opinion, your op. on salesmen and merchants - Traffic's thy god; and thy god confound thee!'

Curse, c. and prediction for a traitor - His treasons will sit blushing in his face..

Curse, c. on unsympathetic associates – Sorrow on thee and all the pack of you that triumph thus upon my misery!

Curse, c. piercing the clouds - Can curses pierce the clouds and enter heaven?

Curse, c. threatened for not keeping an oath. See 'Oath, curse should an o. not be kept - ... And let him ne'er see joy that breaks that oath!'

Curse, c. to a liar - .. may his pernicious soul rot half a grain a day! He lies to the heart.

Curse, c. to both Democrats and Republicans - A plague o' both your houses!

Curse, c. to enemy - More direful hap betide that hated wretch...

Curse, c. to him who brings unpleasant news - Accursed be that tongue that tells me so.

Curse, c. to the slanderers - Sink Rome, and their tongues rot that speak against us.

Curse, c. to the unfair winners - Beshrew the winners, for they play'd me false.

Curse, c. to wars and sex - ... wars and lechery; nothing else holds fashion: a burning devil take them!

Curse, cursing a murderous hand - Cursed be the hand that made these fatal holes!..

Curse, damnation - Let molten coin be thy damnation, thou disease of a friend, and not himself!

Curse, darkness and lack of sun - May never glorious sun reflex his beams upon the country where you make abode..

Curse, desire to c. under any circumstances - Well could I curse away a winter's night..

Curse, fog - The south-fog rot him!

Curse, go to hell - Hie thee to hell for shame, and leave the world, thou cacodemon! there thy kingdom is.

Curse, infectious diseases - All the infections that the sun sucks up from bogs...

Curse, lung eating vultures - Let vultures vile seize on his lungs.

Curse, may that dog die - Cancel his bond of life, dear God, I pray, that I may live to say, the dog is dead.

Curse, minister of hell - Break thou in pieces and consume to ashes thou foul accursed minister of hell.

Curse, misery – your misery increase with your age!

Curse, plague – ...all the plagues that in the pendulous air hung fated over men's faults...

Curse, plague - ... and would send them back the plague could I but catch it for them.

Curse. canker - The canker gnaw thy heart for showing me again the eyes of man.

Curse, plague on murderers - A plague upon you, murderers, traitors all!

Curse, plague plus - Plagues, incident to men, your potent and infectious fevers heap on Athens...

Curse, poison - Poison be their drink!...

Curse, poison - Would poison were obedient and knew my mind..

Curse, quick course on cursing. - ... Forbear to sleep the nights, and fast the days..

Curse, sciatica - Thou cold sciatica cripple our senators...

Curse, sterility - Into her womb convey sterility! Dry up in her the organs of increase.

Curse, the worm of conscience begnaw thy soul. See 'Insults, volley of i. plus curses – stay dog for thou shalt hear me, deadly eye, troubler of world's peace etc.'

Curse, training in cursing. See 'Education, literature, results of teaching - You taught me language and my profit on it is, I know how to curse.'

Curse, variety of skin conditions - .. Itches, blains, sow all the Athenian bosoms; and their crop be general leprosy!

Curse, wishing ignorance and stupidity - The common curse of mankind, folly and ignorance..

Curse, wishing woe. See 'Anger, a. at authorities - .. woe upon ye, and all such false professors!'

Curse, you cause me to c. - .. thou, I fear, has given me cause to curse.

Curse, your enemy shipped to hell - would thou wert shipped to hell, rather than rob me of the people's hearts.

Curses, antidote to c. - .. curses never pass the lips of those that breathe them in the air.

Curses, if curses only work - Would curses kill, as doth the mandrake's groan…

Curses, c. on evil doers. See 'Evil, e. that calls for curses on its doers - … it calls I fear, too many curses on their heads that were the authors.'

Custom, c. as an obstacle to positive change - What custom wills, in all things should we do't, the dust of antique time would lie unswept…

Custom, c. making heart (or mind) impenetrable to sense – … damned custom have not brass'd it so that it is proof and bulwark against sense.

Custom, c. more ignored than followed - … it is a custom more honour'd in the breach than the observance.

Custom, how to reverse a c. or bad habit - That monster, custom, who all sense doth eat…

Dagger, d. of the mind - … art thou but a dagger of the mind, a false creation, proceeding from the heat-oppressed brain?

Daggers, see 'Perception, you want me dead - Thou hidest a thousand daggers in thy thoughts…' *** 'Place, a dangerous p. – where we are there's daggers in men's smiles.

Damage (unexpected) received from a supposedly helpful source - .. from that spring whence comfort seem'd to come discomfort swells..

Damage, d. minimal, only annoyance. See 'Annoyance, enemies creating more a. than damage'.

Damn'd Republicans and Democrats. See 'Curse, c. to both parties - A plague o' both your houses!'

Dance, invitation to d. - … with measure heap'd in joy, to the measure fall.

Dance, marching on hard road imagined as a dance. See lines in 'Positive thinking, how to acquire it, the art of it – Suppose the singing birds musicians… the flowers, fair ladies…'

Dancing days. See 'Time, t. past for entertainment - … for you and I are past our dancing days'.

Dancing perfection. See 'Perfection, p. in action, speech, dance etc. – What you do, still betters what is done. When you speak, sweet, I'd have you do it ever…'

Dancing, reason for not d. – .. I have a soul of lead so stakes me to the ground I cannot move.

Dancing, you don't like to dance. See 'Party, not attracted to parties - … so to your pleasures I am for other than for dancing measures.'

Dandy, arrival of a d. - Came there a certain lord, neat, and trimly dress'd, fresh as a bridegroom.

Dandy. See 'Character, a dandy – He speaks holiday, he smells April and May.'

Danger, avoiding unnecessary d. - .. nor seek for danger where there's no profit.

Danger, courage needed in d. - 'Tis true that we are in great danger, the greater therefore should our courage be.

Danger, d. compared t an approaching storm – When tempest of commotion, like the south…

Danger, d. lurking unexpectedly. See 'Character, quiet but crafty - Smooth runs the water where the brook is deep.'

Danger, d. necessary to achieve safety – Out of this nettle, danger, we pluck this flower, safety.

Danger, d. undertaken for someone else's benefit - Much danger do I undergo for thee.

Danger, dismissing d. unwise – You take a precipice for no leap of danger and woo your own destruction.

Danger, eliminating d. at the beginning. See entries for 'Problem, p. to be tackled before it gets bigger.'

Danger, facing d. as best option - I must go and meet with danger there..

Danger, fearing d. before any evidence, creates danger - To fly the boar before the boar pursues were to incense the boar to follow us…

Danger, facing up to d. – (We) boldly did outdare the dangers of the time

Danger, generalized apprehension. See 'Apprehension, generalized a. of danger – When clouds appear, wise men put on their cloaks…'

Danger, imminent d. and reaction on men – … By a divine instinct men's minds mistrust ensuing dangers…

Danger, mind's ability to sense danger - By a divine instinct men's minds mistrust ensuing dangers..

Danger, on being pre-warned of a danger - For many men that stumble at the threshold are well foretold that danger lurks within.

Dangerous, d. act or information. See 'Information, dangerous and sensitive i. – … matter deep and dangerous, as full of peril and adventurous spirit…'

Dangers, assessment and priority of d. – Thou'ldst shun a bear; but if thy flight lay toward the raging sea…

Dangers, images of mortal d. - Thou mayst hold a serpent by the tongue.

Daring, d. but to a limit - I dare do all that may become a man; who dares do more is none.

Daring. See 'Impossible, nothing i. to the daring - Impossible be strange attempts to those that weigh their pains in sense…

Dark, don't keep me in the d. See 'Answer, request to have an a. - … O, answer me! Let me not burst in ignorance.'

Darkness, d. sharpens the sense of hearing. See 'Nature, night, decreases visibility and sharpens hearing - Dark night that from the eye his function takes, the ear more quick of apprehension makes…'

Darkness, d. as ignorance. See 'Ignorance, i. observed in person - there is no darkness but ignorance'.

Darkness, fear of d. - In the night, imagining some fear, how easy is a bush supposed a bear.

Date with a foreign girl. See 'Foreign girls'

Date, blind d. See entries for 'Expectations'

Date, looking forward to a second d. – this bud of love…may prove a beauteous flower when we next meet.

Dating, a long time without d. - .. For long agone I have forgot to court, besides the fashion of the time is changed.

Day, alternating sunshine and storms. See 'Weather, wild w. conditions – So foul and fair a day I have not seen.'

Day, d. and night reversed. See 'Love, effects of l., reversal of physical phenomena - All days are nights to see till I see thee, and nights bright days when dreams do show thee me.'

Day, black day, beginning of dark period - This day's black fate on more days doth depend; this but begins the woe, others must end.

Day, d. of shame to be eliminated from the calendar – … Nay, rather turn this day out of the week…

Day, d. of victory. See 'Victory, v. that dignifies the times – O, such a day, so fought, so follow'd and so fairly won came not till now to dignify the times…'

Deafness, d. of mad men. See 'Madness,

evidence of m. due to perceived lack of understanding or ability to listen - .. O, then I see that madmen have no ears.'

Deafness, d. to heavenly harmony caused by corrupted nature of man - Such harmony is in immortal souls..

Deafness, strategic d. – … my master is deaf, I am sure he is, to the hearing of any thing good'

Deal, d. with credulous party almost done - I have him already tempering between my finger and my thumb.

Death by inches – … They'll give him death by inches.

Death, advantages of d. - Though death be poor, it ends a mortal woe.

Death, attitude towards d. – … To throw away the dearest thing he owed as 'twere a careless trifle.

Death, d. after an evil life – … what a sign it is of evil life where death's approach is seen so terrible!

Death, d. and suffering equal for any creature – … The sense of death is most in apprehension…

Death, d. as a cave – … the blind cave of eternal night.

Death, d. as a means to beat collectors - .. But the comfort is, you shall be called to no more payments..

Death, d. as a relief to despair - … my joy is death, death at whose name I oft have been afear'd…

Death, d. as a sleep. See 'Sleep, s. of death considered as rest - … After life's fitful fever he sleeps well.'

Death, d. as liberation – … my long sickness of health and living now begins to mend…

Death, d. as preventing miseries. See 'Event, course of e. completely changing your outlook on life - Had I but died an hour before this chance I had lived a blessed time…'

Death, d. as the end of despair - … the arbitrator of despairs, just death, kind umpire of men's miseries.

Death, d. as the only personal asset. See 'Pessimism, p. on life and personal property - … And nothing can we call our own but death and that small model of the barren earth…'

Death, d. attacking the mind - O vanity of sickness! fierce extremes in their continuance will not feel themselves…

Death, d. common to high and low – But kings and mightiest potentates must die, for that's the end of human misery.

Death, d. defeated by fame. See 'Writing, fame and immortality through w. - Death makes no conquest of this conqueror, for now he lives in fame, though not in life.' *** 'Love, endurance of l. through poetry - Not marble, nor the gilded monuments of princes…'

Death, d. defined – … the blind cave of eternal night.

Death, d. defined - …the kingdom of perpetual night

Death, d. following defeat. See 'Defeat, d. acknowledged – … My blood, my want o

Death, d. in imperialistic wars useless - … for a fantasy and trick of fame go to their graves like beds…

Death, d. in poverty. See 'Fortune cruel f. that usually lets man outlive his wealth – … To view with hollow eye and wrinkled brow an age of poverty…'

Death, d. indifferent to status - A man may fish with the worm that hath eat of a king…

Death, d. inevitable – All lovers young, all lovers must consign to thee, and come to dust.

Death, d. inevitable – And live we how we can, yet die we must.

Death, d. inevitable – Death will have his day.

Death, d. inevitable – Golden lads and girls all must, as chimney-sweepers, come to dust.

Death, d. inevitable. See Entries for 'Mortality, m. recognized ' *** Life, end of l.

inevitable'

Death, d. of poor people irrelevant. See 'Class, c. distinction even in death - When beggars die, there are no comets seen…'

Death, d. not feared - … he that hath a will to die by himself fears it not from another.

Death, d. not felt by a habitual drunkard - … insensible of mortality, and desperately mortal.

Death, d. not more painful than separation - There cannot be a pinch in death more sharp than this.

Death, d. preferable if event is true – … if thou teach me to believe this sorrow teach thou this sorrow how to make me die…

Death, d. preferred to a life of infamy. See 'Honor, sense of h. paramount - I beg mortality, rather than life preserved with infamy.'

Death, d. preferable to be away from her - … To die is to be banish'd from myself…

Death, d. preferable to the lack of her love. See 'Life, l. better ended if her l. is missing - My life were better ended by their hate, than death prorogued, wanting of thy love.'

Death, d. preferable to the rule of a wicked politician - More welcome is the stroke of death to me than Bolingbroke to England.

Death, d. wish - .. with thy sharp teeth this knot intrinsicate of life at once untie.

Death, d. with dignity – … The stroke of death is as a lover's pinch, which hurts, and is desired.

Death, d. with dignity. See 'Life, l. unbearable, death as a physician – It is silliness to live when to live is torment…'

Death, d., sleep and dreams - To sleep: perchance to dream: ay, there's the rub…

Death, effects of d. – … and shake the yoke of inauspicious stars from this world-wearied flesh.

Death, egalitarian nature of d. - … mean and mighty, rotting together, have one dust.

Death, fear and other problems eliminated by d. - Fear no more the heat o' the sun..

Death, fear of d. – The weariest and most loathed worldly life…

Death, fear of d. See 'Fear of death, attitude towards it - That life is better life, past fearing death than that which lives to fear'

Death, fear of d. strange - Of all the wonders that I yet have heard…

Death, fear of d. unjustified. See 'Pessimism, fleetness of life - … Yet in this life lie hid more thousand deaths…'

Death, fearful d. versus shamed life - Death is a fearful thing… And shamed life a hateful

Death, feeling near d. See 'Indisposition, major i. or illness - … my cloud of dignity is held from falling with so weak a wind that it will quickly drop.'

Death, grave as a place of peace - … here are no storms, no noise, but silence and eternal sleep.

Death, happy to d. - I am merrier to die than thou art to live.

Death, lightning before d. – How oft when men are at the point of death have they been merry!

Death, mortality a reality. See 'Mortality, m. to be kept in mind - For death remembered should be like a mirror…'

Death, mortuary – … palace of dim night.

Death, no escape from d. - … this fell sergeant, death is strict in his arrest.

Death, noble d. – Mount, mount, my soul! thy seat is up on high…

Death, not afraid to die - … what blessings I have here alive, that I should be afraid to die?

Death, not afraid to die. See 'Threat, t. useless - … spare your threats; The bug which you would fright me with, I seek..

Death, only d. certain, the interim is not - That we shall die, we know; 'tis but the time and drawing days out, that men stand upon.

Death, positive view on d. – … he that cuts off twenty years of life cuts off so many years of fearing death.

Death, ready for d. - … gaunt as a grave,

whose hollow womb inherits nought but bones.

Death, ritual denial of d. See 'Health-care, ritual denial of death - ... sick men, when their deaths be near..'

Death, the right way how to face it – If I must die, I will encounter darkness as a bride…

Death, wishing d. rather than witnessing a dire prediction come true. See 'Prediction, p. in the process of occurring – …Which is so plain that Exeter doth wish his days may finish ere that hapless time.'

Death, words of dying men. See 'Truth, t. in economy of words - Where words are scarce, they are seldom spent in vain.'

Debate, angry and refusal to d. - I will not bandy with thee word for word.

Debate, disagreeing with skill - But Brutus says he was ambitious, and Brutus is an honourable man.

Debate, feisty but friendly d. - Strive mightily, but eat and drink as friends.

Debate, moderating d. See entries for 'Conflict, c. resolution'.

Debate, skillful destruction of opponent's argument - I speak not to disprove what Brutus spoke but here I am to prove what I do know.

Debate. See 'Argument, a. between to contending parties – The bitter clamour of two eager tongues.

Debates, d. instead of action – You are disputing of your generals, one would have lingering wars with little cost…

Debriefing, d. postponed due to length - ... For 'tis a chronicle of day by day not a relation for a breakfast nor befitting this first meeting.

Debt, in deep d. See 'Financial status, resources over-stretched – … he owes for every word.' *** Entries for 'Financial status'.

Debt, insisting on repaying a courtesy - In common worldly things, 'tis call'd ungrateful, with dull unwillingness to repay a debt.

Deceit, d. and treachery rationalized - .. for that is good deceit which mates him first that first intends deceit.

Deceit, detecting d. See 'Man, capable m. able to discern deceit – These eyes… as piercing as the mid-day sun, to search the secret treasons of the world…

Deceit, learning the tricks of d. to avoid it - to avoid deceit, I mean to learn, for it shall strew the footsteps of my rising.

Deceit, no reason to deceive – What in the world should make me now deceive…

Deceit, unaware of d. See 'Innocence, naïveté due to youth - .. the untainted virtue of your years hath not yet dived into the world's deceit…'

Deceit. See entries for 'Appearances, a. deceiving'.

Deception, d. by friends. See 'Treason, invocation, is this possible? - Can this be so, that in alliance, amity and oaths there should be found such false, dissembling guile?'

Deception, d. from false teachers - Thus may poor fools believe false teachers…

Deception, d. to cover foul objectives – … With colours fairer painted their foul ends.

Deception, deceived by a fool . See lines in 'Love, l. making fools of people. .. he that is so yoked by a fool, methinks should not be chronicled for wise.'

Deception, deceptive t. See 'Truth, t. only apparent - the seeming truth which cunning times put on'.

Deception, not caring about being deceived. See 'Pessimism, not even caring about being deceived – … I do not greatly care to be deceived, that have no use for trusting.'

Decimation - … by the hazard of the spotted die let die the spotted.

Decision, acceptance of a d. - Be it as your wisdom will.

Decision, bad d. – Thou hast pared thy wit o' both sides, and left nothing i' the middle.

Decision, bad d. and its consequences. See 'Consequences, c. of a bad decision - You pluck a thousand dangers on your head…'

Decision, bad personnel or management d. - Ah! thus King Henry throws away his crutch before his legs be firm to bear his body.

Decision, bad personnel or management d. - Thus is the shepherd beaten from thy side, and wolves are gnarling who shall gnaw thee first.

Decision, concern about a decision taken too quickly - It is too rash, too unadvise'd, too sudden, too like the lightning…

Decision, d. guided by sight and hearing - … mine eyes and ears, two traded pilots 'twixt the dangerous shores of will and judgement.

Decision, d. making, important matters to be considered before taking a d. - … we would be resolv'd … of some things of weight that task our thoughts…

Decision, d. prompted by passion or revenge - The reasons you allege do more conduce to the hot passion of distempered blood..

Decision, d. that would require more research but even so it would not help - More should I question thee, and more I must, though more to know could not be more to trust.

Decision, impending critical d. generating anxiety. See 'Sleeplessness, nightmares caused by impending critical decision - Between the acting of a dreadful thing and the first motion… '

Decision, one night required to take a d. See 'Night, n. to think it over - A night is but small breath and little pause to answer matters of this consequence'.

Decision, self-defeating d. – What is it, but to make thy sepulchre and creep into it far before thy time?

Decision, you decide - Frame the business after your own wisdom.

Decisions, decisions – To be or not to be - be - that is the question, whether 'tis nobler in the mind to suffer…'

Decisions, bad d. yielding bad results - .. But by bad courses may be understood that their events can never fall out good.

Decisions, rash d. - What to ourselves in passion we propose, the passion ending, doth the purpose lose.

Declaration, d. of admiration and respect - … Burgundy enshrines thee in his heart…

Decrepitude. See entries for 'Age, old a.'

Dedication, d. and spirituality - .. Not dallying with a brace of courtezans, but meditating with two deep divines…

Dedication, total and complete d. - … And all my fortunes at thy foot I'll lay and follow thee…

Deduction, the power of d. - … therefore thou art a sheep.

Deed, a good d. shines in a bad world - … So shines a good deed in a naughty world.

Deed, damned and bloody - It is a damned and a bloody work; the graceless action of a heavy hand…

Deed, horrible d. - … such a deed as from the body of contraction plucks the very soul….

Deed, d. so vile to be unmentioned - The deed, which both our tongues held vile to name.

Deed, d. that cannot be mentioned. See 'What have I done? – I should make very forges of my cheeks that would to cinders burn up modesty…'

Defeat, admitting electoral d. – Thus yields the cedar to the axe's edge…

Defeat, d. acknowledged – … My blood, my want of strength, my sick heart shows, that I must yield my body to the earth.

Defeat, d. acknowledged – Reproach and everlasting shame sits mocking in our plumes.

Defeat, d. acknowledged – Our enemies have beat us to the pit: it is more worthy to leap in ourselves, than tarry till they push us.

Defeat, d. against overwhelming forces – But Hercules himself must yield to odds; and many strokes…fell the hardest-timber'd oak.

Defeat, d. converted into triumph over oneself – … not Caesar's valour hath overthrown Antony, but Antony's hath triumph'd on itself.

Defeat, d. imminent - … our throats are sentenced and stay upon execution.

Defeat, d. or retribution, a metaphor – Thus hath the candle singed the moth…

Defeat, d. that does not mean dishonor - A scar nobly got, or a noble scar, is a good livery of honour; so, belike, is that.

Defeat, putting a good face on d. - I here do give thee that with all my heart which, but thou hast already…

Defeat, your enemy has not won, you have conquered yourself. See 'Winners and losers, loser defeated by himself - Not Caesar's valor hath o'erthrown Antony but Antony's hath triumphed on itself.'

Defects, personal d. sometimes an asset. See 'Shortcomings, sometimes s. prove useful - …full oft 'tis seen, our means secure us, and our mere defects prove our commodities.'

Defence, d. from accusation, justification for rash words - I was provoked by her slanderous tongue..

Defence, d. from general accusation – Let me have some patient leisure to excuse myself.

Defense, d. from general accusation - … Till I have told this slander of his blood how God and good men hate so foul a liar.

Defence, d. from general accusation, look who's talking - .. if thy offences were upon record..

Defence, d. from general accusations – I am a man more sinned against than sinning.

Defence, d. from general accusations - … my name be blotted from the book of life.

Defence, d. from general accusations - Pierced to the soul with slander's venom spear.

Defence, d. from slander – It's slander, whose edge is sharper than the sword..

Defence, d. of criminal demeaning - … every word you speak in his behalf is slander to your royal dignity.

Defence, d. of loved ones natural - … for the poor wren, the most diminutive of birds, will fight, her young ones..

Defiance, d. based on the merit of your services – … My services which I have done the signiory shall out-tongue his complaints.

Defiance, d. compared to cedar's strength. See 'Resistance, strong and unconquerable - As on a mountain top the cedar shows that keep his leaves in spite of any storm.'

Defiance, d. declared - Defiance, traitors, hurl we in your teeth.

Defiance, d. declared in unpleasant circumstances - Though what I am I cannot avoid, yet to be what I would not shall not make me tame.

Defiance, refusal to yield - I had rather chop this hand off at a blow, and with the other fling it at thy face.

Defiance. See entries for 'Accusation, false a.' *** 'Accusation, a. rejected' *** 'Action, justifying honorable a. - … what I did, I did in honour, led by the impartial conduct of my soul…'

Deficit, See 'Budget deficit – … his coffers sound with hollow poverty and emptiness'.

Definition, calling things by their names - We call a nettle but a nettle; and the faults of fools, but folly.

Definition, offensive d, cannot be named - What I cannot name but I shall offend.

Dejection, mood of d. inspired by past and present. See 'Unhappiness, u. and desperation - O, woe is me, to have seen what I have seen, see what I see!'

Delay, avoid d. - Defer no time, delays have dangerous ends.

Delay, d. is time wasted - … in delay we waste our lights in vain, like lamps by day.

Delay, d. generated by fear. See 'Fear, f. generates delay and failure – fearful commenting is leaden servitor to dull delay…'

Delay, d. to be avoided. See 'Action, a. that cannot be delayed - This weighty business will not brook delay.'

Delay. Arriving late at appointment. See 'Apologies for delay'

Delegating, d. power to ratify. See 'Negotiations, delegating power to negotiate - ... take with you free power to ratify, augment, or alter, as your wisdoms best …'

Delight, d. in work. See 'Work, type of w. we like to go to - To business that we love we rise betime and go to it with delight.'

Delights, d. are vain. See 'Education, e. and knowledge, limits of. - … all delights are vain; but that most vain, which with pain purchased doth inherit pain…'

Delights, violent d. not recommended. See 'Pleasure, excessive p. unsafe - These violent delights have violent ends and in their triumph die, like fire and powder, which as they kiss consume.'

Delivery, quick d. on promises made. See 'Promises, p. delivered - Thy promises are like Adonis' gardens that one day bloom'd and fruitful were the next'.

Delusion, d. of righteousness. See 'Exhortation, e. not to feed a delusion - ... Lay not that flattering unction to your soul, that not your trespass, but my madness speaks…'

Demagogy. See 'Popularity, achieving p. with the common man - How he did seem to dive into their hearts with humble and familiar courtesy.'

Demeanor, wondering at a sudden change of d. – (This) leaves me to consider what is breeding that changeth thus his manners.

Democrats and Republicans distasteful. See 'Curse, c. to both Democrats and Republicans - A plague o' both your houses!'

Democracy, evils of d. See 'Politics, democracy and its evils'.

Demonstration, d. of love prevented by circumstances - … have prevented the ostentation of our love, which, left unshown, is often left unloved.

Deniability, accusing the subordinates. See 'Intentions, i. misinterpreted - … some about him have too lavishly wrested his meaning and authority.

Deniability, d., politics and crime - … Being done unknown I should have found it afterwards well done but must condemn it now.

Deniability, how to set it up. See 'Responsibility, shift of responsibility, deniability - It is the curse of kings to be attended by slaves that take their humour as a warrant…' – 'Secret, s. will be disclosed to her

Denial - … contradict thyself and say it is not so.

Denial, absolute d. - As faithfully as I deny the devil.

Denial, complete d. (of a husband) - … Not till God make men of some other metal than earth.

Denial, d. of wrongdoing - The gods throw stones of sulphur on me, if…

Denial, difficulty to deny previous statement – I know your daring tongue scorns to unsay what once it hath deliver'd…

Denial, when you have to say no to a lady - I beseech you, punish me not with your hard thoughts..

Denying an invitation. See 'Invitation, impossible to resist.'

Departure, d. difficult - Can I go forward when my heart is here?

Departure, d. expedited – … aboard, aboard, for shame! The wind sits in the shoulder of your sail…

Departure, d. necessary - … though parting be a fretful corrosive, it is applied to a deathful wound.

Departure, d. of unwelcome g. welcome - You cannot, sir, take from me any thing that I will more willingly part withal: except my life

Departure, forceful d. from a slaughtering place or abandonment of sin in general.

Departure, reason for having to leave - I take it, your own business calls on you and you embrace the occasion to depart.

Depression, general depression leading to total pessimism - … if this were seen, the happiest youth, viewing his progress through…

Depression, general depression leading to total pessimism – … the whips and scorns of time, the oppressor's wrong, the proud man's contumely…

Depression, general depression leading to total pessimism – to-morrow and to-morrow and to-morrow, creeps in this petty pace from day to day…

Depression, in a state of d. – I have… lost all my mirth, forgone all custom of exercises…

Depression, relieved by thinking of her. See 'Psychological uplifting, her positive effect when you are down in the dumps.'

Depression, self-deprecation - I am nothing: or if not nothing to be were better.

Depression, state of d. – A heart as full of sorrows as the sea of sands.

Depression, state of d. – I am wrapped in dismal thinkings.

Depression, state of d. - See 'Heart, h. in misery - … my heart, all mad with misery, beats in this hollow prison of my flesh.' *** 'Wine, w. as an anti-depressant - Give me a bowl of wine, I have not the alacrity of spirit nor cheer of mind that I as wont to have.'

Deprivation, d. of things shows their true value. See entries for 'Appreciation coming too late.'

Description, beautiful beyond d. See 'Woman, w. beyond description - … For her own person, it beggar'd all description.'

Description, beyond d. - I never heard of such another encounter, which lames report to follow it and undoes description to do it.

Description, beyond d. See 'Optimism, overly optimistic - Description cannot suit itself in words to demonstrate the life of such a battle'.

Description, beyond d. See 'Spectacle, wonderful s. that cannot be described - … a sight, which was to be seen, cannot be spoken of…'

Description, self-evident d. - What manner o' thing is your crocodile?…

Description, d. of her perfection would fill volumes - The chief perfections of that lovely dame … would make a volume of enticing lines.

Desert, words to be uttered only in the d. See 'Words, devastating w. - I have words that would be howl'd out in the desert air…'

Disease, making a profit out of d. See 'Workers' compensation for questionable disability - I will turn diseases to commodity'.

Desire, d. contained. See 'Reliability. "Am I going to be safe with you? Can I trust you? Etc.'

Desire, d. expressed – To taste the fruit of yon celestial tree…

Desire, d. increased by obstacles. See 'Obstacles, o. increasing desire –..as all impediments in fancy's course are motives of more fancy'

Desire , d. prompting to promise. See 'Promises, love p. unreliable - I do know when the blood burns, how prodigal the soul lends the tongue vows.

Desire, d. tempting judgment. See 'Judgment, j. tempted by desire – often… mine ear hath tempted judgment to desire.'

Desire, d. to know in advance the outcome of events. See "Prediction, desire to know in advance - O, that a man might know the end of this day's business ere it come…'

Desire, d. to see her. See 'Travel, motivation for traveling to see her - .. my desire, more sharp than filed steel, did spur me on.'

Despair, d. and desperation - … And if I die, no soul will pity me. Nay wherefore should they, since that I myself find in myself, no pity to myself?

Despair, d. and determination to go down fighting – … Blow, wind! come, wrack At least we'll die with harness on our back

Despair, d. and helplessness, 'The wine of life is drawn'. See l

Despair, d. and hopelessness. See 'Hope, h. as a flatterer and parasite - I will despair, and be at enmity with cozening hope: he is a flatterer'.

Despair, d. as the result of a horrible act - If thou didst but consent to this most cruel act, do but despair.

Despair, let the world go to pieces – … let order die! … And darkness be the burier of the dead!

Desperation, d. as the only defense policy – … desperation is all the policy, strength and defence …

Desperation, d. at the easily predictable course of events - .. Which is so plain, that Exeter doth wish his days may finish ere that hapless time.

Desperation, d. leading to desperate acts - O mischief! thou art swift to enter the heart of desperate men.

Desperation, d. out of repressed anger - Now could I drink hot blood, and do such bitter business as the day would quake to look on.

Desperation, total d. – … Holding the eternal spirit against her will in the vile prison of afflicted breath.

Desperation, ready to die - … Thou desperate pilot, now at once run on the dashing rocks thy sea-sick weary bark!

Destiny - What must be shall be. …That's a certain text.

Destiny, accepting the inevitability of d. - … let determined things to destiny hold unbewail'd their way.

Destiny, accepting the inevitability of d. - Are these things then necessities? Then let us meet them like necessities.

Destiny, accepting the inevitability of d. - But He, that hath the steerage of my course direct my sail!

Destiny, accepting the inevitability of d. – Heaven has an end in all.

Destiny, accepting the inevitability of d. - What cannot be eschew'd, must be embraced

Destiny, at odd with our wills - .. Our wills and fates do so contrary run that our devices still are overthrown, our thoughts are ours, their ends none of our own.

Destiny, beyond our control - …the lottery of my destiny bars me the right of voluntary choosing.

Destiny, beyond our control - …ourselves we do not owe; what is decreed must be, and be this so.

Destiny, beyond our control – A greater power than we can contradict hath thwarted our intents.

Destiny, beyond our control – What can be avoided whose end is purposed by the mighty gods?

Destiny, desire to know in advance. See 'Prediction, desire to know in advance - o, that a man might know the end of this day's business ere it come…'

Destiny, d. inscrutable – … how chances mock, and changes fill the cup of alteration with divers liquors!

Destiny, d. involved in marriage and justice. See 'Marriage and sentencing subjects to destiny - The ancient saying is no heresy, hanging and wiving goes by destiny.'

Destiny, d. of the weak – The weakest kind of fruit drop earliest to the ground.

Destiny, d. shaping our ends - … There's a divinity that shapes our ends, rough-hew them how we will.

Destiny, d. unavoidable – All unavoided is doom of destiny.

Destiny, d. unavoidable – 'Tis destiny unshunnable, like death.

Destiny, d. uncontrollable – O vain boast! Who can control his fate?

Destiny, evil event triggering a series of

subsequent disasters. Day, black day, beginning of dark period - This day's black fate on more days doth depend; this but begins the woe, others must end.

Destiny, inappropriate to resist to d. - What fates impose, that men must needs abide, it boots not to resist both wind and tide.

Destiny, mastership of our own d. - Men at some time are masters of their fates, the fault, dear Brutus, is not in our stars...

Destiny, reading the book of fate. See 'Prediction, desire to know in advance - O God! that one might read the book of fate and see the revolutions of the times…'

Destiny, resignation to d. - … there's a special providence in the fall of a sparrow….

Destiny, revolving - The wheel is come full circle.

Destiny, the stars in charge of us - It is the stars, the stars above us, govern our conditions…

Destiny. See 'Will, contrast between our w. and destiny' *** Entries for 'Acceptance'

Destruction, bent on d. See 'Conquest, determination to conquer - Now, Rouen, I'll shake thy bulwarks to the ground.'

Destruction, d. and undoing of previous achievements - Undoing all, as all had never been!

Destruction, hastening towards self-destruction. See 'Anger, a. self-destructive - .. She'll gallop fast enough to her destruction.'

Detective work to find out the scoundrel. – … we'll unkennel the fox.

Determination - What man dare, I dare.

Determination and purpose. See 'Commitments, purposeful c. must be limited in number - It is the purpose that makes strong the vow but vows to every purpose must not hold.'

Determination and resolution. - My will is back'd with resolution, thoughts are but dreams till their effects be tried…

Determination and resolution - We have no friend but resolution, and the briefest end.

Determination and strength failing, common weakness of human nature - … I melt, and am not of stronger earth than others.

Determination, d. in anger – … my intents are savage-wild, more fierce and more inexorable far than empty tigers or the roaring sea.

Determination, d. never to retreat - Him I forgive my death that killeth me when he sees me go back one foot or fly.

Determination, d. not to yield to misfortune. See 'Motivation, m. to stand up to ill fortune - Yield not thy neck to fortune's yoke, but let thy dauntless mind still ride in triumph over all mischance.'

Determination, d. not to sway from the course. See 'Exhortation, e. not to yield to enemy – We will not from the helm to sit and weep, but keep our course, though the rough wind say no..'

Determination, d. or agreement to do anything honorable - I have spirit to do any thing that appears not foul in the truth of my spirit.

Determination, d. shown even in extreme circumstances - I shall show the cinders of my spirits through the ashes of my chance.

Determination, d. to accept suffering - Henceforth I'll bear affliction till it do cry out itself 'enough, enough' and die.

Determination, d. to act - To crown my thoughts with acts, be it thought and done.

Determination to ban f. See 'Fear, determination to ban f. - The mind I sway by and the heart I bear…'

Determination, d. to be remorseless - … make thick my blood, stop the access and passage of remorse…

Determination, d. to conquer fear. See 'Fear, determination to conquer f.'

Determination, d. to face the inevitable - I am tied to the stake, and I must stand the course.

Determination, d. to fight back after a

setback - … make my ill th'advantage of my good.

Determination, d. to fight on. See 'Fight, determination to f. - …I cannot fly, but, bear-like, I must fight the course.'

Determination, d. to fight on - I'll set my teeth and send to darkness all that stop me.

Determination, d. to fight to the very end - And here will Talbot mount, or make his grave

Determination, d. to fight to the very end - I'll fight, till from my bones my flesh be hack'd.

Determination, d. to keep the course. See 'Exhortation, e. not to yield to enemy – We will not from the helm to sit and weep, but keep our course, though the rough wind say no…'

Determination, d. to overcome misfortune. See 'Misfortune, determination to overcome m. - Though fortune's malice overthrow my state, my mind exceeds the compass of her wheel.'

Determination, d. to overcome obstacles - … that is a step on which I must fall down, or else o'er-leap…

Determination, d. to participate to an event or a party even if ill - … Not sickness should detain me.

Determination, d. to proceed against tenuous odds - … my project may deceive me but my intents are fix'd and will not leave me.

Determination, d. to resist by a woman. See 'Resistance, female r. advisable - I see, a woman may be made a fool, if she had not the spirit to resist.'

Determination, d. to speak with courage. See 'Speech, determination to speak with courage - I'll use that tongue I have. If wit flows from it..'

Determination, d. to stamp out hypocrisy. See 'Hypocrisy, determination to stamp it out'.

Determination, d. to take care alone of your own affairs - I will be master of what is mine own.

Determination, d. to the bitter end, no trading dignity for life - I am resolved for death or dignity.

Determination, d. to the end. See 'Mood, combative m. – I am fire and air; my other elements I give to baser life.'

Determination, d. to turn the situation around - Or make my ill the advantage of my good.

Determination, insisting may yield results - He plies her hard; and much rain wears the marble.

Determination, lack of d. occurring often - But what we determine oft we break. Purpose's but the slave to memory, of violent birth, but poor validity.

Determination, no boasting - No boasting like a fool, this deed I'll do before this purpose cool.

Determination, sign of d. until goal accomplished - I vow by heaven these eyes shall never close

Determination, simile - … and much rain wears the marble.

Determination, simile – … many strokes, though with a little axe, hew down and fell the hardest-timbered oak..

Determination, stubbornness, no change of mind – There is no power in the tongue of man to alter me.

Detraction, reaction to detraction or exposure of your faults – … happy are they that hear their detractions and can put them to mending.

Devil, a creature from hell - I think this Talbot be a fiend of hell.

Devil, d. appearing in a deceivingly pleasing shape - … the devil hath power to assume a pleasing shape.

Devil, d. as an ingredient of wine. See 'Wine, teetotaler, reasons for not drinking - Every inordinate cup is unblessed and the ingredient is a devil.'

Devil, d. as the creator of politicians. See 'Opinion, your op. on politicians in general - The devil knew not what he did when he made man politic, he crossed himself by 't.'

Devil, d. telling the truth surprising. See 'Truth, surprise at the devil telling the truth – What, can the devil speak true?'

Devil, how to recognize the d. – By his horns.

Devil, tempted by the d. See 'Temptation, t. by devil - Shall I be tempted of the devil thus?'

Devil, prize winner of devils. See 'Man, worse than the worst of devils – Not in the legions of horrid hell can come a devil more damn'd to top Macbeth.'

Devil, who are you? - What devil art thou, that dost torment me thus?

Dew. See 'Freshness, like dew - .. as fresh as morning dew distilled on flowers.'

Diagnosis, d. based on Galen - … I have read the cause of his effects in Galen

Dialog, d. postponed when hearer in better mood.

Dice. See 'Games, dice - ... and by the hazard of the spotted die…'

Dictatorship, in praise of d. - ..at once pluck out the multitudinous tongue, let them not lick the sweet which is their poison.

Did you hear? See 'News, n. already known to everybody who is not deaf - … every one hears that who can distinguish sound'

Did you just think of this? See 'Proposal, meditated p. - …'tis a studied, not a present thought by duty meditated.'

Did you like the joke? See 'Laughter, laughing to tears -… I must confess, made nine eyes water; but more merry tears the passion of loud laughter never shed.'

Did you like the (musical) performance? See entries for 'Music'.

Did you like the place? (when you did not). See 'Night, nightmare, waking up from a n. - I trembling waked, and for a season after could not believe but that I was in hell...'

Did you make love? See 'Confession, confessing to lust - … served the lust of my mistress' heart, and did the act of darkness with her.'

Did you sleep well? (when you have). See 'Sleep, excellent s. accompanied by pleasant dreams - The sweetest sleep, and fairest-boding dreams that ever enter'd in a drowsy head.' *** Entries for 'Sleep'

Did you sleep well? (when you haven't). See 'Night, nightmare – O, I have pass'

Die, desire to d. - … he hates him much that would upon the rack of this tough world stretch him out longer.

Diet, bad d. See 'Health-care, effects of a bad diet - O, he hath kept an evil diet long, and overmuch consumed his royal person..

Dieting, d. advice – Make less thy body hence, and more thy grace, leave gormandizing

Dieting, how to refuse when offered more food - … dainty bits make rich the ribs, but bankrupt quite the wits.

Dieting, too much sugar, excess brings distaste - ...a surfeit of the sweetest things the deepest loathing to the stomach brings.

Dieting, too much sugar, excess brings distaste. See first lines in 'Advice, a. to love moderately and to avoid excess - The sweetest honey is loathsome in his own deliciousness…'

Difference, d. in type of actions or offices - To offend, and judge, are distinct offices and of opposite nature.

Difficulties, d. easy when known. See 'Problem, p. solving – … all difficulties are but easy when they are known.'

Diffidence as a form of cowardice - I hold it cowardice to rest mistrustful where a noble heart hath pawn'd an open hand in sign of love.

Digestion, good d. See 'Health, good eating habits, good digestion disrupted by arguing - Unquiet meals make ill digestion.'

Dignities, d, not to be renounced. See

'Refusal, r. to compromise - ... nothing but death shall e'er divorce my dignities'

Dinner invitation, answer to - Ay, if I be alive and your mind hold and your dinner worth the eating.

Dinner invitation refused. See 'Invitation, i. refused (to dinner) – I will buy with you, sell with you….but I will not eat with you…'

Dinner time, d.t. as an opportunity to remove attention - .. that you might kill your stomach on your meat and not upon your maid.

Dinner, business discussions better after d. See 'Negotiations, n. better after dinner – … but when we have stuffed these pipes and these conveyances of our blood with wine and feeding…'

Dinner, have d. precede a meeting - Discourse is heavy, fasting; when we have supp'd we'll mannerly demand thee of thy story so far as thou wilt speak it.

Dinner, invitation to a working d. - .. let us sup betimes, that afterwards we may digest our complots in some form.

Dinner, not hungry after d. - Who riseth from a feast with that keen appetite that he sits down?

Dinner. How to pay for dinner, cash or credit card - (I'll pay cash) as far as my coin would stretch..

Diplomacy, adjusting d. - O, pardon me…that I am meek and gentle with these butchers!

Diplomacy, lack of d. See 'Speech, saying the right thing at the wrong time - The truth you speak doth lack some gentleness and time to speak it in.'

Direction, wrong d. – by a pace goes backward, with a purpose it hath to climb.

Disagreement, d. costly - … we'll no longer stay; these words will cost ten thousand lives this day.

Disappearance – … they made themselves air, into which they vanished.

Disappearance, where is he? - …melted into air, into thin air…

Disappointment, d. anticipated - ... this may prove food to my displeasure.

Disappointment, d. arising from reliance on the favors of the great. See 'Reliance, r. on the favor of the great a source of disappointment. - Poor wretches that depend on greatness' favour dream as I have done, wake and find nothing.'

Disappointment, d. expressed in dramatic terms – … make dust our paper and with rainy eyes…

Disapproval, expectation of d. See 'Expression, frowning to be expected - Prepare thy brow to frown.'

Disaster, too late to avoid d. - We see the very wreck that we must suffer and unavoided is the danger now…

Disasters, rationalizing d. – … checks and disasters grow in the veins of actions highest rear'd.

Disbelief, d. about one's mental state and perception - Or sleep I now and think I hear all this?

Disbelief, epitome of d. See 'Wife, no trust in w. – I will rather trust a Fleming with my butter… than my wife with herself.'

Disbelief, suspend your d. See 'Surprise, hold your s. for a moment – Season your admiration for a while.'

Discipline, measured approach in establishing d. - We shall be call'd purgers, not murderers.

Discipline. See 'Exhortation, e. to discipline and expeditiousness - Let's want no discipline, make no delay for, lords, tomorrow is a busy day.'

Disclaimer - .. if I were disposed to stir your hearts and minds to mutiny and rage…

Disclaimer, do not think I am greedy. See 'Greed, g. disclaimed - … I would not have you to think that my desire of having is the sin of covetousness.'

Disclaimer, dramatic d. - The gods throw stones of sulphur on me, if…

Disclosure, complete d. - .. I have unclasped to thee the book even of my secret soul.

Discontent, d. causing stress. See 'Stress, s. caused by discontent - For what's more miserable than discontent?'

Discontent, d. ended. See 'Greetings, end of unhappiness – Now is the winter of our discontent, made glorious summer by this sun of York…'

Discontent, inability to see the good and its pernicious effects – Thou pout'st upon thy fortune and thy love: take heed, take heed, for such die miserable.

Discretion or cowardice. See 'Cowardice, c. or discretion - The better part of valour is, discretion'.

Discretion, d. as a teacher. See 'Action, request for advice on how or what to do - let your own discretion be your tutor.'

Discretion, invitation not to exceed the limits of d. - Let's teach ourselves that honourable stop not to outsport discretion.

Discretion, relying on d. - your discretions better can persuade than I am able to instruct or teach.

Discrimination, nature does not discriminate – The selfsame sun that shines upon his court hides not his visage…

Discrimination, no racial d. – Mislike me not for my complexion…

Disguise, d. and pretence, tools of wicked enemy - Disguise, I see, thou art a wickedness, wherein the pregnant enemy does much…

Disguise, d. discovered - There is a kind of confession in your looks.

Disguise, hypocrisy - … some that smile have in their hearts, I fear, millions of mischiefs.

Disguise, wearing a d. - .. disliken the truth of your own seeming.

Disgust, d. and hatred expressed - Tempt not too much the hatred of my spirit for I am sick when I do look on thee.

Disgust, d. at words heard - I do condemn mine ears that have so long attended thee…

Disgust, d. at words heard - Mine ears, that to your wanton talk attended…

Dish fit for the Gods. See 'Handling, proper h. of an execution or firing- Let's carve him as a dish fit for the gods..'

Dish for the Gods. See 'Woman, dish for the Gods - A woman is a dish for the gods, if the devil dress her not'.

Disinterestedness. See 'Times, good old t, better then, less greed than now - … how well in thee appears the constant service of the antique world…'

Dislike, d. and antagonism - … for I desire nothing but odds with England.

Dislike, d. mixed with contempt - .. I care not for you and am so near the lack of charity to accuse myself--I hate you.

Dislike, d. of speech and person - 'T is not my speeches that you do mislike, but 't is my presence that doth trouble ye.

Dislike, I don't like him - His countenance likes me not.

Dislike, intense d. of a person – I see, lady, the gentleman is not in your books…

Dislike, liking what you don't like - That that likes not you pleases me best.

Dislike, mutual d. expressed - I do desire we may be better strangers.

Dislike, total d. of a person. See 'Character, incompatibility of c. - No contraries hold more antipathy than I and such a knave.'

Dismissal, cold d. - … when we need your use and counsel, we shall send for you.

Disobedience, civil d. See 'Conflict resolution, advice to proceed with caution - .. temperately proceed to what you would thus violently redress.'

Disobedience, civil d. useless – … those cold ways that seem like prudent helps, are very poisonous…

Disobedience, d. justified on moral grounds – Every good servant does not all commands

Disobedience, d. perceived - Worcester, get

1113

thee gone, for I do see danger and disobedience in thine eye.

Disobedience, the cost of d. - … You have obedience scanted and well are worth the want that you have wanted.

Displeasure, d. reduced by knowledge of circumstances - If you did know for what I gave the ring you would abate the strength of your displeasure.

Dispute, d. and disagreement on right and wrong - If that be right which Warwick says is right, there is no wrong, but everything is right.

Dispute, d. that cannot be peacefully resolved - .. the wound that bred this meeting here cannot be cured by words.

Disregard, completely disregarded – … they pass'd by me as misers do by beggars…

Dissension, d. destructive. See Evils, self-created e. - And this same progeny of evils comes from our debate, from our dissension…

Dissension, d. prompting rebellion. See 'Rebellion, r. promoted by perception of dissension - If they perceive dissension in our looks…'

Dissension, strife dangerous - Civil dissension is a viperous worm, that gnaws the bowels of the commonwealth.

Dissimulation - … and wonder greatly that man's face can fold in pleasing smiles such murderous tyranny.

Dissimulation, d. and cunning. See 'Hypocrisy, deceit and cunning - O, what authority and show of truth can cunning sin cover itself withal.'

Dissimulation, d. with words. See 'Words, poisoned w. coated with false niceties - Hide not thy poison with such sugar'd words.'

Dissimulation, devils' technique - When devils will the blackest sins put on, they do suggest at first with heavenly shows…

Dissimulation, enchanting with sweets but poisonous words - I will enchant the old Andronicus with words more sweet, and yet more dangerous

Dissimulation, facial expression not giving away intention – (We will) make our faces vizards to our hearts, disguising what they are.

Dissimulation, lesson in d. - Your face, my thane, is as a book where men may read strange matters…

Dissimulation, pretence, put a show, as if nothing were happening - …and mock the time with fairest show..

Dissimulation, pretence, put a show, as if nothing were happening – … look fresh and merrily let not our looks put on our purposes.

Dissimulation, pretending not to understand. See 'Understanding, sincerity of lack of u. questioned - Your sense pursues not mine or seem so craftily; and that's not good.'

Dissimulation, pretending to know by saying nothing. See 'Character, one who pretends to be thought clever by saying nothing - there are a sort of men whose visages…'

Dissimulation, dissimulating woman. See 'Woman, cruel, serpent - O serpent heart, hid with a flowering face!'

Dissimulation. See also entries for 'Hypocrisy'.

Dissipation, d. of assets for a woman - … He hath given his empire up to a whore…

Dissipation, loss of assets through poor management - Pirates may make cheap worth of their pillage…

Distance (physical) not a problem. "But it is such long way away!" or "Do you mind?" - A true devoted pilgrim is not weary to measure kingdoms with his feeble steps.

Distance, keeping a long d. due to personal dislike - … if there be breadth enough in the world, I will hold a long distance.

Distilled almost to jelly with the act of fear. See 'Fear, effects of f. '

Distinction, d. or promotion misplaced or

unbecoming – It lies as sightly on the back of him as great Alcides' shows upon an ass.

Distraction, no d. please – When holy and devout religious men are at their beads…

Distress, d. causing rudeness. See 'Rudeness, apologies for r. – the thorny point of bare distress hath taken from me, the show of smooth civility…'

Distress, d. emphasized dramatically - ….if the river dry, I am able to fill it with my tears…

Distress, deep d. and reason of- why, say, fair queen, whence springs this deep despair?

Distress. See entries for 'Mind, state of mind'

Disturbance, d. and noise - But with thy brawls thou hast disturb'd our sport.

Diversification, limits to d. See 'Personnel, downsizing - … superfluous branches we lop away, that bearing boughs may live…'

Diversification. See 'Investments, diversification of i. - .. my ventures are not in one bottom trusted'.

Divine, exceeding all natural excellence - I might call him a thing divine, for nothing natural I ever saw so noble.

Divine, goddess of my idolatry - Do not swear at all.. or by thy gracious self, which is the god of my idolatry.

Divine. See 'Woman, dish for the Gods - A woman is a dish for the gods, if the devil dress her not'.

Dizzy, in a d. See 'Stunned, mesmerized, in a trance - My thoughts are whirled like a potter's wheel; I know not where I am, nor what I do.'

Do as you see fit. See 'Decision, you decide - Frame the business after your own wisdom.'

Do I have bad breath? See entry for 'Breath'

Do I look old? See entries for 'Ageless'

Do not saw the air too much with your hand… See 'Gesturing, acting'.

Do it now - no procrastination. See 'Procrastination to be avoided – .. for this 'would' changes, hath abatements and delays as many as there are tongues, are hands, are accidents'

Do not, as some ungracious pastors do … See 'Hypocrisy, practice what you preach - Do not, as some ungracious pastors do… The primrose path of dalliance threads and recks not his own reed.'

Do not hurt me. See 'Reliability. am I going to be safe with you? Can I trust you? Etc. - O fairest beauty, do not fear or fly! for I will touch thee but with reverent hands…'

Do this. See 'Command, c. given with some arrogance, reaction to - When Caesar says 'do this,' it is perform'd.'

Do what I say but not what I do. See 'Preaching, p. versus practice - .. will not you maintain the thing you teach but prove a chief offender in the same?'

Do you agree? See 'Agreement, wholeheartedly in a. - May I never, to this good purpose, that so fairly shows dream of impediment.' *** Other entries for 'Agreement'.

Do you believe in dreams? See 'Dreams, not believing in them - … to trust the mockery of unquiet slumbers.'

Do you believe me? See 'Believability, complete b. – If Jupiter should from yond cloud speak divine things…'

Do you deny this? See 'Denial, absolute d. - As faithfully as I deny the devil.'

Do you forgive me? See 'Forgiveness, f. at something she has done - No more be grieved at that which thou hast done, roses have thorns, and silver mountains mud…'

Do you get angry easily? See 'Anger, a. aroused with difficulty and quickly extinguished – … That carries anger as the flint bears fire, who… shows a hasty spark and straight is cold again.'

Do you hear me? See 'Hearing, do you hear me? – Your tale, sir, would cure deafness.' *** ' Attention, undivided a. - Had I three ears, I'd hear thee.'

Do you know each other? See 'Acquaintance, a. unpleasant - And long to know each other worse…'

Do you like me? See entries for 'Beauty', 'Beautiful' *** 'Bosom, her b. as a coveted place of rest - I might live one hour in your sweet bosom.' *** 'The best of all' *** 'Woman' *** 'Face

Do you like my perfume? See entries for 'Perfume'

Do you like my picture? See 'Woman, real w. better than her picture – so far this shadow doth limp behind the substance.'

Do you like my skin? See "Skin, her beautiful s. - That whiter skin of hers than snow, and smooth as monumental alabaster."

Do you like my sun tan? See 'Woman, w. sun-tanned and/or with brown eyes - … as brown in hue as hazel nuts and sweeter than the kernels.'

Do you like my voice? See 'Voice, her v.

Do you like beer? See 'Beer, do you like b.? - …a quart of ale is a dish for a king.'

Do you like to go to work? See 'Work, type of w. we like to go to - To business that we love we rise betime and go to it with delight.'

Do you like wine? See 'Wine, positive effects of w. – A good sherri-sack hath a two fold operation in it…'

Do you love me? See entries for 'Love, declaration of l.' and other entries for 'Love'. *** 'Universe, rose, unique - For nothing this wide universe I call, save thou my rose, in it thou art my all.'

Do you mean it? See 'Intentions, do you mean it? – Fair Margaret knows that Suffolk doth not flatter, face, or feign.' *** 'Concordance between belief and words used to express it - For things are often spoke and seldom meant…'

Do you mind if I do this? See 'Love, in l. but unpossessive - That god forbid that made me first your slave…'

Do you mind this? See 'Death, d. not more painful than separation - There cannot be a pinch in death more sharp than this.'

Do you mind to do this? See 'Distance (physical) not a problem. "But it is such long way away!" or "Do you mind?" - A true devoted pilgrim is not weary to measure kingdoms with his feeble steps.'

Do you miss me? See 'Presence, 'Do you miss me?' - … Save that my soul's imaginary sight presents thy shadow to my sightless view…'

Do you not know I am a woman? See 'Women, impulsive character of w. - … when I think, I must speak.'

Do you think you will like it? See 'Effort, making an effort to share her taste - I'll look to like, if looking liking move.'

Do you trust me? See 'Friend, trusted f. – (He was) my book wherein my soul recorded the history of all her secret thoughts.'

Do you want still more? See 'Ambition, not satisfied with the plenty already available - Hast thou not worldly pleasure at command, above the reach and compass of thy thought?'

Do you want to hear first the good news or the bad news? See 'News, exhortation to deliver the n. - Pour out the pack of matter to mine ear, the good and bad together.'

Do you want to hear some good news? See 'News, invitation to disclose (good) news - ram though thy fruitful tidings in mine ears, that long time have been barren.'

Do you want to know why? See 'Explanation, do you want to know why? - Ay sir, and wherefore; for, they say, every why hath a wherefore.'

Do you want war? See 'War, do you want war? - … will you again unknit this curlish knot of all-abhorred war?'

Do you watch TV (or radio)? See 'Party, p. sounds out - Let not the sound of shallow foppery enter my sober house.'

Doctors, d. that procured the illness - … careless patient as thou art, commit'st thy anointed body to the cure of those physicians that first wounded thee.

Document, policy statement, message filled with questionable reasons for a dreadful act - … Larded with many several sorts of reasons.

Doer, d. of no good – … The close contriver of all harms…

Does he (or she) still do it? See 'Character, stubborn - … and perversely she persevers so.'

Does she like you? See 'Body, b. language – … sometimes from her eyes I did receive fair speechless messages.'

Dog, beware of venomous dog (figuratively) - O Buckingham, take heed of yonder dog; look, when he fawns he bites..

Dog, d. as the true icon of authority. See 'Opinion, your op. on authority – a dog's obeyed in office'

Dog, d. eating d. See 'Man, m. eating man, just like fish – ..the great ones eat up little ones'.

Dog, sleeping d. See 'Prudence, do not wake a sleeping dog - This butcher's cur is venom mouthed and I have not the power to muzzle him; therefore…'

Dogs, d. preferable to men - … I do wish thou wert a dog that I might love thee something.

Doing good - I never did repent for doing good, nor shall not now.

Doing what needs to be done. See 'Action, need to act notwithstanding possible censure – we must not stint our necessary actions…'

Don't you have enough? See 'Satisfied, but wanting more - … can one desire too much of a good thing?'

Doomsday closing in. See 'Honesty, h. in the world presaging doomsday – … the world's grown honest… Then is doomsday near.'

Door, shut the door. See 'Prevention, p. as key to success and security - Fast bind, fast find, a proverb never stale in thrifty mind.'

Doors, d. opened by money. See 'Money, m. opening the way - … for they say, if money go before, all ways do lie open.'

Double toil and trouble. See 'Effort, hard e. – Double, double toil and trouble; fire burn, and cauldron bubble.'

Double-crosser - Weigh oath with oath, and you will nothing weigh…

Double-talk. See 'Conceit, you do not say what you mean - You speak not as you think, it cannot be.'

Double-standards. See 'Political (and personal) double standards - whiles I am a beggar, I will rail… there is no sin but to be rich..'

Double-speak – And be these juggling fiends no more believed, that palter with us in a double sense

Doubt thou the stars are fire… See 'Love, how much?'

Doubt, beginning to d. See 'Lying, l. based on equivocation – … and begin to doubt the equivocation of the fiend that lies like truth.'

Doubt, d. as a symptom of wisdom - … modest doubt is call'd the beacon of the wise.

Doubt, d. hurting more than certainty. See 'Psychology, doubt hurts more than certainty - doubting things go ill often hurts more than to be sure they do.'

Doubt, d. not considered without evidence. See 'Evidence, e. required before confirming doubt- … I'll see before I doubt; when I doubt, prove.

Doubt, d. or remorse, or awareness of crime - … this even-handed justice commends the ingredients of our poison'd chalice to our own lips.

Doubt, seeding d. and fears – He dives into the king's soul, and there scatters…

Doubts, d. as traitors - Our doubts are traitors and make us lose the good we oft might win by fearing to attempt.

Dove, more of a crow (or a political hawk) than a d. See 'Appearances, a. deceptive or false – Seems he a dove? his feathers are but borrowed…'

Down in the dumps. See entries for 'Depression', 'World, pessimistic view of the w.', 'Melancholy', 'Sadness', 'Pessimism', 'Despair'.

Downsizing. See 'Company, c. downsizes, effect on employees - .. leak'd is our bark and we, poor mates, stand on the dying deck…' *** 'Personnel, downsizing - .. superfluous branches we lop away, that bearing boughs may live..'

Dowry, not marrying for m. – Henry is able to enrich his queen…

Dream and illusion - Thus have I had thee as a dream doth flatter, in sleep a king, but waking, no such matter.

Dream or madness - 'Tis still a dream, or else such stuff as madmen tongue and brain not.

Dream, American d realized - I have lived to see inherited my very wishes…

Dream, bad d. put it down to a bad d. - … think no more of this night's accidents but as the fierce vexation of a dream.

Dream, d. or illusion. See 'Happiness, h, overwhelming and incredible - If it be thus to dream, still let me sleep!'

Dream, d. past recollection or not to be explained – I have had a dream, past the wit of man to say what dream it was…

Dream, d. that inspires confidence and well being - If I may trust the flattering truth of sleep, my dreams presage some joyful news at hand...

Dream, d. too good to be true. See 'True, too good to be t., almost like a dream - This is the rarest dream that ever dull sleep did mock sad fools withal!'

Dream, d. with pleasant forebodings – If I may trust the flattering truth of sleep my dreams presage some joyful news at hand.

Dream, if this is a d. let it continue. See 'Happiness, h, overwhelming and incredible - to the point of questioning if it is an illusion or a dream'.

Dream, it feels like a dream - How like a dream is this I see and hear!

Dream, it feels like a dream -... all this is but a dream, too flattering sweet to be substantial.

Dream, waking from a d., true or pretended - O, where am I?' quoth she, 'in earth or heaven, or in the ocean drench'd, or in the fire?

Dreams, delusions – ... I talk of dreams, which are the children of an idle brain, begot of nothing but vain fantasy.

Dreams, illusions and nightmares - ... it is the weakness of mine eyes that shapes his monstrous apparition.

Dreams, not believing in them - ... to trust the mockery of unquiet slumbers.

Dress, adorned d. eliciting the idea of May and Spring – …she came adorned hither like sweet May…

Dress, compliment for a sparkling dress - The intertissued robe of gold and pearl…

Dress, d. code. See 'Advice, a. on men's wear and fashion - Costly thy habit as thy purse can buy, but not express'd in fancy; rich, not gaudy…'

Dress, d. for success. See 'Advice, a. on men's wear and fashion - Costly thy habit as thy purse can buy, but not express'd in fancy; rich, not gaudy…'

Dress, fitting the d. - The tailor stays thy leisure to deck thy body with his ruffling treasure.

Dress, j

Dress, long d. to be held up - ... lest the base earth should from her vesture chance to steal a kiss.

Dress, white, beautiful and worthy of a fairy queen - ... the queen of all the fairies, finely attired in a robe of white.

Drink, or liquid, disgusting and poisonous - ... leperous distilment; whose effect holds such an enmity with blood of man..

Drink, excessive, see 'Apologies for having drunk too much – it perfumes the blood ere one can say, what's this?'

Drink, going to the bar. See 'Bar, going to b. to find solace in alcohol and company - I will see what physic the tavern affords.'

Drink, invitation to d. until asleep. See 'Party, invitation to p. - .. let's take hand till the conquering wine hath steeped our sense in soft and delicate Lethe.'

Drink, reaction to unpleasant drink. See 'Medicine, swallowing a bitter medicine or unpleasant drink – O true apothecary! Thy drugs are quick.'

Drinking, heavy d. and its effect on the purse - .. you come in flint for want of meat, depart reeling with too much drink..

Drinking, knowing when to stop (drinking) – Let's teach ourselves that honorable stop, not to out-sport discretion.

Drinking, person who is poorly affected by d. See 'Wine, drinking, unable to tolerate strong drinks - ... I have very poor and unhappy brains for drinking…'

Drinks and drinking, see entries for Wine and Beer

Driving a hard bargain. See 'Negotiator, a hard n. and petty to the penny - .. in the way of bargain, mark ye me, I'll cavil on the ninth part of a hair'

Driving under the Influence, not DUI – … I am not drunk now; I can stand well enough, and speak well enough.

Drums, d. of war. See 'War, let there be war – Strike up the drums and let the tongue of war plead for our interest…'

Drunkard. See entries for 'Character, drunkard.'

Drunkenness, d. as a source of illusion – The world turns round.

Drunkenness, d. as a source of illusion – I believe drink gave thee the lie last night'

Drunkenness, d. of group described – … they were red-hot with drinking…

Dulness shown by unfruitful attempt to understanding. See 'Brain, no more raking of the b - Cudgel thy brains no more about it…'

Duped by a fool. See 'Love, not a sign of wisdom - … he who is so yoked by a fool methinks should not be chronicled for wise'.

Dust, worth less than d. See 'Insult, worth less than dust - … You are not worth the dust which the rude wind blows in your face' *** 'Man and his wicked nature - … what is this quintessence of dust? Man delights not me.'

Duty, d. performed formally only - … Others there are who, trimm'd in forms and visages of duty, keep yet their hearts attending on themselves…

Duty, sense of d. and straightforwardness leading to good results – For never anything can be amiss when simpleness and duty tender it.

Dwell I but in the suburbs … See 'Cooling off observed, question for verification - Dwell I but in the suburbs of your good pleasure?'

Eagerness for action, eager and ready to go – I see you stand like greyhounds in the slips, straining upon the start.

Eagerness for action. See 'Action, eagerness for a. – let the hours be short, till fields, and blows, and groans applaud our sport!'

Ears, e. condemned for listening. See entries for 'Disgust, d. at words heard.'

Earth, preventing a lady's dress from being soiled by e. See 'Dress, long d. to be held up - .. lest the base earth should from her vesture chance to steal a kiss.'

Eating and drinking. See 'Philosophy, simple p. - Thou art a scholar; let us therefore eat and drink.'

Eating, good food, antipasto - … Epicurean cooks sharpen with cloyless sauce his appetite.

Eccentricity, above the crowd – … I will not jump with common spirits and rank me with the barbarous multitude.

Echo, e. defined - … the babbling gossip of the air.

Economy, price of hogs affected by

religious conversions - this making of Christians will raise the price of hogs..

Ecstasy. See entries for 'Happiness, h. overwhelming '

Education, a less orthodox view - … corrupted the youth of the realm in erecting a grammar school.

Education, bad e. See 'Example, bad e. and/or bad education – transformed him ape'.

Education, continued e. - … continue your resolve to suck the sweets of sweet philosophy.

Education, e. and knowledge, limits of. - … all delights are vain; but that most vain, which with pain purchased doth inherit pain…

Education, e. and lack thereof - He that hath learned no wit by nature nor art, may complain of good breeding or comes of a very dull kindred.

Education, e. as an addition to personality. See 'Learning, l. as an addition to what we are – Learning is but an adjunct to ourselves, and where we are, our learning likewise is.'

Education, importance of good company. - It is certain that either wise bearing or ignorant carriage is caught, as men take diseases, one of another..

Education, lack of formal education - (I) have been an idle truant, omitting the sweet benefit of time to clothe mine age with angel-like perfection.

Education, literature, results of teaching - You taught me language and my profit on it is, I know how to curse.

Education, not an asset - The clerk of Chatham: he can write and read and cast accompt… O monstrous.

Education, principles of e. – If I had a thousand sons, the first human principle I would teach them…

Education, profitable if pleasurable – No profit grows where is no pleasure taken…

Education. See entries for 'Studying'.

Effect, quick, strong and violent - As violently, as hasty powder fired doth hurry from the fatal cannon's womb.

Effort, hard e. – Double, double toil and trouble; fire burn, and cauldron bubble.

Effort, making an effort to share her taste - I'll look to like, if looking liking move.

Effort, overwhelmed by opposing forces - … as I have seen a swan with bootless labour swim against the tide..

Effort, trying does not hurt - What I can do, can do no hurt to try.

Effort, useless and detrimental - You lay too much pains for purchasing but trouble.

Effort, vain e. See 'Task, t. impossible and unrealistic - … the task he undertakes is numbering sands and drinking oceans dry.' *** 'Impossibility, cooling the sun with a fan - .. you may as well go about to turn the sun to ice…'

Efforts, e. unrewarded or punished – … and like the bees are murdered for our pains.

Efforts, hard e. disregarded or unappreciated - … Have broke their sleep with thoughts, their brains with care, their bones with industry.

Ego boosting, she is a sought after prize - Nor is the wide world ignorant of her worth…

Elbow room (One of everyday expressions from Shakespeare) – … now my soul hath elbow-room…

Elbows, btain in the e. See 'Insult, brainless – … thou hast no more brain in thy head than I have in mine elbows.'

Elections, democratic e. - .. let desert in pure election shine, and, Romans, fight for freedom in your choice.

Elections, e. promises. See 'Politicians' promises, wine for all - … I charge and command that, of the city's cost, the pissing-conduit run nothing but claret wine…'

Elections, electoral commitment – I would with such perfection govern, sir, to excel the golden age.

Election, presidential e. slogan. See 'Enemy, e. to be eliminated - ... the welfare of us all hangs on the cutting short that fraudful man.'

Elements, battling the e. See 'Change, desire for radical c. – Contending with the fretful element…that things might change or cease…'

Elephant, e. as a symbol of uncouthness or lack of manners. See 'Character, uncouth and discourteous - The elephant hath joints, but none for courtesy…'

Eloquence in action, see 'Action, eloquence, eloquence in a.'

Eloquence, characteristic of the eloquent – … on the tip of their persuasive tongue carry all arguments and questions deep…

Eloquence, empty e. See 'Speech, simple s. delivered with modesty better than pompous eloquence - … in the modesty of fearful duty, I read as much, as from the rattling tongue of saucy and audacious eloquence.'

Eloquent lovers not reliable. See 'Lovers, eloquent lovers not reliable - … these fellows of infinite tongue that can rhyme themselves into ladies' favours…'

Embrace, rationale for embracing lady – … the nobleness of life is to do thus…

Embrace, style of embracing - So doth the woodbine the sweet honeysuckle…

Emotion, overpowered by e. – My tears will choke me, if I ope my mouth.

Emotional display. See 'Tears, unmanly and prompted by moving scene - These foolish drops do something drown my manly spirit.'

Emotional reaction - Who can be wise, amazed, temperate and furious….

Emotional reaction, more typical of a woman than a man. See 'Animal, man acting like an a. or woman - thy wild acts denote the unreasonable fury of a beast..'

Emotions, violent e. of grief or joy self-destructive. See 'Man, very emotional m., characteristics of - Where joy most revels, grief doth most lament; grief joys, joy grieves, on slender accident.'

Employees, e. stuck in their career or simple opportunists – You shall mark many a duteous and knee-crooking knave…

Employment, quick resume - … that which ordinary men are fit for, I am qualified in; and the best of me is diligence.

Employment, reason for seeking alternative e. – … their villany goes against my weak stomach and therefore I must cast it up.

Employment, working for a company as opposed to being self-employed - … I am shepherd to another man and do not shear the fleeces that I graze.

Employment, working for someone else - My affairs are servanted to others.

Emulation, e. and imitation. See lines in 'Honor, the narrow path of h. - .. honour travels in a strait so narrow, where one but goes abreast…'

Encouragement, e. uncalled for given the valiant nature of the encouraged – … And yet I do thee wrong to mind thee of it …

Encouragement, e. during distress - let not discontent daunt all your hopes.

Encouragement, self-e. to change doubt to resolution. - Now, York, or never, steel thy fearful thoughts, and change misdoubt to resolution..

Encouraging words. See entries for 'Words, encouraging and reviving'.

End, beginning of the e. – now prosperity begins to mellow and drop into the rotten mouth of death.

End, e. crowned by time. See 'Time, the great arbitrator - …. the end crowns all and that old common arbitrator, Time, will one day end it.'

End, e. crowns the deed – La fin couronne les oeuvres.

End, e. justifies means – All with me's meet that I can fashion fit.

End, e. justifies means – … some kinds of baseness are nobly undergone…

End, e. of the good times. See 'Times, end

of the good t. - .. the bright day is done and we are for the dark'.

End, metaphor for e. See 'Sleep, s. after a hard day - ... the long day's task is done and we must sleep.'

Endless line. See 'Traffic, long line of stalled cars – ... will the line stretch out to the crack of doom?'

Endless speech. See 'Speech, lengthy and annoying - This will last out a night in Russia when nights are longest there.'

Endurance, capable of e. See 'Character, steady and ready to face unfriendly reception - ... to the proof, as mountains are for winds…'

Endurance, e. for man is a necessity. See 'Maturity, m. is everything - Men must endure their going hence, even as their coming hither. Ripeness is all.'

Endurance, your e. at an end - I will no longer endure it, though yet I know no wise remedy how to avoid it.

Enemies, abandoned by friend in the hands of the e. - So flies the reckless shepherd from the wolf…

Enemies, how e. work - know'st thou not that when the searching eye of heaven is hid..

Enemies, planning traps for your e. - My brain more busy than the labouring spider…

Enemies, smiling e. - .. some that smile have in their hearts, I fear, millions of mischiefs.

Enemies, unthinking and unreasonable – … like to village curs bark when their fellows do.

Enemies, weak but annoying e. - For though they cannot greatly sting to hurt, yet look to have them buzz to offend thine ears.

Enemies, why e. are better than friends - ... my friends praise me and make an ass of me…

Enemies, you are all my e., don't trouble me any more - My foes I do repute you every one; so, trouble me no more, but get you gone.

Enemy, beware of the e. See 'Beware, b. of the enemy - Take heed o' the foul fiend!'

Enemy, bitter e. - The devil himself could not pronounce a title more hateful to mine ear.

Enemy, contempt for unworthy e. See 'Challenge, c. by an unworthy enemy - shall I be flouted thus by dunghill grooms?'

Enemy, e. hurt but not destroyed - We have scotch'd the snake, not kill'd it…

Enemy, e. or friend. See 'Friend, f. or enemy? - .. But what compact mean you to have with us? Will you be prick'd in number of our friends…'

Enemy, e. shamed - ... now shall the devil be shamed.

Enemy, e. to be eliminated - ... the welfare of us all hangs on the cutting short that fraudful man.

Enemy, know your real e., don't hurt your friends - ... strike those that hurt, and hurt not those that help.

Enemy, my e. and e. of the truth - ... whom, yet, once more I hold my most malicious foe, and think not at all a friend to truth.

Enemy, recognizing honor in e. - For though mine enemy thou hast ever been high sparks of honour in thee have I seen.

Enemy, resurgence of e. - … Thrusts forth his horns again into the world, which were inshell'd…

Energy, love as an energizer. See 'Love, effects of l., empowerment– … love, first learned in a lady's eyes… gives to every power a double power, above their functions and their offices.'

Engineering, civil e. - ..much more.. should we survey the plot of the situation and the model..

Engineering, civil e. See 'Planning, importance of p. - When we mean to build, we first survey the plot, then draw the model…'

England – E. and her connection with the sea - …your isle, which stands as Neptune's park…

England, E. never conquered – This England never did, nor never shall lie at the proud foot of a conqueror…

England, in praise of E. – The natural bravery of your isle, which stands as Neptune's park…

England, in praise of E. while deploring the current state of affairs – This fortress…This precious stone…bound in with triumphant sea…

England, in praise of the greatness of E. - O England! model to thy inward greatness, like little body with a mighty heart.

England, nationalistic statement - Come the three corners of the world in arms and we shall shock them..

England, protected by the sea against foreign invasion - England, hedged in with the main… that water-walled bulwark…

England, that will never be conquered - This England never did, nor never shall lie at the proud foot of a conqueror…

England, the cliffs of Dover - There is a cliff whose high and bending head looks fearfully in the confined deep.

England, the shores of E. - … that pale, that white faced shore, whose foot spurns back the ocean's roaring tides.

English, e. language marginal. See 'Language, his English marginal – … at the taunt of one that makes fritte

Englishman, proud to be an E. – Where'er I wander, boast of this I can… a trueborn Englishman.

Enmity, e. declared - I do believe induced by potent circumstances, that you are mine enemy.

Enmity, e. unjustified or e. by imitation. See 'Enemies, unthinking and unreasonable – like to village curs bark when their fellows do.

Enmity, mutual e. disguised. See 'Conflict, c. smoldering between two parties - .. there is division although as yet the face of it is covered with mutual cunning.

Enterprise, a daring e. - .. an enterprise of honourable-dangerous consequence.

Entertainment, e. of an honored guest - … your entertain shall be as doth befit our honour and your worth.

Entertainment, endless e. tiring. See 'Tediousness, t. in everything being always the same – If all the year were playing holidays, to sport would be as tedious as to work.'

Entertainment, moderation in e. - It will be pastime passing excellent if it be husbanded with modesty.

Entrapment - I am angling now, though you perceive me not how I give line.

Entrapment. See 'Sting operation - … the play's the thing wherein I'll catch the conscience of the king.'

Entrapment. See 'Plot, a p. and a set-up - A pretty plot, well chosen to build upon!'

Envy, above the reach of e. - Advanced above pale envy's threatening reach, as when the golden sun salutes the morn…

Envy, addressing envious accusers – Now I feel of what coarse metal ye are molded, - envy!

Envy, e. as a monster - That monster envy, oft the wrack of earned praise.

Envy, e. as practiced by the envious - .. Men that make envy and crooked malice, nourishment, dare bite the best.

Envy, e. coupled with ambition - Such men as he be never at heart's ease whiles they behold a greater than themselves, and therefore are they very dangerous.

Envy, e. generated by merit. See 'Merit, m., skills or talent excite envy - … to some kind of men their grace serve them as enemies.'

Envy, e. generates division and confusion. See 'Management, poor m. coupled with bitter in-fighting - .. when envy breeds unkind division, there comes the ruin, there begins confusion.'

Envy, e. mixed with hypocrisy – Follow your envious courses, men of malice…

Envy, e. shown in speech - Sharp

Buckingham unburthens with his tongue the envious load that lies upon his heart.

Envy, e. unloaded and evident. See 'Malice, m. and hate – Beaufort's red sparkling eyes blab his heart's malice…'

Envy, lack of e. See 'Magnanimity, gentlemanship, lack of envy - … for we are gentlemen that neither in our hearts nor outward eyes, envy the great, nor the low despise.

Envy, words or speech prompted by envy – The envious barking of your saucy tongue…

Epitaph, e. kind to the memory of an evil man - Thy ignominy sleep with thee in the grave but not remember'd in thy epitaph!

Epitaph, e. of a disgruntled man – 'Here lies a wretched corse, of wretched soul bereft: seek not my name…

Equality asserted. See 'Authority, king, no different from other men - … the king is but a man, as I am: the violet smells to him as it doth to me.'

Equality among men impossible - …but clay and clay differs in dignity, whose dust is both alike.

Equivocation - … here's an equivocator, that could swear in both the scales against either scale.

Equivocation, misunderstanding, need for accurate wording or expression – … we must speak by the card or equivocation will undo us.

Error, e. admitted and due to youthful inexperience – Those were my salad days when I was green in judgement.

Error, e. due to ignorance, not cunning - … if he be not one that truly loves you that errs in ignorance, and not in cunning..

Error, e. due to misapprehension or misrepresentation - O, hateful error, Melancholy's child! Why dost thou show to the apt thoughts of men the things that are not?

Error, e. in character judgment, acknowledged - What a thrice-double ass was I to take this drunkard for a god…

Error, e. resulting in good results. See 'Fault, f. from which good results occurred - I cannot wish the fault undone, the issue of it being so proper.'

Error, fault, mixed feelings about a fault - There's something in me that reproves my fault…

Errors, e. as a source of experience, sarcastic – … to wilful men the injuries they themselves procure must be their schoolmasters.

Erudition, master of e. – … Thrice famed, beyond all erudition.

Erudition, putting do

Escape, fleeing - … fly, like ships before the wind or lambs pursued by hunger-starved wolves.

Escape. See 'Run, time to r. - like a brace of greyhounds …are at our backs.'

Escape. See 'Safety, escape for s. - .. let us not be dainty of leave-taking, but shift away: there's warrant in that theft which steals itself, when there's no mercy left.'

Establishment, e. run down and poorly managed - … epicurism and lust make it more like a tavern or a brothel than a graced palace.

Esteem, return to a statement of esteem - Your worth is very dear in my regard.

Estimation, e. of people or objects differing among people - I never knew man hold vile stuff so dear.

Eternity, e. as a heritage. See lines 5,6 in 'Fame, f. defeating death and time - … And make us heirs of all eternity.'

Eulogy – He was a man, take him for all in all, I shall not look upon his like again.

Eulogy – Now cracks a noble heart. Good night sweet prince…

Eulogy, e. for a sinner – So may he rest; his faults lie gently on him!

Eulogy, praises - His life was gentle: and the element so mixed in him…

Eulogy. See 'Man, best m. of all – Thou art the ruins of the noblest man that ever lived in the tide of times.' *** 'Man, m. wealthy and powerful – … realms and islands were as plates dropp'd from his pocket.'

Event, course of e. completely changing your outlook on life - Had I but died an hour before this chance I had lived a blessed time…

Event, deprecating an unhappy e. - .. unhappy was the clock that struck the hour.

Event, e. of historical importance - How many ages hence shall this, our lofty scene be acted over, in states unborn…

Event, e. or fact, confirmation of it - If this were so, so were it uttered.

Event, e. remembered even in old age - … all shall be forgot but he'll remember with advantages…

Event, e. that can only be told with shame - may not be without much shame retold.

Event, e. that should have excited more reaction - The breaking of so great a thing should make a greater crack.

Event, evil e. triggering a series of subsequent disasters. See 'Day, black day, beginning of dark period - This day's black fate on more days doth depend; this but begins the woe, others must end.'

Event, extraordinary astronomical event called for – Methinks it should be now a huge eclipse…

Event, greatness of event, next day better than the last - .. Each following day became the next day's master, till the last made former wonders its.

Event, new and amazing e. – 'tis wondrous strange, the like yet never heard of.

Event, outcome of e. not yet decided. See 'Results, r. prematurely assessed - .. the event is yet to name the winner.'

Event, potentially incredible e. - That would be ten days' wonder at the least.

Event, strange e. explained - All this amazement can I qualify…

Events, e. caused when women rule men. See 'Men, m. subjected to women – Why, this it is, when men are ruled by women…'

Events, e. turning out as you wanted - Every thing lies level to our wish.

Events, interpretation of e., how the doubtful draw their conclusions - … how such an apprehension may turn the tide of fearful faction and breed a kind of question in our cause.

Events, mass hysteria turning natural e. distorted into supernatural phenomena - .. they will pluck away his natural cause and call them meteors, prodigies and signs..

Events, not good at predicting e. See 'Forecasting, not good at f. – … much too shallow to sound the bottom of the after-times.'

Events, strange and extraordinary and given favorable interpretation - 'Tis wondrous strange, the like yet never heard of..

Events, strange and extraordinary and given ominous meaning - …And meteors fright the fixed stars of heaven.

Events, strange and extraordinary and given ominous meaning - … stars with trains of fire and dews of blood …

Events, strange and extraordinary and given ominous meaning – … The bay-trees in our country are all wither'd and meteors fright the fixed stars of heaven…

Events, strange and extraordinary and given ominous meaning - … The graves stood tenantless and the sheeted dead…

Events, strange and extraordinary and given ominous meaning - … they say five moons were seen tonight; four fixed and the fifth…

Events, strange and extraordinary and given ominous meaning - A lioness hath whelped in the streets and graves have yawn'd, and yielded up their dead.

Events, stranger and stranger - These are not natural events; they strengthen from strange to stranger.

Event, unbelievable - … it is past the infinite

of thought.

Events, unnatural. See 'Unnatural events as indication of the gravity of the times - ... they are portentous things unto the climate that they point upon'.

Every good servant does not all commands. See 'Disobedience, d. justified on moral grounds'

Every which way you win. See 'Gain assured under any circumstance – Sort how it will, I shall have gold for all.'

Everybody knows me here. See 'Knowledge, man well known in town - Thy very stones prate of my whereabout...'

Every inordinate cup is unblessed and the ingredient is a devil. See 'Wine, teetotaler, reasons for not drinking.

Every subject's soul is his own. See 'Freedom, f. of the soul – Every subject's duty is the king's; but every subject's soul is his own.'

Everything, e. has a reason. See 'Destiny, resignation to d. - ... there's a special providence in the fall of a sparrow....'

Everything, e. or nothing. See 'Victory, v. or nothing - Either our history shall with full mouth speak freely of our acts…'

Evidence, additional supporting e. – ... And this may help to thicken other proofs that do demonstrate thinly.

Evidence, desire to disbelieve the e. - Yet there is a credence in my heart… that doth invert the utmost of eyes and ears…

Evidence, disputing incriminating written e. – My heart is not confederate with my hand.

Evidence, e. lacking or circumstantial – To vouch this, is no proof, without more wider and more overt test.

Evidence, e. required before confirming doubt- ... I'll see before I doubt; when I doubt, prove.

Evidence, e. very clear – ... proofs as clear as founts in July when we see each grain of gravel..

Evidence, e. from the vice squad - … We have here recovered the most dangerous piece of lechery that ever was known in the commonwealth.

Evidence, e. gleaned with direct observation. See 'Decision, d. guided by sight and hearing - ..mine eyes and ears, two traded pilots 'twixt the dangerous shores of will and judgement'.

Evidence, e, heard directly – … and by an auricular assurance have your satisfaction.

Evidence, e. of your worth or action - Well, let my deeds be witness of my worth.

Evidence, e. requested will be provided – … strong circumstances which lead directly to the door of truth…

Evidence, e. required or else - Give me the ocular proof: or by the worth of man's eternal soul..

Evidence, e. showing shame and guilt - That argues but the shame of your offence.

Evidence, example of self-e. - That, that it is, is.

Evidence, let e. prove the point – Let proof speak.

Evidence, visual e. See 'Unbelievable - I might not this believe without the sensible and true avouch of mine own eyes.'

Evidence, we have the e. - The particular confirmation, point to point, to the full arming of the verity.

Evidence. See 'News, conflicting n., not knowing how to react - Such welcome and unwelcome things at once 't is hard to reconcile.'

Evident, clear and e. - 'Tis probable and palpable to thinking.

Evil, consorting with evil to understand and avoid it - … studies his companions like a strange tongue, wherein, to gain the language…

Evil, e. that calls for curses on its doers - … it calls I fear, too many curses on their heads that were the authors.

Evil, doing e. to do good - A little harm done to a great good end…

Evil, e. always remembered more than the good. See entries for 'Remembering, r. the bad more than the good'

Evil, e. compounding with e. - Things bad begun make strong themselves by ill.

Evil, e. destroying virtue – … The adder hisses where the sweet birds sing; what virtue breeds iniquity devours.

Evil, e. generates e. 'base things sire base'. See lines in 'Character, c. and qualities intergenerational - O noble strain! O worthiness of nature! breed of greatness!'

Evil, e. rebounding against its inventor - … Bloody instructions, which, being taught, return, return to plague the inventor.

Evil, e. rebounding against its perpetrators. See 'Consequences, dangerous c. predicted - I told ye all, when ye first put this dangerous stone a-rolling, 'twould fall upon ourselves.'

Evil, effort to find some good in e. advocated. See 'Adversity, some g. can be found in a. - There is some soul of goodness in things evil…' *** 'Determination, d. to turn the situation around - Or make my ill the advantage of my good.'

Evil, epitome of e. See 'Angry, a. at her, the opposite of every good - Thou art as opposite to every good as the Antipodes are unto us or as the south to the septentrion.'

Evil, no e. intended – No man means evil but the devil, and we shall know him by his horns.

Evil, piling e. on e. – .. And do not spread the compost on the weeds, to make them ranker.

Evils, self-created e. - And this same progeny of evils comes from our debate, from our dissension…

Exactly my idea! See 'Man, m. who anticipates our very ideas - My other self, my counsel's consistory, my oracle, my prophet!'

Exaggeration, resentment not called for – Taking bird bolts for cannon bullets

Example, bad e. and/or bad education – :.. a' had him from me Christian; and look, if the fat villain have not transformed him ape

Example, bad e. from authority. See "Judges, j. as thieves - Thieves for their robbery have authority when judges steal themselves.'

Example, power of e. – … inferior eyes, that borrow their behaviour from the great…

Example, role model – For from his metal was his party steel'd..

Examples, e. leading to decisions – Examples gross as earth exhort me…

Excellence, e. declared. See 'Wishes, good w. plus compliment - they are worthy to inlay heaven with stars.'

Excellence, e. has no fear – Things done well and with a care exempt themselves from fear.

Excess, a comparison - Light seeking light doth light of light beguile.

Excess, adding honey to sugar. See 'Beauty, b. and honesty incompatible? – … for honesty coupled to beauty is to have honey a sauce to sugar.'

Excess, e. bad even in excellence - Striving to better, oft we mar what's well.

Excess, e. leads to loathing – They surfeited with honey and began to loathe the taste of sweetness…

Excess, e. leading to corruption - Most subject is the fattest soil to weeds.

Excess, e. leading to restraint. See 'Restraint, r. caused by excess - As surfeit is the father of much fast…'

Excess, e. leading to tediousness. See "Tediousness, t. in everything being always the same – If all the year were playing holidays, to sport would be as tedious as to work.'

Excess, e. not necessary and wasteful once objective is reached - To gild refined gold, to paint the lily… is wasteful and ridiculous excess.

Excess, e. turning vice to virtue and viceversa. See 'Virtue, vice and their relationship - Virtue itself turns vice, being misapplied and vice sometimes is by action dignified.'

Excess, effects of e. - Sweets grown common lose their dear delight.

Excess, invitation to avoid e. See 'Discretion, invitation not to exceed the limits of d. - Let's teach ourselves that honourable stop not to outsport discretion.'

Exchange, e. for the better - … what fool is not so wise to lose an oath to win a paradise?

Exclamation in support of the veracity of (your) following statement. See 'Invocation, i. in the name of truth - As there comes light from heaven, and words from breath, as there is sense in truth, and truth in virtue…'

Exclamation, false conclusion - O most lame and impotent conclusion!

Exclamation, falsehood – Excellent falsehood!

Exclamation, what the dickens - I cannot tell what the dickens his name is…

Excuse, e. for being late or other mishap. See 'Information, i. annoying and unpleasant - Tedious it were to tell, and harsh to hear, sufficeth…'

Excuse, e. often worse than the fault - .. And oftentimes excusing of a fault, …discredit more in hiding of the fault than did the fault before it was so patched.

Excuse, no e. plus insult – Fouler than heart can think thee, thou canst make no excuse current, but to hang thyself.

Excuse, verbosity in e. See 'Breath, out of b. - How art thou out of breath, when thou hast breath to say to me that thou art out of breath?'

Excuses, attempt to cover-up with excuses - Why seek'st thou to cover with excuse that which appears in proper nakedness?

Excusing poor behavior due to haste. See 'Apologies for poor manners due to haste - .. my haste made me unmannerly.'

Excusing poor behavior due to indisposition. See 'Apologies for unruly words caused by indisposition - … impute

his words to wayward sickliness and age in him.'

Executioner, refusing to be the e. - though I wish thy death I will not be the executioner.

Exercise, enough e. for now - Thy exercise hath been too violent for a second course of fight.

Exhausted. See 'Walk, impossibility to w. any further - I can go no further, sir; my old bones ache'

Excitement, more e. from a greater challenge. See 'Proposal, difference between an exciting and an unexciting p. – … the blood more stirs to rouse a lion than to start a hare

Exhortation, e. not be afraid to fail. See 'Failure, dealing with fear of f. - … screw your courage to the sticking-place and we'll not fail.'

Exhortation, e. not to attempt to solve a riddle. See 'Understanding, discouraging attempt to sort out a strange business - Do not infest your mind with beating on the strangeness of this business'

Exhortation, e. not to aggravate a man who is desperate - Tempt not a desperate man.

Exhortation, e. not to feed a delusion - … Lay not that flattering unction to your soul, that not your trespass, but my madness speaks..

Exhortation, e. not to hit a falling man. See 'Mercy, exhortation not to hit a falling man - Press not a falling man too far! 'tis virtue..'

Exhortation, e. not to yield to enemy - … And he that will not fight for such a hope, go home to bed...

Exhortation, e. not to yield to enemy – We will not from the helm to sit and weep, but keep our course, though the rough wind say no..

Exhortation, e. not to yield to enemy - .. With tearful eyes add water to the sea and give more strength to that which hath too much?

Exhortation, e. not to stir up trouble - Your

speech is passion: but, pray you, stir no embers up.

Exhortation, e. redundant - …and yet I do thee wrong to mind thee of it…

Exhortation, e. to act - … be a soldier to thy purpose.

Exhortation, e. to act. See 'Ardor, military a. – O, let the hours be short, till fields and blows and groans applaud our sport!'

Exhortation, e. to act according to intent expressed - .. And let your mind be coupled with your words.

Exhortation, e. to act manfully and forcefully – Be great in act, as you have been in thought

Exhortation, e. to act quickly – … make no delay: we may effect this business yet ere day.

Exhortation, e. to action with stealth - … let's on our way in silent sort: for Warwick and his friends, God and Saint George!

Exhortation, e. to be brave - Hang those that talk of fear.

Exhortation, e. to be concise. See 'Messenger, exhortation to m. to deliver information quickly - Thou comest to use thy tongue; thy story quickly.'

Exhortation, e. to be friendly – … put off these frowns and ill-beseeming semblance for a feast.

Exhortation, e. to calm to reduce confusion - Peace, ho, for shame! confusion's cure lives not in these confusions.

Exhortation, e. to change opinion - … remove the root of his opinion which is rotten as ever oak or stone was sound.

Exhortation, e. to change opinion - Remove your thought; it doth abuse your bosom.

Exhortation, e. to change opinion - … weed your better judgments of all opinion that grows rank in them.

Exhortation, e. to change opinion - I do beseech you, gracious madam, to unthink your speaking…

Exhortation, e. to consider the issue - I would your highness would give it quick consideration, for there is no primer business.

Exhortation, e. to dieting. See 'Dieting, d. advice – Make less thy body hence, and more thy grace, leave gormandizing. '

Exhortation, e. to discipline and expeditiousness - Let's want no discipline, make no delay for, lords, tomorrow is a busy day.

Exhortation, e. to dispel fear - Nay, good my lord, be not afraid of shadows.

Exhortation, e. to fairness - We turn not back the silks upon the merchant, when we have soil'd them…

Exhortation, e. to fight - Now put your shields before your hearts, and fight…

Exhortation, e. to get started and go – Let us go, our corn's to reap, for yet our tithe's to sow.

Exhortation, e. to give information. See 'Speech, exhortation to speak and give information - Be not a niggard of your speech; how goes it?'

Exhortation, e. to inspire. See 'Welcome, w. and exhortation - Give renew'd fire to our extinct spirits.'

Exhortation, e. to know the real enemy. See 'Enemy, know your real e., don't hurt your friends - .. strike those that hurt, and hurt not those that help.'

Exhortation, e. to leave rebellion. See 'Rebellion, exhortation against r. – Unthread the rude eye of rebellion…'

Exhortation, e. to limit facetiousness - … do not play in wench-like words with that which is so serious.

Exhortation, e. to listen and understand a plain message - I pray thee, understand a plain man in his plain meaning.

Exhortation, e. to listen for a little longer – Hear a little further and then I'll bring thee to the present business…

Exhortation, e. to passion - … put fire in your heart and brimstone in your liver.

Exhortation, e. to patience - Be patient, for

the world is broad and wide.

Exhortation, e. to question our motives - Go to your bosom; knock there, and ask your heart what it doth know…

Exhortation, e. to rational behavior - Seal up the mouth of outrage for a while, till we can clear these ambiguities…

Exhortation, e. to redouble the effort – Once more unto the breach, dear friends, once more

Exhortation, e. to speak up. See 'Speech, exhortation to speak and give information'

Exhortation, e. to speak without affectation. See 'Trippingly on the tongue - Speak the speech, I pray you, as I pronounced it to you, trippingly on the tongue.'

Exhortation, e. to unite powers against common foe – … and join our powers and seek how we may prejudice the foe.

Exhortation, e. to the well off. See 'Social issues, exhortation to

Exhortation, e. to use reason - Sweet earl, divorce not wisdom from your honour.

Exhortation, e. to understand the limitations imposed by circumstances - construe the times to their necessities.

Exile, going into e. - … He'll shape his old course in a country new.

Existence, e. and being proven - … as the old hermit of Prague.. said to a niece of King Gorboduc, 'That that is is".

Expect anything from man. See 'Man, m.'s nature unpredictable - .. we know what we are, but know not what we may be.'

Expectations, e. and rapid sequence of events – … every minute is expectancy of more arrivance.

Expectations, e. fed by hope often frustrated by reality - The ample proposition that hope makes in all designs begun on earth below fails in the promised largeness…

Expectations, e. limited. See 'Contentment, the art of c. - I could be bounded in a nutshell, and count myself a king of infinite space.'

Expectations, e. often fail - Oft expectation fails, and most oft there, and most oft there where it most promises…

Expectations, e. poorly placed - … briefly die their joys that place them on the truth of girls and boys.

Expectations, your e. unreasonable – …till all graces be in a woman, one woman shall not come in my grace.

Expedience - Who dares not stir by day must walk by night.

Expedience, e. not sincerity involved - .. it proceeds from policy, not love.

Expedience. See 'Exhortation, e. to understand the limitations imposed by circumstances - Construe the times to their necessities.'

Expenses, excessive e. and personal gain – How, i' the name of thrift, does he rake this together!

Expenses, travel e. See 'Business travel expenses, pretty nifty - … as 't is ever common, that men are merriest when they are from home.'

Experience, direct e. disproving official reports - Experience, O, thou disprov'st report!

Experience, e. acquired through observation - How hast thou purchased this experience? By my penny of observation.

Experience, e. or evidence disproving commonly held notions – Experience, O, thou disprov'st report!

Experience, expensive e. and no other benefit - … unless experience be a jewel that I have purchased at an infinite rate.

Experience, lack of e. alleged for refusing to take on a responsibility - Let there be some more test made of my metal…

Experience, let e. speak - … give experience tongue.

Experience, value of e. and how it is acquired - Experience is by industry achieved and perfected by the swift course of time.

Experience, worldly experience makes a

perfect man- .. he cannot be a perfect man, not being tried and tutored in the world

Experimentation, e. harmless and worth trying – What I can do can do no hurt to try.

Explanation, difficult matter made easy by expert - What impossible matter will he make easy next?

Explanation, do you want to know why? - Ay sir, and wherefore; for, they say, every why hath a wherefore.

Explanation, e. by way of an example - .. I shall tell you a pretty tale; it may be, you have heard it..

Explanation, e. of strange events needing oracle - … some oracle must rectify our knowledge.

Explanation, further e. required - This fierce abridgement hath to it circumstantial branches..

Explanation, pleading for an e. – Lay open…the folded meaning of your words' deceit.

Explanation, rational e. and miracles excluded - … for miracles are ceased…

Explanation, request to be allowed to give an e. See 'Request, r. to be heard – To my unfolding lend your prosperous ear…'

Expletives, e. not used. See entries for 'Speech, restraint from use of expletives due to anger.'

Exploits, young and ready for e. - … in the very May-morn of his youth, ripe for exploits and mighty enterprises.

Exploitation - .. He hath eaten me out of house and home.

Exposition, clear e. - Your exposition hath been most sound.

Exposure, e. of face - … we will draw the curtain and show you the picture…

Expression of sadness misconstrued - My heart is ten times lighter than my looks.

Expression of sadness unsuitable for a p. - … put off these frowns, and ill-beseeming semblance for a feast.

Expression, come on relax - … unknit that threatening unkind brow.

Expression, change in e. denoting loss of favor - … see already how he doth begin to make us strangers to his looks of love.

Expression, change in e. giving away evidence of misdeeds – I'll observe his looks; I'll tent him to the quick: if he but blench…

Expression, e. indicating an offense received - You throw a strange regard upon me, and by that I do perceive it hath offended you.

Expression, e. indicating bad n. – … this man's brow, like to a title-leaf foretells the nature of a tragic volume.

Expression, e. indicating concealment - … didst contract and purse thy brow together, as if thou then hadst shut up in thy brain some horrible conceit.

Expression, e. indicating guilt. See 'Guilt, evidence of g. visible in expression - The image of a wicked heinous fault lives in his eye.'

Expression, e. indicating troubled conscience - The colour of the king doth come and go between his purpose and his conscience…

Expression, e. indicating urgency - How now, good Blunt? thy looks are full of speed.

Expression, e. portending the witnessing of extraordinary events - … So should he look that seems to speak things strange.

Expression, e. provocative. See 'Woman, provocative w. - there's language in her eye, her cheek, her lip, nay, her foot speaks…'

Expression, facial e. articulating its meaning - …to speak that in words which his eye hath disclosed, I only have made a mouth of his eye…

Expression, facial e. clearly supporting the suspicion of bad news – hath by instinct knowledge from others' eyes.

Expression, facial e. compared to visual weather forecasting. See 'News, bad n. inferred by the look of the messenger – men judge by the complexion of the sky..

Expression, facial e. indicating anger - He knits his brow and shows an angry eye..

Expression, facial e. indicating anger - Here comes the queen, whose looks bewray her anger

Expression, facial e. indicating anger - .. The angry spot doth glow on Caesar's brow.

Expression, facial e. indicating bad news. See entries for 'News, bad n. inferred by the look of the messenger' *** 'Expression, e. indicating bad n. – ... this man's brow, like to a title-leaf foretells the nature of a tragic volume.'

Expression, facial e. indicating disapproval. See 'Opinion, your op. on the choice - how like you our choice that you stand pensive, as half malcontent?'

Expression, facial e. indicating discontent, why? See 'Mood, why are you in a bad mood? - .. what's the matter that you have such a February face…'

Expression, facial e. indicating positive traits – ... in thy face I see the map of honour, truth and loyalty.

Expression, facial e. indicating positive traits - ... There is written in your brow, provost, honesty and constancy…

Expression, facial e. indicating sadness, why? - Why are thine eyes fixed to the sullen earth, gazing on that which seems to dim thy sight?

Expression, facial e. indicating sadness, why? – Why droops my lord, like over-ripened corn…

Expression, facial e. indicating tyranny – Upon thy eye-balls murderous tyranny sits in grim majesty, to fright the world.

Expression, facial e. knitting of brows – … knit his brows, as frowning at the favours of the world?

Expression, facial e. misinterpreted - Interpretation will misquote our looks.

Expression, facial e. of unhappiness detected - I see your brows are full of discontent…

Expression, facial e. subject to various readings. See 'Dissimulation, lesson in d. - Your face, my thane, is as a book where men may read strange matters…'

Expression, facial e. to hide intent. See 'Dissimulation, facial expression not giving away intention – (We will) make our faces vizards to our hearts, disguising what they are.'

Expression, facial e. unfriendly - .. the tartness of his face sours ripe grapes.

Expression, facial expression unreliable as an indicator of character. See 'Physiognomy, p. unreliable .. there's no art to find the mind's construction in the face…'

Expression, frowning to be expected - Prepare thy brow to frown.

Expression, guilty e. See 'Disguise, d. discovered - There is a kind of confession in your looks...'

Expression, invitation to a more cheerful e. - Clear up, fair queen, that cloudy countenance.

Expression, looks that kill or revive. See 'Reconciliation, r. effected with a smile - For looks kill love and love by looks reviveth; a smile recures the wounding of a frown.'

Expression, perplexed and amazed e. detected at seeing your attire - ... wherefore gaze this goodly company as if they saw some wondrous monument…

Expression, power of e. tremendous– … these brows of mine, whose smile and frown…able with the change to kill and cure.

Expression, power of e. reduced by pain. See 'Pain, p. limiting power of expression - I'll utter what my sorrows give me leave'.

Expression, sour facial e. habitual when seeing a (figurative) crab - ... you must not look so sour … It is my fashion when I see a crab.

Expression, sour look - Why look you still so stern and tragical?

Expression, telling e. – …I saw his heart in

his face.

Expression, threatening e. See 'Reaction, negative r. – And on my face he turn'd an eye of death.'

Expression, why so serious, what are you thinking about? - … What serious contemplation are you in?

Expression, why so solemn an e.? - Why do you bend such solemn brows on me?

Expression, wild e. observed - Forth at your eyes your spirits wildly peep.

Exquisite, see 'Beauty, radiant - most radiant, exquisite, unmatchable beauty'

Exterior, e. for once agreeing with the interior. See 'Appearances, a. deceiving (usually), but not in this case - .. thou hast a mind that suits with this fair and outward character.'

Eyebrows, aesthetic considerations – … black brows, they say, become some women best…

Eyelids - …behold, her eyelids, cases to those heavenly jewels.

Eyes and voice together - Your eyes are lodestars; and your tongue's sweet air more tunable than lark to shepherd's ear.

Eyes that partake of the miraculous - .. in her eye I find a wonder, or a wondrous miracle.

Eyes with the sparkle of diamonds - I see how thine eye would emulate the diamond: thou hast the right arched beauty of the brow.

Eyes, beauty of e. and eyelids – Her eyelids, cases to those heavenly jewels…

Eyes, beauty of e. to be written about - If I could write the beauty of your eyes, and in fresh numbers number all your graces…

Eyes, e. and cheeks - The lustre in your eye, heaven in your cheek, pleads your fair usage.

Eyes, e. and ears. See 'Decision, d. guided by sight and hearing - …mine eyes and ears, two traded pilots 'twixt the dangerous shores of will and judgement.'

Eyes, e. as deceptive judges. See 'See 'Judgment, poor j. compared to not seeing well - .. our very eyes are sometimes like our judgments, blind!'

Eyes, e. as a source of knowledge - Not from the stars do I my judgment pluck, and yet methinks I have astronomy…

Eyes, e. as instruments of persuasion - Did not the heavenly rhetoric of thine eye, 'gainst whom the world cannot hold argument…

Eyes, e. as painters of her beauty - Mine eye hath play'd the painter and drawn thy beauty's form in table of my heart…

Eyes, e. as spies – If these be true spies which I wear in my head, here's a goodly sight.

Eyes, e. as teachers - For where is any author in the world teaches such beauty as a woman's eye?

Eyes, e. emitting bright light - … her eye in heaven would through the airy region stream so bright, that birds would sing, and think it were not night.

Eyes, e. indicating baseness of character. See 'Character, baseness of c. displayed by the expression – … an eye base and unlustrous as the smoky light that's fed with stinking tallow.'

Eyes, e. like stars – Two of the fairest stars in all the heaven, having some business, do entreat her eyes to twinkle in their spheres till they return.

Eyes, e. like stars – What stars do spangle heaven with such beauty as those two eyes become that heavenly face?

Eyes, e. made red by pain and rage - … With eyes as red as new-enkindled fire.

Eyes, e. made for looking. See 'Attention, object of a., unconcerned about being the object of a. – Men's eyes were made to look, and let them gaze.'

Eyes, e. of a man compared to the e. of an eagle – … an eagle, madam hath not so green, so quick, so fair an eye as Paris hath.

Eyes, e. of the soul. See 'Presence, 'Do you miss me?' - … Save that my soul's imaginary

1133

sight presents thy shadow to my sightless view…'

Eyes, e. on lookout for the ladies - My eyes, my lord, can look as swift as yours…

Eyes, her e. and lids - … the enclosed lights, now canopied under these windows, white and azure laced with blue of heaven's own tinct.

Eyes, her e. as windows to your breast - Mine eyes have drawn thy shape, and thine for me are windows to my breast…

Eyes, her e. weapons of mass destruction - .. there lies more peril in thine eye, than twenty of their swords.

Eyes, incomparably beautiful, shinier than crystal - To what, my love shall I compare thine eye? Crystal is muddy.

Eyes, ladies e. as a source of philosophical learning - From women's eyes this doctrine I derive..

Eyes, open e. but unable to see - You see, her eyes are open. Ay, but their sense is shut.

Eyes, sun interfering with good vision - … my mistaking eyes that have been so bedazzled with the sun.

Eyes, their rejuvenating power – … might shake off fifty, looking in her eyes.

Eyes, wounded by the e. of a lady. See 'Sigh - (my heart) wounded it is, but with the eyes of a lady.'

Face shown or visible after she removes her mask, or a hat or anything which partially or completely hides her face - Fair ladies mask'd are roses in their bud…

Face, beautiful beyond wonder - Her face was to mine eye beyond all wonder.

Face, brighter than the moon - Nor shines the silver moon one half so bright…as doth thy face through tears of mine give light.

Face, expression., beauty, imitating Nature - 'T is beauty truly blent, whose red and white, nature's own sweet and cunning hand laid on.

Face, f. as a book. See 'Dissimulation, lesson in d. - Your face, my thane, is as a book where men may read strange matters…'

Face, f. like sunshine. See 'Sunshine, her face like s. - Vouchsafe to show the sunshine of your face…'

Face, f. saving - How well this yielding rescues thee from shame!

Face, heavenly f. as a cause of various acts, desperate or otherwise - … 'twas thy heavenly face that set me on.

Face, relative value of a f. - Your face hath got five hundred pound a year yet sell your face for five pence and 'tis dear.

Face, sweet expression - Thou hast the sweetest face I ever look'd on.

Fact, a common f. - …is as common as any the most vulgar thing to sense.

Fact, just repeating a well known f. - I speak no more than everyone doth know.

Fact, not fiction. See 'Reality, not appearance - Seems, madam! nay it is; I know not 'seems'.

Facts, knowledge of f. by audience implied - I tell you that which you yourselves do know.

Failure, dealing with fear of f. - … screw your courage to the sticking-place and we'll not fail.

Fair is foul. See 'Values, perversion of v. - Fair is foul, and foul is fair'.

Fair play - … and I would call it, fair play

Faith, broken f. causing rebellion – … unkind usage, dangerous countenance and violation of all faith and troth…

Faithfulness, faithful after saying yes - … they are constant being won: they are burs, I can tell you; they'll stick where they are thrown.

Faithfulness, f. restated - While others fish with craft for great opinion, I with great truth catch more simplicity…

Faithlessness - better have none than plural faith which is too much by one.

Fall, f. from grace. See 'Rejection, reaction to r., emphatic and mildly theatrical – … like the lily, that once was mistress of the field

and flourished I'll hang my head and perish..'
– 'Resig

Fall, f. from greatness - Take but good note, and you shall see in him…

Fall from greatness described – … then was I as a tree whose boughs did bend with fruit: but in one night…

Fall from greatness painful, better not have pomp to begin with – … 'tis a sufferance panging as soul and body's severing.

Fall from greatness, meditation on f. from greatness – … And when you would say something that is sad, speak how I fell.

Fall from grea

Fall from greatness and general reaction - 'Tis certain, greatness, once fall'n out with fortune must fall out with men too…

Fall, f. from greatness sudden - … then in a moment, see how soon this mightiness meets misery.

Fall, f. from greatness. See 'Forgetting, wishing to forget - … that I could forget

Fall, season - … the year growing ancient, not yet on summer's death, nor on the birth of trembling winter.

Fall, season - That time of year thou mayst in me behold…

False claim, claiming a non existent achievement or feat - … the knave bragged of that he could not compass.

False, as f. as - … As false as dicers' oaths.

False, as f. as. See 'Man, m. false - … falser than vows made in wine'

False, f. and cunning. See 'Character, false, cunning, shifting and perverse – I can smile and murder whiles I smile.

False, f. appearances. See entries for 'Appearances, false a.'

False, f. or unbelievable. See 'Character, false or unbelievable - no more faith in thee than in a stewed prune'.

Falsehood, f. of the powerful. stronger than truth of the poor - … Say what you can, my false o'erweighs your true.

Falsehood, f. worse in higher ups than common people - … and falsehood is worse in kings than beggars.

Fame, f. acquired via hard study. See' Time, defeated by fame and honor'.

Fame, f. and achievements - Great is the rumor of this dreadful knight and his achievements of no less account.

Fame, f. defeating death and time - … And make us heirs of all eternity.

Fame, f. preventing oblivion. See 'Oblivion, insurance against o. – … A forted residence 'gainst the tooth of time and razure of oblivion.'

Fame, looking for f. in war - … to win renown even in the jaws of danger and of death.

Fame, looking for f. in war. See 'Militarism, reputation as a volatile commodity - … Seeking the bubble reputation even in the cannon's mouth.'

Fame, f. secured by poetical love lines. See 'Love, l. made immortal by words - So long as men can breath or eyes can see, so long lives this and this gives life to thee.'

Fame, no claim to f. – … our grave, like Turkish mute, shall have a tongueless mouth…

Fame, safety preferable to f. See 'Safety, s. and beer preferable to fame – I would give all my fame for a pot of ale and safety.'

Fancy, f. spurred by obstacles. See 'Obstacles, o. increasing desire --… as all impediments in fancy's course are motives of more fancy.'

Fancy, flight of f. See 'Imagination, i. is rich with strange images – So full of shapes is fancy that it alone is high-fantastical.'

Farewell, f. - … farewell, and better than I fare.

Farewell, f. to beautiful but cruel woman - … Farewell, fair cruelty.

Fashion, f. making suits or dresses useless – … the fashion wears out more apparel than the man

Fashion, f. or custom setting – … we are the makers of manners, Kate…

Fashion, foreign f. See 'Imitation, i. of foreign fashion - … whose manners still our tardy apish nation limps after in base imitation'.

Fashion, getting a new suit. See 'Image building or restoration - I'll be at charges for a looking glass and entertain a score or two of tailors…'

Fashion, new or ridiculous f. easily adopted – New customs, though they be ever so ridiculous.. yet they are followed.

Fashion, opinion on f. See entries for 'Opinion, your op. on fashion'.

Fashion, poorly dressed. See 'Attire, outlandish or wacky - .. so wild in their attire, that look not like the inhabitants o' the earth'.

Fashion, the epitome of fashion and elegance, the glass of fashion and the mold of form. See 'Politician, young aspiring p. - The expectancy and rose of the fair state… the observed of all observers.'

Fast. See entries for 'Speed'.

Fasting, f. after dinner – When you fasted it was presently after dinner…

Fasting, f. as a consequence of excess. See 'Excess, e. leading to restraint. See 'Restraint, r. caused by excess - As surfeit is the father of much fast…'

Fat, admitting to being f. See 'Appearance, haggard, fat – skin hangs about me like a loose gown'.

Fat, being f. as a justification for weakness of character or errors - Thou seest I have more flesh than another man, and therefore more frailty.

Fat. f. man and flotation - … you may know by my size that I have a kind of alacrity in sinking.

Fat, f. man and lust - … till the wicked fire of lust have melted him in his own grease.

Fat, f. men less dangerous than thin – … Yond Cassius has a lean and hungry look.

Fat, f. woman. See 'Woman, a very large w. - ..in what part of her body stands Ireland' – 'Woman, correspondence between w.'s parts and countries' geography'.

Fatal attraction. See 'Attraction, fatal, her voice and shape - mine ear is much enamoured of thy note…'

Fatal vision. See 'Reality and imagination - …art thou but a dagger of the mind, a false creation, proceeding from the heat-oppressed brain.

Fatalism, fatalistic a. to life – … let determined things to destiny hold unbewail'd their way.

Fate(s), see entries for 'Destiny'

Father, f. of fast. See 'Restraint, r. caused by excess - As surfeit is the father of much fast…'

Father, f. of stratagems. See 'Situation, tense s. - … every minute now should be the father of some stratagem: the times are wild.'

Fault, admitting to your fault - I have deserved all tongues to talk their bitterest.

Fault, condemning the f., not the perpetrator – Condemn the fault and not the actor of it.

Fault, f. from which good results occurred - I cannot wish the fault undone, the issue of it being so proper.

Fault, one f. obscuring all other virtues - … the stamp of one defect… shall in the general censure take corruption from that particular fault.

Fault, faults. See entries for 'Error'

Faults, f. as graces, see 'Apologies unnecessary, on the contrary – thou mak'st faults graces that to thee resort'.

Faults, f. improving character. See 'Apologies for past poor behavior - they say best men are moulded out of faults…'

Faults, f. make us human. See 'Man, m's nature, his faults separate him from the Gods - … but you, gods, will give us some faults to make us men.'

Faults, man with many f. – … he hath

faults, with surplus, to tire in repetition.
Faults, f. redeemed by spirit of generosity - ... faults that are rich are fair.
Faults, f. seen in others but not in oneself. See 'Hypocrisy, criticizing one's own faults in others - wilt thou whip thine own faults in other men?'
Faults, little f. to be forgiven. See 'Forgiveness, f. advisable for little faults - If little faults, proceeding on distemper, shall not be wink'd at…'
Faults, women's f. See 'Women, a question about w's faults - …There were none principal; they were all like one another as half pence are…'
Favor, begging for a f. - … But if a humble prayer may prevail
Favor, begging for a f. while declaring your total subservience - and if thy poor devoted servant may but beg one favor at thy gracious hand..
Favor, f. of the great disappointing. See 'Reliance, r. on the favor of the great a source of disappointment. - Poor wretches that depend on greatness' favour dream as I have done, wake and find nothing.'
Favor, f. of the powerful risky – How wretched is that poor man that hangs on princes' favours.
Favor, f. of the wicked easily turns to hate - the love of wicked men converts to fear..
Favor, out of f. with lady - .. you are now sailed into the north of my lady's opinion..
Favor, unable to plead for favors - … Used to command, untaught to plead for favour.
Favorite, crawling into being a f. – …one hath crawl'd into the favour of the king…
Favorite, f. through oratory - … he hath a witchcraft over the king …
Favorite. See 'Position, well positioned at court - ripens in the sunshine of his favour'.
Fed up with comforting efforts - I'll hate him everlastingly that bids me be of comfort any more.
Fed up with self-serving statements. See '

Words, fed up with idle or self-serving w. - I can no longer brook thy vanities'
Fear, afraid of not pleasing – … Ever in fear to kindle your dislike
Fear, determination to conquer f. - The mind I sway by, and the heart I bear, shall never shake with doubt nor shake with fear.
Fear, display of f. a stimulus for coward enemies – … coward dogs most spend their mouths when…
Fear, effects of f. - ... distilled almost to jelly with the act of fear.
Fear, exhortation to dispel fears. See 'Exhortation, e. to dispel fear - Nay, good my lord, be not afraid of shadows.'
Fear, f. arising poor judgment - ... for defect of judgment is oft the sauce of fear.
Fear, f. as a corrupting agent – Fears make devils of cherubims; they never see truly.
Fear, f. as a factor in safety – … best safety lies in fear.'
Fear, f. as a proper reaction to portentous signals from heavens or nature. See 'Heavens, tempting the h. - But wherefore did you so much tempt the heavens?..'
Fear, f. as the reason for defeat - .. nothing routs us but the villany of our fears.
Fear, f. causing treason - …. when our actions do not our fears do make us traitors.
Fear, f. conquered by the presence of an inspiring leader. See 'Presence, p. that inspires confidence and conquers fear - …a largess universal like the sun his liberal eye doth give to every one, thawing cold fear.'
Fear, f. contemptible and cursed passion - Of all base passions, fear is most accursed.
Fear, f. converting into hatred. See 'Management style, fear and government - In time we hate that which we often fear.'
Fear, f. disguised as conscience. See entries for 'Conscience, c. or fear?'
Fear, f. engendered by wrong-doing – … fears, which, as they say, attend the steps of wrong.

Fear, f. generates delay and failure – fearful commenting is leaden servitor to dull delay…

Fear, f. generates disorder - Fear frames disorder, and disorder wounds where it should guard…

Fear, f. guided by reason better than fearless blind reason - Blind fear, that seeing reason leads, finds safer footing than blind reason stumbling without fear..

Fear, f. in leader demeaning - If Caesar hide himself, shall they not whisper… Caesar is afraid'?

Fear, f. in tyrannous leaders increasing with time. See 'Authority, fear in a. grows with time – .. tyrants' fears decrease not, but grow faster than the years'.

Fear, f. increased by rumor. See 'Rumor, effect of r. on fear - Rumour doth double, like the voice and echo, the numbers of the fear'd.'

Fear, f. induced by desire to conform - … reason and respect make livers pale and lustihood deject.

Fear, f. of bad n. See 'News, enough of bad n., dangers of ignoring it - ... if you be afeard to hear the worst then let the worst unheard fall on your bead.'

Fear, f. of criticism to be overcome if there must be progress. See 'Action, need to act notwithstanding possible censure – if we shall stand still in fear our motion...'

Fear, f. of darkness. See 'Darkness, fear of d. - In the night, imagining some fear, how easy is a bush supposed a bear.'

Fear, f. of death, attitude towards it - That life is better life, past fearing death than that which lives to fear.

Fear, f. of death. See entries for 'Death, fear of d.'

Fear, f. of enemy engenders weakness. See entries in 'Complaint, c. after problems useless'

Fear, f. of failure. See 'Failure, dealing with fear of f. - ... screw your courage to the sticking-place and we'll not fail'.

Fear, f. of obstacle unjustified - ... every cloud engenders not a storm.

Fear, f. or compunction – Art thou afeard to be the same in thine own act and valour as thou art in desire?

Fear, f. prompted by imagination - …'tis the eye of childhood that fears a painted devil.

Fear, f. that he/she will yield during negotiations, 'yet do I fear thy nature'. See 'Character, kind, perhaps too much - ... it is too full o' the milk of human kindness…'

Fear, f. unwarranted - Each substance of a grief hath twenty shadows…

Fear, in a state of f. See 'Presentment, p. and fear - I have a faint cold fear thrills through my veins, that almost freezes up the heat of life.'

Fear, mutual f. eliminated by a marriage - … truths would be tales where now half tales be truths.

Fear, no f. to speak out when power is bent on madness. See 'Flattery, power yielding to f. and the obligations of honor - Think'st thou that duty shall have dread to speak when power to flattery bows?…'

Fear, no place for fear in a noble heart. See 'Encouragement, self-e. to change doubt to resolution.'

Fear, nobility, a noble soul is fearless - True nobility is exempt from fear: more can I bear than you dare execute.

Fear, not afraid as compared to an instinctual coward - ... Not a whit, i' faith; I lack some of thy instinct.

Fear, presentment, suspicion. See 'Presentment, premonition - I am surprised with an uncouth fear, a chilling sweat o'er-runs my trembling joints..'

Fear, questioning inappropriate f. - ... why do you start; and seem to fear things that do sound so fair?

Fear, reason for defying f. - fight and die, is death destroying death.

Fear, sweating in f. See 'Time, midnight, sweating at m. - fearful drops stand on my trembling flesh'.

Fear, symptoms or evidence of f. – ... these linen cheeks of thine are counsellors to fear.

Fear, type of f. that is common - ... 'twas a fear which oft infects the wisest.

Fear, useless and an advantage to the enemy – To fear the foe, since fear oppresseth strength, gives in your weakness strength unto your foe.

Fear, whom to f. and whom not to f. - Those that I reverence those I fear, the wise: at fools I laugh, not fear them.

Fearless, confidence overpowering f. See 'Confidence, c. that overcomes any fear – ... all too confident to give admittance to a thought of fear.' *** Entries for 'Courage'

Fears, f. unsubstantiated - .. his fears are shallow, wanting instance.

Feat, f. to be rewarded with honor and commendations - .. the duke shall both speak of it and extend to you what further becomes his greatness..

Feather for each wind that blows. See 'Political convictions, shaky' - I am a feather for each wind that blows…'

February face. See 'Mood, why are you in a bad mood? - ... what's the matter that you have such a February face…'

Feeling, f. of loss and deprivation by enemies - Thus are my blossoms blasted in the bud..

Feeling, f. very sorry - It strains me past the compass of my wits.

Feeling, f. weak. See 'Weak, feeling w. and unprotected – A naked subject to the weeping clouds…'

Feelings, misgivings. See entries for 'Misgivings'.

Feelings, true f. as opposed to hollow f. - Nor are those empty-hearted whose low sound reverbs no hollowness.

Feelings, true f. instead of affectation - ... I am sure my love's more richer than my tongue.

Feet, f. in pain due to long walk or rough path - The ruthless flint doth cut my tender feet.

Feet, tired f. - These feet, whose strengthless stay is numb, unable to support this lump of clay.

Fellows, a pair of worthy f. See 'Wishes, good w. plus compliment - they are worthy to inlay heaven with stars.'

Female, a f. defined - ... with a child of our grandmother Eve a female; or, for thy more sweet understanding, a woman.

Femininity and genetics - Why are our bodies soft and weak and smooth, unapt to toil and trouble in the world…

Feminism, feminist plea for equality of rights in marriage – ... Let husbands know their wives have sense like them…

Feminist, f.'s view of man. See 'Man, m. as dust – Would it not grieve a woman to be overmastered with a piece of valiant dust?'

Few die well that die in a battle. See 'War, who is responsible when participating in a criminal war - ... But if the cause be not good, the king himself hath a heavy reckoning to make…'

Few love to hear the sins they love to act. See 'Sins, unpleasant to hear of one's own s. '

Fetish, f. that takes prisoner the eye - .. this object, which takes prisoner the wild motion of mine eye,, fixing it only here.

Fiction, improbable f. See 'Unbelievable - If this were played upon a stage now I could condemn it as an improbable fiction'.

Fidelity, f. even when losing. See 'Siding with the losing party - …though my reason sits in the wind against me.'

Fight, determination to f. on - ... I cannot fly, but, bear-like, I must fight the course.

Fight, determined to f. for your rights - By words or blows here let us win our right.

Fight, fighting to be right – O virtuous fight when right with right wars who shall be most right.

Fight, f. among equals – Blood hath bought blood and blows have answered blows.

Fight, f. to the end - I'll fight till from my bones my flesh be hack'd.

Fight, f. to the end. - Ring the alarum-bell! Blow, wind! come, wrack! At least we'll die with harness on our back.

Fight, f. to the end. See 'Lion, dying l. still shows his rage - ... and wounds the earth, if nothing else, with rage.'

Fighter, a. committed f. – A stouter champion never handled sword.

Figs. See 'Life, longevity and unusual way of expressing love for it – I love long life better than figs.' *** 'Theft, t. and proper terminology - 'Convey,' the wise call it. 'Steal!' foh! a fico for the phrase!'

Financial analysis discouraging - ...Lord Timon's happy hours are done and past, and his estate shrinks from him.

Financial assistance, f.a. offered for honorable cause - My purse, my person, my extremest means, lie all unlock'd to your occasions.

Financial contribution denied - Who bates mine honour shall not know my coin.

Financial status, cash flow critical – ...his means most short means, his creditors most strait.

Financial status, cash flow critical – His promises fly so beyond his state that what he speaks is all in debt..

Financial status, challenging – I can get no remedy against this consumption of the purse...

Financial status, challenging - 'T is deepest winter in Lord Timon's purse.

Financial status, credit worthiness. See 'Credit worthiness spoiled by uncollected debts - ... my reliances on his fracted dates have smit my credit...'

Financial status, financial irresponsibility - ... the world is but a word: were it all yours to give it in a breath...

Financial status, foreseen weakness in financial position - When every feather sticks in his own wing, Lord Timon will be left a naked gull...

Financial status, on the edge of ruin - ... leaked is our bark and we stand on the dying deck, hearing the surges threat.

Financial status, poverty and contentment. See 'Contentment, c. assured if insensitive to poverty - Poor and content is rich and rich enough...'

Financial status, poverty obvious - ... famine is in thy cheeks, need and oppression starveth in thine eyes...

Financial status, poverty, evidence of poverty - The naked truth of it is, I have no shirt

Financial status, poverty, evidence of poverty - ... for I have no more stockings than legs, nor no more shoes than feet..

Financial status, pressure from collectors - The future comes apace: what shall defend the interim?

Financial status, receivables. See entries for 'Receivables'

Financial status, strained due to overspending - .. By something showing a more swelling port than my faint means would grant continuance...

Financial Status. 'Are you rich?' or 'How much money do you make?' - They are but beggars that can count their worth.'

Financing, f. denied - They have all been touch'd and found base metal...

Financing, lending denied - ... this is no time to lend money, especially upon bare friendship, without security.

Finding an honest Athenian impossible. See 'Honesty, an honest Athenian as a physical impossibility - ... if doing nothing be death by the law...'

Fingers, their enchanting touch - his stubborn buckles, with these your white enchanting fingers touch'd...

Fires, two strong f. compared to two strong characters. See 'Meeting, m. of strong characters - ... where two raging fires meet together, they do consume the thing that feeds upon.'

Firing. See 'Handling, proper h. of an execution - Let's carve him as a dish fit for the gods..'

Fish, cold f. See entries for 'Character, a cold fish'.

Fishing, metaphorically speaking - Bait the hook well; this fish will bite.

Fishing, pleasures of f. (also metaphorically) - The pleasant'st angling is to see the fish.. greedily devour the treacherous bait.

Flatterers. See entries for 'Flattery, f. observed'.

Flatterers, character of f. is always the same - .. this is the world's soul; and just of the same piece is every flatterer's spirit.

Flatterers, f. and flattered. See 'Opinion, your op. on flattery - .. he that loves to be flattered is worthy of the flatterer.'

Flatterers, f. and spreaders of rumor. See 'News, n. incorrect - .. many tales devis'd, which oft the ear of greatness needs must hear by smiling pick-thanks and base newsmongers.'

Flatterers, f. as sponges – take you me for a sponge my lord?

Flatterers, many and stupid - A thousand flatterers sit within thy crown, whose compass is no bigger than thy head.

Flattery - ... you are a gentleman of excellent breeding, admirable discourse…

Flattery, a complete un-flatterer who would not compliment Neptune for his trident. See 'Character, direct to the extreme - … what his breast forges, that his tongue must vent.'

Flattery, extreme f. – … in action how like an angel! in apprehension how like a god…

Flattery, f. and ceremony. See 'Ceremony, c., pomp and flattery useless - .. and what are thou, thou idol ceremony?'

Flattery, f. and praise tied to reward - ... when the means are gone that buy this praise, the breath is gone whereof this praise is made.

Flattery, f. by the intellectual to the rich - ..the learned pate ducks to the golden fool: all is oblique..

Flattery, f. counterproductive - They do abuse the king that flatter him…

Flattery, f. crime, hypocrisy - No vizor does become black villainy so well as soft and tender flattery.

Flattery, f. exposed - You play the spaniel and think with wagging of your tongue to win me.

Flattery, f. in hope of reward - No, let the candied tongue lick absurd pomp, and crook the pregnant hinges of the knee where thrift may follow fawning.

Flattery, f. justified – … when the sweet breath of flattery conquers strife.

Flattery, f. observed – … rain sacrificial whispering in his ears.

Flattery, f. observed and used for advancement – You shall mark many a duteous and knee-crooking knave…

Flattery, f. overlooks sin - A friendly eye could never see such faults..

Flattery, f. physically depicted. See 'Flattery, tools of f. - Serving of becks and jutting-out of bums'.

Flattery, f. rejected - He does me double wrong that wounds me with the flatteries of his tongue.

Flattery, f. useless – … blood that will be thaw'd from the true quality with that which melteth fools…

Flattery, flattered for hating flatterers - ...when I tell him he hates flatterers he says he does, being then most flattered

Flattery, invocation – See 'Invocation, i. to flattery - O, that men's ears should be to counsel deaf, but not to flattery.'

Flattery, leave f. to servile people - … let the candied tongue lick absurd pomp..

Flattery, let there be no limit to your f. - Flatter and praise, commend, extol their graces, though ne'er so black, say they have angels' faces.

Flattery, love of f. leading to financial ruin -

Methinks false hearts should never have sound leg, thus honest fools lay out their wealth on courtsies.

Flattery, no f. – ... do not think I flatter, for what advancement may I hope from thee...

Flattery, power yielding to f. and the obligations of honor - Think'st thou that duty shall have dread to speak when power to flattery bows?...

Flattery, the dews of f. – ... with dews of flattery seducing so my friends.

Flattery, tools of f. - Serving of becks and jutting-out of bums.

Flattery, tools of f. - ..sweet words, low-crooked court'sies and base spaniel-fawning.

Flattery, unable to flatter. See 'Character, unable to flatter, pretend and deceive - because I cannot flatter and speak fair..'

Fleetingness, f. of everything. See 'Time, t. and the inherent limited duration of e

Flesh and blood. See 'Real, compliment, are you real? - But are you flesh and blood? Have you a working pulse?'

Flies. See 'Pessimism, fleetness of life – As flies to wanton boys are we to the gods, they kill us for their sport.'

Fly, killing a f. - ... A deed of death done on the innocent.

Flower, compliment – ... no shepherdess, but Flora peering in April's front.

Flower, the sweetest flower - ... the sweetest flower of all the field.

Flowers - introduction.

Flowers, compliment, like spring-time f. - For thou are pleasant, gamesome... yet sweet as spring-time flowers.

Flowers, fields in flower and romance - Away before me to sweet beds of flowers, Love-thoughts lie rich when canopied with bowers.

Flowers, honeysuckle providing shade - .. honeysuckles, ripen'd by the sun, forbid the sun to enter...

Flowers, lilies and roses. See 'Beauty, b. contending with that of lilies and roses – Of Nature's gifts thou mayst with lilies boast and with the half-blown rose.'

Flowers, lily, comparing yourself to a withering lily. See 'Rejection, reaction to r., emphatic and mildly theatrical – ... like the lily, that once was mistress of the field and flourished I'll hang my head and perish.'

Flowers, lily, painting the lily as an analogy for excess. See 'Excess, e. not necessary and wasteful once objective is reached - To gild refined gold, to paint the lily... is wasteful and ridiculous excess.'

Flowers, marigolds and other f. indicated for middle age men - .. Here's flowers for you, hot lavender...

Flowers, primrose and harebell - ... thou shalt not lack the flower that's like thy face, pale primrose, nor the azured harebell, like thy veins.

Flowers, primroses unmarried - ... pale primroses that die unmarried ere they can behold bright Phoebus in his strength.

Flowers, rose, universe. See 'Universe, rose, unique - For nothing this wide universe I call, save thou my rose, in it thou art my all.'

Flowers, homage of f - Sweets to the sweet

Flowers, violets - ... a violet in the youth of primy nature...

Flowers, violets - ...dim but sweeter than the lids of Juno's eyes..

Flowers, violets – Who are the violets now that strew the green lap of the new come spring?

Flowers, violets. See 'Breath excellent, stolen from the violet - the forward violet thus did I chide..'

Flowers, her beauty exceeding all flowers - More flowers I noted, yet none I could see, but sweet, or colour it had stolen from thee

Flowers, lilies and roses - Nor did I wonder at the lily's white, nor praise the deep vermilion in the rose...

Flowers, roses, lips as r. See 'Lips, l. as roses'

Flowers, roses, women like roses - For

women are as roses, whose fair flower being once display'd, doth fall that very hour.

Flowers, white rose - ... the milk-white rose, with whose sweet smell the air shall be perfumed.

Fly, murder of a f. and considerations thereof - Poor harmless fly! That with his pretty bussing melody..

Follies prompted my love. See 'Blindness, b. of lovers to themselves - But love is blind and lovers cannot see the pretty follies they themselves commit.'

Folly maybe but not childishness - Though age from folly could not give me freedom it does from childishness.

Folly or malice - Either you must confess yourselves wondrous malicious or be accus'd of folly.

Folly, f. as a pretence. See 'See 'Wisdom, w. hidden behind apparent folly - He uses his folly like a stalking horse, and under the presentation of that, he shoots his wit.'

Folly, f. dedicated to her. See 'Love, l. and folly - ... what folly I commit, I dedicate to you.'

Folly, f. to be loyal to fools. See 'Loyalty, l. to fools an act of folly - The loyalty well held to fools does make our faith mere folly.'

Folly, f. in fools vs. folly in wits. See 'Stupidity, s. more striking in a person not normally stupid - Folly in fools bears not so strong a note…'

Folly, see 'Objective, examining the folly required to achieve an o. - the purpose must weigh with the folly'.

Folly, the faults of fools. See 'Definition, calling things by their names - We call a nettle but a nettle; and the faults of fools, but folly.'

Food, bad f. See 'Restaurant, r. with bad food - ... thy food is as hath been belched on by infected lungs'.

Food, fast f. distaste for it – On what I hate I feed not.

Food, f. turning bitter. See 'Jealousy, effects of j. - … the food that to him now is as luscious as locusts, shall be to him shortly as bitter as coloquintida.'

Food, giving priority to spiritual over material f. - The mind shall banquet, though the body pine

Food, questionable f. - … strange flesh which some did die to look on.

Food, virtual f. – (Who can) cloy the hungry edge of appetite by bare imagination of a feast?

Fool, answer to insulting fool. See 'Slander, no s. can come from a fool - .. there is no slander in an allowed fool, though he do nothing but rail'

Fool, do you think I am a fool? – … bear some charity to my wit: do not think it so unwholesome.

Fool, on having been outwitted by a fool. See 'Love, not a sign of wisdom - ... he that is so yoked by a fool, methinks should not be chronicled for wise.".

Fool's paradise – …if ye should lead her into a fool's paradise…

Foolery, amusing f. versus sad experience. See 'Merriment, m. preferable to melancholy - …I had rather have a fool make me merry than experience to make me sad.'

Foolery, clever f. requiring some wit - … to do that well craves a kind of wit.

Foolery, f. universal. See 'Stupidity, s. universal, compared sarcastically to the sun - Foolery, sir, does walk about the orb, like the sun, it shines everywhere.'

Foolery, skill in f. and men who make fools of themselves – … a practice as full of labour as a wise man's art…

Foolish figure. See 'Madness, m. confirmed rhetorically - That he's mad, 'tis true; 'tis true, 'tis pity. And pity 'tis 'tis true.'

Fools, dullness of f. as an opportunity for the clever - … for always the dulness of the fool is the whetstone of the wits.

Fools, f. making bad choices - O, these deliberate fools! when they do choose…

Fools, talents of f. See 'Invocation, ironic i. applicable to fools – God give them wisdom that have it; and those that are fools, let them use their talents.'

Fools, two of them observed approaching - Here comes a pair of very strange beasts which in all tongues are called fools.

Foot, a light f. - O, so light a foot will ne'er wear out the everlasting flint.

Foot, see 'Woman, pretty in foot, lip, eye and well spoken - We say that Shore's wife hath a pretty foot…'

For if our virtues did not go forth of us… See 'Talents, t. to be used – Heaven doth with us as we with torches do, not light them for themselves…'

For never-resting time leads summer on… See 'Summer, s. turning into winter - For never-resting time leads summer on to hideous winter…'

For nimble thought can jump… See 'Thought, power of t. and imagination to travel instantly - For nimble thought can jump both sea and land as soon as think the place where he would be.'

For nothing this wide universe I call… See 'Universe, rose, unique - For nothing this wide universe I call, save thou my rose, in it thou art my all.'

For several virtues have I lik'd several women… See 'Best, compliment, you are the best – Full many a lady I have eyed with best regards…'

For so work the honey bees… See 'Management structure, hierarchical – Obedience: for so work the honey bees…'

For violent fires soon burn out themselves. See 'Vanity, v. and heedlessness in a leader'

For you and I are past our dancing days. See 'Time, t. past for entertainment '

Forbear to judge … See 'Judgment, suspending j. for we all are at fault - Forbear to judge, for we are sinners all.'

Force, f. imposing action - For do we must what force will have us do.

Forebodings, uncertain or bad f. See entries for 'Misgivings', 'Premonition'

Forecast, f. looks good - If consequence do but approve my dream, my boat sails freely, both with wind and stream.

Forecast, f. of war. See 'War, w. predicted - I do believe, statist though I am none, nor like to be, that this will prove a war.

Forecast, gloomy f. - … lend me ten thousand eyes and I will fill them with prophetic tears.

Forecast, positive f. - Last night the very gods show'd me a vision..

Forecasting ability - In nature's infinite book of secrecy a little I can read.

Forecasting and prophetic ability - Methinks I am a prophet new inspired…

Forecasting requested - If you can look into the seeds of time and say which grain will grow and which will not…

Forecasting skills – The spirit of deep prophecy she hath, exceeding the nine sibyls of old Rome..

Forecasting, expressing doubts about someone's forecasts – How far your eyes may pierce I can not tell…

Forecasting, if I am correct… – If secret powers suggest but truth to my divining thoughts…

Forecasting, not good at f. – … much too shallow to sound the bottom of the after-times.

Forecasting, positive f. - My mind presageth happy gain and conquest.

Forecasting, shapes of things to come. See 'Outcome of events detectable in small details at the beginning - And in such indexes, although small pricks to their subsequent volumes…'

Forecasting, total confidence in the forecaster - No prophet will I trust, if she prove false.

Foregone conclusion - But this denoted a foregone conclusion.

Foreign girl, f.g. whom you like and she

1144

speaks some English – …for thy tongue makes Welsh as sweet as ditties highly penn'd….

Foreign girls, admitting to limited knowledge of the lady's native tongue - I shall never move thee in French, unless it be to laugh at me.

Foreign girls, effort at speaking in the lady's native tongue - … in French; which, I am sure, will hang upon my tongue like a new-married wife about her husband's neck..

Foreign girls, Italian girls, irresistible - Those girls of Italy, take heed of them..

Foreign girl, kissing overcoming language barriers – I understand thy kisses and thou mine…

Foreign girls, love overcoming language barriers - … if you will love me soundly with your French heart…

Foreign language, disadvantages of speaking a f.l. - … can he that speaks with the tongue of an enemy be a good counselor, or no?

Foreign language, f.l. expert – (he) speaks three or four languages word for word without book.

Foreign language, knowledge of French a liability - … he can speak French and therefore he is a traitor.

Foreign language, knowledge of Latin a liability - Away with him, away with him! he speaks Latin.

Foreign language, too old to learn a f.l. See 'Age, too old to learn – … Too far in years to be a pupil now.'

Foreign policy, war to cover up internal problems - Be it thy course to busy giddy minds with foreign quarrels.

Foreigner - Not of this country, though my chance is now to use it for my time.

Forewarning, f. advisable – To acquaint you with this evil, that you might the better arm you to the sudden time…

Forgetfulness, strong image of f. See 'Oblivion, o. as a gulf - … in the swallowing gulf of blind forgetfulness and dark oblivion.'

Forgetting - I have forgot all men; then, if thou grant'st thou'rt a man, I have forgot thee.

Forgetting and consequences - I shall forget, to have thee still stand there, remembering how I love thy company.

Forgetting, cannot forget what not remembered – That is not forgot which never did I remember.

Forgetting, event or matter completely forgotten. See 'Oblivion, o. as a gulf - … in the swallowing gulf of blind forgetfulness and dark oblivion.'

Forgetting, f. a part. See 'Part, p. forgotten, like an actor forgetting his p. - Like a dull actor now, I have forgot my part…

Forgetting, f. common to men - But men are men; the best sometimes forget.

Forgetting, f. due to drinking. See 'Wine, w. and forgetfulness - … though I cannot remember what I did when you made me drunk…'

Forgetting, f. everything but the essential. See 'Remembering, r. only the essential - .. from the table of my memory I'll wipe away all trivial fond records.

Forgetting, f. the good under the influence of anger - All this from my remembrance brutish wrath sinfully pluck'd…

Forgetting, f. the most important – Great thing of us forgot!

Forgetting, impossible to f. See 'Memory, impossible to forget - Why should I write this down, that's riveted, screw'd to my memory'.

Forgetting, questioning rhetorically – May this be wash'd in Lethe, and forgotten?

Forgetting, time helps f - … some more time must wear the print of his remembrance out.

Forgetting, tools for f. See 'Wine, w. as a tool for forgetting and making others forget - … memory, the warder of the brain, shall be a fume…'

Forgetting, wishing to forget - .. that I could forget what I have been..

Forgetting. See also entries for 'Oblivion'.

Forgiveness, f. advisable for little faults - If little faults, proceeding on distemper, shall not be wink'd at…

Forgiveness, f. and forgetting - … it hath the excuse of youth and heat of blood

Forgiveness, f. asked for rashness – Forgive my general and exceptless rashness, you perpetual-sober gods!

Forgiveness, f. at something she has done - No more be grieved at that which thou hast done, roses have thorns, and silver mountains mud..

Forgiveness, f. by a king, request for f. - Who am I, ha? .. A gracious king, that pardons all offences malice never meant.

Forgiveness, f. following adversary's repentance – … these words have turn'd my hate to love; and forgive and quite forget old faults.

Forgiveness, f. for looking at other women - … A sin prevailing much in youthful men who give their eyes the liberty of gazing.

Forgiveness, f. granted - The nature of his great offence is dead and deeper than oblivion we do bury the incensing relics of it.

Forgiveness, f. to a recreant – … ten times more beloved than if thou never hadst deserved our hate

Forgiveness, injuries forgotten - The record of what injuries you did us…as done by chance'

Forgiveness, no f. possible. See 'Pity, p. not to be hoped for – as the wolf does of the shepherd' – 'Pity, p. prevented by resentment at offense or injury'.

Forgiveness, plea to be forgiven - … if hearty sorrow be a sufficient ransom for offence, I tender it here.

Forgiveness, self-f. - … at the last do as the heavens have done, forget your evil; with them forgive yourself.

Forgiveness. See entries for 'Defense, d. from accusation'.

Formality asserted, austere regard of control - .. quenching my familiar smile with an austere regard of control.

Formality, no f. in love - Love is not love when it is mingled with regards, that stand aloof from the whole point.

Fortune, a pipe for her fingers. See "Man, m. to be praised who can stand up to the vagaries of fortune - … blest are those whose blood and judgment are so well commingled..'

Fortune, circumstances, reversal of position, is eaten by a worm. See 'Circumstances, c. and status, a complete turn-around - a man may fish with a worm that had eat of a king…'

Fortune, cruel f. that usually lets man outlive his wealth – … To view with hollow eye and wrinkled brow an age of poverty…

Fortune, defying f. - … Fortune knows we scorn her most when most she offers blows.

Fortune, down with f. - Affliction is enamour'd of thy parts…

Fortune, f. biased and unfair - … for those that Fortune makes fair, she scarce makes honest..

Fortune, f. has taken a turn for the worse – Thus hath the course of justice wheel'd about, and left thee but a very prey to time..

Fortune, f. never complete - Will fortune never come with both hands full…

Fortune, f. re-interpreted, she is acting in disguise - … when fortune means to men most good she looks upon them with a threatening eye.

Fortune, f. second to wisdom. See 'Wisdom, w. prevailing over chance - Wisdom and fortune combating together…'

Fortune, f. so far good but… - Thus far our fortune keeps an upward course …but… I spy a black, suspicious, threatening cloud…

Fortune, f. to be praised for good turnout of events - Well, if Fortune be a woman, she's a good wench for this gear.

Fortune, fickle - O fortune, fortune! all men call thee fickle.

Fortune, friendship and their relationship - When Fortune, in her shift and change of mood, spurns down her late beloved…

Fortune, hoping in a redress of f. See first line of 'Death, effects of d. – … and shake the yoke of inauspicious stars from this world-wearied flesh.'

Fortune, gifts of f. uneven and unequal - … the bountiful blind woman doth most mistake in her gift.

Fortune, invocation - Fortune, good night: smile once more: turn thy wheel!

Fortune, luck found in number 3 or in odd numbers - I hope good luck lies in odd numbers.

Fortune, luck will do the selection - .. in a moment, fortune shall call forth out of one side her happy minion..

Fortune, meditation on the fall of f. - This is the state of man; today he puts forth the tender leaves of hope…

Fortune, men show respect and loyalty only to the rich and fortunate - … for men, like butterflies show not their mealy wings but to the summer.

Fortune, mistreated by f. - A man whom both the waters and the wind…have made a ball for them to play upon.

Fortune, modest attitude towards f. – Since you will buckle fortune on my back.. I must have patience to endure the load.

Fortune, moment of unfavorable conditions due to astrological influences - There's some ill planet reigns…

Fortune, on the good side of f. - … Fortune is merry and in this mood will give us any thing.

Fortune, recollection of former f. - … The ruin speaks that sometime it was a worthy building.

Fortune, reversal of f. - … my good stars, that were my former guides, have empty left their orbs..

Fortune, reversal of f. and abandonment by friends - Thy friends are fled to wait upon thy foes and crossly to thy good all fortune goes.

Fortune, reversal of f. and the bright side of it - … and found the blessedness of being little.

Fortune, reversal of f. observed - … I see thy glory like a shooting star fall to the base earth from the firmament.

Fortune, reversal of f. vs. earlier ambitious claims– Now Phaethon hath tumbled from his car…

Fortune, role of f. in love an open question. See 'Love, l. tied to success or fortune? - For 'tis a question left us yet to prove whether love lead fortune, or else fortune love…'

Fortune, scratched by f. - … I am a man whom fortune hath cruelly scratched.

Fortune, sequence of events too good to be true - … (I) am ready to distrust mine eyes, and wrangle with my reason…

Fortune, she is your total f. - … the continent and summary of my fortune.

Fortune, unfriendly to the poor – Fortune, that arrant whore, ne'er turns the key to the poor.

Fortune, when f. down strength shows. See 'Person, worthiness of a p. shown under trial - … in the wind and tempest of her frown, distinction…'

Fortune, wish of good f. - … and fortune play upon thy prosperous helm as thy auspicious mistress!

Fortune's fool – O, I am fortune's fool.

Foul deeds exposed, See 'Hypocrisy, h. and dishonesty exposed - foul deeds will rise though all the world o'erwhelm them, to men's eyes'.

Foul play suspected – All is not well; I doubt some foul play.

Foul whisperings are abroad… See 'Whisperings, w. about bad deeds - Foul whisperings are abroad, unnatural deeds do breed unnatural troubles.'

Fox, f. guarding the chickens. See 'Misjudgment, m. in the selection of a controller, overseer, accountant or similar - .. thou hast entertained a fox, to be the shepherd of thy lambs.'

Frailty, thy name is woman. See 'Woman, female frailty, invocation - Frailty, thy name is woman.'

France, French air prompts bragging - … this your air of France hath blown that vice in me…

France, uncomplimentary remark on F. or any place - France is a dog hole, and it no more merits the thread of a man's foot.

Freedom, as free as - … as free as heart can wish or tongue can tell.

Freedom, as free as - … free as mountain winds.

Freedom, f. as a personal achievement - … every bondman in his own hand bears the power to cancel his captivity.

Freedom, f. fighters or terrorists? - .. So often shall the knot of us be call'd the men that gave their country liberty.

Freedom, f. of the soul – Every subject's duty is the king's; but every subject's soul is his own.

Freedom, f. of the spirit has no obstacles - … Nor stony tower, nor walls of beaten brass…

Freedom, relocation in search of f. – Now go we in content to liberty…

French, a warning against their seductive techniques - Beware of them, Diana; their promises.. are not the things they go under.

French, f. language not understood - Speak 'pardon' as 'tis current in our land; the chopping French we do not understand.

French, knowledge of French a liability. See 'Foreign language, knowledge of French a liability - … he can speak French and therefore he is a traitor.'

French, the French are unreliable - Done like a Frenchman: turn, and turn again!

French, the French are unreliable - … we are in France, amongst a fickle wavering nation.

Freshness, like a rose - she looks as clear as morning roses newly wash'd with dew.

Freshness, like dew - … as fresh as morning dew distilled on flowers.

Friend, dear and honorable f. described. See 'Man, honorable Italian m. – … one in whom the ancient Roman honour more appears…'

Friend, f. or enemy? - .. But what compact mean you to have with us? Will you be prick'd in number of our friends…

Friend, one's soul chooses or elects someone to be a f. – Since my dear soul was mistress of her choice and could of men distinguish…

Friend, trusted f. – (He was) my book wherein my soul recorded the history of all her secret thoughts.

Friends and friendship. See 'Advice, a. on c

Friends, f. amazed and perplexed - … wild amazement hurries up and down the little number of your doubtful friends.

Friends, f. as wealth – I am wealthy in my friends

Friends, f. neglected, reason why. See 'Neglect explained - nor construe any further my neglect that poor Brutus…'

Friends, f. worse than enemies. See 'Enemies, why e. are better than friends - … my friends praise me and make an ass of me…'

Friends, not many words needed among f. - .. 'twixt such friends as we few words suffice.

Friends, ungrateful and mercenary f. - .. left me open, bare for every storm that blows.

Friendship and fortune. See 'Fortune, friendship and their relationship - When Fortune, in her shift and change of mood, spurns down her late beloved…'

Friendship, adoration more than f. See 'Adoration, a. not just friendship - I profess myself her adorer, not her friend.'

Friendship, continued help required and extended to friend - 'T is not enough to help the feeble up, but to support him after.

Friendship, disappointed and disillusionment with friends - O time most accurst, 'mongst all foes that a friend should be the worst!

Friendship, extreme f. - Methinks, I could deal kingdoms to my friends and ne'er be weary.

Friendship, f. and help assured - … If I do vow a friendship, I'll perform it to the last article.

Friendship, f. declared. - I have professed me thy friend, and I confess me knit to thy deserving with cables of perdurable toughness.

Friendship, f. guaranteed by wisdom - The amity that wisdom knits not, folly may easily untie.

Friendship, f. restoring optimism - But if the while I think on thee, dear friend, all losses are restored and sorrows end.

Friendship, f. secondary to love. See "Love, l. prevailing over friendship - Friendship is constant in all other things, save in the office and affairs of love…'

Friendship, f. should show some understanding - A friend should bear his friend's infirmities…

Friendship, f. should show some understanding. See 'Flattery, f. overlooks sin - A friendly eye could never see such faults…'

Friendship, f. shown and extended in difficult circumstances - I am not of that feather to shake off my friend when he most needs me.

Friendship, f. with woman leading to physical relationship - … to mingle friendship far is mingling bloods.

Friendship, questionable and insincere f. – For who not needs shall never lack a friend…

Friendship, strategic f. and tied to wealth - Every man will be thy friend whilst thou hast wherewith to spend..

Friendship, value of f. – ..would most resembled instruments hung up in their cases.

Frigidity, plea to cold lady – Titled goddess.. you are no maiden, but a monument..

From fairest creatures we desire increase… See 'Pregnancy, p. good - From fairest creatures we desire increase, that thereby beauty's rose may never die.'

Frown, f. by a powerful m. - … And who durst smile when Warwick bent his brow?

Frowning, see 'Expression, frowning to be expected - Prepare thy brow to frown.' -- 'Expression, come on relax - … unknit that threatening unkind brow'.

Frustration, f. relieved at the cost of retribution - .. I will ease my heart, albeit I make a hazard of my head.

Full Circle (An everyday expressions from Shakespeare.). See 'Destiny, revolving - The wheel is come full circle'.

Full many a glorious morning… See 'Nature, dawn, sun on the mountains - Full many a glorious morning have I seen, flatter the mountain top with sovereign eye…'

Fully equipped – With all appliances and means to boot…

Fun, f. behind one's back - … persevere, counterfeit sad looks, make mouths upon me when I turn my back..

Funding, inadequate funding for the project – There's but a shirt and a half in all my company…

Furniture, comfortable couch - … couch softer and sweeter than the lustful bed…

Fury, f. prevents rational thinking – Now he'll outstare the lightning … in that mood the dove will peck the estridge.

Fury. See entries for 'Anger', 'Angry', 'Rage'.

Future, attitude towards the f. - … for the life to come, I sleep out the thought of it.

Future, marred by the effect of current events - The woe's to come; the children yet unborn.

Future, sensing the f. in one moment - …and I feel now the future in the instant.

Future, the f. will tell – There are many events in the womb of time, which will be delivered.

Gain, g. assured under any circumstance – Sort how it will, I shall have gold for all.

Gain, g. from crime illusory - ... Who buys a minute's mirth to wail a week? Or sells eternity to get a toy?

Gains, dishonest gains self-destructive. See 'Argument, good a. but honest dealing is best - didst thou never hear that things ill got had ever bad success?'

Gains, ill gotten g. to be maintained with ill deeds - ... and he that stands upon a slippery place must be as boisterously maintain'd as gain'd.

Games, dice - .. and by the hazard of the spotted die...

Gardening, weed pulling – ...I will go root away the noisome weeds, which without profit suck the soil's fertility from wholesome flowers.

Garlic or onions. See 'Breath, how to avoid bad b. - ... eat no onion, nor garlic, for we are to utter sweet breath'

Garments needing to be worn to fit well - ... garments, cleave not to their mould but with the aid of use.

Gaze, turning away your g. - I am no loathsome leper; look on me.

Gem, she is a g. - But 'tis that miracle and queen of gems...

Generosity, an excess in g. a fine weakness - ...faults that are rich are fair.

Generosity, true g. See 'Gratitude, refusing payment or recompense for a previous favor or act of kindness - .. there's none can truly say he gives, if he receives.'

Genius, g. rewarded. See 'Inventiveness, i., wit and geniality rewarded - ...wit shall not go unrewarded while I am king of this country.'

Gentle thou art... See 'Approach, securing a way out - gentle thou art, therefore to be won...'

Gentlemen, true g. See 'Magnanimity, gentlemanship, lack of envy - ... for we are gentlemen that neither in our hearts nor outward eyes, envy the great, nor the low despise.'

Gesturing, acting - ... do not saw the air too much with your hand, thus, but use all gently.

Get rid of him. See entries for 'Kill him'

Gift, unexpected g. - I see, a man here needs not live by shifts, when in the street he meets such golden gifts.

Gifts, g. as means to a young woman's heart - ... trifles, nosegays, sweetmeats, messengers of strong prevailment in unharden'd youth.

Gifts, g. sometimes not welcome - .. to the noble mind rich gifts wax poor when givers prove unkind.

Gifts, poor g. due to poor fortune– ... one out of suits with fortune, that could give more, but that her hand lacks means.

Gifts. See entries for 'Jewelry'.

Girl (wench), looking forward to a chat - ...I love her ten times more than e'er I did: I love her ten times more than e'er I did: O, how I long to have some chat with her!

Girl, bad g. – I have sworn thee fair and thought thee bright who art as black as hell, as dark as night.

Girl, country g. See 'Queen, so to speak - ... she is the queen of curds and cream.'

Girlfriend, changing g. and why. See entries for 'Love, selection criteria for choosing between two loves established'

Girlfriend, g. turning night into day. See 'Night and morning reversed by her presence - 'tis fresh morning with me when you are by at night.'

Girlfriend, when you go out with your friend's g. – See 'Love, l. prevailing over friendship - Friendship is constant in all other things, save in the office and affairs of love...'

Girls, easy going g. warning about them - ... they appear to men like angels of light...

Give me the ocular proof: See 'Evidence, e.

required or else - ... give me the ocular proof: or by the worth of man's eternal soul…'

Give it an understanding, but no tongue. See 'Secret, injunction to keep the matter s. - ... whatsoever else shall hap to-night, give it an understanding, but no tongue.'

Give the devil his due – ... the devil shall have his bargain… : he will give the devil his due.

Giving it away. See 'Disguise, d. discovered - there is a kind of confession in your looks'.

Giving up - ... deeper than did ever plummet sound I'll drown my book.

Glories, days of g. remembered. See 'Fortune, recollection of former f. - ... The ruin speaks that sometime it was a worthy building.'

Glories, the time of past g. – ... in former golden days…

Glory, g. and honor. See 'Introduction, i. to a speaker with impressive background – ... that once trod the ways of glory and sounded all the depths and shoals of honour.'

Glory, g. quickly vanishes. See 'Success, s. always temporary, dangers of over-extension - Glory is like a circle in the water, which never ceaseth to enlarge itself…'

Glory, there is g. in dying for a good cause - He lives in fame that died in virtue's cause.

Glove, wishing to be a g. See 'Cheek, wishing to be a glove to fit her hand to touch her c. .. o, that I were a glove upon that hand…'

Glow. See "Beauty, radiant - most radiant, exquisite, unmatchable beauty'

Glow-worm, its light fading in the light of dawn. See 'Nature, dawn approaching – The glow-worm shows the matin to be near

Go away. See entries for 'Insult, go away'.

Goal, see entries for 'Achievement'.

God! that one might read the book of fate… See 'Prediction, desire to know in advance'

God, g. responsible for victory - Thy arm was here; and not to us, but to thy arm alone, ascribe we all.

God, g's work inscrutable. See 'Results, great r. from small resources - He that of greatest works is finisher, oft does them by the weakest minister.'

Gods, g. dealing with our ignorance. See 'Ignorance, i. of what is really good for us - We, ignorant of ourselves beg often our own harms, which the wise powers deny us for our good…'

Gods, their effects on our power of judgment. See 'Self-destruction compounded by incorrect judgment - ... when we in our own viciousness grow hard... the wise Gods seal our eyes…'

Gods, their qualified assistance - If the great gods be just, they shall assist the deeds of justest men.

Gods, what makes them different from men. See 'Man, m's nature, his faults separate him from the Gods - ... but you, gods, will give us some faults to make us men.'

Gold, comparing a man to g. to test his mettle. See 'Testing, t. the skill or determination of a man – ... now do I play the touch, if thou be current gold indeed.'

Gold, corrupting effects of g. - O thou sweet king-killer, and dear divorce 'twixt natural son and sire!…

Gold, corrupting effects of g. – Thus much of this will make black white, foul fair, wrong right, base noble, old young, coward valiant….

Gold, corrupting even saints. See lines in 'Woman, impregnable – She will not stay the siege of loving terms, nor bide…'

Gold, effects of g. in overlooking a person's liabilities – Hortensio, peace! thou know'st not gold's effect…

Gold, g. as an object of idolatry – What a god's gold, that he is worshipp'd in a baser temple than where swine feed!

Gold, g. as powerful tool of corruption – ... gold were as good as twenty orators and will, no doubt, tempt him to anything.

Gold, g. b

Gold, g. can corrupt authority. See 'Authority, corrupted by gold - .. and though authority be a stubborn bear, yet he is oft led by the nose with gold.'

Gold, power of g. to buy access. – 'Tis gold which buys admittance

Gold. See 'Appearances, a, deceiving – all that glisters is not g

Good and bad, inability to distinguish between g. and bad - … can we not partition make with spectacles so precious 'twixt fair and foul?

Good and bad relative. See 'Thought, t. as the arbiter of good or bad - .. for there is nothing either good or bad, but thinking makes it so.'

Good morning. See 'Time, morning, is it really morning? - Is the day so young?'

Good news and bad news. See

Good news, longing to hear good n. See 'News, invitation to disclose (good) news - ram though thy fruitful tidings in mine ears, that long time have been barren.'

Good night – As sweet repose and rest come to thy heart as that within my breast!

Good night - Enjoy the honey-heavy dew of slumber.

Good night – Fair thoughts be your fair pillow.

Good night – Sleep dwell upon thine eyes, peace in thy breast!

Good night. See entries for 'Salutations and wishes'.

Good night. See 'Separation temporarily postponed - Good night, good night! parting is such sweet sorrow…'

Good reasons must, of course, give place to better. See 'Reasons, good r. yielding to better r. '

Good, finding good in bad - Thus may we gather honey from the weed and make a moral of the devil himself.

Good, from good to bad worse than from bad to good. See 'Bad, from bad to good better than from good to bad - … The lamentable change is from the best; the worst returns to laughter'.

Good, one out of ten - Among nine bad if one be good, there's yet one good in ten.

Good, what g. does not need propping – Good alone is good without a name. Vileness is so…

Good-bye, cordial - If we do meet again, why, we shall smile; if not, why then, this parting was well made.

Good-bye, when she is leaving for a short or long trip, or a shopping excursion - Let all the number of the stars give light to thy fair way.

Good-bye, when you really hate to leave - Good night, good night! parting is such sweet sorrow..

Goodness, g. of character as a preserver of beauty. See 'Beauty, b. preservation and its relationship with goodness of character - the hand that hath made you fair hath made you good…'

Goodness, g. poorly repaid - Undone by goodness! Strange, unusual blood, when man's worst sin is, he does too much good!

Goodness' sake - For goodness' sake, consider what you do..

Good night sweet prince. See 'Eulogy – Now cracks a noble heart. Good night sweet prince…'

Gossip, g. about celebrities - What great ones do, the less will prattle of.

Government, despicable g. or administration. See 'Invocation, despicable administration - hell is empty and all the devils are here.'

Government, foreign g. support of home tyranny - For how can tyrants safely govern home, unless abroad they purchase great alliance?

Government, good ruler defined by the goodness of his g. - … He is a happy king, since he gains from his subjects the name of good by his government.

Government, imperialistic g. See "Foreign

policy, war to cover up internal problems - Be it thy course to busy giddy minds with foreign quarrels.'

Government, puppet g. See 'Subservience - ... and bend the dukedom yet unbow'd... to most ignoble stooping.'

Government, tyrannical g. and its effect on the country,. See 'Country, c. in poor state, only the ignorant smile - ... where nothing, but who knows nothing, is once seen to smile.'

Grace me no grace, nor uncle me no uncle. See 'Courtesy, false c.'

Grace, compared to the best herb in a salad - she was the sweet marjoram of the salad, or rather, the herb of grace.

Grace, men's g. or benevolence or approval momentary. See 'Philosophical considerations. Uselessness of coveting earthly fortunes as fortune is so prone to change - O momentary grace of mortal men which we more hunt for than the grace of God...'

Grace, presence, speech - .. Possess'd with such a gentle sovereign grace, of such enchanting presence and discourse.

Grace, uniqueness, alternate salad comparison. See 'Character, excellent person and one in a thousand – we may pick a thousand salads ere we light on such another herb.'

Graces, her g. and virtues - Her virtues graced with external gifts do breed love's settled passions in my heart...

Graffiti, g. on tree barks - ... and in their barks my thoughts I'll character

Graffiti, questionable romantic g. See 'Poetry, p. of very questionable taste - Let no face be kept in mind but the face of Rosalind.'

Graphics, picture as a substitute - Vouchsafe me yet your picture for my love, picture that is hanging in your chamber.

Graphology, g and an occasion for a compliment – ...and whiter than the paper it writ on is the fair hand that writ.

Gratitude - ... only I have left to say more is thy due than more than all can pay.

Gratitude, beyond g. – ... thou art so far before that swiftest wing of recompense is slow...

Gratitude, commitment to demonstrate g. - ... and creep time ne'er so slow, yet it shall come from me to do thee good.

Gratitude, extent of g. limited by circumstances - ... all my treasury is yet but unfelt thanks.

Gratitude, extent of g. limited by circumstances - My recompense is thanks, and that's all, yet my good will is great, though the gift small.

Gratitude, g. and praise. See 'Praise, p. and gratitude - A god on earth thou art.'

Gratitude, g. and promise of reward - ... If fortune serve me, I'll requite this kindness.

Gratitude, g. expressed and responded to - ... To be acknowledged, madam, is o'erpaid.

Gratitude, g. expressed and responded to. - Too little payment for so great a debt.

Gratitude, g. expressed and responded to - Your presence makes us rich, most noble lord and far surmounts our labour to attain it.

Gratitude, g. and promise of reward to good friends – I count myself in nothing else so happy as in a soul remembering my good friends.

Gratitude, g. expressed for welcome - ... I am not of many words, but I thank you.

Gratitude, g. expressed to team for good work - I thank you all, For doughty-handed are you, and have fought not as you served the cause...

Gratitude, g. expressed with accompanying tears - I have a kind soul, that would give you thanks and knows not how to do it, but with tears.

Gratitude, g. expressed with commitment to a reward - I give thee thanks in part of thy deserts and will with deeds requite thy gentleness.

Gratitude, g. for good news – The gods bless you for your tidings, next …

Gratitude, g. for honor received – I have received much honour by your presence and ye shall find me thankful.

Gratitude, g. recognized and expressed – … within this wall of flesh there is a soul that counts thee her creditor.

Gratitude, g. to Jupiter and stars – Jove and my stars be praised!"

Gratitude, g. towards noble men - .. and thanks to men of noble minds is honourable meed.

Gratitude, modesty in expressing g. – Too little payment for so great a debt

Gratitude, no need to return favor - The service and the loyalty I owe in doing it, pays itself.

Gratitude, refusing payment or recompense for a previous favor or act of kindness - .. there's none can truly say he gives, if he receives.

Grave. See 'Death, grave as a place of peace - … here are no storms, no noise, but silence and eternal sleep.'

Great griefs, I see, medicine the less. See 'Sorrows, graduation in s. '

Greatness, acquisition of g. - Some are born great, some have greatness thrust upon them.

Greatness, advantages of g. questionable – … 'tis better to be lowly born and range with humble livers in content…

Greatness, g. falling with falling fortune - 'T is certain, greatness, once fall'n out with fortune must fall out with men too.

Greatness, g. self-conscious - … greatness knows itself…

Greatness, good-bye g. See 'Fortune, meditation on the fall of f.'– 'Resignations, after resigning or being fired' *** 'Fortune, reversal of f. and the bright side of it' – 'Invocation, misplaced ambition, see the results'

Greatness, longing for g. natural to man. See 'Man, compared to a bird soaring high - .. man and birds are fain of climbing high.'

Greed, g. disclaimed - … I would not have you to think that my desire of having is the sin of covetousness.

Greed, g., covetousness and desire for more - Those that much covet are with gain so fond…

Greed, gold provokes g. – How quickly nature falls into revolt, when gold becomes her object!

Greed, more calling for more - … and my more having would be as a sauce to make me hunger more..

Greed, wanting more - Hast thou not worldly pleasure at command, above the reach or compass of thy thought?

Green-eyed monster. See 'Jealousy, j. as a monster and to be avoided - T'is the green-eyed monster, which doth mock the eat it feeds on'

Greeting, g. an unexpected visitor while you are down in the dumps - What art thou? and how comest thou hither..

Greetings, answer to early morning greetings – What early tongue so sweet saluteth me?

Greetings, end of unhappiness – Now is the winter of our discontent, made glorious summer by this sun of York..

Greetings, g. and wishes - Most excellent accomplished lady, the heavens rain odours on you!

Greyhounds. See 'Men, one word catch all - … in the catalogue ye go for men…' *** 'Run, time to r. - like a brace of greyhounds … are at our backs.' *** 'Eager and ready to go – I see you stand like greyhounds in the slips, straining upon the start.'

Grief, burning g. - …I have that honourable grief lodged here which burns worse than tears drown.

Grief, g. at being forced to resign - You may my glories and my state depose, but not my griefs; still am I king of those.

1154

Grief, demonstrations of g. - And some will mourn in ashes, some coal-black…

Grief, g. and anxiety magnifying fears - … shapes of grief, more than himself, to wail which, look'd on as it is, is nought but shadows of what it is not.

Grief, g. easily turning to joy and viceversa. See 'Man, very emotional m., characteristics of - Where joy most revels, grief doth most lament; grief joys, joy grieves, on slender accident.'

Grief, g. excessive - Some grief shows much of love but much of grief shows some want of wit.

Grief, g. immeasurable - … my particular grief is of so flood-gate and o'erbearing nature …

Grief, g. kept inside – … my grief lies all within and these external manners of laments…

Grief, g. makes time seem long. - … grief makes one hour ten.

Grief, g. softens the mind - Oft have I heard that grief softens the mind…

Grief, g. soothed by grieving, and not cheerful company – Grief best is pleased with grief's society:..

Grief, g. that outlasts death – … my grief stretches itself beyond the hour of death… the unguided days and rotten times that you shall look upon…

Grief, real g. is all inside - … my grief lies all within, and these external manners of laments…

Grievances, g. aired out - Windy attorneys to their client's woes …. let them have scope.

Grievances, ready to listen to g. - … Then in my tent, Cassius, enlarge your griefs and I will give you audience.

Group, g. of bad people agreeing on something bad - Shameful is this league!

Growing up together - … Like to a double cherry, seeming parted, but yet an union in partition.

Guarantee, personal g. – … let the forfeit be nominated for an equal pound of your fair flesh…

Guardian, poor choice of g. See 'Misjudgment, m. in the selection of a controller, overseer, accountant or similar - … thou hast entertained a fox, to be the shepherd of thy lambs.'

Guessing, refusal to g. due to previous mistakes (in guessing) - …I have found my self in my uncertain grounds to fail as often as I guessed.

Guilt, admission of g. and remorse - O Brakenbury, I have done those things, which now bear evidence against my soul.

Guilt, admit your g. and be honest - Now if you can blush and cry guilty, cardinal, you'll show a little honesty.

Guilt, evidence of g. visible in expression - The image of a wicked heinous fault lives in his eye.

Guilt, extreme admission of g. - … Wrong hath but wrong, and blame the due of blame

Guilt, g. evident without need for a verbal confession - … guiltiness will speak, though tongues were out of use.

Guilt, g. for wasting t. See 'Time, sense of guilt at wasting t. - I feel me much to blame so idly to profane the precious time…

Guilt, g. generates fear - So full of artless jealousy is guilt, it spills itself in fearing to be spilt.

Guilt, g. proven by evidence. See 'Evidence, e. showing shame and guilt - that argues but the shame of your offence'.

Guilt, guilty but not through recklessness - … your fault was not your folly.

Guilt, guilty by connivance or fear. See 'Compassion, perfunctory c. cannot exempt from responsibility – … And water cannot wash away your sin.'

Guilt, invitation to admit g. - … bear not along the clogging burthen of a guilty soul…

Guilt, sense of g. – … Though inclination be as sharp as will…

Guilt, tempter or tempted guiltier - The

tempter or the tempted, who sins most, ha?

Guitarist, praising a g. by comparing him to Orpheus. See 'Music, power of m. - ...whose golden touch could soften steel and stones.'

Gullibility. See 'Mass, m. psychology, following thoughtlessly - They'll take suggestion as a cat laps milk; they'll tell the clock to any business that we say befits the hour.

Habit, h. can change character. See 'Character, habit can change c. - for use almost can change the stamp of nature and either quell the devil, or throw him out with wondrous potency.'

Habit, h. formation – How use doth breed a habit in a man!

Habit, not yet used to flattery and submission – ... hardly yet have learn'd to insinuate, flatter, bow, and bend my limbs

Habit, personal h. - ...(I am) one that converses more with the buttock of the night than with the forehead of the morning.

Had I but died an hour... See 'Event, course of e. completely changing your outlook on life'

Hair, a blonde – ... her sunny locks hang on her temples like a golden fleece.

Hair, artificial hair - So are those crisped snaky golden locks ..the skull that bred them in the sepulchre.

Hair, as tempting cobweb - A golden mesh to entrap the hearts of men..

Hair, dealing with thinning hair or baldness. See entries for 'Baldness'

Hair, false h. See 'Wig, not true hair – ... the dowry of a second head, the skull that bred them in the sepulchre.

Hair, h. color as a tool for seduction – Her hair is auburn, mine is perfect yellow: if that be all the difference in his love...

Hair, some gray in it, but you still have the vigor of youth . See 'Age, graying hair does not imply less brain power - .. though grey do something mingle with our younger brown, yet have we a brain…..

Hair, unkempt. See 'Beard, b. unkempt (but also hair) - ...beard made rough and rugged, like to the summer's corn by tempest lodged.

Haircut, no h. for a while - Unscissor'd shall this hair of mine remain.

Halcyon days – Expect Saint Martin's summer, halcyon days…

Halloween, h. material - .. Nature seems dead, and wicked dreams abuse the curtain'd sleep…

Halloween, h. material - Upon the corner of the moon there hangs a vaporous drop profound…

Hand and hand kissing - If I profane with my unworthiest hand this holy shrine, the gentle sin is this - my lips, two blushing pilgrims, ready stand..

Hand, her h. an occasion to extol her beauty - The fairest hand I ever touched! O beauty, till now I never knew thee.

Hand, her h. epitome of whiteness - O, that hand, in whose comparison all whites are ink…

Hand, kissing of h. as a means to be remembered - O, could this kiss be printed in thy hand, that thou mightst think upon this as a seal…

Hand, request to kiss her h. - Behold this man, commend unto his lips thy favouring hand.

Hand, snow-white - ... To the snow-white hand of the most beauteous Lady Rosaline.

Hand, white– as soft as dove's down and as white as it…

Hand, worthy to be kissed by kings – ... a hand that kings have lipped, and trembled kissing.

Handling, proper h. of an execution or firing - Let's carve him as a dish fit for the gods..

Hands, beautiful, like lilies - ... those lily hands tremble, like aspen-leaves, upon a lute, and make the silken strings delight to kiss them.

Hands (metaphor) unstained with kindred

blood - His hands were guilty of no kindred blood, but bloody with the enemies of his kin.

Hands, white - That pure congealed white, high Taurus' snow… turns to a crow, when thou hold'st up thy hand.

Hangover, recovery from. See 'Answering, buying time to answer - the charm dissolves apace… mantle their clearer reason.'

Happiness, feigned h. - I am not merry; but I do beguile the thing I am, by seeming otherwise.

Happiness, h. and its relationship to hope. See 'Hope, h. comparable to actual enjoyment - And hope to joy is little less in joy than hope enjoy'd'.

Happiness, h. at last - And happily I have arrived at the last unto the wished haven of my bliss.

Happiness, h. beyond description - I cannot speak enough of this content; it stops me here; it is too

Happiness, h. beyond endurance - If this be so, the gods do mean to strike me to death with mortal joy.

Happiness, h. described as a human figure dressed in best garments - Happiness courts thee in her best array.

Happiness, h. expressed with silence. See 'Silence, s. as a symptom or evidence of happiness - Silence is the perfectest herald of joy, I were but little happy, if I could say how much.'

Happiness, h. in simplicity - … my crown is called content: a crown it is that seldom kings enjoy.

Happiness, h. not secured by titles or fame - Princes have but their tides for their glories… an outward honour for an inward toil.

Happiness, h. or peace of mind, farewell to - Farewell the tranquil mind! farewell content!

Happiness, h. overwhelming – …this great sea of joys…. drown me with their sweetness.

Happiness, h, overwhelming and incredible - If it be thus to dream, still let me sleep!

Happiness, h. seen through another man's eyes a bitter experience - … how bitter a thing it is to look into happiness through another man's eyes.

Happiness, contrast of happiness with personal unhappiness - the apprehension of the good gives but the greater feeling to the worse.

Happiness, in a state of h. - … turns to a wild of nothing, save of joy..

Happiness, in a state of happy confusion - … there is such confusion in my powers…

Happiness, promise of return to h. - ..The liquid drops of tears that you have shed shall come again, transform'd to orient pearl.

Happiness, road to h. via applied philosophy - … that part of philosophy will I apply that treats of happiness by virtue specially to be achieved.

Happiness, supreme and unsurpassable - … If it were now to die, 't were now to be most happy…

Happiness, unbearable h. - … the gods do mean to strike me to death with mortal joy.

Happy days expected. See 'Halcyon days – Expect Saint Martin's summer, halcyon days…' *** 'Salutations and wishes - Many years of happy days befal …'

Happy that you are here. See 'Presence, giving happiness and pleasure - Your presence glads our days.'

Happy with leftovers - .. I shall think it a most plenteous crop to glean the broken ears after the man that the main harvest reaps.

Happy with yourself - Shine out, fair sun, till I have bought a glass, that I may see my shadow, as I pass.

Harassment, handling of sexual h. - … I am too mean to be your queen, and yet too good to be your concubine.

Harassment, handling of sexual h. - What love, think'st thou, I sue so much to get?..

Harassment, stop harassing me - .. leave to afflict my heart: sorrow and grief have vanquished all my powers.

Hard worker. See 'Dedication, d. and spirituality - .. Not dallying with a brace of courtezans, but meditating with two deep divines…'

Hardiness, h. acquired via a rough life - Plenty and peace breeds cowards: hardness ever of hardiness is mother.

Harmony, heavenly harmony generator. See 'Music, m. queen – This is the patroness of heavenly harmony.'

Harp not on that string. See 'Insist, do not i. - Harp not on that string, madam; that is past.'

Harpy, h. of a woman. See 'Woman, evil w. like a harpy - .. to betray, dost, with thine angel's face seize with thine eagle's talons'. *** 'Woman, anything but talking with her – (Anything) rather than hold three words' conference with this harpy.'

Haste, counting what has not yet been achieved - But yet I run before my horse to market…

Haste, over h. – The mellow plum doth fall, the green sticks fast…

Hat. See 'Ornaments, enhancing a divine beauty - Sweet ornament, that decks a thing divine.'

Hate, h. not deserved - To plead for love deserves more fee than hate.

Hate, just hearing the name. See 'Name, psychosomatic and/or negative reaction at just hearing a n. - I am whipp'd and scourg'd with rods, Nettled and stung with pismires…'

Hate, h. removed and changed in love - ... my heart is purged from grudging hate: and with my hand I seal my true heart's love.

Hate, strong h. replacing strong love. See 'Love, how l. betrayed turns to hate – Sweet love, I see, changing his property turns to the sourest and most deadly hate.'

Hate, you cannot stand any of them - The sight of any of the house of York is as a fury to torment my soul.

Hateful, I hate you as I hate hell - I hate the word, as I hate hell, all Montagues and thee.

Hateful - .. she did confess was as a scorpion to her sight.

Hating just to look at it - It is a basilisk unto mine eye, kills me to look on't.

Hatred, h. declared - I do hate him as I do hell pains.

Hatred, h. expressed in terms of opposites - All form is formless, order orderless, save what is opposite to England's love.

Hatred, h. mixed with pity - ... but that I hate thee deadly I should lament thy miserable state.

Hatred, h. of the world - … had I power, I should pour the sweet milk of concord into hell…

Hatred, mutual h. - … Not Afric owns a serpent I abhor more than thy fame and envy.

Hatred, shared h. – All the commons hate him perniciously… wish him ten fathom deep.

Have we eaten on the insane root… See 'Madness, isn't this m.? – … have we eaten on the insane root that takes the reason prisoner?

Have you forgotten me? See 'Forgetting - I have forgot all men; then, if thou grant'st thou'rt a man, I have forgot thee.'

Have you forgotten this or so & so? See 'Forgetting, cannot forget what not remembered – That is not forgot which never did I remember.'

Have you not finished yet? See 'Patience, p. and time management required - How poor are they that have not patience!…'

Hawk, h. or falcon observed – A falcon, towering in her pride of place.

Hawk, h. or falcon as symbol of the aspirations of man. See 'Man, compared to a bird soaring high - … man and birds are fain of climbing high.'

Hazard of the die. See 'Character, not afraid of taking chances - I have set my life upon a cast and I will stand the hazard of the die.'

He draweth out the thread of his verbosity finer than the staple of his argument. See 'Man, a verbose m.'

He is a very dog to the communalty. See 'Political stand, an extreme right winger - … he is a very dog to the communalty.'

He is well paid that is well satisfied…See 'Satisfaction, s. as payment.'

He jests at scars that never felt a wound. See 'Love, l.'s pains not to be laughed at'

He hath eaten me out of house and home. See 'Exploitation - .. He hath eaten me out of house and home'.

He's winding up the watch of his wit. See 'Speech, gaining time before speaking up - … he's winding up the watch of his wit, by and by it will strike.'

He that will have a cake out of the wheat, must tarry the grinding. See 'Persistence, your persistence has paid off '

He tires betimes, who spurs too fast betimes. See 'Vanity, v. and heedlessness in a leader'

Head-piece, heavy hp - … if their heads had any intellectual armour, they could never wear such heavy head pieces.

Health, banning of obesity - I'll exhibit a bill in parliament for the putting down of fat men.

Health, banter about state of h. See 'Soundness, different kind of s. - .. not as one would say, healthy; but so sound as things that are hollow.'

Health, care an enemy to good h. - I am sure care's an enemy to life.

Health, dieting. See 'Dieting, how to refuse when offered more food - … … dainty bits make rich the ribs, but bankrupt quite the wits.'

Health, good eating habits, good digestion disrupted by arguing - Unquiet meals make ill digestion.

Health, laughter as a medicine - With mirth and laughter let old wrinkles come and let my liver rather heat with wine…

Health, on being sound. See 'Soundness, different kind of s. - .. not as one would say, healthy; but so sound as things that are hollow'

Health, physical and mental h. of leader key to safety - The lives of all your loving complices lean on your health..

Health, poor h. attributable to poor diet. See 'Health-care, effects of a bad diet - O, he hath kept an evil diet long, and overmuch consumed his royal person..'

Health care, a good psychologist – … The quiet of my wounded conscience, thou art a cure fit for a king.

Health-care, advantages of lightheartedness or positive thinking. See 'Age. Longevity promoted by lightheartedness - a light heart lives long.'

Health-care, advice and medicine can ensure recovery. See 'Company, commercial c. in poor but recoverable shape - It is but as a body yet distemper'd, which to his former strength may be restored.'

Health-care, avoiding too much sugar. See 'Dieting, too much sugar, excess brings distaste - …a surfeit of the sweetest things the deepest loathing to the stomach brings.'

Health-care, bad doctors. See 'Doctors, d. that procured the illness - … careless patient as thou art, commit'st thy anointed body to the cure of those physicians that first wounded thee.'

Health-care, beef harmful. See 'Vegetarian, better to be a v. - … but I am a great eater of beef, and I believe that does harm my wit.'

Health-care, ease at getting upset as a cause for hepatitis – Why should a man sleep when he wakes and creep into the jaundice by being peevish?

Health-care, effects of a bad diet - O, he hath kept an evil diet long, and overmuch consumed his royal person.

Health-care, exposure to night cold air

unadvisable if already affected by a respiratory ailment – To dare the vile contagion of the night.

Health-care, exposure to night temperature. See 'Night, stormy n. hard to bear - The tyranny of the open night's too rough for nature to endure.'

Health-care, herbal remedies – Within the infant rind of this small flower …

Health-care, mental - … a turn or two I'll walk, to still my beating mind.

Health-care, nutrition - Things sweet to taste prove in digestion sour.

Health-care, nutrition – A little more than a little, is by much too much.

Health-care, nutrition. See entries for 'Dieting'.

Health-care, positive mental attitude a tool to longevity. See 'Melancholy, m. an evil influence and an enemy to health – … frame your mind to mirth and merriment, which bars a thousand harms, and lengthens life.'

Health-care, psychological, temperance. See 'Temperance, t. as a cure - … temperance; that's the appliance only which your disease requires.'

Health-care, recreation necessary for healthy life - Sweet recreation barred, what doth ensue…

Health-care, request for psychological remedy – Canst thou not minister to a mind diseased…

Health-care, rest as medicine - Our foster-nurse of nature is repose, the which he lacks

Health-care, ritual denial of death - … sick men, when their deaths be near…

Health-care, upset stomach - Prithee, do not turn me about; my stomach is not constant.

Health-care, vegetarianism to preserve intelligence. See 'Vegetarian, better to be a v. - .. but I am a great eater of beef, and I believe that does harm my wit'.

Health-care, walking. See 'Walking, w. as a relaxation exercise - … a turn or two I'll walk to still my beating mind.'

Health-care, wine as an anti-depressant. See 'Wine, w. as an anti-depressant - Give me a bowl of wine, I have not the alacrity of spirit nor cheer of mind that I as wont to have.'

Health-care, wounded. See 'Wounded and in need of a band aid - But I am faint, my gashes cry for help'

Hearing, h. improved by darkness. See 'Nature, night, decreases visibility and sharpens hearing - Dark night that from the eye his function takes, the ear more quick of apprehension makes…'

Hearing, do you hear me? – Your tale, sir, would cure deafness.

Hearing with eyes. See 'Love, detection possible without verbal evidence - O learn to read what silent love hath writ…'

Heart, h. corrupted by custom – … if damned custom have not brass'd it so that it is proof and bulwark against sense.

Heart, h. in misery - … my heart, all mad with misery, beats in this hollow prison of my flesh.

Heart, h. in turmoil - ... the windy tempest of my heart

Heart, h. of stone. See 'Rejection, heart of stone - I have said too much unto a heart of stone…'

Heart, h. overwhelmed by passion. See 'Passion overwhelming the heart - Why does my blood thus muster to my heart…'

Heart, h. turned to stone. See entries for 'Pity, pitiless, heart turned to stone' *** 'Cruelty'

Heart, h. wounded by eyes of lady. See 'Sigh - (my heart) wounded it is, but with the eyes of a lady.'

Heart, heartbreaking discovery - This blows my heart if swift thought break it not, a swifter mean shall outstrike thought.

Heart, positive self appraisal and advertisement - … a good heart, Kate, is the sun and the moon…

Heart, question about heartlessness – Is

there any cause in nature that makes these hard hearts?

Heart, sad h. and in a state of depression.. See 'Sadness, s. and misery'.

Heart, voice of the h. - What my tongue dares not, that my heart shall say…

Heartbreak - O heart, heavy heart, why sigh'st thou without breaking?

Heartlessness. See 'Indifference, heartlessness – .. you recount your sorrows to a stone.'

Heat, virtual h. – (Who can) wallow naked in December snow by thinking on fantastic summer's heat?

Heaven on earth - A heaven on earth I won, by wooing thee.

Heaven walking on earth - Here comes the countess: now heaven walks on earth.

Heaven, she makes heaven light up. See 'Party, many fine ladies expected - look to behold this night earth treading stars, that make dark heaven light.'

Heavenly powers, obedience to h. powers - We cannot but obey the powers above us.

Heavens, h. restraining the extremes of inhumanity - … Humanity must perforce prey on itself like monsters of the deep.

Heavens, tempting the h. - But wherefore did you so much tempt the heavens?..

Hell, automatic insurance protection - … the devil will not have me damned, lest the oil that's in me should set hell on fire.

Hell, ready to go to h. See 'Punishment and condemnation - My hour is almost come, when I to sulphurous and tormenting flames must render up myself.'

Hell, you make earth hell - …Thou camest on earth to make the earth my hell.

Help, asking to put a word on your behalf - … let me have thy voice in my behalf.

Help, determination to h. beyond what one would do for him/herself – What I can do I will; and more I will than for myself I dare.

Help, h. assumed but not certain. See 'Speculation, s. on uncertain help or aid, unwise – Conjecture, expectation, and surmise of aids incertain should not be admitted.'

Help, h. assured - what I can help thee to, thou shalt not miss.

Help, h. denied. See 'Financing, f. denied - They have all been touch'd and found base metal…'

Help, h. continued for the weak. See 'Friendship, continued help required and extended to friend - 'T is not enough to help the feeble up, but to support him after.'

Help, h. inadequate - The help of one stands me in little stead.

Help, h. limited. See 'Pity, no other help possible but p. - No good at all that I can do for him, unless you call it good to pity him.'

Help, h. offered - … tell thy grief, it shall be eased, if France can yield relief.

Help, h. on the way - Be not dismay'd for succour is at hand.

Help, h. sought from heavens to escape from dreadful place - … some heavenly power guide us out of this fearful country.

Help, request for h. and counsel. See 'Advice, request for a. from capable person - Counsel me Tranio, for I know thou canst…'

Help, request for h. unexpectedly rejected - … shut his bosom against our borrowing prayers.

Help, seeking h. in secret - … and thence it is that I to your assistance do make love: masking the business from the common eye for sundry weighty reasons.

Help, unreliable h. See 'Ally, shaky a. - What shalt thou expect, to be depender on a thing that leans'.

Helplessness, h. due to circumstances. See 'Measure, inevitable m. - There is no help; the bitter disposition of the time will have it so.'

Helter-Skelter – And helter-skelter have I rode to thee…

Hepatitis, h. or liver problems. See 'Health-care, ease at getting upset as a cause for hepatitis – Why should a man sleep when he wakes and creep into the jaundice by being peevish?'

Herb, see Character, excellent person and one in a thousand – we may pick a thousand salads ere we light on such another herb.'

Herb, herbal medicine. See 'Medicine, alternative m, efficacy of - mickle is the powerful grace, that lies in plants, herbs, stones, and their true qualities…'

Heroism, victory or death. See "Victory, v. or nothing - Either our history shall with full mouth speak freely of our acts…'

Hesitation, h. to deliver n. or unusual information. See 'News, information, hesitation to deliver - I should report that which I say I saw but know not how to do it.'

Hiding something - … the quality of nothing hath not such need to hide itself…

History, h. is but our opinion on events, (or someone else's). See 'Interpretation, i. is all - So our virtues lie in the interpretation of the time.. One fire drives out one fire; one nail, one nail… '

History, h. written by the winner. See 'Victory, v. makes everything seem good - nothing can seem foul to those that win'.

History, each man has a h. See 'Life, l.'s history of a person as a predictor of future performance – There is a history in all men's lives'.

History, h. being made. See 'Event, e. of historical importance - How many ages hence shall this, our lofty scene be acted over, in states unborn..'

History, incredible h. – If I should tell my history, it would seem like lies disdained in the reporting.

History, knowledge of h. valuable. See 'Age, a. inevitably engenders wisdom - .. Instructed by the antiquary times, he must be, he is, he cannot be but wise.'

History, short period of h. but pregnant with consequences - Small time, but in that small most greatly lived this star of England.

Holiday, continuous h. tedious. See 'Tediousness, t. in everything being always the same – If all the year were playing holidays, to sport would be as tedious as to work.'

Homeland security. See 'Paranoia - There is a plot against my life, my crown; all's true that is mistrusted' *** "Conspiracy – … Open-eyed conspiracy his time doth take …'

Honest, sometimes h. See 'Character, c. occasionally honest - though I am not naturally honest, I am so sometimes by chance.'

Honesty, an honest Athenian as a physical impossibility - … if doing nothing be death by the law...

Honesty, h. a rare quality - .. to be honest, as this world goes, is to be one man picked out of ten thousand.

Honesty, h. as a fault - Every man has his faults, and honesty is his; I have told him on it; but I could never get it from it.

Honesty, h. as a liability. See 'Invocation, i. about honesty - O wretched fool, that livest to make thine honesty a vice!' *** 'World, pessimistic view of the w. and its inherent evil - I am in this earthly world; where to do harm is often laudable…'

Honesty, h. as a questionable virtue - … what a fool Honesty is! and Trust, his sworn brother, a very simple gentleman!

Honesty, h. best legacy - …and no legacy is so rich as honesty.

Honesty, h. compatible with wisdom? See 'Behavior, wise or honest - I should be wise, for honesty's a fool and loses that it works for.'

Honesty, h. emptying threats. See 'Threats, idle t. - There is no terror, Cassius, in your threats…'

Honesty, h. in the world presaging doomsday – … the world's grown honest… Then is doomsday near.

1162

Honesty, h. must in the end win. See 'Angels, a. are a. even if some of them become rotten - Angels are bright still, though the brightest fell…'

Honesty, h. not safe – Take note, take note, O world, to be direct and honest is not safe.

Honesty, h. over wisdom - .. Methinks thou art more honest now than wise..

Honesty, h. unsuspecting of dishonesty – .. unstain'd thoughts do seldom dream on evil

Honesty, h. vs. corruption. See 'Corruption, c. no better than honesty - corruption wins no more than honesty.'

Honesty, no h. left in the world. See 'World, pessimistic view of the w., no honesty left - We need no grave to bury honesty: there is not a grain of it the face to sweeten of the whole dungy earth.'

Honor, a man of exemplary h. – Honour stuck upon him as the sun in the grey vault of heaven.

Honor, a man of h. to whom praise is due - The theme of honour's tongue.

Honor, can h. and politics co-exists? – … In peace what each of them by the other lose that they combine not there.

Honor, death preferable to loss of h. See 'Honor, sense of h. paramount - I beg mortality, rather than life preserved with infamy'

Honor, h. above all – .. honour we love, for who hates honor hates the gods above.

Honor, h. above all – 'tis not my profit that does lead mine honor, mine honour, it.

Honor, h. above all – … But, if it be a sin to covet honor I am the most offending soul alive.

Honor, h. above all – I love the name of honor more than I fear death.

Honor, h. above all – if I lose mine honor I lose myself.

Honor, h. above all – Life every man holds dear; but the dear man holds honour far more precious dear than life.

Honor, h. and class showing through notwithstanding mean attire. See 'Wealth relative, real w. is in the mind - .. for 'tis the mind that makes the body rich…'

Honor, h. and credit at stake - Thereon I pawn my credit and mine honour.

Honor, h. as motive for murder, not hate – … For nought I did in hate, but all in honour.

Honor, h. inseparable part of life - Mine honour is my life; both grow in one: take honour from me, and my life is done.

Honor, h. inspiring what chances to take – Mine honour keeps the weather of my fate.

Honor, h. not related to garments. See lines 3.4 in 'Wealth relative, real w. is in the mind - .. for 'tis the mind that makes the body rich…'

Honesty, h. not safe – Take note, take note, O world, to be direct and honest is not safe.

Honor, h. potentially lost – (It) would bark your honour from that trunk you bear…

Honor, h. preferred to love. See 'Love, l. preferred over power - He after honour hunts, I after love…'

Honor, if you have h. show it - If you were born of honour, show it now, if put on you…

Honor, man who is tops for h. – … Upon his brow shame is ashamed to sit, for 'tis a throne where honour…

Honor, meaning of h. and standing up when h. is at stake - Rightly to be great is not to stir without great argument..

Honor, sense of h. paramount - I beg mortality, rather than life preserved with infamy.

Honor, share of h. See 'People, the fewer the better for a great enterprise - … the fewer men, the greater share of honour.

Honor, the narrow path of h. - … honour travels in a strait so narrow, where one but goes abreast…

Honorable man. See 'Debate, disagreeing with skill - but Brutus says he was ambitious, and Brutus is an honourable man.'

Hope, abandoning h. -….I will put off my hope and keep it no longer for my flatterer.

Hope, caution about unwarranted h. – … a cause on foot lives so in hope as in an early spring we see the appearing buds…

Hope, concern about h., will it really happen? - I sometimes do believe, and sometimes do not, as those that fear they hope, and know they fear.

Hope, confident in better days ahead. See 'Happiness, promise of return to h. - ..The liquid drops of tears that you have shed shall come again, transform'd to orient pearl.'

Hope, glimmer of h. spied – … even through the hollow eyes of death I spy life peering…

Hope, glimmer of h. spied - I do spy a kind of hope which craves as desperate an execution as that is desperate which we would prevent.

Hope, h. against evidence. See 'Evidence, desire to disbelieve the e. - yet there is a credence in my heart… that doth invert the utmost of eyes and ears…'

Hope, h. as a flatterer and parasite - I will despair, and be at enmity with cozening hope: he is a flatterer

Hope, h. as a weapon against adversity - Till then fair hope must hinder life's decay.

Hope, h. as an asset of lovers. See 'Rejection, handling of r. - Hope is a lover's staff, I'll walk hence with that and manage it against despairing thoughts.'

Hope, h. as the refuge of the distressed - The miserable have no other medicine but only hope.

Hope, h. as the supporting staff of a lover. See 'Rejection, handling of r. - Hope is a lover's staff, I'll walk hence with that and manage it against despairing thoughts.'

Hope, h. comparable to actual enjoyment - And hope to joy is little less in joy than hope enjoy'd

Hope, h. in a new president - shall convert those tears by number into hours of happiness.

Hope, h. in a person crashed - the hopes we have in him touch ground.

Hope, h. in men misguided. See 'Philosophical considerations. Uselessness of coveting earthly fortunes as fortune is so prone to change - O momentary grace of mortal men which we more hunt for than the grace of God…'

Hope, h. making kings out of common men - True hope is swift, and flies with swallow's wings.

Hope, h. misplaced - … do not satisfy your resolution with hopes that are fallible.

Hope, h. never hurts -… it never yet did hurt to lay down likelihoods and forms of hope.

Hope, h. revived - how thy words revive my heart.

Hope, h. shattered, exclamation - O my breast, thy hope ends here.

Hope, h. worth fighting for. See 'Exhortation, e. not to yield to enemy - … And he that will not fight for such a hope, go home to bed…'

Hope, sparkles of h. See 'Reformation, symptoms of reformation – I see some sparks of better hope…'

Hopelessness, beyond help - "(We must not)… esteem a senseless help when help past sense we deem.

Hopelessness, h. and helplessness - Hopeless and helpless doth Aegeon wend….

Hopelessness. See 'Hope, h. shattered, exclamation - O my breast, thy hope ends here'.

Hopelessness. See 'Medicine, doctors, skeptical about doctors - … under whose practises he hath persecuted time with hope…'

Horizon, h. at sea, sky and water blended – … to throw out our eyes…even till we make the main and the aerial blue an indistinct regard.

Horror, horror, horror. See 'Invocation,

horror. - … Tongue nor heart cannot conceive nor name thee!'

Horrors, house of h. See 'Revelation, startling r. – I could a tale unfold whose lightest word would harrow up thy soul, freeze thy young blood…'

Horse, excellent h. - It is the prince of palfreys; his neigh is like the bidding of a monarch…

Horse, horses compared to hollow men. See 'Men, characteristics of hollow m. - … hollow men, like horses hot at hand make gallant show and promise of their mettle…'

Horse, happy h. because of its rider – O happy horse, to bear the weight of Antony!

Horse, my kingdom for a h. See 'Transportation, t. needed quickly - A horse! A horse! My kingdom for a horse. '

Horse, proudly striding h. See 'Walk, walking proudly by a horse, but applicable also to men – So proudly as if he disdain'd the ground.'

House, dwelling, not necessarily reflecting the mind of the dwellers - … nor measure our good minds by this rude place we live in.

Horse, only talking of horses. See 'Subject, obsessive subject of conversation, horse - … he doth nothing but talk of his horse.'

House, compliment on a h. you are visiting – 'Fore God, you have here a goodly dwelling and a rich.

House, reason for going somewhere else when not welcome in your own h. - … Since mine own doors refuse to entertain me…

Household words - …our names, familiar in his mouth as household words.

Housing, h. unsuitable to rank or circumstance, poor living conditions, hotel comment, travel - … call you that keeping… that differs not from the stalling of an ox?

Hotel, looking for a h. in the evening – Now spurs the lated traveller apace to gain the timely inn.

How absolute the knave is… See 'Equivocation, misunderstanding, need for accurate wording or expression – … we must speak by the card or equivocation will undo us.'

How can I help you? See entries for 'Service, at her complete s. '

How are things? when things are going well. See 'Events, e. turning out as you wanted - every thing lies level to our wish.'

How are you? Answer to question, anxious. See 'Anxiety, state of a., hope and fear mixed - I feel such sharp dissension in my breast…' *** Other entries for 'Anxiety'.

How are you? Answer to question, better now that you ask - The better that it pleases your good worship to ask.

How are you? Answer to question, in good spirits. See 'Mind, state of

How are you? Answer to question, in the dumps. See 'Distress, d. emphasized dramatically - …if the river were dry, I am able to

How are you? Answer to question, in the middle - Like to the time of the year between the extremes of hot and cold, he was nor sad nor merry.

How are you? Answer to question, in the middle - Happy, in that we are not overhappy; on Fortune's cap we are not the very button.

How are you? Answer to question, uncommitted, (bank and shoal of time). See comment to 'Speed, let's do it quickly - If it were done when 't is done, then 't were well it were done quickly.'

How are you? Answer to question, worried. See 'Lover, l's absence justified - I have this while with leaden thoughts been pressed…' *** 'Anxiety, a. till return - … till you do return, I rest perplexed with a thousand cares.'

How are you? (well if she is well). See 'Well being, everything is OK if she is OK - … for nothing can be ill, if she be well.'

How are the negotiations progressing? See 'Deal, d. with credulous party almost done - I have him already tempering between my finger and my thumb.'

How are your finances? See 'Financial status, challenging – I can get no remedy against this consumption of the purse…'

How can I thank you? See 'Gratitude, g. expressed and responded to - … To be acknowledged, madam, is o'erpaid.' *** Entries for 'Gratitude'

How can you say this? See 'Fact, just repeating a well known f. - I speak no more than everyone doth know.'

How could they do this? See 'Stupidity, s. universal, compared sarcastically to the sun - Foolery, sir, does walk about the orb, like the sun, it shines everywhere.'

How could you possibly associate with people like that? See 'Company, rationalization for having frequented the wrong crowd - The strawberry grows underneath the nettle… fruit of baser quality.'

How did you sleep? See 'Dream, d. that inspires confidence and well being - If I may trust the flattering truth of sleep, my dreams presage some joyful news at hand…'

How do you feel? See 'Music, melody lulling to

How do you like the food? See 'Eating, good food, antipasto - … Epicurean cooks sharpen with cloyless sauce his appetite.'

How do you react to criticism? See 'Advice, a. on talking and listening - Give every man thy ear, but few thy voice, take each man's censure, but reserve thy judgment.'

How every fool can play upon the word. See 'Words, silly w., playing with w., - …and discourse will grow commendable only in parrots.'

How ill white hairs become… See 'Age, old a. should be more serious - Now ill white hairs become a fool and jester.'

How is it going? See 'World, pessimistic view of the w. – it wears as it grows.'

How is your love life? See 'Love, account of your love life boring - My tales of love were wont to weary you; I know you joy not in a love discourse.' *** First line in 'Love, obstacles increase passion - The more thou damm'st it up, the more it burns.'

How long did it last? See 'Time, counting numbers to measure t. – Stay'd it long?… While one with moderate haste might tell a hundred.

How many ages hence shall this, our lofty scene be acted over, in states unborn… See 'Event, e. of historical importance'

How much do you love me? See entries for 'Love, how much?'

How much do your services cost? See 'Payment, p. after service – When I have chased all thy foes from hence, then will I think upon a recompense.'

How much money do you make? See 'Financial Status - They are but beggars that can count their worth.' *** Entries for 'Salary'

How oft the sight of means… See 'Crime, c. prompted by opportunity - How oft the sight of means to do ill deeds makes ill deeds done.'

How old are you? See entries for 'Age'

How quick do you want it? See 'Effect, quick, strong and violent - As violently, as hasty powder fired doth hurry from the fatal cannon's womb.'

How soon can you be there? See 'Speed, arriving very quickly at location - I am there before my legs.' *** Entries for 'Speed'

How sweet the moonlight sleeps upon this bank! See 'Moonlight, by the m.'

How weary, stale, flat and unprofitable. See 'Pessimism, sadness on a grand scale - How weary, stale, flat and unprofitable seem to me all the uses of this world!…'

How well do you know him? See 'Acquaintance, a. superficial - we know each other faces; but for our hearts…'

How would you wish to pay? See 'Dinner. How to pay for dinner, cash or credit card –

(I'll pay cash) as far as my coin would stretch…'

Human nature, follow the fortunate, abandon the unfortunate - Men shut their doors against the setting sun.

Human nature, h.n. common to even kings - I live with bread like you, feel want, taste grief, need friends..

Human nature, recognizing the value of what we have only after losing it. See entries for 'Appreciation coming too late'

Human nature, reason balancing instinct - If the balance of our lives had not one scale of reason to poise another of sensuality..

Human nature, animals better than men. See entries for 'Animals, a. better than men'.

Human nature, baseness of h.n. See 'Invocation, i. and curse to the baseness of human nature - Fly, damned baseness to him that worships thee.'

Human nature, despicable and similar to the spirit that inspires flattery.

Human nature, pessimism about its stupidity. See 'Stupidity, s. universal, compared sarcastically to the sun - Foolery, sir, does walk about the orb, like the sun, it shines everywhere.'

Human nature, pessimism about h.n. – I set it down, that one may smile, and smile, and be a villain; at least I'm sure it may be so in Denmark.

Humanity, common trait of h. – One touch of nature makes the whole world kin…

Humanity, h. perverted if crimes against h. go unpunished. See 'Heavens, h. restraining the extremes of in-humanity - … Humanity must perforce prey on itself like monsters of the deep.'

Humiliation, reaching the bottom of h. – I have sounded the very base-string of humility.

Humility, h. leading to safer life - And often, to our comfort, shall we find the sharded-beetle in a safer hold…

Humor, truth in h. - Jesters do oft prove prophets.

Humor. See 'Witticism, humor as a double edges sword - A sentence is but a cheveril glove to a good wit; how quickly the wrong side may be turned outward!'

Hunger, feeling incredibly hungry – I am so hungry that if I might have a lease of my life for a thousand years I could stay no longer.

Hunger, feeling hungry - I am weak with toil, yet strong in appetite.

Hunger, h. not appeased by imagining food - "(who can) cloy the hungry edge of appetite by bare imagination of a feast?

Hunger, h. to be appeased, food coming - …but if thou diest before I come, thou art a mocker of my labour.

Hunger, hungry and looking for anything as long as it is healthy food - … get me some repast; I care not what so it be wholesome food.

Hunger, poverty and resentment - … for the gods know, I speak in hunger for bread, not in thirst for revenge…

Hunger, when in love not important but…- .. though the chameleon love may feed on air, I am one that is nourished by my victuals, and would fain have meat.

Hurricane, more noise than a h. – … the dreadful spout which shipmen do the hurricano call …

Hurt, minimizing h. See 'Modesty, just a scratch - Scratches with briers, scars to move laughter only.'

Hurt, you hurt me - Thou stickest a dagger in me.

Husband, declaration of husband's rights - Such duty as the subject owes the prince even such a woman oweth to her husband.

Hygiene, good manners require hand-washing – When good manners shall lie all in one or two men's hands and they unwashed…

Hypocrisy, accusing others of one's mischiefs - The secret mischiefs that I set abroach I lay unto the grievous charge of others.

Hypocrisy, counseling a hypocrite to put up a show. See 'Pretence, no for yes - Play the maid's part, still answer nay, and take it.'

Hypocrisy, criticizing one's own faults in others - Wilt thou whip thine own faults in other men?

Hypocrisy, determination to stamp it out - Now step I forth to whip hypocrisy.

Hypocrisy, deceit and cunning - O, what authority and show of truth can cunning sin cover itself withal.

Hypocrisy, deceit and disguise under a virtuous appearance. See entries for 'Appearances, a. deceptive or false'.

Hypocrisy, devils mask sin with good appearance - When devils will the blackest sins put on, they do tempt at first with heavenly shows..

Hypocrisy, false conclusion from a righteous example - The devil can cite scriptures for his purpose…

Hypocrisy, flimsy excuses to deny help - How fairly this lord strives to appear foul.

Hypocrisy, h. and cunning will eventually be discovered - Time shall unfold what plighted cunning hides, who cover faults at last shame them derides

Hypocrisy, h. and dishonesty exposed - foul deeds will rise though all the world o'erwhelm them, to men's eyes.

Hypocrisy, double standards. See 'Political (and personal) double standards - whiles I am a beggar, I will rail… there is no sin but to be rich…'

Hypocrisy, h. and double standards condemned - Shame to him whose cruel striking kills for faults of his own liking!

Hypocrisy, h. and feigned kindness - How courtesy would seem to cover sin when what is done is like a hypocrite….

Hypocrisy, h. and self-illusion - .. with devotion's visage and pious action we do sugar o'er the devil himself.

Hypocrisy, h. covering vice - There is no vice so simple but assumes some mark of virtue on his outward parts.

Hypocrisy, h. defined - your virtue hath a licence in't.

Hypocrisy, h. in prayers – His prayers are full of false hypocrisy…

Hypocrisy, h. in religion - .. In religion, what damned error….hiding the grossness with fair ornament?

Hypocrisy, h. in religion. - How canst thou urge God's dreadful law to us when thou hast broke it in so dear degree?

Hypocrisy, h. in seeming a saint - .. And thus I clothe my naked villany.. and seem a saint, when most I play the devil…

Hypocrisy, h. in speech aimed at obtaining objective. See 'Meaning, m. misinterpreted – … to have what we would have we speak not what we mean.'

Hypocrisy, h. in writing - A huge translation of hypocrisy, vilely compiled….

Hypocrisy, h. masking vice - There is no vice so simple but assumes some mark of virtue.

Hypocrisy, h. to cover treason - How smooth and even they do bear themselves!…

Hypocrisy, hiding sin as a form of conscience. See 'Conscience, false c. - … their best conscience is not to leave it undone, but keep it unknown'.

Hypocrisy, political h. See 'Equivocation - … here's an equivocator, that could swear in both the scales against either scale.'

Hypocrisy, practice what you preach - Do not, as some ungracious pastors do… The primrose path of dalliance threads and recks not his own reed.

Hypocrisy, preaching but not practising. See 'Preaching, p. versus practice - .. will not you maintain the thing you teach but prove a chief offender in the same?'

Hypocrisy, pretending not to aspire to riches or high position. See 'Virginity, v. potentially traded for high life – I would… and so would you for all this spice of your hypocrisy.'

Hypocrisy, show of virtue - So smooth he daub'd his vice with show of virtue.. he lived from all attainder of suspect.

Hypocrisy, unfelt sorrow - To show an unfelt sorrow is an office which the false man does easy.

Hypocrisy, vice and h. – There is no vice so simple, but assumes some mark of virtue in its outward parts…

Hypocrisy. See also entries for 'Dissimulation'.

Hypocrite, address to a h. - Thou wolf in sheep's array.

Hypocrite, no h. See 'Pride, p. in lacking hypocritical skills - … for want of that for which I am richer, a still-soliciting eye…'

I am a man more sinned against than sinning. See 'Defence, d. from general accusations'

I am as constant as the northern star… See 'Credentials, establishing your c'

I am at war 'twixt will and will not. See 'Indecision, i. between two courses of action'

I am not in the giving vein to-day. See 'Solicitations, answer to telephone s.'

I am not in the roll of common men. See 'Praise, self-p. or praise of speaker'

I am one, my liege, whom… See 'Attitude, a. towards the world, hating it – one… whom the vile blows and buffets of the world…'

I am not covetous for gold. See 'Self-assessment – I am not covetous for gold…'

I am sorry (by a woman). See 'Perfection, p. even in her shortcomings - She spoke and panted that she made defect perfection.'

I am tied to the stake, and I must stand the course. See 'Determination, d. to face the inevitable'

I beg cold comfort. See 'Thirst, parched lips begging for water - … entreat the north to make his bleak wind kiss my parched lips…'

I can get no remedy against this consumption of the purse. See 'Financial status, challenging'

I can't live without you. See 'Absence, a. felt - Is it thy will, thy image should keep open my heavy eyelids to the weary night?'

I dare do all that may become a man; who dares do more is none. See 'Daring, d. but to a limit'

I do desire we may be better strangers. See 'Dislike, mutual d. expressed - I do desire we may be better strangers.'

I do not want to get pregnant. See entries for 'Pregnancy, p. good'.

I do not want to hear of that place. See 'Sicily, (or any country) out of mind – Of that fatal country.. pr'ythee speak no more; whose very naming punishes me with the remembrance.'

I grant (sweet love) thy lovely argument… See 'Writing, excusing your poor means to extol her charms - I grant (sweet love) thy lovely argument deserves the travail of a worthier pen.'

I hate to do this. See 'Crying, c. impossible notwithstanding the pain but.. – …weep I cannot, but my heart bleeds..'

I have lost the immortal part of myself and what remains is bestial. See 'Reputation, r. lost.'

I have neither wit, nor words, nor worth… See 'Oratory, lack of o. claimed'

I have no other reason but a woman's reason. See 'Woman, w.'s intuition'

I have not slept one wink. See 'Anxiety, a. at doing something you don't like but must do - Since I receiv'd command to do this business I have not slept a wink.'

I have seen better faces in my times than stands on any shoulder… See 'Character, self-defined, straight, direct and who does not like any of the company around him - .. 'tis my occupation to be plain…'

I have set my life upon a cast and I will stand the hazard of the die. See 'Character, not afraid of taking chances.'

I have very poor and unhappy brains for

drinking. See 'Wine, drinking, unable to tolerate strong drinks.'

I hold it cowardice…See 'Diffidence as a form of cowardice - I hold it cowardice to rest mistrustful where a noble heart hath pawn'd an open hand in sign of love.'

I hope good luck lies in odd numbers. See 'Fortune, luck found in number 3 or in odd numbers.'

I know I am right. See 'Truth, t. evident and on my side - I'll maintain my words on any plot of ground on Christendom'.

I like not fair terms and a villain's mind. See 'Suspicion, s. at terms offered by a crook'

I see you stand like greyhounds in the slips. See 'Eagerness for action, eager and ready to go – I see you stand like greyhounds in the slips, straining upon the start.'

I will praise any man that… See 'Praise, accepted and returned, responding to praise - I will praise any man that will praise me.'

I will remember what you said, See 'Promise, p. to remember what you have been told - ..'Tis in my memory lock'd and you yourself shall keep the key of it.

I will write to you. See 'Writing, assurance of continued communications - I will omit no opportunity that may convey my greetings, love, to thee'.

I wish I could be th

I would rather be…. See cross references in 'Anything, a. but this.'

Ice, icy reception. See 'Reaction, cold r. – thou art all ice, thy kindness freezeth.'

Idea, stuck on an i. See 'Opinion, op. or idea, stuck on an op. or idea and unable to change it - ..you may as well forbid the sea to obey the moon..'.

Idea, mad, odd or ridiculous i. See 'Dagger, d. of the mind - .. art thou but a dagger of the mind, a false creation, proceeding from the heat-oppressed brain?'

Ideas, good i. rejected by some politicians. See 'Wisdom, w. and goodness not for the vile - Wisdom and goodness to the vile seem vile, filths savour but themselves.'

Ideas, heretical i. - … new new opinions, divers and dangerous; which are heresies…

Ideas, new i. to be rewarded - Search out thy wit for secret policies, and we will make thee famous through the world.

Identification, are you so and so? - If I do not usurp myself, I am.

Identification, characteristics - More than I seem, and less than I was born to..

Identification, who is who? – How may a stranger to those most imperial looks know them from the eyes of other mortals?

Identity, searching for self-identity. See 'Self-identity in question - Who is it that can tell me who I am?

Ides of March. See 'Careful now, the ides of March, impending danger'.

Idleness, i. harmful - Ten thousand harms, more than the ills I know my idleness doth hatch.

Idolatry, goddess of my i. See Divine, goddess of my idolatry.'

Idolatry, i. misplaced - …idol of idiot worshippers.

Idolatry, i. the means, not the end. See 'Means, idolizing means rather than end, wrong - …'tis mad idolatry to make the service greater than the god.'

If all the year were playing holidays… See 'Tediousness, t. in everything being always the same – If all the year were playing holidays, to sport would be as tedious as to work.'

If circumstances lead me … See 'Truth, you are determined to find the t. - If circumstances lead me, I will find where truth is hid, though it were hid indeed within the centre.'

If I could write the beauty… See 'Eyes, beauty of e. to be written about - If I could write the beauty of your eyes, and in fresh numbers number all your graces…'

If thou remember'st not… See 'Love, includes making a fool of yourself - If thou remember'st not the slightest folly that ever love did make thee run into thou hast not loved.'

If you can look into the seeds of time… See 'Forecasting requested - If you can look into the seeds of time and say which grain will grow and which will not…'

If you have tears… See 'Introduction, i. to a presentation - If you have tears, prepare to shed them now…' *** 'Sadness, license to cry - Those that can pity, here may, if they think it well, let fall a tear; the subject will deserve it.'

If, the power of 'If' as a peacemaker - Your 'If' is the only peacemaker; much virtue in 'If'.

Ignorance, advantage of not knowing - … There may be in the cup a steep'd, and one may drink, depart and yet partake no venom…

Ignorance, advantage of not knowing – He that is robbed, not wanting what is stolen…

Ignorance, i. decried – O gross and miserable ignorance!

Ignorance, i. observed in person - There is no darkness but ignorance.

Ignorance, i. of an unread man. See lines in 'Man, clearly not an intellectual - He is only an animal, only sensible in the duller parts…'

Ignorance, i. of what is really good for us - We, ignorant of ourselves beg often our own harms, which the wise powers deny us for our good…

Ignorance, i. shown - you speak, Lord Mowbray, now you know not what.

Ignorance, i. vs. knowledge - … ignorance is the curse of God, the wing wherewith we fly to heaven.

Ignorance, invocation in disgust. See 'Invocation, i. to ignorance - O thou monster Ignorance, how deformed dost thou look!'

Ignorance, lack of self knowledge. See 'Insult, lack of self-knowledge - … asses… that you ask me what you are, and do not know yourselves.'

Ignorance, pain of knowing too little - I swear 'tis better to be much abused than but to know't a little.

Ignorance, planned i. to escape guilt - I will not reason what is meant hereby, because I will be guiltless of the meaning.

Ignorance, you don't know what you are talking about - thou knowest not what thou speak'st

Ill-weav'd ambition… See 'Invocation, misplaced ambition, see the results - Ill-weav'd ambition, how much art thou shrunk!'

Illness, I. beyond the power of medicine. See 'Medicine, illness beyond power of m. - … labouring art can never ransom nature.' *** Entries for 'Medicine, limits of m.'

Illness, i. not an obstacle to participation. See 'Determination, d. to participate to an event or a party even if ill - … Not sickness should detain me.'

Illness, i. not relieved by company. See 'Character, c. self-described as not sociable - ..society is no comfort to one not sociable'.

Illness, see entries for 'Disease', 'Indisposition'.

Illusion, I am so happy, is this a dream? See 'Happiness, h, overwhelming and incredible - If it be thus to dream, still let me sleep!'

Illusion, exchanging imagination for reality. See "Sorrow, causing madness and misjudgment - .. grief hath so wrought on him, he takes false shadows for true substance.'

Illusion, i. leading to confusion – … the strength of their illusion shall draw him on to his confusion.

Illusion, optical i - Mine eyes are made the fools o' the other senses.

Illness, i. not relieved by company. See 'Character, c. self-described as not sociable - ..society is no comfort to one not sociable'.

Illusion, state of i., invocation - .. and here we wander in illusions some blessed power deliver us from hence.

Illusions, constructs of the mind - Sometimes we see a cloud that's dragonish…

Illusions, end of i. See first line in 'Retirement, retiring and giving up your secrets – … And deeper than did ever plummet sound I'll drown my book.'

Illusions, i. brought on by grief and fear. See 'Grief, g. and anxiety magnifying fears - … shapes of grief, more than himself, to wail which, look'd on as it is, is nought but shadows of what it is not.'

Illusions, results of i. See 'Shadows, rewarded with s. - some there be that shadows kiss, such have but a shadow's bliss.

Image building or restoration - I'll be at charges for a looking glass and entertain a score or two of tailors…

Image building, too much effort - You might have been enough the man you are with striving less to be so.

Image, happy about your i. - Shine out, fair sun, till I have bought a glass, that I may see my shadow as I pass.

Image, i. appearing as seen at first - … thy image doth appear in the rare semblance that I loved it first.

Image, i. of strength. See 'Attitude, posture and its importance - Let not the world see fear and sad distrust… threaten the threatener…'

Image, the power of i. to deceive and corrupt - O place! O form! How often dost thou with thy case, thy habit, wrench awe from fools…

Imagination, appeal to the i. to visualize events when graphics are missing - … Still be kind and eke out our performance with your mind.

Imagination, commonality among lunatic, lover & poet . See 'Profession, what do you do for a living? - As my imagination bodies forth the forms of things unknown…

Imagination, conceit, lack of realism - Conceit in weakest bodies strongest works.

Imagination, figment of the i. – This the very coinage of your brain…

Imagination, help for the i. See 'Supplement, s. to help imagination - Give me an ounce of civet, good apothecary, to sweeten my imagination.

Imagination, i. as the seat of perversion. See 'Perversion, p. of the imagination - O, deeper sin than bottomless conceit can comprehend in still imagination!'

Imagination, i. is rich with strange images – So full of shapes is fancy that it alone is high-fantastical.

Imagination, imagining that thoughts are people – My brain I'll prove the female to my soul…

Imagination, man of i. - … these are begot in the ventricle of memory…

Imagination, not a substitute of reality - O, who can hold a fire in his hand by thinking on the frosty Caucasus?..

Imagination, product of a distorted brain. See 'Dagger, d. of the mind - .. art thou but a dagger of the mind, a false creation, proceeding from the heat-oppressed brain?'

Imagination, product of the i. - … the baseless fabric of your vision.

Imagination, seeing a fleet - … behold the threaden sails, borne with the invisible and creeping wind…

Imagination, use of i. prompted - … the quick forge and working-house of thought.

Imitation, do not imitate stupidity. See 'Stupidity, s. not to be imitated, don't copy the fool - If the enemy is an ass and a fool, and a prating coxcomb…'

Imitation, i. of foreign fashion - … whose manners still our tardy apish nation limps after in base imitation.

Immortality, desire for i. – I have immortal longings in me.

Immortality, acquisition of I. See entries for 'Fame'.

Impartiality, I'll be impartial -… nor partialize the unstooping firmness of my upright soul.

Impatience, its privilege - ... impatience hath his privilege.

Impatience, i. for action - Imagination of some great exploit drives him beyond the bounds of patience.

Impatience, i. in words reprimanded. See 'Speech, showing impatience and a self-centered personality – tying thine ear to no tongue but thine own'.

Impatience, i. observed – ... a very little thief of occasion will rob you of a great deal of patience

Impatience, see entries for 'Patience'

Impatience, signs of i. – hoping it was but an effect of humour, which sometimes hath his hour with every man.

Impatience. See entries for 'Anticipation'.

Imperialistic policies. See 'Wickedness, w. painted in fair colors - .. with colours fairer painted their foul ends'.

Implementation, careful i. - by cold gradation and well-balanced form.

Impossibility to make a man change his mind - ... you may as well forbid the sea for to obey the moon...

Impossibility to soften a hard heart - You may as well forbid the mountain pines...

Impossibility, cooling the sun with a fan - .. you may as well go about to turn the sun to ice...

Impossibility, making the impossible happen. See 'Invocation, if this happens then.. - Then let the pebbles on the hungry beach fillip the stars...'

Impossible, dreaming on the i. – Flattering me with impossibilities...

Impossible, nothing i. to the daring - Impossible be strange attempts to those that weigh their pains in sense...

Imprecation. See entries for 'Invocation'.

Impressed, amazed (positively) - This is a most majestic vision, and harmoniously charming.

Improbable fiction. See 'Unbelievable – if played on stage it would be rated as improbable fiction.'

Improvement of the situation expected with time. See 'Time, improvement expected with time - ... the time will bring on summer when briars shall have leaves as well as thorns...'

Improvisation, i. as a sign of wit. See 'Workers' compensation for questionable disability - ... A good wit will make use of any thing..'.

Impudence, shamelessness – What, canst thou say all this, and never blush

In my heart of hearts. See 'Man, m. not enslaved by passion a commendable exception - Give me that man that is not passion's slave...'

In my mind's eye. See "Vision, intuition - In my mind's eye, Horatio'.

In the reproof of chance lies the true proof of men. See 'Chance, temper of man shown when handling reversals'.

In time we hate that. See "Management style, fear and government - In time we hate that which we often fear.'

Intuition, vision. See 'Vision, intuition - In my mind's eye, Horatio'

Inability, i. to appreciate what we have. See 'Appreciation coming too late - .. . for it so falls out that what we have we prize not the worth...'

Inarticulate. See 'Opinion, your op. on an inarticulate man – Dull of tongue'.

Income, see entries for 'Financial Status'

Inconveniences, daily i. defined. See 'L

Indecision, i. between two courses of action - .. 't is with my mind as with the tide... running either way.

Indecision, i. between two courses of action - ... like a man to double business bound, I stand in pause where I shall first begin and both neglect.

Indecision, i. between two courses of action - ... I am at war 'twixt will and will not.

Indecision, i. due to confusion in the mind - My thoughts are whirled like a potter's wheel;

I know not where I am, nor what I do.

Indecision, state of i. – Her tongue will not obey her heart nor can her heart inform her tongue.

Indecision, i. to act,, wisdom or fear? - … A thought which, quarter'd, hath but one part wisdom and ever three parts coward, I do not know.

Indecision. See 'Doubts, d.

Independence, i. of thought. See 'Freedom, f. of the soul – Every subject's duty is the king's; but every subject's soul is his own.'

Indifference, heartlessness – … you recount your sorrows to a stone.

Indifference, indifferent to someone's praise or hatred - … his curses and his blessings touch me alike, they're breath I not believe in

Indifference, seeming i. at tragedy - … And look upon, as if the tragedy were play'd in jest by counterfeiting actors?

Indignation – … his indignation derives itself out of a very competent injury

Indignation, hold back outrage until facts are clear - seal up the mouth of outrage for a while..

Indignation, i. at a bad deed – O, forfend it, God, that souls refined should show so heinous, black, obscene a deed.

Indignation, i. at the idea – Throw your vile guesses in the devil's teeth…

Indignation, i. mixed with threats - the cannons have their bowels full of wrath..

Indignation. See 'Language, no correct l. adequate to describe the fault - … There is not chastity enough in language without offence to utter them.'

Indignities, i. not recounted for decency – Many more there are which … I will not taint my mouth with.

Indiscretion, sometimes i. pays off – Our indiscretion sometimes serves us well.

Indisposition or illness causing poor behavior or mood. See 'Apologies for behavior caused by indisposition - … we are not ourselves when nature being oppress'd commands the mind to suffer with the body.'

Indisposition, confined by i. – An untimely ague stay'd me a prisoner in my chamber…

Indisposition, feeling out of sorts - …to deal plainly, I fear I am not in my perfect mind.

Indisposition, i. causing unruly language. See 'Apologies for unruly words caused by indisposition - … impute his words to wayward sickliness and age in him.'

Indisposition, i. not relieved by company. See 'Character, c. self-described as not sociable - ..society is no comfort to one not sociable'.

Indisposition, major i. or illness - … my cloud of dignity is held from falling with so weak a wind that it will quickly drop.

Indisposition, minor i. - .. I am not very sick since I can reason of it

Indisposition, minor i. affecting overall behavior - .. let our finger ache, and it indues our other healthful members even to that sense of pain.

Indisposition, momentary i. – The fit is momentary; upon a thought he will again be well.

Indivisible, always together – No more can I be sever'd from your side than can yourself yourself in twain divide.

Inequality. See 'Tyranny, t. of individual or corporations – … and we petty men walk under his huge legs and peep about to find ourselves dishonourable graves…' *** Entries for 'Social issues'

Inevitable, facing the i. See 'Courage, exhortation to c. - what cannot be avoided, 't were childish weakness to lament or fear.' *** Entries for 'Destiny'.

Infidelity, lax views on i. - … who would not make her husband a cuckold to make him a monarch?

Infidelity, no tolerance for i. - I had rather be a toad and live upon the vapour of a dungeon, than …

Inflexibility. See entries for 'Success, s.

impossible given the man and the circumstances ' *** 'Impossibility to make a man change his mind - ... you may as well forbid the sea for to obey the moon...'

Information, amusing i. delivered while walking - And, as we walk along, I dare be bold with our discourse to make your grace to smile.

Information, attention riveting i. See 'Hearing, do you hear me? – Your tale, sir, would cure deafness.'

Information, concern about reporting certain i. See 'Messenger, m. fearful to report information - I should report that which I say I saw but know not how to do it'.

Information, confidential i. and for one person only - My matter hath no voice, lady, but to your own most pregnant and vouchsafed ear.

Information, dangerous and sensitive i. – ... matter deep and dangerous, as full of peril and adventurous spirit...

Information, fishing for i. - I am angling now, though you perceive not how I give line.

Information, i. annoying and unpleasant - Tedious it were to tell, and harsh to hear, sufficeth...

Information, i. given away indirectly. See 'Secret, s. information given away indirectly – Thou shalt never get such a secret from me but by a parable.'

Information, i. is money - Open your purse, that the money, and the matter be at once delivered.

Information, i. not wanted or sought (in the past) - More to know did never meddle with my thoughts.

Information, i. requested and believed interesting - Inform us of thy fortunes; for it seems they crave to be demanded.

Information, i. that must be kept secret. See 'Secret, information that must be kept s. – dwell darkly with you'.

Information, i. to be made public for security - This must be known, which, being kept close, might move more grief to hide...

Information, importance of packaging i. - I fear my Julia would not deign my lines receiving them from such a worthless post.

Information, important i. not to be withheld from friend – ... and makest his ear a stranger to thy thoughts.

Information, last to know - Nimble mischance, that art so light of foot... and am I last that knows it?

Information, no i. disclosed about what you intend to do next - ... What course I mean to hold shall nothing benefit your knowledge.

Information, no more i. - Seek to know no more.

Information, plea to be given critical i. - If you know aught which does behoove my knowledge..

Information, questioning the source of the i. - ... from whence you owe this strange intelligence?

Information, revealing so far kept secret personal i. - ... who shall be true to us when we are so unsecret to ourselves?

Information, sensitive and to remain secret - I am to break with thee of some affairs that touch me near..

Information, sensitive i. - That which I would discover, the law of friendship bids me to conceal.

Information, sensitive i. See 'Confidence, c. among trusted friends - .. We three are but thyself; and, speaking so, thy words are but as thoughts; therefore, be bold'

Information, twisted in one's favor - ... your manner of wrenching the true cause the false way.

Inhumanity. See 'Insult, man like animal according to the theories of Pythagoras - Thou almost make'st me waver in my faith, to hold opinion with Pythagoras...'

Ingratitude, addressing the ingrate as wasps - Injurious wasps! to feed on such sweet honey and kill the bees, that yield it, with your sting.

Ingratitude, comparing one's unrewarded efforts to bees killed on their return to the beehive. See 'Efforts, e. unrewarded or punished – … and like the bees are murdered for our pains.'

Ingratitude, i. as a deformity - In nature there's no blemish but the mind…

Ingratitude, i. despicable and beyond description - … and cannot cover the monstrous bulk of this ingratitude with any size of words.

Ingratitude, i. dishonorable - My honour would not let ingratitude so much besmear it.

Ingratitude, I. for services rendered in the past. See "Time, t. and ingratitude - Time hath, my lord, a wallet in his back wherein he puts alms for oblivion…'

Ingratitude, i. from friends - What viler thing upon the earth than friends..

Ingratitude, i. hateful – I hate ingratitude more in a man, than lying, vainness, babbling, drunkenness..

Ingratitude, i. observed - .. 'tis call'd ungrateful, with dull unwillingness to repay a debt which with a bounteous hand was kindly lent.

Ingratitude, i. of the masses monstrous – Ingratitude is monstrous and for the multitude to be ungrateful…

Ingratitude, i. tied to aging - These old fellows have their ingratitude in them hereditary..

Ingratitude, i. tied to loss of fortune - … when they once perceive the least rub in your fortunes, fall away like water from ye…

Ingratitude, i. to be deprecated - … see the monstrousness of man when he looks out in an ungrateful shape.

Ingratitude, i. towards parents despicable - How sharper than a serpent's tooth it is to have a thankless child!

Ingratitude, i. worse than treason - Ingratitude, more strong than traitors' arms…

Ingratitude, invocation to filial i. - Ingratitude, thou marble-hearted fiend…

Ingratitude, invocation to i. - And thou, all-shaking thunder, smite flat the thick rotundity o' the world…

Ingratitude, invocation to i. - Blow, blow, thou winter wind. thou art not so unkind as man's ingratitude.

Ingratitude, show of i. - … small thanks for my labour.

Initiative. See 'Self-reliance, remedies to be found within ourselves - Our remedies oft in ourselves do lie which we ascribe to heaven.' – 'Impossible, nothing i. to the daring - Impossible be strange attempts to those that weigh their pains in sense…'

Injunction, do no return empty handed - Be clamorous and leap all civil bounds, rather than make unprofited return.

Injunction, stay away - Come not within the measure of my wrath.

Injunction, stay out of this - Come not between the dragon and his wrath.

Injuries, i. as a source of experience. See 'Errors, e. as a source of experience, sarcastic – … to wilful men the injuries they themselves procure must be their schoolmasters'.

Injuries, i. causing anger. See 'Anger, a. caused by sustained unjust treatment or injuries - whose bosom burns with an incensed fire of injuries'.

Injuries, i. forgotten. See 'Forgiveness, injuries forgotten - The record of what injuries you did us…as done by chance'

Injustice, i. through corrupted witnesses. See 'Corruption, corrupted witnesses - … at what ease might corrupt minds procure knaves as corrupt to swear against you?…'

Injustice, i. under the cover of law. See 'Law, corruption of the l, - what plea so tainted and corrupt… being seasoned with a gracious voice'.

Injustice, justice unequally applied - Some

rise by sin and some by virtue fall…

Injustice, revenge for injustices - .. even for revenge mock my destruction!

Injustice, unjust accusations and attack on the weak – .. A staff is quickly found to beat a dog.

Injustice, using tools of injustice to correct wrongs – But such is the infection of the time that for the health and physic of our right…

Innocence, claim of no responsibility for violent crime - This hand of mine is yet a maiden and an innocent hand, not painted with the crimson spots of blood.

Innocence, condemning the innocent through prejudice and false accusation. See 'Condemnation, c. of an innocent man through prejudice – … that dye is on me which makes my whitest part black.'

Innocence, declaration of i. - … as innocent… as is the sucking lamb or harmless dove.

Innocence, declaration of i. - A heart unspotted is not easily daunted.

Innocence, declaration of i. – I here protest, in sight of heaven, and by the hope I have of heavenly bliss, that…

Innocence, declaration of i. - These hands are free from guiltless bloodshedding…

Innocence, i. against false accusations. See 'Accusation, false a. innocence will triumph – Innocence shall make false accusation blush.

Innocence, i. and naivete - … we knew not the doctrine of ill-doing, nor dream'd that any did.

Innocence, i. claimed - Heaven lay not my transgression to my charge!

Innocence, i. claimed and complaint about slander - … howsoever rude exteriorly, is yet the cover of a fairer mind …

Innocence, i. claimed and complaint about slander. See 'Slander, record of calumnies against you – … none stands under more calumnious tongues than I myself.'

Innocence, i. giving courage - The trust I have is in my innocence and therefore am I bold and resolute.

Innocence, I. not afraid of judgment. See 'Judgment, no fear of j. - What judgment shall I dread, doing no wrong?'

Innocence, i. not immune from undeserved punishment – Some innocents 'scape not the thunderbolt.

Innocence, i. of murder and treason - These hands are free from guiltless blood-shedding..

Innocence, i. proclaimed by silence. See 'Silence, s. as proof of innocence - The silence often of pure innocence persuades, when speaking fails.'

Innocence, i. unsuspecting - … unstain'd thoughts do seldom dream on evil.

Innocence, i. will be proven - … innocence shall make false accusation blush and tyranny and tyranny tremble at patience.

Innocence, innocent and not ashamed to denounce crime - … my true eyes have never practised how to cloak offences with a cunning brow.

Innocence, innocent of any offense. See Offense, no o. done to anyone - … my remembrance is very free and clear from any image of offence done to any man.'

Innocence, innocent of any wrongdoing and non violent of character - I never killed a mouse, nor hurt a fly…

Innocence, naïveté due to youth - .. the untainted virtue of your years hath not yet dived into the world's deceit…

Innocence, the strength of i. - The trust I have is in mine innocence and therefore am I bold and resolute.

Innocence, what is my fault? – What is my offence? Where are the evidence that do accuse me?…

Innuendoes, straight t. preferable to i. See 'Ignorance, pain of knowing too little - I swear 'tis better to be much abused than but to know't a little.'

Insanity. See entries for 'Madness' ***

'Apologies for behavior caused by indisposition - ... we are not ourselves when nature being oppress'd commands the mind to suffer with the body.'

Insincere, see 'Words, reaction to w. without meaning or sincerity - Words, words, mere words, no matter from the heart...'

Insincerity, i. suspected. See 'Suspicion, s. that show of love is insincere - ... you may think my love was crafty love and call it cunning.'

Insinuation. See 'Expression, e. indicating concealment - ... didst contract and purse thy brow together, as if thou then hadst shut up in thy brain some horrible conceit.'

Insist, do not i. - Harp not on that string, madam; that is past.

Insistence, insisting speech. See 'Speech, annoying, boisterous and loud – You cram words into mine ear against the stomach of my sense.'

Insistence, warning about further insisting - ..urge it no more on height of our displeasure…

Insistence. See 'Justification for insisting even after she said 'no' - ... maids in modesty, say 'No' to that which they would have the profferer construe 'Ay''.

Insisting, request not to insist on the same subject – harp not on that string.

Insolence, intolerable i. – … His insolence is more intolerable than all the princes in the land beside.

Insolence, questioning with i. - With many holiday and lady terms he question'd me.

Insolence, reaction to i. - ... his insolence draws folly from my lips.

Insolence. See 'Words, evil w. aggravating weight of evil act - Ill deeds are doubled with an evil word.'

Insomnia – Not enjoying the golden dew of sleep.

Insomnia. See entries for 'Sleep', 'Sleeplessness'

Inspiration, a powerful Muse required before starting a speech - O for a Muse of fire, that would ascend the brightest heaven of invention!

Inspiration, how i. works - ...the fire i' the flint shows not till it be struck.

Inspiration, she is a source of i. and poetry - Never durst poet touch a pen to write…

Inspiration, she is a superb source of i. - How can my Muse want subject to invent, while thou dost breathe..

Inspiration, she is capable of performing miracles - .. chosen from above, by inspiration of celestial grace..

Inspiration, she is the 10th Muse - Be thou the tenth Muse, ten times more in worth than those old nine which rhymers invocate..

Instinct, i. prevailing over the dictates of law - …the brain may devise laws for the blood…

Instinct, i. revealing character - .. 'Tis wonder that an invisible instinct should frame them to royalty unlearn'd.

Instructions, hope that i. will remove folly. See 'Training, t. or good sense overcoming ignorance or folly - and let instructions enter where folly now possesses.'

Instruments of darkness. See 'Appearance, a. of truth hiding a deeper and malicious purpose - ... to win us to our harm the instruments of darkness tell us truths..'

Insubordination, youthful i. - ...bristle up the crest of youth against your dignity.

Insubordination. See 'Language, insubordination in l. - ... Language unmannerly, yea, such which breaks the sides of loyalty and almost appears in loud rebellion.'

Insult, a dog, a bloodhound - ... That dog, that had his teeth before his eyes, to worry lambs and lap their gentle blood.

Insult, a longwinded speaker of nonsense - What cracker is this ass, that deafs our ears with this abundance of superfluous breath.

Insult, absolute devil - Not in the legions of horrid hell can come a devil more damn'd in

1178

evil to top Macbeth.

Insult, all noise, no substance - The empty vessel makes the greatest sound.

Insult, answer to insult of being a fool - Thou art not altogether a fool ... Nor thou altogether a wise man...

Insult, arch-villain and more – ... but he's more, had I more name for badness.

Insult, ass - Asses are made to bear, and so are you.

Insult, ass, i. delivered sarcastically - ... what a thing it is to be an ass!

Insult, beast – The very best at a beast, my lord, that ever I saw.

Insult, beshrew your heart.

Insult, better be a dog - I had rather be a dog and bay the moon than such a Roman.

Insult, better to be an animal than Menelaus - ... but to be Menelaus, I would conspire against destiny.

Insult, blisters on tongue - blistered by thy tongue, for such a wish!

Insult, blood-suckers - A knot you are of damned blood-suckers!

Insult, brain - ... as dry as the remainder biscuit after a voyage....

Insult, brainless - ... in such a barren rascal....that has no more brain than a stone.

Insult, brainless – ... thou hast no more brain in thy head than I have in mine elbows.

Insult, brainless. See 'Character, brainless – not Hercules could have knock'd out his brains, for he had none.

Insult, butcher, blood thirsty - Thou wast provoked by thy bloody mind, that never dreamt on aught but butcheries.

Insult, chicken hawk - Foul-spoken coward, that thunder'st with thy tongue...

Insult, cow in June - .. The breese upon her, like a cow in June, hoist sails and flies.

Insult, coward. See 'Insult, coward. See 'Cowardice, c. evident – .. there's no more valour in that Poins, than in a wild duck.'

Insult, coward - Coward, that thunder'st with thy tongue, and with thy weapon nothing darest perform!

Insult, coward - You are the hare of whom the proverb goes, whose valour plucks dead lions by the beard.

Insult, cowards - Souls of geese, that bear the shapes of men.

Insult, cowards, thief, thieves - ... he hath a killing tongue and a quiet sword... steal anything, and call it purchase... few bad words are matched with few good deeds.

Insult, creditors, imprecation – They have e'en put my breath from me, the slaves...

Insult, crooked - .. foul indigested lump, as crooked in thy manners as thy shape.

Insult, curse – Let vultures gripe thy guts!

Insult, curse of universal illness - Of man and beast the infinite malady crust you quite o'er!

Insult, deceit, compared to actions by crocodile - ... as the mournful crocodile with sorrow snares relenting passengers..

Insult, devil - Hell's black intelligencer.

Insult, dog - Away, inhuman dog! unhallow'd slave.

Insult, dog - It is the most impenetrable cur hat ever kept with men.

Insult, dog and abuser of patience - Out dog! out, cur! thou drivest me past the bounds of maiden's patience.

Insult, dog and retort - Thy mother's of my generation: what's she, if I be a dog?

Insult, dog and viper - ... egregious dog? O viper vile!

Insult, dog from Crete - O hound of Crete!

Insult, either ignorant by decrepitude or a fool - Either thou art most ignorant by age or thou wert born a fool.

Insult, envious tongue - .. the envious barking of thy saucy tongue.

Insult, evil, one for whom goodness is poison – All goodness is poison to thy stomach.

Insult, fat –... thou globe of sinful

continents…

Insult, fat and dishonest man. See 'Character, untruthful and dishonest - no room for faith, truth, nor honesty in this bosom of thine'

Insult, fawning greyhound. See 'Kindness, false k. - .. what a candy deal of courtesy this fawning greyhound then did proffer me!'

Insult, fit only for hell - .. thou unfit for any place but hell.

Insult, fool, response and maxim - Better a witty fool than a foolish wit.

Insult, goat - Thou damned and luxurious mountain goat.

Insult, go away - Go, base intruder! overweening slave!

Insult, go away, direct your feet - .. but direct thy feet where thou and I henceforth may never meet.

Insult, go away, I cannot stand you - Fellow, be gone: I cannot brook thy sight, this news hath made thee a most ugly man

Insult, go away – Take thy face hence.

Insult, good for nothing - To say nothing, to do nothing, to know nothing, and to have nothing..

Insult, hang thyself or equivalent - No, I will do nothing to thy bidding; make thy request to thy friend.

Insult, hatred plus - I hate thee, pronounce thee a gross lout, a mindless slave.

Insult, hell as a destination - ..would thou wert shipp'd to hell.

Insult, i. and curse - Blasts and fogs upon thee!

Insult, i. and curse – You herd of boils and plagues .. that you may be abhorr'd further than seen..

Insult, i. followed by threat - Base dunghill villain and mechanical..

Insult, i. given and returned – Dost dialog with your shadow?

Insult, i. plus threat - Abominable Gloucester, guard thy head; for I intend to have it ere long.

Insult, i. to a group, incapable of thought - . …when you speak best unto the purpose, it is not worth the wagging of your beards.

Insult, i. to a group, sickening conversation - … more of your conversation would infect my brain, being the herdsmen of the beastly plebeians.

Insult, i. to flattering parasites - Live loathed and long, ..affable wolves…

Insult, i. to individual and his followers - (Thou) idol of idiot-worshippers.

Insult, i. to masses considered as despicable - You common cry of curs! whose breath I hate as reek of the rotten fens..

Insult, i. to rebellious group - … dissentious rogues that, rubbing the poor itch of your opinion, make yourselves scabs.

Insult, ignorance - .. Would the fountain of your mind were clear again, that I might water an ass at it.

Insult, ignorant – There will be little learning die, then, that day thou art hanged.

Insult, ignorant. See 'Ignorance, i. observed in person - there is no darkness but ignorance.'

Insult, in your place I would dispose of myself - Were I like thee, I'd throw away myself.

Insult, injurer of heaven and earth - Thou monstrous injurer of heaven and earth!

Insult, lack of self-knowledge - … asses… that you ask me what you are, and do not know yourselves.

Insult, lascivious, wanton, a shame to the profession - .. Lascivious, wanton, more than well beseems a man of thy profession and degree.

Insult, last letter of the alphabet - Thou whoreson zed, thou unnecessary letter…

Insult, liar – … the lyingest knave in Christendom.

Insult, liar – … Within these forty hours Surrey durst better have burnt that tongue than said so

Insult, liar - I say, thou liest and will maintain what thou hast said is false…
Insult, liar - In thy foul throat thou liest.
Insult, liar - Thou liest, malignant thing!…
Insult, liar – Through the false passage of thy throat thou liest.
Insult, liar - You lie, up to the hearing of the gods.
Insult, liar, defense from accusation - Thou speakest it falsely, as I love mine honour.
Insult, lips – thy lips to rot off.
Insult, man like animal according to the theories of Pythagoras - thou almost make'st me waver in my faith, to hold opinion with Pythagoras…
Insult, minister of hell - .. ..thou dreadful minister of hell!"
Insult, miscellany of I, liar, hound, braggart.
Insult, murderer - Pernicious blood-sucker of sleeping men!
Insult, negative qualification, ass - .. if thou be'st not an ass, I am a youth of fourteen.
Insult, no honesty, no honor - You have as little honesty as honour.
Insult, not fit to be in the company of honest men - Fie on thee wretch! 'tis pity that thou livest to walk where any honest men resort.
Insult, not worth another word - You are not worth another word, else I'd call you knave.
Insult, nymphomaniac – … you are more intemperate in your blood than Venus …
Insult, opinion defining the man - .. An all men were o' my mind wit would be out of fashion.
Insult, opinion of a person - God made him, and therefore let him pass for a man.
Insult, owl of death – Thou ominous and fearful owl of death.
Insult, out of my sight - Out of my sight! Thou dost infect mine eyes.
Insult, pestilence - A pestilence on him!
Insult, pestilence - A pestilence on him!
Insult, plague – .. thou wast born to be a plague to men.
Insult, poison - Thou'rt poison to my blood.
Insult, retort to i. – Look in a glass, and call thy image so.
Insult, reversing the direction of the i. - Look in a glass, and call thy image so.
Insult, scorn, insult, arrogant villain, pretender - Small things make men proud..
Insult, seeing your face is like hell - I never see thy face, but I think of hell-fire.
Insult, slanderers and injurers - Thou monstrous slanderer of heaven and earth! …
Insult, snake - … with doubler tongue than thine, thou serpent, never adder stung.
Insult, son of a bitch and villain plus an ass - Thou art sensible in nothing but blows, and so is an ass.
Insult, stupid – … who wears his wit in his belly and his guts in his head
Insult, stupid, not very bright. See 'Tewksbury mustard, see 'Character, not very bright – … his wit is as thick as Tewksbury mustard.'
Insult, totally unmannered - .. ungracious wretch, Fit for the mountains and the barbarous caves… out of my sight!
Insult, traitor - … from the extremest upward of thy head to the descent and dust below thy foot…
Insult, traitors - O villains, vipers, damn'd without redemption!..
Insult, untrustworthy - .. of no more trust than love that's hired.
Insult, veiled i., prostitutes. See 'Words, refraining from using abusive w., veiled insult - .. I know you what you are… am most loath to call your faults as they are named.'
Insult, venomous toad or lizard - .. mark'd by the destinies to be avoided as venom toads, or lizards' dreadful stings.
Insult, villain - I know thee well: a serviceable villain…
Insult, villain and murderer - .. thou bloodier

villain than terms can give thee out!

Insult, wicked man – A very tainted fellow and full of wickedness.

Insult, wishing never to see a person again - If I hope well, I'll never see thee more.

Insult, worth less than dust - … You are not worth the dust which the rude wind blows in your face.

Insult, worthless - .. vile thing, let loose..

Insult, worthy of indignity - … with all my heart; and thou art worthy of it.

Insult, you are vane and untrustworthy - I trust I may not trust thee; for thy word is but the vain breath of a common man.

Insult, you don't know what you are talking about. See 'Ignorance, i. shown - you speak, Lord Mowbray, now you know not what.

Insults, a medley of i. – I had rather a beggar's dog, clean enough to spit upon.

Insults, a volley of i. – … cunning but in craft, crafty but in villany.

Insults, a volley of i. - Slave, soulless villain, dog.

Insults, volley of i. plus curses – Stay dog for thou shalt hear me, deadly eye, troubler of world's peace etc.

Insults, volley of i. – Trunk of humours, hutch of beastliness, parcel of dropsies etc.

Insurance, self-i. to pay for requirements of old age - … When service should in my old limbs lie lame and unregarded age in corners thrown.

Insurrection, see entries for 'Rebellion'.

Integrity or second stage after introduction - … my integrity never knew the craft that you do charge men with…

Integrity, i. still a value even if not practiced. See 'Angels, a. are a. even if some of them become rotten - Angels are bright still, though the brightest fell..'

Integrity, no change of mind – … nothing alter'd: what I was, I am

Integrity. See 'Character, c. observed in a person that reveals his history - … there is a kind of character in thy life…' ***
'Expression, facial e. indicating positive traits - … There is written in your brow, provost, honesty and constancy…'

Intellectuals, i. as caterpillars - All scholars, lawyers, courtiers, gentlemen, they call false caterpillars..

Intellectuals, the opposite of i. - Hard-headed men, that work in Athens here, which never laboured in their minds till now.

Intelligence services, vacuum in the i. s. - Where hath our intelligence been drunk? Where hath it slept?

Intelligence, i. available and confirmed - … and the particular confirmations, point from point, to the full arming of verity.

Intelligence, i. inspired by madness. See 'Madness, m. inspiring feats of intelligence - … a happiness that often madness hits on, which reason and sanity …' *** 'Madness, method in m. - Though this be madness, yet there is method in it'

Intelligence, gathering and sifting i. - Your bait of falsehood takes this carp of truth…. By indirections find directions out

Intemperance, i. without limits - … But there is no bottom, none to my voluptuousness.

Intemperance, see 'Lust, intemperance leading to disaster - Boundless intemperance in nature is a tyranny…'

Intent, evil i. to remain hidden – Stars hide your fires, let not light see my black and deep desires.

Intentions, do you mean it? – Fair Margaret knows that Suffolk doth not flatter, face, or feign.

Intentions, good i. gone awry - We are not the first who with best meaning have incurred the worst.

Intentions, i. misinterpreted - … some about him have too lavishly wrested his meaning and authority.

Intentions, i. that did not materialize – Thoughts are no subjects, intents but merely thoughts.

Intentions, treacherous. See 'Treason, treacherous intentions - ... so Judas kiss'd his master; and cried 'all hail!' whenas he meant all harm.'

Intentions, wicked i. shown in the type of question and type of answer - ... you question with a wicked tongue.

Interest, i. in knowing person better - .. I desire more acquaintance of you.

Interest, personal i. reply to statement indicating interest - .. I shall study deserving

Interpretation, i. is all - So our virtues lie in the interpretation of the time.. One fire drives out one fire; one nail, one nail…

Interpretation, i. of events. See 'Events, interpretation of e., how the doubtful draw their conclusions - .. how such an apprehension may turn the tide of fearful faction and breed a kind of question in our cause.

Interpretation, i. of events depending on the interpreter - ... but men may construe things after their fashion clean from the purpose of the things themselves.

Interpretation, wrong interpretation of events - … you take things ill which are not so…

Interrogation, harsh i. See 'Answer, on the point of giving reluctantly a nasty answer - will you tear impatient answers from my gentle tongue?'

Interruption, someone interrupts your speech. See entries for 'Speech, interruption of s.'

Interruption. See 'Man, tyrannical - ... and like the tyrannous breathing of the north shakes all our buds from growing.'

Introduction, avoiding nausea in the audience. See 'Sea-crossing, virtual s.-c. - ... charming the narrow seas to give you gentle pass…'

Introduction, exhortation to the audience to use their imagination - …Yet sit and see, minding true things by what their mockeries be.

Introduction, exhortation to the audience to use their imagination - …Yet sit and see, minding true things by what their mockeries be.

Introduction, subject of your talk specially important. See 'Inspiration, a powerful Muse required before starting a speech - O for a Muse of fire, that would ascend the brightest heaven of invention!'

Introduction, i. of a VIP - … But pardon, gentles all the flat unraised spirits…

Introduction, i. to a point or an argument, with irony and sarcastic affectation - ... in good faith, in sincere verity, under the allowance of your great aspect…

Introduction, i. to a presentation - ... And let me speak to the yet unknowing world how these things came about.

Introduction, i. to a presentation - As an unperfect actor on the stage, who with his fear is put besides his part…

Introduction, i. to a presentation - If you have tears, prepare to shed them now…

Introduction, i. to a presentation after a previous good speaker. See 'Speech, speaking after a well known or skillful speaker - As in a theatre, the eyes of men, after a well grac'd actor leaves the stage…'

Introduction, i. to a presentation anticipating momentous information. See 'Masters, I am to discourse wonders'

Introduction, i. to a presentation describing the fall of a man or of an idea. See 'Fall, f. from greatness - … then in a moment, see how soon this mightiness meets misery.

Introduction, i. to a presentation that contains some real or ironic sadness inducing material. See 'Sadness, license to cry - Those that can pity, here may, if they think it well, let fall a tear; the subject will deserve it.'

Introduction, i. to a presentation where subject very important. See 'Inspiration, a powerful Muse required before starting a speech - O for a Muse of fire, that would ascend the brightest heaven of invention!'

Introduction, I. to a presentation where subject is sad. See 'Sadness, license to cry - Those that can pity, here may, if they think it well, let fall a tear; the subject will deserve it.'

Introduction, i. to a presentation, stage-fright. See 'Speech, stage-fright - As an unperfect actor on the stage who with his fear is put besides his part…'

Introduction, i. to a seminar. See 'Seminar, introduction to a s. - Here let us breathe, and haply institute a course of learning, and ingenious studies.'

Introduction, i. to a speaker whose achievements will always be remembered. See ' Time, almost forever – …When time is old and hath forgot itself, when water drops have worn the stones of Troy..'

Introduction, i. to a speaker of great reputation – (a) man whose glory fills the world with loud report.

Introduction, i. to a speaker with an impressive background – … that once trod the ways of glory and sounded all the depths and shoals of honour.

Introduction, i. to a top performer. See 'Performance, p. beyond description - .. his deeds exceed all speech.'

Introduction, i. to a trend setter. See 'Trend, trend setter - … the mark and glass, copy and book that fashion'd other.'

Introduction, i. to the last part of a presentation - .. To show our simple skill that is the true beginning of our end.

Introduction, impossible to describe all her/his accomplishments in a short time - Turning the accomplishment of many years into an hour-glass..

Introduction, introducing and expert. See 'Explanation, difficult matter made easy by expert - What impossible matter will he make easy next?'

Introduction, introducing yourself after the end of a presentation by a good speaker. See 'The audience applauded at length the speaker just before it is your turn to speak'.

Introduction, invited to tell something about yourself. See entries for 'Credentials' - 'Who are you?' - 'Defence, d. from general accusations – I am a man more sinned against than sinning.'

Introduction, request to accept the limitations of the presentation and choreography - Piece out our imperfections with your thoughts…

Introduction, sad subject. See 'Sadness, license to cry - Those that can pity, here may, if they think it well, let fall a tear; the subject will deserve it'.

Introduction, self-introduction – Am bold to show myself a forward guest.. to make mine eye the witness of that report which I so oft have heard.

Introduction, self-introduction - I prithee, pretty youth, let me be better acquainted with thee.

Introduction, self-introduction to pretty lady - … Be not offended, nature's miracle, thou art allotted to be ta'en by me.

Introduction, self-introduction, modest – If one so rude and of so mean condition may pass into the presence of a king.

Introduction, you will be brief - I will be brief, for my short date of breath is not so long as is a tedious tale.

Introduction, you will be brief - O' Sir, 't is better to be brief than tedious.

Introduction, you will be brief - Since brevity is the soul of wit and tediousness the limbs and outward flourishes, I will be brief.

Introduction. See also entries for 'Presentation'

Intuition, female i. See 'Woman, w.'s intuition - I have no other reason but a woman's reason.'

Intuition, general i. - There is a thing within my bosom tells me…

Intuition, I. overpowered by sentiment. See "Siding with the losing party - …though my reason sits in the wind against me.'

Intuition, seeing through appearance - It may be so; but yet my inward soul persuades me it is otherwise.

Intuition, sudden i. about the future. See 'Future, sensing the f. in one moment - …and I feel now the future in the instant.'

Invention, extraordinary power of i. required to properly describe her – O for a Muse of fire, that would ascend the brightest heaven of invention.

Inventiveness, i., wit and geniality rewarded - …wit shall not go unrewarded while I am king of this country.

Investigation, launching an I. See 'Truth, you are determine

Investments, diversification of i. - .. my ventures are not in one bottom trusted.

Invincibility - I will not be afraid of death and bane till Birnam forest come to Dunsinane.

Invitation, i. impossible to resist - … There is no tongue that moves, none, none in the world so soon as yours could win me.

Invitation, i. not to mourn – No longer mourn for me when I am dead…

Invitation, i. refused - I have heard it said, unbidden guests are often welcomest when they are gone.

Invitation, i. refused (to dinner) – I will buy with you, sell with you….but I will not eat with you…

Invitation, i. to be frank and plain - Therefore with frank and with uncurbed plainness tell us the Dauphin's mind'.

Invitation, i. to butchery - The lamb entreats the butcher: where's thy knife

Invitation, i. to cold lady to warm up – …descend; be stone no more; approach.

Invitation, i. to dinner and to freedom from care - Let's to supper, come, and drown consideration.

Invitation, I. To eat at fast food place. See 'Food, fast f. distaste for it – On what I hate I feed not.'

Invitation, I. to give information about self. See 'Life, longing

Invitation, i. to leave out all niceties and pretenses - Lay by all nicety and prolixious blushes that banish what they sue for.

Invitation, i. to return soon – O thou that dost inhabit in my breast, leave not the mansion so long tenantless.

Invitation, i. to speak clearly. See entries for 'Speech, clarity of language/meaning requested' and 'Speech, clarity of meaning requested'.

Invitation, i. to speak openly - Say as you think, and speak it from your souls.

Invitation, i. to speak openly. See 'Speak, s. openly, not to mince words - give thy worst of thoughts the worst of words.'

Invitation, i. to speak openly among trusted friends. See 'Confidence, c. among trusted friends - … We three are but thyself; and, speaking so, thy words are but as thoughts; therefore, be bold.'

Invitation, i. to tell good news. See 'News, invitation to disclose (good) news - ram though thy fruitful tidings'.

Invitation, i. to travel - I rather would entreat thy company to see the wonders of the world abroad.

Invitation, i. to wife to sit near you - Come, madam wife, sit by my side and let the world slip: we shall ne'er be younger.

Invitation, i. to your place when you know that your place is in a state of disarray - We will give you sleepy drinks, that your senses, unintelligent of our insufficiency..

Invitation, your hand - Your hand, my Perdita, so turtles pair, that never mean to part.

Invocation - Fire and brimstone!

Invocation, accursed hour - Let this pernicious hour stand aye accursed in the calendar.

Invocation, anger - O, were mine eyeballs into bullets turned, that I, in rage, might shoot them at your faces.

Invocation, blood turn to jelly. See 'Anger,

a. at news that makes the blood curdle, invocation'.

Invocation, boldness. See 'Psychology, self-encouragement to boldness - Boldness be my friend, arm me audacity from head to foot.'

Invocation, by this and by that - By Jove that thunders!

Invocation, by this and by that – By my troth.

Invocation, by this and by that - By that fair sun which shows me where thou stand'st.

Invocation, by this and by that – By the fire that quickens Nilus' slime.

Invocation, by this and by that – By the grace of Grace

Invocation, by this and by that - By the roses of the spring.

Invocation, by this and by that – By the sacred radiance of the sun.

Invocation, by this and by that – By the salt wave of the Mediterranean.

Invocation, by this and by that - By the sky that hangs above our heads I like it well.

Invocation, by this and by that - By these blessed candles of the night..

Invocation, by this and by that – By two-headed Janus.

Invocation, by this and by that - By yond marble heaven.

Invocation, by this and by that – For all the mud in Egypt…

Invocation, by this and by that - Now, by the death of Him that died for all…

Invocation, by this and by that. See 'Love, string of compliments - … bright eyes, by her high forehead and her scarlet lip, by her fine foot, straight leg and quivering thigh…'

Invocation, damned letter - O damn'd paper! Black as the ink that's on thee!

Invocation, delivery from illusions – See 'Illusion, state of i., invocation - .. and here we wander in illusions some blessed power deliver us from hence.'

Invocation, despair – Now let hot Aetna cool in Sicily and be my heart an ever-burning hell!

Invocation, despicable administration - Hell is empty and all the devils are here.

Invocation, deviant mood – Can it be that so degenerate a strain as this should once set footing in your generous bosoms?

Invocation, end - Sun, hide thy beams! Timon hath done his reign.

Invocation, fortune. See 'Fortune, invocation - Fortune, good night: smile once more: turn thy wheel!'

Invocation, happiness in love – O Love, be moderate, allay thy ecstasy… make it less for fear I surfeit.

Invocation, heaven's doings. See 'Invocation, i. against unfair heaven - … that heaven should practise stratagems upon so soft a subject as myself!'

Invocation, horror. - … Tongue nor heart cannot conceive nor name thee!

Invocation, i. about honesty - O wretched fool, that livest to make thine honesty a vice!

Invocation, i. after feeling shame - Let life be short; else shame will be too long.

Invocation, i. against adverse Fortune - … let me rail so high that the false housewife Fortune break her wheel, provoked by my offence.

Invocation, i. against enemies – Earth, yield stinging nettles to mine enemies…

Invocation, i. against ignorance. See 'Ignorance, i. decried – O gross and miserable ignorance!'

Invocation, i. against questionable experts or presumptuous authorities. See 'Anger, a. at authorities - … woe upon ye, and all such false professors!'

Invocation, i. against the heavens for their doings - Hung be the heavens with black, yield day to night!…

Invocation, i. against time – … Thou ceaseless lackey to eternity…

Invocation, i. against rascals – … And put in every honest hand a whip to lash the rascals naked through the world…

Invocation, i. against tyranny. See 'Tyranny, invocation in helplessness - O nation miserable, with an untitled tyrant bloody-scepter'd…'

Invocation, i. against unfair heaven - … that heaven should practise stratagems upon so soft a subject as myself!

Invocation, i. against war and current times. - O, pity, God, this miserable age!…

Invocation, i. and curse to the baseness of human nature - Fly, damned baseness to him that worships thee.

Invocation, i. and satisfaction at the success of your scheme – Work on, my medicine, work!

Invocation, i. for inspiration - Assist me, some extemporal god of rhyme…

Invocation, i. for lover to come – … Come, thou day in night; for thou wilt lie upon the wings of night whiter than new snow on a raven's back.

Invocation, i. for night to come - .. Come, thick night, and pall thee in the dunnest smoke of hell…

Invocation, i. for patience, need for p. - You heavens, give me that patience, patience I need!

Invocation, i. for the world to end - O, let the vile world end and the premised flames of the last day…

Invocation, i. for thunder - O that I were a god, to shoot forth thunder upon these paltry, servile, abject drudges!

Invocation, i. in amazement - All seeing heaven, what a world is this!

Invocation, i. in the name of all the Gods at once. See first line of 'Popularity, p. questioned'

Invocation, i. in the name of truth - As there comes light from heaven, and words from breath, as there is sense in truth, and truth in virtue…

Invocation, i. in the way of assurance - Heaven and fortune bar me happy hours! …

if …

Invocation, i. not to bear or tolerate the horrible - O, horrible! O, horrible! most horrible! If thou hast nature in thee, bear it not.

Invocation, i. of desperation - Hath no man's dagger here a point for me?

Invocation, i. prompted by government's evil deeds - Woe, woe for England! not a whit for me.

Invocation, i. that faults of kings be not hidden - … heaven forbid that kings should let their ears hear their faults hid!

Invocation, i. to affirm that truth is on your side. See 'Truth, t. evident and on my side - By him that made me, I'll maintain my words on any plot of ground on Christendom.'

Invocation, i. to angels and superior powers – Angels and ministers of grace defend us!

Invocation, I. to a tought world. See 'World, a tough w. to live in - O, how full of briers is this working-day world.'

Invocation, i. to an oath maintained - Let nature crush the sides o' the earth together and mar the seeds within!

Invocation, i. to bullets, do not hit - O, you leaden messengers, that ride upon the wicked speed of fire…

Invocation, i. to comets and physical phenomena - yield day to night! Comets, importing changes of times and states..

Invocation, i. to conscience. See 'Conscience, tormenting c. – O coward conscience, how dost thou afflict me.'

Invocation, i. to constancy - O constancy, be strong upon my side, set a huge mountain 'tween my heart and tongue!

Invocation, i. to cruelty. See 'Cruelty, invocation to c. by a woman – Come, you spirits that tend on mortal thoughts, unsex me here…

Invocation, i. to flattery - O, that men's ears should be to counsel deaf, but not to flattery.

Invocation, i. to fortune. See entries for 'Fortune, invocation'

Invocation, i. to God - God befriend us, as our cause is just!

Invocation, i. to gold as a corrupter. See 'Gold, corrupting effects of g. - O thou sweet king-killer, and dear divorce 'twixt natural son and sire!…'

Invocation, i. to hard times – O heavy times, begetting such events!

Invocation, i. to heaven addressing the character of a person. See 'Suspicion, s. rejected - Heaven make you better than your thoughts!'

Invocation, i. to heavens that tolerate the victory of hell – Heavens, can you suffer hell so to prevail?

Invocation, i. to ignorance - O thou monster Ignorance, how deformed dost thou look!

Invocation, i. to mischief. See 'Desperation, d. leading to desperate acts - O mischief, thou art swift to enter in the thoughts of desperate men!'

Invocation, i. to one's own power of prediction - O my prophetic soul!

Invocation, i. to quench thirst and heat . See 'Thirst, parched lips begging for water - … entreat the north to make his bleak wind kiss my parched lips…'

Invocation, i. to the Gods – Gods and goddesses, all the whole synod of them!

Invocation, i. to the world and its vicissitudes – World, world, O world! But that thy strange mutations make us hate thee…

Invocation, i. to heaven not to see men's evil acts - O, you powers! that give heaven countless eyes to view men's acts.

Invocation, i. to heaven that I am telling the truth - Heaven be the record to my speech.

Invocation, i. to heaven to send down justice. See 'Justice, no j. on earth – invocation to heaven to send down justice'.

Invocation, i. to heaven, that what is feared be not true - Grant, heavens, that which I fear prove false!

Invocation, i. to honest p. See 'Power, invocation for honestly acquired p. - O, that estates, degrees and offices were not derived corruptly…'

Invocation, i. to ingratitude. See entries for 'Ingratitude, invocation to i.'

Invocation, i. to Jove for hope – Great Jove… give renew'd fire to our extinct spirits.

Invocation, i. to nature as a supreme ruler, also answer to a request from your girlfriend - Thou, nature, art my goddess; to thy law my services are bound.

Invocation, i. to Neptune to calm a sea and thunder storm - … rebuke these surges, which wash both heaven and hell…

Invocation, i. to predict the future. See entries for 'Prediction, desire to know in advance'

Invocation, i. to revenge - Arise, black vengeance, from thy hollow cell!

Invocation, i. to self-safety in combat - God keep lead out of me! I need no more weight than mine own bowels.

Invocation, i. to stormy skies - Yet cease your ire, you angry stars of heaven!…

Invocation, i. to success in the pursuit of love - Love, lend me wings to make my purpose swift..

Invocation, i. to the gods for justice - We will solicit heaven and move the gods to send down Justice for to wreak our wrongs.

Invocation, i. to the moon, massive depression - O sovereign mistress of true melancholy,…

Invocation, i. to the world and its vicissitudes – World, world, O world! But that thy strange mutations make us hate thee…

Invocation, i. to thunder - And thou, all-shaking thunder, smite flat the thick rotundity o' the world!

Invocation, i. to time as a problem solver - O time, thou must untangle this, not I; it is too hard a knot for me to untie.

Invocation, i. to utter falsehood - Let all untruths stand by thy stained name and they'll seem glorious.

Invocation, I. to war. See 'War, let there be war - O war, thou son of hell, whom angry heavens do make their minister…'

Invocation, if I ever have done anything like this then... See 'Anger, a. at news that makes thee blood curdle, invocation - .. then my best blood turn to an infected jelly.'

Invocation, if real merit were rewarded and not theft.

Invocation, if this happens then... - Then let the pebbles on the hungry beach fillip the stars…

Invocation - … in the names of all the gods at once

Invocation - In the name of something holy…

Invocation, ironic i. applicable to fools – God give them wisdom that have it; and those that are fools, let them use their talents.

Invocation, let the sky rain potatoes - Let the sky rain potatoes; let it thunder to the tune of Green Sleeves

Invocation, let's go, I am upset - O, come away! My soul is full of discord and dismay.

Invocation, madness generalized - Mad world! mad kings! mad disposition!

Invocation, misplaced ambition, see the results - Ill-weav'd ambition, how much art thou shrunk!

Invocation, mistrust in human nature – Grant I may never prove so fond, to trust man on his oath or bond.

Invocation, no honesty among thieves - .. a plague upon it when thieves cannot be true one to another!

Invocation, no pity in the clouds - Is there no pity sitting in the clouds that sees into the bottom of my grief?

Invocation, obstinacy - Let it be virtuous to be obstinate.

Invocation, protection from shame - The gods defend him from so great a shame!

Invocation, rain as tears - Dissolve, thick cloud, and rain; that I may say, the gods themselves do weep!

Invocation, rascals to be punished - And put in every honest hand a whip to lash the rascals naked through the world..

Invocation, rather this than… - May that ground gape and swallow me alive…

Invocation, reluctance to shut up. See 'Silence, self-enforced - It is not nor it cannot come to good: but break, my heart; for I must hold my tongue.'

Invocation, retraction of statement. See 'Meaning, denial of meaning, invocation - Now the witch take me, if I meant it thus!'

Invocation, revenge - "I am Revenge: sent from the infernal kingdom, to ease the gnawing vulture of thy mind…'

Invocation, shame - Live in thy shame, but die not shame with thee!

Invocation, shamelessness - O shame, where is thy blush!

Invocation, skepticism about human nature - O, what men dare do! what men may do! what men daily do! not knowing what they do!

Invocation, stars - See 'Intent, evil i. to remain hidden – stars hide your fires, let not light see my black and deep desires.'

Invocation, state of country – Bleed, bleed, poor country! Great tyranny! lay thou thy basis sure…

Invocation, stones in heaven - Are there no stones in heaven but what serve for thunder?

Invocation, sun – O sun, Burn the great sphere thou movest in!

Invocation, that heaven may not see disgusting acts - O you powers that give heaven countless eyes to view men's acts…

Invocation, thunder in the mouth – O, that my tongue were in the thunder's mouth! Then with a passion would I shake the world.

Invocation, time, short time for good-byes -

Injurious time now with a robber's haste…

Invocation, unholy alliance. See 'Alliance, unholy a. - O inglorious league!'

Invocation, unkind hour - Ah, what an unkind hour is guilty of this lamentable chance!

Invocation, war. See 'War, let there be war - O war, thou son of hell, whom angry heavens do make their minister…'

Invocation, why does it fall to me to do this! - The time is out of joint - O cursed spite, that ever I was born to set it right.

Invocation, wish to disappear. See 'Pessimism, life - "O, that this too too solid flesh would melt thaw and resolve itself into a dew'

Invocation, you never said anything more inappropriate or untrue. See 'Speech, completely unbecoming – you never spoke what did become you less'

Irish Wolves. See 'Music, distasteful or that you do not like - .. 'tis like the howling of Irish wolves against the moon.'

Irrelevance, bound to i. - ... snapper-up of unconsidered trifles.

Is he asleep? See 'Sleep, someone fast asleep - As fast lock'd up in sleep as guiltless labour when lies starkly in the traveller's bones.'

Is he asleep? See 'Sleep, someone fast asleep - As fast lock'd up in sleep as guiltless labour when lies starkly in the traveller's bones.'

It is the east, and Juliet is the sun. See 'Light, l. through a window – … what light through yonder window breaks? It is the east…'

Is it thy will thy image... See 'Mind, always on your mind - Is it thy will thy image should keep open my heavy eyelids to the weary night?'

Is it true? See 'True, absolutely and emphatically t. - As certain as I know the sun is fire.' *** 'Truth, t. emphatically asserted – … never man sigh'd truer breath.' *** Other entries for 'Truth'

Is it you? See 'Voice, v. recognition - ... if you knew his pure heart's truth, you would quickly learn to know him by his voice.'

Issue, outcome of political i. or debate uncertain – This battle fares like to the morning's war…

It is a custom more honour'd in the breach than the observance. See 'Custom, c. more ignored than followed'

It is not nor it cannot come to good. See 'Silence, self-enforced - It is not nor it cannot come to good: but break, my heart; for I must hold my tongue.'

Is this a good time? See 'Time, appropriate t. for whatever needs to be done – Every time serves for the matter that is then born in it.'

Is this a dagger which I see before me? See 'Reality and imagination - …art thou but a dagger of the mind, a false creation, proceeding from the heat-oppressed brain.'

It smells to heaven. See 'Crime, extreme c. - O, my offence is rank it smells to heaven.'

Issue, very clear i. - … as clear as is the summer's sun..

Jargon, people who use jargon - They have been at a great feast of languages, and stolen the scraps.

Jealousy, a standard accompaniment of love - ... love, thou know'st, is full of jealousy.

Jealousy, characteristic of j. and of the jealous – … They are not ever jealous for the cause but jealous for they are jealous…

Jealousy, effects of j. - … the food that to him now is as luscious as locusts, shall be to him shortly as bitter as coloquintida.

Jealousy, evidence of deceit invented - These are the forgeries of jealousy.

Jealousy, j. and suspicion eliminated. See 'Suspicion, s. removed and trust restored - I rather will suspect the sun with cold than thee with wantonness'.

Jealousy, j. as a monster and to be avoided - T'is the green-eyed monster, which doth mock the eat it feeds on.

Jealousy, j. as a poison - The venom clamour of a jealous woman poisons more deadly than a mad dog's tooth.

Jealousy, j. barring sleep - .. Nor all the drowsy syrups of the world shall ever medicine thee to that sweet sleep which thou owed'st yesterday.

Jealousy, j. beyond the reach of judgment - … a jealousy so strong that judgment cannot cure.

Jealousy, j. left to the fools - How many fond fools serve mad jealousy.

Jealousy, j. prompting madness in the man subjected to it. - … thy jealous fits have scared thy husband from the use of wits.

Jealousy, jealous and passionate - I will be more jealous of thee than a Barbary cock-pigeon over his hen…

Jealousy, no j. – Nor dare I question with my jealous thought…

Jealousy, trifles make the jealous jealous - Trifles light as air are to the jealous confirmation strong as proofs of holy writ.

Jest, see entries for 'Joke'

Jesters, j. as accurate predictors of events. See 'Humor, truth in h. - Jesters do oft prove prophets.'

Jewel, like an expensive jewel - … she hangs upon the cheek of night as a rich jewel in an Ethiop's ear..

Jewel, reputation as a jewel. See 'Reputation, r. more valuable than earthly goods – Good name in man and woman, dear my lord, is the immediate jewel of their souls…'

Jewelry, gifts large and small - … Dumb jewels often, in their silent kind, More than quick words, do move a woman's mind.

Jewelry, value of j. depending on fancy - … Or stones whose rates are either rich or poor as fancy values them.

Jewelry, value of discount jewel increased by the charm of the wearer – You mend the jewel by the wearing it.

Job, no j. is dishonorable. See 'Perception, p. determining judgment – This service is not service, so being done but being so allow'd.'

Joining the party – The swallow follows not summer more willing than we your lordship

Joke, a j. you don't find funny - This jest is dry to me.

Joke, determining if a j. is good or not - A jest's prosperity lies in the ear of him that hears it…

Joke, j. inappropriate. See 'Love, l.'s pains not to be laughed at - He jests at scars that never felt a wound.'

Joke, answer to a joke on you. See 'Insult, lips – thy lips to rot off.'

Joke, more nonsense than a j. - These are old fond paradoxes, to make fools laugh in the alehouse.'

Joke, poor j. - His jest will savour but of shallow wit, when thousands weep, more than did laugh at it.

Joke, semi-ironic reaction to j. – I will bite thee by the ear for that jest.

Jokes, amusing deliverer of j. See 'Character, a humorous c. - … When I am dull with care and melancholy lightens my humour with his merry jests.'

Jokes, j. inappropriate to the moment or situation - .. these jests are out of season; reserve them till a merrier hour than this.

Jokes, no time for joking - … 't is no time to jest, and therefore frame your manners to the time.

Jokes, no time for joking - … do not play in wench-like words with that which is so serious.

Jokes, no time for joking - Reply not to me with a fool-born jest…

Jokes, not in the mood for j. - I am not in a sportive humour now; tell me and dally not, where is the money?

Jokes, the butt of others' jokes - … the brain of this foolish-compounded clay, man, is not able to invent..

Joking, freedom to joke depending on class. See 'License, l. to use humor limited - Great men may jest with saints; 'tis wit in them but in the less foul profanation.'

Joking, leave me out of it - Make yourself mirth with your particular fancy, and leave me out on it.

Judas. See 'Treason, treacherous intentions - ... so Judas kiss'd his master; and cried 'all hail!' whenas he meant all harm.'

Judge, thief, which is which? - ... change places; and, handy-dandy, which is the justice, which is the thief?

Judges, j. as thieves - Thieves for their robbery have authority when judges steal themselves.

Judgment, agreeing with the judge – A Daniel come to judgment! yea, a Daniel!

Judgment, biased j. See entries for 'Remembering, r. the bad more than the good'.

Judgment, fear of final j. – The urging of that word 'judgment' hath bred a kind of remorse in me.

Judgment, inability to assess the situation - You smell this business with a sense as cold as is a dead man's nose.

Judgment, j. and offence are not the same thing – To offend, and judge, are distinct offices and of opposed natures.

Judgment, j. as the mark of man - .. poor Ophelia, divided from herself and her fair judgment, without the which we are pictures, or mere beasts.

Judgment, j. tempted by desire – often… mine ear hath tempted judgment to desire.

Judgment, j. vanished - O judgment, thou art fled to brutish beasts and men have lost their reason.

Judgment, men's j. affected by circumstances and showing their character - …I see men's judgments are a parcel of their fortunes…

Judgment, no fear of j. - What judgment shall I dread, doing no wrong?

Judgment, poor j. compared to not seeing well - ... our very eyes are sometimes like our judgments, blind!

Judgment, refraining from j. – ... in these nice sharp quillets of the law, good faith, I am no wiser than a daw.

Judgment, skepticism about people's j. – All that follow their noses are led by their eyes but blind men…

Judgment, suspending j. for we all are at fault - Forbear to judge, for we are sinners all.

Judgment, unjust j. See 'Law, unjust l. - ... if I shall be condemn'd upon surmises... I tell you 'tis rigor and not law.'

Judgment, unfair sentence and war on literacy - .. because they could not read, thou hast hanged them…

Judgment, without j. - Sense, sure, you have, else could you not have motion, but…

Judgment. See entries for 'Retribution'.

July, J. as a term of reference for clarity. See 'Evidence, e. very clear – ... proofs as clear as founts in July when we see each grain of gravel...'

Justice, bringing offenders to j. - ..and poise the cause in justice's equal scales, whose beam stands sure, whose rightful cause prevails

Justice, corruption of j. by commercial interests - In the corrupted currents of this world, offence's gilded hand may shove by justice...

Justice, fitting the law to the will of the powerful - ... Bidding the law make court'sy to their will, hooking both right and wrong to the appetite…

Justice, God as incorruptible judge - Heaven is above all yet; there sits a judge that king can corrupt.

Justice, gold buys j. - Plate sin with gold and the strong lance of justice hurtless breaks…

Justice, hope in j. after death – My comfort is that heaven will … plague injustice with the pains of hell.

Justice, j. of the Gods. See 'Retribution, divine r. - The gods are just, and of our pleasant vices make instruments to plague us.'

Justice, j. standing between right and wrong. See 'Leadership, consequences of a lack of l.

– Strength should be lord of imbecility...right and wrong...should lose their names...'

Justice, j. unevenly applied. See 'Injustice, justice unequally applied - Some rise by sin and some by virtue fall...'

Justice, misapplied and arbitrary, time for revolution - ... now breathless wrong shall sit and pant in your great chairs of ease...

Justice, mocked by the presence of laws that are not enforced. See 'Laws, l. disregarded – I have seen corruption boil and bubble till it o'er-run the stew...'

Justice, no j. on earth. See 'Invocation, i. to the gods for justice - We will solicit heaven and move the gods to send down Justice for to wreak our wrongs.'

Justice, no j. possible from the very author of the crime - ... You bid me seek redemption of the devil.

Justice, pretence of j. to justify selfish gain - .. and by this face this seeming brow of justice, did he win..

Justice, purchased and corrupted by money. See 'Justice, gold buys j. - Plate sin with gold and the strong lance of justice hurtless breaks...'

Justice, right and wrong lost when there is no principle - Force should be right; or rather, right and wrong, between whose endless jar justice resides...

Justice, j. tainted - ... craft, being richer than innocency, stands for the facing

Justification for insisting after a rejection - A woman sometimes scorns what best contents her.

Justification for insisting even after she said 'no' - ... maids in modesty, say 'No' to that which they would have the profferer construe 'Ay".

Justification for insisting even after she said 'no' – Things out of hope are compass'd oft with venturing, chiefly in love.

Justification, request for j. for change of heart and feeling - ... when was the hour I ever contradicted your desire...

Justification, self j. - I hope this reason stands for my excuse.

Kill him - ...Off with the crown, and with the crown his head...

Kill him – ...to the Tower and chop away that factious pate of his.

Kill me if I go back. See 'Determination, d. never to retreat - Him I forgive my death that killeth me when he sees me go back one foot or fly.'

Killing, k. in self-defense. See 'Self-defense, killing in s-d - To kill, I grant, is sin's extremest gust but, in defence, by mercy, 'tis most just.'

Killing, unjust k. breeds revenge - ... to end one doubt by death revives two greater in the heirs of life.

Kindness always, I am always kind - For Caesar cannot live to be ungentle.

Kindness conducive to love more than external appearance - Kindness in women, not their beauteous looks shall win my love.

Kindness, false k. - ... what a candy deal of courtesy this fawning greyhound then did proffer me!

Kindness, k. and thoughtfulness rewarded. See 'Woman, thoughtful and gentle w. - You bear a gentle mind, and heavenly blessings follow such creatures.'

Kindness, k. applied even to the wicked - ... for I am one of those gentle ones that will use the devil himself with courtesy.

Kindness, k. misplaced and bestowed on a snake - Why strew'st thy sugar on that bottled spider...

Kindness, k. more effective than arrogance to achieve results. See 'Request, more successful made with kindness than with arrogance – You may ride with one soft kiss a thousand furlongs ere with spur we heat an acre.'

Kindness, k. more effective than rudeness to achieve results - What thou wilt, thou rather shalt enforce it with thy smile, than hew to it with thy sword.'

Kindness, k. more effective than rudeness to achieve results - Your gentleness shall force more than your force move us to gentleness.

Kindness, k. poorly repaid - Who, then, dares to be half so kind again? For bounty, that makes gods, does still mar men.

Kindness, lack of k. See 'Ingratitude, i. as a deformity - In nature there's no blemish but the mind,…'

King of infinite space. See 'Contentment, the art of c. - I could be bounded in a nutshell, and count myself a king of infinite space,'

King, fall of king affects everyone and everybody. See 'Management, m. changes at the top and consequences – The cease of majesty, but, like a gulf doth draw what's near it with it…'

King, how nice to be a k. - … how sweet a thing it is to wear a crown.

King, k. that shares the pain of his subjects – Much is your sorrow; mine ten times so much.

King, k's approval ratings to a minimum – … For yet may England curse my wretched reign

King, k.'s power in the name itself – Is not the king's name twenty thousand names?

King, kingly power unshakable. See 'Position, p. felt secure due to tenure - Not all the water in the rough, rude sea can wash the balm from an anointed king…'

King. See 'Appearance, kingly - … every inch a king'

Kings, authority, lying. See 'Falsehood, f. worse in higher ups than common people - … and falsehood is worse in kings than beggars.'

Kings, authority, making their own laws - Kings are the earth's gods: in vice their law is their will…

Kings, authority, vices of k. better kept secret - Who has a book of all that monarchs do, he's more secure to keep it shut, than shown…

Kings, k. just like other people. See 'Human Nature, h.n. common to even kings - I live with bread like you, feel want, taste grief, need friends..'

Kings, supreme power of k. - … such is the breath of kings

Kiss of death, figuratively speaking – Thus with a kiss I die.

Kiss of welcome. See 'Welcome, w. kiss. - I can express no kinder sign of love, than this kind kiss.'

Kiss, longing for a k. – Never did passenger in summer's heat more thirst for drink than…

Kisses, cold k. – … a nun of winter's sisterhood kisses not more religiously…

Kissing, compared to the sun kissing a rose - So sweet a kiss the golden sun gives not to those fresh morning drops upon the rose.

Kissing, invitation to kiss - Touch but my lips with those fair lips of thine..

Kissing, invitation to mix kissing with gentle words - … speak fair words, or else be mute: give me one kiss…

Kissing, invitation to sit down and kiss - Here come and sit, where never serpent hisses..

Kissing, k. a princess – O, le me kiss this princess of pure white, this seal of bliss!

Kissing, prepared extremities for kissing - I know a lady in Venice would have walked barefoot to Palestine for a touch of his nether lip.

Kissing, the first kiss – The tender spring upon thy tempting lip shows thee unripe; yet mayst thou well be tasted.

Kneeling, k. for request - … with no softer cushion than the flint, I kneel before thee.

Knife. See 'Tool, t. of destruction not used - Hence, vile instrument! Thou shalt not damn my hand' – 'Depression, general depression leading to total pessimism – whips and scorns of time'.

Knock, hard k. on door - .. That spirit's possessed with haste that wounds the unsisting postern with these strokes.

Knock, hard k. on door - What's he that knocks as he would beat down the gate?

Knock, knock! - Knock, knock, knock! Who's there, i' the name of Beelzebub?

Knots, k. as representation of obstacles. See 'Expectations, e. fed by hope often frustrated by reality - The ample proposition that hope makes in all designs begun on earth below fails in the promised largeness…'

Knowledge, bookish k. ineffective – Small have continual plodders ever won save base authority from others' books.

Knowledge, man well known in town - Thy very stones prate of my whereabout..

Knowledge, k. by fame, hearsay and reputation - this famous Duke of Milan of whom so often I have heard renown but never saw before.

Knowledge, search for k. - … and with satiety seeks to quench his thirst.

Knowledge, she is the absolute source of your k. - But thou art all my art, and dost advance as high as learning, my rude ignorance.

Label, l. should be irrelevant. See 'Name, n. or label, irrelevant - … That which we call a rose by any other name would smell as sweet.'

Label, power of the label – …the king's name is a tower of strength.

Label, power of the label. See 'Image, the power of i. to deceive and corrupt - O place! O form! How often dost thou with thy case, thy habit, wrench awe from fools…'

Labor, description of repetitive work – … from the rise to set sweats in the eye of Phoebus and all night…

Labor, heavy lifting, offer to carry her suitcase - I'd rather crack my sinews, break my back than you such dishonour undergo as I sit lazy by.

Labor, value of manual l. – … for there's no better sign of a brave mind than a hard hand.

Labor, ultimate uselessness of patient l. – … they say, all the yarn she spun in Ulysses'

absence did but fill Ithaca full of moths.

Ladies, beautiful l. See 'Party, many fine ladies expected - look to behold this night earth treading stars, that make dark heaven light.'

Ladies, l's man and yet not – I'll make my heaven in a lady's lap, and deck my body in gay ornaments…

Lady, apologies to l. for having caused offence. See 'Apologies to lady for having caused offense - .. to make a sweet lady sad is a sour offence.'

Lady, l. killer – … a lady in Venice would have walked barefoot to Palestine for a touch of his nether lip.

Lady, l. killer - … sometimes the beam of her view gilded my foot, sometimes my portly belly.

Lady, l. killer - This gallant pins the wenches on his sleeve; had he been Adam, he had tempted Eve.

Lady, l. killer - This is the flower that smiles on every one to show his teeth as white as whale's bone.

Lady, l. killer. See also entries for 'Casanova'.

Lady, l. who behaved rottenly towards you - For sweetest things turn sourest by their deeds…

Laid on with a trowel - Well said: that was laid on with a trowel.

Lamb, more a wolf than a l. See 'Appearances, a. deceptive or false – Seems he a dove? his feathers are but borrowed…'

Lamb, skin of l. used for malicious purposes. See 'Lawyers, tricks of l. - Is not this a lamentable thing, that of the skin of an innocent lamb… should undo a man?'

Lamentation, no need for help in l. - Give me no help in lamentation; I am not barren to bring forth complaints..

Lamentations, generating l. - I am your sorrow's nurse, and will pamper it with lamentations.

Lamentations. See entries for 'Grievances'
*** Entries for 'Complaint, c. after problems

useless'

Land, l. preferable to sea - ... would I give a thousand furlongs of sea for an acre of barren ground...

Land, value of l. lowered - ... you may buy land now as cheap as stinking mackerel.

Language, hackers of English – ... let them question: let them keep their limbs whole and hack our English.

Language, his English marginal – ... at the taunt of one that makes fritters of English.

Language, insubordination in l. - .. Language unmannerly, yea, such which breaks the sides of loyalty and almost appears in loud rebellion.

Language, l. barriers, foreign tongues. See entries for 'Foreign girls'.

Language, l. education. See 'Education, literature, results of teaching - You taught me language and my profit on it is, I know how to curse.'

Language, l. of peasants – Talk like the vulgar sort of market men...

Language, no correct l. adequate to describe the fault - ... There is not chastity enough in language without offence to utter them.

Language, risqué l. justified - ... If I chance to talk a little wild, forgive me, I had it from my father.

Language, ununderstandable l. See entries for 'Speech, nonsensical or meaningless.'

Language, watch your l. See 'Speech, language, watch your language - Take heed, be wary how you place your words.'

Lark. See 'Music, m. of the lark – the lark, whose notes do beat the vaulty heaven so high above our heads.' *** 'Music, unpleasant and discordant - ...Straining harsh discords and unpleasing sharps.'

Lascivious remark – That's a lascivious apprehension.... So thou apprehendest it: take it for thy labour.

Last, not being the l. better than nothing - not being the worst stands in some rank of praise.

Last to know. See 'Information, last to know - Nimble mischance, that art so light of foot... and am I last that knows it?'

Latin, adequacy in L. - Satis quod sufficit.

Latin, few words as a sign of wisdom - Vir sapit, qui pauca loquitur.

Latin, incorrect L. - I smell false Latin.

Latin, Ira furor brevis est (ire is a short fury). See 'Character, c. always angry – ira furor brevis est, but yond' man is ever angry.' *** Introduction an entries for 'Anger'

Latin, l. as a liability. See 'Foreign language, knowledge of Latin a liability - Away with him, away with him! he speaks Latin.'

Latin, l. for the lower middle classes - 'Hang-hog' is Latin for bacon, I warrant you.

Latin, no l. please we are British – ... no Latin; I am not such a truant since my coming as not to know the language I have lived in...

Laugh, laughable matter or character - If you desire the spleen, and will laugh yourself into stitches, follow me.

Laughing, l. matter for a long time - ...argument for a week, laughter for a month and a good jest for ever.

Laughing, reasons for not l. - ... and for mine own part, I durst not laugh, for fear of opening my lips and receiving the bad air.

Laughter as a medicine. See 'Health, laughter as a medicine - With mirth and laughter let old wrinkles come and let my liver rather heat with wine...'

Laughter, fit of l. - I am stabbed with laughter.

Laughter, forced l. - ... the heaving of my lungs provokes me to ridiculous smiling.

Laughter, l. not called for - Laughest thou, wretch? thy mirth shall turn to moan.

Laughter, l. provoked by a funny character. See 'Character, funny c. - I warrant thou art a merry fellow.'

Laughter, laughing to tears -... I must confess, made nine eyes water; but more merry tears the passion of loud laughter never shed.

Laughter, opportunity for l. not to be missed - I will not give my part of this sport for a pension of thousands to be paid by the Sophy.

Laughter, people who always l. See 'Character, always laughing and does not taking things seriously - are of such sensible and nimble lungs that they always use to laugh at nothing.'

Laughter, refractory to l. See 'Wine, w. as an ingredient for a sense of humor - .. nor a man cannot make him laugh; but that's no marvel, he drinks no wine.'

Law, anarchy as a consequence of unjust law – When law can do no right, let it be lawful that law bar no wrong.

Law, authorities making their will the l. - … bidding the law make court'sy to their will…

Law, corruption of the l, - what plea so tainted and corrupt… being seasoned with a gracious voice.

Law, l. acts on what is visible – What's open made to justice, that justice seizes… The jewel that we find, we stoop and take't…

Law, l. and order – There is a law in each well-order'd nation to curb those raging appetites…

Law, l. and precedent – 'Twill be recorded for a precedent, and many an error by the same example…

Law, l. discriminatory and against the poor - … here's a fish hangs in the net….

Law, l. maybe right but judges questionable - … (the law) has done upon the premises, but justice, but those that sought it I could wish more christians.

Law, l. must be enforced - We must not make a scarecrow of the law..

Law, l. not allowing for justification - I cannot justify whom the law condemns.

Law, l. to repress base passions - There is a law in each well ordered nation, to curb these raging appetites…

Law, l. vs. personal will - I have been a truant to the law.

Law, precedent in l. – … no power in Venice can alter a decree established: 'twill be recorded for a precedent…

Law, punishment as a deterrent – Those many had not dared to do that evil…

Law, rules of law abolished - The wild dog shall flesh his tooth on every innocent.

Law, trial jury may include criminals – The jury, passing on the prisoner's life, may in the sworn twelve have a thief or two…

Law, unjust l. - … if I shall be condemn'd upon surmises… I tell you 'tis rigor and not law.

Laws, l. on the book but not enforced – … the enrolled penalties which have, like unscour'd armour, hung by the wall…

Laws, l. disregarded – I have seen corruption boil and bubble till it o'er-run the stew…

Laws, l. to be enforced - …our decrees, dead to infliction, to themselves are dead…

Laws, questionable effects of repressive l. against licentious behavior - …. it is impossible to extirp it quite, friar, till eating and drinking be put down.

Lawyers, l. debate mightily but remain friends. See 'Debate, feisty but friendly d. - strive mightily, but eat and drink as friends.'

Lawyers, tricks of l. - Is not this a lamentable thing, that of the skin of an innocent lamb… should undo a man?

Lawyers. See 'Opinion, your op. on lawyers - The first thing we do, let's kill all the lawyers.'

Leader, l. loved until in power, loosing leader missed. See addition to 'Opinion, your op. on crowds and masses - This common body, like to a vagabond flag upon the stream, goes to and back…'

Leader, metaphor for a l. – When that the general is not like the hive…what honey is expected?

Leader, new l. inexperienced or tyrannical. See 'Behavior, tyrannical b. of a newly appointed leader - fault and glimpse of newness'.

Leaders, l. and followers. See 'Management, m. and managers - We cannot all be masters, nor all masters cannot be truly follow'd.'

Leadership, consequences of a lack of l. – Strength should be lord of imbecility…right and wrong…should lose their names…

Leadership, consequences of an absent leader - Indeed a sheep doth very often stray if the shepherd be awhile away

Leadership, l. indispensable - …and knowing this kingdom is without a head..

Leadership, wishing for a l. change - … a swift blessing may soon return to this our suffering country..

Learning, a man of commendable l. - …learning, the greatness whereof I cannot enough commend.

Learning, in awe at learning. See 'Advice, a. welcome and praised, along with praise of learning - I could have stay'd here all the night to hear good counsel: O, what learning is!'

Learning, l. as an addition to our personality – Learning is but an adjunct to ourselves, and where we are, our learning likewise is.

Learning, power of l. - O this learning, what a thing it is.

Learning, power of l. better displayed after a drink – … and learning a mere hoard of gold kept by a devil, till sack commences it and sets it in act and use.

Learning the ways of the world. See 'Deceit, learning the tricks of d. to avoid it - to avoid deceit, I mean to learn, for it shall strew the footsteps of my rising.'

Leaving the country - Then thus I turn me from my country's light.

Leftist Declarations. See 'Social issues, proletariat's point of view - .. the leanness that afflicts us, the object of our misery… our sufferance is a gain to them' *** 'Hunger

Legality, l. upside down. See 'Di

Leg pulling, response to l.p.– Make yourself mirth with your particular fancy and leave me out on't.

Legs, tired l. See 'Walking, tired of w. - My legs can keep no pace with my desires, here will I rest me…'

Lend me your ears. See 'Request to be heard - … Countrymen, lend me your ears…'

Lenity. See entries for 'Mercy'.

Leperous distilment. See 'Wine, w. of horrible quality – (A) leperous distilment, whose effect holds an enmity with blood of man.'

Lesson, l. given was understood - I shall th'effect of this good lesson keep as watchman to my heart.

Let me not to the marriage of true minds… See 'Love, unshakable and beyond any obstacle - Let me not to the marriage of true minds admit impediments.'

Let your own discretion be your tutor. See 'Action, request for advice on how or what to do'

Let's do it quickly. See 'Exhortation, e. to act quickly – … make no delay:: we may effect this business yet ere day.'

Let's get out of here – … To seek the empty, vast and wandering air.

Let's go inside. See 'Health-care, exposure to night temperature - The tyranny of the open night's too rough for nature to endure.

Let's make dust our paper and with rainy eyes… See 'Disappointment, d. expressed in dramatic terms'

Let's purge this choler without letting blood. – See 'Peace, p. making efforts.'

Letter, ending of l. - Your ladyship's in all desired employment.

Letter, ending of love's letter. See 'Love, l. letter ending – Thine own true knight, by day or night…'

Letter, l. too long - The letter is too long by half a mile.

Letter, l. written immediately fresh from receiving ideas and inspiration - I'll write straight; the matter's in my head and in my

1198

heart.

Letter, silly l. - What plume of feathers is he that indited this letter?

Letters, see 'Writing, letters anxiously awaited - ...and with mine eyes I'll drink the words you send though ink be made of gall.'

Letters, see 'Writing, letters anxiously awaited - ...and with mine eyes I'll drink the words you send though ink be made of gall.'

Liability, small defect overshadowing all other virtues. See 'Fault, one f. obscuring all other virtues - ... the stamp of one defect... shall in the general censure take corruption from that particular fault.'

Liar, a breaker of promises - He professes no keeping of oaths; in breaking them he is stronger than Hercules.

Liar, a well known l. - He's quoted for a most perfidious slave, whose nature sickens, but to speak the truth.

Liar, an endless l. - An infinite and endless liar.

Liar, an endless l. who once makes an exception - This is the first truth that ever thine own tongue was guilty of.

Liar, habitual l. –... and every third word a lie.

Liar, imaginative l. - … return with an invention and clap upon you two or three probable lies.

Liar, making allowances for some lies and punishment for an incorrigible l. – … and uses a known truth to pass a thousand nothings …

Liar, pathologic l. - .. and swear the lies he forges.

Liar, twenty times a l. – If thou deny'st it twenty times, thou liest…

Liar. see 'Character, liar - .. he will lie, sir, with such volubility, that you would think truth were a fool.'

Liars – men of less truth than tongue.

Liberality, l. excessive - ... Plutus the God of gold is but his steward.

Liberty, fighting to maintain one's l. - We'll mingle our bloods together in the earth, from whence we had our being and our birth.

Library, l. as a dukedom. See 'Character, bookworm – ...my library was dukedom large enough.'

License, l. to use humor limited - Great men may jest with saints; 'tis wit in them but in the less foul profanation.

License, l. without punishment - ... when evil deeds have their permissive pass and not the punishment.

Lies, l. from a fat man - These lies are like the father that begets them; gross as a mountain, open, palpable.

Lies, l. well constructed - .. lies well steeled with weighty arguments.

Lies, letter or document filled to the brim with l. - .. and as many lies as will lie in thy sheet of paper, although the sheet were big enough for the bed of Ware..

Lies, manufacturing l. – .. made such a sinner of his memory to credit his own lie.

Lies, marketing l. – Let me have no lying: it becomes none but tradesmen.

Lies, quaint l. - .. and tell quaint lies how honourable ladies sought my love.

Lies, the seven degrees of lying – Reply churlish... reproof valiant... counter-cheque quarrelsome…

Life, a combination of good and bad - The web of our life is of a mingled yarn, good and ill go together..

Life, an alternation of joys and sorrows - Thus sometimes hath the brightest day a cloud; and after summer evermore succeeds…

Life, desire for a l. with love and honor – Love they to live that love and honour have.

Life, end of l. – My life is run his compass.

Life, everything has an end - All that lives must die passing through nature to eternity.

Life, everything has an end – We cannot hold mortality's strong hand.

Life, finding l. tedious. See ' 'Mood, pessimistic, life tedious - There's nothing in this world can make me joy: life is as tedious as a twice-told tale, vexing the dull ear of a drowsy man.'

Life, fleetness of l. See entries for 'Pessimism, fleetness of life'.

Life, humble l. as a blessing. See 'Fortune, reversal of f. and the bright side of it - ... and found the blessedness of being little.'

Life, getting to the Autumn of life - I have lived long enough: my way of life is fallen into the sear, the yellow leaf.

Life, golden rule for l. See 'Balance, in praise of balanced life - ... they are as sick that surfeit with too much, as they that starve with nothing.'

Life, inherent weakness of l. See 'Pessimism, limits of self-importance - ... Infusing him with self and vain conceits, as if this flesh, which walls about our life were brass impregnable.'

Life, l. after death. See 'Life, uncertainty of the afterlife and its influence on our behavior - The undiscovered country from whose bourn no traveler returns - puzzles the will...'

Life, l. and death, values reversed - To sue to live, I find I seek to die...

Life, l. as a battle - Strives in his little world of man to out-scorn the to-and-fro-conflicting wind and rain.

Life, l. as a stage for fools - When we are born we cry that we are come to this great stage of fools.

Life, l. as a tangled knot. See 'Death wish - .. with thy sharp teeth this knot intrinsicate of life at once untie'.

Life, l. as an hourly progress towards death – ... That we the pain of death would hourly die, rather than die at once!

Life, l. at court or in a corporation compared to country life - ... what lies I have heard! Our courtiers say all's savage but at court..

Life, l. better ended if her l. is missing - My life were better ended by their hate, than death prorogued, wanting of thy love.

Life, l. driven by a sense of honor. See 'Honor, h. above all – Life every man holds dear; but the dear man holds honour far more precious dear than life.'

Life, l. in the country as opposed to l. in a corporation - ... and we will fear no poison, which attends In place of greater state.

Life, l. in the country as opposed to l. in a corporation - ... prouder than rustling in unpaid-for silk.

Life, l. in the country, advantages of – Lord, who would live turmoiled in the court, and may enjoy such quiet walks as these?...

Life, l. inherently short and lasting but a moment - ... And a man's life's no more than to say 'One.'

Life, l. inherently short and reminded of it. See 'Warning, gratitude for the w. – I thank thee who hath taught my frail mortality to know itself...'

Life, l. inside a corporation or the Washington belt – ... the art of the court as hard to leave as keep...

Life, l. is but a questionable commodity - Reason thus with life - If I do lose thee, I do lose a thing that none but fools would keep...

Life, l. made impossible without means to make a living. See 'Living means - ... you take my life when you do take the means whereby I live...

Life, l. lived according to nature - ... tongues in trees, books in the running brooks.

Life, l. unbearable, death as a physician – It is silliness to live when to live is torment...

Life, l's but a walking shadow. See 'Depression, general depression leading to total pessimism – to-morrow and to-morrow and to-morrow...'

Life, l's chronic unhappiness - Happy thou art not; for what thou hast not, still thou strivest to get...

Life, l.'s history of a person as a predictor of

future performance – There is a history in all men's lives.

Life, l's inherent fleetingness, comforts for the concept of mortality - … a breath thou art, servile to all the skyey influences, that dost this habitation…

Life, l's objectives and the consequences of excessive ambition for wealth - Honour for wealth; and oft that wealth doth cost the death of all, and all together lost.

Life, l.'s problems and the uncertainty of the afterlife. See 'Depression, general depression leading to total pessimism,' whips and scorns of time'.

Life, l.'s progress and decay in a nutshell. See 'Time, devastating effects of t. - … And so, from hour to hour, we ripe and ripe, and then…'

Life, l's story, invitation to speak about his/her/their l. – Part performed in this wide gap of time.

Life, l's story. See 'Biography, invitation to tell his/her life story – I long to hear the story of your life'

Life, l's uncertainties - …(The) other incident throes that nature's fragile vessel doth sustain in life's uncertain voyage.

Life, life-style not commensurate with means – … whose humble means match not his haughty spirit.

Life, life-style not commensurate with means - … whose large style agrees not with the leanness of his purse.

Life, longevity and unusual way of expressing love for it – I love long life better than figs

Life, longevity. See entries for 'Age, longevity'.

Life, longing to hear her life story - I long hear the story of your life, which must take the ear strangely.

Life, manly approach to unexpected events, however rough - Come what come may, time and the hour runs through the roughest day.

Life, married l. affecting negatively behavior of men and women - Men are April when they woo, December when they wed.

Life, misspent. See 'Music, m. without rhythm compared to life misspent - … how sour sweet music is, when time is broke and no proportion kept!! So is it in the music of men's lives.'

Life, outlook on life suddenly changed. See 'Event, course of e. completely changing your outlook on life - Had I but died an hour before this chance I had lived a blessed time…'

Life, no control on l. See second and third line in 'Expression, why so solemn an e.? - Why do you bend such solemn brows on me?…'

Life, not really a l. - Canst thou believe thy living is a life, so stinkingly depending?

Life, personal view of l., afraid of oneself - I had as lief not be, as live to be in awe of such a thing as I myself.

Life, pessimistic view of l. - … each hour's joy wrecked with a week of teen.

Life, pessimistic view of l. - Comfort's in heaven; and we are on the earth.

Life, pessimistic view of l. - This world to me is like a lasting storm.

Life, pessim

Life, rationalization against 'death with dignity' advocates - … The weariest and most loathed worldly life…is a paradise to what we fear of death'

Life, reasons for hanging on to l. - O, our lives' sweetness! That we the pain of death would hourly die…

Life, rough l. See 'Hardiness, h. acquired via a rough life - Plenty and peace breeds cowards: hardness ever of hardiness is mother'.

Life, short and therefore to be well lived - … the time of life is short! To spend that shortness basely were too long.

Life, simple l. - … and the greatest of my pride is to see my ewes graze, and my lambs suck.

Life, simple country l., advantages of – Here feel we but the penalty of Adam…

Life, simple country l., advantages of – … Is far beyond a prince's delicates,… when care, mistrust, and treason waits on him.

Life, simple l. preferable - Hath not old custom made this life more sweet than that of painted pomp?

Life, simple country life preferable to rat-race - Gives not the hawthorn bush a sweeter shade… to shepherds, looking on their silly sheep..

Life, spent wasting time. See 'Time, admitting to having wasted it - I wasted time and now doth time waste me.'

Life, surrounded by sleep and partaking of dream experience - We are such stuff as dreams are made on, and our little life is rounded with a sleep.

Life, time of l. limited. See 'Time, survival t. limited - The sands are number'd that make up my life.'

Life, tired of l. – I am so out of love with life that I will sue to be rid of it.

Life, the act of living – … live the lease of nature, pay his breath to time and mortal custom.

Life, uncertainty of l. – What surety of the world, what hope, what stay, when this was now a king, and now is clay?

Life, uncertainty of the afterlife and its influence on our behavior - The undiscovered country from whose bourn no traveler returns - puzzles the will..

Lifestyle, desired l. not commensurate to available means - … a discontented gentleman whose humble means match not his haughty spirit.

Lifestyle, l. change for the bettering of the mind. See 'Self-improvement - …all dedicated to closeness and the bettering of my mind.'

Lifestyle, not bothered by ambition for public office – Let those who are in favour with their stars…

Lifestyle, shunning crowds – … I have ever loved the life removed and held in idle price to haunt assemblies…

Light, l. through a window – … what light through yonder window breaks? It is the east…

Lightning, outstaring the l. See 'Fury, f. prevents rational thinking – Now he'll outstare the lightning … in that mood the dove will peck the estridge.'

Lightning-thunderbolt, if you could deliver it. See 'Wish, w. to possess the power of lightning-thunderbolt - If I had a thunderbolt in mine eye, I can tell who should down.'

Like as the waves … See 'Time, passing of t. inevitable –Like as the waves make towards the pebbled shore, so do our minutes hasten to their end…'

Lilies that fester smell far worse than weeds. See 'Lady, l. who behaved rottenly towards you - For sweetest things turn sourest by their deeds…'

Lily, like the lily… See 'Rejection, reaction to r., emphatic and mildly theatrical – … like the lily, that once was mistress of the field and flourished I'll hang my head and perish.'

Lily, to paint the l. See 'Excess, e. not necessary and wasteful once objective is reached - To gild refined gold, to paint the lily… is wasteful and ridiculous excess.'

Lion, dying l. still shows his rage - … and wounds the earth, if nothing else, with rage.

Lips, bewitching - you have witchcraft in your lips…

Lips, delivering immortal blessings - … and steal immortal blessing from her lips…

Lips, doors of breath – o you the doors of breath, seal with a righteous kiss a dateless bargain.

Lips, l. and cheeks. See 'Beauty, b. shown in color of lips and cheeks - … beauty's ensign… is crimson in thy lips and in thy cheeks.'

Lips, l. and fresh breath - Here are sever'd lips parted with sugar breath…

Lips, l. like roses - Their lips were four red roses on a stalk.

Lips, l. made for kissing not insulting. See "Rejection, rebuttal to rejection or harsh words - Teach not thy lip such scorn; for it was made for kissing, lady, not for such contempt.'

Lips, moving in discontent - ..whose restraint doth move the murmuring lips of discontent.

Lips, plus nose plus cheeks – lily lips, this cherry nose, these yellow cowslip cheeks.

Lips, smooth - ..Diana's lip is not more smooth and rubious.

Lips, tempting - O, how ripe in show thy lips, those kissing cherries, tempting grow!

Listen to me. See entries for 'Request, r. to be heard' *** 'News, believability of a story - ... And let us once again assail your ears that are so fortified against our story.' *** 'Advice, listen to my a. - ... fasten your ear on my advisings…'

Listening, are you l.? - ... how is't with you, that you do bend your eye on vacancy and with the incorporal air do hold discourse?

Listening, eager l. – and with a greedy ear devour up my discourse.

Listening, prepared to listen - What you have said I will consider; what you have to say I will with patience hear.

Listening, unable to listen as a disease – ... it is the disease of not listening… that I am troubled withal.

Listening, you are not l. - You start away and lend no ear unto my purposes.

Little, content with very little, a smile sufficient - .. loose now and then a scattered smile, and that I'll live upon.

Living means - ... you take my life when you do take the means whereby I live…

Load, heavy (metaphorical) load to carry - I was not made a horse and yet I bear a burthen like an ass.

Lobbying, expression of lobbying intent – I come to whet your gentle thoughts on his behalf.

Lobbying, l. generally successful. See 'Praise, praising the criminal if advantage drawn from him – A giving hand, though foul, shall have fair praise.'

Lobbying, tools for l. See 'Gold, power of g. to buy access. – 'Tis gold which buys admittance…' *** Entries for 'Gold, corrupting effects of g. '

Lobbyist, l. defined – (he who has access to)… the perfumed chambers of the great…

Loan, l. not advisable. See "Opinion, your op. on money, handling of, borrowing and lending - Neither a borrower nor a lender be..."

Location, remote l. - … some forlorn and naked hermitage, remote from all the pleasures of the world…

Location, secluded l. where to discuss private matter – We are too open here to argue this, let's think in private more.

Logic, lack of l. – How now, how now, chop-logic!

Loneliness, feeling alone – Now my soul's palace is become a prison.

Longevity. See entries for 'Age. Longevity'.

Look carefully! – The fringed curtain of thine eye advance and say what thou seest yond.

Look who is talking. See 'Defense, d. from general accusation, look who's talking - ... if thy offences were upon record…'

Look, angry l. – ... so looks the chafed lion upon the daring huntsman that has gall'd him

Look, angry l. not justified. - Why do you bend such solemn brow on me? Think you I bear the shears of destiny?…

Look, appearance, worried l. - What watchful cares do interpose themselves betwixt your eyes and night?

Looks, admitting to unprepossessing personal l. See entries for 'Modesty, admitted m. of personal looks'

Looks, killing l. - ... my love well knows her pretty looks have been mine enemies…

1203

Looks, sour l. See 'Man, m. causing heartburn at sight - ... I never can see him, but I am heart burned an hour after.'

Looks. See entries for 'Expression'.

Lord, what fools these mortals be! See 'Men, their folly.'

Lose, every which way you lose – Whoever wins, on that side shall I lose…

Loser, sticking with the l. See 'Siding with the losing party - ...though my reason sits in the wind against me.'

Losing, l. gracefully - ... adieu. I have too grieved a heart to take a tedious leave: thus losers part.

Losses due to ignorance - With very ignorance; we have kiss'd away kingdoms and provinces.

Lost, l. in the world - I to the world am like a drop of water that in the ocean seeks another drop.

Love is blind. See 'Blindness, b. of lovers to themselves - But love is blind and lovers cannot see the pretty follies they themselves commit.'

Love, a folly – Love is a folly bought with wit, or else a wit with folly vanquished.

Love, a folly supported by written evidence – And writers say, as the most forward bud is eaten by the canker ere it blow…

Love, a masochistic exercise – To be in love, where scorn is bought with groans…

Love, account of your love life boring - My tales of love were wont to weary you; I know you joy not in a love discourse.

Love, acknowledging signs of l. reciprocated - … yet my blood begins to flatter me that thou dost…

Love, always at first sight, see entries for 'Love, l. at first sight'.

Love, always thinking of her – My thoughts do harbour with my Silvia nightly and slaves they are to me that send them flying…

Love, anticipating her desires. See 'Love, detection possible without verbal evidence - O learn to read what silent love hath writ…'

Love, appeal of l. inversely proportional to appeal of books to schoolboys - Love goes toward love, as schoolboys from their books..

Love, argument for accepting your courtship - Torches are made to light, jewels to wear…

Love, argument for her saying yes without extended delays – .. Thou by thy dial's shady stealth mayst know time's thievish progress to eternity.

Love, attraction, gem. See 'Gem, she is a g. - But 'tis that miracle and queen of gems..

Love, beautiful particularly yesterday. See 'Beautiful, particularly yesterday - .. she looked yesternight fairer than ever I saw her look, or any woman else.'

Love, being in l., virtue or fault? - …'T is a fault I will not change for your best virtue.

Love, beware of hasty proposals - .. A time, methinks, too short to make a world-without-end bargain in.

Love, blindness of l. impairing clear vision - If you love her, you cannot see her…

Love, bound by l. See 'Passion, tied up by p. - ... faster bound to Aaron's charming eyes than is Prometheus tied to Caucasus.

Love, case of reversed roles – The dove pursues the griffin…

Love, changes effected by l. not all positive – … thou made me neglect my studies, lose my time.

Love, characteristics of a man in love – … and every thing about you demonstrating a careless desolation.

Love, characteristics of l. - … love is full of unbefitting strains, all wanton as a child…

Love, characteristics of l., both gentle and rough – Alas, that love, so gentle in his view, should be so tyrannous and rough in proof!

Love, chaste l. inspired by gratitude. See 'Harassment, handling of sexual h. - What love, think'st thou, I sue so much to get?…'

Love, cold l. easily supplanted - This weak impress of love is as a figure trenched in ice...

Love, command to l. - Put off your maiden blushes, avouch the thoughts of your heart...

Love, compared to an impatient and acquisitive child –.. Love is like a child, that longs for every thing that he can come by.

Love, compared to being thirsty in a summer's day - Never did passenger in summer's heat...

Love, comparing her to Venus. See 'Venus, compared to V., worthy of worship - Bright star of Venus, fall'n down on earth, may I reverently worship thee enough?'

Love, complete l. - I love you with so much of my heart that none is left to protest.

Love, complete possession - One half of me is yours, the other half yours...

Love, completely ruled by her – ... this lovely face ruled like a wandering planet, over me.

Love, consolation prize - .. but one fair look; a smaller boon than this I cannot beg..

Love, crossing distances for l. See 'Distance (physical). "But it is such long way away!" or "Do you mind?" - A true devoted pilgrim is not weary to measure kingdoms with his feeble steps.'

Love, curse of l. See 'Rejection, curse of love - .. 'tis the curse in love, and still approved, when women cannot love where they're beloved!'

Love, darkness more suitable for l. - Blind is his love and best befits the dark.

Love, declaration of l. - ... And run through fire I will for thy sweet sake...

Love, declaration of. l. - ... Behold the window of my heart, mine eye...

Love, declaration of l. - I speak no more than what my soul intends...

Love, declaration of. l. - ... Mine own self's better part; mine eye's clear eye, my dear heart's dearer heart...

Love, declaration of l. See 'Love, how much? – Doubt thou the stars are fire...'

Love, declaration of l. in writing. See 'Writing, using w. before telling the matter in speech - O let my books be then the eloquence...'

Love, deep in it, denial useless - Invention is ashamed, against the proclamation of thy passion

Love, demonstration of l. prevented by circumstances. See 'Demonstration, d. of love prevented by circumstances - ... have prevented the ostentation of our love, which, left unshown, is often left unloved.'

Love, detection possible without verbal evidence - O learn to read what silent love hath writ...

Love, determination to win her – (I would)... mock the lion when he roars for prey to win thee, lady.

Love, determination to win her - He plies her hard; and much rain wears the marble.

Love, difference between l. and lust – Love comforteth like sunshine after rain...

Love, different points of view on whether darkness is conducive to l. - ... If love be blind, love cannot hit the mark.

Love, direct declaration of l. - ... I know no ways to mince it in love, but directly to say 'I love you'

Love, divided between two loves. S

Love, effects of l. overpowering - The strongest, love ill instantly make weak...

Love, effects of l. recollected, drive to extremity - ... and truly in my youth I suffered much extremity for love...

Love, effects of l., empowerment– ... love, first learned in a lady's eyes... gives to every power a double power, above their functions and their offices.

Love, effects of l., ennoblement – Things base and vile, holding no quantity, love can transpose to form and dignity.

Love, effects of l., reversal of physical phenomena - All days are nights to see till I see thee, and nights bright days when dreams do show thee me.

Love, effects on words and expression - ... his words are a very fantastical banquet, just so many strange dishes.

Love, endurance of l. through poetry - Not marble, nor the gilded monuments of princes…

Love, evidence suggesting that he is in l. - Methinks he looks as though he were in love.

Love, favor to the loved one, or effort or sacrifice. See 'Woman, w. as a prize – … the prize of all too precious you'.

Love, fickle l. recognized - O, she knew well thy love did read by rote and could not spell

Love, food to the mind - So are you to my thoughts as food to life, or as sweet-seasoned showers are to the ground.

Love, gods transforming themselves into beasts for l. See 'Attire, justifying your curious attire or transformation - the gods themselves.. have taken the shapes of beasts upon them.'

Love, great l. concerned about little things - Where love is great, the littlest doubts are fear..

Love, her extraordinariness as a reason for your loving her - What made me love thee? let that persuade thee, there's something extraordinary in thee.

Love, how l. betrayed turns to hate – Sweet love, I see, changing his property turns to the sourest and most deadly hate.

Love, how much? – Doubt thou the stars are fire…

Love, how much? - I love you with so much of my heart that none is left to protest.

Love, how much? – let him (Cupid) be judge how deep I am in love.

Love, how much? – My bounty is as boundless as the sea, my love as deep…

Love, how much? - Neither rhyme nor reason can express so much.

Love, how much? - There's beggary in the love that can be reckoned.

Love, how much? - With admirations, with fertile tears, with groans that thunder love, with sighs of fire.

Love, how much? Deflecting the question - They are but beggars that can count their worth, but my love...

Love, how much? Exceeding power of words to express it - … more than words can witness, or your thoughts can guess.

Love, how much? Immeasurable - I love you more than words can wield the matter…

Love, how much? Very deeply - … it cannot be sounded; my affection hath an unknown bottom, like the bay of Portugal.

Love, I would do anything for you -

Love, if not l. at least give me your picture. See 'Graphics, picture as a substitute - Vouchsafe me yet your picture for my love, picture that is hanging in your chamber.'

Love, if you love tell me what you think - … If thou dost love me, show me thy thought.

Love, in l. but unpossessive - That god forbid that made me first your slave…

Love, includes making a fool of yourself - If thou remember'st not the slightest folly that ever love did make thee run into thou hast not loved.

Love, insisting after a rejection. See entries for 'Justification for insisting even after she said 'no'.

Love, its permanence via the printed medium. See 'Love, l. long lasting even after beauty is a thing of the past - Yet, do thy worst old Time; despite thy wrong, my love shall in my verse ever live young.'

Love, l. affecting mental and physical condition - ... stabbed with a white wench's black eye...

Love, l. altering mental condition. See 'Mental condition, dramatically altered by love - .. stabbed with a white wench's black eye..

Love, l. and codependence. See 'Codependence, c. to be avoided - There lives within the very flame of love…'

Love, l. and eloquence. See 'Word, w. power, key to seduction - That man that hath a tongue, I say, is no man if with his tongue he cannot win a woman.'

Love, l. and flattery, plea to be flattered - O flatter me, for love delights in praises.

Love, l. and folly - … what folly I commit, I dedicate to you.

Love, l. and folly as a natural association - … but as all is mortal in nature, so is all nature in love, mortal in folly.

Love, l. and its association with flowers - Away before me to sweets beds of flowers; love-thoughts lie rich, when canopied with bowers.

Love, l. and its connection with music. See entries for 'Music, request for m. as food of love '

Love, l. and its detrimental effect on education. See 'Love, changes effected by l. not all positive – … thou made me neglect my studies, lose my time.'

Love, l. and moderation. In praise of moderation in l. - .. Therefore, love moderately; long love doth so; too swift arrives as tardy as too slow.

Love, l. and priorities - …this is my answer, not that I loved Caesar less, but that I loved Rome more.

Love, l. and silence - Fire, that's closest kept, burns most of all.

Love, l. as a fever – My love is as a fever, longing still for that which longer nurseth the disease..

Love, l. as a fiery spirit – Love is a spirit all compact of fire

Love, l. as a generator of tears and sighs. See entries for 'Sigh. Why are you sighing?'

Love, l. as a joining of hearts - .. my heart unto yours is knit so that but one heart we can make of it.

Love, l. as a location finder - By whose direction found'st thou out this place? .. By love, that first did prompt me to inquire..

Love, l. as an antidepressant. - … thy sweet love remembered such wealth brings…

Love, l. as an appetite suppressant. See 'Hunger, when in love not important but…-.. though the chameleon love may feed on air, I am one that is nourished by my victuals, and would fain have meat.'

Love, l. as madness - Love is merely a madness, and, I tell you…

Love, l. as the birth of conscience – Love is too young to know what conscience is; yet who knows not conscience is born of love?

Love, l. as the supreme source of poetical inspiration. See 'Inspiration, she is a source of i. and poetry - Never durst poet touch a pen to write…'

Love, l. asserted unenthusiastically - … nothing do I see in you… that I can find should merit any hate.

Love, l. at first sight - …How now! Even so quickly may one catch the plague?

Love, l. at first sight - …that maid whose sudden sight hath thrall'd my wounded eye.

Love, l. at first sight - …the very instant that I saw you, did my heart fly to your service.

Love, l. at first sight – …there was never any thing so sudden but…

Love, l. at first sight - Who ever loved that loved not at first sight?

Love, l. at first sight, effects of – O, when mine eyes did see Olivia first, methought she purged the air of pestilence!…

Love, l. best at night. See "Time, t. for love, night more suitable -… if love be blind, it best agrees with night."

Love, l. blind to lover's shortcomings. See 'Love, true l. extremely forgiving - So true a fool is love that in your will…'

Laughter, l. cannot destroy pain - Mirth cannot move a soul in agony.

Love, l. causing sleeplessness - Love hath chased sleep from my enthralled eyes and made them watchers of mine own heart's sorrow.

Love, l. compared to a shadow - 'Love like a shadow flies when substance love pursues…

Love, l. compared to an April day - O, how this spring of love resembleth the uncertain glory of an April day…

Love, l. compared to the magnetic center of the earth - … the strong base and building of my love is as the very centre of the earth…

Love, l. concealed. See 'Shyness, love concealed - She never told her love, but let concealment, like a worm in the bud…'

Love, l. detected - I do spy some marks of love in her.

Love, l. diminishing in certain circumstances. See 'Codependence, c. to be avoided - There lives within the very flame of love…'.

Love, l. enabling flight - A lover may bestride the gossamer, that idles in the wanton summer air, and yet not fall..

Love, l. eternal – … eternal love in love's fresh case weighs not the dust and injury of age…

Love, l. even changing the behavior of gods. See 'Attire, justifying your curious a. or transformation - the gods themselves.. have taken the shapes of beasts upon them.'

Love, l. felt but kept hidden - I have loved you night and day for many weary months.

Love, l. for her above all else – … were I crown'd the most imperial monarch… had force and knowledge more than was ever man's…

Love, l. hidden and undeclared - … thus, Indian like, religious in mine error, I adore the sun…

Love, l. impossible but unavoidable - I know I love in vain, strive against hope..

Love, l. impossible to hide – A murderous guilt shows not itself more soon than love that would seem hid…

Love, l. in any conditions – Had I no eyes but ears, my ears would love that inward beauty and invisible…

Love, l. incompatible with reason - … to say the truth, reason and love keep little company together now-a-days.

Love, l. incompatible with wisdom - …for to be wise and love exceeds man's might; that dwells with gods above..

Love, l. independent of wealth. See 'Wealth, w. in poverty - … that art most rich, being poor, most choice, forsaken; and most loved, despised.'

Love, l. inspired by dangerous accomplishments – She loved me for the dangers I had pass'd…

Love, l. inspiring reactions opposite to what they should be – (Love) shall suspect where is no cause of fear, it shall not fear where it should most mistrust.

Love, l. inspiring wordiness - Thou wilt be like a lover, presently and tire the hearer with a book of words.

Love, l. keeps him enchained - … his mistress did hold his eyes locked in her crystal looks.

Love, l. kept platonic - I never tempted her with word too large… bashful sincerity and comely love.

Love, l. leading to extreme and desperate undertakings. See 'Passion, effects of strong p. - This is the very ecstasy of love, whose violent property fordoes itself and leads the will to desperate undertakings.'

Love, l. lessons - You must lay lime to tangle her desires by waiful sonnets…

Love, l. linked to hair color. See 'Hair, h. color as a tool for seduction – Her hair is auburn, mine is perfect yellow: if that be all the difference in his love…'

Love, l. long lasting even after beauty is a thing of the past - Yet, do thy worst old Time; despite thy wrong, my love shall in my verse ever live young.

Love, l. made immortal by words - So long as men can breath or eyes can see, so long lives this and this gives life to thee.

Love, l. makes time pass quickly - A summer's day will seem an hour but short being wasted in such time-beguiling sport.

Love, l. making with a divine lady – … not yet made wanton the night with her; and she is sport for Jove.

Love, l. misplaced – …dotes in idolatry upon this spotted and inconstant man.

Love, l. moderately. See 'Advice, a. to love moderately and to avoid excess - ... too swift arrives as tardy as too slow.'

Love, l. never smooth - ... the course of true love never did run smooth

Love, l. not ambition as a driving force - No blown ambition doth our arms incite but love, dear love.

Love, l. not sincere or true l. See 'Formality, no f. in love - Love is not love when it is mingled with regards, that stand aloof from the whole point.'

Love, l. of self prompted by seeing her – ... I beheld myself drawn in the flattering table of her eye.

Love, l. by wicked men converting into fear and hatred. See 'Favor, f. of the wicked easily turns to hate - the love of wicked men converts to fear…'

Love, l. is not love. See 'Formality, no f. in love - Love is not love when it is mingled with regards, that stand aloof from the whole point.' *** lines in 'Love, unshakable and beyond any obstacle - Let me not to the marriage of true minds admit impediments.'

Love, l. preferred over power - He after honour hunts, I after love…

Love, l. prevailing over friendship - Friendship is constant in all other things, save in the office and affairs of love...

Love, l. prevailing over friendship - O, but I love his lady too too much, and that's the reason I love him so little.

Love, l. prompted by description. See 'Judgment, j. tempted by desire – Yet I confess that often ere this day, mine ear hath tempted judgment to desire.'

Love, l. prompting oratory - My tongue could never learn sweet smoothing words; but now thy beauty is propos'd my fee..

Love, l. proposal. See 'Proposal, detailed p. on sharing pillows - One turf shall serve as pillows to us both….'

Love, l. put to a test - ... If frosts and fasts, hard lodging and thin weeds nip not the gaudy blossoms of your love..

Love, l. replaced. See 'Replacement, you loved her first and suddenly you love another - Even as one heat another heat expels, or as one nail by strength drives out another…'

Love, l. re-stated. See 'Blood, lady as dear as own b. - ... as dear to me as the ruddy drops that visit my sad heart.'

Love, l. so deep, chaos without it - ... and when I love thee not chaos is come again.

Love, l. spontaneous or sought - Love sought is good, but given unsought is better.

Love, l. tender or rough? - .. it is too rough, too rude, too boisterous; and it pricks like thorn.

Love, l. tested by time – ... love is begun by time and …time qualifies the spark and fire of it.

Love, l. tied to success or fortune? - For 'tis a question left us yet to prove whether love lead fortune, or else fortune love…

Love, l. travelling at the speed of thought - ... love's heralds should be thoughts, which ten times faster glide than the sun's beams…

Love, l. unrequited, how looking at other ladies does not help - ... What doth her beauty serve, but as a note where I may read who pass'd that passing fair?

Love. l. unrequited, technique for forgetting - O, teach me how I should forget to think. .. By giving liberty unto thine eyes..

Love, l. unstoppable, beyond any limit - For stony limits cannot hold love out, and what love can do, that dares love attempt.

Love, l. waning or melted away -- ... my love is thaw'd, which, like a waxen image, 'gainst a fire bears no impression of the thing it was.

Love, l.'s downside - Love is a smoke made with the fume of sighs…

Love, l's effects on young and old respectively – How love makes young men thrall and old men dote…

Love, l.'s letter ending – Thine own true knight, by day or night…

Love, l.'s pains not to be laughed at - He

jests at scars that never felt a wound.

Love, l.'s pleasures recalled - Eternity was in our lips and eyes, bliss in our brows' bent.

Love, l.'s power to wound when feelings are not reciprocated - … then shall you know the wounds invisible that love's keen arrows make.

Love, l.'s redemptive effects on men of questionable character - … base men being in love have then a nobility in their natures more than is native to them.

Love, l.'s promises unreliable. See entries for 'Promises, love promises unreliable'

Love, l.'s psychological effects, generator of poetical spirit - … it hath taught me to rhyme, and to be melancholy…

Love, l.'s remarkable power of transformation - O powerful love! that, in some respects, makes a beast a man, in some other, a man a beast.

Love, l.'s revenge for having undervalued it – … it is a plague that Cupid will impose for my neglect…

Love, l.'s revenge for having undervalued it - I have done penance for contemning love…

Love, l' s strategy when courting a rich woman – … I found thee of more value than stamps in gold or sums in sealed bags…

Love, l.'s trials - …if frosts and fasts, hard lodging and thin weeds nip not the gaudy blossoms of your love…

Love, l.'s voice and its divine harmony - when Love speaks, the voice of all the gods makes heaven drowsy with the harmony.

Love, l's vows like music – And I… that suck'd the honey of his music vows…

Love, l.'s yearnings not abated by words - Didst thou but know the inly touch of love…

Love, lack of attraction suggesting abandonment of pursuit - ..if there be no great love in the beginning..

Love, lack of l. for own self prevents loving others - Love loving not itself none other can.

Love, loveless, there is no creature loves me.

See 'Despair, d. and desperation - .. And if I die, no soul will pity me. Nay wherefore should they, since that I myself find in myself, no pity to myself?'

Love, lover compared to a book - This precious book of love, this unbound lover, to beautify him, only lacks a cover.

Love, lovers' looks as food - O, know'st thou not his looks are my soul's food?

Love, making fools of people. … he that is so yoked by a fool, methinks should not be chronicled for wise.

Love, making l. not war. - … He capers nimbly in a lady's chamber to the lascivious pleasing of a lute…

Love, more under the control of heavens than anything else - In love, the heavens themselves do guide the state. Money buys land and wives are sold by fate.

Love, mutual l. visible – …or both dissemble deeply their affections.

Love, never so much l. - I never loved myself, till now infixed I beheld myself, drawn in the flattering picture of her eye.

Love, no trial too difficult – … to weep seas, live in fire, eat rocks…

Love, not a sign of wisdom - … he that is so yoked by a fool, methinks should not be chronicled for wise.

Love, obstacles increase passion - … the current that with gentle murmur glides, thou know'st, being stopp'd, impatiently doth rage…

Love, offerings of sacrifices - Say that upon the altar of her beauty you sacrifice your tears, your sighs, your heart.

Love, plea for l. - see 'Words, w. of love, prompted by her beauty - My tongue could never learn sweet smoothing words…'

Love, plea for l. not to be ridiculed - … but, good Kate, mock me mercifully…

Love, pleading for l's sake, a play on words - For wisdom's sake, a word that all men love..

Love, poetry and madness - The lunatic, the lover and the poet are of imagination all compact.

Love, poor performance in l. See '

Love, pregnancy and agricultural references – ... As those that feed grow full, as blossoming time ...

Love, presence of lady turning night into morning. See 'Night and morning reversed by her presence - 'tis fresh morning with me when you are by at night.'

Love, prosperity an essential ingredient for l. - Prosperity's the very bond of love, whose fresh complexion and whose heart together affliction alters.

Love, ready to take any abuse for her l. – Such is my love, to thee I so belong, that for thy right myself will bear all wrong.

Love, reasons for l. uncertain – ... love's reason's without reason.

Love, reasons for l. unexplainable – Ask me no reason why I love you.

Love, reasons for l. See entries for 'Pregnancy, p. good'.

Love, reasons for not refusing it - Affection is a coal that must be cool'd...

Love, reasons for not refusing it – Beauty within itself should not be wasted...

Love, reasons for not refusing it – Torches are made to light, jewels to wear...

Love, rejection as l.'s curse. See 'Rejection, curse of love - .. 'tis the curse in love, and still approved, when women cannot love where they're beloved!'

Love, restating your love with a touch of modesty - So all my best is dressing old words new.

Love, selection criteria for choosing between two loves established - The will of man is by his reason sway'd...

Love, selection criteria for choosing between two loves established - Who will not change a raven for a dove?

Love, she is perfect. See entries for 'Perfection'.

Love, she said yes – As doubtful whether what I see be true until confirm'd, sign'd, ratified by you.

Love, showing signs of being in l. - Methinks he looks as though he were in love

Love, sign of l. unexpected when abandoned by all - For 'tis a sign of love; and love to Richard is a strange brooch in this all-hating world.

Love, signs of l. unmistakable - ... he is far gone, far gone: and truly in my youth I suffered much extremity for love; very near this.

Love, signs of l. unmistakable – ... if he love her not and be not from his reason fall'n thereon...

Love, signs or evidence of being in l. – If he be not in love with some woman, there is no believing old signs...

Love, signs or evidence of l. - ... might not beteem the winds of heaven visit her face too roughly.

Love, sincerity in expressing it – I am too fond, and therefore thou mayst think my 'havior light: but trust me...

Love, strength of l. in youth - ... Our blood to us, this to our blood is born..

Love, string of compliments - .. bright eyes, by her high forehead and her scarlet lip, by her fine foot, straight leg and quivering thigh..

Love, strong l. but unwise – (I am) one that loved not wisely but too well.

Love, sudden l. realized only after personal experience - ... till I found it to be true I never thought it possible or likely.

Love, symptoms of something going on – ... whispering... meeting noses... horsing foot on foot...

Love, the right man not yet found (or woman by changing one word) - .. I never yet beheld that special face which I could fancy yet more than any other.

Love, the state of being in l. – It is to be all made of sighs and tears...

Love, time as the test of l. See 'Time, t. as

the test of love – .. I know love is begun by time, and that I see, in passages of proof, time qualifies the spark and fire of it.

Love, to die for l. not proven by historical evidence - ... men have died from time to time and worms have eaten them, but not for love.

Love, totally taken by her. See 'Conquest accomplished, totally overwhelmed - ... My heart and hands thou hast at once subdued.'

Love, transfixed by l. – for never gazed the moon upon the water as he'll stand and read as 'twere my daughter's eyes.

Love, true l. extremely forgiving - So true a fool is love that in your will...

Love, unshakable and beyond any obstacle - Let me not to the marriage of true minds admit impediments.

Love, waiting for your l. to arrive - I'll go find a shadow and sigh till he come.

Love, will not l. until perfect woman is found. See 'Expectations, your e. unreasonable – ... till all graces be in a woman, one woman shall not come in my grace.'

Love, wishing to be near. See 'Travel, motivation for traveling to see her - .. my desire, more sharp than filed steel, did spur me on.'

Love, you are glad she is yours. See "Pride, p. in possession. 'Are you glad that you married me?' – (I am) as rich in having such a jewel as twenty seas, if all their sand were pearl...'

Love, your l. and her pride - I love thee so, that, maugre all thy pride, nor wit nor reason can my passion hide.

Love, your l. as your empress - ... empress of my soul, which never hopes more heaven than rests in thee.

Love, your reaction after she said she loves you – See 'Happiness, in a state of happy confusion - .. there is such confusion in my powers..'

Love. See also entries for 'Passion'.

Loved not wisely, but too well. See 'Love, strong l. but unwise – (I am) one that loved not wisely but too well.'

Lover, absence of l. unbearable - ... and lovers' absent hours more tedious than the dial eight score times? O weary reckoning.

Lover, l's absence justified - I have this while with leaden thoughts been press'd:...

Lover, sighing characteristics of a l. - ... as true a lover as ever sigh'd upon a midnight pillow.

Lovers, blindness of l. See 'Blindness, b. of lovers to themselves - but love is blind and lovers cannot see the pretty follies they themselves commit.'

Lovers, eloquent l. not reliable - ... these fellows of infinite tongue that can rhyme themselves into ladies' favours...

Lovers, l. always punctual – ... for lovers ever run before the clock.

Lovers, l. always punctual – Lovers break not hours unless it be to come before their time.

Lovers, l. arriving holding hands - ... Like to a pair of loving turtle-doves that could not live asunder day or night.

Lovers, l. like turtles. See 'Invitation, your hand - Your hand, my Perdita, so turtles pair, that never mean to part.'

Lovers, l. observed fostering romantic inclinations - The sight of lovers feedeth those in love.

Lovers', l's stories, tedious. See 'Story, long boring s. and its effect on the audience – ... their copious stories oftentimes begun end without audience and are never done.'

Lovers, odd behavior of l. - It is as easy to count atomies as to resolve the propositions of a lover.

Loving skills, apologizing for lack of l.s. – For I am rough and woo not like a babe.

Loyalty, l. to fools an act of folly, pros and cons - The loyalty well held to fools does make our faith mere folly, yet...'

Loyalty, l. to the losing party. See 'Siding

with the losing party - …though my reason sits in the wind against me.'

Loyalty, no l. left – O, where is loyalty? If it be banish'd from the frosty head, where shall it find a harbour in the earth?

Luck, bad l. See 'Adversity, affected by a. – A man I am cross'd with adversity.' *** "Attitude, a. towards the world, hating it – one… whom the vile blows and buffets of the world…' *** Entries for 'Fortune'.

Luck. See 'Games, dice - … and by the hazard of the spotted die…' *** "Character, not afraid of taking chances - I have set my life upon a cast and I will stand the hazard of the die' *** Entries for 'Fortune'

Lunatic, the lover and the poet. See 'Profession, what do you do for a living? - As my imagination bodies forth the forms of things unknown..' *** 'Love, poetry and madness - The lunatic, the lover and the poet are of imagination all compact.'

Lust and a fat man. See 'Fat man and lust - … till the wicked fire of lust have melted him in his own grease'.

Lust, evidence of lustful intents – … an index and obscure prologue to the history of lust and foul thoughts.

Lust, intemperance leading to disaster - Boundless intemperance in nature is a tyranny…

Lust, l. checked by reason – … but we have reason to cool our raging motions…

Lust, l. compared to virtue - .. So lust, though to a radiant angel link'd, will sate itself in a celestial bed and prey on garbage.

Lust, l. triggered by first kisses – And having felt the sweetness of the spoil, with blindfold fury she begins to forage…

Lust, l. versus love. See 'Love, difference between l. and lust – Love comforteth like sunshine after rain…'

Lust, perhaps reprehensible but inevitable - All this the world well knows yet none knows well to shun the heaven that leads men to this hell.

Lust, seemingly rational reasons for justifying l – O strange excuse, when reason is the bawd to lust's abuse!

Lust. See 'Confession, confessing to lust - … served the lust of my mistress' heart, and did the act of darkness with her.

Lust. See 'Intemperance, i. without limits - … But there is no bottom, none to my voluptuousness.'

Lying or rather admitting to it - If I could add a lie unto a fault, I would deny it.

Lying, am I compelled to lie? - Must I, with my base tongue give to my noble heart a lie, that I must bear?

Lying, I do not mean to say you're lying - Now much beshrew my manners and my pride if Hermia meant to say Lysander lied.

Lying, l. about impossibility and fear - … Cannot, is false, and that I dare not, falser…

Lying, l. as a trait of old age. See 'Age, a. and lying - Lord, lord, how subject we old men are to this vice of lying.'

Lying, l. based on equivocation – … and begin to doubt the equivocation of the fiend that lies like truth.

Lying, penalty for l. – If thou speak'st false, upon the next tree shalt thou hang alive till famine cling thee…

Lying, will you lie for me? - If a lie may do thee grace, I'll gild it with the happiest terms I have.

Lying. See 'Truth and lying accurately defined - … whose tongue soe'er speaks false not truly speaks; who speaks not truly, lies.' *** Entries for 'Lies'.

Lyrics that will not win you a Grammy. See 'Spring, season for love and birds – When birds do sing, hey ding a ding, ding: sweet lovers love the spring.'

Machiavel. See antries for 'Character, false, cunning' *** 'Counterfeit, c. skills – … ghastly looks are at my service, like enforced smiles and both are ready in their offices at any time, to grace my stratagems.'

Macho man or unstoppable skirt chaser -

She is a woman, therefore may be woo'd; she is a woman, therefore may be won…

Macho man, successful with women - … a dangerous and lascivious boy, who is a whale to virginity..

Mad, how mad? - Mad as the sea and wind, when both contend which is the mightier.

Mad, this guy is mad. See 'Madness, m. conclusively defined - … Mad I call it; for, to define true madness, what is 't but to be nothing else but mad?'

Madness, charge of madness rejected - … it is not madness that I have utter'd: bring me to the test…

Madness, evidence of m. due to perceived lack of understanding or ability to listen - .. O, then I see that madmen have no ears.

Madness, isn't this m.? – … have we eaten on the insane root that takes the reason prisoner?

Madness, m. caused by sorrow. See 'Sorrow, causing madness and misjudgment - .. grief hath so wrought on him, he takes false shadows for true substance.'

Madness, m. conclusively defined - .. Mad I call it; for, to define true madness, what is 't but to be nothing else but mad?

Madness, m. confirmed rhetorically - That he's mad, 'tis true; 'tis true, 'tis pity. And pity 'tis 'tis true.

Madness, m. in men due to astronomical factors - It is the very error of the moon; she comes more nearer earth than she was wont and makes men mad.

Madness, m. in VIPs of concern - Madness in great ones must not unwatch'd go.

Madness, m. inspiring feats of intelligence - … a happiness that often madness hits on, which reason and sanity …

Madness, m. that has all the traits of sanity - .. her madness hath the oddest frame of sense..

Madness, m. typical of summer, but applicable or attributable to other seasons -.. this is very midsummer madness.

Madness, method in m. - Though this be madness, yet there is method in it

Madness, obvious mad behavior prompting lack of manners - be Kent unmannerly when Lear is mad.

Madness, you are mad - … thou art essentially mad, without seeming so.

Madness, exhortation not to be considered mad - … neglect me not, with that opinion that I am touch'd with madness.

Madness, wishing to be mad to forget/avoid pain - I am not mad, I would to heaven I were…

Madness, wishing to be mad to forget/avoid pain -… better I were distract, so should my thoughts be severed from my griefs…

Madness, wishing to be mad to forget/avoid pain – Preach some philosophy to make me mad…

Magic power. See 'Power, magic p. - I have bedimm'd the noontide sun, call'd forth the mutinous winds…'

Magic, a wonderful art to be sanctioned by law - If this be magic, let it be an art as lawful as eating.

Magic, black m. - … practises of cunning hell.

Magic, black m., a practitioner of black m. - … an abuser of the world, a practiser of arts inhibited and out of warrant.

Magnanimity, gentlemanship, lack of envy - … for we are gentlemen that neither in our hearts nor outward eyes, envy the great, nor the low despise.

Mailing, mass m. - … Thousand of these letters, writ with blank space for different names.

Make war, not love. See 'Villain, lover or v. - … since I cannot prove a lover … I am determined to prove a villain.'

Make-up, neglected – …since she did neglect her looking glass.

Malcontent, primacy in unhappiness – Thou art the Mars of malecontents.

Malice, m. and envy. See 'Envy, e. mixed with hypocrisy – Follow your envious courses, men of malice…' *** 'Envy, e. as practiced by the envious - … Men that make envy and crooked malice nourishment, dare bite the best.'

Malice, m. and hate – Beaufort's red sparkling eyes blab his heart's malice..

Malice, m. distorting truth. See 'Truth, t. destroyed by malice – it must appear that malice bears down truth'

Malice, m. expressed - … the venomous malice of my swelling heart.

Malice, m. expressed in sarcastic remarks - Ill will never said well.

Malice. See 'Character, c. without malice - I lack iniquity some times to do me service.'

Man and his wicked nature - … use every man after his desert, and who should 'scape whipping?

Man and his wicked nature - …what is this quintessence of dust? Man delights not me.

Man and his wicked nature – All is oblique, there is nothing level in our cursed natures but direst villainy.

Man and his wicked nature – Is man no more than this?

Man and his wicked nature – There's no trust, no faith, no honesty in man..

Man and his wicked nature - Who lives that's not depraved or depraves?

Man and his wicked nature - …what is this quintessence of dust? Man delights not me.

Man and his wicked nature. See entries for 'Slander, calumny unavoidable'

Man, a bad m. all around - From forth the kennel of thy womb hath crept a hell-hound….

Man, a brave m. - … to grace this latter age with noble deeds.

Man, a dangerous m. – …full of danger is the Duke of Gloucester.

Man, a drunkard – … drunk many times a day, if not many days entirely drunk.

Man, a hated m. – All the commons hate him perniciously and … wish him ten fathom deep.

Man, a m. called Pompey Bum – … and your bum is the greatest thing about you…

Man, a noble m. - The noblest mind he carries that ever govern'd man.

Man, a verbose and annoying m. – … such a deal of skimble-skamble stuff as puts me from my faith.

Man, a verbose and nonsensical m. – See 'Character, c. who says a lot of nonsense - Gratiano speaks an infinite deal of nothing…'

Man, a verbose m. – He draweth out the thread of his verbosity finer than the staple of his argument.

Man, a verbose or fast talking m. – a gentleman... that loves to hear himself talk, and he will speak more in a minute…

Man, able to stir things up - .. when he meant to quail and shake the orb he was as rattling thunder.

Man, all show, no brain - What a pretty thing man is, when he goes in his doublet and hose..

Man, an absolutely trustworthy and loving m. - His words are bonds, his oaths are oracles…

Man, antisocial - …he does neither affect company, nor is he fit for't, indeed.

Man, anything but this m. – See 'Insult, better to be an animal than Menelaus - .. but to be Menelaus - I would conspire against destiny.'

Man, bad m. exceedingly so – … a thing too bad for bad report.

Man, base and worthless - … from whose so many weights of baseness cannot a dram of worth be drawn.

Man, best m. of all – Thou art the ruins of the noblest man that ever lived in the tide of times.

Man, capable m. able to discern deceit – These eyes… as piercing as the mid-day sun, to search the secret treasons of the world…

Man, cheap, stingy and vulgar bargain hunter - So worthless peasants bargain for their wives…

Man, clearly not an intellectual - He is only an animal, only sensible in the duller parts.

Man, compared to a bird soaring high - … man and birds are fain of climbing high.

Man, comparing unfavorably one m. to another - Romeo's a dishclout to him.

Man, convinced, almost c. - … three parts of him is ours already, and the man entire upon the next encounter yields him ours.

Man, corrupt m. - … smacking of every sin that has a name.

Man, cruel and a pest since birth - Teeth hadst thou in thy head when thou wast born to signify thou camest to bite the world.

Man, dangerous and to be avoided – … if my name were liable to fear, I do not know the man I should avoid so soon as that spare Cassius.

Man, despicable m. and a danger to the nation – … whose filth and dirt troubles the silver spring where England drinks.

Man, difficult to classify. See 'Classification, c. of man uncertain – That which you are my thoughts cannot transpose.'

Man, disconnected m. – … he hath the joints of every thing, but everything so out of joint…

Man, dissimulating m. – O serpent heart, hid with a flowering face!

Man, dissolute m. - … he fishes, drinks, and wastes the lamps of night in revel…

Man, dull m. See 'Insult, brain - … as dry as the remainder biscuit after a voyage….' *** 'Understanding, thick of u. - … thou wert not wont to be so dull…'

Man, easily irritated - .. thou wilt quarrel with a man that hath a hair more, or a hair less, in his beard, than thou hast.

Man, easily quarrelsome after a few drinks – … as full of quarrel and offence as my young mistress' dog.

Man, evil m. - .. he is born with teeth!' and so I was; which plainly signified that I should snarl and bite and play the dog.

Man, extraordinary m. - He sits 'mongst men like a descended god..

Man, extremely undernourished man, but lusty – He was the very genius of famine…

Man, gentleman described - A gentleman of noble parentage, of fair demesnes..

Man, good man meaning commercially reliable or solvent – … my meaning in saying he is a good man is to have you understand me that he is sufficient.

Man, harmless m. - I took him for the plainest harmless creature….

Man, his nature debased by materialism. See 'Sleep, s. unprofitable - What is a man, if his chief good and market of his time be but to sleep and feed? a beast, no more'

Man, hollow m., play on words with 'sound'. See 'Soundness, different kind of s. - .. not as one would say, healthy; but so sound as things that are hollow.'

Man, honest and acute judge of human nature – (a fellow) of exceeding honesty and knows all qualities with a learned spirit…

Man, honest but not very intelligent - .. an honest fellow enough.. but he has not so much brain as earwax.

Man, honorable Italian m. – … one in whom the ancient Roman honour more appears…

Man, hungry, oppressed and despised. See 'Financial status, poverty obvious - ..famine is in thy cheeks, need and oppression starveth in thine eyes…'

Man, m's inherent oddity – … every man is odd.

Man, inhuman - He's opposite to humanity.

Man, inveterate sinner. See 'Sin, s. not occasional, but chronic - Thy sin's not accidental, but a trade.'

Man, larger than life, doer of good and poorly repaid - O monument and wonder of good deeds evilly bestow'd!

Man, m. and his qualities, salt and spice – Is not birth, beauty… the spice and salt that seasons a man?

Man, m. arriving in force and fanfare - … In thunder and in earthquake, like a Jove…

Man, m. as a slave of chance. See 'Character, fatalistic – we profess ourselves to be the slaves of chance, and flies of every wind that blows.'

Man, m. as dust – Would it not grieve a woman to be overmastered with a piece of valiant dust?

Man, m. as paragon of animals – What a piece of work is a man!…

Man, m. believed to be plain and harmless - I took him for the plainest harmless creature..

Man, m. believed to be rich. See 'Rumor, wealth – It is noised he hath a mass of treasure'.

Man, m. causing heartburn at sight - ..I never can see him, but I am heart burned an hour after.

Man, m. courageous to the end – Undaunted spirit in a dying breast!

Man, m. damned – Mark'd with a blot, damn'd in the book of heaven.

Man, m. discredited and speaking nonsense - .. will you credit this base drudge's words that speaks he knows not what?

Man, m. eating man, just like fish – ..the great ones eat up little ones.

Man, m. false - … falser than vows made in wine

Man, m. fashionable and courtly. See 'Politician, young aspiring p. - The expectancy and rose of the fair state… the observed of all observers.'

Man, m. heaped with honors – And sounded all the depths and shoals of honour…

Man, m. honest if slow witted - … his wits are not so blunt as, God help, I would desire they were…

Man, m. genetically predisposed to crime - A fellow … quoted and sign'd to do a deed of shame.

Man, m. in full form and perfect shape - As full of spirit as the month of May.

Man, m. in general, constitutionally unreliable – Man is a giddy thing and this is my conclusion.

Man, m. in shape but with traits of an animal - Never did I know a creature, that did bear the shape of man..

Man, m. made poor by fortune. See 'Who are you? - A most poor man, made tame to fortune's blows…'

Man, m. master of his destiny. See 'Destiny, mastership of our own d. - Men at some time are masters of their fates, the fault, dear Brutus, is not in our stars…'

Man, m. never completely above board - Who has a breast so pure, but some uncleanly apprehensions…

Man, m. not afraid of noise and challenging situations in general. See 'Resistance, power of r. to noise acquired via repeated trials - Think you a little din can daunt mine ears?'

Man, m. not enslaved by passion a commendable exception - Give me that man that is not passion's slave…

Man, m. not shaken by extraordinary natural phenomena – Are not you moved, when all the sway of earth shakes like a thing unfirm?

Man, m. old and hungry. See 'Age, a. and hunger - Oppress'd with two great evils, age and hunger'.

Man, m. of good qualities - A man of good repute, carriage, bearing, and estimation

Man, m. of good qualities - A man of sovereign parts he is esteem'd, well fitted in arts, glorious in arms.

Man, m. of honorable mind and of behavior with women - … he bears an honourable mind and will not use a woman lawlessly.

Man, m. of learning. See 'Learning, a man of commendable l. - … learning, the greatness whereof I cannot enough commend'.

Man, m. of noble character - .. a nobler sir

ne'er lived 'twixt sky and ground.

Man, m. of perfection - … the sole inheritor of all perfections that a man may owe…

Man, m. of physical substance – … think of that,--a man of my kidney …

Man, m. of quick wit - I do say thou art quick in answers…

Man, m. of solid character and fiber – … whose solid virtue the shot of accident, nor dart of chance…

Man, m. particularly skillful in his profession or trade and still OK - … most profound in his art and yet not damnable.

Man, m. passionate and fiery - Why should a man whose blood is warm within…

Man, m. prone to mischief – … as prone to mischief as able to perform it.

Man, m. prone to mischief - There's mischief in this man.

Man, m. prone to mischief. See 'Character, evil and beyond description - … For mischiefs manifold and sorceries terrible to enter human hearing.'

Man, qualified only for menial responsibilities – This is a slight unmeritable man, meet to be sent on errands.

Man, m. restraining himself against his won advantage - I lack iniquity sometimes to do me service.

Man, m. shipwrecked (materially or metaphorically) - A man whom both the waters and the wind…

Man, m. subject to constant mood changes - … his humour was nothing but mutation…

Man, m. thin and lusty – … was the very genius of famine; yet lecherous as a monkey…

Man, m. to be avoided. See 'Insult, venomous toad or lizard - .. mark'd by the destinies to be avoided as venom toads, or lizards' dreadful stings.'

Man, m. to be praised who can stand up to the vagaries of fortune - .. blest are those whose blood and judgment are so well commingled..

Man, m. wealthy and generous - O, he's the very soul of bounty.

Man, m. wealthy and powerful – … realms and islands were as plates dropp'd from his pocket.

Man, m. who can explain difficult things. See 'Explanation, difficult matter made easy by expert - What impossible matter will he make easy next?'

Man, m. well connected who knows what is going on in politics - .. those that know the very nerves of state.

Man, m. who anticipates our very ideas - My other self, my counsel's consistory, my oracle, my prophet!

Man, m. who does not want to be found - .. 'tis in vain to seek him here that means not to be found.

Man, m. who hates peace. See entries for 'Warmonger, w's frame of mind '

Man, m. who never laughs. See 'Wine, w. as an ingredient for a sense of humor - .. nor a man cannot make him laugh; but that's no marvel, he drinks no wine.'

Man, m. who never retreats - … Whose warlike ears could never brook retreat

Man, m. who promises but does not deliver - … he writes brave verses, speaks brave words, swears brave oaths, and breaks them bravely.

Man, m. wielding great political power – (No one) dares stir a wing, if Warwick shake his bells.

Man, m with a big mouth - Here's a large mouth indeed that spits forth death, and mountains, rocks, and seas…

Man, m. with a keen sense of humor - His eye begets occasion for his wit…

Man, m. with many faults. See 'Faults, man with many f. – … he hath faults, with surplus, to tire in repetition.' *** 'Character, compound of all faults - a man who is the abstract of all faults that all men follow.'

Man, m. with self-asserted composition skills – … motions, revolutions: these are begot in the ventricle of memory…

Man, m. without manners. See 'Insult, totally unmannered - … ungracious wretch, fit for the mountains and the barbarous caves… out of my sight!'

Man, m's nature but a collection of dust – Thou art not thyself, for thou exist'st on many a thousand grains that issue out of dust.

Man, m.'s nature compared to the nature of plants. See 'Man, m.'s nature, a conflict of good and bad - … Two such opposed kings encamp them still in man as well as herbs, grace and rude will…'

Man, m.'s nature disappointing– Is man no more than this?

Man, m's nature subject to unpredictable changes – Thou art not certain, for thy complexion shifts to strange effects after the moon.

Man, m.'s nature unable to appreciate the harmony of the universe. See 'Deafness, d. to heavenly harmony caused by corrupted nature of man - Such harmony is in immortal souls..'

Man, m.'s nature unpredictable - .. we know what we are, but know not what we may be.

Man, m.'s nature volatile - … such summer-birds are men.

Man, m.'s nature, a conflict of good and bad - … Two such opposed kings encamp them still in man as well as herbs, grace and rude will…

Man, m.'s nature, his faults separate him from the Gods - … but you, gods, will give us some faults to make us men.

Man, m's qualifications questioned - But he's a tried and valiant soldier… So is my horse, Octavius…

Man, new rich and self-made - … a man, they say, that from very nothing, and beyond the imagination of his neighbours, is grown into an unspeakable estate.

Man, perception establishing his value - And not a man, for being simply a man hath any honour..

Man, perfect m. See 'Experience, worldly experience ma

Man, pitiless. See entries for 'Pity, pitiless'

Man, politically broken and seeking a quiet life – … An old man, broken with the storms of state…

Man, politically powerful and dangerous man – … this imperious man will work us all from princes into pages…

Man, politically very powerful - .. this is he that moves both wind and tide.

Man, qualities of a complete m. - … they are both the varnish of a complete man.

Man, question about man's stability of mind – Are his wits safe? is he not light of brain?

Man, right m. not yet found. See 'Love, the right man not yet found (or woman by changing one word) - .. I never yet beheld that special face which I could fancy yet more than any other.'

Man, self-conscious and somewhat full of himself - Full of wise saws and modern instances.

Man, self-supporting and living within his means – I earn that I eat; get that I wear.

Man, simple-minded m. – How green you are and fresh in this old world

Man, something wrong with his brain - .. for, sure, the man is tainted in's wits.

Man, strain of m. debased - The strain of man's bred into baboon and monkey.

Man, temper of m., when it really shows. See 'Chance, temper of man shown when handling reversals – In the reproof of chance lies the true proof of men.'

Man, type of m. better to a friend than enemy - I had rather have such men my friends than enemies.

Man, tyrannical - … and like the tyrannous breathing of the north shakes all our buds from growing.

Man, very emotional m., characteristics of - Where joy most revels, grief doth most

1219

lament; grief joys, joy grieves, on slender accident.

Man, very thin out of constitution or hunger - … was so forlorn, that his dimensions to any thick sight were invincible...

Man, well poised m. - … stuffed with all honourable virtues

Man, wicked and villainous - The multiplying villanies of nature do swarm upon him.

Man, witty m. See 'Character, with a sense of humor - .. the world's large tongue proclaims you for a man replete with mocks.'

Man, worse than the worst of devils – Not in the legions of horrid hell can come a devil more damn'd to top Macbeth.

Man, m. with a cutting wit - … a sharp wit matched with too blunt a will…

Man, unfriendly m. See 'Character, unfriendly – … nothing but himself which looks like man is friendly with him.' *** "Expression, facial e. unfriendly - .. the tartness of his face sours ripe grapes.'

Man, unmusical m. not to be trusted. See 'Music, distrust for men who do not like music - The man that hath no music in himself… is fit for treasons, stratagems and spoils.'

Man, young and always sad - I fear he will prove the weeping philosopher when he grows old…

Man, young and intelligent - … I never knew so young a body with so old a head.

Man, young but experienced – his years but young, but his experience old..

Man, young but experienced - How much more elder art thou than thy looks!

Management structure, hierarchical – Obedience: for so work the honey bees…

Management style, fear and government - In time we hate that which we often fear.

Management style. See 'Touch, soft t. better than heavy hand - … when lenity and cruelty play for a kingdom, the gentler gamester is the soonest winner.'

Management, challenges of top m. See 'Sleeplessness caused by the weight of your responsibilities - Uneasy lies the head that wears a crown.

Management, m. and leadership crucial - The heavens themselves, the planets and this centre…

Management, m. and managers - We cannot all be masters, nor all masters cannot be truly follow'd.

Management, m. changes at the top and consequences – The cease of majesty, but, like a gulf doth draw what's near it with it…

Management, m. changes at the top. See 'Hope, h. in a new ruler - shall convert those tears by number into hours of happiness'.

Management, m. conflict, conflicting personalities – Two stars keep not their motion in one sphere…

Management, m. strength shown in trying circumstances - (Did you not say) …That common chances common men could bear…

Management, m's chronic stress – I leap into the seas, where's hourly trouble for a minute's ease.

Management, metaphor for good management and good manager - His bark is stoutly timber'd, and his pilot of very expert and approved allowance

Management, mixed m. and conflicting authorities - ...and my soul aches to know, when two authorities are up, neither supreme…

Management, multiple lines of command unmanageable - How in one house should many people under two commands hold amity?

Management, poor m. coupled with bitter in-fighting - .. when envy breeds unkind division, there comes the ruin, there begins confusion.

Management, unfit for m. - … how should you govern any kingdom,

Management, upper m. position unwanted.

See 'Authority, executive position, suffered, not wanted - was never subject long'd to be a king...'

Management, upward mobility stunted - ... Farewell the hopes of court! my hopes in heaven do dwell

Manager, how to recognize the m. - ... which is the head lady?

Manager, m. newly appointed wanting to make his mark. See 'Behavior, tyrannical b. of a newly appointed leader – Whether it be fault and glimpse of newness…'

Manager, m. pushed by crafty subordinate. See 'Power, where real power is - ... As doth a sail, fill'd with a fretting gust, command an argosy to stem the waves.'

Manager, m. that is followed without enthusiasm - Those he commands move only in command, nothing in love.

Manager, m. unable to manage. See 'Authority, a. proclaimed – Let them obey, that know not how to rule…

Mankind, admiration of m. (ironic) - ... O brave new world that has such people in it.

Manners, I thought you more gentleman than you are - ... perforce I must confess I thought you lord of more true gentleness.

Manners, m. over murder (part of a threat) – ... the cool and temperate wind of grace o'erblows the filthy and contagious clouds…

Manners, self-training in m. - …he has been yonder i' the sun practising behavior to his own shadow…

Manners, pleasant approach achieves better results than arrogance. See 'Kindness, k. more effective than rudeness to achieve results - What thou wilt, thou rather shalt enforce it with thy smile, than hew to it with thy sword.'

Manners. See 'Apologies for poor manners due to haste - ... my haste made me unmannerly.'

Marketing lies. See 'Lies, marketing l. – Let me have no lying: it becomes none but tradesmen'.

Marriage, combination unusual or plainly mad - Such a mad marriage never was before.

Marriage, happily m. at last. See 'Achievement, happily married to the woman of choice – And happily I have arrived at last unto the wished haven of my bliss'.

Marriage, in praise of m. – But earthly happier is the rose distill'd….

Marriage, joys of m. – ... the sweet silent hours of marriage joys.

Marriage, m. and sentencing subjects to destiny - The ancient saying is no heresy, hanging and wiving goes by destiny.

Marriage, m. between upper and lower class - ... we marry a gentler scion to the wildest stock...

Marriage, m. proposal that should be accepted. See 'Opportunity, advice to seize on the o. – Sell when you can: you are not for all markets.'

Marriage, m. unsuited to military life - A soldier is better accommodated than with a wife.

Marriage, negative view of m. - A young man married is a man that's marr'd.

Marriage, not marrying her under any circumstance – ... were my state far worser than it is, I would not wed her for a mine of gold.

Marriage, quick m. statistically unsuccessful - ... hasty marriage seldom proveth well.

Marriage, spontaneous vs. forced m. - For what is wedlock forced but a hell, an age of discord and continual strife?

Marriage, the state of being m. – ... the true concord of well-tuned sounds, by unions married.

Married life and related behavioral modification. See 'Life, married l. affecting negatively behavior of men and women - men are April when they woo, December when they wed.'

Masochism, against m. - all delights are vain; but that most vain, which with pain purchased doth inherit pain.

Masochism, m. for love – … dart thy skill at me… cut me to pieces with thy keen conceit.

Masochism, masochistic solution. See 'Solution, masochistic solution to problem observed - Methinks you prescribe to yourself very preposterously.'

Mass, m. behavior – … they threw their caps as they would hang them on the horns o' the moon…

Mass, m. behavior. See 'Committee, portrait of a c. and its characteristic confusion – … truly I think if all our wits were to issue out of one skull, they would fly east, west…'

Mass, m. manipulation - … patient fools, whose children he hath slain their base throats tear …

Mass, m. movement. See 'Avalanche, formation of an a., metaphor for a revolution - ..as a little snow, tumbled about anon becomes a mountain'.

Mass, m. psychology – Look, how the world's poor people are amazed at apparitions, signs and prodigies…

Mass, m. psychology, following thoughtlessly - They'll take suggestion as a cat laps milk; they'll tell the clock to any business that we say befits the hour.

Mass, m. psychology, masses needing excitement - … And quietness, grown sick of rest, would purge by any desperate change.

Masses and their behavior. See entries for 'Opinion, your op. on crowds and masses'

Masses, appealing to the m. See 'Action, eloquence in a. – for in such business action is eloquence.'

Masses, crowds at all windows driven by curiosity – You would have thought the very windows spake…

Masses, grumbling m. defined – This inundation of mistemper'd humour.

Masses, insult to m. See 'Insult, i. to masses considered as despicable - You common cry of curs! whose breath I hate as reek of the rotten fens…'

Masses, m. contemptible - …The breath of garlic-eaters!

Masses, m. in confusion – … like a flight of fowl, scatter'd by winds and high tempestuous gusts

Masses, ingratitude of m. See 'Ingratitude, i. of the masses monstrous – Ingratitude is monstrous and for the multitude to be ungrateful…'

Masses, mass excitement - .. so many greedy looks of young and old..

Masses, not counting yourself as part of the masses. See 'Eccentricity, above the crowd – … I will not jump with common spirits and rank me with the barbarous multitude.'

Masses, pitiless - .. had not God, for some strong purpose, steel'd the hearts of men..

Masses, working the m - … Wooing poor craftsmen with the craft of smiles.

Masses, working the m. using applause as a tool – This general applause and loving shout argues your wisdoms and your love to Richard.

Master of ceremonies, calling for the m.o.c. - Where is our usual manager of mirth?"

Masters and followers. See 'Management, m. and managers - We cannot all be masters, nor all masters cannot be truly follow'd.'

Match, m. beyond hope or impossible - The hind that would be mated by the lion must die for love.

Match, mad m. - Of all mad matches never was the like.

Materialism, m. to the extreme. See "Sleep, s. unprofitable - What is a man, if his chief good and market of his time be but to sleep and feed? a beast, no more'

Mathematics, applied m. See 'Advice, a. on how to apply knowledge and the arts - Music and poesy use to quicken you…'

Mathematics, elegant m. - … one more than two…which the base vulgar do call, three.

Mathematics, error in calculations - .. it

were pity you should get your living by reckoning.

Mathematics, not a strength - ..cannot take two from twenty, for his heart and leave eighteen

Mathematics, not a strength - I am ill at reckoning: it fitteth the spirit of a tapster.

Mathematics, questionable m. - A horse and a man is more than one and yet not many.

Matter, m. clear, evident, without question. See 'Truth, t. evident and on my side – The truth appears so naked on my side, that any purblind eye may find it out.'

Matter, more m. than you can understand. See 'Supernatural, existence of the s. a clear fact. - There are more things in heaven and earth, Horatio, than are dreamt of in your philosophy.'

Matters, leave m. as they are - … wake not a sleeping wolf.

Matters, weighty m. to consider - … some things of weight that task our thoughts…

Maturity, m. is everything - Men must endure their going hence, even as their coming hither. Ripeness is all.

May, M. as the month of love - Love, whose month is ever May.

May, compared to December. See 'Beauty, comparing beauties - .. exceeds her as much in beauty as beauty as the first of May doth the last of December'.

May, ladies compared to M. when being courted . See 'Life, married l. affecting negatively behavior of men and women - Men are April when they woo, December when they wed'.

May, M. as an image of being in perfect shape. See 'Man, m. in full form and perfect shape - as full of spirit as the month of May'.

Meadow, m. in bloom – I know a bank where the wild thyme blows…

Meaning, m. misinterpreted – to have what we would have we speak not what we mean.

Meaning, m. misinterpreted, invocation - Now the witch take me, if I meant it thus!

Meaning, m. misinterpreted, plea not to misinterpret m. – Construe my speeches better, if you may.

Meaning, m. misinterpreted. See 'Misinterpretation, exhortation not to misinterpret meaning - Be not so hasty to confound my meaning.'

Means, end jusifies m. See entries for 'End, e. justifies means'

Means, idolizing means rather than end, wrong - …'tis mad idolatry to make the service greater than the god.

Means, m. appropriate to objectives - What need the bridge much broader than the flood?

Measure for measure. See 'Revenge, measure for measure – like doth quit like and Measure still for Measure'.

Measure, inevitable m. - There is no help; the bitter disposition of the time will have it so.

Media, importance of having the support of the m. See 'Artists, a. as a representing their times - … they are the abstract and brief chronicles of the time…'

Media, importance of having the support of the m. See 'Artists, a. as a representing their times - … they are the abstract and brief chronicles of the time…'

Media, m. control – (Antonio) set all hearts i' the state to what tune pleased his ear.

Media, m. deceiving their audience. See 'Deception, d. from false teachers - Thus may poor fools believe false teachers…'

Media, m. defined if you believe it. See 'Politics, representatives of the people despised - The tongues of the common mouth'

Medicine, alternative m, efficacy of - mickle is the powerful grace, that lies in plants, herbs, stones, and their true qualities…

Medicine, beyond the power of m. - This disease is beyond my practise.

Medicine, bitter m. but necessary - They

love not poison, that do poison need.

Medicine, effective within 24 hours - (before) four and twenty times the pilot's glass hath told the thievish minutes how they pass…

Medicine, doctor, an excellent and honest doctor – … whose skill … would have made nature immortal.

Medicine, doctors, skeptical about doctors - … under whose practises he hath persecuted time with hope…

Medicine, excellent m. - … that's able to breathe life into a stone.

Medicine, good for patient but refused by the doctor - …a potion unto me, that thou wouldst tremble to receive thyself.

Medicine, healing, confidence in one's ability to heal - My art is not past power nor you past cure.

Medicine, healing, time as a healer. See 'Time, healing properties of t. - Time is the nurse and breeder of all good.'

Medicine, hypothetical m. requested – If thou couldst, doctor… find her disease and purge it to a sound and pristine health…

Medicine, illness beyond power of m. - … labouring art can never ransom nature.

Medicine, limits of m. - … By medicine life may be prolong'd, yet death will seize the doctor too.

Medicine, m. as poison. See 'Opinion, your op. on doctors, you do not trust them - his antidotes are poison'.

Medicine, limits of m., it cannot defeat mortality - …if knowledge could be set up against mortality

Medicine, m. for the ills of the world. See 'World, medicine for the ills of the w. - … and I will through and through cleanse the foul body of the infected world if they will patiently receive my medicine.'

Medicine, metaphor, m. against costume - .. 'Tis time to give 'em physic, their diseases are grown so catching

Medicine, prescription, effective, take it –

… prescriptions of rared and proved effects.

Medicine, skeptical about medicinal remedy – Throw physic to the dogs; I'll none of it.

Medicine, swallowing a bitter medicine or unpleasant drink – O true apothecary! Thy drugs are quick.

Meditating on the mystery of things - … and take upon's the mystery of things…

Meditation, lamenting an interrupted m. - How dare you thrust yourselves into my private meditations?

Meditation, m. helped to find a solution. See 'Problem, solution of p. found after meditation - Thus hulling in the wild sea of my conscience, I did steer towards this remedy.'

Meeting, announcing an important m. - Let's briefly put on manly readiness and meet in the hall together.

Meeting, called in by the boss. See lines in 'Boss, b. calls you in and you imagine the worst – … Hear it not, Duncan; for it is a knell that summons thee to heaven or to hell.'

Meeting, calling a m. at night – Now sit we close about this taper here and call in question our necessities.

Meeting, difficult but not impossible to get participants together - … but mountains may be removed with earthquakes, and so encounter.

Meeting, electric and stormy m. predicted - … fire and water, when their thundering shock at meeting tears the cloudy cheeks of heaven.

Meeting, invitation to sit down and talk - Then sit we down, and let us all consult.

Meeting, joining a contentious m. when is finished – To the latter end of a fray and the beginning of a feast…

Meeting, m. adjourned due to late hour. See 'Sleep, s. or rest, time to adjourn the meeting - The deep of night is crept upon our talk and nature must obey necessity…'

Meeting, m. of strong characters - … where

two raging fires meet together, they do consume the thing that feeds upon.

Meeting, m. of VIPs - Here is like to be a good presence of Worthies.

Meeting, material not to be discussed at first m. See 'Debriefing, d. postponed due to length - ... For 'tis a chronicle of day by day not a relation for a breakfast nor befitting this first meeting.'

Meeting, quiet m. where no one speaks - We meet like men that have forgot to speak.

Meeting, scheduling the next m. - When shall we three meet again? In thunder, lightning or in rain?

Meeting, she arrives for the appointment before you do - It gives me wonder great as my content to see you here before me.

Meeting, surprise at meeting him/her unexpectedly – In the name of truth, are you fantastical or that indeed which outwardly you show?

Meeting, surprise at meeting him/her unexpectedly – ... is it fantasy that plays upon our eyesight?

Meeting, the fourth participant arrives late at the m. - The fox, the ape and the bumble bee..

Melancholy, m. an evil influence and an enemy to health – ... frame your mind to mirth and merriment, which bars a thousand harms, and lengthens life.

Melancholy, personal m. explained - ... it is a melancholy of mine own, compounded of many simples...

Melancholy, sadness, invocation. - O, melancholy, who ever yet could sound thy bottom?

Melancholy, in a m. mood - ...besieged with sable-coloured melancholy...

Melancholy, in a m. mood. See 'Depression, in a state of d. – I have... lost all my mirth, forgone all custom of exercises...'

Memory, impossible to forget - Why should I write this down, that's riveted, screw'd to my memory.

Memory, indistinct and vague recollections - I remember a mass of things, but nothing distinctly.

Memory, m. recollections - What seest thou else in the dark backward and abysm of time?

Memory, praising good m. – ... praise be given to your remembrance.

Memory, vague recollection only. See 'Recollection, vague r. only – T'is far off and rather like a dream than an assurance that my remembrance warrants.'

Men, characteristics of hollow m. - .. hollow men, like horses hot at hand make gallant show and promise of their mettle...

Men, contempt for men in general to the point of purposely forgetting their existence - ... if thou grantest thou art a man, I have forgot thee.

Men, enemies and angry at each other. See 'Anger, two characters angry at each other - in rage deaf as the sea, hasty as fire.'

Men, envious m. See 'Envy, e. as practiced by the envious - ... Men that make envy and crooked malice nourishment, dare bite the best.'

Men, fallen men with a noble mind to be respected - ... men so noble, however faulty, yet should find respect for what they have been...

Men, fat m. are harmless, lean m. are dangerous - ... Yond Cassius hath a lean and hungry look; he thinks too much: such men are dangerous.

Men, fat m. disliked - I shall think the worse of fat men, as long as I have an eye to make difference of men's liking.

Man, fat m., questions on his arrival – ... this whale, with so many tuns of oil in his belly...

Men, m. blind to their own faults - Men's faults do seldom to themselves appear, their own transgressions partially they smother...

Men, m. generally unreliable - Trust none, for oaths are straws, men's faiths are wafer-cakes...

Men, m. inspiring an age and moment - …the choice and master spirits of this age.

Men, m. of few words - … he hath heard that men of few words are the best men …

Men, m. of strong temper - …brave conquerors… that war against your own affections

Men, m. put down constitutionally. See 'Women, bill of rights for women - I'll exhibit a bill in the parliament for the putting down of men.'

Men, m. subjected to women – Why, this it is, when men are ruled by women…

Men, m. superior to women – … Men, more divine, the masters of all these…

Men, m. taking advantage of women – 'Tis not a year or two shows us a man: they are all but stomachs, and we all but food…

Men, m. versus women, women more steady than m. - However we do praise ourselves, our fancies are more giddy and unfirm…

Men, m. who talk in their sleep. See 'Sleep, talking while asleep - There are a kind of men so loose of soul, that in their sleeps will mutter their affairs'.

Men, mad men to be recovered in a mental institution - … I know it by their pale and deadly looks; they must be bound and laid in some dark room.

Men, malicious m. - Follow your envious courses, men of malice.

Men, one word catch all - … in the catalogue ye go for men…

Men, their folly - Lord, what fools these mortals be!

Men's judgments are a parcel of their fortunes… See 'Judgment, men's j. affected by circumstances and showing their character - ..I see men's judgments are a parcel of their fortunes…'

Mental condition affected by love. See 'Love, l. affecting mental condition - .. stabbed with a white wench's black eye..'

Mercy, benefits of using mercy with justice - … and earthly power doth then show likest God's when mercy seasons justice.

Mercy, exhortation not to hit a falling man - Press not a falling man too far! 'tis virtue..

Mercy, m. a sign of nobility - sweet mercy is nobility's true badge.

Mercy, m. as a stimulus to crime. See 'Crime, c. emboldened by clemency - … nothing emboldens sin so much as mercy.'

Mercy, m. becoming to the great – No ceremony…become them with one half so good a grace as mercy does.

Mercy, m. dangerous - .. And what makes robbers bold but too much lenity?

Mercy, m. engendering more sin or rebellion - …more sins for this forgiveness prosper may.

Mercy, m. obtained with honest methods - Ignomy in ransom and free pardon are of two houses…

Mercy, no m. for killers – Mercy but murders, pardoning those that kill.

Mercy, plead for m. - … behold my sighs and tears and will not once relent?

Mercy, quality of m. - … It droppeth as the gentle rain from heaven…

Mercy, reasons against m. – Mercy is not itself, that oft looks so, pardon is still the nurse of second woe.

Mercy, reasons for m. – … in the course of justice, none of us should see salvation…

Mercy. See also entries for 'Pity' and 'Compassion'.

Merger. See 'Alliance, a. between two strong companies - … two such silver currents, when they join do glorify the banks that bound them in.'

Merit, m., skills or talent excite envy - … to some kind of men their grace serve them as enemies.

Meritocracy advocated - From lowest place when virtuous things proceed…

Meritocracy advocated – … honours thrive when rather from our own acts we them derive than our fore-goers.

Meritocracy. See 'Character, ambitious and weaving his own web for success - ... the force of his own merit makes his way.'

Merriment, m. not a good response to situation - ... this merry inclination accords not with the sadness of my suit

Merriment, m. preferable to melancholy - ...I had rather have a fool make me merry than experience to make me sad.

Merry as the day is long. See 'Pleasures, p, of a simple life – If I kept sheep, I should be as merry as the day is long.'

Mesmerizing effects of love. See 'Love, l. keeps him enchained - .. his mistress did hold his eyes locked in her crystal looks.'

Mess, tangled m. See 'Situation, s. tangled - What an intricate impeach is this!'

Message or request, same m. or request annoying - If it be aught to the old tune… it is as fat and fulsome to mine ear..

Message, acknowledging pleasant m. - Thou sing'st sweet music.

Message, ignoring written m. irrelevant - … I know they are stuff'd with protestations and full of new-found oaths…

Message, insisting on delivering a m. See 'Speech, insisting on delivering a s. - … I would be loath to cast away my speech, for besides that it is excellently well penned…'

Message, listen carefully. See 'Request to be heard, important message coming - ... lend thy serious hearing to what I shall unfold.'

Message, m. or news that are good to hear – Thou sing'st sweet music.

Message, plain m. See 'Exhortation, e. to listen and understand a plain message - I pray thee, understand a plain man in his plain meaning.'

Message, serious but delivered lightly - If seriously I may convey my thoughts in this my light deliverance.

Messenger, advise to a breathless m. - Let your breath cool yourself, telling your haste.

Messenger, exhortation to m. to deliver information quickly - Thou comest to use thy tongue; thy story quickly.

Messenger, guiltless m. - I am but as a guiltless messenger.

Messenger, m. better than the author of the message - a horse to be ambassador to an ass.

Messenger, m. brings good news when times are not so good. See 'News, messenger bringing good news at a bad time - O Westmoreland, thou art a summer bird'.

Messenger, m. fearful to report information - I should report that which I say I saw but know not how to do it.

Messenger, m. not needed – I shall not need transport my words by you, here comes his grace in person.

Messenger, m. unwelcome. See entries for 'News, unwelcome n. makes messenger unwelcome'.

Messenger, punishing the m - ... reason with the fellow before you punish him..

Messenger, reprimanding the m. for the bad n. - How dares thy harsh rude tongue sound this unpleasing news?

Methinks it were a happy life … See 'Anonymity, pleasures of a. - Methinks it were a happy life to be no better than a homely swain…'

Method, m. in madness. See 'Madness, method in m. - Though this be madness, yet there is method in it'

Middle ground, no middle ground – no midway 'twixt these extremes at all.

Militarism, reputation as a volatile commodity - … Seeking the bubble reputation even in the cannon's mouth.

Milk, adversity's sweet milk, philosophy. See 'Philosophy, p. as a remedy to adversity - I'll give thee armour to keep off that word, adversity's sweet milk, philosophy.'

Milk, m. of human kindness. See 'Character, kind, perhaps too much - ... it is too full o' the milk of human kindness…'

Milk, sweet m. of concord. See 'Power, p. used to war and plunder - … had I power, I should pour the sweet milk of concord into hell…'

Mind diseased. See 'Health-care, request for psychological remedy – Canst thou not minister to a mind diseased…'

Mind, always on your mind - Is it thy will thy image should keep open my heavy eyelids to the weary night?

Mind, always on your m. - Weary with toil, I haste me to my bed, the dear repose for limbs with travel tired..

Mind, change of m. after words heard directly - Either she hath bewitch'd me with her words or nature makes me suddenly relent.

Mind, decision to change your mind on something very important - Let us once lose our oaths to find ourselves…

Mind, impossible to change a man's m. See 'Impossibility to make a man change his mind - .. you may as well forbid the sea for to obey the moon…'

Mind, m. affected when body is ill. See 'Apologies for behavior caused by indisposition - ... we are not ourselves when nature being oppress'd commands the mind to suffer with the body.'

Mind, m. ready? See 'Action, ready for a. if mind is ready - All things are ready, if our minds be so.'

Mind, muddled m. due to problems unspoken of - … and in such cases men's natures wrangle with inferior things, though great ones are their object.

Mind, no change of mind ever. See 'Determination, stubbornness, no change of mind – There is no power in the tongue of man to alter me.'

Mind, only the m. to blame. See 'Ingratitude, i. as a deformity - In nature there's no blemish but the mind…'

Mind, out of his mind – ... his pure brain ... doth, by the idle comment that it makes, foretell the ending of mortality.

Mind, simple m. See 'Understanding, u. showing no specific education – …an understanding simple and unschooled.'

Mind, state of m. – Are his wits safe? is he not light of brain?

Mind, state of m. 'where am I?' - Am I in earth, in heaven or in hell….

Mind, state of m. full of doubts and fears – … now I am cabin'd, cribb'd, confined, bound in to saucy doubts and fears.

Mind, state of m. in good spirits – … all this day an unaccustom'd spirit lifts me above the ground with cheerful thoughts

Mind, state of m. in mutiny - There is a mutiny in his mind.

Mind, state of m. in turmoil - .. the tempest in my mind doth from my senses take all feeling else save what beats there.

Mind, state of m. in turmoil before having to do something unpleasant. See 'Sleeplessness, nightmares caused by impending critical decision - Between the acting of a dreadful thing and the first motion…'

Mind, state of m. thinking about nothing and sad - … though, in thinking, on no thought I think.

Mind, state of mind, troubled - My mind is troubled, like a fountain stirred and I myself see not the bottom of it.

Mind, state of m. weariness as a weakness - … it discolours the complexion of my greatness to acknowledge it.

Mine eyes are made the fools… See 'Illusion, optical illusion - Mine eyes are made the fools o' the other senses.'

Mine own flesh and blood - … if thou be Launcelot, thou art mine own flesh and blood

Miracles, m. no longer possible. See 'Explanation, rational e. and miracles excluded - … for miracles are ceased…'

Miracle, m. worker. See 'Appointment, a. from above, appointee expected to work miracles - … chosen from above by inspiration of celestial grace to work exceeding miracles on earth.'

Miracles, possibility of m. not to be excluded - They say miracles are past..

Mirror, inability to see himself without one. See 'See 'Appearance, did you see how you look? – No…. for the eye sees not itself but by reflection, by some other things.'

Mirror, m. not showing your age if… See "Age. You are a bit older than she is - My glass shall not persuade me I am old as long as youth and thou are of one date.'

Mirror, m. showing her beauty better than your words can express – And more, much more than in my verse can sit…

Mirror. See Image building or restoration - I'll be at charges for a looking glass ..'*** 'Happy with yourself - Shine out, fair sun, till I have bought a glass'

Misanthropy, m. questioned – Is man so hateful to thee that art thyself a man?

Misanthropy, self as the only friend – … nothing but himself which looks like man is friendly with him.

Misanthropy. See 'Dogs, d. preferab

Mischief, m. committed out of desperation. See 'Desperation, d. leading to desperate acts - O mischief! thou art swift to enter the heart of desperate men.'

Mischief, m. maker. See entries for 'Man, m. prone to mischief'

Mischief, m. stirred. See 'Revolution, r. ignited - Mischief, thou art afoot, take thou what course thou wilt.'

Mischief, m. turning on the miscreant - What mischiefs work the wicked ones heaping confusion on their own heads thereby.

Miscommunications - … we understand not one another: I am too courtly and thou art too cunning.

Misfortune, m. and its effect on general attire and clothing. See 'Clothing, foul and in need of changing, a bath needed too - I have held some familiarity with fresher clothes.'

Misconduct, m. as a front - I'll so offend, to make offence a skill; redeeming time when men think least I will.

Misconduct, m. justified – … in the state of innocency Adam fell…

Misfortune, affected by m. – … wayward fortune did malign my state…

Misfortune, determination to overcome m. - Though fortune's malice overthrow my state, my mind exceeds the compass of her wheel.

Misfortune, determination to overcome m. - See "Motivation, m. to stand up to ill fortune - Yield not thy neck to fortune's yoke, but let thy dauntless mind still ride in triumph over all mischance.'

Misfortune, m. affecting manners and judgment - … for his wits are drown'd and lost in his calamities.

Misfortune, setback - My stars shine darkly over me

Misfortune. See entries for 'Fortune' *** 'Fall, f. from grace' *** 'Fall, f. from greatness'

Misfortunes piling up - When sorrows come, they come not single spies, but in battalions!

Mishaps, m. or dangers accumulating. See 'One thing after another - Like to a ship that, having 'scaped a tempest is straightway calm'd and boarded with a pirate.

Misgivings, bad feelings about an occurrence - … in the gross and scope of my opinion this bodes some strange eruption to our state.

Misgivings, gutsy negative feelings - I know not what may fall; I like it not.

Misgivings, m. about the future - … my mind misgives some consequence yet hanging in the stars.

Misinterpretation, exhortation not to misinterpret meaning - Be not so hasty to confound my meaning.

Misinterpretation, wrong interpretation of events - .. you take things ill which are not so.

Misjudgment, m. in the selection of a

controller, overseer, accountant or similar - .. thou hast entertained a fox, to be the shepherd of thy lambs.

Misjudgement, transposition of values - .. What we oft do best.. , is not ours, or not allow'd; what worst ..is cried up for our best act.

Misnomer – Benefactors? Well; what benefactors are they? Are they not malefactors?

Mission, going alone if companions fearful - ... But if you faint, as fearing to do so, stay and be secret, and myself will go.

Mission, m. accomplished - If to have done the thing you gave in charge beget your happiness…

Mission, m. important and confidential - .. And my appointments have in them a need, greater than shows itself at the first view..

Mistake me? No it's you who are mistaken - .. But thou mistakest me much to think I do.

Mistake, admitting m. without lying - If I could add a lie unto a fault, I would deny it.

Mistakes, admitting to honest m. See 'Shortcomings, admitting to one's own s. - If ever I were wilful-negligent it was my folly…' *** 'Entries for 'Error'.

Mistrust, congenital m. See 'Paranoia - There is a plot against my life, my crown; all's true that is mistrusted.'

Mistrust, m. rejected. See 'Warning, response to w. that indicates mistrust – Make me not offended in your distrust.'

Mistrust, total – I will no more trust him when he leers, than I will a serpent when he hisses.

Mistrust, m. uncalled for. See 'Diffidence as a form of cowardice - I hold it cowardice to rest mistrustful where a noble heart hath pawn'd an open hand in sign of love.'

Misunderstanding. See 'Equivocation, misunderstanding, need for accurate wording or expression – … we must speak by the card or equivocation will undo us.'

Mockery, displaying one's scars deserving ridicule - ... to such as boasting show their scars a mock is due.

Mockery, reaction to mild mockery - You do blaspheme the good in mocking me.

Moderation, in praise of m. See "Balance, in praise of balanced life - … they are as sick that surfeit with too much, as they that starve with nothing.'

Moderation, m. urged in criticism - ... deal mildly with his youth; for young hot colts being raged do rage the more.

Moderation, m. urged in debate. See entries for 'Conflict, c. resolution'.

Moderation, m. urged in upbraiding - Forbear sharp speeches to her…

Modesty in poetry. See 'Poetry, disavowal of poetical skills compensated by general strength in other areas.'

Modesty in your ability to adequately praise her beauty in words. See 'Praise, tongue too earthly to sing of her celestial beauty - …this wrong that sings heaven's praise with such an earthly tongue.'

Modesty in your ability to adequately praise her beauty in writing. See 'Writing, excusing your poor means to extol her charms - I grant (sweet love) thy lovely argument deserves the travail of a worthier pen..'

Modesty praised. See 'Plainness moving more than eloquence - Thy plainness moves me more than eloquence.'

Modesty strategically applied. See 'Boss, never outshine him. Modesty strategically applied'.

Modesty, absence not felt - My worth unknown, no loss is known in me.

Modesty, admitted m. of personal looks – … so lamely and unfashionable that dogs bark at me as I halt by then.

Modesty, admitted m. of personal looks – … not shaped for sportive tricks, nor made to court an amorous looking-glass…

Modesty, admitted m. of personal looks – I am as ugly as a bear, for beasts that meet me run away in fear

Modesty, admitted m. of personal looks - (a fellow)… that never looks in his glass for love of any thing he sees there…"

Modesty, admitting to m. of descent or skill - … I am by birth a shepherd's daughter, my wit untrain'd in any kind of art.

Modesty, admitting to one's own weakness. See 'Determination and strength failing, common weakness of human nature - … I melt, and am not of stronger earth than others.'

Modesty, comment on a modest comment of hers - Words sweetly placed and modestly directed.

Modesty, commitment expressed with m. - … We'll strive to bear it for your worthy sake to the extremest edge of hazard.

Modesty, declaration of declining power. See 'Power, declining p. – Now my charms are all o'erthrown and what strength I have's mine own…'

Modesty, deeds as their own reward - … rewards his deeds with doing them, and is content to spend the time to end it.

Modesty, disclaimer of ability. See 'Promotion, p. refused – I had rather hide me from my greatness, being a bark to brook no mighty sea…'

Modesty, false m. See 'Arrogance, a. behind false modesty - … but your heart is cramm'd with arrogancy, spleen and pride.'

Modesty, Jupiter is responsible for my success, not I. - Well, Jove, not I, is the doer of this, and he is to be thanked.

Modesty, just a scratch - Scratches with briers, scars to move laughter only.

Modesty, justifying the display of some skill - Heaven doth with us as we with torches do, not light them for themselves…

Modesty, lack of oratorical skills. See 'Oratory, lack of o. claimed - .. I have neither wit, nor words, nor worth.'

Modesty, m. about your achievements - … my endeavors have ever come too short of my desires.

Modesty, m. at a ceremony to celebrate your achievements - … It is a part that I shall blush in acting.

Modesty, m. at a compliment - It is your grace's pleasure to commend, not my desert.

Modesty, m. at recounting one's exploits - I have some wounds upon me, and they smart to hear themselves remember'd.

Modesty, m. at your new high responsibility - This new and gorgeous garment, majesty…

Modesty, m. by denial of personal merit - .. But most it is presumption in us when the help of heaven we count the act of men.

Modesty, m. characteristic of a wise person - … there's not one wise man among twenty that will praise himself.

Modesty, m. expressed - Your praises are too large.

Modesty, m. gently reprimanded – Too modest are you, more cruel to your good report…

Modesty, m. hurt by disclosure of feats - … we wound our modesty and make foul the clearness of our deservings, when of ourselves we publish them

Modesty, m. in a woman as temptation for a seducer - … modesty may more betray our sense than woman's lightness?

Modesty, m. in making a request. See 'Character, modest but strong and reliable - I cannot gasp out my eloquence, nor I have no cunning in protestation…'

Modesty, m. in introduction - … Further to boast were neither true nor modest, unless I add, we are honest.

Modesty, m. in judging on legal matters. See 'Judgment, refraining from j. – … in these nice sharp quillets of the law, good faith, I am no wiser than a daw.'

Modesty, m. in poetry. See 'Po

Modesty, m. in possession – … this thing of darkness acknowledge mine.

Modesty, m. in praising your own performance. See 'Presentation. Epilogues to p. - Thus far, with rough and all-unable pen

1231

our bending author hath pursued the story..

Modesty, m. in reporting. See 'Reporting, r. falling short of representing action - .. the tract of every thing would by a good discourser lose some life, which action's self was tongue to.'

Modesty, m. in victory - Praised be God, and not our strength, for it!

Modesty, m. in your sense of humor. See 'Wit, unaware of one's own wit – I shall ne'er be ware of mine own wit till I break my shins against it.'

Modesty, m. observed – It is the witness still of excellency to put a strange face on his own perfection.

Modesty, m. shown in a refusal to sing again. See Don Pedro's comment in 'Music, singing, refusal to sing - ... tax not so bad a voice, to slander music any more than once...'

Modesty, no m. here. See entries for 'Praise, self-p.'

Modesty, refusal to be praised - I had rather have my wounds to heal again, than hear say how I got them.

Modesty, refusal to teach an expert - To teach a teacher ill beseemeth me.

Modesty, responding to praise for your writings or presentation. See 'Love, restating your love with a touch of modesty - all my best is dressing old words new.'

Modesty, responding to praise of your good company - Of much less value is my company than your good words.

Modesty, self-doubt - ..I do not call your faith in question so mainly as my merit..

Modesty, self-praise to be avoided - The worthiness of praise distains his worth, if that the praised himself bring the praise forth.

Modesty, self-praise to be avoided - This comes too near the praising of myself, no more of it.

Modesty, self-praise, awareness of self-praise and enough of it - ... methinks I do digress too much citing my worthless praise..

Modesty, self-praise, knowing the limitations of self-praise - ... Though I lose the praise of it by telling…

Modesty, shying away from excessive praise - You shout me forth in acclamation hyperbolical…

Modesty, total m. – The full some of me is sum of nothing.

Modesty, unable to judge between two sides. See 'Judgment, refraining from j. – .. in these nice sharp quillets of the law, good faith, I am no wiser than a daw.'

Moment, critical m. See 'Action, urgent a. required against enemy - The land is burning; Percy stands on high, and either we or they must lower lie.'

Money, anything for a buck. See 'Woman, search for a w. woman - … nothing comes amiss, so money comes withal'.

Money, corrupting and falsifying power of m. See

Money, contempt for m. worshipers . See 'Payment, refusing to be p. – All gold and silver rather turn to dirt, as 'tis no better reckon'd, but of those who worship dirty gods.'

Money, m. and conscience. See 'Conscience, c. lost to money - ... in the Duke of Gloucester's purse.'

Money, m. covers up faults or liabilities - O, what a world of vile ill-favoured faults look handsome in three hundred pounds a year!

Money, m. only partial motive - For me, the gold of France did not seduce..

Money, m. opening the way - … for they say, if money go before, all ways do lie open.

Money, m. overrides any other consideration – … nothing comes amiss, so money comes withal.

Money, m. poisonous and murderous effects of m. - There is thy gold, worse poison to men's souls…

Money, m. to assassinate foreign leaders. See 'Traitors, t. corrupted by m. - A nest of hollow bosoms which he fills with treacherous crowns.'

Monitoring, you are observing someone's behavior – I have eyes upon him and his affairs come to me on the wind.

Monotony, change from m. See 'Change, need for c. from monotony. See 'Tediousness, t. in everything being always the same – If all the year were playing holidays, to sport would be as tedious as to work.'

Monster, (figurative) that leads man to madness – … some other horrible form which might deprive your sovereignty of reason…

Monster. See 'Thing of darkness. See 'Modesty, m. in possession – … this thing of darkness acknowledge mine.'

Mood, aloofness due to personal reasons - … if I have veil'd my look, I turn the trouble of my countenance merely upon myself.

Mood, bad m epidemic – It is foul weather in us all, good sir when you are cloudy.

Mood, change in m. observed - … I have not from your eyes that gentleness and show of love as I was wont to have.

Mood, combative m. – I am fire and air; my other elements I give to baser life.

Mood, depressed m. followed by an uplifting – When in disgrace with fortune and men's eyes…

Mood, diagnosis. See 'Impatience, signs of i. – Hoping it was but an effect of humour, which sometimes hath his hour with every man.

Mood, in a good m. and ready to say yes - I am in a holiday humour, and like enough to consent.

Mood, in a merry m. - I am glad to see you in this merry vein…

Mood, in a poor m. - Vexed I am, of late, with passions of some difference, conceptions only proper to myself, which give some soil, perhaps to my behaviours.

Mood, in a poor m. – … my lord leans wondrously to discontent: his comfortable temper has forsook him…

Mood, pessimistic, life tedious - There's nothing in this world can make me joy: life is as tedious as a twice-told tale, vexing the dull ear of a drowsy man.

Mood, pessimistic. See entries for 'Pessimism'

Mood, subject to constant mood changes. See 'Man, m. subject to constant mood changes - … his humour was nothing but mutation…'

Mood, tormented and seeking a way out of a problem or dilemma - … like one lost in a thorny wood, that rends the thorns and is rent with the thorns, seeking a way and straying from the way..

Mood, tormented by indecision. See entries for 'Indecision, I. between two courses of action'.

Mood, unable to be happy. See 'Pessimism, unable to be happy - He that commends me to mine own content, commends me to do the thing I cannot get.'

Mood, unhappy - .. I show more mirth than I am mistress of.

Mood, why are you in a bad mood? - … what's the matter that you have such a February face…

Mood, why are you still in a bad mood? - How is it that the clouds still hang on you?

Moon, m. envious of her beauty - Arise, fair sun, and kill the envious moon, who is already sick with grief, that thou her maid art far more fair than she.

Moon, m. to be excluded from swearing. See 'Reassurance, answer to demands for r. – O, swear not by the moon, the inconstant moon, that monthly changes in her circle orb…'

Moonlight, by the m. – How sweet the moonlight sleeps upon this bank!

Morality, m. relative. See 'Thought, t. as the arbiter of good or bad - .. for there is nothing either good or bad, but thinking makes it so.'

More flowers I noted… See 'Flowers, her beauty exceeding all flowers - More flowers I noted, yet none I could see, but sweet, or colour it had stolen from thee.'

More matter with less art. See 'Substance, come to the point - More matter, with less art.'

More sinned against than sinning. See 'Defence, d. from general accusations - more sinned against than sinning'.

More than hits the eye. See 'Supernatural, existence of the s. a clear fact. - There are more things in heaven and earth, Horatio, than are dreamt of in your philosophy.'

Morning, an early start - This morning, like the spirit of a youth that means to be of note, begins betimes.

Morning. See entries for 'Time, in the morning'.

Mortality, m. recognized – Even so must I run on, and even so stop…

Mortality, m. recognized - Thou know'st 'tis common; all that lives must die passing through nature to eternity.

Mortality, m. recognized - Well, we were born to die.

Mortality, m. to be kept in mind - For death remembered should be like a mirror…

Mortality, time must have a stop. See 'Thought, t. as the slave of life, expressing pessimism - … thought's the slave of life, and life time's fool; and time, that takes survey of all the world, must have a stop.'

Motion, what moves catches the attention - … things in motion sooner catch the eye than what not stirs.

Motivation, m. to stand up to ill fortune - Yield not thy neck to fortune's yoke, but let thy dauntless mind still ride in triumph over all mischance.

Motivation, m. to victory against the odds. See 'Victory, confidence in v. against odds - … though the odds be great, I doubt not, uncle, of our victory.'

Motives. See 'Plot and motives clear to see but no one speaks out of fear - … Who is so gross that cannot see this palpable device?..'

Motley crew. See 'Personnel, crew, a motley crew - A crew of patches, rude mechanicals, that work for bread upon the Athenian walls.'

Mountains, high m. described – … rocks and hills whose heads touch heaven.

Mouth, big m. See 'Man, m with a big mouth - Here's a large mouth indeed that spits forth death, and mountains, rocks, and seas…'

Mouth, sweet and heavenly - The heavenly moisture, that sweet coral mouth…

Moved by plea or request. See 'Determination and strength failing, common weakness of human nature - … I melt, and am not of stronger earth than others.'

Mum's the word. See 'Secrecy, s. essential - Seal up your lips, and give no words but mum!

Murder, foul m. – Murder most foul, as in the best it is; but this most foul, strange and unnatural

Murder, m. cannot be concealed – For murder, though it have no tongue, will speak with most miraculous organ.

Murder, m. cannot be erased - Here's the smell of the blood still: all the perfumes of Arabia will not sweeten this little hand.

Murder, m. cannot be pardoned. See 'Mercy, no m. for killers – Mercy but murders, pardoning those that kill.

Murder, m. discovered – For murder, though it have no tongue, will speak with most miraculous organ.

Murder, m. has no excuses - … he forfeits his own blood that spills another.

Murder, m. on the point of being consumed. See lines in 'Halloween, h. material - .. Nature seems dead, and wicked dreams abuse the curtain'd sleep…'

Murder, no m. of boys or civilians - … murder not this innocent child, lest thou be hated both of God and man!

Murder. See 'Revenge, request to r. murder - Revenge this foul and most unnatural murder.'

Muse, source of inspiration. See 'Inspiration, she i

Music, a superb artist – Every thing that heard him play…

Music, beautiful and restful - Most heavenly music! It nips me unto listening…

Music, calling for m. while depressed – Let there be no noise made…will whisper music to my weary spirit.

Music, contempt for music, pop, rap or country - I had rather be a kitten, and cry - mew, than one of these same metre ballad-mongers.

Music, delightful m. and performance - .. my ears were never better fed with such delightful pleasing harmony.

Music, disharmony, lack of balance, metaphor - …how sour sweet music is, when time is broke, and no proportion kept.

Music, dislike for bag-pipes - .. and others, when the bagpipe sings i' the nose cannot contain their urine.

Music, distasteful or that you do not like - .. 'tis like the howling of Irish wolves against the moon.

Music, distrust for men who do not like music - The man that hath no music in himself… is fit for treasons, stratagems and spoils.

Music, effect of m. recalling images and scent of violets - … like the sweet sound that breathes upon a bank of violets.

Music, excellent performance - …true concord of well tuned sounds.

Music, extraordinary power of m. to humanize even things - Since nought so stockish, hard and full of rage…

Music, invitation to an evening of m. by the moonlight. See 'Moonlight, by the m. – how sweet the moonlight sleeps upon this bank."

Music, lady who plays or sings to you – (I am) lulled with the sound of sweetest melody.

Music, m. and its mixed power to be good and bad - … music oft hath such a charm to make bad good, and good provoke to harm.

Music, m. as solace - In sweet music is such art; killing care and grief of heart

Music, m. as solace - Take thy lute, wench; my soul grows sad with troubles: sing and disperse them.

Music, m. composer complimenting himself - ..I framed to the harp…and gave the tongue a helpful ornament.

Music, m. dramatically improving when it stops – … the general so likes your music, that he desires you… to make no more noise with it.

Music, m. even tames animals - … Their savage eyes turn'd to a modest gaze by the sweet power of music.

Music, m. in good news. See 'News, uncertain nature of the n. detected by the expression of the messenger - Though news be sad, yet tell them merrily; if good, thou shamest the music of sweet news..'

Music, m. of the lark – the lark, whose notes do beat the vaulty heaven so high above our heads.

Music, m. or singing produced by a mermaid calming the sea - … the rude sea grew civil at her song and certain stars shot madly from their spheres….

Music, m. ordered to relieve sadness - Take thy lute, wench: my soul grows sad with troubles; sing and disperse 'em..

Music, m. queen – This is the patroness of heavenly harmony.

Music, m. suitable to evening - How still the evening is, as hush'd on purpose to grace harmony.

Music, m. that induce sadness - I am never merry when I hear sweet music.

Music, m. that inspires sadness – Music to hear, why hear'st thou music sadly?

Music, m. that speaks to the heart – … It gives a very echo to the seat where Love is throned.

Music, m. to be played during a lottery extraction or similar - Let music sound while he doth make his choice…

Music, m. without rhythm compared to life misspent - … how sour sweet music is, when time is broke and no proportion kept!! So is it in the music of men's lives

Music, power of m. - …whose golden touch could soften steel and stones.

Music, power of m. to soothe the spirit – (When) doleful dumps the mind oppress then music with her silver sound with speedy help doth lend redress.

Music, power of m. See 'Voice, her excellent singing v. - … Uttering such dulcet and harmonious breath that the rude sea grew civil at her song…'

Music, purpose of m. - … to refresh the mind of man after his studies or his usual pain.

Music, questionable musical execution - … I count it but time lost to hear such a foolish song.

Music, request for m. as food of love – If music be the food of love, play on…

Music, request for m. as food of love – … music, moody food of us that trade in love.

Music, singing and the effect of string instruments - Is it not strange, that sheep's guts, should hale souls out of men's bodies.

Music, singing, refusal to sing - … tax not so bad a voice, to slander music any more than once…

Music, singing, warning that music or singing will be below standards - … There's not a note of mine that's worth the noting.

Music, soft m. suitable to atmosphere. See 'Moonlight, by the m. – how sweet the moonlight sleeps upon this bank'

Music, uneducational type of m. - Lascivious metres, to whose venom sound the open ear of youth doth always listen.

Music, unpleasant and discordant - …Straining harsh discords and unpleasing sharps.

Music, why good music has a silver sound - …I say 'silver sound,' because musicians sound for silver.

Music, words of love like m - How silver sweet sound lovers' tongues by night like softest music to attending ears!

Music. See also entries for 'Voice'.

Musician, extraordinary m. - … To his music, plants and flowers ever sprung…

Musicians, 'in' joke for m. – … Marry, sir, because silver hath a sweet sound.

Mutability, love tied to m. of events. See 'Love, l. tied to success or fortune? - For 'tis a question left us yet to prove whether love lead fortune, or else fortune love…'

Mutability, unpredictable m. of events. See 'Destiny, d. inscrutable – … how chances mock, and changes fill the cup of alteration with divers liquors!'

My glass shall not persuade me… See 'Age. You are a bit older than she is - My glass shall not persuade me I am old as long as youth and thou are of one date.'

My heart upon my sleeve. See 'My heart upon my sleeve - But I will wear my heart upon my sleeve….'

Mystery of things. See 'Meditating on the mystery of things - … and take upon's the mystery of things…' *** 'Supernatural, existence of the s. a clear fact. - There are more things in heaven and earth, Horatio, than are dreamt of in your philosophy.'

Naivete, innocence - You speak like a green girl, unsifted in such perilous circumstance.

Naivete, n. observed - How green you are and fresh in this old world!

Name, hateful n. - The devil himself could not pronounce a title more hateful to mine ear.

Name, n. appropriately chosen - O how that name befits my composition!

Name, n. hated. See 'Hateful, I hate you as I hate hell - I hate the word, as I hate hell, all Montagues and thee.' *** 'Character, dramatic change in c. - This tyrant, whose sole name blisters our tongues was once thought honest.'

Name, n. or label, irrelevant - ... That which we call a rose by any other name would smell as sweet.

Name, hearing n. is a source of pleasure - ... and every tongue that speaks but Romeo's name, speaks heavenly eloquence.

Name, hesitation to self-introduction – By a name I know not how to tell thee who I am.

Name, is this your name? - Simple, you say your name is? Ay, for fault of a better.

Name, play on n., Pompey the Great - ... your bum is the greatest thing about you; so that, in the beastliest sense

Name, power in a n. See 'Label, power of the label – ...the king's name is a tower of strength.

Name, psychosomatic and/or negative reaction at just hearing a n. - I am whipp'd and scourg'd with rods, Nettled and stung with pismires...

Name, psychosomatic and/or negative reaction at just hearing a n. See 'Character, dramatic change in c. - This tyrant, whose sole name blisters our tongues was once thought honest.'

Name, unpleasant n. due to past occurrences - ... A name unmusical to the Volscians' ears and harsh in sound to thine.

Narration, beginning of a narration of a fact - .. And let me speak to the yet unknowing world how these things came about.

Narrative, gap in the n. See 'Time, gap in the narrative - ... Impute it not a crime to me or my swift passage... and leave the growth untried of that wide gap.'

Natural medicine. See 'Medicine, alternative m, efficacy of - mickle is the powerful grace, that lies in plants, herbs, stones, and their true qualities...'

Nature hath framed strange fellows in her time. See 'Characters, of all sorts'

Nature, air, welcome to the air - ... Welcome, then, thou unsubstantial air that I embrace.

Nature, air. See 'Let's get out of here – ... To seek the empty, vast and wandering air.'

Nature, clouds obscuring the sun. See analogy in 'Sigh, s. of distress fogging up the sky – ... with our sighs we'll breathe the welkin dim...'

Nature, clouds spoiling a clear sky - The more fair and crystal is the sky the uglier seem the clouds that in it fly.

Nature, dawn announced by the cock. See 'Time, in the morning - ... the cock, that is the trumpet to the morn, doth with his lofty and shrill-sounding throat awake the god of day.'

Nature, dawn approaching - ... night's swift dragons cut the clouds full fast, and yonder shines Aurora's harbinger...

Nature, dawn approaching - ... the gentle day before the wheels of Phoebus, round about dapples the drowsy east with spots of grey.

Nature, dawn approaching – The glow-worm shows the matin to be near...

Nature, dawn at sea - ... the eastern gate ... turns into yellow gold his salt green streams.

Nature, dawn in the company of a fine lady to be complimented.

Nature, dawn of a cloudy day - ...yon grey clouds that fret the clouds are messengers of day.

Nature, dawn, an hour before dawn - ... an hour before the worshipped sun..

Nature, dawn, aurora - ... the all-cheering sun should in the furthest east begin to draw..

Nature. dawn, before d. - Ere the sun advance his burning eye, The day to cheer and night's dank dew to dry...

Nature, dawn, just breaking - The silent hours steal on and flaky darkness breaks within the east.

Nature, dawn, lights showing on clouds - ... what envious streaks do lace the severing clouds in yonder east.

Nature, dawn, smiling morning - The grey-eyed morn smiles on the frowning night, chequering the eastern clouds with streaks of light..

Nature, dawn, night fled - The day begins to break, and night is fled..

Nature, dawn, one hour before dawn - The hour before the heavenly-harness'd team..

Nature, dawn, planet Venus waking up shepherd – Look, the unfolding star calls up he shepherd.

Nature, dawn, sun and its gracious light – Lo in the orient when the gracious light..

Nature, dawn, sun on the mountains - Full many a glorious morning have I seen, flatter the mountain top with sovereign eye…

Nature, dawn, uncertainty or conflict between dark and light – … When dying clouds contend with growing light…

Nature,

Nature, deep forest – The trees, though summer, yet forlorn and lean…

Nature, earthquakes explained - Diseased nature oftentimes breaks forth in strange eruptions..

Nature, everything found in n. See 'People, there are all sorts of p. – Nature hath meal and bran, contempt and grace.'

Nature, extraordinary exceptional events - … and I have seen the ambitious ocean swell and rage and foam…

Nature, frost on flowers - … hoary-headed frosts fall in the fresh lap of the crimson rose.

Nature, in between night and morning - What is the night?… Almost at odds with morning, which is which.

Nature, inappropriate to alter the dictates of nature. See 'Authority, rarely to be questioned - for few men rightly temper with the stars.'

Nature, light through the trees – The green leaves quiver with the cooling wind.

Nature, lightning - Jove's lightnings, the precursors of the dreadful thunder-claps.

Nature, lightning and thunder. See 'Arrival, fearful a. - He came in thunder; his celestial breath was sulphurous to smell.'

Nature, moon shining bright and creating romantic environment - The moon shines bright: in such a night as this, when the sweet wind did gently kiss the trees…

Nature, morning – But, soft! methinks I scent the morning air.

Nature, morning, announced by the crows - …the busy day, waked by the lark, hath roused the ribald crows…

Nature, morning - … the morning steals upon the night melting the darkness..

Nature, morning giving way to afternoon - See how the morning opes her golden gates…

Nature, morning - … from whose silver breast the sun ariseth in his majesty.

Nature, morning, when the golden sun salutes the morn. See 'Envy, above the reach of e. - Advanced above pale envy's threatening reach, as when the golden sun salutes the morn…'

Nature, n. as a personal goddess. See 'Invocation, i. to nature as a supreme ruler, also answer to a request from your girlfriend - Thou, nature, art my goddess; to thy law my services are bound.'

Nature, n. at its best - The birds chant melody on every bush… green leaves quiver with the cooling wind…

Nature, n. does not discriminate. See 'Discrimination, nature does not discriminate – The selfsame sun that shines upon his court hides not his visage.'

Nature, night - … horrid night, the child of hell.

Nature, night - … when the searching eye of heaven is hid behind the globe…

Nature, night - The dragon wing of night o'erspreads the earth.

Nature, night - The night comes on, and the

bleak winds do sorely ruffle…

Nature, night, decreases visibility and sharpens hearing - Dark night that from the eye his function takes, the ear more quick of apprehension makes…

Nature, northern star - The skies are painted with unnumber'd sparks… but there is but one in all doth hold his place.

Nature, not quite dawn, not quite night – Almost at odds with morning, which is which.

Nature, only n. has the power of improving itself - … nature is made better by no mean but nature makes that mean.

Nature, portentous events explained - … they are portentous things unto the climate that they point upon.

Nature, sea and crested waves - The watery kingdom, whose ambitious head spits in the face of heaven.

Nature, sea and sky indistinct to the eye. See 'Horizon, h. at sea, sky and water blended – … to throw out our eyes…even till we make the main and the aerial blue an indistinct regard.'

Nature, sea waves compared to time. See 'Time, passing of t. inevitable –Like as the waves make towards the pebbled shore, so do our minutes hasten to their end…'

Nature, shadow of honeysuckles - … honeysuckles, ripen'd by the sun…

Nature, signs of tempest - the southern wind doth play the trumpet to his purposes.

Nature, sky - The skies are painted with unnumber'd sparks..

Nature, sky, s. as the floor of heaven and stars as patines of gold. See 'Moonligh

Nature, storm approaching. See 'Danger, d. compared t an approaching storm – When tempest of commotion, like the south…'

Nature, storm brewing - … yond same black cloud, yond huge one, looks like a foul bombard that would shed his liquor.

Nature, storm, the creation of a s. – For raging wind blows up incessant showers and when the rage allays, the rain begins.

Nature, stormy day - … like an unseasonable stormy day which makes the silver rivers drown their shores…

Nature, stormy sea – … the sea puff'd up with winds rage like an angry boar chafed with sweat.

Nature, stormy sea – … the visitation of the winds who take the ruffian billows by the top…

Night, stormy sea - … the wrathful skies gallow the very wanderers of the dark and make them keep their caves…

Nature, stormy sea – When I have seen the hungry ocean gain advantage on the kingdom of the shore.

Nature, stormy sea. See 'Wind, extremely strong w. – Methinks the wind hath spoke aloud at land…'

Nature, sunrise - The morn, in russet mantle clad walks o'er the dew of yon high eastern hill

Nature, sunrise with threatening clouds - … as doth the blushing discontented sun from out the fiery portal of the east…

Nature, sunset – … the world's comforter, with weary gait his day's hot task hath ended in the west.

Nature, sunset delayed - The sun of heaven methought was loath to set but stay'd and made the western welkin blush.

Nature, sunset, almost night - Night, whose black contagious breath already smokes about the burning crest…

Nature, sunset, at sea – The gaudy, blabbing and remorseful day is crept into the bosom of the sea.

Nature, sunset, before s. - … ere the weary sun set in the west.

Nature, sunset, beginning of - The sun begins to gild the western sky.

Nature, sunset, golden s. boding well for tomorrow - The weary sun hath made a golden set and by the bright track of his fiery car…

Nature, sunset, light dimming – Light thickens and the crow makes wing to the rooky wood.

Nature, sunset, immediately after s. - The sun no sooner shall the mountains touch.

Nature, sunset, still some light - The west yet glimmers with some streaks of day…

Nature, sunset, with signs of impending storm - Thy sun sets weeping in the lowly west, witnessing storms to come, woe and unrest.

Nature, things observed from above - … the murmuring surge, that on the unnumber'd idle pebbles chafes cannot be heard so high.

Nature, things seen from above – The crows… show scarce so gross as beetles.

Nature, tides – … the beached verge of the salt flood who once a day with his embossed froth…

Nature, thunder - …as thunder when the clouds in autumn crack.

Nature, weather, cold - The air bites shrewdly; it is very cold.

Nature, weather, fearful w. – the strange impatience of the heavens.

Nature, weather, very foul weather, hurricane etc. – Diseased nature oftentimes breaks forth in strange eruptions.

Nearness, wishing to be near loved one - If the dull substance of my flesh were thought…

Necessity, brother to n. - I am sworn brother, sweet, to grim Necessity….

Necessity, n. as a virtue - Teach thy necessity to reason thus; there is no virtue like necessity.

Necessity, n. changing the appearance of things – The art of our necessities is strange, that can make vile things precious.

Necessity, n. overriding commitments and other concerns – Necessity will make us all forsworn…

Necessity, n. as a sharp reminder – Necessity's sharp pinch!

Necessity, political n. and drive for power - … necessity so bow'd the state hat I and greatness were compell'd to kiss.

Neglect, completely neglected. See 'Disregard, completely disregarded – … they pass'd by me as misers do by beggars…'

Neglect, n. explained - nor construe any further my neglect that poor Brutus..

Neglect, n. resulting in trouble. See 'Omission, o. of responsibility dangerous - Omission to do what is necessary seals commission to a blank of danger…'

Negligence, invocation - O negligence! Fit for a fool to fall by!

Negotiations, delegating power to negotiate - … take with you free power to ratify, augment, or alter, as your wisdoms best …

Negotiations, n. better after dinner – … but when we have stuffed these pipes and these conveyances of our blood with wine and feeding

Negotiations, n. craftily conducted - .. this swift business I must uneasy make, lest too light winning make the prize light.

Negotiations, no deal - No, he shall not knit a knot in his fortunes with the fingers of my substance.

Negotiator, a hard n. and petty to the penny - … in the way of bargain, mark ye me, I'll cavil on the ninth part of a hair'

Neighbor, unreliable n. - … the Scot, who hath been still a giddy neighbour to us.

Neither a borrower nor a lender be. See 'Opinion, your op. on money, handling of, borrowing and lending - Neither a borrower nor a lender be…'

Neither here nor there. See 'Classification, unclassifiable - 'Tis neither here nor there.'

Neither rhyme nor reason. See 'Love, how much? - Neither rhyme nor reason can express so much'

New rich, weaknesses of the new rich - … beggars mounted run their horse to death.

News, bad n. – … uneven and unwelcome

1240

news…

News, bad n. and reluctance to deliver it - Let not your ears despise my tongue for ever, which shall possess them with the heaviest sound that ever yet they heard.

News, bad n. as a dagger. See 'Hurt, you hurt me - Thou stickest a dagger in me.'

News, bad n. bearer - … thou art the midwife to my woe.

News, bad n. causing the reader to pale - … that steals the colour from Bassanio's cheek.

News, bad n. circulating – There's villanous news abroad.

News, bad n. delivered smiling. See 'Rejection, she says no with a smile that hurts more than soothes - Thou cuttest my head with a golden axe and smil'st upon the stroke that murders me.'

News, bad n. fitting the night - … news fitting to the night, black, fearful, comfortless and horrible.

News, bad n. inferred by the look of the messenger - … full of careful business are his looks!

News, bad n. inferred by the look of the messenger – … whose heavy looks foretell some dreadful story hanging on thy tongue?

News, bad n. inferred by the look of the messenger - A fearful eye thou hast. Where is that blood, that I have seen inhabit in those cheeks?

News, bad n. inferred by the look of the messenger and delivered slowly – men judge by the complexion of the sky the state and inclination of the day..

News, bad n. inferred by the look of the messenger - the nature of bad news infects the teller

News, bad n. inferred by the look of the messenger - … the whiteness in thy cheek is apter than thy tongue to tell thy errand.

News, bad n. like a cold wave - … as flowers with frost or grass beat down with storms.

News, bad n. recounted – … at each word's deliverance, stab poniards in our flesh till all were told…

News, bad n. unwelcome – Though it be honest, it is never good to bring bad news..

News, barely capable to hear the n. – My heart hath one poor string to stay it by…

News, believability of a story - … And let us once again assail your ears that are so fortified against our story.

News, better than expected - … I have better news in store for you than you expect.

News, chilling n. - Ay, by my faith, that bears a frosty sound.

News, condensing the n. - Short tale to make…

News, conflicting n., not knowing how to react - Such welcome and unwelcome things at once 't is hard to reconcile.

News, devastating n. See 'Words, devastating w. - I have words that would be howl'd out in the desert air…'

News, difficult to be delivered - .. the news I bring is heavy in my tongue.

News, encouraging n. - … Lines of fair comfort and encouragement.

News, enough of bad n., dangers of ignoring it - … if you be afeard to hear the worst then let the worst unheard fall on your bead.

News, everybody knows it already - I speak no more than every one doth know.

News, exhortation to deliver the n. - Pour out the pack of matter to mine ear, the good and bad together.

News, extraordinary n. beyond the power of songwriters – … such a deal of wonder is broken out within this hour that ballad-makers cannot be able to express it

News, extraordinary, wonder inducing n. See 'Wonder, w. inducing news - 'tis the rarest argument of wonder that hath shot out in our latter times.'

News, good and bad - ..that is the best news … is colder tidings, yet they must be told.

News, good n. – (News) such as fill my heart with unhoped joys.

News, good news brought in by messenger – … he hath brought us smooth and welcome news.

News, good n. delivered by a bad guy - Did ever raven sing so like a lark, that gives sweet tidings of the sun's uprise?

News, good news. See 'Message, m or news that are good to hear – singest sweet music'

News, heavy n. and a heavy heart - .. this heavy act with heavy heart relate.

News, hesitation to give the n. - I am loath to tell you what I would you knew.

News, I have reported all I know - The sum of all I can I have disclosed

News, information, hesitation to deliver - I should report that which I say I saw but know not how to do it.

News, invitation to disclose (good) news - Ram though thy fruitful tidings in mine ears, that long time have been barren.

News, messenger bringing good news at a bad time - O Westmoreland, thou art a summer bird.

News, n. already known and not extraordinary – There needs no ghost, my lord, come from the grave to tell us this.

News, n. already known to everybody who is not deaf - … every one hears that who can distinguish sound.

News, n. carrier spotted and a notorious gossip - …(news) which he will put on us as pigeons feed the young.

News, n. delivered without spin – I will a round unvarnish'd tale deliver…

News, n. depressing – I hang the head as flowers with frost.

News, n. eagerly expected and requested - I stand on fire, come to the matter.

News, n. fast reaching destination – Thither go these news, as fast as horse can carry them.

News, n. gathered from hearsay - … this from rumour's tongue I idly heard; if true or false, I know not.

News, n. hotly and widely discussed – … men's mouths are full of it.

News, n. incorrect - .. many tales devis'd, which oft the ear of greatness needs must hear by smiling pick-thanks and base newsmongers.

News, n. leaked but not public - .. and may be left to some ears unrecounted

News, n. of an insurrection - .. and all goes worse than I have power to tell.

News, n. reported faithfully - All my reports go with the modest truth, nor more nor clipp'd, but so.

News, n. strange almost a tale - His is the strangest tale that ever I heard.

News, n. tedious and unpleasant. See "Information, i. annoying and unpleasant - Tedious it were to tell, and harsh to hear, sufficeth…'

News, n. that is neither good nor bad - None good, my liege, to please you with the hearing..

News, no pleasure in delivering it - Little joy have I to breathe this news, yet what I say is true.

News, not speculation but fact - I speak not this in estimation as what I think might be…

News, nothing new - there is no news at court, sir; but the old news.

News, promise requested to advise of one's whereabouts - … let me hear from thee, for wheresoe'er thou art in this world's globe…

News, punishment for bringing unpleasant news. See 'Punishment, p. for bringing unpleasant news - Thou shalt be whipp'd with wire, and stew'd in brine"

News, questionable – .. is so like an old tale, that the verity of it is in strong suspicion.

News, ready to receive the bad n. – Glad am I that your highness is so arm'd to bear the tidings of calamity.

News, ready to receive the bad n. - Mine ear is open and my heart prepared

News, refusal to listen to any more n. good or bad - My ears are stopt and cannot hear good news, so much of bad already hath possess'd them.

News, source of it apparently reliable – A gentleman well bred and of good name…

News, string of bad n. but they cannot be ignored. See 'News, enough of bad n., dangers of ignoring it - … if you be afeard to hear the worst then let the worst unheard fall on your bead.'

News, thanks for the good n. See 'Gratitude, g. for good news – the gods bless you for your tidings, next …

News, the n. is true – It is true, without any slips of prolixity or crossing the plain highway of talk.

News, time dense with n. See 'Time, t. pregnant with news - With news the time's with labour, and throes forth each minute, some.'

News, unbelievable n. were it not for the evidence - …That which I shall report will bear no credit, were not the proof so nigh.

News, uncertain nature of the n. detected by the expression of the messenger - Though news be sad, yet tell them merrily; if good, thou shamest the music of sweet news..

News, unwelcome n. makes messenger unwelcome - … the first bringer of unwelcome news hath but a losing office.

News, unwelcome n. makes messenger unwelcome - … harm within itself so heinous is as it makes harmful all that speak of it.

Night and morning reversed by her presence - 'tis fresh morning with me when you are by at night.

Night, best suited for work at hand - Deep night, dark night, the silent of the night…

Night, deep of n. See 'Sleep, s. or rest, time to adjourn the meeting - The deep of night is crept upon our talk and nature must obey necessity…'

Night, effects of a cold n. - This cold night will turn us all to fools and madmen.

Night, face of lover eliminating night's darkness - "It is not night when I do see your face…

Night, n. and reduced visibility – (the) smoke and dusky vapours of the night…

Night, n. as bright as noon meaning that love cannot be hidden. See 'Love, l. impossible to hide – A murderous guilt shows not itself more soon than love that would seem hid…'

Night, n. as the jaws of darkness. See end lines in 'Confusion, how quickly things become confused -… so quick bright things come to confusion.'

Night, n. better suited for love. See 'Time, t. for love, night more suitable -… if love be blind, it best agrees with night.'

Night, n. holding record of strange events - .. I have seen hours dreadful and things strange; but this sore night..

Night, n. meandering not recommended, See 'Health-care, exposure to night cold air unadvisable if already affected by a respiratory ailment – to dare the vile contagion of the night.'

Night, n. to think it over - A night is but small breath and little pause to answer matters of this consequence.

Night, nightmare – O, I have pass'd a miserable night, so full of ugly sights, of ghastly dreams.

Night, nightmare, waking up from a n. - I trembling waked, and for a season after could not believe but that I was in hell,..

Night, preferring n. to day – … let us be Diana's gentlemen of the shade, minions of the moon.

Night, preferring n. to day - … we that take purses go by the moon and the seven stars.

Night, professional night revelers - .. being governed, as the sea is, by our noble and chaste mistress the moon..

Night, rough n. See 'Comparison, night beyond c. - … My young remembrance cannot parallel a fellow to it'.

Night, slowly passing - .. the cripple tardy-gaited night, who .. doth limp so tediously away.

Night, starry n. – the floor of heaven is thick inlaid with patines of bright gold…

Night, stormy n. hard to bear - The tyranny of the open night's too rough for nature to endure.

Night, stormy or unpleasant, no suitable for going out - … things that love night love not such nights as these.

Night, wish for n. to come – Come, civil night, thou sober-suited matron, all in black.

Nightingale, n. as a companin to melancholy. See 'Country living, in praise of country living - … Here can I sit alone, unseen of any and to the nightingale's complaining notes…'

Nightmare. See 'Night, nightmare – O, I have pass'd a miserable night, so full of ugly sights, of ghastly dreams.'

Nightmares, no fear from nightmares - Let not our babbling dreams affright our souls…

No boasting like a fool… See 'Determination, no boasting - No boasting like a fool, this deed I'll do before this purpose cool.'

No comment. See 'Comment, no c. - .. what he is indeed, more suits you to conceive than I to speak of'.

No more be grieved at… See 'Forgiveness, f. at something she has done - No more be grieved at that which thou hast done, roses have thorns, and silver mountains mud…'

No profit grows… See 'Education, profitable if pleasurable – No profit grows where is no pleasure taken…'

No sooner met but they looked, no sooner looked but they loved… See 'Love, l. at first sight – …there was never any thing so sudden but…'

No, unable to say 'no' to women. See 'Character, unable to say 'no' to women - … whom ne'er the word of 'No' woman heard speak.'

Nobility, n. and mercy. See 'Mercy, m. a sign of nobility - sweet mercy is nobility's true badge.'

Nobility, n. exempt from fear. See 'Fear, nobility, a noble soul is fearless - True nobility is exempt from fear: more can I bear than you dare execute.'

Noise, injunction to cut out noise - Silence that dreadful bell: it frights the isle from her propriety.

Noise, loud n. generated via arguing – … mortal ears might hardly endure the din.

Noise, make absolutely no n. - .. tread softly, that the blind mole may not hear a foot fall.

Noise, n. and motion catching attention. See ''Motion, what moves catches the attention - … things in motion sooner catch the eye than what not stirs.'

Noise, n. as loud as. See 'Woman, loud and contentious w. - … she chide as loud as thunder when the clouds in autumn crack.'

Noise. See 'Insult, all noise, no substance - The empty vessel makes the greatest sound'.

None of woman born. See 'Unassailable - … laugh to scorn the power of man for none of woman born shall harm Macbeth'

Nonsense, n. banned from your house. See 'Party, p. sounds out - Let not the sound of shallow foppery enter my sober house.'

Nonsense, stop talking n. – Peace, peace, Mercutio, peace! Thou talk'st of nothing

Nonsense, stop the n. - … leave thy vain bibble babble.

Nonsense. See entries for 'Speech, nonsensical or meaningless.'

Nor did I wonder at the lily's white… See 'Flowers, lilies and roses - Nor did I wonder at the lily's white, nor praise the deep vermilion in the rose….'

Nor stony tower, nor walls of beaten brass… See 'Freedom, f. of the spirit has no obstacles - … Nor stony tower, nor walls of beaten brass…'

Northern climate. See 'Climate, northern c. - … the north, where shivering cold and sickness pines the clime.'

Nose, importance of the olfactory sense - …

a good nose is requisite also, to smell out work for the other senses.

Noses, comment on those who follow their n. See 'Judgment, skepticism about people's j. – All that follow their noses are led by their eyes but blind men…'

Nostalgia, regret - When to the session of sweet silent thought, I summon up remembrance of things past…

Not all the water in the rough, rude sea can wash the balm from an anointed king. See 'Position, p. felt secure due to tenure.'

Not being the worst stands in some rank of praise. See 'Last, not being the l. better than nothing'

Not Caesar's valour hath… See 'Winners and losers, loser defeated by himself - Not Caesar's valor hath o'erthrown Antony but Antony's hath triumphed on itself'

Not from the stars do I my judgment… See 'Eyes, e. as a source of knowledge - Not from the stars do I my judgment pluck, and yet methinks I have astronomy…'

Not marble, nor the gilded monuments… See 'Love, endurance of l. through poetry - Not marble, nor the gilded monuments of princes…'

Notes, note-taking – Notes, note-taking – Fery goot: I will make a prief of it in my note-book.

Notes, note-taking – I will set down what comes from her, to satisfy my remembrance the more strongly.

Notes, reason for not taking n. See 'Forgetting, impossible to f. See 'Memory, impossible to forget - Why should I write this down, that's riveted, screw'd to my memory'.

Nothing more to say. See 'Speech, argument exhausted - do what you will; your wisdom be your guide'.

Nothingness, learning to accept to be nothing. See 'Peace, p. of the soul, only learning to become nothing can provide some comfort - Nor I nor any man that but man is, with nothing shall be pleased, till he be eased with being nothing.'

Novelty, a

Novelty, fear of n. See 'Custom, c. as an obstacle to positive change - What custom wills, in all things should we do't, the dust of antique time would lie unswept…'

Numbers, n. unnecessary - Spare your arithmetic.

O call back yesterday, bid time return… See 'Time, call back t.'

O change thy thought… See 'Quarrel, exhortation to change attitude - O change thy thought, that I may change my mind…'

O fearful meditation, where alack… See 'Writing, power of printed message - … in black ink my love may still shine bright.'

O for a horse… See 'Transportation, fast t. needed – O, for a horse with wings!'

O for a muse of fire. See 'Inspiration, a powerful Muse required before starting a speech - O for a Muse of fire, that would ascend the brightest heaven of invention!'

O hard condition, twin born of greatness. See 'Power, the downside of p. - .. . subject to the breath of every fool, whose sense no more can feel, but his own wringing.'

O hateful error, Melancholy's child! Why dost thou show to the apt thoughts of men the things that are not? See 'Error, e. due to misapprehension or misrepresentation'.

O he sits high in all the people's hearts. See 'Perception, craftiness can make bad appear good - … His countenance, like richest alchemy will change to virtue and to worthiness.'

O judgment, thou art fled to brutish beasts … See 'Judgment, j. vanished - O judgment, thou art fled to brutish beasts and men have lost their reason.'

O learn to read what silent love… See ' 'Love, detection possible without verbal evidence - O learn to read what silent love hath writ…'

O my prophetic soul! See 'Invocation, i. to

one's own power of prediction - O my prophetic soul!'

O sleep. See 'Sleeplessness, invocation - O sleep, O gentle sleep, nature's soft nurse…

O tiger's heart… See 'Angry, a. at her, compared to a tiger in disguise - O tiger's heart wrapt in a woman's hide!...'

O that a man might know the end… See 'Prediction, desire to know in advance - o, that a man might know the end of this day's business ere it come…'

O that this too too solid flesh… See 'Pessimism, life - "O, that this too too solid flesh would melt thaw and resolve itself into a dew'

O weary reckoning! See 'Lover, absence of l. unbearable - … and lovers' absent hours more tedious than the dial eight score times? O weary reckoning.'

O what men dare do! what men may do! what men daily do! not knowing what they do! See 'Invocation, skepticism about human nature'

O wonderful, when devils tell the truth. See '.Anger, even her a. is an occasion for admiration - … wonderful when angels are so angry.'

Oak, old o. also metaphor for old age – … an oak, whose boughs were moss'd with age and high top bald with dry antiquity.

Oath - … by this pale queen of night I swear…

Oath, all sort of bad things may happen to me if… - … myself myself confound!… if

Oath, commitment not to break an o. however unpalatable. See 'Agreement, abiding by the majority decision or a., even if you do not like the terms - … although I seem so loth, I am the last that will last keep his oath.'

Oath, curse should an o. not be kept - … And let him ne'er see joy that breaks that oath!

Oath, excuse for breaking an o. - … but, for a kingdom, any oath may be broken

Oath, excuse for breaking an o. - …The truth is then most done not doing it

Oath, excuse for breaking an o. - An oath is of no moment, being not took before a true and lawful magistrate…

Oath, excuse for breaking an o. - It is great sin to swear unto a sin..

Oath, excuse for breaking an o. - To keep that oath were more impiety than Jephthah's, when he sacrificed his daughter.

Oath, no o. needed - do not stain the even virtue of our enterprise…

Oath, no reason could make me break this o. - … (not) for all the sun sees or the close earth wombs…

Oath, promise to keep it. See 'Promise, solemn p. – And I will die a hundred thousand deaths, ere break the smallest parcel of this vow.'

Oath, reason why oath will be broken – If I break faith, this word shall speak for me, I am forsworn on 'mere necessity'.

Oaths, a habitual breaker of oaths, also applicable to promises. See 'Liar, a breaker of promises - He professes no keeping of oaths; in breaking them he is stronger than Hercules.'

Oaths, not easily given to pronounce o. but maintaining them when given – .. I never use till urged, nor never break for urging.

Oath, resolution broken - … Breaking his oath and resolution, like a twist of rotten silk.

Oath, solemn o. taken – … In the due reverence of a sacred vow I here engage my words.

Oath, swearing by the moon not recommended. See 'Reassurance, answer to demands for r. – O, swear not by the moon, the inconstant moon, that monthly changes in her circle orb…'

Oath, sworn o. invalid if the premises of the o. are false – … if you swear by that that is not, you are not forsworn.

Oaths, many o. unnecessary. See 'Truth, simple t. not requiring oaths - 'T is not the many oaths that make the truth, but the plain single vow, that is vow'd true.'

Oaths, men's p. unreliable. See 'Men, m. generally unreliable - Trust none, for oaths are straws, men's faiths are wafer-cakes…'

Oaths, no o. needed. See 'Truth, simple t. not requiring oaths - 'T is not the many oaths that make the truth, but the plain single vow, that is vow'd true.'

Oaths, o. unnecessary between gentlemen - I'll take thy word for faith, not ask thine oath…

Oaths, unreliable o. or vows - … those mouth-made vows which break themselves in swearing.

Obedience, complete o. - I am your shadow, my lord; I'll follow you

Obedience, immediate o. - Proud of employment, willingly I go.

Obedience, o. and execution – … Performance shall follow.

Obedience, o. and the ideal capitalist system - … for so work the honey-bees…

Obedience, o. by master demanded. See 'Task, t. carried out but reluctantly - Thither I must, although against my will, for servants must their masters' minds fulfil.'

Obedience, o. declared - my voice shall sound as you do prompt mine ear.

Obedience, o. or responsibility? - … our obedience to the king wipes the crime of it out of us

Obedience, o. to authority as justification of crime - My commission is not to reason of the deed, but do it.

Obedience, passive o. expected – It fits thee not to ask the reason why because we bid it…

Obedience, we'll do as you say - Well hast thou lesson'd us; this shall we do.

Obesity, hell no place for fat men - I think, the devil will not have me damned, less the oil that is in me should set hell on fire.

Obesity, o. caused by stress - … when I was about thy years… I was not an eagle's talon in the waist…

Obesity, obese man in Windsor - .. What tempest, I trow, threw this whale, with so many tons of oil in his belly, ashore in Windsor?

Obesity, proposal for law against o. See 'Health, banning of obesity - I'll exhibit a bill in parliament for the putting down of fat men'.

Object, o. of admiration. See 'Cheeks and hands - … this cheek to bathe my lips upon.. this hand, whose touch… would force the feeler to an oath of loyalty… this object which takes prisoner the wild motion of mine eye.'

Objective, examining the folly required to achieve an o. - … in everything the purpose must weigh with the folly.

Objective, now I understand your o. – Now I see the bottom of your purpose.

Objectives, finally stating your o. - … here is the heart of my purpose.

Objectives, focus on the o. – … let every man now task his thought that this fair action may on foot be brought.

Objectives, means to achieve o. – … to load our purposes with what they travail for.

Objectives, o. achieved by dogged determination and solving problem in little steps . See 'Defeat, d. against overwhelming forces – But Hercules himself must yield to odds; and many strokes…fell the hardest-timber'd oak'.

Objectives, o. better achieved if a woman calls. See 'Woman, young w. and a natural persuader - … for in her youth there is a prone and speechless dialect, such as move men.'

Objectives, o. of a plea - Was't not to this end that thou began'st to twist so fine a story?

Objectives, o. of study. See 'Studying, objective of s. - … that to know, which else we should not know…'

Objectives, o. achieved with humble tools -

What poor an instrument may do a noble deed!

Objectives, o. versus conscience - The colour of the king doth come and go between his purpose and his conscience…

Obligations, no o. and no love - I owe him little duty, and less love.

Oblivion, insurance against o. – … A forted residence 'gainst the tooth of time and razure of oblivion.

Oblivion, o. as a gulf - … in the swallowing gulf of blind forgetfulness and dark oblivion.

Oblivion, o. prevented through wri

Oblivion. See entries for 'Forgetting'

Oblivion. See 'Time, t. and ingratitude - Time hath, my lord, a wallet in his back wherein he puts alms for oblivion…'

Observation, concurring with an o. - Thou but rememberest me of mine own conception..

Observation, careful o. by a person - But there's more in me than thou understand'st. Why dost thou so oppress me with thine eye?

Observation, careful o. of a person – I have with exact view perused thee..

Observation, direct o. more trustworthy than official reports – Let every eye negotiate for itself and trust no agent.

Observation, insincere or exaggerated reaction - The lady protests too much, methinks.

Observation, intelligent o. always yield some benefit – … to apprehend thus, draws us a profit from all things we see.

Observation, o. leading to experience. See 'Experience, e. acquired through observation - How hast thou purchased this experience? By my penny of observation.

Obstacles, all o. removed – … And all the clouds that lour'd upon our house, in the deep bosom of the ocean buried.

Obstacles, intention not to put obstacles. See 'Agreement, wholeheartedly in a. - May I never, to this good purpose, that so fairly shows dream of impediment.'

Obstacles, o. increasing desire --...as all impediments in fancy's course are motives of more fancy.

Obstacles, see 'Determination, d. to overcome obstacles - … that is a step on which I must fall down, or else o'er-leap…

Obstacles, two obstacles in succession. See 'One thing after another - Like to a ship that, having 'scaped a tempest is straightway calm'd and boarded with a pirate.'

Occasion, torrent of o., circumstances forcing action. See 'Rebellion, reasons and occasions for a r. - We see which way the stream of time doth run… the rough torrent of occasion.'

Occupation, stock breeding - …to get your living by the copulation of cattle.

Occurrence, rare o. - It is no act of common passage, but a strain of rareness.

Odds, o. overwhelmingly unfavorable - .. But now 't is odds beyond arithmetic.

Odds, yielding to o. See 'Defeat, d. against overwhelming forces – But Hercules himself must yield to odds; and many strokes…fell the hardest-timber'd oak.'

Odor, unpleasant – … I do smell all horse-piss; at which my nose is in great indignation.

Odor, unpleasant and offensive to nostrils - … there was the rankest compound of villanous smell, that ever offended nostril.

Offense, charge of o. rejected - Never so much as in a thought unborn did I offend your highness.

Offense, if any o. done that's the end of it - I will no further offend you than becomes me for my good.

Offense, no o. done to anyone - … my remembrance is very free and clear from any image of offence done to any man.

Offence, o. forgotten – … his great offence is dead and deeper than oblivion we do bury…

Offense, o. will not be rewarded - Who bates mine honour, shall not know my coin.

Offense, offending the law as a front. See 'Misconduct, m. as a front - I'll so offend, to make offence a skill; redeeming time when men think least I will.'

Offer, o. unacceptable - This proffer is absurd and reasonless.

Office, o. functions better when you are not there - They prosper best of all when I am thence.

Office, qualifications for o. See 'Politics, qualification for office – ..Outcake or Seacoal for they can read and write'.

Office, untidy state of o. See 'Shop, s. not in tip-top conditions - and about his shelves a beggarly account of empty boxes.'

Office holders, often of questionable merit or qualifications - O, that estates, degrees and offices were not derived corruptly…

Old tune annoying. See 'Message or request, same m. or request annoying - If it be aught to the old tune… it is as fat and fulsome to mine ear…'

Omen, o. characterizing an evil man – The owl shriek'd at thy birth,--an evil sign…

Omission, o. does not mean giving up - Omittance is no quittance.

Omission, o. of responsibility dangerous - Omission to do what is necessary seals commission to a blank of danger..

Omnipotence, God works in inscrutable ways. See 'Results, great r. from small resources - He that of greatest works is finisher, oft does them by the weakest minister.'

One doth not know how much an ill word may empoison liking. See 'Words, power of w. to poison relationships.'

One fell swoop

One thing after another - Like to a ship that, having 'scaped a tempest is straightway calm'd and boarded with a pirate.

Onion, tears caused by an o. See 'Crying not called for, on the contrary - the tears live in an onion that should water this sorrow.'

Onion. See entries for 'Breath' *** 'Garlic'

Openness, invitation to o. - Out with it boldly; truth loves open dealing.

Openness, no need for secrecy - There's nothing I have done yet, of my conscience, deserves a corner

Operation, covert o. See 'Intelligence, gathering and sifting i. - Your bait of falsehood takes this carp of truth…. By indirections find directions out'

Opinion, acquired excellent o. - … I have bought golden opinions from all sorts of people.

Opinion, change your opinion. See entries for 'Exhortation, e. to change opinion - … remove the root of his opinion which is rotten as ever oak or stone was sound.'

Opinion, comparing o. - I will hear Cassius; and compare their reasons, when severally we hear them rendered.

Opinion, concerned about what people think of you. See 'Care, too much c. about worldly opinion counterproductive - You have too much respect upon the world, they lose it that do buy it with much care.'

Opinion, op. directs the course of events - … opinion, a sovereign mistress of effects…

Opinion, own o. as law. See 'Character, c. treacherous and false - … and be ever double in his words and meaning.'

Opinion, emphatic exhortation to discard an o.– … be cured of this diseased opinion.

Opinion, false o. strangely acquired - … what a strange infection is fall'n into thy ear!

Opinion, good o. lost - … you are now sailed into the north of my lady's opinion.

Opinion, good o. regained - Thou hast redeem'd thy lost opinion.

Opinion, o… as foolish. See 'Appearances, outside a. leading to false judgment - Opinion's but a fool, that makes us scan the outward habit by the inward man.'

Opinion, o. of others to be disregarded – A plague of opinion! a man may wear it on both sides, like a leather jerkin.

Opinion, o.. or idea, stuck on an op. or idea

and unable to change it - …you may as well forbid the sea to obey the moon…`

Opinion, o. poll negative - I find the people strangely fantasied… not knowing what they fear, but full of fear.

Opinion, o.. poll worse than before - The faiths of men ne'er stained with revolt, fresh expectation troubled not the land …

Opinion, o. polling. See 'Speech, s. and opinion polling – there shall I try in my oration, how the people take..'

Opinion, public o. gained by the appearance of maturity in the shape of an elder person - .. his silver hairs will purchase us a good opinion…

Opinion, what is your o.? (case when you approve) - The image of it gives me content already…

Opinion, your op. delivered simply - I'll show my mind according to my shallow simple skills.

Opinion, your op. firm and immovable - … is the opinion, that fire cannot melt out of me; I will die in it at the stake.

Opinion, your op. on a man who could be better - He's that he is: I may not breathe my censure, what he might be..

Opinion, your op. on a man who is rich but shallow - Well of his wealth; but of himself, so, so.

Opinion, your op. on a man whose clothing lacks coordination – How oddly he is suited! I think he bought his doublet in Italy, his round hose in France…

Opinion, your op. on a specific man – … know him noble, of great estate, of fresh and stainless youth..

Opinion, your op. on ambition. See 'Character, ambition - for the very substance of the ambitious is merely the shadow of a dream'.

Opinion, your op. on an inarticulate man – dull of tongue.

Opinion, your op. on authority – …There thou mightst behold the great image of authority: a dog's obeyed in office.

Opinion, your op. on authority – …..man, proud man, dressed in a little brief authority…

Opinion, your op. on crowds and masses - … Commanded always by the greater gust; such is the lightness of you common men.

Opinion, your op. on crowds and masses - … subject to the breath of every fool… See 'Power, the downside of p. - .. . subject to the breath of every fool, whose sense no more can feel, but his own wringing.'

Opinion, your op. on crowds and masses – … your affections are a sick man's appetite …

Opinion, your op. on crowds and masses – An habitation giddy and unsure hath he, that buildeth on the vulgar heart.

Opinion, your op. on crowds and masses – He that trusts to you, where he should find you lions, finds you hares…

Opinion, your op. on crowds and masses – The beast with many heads…

Opinion, your op. on crowds and masses – The blunt monster with uncounted heads.

Opinion, your op. on crowds and masses - The fool multitude, that choose by show…

Opinion, your op. on crowds and masses - The mutable, rank-scented many.

Opinion, your op. on crowds and masses – (They) can judge as fitly of his worth as I can of those mysteries which heaven will not have earth to know.

Opinion, your op. on crowds and masses - This common body, like to a vagabond flag upon the stream, goes to and back..

Opinion, your op. on crowds and masses – Was ever feather so lightly blown to and fro as this multitude?

Opinion, your op. on crowds and masses – With every minute you do change a mind

Opinion, your op. on crowds and masses - Worship shadows and adore false shapes.

Opinion, your op. on crowds and masses, mass psychology - … if they love they know not why, they hate upon no better a ground.

Opinion, your op. on crowds and masses, always siding with the winner - The common people swarm like summer flies and whither fly the gnats but to the sun?

Opinion, your op. on crowds and masses, blindly applauding the last mountebank - ... when you saw his chariot but appear, have you not made an universal shout….

Opinion, your op. on crowds and masses, never depend on their favor - He that depends upon your favours, swims with fins of lead..

Opinion, your op. on crowds and masses, slippery, unable to know who is good - — whose love is never linked to the deserver.

Opinion, your op. on crowds and masses, using eyes, not judgment - He is loved of the distracted multitude, who like not in their judgement, but their eyes.

Opinion, your op. on crowds and masses. See 'Army, ragged a. or unruly mass - ... His army is a ragged multitude of hinds and peasants, rude and merciless.'

Opinion, your op. on doctors, you do not trust them - … trust not the physician; his antidotes are poison.

Opinion, your o. on fashion – Seest thou not, I say, what a deformed thief this fashion is?…

Opinion, your op. on fashion (new, foreign and trendy) - .. is not this a lamentable thing, grandsire, that we should be thus afflicted with these strange flies..

Opinion, your op. on fashion. See 'Advice, a. on men's wear and fashion - Costly thy habit as thy purse can buy, but not express'd in fancy; rich, not gaudy…'

Opinion, your op. on flattery - … he that loves to be flattered is worthy of the flatterer.

Opinion, your op. on friendship and its value. See 'Advice, a. on cultivating friendship - Those friends thou hast, and their adoption tried, grapple them to thy soul with hoops of steel.'

Opinion, your op. on lawyers - The first thing we do, let's kill all the lawyers.

Opinion, your op. on medicine. See 'Opinion, your op. on doctors, you do not trust them - his antidotes are poison.'

Opinion, your op. on money, handling of, borrowing and lending - Neither a borrower nor a lender be..

Opinion, your op. on painting. See 'Painting, inherent value of the art of p. – … the painting is almost the natural man…'

Opinion, your op. on politicians in general - The devil knew not what he did when he made man politic, he crossed himself by 't.

Opinion, your op. on power, pomp and prestige - ... what is pomp, rule, reign, but earth and dust?...

Opinion, your op. on profusely given thanks - ... when a man thanks me heartily…

Opinion, your op. on salesmen and merchants - Traffic's thy god; and thy god confound thee!

Opinion, your op. on sociological issues, minimum wage - O, reason not the need: our basest beggars are in the poorest thing superfluous..

Opinion, your op. on specific man, bad in himself and worse when drunk - … when he is best, he is a little worse than a man and when he is worst, he is little better than a beast.

Opinion, your op. on the choice - how like you our choice that you stand pensive, as half malcontent?

Opinion, your op. on the newly rich - ... 'tis a common proof that lowliness is young ambition's ladder..

Opinion, your op. on who is the best man - … of many good I think him best.

Opinion, your op. on women. See 'Women, w. compared to German clocks - A woman, that is like a German clock, still a-repairing, ever out of frame, and never going a-right…'

Opinion, your poor op. of a man. See 'Insult, opinion of a person - God made him, and therefore let him pass for a man'.

Opportunist. See 'Character, c. slippery and opportunist - ... a slipper and subtle knave, a finder of occasions.'

Opportunists. See 'Duty, d. performed formally only - .. Others there are who, trimm'd in forms and visages of duty, keep yet their hearts attending

Opportunity, advice to seize on the o. – Sell when you can: you are not for all markets.

Opportunity, crime of o. - 'O Opportunity, thy guilt is great!..

Opportunity, favorable conditions. See 'Astrology, astrological conditions favorable - I find my zenith doth depend upon a most auspicious star…'

Opportunity, men's different behavior with o. - ... O heavens, what some men do, while some men leave to do!.

Opportunity, o. dependent on right time and availability - ... advantage, which doth ever cool in the absence of the needer.

Opportunity, o. missed through lack of judgment - ... defect of judgement to fail in the disposing of those chances which he was lord of'.

Opportunity, o. not to be rejected due to pessimism. See 'Action, doing the best with the means available - The means that heaven yields must be embraced and not neglected.'

Opportunity, o. offered and rejected - Who seeks, and will not take when once 'tis offered, shall never find it more.

Opportunity, poor chance of paying back for goods or services received - ... thou prun'st a rotten tree that cannot so much as a blossom yield…

Opportunity, the world as a source of o - …then the world's mine oyster.

Opportunity, the world as a source of o. - There's place and means for every man alive.

Opportunity, waiting for the o. - … there I am till time and vantage crave my company.

Opportunity, why it should not be missed - There is a tide in the affairs of men, which, taken at the flood, leads on to fortune, omitted….

Opposition, o. without reason – … though you bite so sharp at reasons you are so empty of them.

Opposition, strong and malicious – … potently opposed; and with a malice of as great size.

Oppression, o. and unfair working conditions – … I have served him from the hour of my nativity to this instant…

Oppression, resistance to o. See 'Prevarication on anyone will prompt vengeance - the smallest worm will turn being trodden on.'

Optimism, overly optimistic - Description cannot suit itself in words to demonstrate the life of such a battle.

Optimism, over o. disastrous - .. And so, with great imagination proper to madmen, led his powers to death and winking leap'd into destruction.

Orator, being an orator on someone else's behalf. See 'Speech, s. to further someone else's cause - .. I'll play the orator as if the golden fee for which I plead were for myself.'

Oratory, a subtle orator and a pliable listener - ... For Warwick is a subtle orator, and Lewis a prince soon won with moving words.

Oratory, o. by women convincing. See 'Women, their persuasive power greater than men's oratory - .. when a world of men could not prevail with all their oratory, yet hath a woman kindness over-ruled.

Oratory, lack of o. claimed - ... I have neither wit, nor words, nor worth...

Oratory, lack of o. claimed - Rude am I in my speech, and little bless'd with the soft phrase of peace.

Oratory, lack of o. claimed but … - … little shall I grace my cause in speaking for myself. Yet, by your gracious patience…

Oratory, working up the crowd – You are not wood, you are not stones, but men …

Orders, disobeying o. for the safety of the

orderer - They say, in care of your most royal person.. and therefore do they cry, though you forbid.

Organization, creativity of an o. - … This teeming womb of royal kings …

Organization, o. on the point of sinking - … leak'd is our bark and we, poor mates, stand on the dying deck..

Organization, perfect management o. such as the bees - … So may a thousand actions, once afoot. end in one purpose…

Ornament, o. a

Ornaments, enhancing a divine beauty - Sweet ornament, that decks a thing divine.

Ornaments, to make a goddess angry - Your laboursome and dainty trims, wherein you made great Juno angry.

Orwellian words. See 'Words, w. used to twist meaning - I can yield you no reason without words; and words are grown so false, I am loth to prove reason with them.'

Our basest beggars are in the poorest things superfluous… See 'Opinion, your op. on sociological issues, minimum wage'.

Our content is our best having . See 'Contentment, c. as the best asset'

Our virtues lie in the interpretation of the time. See 'Virtue, perception of v. depending on contemporary culture – So our virtues lie in the interpretation of the time.'

Our wills and fates … See 'Destiny, at odd with our wills - … Our wills and fates do so contrary run that our devices still are overthrown, our thoughts are ours, their ends none of our own.'

Out, damned spot! out, I say! See 'Washing a persistent stain - Out, damned spot! out, I say.'

Outburst, puzzled at o. – … what means this passionate discourse…

Outcast, I am an o. See 'Attitude, a. towards the world, hating it – one… whom the vile blows and buffets of the world…'

Outcome of events detectable in small details at the beginning - And in such

indexes, although small pricks to their subsequent volumes…

Outcome, happy o. after a hard trial - …and if it end so meet, the bitter past, more welcome is the sweet.

Outrage, see entries for 'Indignation'.

Overconfidence, see entries for 'Confidence'.

Overweight and underfunded. See 'Character, overweight and underfunded - our means are very slender, and your waist is great..'

Ovid, in praise of O. – … the elegancy, facility, and golden cadence of poesy…

Owner, o. dignifying his possession. See 'Value, v. of object enhanced by owner - .. things of like value differing in the owners are prized by their masters…'

Ownership by implication - … when France is mine and I am yours, then yours is France and you are mine.

Ownership pre-established and without question - .. To try if that our own be ours or no.

Packaging. See 'Information, importance of packaging i. - I fear my Julia would not deign my lines receiving them from such a worthless post.'

Pain, extreme pain, like separating body and soul. See 'Fall from greatness painful, better not have pomp to begin with – … 'tis a sufferance panging as soul and body's severing.'

Pain, p. better endured by him who does nor feel it – He bears the sentence well that nothing bears..

Pain, mental p. - … I am bound upon a wheel of fire, that mine own tears do scald like moulten lead.

Pain, mental p. - These miseries are more than may be borne. To weep with them that weep doth ease some deal..

Pain, mental p. absolute - Nothing so heavy as these woes of mine.

Pain, mental p. aggravated by being

concealed - Sorrow concealed, like an oven stopp'd doth burn the heart to cinders where it is.

Pain, mental p. and degrees of it. See 'Positive thinking and defiance towards setbacks – woe doth the heavier sit, where it perceives it is but faintly borne.'

Pain, mental p. at thinking of the future – … when I do shape in forms imaginary the unguided days and rotten times…

Pain, mental p. increased by impossibility to verbalize it - … the heart hath treble wrong when it is barr'd the aidance of the tongue…

Pain, mental p. leading to illusions, shadows for true substances. See 'Sorrow, causing madness and misjudgment - .. grief hath so wrought on him, he takes false shadows for true substance.'

Pain, mental p. leading to incoherent speech - Sorrow and grief of heart makes him speak fondly, like a frantic man.

Pain, mental p. leading to madness - Extremity of griefs would make men mad.

Pain, mental p. not realized by other party – … thou wouldst not think how ill all's here about my heart.

Pain, mental p. reduced by seeing other sufferers - When we our betters see bearing our woes, we scarcely think our miseries our foes…

Pain, mental p. relieved by talking about it - Give sorrow words: the grief that does not speak...

Pain, mental p. relieved by talking about it. See 'Grievances, g. aired out - windy attorneys to their client's woes …. let them have scope.'

Pain, mental p. that is both proud and cannot be supported by anything smaller than the earth.

Pain, mental p., greater suffering makes us insensitive to the lesser - … where the greater malady is fix'd the lesser is scarce felt.

Pain, mental p., stones as a better audience than people - … I tell my sorrows to the stones; who, though they cannot answer my distress, yet in some sort they are better than the tribunes..

Pain, mental p., use of reason as a palliative - … If not a present remedy, at least a patient sufferance.

Pain, p. and sorrow altering perceptions - Sorrow breaks seasons and reposing hours, makes the night morning, and the noon-tide night.

Pain, p. at having to say this – I grieve at what I speak and am right sorry to repeat what follows.

Pain, p. felt by ourselves vs

Pain, p. internalized and invisible – .. the unseen grief that swells with silence in the tortured soul…

Pain, p. limiting power of expression - I'll utter what my sorrows give me leave.

Pain, p. of death equal for everyone. See 'Death, d. and suffering equal for any creature – … The sense of death is most in apprehension…'

Pain, p. or wrong, describing it not a cure – …if it should be told, the repetition cannot make it less…

Pain, p. repressed more hurtful - Sorrow concealed, like an oven stopped, doth burn the heart to cinders where it is.

Pain, p. scorned at doubly painful - … sorrow flouted at is double death

Pain, p. soothed when shared with others - Grief best is pleased with grief's society…

Pain, p. suffered by accused party contradicting alleged motives - Never did base and rotten policy colour her working with such deadly wounds.

Pain, p. that cannot be comforted - …men can counsel, and speak comfort to that grief which they themselves do not feel.

Pain, painful event, seeing it has greater impact than hearing about it - - To see sad sights moves more than hear them told…

Pain, see 'Advice, uselessness of a. when in pain - every one can master a grief, but he that has it.'

Pain, tears repressed but heart aches - Weep I cannot, but my heart bleeds.

Pains, p. yielding trouble. See 'Effort, useless and detrimental - You lay too much pains for purchasing but trouble.'

Painting, inherent value of the art of p. – ... the painting is almost the natural man...

Painting, p. better than words to explain a concept - A thousand moral paintings I can show..

Painting, your positive opinion on a p. – I will say of it, it tutors nature..

Paleness, inquiring about the reasons of her p. - How chance the roses there do fade so fast?

Paleness, p. caused by reading unpleasant news. See 'News, bad n. causing the reader to pale - .. hat steals the colour from Bassanio's cheek'.

Paleness, the act of becoming pale – chased your blood out of appearance?

Panhandling, profitable p. See 'Welfare, excesses of w. - ... here's them in our country of Greece gets more with begging than we can do with working'.

Paper bullets of the brain. See 'Sarcasm, retort to s. – ... shall quips, and sentences, and these paper bullets of the brain...'

Parable, disclosing information by way of a parable or comparison. See "Secret, s. information given away indirectly – Thou shalt never get such a secret from me but by a parable.'

Paradise, a comparison - .. O nature! What hadst thou to do in hell when thou didst bower the spirit of a fiend...

Paradise, a statement. See 'Body, celestial b. - ... body as a paradise, to envelop and contain celestial spirits.'

Paradox, criticism followed by imitation - ... after he hath laughed at such shallow follies in others... will become the argument of his own scorn, by falling in love.

Paradox, explaining a failure, infinite will, finite reality - This is the monstruosity in love, lady - that the will is infinite, and the execution confined..

Paradox, using p. as a tool for spin. See 'Spin, how to re-interpret reality - You undergo too strict a paradox striving to make an ugly deed look fair.'

Paradoxes, as means to obtain a cheap laugh. See 'Joke, more nonsense than a j. - These are old fond paradoxes, to make fools laugh in the alehouse.'

Paranoia - There is a plot against my life, my crown; all's true that is mistrusted.

Parasites. See 'Character, c. only interested in gain and therefore unreliable - That sir

Pardon, asking for p. before uttering a dissenting voice. See 'Politeness, p. in asking for pardon - Pardon me, if you please; if not, I, pleased not to be pardon'd, am content withal.'

Pardon, p. befitting a king – The word is short, but not so short as sweet...

Pardon, p. granted to thief while he retains the loot – May one be pardon'd and retain the offence?

Pardon, p. reasonable – I do think that you might pardon him and neither heaven nor man grieve at the mercy.

Pardon, royalty of p. - ... how royal 'twas to pardon when it was less expected.

Pardon. See entries for 'Mercy'

Part, p. forgotten, like an actor forgetting his p. - Like a dull actor now, I have forgot my part...

Part, easy p. to learn and play, roaring lion - ... You may do it extempore, for it is nothing but roaring.

Part, unsuitable p. in a play – ... let not me play a woman; I have a beard coming.

Participation, p. in the scheme or debate inevitable - I see the play so lies that I must bear a part.

Parting, p. with promise of fidelity – Here is my hand for my true constancy...

Parting, p. without words. See 'Truth, t.

supported by facts not words - ... truth hath better deeds than words to grace it.'

Parting. See 'Good night, good night! parting is such sweet sorrow, that I shall say-good night till it be morrow!' *** Invocation, t

Party, invitation to p. - ... let's take hand till the conquering wine hath steeped our sense in soft and delicate Lethe.

Party, let's party - ... we will begin these rites as we do trust they'll end in true delights.

Party, many fine ladies expected - look to behold this night earth treading stars, that make dark heaven light.

Party, not attracted to parties - ... so to your pleasures I am for other than for dancing measures.

Party, opening the p. - Prepare for mirth, for mirth becomes a feast...

Party, p. attended by fools and parasites - ... to see meat fill knaves, and wine heat fools

Party, p. sounds out - Let not the sound of shallow foppery enter my sober house.

Party, p. spoiler - You have displaced the mirth, broke the good meeting..

Party, p. time, celebration - .. let us banquet royally after this golden day of victory.

Party, p. time, celebration - My banquet is to close our stomachs up... sit down; for now we sit to chat as well as eat.

Party, partying till and after midnight - ... fill our bowls once more; let's mock the midnight bell.

Party, partying with good wine, welcome and company - ... good company, good wine, good welcome can make good people.

Party, sad face at a p. See 'Expression of sadness unsuitable for a p. - ... put off these frowns, and ill-beseeming semblance for a feast.'

Party, speeding to p. considering the charm of the participants – The very thought of this fair company.

Party, toasts and request to be merry - ... that noble lady or gentleman that is not freely merry...

Party, victory p. - And now what rests but that we spend the time with stately triumphs, mirthful comic shows..

Partying, limits to p. See 'Drinking, knowing when to stop (drinking) – Let's teach ourselves that honorable stop, not to out-sport discretion.'

Passion, behavior inspired by p. - ... the brain may devise laws for the blood, but a hot temper leaps o'er a cold decree.

Passion, self-compounding, clearly in love with him - .. she would hang on him as if increase of appetite had grown by what it fed on.

Passion, desire to hear and to see her eyes - ... do I love her, that I desire to hear her speak again and feast upon her eyes?

Passion, effects of strong p. - This is the very ecstasy of love, whose violent property fordoes itself and leads the will to desperate undertakings.

Passion, generating irrational belief (in oneself or in what said) - Methinks his words do from such passion fly, that he believes himself.

Passion, noble p. observed – ... this noble passion, child of integrity ...

Passion, p. elicited by her virtue and graces. See 'Graces, her g. and virtues - Her virtues graced with external gifts do breed love's settled passions in my heart...'

Passion, p. instantly developed - .. if he be married, my grave is like to be my wedding bed.

Passion, p. irresistible. See 'Character, passion, c. that cannot resist passion - I confess it is my shame to be so fond; but it is not in my virtue to amend it.'

Passion, p. overwhelming the heart - Why does my blood thus muster to my heart,...

Passion, power of p. to overcome obstacles - ... passion lends them power, time means, to meet, tempering extremities with extreme sweet.

Passion, tied up by p. - ... faster bound to Aaron's charming eyes than is Prometheus tied to Caucasus.

Passion, too strong, almost unbearable - .. some joy too fine, too subtle potent, turned too sharp in sweetness, for the capacity of my ruder powers…

Passion, too strong, almost unbearable - .. some joy too fine, too subtle potent, turned too sharp in sweetness, for the capacity of my ruder powers…

Passionate man. See 'Man, m. passionate and fiery - Why should a man whose blood is warm within…'

Past, happy p. as a dream - ... learn, good soul, to think our former state a happy dream...

Past, rationalizing your bumpy p. See 'Company, rationalization for having frequented the wrong crowd - The strawberry grows underneath the nettle… fruit of baser quality ' *** 'Apologies for past poor behavior - they say best men are moulded out of faults...'

Past, request not to insist on a subject past and already dealt with. See 'Insisting, request not to insist on the same subject – harp not on that string'.

Patching, p. never restore original. See 'Virtue, sin and their interrelationship, maxim - Any thing that's mended is but patched'

Patience, abuser of p. See 'Insult, dog and abuser of patience - Out dog! out, cur! thou drivest me past the bounds of maiden's patience'.

Patience, against p. – Patience is for poltroons.

Patience, asking for a little p. - ... I shall crave your forbearance a little.

Patience, asking for p. or a raise - I am much too venturous in tempting of your patience…

Patience, calm down - ... Sheath thy impatience; throw cold water on thy choler.

Patience, calm down – ... Upon the heat and flame of thy distemper sprinkle cool patience.

Patience, compared to a tired horse - ... though patience be a tired mare, yet she will plod.

Patience, counseling p. to sorrow useless - … 'tis all men's office to speak patience to those that wring under the load of sorrow…

Patience, p. in accepting suffering. See 'Determination, d. to accept suffering - Henceforth I'll bear affliction till it do cry out itself 'enough, enough' and die.'

Patience, endowed with the utmost p. - Were I as patient as the midnight sleep, by Jove, 'twould be my mind!

Patience, exhortation to p. - ... with patience calm the storm while we bethink a means to break it off.

Patience, exhortation to p. - I pray thee, sort thy heart to patience..

Patience, exhortation to p. See 'Exhortation, e. to patience - Be patient, for the world is broad and wide.'

Patience, p. and time management required - How poor are they that have not patience!…

Patience, p. as a palliative – I have her sovereign aid and rest myself content.

Patience, p. as a questionable remedy. See 'Anger, are you patient? - Patience is sottish, and impatience does become a dog that's mad.'

Patience, p. as a weapon against bad fortune – What cannot be preserved when fortune takes…

Patience, p. invoked. See 'Invocation, i. for patience, need for p. - You heavens, give me that patience, patience I need!'

Patience, p. lost - ... quite besides the government of patience

Patience, p. or cowardice? - That which in mean men we entitle patience is pure cold cowardice in noble breasts.

Patience, p. requested - .. If you'll bestow a

small (of what you have little) patience..

Patience, p. required and a virtue. See 'Patience, p. and time management required - How poor are they that have not patience!…

Patience, p. required until horoscope improves. See 'Fortune, moment of unfavorable conditions due to astrological influences - There's some ill planet reigns…'

Patience, p. should rule misfortune - … let mischance be slave to patience.

Patience, p. strained - Who can be patient in such extremes?

Patience, p. strained. See 'Thought, forced to think the unthinkable – (You) prick my tender patience, to those thoughts which honour and allegiance cannot think.'

Patience, p. waiting for better times. See 'Fortune, moment of unfavorable conditions due to astrological influences - There's some ill planet reigns…'

Patience, p. with authority strained - How long shall I be patient? ah, how long shall tender duty make me suffer wrong?

Patience, reluctantly silent – I will be the pattern of all patience, I will say nothing.

Patience, resigned to the situation and bearing it with p. and melancholy - … And with a green and yellow melancholy, she sat like Patience on a monument…

Patience, rhetorical self-analysis - Why have I patience to endure all this?

Patience, running out of p. - The devil take Henry of Lancaster and thee! patience is stale, and I am weary of it.

Patience, temperance. See 'Temperance, t. as a cure - … temperance; that's the appliance only which your disease requires.'

Patriotism – … But yet I love my country, and am not one that rejoices in the common wreck…

Patronage, p. unreliable. See 'Philosophical considerations, uselessness of coveting patronage as patronage is so prone to change - O momentary grace of mortal men which we more hunt for than the grace of God…'

Pause, relaxation after victorious struggle - … good fortune bids us pause, and smooth the frowns of war with peaceful looks.

Payment method. See 'Dinner. How to pay for dinner, cash or credit card - (I'll pay cash) as far as my coin would stretch..'

Payment, p. after service – When I have chased all thy foes from hence, then will I think upon a recompense.

Payment, refusing to be p. – All gold and silver rather turn to dirt, as 'tis no better reckon'd, but of those who worship dirty gods.

Payment, satisfaction. See 'Satisfaction, s. as payment. - He is well paid that is well satisfied…'

Payroll, meeting the p. – … there is remuneration; for the best ward of mine honour is rewarding my dependents.

Peace, calling for p. - … let your drums be still for here we entertain a solemn peace.

Peace, calling for p. - Peace, peace, for shame, if not for charity.

Peace, exhortation to stop arguing - .. cease these jars, and rest your minds in peace.

Peace, let's have some p. See 'Pause, relaxation after victorious struggle - .. good fortune bids us pause, and smooth the frowns of war with peaceful looks.'

Peace, false words of p. See 'Words, false w. of peace - I speak of peace, while covert enmity..'

Peace, in praise of p. - … dear nurse of arts, plenties and joyful births.

Peace, inconsistency of p. proposal – What, drawn and talk of peace?

Peace, inner p. felt. - … I feel within me a peace above all earthly dignities, a still and quiet conscience.

Peace, inner p., self-created disruption of one's inner peace - … put rancours in the vessel of my peace.

Peace, invitation to p. - … tame the savage spirit of wild war

Peace, invocation and wishes for p. - …

poor and mangled peace, dear nurse of arts and joyful births…

Peace, offer of p. - His glittering arms he will commend to rust…

Peace, p. advocated between France and England - .. combine the blood of malice in a vein of league and not to spend it so unneighbourly.

Peace, p. after rebellion - Our peace will, like a broken limb united grow stronger for the breaking.

Peace, p. among equals - … It was both impious and unnatural, that such cruelty and bloody strife should reign among professors of one faith.

Peace, p. and harmony sanctioned by the highest powers - The fingers of the powers above do tune the harmony of this peace.

Peace, p. and reconciliation - … to the brightest beams distracted clouds give way..

Peace, stating the end of a quarrel. See 'War, end of war or quarrel - Grim-visaged war hath smooth'd his wrinkled front…'

Peace, p. as the goal of war - … cheerly on, courageous friends to reap the harvest of perpetual peace by this one bloody trial of sharp war.

Peace, p. at last - Now civil wounds are stopp'd, peace lives again that she may long live here, God say amen.

Peace, p. considered as a conquest and a victory – A peace is of the nature of a conquest ; for then both parties nobly are subdued…

Peace, p. declared – The edge of war, like an ill-sheathed knife, no more shall cut his master.

Peace, p. making efforts - Let's purge this choler without letting blood.

Peace, p. of mind lost. See 'Happiness, h. or peace of mind, farewell to - Farewell the tranquil mind! farewell content!'

Peace, p. of the soul, only learning to become nothing can provide some comfort - Nor I nor any man that but man is, with nothing shall be pleased, till he be eased with being nothing.

Peace, p. promised - My tongue shall hush again this storm of war and make fair weather in your blustering land.

Peace, p. proposal. See 'Speech, bringing a message of peace and substance - I hold the olive in my hand: my words are full of praise as matter.'

Peace, peaceful resolution, too late for a peaceful resolution. See 'Dispute, d. that cannot be peacefully resolved - … the wound that bred this meeting here cannot be cured by words.'

Peace, shaky p. - This late dissension, grown betwixt the peers burns under feigned ashes of forged love..

Peacock, p. as an image of vanity. See 'Concession, tolerate your adversary's temporary glory - Let frantic Talbot triumph for a while and like a peacock sweep along his tail…'

Peasants, p. talk. See 'Language, l. of peasants – Talk like the vulgar sort of market men…'

Peerless, without comparison - .. the most peerless piece of earth, I think, e'er the sun shone bright on.

People, love of the p. to a limit – … I love the people but do not like to stage me to their eyes…

People, the fewer the better for a great enterprise - … the fewer men, the greater share of honour.

People, there are all sorts of p. – Nature hath meal and bran, contempt and grace.

Perception, craftiness can make bad appear good - … His countenance, like richest alchemy will change to virtue and to worthiness.

Perception, giving the right spin to an event by using the right words – … but now the bishop turns insurrection to religion.

Perception, mis-perception. See 'Illusion, optical illusion - Mine eyes are made the fools o' the other senses.'

Perception, p. determining judgment – This service is not service, so being done but being so allow'd.

Perception, p. of current times. See 'Time, present t. bad, past and future OK – O thoughts of men accurst! Past and to come seem best, things present, worst.'

Perception, visual p. flawed and admitted to, See 'Illusion, optical illusion - Mine eyes are made the fools o' the other senses.'

Perception, you want me dead - thou hidest a thousand daggers in thy thoughts…

Perfection, astrological contribution to her perfection - … The senate-house of planets all did sit to knit in her their best perfections

Perfection, conditions to avoid in order to achieve p. - For he's no man on whom perfections wait….

Perfection, divine p. in a woman. See 'Woman, perfect - Divine perfection of a woman'.

Perfection, her p. unbelievable - Who will believe my verse in time to come…

Perfection, her p. unparalleled - … her, whom, we know well the world's large spaces cannot parallel.

Perfection, p. compounding with p. - .. each your doing, so singular in each particular… that all your acts are queens.

Perfection, p. even in her shortcomings - She spoke and panted that she made defect perfection.

Perfection, p. in action, speech, dance etc. – What you do, still betters what is done. When you speak, sweet, I'd have you do it ever…

Perfection, p. never total – … no perfection is so absolute, that some impurity doth not pollute

Perfection, p. that excludes any possibility of evil - There's nothing ill can dwell in such a temple…

Perfection, the description of her p. would fill volumes - The chief perfections of that lively dame… would make a volume of enticing lines..

Perfection, wishing no one else but her -… nor can imagination form a shape beside yourself, to like of

Perfection, woman unique in p. See 'Woman, unique in perfection – her whose worth makes other worthies nothing'.

Perfection, worthy of a king - … all her perfections challenge sovereignty; one way or other, she is for a king.

Performance, effectiveness of p. depending on quality of choreography or suitable setting. - The nightingale, if she should sing by day..

Performance, judgment of p. arbitrary. See 'Virt

Performance, outdoing previous p. - … he hath in this action outdone his former deeds doubly.

Performance, p. beyond description - … his deeds exceed all speech.

Performance, p. contrary to expectations. See 'Men, characteristics of hollow m. - … hollow men, like horses hot at hand make gallant show and promise of their mettle…'

Perfume, excellent scent – A delicate odour… as ever hit my nostrils.

Perfume, p. that even makes the winds love-sick – … and so perfumed that the winds were love-sick with them.

Perfumes of Arabia. See 'Murder, m. cannot be erased - Here's the smell of the blood still: all the perfumes of Arabia will not sweeten this little hand.'

Perjury, p. punished – Thus pour the stars down plagues for perjury.

Perjury, what punishment for p. - What scourge for perjury can this dark monarchy afford false Clarence?

Permission to speak. See 'Speech, using permission to speak - .. since you have given me leave to speak, freely will I speak'.

Perseverance, in praise of p. - … perseverance, dear my lord keeps honour bright…

Perseverance, p. against a set back - Do not, for one repulse, forego the purpose that thou resolved to effect.

Persistence, failure. positive attitude - … the protractive trials of great Jove to find persistive constancy in men.

Persistence, your persistence has paid off - He that will have a cake out of the wheat, must tarry the grinding.

Person, a dangerous p. See 'Sym

Person, a rude p. - … a rude despiser of good manners, that in civility thou seem'st so empty.

Person, arrival of a gullible p. to be made fun of - … here comes the trout that must be caught with tickling.

Person, compliments to a witty p. - …forms… begot in the ventricle of memory…

Person, deceitful but beautiful - O that deceit should dwell in such a gorgeous palace.

Person, hateful p. due to the news he brings. See 'News, unwelcome n. makes messenger unwelcome - … harm within itself so heinous is as it makes harmful all that speak of it.'

Person, p. best of all (applies to both woman and man) - … and was the best of all among the rar'st of good ones.

Person, p. helpful with your distress. See 'Comfort, recognizing a person for his/her help - Thou art all the comfort the gods will diet me with'.

Person, undefinable - … Why an otter?… she's neither fish nor flesh…

Person, p. who inspires hope - … Their very heart of hope.

Person, p's comparative worth - To me he seems like diamond to glass.

Person, self-defined kind p. See 'Kindness, k. applied even to the wicked - .. for I am one of those gentle ones that will use the devil himself with courtesy.'

Person, symptoms of a dangerous p. See 'Symptoms, s. of a potentially dangerous person - … He reads much; he is a great observer, and he looks quite through the deeds of men'.

Person, worthiness of a p. shown under trial - … in the wind and tempest of her frown, distinction…

Personality, multiple p. - thus play I in one person many people and none contented.

Personnel, background analysis as a good indicator of performance. See 'Life, l.'s history of a person as a predictor of future performance – there is a history in all men's lives…'

Personnel, candidate not qualified. See 'Man, qualified only for menial responsibilities – This is a slight unmeritable man, meet to be sent on errands.'

Personnel, crew, a motley crew - A crew of patches, rude mechanicals, that work for bread upon the Athenian walls.

Personnel, downsizing - … superfluous branches we lop away, that bearing boughs may live…

Personnel, employees stuck in their growth path. See 'Employees, e. stuck in their career or simple opportunists – You shall mark many a duteous and knee-crooking knave…'

Personnel, more people needed - Never so few, and never yet more need.

Personnel, p. not in good shape - The stuff we have, a strong wind will blow to pieces.

Personnel, unskilled p. - Hard-handed men… which never labour'd in their minds till now.

Personnel, warning to a chronic complainer. See 'Threat, t. towards complaining employee - If thou more murmur'st, I will rend an oak and peg thee in his knotty entrails…'

Persuader, absolute p. - This is a creature, would she begin a sect, might quench the zeal…

Persuasion, all efforts to persuade useless – I have laboured for the poor gentleman to the extremest shore of my modesty.

1261

Persuasion, amenable or not to p. See 'Heart, h. corrupted by custom – … if damned custom have not brass'd it so that it is proof and bulwark against sense.'

Persuasion, p. and sugared words - … By fair persuasions, mix'd with sugar'd words, we will entice the duke of Burgundy…

Persuasion, p. obtained with honey words - .. my woman's heart grossly grew captive to his honey words.

Persuasion, p. or suggestion that achieves the opposite result - Has almost charmed me from my profession, by persuading me to it.

Persuasion, persuaded by a woman - .. As prisoners to her womanly persuasion.

Persuasion, persuaded. See 'Convinced, convincing argument - His words do take possession of my bosom.'

Persuasion, persuasive power of women. See 'Woman, young w. and a natural persuader - … for in her youth there is a prone and speechless dialect, such as move men.'

Perversion, p. of the imagination - O, deeper sin than bottomless conceit can comprehend in still imagination!

Pessimism about human nature. See entries for 'Human nature, pessimism on h.n.'

Pessimism, comfort only in heaven - Comfort's in heaven; and we are on earth where nothing lives, but crosses, cares and grief.

Pessimism, down in the dumps remembering the past - And weep afresh love's long since cancell'd woe…

Pessimism, down in the dumps. See entries for 'World, pessimistic view of the world'

Pessimism, enough ugliness on earth to stir to mutiny the mildest man. See 'World, pessimistic view of the w. – enough to stir a mutiny in the most quiet'.

Pessimism, fleetness of life - … Yet in this life lie hid more thousand deaths…

Pessimism, fleetness of life – As flies to wanton boys are we to the gods, they kill us for their sport.

Pessimism, life – O world, but that thy strange mutations make us hate thee life would not yield to age.

Pessimism, life - O, that this too too solid flesh would melt thaw and resolve itself into a dew!

Pessimism, life as a stage for fools. See 'Life, l. as a stage for fools - When we are born we cry that we are come to this great stage of fools.'

Pessimism, life tedious as a tale told twice. See 'Mood, pessimistic, life tedious - There's nothing in this world can make me joy: life is as tedious as a twice-told tale, vexing the dull ear of a drowsy man.'

Pessimism, limits of self-importance - … Infusing him with self and vain conceits, as if this flesh, which walls about our life were brass impregnable.

Pessimism, nobody will pity me. See 'Despair and desperation'.

Pessimism, not even caring about being deceived – … I do not greatly care to be deceived, that have no use for trusting.

Pessimism, nothing left that is important after an important person gone - … and there is nothing left remarkable beneath the visiting moon.

Pessimism, p. on life and personal property - … And nothing can we call our own but death and that small model of the barren earth…

Pessimism, p. to the point that death is tolerable - The stroke of death is as a lover's pinch, which hurts, and is desired.

Pessimism, p. to the point that death is tolerable. See 'Peace, p. of the soul, only learning to become nothing can provide some comfort - Nor I nor any man that but man is, with nothing shall be pleased, till he be eased with being nothing.'

Pessimism, sadness on a grand scale - How weary, stale, flat and unprofitable seem to me all the uses of this world!...

Pessimism, unable to be happy - He that commends me to mine own content, commends me to do the thing I cannot get.

Pessimism, world will not feel my loss - … I shall do my friends no wrong, for I have none to lament me…

Phantasy. See entries for 'Imagination'

Pharmaceutical industry and doctors. See 'Opinion, your op. on doctors, you do not trust them - his antidotes are poison.'

Philosophical considerations, unwillingness to take responsibility for our mistakes - This is the excellent foppery of the world…'

Philosophical considerations, uselessness of coveting patronage as patronage is so prone to change - O momentary grace of mortal men which we more hunt for than the grace of God…

Philosophy, p. and common sense - … and that he that wants money, means and content is without three good friends.

Philosophy, p. and tooth ache - … there was never yet philosopher, that could endure the tooth-ache patiently.

Philosophy, p. as a remedy to adversity - I'll give thee armour to keep off that word, adversity's sweet milk, philosophy.

Philosophy, p. as a tool for happiness. See 'Happiness, road to h. via applied philosophy - … that part of philosophy will I apply that treats of happiness by virtue specially to be achieved.'

Philosophy, simple p. - Thou art a scholar; let us therefore eat and drink.

Philosophy, simple p. of life - … I will live so long as I may, that's the certain of it…

Philosophy, theory vs. practice - Of your philosophy you make no use, if you give place to accidental evils.

Philosophy, there is a reason for everything - There is occasions and causes why and wherefore in all things.

Phrases, good p. appreciated – good phrases are surely, and ever were, very commendable.

Physician, a p. faithful to the calling and not attracted by riches - .. a more content in course of true delight than to be thirsty after tottering honour…

Physiognomy, a person whose feelings are easily detected by his expression - .. For by his face straight shall you know his heart.

Physiognomy, expression telling – In many's looks the false heart's history is writ in moods and frowns and wrinkles strange..

Physiognomy, expression telling – see 'Expression, telling e. – heart in his face' and other entries for 'Expression, facial e'.

Physiognomy, p. unreliable - There's no art to find the mind's construction in the face…

Picture, loving her p. to extremes – O thou senseless form, thou shalt be worshipp'd, kiss'd, loved and adored!

Picture. See 'Woman, real w. better than her picture – so far this shadow doth limp behind the substance'.

Pilates, like Pontius Pilate. See 'Compassion, perfunctory c. cannot exempt from responsibility – … And water cannot wash away your sin.'

Pirates, thieves who argue on how to split the loot - Hear me, you wrangling pirates, that fall out in sharing that which you have pill'd from me!

Pity, hints of p. observed - My friend, I spy some pity in thy looks.. ..a begging prince what beggar pities not?

Pity, lack of p. See 'Politics, p. above conscience - Men must learn now with pity to dispense, for policy sits above conscience.'

Pity, no feeling of p. - Think but upon the wrong he did us all and that will quickly dry thy melting tears.

Pity, no other help possible but p. - No good at all that I can do for him, unless you call it good to pity him.

Pity, no pity? – Will nothing turn your unrelenting hearts?

Pity, no p. expected - ..O let no noble eye profane a tear for me, if I be gored with Mowbray's spear.

Pity, pitiful case moving even a monster – … it is a pity would move a monster.

Pity, p. and hatred. See 'Hatred, h. mixed with pity - ... but that I hate thee deadly I should lament thy miserable state.'

Pity, p. and the law - .. pity is the virtue of the law and none but tyrants use it cruelly.

Pity, p. inspired by experience. See 'Who are you? - A most poor man, made tame to fortune's blows…'

Pity, p. leading to a pardon - Say 'pardon,' king; let pity teach thee how; the word is short, but not so short as sweet.

Pity, p. not to be hoped for – … the people deserve such pity of him as the wolf does of the shepherd.

Pity, p. or tenderness, how to prevent it - Not of a woman's tenderness to be, requires nor child nor woman's face to see.

Pity, p. prevented by resentment at offense or injury - .. his injury the gaoler to his pity.

Pity, p. uncalled for. See 'Strike, pre-emptive s. - who 'scapes the lurking serpent's mortal sting.'

Pity, pitiless – ... be your heart to them as unrelenting flint to drops of rain.

Pity, pitiless, heart turned to stone and hurting hands when struck - My heart is turned to stone; I strike it, and it hurts my hand.

Pity, pitiless, heart turned to stone and remaining stony - My heart is turn'd to stone, and, while't is mine it shall be stony.

Pity, pitiless – … and pluck commiseration of his state from brassy bosoms and rough hearts of flint.

Pity, pitiless – … no hoped-for mercy with the brothers more than with ruthless waves, with sands and rocks.

Pity, pitiless – Tear-falling pity dwells not in this eye.

Pity, pitiless. See 'Character, merciless - .. there is no more mercy in him than there is milk in a male tiger.'

Pity, pitiless adversary. See 'Adversary, inhuman and pitiless - A stony adversary, an inhuman wretch..

Pity, pitiless as shown by deeds – Were thy heart as hard as steel as thou hast shown it flinty by thy deeds..

Pity, pitiless masses. See 'Masses, pitiless - .. had not God, for some strong purpose, steel'd the hearts of men…'

Pity. See entries for 'Mercy'.

Place, a dangerous p. – Where we are there's daggers in men's smiles.

Place, haunted p. to get away from - There's none but witches do inhabit here and therefore 'tis high time that I were hence.

Place, a nice p. to go to - I know a bank where the wild thyme blows…

Place, a nice p. to stay – … the air nimbly and sweetly recommends itself unto our gentle senses.

Place, a nice p. to stay – I like this place and willingly could waste my time in it.

Place, horrible p. from which you hope to get away ASAP. See 'Help, h. sought from heavens to escape from dreadful place - … some heavenly power guide us out of this fearful country.'

Place, horrible p. referred to. See 'Night, nightmare, waking up from a n. - I trembling waked, and for a season after could not believe but that I was in hell…'

Place, p. of birth, if nearby, where were you born? - Not three hours' travel from this very place.

Place, p. suitable to melancholy musings - Let us seek out some desolate shade and there weep our sad bosoms empty.

Place, residence, temporary safe heaven - .. we'll feast here awhile, until our stars that frown lend us a smile.

Places, all p. beautiful. See 'Positive thinking, how to acquire it, the art of it – all places.. are to a wise man ports and happy havens.'

Plain speaking. See 'Character, self-defined, straight, direct and who does not like any of the company around him - .. 'tis my occupation to be plain'

Plainness moving more than eloquence - Thy plainness moves me more than eloquence.

Plan, contingency p. - ... since the affairs of men rest still uncertain let's reason with the worst that may befall.

Plan, contingency p. – ... this project should have a back or second, that might hold, if this should blast in proof.

Plan, p. disapproved – Uneven is the course, I like it not.

Plan, p. must have no holes to succeed - ... and stop all sight-holes, every loop from whence the eye of reason may pry in upon us.

Plan, p. of deceit – ... Knavery's plain face is never seen till used.

Plan, p. to be carried out with care and secrecy - And that's not suddenly to be performed, but with advise and silent secrecy.

Plan, p. to remain confidential - What course I mean to hold shall nothing benefit your knowledge, nor concern me the reporting.

Plan, strategy for upward mobility - ... And, when I spy advantage, claim the crown for that's the golden mark I seek to hit.

Plans, evil p. fall back on the evil planners - ... purposes mistook fall'n on the inventors' heads.

Planetary influence. See 'Philosophical considerations. Unwillingness to take responsibility for our mistakes - This is the excellent foppery of the world…'

Planning, call for strategic p. by experts - Call for our chiefest men of discipline to cull the plots of best advantages.

Planning, importance of p. - When we mean to build, we first survey the plot, then draw the model..

Planning, p. and preparation. See 'Preparations, p. for action - ... (Let) all things thought upon ... add more feathers to our wings.'

Planning, p. and reflection advised before action - ... determine on some course, more than a wild exposure to each chance that starts i' the way before thee.

Planning, putting it on paper - Give me some ink and paper in my tent: I'll draw the form and model of our battle.

Plans if you haven't made any. See 'Character, fatalistic – We profess ourselves to be the slaves of chance, and flies of every wind that blows.'

Play, it was just a play. See first lines in 'Retirement, retiring and giving up your secrets – ... And deeper than did ever plummet sound I'll drown my book.'

Play, reasons for unfavorable review of a p. See 'Presentation. Epilogues to p. - 'Tis ten to one this play can never please all that are here…'

Playboy mission statement. See 'Ladies, l's man and yet not – I'll make my heaven in a lady's lap, and deck my body in gay ornaments.'

Playboy. See entries for 'Lady, l. killer.' *** 'Casanova'.

Playing hard-to-get and why - ... If I confess much, you will play the tyrant.

Playing hard-to-get - Or if thou think'st I am too quickly won, I'll frown, and be perverse, and say thee nay.

Playing hard-to-get. See entries for 'Pretence, no for yes'

Plea, introduction to a 'not guilty' p. - ... it shall scarce boot me to say 'not guilty:' mine integrity being counted falsehood…

Plea, p. for being understood - If ever from your eyelids wiped a tear, and know what it is to pity and be pitied..

Plea, p. for frankness and direct talk. See 'Invitation, i. to be frank and plain - Therefore with frank and with uncurbed plainness tell us the Dauphin's mind'.

Plea, p. for gentle refusal. See 'Rejection,

plea for gentle refusal - Say that you love me not, but say not so in bitterness…'

Plea, plea of not guilty of questionable use – … it shall scarce boot me to say 'not guilty:' mine integrity being counted falsehood…

Plea, p. to be heard. See entries for 'Request, r. to be heard'.

Plea, pleading for a good cause - If his occasions were not virtuous, I should not urge it half so faithfully.

Pleading for love. See 'Hate, h. not deserved - To plead for love deserves more fee than hate.'

Pleasure, excessive p. unsafe - These violent delights have violent ends and in their triumph die, like fire and powder, which as they kiss consume.

Pleasure, no profit in education if not accompanied by the p. of learning. See 'Education, profitable if pleasurable – No profit grows where is no pleasure taken..'

Pleasure, p. always gained through pain. See entries for 'Achievement, a. requires effort'

Pleasure, p. and revenge as great motivators - … pleasure and revenge have ears more deaf than adders to the voice of any true decision.

Pleasure, p. offered and misinterpreted - … your pleasure?… That you might know it, would much better please me…

Pleasures, brief p. of life - The sweet degrees that this brief world affords.

Pleasures, p, of a simple life – If I kept sheep, I should be as merry as the day is long.

Pleasures, priorities in p. - But that a joy past joy calls out on me, it were a grief, so brief to part with thee.

Pleasures, vanity of p., especially some. See 'Masochism, against m. - all delights are vain; but that most vain, which with pain purchased doth inherit pain.'

Plot, p. and motives clear to see but no one speaks out of fear - … Who is so gross that cannot see this palpable device?..

Plot, political p. clear to anyone that is interested - … all that dare look into these affairs see this main end…

Plutocrats, p. as whales - I can compare our rich misers to nothing so fitly as to a whale…

Poem, ready p. for the purpose - I have a sonnet that will serve the turn…

Poetical. See 'Character, wishing for a poetical c. – Truly, I would the gods had made thee poetical.'

Poetry, bad p. – This is the very false gallop of verses; why do you infect yourself with them?

Poetry, contempt of poetry or lyrics in general - … Nothing so much as mincing poetry, 't is like the forced gait of a shuffling nag.

Poetry, difficulty in finding a suitable rhyme - … I can find out no rhyme to 'lady' but 'baby..

Poetry, disavowal of poetical skills compensated by general strength in other areas - I have no strength in measure, yet a reasonable measure in strength.

Poetry, equally applicable to women or horses - I once writ a sonnet in his praise and began thus: 'Wonder of nature'…

Poetry, futility of p. – A speaker is but a prater; a rhyme is but a ballad.

Poetry, good p. – The elegancy, facility, and golden cadence of poesy.

Poetry, love p. enduring the test of time. See 'Love, endurance of l. through poetry - Not marble, nor the gilded monuments of princes…'

Poetry, love p. not necessarily true – … the truest poetry is the most is most feigning…

Poetry, no p. if not inspired by love. See 'Inspiration, she is a source of i. and poetry - Never durst poet touch a pen to write…'

Poetry, p. as a tool for seduction - You must lay lime to tangle her desires by wailful sonnets..

Poetry, p. of very questionable taste - Let no face be kept in mind but the face of Rosalind.

Poetry, power of p. - much is the force of heaven-bred poesy.

Poetry, very poor verses or text - some of them had in them more feet than verses would bear.

Points of view, comparing them. See 'Opinions, comparing o. - I will hear Cassius; and compare their reasons, when severally we hear them rendered.'

Poison, medicine as poison. See 'Opinion, your op. on doctors, you do not trust them - his antidotes are poison'.

Poison, metaphorical, not loved by those who need it. See 'Medicine, bitter m. but necessary - They love not poison, that do poison need.'

Poison, metaphorical. See 'Attitude, positive and defiant towards adversity – in poison there is physic'.

Poison, poisonous drink - … in the porches of my ears did pour the leperous distilment.

Police officer, a hard p.o. - One whose hard heart is button'd up with steel…

Police officer, plea with a p.o. See 'Pity, hints of p. observed - My friend, I spy some pity in thy looks.. ..a begging prince what beggar pities not?'

Police officer, response to a p.o. - What wilt thou do, peevish officer? Hast thou delight to see a wretched man do outrage and displeasure to himself?

Policy, imperialistic p. – France being ours, we'll bend it to our awe, or break it all to pieces…

Policy, lack of sincerity. See 'Expedience, e. not sincerity involved - .. it proceeds from policy, not love'.

Politeness, p. in asking for pardon - Pardon me, if you please; if not, I, pleased not to be pardon'd, am content withal.

Political appeal for the discontented - … creeps apace into the hearts of such as have not thrived upon the present state…

Political (and personal) double standards - whiles I am a beggar, I will rail… there is no sin but to be rich…

Political change, time for p.c. See 'Remedies, extreme r. required - … The present time's so sick that present medicine must be ministered or overthrow incurable ensues.'

Political choice limited. See 'Choice, deprived of c. – I may neither choose whom I would nor refuse whom I dislike'.

Political conditions intolerable. See 'Conditions, political c intolerable – Brutus had rather be a villager than to repute himself a son of Rome…

Political convictions, shaky' - I am a feather for each wind that blows.

Political correctness. See 'Opinion, your op. on politicians in general - The devil knew not what he did when he made man politic, he crossed himself by 't.'

Political correctness and political skills – … manhood is melted into courtesies, valour into compliment, and men are only turned into tongue…

Political hypocrisy. See 'Equivocation - … here's an equivocator, that could swear in both the scales against either scale.'

Political naivete. See 'Wishful thinking, political w.t. – … My pity hath been balm to heal their wounds…'

Political opponent. See entries for 'Adversary'.

Political situation, pessimism about present ruler - It is a reeling world, indeed, my lord; and I believe twill never stand upright..

Political staffers – … gallants, that fill the court with quarrels, talk, and tailors.

Political stand, an extreme right winger - … he is a very dog to the commonalty.

Political strategies, common enemy abating intestine differences – … how the fear of us may cement their divisions and bind up the petty difference…

Political uncertainty. See 'Uncertainty, political u. - … I fear 'twill prove a giddy world.'

Politician, crooked p. See 'Confession, confessing to sins - ...false of heart, light of ear, bloody of hand; hog in sloth, fox in stealth, wolf in greediness...'

Politician, honest p. as an exception - He's one honest enough: would all the rest were so!

Politician, p. previously thought honest. See 'Character, dramatic change in c. - this tyrant, whose sole name blisters our tongues was once thought honest'

Politician, p. who fleeced the treasury - ... Lord Say hath gelded the commonwealth, and made it an eunuch.

Politician, p's ascent to power. See 'Position, p. achieved through crooked means - God knows... by what by-paths and indirect crooked ways I met this crown.'

Politician, young aspiring p. - The expectancy and rose of the fair state... the observed of all observers.

Politicians, deceitful - ... And like a scurvy politician, seem to see the things thou dost not.

Politicians, p. who reject good or socially beneficial ideas. See "Wisdom, w. and goodness not for the vile - Wisdom and goodness to the vile seem vile, filths savour but themselves.'

Politicians. See 'Honesty, h. as a questionable virtue - ... what a fool Honesty is! and Trust, his sworn brother, a very simple gentleman!'

Politicians' promises, habitual - Promising is the very air o' the time: it opens the eyes of expectation...

Politicians' promises, price reductions and more plentiful manufactured products - There shall be in England seven halfpenny loaves sold for a penny...

Politicians' promises, wine for all - ... I charge and command that, of the city's cost, the pissing-conduit run nothing but claret wine...

Politicians' promises. See 'Liar, a breaker of promises - He professes no keeping of oaths; in breaking them he is stronger than Hercules.'

Politics, democracy, defects of d., lack of clear objectives - ... purpose so barred, it follows, nothing is done to purpose.

Politics, democracy, evils of d. - .. Where one part does disdain with cause, the other insult without all reason..

Politics, dictatorship. See 'Dictatorship, in praise of d. - ..at once pluck out the multitudinous tongue, let them not lick the sweet which is their poison.'

Politics, hating p. - ...for policy I hate: I had as lief be a Brownist as a politician.

Politics, p. above conscience - Men must learn now with pity to dispense, for policy sits above conscience.

Politics, p. as a gift from hell - ... the devil knew not what he did when he made man politic, he crossed himself by it.

Politics, p. in a well run state - There is a mystery (with whom relation durst never meddle) in the soul of state..

Politics, power, role of foul play - A sceptre, snatched with an unruly hand..

Politics, qualification for office – ..Outcake or Seacoal for they can read and write.

Politics, reaganomics. See 'Reaganomics, trickle down economics, the belly as a metaphor for the super-rich - 'True is it, my incorporate friends,' quoth he, 'That I receive the general food at first'...'

Politics, representatives of the people despised - the tongues of the common mouth: I do despise them

Politics, right wing p. - I tell you, friends, most charitable care have the patricians of you...

Pollution, p. of character. See 'Appearances, a. deceiving (usually), but not in this case - ... thou hast a mind that suits with this fair and outward character.'

Pomp and circumstance. See lines in 'Happiness, h. or peace of mind, farewell to -

Farewell the tranquil mind! farewell content!'.

Pomp, the p. that surrounds power – … the tide of pomp that beats upon the high shore of this world.

Pomp, power and prestige. See 'Opinion, your op. on power, pomp and prestige - … what is pomp, rule, reign, but earth and dust?…'

Poor and content. See 'Contentment, c. assured if insensitive to poverty - poor and content is rich and rich enough'.

Poor Brutus with himself at war… See 'Neglect, n. explained - Nor construe any further my neglect that poor Brutus…'

Poor but noble. See 'Character, noble though poor, of noble lineage - though wayward fortune did malign my state…'

Poor, no notice of p. when they die. See 'Class, c. distinction even in death - When beggars die, there are no comets seen…'

Pope, the p's rotten policies and sale of indulgences - .. are led so grossly by the meddling priest.

Popularity, achieving p. with the common man - How he did seem to dive into their hearts with humble and familiar courtesy.

Popularity, p. questioned - Upon what meat doth this our Caesar feed, that he is grown so great?

Popularity. See 'Opinion, your op. on crowds and masses, using eyes, not judgment - He is loved of the distracted multitude, who like not in their judgement, but their eyes'

Portrait, p. of a lady observed with mild vanity – …And yet the painter flattered her a little, unless I flatter with myself too much.

Position, p. achieved through crooked means - God knows… by what by-paths and indirect crooked ways I met this crown.

Position, p. felt secure due to tenure - Not all the water in the rough, rude sea can wash the balm from an anointed king…

Position, precarious p. physical and metaphorical – … I stand as one upon a rock environ'd with a wilderness of sea…

Position, secure p. defined - Whole as the marble, founded as the rock…

Position, well positioned at court – (He) sits within a monarch's heart and ripens in the sunshine of his favour.

Positive outcome - All's well that ends well.

Positive thinking about exile - … suppose devouring pestilence hangs in our air and thou art flying to a fresher clime.

Positive thinking and defiance towards setbacks – For gnarling sorrow hath less power to bite the man that mocks at it and sets it light.

Positive thinking and defiance towards setbacks – Woe doth the heavier sit, where it perceives it is but faintly borne.

Positive thinking induced by comparing our conditions with others who are worse off. See 'Conditions, current place and c. not as bad as others' - This wide and universal theatre presents more woeful pageants.'

Positive thinking ineffective. See 'Imagination, not a substitute of reality - O, who can hold a fire in his hand by thinking on the frosty Caucasus?..

Positive thinking, how to acquire it, the art of it – All places… are to a wise man ports and happy heavens.

Positive thinking, how to acquire it, the art of it – Suppose the singing birds musicians… the flowers, fair ladies…

Positive thinking. See 'Comfort, exhortation to see things positively – put color in thy cheek'.

Pound of flesh. See 'Guarantee, personal g. – … let the forfeit be nominated for an equal pound of your fair flesh…'

Poverty, a case for p. - Who would not wish to be from wealth exempt…

Poverty, p. as a social disease – … A dedicated beggar to the air, with his disease of all-shunn'd poverty…

Poverty, p. prevailing over will – My poverty, but not my will, consents.

Poverty. See entries for 'Financial Status'

Power, abuse of p. - The abuse of greatness is, when it disjoins remorse from power.

Power, analysing one's and the enemy's resources. See 'Balance of power, examination of – I have in equal balance justly weigh'd…and find our griefs heavier than our offences.'

Power, declining p. – Now my charms are all o'erthrown and what strength I have's mine own…

Power, disappointment with p. - I'll give my jewels for a set of beads, my gorgeous palace for a hermitage..

Power, dreaming of p. - ... I do but dream on sovereignty; like one that stands upon a promontory..

Power, effects of uncontrolled p. – … And appetite, an universal wolf … must make perforce an universal prey…

Power, high places, long falls, powerful shattered to pieces - They that stand high have many blasts to shake them…

Power, invocation for honestly acquired p. - O, that estates, degrees and offices were not derived corruptly…

Power, lust for p. as a psychological compensation - Then, since this earth affords no joy to me… I'll make my heaven to dream upon the crown.

Power, magic p. - I have bedimm'd the noontide sun, call'd forth the mutinous winds…

Power, misapplied or abused p. is self-defeating - .. The hardest knife ill-used doth lose his edge.

Power, one way to use p. - And when the lion fawns upon the lamb, the lamb will never cease to follow him.

Power, p. acquired with b. unstable. See 'Blood, power acquired with b. unstable - There is no sure foundation set on blood.. No certain life achieved by others' death'

Power, p. broker - … For who lived king, but I could dig his grave?

Power, p. broker - Proud setter up and puller down of kings!

Power, p. broker - Thou setter up and plucker down of kings.

Power, p. broker. See 'Man, politically very powerful - … this is he that moves both wind and tide.'

Power, p. in the hands of the contemptible - More pity that the eagle should be mew'd, while kites and buzzards prey at liberty.

Power, p. of time. See 'Time, all encompassing power of t. – It is in my power to o'erthrow law and in one self-born hour to plant and o'erwhelm custom.'

Power, p. provokes fear – .. great men tremble when the lion roars.

Power, p. used appropriately and inappropriately – … it is excellent to have a giant's strength..

Power, p. used to war and plunder - … had I power, I should pour the sweet milk of concord into hell..

Power, p. vs. love. See 'Love, l. preferred over power - He after honour hunts, I after love…'

Power, p.'s precedence over custom - … nice customs curtsy to great kings …

Power, persuasive p. of beauty. See 'Beauty, persuasive power of b. - Beauty itself doth of itself persuade the eyes of men without an orator'.

Power, privilege of p. to give no explanations - The cause is in my will.

Power, source of p. more pain than joy - … As brings a thousand-fold more care to keep than in possession any jot of pleasure.

Power, special p. of affection - Affection! thy intention stabs the centre…

Power, the downside of p. - .. subject to the breath of every fool, whose sense no more can feel, but his own wringing.

Power, where real power is - … As doth a sail, fill'd with a fretting gust, command an argosy to stem the waves.

Power, where real power is - ... for, as I hear

you that are king, though he doth wear the crown.

Praise - … I never heard a man of his place, gravity and learning…

Praise for performance - .. his deeds exceed all speech: he ne'er lift up his hand but conquered.

Praise, accepted and returned, responding to praise - I will praise any man that will praise me.

Praise, agreement in p. - Quick is mine ear to hear of good towards him.

Praise, how p. can accomplish objectives more easily than reprimand - Our praises are our wages…

Praise, importance of p., insisting in praising her - … one good deed, dying tongueless slaughters a thousand waiting upon that.

Praise, indirect self-praise by accusing another of poor judgment - You praise yourself by laying defects of judgement to me..

Praise, knowing the limitations of self praise. See 'Modesty, self-praise, knowing the limitations of self-praise - … Though I lose the praise of it by telling…'

Praise, p. and endorsement - I know the gentleman to be of worth and worthy estimation and not without desert so well reputed.

Praise, p. and gratitude - A god on earth thou art.

Praise, p. as well as defense from accusation - To banish him that struck more blows for Rome than thou hast spoken words?

Praise, p. bought with flattery insincere. See 'Flattery, f. and praise tied to reward - .. when the means are gone that buy this praise, the breath is gone whereof this praise is made.'

Praise, p. by comparison - … and make your chronicles as rich with praise as is the ooze and bottom of the sea with sunken wreck and sumless treasuries.

Praise, p. by the enemy acceptable. See last three lines in 'Modesty, self-praise to be avoided - The worthiness of praise distains his worth, if that the praised himself bring the praise forth.'

Praise, p. cannot create beauty - Where fair is not, praise cannot mend the brow.

Praise, p. deserved – You shall not be the grave of your deserving.. 'twere a concealment worse than a theft... to hide your doings…

Praise, p. deserved and not to be hidden - … A forted residence 'gainst the tooth of time and the razure of oblivion.

Praise, p. for achievements - The heavens through you, increase our wonder and set up your fame forever.

Praise, p. for noble behavior - A noble temper dost thou show in this…

Praise, p. lavished - … every one her own hath garnished with such bedecking ornaments of praise.

Praise, p. misapplied, paid to approve - When we for recompense have praised the vile..

Praise, p. not as good as correction. See 'Enemies, why e. are better than friends - .. my friends praise me and make an ass of me…'

Praise, p. not flattery - .. the words I utter let none think flattery, for they'll find 'em truth.

Praise, p. of beauty. See Beautiful, beyond any praise - You will find she will outstrip all praise..'

Praise, p. of friends - I have told more of you to myself..

Praise, p. of nobility of mind. See 'Man, a noble m. - The noblest mind he carries that ever govern'd man.'

Praise, p. rekindling memory – praising what is lost makes the remembrance dear.

Praise, p. to a man of honour. See 'Honor, a man of h. to whom praise is due - the theme of honour's tongue.'

Praise, praising the creativity of a team. See 'Organization, creativity of an o. - … This teeming womb of …'

Praise, praising the criminal if advantage drawn from him – A giving hand, though foul, shall have fair praise.

Praise, proper response to praise – 'Tis the best brine a maiden can season her praise in.

Praise, refusal to be p. – He had rather venture all his limbs for honour…

Praise, self-p. - So much for praising myself, who, I myself will bear witness, is praiseworthy.

Praise, self-p. justified - … to be the trumpet of his own virtues, as I am to myself.

Praise, self-p. or praise of speaker – And all the courses of my life do show I am not in the roll of common men.

Praise, self-p. to be avoided. See 'Modesty, m. characteristic of a wise person - … there's not one wise man among twenty that will praise himself.'

Praise, tongue too earthly to sing of her celestial beauty - ..this wrong that sings heaven's praise with such an earthly tongue.

Praise, why extended p. is justified. See 'Speech, introduction to a flattering or praising s. - Lend me the flourish of all gentle tongues.'

Praising, p. while blaming – …but breathe his faults so quaintly that they may seem the taints of liberty…

Prank. See entries for 'Trick'

Prayer, need for p. to better one's conditions. See 'Solitude, wanting to be alone - … leave me to my self to-night, For I have need of many orisons to move the heavens to smile upon my state.'

Prayer, praying for what is wrong or counterproductive. See "Ignorance, i. of what is really good for us - We, ignorant of ourselves beg often our own harms, which the wise powers deny us for our good…'

Prayers, conflict of p. for opposite ends - .. our prayers do out-pray his…

Prayers, hypocritical p. See 'Hypocrisy, h. in prayers – His prayers are full of false hypocrisy…'

Preaching, p. versus practice - .. will not you maintain the thing you teach but prove a chief offender in the same?

Precedent, p. in law. See 'Law, precedent in l. – … no power in Venice can alter a decree established: 'twill be recorded for a precedent…'

Precision, p. shooting - … and like an arrow shot from a well-experienced archer hits the mark..

Prediction, desire to know in advance - O God! that one might read the book of fate and see the revolutions of the times…

Prediction, desire to know in advance - O, that a man might know the end of this day's business ere it come…

Prediction, dire p. – The time will come, that foul sin shall break into corruption.

Prediction, dire p. - The time shall not be many hours of age.. .

Prediction, dire p. - The woe's to come; the children yet unborn shall feel this day as sharp to them as thorn.

Prediction, p. in the process of occurring – …Which is so plain that Exeter doth wish his days may finish ere that hapless time.

Prediction, predicting what party is going to say - … his embassy, which I could with a ready guess declare…

Predictions. See entries on 'Forecasting'

Predictors, p. of developments. Se

Pregnancy, causes of. and evidence – … it chances the stealth of our most mutual entertainment …

Pregnancy, p. good - Lady, you are the cruel'st she alive, if you will lead these graces to the grave…

Pregnancy, p. good - From fairest creatures we desire increase, that thereby beauty's rose may never die.

Prejudice, exhortation to clear p. - … weed your better judgements of all opinion that grows rank in them.

Prejudice, inability to believe in exceptional performance - You judge it straight a thing impossible to compass wonders but by help of devils.

Prejudice, warped view of reality - … warp'd the line of every other favour scorn'd a fair colour …

Premise, conclusion does not follow p. See 'Conclusion, c. does not follow from premise - … there is no consonancy in the sequel.'

Preoccupation. See 'Mood, in a poor m. - Vexed I am, of late, with passions of some difference

Preparations, p. for action - … (let) all things thought upon … add more feathers to our wings.

Prepared for the worst. See 'Anxious while waiting for her answer – Thus ready for the way of life or death I wait the sharpest blow.'

Prepared to do anything for her. See 'Beauty as a determining factor - your beauty was the cause of that effect…'

Presence, 'Are you here?' – No, no, I am but shadow of myself.

Presence, 'Do you miss me?' - … Save that my soul's imaginary sight presents thy shadow to my sightless view..

Presence, giving happiness and pleasure - Your presence glads our days.

Presence, her p. your light and only joy - What joy is joy if Sylvia is not by? Unless it be to think that she is by and feed upon the shadow of perfection…

Presence, inquiry on physical presence – Is Horatio there?… A piece of him

Presence, missing her p. See 'Anxiety, obsession, missing her presence - how can I then return in happy plight, that am debarred the benefit of rest?…'

Presence, p. that inspires confidence and conquers fear - …a largess universal like the sun his liberal eye doth give to every one, thawing cold fear.

Presence, physical p. crucial for success - The present eye praises the present object.

Present, impact of the p. moment – Each present joy or sorrow seems the chief.

Presentation, complimenting a member of the audience who asked a good question - Well demanded, wench: my tale provokes that question.

Presentation, plea for patience from audience – … with patient ears attend, what here shall miss, our toil shall strive to mend.

Presentation, requesting audience to be patient before coming to the point. See 'Exhortation, e. to listen for a little longer – Hear a little further and then I'll bring thee to the present business…'

Presentation, skipping intermediate sections of a p. - Then brook abridgment, and your eyes advance…

Presentation, you have lost or mislaid the graphic material you needed. See 'Introduction, request to accept the limitations of the presentation and choreography - Piece out our imperfections with your thoughts…'

Presentation, you have lost or mislaid the graphic material you needed. See 'Introduction, request to accept the limitations of the presentation and choreography - Piece out our imperfections with your thoughts…'

Presentation. Epilogues to p. - … If I were a woman I would kiss as many of you as had beards that pleased me…

Presentation. Epilogues to p. - … thanks to all at once and to each one.

Presentation. Epilogues to p. – First my fear; then my courtesy; last my speech…

Presentation. Epilogues to p. – Gentle breath of yours my sails must fill, or else my project fails…

Presentation. Epilogues to p. - Gentles, do not reprehend, if you pardon, we will mend.

Presentation. Epilogues to p. – If it be true that 'good wine needs no bush'…

Presentation. Epilogues to p. - If we shadows have offended think but this, (and all is mended)…

Presentation. Epilogues to p. – My tongue is weary; when my legs are too, I will bid you good night.

Presentation. Epilogues to p., inviting questions from the audience. See 'Question, answering q. - Ask me what question thou canst possible, and I will answer unpremeditated.'

Presentation. Epilogues to p. See 'Salutations, ending salutations - Be free, and fare thou well!' *** Power, reduced personal

Presentation. Epilogues to p. - So, on your patience evermore attending..

Presentation. Epilogues to p. - Thus far, with rough and all-unable pen our bending author hath pursued the story..

Presentation. Epilogues to p. - 'Tis ten to one this play can never please all that are here..

Presentation. Epilogues to p., asking for pardon – … my fear is your displeasure; my courtesy, my duty; and my speech, to beg your pardons.

Presentation. Epilogues to p., end of magic. – … But this rough magic I here abjure…

Presentation. Epilogues to p., modesty. See 'Modesty, m. in praising your own performance - Thus far, with rough and all-unable pen our bending author has pursu'd the story.'

Presentation. Epilogue to p., should I run? – If my tongue cannot entreat you to acquit me, will you command me to use my legs?

Presentation. Introductions to p. See entries for 'Introduction'.

Presentation, lack of special effects for the p. - Think, when we talk of horses, that you see them…

Presentation, modesty in p. – If you look for a good speech now, you undo me: for what I have to say is of mine own making..

Presentment, p. and fear - I have a faint cold fear thrills through my veins, that almost freezes up the heat of life.

Presentment, premonition - I am surprised with an uncouth fear, a chilling sweat o'er-runs my trembling joints…

Presentment, premonition, fearful p. – … methinks, some unborn sorrow, ripe in fortune's womb is coming towards me…

Presentment, premonition, instant awareness of future consequences. See 'Future, marred by the effect of current events - The woe's to come; the children yet unborn.'

Presume not that I am … See 'Character, radical change in c. - presume not that I am the thing I was.'

Presumption, p. of knowledge. See 'Miracles, possibility of m. not to be excluded - They say miracles are past…'

Presumption. See 'Modesty, m. by denial of personal merit - … But most it is presumption in us when the help of heaven we count the act of men.'

Pretence, exhortation to p. See 'Virtue, how to acquire it - Assume a virtue, if you have it not.'

Pretence, no for yes - Play the maid's part, still answer nay, and take it.

Pretence, no for yes. See 'Justification for insisting even after she said 'no' - … maids in modesty, say 'No' to that which they would have the profferer construe 'Ay'.

Pretence, p. of amity. See 'Peace, shaky p. - This late dissension, grown betwixt the peers burns under feigned ashes of forged love…'

Pretence, pretending to be silly - … as gardeners do with ordure hide those roots that shall first spring..

Pretence, see 'Disguise, d. and pretence, tools of wicked enemy - Disguise, I see, thou art a wickedness, wherein the pregnant enemy does much…'

Pretence. See also entries for 'Dissimulation', 'Hypocrisy'

Pretext, p. for personal attack - … my pretext to strike at him admits a good construction.

Pretty, answer to 'Am I pretty?' – … if ladies be but young and fair they have the gift to know it.

Pretty, answer to 'Am I pretty?' – as a fair day in summer…

Pretty, as well as wise – … fair and wise is she; the heaven such grace did lend her, that she might admired be

Pretty, more than the word can express plus - … she is fair, and, fairer than that word, of wondrous virtues.

Pretty, the prettiest of all - the prettiest Kate in Christendom.

Prevarication on anyone will prompt vengeance - the smallest worm will turn being trodden on.

Prevention, p. as key to success and security - Fast bind, fast find, a proverb never stale in thrifty mind.

Prevention. See entries for 'Problem, p. to be tackled before it gets bigger'

Pride, cooling effect of p. - … And, may I say to thee, this pride of hers, upon advice, hath drawn my love from her.

Pride, downside of p. – … pride, which out of daily fortune ever taints the happy man.

Pride, excessive p. a personal liability – Pride, haughtiness, opinion and disdain… loseth men's hearts and leaves behind a stain…

Pride, extreme p. - He wants nothing of a god but eternity and a heaven to throne in.

Pride, p. and ambition - Pride went before, ambition follows him.

Pride, p. as a trait of women - … it was Eve's legacy, and cannot be ta'en from her.

Pride, p. augmented by flattery. See 'Arrogance, a. promoted by submission - supple knees feed arrogance, and are the proud man's fees.'

Pride, p. distasteful. See ' 'Character, arrogant, supercilious, hateful - I do hate a proud man, as I hate the engendering of toads'.

Pride, p. in lacking hypocritical skills - … for want of that for which I am richer, a still-soliciting eye…

Pride, p. in possession. "Are you glad that you married me?" - .. as rich in having such a jewel as twenty seas, if all their sand were pearl…

Pride, p. maintained even during pain - I will instruct my sorrows to be proud, for grief is proud, and makes his owner stout.

Pride, p. misguided - … He that is proud eats up himself: pride is his own glass, his own trumpet, his own chronicle..

Pride, p. reducing consideration (for the proud man) - … could be content to give him good report fort, but that he pays himself with being proud

Pride, p., ambition and envy as agents of mutual hatred - .. the eagle-winged pride of sky-aspiring and ambitious thoughts…set on you to wake our peace..

Pride, poverty no barrier to personal p. - O, world, how apt the poor are to be proud!

Pride. See entries for 'Character, proud'

Princes, p. as models of authority. See 'Authority, a. of princes and signs of respect due to them - … for princes are a model, which heaven makes like to itself…'

Priorities, choosing to stay here – let Rome in Tiber melt, and the wide arch of the ranged empire fall!…

Priorities, safety over fame. See 'Safety, s. and beer preferable to fame – I would give all my fame for a pot of ale and safety.'

Prison, forgetting being in a prison - .. it made my imprisonment a pleasure; ay, such a pleasure as incaged birds…

Prisoner of oneself. See 'Loneliness, feeling alone – Now my soul's palace is become a prison.'

Privacy, disregard for p. acknowledged - Saucy controller of our private steps.

Prize, p. well worth fighting for, compliment – See 'Perfection, her p. unparalleled - .. her, whom, we know well the world's large spaces cannot parallel.'

Problem, diagnosis of p. incorrect. See 'Exhortation, e. not to feed a delusion - .. Lay not that flattering unction to your soul, that not your trespass, but my madness speaks…'

Problem, how by avoiding a p. you created one greater - Thus have I shunn'd the fire for fear of burning and drench'd me in the sea, where I am drown'd.

Problem, gradual approach to p. solving – … to climb steep hills requires slow pace at first

Problem, p. solver - Turn him to any cause of policy, the Gordian knot of it he will unloose, familiar as his garter.

Problem, p. solving – … all difficulties are but easy when they are known.

Problem, p. solving, effort at solving problem appreciated but.. - … the care you have of us, to mow down thorns that would annoy our foot, is worthy praise…

Problem, p. to be tackled before it gets bigger – A little fire is quickly trodden out, which being suffered, rivers cannot quench.

Problem, p. to be tackled before it gets bigger – Now 'tis the spring, and weeds are shallow-rooted…

Problem, solution of p. found after meditation - Thus hulling in the wild sea of my conscience, I did steer towards this remedy.

Problems, p. not solved by complaints. See entries for 'Complaint, c. after problems useless'

Procrastination to be avoided – … for this 'would' changes, hath abatements and delays as many as there are tongues, are hands, are accidents.

Prodigality. See 'Wealth, high income not a cert

Profession, argument to use to justify a disreputable p. – What would you have me do? go to the wars…

Profession, not the top of professions – (I) work for bread upon the Athenian walls.

Profession, See 'Man, m. particularly skillful in his profession or trade and still OK - … most profound in his art and yet not damnable.'

Profession, what do you do for a living? - As my imagination bodies forth the forms of things unknown..

Professions that include many thieves. See 'Thieves, t. in high places - .. there is boundless theft in limited professions.'

Profit, no profit for anyone. See 'Wind, venture without profit - Ill blows the wind that profits nobody.'

Profit, p. derived from understanding - … to apprehend thus, draws us a profit from all things we see.

Profit, p. from learning – See 'Education, profitable if pleasurable – No profit grows where is no pleasure taken...'

Profit, p. worship – Gain, be my lord, for I will worship thee.

Profit, speaking against one's own interest - I speak against my present profit, but my wish hath a preferment in 't.

Profiteers. See 'Flatterers, f. as sponges – take you me for a sponge my lord?'

Profligacy, p. blind - 'Tis pity bounty had not eyes behind..

Profligacy, p. short lived - His rash fierce blaze of riot cannot last, for violent fires soon burn out themselves…

Progeny, p. worse than parents - Good wombs have borne bad sons.

Project management and how to approach it. See 'Planning, importance of p. - When we mean to build, we first survey the plot, then draw the model..'

Promise, commitment to maintain a p. - I am the master of my speeches, and would undergo what's spoken.

Promise, commitment to maintain a p. - My hand to thee; mine honour on my promise.

Promise, p. or commitment of questionable sincerity. See Rejection, warning about your character plus you don't like her - … do not fall in love with me, for I am falser than vows made in wine..'

Promise, p. to comply with command - I'll not fail, if I live.

Promise, p. to remember what you have been told - ... 'Tis in my memory lock'd and you yourself shall keep the key of it.

Promise, p. to repay for help received - ... if that ever my low fortune's better I'll your bounties; till then rest your debtor.

Promise, solemn p. – And I will die a hundred thousand deaths, ere break the smallest parcel of this vow.

Promises, alluring p. to a mature adult - .. I can smooth and fill his aged ear with golden promises..

Promises, love p. unreliable - ... the oath of a lover is no stronger than the word of a tapster…

Promises, love p. unreliable - …the strongest oaths are straw to the fire in the blood.

Promises, love p. unreliable - … Thou mayst prove false; at lovers' perjuries they say, Jove laughs.

Promises, love p. unreliable - I do know when the blood burns, how prodigal the soul lends the tongue vows.

Promises, love p. unreliable - Men's vows are women's traitors.

Promises, more than can be delivered – I charge and command that, of the city's cost, the pissing conduit run nothing but claret wine..

Promises, more than can be delivered. See 'Politicians' promises, habitual - Promising is the very air o' the time: it opens the eyes of expectation…'

Promises, more than can be delivered - They say all lovers swear more performance than they are able…

Promises, more than can be delivered. See 'Politicians' promises, wine for all -

Promises, p. not delivered - His promises were, as he then was, mighty, but his performance…'

Promises, p. not delivered – … your words and performances are no kin together.

Promises, p. not kept - … That keep the word of promise to our ear and break it to our hope.

Promises, p. quickly delivered - Thy promises are like Adonis' gardens that one day bloom'd and fruitful were the next.

Promises, p. too good to be true. See 'Fool's paradise – …if ye should lead her into a fool's paradise…'

Promotion, p. given according to whim - … Preferment goes by letter and affection, and not by old gradation…

Promotion, p. promised - … I will be the man yet that shall make you great.

Promotion, p. refused – I had rather hide me from my greatness, being a bark to brook no mighty sea..

Promotion, p. through slander – … many so arrive at second masters upon their first lord's neck.

Promotion, p. undeserved to a man not suited to the job. See 'Distinction, d. or promotion misplaced or unbecoming – It lies as sightly on the back of him as great Alcides' shows upon an ass.'

Proof. See entries for 'Evidence'.

Propaganda, economy is great – Here is everything advantageous to life… save means to live.

Proposal, dangerous p. - Into what dangers would you lead me, Cassius..

Proposal, detailed p. on sharing pillows - One turf shall serve as pillows to us both….

Proposal, difference between an exciting and an unexciting p. – .. the blood more stirs to rouse a lion than to start a hare.

Proposal, love p. See 'Love, beware of hasty proposals - .. A time, methinks, too short to make a world-without-end bargain in.'

Proposal, meditated p. - …'tis a studied, not a present thought by duty meditated.

Prosperity, a satire on p. – … the softness of prosperity, with a discovery of the infinite flatteries that follow youth and opulency.

Prosperity, a wish for p. See 'Toast, t. and wish, prosperity - Now the fair goddess, Fortune fall deep in love with thee. Prosperity be thy page!'

Prosperity, end of p. See 'End, beginning of the e. – now prosperity begins to mellow and drop into the rotten mouth of death.'

Prosperity, p. and its relation to love. See 'Love, prosperity an essential ingredient for l. - Prosperity's the very bond of love, whose fresh complexion and whose heart together affliction alters.'

Prostitute – a creature of sale

Protection, offer of p. - My bosom as a bed shall lodge thee till thy wound be thoroughly heal'd.

Prove me wrong. See 'Agree or prove me wrong - Reprove my allegations if you can; or else conclude my words effectual.'

Providence, luck of possession - She is mortal, but, by immortal providence, she is mine.

Providence, p. acting irrespective of our will. See 'Destiny, d. shaping our ends - … There's a divinity that shapes our ends, rough-hew them how we will.'

Providence, p. and previdence of the Gods. See 'Ignorance, i. of what is really good for us - We, ignorant of ourselves beg often our own harms, which the wise powers deny us for our good…'

Provocation, response to p. – … we can (not) let our beard be shook with danger and think it pastime.

Prudence, better keep what we have than lose everything - …I'll rather keep hat which I have, than, coveting for more…

Prudence, do not wake a sleeping dog - This butcher's cur is venom mouthed and I have not the power to muzzle him; therefore..

Prudence, never underestimate enemy or competition - In cases of defence, 't is best to weigh the enemy more mighty than he seems…

Prudence, p. advisable rather than unrealistic optimism – The man that once did sell the lion's skin while the beast liv'd…

Prudence, p. advised - It fits us then to be as provident as fear may teach…

Prudence, p. in giving confidence and being generous - ..where you are liberal of your loves and counsels be sure you be not loose...

Psychological, p. help needed - the immortal part needs a physician.

Psychological uplifting, her positive effect when you are down in the dumps. See 'Love, l. as an antidepressant. - … thy sweet love remembered such wealth brings…'

Psychological uplifting, positive effects of thoughts about a friend - … But if the while I think on thee, dear friend, all losses are restored and sorrows end.

Psychology, contradictions in personality. See 'Personality, multiple p. - thus play I in one person many people..'

Psychology, doubt hurts more than certainty - Doubting things go ill often hurts more than to be sure they do.

Psychology, reverse p., turning her shortcomings into virtues and qualities - … Say that she rails; why, then I'll tell her plain she sings as sweetly as a nightingale…

Psychology, self-analysis, See 'Self-analysis, I wish you would look at yourselves - O, that you could turn your eyes towards the napes of your necks…'

Psychology, self-encouragement to boldness - Boldness be my friend, arm me audacity from head to foot.

Psychology, self-knowledge key to knowing others - … to know a man well, were to know himself.

Psychology, winning encouraging - Winning will put any man into courage.

Pub, going to the p. See 'Bar, going to b. to find solace in alcohol and company - I will see what physic the tavern affords.'

Punctuality, p. important - better three hours too soon than a minute too late.

Punctuality, p. in lovers. See entries for 'Lovers always punctual'.

Punishment and condemnation - My hour is almost come, when I to sulphurous and tormenting flames must render up myself.

Punishment, no p. strong enough - If it be true, all vengeance comes too short which can pursue the offender.

Punishment, p. announced - And where the offence is let the great axe fall.

Punishment, p. for bringing unpleasant news - Thou shalt be whipp'd with wire, and stew'd in brine, smarting in lingering pickle.

Punishment, p. for not celebrating. See 'Welcome, a 100 thousand welcomes - ... A curse begin at

Punishment, p. occurring through our vices – See 'Retribution, divine r. - The gods are just, and of our pleasant vices make instruments to plague us'.

Punishment, poison - If you have poison for me, I will drink it.

Punishment, restraint advised in p. – Let us be keen, and rather cut a little than fall and bruise to death.

Punishment, self-p. and revenge. See 'Repentance, r. accompanied by a request for punishment - ... Choose your revenge yourself; Impose me to what penance your invention…'

Punishment, selective p., only for the leaders - We, as the spring of all, shall pay for all

Punishment, suggested p. is castration - An they were sons of mine, I'd have the whipped; or I would send them to the Turk, to make eunuchs of.

Purchasing and bargaining. See 'Bargaining, dispraising the value of what you wish to buy - ... you do as chapmen do dispraise the thing that you desire to buy…'

Puritans, dislike for p. - O, if I thought that I'ld beat him like a dog!

Purpose, p. forgotten. See 'Determination, lapses in d. occurring often - ... But what we determine oft we break. Purpose's but the slave to memory, of violent birth, but poor validity.'

Purpose, p. to weighed against the consequences. See 'Objective, examining the folly required to achieve an o. - ... in everything the purpose must weigh with the folly.' *** Other entries for 'Ovjective', 'Objectives'

Purpose, plea to guess an evil p. to be executed – ... if that thou couldst see me without eyes, hear me without thine ears …

Purpose, unwavering p. – I am constant to my purpose.

Purposes mistook fall on the inventor's head. See 'Plans, evil p. fall back on the evil planners - ... purposes mistook fall'n on the inventors' heads.'

Pursuit, p. more fun than possession. See 'Chase, enjoyment greater in the chase - All things that are, are with more spirit chased than enjoyed.'

Pursuit, p. of enemy. See 'Victory, taking advantage of the v., pursuing the enemy – Let us score their backs ... 'Tis sport to maul a runner.'

Put your discourse into some frame. See 'Answer, irrelevant a. - ... put your discourse into some frame and start not so wildly from my affair.'

Pythagoras. See "Insult, man like animal according to the theories of Pythagoras - thou almost make'st me waver in my faith, to hold opinion with Pythagoras…'

Qualifications, q. for office - ... Hugh Otecake, sir, or George Seacole; for they can write and read.

Qualifications, what are your q.? See 'Employment, quick resume - ... that which ordinary men are fit for, I am qualified in; and the best of me is diligence.

Quarrel, dispute and conflict resolution - ... to leave this keen encounter of our wits and fall something into a slower method.

Quarrel, dispute and conflict resolution -

Now for the love of love and her soft hours let's not confound the time with conference harsh.

Quarrel, dissension, lack of harmony - How irksome is this music to my heart when such strings jar, what hope of harmony?

Quarrel, exhortation to change attitude - O change thy thought, that I may change my mind…

Quarrel, not really a q. - No quarrel, but a slight contention.

Quarrel, plea for restraint from q. - Forbear sharp speeches to her: she's a lady so tender of rebukes that words are strokes…

Quarrel, plea to stop q. – Cease, cease these jars and rest your minds in peace

Quarrel, plea to stop q. - Quarrel no more, but be prepared to know the purposes I bear.

Quarrel, q. about trifles as a symptom of man's madness - … what madness rules in brainsick men, when for so slight and frivolous a cause…

Quarrel, q. brewing. See 'Conflict, c. smoldering between two parties - … there is division although as yet the face of it is covered with mutual cunning.'

Quarrel, q. ended. See 'War, end of war or quarrel - Grim-visaged war hath smooth'd his wrinkled front…'

Quarrel, q. unjustified - In a false quarrel there is no true valour.

Quarrelsome man. See entries for 'Man, easily irritated'.

Queen, like a Grecian Q. - He brought a Grecian queen, whose youth and freshness wrinkles Apollo's and makes stale the morning.

Queen, so to speak - …she is the queen of curds and cream.

Queen, woman with all the traits of a queen – She had all the royal makings of a queen…

Question, answering q. - Ask me what question thou canst possible, and I will answer unpremeditated.

Question, apologizing for a posing a silly question - I will be a fool in question, hoping to be the wiser by your answer.

Question, insisting on receiving an answer - …I pry'thee take the cork out of thy mouth, that I may drink thy tidings.

Question, insisting on receiving an answer, who is it? – I pray thee now, with most petitionary vehemence…

Question, q. that cannot be answered as it is outside the scope of the interview – I can say little more than I have studied, and that question's out of my part.

Question, tricky q. See 'Intentions, wicked i. shown in the type of question and type of answer - .. you question with a wicked tongue.'

Quibbler. See "Words, rehearsed w

Quillets of the law. See 'Judgment, refraining from j. – .. in these nice sharp quillets of the law, good faith, I am no wiser than a daw'

Quintessence of dust. See 'Man and its wicked nature - .. what is this quintessence of dust? Man delights not me.'

Racial discrimination. See "Discrimination, no racial d. – Mislike me not for my complexion…'

Racket, a good racket – .. It is an honorable kind of thievery.

Radiance, r. described – … like a wreath of radiant fire on flickering Phoebus' front.

Radiant, exquisite, unmatchable. See 'Beauty, radiant - most radiant, exquisite, unmatchable beauty'

Rage, calm down. See 'Patience, calm down – … Upon the heat and flame of thy distemper sprinkle cool patience.'

Rage, cool your language - Put not your worthy rage into your tongue one time will owe another.

Rage, effects of r. - … men in rage strike those that wish them best.

Rage, r. compared to a labyrinth - … lost in the labyrinth of thy fury!"

Rage, r. compared to a storm. See 'Nature,

stormy day - ... like an unseasonable stormy day which makes the silver rivers drown their shores…'

Rage, r. compared to a storm and the noise it generates. See 'Noise, loud n. generated via arguing – ... mortal ears might hardly endure the din.'

Rage, r. not conducive to wisdom – He's in his fit now and does not talk after the wisest…

Rage. See entries for 'Anger', 'Angry'

Raise, asking for a r. - Now, princes, for the service I have done you, the advantage of the time prompts me aloud to call for recompense.

Raise, asking for a r. after multiple grand promises yet unfulfilled - I do beseech you, as in way of taste…

Raise, need for a r. See entries for 'Financial status, cash flow critical' *** 'Financial status, challenging'

Raise, salary r. See cross references at 'Salary, s. issues'.

Ransom, r. terms dishonorable – … lawful mercy is nothing kin to foul redemption.

Rare occurrence. See 'Occurrence, rare o. - It is no act of common passage, but a strain of rareness'.

Rareness, a rare a. See 'Act, uncommon a. and showing loyalty - it is no act of common passage but a strain or rareness'.

Rascal by profession. See 'Background, checkered professional b. - … having flown over many knavish professions…'

Rat race, abandoning the r.r. See 'Retirement – … to forswear the full stream of the world and to live in a nook merely monastic'

Ratings, low rating better than worst. See 'Last, not being the l. better than nothing - not being the worst stands in some rank of praise.'

Reaction, cold r. – thou art all ice, thy kindness freezeth.

Reaction, emotional r. See entries for 'Emotional Reaction'

Reaction, exaggerated r. See 'Observation, insincere or exaggerated reaction - The lady protests too much, methinks.'

Reaction, negative r. – And on my face he turn'd an eye of death.

Reaction, r. to a very strange suggestion - … whose horrid image unfix my hair and make my seated heart knock at my ribs.

Read not my blemishes in the world's report. See 'Character, promise of self-reformation - … that to come hall all be done by the rule.'

Reading, not being able to read on due to unhappiness - Some sudden qualm hath struck me at the heart..

Reading, r. and writing natural - .. to write and read comes by nature.

Reading, r. as a key to knowledge and understanding – He reads much; he is a great observer and he looks quite through the deeds of men.

Reading, r. through the lines. See 'Speech, simple s. delivered with modesty better than pompous eloquence - … in the modesty of fearful duty, I read as much, as from the rattling tongue of saucy and audacious eloquence.'

Reading, what are you r.? – Words, words, words.

Ready for action. See entries for 'Action, ready for a.'

Ready for everything. See 'Anxious while waiting for her answer – Thus ready for the way of life or death I wait the sharpest blow.'

Reaganomics, trickle down economics, the belly as a metaphor for the super-rich - 'True is it, my incorporate friends,' quoth he, 'That I receive the general food at first'…

Real, compliment, are you real? - But are you flesh and blood? Have you a working pulse?

Real estate cheap. See 'Land, value of l. lowered - … you may buy land now as cheap as stinking mackerel.'

Realism, exhortation to realism. See 'Exhortation, e. to understand the limitations imposed by circumstances - Construe the times to their necessities.'

Realism, r. counseled - … speak with possibilities and do not break into these deep extremes.

Reality and imagination - …art thou but a dagger of the mind, a false creation, proceeding from the heat-oppressed brain.

Reality and re-interpretation. See 'Spin, how to re-interpret reality - You undergo too strict a paradox striving to make an ugly deed look fair.'

Reality, not appearance - Seems, madam! nay it is; I know not 'seems'.

Reason not the need. See 'Opinion, your op. on sociological issues, minimum wage - O, reason not the need: our basest beggars are in the poorest thing superfluous…'

Reason vs. instinct or sensuality. See 'Human nature, reason balancing instinct - If the balance of our lives had not one scale of reason to poise another of sensuality…'

Reason, are you blind to reason? - … is your blood so madly hot, that no discourse of reason… can qualify the same?

Reason, argument against r. and respect. See 'Fear, f. induced by desire to conform - … reason and respect make livers pale and lustihood deject.'

Reason, doubts about one's reasoning – (What is) that makes me reasonless to reason thus?

Reason, lack of r. displayed - … is your blood so madly hot that no discourse of reason…

Reason, r. and fear. See entries for 'Fear'

Reason, r. applied to passion - … For those that mingle reason with your passion…

Reason, r. as a check on low appetites. See 'Lust, l. checked by reason – … but we have reason to cool our raging motions…'

Reason, r. as a palliative for pain. See 'Pain, use of reason as a palliative - … If not a present remedy, at least a patient sufferance.'

Reason, r. for everything. See 'Philosophy, there is a reason for everything - There is occasions and causes why and wherefore in all things'.

Reason, r. good enough – I have no exquisite reason but reason good enough.

Reason, r. secondary to will. See 'Will, w. prevailing over reason – … that would make his will lord of his reason.'

Reason, use of r. See 'Exhortation, e. to use reason - Sweet earl, divorce not wisdom from your honour'.

Reasoning obvious, not an utterer of great truths - … a great cause of the night is lack of the sun.

Reasons, good and weighty - … if thou ask me why, sufficeth, my reasons are both good and weighty.

Reasons, good r. yielding to better r. - Good reasons must, of course, give place to better.

Reasons, irrational r. See 'Answer, retort to irrational a. - Your reasons are too shallow and too quick.'

Reasons, questionable r. in writing . See 'Document, policy statement, message filled with questionable reasons for a dreadful act - … Larded with many several sorts of reasons.'

Reasons, r. for love uncertain. See entries for 'Love, reasons for l. uncertain'.

Reasons, r. that do not hold. See 'Decision, d. prompted by passion or revenge - The reasons you allege do more conduce to the hot passion of distempered blood..'

Reasons, strong r. See 'Agreement, a. on a course of action – Strong reasons make strong actions.'

Reassurance, answer to demands for r. – O, swear not by the moon, the inconstant moon, that monthly changes in her circle orb…

Rebellion, exhortation against r. – Unthread the rude eye of rebellion..

Rebellion, justification for r. – (he) broke oath on oath, committed wrong on wrong…

Rebellion, justification for r. - … (we) find

our griefs heavier than our offences.

Rebellion, making r. seem good. See 'Treason, accusation of t. – never did insurrection want such water colours.'

Rebellion, measures to quench r. - Stop their mouths with stubborn bits and spur them till they obey the manage.

Rebellion, r. as a vulture – … the vulture of sedition feeds in the bosom of such great commanders…

Rebellion, r. caused by heavy taxation – … Unfit for other life, compell'd by hunger and lack of other means…

Rebellion, r. in the air. See 'Times, rebellious t. - Rich men look sad and ruffians dance and leap…'

Rebellion, r. made more palatable by religion – See 'Perception, giving the right spin to an event by using the right words – … but now the bishop turns insurrection to religion.'

Rebellion, r. promoted by perception of dissension - If they perceive dissension in our looks…

Rebellion, reasons and occasions for a r. - We see which way the stream of time doth run… the rough torrent of occasion.

Rebellion, stirring a r. - … ruffle up your spirits and put a tongue in every wound of Caesar…

Receivables, poor chances of collection - .. if money were as certain as your waiting, 't were sure enough.

Receivables, r. must be collected immediately - Immediate are my needs; and my relief must not be tossed and turned to me in words…

Reception, cold r. See 'Reaction, cold r. – thou art all ice, thy kindness freezeth.'

Recipe, r. for the powerful and super-rich. See 'Social issues, exhortation to

Recognition, r. due. See 'Praise, p. deserved and not to be hidden - O, your desert speaks loud; and I should wrong it…'

Recognition, unfair r. resulting from the passage of time- … And give to dust that is a little gilt more laud than gilt o'er-dusted.

Recognizing , reason for not r. someone – .. I fear I am not in my perfect mind. Methinks I should know you.

Recollection, vague r. only – T''is far off and rather like a dream than an assurance that my remembrance warrants.

Recommendation, seeking a r. for a third party. See 'Lobbying, expression of lobbying intent – I come to whet your gentle thoughts on his behalf.'

Reconciliation, all resentment gone. See 'Words, w. that remove any resentment - Each word thou hast spoke hath weeded from my heart a root of ancient envy.'

Reconciliation, r. effected with a smile - For looks kill love and love by looks reviveth; a smile recures the wounding of a frown.

Recreation, r. to put away care - What sport shall we devise here in this garden, to drive away the heavy thought of care?

Recreation. See 'Health-care, recreation necessary for healthy life - Sweet recreation barred, what doth ensue…'

Recrimination, self-recrimination – …my very hairs do mutiny, for the white reprove the brown for rashness…

Redress, need for immediate r. - The shame itself doth speak for instant remedy.

Redress, r. or positive a. promised - .. and wherein it shall appear that your demands are just..

Redress, wish for the undoing of wrongs – (He) hath given me some worthy cause to wish things done, undone.

Reform, determination to r. – … I survive, to mock the expectations of the world; to frustrate prophecies…

Reform, radical r. See 'Animals, a. better than men'.

Reformation, r. of character. See 'Character, c. reformed - consideration, like an angel cam

Reformation, pleasure of being reformed.

1283

See 'Repentance, pleasure of r. - .. I do not shame to tell you what I was, since my conversion so sweetly tastes, being the thing I am.'

Reformation, symptoms of r. observed – I see some sparks of better hope…

Refusal, r. for a good reason – …I hope this reason stands for my excuse.

Refusal, r. of help or brokerage - … give me leave to play the broker in mine own behalf …

Refusal, r. to budge - .. I will not budge for no man's pleasure.

Refusal, r. to compromise - … nothing but death shall e'er divorce my dignities

Refusal, r. to do something distasteful – Not for all this land would I be guilty of so deep a sin.

Refusal, r. to give up – I was not born a yielder.

Refusal, r. to have patience or to yield to command - … my tongue, though not my heart, shall have his will.

Refusal, r. to serve a murderer - … nor attend the foot that leaves the print of blood where'er it walks.

Regret, manifestation of r. See 'Tears, t. on hand - Give me thy hand that I may dew it with my mournful tears.'

Regret, r. at confirming truthfulness of event - I am sorry I should force you to believe that which I would to God I had not seen.

Regret, r. corrosive for things that cannot be changed - Care is no cure, but rather corrosive, for things that are not to be remedied.

Regret, r. past to be forgotten - Let us not burden our remembrance with a heaviness that's gone.

Regret, r. without remedy useless. See 'Attitude, a. towards what is past and cannot be changed – Things without all remedy should be without regard...'

Regrets, no r. See 'Fault, f. from which good results occurred - I cannot wish the fault undone, the issue of it being so proper.'

Rejection, answer to rejecting words - … Get thee to yond same sovereign cruelty.

Rejection, causing tears. See 'Disappointment, d. expressed in dramatic terms – … make dust our paper and with rainy eyes…'

Rejection, curse of love - .. 'tis the curse in love, and still approved, when women cannot love where they're beloved!

Rejection, cut it out - Dismiss your vows, your feigned tears, your flattery…

Rejection, despair at her r. - .. thus I turn me from my country's light to dwell in solemn shades of endless night.

Rejection, despair at her words - .. if words be made of breath and breath of life, I have no life to breathe what thou hast said to me.

Rejection, despair, night and day reversed - .. dark shall be my light and night my day.

Rejection, handling of r. - Hope is a lover's staff, I'll walk hence with that and manage it against despairing thoughts.

Rejection, no chance of a change of heart - Remove your siege from my unyielding heart; to love's alarms it will not ope the gate.

Rejection, r. and dismissal - … dismiss'd me this with his speechless hand.

Rejection, r. in all circumstances - Had I been seized by a hungry lion, I would have been a breakfast to the beast..

Rejection, r. in principle - I had rather hear my dog bark at a crow, than a man swear he loves me.

Rejection, r. increasing rather than decreasing desire - If the scorn of your bright eyes have power to raise such love in mine…

Rejection, r. only apparent. See 'Justification for insisting even after she said 'no' - … maids in modesty, say 'No' to that which they would have the profferer construe 'Ay".

Rejection, r. with hurtful words. See 'Speech, disappointment or despair at her words - .. thou hast cleft my heart in twain.'

Rejection, continuing to love her as a shadow - For since the substance of your perfect self is else devoted… to your shadow will I make true love.

Rejection, heart of stone - I have said too much unto a heart of stone…

Rejection, plea for gentle refusal - Say that you love me not, but say not so in bitterness…

Rejection, plea not to be rejected - Rebuke me not for that which you provoke, the virtue of your eye must break my oath.

Rejection, plea to get and keep at least her picture. See 'Graphics, picture as a substitute - Vouchsafe me yet your picture for my love, picture that is hanging in your chamber.'

Rejection, r. fostering even stronger passion - …the more she spurns my love, the more it grows and fawneth on her still.

Rejection, reaction to r., emphatic and mildly theatrical – … like the lily, that once was mistress of the field and flourished I'll hang my head and perish.

Rejection, reason for not taking 'no' for an answer – For scorn at first makes after-love the more..

Rejection, rebuttal to rejection or harsh words - Teach not thy lip such scorn; for it was made for kissing, lady, not for such contempt.

Rejection, she says no with a smile that hurts more than soothes - Thou cuttest my head with a golden axe and smil'st upon the stroke that murders me.

Rejection, warning about your character plus you don't like her - … do not fall in love with me, for I am falser than vows made in wine..

Relationship, indications of a deeper r. - … to be paddling palms and pinching fingers … and making practised smiles…

Relationship, r. beyond repair - … past hope, past cure, past help!

Relax, invitation to r. See 'Expression, come on relax - .. unknit that threatening unkind brow'.

Reliability, r. and innocence claimed - O, take the sense, sweet, of my innocence!…

Reliability, am I going to be safe with you? Can I trust you? Etc. – I shall never melt mine honour into lust.

Reliability, am I going to be safe with you? Can I trust you? Etc. - … my desires run not before mine honour…

Reliability, am I going to be safe with you? Can I trust you? Etc. - … the strong'st suggestion… shall never melt mine honour into lust.

Reliability, am I going to be safe with you? Can I trust you? Etc. - The white-cold virgin snow upon my heart abates the ardour of my liver.

Reliability. am I going to be safe with you? Can I trust you? Etc. - O fairest beauty, do not fear or fly! for I will touch thee but with reverent hands…

Reliability. See 'Lust, intemperance leading to disaster - Boundless intemperance in nature is a tyranny…'

Reliable people needed - Natures of such deep trust we shall much need.

Reliance, r. on the favor of the great a source of disappointment. - Poor wretches that depend on greatness' favour dream as I have done, wake and find nothing.

Relief, cheering up - I'll take the winter from your lips, fair lady.

Relief, e. at not to having to do what you dislike - I am best pleased to be from such a deed.

Religion, questionable religious character or motives – Name not religion, for thou lovest the flesh…

Religion, religious hypocrites – … and sweet religion makes a rhapsody of words.

Religion, religious spin to justify rebellion or other action. See 'Perception, giving the right spin to an event by using the right words – … but now the bishop turns insurrection to religion.'

Remedies, extreme r. required - ... Diseases desperate grown by desperate appliances are relieved or not at all.

Remedies, extreme r. required - ... The present time's so sick that present medicine must be ministered or overthrow incurable ensues.

Remedies, extreme r. required – ... those cold ways, that seem like prudent helps, are very poisonous where the disease is violent.

Remedies, r. to be found within ourselves. See 'Self-reliance, remedies to be found within ourselves - Our remedies oft in ourselves do lie which we ascribe to heaven.'

Remedy, advice on possible r. after identifying a problem - The nature of the sickness found, Ulysses, what is the remedy?

Remedy, every r. will be tried - ... nothing we'll omit that bears recovery's name.

Remedy, r. painful but better than death – ... though parting be a fretful corrosive, it is applied to a deathful wound.

Remedy, r. to confusion. See 'Confusion, remedy for c. is not more c. - .. confusion's cure lives not in these confusions.'

Remedy, r. worse than the disease – So play the foolish throngs with one that swoons…

Remedy, taking r. before the problem spreads - ... and stop the rage betime, before the wound do grow uncurable..

Remembering, r. only the essential - ... from the table of my memory I'll wipe away all trivial fond records.

Remembering, r. others' efforts on your behalf – ... your pains are register'd where every day I turn the leaf to read them.

Remembering, r. the bad more than the good - Men's evil manners live in brass; their virtues we write in water.

Remembering, r. the bad more than the good - The evil that men do lives after them, the good is oft interred with their bones.

Remorse - Will all great Neptune's ocean wash this blood clean from my hand?

Remorse, determination to be remorseless. See 'Determination, d. to be remorseless - ... make thick my blood, stop the access and passage of remorse…'

Remorse, false r., false tears - Trust not those cunning waters of his eyes…

Remorse, r. and fear – I am afraid to think what I have done, look on't again I dare not.

Remorse, r. and guilt. See 'Guilt, admission of g. and remorse - O Brakenbury, I have done those things, which now bear evidence against my soul.

Remorse, r. and self-awareness - To know my deed, 'twere best not know myself.

Remorse, r. at remembering - How sharp the point of this remembrance is!

Remorse, wish to undo what done - Were I the chief lord of all this spacious world I'd give it to undo the deed.

Remorse. See also entries for 'Repentance'.

Remuneration. See 'Salary, meager s. - Remuneration! O, that's the Latin word for three farthings'

Repair, ethical r. does not erase record of fault. See 'Virtue, sin and their interrelationship, maxim - Any thing that's mended is but patched : virtue that transgresses is but patched with sin; and sin that amends is but patched with virtue.'

Repeat, ask her to r. what she said – ... speak again, bright angel! for thou art as glorious to this night …

Repentance, insincere r. - My words fly up, my thoughts remain below, words without thoughts never to heaven go.

Repentance, invitation to repent – ... Repent what's past; avoid what is to come…

Repentance, pleasure of r. - .. I do not shame to tell you what I was, since my conversion so sweetly tastes, being the thing I am.

Repentance, r. accompanied by a request for punishment - ... Choose your revenge yourself; Impose me to what penance your invention…

Repentance, r. for brutal act - Were I chief

lord of all this spacious world, I'ld give it to undo the deed.

Repentance, r. for despicable action - O would the deed were good, for now the devil, that told me I did well, says that this deed is chronicled in hell

Repentance, r. for the only good act ever done. See 'Character, evil, totally and absurdly e. – repenting for one in a lifetime good deed.

Repentance, r. questionable – … Words without thoughts never to heaven go.

Repentance, r. to be accepted - Who by repentance is not satisfied is nor of heaven nor earth..

Repentance, r. useless and ineffective – … betake thee to nothing but despair. A thousand knees…

Repentance, willingness to repent questionable - … if my wind were but long enough to say my prayers, I would repent.

Repetition, r. in small steps leading to results. See 'Determination, simile – … many strokes, though with a little axe, hew down and fell the hardest-timbered oak..'

Repetition, r. ineffective and counterproductive - This act is as an ancient tale new told and in the last repeating troublesome…

Replacement, you loved her first and suddenly you love another - Even as one heat another heat expels, or as one nail by strength drives out another…

Reply, anxiously awaiting for her r. - .. expecting thy reply, I profane my lips on thy foot..

Reply, r. approved of – …'tis a loving and a fair reply.

Reply, unable to sustain the verbal attack - You have too courtly a wit for me; I'll rest.

Reply, wanting to r. See 'Speech, interruption of s. - Shall I hear more or shall I speak at this?'

Report, false r. - … let not his report come current for an accusation…

Report, he is doing very well - Report speaks goldenly of his profit.

Report, handing your r. to your boss. See second comment to 'Love, endurance of l. through poetry - Not marble, nor the gilded monuments of princes…

Report, praise or irony on a r. See comments to 'Love, endurance of l. through poetry - Not marble, nor the gilded monuments of princes…'

Repression, violent r. leading to vengeance - … to end one doubt by death revives two greater in the heirs of life.

Reprimand, complaint about being reprimanded - … it is not meet that every nice offence should bear his comment.

Reprimand, invitation to r. – … taunt my faults with such full licence as both truth and malice have power to utter.

Reprimand, r. causing a fall in mental energy - you do draw my spirits from me, with new lamenting ancient oversights.

Reprimand, r. deserved. See 'Fault, admitting to your fault - I have deserved all tongues to talk their bitterest.'

Reprimand, r. for going down and not fighting – … wilt thou, pupil-like, take thy correction mildly…

Reprimand, reprimanding impatience in speech. See 'Speech, showing impatience and a self-centered personality – tying thine ear to no tongue but thine own.

Reprimand, speed and the negligent - Celerity is never more admired than by the negligent.

Reproach, undeserved r. - I never knew yet but rebuke and cheque was the reward of valour.

Reproduction, r. suggested when mother is so beautiful. See entries for 'Pregnancy, p. good.'

Repugnance. See 'Anything, a. but this.'

Reputation, man of great r. See 'Introduction, i. to a speaker of great reputation – (A) man whose glory fills the world with loud report.'

Reputation, man spoken of highly – … there's wondrous things spoke of him.

Reputation, poor r. in the world – … we in the world's wide mouth live scandalized and foully spoken of.

Reputation, r. as a man with a sharp tongue - … the world's large tongue proclaims you for a man replete with mocks…

Reputation, r. as a questionable value - Reputation is an idle and most false imposition: oft got without merit, and lost without deserving..

Reputation, r. at stake - … my reputation is at stake, my fame is shrewdly gored.

Reputation, r. at stake - This touches me in reputation.

Reputation, r. established with the most reputable - … your name is great in mouths of wisest censure.

Reputation, r. lost - … I have lost the immortal part of myself and what remains is bestial.

Reputation, r. more valuable than earthly goods – Good name in man and woman, dear my lord, is the immediate jewel of their souls…

Reputation, r. poor. See entries for 'Defence, general d. from general accusations.'

Reputation, r. ruined - … the benefit which thou shalt thereby reap is such a name, whose repetition will be dogg'd with curses.

Reputation, r. sought in the military. See 'Militarism, reputation as a volatile commodity - … Seeking the bubble reputation even in the cannon's mouth.'

Reputation, r. tarnished by inaction - If thou wouldst not entomb thyself alive and case thy reputation in thy tent..

Reputation, value placed on r. - The purest treasure mortal times afford…

Reputation, what type of r. - How is the man esteemed here in the city?…

Reputation, wishing that r. could be purchased – I would to God thou and I knew where a commodity of good names were to be bought.

Request, emphatic r. due to strained circumstances - He asks of you that never used to beg.

Request, negative response to r. - They froze me into silence.

Request, r. granted - I will both hear and grant you your requests.

Request, more successful made with kindness than with arrogance – You may ride with one soft kiss a thousand furlongs ere with spur we heat an acre.

Request, r. for dialog – … a word with you … A hundred, if they'll do you any good.

Request, r. granted conditionally - Ay, if thou wilt say 'ay' to my request, no if thou dost say 'no' to my demand'

Request, r. not to insist. See 'Insisting, request not to insist on the same subject – harp not on that string'.

Request, r. of a lady not motivated by sexual motive or impropriety – I therefore beg it not to please the palate of my appetite…

Request, r. or plan, is it reasonable? - Well, what is it? is it within reason and compass?

Request, r. that can be easily accommodated – To do this is within the compass of man's wit…

Request, r. to be heard – Friends, Romans, countrymen, lend me your ears.

Request, r. to be heard – Hear me with patience but to speak a word.

Request, r. to be heard – Lend favourable ear to our requests…

Request, r. to be heard - Sweet royalty, bestow on me the sense of hearing.

Request, r. to be heard – To my unfolding lend your gracious ear…

Request to be heard, important message coming - … lend thy serious hearing to what I shall unfold.

Requests, r. from women. See 'Women,

requests from w. bound to be gratified - … when maidens sue, men give like gods; but when they weep and kneel…'

Reserve, rationale for being somewhat reserved at first - Therefore this maxim out of love I teach..

Rescue, refusing the rescuer – Had I been seized by a hungry lion, would have been a breakfast to the beast…

Residence, see entries for 'Place'

Resignation, r. or revenge, rhetorical question - Shall we go throw away our coats of steel and wrap our bodies in mourning gowns..

Resignation, r. to destiny. See entries for 'Destiny', also last two lines in 'Cheer up - Cheer your heart, be you not troubled with the time…'

Resignation, r. to fate - … I embrace this fortune patiently since not to be avoided it falls on me.

Resignation, r. to fate – … stoop with patience to my fortune

Resignation, r. to fate. See 'Adversity, turning a. around - … that can translate the stubbornness of fortune into so quiet and so sweet a style.'

Resignations, after resigning or being fired – I have touched the highest point of all my greatness, and from that full meridian of my glory…

Resignations, going somewhere else - … I turn my back: there is a world elsewhere.

Resistance - A thousand more mischances than this one have learn'd me how to brook this patiently.

Resistance, female r. advisable - I see, a woman may be made a fool, if she had not the spirit to resist. "I see, a woman may be made a fool,

Resistance, power of r. to noise acquired via repeated trials - Think you a little din can daunt mine ears?

Resistance, r. to aggression – To whom do lions cast their gentle looks?

Resistance, strong and unconquerable - As on a mountain top the cedar shows that keep his leaves in spite of any storm.

Resolution, changing doubt to r. See 'Encouragement, self-e. to change doubt to resolution. - Now, York, or never, steel thy fearful thoughts, and change misdoubt to resolution…'

Resolution. See entries for 'Determination'.

Resources, physical r. strained - As two spent swimmers, that do cling together and choke their art.

Resources, r. or weapons in the wrong hands - You put sharp weapons in a madman's hands.

Respect and contempt - Those that I reverence, these I fear, - the wise…

Respect, excessive r. of the world counterproductive. See 'Care, too much c. about worldly opinion counterproductive - You have too much respect upon the world, they lose it that do buy it with much care.

Respect, feigned r. - Love talks with better knowledge, and knowledge with dearer love.

Respect, r. not learned - never learn'd the icy precepts of respect, but follow'd the sugar'd game before thee.

Response, available for a positive response - … I am not made of stone but penetrable to your kind entreaties…

Response, explanation for a slow or lacking r. - … a tardiness in nature which often leaves the history unspoke that it intends to do.

Response, uncertain r. to a certain type of request - I cannot tell if to depart in silence or bitterly to speak in your reproof..

Responsibility, I was not responsible. See 'Innocence, i. claimed - Heaven lay not my transgression to my charge!'

Responsibility, making an authority face his r. See 'Sting operation - … the play 's the thing wherein I'll catch the conscience of the king.'

Responsibility, r. limited - … your fault was

not your folly.

Responsibility, r. shifted. See 'Philosophical considerations. Unwillingness to take responsibility for our mistakes - This is the excellent foppery of the world…'

Responsibility, r. shifted, deniability - It is the curse of kings to be attended by slaves that take their humour as a warrant…

Responsibility, taking the fall - Upon mine honour, I will stand betwixt you and danger.

Rest, r. as a medicine. See 'Health-care, rest as medicine - Our foster-nurse of nature is repose, the which he lacks.'

Rest, r. badly needed – … And spite of spite needs must I rest awhile

Rest, r. disturbed or interrupted - Who doth molest my contemplation?

Rest, r. needed – … and nature does require her times of preservation …

Rest, r. needed. - I lay me down a little while to breath; …and, spite of spite, needs must I rest a while.

Rest, r. not to be interrupted - .. life-preserving rest, to be disturb'd, would mad or man or beast.

Restaurant, r. with bad food - … thy food is as hath been belched on by infected lungs.

Restraint, r. caused by excess - As surfeit is the father of much fast…

Results, better r. through kindness. See 'Kindness, k. more effective than rudeness to achieve results - What thou wilt, thou rather shalt enforce it with thy smile, than hew to it with thy sword.'

Results, great r. from small resources - He that of greatest works is finisher, oft does them by the weakest minister.

Results, poor personal r. acknowledged – How my achievements mock me!

Results, positive r. in the end - All's well that ends well, yet; though time seems so adverse, and means unfit.

Results, positive results shown and a challenge to him who can do better - He that knows better how to tame a shrew, now let him speak: 'tis charity to show.

Results, r. not immediate. See 'Plan, p. to be carried out with care and secrecy - And that's not suddenly to be performed, but with advise and silent secrecy.'

Results, r. of venture. See 'Venture, v. delivered what predicted - .. what hath then befallen, or what hath this bold enterprise brought forth..'

Results, r. prematurely assessed - .. the event is yet to name the winner

Retaliation, r. promised - …we shall your tawny ground with your red blood discolour.

Retaliation, threat of r. – and withal thrust these reproachful speeches down his throat…

Retirement, desire to r. before becoming useless - … let me not live, quoth he, after my flame lacks oil…

Retirement, ending to a r. speech. See 'Invocation, end - Sun, hide thy beams! Timon hath done his reign.'

Retirement, ending to a r. speech. See 'Power, declining p. – Now my charms are all o'erthrown and what strength I have's mine own…'

Retirement, 'I have retired'. See 'Presentation. Epilogues to p., end of magic. – … But this rough magic I here abjure…'

Retirement, plans for r. - And thence retire me to my Milan, where every third thought shall be my grave.

Retirement, r. announced - … and 'tis our fast intent to shake all cares and business from our age…

Retirement, r. planned to be spent in peace – For mine own part, I could be well content to entertain the lag-end of my life with quiet hours.

Retirement, r. to a secluded life – … to forswear the full stream of the world and to live in a nook merely monastic.

Retirement, retiring and giving up your secrets – … And deeper than did ever plummet sound I'll drown my book.

Retouching of picture or painting - And yet the painter flatter'd her a little, unless flatter with myself too much.

Retreat? Never again - ... Charge! upon our foes but never once again turn back and fly.

Retreat? Never again - Never may he live to see a sunshine day that cries 'Retire', if Warwick bid him stay.

Retribution, divine r. - The gods are just, and of our pleasant vices make instruments to plague us.

Retribution, r. for wrongs inflicted by authorities. See "Justice, misapplied and arbitrary, time for revolution - ... now breathless wrong shall sit and pant in your great chairs of ease...'

Retribution, friends and enemies handled - ... all friends shall taste the wages of their virtue.

Retribution, time as an administrator of justice - ... and thus the whirligig of time brings in his revenges.

Retribution, wish pronounced in jest has become true - ... And given in earnest what I begg'd in jest.

Retrospection. See 'Nostalgia, regret - When to the session of sweet silent thought, I summon up remembrance of things past...'

Return, see 'Invitation, i. to return soon – O thou that dost inhabit in my breast, leave not the mansion so long tenantless'.

Return, r. from a foreign assignment - (I) sighed my English breath in foreign clouds, eating the bitter bread of banishment.

Return, r. home or to base – ... as the bark that hath discharged his fraught, return with precious lading to the bay..

Return, r. home or homebase - ... to England then: where ne'er from France arrived more happy men.

Return, your r. guaranteed. See 'Priorities, choosing to stay here – let Rome in Tiber melt, and the wide arch of the ranged empire fall!...'

Return? Not a chance - No, rather I abjure all roofs, and choose to wage against the enmity o' the air...

Revelation, startling r. – I could a tale unfold whose lightest word would harrow up thy soul, freeze thy young blood...

Revenge, crime eliciting the vengeance of heaven – ... Will cry for vengeance at the gates of heaven.

Revenge, culprit should have thousands of lives - O, that the slave had forty thousand lives! One is too poor, too weak for my revenge.

Revenge, determination to seek r. - ... I'll never pause again, never stand still, till either death hath closed these eyes of mine or fortune given me measure of revenge.

Revenge, determination to seek r. - From this time forth my thoughts be bloody, or be nothing worth!

Revenge, equal treatment when roles are reversed - The villany you teach me, I will execute...

Revenge, exhortation to r. - O, let no words, but deeds, revenge this treason!

Revenge, God's vengeance predicted – ... my master, God omnipotent is mustering in his clouds on our behalf armies of pestilence.

Revenge, hope of r. - Hope of revenge shall hide our inward woe.

Revenge, indiscriminate r. See 'Anger, behavior of crowd's anger - ... like an angry hive of bees that want their leader, scatter up and down...'

Revenge, invocation. See 'Invocation, stones in heaven - Are there no stones in heaven but what serve for thunder?'

Revenge, justice from heaven - We will solicit heaven and move the gods to send down Justice for to wreak our wrongs.

Revenge, measure for measure – like doth quit like and Measure still for Measure.

Revenge, measure for measure - Measure for measure must be answered.

Revenge, no limits to r. - Revenge should have no bounds.

Revenge, no limits to the desire for r. – Had all his hairs been lives, my great revenge had stomach for them all.

Revenge, no tears but only revenge. See 'Tears, t. banned and substituted by revenge - To weep is to make less the depth of grief: tears, then, for babes; blows and revenge for me.'

Revenge, only satisfaction in r. – … I shall never come to bliss till all these mischiefs be return'd again…

Revenge, plea to refrain from r. – Stay thy revengeful hand; thou hast no cause to fear

Revenge, prepared to die to seek r. – … I'll empty all these veins and shed my dear blood drop by drop in the dust…

Revenge, r. advocated – Be comforted: let's make us medicines of our great revenge, to cure this deadly grief.

Revenge, r. against a killer – Every man's conscience is a thousand swords…

Revenge, r. against false accusations. See 'Defence, d. from general accusations - pierced to the soul with slander's venom spear.'

Revenge, r. against injustice. See 'Injustice, revenge for injustices - .. even for revenge mock my destruction!'

Revenge, r. and justice – .. blood, like sacrificing Abel's, cries even from the tongueless caverns of the earth to me for justice and rough chastisement.

Revenge, r. brewing - Vengeance is in my heart, death in my hand, blood and revenge are hammering in my head.

Revenge, r. call for r. - …shall we bite our tongues, and in dumb shows pass the remainder of our hateful days?

Revenge, r. coupled with pleasure. see 'Pleasure, p. and revenge as great motivators - .. pleasure and revenge have ears more deaf than adders to the voice of any true decision.'

Revenge, r. on a fat man - … for revenged I will be, as sure as his guts are made of puddings.

Revenge, r. or tricks against lechers OK - Against such lewdsters and their lechery those that betray them do no treachery.

Revenge, r. planned - My thoughts are ripe in mischief…

Revenge, r. promised - And they shall feel the vengeance of my wrath.

Revenge, r. promised – I will have such revenges on you both… they shall be the terrors of the earth.

Revenge, r. promised on everyone - Clarence, thy turn is next, and then the rest, counting myself but bad till I be best.

Revenge, r. prompted by grief - Be this the whetstone of your sword: let grief convert to anger…

Revenge, r. reminded - How all occasions do inform against me, and spur my dull revenge!

Revenge, r. threatened - I'll be revenged on the whole pack of you.

Revenge, raven as an emblem of r. - The croaking raven doth bellow for revenge.

Revenge, request to r. murder - Revenge this foul and most unnatural murder.

Revenge, sorrow preventing r. - I have not another tear to shed.. then which way shall I find Revenge's cave?

Revenge, terrible r. threatened - Thou hadst been better have been born a dog than answer my waked wrath!

Revenge, total masochism until r. accomplished - … Never to taste the pleasures of the world.. till I have set a glory to this hand by giving it the worship of revenge.

Revenge, violent r. promised. See 'Violence, v. threatened - .. (I'll) make a quagmire of your mingled brains.'

Revenge, vowing r. for unfair termination - My ashes, as the phoenix, may bring forth a bird that will revenge upon you all.

Revenge, war for r. See 'War, w. and revenge - … let slip the dogs of war that this foul deed shall smell above the earth…'

Revenge. See 'Virtue, v. nobler than revenge - ..the rarer action is in virtue than in revenge.'

Revenge. See 'Invocation, revenge - "I am Revenge: sent from the infernal kingdom, to ease the gnawing vulture of thy mind…'

Reverence, r. as the angel of the world. See lines in 'Death, egalitarian nature of d. - .. mean and mighty, rotting together, have one dust.'

Reversal, r. of previous achievements. See 'Destruction, d. and undoing of previous achievements - Undoing all, as all had never been!'

Revolution, call for r. See 'Justice, misapplied and arbitrary, time for revolution - .. now breathless wrong shall sit and pant in your great chairs of ease…'

Revolution, call for violent action when peaceful demonstrations ineffective - .. those cold ways that seem like prudent helps, are very poisonous where the disease is violent.

Revolution, discontent leading to r. - … move the murmuring lips of discontent to break into this dangerous argument.

Revolution, how a revolution gets started - … kiss the lips of unacquainted change and pick strong matter of revolt and wrath..

Revolution, military strategy reversed - … we in order when we are most out of order.

Revolution, r. ignited - Mischief, thou art afoot, take thou what course thou wilt.

Revolution, r. in the offing. See 'Social issues, strength in numbers and justice of claim - They say poor suitors have strong breaths; they shall know we have strong arms too.'

Revolutions, why r. fail – … and delight to live in slavery to the nobility.

Reward, promise of r. See 'Gratitude, g. and promise of reward - .. If fortune serve me, I'll requite this kindness'.

Reward, great r. promised – I'll set thee in a shower of gold, and hail rich pearls upon thee.

Reward, promise of r. improving performance .. And if we thrive, promise them such rewards as victors wear at the Olympian games..

Reward, r. for courage. See 'Courage, reward goes to the courageous - .. fearless minds climb soonest unto crowns.'

Reward, r. for wit. See 'Inventiveness, i., wit and geniality rewarded -…wit shall not go unrewarded while I am king of this country.'

Reward, r. given only when merited - … our head shall go bare till merit crown it.

Reward, r. in the action itself. See 'Gratitude, no need to return favor - The service and the loyalty I owe in doing it, pays itself.'

Reward, r. promised for success - .. If thou proceed as high as word, my deed shall match thy deed.

Rhetoric, all smoke, no substance - Sweet smoke of rhetoric.

Rhetoric, imperialist r. - … the signs of war advance, no king of England, if not king of France.

Rhyme and reason - … in despite of the teeth of all rhyme and reason, that they were fairies.

Rhyme or reason. See 'Love, how much? - Neither rhyme nor reason can express so much'

Ridicule, being made an object of r. – A fixed figure for the time of scorn to point his slow unmoving finger at.

Ridicule, being made an object of r. - I see you all are bent to set against me for your merriment…

Ridicule, recognizing that one is made object of r. - I do begin to perceive that I am made an ass…

Right and wrong, sense of r. and wrong lost. See 'Justice, right and wrong lost when there is no principle - Force should be right; or rather, right and wrong, between whose endless jar justice resides…'

Right and wrong. See 'Dispute, d. and

disagreement on right and wrong - If that be right which Warwick says is right, there is no wrong, but everything is right.

Right thing at the right time. See 'Appropriateness, the right thing at the right time – roses in May and snow in winter'.

Rightly to be great … See 'Honor, meaning of h. and standing up when h. is at stake - Rightly to be great is not to stir without great argument…'

Ripeness is all. See 'Maturity, m. is everything - Men must endure their going hence, even as their coming hither. Ripeness is all.'

Rise, an early rise to launch into an adventure - The day shall not be up so soon as I to try the fair adventure of tomorrow.

Risk, desperate r. but confidence in its success – thou this to hazard, needs must intimate Skill infinite, or monstrous desperate…

Risk, question about r. - … to set so rich a main on the nice hazard of one doubtful hour?

Risk, risking all on one speculation - to set so rich a main on the nice hazard of one doubtful hour.

Risks, not afraid to take r. - I do not set my life in a pin's fee.

Risks, r. inherent to transportation or trade at large – but ships are but boards, sailors but men.

Robbery, r. by judges. See 'Judges, j. as thieves - Thieves for their robbery have authority when judges steal themselves.'

Robbery, victim of r. See 'Attitude, positive a. in reversals - The robb'd that smiles steals something from the thief...'

Role model. See 'Example, role model – From his metal was his party steeled'.

Rome as a wilderness of tigers. See 'Cruelty, c. in Rome - Rome is but a wilderness of tigers'

Romeo, old r. See 'Age, a. placing a limit to the display of gallantry - … One that is well-nigh worn to pieces with age to show himself a young gallant.'

Roof decorations - The roof o' the chamber with golden cherubins is fretted.

Rose. See ' Universe, rose, unique - For nothing this wide universe I call, save thou my rose, in it thou art my all.'

Rude. See 'Person, a rude p. - … a rude despiser of good manners, that in civility thou seem'st so empty.'

Rudeness, apologies for r. – the thorny point of bare distress hath taken from me, the show of smooth civility…

Rudeness, r. explained - This rudeness is a sauce to his good wit…

Rudeness, r. not as effective as kindness. See 'Kindness, k. more effective than ru

Rudeness, r. to be avoided. See 'Advice, a. not to be rude or patronizing – (haughtiness) …leaves behind a stain…'

Rudeness, r. undeserved - What have I done, that thou darest wag thy tongue in noise so rude against me?

Rule, authoritarian r. – … from them take their liberties; make them of no more voice than dogs…

Rule, authoritarian rule - … my mouth shall be the parliament of England

Rule, golden r. applied to life. See 'Balance, in praise of balanced life - … they are as sick that surfeit with too much, as they that starve with nothing.'

Ruler, a good r. See 'Government, good ruler defined by the goodness of his g. - … He is a happy king, since he gains from his subjects the name of good by his government.'

Ruler, bad r. See 'Rebellion, justification for r. – (he) broke oath on oath, committed wrong on wrong…'

Rumor, effect of r. on fear - Rumour doth double, like the voice and echo, the numbers of the fear'd.

Rumor, r. defined and its effect on the masses - rumor is a pipe blown by surmises, jealousies, conjectures.

Rumor, r. fabricating slander – Upon my tongue continual slanders ride, the which in every language I pronounce..

Rumor, r. increases fear - Rumor doth double, like the voice and echo the numbers of the fear'd.

Rumor, r. spread by political enemies. See 'News, n. incorrect - .. many tales devis'd, which oft the ear of greatness needs must hear by smiling pick-thanks and base newsmongers.'

Rumor, r. that must be stopped - … stop the rumor, and allay those tongues that durst disperse it.

Rumor, so far it is only r. - I mean the whispered ones, for they are yet but ear-kissing arguments.

Rumor, wealth – It is noised he hath a mass of treasure.

Rumors, suspicious r. See 'Whisperings, w. about bad deeds - Foul whisperings are abroad, unnatural deeds do breed unnatural troubles.'

Run, time to r. - like a brace of greyhounds ..are at our backs.

Running as fast as you can - I drink the air before me, and return or ere your pulse twice beat.

Running as fast as you can – ..I have speeded here with the extremest inch of possibility.

Sadness, extreme s. See 'Disappointment, d. expressed in dramatic terms – …make dust our paper and with rainy eyes…'

Sadness, hyperbolic. See 'Distress, d. emphasized dramatically - …if the river were dry, I am able to fill it with my tears…'

Sadness, imprisoned within oneself - Now my soul's palace is become a prison.

Sadness, license to cry - Those that can pity, here may, if they think it well, let fall a tear; the subject will deserve it.

Sadness, s. and misery - … my heart, all mad with misery, beats in this hollow prison of my flesh.

Sadness, s. arising from business cares – … had I such venture forth, the better part of my affections would be with my hopes abroad…

Sadness, s. detected - …even in the glasses of thine eyes I see thy grieved heart.

Sadness, s. induced by music. See entries for 'Music, m. that induce sadness '

Sadness, s. making time pass slowly. See 'Time, sadness making hours long - what sadness lengthens Romeo's hours? Not having that…'

Sadness, s. misconstrued. See 'Expression of sadness misconstrued - My heart is ten times lighter than my looks.'

Sadness, s. not the natural condition for love - Venus smiles not in a house of tears,

Sadness, s. prompting tears - .. my heart is drown'd with grief whose flood begins to flow within mine eyes.

Sadness, s. reinforced by inducing s. in others – Griefs of mine own lie heavy in my breast…

Sadness, sad and not knowing why - In sooth, I know not why I am so sad, it wearies me…

Safety, escape for s. - … let us not be dainty of leave-taking, but shift away: there's warrant in that theft which steals itself, when there's no mercy left.

Safety, questionable s. - … such safety finds the trembling lamb environed with wolves.

Safety, s. and beer preferable to fame – I would give all my fame for a pot of ale and safety.

Safety, s. first before questioning danger - …'tis safer to avoid what's grown than question how 'tis born.

Safety, s. not achieved by task half accomplished - Nought's had, all's spent where our desire is got without content…

Safety, s. through danger. See 'Danger, d. necessary to achieve safety – out of this nettle, danger, we pluck this flower, safety.'

Safety, s. warning. See 'Security, false sense of s. - … If thou beest not immortal look about you: security gives way to conspiracy.'

Salad days, see 'Error, e. admitted and due to youthful inexperience – Those were my salad days when I was green in judgement.'

Salad, see 'Character, excellent person and one in a thousand – we may pick a thousand salads ere we light on such another herb.'

Salary, how much money do you make? See 'Financial Status - They are but beggars that can count their worth.'

Salary, meager s. - Remuneration! O, that's the Latin word for three farthings

Salary, meager s. and visible ribs - .. you may tell every finger I have with my ribs.

Salary, s. issues. See 'Advance, applying for an advance or raise - I do beseech you, as in the way of tast

Salutations – Hail, you anointed deputies of heaven!

Salutations and wishes - … all joy befall your grace and you.

Salutations and wishes - Be free, and fare thou well!

Salutations and wishes - Bliss be upon you!

Salutations and wishes – … fair be all thy hopes and prosperous be thy life in peace and war.

Salutations and wishes - Fair thoughts and happy hours attend on you.

Salutations and wishes - Health and fair time of day; joy and good wishes.

Salutations and wishes - Many years of happy days befal …

Salutations and wishes - Sir, I commend you to your own content.

Salutations and wishes – The best and wholesomest spirits of the night envelope you.

Salutations and wishes – The gentleness of all the gods go with thee.

Salutations and wishes – The goodness of the night upon you, friends.

Salutations and wishes - The grace of heaven, before, behind thee, and on every hand enwheel thee round!

Salutations and wishes - The heavens give safety to your purposes!

Salutations and wishes, could also be sarcastic – … I leave you to the protection of the prosperous gods…

Salutations and wishes, stand in the smile of heaven. See 'Circumstances, favored by c. – (standing in) …the smile of heaven.'

Salutations and wishes. See also entries for 'Toast'.

Salutations, s and greetings quick due to time constraints - The time will not allow the compliment which very manners urges.

Salutations, s. in a rush due to urgency. See 'Ceremonies, no time for c. even if friends meet again after a long time - ..the leisure and the fearful time cuts off the ceremonious vows of love..'

Salutations, s. to a group - Good morrow to this fair assembly.

Salutations, s. to the earth – Dear earth, I do salute thee with my hand…

Salutations, s. with sadness - More health and happiness betide my liege than can my care-tuned tongue deliver him.

Salutations, till next time – This bud of love, by summer's ripening breath, may prove a beauteous flower when we next meet.

Salutations, wishes for a rain of fragrances - … the heavens rain fragrances on you.

Salutations. See also entries for 'Good-bye'.

Sanity, s. rather than madness. See 'Madness, m. that has all the traits of sanity - .. her madness hath the oddest frame of sense..'.

Sarcasm, retort to s. – … shall quips, and sentences, and these paper bullets of the brain…

Sarcasm, retort to s. – … wit larded with malice.

Sarcasm, s. rejected. See 'Words, wasted

breath - Never did mockers waste more idle breath.'

Satire, impervious to s. – ... a college of wit-crackers cannot flout me out of my humour.

Satisfaction, s. as payment. - He is well paid that is well satisfied...

Satisfaction, s. for the way things turned out – We have cause to be glad that matters are so well digested.

Satisfaction, self s. - Thus have I politicly begun my reign.

Satisfied, but wanting more - ... can one desire too much of a good thing?

Saved, reasons to be grateful - ... then wisely, good sir, weigh our sorrow with our comfort.

Saving, s. as a virtue – And thrift is blessing, if men steal it not.

Say it is not so. See 'Denial - ... contradict thyself and say it is not so'.

Saying, a s. well worth remembering – There was never a truer rhyme.

Scar, s. nobly got a mark of honor. See 'Defeat, d. that does not mean dishonor - A scar nobly got, or a noble scar, is a good livery of honour; so, belike, is that.'

Scarecrow, s. of the law. See 'Law, l. must be enforced - We must not make a scarecrow of the law...'

Schedule, s. to adhere to - Stick to your journal course: the breach of custom is breach of all.

Scholarly considerations, identifying a scholar. See 'Philosophy, simple p. - Thou art a scholar; let us therefore eat and drink.'

Sciatica, wishing to inflict s. See 'Curse, sciatica - Thou cold sciatica cripple our senators...'

Scientists, s. explaining the supernatural – ... we have our philosophical persons, to make modern and familiar...

Scorn, reaction to s. - What means this scorn, thou most untoward knave?

Scorpion, s's nest to be avoided - .. Seek not a scorpion's nest.

Scoundrel, a congenital s. See 'Sin, s. not occasional, but chronic - Thy sin's not accidental, but a trade.'

Scoundrels, euphemism. See 'Night, preferring n. to day – ... let us be Diana's gentlemen of the shade, minions of the moon'

Scoundrels, s. around – ... there are cozeners abroad; therefore it behoves men to be wary.

Scoundrel, s. constant to his calling – ... and therein am I constant to my profession.

Screw your courage to the sticking-place. See 'Failure, dealing with fear of f. - ... screw your courage to the sticking-place and we'll not fail.'

Scruples, no s. - Let me, if not by birth, have lands by wit: all with me's meet that I can fashion fit.

Sculpture, divine s. – ...a piece many years in doing and now newly performed by that rare Italian master, Julio Romano...

Sea, see entries for 'Nature, sea'

Sea, wild s. as a metaphor for a troubled conscience. See 'Conscience, debating within one's c. – ... Thus hulling in the wild sea of my conscience...'

Sea-crossing, virtual s.-c. - ... charming the narrow seas to give you gentle pass...

Sea-sickness. See 'Land, l. preferable to sea - ... would I give a thousand furlongs of sea for an acre of barren ground...'

Search, s. bound to be useless. See 'Man, m. who does not want to be found - .. 'tis in vain to seek him here that means not to be found.

Search, searching with no hope to find - ... Hopeless to find, yet loath to leave unsought...

Season your admiration for a while. See 'Surprise, hold your s. for a moment '

Seasoning, s. by time. See 'Time, give it time to mature, t. as a seasoning agent - How many things by season season'd are...'

Seclusion, total s. - Out of all eyes, tongues, minds and injuries.

Secrecy, impossible to break it if secret is not known - ...thou wilt not utter what thou dost not know.

Secrecy, s. advisable on the sins of authorities. See 'Kings, authority, vices of k. better kept secret - Who has a book of all that monarchs do, he's more secure to keep it shut, than shown…'

Secrecy, s. assured - .. the secrets of nature have not more gift in taciturnity.

Secrecy, s. assured - When you have spoken it, 't is dead, and I am the grave of it.

Secrecy, s. assured. See 'Rejection, despair at her words - ... if words be made of breath and breath of life, I have no life to breathe what thou hast said to me.'

Secrecy, s. demanded - … such things that want no ear but yours.

Secrecy, s. essential - Seal up your lips, and give no words but - mum!

Secrecy, s. required, secret to be kept - ... stall this in your bosom.

Secrecy, s. required for various reasons. See 'Help, seeking h. in secret - ... and thence it is that I to your assistance do make love: masking the business from the common eye for sundry weighty reasons.'

Secret, I will keep the s. - ...your mute I'll be; when my tongue blabs, then let mine eyes not see!

Secret, information that must be kept s. – ... I will tell you a thing, but you shall let it dwell darkly with you.

Secret, injunction to keep the matter s. - ... whatsoever else shall hap to-night, give it an understanding, but no tongue.

Secret, s. information given away indirectly – Thou shalt never get such a secret from me but by a parable.

Secret, s. matters - For I would commune with you of such things that want no ear but yours.

Secret, s. will be disclosed to her after the (successful) event - - Be innocent of the knowledge, dearest chuck, till thou applaud the deed.

Secret, s. that must be well kept - …'tis a secret must be locked within the teeth and the lips.

Secret, weighty s. - This secret is so weighty, 't will require a strong faith to conceal it.

Secrets, s. of the heart, promise to reveal them - … and by and by thy bosom shall partake the secrets of my heart.

Security, achieving s. through initial risk. See 'Danger, d. necessary to achieve safety – out of this nettle, danger, we pluck this flower, safety.'

Security, false sense of s. - … If thou beest not immortal look about you: security gives way to conspiracy.

Security, sense of s. always questionable - …security is mortals' chiefest enemy.

Seducer, great s. - He is the bluntest wooer in Christendom.

Seducer, requisites of a s. - … the knave is handsome, young, and hath all those requisites in him…

Seduction, a viewpoint on s. – … when you have our roses, you barely leave our thorns to prick ourselves…

Seduction, flattery as a tool of s. See 'Flattery, let there be no limit to your f. - Flatter and praise, commend, extol their graces, though ne'er so black, say they have angels' faces.'

Seduction, lesson in s. – ...you must seem to do that fearfully which you commit…

Seduction, seductive pow

Seduction, s. techniques – He hath studied her will, and translated her will, out of honesty into English.

Seduction, tools of s. - … a speeding trick to lay down ladies, a French song and a fiddle has no fellow.

Seduction, tools of s. See 'Cupid, C's varied mode of operation - .. loving goes by haps, some Cupid kills with arrows, some with traps.'

Seeing, greater impact than hearing of a painful event. See 'Pain, painful event, seeing it has greater impact than hearing about it - - To see sad sights moves more than hear them told…'

Seeing, s. is believing - If there be truth in sight..

Seeing, s. is believing - If you dare not trust that you see, confess not that you know.

Seems, madam… See 'Reality, not appearance - Seems, madam! nay it is; I know not 'seems'.

Selection, desire to select independently - … in such a business give me leave to use help of mine own eyes.

Selection, s. limited – … there's small choice in rotten apples.

Self-accusation - ..I have done ill, of which I do accuse myself so sorely, that I will joy no more.

Self-analysis, I wish you would look at yourselves - O, that you could turn your eyes towards the napes of your necks…

Self-assertion encouraged - Self-love, my liege, is not so vile a sin as self-neglecting.

Self-assertion to remove self-doubt - … to be afeard of my deserving were but a weak disabling of myself.

Self-assessment - A man that fortune's buffets and rewards hast ta'en with equal thanks.

Self-assessment - I am myself indifferent honest; but yet I could accuse me of such things that it were better my mother had not borne me…

Self-assessment – I am not covetous for gold…

Self-assessment – Though I am not splenitive and rash, yet have I something in me dangerous.

Self-awareness difficult. See 'Mirror, inability to see himself without one - … the eye sees not itself but by reflection…'

Self-defence, killing in s-d - To kill, I grant, is sin's extremest gust but, in defence, by mercy, 'tis most just.

Self-defense, killing in s-d. justified – Who cannot condemn rashness in cold blood?…

Self-defence, s-d and parental defense - Unreasonable creatures feed their young… make war with him that climb'd unto their nest…

Self-defense. See 'Prevarication on anyone will prompt vengeance - the smallest worm will turn being trodden on.'

Self-government. See 'Body, our bodies as gardens and our wills as gardeners - … Our bodies are our gardens…'

Self-denial, s.d. as a sign of wisdom – The greatest virtue of which wise men boast is to abstain from ill, when pleasing most

Self-destruction, s.d. compounded by incorrect judgment - … when we in our own viciousness grow hard.. the wise Gods seal our eyes…

Self-effacement and blame at having been betrayed by false appearances – What a thrice-double ass was I, to take this drunkard for a god…

Self-effacement and pessimistic view of own self – What should such fellows as I do crawling between earth and heaven?

Self-effacement and request for punishment. See 'Punishment, poison - If you have poison for me, I will drink it.'

Self-effacement, emphatic, beating your own head – … Beat at this gate, that let thy folly in.

Self-effacement, making sport of ones misery - … misery makes sport to mock itself

Self-evidence. See 'Evidence, example of self-e.'

Self-identity in question - Who is it that can tell me who I am?

Self-illusion. See 'Hypocrisy and self-illusion - .. with devotion's visage and pious action we do sugar o'er the devil himself'.

Self-improvement - …all dedicated to

closeness and the bettering of my mind.
Self-improvement. See 'Lifestyle change – dedication to the bettering of the mind'
Self-introduction. See entries for 'Introduction, self-I.' *** 'Body language'
Self-interest, bias of the world - That smooth-fac'd gentleman, tickling commodity, commodity, the bias of the world.
Self-knowledge key to knowing others. See 'Psychology, self-knowledge key to knowing others - .. to know a man well, were to know himself.'
Self-loathing – … one unperfectness shows me another, to make me frankly despise myself.
Self-love, s-l admitted as a sin - Sin of self-love possesseth all mine eye, and all my soul, and all my every part…
Self-love, s-l. better than self-neglect - Self-love, my liege, is not so vile a sin as self-neglecting.
Self-love, s-l or self-respect as a pre-requisite for loving others. See 'Love, lack of l. for own self prevents loving others - Love loving not itself none other can.'
Self-praise. See entries for 'Modesty, self-praise' - 'Praise, self-praise'
Self-punishment - thou gavest them the rod, and put'st down thine own breeches
Self-punishment, desire for s-p.. See 'Invocation, i. to the moon, massive depression - O sovereign mistress of true melancholy,…'
Self-punishment, s.p. invoked – Hang there like a fruit, my soul, till the tree die!
Self-punishment, s.p. invoked – … roast me in sulphur! Wash me in steep-down gulfs of liquid fire!
Self-recrimination - My very hairs do mutiny, for the white reprove the brown for rashness…
Self-reliance, remedies to be found within ourselves - Our remedies oft in ourselves do lie which we ascribe to heaven.
Seminar, introduction to a s. - Here let us breathe, and haply institute a course of learning, and ingenious studies.
Sense of humor. See 'Character, with a sense of humor - .. the world's large tongue proclaims you for a man replete with mocks.' – 'Man, m. with a keen sense of humor - His eye begets occasion for his wit…' *** Entries for 'Wit'
Sense, sure, you have… See 'Judgment, without j. - Sense, sure, you have, else could you not have motion, but…'
Senselessness. See 'Eyes, open e. but unable to see - You see, her eyes are open. Ay, but their sense is shut.' Entries for 'Speech, nonsensical or meaningless' and 'Nonsense'
Sentence, reaction to a s. - He bears the sentence well that nothing bears…
Sentence, waiting for the s. See 'Anxious while waiting for her answer – Thus ready for the way of life or death I wait the sharpest blow'.
Separation, s. temporarily postponed - Good night, good night! parting is such sweet sorrow, that I shall say-good night till it be morrow!
Separation, s. between church and state – Where we do reign, we will alone uphold…
Separation, s. concurrent with spiritual presence - Our separation so abides, and flies, that thou, residing here, go'st yet with me…
Separation, s. in harrowing circumstances - I doubt it not; and all these woes shall serve for sweet discourses in our time to come.
Separation, s. temporarily postponed - Good night, good night! parting is such sweet sorrow, that I shall say-good night till it be morrow!
Separation, not wanting to leave - I have more care to stay than will to go.
Separation, you or she leave for a trip. See 'Goodbye, when she is leaving for a short or long trip, or a shopping excursion - Let all the number of the stars give light to thy fair

way.'

Serious, solemn man who never laughs. See 'Wine, w. as an ingredient for a sense of humor - .. nor a man cannot make him laugh; but that's no marvel, he drinks no wine.'

Serious message in light delivery. See 'Message, serious but delivered lightly - If seriously I may convey my thoughts in this my light deliverance.'

Serpent heart. See 'Woman, cruel, serpent - O serpent heart, hid with a flowering face!'

Service, at her complete s. - ... sworn by your command, which my love makes religion to obey…

Service, at her complete service – Being your thy slave what should I do but tend upon the hours and times of your desire?

Service, at her complete service – I am thus early come to know what service it is your pleasure to command me in.

Service, at her complete service – I come to answer your pleasure.

Service, at her complete service – I will live in thy heart, die in thy lap, and be buried in thy eyes…

Service, at the king's s. - ... service shall with steeled sinews toil, and labour shall refresh itself with hope…

Service, at your s. – Thy humble servant vows obedience and humble service till the point of death.

Service, at your service - ... I will be correspondent to command and do my spiriting gently.

Service, at your service, ask me to do anything you want - I come to answer thy best pleasure; be't to fly, to swim, to dive into the fire…

Service, commitment to trustful service and looking forward to it - You never had a servant to whose trust your business was more welcome.

Service, holding up her long dress to avoid soiling it. See 'Dress, long d. to be held up.'

Service, ready to provide best possible s. – … we are ready to use our utmost studies in your service

Service, s. inspired by respect and loyalty. See 'Gratitude, no need to return favor - The service and the

Service, s. offered as a token of love - … impose some service on me for thy love.

Service, s. requested and offered - I am thus early come, to know what service it is your pleasure to command me in.

Service, s. without expectation of reward - .. do not look for further recompense than thine own gladness that thou art employed.

Services, s. rendered to be recognized. See 'Defiance, d. based on the merit of your services – ... My services which I have done the signiory shall out-tongue his complaints.'

Servility, following the leader – The swallow follows not summer more willing than we your lordship.

Sex and aging. See 'Age, sex and aging - Is it not strange that desire should so many years outlive performance?'

Sex appeal of modesty. See 'Modesty, m. in a woman as temptation for a seducer' – 'Modest and virtuous women greater tempters than lascivious ones'.

Sex identity difficult, masculine looking women - .. you should be women, and yet your beards forbid me to interpret that you are so.

Sex, desire for s. – My poor body, madam, requires it: I am driven on by the flesh…

Sex, hot s. - ... till strange love, grown bold think true love acted simple modesty.

Sex, indications of mutual attraction leading to s. - When these mutualities so marshal the way…

Sex, s. and desire. See 'Forgiveness, f. for looking at other women - … A sin prevailing much in youthful men who give their eyes the liberty of gazing.'

Sex, s. and the military. See 'Curse, c. to wars and sex - … wars and lechery; nothing else holds fashion: a burning devil take them!'

Sex, s. as a restorer of spirits - … Make love's quick pants in Desdemona's arms give renew'd fire to our extincted spirits.

Sex, s. having long historical precedents – All sects, all ages smack of this vice…

Sex, s. postponed - … though Venus govern your desires, Saturn is dominator over mine.

Sex, symptoms of mutual attraction - … they met so near with their lips that their breaths embraced together.

Sex, when he does not seem interested – Why hast thou lost the fresh blood in thy cheeks and given my treasures and my rights of thee…

Sexual advances rationalized. See "Approach, securing a way out - gentle thou art, therefore to be won…'

Sexual appetite. See 'Appetite, sexual a. as a motive denied – (I) therefore beg it not, to please the palate of my appetite…'

Sexual desire waning – … I begin to love, as an old man loves money, with no stomach.

Sexual education - .. the lesson is but plain and once made perfect, never lost again.

Sexual embrace. See 'Embrace, rationale for embracing lady – … the nobleness of life is to do thus…'

Sexual fantasy – That's a fair thought to lie between maids' legs.

Sexual harassment - Fit thy consent to my sharp appetite…

Sexual intercourse - … conflict such as was supposed the wandering prince and Dido once enjoy'd.

Sexual intercourse – … Groping for trouts in a peculiar river

Sexual intercourse - … I liked her and boarded her i' the wanton way of youth.

Sexual intercourse – … the deed of darkness.

Sexual intercourse – … your daughter and the Moor are now making the beast with two backs.

Sexual intercourse - He thinks … that you have touch'd his queen forbiddenly.

Sexual intercourse and related punishment - Why should he die, sir? … filling a bottle with a tundish

Sexual intercourse suspected – I am doubtful that you have been conjunct…

Shadow, loving a s. See 'Rejection, continuing to love her as a shadow - For since the substance of your perfect self is else devoted… to your shadow will I make true love.'

Shadows, rewarded with s. - Some there be that shadows kiss, such have but a shadow's bliss.

Shaky support base. See entries for 'Opinion, your op. on crowds and masses'

Shame, an event that can only be spoken of with shame. See 'Event, e. that can only be told with shame - may not be without much shame retold.'

Shame, curious as to how the shameless can avoid s. – What trick, what device, what starting-hole, canst thou now find out to hide thee…

Shame, exempt from s. - … upon his brow shame is ashamed to sit.

Shame, hope that in future shameful man will acquire the sense of s. See 'Invocation, shame - Live in thy shame, but die not shame with thee!'

Shame, s. calling for instant remedy. See last lines in 'Establishment, e. run down and poorly managed - … epicurism and lust make it more like a tavern or a brothel than a graced palace.'

Shame, shameful acts and behavior – Heaven stops the nose at it and the moon winks…

Shame, shameful acts by a shameless character – … Were shame enough to shame thee, wert thou not shameless.

Shame, shamelessness. See 'Invocation, shamelessness - O shame, where is thy blush!'

Shameless, saying this without blushing?

See 'Impudence, shamelessness – you never blush at this?'

Shape, in perfect s. and full form. See 'Man, m. in full form and perfect shape - as full of spirit as the month of May'.

Sharper than a serpent's tooth. See 'Ingratitude, i. towards parents despicable - How sharper than a serpent's tooth it is to have a thankless child!'

She is leaving for a trip. See 'Invitation, i. to return soon – O thou that dost inhabit in my breast, leave not the mansion so long tenantless.'

She's just got out of the shower. See 'Freshness, like dew - .. As fresh as morning dew distilled on flowers.'

Sheep. See 'Deduction, the power of d. - ..therefore thou art a sheep.' – 'Strength, s. relative, wolf and sheep - ... I know he would not be a wolf but that he sees the Romans are but sheep.'

Shepherdess, if she were a shepherdess - I should leave grazing, were I of your flock, and only live by gazing.

Ship, compliment, like Helen of Troy - .. she is a pearl, whose price hath launched above a thousand ships, and turn'd crown'd kings to merchants.

Shoes, putting on s. on the wrong foot – … slippers, which his nimble haste had falsely thrust upon contrary feet.

Shop, s. not in tip-top conditions -… and about his shelves a beggarly account of empty boxes

Short shrift - … make a short shrift.

Shortcomings, admitting to one's own s. - If ever I were wilful-negligent it was my folly…

Shortcomings, sometimes s. prove useful - …full oft 'tis seen, our means secure us, and our mere defects prove our commodities.

Shout, loud shout. See 'Opinion, your op. on crowds and masses, blindly applauding the last mountebank - ... when you saw his chariot but appear, have you not made an universal shout…'

Shot, accurate s. See 'Precision, p. shooting - … and like an arrow shot from a well-experienced archer hits the mark..'

Shut up! See 'Speech, be quiet'

Shyness and speechlessness, you are unable to speak - What passion hangs these weights upon my tongue?

Shyness, love concealed - She never told her love, but let concealment, like a worm in the bud…

Sick, s. of the world. See 'World, pessimistic view of the w. - I am sick of this false world, and will love nought but even the mere necessities upon 't.

Sickness, s. doubtful - Many do keep their chambers are not sick.

Sickness, s. will not prevent you from going to the party. See 'Determination, d. to participate to an event or a party even if ill - … Not sickness should detain me.'

Sicily, (or any country) out of mind – Of that fatal country.. pr'ythee speak no more; whose very naming punishes me with the remembrance.

Siding with the losing party - …though my reason sits in the wind against me.

Sigh - (my heart) wounded it is, but with the eyes of a lady.

Sigh - .. adding to clouds more clouds with his deep sighs

Sigh - Wherefore breaks that sigh from the inward of thee?

Sigh, s., of distress fogging up the sky – … with our sighs we'll breathe the welkin dim…

Sight, a horrible s. - .. the object poisons sight; let it be hid.

Sight, heart-rendering - O thou side-piercing sight.

Sight, heart warming and cheering s. - thy sight, which should make our eyes flow with joy, hearts dance with comfort.

Sight, not seeing straight - Methinks I see these things with parted eye, when every thing seems double.

Sight, pitiful s. especially in an authority – A sight most pitiful in the meanest wretch...

Sight, ugly s. – ... most lamentable to behold.

Sight, unbearable sight - The sight of any of the house of York is as a fury to torment my soul.

Sight, unpleasant s. - ... to see this sight, it inks my very soul.

Sightseeing, acquiring knowledge of the town via s. - .. you beguile the time and feed your knowledge with viewing of the town.

Sightseeing, looking at people - ... we'll wander through the streets and note the qualities of people.

Sightseeing, s. suggestion, especially museums - ... let us satisfy our eyes with the memorials and the things of fame..

Sightseeing - ...I'll view the manners of the town...

Sightseeing - ...I will go lose myself and wander up and down to view the city.

Signal, momentous s. See 'Boss, b. calls you in and you imagine the worst – ... Hear it not, Duncan; for it is a knell that summons thee to heaven or to hell.

Silence, admired and meaningful – I like your silence, it the more shows off your wonder.

Silence, affected s. to imply wisdom. See 'Character, one who pretends to be thought clever by saying nothing - there are a sort of men whose visages...'

Silence, better keep quiet about the whole thing - It is enough you know; and it is fit what being known grows worse, to smother it.

Silence, criticized and unendorsed - ... for silence is only commendable in a neat's tongue dried and a maid not vendible.

Silence, discretion, s. advised - .... Bosom up my counsel, you'll find it wholesome.

Silence, exhortation to s. - Cry 'holla' to thy tongue, I prithee; it curvets unseasonably.

Silence, frozen into s. - They froze me into silence.

Silence, no answer to any question, remaining speechless - ... From this time forth I never will speak word.

Silence, nothing else to say - The rest is silence.

Silence, preferring s. to lying - I had rather seal my lips, than, to my peril, speak that which is not.

Silence, prompting to speak. See 'Speech, nothing said, silence, prompting to speak - Nothing will come of nothing, speak again.'

Silence, reason for s. – ... our argument is all too heavy to admit much talk.

Silence, s. as a symptom or evidence of happiness - Silence is the perfectest herald of joy, I were but little happy, if I could say how much.

Silence, s. as proof of innocence - The silence often of pure innocence persuades, when speaking fails.

Silence, s. commented on – ... methought her eyes had lost her tongue.

Silence, s. imposed - ... be you silent and attentive too, for he that interrupts him shall not live.

Silence, s. not a symptom of indifference - I hear, yet say not much, but think the more.

Silence, s. observed in person - ... thou hast spoken no word all this while.

Silence, s. of truth. See 'Truth, sometimes it cannot be told, conflict - ... That truth should be silent I had almost forgot.'

Silence, s. to prevent boring audience. See 'Excess, effects of e. - Sweets grown common lose their dear delight'

Silence, self-enforced - It is not nor it cannot come to good: but break, my heart; for I must hold my tongue.

Silence, self-imposed but reluctantly. See 'Patience, reluctantly silent - I'll be the pattern of all patience, I will say nothing.'

Silence, self-imposed in the circumstances - My heart is great; but it must break with silence…

Silence, silent for pretence. See 'Character, one who pretends to be thought clever by saying nothing - there are a sort of men whose visages…'

Silence, speaking in s. See 'Speech, s in silence - I'll speak to thee in silence'.

Silence, unable to answer - I am perplex'd, and know not what to say.

Silence, when you really would like her to be quiet. See 'Speech, be quiet – … for the benefit of silence would thou wert so too!'

Silliness or foolery repeated - … you see, sir, your fooling grows old, and people dislike it.

Similarity between two people, twins - An apple cleft in two is not more twin than these two creatures.'

Simile, s. not appreciated – Thou hast the most unsavoury similes.

Simile. s. OK but somewhat gross – A good swift simile, but something currish

Simony, assigning positions for bribes - … Cassius, you yourself are much condemn'd to have an itching palm.

Simplicity, proud of your s. See 'Faithfulness, f. restated - While others fish with craft for great opinion, I with great truth catch more simplicity…'

Simplicity, s. in giving away information – The flat transgression of a schoolboy…

Simplicity, value of s. See 'Duty, sense of d. and straightforwardness leading to good results – For never anything can be amiss when simpleness and duty tender it.'

Sin of self-love … See 'Self-love, s-l admitted as a sin - Sin of self-love possesseth all mine eye, and all my soul, and all my every part…'

Sin, cannot put a gloss on s. - You cannot make gross sins look clear

Sin, doubtful gains of s. - What win I, if I gain the thing I seek?…

Sin, rationale for s. - .. in the state of innocency Adam fell; and what should poor Jack Falstaff do in the days of villany?

Sin, s. not occasional, but chronic - Thy sin's not accidental, but a trade.

Sincere. See entries for 'Credentials, sincerity'

Sincerity, doubts about s. - I would I knew thy heart. – 'tis figured in my tongue.

Sincerity, question about s. - Speakest thou from thy heart? .. And from my soul too; or else beshrew them both.

Sincerity, s. as opposed to appearance – … they are actions that a man might play, but I have that within which passeth show…

Sincerity, s. emphatically stated in comparison with s. of opposing party. See 'Words, sincere w. - … his words come from his mouth, ours from our breast.'

Sincerity, s. of expression. See 'Invitation, i. to speak openly - Say as you think, and speak it from your souls.'

Sincerity, s. preferable to affected ceremony - Me rather had my heart might feel your love than my unpleased eye see your courtesy.

Sincerity, s. stated - I want that glib and oily art to speak and purpose not…

Sincerity, spoken sincerely - … and believe in heart that what you speak is in your conscience wash'd as pure as sin with baptism.

Sincerity, time to be sincere - The weight of this sad time we must obey, speak what we feel, not what we ought to say.

Sincerity, verifying a person's s. - But tell me true, for I must ever doubt…

Sincerity, words from the heart. See 'Words, sincere w. - .. his words come from his mouth, ours from our breast.'

Singer, a poor s. - An he had been a dog that should have howled thus, they would have hanged him.

Singing, pleasure to be sung to - … and she will sing the song that pleaseth you…

Singing, refusal to sing. See 'Music, singing, refusal to sing - … tax not so bad a voice, to slander music any more than once…'

Single - … thou consumest thyself in single life.

Sinful. See 'Man, corrupt m. - … smacking of every sin that has a name.'

Sinned against more than sinning. See entries for 'Defence from accusation'

Sinner, inventive s. – … commit the oldest sins the newest kind of ways…

Sins. See 'Confession, confessing to sins - … false of heart, light of ear, bloody of hand; hog in sloth, fox in stealth, wolf in greediness…'

Sins, unpleasant to hear of one's own s - few love to hear the sins they love to act.

Situation, acceptance (with some reservation) of a situation that cannot be changed - … I must excuse what cannot be amended.

Situation, accurate assessment of the s. - … Be it art or hap he hath spoken true.

Situation, from one bad s. to another - … Thus must I from the smoke into the smother…

Situation, general s. that you don't like - Uneven is the course, I like it not.

Situation, s. advantageous whatever the outcome - … my end can make good use of either…

Situation, s. confused and out of control. See "Invocation, despicable administration - hell is empty and all the devils are here.'

Situation, s. deteriorating, welcome overstayed - … methinks my favour here begins to warp.

Situation, s. dire and without cure – Bootless are plaints, and cureless are my wounds.

Situation, s. irreparable. See 'Relationship, r. beyond repair - … past hope, past cure, past help!'

Situation, s. redressed by hard means - … for the health and physic of our right we cannot deal but with the very hand of stern injustice and confused wrong.

Situation, s. tangled - What an intricate impeach is this!

Situation, tense s. - … every minute now should be the father of some stratagem: the times are wild.

Situation, uncertain s. and feeling uneasy about the outcome. See 'Feeling, gutsy negative f. - I know not what may fall; I like it not.'

Skepticism, excessive s. See 'Prejudice, inability to believe in exceptional performance - You judge it straight a thing impossible to compass wonders but by help of devils.'

Skepticism, s. about reported information or report, wanting to verify personally, See 'Observation, direct o. more trustworthy than official reports – Let every eye negotiate for itself and trust no agent.'

Skepticism, s. on the current state of affairs - When clouds appear, wise men put on their cloaks…

Skepticism, s. on the value of offered help - …to esteem a senseless help, when help past sense we deem.

Skin, her beautiful s. - That whiter skin of hers than snow, and smooth as monumental alabaster.

Skirt-chaser. See 'Character, skirt chaser - he woos both high and low, both rich and poor…'

Sky. See entries for 'Nature, sky'

Skyscrapers, s. described – (Tarsus) Whose towers bore heads so high they kiss'd the clouds.

Slander, being the object of s. - So shall my name with slander's tongue be wounded.

Slander, being the object of s. - To be a queen, and crown'd with infamy!

Slander, being the object of s. See 'Defence, d. from general accusations - pierced to the soul with slander's venom spear.' – 'Defence, d. from slander – it's slander, whose edge is sharper than the sword…'

Slander, calumny unavoidable – be thou as chaste as ice, as pure as snow, thou shalt not escape calumny.

Slander, calumny, unavoidable - No might nor greatness in mortality can censure 'scape..

Slander, killed by s. – Done to death by slanderous tongues…

Slander, no s. can come from a fool - .. there is no slander in an allowed fool, though he do nothing but rail

Slander, permanent characteristic of s. - For slander lives upon succession, for ever housed where it gets possession.

Slander, calumny, virtue not immune to s. - ..Virtue itself scapes not calumnious strokes..

Slander, record of calumnies against you – … none stands under more calumnious tongues than I myself.

Slander, s. as a tool of self-advancement – … some eternal villain… to get some office… have not devised this slander…

Slander, s. burning virtue – … calumny will sear virtue itself.

Slander, s. generated by rumor. See 'Rumor, r. fabricating slander – upon my tongue…'

Slander, s.'s venom spear. See 'Defence, d. from general accusations - pierced to the soul with slander's venom spear.'

Slander, sting of s. – … slander, whose sting is sharper than the sword's..

Slander, transported like poison - ..slander whose whisper o'er the word's diameter, as level as the cannon to his blank..

Slanderer, reaction to a s. - O, fie upon thee, slanderer!

Slanderer. See 'Character, slanderer, habitual slanderer - a slave whose gall coins slanders like a mint.'

Slanderers, s. to be punished. See 'Invocation, i. against rascals – … And put in every honest hand a whip to lash the rascals naked through the world…'

Slender, s. in former years. See 'Obesity, o. caused by stress - … when I was about thy years… I was not an eagle's talon in the waist…'

Sleep, s. creeping in - … o'er their brows death-counterfeiting sleep with leaden legs…

Sleep, s. or rest, time to adjourn the meeting - The deep of night is crept upon our talk and nature must obey necessity…

Sleep, 'Are you asleep?' - I have been broad awake two hours and more.

Sleep, able to s. in any conditions. See 'Nature, sea storm – and in the visitation of the winds, who take the ruffian billows by the top curling their monstrous heads'.

Sleep, before closing eyes and going to sleep – Ere I let fall the windows of mine eyes.

Sleep, denied to persons with great power and responsibility - Canst thou, O partial sleep, give thy repose to the wet sea-boy in an hour so rude…

Sleep, drowsiness - What a strange drowsiness possesses them!

Sleep, end of s. - … shake off the golden slumber of repose.

Sleep, excellent s. accompanied by pleasant dreams - The sweetest sleep, and fairest-boding dreams that ever enter'd in a drowsy head.

Sleep, feeling sleepy - Night hangs upon mine eyes; my bones would rest, that have but labour'd to attain this hour.

Sleep, feeling sleepy - Thou art inclined to sleep; 'tis a good dulness…

Sleep, feeling very sleepy. See 'Sleep, sound s., invocation. - … sleep, thou ape of death, lie dull upon her.'

Sleep, feeling very sleepy, mood of the believer - Sleep hath seized me wholly, to your protection I commend me, gods.

Sleep, lack of care promoting sound sleep – Thou hast no figures nor no fantasies, which busy care draws in the brains of men…

Sleep, lack of sleep creating anxiety - You lack the season of all natures, sleep.

Sleep, miserable and affected by nightmares - O, I have pass'd a miserable night, so full of ugly sights, of ghastly dreams.

Sleep, heaviness of soul - My soul is heavy,

and I fain would sleep.

Sleep, invocation to s. - ...sleep... steal me awhile from mine own company.

Sleep, prayer before s. – To thee I do commend my watchful soul, let fall the windows of mine eyes.

Sleep, s. after a hard day - ... the long day's task is done and we must sleep.

Sleep, s. as a tooth-ache reliever - Indeed, sir, he that sleeps feels not the tooth-ache.

Sleep, s. as rest - The crickets sing, and man's o'er-labour'd sense repairs itself by rest.

Sleep, s. fostered by music. See 'Music, melody lulling to sleep - lull'd with sound of sweetest melody'.

Sleep, s. habits influenced by lifestyle – Weariness can snore upon the flint, when resty sloth finds the down pillow hard.

Sleep, s. induced by a boring speaker - The best of rest is sleep and that thou oft provokest.

Sleep, s. induced by a lengthy s. See 'Story, reaction to a lengthy account - The strangeness of your story put heaviness in me.'

Sleep, s. interruption common with soldiers - ... 'tis the soldiers' life to have their balmy slumbers waked with strife.

Sleep, s. of death considered as rest - ... After life's fitful fever he sleeps well.

Sleep, s. or nap required to restore strength - I'll strive with troubled thoughts to take a nap..

Sleep, s. patterns and logic whereby late sleep is actually early rising - ... not to be abed after midnight is to be up betimes.

Sleep, s. prevented by care - ... and where care lodges, sleep will never lie.

Sleep, s. unprofitable - What is a man, if his chief good and market of his time be but to sleep and feed? a beast, no more.

Sleep, singing her to s. - Many a time he danc'd thee on his knee sung thee asleep, his loving breast thy pillow.

Sleep, sleeping remedy while lover is absent - Give me to drink mandragora that I might sleep out this great gap of time.

Sleep, someone fast asleep - As fast lock'd up in sleep as guiltless labour when lies starkly in the traveller's bones.

Sleep, soothing properties of s. - ... sleep that knits up the ravell'd sleeve of care…

Sleep, soothing properties of s., when it comes – It seldom visits sorrow; when it doth, it is a comforter.

Sleep, sound s., invocation. - … sleep, thou ape of death, lie dull upon her.

Sleep, sung to s. See 'Singing, pleasure to be sung to - ... and she will sing the song that pleaseth you…

Sleep, talking while asleep - There are a kind of men so loose of soul, that in their sleeps will mutter their affairs.

Sleep, talking while asleep – … infected minds to their deaf pillows will discharge their secrets.

Sleep, tired and in need of immediate s. - … Faintness constraineth me to measure out my length on this cold bed.

Sleep, too early to get up. See 'Awakening, too early to get up - … it argues a distempered head so soon to bid good morrow to thy bed.'

Sleep, troubled s. but better in the morning - I have been troubled in my sleep this night, but dawning day new comfort hath inspired.

Sleep, very sound s. - Though we seemed dead, we did but sleep.

Sleep, wish that s. could erase worries - I wish mine eyes would, with themselves, shut up my thoughts.

Sleeplessness caused by inner conflict - … in my heart there was a kind of fighting, that would not let me sleep.

Sleeplessness caused by

Sleeplessness caused by the weight of your responsibilities - … Can sleep so soundly as the wretched slave, who with a body fill'd and vacant mind..

Sleeplessness caused by the weight of your responsibilities - Uneasy lies the head that wears a crown.

Sleeplessness, s. caused by great responsibility - O polish'd perturbation! golden care! That keep'st the ports of slumber open wide…

Sleeplessness, invocation - O sleep, O gentle sleep, nature's soft nurse…

Sleeplessness, nightmares caused by impending critical decision - Between the acting of a dreadful thing and the first motion…'

Sleepwalking. - … A great perturbation in nature, to receive at once the benefit of sleep and do the effects of watching.

Smell, bad. See 'Odor, unpleasant.'

Smile, false s. See 'Character, false, cunning, shifting and perverse – I can smile and murder whiles I smile.' *** 'Disguise, hypocrisy - … some that smile have in their hearts, I fear, millions of mischiefs.'

Smile, forced s. with wrinkles. See 'Character, a hypocrite with a false smile - .. he does smile his face into more lines than are in the new map…'

Smile, hurtful. See 'Rejection, she says no with a smile that hurts more than soothes - Thou cuttest my head with a golden axe and smil'st upon the stroke that murders me.

Smile, mixed with a bit of sadness – Nobly he yokes a smiling with a sigh…

Smile, s. that hides sadness. See 'Sorrow, s. concealed behind a smile - … sorrow, that is couch'd in seeming gladness…'

Smiles, affected s. See 'Place, a dangerous p. – where we are there's daggers in men's smiles.

Small things make inferior men proud. See 'Insult, scorn, insult, arrogant villain, pretender'

Smooth runs the water. See 'Character, quiet but crafty - Smooth runs the water where the brook is deep.'

Snake, poisonous s. – His biting is immortal; those that do die of it do seldom or never recover.

Snake, s. preparing to attack - I fear me you but warm the starved snake, who, cherish'd in your breasts, will sting your hearts.

Snapper-up of unconsidered trifles. See 'Irrelevance, bound to i.'.

Snoring, snores with a meaning - Thou dost snore distinctly; there's meaning in thy snores

Snow that cools liver. See 'Reliability. "Am I going to be safe with you? Can I trust you? Etc.'

So far so good. See 'Fortune, f. so far good but..- Thus far our fortune keeps an upward course… but…I spy a black, suspicious, threatening cloud…'

So are you to my thoughts … See 'Love, food to the mind - So are you to my thoughts as food to life, or as sweet-seasoned showers are to the ground.'

Social issues, allowing people more than the bare necessities. See 'Opinion, your op. on sociological issues - minimum wage'.

Social issues, deprivation of means to live. See 'Life, l. made impossible without means to make a living. See 'Living means - … you take my life when you do take the means whereby I live…'

Social issues, exhortation to the better offs to think of the poor - … Expose thyself to feel what wretches feel that thou mayst shake the superflux to them…

Social issues, have the rich feel the sting of poverty - … so distribution should undo excess, and each man have enough.

Social issues, poor discriminated by the law. See 'Law, l. discriminatory and against the poor - … here's a fish hangs in the net….'

Social issues, proletariat's point of view - … the leanness that afflicts us, the object of our misery… our sufferance is a gain to them.

Social issues, strength in numbers and justice of claim - They say poor suitors have strong breaths; they shall know we have strong arms too.

Social issues, the rich care for the poor. See 'Politics, right wing p. - I tell you, friends, most charitable care have the patricians of you…'

Social position a handicap - … whose state is such that cannot choose but lend and give where she is sure to lose.

Social reforms and lawyers. See 'Opinion, your op. on lawyers - The first thing we do, let's kill all the lawyers.'

Social security. See 'Opinion, your op. on sociological issues, minimum wage - O, reason not the need: our basest beggars are in the poorest thing superfluous…'

Society, s. as the happiness of life - … for society, saith the text, is the happiness of life

Society, state of s. - … there is so a great a fever on goodness, that the dissolution of it must cure it. Novelty is only in request…

Soldier, a s. cannot weep. See 'Character, strong, unable to weep - I am a soldier, and unapt to weep, or to exclaim on fortune's fickleness.

Soldier, inconveniences of a s.'s life. See 'Sleep, s. interruption common with soldiers - … 'tis the soldiers' life to have their balmy slumbers waked with strife.'

Soldier, life of a s. – … all thy living lie in a pitched field.

Solicitations, answer to telephone s. – I am not in the giving vein to-day.

Solitude, need to be alone for a while, need for space - I and my bosom must debate awhile and then I would no other company.

Solitude, request to be left alone – I do beseech thee, grant me this, to leave me but a little to myself.

Solitude, s. and melancholy. See 'Country living, in praise of country living - … Here can I sit alone, unseen of any and to the nightingale's complaining notes…'

Soldier, s. and warring spirit – He that is truly dedicate to war hath no self-love…

Soldier, s. in love – … we are soldiers, and may that soldier a mere recreant prove…

Solitude, s. preferable – … I am best when least in company.

Solitude, wanting to be alone - … I must think of that which company would not be friendly to.

Solitude, wanting to be alone - … leave me to my self to-night, For I have need of many orisons to move the heavens to smile upon my state.

Solitude, wanting to be alone - … she hath abjured the company and sight of men.

Solution, any better s.? See 'Taming of a shrew, any better solution to tame a woman? - He that knows better how to tame a shrew…'

Solution, desperate s., anything better than this – Bid me lurk where serpents are, chain me with roaring bears.

Solution, masochistic solution to problem observed - Methinks you prescribe to yourself very preposterously.

Some rise by sin and some by virtue fall… See 'Injustice, justice unequally applied'

Something is rotten in the state of Denmark. See 'State of affairs, rotten state of affairs - Something is rotten in the state of Denmark'

Something wicked this way comes. See 'Arrival, a. of unpleasant or unwelcome character - By the pricking of my thumbs, something wicked this way comes.'

Song, a love s. See 'Music, m. that speaks to the heart – … It gives a very echo to the seat where Love is throned.'

Soon, too soon for action. See 'Haste, over h. – The mellow plum doth fall, the green sticks fast…'

Sorrow, causing madness and misjudgment - … grief hath so wrought on him, he takes false shadows for true substance.

Sorrow, disappointment, attitude towards s. See entries for 'Positive thinking'.

Sorrow, faked s. - … windy suspiration of forced breath.

Sorrow, one s. after another - One sorrow never comes but brings an heir, that may succeed as his inheritor.

Sorrow, one's s. greater than another's – If ancient sorrow be most reverend give mine the benefit of seniory…

Sorrow, s. concealed behind a smile - … sorrow, that is couch'd in seeming gladness…

Sorrow, s. inspiring desire for death – … Teach thou this sorrow how to make me die

Sorrow, s. preventing revenge. See 'Revenge, sorrow preventing r. - I have not another tear to shed.. then which way shall I find Revenge's cave?'

Sorrow, s. reduced by positive thinking. See 'Positive thinking and defiance towards setbacks – for gnarling sorrow hath less power to bite the man that mocks at it and sets it light.'

Sorrow, s. unfelt. See 'Hypocrisy, unfelt sorrow - To show an unfelt sorrow is an office which the false man does easy'.

Sorrow. See entries for 'Pain' *** 'Grief'

Sorrows, graduation in s. - Great griefs, I see, medicine the less.

Sorrows, s. coming all together. See 'Misfortunes piling up - When sorrows come, they come not single spies, but in battalions!'

Sorry, excusing yourself. See entries for 'Apologies'

Sorry, very sorry. See 'Feeling, f. very sorry - It strains me past the compass of my wits.'

Soul, guilty s. See 'Guilt, invitation to admit g. - … bear not along the clogging burthen of a guilty soul…'

Soul, independence of the s. See 'Freedom, f. of the soul – Every subject's duty is the king's; but every subject's soul is his own.'

Soul, s. as the housing for the mind. See 'Mind, out of his mind – … his pure brain .. doth, by the idle comment that it makes, foretell the ending of mortality'…

Soul, s. makes her own decisions. See 'Friend, one's soul chooses or elects someone to be a f. – Since my dear soul was mistress of her choice and could of men distinguish…'

Soundness, different kind of s. - … not as one would say, healthy; but so sound as things that are hollow.

Sounds, gentle sounds propitious to love - Whiles hounds and horns and sweet melodious birds be unto us as is a nurse's song…

Spade, calling a s. as s. See 'Definition, calling things by their names - We call a nettle but a nettle; and the faults of fools, but folly.'

Speak the speech. See 'Trippingly on the tongue - Speak the speech, I pray you, as I pronounced it to you, trippingly on the tongue.'

Speak, double s. - And be these juggling fiends no more believed, that palter with us in a double sense…

Speak, exhortation to s. – … If thou hast any sound, or use of voice, speak to me.

Speak, s. if you love me. See 'Love, if you love tell me what you think - … If thou dost love me, show me thy thought.'

Speak, s. openly, not to mince words - Give thy worst of thoughts the worst of words.

Speak what we feel. See 'Sincerity, time to be sincere - The weight of this sad time we must obey, speak what we feel, not what we ought to say.'

Speaker, boring and longwinded s. See 'Insult, a longwinded speaker of nonsense - What cracker is this ass, that deafs our ears with this abundance of superfluous breath.'

Speaker, excellent s. - … we, almost with ravish'd listening, could not find his hour of speech a minute.

Speaker, pleasant and delightful – … your fair discourse hath been as sugar.

Speaker, tedious s. - As tedious as a tired horse, a railing wife.

Speaker, what discourages a s. - … that contempt will kill the speaker's heart and quite divorce his memory from his part

Speaking frankly - Speak frankly as the wind.

Speaking the truth unintentionally. See 'Truth, t. unexpectedly uttered - …you have spoken truer than you purposed…'

Speaking to oneself - … with the incorporal air do hold discourse…

Speaking to oneself. See 'Vanity, v. or not? - it is not vain-glory for a man and his glass to confer in his own chamber.'

Speaking, public s., techniques of. See 'Gesturing, acting - .. do not saw the air too much with your hand, thus, but use all gently…'

Speaking, thinking carefully before s. See 'Words, weighing w. before speaking - …(thou) weigh'st thy words before thou givest them breath…'

Spectacle, a sad s. – The saddest spectacle that e'er I view'd.

Spectacle, wonderful s. that cannot be described - … a sight, which was to be seen, cannot be spoken of.

Speculation, s. on uncertain help or aid, unwise – Conjecture, expectation, and surmise of aids incertain should not be admitted.

Speech, annoying, boisterous and loud – You cram words into mine ear against the stomach of my sense.

Speech, argument exhausted - Do what you will; your wisdom be your guide.

Speech, be quiet - Be silent, boy; I profit not by thy talk.

Speech, be quiet – … for the benefit of silence would thou wert so too!'

Speech, better to be brief. See entries for 'Introduction. You will be brief'.

Speech, blunt speaking - …but mark me: to be received plain, I'll speak more gross.

Speech, brevity of s. promised - My short date of breath is not so long as is a tedious tale.

Speech, bringing a message of peace and substance - I hold the olive in my hand: my words are full of praise as matter.

Speech, change suggested in s. for the good of the speaker - … mend your speech a little lest you may mar your fortunes.

Speech, clarity in language requested - Ay, is it not a language, I speak?

Speech, clarity of language requested - A strange tongue makes my cause more strange, suspicious; pray, speak in English.

Speech, clarity of meaning requested – Be plain, good son, and homely in thy drift; riddling confession finds but riddling shrift.

Speech, clarity of meaning requested - Be plainer with me; let me know my trespass by its own visage…

Speech, comment on a good dinner s. - … your reasons at dinner have been sharp and sententious..

Speech, concision, be brief - If you be not mad, be gone; if you have reason, be brief:…

Speech, content of s. wiser than speaker realizes - Thou speakest wiser than thou art 'ware of.

Speech, determination to speak with courage - I'll use that tongue I have. If wit flows from it..

Speech, determined to speak and tell the truth - I will speak as liberal as the north, let heaven and men and devils, let them all…

Speech, disappointment or despair at her words - .. thou hast cleft my heart in twain

Speech, discouraging inflammatory s. See 'Exhortation, e. not to stir up trouble - Your speech is passion: but, pray you, stir no embers up.'

Speech, dislike of manner of s. more than content - I do not much dislike the matter, but the manner of his speech.

Speech, double speak or double tongue - you have a double tongue within your mask.

Speech, endings generic. See entries for 'Epilogue'.

Speech, exhortation to be brief to a girl-messenger - … be brief, my good she-Mercury

Speech, exhortation to speak and give information - Be not a niggard of your speech; how goes it?

Speech, exhortation to speak in mild tone - Speak sweetly, man, although thy looks be sour.

Speech, exhortation to speak properly - ... keep a good tongue in your head.

Speech, exhortation to speak without affectation. See 'Trippingly on the tongue - Speak the speech, I pray you, as I pronounced it to you, trippingly on the tongue.'

Speech, futility of speech. See 'Poetry, futility of p. – A speaker is but a prater; a rhyme is but a ballad.'

Speech, gaining time before speaking up - ... he's winding up the watch of his wit' by and by it will strike.

Speech, her words have completely overcome your resistance - I am vanquished; these haughty words of hers have batter'd me like roaring cannon-shot..

Speech, how or where did you learn all this - Where did you study all this goodly speech?

Speech, hurtful s. but within limits - I will speak daggers to her, but use none.

Speech, hurtful s. - Runs not this speech like iron through your blood?

Speech, incomprehensible s. and its correction - ... but wouldst gabble like a thing most brutish, I endow'd thy purposes with words that made them known.

Speech, insisting on delivering a s. - ... I would be loath to cast away my speech, for besides that it is excellently well penned…'

Speech, interruption of s. - Shall I hear more or shall I speak at this?

Speech, interruption of s. impolite - It is not well done, mark you now, to take the tales out of my mouth, ere it is made an end and finished.

Speech, interruption of s. not allowed. See 'Silence, s. imposed - .. be you silent and attentive too, for he that interrupts him shall not live.'

Speech, introduction to a flattering or praising s. - Lend me the flourish of all gentle tongues.

Speech, irritating content and incorrect English - … here will be an old abusing of God's patience, and the king's English.

Speech, lack of substance. See 'Rhetoric, all smoke, no substance - Sweet smoke of rhetoric.'

Speech, language, watch your language - Take heed, be wary how you place your words.

Speech, lengthy and annoying - This will last out a night in Russia when nights are longest there.

Speech, loud speaking, lower your voice - Thou but offend'st thy lungs to speak so loud.

Speech, melancholy mood not engendering cheerful s. - A heavy heart bears not a nimble tongue.

Speech, moving s. - This speech of yours hath moved me and shall perchance do good.

Speech, news, invitation to be clear and without riddles. See 'Speech, why giving me the run around? - What need'st thou run so many miles about when thou mayst tell thy tale the nearest way?'

Speech, nonsensical or meaningless - ... senseless speaking or a speaking such s sense cannot untie.

Speech, nonsensical or meaningless - ... this learned constable is too cunning to be understood.

Speech, nonsensical or meaningless - This is the silliest stuff that ever I heard

Speech, nonsensical or meaningless. See 'Dream or madness - 'Tis still a dream, or else such stuff as madmen tongue and brain not.'

Speech, nothing said, silence, prompting to speak - Nothing will come of nothing, speak again.

Speech, overwhelmed by speaker who does

not allow you to put a word in. See 'Character, one that always speaks and does not let anyone else put a word in - ... keep me company but two years more thou shalt not know the sound of thine own tongue.'

Speech, painful to speak - My heart is heavy, and mine age is weak.

Speech, pessimistic and unpleasant to make - ... discomfort guides my tongue and bids me speak of nothing but despair.

Speech, plea to stop hurtful s. - O, speak to me no more; these words, like daggers, enter in mine ears.

Speech, poor s. and poor action. See 'Speech, poor s. and poor action. See 'Insult, cowards, thief, thieves - ... he hath a killing tongue and a quiet sword... steal anything, and call it purchase.. few bad words are matched with few good deeds.'

Speech, prevented by tears. See 'Tears, t. that prevent speech - ... my tears, the moist impediments unto my speech.'

Speech, reaction (mildly ironic) at her reprimands or statements of principle - Well know they what they speak, that speak so wisely.

Speech, refraining from making inflammatory statements - With silence, nephew, be thou politic...

Speech, request to speak - I'd crave a word or two, the which shall turn you to no further harm than so much loss of time.

Speech, restraint from use of expletives due to anger – More bitterly could I expostulate...

Speech, restraint from use of expletives due to anger – ...the fair reverence of your highness curbs me from giving reigns and spurs to my free speech.

Speech, risks of free s. - ... And stood within the blank of his displeasure for my free speech!

Speech, s. and opinion polling – ... there shall I try in my oration, how the people take...

Speech, s. can undo the speaker - ... many a man's tongue shakes out his master's undoing.

Speech, s. completely unbecoming – You never spoke what did become you less than this.

Speech, speaking in jargon. See 'Jargon, people who use jargon - They have been at a great feast of languages, and stolen the scraps.'

Speech, s. in silence - I'll speak to thee in silence.

Speech, s. not easily forgotten – His speech sticks in my heart.

Speech, s. of envy. See 'Envy, e. shown in speech - Sharp Buckingham unburthens with his tongue the envious load that lies upon his heart.'

Speech, s. that gives pain. See 'Pain, p. at having to say this – I grieve at what I speak and am right sorry to repeat what follows.'

Speech, s. that shows the lowliness of birth or status – Shamest thou not...to let thy tongue detect thy base-born heart?

Speech, s. to further someone else's cause - .. I'll play the orator as if the golden fee for which I plead were for myself.

Speech, s. unpunished because of position of speaker - ... This tongue that runs so roundly in thy head, should run thy head from thy unreverent shoulders.

Speech, saying the right thing at the wrong time - The truth you speak doth lack some gentleness and time to speak it in.

Speech, short and clear s. makes it well accepted - Your plainness and your shortness please me well.

Speech, shortened by circumstances of urgency - More than I have said... the leisure and enforcement of the time forbids to dwell upon.

Speech, showing impatience and a self-centered personality – ... tying thine ear to no tongue but thine own.

Speech, simple s. delivered with modesty better than pompous eloquence - ... in the modesty of fearful duty, I read as much, as from the rattling tongue of saucy and audacious eloquence.

Speech, speak no more - O, speak no more! for I have heard too much.

Speech, speaking after a well known or skillful speaker - As in a theatre, the eyes of men, after a well grac'd actor leaves the stage…

Speech, speaking simply and honestly - I speak as my understanding instructs me and as mine honesty puts it to utterance.

Speech, speaking your mind emphatically - .. unloose thy long-imprison'd thoughts and let thy tongue be equal with thy heart.

Speech, stage-fright - As an unperfect actor on the stage who with his fear is put besides his part…

Speech, strange, tangled and incoherent way of expressing oneself . See 'Love, effects on words and expression - ... his words are a very fantastical banquet, just so many strange dishes.'

Speech, strange way of expressing oneself - He speaks not like a man of God's making.

Speech, summarizing the sequence and course of events - I carry winged time post on the lame feet of my rhyme.

Speech, tangled s. – His speech was like a tangled chain; nothing impaired, but all disordered.

Speech, unable to speak due to tears - My heart is not compact of flint and steel..

Speech, unable to speak due to vexation and frustration - Vexation almost stops my breath.

Speech, unable to speak or cry due to anger and desire for vengeance. See 'Tears, anger and thirst for revenge preventing t. and speech – For self-same wind that I should speak withal, is kindling coals that fire all my breast.'

Speech, understandable language or statement - You speak a language that I understand not.

Speech, undiplomatic mode of speaking - ... (he) is ill school'd in boulted language; meal and bran together he throws without distinction.

Speech, using permission to speak - .. since you have given me leave to speak, freely will I speak.

Speech, warning an enemy not to shame himself with his s. - Be not thy tongue thy own shame's orator.

Speech, well said – That's worthily as any ear can hear.

Speech, well said - Thou dost speak masterly.

Speech, well said but not changing the situation. See 'Words, w. that are no deeds - ... 'Tis a kind of good deed to say well and yet words are no deeds.'

Speech, well said or very appropriate - ... thou never spokest to better purpose.

Speech, why giving me the run around? - What need'st thou run so many miles about when thou mayst tell thy tale the nearest way?

Speech, wine and its effect on women's speech - The red wine first must rise in their fair cheeks, my lord; then we shall have 'em talk us to silence.

Speech, witticism misplaced or to be stopped - This civil war of wits..

Speech, words well said - 'Tis most nobly spoken.

Speechless - His tongue is now a stringless instrument.

Speechless - Within my mouth you have engaol'd my tongue.

Speechless in wonder. See 'Silence, admired and meaningful – I like your silence, it the more shows off your wonder.'

Speechless, awed in wonder – I am so attired in wonder I know not what to say.

Speechless, early in the morning. See 'Answering, buying time to answer - the charm dissolves apace... mantle their clearer reason'

Speechless, made speechless by her princely beauty - ... beauty's princely majesty is such, confounds the tongue, and makes the senses rough.

Speechless, plainly amazed - I am amazed and know not what to say.

Speechless, s. for happiness. See 'Happiness, h. beyond description - I cannot speak enough of this content; it stops me here; it is too much of joy.'

Speechless, stunned by her love - Madam, you have bereft me of all words, only my blood speaks to you in my veins…

Speechless, stunned by her beauty - You have bereft me of all words, lady.

Speed, amazing s. - I go, I go; look, how I go swifter than arrow from the Tartar's bow.

Speed, amazing s. - I'll put a girdle around the earth in forty minutes.

Speed, arriving very quickly at location - I am there before my legs.

Speed, command to be quick - Be Mercury, set feathers to thy heels …

Speed, faster than lightning. See 'Nature, lightning - Jove's lightnings, the precursors of the dreadful thunder-claps.'

Speed, let's do it quickly - If it were done when 't is done, then 't were well it were done quickly.

Speed, need for s. acknowledged - The spirit of the time shall teach me speed.

Speed, s. admired by the negligent. See 'Reprimand, speed and the negligent - Celerity is never more admired than by the negligent.'

Speed, d. of thought. See 'Thought, power of t. and imagination to travel instantly - For nimble thought can jump both sea and land as soon as think the place where he would be.'

Speed, speedy exit – as swift as swallow flies.

Speed, you can only run so fast. See entries for 'Running as fast as you can'.

Spelling, poor s. - What call you the town's name where Alexander the pig was porn?

Spin, hypocrisy, posturing - … With colours fairer painted their foul ends

Spin, how to re-interpret reality - You undergo too strict a paradox striving to make an ugly deed look fair.

Spin, interpreting the news. See 'Discipline, measured approach in establishing d. - We shall be call'd purgers, not murderers.'

Spin, positive s. on bad luck. See 'Fortune, f. re-interpreted, she is acting in disguise - … when fortune means to men most good she looks upon them with a threatening eye.'

Spin, posturing - … with forged quaint conceit to set a gloss upon his bold intent…

Spirit, invincible power of the s. See 'Freedom, f. of the spirit has no obstacles - … Nor stony tower, nor walls of beaten brass…'

Spirit, keeping up a good s. - And like the watchful minutes to the hour…

Spirit, s. undaunted. See 'Determination, d. shown even in extreme circumstances - I shall show the cinders of my spirits through the ashes of my chance.'

Sport, wrestling not a s. for ladies – … it is the first time that ever I heard breaking of ribs was sport for ladies.

Sport. See 'Battle, b. of the wits - there is no such sport, as sport by sport overthrown.'

Spring, looking like the s. – See where she comes, apparell'd like the spring.

Spring, s. and April - ….the spring, when proud-pied April dress'd in all his trim..

Spring, season for love and birds – When birds do sing, hey ding a ding, ding: sweet lovers love the spring.

Spy, private investigator - Saucy controllers of our private steps!

Squalor, living in physical and moral squalor. See 'Life, not really a l. - Canst thou believe thy living is a life, so stinkingly depending?'

Staff to beat a dog. See 'Injustice, unjust accusations and attack on the weak – .. A staff is quickly found to beat a dog.'

Stain, character's stain standing out. See 'Nature, clouds spoiling a clear sky - the more fair and crystal is the sky the uglier seem the clouds that in it fly.'

Stain, s. of crime unerasable. See 'Murder, m. cannot be erased - Here's the smell of the blood still: all the perfumes of Arabia will not sweeten this little hand.'

Stain, s. on a person's character - … it doth confirm another stain, as big as hell can hold …

Stalemate, s. between two equal powers - Blood hath bought blood, and blows have answered blows..

Standards, double s., hypocrisy. See 'Political (and personal) double standards - whiles I am a beggar, I will rail… there is no sin but to be rich…'

Star, s. versus sun, divided between two loves - At first I did adore a twinkling star, but now I worship a celestial sun.

Star, compliment. See 'Party, many fine ladies expected - look to behold this night earth treading stars, that make dark heaven light.'

Stars, s. determining our fate. See 'Destiny, stars in charge of us - It is the stars, the stars above us, govern our conditions…'

Stars, unpropitious s. See 'Misfortune, setback - My stars shine darkly over me'

Start line, at the start line - the game's afoot, England and St. George.

State of affairs, rotten state of affairs - Something is rotten in the state of Denmark

State of affairs, state diseased - You perceive the body of our kingdom how foul it is …

State of distress, cold and hungry - (I am) a man thronged up with cold, my veins are chill..

State of mind. See entries for 'Mind, state of m.'

Statement, making a formal s. - Let me be recorded by the righteous gods..

Statement, s. inappropriate and untrue. See 'Speech, s. completely unbecoming – you never spoke what did become you less than this.

Statements, s. worthy of an alehouse. See 'Joke, more nonsense than a j. - These are old fond paradoxes, to make fools laugh in the alehouse.'

Status, concern about s. excessive. See 'Care, too much care about worldly opinion counterproductive - You have too much respect upon the world, they lose it that do buy it with much care'.

Stay out of this. See 'Injunction, stay out of this - Come not between the dragon and his wrath.'

Stench. See entries for 'Odor, unpleasant'.

Sting operation - … the play's the thing wherein I'll catch the conscience of the king.

Stomach, s. ache. See 'Ache, stomach ache - There is so hot a summer in my bosom…'

Stomach, upset s. See 'Health-care, upset stomach - Prithee, do not turn me about; my stomach is not constant.'

Stones, not made of s. See 'Response, available for a positive response - … I am not made of stone but penetrable to your kind entreaties…'

Stones, s. more sympathetic than people – A stone is soft as wax,--tribunes more hard than stones…

Stop quarreling. See 'Quarrel, not really a q. - No quarrel, but a slight contention'

Storm, battling a s. See 'Life, life as a b. - Strives in his little world of man to out-scorn the to-and-fro-conflicting wind and rain.'

Storm, braving a s. – … to stand against the deep dread-bolted thunder?

Storm, indifferent to s. See 'Man, m. not shaken by extraordinary natural phenomena – Are not you moved, when all the sway of earth shakes like a thing unfirm?'

Storm, s. (metaphor for vexation) unavoidable - … we hear this fearful tempest sing, yet see no shelter to avoid the storm.

Story, if same story I don't like it - If it be

aught to the old tune, my lord, it is as fat and fulsome to mine ear, as howling after music.

Story, long boring s. and its effect on the audience – … their copious stories oftentimes begun end without audience and are never done.

Story, pitiful s. to tell – And if thou tell'st the heavy story right, upon my soul, the hearers will shed tears…

Story, reaction to a lengthy account - The strangeness of your story put heaviness in me.

Story, s. with record in painfulness – … never was a story of more woe than this of Juliet and her Romeo.

Story, sad s. to be told - … And in this harsh world draw thy breath in pain, to tell my story.

Strange, isn't it strange? - As strange as the thing I know not.

Strange bedfellows. See 'Adversity, a. assembles strange characters - .. misery acquaints a man with strange bedfellows.'

Strategy, s. for kingly popularity - … my state, seldom but sumptuous, showed like a feast…

Strategy, s. not to fight but fight if provoked - The sum of all our answer is but this…

Strategy, s. requires to stop and avoid any uncertainty – …(stop) every loop from whence the eye of reason may pry in upon us.

Strength, inside s. as opposed to outward show. See 'Trend setting by bucking the t. - To shame the guise o' the world, I will begin the fashion, less without and more within.

Strength, s. deriving from doing the right thing - ..Thrice is he arm'd, that hath his quarrel just..

Strength, s. in moderation – … if, with the sap of reason you would quench, or but allay, the fire of passion.

Strength, s. relative – … Troy in our weakness stands, not in her strength.

Strength, s. relative, wolf and sheep - … I know he would not be a wolf but that he sees the Romans are but sheep.

Strength, strong and resistant, as a cedar – See 'Resistance, strong and unconquerable - As on a mountain top the cedar shows that keep his leaves in spite of any storm.'

Strength. See also entries for 'Strong'

Strengthening, image of s. - …join you with them, like a rib of steel to make strength stronger.

Strengths, s. neutralizing themselves - One fire drives out one fire: one nail, one nail.

Stress, influence of s. on longevity - Shorten my days thou canst with sullen sorrow.

Stress, s. caused by discontent - For what's more miserable than discontent?

Strike, at the point of s. See 'Complaint, c. to the point of breaking, union's grievances – Know that our griefs are risen to the top and now at length they overflow their banks.' *** 'Justice, misapplied an

Strike, pre-emptive s. - Who 'scapes the lurking serpent's mortal sting.

Strong, as strong as - … As doth a rock against the chiding flood…

Strong, feeling s. – A thousand hearts are great within my bosom…

Stubbornness, s. becoming folly after reaching a limit - … And manhood is called foolery, when it stands against a falling fabric.

Study. See entries for 'Education'

Studying, against studying as mere erudition – Study is like the heaven's glorious sun that will not be deep-search'd with saucy looks…

Studying, bad effects of long s. - .. universal plodding poisons up the nimble spirits in the arteries..

Studying, limitation of s. and theoretical knowledge - … while it doth study to have what it would, it doth forget to do the thing it should

Studying, objective of s. - … that to know, which else we should not know…

Studying, passion for s. - ... transported and rapt in secret studies.
Stunned, mesmerized, in a trance - My thoughts are whirled like a potter's wheel; I know not where I am, nor what I do.
Stupidity, s. more striking in a person not normally stupid - Folly in fools bears not so strong a note...
Stupidity, s. not to be imitated, don't copy the fool - If the enemy is an ass and a fool, and a prating coxcomb...
Stupidity, s. universal, compared sarcastically to the sun - Foolery, sir, does walk about the orb, like the sun, it shines everywhere.
Subservience - ... and bend the dukedom yet unbow'd... to most ignoble stooping.
Substance, come to the point - More matter, with less art.
Substance, prevailing over form - ... is the adder better than the eel, because his painted skin contents the eye?
Subject, inquiring about secretly discussed s. – What were't worth to know the secret of your conference?
Subject, obsessive subject of conversation, horse - ... he doth nothing but talk of his horse...
Substitute, s. not as good as the original. See 'Vice-President, VP's importance dimmed when President returns - So doth the greater glory dim the less...'
Success, promised s. certain - ... doubt not but success will fashion the event in better shape than I can lay it down in likelihood.
Success, s. achieved through damaging policies - By devilish policy art thou grown great...
Success, s. always temporary, dangers of over-extension - Glory is like a circle in the water, which never ceaseth to enlarge itself...
Success, s. depending on a specific condition - ... our fortune lies upon this jump.
Success, s. depending on judgment. See 'Judgment, men's j. affected by circumstances and showing their character - ...I see men's judgments are a parcel of their fortunes...'
Success, s. impossible given the man and the circumstances. See 'Impossibility, cooling the sun with a fan - ... you may as well go about to turn the sun to ice...'
Success, s. impossible given the man and the circumstances –You may as well go stand upon the beach and bid the main flood bate his usual height...
Success, s. voiding complaints. See 'Defiance, d. based on the merit of your services – ... My services which I have done the signiory shall out-tongue his complaints.'
Success, s. through deceit - ... their deceit, contrived by art and baleful sorcery
Successes, past s. irrelevant - O, let not virtue seek remuneration for the thing it was....
Such is my love, to thee I so belong... See 'Love, ready to take any abuse for her l. – Such is my love, to thee I so belong, that for thy right myself will bear all wrong.'
Suddenness as a string of comparisons - ... momentary as a sound, swift as a shadow, short as any dream...
Suffering, insensible to s. – ... if you can be merry then, I'll say a man may weep upon his wedding-day.
Suffering, s. as a badge of valor – He's truly valiant that can wisely suffer...
Suffering, strategy against s. See entries for 'Positive thinking'.
Suggestion, horrible s. See 'Reaction, r. to a very strange suggestion - ... whose horrid image unfix my hair and make my seated heart knock at my ribs.'
Suicide, ethical issues – ... is it sin to rush into the secret house of death ere death dare come to us?
Suicide, s. always an option - ...life, being weary of these worldly bars, never lacks power to dismiss itself...

Suicide, s. as a liberation prevented – Is wretchedness deprived that benefit, to end itself by death?

Suicide, s. as a way out – … it is great to do that thing that ends all other deeds …

Suicide, s. as an act of desperation. See 'Desperation, ready to die - … Thou desperate pilot, now at once run on the dashing rocks thy sea-sick weary bark!'

Suicide, s. as freedom. See 'Freedom, f. as a personal achievement - … every bondman in his own hand bears the power to cancel his captivity.'

Suicide, s. vs. resignation to events. See 'Acceptance, a. of what may come - I do find it cowardly and vile for fear of what might fall…'

Summarizing – There's the short and the long of it.

Summer, like a s. day but only better - Shall I compare thee to a Summer's day? Thou art more lovely and more temperate..

Summer, not yet fall, not yet winter - … the year growing ancient, not yet on summer's death, nor on the birth of trembling winter.

Summer, s. registers statistically more crimes. See 'Weather, hot w. and its effects on temper - .. if we meet, we shall not 'scape a brawl; for now, these hot days, is the mad blood stirring.'

Summer, s. turning into winter - For never-resting time leads summer on to hideous winter…

Summer, s's distillation. See 'Age. Looking good for your age - …but flowers distilled though they with winter meet, lose but their show, their substance still lives sweet.'

Sun, s. contributing to celebrations. See 'Celebration, day of c. when even the sun contributes to the glory - … to solemnize this day, the glorious sun stays his course…'

Sunbeam, her beauty compared to the reflection of sunbeams on water - As plays the sun upon the glossy streams, twinkling another counterfeited beam..

Sunset, s., music and dessert. See lines 2,3 of 'Counsel, impact of c. from a man nearing death - More are men's ends mark'd than their lives before…'

Sunset. See entries for 'Nature, sunset'.

Sunshine, her face like s. - Vouchsafe to show the sunshine of your face…

Supernatural, existence of the s. a clear fact. - There are more things in heaven and earth, Horatio, than are dreamt of in your philosophy.

Superstition. See 'Mass, m. psychology – Look, how the world's poor people are amazed at apparitions, si

Supplement, s. to help imagination - Give me an ounce of civet, good apothecary, to sweeten my imagination.

Supply and demand economics. See 'Economy, price of hogs affected by religious conversions - this making of Christians will raise the price of hogs…'

Sure, are you sure? - Yea, as sure as I have a thought, or a soul.

Sure, are you sure? See 'Invocation, i. to an oath maintained - Let nature crush the sides o' the earth together and mar the seeds within!'

Surge, sea s. See 'Nature, things observed from above - … the murmuring surge, that on the unnumber'd idle pebbles chafes cannot be heard so high.

Surprise, extreme s. – … (You) surprise me to the very brink of tears.

Surprise, hold your s. for a moment – Season your admiration for a while.

Surprise, s. at meeting someone unexpectedly. See entries for 'Meeting, surprise at meeting him/her unexpectedly'.

Surprise, s. or wonder at meeting her or at her reaction - Am I in earth, in heaven, or in hell?…

Suspense, state of s. See 'Sleeplessness, nightmares caused by impending critical decision - Between the acting of a dreadful thing and the first motion… '

Suspicion, evidence of s. from expression - See, what a ready tongue suspicion hath!…
Suspicion, I suspect it is you - I do suspect thee very grievously.
Suspicion, mutual s. - Each jealous of the other, as the stung are of the adder.
Suspicion, reason to be suspicious - The bird that hath been limed in a bush with trembling wings misdoubteth every bush.
Suspicion, s. always follow a previous suspect - Suspicion all our lives shall be stuck full of eyes…
Suspicion, s. as a biting hurt inside the body – … the thought whereof doth, like a poisonous mineral, gnaw my inwards…
Suspicion, s. at terms offered by a crook - I like not fair terms and a villain's mind.
Suspicion, s. in a person – …but yet have I a mind that fears him much..
Suspicion, s. in a person – …our fears in Banquo stick deep.
Suspicion, s. of bad news. See 'Expression, e. clearly supporting the suspicion of bad news – hath by instinct knowledge from others' eyes'.
Suspicion, s. of cooking the books rejected. See 'Accounting, a. above board, request for an audit -.. call me before the exactest auditors…'
Suspicion, s. rejected - Heaven make you better than your thoughts!
Suspicion, s. removed and trust restored - I rather will suspect the sun with cold than thee with wantonness.
Suspicion, s. sign of guilty mind - Suspicion always haunts the guilty mind, the thief doth fear each bush an officer.
Suspicion, s. that show of love is insincere - … you may think my love was crafty love and call it cunning.
Suspicion, shame on the suspicious – Honi soit qui mal y pense.
Suspicion, will to consider s. as truth – …I know not if't be true; but I for mere suspicion in that kind will do as if for surety.
Swearing, invitation not to swear. See 'Divine, goddess of my idolatry - Do not swear at all.. or by thy gracious self, which is the god of my idolatry.'
Swearing, s. as a sign of strong manhood - … a terrible oath, with a swaggering accent sharply twanged off…
Swearing, s. by the moon. See 'Reassurance, answer to demands for r. – O, swear not by the moon, the inconstant moon, that monthly changes in her circle orb…'
Swearing. See entries for 'Oaths'.
Sweat - Falstaff sweats to death and lards the lean earth as he walks along…
Sweet are the uses of adversity. See 'Adversity, a. put to good use - Sweet are the uses of adversity…'
Sweet to the sweet. . See 'Flowers, homage of f - Sweets to the sweet'
Sweets, too many s. revolting. See 'Excess, e. leads to loathing – They surfeited with honey and began to loathe the taste of sweetness…'
Swift as a shadow. See 'Confusion, how quickly things become confused -.. so quick bright things come to confusion.'
Syllogism, s. applied - … if thou never wast at court, thou never sawest good manners…
Sympathy, fed up with s. See 'Fed up with comforting efforts - I'll hate him everlastingly that bids me be of comfort any more.'
Sympathy, false s. - Came he right now to sing a raven's note whose dismal tune bereft my vital powers.
Symptoms, s. observed but not conclusive - … many likelihoods informed me of this before, which hung so tottering in the balance..
Symptoms, s. of a potentially dangerous person - .. He reads much; he is a great observer, and he looks quite through the deeds of men.
System, corrupt s. cannot correct its own mistakes - … correction lieth in those hands which make the fault we cannot correct…

1321

System, s. or device suitable to your purpose – … here an engine fit for my proceeding.

'T is well said again… See 'Words, w. that are no deeds - … 'Tis a kind of good deed to say well and yet words are no deeds.'

Table talk - … let it serve for table-talk' then… I shall digest it.

Tailor, t. ready to fit suitable dress for beautiful woman. See 'Dress, fitting the d. - The tailor stays thy leisure to deck thy body with his ruffling treasure.'

Tailor, using a t.'s skill to enhance your image. See 'Image building or restoration - I'll be at charges for a looking glass and entertain a score or two of tailors…'

Taint, a fault that obscures other virtues - … the dram of base doth all the noble substance often dout to his own scandal.

Tale, t. illustrating idea. See 'Explanation, e. by way of an example - … I shall tell you a pretty tale; it may be, you have heard it.

Tale, strange t. See 'News, n. strange almost a tale - his is the strangest tale that ever I heard.'

Talents, t. or qualities misused – all his virtues, not virtuously on his own part beheld, do in our eyes begin to lose their gloss.

Talents, t. to be used – Heaven doth with us as we with torches do, not light them for themselves…

Talk, all t. and no substance – … mere prattle, without practise…

Talk, I wish to talk to you - Vouchsafe me a word; it does concern you near.

Talk, idle talk, let's put a stop to it - .. no more of this unprofitable chat.

Talk, invitation to straight t. however negative - Speak to me home, mince not the general tongue…

Talk, let me talk to you - Hie thee hither that I may pour my spirits in thine ear.

Talk, subject t. when old - … when we shall hear the rain and wind beat dark December

Talk, table t. See 'Table talk - … let it serve for table-talk' then… I shall digest it.'

Talk, talk is no action - … we will not stand to prate, talkers are no doers.

Talk, talking seriously now - But, turning these jests out of service, let us talk in good earnest.

Talker, compulsive t. – … what a spendthrift is he of his tongue!

Talker, idle t. – See 'Character, c. who says a lot of nonsense - Gratiano speaks an infinite deal of nothing…'

Taming of a shrew, any better solution to tame a woman? - He that knows better how to tame a shrew…

Task, heavy t. imposed, to speak of your pain - A heavier task could not have been imposed than I to speak my griefs unspeakable.

Task, need to finish the t. after initial success – let us not leave till all our own be won.

Task, proud to carry it out - This shall I undertake, and 't is a burden, which I am proud to bear.

Task, t. better fitted to a woman. See 'Woman, task better left to a w. – the office becomes a woman best.'

Task, t. carried out but reluctantly - Thither I must, although against my will, for servants must their masters' minds fulfil.

Task, t. impossible and unrealistic - … the task he undertakes is numbering sands and drinking oceans dry.

Task, t. still incomplete - We are yet but young in deed.

Task, t. that can be completed with very little effort - … for very little pains will bring this labour to a happy end.

Task, t. will be accomplished – … by the grace of Grace we will perform in measure, time and place.

Task, willingness to undertake an unpleasant t. - Many can brook the weather, that love not the wind.

Tavern, going to the t. See 'Bar, going to b.

to find solace in alcohol and company - I will see what physic the tavern affords.'

Taverns, drawback of t. - … no more tavern bills; which are often the sadness of parting as the procuring of mirth..

Tax, t. collection – We are inforced to farm our royal realm; the revenue whereof shall furnish us… large sums of gold

Tax, t. collector, how to handle a tax c. – My riches are these poor habiliments…

Tax, t. revolt - we will nothing pay for wearing our own noses.

Taxation, t. causing revolt. See 'Rebellion, r. caused by heavy taxation – … Unfit for other life, compell'd by hunger and lack of other means…'

Taxation, t. recipe of hatred – Their love lies in their purses and whoso empties them by so much fills their hearts with deadly hate.

Taxes, overbearing t. – … These exactions … are most pestilent to the bearing…

Teacher, a t. of teachers - She seems a mistress to most that teach.

Teacher, praising the t. that had such an outstanding student. See 'Erudition, master of e. – … Thrice famed, beyond all erudition.'

Teacher, teaching a t. not appropriate. See 'Modesty, refusal to teach an expert - to teach a teacher ill beseemeth me'.

Teachers, treacherous t. See 'Deception, d. from false teachers - Thus may poor fools believe false teachers…'

Tediousness, t. of lovers' stories. See 'Story, long boring s. and its effect on the audience – … their copious stories oftentimes begun end without audience and are never done.'

Tediousness. See 'Speech, lengthy and annoying - This will last out a night in Russia when nights are longest there.'

Tear, fall not a t. See 'Cry, do not cry – fall not a tear'.

Tears unbecoming - … he weeps like a wench that hath shed her milk.

Tears, anger and thirst for revenge preventing t. and speech – For self-same wind that I should speak withal, is kindling coals that fire all my breast.

Tears, compared to pearls – a sea of melting pearls.

Tears, difficult to hold back t. - Beshrew me, but his passions move me so, that hardly can I check my eyes from tears.

Tears, drying off her t. - Let me wipe off this honorable dew that silverly doth progress on thy cheeks.

Tears, false t. See 'Character, false, cunning, shifting and perverse – I can smile and murder whiles I smile.' *** 'Remorse, false r., false tears - Trust not those cunning waters of his eyes…'

Tears, false t., induced by onions - An onion will do well for such a shift; which in a napkin being close conveyed, shall in despite force a watery eye.

Tears, flood of t. from a person who usually does not cry - … drop tears as fast as the Arabian trees their medicinal gum.

Tears, moved to t. - Beshrew me, but his passion moves me so that hardly can I cheque my eyes from tears.

Tears, not called for - Back, foolish tears, back to your native spring, your tributary drops belong to woe…

Tears, not conducive to love. See 'Sadness, s. not the natural condition for love - Venus smiles not in a house of tears.'

Tears, prophetic. See 'Forecast, gloomy f. . – … lend me ten thousand eyes and will fill them with prophetic tears.'

Tears, sarcastic promise of t. - Lend me a fool's heart and a woman's eyes and I'll beweep…

Tears, shedding t. - Let my tears stanch the earth's dry appetite.

Tears, t. and sighs. See 'Sigh - Wherefore breaks that sigh from the inward of thee?'

Tears, t. banned and substituted by revenge - To weep is to make less the depth of grief: tears, then, for babes; blows and revenge for me.

Tears, t. beginning to flow - my heart is drowned with grief whose flood begins to flow within mine eyes.

Tears, t. brought in by tragedy – ... what showers arise, blown with the windy tempest of my heart.

Tears, t. down the beard - His tears run down his beard, like winter's drops from eaves of reeds.

Tears, t. in an onion. See 'Crying not called for, on the contrary - the tears live in an onion that should water this sorrow.'

Tears, t. in great volume – ... one whose subdued eyes drop tears as fast as the Arabian trees their medicinal gum.

Tears, t. ineffective though they show empathy - ... tears show their love, but want their remedies...

Tears, t. of joy – Better to weep at joy than to joy at weeping.

Tears, t. of joy – I am a fool to weep at what I am glad of.

Tears, t. of laughter. See 'Laughter, laughing to tears -... I must confess, made nine eyes water; but more merry tears the passion of loud laughter never shed.'

Tears, t. of love – The April 's in her eyes: it is love's spring...

Tears, t. on hand - Give me thy hand that I may dew it with my mournful tears.

Tears, t. pouring out like heavy rain - And with the southern clouds contend in tears, theirs for the earth's increase, mine for my sorrows.

Tears, t. prompted by

Tears, t. that prevent speech - ... my tears, the moist impediments unto my speech.

Tears, t. that prevent speech – He has strangled his language in his tears.

Tears, t. transformed into orient pearls. See 'Happiness, promise of return to h. - ...The liquid drops of tears that you have shed shall come again, transform'd to orient pearl...'

Tears, unmanly and prompted by moving scene - These foolish drops do something drown my manly spirit.

Tears, unstoppable - Mine eyes cannot hold out water, methinks.

Tears, unstoppable t. at a moving sight – ... And all my mother came into mine eyes and gave me up to tears.

Tediousness, t. in everything being always the same – If all the year were playing holidays, to sport would be as tedious as to work.

Teen-agers, complaint against t-a. – I would there were no age between sixteen and three-and-twenty, or that youth would sleep out the rest...

Telemarketers, soliciting t. See 'Solicitations, answer to telephone s. – I am not in the giving vein to-day.'

Telephone, who is calling – Your servant and your friend, one that attends your ladyship's command.

Tell me something about yourself. See entries for 'Self-assessment' *** 'Char

Telling it like it is. See 'Oratory, lack of o. claimed but ... - ... little shall I

Temper, explaining a loss of t. - Thou must not take my former sharpness ill...

Temperance, one who does not know it - Though you can guess what temperance should be, you know not what it is.

Temperance, t. as a cure - ... temperance; that's the appliance only which your disease requires.

Temptation, t. arising from hearing tempting information - ... For by our ears our hearts oft tainted be.

Temptation, t. by devil - Shall I be tempted of the devil thus?

Temptation, t. different from sin - 'Tis one thing to be tempted, Escalus, another thing to fall.

Temptation, t. in the form of a fair and modest girl – O cunning enemy, that, to catch a saint, with saints dost bait thy hook!

Temptation, t. taking up false appearances - Devils soonest tempt, resembling spirits of light

Temptation, t. to steal. See 'Thieves, temptation to steal – Rich preys make true men thieves.'

Temptation, overconfidence in our ability to resist t. See 'Confidence, overconfidence challenges the frailty of our powers - And sometimes we are devils to ourselves…'

Temptation. See 'Guilt, tempter or tempted guiltier - The tempter or the tempted, who sins most, ha?" *** 'Crime, c. prompted by opportunity - How oft the sight of means to do ill deeds makes ill deeds done'.

Temptations, t. of the world. See line 3 in 'Men, m. of strong temper - …brave conquerors… that war against your own affections.'

Tennis-court of life. See 'Fortune, mistreated by f. - A man whom both the waters and the wind…have made a ball for them to play upon'.

Termination - .. thus part we rich in sorrow, parting poor.

Termination, revenge for unfair t. See 'Revenge, vowing revenge for being terminated unfairly - My ashes, as the phoenix, may bring forth a bird that will revenge upon you all.'

Terminator – … he was a thing of blood, whose every motion was timed with dying cries.

Terrorists, t. or freedom fighters. See 'Freedom, f. fighters or terrorists? - … So often shall the knot of us be call'd the men that gave their country liberty'.

Testing, t. the skill or determination of a man – … now do I play the touch, if thou be current gold indeed.

Tewksbury mustard, see 'Character, not very bright – … his wit is as thick as Tewksbury mustard.'

Thank me no thankings. See 'Thanks rejected - Thank me no thankings, nor, proud me no prouds.'

Thank you for unexpected visit, answer or honor - My poor house to visit it is a surplus of your grace, which never my life may last to answer.

Thank you. See entries for 'Gratitude, g. expressed and responded to'

Thankful, great cause to be t. - .. we have all great cause to give great thanks.

Thanks but no thanks - Proffers not took, reap thanks for their reward.

Thanks but no thanks (to a proposal of questionable morality or legality). See 'Gain, g. from crime illusory - … Who buys a minute's mirth to wail a week? Or sells eternity to get a toy?'

Thanks profusely given. See 'Opinion, your op. on profusely given thanks - … when a man thanks me heartily…'

Thanks rejected - Thank me no thankings, nor, proud me no prouds.

Thanks to all. See 'Epilogue to a presentation'.

Thanks, follow up to 'thank-you' and alternatives to 'you welcome'. See entries for 'Gratitude, g. expressed and responded to'.

Thanks, multiple t. - I can no more answer make, but thanks and thanks, and ever thanks.

That one may smile, and smile, and be a villain. See 'Human nature, pessimism about h.n. – I set it down, that one may smile, and smile, and be a villain; at least I'm sure it may be so in Denmark.'

That time of year… See 'Age, admitting to being old - That time of year thou mayst in me behold…'

The all of all - The very all of all is…

The be-all and end-all. See 'Act, extreme a. shaping all things to come - this blow be the be-all and the end-all here..'

The best of all. See 'Woman, best of all - She excels each mortal thing upon the dull earth dwelling.' *** 'Woman, perfect - Divine perfection of a woman.' *** 'Entries for

'Best, compliment, you are the best.'

The better part of valour ... See 'Cowardice, c. or discretion - The better part of valour is, discretion'.

The cause is in my will. .See 'Power, privilege of p. to give no explanations'

The constant service of the antique world... See 'Times, good old t, better then, less greed than now - ... how well in thee appears the constant service of the antique world...'

The course of true love never did run smooth . See 'The course of true love never did run smooth . See 'Love, l. never smooth - ... the course of true love never did run smooth.'

The devil can cite scriptures for his purpose... See 'Hypocrisy, false conclusion from a righteous example.'

The end crowns all and that old common arbitrator, Time, will one day end it. See 'Time, the great arbitrator'

The expense of spirit in a waste of shame... See 'Lust, perhaps reprehensible but inevitable - All this the world well knows yet none knows well to shun the heaven that leads men to this hell.'

The fewer men ... See 'People, the fewer the better for a great enterprise - ... the fewer men, the greater share of honour.'

The lady doth protest too much. See 'Affectation – the lady doth protest too much, methinks.'

The lowest and most dejected thing of fortune. See 'Bad, from bad to good better than from good to bad - ... The lamentable change is from the best; the worst returns to laughter.'

The man that hath no music in himself... is fit for treasons, stratagems and spoils. See 'Music, distrust for men who do not like music.'

The means that heaven yields... See 'Action, doing the best with the means available - The means that heaven yields must be embraced and not neglected.'

The milk of human kindness. See 'Character, kind, perhaps too much - .. it is too full o' the milk of human kindness..'

The miserable have no other medicine but only hope. See 'Hope, h. as the refuge of the distressed'

The most unkindest cut of all. See 'Unfairness, extreme u. – This was the most unkindest cut of all.'

The play's the thing. See 'Sting operation - ... the play 's the thing wherein I'll catch the conscience of the king..

The rich are getting richer. See 'Social issues, proletariat's point of view - .. the leanness that afflicts us, the object of our misery... our sufferance is a gain to them.'

The robbed that smiles steals something from the thief... See 'Attitude, a. towards what is past and cannot be changed - To mourn a mischief that is past and gone...'

The short and the long of it (one of everyday expressions from Shakespeare). See 'Summarizing – There's the short and the long of it.'

The taste of sweetness. See 'Excess, e. leads to loathing – They surfeited with honey and began to loathe the taste of sweetness...'

The tender leaves of hope. See 'Fortune, meditation on the fall of f. - This is the state of man; today he puts forth the tender leaves of hope...'

The time of life is short!... See 'Life, short and therefore to be well lived - ... the time of life is short! To spend that shortness basely were too long.'

The time is out of joint. See 'Correction, regret for having to take corrective action – that ever I was born to set it right.'

The violet smells to him... See 'Authority, king, no different from other men - ... the king is but a man, as I am: the violet smells to him as it doth to me."

The web of our life... See 'Life, a combination of good and bad - The web of our life is of a mingled yarn, good and ill go together…'

The weight of this sad time we must obey, speak what we feel, not what we ought to say. See 'Sincerity, time to be sincere'

The woman's part in me. See 'Women, w. as repositories of vice - .. Could I find out the woman's part in me!'

The world's mine oyster. See 'Opportunity, the world as a source of o - …then the world's mine oyster'.

Theater, plays, their purpose. See 'Art and theatrical representation – … the purpose of playing… to hold, the mirror up to nature…'

Theft, t. and proper terminology - 'Convey,' the wise call it. 'Steal!' foh! a fico for the phrase!

Theft, t. as purchase. See 'Insult, cowards, thief, thieves - … he hath a killing tongue and a quiet sword… steal anything, and call it purchase… few bad words are matched with few good deeds.'

Theft, t. probably unnoticed – … easy it is of a cut loaf to steal a shive, we know.

Theory and practice, from one to the other - … the art and practic part of life must be the mistress to this theoric.

Theory and practice, their difference - … they would be better if well followed.

Theory and practice, their difference - I can easier teach twenty what were good to be done..

Theory and practice, their difference - If to do were as easy as to know what were good to do..

There are many events in the womb of time, which will be delivered. See 'Future, the f. will tell.'

There are more things in heaven and earth… See 'Supernatural, existence of the s. a clear fact. - There are more things in heaven and earth, Horatio, than are dreamt of in your philosophy.'

There is a history in all men's lives… See 'Life, l.'s history of a person as a predictor of future performance – there is a history in all men's lives.'

There's no art to find the mind's construction in the face… See 'Physiognomy, p. unreliable'

There is some soul of goodness …See 'Adversity, some g. can be found in a. - There is some soul of goodness in things evil…

There is a tide in the affairs of men. See 'Opportunity, why it should not be missed - There is a tide in the affairs of men, which, taken at the flood, leads on to fortune, omitted….'

There is nothing good or bad. See ''Thought, t. as the arbiter of good or bad - .. for there is nothing either good or bad, but thinking makes it so.'

There is occasions and causes… See 'Philosophy, there is a reason for everything - There is occasions and causes why and wherefore in all things.'

There shall be in England… See 'Politicians' promises, price reductions and more plentiful manufactured products - There shall be in England seven halfpenny loaves sold for a penny'

There's a divinity that shapes our ends… See 'Destiny, d. shaping our ends - … There's a divinity that shapes our ends, rough-hew them how we will.'

There's a special providence… See 'Destiny, resignation to d. - … there's a special providence in the fall of a sparrow…'

There's the rub. See 'Death, d., sleep and dreams - To sleep: perchance to dream: ay, there's the rub…'

Therefore my age is as lusty as winter, frosty, but kindly. See 'Age. You admit that you are old but explain why and how you have maintained your youthful strength – Though I look old yet I am strong and lusty…'

These fellows of infinite tongue… See 'Lovers, eloquent lovers not reliable - … these fellows of infinite tongue that can

1327

rhyme themselves into ladies' favours…'

They say best men are moulded out of faults… See 'Apologies for past poor behavior '

Thief, qualifications for a t. – … to have an open ear, a quick eye, and a nimble hand, is necessary for a cut-purse…

Thievery, recognized as such but tolerable. See 'Racket, a good racket – .. It is an honorable kind of thievery.'

Thievery, t. universal – The sun's a thief, and with his great attraction…

Thieves, comparing your winning enemies to t. - So triumph thieves upon their conquer'd booty…

Thieves, euphemistic definition - We are not thieves, but men that much do want.

Thieves, no honesty. See 'Invocation, no honesty among thieves - … a plague upon it when thieves cannot be true one to another!'

Thieves, t. in high places - … there is boundless theft in limited professions.

Thieves, temptation to steal – Rich preys make true men thieves.

Thieving, when t. justified. See 'Judges, j. as thieves - Thieves for their robbery have authority when judges steal themselves.'

Thieving. See 'Character, coward and thieving – … they will steal any thing, and call it purchase'.

Thing of darkness. See 'Modesty, m. in possession – … this thing of darkness acknowledge mine.'

Things change all the time. See 'Destiny, d. inscrutable – ... how chances mock, and changes fill the cup of alteration with divers liquors!'

Things done well. See 'Excellence, e. has no fear – things done well and with a care exempt themselves from fear.'

Thing inconsequential. See 'Bubbles - The earth hath bubbles, as the water has and these are of them.'

Things that do not go together - … they do no more adhere and keep place together than

the Hundredth Psalm to the tune of 'Green Sleeves'.

Thinking, t. about nothing. See 'Mind, state of m. thinking about nothing and sad - … though, in thinking, on no thought I think.'

Thinking, t. before speaking. See 'Words, t. before speaking - I know thou'rt full of love and honesty, and weigh'st thy words before thou giv'st them breath.'

Thinking, t. quickly - Faster than spring-time showers comes thought on thought…

Thirst, parched lips begging for water - … entreat the north to make his bleak wind kiss my parched lips..

This comes too near the praising of myself, no more of it. See 'Modesty, self-praise to be avoided.'

This is the excellent foppery of the world… See 'Philosophical considerations, unwillingness to take responsibility for our mistakes - This is the excellent foppery of the world…'

Thou cuttest my head with a golden axe. See 'Rejection, she says no with a smile that hurts more than soothes - Thou cuttest my head with a golden axe and smil'st upon the stroke that murders me.'

Thou for whom Jove would swear … See 'Beauty, b. superior even to a goddess - Thou for whom Jove would swear Juno but an Ethiope were…'

Thou mak'st faults graces that to thee resort. See 'Apologies unnecessary, on the contrary.'

Thou speakest wiser… See 'Speech, content of s. wiser than speaker realizes - Thou speakest wiser than thou art 'ware of.'

Thought, evil t. to be banned. See 'Suspicion, shame on the suspicious – Honi soit qui mal y pense.'

Thought, forced to think the unthinkable – (You) prick my tender patience, to those thoughts which honour and allegiance cannot think.

Thought, monstrous t. kept hidden - … As if there were some monster in his thought too hideous to be shown.

Thought, power of t. and imagination to travel instantly - For nimble thought can jump both sea and land as soon as think the place where he would be.

Thought, reticence to disclose or trust one's t. – Utter my thoughts? Why, say they are vile and false…

Thought, speed of t. - … In motion of no less celerity than that of thought.

Thought, t. absent from non-thinkers - … for cogitation resides not in that man that does not think it.

Thought, t. as the arbiter of good or bad - … for there is nothing either good or bad, but thinking makes it so.

Thought, t. as the slave of life, expressing pessimism - … thought's the slave of life, and life time's fool; and time, that takes survey of all the world, must have a stop.

Thought, t. is no action. See 'Determination and resolution. - My will is back'd with resolution, thoughts are but dreams till their effects be tried…'

Thought, t. not to be considered - O monstrous fault, to harbour such a thought! **are** but d

Thoughts, ambitious t. See 'Ambition, ambitious thoughts - Thoughts tending to ambition, they do plot unlikely wonders…'

Thoughts, harboring murderous t. See 'Perception, you want me dead - thou hidest a thousand daggers in thy thoughts…'

Thoughts, morbid or self-destructive t. to be avoided - You do unbend your noble strength, to think so brainsickly of things.

Thoughts, t. better expressed in writing. See 'Writing, w. preferred to speech - I'll call for pen and ink, and write my mind.'

Thoughts, t. compared to people - … And these same thoughts people this little world..

Thoughts, t. of ambition. See 'Ambition, ambitious thoughts - Thoughts tending to ambition, they do plot unlikely wonders…'

Thoughts, t. of consolation. See

'Consolation, thoughts of c. in sharing misfortunes - … that they are not the first of fortune's slaves…'

Thoughts, t. running wild - My thoughts were like unbridled children, grown too headstrong for their mother.

Thoughts, t. to rationalize a personal situation. See 'Consolation, thoughts of c. in sharing misfortunes - … that they are not the first of fortune's slaves…'

Threat, friendly t. if he does not celebrate. See 'Celebrations, c. for victory or any happy event - And he that throws not up his cap for joy…'

Threat, I will remember you - I'll note you in my book of memory to scourge for this apprehension.

Threat, not an idle t. - It is the Prince of Wales that threatens thee who never promiseth but he means to pay…

Threat, proper reaction to a t. See 'Attitude, posture and its importance - Let not the world see fear and sad distrust… threaten the threatener…'

Threat, t. from an angered friend - Do not presume too much upon my love, I may do that I shall be sorry for.

Threat, t. of blood and revenge - … I'll use the advantage of my power and lay the summer's dust with showers of blood…

Threat, t. of violence. See 'Violence, v. threatened - .. (I'll) make a quagmire of your mingled brains.'

Threat, t. of whipping etc. See 'Punishment, p. for bringing unpleasant news - Thou shalt be whipp'd with wire, and stew'd in brine, smarting in lingering pickle.'

Threat, t. to have his head. See 'Insult, i. plus threat - Abominable Gloucester, guard thy head; for I intend to have it ere long.'

Threat, t. towards complaining employee - If thou more murmur'st, I will rend an oak and peg thee in his knotty entrails…

Threat, t. useless - … spare your threats; The bug which you would fright me with, I seek..

Threat, t. useless - How I scorn these useless threats.

Threat, verbal t. - I wear not my dagger in my mouth.

Threats, idle t. - There is no terror, Cassius, in your threats…

Threats. See entries for 'Warning'.

Thrift, t. as a virtue under certain conditions - … And thrift is blessing, if men steal it not.

Thunder, t. as a metaphor for loud voice - To tear with thunder the wide cheeks o' the air.

Thus credulous fools are caught. See 'Invocation, i. and satisfaction at the success of your scheme – Work on, my medicine, work!

Thus have I had thee… See 'Dream and illusion - Thus have I had thee as a dream doth flatter, in sleep a king, but waking, no such matter.'

Thus ornament is but the guiled shore… See 'Appearances, a. deceptive or false – Ornament… the seeming truth which cunning times put on to entrap the wisest.'

Thus yields the cedar to the axe's edge… See 'Defeat, admitting electoral d. – Thus yields the cedar to the axe's edge…'

Thy own wish wish I thee in every place! See 'Toasts, t. to health and realization of wishes- Sweet health and fair desires consort your grace…'

Time - … the lazy foot of time

Time - … the tooth time, gnawing image of t. See 'See 'Oblivion, insurance against o. – … A forted residence 'gainst the tooth of time and razure of oblivion.'

Time, about nine o'clock - … labouring for nine.

Time, admitting to having dropped out of school. See 'Education, lack of formal e. - (I) have been an idle truant, omitting the sweet benefit of time to cloth mine age with angel-like perfection'

Time, admitting to having wasted it - I wasted time and now doth time waste me.

Time, all encompassing power of t. – It is in my power to o'erthrow law and in one self-born hour to plant and o'erwhelm custom.

Time, almost forever – … When time is old and hath forgot itself, when water drops have worn the stones of Troy..

Time, appropriate t. for whatever needs to be done – Every time serves for the matter that is then born in it.

Time, beautiful for all t. See 'Beauty transcending the limitations of time – When in the chronicle of waster time…'

Time, bedtime as a matte

Time, buying t. until conditions improve - … there am I, till time and vantage crave my company.

Time, call back t. - O, call back yesterday, bid time return…

Time, characteristics of past and future – What's past and what's to come is strew'd with husks and formless ruin of oblivion.

Time, clock. See 'Clock, sound of c. striking hours painful - … the sound that tells what hour it is…'

Time, consciousness of wasted t. - The clock upbraids me with the waste of time

Time, counting numbers to measure t. – Stay'd it long?… While one with moderate haste might tell a hundred.

Time, defenseless against t. – Nothing 'gainst Time's scythe can make defence.

Time, destructive nature of t. – … Love, friendship, charity, are subjects all to envious and calumniating time…

Time, devastating effects of t. - … And so, from hour to hour, we ripe and ripe, and then…

Time, dinner t. about 6 PM – … when… men sit down to that nourishment which is called supper.

Time, everything in good t. – … there's a time for all things.

Time, exhortation to t. not to damage her beauty - But I forbid thee one most heinous crime, o carve not with thy hours my love's fair brow..

Time, gaining time before answering. See 'Speech, gaining time before speaking up - .. he's winding up the watch of his wit' by and by it will strike.' -- 'Speechless, stunned by her beauty - you have bereft me of all words, lady.'

Time, gap in the narrative - ... Impute it not a crime to me or my swift passage... and leave the growth untried of that wide gap.

Time, give it time to mature, t. as a seasoning agent - How many things by season season'd are…

Time, healing properties of t. - Time is the nurse and breeder of all good.

Time, his or her presence makes t. pass quickly - He makes a July's day short as December..

Time, improvement expected with time - … the time will bring on summer when briars shall have leaves as well as thorns...

Time, in one year - ... until the twelve celestial signs have brought about the annual reckoning.

Time, in the afternoon, a. redefined – …, in the posteriors of the day, which the rude multitude call afternoon.

Time, in the early morning - ... look love, what envious streaks do lace the severing clouds in yonder east.

Time, in the early morning - The early village-cock hath twice done salutation to the morn.

Time, in the morning - ... the cock, that is the trumpet to the morn, doth with his lofty and shrill-sounding throat awake the god of day.

Time, in the morning - …when the morning sun shall rise his car above the border of this horizon.

Time, in the morning, golden sun saluting the m. See 'Envy, above the reach of e. - Advanced above pale envy's threatening reach, as when the golden sun salutes the morn…'

Time, in the morning, in the country with good weather - The hunt is up, the morn is bright and grey, the fields are fragrant, and the woods are green.

Time, invocation against t. See 'Invocation, i. against time - … Thou ceaseless lackey to eternity.'

Time, is this a good time? See 'Conflict, not a time for c. – 'Tis not a time for private stomaching…'

Time, late night t. making it early morning - … it is so very very late, that we may call it early by and by.

Time, let's concentrate on the present – Let's take the instant by the forward top…. The inaudible and noiseless foot of time…

Time, let's wait a bit longer - Let two summers wither in their pride..

Time, long t. in a word - How long a time lies in one little word!...

Time, meeting the challenges of t. See 'Attitude, a. towards challenges ahead - … And meet the time as it seeks us.'

Time, midday - …the bawdy hand of the dial is now upon the prick of noon.

Time, midday – Now is sun upon the highmost hill of this day's journey

Time, midnight - The iron tongue of midnight hath told twelve.

Time, midnight, close to m. - … it draws near the season wherein the spirit held his wont to walk.

Time, midnight, sweating at m. - It is now dead midnight. Cold fearful drops stand on my trembling flesh.

Time, more t. required to finish a project. See 'Patience, p. and time management required - How poor are they that have not patience!…'

Time, morning, is it really morning? - Is the day so young?

Time, night t. – … when creeping murmur and the poring dark fills the wide vessel of the universe.

Time, night t. - In the dead vast and middle

of the night

Time, night t.– 'Tis now the very witching time of night, when churchyards yawn…

Time, night t. See 'Halloween, h. material - … Nature seems dead, and wicked dreams abuse the curtain'd sleep…' *** 'Moonlight, by the m. – How sweet the moonlight sleeps upon this bank!' *** Entries for 'Nature, night'.

Time, night t. and very late, t. for rest – See 'Sleep, s. or rest, time to adjourn the meeting - The deep of night is crept upon our talk and nature must obey necessity…'

Time, night t. as the end of day at sea. See 'Nature, sunset, at sea – The gaudy, blabbing and remorseful day is crept into the bosom of the sea.'

Time, n. t. for rest – … times to repair our nature with comforting repose…

Time, no t. to be lost with an importune caller - … We hold our time too precious to be spent with such a babbler.

Time, not a good t. See 'Misfortune, setback - My stars shine darkly over me'

Time, observing t. passing - When I do count the clock that tells the time…

Time, passing of t. inevitable –Like as the waves make towards the pebbled shore, so do our minutes hasten to their end...

Time, passing t. carelessly - … and fleet the time carelessly, as they did in the golden world..

Time, precious short t. - … The time 'twixt six and now must by us both be spent most preciously.

Time, present t. bad, past and future OK – O thoughts of men accurst! Past and to come seem best, things present, worst.

Time, punctuality. See 'Punctuality important. You are early! Better too soon than too late'.

Time, relentlessly advancing, compared to a thief - Time comes stealing on by night and day.

Tine, sadness. extending the perception of time - … sad hours seem long.

Time, sadness making hours long - what sadness lengthens Romeo's hours? Not having that…

Time, searching for some entertainment to pass the t. - How shall we beguile the lazy time, if not with some delight?

Time, sense of guilt at wasting t. - I feel me much to blame so idly to profane the precious time…

Time, spending it in a wood under the trees - … Under the shade of melancholy boughs lose and neglect the creeping hours of time.

Time, sundown - The day begins to break, and night is fled whose pitchy mantle over-veiled the earth.

Time, survival t. limited - The sands are number'd that make up my life.

Time, t. all encompassing ruler - … Time's the king of men, for he's their parent, and he is their grave and gives them what he will, not what they crave

Time, t. and dec

Time, t. and ingratitude - Time hath, my lord, a wallet in his back wherein he puts alms for oblivion…

Time, t. and mortality. See 'Thought, t. as the slave of life, expressing pessimism - … thought's the slave of life, and life time's fool; and time, that takes survey of all the world, must have a stop.'

Time, t. and the inherent limited duration of everything - When I consider everything that grows holds in perfection but a little moment…

Time, t. and urgency - We are time's subjects, and time bids be gone.

Time, t. as 'cormorant devouring time'. See lines in 'Fame, f. defeating death and time - … And make us heirs of all eternity.'

Time, t. as a dark entity. See 'Memory, m. recollections - What seest thou else in the dark backward and abysm of time?'

Time, t. as a fashionable host. See 'Time, t. erasing impact of action - … time is like a fashionable host that slightly shakes his parting guest by the hand…'

Time, t. as a justice provider – Yet heavens are just, and time suppresseth wrongs.

Time, t. as a justice provider. See 'Retribution, time as an administrator of justice - … and thus the whirligig of time brings in his revenges.'

Time, t. as a mellowing of characters. See 'Character, mellowed by time - .. mellow'd by the stealing hours of time.'

Time, t. as a problem solver. See 'Invocation, i. to time as a problem solver'

Time, t. as a thief. See 'Invocation, time, short time for good-byes - Injurious time now with a robber's haste…' *** 'Character, mellowed by time - .. mellow'd by the stealing hours of time.'

Time, t. as the father of stratagems. See 'Situation, tense s. - … every minute now should be the father of some stratagem: the times are wild.'

Time, t. as the test of love – … I know love is begun by time, and that I see, in passages of proof, time qualifies the spark and fire of it.

Time, t. causes past good deeds to be forgotten. See 'Recognition, unfair r. resulting from the passage of time - … And give to dust that is a little gilt more laud than gilt o'er-dusted.'

Time, t. defeated by fame and honor, (spite of cormorant devouring time…) See 'Fame, f. defeating death and time - … And make us heirs of all eternity.'

Time, t. described as a dark and fathomless entity. See 'Memory, m. recollections - What seest thou else in the dark backward and abysm of time?'

Time, t. erasing impact of action - … time is like a fashionable host that slightly shakes his parting guest by the hand…

Time, t. for love, night more suitable -… if love be blind, it best agrees with night.

Time, t. for meeting or request inappropriate - The time is unagreeable to this business..

Time, t. for rest - … times to repair our nature with comforting repose.

Time, t. handled differently by different people - Time travels in divers paces with divers persons.

Time, t. helps to forget. See 'Forgetting, time helps f - … some more time must wear the print of his remembrance out.

Time, t. management, t. wasted – …thus we play the fools with the time and the spirits of the wise sit in the clouds and mock us.

Time, t. needed to think before deciding, sleeping it over. See 'See 'Night, n. to think it over - A night is but small breath and little pause to answer matters of this consequence.'

Time, t. oblivious to the nature of events. See "Life, manly approach to unexpected events, however rough - Come what come may, time and the hour runs through the roughest day.'

Time, t. of day - I see no reason why thou shouldst be so superfluous to demand the time of the day.

Time, t. passing and a sense of urgency - The hour steals on; I pray you, sir, dispatch

Time, t. passing quickly - Four days will quickly steep themselves in nights…

Time, t. passing without noise or trace - The inaudible and noiseless foot of time.

Time, past and next. See 'Continuation, going to the next step - … to perform an act whereof what's past is prologue.'

Time, t. past for entertainment - … for you and I are past our dancing days.

Time, t. past forgotten, future uncertain - What's past and what's to come is strew'd with husks…

Time, t. poorly spent and not dedicated to education. See "Education, lack of formal e. - (I) have been an idle truant, omitting the sweet benefit of time to cloth mine age with angel-like perfection'

Time, t. pregnant with news - With news the time's with labour, and throes forth each minute, some.

Time, t. required for forgetting. See 'Forgetting, time helps f - ... some more time must wear the print of his remembrance out.'

Time, t. seems short when passed in pleasurable undertakings - Pleasure and action make the hours seem short.

Time, t. self-described - I, that please some, try all, both joy and terror..

Time, t. spent idly while danger at hand - ... When tempest of commotion, like the south borne with black vapour...

Time, t. spent leisurely - ... under the shade of melancholy boughs lose and neglect the creeping hours of time.

Time, t. spoiler of beauty defeated by power of written lines. See 'Writing, power of printed message - ... in black ink my love may still shine bright.'

Time, t. troublesome - The time is troublesome.

Time, t. will uncover the guilty. See 'Hypocrisy, h. and cunning will eventually be discovered - Time shall unfold what plighted cunning hides, who cover faults at last shame them derides.'

Time, t.'s tasks or characteristics - 'Time's glory is to calm contending kings...

Time, the great arbitrator - .... the end crowns all and that old common arbitrator, Time, will one day end it.

Time, the right thing at the right time. See 'Appropriateness, the right thing at the right time – at Christmas I no more desire a rose..'

Time, three years since last meeting - Three April perfumes in three hot Junes burn'd...

Time, two hours ago - Since when, my watch hath told me, toward my grave I have travelled but two hours.

Time, unsuitable t. for receiving visits - If I might beseech you, gentlemen, to repair some other hour..

Time, up late, up early - I am glad I was up so late; for that's the reason I was up so early.

Time, within one day - Ere twice the horses of the sun shall bring…

Time, within one day. See 'Medicine, effective within 24 hours - (before) four and twenty times the pilot's glass hath told the thievish minutes how they pass…'

Time, within one hour - ... ere the glass, that now begins to run finish the process of his sandy hour.

Time, within two weeks - Ere a fortnight make me elder.

Times, bad and in need of a remedy. See entries for 'Remedies, extreme r. required'

Times, bad times – 'Tis the times' plague, when madmen lead the blind.

Times, bad times - … these days are dangerous, virtue is chock'd with foul ambition…

Times, bad times, infected, as a pestilence. See 'Injustice, using tools of injustice to correct wrongs – But such is the infection of the time that for the health and physic of our right…'

Times, best t. are past. See 'World, pessimistic view of the w. - We have seen the best of our time: machinations, hollowness, treachery, and all ruinous disorders…

Times, better when they were worse. See 'Time, present bad, past and future OK – O thoughts of men accurst! Past and to come seem best, things present, worst.'

Times, degeneracy of t. when values are reversed - ... the world is grown so bad that wrens make prey where eagles dare not perch…

Times, degeneracy of t. when values are reversed. See 'Values, v. reversed – In the fatness of these pursy times, virtue itself of vice must pardon beg…'

Times, end of the good t. - ... the bright day is done and we are for the dark.

Times, end of the good t. See 'Financial analysis discouraging - ..Lord Timon's happy hours are done and past, and his estate shrinks from him.'

Times, good old t., better then, less greed than now - ... how well in thee appears the constant service of the antique world...

Times, good old t., less selfishness detectable in previous times

Times, good old t., less selfishness detectable in previous times - Thou art not for the fashion of these times, where none will sweat but for promotion.

Times, hard t. ahead - The storm is up and all is on the hazard.

Times, out of joint. See 'Correction, regret for having to take corrective action – O cursed spite, that ever I was born to set it right.'

Times, rebellious t. - Rich men look sad and ruffians dance and leap...

Times, rotten

Times, wild t. – Contention like a horse.. bears down all before him.

Timing, importance of being first - Fruits that blossom first will first be ripe.

Tired of walking. See 'Walking, tired of w. - My legs can keep no pace with my desires, here will I rest me…'

Tired. See 'Weariness, tired, at the end of your rope - ... the last hour of my long weary life is come upon me.'

Title, crown and content - My crown is call'd content, a crown is it that seldom kings enjoy.

Title, job t. magnified - Thou art a cobbler, art thou?... I am, indeed, sir, a surgeon to old shoes.

Titles, all t. no substance – ... no better than an earl. Although in glorious titles he excel.

To be or not to be. See 'Decisions decisions – To be or not to be - be - that is the question, whether 'tis nobler in the mind to suffer…'

To business that we love we rise ... See 'Work, type of w. we like to go to - To business that we love we rise betime and go to it with delight.'

To me fair friend you never can be old, for as you were... See 'Ageless'

To thine own self be true. See 'Advice, a. on strength of character - .. to thine own self be true, and it must follow, as the night the day, thou canst not then be false to any man.'

Toast, dinner and health - Now, good digestion wait on appetite and health on both!

Toast, drinking down unkindness - ... I hope we shall drink down all unkindness.

Toast, generic, drink - I drink to the general joy o' the whole table.

Toast, joining in a t. - I'll drink to her, as long as there is a passage in my throat and drink in Illyria.

Toast, proposing a t. - Be large in mirth; anon we'll drink a measure the table round.

Toast, t. and wish, prosperity - Now the fair goddess, Fortune fall deep in love with thee. Prosperity be thy page!

Toast, t. to an agreement reached. See 'Action, a. that promises to be successful - .. rich advantage of a promised glory as smiles upon the forehead of this action.'

Toast, t. to health and realization of wishes- Sweet health and fair desires consort your grace..

Toast, t. with water - ... Here's that which is too weak to be a sinner, honest water…

Toast. See also entries for 'Salutations and wishes'.

Tolerance, no t. for abuse. See 'Zero tolerance – I will be deaf to pleading and excuses, nor tears nor prayers shall purchase out abuses.'

Tomorrow, and tomorrow, and tomorrow. See entries for 'Depression, general depression leading to total pessimism'.

Tongue, a witching t. - .. he has witchcraft over the king in his tongue.

Tongue, experienced t. See 'Advice, listen to experienced a. - knit all the Greekish ears to his experienced tongue'

Tongue, leading speaker into peril -

1335

….tongue… you prattle me into these perils.

Tongue, malicious - … struck me with her tongue, most serpent-like, upon the very heart.

Tongue, native t. no longer of use - And now my tongue's use is to me no more than an unstrung viol or a harp…

Tongue, poisonous t. See 'Angry, a. at her compared to a she-wolf - She-wolf of France, but worse than wolves of France, whose tongue more poisons than the adder's tooth.'

Tongue, sharp t. – Thy wit is a very bitter sweeting; it is almost a sharp sauce.

Tongue, sharp t. See 'Reputation, r. as a man with a sharp tongue - … the world's large tongue proclaims you for a man replete with mocks…'

Tongue, women's t. See 'Women, power of w's tongue - The tongues of mocking wenches are as keen as is the razor's edge invisible..'

Tongue. See 'Word, w. power, key to seduction - That man that hath a tongue, I say, is no man if with his tongue he cannot win a woman. *** '

Tongue. See "Speechless, made speechless by her princely beauty - .. beauty's princely majesty is such,

Too good to be true. See 'True, too good to be t., almost like a dream - This is the rarest dream that ever dull sleep did mock sad fools withal!

Too many unqualified managers. See 'Times, degeneracy of t. when values are reversed - .. the world is grown so bad that wrens make prey where eagles dare not perch.'

Too much of a good thing (one of everyday expressions from Shakespeare). See 'Satisfied, but wanting more - … can one desire too much of a good thing?'

Tool, humble t. achieving objectives. See 'Objectives, o. achieved with humble tools - What poor an instrument may do a noble deed!

Tool, t. of destruction not used - Hence, vile instrument! Thou shalt not damn my hand.

Tooth of time. See 'Oblivion, insurance against o. – … A forted residence 'gainst the tooth of time and razure of oblivion.'

Tooth-ache. See 'Philosophy, p. and tooth ache - ... there was never yet philosopher, that could endure the tooth-ache patiently.'

Tooth-ache. See 'Sleep, s. as a tooth-ache reliever - Indeed, sir, he that sleeps feels not the tooth-ache.'

Torment, mental t. – O, full of scorpions is my mind…

Torture, inner torture - … the thought whereof doth, like poisonous mineral, gnaw my innards.

Touch, soft t. better than heavy hand - … when lenity and cruelty play for a kingdom, the gentler gamester is the soonest winner.

Tourism, see entries for 'Sightseeing'.

Tower of strength. See 'Label, power of the label – … the king's name is a tower of strength.'

Town, bad t, bad place. - They say this town is full of cozenage… dark working sorcerers…

Track record. See 'Life, l.'s history of a person as a predictor of future performance – there is a history in all men's lives.'

Trade, offensive t. See 'Definition, offensive d, cannot be named - What I cannot name but I shall offend.'

Trading security for untested chance - …and give up yourself merely to chance and hazard from firm security.

Traffic, long line of stalled cars – … will the line stretch out to the crack of doom?

Training, t. or good sense overcoming ignorance or folly - and let instructions enter where folly now possesses.

Trait, t. common to all men. See 'Humanity, common trait of h. – One touch of nature makes the whole world kin…'

Traits, natural t. See 'Character, c. showing natural traits - how hard it is to hide the sparks of nature.'

Traitor in full - by day and night he's traitor to the height.
Traitor, skilled at twisting the truth - A subtle traitor needs no sophister.
Traitors, how to recognize them – … Why, one that swears and lies…
Traitors, t. corrupted by m. - A nest of hollow bosoms which he fills with treacherous crowns.
Traitor, t. given the means to attack. See 'Snake, s. preparing to attack - I fear me you but warm the starved snake, who, cherish'd in your breasts, will sting your hearts.'
Traitor. See 'Curse, c and prediction for a traitor - His treasons will sit blushing in his face..' *** Entries for 'Insult, traitor'
Traitors, t. purging treason with words - Thus do all traitors: if their purgation did consist in words they are as innocent as grace itself…
Traitors, t. without knowing it. - But cruel are the times, when we are traitors and do not know ourselves…
Trance, in a t. - … Like our strange garments, cleave not to their mould but with the aid of use.
Transformation, t. and new position in society – … And now is this vice's dagger become a squire.
Transformation, t. of character. See 'Character, transformed dramatically - … nor the exterior nor the inward man resembles that it was.'
Transformation, your t. as the effect of love at first sight. See 'Love, love at first sight, effects of – O, when mine eyes did see Olivia first, methought she purged the air of pestilence!…'
Transportation, fast t. needed – O, for a horse with wings!
Transportation, t. needed quickly - A horse! A horse! My kingdom for a horse.
Traps, t. for enemies - My brain more busy than the labouring spider weaves tedious snares to trap mine enemies.

Travel, against t. – … to have seen much and to have nothing, is to have rich eyes and poor hands
Travel, better at home than travelling – … when I was at home, I was in a better place: but travellers must be content.
Travel, have a good trip and return happy – Lead forth and bring you back in happiness!
Travel, have a good trip and wish me with you - … wish me partaker in thy happiness when thou dost meet good hap.
Travel, departure expedited. See 'Departure, d. expedited – … aboard, aboard, for shame! The wind sits in the shoulder of your sail…'
Travel, invitation. See 'Travel, invitation. See 'Invitation, i. to travel - I rather would entreat thy company to see the wonders of the world abroad.'
Travel, motivation for traveling to see her - … my desire, more sharp than filed steel, did spur me on.
Travel, seaport, airport, accompanying guest to seaport or airport - We'll bring your grace even to the edge o' the shore..
Travel, separation but you will think of her - … the time shall not outgo my thinking of you.
Travel, statement of will to be a t. companion - The swallow follows not summer more willing than we your lordship.
Travel, t. always a positive experience. See 'Positive thinking, how to acquire it, the art of it – All places… are to a wise man ports and happy havens.'
Travel, t. in good company. See 'Company, good c. making time and travel seem shorter - .. And yet your fair discourse hath been as sugar, making the hard way sweet and delectable'.
Travel, t. in youth an important educational tool - .. Which would be great impeachment to his age in having known no travel in his youth.
Travel, wishing a successful trip. See 'Wishes, w. of success during a travel away

from home - Upon your sword sit laurel victory and smooth success be strewed before your feet.'

Travellers must be content. See 'Travel, better at home than travelling – … when I was at home, I was in a better place: but travellers must be content.'

Treachery, excellence in t. – And whatsoever cunning fiend… hath got the voice in hell for excellence.

Treason, accusation of t. – … never did insurrection want such water colours.

Treason, condemnation for t. unjust – Condemn'd to die for treason, but no traitor.

Treason, invocation, is this possible? - Can this be so, that in alliance, amity and oaths there should be found such false, dissembling guile?"

Treason, previous t. always to cause suspicion. See 'Suspicion, s. always follows a previous suspect - Suspicion all our lives shall be stuck full of eyes…'

Treason, t. and murder - Treason and murder ever kept together…

Treason, t. hidden behind pretence. See 'Hypocrisy, h. to cover treason - How smooth and even they do bear themselves!…'

Treason, t. for money - That he should, for a foreign purse, so sell his sovereign's life to death and treachery.

Treason, treacherous intentions - … so Judas kiss'd his master; and cried 'all hail!' whenas he meant all harm.

Treason, unexpected t. from a friend hurting more - The private wound is deepest.

Treason, victim feeling t. sharply. See 'Deception, d. from false teachers - Thus may poor fools believe false teachers…'

Treasons, secret t. of the world. See 'Man, capable m. able to discern deceit – These eyes… as piercing as the mid-day sun, to search the secret treasons of the world…'

Treatment, care of details and pleasant t. promised - … And pluck the wings from painted butterflies, to fan the moonbeams from his sleeping eye.

Treatment, ignoble t. – … noble uncle, thus ignobly used.

Treatment, pleasant treatment - … and she will sing the song that pleaseth you, and on your eyelids crown the god of sleep.

Treatment, reasons for treating her well - The lustre in your eye, heaven in your cheek pleads your fair usage.

Treaty, t. unfavorable to the losing party – What good condition can a treaty find in the part that is at mercy?

Trend setting by bucking the t. - To shame the guise o' the world, I will begin the fashion, less without and more within.

Trend, trend setter - … the mark and glass, copy and book that fashion'd other.

Trepidation, see 'Anxious while waiting for her answer – Thus ready for the way of life or death I wait the sharpest blow.' *** 'Bated breath - With bated breath and whispering humbleness…' *** entries for 'Anxiety'.

Trial, jury t. See 'Law, trial jury may include criminals – The jury, passing on the prisoner's life, may in the sworn twelve have a thief or two…'

Trick, good t. - … it is admirable pleasures, and fery honest knaveries.

Trick, laughter inducing t. not to be missed. See 'Laughter, opportunity for l. not to be missed - I will not give my part of this sport for a pension of thousands to be paid by the Sophy.'

Trick, self-effacement after having been the butt of a prank – … if I be served such another trick, I'll have my brains ta'en out and buttered…

Trifles, a person concerned with t. See 'Irrelevance, bound to i. - … snapper-up of unconsidered trifles.'

Trifles or trivia, quarreling about t. See 'Quarrel, q. about trifles as a symptom of man's madness - … what madness rules in brainsick men, when for so slight and frivolous a cause...'

Trifling, no t. See entries for 'Jokes, no time for joking. '

Trip, have a good trip. See entries for 'Travel, have a good trip' *** 'Goodbye, when she is leaving for a short or long trip, or a shopping excursion - Let all the number of the stars give light to thy fair way.'

Trippingly on the tongue - Speak the speech, I pray you, as I pronounced it to you, trippingly on the tongue.

Trivia, do away with t. See 'Exhortation, e. to limit facetiousness - ... do not play in wench-like words with that which is so serious.'

Trivia, t. and trifles – ... Triumphs for nothing and lamenting toys is jollity for apes and grief for boys.

Trouble, what is troubling you? See 'Unhappiness, asking for reasons of u. - .. make me acquainted with your cause of grief.'

Troubles, t. affecting all. See 'Conditions, current place and c. not as bad as others' - This wide and universal theatre presents more woeful pageants...'

Truant. See 'Education, lack of formal education - (I) have been an idle truant, omitting the sweet benefit of time to clothe mine age with angel-like perfection.'

True, absolutely and emphatically t. - As certain as I know the sun is fire.

True, as true as Troilus - ... truth tired with iteration, as true as steel, as plantage to the moon...

True, is this t.? See 'Honor, h. and credit at stake - Thereon I pawn my credit and mine honour.'

True, too good to be t., almost like a dream - This is the rarest dream that ever dull sleep did mock sad fools withal!

Trust, can I trust you? See entries for 'Reliability, "Am I going to be safe with you?'

Trust, declaration of t. See 'Diffidence as a form of cowardice - I hold it cowardice to rest mistrustful where a noble heart hath pawn'd an open hand in sign of love.

Trust, no t. for him who has already proven untrustworthy - ... trust not him that hath once broken faith

Trust, skepticism in the face of deceitful friends - Who should be trusted, when one's own right hand is perjured to the bosom?

Trust, t. in divine powers. See 'Destiny, accepting the inevitability of d. - But He, that hath the steerage of my course direct my sail!'

Trust, t. in group's courage or intelligence misplaced. See 'Opinion, your op. on crowds and masses – He that trusts to you, where he should find you lions, finds you hares...'

Trust, t. misplaced as a form of madness – He's mad that trusts in the tameness of a wolf....

Trust, t. or deception. See 'on or trust, indifference to either - I do not greatly care to be deceived that have no use for trusting'.

Trust, t. restored. See 'Suspicion, s. removed and trust restored.

Truth and lying accurately defined - ... whose tongue soe'er speaks false not truly speaks; who speaks not truly, lies.

Truth, an enemy of the t. See 'Enemy, my e. and e. of the truth'.

Truth, appearance of t. See 'Appearance, a. of truth hiding a deeper and malicious purpose - .. to win us to our harm the instruments of darkness tell us truths...'

Truth, assurance about one's own credibility - Believe my words for they are certain and unfallible.

Truth, assurance of t. emphatically stated – If I tell thee a lie, spit in my face, call me horse.

Truth, dangerous t., trying to prove it may be fatal –I have uttered truth which, if you seek to prove, I dare not stand by.

Truth, determined to tell the t. See 'Speech, determined to speak and tell the truth - I will speak as liberal as the north, let heaven and men and devils, let them all...'

Truth, emphatic statement of truth-telling - ... for what I speak my body shall make good upon this earth or my divine soul answer it in heaven.

Truth, evident and yet unseen - ... though the truth of it stands off as gross as black and white, my eye will scarcely see it.

Truth, extracting t. from falsehood via torture - Bitter torture shall winnow the truth from falsehood.

Truth, extraordinary t. at first glance unbelievable - Most true, if ever truth were pregnant by circumstance...

Truth, ignorant of the t. See 'Accusers, attitude towards a. and you are innocent - I am richer than my base accusers.'

Truth, in the name of truth. See 'Invocation, i. in the name of truth - As there comes light from heaven, and words from breath, as there is sense in truth, and truth in virtue...'

Truth, painful t. not told - ... sick men, when their deaths be near no news but health from their physicians know.

Truth, simple t. not requiring oaths - 'T is not the many oaths that make the truth, but the plain single vow, that is vow'd true.

Truth, sometimes it cannot be told, conflict - ... That truth should be silent I had almost forgot.

Truth, surprise at the devil telling the truth – What, can the devil speak true?

Truth, t. and openness. See 'Openness, invitation to o. - Out with it boldly; truth loves open dealing'.

Truth, t. confers calmness of spirit - Truth hath a quiet breast.

Truth, t. destroyed by malice – ... it must appear that malice bears down truth.

Truth, t. emphatically asserted – ... never man sigh'd truer breath.

Truth, t. emphatically maintained. See 'Exclamation in support of the veracity of (your) following statement – As there comes light from heaven and words from breath.'

Truth, t. evident and on my side - I'll maintain my words on any plot of ground on Christendom.

Truth, t. evident and on my side – The truth appears so naked on my side, that any purblind eye may find it out.

Truth, t. in economy of words - Where words are scarce, they are seldom spent in vain.

Truth, t. incomplete or inaccurate - Though thou speak'st truth methinks thou speak'st not well.

Truth, t. is not slander - That is no slander, sir, which is a truth.

Truth, t. is on my side - ...And on my side truth so well apparell'd, so shining and so evident..

Truth, t. is t. however they may try to twist it - ... truth is truth to the end of reckoning.

Truth, t. needs no embellishment – Truth needs no colour... beauty no pencil

Truth, t. not seen or perceived - ... he doth but mistake the truth totally.

Truth, t. only apparent - The seeming truth which cunning times put on.

Truth, t. painful not told - ... sick men, when their deaths be near no news but health from their physicians know.

Truth, t. passed on through the ages – Methinks the truth should live from age to age as 'twere retail'd to all posterity...

Truth, t. presented without diplomacy. See 'Speech, saying the right thing at the wrong time - The truth you speak doth lack some gentleness and time to speak it in.'

Truth, t. supported by facts not words - .. truth hath better deeds than words to grace it.

Truth, t. that cannot be told - Truth's a dog must to kennel; he must be whipped out...

Truth, t. told, end of story - Some such thing I said and said no more but what my thoughts did warrant me was likely.

Truth, t. unexpectedly uttered - ...you have spoken truer than you purposed...

Truth, this is the absolute t. - Mark what I say, which you shall find by every syllable a faithful verity.

Truth, you are determined to find the t. - If circumstances lead me, I will find where truth is hid, though it were hid indeed within the centre.

Truthful, a person who appears t. See 'Character, c. of a person who seems truthful - .. thou seem'st a palace for the crown'd truth to dwell in.' *** 'Character, c. truthful and simple - I am as true as truth's simplicity and simpler than the infancy of truth.'

Truthfulness, t. confirmed - ... what truth can speak truest (shall be) not truer than Troilus.

Truthfulness, t. confirmed - Heaven be re the record to my speech.

Turmoil, what is happening? – ... Are we turn'd Turks, and to ourselves do that which heaven hath forbid the Ottomites?

Turpitude, rewarding t. - ... my turpitude thou dost so crown with gold!

Two people absolutely identical. See 'Similarity between two people, twins - An apple cleft in two is not more twin than these two creatures.'

Tyranny, act of t. – ... nothing less than bloody tyranny

Tyranny, difference between t. and justice. See 'Belief, consistency of b. - ... were he meal'd with that which he corrects, then were he tyrannous...'

Tyranny, invocation in helplessness - O nation miserable, with an untitled tyrant bloody-scepter'd...

Tyranny, t. of individual or corporations – ... and we petty men walk under his huge legs and peep about to find ourselves dishonourable graves...

Tyranny. See 'Country, c. under yoke - I think our country sinks beneath the yoke...' *** 'Expression, facial e. indicating tyranny – Upon thy eye-balls murderous tyranny sits in grim majesty, to frig

Tyrant, almost a t. – ... I'll not call you tyrant but.... something savours of tyranny and will ignoble make you...

Tyrant, praying for deliverance from a t. – ... this imperious man will work us all from princes into pages...

Tyrant, t. killing those who helped him succeed – One raised in blood, and one in blood establish'd...

Tyrant, t. once an honest person. See 'Character, dramatic change in c. - This tyrant, whose sole name blisters our tongues was once thought honest.'

Tyrants, fearful t. See 'Authority, fear in a. grows with time – ... tyrants' fears decrease not, but grow faster than the years'.*** 'Strength, s. relative, wolf and sheep - ... I know he would not be a wolf but that he sees the Romans are but sheep.'

Tyrants, t. followed but not loved. See 'Manager, m. that is followed without enthusiasm - Those he commands move only in command, nothing in love...'

Tyrants, t. foreign policy. See 'Government, foreign g. support of home tyranny - For how can tyrants safely govern home, unless abroad they purchase great alliance?'

Tyrants, t.'s fears. See 'Authority, fear in a. grows with time – ... tyrants' fears decrease not, but grow faster than the years.'

Tyrants, seemingly kind. See 'Authority, smiling authorities to be feared - 'T is time to fear, when tyrants seem to kiss'.

Ugliness in men. See 'Appearance, a. improving with age, ugliness in men as an advantage - I was created with a stubborn outside...'

Ugliness, u. not changed by praise - Where fair is not, praise cannot mend the brow.

Ugliness, u. of self acknowledged. See entries for 'Modesty, admitted m. of personal looks'.

Unable to assess the situation. See 'Judgment, inability to assess the situation - You smell this business with a sense as cold as is a dead man's nose'.

Unassailable - … laugh to scorn the power of man for none of woman born shall harm Macbeth

Unbelievable - … 'tis but our fantasy, and will not let belief take hold of him.

Unbelievable - I might not this believe without the sensible and true avouch of mine own eyes.

Unbelievable - If this were played upon a stage now I could condemn it as an improbable fiction.

Unbelievable character. See 'Character, false or unbelievable - no more faith in thee than in a stewed prune'.

Unbelievable event. See 'Event, unbelievable - … it is past the infinite of thought.'

Unbelievable news. See 'News, unbelievable were it not for the evidence - ..That which I shall report will bear no credit, were not the proof so nigh.'

Unbelievable sight - … speak; we will not trust our eyes without our ears…

Unbelievable, can this be true? - What fire is in my ears? can this be true?

Unbelievable, can this be true? - Are these things spoken? or do I but dream?

Unbelievable, cannot believe their (or my) eyes – … scarse think their eyes do offices of truth, their words are natural breath.

Unbelievable, can this be true? – Stand I, even so, as doubtful whether what I see be true…

Unbidden guests are often welcomest…' Invitation, i. refused - I have heard it said, unbidden guests are often welcomest when they are gone.'

Uncertainty, end unknown - … and the end of it unknown to the beginning.

Uncertainty, political u. - … I fear 'twill prove a giddy world.

Uncertainty, u. about what to do next. See entries for 'Indecision, i. between two courses of action'.

Underrating, underestimation – … holding a weak supposal of our worth.

Understanding , maybe you understand now - But now you partly may perceive my mind.

Understanding, discouraging attempt to sort out a strange business - Do not infest your mind with beating on the strangeness of this business.

Understanding, limited u. - a knavish speech sleeps in a foolish ear.

Understanding, one who does not understand…- I think his understanding is bereft!

Understanding, sincerity of lack of u. questioned - Your sense pursues not mine or seem so craftily; and that's not good.

Understanding, thick of u. - … thou wert not wont to be so dull…

Understanding, total lack of u. of the situation. See 'Truth, t. not seen or perceived - .. he doth but mistake the truth totally.'

Understanding, u. impossible due to words spoken unintelligibly in anger. See 'Anger, a. detected but inexplicable – I understand a fury in your words but not the words.'

Understanding, u. showing no specific education – …an understanding simple and unschooled.

Undoing work previously accomplished with hardship - Undoing all, as all had never been!

Uneasy lies the head … See 'Sleeplessness caused by the weight of your responsibilities - Uneasy lies the head that wears a crown.'

Unemployment, u. soon ending - … But long I will not be Jack out of office…

Unexpected meeting. See entries for 'Meeting, surprise at meeting him/her unexpectedly – In the name of truth, are you fantastical or that indeed which outwardly you show?'

Unfairness, extreme u. – This was the most unkindest cut of all.

Unforgettable. See 'Speech, s. not easily

forgotten – His speech sticks in my heart.'
*** 'Promise, p. to remember what you have been told - ... 'Tis in my memory lock'd and you yourself shall keep the key of it.'

Unhappiness, asking for reasons of u. - ... make me acquainted with your cause of grief.

Unhappiness, impossible to be understood by those who do not feel it - Thou canst not speak of that thou dost not feel.

Unhappiness, u. and desperation – O limed soul, that, struggling to be free, art more engaged!

Unhappiness, u. and desperation - O, woe is me, to have seen what I have seen, see what I see!

Unhappiness, u. detected. See 'Expression, e. expressing unhappiness - I see your brows are full of discontent..'

Unhappiness. See 'Happiness, contrast of happiness with personal unhappiness - the apprehension of the good gives but the greater feeling to the worse'.

Unkindness, u. destructive – Unkindness may do much and his unkindness may defeat my life.

Unity, u. of effort – So may a thousand actions, once afoot end in one purpose...

Universe, rose, unique - For nothing this wide universe I call, save thou my rose, in it thou art my all.

Unkindness, See 'Ingratitude, i. as a deformity - In nature there's no blemish but the mind…'

Unmatchable, see 'Beauty, radiant - most radiant, exquisite, unmatchable beauty'

Unmentionable, u. something – Why, I cannot name't but I shall offend

Unmovable. See 'Determination, stubbornness, no change of mind – There is no power in the tongue of man to alter me.'

Unnatural events as indication of the gravity of the times - ... they are portentous things unto the climate that they point upon.

Unpleasantness, tolerated for her sake - many can brook the weather that love not the wind.

Unsalvageable, not worth looking for the salvageable - He could not stay to pick them in a pile of noisome musty chaff…]

Unspeakable crimes. See entries for 'Crime' and 'Crimes'

Unstoppable and ferocious - … from face to foot he was a thing of blood …

Unthink your speaking. See 'Exhortation, e. to change opinion - I do beseech you, gracious madam, to unthink your speaking…'

Unthinkable, u. that I would do this - If ever I did dream of such a matter, abhor me.

Untrustworthy – I will trust as I will adders fang'd.

Upbraiding, gentle u. urged. See 'Moderation, m. urged in upbraiding - Forbear sharp speeches to her...'

Upward mobility. See 'Transformation and new posi

Urgency - It requires swift foot.

Urgency. See 'Time, t. and urgency - we are time's subjects, and time bids be gone'. *** Entries for 'Action'.

Urgency, complying with urgent request. See 'Speed, need for s. acknowledged - The spirit of the time shall teach me speed.'

Urgent business, u. action required - … haste is needful in this desperate case.

Urgent business, u. action required - Our hands are full of business: let's away..

Urgent business, u. action required. See 'Action, a. requiring urgent and strong response – 't is not sleepy business but must be look'd to speedily…'

Use every man … See "Man and his wicked nature - ... use every man after his desert, and who should 'scape whipping?'

Uselessness, ultimate u. of labor. See 'Labor, ultimate uselessness of patient l. – .. they say, all the yarn she spun in Ulysses' absence did but fill Ithaca full of moths'.

Vacation, effects of not taking a v. See

'Health, recreation necessary for healthy life - Sweet recreation barred, what doth ensue…'

Vale of years. See entries for 'Age, admitting to being old'

Valiant dust. See 'Man, m. as dust – Would it not grieve a woman to be overmastered with a piece of valiant dust?'

Valor, no v. in a false quarrel. See 'Quarrel, q. unjustified - In a false quarrel there is no true valour.'

Valor, no v. in fighting a dog - What valour were it, when a cur doth grin for one to thrust his hands between his teeth…character, c. p

Valor, v. and discretion. See 'Cowardice, c. or discretion - The better part of valour is, discretion'.

Valor, v. as the chiefest virtue. See 'Courage, c. the number one virtue - … valour is the chiefest virtue and most dignifies the haver.'

Valor, v. in adversary acknowledged. See 'Adversary, paying homage to a valiant a. - His valour shown upon our crests to-day hath taught us to cherish such high deeds even in the bosom of our adversaries.'

Value, different v. placed on possessions by thieves and rightful owners – Pirates may make cheap pennyworths of their pillage…

Value, perception of v. and relative v. of useful and useless things - … Nature, what things there are most abject in regard, and dear in use!

Value, v. of object enhanced by owner - … things of like value differing in the owners are prized by their masters…

Value, v. resides in perception - What is aught, but as 'tis valued?

Value, valueless - … not worth my thinking.

Values, perversion of v. - Fair is foul, and r.

Values, v. reversed – In the fatness of these pursy times, virtue itself of vice must pardon beg…

Vanished, persons v. - … Into the air; and what seem'd corporal melted as breath into the wind.

Vanity, v. and heedlessness in a leader - … he tires betimes, who spurs too fast betimes.

Vanity, v. displayed and observed - … what a sweep of vanity comes this way!

Vanity, v. or not? - it is not vain-glory for a man and his glass to confer in his own chamber.

Vanity, v. punished. See 'Character, pompous, an ass - for it will come to pass that every braggart shall be found an ass.'

Vanity, wanting others to believe to be sought after - … You see, my good wenches, how men of merit are sought after…

Vegetables, unpalatable v. - … mixture rank, of midnight weeds collected…

Vegetarian, better to be a v. - … but I am a great eater of beef, and I believe that does harm my wit.

Vegetarianism, plenty of natural nutrients available – … The bounteous housewife, nature, on each bush lays her full mess before you…

Venom, v. useful under certain conditions – … like the toad, ugly and venomous, wears yet a precious jewel in his head.

Venture, profitless c. See 'Wind, venture without profit - Ill blows the wind that profits nobody'.

Venture, risky v. but undertaken – We knew that we ventured on such dangerous seas that if we wrought our life 'twas ten to one…

Venture, v. capital. See 'Capital, no raising capital by corruption - … I can raise no money by vile means…'

Venture, v. delivered what predicted - … what hath then befallen, or what hath this bold enterprise brought forth..

Venus, compared to V., worthy of worship - Bright star of Venus, fall'n down on earth, may I reverently worship thee enough?

Venus, love's soul - .. the heartbreak of beauty, love's invisible soul.

Veracity. See 'Believability, complete b. – If Jupiter should from yond cloud speak divine things…' *** Entries for 'Truth'

1344

Verbal self-defence, 'why don't you answer?' - Why bear you these rebukes and answer not?

Verbose. See 'Love, l. inspiring wordiness - Thou wilt be like a lover, presently and tire the hearer with a book of w

Viagra, a case for V. See 'Age, sex and aging - Is it not strange that desire should so many years outlive performance?'

Vice, abhorrent v. - There is a vice that most I do abhor, and most desire should meet the blow of justice.

Vice, v. as the excess of virtue. See 'Virtue, vice and their relationship - Virtue itself turns vice, being misapplied and vice sometimes is by action dignified.'

Vice, v. counterbalanced by virtue – … his vice is to his virtue a just equinox

Vice, v. masked by hypocrisy. See 'Hypocrisy, h. covering vice - There is no vice so simple but assumes some mark of virtue'.

Vice, v. unchecked tends to spread - … vice repeated's like the wandering wind, blows dust in others' eyes, to spread itself.

Vice-President, VP's importance dimmed when President returns - So doth the greater glory dim the less…

Victim, blaming the v. See 'Injustice, unjust accusations and attack on the weak – .. A staff is quickly found to beat a dog.'

Victim, smiling v. reduces impact of theft. See 'Attitude, positive a. in reversals - The robb'd that smiles steals something from the thief…'

Victory, a great v. - … It is a conquest for a prince to boast of.

Victory, confidence in v. against odds - … though the odds be great, I doubt not, uncle, of our victory.

Victory, proud of one's v. - … may justly say, with the hook-nosed fellow of Rome, 'I came, saw, and overcame'.

Victory, still not believing to have won - … Giddy in spirit, still gazing in a doubt whether these pearls of praise be his or no…

Victory, taking advantage of the v., pursuing the enemy – Let us score their backs … 'Tis sport to maul a runner.

Victory, v. celebrations - … and let's away, to part the glories of this happy day.

Victory, v. celebrations. See 'Party, p. time, celebration - … let us banquet royally after this golden day of victory.'

Victory, v. dedication – And with submissive loyalty of heart, ascribes the glory of his conquest…

Victory, v. makes everything seem good - Nothing can seem foul to those that win.

Victory, v. on the cheap - So great a day as this is cheaply bought.

Victory, v. or death. See 'War, cry to w. – … let our bloody colours wave! And either victory, or else a grave.'

Victory, v. or nothing - Either our history shall with full mouth speak freely of our acts…

Victory, v. proclaimed and confidence in the future – This day is ours, as many more shall be.

Victory, v. remembered in future ages – Saint Alban's battle won by famous York shall be eternized in all age to come.

Victory, v. that dignifies the times – O, such a day, so fought, so follow'd and so fairly won came not till now to dignify the times..

Victory, v. through peace. See 'Peace, p. considered as a conquest and a victory – both parties nobly are subdued'.

Victory, v. unfairly obtained. See 'Curse, c. to the unfair winners - Beshrew the winners, for they play'd me false.'

Victory, winner, w. takes all – … the fall of either makes the survivor heir of all.

Victory. See 'Modesty, m. in victory - Praised be God, and not our strength, for it!'

Views, heretical v. suspicious. See 'Ideas, heretical i. - … new opinions, divers and dangerous; which are heresies…'

Villain, lover or v. - ... since I cannot prove a lover ... I am determined to prove a villain.

Villain, the word of a v. - Some villain, ay, and singular in his art, hath done you both this cursed injury.

Villain, v's mind. See "Suspicion, s. at terms offered by a crook - I like not fair terms and a villain's mind.'

Villany, extreme v. - A very excellent piece of villany.

Villany, self-effacement – I am alone the villain of the earth.

Villany, v. and corruption. See 'Corruption, the price of c. - Is it possible that any villany should be so dear?...'

Villany, v. beyond v. See 'Character, villainous with an Oscar for villainy - .. he hath out-villained villainy so far, that the rarity redeems him.'

Violence, v. and cruelty rationalized - ...men are as the time is: to be tender-minded does not become a sword.

Violence, v. threatened - .. (I'll) make a quagmire of your mingled brains.

Violent effect. See 'Effect, quick, strong and violent - As violently, as hasty powder fired doth hurry from the fatal cannon's womb.'

Violet, breath. See ' Breath excellent, stolen from the violet - the forward violet thus did I chide...

Violets, scent of v. compared to fine music. See 'Music, effect of m. similar to scent of violets - ... like the sweet sound that breathes upon a bank of violets'

Violets. See entries for 'Flowers, violets'.

Virginity as a waste - ..for beauty starved with her severity cuts beauty off from all posterity

Virginity, determination to keep it at all costs - If fires be hot, knives sharp, or waters deep, untied I still my virgin knot will keep.

Virginity, exhortation to v. - ...but if thou dost break her virgin-knot before all sanctimonious ceremonies...

Virginity, loss of v. not recommended – ... weigh what loss your honour may sustain ...

Virginity, negative characteristics of v. – ... earthlier happy is the rose distill'd...

Virginity, negative characteristics of v. - ... virginity is peevish, proud, idle, made of self-love...

Virginity, not politically correct - It is not politic in the commonwealth of nature, to preserve virginity.

Virginity, time dependent value of v. - 'Tis a commodity will lose the gloss with lying; the longer kept, the less worth.

Virginity, v. as a dried fruit – ...your old virginity, is like one of our French withered pears, it looks ill, it eats drily...

Virginity, v. potentially traded for high life – I would... and so would you for all this spice of your hypocrisy.

Virtue itself of vice must pardon beg... See 'Values, v. reversed – In the fatness of these pursy times, virtue itself of vice must pardon beg...'

Virtue, how to acquire it - Assume a virtue, if you have it not.

Virtue, perception of v. depending on contemporary culture – So our virtues lie in the interpretation of the time.

Virtue, re

Virtue, sin and their interrelationship, maxim - Any thing that's mended is but patched : virtue that transgresses is but patched with sin; and sin that amends is but patched with virtue.

Virtue, v. and smartness as assets - ... Virtue and cunning were endowment greater than nobleness and riches...

Virtue, v. as opposed to lust – But virtue, as it never will be moved...

Virtue, v. asking forgiveness of vice. See 'Values, v. reversed – In the fatness of these pursy times, virtue itself of vice must pardon beg...'

Virtue, v. inspires courage - Virtue is bold and goodness never fearful.

Virtue, v. nobler than revenge - ..the rarer

1346

action is in virtue than in revenge.

Virtue, v. on one side of the equinox, separating it from vice. See 'Vice, v. counterbalanced by virtue – … his vice is to his virtue a just equinox…'

Virtue, vice and their relationship - Virtue itself turns vice, being misapplied and vice sometimes is by action dignified.

Visibility, advantages for authorities of not being seen too often - … Such as is bent on sun-like majesty when it shines seldom in admiring eyes.

Vision, intuition - In my mind's eye, Horatio.

Vision, majestic v. See 'Impressed, amazed (positively) - This is a most majestic vision, and harmoniously charming'.

Vision, v. affected by overly bright sun. See 'Eyes, sun interfering with good vision - … my mistaking eyes that have been so bedazzled with the sun.'

Visit, cutting v. short due to priorities. See 'Pleasures, priorities in p. - But that a joy past joy calls out on me, it were a grief, so brief to part with thee.'

Visit, thank you for your

Visit, v. or call, reason for – I come, in kindness and unfeigned love…to crave a league of amity.

Visual error or miscalculation. See 'Illusion, optical illusion - Mine eyes are made the fools o' the other senses.'

Vocation, following one's v. natural – 'tis no sin for a man to labour in his vocation.

Voice, her excellent singing v. - … Uttering such dulcet and harmonious breath that the rude sea grew civil at her song…

Voice, her v. creating a heavenly harmony - … had he heard the heavenly harmony which that sweet tongue hath made.

Voice, her v. delightful, like a melodious bird - O, that delightful engine of her thoughts, that blabb'd with such pleasing eloquence …

Voice, her v. feminine – … gentle and low, an excellent thing in a woman.

Voice, her v. harmonious and irresistible - The harmony of your tongue hath into bondage brought my too diligent ear.

Voice, comparing her to a nightingale – My nightingale…

Voice, her v. like music and with a foreign accent - … for thy voice is music and thy English broken…

Voice, her v. makes the ears hungry for it - .. another Juno, who starves the ears she feeds and makes them hungry, the more she gives them speech.

Voice, her v. soothing - O! she will sing the savageness out of a bear.

Voice, loud v. See 'Thunder, t. as a metaphor for loud voice - To tear with thunder the wide cheeks o' the air.'

Voice, provocative v. – And when she speaks, is it not an alarum to love?

Voice, v. as pleasure, honeyed sentences - … when he speaks, the air, a charter'd libertine, is still….

Voice, v. unmistakable - The shepherd knows not thunder from a tabour…

Voice, v. recognition - … if you knew his pure heart's truth, you would quickly learn to know him by his voice.

Voice, v. recognition - My ears have not yet drunk a hundred words of that tongue's utterance, yet I know the sound.

Voice, v. unmistakable - The shepherd knows not thunder from a tabour…

Voice. See also entries for 'Music'.

Vow. See 'Commitments, purposeful c. must be limited in number - It is the purpose that makes strong the vow but vows to every purpose must not hold.' *** Entries for 'Oaths'

Wage, minimum wage. See 'Opinion, your op. on sociological issues, minimum wage - O, reason not the need: our basest beggars are in the poorest thing superfluous…'

Wager, w. of life to sustain an opinion - …to wager she is honest lay down my soul at stake.

Waiting, w. anxiously for an answer. See 'Anxious while waiting for her answer – thus ready for the way of life or death I wait the sharpest blow.'

Wake-up, invitation to an early rising - Stir with the lark to-morrow, gentle Norfolk.

Wake up, metaphor - Trumpet, blow loud, send thy brass voice through all these lazy tents.

Waking up early, reaction to being woken up too early - What misadventure is so early up that calls our person from our morning's rest?

Waking up early, possible reasons why - .. thy earliness doth me assure thou art up-roused by some distemperature; or if not so, then here I hit it right…

Waking up, why so early? – It argues a distempered head so soon to bid good morrow to thy bed

Walk, a w. proposed. See 'Sightseeing, looking at people - … we'll wander through the streets and note the qualities of people.'

Walk, impossibility to w. any further - I can go no further, sir; my old bones ache.

Walk, tiresome country w. – These high wild hills and rough uneven ways draws out our miles…

Walk, unable to w. See 'Feet, tired f. - These feet, whose strengthless stay is numb, unable to support this lump of clay.'

Walk, walking proudly by a horse, but applicable also to men – So proudly as if he disdain'd the ground.

Walking, tired of w. - My legs can keep no pace with my desires, here will I rest me…

Walking, w. as a relaxation exercise - … a turn or two I'll walk to still my beating mind.

War - … to open the purple testament of bleeding war…

War, call to battle – … set the teeth and stretch the nostril wide…

War, cold w. strategy – … frowns, words and threats shall be the war that Henry means to use.

War, cry to w. – … let our bloody colours wave! And either victory, or else a grave.

War, declaring w. - Turning the word to sword and life to death.

Wars, destructive effects of w. – … wasteful war shall statues overturn and broils root out the work of masonry.

War, do you want war? - … will you again unknit this curlish knot of all-abhorred war?

War, end of w. or quarrel - Grim-visaged war hath smooth'd his wrinkled front…

War, imperialistic w. See 'Death, d. in imperialistic wars useless - … for a fantasy and trick of fame go to their graves like beds…'

War, in praise of w. – This peace is nothing, but to rust iron, increase tailors, and breed ballad-makers…

War, let there be war - O war, thou son of hell, whom angry heavens do make their minister…

War, let there be war - Sound all the lofty instruments of war…

War, let there be war – Strike up the drums and let the tongue of war plead for our interest…

War, need to be certain that w. is necessary before declaring it - Therefore take heed… how you awake our sleeping sword of war'.

War, outcome of w. uncertain – … Thou know'st, great son, the end of war's uncertain.

War, questionable rewards of w. See 'Profession, argument to use to justify a disreputable p. – What would you have me do? go to the wars…'

War, ready for w. – the cannons have their bowels full of wrath.

War, threat of w. See 'Threat, t. of blood and revenge - … I'll use the advantage of my power and lay the summer's dust with showers of blood…'

War, who is responsible when participating in a criminal war - … But if the cause be not good, the king himself hath a heavy reckoning to make

War, w. and peace, requiring different behavior. See 'Behavior, b. appropriate to peace and war - ... modest stillness and humility… then imitate the action of the tiger…'

War, w. bloody and unnatural - ... I always thought it was both impious and unnatural that such immanity and bloody strife…

War, warmongering breath - Your breath first kindled the dead coal of wars..

War, w. and revenge - ... let slip the dogs of war that this foul deed shall smell above the earth…

War, w. in progress – … the nimble gunner with linstock now the devilish cannon touches…

War, w. justified for a noble cause – The peace of heaven is theirs, that lift their swords in such a just and charitable war.

War, w. justified if intent is just – The arms are fair when the intent of bearing them is just.

War, w. leader and charismatic following – He is their god: he leads them like a thing made by some other deity than nature…

War, w. pending. See 'Times, rebellious t. - Rich men look sad and ruffians dance and leap…'

War, w. predicted - I do believe, statist though I am none, nor like to be, that this will prove a war.

War, w. preferable to love - He wears his honour in a box unseen…

War, w. prevention - This might have been prevented and made whole with very easy arguments of love…

War, w. unsought but forced on us - made us doff our easy robes of peace.

War, w. useless – …and shows no cause without why the man dies.

War, w. useless - …the toil of war, a pain that only seems to seek out danger…

War, w. useless - …We go to gain a little patch of ground that hath in it no profit but the name.

Wars, imperialistic w. See 'Foreign policy, war to cover up internal problems - Be it thy course to busy giddy minds with foreign quarrels.'

Warmonger, w's frame of mind - I, in this weak piping time of peace have no delight to pass away the time.

Warmonger, w's frame of mind. See 'War, in praise of w. – This peace is nothing, but to rust iron, increase tailors, and breed ballad-makers…'

Warning – stop being a portent of broached mischief to the unborn times.

Warning, gratitude for the w. – I thank thee who hath taught my frail mortality to know itself

Warning, response to w. that indicates mistrust – Make me not offended in your distrust.

Warning, safety w. better leave this place - Hie thee from this slaughter-house, lest thou increase the number of the dead.

Warning, stay away. See 'Injunction, stay out of this - come not between the dragon and his wrath.'

Warning, you'll hear from me - The thunder of my cannon shall be heard.

Warning, w. against lying. See 'Lying, penalty for l. – If thou speak'st false, upon the next tree shalt thou hang alive till famine cling thee…'

Warning, w. against a malicious character. See 'Character, malicious with everyone - ..the king.. is not quite exempt from envious malice of thy swelling heart.'

Warning, w. lest the pain inflicted on others may fall on the inflicters - Take heed, for heaven's sake, take heed, lest at once the burthen of my sorrows fall upon ye.

Warning, w. not to be taken in by misleading words. See 'Words, smooth and treacherous - ... let not his smoothing words bewitch your hearts; be wise and circumspect.

Warning, w. not to use the memory of great men to justify or add mischief - ... let 'em look they glory not in mischief, nor build their evils on the graves of great men...

Warning, w. of doing evil - Whilst I can vent clamour from my throat I'll tell thee thou dost evil.

Warning. See 'Anger, a. boiling up to the point of explosion - The bow is bent and drawn, make from the shaft.' *** Entries for 'Threat'. *** 'Beware, b. of the enemy - Take heed o' the foul fiend!'

Wash, in need of a w. - As black as Vulcan in the smoke of war.

Washing a persistent stain - Out, damned spot! out, I say.

Wasps, w. as a symbol of ingratitude. See 'Ingratitude, addressing the ingrate as wasps - Injurious wasps! to feed on such sweet honey and kill the bees, that yield it, with your sting.'

Waste, determination to eliminate w. - The caterpillars of the commonwealth, which I have sworn to weed and pluck away.

Waste, w. by excess. See 'Excess, e. not necessary and wasteful once objective is reached - To gild refined gold, to paint the lily... is wasteful and ridiculous excess.'

Waste, w. of time. See 'Time

Watch your language. See 'Watch your language. See 'Speech, language, watch your language - Take heed, be wary how you place your words.'

Watch, without a w. at night - I cannot, by the progress of the stars give guess how near to day.

Water, toast to w. in praise of water against wine – See 'Toast, t. with water - ... Here's that which is too weak to be a sinner, honest water...'

Waves, ocean stormy w. See 'Nature, stormy sea – When I have seen the hungry ocean gain advantage on the kingdom of the shore.

Waves, playing with the w. at the beach. See 'Beach, entertainment on the beach - ... chase the ebbing Neptune and do fly him when he comes back'

Waves, w. as a metaphor for the passing of time. See 'Time, passing of t. inevitable –Like as the waves make towards the pebbled shore, so do our minutes hasten to their end...

We are such stuff as dreams are made on. See 'Life, surrounded by sleep and partaking of dream experience - We are such stuff as dreams are made on, and our little life is rounded with a sleep.'

We have seen better days - True is it that we have seen better days..

We ignorant of ourselves... See 'Ignorance, i. of what is really good for us - We, ignorant of ourselves beg often our own harms, which the wise powers deny us for our good...'

We must not stint our necessary actions... See 'Action, need to act notwithstanding possible censure – We must not stint our necessary actions...'

Weak, compared to a twist of rotten silk. See 'Oath, resolution broken - ... Breaking his oath and resolution, like a twist of rotten silk.'

Weak, feeling w. and unprotected – A naked subject to the weeping clouds...

Weak, the w. always loses. See 'Injustice, unjust accusations and attack on the weak – .. A staff is quickly found to beat a dog.'

Weakness, group w. , in a weak position - ... our lances are but straws, our strength as weak, our weakness past compare...

Weakness, perception of w. - This milky gentleness and course of yours...

Weakness, w. and strength relative. See entries for 'Strength'.

Weakness, w. and/or shyness - I am weaker than a woman's tear.

Wealth relative, real w. is in the mind - ... for 'tis the mind that makes the body rich...

Wealth, accumulation of questionable w. – ... they have engrossed and piled up the canker'd heaps of strange-achieved gold.

Wealth, advantages of lack of w. See 'Poverty, a case for p. - Who would not wish to be from wealth exempt..'

Wealth, a wealthy man. See 'Liberality, l. excessive - ... Plutus the God of gold is but his steward'.

Wealth, consequences of hunger for w. See 'Life, l's objectives and the consequences of excessive ambition for wealth - Honour for wealth; and oft that wealth doth cost the death of all, and all together lost.'

Wealth, excessive ambition for w. self-destructing – ...And this ambitious foul infirmity, in having much, torments us with defect...

Wealth, high income not a certificate of intelligence when coupled with prodigality - ... but he'll have but a year in all those ducats: he's a very fool and prodigal.

Wealth, indifferent to the display of w. – Such outward things dwell not in my desires.

Wealth, the downside of w. - Who would not wish to be from health exempt since riches point to misery and contempt.

Wealth, w. accumulated via the cover of thrift – ... How, i' the name of thrift does he rake this together!

Wealth, w. in poverty - ... that art most rich, being poor, most choice, forsaken; and most loved, despised.

Wealth, w. not a recipe for happiness. See 'Contentment, assured if insensitive to poverty - Poor and content is rich and rich enough...'

Wealth, w. of no use to old age - ... when thou art old and rich, thou hast neither heat, affection, limb, nor beauty...

Wealth, w. of no use to old age. See 'Age, a. incapable of enjoying wealth – 'The aged man that coffers-up his gold is plagued with cramps and gouts and painful fits...'

Wealth, w. unloaded by death – If thou art rich, thou'rt poor for, like an ass whose back with ingots bows...

Wealth. See 'Financial Status - They are but beggars that can count their worth.'

Weariness can snore upon the flint... See 'Sleep, s. habits influenced by lifestyle – weariness can snore upon the flint, when resty sloth finds the down pillow hard.'

Weariness, tired, at the end of your rope - ... the last hour of my long weary life is come upon me.

Weariness. See 'Mind, state of m. weariness as a weakness - ... it discolours the complexion of my greatness to acknowledge it.'

Weary with toil... See "Mind, always on your mind - Weary with toil, I haste me to my bed, the dear repose for limbs with travel tired...'

Weather, hot w. - too hot the eye of heaven shines.

Weather, hot w. and its effects on temper - ... if we meet, we shall not 'scape a brawl; for now, these hot days, is the mad blood stirring.

Weather, see also entries for 'Nature, weather'.

Weather, storm, walking under the storm - ... have walk'd about the streets submitting me unto the perilous night...

Weather, unreliable w. and w. patterns - The spring, the summer, the chiding autumn, angry winter, change their wonted liveries...

Weather, wild w. conditions – So foul and fair a day I have not seen.

Weather, w. as an impartial arbiter - ... the selfsame heaven that frowns on me looks sadly upon him.

Weather, w. conditions, extreme – In winter's cold and summer's parching heat...

Weather, w. conditions threatening - ... the skies look grimly, and threaten present blusters.

Weather, w. conditions unsuitable to walking - ... this disturbed sky is not to walk in.

Weather, w. prediction, derived from sky observations - Men judge by the complexion of the sky the state and inclination of the day.

Weather, w. predictions incorrect - Why didst thou promise such a beauteous day and make me travel forth without my cloak…

Weeding, literal and metaphorical. See 'Gardening, weed pulling – …I will go root away the noisome weeds, which without profit suck the soil's fertility from wholesome flowers.'

Weeds, w. as analogy of problem to be solved. See 'Problem, p. to be tackled before it gets bigger – Now 'tis the spring, and weeds are shallow-rooted...'

Welcome - … as welcome… as I have words to bid you…

Welcome - The night to the owl and morn to the lark less welcome.

Welcome, a 100 thousand welcomes - … A curse begin at the very root of his heart, that is not glad to see thee!

Welcome, anything you want - … welcome: if thou wantest any thing, and wilt not call, beshrew thy heart

Welcome, going behind formality - You are very welcome to our house, it must appear in other ways than words…

Welcome, rhetorical w. – Welcome, a curse begin at very root on's heart…'

Welcome, sincere w. - .. but when you depart from me, sorrow abides, and happiness takes his leave.

Welcome, w. as spring to earth - … Welcome hither, as is the spring to the earth.

Welcome, w. given in strained circumstances. See 'Alliance, a. weak in power but heartfelt - I give you welcome with a powerless hand but with a heart full of unstained love.'

Welcome, w. in humbleness. See 'Invitation, i. to your place when you know that your place is in a state of disarray - We will give you sleepy drinks, that your senses, unintelligent of our insufficiency…'

Welcome, w. kiss. - I can express no kinder sign of love, than this kind kiss.

Welcome, w. overstayed. See 'Situation, s. deteriorating, welcome overstayed - .. methinks my favour here begins to warp.'

Welcome, w. to our house - All our services in every point twice done, and then done double..

Welcome, w. with friendly threat – … welcome: if thou wantest any thing, and wilt not call, beshrew thy heart.

Welcoming compliments - …the appurtenance of welcome is fashion and ceremony..

Welfare, consideration for your w. noted. See 'Problem, p. solving, effort at solving problem appreciated but.. - .. the care you have of us, to mow down thorns that would annoy our foot, is worthy praise..'

Welfare, excesses of w. - … here's them in our country of Greece gets more with begging than we can do with working.

Welfare, w. hinging on electoral changes. See 'Enemy, e. to be eliminated - .. the welfare of us all hangs on the cutting short that fraudful man.'

Well being, everything is OK if she is OK - … for nothing can be ill, if she be well.

Well said. See 'Speech, words well said - 'Tis most nobly spoken'.

What a candy deal of courtesy… See 'Kindness, false k. - … what a candy deal of courtesy this fawning greyhound then did proffer me!'

What are you doing? See 'Dedication, d. and spirituality - … Not dallying with a brace of courtezans, but meditating with two deep divines…'

What are you doing now? See 'Education, continued e. - …

What are you doing in your retirement? See 'Time, passing t. carelessly - and fleet the time carelessly, as they did in the golden world…'

What are you going to do next? See 'Chance, taking your c. for a while - … let myself and fortune tug for the time to come.'

What are you going to do now that you have been fired? See 'Determination, d. shown even in extreme circumstances - I shall show the cinders of my spirits through the ashes of my chance.'

What are you here for? See 'Visit, v. or call, reason for – I come, in kindness and unfeigned love…to crave a league of amity.'

What are you talking about? See 'Subject, inquiring about discussed s. – What were't worth to know the secret of your conference?'

What are you thinking about? See 'Expression, why so serious, what are you thinking about? - … What serious contemplation are you in?' *** 'Mind, state of mind, thinking about nothing and sad - … though, in thinking, on no thought I think.'

What are your plans? See 'Character, fatalistic – We profess ourselves to be the slaves of chance, and flies of every wind that blows.'

What are your str

What can be avoided…See 'Destiny, beyond our control – What can be avoided whose end is purposed by the mighty gods?'

What can you do for us? See 'Daring, d. but to a limit - I dare do all that may become a man; who dares do more is none.'

What custom wills, in all things… See 'Custom, c. as an obstacle to positive change - What custom wills, in all things should we do't, the dust of antique time would lie unswept…'

What did he say? See 'Definition, offensive d, cannot be named - What I cannot name but I shall offend.'

What did you do at college? See 'Youth, y. potentially misspent - … thou wouldst have plunged thyself in general riot; melted down thy youth in different beds of lust…'

What did you think of lady XY? See 'Woman, w. beyond description - … For her own person, it beggar'd all description.'

What do you do for a living? See "Life, l. as a battle - Strives in his little world

What do you drink? See 'Wine, w. preferred – The juice of Egypt's grape shall moist this lip.'

What do you have to say? See 'Words, w. comforting, true, honest – I do come with words as medicinal as true…'

What do you know of him? See 'Character, a respectable person - common speech gives him a worthy pass.'

What do you like? See 'Character, likes and dislikes, a temperate man immune to mass media and events - rather rejoicing to see another merry…'

What do you like in me? See 'Invention, extraordinary power of i. required to properly describe her – O for a Muse of fire, that would ascend the brightest heaven of invention.' *** Entries for 'Beauty', 'Complexion', 'Woman'

What do you mean? See 'Opinion, your op. delivered simply - I'll show my mind according to my shallow simple skills.'

What do you think? See 'Opinion, your op. delivered simply - I'll show my mind according to my shallow simple skills.'

What do you think it's worth? See 'Value, valueless - … not worth my thinking.'

What do you think of him/her (ne

What do you think of her (positive)? See 'Adoration, a. not just friendship - I profess myself her adorer, not her friend.' *** Select from entries for 'Opinion', 'Character', 'Woman', 'Beauty'.

What do you think of him? (positive) See 'Opinion, your op. on a specific man – … know him noble, of great estate, of fresh and stainless youth…' *** Select from entries for 'Opinion', 'Character', 'Man'

What do you think of him? (proud man). See entries for 'Character, proud'.

What do you think of him? (sarcastic). See 'Flattery, extreme f. – … in action how like an angel! in apprehension how like a god…'

What do you think of me? See 'Divine, exceeding all natural excellence - I might call him a thing divine, for nothing natural I ever saw so nob

What do you think of my idea/plan? See 'Opinion, what is your o? (case when you approve) - The image of it gives me content already…'

What do you think of it? See 'Opinion, what is your o.? (case when you approve) - The image of it gives me content already…'

What do you think of them? See 'Men, one word catch all - ... in the catalogue ye go for men…'

What do you think of this hot weather? See 'Weather, hot w. - too hot the eye of heaven shines.'

What do you think of women? See 'Woman, dish for the Gods - A woman is a dish for the gods, if the devil dress her not.' *** 'Women, w.

What do you think will happen? See 'Future, the f. will tell – There are many events in the womb of time, which will be delivered.'

What do you want? See 'Approach, securing a way out - She's beautiful, and therefore to be woo'd…'

What do you want to do? See 'Determination, d. to the bitter end, no trading dignity for life - I am resolved for death or dignity.'

What fools these mortals be. See 'Men, their folly - Lord, what fools these mortals be!'

What happened to so and so? See 'Report, he is doing very well - Report speaks goldenly of his profit.'

What have I done? – I should make very forges of my cheeks that would to cinders burn up modesty…

What have I done? See 'Rudeness, r. undeserved - What have I done, that thou darest wag thy tongue in noise so rude against me?'

What have you done? See 'Secret, s. will be disclosed to her after the (successful) event - Be innocent of the knowledge, dearest chuck, till thou applaud the deed.'

What is a man, if his chief good… See 'Sleep, s. unprofitable - What is a man, if his chief good and market of his time be but to sleep and feed? a beast, no more.'

What is the problem? See 'Distress, deep d. and reason of- why, say, fair queen, whence springs this deep despair?'

What is the time? S

What is worrying you? See 'Words, painful and pressing on memory – .. it presses to my memory like damned guilty deeds to sinners' minds.'

What's wrong with him/her? See 'Women, a question about w's faults - …There were none principal; they were all like one another as half pence are…'

What is your financial condition? See entries for 'Financial status'.

What is your education? See 'Writing, w. skills not always an asset - ... I have been so well brought up that I can write my name…'

What is your experience? See 'Experience, value of e. and how it is acquired - Experience is by industry achieved and perfected by the swift course of time.' and other entries for 'Experience'

What is your hobby? See 'Ladies, l's man and yet not – I'll make my heaven in a lady's lap, and deck my body in gay ornaments…'

What is your name? See 'Expression, frowning to be expected - Prepare thy brow to frown.'

What is your philosophy? See 'Invocation, i. to nature as a supreme ruler, also answer to a request from your girlfriend - Thou, nature, art my goddess; to thy law my services are

What is your reason? See 'Reason, r. good enough – I have no exquisite reason but reason good enough.' *** 'Woman, w.'s intuition - I have no other reason but a woman's reason.' *** Entries for 'Intuition'.

What is your taste in clothnig? See 'Advice, a. on men's wear and fashion - Costly thy habit as thy purse can buy, but not express'd in fancy; rich, not gaudy…'

What is your title? See 'Title, crown and content - My crown is call'd content, a crown is it that seldom kings enjoy.'

What made you come here? See 'Adventure, move prompted by a sense of a. – Such wind as scatters young men through the world.'

What need the bridge much broader than the flood? See 'Means, m. appropriate to objectives.'

What shall we do? See 'Discretion, relying on d. - your discretions better can persuade than I am able to instruct or teach.' *** 'Action, request for advice on how or what to do - let your own discretion be your tutor.'

What should we do with him? See 'Kill him - …Off with the crown, and with the crown his head…'

What should we speak of when we are as old as you… See 'Talk, subject t. when old - … when we shall hear the rain and wind beat dark December'

What the dickens. See 'Exclamation, what the dickens - I cannot tell what the dickens his name is…'

What we oft do best… See 'Misjudgement, transposition of values - … What we oft do best... is not ours, or not allow'd; what worst … is cried up for our best act.'

What to ourselves in passion we propose. See 'Decisions, rash d. - What to ourselves in passion we propose, the passion ending, doth the purpose lose.'

What type of person is he? See 'Comment, no c. - … what he is indeed, more suits you to conceive than I to speak of.'

What will other people think? See 'Opinion, o. of others to be disregarded – A plague of opinion! a man may wear it on both sides, like a leather jerkin.'

What will you be doing after your retirement? See entries for 'Retirement'.

What will you do next? See 'Information, no i. disclosed about what you intend to do next - … What course I mean to hold shall nothing benefit your knowledge.'

What will you do this week end? See 'Country living, in praise of country living - .. Here can I sit alone, unseen of any and to the nightingale's complaining notes…' – Entries for 'Sightseeing'.

What will you do, (after your resignations). See 'Exhortation, e. to patience - Be patient, for the world is bro

What would you like to have? See 'Music, request for m. as food of love – … music, moody food of us that trade in love.'

Whatever happened to your other girlfriend? See 'Star, s. versus sun, divided between two loves - At first I did adore a twinkling star, but now I worship a celestial sun.'

What's done is done. See 'Attitude, a. towards what is past and cannot be changed – things without all remedy should be without regard…' *** 'Actions, past a. cannot be remedied – Look, what is done cannot be now amended, men shall deal unadvisedly sometimes…'

What's in a name? See 'Name, n. or label, irrelevant - … That which we call a rose by any other name would smell as sweet.'

What's in it for you? See 'Modesty, deeds as their own reward - ... rewards his deeds with doing them, and is content to spend the time to end it.'

What's past is prologue. See 'Continuation, going to the next step - … to perform an act whereof what's past is prologue.'

When I consider everything that grows… See 'Time, t. and the inherent limited duration of everything - When I consider everything that grows holds in perfection but a little moment...'

When I have seen… See 'Nature, stormy sea – When I have seen the hungry ocean gain advantage on the kingdom of the shore.'

When in disgrace with fortune and men's eyes. See 'Psychological uplifting, her positive effect when you are down in the dumps – When in disgrace with fortune and men's eyes…'

When love begins to sicken and decay… See 'Cooling off observed, general truth - When love begins to sicken and decay, it useth an enforced ceremony.'

When my glass… See 'Age. You are old and you may as well admit it – When my glass shows me myself indeed…'

When my love swears that she is made of truth. See 'Age. You are old, you know it, she tells you that you are young and you pretend to believe it.'

When our actions do not our fears do make us traitors. See 'Fear, f. causing treason'

When our actions do not our fears do make us traitors. See 'Fear, f. causing treason'

When shall we three meet again? See 'Meeting, scheduling the next m. - When shall we three meet again? In thunder, lightning or in rain?'

When she is angry. See 'Anger, even her a. is an occasion for admiration - … How wonderful when angels are so angry.'

When sorrows come … See 'Misfortunes piling up - When sorrows come, they come not single spies, but in battalions!'

When the age is in, the wit is out. See 'Age. Its effects on intelligence'.

When to the session of sweet silent thought. See 'Nostalgia, regret - When to the session of sweet silent thought, I summon up remembrance of things past…'

Where are you from? See 'Foreigner - Not of this country, though my chance is now to use it for my time.'

Where are you going? See 'Let's get out of here – … To seek the empty, vast and wandering air.'

Where did he go? See entries for 'Disappearance'

Where did you hear of this? See 'News, n. gathered from hearsay - … this from rumour's tongue I idly heard; if true or false, I know not.'

Where did you see this? See 'Vision, intuition - In my mind's eye, Horatio.'

Where do you live? See 'Location, remote l. - … some forlorn and naked hermitage, remote from all the pleasures of the world…'

Where is he? See 'Absent, cannot find him - I think he be transform'd into a beast for I can no where find him like a man.'

Where is he/she? - I know not where; but wheresoever, I wish him well.

Whiles I am a beggar, I will rail … See 'Political (and personal) double standards - whiles I am a beggar, I will rail… there is no sin but to be rich…'

Whipping, w. deserved by all. See 'Man and his wicked nature - … use every man after his desert, and who should 'scape whipping?'

Whisperings, w. about bad deeds - Foul whisperings are abroad, unnatural deeds do breed unnatural troubles.

Whistle-blowers, put down by authority. See 'Authority, a. using its power to discredit accusers and whistle blowers - … no particular scandal once can touch but it confounds the breather.'

White, whiter than w. See 'Invocation, i. for lover to come – .. come, thou day in night; for thou wilt lie upon the

Who are you? – …I am that merry wanderer of the night.

Who are you? - A most poor man, made tame to fortune's blows…

Who are you? - What man art thou that thus bescreen'd in night so stumblest on my counsel?

Who are you? See 'Devil, who are you? - What devil art thou, that dost torment me thus'. *** 'Defense, d. from general accusations – I am a man more sinned against than sinning'

Who are you? See 'Identification, characteristics - More than I seem, and less than I was born to…' *** 'Man, m. shipwrecked (materially or metaphorically) - A man whom both the waters and the wind…' *** 'Name, hesitation to self-introduction – By

Why are you doing this? See 'Woman, w. as a prize – … the prize of all too precious you'

Why are you not running for office? See 'Lifestyle, not bothered by ambition for public office – Let those who are in favour with thei

Why are you not taking notes? See 'Memory, impossible to forget - Why should I write this down, that's riveted, screw'd to my memory.'

Why are you sighing? See 'Sigh - (my heart) wounded it is, but with the eyes of a lady.'

Why can't you sleep? See 'Sleeplessness caused by the weight of your responsibilities - Uneasy lies the head that wears a crown.' *** Entries for 'Sleeplessness'

Why did you do this? See 'Face, heavenly f. as a cause of various acts, desperate or otherwise - … 'twas thy heavenly face that set me on.'

Why did you stop reading? See 'Reading, not being able to read on due to unhappiness - Some sudden qualm hath struck me at the heart…'

Why didst thou promise… See 'Weather, w. predictions incorrect - Why didst thou promise such a beauteous day and make me travel forth without my cloak…'

Why do you look so sad? See 'Expression of sadness misconstrued - My heart is ten times lighter than my looks.' *** Entries for 'Depression'

Why do you look so sad, (or upset or serious)? See 'Expression, sour facial e. habitual when seeing a (figurative) crab - … you must not look so sour … It is my fashion when I see a crab.'

Why do you want to be elected? See 'Immortality, desire for i. – I have immortal longings in me.'

Why don't you dance? See 'Dancing, reason for not d. – … I have a soul of lead so stakes me to the ground I cannot move.'

Why don't you drive a Mercedes? See 'Eccentricity, above the crowd –… I will not jump with common spirits and rank me with the barbarous multitude.'

Why don't you like him? See 'Dislike, I don't like him - His countenance likes me not.'

Why don't you look at me? See 'Gaze, turning away your g. - I am no loathsome leper; look on me.'

Why don't you say anything? See entries for 'Silence'.

Why don't you like to go to a discotheque? See 'Masochism, against m. - all delights are vain; but that most vain, which with pain purchased doth inherit pain.'

Why are you not talking? See 'Silence, s. as a symptom or evidence of happiness - Silence is the perfectest herald of joy, I were but little happy, if I could say how much.'

Why are you unhappy? See 'Character, c. pessimistic by nature - His discontents are unremoveably coupled to nature.' *** 'Unhappiness, asking for reasons of u. - … make me acquainted with your cause of grief.' *** Other entries for 'Unhappiness'.

Why change? (reason for) See 'Custom, c. as an obstacle to positive change - What custom wills, in all things should we do't, the dust of antique time would lie unswept…'

Why change? (accepting but somewhat critical). See 'Society, state of s. - … there is so a great a fever on goodness, that the dissolution of it must cure it. Novelty is only in request…'

Why should you be different from others? See 'Nature, northern star - The skies are painted with unnumber'd sparks… but there is but one in all doth hold his place.'

Wickedness, w. painted in fair colors - … with colours fairer painted their foul ends.

Wife, answer to an angry w. - To offer war where they should kneel for peace

Wife, choosing a w. independently. See 'Selection, desire to select independently - … in such a business give me leave to use help of mine own eyes.' *** 'Refusal, r. of help or

1357

brokerage - … give me leave to play the broker in mine own behalf …'

Wife, complaining w. 'You do nothing in the house' – … for thy maintenance commits his body to painful labour….

Wife, compliment. See 'Best, compliment, she is the best wife – … kings might be espoused to more fame but king nor peer to such a peerless dame.'

Wife, constancy of her love. See 'Constancy, c. of wifely love – …like a jewel, has hung twenty years about his neck, yet never lost her lustre…'

Wife, duties of a w. obedience as a subject to a prince - .. such duty as the subject owes the prince..

Wife, no trust in w. – I will rather trust a Fleming with my butter… than my wife with herself.

Wife, praise for a good w. – O ye gods, render me worthy of this noble wife

Wife, w. asking husband 'what do you want from me'? See lines in 'Husband, declaration of husband's rights - Such duty as the subject owes the prince even such a woman oweth to her husband.'

Wife, w. that routinely outspeaks her husband - When she will take the rein I let her run but she'll not stumble.

Wife, wives' merriment not incompatible with their honesty – Wives may be merry, and yet honest too.

Wig, false hair – … the dowry of a second head, the skull that bred them in the sepulchre.

Wild-goose chase - Nay, if thy wits run the wild-goose chase, I have done.

Wilderness of tigers. See 'Cruelty, c. in Rome - Rome is but a wilderness of tigers'

Will you always lo

Will you be good to me? See 'Treatment, care of details and pleasant t. promised - … And pluck the wings from painted butterflies, to fan the moonbeams from his sleeping eye.'

Will you be true? See 'Faithfulness, f. restated - While others fish with craft for great opinion, I with great truth catch more simplicity…'

Will you change your mind? See 'Determination, stubbornness, no change of mind – There is no power in the tongue of man to alter me.'

Will you come? See 'Determination, d. to participate to an event or a party even if ill - … Not sickness should detain me.'

Will you come back? See 'Return? Not a chance - No, rather I abjure all roofs, and choose to wage against the enmity o' the air…'

Will you come to dinner? See 'Dinner invitation, answer to - Ay, if I be alive and your mind hold and your dinner worth the eating.'

Will you come with me? See 'Joining the party – The swallow follows not summer more willing than we your lordship.' *** 'Obedience, complete o. - I am your shadow, my lord; I'll follow you'

Will you do exactly what I told you to do? See 'Commitment, c. to execute o. to the fullest - … thy commandment all alone shall live within the book and volume of my brain, unmix'd with baser matter.'

Will you do this? See entries for 'Command

Will you do this for me? See 'Service, at her complete s. – Being your slave what should I do but tend upon the hours and times of your desire?' *** 'Character, unable to say 'no' to women - … whom ne'er the word of 'No' woman heard speak.'

Will you forgive me? See 'Love, true l. extremely forgiving - So true a fool is love that in your will…' *** Entries for 'forgiveness'.

Will you give to organization (or other)? See 'Solicitations, answer to telephone s. – I am not in the giving vein to-day.'

Will you really do it?' See 'Promise, solemn p. – And I will die a hundred thousand deaths, ere break the smallest parcel of this vow.'

Will you go to XY's party? See 'Party, p. attended by fools and parasites - ... to see meat fill knaves, and wine heat fools'

Will, making personal w. the law. See 'Law, l. vs. personal will - I have been a truant to the law....'

Will, mind over matter notwithstanding a state of debility – And like the rich hangings in a homely house.

Will, our w. at odds with destiny. See 'Destiny, at odd with our wills - ... Our wills and fates do so contrary run that our devices still are overthrown, our thoughts are ours, their ends none of our own.'

Will, w., not impossibility or cowardice. See 'Lying, l. about impossibility and fear - ... Cannot, is false, and that I dare not, falser…'

Will, w. or fancy prevailing over reason - .. if my reason will thereto be obedient, I have reason…

Will, w. prevailing over reason – … that would make his will lord of his reason.

Will, w. to live gone. See 'Die, desire to d. - … he hates him much that would upon the rack of this tough world stretch him out longer.'

Wind and tide. See 'Destiny, inappropriate to resist to d. - What fates impose, that men must needs abide, it boots not to resist both wind and tide.' *** 'Man, politically very powerful - .. this is he that moves both wind and tide.'

Wind, extremely strong w. – Methinks the wind hath spoke aloud at land…

Wind, venture without profit - Ill blows the wind that profits nobody.

Winds, sheltering her from harsh weather conditions. See 'Love, signs or evidence of l. - .. he might not beteem the winds of heaven visit her face too roughly.'

Wine, drink as a warmer-upper - Come, let me pour some sack to the Thames water; for my belly's as cold..

Wine, drinking, unable to tolerate strong drinks - ... I have very poor and unhappy brains for drinking...

Wine, drinking, unable to tolerate strong drinks - It's monstrous labor when I wash my brain and it grows fouler.

Wine, drunkenness, see 'Apologies for having drunk too much – it perfumes the blood ere one can say, what's this?'

Wine, effects of w. - ... it raises the greater war between him and his discretion

Wine, effects of w. - … mine own tongue splits what it speaks.

Wine, evil effects of w. - O God, that men should put an enemy in their mouths to steal away their brains!…

Wine, good but devastating. See 'Apologies for having drunk too much – it perfumes the blood ere one can say, what's this?'

Wine, good w. – Good wine is a good familiar creature if it be well used; exclaim no more against it.

Wine, invitation to drink until falling asleep. See 'Party, invitation to p. - ... let's take hand till the conquering wine hath steeped our sense in soft and delicate Lethe.'

Wine, medium to get a girl talking. See 'Speech, wine and its effect on women's speech'

Wine, negative effects of w. - … and drink, sir, is a great provoker of three things.

Wine, no water in it - (I am) one that loves a cup of hot wine with not a drop of allaying Tiber in't.

Wine, positive effects of w. – A good sherri-sack hath a two fold operation in it…

Wine, promises made under the influence unreliable. See 'Man, m. false - … falser than vows made in wine'

Wine, refusing more e. or drink - I am unfortunate in the infirmity, and dare not task my weakness with any more.

Wine, see also entries for 'Drink' and 'Drunkenness'

Wine, selecting the company with whom to

get drunk - …if I be drunk, I'll be drunk with those that have the fear of God, and not with drunken knaves.

Wine, stop drinking. See 'Drinking, knowing when to stop (drinking) – honorable stop'

Wine, teetotaler, reasons for not drinking - Every inordinate cup is unblessed and the ingredient is a devil.

Wine, toasting with water instead of w. See 'Toast, t. with water - … Here's that which is too weak to be a sinner, honest water…'

Wine, unacceptable statements made under the effects of w. - … we consider it was excess of wine that set him on…

Wine, w. and forgetfulness - … though I cannot remember what I did when you made me drunk…

Wine, w. and its effect on women. See 'Speech, wine and its effect on women's speech - The red wine first must rise in their fair cheeks, my lord; then we shall have 'em talk us to silence.'

Wine, w. as a catalyst for reconciliation - Give me a bowl of wine. In this I bury all unkindness.

Wine, w. a catalyst for the display of learning. See 'Learning, power of l. better displayed after a drink – … and learning a mere hoard of gold kept by a devil, till sack commences it and sets it in act and use.'

Wine, w. as a psychosomatic remedy against anger or depression – He shall taste of my bottle: if he have never drunk wine afore…

Wine, w. as a support for speech - … give me some wine, and let me speak a little.

Wine, w. as a tool for forgetting and making others forget - … memory, the warder of the brain, shall be a fume…

Wine, w. as an anti-depressant - Give me a bowl of wine, I have not the alacrity of spirit nor cheer of mind that I as wont to have.

Wine, w. as an ingredient for a sense of humor - … nor a man cannot make him laugh; but that's no marvel, he drinks no wine.

Wine, w. as an instrument of the devil – O thou invisible spirit of wine, if thou hast no name to be known by, let us call thee devil.

Wine, w. as the distillate of summer - But flowers distilled though they with winter meet…

Wine, w. of life. See 'Event, course of e. completely changing your outlook on life - Had I but died an hour before this chance I had lived a blessed time…'

Wine, w. or drink of horrible quality – (A) leperous distilment, whose effect holds an enmity with blood of man.

Wine, w. preferred – The juice of Egypt's grape shall moist this lip.

Wine. See entries for 'Drunkenness'

Winking. See 'Awareness, a. declared and pointed out – I see things too although you judge I wink.'

Winners and losers, loser defeated by himself - Not Caesar's valor hath o'erthrown Antony but Antony's hath triumphed on itself

Winter of our discontent. See 'Greetings, end of unhappiness – Now is the winter of our discontent, made glorious summer by this sun of York..'

Winter, it feels like w. when she is away – Yet seem'd it winter still, and, you away, as with your shadow I with these did play.

Winter, w. as a tamer (mellowing agent) of spirits - … thou know'st, winter tames man, woman and beast.

Winter, w. nights, a method of spending them – In winter's tedious nights sit by the fire…

Winter. See 'Summer turning into Winter'

Win-win situation through a stratagem - … the doubleness of the benefit defends the deceit from reproof.

Wisdom, request to deliver w. – … now unmuzzle your wisdom.

Wisdom, showing lack of wisdom but not lack of nobility - Unwisely, not ignobly, have I given.

Wisdom, w. absorbed with nursing milk - Were not I thine only nurse, I would say thou hadst suck'd wisdom from thy teat.

Wisdom, w. and age. See 'Age, a. inevitably engenders wisdom'.

Wisdom, w. and goodness not for the vile - Wisdom and goodness to the vile seem vile, filths savour but themselves.

Wisdom, w. and self-denial. See 'Self-denial, s.d. as a sign of wisdom – The greatest virtue of which wise men boast is to abstain from ill, when pleasing most'

Wisdom, w. as a lack of irrational haste. See 'Wisdom, w. in caution with expectations - ...and modest wisdom plucks me from over-credulous haste.'

Wisdom, w. as the support of true friendship. See 'Friendship, f. guaranteed by wisdom - The amity that wisdom knits not, folly may easily untie.'

Wisdom, w. beyond a doubt - I doubt not of your wisdom.

Wisdom, w. exemplary – ... whose wisdom was a mirror to the wisest

Wisdom, w. hidden behind apparent folly - He uses his folly like a stalking horse, and under the presentation of that, he shoots his wit.

Wisdom, w. in caution with expectations - ...and modest wisdom plucks me from over-credulous haste.

Wisdom, w. in the young dangerous to themselves - So wise so young, they say, do never live long.

Wisdom, w. invoked. See 'Invocation, ironic i. applicable to fools – God give them wisdom that have it; and those that are fools, let them use their talents.'

Wisdom, w. only apparent and misguided - 'The fool doth think he is wise but the wise man knows himself to be a fool.

Wisdom, w. prevailing over chance - Wisdom and fortune combating together...

Wisdom, words of w. to oneself, avoiding messy situation – ... But, Suffolk, stay; thou mayst not wander in that labyrinth...

Wisdom, yielding to w. - To wisdom he's a fool that will not yield.

Wish, w. expressed in jest becomes true. See 'Retribution, wish pronounced in jest has become true - ... And given in earnest what I begg'd in jest.'

Wish, w. to possess the power of lightning-thunderbolt - If I had a thunderbolt in mine eye, I can tell who should down.

Wishes and salutations, see entries for 'Salutations and Wishes'.

Wishes, good w. plus compliment - Wishes, good w. plus compliment - they are worthy to inlay heaven with stars.

Wishes, have a good trip. See 'Goodbye, when she is leaving for a short or long trip, or a shopping excursion - Let all the number of the stars give light to thy fair way.'

Wishes, shared w. See 'Agreeing, a. with wish or proposal - My vows are equal partners with thy vows.'

Wishes, w. for a happy day - The gods make this a happy day to Antony!

Wishes, w. for a long life - ... let Aeneas live ... thousand complete courses of the sun!

Wishes, w. for a long life – ... may he live longer than I have time to tell his years!

Wishes, w. for a repetition of success - And more such days as these to us befall!

Wishes, w. of happiness - Let grief and sorrow still embrace his heart that doth not wish you joy!

Wishes, w. of happiness ever increasing - ... that our loves and comforts should increase even as our days do grow.

Wishes, w. of getting what is desired - God send every one their heart's desire!

Wishes, w. of joy – Let grief and sorrow still embrace his heart that doth not wish you joy.

Wishes, w. of peace and prosperity - Enrich the time to come with smooth-faced peace...

Wishes, w. of success during a travel away from home - Upon your sword sit laurel victory and smooth success be strewed before your feet.

Wishes, w. that facts may follow words – … and ever may your highness yoke together… my doing well with my well saying.

Wishes, w. that facts may follow words - … And your large speeches may your deeds approve…

Wishes, w. to have the power of persuasion - God give thee the spirit of persuasion and him the ears of profiting.

Wishful thinking, political w.t. – … My pity hath been balm to heal their wounds…

Wit, lack of w. shown in bad decision. See 'Decision, bad d. – thou hast pared thy wit o' both sides, and left nothing i' the middle.'

Wit, person capable to use w. to turn bad into good situations. See 'Workers' compensation for questionable disability - … A good wit will make use of any thing …'

Wit, sarcasm on someone's wit - Thy wit is as quick as the greyhound's mouth; it catches.

Wit, unaware of one's own wit – I shall ne'er be ware of mine own wit till I break my shins against it.

Wit, w. admired - I like thy wit well, in good faith.

Wit, w. against self invited. See 'Masochism, m. for love – … dart thy skill at me… cut me to pieces with thy keen conceit.'

Wit, w. concealed. See 'Wisdom, w. hidden behind apparent folly - He uses his folly like a stalking horse, and under the presentation of that, he shoots his wit.'

Wit, w. ill directed and punished - See now, how wit may be made a Jack-a-lent, when 'tis upon ill employment.

Wit, w. somewhat overwhelming - Your wit's too hot, it speeds too fast, 'twill tire.

Wit, w. that cannot be understood - When a man's verses cannot be understood, nor a man's good wit seconded with the forward child Understanding…

Wit, witless. See 'Character, not very bright – … his wit is as thick as Tewksbury mustard.'

Wit, witty and target of wits. See 'Jokes, the butt of others' jokes - … the brain of this foolish-compounded clay, man, is not able to invent…'

Wit, witty f. vs. foolish wit. See 'Insult, fool, response and maxim - Better a witty fool than a foolish wit.'

Wit, witty man. See 'Character, man with a jovial disposition - … a merrier man, within the limit of becoming mirth, I never spent ' *** 'Workers' compensation for questionable disability - … A good wit will make use of any thing …'

Wit. See entries for 'Folly'

Wit, wits that make fools of themselves – None are so surely caught, when they are catch'd, as wit turn'd fool…

Witches, recognizable by their attire. See 'Attire, outlandish or wacky - … so wild in their attire, that look not like the inhabitants o' the earth'

Witches, uncertainty about their sex. See 'Sex identity difficult, masculine looking women - .. you should be women, and yet your beards forbid me to interpret that you are so.'

Witchcraft, excellent w. - …fresh piece of excellent witchcraft.

Witchcraft, w. in language. See 'Favoritism, f. through oratory - … he hath a witchcraft over the king …'

Witchcraft. See 'Lips, bewitching - you have witchcraft in your lips…'

Witnesses, corrupted w. See 'Corruption, corrupted witnesses - … at what ease might corrupt minds procure knaves as corrupt to swear against you?...'

Wits, w. willfully lost - … thou hast pared thy wit o' both sides and left nothing i' the middle.

Witticism, humor as a double edges sword - A sentence is but a cheveril glove to a good wit; how quickly the wrong side may be turned outward!

Woe. See entries for 'Positive thinking and defiance towards setbacks'.

Woe is me. See 'Unhappiness, u. and desperation - O, woe is me, to have seen what I have seen, see what I see!'

Wolf. See 'Anger. Angry at h

Wolves, w. greedily expecting to assault the prey. See 'Decision, bad personnel or management d. - Thus is the shepherd beaten from thy side, and wolves are gnarling who shall gnaw thee first.'

Woman, a cold w. – I would have thought her spirit had been invincible against the assaults of affection.

Woman, a cold w. – ... spoke with her but once and found her wondrous cold.

Woman, a physically strong, fighting w. See 'Amazon, an a. - .. thou art an Amazon and fightest with the sword of Deborah.'

Woman, amazement, a. at her change in character - ... I would have I thought her spirit had been invincible against all assaults of affection.

Woman, anything but talking with her – (Anything) rather than hold three words' conference with this harpy.

Woman, assessment of a fair and silly w. – She never yet was foolish that was fair...

Woman, assessment of a fair and wise w. – If she be fair and wise, fairness and wit...

Woman, assessment of an ugly and silly w. – There's none so foul and foolish thereunto...

Woman, beautiful - ... As silver-voiced; her eyes as jewel-like and cased as richly...

Woman, beautiful – ... gorgeous as the sun at midsummer.

Woman, beautiful and to be courted. See entries for 'Approach, securing a way out '.

Woman, best of all - She excels each mortal thing upon the dull earth dwelling.

Woman, conceding to a w. See 'Bewi

Woman, correspondence between w.'s parts and countries' geography - Scotland, France, etc.

Woman, cruel - ... Pierced through the heart with your stern cruelty...

Woman, cruel, farewell to cruel w. See 'Farewell, f. to beautiful but cruel woman - ...Farewell, fair cruelty.'

Woman, cruel, killer - Fly away, fly away breath, I am slain by a fair cruel maid.

Woman, cruel, serpent - O serpent heart, hid with a flowering face!

Woman, determined w. See 'Character, woman, ambitious w. - .. being a woman, I will not slack to play my part in Fortune's pageant.'

Woman, dish for the Gods - A woman is a dish for the gods, if the devil dress her not.

Woman, evil w. – ... she hath lived too long to fill the world with vicious qualities.

Woman, evil w., like a harpy - ... with thine angel's face seize with thine eagle's talons.

Woman, female frailty – ... as the glasses where they view themselves; which are as easy broke as they make forms.

Woman, female frailty, invocation - ... how weak a thing the heart of woman is.

Woman, female frailty, invocation - Frailty, thy name is woman.

Woman, getting to a young w.'s heart. See 'Gifts, g. as means to a young woman's heart - ... trifles, nosegays, sweetmeats, messengers of strong prevailment in unharden'd youth'.

Woman, happy the man who will marry her - ... Happier the man, whom favourable stars allot thee for his lovely bed-fellow!

Woman, hard and harsh w. or crying - A woman mov'd is like a fountain troubled...

Woman, ideal w. - ... a shop of all the qualities that man loves woman for.

Woman, impossible w. - Her only fault (and that is fault enough) is that she is intolerable curst... I would not wed her for a mine of gold.

Woman, impregnable – She will not stay the siege of loving terms, nor bide..

Woman, in deep trouble – She is fallen into a pit of ink!

Woman, inestimable and powerful – … she is a pearl, whose price hath launch'd above a thousand ships…

Woman, jealous w. See entries for 'Jealousy'.

Woman, large w. - … in what part of her body stands Ireland.

Woman, large w. after an unwilling male - She is too big, I hope, for me to compass.

Woman, life of married life preferable to that of a nun. See 'Marriage, in praise of m. – But earthly happier is the rose distill'd.…'

Woman, list of her lovable qualities - Beshrew me but I love her heartily, for she is wise, if I can judge of her…

Woman, modest w. more attractive than immodest w. See 'Modesty, m. in a woman as temptation for a seducer - … modesty may more betray our sense than woman's lightness?'

Woman, moved by w's tears - At a few drops of women's rheum.. he sold the blood and labour of our great action.

Woman, noisy and shrew-like, no deterrent. See 'Resistance, power of r. to noise acquired via repeated trials - Think you a little din can daunt mine ears?'

Woman, not to be trusted to keep a secret. See 'Secrecy, impossible to break it if secret is not known - …thou wilt not utter what thou dost not know.'

Woman, perfect - divine perfection of a woman.

Woman, perfect w and beyond description. See 'Beauty, b. exceeding power of the pen to describe it - … a maid that paragons description and wild fame; one that excels the quirks of blazoning pens…'

Woman, perfect w. everything OK with her - … Whom every thing becomes, to chide, to laugh, to weep …

Woman, perfection in a w. See related entries for 'Perfection' *** 'Best, compliment, you are the best .'

Woman, persuaded by a w. See 'Persuasion, persuaded by a woman - .. As prisoners to her womanly persuasion.'

Woman, preferring one w. to another suddenly. See 'Replacement, you loved her first and suddenly you love another - Even as one heat another heat expels, or as one nail by strength drives out another…'

Woman, pretty in foot, lip, eye and well spoken - We say that Shore's wife hath a pretty foot,…

Woman, pretty w, seen dancing, who is she? – What lady is that, which doth enrich the hand of yonder night?

Woman, pretty, witty and wild – I know a wench of excellent discourse, pretty and witty…

Woman, proud and haughty w. - Nature never framed a woman's heart of prouder stuff than that of Beatrice…

Woman, proud w. See 'Queen, so to speak - …she is the queen of curds and cream.'

Woman, provocative - there's language in her eye, her cheek, her lip, nay, her foot speaks…

Woman, provocative w. - What an eye she has! methinks it sounds a parley of provocation.

Woman, provocative w. and available - I spy entertainment in her.

Woman, real w. better than her picture – So far this shadow doth limp behind the substance.

Woman, rich w. - … she is a region in Guiana, all gold and bounty.

Woman, search for a wealthy w. - … nothing comes amiss, so money comes withal.

Woman, spiritual deformity in a w. worse. See 'Character, evil c. in a woman worse than in an enemy – Proper deformity seems not in the fiend so horrid as in woman.'

Woman, spiteful and sharp tongued - She speaks poniards, and every word stabs…

Woman, splendid and majestic - What

peremptory eagle-sighted eye dares look upon the heaven of her brow…

Woman, sweet w. - … she is sweeter than perfume itself.

Woman, sweetest w. in the world - … the world hath not a sweeter creature

Woman, task better left to a w. – The office becomes a woman best.

Woman, the opposite of a w. – Women are soft, mild… thou … rough, remorseless

Woman, trust in w. unjustified – Mine eyes were not in fault, for she was beautiful…

Woman, waiting for the perfect w. See 'Expectations, your e. unreasonable – … till all graces be in a woman, one woman shall not come in my grace.'

Woman, thoughtful and gentle w. - You bear a gentle mind, and heavenly blessings follow such creatures.

Woman, totally incorruptible –… she would make a puritan of the devil, if he should cheapen a kiss of her.

Woman, unable to say 'no' to a woman. See 'Character, unable to say 'no' to women - … whom ne'er the word of 'No' woman heard speak.'

Woman, undaunted by w's shrewish character - Think you a little din can daunt mine ears?…

Woman, unimaginably cunning w. – She is cunning past man's thought.

Woman, unique in perfection – Her whose worth makes other worthies nothing.

Woman, unpredictable - Who is 't can read a woman?

Woman, unsuitable words for a w. See 'Words, not w. for a woman - …'Tis not for you to hear what I can speak..'

Woman, what she is to you - The fountain from the which my current runs…

Woman, with mannish manners - A woman impudent and mannish grown…

Woman, w. admired by all - the observed of all observers. See 'Politician, young aspiring p. - The expectancy and rose of the fair state… the observed of all observers.'

Woman, w. admired for beauty and honor – I have perused her well, beauty and honour in her are so mingled…

Woman, w. as a jewel. See 'Pride, p. in possession. "Are you glad that you married me?" - .. as rich in having such a jewel as twenty seas, if all their sand were pearl…'

Woman, w. as a prize – … the prize of all too precious you.

Woman, w. beautiful, as a sunbeam. See 'Sunbeam, her beauty compared to the reflection of sunbeams on water - As plays the sun upon the glassy streams, twinkling another counterfeited beam…'

Woman, w. beautiful, bewitching and sexy - Let witchcraft join with beauty, lust with both!

Woman, w. beautiful, confounds speech. See 'Speechless, made speechless by her princely beauty - .. beauty's princely majesty is such, confounds the tongue, and makes the senses rough.'

Woman, w. beautiful, even the air would go and see her - … the air; which, but for vacancy had gone to gaze on Cleopatra too…

Woman, w. beautiful, prompts courting. See 'Approach, securing a way out - she's beautiful, and therefore to be woo'd…'

Woman, w. beyond description - … For her own person, it beggar'd all description.

Woman, w. believed chaste - … as chaste as unsunn'd snow.

Woman, w. chaste – … chaste as the icicle that curdied by the frost from purest snow…

Woman, w. defined - … a child of our grandmother Eve, a female.

Woman, w. difficult to read - You are such a woman! one knows not at what ward you lie…

Woman, w. helpful during negotiations – … when maidens sue men give like gods…

Woman, w. helpful during negotiations –

Haply a woman's voice may do some good...

Woman, w. like a queen. See entries for 'Queen'

Woman, w. looking like the Spring. See 'Spring, looking like the s. – See where she comes, apparell'd like the spring.'

Woman, w. loud and contentious w. - ... she chide as loud as thunder when the clouds in autumn crack.

Woman, w. lovely and fragrant to the extreme – (Thou) who art so lovely fair and smell'st so sweet...

Woman, w. misjudged – Mine eyes were not in fault, for she was beautiful...

Woman, w. of superior intelligence. See section of 'Mathematics, not a strength - ..cannot take two from twenty, for his heart and leave eighteen'.

Woman, w. reserved and bashful – A pudency so rosy the sweet view on't might well have warm'd old Saturn.

Woman, w. sun-tanned and/or with brown eyes - ... as brown in hue as hazel nuts and sweeter than the kernels.

Woman, w. super chaste – ... in strong proof of chastity well arm'd...

Woman, w. super chaste – He spake of her, as Dian had hot dreams...

Woman, w. tempting in her modesty. See 'Modesty, m. in a woman as temptation for a seducer'.

Woman, w. that keeps the books and is arbiter of economic decisions - ... the report goes she has all the rule of her husband's purse.

Woman, w. that yields real power. See 'Power, where real power is - .. for, as I hear you that are king, though he doth wear the crown.'

Woman, w. universally admired and pursued. See 'Ego boosting, she is a sought after prize - Nor is the wide world ignorant of her worth...'

Woman, w. unmarried and pregnant – ... a gentlewoman of mine, who, falling in the flaws of her own youth hath blister'd her report.

Woman, w. unmoved by extraordinary events - ... you can behold such sights and keep the natural ruby of your cheeks.

Woman, w. who does not like bearded men - ... I could not endure a husband with a beard on his face...

Woman, w. who turns men off - So turns she every man the wrong side out ...

Woman, w. worthy of a king. See 'Perfection, worthy of a king - ... all her perfections challenge sovereignty; one way or other, she is for a king.'

Woman, w.'s character altered by anger - O, when she's angry, she is keen and shrewd!...

Woman, w.'s intuition - I have no other reason but a woman's reason.

Woman, w.'s power to move - ... Her sighs will make a battery in his breast, her tears will pierce into a marble heart.

Woman, w's pride congenital. See 'Pride, p. as a trait of women - ... it was Eve's legacy, and cannot be ta'en from her.'

Woman, w.'s reputation, r. or character marred by sin – ... falling in the flaws of her own youth hath blister'd her report.

Woman, witty - Thou wert as witty a piece of Eve's flesh as any in Illyria

Woman, young w. and a natural persuader - ... for in her youth there is a prone and speechless dialect, such as move men.

Womb, w. redefined - ... that nest of spicery...

Women as weapons of mass destruction - This fell whore of thine hath in her more destruction than thy sword, for all her cherubim look.

Women, a question about w's faults - ...There were none principal; they were all like one another as half pence are...

Women, anti-feminist logic - Why are our bodies soft, and weak, and smooth, unapt to toil, and trouble in the world...

Women, anti-feminist statement - ... know

he is the bridle of your will…

Women, light w. argument against them– It is written, they appear to men like angels of light…

Women, bill of rights for women - I'll exhibit a bill in the parliament for the putting down of men.

Women, changelings even in vice - … For even to vice they are not constant but are changing still…

Women, contiguity of w. at table to be avoided - Two women placed together makes cold weather.

Women, disparaging generalizations – … you are pictures out of doors…

Women, giving thought precedence to action. See 'Thought, t. preceding action - so do all thoughts, they are winged'.

Women, impulsive character of w. - … when I think, I must speak.

Women, looking at other w. See 'Forgiveness, f. for looking at other women - … A sin prevailing much in youthful men who give their eyes the liberty of gazing.'

Women, masculine looking. See 'Sex identity difficult, masculine looking women'.

Women, modest and virtuous w. have greater appeal than lascivious ones - Most dangerous is that temptation that doth goad us on to sin in loving virtue…

Women, negative effects of w, ruling men. 'See 'Men, m. subjected to women – Why, this it is, when men are ruled by women…'

Women, not trusting w. See 'Bachelorhood, justification for b. - Because I will not do them the wrong to mistrust any, I will do myself the right to trust none…'

Women, over-feminist w. – I am ashamed that women are so simple to offer war where they should kneel for peace…

Women, power of w's tongue - The tongues of mocking wenches are as keen as is the razor's edge invisible..

Women, requests from w. bound to be gratified - … when maidens sue, men give like gods; but when they weep and kneel…

Women, some reasons for disliking other women. See entries for 'Best, compliment'.

Women, submissive role of w. - I am asham'd that women are so simple to offer war, where they should kneel for peace..

Women, talkativeness of w. unstoppable - .. thou are worthy to be hang'd, that wilt not stay her tongue…

Women, the fun is in the chase - Women are angels wooing, things won are done, joy's soul lies in the doing.

Women, their difficulty to keep things to themselves - How hard it is for women to keep counsel.

Women, their judgment swayed by appearances - … the error of our eye directs our mind…

Women, their persuasive power greater than men's oratory - … when a world of men could not prevail with all their oratory, yet hath a woman kindness over-ruled.

Women, their verbal persuasive skills - These women are shrewd tempters with their tongues.

Women, Venetian w. See 'Conscience, false c. - … their best conscience is not to leave it undone, but keep it unknown.'

Women, very uncomplimentary view - Down from the waist they are Centaurs, though women all above…

Women, w. as repositories of vice - .. Could I find out the woman's part in me!

Women, w. compared to German clocks - A woman, that is like a German clock, still a-repairing, ever out of frame, and never going a-right…

Women, w. compared to roses - For women are as roses, whose fair flower, being once displayed, doth fall that very hour.

Women, w. vs. men. See 'Men versus women, women more steady than m.'

Women, w.'s reaction in trying circumstances – … women are not in their best fortunes strong; but want will perjure…

Wonder, audience awestruck. See 'Audience, quiet or unreceptive - … like dumb statues or breathing stones.'

Wonder, events eliciting w. See entries for 'Events, strange'

Wonder, w. beyond power of written description – One that excels the quirks of blazoning pens.

Wonder, w. inducing news - 'tis the rarest argument of wonder that hath shot out in our latter times.

Wonder, w. that leaves you speechless, See 'Speechless, awed in wonder – I am so attired in wonder I know not what to say.'

Wonders, w. to be described – Masters, I am to discourse wonders.

Word, compressing in itself and expressing a very long time - How long a time lies in one little word!

Word, convinced about the accuracy of the w. – I will maintain the word with my sword…

Word, w. power, key to seduction - That man that hath a tongue, I say, is no man if with his tongue he cannot win a woman.

Wordiness. See entries for 'Talker' *** 'Character, wordy - … what a spendthrift is he of his tongue!' *** 'Verbose'

Words to the heat of deed… See 'Actions, a. speak more than words - Words to the heat of deeds too cold breath gives.'

Words, absolutely true. See 'Truth, assurance about one's own credibility - Believe my words for they are certain and unfallible.'

Words, abuse and Orwellian use of w. – … they, that dally nicely with words, may quickly make them wanton.

Words, abusive. See 'Annoying, arrogant and unpleasant to hear – She does abuse our ears…'

Words, acknowledgment of pleasing w.– I thank thee, Meg; these words content me much.

Words, apologies for w. said. See 'Apologies for words unruly words caused by indisposition - … impute his words to wayward sickliness and age in him.'

Words, array of good w. uttered by a fool - The fool has planted in his memory an array of good words.

Words, barrage of w, many and inconsequential - A fine volley of words, gentlemen, and quickly shot off.

Words, barrage of w. - I was never so bethump'd with words since I first call'd my brother's father dad

Words, barrage of w. - What craker is this same that deafs our ears with this abundance of superfluous breath?

Words, battery of words that persuade, convince and motivate. See 'Speech, her words have completely overcome your resistance - I am vanquished; these haughty words of hers have batter'd me like roaring cannon-shot…'

Words, carrying bad news or offensive or poorly written - Here are a few of the unpleasant'st words that ever blotted paper.

Words, cruel w. delivered diplomatically. See 'Rejection, she says no with a smile that hurts more than soothes - Thou cuttest my head with a golden axe and smil'st upon the stroke that murders me.'

Words, deceiving w. – They shoot but calm words folded up in smoke…

Words, despicable w. but well crafted - Ignominious words, though clerkly couched.

Words, devastating w. - I have words that would be howl'd out in the desert air…

Words, devious w. used in questioning - With many holidays and lady terms he question'd me.

Words, encouraging and acknowledged as such - O Clifford, how thy words revive my heart!

Words, encouraging and reviving – Those gracious words revive my drooping thoughts.

Words, encouraging and reviving w. – These words, these looks, infuse new life in me.

Words, evil w. aggravating weight of evil act

- Ill deeds are doubled with an evil word.

Words, excellent and well put w. - these words become your lips as they pass through them.

Words, false w. of peace - I speak of peace, while covert enmity under the smile of safety wounds the world.

Words, fed up with idle or self-serving w. - I can no longer brook thy vanities

Words, fed up with soothing w. of comfort. See 'Fed up with comforting efforts - I'll hate him everlastingly that bids me be of comfort any more.'

Words, few w. more likely to achieve the desired effect. See 'Truth, t. in economy of words - where words are scarce, they are seldom spent in vain.'

Words, fighting with w. at first. See 'Battle, b. strategy, diplomacy first, arms later - ... let's fight with gentle words...'

Words, foul w. ending deductively into foul b. - Foul words is but foul wind…

Words, good w. vs. bad action - Good words are better than bad strokes…

Words, hurting w. – … your words, they rob the Hybla bees and leave them honeyless

Words, insincere w. See 'Repentance, insincere r. - My words fly up, my thoughts remain below, words without thoughts never to heaven go.' *** 'Religion, r. allegiance just in words – … and sweet religion makes a rhapsody of words.'

Words, killing w. See 'Rejection, despair at her words - .. if words be made of breath and breath of life, I have no life to breathe what thou hast said to me.'

Words, no mincing of w. - If I prove honey-mouth'd let my tongue blister…

Words, no w. available in language to express indignation - there is no chastity enough in language without offence, to utter them

Words, not many words needed among friends. See 'Friends, not many words needed among f. - .. 'twixt such friends as we few words suffice.'

Words, not w. for a woman - …'Tis not for you to hear what I can speak..

Words, painful and pressing on memory – .. it presses to my memory like damned guilty deeds to sinners' minds.

Words, painful w. – These words are razors to my wounded heart.

Words, painful w. – These words of yours draw life-blood from my heart.

Words, perfunctory - ..(speak to them) with such words that are but roted in your tongue..

Words, plea to stop hurtful w. See 'Speech, plea to stop hurtful s. - O, speak to me no more; these words, like daggers, enter in mine ears.

Words, poisoned w. coated with false niceties - Hide not thy poison with such sugar'd words.

Words, pompous w. - To divide him inventorially would dizzy the arithmetic of memory…

Words, power of w. to poison relationships - … one doth not know how much an ill word may empoison liking.

Words, quick wit recognized - I would my horse had the speed of your tongue, and so good a continuer.

Words, rash w. caused by reaction to unfair accusation. See 'Accusation, defense from a., justification for rash words – slanderous tongue'.

Words, reaction to w. heard. See 'Disgust, d. at words heard'.

Words, reaction to w. without meaning or sincerity - Words, words, mere words, no matter from the heart…

Words, refraining from using abusive w., veiled insult - … I know you what you are… am most loath to call your faults as they are named.

Words, rehearsed w. planted in memory - The fool hath planted in his memory an army of good words.

Words, relative harmlessness of w. - But words are words, I never yet did hear…

Words, silly w., playing with w., - …and discourse will grow commendable only in parrots.

Words, sincere w. - .. his words come from his mouth, ours from our breast.

Words, smooth and treacherous - Let not his smoothing words bewitch your hearts; be wise and circumspect.

Words, stinging w. - Ah, what sharp sting are in her mildest words!

Words, taking back words just uttered - What then he said, so he unsay it now.

Words, thinking before speaking - I know thou'rt full of love and honesty, and weigh'st thy words before thou giv'st them breath.

Words, unconvincing w. - Out idle words, servants to shallow fools!

Words, unintelligible w. See "Anger, a. detected but inexplicable – I understand a fury in your words but not the words.'

Words, using strange w. See 'Speech, strange way of expressing oneself – .. his words are a very fantastical banquet, like many strange dishes.'

Words, weighing w. before speaking - …(Thou) weigh'st thy words before thou givest them breath…

Words, weight of w. depending on the their utterer - That in the captain's but a choleric word which in the soldier is flat blasphemy.

Words, w. cannot remove pain. See 'Pain, p. that cannot be comforted - …men can counsel, and speak comfort to that grief which they themselves do not feel… Charm ache with air and agony with words.'

Words, w. comforting, true, honest – I do come with words as medicinal as true…

Words, w. of love, prompted by her beauty - My tongue could never learn sweet smoothing words…

Words, w. not enough, truth is important - … it is not enough to speak, but to speak true.

Words, w. not enough, truth is important - … it is not enough to speak, but to speak true.

Words, w. not enough to stop love. See 'Love, l.'s yearnings not abated by words - Didst thou but know the inly touch of love…'

Words, w. that are no deeds - … 'Tis a kind of good deed to say well and yet words are no deeds.

Words, w. that please the audience - But what care I for words? yet words do well, when he that speaks them pleases those that hear.

Words, w. that remove any resentment - Each word thou hast spoke hath weeded from my heart a root of ancient envy.

Words, w. used to twist meaning - I can yield you no reason without words; and words are grown so false, I am loth to prove reason with them.

Words, w. uttered but not meant - … syllables of no allowance to your bosom's truth.

Words, w. well said and showing modesty and discretion. See 'Modesty, comment on a modest comment of hers - Words sweetly placed and modestly directed.'

Words, wasted breath - Never did mockers waste more idle breath.

Words, wild and somewhat senseless - .. These are but wild and whirling words.

Words, wounding w. - They wound my thoughts worse than sword my flesh.

Words, your w. have no effect on me - Thy words move rage and not remorse in me.

Work, available for w. - … If it be man's work, I'll do 't.

Work, back to hard w. after some rest. See 'Punishment and condemnation - My hour is almost come, when I to sulphurous and tormenting flames must render up myself.'

Work, enough of idle talk - … there are throats to be cut and works to be done

Work, it does not matter if it is hard w.

provided we like it - The labour we delight in physics pain.

Work, type of w. we like to go to - To business that we love we rise betime and go to it with delight.

Work, what type of w. can you do? – ... If it be man's work, I'll do 't

Work, working overtime while other sleep - ... constrain'd to watch in darkness, rain and cold.

Workers' compensation for questionable disability - ... A good wit will make use of any thing: I will turn diseases to commodity.

Working day world. See 'World, a tough w. to live in - O, how full of briers is this working-day world.'

Working hard in all sorts of conditions. See 'Weather, w. conditions, extreme – In winter's cold and summer's parching heat...'

Working late or at night – ... some must watch, while some must sleep...

World, w. a dangerous place – I am amazed, methinks, and lose my way among the thorns and dangers of this world.

World, a slippery place – O world, thy slippery turns!

World, a tough w. to live in - O, how full of briers is this working-day world.

World, conditions of the w. See 'Conditions, current place and c. not as bad as others' - This wide and universal theatre presents more woeful pageants.'

World, hating it and reasons why. See 'Attitude, a. towards the world, hating it – one.. whom the vile blows and buffets of the world...'

World, medicine for the ills of the w. - .. and I will through and through cleanse the foul body of the infected world if they will patiently receive my medicine.

World, pessimistic view of the w. – ... what is in this world but grief and woe?

World, pessimistic view of the w. – A bawdy planet, that will strike where 'tis predominant...

World, pessimistic view of the w. - Earth, yield me roots! Who seeks for better of thee, sauce his palate thy most operant poison.

World, pessimistic view of the w. - I am sick of this false world, and will love nought but even the mere necessities upon 't.

World, pessimistic view of the world – I 'gin to be aweary of the sun and wish the estate o' the world were now undone.

World, pessimistic view of the w. - It wears as it grows.

World, pessimistic view of the w. – There is enough written upon this earth to stir a mutiny in the most quiet.

World, pessimistic view of the w. - We have seen the best of our time: machinations, hollowness, treachery, and all ruinous disorders...

World, pessimistic view of the w. and its inherent evil - I am in this earthly world; where to do harm is often laudable..

World, pessimistic view of the w. See 'Life, a combination of good and bad - The web of our life is of a mingled yarn, good and ill go together..' *** 'Pessimism, p. to the point that death is tolerable - The stroke of death is as a

World, pessimistic view of the w., a congregation of vapors – It goes so heavily with my disposition that this goodly frame, the earth..

World, pessimistic view of the w., just a stage - I hold the world but as the world, Gratiano; a stage where every man must play a part..

World, pessimistic view of the w., no honesty left - We need no grave to bury honesty: there is not a grain of it the face to sweeten of the whole dungy earth.

World, she is the w. - ... for where thou art, there is the world itself.

World, w. dispensing troubles to all. See 'Conditions, current place and c. not as bad as others - This wide and universal theatre presents more woeful pageants...'

World, w. hostile to goodness - O, what a world this is, when what is comely envenoms him that bears it.

World, w's deceit. See 'Innocence, naïveté due to youth - ... the untainted virtue of your years hath not yet dived into the world's deceit...'

Worm, w. or metaphor for small creature reacting in self-defense - The smallest worm will turn being trodden on.

Worms. See 'Love, to die for l. not proven by historical evidence - ... men have died from time to time and worms have eaten them, but not for love.'

Worship, question in the form of a compliment - Bright Star of Venus, fallen down on earth, how may I reverently worship thee enough?

Worst, the extreme of w. - And worse I may be yet: the worst is not so long as we can say 'This is the worst'.

Worth, w. depending on value – What is aught, but as 'tis valued?

Worthless person. See 'Insult, worth less than dust - ... You are not worth the dust which the rude wind blows in your face'.

Wound, nothing to bother about - And God forbid a shallow scratch should drive the Prince of Wales from such a field as this..

Wounded, w. and in need of a band aid - But I am faint, my gashes cry for help.

Wounded, w. figuratively by a friend. See 'Treason, unexpected t. from a friend hurting more - The private wound is deepest.'

Wounds, w. caused by love. See 'Love, l.'s power to wound when feelings are not reciprocated - ... then shall you know the wounds invisible that love's keen arrows make.'

Wounds, w. self-inflicted hard to heel - Those wounds heal ill that men do give themselves.

Wrinkles, in need of a face lift. See 'Character, a hypocrite with a false smile - .. he does smile his face into more lines than are in the new map…'

Writing the beauty of her eyes. See entries for 'Eyes, beauty of e.'

Writing, assurance of continued communications - I will omit no opportunity that may convey my greetings, love, to thee.

Writing, commitment to write frequently. See 'Commitment, c. to writing - Who's born that day when I forget to send to Antony shall die a beggar'.

Writing, confidence in your w. power - Your beauty shall in these black lines be seen, and they shall live, and you in them still green.

Writing, decision to write in prose after questioning your own poetical skills - I fear these stubborn lines lack power to move… These numbers will I tear, and write in prose

Writing, excusing your poor means to extol her charms - I grant (sweet love) thy lovely argument deserves the travail of a worthier pen...

Writing, fame and immortality through w. - Death makes no conquest of this conqueror, for now he lives in fame, though not in life.

Writing, letters anxiously awaited - ..and with mine eyes I'll drink the words you send though ink be made of gall.

Writing, power of printed message - .. in black ink my love may still shine bright.

Writing, using w. rather than speech - O let my books be then the eloquence…

Writing, what are you w. – O, know, sweet love, I always write of you…

Writing, w. preferred to speech - I'll call for pen and ink, and write my mind.

Writing, w. skills not always an asset - ... I have been so well brought up that I can write my name…

Written evidence. See 'Evidence, disputing incriminating written e. – My heart is not confederate with my hand.'

Wrong, w. compounded - ... thus to persist in doing wrong extenuates not wrong.

Wrong, w. suffered inhibits any pity. See 'Pity, no feeling of p. - Think but upon the wrong he did us all and that will quickly dry thy melting tears.'

Wrongs, great w. leading to barbarism. See 'Heavens, h. restraining the extremes of inhumanity - ... Humanity must perforce prey on itself like monsters of the deep.'

Wrongdoing. See 'Denial, d. of wrongdoing - The gods throw stones of sulphur on me, if...'

Yielding to wisdom. See 'Wisdom, yielding to w. - To wisdom he's a fool that will not yield.'

Yond Cassius has a lean and hungry look. See 'Fat, f. men less dangerous than thin – ... Yond Cassius has a lean and hungry look.'

You are always on my mind, see 'Mind, always on your mind - Weary with toil, I haste me to my bed, the dear repose for limbs with travel tired...'

You are not hungry any more? See 'Dinner, not hungry after d. - Who riseth from a feast with that keen appetite that he sits down?'

You came home too late. See 'Sleep, s. patterns and logic whereby late sleep is actually early rising - .. not to be abed after midnight is to be up betimes.'

You have a sense of humor. See 'Wit, unaware of one's own wit – I shall ne'er be ware of mine own wit till I break my shins against it.'

You have changed. See 'Beauty, b. declining with age or unforeseen circumstances - And every fair from fair sometime declines...'

You undergo too strict a paradox. Seen 'Spin, how to re-interpret reality - You undergo too strict a paradox striving to make an ugly deed look fair.'

You don't know what you are talking about. See 'Ignorance, i. shown - you speak, Lord Mowbray, now you know not what.'

You lie. See entries for 'Insult, liar'.

You write so well. See 'Reading, r. and writing natural - ... to write and read comes by nature.'

You taught me language ... See 'Education,

literature, results of teaching - You taught me language and my profit on it is, I know how to curse.'

Young and ready for greatness - ... ripe for exploits and mighty enterprises.

Your face, my thane, is as a book where men may read strange matters... See 'Dissimulation, lesson in d.'

Youth and rebellion - ... natural rebellion, done in the blaze of youth..

Youth, a dangerous time, prudence counseled - ... and in the morn and liquid dew of youth contagious blastments are most imminent.

Youth, a dangerous time, prudence counseled - ... keep you in the rear of your affection...

Youth, a young person – he wears the rose of youth upon him.

Youth, carefree attitude in your younger days - ... two lads that thought there was no more behind...

Youth, characteristics of youth's behavior - ... wanton, wild and usual slips as are companions noted...

Youth, levity of y. recollected - Our own precedent passions do instruct us..

Youth, lifestyle or regimen unsuitable to y. - To fast, to study and to see no woman.

Youth, restricting y. ineffective - Young blood doth not obey an old decree.

Youth, stage of y. - His May of youth and bloom of lustihood.

Youth, strict impositions on y. ineffective. See 'Instinct, i. prevailing over the dictates of law - ...the brain may devise laws for the blood...'

Youth, y. generally unreliable. See 'Expectations, e. poorly placed - .. briefly die their joys that place them on the truth of girls and boys.'

Youth, y. always craving for novelty - ... younger spirits, whose apprehensive senses all but new things disdain..

Youth, y. and travel. See 'Travel, t. in youth

an important educational tool - .. Which would be great impeachment to his age in having known no travel in his youth.'

Youth, y. potentially misspent - ... thou wouldst have plunged thyself in general riot; melted down thy youth in different beds of lust…

Youth, y. shortened by recklessness - For though the camomile, the more it is trodden on, the faster it grows, yet youth, the more it is wasted, the sooner it wears.

Youth, y. spent in idleness - …wear out thy youth with shapeless idleness.

Youth, y. spent in prison – … And hath detain'd me all my flowering youth within a loathsome dungeon…

Youthful insubordination. See 'Insubordination, youthful i. - …bristle up the crest of youth against your dignity'.

Youth, y. unable to follow good counsel – … such a hare is madness the youth, to skip o'er the meshes of good counsel the cripple.

Zed. See 'Insult, last letter of the alphabet - Thou whoreson zed, thou unnecessary letter…'

Zero tolerance – I will be deaf to pleading and excuses, nor tears nor prayers shall purchase out abuses.

Summary of Plays and Poems

ALL'S WELL THAT ENDS WELL
Helena loves Count Bertram and lives in Roussillon with the Countess, Bertram's mother. Helena is the daughter of a famous deceased physician – on her initiative she goes to Paris and cures the king of a grave illness when all other doctors had lost hope. As a reward, she asks the king to let her select a husband among the noblemen at court and of course she picks Bertram. He cannot refuse the king's order and marries her but abandons her immediately because she is below his station. He tells her that she will become his true wife if and when she will manage to get hold of the ring he wears on his finger. Whereupon Bertram, who behaves like an ass, goes to Florence to battle the Sienese, accompanied by his cowardly and equally asinine friend Parolles. In Florence Bertram tries to seduce Diana. But Helena, who had followed Bertram at a distance through his meandering, arranges to take the place of Diana when Bertram will arrive for a romantic rendezvous. Helena gets the ring, Bertram repents, the king forgives, Diana gets a dowry, Parolles is shamed and all ends well. All the while the Clown, the nobleman Lafeu and other lords poke fun at Parolles.

ANTONY AND CLEOPATRA
Antony moves in with sexy Cleopatra in Alexandria (Egypt) after abandoning wife Fulvia in Rome. Besides lust, Antony loves power. Caesar (Octavian) calls him back to Rome where the situation is uncertain and Pompey is stirring some trouble. In Rome Caesar, Lepidus and Antony strike a deal with Pompey and Antony marries Octavia, Caesar's sister. It is a political marriage and Antony soon drops Octavia and returns to Cleopatra. Caesar gives chase. Distracted by Cleopatra, Antony loses both at sea and on land and kills himself. In the end Caesar socks it to Antony, Lepidus and Pompey. Cleopatra is spared but she fears being dragged to Rome due to the Romans having very bad breath. A poisonous snake is smuggled in her palace and she uses it to end her days.

AS YOU LIKE IT
In a coup Frederick unseats Duke Senior, who then escapes to the forest of Arden with some congenial friends. Rosalind, Duke Senior's daughter, must also escape to the forest along with Celia, Frederick's daughter who dislikes her bossy and cruel father. Rosalind loves Orlando who knocked out Charles in a wrestling match. Orlando has enemies and also flees to the same forest. Rosalind disguises herself as a boy and rents lodgings from Corin the shepherd. Rosalind meets Orlando who is either blind or stupid and does not recognize the disguise. 'Rosalind' the boy asks Orlando to woo her as if she were Rosalind the girl. Meanwhile Phebe, a shepherdess rejects the advances of Silvius, a shepherd and falls in love with 'Rosalind' the boy. Touchstone, the clown likes Audrey, a country girl and steals her away from her country admirer William. Oliver, Orlando's evil brother tries to find Orlando in the forest but finds Celia instead and falls in love with her whereupon he repents. Orlando writes pitiful verses and graffiti to celebrate his love for Rosalind. In the end Rosalind throws off her disguise and puts some order in all these relationships. Rosalind marries Orlando, Oliver marries Celia, Phebe marries Silvius, Touchstone marries Audrey. Jacques, the skeptic who has had enough of all this retires to the forest probably for good.

COMEDY OF ERRORS
The twins Antipholus of Ephesus and Antipholus of Syracuse have also twin servants, Dromio of Ephesus and Dromio of Syracuse. The Antipholi were shipwrecked in infancy, rescued and raised separately in Ephesus and Syracuse. Their father Aegeon goes to Ephesus looking for his lost son and is arrested as an illegal alien. Antipholus S also goes to Ephesus looking for his brother. Extreme confusion follows due to continued instances of mistaken identity, including Adriana, wife of Antipholus E. and her sister Luciana. Eventually Antipholus S. takes refuge in a convent whose abbess turns out to be his

mother Emilia. The duke intervenes, Aegeon is freed, the confusion is cleared and the family is reunited.

CORIOLANUS
Caius Marcius is the archetypal right wing red neck. Having won over the Volsces at Corioli he is given the title of Coriolanus. He hates the working class. Left wing tribunes Sicinius and Brutus reciprocate and rouse the mob against him. His mother Volumnia, wife Virgilia and senator Menenius try to instill some moderation into Coriolanus without success. He is banished from Rome and joins the Volsces out of revenge, offering to fight for his former arch-rival and Volscean leader Tullus Aufidius. Menenius tries to dissuade Coriolanus from fighting against Rome but fails. Volumnia and Virgilia have better luck and Coriolanus relents. Now the Volsces are angry, consider him a traitor and kill him.

CYMBELINE
Cymbeline is king of England and Imogen, his daughter is married to Posthumus. Her stepmother and evil queen wants her to marry Cloten, her asinine son from a previous marriage. To achieve this she has Posthumus exiled to Rome. There he meets Iachimo and enters into a wager about Imogen's chastity. Iachimo travels to England, surreptitiously sneaks into Imogen's bedroom while she is asleep and gathers evidence that convinces Posthumus of her infidelity. Posthumus instructs by letter his servant Pisanio to kill Imogen. Instead, Pisanio helps her escape disguised as a boy. She takes refuge in the forest with Guiderius and Arviragus, her brothers, though she does not know it. Yes, because prior to the play, Belarius, a banned lord, had kidnapped and raised Cymbeline's sons. Cloten chases Imogen and is killed by Guiderius. Imogen drinks a powerful sleeping potion and is given for dead by her brothers. Caius Lucius, who has come from Rome to fight Cymbeline over owed taxes, finds Imogen. The British defeat the Romans, thanks to the valor of Posthumus (who initially came back with Lucius), Guiderius and Arviragus. The evil queen dies, Guiderius and Arviragus are returned to their father, the king, and the super-innocent Imogen gets back with Posthumus.

HAMLET
Claudius poisons and kills his brother king of Denmark, thus becoming king himself and quickly marries the widowed queen. The dead king shows up as a ghost first to the guards then to Hamlet friend's Horatio then to Hamlet, the dead king's son. The ghost tells Hamlet about the murder and asks him to be revenged. Hamlet complies while assailed and troubled by doubt and depression. To establish the king's guilt Hamlet produces a play where the slaying is accurately reproduced and watches the disturbed reaction of the king. Then Hamlet feigns madness and Polonius, the king's counselor attributes it to Hamlet's love for Ophelia, Polonius' beautiful daughter. The king wants to have Hamlet wasted and sends him to England in the company of Rosencrantz and Guildenstern, two counselors. But the plot fails and Hamlet is back in Denmark. While upbraiding the queen, his mother, Hamlet notices someone spying behind a curtain. It's Polonius and Hamlet kills him. Ophelia goes mad. Laertes, Polonius's son returns from France to avenge his father's death. The king uses Laertes to finally get rid of Hamlet and organizes a rapier match featuring Laertes versus Hamlet. Laertes' rapier is dipped in poison. Should Laertes lose, some poisoned wine is ready for Hamlet to drink in celebration of his victory. But the plan miscarries - in the duel both Hamlet and Laertes manage to wound each other with the poisoned rapier. The queen ends up drinking the poisoned wine. Before dying Laertes tells Hamlet of the king's plot, whereupon Hamlet kills the king before dying himself.

JULIUS CAESAR
Caesar has become the supreme ruler of Rome, beloved by the masses, always ready to praise and idolize the latest ruler.

Cassius, moved probably more by envy than love of democracy convinces Brutus that Caesar is a destroyer of freedom and must be eliminated. Brutus, Cassius and other conspirators hatch an assassination plot. Caesar disregards omens and warnings and goes to the Senate where he is duly killed. First Brutus addresses the mob, the Antony follows and craftily manages to inflame the masses who turn against the conspirators. The conspirators fly and Antony, Caesar (Octavian) and Lepidus take charge. Antony and allies defeat the conspirators at Philippi, where Brutus and Cassius kill themselves when they see that all is lost

KING JOHN
King John (the one of the *magna charta*) proves here to be an authentic SOB. He usurps the throne that legitimately belongs to his young nephew Prince Arthur. King Philip of France supports the rights of Arthur along with Arthur's mother Constance. But Elinor, King John's mother of course supports the rights of his son. There is a war in France between King John and King Philip after which a tenuous piece is established. Pandulph, the Pope's legate arrives to stir trouble and there is war again. King John captures young Arthur and imprisons him in a castle. Hubert de Burgh is contracted to murder Arthur but repents at the last moment. Arthur tries to escape by jumping from the castle ramparts but falls to his death. The people think that King John was responsible, bringing the country on the verge of civil war. Eventually the French invade England and the English unite to defeat the French. King John is finally poisoned.

KING HENRY IV PART 1
After having unseated his predecessor (see Richard II), Bolingbroke (Henry IV) is well established on the throne of England. His son, the Prince of Wales and future Henry V has a totally different character. He prefers the company of the fat and disreputable Falstaff rather than pursuing the duties of a would-be monarch. But hints are given throughout the play that the truly noble and strong character of the future Henry V will surface after a period of youthful intemperance.
To demonstrate how coward Falstaff really is, the Prince of Wales organizes a caper at Gadshill. Falstaff will rob some travelers. Afterwards the Price of Wales and Poins (disguised) will ambush Falstaff and company.
Falstaff is exposed but he has always an excuse. Meantime rebellion is brewing, the key rebels being led by the wild and hot tempered Hotspur (Lord Percy), Mortimer, Glendower of Wales and Douglas of Scotland.
At the battle of Shrewsbury the prince of Wales kills Hotspur and the rebels are defeated. Falstaff pretends that it was he who killed Hotspur whereas Hotspur was already dead.

KING HENRY IV PART 2
In Henry IV part 1, the Prince of Wales defeated a rebellion after killing the boisterous Hotspur. But there are other rebels, Mowbray and Hastings, led by Scroop, the Archbishop of York. Prior to another battle the rebels parley with John, the Prince of Lancaster, brother of the King of Wales. In a treacherous move, Lancaster arrests the rebels who are subsequently executed. In the meantime, the Prince of Wales still keeps company with the rowdy Falstaff and the Eastcheap crowd, Bardolph, Peto, Poins, Mistress Quickly and Toll Tearsheet (the names are all indicative). Falstaff is in charge to recruit a platoon of losers. In the meantime, he manages to extract money from his old acquaintance Justice Shallow, promising him advancement at court after the Prince of Wales becomes king. Henry IV dies and the Prince of Wales ascends to the throne as Henry V. He immediately reforms and turns around completely, rejects Falstaff and bans him from court. Before dying, Henry IV, counsels his successor to start foreign wars to deflect attention from domestic problems, a policy followed successfully ever since by various totalitarian and not totalitarian governments and leaders.

KING HENRY V
Henry V, the son of Henry IV is now king of England and, following the advice of his father, wages war in France. He is prompted by the bishops who explain very lengthily why Henry V has a claim to France. The priests really aim at avoiding taxation and lure Henry V into believing that the conquest of France will yield much greater revenue than what could be derived by taxing the church. In France, Henry V first captures Harfleur then wins the battle of Agincourt and finally woes and marries Katharine, the daughter of the king of France. He is now king of both England and France. The honest and somewhat hard headed Welsh Captain Fluellen, provides amusement by murdering the language with his expressions. Some of the Eastcheap gang shows up in France, including Pistol, Nym and Bardolph. Pistol has married Mistress Quickly. Events show their general cowardice and ineptitude.

KING HENRY VI , PART 1
The play covers the period from 1422, death of Henry V to 1444, year of the marriage between Henry VI, his son to Margaret, daughter of Reignier, king of Naples. Joan of Arc has freed the city of Orleans, besieged by the English. The English champion Talbot is killed near the city of Angiers. But the English regroup and manage to capture Joan of Arc, unceremoniously represented here as a witch and a harlot. Suffolk arranges the marriage between Margaret and Henry VI thereby assuring a temporary peace between England and France. The English squabble among themselves and the parties divide themselves between the York faction (white rose) and the Lancastrian faction (red rose) – the symbols associated with the War of the Roses. Somerset (a Lancastrian) and Plantagenet (a Yorkist) have a dispute and other lords are asked to decide who is right. But the lords remain silent. Plantagenet suggests that those who agree with him pluck a white rose (they are in the Temple gardens in London). In turn Somerset suggests that those who agree with him pluck a red rose.

KING HENRY VI , PART 2
Henry VI marries Margaret of Anjou, (1445), thanks to the good offices of the duke of Suffolk who may or may not be the Queen's lover. Intrigues and squabbles continue at court where the Duke of York (Richard Plantagenet) is plotting against the king who is supported by his uncle the duke of Gloucester and Lord Protector. Suffolk and Beaufort, cardinal of Westminster, hate the Duke of Gloucester. Gloucester is accused of treason and is found murdered, then Beaufort also dies of natural causes. Suffolk is banned and killed by pirates. Eventually the duke of York defeats the army of the king at St. Alban's. Meanwhile, John Cade a commoner starts a communist rebellion in London, hoping to kill all lawyers and grammar teachers, as he hates education in principle.

KING HENRY VI , PART 3
Henry VI agrees to name Richard Plantagenet, duke of York successor to the throne thus depriving Henry's own son of the right to the throne. But feisty queen Margaret has other ideas than her peace-loving husband. Richard is killed at the battle of Wakefield. Edward, Richard's son continues to fight against the army of Henry VI who is defeated at Towton. Edward is crowned as Edward IV. Henry VI repairs to Scotland but is captured and imprisoned. Warwick goes to France to arrange a marriage between Edward IV and the French king's sister. While Warwick is in France, Edward IV falls in love with the Lady Grey and marries her. Warwick is mad, allies himself with the French and invades England. Warwick, in history referred to as the kingmaker, restores Henry VI to the throne. Edward IV fights back, defeats and kills Warwick at the battle of Barnet. Henry VI is captured, imprisoned again and this time murdered by the Duke of Gloucester, brother of Edward IV and later to become King Richard III.

KING HENRY VIII

Henry VIII is married with Katharine of Aragon - his Prime Minister is the ambitious Cardinal Wolsey. The duke of Buckingham opposes Wolsey but Wolsey schemes to have Buckingham tried for treason and executed. Katharine does not produce a male heir to the throne. Meanwhile Henry VIII develops a passion for Anne Boleyn and tries to find plausible reasons to divorce Katharine. Wolsey schemes with the Pope to prevent the divorce. Archbishop Cranmer instead follows the wishes of the king. Wolsey is stripped of title, power and possessions after compromising letters to the Pope are intercepted. Henry VIII marries Anne Boleyn. Cranmer is master of ceremonies at the baptism of Elisabeth (the future Elisabeth I) and foretells all Elisabeth's virtues and benefits deriving to England from her future reign. The play, no doubt, was intended to be attended by Queen Elisabeth I herself and some flattery never hurts.

KING LEAR

Lear, king of Britain, has decided to abdicate and to divide his kingdom and possessions among his three daughters, Regan, Goneril and Cordelia in proportion to how much each of them loves him. The false Regan and Goneril declare great love, Cordelia refuses to stoop to this un-sincere spectacle. Lear disowns her and she marries the King of France who loves her for what she is and not for what she has inherited. Kent opposes Lear's action and is immediately banished though he later returns to help Lear. Regan and Goneril renege on their plea of filial love and refuse any assistance to Lear who wanders away in a storm, angry and disgusted. Gloucester has two sons Edgar and the bastard Edmund. Edmund plots to discredit Edgar who is banished. Cordelia returns with French forces to rescue Lear. Cornwall, Regan's husband suspects Gloucester of having orchestrated the invasion and blinds him. Gloucester's good son Edgar finds his father and rescues him from suicide. Lear and Cordelia are captured by Cornwall's forces, Cordelia is hanged and Lear dies of heartbreak. The good Edgar kills the evil Edmund. The good Cordelia, the evil Regan plus all the other evil characters also die.

KING RICHARD II

Richard II is the first of the historical plays covering the reigns of Richard II, Henry IV, Henry V, Henry VI, Richard III. The play covers the two-year period 1398 to 1400. Henry (Bolingbroke) accuses Mowbray of treason and challenges him to a duel. Richard II intervenes and sends both in exile. At the death of John of Gaunt, Bolingbroke's father, Richard also forfeits Gaunt's estate. While Richard is in Ireland Bolingbroke return to England with an army and gathering allies among the malcontents manages to dethrone Richard II and imprisons him at Pomfret castle where he is killed. Bolingbroke is crowned King Henry IV.

KING RICHARD III

Richard has set his mind on becoming king and eliminates anyone who is in his way. After killing the previous king Henry VI, he has Clarence, his own brother murdered and manages to marry Clarence's widowed wife Anne, with a view toward political advantage. Later when king Edward IV dies, he murders all the queen's allies as well as the unwary Hastings. Next in line to be killed are the young Prince of Wales and his brother. Buckingham helped Richard with the initial killings but refuses to kill the boys and turns against Richard. Buckingham is the next to be executed, as well as the two boys. Richard is now King. He attempts to marry Elizabeth, daughter of the dead king Edward IV, but revolt is brewing. The Earl of Richmond engages Richard's forces at Bosworth Field. Richard is defeated and killed. Richmond ascends to the throne as King Henry VII. Historically, the play covers the years from 1471 to 1485.

LOVE'S LABOURS LOST
Ferdinand, king of Navarre decides to devote himself to study along with friends Biron, Longaville and Dumain. To study with diligence, they vow to avoid completely the company of women for 3 years. But the Princess of France arrives for a visit, along with ladies in waiting Rosaline, Maria, Katharine and attendant lords Boyet and Mercado. Ferdinand falls in love with the Princess and his friends with the ladies of the Princess' train. It's good bye to abstinence. Don Armado, a pedant, courts Jaquenetta, a maid who does not understand what he is talking about. Page Moth, clown Costard, schoolmaster Holofernes, curate Nathaniel and constable Dull manage to poke fun at pedantry and affectation of language.

MACBETH
Three witches show up in Macbeth and Banquo's presence, after Macbeth has just defeated a rebellious Scottish feudal lord. They forecast that in time Macbeth will be king and Banquo the direct relative of a king. The predictions prompt Macbeth to commit a string of murders with the agreement, assistance and connivance of his ambitious wife, Lady Macbeth. First he kills King Duncan who is guest at Macbeth's castle, along with his guards, then he kills Banquo, then the wife and children of Macduff, a Scottish nobleman, following another prediction of the witches. Macbeth is confident that the predictions will come true. The witches also said that no person born of a woman will kill Macbeth and that he will be safe until a forest will actually move towards his castle, 'till Birnan wood come to Dunsinane'.
Lady Macbeth goes mad and dies and Malcolm's forces attack Macbeth's castle. Soldiers use tree branches to hide themselves and disguise their advance, giving the overall impression of a moving forest. Finally, Macbeth is slain by Macduff who, having been born with a Cesarean operation was 'none of woman born'.

MEASURE FOR MEASURE
The Duke of Vienna pretends to go on a discovery trip and leaves Angelo in charge. Angelo is a strict enforcer of chastity laws. Claudio is condemned to death for having seduced Juliet. Isabella, Claudio's sister, pleads with Angelo to spare her brother's life. The hypocrite Angelo offers to spare Claudio's life if Isabella will yield to him. Isabella refuses. The duke of Vienna wearing a disguise hatches a plot. Isabella will pretend to agree to Angelo's advances but at the last moment Isabella will be substituted by Mariana. Mariana is Angelo's fiancée but he previously refused to marry her because she is poor. The plot succeeds but Angelo recants on his promise and confirms Claudio's death sentence. The Duke manages to stop the execution then, throwing away the disguise, unmasks Angelo's treachery and hypocrisy. In the end Angelo escapes punishment and marries Mariana. Claudio marries Juliet and the Duke, impressed by Isabella's beauty and virtue, marries her. Other characters are Escalus, a faithful lord and Lucius, a somewhat asinine courtier.

MERCHANT OF VENICE
Bassanio loves Portia but needs money to compete with other suitors. The deal, (established by her dead father), is that Portia will marry him who solves a puzzle. Bassanio borrows money from Antonio, a merchant, who, due to temporary unfavorable circumstances, must borrow from Shylock, a Jewish usurer. If Antonio defaults on the payments, the contract calls for a pound of flesh to be cut off Antonio. Bassanio solves the riddle and marries Portia. In the meantime Antonio's ships are given for lost and he cannot repay the debt in time. Bassanio, the duke of Venice and others try to convince Shylock to accept 3 times the original payment but Shylock is immovable – he wants Antonio's blood. Portia, disguised as a male attorney comes up with a legal argument, the pound of flesh must be cut without one drop of blood as blood was not in the contract, only flesh. Antonio wins the case and Shylock must lick his own wounds. His daughter

Jessica, in the meantime, has married Lorenzo, a friend of Bassanio. Launcelot, a servant to Shylock and then of Bassanio and the loquacious Gratiano provide some additional merriment.

MIDSUMMER NIGHT'S DREAM
Hermia loves Lysander but her father has decreed that she must marry Demetrius or else she will be executed as per Athenian law. Hermia and Lysander elope in a forest. Meanwhile Helena loves Demetrius and convinces him to follow Hermia and Lysander. Oberon, king of the fairies wants his servant Puck to administer a magic filter to the appropriate parties so that Demetrius will love Helena. But the application of the filter goes wrong and now both Lysander and Demetrius love Helena, who thinks they make fun of her. In the end matters get sorted via a correct application of the potion. In the meantime Oberon plays a trick on Titania and gives her the same magic drink whereby the patient goes to sleep and falls in love with the first person he or she sees on waking up. A group of actors is rehearsing a play in the forest and one of the actors is Bottom who in the play the part and wears the head of an ass. On waking up Titania sees Bottom and falls in love with him. Eventually the spell is broken and the actors perform the play to celebrate the wedding of Theseus and Hyppolita.

MUCH ADO ABOUT NOTHING
Hero loves Claudio and is engaged to marry him. Benedick is a staunch bachelor, Beatrice is a quick-witted woman who has a general poor opinion of men. Their friends hatch a plot whereby Benedick will overhear Beatrice's secret monologues and viceversa. It turns out that Benedick and Beatrice are in love. The evil Don John wants to wreak havoc and convinces Margaret, Hero's maid to dress up as Hero and make it appear as if Hero had another lover. Claudio falls for the trick and repudiates Hero, who is given for dead. But two constables, Dogberry and Verges overhear two of Don John's henchmen discuss the evil deed planned with the help of the maid Margaret. Dogberry reports the matter to the Prince, Claudio repents and agrees to marry Hero's cousin, but it turns out that Hero's cousin is actually Hero. The original wedding takes place - Claudio, Hero along with Benedick and Beatrice live happily thereafter.

OTHELLO
Othello, a Moor in the Venetian army has married Desdemona against the wishes of her father Brabantio. Othello has promoted Cassio over Iago. Corroded by envy, Iago plots his revenge. Cassio cannot tolerate alcohol. Iago manages to get Cassio drunk whereby Cassio misbehaves and Othello relieves him from his position in the army. Iago suggests to Cassio to ask Desdemona to plead with Othello on Cassio's behalf. In the meantime Iago skillfully manages to inculcate jealousy in Othello and concocts false evidence to prove that Desdemona was unfaithful. Iago asks his wife Emilia (Desdemona's maid) to steal a handkerchief from Desdemona then asks Othello to ask Desdemona for the fine handkerchief that Othello had given Desdemona as a gift. Convinced of her infidelity Othello kills Desdemona but Emilia immediately reveals what happened. Iago kills Emilia. Othello kills himself and Iago is arrested and taken away to face up to his crimes.

PERICLES, PRINCE OF TYRE
Pericles travels to Antioch to solve a riddle knowing that if he does he will marry the King of Antioch's daughter. If he does not he will be killed. Pericles solves the riddle that, however, contains evidence of the incestuous relationship between Antioch and his daughter. Pericle's life being now in danger, he runs from Antioch and also leaves Tyre in the hands of the faithful Helicanus. Pericles is shipwrecked in Pentapolis where he wins a tourney and marries the king's daughter Thaisa. He then sails back to Tyre but is shipwrecked again while at the last moment during the storm Thaisa delivers a baby girl called Marina. Thaisa is given up for dead but unbeknown to Pericles, is rescued in

Ephesus by a miracle-performing doctor and enters Diana's temple as a priestess. Pericles leaves Marina in the hands of Cleon and Dioniza at Tarsus. Marina is brought up at Tarsus along with Cleon and Dioniza's own daughter. Envious of Marina's beauty, Dioniza plans to kill Marina. At the last moment pirates capture Marina and sell her to a brothel keeper in Mytilene. Through her virtue she manages to win her freedom. Lysimachus, governor of Mytilene, is so impressed by Marina that he asks her to marry him. In the meantime Pericles, almost mad with grief, arrives in Mytilene. Marina is called to speak to Pericles, whereupon he recognizes her and recovers his senses. In a vision he sees that Thaisa is alive in Ephesus, goes there, find his lost wife and the family is re-united.

ROMEO AND JULIET
Romeo, a Montague, loves Juliet, a Capulet but their respective families hate each other. Romeo secretly marries Juliet with the help of Friar Lawrence. Soon afterwards the Capulet Tybalt slays the Montague Mercutio and in the ensuing duel Romeo kills Tybalt and must run for his life from Verona to Mantua. Meanwhile Juliet's father wants her to marry Paris and she is in a bind. Friar Lawrence comes to her assistance by giving her a potion that will cause her to fall into a sleep similar to death. Romeo then would arrive from Mantua and carry her away while others assume that Juliet is dead. But things go awry. Romeo hears of Juliet's alleged death and travels to her tomb where he finds Paris and kills him. Then believing Juliet to be dead, Romeo poisons himself at Juliet's side. Julie wakes up, finds Romeo dead and kills herself in turn.

THE MERRY WIVES OF WINDSOR
Falstaff courts simultaneously the merry wives of Windsor Mrs. Ford and Mrs. Page hoping to obtain all kinds of benefits. They become aware of Falstaff's scheming and decide to ridicule him. Mrs. Ford sets up a rendezvous, Mr. Ford appears, Falstaff hides in a basket of dirty linen and is dumped into the river. In a second pretence date with Mrs. Ford, Falstaff escapes disguised as an old woman and beaten by Mr. Ford. In the third and final meeting the poor Falstaff is pinched and ridiculed by a bunch of faked fairies. Throughout all this Anne, pretty daughter of Mrs. Page, is courted by Slender, a good-for-nothing, Dr. Caius, a pompous servant to Mistress Quickly and young Fenton. Anne loves Fenton and elopes with him. Rumor has it that Queen Elizabeth herself asked Shakespeare to write a play in which Falstaff was in love.

THE TAMING OF THE SHREW
An English lord finds Christopher Sly a tinkerer, dead drunk. The lord has Sly dressed in fancy clothes and arranges for Sly to be attended by obsequious servants. When Sly wakes up the servants convince him that he is actually a nobleman and organize the proper play (The Taming of the Shrew), for his delectation and amusement.
Young Hortensio loves Bianca who is also courted by the old Gremio and by Lucentio. But Baptista, Bianca's father will not allow Bianca to be married before the elder sister Katharina is married. Katharina is a shrew who immediately scares away all suitors. In comes Petruchio who likes Katharina and assures all relevant parties that he knows how to handle her. In the meantime Bianca needs a music teacher. Petruchio sponsors Hortensio, but Lucentio also wants to be Bianca's teacher. In a complex plot involving competition and disguises Bianca finds herself courted by Gremio, an old gentleman, Hortensio who will disguise himself as a music-teacher, Lucentio, disguised as a school-master and Tranio, servant of Lucentio and disguised as Lucentio. Petruchio's initial strategy with Katharina is to praise her when she rather expects to be scolded - Katharina will marry Petruchio. Now Bianca will marry one of her actually (3) suitors, Hortensio, old Gremio or young Lucentio. Hortensio and Lucentio deliver love messages to Bianca in competition with each other. Meanwhile Tranio (disguised as Lucentio), and old Gremio also bid for Bianca's hand, prompted by her father Baptista who is present at the

bid. Petruchio is late at his wedding with Katharina, behaves very oddly and carries her away immediately after the ceremony. He now becomes as shrewish as Katharina pretending that his shrewishness is the result of his passion for her. He starves her and forces to accept whatever he says or commands - everything being done in the name of love. In the end Katharina is tamed, accepts his love and becomes the perfect wife. Lucentio elopes with Bianca and the defeated Hortensio marries a widow. Finally Katharina (the ex-shrew) delivers a lecture to other married ladies on how to be the perfect wife (according to the standards of the time).

THE TEMPEST
Antonio, with the help of Alonso, king of Naples, usurps the dukedom from his brother Prospero who escapes to a magic island with young daughter Miranda. Prospero has learned magic and hired as indentured servants Ariel, a spirit, and Caliban a brute monster, son of the witch Sycorax. A storm shipwrecks on the island Antonio along with Alonso, Ferdinand (Alonso's son), Sebastian (Alonso's brother), and other courtiers. Ferdinand, lost in a different part of the island meets with Miranda and they instantly fall in love. Caliban meets with the shipwrecked Stephano, a butler and Trinculo, a servant. They plot to dethrone Prospero from his kingdom of the island, but they are easily unmasked and ridiculed. In the meantime the evil Antonio tries to persuade Sebastian to kill Alonso in his sleep and get the throne of Naples but the plot fails. In the end Ferdinand marries Miranda, Antonio repents, Prospero's rights are restored, Ariel is freed for good and Prospero gives up magic.

THE WINTER'S TALE
Polixenes, king of Bohemia visits his old friend Leontes, king of Sicilia. During the visit Leontes, without any evidence, believes that his wife Hermione has an affair with Polixenes. Camillo, Leonte's minister, defends Hermione but must flee for his life to Bohemia along with Polixenes. Leontes imprisons his wife who just delivered a baby girl, Perdita. Leontes believes that Perdita is not his daughter and orders Antigonus, a Sicilian lord, to expose the baby. Instead, Antigonus abandons Perdita on a remote coast of Bohemia before being killed by a bear. Meanwhile in Sicilia an oracle returns a verdict proving that Hermione is absolutely innocent and that if the newly born baby is not found Leontes will die heirless. The prediction is reinforced by the sudden death of Mamilius, Leonte's other son. Leontes repents and bitterly regrets his jealousy.
Meantime a shepherd finds Perdita in Bohemia and raises her as his own daughter. Sixteen years later Florizel, Polixenes' son, finds Perdita and falls in love with her. Polixenes strongly disapproves of a king's son marrying a shepherd's daughter. But Polixenes and Perdita flee to Sicilia with the help of Camillo who longs for home. The shepherd reveals to Polixenes how he found Perdita and produces documents proving her to be the daughter of Hermione, queen of Sicily. Polixenes himself travels to Sicily, now happy with his son's choice. Paulina, Antigonus' wife, invites the repented Leontes to examine a statue that is a life-like representation of the allegedly deceased Hermione. But the statue is actually the real Hermione and everyone is happy. Autolycus, a pedlar with a penchant for scams provides further merriment.

TIMON OF ATHENS
The overgenerous Timon has no concept of accounting or budgeting and runs into debt notwithstanding the warnings of faithful friend Flavius and the scolding of the cynic and rogue philosopher Apemantus. None of Timon's former friends who yet benefited from his generosity want to help him. Timon gathers his flattering and ungrateful friends to a last banquet where he throws water at them, then departs for the woods to live as a hermit. Alcibiades, an Athenian general visits with Timon - later he becomes ruler of the city after the ungrateful Athenian senators managed to make him (Alcibiades) mad. Timon dies alone in the woods, completely disillusioned with the world.

TITUS ANDRONICUS
This is the goriest play of all. Titus Andronicus, winner of the Goths, sacrifices to the gods the son of Tamora, their queen. In turn Tamora marries Saturninus, emperor of the Romans and manages to have two of Titus' sons beheaded, his son in law Bassanio killed and his daughter Lavinia raped and mutilated. Next Titus slays Tamora's sons who raped and mutilated Lavinia and serves them as a meal to the unsuspecting Tamora. At the same banquet Titus kills Tamora, Saturninus kills Titus and Lucius, another of Titus' sons kills Saturninus. Aaron, a champion of wickedness and Tamora's lover meets his end proud of his non-repentance.

TROILUS AND CRESSIDA
In Troy Troilus loves Cressida, whose father has defected to the Greeks. Through the offices of Pandarus, her uncle, Troilus gets Cressida and they exchange vows of eternal love. But there is an exchange of prisoners and Cressida is led to the Greek camp to join her father and immediately becomes the mistress of Diomedes. In Troy there is a debate on whether to return Helen to the Greeks and stop the war. Meanwhile in the Greek camp, the invincible Achilles is sulking. Ulysses wily manages to prick Achilles' pride. Achille fights with Hector and slays him. Among the Greeks, the wise and old Nestor offers words of wisdom and the skeptical Thersites words of contempt.

TWELFTH NIGHT
As in 'The Tempest' and 'Pericles', a shipwreck is a key event in the plot of 'Twelfth Night'. The lookalike twins Sebastian and Viola are shipwrecked and separated on the coast of Illyria. Viola disguised as a man and calling him/herself Cesario finds employment with Orsino, the Duke of Illyria. Orsino uses Viola/Cesario to woo Olivia, but Olivia rejects Orsino's advances and falls in love with Viola/Cesario, or rather with Cesario not knowing that he is a she. Antonio, master of the shipwrecked boat looks for Sebastian who has gone sightseeing and meets instead with Viola/Cesario whom he takes for Sebastian. The Duke's officers arrest Antonio who accuses the alleged Sebastian of ingratitude. Sebastian meets with Olivia who, believing him to be Viola/Cesario marries him. Later, when Olivia meets the true Viola/Cesario, Viola denies that there was ever a marriage and the Duke is upset at the presumed betrayal of Viola/Cesario. Eventually the twins show up together, the mystery is solved and Viola marries the Duke. In the meantime Sir Toby Belch, Olivia's uncle and Sir Andrew Aguecheek concoct a bitter joke against Malvolio, Olivia's pompous butler. Malvolio receives a faked letter in which Olivia promises her love to him whereupon he proceeds to make an ass of himself. Olivia thinks that Malvolio is insane and he ends up in prison. Malvolio is eventually released and promises vengeance on the pranksters who tricked him.

TWO GENTLEMEN FROM VERONA
In Verona Proteus loves Julia. His friend Valentine is dispatched to Milan to gain experience in the world and there he falls in love with Sylvia, daughter of the Duke of Milan. Sylvia reciprocates. Proteus' father also dispatches his son to Milan to gain experience as an intern with the Duke of Milan. Proteus quickly forgets Julia and falls in love with Sylvia. The Duke wants Sylvia to marry the spineless but wealthy Thurio. Proteus then plays a dirty trick on Valentine to remove him from Sylvia. Proteus tells the Duke that Sylvia and Valentine plan to elope. The angry Duke bans Valentine from Milan but Sylvia rejects Proteus' advances. In the meantime Julia arrives in Milan disguised as a man and is hired by Proteus to woo Sylvia on his behalf. Accompanied by the old and trusted Eglamour, Sylvia escapes into a forest where she knows Valentine has taken refuge. Proteus chases Sylvia and wants to take her by force but at the critical moment Valentine shows up and saves her from Proteus. The Duke equally arrives on the

scene with Thurio. Thurio is shamed for his cowardice and the Duke consents to the marriage of Valentine to Sylvia. Proteus repents and will marry Julia after all.

SONNETS

While all the plays refer to historical or imaginary events, the Sonnets touch Shakespeare's life directly. The Sonnets have been the subject of extended debates and speculations. There are three characters involved, the very handsome youth to whom some sonnets are dedicated, the so called Dark Lady to whom some other sonnets are addressed, and of course, Shakespeare who wrote them. That a handsome youth be the subject of love lines has fueled speculation that Shakespeare was homosexual. But it seems clear that his love for the youth appears to be purely spiritual – how else would he (Shakespeare) prompt, in the Sonnets, the youth to marry so that he may have children and therefore generate a good copy of himself? Besides, what about the Dark Lady? By re-ordering the Sonnets and other research, historians have concluded that the Dark Lady was a married woman and Shakespeare her lover. At some time, Shakespeare introduced the Dark Lady to the handsome youth and the two of them betrayed Shakespeare. Today we would define this a curious 'menage a' trois'. It does not really matter. Taken together, the Sonnets are universally acknowledged as the most beautiful love poem ever written.

VENUS AND ADONIS

If the events described in this poem were to happen today, Venus could be arrested and tried for corruption of a minor and sexual harassment. Venus catches a glimpse of Adonis who is hunting and immediately falls in love with him. But notwithstanding all her charms and entreaties he does not yield. He claims to be under age and uninterested. Eventually Adonis takes off on his horse to hunt a wild boar, but the boar kills Adonis. Where Adonis' blood is spilled a new flower arises, the anemone. Venus retires to Paphos for meditation and counseling.

RAPE OF LUCRECE

Tarquinius Superbus (an Etruscan-Roman king) sets siege to the city of Ardea (Italy) along with Roman nobles and his son Sextus Tarquinius. During a social get-together the besiegers bet on whose wife is the most chaste. Collatine extols the virtue and the beauty of his wife. Sextus Tarquinius inflamed by the description of Lucrece' beauty, manages to call at Lucrece's house while Collatine is fighting. During the night he treacherously steals into her chamber, rapes her and departs. The distraught Lucrece sends messengers to her father and her husband Collatine. They arrive - finding Lucrece wearing a mourning dress they ask what is the cause of her sorrow. Lucrece explains the facts and makes her them promise that they will revenge her, whereupon she stabs herself and dies. Father, husband and their allies bring Lucrece's body to Rome and move the people to ban all the Tarquins from Rome. Rome then becomes a Republic (509 AC),